AMERICAN WRITERS

AMERICAN WRITERS

JAY PARINI
Editor

SUPPLEMENT XXVI

CHARLES SCRIBNER'S SONS
A part of Gale, Cengage Learning

GALE
CENGAGE Learning·

Farmington Hills, Mich • San Francisco • New York • Waterville, Maine
Meriden, Conn • Mason, Ohio • Chicago

GALE
CENGAGE Learning®

American Writers Supplement XXVI

Editor in Chief: Jay Parini

Project Editor: Lisa Kumar

Permissions: Moriam Aigoro

Composition and Electronic Capture: Gary Leach

Manufacturing: Rhonda Dover

920.03
Ame

For product information and technology assistance, contact us at
Gale Customer Support, 1-800-877-4253.
For permission to use material from this text or product,
submit all requests online at
www.cengage.com/permissions
Further permissions questions can be emailed to
permissionrequest@cengage.com

LIBRARY OF CONGRESS CATALOGING-IN-PUBLICATION DATA

American writers: a collection of literary biographies / Leonard Unger, editor in chief.
  p. cm.
  The 4-vol. main set consists of 97 of the pamphlets originally published as the University of Minnesota pamphlets on American writers; some have been rev. and updated. The supplements cover writers not included in the original series.
  Supplement 2, has editor in chief, A. Walton Litz; Retrospective suppl. 1, c. 1998, was edited by A. Walton Litz & Molly Weigel; Suppl. 5–26 have as editor-in-chief, Jay Parini.
  Includes bibliographies and index.
  Contents: v. 1. Henry Adams to T.S. Eliot — v. 2. Ralph Waldo Emerson to Carson McCullers — v. 3. Archibald MacLeish to George Santayana — v. 4. Isaac Bashevis Singer to Richard Wright — Supplement[s]: 1, pt. 1. Jane Addams to Sidney Lanier. 1, pt. 2. Vachel Lindsay to Elinor Wylie. 2, pt. 1. W.H. Auden to O. Henry. 2, pt. 2. Robinson Jeffers to Yvor Winters. — 4, pt. 1. Maya Angelou to Linda Hogan. 4, pt. 2. Susan Howe to Gore Vidal — Suppl. 5. Russell Banks to Charles Wright — Suppl. 6. Don DeLillo to W. D. Snodgrass — Suppl. 7. Julia Alvarez to Tobias Wolff — Suppl. 8. T.C. Boyle to August Wilson. — Suppl. 11 Toni Cade Bambara to Richard Yates.
  ISBN 978-0-684-32506-4
  1. American literature—History and criticism. 2. American literature—Bio-bibliography. 3. Authors, American—Biography. I. Unger, Leonard. II. Litz, A. Walton. III. Weigel, Molly. IV. Parini, Jay. V. University of Minnesota pamphlets on American writers.

PS129 .A55
810'.9
[B]   73-001759

ISBN-13: 978-0-684-32506-4

This title is also available as an e-book.
ISBN-13: 978-0-684-32507-1
Contact your Gale, Cengage Learning sales representative for ordering information.

Charles Scribner's Sons an imprint of Gale, Cengage Learning
27500 Drake Rd.
Farmington Hills, MI 48331-3535

Printed in Mexico
1 2 3 4 5 6 7 19 18 17 16 15

Acknowledgments

The editors wish to thank the copyright holders of the excerpted criticism included in this volume and the permissions managers of many book and magazine publishing companies for assisting us in securing reproduction rights. Following is a list of the copyright holders who have granted us permission to reproduce material in this volume of *American Writers*. Every effort has been made to trace copyright, but if omissions have been made, please let us know.

COPYRIGHTED EXCERPTS IN *AMERICAN WRITERS*, VOLUME 26, WERE REPRODUCED FROM THE FOLLOWING SOURCES:

ANDREWS, RAYMOND. Perry, Pam, "Novella of Rural South Tell Some Painful Truths," *Atlanta Journal-Constitution*, November 10, 1991.

BISS, EULA. "Barry," *Hanging Loose 74*, Hanging Loose Press, 1999. / "In the Syntax: Rewriting Joan Didion's 'Goodbye to All That'," *Fourth Genre: Explorations in Nonfiction* 13(1), Michigan State University Press, Spring 2011, pp. 133, 135, 136, 137. / "Living Together, a Letter," *Massachusetts Review* 45(2), The Massachusetts Review Inc., Summer 2004, pp. 394-395. / "My Mother," *Hanging Loose 74*, Hanging Loose Press, 1999. / "Notes on 'All Apologizes'," *Notes from No Man's Land*, Graywolf Press, 2009, p. 221. / "Notes On 'Goodbye to All That'," *Notes from No Man's Land*, Graywolf Press, 2009, pp.207-208. / "Notes On 'Time and Distance Overcome'," *Notes from No Man's Land*, Graywolf Press, 2009, p. 202. / "Team Blue/Team Square: Revisiting the Lyric and the Narrative," *American Poet*, Academy of American Poets, 2005, pp. 11-12. / "The Price of Poetry," *Massachusetts Review* 42(1), The Massachusetts Review Inc., Spring 2001. / Excerpts from *The Balloonists*, Hanging Loose Press, 2002, pp. 13,

14, 18, 19, 39, 70, 72. / From "Mission Statement," *Race Traitor*, Race Traitor Journal of the New Abolitionism. / Skurnick, Lizzie, "Personal Yet Dazzlingly Eclectic 'Notes' On Race," National Public Radio, March 23, 2009. / Wyce, Marion, review of *Notes from No Man's Land*, *Literary Review* 53(2), Fairleigh Dickinson University, 2009. / Polito, Robert, "Judges Afterword," *Notes from No Man's Land*, Graywolf Press, 2009, p. 227. / Scott, Whitney, review of *The Balloonists*, Booklist, American Library Association, May 15, 2005.

DAVISON, PETER. Dedication, *The Breaking of the Day*, Yale University Press, 1964. / "Fawn," *Barn Fever and Other Poems*, Atheneum, 1981, p. 15. / "Is Anything Wrong?," *Walking the Boundaries: Poems 1957-1974*, Atheneum, 1974, p. 66. / "No Escape," *Breathing Room*, Alfred A. Knopf, 2000. / "Not Forgotten: Dream," *The Breaking of the Day*, Yale University Press, 1964. / "Our Eyes," *The Poems of Peter Davison: 1957-1995*, Alfred A. Knopf, 1995, p. 309. / "Passages for Puritans," *The Poems of Peter Davison: 1957-1995*, Alfred A. Knopf, 1995, p. 73. / "Walking the Boundaries: North by the Creek," *Walking the Boundar-*

ACKNOWLEDGEMENTS

ies: Poems 1957-1974, Atheneum, 1974, p. 93. / "Zenith: Walker Creek," *A Voice in the Mountain,* Atheneum, 1977, p. 5. / Hass, Robert, "Meditation at Lagunitas," *Praise,* HarperCollins, 1999, p. 4.

GANSWORTH, ERIC. "Artist's Statement," *Nickel Eclipse,* Michigan State University Press, 2000, pp. xiii-xiv. / "Dakota (IV)," *A Half-Life of Cardio-Pulmonary Function,* Syracuse University Press, 2008, p. 112. / "Eric Gansworth," amerinda.org, American Indian Artists Inc. / "Finding a Voice from Home: Louise Erdrich's *Love Medicine,*" *Conversations on Jesuit Higher Education* 30(25), Marquette University, October 1, 2006, p. 34. / "Introduction," *From the Western Door to the Lower West Side,* White Pine Press, 2009. / "It Goes Something Like This," *Nickel Eclipse,* Michigan State University Press, 2000. / "On Meeting My Father in a Bar for the First Time," *Nickel Eclipse,* Michigan State University Press, 2000, p. 116. / "The Gifts of Our Fathers," *Nickel Eclipse,* Michigan State University Press, 2000, pp. 46-47. / title poem, *A Half-Life of Cardio-Pulmonary Function,* Syracuse University Press, 2008, p. 3. / "Toronto, More or Less, in Fifteen Years," *Nickel Eclipse,* Michigan State University Press, 2000, p. 121. / "While Hendrix Played a Solo: 'Burning of the Midnight Lamp'," *From the Western Door to the Lower West Side,* White Pine Press, 2009. / "2010 Native American $1 Coin," United States Mint. / Andracki, Thaddeus, review of *If I Ever Get Out of Here, Bulletin of the Center for Children's Books* 67(1), Johns Hopkins University Press, September 2013, p. 19.

GOODMAN, ALLEGRA. "Onionskin," *New Yorker,* April 1, 1991, p. 29. / "Rereading: Pemberly Previsited," *American Scholar* 73(2), The American Scholar, Spring 2004, pp. 142-145. / *Paradise Point,* The Dial Press, 2001, p. 360. / Browning, Dominique, "The Insatiable Years," *New York Times Book Review,* July 25, 2010, BR10. / Schuessler, Jennifer, "Looking for Love," *New York Times,* March 11, 2001. / Hacker, Randi, "In Short," *New York Times,* September 10, 1989, BR26.

HAYES, ALFRED. "As a Young Man," *Wel-* *come to the Castle: Poems by Alfred Hayes,* Harper &Brothers, 1950, p. 44. / "Comrade Poets," *New Masses,* April 1933. / "Into the Streets May First," *New Masses,* May 1934. / "The Sour Note," *Welcome to the Castle: Poems by Alfred Hayes,* Harper &Brothers, 1950, p. 82. © 1950 HarperCollins. / Excerpt from *Just Before the Divorce,* Atheneum, 1968, p. 24. © 1968 Simon &Schuster, Inc. / "A Nice Part of Town," *The Big Time,* Howell, Soskin, 1944, p. 98. / "In a Coffee Pot," *Partisan Review* 1(1), 1934, p. 15. / "Underground," *The Big Time,* Howell, Soskin, 1944, p. 80.

HUDDLE, DAVID. "1953 Dodge Coronet," *Blacksnake at the Family Reunion,* Louisiana State University Press, 2012, p. 5. / "A Brief History of My Mother's Temper," *Summer Lake: New and Selected Poems,* Louisiana State University Press, 1999, pp. 155, 162. © 1999 Louisiana State University Press. / "April Saturday," *Grayscale,* Louisiana State University Press, 2004, pp. 16, 18. / "Circus," *Grayscale,* Louisiana State University Press, 2004, p. 56. / "Confessions," *Summer Lake: New and Selected Poems,* Louisiana State University Press, 1999, p. 128. © 1999 Louisiana State University Press. / "Crossing New River," *Grayscale,* Louisiana State University Press, 2004, p. 12. / Dedication for section "New Poems: What You Live For," *Summer Lake: New and Selected Poems,* Louisiana State University Press, 1999. / "Going, 1960-1970," *Paper Boy,* University of Pittsburgh Press, 1979, p. 52. / "Hard Drive," *Blacksnake at the Family Reunion,* Louisiana State University Press, 2012, p. 33. / "Huddle Brothers, Ivanhoe, Virginia; Circa 1963," *Grayscale,* Louisiana State University Press, 2004, p. 2. © 2004 Louisiana State University Press. / "In My Other Life," *Blacksnake at the Family Reunion,* Louisiana State University Press, 2012, p. 36. / "Inheritance," *Grayscale,* Louisiana State University Press, 2004, p. 6. / "Introduction," A David Huddle Reader: Selected Prose and Poetry, University Press of New England, 1994, pp. 1-4. / "Linguistics 101," *Blacksnake at the Family Reunion,* Louisiana State University Press, 2012, p. 52. / "Model Father," *Summer Lake: New and Selected Poems,* Louisiana State University Press, 1999, p.

ACKNOWLEDGEMENTS

138. © 1999 Louisiana State University Press. / "Nerves," Stopping by Home, Peregrine Smith Books, 1988, p. 2. / "Never Been," *Summer Lake: New and Selected Poems,* Louisiana State University Press, 1999, pp. 168-169. / "Party Poem," The Nature of Yearning, Peregrine Smith Books, 1992, p. 17. / "Picture," *Summer Lake: New and Selected Poems,* Louisiana State University Press, 1999, p. 135. / "Pity," Glory River, Louisiana State University Press, 2008, p. 29. © 2008 Louisiana State University Press. / "Quiet Hour," The Nature of Yearning, Peregrine Smith Books, 1992, p. 24. / "Summer Lake," The Nature of Yearning, Peregrine Smith Books, 1992, p. 28. / "The House," Stopping by Home, Peregrine Smith Books, 1988, p. 16. / "The Husband's Tale," *Blacksnake at the Family Reunion,* Louisiana State University Press, 2012, p. 39. / "The Poem, The Snow, Jane Goodall, The Vase of Daffodils," *Grayscale,* Louisiana State University Press, 2004, p. 32. / "Thinking about My Fathers," The Nature of Yearning, Peregrine Smith Books, 1992, p. 47. / "This Morning," *Blacksnake at the Family Reunion,* Louisiana State University Press, 2012, p. 6. / title poem, *The Nature of Yearning,* Peregrine Smith Books, 1992, pp. 5,6,8,9. © 1992 Peregrine Smith Books. / "Two Facts," *Stopping by Home,* Peregrine Smith Books, 1988, p. 16. / "Visit of the Hawk," *The Nature of Yearning,* Peregrine Smith Books, 1992, p. 10. / "Weather Report," *Blacksnake at the Family Reunion,* Louisiana State University Press, 2012, p. 47. / "What the Stone Says," *Blacksnake at the Family Reunion,* Louisiana State University Press, 2012, pp. 13-14. © 2012 Louisiana State University Press. / *Stopping by Home,* Peregrine Smith Books, 1988, p. 45. © 1988 Peregrine Smith Books. / *Stopping by Home,* Peregrine Smith Books, 1988, p. 52. © 1988 Peregrine Smith Books. / Haggas, Carol, review of *Nothing Can Make Me Do This, Booklist* 108(4), American Library Association, October 15, 2011, p. 18; review of *The Faulkes Chronicles, Booklist* 110(22), American Library Association, August 1, 2014, p. 33. / Sabol, Cathy, review of *The Writing Habit: Essays, Library Journal* 117(6), May 1, 1992. / Allen, Frank, review of *Summer Lake, Library Journal* 124(12), July 1999, p. 94. / Review of *Summer Lake, Virginia Quarterly* 76(1), University of Virginia, Winter 2000, A27. / Review of *The Nature of Yearning, Virginia Quarterly* 68(4), University of Virginia, Autumn 1992. / Review of *The Story of a Million Years, Publishers Weekly,* Pwxyz LLC, October 2, 2000. / Review of *The Story of a Million Years, New Yorker,* Conde Nast, September 27, 1999, p. 96. / Washburn, Keith E., review of *Paper Boy, Library Journal* 104(3), Feb 1, 1999, p. 406. / Hutchinson, Paul E., review of *Intimates, Library Journal* 117(18), November 1, 1992, p. 120. / Ratner, Rochelle, review of *A David Huddle Reader: Selected Prose and Poetry,* Library Journal 118(21), December 15, 1993. / Kessler, Rod, review of *Tenorman, Harvard Review,* Vol. 10, Houghton Library at Harvard University, Spring 1996, p. 230. / Balitas, Vincent D., review of *Stopping by Home, Library Journal* 114(4), March 1, 1989, p. 73. / Portis, Virginia Rowe, review of *A Dream with No Stump Roots in It, Library Journal* 100(12), June 15, 1975, p. 1240.

JOHNSON, HELENE. "A Missionary Brings a Young Native to America," *Helene Johnson: Poet of the Harlem Renaissance,* Verner D. Mitchell, ed., University of Massachusetts Press, 2000, p. 43. © 2000 University of Massachusetts Press. / "Cui Bono?," *Helene Johnson: Poet of the Harlem Renaissance,* Verner D. Mitchell, ed., University of Massachusetts Press, 2000, p. 44. © 2000 University of Massachusetts Press. / "Foraging," *Helene Johnson: Poet of the Harlem Renaissance,* Verner D. Mitchell, ed., University of Massachusetts Press, 2000, p. 69. © 2000 University of Massachusetts Press. / "Futility," *Helene Johnson: Poet of the Harlem Renaissance,* Verner D. Mitchell, ed., University of Massachusetts Press, 2000, p. 31. © 2000 University of Massachusetts Press. / "He's About 22. I'm 63," *Helene Johnson: Poet of the Harlem Renaissance,* Verner D. Mitchell, ed., University of Massachusetts Press, 2000, pp. 72-73. © 2000 University of Massachusetts Press. / "Invocation," *Helene Johnson: Poet of the Harlem Renaissance,* Verner D. Mitchell, ed., University of Massachusetts Press, 2000, p. 46. © 2000 University of Massachusetts Press. / "Magula," *Helene Johnson: Poet of the Harlem*

ACKNOWLEDGEMENTS

Renaissance, Verner D. Mitchell, ed., University of Massachusetts Press, 2000, p. 34. © 2000 University of Massachusetts Press. / "My Race," *Helene Johnson: Poet of the Harlem Renaissance,* Verner D. Mitchell, ed., University of Massachusetts Press, 2000, p. 24. © 2000 University of Massachusetts Press. / "Plea of a Plebian," *Helene Johnson: Poet of the Harlem Renaissance,* Verner D. Mitchell, ed., University of Massachusetts Press, 2000, p. 61. / "Sonnet to a Negro in Harlem," *Helene Johnson: Poet of the Harlem Renaissance,* Verner D. Mitchell, ed., University of Massachusetts Press, 2000, p. 40. © 2000 University of Massachusetts Press. / "War," *Helene Johnson: Poet of the Harlem Renaissance,* Verner D. Mitchell, ed. University of Massachusetts Press, 2000, p. 78. © 2000 University of Massachusetts Press. / "Why Do They Prate?," *Helene Johnson: Poet of the Harlem Renaissance,* Verner D. Mitchell, ed., University of Massachusetts Press, 2000, p. 53. © 2000 University of Massachusetts Press. / McGrath, Abigail, "Afterword: A Daughter Reminisces," *Helene Johnson: Poet of the Harlem Renaissance,* Verner D. Mitchell, ed., University of Massachusetts Press, 2000, pp. 123, 124, 125, 127. / Millay, Edna St. Vincent, "To a Calvinist in Bali," *Collected Poems of Edna St. Vincent Millay,* Harper &Row, 1956, p. 329.

KITTREDGE, WILLIAM. "Learning to Think," *Taking Care: Thoughts on Storytelling and Belief,* Scott Slovic ed., Milkweed Editions, 1999, pp. 32, 33, 36, 38, 39. / Ott, Bill, Review of *The Next Rodeo, Booklist* 104(9-10), American Library Association, January 1, 2008, p. 34.

McBRIDE, JAMES. "Author's Note" (hardcover edition), *Song Yet Sung,* Riverhead Books, 2008, p. 356. / Prologue, *The Good Lord Bird,* Riverhead Books, 2013, p. 1.

NGUYEN, BICH MINH. "Author's Note," *Stealing Budda's Dinner: A Memoir,* Penguin Books, 2007, p. 255. / "Goodbye to My Twinkie Days," *New York Times,* November 17, 2012, A23. / "Thanksgiving About Gathering of Traditions, Essayist Says," *PBS Newshour,* NewsHour Productions LLC, November 23, 2006. /

Hagestadt, Emma, "Short Girls, By Bich Minh Nguyen," *Independent,* September 25, 2009. / Kalb, Deborah, "Q&A with Writer Bich Minh Nguyen," *Haunting Legacy,* August 1, 2012. / Kempf, Andrea, "Short Girls," *Library Journal* 134(12), July 2009, p. 86. / Malandrinos, Cheryl, "Q&A with Bich Minh Nguyen, author of Pioneer Girl," *The Busy Mom's Daily Blog,* March 5, 2014. / Marra, Anthony, "Pioneer Girl," *SFGate,* Hearst Newspapers, February 7, 2014. / Mudge, Alden, "Bich Minh Nguyen: From Vietnam to Wilder's Little House," *BookPage,* BookPage and ProMotion, Inc., February 2014. / Tran, Sharon, "Pioneer Girl: A Novel by Bich Minh Nguyen," *Amerasia Journal* 40(1), UCLA Asian American Studies Center Press, 2014, pp. 116-117.

OPPEN, GEORGE. "1," *George Oppen: New Collected Poems,* Michael Davidson, ed.,, New Directions, 2008, p. 6. © 2008 New Directions. / "11 (A Narrative)," *George Oppen: New Collected Poems,* Michael Davidson, ed., New Directions, 2008, p. 156. © 2008 New Directions. / "11 (Of Being Numerous)," *George Oppen: New Collected Poems,* Michael Davidson, ed., New Directions, 2008, p. 169. © 2008 New Directions. / "18 (Of Being Numerous)," *George Oppen: New Collected Poems,* Michael Davidson, ed., New Directions, 2008, p. 173. © 2008 New Directions. / "18," *George Oppen: New Collected Poems,* Michael Davidson, ed., New Directions, 2008, p. 173. / "19," *George Oppen: New Collected Poems,* Michael Davidson, ed., New Directions, 2008, p. 173. / "32 (Of Being Numerous)," *George Oppen: New Collected Poems,* Michael Davidson, ed., New Directions, 2008, p. 183. © 2008 New Directions / "33 (Of Being Numerous)," *George Oppen: New Collected Poems,* Michael Davidson, ed., New Directions, 2008, pp. 183-184. © 2008 New Directions. / "37 (Of Being Numerous)," *George Oppen: New Collected Poems,* Michael Davidson, ed., New Directions, 2008, p. 186. / "4 (Route)," *George Oppen: New Collected Poems,* Michael Davidson, ed., New Directions, 2008, p. 194. © 2008 New Directions. / "4 Anniversary Poem (Some San Francisco Poems)," *George Oppen: New Collected Poems,* Michael Davidson, ed., New Directions, 2008, p. 227. ©

ACKNOWLEDGEMENTS

2008 New Directions. / "40 (Of Being Numerous)," *George Oppen: New Collected Poems,* Michael Davidson, ed., New Directions, 2008, p. 188. / "7 (Of Being Numerous)," *George Oppen: New Collected Poems,* Michael Davidson, ed., New Directions, 2008, p. 166. © 2008 New Directions. / "9 (of Being Numerous)," *George Oppen: New Collected Poems,* Michael Davidson, ed., New Directions, 2008, p. 167. / "Birthplace: New Rochelle," *George Oppen: New Collected Poems,* Michael Davidson, ed., New Directions, 2008, p. 55. © 2008 New Directions. / "Eclogue," *George Oppen: New Collected Poems,* Michael Davidson, ed., New Directions, 2008, p. 39. © 2008 New Directions. / "From a Phrase of Simone Weil's and Some Words of Hegel's," *George Oppen: New Collected Poems,* Michael Davidson, ed., New Directions, 2008, p. 211. © 2008 New Directions. / "From Virgil," *George Oppen: New Collected Poems,* Michael Davidson, ed., New Directions, 2008, p. 104. © 2008 New Directions. / "I (Blood from the Stone)," *George Oppen: New Collected Poems,* Michael Davidson, ed., New Directions, 2008, p. 52. © 2008 New Directions. / "II (Blood from the Stone)," *George Oppen: New Collected Poems,* Michael Davidson, ed., New Directions, 2008, p. 52. / "III (Blood from the Stone)," *George Oppen: New Collected Poems,* Michael Davidson, ed., New Directions, 2008, p. 53. © 2008 New Directions. / "IV (Blood from the Stone)," *George Oppen: New Collected Poems,* Michael Davidson, ed., New Directions, 2008, pp. 53-54. © 2008 New Directions. / untitled, *George Oppen: New Collected Poems,* Michael Davidson, ed., New Directions, 2008, p. 13. © 2008 New Directions. / "Of Being Numerous," *George Oppen: New Collected Poems,* Michael Davidson, ed., New Directions, 2008, p. 163. / "Psalm," *George Oppen: New Collected Poems,* Michael Davidson, ed., New Directions, 2008, p. 99. © 2008 New Directions. / "Return," *George Oppen: New Collected Poems,* Michael Davidson, ed., New Directions, 2008, p. 48. / "Song, The Winds of Downhill," *George Oppen: New Collected Poems,* Michael Davidson, ed., New Directions, 2008, p. 220. © 2008 New Directions. / "Survival: Infantry," *George Oppen: New Collected Poems,* Michael Davidson, ed., New Directions, 2008, p. 81. © 2008 New Directions. / "The Crowded Countries of the Bomb," *George Oppen: New Collected Poems,* Michael Davidson, ed., New Directions, 2008, p. 78. © 2008 New Directions. / "Til Other Voices Wake Us," *George Oppen: New Collected Poems,* Michael Davidson, ed., New Directions, 2008, p. 286. © 2008 New Directions. / "Time of the Missle," *George Oppen: New Collected Poems,* Michael Davidson, ed., New Directions, 2008, p. 70. / "Tourist Eye," *George Oppen: New Collected Poems,* Michael Davidson, ed., New Directions, 2008, p. 65. / untitled, *George Oppen: New Collected Poems,* Michael Davidson, ed., New Directions, 2008, p. 5. © 2008 New Directions. / "World, World," *George Oppen: New Collected Poems,* Michael Davidson, ed., New Directions, 2008, p. 159. © 2008 New Directions. / "The Forms of Love," *George Oppen: New Collected Poems,* New Directions, 2008, p. 106. / Maritain, "epigraph to Eclogue," *George Oppen: New Collected Poems,* Michael Davidson, ed., New Directions, 2008, p. 38. / Lukas, Michael, review of *Notes from No Man's Land, Georgia Review* 63(3), Board of Regents of the University System of Georgia, Fall 2009, pp. 536-537.

List of Subjects

Introduction   xiii

List of Contributors   xv

RAYMOND ANDREWS   1
Emily Wright

NATHAN ASCH   17
Robert Buckeye

HENRY BESTON   31
Dan Brayton

EULA BISS   45
Jen Hirt

PETER DAVISON   61
Guy Rotella

DEGANAWIDA, THE PEACEMAKER   81
Christopher Buck

ERIC GANSWORTH   101
Elizabeth DeLaney Hoffman

ALLEGRA GOODMAN   117
Sanford Pinsker

ALFRED HAYES   133
Robert Buckeye

DAVID HUDDLE   147
Ann McKinstry Micou

HELENE JOHNSON   163
Eleanor Wakefield

WILLIAM KITTREDGE   177
Susan Carol Hauser

JAMES McBRIDE   191
Allen Guy Wilcox

BICH MINH NGUYEN   207
Kathleen Pfeiffer

GEORGE OPPEN   223
Anton Vander Zee

JOHN KENNEDY TOOLE   239
Jeffrey Bickerstaff

KATHERINE VAZ   255
Nancy Bunge

CAROLYN WELLS   271
Windy Counsell Petrie

Cumulative Index   289

Introduction

Carlos Fuentes, the Mexican novelist, once said with some irritation: "Don't classify me. Read me. I'm a writer, not a genre." As it happens, most of the writers we discuss in this supplement of *American Writers* are difficult, if not impossible, to classify by genre. To a surprising degree, in fact, this has been true of many of the writers we have treated since the series began. American writers have almost always liked to range widely, moving away from genre, crossing boundaries, and working against the grain of fixed impressions or the expectations that genres seem to demand from an author.

American Writers itself, as a publishing project, began with a series of critical and biographical monographs that came out between 1959 and 1972. The *Minnesota Pamphlets on American Writers* were clearly written, smart, and informative, treating ninety-seven American writers in a format and style that attracted a considerable following of readers. These articles on major writers proved invaluable to a generation of students and teachers, who found they could depend on them for reliable, deeply thoughtful, often penetrating critiques. The notion of reprinting the articles occurred to Charles Scribner, Jr. (1921-1995), the well-known publisher. Four substantial volumes titled *American Writers: A Collection of Literary Biographies* appeared in 1974.

Since then, twenty-six supplements have followed, focusing on well over two hundred American writers in any number of genres—novelists and writers of short stories for adults and children, poets, essayists, autobiographers, dramatists, critics, travel writers and screenwriters. The goal has been consistent: to provide clear, informative essays aimed at the general reader, which includes students in high school and college. As anyone looking through this new collection will notice, these essays often rise to a high level of craft and critical vision, yet they aim to introduce a writer of note in the history of American literature, offering a sense of the scope and nature of the career under review. The relevant biographical and historical backgrounds are also provided, putting the work itself in a living context.

The authors of these articles have published in their fields, and several are well-known. As anyone glancing through this volume will observe, they have been held to the highest standards of good writing and intelligent scholarship. The essays each conclude with a select bibliography intended to direct the reading of those who wish to pursue the subject further.

As noted above, few of the authors we engage here have specialized in one genre, although most are better known in one field or another. Among those who seem most at home in fiction are Raymond Andrews, the African-American novelist, Nathan Asch, who wrote four novels as well as nonfiction, Eric Gansworth, who is also poet visual artist, Allegra Goodman, who moves easily between novels and short stories, Alfred Hayes, the author of novels, poetry, and screenplays, James McBride, a novelist and memoirist, Bich Minh Nguyen, author of novels and nonfiction, John Kennedy Toole (who died too young to try his hand at other genres), Katherine Vaz, author of novels and short stories, and the vastly prolific Carolyn Wells, who wrote dozens of novels for adults and children as well as some popular light verse.

We discuss three writers who have tended to focus in the area of nonfiction: Henry Beston, William Kittredge, and Eula Biss. Beston was mainly a nature writer, while Kittredge has moved easily between nonfiction and fiction, an

INTRODUCTION

apparent master of both genres. Biss has ranged widely over the field of nonfiction, winning a National Book Critics Circle Award in 2009 for a major book of critical essays on race in America.

Even the poets we deal with here have moved among genres. David Huddle is as much a poet as a novelist and writer of stories and essays. Peter Davison wrote mainly poems, but he was a shrewd critic and autobiographer as well. George Oppen was almost exclusively a poet, but he was closely involved with political movements in the period between the wars, and he was a publisher and founder of the Objectivist Movement, which had its heyday in the thirties. Helene Johnson was a poet of the Harlem Renaissance, although she wrote stories as well as poems, publishing in the twenties and early thirties.

One of the most unusual pieces in this collection treats the nearly legendary Native American figure, Deganawida, a founder of the Iroquois Confederacy who has become a kind of spiritual father to many Native American writers. He was influential in establishing the code known as the Great Peace, a highly evolved piece of political thinking.

Most of the authors discussed in these pages have been written about in newspapers, magazines, and journals, but few have had the kind of focused attention they deserve. The articles collected here represent, in many cases, a first pass at sustained critical attention. Their work is, however, important, and merits the kind of close readings afforded here, which we hope will send readers back to the work itself.

—JAY PARINI

Contributors

Jeffrey Bickerstaff. Jeffrey Bickerstaff received his Ph.D. from Miami University of Ohio. He currently teaches writing and literature at Johnson State College and the Community College of Vermont. His research interests include representations of American politics in literature and film. JOHN KENNEDY TOOLE

Dan Brayton. Dan Brayton teaches at Middlebury College, where he is Associate Professor in the Department of English and American Literatures and the Program in Environmental Studies. He earned his doctorate from Cornell University in 2001. His book, *Shakespeare's Ocean: An Ecocritical Exploration,* published in 2012 by the University of Virginia Press, won the 2012 Northeast Modern Language Association Book Prize. He has also published an edited volume, *Ecocritical Shakespeare* (Ashgate 2011; with Lynne Bruckner) and numerous articles. In addition, he teaches for SEA Semester aboard sailing vessels in the Atlantic, Pacific, and Caribbean. HENRY BESTON

Christopher Buck. Christopher Buck, independent scholar and Pittsburgh attorney, publishes broadly in American studies, Native American studies, African American studies, religious studies, Islamic studies, and Baha'i studies. He is author of the books *God and Apple Pie* (2015), *Religious Myths and Visions of America* (2009), *Alain Locke: Faith and Philosophy* (2005), *Paradise and Paradigm* (1999), *Symbol and Secret* (1995/2004), and *Religious Celebrations* (co-author, 2011). He contributed book chapters to *'Abdu'l-Bahá's Journey West* (2013), *The Blackwell Companion to the Qur'an* (2006/ 2015), *The Islamic World* (2008), *American Writers* (2004/2010/2015), and *British Writers*

(2014), and has published various journal and encyclopedia articles as well. DEGANAWIDA, THE PEACEMAKER

Robert Buckeye. Robert Buckeye is author of four works of fiction, *Pressure Drop, The Munch Case, Left,* and *Still Lives,* as well as *Re: Quin* (Dalkey Archive Press, 2013), a study of English novelist Ann Quin; and a history of staff at Middlebury College. He has also published fiction, articles and reviews on literature, film and art in magazines. For more than thirty years he was Abernethy Curator of American Literature and College Archivist at Middlebury College. NATHAN ASCH; ALFRED HAYES

Nancy Bunge. A professor at Michigan State University, Nancy Bunge has also held senior Fulbright lectureships at the University of Vienna, the Free University of Brussels, the University of Ghent and the University of Siegen. Her essays have appeared in places like *Poets & Writers Magazine, the Writers Chronicle,* and the *Chronicle of Higher Education;* her most recent book is *The Midwestern Novel: Literary Populism from Huckleberry Finn to the Present.* KATHERINE VAZ

Susan Carol Hauser. Susan Carol Hauser is an essayist, poet and natural history writer with twelve books, most recently *Wild Rice: An Essential Guide to Cooking, Harvesting and History* and *Wild Sugar: The Pleasures of Making Maple Syrup.* Her grants and awards include a 2010 McKnight Artist Fellowship-Loft Award in Poetry and 2011 and 2015 Minnesota State Arts Board Artist Initiative Grants for Nonfiction. She is co-editor of *A Guide to the North Country National Scenic Trail in Minnesota*

CONTRIBUTORS

which received a 2014 award from the national North Country Trail Association. WILLIAM KITTREDGE

Jen Hirt. Jen Hirt is an assistant professor of creative writing at Penn State Harrisburg. She is the author of the memoir *Under Glass: The Girl With a Thousand Christmas Trees* (University of Akron 2010) and the Pushcart Prize-winning essay "Lores of Last Unicorns." Her essays have received grants and fellowships from the Pennsylvania Council on the Arts, Bernheim Arboretum, and the Ohioana Library. EULA BISS

Elizabeth DeLaney Hoffman. Elizabeth DeLaney Hoffman edited *American Indians and Popular Culture* (Praeger, 2012), a two-volume collection of essays that seeks to help readers understand American Indians by analyzing their relationships with the popular culture of the United States and Canada. She has been an editor for academic presses (books and journals) for over a decade. She teaches English at Athens Technical College in Athens, Georgia. ERIC GANSWORTH

Ann McKinstry Micou. Ann McKinstry Micou is a writer who lives in Montclair, New Jersey; she received a D.Litt. from Drew University in 2014. She is the author of a trilogy of reference books about the role and importance of place in fiction set in Vermont. Her essay on Howard Frank Mosher appears in *American Writers, Supplement XXII* (2011). DAVID HUDDLE

Windy Counsell Petrie. Windy Counsell Petrie (Ph.D., University of Delaware, 2001) is Associate Professor and Chair of English at Colorado Christian University. Her research focuses on the overlapping territories and techniques of autobiography and fiction. In 2006, she served as a Fulbright Scholar to Lithuania, lecturing on representations of exile in nineteenth- and twentieth-century novels as well as the roles of female and African-American authors in American literary history. Her most recent publications examine autobiog-

raphy as rhetoric as well as autobiographical and fictional depictions of expatriatism in the early twentieth century. CAROLYN WELLS

Kathleen Pfeiffer. Kathleen Pfeiffer, Ph.D. is professor and chair of English at Oakland University in Rochester, Michigan. Her books include *Brother Mine: The Correspondence of Jean Toomer and Waldo Frank* (2010) and *Race Passing and American Individualism* (2003). She has edited and written the introductions to the re ???? issues of two Harlem Renaissance novels, Carl Van Vechten's *Nigger Heaven* (2000) and Waldo Frank's *Holiday* (2003). In 2012, she was awarded the Kresge Artist Fellowship in Literary Arts. BICH MINH NGUYEN

Sanford Pinsker. Sanford Pinsker is an emeritus professor of Humanities at Franklin and Marshall College. He currently lives in south Florida where he continues to read and write about contemporary American literature. ALLEGRA GOODMAN

Guy Rotella. Guy Rotella is emeritus professor of English at Northeastern University. He has published widely on modern and postmodern poetry, including essays in *American Literature* and *Contemporary Literature*. His most recent book is *Castings: Monuments and Monumentality in Poems by Elizabeth Bishop, Robert Lowell, James Merrill, Derek Walcott, and Seamus Heaney.* PETER DAVISON

Anton Vander Zee. Anton Vander Zee is Assistant Professor of English at the College of Charleston. With a primary interest in poetry and poetic, he co-edited and introduced the edited collection *A Broken Thing: Poets on the Line* (U. of Iowa Press) and has published on a range of writers, from John Milton and Walt Whitman to Wallace Stevens and contemporary poets such as C. K. Williams and Mary Ann Samyn. GEORGE OPPEN

Eleanor Wakefield. Eleanor Wakefield is a Ph.D. candidate in American poetry at the University of Oregon. Her research interests

CONTRIBUTORS

include the history of the sonnet, twentieth-century poetry, and philosophy in poetry. She teaches composition and literature at the UO and also teaches dance classes in the Eugene area. HELENE JOHNSON

Allen Guy Wilcox. Allen Guy Wilcox was born in Cooperstown, New York, and grew up on his parents' farm in the Mohawk Valley. Educated at Middlebury College, he has lived in Brooklyn, New York since 2005. He is a regular contributor to the *Brooklyn Rail.* JAMES McBRIDE

Emily Wright. Emily Wright is professor of English at Methodist University, where she teaches composition, women's studies, and southern literature. She became interested in the works of Raymond Andrews when she worked with him as his editor at Peachtree Publishers in Atlanta, Georgia. RAYMOND ANDREWS

AMERICAN WRITERS

RAYMOND ANDREWS

(1934—1991)

Emily Wright

RAYMOND ANDREWS WAS born into a sharecropping family in rural Morgan County, Georgia, on June 6, 1934. As an adult, he traveled to the Midwest, the Far East, New York City, and Europe. But it was in rural Clarke County, Georgia, just one county removed from his birthplace, that he ended his life with a self-inflicted bullet wound on November 25, 1991.

At the time of his death, rumors abounded as to why Andrews killed himself at the age of fifty-seven. There was talk of an unsuccessful love affair, health problems, financial problems, housing issues. Andrews may have had several reasons to be depressed. However, a major cause of his despair was that his writing had not garnered him the recognition or the remuneration he expected, needed, and deserved.

Andrews attributed this lack of reward primarily to the subject matter of his works: life among rural African Americans in the southern United States in the early twentieth century. Andrews wrote about the people he knew from his childhood: the African Americans who did not go north during the Great Migration but instead stayed at home in the rural South. Andrews felt that this group had been neglected by historians and writers alike; with the exception of Zora Neale Hurston, he felt, African American writers had turned their backs on their southern roots, embarrassed by the poverty, lack of education, and racial oppression experienced by their relatives in that region. Andrews, by contrast, like Hurston, celebrated the vibrancy and richness of southern black folk life, and although racial oppression certainly appears in his novels, it does not take center stage. As Andrews wrote in a piece titled "The Necessity of Blacks' Writing Fiction About the South," speaking of his own childhood, "I knew we were victims ... yet knew we were much more. And this 'more' was what I wanted to write about" (p. 297). Therefore, his work focuses less on oppression than on the colorful characters, lively escapades, and complicated family dynamics of a southern black community—and just as Hurston was marginalized in her day for her similar focus, so Andrews felt he was similarly marginalized.

If Andrews invites comparison with Hurston, he also brings to mind William Faulkner. Like Faulkner, Andrews turned to his own "postage stamp of native soil" for the material of his fiction, mining his own family and local history to create his mythical landscape—Muskhogean County, modeled on Andrews' home county. Like Faulkner's Yoknapatawpha County, Muskhogean County is peopled by a large, intersecting cast of colorful characters with complex stories, and, like Faulkner, Andrews told those stories in a unique and original prose style. Andrews contributed to American literature not only by relating the little-understood history of southern rural black people but also by describing that history in an utterly original voice.

Ultimately, it is Andrews' unique narrative perspective, rambunctious "speakerly" voice, and intertextual resonances that account for his appeal. A completely self-taught writer who absorbed a myriad of popular-culture influences while growing up, Andrews produced fiction that is part Saturday matinee, part Sunday cartoon, and part tall tale, with a dash of film noir and a pinch of Zane Gray, a lot of Faulkner, some Hurston, a church service here and there, and a generous helping of François Rabelais. This lively mix of influences results in prose that is highly pleasurable to read. At its best, Andrews' prose rocks, it rollicks, it bounces—from character to character and scene to scene, his energetic

1

storytelling voice bringing character and scene to life with a flick of the pen before moving on to the next plot point, the next vivid scenario, the next colorful character. As *Kirkus Reviews* put it in a review of *Jessie and Jesus and Cousin Claire* (August 15, 1991), reading an Andrews novel is "like listening to a country-store denizen on speed."

Underneath this engaging comic vision lies a seething anger and bitterness, however, for Andrews had an ax to grind—not so much about being black in a white world as about being half-caste in a black-white world. As a very light-skinned black man, Andrews suffered at the hands of both whites and blacks, and his works as a whole explore the pain inflicted on mixed-race people. Andrews considered this his main theme, and he had serious things to say about it. Alongside that seriousness, however, was Andrews' palpable affection for his characters and amusement at their antics—and nowhere is that affection and amusement more apparent than when he described his own family and childhood in the early decades of the twentieth century. That is the material of *The Last Radio Baby*, the first volume of his memoir.

EARLY YEARS: THE LAST RADIO BABY

Described by *People* magazine as "a cross between *Roots* and *A Prairie Home Companion*," *The Last Radio Baby* (1990) begins with Andrews' grandparents, who met around the turn of the twentieth century. His grandmother, Jessie Rose Lee Brightwell, was reportedly called Jessie Rose Lee Wildcat Tennessee by her father. Part Native American, part white, and part black, Jessie married a black man named Eddie Andrews, but he faded into the background when Jessie became the mistress of the county's most prominent white man, Jim Orr. Orr, who never married, kept Jessie as his mistress, giving her land, a house, and even servants. She in turn became a kind of matriarch to the black community, with whom she generously shared her wealth. Orr never acknowledged Andrews as his grandson but did exhibit interest in him. He saved

his old newspapers and other materials for Andrews to read, and as Andrews grew older, the two spent more and more time together, reading, listening to the radio, and talking.

Orr and Jessie's second-oldest son, George Cleveland, was Raymond Andrews' father. He married Viola Crawford Perryman, who came from a family that valued education and who insisted that her children go to school whenever they could be spared from farm work. She also encouraged them to spend time reading and writing at home. Andrews' father did not support his children's education, fearing it would unsuit them for their lives as sharecroppers, but he was an avid reader, as was the entire family. Much of the family's reading consisted of newspapers and other periodicals, especially the *Atlanta Constitution* and the "colored" papers: the *Chicago Defender*, the *Pittsburgh Courier*, and the *Atlanta Daily World*. As he moved into his teen years, Andrews discovered novels. He began with series such as the Nancy Drew and Tom Swift novels and eventually moved on to genre fiction, becoming an avid reader of detective novels, mystery fiction, and westerns.

The Andrews family was not only bookish but also artistic. Viola supplied her children with drawing materials and encouraged them to follow the example of their father, George, an avid "drawer" who drew on everything from the dirt in the front yard to the sides of abandoned barns. The most artistic of the Andrews children was Raymond's next-oldest brother, Benny, who enjoyed creating his own comic books. As Andrews explained in his memoir, he helped Benny with his comic books by supplying him with appropriate images from the stockpile he kept under his bed, where he had cardboard boxes stuffed with "the funnies, the movie, sport, and radio sections of the newspapers, funny books, movie, radio, and sport magazines, football scrapbooks, and detective, mystery, and western (predominantly paperback) novels" (p. 78).

In addition to reading—and re-reading—everything he could get his hands on, Andrews went to Madison every chance he got to see the "picture show." This was the start of an interest

in film that was only surpassed by his enthusiasm for sports. Beginning with the Joe Louis fights he and his community listened to on the radio, Andrews developed an encyclopedic knowledge of sports history, especially baseball and basketball history. He also enjoyed playing baseball with playmates, although, as he describes his community's version of baseball in *The Last Radio Baby*, the rules were rather different from the official ones. This was even more the case with football, which, according to his first published piece, "A Football Rebellion in Backwoods Georgia," he and his brother Benny introduced, in radically modified form, to his home community.

In *The Last Radio Baby*, Andrews described a missing piece of American history: the daily doings of rural blacks in the Deep South in the 1930s and 1940s. As Andrews describes this world, it is filled with brothers, sisters, aunts, uncles, cousins, possum hunts, hog killings, superstitions, funerals, church revivals, courtship rituals, and, always, work. Over the course of his childhood, Andrews worked at sawmills, in peach orchards, and in cotton fields (although he was a notoriously slow cotton picker because he was always busy daydreaming or acting out scenes from movies instead of picking cotton). This was Andrews' world until the age of fifteen, when he went to live in Atlanta.

TEENAGE YEARS: ONCE UPON A TIME IN ATLANTA

By 1949 Raymond's oldest brother, Harvey, had gone to live at the Butler Street YMCA in Atlanta, where he attended Booker T. Washington High School at night. In December of that year, Raymond joined Harvey, an experience he recounted in the second volume of his autobiography, *Once Upon a Time in Atlanta*, published in 1998, after his death.

During this period, Andrews worked at a variety of jobs during the day and attended high school at night. Although he managed to graduate, he exhibited little interest in school, preferring to spend his time in movie theaters and at ballgames (an important memory was seeing Jackie Robinson play baseball for the Dodgers); attending to the lively doings on Auburn Avenue, or "Sweet Auburn," the commercial center of the black section of Atlanta; and listening to the R&B music emanating from nightclubs up and down Decatur Street. In Atlanta, Andrews encountered black-owned business, all-black radio stations, even black policemen. At the same time that he was empowered by this experience, he also experienced racial conflict—not just because he was black but also because he was a light-skinned African American.

Andrews was so light-skinned that he was frequently taken for white. For this reason, he did not exercise the kind of vigilance darker-skinned blacks learned to exercise. He entered all-white theaters at times, strolled about in white neighborhoods with impunity, and failed to take the precaution of sitting at the back of the bus. It was not that he wanted to pass as white so much as that he often did pass as white without even thinking about it. And then, one day, while Andrews was taking a bus to work, a white woman insisted that he move to the back. Andrews was thoroughly humiliated. As he put it in his memoir, "Thus on that early Saturday morning I, publicly, ceased to be a person and became a 'colored' person" (p. 57).

From that time forward, Andrews only rode buses in the black areas of town, and when he did, he sat in the very last seat—because otherwise, black passengers, taking him for white, tried to sit behind him. This difficulty of placement plagued Andrews throughout the remainder of his life and was evident in his adolescent sex life as well: at one point in Atlanta he had an affair with a white woman that he had to work very hard to keep secret, but when he tried to date black girls, their parents often considered him too white. In Atlanta, Andrews discovered not only racism directed by whites toward blacks but also "colorism"—prejudice based on color within the black community. He claimed that neither whites nor blacks wanted him around because with either group, he had to be "explained." "But," he went on, "I always had to be *somewhere*" (p. 96).

RAYMOND ANDREWS

YOUTH AND ADULTHOOD

Problems related to skin color continued to plague Andrews in the military. Following once again in the footsteps of his older brothers, in 1952 Andrews enlisted in the U.S. Air Force and served in the Korean War, the first American war in which the military was integrated. There Andrews continued to cause confusion due to his light skin. When inducted, he was initially mistaken as white, and at one point, while traveling across the country with a white friend, he accidentally ended up at a Ku Klux Klan rally. Fortunately, by keeping his hat on despite pressure to remove it, he managed to escape the rally without anyone discovering that he was black.

After four years in the Air Force, in 1957 Andrews enrolled as a freshman at Michigan State University. While there, he had his first encounter with "literary" writers. As he later wrote his roommate, the fiction writer and poet Gary Gildner, up until his time at MSU he had considered Zane Grey and Erle Stanley Gardner to be great writers and *Peyton Place* to be a classic, but in college he first learned about writers such as Ernest Hemingway, F. Scott Fitzgerald, and Sinclair Lewis. As he later wrote Gildner, "It was only after leaving MSU that I started to read *real* writers" (Gildner, p. 435). He also apologized to Gildner for having "passed" as white while at MSU. As he explained, it wasn't so much that he intended to mislead people as that he didn't feel it was appropriate to make an issue of his race, especially since the people whom he enjoyed spending time with inevitably told him that they didn't care about his race anyway.

Perhaps partly due to discomfort around this issue but also due to lack of funds, he left MSU in 1958 and moved to New York, where he soon got a job with KLM Airlines—a position that he held for more than eight years and that enabled him to travel and live in Europe. Upon arriving in New York, he had thoughts of attending New York University, but that didn't work out, and therefore his sparse schooling came to an end.

Andrews was always self-conscious about his lack of education. As he explained in an interview with William Walsh, "Most people didn't know how to read where I came from let alone think about writing" (p. 24). He added that his childhood schooling had been weak and intermittent, and he expressed anxiety about his ignorance of grammar and punctuation. As he told interviewer Elfriede Kristwald,

> The thought of becoming a writer was always with me. But for years, it was kept at bay by my fear of grammar. My Georgia schooling had been poor and I didn't feel that it had gotten significantly better in college…. But then, the overpowering urge to write won out and forced me—at age 32—to put all those words on paper, regardless of the grammar. So, po' English and all, here I is!
>
> (pp. 102–103)

Andrews turned thirty-two in 1966, and this was the year when his need to write "erupted," as he put it. "Apparently, like a volcano, the pressure [to write] was building up inside of me. You could say, almost in an orderly fashion. But when it reached a certain level, it surfaced so suddenly and so dramatically that it could be called an 'eruption,'" he told Kristwald (p. 103). As a result of this eruption, and with the encouragement of his new wife, Adelheid (Heidi) Wagner, whom he married in 1966, Andrews quit his job at KLM Airlines and began devoting himself to writing. In *Sports Illustrated*, he had read a nostalgic piece set in a small Canadian town, and this experience encouraged him to think that perhaps he could publish something about his own small-town background. The result was "A Football Rebellion in Backwoods Georgia." When *Sports Illustrated* accepted the article, Andrews' career had begun.

Between 1966 and 1980, Andrews wrote the three volumes of the Muskhogean County trilogy and a variety of unpublished writings, including the novel "Ninety-Nine Years and a Dark Day," which is based on the history of his mother's side of the family. However, he had great difficulty finding a publisher. In later years Andrews joked, in typical self-deprecating fashion, that his manuscripts were returned to him so quickly, he thought the editors must be working at his local post office. While writing and circulating manuscripts, Andrews worked at various odd jobs and traveled back and forth from New York to Europe with his Swiss wife. Eventually, after a decade of

effort, Andrews found a publisher when Dial Press accepted *Appalachee Red.*

THE MUSKHOGEAN COUNTY TRILOGY, VOLUME 1: APPALACHEE RED

In the Kristwald interview, Andrews explained that when his need to write "erupted," the result was *Appalachee Red* (1978). Referring to the novel as "that 'Krakatoa,'" he explained, "It was a time when I had bottled up thoughts, ideas and experiences and when all of that suddenly flowed out of me" (p. 103). The result was a novel that, he said, he could never write again.

Appalachee Red begins in 1918 in a small town in north Georgia, Appalachee. A black man, Big Man Thompson, has been wrongly sentenced to a year in jail. In his absence his wife, Little Bit, is pressured into having sex with her employer's son, John Morgan. She becomes pregnant and delivers a "red" (near-white) baby, whom she sends away to Chicago to be raised by a sister. Many years later, an encounter with a racist sheriff results in Big Man's death and Little Bit's premature delivery of their only child, Blue Thompson—so named because, as his mother says of the infant, "hit's so black, hit's blue" (p. 52).

Years later, on Thanksgiving Day 1945, a mysterious stranger arrives in town. A huge, light-skinned black man, he is christened "Appalachee Red," and the mere sight of him fills the Appalachee citizens with unease. Setting up shop in "Dark Town," where the darker-skinned blacks live, Red opens a combined gambling casino, liquor store, and dance hall, which he operates with his lover, Baby Sweet, and a colorful cast of characters: Big Apple, who claims to be a "brown-skinned Jew"; Snake, a roughneck from Hard Labor Hole who becomes Red's chauffeur; and Darling Pullman, the gay man, or "punk," who becomes Red's cook and who is adored by another of Red's employees, the ever-giggling Mary Mac Mapp.

Over the years, Red attains mythic status in the minds of the black and white communities alike. In keeping with the ominous passages from Revelations that begin each section of the novel, Red is presented in apocalyptic terms, as a harbinger of death and justice. He is unnervingly silent and rarely ever seen. Aside from his companion, Baby Sweet, the only townspeople Red seems interested in are Blue and Little Bit Thompson. As Blue enters his teenage years, Red gives him employment and then offers to finance Blue's college education. While Blue is at college, Red makes sure that Little Bit is taken care of.

The story climaxes when Little Bit dies and Blue, now a civil rights activist, returns to Appalachee. Blue stages a sit-in and winds up in jail. Red goes to see him there, and it comes out that the two men are half-brothers, both sons of Little Bit Thompson. As the narrative leads up to her funeral (scheduled for November 22, 1963, the day of John F. Kennedy's assassination), the focus shifts from the black to the white side of Red's family. At this point the reader learns that every Sunday since his arrival in 1945, Red has driven to the foot of Morgan Hill and stood for a while, smoking a cigarette and staring up the hill at the mansion from which Roxanne Morgan, his white half-sister, has stared back in fascination. Over the years, she has become obsessed with Red, and at the funeral, she ends up throwing herself into Red's black Cadillac. Red and Roxanne are last seen driving out of town, and after their departure Sheriff White, the killer of Big Man Thompson, is found dead at Red's Café.

With this first novel in the Muskhogean County trilogy, Andrews presented himself as a kind of literary folk artist. His meandering plot, lack of focus on a particular character or theme, and oddly unmediated narrative perspective reflected, perhaps, his lack of education. These problems repelled some reviewers, such as Alan Ryan of the *Los Angeles Times*, who faulted Andrews for his "failure of craftsmanship." Most reviewers, however, while noting flaws, were intrigued by the bold, fresh, witty, and in some ways very sophisticated quality of Andrews' writing. For example, Bud Foote of the *Detroit News* wrote that, despite the book's "shortcomings," this was "a first novel of power and skill and mystery" (November 19, 1978). Similarly,

the *Guardian*, while describing the novel as "a shade long-winded," admired its "drive and style" and the way the author "keeps three balls in the air—mysterious, sinister, darkly comic" (January 24, 1980). The *Chicago Tribune* also admired its "fusion of racy comedy and horror or pathos" (November 12, 1978), and *Kirkus Reviews* (August 15, 1991) appreciated Andrews' "inexhaustible energy for storytelling."

Most critics were completely swept away by that energy, becoming caught up in the story Andrews was telling and in the lively, humorous, bawdy, suspenseful way he told it. Charles H. Gold of the *Chicago Sun-Times,* for example, raved about the "dazzling virtuosity" of the novel and concluded, "It's that rare thing—a great book" (October 29, 1978). Most reviewers welcomed Andrews as a fresh new voice with a unique story to tell: that of rural and small-town southern blacks in the first half of the twentieth century. The *San Francisco Sunday Examiner & Chronicle*, for example, praised *Appalachee Red* for telling a "solid, truthful, and evocative story whose time has finally come" (December 17, 1978). Fran Podulka of the *Milwaukee Journal* claimed that as a work of "social history," the novel could become a "classic" (November 26, 1978).

In general, the reviewers praised *Appalachee Red* and its author and agreed that the novel was a deserving winner of the James Baldwin Prize, awarded in 1979 by the Dial Press, Baldwin's publisher. They also appreciated its illustrations, contributed by Andrews' brother Benny, who had by this time completed his undergraduate degree at the Art Institute of Chicago and established himself as a successful painter, collage artist, and activist on behalf of African American art. In his suggestive line drawings, Benny sought to do figuratively what Raymond was doing in words—capture the look and feel of the rural South in the 1930s, '40s, and '50s. Featuring such scenes as peach pickers dancing ecstatically in an orchard, a family sitting down to cornbread and milk, a farmer trudging behind his mule, or a nattily dressed chauffeur leaning up against a Cadillac, Benny's drawings capture the mood and flavor of the rural South, from its good-timing men and women to its rustic farm families. Like Raymond's writing, Benny's drawings are energetic, vivid, and witty, providing an important visual context for Raymond's prose. Not only *Appalachee Red* but all of Raymond's works were illustrated by Benny, in a collaboration that lasted even after Raymond's death.

THE MUSKHOGEAN COUNTY TRILOGY, VOLUME 2: ROSIEBELLE LEE WILDCAT TENNESSEE

The second volume of the Muskhogean County trilogy (1980) is anomalous; although it is tangentially linked to the events of volumes 1 and 3, in fact it interrupts a story that begins in *Appalachee Red* and ends in *Baby Sweet's*, the trilogy's third volume. In this second novel, Andrews takes a break from the story he started in volume 1 to tell another story—that of his own family.

As its title indicates, the novel's focus is on Andrews' grandmother, reportedly nicknamed "Jessie Rose Lee Wildcat Tennessee" by her father. Here Andrews tells of her mysterious arrival in the area, her lifelong attachment to a wealthy white man, her nurturing but controlling relationship with her black neighbors, and her four children and their families. In part 1 Andrews uses an omniscient perspective to establish the basic facts of Jessie/Rosiebelle's life, but in part 2 he uses a limited omniscient perspective. In most of part 2 the center of consciousness is Speck, a stand-in for Andrews' father, George Andrews, and toward the very end of part 2, the narrative perspective shifts briefly to the son of Speck/George—Richmond, who is Raymond Andrews himself. From these points of view, we learn about the four children of Jessie/Rosiebelle as of the day she announces that she will die.

As the afternoon moves into evening, everyone in the community comes to pay his or her respects, including such vivid characters as Crazy Coot the photographer; Cousin Tater and his possum-hunting pig, Roosevelt; and Tree, so called because of his height and his tendency to fall over, smashing everything around him. As the evening turns into night, the narrative moves from one character to another, describing each

one's increasingly frenetic actions and intensifying emotions. As Rosiebelle's death approaches, the atmosphere becomes more and more carnivalesque, concluding in a wild buck dance under the moonlight and driving Rosiebelle's son Sugar Boy into the arms of Betty Jean Prickard, daughter of the poor white "hillbilly" family living across the road. As Speck "buckdances" and "hambones" to the tune of Sugar Boy's harmonica, Sugar Boy becomes mesmerized by the sight of Betty Jean, playing her guitar across the road:

> Meantime, Sugar Boy was totally unaware of everything going on around him, and with the crowd whooping him on at his back, paying no attention to anyone now but him and the hillbilly gal. He just kept blowing his harp across at Betty Jean, and by now she was picking her guitar right back at him, while to her comely rear her folks were standing, sitting, and squatting on the porch and stoop and in the front yard of their darkened house.... fervidly hooting and hollering her on in the Saturday-night battle that was building up between the ... mean and low-down blues-blowing harp and their toetapping, knee-slapping, authentic fork-of-the-chick-style guitar. And now with sore lips and a tired tongue, Sugar Boy, both hands cupped tightly, just kept right on blowing and slobbering all over that overheated, moaning, groaning, hot-sounding harp, and kept staring feverishly over across the road at that pretty-as-peach-pie hillbilly gal, who was playing just as hard and as hot right straight back across at him, with her fiery fingers gripping the long neck of that ol' guitar like if she was to loosen her hold upon it just one mite that strange-looking Nigra man looming over across the road would slip away from her forever. Blow on, Sugar Boy, blow on! Pick it, Berry Jean, pick it! Lord, have mercy! San Antone!
>
> (pp. 217–218)

Not long after this scene, Rosiebelle comes off her deathbed to restore order, and what is described in *Baby Sweet's* as a "strange, sad, happy, crazy sort of night" (p. 153) comes to an end with Rosiebelle's death.

Rosiebelle Lee Wildcat Tennessee is a fictionalized version of Andrews' childhood as depicted in *The Last Radio Baby*. Arguably, it contains some of Andrews' best writing. Andrews himself said that after producing *Appalachee Red* in a kind of frenzy of bottled-up ideas and energy, he

settled into becoming a better writer. "By the time I got around to writing my second book, *Rosiebelle*, the seas were much calmer," he told Kristwald. "Following that 'Krakatoa,' things had settled down and that allowed me to ... write better" (p. 103). Indeed, in this novel, Andrews seems particularly relaxed, particularly on top of his game stylistically, writing with confidence and aplomb in a manner alternately sophisticated and colloquial. As a result, reviewers responded with even more enthusiasm for Andrews' stylistic mastery than they had expressed for his first novel. As David Heaton of the Cleveland *Plain Dealer* put it, Andrews' style "mixes hilarious epigrammatic idioms with lilting transcontinental sentences, a style that blends elegant with colloquial diction, sacred with profane exclamation" (August 3, 1980). The *Washington Post* described the novel as "totally captivating" (July 6, 1980), and the *Chicago Tribune Book World* (February 8, 1981) labeled it "a very distinguished novel."

However, just as Andrews employed a digressive technique within each volume of the trilogy, so this novel in its entirety is a digression, sharing little in common with the other two volumes of the trilogy except for a few characters. At the end of the novel, though, a link is made in the form of Betty Jean Prickard and Sugar Boy, who are last seen having sex in a ditch under the moonlight. That event leads to volume 3, which picks up directly after the events of *Appalachee Red*.

THE MUSKHOGEAN COUNTY TRILOGY, VOLUME 3: BABY SWEET'S

Part 1 of *Baby Sweet's* (published in 1983) begins in 1966, three years after the disappearance of Appalachee Red and his half-sister, Roxanne Morgan. In those three years, Baby Sweet has languished, and so has Red's Café. Its illegal components have been closed, leaving only the café itself, where, as a result of integration, fewer customers come to dine. Into this situation comes John Morgan, Jr., son of the original John Morgan who had impregnated Little Bit Thompson and produced Appalachee Red—and thus, unbeknownst to him, Appalachee Red's half-brother.

John Junior proposes that he and Baby Sweet turn Red's Café into a brothel.

The narrative then flashes back to 1944, when John Junior had encountered Betty Jean Prickard on her way out of town with the baby she had borne by Sugar Boy. Her father has banished her from their home because of her half-black bastard baby, and she is heading for Atlanta in the hopes of becoming a country music star. John Junior, struck by her plight, gives her money and a ride to the highway.

After describing this encounter, the narrative goes on to detail the life of John Junior, who devotes himself to countercultural rebellion against his father's expectations, becoming an artist, dilettante, and bohemian before finally abandoning his beatnik lifestyle, getting married, donning a suit, and becoming mysteriously enmeshed with the rowdy, redneck element in nearby Yankee Town. This enmeshment somehow produces John Junior's idea of opening a house of prostitution with Baby Sweet in what was formerly Red's Café. He enlists the aid of a pimp named Slick in acquiring three prostitutes with whom to open up the brothel.

Part 2 returns to the present day and the opening of Baby Sweet's. As the day progresses, the cast of characters assembles. Still in place are several characters introduced in *Appalachee Red*: Baby Sweet herself, the "black Jew" Big Apple, the "punk" Darling Pullman, his admirer Mary Mae Mapp, and the ever-present chorus of onlookers sitting on the porch of Blackshear's funeral parlor across the street. New on the scene are the first two prostitutes hired for the occasion, Fig and Lana Lips; T Cake, the old prostitute who had serviced the community for years before the opening of Baby Sweet's; the Pink Pickup Sisters, a suspected lesbian couple who drive a pink truck; Leroyrogers, who has the largest penis in town; and Rob and Rick Bash, two soldiers trying to lose their virginity before getting married.

As is typical, Andrews presents a number of colorful characters in the process of telling his story. However, the focus is on one character in particular: the "Third Whore" hired to work at Baby Sweet's, Lea, who turns out to be the child

of Sugar Boy and Betty Jean Prickard. In an awkward narrative turn, Lea's entrance into Muskhogean County is described from an omniscient perspective, then retold from Lea's perspective as she pours out her heart to Baby Sweet. Lea also tells Baby Sweet about her childhood and then retells that same information from her mother's perspective as she narrates to Baby Sweet the story her mother had told her before dying. Given that each new version adds little information to previous ones, this nested narration does not work in the way that it does in, say, Faulkner's *Absalom, Absalom!* In other ways, though, *Baby Sweet's* offers an interesting gloss on that very Faulkner novel. Whereas in *Absalom, Absalom!* an unacknowledged half-black brother is prevented from engaging in incest and miscegenation with his white sister, in *Baby Sweet's* it transpires that the half-black brother Red has succeeded in engaging in incest and miscegenation with his white half-sister, Roxanne Morgan, with the result that Roxanne has a mixed-race child by her own half-brother.

The Red-Roxanne plot is not the main focus of *Baby Sweet's*, however. According to Andrews in his preface, this is Lea's novel, not Appalachee Red's, Roxanne's, or, despite its title, Baby Sweet's. It is Lea's voice that dominates part 2 of the novel, where she narrates the devastating effects on her mother of having a mixed-race baby and the hardships endured by Lea herself for being neither white nor black. It is easy to imagine that Andrews spoke for himself here as he described Lea's growing up in the 1950s and '60s, and perhaps for that reason, the writing becomes strident and the voices fall flat. Also, Andrews' technique of focusing the latter third of his texts on a specific event is not as well handled as in the first two volumes of the trilogy. As Andrews builds toward the opening of Baby Sweet's brothel, he not only switches back and forth among various characters, as he had done toward the end of volumes 1 and 2, but he also switches back and forth among texts, incorporating snippets of a newspaper article about the elder Morgans' fortieth wedding anniversary; bits and pieces of a folk song; and verses of "The Signifying Monkey." This accumulation of texts begins

to seem frenetic, overdone, especially since, at the same time, descriptions of sexual matters become increasingly frequent and vulgar, resulting in an almost confrontationally insistent emphasis on the sweating, groaning, grunting, ejaculating body.

In fact, the novel ends with a sex act, when John Morgan, Sr., dies of a heart attack while having sex with Lea. By this time Lea has achieved healing through reconnection with her Muskhogean County relatives and has decided to renounce her bitterness along with her life as a prostitute. However, she agrees to have sex with one last customer—John Senior. At the end of *Baby Sweet's*, John Senior discovers that Red, the father of his grandchild, is not only a black man but also his own son. Shortly after this discovery, he dies atop Lea, and thus Andrews forces the narrative to a neat conclusion—a new business for Baby Sweet and John Junior, a new life and family for Lea, and the Faulkneresque conclusion of the saga of miscegenation that began in *Appalachee Red*.

Throughout the second half of *Baby Sweet's*, one feels Andrews reaching toward Faulkner in several different ways. It is while reading *Baby Sweet's* that the Andrews enthusiast begins to want to do what has been done for Faulkner and his fictional county: create a map of the county and genealogy charts for each of its major families: the "hillbilly" Prickards, the nouveau-rich white Thompson family, the tragic black Thompson family, the wealthy Morgan family, the formerly wealthy MacAndrew family, the mean, racist White family, and the mixed-race family resulting from the union of Rosiebelle Lee and Mr. Mac. These families and their interrelationships form the fabric of Muskhogean County, much as Faulkner's Sartorises and Compsons and Snopeses do in Yoknapatawpha. In this novel one can feel Andrews' desire to achieve the kind of scope Faulkner achieved and to present a complete sociological history of his county from the 1930s through the 1960s.

The results of his effort were somewhat mixed, but on the whole, the novel was well received. Carolyn Banks of the *Los Angeles Times* gently chided it for "expository overload" (June 26, 1983), David Guy, in *Washington Post Book World,* acknowledged some plotting and narration problems, but he went on to say, "One reads Andrews, however, for his raucous and robust humor, his really profound knowledge of the South, his ultimately accepting and benign vision ... and most of all for the entertaining voice that tells the stories" (July 31, 1983). Similarly, in the *New York Times Book Review*, Frederick Busch acknowledged both verbal clichés and psychological opaqueness in *Baby Sweet's* but pointed out that these are qualities found in the best of blues music and in every "backporch or barroom tale." Likening Andrews' prose to song, he concluded that "it is the music of Mr. Andrews's narrative that makes this book a pleasure to read" (July 24, 1983).

With the end of *Baby Sweet's*, Andrews had finished spinning the yarn he had begun in *Appalachee Red*, and for several years after completing the trilogy, he produced no new works. *Baby Sweet's* was published in 1983, but the novel was apparently completed by 1980, when Andrews was divorced, for Andrews later wrote to a friend that he did no writing after the divorce. While the separation from Heidi was amicable, it evidently derailed Andrews emotionally and creatively, for as he later wrote, "I *wasn't* [writing] ... in New York following my divorce when I went on a spree trying to make up for lost lovings and nearly got lost myself" (Gildner and Andrews, p. 462). In addition to losing his wife, Andrews was also losing his publisher, Dial Press, which was being dissolved by its parent company, Doubleday. Fortunately, however, after a few unproductive years, Andrews began writing again.

THE ATHENS YEARS

In 1984, when Andrews was fifty years old, he left New York and returned to Georgia determined to "get started again," as he put it in the interview with William Walsh (p. 26). At this time his older brother Benny, who continued to illustrate his novels, built a summer studio on a plot of land near Athens, Georgia, and Raymond began to spend winters there, using Benny's New York

apartment in the summers, when Benny and his family were in Georgia. Having worked since the age of six, when he entered the cotton fields, and having held numerous jobs throughout his life, Andrews was determined to support himself entirely through his writing. Although he was ultimately not able to do that, he did accomplish quite a bit in the last seven years of his life. In addition to writing two novellas and two volumes of his memoir, he also had publishing success. The Muskhogean County trilogy, out of print by this time, was reprinted by the University of Georgia Press in 1988 and 1989, by which time Andrews had developed a relationship with Peachtree Publishers, which published *The Last Radio Baby* in 1990 and *Jessie and Jesus and Cousin Claire* in 1991.

During these years, Andrews published essays and reviews, gave lectures and readings, participated in writing workshops, and gathered a devoted following around Athens and Atlanta. He also made some appearances with his brother Benny, such as an exhibit at the Wendell Street Gallery in Cambridge, Massachusetts, in May and June 1990, and with other members of his family as well. By this time his father had begun to achieve local recognition as a folk artist known as "the Dot Man," and his mother, who had written a weekly column on religion for an Atlanta bulletin, had also published a short story in a literary magazine. The remarkable creativity of the Andrews family was celebrated in several venues, including a Georgia library program titled "The Andrews Family of Morgan County: Arts and Letters in Rural Georgia" that was presented at regional libraries.

Through these appearances and recognitions, Andrews added to his circle of friends and admirers, while he also maintained an active writing schedule. Unfortunately, however, these career advances were not matched by remuneration. Andrews' publications had never yielded much profit, and this was increasingly a source of frustration and anxiety. His letters from the late 1980s reveal considerable financial stress, as well as increasing reliance on Benny for financial assistance. Eventually, Benny came to feel that Raymond was taking advantage of him for lodg-

ing and for money. A series of letters between the brothers addressed this concern, culminating in a letter of June 26, 1991, in which Benny asked Raymond to move out of the Athens house by Thanksgiving, when Benny was to arrive in Georgia from New York. On November 25, the day of Benny's arrival, Andrews shot himself in the back yard of the Athens house.

Andrews left a letter to Benny in which he claimed that his reason for committing suicide was primarily financial. He had had a surgical procedure of some sort the previous year and was having difficulty paying the bills. The nature of his surgery is unknown, as is the cause of the pain in his "joints and digestive system" that he mentions in his final letter. In that letter he explained that he refused to seek medical help because of the cost, preferring that any money his works might make go back into Benny's house or to his siblings' children. His final words were calm and uncomplaining; he thanked Benny for allowing him to spend his last years writing, expressed his love for his family, and asserted that he had no regrets.

Raymond's self-effacing and appreciative suicide letter does not tell the whole story. Those who knew Andrews around the time of his death know that he felt a professional rivalry with Benny, who had achieved a level of recognition and financial success that Raymond, working in a less accessible medium and without the benefit of formal training, simply could not achieve. This disparity galled Andrews, especially since its result was poverty. Although he accepted responsibility for the situation in which he found himself ("I chose this life myself ... and don't regret one moment of it," he wrote in his last letter), in conversations and interviews that took place in the late 1980s, he expressed frustration that his books had been marginalized by a literary establishment uninterested in rural African Americans, uncomfortable with the theme of miscegenation, and uncertain as to how to categorize and market his unusual books. Despite his frustration, however, his final letter, as well as a series of short final notes he left with various kinds of instructions, were written in typi-

cally self-effacing, courteous, even humorous tones.

Andrews' humor, humility, and gentleness were some of the qualities that attracted a devoted following of friends, editors, publishers, literature professors, and fellow writers who after his death organized a variety of tributes to honor him and his body of work: a memorial service on February 8, 1992, at the Atlanta–Fulton County Public Library; a place in a literary exhibit mounted at the same library in 1994 for the Olympic Games; posthumous publication of the second volume of Andrews' memoir, *Once Upon a Time in Atlanta*, by the *Chattahoochee Review* in 1998; a 2007 symposium on Andrews at Methodist University in Fayetteville, North Carolina; an event titled "Once Upon a Time in Athens: The Legacy of Raymond Andrews," sponsored by the *Georgia Review*, in October 2010; the production of an independent documentary film about Andrews titled *Somebody Else, Somewhere Else: The Raymond Andrews Story*, by Jesse Freeman, which aired on Georgia Public Broadcasting in 2010; and the publication of a special issue of the *Georgia Review* in fall 2010 devoted to Andrews, which includes tributes to Andrews by some of his more prominent friends and admirers as well as selections from two otherwise unpublished works. A final tribute was Andrews' receipt of the American Book Award from the Before Columbus Foundation. Andrews received this award in 1992 for *Jessie and Jesus and Cousin Claire*, which was published in 1991, just a few months after his death.

If it were not for this last work of Andrews', his suicide would make more sense. In all of his previous works, he had exploited his own family history, his childhood, and his teenage years to present a series of engaging novels and memoirs about southern African Americans in the first half of the twentieth century. Each of his works had revisited that same time and place from a different angle, and it was beginning to seem that he had nothing more to say—that he had already made whatever contribution to American literature he was going to make. If this had indeed been the case, his suicide, however tragic, would have possessed a certain logic. However, tidy conclusions about Andrews' oeuvre are obliterated by *Jessie and Jesus and Cousin Claire*.

JESSIE AND JESUS AND COUSIN CLAIRE

Andrews' last work of fiction—consisting of the novellas "Jessie and Jesus" and "Cousin Claire"—marked an entirely new direction. While these novellas pick up where the Muskhogean County trilogy left off, in the late 1960s and 1970s, references to Muskhogean County places and people are minimal. And while the text as a whole provides fascinating insights into the rise of a southern black middle class, here Andrews' interest is not sociological or genealogical but psychological.

Each novella focuses on a young black woman who has been damaged by her father in particular and patriarchal values in general. Jessie's father fatally wounds her by showing preference to her brothers, and Cousin Claire's father abandons her. Each woman, in turn, develops a hard-hearted determination to get her way and achieve revenge. In her efforts to monopolize her father's love—and his property— Jessie is responsible for several deaths and one castration. In her effort to achieve revenge on her father's first love, Luella, and to get her hands on Luella's house, Cousin Claire kills Luella herself, Luella's daughter-in-law, and Luella's husband. However, both women are ultimately unsuccessful in their aims. Jessie's plan is sabotaged when her best friend bears a second son by Jessie's father, thus supplying him with a new male heir, and Claire's plan is sabotaged by the appearance of her father's other abandoned daughter, Cousin Claudia.

These stories are tragedies; as is always the case with Andrews, real human injustice lies at the core of the story. In the trilogy, the injustices have to do with race; in the novellas, they are gender related. But as with the trilogy, the fundamental tragedy is delivered in a kind of exaggerated, almost cartoonlike manner that adds elements both of comedy and of unreality, rendering the narratives more like morality plays or allegories than like novels in the realistic tradition. At the same time, however, in the character of

Jessie Mitchell, Andrews achieves what may be his most astute—and realistic—character analysis.

Jessie Mitchell reminds one of Appalachee Red. Both are menacing, mysterious, and motivated by revenge: Red for his father's rejection of him on the basis of his race, and Jessie for her father's rejection of her on the basis of her sex. However, Appalachee Red is seen entirely from the outside; he has no psychological depth beyond what the reader might imagine him to have. Not unlike Charles Bon in Faulkner's *Absalom! Absalom!* he is more symbol than character, representing the return of the repressed, the avenging angel seeking retribution for the racial and familial crimes of the father. Jessie, on the other hand, is a much more rounded character. Vulnerable, capable of affection, loyalty, and guilt, and usually unaware of her own motivations, Jessie is dangerous in the way real people can become dangerous when they are hurt and proceed to act out their pain without self-awareness. Claire of "Cousin Claire" is a flatter character, reminiscent of Lea in *Baby Sweet's*, but Jessie Mitchell of "Jessie and Jesus" reflects a psychological depth that is new in Andrews' writing. Also new for Andrews is the heavy reliance on dialogue in these two novellas. Whereas Andrews' earlier attempts at dialogue were few and awkward, in the novellas the characters reveal themselves largely through convincing, well-handled conversations. Finally, whereas his other texts had been long, loose, and episodically structured, each of the novellas is short and tightly focused.

Perhaps because of Andrews' death shortly before its publication, *Jessie and Jesus and Cousin Claire* was not as widely reviewed as his earlier works. However, the reviews that did come out were positive. *Kirkus Reviews* appreciated the novellas for their "colorful characters and roller-coaster plotline[s]" (October 1, 1991); Al Young in the *Washington Post Book World* (February 16, 1992) described them as "a pair of eccentric, spellbinding yarns"; and Pam Perry in the *Atlanta Journal Constitution* praised their "dark comic power that deftly combine tragedy and farce to reveal deep undercurrents of emotional truth" (November 10, 1991).

In *Jessie and Jesus and Cousin Claire*, Andrews proved that as a writer he could grow and develop in interesting ways. Unfortunately that was not to be. However, through the six book-length works he published, he made an important contribution to American social history and contributed an absolutely original voice and style to American literature. In the years since his death, a number of critics have examined this legacy.

LEGACY: ANDREWS AS HISTORIAN

From the beginning, Andrews has been appreciated as a social historian. His entertaining descriptions of the everyday lives of rural and small-town African Americans offer readers a rare glimpse into a time, place, and population that had been given short shrift by other black writers, who, with the exception of Zora Neale Hurston, viewed the area from a distance, and often disparagingly. The people about whom Andrews writes—the southern black peasantry of the first half of the twentieth century—have tended to be thought of as lacking the will or the ability to move north to the "promised land" during the Great Migration and thereafter. As Brennan Collins shows in his dissertation, "'Forsaking the Promised Land,'" Andrews and Hurston were unique among black writers for possessing what Brennan calls an "in-group southern perspective" rather than the expatriate, northern perspective of most black writers. Although Andrews paid more attention than Hurston to important historical events, especially the Great Migration and the civil rights movement, like Hurston he viewed these events entirely from a rural, southern perspective.

Andrews recognized his kinship with Hurston, and he also recognized their shared marginalization. As Collins and other critics have shown, Hurston's focus on the southern black peasantry was not well taken by the black intelligentsia of her time, and she was marginalized by the Harlem Renaissance literati as a result. Andrews felt that he was being similarly margin-

alized for not writing about the kinds of African Americans New York publishers expected to encounter. In Andrews' unpublished novel "Ninety-Nine Years and a Dark Day," the character Richmond Crawford, a writer and thinly disguised stand-in for Andrews himself, complains that what he calls the "Northeast Elite," which controls the publishing world, "honestly believ[es] the overwhelming majority of blacks to be inner city/ghetto/drug victims. Finding it impossible to envision any black living outside of such an environment, publishers have difficulties dealing with my type of writing, involving the lives of small town and rural black folk" (p. 292). In the publishers' view, Richmond/Raymond asserts, all African Americans can be divided into two types: "the sympathetic—the noble servant savage" and "the pathetic—society's-fault junkie" (p. 292). This oversimplification should be corrected, Andrews thought, and it should be corrected through the writing of fiction. In "The Necessity of Blacks' Writing Fiction About the South," Andrews wrote,

> It is, I strongly feel[,] important for blacks to write fiction about the South. I say fiction because practically all of the books I've seen written about the South by blacks have been nonfiction, mostly black history. I am a history buff, so I know history is very important. Yet in wanting to learn about the everyday lives and thoughts of everyday people from any given society of any given people (and this includes black folks), nothing—I repeat, nothing—tells more about these people than does the fiction of the particular day. History written in 1991 rarely, if ever, captures the feel of 1891.
>
> (p. 297)

Not only Andrews' fiction but also his memoirs (which read like fiction) "capture the feel" of his and his family's rural, southern roots. In the process, his texts not only relay entertaining stories about entertaining characters; they also provide fascinating insight into historical events that have otherwise only been related from an outsider perspective. In Andrews' novels, we get the inside view on how the black community was affected by Reconstruction, the boll weevil, the cotton-picking machine, civil rights activism, integration, and, especially, miscegenation. Andrews describes how the split between light- and dark-skinned blacks passed down through the generations, affecting everything from class status to gender relations to the physical layouts of the "colored" sections of towns. The insights provided are often unexpected and always interesting, and in this way Andrews' novels constitute valuable historical documents.

However, the writings of Raymond Andrews are not historical documents, nor are they even realistic in the literary sense of the word. In fact, it has proven difficult for critics to determine exactly what they are and precisely how to characterize them. Speaking of the odd "angle of vision" (p. 287) from which Andrews tells his stories, Richard Bausch, in his afterword to *Appalachee Red*, concludes, "I know of nothing quite like it in American literature" (p. 288).

LEGACY: ANDREWS AS WRITER

In part, Andrews' originality stems from the oral aspects of his writing style. As Collins shows in his article "Raymond Andrews as Griot," Andrews produced what Henry Louis Gates, Jr., called "speakerly" rather than "writerly" texts, writing in free indirect discourse and incorporating African American oral techniques such as testifying and call and response. He also structured his novels as a storyteller would do, moving back and forth in time and from character to character as he narrates the life of the southern black community. Andrews has been criticized for this meandering, but as Collins points out, these apparent digressions actually "represent a rhetorical strategy that allows Andrews to fulfill the duties of the griot" (p. 2), which, according to Geneva Smitherman, are to maintain "tribal history" by presenting "composite word pictures of the culture, belief, ethics, and values of the tribe" (qtd. in "Griot," p. 2). This is very much the function Andrews serves.

While these speakerly elements partially account for Andrews' originality, however, they do not entirely do so. The experience of reading Andrews' texts is not as simple as being told long and interesting stories by a wise old storyteller. As Trudier Harris puts it, "lots of writers are good storytellers. With Andrews, the distinction is in the dual roles he plays as creator

and spectator, or as writer and voyeur" (p. 198). Analyzing *Baby Sweet's* in particular, Harris shows how Andrews participates in his texts not only as their creator but also as a spectator of his own creation and as a "shadow character" (p. 201) who views the events of his stories along with the other characters. This creates a number of unusual effects, one of which is a unique blend of humor and horror. As numerous reviewers and critics have pointed out, Andrews describes terrible injuries done to blacks by whites, and he does so honestly and straightforwardly, but his humorous perspective is never far behind his descriptions of brutality. Thus Harris describes him as "perhaps a lone representative of an African American writer who can be just as humorous in claiming the South as he can be critical in his indictments of it" (p. 196).

One of the sources of Andrews' humor is his obvious enjoyment of his own storytelling. Harris contends that while other black writers were motivated by a mission of racial uplift, Andrews' mission was pleasure—and, furthermore, his own pleasure. "I contend," wrote Harris, "that Andrews is having such a good time [telling his stories] that he could give a flying flip about whether or not we come along for the ride" (p. 198). It appears that he could also give a flip about the rules of narrative technique. According to those rules, a third-person narrative should employ a carefully constructed narrative persona, and the narrator should "speak" in a controlled and consistent voice. This is not the case in Andrews' novels, where the narrator speaks for Andrews himself, complete with snide remarks, occasional grammar errors, and at times anachronistic slang.

One suspects that Andrews—who never took a creative writing class or enrolled in a workshop and studied little, if any, literature in a formal way—did not fully understand the acceptable options for narrative perspective (first-person, limited omniscient, etc.) or the ground rules for remaining within the selected perspective. Later in life, when an interviewer asked him a sophisticated question about his narrative technique in *Appalachee Red*, he responded, "I don't know about technique. I always have a story to tell,

and I tell it the best way I know how to" (Kristwald, p. 103). Like a folk, or outsider, artist, Andrews departs from accepted practice in several ways but achieves a freshness and originality despite—and in part because of—these departures.

A final element of originality in Andrews is the way he blends social realism with … something else. For Trudier Harris, this "something else" is a mythical quality. As she writes in her essay "Chocklit Geography: Raymond Andrews's Mythical South," instead of realistically representing history, Andrews created a mythical landscape, a larger-than-life world in which he placed characters modeled on legendary figures in American folklore. For Michael Kreyling, on the other hand, such images from folk culture are just some of the "invented meanings" that Andrews puts into play with each other. Kreyling argues that Andrews' works are not about "life" but about the "adroit manipulation" of "signs and tropes" familiar to readers from other literary contexts (pp. 287, 288). For Kreyling, Andrews is up to something other than just telling stories. Larger-than-life characters like Appalachee Red, symbols like the White House (the name of the building in which Red and Baby Sweet locate their businesses), historical references such as the conclusion of *Appalachee Red* on the day when John F. Kennedy was assassinated — all of these elements point to larger meanings for Andrews' texts.

One of the more fruitful readings of this larger meaning is offered by Meghan Lydon, who compares Andrews to Toni Morrison. Pointing out that Morrison has been praised for putting her works in dialogue with the larger American culture, Lydon argues that Andrews was "similarly engaged in reconsidering and rewriting American history to incorporate unrecorded black experience" (p. 57). Lydon traces allusions to national and international events and issues in Andrews' texts and argues that his fiction is concerned not only with what it is to be African American but also with what it is to be American. This is especially the case in *Appalachee Red*, which is "filled with references to money, cowboys and Indians, Thanksgiving, Wall Street,

Uncle Sam, the White House, baseball, red, white, and blue, and the American Dream" (p. 74).

Lydon's is the most sustained effort to put Andrews in a national and international literary context, but she is not the only critic to have done so. At various points, various critics have compared him not only to the African American writers Zora Neale Hurston, Langston Hughes, Jean Toomer, Richard Wright, Ralph Ellison, Randall Kenan, Alice Walker, and Toni Morrison, and not only to the southern writers William Faulkner, Flannery O'Connor, and Eudora Welty, but also to the white American writers Herman Melville, Mark Twain, John Steinbeck, and Washington Irving. Other reviews have expanded their comparisons to British writers, including Geoffrey Chaucer, Henry Fielding, Charles Dickens, William Makepeace Thackeray, and Ben Jonson, as well as to older European writers like François Rabelais, Giovanni Boccaccio, and Sophocles.

The tendency to compare Andrews with other authors is pronounced in Andrews criticism, drawing attention to itself. It is as if the critics are casting about, grasping at straws, trying to find a way to make literary-critical sense of the way Andrews wrote. Friend, admirer, and fellow author Mary Hood seems to be poking fun at that tendency when, in just one paragraph, she compares Andrews to Dante, Boccaccio, Lope de Vega, Cervantes, Rabelais, Balzac, Saroyan, Caldwell, Faulkner, Hurston, and Steinbeck (p. 488). In fact, she is not poking fun but rather paying tribute to the myriad of sources upon which Andrews drew and to the artistry of his work. To these influences, she might well have added church services, cartoons, comic strips, and westerns, for Andrews was influenced by a strange mix of high and low culture, just as his writing strangely mixed comedy and tragedy, sophisticated vocabulary with shaky grammar, realistic historical accounts with myth.

As Jeffrey Folks put it, Andrews' writing is "absolutely original" (p. 74)—and Andrews knew it. As self-conscious as he was about his weak schooling, Andrews believed in himself and his work. His papers include a long letter dated May 17, 1971, from the agent Scott Meredith in which Meredith expressed admiration for many aspects of Andrews' work but ultimately declined interest in representing Andrews because Andrews did not follow the rules of novel writing. Meredith then proceeded to instruct Andrews on how he should revise his manuscript along more traditional novelistic lines. Attached to this letter is a note, clearly written by Andrews, in which he writes, "WHAT YOU SEE IS WHAT YOU GET / (AND YOU AIN'T SEEN NOTHING YET)," signed "APPALACHEE RED, ET AL" (qtd. in Collins 2005, p. 113). For an untutored, if not unlettered, writer with just one publication to his name—a short essay in *Sports Illustrated*—and a host of rejection slips in his drawer, this shows remarkable confidence on Andrews' part.

Fortunately for American literature, Andrews did what he told all aspiring writers to do: "Don't let anybody stop you," he advised. "The main thing is just to tell your story. Tell the story how you want to tell it, and that is all that writing is about" ("Blue Plate Interview," p. 27). Andrews told the stories he wanted to tell, and he told them the way he wanted to tell them. Even though few people seemed interested, he wrote about rural southern blacks in the early part of the twentieth century. Even though readers found the topic uncomfortable, he wrote about the complicated psychological, sociological, and economic effects of miscegenation. Although he felt that other black writers didn't want him to, he wrote about African Americans just as he knew them to be, sinners as well as saints, warts and all. And he wrote about these things the way he wanted to write about them, even though doing so involved breaking some creative-writing rules along the way. The result is a delightful and important contribution to American literature.

Selected Bibliography

WORKS OF RAYMOND ANDREWS

FICTION

Appalachee Red. New York: Dial, 1978. Reprinted, Athens: University of Georgia Press, 1987, with an afterword by

Richard Bausch. (All citations are to this edition.)

Rosiebelle Lee Wildcat Tennessee. New York: Dial, 1980. Reprinted, Athens: University of Georgia Press, 1988, with a foreword by Mary Hood. (All citations are to this edition.)

Baby Sweet's. New York: Dial, 1983. Reprinted, Athens: University of Georgia Press, 1988, with an afterword by Philip Lee Williams. (All citations are to this edition.)

Jessie and Jesus and Cousin Claire. Atlanta, Ga.: Peachtree, 1991.

"Ninety-Nine Years and a Dark Day." Unpublished novel. Raymond Andrews Papers. Manuscript, Archives, and Rare Book Library, Emory University.

MEMOIRS

The Last Radio Baby. Atlanta: Peachtree, 1990.

Once Upon a Time in Atlanta. Special issue, *Chattahoochee Review* 18, no. 2 (winter 1998).

SHORT WRITINGS

"A Football Rebellion in Backwoods Georgia." *Sports Illustrated*, November 7, 1966.

"Black Boy and Man in the Small-Town South." *Atlanta Journal-Constitution,* July 18, 1988, pp. 50–53. Reprinted in *The Prevailing South: Life and Politics in a Changing Culture*. Marietta, Ga.: Longstreet Press, 1988. Pp. 170–183.

"The Necessity of Blacks' Writing Fiction About the South." *African American Review* 27, no. 2:297–299 (summer 1993). (Posthumous publication.)

PAPERS

Raymond Andrews Papers. Manuscript, Archives, and Rare Book Library, Emory University, Atlanta, Georgia.

CORRESPONDENCE

Andrews, Benny, letter to Raymond Andrews. June 26, 1991. Box 2, folder 7, Raymond Andrews Papers, Manuscript, Archives, and Rare Book Library, Emory University.

Andrews, Raymond, letter to Benny Andrews. November 25, 1991. Box 15, folder 7, Raymond Andrews Papers, Manuscript, Archives, and Rare Book Library, Emory University.

Gildner, Gary, and Raymond Andrews. "'What a Nice Surprise': A Correspondence." *Georgia Review* 64, no. 3:446–476 (fall 2010).

Meredith, Scott, letter to Raymond Andrews. May 17, 1971. Box 29, folder 17, Raymond Andrews Papers, Manuscript, Archives, and Rare Book Library, Emory University.

CRITICAL AND BIOGRAPHICAL STUDIES

Collins, Brennan. "'Forsaking the Promised Land': Raymond Andrews and the Many African-American Literary Perspectives on the South." Ph.D. dissertation, Georgia State University, Atlanta, 2005.

———. "Raymond Andrews as Griot: Privileging Southern Black Communities through Oral Storytelling and Cultural History." *American Studies Journal* 56 (2012). http://www.asjournal.org/?p=476

Folks, Jeffrey J. "'Trouble' in Muskhogean County: The Social History of a Southern Community in the Fiction of Raymond Andrews." *Southern Literary Journal* 30, no. 2:67–74 (1998).

Gildner, Gary. "Remembering Raymond Andrews." *Georgia Review* 64, no. 3:424–445 (fall 2010).

Harris, Trudier. "No Fear; or, Autoerotic Creativity: How Raymond Andrews Pleasures Himself in *Baby Sweet's*." In *The Scary Mason-Dixon Line: African American Writers and the South*. Baton Rouge: Louisiana State University Press, 2009. Pp. 195–206.

Harris-Lopez, Trudier. "Chocklit Geography: Raymond Andrews's Mythical South." In *South of Tradition: Essays on African American Literature*. Athens: University of Georgia Press, 2002. Pp. 37–53.

Hood, Mary. "Laughs Last." *Georgia Review* 64, no. 3:477–494 (fall 2010).

Kreyling, Michael. *Inventing Southern Literature*. Jackson: University Press of Mississippi, 1998.

Lydon, Meghan. "'The American Dream—and Black Man's Nightmare': Remaking America in Raymond Andrews's Fiction." *South Atlantic Review* 71, no. 3:57–75 (summer 2007).

INTERVIEWS

"Blue Plate Interview: Raymond Andrews." *Blue Plate Special* 1, no. 4:26–27 (spring 1990).

Kristwald, Elfriede H. "Interview with Raymond Andrews." *Catalyst*, fall 1989, pp. 102–107.

Walsh, William J. "Raymond Andrews." In *Speak So I Shall Know Thee: Interviews with Southern Writers*. Jefferson, N.C.: McFarland, 1990. Pp. 24–30.

NATHAN ASCH

(1902—1964)

Robert Buckeye

NATHAN ASCH CARRIES the half-century of American writing that put modernism on its back in his own life: his escape from America after the First World War to Paris; his return only to retreat from the mainstream in places America had passed by; his search, thumb out, in the back of the bus, behind a wheel, in a boxcar, for what cannot be found, the length and breadth of America scrolling by.

His is a modernist aesthetic in which we can trace the marks of John Dos Passos, Ernest Hemingway, and James Joyce. His is also a political-left sensibility that rejects mainstream America, if not the American dream, as much as it can't let them go. His last two books, *The Valley* (1935) and *The Road: In Search of America* (1937), are stations of the cross of the Passion America lives.

In *The Road*, Asch writes of Myrtle, a woman he meets in Dallas. "She was romantic ... had gone to the movies ... hoped against hope" and

> instinctively she was drawn to a kid of her kind; Myrtle got herself a young whistling fellow, climbed into his rickety car, went careening around corners hell bent for pleasure and not quite so worried—she had even forgotten what she was riding for. Of course she remembered later, in the beer flat, lying hurt and weeping; "What did you want to do me that way for?"
>
> (*The Road*, p. 32)

She is going to Hibbing. She is going to Walla Walla. She is going "to be near a boy friend who had been sent up for four years. She would wash dishes in a rooming house. She was sitting in a dance hall in Denver, going next day on to Salt Lake City. She didn't know what she was going to do, but she had a ticket" (p. 33).

It is a story, Asch says, that has been done countless times in magazines and movies, but he begins to write it nevertheless, names her Jessie, but tears it up because, he realizes, it is not possible for him to write about her.

> She stands on the street in Dallas, unwanted, unloved, the most sorry, the most pitiful figure that I know and there is nothing I can do about her.
>
> (p. 35)

> And in Los Angeles on Santa Monica Boulevard. All over America when the season ended, when times went bad, Myrtle was fired from the nickel store, from the hat shop, from the textile mill, from the collar factory.
>
> (p. 33)

> Myrtle wasn't fiction. She existed.
>
> (p. 33)

If Asch stands aside from Myrtle, he also stands alongside her, even though he was never at home in America. He was born in Warsaw on July 10, 1902, and moved to Paris in 1912, where as a boy he met Marc Chagall and Jules Pascin. In 1915 the family moved again because of the First World War, this time to Staten Island. Asch studied at Syracuse and Columbia Universities and worked as a stockbroker in Manhattan before leaving for Paris in 1923. In 1926 he returned to America, not to leave again except for service in Europe during the Second World War.

Asch was never at home anywhere. He was a secular Jew, who never felt himself to be either American or European. In 1930 he applied for a Guggenheim Fellowship to visit relatives in Poland and elsewhere in Europe. "The problem to be examined is one of rootlessness. Most writers, like most people, have within them the memory of a home," he wrote in his application, concluding, "It is a quality the writer of this statement does not possess" (Berthoff, p. xv). A year later, after a trip to France to visit his parents, he wrote Malcolm Cowley:

I am not American, and probably if I never went back to Europe and lost all contact with it, and remained in America I would still never be an American. Which probably explains why they read me in Germany and Russia more than they do here. But the curious thing is that I love this place and feel no sympathy for Eastern Europe.... I feel clean in America and not in Germany.... So you see I have no place anywhere, ... I love America, and am not an American, not liked by Americans.

(Mills, 1984, p. 5)

His father, Sholem Asch, was a popular novelist in America whose straightforward narratives Asch could never write. He had crossed over, as his father never would in America, but it was the father, not the son, who made a home for himself in the New World. At the end of his life, Nathan Asch planned a series of novels collectively titled "Marginal Man." In *Love in Chartres* (1925), the writer, whose story is Asch's own, is never named, and the narrators of his last two books, *The Valley* and *The Road*, are nameless.

Myrtle may not have known what she was going to do—she is futureless we might say—but she had a ticket, even if she does not know where it will take her. Asch never did. When he looks at her to see who she is—the enigma that is her life—he can only see his own solitude: "The absence of a place," Jacques Rancière writes, "for a relation between two equally abandoned beings" (*Short Voyages*, p. 94). Asch's friend Josephine Herbst reported that he came back from Europe with a haunted look.

For those left behind, the consolations of art and empathy are of little comfort, and Asch refuses to compromise Myrtle by offering them, understanding that for him to fictionalize her is, in effect, to use if not exploit her. He denies us compensation—what art does so well—for what cannot be compensated. We might say Asch describes her, but he does so in order that she might speak.

"Culture is a weapon that's used against us," notes Dave Thomas of the band Pere Ubu, if you go against the grain, stand outside, can't get off the floor; a club to keep those kept down kept down. The culture Thomas refers to here is, of course, high culture that keeps those without it outside, put down, refused or denied, which both

explains and justifies why we keep them in their place.

We are not talking of art here. Or perhaps the only art possible. Asch may have walked alongside Hemingway, Joyce, Ford Madox Ford (who first published him in 1924 in *Transatlantic Review*), Morley Callaghan, Kay Boyle, Hart Crane, Cowley, and Herbst, but he sat next to Myrtle on the bus, talked to her, brought her coffee. If modernism gave him the tools, it took the Thirties to give him his subject, even though there are intimations of it in his first three books. What speaks in his writing is as much the agonized cry of America as it is Asch.

THE OFFICE

Asch's first novel, *The Office*, was published in 1925, the same year that *In Our Time, The Great Gatsby, Manhattan Transfer, An American Tragedy*, and *A Draft of XVI Cantos* were published. In all of these books the need to leave home for New York or Paris is the catalyst. There was a hunger for a new world and a new way to write it, and it could not be found at home.

The novel is a series of sketches of life in a Wall Street firm that has gone bankrupt, an episodic montage, much like Dos Passos' *Manhattan Transfer*, of the corrosive effects of capitalism and a kitsch version of the American dream reinforced daily on every billboard and in every radio song. It is, James T. Farrell wrote in *New Masses*, "an impressionistic description of the boom-time office that is, in effect, symphonic."

In the chapter "The Voice of the Office," Asch strings together the voices that move the work of the office forward in a hyper-staccato drone, harsh, savage, a fingernail scratched across glass: talk of stock prices and options, the relentless whine of the ticker tape, telephones ringing and answered, parenthetical asides about women, coworkers, this evening, as the day plunges forward less to any conclusion than to an end. Everyone has his story, but in the office the only story is that of the office, not those who work in it.

For some, work in the office has been an opportunity, and when it fails they confront a bleak future they thought they had escaped. They return home to fathers, wives, or friends, some having become drunk first, because there is no other place to go. For some, work is not what they like (they would just as soon not work), and the failure of the Wall Street firm gives them, if but for a moment, the freedom they desire. For some, it is how things are. Every few years they must look for another job.

In "Gertrude Donovan," Asch employs stream of consciousness to tell us what Donovan thinks about work, what she dreams, how she feels about the way men look at women: "The manager would first look at her legs, then at her neck. He would measure her with his eyes. The old look ... as if you were lying naked on the bed waiting for them" (*The Office*, p. 29).

On her way home the day her work as a stenographer on Wall Street ends, Donovan passes by the movie theater, ice cream parlor, and hardware store in her neighborhood, formative places of her youth where, after a movie or ice cream, her boyfriend would take her into his arms, "and they would seek something which they did not understand, and did not know where to find it" (p. 41).

When she reaches home and dresses in her bedroom for the man she does not love but will marry, confusing him for the moment when he asks her to marry him with Harry Widener, the senior partner at the brokerage, who is "a rare drug that she needed" (p. 37), she thinks, "She had no place in the room where she was" (p. 49). Harry Widener, for his part, fantasizes for a moment of a life as a worker living with Gertrude Donovan, as she does of a life with him.

Here, as in his next two books, *Love in Chartres* and *Pay Day* (1930), home prevents one from living. If Donovan's work and that of Jim Cowan in *Pay Day* are deadening, we must see, nevertheless, that it offers the possibility of a life better than the one at home. The unnamed woman of *Love in Chartres* goes to France because at home there is no life. Their attitude is little different from that of Hemingway and F. Scott Fitzgerald, who also left home, although with goals clear in ways that theirs are not.

Marc Kranz, one of those cashiered, will leave Wall Street for Paris to write. His writing, he tells himself, will be in a language to match the times:

> He would sing a song of speed, of energy, in which would be mixed the automobile horns, and the tick-tick of the ticker. It would be full of blows from the boxer's glove, and of hits from the bat of the ball player, and of the noise of a policeman's stick as it strikes the head of a wayward drunk.
>
> (p. 100)

On his last day of work at the brokerage, he is told by his supervisor that he can now be the poet he wants to be. Kranz understands, however, that for his generation to write, it first had to leave America, which did not provide what it needed, even if American would be that generation's subject.

Esther Thomas has been forced to work after her family in a small town in upstate New York lost their money, and she not only despises those she works with but also the firm itself because she feels neither those in the office nor the office itself ever do anything right. She keeps to herself, wanting nothing more than to be alone. When she returns to her apartment the day the firm closes, she hears a neighbor making love to a man in the next apartment, but as she listens to them she inexplicably feels the man is making love to her and for the first time experiences sexual pleasure, if only vicariously, alone, in her bed.

The first thing Robert Michelet does when he leaves the office is to go to an attractive woman friend of his father's to ask her to intercede for him with his father. He does not want to work and wants his father to support him. The woman dismisses him, saying Michelet never cared for her, only her body. Afterward he and a friend pick up two women, one of whom says she is an actress and hopes Michelet can support her. They spend the night together.

Mr. Read, who had convinced partners to provide financial support for him to manage the office that has failed, waits in a hotel lobby for a

meeting with potential backers for another firm. He notices an attractive woman in a black satin dress also waiting, for a man he thinks, and imagines what life with her would be like.

Kranz, in the subway on his way home, sees a girl show more of her leg to him and imagines he will leave the train when she does and follow her home. Some of the clerks spend their last paycheck drinking and eating at a good restaurant before going to a whorehouse.

When what fails fails we turn to what first turned us, whether that be the woman, the man, the mother or father. The unconscious, as Freud reminds us, made up of desires and impulses of mostly a sexual if not destructive nature, asserts itself in those who work in the office the day it closes. Love may be what they need, but the day the firm fails, what passes for love is anything but what they need.

If, in his later writing, Asch abandons the expressionism of the early chapters of *The Office*—his rapid-fire use of the dash, repetition, cinematic montage, detail piled on detail, image after image in a kaleidoscopic, unrelenting rush—he will also abandon, if you will, love as the patriarchal love men practice. Myrtle standing on a street in Dallas is not the woman Kranz sees in the subway, Helen the waitress in Manhattan who Jim Cowan desires on pay day, Martha Akin dancing naked in the road in the Valley.

LOVE IN CHARTRES

In *Love in Chartres* (1927), Asch writes of Marc Kranz and a young woman he meets whose father is a successful businessman—let us say it is the girl Kranz sees in the subway—who have each come to France to find a way to live that neither can find in America. He, to write. She, because "she had looked for ideas [in America], and she found gossip" (*Chartres*, p. 17). In their search, they are both drawn to Chartres, seeing in its cathedral, as Henry Adams had, an embodiment of a spirit lacking at home.

They meet there, fall in love, move in together. *Love in Chartres* is a graceful, youthful account of first love, told without sentimentality.

Asch may continue to utilize the modernist techniques he employed in *The Office* to capture the kaleidoscopic rush of life in Manhattan, but he does so here to calibrate the wild, unruly sweep of desire crashing against fear and uncertainty.

There is the girl. There is his writing. The writer knows he has been alone for a long time and has come to France as much to escape his loneliness as to write. She shows him how he can live without writing when he had thought writing was the only thing, even if he agonizes over what it should be. The more she does to make it possible for him to write, however, the more he feels trapped.

Increasingly he leaves the apartment to drink in cafés, avoiding both his writing and her. He comes to understand that it had been first the Chartres cathedral, then his love for her, and at last drink, which were roadblocks he put in the way of writing. So what must he do? He leaves for Paris, telling her it is temporary and that when he returns with a manuscript they will marry. In Paris, he is able to write and realizes that despite his love for her he cannot write as long as they are together.

She knows he will not come back. Like Gertrude Donovan, she realizes she has no place in the room where she is and returns to an America that will never be what she wants, leaving the place she thought would be her life when she met him in the cathedral in Chartres. Perhaps she would never find it no matter how much she looked.

As accomplished as *Love in Chartres* is, the writing of it complicated matters for Asch. His protagonist fears that the woman he loves will think that he can only be alone, that he is no more than a stranger to everyone, and in writing the book Asch began to question whether he himself could walk down the road with anyone or ever be at home anywhere. He would divorce Lysel Ingerwesen, the woman he met in France and wrote about in *Love in Chartres*, three years after their return to America.

From the beginning, Asch questioned the project his life would follow. In *The Office*, on his way to Wall Street one day, Kranz climbs

aboard an abandoned vessel to watch the life of the city rush by, "a rhapsody of strength and speed" (p. 96). He tells himself that this is what he will write, but in a moment is unsure and asks himself "whether the accomplishment of many was worth the suffering of a few.... Whether to be able to create thoughts, he could ruin another, who in a crowd, counted for nothing" (p. 97).

Asch may not have found his subject yet, as one reviewer wrote, but he has had his first glimpse of Myrtle, although he has not yet seen her. In *Love in Chartres*, he may drag out old, tired chestnuts of writing—the writer has no life but that of writing, solitude is his state, love prevents him from writing—only to discover on his return to America that he has found his subject and that it trumped the modernism he drank in at the Dome in Paris sitting at the feet of Ford and Hemingway. He may have thought that what mattered was the way of telling it but learns that the only way he can tell it is not to say what he cannot say. By not being able to write about Myrtle, he opens up a space in which the speech that has been taken from her may be heard.

PAY DAY

In 1928 Asch and Lysel were living in two rooms in Mrs. Turner's boardinghouse in Patterson, New York, in what once had been a roadhouse, sleeping on a wrapped-over mattress on the floor, next door to Hart Crane. Crane was working on *The Bridge*, playing Dvořák's *New World Symphony* over and over while he wrote. Nicola Sacco and Bartolomeo Vanzetti had been executed the year before. Wall Street was to crash a year later. At Mrs. Turner's, Crane gave parties at which everyone drank bootleg liquor, shouted (but not to anyone), danced (but not with anyone). "Anything went there," Asch commented later, "because nothing was important, nothing mattered" ("Nathan Asch Remembers," p. 281).

If his unsettled, sometimes chaotic, life in Patterson became material Asch used in *The Valley* (1935), it also shaped *Pay Day*, the novel he was writing at the time, and so too did Crane's *The Bridge* and the deaths of Sacco and Vanzetti,

which are central to the novel and crucial to our understanding of it. ("Today," Asch wrote, "when I read passages in *The Bridge,* I shiver because I seem to hear again Hart's voice" ["Nathan Asch Remembers," p. 281].) *The Bridge* brought Asch back to the dream of America first seen in the Statue of Liberty as the ship neared New York harbor; the execution of Sacco and Vanzetti to its failure.

Pay Day (1930) is the only novel of Asch's in which he himself does not play a part. In *The Office*, Marc Kranz is based on Asch's experience in Wall Street. *Love in Chartres* is the story of how Asch met Lysel. In *The Valley* and *The Road*, the narrator is Asch. Why he does not assume a role as character or narrator in *Pay Day* may have to do with his experience of those he met in the Valley: the endless sounds of Dvořák coming through the walls of Mrs. Turner's boardinghouse and Crane reading passages of *The Bridge* to him; the execution of Sacco and Vanzetti, the Wall Street crash. Asch could no longer write about America as he had seen it from Europe in *The Office* and *Love in Chartres*. He would not see until later that what was happening in America would make him the writer he was to become.

For Jim Cowan, an office clerk, pay day is the day he can take a girl out, drink and dance with her, and, if she is willing, sleep with her. It is the only thing he lives for. Whether he is in the office, on the subway, or the street, his glance undresses every woman he sees. Helen, a waitress at the luncheon where he eats, is the woman he fantasizes he will sleep with this evening, but pay day becomes less a journey to the end of night than a *Walpurgisnacht*.

Cowan takes Helen to the movies, a dance hall afterward, gets drunk, loses her to another man, meets a woman whose sister is with a state senator, passes out, is dumped by them, meets the high school friend who earlier in the evening had taken Helen from him, breakfasts with him, returns home at dawn. Everything flashes by: Cowan in the subway, on the L, a shuttle train, a taxi, rushing toward what everyone in the city rushes toward but which he never finds. (Asch may have seen Charlie Chaplin's *Pay Day,* in

which Chaplin's misadventures mimic Cowan's own.)

The only moments Cowan feels alive are those in his head: internal monologues he has with himself; fantasies that obsess him; dreams of power and success undercut by fears of failure. In a scene reminiscent of Joyce's Nighttown, he imagines himself arraigned in a front of a judge for a crime he did not commit. His mother is in the courtroom and at one point she and the judge dance closely together—the government and family in each other's arms aligned against him.

Cowan is afraid to say what he wants to say, and when he does say anything, it comes out wrong. He does not do what he wants to do, unless it is a visceral, knee-jerk reaction to protect himself. Resentment drives him, failure defines him, anger lives in him; violent, dark revolts of his being against the way things are: "He was born wrong, he lived wrong, he was wrong" (*Pay Day*, p. 81).

At the still point of the storm is a movie Cowan and Helen see, presumably some travelogue about America put on the screen before the feature film. It begins at dawn on the East Coast with waves breaking over surf and ends at the Pacific Ocean with white crests breaking under moonlight.

> On the side of a hill cattle, huddled together, stood sleeping.
>
> A dog barked.
>
> In a white birch wood the rain fell.
>
> An express train rushed through the fog. The curtained aisle of the sleeping car was empty. In the smoking compartment the porter slept curled on the seat.
>
> A baby cried.
>
> The doorman of a night club helped a tired party of four, in evening clothes, into an automobile.
>
> Off Pittsburgh white-hot blast furnaces threw flares into the sky.
>
> (p. 133)

The movie is America as Whitman sees it in *Leaves of Grass*. Asch's description of the film is

thirty pages long, nearly one-sixth of the book. Before the movie begins, he describes Cowan looking at the attractive woman sitting next to him, hearing what the man she has come in with says, thinking about what his evening with Helen will be like, but when the movie begins, Cowan, Helen, and the couple sitting next to them fade, disappear. It is an extraordinary moment, unlike anything in American fiction, as if *Leaves of Grass* channeled through Crane's *The Bridge* permitted Asch to see in the Manhattan whose mean streets Herman Melville's Pierre walked before Cowan did that so too did Whitman.

The movie stops the narrative movement of *Pay Day*, disrupts it, permits it to stand by itself, unmediated. Its interruption, an intervention if you will, blocks narrative movement and counteracts the illusion fiction creates, permitting another world to enter. We must see a day in the life of Jim Cowan in relationship to the America the movie establishes.

In a speakeasy afterward, Cowan hears a drunk talk about a movie he has seen. "It hasn't got a story," he says. "It hasn't got a plot. You can come in one minute and go out the next, and you wouldn't miss anything."

> You got to have a story, don't you? You can't look at a picture, where there ain't some guy trying to get a girl to go to bed with him, and then a big fairy comes in, and saves her from fate worse than death. You can't look when somebody's trying to be honest and show you the country you're living in, how it looks, and what's in it.
>
> (p. 172)

Asch never had a story, any more than the movie Cowan and Helen see has one, although it is the one everyone knows. If he would find it impossible to write about Myrtle later, it has to do not only with her but also with how the talk in the Café du Dome in Montparnasse in the twenties ended writing as it had been practiced. Any story one could tell was no longer *the* story, but one contradicted, qualified, or overshadowed by the stories around it one did not tell or know.

One could only pull different threads together, grasp the contingent, establish relationship through juxtaposition. It was a poetics of the

fragmentary, Ezra Pound's "rose in the steel dust," a way of writing, of dreaming of writing: how a detail becomes a lens through which we read a civilization; an image the manifestation of a concept; a street song the summary not only of a life but of a people. In *Pay Day*, as in *The Valley* and *The Road: In Search of America*, you can't look, as the man in the speakeasy says, when Asch shows us the country we live in.

Sacco and Vanzetti follow Cowan through the day. Newsboys shouting the news, holding up headlines of papers, people talking about them. In the subway, Cowan thinks, "they were Reds, and they were wops, and they raised hell, and now they had to pay for it" (p. 32). After the movie he is asked whether the newsreel had Sacco and Vanzetti pictures in it. In the speakeasy, a reporter tells a state senator that they're murdering two men in Boston. They're Bolsheviks, the state senator replies. There's no place for them in America. In a taxi, a cabbie says he'd be willing to give his life for them because he's got nothing to live for anyway. On the train on his way home, a man sitting next to Cowan says, "What if I stood before this car and told the people here a terrible injustice, and awful crime, had been committed" (p. 253).

There are moments in time that define a people. In America the minutemen at Lexington, Abraham Lincoln's Gettysburg Address, American soldiers raising the flag at Iwo Jima are such moments. For the Left, we might add Haymarket, the Abraham Lincoln Brigade, 1968. In 1921 two immigrant Italian anarchists, one a shoemaker, the other a fish peddler, were found guilty of the murders of a shoe company paymaster and a security guard in South Braintree, Massachusetts, in a trial that was widely regarded as flawed and unfair. "It came to be seen as a decisive test of basic American principles," Werner Berthoff writes, "in particular the principle of equal justice before the law" (p. xviii). Six years later, thousands and tens of thousands protested in Boston, New York, Paris, Berlin, Madrid, and Moscow at the refusal of Judge Webster Thayer, Governor Alvan Fuller, the Supreme Court, and finally President Calvin Coolidge to halt the executions of the two immigrants.

Herbst called the executions of Sacco and Vanzetti "A Year of Disgrace." It was, Katherine Anne Porter, wrote, "one of the important turning points in the history of this country" ("Never-Ending Wrong," p. 38). "The beginning of the end," Lola Ridge said; "we have lost something we shan't find again" (qtd. in Porter, p. 57). "All right," Dos Passos wrote in *U.S.A.*, "we are two nations."

In *Pay Day*, Asch refuses to take a stand about Sacco and Vanzetti, although it is clear that he supports them. (He wrote for *New Masses* and was friends with Leftists, particularly Josephine Herbst. In the forties, Asch's second wife, Carol Tasker Miles, was suspended from her government job by the House Un-American Activities Committee, which examined Asch's left-wing activities.) Instead, he shows to what extent not only Sacco and Vanzetti's trial but also their lives trigger knee-jerk reactions about the contradictions that define us as a people. In this sense, the voices of newspapers and people about two Italian immigrants throughout the day and night of their deaths serve less as a chorus than a street song everyone hears. It speaks, in ways we do not always understand, of what everyone knows. We hear it without having to hear it.

Pay Day is no more and no less than a mass for Sacco and Vanzetti; a dirge for Jim Cowan; a requiem for the promise of America seen in the movie that is, like Jay Gatsby's green light, "the orgiastic future that year by year recedes before us" (Fitzgerald, p. 189).

THE VALLEY

A moment arrived when a border was crossed. Asch was living in a hotel in Brooklyn near the Navy Yard, separated from Lysel, working on the book that would be *The Valley* (1935). Crane, who lived nearby to pick up sailors at the Yard, would stop by after a night with one of his loves, "while one of his eyes was almost bursting out of its socket and surrounded by a pulpy, bloody mass of flesh, and strips of bandage would try to hide the places where he'd been slashed with a knife" ("Nathan Asch Remembers," p. 281).

On a trip back to the Valley to see his child, who was living with Lysel, Asch took Crane along. Writes Asch: "We got into a discussion on the subject of—of all things—is there a simple explanation for us all? Is there a synthesis?—with Hart scornfully demanding, 'Where is it? What is it like?'" ("Nathan Asch Remembers," p. 281).

The unnamed narrator of Asch's novel has come to the Valley with his wife to write. Some of those who settled the Valley are long gone, although their houses still bear their names. Others have foundered and can neither leave nor live. Those who have come later seek a new life, solitude, oblivion. Some are landowners who escape the city weekends for rustic beauty. Those who have been in the Valley from the beginning grudgingly tolerate, if not resent and despise, those who have come later and have no idea what life in the Valley is like.

The writer doesn't have to be in the Valley, even if increasingly he does not know why he is. He and his wife visit neighbors, hear what they say about themselves and others, listen to the postman. Their lives are not his and are, for the most part, little more than an inventory of failure, defeat, and loss, but the longer he stays the less sure he is.

Old Man Preston lives with Sue Briggs in the Schoolhouse. He drinks and damns everyone with every word he speaks: Henderson, a New York lawyer who comes to the Valley on weekends, most of all. Briggs scrapes dirt roads with two horses when they need to be scraped, but otherwise does little but get Preston a drink when he wants one. Mrs. Henderson feels she needs to civilize Briggs but fails, and in anger at her failure accuses Briggs of sleeping with Preston, whom she sees to be a lecherous old man. Briggs says he's her father. Everyone believes the story Mrs. Henderson tells. Sue Briggs had never said before that Preston was her father. Mrs. Henderson must have said something to the postman.

Stefan Marny and his wife, Leokadia, have come with their children from Poland to the Parker House, having been sold a bill of goods by an unscrupulous agent selling passage to America. The farm is not manageable, its house

a ruin. Children are born as regularly as the seasons, but one day Leokadia is kicked in the belly by a cow and dies. One son leaves to become a priest, another is jailed for his crimes. One daughter becomes a burlesque queen in New York, another, the oldest, mothers the remaining children and replaces her mother in her father's bed.

Mac, an Irishman, and Sarah, a Jew, live at the Merritt Farm. They had come to the Valley from New York because his lungs are bad and air in the city had not been good for him. Sarah becomes pregnant and Mac returns to New York to work in order to support the baby. Mrs. Merritt, who has rented the farm to them, helps Sarah give birth. When Mac returns, he discovers that he has been shut out by the bond the women have established. He returns to New York to write. Sarah and the child go to Europe, brought by her family for the season in Biarritz, picking up a divorce in Paris on the way.

Arthur Cassou is at the Swanson Place on Rattlesnake Mountain living as a bootlegger, less to sell liquor than to drink it himself. He is a former army officer who had won the Congressional Medal of Honor during the First World War, got drunk in New York after the war and assaulted a woman, only to be saved from prison because of his medal. Cassou's wife has come to join him, a woman, the writer tells his wife, he must have met in a dive while he was drunk. Cassou has come to Rattlesnake Mountain to drink himself to death.

Martha Akin lives in Twin Houses. Twenty years after his first wife killed herself, Jeremiah Akin had gone to Boston and brought Martha back to be his second wife. He had found her, so the story goes, naked outside a bordello in Boston. On their wedding night, Akin's drunk father asserted bridal rights. No one knows why what happened happened, but they do not have to know what they do not know. At some point Jeremiah began to hate her. It was the house, they say. It was her, they say. She was young. She was mad. "She didn't wear no clothes at all, she wore out four hired men" (*The Valley*, p. 66). One day Jeremiah hangs himself. Martha leaves for Europe with money from the estate.

But all this was told to us as fact, and perhaps it is not true. Dorothy and I heard the story of Martha Akin from different people, men and women, drunk and sober, in various times and moods; and some, no question, lied, exaggerated, made of Martha something much crazier than she really was.

(p. 76)

Whatever the writer knows is less what he sees than what he hears, what everyone knows but feels no need to explain. Do you remember that? they ask. No, this was more terrible, they answer. That's what I remember, one says. I heard it from the servants. I saw a photograph in a New York paper. I heard it from the postman. The Schoolhouse is not a Schoolhouse and no one remembers when it was. The Parker of the Parker House has faded into the mists of time.

Old John Turner repairs fences on his land for no reason since the farm is no longer active, lifting heavy stones that had been dislodged by wind, frost, and years. "No one today could make the patchwork design with stone that the first settlers could," Asch writes, "but Old John Turner did" (p. 42). Warren Davis, a painter the writer had met before at the Dome in Montparnasse, tells him that he could not find in any other place what he finds in the Valley. He marries Turner's daughter, paints *The Valley*, but returns to Paris with his wife.

The writer may have talked to Davis in the Dome, but he will never be part of the Valley as Davis is. He sees Old John Turner to be intimately part of this world in a way he knows he will never be. It would seem, however, that his life, as much as he believes it to be unlike other lives in the Valley, is, in fact, little different. He leaves, just as others do: Davis and his wife for Europe, Mac for New York, Sarah for Biarritz, Martha Akin for Europe, Maria, the Marny daughter, for the New York burlesque stage. Whatever life had been in the Valley was no life at all.

In *The Valley*, Asch includes chapters on the seasons, the car and horse the writer buys, Moses, the cat he acquires, as if merely an account of an event is its meaning, as if anything in the Valley contains in itself its story. Fact, memory, hearsay, questions, fantasy, conjecture, desire circle around one another, becoming the stories of the

Valley, deepening over time; story becomes legend and legend history. "The side of truth," Rancière writes, "is where the spoken words are no longer written on paper or on the wind, but engraved in the texture of things" (*Names of History*, p. 57).

Asch will remember his deep feelings of homelessness. He was as marginal as the title of his last unfinished work, "Marginal Man," but in the Valley, he was no more abandoned than anyone else. There was no place for him but the place he had.

He will remember its women. Martha Akin, made mad by her husband, who "sat on the grass at night and hummed in the moonlight, danced in the road, forgot to put her clothes on in the daytime, forget to take them off at night" (p. 72). Mrs. Ferris, who is beaten by her husband when he is at home. "Her body remembered his blows," Asch writes, "while her mind was lonely; and sometimes it was the mind that was afraid, and perhaps her body wanted him" (p. 161). The unanswered relationship between Sue Briggs and Old Man Preston. Maria on the burlesque stage in New York. Jennie, the oldest Marny daughter, replacing her mother in her father's bed.

He will remember the pulpy, bloody mass of Crane's face and the strips of bandage where he had been slashed with a knife; and he would find Myrtle in the women in the Valley. One told him the cost of *The Bridge*; the other that of silence. If Asch shivered at the sound of Crane's voice reading the poem to him, did not Crane also at what the cost of writing it had been? If Asch is silenced by his inability to write about Myrtle, the failure of language to speak in the face of what is, what did she see when she saw him? How does the writer justify himself in her eyes? Where is it? What is it? he will remember Crane asked.

If Asch wrestles with these questions in *The Valley*, he would find their answers in *The Road: In Search of America*. The episodes and events of *The Valley* may block and contradict the stories Asch might construct, but he silences himself in *The Road* so that the silenced might be heard. If *The Office* and *Love in Chartres* chart the postwar exodus of American writers to Europe after the

First World War, *The Valley* and *The Road* anticipate the search for a new life, if not America itself, that we see in Jack Kerouac's *On the Road*, Clancy Sigal's *Going Away*, Gilbert Sorrentino's *The Sky Changes*, Dennis Hopper's *Easy Rider*, Robert Kramer's *Milestones* and *U.S. 1*. If Asch's road trips are like those that followed them, they are also reports from a land in which Asch could neither live nor write.

The day the writer's car dies, Asch writes, "Before we reached [the house], I turned off the road, drove the car onto an abandoned field, and I left it there" (*The Valley*, p. 117). Writing in America always begins at the end of the road.

THE ROAD: IN SEARCH OF AMERICA

In 1936 Asch was living in a chicken coop on Josephine Herbst's rented farm in Erwinna, Pennsylvania, and writing *The Road*, which he would dedicate to Herbst. Behind him was a four-month trip cross country by bus. "What I wanted to see was America as it was," he writes, "not as I might want it to be" (*The Road*, p. 58). His trip told him not only what the country was but also the kind of a writer it needed. It reminded him that he was a man without a country.

The Road begins with Asch leaving from Washington at dawn, passing by the Washington Monument. "I was going to drift in the entire country," he writes. "I was going to lose myself in it" (*The Road*, p. 16). If his trip has an itinerary—he goes south, west toward the Southwest, across the Great Plains until he reaches the Far West before heading back east across the top of the country—increasingly it becomes a drift determined by who he meets, where he is, what happens. At one place, he stays longer than he anticipated. At another, he leaves without a second thought. Such travel can never be planned or directed, except as aimlessness itself directs attention. Drifting encounters possibilities that planning prevents. Triptiks always tell you what they want you to know.

"It is not possible to sleep in a bus," he writes. "Everything the huge wheels meet upon the road is transferred, is applied to the sitting body, and you vibrate and shake; and at night when there is no distracting scenery you sit and try to doze; and you feel the road" (p. 8). At such moments the configuration of a place is made manifest in a way speech cannot answer.

Asch stays in a flophouse, a sharecropper's shack, the home of a university professor and an automotive engineer. He descends into coal mines, lives with loggers in the Pacific Northwest, goes with a former pimp into the red light district of Memphis, attends union meetings, seeds fields on a tractor with a farmer, works with a sheepherder, visits a prison, observes an operation on a woman with breast cancer.

He sees poverty everywhere: "in doorways lay these men's future, lay what they would become: junk, with still beating arteries, huddled in doorways" (p. 185). Racism is rampant. Banks own everyone and everything.

He documents, as Jacob Holdt did in his book of photographs *American Pictures: A Personal Journey Through the American Underclass* (1985), the rich alongside the poor, able, as Holdt was, to talk to and live with both a university professor and a sharecropper, a banker and a union organizer, a farmer and an engineer.

He is always on the move, one place following another—not only Asch, but also America, the road its life. "I began to see the entire country," Asch writes, "with its maze of road, twining, twisting, entering everywhere. I saw the million automobiles, and trains, and buses, and people walking on the road, all trying to get somewhere" (p. 140). As if there is no home in America but the road, no goal but the next ridge, no life but that of the nomad, if not the immigrant or exile.

Places assert themselves, with people being formed by where they live, the cities themselves taking on human form, as Rudolph Wurlitzer would envisage years later in *Flats* (1970). If Wurlitzer places his people, each one named after the city where they lived, in camps after a nuclear holocaust in America, Asch sees the Depression as no less a holocaust. Atlanta is "a painted, elegant parasite" (p. 44); Central City, Colorado, a killed town; Garland, Arkansas, the meanest town. There was no story in Hamtramck,

Michigan. Tulsa didn't dream. And up in Montana, he writes, "Human? That word meant nothing in Butte" (p. 200).

In Winston-Salem, he tells himself that he will write a novel about what has happened in the city. He imagines Jake, a young Negro, arriving at night with nowhere to stay, but knowing that any family that employs black servants houses them in small houses behind the main ones. Jake must take a chance and knock on the door of one of the servants' homes. Asch imagines a Mr. and Mrs. Miller who do not get along and no longer have servants. When Mrs. Miller wants to get away from her husband she sleeps in the empty servant's home. Jake knocks and enters and sees Mrs. Miller sleeping in bed.

Asch cannot write this story, because this is not what happened in Winston-Salem. He refuses to turn what he has seen into fiction or imagine what he has not seen.

> One of the reasons I have not been able to write this novel is that there is a girl haunting me. For the last two years, whenever I begin to do any work, write a short story, think about a novel, begin to trace the pattern of a play, this girl stands between me and any other thoughts, sharp, distinct, and not insistent, because there is nothing insistent about her passive greyness; still she is alive, existing and somehow more important than any other figures forming in my mind—perhaps because she is already formed. I have seen her, known her, I think I understand her, and although I've tried I cannot write about her....
>
> (p. 30)

> While I was riding in the bus through America, sometimes Myrtle sat in the seat beside me.
>
> (p. 33)

On the way to Richmond, she is Jerry, a dancer in a Broadway nightclub, going to see her gambler brother in Miami. In Oklahoma, she is Mary, who at sixteen had been raped by the teenage son of the richest man in town. She was innocent, a victim, but had to leave town because the town wants nothing more to do with her. On the way to Salt Lake City, she is Marcheta. "That first night in the bus," Asch writes, "she was just a crazy and not very attractive person who had attached herself to me" (p.

148). They travel together to Reno and share a rented room in San Francisco. "She talked all the time, and often she put her facts in the wrong places, but everything she said was true" (p. 148).

In Chicago, she is Cynthia, whom he meets in a taxi dance hall. Her husband is in jail for drugs. They drink and Asch goes home with her, but she has to leave to see a man. At four in the morning, a girl comes in. She works in a radio assembly plant, but is not old enough yet to be a taxi dancer, which pays better than work wiring radios.

What Asch has experienced on his trip has undone him and he cannot get his hands around it. America has overwhelmed him in ways he could not have anticipated. In Oklahoma, he encounters a dust storm that has obscured the sun for several weeks. At the Donner Pass, he walks ahead of the bus to clear stones from its path during a snowstorm. In Reno, he says, he went mad. All the facts are in the wrong places, but they are true.

What is the writing of the undone? How does one say that the meaning lay in how one felt the road while on a bus? How does one say that if the road is America, where can one be at home? How does one say that Myrtle standing on a street corner in Dallas says all there is to say?

In the Ozarks, Asch stays at the house of an old, blind woman, who tells him that when her daughter comes home she will cook dinner for him, but if she sings to him before her daughter returns, he will forget his hunger. Her past and tradition were in stories and songs, Asch notes after hearing her sing. That evening Clarabelle, the daughter, takes him to a square dance in the kitchen of a house.

> The fiddler played his version of a foxtrot, and couples started to dance, and I also tried, but I could not recognize the rhythm, nor lead. They had made of the foxtrot something their own.
>
> (p. 84)

In northern Colorado, Asch joins two union organizers at a meeting to organize Mexican beet workers. One of them, Aragon, a Native Ameri-

can, tells the workers what they know but cannot articulate, as the white organizer could not.

> I seemed to feel what he said more in the pauses between his words, in the silence which he, a man not really fitted for speech but more for doing, needed to arrange his thoughts.
>
> (p. 129)

In Paris, Asch may have asked, as Paul Cézanne did, "if modernism is really possible, at the highest pitch, without a utopian hope or belief that the process of representation might remake the world and our knowledge of it" (Clark, p. 135). By the time Asch has lived in the Valley and traveled by bus across America, felt the road under him, seen its traffic, as James Ballard does in David Cronenberg's film *Crash*, he knows the world cannot be remade and he can write about it only as those who don't speak have shown him: the old, blind woman who sings to make him forget hunger; the fiddler who has made of the foxtrot something his own (as so many American writers have made of English and European literature); Aragon, whose silence must be heard.

This story cannot be told without Myrtle. She has taught Asch what he does not know, given him life—initiated him. If the world cannot be remade, Myrtle, standing on a street in Dallas or in Santa Monica, on her way to Hibbing, Chicago, Denver, Salt Lake, Walla Walla, shows him how it might. "To bring forth new flowers on graves," Rancière writes, "the historian must constantly return to an always living source" (*Short Voyages*, p. 85).

The Road: In Search of America is the story of a voyage, one that began when Asch left New York for Paris in the twenties only to return to America in the thirties, which gave him glimpses of other worlds, taught him who he was, and made him the only writer he could be.

CONCLUSION

The Road was the last novel Asch wrote that was published. In a review in *New Masses*, Alvah C. Bessie dismissed it as soft:

> Accurate as his observations may be, his purpose and his observation would have taken on real impact if he had tried to feel a little less and think a little more, and then say what he had thought. The reader of this book will be continually harassed by a feeling of softness in the writer—there is no other word for it—a softness that skirts the edges of sentimentalism.... it is not enough to say, merely by implication, "This is rotten." The time has come for us to say forthright: "This is rotten and we will change it!"
>
> (p. 23)

Asch would always be dismissed by those on the Left, as Meridel Le Sueur sometimes was, because he did not hew the party line. As much a friend of his as Herbst considered herself, she did not take Asch seriously. He is considered an acolyte of Hemingway and Ford, a writer influenced by Dos Passos and Joyce, but who influenced no one. Barbara Foley, Walter B. Rideout, and Michael Denning do not discuss him in their accounts of the thirties.

In *The Road*, Asch writes, "It didn't matter whether I wrote a book or not," after hearing a drunk white man call a black female stripper "a pretty baboon" (p. 59). But it did and Asch writes it. *The Road* is less "soft," as Bessie calls it, than of a texture yet to be understood.

We must ask further how one lives with the book one writes. How did Crane follow *The Bridge*, Malcolm Lowry *Under the Volcano*, Asch *The Road: In Search of America*?

In 1939 Asch married Carol Tasker Miles and moved to Saratoga Springs, New York. In 1941, at age thirty-nine, he enlisted in the U.S. Army Air Force and flew missions over Europe as a bomber sergeant. (Miles joined the Women's Army Corps.) After the war, they bought a house in Mill Valley, California. Asch wrote, made furniture, taught writing to adults. He published in the *New Yorker, New Republic, Commentary*. He completed two novels of his projected "Marginal Man" series, "Paris Is Home" and "London Is a Lonely Town," but did not revise them after they were rejected. Two novellas, "The Shrewd and the Mad" and "The Livelong Day," and another novel, "Celia," were also rejected by publishers.

In 1964, Asch died from lung cancer.

Selected Bibliography

WORKS OF NATHAN ASCH

NOVELS

The Office. New York: Harcourt, Brace, 1925.

Love in Chartres. New York: Boni, 1927.

Pay Day. New York: Brewer & Warren, 1930.

The Valley. New York: Macmillan, 1935.

The Road: In Search of America. New York: Norton, 1937.

ARTICLES AND STORIES

"The Voice of the Office." *Transatlantic Review* 1:414–420 (June 1924).

"Marc Kranz." *Transatlantic Review* 2:144–153 (August 1924).

"Gertrude Donovan." *Transatlantic Review* 3:608–622 (December 1924).

"In the Country." In *The American Caravan.* Edited by Van Wyck Brooks and others. New York: Macaulay, 1927. Pp. 515–525.

"Dying in Carcassone." *Forum* 84:305–310 (November 1930).

"Cross Country Bus." *New Republic,* January 15, 1934, pp. 301–314.

"Route 61." *New Republic,* January 15, 1936, p. 380.

"Record of a Generation." *New Masses,* February 4, 1936, pp. 23–24.

"A Home for Emma." *Yale Review* 31:350–374 (December 1941).

"Mary." *Contact,* August 8, 1942, pp. 18–44.

"Inland Western Sea." *New Yorker,* April 29, 1950, pp. 29–35.

"The Nineteen Twenties: An Interior." *Paris Review* 6:82–92 (summer 1954).

"My Father and I." *Commentary* 39:55–65 (January 1965).

"In Search of America." In *The Thirties: A Time to Remember.* Edited by Don Congdon. New York: Simon & Schuster, 1962. Pp. 284–306.

"Nathan Asch Remembers Ford Madox Ford, Sam Roth, and Hart Crane." In *Dictionary of Literary Biography Yearbook 2002.* Edited by Matthew J. Bruccoli, George Garrett, and George Parker Anderson. Detroit: Gale, 2003. Pp. 271–281.

PAPERS

Manuscripts, letters, and other memorabilia are in the Nathan Asch Collection, Dacus Library, Winthrop College, Rock Hill, South Carolina. Asch's letters to Malcolm Cowley are with the Cowley papers at the Newberry Library, Chicago.

CRITICAL AND BIOGRAPHICAL STUDIES

Beaver, Harold. "Proletarian or Not?" *Times Literary Supplement*, May 17, 1990, p. 7.

Berthoff, Werner. Introduction to *Pay Day.* Detroit: Omnigraphics, 1990. Pp. iii–xxxvii.

Bessie, Alvah C. "American Byways." *New Masses,* June 22, 1937, pp. 22–23.

Callaghan, Morley. *That Summer in Paris.* New York: Coward-McCann, 1963.

Cowley, Malcolm. *Exile's Return.* New York: Viking, 1966.

———. *A Second Flowering: Works and Days of the Lost Generation.* New York: Viking, 1973.

———. *And I Worked at the Writer's Trade: Chapters of Literary History, 1918–1978.* New York: Viking, 1978.

Farrell, James T. "A Connecticut Valley." *New Masses,* September 10, 1935, p. 28.

Langer, Elinor. *Josephine Herbst.* New York: Warner Books, 1984.

Mills, Eva B. "Nathan Asch." In *American Writers in Paris, 1920–1939.* Edited by Karen Lane Rood. *Dictionary of Literary Biography.* Vol. 4. Detroit: Gale Research, 1980. Pp. 14–15.

———. "Nathan Asch." In *Twentieth-Century American-Jewish Fiction Writers.* Edited by Daniel Walden. *Dictionary of Literary Biography.* Vol. 28. Detroit: Gale Research, 1984. Pp. 3–8.

OTHER SOURCES

Clark, T. J. *Farewell to an Idea.* New Haven, Conn.: Yale University Press, 1999.

Fitzgerald, F. Scott. *The Great Gatsby.* New York: Simon & Schuster, 1995.

Pere Ubu. *Pennsylvania.* Portland, Ore.: Tim/Kerr Records, 1998. T/K155-2.

Porter, Katherine Anne. "The Never-Ending Wrong." *Atlantic* 239, no. 6:37–64 (June 1977).

Rancière, Jacques. *The Names of History: On the Poetics of Knowledge.* Minneapolis: University of Minnesota Press, 1994.

———. *Short Voyages to the Land of the People.* Stanford, Calif.: Stanford University Press, 2003.

HENRY BESTON

(1888—1968)

Dan Brayton

A BEST-SELLING author widely familiar to twentieth-century American readers, Henry Beston is remembered today for a single work of nonfiction, *The Outermost House* (1928). Beston's name and legacy remain closely associated with a particular region of the United States: Cape Cod, Massachusetts. *The Outermost House* is a lyrical memoir of the author's experiences living in a small cabin dubbed "the Fo'castle," situated in the dunes between the outer beach and Nauset Marsh in the town of Eastham. This Thoreauvian narrative of relative solitude (although Beston disliked being compared to Thoreau), in which the author bears witness to the wonders of the natural world, captured the imagination of several generations of American readers and produced a groundswell of public opinion in favor of conserving the landscape it celebrates. Part natural history essay, part philosophical tract, this brief work of nonfiction propelled its author to immediate and lasting fame and contributed to the creation of the Cape Cod National Seashore (Massachusetts). Today Beston is remembered as one of the forebears of the modern environmental movement in the United States, not merely for the impact of his work on Rachel Carson—perhaps the most significant American environmental writer of the twentieth century, who singled out *The Outermost House* as a major influence on her own best-selling books on the sea—but also because of his lasting contribution to the American literature of place.

Because none of his other books achieved anything like the fame of *The Outermost House*, Beston is remembered as something of a one-hit wonder, yet he also wrote more than a dozen other books in his lifetime, ranging from wartime journalism to fairy tales for children. His oeuvre, written between the start of the First World War

and the author's death in 1968 (one more of his books appeared posthumously in 1970), reveals an unquenchable love of the natural world, children, storytelling, and the changing of the seasons as well as a sharp eye for the human impact on the environment and, conversely, a deep appreciation for the ability of the natural world to renew and transform humanity. These are the major themes of his best writings, particularly of his greatest book, *The Outermost House*, one of the foremost contributions to American environmental literature.

Beston's name belongs squarely within a literary genealogy of nonfiction writers committed to celebrating specific regional landscapes that includes Henry David Thoreau, Mary Austin, Aldo Leopold, Edward Abbey, Annie Dillard, Gretel Ehrlich, and Rick Bass, among other noted American environmental writers. It is therefore somewhat surprising that Beston should now be increasingly obscure and his writings neglected. The cause of this decline lies in part with historical changes in literary taste; partly, however, the origins of Beston's current relative obscurity can be found in the author's biography.

LIFE

Still more obscure than Beston's lesser-known literary works is his early biography, largely because of his lifelong reticence toward discussion or writing of himself. Henry Beston Sheahan was born on June 1, 1888, in Boston, Massachusetts, to an Irish American physician father, Joseph Maurice Sheahan, and a French mother, Marie Louise Beston Sheahan. The author grew up in Quincy, Massachusetts, with his one brother, George. The parents, Joseph and Marie Louise, met when the former was studying

medicine in Paris. They subsequently settled in Quincy, where Joseph established his medical practice. In this context the young Henry had a relatively privileged childhood. After attending Adams Academy in Quincy, he entered Harvard College, where he earned his B.A. (1909) and M.A. (1911) in English. Fluent in French as well as English, the young Henry B. Sheahan grew up speaking both languages at home. He moved to Lyon, France, shortly after graduating from Harvard. In France he taught for a brief time at the University of Lyon. During this prewar period of his life the future author spent much of his time in the village of Ste. Catherine-sous-Rivière, outside of Lyons. It was here, more than anywhere else in his young life, that he developed an appreciation for the natural environment. As he wrote much later in life, in a book titled *Especially Maine*, Ste. Catherine was "the first place in which I encountered and knew and loved the earth" (p. 48). It certainly was not the last. His experiences in France were foundational for his later writing.

After a year in France, Henry Beston Sheahan returned to teach for a brief stint in the English Department at Harvard in 1914, but with the outbreak of World War I he returned to France under the auspices of the American Field Service. There, in the summer of 1915 he became, like his literary contemporaries and countrymen Ernest Hemingway, John Dos Passos, and E. E. Cummings, a wartime ambulance driver. Living in the country where his mother was born, Henry possessed a powerful linguistic advantage, for his French language skills allowed him to understand his surroundings at a depth unavailable to his monolingual peers. The young writer's bilingual and bicultural identity gave him an unusual purchase on the English language, for his distinctive literary voice clearly owes much to the diction, syntax, and rhythms of French prose.

The protracted international conflict also known variously as the Great War and the War to End All Wars bequeathed many horrors to the twentieth century, including widespread shell shock (post-traumatic stress disorder), the destruction of an entire generation of young men, an influenza pandemic, a global economic crisis and the subsequent rise of European fascism, and public disillusionment with the motives of politicians and military leaders. In terms of the scale of destruction, human and environmental, and the use of modern, industrial technology to execute outdated military tactics and often obscure geopolitical objectives, nothing quite like World War I had occurred before in human history. With its machine guns (invented decades earlier but put into widespread use in the trenches), flamethrowers, airplane duels, mustard gas, and massive-scale environmental and human destruction, the Great War shocked the people who survived it. The devastating social, psychological, and environmental effects of the war have been amply chronicled by historians and novelists alike; the young Irish-Franco-American writer from Massachusetts would soon contribute to this body of literature.

The future best-selling author who would be known as Henry Beston served in several of the war's most devastating battles, including Bois le Prêtre and Verdun, witnessing some the worst trench warfare at first hand. In 1916, as the scale of warfare grew and its destructiveness intensified, Henry was moved to the northern French town of Verdun, until then a relatively quiet city in the provinces. He arrived there in February, just in time for the onset of a massive German offensive that would last for several months and cause staggeringly high casualties on both sides. The unthinkable violence of the months of intensive warfare around Verdun marked the young writer's consciousness in ways that he would only be able to process years later. Describing the events of this phase of the war for readers on the other side of the Atlantic presented a challenge to the aspiring journalist. In 1916 Henry recounted some of these experiences in his first book, *A Volunteer Poilu*, and in two articles that were published in the *Atlantic Monthly*, "Verdun" and "The Vineyard of Red Wine." These pieces helped to shape American awareness of the horrors transpiring in the trenches of northwestern France in the months prior to the entry of the United States itself into the war in April 1917.

The future author and young expatriate next began to work as a press representative for the U.S. Navy, assigned to the submarine corps. As the sole American journalist to travel with the British Grand Fleet, he witnessed the worst of naval warfare, just as he had experienced the worst of terrestrial warfare in northwestern France a short while earlier. While on assignment with the British Grand Fleet he witnessed the torpedoing and sinking of an American destroyer by a German U-boat, an episode recounted in his second book, *Full Speed Ahead: Tales from the Log of a Correspondent with Our Navy*, published in 1919, soon after the war's end. Whereas the author of the earlier wartime works had been Henry Beston Sheahan, as the war continued he dropped his father's family name and began signing his works, including *Full Speed Ahead*, as "Henry B. Beston." (Within a few years he would drop the middle initial "B," which didn't actually stand for anything.) This change causes some confusion among his readers, and among those who teach his writings, for both names denote the same author, but this fact has often been overlooked. The change was significant in another respect, for Beston's wartime works contain little of the fanciful imagination and tender concern for the natural world evinced by his later stories for children and by his environmental writings. Henry Beston emerged from the First World War a different man, in some respects, from Henry Sheahan.

After the war he returned to the United States and turned his literary activities to writing fairy tales for children. The reason for this imaginative turn, and for dropping his father's family name, has been examined by admirers and biographers ever since. Suffice here to note that Beston was at this time suffering from what he would later describe as a spiritual crisis after the traumatic events he had experienced in the war. Indeed, it is reasonable to describe Beston as a post-traumatic writer in this phase of his life; his turn to imaginative stories and to the wonders of nature accompany a critical attitude toward human constructs. As Beston's biographer Daniel Payne points out, it took some time for Beston to process the full effect of World War I on his consciousness (*Henry Beston Society Program #1*). When he did, Beston retained a genuine and lasting aversion to mechanized and market-ready warfare.

Only a year after the war's end Beston published a book that could hardly have differed more from wartime journalism, *The Firelight Fairy Book* (1919). This collection of tales for children evoked the popular fairy tale books of Andrew Lang—*The Orange Fairy Book*, *The Blue Fairy Book*, and the like. Beston's fairy tales reveal the workings of an imagination spurred by a love for innocence, wonder, and the natural world. This new literary tack proved to be rewarding in the short term, for Beston's next book was *The Starlight Wonder Book* (1923), followed by *The Book of Gallant Vagabonds* in 1925, a collection of biographical descriptions of famous travelers in history, from the early New England settler Thomas Morton to the French poet Arthur Rimbaud and the world traveler John Ledyard. Beston dedicated this book to his friend "Young Teddy" Roosevelt, son of the twenty-sixth president. This was followed by *The Sons of Kai: The Story the Indian Told* in 1926. Neither achieved much critical success.

During this period Beston also worked as an editor at the *Living Age*, a literary magazine associated with the *Atlantic Monthly*, perhaps the foremost magazine in the United States at the time. Being an editor did not entirely suit Beston; even as he edited manuscripts, he dreamed of writing something different, a serious work to which he could dedicate all his talent. Around this time Beston met the celebrated author of children's books Elizabeth Jane Coatsworth (1893–1986)—who would eventually become his wife, lifelong companion, and the mother of their two daughters—at a party in Boston. Like Beston, Coatsworth was already well established when they met, an accomplished author who would in 1931 be awarded the Newbery Medal, the most prestigious annual prize for American children's book writers, for her book *The Cat Who Went to Heaven* (1930). Also like Beston, Coatsworth wrote imaginative stories for children that often emphasized the wonders of the natural world. Between the time they first met and their

marriage in 1929, Beston and Coatsworth were both hard at work. With her encouragement, he—still recovering from his wartime experiences—spent considerable time at the beach in Eastham, Massachusetts (where some of *The Book of Gallant Vagabonds* was composed), then a remote part of the peninsula of Cape Cod, having received an assignment to write an article on the Coast Guardsmen who patrolled the beaches of the outer Cape on foot.

The particular mix of Cape Cod's physical geography, flora, fauna, and high-energy coastal ecosystem appealed powerfully to Beston. Enamored by the seabirds, beach, surf, storms, and the sparse local human population, he found in rural Cape Cod a redemptive landscape where nature's rhythms held the power of spiritual renewal by means of connecting humans to the elemental forces of nature. After repeated trips to the Cape, Beston grew so attached to his sandy haunts that he hired a local carpenter, Harvey Moore, to construct a twenty-by-sixteen wood frame cottage on a narrow sandspit between marsh and open sea at Nauset Beach, in the town of Eastham, in the spring of 1925. The author subsequently dubbed this small cottage the Fo'castle, after the term used to describe the sailors' quarters on a ship. His experiences living there and interacting with the local people, flora, and fauna during this time provided the material for *The Outermost House*. He did not live in Eastham full-time because he and Coatsworth were spending more and more time together. She nevertheless told him that, before she would marry him, Beston must finish the book about Cape Cod, saying, "No book, no marriage" (qtd. in McKibben, ed., *American Earth*, p. 205). For that, and for much else, readers of *The Outermost House* owe her a debt of gratitude.

It is impossible to avoid drawing parallels between *The Outermost House* and the writings of an earlier American writer, Henry David Thoreau. As much as Beston would later shrug off comparisons between his own life and works and those of Thoreau, the parallels between their two masterpieces are too obvious, and numerous, to ignore. Both authors had French heritage; both hailed from eastern Massachusetts; both enjoyed solitude; both lived in a small, secluded cabin near the water's edge; both celebrated the natural world while leveling a critical eye at humanity; both enjoined their readers to seek spiritual transformation by observing natural processes. Both men wrote superb and transformative works of nonfiction. A solitary writer communing intensely with the natural world, living in a small cabin and meditating on the spiritual value of solitude and elemental things—these are the key ingredients of Beston's masterpiece, and of Thoreau's *Walden*. Thoreau lost his brother John before retreating to the woods; Beston endured the horrors of trench warfare. Also like Thoreau before him, Beston distilled two years' worth of living simply in a cabin into a memoir purporting to describe the passage of one year in that place. Both authors sought seclusion, although neither was entirely solitary. Both wrote passionately about the dangers of losing touch with elemental things, and both produced books that read like secular sermons directed at spiritual renewal. Yet neither man was a recluse, and we should not think of either as champions of wilderness in the manner of John Muir, for example, or Anne LaBastille—nature writers who wrote about wilder places than Thoreau or Beston celebrated. In fact, like Thoreau visiting the Emersons on Sundays, Beston frequently left his cottage retreat and ventured into the company of others, both at the nearby Coast Guard station and, on occasion, in Boston.

Yet the differences between the two writers are as revealing as their similarities. Beston considered Thoreau to be something of a heartless ascetic and resisted being compared to his predecessor because of their temperamental contrast. Thoreau was hermetic, edgy, and awkward around women; he never married and prided himself on his own physical "purity." Beston, in contrast, would find happiness as Thoreau never did, fathering two children and sharing his life with a women every bit his intellectual and literary equal. While Thoreau remained underappreciated and little known in his own lifetime, Beston found an appreciative reading public immediately upon the publication of his magnum opus and lived long enough to

reap the fruits of his own literary success. Thoreau never did, nor did he live to bask in the fame his writings would garner him; he died a bachelor in his forties. The similarities between the two men and their books are many but fraught with complexity.

When Beston and Coatsworth were married in 1929, the two were old by the standards of the time, he forty-one and she thirty-six. They lived together for a time on Boston's South Shore (the southern side of Massachusetts Bay) in Hingham, Massachusetts, not far from Quincy, the site of Henry's childhood home. In this respect Beston's life resembled those of many Irish Americans of this era whose families had settled in the Boston area; to this day the South Shore is jocularly referred to as the Irish Riviera. But the mature Beston was as uncomfortable with suburban life as he was with the name Sheahan, and life in Hingham did not suit him or his wife. They longed for more space and readier access to the natural world to which they were both profoundly attached. After the births of their daughters, Margaret (b. 1930) and Catherine (1932–2013), the couple began to spend more and more time with friends in mid-coast Maine, far from the ravages of the ever-expanding twentieth-century metropolitan sprawl.

One day while visiting his friend Jake Day aboard Day's houseboat on Damariscotta Lake, not far from Boothbay, Beston learned from his friend of a property for sale nearby known as Chimney Farm. It consisted of an old farmhouse near Damariscotta Lake in Nobleboro; Elizabeth liked the idea, and they decided to buy it and move north. There they would remain for the rest of their lives, raising their two daughters, continuing to write, and striving to live a mindful life in harmony with the natural world; and there they are buried, their gravestones not far from the farmhouse. As refugees from the East Coast megalopolis seeking refuge in rural Maine, Beston and Coatsworth can be seen, in hindsight, as early members of the back-to-the-land movement that would send many Americans to rural regions of the country, including northern New England, throughout the 1960s and 1970s. Like Helen and Scott Nearing, authors of *The Good*

Life, whose living style in Vermont and then Maine would become the basis for a spiritual movement centered on simplicity and a reverence for nature, Beston and Coatsworth built a life that was at once more traditional and less "plugged in," as we would say today, than what was on offer in this country's cities and suburbs during the middle decades of the twentieth century.

"What do you do after you write *Moby-Dick?*" asks the scholar Daniel Payne, comparing Beston's magnum opus to Herman Melville's and in doing so pointing out that *The Outermost House* was so successful it may have had a temporary crippling effect on Beston's writing (*Henry Beston Society Program #1*). In the next phase of Beston's life, he and Coatsworth raised their children and continued writing books. After a slow start (due to the onset of the Great Depression), sales of *The Outermost House* burgeoned and created a fulfilling and challenging new role for the now famous American nature writer. Although he contemplated writing a sequel about Cape Cod, Beston dragged his heels and later abandoned the project; instead, his next book, *Herbs and the Earth* (1935), explored the history and uses of common household herbs. This book can been seen as the work of a naturalist settling into life on the mid-Maine coast, where the winter ice sometimes did not melt off the local ponds until early June. It is a fine, quiet book, but it is no masterpiece.

At their Chimney Farm home Beston and Coatsworth strove to live up to the ideals articulated in *The Outermost House*—simplicity, fecundity, and harmony with the earth. One way they did this was by growing herbs, "the oldest group of plants known to gardeners," as Beston calls them in *Herbs and the Earth* (p. xvii). At the farmhouse in Nobleboro, Beston had a study that also doubled as a room for herb storage. It is no surprise, then, that he would choose to write a book about humanity's ancient connection to a set of plants. The book is no scientific treatise or farming manual; it is, rather like *The Outermost House*, a natural history essay exploring the uses and meanings of the vegetable kingdom. At its heart lies an argument familiar to readers of

Beston's earlier and better-known book. He claims that

> it is only when we are aware of the earth and of the earth as poetry that we truly live.... It is this earth which is the true inheritance of man, his link with his human past, the source of his religion, ritual and song, the kingdom without whose splendor he lapses from his mysterious estate of man to a baser world which is without the other virtue and the other integrity of the animal.

(pp. 4–5)

The "baser world" into which a disconnected humanity may lapse is easily identified as the modern industrial society from which Beston sought refuge, a world in which "there is no nature for a naturalist to see, there are no birds save, 'the Spotted Chevrolet and the Greater and Lesser Buick,'" and industrialized society, like industrial warfare, tends toward the destruction of earth and humanity alike (*Especially Maine*, p. 72).

For Beston, cultivating an herb garden could help to restore harmony between humankind and the earth, and a historically aware appreciation for those special plants that human cultures have long valued was part of this restoration. *Herbs and the Earth,* then, is an antimodern book, a cultural and agricultural critique of modern humanity's material excesses and spiritual impoverishment. It is noteworthy in this respect that Beston handwrote his manuscripts instead of typing them, preferring the directness of his method to the mechanical clattering of a writing machine. This was a laborious way to write books, but it was consistent with Beston's overarching commitment to simplicity and painstaking care for material things.

For decades readers have wondered why Beston failed to build on the success of *The Outermost House* by writing another book equal to it. Explanations vary. His slow, painstaking composition process and extremely high standards for his own work led him to revise his work continuously. Writing did not come easily, but as a successful author Beston could not and did not stop writing altogether; he continued to write books of nonfiction, some of them quite good. But never again did Beston achieve the success

he reached with *The Outermost House*, his subsequent works failing, one after another, to achieve its popularity and impact. But such was the popularity of his best-known book that Beston remained in the public eye for the rest of his life and continued to give talks, receive honorary degrees, and publish short pieces in various publications. Together he and Coatsworth lived the life of a successful literary couple, and their devotion to literature and to each other rubbed off on others—countless readers of their books and those whose lives they touched in person. Their daughter Catherine, who would be known to readers as Kate Barnes as an adult, would be appointed the state of Maine's first poet laureate in 1996.

In the decades following the publication of *The Outermost House*, honorary degrees were conferred on Beston by some of the most prestigious academic institutions in the United States, including Bowdoin College, Dartmouth College (where Beston lectured regularly), and the University of Maine. The Harvard chapter of Phi Beta Kappa made him an honorary member of the society, and *Audubon Magazine* named Beston an honorary editor. A special twentieth-anniversary issue of *The Outermost House* was published in 1948. In 1954 Beston was elected a member of the American Academy of Arts and Sciences, which awarded him in 1960 with the Emerson-Thoreau Medal, an honor that only Robert Frost and T. S. Eliot had received before him.

Beston's public influence in the latter half of the twentieth century was not limited to the honors conferred upon him; it also encompassed public recognition for his gifts to the American public. In 1959 Beston donated his cabin, the Fo'castle, to the Massachusetts Audubon Society, and, in a culminating moment five years later, the building was dedicated as a National Literary Landmark at a ceremony with many influential public figures in attendance. The dedicatory plaque, signed by Governor Endicott Peabody of Massachusetts and Secretary of the Interior Stewart Lee Udall, contained the words: "'The Outermost House' in which Henry Beston, author-naturalist, wrote his classic book by that

name wherein he sought the great truth and found it in the nature of man. This plaque dedicated October 11, 1964, by a grateful citizenry." Beston himself was present to acknowledge the honor. With his health failing, this was one of the last trips he would make away from Chimney Farm.

On April 15, 1968, Henry Beston died at his home in Nobleboro, leaving his wife, who would survive him by decades, and their two daughters, Margaret and Catherine (Kate). A decade later, and almost exactly a half-century after the *The Outermost House* was first published, a storm surge caused by a massive winter storm locally known as the Blizzard of 1978 produced unusually high tides in the month of February. The narrow sandspit of Nauset Beach was heavily eroded by the high water and heavy surf: new cuts through the spit were made, and the Fo'castle was swept out to sea. For some readers this loss was tragic, while for others the loss of Beston's cabin was a fittingly natural end. It was not so much this cottage, after all, as the beach and its memorialization in *The Outermost House* that appeals to the throngs of visitors that continue to flock to the site. Signs placed by the National Park Service on the boardwalk at Coast Guard Beach honor Beston's legacy. As Nan Turner Waldron, a devoted follower of Beston's who sought refuge in the Fo'castle in the 1970s, wrote: "Many know the book, some carry it with them. Still they come, pilgrims of a sort—stirred by his sense of wonder but drawn by his vision of hope." These two qualities, wonder and hope, breathe from every page of *The Outermost House.* Readers continue to imbibe both from their literary source.

THE OUTERMOST HOUSE

When Beston published *The Outermost House* he "was forty years old, a writer and editor at the midpoint of an accomplished if rather obscure literary career," as Payne has noted (*American Nature Writers*, p. 107). The book's publication would be the turning point in his career, catapulting him into the highest echelon of American writers and garnering him the publicity, honors, and wealth that so many writers crave yet few attain. Today, after nearly a century in print and numerous editions, *The Outermost House* is widely considered a classic of American nature writing, regional literature, and the literature of place. It is frequently taught in college courses alongside the writings of Ralph Waldo Emerson, John Burroughs, Thoreau, Muir, Abbey, and Dillard. It is a remarkable work of descriptive nonfiction, part memoir, part chorography (place writing), and part philosophical meditation on the human value of nature's gifts. It is a highly developed natural history essay as well as a meditation on revaluing the gifts of the biophysical environment. Beston immersed himself in the natural world with a passionate attentiveness that resonates on every page of *The Outermost House.* Although he was quite myopic and hard of hearing as well, Beston wrote of sand, wind, water, birds, and storms with a rapturous attachment that makes for a compelling reading experience.

The Outermost House is first and foremost a book about the beach. Beston's beach, however, is no mere recreational space; it is a springboard into the natural world and a window onto geologic time and the workings of nature. In Beston's prose the beach becomes a stage for life itself, human and nonhuman, full of drama and latent meaning. He writes, "To understand this great outer beach, to appreciate its atmosphere, its 'feel,' one must have a sense of it as the scene of wreck and elemental drama" (*Outermost House*, p. 165; all quotations are from the 1989 Penguin Books edition). With Nauset Marsh behind his cottage and the Atlantic Ocean at his doorstep, Beston mapped in exquisite prose the ever-changing boundary between ocean and sand that marks the shoreline of lower Cape Cod at Eastham. The first chapter, with its evocative description of the physical geography of Cape Cod, evokes Elizabethan chorography with its careful narrative description of the physical geography of the region combined with a celebratory tone. Beston's narrative persona combines philosophical and moral seriousness with anecdotal intimacy—he seems, at first reading, like a somewhat confessional preacher intent on finding deep meaning in everything he sees and feels.

Right away Beston tells the reader, "I built myself a house upon the beach" (p. 6), and situates us there by personifying the sea to evoke geologic time:

> At the foot of this cliff a great ocean beach runs north and south unbroken, mile lengthening into mile. Solitary and elemental, unsullied and remote, visited and possessed by the outer sea, these sands might be the end or the beginning of the world. Age by age, the sea here gives battle to the land; age by age, the earth struggles for her own, calling to her defence her energies and her creations, bidding her plants steal down upon the beach, and holding the frontier sands in a net of grass and roots which the storms wash free. The great rhythms of nature, to-day so dully disregarded, wounded even, have here their spacious and primeval liberty; cloud and shadow of cloud, wind and tide, tremor of night and day.
>
> (p. 2)

Notice how Beston's lyrical prose employs the tools of the poet. In this passage the alliteration of "dully disregarded" resonates with the *d*'s in "to-day" and "wounded," thuddingly driving home the notion of our alienation from the natural world. At the same time, the gentle personification of the earth suggests a healing agency in natural processes. Beston's sharp eye notes the ways in which natural cycles form a kind of sensory symphony for the careful observer. One word in particular jumps out from this description of setting, the descriptor "elemental." It is Beston's favorite adjective, and he uses it again and again to describe the fundamental aspects of the given world with which modern humanity has lost touch. It is a word that suggests a deep hidden connection between nature's rhythms and human life.

The Outermost House is laden with passages memorable for their intellectual seriousness, arresting visual images, and impassioned calls for a change in our conventional attitudes toward the natural world. After setting the scene for his solitary sojourn, Beston describes his humble shingled cottage in detail, its construction and situation, as well as his manner of living in it, introducing the special combination of wonder toward nature and weariness toward civilization that he retains throughout the narrative. Next he

recounts how his short visit to the beach in 1926 turned into a longer sojourn:

> The fortnight ending, I lingered on, and as the year lengthened into autumn, the beauty and mystery of this earth and outer sea so possessed and held me that I could not go. The world to-day is sick to its thin blood for lack of elemental things, for fire before the hands, for water welling from the earth, for air, for the dear earth itself underfoot. In my world of beach and dune these elemental presences lived and had their being, and under their arch there moved an incomparable pageant of nature and the year.
>
> (p. 10)

Again we encounter the striking descriptive term "elemental," which signals the author's criticism of industrial modernity. The term signifies for Beston a direct physical connection with the material universe, with the given, bedrock, nonanthropogenic substances and forces of this world: water, fire, sand, surf, wind, night, and the seasons. Such passages as the above reveal the combination of lyrical prose and spiritually inflected appreciation for the natural environment that characterize the entirety of *The Outermost House*.

Robert Finch and John Elder make the claim that Beston's "style has a sensual and rhythmic richness unsurpassed in the genre [of nature writing]," yet Beston is cagey about his literary forebears, many of whom are clearly French (*Nature Writing*, p. 366). At one point in the narrative he notes that "our whole English tradition neglects smell," while, by contrast, "one can scarcely read ten lines of any French verse without encountering the omnipresent, the inevitable *parfum*" (*Outermost House*, p. 190). Clearly this cultural allegiance to things French is not merely olfactory but also literary. While the sole philosopher Beston mentions by name in the text of *The Outermost House* is René Descartes, and then quite critically, it is clear that he was influenced by the meditative and mellifluous prose of the eighteenth-century French philosophe Jean-Jacques Rousseau, both thematically and stylistically. One cannot help hearing the echoes of Rousseau in such passages as this:

> The flux and reflux of ocean, the incomings of waves, the gatherings of birds, the pilgrimages of

the peoples of the sea, winter and storm, the splendour of autumn and the holiness of spring—all these were part of the great beach. The longer I stayed, the more eager I was to know this coast and to share its mysterious and elemental life.

(p. 10)

This passage echoes Rousseau down to the very word choice: "flux and reflux" is in fact a direct translation of the same phrase used in French by the great philosophe in his late book *Reveries of a Solitary Walker*. Indeed, Beston's prose is in some respects markedly French, its lyricism evoking the prose poems of Charles Baudelaire far more than the assertive optimism of Ralph Waldo Emerson or the edgy moralizing of Thoreau. Like the prose in Rousseau's *Reveries*, the writing in *Outermost* mixes lyrical prose descriptions of rambles in the countryside with flights of high philosophy. Both works blend memoir with empirical first-person micro-travelogue, and both narratives interweave chapters that can be read as freestanding philosophical essays on the value and significance of the natural world. In his mastery of the first-person essay genre, Beston also owes a debt to another great French essayist-philosopher, the Renaissance luminary Michel de Montaigne, whose *Essays* established the nonfiction prose essay as a legitimate philosophical genre.

Beston's main rhetorical strategy is to describe natural phenomena—the passage of migratory birds, the sounds of the pounding surf, the flight of a deer from marauding dogs, the drama of shipwreck on the coast—with great precision and lyricism from his own eyewitness perspective on the beach, and then to introduce a philosophical idea that he develops through the lens of rapt attention toward nature's splendor. His observations combine amateur natural history with spiritual contemplation and speculative flights of fancy about the alienation of modern humanity from the physical environment; these disparate elements are linked together by a framing narrative of a solitary sojourn at the edge of the sea. It is a strategy that has proven particularly effective for generations of American nature writers, and the *Outermost House* contains many unusually memorable and quotable passages of descriptive prose.

As the narrative proceeds, the reader is swept up by the combination of superbly crafted descriptive prose and deeply personal philosophical fervor that characterizes Beston's writing at its best. One of Beston's achievements in this book is to transcend the quotidian description of the beach sojourn by raising a series of challenges to modern lifestyles—challenges posed, at first, in the form of simple observations. For instance, one of the most celebrated of these passages in *The Outermost House* begins as a description of the flight of a flock of shorebirds that the author observes on one of his walks along the beach. How, he wonders, do they fly so closely together, coordinating their takeoffs and landings with such careful synchronicity? Have we truly, he wonders, understood birds—and animals more generally?

We need another and a wiser and perhaps a more mystical concept of animals. Remote from universal nature, and living by complicated artifice, man in civilization surveys the creature through the glass of his knowledge and sees thereby a feather magnified and the whole image in distortion. We patronize them for their incompleteness, for their tragic fate of having taken form so far below ourselves. And therein we err, and greatly err. For the animal shall not be measured by man. In a world older and more complete than ours they move finished and complete, gifted with extensions of the senses we have lost or never attained, living by voices we shall never hear. They are not brethren, they are not underlings; they are other nations, caught with ourselves in the net of life and time, fellow prisoners of the splendour and travail of the earth.

(p. 25)

This passage is striking for its intellectual seriousness and stylistic power. The moral vision Beston gleans from observing the synchronized motions of a flock of shorebirds is couched in exquisitely cadenced English. His attentiveness to the denizens of the coast, whether gulls, terns, eagles, marsh hawks, semipalmated and piping plovers, jaegers, skates, gannets, puffins, alewives, sharks, muskrats, protozoans, sailors, or Coast Guardsmen, is everywhere characterized by an insistence on the possibility of spiritual transformation by means of fresh encounters with the natural world.

The argument appears simple: we fail to understand nonhuman life forms, and life itself, because we too slavishly follow Descartes in seeing animals as machines motivated by merely instinctual forces. By reducing nonhuman life to the soulless status of the machine, we evacuate the spiritual content of the nonhuman world. In so doing we not only look down on other animal life forms; we also denigrate ourselves by detaching our own lives from the greater mystery of life itself. Instead of seeing animals as lesser beings than ourselves, Beston affirms, we should see them as "other nations," creatures radically different from ourselves who nonetheless have their own integrity, their own rules, habits, and patterns that we simply do not fully understand and, therefore, that we should respect instead of denigrating. As Payne astutely summarizes the point, "Beston rejected the traditionally anthropocentric worldview of western civilization and replaced it with a biocentric one that extended a respectful sympathy for other species" (*American Nature Writers*, p. 111). This respect for all living things is palpable throughout *The Outermost House*.

After enjoining readers to reconsider our conceptions of the animal kingdom, Beston goes on to describe other "elemental" features of the natural world. It is this keen observation of everyday natural phenomena, so careful and attentive that the dynamics of these phenomena seem as if reborn, that stands out in Beston's writing. This attentiveness reaches a crescendo in chapter 3, "The Headlong Wave," which begins with the author declaring that he will attempt something never before essayed by a writer—to describe the sound of surf breaking on a beach in all its musical complexity. This he does, and it is a bravura performance of rhetorical description that brilliantly evokes the symphonic combinations of sounds caused by breaking waves. Consider the following passage, in which Beston tunes his voice to the natural forces that enthrall him:

> The sea has many voices. Listen to the surf, really lend it your ears, and you will hear in it a world of sounds: hollow boomings and heavy roarings, great watery tumblings and tramplings, long hissing seethes, sharp, rifle-shot reports, splashes, whispers, the grinding undertone of stones, and sometimes vocal sounds that might be the half-heard talk of people in the sea. And not only is the great sound varied in the manner of its making, it is also constantly changing its tempo, its pitch, its accent, and its rhythm, being now loud and thundering, now almost placid, now furious, now grave and solemn-slow, now a simple measure, now a rhythm monstrous with a sense of purpose and elemental will.

(p. 44)

Not bad for a writer with poor hearing. Here he makes excellent use of his descriptive powers, transmuting empirical observations into sentences with their own distinct musicality. This passage also encodes an intertextual allusion to Shakespeare's tragedy *Julius Caesar*, with the injunction to "lend [the surf] your ears." Although the emphasis, here as elsewhere, is on the freshness of direct observation, Beston's observations are frequently made in a highly allusive style in which a great deal of the author's education lies distilled.

From Gilbert White to Gretel Ehrlich, nature writers have excelled at describing natural phenomena, yet few have attained the sheer descriptive force that Beston achieves in his most memorable passages. *The Outermost House* contains virtuosic descriptions of storms on the coast, rain, sleet, and snows, as well as vivid accounts of shipwrecks that he either witnessed or heard about from locals. He also describes interactions with the Coast Guardsmen who traverse the sands between Eastham and Truro, their conversation, lives, and hardships. In one vivid vignette he recounts observing a deer that is chased by two dogs, as it finds sanctuary by swimming across part of the Nauset Marsh to a tidal island. A storm arises, and the deer remains marooned on the island. Later, as it attempts to swim ashore to the mainland, it is buffeted by large, floating chunks of ice. Fortunately, the author reveals that he is not the only witness of the deer's plight; several Coast Guardsmen arrive in a small boat and help the deer ashore, where it presumably returns to the safety of the woods. These kindly guardians of the beach prove to be nature's stewards too in this episode, and their generosity toward the beset deer redeems the

viciousness of the dogs that chased it in the first place.

Unlike many more recent works of environmental literature, there is little direct criticism of humanity in *The Outermost House*, or of the anthropogenic degradation of the environment. Beston's narrative is no environmentalist's harangue about the causes of and solutions to particular issues, nor does it stake out specific ideological positions on hot-button issues. The way Beston stakes out a moral high ground for environmental writing is by maintaining a tone of wonder and reverence throughout the narrative—a disposition toward the cosmos (stars in the night sky, for example) and toward living flora and fauna. The reader cannot help being struck by Beston's deep respect for his fellow humans at the beach as well, especially for the hardworking Coast Guardsmen he singles out for praise. Above all, Beston's narrative persona is that of a caring, attentive person who listens to the wind and pays minute attention to the dynamics of natural processes—the sound of waves breaking on the beach, the collective motions of birds in flight, the appearance of sand dunes in all seasons.

But a deep undercurrent of criticism directed toward anthropocentrism and its environmental effects can be discerned nonetheless. In spite of its tone of reverence, the narrative subtly and persistently critiques the spiritual and material depredations of our modern, materialistic, market-obsessed lifestyle. Like *Walden*, *The Outermost House* celebrates simplicity and rejects the exploitative dimensions of consumer society; unlike Thoreau, however, Beston prefers to couch his critique of industrial modernity in passages that celebrate nature's wonders. When Beston offers a direct account of oil pollution in the marine environment he also reminds us of the awesome power of the sea. When he describes how the practice of transferring fuel to freighters leads to spills and recounts the plight of doomed seabirds covered in oil, he draws the reader in with details about his attempts to adopt unruly birds. Similarly, he condemns light pollution obliquely by praising the beauty of the night sky, which, he notes, humans can only fully appreciate far from the artificial lights that obscure it. In these sections of the book it is clear that Beston is deeply concerned about civilization's drift away from the natural world, from "elemental things," which he blames on our growing addiction to technology and material complexity. The conundrums of the animal kingdom, the darkness of the night sky, the destructive power of a storm at sea, the effects of winter on the frozen sand—these are some of the topics that Beston investigates in order to suggest that nature's apparent harshness and incomprehensibility in fact contribute to the mystery and wonder of the earth.

It is no surprise, therefore, that in chapter 8, "Night on the Great Beach," the reader is exhorted to reconsider his or her attitude toward darkness itself. For, Beston argues, "to-day's civilization is full of people who have not the slightest notion of the character or the poetry of night, who have never even seen night" (p. 176). Such a monstrous alienation from diurnal reality brings the narrator to one of his very few direct, negative judgments: "to live thus, to know only artificial night, is as absurd and evil as to know only artificial day" (p. 176). This is as final and critical a pronouncement as Beston makes, and it stands out in the narrative for its harshness. Yet he then goes on, in one of his characteristic rushes of melodious prose, to address the reader with an exhortation:

> Learn to reverence night and to put away the vulgar fear of it, for, with the banishment of night from the experience of man, there vanishes as well a religious emotion, a poetic mood, which gives depth to the adventure of humanity. By day, space is one with the earth and with man—it is his sun that is shining, his clouds that are floating past; at night, space is his no more. When the great earth, abandoning day, rolls up the deeps of the heavens and the universe, a new door opens for the human spirit, and there are few so clownish that some awareness of the mystery of being does not touch them as they gaze. For a moment of night we have a glimpse of ourselves and of our world islanded in its stream of stars—pilgrims of mortality, voyaging between horizons across eternal seas of space and time. Fugitive though the instant be, the spirit of man is, during it, ennobled by a genuine moment of emotional dignity, and poetry makes its own both the human spirit and experience.

(p. 176)

This is a hymn to the night sky and a plea to abandon anthropocentrism; it is a metaphysics of nature, night, and life based on no system or orthodoxy but, rather, based on awe for all life.

Near the end of *The Outermost House* the narrator recounts seeing a young man swimming naked in the surf. In a rare (but by no means unique) moment of narrative focus on a human figure in the seascape, the reader beholds the arresting image of a body-surfing young man "standing naked on the steep beach, his feet in the climbing seethe" (p. 215). After describing the repeated dives the young man makes into the surf, the narrator reflects:

> It was all a beautiful thing to see: the surf thundering across the great natural world, the beautiful and compact body in its naked strength and symmetry, the astounding plunge across the air, arms extended ahead, legs and feet together, the emerging stroke of the flat hands, and the alternate rhythms of the sunburned and powerful shoulders.
>
> (p. 216)

What strikes the reader about this passage is the impersonal description of the young swimmer, whose actions, recounted by an impersonal and presumably distant observer, are not presented as being specifically human; they could be the movements of any intertidal animal. First, the swimmer is a not a person with an identity but an unnamed "body"; second, instead of using the third-person masculine possessive "his" we are treated to descriptions of "the beautiful and compact body," "the flat hands," and "the sunburned and powerful shoulders." What jumps out at us is the depersonalizing use of the definite article "the." This youth is de-individuated, perhaps even dehumanized to some extent; observing the young man at second hand the reader is reminded of the book's previous descriptions of animals of all kinds.

This impersonal description evokes a scientist's field journal; it is a record of empirical observations. One effect of this descriptive strategy is to render the image of a human body leaping in the surf a picture of stunning harmony between human life and the marine environment. Like a seal frolicking in the surf, the young man becomes a creature at one with nature. Yet it is precisely the physicality of the youth and his oneness with the surf that defines his humanity for Beston, who "watch[es] this picture of a fine human being free for the moment of everything save his own humanity and framed in a scene of nature" (p. 216). In this instance, humanity is defined as the ability to connect and commune with the physical environment, with nature and its forces. As if to emphasize the symbolic dimensions of this vignette, Beston ends chapter 9 with deliberate symbolism: "My swimmer having gone his way, out of a chance curiosity I picked the top of a dune goldenrod, and found at the very bottom of a cocoon of twisted leaves the embryo head of the late autumnal flower" (p. 217). The imagery of renewal cannot be overlooked: like the youth in the surf, the flowering goldenrod offers the prospect of revitalization and renewal.

In the final chapter of *The Outermost House*, "Orion Rises on the Dunes," Beston provides the reader with a series of self-reflexive summations of what he has learned in a year at the beach. Posing the question of what he has learned "of Nature" in "so strange a year," he offers this answer:

> I would answer that one's first appreciation [of nature] is a sense that the creation is still going on, that the creative forces are as great and as active today as they have ever been, and that to-morrow's morning will be as heroic as any of the world. Creation is here and now. So near is man to the creative pageant, so much a part is he of the endless and incredible experiment, that any glimpse he may have will be but the revelation of a moment, a solitary note heard in a symphony thundering through debatable existences of time. Poetry is as necessary to comprehension as science.
>
> (p. 220)

This is a decidedly heterodox statement—at least, from the point of view of organized religion. Far from being the finite act of a creator-deity whose worked extended over six days and one supplementary day of rest, the creation—the earth's creation—is not complete but ongoing. This argument, of course, gestures to evolution and ecological processes as ongoing developments that unfold in time. What we call nature, asserts Henry Beston, cannot be defined in the past tense;

it is the lived experience of a cosmic "experiment" far grander than ourselves.

BESTON'S LEGACY

Nature writing has played a significant role in land conservation and environmental legislation in the United States, although many nature writers wish that they could have a more direct impact on policy decisions, especially those pertaining to conservation. The writings of John Muir provided the inspiration for the national parks movement. Thoreau's *Walden* lies behind the present trust that conserves the waters of Walden Pond and the surrounding landscape. Henry Beston's *The Outermost House* contributed to this tradition by inspiring a generation of lawmakers and voters at precisely the right historical moment. On August 7, 1961, President John F. Kennedy signed a bill, passed by both houses of Congress, into law establishing the Cape Cod National Seashore. This was an area consisting of some 44,000 acres comprising ponds, marshes, swamps, upland woods, and approximately forty miles of outer Cape Cod beach stretching from Chatham, at its southern end, to Provincetown in the north. The new National Seashore would be administered by the U.S. National Park Service. A clearer example of the power of literature to effect environmental change could hardly be found, for the establishment of the Cape Cod National Seashore can be linked directly to the popularity of Beston's best-known book.

Although writers and politicians long before the 1960s had initiated efforts to preserve the landscape of the Outer Cape, it was not until the rise of John F. Kennedy that propitious political conditions would make it happen. As a senator from Massachusetts, Kennedy had supported the plan for the National Seashore with his colleague Senator Leverett Saltonstall, only to have the initiative stall out during the Eisenhower administration. As a newly elected president, however, Kennedy, who had spent much of his boyhood in the nearby town of Hyannis, just south and west of the region to be preserved, enthusiastically signed the bill into law.

Kennedy's influential secretary of the interior Stewart Udall, who spearheaded the creation of a number of national parks and landmarks as well as promoting considerable new environmental legislation, was charged with overseeing the acquisition of approximately sixty-nine square miles of public land and managing the new park. For over five decades the Seashore has provided recreation for human visitors and refuge for both endemic and migratory wildlife. Today the Seashore receives more than 4 million visitors each year. Although the Fo'castle no longer stands on narrow Nauset Beach, *The Outermost House* remains a literary monument for readers and visitors inspired by Beston's finest work.

Selected Bibliography

WORKS OF HENRY BESTON

BOOKS

A Volunteer Poilu. Boston: Houghton Mifflin, 1916.

Full Speed Ahead: Tales from the Log of a Correspondent with Our Navy. Garden City, N.Y.: Doubleday, Page, 1919.

The Firelight Fairy Book. Boston: Atlantic Monthly Press, 1919.

The Starlight Wonder Book. Boston: Atlantic Monthly Press, 1923.

The Book of Gallant Vagabonds. New York: Doran, 1925.

The Sons of Kai: The Story the Indian Told. New York: Macmillan, 1926.

The Outermost House: A Year of Life on the Great Beach of Cape Cod. Garden City, N.Y.: Doubleday, Doran, 1928.

Herbs and the Earth. Garden City, N.Y.: Doubleday, Doran, 1935.

Five Bears and Miranda. With Elizabeth Jane Coatsworth. New York: Macmillan, 1939.

The Tree That Ran Away. New York: Macmillan, 1941.

The St. Lawrence. New York: Farrar & Rinehart, 1942.

Northern Farm: A Chronicle of Maine. New York: Rinehart, 1948.

Henry Beston's Fairy Tales. New York: Aladdin, 1952.

Chimney Farm Bedtime Stories. With Elizabeth Jane Coatsworth. New York: Holt, Rinehart and Winston, 1966.

Especially Maine: The Natural World of Henry Beston from

Cape Cod to the St. Lawrence. Brattleboro, Vt.: S. Greene Press, 1970.

As Editor

American Memory: Being a Mirror of the Stirring and Picturesque Past of Americans and the American Nation. New York: Farrar & Rinehart, 1937.

White Pine and Blue Water: A State of Maine Reader. New York: Farrar, Straus, 1950.

Articles

"Verdun." *Atlantic Monthly* 118 (July 1916).

"Vineyard of Red Wine." *Atlantic Monthly* 118 (August 1916).

"With the American Submarines." *Atlantic Monthly* 122 (November 1918).

"The Wardens of Cape Cod." *World's Work* 47 (December 1923).

"Night on a Great Beach." *Atlantic Monthly* 141 (June 1928).

"Garden Escapes." *House Beautiful* 78 (November 1936).

"Some Birds of a Maine Lake." *Audubon Magazine* 45 (September 1943).

"Sister Swallow, Beloved Bird of Europe." *Audubon Magazine* 46 (July 1944).

"Spring Comes to the Farm." *Progressive* 12 (May 1948).

"End of a Farm Summer." *Progressive* 12 (October 1948).

"Summer Regained." *Progressive* 14 (June 1950).

"Season of Splendor." *Progressive* 14 (November 1950).

Papers

Beston Family Papers, 1899–1977. George J. Mitchell Department of Special Collections & Archives, Bowdoin College Library, Brunswick, Maine.

CRITICAL AND BIOGRAPHICAL STUDIES

Coatsworth, Elizabeth Jane. *Personal Geography: Almost an Autobiography.* Brattleboro, Vt.: S. Greene, 1976.

Federman, Donald. "Toward an Ecology of Place: Three Views of Cape Cod." In *Colby Library Quarterly* 13, no. 3:209–222 (1977).

Finch, Robert, and John Elder, eds. *Nature Writing: The Tradition in English.* New York: Norton, 2002.

Lorenz, Clarissa M. "Henry Beston: The Outermost Man." *Atlantic Monthly* 242:107–110 (October 1978).

Lyon, Thomas J. *This Incomperable Lande: A Book of American Nature Writing.* Boston: Houghton Mifflin, 1989.

McKibben, Bill, ed. *American Earth: Environmental Writing Since Thoreau.* New York: Literary Classics of the United States, 2008.

Paul, Sherman. "Coming Home to the World: Another Journal for Henry Beston." In his *For Love of the World: Essays on Nature Writers.* Iowa City: University of Iowa Press, 1992. Pp. 111–134.

Payne, Daniel G. "Henry Beston (1888–1968)." In *American Nature Writers,* vol. 1. Edited by John Elder. New York: Scribners, 1996. Pp.107–120.

———. *Henry Beston Society Program #1: Daniel Payne Interview.* https://www.youtube.com/watch?v=SbUFbML3cbo

Spencer, Maryellen. "Henry Beston (1888–1968): A Primary Checklist." *Resources for American Literary Study* 12, no. 1:49–63 (spring 1982).

Waldron, Nan Turner. *Journey to the Outermost House.* Bethlehem, Conn.: Butterfly & Wheel, 1991.

Wild, Peter. "Henry Beston's *The Outermost House.*" *North Dakota Quarterly* 55, no. 1:188–195 (winter 1987).

EULA BISS

(1977—)

Jen Hirt

THE WOVEN LYRICAL essays and strange prose poems of Eula Biss have been making readers stop and think since 2001, when publishers took note of her unique style and invited her into the emerging world of the creative nonfiction essay. Her critical acumen has been compared to her literary predecessors Joan Didion (b. 1934), Susan Sontag (1933–2004), and Rebecca Solnit (b. 1961), three nonfiction writers known for their ability to explain elements of American culture with profound precision. But what makes Biss different from her female literary forebears, other than the fact that she's from a different genera-tion (one that cannot help but critique society through a post-9/11 lens, even if the watershed moment remains unmentioned in her work) is the brevity of her writing and its kinship with poetry and metaphor. It would be accurate to label Biss as a lyrical essayist. It would also be accurate to call her a prose poet. And a reader need only take one glance at her detailed endnotes in two of her three books to realize she is an ac-complished researcher with streetwise journalism skills as well. She can make a political argument as soundly as she can write a description or a verse that seems to be straight out of the 1960s language-poet movement. Simply put, Eula Biss is an intellectual prose writer who is less con-cerned with genres, categories, characters, and narrative and more concerned with letting language do its job, which is not so much to explain or clarify but to illuminate peculiar juxtapositions and startling metaphorical connections.

In a 2014 interview with the online magazine *Numero Cinq* she said she was "heavily influ-enced by poetry, and I was lucky to be reading Adrienne Rich and Sylvia Plath as I was finding my way as a young writer. I count that as one of the reasons why I think of personal narrative … as a perfectly viable space for intellectual exploration." In the same interview, she cited the novelists William Faulkner and Marilynne Robinson (a former professor of Biss's) as major influences as well, in particular their adherence to the idea that reading literature (and writing it) gets us closer to the consciousness of others. This is important for Biss because one of her reliable themes across all three of her books is her struggle with how separate we really are from anyone else. Her conclusion, again and again, is that while we like to think we are autonomous, that way of seeing ourselves (and others) is fraught with error, and it needs to be questioned. Her first book, *The Balloonists* (2002), dealt with this on a personal level, and she looked closely at her parents' divorce and her own entrance into a serious relationship and marriage. Her second book, *Notes from No Man's Land* (2009), shifted the debate to race, presenting a slew of unusual research meant to make us think about ethnic perceptions in America. Her third book, *On Im-munity: An Inoculation* (2014),took the individual-versus-society debate to the volatile field of childhood vaccinations.

Through all these publications, Biss has remained in the upper echelons of young prose writers, having won many prestigious grants and awards in her thirties (honors often given to writ-ers twice her age). She lives in Evanston, Illinois, and is a professor at Northwestern University.

EARLY LIFE, COLLEGE, AND FIRST PUBLICA-TIONS

Eula Ruth Biss was born on August 9, 1977, in Rochester, New York, to Roger T. Biss, a physi-cian, and Ellen Graf, a writer and sculptor. She

was the eldest of four children: a sister, Mavis; a brother, Athan, and the youngest sibling, a sister named Paroda.

Biss's formative years were defined by fluid racial and ethnic identities that altered what would have otherwise been a mainstream white upbringing. Her parents divorced when Biss was still young. Her mother eventually lived with a black man devoted to the West African religion of Yoruba, so Biss and her siblings often experienced the art, dancing, music, and rituals of the religion. Later, her mother married a Chinese man she met on a blind date in China. Biss had moved on to college by the time the Chinese stepfather arrived, but on visits home she was still a part of a cultural exchange that was defined in part by the double language barrier of Biss's mother not speaking Chinese and her new husband not speaking English. This time in Biss's life is not something she has directly written about at length, but it was documented in her mother's memoir, *The Natural Laws of Good Luck* (2009). In addition, Biss had a close relationship with a cousin from her mother's side who had a white mother (Biss's aunt) and a black father. Biss and her cousin would eventually room together in Brooklyn, New York, at the turn of the century, a time and place that further energized her critiques of identity.

Her first publication, earned while she was still a Hampshire College undergraduate living in Amherst, Massachusetts, was the 1998 short story "Team Players," published by *Race Traitor*, a radical 'zine based in Cambridge, Massachusetts. Set in a college dorm room, the story features an unnamed female narrator listening to a Jewish classmate, Nick, tell a disturbing story about the time in high school when his friends began randomly beating black people and Nick watched it happen. The story is primarily Nick's monologue, with only a handful of quiet clues about how the narrator, who may or may not be based on Biss, is reacting. The narrator listens, filling in sensory details and trying to assess if Nick is racist (for going along) or not (for not beating anyone). She wonders if she should comfort Nick when he seems on the verge of tears after revealing that one of the boys beat a young girl. Nick wraps up the story by revealing that a father of one of the friends was abusive and racist, a detail that seems to allow Nick to rationalize the violence. In the conclusion, Nick admits that the situation was uncomfortable yet he didn't leave. The story stops abruptly (a style that would come to define Biss's later works) with dialogue from Nick that reveals the origin of the title: "Part of this group, you know, everyone's slapping high fives, all team players, all friends" (p. 38).

When read through the lens of everything else Biss would eventually write, "Team Players" stands as an early awareness of how peer pressure feeds into racism and violence. Her choice to put her name in *Race Traitor* is telling too. *Race Traitor* published features, reviews, unsigned editorials, and letters all focusing on some aspect of its neo-abolitionist mission statement, which was that it wanted to "serve as an intellectual center for those seeking to abolish the white race" (p. 121). This is an extremist goal that Biss in the twenty-first century would probably not support in the literal sense, although questions about white privilege guided her second book, *Notes from No Man's Land,* which won the National Book Critics Circle Award for Criticism in 2010.

Biss graduated from Hampshire College in 1999 with a B.A. in nonfiction writing. She moved to Brooklyn, where she had an editorial internship at *Bomb* magazine for three issues (fall 1999 to spring 2000). *Bomb* bills itself as a magazine of interviews among artists of all types. Biss was involved with issues that included luminaries such as the filmmaker Errol Morris, performance artist Laurie Anderson, novelist Oscar Hijuelos, and poet Yusef Komunyakaa. She mentions the job only in passing in her essay "Goodbye to All That" in *Notes from No Man's Land*. "I proofread just long enough to learn proofreader's marks, I did transcriptions now and then, I opened mail" (p. 63). She also briefly held a job as an editorial assistant in nonfiction at HarperCollins Publishers from 1999 to 2000, which she described in "Goodbye to All That" as "by far the most menial work I ever did in the city. I remember it mostly as a series of pointless trips in elevators" (p. 63).

Biss also taught during this time for the DreamYard Project, an arts center that implemented artistic outreach programs into the underfunded public schools of the Bronx and Harlem. She wrote about the experience in her essay "Watch Out for Landmines," published many years later in the fall 2005 issue of *Columbia: A Journal of Literature and Art* (and then revised and included as "Land Mines" in *Notes from No Man's Land*). In the 2005 version, Biss elaborates on two narrative threads: first, how emancipation contributed to the structure of the public school system, and second, how she handles and mishandles a bullying situation in her classroom, where she is struggling as a young teacher. The essay contains piercing criticism: "Northerners set up one of the first widespread systems of public education in the South … [which is] the method we use to manage large populations of our own people who frighten us" (p. 136). The essay also contains poignant self-criticism and dark humor. As the bullying takes over her classroom, Biss tries to engage the preteen students in a discussion where they reflect on how it feels to be called a bad name (in an effort to get them to stop calling one classmate "gay"). The discussion falls apart, however, and Biss reflects that her lesson plan was "designed to manipulate how my students thought. I wanted to make them more liberal-minded—I wanted to make them more like me" (p. 140). The essay's conclusion starts with a line that perhaps sums up why Biss left the job: "During my first year of teaching, I found that I said 'Quiet!' more than anything else" (p. 141).

As a final foray into her postcollegiate world of work, and no doubt to make ends meet in the expensive city, she held down random jobs, including one as a garden inspector for the parks department, a task she wrote about in the essays "Goodbye to All That" and "No Man's Land" in *Notes from No Man's Land*. The parks job took her through "some of the city's most notorious neighborhoods; in Bed-Stuy, in East New York, in Spanish Harlem, in Washington Heights. That was before I knew the language of the city, and the codes, so I had no sense that these places were considered dangerous" (p. 152). It would

take Biss almost a decade to begin publishing the race-themed essays that grew out of her time in Brooklyn. She stepped away from the subculture of radical race 'zines to find a different home with one of the most venerable small press journals in America, *Hanging Loose*, a Brooklyn-based literary journal that would end up launching her career as a lyrical prose poet rather than a political agitator.

In 1999, issue 74 of *Hanging Loose* published a trio of prose poems by Biss: "My Mother," "My Father," and "Barry," which refers to her mother's boyfriend who practiced the Yoruba faith. Grounded in what are likely autobiographical observations, each is a roughly half-page anecdote about a moment that defined Biss's relationship with each guardian. In "My Mother," Biss and her mother catch and slaughter chickens. Biss doesn't shy away from any details, a skill that will make her later work achingly unique. For example, she writes of the moment of disembowelment: "The yellow fat, the blue kidneys, hard like eggs, the deep brown heart, tiny, the pink lungs…. I slip my hand into the cavity, warm and wet like a woman" (p. 19). In "My Father," the reader is dropped in medias res to the moments after some sort of accident where, with the father bleeding from his chin, Biss must remove his shirt and tie his shoes and get him to a hospital. The piece is detached and cool, with Biss referring to snippets of sublime moments—heat lightning, dead wasps, white buttons on a blue shirt (p. 20). Finally, in "Barry," Biss-as-narrator is on the sidelines watching Barry go through a series of dental appointments to get dentures, but the "country dentist" is not sensitive to Barry's request for "the darkest pigment" (p. 21). When the dentures arrive with bright pink fake gums that look glaringly awkward against Barry's dark lips, Biss writes that Barry "composed letters to the dentist while he scraped stinking goatskins and pulled drum strings tight" (p. 21). Taken together, the three prose poems display talent for showing the odd and touching details of how these adults influenced her early years.

Her next set of prose poems also appeared in *Hanging Loose*, this time in issue 77 in 2000.

Succinct and sparse on the pages at just a couple paragraphs or sentences apiece, the four poems are "Cradle Me," "Noah," "The Sidewalk," and "In the Park," which weighs it at just thirty-one words (making it her shortest published piece). In the style of her first *Hanging Loose* submissions, these too capture intimate moments grounded in almost hallucinogenic, ethereal detail. What they add, however, is a sense of loss, as the narrator in each recounts some sort of longing—for inaccessible places, for simpler times, for objects, for relationships. The brief pieces are bright in their detail, yet because they are so short, they lack the magnitude of her other work, and might even be justifiably read as excerpts from a journal or diary.

A year later, in 2001, Biss had a couple of big breaks. First, she worked as an instructor at her alma mater, Hampshire College, where she taught introductory creative writing workshops through Hampshire's unique between-terms offerings (where students and community members can take intensive weeklong classes with successful alums). Second, she had a piece accepted at the *Massachusetts Review*. Her essay "The Price of Poetry" appeared in the spring 2001 issue, and it is her earliest work that clearly fits in to her fragmented layering of thematically related ephemera. In the piece, she alternates stories of a visit to Emily Dickinson's homestead, the story of the time her computer's hard drive died (erasing a year's worth of writing), meditations on what poetry is worth, and two peculiar sections, one about childhood painkillers and the other about archival-quality photography supplies. All tap in to a larger point about preservation and protection. "After all the efforts to preserve and protect and document the poetry and furniture and clothing of Emily Dickinson, has her love of the present moment survived?" (p. 11). Biss also admits, "I enjoy the gasps people make when I tell them I lost everything. It makes up for some other pain that is not as easily named" (p. 10). The piece is provocative and unsettling, two hallmarks of Biss's future work soon to hit a wider audience. And given that Biss would eventually attain critical and financial success (winning almost all the major grants available to creative writers), it is somewhat ironic that this early publication danced with the literal value our culture places on poetry and poets.

TAKING OFF WITH THE BALLOONISTS

The year 2002 was productive for Biss, who left Brooklyn (and Hampshire College, where she was still running weeklong workshops as an alumna) for a stint in San Diego, California, as a part-time staff member of the small newspaper *Voice and Viewpoint*, where she wrote articles and took photos. She also took Spanish-language classes at a community college and in Ensenada, Mexico (across the border in the Baja California region), events all recounted in "Letter to Mexico" in *Notes from No Man's Land*.

She published three more poems in *Hanging Loose*, a piece in *Jubilat*, and her first book, *The Balloonists*. The pieces in *Hanging Loose* 81 (2002) are odd little poems all having to do with sound, a project Biss did not continue with in her later work. In contrast, the essay in *Jubilat*, "How to Love a Bicycle," is, like much of her future award-winning work, a segmented meditation on seemingly unrelated topics that, by the end, have fallen under Biss's spell of making metaphorical connections. The forty-four short sections (just over five pages in the journal) cover classified ads, her bike, machines, marriage, mothers, and what it means to love something. It is worth noting that "How to Love a Bicycle" is Biss's only nonfiction piece to comment on her mother's sudden marriage to the Chinese man. Biss writes, "My mother recently married. Her kung fu teacher offered to take her to China if she would meet his brother-in-law. She went to China and she came back married. My mother is not like your mother" (pp. 28–29).

As peculiar as the bicycle essay seems, it was Biss's first book, *The Balloonists* (Hanging Loose Press, 2002) that really put her on the experimental map of the blurred country between poetry and prose. The book is about how we tell ourselves about relationships, especially how we tell the story of a marriage. It is only seventy-two pages long and reads like a long fragmented

essay (or an even longer prose poem) with five or six section breaks per page. There are also nine pages where the text, italicized, has a box around it. A prelude, helpfully titled "The Box," is written like a play or script, with the characters of Mother, Aunt, Uncle, Grandmother, Father, and many unattributed lines that could be Biss or some other narrator. In addition, the prelude contains italicized sections that are only about plane crashes and the recovery of the black boxes (which, Biss notes with delight, are orange, not black). Some pages are half-empty; one page has only one sentence. Finally, the cover of the book is an actual photograph of a silver hot-air balloon landing—the Breitling Orbiter 3, with Bertrand Piccard and Brian Jones at the controls, finishing their 1999 round-the-world nonstop flight, the first ever.

In the prelude, various family members recount how "the mother" (who, by all details, appears to be Biss's actual mother, Ellen Graf) came to marry "the father" (referred to as Roger, a doctor, like Biss's actual father) and go to college, start a family, then get a divorce. Since the prelude is woven with startling information about plane crashes and the recovery of data (including Biss reprinting parts of transcripts of pilots talking as the crash happens), it takes on an ominous tone, even though Biss points out that the National Transportation Safety Board redacts most emotional material from the transcripts. She writes, "One pilot sang a lullaby as his plane went down" (p. 14), and, perhaps more disturbingly, "There is no way of knowing exactly what the pilots are doing during the silences on the recordings. Reading their instruments? Manipulating the controls? Looking out the window?" (p. 13).

The nine pages of boxed italicized text can be read alone or as part of the main narrative. Read alone, they clearly work to show the young Biss contemplating what it means to commit to someone in a marriage, and what happens to sincerity when the marriage fails. She writes, "I think of a married person as a kind of specialist" (p. 18). She cites and subverts Joan Didion's famous line "We tell ourselves stories in order to live" when she follows it up with "We also live

by the stories we tell" (p. 19). The one-sentence page, then, is: "Are we going to keep living the same stories our parents lived?" (p. 39). Surrounded by blank space, it resonates as the turning point in the book. The final page of boxed italicized text concludes that "stories are only true if we believe them. Or if we live them. It is unclear where our parents' stories end and where our stories begin" (p. 70).

Meanwhile, among these nine pages, Biss drops a barrage of images, observations, stories, conversations, questions, and fragments of memory. They sometimes (but not always) connect in a narrative sense, and, like her early publications in *Hanging Loose* and the bicycle essay in *Jubilat*, they make the most unexpected thematic partnerships, a sort of collage of contemplations. *The Balloonists* eventually solidifies into thoughts on women, feminism, and relationships. The last paragraph is:

> So many fairy tales have been changed. They have been adapted for movies. The stories have been rewritten so that the woman who steps out of the ocean, perfect and naked, does not slip back into the skin of a seal. Cartoon fairy tales end in a shower of flower petals falling over a wedding as the credits begin. They should end with the woman disappearing into the sea.
>
> (p. 72)

The Balloonists received a brief review that year in *Booklist*. Reviewer Whitney Scott comments that "Biss' slender debut collection is as spare as a Japanese watercolor" (p. 1568). Scott goes on to explain that a high point of the book is Biss's ability to draw subtle connections between redacted emotion from crash transcripts and how families also cut certain emotional aspects of their private stories. In 2009, when Biss's second book was released, the National Public Radio commenter Lizzie Skurnick prefaced her online review with a brief look back at *The Balloonists*. Skurnick said, "Arresting and singular, its flat, affectless recounting of seemingly disparate events could have been mind-numbing but for the author's dazzlingly intuitive leaps, in which these odd juxtapositions lead to startling illumination."

Aside from these and a few other short reviews, Biss's first collection attracted little critical attention. Biss, who prior to 2014 did not frequently grant interviews, finally said in an online 2014 interview with the National Endowment for the Arts that "I had already drafted the manuscript [of *The Balloonists*] ... by the time I graduated college, but I had no idea what to do with it.... The editors at *Hanging Loose* ... gave me the encouragement I needed to keep writing, though it would be another ten years before I felt that I had established myself as a writer." *The Balloonists*, then, might best be seen as a precocious first book from a wildly talented young writer who knew full well how to compose her unusual lyrical arguments. Why it didn't receive wider critical acclaim has to do, most likely, with numbers. With around a quarter-million books published that year, many critics would have simply overlooked a first-time author and her seventy-two-page prose poem from a small independent press out of Brooklyn.

The encouragement from *Hanging Loose* Press might have been small, but it started the momentum Biss needed. She also got financial encouragement in 2002 from the Rona Jaffe Foundation, which awarded her a $10,000 Rona Jaffe Writers' Foundation Award. The annual award goes to talented female writers who are early in their career.

Finally, the publication of *The Balloonists* helped secure Biss a spot at the University of Iowa, where she enrolled in 2003, moving to Iowa City, a place that would help round out her experiences with race, ethnicity, and regions—themes that would appear in her second book, *Notes from No Man's Land.*

BISS IN THE HEARTLAND: THE UNIVERSITY OF IOWA

Biss attended the University of Iowa from 2003 to 2006 while she worked on her M.F.A. degree in nonfiction, drafted the essays that would find their way to *Notes From No Man's Land,* and taught college courses as a graduate assistant. While the University of Iowa's graduate writing programs are generally lumped together as the "Iowa Writer's Workshop," the famed two-year workshop, which has been running since 1936, is for fiction writers and poets only. In comparison, nonfiction candidates for an M.F.A. in the nonfiction writing program (which started in 1974) have three years to complete a thesis. It was in the nonfiction writing program that she met John Bresland (also pursuing an M.F.A. in nonfiction), whom she would marry, and it was here that she began to garner more grants and awards for her writing, as well as more prominent publications. To start off her graduate school career, she won a 2003 Barbara Deming Memorial Fund Grant, a Ludwig Vogelstein Foundation Grant, and a 2003 Iowa Arts Scholarship.

An obscure piece titled "A History of the Blues" appeared in the defunct poetry journal *Chase Park* in early 2003. The six-page prose poem seems to have originated out of Biss's study of the book *Blues Legacies and Black Feminism* by Angela Davis. Biss weaves statements from Davis, lyrics sung by Gertrude "Ma" Rainey (making this piece the first time Biss would use song lyrics as part of her thematic segmenting), and Biss's experience being the sole woman around groups of male musicians or male writers. She writes of her inability to play or even comprehend the technical aspects of composing music, yet she is drawn to it. "I love to watch musicians on stage with their cables ... I want them and I want all their cables. I want their authority on stage. I want their command of the room" (p. 83).

Biss had another obscure publication that year as well, in another magazine that went out of print. Her prose poem "These Nerves (England, 2002)" was published by *La Petite Zine*, an online literary magazine that started in 1999 and ceased in 2011. It appeared in issue 13, summer 2003. It was published alongside three poems from David Lehman, who would go on to be the longtime series editor of *Best American Poetry*. "These Nerves" winds together three narratives in six short sections: a visit to a museum's anatomy exhibit; case notes of someone named G.L., who "has reported being unable to feel below her nose"; and a conflict with someone

identified as "B," who seems to dislike the exhibit.

It was after the publication of "These Nerves" that Biss's focus shifted from prose poems to longer essays. While she has continued to publish the occasional poem, 2003 was when she started publishing far more essays.

One of her first essays to earn wider critical acclaim was "The Only Professional Player of the Toy Piano, Margaret Leng Tan," which won second place in the *Bellingham Review*'s contest for the Annie Dillard Award for Creative Nonfiction. It appeared in issue 52 (winter/spring 2003) and was then reprinted by *Harper's* (as "This Is Not a Toy"). The reprint in *Harper's* immediately put Biss on the national map of innovative nonfiction writers.

The essay is similar to Biss's prior work in that it makes use of a fractured, segmented form. But it is different in how it refocuses Biss's interests away from deep examinations of the personal (and family) and instead focuses on a one-of-a-kind celebrity, Margaret Leng Tan. She was a musician from Singapore who struggled as a teen at Juilliard (but was the first woman to earn a doctoral degree there) and as a result took up the toy piano instead of the grand piano. Biss's commentary covers toys, feminism, entertainment, experimental music, and devotion to practice. Biss repeats the lament and mantra, "I saw her play only once" (pp. 75, 76, 78, 79). Biss also includes a statement from Tan: "'I've expanded by contracting,' she said. 'Life is full of marvelous contradictions'"(p. 75). It's a statement that Biss no doubt identified with in many ways. At the end of the piece, Biss riffs on Tan's status as "the only player of the toy piano" in a brilliant conclusion that is written as a fictional monologue for Tan:

> But I am the only professional enjoyer of jet sounds. I am the only professional hitter of catfood cans with chopsticks. I am the only professional blower of soda bottles. I am the only professional jumper on the hollow squares of the sidewalk. I am the only professional twanger of rubber bands. I am the only professional player of the toy piano.
>
> (p. 80)

In 2004 Biss had a second piece published in the *Massachusetts Review*, a short story titled "Living Together: A Letter." It has the same tone as her earlier prose poems and essays, but it was published as fiction—a detail that would be hard to know were it not for the table of contents in the journal. (To complicate matters, some academic databases have mislabeled it as a poem.) In the short story, an unnamed female narrator is struggling with a male partner's desire to be with her more often, even though they already share an apartment. The narrator thinks, "I'm afraid you don't understand what I mean when I say I want to be alone," and "I have learned, like many young women, to be constantly attentive. Which leaves me never alone.... I know that people think there is something sad and wrong about a woman who is by herself. Maybe there is also something hated" (p. 394).

"THE PAIN SCALE," *NORTHWESTERN UNIVERSITY, AND THE GRAYWOLF PRIZE*

By 2005 Biss had fine-tuned the lyrical essay style she had come to Iowa to practice. She published one more short prose poem, the three-paragraph "Dear Smoker," in issue 87 of *Hanging Loose,* her longtime go-to magazine. She also published an essay discussed earlier, "Watch Out for Landmines," in the fall 2005 edition of *Columbia: A Journal of Literature and Art.* But most notably, this year marked the period where she published one of her most anthologized and discussed essays, "The Pain Scale."

"The Pain Scale" first appeared in the *Seneca Review* and was quickly picked up for reprint by *Harper's* (Biss's second reprint with them). The essay is about the different ways to quantify pain, an idea that came to Biss due to her own struggles with chronic pain. When visiting doctors, she was often asked to rate her pain on a scale of zero to ten. The simplicity of the scale (often rendered with the cartoon drawings of the Wong-Baker Faces Scale showing degrees of pain, images reprinted as illustrations in her article) conflicted with her critical questioning of how a number could represent something so subjective. "Like the advanced math of my

distant past, determining the intensity of my own pain is a blind calculation. On my first attempt, I assigned the value of ten to a theoretical experience—burning alive. Then I tried to determine what percentage of the pain of burning alive I was feeling" (p. 11). She settles on 30 percent, then calculates that down to a three on a scale of zero to ten. But the physical reality of that level of pain doesn't seem to translate to a number. Biss describes it as "Three. Mail remains unopened. Thoughts rarely follow to their conclusions. Sitting still becomes unbearable after one hour. Nausea sets in" (p. 11). Her father, who is a physician, dismisses pain of this number and tells her to treat it with aspirin.

Ever alert to the quiet absurdities of science, Biss notes in the essay that as physicians improved their pain scales, researchers then also wanted patients not only to rate their pain but also to look at multiple pain scales and pick the easiest one. "The patients," she writes with just the slightest hint of mockery, "were not invited to rate the experience of the rating" (p. 14).

Typical to her style, Biss infuses "The Pain Scale" with fascinating research such as the Beaufort scale (wind strength ratings), Galileo's geometric mapping of Hell's actual entrance, the Reverend James Chase's definition of suffering (it is "the story we tell ourselves of our pain" [p. 22]), and notions of the golden rectangle and the divine ratio. She then juxtaposes these snippets of research with her own astute insight, such as, "The pain scale measures only the intensity of pain, not the duration. This may be its greatest flaw" (p. 19). Later in the essay, she differentiates pain from suffering. "I rated my pain as a three. Having been sleepless for nearly a week, I rated my suffering as a seven" (p. 22).

A new structural strategy in "The Pain Scale" has to do with how Biss organizes the sections. Instead of just using her typical segmented style with plenty of blank space between ideas, she adds one more layer—the actual pain scale. The first section corresponds with "0" or "No Pain," and that is the section's subheading. There is also an arrow pointing to the right, indicating that we will progress through the numerical scale. The sections then proceed with 1–9, with the numbers serving as subheadings and arrows pointing left and right (up and down the scale, back and forth through the essay). When the essay concludes with 10, Biss adds the phrase "The Worst Pain Imaginable," and revisits her earlier discussion of the problems of starting the scale with zero, which is that "it does not behave like a number. It does not add, subtract, or multiply like other numbers" (p. 5), an allusion to how pain does not behave like other sensations. She notes that "10" contains a zero (so how can it behave like the other numbers?), and that "there is no tenth circle in Dante's Hell." There is a penultimate anecdote where she and her father dream up an improved pain scale, one that is both whimsical and disturbing as it rates "what patients would be willing to do to relieve their pain" (p. 24). The essay ends with a fact about the aforementioned Beaufort wind scale, whose "10" is not a number at all but just the phrase "destruction occurs," an event Biss parallels with suicide due to unbearable chronic pain, "bringing us, of course, back to zero" (p. 25).

Beside being lauded as a triumph of criticism, lyricism, research, and even feminism, "The Pain Scale" gained attention in international academic circles because of how it could be used to enlighten physicians, therapists, and counselors. In 2011 the *Journal of Literary & Cultural Disability Studies*, out of Liverpool University in England, published Susannah B. Mintz's article "On a Scale of 1 to 10: Life Writing and Lyrical Pain," which argues that because of Biss's phenomenal essay, we should now consider the "lyric essay [to be] pain's most suitable autobiographical genre" (p. 245). Mintz comments on how Biss's structure (blank space, segments) underscores her theme. "Gaps in the prose remind us of the inarticulable sensations of pain, the silence it commands, but Biss's short paragraph structure also suggests, unexpectedly, the opposite—that *without* pain there is no language" (p. 246). Mintz also highlights what Biss was able to see, a situation many doctors could not see: "A pain scale … is both a fiction and a fixative. Asked to rate pain according to numbers meaningful only in relation to each other or to abstracted qualifiers, patients must create a

story that bears no real or absolute relation to physical sensation" (p. 248). Finally, Mintz argues that Biss's essay provides a sort of turning point in studies of pain management, because of "its demonstration of a person carrying on with pain, even if pain dominates this particular 'moment'—or the series of fragmented moments that a lyric essay will necessarily gather.... The essay *sustains* pain, as if its purpose is not at all to assuage but rather to perpetuate it" (p. 254). She concludes that Biss helps us realize that pain is not so much about definition as it is about transformation. "The lyric essay is our perfect autobiographical form: profound, emotionally resonant, thoughtful, urgent, discontinuous, whole" (p. 257).

A religious scholar, Philip Browning Helsel, cited Biss's "The Pain Scale" in a 2009 article, "Simone Weil's Passion Mysticism: The Paradox of Chronic Pain and the Transformation of the Cross," published in *Pastoral Psychology*. In his discussion of pain as a state of loneliness, he mentions how Biss's experience with the numerical pain scale creates isolation (not the intended partnership with a physician) because it asks her to negate her experience (determining what number her pain "is" by determining what numbers it "is not").

> Biss's writing is a form of apophaticism [the theology that God is unknowable], because it explores the manner in which medical quantification of pain is an illusion, and in fact a method of managing anxiety about the pain. As a person whose pain fell outside of the traditional qualifications of illness and cure, Biss articulates the void which is implied in the experience of being outside these communities.
>
> (p. 57)

Finally, a third scholarly publication, *Biography: An Interdisciplinary Quarterly* published Leigh Gilmore's analysis of pain narratives in "Agency Without Mastery: Chronic Pain and Posthuman Life Writing" in its January 2012 issue, an analysis which mentioned Biss's "The Pain Scale" in passing and in context with other works about chronic pain. Gilmore points out that writers like Biss (who are approaching the description of chronic pain in new and unusual ways) are "challeng[ing] the hallmarks of autobi-

ography that tie it to humanism" (p. 83). She groups Biss's essay as part of the "archive of pain narratives," written by people who "feel cast out of the discourse" (p. 83). But since "The Pain Scale" is a work of short creative nonfiction, it stands apart from self-help books, New Age healing publications, or book-length memoirs about chronic pain.

In addition to those noted scholarly citations, "The Pain Scale" was anthologized in a composition textbook intended for first-year college students (*Ways of Reading: An Anthology of Writers,* 9th ed.), as well as *The Best Creative Nonfiction* (2007) and the *Touchstone Anthology of Contemporary Nonfiction: Work from 1970 to the Present* (2007). It was also reprinted in *Twentysomething Essays by Twentysomething Writers* (2006).

While "The Pain Scale" is arguably Biss's most recognized essay in a cross-discipline sense, another 2005 essay, "Goodbye to All That," earned her much admiration in literary circles, so much so that it received an honorable mention in the 2006 Pushcart Prize anthology, which is a "best of the small presses" award. "Goodbye to All That," first published in the *North American Review*, is an homage to the nonfiction great Joan Didion, because it is a clever rewrite of (and argument with) Didion's 1967 essay of the same title, which itself was based on a third memoir with the title, the book *Goodbye to All That*, published in 1929 by Robert Graves. His memoir was about World War I; Didion's essay was about leaving New York City; Biss's essay is about both moving to New York City and leaving it. In the version of the essay published in *Notes from No Man's Land*, she writes,

> I have to explain to you why I no longer live in New York, but first I have to explain to myself why I stayed so long. Because what I want to say about living there is that it is not, as the mythology goes, more real than any place else. In some ways, it is less.
>
> (p. 61)

Biss's contention with New York City is how over-imagined and over-storied it is, and as a result, people who live there (herself included) seem to resent it yet cling to its promises and

tolerate its difficulties. She navigates Brooklyn and Manhattan on her bicycle, a fantastic way for her to see the sordid and sublime sights, such as a legless homeless person harassed by cops (p. 64) and a dead cat in barrel (p. 69), as well as the expensive objects and places she will never be able to afford. She confronts the realities of what she can afford—at first, a tiny apartment with, unexpectedly, no refrigerator. When, in the second paragraph of the essay, she fabricates a story about having a potential refrigerator stolen, she immediately recants it in the third paragraph of the essay: "But that is not the way it really happened. That is how I learned to tell the story of my life in New York. I learned to make my experience of being young and new to the city sound effortless and zany. It was not" (p. 58).

When the essay was included in *Notes from No Man's Land* in 2009, Biss included an endnote explaining all the allusions to Didion, from the title to sentence structure to wordplay. "For instance, in her essay Didion writes: 'Nothing was irrevocable; everything was within reach.' And in mine I write: 'Everything was irrevocable, and nothing was within reach'" (p. 207). Biss also discusses an exercise for young writers, where they copy, word for word, the work of a writer they admire. When Biss set out to do this with Didion's essay, Biss found that "Didion's experience of being young in New York was so different from mine that I found I could not rewrite her essay without changing the words" (p. 208).

In 2011, a full six years after the initial publication of the essay, Biss wrote a longer analysis of it in the spring issue of *Fourth Genre: Explorations in Nonfiction*. "In the Syntax: Rewriting Joan Didion's 'Goodbye to All That'" appeared in *Fourth Genre's* "Writer as Reader" section, a quarterly feature of writers commenting on the intricacies of close reading. In discussing her own attempts to copy Didion (and Didion's attempts to copy Ernest Hemingway), Biss looks at syntax (the arrangement of phrases), observing that "some elements of syntax may be learned, evidently, some may be borrowed, but syntax cannot be copied. It is too fragile to bear transport, even syntax that seems, as Didion's

has always seemed to me, carved of marble" (p. 135). Biss concludes that when one looks at syntax, "we are best instructed that authors' lives ... need only provide a terrain over which their minds can move nimbly, forging a syntax that the rest of us may use as a map for our own thinking" (pp. 136–137). It's a nice conclusion that circles back to Biss's beginning of the analytical article, where she states that, given the opportunity, she would want Didion to "guide me through the architecture of hell.... She has already provided the most comprehensive tour of the damned I am likely to experience in this lifetime" (p. 133).

Biss ended 2005 with two more major steps toward securing herself as a leading voice in American creative writing. First, she cofounded Essay Press with Catherine Taylor (a professor at Ithaca College) and Stephen Cope (an experimental poet, musician, and instructor at various colleges near Ithaca, New York). True to Biss's own style, they planned to publish long-form experimental essays (roughly the length of a novella) in order to challenge the limits of what nonfiction would accomplish.

Second, she published an odd craft essay cowritten with the poet Matthew Zapruder. "Team Blue/Team Square: Revisiting the Lyric and the Narrative" appeared in the 2005 annual edition of *American Poet*. At the time, Zapruder (who would earn critical acclaim with *Come On All You Ghosts* in 2010), had published one book, *American Linden,* and was just ending his pet project, Verse Press, which he was changing to Wave Books. He was, and is, a frequent collaborator. Although the piece has two authors, it is written in first-person singular, with neither Biss nor Zapruder making any overt reference to who was asserting which ideas in the essay. Essentially discussing the different meanings of "lyric" and "narrative," Biss and Zapruder write, "The confusion was that, yes, each word has been transformed by misuse and imprecision into a battle flag, and that each flag gets waved around in implacable opposition to the other" (p. 11). The essay is also about a visit to a dim sum restaurant, where a lazy Susan proves inadequate for the group's dining needs and a fierce karaoke

competition beckons. Amusing descriptions of the food problems and karaoke-scheming butt up against theoretical throwdowns about the narrative and the lyric, such as

> As a descriptor, lyric seems to address the surface of a poem, and narrative seems to address the shape. Calling a poem lyric is like calling it blue. And calling it narrative is like calling it square. But our friends at the dinner table were in the process of dividing themselves into Team Blue and Team Square in order to better compete in karaoke.
>
> (p. 11)

The short essay stands as an example of how Biss preferred to explain her nonfiction technique via example, not instruction. So "Team Blue/Team Square: Revisiting the Lyric and the Narrative" is at once a lyric essay and a narrative essay and a craft essay about how to write about the writing of lyric and narrative poetry or essays. Biss and Zapruder conclude that the differences in "terminology might not be problematic, except for the fact that stylistic differences have devolved into value judgments.... Aren't we all radical experimenters the moment we open our mouths?" (p. 12).

Biss's prominence on all levels of creative writing—as editor, as critic, as author—made the next few years ones of seemingly easy promotions. Biss graduated from the University of Iowa in 2006 and was immediately hired as an artist in residence at Northwestern University in Chicago. From 2006 through 2008 she published many essays that would ultimately end up in her first essay collection, *Notes from No Man's Land*. And while a few have already been discussed in this article, the entire book is worth its own discussion.

Notes from No Man's Land was the winner of the 2008 Graywolf Press Nonfiction Prize, and it was published in 2009 by the esteemed small press, which had been focusing on contemporary nonfiction since the prize's inception in 2005. The writer Robert Polito, who served as the judge that year, commented in his "Judge's Afterword" that he couldn't recall the last time he "found a new book of essays so canny, so casually smart" (p. 227). He added, "Her voice embraces a devastating mix of insistence and quandary, as

though she is despairing and pressing on simultaneously" (p. 227). *Notes from No Man's Land* received regional attention when one of the essays won an Illinois Arts Council Literary Award in 2009 and the entire book won the Chicago Public Library 21st Century Literary Award in 2010. But it went on to impress a much larger audience than just the small-press aficionados and regional fans; it won the 2010 National Book Critics Circle Award for Criticism, no small feat given that the criticism award often goes to established journalists or historians, not young essayists with a slew of prose poems to their credit.

Compared with the slender *Balloonists*, the 230-page *Notes from No Man's Land* is an entirely different beast in terms of length, but it is very similar in style to everything she'd done before, that style being a lyrical, fragmented weaving of seemingly unconnected passages that do eventually, by Biss's talented hand, come together. The thirteen essays are divided into five sections: a beginning "Before" and a concluding "After," with regional categories in between, designating Biss's residencies in the prior decade ("New York," "California," and "The Midwest.") In a "Notes" section at the back, Biss gives brief discussions of the intent or process behind each essay. This is, however, not a memoir of place, nor is it even a straightforward memoir. Subtitled *American Essays*, it is a powerful and singular commentary on race in America.

It starts with one of her more daring essays, "Time and Distance Overcome," which was first published in the *Iowa Review* in 2008. Initially about the invention of and dissemination of telephone poles across the landscape, the odd essay takes a critical turn when Biss writes, in her characteristically abrupt and segmented style, that starting in 1898, white people started using telephone poles as a way to lynch black people. After a long and horrific list that reads somewhat like coroners' reports on the facts of the telephone pole lynchings, Biss makes an observation midway through the essay:

> The poles, of course, were not to blame. It was only coincidence that they became convenient as gallows, because they were tall and straight, with a

crossbar, and because they stood in public places. And it was only coincidence that the telephone poles so closely resembled crucifixes.

(p. 8)

And while the essay ends, of course, there is not really a conclusion. Biss stops with a strange anecdote: "One summer, heavy rains fells in Nebraska and some green telephone poles grew small leafy branches" (p. 11).

In her "Notes" at the end of the book, Biss gives important insight about her intentions behind "Time and Distance Overcome." She says, "I began my research for this essay by searching for every instance of 'telephone pole' in the *New York Times* from 1880 to 1920, which resulted in 370 articles" (p. 202). As she methodically read every article, she noticed the pattern of lynchings, and her essay redefined itself. "Time and Distance Overcome" was named a notable essay of 2008 in *Best American Essays 2009,* and it went on to win a Pushcart Prize as one of the best small-press essays of 2008, an honor Biss had been chasing for the two years since "Goodbye to All That" had gotten a Pushcart honorable mention.

With such a startling essay opening the collection, one might think that other essays could not reach that bar, but they do. In "Relations," Biss uses her reporter skills to convey the details of a white woman artificially inseminated with her own white embryo and then, accidentally, also inseminated with an embryo from a black couple, resulting in twins of different races. The essay circles around definitions and anecdotes of parenthood and racial identity with Biss asserting that "Race is a social fiction. But it is also, for now at least, a social fact" (p. 17). The "no man's land" of the title, she says, is the space we find ourselves in when we are "between two racial identities" (p. 17). All of her essays touch on this. "Land Mines" (previously discussed) is about race and education. "Black News" is an account of Biss's time reporting in California. "No Man's Land" refers to Biss and Bresland's first neighborhood in Chicago, Rogers Park, colloquially known at the turn of the century as "No Man's Land" because it was an unimproved rough area between Evanston and Chicago. When

the two move there it is still blighted with crime, but since it is across the street from Lake Michigan (where Biss loves to swim), and since it is affordable, she and Bresland settle in. The final essay, "All Apologies" (which seems to allude to the song of the same title by the 1990s Seattle grunge band Nirvana), is a closing variation on her research technique that led to "Time and Distance Overcome." In her "Notes," Biss explains, "Much of the information in ["All Apologies"] was produced by a search for the word 'apology' in national newspapers from the part thirty years" (p. 221). And that is exactly what the essay is—a collage of apologies, from the political to the personal. She ends with, "I apologize for slavery. It wasn't me, true. But it might have been my cousin" (p. 199).

Michael Lukas wrote a review of *Notes from No Man's Land* in the fall 2009 issue of the *Georgia Review.* "With a surgical-grade prose and an earnest, unrelenting pursuit of uncomfortable truths, Biss explores what it means to live in America … Although Biss rarely draws hard and fast conclusions, her essays open new spaces of inquiry" (p. 536). Lukas has obvious admiration for the book, but he does point out one weakness, which has to do with an omission that seems intentional. "I question why she never once mentions her experience as a student at Hampshire College, and I struggle with the willful instigation and hyperbole of lines such as 'My skin is white, but I still have the ravaged blood of Africa in me'" (p. 537). However, despite what he sees as her failure to reveal her privileged status, Lukas concludes that "*Notes from No Man's Land* is a necessary and troubling work that traces the undulations of the color line" (p. 537).

Melissa Goldthwaite, reviewing the book in *American Book Review*, also drew attention to a weak point, which is that some of the essays only make complete sense after one reads the explanatory note at the end of the book. Goldthwaite argues that Biss should have worked harder to put the "cogent reflection" found in the endnotes into the essays themselves (p. 11). But like Lukas, she concludes that "Biss offers a complex collage of racial experience in America."

Marion Wyce, writing for the *Literary Review*, noted that Biss leads "us into no man's land by uncovering how we're already there" (p. 213). Taking a different view from Lukas, Wyce writes that "as a white woman from a multiracial family who grew up with African traditions, Biss interrogates her own whiteness and the privileges it confers on her but finds no easy answers" (p. 213).

A final review by Sarah Salter was published in the spring 2010 edition of *Prairie Schooner*. She was so struck by Biss's fascination with white privilege and institutionalized racism that she was compelled to admit that "the revelation of Biss's white skin surprises the reader. This surprise allows for a reflection on our most basic presumptions about racial solidarity, which may leave one feeling implicated in a convenient assumption. By undermining the racial poise of her readers, Biss successfully begins her study" (p. 171). Like the other reviewers, Salter had nothing but praise for Biss's ability to make meaning of juxtapositions, as well as her lyrical prowess with phrases: "Biss's beautiful prose ... evoke[s] complex emotional responses (despair, delight, and disgust all have a place)" (p. 171). And whereas Wyce, in the previous review, concludes that Biss "finds no easy answers" by the end of the book, Salter has a different read. "By the close of this nuanced collection, Biss has forgiven her younger self for this oversimplification [in reference to a childhood toy, a black-skinned doll Biss called 'Black Doll'] and seems almost comfortable in her own white skin" (p. 172).

Notes from No Man's Land continues to be a prominent essay collection on race in America. Macmillan Publishers (known for college textbooks) has listed it as a recommended book for first-year common reading programs in colleges. As late as 2013, major universities such as Washington University, Kansas State University, and Wheelock College chose it as the one book that every first-year student would read and discuss, despite that fact that it had been published more than three years earlier, a testament to Biss's ability to write lyric essays that remain relevant and accessible.

The success of *Notes from No Man's Land* earned Biss a promotion at Northwestern University, where she went from an artist in residence to a "continuing lecturer" position. More importantly, however, the book earned Biss the trio of financial-support fellowships that most creative writers aspire their entire lives to receive. She won a $25,000 National Endowment for the Arts Literature Fellowship, a Howard Foundation Fellowship (which changes in value year to year, but is generally around $30,000) and a Guggenheim Memorial Foundation Fellowship (also at least $30,000), all of which she won in 2011. The financial support provided by the grants allowed her to focus on her third book—a book about the controversial subject of childhood immunizations.

ON IMMUNITY, ON ARGUMENTS, ON LYRICISM

Biss and Bresland had a child in 2009, a son named Juneau, and it was his birth that inspired Biss's third book, *On Immunity: An Inoculation*, published in 2014. As the H1N1 flu virus spread through the United States in 2009, and as Biss held her infant son, she watched the news for updates on how people were taking steps to avoid the virus.

> It all became part of the landscape of new motherhood, where ordinary objects like pillows and blankets have the power to kill a newborn. Colleges were daily sterilizing every "high-touch" surface, while I was nightly boiling every object my child put in his mouth. It was as if the nation had joined me in the paranoia of infant care.
>
> (p. 7)

That situation, compounded with having had an unexpected blood transfusion when she gave birth and the dilemma of whether or not to fully vaccinate her son, led Biss to research all aspects of disease, immunization, and vaccinations, which had become a highly charged topic owing to the widespread belief that vaccinations caused an increase in autism spectrum disorders.

To understand the researched density of *On Immunity*, one has only to look at the documentation, which includes sixty-five pages of detailed

endnotes and eleven pages of bibliographic notes from well over fifty sources on the immunity debate. But *On Immunity* is not a long research paper, nor is it a medical text, nor is it a general nonfiction book. True to Biss's style, it merges her pitch-perfect lyricism with startling facts and the conviction of a new parent desperately searching for evidence to help her make the right decision about her son's health.

One of the unique strengths of the book is Biss's decision to analyze nineteenth-century germ theory, its connection to Bram Stoker's *Dracula,* and how a subconscious connection remains, in the twenty-first century, between vampires and vaccinations. It leads her to a question that guides the book: "Do we believe vaccination to be more monstrous than disease?" (p. 16). She layers her research with personal stories about the trials of childhood illness (Juneau, it turns out, suffers severe allergies, as well as a scary but common bout with croup) and her own evolving awareness of the importance of vaccinations. In writing that is clear and powerful beyond all else she has written, she takes the side of "herd immunity," which becomes the call to action of the book.

> If we imagine the action of a vaccine not just in terms of how it affects a single body, but also in terms of how it affects the collective body of a community, it is fair to think of vaccination as a kind of banking of immunity. Contributions to this bank are donations to those who cannot or will not be protected by their own immunity. This is the principle of *herd immunity*, and it is through herd immunity that mass vaccination becomes far more effective than individual vaccination.
>
> (p. 19)

Later in the book, Biss broaches the fact that, historically, women (such as peasants and midwives) have long known how to inoculate their children, as it was simply part of the regimen of folklore passed down from generation to generation. But as female healers were seen (unfairly) as working in tandem with the occult or under the influence of superstitions, male doctors soon claimed the realm of medicine, drastically changing the public's perceptions of healing, prevention, and authority (p. 68). Biss acknowledges that, now,

> paternalism has fallen out of favor in medicine.... But how we should care for other people remains a question.... *Autonomy* is usually imagined as the alternative to paternalism. But in what is sometimes called the "restaurant model" of medicine, the paternalism of doctors has been replaced by the consumerism of patients.... The idea that the patient is always right, imported to medicine, is a dangerous dictum.
>
> (pp. 98–99)

One of the strongest parts of the book is when Biss, through dogged research, uncovers the fact that the term "conscientious objector," which most of us associate with refusing to go to war, was originally applied to people who refused vaccinations after, in theory, much conscientious soul-searching. "This was an intentional decision made by caring parents," explains Biss. "[They wanted to] distinguish themselves from negligent parents" (p. 118). Biss uses the research to underscore the fact that in the twenty-first century, many parents who decide not to vaccinate their children identify as liberal and highly educated, a subculture Biss puts herself into all too easily—and it's a subculture many of her readers will see themselves in, as well. True to her style of offering no easy answers, Biss says, "If we owe the existence of this nation in some part to compulsory inoculation, we also owe some of its present character to the resistance against compulsory vaccination" (p. 120). Biss's ultimate conclusion comes straight of out of her poetry background. "We are each other's environment. And Immunity is a shared space—a garden we tend together" (p. 163).

The journalist Kevin Nance, reviewing the book online for the *Chicago Tribune* in September 2014, called it a "kaleidoscopic work that combines a survey of the science and history of vaccination with personal reflection, literary criticism, and a study of the ancient and latter-day mythologies that hover over and around the issue like a fog." He also interviewed Biss's editor at Graywolf Press, Jeffrey Shotts, who described the book as "part extended essay or memoir, part cultural criticism and narrative nonfiction; parts of it feel not unlike a poem."

It's an apt description not only for *On Immunity* but for all of Biss's published work. The

style will likely continue to define her future writings (and since she was only thirty-seven years old at the time *On Immunity* was published, there will undoubtedly be more stellar work from her). Among all American creative nonfiction writers, Eula Biss's intellect and prowess with organizing research and insight set her apart, and yet the defining characteristics of her work clearly link her to the lineage of thought-provoking nonfiction writers who seek to convey more than their own personal story.

Selected Bibliography

WORKS OF EULA BISS

BOOKS
The Balloonists. Brooklyn, N.Y.: Hanging Loose Press, 2002.

Notes from No Man's Land. Minneapolis, Minn.: Graywolf Press, 2009.

On Immunity: An Inoculation. Minneapolis, Minn.: Graywolf Press, 2014.

ESSAYS
"The Price of Poetry." *Massachusetts Review* 42, no. 1:9–11 (2001).

"How to Love a Bicycle." *Jubilat* 16, no. 6:24–29 (2002).

"These Nerves (England, 2002)." *La Petite Zine,* 2003. http://lapetitezine.org/EulaBiss.htm

"The Only Professional Player of the Toy Piano." *Bellingham Review* 26, no. 1:74–80 (2003).

"A History of the Blues." *Chase Park* 4:82–88 (2003).

"The Pain Scale." *Seneca Review* 35, no. 1:5–25 (2005).

"Watch Out for Land Mines." *Columbia: A Journal of Literature and Art* 42:136–141 (2005).

"The Voice Box: Our Opera of High and Low." *Columbia: A Journal of Literature and Art* 45:150–164 (2008).

"Short Talks on the Midwest." *Third Coast,* fall 2010, pp. 169–170.

"Ode to Everything." *Requited* 11 (2010). http://requitedjournal.com/index.php?/form/eula-biss-and-john-bresland/ (Video essay.)

PROSE POEMS
"My Mother." *Hanging Loose* 74:19 (1999).

"My Father." *Hanging Loose* 74:20 (1999).

"Barry." *Hanging Loose* 74:21 (1999).

"Cradle Me." *Hanging Loose* 77:6 (2000).

"Noah." *Hanging Loose* 77:6 (2000).

"The Sidewalk." *Hanging Loose* 77:7 (2000).

"In the Park." *Hanging Loose* 77:7 (2000).

"Field Guide to Birds of the City." *Both* online (2001).

"Counting." *Both* online (2001).

"Yesterday's Paper." *Rattapallax* 6 online (2001).

"Composition #1." *Hanging Loose* 81:11 (2002).

"Compact Disk for Alice Mary, Titled: What You Sound Like When You're Sleeping." *Hanging Loose* 81:12 (2002).

"Sound Dictionary." *Hanging Loose* 81:13 (2002).

"Dear Smoker." *Hanging Loose* 87:28 (2005).

"All the Words." *American Poet* 29:13 (2005).

"The Donut Project." *American Poet* 29:14 (2005).

"Babylon." *Hanging Loose* 93:14 (2008).

SHORT STORIES
"Team Players." *Race Traitor* 8:31–38 (1998).

"Living Together: A Letter." *Massachusetts Review* 45, no. 2:392–395 (2004).

OTHER WORKS
"Team Blue/Team Square: Revisiting the Lyric and the Narrative." *American Poet* 29:11–12 (2005).

"First Person Singular: An African Master Recedes Behind His Own Myth." *Columbia Journalism Review,* September–October 2009, pp. 60–61.

"In the Syntax: Rewriting Joan Didion's 'Goodbye to All That.'" *Fourth Genre: Explorations in Nonfiction* 13, no. 1:133–137 (2011).

"Reading 'On Trout.'" In *Understanding the Essay.* Edited by Patricia Foster and Jeffrey Lyn Porter. Peterborough, Ont.: Broadview Press, 2012.

CRITICAL AND BIOGRAPHICAL STUDIES
Gilmore, Leigh. "Agency Without Mastery: Chronic Pain and Posthuman Life Writing." *Biography* 35, no. 1:83–98 (2012).

Goldthwaite, Melissa. "A Collage of Crots." *American Book Review* 33, no. 2:11 (2012).

Helsel, Philip Browning. "Simone Weil's Passion Mysticism: The Paradox of Chronic Pain and the Transformation of the Cross." *Pastoral Psychology* 58:55–63 (2009).

Lukas, Michael. "*Notes from No Man's Land* by Eula Biss." *Georgia Review* 63, no. 3:536–537 (2009).

Mintz, Susannah B. "On a Scale from 1–10: Life Writing and Lyrical Pain." *Journal of Literary & Cultural Disability Studies* 5, no. 3:243–260 (2011).

Pettice, Mary. "Slipperiness of Identity." *American Book Review* 31, no. 4:17–18 (2010).

Salter, Sarah. *"Notes from No Man's Land* by Eula Biss; *;Poor Man's Provence;* by Rheta Grimsley Johnson." *Prairie Schooner* 84, no. 1:170–173 (2010).

Scott, Whitney. "Eula Biss: *The Balloonists.*" *Booklist,* May 15, 2002, p. 1568.

Skurnick, Lizzie. "Personal Yet Dazzlingly Eclectic 'Notes' on Race." *National Public Radio Books,* March 23, 2009.

Wyce, Marion. *"Notes from No Man's Land*: American Essays." *Literary Review* 53, no. 1:212–213 (2009).

INTERVIEWS

Beete, Paulette. "Art Talk with Eula Biss." Art Works Blog, *National Endowment for the Arts,* August 27, 2014. http://arts.gov/art-works/2014/art-talk-eula-biss

Carroll, Nikki, and Amanda Giracca. "Influence, Chaos, and the Art of Open-Ended Research: An Interview and Q&A with Eula Biss." *Hot Metal Bridge,* March 23, 2012. http://hotmetalbridge.org/archivelinks/conflict-confluence/influence-chaos-and-the-art-of-open-ended-research-an-interview-and-qa-with-eula-biss/

Nance, Kevin. "Eula Biss Discusses *On Immunity.*" *Chicago Tribune,* September 19, 2014. http://www.chicagotribune.com/lifestyles/books/ct-prj-on-immunity-eula-biss-20140919-story.html#page=1

Segal, Adam. "We Do Not Know Alone: Interview with Eula Biss." *Numero Cinq* 5, no. 8: (2014). http://numerocinqmagazine.com/2014/08/12/we-do-not-know-alone-interview-with-eula-biss-adam-segal/

Shier, Mike. "Gravitating Toward Between-ness or Both-ness." *Coastlines,* 2012. https://fau.edu/coastlines/pdf/Eula%20Biss.pdf

PETER DAVISON

(1928—2004)

Guy Rotella

PETER DAVISON'S REPUTATION rests most firmly on the ten books of poetry he published from 1964 to 2000. It has other sturdy supports as well. In addition to writing verse, Davison did important work as a memoirist, essayist, editor, reviewer, literary chronicler, and literary gatekeeper, and he was a vital figure in the publishing and cultural life of Boston from the mid-1950s until his death in 2004. Davison was the poetry editor of the influential magazine the *Atlantic* for several decades, working with many of the important poets of the time. His 1994 book *The Fading Smile* is an engaging firsthand account of poetry and poets in Boston in the half-decade from 1955 to 1960. His trenchant essays on poetry and poetics are collected in *One of the Dangerous Trades* (1991), along with reviews and self-appraisals. As an editor at Houghton Mifflin, where he had his own imprint, and before that at the Atlantic Monthly Press, where he was also for many years the director, Davison had a keen eye for both quality and commercial viability across many genres and subjects. His 1973 autobiography, *Half Remembered*, insightfully explores his development as a man and poet against the shifting social circumstances of his time, including the corporate fifties, the counterculture of the sixties, and the women's movement of the seventies. As this list of activities suggests, in addition to being a poet, Peter Davison was a live and lively specimen of a species supposedly extinct in his day, the man of letters. He was a singer and sometime actor, too, and what Cullen Murphy called his "theatrical sociability" brought together Bostonians of many sorts: jurists, activists, reporters, scholars, politicians, and architects, as well as literary people. Davison's career in publishing preceded his work as a poet and provided an important framework for it, as did his social engagement, reach, and range. In a period when poetry emphasized introspection, shifted away from traditional toward experimental modes, and had a narrowed, frequently academic context and audience, Davison's verse, although often candidly personal, retained formal and public dimensions and sought a general readership. Artfully crafted, it has the verve, perspicacity, and scope of a life intensely lived and intensely examined in both private and broadly cultural terms.

More than once, Peter Davison quoted approvingly these lines from Robert Hass's "Meditation at Lagunitas": "All the new thinking is about loss. / In this it resembles all the old thinking" (*Praise*, p. 4, HarperCollins, 1999). And loss, that old news that stays news and mocks novelty, is one of Davison's great poetic subjects. He treats it, as he does much else, with the refusal of the "meliorative chorus" he praised in the works of the Canadian writer Farley Mowat. That is to say, Davison is frequently an elegist: he affectingly mourns the deaths of his parents and his first wife, for instance, and he records ecological and historical desolations, but he typically does so without the ameliorating consolations of philosophical, religious, or political faith. His concern is with facts, with the feelings and imaginings they generate, and with the attempt to align all three, so that they reflect, correct, and honor one another. Davison thought of poetry in terms he learned from Robert Frost: with regard to technique, as more or less a matter of strict or loose iambics either rhymed or blank (i.e., not rhymed), and with regard to content, procedure, and outcome, as a figure of the will braving alien entanglements. Those entanglements take many forms in Davison's work: the struggle to utter truth within the constraints of poetic form, the intricacies of family inheritance, divisions within the self, the gulf between wakefulness and

PETER DAVISON

dreams, rents in the fabric of society and nature, and the inevitability of suffering, separation, death, and grief. And Davison knew that the will facing those entanglements could become an entanglement itself, precisely because of its impulse to disentangle, to simplify or ignore facts, to resolve complications, to lay blame. In this too Davison recalls Frost. He prefers griefs to grievances; he seeks to know and confront experience and his responses to it in all their (often contradictory) intricacies rather than to solve, resolve, or otherwise offer falsifying solace for them. "Passages for Puritans" in Davison's second book (*The City and the Island*, 1966) gives memorable early expression to his vision: it concludes with an ancient trope, the metaphor of the poet as a singing bird. The bird sings, as Davison thinks the poet must, of life as an irresolvable skein of joy and terror: the sweet lift of air; the threats of hawk and fox—and all of this, pleasure and pain, and drives and desires both noble and not, is framed by the inevitable fact of eventual death, figured here as a mound of feathers on a hill. Braving such entanglements, the bird-poet does what it can to keep a grip on the swaying branch of the world and sing.

Davison's poetic career can be divided into phases. His first three books of poems are largely psychological in matter and method. They confront his divided family inheritance, his psychic difficulties, and the death of his mother. The next three, following the death of his father, a happy marriage, fatherhood, and the purchase of his beloved West Gloucester, Massachusetts, saltwater farm, focus on landscape and on natural and historical processes. The last four books, after the death of his first wife and his second marriage, stress the mysteries of the self's involvement in time, often with an ecological emphasis. Elegies, unsoftened by the usual consolations but not, finally, unconsoling, connect all of Davison's volumes; however, because he came late to writing poetry (although not to poetry itself) and because so much of his writing reflects the facts of his personal and public life, discussion of the life can help to prepare for comments on the work.

BIOGRAPHY

Peter Davison was born on June 27, 1928, in New York City. His father, the English poet Edward Davison, had been born poor and out of wedlock, but on the strength of a fine singing voice he became a chorister in the Church of England and went on to the Royal Navy, the University of Cambridge, and a career as a poet. Working as a lecturer and editor, he came to the United States to marry Davison's mother, Natalie Weiner, whom he had met when she was traveling in England. She had grown up in an affluent and assimilated Jewish home on Manhattan's Upper West Side. The religious, economic, and ethnic divisions implied by this pairing provided grist for young Davison's struggles with identity and, eventually, with material for verse. As a child, Davison lived briefly in Peekskill and Ossining, New York, but in 1935, when his father's lecture fees dried up with the Great Depression and he turned to college teaching, the family moved to Boulder, Colorado. Edward Davison taught at the university there, and Davison's parents directed the annual summer sessions of the school's Writers' Conference in the Rocky Mountains. Situated at the edge of mountains and plains, where dryness struggled endlessly for moisture, Boulder was Davison's boyhood home, a place of confrontation where he met with success in the classroom and tested his physical capacities in mountain climbing expeditions and school sports, and where the complications of his family inheritance began to weigh on him. He learned of his Jewish ancestry from a schoolmate, not at home; it made his mother seem to have deprived and misled as well as nourished him.

Davison's sense of his father was still more dangerously entangled. Edward Davison taught his son to read and enriched his life with a nearly worshipful sense of the great storehouse of English poetry, much of which his father had by heart and recited with an authority, resonance, and interpretative command the son would later liken to the skills of Dylan Thomas, considered the era's greatest public performer of verse. His father's stature and the near-religious importance of the arts, especially music, and above all poetry, in young Davison's life and imagination were

62

reinforced by the presence in his home of the many musicians and poets who stayed with Davison's parents when they visited the Boulder campus, Robert Frost and Robert Penn Warren among them. At the same time, though, Davison began to see that his father now more often talked about poetry than actually wrote it. His vital gift seemed to his son to have been lost or wasted, perhaps betrayed. Davison later guessed his father suspected that modernist innovations had made irrelevant his facility with traditional forms and moody pastorals. For the father, his course in those years and after from poet to teacher to administrator felt like diminishment and was a source of disappointment, anger, and increasingly heavy drinking. For the family, home life was fraught, a setting for loud and vengeful quarrels. For the son, writing poetry became something greatly to be desired and greatly to be feared: Davison would not compose his own first poems until he was nearly thirty. Meanwhile, in more general terms, Davison felt his early family life had taught him to hide his strengths under weaknesses (feigning illness to secure his mother's love) and to hide his weaknesses under strengths (scrambling for victories in school and sports to command his father's approval). Later, self-examination and psychoanalysis convinced him he had learned at his peril to ignore his own desires, repress his feelings, perform for a real or imagined audience rather than himself, and fail to reciprocate the love of others. It would take some years for him to work through these matters and find a place in the world and in writing.

Meanwhile, Davison's outward life had the hallmarks of success. Sent to board at the Fountain Valley School in Colorado Springs he excelled as a student. In the historic wartime summer of 1944 he served as a page in the U.S. Senate. In 1945 he entered Harvard College, where he studied poetry with estimable teachers—Walter Jackson Bate, I. A. Richards, and Howard Mumford Jones—and sang in choral concerts conducted by such luminaries as Serge Koussevitzky and Leonard Bernstein. After graduation (and a violent quarrel in which he struck his father to protect his mother and sister), he spent a year at the University of Cambridge,

supported by one of the first Fulbright awards for study abroad (quarrels aside, he loyally applied to his father's college, St. John's). Davison made friends at Cambridge, including the playwright Peter Shaffer; during vacations he traveled independently in England, Italy, and elsewhere in Europe; and he had his first love affairs. In 1950 he returned to New York as a junior editor at the important publisher Harcourt, Brace (in those years, the company issued work by E. E. Cummings, E. M. Forster, and T. S. Eliot, for instance). Davison was a "first reader," responsible for culling the so-called slush pile of unendorsed manuscript submissions, and he set out to learn the publisher's trade that would become his professional career and allow him to serve the written word his childhood had taught him to revere. But for all of this, Davison reported, in 1950 he still felt self-repressed, unable to experience or express his feelings in writing or otherwise, without a clear or stable identity, haunted by his parents, amorous but unable to love, stymied.

Davison stayed five years in New York with Harcourt, Brace, and he came to know his mother's Jewish family there and to develop some sense of her and their milieu. Meanwhile, his residence and work in the city were interrupted by two years of army service, when he was drafted in 1951 at the height of the Korean War. He spent his service time stateside. His unit was the Second Loudspeaker and Leaflet Company, stationed at Fort Riley, Kansas. Its task was tactical psychological warfare, the use of propaganda to induce the enemy to surrender: as he drily summarized the matter in *Half Remembered*, "Unfortunately nobody knows how to do this" (p. 142). In part, Davison found his military experience salutary: he enjoyed his exposure to the richness of American speech as used by men of widely divergent backgrounds, took pleasure in the physical and outdoor aspects of his training, and learned something about how to turn hardship into humor and to muster and apply authority. At the same time, he became disgusted by his efforts to join wholeheartedly in the heavy drinking, sexually predatory activities of after-hours life in the camp. The result was crisis—

and conversion. He found an Episcopal church (an American version of his father's Anglican Church of England); he made a public confession and was baptized and confirmed. The comfort was real: the poetry and music of the rites helped reconnect him to the things his parents had taught him are sacred, and he felt he had recovered his inner life. But it was finally faith in art and not religious faith that mattered. His pious observances soon dwindled; as he recalled, "I proved no exception to the rule that intellectuals make untrustworthy converts" (p. 149).

Back in New York, Davison struggled to write. He couldn't, and he felt "infected" by his "incapacity" (p. 152), which he later saw as symptomatic not only of his own psychic struggles but also of the self-repression a fifties corporate culture increasingly intent on image-making demanded of its suitors in exchange for security and success. He had developed professional competence in the publishing business but again felt he had lost the way to his inmost self. This, with the catalysts of seismic shifts at Harcourt, Brace and an intensifying dislike of the city, encouraged Davison to leave New York in 1955, return to Cambridge, Massachusetts, and take an editorial position at Harvard University Press. It was then that Davison had a brief, intense, and, for him at least, disturbing affair with the poet Sylvia Plath; he would revisit the experience often in poems and reviews, chronicle and memoir, trying to do justice to the voraciousness of her personality and the incandescence of her art, and to his own sense of attraction and repulsion, injury and awe. Unable to write, Davison threw himself into other things: singing, ballet lessons, touch football. He became involved with the Poets' Theatre and acted the part of the hero-fool Alceste in Richard Wilbur's translation of Molière's seventeenth-century comedy *The Misanthrope*. The experience proved transformative. Davison felt that reciting Wilbur's lines helped teach him poetry as athletic discipline: sensory, intellectual, physical. Soon, that discipline would join other events—three years of intensive psychoanalysis, work with a manuscript of poems by Stanley Kunitz—to free him to write.

In the meantime, in 1956, Davison received and accepted an offer to join the editorial staff of the Atlantic Monthly Press in Boston. He stayed for twenty-nine years, fifteen of them as director, and he published there (under the Little, Brown imprint) and afterward at Houghton Mifflin, many commercially successful and prizewinning books, among them American editions of the Tintin adventures, *Eskimos, Chicanos, Indians* by Robert Coles, *The Kennedy Imprisonment* by Garry Wills, *Beautiful Swimmers* by William Warner, *New and Selected Things Taking Place* by May Swenson, *Blue Highways* by William Least Heat Moon, *American Primitive* by Mary Oliver, *A Dangerous Place* by Daniel Patrick Moynihan, and *The Undiscovered Self* by Carl Jung. In the fall of 1958, at the time of Natalie Weiner Davison's final illness and just before her difficult death from cancer, Davison met Jane Auchincloss Truslow; he found her diffident charm captivating and they married the following spring. He said that psychotherapy had taught him how to love and how to work. His marriage to Jane Truslow demonstrated the former; the emergence of poetry writing in his life proved the latter.

Davison specifies quite exactly the moment when he began to write. On an August Sunday afternoon in 1957, he was reading, in manuscript, preparatory to its publication, *The Selected Poems of Stanley Kunitz*. Impelled by the resonance of Kunitz's astringent verse, he found himself writing his first successfully completed poem. Called "The Winner," it evokes the mind's Pyrrhic victory in silencing the adult expression of remembered childhood pain, but does so in a way that gives utterance to what has supposedly been censored. The poem's autobiographical and psychological drama established the terms and content of Davison's early work.

The Davison marriage was a happy one. They had two children, a son, Angus, and a daughter, Lesley. With funds from an inheritance, they purchased a saltwater farm in West Gloucester, dividing their time between it and homes in Cambridge and, later on, Boston. Davison felt refreshed by the physical labor the farm required and by his recovery of the invigorating contact

with the natural world he'd mostly lost since his Colorado childhood. His career in publishing flourished, and his poetry did too. In 1964 Dudley Fitts selected Davison's first book, *The Breaking of the Day*, for inclusion in Yale's famous younger poets series. Two years after that, Davison published a second collection of poems, *The City and the Island*, and four years later a third, *Pretending to Be Asleep*.

In addition to these familial and professional developments, an important factor in Davison's life in the years leading up to his first book was his friendship with Robert Frost. Davison first met Frost in 1935 in Coral Gables, Florida, when Davison was a child and his father taught for a time in Miami; he encountered him again at the writers' conference his parents directed in Boulder. When Davison entered Harvard in 1945, his father took him to visit the aging Frost, who was then living part of each year on Brewster Street in Cambridge. For the next eighteen years, until Frost's death in 1963, the two met twenty or thirty times, usually for dinner at one or the other's home. Their conversations during and after meals and on the long nocturnal walks between houses Frost favored in those days meant a great deal to Davison as examples of how to live a poet's life. He characterized their relationship several times in prose, memorably depicting Frost's compelling, exploratory way of talking, including the expressive hand gestures Davison likened to both splitting kindling with a hatchet and conducting music. As with Frost's sense of poetry as prowess, this fusion of the physical and aesthetic with the intellectual in Frost's personal and poetic performance reinforced Davison's experience speaking Wilbur's version of Molière on stage. When he published his first book in the year after Frost's death, the dedication was double: in memory of Robert Frost, and for Edward Davison. The sense of dual paternal obligations incurred and repaid resonates with mixed feelings; his inherited poetic gift once taken up, Davison would keep it intact for life, as Frost did too and Davison's father could not.

To return to chronology, Davison's father died in 1970. His ashes were scattered from a granite cliff on his son's farm, facing a salt marsh.

A year later, Davison's elegy for him was published in a fine press limited edition. In 1972 Davison took on the poetry editorship of the *Atlantic* (a position he continued to hold even after his move to Houghton Mifflin and retained into the twenty-first century); in 1973 the memoir *Half Remembered* appeared, recording his family, school, and early professional life and his breakthrough into writing. Meanwhile, Jane Davison began a writing career of her own. She edited a companion cookbook to a public television program in 1973 and wrote *This Old House* to accompany the perennial series then hosted by Bob Vila. It came out in 1980, as did her feminist study of women and houses, *The Fall of a Doll's House*. These developments, including the family's increasing commitments to life on the West Gloucester farm (Davison began part-time farming, there in 1975, keeping pigs, sheep, goats, and geese), are all reflected in Davison's next collections of poems. The natural world of the farm and the elegy for his father are centerpieces of *Walking the Boundaries* (1974). The title of *A Voice in the Mountain* (1977) signals Davison's renewed interest in the obscured voices of women, influenced by the feminism of the seventies, the matriarchal line of his mother's Jewish family, and his wife's emerging independence, reflected in the subject of her most significant book. By the late seventies, their children schooled and grown, the couple had barely decided to move full-time to their farm when Jane, her new midlife career just launched, was diagnosed with breast cancer. She died in July of 1981, at forty-nine. Davison was fifty-three and, as he put it, "reeling with grief" (*Half Remembered*, p. 262).

He again sought and found help in psychotherapy, and, fearing too luxurious forms of mourning, threw himself into the distractions of paid and volunteer work: editing, traveling to meet with authors and give poetry readings, raising funds for Yaddo (the writers' retreat in New York), and serving the National Endowment for the Arts. Eight months later, he began spending time with the noted Boston architect Joan Edelman Goody, recently widowed. In 1984, they married at Agassiz House in Cambridge, which

PETER DAVISON

she had renovated for Radcliffe College and where he had once acted in a play. They divided their time between her house at the foot of Beacon Hill in Boston and his farm in West Gloucester until Davison's death of pancreatic cancer on December 29, 2004.

In 1985 Davison had left the Atlantic Monthly Press and taken up his own imprint, Peter Davison Books, at Houghton Mifflin. Some of the writers he had worked with before stayed with him, including the poets William Matthews and Rodney Jones, but many of his Houghton Mifflin authors were women: Anne Stevenson, Diane Wood Middlebrook, Agnes de Mille, and the poets Ai and May Swenson among them. Meanwhile, Davison continued to publish: books of poems (*Barn Fever*, *Praying Wrong*, *The Great Ledge*, *The Poems of Peter Davison*, and *Breathing Room* from 1981 through 2000), an expanded edition of *Half Remembered* and his collected essays and reviews (both in 1991), and *The Fading Smile*, chronicling the Boston poetry scene of the second half of the fifties (in 1994). It was a richly productive life.

PROSE

Davison's first prose book, *Half Remembered*, traces his life to 1970; it was written in Rome during a self-funded sabbatical from publishing and with the support of an award from the National Institute of Arts and Letters. Much of its content is conveyed in the biographical sketch above. In later years, Davison would come to regard the memoir as too self-castigating. He is hard on himself in it, and the book's psychological emphasis on family dynamics, dreams, and self-scrutiny can sometimes seem guiltily excessive, although it is very much in keeping with the period (for many American intellectuals in the fifties and sixties, psychotherapist and couch replaced priest and altar). In any case, the book remains a compelling narrative of the poet's coming of age, incisive in its observations and its insights. Davison's sharp-eyed portraits of his parents are tempered by love and understanding as well as by puzzlement and anger. He conveys his mother's beauty, musicality, social verve, and

political commitments as fully as her role in the family's intensifying unhappiness and quarrels, suggesting that the expectations of easy affluence she'd imbibed in childhood exacerbated the tensions rising from his father's loss of poetic vocation and declining prospects. He frankly describes his father's self-pity and rage as his talent failed and his career faltered, yet gratefully honors the generosity with which he bequeathed his literary gifts, perceiving their relationship in Oedipal terms, with the father as endower and competitor and the son as acolyte, thief, and ritual slayer. Such matters, as with his mixed Anglican and Jewish inheritance, would provide vital material for Davison's early poetry, and the memoir lays out their sources with clarity and power. The book's most important story, of course, is the tale of Davison's inability or repressed ability to write and his eventual breakthrough into creativity. It remains to note his skill in representing people, places, and social change: portraits of Robert Penn Warren swimming, of Frost talking, of Plath yearning to publish; a sense of prewar Boulder, of prep school sexual and other competitions, of the Senate chamber at the end of World War II, and of Harvard in the years when returning war veterans transformed it—these accompany glimpses of the publishing world as it shifted toward corporate control, of the altering ambience of Cambridge during the youth movement of the sixties, of the revelations of seventies feminism. Those create the context for Davison's coming of age as person and poet. Meanwhile, the memoir's title, with its implication that memory and invention overlap and may falsify experience as well as record it, hints at Davison's sense that artistry can obscure as well as reveal, an important undercurrent in his poems. In 1991 Davison published a revised edition of *Half Remembered*, leaving the original story intact, but expanding it with a new preface, afterword, and photographs. It brings his autobiography up to date with the details of his marriage and his family and professional lives, his first wife's death, and his second marriage, and it reframes the original edition's tone and judgments from a greater chronological and cooler emotional distance. Along with stories of happiness and

success, the new material has its own quota of suffering and pain, but these are managed now with less anxiety or guilt and with the mature sense of balance, purpose, and dedication the first edition showed the poet beginning to achieve. The afterword's discussion of his late-life reconciliation of what had once seemed his divided Christian and Jewish ancestry is exemplary.

While working as an editor and poet, Davison also produced a good deal of other writing, including essays on poetry and publishing, book reviews, and appraising portraits of himself and others. Many of these were collected in 1991 in *One of the Dangerous Trades: Essays on the Work and Workings of Poetry*. The book throws light on Davison's poetic practices and preferences, reveals his discriminating eye and ear, and demonstrates his gift for incisive, sometimes tart evaluation and expression. From the perspective of his position in the competitive, economically driven world of publishing, he distrusts the deepening dependence in his era of poetry and poets on academic and governmental institutions. He dislikes what he judges the period's discarding of the legacies of rhyme and meter, of intricate syntax, and of memorability as a test of poetic quality. He decries the nearly exclusive preference for the present tense and indicative mood in the poetry of his time. This can be merely cranky, but it can prove insightful as well: praising the complexities of rhyme, meter, syntax, and logical sequence in poems by Geoffrey Hill, Davison shows that Hill's traditional commitments are subversive, not conservative, "like entering a church in order to strip it of its treasures" (p. 14). The implied point that formal choices need not correlate with political stances is salutary. Davison can be a good guide to his near contemporaries. He identifies the struggle between personal and imperial voices in the work of Robert Lowell, for instance, and captures James Dickey's drive to wrench heaven down to earth. Often his portraits enliven liveliness, as when he shows Randall Jarrell "flushing out" and "shooting down" "like a blue-ribbon duck hunter" the fumbling queries of a post-poetry reading question period (p. 29). Meanwhile, Davison's

praise for such predecessors as Thomas Hardy, Robert Frost, and Edwin Muir reveals not only preferences but influences too.

A section of the book called "Admirations" includes portraits of Frost referred to earlier and several reviews of books by Sylvia Plath (these praise her best work but dislike the cult of the poet-suicide that grew up around her, notice her vaulting ambition, and excoriate the greedy, often distorting posthumous publication by others of her weaker writings). A piece on Wallace Stevens shows Davison a little deaf to the emotional and public resonance of poems he finds monotonously fluent and hermetically private, while the elegant narrative of Davison's trip to Vermont to attend Robert Penn Warren's funeral reveals much about that poet's writing and milieu. Discussing Stanley Kunitz at eighty, Davison—Kunitz' editor for nearly thirty years—says he never edited a line; his respect for the senior poet includes intense and emulative admiration for Kunitz' patient vigils in wait for unpredictable thrusts of transforming internal growth. If Davison misses some of the intensities in Elizabeth Bishop later commentators have revealed, he notices early on her sinister interiors and harmonious exteriors, lack of overt ambition, and wit and sophistication. His summary of Philip Larkin's verse remains tellingly precise; its inclusion of cultural and historical as well as literary frameworks is characteristic of Davison's untheoretical but worldly criticism: "Larkin's poetry rings the knell on the white man's triumph, on the arts and riches of the island kingdom, on a culture of which he regarded himself as one of the last qualified, yet impotent, stewards" (p. 126).

Davison's reviews of his fellow poets sometimes provide more insight than scholarly literary histories. Discussing Lowell's famous metaphor of poetry as "raw" or "cooked," he shows how soon those terms became obsolete, as antiformalists quickly sought alternate shapes and formalists moved to shake up traditions. The insight applies to Davison's loosened formalism too. Davison's early estimates of James Merrill ("a gifted makeup artist" [p. 136]), W. S. Merwin (one of "the new inventors of silence" [p. 149]), May Swenson, A. R. Ammons, Galway Kinnell,

James Wright, Robert Hass, and others remain convincing, as do his discussions of L. E. Sissman, whose urbane narrative poems Davison edited for publication in 1978, and Lucia Perillo, whose first book he selected and introduced for the Samuel French Morse Poetry Prize in 1989 and whose subsequent achievements validate his judgment. The final section of *One of the Dangerous Trades* is called "Self-Appraisal." It includes a piece on Davison's writing practices: instructively wry, he observes that, with respect to having time to write, "You can never have enough; yet it is quite possible to have too much" (p. 179). The essay "Self-Portrait" anticipates the afterword included in the revised edition of *Half Remembered*, while the transcript of a 1985 radio interview includes Davison's suggestion that the art of poetry might be called the art of "praying wrong." Hopeful and wary, the phrase titles one of his books.

Davison's final prose work is *The Fading Smile: Poets in Boston, from Robert Frost to Robert Lowell to Sylvia Plath, 1955–1960*, published in 1994. It chronicles that brief half-decade when Boston and New England once more seemed the hub of American poetry they had been in the nineteenth century. It is a collective portrait, featuring Frost as presiding modernist giant, with close-ups of Richard Wilbur, W. S. Merwin, Maxine Kumin, Donald Hall, Philip Booth, Anne Sexton, Sylvia Plath, Adrienne Rich, L. E. Sissman, Stanley Kunitz, Robert Lowell, and Davison himself, and with snapshots of the Poets' Theatre, John Holmes, Richard Eberhart, George Starbuck, and several others. The book takes up its gallery of individual writers in sequence, but it treats their complicated interactions at parties, readings, and workshops, their friendships, liaisons, and rivalries, their shared circumstances and varied attainments in a braided narrative thick with detail and anecdote. It resists representative excerption but is a treasure trove for biographers and literary and cultural historians, an eyewitness account enriched by research and probing interviews. Its main achievement is to capture, in lively, intimate, and un-awed prose, the personalities, venues, relationships, and ambience of a transformative moment in American literary history, a moment when poets of widely divergent talents and styles shared a profound and disturbing sense that not only their poetry but they themselves and the terms of their access to and representation of experience had become encrusted with falsifying inherited conventions and, stymied and stultified, were in desperate need of renewal. Lowell famously called for "some breakthrough back into life"; more melodramatic, Sexton repeated Franz Kafka's view that a book should serve as an ax for the frozen sea within us. With Wilbur as an exception in this and other things, problems with fathers occur again and again in the lives and work of these poets, both literally and as a sign of damaging inheritances of every kind: familial, political, and cultural, and including received codes of race, class, sexuality, and the roles associated with gender. The difficulties are usually framed in psychological terms, as is the response. This is typically a matter of writing personal (rather than impersonal and therefore supposedly universal) poetry, poetry that more or less openly reveals extreme experiences and behaviors, and does so in hope of relief, on the model of the psychotherapeutic session (or its predecessor, confession). As to the degree and nature of the revelations involved, Davison says nicely that where the New York and San Francisco Beats went naked, the more prudent Boston poets changed their clothes.

POETRY: 1957–1970

Davison's early personal and psychological poetry is of a piece with the work of the time, place, and poets *The Fading Smile* treats, but it has other features as well. His first book, *The Breaking of the Day* (1964), takes its title from the Genesis story of Jacob wrestling with an angel in search of a blessing. Wrestling is an apt image for the book's emphasis on struggle and confrontation, but whatever blessing it wins has more to do with hard and unforgiving self-knowledge than with saving or soothing forms of religious or other grace. While the title poem talks fretfully of competing faiths, the book's reference frames are more those of psychic

identity and familial, social, and sexual behavior than of theology. Davison's memoir guiltily insists on his inability to reciprocate the love of others emotionally as well as physically in the affairs that preceded his marriage. Several poems in *The Breaking of the Day* reflect such failures, some in directly personal terms, others more obliquely. "'True Feeling Leaves No Memory,'" "At the Site of Last Night's Fire," and "Goodbye" all depict self-centered love affairs gone cold, the barren chill that descends when, lust expended, only ash remains. The phantasmagoria of "After a Nightmare" carries the Freudian view that a child's unresolved desires for its mother may poison or distort later sexual relations. For all their aesthetic distance, these poems have at least the feel of autobiographical reporting. Other poems on similar subjects are more remote. Whether they displace the poet's own experience and feelings into portraits or reflect his scrutiny of others, they repeatedly represent love and desire as blocked and perverted. Offered love, the frightened boy in "The Firstling" fails to respond and is shamed and unmanned. In "Summer School," adulterous scholars fatten lewdly on one another, their studied appetites grim with self-absorption. "Artemis" compounds sex with death. And in "The Peeper," a voyeur, cringing from actual flesh, prefers to see it only through protective glass, thereby avoiding change as well as intimacies like touch and taste and smell. There is more than a hint of sexual guilt or disgust in these poems, the sort of thing the later sixties imagined doing away with, but there are elements of frank self-appraisal, accurate social observation, and satirical correction, too, an implicit preference for more natural and healthier relations.

Troubled sexuality is a major concern of *The Breaking of the Day*, as of much of the psychologically based poetry of the late fifties and early sixties. The book also reflects the period's interest in extreme psychological states, including mental illness: "To a Mad Friend" seems addressed to the manic-depressive Robert Lowell and claims kinship with him. Davison's concern with his own psychological state is most apparent in poems that depict a fractured self, espe-

cially the volume's explicitly autobiographical title poem. In eight sections, "The Breaking of the Day" records Davison's misery at his divided circumstances: his parents bequeathed him Christian and Jewish ancestry but could not or would not help him comprehend it; conversion saved him from degradation in Kansas but he subsequently lost to secularism both his belief in Christian redemption and his Jewish lifeline; the currency of his father's gift of words was deflated by squandering and silence. The poem's biblically charged language is everywhere marked by extremity and abasement: the poet suffers darkness at noon in a world where weather is a bludgeon; his hide blisters and burns; his mind is cracked. Diminished in every way, crippled and staggering, and with his language reduced to howls and curses, he stammers out part of a prayer to a fragmented god. This is desolation but not surrender. Body and mind are shattered, religious faith is in fragments, speech falters, yet efforts to understand, to move and think, and to utter meaningful words persist as the poet wrestles with his fate. The poem's final section, called "Delphi," holds out hope: perhaps the trust of the ancient Greeks in art, prophecy, or rigorous self-knowledge can replace lost faiths. Those things too prove damaged: the springs of poetic inspiration "gush" (an ambiguous word that takes back much of what it gives); oracles are bribed and confusion garbles omens (vultures are mistaken for eagles); mere knowledge is insufficient. The poem's closing words are desperate, but the bleakness is not entirely despairing. Bereft of resolving wholeness, the poet maintains a resolute wrestler's hold on the fragments, parts, and halves he owns.

Several poems in the volume vary and lighten the nearly abject tone of "The Breaking of the Day." "Late Summer Love Song" gratefully welcomes erotic joy. "The Star Watcher" emulates Frost's "talk-songs" in order knowingly to praise him. "Hunger" plays at epigram, and other poems have satiric or gentler humor (some reflect the sentimentality, forced wit, and awkward diction that now and then mar Davison's usually well-made work). "Winter Sunrise" and "Peripheral Vision" state a preference for honest complica-

tion and confusion over artificially arranged perfection, a preference Davison's later work develops, as it also develops the uncompromising but uncertain moral exploration of "The Massacre of the Innocents." Throughout the book Davison demonstrates technical facility. If he avoids the refreshing gymnastic experiments such contemporaries as Allen Ginsberg and John Ashbery were then performing, he renovates traditional forms and effects (quatrains, sonnets and double sonnets, dramatic monologues, choruses and refrains) and shows skill in managing metrical substitution, rhyme's pairing of predictability and surprise, and the mixing together of slightly elevated with ordinary cadences and vocabulary for dramatic impact.

Together with the title poem, the finest achievement of *The Breaking of the Day* is a trio of poems on the death of Davison's mother from cancer in 1959. As he says in *Half Remembered*, the disease took her vitality, then her equanimity, and then her speech; her suffering was so great she asked her son to help her die. The poems on this scarifying event are of different kinds. "Not Forgotten" is an elegy in five parts, spoken in the poet's voice. The irregular lines and fumbling rhythms of the opening passage convey the distorting pain of Natalie Davison's death and the suffering of her family as they witness it. The second section recounts a macabre dream, surreally comic, in which the son, called on to pronounce his mother's eulogy before assembled mourners, finds himself speechless and without resources, no notes, no "Oxford Book of Consolations." Desperate, he improvises, dancing on her coffin and imagining her drumming her toes in reply from beneath the coffin lid. The dream is dreadful in its way. Its bizarre impropriety reflects Davison's guilt, anger, grief, and wordless incapacity in the face of loss, and the missing Oxford book indicates the poverty of inherited codes of solace. But the poet's nightmarish dance also restores contact; his mother responds to his gesture. Still howling with grief, the next part of the poem moves closer to metrical balance, and the fourth section, although it presents the poet wracked with guilt at his inability to grant his mother's plea to help her die,

achieves iambic regularity in rhyming quatrains. This counterpointing of form and content, of chaotic feelings and increasingly orderly shaping, conveys grief's need for and resistance to conventional comfort, and it suggests the capacities and limitations of poetic art to provide them. It prepares for the entangled closing passage. The poet's world is diminished by loss: colorless, dull, diluted, and small. The grand religious, philosophical, or natural consolations associated with traditional elegy are unavailable to him. Even so, his grief is quieted. Now he addresses his mother intimately as "you," not "her" or "she" as before; memories of her singular beauty and presence arise and abide. These things are threatened, too, by literal absence and looming forgetfulness. As in "The Breaking of the Day," what remain are intricate mixed feelings that respect experience and resist solution, comfort, or simplification.

Two additional poems address Natalie Davison's death. "Finale: Presto" is an accomplished dramatic monologue in the mother's voice. It allows frank and courageous, unsoftened expression of her desire to die in the face of her extremity. Where there is some assuagement in the image of her dying like an otter slipping into a pond in "Not Forgotten," in this still tougher-minded poem she departs her body like water spilled from a jug. "The Death of the Virgin (Rembrandt)" goes further. Its meditation on the famous painting is also autobiographical. It insists that death is a bitter end, not a miraculous transformation. Solace in Davison's work is absent, unavailing, or under threat. His urgent confrontations with situations that traditionally demand it have their own strict virtue.

Advance or consolidation can make a second book compelling, but the hard-earned commitment to irresolvable complications that gives *The Breaking of the Day* its drive and conviction is more apt to stall than to power Davison's *The City and the Island*, published in 1966. The traditional crafts of meter, rhyme, and organizing stanza forms still serve him there. And the entangled meanings and feelings symbolized by the moralized landscapes named in the book's title convey the knotted sense of reality so central

to his vision: the city represents desirable security and sociability but also stifling regimentation; the island signals invigorating freedom and adventure but also the terrors of exposure, risk, and isolation. Too often, though, these matters seem abstract and programmatic, their roots obscured. The poems depict a person caught between the satisfactions and snares of routine and the temptations and fearfulness of freedom (in the city, he longs for the island; arrived there, he aches to return). This might reflect Davison's situation as he moved from the delights and disgruntlements of bachelorhood into the expansive pleasures and restricting obligations of marriage, parenthood, and work at the office. Perhaps they portray less conventional dilemmas: psychological obsession, the compulsive confronting of impossible choices. The poems' repeated and tormented twists and turns imply that, and it might be confirmed by stories and dreams of times at sea related in *Half Remembered,* and by the memoir's larger psychic self-portrait. In any case, the poems' sources in experience are often opaque, perhaps in an effort to make the particular universal. Mythic elements, parallels with Odysseus, for instance, suggest a generalizing impulse, but they seem weakly integrated here and out of scale. Davison has already written stronger poems of private psychic struggle; he will later produce better poems of generalized social and moral investigation.

Other things in the book reward attention. There are mildly amusing poems on office sexual and power politics ("Lucifer Ashore," "Lunch at the Coq D'Or") and satiric thrusts at serial philandering, coy virginity, and cults of pain ("The Collector," "Intacta," and "One of the Muses"). "Epitaph for S.P." is a stringent portrait of Sylvia Plath's uneven fires, its aching brevity a gloss on her abbreviated life. "The Light of the Body" makes eerie good use of a varied refrain. "Galop" has social and metrical wit, while a poem on portrait painting explores the gap between art's fleshly source and artificial surface. "The Destroyer" and "The Fire in the House" reveal perils haunting supposedly safe domestic settings. The best poems in the book stand more or less apart from the city-island structure. In

"Easter Island: The Statues Speak," buried gods threaten those who seek to revive them. "Eurydice in Darkness" and "Mary Magdalene at Easter" acidly revise male-centered resurrection myths from more pragmatist women's perspectives. "Having Saints" imagines divinities more earthy than transcendent; its sense of human limitations is newly fond and forgiving. "Gifts" introduces ideas about gifts and praying important to Davison's later work, and all of these poems prefer the flawed realm of the here and now to the purported perfections of other worlds, whether cities, islands, or somewhere else.

Pretending to Be Asleep (1970) is a book of public and private desolations, tempered by its skilled use of formal versification, political astuteness, clear-eyed self-appraisal, and continuing attention to all the entangled strands a life in the world comprises. It restores the personal sources of distress obscured in its predecessor. The book's eponymous central section is as relentless and castigating a self-portrait as the one in the near contemporary memoir *Half Remembered.* Davison indicts himself again and again as a blocked and evasive pretender hiding defensively from his own and others' scrutiny. The thoroughness and precision of his cross-examination argues otherwise. The result is a kind of hung jury; it imagines at least the possibility of judgments more accurate than extremes of execution or exculpation. As in *Half Remembered*, the self's struggles enable the writing they once prevented and still make hard to do.

More public concerns focus the first section of *Pretending to Be Asleep.* A poem on the Robert Kennedy assassination, "Visions and Voices," despairs at the state of the nation, facing squarely the failures of press and people properly to estimate and respond to Kennedy's flaws and virtues. "The Gun Hand" paints a violent American culture at home and in Vietnam. "Forked Tongue" shows politicians using money and guilt to manipulate the system, "Plausible Man" pictures corporate soullessness, and "The Pleaders" echoes the persistent but powerless voice of citizens governed and oppressed by elites who presume to know what's good for them. None of

these poems imagines such things are likely to alter very much. One poem promotes indifference, but as an anti-apocalyptic anodyne too dulling to be a solution. The book's third and final section returns to personal themes of parentage and failed love. "Old Photograph" again mourns hopelessly Davison's loss of his mother, while "Words for My Father" revisits the son's sense of a damaged poetic inheritance. There, though, by way of paternal and filial exchanges effectively echoing the *Odyssey*, the son offers accommodation, returning gratefully the gift of words his father gave him. Two other fine poems also merit mention, one from early in the book, the other its last. In rhymed and slant-rhymed couplets, "Making Marks" bitingly inscribes the forensic signature of a poet's way with words and speech. "Stumps" describes sprouts rising from the roots of felled trees as a cogent metaphor for the unexhausted but weakening persistence of the past, so far Davison's defining subject but beginning now to loosen if not release its grip on him.

POETRY: 1970–1981

Published in 1974, *Walking the Boundaries* is both a summary and a fresh start; it follows a selection of poems from Davison's first three volumes with twenty-five new ones. He rightly judged it the book in which he hit his stride as a poet. Davison's marriage and children, his achievements as poet and publisher, and the labors and pleasures of life on the West Gloucester farm seem to have relieved his obsession with the past and his bouts of self-castigating depression. Davison's metrical and formal rigors relax here as well. The conventional use of capital letters to head every new line of verse is dropped, rhyme is rare, and the vocabulary and phrasing of the poems come nearer those of speech. Even as it presses closer to acknowledging that what we think of as knowledge is a form of ignorance, Davison's voice is increasingly assured. The world remains for him a place of alien entanglements without trustworthy solutions or lasting consolation, but it has greater room for compensatory pleasures, including those of marital and family love, of a beloved place,

and of poetic making. His effort to resist simplification and to express all of the multiple and conflicting facts and implications of experience continues in poems of greater range and reach.

Davison still writes poems of psychological disturbance and failed love. In "Bed Time," insomnia signals mental distress; suicides multiply in "The Obituary Writer"; a wound in "Bandages" refuses to heal. "London 1972: Silent Zone" and "Embraces" revisit love affairs made sordid by lack of feeling. But these matters and memories no longer overwhelm the poet and are often relieved by the presence in his life of selfless love (see "Doors" and the final section of "Embraces") and by his own greater independence and self-reliance (see the announcement in "Standing Fast: Fox into Hedgehog" that he is leaving behind a more evasive and frenetic self, knows what he knows, and intends to stand his ground).

Davison's elegy for his father takes its title from one of his father's poems (he again returns as a gift the gift of words his father gave him). In six sections arranged by reverse chronology, "Dark Houses" writes Edward Davison back from death toward youth and promise. As he has before, Davison insists on an accurate record and assessment of his father's failures and decline, his squandered talent and drink-fueled rages. But now these are more nearly matters of description than accusation. Understanding replaces or modifies judgments, and the son responds with compassion and poise to memories that once had made him wretched. His father abandoned poetry, but Davison refuses to charge him with desertion. If the poems his father did write are escapist, out of touch with the depths of life, perhaps this is so because writing for him was a way to escape his childhood poverty and sense of shame. A ritual seventh section returns to the present. The father's ashes are ceremonially scattered from a cliff on the son's saltwater farm, a place his father cared for but that is not quite his own. The effect is bittersweet. Unpleasant facts preclude complete forgiveness; there is no home to come to; death is real; and no transcendent faith confers consolation. Yet the son's composure and compositional effort, his attention both to harsh reality

and alleviating gestures is an achievement. It lays his ghosts.

Walking the Boundaries is framed and interleaved by its four-part title poem. A major development occurs there: a shift away from psychological poetry toward poems of landscape and the natural world. The poet's increased personal stability in this book stems partly from a settled sense of place, and "Walking the Boundaries" is firmly organized by the solidity of compass points, the permanence of the changing seasons, and the reliable landmarks of Davison's farm. Natural descriptions in his earlier poems are typically abstract and symbolic; here meaning arises gradually from physical realities attentively observed and represented. "Walking the Boundaries: West by the Road" describes the annual turn from fall toward winter. Plants and animals hoard and hunker down. Without panic, complaint, or dreams of salvation, life burrows, ducks, hangs on, and takes its chances. The quiet implication is that, faced with inevitable loss and suffering and death, we might do the same. This and the poem's next two sections convey abiding love for a place that constantly changes yet remains persistent. The farm grounds the poet's being in ways his wife's love also does (see the aptly titled "Ground"). The final section of "Walking the Boundaries" goes north by the creek. It achieves the finest expression of Davison's central vision in his work so far. The season is early spring, at dusk, the time of the male woodcock's nuptial flight. Davison describes the woodcock's helical upward soaring and its accompanying song with emulative patience and precision. Despite its drab, earthbound appearance, the bird carries itself higher and higher, rising on the updraft of its song until it reaches a boundary or limit and comes back down: comes down but is not defeated. It soars, sings, and descends again. Wholly itself, it becomes a sign of the human condition as Davison sees it. Caught between earth and the heavens, daylight and night, birth and death, real boundaries we cannot cross into any place that is perfect or transcendent, we still can push to reach beyond our powers, accepting and resisting our circumstances, making music that, however awkwardly,

climbs skyward. The combination of hampered striving, elevating lift, and impassable limitation in this clambering effort defines Davison's view of things and his skill in conveying it.

Davison's most varied volume to date, *A Voice in the Mountain*, appeared in 1977, a year after the nation's bicentennial celebration. Perhaps that event occasioned some of the book's ambitious treatment of large-scale political, economic, social, and historical matters. One anticolonial poem attacks England's imperialist insularity in a distant echo of the American Revolution. "Toward an Understanding of the Public Life" chides a national political class out of touch with ordinary experience and habituated to evading judgment. The section of "House Holding" called "The New World" presents the American immigrant experience without the varnish of nostalgia or self-regarding national myth. "Haskell's Mill" is about a ruined Gloucester landmark. Although occasionally marred by mawkish diction, it forcefully reflects a bicentennial interest in local history and smartly treats the national shift from rural to urban life and economy without romanticizing one or damning the other, since all these forms are driven by exigencies of trade and profit. The explicitly titled "Bicentennial" offers a Frost-like version of New England history: woods now close in to retake the land colonial and federal farmers cleared, troubling national narratives of settlement and expansion. Large cultural generalizations are at work in many other poems, regardless of their subjects. For instance, "The Fall of the Dolls' House" refers to the seismic shift from the Enlightenment harmonies of Denis Diderot and Isaac Newton to the post-Enlightenment dissonance of Karl Marx and Sigmund Freud. Here as elsewhere Davison insists that whatever freedom we may have, we are formed and constrained by our time and place, by cultural context and the history of ideas as well as family inheritance. Davison's particular family inheritance is the subject of the poem, but it makes clear that larger public frameworks condition private history.

One of those frameworks has to do with the roles a given society or culture assigns to gender,

and *A Voice in the Mountain* reflects some lessons of seventies feminism. "The Fall of the Dolls' House" examines the power differentials, places, possibilities, and limits set for women, men, and children by patriarchal myths about family arrangements and positions, the sorts of things a doll house, like other toys and stories, represents and teaches. The "Radiant City" and "Strict Construction" sections of "House Holding" also stress that although things may be changing, women are mostly condemned to inhabit structures designed by men for their own convenience but described as though they were inevitable, permanent, and natural, a system in which homes themselves can be nearly escape-proof prisons, places of containment and possession masquerading as sites of benevolent protection. In technical terms, *A Voice in the Mountain* continues some of the more relaxed patterns of *Walking the Boundaries*, but several poems return to earlier formal rigors: there is more blank verse than free verse; a number of poems are in rhymed or unrhymed quatrains; "Lamia" is a polished Italian sonnet and "Creatures of the Genitive" is a sestina. By this stage in his career, Davison's technical palette comprises many colors, knives, and brushes.

A Voice in the Mountain varies its subjects as well as its techniques. One poem depicts a cathedral drowned by secular smugness. "Day of Wrath" howls with irredeemable desolation. "Jesus Shaves" is comically epigrammatic. "Gratified Desire" takes a satirical swipe at the life of the mathematician, philosopher, social activist, and lover Bertrand Russell. Two poems, "The Genie in the Bottle" and "The Poem in the Park," confirm the sexual sources of writing; another, "La Bocca della Verità," defends poetry: its sort of feigning tells the truth. Concepts of orthodoxy and heterodoxy, order and entropy, matter and antimatter inform the inverted wit of "The Hanging Man." A lovely elegy for the poet L. E. Sissman revisits one of Davison's vital themes, the inseparable entanglement within experience of life with death, order with disorder, elegance with mess. Its title, "The Compound Eye," indicates the kind of intricately inclusive vision Davison prefers, as does its praise of

"sweet disorder" (in Robert Herrick's famous phrase).

Many fine poems in *A Voice in the Mountain* develop the mode of natural description and conceptual speculation begun in *Walking the Boundaries*. "Skiing by Moonlight" shows wild nature retaking by night the realms that daylight lets us think we own. "Cross Cut" describes the felling of a dying tree; it quietly echoes Davison's guilt at his failure to help his mother out of life and shows how effectively psychic and natural landscapes come together in his later work. "Zenith: Walker Creek" evokes the height of summer. Time seems suspended in mellow days rich with relaxation, satisfaction, and fulfillment. Then reality and Davison's signature sense of things intrude: change and loss tick at the core of human and natural seasons; perfection is always transient and incomplete. The poem's tone abruptly shifts. Excessive heat and the hungry anger of insects suggest natural violence and human passions. Facts dissolve contentment. Echoing the Frost poem called "The Exposed Nest," "Making Much of Orioles" faces similar entanglements. The poet fells a diseased elm tree. Lopping its branches, he finds an oriole nest. Frightened and hungry, the chicks still cheep inside it. He tries to save them, tying the limb with the nest to a branch in a nearby cherry, out of predators' reach. Coaxed by the poet's mimic whistling, or by accident or instinct, the parent birds find and feed their young despite their alien position. The nestlings fledge. This is a victory of sorts, the will overcoming circumstances, loss defeated. To celebrate, the poet retrieves the nest on its branch and keeps it like a trophy in his room. But time and reality temper his proprietary sense of triumph. The orioles move on. He knows nothing of larger outcomes. The commemorative branch and nest get tossed behind a lilac bush. The poem just stops, before it makes *too* much of orioles. For Davison, the act of intervention the poem records, like every human effort to press against natural limits, encounters boundaries it cannot cross. "Thanksgiving" expresses a similarly calm and inclusive view of life's irresolvable complications. Davison returns to the subject of his family inheritance; its milk is

nourishing and bitter, an intricacy that hurts him still but no longer overwhelms him. In later work the poem's reminder that "gift" means "marriage" in Swedish and "poison" in German joins his nuanced sense of "praying wrong" to characterize Davison's compelling vision.

Barn Fever appeared in 1981, after Jane Davison's breast cancer diagnosis but before her death that summer. Several poems in its opening section follow precedents *A Voice in the Mountain* laid down. For example, "Haskell's Mill" sets the pattern for the title poem's encompassing historical and cultural concerns. Laconic and expansive, it relates the long history of the barn on Davison's Gloucester farm in achieved New England accents; it tells a representative tale of agricultural decline. "Barn Fever" mourns the suburbs' invasion of the country, a process the poet's ownership of the place admittedly fosters, and it regrets the accompanying loss of a way of life and of meaningful patterns of craftsmanship and land use. Its sorrow is tempered by a realistic sense that change is the nature of things and by the poet's modest holding action: by making repairs and through part-time animal husbandry and writing, he conserves for a while some part of what will disappear. "Fawn" recalls "Making Much of Orioles." Ill or injured, a young deer is nurtured back to health and released to the wild. The pleasure of having saved it is intertwined with Davison's signature tough-mindedness about the limitations of knowledge—and with wistful hope: while there is no way of knowing if the fawn survived the winter, the season was a mild one. Similar intricacies focus the remarkable "Lambkill," another name for sheep laurel, a common meadow plant sometimes poisonous to livestock. Sheep are introduced into an overgrown meadow; browsing, they reduce its tangled growth to lawnlike pasture. In the process, a young ram, despite every effort to save him, dies from having eaten lambkill. As in all of Davison's finest nature writing, the story quietly releases metaphors with human implications: however attractive regular patterns and clarity may be, something deadly lurks in our hunger to make the inscrutable simple. Technical aspects of *Barn Fever* mirror the lesson. There are poems in conventional forms: a

few in symmetrical stanzas, rhymed and unrhymed quatrains, a villanelle; these are mixed with blank verse poems in tight or loose iambics and with free verse.

Much in *Barn Fever* is grounded in the facts of farm life. The poems gathered under the heading "The Sound of Wings" are less tethered; freed toward the flights and heights of transcendence, their mysterious, sometimes mystical language strikes a new note in Davison's work. Finally, though, these poems are also grounded in earthly specifics, including those of Davison's Colorado boyhood and more recent travels. The final section of "Atmospheres," for instance, uses metaphors drawn from pottery making to depict the human condition. We carry the clay of our unfired flesh through a world that awaits its decay. No kiln hardens us into permanence. The drift of change transforms us into other transient things, snowflakes or vapor. The third section of *Barn Fever*, "Men Working" includes poems of social observation and satire. "The Laughter of Women" reveals a comically wounded masculinity, for instance, and "Short Weight" attacks the usurpation of language by advertisers and governments who use it to sell lies.

Each section of *Barn Fever* is headed by a definition of the word "gift" that provides a kind of keynote: for the farm poems, the definition relates to property and ownership; for "The Sound of Wings," to divine endowments; and for the satiric "Men Working," to bribery. The definitions introducing the closing section are those first used in "Thanksgiving": in Swedish, "gift" means "marriage"; in German, "poison." Like the section's title, "Mixed Blessings," these competing, intricately related terms establish the tone for poems of troubled, guilty, threatened, and abiding love, some of them private, others set in the more universal public realms of fairy tale, myth, and epic. Each is remarkable, including "Wordless Winter," an eight-part response to Jane Davison's soon to be fatal illness. The opening poems of the sequence characterize the poet's anxiety, guilt, and depression; in one, the absence of Davison's usually meticulous punctuation conveys his derangement. Other sections define inner with outer weather (a frozen drought) and

portray his hopes for his wife's survival (those are dashed by insistent funeral images of prayers and tears and shovels, revealing his deepest fear). In another, battle language praises Jane Davison's courage and resistance. Its title, "Stalemate," indicates a standoff, but the dismal pun is terrifying. The poet is wordless and clenched, unable to write. The final poem of *Barn Fever* is equally foreboding. In it, the natural cycle is a sink of indifference, not a source of comfort.

POETRY: 1981–2000

Praying Wrong (1984) has a dozen new poems gathered under the heading "The Vanishing Point," a phrase that implies both irredeemable loss and artistic perspective and control. The book also includes a generous selection from Davison's first six volumes. The selected poems are occasionally revised ("Haskell's Mill" is improved, for instance), and they are often rearranged in ways that reveal new relationships among them, an effect in keeping with Davison's lifelong practice of structuring his books to avoid miscellany and provide overarching patterns of drama, narrative, or argument. *Barn Fever* closes darkly; after that, and the grievous loss of Jane Davison's death in 1981, the new poems of *Praying Wrong* begin with hobbled recovery. The poet has survived his wordless winter, as "Wintering Over," the opening poem, suggests. Although the warmer sun of the new season is barely established and the self is worn and weathered, Davison reaffirms his poetry's commitment to rummage in the attic of language, acknowledge the constancy of change, and connect the past and future. As those chronic terms imply, several of these poems focus on the mysteries of living within the flawed world of time and alteration while nonetheless being spurred by desires for permanence and perfection.

Dying and death are ultimate signs of change and limitation, and the last of the new poems in *Praying Wrong* is "Nothing Sudden," a beautifully modulated elegy for the poet's wife, who died of cancer after two slow years of irreversible decline. The funeral rites are gracious, her ashes buried, her first name carved in the granite cliff on the farm. But memory is the only available consolation: sorrowing recollections of her intimate touch, her beauty and courage. And memory fades. Like Orpheus, the poet lacks the power to reclaim his bride. He holds a remnant lock of her graying hair; the adjective insists on unrelenting processes of aging and decay. The surrounding world persists: woods and grasses, birds at the feeder, but these are a theater of change and remember nothing.

Between the reaffirmation of "Wintering Over" and the finalities of "Nothing Sudden" there are poems on father-and-son and father-and-daughter relationships, and several poems explore the strangeness of living in time and address the lures and hazards of perfection. The title poem of the new poems section portrays an instant after nightmare, when, at the turn of the year, time seems to pause for an extended moment before it begins again to coast or scramble forward. It has no destination, just direction. Mysteriously, it holds and carries and assesses us before it leaves us behind and moves on. Two poems, "The Housewife's Paradise" and "Low Lands," consider painters who transform the actual world to confer dimensions of perfection or transcendence on it. Neither transformation is ultimately convincing. In "Questions of Swimming, 1935" the distant shore is earthly, not the otherworld or heaven such words conventionally conjure. As usual in Davison, these poems stop short at impassable boundaries or limits. Yet their feel is slightly different than before, as though a door between this world and some almost palpable, nonexistent elsewhere were held ajar for a flickering moment before being firmly shut. This is especially so in the superb poem "Crossing the Void," dedicated to Stanley Kunitz. The journey it calls for is impossible but required. A deeply frightened figure forces himself outward on a half-built bridge to nowhere visible or known yet hauntingly all but present; confronting nothingness and wholly ungrounded, he feels himself drowning, sea boots filled, planking awash and sinking. Perhaps the poet's humble sense of praying wrong, of asking for gifts as though he had none coming, of accepting gifts, including poems, as nurturing apples that are also always poisoned,

offers some slender, temporary margin of protection against such terminal undoing.

The Great Ledge appeared in 1989. It uses Davison's well-established techniques: poems rhymed or blank with a tight or loose iambic pulse, occasional forays in free verse. Its subjects are widely varied, but in mostly familiar ways. A poem for a grandchild meditates on the mysteries of heredity and environment, nature and nurture. "Peaches" indulges sweetly the fleshy play of language. Several poems reflect travel, to Lombardy, Paris, Puerto Rico. "Stretto" makes music out of music. There are fond elegies for a family dog and for a child dead as an infant. A set of literary portraits satirizes self-indulgent memoirists and self-important professors, praises the poet and translator of Homer, Robert Fitzgerald, and calibrates once more Davison's response to Sylvia Plath (see the earlier poems "Epitaph for S.P.," "The Heroine," and perhaps "Artemis" as well, and, in *Breathing Room*, the later poems "Sorry" and "A Ballad"). Intimations of both growth and guilt appear in the poet's self-portrait "At Sixty." "Cramped Quarters" revisits his maternal Jewish heritage and its attendant obligations, and "Mother and Child #3" returns to his mother's death and to memory's uses and limits. There are poems on cracks in the universe and the sleep of birds, as well as an acrid and funny set of oracular stock replies to a list of sample questions. Many of these poems are successful, but the true excellence of *The Great Ledge* lies elsewhere: in poems on Davison's continuing grief for Jane and on the joys of his new marriage to Joan Edelman Goody, and in several poems on history and ecology—the last continue and expand directions set out in *A Voice in the Mountain* and *Barn Fever*.

"Equinox 1980" opens the book. It describes the sweet, still, changeless, unruffled, shimmering day when, in the summer before her death, the poet and his first wife took their final kayak trip together into the salt marsh near their farm. Like the equinox, both the occasion and the poem poise trembling at a turning point. They brim with something like perfection; within perfection rises all that entangles and contests it: the poem's past tense resonates with loss; the word "wake-

fall" hints at endings as well as new beginnings; the incoming tide smudged the water's spotless mirror; the marsh grass was ripe but already gone to seed; the couple's elegant craft was slender and light but forebodingly frail. The following poem, "Second Nesting," is a nuptial poem for the poet's new wife. Its tone is both more and less fresh and more and less grave than that of "Equinox." It might be called mature, celebrating each partner's second marriage as a surplus to what went before, or as a repetition with a difference, not, in any case, as a matter of substitution or replacement (see "The Face in the Field" for confirmation). This occasion also has entangling complications: the season is late summer although the couple call it spring; they will need all they have learned before of joy and comfort to fend off future dangers; it will take significant effort to mold each room to the shape of shelter (a handsome sidelong tribute to Joan Goody's architectural skill). If there is something in all of this of late-life love as a matter of deliberate decision more than of being swept away by first fine careless rapture, the couple's conscientious choosing also has about it some of the certainty of instinct, as the homely and erotic metaphor of nesting nicely implies. Together the two poems gracefully navigate a delicate transition.

Other poems in *The Great Ledge*, especially the title poem and "Keeping Accounts," continue the treatment of material and cultural history begun in earlier books. The latter follows "Bicentennial" in showing how failures of settlement unsettle national narratives and their excessive confidence. "The Great Ledge," like "Barn Fever," uses Davison's West Gloucester farm (here, its imposing landmark granite cliff) to tell an expansive tale of cultural, national, and natural change. It reaches back through colonial and later U.S. history to the Native American past and still deeper geological and glacial strata, while also reaching forward to a post-human future when events will submerge, erode, or otherwise erase even the ledge's seemingly immutable permanence. One of Davison's finest poems in this vein, "The Great Ledge" imitates Frost's "Directive" (each has an enormous timescale, tells tales of cultural design, construction, and

ruin, and features children's toys as fragile signs of human presence and creation). It also revises "Directive," toning down the literary, religious, and mythic aspects of Frost's great poem to direct us more quietly still to accept the root entanglement of life with loss without either consoling hopes of recovered wholeness or confused despair. Another important theme in *The Great Ledge* is ecological degradation. An excerpt from an 1852 letter from Chief Seattle to the U.S. president provides its epigraph; it reads, in part, "The earth does not belong to man, man belongs to the earth." "The Great Ledge" echoes this conservationist vision: in tune with natural conditions, the farmer who sited Davison's house positioned it so well that breezes cool it in summer and prevailing winds in winter sweep its driveway clear of snow, but now, slaves having been landed and native peoples overwhelmed, the buffalo herds are gone, the nation is paved, and the shining seas are a sump for poisons. A similar angry disgust with environmental rapaciousness fuels "Ye Have Your Closes" and the "Valtellina" section of "Cracks in the Universe."

Dedicated to his father (with filial piety, its title imitates the title of his father's final book), *The Poems of Peter Davison* (1995) collects the earlier poems Davison chose then to preserve; it also includes twenty-two new poems, titled "Harmonics" and dedicated to his mother. Some of those are relatively slight, like five-finger exercises meant to keep the poet's hand in, his talents tuned up and limber, perhaps during illness. One poem wittily records an endoscopy procedure's exposure of inner lights. Another repeats the theme of cultural change in a landscape, comparing Florida oleanders to New England cedars, both harbingers of impending alteration. Several poems make mince of narcissists, philanderers, and other wayward lovers. A few report disturbing dreams. One borrows a phrase applied to Elizabeth Bishop in a Davison book review to describe her with considerable precision as an "unfrocked governess." And one fiddles like Frost's "New Hampshire" with Davison's New York roots and their transplantation to New England. Five of the new poems have more permanent importance. "Under the

Roof of Memory" is a tender and aching, self-questioning sequence for Jane. In alternately rhyming quatrains, the poem "In Quercy, 1993" repays Davison's debt to Thomas Hardy's dry-eyed, wrenching poems of private and historical grieving. "The Black Aspen" honors Robert Penn Warren and stakes Davison's own claim to being struck by poetic lightning. "The Silent Piano" evokes the instrument inherited from his mother and now no longer played; matching memory to harmonics, its held note vibrates with sounds time damps and stills. "Our Eyes" is especially powerful. It uses photographs and other artwork hung in the poet's study to compose a retrospective family gallery and a self-portrait of the artist; Davison depicts himself as a developer in a darkroom mixing the chemicals that only seem to fix unfixable life, a fine summation of his composed and troubled family writing.

Davison concludes his final book, *Breathing Room,* published in 2000, by repeating its opening poem in italics. The effect is a circle-closing refusal of both surrender and escape; it reflects once more the poet's commitment to honor and stand up to life's entanglements. Atmospheres of relaxed and ruminative ease, of summing up, and of approaching death distinguish the book, as does a late last flourish of formal innovation. Although a few poems curtail or expand the predominant pattern or take other shapes, most poems in *Breathing Room* fit neatly on a single page, using a form of Davison's invention: twenty-five lines arranged in seven triplets and a closing quatrain. Symmetrically indented, they sift and dance and tumble down the page as though to match the pace of the poet's introspection, discovery, and compositional effort and achievement as he works. The form recalls a little the so-called triadic foot employed in later work by William Carlos Williams, and has some of Williams' emphasis on process, but it also has the greater regularity and polish and some of the asperity, emotional intellection, speed, and compression associated with Dante's terza rima. Meanwhile, the five sections into which *Breathing Room* is divided are headed by phrases taken from the passage of Shakespeare's *Measure for Measure* that T. S. Eliot used as the epigraph to

"Gerontion." These further emphasize the volume's sense of aging and death as more natural than alarming. A brief introduction relays as intention what the book's best poems and their novel form accomplish: to contain experience but not to constrain it.

Many poems in *Breathing Room* revisit familiar subjects and themes with heightened equanimity. One displays again the competing parties of the poet's fractured self; careless idealist and calculating pragmatist, they contend here less as foes than confederates. Several poems record childhood and later memories: an encounter with the Dust Bowl on a family drive to Colorado in the 1930s; a boy's solitary play as respite from household woes; early sexual fumbling. Others recall once more his father's voice and his mother's life and death. There are also poems on current matters of illness and recovery, as well as reports from the frontiers of aging, where memory persists as a sort of enriching sixth sense but also sometimes falters. Writing and language are the subject of "These Days," "Prayer to the Verb," "Glittering Trout," and "Under the Language Sea." Those confirm and sometimes happily reach the elusive goal of poetry: to grasp the throbbing pulse of life but not so tightly as to crush it. "Getting over Robert Frost" announces Davison's late arrival at a vision of life more comic than melancholy or tragic. There are poems about walking paths and foxes, ruffed grouse and snapping turtles. Matters of altering land use and ecological vision recur in "Farmer & Wife" and "Falling Water"; the latter creates a lovely rhythmic counterpart to the great earth-nurturing water cycle of rain and flow and evaporation. Other public issues arise in "For Lack of a Treaty," where both birds and warplanes fly in the air of the Golan Heights, and in "Villa dei Pini," where even the most peaceful and cultivated landscape is seen to rest on layers of piracy, religious conflict, slavery, and war. At their frequent best, these poems fulfill Davison's late attempt to encounter "possibility just as it / flowers into the actual" and his lifelong effort to attend to all of reality's competing and intertwining strands—to hear, in the terms of "Breathing Room," his last book's title poem, both the clamor of the earth and cosmic silence.

Davison alludes to Homer's *Odyssey* more often than to any other book except the Bible. The mid-career poem "On Ithaka" reminds us that Odysseus remains entangled by tasks and troubles even after his triumphant return to his home island and its attendant restorations, reunions, and ritual purifications. Elsewhere Davison refers in both prose and verse to the moment when King Alkinoös of the Phaiakians, to whom Odysseus has just told his traveler's tale of trials surmounted and survived, praises his guest as a poet, saying he has related both his own and his people's troubles with the art and honesty of a man who knows the world. Troubled and composed, artful, candid, and worldly, Peter Davison merits a similar report.

Selected Bibliography

WORKS OF PETER DAVISON

POETRY

The Breaking of the Day. New Haven, Conn., and London: Yale University Press, 1964.

The City and the Island. New York: Atheneum, 1966.

Pretending to Be Asleep. New York: Atheneum, 1970.

Dark Houses. Cambridge, Mass.: Halty-Ferguson, 1971.

Walking the Boundaries: Poems 1957–1974. New York: Atheneum, 1974.

A Voice in the Mountain. New York: Atheneum, 1977.

Barn Fever and Other Poems. New York: Atheneum, 1981.

Praying Wrong: New and Selected Poems, 1957–1984. New York: Atheneum, 1984.

The Great Ledge. New York: Knopf, 1989.

The Poems of Peter Davison, 1957–1995. New York: 1995.

Breathing Room. New York: Alfred A. Knopf, 2000.

PROSE

Half Remembered: A Personal History. New York: Harper & Row, 1973. Rev. ed., with a new preface, afterword, and photographs, Brownsville, Ore.: Story Line Press, 1991.

One of the Dangerous Trades: Essays on the Work and Workings of Poetry. Ann Arbor: University of Michigan Press, 1991.

The Fading Smile: Poets in Boston, 1955–1960, from Robert Frost to Robert Lowell to Sylvia Plath. New York: Kopf, 1994.

AUDIO RECORDING

New Letters on the Air: Peter Davison. Kansas City: University of Missouri, 1983.

AS EDITOR

Hello Darkness: The Collected Poems of L. E. Sissman. Boston: Little, Brown, 1978.

The World of Farley Mowat. Boston: Little, Brown, 1980.

PAPERS

Peter Davison Papers, circa 1938–2005. Beinecke Rare Book and Manuscript Library, Yale University, New Haven, Connecticut.

CRITICAL AND BIOGRAPHICAL STUDIES

Barber, David. "A Life's Work: Remembering Peter Davison." *Atlantic* 295:11 (April 2005).

Briggs, Edward. "Middle-Point Reflections." *Boston Globe,* August 31, 1973, p. 17.

Cotter, James Finn. Review of *A Voice in the Mountain. Hudson Review* 31:209 (spring 1978).

Fitts, Dudley. Foreword to *The Breaking of the Day.* New Haven, Conn.: Yale University Press, 1964. Pp. vii–x.

Flint, R. W. Review of *Praying Wrong. New York Times Book Review,* January 27, 1985, pp. 18–19.

Galler, David. "Three Recent Volumes." *Poetry* 110:269 (August 1967).

Harlan, Megan. Review of *Breathing Room. New York Times Book Review,* December 24, 2000.

McClatchy, J. D. Review of *Praying Wrong. Hudson Review* 38:157 (spring 1985).

Parini, Jay. "In the Presence of What Is There: Wendell Barry and Peter Davison." *Virginia Quarterly Review* 54:762–768 (autumn 1978).

Pettingill, Phoebe. Review of *A Voice in the Mountain. New Leader* 61:17–18 (January 2, 1978).

Rotella, Guy. *Three Contemporary Poets of New England: William Meredith, Philip Booth, and Peter Davison.* Boston: Twayne, 1983.

Sandy, Stephen. Review of *Barn Fever. Poetry* 140:293 (August 1982).

Stitt, Peter. Review of *A Voice in the Mountain. Georgia Review* 32:474–475 (summer 1978).

Swenson, May. Review of *The Breaking of the Day. Quartet* 3:29–30 (spring 1967).

———. "Cheek by Jowl: Eight Poets." *Southern Review* n.s. 7:958 (1971).

Young, Vernon. "Raptures of Distress." *Parnassus: Poetry in Review* 3:75–89 (spring–summer 1979).

DEGANAWIDA, THE PEACEMAKER

(c. 1150 CE: Native traditional/academic; c. 1450–1550 CE: non-Native academic)

Christopher Buck

DEGANAWIDA, A NAME traditionally considered too sacred to pronounce (yet fine in printed form), is respectfully referred to as "the Peacemaker" by the Iroquois people, who are more properly known as the Haudenosaunee ("People of the Longhouse"). The Iroquois were aboriginal inhabitants of lands bordering Lakes Huron, Erie, and Ontario and the St. Lawrence River, an area comprising nearly all of present-day New York State, part of Pennsylvania, and southern Ontario and Quebec. The Peacemaker is a legendary yet historical figure, memorialized in traditions held to be sacred by indigenous peoples among the Iroquois Nations—and, generally, among Native Americans and Native Canadians today. This article takes a look at the Deganawida epic, a cycle of narratives that exists in some forty versions—composites of Iroquois sophiology, as it were—recorded largely as part of a process of Haudenosaunee survival and revival, culturally, spiritually, and politically.

The version privileged here is titled *Concerning the League*, translated by the linguist Hanni Woodbury in collaboration with two native speakers of Onondaga, the late Reg Henry and the late Harry Webster. This version (hereafter abbreviated *CL* in page references) provides a direct, authentic link to the past. Other major versions will be referred to as well.

WIDENING THE AMERICAN CANON: ORATURE AS LITERATURE

It may surprise readers to characterize Deganawida (a.k.a. Tekanawita? and other variant spellings) as an "American writer." Yes, the Peacemaker was "American" in that he was a Native American—and possibly Native Canadian, that is, a "dual citizen," if his Canadian birth "on the northerly side of the lake, Lake Ontario" (*CL*, p. 2) has any credence—and was certainly a Native North American. (Obviously the United States and Canada, as nations, did not exist during the founding of the Confederacy.) Not being a "writer" in the traditional sense, the Peacemaker was a charismatic figure—orator, author, and author of a living tradition. Thus, Deganawida, the Peacemaker, with the assistance of Hiawatha and Jigonsaseh (the leader of the corn-planting "Cultivators," also called the "Peace Queen"), united five warring Haudenosaunee (Iroquois) nations into a formidable and enduring federation—a consensus-based matrilineally hereditary federal council of fifty chiefs ("sachems," or spokesmen), each appointed by local councils of clan matrons, with protocols rooted in "Condolence" ceremonies that served as a vehicle for political decision-making. Never would Deganawida have been able to accomplish this had he and his illustrious cohorts not met face-to-face with the warlords of belligerent tribes and skillfully persuaded them to become close allies, replacing war with a sophisticated system of peaceful conflict resolution by democratic consultation and collective decision-making. Barbara Mann refers to Deganawida, Hiawatha, and Jigonsaseh as "the peace trio" (*Iroquoian Women*, p. 38). J. N. B. Hewitt, for instance, speaks of the peace trio as "the swart statesmen Dekanawida [*sic*], Hiawatha, and ... the equally astute stateswoman Djigonsasen [*sic*], a chieftainess of the powerful Neutral Tribe" ("Some Esoteric Aspects," p. 322).

DEGANAWIDA, THE PEACEMAKER

Some may disagree with characterizing the Peacemaker as a [Native] "American writer," since the Deganawida epic is *about* him, not *by* him. However, the latter could not have happened without the former. In that sense, the "message" and the "history" contained in the Deganawida epic may be said to have been "authored" by Deganawida. Since the Deganawida epic qualifies as oral literature (and arguably as sacred literature), an analogy may be drawn with the traditional ascription of Moses as the traditional "author" of the Torah (i.e., "The Five Books of Moses"), even though, as one early Jewish Christian document argued, referring to Deuteronomy 34:6, "But how could Moses write that 'Moses died'?" (*Pseudo-Clementine Homilies*, chap. 47). The *Oxford English Dictionary* defines "author," in part, as "A creator, cause, or source." One literary example given is this: "The author of our religion." If the semantic penumbra of "writer" adumbrates this sense of its synonym, "author," then a case can be made. That said, provisions of the Great Law were preserved on wampum belts (freshwater shells strung together), a form of communication which, like writing, used visual symbols to convey information and aid memory. So transmission was not entirely oral. (See Barbara Mann, "The Fire at Onondaga: Wampum as Proto-Writing.")

The Peacemaker's inclusion in the *American Writers* series is justified if "orature" is accepted as "literature." Compositions in languages lacking writing can be designated as "oral literature." Literary productions in most indigenous languages remain predominantly "oral" in character until print technology brings them to the threshold of "writing." "Oral literature" therefore becomes "orature" with the emergence of print technology as a means of literary dissemination, once such languages are committed to print. The *Oxford English Dictionary* defines "orature" as a "body of poetry, tales, etc., preserved through oral transmission as part of a particular culture, esp. a preliterate one." Thus the Deganawida epic, better known as the "Great Law of Peace," is orature here being recognized as part of the American literary canon.

That said, in Hanni Woodbury's translation, *Concerning the League*, a stock introductory formula is used to directly quote the Peacemaker. The recurrent phrase "Thereupon Tekanawita? said," occurs 191 times (present writer's count). This phrase is a literary device used in Iroquoian texts to distinguish temporal sequencing from declarative statements. Non-Native academics generally do not take this formula literally as indicating direct quotations by the Peacemaker. However, many, if not most, Native American and Native Canadian authorities tend to accept the statements attributed to Deganawida as substantially authentic transmissions of his teachings.

The Deganawida epic, moreover, belongs to world literature. Enter the Peacemaker among the men and women of American and world literature, as a man of wisdom. The Deganawida cycle is an originary voice that stories America before America was "America"—originally called "Turtle Island" by the Iroquois themselves. Deganawida may therefore be considered to be a venerable "American writer" (orator/author of oral/written tradition) of history and culture, as a *maker* of history and culture, long before American literati came on the scene.

Some regard the Peacemaker as the founder (along with Hiawatha and Jigonsaseh) of the first New World democracy. In this sense, not only is Deganawida a truly American orator/author in the indigenous sense but is equally "American" given the extraordinary value that America attaches to democracy. That said, the notion of the Peacemaker as an "American writer" (orator/author) fails to do justice to so powerful a personality, who, by his inspired vision, charismatic influence, and skillful diplomacy, "wrote" history and revolutionized a culture, which survives today as a lived legacy. Given these reasons, recognition of Deganawida as an "American writer" is both justified and timely.

Equally at issue, however, is the question of how this canonization of the Peacemaker comports with the views of Native Americans and Native Canadians. What justification for this cultural appropriation, this impingement on all things indigenous, this infringement, as it were,

of sacred indigenous tradition, which is so culturally sensitive? By what right can the non-Native present writer presume to profane (i.e., to publicly render secular) a sacred oral tradition? The Iroquoian ethnologist Michael K. Foster, curator emeritus of the Canadian Museum of Civilization, recounts how Chief Jacob ("Jake") Thomas (d. 1998), a prominent proponent and interpreter of Haudenosaunee culture, justified this profanation/translation to the non-Native world when, in September 1992 on the Six Nations Reserve near Brantford, Ontario, he took the unprecedented step of reciting the Great Law in English (drawing much indigenous indignation thereby), in a nine-day event on the grounds of his home, which attracted national media coverage. Among the some two thousand people present, a large number of these listeners were white, not Iroquois. During the summer of 1994 Chief Thomas repeated the event. Responding to criticism, he offered this justification, according to Foster:

> I think the white man needs to understand. It isn't that he's going to take the law and use it himself.... They already did! The 13 colonies already took the Great Law for their so-called Constitution. So what should we be afraid of? ... If they want to learn it, they have a right to. That should have been done 500 years ago, to study and respect the Confederacy. Maybe we wouldn't have the problems we have today if they would have studied our people, and [would now] understand and honor and respect [us].
>
> (Foster, "Jacob Ezra Thomas," p. 227)

It is in the spirit of this advice that the following epitome of the life and teachings (i.e. oral "writings") of the Peacemaker are here presented. In so doing, this is not intended as exploitation of Native American spiritual traditions. It is not a "theft of spirit." Rather, it is recognition of the universality and contemporary relevance of the Peacemaker's enunciation of "the Good Message, also the Power and the Peace."

The Iroquois were known for their political genius, which impressed Benjamin Franklin and continues to be noted by the U.S. government to this day. In 2010, for instance, the U.S. Mint issued its Native American one-dollar coin, featuring, on the reverse, an image of the "Hiawatha Belt," with five arrows bound together, along with the inscriptions "Haudenosaunee" ("People of the Longhouse") and "Great Law of Peace." The official description reads, in part:

> The Haudenosaunee Confederation, also known as the Iroquois Confederacy of upstate New York, was remarkable for being founded by 2 historic figures, the Peacemaker and his Onondaga spokesman, Hiawatha, who spent years preaching the need for a league. The Peacemaker sealed the treaty by symbolically burying weapons at the foot of a Great White Pine, or Great Tree of Peace, whose 5-needle clusters stood for the original 5 nations: Mohawk, Oneida, Onondaga, Cayuga and Seneca.
>
> (U.S. Mint, "2010 Native American $1 Coin")

The mastermind behind Iroquoian political genius was Deganawida, assisted by Hiawatha (no resemblance to Henry Wadsworth Longfellow's poetic fiction) and Jigonsaseh (whose presence assured a male-female equilibrium in the League's governance system). According to Chief John Arthur Gibson's 1899 version (pp. 34–60), Hiawatha was a former cannibal whom Deganawida won over and who then became the latter's spokesman. (In Gibson's 1912 version, the cannibal is not named.) Together, Deganawida, Hiawatha, and Jigonsaseh established the Iroquois League, uniting the "Five Nations" (Mohawk, Oneida, Onondaga, Cayuga, and Seneca) into a powerful confederacy, into which the Tuscaroras, after a gradual migration that began in 1714, were adopted in 1722 (now the "Six Nations"), with the Tuteloes and Nanticokes added to the "Longhouse" (the grand metaphor for the League) in 1753, and protection extended to the Delawares and others. The territory under the sway of the Iroquois League was vast, as James A. Tuck notes in *Scientific American*:

> Five tribes of the Iroquois confederacy were, from west to east, the Senecas, the Cayugas, the Onondagas, the Oneidas and the Mohawks. At the beginning of the 18th century their power extended from Maine to Illinois and from southern Ontario to Tennessee. The Tuscaroras became the sixth after being ousted by white settlers in the Carolinas.
>
> ("The Iroquois Confederacy," p. 36)

Arthur Gajarsa, circuit judge on the U.S. Court of Appeals for the Federal Circuit (1997–2012), in *Banner v. United States* (2001), noted:

DEGANAWIDA, THE PEACEMAKER

The Iroquois Confederacy, or Haudenosaunee, is believed to have been formed in the fifteenth century when the legendary Hiawatha and the Great Peacemaker united the warring eastern Native American tribes. Prior to European colonization, the Iroquois Confederacy exercised active dominion over nearly thirty-five million acres, most of what is now the states of New York and Pennsylvania, and was considered the most powerful peacekeeping force of Native Americans east of the Mississippi River.

(Banner v. United States, 238 F.3d at p. 1350)

In New York, Archibald Kennedy and James Parker (Benjamin Franklin's printing partner) published a pamphlet, *The Importance of Gaining and Preserving the Friendship of the Indians to the British Interest Considered* (1751), calling for the Iroquois Six Nations to be federated with the colonies. In his letter, dated March 20, 1751, to James Parker, Benjamin Franklin held up the Iroquois confederacy as a model of good governance:

> It would be a very strange Thing, if six Nations of ignorant Savages should be capable of forming a Scheme for such an Union, and be able to execute it in such a Manner, as that it has subsisted Ages, and appears indissoluble; and yet that a like Union should be impracticable for ten or a Dozen English Colonies, to whom it is more necessary, and must be more advantageous; and who cannot be supposed to want an equal Understanding of their Interests.

(Papers of Benjamin Franklin, vol. 4, pp. 118–119)

Having justified the significance and importance of Deganawida as an "American writer" (orator/author of oral/written tradition) in the grand sense of the word, a word regarding methodology: The present author has adopted and adapted a new methodology called "tribalography," which is still under development, and so may mean slightly different approaches depending on the scholar. In her highly influential article "The Story of America: A Tribalography," LeAnne Howe explains:

> Native stories are power. They create people. They author tribes. America is a tribal creation story, a tribalography.... I am suggesting that when the European Founding Fathers heard the stories of how the Haudenosaunee unified six individual tribes into an Indian confederacy, they created a docu-

ment, the U.S. Constitution, that united immigrant Europeans into a symbiotic union called America.

(pp. 29, 37)

Tribalography, as understood by the present writer, recognizes that traditional narratives are formative (culturally foundational), performative (ceremonially recited), and transformative (spiritually and socially revitalizing). They represent the past in the present. Fact and fiction synthesize into the grand, collective tradition, admixed with legendary and mythic elements (not unlike the "magical realism" of Gabriel García Márquez), integrating symbolically mnemonic accounts, where cosmogony (origin of universe) functions as sociogony (origin of society), in a sacred embrace of physical and metaphysical epistemology that characterizes Native American perspectives. In other words, while there is no way to definitively recapture "pre-contact" history by way of "post-contact" sources, a consensus, for the most part, has emerged that the Peacemaker was a historical figure.

HISTORICITY OF THE PEACEMAKER

Without considering Native Americans, one cannot understand the early development of North America. Enter the Peacemaker. Legends are historically rooted and culturally bound. As such, Deganawida is not an ethnographic curiosity but a living cultural presence. The overmastering fact in the history of the Iroquois is the dominance and centrality of the "Longhouse" tradition based upon the Peacemaker cycle. Phenomenologically, the Deganawida epic—most notably *Concerning the League*, dictated by Chief John Arthur Gibson in 1912—compares favorably with the sacred scripture in the world's great religions and, as such, belongs to world literature.

Most ethnologists and linguists have assumed that Deganawida was a historical figure and use the term "tradition" for that reason. A solid intellectual approach is that the Peacemaker ought to be treated as phenomenologically parallel to the founders of world religions—such as Buddha, Moses, Christ, Muhammad, or Bahá'u'lláh. By adopting this approach, the Deganawida epic, in

its several versions, is understood as a sacred or "enlightened" tradition within the Haudenosaunee worldview, with an appreciation of the irreducible historical dimension of the Peacemaker as founder (variants and possible embellishments within the collective tradition notwithstanding). For the Peacemaker gave supernatural sanction to the League that he and Hiawatha founded, "because the Great Spirit never planned for humans to hurt one another nor to slaughter one another" (*CL*, p. 106). While the historicity of the Peacemaker is widely accepted by scholars, dating varies. By analogy, such dating presents problems akin to the so-called "quest for the historical Jesus."

All religions are influenced by subsequent events. As such, there is no single pristine account of the Peacemaker, uninflected by various outside influences, be they Christian or otherwise. Traditionally, however, a plurality of Deganawida traditions are considered to be simultaneously true. That said, the Gibson-Goldenweiser version (see below) has been widely acknowledged as the best version extant, in that it is structured faithfully to how it was ceremonially recited and ritually performed in the present.

So what is the most tenable date of Deganawida? Arguably the most widely accepted date among academics is c. 1450 CE. In "The Long Peace Among Iroquois Nations," Neta C. Crawford, after reviewing traditional sources and scholarly literature, concludes that

> it seems likely that the League of the Iroquois was formed well before the five original nations came into contact with European explorers and settlers.... The negotiations for the formation of the League were probably concluded around 1450, about 85 years before the Mohawks, in the League members' first direct contact with Europeans, met Cartier on the Saint Lawrence.
>
> (p. 351)

Similarly, Jon Parmenter, in his *The Edge of the Woods: Iroquoia, 1534–1701*, holds that plausible dates for the historical Peacemaker, where the date of "founding" can be interpreted as the initiation of diplomacy by the Peacemaker and Hiawatha, could be anywhere circa 1400–1550, while the League formation itself was a lengthy

process that took place over generations. Taking Crawford's and Parmenter's best estimates together, the date range for the historical Peacemaker becomes c. 1450–1550.

That date range is not the final word on the subject, however, for what about "ethnohistory"? What does Haudenosaunee tradition have to say about the question of when the Great League was founded, and why is that tradition important? The answer is as political as it is academic: indigenous scholars and activists are reclaiming the right to their own history. So the date range that extends to the mid-1500s may soon be regarded, by the Iroquois at least, as racist history. The Haudenosaunee see insisting on the post-contact date (after Columbus) as colonializing their history.

In principle (legally, at least), oral tradition should be taken far more seriously. As of March 21, 2014, U.S. federal law, as put forth in the Native American Graves Protection and Repatriation Act (NAGPRA), now recognizes that oral tradition is accepted as admissible on a par with expert opinion:

> Where cultural affiliation of Native American human remains and funerary objects has not been established in an inventory prepared pursuant to section 5 [25 USCS § 3003], or the summary pursuant to section 6 [25 USCS § 3004], ... such Native American human remains and funerary objects shall be expeditiously returned where the requesting Indian tribe or Native Hawaiian organization can show cultural affiliation by a preponderance of the evidence based upon geographical, kinship, biological, archaeological, anthropological, linguistic, folkloric, oral traditional, historical, or other relevant information or expert opinion.
>
> (25 USCS § 3005(a)(4))

One Haudenosaunee (Iroquois) voice is that of Barbara Alice Mann, associate professor in the Honors Department of the University of Toledo and also an Ohio Bear Clan Seneca, who would therefore be considered an expert in more than one sense as defined by NAGPRA, given her command of the oral tradition, documentary evidence, and the scholarly literature. At the polar opposite are the reductionist views of the anthropologist William A. Starna, professor emeritus at the State University of New York College at

Oneonta. This intellectual landscape—a hyper-critical minefield—is difficult to map, because the claims are so territorial, with so much heritage and history at stake.

At issue is a central question: was the League "pre-contact" (before Europeans arrived on the American scene), or was it "post-contact"? The earliest date posited for the formation of the Iroquois Confederacy is August 31, 1142, during which a "Black Sun" (total eclipse) occurred right before the League was finally and fully established. This date has been proposed by Barbara Mann and Jerry Fields, an astronomer, in "A Sign in the Sky: Dating the League of the Haudenosaunee." According to Mann and Fields, the Peacemaker, along with Hiawatha and Jigonsaseh, flourished in the twelfth century. This is squarely based on a Seneca legend which holds that, during a ratification council held at Ganondagan (near modern-day Victor, New York), a solar eclipse coincided with the Senecas' decision to join the League. In William W. Canfield's comment on a parallel traditional account, as told to him by "the Cornplanter" (a warrior, Seneca chief, and major Iroquois leader of the late eighteenth century), he cites both the Cornplanter and Chief Governor Blacksnake as authorities for the Seneca eclipse tradition:

> The legend of its formation here published is not only based upon what was considered reliable authority by Cornplanter, but has also the sanction of that other noted Seneca chief, Governor Blacksnake (the Nephew), who was contemporaneous with Cornplanter.... These chiefs both claimed to have seen a string of wampum in their early years that placed the formation of the confederacy at a time when there occurred a total eclipse of the sun—"a darkening of the Great Spirit's smiling face"—that took place when the corn was receiving its last tillage, long before events that could be reliably ascribed to the year 1540.
>
> (Canfield, "Notes to the Legends,"
> *The Legends of the Iroquois*, pp. 205–206)

The same traditional/astrophysical approach was used by Dean Snow to arrive at the Julian calendar date of June 28, 1451, by adopting the date of a later solar eclipse. (See "Dating the Emergence of the League of the Iroquois: A Reconsideration of the Documentary Evidence.") Such an eclipse could easily be interpreted as a divine portent of cosmic and therefore historical significance.

The latest date for the formation of the Iroquois Confederacy has been put forward by Starna, who postulates that "the genesis of the League is tied directly to the arrival of the Dutch [in 1609] and the trade at Fort Nassau [1613–14]" (p. 321). Henry Hudson, an English navigator in the service of the Dutch East India Company aboard the ship *Half Moon*, discovered the Delaware Bay and River, according to the journal kept by his first officer, on August 28, 1609. According to Starna (pp. 285–286), the earliest documentary mention of a version of the name "Deganawida" is found in *A Dictionary of the Mohawk Language* produced sometime in the period 1743–1748 by Johann Christopher Pyrlaeus, a German-born Moravian missionary. Pyrlaeus' informant was an elderly Mohawk man, Sganarády. While Starna recognizes the Deganawida epic's "status as a sacred text" (p. 320), he does not accord it much historical value. Starna, moreover, holds that, once the Deganawida epic is set aside, nothing in the historical or archaeological record confirms the existence of the League before contact; in other words, that "the impetus for and timing of the formation of the League ... cannot be satisfactorily answered solely on the basis of the Deganawidah epic" (p. 315), and that it is too much to expect historians to accept a sacred narrative of events so deep in the past without independent evidence.

Even if one does not accept the date of August 31, 1142, proposed by Mann and Fields, they make a powerful and compelling argument against dating the formation of the League as a response to Europeans in the mid-sixteenth century and beyond:

> We know who "the enemy" was during the mid-sixteenth century: the Europeans. We also know who "the enemy" was in League tradition: the cannibal cult. At no point does League tradition state that the cannibals were Europeans; quite the opposite, the cannibals were an absolutely Native group. If the mid-sixteenth century claim is to stand, its advocates must demonstrate that the cannibals and the Europeans are one and the same. They must

also explain why the Keepers seem unaware of this extraordinary fact.

(p. 110)

DEGANAWIDA EPIC: VERSIONS BY LANGUAGE

Although the chronological focus of the sundry Peacemaker traditions (collectively referred to as the Deganawida epic) is essentially "pre-contact," the primary sources are "post-contact."

Native-Authored English Versions: As previously stated, more than forty versions (oral and written) of the Deganawida epic exist (Kimura, p. 49). All are honored as "authoritative" among Iroquois communities and speakers. Perhaps the most truly representative tradition is the Chiefs' version (English-only), "written from dictation by the ceremonial Chiefs" from each of the Six Nations. These chiefs were Peter Powless (Mohawk), Nicodemus Porter (Oneida), William Wage and Abram Charles (Cayuga), John Arthur Gibson (Seneca), Thomas William Echo (Onondaga), and Josiah Hill (Tuscarora), with J. W. M. Elliott serving as secretary, along with Chief Hill. The chiefs' version was promulgated on August 17, 1900, at the Six Nations Reserve in Ontario, Canada, where, in 1874, Loyalist Mohawks and their confederated allies followed Joseph Brant to the banks of the Grand River near Brantford, Ontario. There, the Six Nations reconstituted the old League.

This endorsed version, promulgated "by the authority of the Six Nations Council," represents a synthesis of parallel traditions. Of these eight leaders, Gibson (1850–1912) was arguably the most influential. In 1872, at age twenty-three, Gibson was appointed a Seneca chief, having inherited his title, Kanyataiyo ("Beautiful Lake"), from his mother's side. At thirty-one, Gibson suddenly became blind due to an injury suffered during a lacrosse match, a sport invented by the Iroquois. From then on, Gibson's nephew would typically escort and assist him. As one of the approximately 20 percent of the Grand River Iroquois who followed the Longhouse religion, Seneca was Gibson's mother tongue. Although his English was excellent, he spoke mostly in Onondaga. (While his wife would address him in

Cayuga, he would reply in Onondaga.) Gibson could, at will, converse with visiting Oneida chiefs. Occasionally Chief Gibson performed rituals in Mohawk. He knew some Tuscarora as well. Chief Gibson was trained as a ceremonialist under the oldest living Onondaga fire-keeper at that time (Fenton, 1962, p. 286.) Besides the Chiefs' version, there is the 1899 Gibson-Hewitt version and the 1912 Gibson-Goldenweiser version. (See below.)

The Chiefs' version was compiled in English in 1900 ("or composed in one of the Iroquois languages and then translated by them into English—the exact method used is not known," according to Hanni Woodbury in her introduction to *Concerning the League* [p. xvi, n. 12]). It was published as *Traditional History of the Confederacy of the Six Nations* in 1912 by Duncan C. Scott, superintendent of Indian Affairs in Canada. Arthur C. Parker (Seneca, but who did not speak any Iroquoian languages) published *The Constitution of the Five Nations* (1916), in which he combined the Chiefs' version—reviewed, corrected, and revised by Albert Cusick (Onondaga-Tuscarora)—with the Iroquois code of laws set down by Seth Newhouse ("Da-yo-de-ka-ne," Mohawk-Onondaga) in "Indian English," corrected by Cusick. Parker edited Newhouse's code of laws by reorganizing the sections to more closely resemble the U.S. Constitution. Oddly, Parker does not cite Scott's prior publication of the Chiefs' version.

Twice previously, the chiefs had rejected Seth Newhouse's 1885 Native-English version of the Peacemaker narrative, *Cosmogony of the Iroquois Confederacy*, for which he wanted to be paid and which called into question certain titles of chieftainship and some of the Council's procedures as well. A true Mohawk patriot, Newhouse translated his *Cosmogony* into Mohawk, possibly with Hewitt's assistance. It languishes as an unpublished manuscript.

The Chiefs' version was promulgated ostensibly for the purpose of preserving the Peacemaker tradition for posterity. Why English? Theoretically, while the Chiefs' version could have been set forth in an Iroquoian language, as a practical matter, English was preferred since "birth speak-

ers" of indigenous languages were fast disappearing. Moreover, this project was also concerned with legitimacy. This is indicated by the text's noting that "the installation of the Lords or Chiefs as rulers of the people, laid down in these unwritten rules hundreds of years ago, is still strictly observed and adhered to by the Chiefs of the Six Nations and people" (p. 196). Not only was the Chiefs' version an anticolonial project, it was one of self-empowerment as well, particularly as a bulwark against Canadian colonial and assimilation policy. According to Takeshi Kimura (p. 62), the Chiefs' version is best understood as a response to a self-sovereignty dispute between the Canadian Department of Indian Affairs and the matrilineally hereditary Six Nations Council "in order to justify the political authenticity of the chiefs' council." That there was a clear need to establish and maintain such legitimacy is illustrated by the fact that, in 1924, the Canadian government abrogated the authority of the Six Nations Council. Establishing the League tradition in an authoritative, written version was an act of covert resistance against overt coercion into U.S.- and Canadian-friendly tribal councils—in other words, a "settler" oppression tactic.

This is not to say that the Chiefs manipulated and recast tradition beyond recognition in light of these exigent historical circumstances, especially since such updating is itself traditional. As social agents, anchored in time and place, the Chiefs obviously had reasons—a complex of motives—for producing an endorsed version of the Peacemaker epic in English, since doing so was far from customary and traditionally would have been frowned upon. Thus the Chiefs' version was not only culturally and religiously significant but had political, economic, and juridical dimensions as well. By providing an authoritative narrative of the Longhouse tradition to the Department of the Indian Affairs and to outsiders generally, the Chiefs' version was intended for the public. This rendition was not an "invention," since the Peacemaker tradition was a long-standing and venerable one. That said, Parker's version crucially included women's sections, which are missing from other traditions, because men spoke of men's tradition and women spoke of women's tradition. Scholars have not quite grasped that fact, although Barbara Mann's work has drawn attention to this problem and to the need to hear *both* traditions to regain a full perspective.

According to Kimura (pp. 181–182), the Chiefs' version was promulgated "for the purpose of authorizing and legitimating a political structure." Specifically, "the matrilineally hereditary council's primary intention was to persuade the Department of Indian Affairs to accept the legitimacy of their special status." To achieve that objective, a process of "reconstructing tradition" was involved. This reconstruction was essentially an act of reconstituting and codifying a somewhat fluid tradition into a solid framework, vested with the stamp of authority by representatives of the Six Nations.

In their "introductory remarks" of August 17, 1900, Chiefs Josiah Hill (Six Nations Council) and J. W. M. Elliott (secretary of the Ceremonial Committee on Indian Rites and Customs) acknowledge that some of the miraculous feats ascribed to the Peacemaker may betray some Jesuit influence (p. 197). According to Darren Bonaparte, however, the birth of the Peacemaker has precedents not only in Christianity, but also in the Iroquois creation story, where Sky Woman and her virgin daughter may have been recast as Deganawida's grandmother and mother. In either case, Kimura (p. 63) states that this foreword was probably prepared by the *Christian* chiefs (not individually identified), since certain characterizations in the Chiefs' prefatory remarks—such as "much modified" (p. 196), "past mythological legends," "crude (religious) belief," and "transition from a state of paganism to that of civilization and christianity" (p. 197)—could *not* have been made by the traditional Longhouse chiefs. Some of the Christian chiefs strongly advocated an elective rather than matrilineally hereditary tribal council, for instance. Although united for the purpose of producing the Chiefs' version, the preface raises some questions that must remain unanswered until the perspective of each of the eight ceremonial Chiefs is analyzed. That said, the preface may well be an instance of "double-voicing" (what W. E. B. Du Bois called

DEGANAWIDA, THE PEACEMAKER

"double-conscientiousness"), in which an oppressed group speaks in language that the oppressive power would respond to.

Other Native-English versions—beginning with the 1885 version by Seth Newhouse—are cited in the selected bibliography below. Native-language versions are listed, by language, at the end of this article as well. A brief overview of these versions in indigenous languages is provided as follows:

Onondaga Versions: In 1888, Chief John Buck, Sr. (a fourth-generation Onondaga chief, fire-keeper, and wampum-keeper), dictated in Onondaga, a critically endangered language, his version of the League tradition to the ethnographer J. N. B. Hewitt at the Six Nations Reserve, Ontario, Canada. Hewitt was part Tuscarora and had a good command of the Onondaga and Mohawk languages. (It was Hewitt, a founder of the American Anthropological Association, who in 1887 definitively established the connection of Cherokee with the Iroquoian family of languages.) The original is preserved as MS 3130, National Anthropological Archives, Smithsonian Institution. A translation of Chief Buck's was published by Hewitt in 1892. This version, albeit anomalously, ascribes certain events to Hiawatha instead of Deganawida. Oddly, this version refers to the "Seven Nations."

Now we come to the preeminent—and perhaps definitive—version of the peacemaker epic. A renowned speaker in the Longhouse, the Seneca chief John Arthur Gibson has already been introduced above. Chief Gibson assiduously followed the time-honored method of committing oral traditions to memory. From youth, Gibson took every possible opportunity to hear recitals from his elders, which, over time, he learned by heart, bit by bit. Stock phrases and word-for-word repetitions, as obvious memory aids, are very typical of oral literature. (Improvisation is not acceptable in the strict *performance* of a sacred narrative. Although the main *action* can never be changed, certain details in the *narrative* can fluctuate, depending on the era and the telling.

And so, in 1899, at the Six Nations Reserve, Chief Gibson dictated, in Onondaga, a version of the League tradition to J. N. B. Hewitt. Known as the Gibson-Hewitt version, this manuscript is preserved as MS 2316, National Anthropological Archives, Smithsonian Institution (189 typescript pages). The 1899 recitation is a shortened version in that it does not relate the great ceremony for condoling deceased chiefs and raising their successors in their stead. This version, it should be noted, is distinct from the Chiefs' version (1900), which was dictated in English, not Onondaga.

In 1912 Chief Gibson dictated his fuller version of the League tradition to the anthropologist Alexander Aleksandrovich Goldenweiser (born in Kiev) at the Six Nations Reserve. This "Gibson-Goldenweiser" version was transcribed in the first part of the twentieth century, when recording technology was unavailable. This undertaking was completed just four months before Chief Gibson suddenly died of a stroke on November 1, 1912. The original manuscript (529 pages on lined legal pads) is archived as III-I-116M in the Canadian Ethnology Services Archives, Canadian Museum of Civilization, Hull, Québec. Taken together, the Gibson-Hewitt (1899) and the Gibson-Goldenweiser (1912) versions represent "the most satisfactory single native account of the League" (Fenton, p. 158).

Oneida Versions: On June 22, 1971, Damas Elm (ninety-three-year-old Oneida elder of Southwold, Ontario) recited "The Story of Deganawida" in the Oneida language. This version was recorded on magnetic tape. The text was transcribed by the linguist Floyd G. Lounsbury with the assistance of Damas Elm on June 23–28, 1971. It remains unpublished. The archival files are difficult to access since they are deemed "culturally sensitive."

Another Oneida version is that recited by Chief Robert Brown (a.k.a. Anahalihs ["Great Vines"]), Bear Clan chief of the Oneida tribe, translated by Brown and Clifford F. Abbott of the University of Wisconsin–Green Bay and edited by Randy Cornelius (Tehahuko'tha), also of the Sovereign Oneida Nation of Wisconsin. It appears that Brown's recitation closely parallels, if not depends heavily upon, Gibson's 1912 Onondaga version, such that it may be fair to say that Brown was recasting Gibson's work into Oneida.

But there are significant differences as well. Although not formally published, this version is currently available on the Internet.

Mohawk Versions: Chief Seth Newhouse produced a typescript translation of the Mohawk version of the "The Great Law of Peace," as the Peacemaker cycle is also known. This Newhouse document is archived as MS 3490, National Anthropological Archives, Smithsonian Institution. The translation is titled *Constitution of the Confederacy by Dekanawidah: Collected and Translated from* [the] *Mohawk Text by Chief Seth Newhouse.* Digital scans of all forty-three pages of the translation are available online. A bilingual Mohawk-English version was published in 1993 by Ohontsa Films.

Cayuga Version: The ethnographer J. N. B. Hewitt committed to writing the "Cayuga version of the Deganawida legend 1890," cataloged as MS 1582, National Anthropological Archives, Smithsonian Institution. Digital scans of all seventeen pages are available online. (See bibliography.)

Non-Native English Version: In January 1946 the University of Pennsylvania Press published Paul Wallace's *White Roots of Peace.* See discussion of this book below.

DEGANAWIDA EPIC: STRUCTURAL ANALYSIS

Comparing the major versions, Christopher Vecsey identifies twenty-two key structural elements common to the majority of extant versions of the Deganawida epic. To give the reader a fair impression, Christopher Vecsey's twenty-two elements may be cited as a structural framework of analysis. As Vecsey observes: "No one version contains every episode, although Gibson's 1899 manuscript comes the closest to completeness" (p. 82). From a traditional (plurality) perspective, these episodes enjoyed reciprocity as simultaneously true. Gibson simply put together all the versions he had heard, which is allowed in indigenous tradition. Vecsey wrote this in 1986, before Hanni Woodbury published her translation of *Concerning the League* in 1992. The Gibson-Goldenweiser version (*Concerning the League* [CL], translated by Hanni Woodbury et al.) has most of these core elements (as summarized by the present writer), with headings by Vecsey, as noted:

(1) "The Migration and Separation of the People" (Vecsey, pp. 82–83): This element is absent in the Gibson-Goldenweiser version.

(2) "The Birth and Growth of Deganawida" (Vecsey, p. 83): In the distant past, war and blood revenge plagued the Mohawk homeland on the northern shore of Lake Ontario (in what is now Canada), where warriors, ruthlessly and relentlessly, killed and scalped inhabitants of settlements across forest and countryside. (This may be a Western interpolation. According to Mann, the war was the overthrow of the Mound Builder priesthood.) To escape the dangers of this ongoing onslaught, a mother ("End of the Field") takes her daughter ("She Walks Ahead") away from her people and migrates to a remote area of the bush, where the two do not see another human being for a long time.

Later on, the mother discovers that her daughter is pregnant and demands to know who the father is. The daughter has no idea. The old woman, sure that her daughter is lying, grows angry, and the two are estranged until a messenger from the Great Spirit appears and tells the mother that her daughter is about to have a divine birth. (This is patent Christianization, since the Haudenosaunee traditionally do not value "virgins" and "virgin birth" stories.) They should call the boy Tekánawí·ta'; [Deganawida], whose mission will be to bring about peace. The boy grows rapidly, a sign of supernatural origin or powers (*CL*, pp. 1–14).

(3) "The Journey to the Mohawks, the Situation, and the Mission Explained" (Vecsey, p. 84): When the boy becomes a young man, his mother and grandmother return home, where he announces to their people the Good Message, the Power, and the Peace. After the Peacemaker tells the village's children of his mission, the older women spread the news, and a day is appointed for the Peacemaker to speak to the elders (*CL*, pp. 15–36). This is his message, which the chief and elders accept:

> Thereupon Tekanawita? [Deganawida] stood up in the center of the gathering place, and then he said,

"First I will answer what it means to say, 'now it is arriving, the Good Message.' This indeed, is what it means: When it stops, the slaughter of your own people who live here on earth, then everywhere peace will come about, by day and also by night, and it will come about that as one travels around, everyone will be related. Then, indeed, [?]in future days to come.

Now again [?], secondly, I say, 'now it is arriving, the power,' and this means that the different nations, all the nations, will become just a single one, and the Great Law will come into being, so that now all will be related to each other, and there will come to be just a single family, and in the future, in days to come, this family will continue on.

Now in turn, the other, my third saying, 'Now it is arriving, the Peace,' this means that everyone will become related, men and also women, and also the young people and the children, and when all are relatives, every nation, then there will be peace as they roam about by day and also by night. Now, also, it will become possible for them to assemble in meetings. Then there will be truthfulness, and they will uphold hope and charity, so that it is peace that will unite all the people, indeed, it will be as though they have but one mind, and they are a single person with only one body and one head and one life, which means that there will be unity. Moreover, and most importantly, one is going to assembly in meetings where it will be announced that all of mankind will repent of their sins, even evil people, and in the future, they will be kind to one another, one and all. When they are functioning, the Good Message and also the Power and the Peace, moreover, these will be the principal things everybody will live by; these will be the great values among the people."

(CL, pp. 36–41)

This episode is omitted in the Chiefs' version and in the Gibson-Hewitt version.

(4) "The Cannibal Converts" (Vecsey, p. 84): After returning to their camp in the bush, the Peacemaker carves a canoe of white stone. He sets out on his mission. He first encounters a Mohawk who had fled for safety from the bloodshed, and the Peacemaker tells the Mohawk to announce his forthcoming arrival and mission to the chief. Peacemaker then encounters a cannibal, the story of which is one of the most famous episodes (*CL*, pp. 78–90) of the Peacemaker epic:

After Tekanawita? had departed in that direction he came to a house belonging to a cannibal who had his house there. Then Tekanawita? went close to the house. Then, when he saw the man coming out, departing, sliding down the hill to the river, and dipping water, thereupon Tekanawita? hurriedly climbed onto the house to the place where there was a chimney for the smoke to escape; he lay down on his stomach and looking into the house he saw that the task of breaking up meat and piling it up had been completed.

Then the man returned, and he was carrying a drum of water in it. Thereupon he poured it into a vessel, put meat into the liquid, and hung the vessel up over the fire until it boiled. Moreover, the man watched it, and when it was done, he took down the vessel placing it near the embers. Thereupon he said, "Now indeed it is done. Moreover, now I will eat." There upon he set up a seat, a bench, thinking that he will put it on there when he eats. Thereupon he went to where the vessel sat, intending to take the meat out of the liquid, when he saw, from inside the vessel, a man looking out.

Thereupon he moved away without removing the meat, and sat down again on the long bench, for it was a surprise to him, seeing the man in the vessel. Thereupon he thought, "Let me look again." Thereupon he, Tekanawita?, looked again from above where the smoke hole was, again causing a reflection in the vessel, and then the man, standing up again, went to where the vessel sat, looked into the vessel again, saw the man looking out, and he was handsome, he having a nice face. Thereupon the man moved away again and he sat down again on the long bench, and then he bowed his head, pondering and thinking, "I am exceedingly handsome and I have a nice face; it is probably not right, my habit of eating humans. So I will now stop, from now on I ought not kill humans anymore."

(CL, pp. 78–83)

Hiawatha mistakes the Peacemaker's face, which is reflected in the pot, for his own. In the Gibson-Hewitt version, the Peacemaker gives the former cannibal the name Hiawatha, who is then sent to a settlement to announce the coming of "the Good Message, and the Power, and the Peace." However, in the Gibson-Goldenweiser version (Vecsey, p. 84, citing the Gibson-Hewitt version, pp. 34–60), the cannibal remains unnamed, and the Peacemaker confers the name "Hiawatha" on the great warrior and chief of the next Mohawk settlement. (See also *White Roots of Peace*, pp. 42–45.) If analyzed sociologically, this episode

may indicate a transition from cannibalism (especially by Mound Builder priests among the Ohio Iroquois) to crop farming and deer hunting.

(5) The "Mother of Nations Accepts Deganawida's Message" (Vecsey, p. 84): Arriving at the waterfalls on the eastern side of the river, the Peacemaker encounters "Fat Face" (the traditional name is most commonly spelled "Jigonsaseh"), the head mother of the Senecas, who became the Head Mother of the League. The Peacemaker chides her for feeding the warriors, thereby aiding and abetting warfare. After converting her to his message, he sends Fat Face to travel east, to announce his arrival in three days (which is really three years) (*CL*, pp. 90–94). On the role of women who carry the traditional title of "Jigonsaseh," Barbara Mann notes that the Head Clan Mothers of the League were the title-keepers (and also lineage-keepers):

> The Jigonsaseh ... allowed or disallowed passage of war parties, thus giving them tacit veto power over warfare. Because federal officials could be put forward only by their respective Clan Mothers, and could be impeached by them, Clan Mothers effectively controlled the national agenda: Federal officials of the two Brotherhoods (Congress) and the Firekeepers (the Executive Branch) considered matters at a national level only after they had already been discussed, approved, and forwarded by the "women's councils," i.e., the Clan Mothers in their own councils.
>
> ("The Lynx in Time," p. 440; see also Mann, *Iroquoian Women*, chap. 3)

Seneca Chief Cornplanter refers to the office of those who succeeded Jigonsaseh (who, according to parallel traditional accounts, would, and did, carry the title of "the Jigonsaseh") as the "Peacemaker Queen," among the Seneca. (Cornplanter, qtd. in Canfield, "The Peacemaker," *The Legends of the Iroquois*, pp. 149–154.) Barbara Mann stresses the traditional importance of this office. She also laments the fact that it was largely forgotten, due to American and Canadian policies of forced assimilation, and further obscured by Western scholarship, which has simply failed to appreciate the importance of the "Peace Queen" and those who held her office, in succeeding generations, among the Iroquois nations. Speaking of the original Jigonsaseh, Mann notes: "Her

negotiations with the Peacemaker and her personal centrality and ending the Second Epochal war resulted in the women's sections of the Iroquois Constitution, twenty-three of the one hundred seventeen clauses, according to Renée Jacobs' count" (*Iroquoian Women*, p. 155).

(6) "The Prophets Prove Their Power" (Vecsey, p. 84): The Peacemaker proceeds to a Mohawk settlement. He camps on the outskirts overnight, and awaits invitation. The next day, the chief sends scouts, calls a meeting, and invites the Peacemaker to deliver his message. The chief accepts, yet "the Great Warrior and his deputy" express hesitation, challenging Deganawida to a test to see if he is endowed with supernatural power. The Peacemaker climbs a great tree, perched precipitously over a deep gorge. The Great Warrior's men then cut down the tree. Deganawida plunges into the river's turbulent waters below and disappears. The next morning, a young man sees smoke rising from the edge of the cornfield, which turns out to be where the Peacemaker is encamped, and the chief, Great Warrior, and deputy are now convinced of the Peacemaker's power to accomplish his mission (*CL*, pp. 95–130).

(7) "Tadadaho the Wizard Prevents Peace" (Vecsey, p. 85): The Peacemaker proceeds eastward. "First I will go to the dangerous place, where we two will converse, the Great Witch [or 'Sorcerer'] and I." If the Wizard accepts, they will hear a great voice announcing this, at which time the meeting should be convened at "Standing Stone" [the Oneida nation] (*CL*, pp. 130–132).

(8) "Hiawatha's Relatives Are Killed" (Vecsey, p. 85): Meanwhile, Hiawatha's eldest daughter has taken ill and died. Then the next daughter succumbs. To console him, the young warriors divert Hiawatha's attention by putting on a game of lacrosse. During the game, his third daughter, the youngest of the three and pregnant, goes to the river to bathe. On her way back, the warriors see a great bird flying low overhead. In their zeal to seize it, they collide with the last daughter, whose injuries are fatal (*CL*, pp. 132–138).

DEGANAWIDA, THE PEACEMAKER

(9) "Hiawatha Mourns and Quits Onondaga" (Vecsey, p. 86): Heartbroken, Hiawatha departs. He goes to a cornfield, builds a lean-to, and lights a fire to camp overnight (*CL*, p. 139).

(10) "Hiawatha Invents Wampum" (Vecsey, p. 86): At his camp, Hiawatha cuts and cores sumac branches (later described as "basswood," identified as elderberry in the Chiefs' version) into short sticks, hooks them onto a horizontally suspended rod, and gazes at them (*CL*, pp. 140–141). This is the origin of the "Welcome at the Woods' Edge" wampum. Since wampum already existed and was widely used, what Hiawatha actually invented—or rather, revivified—were the Condolence speeches.

(11) "Hiawatha Gives the Mohawks Lessons in Protocol" (Vecsey, pp. 86–87): Puzzled at seeing this, the man guarding the cornfield reports to the chief, who sends two scouts to invite Hiawatha to the chief's house. They address Hiawatha three times. No response. On hearing this, the chief guesses what's expected. Cutting shafts from feathers, he arranges these in similar fashion. When the scouts then present these to Hiawatha, he accepts the chief's overture, saying: "This is right and I accept it." (This is the origin of the "Invitation Wampum," which is part of "forest diplomacy.") The chief calls a meeting. Hiawatha relates what transpired among the Mohawks and announces the Peacemaker's imminent arrival (*CL*, pp. 141–171).

(12) "Deganawida Consoles Hiawatha" (Vecsey, p. 87): This element appears to be absent in the Gibson-Goldenweiser version.

(13) "Deganawida and Hiawatha Join Oneidas, Cayugas, and Senecas to Mohawks" (Vecsey, p. 87): The Peacemaker arrives in the middle of the night, tells Hiawatha he has been to Onondaga, where he announced his mission to the "Great Sorcerer," and from there proceeded to the "Great Mountain" (a Seneca settlement) as well. The Peacemaker's unobserved arrival astonishes the inhabitants of Standing Stone [Oneidas], who take council, where Deganawida proclaims his message. They accept.

Meanwhile, the Great Sorcerer (by whom Tadadaho is likely meant), now growing impatient, shouts a great shout, heard all over the world.

Deganawida then sends two messengers to "look for smoke." They transform into hawks, see the smoke rising, and change back into humans. They see a man smoking a large pipe, who is the chief of the "Big Pipe People" (the Cayugas). He accepts the Peacemaker's message. The messengers proceed to the "Great Mountain."

The Senecas remain unconvinced. So the Peacemaker goes to them, and finds them split into two factions. The chiefs accept, although the warriors do not (*CL*, pp. 141–222).

(14) "Scouts Travel to Tadadaho" (Vecsey, p. 87): Deganawida and Hiawatha launch the stone canoe to cross the great lake. Representatives from the Mohawk, Oneida, Cayuga, and Seneca nations embark, climb aboard. Hiawatha paddles. In the middle of the lake, the Sorcerer shouts, "Is it time yet?" This stirs up a fierce gale, with great waves threatening to capsize the canoe. Then the Peacemaker commands, "Rest wind!" The Sorcerer shouts again, stirring up a great whirlwind. Deganawida then says, "Stop wind!" and calms the tempest (*CL*, pp. 223–225).

(15) "The Nations March to Tadadaho, Singing the Peace Hymn" (Vecsey, pp. 87–88): This element evidently is absent from the Gibson-Goldenweiser version as well.

(16) "Deganawida and Hiawatha Transform Tadadaho" (Vecsey, p. 88): At last they reach the "Great Sorcerer" (i.e., Tadadaho). "They observed that all over his head beings were writhing—it was like snakes, his hair, and his fingers were gnarled—all over they were writhing, nor was he about to talk. Thereupon they saw something hanging on him" (*CL*, p. 228). The Peacemaker then sends Hiawatha to fetch "Fat Face" (Jigonsaseh), now called "our mother, the Great Matron." She arrives. A "grand council" convenes. The Peacemaker proposes the following to the Great Sorcerer:

> Now, indeed, all of them have arrived, they of the four nations, that is, the Mohawks and the Oneidas and the Cayugas and the Senecas; they are the ones who have accepted the Good Message and the Power and the Peace, that which will now function: the Great Law. Moreover, everything reposes there, the minds of the several nations, and as to you, they place before you their proposition that it is to be you who is the title bearer, and the Great Chief,

and you also are to be the fire keeper at the place where we will kindle the fire, whose rising smoke will pierce the sky. Then one will see it in all of the settlements on earth.

(CL, pp. 230–232)

So, after the uniting of four nations (Mohawks, Oneidas, Cayugas, and Senecas), the allegiance of one more remains to be won: the Onondagas, led by the Great Sorcerer (still, at this point in the saga, unnamed). The Peacemaker then proclaims:

> "Now moreover, it is accomplished; now she has arrived, our mother, the Great Matron whose name is [Tsikonhsahsen]; now she has accepted the Good Message, and this, moreover, is what you should confirm and adopt, the Great Law, so that she may place antlers on you, our mother, and they shall together form a circle, standing alongside your body." ... "Now you are looking at all of the ones who will be standing with you." Thereupon the man bowed his head. Thereupon his hair stopped writhing and all of his fingers became quiet. Thereupon Tekanawita? said, "Now, indeed, it is functioning, the Peace." Thereupon the man spoke up saying, "Now I confirm the matter, I accept the Good Message and the Power and the Peace."

(CL, pp. 232–234)

In this dramatic scene, the Great Sorcerer bows his head in humble, yet grand, acquiescence. His hair stops writhing. His fingers uncurl. Unseethed, he accepts the message. Then the Peacemaker strokes the Sorcerer's head, straightens his fingers, while others disentangle the objects hanging from his shoulders. The Sorcerer is now righted, his humanity restored *(CL, pp. 226–235)*.

(17) "Deganawida and Hiawatha Establish Iroquois Unity and Law" (Vecsey, p. 88): The Peacemaker then summons Jigonsaseh, the Great Matron, whom he recognizes as a "Great Chief." Together with Jigonsaseh, Deganawida places a crown of antlers (a symbol of authority) on the Sorcerer's head. The Peacemaker confers on the Sorcerer the title "Thatotaho'." Antlers are then placed on the other chiefs *(CL, pp. 235–251)*.

(18) "Deganawida and Hiawatha Establish League Chiefs and Council Polity" (Vecsey, pp. 88–89): After the Peacemaker sets forth rules of

order for the operation of good governance among the Five Nations, Hiawatha then invites the recalcitrant Seneca warrior chief ("the Great Warrior") and his deputy, who are brought to the council to hear the Peacemaker's message. He offers them the special authority over all of the League's warriors, and also offers them the post of "Doorkeepers." The Great Warrior accepts, whereupon the Peacemaker gives thanks by reciting a short version of the Thanksgiving Address:

> Thereupon Tekanawita? stood up, saying, "The Great Power came from up in the sky, and now it is functioning, the Great Power that we accepted when we reached consensus. So now our house has become complete. Now, therefore, we shall give thanks, that is, we shall thank the Creator of the earth, that is, he who planted all kinds of weeds and all varieties of shrubs and all kinds of trees; and springs, flowing water, such as rivers and large bodies of water, such as lakes; and the sun that keeps moving by day, and by night, the moon, and where the sky is, the stars, which no one is able to count; moreover, the way it is on earth in relation to which no one is able to tell the extent to which it is to their benefit, that is the people whom he created and who will continue to live on earth. This, then, is the reason we thank him, the one with great power, the one who is the Creator, for that which will now move forward, the Good Message and the Power and the Peace; the Great Law."

(CL, pp. 294–296)

The Peacemaker then lays out the specific laws of good governance by which the Confederacy will function. Women become the proprietors of lordship titles *(CL, pp. 294–326)*.

(19) "The Confederacy Takes Symbolic Images" (Vecsey, p. 89): The Peacemaker establishes the central hearth, being the council fire. They plant a great white pine ("Great Tall Tree Trunk") named, in Woodbury's translation, as the "Great Long Leaf," which puts forth four white roots ("Great White Root[s]") extending east, west, north, and south *(CL, pp. 296–297)*. Arrows are bound together by the sinew of a deer, to represent the Confederacy's strong bond *(CL, pp. 300–309)*: "for this bundle, made of five arrows, is impossible to break, and it is impossible to bend it" *(CL, p. 306)*.

Later, on his way home, Hiawatha comes upon a lake, on which a group of ducks are

floating. When the ducks take notice, they fly off, magically lifting all of the water from the lake. On the lake bed, Hiawatha sees "white objects" (that is, shells; *CL*, p. 326) that remind him of his first wampum of sumac sticks. He then collects the white shells and puts them into a pouch of fawn skin, and places these objects near the central fire, to serve as symbols of the Great Law (*CL*, pp. 326–330). According to Mann ("The Fire at Onondaga: Wampum as Proto-Writing"), wampum was a full writing system, whose characters were immediately readable by any wampum reader.

(20) "The League Declares Its Sovereignty" (Vecsey, pp. 89–90): This element is absent in the Gibson-Goldenweiser version as well.

(21) "The Condolence Maintains the Confederacy" (Vecsey, p. 90): The Peacemaker sets forth clear laws of succession to the matrilineally hereditary titles of the Confederacy, with ceremonies for mourning the passing of a former chief and installing his replacement. The League is constituted by fifty chiefs, upon each and every one of whom is bestowed, by the head clan mothers (each of whom bears the position title of "Jigonsaseh," after the Great Matron), a matrilineally hereditary title (*CL*, pp. 237–250). The Condolence ceremonies are then set forth, in considerable detail and at great length. These solemn rites of passage are followed by installation ceremonies to induct a successor to the deceased chief (*CL*, pp. 486–701).

(22) "Deganawida Departs" (Vecsey, p. 90): This element appears to be absent in the Gibson-Goldenweiser version as well. In other words, there is no departure scene in *Concerning the League*. Certain other versions feature the Peacemaker's farewell prophecy.

THE PEACEMAKER'S MESSAGE

As Kathryn Muller points out (p. 22, n. 5), the Gibson-Goldenweiser version is unique in that it refers to the "Good Message, Power and Peace" (Onondaga: *kaihwíyóh, ka'tshátstéhsæ'* and *skęëé'nų'*) as three distinct concepts, whereas the Chiefs' version refers to the "the message of the good news of Peace and Power." According to

Barbara Mann (personal communication, September 3, 2014), these are traditionally referred to as the "Three Pillars," since "three" is the indigenous number meaning "pay attention"; therefore, the Chiefs' version, in giving two, not three such "pillars," reveals its Christianization. However, the Oneida version recited by Chief Robert Brown of the Wisconsin Oneida Nation (who is considered a national treasure), echoes this formulation: "First, what is the meaning of 'good message' and second what is the meaning of 'power' and then third what is the meaning of 'peace has now arrived'?" (Brown, pp. 46–47). So, in the final analysis, this may be a distinction without a difference.

Translator Hanni Woodbury characterizes the "Good Message, Power and Peace" as the "three Great Words" (*CL*, p. 61 and n. 61-1.) In *Concerning the League*, "the Good Message, Power and the Peace" occurs only once (p. 63). But its variations are numerous. "Good Message and the Power and the Peace" is the expression most commonly met with (37 times). "Good Message" comes up 112 times. "Peace" (also capitalized) occurs 114 times. "Power" is found 85 times. The three great words, summed up, is the "Great Law" (16 times).

In Chief Brown's Oneida version, the Peacemaker gives the following explanation to a Mohawk chief (a former cannibal), to whom he gives the name "Two Matters":

["Two Matters"] "Who are you and where did you come from?"

[The Peacemaker] Then he said, "I am the Peacemaker and from the north I have come.… The Creator sent me here on earth. The Creator appointed me to lecture people on what they are doing.…

Now I will tell you what message the Creator send [sent] with me of what there will be on earth. He intended everyone to have a good mind on the earth you travel. He thought there would be reasons. First, he intended all the peopled [people] should be having peaceful thoughts in their minds. Then love will come from that. If their thinking is not peaceful then they will not have love. And if they do have love then from it will come compassion and if they have no love, then they won't have any compassion.

Each and every one of you has the power. Whatever power you have comes from what you have thought. Then that comes from a good mind. He intended you all to be helping each other. You people should not be arguing."

(The Great Law of Peace, pp. 28–31)

This explanation appears to be a gloss on the "Good Message," which gives rise to the "good mind," from which, through force of thought, arise feelings of peace, love, compassion, and altruism.

That said, further distinctions have been made. In the popular non-Native English version, Paul Wallace's *White Roots of Peace,* originally published by the University of Pennsylvania Press in 1946 and considered a classic of Native lore, the Peacemaker elaborates on "the Good News of Peace and Power" as follows:

So Deganawidah passed from settlement to settlement, finding that men desired peace and would practice it if they knew for a certainty that others would practice it, too.

But first, after leaving the hunters, Deganawidah sought the house of a certain woman who lived by the warriors' path which passed between the east and the west.

When Deganawidah arrived, the woman placed food before him and, after he had eaten, asked him his message.

"I carry the Mind of the Master of Life," he replied, "and my message will bring an end to the wars between east and west."

"How will this be?" asked the woman, who wondered at his words, for it was her custom to feed the warriors passing before her door on their way between the east and the west.

"The Word that I bring," he said, "is that all peoples shall love one another and live together in peace. This message has three parts: Righteousness and Health and Power—*Gáiwoh,* *Skénon,* *Gashasdénshaa.* And each part has two branches.

Righteousness means justice practiced between men and between nations; it means also a desire to see justice prevail.

Health means soundness of mind and body; it means also peace, for that is what comes when minds are sane and bodies cared for.

Power means authority, the authority of law and custom, backed by such force as is necessary to make justice prevail; it means also religion, for justice enforced is the will of the Holder of the Heavens and has his sanction."

"Thy message is good," said the woman; "but a word is nothing until it is given form and set to work in the world. What form shall this message take when it comes to dwell among men?"

"It will take the form of the longhouse," replied Deganawidah, "in which there are many fires, one for each family, yet all live as one household under one chief mother. Hereabouts are five nations, each with its own council fire, yet they shall live together as one household in peace. They shall be the Kanonsiónni, the Longhouse. They shall have one mind and live under one law. Thinking shall replace killing, and there shall be one commonwealth."

(Wallace, *White Roots of Peace,* pp. 39–40)

This version of the Peacemaker's message is one of the most widely cited today, being the easiest for Westerners to follow. The above passage, or a substantial part of it, appears on various Native American and Native Canadian Web sites as well. Who are the sources of authority for Wallace's variation on Deganawida's "gospel"? Paul Wallace, a literary historian, credits Chief William D. Loft, to whose memory Wallace dedicates his book. Conversant in five of the Iroquoian languages, Chief Loft, Mohawk of Caledonia, was Speaker of the Six Nations Council at Grand River, 1917–1918, and a noted orator of Haudenosaunee traditions and stories in the 1920s and 1930s. Another source may be the Gibson-Goldenweiser version, which Wallace read in a draft translation that was begun by Hewitt and completed by William Fenton, with Simeon Gibson (son of John Arthur Gibson), archived in the Smithsonian Institution's National Anthropological Archives. (MSS. 1517b, c.) Yet another source may be J. N. B. Hewitt, who gave a paper at the International Congress of Americanists held in Washington in December 1915 on "Some Esoteric Aspects of the League of the Iroquois," published in 1917.

Here, the three words that epitomize the essence of the Peacemaker's message—*Gáiwoh*

("Righteousness"), *Skénon* ("Health"), *Gashas-dénshaa* ("Power")—correspond to their respective Onondaga equivalents: *kaihwíyóh* ("Good Message"), *skẹé'nụ'* ("Peace"), *ka'tshátstéhsæ'* ("Power"). Evidently, Professor Wallace has taken artistic license with these sacred terms of art, reconfiguring the "Good Message, Peace, and Power" as "Righteousness, Health, and Power." Thus, "Good Message" becomes "Righteous-ness." "Peace" becomes primarily "Health" and only secondarily "peace" (i.e., "also peace, for that is what comes when minds are sane and bodies cared for"). In the Gibson-Goldenweiser version, "health" occurs only twice, and only in relation to a person's individual health (*CL*, pp. 13, 448), whereas "righteousness" is absent entirely. Such a shift in emphasis is scarcely warranted by the 1912 text. Since Deganawida is revered as the "Peacemaker," whose purpose was to unite five warring Iroquois tribes into "the League of the Great Law" (*CL*, pp. 310–311) by means of the "the Good Message, the Power, and the Peace," it would seem odd to rename these three great words as "Righteousness, Power, and Health."

Christopher Jocks (Mohawk), in his article "Living Words and Cartoon Translations," implicitly takes a jaundiced view of this variation (or outright alteration of the original message), but stops short of outright criticism (i.e., "I cite this modern exegesis not in order to criticize its accuracy … but to demonstrate how deeply a tradition in translation may draw from very different realms of discourse in the process of recontextualizing itself in the target language" [pp. 225–226]). Invoking the Mohawk terms of art, Jocks notes that the first two terms in "the phrase, *skén-:nen, ka'shatsténhsera, karihríio*, or its equivalent" are "easily glossed as 'peace,' and either 'power' or 'strength,' respectively." "'Good message,'" Jocks hastens to add as to the third term, "is the most direct rendering of the word's composition" (p. 225). These key words are transmogrified, if not mutated, in their transposition from source language to target language in translation, in a process that Jocks calls "the 'cartooning' of culture" where "the link with the living tradition based on enactment is seriously

endangered" (p. 230). In so criticizing the recasting of the Peacemaker's message, Jocks demonstrates how the "appropriation" of Native American spirituality implicates ethical, political, and hermeneutical issues. (See also Jocks's "Spirituality for Sale.")

However, the sixfold explication of the Peacemaker's three core principles evidently goes back to Hewitt, who wrote:

> The founders of the league, therefore, proposed and expounded as the requisite basis of all good government three broad "double" doctrines or principles. The names of these principles in the native tongues vary dialectically, but these three notable terms are expressed in Onondaga as follows: (1) *Ne'´´ Skĕñ´no^n*, meaning, first, sanity of mind and the health of the body; and, second, peace between individuals and between organized bodies or groups of persons. (2) *Ne'´´ Gaii'hwiyo'*, meaning, first, righteousness in conduct and its advocacy in thought and speech; and, second, equity or justice, the adjustment of rights and obligations. (3) *Ne'´´ Gă's'hasdĕ^n'´sä'*, meaning, first, physical strength or power, as military force or civil authority; and, second, the orenda or magic power of the people or of their institutions and rituals, having mythic and religious implications. Six principles in all. The constructive results of the control and guidance of human thinking and conduct in the private, the public, and the foreign relations of the peoples so leagued by these six principles, the reformers maintained, are the establishment and the conservation of what is reverently called *Ne'´´ Gayanĕñ'sä'gō´nă'*—, i.e. the Great Commonwealth, the great Law of Equity and Righteousness and Well-being, of all known men. It is thus seen that the mental grasp and outlook of these prophet-statesman and states-women of the Iroquois looked out beyond the limits of tribal boundaries to a vast sisterhood and brotherhood of all the tribes of men, dwelling in harmony and happiness. This indeed was a notable vision for the Stone Age of America.
>
> ("A Constitutional League of Peace," p. 541)

Thus, it would appear that Paul Wallace's elaboration of the Peacemaker's message depends on Hewitt, who reflects the central Iroquois view of a twinned cosmos.

CONCLUSION

The Deganawida epic, in its sundry versions, belongs to world literature. It can be regarded as

a foundational American text, both in the pre-contact and post-contact periods. Its authenticity is unimpeached, and its magical realism granted as edifying embellishment. Few would doubt its historical core, much less its cultural significance. The influence of the Peacemaker—and that of the Confederacy founded on its principles, organization, and laws he expounded—is a matter of debate. The foremost proponents of the Iroquois influence thesis are Donald A. Grinde, Jr., and Bruce E. Johansen in their book *Exemplar of Liberty: Native America and the Evolution of Democracy*, with a foreword by Vine Deloria, Jr.

On October 4, 1988, during the 100th Congress, the U.S. House of Representatives passed House Concurrent Resolution 331 (H.Con.Res. 331) by a vote of 408–8. Then, on October 21, 1988, the Senate approved Senate Concurrent Resolution 76 (S.Con.Res.76, identical to H.Con. Res. 331), by unanimous voice vote. The joint resolution reads, in part:

> Whereas the original framers of the Constitution, including, most notably, George Washington and Benjamin Franklin, are known to have greatly admired the concepts of the Six Nations of the Iroquois Confederacy;
>
> Whereas the confederation of the original Thirteen Colonies into one republic was influenced by the political system developed by the Iroquois Confederacy as were many of the democratic principles which were incorporated into the Constitution itself
> ...
>
> RESOLVED BY THE HOUSE OF REPRESENTATIVES (THE SENATE CONCURRING), That—
>
> (1) the Congress, on the occasion of the two hundredth anniversary of the signing of the United States Constitution, acknowledges the contribution made by the Iroquois Confederacy and other Indian Nations to the formation and development of the United States; ...

And so LeAnne Howe may be right after all, when she states: "America is a tribal creation story, a tribalography.... When the European Founding Fathers heard the stories of how the Haudenosaunee unified six individual tribes into an Indian confederacy, they created a document, the U.S. Constitution, that united immigrant Europeans into a symbiotic union called America." The Deganawida epic is formative in that it is the founding "document" of the Iroquois League. It is performative in that it remains in practice to this day. It is transformative in that it decolonizes and revisions our conception of America's origins.

Selected Bibliography

DEGANAWIDA EPIC

NATIVE-AUTHORED ENGLISH VERSIONS

"The Legend of the Peacemaker, Part 1." Ohsweken, Ont.: Jake Thomas Learning Centre, 1991.

Newhouse, Seth (Da-yo-de-ka-ne). *The Original Literal Historical Narratives of the Iroquois Confederacy; or, The Birch Bark Canoe.* American Philosophical Society, Microfilm No. 348, 1885. (Also titled *Cosmogony of the Iroquois Confederacy.*)

Parker, Arthur C. "The Constitution of the Five Nations or The Iroquois Book of the Great Law." *New York State Museum Bulletin* 184:7–118 (April 1, 1916).

———. "The Origin of the Long House." In *Seneca Myths and Folk Tales.* Buffalo, N.Y.: Buffalo Historical Society, 1923. Pp. 403–406. (As told by Delos B. Kittle, or "Chief Big Kittle," Cattaraugus Reservation, January 1905. Another "Native-English" version, as it does not appear to be translated directly from a Seneca text.)

Scott, Duncan C., presenter. Prepared by a Committee of the Chiefs. *Traditional History of the Confederacy of the Six Nations.* Ottawa: Royal Society of Canada, 1912. (*Proceedings and Transactions of the Royal Society of Canada,* 3rd ser., 5:195–246 [1911]).

Thomas, Chief Jacob E. "Appendix: Gayanashagowa." In "The Formation of the League of the Haudenosaunee (Iroquois): Interpreting the Archaeological Record Through the Oral Narrative Gayanashagowa," by Sandra Erin Atkins. Master's thesis, Trent University, Peterborough, Ontario, 2002. Pp. 146–212. (A detailed description of Chief Jacob Thomas' version of *Gayanashagowa* presented September 19–27, 1992, in Ohsweken, Ontario.)

ONONDAGA VERSIONS

The Gibson-Goldenweiser Version: John Arthur Gibson, *Concerning the League: The Iroquois League Tradition as Dictated in Onondaga by John Arthur Gibson.* Newly Elicited, Edited and Translated by Hanni Woodbury in

Collaboration with Reg Henry and Harry Webster on the Basis of A. A. Goldenweiser's Manuscript. Memoir 9. Winnipeg, Man.: Algonquian and Iroquoian Linguistics, 1992. (Based on "Original text of the Gibson-Goldenweiser version of the Deganawidah epic comprising 20 of Goldenweiser's notebooks." 529 pages original text. Control no. III-I-116M R. Accession no. 77/130 [formerly cataloged as MS 1252.5], Canadian Ethnology Service Archives, Canadian Museum of Civilization, Hull, Québec.)

The Gibson-Hewitt Version: John Arthur Gibson, *Original Pencil Texts of the Deganawida Legend* (1899). MS 2316, National Anthropological Archives, Smithsonian Institution. Digital scans available online at http://siris-archives.si.edu/ipac20/ipac.jsp?&profile=all&source=˜!si archives&uri=full=3100001˜!83496˜!0#focus For typed transcript (also in Onondaga) see MS 1517(a), National Anthropological Archives, Smithsonian Institution.

Hewitt, J. N. B. "Legend of the Founding of the Iroquois League." *American Anthropologist* 5, no. 2:131–148 (April 1892). (Translation of Chief John Buck's 1888 Onondaga version.)

ONEIDA VERSION

Elm, Demus. *The Story of Deganawida.* Recited in Oneida, 1971. Floyd Glenn Lounsbury Papers. Mss.Ms.Coll.95. Box 42–43. c. 925 pages; 8 folders. Philadelphia: American Philosophical Society. http://amphilsoc.org/mole/view?docId=ead/Mss.Ms.Coll.95-ead.xml (Includes Lounsbury's transcripts of the recording, some translation, text in interlinear form [Oneida and English]).

MOHAWK VERSIONS

Brown, Chief Robert (a.k.a. Anahalihs ["Great Vines"]), Bear Clan chief of the Oneida tribe; cultural advisor, Sovereign Oneida Nation of Wisconsin. *The Great Law of Peace.* Interlinear Oneida transcription and English translation. Translated by Chief Brown and Clifford F. Abbott (University of Wisconsin–Green Bay) and edited by Randy Cornelius (Tehahuko'tha). Available online at http://www.oneidanation.org/uploadedFiles/Kayantlako-1-O-E-ed.pdf and http://www.oneidanation.org/uploadedFiles/Kayantlako-2-O-E-ed.pdf

Newhouse, Seth. *Translation of the Mohawk Version of the Constitution of the League.* MS 3490, National Anthropological Archives, Smithsonian Institution, 1937. 43 pages. Typescript titled *Constitution of the Confederacy by Dekanawidah. Collected and Translated from Mohawk Text by Chief Seth Newhouse.* Digital scans available online at http://collections.si.edu/search/slide show_embedded?xml=%22 http://sirismm.si.edu/naa/viewer/3490_Gallery/viewer_3490.xml%22 (A bilingual Mohawk-English version was published in 1993 by Ohontsa Films.)

CAYUGA VERSION

Hewitt, J. N. B. "Cayuga Version of the Deganawida Legend 1890." MS 1582, National Anthropological Archives, Smithsonian Institution. 17 pages. Digital scans online at http://collections.si.edu/search/results.htm?q=record_ID%3Asiris_arc_83486&repo=DPLA

NON-NATIVE ENGLISH VERSION

Wallace, Paul A. W. *White Roots of Peace: Iroquois Book of Life.* Santa Fe, N.M.: Clear Light, 1998. (Originally published Philadelphia: University of Pennsylvania Press, 1946.)

ACKNOWLEDGMENTS

The author acknowledges the ideas, edits, corrections and encouragement of the following individuals, whose astute input has greatly enhanced the quality of this article: (1) Barbara Alice Mann, Ph.D. (Native American, Ohio Bear Clan Seneca), associate professor, Honors Department, University of Toledo, author of *Iroquoian Women: The Gantowisas* (New York: Peter Lang, 2000, 3rd printing, 2006); (2) Donald A. Grinde, Jr., Ph.D. (Native American), professor, Department of Transnational Studies, University at Buffalo, the State University of New York, editor and author, *A Political History of Native Americans* (Thousand Oaks, Calif.: CQ Press/Sage, 2002 [Choice Outstanding Academic Title 2003]); (3) Bruce E. Johansen, Ph.D., Jacob J. Isaacson University Research Professor, Communication and Native American Studies, University of Nebraska at Omaha, author of *Encyclopedia of the American Indian Movement* (Santa Barbara, Calif.: ABC-CLIO/Greenwood, 2013); (4) Clifford F. Abbott (linguist), professor of information and computing science at the University of Wisconsin–Green Bay, author of *Oneida Teaching Grammar* (University of Wisconsin–Green Bay, 2006); and (5) Steven Kolins, M.S., technical support specialist in the University Library, University of North Carolina at Chapel Hill, published writer of encyclopedic articles.

CRITICAL STUDIES

Bernier, Jonathan. "The Quest for the Historical Tekanawi·ta': Oral Tradition and the Founding of the Iroquois League." *Totem* 11, no. 1:80–84 (2003).

Bonaparte, Darren. *Creation and Confederation: The Living History of the Iroquois.* Akwesasne, Que., and Akwesasne, N.Y.: Wampum Chronicles, 2006.

Campbell, William J. "Seth Newhouse, the Grand River Six Nations, and the Writing of the Great Laws." *Ontario History* 96, no. 2:183–202 (autumn 2004).

Canfield, William W. "The Peacemaker" and "Notes to the Legends." In *The Legends of the Iroquois, Told by "The Cornplanter": From Authoritative Notes and Studies.* New York: A. Wessels, 1904 [1902]. Pp. 149–154, 203–211.

Crawford, Neta C. "The Long Peace Among Iroquois Nations." In *War and Peace in the Ancient World*. Edited by Kurt A. Raaflaub. Malden, Mass., and Oxford: Blackwell, 2007. Pp. 348–368.

Dennis, Matthew. "Deganawidah and the Cultivation of Peace: Iroquois Ideology, Political Culture, and Representation." In *Cultivating a Landscape of Peace: Iroquois-European Encounters in Seventeenth-Century America*. Ithaca, N.Y.: Cornell University Press, 1995. Pp. 76–118.

Fenton, William N. "Seth Newhouse's Traditional History and Constitution of the Iroquois Confederacy." *Proceedings of the American Philosophical Society* 93, no. 2:141–158 (May 16, 1949).

———. "'This Island, the World on the Turtle's Back.'" *Journal of American Folklore* 75, no. 298:283–300 (October–December 1962).

Foster, Michael K. "Jacob Ezra Thomas: Educator and Conservator of Iroquois Culture." *Histories of Anthropology Annual* 1:219–245 (2005).

Franklin, Benjamin. *The Papers of Benjamin Franklin*. Vol. 4, *July 1, 1750 through June 30, 1753*. Edited by Leonard W. Labaree. New Haven, Conn.: Yale University Press, 1961.

Grinde, Donald A., Jr., and Bruce E. Johansen. *Exemplar of Liberty: Native America and the Evolution of Democracy*. Los Angeles: UCLA American Indian Studies Center, 1991.

Hewitt, J. N. B. (John Napoleon Brinton). "Some Esoteric Aspects of the League of the Iroquois." *Proceedings of the 19th International Congress of Americanists, Held at Washington, Dec. 27–31, 1915* (1917). Pp. 322–326.

———. "The Constitution of the Five Nations; Traditional History of the Confederacy of the Six Nations; Civil, Religious, and Mourning Councils and Ceremonies and Adoption of the New York Indians." *American Anthropologist*, n.s., 19, no. 3:429–438 (1917).

———. "A Constitutional League of Peace in the Stone Age of America: The League of the Iroquois and Its Constitution." *Annual Report of the Board of Regents of the Smithsonian … 1918*. Washington, D.C.: U.S. Government Printing Office, 1920. Pp. 527–545.

Howe, LeAnne. "The Story of America: A Tribalography." In *Clearing a Path: Theorizing the Past in Native American Studies*. Edited by Nancy Shoemaker. New York and London: Routledge, 2002. Pp. 29–48.

Jocks, Christopher. "Living Words and Cartoon Translations: Longhouse 'Texts' and the Limitations of English." In *Endangered Languages: Language Loss and Community Response*. Edited by Lenore A. Grenoble and Lindsay J. Whaley. Cambridge, U.K., and New York: Cambridge University Press, 1998. Pp. 217–233.

Jocks, Christopher Ronwanièn:te. "Spirituality for Sale: Sacred Knowledge in the Consumer Age." In *Native American Spirituality: A Critical Reader*. Edited by Lee Irwin. Lincoln: University of Nebraska Press, 2000. (Originally published in *American Indian Quarterly* 20, nos. 3–4:415–431 [1996].)

Johansen, Bruce Elliott, and Barbara Alice Mann, eds. *Encyclopedia of the Haudenosaunee (Iroquois Confederacy)*. Westport, Conn.: Greenwood, 2000.

Kimura, Takeshi. "The Native Chief's Resistance Through Myth: A Historical and Religious Study of a Myth." Ph.D. dissertation, University of Chicago, 1998.

Mann, Barbara A. "The Fire at Onondaga: Wampum as Proto-Writing." *Akwesasne Notes* 1, no. 1:40–48 (spring 1995).

———. "The Lynx in Time: Haudenosaunee Women's Traditions and History." *American Indian Quarterly* 21, no. 3: 423–449 (summer 1997).

———. *Iroquoian Women: The Gantowisas*. New York: Peter Lang, 2006.

Mann, Barbara A., and Jerry L. Fields. "A Sign in the Sky: Dating the League of the Haudenosaunee." *American Indian Culture and Research Journal* 21, no. 2:105–163 (August 1997).

Merriam, Kathryn Lavely. "The Preservation of Iroquois Thought: J. N. B. Hewitt's Legacy of Scholarship for His People." Ph.D. dissertation, University of Massachusetts, Amherst, 2010.

Muller, Kathryn V. "Holding Hands with Wampum: Haudenosaunee Council Fires from the Great Law of Peace to Contemporary Relationships with the Canadian State." Ph.D. dissertation, Queen's University (Kingston, Ont.), 2008.

Parmenter, Jon. *The Edge of the Woods: Iroquoia, 1534–1701*. East Lansing: Michigan State University Press, 2010.

Snow, Dean. "Dating the Emergence of the League of the Iroquois: A Reconsideration of the Documentary Evidence." In *A Beautiful and Fruitful Place: Selected Rensselaerswijck Seminar Papers*. Edited by Nancy Anne McClure Zeller. Albany, N.Y.: New Netherland, 1991. Pp. 139–143.

Starna, William A. "Retrospecting the Origins of the League of the Iroquois." *Proceedings of the American Philosophical Society* 152, no. 3:279–321 (September 2008).

Tooker, Elizabeth. "The League of the Iroquois: Its History, Politics, and Ritual." In *Handbook of North American Indians*. Vol. 15, *Northeast*. Edited by Bruce G. Trigger. Washington, D.C.: Smithsonian Institution, 1978. Pp. 418–441.

Tuck, James A. "The Iroquois Confederacy." *Scientific American* 224, no. 2:32–42 (February 1971).

U.S. Mint. "2010 Native American $1 Coin." http://www.usmint.gov/mint_programs/nativeamerican/?action=2010NADesign

Vecsey, Christopher. "The Story and Structure of the Iroquois Confederacy." *Journal of the American Academy of Religion* 54, no. 1: 79–106 (spring, 1986).

ERIC GANSWORTH

(1965—)

Elizabeth DeLaney Hoffman

THE AMERICAN INDIAN writer and visual artist Eric Gansworth is an enrolled member of the Onondaga Nation (People of the Hills) who was born and raised on the Tuscarora Indian reservation in western New York, near Niagara Falls. This convergence of two tribes, two cultures, and two artistic media has made Gansworth a successful novelist, poet, playwright, and short-story writer whose paintings often illustrate his written words. As of 2015 Gansworth had published five novels (*Indian Summers, Smoke Dancing, Mending Skins, Extra Indians*, and *If I Ever Get Out of Here*); three collections of poetry (*Nickel Eclipse: Iroquois Moon, A Half-Life of Cardio-Pulmonary Function*, and *From the Western Door to the Lower West Side* [with Milton Rogovin]); one nonfiction/poetry work (*Breathing the Monster Alive*); four plays (*Re-Creation Story, Patriot Act, Home Fires and Reservation Roads*, and *Rabbit Dance*); and was the editor of a collection of essays (*Sovereign Bones: New Native American Writing*).

Gansworth's writing develops from his life on the reservation, surrounded by family and friends, traditional stories, and the culture of the Haudenosaunee (People of the Longhouse), sometimes referred to as the Six Nations of the Iroquois. The Onondaga and the Tuscarora are both members of the Haudenosaunee. These circumstances of his early life led to displacement and exclusion, a theme that resounds throughout much of his work. As Onondaga people living on the Tuscarora Reservation, he and his family were not often afforded amenities and services given to enrolled members of the Tuscarora Nation. The irony of exclusion that Gansworth explores in his work stems from the Tuscarora themselves, who became affiliated with the Haudenosaunee in the 1700s and were not part of the original five-member confederacy. They fled persecution in North Carolina and joined the other five tribes as equal members. Paradoxically, Gansworth's family members live on the Tuscarora Reservation and share Tuscarora culture, but remain outsiders as Onondaga.

The connection to Haudenosaunee culture is undeniable. Gansworth's prose, poetry, and paintings reflect the strong matrilineal line, the creation story, and the importance of wampum. In "Border Crossings: An Interview with Eric Gansworth" by Oliver de la Paz and John Lloyd Purdy, Gansworth explains the importance of the purple and white wampum beads that appear in his writing and painting: "These beads, when woven into belts, use symbols and sequences to engage the act of remembering, forcing each member of the culture to commit certain things to memory, in essence, to be individually responsible for cultural memory" (p. 174). Another Haudenosaunee symbol of survival that pervades Gansworth's work is the Three Sisters—corn, beans, and squash—who appear as characters and in illustrations.

Reservation culture is at the heart of Gansworth's writing. In an interview on the *Crazy QuiltEdi* blog, Gansworth states that he grew up "wholly on a reservation. When writers who did not grow up in indigenous communities oversaturate their fictional worlds in some hard core 'Native spirituality' culture, totally at odds with any reservation I've ever been to, I feel an obligation to document the indigenous experiences as I know it." The result is writing that is imbued by the personalities, politics, language, and music of the rez. Place is important as well: Gansworth's reservation is his own—Tuscarora—not some imagined pan-reservation. The people are Onondaga, Tuscarora, and white. The food is corn soup

and fry bread. The politics are historically accurate and often divisive. One of the biggest controversies to appear in his work came in the mid-twentieth century when 550 acres of Tuscarora reservation land were sold by tribal sachems for a reservoir that would generate hydroelectric power from the Niagara River. The construction of the reservoir, or "the dike" as Gansworth and his characters call it, displaced many families; in his writing, the dike remains a place of family and memory, a huge, concrete metaphor of survival. In R. D. Pohl's article in *Buffalo Spree*, Gansworth declares: "The reservoir is the perfect metaphor for Indian life in America. It is a displacement device, with strictly defined yet permeable borders, where life thrives despite the artificiality."

There is also an important confluence in Gansworth's writing between reservation culture and popular culture. De la Paz and Purdy tackle this topic in "Writing the Rez: Popular Obsessions in the Works of Eric Gansworth," arguing that his "canon is woven through with elements of American popular culture: in some instances, the references are overt, in others covert; but in all, they are handled with a playfulness that works on several levels of irony and satire, with many targets as their goal" (pp. 155–156). Gansworth's childhood was full of movies, especially the horror genre, including *The Legend of Boggy Creek*, a B movie about Bigfoot which is central to his 2006 nonfiction/poetry collection *Breathing the Monster Alive*.

Even more importantly, music—mostly classic rock and roll, including the Beatles, Pink Floyd, Rush, and Queen—is at the heart of his work. Gansworth had very little money growing up, but when he found a few bucks, he spent it not on clothing or toys but on record albums. In the De la Paz and Purdy interview, Gansworth professes that he "learned poetic devices ... and the ultimate lesson of being moved by words ... from rock music" (p. 162). This music is the soundtrack to Gansworth's writing; on the *Native American Literature Symposium Blog*, Gansworth even likens his completing a piece of writing to a favorite song: "It has to pull every sentence on the previous 300 or so pages together into a satisfying resonance, like that lingering piano chord at the end of the Beatles 'A Day in the Life.'" Music literally becomes part of the young adult offering *If I Ever Get Out of Here* (2013)—the novel's title and chapter titles are all riffs on Paul McCartney and Wings songs, and Gansworth includes both a playlist and a discography at the end of the book.

Eric Gansworth was a visual artist before he was a writer. He could draw well as a kid and focused his talents not on Indian culture but on pop culture icons like Spiderman and Batman. On Amerinda.org, the website of American Indian Artists Inc., Gansworth explains the transition from painter to writer: "I continued to draw, and advanced to painting, when I got a job in high school and could afford paints and brushes. I found after a while that the stories I was trying to tell in my paintings were becoming too busy and complicated, so I tried writing them— sometimes as well as, sometimes instead of, painting them." Many of these paintings appear as the covers of his books, or as illustrations within. The paintings reflect the plot, characters, and themes of his work—they are reflections of the reservation life he knows.

Gansworth received an associate's degree at a local community college, followed by bachelor's and master's degrees at a nearby state university, but he had read only one American Indian author for a class during his entire time as a student. Outside of school, he read Ted C. Williams (Tuscarora), Louise Erdrich (Anishinaabe), Leslie Marmon Silko (Laguna), and others. On Amerinda.org, Gansworth states that their novels kept him connected to the reservation while he was away at school, but they also helped him realize the depth and richness of his reservation life and this led him to writing. In a 2005 interview with Christopher Teuton, Gansworth emphasizes that "to be adaptable and true to one's identity is a tough business, but Indians in this country have done a pretty impressive job of it, so my work, to a large degree, celebrates that ingenuity" (p. 32).

Louise Erdrich, winner of the National Book Award in 2012, was an inspiration for Gansworth, and this is apparent in his writing. In an essay in

Conversations on Jesuit Higher Education, Gansworth asserts she was a muse: "I heard Erdrich's voice, strong and clear, recognized its celebratory tone and decided then to speak as well, finding the determination to add my voice, as it were, to the chorus of indigenous writers." Like Erdrich's, Gansworth's fiction focuses on his home reservation and the people he knows, favors chapters with alternating narrators, and often uses female narrators (as Erdrich does with men).

In his own writing, Gansworth crosses borders between the reservation and the white world, using versions of real people to populate these spaces. He and his family are usually represented as characters in his novels and plays and speakers in his poetry. Gansworth brings readers into his world, showing them contemporary American Indians and their white counterparts. History, politics, love, and death walk alongside. There is struggle—the truth and memory of American Indian history in this country is laid bare in his work—but there is also joy and survival.

LIFE

Eric Gansworth was born on February 28, 1965, on the Tuscarora Indian reservation near Niagara Falls, New York. He is the youngest of seven children who lived with his mother, his father being largely absent. His mother was the center of his family, the strength that kept them together. She worked from the time she was twelve as a servant, cleaning houses for white families in the nearby posh village of Lewiston. In the interview by Oliver de la Paz and John Lloyd Purdy, Gansworth also explains how his mother's concern did not stop with her own children—she cared for her parents before they died, and her developmentally disabled brother lived in the house with them as well.

Their poverty was profound. His mother could afford only one pair of pants and one shirt per child every school year, and meals often consisted of lettuce and mayonnaise sandwiches and ketchup soup. They lived in a reservation house that was more than a hundred years old.

Gansworth's house makes several appearances in his work; he says the house was "wired by extension cords from one existing outlet box, and had no running water. We got our water from buckets we filled at a cast-iron hand-pump behind the house, which periodically was contaminated with kerosene" (De la Paz and Purdy, "Border Crossings," p. 175). The lack of indoor plumbing also forced his large family to use an outhouse. Despite this crushing poverty, Gansworth and his siblings were happy, healthy, and loved—all owing to his mother's determination. One tragic moment that reappears in Gansworth's work is when his family's house was destroyed in a fire; he movingly re-creates this fire and its consequences in the 2005 novel *Mending Skins*.

Gansworth's formal education began at the Tuscarora Indian School, where he learned the Tuscarora language, much of which he forgot as a teenager. Art was an outlet for him as a child. He was known as the kid who could draw, and that talent has led him ultimately to many exhibitions and galleries. As a visual artist, he had his first solo exhibition at the Olean Public Library in western New York in 1999. Later, an expanded show was held at the Castellani Art Museum at Niagara University. Career-spanning shows have been produced at Westfield State University in Massachusetts and the State University of New York at Oneonta. Paintings that appear in his books have been exhibited at Colgate University and other galleries across New York State. One of his paintings was used as the cover for *First Indian on the Moon*, a poetry collection by Sherman Alexie (Spokane/Coeur d'Alene).

Gansworth left the reservation to attend Niagara County Community College, where he earned an associate's degree in electroencephalography, or the study of brain waves. This career path stemmed from his desire to learn something valuable and profitable. During this time, however, he continued to study writing and literature; on Amerinda.org, he reveals that once he had the degree—a means to survive if need be—he began to write more seriously. He later received his bachelor of arts in English (1989) and master of arts in English (1990) from the State University of New York College at Buffalo. Gansworth

worked at Niagara County Community College, teaching as an assistant professor of English. Presently, he is professor of English and Lowery Writer-in-Residence at Canisius College in Buffalo.

His novels are award winning: *Mending Skins* won the PEN Oakland Josephine Miles National Literary Award for Fiction in 2006, and *Extra Indians* was a winner of the American Book Award in 2011. His work has also appeared in such journals as the *Kenyon Review*, *Cream City Review*, *Boston Review*, *Short Story*, and *Cold Mountain Review*. He is a member of the Wordcraft Circle of Native Writers and Storytellers and the Native Writers' Circle of the Americas. In 2008 and 2014 he was a keynote speaker at the Native American Literature Symposium, and in 2013 he was invited to speak at the National Book Festival on the National Mall in Washington, D.C.

Eric Gansworth took his passions of writing and visual art and left the reservation to find education and work, but he is rarely far from Tuscarora. On Amerinda.org, he says that while he continues to live and work "off the reservation, about ten minutes away, by car, [his] connections remain strong." His home, his family, and his Haudenosaunee culture all remain strongly present in his words and his paintings.

NOVELS

Gansworth's first novel, *Indian Summers* (1998), is set on the Tuscarora Reservation in the summer of 1992 and introduces major characters and themes that will reappear throughout his later work. Family, community, culture, land—and the politics of its destruction—are evident here, shown through the main narrator, Floyd Page, whose chapters alternate with an unnamed narrator. Floyd, a Tuscarora Indian and construction worker, has recently suffered head trauma and consequent memory loss after diving into the reservoir—or "the dike" as it is known on the rez. The reservoir is the political center of the novel; its existence is due only to the agreement brokered by New York State to acquire Tuscarora land for power production. It is a place of swim-

ming fun, a place to meet and drink, but its symbolic concrete is impossible to hide.

The plot centers on the importance of intergenerational community among Native people. The elders, especially, figure largely in Floyd's life as reminders of the past and the Haudenosaunee culture, and they eventually help bring Floyd back into the Longhouse religion. Flashbacks abound, full of childhood mischief and adventure. Gansworth also balances the reservation poverty with the richness of family and culture—all borrowed from his own life at Tuscarora.

Gansworth incorporated his first published short story—"The Ballad of Plastic Fred" published in *Growing Up Native American* (1993)—into the novel. It introduces the character of Fred Howkowski (a.k.a. Frederick Eagle Cry), a Tuscarora Vietnam War veteran who leaves the rez to find fame in Hollywood. Floyd and his cousins play with plastic Indian figures—one, which resembles the characters Fred played in movies, is named in his honor. (The book's cover is a Gansworth painting that features Plastic Fred in warrior mode.) The character of Plastic Fred and its attendant symbolism reappear in much of Gansworth's later work, combining the cultural desire to flee the reservation for a better life with the pop culture cliché of the silent, stoic Indian of so many westerns. *Indian Summers* is a fine beginning to Gansworth's career as novelist: the characters are likable, humor balances the despair, and it is a worthy introduction to his home and family on the reservation.

Smoke Dancing (2004), Gansworth's second novel, delves deeply into the Tuscarora tribal/political struggle between progressives and traditionalists. This novel has a much different feel from that of *Indian Summers*; here, there is anger, hatred, division, and violence. Gansworth uses his own intertribal situation to good effect, exploring how the Tuscarora power structure denies basic rights and inclusion for people from other tribes, like the Onondaga. These people, who live and dance with the Tuscarora, love and marry them, are ostracized in deadly ways—denied clean water, electricity, and emergency services. In the novel, this exclusion is balanced

delicately by dance: traditional dancers maintain their love and respect of the Tuscarora culture through their art.

The novel is organized both in parts named for the traditional Rabbit Dance, Standing Quiver Dance, and Smoke Dance, and by boxing references (Round One, Round Two, and so on). The juxtaposition is striking, and Gansworth deftly shows his characters' struggles to find equilibrium in their lives. This is a work of fiction, but Gansworth does note that "actual locations, legal agreements, and historic events are part of this work's backdrop" (p. x).The novel's cover painting, *The Three Sisters*, sets the tone for the reader: the image is of the Haudenosaunee Three Sisters—corn, beans, and squash—entwined by both a purple wampum belt and a gasoline hose/nozzle. The conflict in *Smoke Dancing* is about survival: traditionalists on the reservation fight against the entrepreneurial intrusion of the more progressive Indian businesses of tax-free cigarettes and gasoline. While this conflict escalates in the most divisive and violent ways, Gansworth keeps the undercurrent of dance throughout.

As in his first novel, Gansworth fills his pages with many characters, several of whom alternately narrate chapters. Fiction Tunny, whose birth name is Patricia, is the main character—a strong, beautiful, traditional dancer who is the last in a line of Onondaga residents living at Tuscarora. Her tribal affiliation has caused her grief, especially since her mother died because of sewage in their well water. Fiction's father, the other central character, is Tuscarora tribal chief Jacob "Bud" Tunny. As his unrecognized, illegitimate daughter, Patricia legally changes her name to "Fiction" because, as she says, "at the heart of fiction is where the truth sleeps" (p. 1). The relationship between father and daughter is strained at best, violent and disturbing at worst. Chapter 3 contains Bud's account of the fight he has with Fiction, after he refuses to allow her to possess the land owned by her late Onondaga mother. The fourth chapter is Fiction's account, and it is shocking in its violence and viciousness. She is badly beaten: "My body is the map of my father's insanity" (p. 49). In revenge, Fiction sews a beautiful velvet dance dress, beading her

bruises onto the dress in the form of roses. She wears it to a Social Dance and humiliates her father in public. Bud's violence escalates, and he seeks further revenge—simply at first by turning off her utilities, and later senselessly by burning down her trailer. Their battles ultimately end with Bud being removed as chief of the tribe. Finally, Fiction becomes Patricia again, finding love and redemption.

Bud's anger is not limited to Fiction; he clashes with Mason Rollins, a progressive Tuscarora businessperson who refuses to allow the tribe to dictate his desire to make money for himself and the Nation. Mason is determined to use treaty laws to sell tax-free smokes and gas on the rez, something some traditional tribal members and Bud Tunny supporters dislike. The intertribal conflict escalates when Bud—ironically of mixed-blood and Christian heritages—signs an agreement allowing New York State troopers jurisdiction over the reservation in order to maintain tribal purity. This complete relinquishment of tribal sovereignty leads to violent clashes, pitting friends and family against each other. According to John Purdy, in his essay "Rewriting Tradition in the Digital Era: The Vision of Eric Gansworth," Gansworth's symbolism in *Smoke Dancing* asks a fundamental question: "How does one negotiate change: the world of what was with the one of the moment?" (p. 154). One answer is seen in Mason's building a mega gas mart and smoke shop; with his earnings, Mason offers employment, health insurance, clean water, and a community center to all residents of the reservation, not just Tuscarora tribal members.

Throughout the novel, dance is apparent—the need and talent for it, its deeply rooted connection to culture. The older dancers make way for the younger, the future leaders of the tribe who will be thoughtful and inclusive. The book ends with one of these dancers saying, "Tradition is one thing, but tradition at the cost of the people is no tradition at all" (p. 234). Drumbeats and dance are at the heart of Gansworth's novel, overcoming the misguided anger and violence that threaten at every turn.

Gansworth's third novel, *Mending Skins* (2005), returns to the more peaceful reservation of *Indian Summers*. The novel spans the years 1957–2002, and Gansworth reintroduces some characters, especially Fred Howkowski, and builds complex relationships among familiar people from his other novels. Gansworth integrates his artwork into the text in a much more structured way: the novel begins with a collage of nine paintings called *Patchwork Life (1)*, each one related to later events. As Elizabeth Archuleta states in the *Kenyon Review*, "Each of the images that open the novel becomes a snapshot in time, representing love and loss, mourning and grief, and the ubiquitous Indian stereotype in Hollywood and material culture" (p. 171). The collage can also be seen as a nine-patch quilt, symbolic in the novel as a means of tearing apart the old and assembling something new, different, and stronger. The novel's structure reflects this emphasis on quilting and sewing; it is divided into three sections of three chapters each, surrounded by "Border" chapters. The "mending" of the book's title blends with section titles—all gerunds—that also refer to "Cutting Patterns," "Hiding Seams," and "Fraying Threads." Gansworth fabricates this family quilt, patterned with great love and deep sadness.

Once again, there are multiple narrators in this novel, including those of the two poignant "Border" chapters. The first "Border" narrator is Fred Howkowski's posthumous voice at his own grave that enumerates the people throwing dirt on his coffin. The second "Border" is a series of first-person accounts of a terrifying house fire caused by two brothers driving a car that literally flies into the house, bursts into flames, and ignites some propane tanks. (The details are based on the fire that destroyed Gansworth's own family home.)

The main character in *Mending Skins,* Shirley Mounter, is the thread that weaves together all the characters' lives. She is many things: a strong, independent woman; a wife with many children and a useless, often violent husband; a mother figure to the young Fred Howkowski; a mother to Annie Boans, her youngest child and a professor whose academic career focuses on Indian stereotypes and Fred's film career; a lover to Tommy Jack McMorsey, Fred's Vietnam War buddy who eventually raises Fred's son, T. J.; and a savior to Martha Boans, whose house is destroyed by the fire. Susan Bernardin, in "As Long as the Hair Shall Grow: Survivance in Eric Gansworth's Reservation Fictions," describes Shirley's wisdom as fixed in humor and resilience, radiating from the reservation, the center, the place everyone returns to eventually. Even Shirley returns, after years of living in Niagara Falls, when her reservation house is lost to the reservoir.

Through Annie Boans and T. J. McMorsey, Gansworth adds a different perspective in this novel—the academic study of American Indians. Annie is a serious academic, refuses to live on the reservation, and according to Bernardin, she is humorless. She is the polar opposite of her familial and gracious mother. T. J. McMorsey, an actor and professor of theater, returns to the reservation, looking for the connection to his father and his culture. He reminds Shirley not only of Fred—who eventually commits suicide in Hollywood—but also of his adoptive father, Tommy Jack, to whom Shirley was devoted. Their meetings were sporadic but their love was deep and true.

Odd circumstances bring together, separate, and bring together again the friendship between Shirley Mounter and Martha Boans. Shirley's husband sells their house to the Boanses, and this is the house eventually destroyed by fire. Annie marries Martha's son, cementing relations. After the fire, Martha must recuperate from her physical injuries, but the psychological scars heal only with Shirley's insistence on sewing and quilting. Shirley describes helping Martha mend by "reconstructing her life in the way only a woman who has lost nearly everything can" (p. 128). Gansworth's talent lies in stitching together these stories of on- and off-reservation life, deep love and even deeper grief, as well as tough female characters who survive despite everything. This work is fiction, but it is not a big leap to see Eric Gansworth's own mother and her strengths on these pages.

Gansworth's fourth novel, *Extra Indians* (2010), builds upon his previous novels, deepening parent-child relationships and divulging secrets. The novel reunites readers with Tommy Jack McMorsey and his adopted son, T. J. McMorsey, as well as Shirley Mounter and her daughter, Annie Boans. At the center of all their lives remains Fred Howkowski, the Hollywood "extra Indian" whose departure from the reservation ends not in film success but in a lonely and tragic suicide.

In his author's note, Gansworth explains that the inspiration for the novel is the true story of a Japanese tourist who came to North Dakota in 2001 to look for the buried ransom money from the movie *Fargo*. The woman believed the opening credits' statement that the film is a true story, and her search for movie money on the frozen prairie ended up killing her. Gansworth says, "This woman's experiences awoke in me a better understanding of where dreams become dangerous" (p. 313). The other part of the inspiration is embedded in readers' reactions to "The Ballad of Plastic Fred"—reprinted in his first novel *Indian Summers*. Fred Howkowski "kept showing up, a ghost wandering at the fringes" of Gansworth's work, and he decided to tell Fred's whole story in *Extra Indians* (p. 315).

With Fred the actor as the focal point, the novel's structure reflects moviemaking: "Prologue," "Act One: Lights," "Act Two: Camera," "Act Three: Action," and "Epilogue: Credits Roll." The chapter titles within each act also have film references—and again the narrators alternate between the characters, this time Tommy Jack and Annie. Uncharacteristically, the publisher's cover illustration for this novel is the first one that is not a Gansworth painting; inside the novel, however, are a series of plot-related paintings.

Gansworth reveals what dedicated readers already suspect: the two narrators, Tommy Jack and Annie, are father and daughter. The details of their relationship are disclosed through flashbacks framed around Tommy Jack: his service in Vietnam with Fred; his love affair with Shirley; his post-Shirley life with his wife and newly adopted son, T. J.; his role in Fred's life and death. For *Extra Indians*, Gansworth has chosen a white protagonist, Tommy Jack, a person whose race is remarkable only to Annie. As an American Indian academic whose specialty is American Indians in film, she is upset when she discovers that she is half-white and that her authenticity has been compromised. For Gansworth, Tommy Jack allows readers to understand white–American Indian relationships from a different perspective: he is friend, lover, and father—not a white friend, white lover, or white father. Annie brings race to the forefront.

The best parts of this novel surround Fred Howkowski. Gansworth does a fine job of balancing the real man with the soldier, the actor, and eventually the victim of suicide; the sections about Fred, or those in his own words, are poignant. He is missed by everyone. Fred's life has a typical trajectory for many Native men in the mid-1960s: he is drafted to serve in Vietnam, comes home a changed person, leaves the reservation in order to survive, and eventually succumbs to depression and suicide far from home. Throughout the novel, Tommy Jack describes meeting Fred and becoming fast friends in the jungles of Vietnam; Fred's stories of home and a photo he has of Shirley lead Tommy Jack to love her long before he ever meets her. Without Fred, Tommy Jack has no love, no son, and no true friend.

Gansworth also indulges his own familiarity with academic pursuits. Ever the scholar, Annie is driven to discover something groundbreaking about Fred, something that will benefit her career. When Annie and T. J. inquire more about Fred, as academic subject and father, respectively, Tommy Jack reveals truths about their friendship. He also offers artifacts Fred left behind in Hollywood: letters to T. J. and Tommy Jack, an eagle feather from a medicine man on the rez, and most interesting for Annie, a reel-to-reel tape of Fred's only speaking part in a film. Fred suffers in Hollywood—cast as the titular extra Indian, never becoming the star he had hoped to be. The tape of him speaking on camera is old and too degraded to hear: "He sounded as if he had somehow learned to breathe underwater and was speaking from there, a voice like air bubbles pop-

ping on the water's surface, maybe the voice of a drowning man, nonsense words, that desperation just before the last held breath leaves his lungs" (p. 256). Gansworth's strong statement here—grounded both in his role as professor and a longtime devotee of popular culture and movies—is about silence and the American Indian on film. Film vaults are filled with westerns, lead actors who are white men and women in redface—and in the shadows behind them, the silent, stoic Indian like Fred, mouth open but producing no sound for audiences to hear.

Tommy Jack's retelling of Fred's descent into madness is heartbreaking, interspersed with Fred's own dark visions and rambling statements that his friends cannot parse. Gansworth's best character is haunted by ghosts from home, from Vietnam, from the big screen. Fred kills himself after spiraling into a place of desperate filth and disillusionment. He has kept a notebook, and Tommy Jack gives Annie and T. J. a copy. For Tommy Jack, "that book suggested the possibility of missed responsibility, the possibility that one could have made a difference" (p. 289); the guilt he feels is palpable but misguided. No one could have saved Fred; in his mind, suicide was a means not only to stop the pain but to get Tommy Jack back to the rez to see Shirley. Even in death, Fred put other people first.

Gansworth's novel is a departure in some ways—there is less reservation and more time spent away from that home, that center of family and culture. Tommy Jack, remembering Fred, reminds readers of all the routes Fred had taken in his life—to safety in war, to Hollywood—but he "just could not find that path back home" (p. 141).

Gansworth's novel *If I Ever Get Out of Here* (2013) is of the "young adult" variety, and it is a delight. In it, Lewis Blake tells his own story about being a smart kid who lives in desperate poverty on the Tuscarora Reservation in western New York. He is the only Indian kid in the "brainiac classes" at his junior high, and he faces racial discrimination and constant bullying. The novel centers on an unexpected friendship between Lewis and George Haddonfield, a recently arrived Air Force brat who lives on the nearby base and loves music. He doesn't mind that Lewis is an Indian, let alone a smart one. They both love the Beatles and build their friendship around rock and roll.

The novel opens in 1975, a magical time when great rock music could save young kids—like Lewis, George, and Gansworth himself—from the likes of Donna Summer and the Bee Gees. Rock music is a mainstay in Gansworth's work, and here he writes about what he liked as a kid: the Beatles, Queen, Rush, and a post-Beatles Paul McCartney with his band Wings. *If I Ever Get Out of Here* is imbued with this music, from the title (a line from a Wings song), to the black-and-white illustrations based on album covers throughout the novel, to the importance music holds in Lewis' difficult life. Gansworth also includes a playlist and discography at the end of the book.

Gansworth faced a challenge in breaking into the young adult market, especially with a period piece set on an Indian reservation. In an interview on the *Crazy QuiltEdi* blog, Gansworth explains that "the most challenging thing was to strip away a lot of that tonal, interior detail and memory, in order to bring the plot to the forefront." He also discusses how the title, *If I Ever Get Out of Here*, refers to middle school but "also about the ways we, at that age, are so vulnerable and trapped by circumstance.… the 'Here' isn't just the physical setting of the school, but also that awkward stage between the formative years of childhood and the freedoms of charting our own courses as adults." This novel has been compared to Sherman Alexie's successful—and often banned—young adult novel, *The Absolutely True Diary of a Part-Time Indian* (2007). Both Alexie and Gansworth refrain from the "buckskin and feathers" genre, choosing to write about real Indian teenagers' experiences on real reservations. Thaddeus Andracki, in a review of *If I Ever Get Out of Here*, calls it "a more delicate exploration" of young male friendship than Alexie's book, and says that "kids with sensitive souls are most likely to flock to this compassionate tale." Debbie Reese (Nambe Pueblo), a librarian and scholar whose work and blog focuses on American Indians in

children's literature, claims that Gansworth's novel is "a rare but honest look at culture and how people from vastly different upbringings and identities can clash. And dance. And laugh."

Lewis Blake is a wonderful narrator. Gansworth creates a kid who is likable, funny, smart, and devoted to his family. Andracki states succinctly that "Lewis has a strong narrative voice in spite of his insecurities—he understands the limitations that have been placed upon him, and he's got gumption and intelligence to deal with them." The reader roots for Lewis from page one. Before the new school year starts, he cuts off his braid, hoping in vain to fit in better. However, the resultant military-style haircut his mom has to inflict on him may have allowed George to see an oddly kindred spirit. Lewis' older brother, Albert, a Vietnam veteran, adds to the underlying motif of military service in the novel. Lewis lives with his mom, who cleans white folks' houses, and he shares a room and record player with Albert. They own no car, and their house is nearly uninhabitable, especially in the winter when snowdrifts fill the kitchen. But Lewis has music for his escape, and once he meets George at school, he has an immediate friend. This is where Gansworth digs to the heart of the problem: poverty and race are two things Lewis cannot overcome, but with George's help, he can get through just about anything else.

George is a good friend to Lewis, introducing him to music—the Queen album *A Night at the Opera*, and a trip to Toronto for a Wings concert. He also shows him, with no malicious intent, how the other half lives. He has two upper-middle class parents who live together in a nice house. This is everything Lewis does not have. Poverty is central to Lewis' life, and he lies to George to prevent him from visiting by telling him that is mother is a spiritual healer who cannot have white people in the house. This lie, though funny, is desperate and heartbreaking. The notorious Blizzard of '77 near Buffalo hits the reservation, and to Lewis' horror, George and his dad must seek shelter there when the roads are impassable. Lewis knows that George will come to the house and "we would be proven to live in this scandalously broken place we'd always kept a secret from any white person we'd ever met" (p. 312). Gansworth makes this fear of discovery real through Lewis' despair and deceit. George and his dad are shocked at the conditions Lewis and his family live in, but they are compassionate and kind, picking up shovels to clear the kitchen.

Race is dealt with through important scenes of Lewis being bullied and harassed, not only by students but by teachers and administrators as well. Lewis is beaten up regularly. Alone, he tries to fend off an attacker from twice-daily thrashings and then follows anti-bullying protocol: he confides in teachers, the principal, and the guidance counselor for rez kids, but Lewis gets no relief. He says, "I'd been dumped off every day among the white people and forced to find my own way out, encountering indifferent teachers, isolation, and now active violence" (p. 207). Gansworth's biting commentary on race and intolerance in the education system is strong and honest thanks to Lewis' realistic attempts to save himself when no one else will. He eventually stops going to school, demanding personal safety. Later Lewis learns the bully is gone and that George and his father have had a hand in removing the menace from Lewis' life.

If I Ever Get Out of Here deals with the nuances of racial intolerance and violence. Gansworth uses the planetary cover art for the new Wings album *Venus and Mars* as a musical simile; Albert explains that Venus is like the white planet where George lives, and the red planet of Mars is like the rez. Lewis is not surprised that his best and truest friend saved him, but that his white friend saved his red hide. He says, "I wanted to try to navigate both planets, make choices within both worlds, not have to choose one to love and one to hate" (p. 311).

Friendship triumphs, but only for a while. Gansworth closes the novel with George moving when his dad gets new orders to report immediately to Texas. George explains that leaving is what they—Air Force kids—do; Lewis knows his situation—reservation kids—is the opposite: "*Never leaving is what we do. It's* our *way of life*" (p. 340).

ERIC GANSWORTH

POETRY

"*Nickel Eclipse: Iroquois Moon* is a concept album, inspired by my brother, Haudenosaunee history and culture, 'The Dark Side of the Moon,' 'The Wall,' the U.S. Mint, wampum, and probably a whole host of other influences" (p. 41). Christopher Teuton's 2005 interview with Eric Gansworth produced this description of the seemingly disparate things that inspired the poetry and illustrations for Gansworth's first poetry collection, published in 2000. However, readers of Gansworth's work will quickly recognize the harmony in the confluence of Pink Floyd's music and Haudenosaunee culture.

The paintings in *Nickel Eclipse: Iroquois Moon* that introduce each section are essential to the structure of the book. According to Gansworth's "Artist's Statement," the book merges "personal history and cultural history," and the poems are organized through a "parallel series of narrative paintings" that integrate Haudenosaunee history and their culture's lunar calendar (p. xiii). Gansworth superimposes the buffalo (Indian head) nickel onto the moon in his paintings, and as the book progresses, the eclipse in the title is revealed. He says, "the buffalo first obscures the Indian from view, and then, as occurs in all eclipses, it eventually passes, and allows the Indian to experience a resurgence" (p. xiii). Gansworth returns to his cultural collection of images, including wampum beads, strawberries, the Three Sisters; each accompanies the lunar coin and a Haudenosaunee month of the year. Images of wampum, for example, begin as only a few beads, with additional strands appearing, until there is infinite wampum; cultural images coincide with the eclipse, and, Gansworth says, "together, they represent the strengths and difficulties of the identity during each of the historical phases chronicled" (p. xiv).

Gansworth's poetry is personal, full of family and reservation friends, fire, alcoholism, and tragedy. His father appears in these poems, a figure largely missing from Gansworth's life and work. In "The Gifts of Our Fathers," the poet describes what he remembers most about his father: "the years of shit and yelling and drunken nights," and "pretending I recalled a time / he lived with us ..." (p. 46, 47). One of the strongest poems in *Nickel Eclipse: Iroquois Moon*—"On Meeting My Father in a Bar for the First Time"—recalls a time when someone points out Gansworth's father and asks if "that guy is anything" to him. The answer is moving and sad in its honest anger: "I shake my head / sipping and laughing / and turn my back / on the form I had stepped over / passed out in the doorway / reeking of piss and betrayal" (p. 116). The harshness of reservation life is painted in words throughout this collection—desperate living conditions, and the funerals of those who died too young and too drunk. In "Toronto, More or Less, in Fifteen Years," Gansworth describes a chance meeting with an Indian prostitute on a corner in Toronto, sharing nothing more than a moment together, enjoying memories of dark roads on the rez, "until the light changes, and we are / no longer red together" (p. 121). There is always hope in Gansworth's words, delicately balancing the tragedy surrounding him.

The section titled "The Cold Moon" revisits the house fire that destroyed his family home on the reservation. Later, Gansworth's grandparents appear in a complementary poem that closes the collection. "It Goes Something Like This" is the story of how his grandparents allegedly met on the New Jersey boardwalk on their way to the Carlisle Indian School. They meet and sing a Tuscarora Social song, but Gansworth questions the validity of this family anecdote. He realizes they probably met while emptying the headmaster's chamber pot at Carlisle, but he is satisfied with their version: "Sometimes the story is / enough to bring me home" (p. 185). Home and family, love and loss, are all at play here in *Nickel Eclipse: Iroquois Moon*. As the buffalo moves across the moon, the Indian resurges, hopeful.

In 2008 Gansworth published *A Half-Life of Cardio-Pulmonary Function: Poems and Paintings*. Like *Nickel Eclipse: Iroquois Moon*, this poetry collection relies heavily on corresponding words and visual images. Gansworth includes twelve paintings in the color of wampum (purple and white), including the cover, where his nieces portray the Three Sisters. Added to the

mix of word and image is Gansworth's connection to popular culture. His artist's statement, titled "Cross-PolliNation," states, "my relationships with popular culture and indigenous culture were living ones," and he includes recognizable companions in this collection: movies, Pink Floyd, and the Beatles, among others (p. xv). Christopher Teuton's review in the *Kenyon Review* sees Gansworth's use of word and image as reimagining indigenous tradition: "... the oral, written, and graphic juxtapose each other as they do in communities in which we live, shaped by wampum as well as American pop culture, the Three Sisters as well as our visual imagination" (p. 225).

As in much of his other work, Gansworth's attention to structure is resolute. He creates a schema by coupling the paintings with the poems to create a multilayered, multimedia dialogue with the reader. The structure in *A Half-Life of Cardio-Pulmonary Function* is complex. The title pumps and beats, and the sections of the book reflect that process: "Inspiration," "Beat," "Pause," "Beat," and "Expiration." In Oliver de la Paz's and John Lloyd Purdy's "Writing the Rez: Popular Obsessions in the Works of Eric Gansworth," these poems "have the strong and steady endurance of a heartbeat ... a tonal ebb and flow, matching the systole and diastole of a heartbeat" (p. 164). Medical images of lungs and hearts in the paintings reflect the book's biological and medical nature. In "Cross-PolliNation," he also explains the poetic connection to his degree in electroencephalography, the study of brainwaves: "there are complicated secrets in all of our unseen worlds ... people want to know the secrets of our dreams, to grasp the mechanisms of our endurance" (pp. xvi–xvii). Susan Bernardin's review of *A Half-Life of Cardio-Pulmonary Function* describes the complexity of Gansworth's title as a "fusion of physiological and emotional language [that] feeds the book's preoccupation with temporality and mortality" (p. 123). Christopher Teuton focuses on the concept of "half-life" as "that which decays, decreases, and is lost over time, and that which continues regardless" (p. 223).

The poems in this collection grow out of those notions of endurance and mortality, espe-cially as they pertain to loss and grief. Again, Gansworth revisits the house fire, but he also delves into the death of his oldest brother in 2000. The hurt and heartache are tempered on these pages by humor, which Gansworth sees as "the key to survival" (p. xviii). The eponymous first poem is a good example of Gansworth's poetic style. Christopher Teuton's review of the collection describes it as "a three-page sentence with tumbling enjambments" (p. 221). The breathless nature of this poem also combines humor and reservation angst in the poet's voice, as a teenaged boy who desires cologne but cannot afford it. He wanted to be "the Calvin Klein Man," not "the My Drafty House Is Warmed Badly / by Kerosene Heaters Man" (p. 3).

"The Rain, the Rez, and Other Things" is a six-part poem dealing with the death of his older brother. This death was very difficult for Gansworth, who was not living at home at the time, and was estranged from his brother by the geography of living off the reservation. Pop culture floods many of the poems, bringing to bear Gansworth's obsession yet again. The Land O' Lakes Indian butter girl makes an appearance, as do rock concerts and his favorite musicians. In "(Not) Born in the U.S.A."—a ten-part poem about Bruce Springsteen—the poet describes how the Boss and his music help reveal the physical and political distance between Gansworth and a friend. Gansworth also visits the Dakota, the apartment building where John Lennon was murdered. The Beatles' significance is not lost on the Gansworth faithful, and this pilgrimage is expected. He is disappointed not to see Yoko Ono, and in "Dakota (IV)," he is sad to find the Strawberry Fields memorial is "indeed a place / of absence" (p. 112).

The collection ends with a section called "Expiration," and a ten-part poem called "Learning to Speak," in which Gansworth returns to the basics—breathing, heart pumping, life. Memory is essential to this poem in its repetition of lines from his previous poems. He asks his reader to remember; the mechanism of endurance is inextricable from memory—people must remember and carry on. Survival depends on it.

From the Western Door to the Lower West Side (2010) is a collaboration with the social documentary photographer Milton Rogovin, who asked Gansworth to write poems to accompany a series of photos of American Indians in western New York; the photos were made both on the nearby Seneca reservations and in the urban setting of Buffalo. Rogovin's style of photography made the poet's task difficult; Rogovin never posed his subjects, allowing them to interact with their surroundings naturally. In turn, and out of respect, Gansworth's poetry had to "complement, but never interfere, never presume to speak for what was already so eloquently stated in the images themselves" (Introduction, p. 14). According to Jeanetta Calhoun Mish's review in *World Literature Today*, "The cultural baggage attached to social documentary alone is daunting; adding on the historical misrepresentation of Native peoples by non-Native photographers could be overwhelming, especially for a poet deeply engaged with his tribal identity."

The title of the book comes from the geographical position in Haudenosaunee culture of the Seneca Nation of Indians as "Keepers of the Western Door." Their role was to protect the western door of the Longhouse; "the lower west side" refers to the poverty-stricken Buffalo neighborhood where Rogovin photographed some of his subjects for forty years. Rogovin's black-and-white photographs are similar metaphorically to the Two Row wampum that guides Gansworth's work: the two rows of beads represent two canoes (Native and colonist), gliding side by side as equals, never interfering with each other. Gansworth states in his introduction that Milton Rogovin's images were "the antitheses of formal studio portraiture manipulation" (p. 14). They show men, women, children, and elders of the Seneca Nation pausing in their everyday duties: fixing cars, sitting on porches, taking part in Iroquois socials. They are not Edward Curtis' posed Indians, a disappearing race. And as Mish states, "because [Rogovin] returned to his subjects over the forty-year period, the collection, rather than presenting a static series of objectified images, has a narrative drive that suggests continuity and change."

This narrative led Gansworth to agree to the collaboration. Ekphrastic poetry can often be derivative, but Gansworth's decision not to speak for the photos' subjects helps make these poems richer. As Mish notes, Gansworth is especially successful when he interprets a chronological or thematic series. For example, in a series of three photos taken over several years, a young Seneca couple sits in their apartment; the walls in each photo are adorned with different Jimi Hendrix posters. Gansworth's accompanying poem, "While Hendrix Played a Solo: 'Burning of the Midnight Lamp,'" plays on Hendrix's "Purple Haze" and joins it with the Haudenosaunee wampum: "Jimi filled the night / with a haze so purple it rivaled / the wampum beads these two would know / as surely as their own names" (p. 72). Mish concludes her review by focusing on Gansworth's addition of "emotional depth and cultural information" to Rogovin's photographs, and calls this "a testament to the poet because the photographs are compelling objects in their own right."

NONFICTION

Eric Gansworth's obsession with Bigfoot made its way from the Tuscarora Reservation to Fouke, Arkansas, and now resides in *Breathing the Monster Alive* (2006). The book's front and back cover illustrations depict several moments from the book through Gansworth's color paintings (inside several are reproduced in black and white). These paintings are a departure from those in his other books; here, there are no Indian themes or symbols. Colors are primary, occasionally Day-Glo, and the subject is entirely Bigfoot. The nonfiction sections tell the story of how this book came to be and how Gansworth's fixation with Bigfoot started. When he was eight, he "saw" the low-budget movie *The Legend of Boggy Creek*—about a monster living in the woods outside Fouke, Arkansas; actually, he only saw the trailers on television and was so afraid that he was unable to watch the film. Yet this film stuck with him, and his obsession never waned; *Breathing the Monster Alive* is the interesting result.

Pop culture in the 1970s produced Bigfoot-mania though Roger Patterson's fuzzy forest film clip of Bigfoot, tabloid stories of encounters, and the movie from Fouke. Gansworth was simultaneously drawn into and scared by stories of this hairy monster. His reservation house abutted a deep wooded area, and Haudenosaunee culture is replete with supernatural beings. The convergence of popular and reservation culture fostered this long fascination with Bigfoot. Twenty years later, he watched the B movie, and it was as awful as he imagined—low quality, not scary, no suspense. In 2002 he traveled to Fouke, finding more Bigfoot tchotchkes than fear or danger. Despite these findings, he traveled there three more times, and on the last trip, he was shown the large unidentifiable skeletal remains of something, but that something was not Bigfoot. Gansworth recognizes the faith in mythology to which the folks in Fouke hold fast; the similarities to Native culture resonate in the book.

Breathing the Monster Alive deals with fear and the unknown in the book's poetry as well; Gansworth writes poems in the fictionalized persona of Fouke resident Jasper Applebee and states that Jasper's voice captures "the possibilities of other lives, other secrets, other places where someone has tried to shine a probing beam on a place where shadows and light take turns equally" (p. 4). Through poetic comparisons of Bigfoot to the Shroud of Turin and Noah's Ark, Gansworth's monster becomes a source of belief, of faith, just as valid as a religion—Christian or Native.

EDITORIAL WORK

The 2007 anthology *Sovereign Bones: New Native American Writing*—a companion to *Genocide of the Mind: New Native American Writing,* edited by MariJo Moore (Cherokee)—is the only editorial work Eric Gansworth has done to date. The focus, combining nonfiction and artwork, is on thirty writers and artists and their ongoing fight to help Native people retain their distinct identities. Gansworth has included some of the big names expected in such anthologies—Simon Ortiz (Acoma), Louise Erdrich, Sherman Alexie—and their offerings are good additions, especially Ortiz' fine discussion of indigenous language, being, and place. "From the Reservation to *Dawn of the Dead* to James Dickey and Back Again" is Gansworth's own personal essay about the six books he had in his reservation house as a child and how they helped shape him as a writer: "I, like many writers, am creating the novelization of a life, trying to remain as faithful to the narrative, but within the confines of a different medium" (p. 88). In her review of *Sovereign Bones*, Amy Ware states that despite some weaknesses in organization, "*Sovereign Bones* complements the artistic work of its contributors and testifies to the larger struggles that Native artists face in developing art that accurately and adequately distinguishes both its creator and her or his tribal nation" (p. 111).

PLAYS

Gansworth's play *Re-Creation Story* was selected to be part of the Public Theater's second annual Native Theater Festival and had a stage reading at the theater in New York City in November 2008. This multimedia play does something slightly dangerous on the surface: it retells the Haudenosaunee creation story of how Skywoman fell through a hole in the sky and was saved by animals and birds. Her arrival resulted in the creation of the North American continent on the back of a great turtle. Turning this story into a play might be seen as simply irreverent or, more possibly, offensive to some traditional Native people. In Tom Pearson's conversation with the playwright in the *Native Theater Festival Online Journal,* Gansworth addresses the questions, "Who has ownership of this story, and who can tell it, and under what circumstances?" The Haudenosaunee creation story has been previously transformed into visual art—by Gansworth himself—and has been retold in books. In a post-show discussion also published in the *Native Theater Festival Online Journal,* Gansworth stated that "pushing a story like this forward into a contemporary place is all about the survival of a culture."

One way that Gansworth moves this story forward is by showing how the creation story functions in his own life. To do this, he shares

various versions of this story through the eyes of his main character, Eric Gansworth, an insecure professor who stands at a podium tasked with telling the creation story to a college class. The creation story is at the center of the play, but whirling around the character of Gansworth is fear of failure, lack of confidence, and doubt. He knows he is not a storyteller, and he has been given three hours to fill with his retelling. The actual retelling of Skywoman's story takes up only a brief time; the rest of the play moves among academia, reservation culture, memory, and family. No matter how much he wishes to leave, however, Eric Gansworth remains center stage. He has backup, however, in the form of a PowerPoint that continuously runs behind his podium. On the screen is a mix of Gansworth's own paintings, pop culture references, and snarky comments meant to bring him back to his point; the electronic overlay helps balance the traditional and the contemporary.

Part of the creation story is the birth of the twins, whom Gansworth calls "the good mind" and "the bad mind": one embodies flowers and the day, the other thorns and night. This duality in the beginning of Haudenosaunee culture is mirrored throughout Gansworth's play; he struggles mightily with his task and his inability to tell the story the way he wants, moving from simply retelling the story of the beginning to an important personal ending in the death of his mother. In Gansworth's *Re-Creation Story*, creation is balanced—there is good and bad, life and death, storytelling jitters and successful conclusions.

The play *Patriot Act* had its first staged reading at the State University of New York at Oneonta in February 2011 with the Grammy Award–winning singer-songwriter Joanne Shenandoah (Oneida) as the lead actor. The play is set in Niagara Falls and is an exploration of identity and borders, both cultural and political. After the September 11 attacks, border crossing—something guaranteed for the Haudenosaunee by long-standing treaties—became more difficult.

In April 2011 a multimedia performance of *Home Fires and Reservation Roads* (which grew from a residency Gansworth received through a diversity grant) was staged at the State University of New York at Oneonta. According to Gansworth's summary on his website, this play—using monologue, actors, musicians, projections, animation, visual art, and photography—is "an autobiographical piece on the nature of generational and cultural memory … shaped around conflicted memories of a family homestead and the lives lived within its walls." The house fire that destroyed Gansworth's family home on the Tuscarora Reservation is central to this play.

Rabbit Dance, a one-act play commissioned by Ohio Northern University for its Ninth Annual International Play Festival, premiered in April 2011. The play, set at Niagara Falls State Park, involves a single encounter between two Haudenosaunee bead workers and two white teenagers from the city of Niagara Falls. On his website, Gansworth says, "the play explores issues of treaty rights, stereotypes, and generational domestic violence."

UNCOLLECTED WORKS

Eric Gansworth's uncollected short stories, poems, and nonfiction have been widely published. Short stories include "My Good Man" (*Boston Review*, 2005), "True Crime" (*Kenyon Review*, 2006), and "Amber" (*Short Story*, 2010); all focus on young American Indian characters dealing with difficult childhoods. His poetry has been published extensively in print magazines and online; some offerings include "'We Had Some Good Times Anyway'" (*Superstition Review*, 2010), "Summons" (*Kenyon Review*, 2010), and "Origin Story" (*Cream City Review*, 2014). In these poems, Gansworth revisits his relationship with this mother, as well as his own early detour into the science of electroencephalography. Gansworth's nonfiction often focuses on Native identity; selections include "Identification Pleas" (in *Genocide of the Mind*, 2003); "American Heritage" (in *Eating Fire, Tasting Blood*, 2006); "Thinking in Subversion" (*American Indian Quarterly*, 2006); "Passing Ports and Crossing Walks" (in *A Usable Past*, 2010); and "You, Too, Will Have This Printed Word (World) of Your Own" (in *Maurice Kenny: Celebrations of a Mohawk Writer*, 2011).

CONCLUSION

Even occasional readers of Eric Gansworth's prose or poetry and viewers of his paintings come to recognize certain places and themes in his work. The Tuscarora Reservation, western New York, the U.S.-Canadian border, Toronto—these places feel like home to Gansworth's audience. His prose, especially, is inviting; his fiction focuses on hardships—poverty, violence, and suicide—but it is always tempered by a firm belief in hope, endurance, and survival. Gansworth and his family are front and center, thinly disguised, their personal triumphs and tragedies set forth on the page. Gansworth's life is his work, and vice versa. His paintings—his first medium—are integrated beautifully into his prose and poetry. Even his plays involve these visual images. Most importantly, his work is connected—indisputably, consistently—with his Haudenosaunee culture. Gansworth writes about the difficulties of being an Onondaga on the Tuscarora Reservation, but the reliance on his culture for images, myths, metaphors, and strength is unquestioned. He is not a "buckskins and feathers" writer; his work is filled with the reality of Native people who often face seemingly insurmountable obstacles but overcome them, with their culture firmly set in their minds and hearts. Intertwined with his Indian culture is American popular culture; Gansworth's obsession with movies and music appears everywhere, creating cross-generational, cross-cultural layers. Gansworth's oeuvre has gifted us with Plastic Fred, Lewis and his snow-filled kitchen, Fiction Tunny and her dress of bruises, and dozens more memorable characters, whose stories are poignant, funny, and worth sharing.

Selected Bibliography

WORKS OF ERIC GANSWORTH

NOVELS

Indian Summers. East Lansing: Michigan State University Press, 1998.

Smoke Dancing. East Lansing: Michigan State University Press, 2004.

Mending Skins. Lincoln: University of Nebraska Press, 2005.

Extra Indians. Minneapolis: Milkweed, 2010.

If I Ever Get Out of Here. New York: Arthur A. Levine Books, 2013.

POETRY

Nickel Eclipse: Iroquois Moon. East Lansing: Michigan State University Press, 2000.

A Half-Life of Cardio-Pulmonary Function. Syracuse, N.Y.: Syracuse University Press, 2008.

From the Western Door to the Lower West Side. With Milton Rogovin. Buffalo, N.Y.: White Pine, 2010.

PLAYS

Re-Creation Story. Second Native Theater Festival, Public Theater, New York City, November 2008.

Patriot Act. Identity Play Series, State University of New York at Oneonta, February 2011.

Home Fires and Reservation Roads. Goodrich Theater, State University of New York at Oneonta, April 2011.

Rabbit Dance. Ninth Annual International Play Festival, Ohio Northern University, April 2011.

ANTHOLOGIES

"The Ballad of Plastic Fred." In *Growing Up Native American*. Edited by Patricia Riley. New York: Avon Books, 1993. Pp. 325–333.

"The Raleigh Man." In *Blue Dawn, Red Earth: New Native American Storytellers*. Edited by Clifford E. Trafzer. New York: Anchor Books, 1996. Pp. 197–206.

"Unfinished Business." In *Nothing but the Truth: An Anthology of Native American Literature*. Edited by John L. Purdy and James Ruppert. Upper Saddle River, N.J.: Prentice Hall, 2001. Pp. 240–249.

"Identification Pleas." In *Genocide of the Mind: New Native American Writing*. Edited by MariJo Moore. New York: Nation Books, 2003. Pp. 269–279.

"American Heritage." In *Eating Fire, Tasting Blood: An Anthology of the American Indian Holocaust*. Edited by MariJo Moore. New York: Thunder's Mouth Press, 2006. Pp. 267–277.

"Passing Ports and Crossing Walks." In *A Usable Past: Tradition in Native American Arts and Literature*. Edited by Simone Pellerin. Bordeaux, France: Presses Universitaires de Bordeaux, 2010. Pp. 137–145.

"You, Too, Will Have This Printed Word (World) of Your Own." In *Maurice Kenny: Celebrations of a Mohawk Writer*. Edited by Penelope Myrtle Kelsey. Albany: State University of New York Press, 2011. Pp. 7–13.

SHORT STORIES

"My Good Man." *Boston Review* 30, no. 1:41–43 (2005). http://www.bostonreview.net/gansworth-my-good-man

"True Crime." *Kenyon Review* 28, no. 4:80–91 (2006).

"Amber." *Short Story* 18, no. 1:10–22 (2010).

UNCOLLECTED POEMS

"'We Had Some Good Times Anyway.'" *Superstition Review: An Online Literary Magazine*, 2010.

"Summons." *Kenyon Review*, 32, no. 1:67–68 (2010).

"Origin Story." *Cream City Review* 38, no. 1:54–56 (2014).

NONFICTION

Breathing the Monster Alive. Treadwell, N.Y.: Bright Hill, 2006. (Nonfiction/poetry.)

"Finding a Voice from Home: Louise Erdrich's *Love Medicine*." *Conversations on Jesuit Higher Education* 30, article 25:33–34 (2006). http://epublications.marquette.edu/cgi/viewcontent.cgi?article=1210&context=conversations

"Thinking in Subversion." *American Indian Quarterly* 30, nos. 1–2:153–165 (2006).

AS EDITOR

Sovereign Bones: New Native American Writing. New York: Nation Books, 2007.

CRITICAL AND BIOGRAPHICAL STUDIES

Archuleta, Elizabeth. "Survival, Transformation, and Renewal in *Mending Skins*." *Kenyon Review* 32, no. 1:170–174 (winter 2011).

Bernardin, Susan. "As Long as the Hair Shall Grow: Survivance in Eric Gansworth's Reservation Fictions." In *Survivance: Narratives of Native Presence*. Edited by Gerald Vizenor. Lincoln: University of Nebraska Press, 2008. Pp. 123–145.

De la Paz, Oliver, and John Lloyd Purdy. "Writing the Rez: Popular Obsessions in the Works of Eric Gansworth." In *American Indians and Popular Culture*. Vol. 2, *Literature, Arts, and Resistance*. Edited by Elizabeth DeLaney Hoffman. Santa Barbara, Calif.: Praeger, 2012. Pp. 155–172.

"Eric Gansworth." Amerinda Inc. http://amerinda.org/newsletter/5-3/eric.html

Eric Gansworth website. http://www.ericgansworth.com/

Purdy, John Lloyd. "Rewriting Tradition in the Digital Era: The Vision of Eric Gansworth." In *A Usable Past: Tradition in Native American Arts and Literature*. Edited by Simone Pellerin. Bordeaux, France: Presses Universitaires de Bordeaux, 2010. Pp. 147–159.

Weagel, Deborah. "Image as Text, Text as Image: Quilts and Quiltmaking in Eric Gansworth's *Mending Skins*." *Studies in American Indian Literatures* 23, no. 1:70–95 (2011).

REVIEWS

Andracki, Thaddeus. Review of *If I Ever Get Out of Here*. *Bulletin of the Center for Children's Books* 67, no. 1:19 (2013).

Bernardin, Susan. Review of *A Half-Life of Cardio-Pulmonary Function*. *Studies in American Indian Literatures* 22, no.1:121–125 (2010).

Mish, Jeanetta Calhoun. Review of *From the Western Door to the Lower West Side*. *World Literature Today* 84, no. 3:75 (2010).

Reese, Debbie. "What I Like About Eric Gansworth's *If I Ever Get Out of Here*." American Indians in Children's Literature blog, May 29, 2013. http://americanindiansinchildrensliterature.blogspot.com/2013/05/what-i-like-about-eric-gansworths-if-i.html

Teuton, Christopher B. "Embodying Life in Art." *Kenyon Review* 32, no. 1:218–225 (2010). (Review of *A Half-Life of Cardio-Pulmonary Function*.)

Ware, Amy. Review of *Sovereign Bones*. *Studies in American Indian Literatures* 20, no. 4:108–111 (2008).

INTERVIEWS

De la Paz, Oliver, and John Lloyd Purdy. "Border Crossings: An Interview with Eric Gansworth." In *A Usable Past: Tradition in Native American Arts and Literature*. Edited by Simone Pellerin. Bordeaux, France: Presses Universitaires de Bordeaux, 2010. Pp. 162–176.

"Male Monday: Eric Gansworth." *Crazy QuiltEdi*, November 11, 2013. https://campbele.wordpress.com/2013/11/11/male-monday-eric-gansworth/

Pearson, Tom. "A Conversation with Playwright Eric Gansworth." *Online Journal of the Public Theater's Native Theater Festival*, January 26, 2009. http://thenativetheaterfestival.blogspot.com/2009/01/conversation-with-playwright-eric.html

Pohl, R. D. "Native Son." *Buffalo Spree*, December 2005. http://www.buffalospree.com/buffalospreemagazine/archives/2005_12/1205nativeson.html

"Q&A with Eric Gansworth." *Many Voices, One Center*, Native American Literature Symposium blog, September 15, 2011. http://nativelit.wordpress.com/2011/09/15/qa-with-eric-gansworth/

"*Re-Creation Story*: Post-Show Discussion Transcription." *Online Journal of the Public Theater's Native Theater Festival*, January 26, 2009. http://thenativetheaterfestival.blogspot.com/2008/12/re-creation-story-post-show-discussion.html

Teuton, Christopher B. "A Conversation with Eric Gansworth." *Cold Mountain Review* 34, no. 1:31–44 (2005).

ALLEGRA GOODMAN

(1967—)

Sanford Pinsker

ALLEGRA GOODMAN IS the very definition of a precocious writer. The winner of various scholastic writing contests when she was a student at Punahou School in Honolulu (the same elite prep school that Barack Obama attended), she published a story in a prestigious national magazine when she was a freshman at Harvard. She then went on to publish a collection of her short stories before she graduated. She has been a steady and impressive writer ever since.

Allegra Goodman was born in Brooklyn, New York, on July 5, 1967, to Lenn and Madeleine Goodman. When she was two, the family moved to Hawaii, where her father was a professor of philosophy at the University of Hawaii and her mother a geneticist who eventually became head of the university's women's studies program.

These facts are important to the way Goodman's career developed. Had her parents remained in Brooklyn, she would have had a childhood similar to dozens and dozens of other Jewish American writers. Given her prodigious talent, there is little doubt that Goodman would have succeeded as a writer, but because place is so central to her work, growing up in Brooklyn would have produced quite different fiction.

In certain sections of Brooklyn, it is possible to grow up "Jewish" and to feel that one is part of the majority. One's teachers are, in large part, Jewish, one's friends are Jewish, and most of all, one's immediate environs seem "Jewish." That was not true of Goodman's childhood in Hawaii, where Jews were a distinct minority in a polyglot culture and where exoticism took on whole new meanings. In much the same way that a generation of Jewish American immigrants were strangers in strange land, who subsequently went on to tell the story of how they assimilated to, and

were successful in, America, Goodman was a semi-outsider in Hawaii. But with this important difference: Goodman saw Jewishness from the inside out rather than from the outside in. Her Jewish characters have their foibles (how could they not?) but are bathed in a gentle satire that is never mean-spirited. Goodman is too entwined with other Jews for that.

As a child of academics, Goodman was surrounded by books and sophisticated ideas. She first read Jane Austen's *Pride and Prejudice* when she was nine years old, and while she was hardly a trained reader, what she remembers about the experience is instructive. Writing in the pages of *American Scholar* in 2004, Goodman put it this way:

> There was a good deal in the book I was too young to understand. I skipped over hard words and long epistolary passages. Nuances of character and the delicate mechanics of plot were lost on me. Like a water insect I skated the surface of the text, scarcely dimpling the rippling current underneath. But I do remember laughing as I read. "Come here, child," Mr. Bennet tells Elizabeth, after her mother orders her to reconsider the odiously officious Mr. Collins. "An unhappy alternative is before you.... From this day you must be a stranger to one of your parents. Your mother will never see you again if you do not marry Mr. Collins, and I will never see you again if you do." I understood that wry proposition perfectly. If nothing else, Austen's buoyant wit came through.
>
> (p. 142)

Goodman goes on to explain that subsequent readings of *Pride and Prejudice*—when she was in high school and, later, in college—gave Austen's technical skill and enormous subtlety its due, but while these elements can be taught, an instinctive appreciation for Austen's delicious wit is another matter altogether. What Goodman recognized, as she read *Pride and Prejudice* for

the first time in the small women's studies library at the University of Hawaii, is this: life is filled with moments best understood through a certain sense of humor.

Goodman was not only a precocious reader, she was also a precocious writer. Best of all, she had an eye for the small, disarming detail that could make a character squirm. In other hands, this talent might have taken a sour turn, as it often does when oppositional characters are little more than punching bags. Goodman's stories avoid this trap and, instead, show us how Austen's social satire can be applied to the contemporary world.

TOTAL IMMERSION

Goodman's first collection, *Total Immersion* (1989), contains "Variant Text," a story she wrote during the summer following her graduation from high school. She sent the tale to *Commentary* magazine, which at that time was as influential as it was selective. There was scant space for fiction, but the editors felt an obligation to showcase certain very talented Jewish American writers. Allegra Goodman was one of them. The collection was reprinted in 1998 with some minor textual revisions and shifting around of some of Goodman's stories.

"Variant Text" does not look or feel as if it were written by somebody who had yet to attend a college class. Here is a sample paragraph from its opening section:

> Beatrix has been exhausting herself. She is in London for the topology conference. As soon as she comes back Sunday, she will have to prepare her paper for Majorca. These conferences are always a strain and raise numerous logistical problems. Beatrix's parents, living upstairs, would seem the logical choice for baby-sitting, but they are really no longer able to control the kids—especially now that Adam can walk. Aunt Clare is out of the question.
>
> (*Total Immersion*, 1989, p. 65)

The tale of academics precariously balancing teaching schedules and children is not what eighteen-year-olds normally write about. Rather,

they are more likely to write (usually predictable) stories about a painful coming-of-age, or how it was the day their parents divorced. Goodman not only concentrates on an adult world but she does so in ways that balance social satire with strains of empathy. The eleven stories collected in *Total Immersion* reveal a writer able to leapfrog over predictable postures (anger, exasperation, and perhaps most of all, smug self-righteousness) toward a compassion wise beyond her years.

Theodore Solotaroff, the influential editor at Harper & Row who shepherded Goodman's first stories into print, played a major role in expanding the parameters of contemporary Jewish American fiction. Goodman fit the bill because whether her stories were set in Hawaii, England, or the United States, they reflect what Solotaroff meant in 1988 when he talked about an "uncanny replication of the precarious, unstable, hemmed-in, contentious, revered conditions of the Diaspora that have all but disappeared in America" (p. 1). Perhaps this telling comment from "Oral History," a story in which a troubled young graduate student tries desperately to prod her research subject into saying the fashionable, politically correct things she wants to record, will explain Solotaroff's decision:

> "When I speak of oppression [the young interviewer explains] here's what I mean. As a member of the European rising bourgeoisie, and as a woman, did you feel that your ambition was stifled in Vienna?"
>
> "I was a *little girl*," Rose protests. "This was before the first war, you remember. Don't make me out a *completely* desiccated old fool. Besides, we were Jewish. That's why we came here."
>
> "So, you were really part of the Jewish intellectual elite. Is that a good description of the family?"
>
> "I had six brothers," Rose says thoughtfully. "Some were smart, some weren't."
>
> (pp. 3–4)

Or this description, from "Variant Text," of a progressive Orthodox day school in England:

> There is no jungle gym or slide or swing set. Instead, an enormous complex of smooth wood has been built in the shape of an amino-acid chain. All

the classroom furniture is made of natural woods and fibers. There are seven computer terminals, with full color capability and joysticks. The art center is decorated with laminated Chagall posters. It is here Adam fingerpaints, listens to Bible stories, plants pumpkin seeds, and during naptime learns deep relaxation on the futon rolled up in his cubbyhole. In the junior school Attalia will soon be sitting in a circle of tiny chairs for Good/Bad Talk. On the blackboard Ms. Nemirov has printed today's question:

Hashem [God] or Darwin?

YOU

Decide

(pp. 70–71)

Some would argue that a "progressive Orthodox school" is an oxymoron; others will insist that science and religion can and do coexist, but Goodman's point is less theological than it is a satiric poke at an all-too-earnest childhood education. "YOU decide" is an empty choice, one as hokey as the education the children have thus far received.

Still, Goodman's tone is not as harsh to the well-meaning as it might have been. A young Philip Roth, in "The Conversion of the Jews," for example, knew how to give synagogue Hebrew schools the drubbing he felt they deserved. And much the same things are true in terms of the elderly. In his twenties (this changed when he grew older), Roth knew how to exasperate his elders; by contrast, Goodman's elderly protagonists can more than hold their own, especially when pitted against the politically correct. In "Oral History," an effort to give the past an appropriately Marxist-feminist configuration takes surprising turns. Alma Renquist, perennial graduate student and ambivalently dutiful daughter, may imagine that she is the interviewer, and that Rose Markowitz, one of life's heartier, more intriguing survivors, is her "subject," but Goodman's story suggests otherwise. Despite the enormous differences in ethnic background, education, and not least of all, age, Alma and Rose are at bottom secret sharers. Their respective stories intertwine until Rose not only becomes the "asker," but also the impetus that

forces Alma to see the hollowness of her fashionable academic talk. As Rose talks about her family's objections to a man she was "sweet on" in her youth, she notices a change in Alma:

"But you look terrible! What is it, dear? You haven't said a word. What was that?"

"Nothing," Alma whispers. "My boyfriend left...."

Rose considers Alma's case a moment. "Well," she concludes, "if he was Jewish, it was a good thing you parted. If you had married, it would have broken his mother's heart! Anyway, they all thought he was no good. It turned out they were right, too. So I had to come back home. Can you imagine? Don't cry, dear. It was only my first marriage. It was very sad, but you know, somehow I lived through it! Don't feel bad."

(pp. 24–25)

That Rose conflates past and present or confuses Alma's scenario with aspects of her own is true enough, but Goodman's point may be that the language of "story" is superior to psychobabble. It also suggests something about the satiric directions that social realism can take in an age that often threatens to replace "character" with category, the conflicted heart with the jargon-filled head.

The indomitable matriarch Rose Markowitz will make a future appearance in Goodman's fiction when a slightly revised "Oral History" becomes the opening story of *The Family Markowitz* (1996), Goodman's continuing portrait of Rose's vivid, altogether memorable clan. When J. D. Salinger chronicled the cerebral/mystical adventures of his Glass family, he paid scant attention to the dictates of realism; by contrast, Goodman's Markowitz family is as recognizable as those assembled around a Thanksgiving dinner table—*anybody*'s Thanksgiving dinner table. There are plenty of bruised feelings to pass around, along with apologies and forgiveness. There is a certain amount of bright talk (the Markowitz clan contains more than its fair share of academics) and Jewish references, but, at bottom, these people manage to strike a balance between the particular and the universal.

In "Wish List," Goodman dramatizes yet another permutation of the conflict between the

abstract and the concrete. This time, her satiric target is the prestigious Wantage Centre, an Oxford University think tank specializing in Middle Eastern thought. To its cushy surroundings and ultra-airy thought comes Edward Markowitz, one of Rose's two sons and a Georgetown expert on terrorism. He is hard at work on a projected book titled *Terrorism: A Civilized Creed*, well aware that many—including the institute director—might regard the title as "provocative," but also that it's meant to be provocative:

> Terrorism must be understood as part of an ethical code. To study terrorism with any dispassion, we have to begin from the understanding that it is a logical, rational, and ethically valid form of action. The real issue in the Middle East is cultural absolutism—something we must recognize in ourselves as well as in Arab nations.
>
> (p. 97)

Not surprisingly, Professor Markowitz's quest for dispassionate study takes theoretical turns that leave the human side of terrorism far behind. Goodman insists that "life" trumps theory every time, and so when he delivers his highbrow talk to the center's distinguished visitors, as well as to a "tour group of seniors from Temple Beth Shalom in Cleveland," the result is a study in mixed communication as befuddled as Markowitz could set into motion. Ed begins his lecture:

> "One man's terrorist is another man's freedom fighter." He looks up mildly at his audience. Suddenly Tiki Sofer stands up.
>
> "I object!" she screams.
>
> Ed sighs. "I assumed," he says, "that I wouldn't have to delve into relativist methodology. All right, let's backtrack. Let's take a look at what cultural relativism means. When a man—"
>
> "I object," Tiki repeats, still standing. "I object to you using the male noun."
>
> "Oh, I see," says Ed, relieved. "Thank you. I was afraid we were going to have to deal with some epistemological stuff here. Well, there you go. All right, once more, with feeling. One person's terrorist is another person's freedom fighter."
>
> (p. 117)

"Wish List" deftly—and satirically—captures what happens when academic discourse is strangled by political correctness. Tiki Sofer is a caricature who insists that all nouns be gender neutral, and Professor Markowitz is so committed to cultural relativism that he sees a forest without specific trees. What both of them badly miss—and what the Wantage Centre overlooks in its desperate effort to stay afloat as a swank watering hole for erudite academics—is that terrorists deal in death rather than abstractions. Death, as it were, period.

This horrific truth is what Professor Markowitz finally discovers when he finds himself in the middle of a telephone interview with a reporter from National Public Radio:

> "Hello, Professor Markowitz? This is Peter Henkey from NPR in Washington. We've been discussing tonight's hijacking with several specialists, and we would like to ask you for your insights...."
>
> Ed shakes himself. "Perhaps the most important motive for a Shiite terrorist is his belief in the rise of Islam through jihad. This term is commonly mistranslated as 'holy war,' but the actual meaning of the Arabic word is 'moral struggle.' As for the mind of the guerilla fighter, I would like to stress that terrorist tactics are justified for him by his extreme dedication to communal mores.... We must take a closer look at what terrorism means on a deeper level than the ideological—the human level, if you will...."
>
> "Three killed in the last hour," the announcer recaps for the radio audience.
>
> "It's unspeakable," Ed whispers.
>
> (pp. 118–119)

The title story of Goodman's first collection is a study of "conversion," or more accurately, conversions. Barbara Ruth Bloom marries a Sikh and converts. Later, the marriage over, she seeks out Rabbi Siegel for lessons in Judaism and yet another conversion:

> Now she wanted to learn. So she studied for conversion with Rabbi Siegel. He was incredible. He said that she didn't need conversion, so they called it a confirmation ceremony, and since we don't have a *mikveh* here, she immersed herself out in the waves at Sandy Beach.
>
> (p. 243)

"Immersion" acts as a charged word here, not only in the story itself but also in the collection as a whole. For whether Goodman's protagonists find themselves amid the dizzying pluralism of Hawaii or in an England where Orthodoxy exists in an uneasy tension with Anglophilism, the prospects of being swamped—or a total immersion into the unfamiliar—always looms as a possibility. Small wonder, then, that *Total Immersion* ends on an ironic note, as a struggling French teacher ponders the prospect of her students doing much more poorly than those of a fellow teacher, only to discover that one of her pupils has won third place on a National Council of French Teachers exam:

> Sandra bounds into her next class. Smiling joyously, she passes back the heavily corrected midterms. She wants to congratulate the third-place national champion in front of all the students, but Ginnie is absent. Sandra contents herself with trying to encourage her depressed class. "Improvement counts," she reminds them. "You can redeem yourselves on the final."
>
> (pp. 253–254)

Goodman chooses her words with care, and there is reason to believe that "redeem" is no exception—as a term not only appropriate to the circumstances of "total immersion" but also to redemption itself. For redemption, in all of Goodman's permutations—the satiric as well as the sympathetic, the ironic and the reverential—is what *Total Immersion* is about.

Total Immersion was published in June 1989, the same time that Goodman graduated magna cum laude from Harvard. (Goodman would release a revised version of the book in 1998, replacing "Oral History" and one other story with two newer ones that had been published in the *New Yorker*, "Onionskin" and "The Closet.") With the exception of some carping remarks in the pages of the *New York Times Book Review* by Randi Hacker, who felt that Goodman's characters "express themselves far too academically to elicit much sympathy," most reviewers followed the lead of Elaine Kendall of the *Los Angeles Times,* who called Goodman's collection "an astonishing display of virtuosity," and *Newsday* reviewer Francine Prose, who made it clear that

Goodman "has observed as deeply as many writers can hope to do in a lifetime." Goodman was showered with praise from the Jewish press as well as from mainstream newspapers and magazines. To the serious literary world, a star had been born.

THE FAMILY MARKOWITZ

The Family Markowitz (1996) is dedicated to "David" [Karger], a math major and Goodman's beau during their undergraduate years at Harvard. They were married shortly after graduation and spent a year in England as David Karger studied advanced mathematics as a Churchill Fellow at Cambridge. Following this stint abroad, both Goodman and Karger enrolled in graduate programs at Stanford. While there, Goodman continued to weave charming tales of the Markowitzes into a book.

Family sagas give writers a chance to explore generational similarities and differences, the force of tradition or the lack thereof, and perhaps most important of all, how the arc of history affects a representative family. Each member of the Markowitz family constitutes a response to assimilation, to freedom, and to the possibility of possibilities.

The Family Markowitz is longer on small nuances than it is on large explosions of plot. Little happens as one story interweaves with another, although a sense of the family and its widely diverting tributaries does emerge. Perhaps no single story exhibits the full range of the family's attitudes toward Judaism and Jewish life, assimilation and sexual independence, better than "The Wedding of Henry Markowitz."

Henry Markowitz is defined by his passions and his assorted stuff:

> Henry sits at the oval claw-foot table, expandable to seat twelve—his find at a Wantage estate sale, a jewel of Victoriana, refinished down to its griffin feet. It's big but it's the table he always wanted, and that's why he bought it. He simply hired piano movers. The flat is full of his discoveries, his rare books, and his antique decanters. There is a special case for his maps, his charts of the heavens. He designed it and had it built by a cabinetmaker.

Everything fits; the colors are warm library hues, deep green and cinnabar.

(p. 72)

Henry is certainly fussy, and there are more than a few suggestions that he might be homosexual— all of which puts quotation marks around his "wedding." Henry's mother, Rose, his younger brother, Ed, and Ed's wife, Sarah, have flown from America to attend this wedding in Britain. Ed, the terrorism expert, makes no bones about how difficult it was to alter his overextended schedule, and his mother is concerned that the bride-to-be is a non-Jew and (gasp!) there might be a priest at the wedding ceremony.

The brothers Markowitz are so divergent, so incompatible, that in another place and time they might have populated a novel by Fyodor Dostoyevsky. Henry has long ago abandoned the vulgarities of America, both in its academic institutions and its general cultural landscape, for a life of representing Laura Ashley by day and poring over his requisite treasures (ancient maps, old books, etc.) by night. As Ed puts it with barely disguised exasperation: "I walk into his apartment and he's still doing *Brideshead Revisited,* with those brocades and those clocks! Those rotting leather bindings. His eighteenth-century *peklach* " (p. 78).

"Small bundles" is the translation of the Yiddish word *peklach,* and Ed uses the term to suggest just how reduced in size and importance Henry's prized possessions actually are. Yiddish is a salty language and perfect for pulling down vanities. It is also a way to measure the cultural distance between the two brothers.

Henry returns the favor by counting the ways that England is superior to America in ways both big and small. Consider, for example, what Henry observes about the place cards for his wedding dinner:

> "What do you think of these?" he asks, holding up the place cards. "We had the calligrapher who did the addresses for the invitations. The printing was a nightmare, of course. There are scarcely any engravers left. Would you believe invitations these days are nearly all done thermally? Run your finger over the verso and you can feel the difference."

(p. 73)

Even though everything about Henry's overly refined taste suggests that he is gay (or at least leaning in that direction), and even though the family "knows" (how could it not?), Henry's sexuality remains shrouded in secrecy and silence.

Granted, Henry's choice of a bride—an administrator at Oxford—may complicate the long-held family arithmetic, but since husband and wife share the same passion for old books and interior decoration, what was once regarded as an unlikely match indeed looks as if it were made in heaven. Moreover, Henry is genuinely happy—and eventually so is the rest of the Markowitz family, for bickering is one thing and reconciliation is another:

> Henry carries Rose's piece [of wedding cake] out for her himself, along with some strawberries. "Thank you, dear," she says.
>
> "Thank you for coming," he tells her, and his voice shakes.

(p. 99)

The final story in the collection, "One Down," also narrates a Markowitz wedding, but with twists that sharply differentiate it from Henry's nuptials. In Henry's case, marrying outside the faith was an issue (especially for Rose). In *One Down,* however, it is the wedding couple's shared Orthodoxy that becomes an issue.

As plans for a wedding uniting Jonathan Schwartz and Ed's daughter Miriam proceed, Ed, the terrorism expert and staunch liberal, is defined by his obsession with the Middle East. So it takes only what he considers to be a stupid, ill-considered letter to the *New York Times* to set him off:

> "Sarah," Ed calls from the living room, "listen to this. 'The Palestinian will hate Israel no matter what Israel does. Give land for peace and you will give up all the security Israel has won in previous wars. A Palestinian state will be a launching pad and a suicide, mandated by America, which I compare to Dr. Kevorkian helping the patient go under to put him out of his misery.'"

(p. 236)

The author of this diatribe is none other than Zaev Schwartz, the father of the groom.

Nor do Ed's wedding troubles end there, for "Miriam and Jon in their young-blood traditionalism are having an Orthodox wedding with *glatt* kosher food, a very young and baleful Orthodox rabbi, and separate dancing circles for men and women" (p. 240). For Ed, a father-daughter dance is part—indeed, a traditional part—of a Jewish wedding, and now that moment has been trumped by Miriam's newly discovered Orthodoxy.

Goodman understands, as perhaps only a writer can, the ways that exasperation can wear many faces; she also knows how to fashion characters from flesh and blood rather than from cardboard. She finds the familiar in the strange and the strange in the familiar. This applies equally to Zaev's politics and Miriam's Orthodoxy.

Ed and Zaev are never going to agree about policies in the Middle East (although each tries to worm in a strident opinion during their respective wedding toasts). What they agree about, however, is their disdain for Orthodoxy.

As it turns out, Ed does, in fact, get his wedding dance with Miriam, and the in-laws manage to get through a rehearsal dinner and a wedding without *too* many fireworks. Goodman's weddings end in complicated gestures of reconciliation and even of love. They are, in short, quite unlike the satiric, no-holds-barred nuptials in Philip Roth's *Goodbye, Columbus*.

Goodman's Jewishness was often puzzling to reviewers and critics, coming as it did at a time when the most notable Jewish American writers of the time (Roth, Saul Bellow, Bernard Malamud, etc.) made much of the fact that they were primarily American writers. As Gloria Cronin points out in an article contained in *Daughters of Valor: Contemporary Jewish American Women Writers*:

> Goodman, unlike many American Jewish writers, willingly accepts the label *Jewish American writer* and indicates that she resides somewhere between a Conservative and Orthodox viewpoint. She writes out of the richness of historical Jewishness, her community, and her literary, scriptural, and Jewish theological traditions. Her work resonates with psalms and liturgical phrases, Jewish family relationships and a general Jewish presence.
>
> (p. 248)

Cronin accurately ticks off the layers of allusion and meaning that give *The Family Markowitz* both its charm and substance.

KAATERSKILL FALLS

Set in the mid-1970s, *Kaaterskill Falls* (1998), Goodman's first novel, is as much about place as it is about people. In this sense, Kaaterskill Falls is a character, one that represents freedom from New York City's oppressive heat and crowded apartments. Kaaterskill Falls is one of the bungalow cottage communities in the Catskill Mountains to which urban Jews flee as soon as they are financially able to do so. They return, summer after summer, wives and children for the entire week, with husbands largely confined to weekend visits. What abides in such a world is Jewish law and the naturalistic setting of Kaaterskill Falls. It is the latter, the natural landscape as not experienced in New York City, that gives Goodman's novel its special dimension:

> Carefully … the girls climb down the long dirt path into the gorge. They climb all the way down from the park to where the falls pour louder and louder into great pools of rippling water, green and brown. The rock pools are cool under the waterfall. Elizabeth and Chani and Ruchel take off their shoes and socks and stand in the shallowest water, smooth mossy pebbles stroking the soles of their bare feet.
>
> (p. 69)

But for all its similarities to other Catskill colonies, the one formed at Kaaterskill Falls is unique: it is populated by ultra-Orthodox (not Hasidic) Jews who follow the teachings of the ultra-strict Rav Elijah Kirshner. As the present writer pointed out when Goodman's novel first appeared ("Kosher Delights," 1998), religiously observant Jews played a role (of sorts) in Jewish American fiction long before Allegra Goodman published *Total Immersion* and *The Family Markowitz*. But for her, observant Jews were not automatically relegated to the sidelines or turned into condescending jokes as in the bulk of Jewish American fiction from Abraham Cahan's *The Rise of David Levinsky* (1918) onward; rather, she brought to neo-Orthodox Jewish life both an

insider's sensibility and a writerly understanding of how to construct literary characters.

Kaaterskill Falls not only continues this beat but also expands it by re-creating the world of upstate New York bungalow colonies during the seventies. For those who associate the Catskills with Borscht Belt cutups and secular, increasingly assimilated Jews, Goodman's tale of the clash between Yankee year-rounders and ultra-Orthodox summer people, known as the Kirshners, plunges readers into a world where flesh-and-blood Jewish characters can have deeply held religious convictions as well as vulnerable human dimensions. (As Lene Schøtt-Khristensen explains, "The Kirshners, whose beliefs are probably based on the 19th century teachings of the real Samson Raphael Hirsch, escaped from Germany to America just before Kristallnacht" [p. 27].) The result is a novel that, however quiet, however subtly understated, is filled with ambition. Not only does Goodman include a wide array of characters (Jewish and non-Jewish alike) and their respective motivations, but, equally impressive, she creates a world that gives the natural wonder of Kaaterskill Falls its full due. In short, occasions to admire the shape and ring of Goodman's sentences abound.

But what will strike most readers is the way Goodman's novel makes the neo-Orthodox look simultaneously exotic and familiar. With the possible exceptions of Chaim Potok and Nessa Rapoport, it is hard to think of a single Jewish American novelist who sets scene after scene in a synagogue or who can describe the religious sensibilities of the neo-Orthodox in such concrete, non-treacly detail. Here, for example, is Goodman's initial description of Elizabeth Schulman, a character who will ultimately loom very large in daily life as Kirshner Jews live it:

> For her religion is a habit, ritual so commonplace, that she takes it for granted. She worships God three times a day in her room, and while she would never say she felt a familiarity with her Creator, the prayers are familiar, and she's used to approaching him. The sacred isn't mysterious to her, and so she romanticizes the secular.
>
> (p. 54)

Rav Kirshner represents religious tradition as it seeks to influence (and hold power over) his followers. None of this comes quickly; it changes over time, slowly and inevitably:

> With the passing years, the Rav has guided his community into a life of increasing restrictions. He has moved in his exegesis of Jewish law toward an interpretation ever more bounded and punctilious.... irrevocably, the Rav is drawing his people after him, in study, in word and deed, into a realm of obscurantism, a life encumbered and weighed down by tradition and endless layers of legalism and strict observance.
>
> (p. 31)

General readers might (reasonably) conclude that the Rav has created a cult of personality around himself, but his followers would insist that theirs is a community bound together by tradition and law. True, the law is interpreted with increasing strictness, and, even truer, the fences that separate them from modernity are ever wider and it is less Rav Kirshner the man as it is Rav Kirshner the teacher who captivates them. To live within boundaries is, for many, a joy rather than a burden.

It is hardly surprising that we focus on Elizabeth, who later fixes on a project to open a small general store that will provide kosher food for summer residents, for she is a restless spirit. Her project has merit because it would reduce the complications of bringing requisite food to Kaaterskill Falls.

The project also speaks to Elizabeth's predilection to push against the envelope. Where Goodman's account differs from previous fiction is that Elizabeth remains part of the Kirshner community even after the old rebbe dies and his stickler son yanks her license. For Goodman, a character living within limitations—and disappointment—is at least as interesting a fictional possibility as a protagonist who leaves a strict religious tradition for the secular attractions of a wider world. Potok made the latter plot his stock in trade, offering up a world of study, commandment and observance that his more sensitive characters melodramatically reject.

By contrast, Goodman is both wiser and more truthful. When the old Rav Kirshner feels his life slipping away, he must choose which of his two sons will replace him: one is uncompromisingly

pious, the other more brilliant but also more worldly. At first glance, the scenario sounds for all the world like a recycling of Potok's *The Chosen,* but in the final analysis it is not. For what Goodman means to explore is the emotions that churn beneath the surface and that give her characters fully rounded dimensions. Rav Kirshner, for example, is "no mystic" (which is to say, he is not a Hasid). "He is a rationalist, interested in law, not myth" (p. 99), and his leadership is based on his deep-seated belief that his disciples' way is already "laid out for them; they must seek guidance by learning halachah" (Jewish law). He belongs to the world of Misnagdim, scholar-teachers of the eighteenth and nineteenth centuries who fiercely opposed what they thought were the excesses of the Hasidim. Still, he agonizes, as does Elizabeth and, indeed, most of the other families Goodman assembles each summer at Kaaterskill Falls. What is not in doubt, however, is the neo-Orthodoxy that defines them simultaneously as a community and as individual selves. Sometimes Goodman's descriptions are packed with gentle ironies, as when one character's parents are described this way:

> Andras's parents taught him that if you are going to be religious, you have to do it all, observing every holiday and law. They believed that when it comes to God, you can't do things by halves—which was why they did nothing.
>
> (p. 38)

Jewish American literature is filled with scenes, usually comic, that take place around the family dinner table or at a local delicatessen; but none can match what Goodman gives us in the texture and smell of kosher cooking. The women in her large families are not only extraordinary bakers and cooks, they are exquisite representations of how to properly present a Sabbath meal. Few putatively "Jewish novels" manage the tricky business of giving equal weight to substance and style. Kaaterskill Falls does—and does so brilliantly.

As Elizabeth discovers, it is one thing to open a general store specializing in kosher foodstuffs (approved by the rebbe) and quite another to cater a birthday party using food from a (kosher) supplier outside the rebbe's purview. Non-Orthodox readers may have a problem understanding how grave Elizabeth's overreaching is, but to the members of the community, and especially, the new, young rebbe, what she did requires sharp discipline: she can no longer operate her grocery store.

In other hands, the seemingly harsh judgment would have been enough to make Elizabeth leave. That, after all, is what happens in novels about women caught in the yoke of Orthodox law. Feminism, Jewish or otherwise, demands no less. But Goodman is truer to the people she writes about. Elizabeth does not leave; rather, she accepts the burden of the decree against her and, later, soothes herself in the blessing of a new child. As Schøtt-Khristensen observes, Elizabeth's conflict never takes on the proportions of a real crisis.

When the book closes, Elizabeth has just given birth to her sixth daughter, who turns out to be a blessing after all, and she is allowed a modest new beginning; she is about to begin a new job in a grocery store in the neighborhood. Goodman chooses not to blow up the conflict; rather, she tones it down, as if intentionally resisting the reader's yearning for a great romantic drama.

Kaaterskill Falls was a finalist for National Book Award and won Goodman an Edward Lewis Wallant Award for fiction. Some readers balked that there wasn't enough "there, there" in term of plot or even energy, but the quiet novel won admirers who appreciated the three-dimensional surfaces Goodman gave to strictly observant Jews.

PARADISE PARK

Readers first met the over-the-top Sharon Spiegelman in the *New Yorker* story titled "Onionskin" (April 1, 1991), which was later included as one of the new stories in Goodman's revised version of her collection *Total Immersion* in 1998. It takes the form of a long, uneven letter. The result is an extended exercise in modulations of voice that range from the self-serving and manipulative to the confessional and self-abasing. Rendered as a

letter to her religious studies professor, Sharon means to "tell all"—from why she disrupted Dr. Freidell's class to why her rambling document should stand for her final paper in the course.

For Sharon, her letter represents nothing less than her current research and thought into religion itself. In less skillful hands, Sharon might be written off as mentally unstable and referred to the counseling service; but she is more, much more, than this:

> This is to apologize [Sharon's letter begins] if I offended you in class a few weeks ago, though I realize that you probably forgot the whole thing by now. I was the one who stood up and said "Fuck Augustine." What I meant was I didn't take the class to read him. I took it to learn about religion—God, prayer, ritual, the Madonna mother-goddess figure, forgiveness, miracles, sin, abortion, death, the big moral concepts.... the point is, when you've been through marriage kids, jobs, welfare, and the whole gamut and you come back to school you're ready for the real thing, and as far as I'm concerned Augustine's Conception of the Soul or whatever is not it. What is "it"? you're asking—well, that's what I came to find out, so you tell me. Obviously what you are paid for is to deal with the big religious issues and you are not dealing with them, which is what I was trying to point out when I made that remark in class, which I apologize for tonewise but not for my feelings behind it.
>
> (*Total Immersion* 1998, pp. 1–2)

Goodman is still close enough to the student experience to know just how weighty the term "final" can be, but she also knows that the term carries eschatological baggage, that it speaks to the end of days rather than the end of semesters.

Sharon concludes her long accusatory-explanatory letter with the desperate hope that her professor will be sufficiently moved to count her letter as a term paper. That he does not is as true as Sharon's feeling that she is a person more sinned against than sinning.

The Sharon we meet in *Paradise Park* (2001) is fashioned from the same exasperating cloth. As Jennifer Schuessler put it in her *New York Times* review, "you've got to pity the poor soul who gets stuck sitting next to her on a bus." Schuessler goes on to point out that "the challenge with a questing first-person narrator is to give him or her a voice the reader wants to fol-

low into the wilderness of a made-up world, and one that allows us to see more of the tale than the teller does.... Sharon's got the voice all right; the novel is a bright bauble of clear, rain-washed prose and low-key humor."

Nothing could be further from the self-absorbed Sharon than the solidly successful Allegra Goodman. The practice of mild, retiring writers imagining their polar opposites is hardly new. The frumpy Ian Fleming was never confused with his signature creation, the dashing James Bond, England's rakish spy; and Joyce Carol Oates makes regular excursions into the lives of downtrodden, desperate characters who do not at all resemble the bookish Ms. Oates. Sharon Spiegelman is Goodman's psychic journey into the Other.

Sharon finds herself at Martin Buber Temple both as student and teacher. She teaches a folk dancing class to the ladies of the temple and tries to find her Jewish self along with a rag-tag assortment of students under the guidance of Rabbi Siegel. Sharon's insistent voice tells it all, everything we need to know about the possibilities that life (Jewish or otherwise) in Hawaii promises, and about Sharon herself:

> Having no educational goals, boyfriends, or visions—I just eddied. I got no exercise, apart from teaching the ladies at the temple, and I guess that didn't count, since in class I never broke a sweat. Rabbi Siegel's class petered out. Matthew converted, and Alyssa had her bat mitzvah, so they stopped coming. Fred was working a lot, and as for me—I didn't have any great excuse.
>
> (p. 193)

Sharon is a study in passive aggression: she gives ground with one hand, and more than takes away whole territories with the other. The novel opens with Sharon as a folk dancer of reasonable talent; she could have done this for many years (had her wanderlust allowed her), but soon we are following Sharon on oceanographic expeditions, to various spots on the water and to jungles. If *Kaaterskill Falls* is quiet, reflective, and altogether given over to nuance, *Paradise Park* is noisy and full of Sharon free-spiritedness. For most of her career, Goodman studiously avoided writing about her generation, much less about herself;

Paradise Park is a notable exception, although nobody could ever confuse the flakey Sharon with the steady, laser-focused Goodman.

It is easy, perhaps too easy, to tire of Sharon's self-serving, long-winded declarations. We process her predictable arguments and write Sharon down as the malingerer she is. At the same time, however, Sharon's search for God has an authentic ring, and as Schuessler puts it:

> It's in the Greater Love Salvation Church that Sharon first reads the Song of Solomon, interpreted by some in the Christian tradition as the expression of Christ's longing for the church. The Song of Songs, as it is known in the Jewish tradition, recurs throughout the book, an expression of the soul's longing for God and the earthly lover's longing for the beloved. In Allegra Goodman's ebullient, bittersweet, plaintive Song of Sharon, the heroine's true achievement is finding poetry in the prosaic business of becoming who she's been all along.

Sharon, the seeker, seeks out a wide range of spiritual solutions. She comes in contact with a group of Bialystoker Hasidim (a fictitious sect closely resembling the real-life Lubavitcher Hasidim) who take her under their large, protective wing. They recognize Sharon's yearning for godliness and find that she is a perfect prospect for the "Jewish reconversions" they perform. Study, prayer, and a life lived according to Law is the regimen Sharon willingly undergoes, and the results are impressive: she is no longer the wacky Sharon she was.

In due course Sharon moves to Crown Heights, Brooklyn, the world headquarters of the Bialystoker movement, and she eagerly does her best to fit into this world. At one point, Sharon attends a wedding where she meets Mikail, the man who will become her *bashert* (intended). He is a Russian-Jewish immigrant whose "genius" as a musician is matched by his oversize bad luck. He struggles, but that makes him even more attractive in Sharon's eyes.

The trouble comes when Mikail's "Jewish" credentials are questioned. Was his mother's conversion in Russia "legitimate"? Such matters, according to the Bialystokers, must be carefully researched because if there are doubts about the mother, then there are necessarily doubts about the son. Until these technical issues are solved, the wedding must be postponed.

Sharon is not convinced, and so Goodman creates another instance where a Jewish woman comes into conflict with the strict boundaries of Law. True, the Bialystokers *seem* looser, more joyful than were the stern summer residents of Kaaterskill Falls; but Sharon soon learns that they can also be an uncompromising bunch:

> "God willing we will find proof." Mrs. Karinsky said fervently.
>
> "Then there will be no problem."
>
> I [Sharon] looked at the two of them. "You want me to wait for some kind of document search?" I asked them.
>
> "Yes," Dr. Karinsky said.
>
> "Isn't there any other way?" my voice wobbled.
>
> "Of course, Mikhail can convert." Mrs. Karinsky brightened a little.
>
> "Convert? To his own religion?"
>
> "He could go before the *bais din*," Dr. Karinsky said, meaning the rabbinical court.
>
> "And how long would that take?"
>
> "Maybe only six months!"
>
> (p. 307)

Sharon, being Sharon, has no intention of waiting another minute, much less six months. Mikhail is her *bashert*, he is Jewish, documents or no, and she desperately wants to marry him. The Bialystokers don't understand because technicalities drown out human feelings. At least that is how Sharon puts the matter to herself. Unlike Elizabeth in *Kaaterskill Falls*, she will *not* submit.

Later, she and Mikhail join a *havurah* (fellowship group), but find that its loose structure allows other members to rattle on about personal matters that have nothing to do with prayer. Once again, Goodman proves herself a master at balancing the assets and liabilities of various

religious groups: Sharon's Hawaiian is too bland, too vanilla; the Bialystokers suggest a more serious commitment to Judaism, but one that is (to her mind) more focused on who is (or is not) authentically Jewish, and who can perform a conversion that meets their rigid standards; and even *havurah* groups can be spiritually disappointing.

Paradise Park ends where it begins, with Sharon folk dancing with her old partner, Gary. He is now part of a Jewish foundation, and he does what he can to bring a measure of Jewishness to their lives. But he is hardly optimistic about how effective Jewish folk dancing can be. Assimilation is a hard fact that does not go away because people wish it to. On the other hand, something positive does happen as Sharon joins the dance circle and sings the words of a Hebrew song:

> Mikhail and I, and Zohar [their son] in the backpack, were dancing along among the couples, and the dance really was easy. Unlike my ladies Lilian and Henny and Estelle, Mikhail had no trouble with the steps. We were dancing the choruses and last verses. The taper was winding down. Only then I realized that very quietly, without even intending to, I'd been singing along. And it was Hebrew poetry on my lips, but I understood exactly what I was singing, I knew all the words.

(p. 360)

To unite Sharon with her elusive soul—and in a thoroughly episodic moment no less—is an easy trick, but Goodman makes the novel's many loose threads cohere.

INTUITION

Intuition (2006) takes on the slippery slopes of how we know what we know and how we can assemble the scientific data to prove this. Its setting is a research laboratory, most of which are highly competitive hothouse worlds where research assistants hope to find the Next Big Thing, or short of that, enough promise in a project to warrant more funding. In Goodman's lab, the atmosphere among her diverse group of postdocs (a significant sprinkling of Asians, along with Jews, and some just plain folks) is intense,

and there are times when the scientific method itself (seemingly) gets short shrift. *Intuition* pivots around the possibility, the "hunch," that one research assistant has fudged his results on what looks for the entire world like a cure for cancer. In other hands, the rightness or wrongness of research would drive the plot until readers were enlightened about who the villain was and who the hero was. But Goodman's novel is ambivalent, elusive, and altogether more compelling. Goodman is well aware that human beings do not move in the predictable manner of rats in a research experiment. Something in the human condition always alters the results—and in ways that even the brainiest scientist could not have predicted.

Robin begins to form her suspicions about Cliff's research as a hunch, as an "intuition," because even a family wedding cannot block out her deepest thoughts:

> And then, inexorably, her mind turned to Cliff. She could not stop questioning his data in her mind. There had been a time she'd searched his face to judge his moods. She'd watched him watch other friends, or even women he hardly knew, and wondered constantly what he felt and thought. Now, however, she was consumed with curiosity about what he'd done.

(p. 172)

"Consumed" is the charged word in this revealing paragraph because it makes clear that Robin is as culpable as Cliff. The reader's "intuition" says that her response is as much driven by thwarted love as it is by curiosity.

Goodman plays these characters against one another in an intricate Morris dance that turns *Intuition* into scientific suspense novel. If readers are wary about trusting Cliff—and his too-good-to-be-true data—they are equally put off by Robin's overly zealous investigations. Sue Halpern, writing in the pages of the *New York Times*, pointed out that Robin "makes an annoying heroine. She's whiny and plodding, and her relentless pursuit of the truth is strangely reductive: it makes her seem small."

But if she is "small" (or, to a reviewer, seems so), Robin is certainly persistent, and her rigorously detailed detective work is designed to keep readers on the edge of their seats:

Darting inside the lab, she flicked on the fluorescent undercabinet lights, and found her copy of the journal article on her desk. Then she reached for Cliff's lab book and riffled through its alternating white and yellow pages, devouring the numbers there.

She had looked at most of this before, but now she compared his notes to the printed data in the article. Her heart was galloping; her lungs cramped and strained at the tight bodice of her dress. There is nothing here, she told herself. Still, she checked the numbers in each table. Meticulous as a scientific bookkeeper, she combed through the raw data and final draft. Line by line she audited Cliff's accounts. She took a deep breath and closed the book. There were no discrepancies.

(p. 174)

Robin's galloping heart and straining bodice are the stuff of lazy, altogether predictable word choices, but they are the exception rather than the rule. Goodman knows how to tell an arresting story, even one in which Cliff is cast, in *People* magazine, as the young man who might just cure cancer. Publicity, as lab codirector Sandy Glass well knows, is what generates the hard cash that keeps the lights on and the Bunsen burners firing. Cliff is a rainmaker of the first order, and that is why it is vital that his article in the prestigious journal *Nature,* which may have been rushed into print, is "true."

Intuition is about scientists rather than about science. The novel begins with a Christmas party that not only introduces the novel's ensemble cast of laboratory researchers but also their fears—collective and individual—that they soon may cease to be employed. Pink slips are never far from a lab assistant's purview, and the party only deepens the fears hidden just beneath the jolly surfaces.

Still, despite the focus on the researchers, the scientific method itself provides the novel's backdrop at the same time it is at the very center of the novel's controversies. According to the scientific method, laboratory results must be duplicable in lab after lab; Cliff begins to suspect that his research is in trouble when lab after lab cannot replicate his results. Small wonder that many start to suspect that Cliff has fudged his data, which would have severe consequences not only for Cliff but also for the Mendelssohn-Glass laboratory.

Robin makes her own discoveries, and hers are the proper stuff of fiction and fictional characters:

This [discovery] was not jealousy, or falling out of love. This was knowledge of Cliff and what he'd done. They could warn her all they wanted; she'd broken through to her own chamber of discovery; she knew what she knew. She was no longer suffocating, weak and anguished with his success; but moving freely, beyond his gravitational field, fired by convictions of greater force. She knew he had misrepresented his findings, and even if that knowledge was awkward and inelegant, unacceptable, she would still trust and use her intuition.

(p. 220)

Robin's epiphany is complicated by the counter-arguments the novel stacks against her. The relationship between the lab's directors, Sandy Glass and Marion Mendelssohn, is strained because he and she are polar opposites. They agree to disagree, which, under the circumstances, is perhaps the best they can do.

The novel ends with Sandy Glass and Marion Mendelssohn taking stock of where the last months have taken them. Sandy misses Marion, and Marion misses Sandy. Goodman recounts their respective regrets but, as always with Goodman, she adds a few touches that give her fiction a subtle complexity. In the final scene, Marion delivers a talk at a conference on the West Coast. She is not the keynote speaker, and she has trouble (initially) with her props and her voice. But she gets past these, and during the question-and-answer period she makes it clear how far she has come:

She took a sip of water and watched Ginsburg [a competitor] scribbling furiously, and then gazed at her former postdoc, her rebellious child with her hand raised. What do you need now? Marion asked herself. Strange, she'd never posed the question that way before. She'd always considered what her postdoc demanded, what she did or did not deserve. What did she need? That was the puzzle, but as was so often the case, framing the question properly went a long way. What did she need? In that calm, clear, nearly joyous moment after her talk, the answer began to come to Marion. Ah, yes, of

course, she thought with some surprise. And she called on Robin.

(p. 344)

Because there are important matters at stake, cancer research being only one of them, *Intuition* is not, ultimately, a tempest in a teapot, no matter how petty the lab's quarrels become. Goodman knows how to draw quirky characters; in this novel she shows that even nerdy scientists can be well-rounded, fully believable characters.

THE COOKBOOK COLLECTOR

Goodman first read Jane Austen's *Pride and Prejudice* as a young girl, and she continues to read Austen as an adult fiction writer. *The Cookbook Collector* (2010) is an homage to another Austen novel, *Sense and Sensibility*, and to its leading characters, the sisters Elinor and Marianne Dashwood. At the end of Austen's novel of manners, she leaves it unclear whether or not sense and sensibility, represented by the Dashwood sisters, have been merged.

Much the same is true for Goodman's novel, which tests the limits of the romantic temperament in Jessamine ("Jess") Bach and of the analytical temperament of her older sister, Emily. At twenty-eight, Emily is the CEO of a start-up data storage company called Veritech. The name, which means "truth in technology," is cutting edge; Emily is where it's at. By contrast, the twenty-three-year-old Jess is where it once was: she is a grad student in comparative literature and more likely to hand out leaflets for environmental groups than to shop for expensive clothing. Both sisters are interesting but entirely different, and that is where the comparisons to *Sense and Sensibility* come in. Emily is more sense than she is sensibility; Jess is more sensibility than she is sense.

Goodman's narrative voice keeps track of the sisters and the plot that thickens around them without becoming overly judgmental. Here is how the narrator describes the two sisters having lunch in Berkeley:

Jess had a theory about everything, but her ideas changed from day to day. It was hard for Emily to

remember whether her sister was primarily feminist or environmentalist, vegan or vegetarian. Did she eat fish, or nothing with a face?

(p. 4)

And later:

The sisters' voices were almost identical, laughing mezzos tuned in childhood to the same pitch and timbre. To the ear, they were twins; to the eye, nothing alike. Emily was tall and slender with her hair cropped short. She wore a pinstriped shirt, elegant slacks, tiny, expensive glasses.... Jess was small and whimsical. Her face and mouth were wider than Emily's, her cheeks rounder, her eyes greener and more generous.

(p. 5)

Much of the plot revolves around the rising—and falling—fortunes of Emily's tech company. Becoming wealthy, even if it is a fortune on paper, is now part of the landscape, and 1999, when the novel opens, was surely a time as giddy as the 1920s before the great stock market crash. Goodman had followed such ups and downs before, when Cliff and Robin went through their respective paces in *Intuition*; in *The Cookbook Collector*, we watch anxiously (often over Emily's shoulder) as Veritech's growth implodes, and what once was no longer is.

Jess, stranded on the shoals of a perpetually unfinished dissertation, divides her time between stints of environmental activism (her boyfriend is king of the tree huggers) and part-time work in a bookstore called Yorick's. It is there that she comes into contact with the fabulously rare, and valuable, cookbook collection that gives the novel its title. Writing in the pages of the *Guardian*, Francine Prose ties the sisters' very different locales and lifestyles to the central issue of ambition: "Despite the distance between the sisters' milieus, both of their fates hinge on scenarios in which enthusiasm, ambition and rather less attractive motives persuade someone to take a moral shortcut." At such scattered moments, Goodman could have taken an arch, judgmental tone; but she doesn't. Instead, her narrative voice points out these lapses in light jabs packed with gentle satire.

At the same time, Goodman has some important things to say about American culture in the

boom-and-bust Silicon Valley years, and about America itself post-9/11. Jess keeps crossing paths with Rabbi Helfgott, a Bialystoker rabbi who knows about the latest computers and potential real estate deals along with Torah and Talmud. Unlike the Bialystokers that Sharon found too dryly legalistic in *Paradise Park*, Rabbi Helfgott is warm, lovable, and, as his name suggests, "helpful." He lends Jess money so that she can invest in her sister's IPO at the same time that his litany of "When?" implies both the messianic urge and the way that time is moving rapidly through their lives. Jess hears her biological clock ticking and wonders what will happen with her boss George Friedman, his lovingly restored house, and his newfound cache of ancient cookbooks.

Emily's intended turns out to be a cad who (conveniently?) dies as a passenger on one of the commandeered planes that slam into the World Trade Center. In retrospect, Rabbi Helfgott's persistent "When?" finds an ironic counterpart in that fateful day in 2001. Destiny has a very different hand for Jess to play, as the cookbooks she is meticulously cataloging take on a life of their own. Focusing on this aspect of the novel, Dominique Browning points out in her *New York Times* review that this

> cache of cookbooks becomes the bonding medium for Jess and George. A mysterious, ashen-faced, gray-eyed woman with long gray hair—a veritable shade—arrives at the shop one day with a request that George inspect a collection of 823 cookbooks left to her by her uncle, a lichenologist. She had promised the old man she wouldn't sell his books, but she can't afford to honor that agreement. They've been stored in his kitchen: every cabinet and shelf, even the oven, is stuffed with ancient, valuable cookbooks. Clippings, drawings and notes, held with rusting paper clips, are jammed into their pages.

Although George seems the lifelong bachelor type, he is happy to marry Jess, and Jess is happy to marry him. For all its twenty-first-century knowingness, *The Cookbook Collector* is, essentially, a nineteenth-century novel, one sturdy enough, in both technical plot devices and essential vision, to belong in the same paragraph with Austen.

Allegra Goodman earned a wide public audience in her early twenties, and while that story is remarkable, her subsequent career at the writing desk has been even more impressive. "Potential" is a double-sided term: one side acknowledges the achievement we expect while the other side makes it all too clear that early talent often goes unfulfilled. Goodman is an illustrative case of a young writer who keeps getting better.

Selected Bibliography

WORKS OF ALLEGRA GOODMAN

SHORT STORY COLLECTIONS
Total Immersion. New York: Harper & Row, 1989. Revised, New York: Delta, 1998 (includes two new stories, "Onionskin" and "The Closet").

The Family Markowitz. New York: Farrar, Straus & Giroux, 1996.

NOVELS
Kaaterskill Falls. New York: Dial Press, 1998.

Paradise Park. New York: Dial Press, 2001.

Intuition. New York: Dial Press, 2006.

The Other Side of the Island. New York: Razorbill, 2008. (Young adult novel.)

The Cookbook Collector. New York: Dial Press, 2010.

ARTICLE
"Rereading: Pemberly Previsited." *American Scholar* 73, no. 2:142–145 (spring 2004).

CRITICAL STUDIES
Cronin, Gloria L. "Immersions in the Postmodern: The Fiction of Allegra Goodman." In *Daughters of Valor: Contemporary Jewish American Women Writers*. Edited by Jay L. Halio and Ben Siegel. Newark: University of Delaware Press, 1997.

———. "Seasons of Our (Dis)Content, or Orthodox Women in Walden: Allegra Goodman's *Kaaterskill Falls*." In *Connections and Collisions: Identities in Contemporary Jewish-American Women's Writing*. Edited by Lois E. Rubin. Newark: University of Delaware Press, 2005.

Kraven, Jeraldine R. "Wandering in the Contact Zone: Tradi-

tion and Modernity in Allegra Goodman's *Kaaterskill Falls*." *CEA Critic* 72, no. 2:23–36 (winter 2010).

Pinsker, Sanford. "Satire, Social Realism, and Moral Seriousness: The Case of Allegra Goodman." *Studies in American Jewish Literature* 11, no. 2: 180–192 (fall 1992).

Schøtt-Khristensen, Lene. "Allegra Goodman's *Kaaterskill Falls*: A Liturgical Novel." *Studies in American Jewish Literature* 24:22–41 (2005).

Socolovsky, Maya. "Land, Legacy, and Return: Negotiating a Post-Assimilationist Stance in Allegra Goodman's *Kaaterskill Falls*." *Shofar: An Interdisciplinary Journal of Jewish Studies* 22, no. 3:26–42 (spring 2004).

Solotaroff, Ted. "American-Jewish Writers: On Edge Once More." *New York Times Book Review*, December 18, 1988, pp. 1, 11–12.

REVIEWS

Browning, Dominique. "The Insatiable Years." *New York Times Book Review*, July 23, 2010. (Review of *The Cookbook Collector*.) http://www.nytimes.com/2010/07/25/books/review/Browning-t.html?pagewanted=1&src=tp

Hacker, Randi. "*Total Immersion*." *New York Times Book Review*, September 10, 1989, p. 26.

Halpern, Sue. "Scientific Americans." *New York Times Book Review*, March 5, 2006. (Review of *Intuition*.) http://www.nytimes.com/2006/03/05/books/review/05halpern.html?_r=0

Kendall, Elaine. "Bagels and Leis: An Ethnic Potpourri of Odd Couple." *Los Angeles Times*, July 27, 1989. (Review of *Total Immersion*.) http://articles.latimes.com/1989-07-27/news/vw-45_1_book-review

Pinsker, Sanford. "Kosher Delights." *Washington Post*, August 16, 1998, p. X05. (Review of *Kaaterskill Falls*.)

Prose, Francine. Review of *Total Immersion*. *Newsday*, May 20, 1989.

———. "*The Cookbook Collector* by Allegra Goodman." *Guardian*, April 17, 2011. http://www.theguardian.com/books/2011/apr/17/cookbook-collector-allegra-goodman-review

Schuessler, Jennifer. "Looking for Love." *New York Times*, March 11, 2001. (Review of *Paradise Park*.) (https://www.nytimes.com/books/01/03/11/reviews/010311.11schuest.html

ALFRED HAYES

(1911—1985)

Robert Buckeye

DURING THE 1930s the children of those who had crossed the Atlantic for better lives only to slave on the factory floor, descend into mines, or crowd sweat shops had come of age; they were Polish, German, Italian, Jewish, and Irish and wrote of the America they knew. John Dos Passos and Theodore Dreiser may have preceded them, but their situations were not the same. Dos Passos was, after all, a Harvard graduate. If their writing was at first resisted, once it asserted itself, it could not, nevertheless, put its past aside. These writers may have gained a place at the table but knew they did not belong there. If they could not forget where they had come from, America would not permit them to do so if they could.

In Alfred Hayes's 1953 novel, *In Love,* a writer approaching middle age goes to Atlantic City for a weekend with a woman in her twenties to salvage the love they might have lost. "It's wonderful to get away," she says. "From what?" he asks. "Us. Them. It," she says (*In Love*, p. 138). In one form or another, "us," "them," and "it" became the subjects of the new, more democratic American writing. "Us" are those who cannot live, denied by "them" of what should be theirs. "It" may be the Depression, the Second World War, America itself.

At the end of a disastrous weekend in Atlantic City, the writer and woman return to New York City, their love shattered. "I'll tell you what's wrong," he says. "What?" she asks. "Us. Them. It," he says (p. 157). If they thought that going to Atlantic City would help them at least momentarily escape their lives, they know on their return that no escape is possible. It is the subtext of these new American writers and, in particular, that of Alfred Hayes. "Us" had been ignored and would be ignored no longer. "Them" was seen as never before. "It" could be understood but not grasped.

LIFE

Alfred Hayes was born on April 17, 1911, of Jewish parents in a London ghetto. His father had fought in the Russo-Japanese War, played a wind instrument, but became a barber in order to work. His mother came to England from Austria-Hungary. Her father had been a butcher. Several months before the beginning of the First World War they left England for America, at first living in Harlem, later the Bronx. Hayes went to public school in Harlem and graduated from the High School of Commerce. For six months he attended the City College of New York. His father wanted him to be an accountant.

During the thirties, Hayes took whatever jobs he could. He worked nights as a copyboy for the *New York American* and later as a crime reporter at the Old Federal Building in New York for the *Daily Mirror*. He was briefly a movie critic for *Friday*. He was also a waiter, delivery boy, process server, briefly a bootlegger. He pitched hay on a farm in Connecticut. In Harrisburg, Pennsylvania, he worked for a union. He went to Pittsburgh for work but there was no work in Pittsburgh. In the Depression there was no work anywhere. He and his first wife, Gertrude, lived on St. Mark's Place in Greenwich Village.

In 1928 he had joined the Young Communist League. Soon he became a member of the John Reed Club, only to leave it for the less doctrinaire Revolutionary Writers Federation. His work in one leftist organization or another gave him opportunities to write. He became an editor of *Partisan Review*. His poem "In a Coffee Pot" was published in its first issue, in 1934, and

selected for inclusion in *Proletarian Literature in the United* States (1935). He wrote a cultural column for *Daily Worker*. In Harrisburg, he wrote a radio drama script for the International Ladies' Garment Workers' Union. One of his poems, "Into the Streets May First," was set to music by Aaron Copland and printed in *New Masses* in 1934.

He read poetry and produced plays at the left-wing Camp Unity in Wingate, New York. At the camp in the summer of 1936, he showed his poem "Joe Hill" to Earl Robinson, who set it to music and performed it the next day. It was published in the *Daily Worker* weeks after Robinson performed it. (The poem, made iconic through Joan Baez's performance of the song, may be his best-known, though few know he wrote it.) In 1938 he adapted Erskine Caldwell's 1935 novel *Journeyman* for the Broadway stage. He also worked for the Federal Writers Project. In *New Masses*, Orrick Johns hailed him: "There was Alfred Hayes, dark, Dantean, witty, conscious to imperiousness that he personifies a new sort of 'young generation,' the lyric poet of the New York working class, the strike front, the writer of sketches that bite into memory" (Green, p. 86).

Soon, however, he began to argue that the Communist cultural movement should not demand ideological orthodoxy of its writers. In conversation with Kenneth Fearing in 1937, he criticized the party stand during the Spanish Civil War. After the Moscow purge trials of 1936–1938, Hayes ended any association with Communism. "I made a political blind date," he notes sardonically, "and maybe the dame ain't nothing like she sounded over the phone" (Wald, p. 217).

During World War II, Hayes served in the Special Services branch of the U.S. Army in Italy from 1943 to 1945. After the war, he stayed and was one of the screenwriters for Roberto Rossellini's film *Paisan* (1946) and contributed dialogue for Vittorio De Sica's *Bicycle Thieves* (1948). His first novel, *All Thy Conquests,* about the war in Italy, was published in 1946. When he returned to America he wrote screenplays for Warner Bros., Twentieth Century–Fox, and RKO while continuing to write his own fiction and

poetry. He lived in Hollywood with his second wife, Marietta, and their four children.

He would write nine novels and three books of poetry (which did not include the caustic, blunt, political poems he wrote in the thirties for *Dynamo, New Masses,* and *Partisan Review*). He wrote screenplays for Fritz Lang and Fred Zinnemann. Among his film credits are *Clash by Night, Island in the Sun, Human Desire, A Hatful of Rain,* and *The Left Hand of God*. Later he also wrote for television, including episodes for *The Alfred Hitchcock Hour, The Twilight Zone,* and *Mannix*.

In a 1982 interview with Gwen Gunderson, Hayes remembered he had written the poem "Joe Hill" one morning when he was nineteen while still living with his parents in the Bronx. He did not say how or when Joe Hill came to mind—it had "not [been] pre-meditated—conscious" (qtd. in Green, p. 90). The folklorist Archie Green wrote several letters to Hayes about his Joe Hill poem, but he did not answer. One year before Hayes's death from meningitis on August 14, 1985, Green called him to ask about the poem. Hayes hung up.

Those who had come to America and succeeded, as Hayes certainly had, seemed to have put the past behind them. They had not. They never would. In that same 1982 interview, Hayes would not only remember the morning he had written "Joe Hill," but also the room in which he had written it. A small room that overlooked an airshaft. A narrow, single bed. A table. An airshaft, room, bed, and table he would not forget.

ITALY

> He could not understand the dramatic thing I made of the Italian landscape, or even understand why it should disturb me so much that I had come to realize that I had lived for thirty years in a country in which there was no place I could think of with the particular warmth or the spontaneous affection that a road in the *compagna* [*campagna*] or a grove of trees or the low hills visible from where we sat stirred in me.
>
> (*The Temptation of Don Volpi,* p. 8)

In a poem about the Second World War, "—As a Young Man," Hayes refers to a portrait

(photograph?) of a young man, likely Hayes, in 1934 when he was twenty-three, ten years before he fought in the war. He remembers the life he had then, the memories of who fought in Spain and how men stood in the rain during the Lawrenceville strike, and the girls, the talk of Henri Matisse and Karl Marx, all blown away by "The heat of a village in Europe / And death closing in" (collected in *Welcome to the Castle*, p. 44). Those who fought in the war came back to America different men. They may have been boys when they left. They were not boys when they came home. Hayes had come to America at age two, the son of Jewish parents. He returned to Europe at age thirty-two to defend Jews.

Hayes remained in Italy after the war as a member of the occupation forces. He became fluent in Italian, worked as a museum guide for the occupation army, and met and worked with the filmmakers Roberto Rossellini and Vittorio De Sica. When he returned to America he worked for Hollywood studios writing scripts. He also returned with the knowledge that his immigrant background had not made him fully American. His sensibility would remain more European than American. His first two novels, *All Thy Conquests* (1945) and *The Girl on the Via Flaminia* (1949), and his novella *The Temptation of Don Volpi* (1960), are set in Rome during the war.

All Thy Conquests is not a story as much as it is stories, some of them interrelated, episodic in nature as if it were a newsreel, of American soldiers and Italians, particularly of one Fascist charged with the executions of hundreds, set in a Rome the Germans have left. Its first chapter, titled "Chorus," describing reactions of Italians outside a courthouse to the trial of the Fascist, suggests that the book may have overtones of a Greek tragedy. But while what follows may be defeat and loss, it is not catharsis.

The novel shows the influence of Ernest Hemingway in its use of repetition and simple, declarative sentences; of John Dos Passos in its "The Liberated City" sections, reminiscent of his use of the "Camera Eye" in *U.S.A.*; and of James Joyce in its use of interior monologue.

American soldiers are conquerors, far from home, lonely, lost, naive, and they assume, without understanding why, that to the conqueror go the spoils. Life in Italy had been awful under the Germans because Italians were under the boot of the conqueror. It seems worse under Americans because Italians have been liberated and nothing has changed. Impoverished, defeated Italians without work or possibility wait at the Colosseum to beg from American soldiers who have come to see that landmark. Italian women are forced to see that their bodies are commodities for sale when nothing else sells. As one Italian says, "History: history had become a pair of shoes" (*All Thy Conquests*, p. 35). The Fascist on trial who was born poor with no way up or out imagines himself asking the prosecutor, "What would you have done in my place?"

"What would you do?" is not a question American soldiers ask themselves, if it is one every Italian must ask. Harry, an American soldier, meets Francesca, an Italian girl, believes he has fallen in love with her, leaves to fight farther north, returns, searches endlessly for her, and one night, forced by another soldier to see a prostitute so that he might forget Francesca, meets her in a room in a bordello. Another American soldier, Captain Pollard, sleeps with Antoinette, also American, whose husband is in England. When her husband comes to Rome and she stays with him, Pollard is devastated. For the first time, he is in love. Later, drunk, he is mugged, robbed and stripped by Italians at the Colosseum.

A third soldier, Grigorio, sees Carla, makes her pregnant, tells her that she should get an abortion. He cannot marry her because he is already married. She had only slept with him because she loved him. In circumstances that are threatening—war, a strange place, a language they do not understand—sex becomes an escape for American soldiers. "The fantasy of liberated sex," Jacques Rancière writes, "recover[s] the innocence of childhood" (*Short Voyage*, p. 96).

In Italy during the war, who we are is not "them," but "them" may suddenly become "us." When the crowd drags the Fascist out of the court and brutalizes him at the end of the book, the anger and frustration of the people, the defeats and suffering they've had to endure, boil over. It

was not they, they think, who had brought Italy to its defeat. Who we are and who they are thus cannot be determined unless we understand the context. At one point Hayes describes American soldiers on a street. They are at once conquerors and conquered. "The people," Rancière writes, "are first of all a way of framing" (p. 113).

> [The American soldiers] had no share in the life of the country, only in the destruction of it. They looked enviously and bitterly at the officers of their own army and country who sat, with women, in the cane chairs outside the cafés. The officers were clean with a cleanness they could not achieve; their women were invariably pretty. They seemed, to the soldiers whose armpits were stained with their own sweat, to possess a whole world of privileges they were denied. They looked at the women, at their legs and at their breasts; they looked at their floating hair; they looked at their tanned and naked arms lying on the tabletops. They looked at them with the hard obscene stare of convicts.
>
> (*All Thy Conquests*, p. 137)

If *All Thy Conquests* is many stories that are one story, *The Girl on the Via Flaminia* (1949) is one story that is like so many stories of its kind, even if this one story is not the so many other stories that are like it. This novel about a man and a woman brought together by irreconcilable needs—often seen to be a love story, even though they live together without being lovers—became the most successful book Hayes wrote. Hayes had first written the novel as a play and after the success of the book transformed it back into a play, which was performed first at the Circle in the Square theater in New York, later on Broadway. It was later adapted as a movie, *Act of Love*.

Robert (Roberto) is an American soldier, away from home, lonely, in need of a woman. He had never been away from home. "A good American stayed home," he says, "and discovered the beauties of Buffalo" (*Via Flaminia*, p. 32). He can go to a prostitute, but he wants something more than paid sex, even if he will pay for what he wants. "I thought I would just be exchanging something somebody needed for something I needed. Something somebody wanted for something I wanted," he says (p. 91).

Lisa is an Italian woman, who no longer lives as she likes but as she must. Nina, an Italian woman kept by an American officer, convinces Lisa that to live with an American soldier will permit her to live as she cannot now. The soldier will pay the rent, bring food, and, of course, be her husband in everything but the marriage document. "Everything now is such an arrangement," she says (p. 22). Lisa agrees to the arrangement, even if she despises Americans and can't make love to a stranger. Everyone believes nothing matters anymore, and if she believes something still does, it does not change anything.

One learns to make love to a stranger, Nina tells her, but Lisa answers bitterly, "He'll feed me because he's won the war, and that's part of the arrangement, and then after he's fed me we'll go to bed, because that's part of the arrangement" (p. 22). She understands that she has let herself be bought, that she is a commodity to be exchanged, but she will not consummate their relationship. Robert does not demand she exchange it, despite the terms of their agreement, unless she chooses to give it on her own.

One Sunday he takes her in a jeep to Lake Bracciano. In the glances, comments, and stones thrown at them on the way, she sees what Italians think of her. "We do finally what we thought we were incapable of doing," she thinks, "and it is less than we thought the doing would be, and at the same time more" (p. 94). Police discover that Robert and Lisa have no marriage papers, and Lisa is forced to register as a prostitute. She must carry a prostitute's card on her at all times and undergo periodic examinations.

Those who live in the house on Via Flaminia whose room Robert has rented function as a chorus, as do the voices of Italians in the opening chapter of *All Thy Conquests*. Adele, wife and mother, tells Lisa to escape, go to America with Roberto. There is nothing left in Europe. Antonio, the son, an officer who fought for Italy in Africa, despises Italian women who prostitute themselves. Ugo, husband and father, asks Roberto what Lisa will do tomorrow now that she is registered as a prostitute. Whose responsibility is it?

The weeks they have shared a room without sharing it has changed Robert and Lisa. Talk that only circled back on itself or stopped because it was not heard begins to be heard. The something for Robert is not the Lisa he has come to know; not just somebody—some body—as he has learned. Robert is not just any American soldier Lisa despises, somebody who is any body, as she too has learned. He will do anything to help her, he says. Why? she asks. Because, he answers. Pity, she says. Call it what you want, he says. (Their different circumstances lead them to what Rancière calls "the impossibility of reciprocity and the discourse it contains" [p. 91].)

"She was hungry, I was lonely, that's the story," Robert says (p. 129). The story that is the story is not the one it has become. They both want love, even if it cannot be with each other. One desires what the other cannot give. One gives what the other cannot accept. One cannot do what one cannot do. There may be love without love.

Lisa goes to the bridge over the Tiber River where so many women have prostituted themselves or in despair drowned themselves. Robert runs after her. Men playing cards in wine shops, prostitutes keeping appointments, drivers waiting at their carriages for fares look up only to look away. "It was only a soldier running" (p. 153).

We do not know what happens to Lisa. We do know that her moral principles and integrity prevent her from living in the world. The Tiber River waits—the only answer there seems to be. We do not know how far Robert runs, whether he finds Lisa or not, what would happen if he did. We do know that the beauties of Buffalo are no longer what they were.

The Temptation of Don Volpi (1960), written while Hayes was in Hollywood, looks back on his Italian experience during the war. Alfredo, a Jewish American officer, brings soldiers as part of an education program to see catacombs at St. Cecilia's monastery. He meets Don Volpi, a priest who had fought with the Italian army in Africa and then later served with partisans in the resistance.

Ten years before he became a priest, Don Volpi had a tempestuous relationship with a woman, Anna, that ended when he stabbed himself in the chest with her scissors. "That was the path love took," Alfredo thinks after Don Volpi tells him the story. "Downwards; into a darkness and a hatred of one's self, and cruelty toward what one loved" (*The Temptation of Don Volpi*, p. 33). He had become a priest in denial of his desire for the sensuous, carefree, casual life that Anna lives.

One day Don Volpi meets Anna and afterward can no longer rest, tormented by the desire that had driven him to her in the first place. He goes to her, kneels in front of her, embraces her knees. "It was submission, that's what the ecstasy and the tears were about," Alfredo tells his lover Liliane, an Italian woman half his age, "submission to his own torment" (p. 49). Anna's knees are a sign of Don Volpi's error, of his having put flesh above spirit; and his embrace of them, in some twisted logic, is forgiveness. Anna flees in tears. "For whatever reasons: shame, horror, the movement in the very depth of things which rejects being knelt to.... The spirit goes on its knees to God, but the flesh can't abide a devotion of that kind" (pp. 54, 55).

Liliane is the only woman Alfredo has been happy with, and when he leaves to return to America, he is sure that he will come back to her. That's another story, he says. A story that Hayes will write the rest of his life: of forty-year-old men who have seen too much of life, who no longer believe what they once believed and do not think that the twenty-something women will be what they have missed, even if what they have at the moment is both more and less than talk of Marx and Matisse ever was, and far less regrettable than the cost of the comfortable life they now have. The women are real as they are not.

POLITICS

Shadow of Heaven (1947), published between *All Thy Conquests* and *The Girl on the Via Flaminia*, looks back to Hayes's work with garment workers in Harrisburg, Pennsylvania, in the thirties, although it takes place after the Second World

War. It is his only novel to take up the issues of class that he fought for in the thirties.

Harry Oberon, a forty-year-old union organizer and representative for garment workers in Pennsylvania, has done his job a long time—perhaps, he thinks, too long—and he no longer has any illusions about it, even though he believes it must be done. Every day he addresses the complaints and questions of workers, argues with owners and bosses. Someone comes into the office. A phone rings. He is at a conference, a committee meeting, a labor negotiation. The patience of impatience drives him. The failure of failure dogs him. The anger of his anger is a source of good. The loneliness of the alone cannot be escaped. "For a long time something had been going wrong—as though under the skin the nerves were dying; as though the ability to feel was becoming so much less; a growing sense of darkness inside" (*Shadow of Heaven*, p. 72).

It can no longer be contained. It? Everything. Oberon must speak of it—what has happened, is happening, what is wrong, what is right, what must be made right, who we are, who we are not, who we must be. He speaks of it to Margaret, the woman he has seen for three months; to his doctor, to students interested in radical politics, union workers, bosses, bartenders, anyone. He talks too much, he says, but his thoughts follow him like a faithful dog. He must speak of them endlessly. The more he does the less he feels, he says, but he cannot stop.

> It had been a generation that had somehow never had the opportunity to become men. It had remained a generation of violent boys. The boys had made terrible efforts to become men and they had died in Spain trying to become men and had violently attacked their own society in their effort to become men. Then the war's coming had more or less ended them as a generation and their historical importance had dwindled and been absorbed by the importance of the war.... Those of them who survived still seemed even at forty to possess much of the nature of boys.
>
> (pp. 143–144)

> Not failing was having money, and I hated money, and I also hated not having money and I hated needing money. When I grew up the idea was not to

fail, like my father, but also not to succeed. Not to submit, but also not to exploit.

(p. 174)

He remembers the day the national guard shot three loom fixers in the Saylesville cemetery. He remembers the day during the Lawrenceville strike that two cars followed him. Looking for help, he goes to the farmhouse of two sisters who work in one of the shops he is organizing. He calls the sheriff and state police, but they will do nothing. The sisters' father, a former miner, asks the men following Oberon what they want. The dirty Jew, they say. The miner stands outside on the porch with a shotgun. His wife is out back with another gun. In an hour thirty miners arrive. His ten-year-old daughter had gone across the mountain to get them. Slepowicz was their name, he tells Margaret. At some point he will go back: "The little blondie would be all grown up now; how was the old man? He must go down to the pits, Miller must be still there, they were the people he loved if he loved anybody at all" (pp. 131–132).

He tells himself he cannot be with Margaret. He is educated. She is not. He is middle class. She is working class. Even if she is from the world he wants to be his. He tells himself he should be with her. She may have no future, but when he looks at her he sees what might be possible. "A woman like Margaret was real, and being with her and making love to her would restore that sense of lost reality" (p. 147). When they make love, "a terribleness came out of her" that he recognizes in himself (p. 52).

Margaret is married to a man she does not love, but knows that if she is to find a man she loves it must be a man like Oberon, even if at times he dismisses her, cares only for his work, treats her as no more than a convenience: "Harry's a man, he's smart, he doesn't let them step all over him, he's educated. I don't have to be ashamed or feel small when I'm with him" (p. 81).

One night at Margaret's apartment Oberon hears a siren and leaps out of bed. She does not understand what has frightened him, and it frightens her. When he sees the look on her face, he understands what it would be like for her to

have a life with him and tells her to get somebody young, someone not burned out, someone who doesn't get the shakes when he hears a siren.

A politician asks Oberon to organize labor in the state for the upcoming election. They will pay well. (When Oberon mentions the sum to Margaret, she asks who he has to murder to be paid that much. Me, he answers.) Oberon turns him down. He will not be bought.

One of his students brings a war widow to him, the daughter-in-law of the owner of the shop whose workers Oberon has organized. She will be able to talk to Oberon, they say, he will listen, understand. It is less talk she needs than a man; every night in her bed it is "wanting wanting wanting it did not matter who anymore" (p. 192). She comes back, wants to sleep with him. Oberon turns her down. It would not be right, he tells her.

He can no longer do what he should do. It has been too much for far too long. He needs to escape, to be alone. It becomes an obsession. He ends his relationship with Margaret.

The shop owner refuses to believe that Oberon did not seduce his daughter-in-law. He asks Margaret to sign a paper saying Oberon tried to rape her. If she does, she will be paid more for her work. Margaret tells Oberon that she will not sign the paper, if he loves her. It is not a question of love, he says.

> Don't do it for me. Do it because you work. Do it because if you sign that affidavit you'll always remember signing, and you won't like what you remember and the revenge won't taste as good as you think it will. Don't do it for me. Do it because not to sign will make you more than you are and to sign it will make you less.
>
> (p. 261)

Abruptly Oberon kisses Margaret, as Robert had kissed Lisa in *The Girl on the Via Flaminia* before she ran from him. Is this what she wants? he asks Margaret. Yes, she answers. "This and this and this and this" (p. 263). They do not realize until too late that they have accidentally released the brake of the car and are heading toward tracks and an onrushing train. Margaret dies. Oberon survives. In the hospital, he thinks,

"there were no triumphs. All triumphs were lies. There was only the education of defeat" (p. 277).

Shadow of Heaven is the last gasp of the radicalism of Alfred Hayes, but its defeat is nevertheless its triumph, for defeat understands what triumph never will. The book is a labor of mourning—of what life gives, what it takes away, what remains. There can be no labor without love, it says. For only love educates. He would remember Margaret. He would remember Slepowicz. In *Shadow of Heaven*, Hayes opens up a place in which those who do not count are counted.

The year the novel was published, the House Un-American Activities Committee was holding hearings in Washington. The Hollywood Ten were called, including Dalton Trumbo and Albert Maltz, writers Hayes must have known. Charlie Chaplin, Bertolt Brecht, and Paul Robeson left for Europe so they would not have to testify. George Oppen went to Mexico. Hayes would not write a *Shadow of Heaven* again.

HOLLYWOOD AND NEW YORK

> I went back to my difficulties of dealing with a landscape that lacked love. I worked with the belief that it was possible to find something else in that landscape which might prove to be important. I grew used to not experiencing happiness: it seemed a normal condition in my country.
>
> (*The Temptation of Don Volpi*, p. 55)

Hayes's next two novels, *In Love* (1953) and *My Face for the World to See* (1958), are first-person narratives told by forty-year-old male writers about their relationships with women half their age. The men may be well off, but their lives are not what they want them to be. Writing is not what the writing should be. Money does not bring them happiness. The women had left home to come to New York and Hollywood because home had not given them what they need. If the city does not give it to them, they will not go back. Home was never home. Only the city is possible. Although Hayes is no longer the radical he was in the thirties, he would continue to question the neoliberal imperative that money determines hap-

piness, even if it permits these men to live as they do and provides these women the security they seek.

The unnamed narrator of *In Love* tells a young woman at a café in New York how he had been in love with a woman her age. He always thought he would find love, but must have done something he did not understand, something that could not be taken back. Whatever it was he had lost it, it was hard to describe, some sense of permanent loss, but he knows that it is four o'clock, drinks have arrived; it can be "an afternoon in which something apparently happens" (*In Love*, p. 4). It is a story he has told before. One that, as young as this woman is, particularly because she is young, she has heard before. One that we hear every day in cafés and bars.

He wants a simple, uncomplicated relationship, a fixed and unvarying idyll, he says, that will not radically change his life; not to be free from the world but to be in control of it. She wants everything but feels she has nothing. She had been married at eighteen and left her child with family in Oak Park, Illinois. She is not smart enough, she says, not wise, but when she lies on the studio couch in her apartment she knows she will be the woman she dreams of and that when she is she will be happy.

She remembers, she insists on, everything about the first time they had gone out. Snow was falling, the cab was heated, its meter ticked, they held hands. Perhaps, he thinks when she speaks of it, "it was the anticipation, that moment sustained by the drive home, when one is in a taxi with a stranger who is about to be transfigured into a lover" (p. 26).

One night, friends take her to a club. A man is attracted to her and asks her to dance. He offers her a thousand dollars if she will sleep with him. She tells the narrator of the offer. It would not affect her love for him, she says. But she can't do it. It would not be right. He will say later that what he thought to be an inconsequential gesture—"this nothing"—would be the cause of everything.

She loves him, and what is an idyll, if not convenience, for him is no longer sufficient for her. She needs to hear him say he loves her, and when he does not, she goes to Howard, the man who offered a thousand dollars. He is rich, always right, she says, violent about politics. He knows the value of a thousand dollars. "A suit of clothes," the narrator thinks. "Something in a chair." All that he despises, but from a world, nevertheless, he believes to be superior to his own. He does not think anything will happen with Howard, but when something does, he realizes that he is in love with her, and his failure to hold her "was simply one more of the failures I had to endure in the struggle with that world" (p. 115).

He goes to her, one last time he thinks, but when he kisses her on the neck he sees the marks of Howard's teeth. Three months later she calls him at three in the morning. The moment he enters her apartment he kneels before her. (He thinks later that Howard would not kneel at the sight of her. "His money held him up like a corset" [p. 180]). They go to the Jersey shore together for a weekend but it is a disaster.

What happens keeps on happening. She goes back to Howard to become his wife. The narrator calls her and says he will write a letter to Howard that will compromise her if she does not sleep with him. Howard offered her a thousand dollars to do it, he says. He asks only for a letter. It seems a fair trade. "The sense mounted in me," he thinks, "of having become something I was not, of having some creature emerge who inhabited me but was not me and who appeared only when I suffered" (p. 182).

She knows he will not send the letter. She knows the kind of man he is would not send the letter nor force her to sleep with him. They might see one another, she says. She will be married to Howard. He can remain her lover. They have learned things about themselves they did not know before. He had been incapable of love and has learned what he would do to keep a love he no longer has. She is no longer the girl from Oak Park who only wanted love, happiness, a good marriage, a second child.

On the way home from their disastrous weekend in Atlantic City, he had said, "I'll tell you what's wrong.... Us. Them. It" (p. 157).

Whatever remains of Hayes's radical thirties beliefs we hear in the disillusion and despair of those words. "Us": those without wealth. "Them": the world of wealth. "It": life in America. "A landscape that lack[s] love … a normal condition in my country" (*The Temptation of Don Volpi*, p. 55).

By the time Hayes wrote *In Love* he had moved away from the clipped, austere writing of Hemingway and the newsreel montage character-istic of Dos Passos to the more nuanced prose of Henry James and its examination of the complexi-ties of self. Hayes's forty-year-old man, with his twenty-something woman, is a characteristic Jamesian figure whose experience and knowledge offer possibilities for the young woman even if he is disillusioned, if not cynical, as James's middle-aged men are not. We may say that *In Love* is Hayes's "The Beast in the Jungle".

The face of *My Face for the World to See* (1958) is that of a young woman who at one time thought hers would be the face seen in theaters across the country but no longer does. The face is also that of a no longer young writer who thought he would go his own way in Hollywood.

Hollywood for her is necessary. Even if she does not become an actress, her life is preferable to a life with a husband and child in her hometown. It is the only way she can live. Hol-lywood for him is an escape from an unhappy marriage in New York, although it does little more than pay the bills. "There was just some-thing invisible, I found, about everybody who lived in the town" (*My Face for the World to See*, p. 10).

They are alone. He, because being alone is what he wants, "the one active passion I had left now" (p. 15). An obsession. She, because when she is drunk things happen she can't predict, but when she sobers up she faces consequences she does not want.

Bored one night at a Hollywood party, he goes out onto the porch of the house to see the ocean, as Nathanael West's Midwesterners had. He sees a "girl, a pretty girl," in shorts, a Basque shirt, a yachting cap on her head, carrying in one hand a cocktail glass. "Her legs had, in the very tight shorts, and in the darkness, a special white-ness" (p. 2). She holds the glass up as if it were a chalice. It is the beginning of a Hollywood movie he might have written and one she has seen more than once. "I assumed she was perfectly aware of the composition" (p. 2).

When she drinks from the glass and walks into the ocean the scene shifts. A wave breaks and she goes under. He jumps off the porch to save her. On the sand, he straddles her and pumps water out of her. He feels silly. The position is obscene. When she calls him later to thank him, she does not speak of suicide. He remembers that on the sand she kept trying to say something. What happened seems to have had a strange ef-fect on him. She'd lain exposed on the sand. He had straddled her. "An intimate act, and a relationship of a kind had come into existence between us" (p. 18).

She was the successful daughter who had gone away from home, but she got no parts she auditioned for and had no loves except married men. He can no longer go to bed with his wife and does not understand why he stays married. When he manages to get her an audition at a studio, she fails miserably and afterward looks at him with hatred. "I knew, of course, the contours of the pit into which she was looking. I'd looked into it in my own time; the pit of one's own incapabilities. It never really closed over" (p. 113).

He tries to say something to reassure her. She is beautiful, her silk blouse glimmers, the candle flickers, fades, the record on the stereo plays over and over. He tells her he loves her. And freezes. "The relationship that hangs upon the desire of another that does not know itself," Rancière says (p. 88).

A man sees a pretty woman and saves her. His marriage is on the rocks. A woman in need of saving sees a man who is kind, who listens. It cannot be any other way. She is desperate. He does not understand that he is desperate until she shows him he is. He knows it will not work.

She shouldn't sleep with anybody if she doesn't wish them to know her secrets. It was something more than her nakedness: more than the exhaustion after love. She was in the bed as she would be in a

ALFRED HAYES

ditch or a field. She slept like someone who could not go any further and had already come too far.

(*My Face for the World to See*, p. 80)

He knows it will not work but does not end the relationship until his wife tells him that she is coming to visit. At a restaurant for their last dinner the young woman savages him. She may have slept with a grocery boy, she says, a girl in San Francisco, a bartender, an eight-year-old boy, more, many more, but the writing he does for the studio makes him as much a whore as she is. He does not believe what she has said about herself, but knows that what she has said about him is true. She drinks and does not stop drinking. When she goes to the bathroom, she disappears. When he cannot find her he goes home.

Later that night she knocks on his door, berates him for leaving her at the restaurant, hallucinates about a Phillip who beat her, a Marsha who is not there, and him, who is, but she does not see whoever has been paid by the studios to follow her. She knows that everyone she meets is in the pay of the studio to keep tabs on her. Her madness is chilling. She goes into the bathroom, breaks a glass, slits her wrists. He calls Charlie, who had hosted the party where she had walked into the ocean. Charlie is the man who takes care of things. They take her to her apartment, call her psychiatrist, go to Romanoff's so that everyone will see them.

> It was, after all, their world and sooner or later I had to live in it on the only possible terms: theirs. It was a delusion that I could make my own. The self-deception had been that any terms but theirs could exist. I did not want to be again that coldwater-flat hero, keeping myself neat and unimpaired on the subway at the five o'clock rush hour.
>
> (p. 180)

He tries to explain to Charlie why she tried to commit suicide (a second time), mentions the prize she sought, the apple at the end of the branch, like the green light that Jay Gatsby saw at the end of Daisy's dock, that sends us from Hoboken to Hollywood, Niantic to New York. "For in the end, that was where the injustice of it lay: that it was visible, that it was there, on that branch, that it was reachable, that it was close or seemingly close" (p. 178).

That she—and those like her—refuse to be what they can. That he—and those like him—will not be what they can. Their dark side, subterranean passages and blasted nights of the soul. Their dank root. Hayes goes where other writers of his generation will not. *My Face for the World to See* is merciless. The face we face that we turn away from.

"America is a story and a place," writes Greil Marcus (p. 6). Its story is never more than what it is in Hollywood; the place of all places in the American psyche. "The American blessing or curse—the terror or embrace that is found as a reward—is to live out that absolute, or live in its shadow" (p. 19).

The End of Me (1968) is a book of the sixties: of the generation that fought during the Second World War and is now middle-aged; and of the one born during the war that has now come into its own. Asher is fifty-one. His nephew, Michael, is twenty-six. "Every generation arrives on the scene with its particular hunger," Walter Benjamin notes (p. 307), but Asher does not understand what Michael's hunger is. These kids are not what kids were like in Asher's day. Asher is John Updike's Rabbit Angstrom in the last novel of his Rabbit trilogy, *Rabbit Is Rich*. They both have come to understand what "over thirty" means.

Asher is a Hollywood screenwriter whose second wife is sleeping with her tennis partner. He abruptly leaves for New York, where he spent the first thirty-five years of his life. "I wanted to be lost," Asher says. "I wanted to be effaced. I wanted a place that could suck the pain out" (*The End of Me*, p. 5). New York is home. It is the past.

An aunt asks him to talk to Michael, who is a poet. Once he reads Michael's abrasive and suffocating writing, however, language that lashes out, howls, every other word an obscenity, he feels put up against the wall. "The sex he celebrated took place in a world not quite my world: it seemed more destructive, more finally poisoned" (p. 59).

Michael reads Arthur Rimbaud, Boris Pasternak (the poetry), *Indian Love Lyrics,* and thinks Asher would not understand what interests him.

Asher feels dismissed by Michael. His trip to Japan to momentarily step aside from a failing career is seen by the boy to be no more than tourism. He hires Michael, who does not seem to work, to stroll with him through his past in New York so that Michael might understand what made Asher who he is. A naive notion, he soon realizes.

Michael has a girlfriend, Aurora, a law student, whom Asher, like all middle-aged men in Hayes's writing, finds attractive. He soon discovers that Michael and Aurora lie as it suits them, take on whatever roles they need for the games they play, and that he has become the ball to be kicked around in their next game.

At one point Aurora tells Asher she is pregnant. He provides money for the abortion, but, as it turns out, she is not pregnant. It was just another of the games they had planned for him. Later he discovers that they had cut out the heads of Washington, Lincoln, Jackson, and Grant on the bills he had given Aurora and pasted them over his own head in pictures contained in the scrapbook of his life he had shown them.

He does not understand why they play the games they do, but he cannot miss this one. "I wasn't any of the things I'd thought I'd been. I was merely money" (p. 177). Asher goes to the window and sees what is outside: "Everything went by. Nothing went by. I went by" (p. 178). He had come to New York so that the past might erase the present but learns that the present has done away with the past.

If the book is one more example in Hayes's work of the devastation money causes, it is also the requiem of a writer who is no longer what he once was. The man who in the thirties opposed capitalism lives by it in the sixties. He had been bought like the women in Rome during the war.

The Stockbroker, the Bitter Young Man, and the Beautiful Girl (1973) ends in the death of the young man but feels as if rigor mortis had already set in. The disaster that was Vietnam was reaching its end. The sixties had come and gone and we did not know what it left behind. Hayes had been writing for forty years. The title of this book does no more than recapitulate his obsessions: money and class; an unhappy man; a beautiful

girl. The writing is slapdash, tired. It was Hayes's last novel and not a fitting final act. It was published only in England and reviews were not favorable.

Ten years before the young man of the title, Arthur Lewis, flies to Switzerland, he had been drawn in by the beautiful girl, Phyllis Zura, to be her rent-a-lover so that the man she loves, the stockbroker Jay Richards, will divorce his wife, an Oklahoma oil heiress, and marry her. At the hotel in St. Andreas, Arthur sees Phyllis and Jay. (We do not know why he has come to Switzerland. Phyllis has married someone else and Jay remains married, but they are still lovers.)

Arthur is still in love with Phyllis. Jay continues to remind Arthur that he has always denied him recognition of his life. Jay does not miss any chance to tell Arthur that he does not have the life he has. Jay is rich. He has Phyllis. He does what he wants. Jay forces Arthur, who has never skied before, to ski. He crashes. His last words before he dies are:

> Fuck you, Arthur Lewis screamed. And the cold mountains, the light-year, the pattern in space, echoed back: Fuck you.
>
> (*Stockbroker*, p. 157)

The last words that a boy from the Bronx would say. The last words that the man who was no longer the boy would reclaim, in despair, in this, his last novel. Hayes continued to write poetry but never sent anything out to be published.

POETRY

There were no books in Hayes's home when he was growing up. He preferred the company of cabdrivers in pool halls, liked to gamble. He dropped out of college after six months. He began to steal books because he could not afford to buy them. He read Hart Crane, William Carlos Williams, T. S. Eliot, Ezra Pound. His friends were poets: Sol Funaroff, Herman Spector, and, in particular, Kenneth Fearing, whose politics he shared until the Moscow Trials of the late 1930s caused Hayes to go his own way.

His is a modernist sensibility masked, if not concealed, by his leftist politics of the thirties

and later by his novels of the war in Italy and writings set in Hollywood and New York after the war. The only novelist he mentions is William Faulkner. He saw him at the Players restaurant in West Hollywood.

The first poems Hayes published in the thirties in the *New Masses*, *Dynamo*, and *Partisan Review* are, as their titles tell us, in service of a movement, that of the Communist Left in America: "Into the Streets May First," "Comrade Poets," "May First." Their language is rushed, breathless, urgent; harsh, bitter yet incantatory; language of the streets reminiscent of Alexander Blok's *Twelve* (1918). Their language is, above all, a weapon: "We hurl the bright bombs of the sun"; "The moon like a hand grenade"; "Poised as a song with a hammer" (*New Masses*, May 1934 and April 1933).

Hayes told Granville Hicks that his poem "In a Coffee Pot" was "the first poem I know of in the movement which attempted to create a realistic, representative experience of my generation—a generation which is a decisive factor in the growth of revolutionary consciousness" (qtd. in Wald, p. 218).

When *The Big Time* (1944), his first book of poetry, was published, he included none of the political poems he wrote in the thirties. He would not permit them to be published. His poetry remains bleak in this volume, but it now focuses more narrowly on the struggle between the sexes. One poem, though, is a dramatic monologue about Julius Caesar at Epirus, which marks a shift from his earlier tropes—such as an unemployed man sitting in a café or a solitary woman at a window in her apartment, as if in an Edward Hopper painting—to more classical tropes of poetry, scenes from Rome, Greece, mythology.

Another poem, "A Nice Part of Town," that describes changes in New York is reminiscent of Genevieve Taggard's poem of New York, "All Around the Town." In "Underground," Hayes sees the hopelessness and despair of those on the subway on their way to work.

Welcome to the Castle (1950) recapitulates the subjects of his first novels. Half of the poems are about the war in Italy ("The killing went on and it was cold that winter" [p. 19]), but a number of these poems are transformed into dramatic monologues of ancient Romans in scenes of war and loss. The war will not go away, even if it must be seen in someone else's life from a distant past. The women are there, as they always are; love is as difficult as ever, if not impossible. His poems here are strikingly like and as good as the wartime poems of Anthony Hecht. The other half of the poems are about the soldier's return to a suddenly rich, profit-driven America that has no place for him. The only song he can sing: "Whimpers, loneliness, despair—A music squeezed from unmusical things" (p. 82).

Just Before the Divorce (1968), published the same year as *The End of Me*, bookends that volume. It looks back on the poet's life as Asher does in the novel, to his childhood, his father the barber, memories of war, his new life as a tourist in France and Japan, a house in California. He asks what has happened to this man, who or what has worked on him.

CONCLUSION

We cannot place Alfred Hayes, and because we cannot, he has no place at the table. As a young man he was addicted to pinball machines and pool halls. He talked to cabdrivers. His poems of the thirties were proletarian. He wrote scripts on demand for Hollywood. He thought his novels were commercial, although only one of them, *The Girl on the Via Flaminia*, sold well. His vision was seen to be dark, cynical some would say, disillusioned; a sensibility more European than American. The man who had come out of Harlem and the Bronx, served in Italy during the Second World War, labored in the vineyards of Hollywood, and traveled to Kyoto and Paris was no longer the one who picked up a pool cue and chalked it.

In an interview late in life, Hayes considered his novels to be different from those written at the time. People read, but he didn't understand what they made of what they read. So much of it was a bore, flat. It is a damnation out of Ezra Pound, Wyndham Lewis, and D. H. Lawrence, for Hayes's work was modernist. If at first it came out of Blok and Vladimir Mayakovsky, it

would later define itself through Edith Wharton and Henry James. Hayes is, as Martin Schifino writes in the *Times Literary Supplement,* "an archaeologist of the everyday." He would see William Faulkner across the room in the Players restaurant and know they knew where they were.

Selected Bibliography

WORKS OF ALFRED HAYES

FICTION

All Thy Conquests. New York: Howell, Soskin, 1946.
Shadow of Heaven. New York: Howell, Soskin, 1947.
The Girl on the Via Flaminia. New York: Harper, 1949.
In Love. New York: Harper, 1953.
My Face for the World to See. New York: Harper, 1958.
The Temptation of Don Volpi. New York: Atheneum, 1960.
The End of Me. New York: Atheneum, 1968.
The Stockbroker, the Bitter Young Man, and the Beautiful Girl. London: Gollancz, 1973.

POETRY COLLECTIONS

The Big Time. New York: Howell, Soskin, 1944.
Welcome to the Castle. New York: Harper, 1950.
Just Before the Divorce. New York: Atheneum, 1968.

DRAMA

Journeyman. (Play.) Adapted from the novel by Erskine Caldwell. Fulton Theatre, New York City, 1938.
Tis of Thee. (Musical.) Music by Alex North, book by Sam Locke, lyrics by Alfred Hayes. Maxine Elliott's Theatre, New York City, 1940.
The Girl on the Via Flaminia. (Play.) Circle in the Square and 48th Street Theatre, New York City, 1954. (Adapted for film as *Act of Love,* United Artists, 1953.)

SCREENPLAYS

Paisan. With Federico Fellini, Roberto Rossellini et al. OFI, 1949.
Teresa. Story by Alfred Hayes and Stewart Stern. MGM, 1951.
Clash by Night. From the play by Clifford Odets. RKO, 1952.
Human Desire. From the novel by Émile Zola. Columbia, 1954.

The Left Hand of God. From the novel by William E. Barrett. Warner Bros., 1955.
A Hatful of Rain. From the play by Michael V. Gazzo. Twentieth Century–Fox, 1957.
Island in the Sun. From the novel by Alec Waugh. Twentieth Century–Fox, 1957.
These Thousand Hills. From the novel by A. B. Guthrie, Jr. Twentieth Century–Fox, 1959.
The Mountain Road. From the novel by Theodore H. White. Columbia, 1960.
Joy in the Morning. From the novel by Betty Smith. MGM, 1965.
The Double Man. From the novel *Legacy of a Spy* by Henry S. Maxfield. Warner Bros., 1967.
The Blue Bird. From the play *L'Oiseau bleu* by Maurice Maeterlinck. Twentieth Century–Fox, 1976.

POEMS

"Joe Hill" ["I Dreamed I Saw Joe Hill Last Night"]. Song adaptation, with Earl Robinson. *Daily Worker,* September 4, 1936.
"Comrade Poets." *New Masses.* April 1933, p. 22.
"In a Coffee Pot." *Partisan Review* 1:12–15 (February–March 1934).
"Into the Streets May First." Song adaptation, with Aaron Copland. *New Masses,* May 1934, pp. 16–17.

CRITICAL AND BIOGRAPHICAL STUDIES

Aldridge, John W. *After the Lost Generation: A Critical Study of the Writers of Two Wars.* New York: McGraw-Hill, 1951.
Bailey, Paul. "Chronicles of Dust and Sin." *Guardian,* October 28, 2005. http://www.theguardian.com/books/2005/oct/29/featuresreviews.guardianreview10
Beach, Joseph Warren. *Obsessive Images; Symbolism in Poetry of the 1930s and 1940s.* Minneapolis: University of Minnesota Press, 1960.
Cowley, Malcolm. *The Dream of the Golden Mountains: Remembering the 1930s.* New York: Viking Press, 1980.
Contemporary Authors Online. "Alfred Hayes." (Interview, August 18, 1980.) Detroit: Gale, 2015.
Fourth Street Review. Review of *In Love.* June 17, 2013. http://fourthstreetreview.com/2013/06/17/in-love-by-alfred-hayes/
Green, Archie. *Wobblies, Pile Butts, and Other Heroes.* Urbana: University of Illinois Press, 1993.
Lezard, Nicholas. Review of *My Face for the World to See. Guardian,* August 6, 2013. http://www.theguardian.com/books/2013/aug/06/my-face-world-see-review
Raphael, Frederic. Introduction to *In Love.* New York: New York Review Books, 2007.

Schifino, Martin. "Well-Bred Rebel." *Times Literary Supplement,* October 4, 2013.

Thomson, David. Introduction to *My Face for the World to See*. New York: New York Review Books, 2013.

Wald, Alan M. *Exiles from a Future Time: The Forging of the Mid-Twentieth-Century Literary Left*. Chapel Hill: University of North Carolina Press, 2002.

OTHER SOURCES

Benjamin, Walter. *The Arcades Project*. Edited by Rolf Tiedemann. Cambridge, Mass.: Belknap Press, 1999.

Marcus, Greil. *The Shape of Things to Come: Prophecy and the American Voice*. London: Faber, 2006.

Rancière, Jacques. *Short Voyages to the Land of the People*. Stanford, Calif.: Stanford University Press, 2003.

DAVID HUDDLE

(1942—)

Ann McKinstry Micou

DAVID HUDDLE, AN award-winning writer and distinguished teacher, had published twenty books as of 2015—seven collections of poetry, six volumes of short fiction, four novels, two compilations of essays, and one reader of selected prose and poetry. For the novel *The Story of a Million Years*, he received the Distinguished Book of the Year award from *Esquire* and Best Book of the Year citation from the *Los Angeles Times Book Review*, both in 2000. *Nothing Can Make Me Do This* won the Emyl Jenkins Sexton Literary Award for Fiction of the Library of Virginia in 2012. *Blacksnake at the Family Reunion* garnered the PEN New England Award for Poetry and was a finalist for the Library of Virginia Award for Poetry, both in 2013.

Huddle's compassionate, honest, and accessible narratives were nurtured in his southern childhood, matured in his youthful tour in Vietnam, and seasoned in a northern climate. His work is elegant in its clarity, poignant in its intimacy, and shapely in its form. He contemplates the intricacies of human relationships—son and extended family, husband and wife, and father and daughters. In the imagery of Huddle's poetry and prose, light is everywhere: it shines on the faces of his characters and emanates from them; it penetrates the dark interiors of their lives, illuminating their secrets, their amatory longings, their shame. Among influences, he points to Ernest Hemingway's and William Faulkner's concern for "the external world" and John Cheever's and Raymond Carver's "interest in internal thoughts" (Hallenbeck interview).

LIFE

David Ross Huddle was born on July 11, 1942, in Ivanhoe, Virginia, a tiny Appalachian town on the New River in Wythe County. His father, Charles Richard Huddle, Jr. (1911–1986), became manager for National Carbide Company's manufacturing plant; he was "a good listener and a compassionate person" ("Out of Ivanhoe," p. 181). His mother, Mary Francis Akers Huddle (1919–1999), was fifteen years old when she married Charles: "She spent hours / talking quietly— / she could listen— // and she liked us" (*Summer Lake*, p. 155). Huddle's brothers were Charles Richard Huddle III and William Royal Huddle. He traveled by school bus from Ivanhoe to Wytheville, where he attended the consolidated high school, played saxophone in the band, and had a superb English teacher, who gave him "the skills to become a writer" ("Out of Ivanhoe," p. 181).

Huddle attended the University of Virginia, dropped out, and joined the U.S. Army, serving from 1964 to 1967 as a paratrooper in Germany and a military intelligence specialist in Vietnam; promoted to sergeant, he received the Bronze Star. The first stories he published, "Rosie Baby" (*Georgia Review*, 1969) and "The Interrogation of the Prisoner Bung by Mister Hawkins and Sergeant Tree" (*Esquire*, 1971), were set in Vietnam. Rowe Portis called the latter "as good a story as anyone has written about the war in Vietnam" (*Library Journal*, p. 1240). Huddle writes that "my first two short stories made it into print mostly because they were about the Vietnam War" ("Got to Go to That War," p. 195).

He returned to the University of Virginia to earn his B.A. degree, followed by an M.A. in English from Hollins College in 1969 and an M.F.A. from Columbia University in 1971. Huddle says, "I couldn't have become a writer without the two graduate writing programs that I went through. I needed that time to be able to

believe that I could be a writer, to have people treat me as if I were a writer" (Hudgens et al., p. 1). In 1968 he married Lindsey Massie, an attorney; the couple had two daughters, Bess and Molly. His domestic life "has deepened my understanding of just about everything" (Eder and Donovan).

From 1971 until 2009 Huddle taught literature and creative writing at the University of Vermont in Burlington. He was a faculty member at the Rainier Writing Workshop at Pacific Lutheran University and the Bread Loaf School of English. He has taught at the University of Idaho; Goddard, Warren Wilson, and Middlebury Colleges; and the Bread Loaf Writers' Conference. He also wrote early every morning, with a cup of coffee "so hot I can barely sip it" (*Grayscale*, p. 6). After his retirement from UVM, he was Distinguished Visiting Professor of Creative Writing at Hollins College in Virginia. In Tennessee, he held the 2012–2013 Roy Acuff Chair of Excellence in the Creative Arts at Austin Peay State University and in 2014 joined the Sewanee School of Letters faculty. Burlington has remained home to him and his wife.

The National Endowment for the Arts awarded him two fellowships in literature; he also received fellowships from Yaddo and the Bread Loaf Writers' Conference. He received the *Michigan Quarterly Review*'s Lawrence Foundation Prize for the Short Story and the *Mid-American Review*'s James Wright Prize for Poetry. His native state has celebrated his work: he has received an honorary doctorate from Shenandoah University and a fellowship from Virginia Center for the Creative Arts, and was named "20th Century Virginia Author" by the Library of Virginia.

More than two hundred of his works have appeared in periodicals and anthologies, including the *American Scholar, Antioch Review, Best American Stories, Contemporary Poetry of New England, Esquire, Harper's, Harvard Review, The Jazz Fiction Anthology, Kenyon Review, New England Review, New Yorker, New York Times Book Review, Playboy, Southern Review, Yale Review,* and *Vietnam Anthology: American War Literature.*

POETRY

In *Southern Writers*, Owen W. Gilman, Jr., writes, "In the guise of poet, Huddle embraces Sir Walter Scott's Ivanhoe impulse, repeatedly bringing his Virginia origins up close for loving reconsideration" (p. 205). Huddle says that his first collection, *Paper Boy* (1979), was "written almost just to say I can do this, I will do this" (Garrett, p. 248). His poems are tender, disappointed, empathetic, appreciative, apologetic, intimate, and autobiographical As he told Christina Arregoces of *Superstition Review*, "A major portion of my writing draws from my past." *Paper Boy* is "pretty close to one hundred percent autobiography." These narrative poems are colloquial and detailed, filled with small-town characters who are not caricatures but fully drawn individuals. He is interested in "writing poems in sequences" (Hudgens et al., p. 9).

The poems in *Paper Boy* salute his parents: his mother grew up in the house they live in; his father, across the field. As a boy, Huddle delivers the *Roanoke Times* and, with his proceeds, buys a gold-plated trumpet. Twin brothers drown when he is in the fifth grade, a recurring motif in "Crossing New River" (*Grayscale*), "Poison Oak" (*Only the Little Bone*), *La Tour Dreams of the Wolf Girl*, and *The Faulkes Chronicle*. "Threshing Wheat" foreshadows a similar scene in "Dirge Notes" (*Only the Little Bone*). In another episode that stays with Huddle, his father is devastated over the terrible burning of one of his employees in an accident at the plant, retold in "Burned Man" (*Blacksnake*) and "The Undesirable" (*Only the Little Bone*). In "Mrs. Green," he longs to see the inside of the house belonging to a sympathetic woman to whom he delivers papers. In "Going 1960–1970," Huddle touches affectingly on slivers of his life—news about his dying grandfather, attending the University of Virginia, going to Germany and Vietnam, and his father's dancing with his mother before three hundred people at a wedding ("I'd / been through enough of a / war to know courage / when I saw it," p. 52). At his grandfather's funeral, he sees his father cry for the first time. In *Library Journal*, Keith Washburn noted Huddle's "ability to

select the small detail that makes a poem compelling rather than ordinary" (p. 406).

The poems in the first section of *Stopping by Home* (1988), "Tour of Duty," concern Huddle's experiences in Vietnam. In "Entry," he is the novice in tan; the men in green have M16s slung on their backs "like toys" (p. 3). In "Nerves," he says he never shot anyone because he was an interrogator, but he remembers the women, children, and old men—"shame is natural, wear it, every day" (p. 37). "Theory" tells of living first in holes, then in hooches. "Smoke" summons the memory of the incineration of human waste from the outhouses. In "Work," Huddle's assignment as an interrogator with the help of the interpreter Sergeant Tri is the seed of Huddle's stunning short story "The Interrogation of the Prisoner Bung by Mister Hawkins and Sergeant Tree."

The second section, "Album," is dedicated to his mother. He evokes the day his father arrives at his mother's house in white tennis flannels. As an adult, Huddle remembers ascending the stairs of the white clapboard house, astounded to think that once, as a small girl, his mother climbed these very stairs, "light slanting / down from the high window" (p. 16). She loses her first baby; he imagines them together, "the light falling / in slats into that upstairs bedroom" (p. 16). The school does not have a real basketball court, a team, or uniforms, and is scorned by its opponents. He feels terrible regret for hitting one of his brothers in the face with an icicle.

The third section focuses on his father's struggle with emphysema, in and out of the hospital. Huddle is beset by remorse for living far away; he arrives for a visit and cannot wait to leave. His word for departing, "scuttle" (p. 31), reveals his shame: his father is sick and he cannot stand being around him. He can hardly bear the change from the father he knew to this "babbling monster" (p. 40). Sometimes his father makes sense: he quietly tells his son to turn on the light so the latter can read. Huddle remembers once asking his father about homosexuals; his father looks up the word in a dictionary. "This will tell you everything / you need to know about the time and / place I grew up in and the kind /

of family we were" (p. 45). He understands that "Books was what they put their faith in" (p. 46). The telephone call comes from the hospital. He can say the words: "I say my father was / here. I say he lived thousands of strong days. / I know he got sick. My / father // died" (p. 52). Vincent Balitas in *Library Journal* found the collection "important because of its sequence of poems about Vietnam."

The poems in *The Nature of Yearning* (1992) belonged to his English professor/poet in an unpublished novel; he "stole the good ones" for this collection (*Reader*, p. 2). Its title is a synecdoche for much of his oeuvre—a longing for love and understanding, for sunlight and uncovering truth, for nature and family. In "Local Metaphysics," the children visit Miss Ossie Price to confirm that she did not burn up in a fire, which may be a true story or one the mother makes up later. In "Eastern Standard," Grandmama Huddle, as a matter of principle, refuses to change her clocks to accommodate daylight savings. The title poem is a paean to Vermont's seasons: August "swells with warmth / the garden would burst" (p. 5); in October, "the trees were pure / fire for two weeks" (p. 6); in February, "the ice builds its kingdom / and holds against what fire we have left love" (p. 8); in March, "the trees / are just bones they shiver" (p. 8); in April, "the earth is sunlight" (p. 9). In "Visit of the Hawk," he calls his wife to see the bird. They stick their heads out the skylight and "[brush] against each other / most pleasantly" (p. 10), recalling the transcendent moment in the short story "The Mean Mud Season," when the narrator looks out the skylight with his daughter, "bumping shoulders with Victoria" (*High Spirits*, p. 219). Huddle thinks happily of an old home movie with his thin young father who "smiled at" and "lifted up [his baby] to the sun ... and wanted me / right here in this world" (p. 47).

A sequence of poems illustrates the recurring theme of out-of-step lovers. In "Party Poem," a woman he hardly knows tells him cryptically, "There's this secret / everybody knows and nobody / ever tells" (p. 17). "Quiet Hour" summons up the time after the children have left the table and, in the silence, it would be easy for the

parents to talk about separating, about how "to share the children" (p. 24). In "Music," the couple is going through such a bad time they cannot bear one more day together. In "Summer Lake," a husband and wife watch "the slow coming of dusk over the water" (p. 28): he is "aching," she is "soul-tired" (p. 28). They listen to an accordion player on the Lake Champlain ferry and hear the music afterward. In "Love and Art," a couple at the art gallery is not on the same wavelength: she is enthralled, he buys postcards. When he returns to find her, she is "smiling into the light" (p. 39). This common motif of being out of step or off-key recurs in *Tenorman* and *Not: A Trio. Virginia Quarterly Review* found that the "poems come to us casually, like the voice of an old friend."

In *Summer Lake: New and Selected Poems* (1999), Huddle dedicates "What You Live For" to his mother, an Alzheimer's patient "dying away from home." "A Brief History of My Mother's Temper" ends: "it takes almost / a lifetime to / appreciate / one clear, bright day. / Mother, I wish / you this day's light" (p. 162). "Men's Sauna," Huddle told Brian Brodeur, is "a very autobiographical piece of writing," written within days of the experience: he becomes enraged with a fat, unattractive man's ignoring his little boy's needs. Huddle said that the "generating force of this poem—and most of my writing—is 'moral and ethical anxiety'" (Brodeur). "Military Parachuting Exercise" lists nine jump commands (p. 116), also referred to in "Save One for Mainz" (*Only the Little Bone*, p. 151). In "Two," a pair of Chinese women walk together. Their song is a "*moving puzzle of light*" (p. 123).

In "Confessions," Monkey Dunford, a "Holy Roller" and his grandfather's hired man, also appears in *Paper Boy*. Huddle knows he condescended to Monkey and is ashamed; he now realizes "how he was / my teacher, and how until I die / I'll be his / disciple" (p. 128). "Picture" is another salute to his grandfather, who "let me witness / who he was" (p. 135). In "Model Father," he spends hours with his father gluing small pieces of balsa "without much regard / for whether or not what / we made would fly" (p.

138). In "Basket," his mother is in a nursing home in Georgia, trying to do needlepoint, as was her custom. She is dismayed to think she has lost her basket; she calms down, her "coiled cobra"—her dementia—beside her (p. 144). "The Episode" details a familiar litany of her Alzheimer's—she calls the sheriff to tell him her boys are missing (they are long grown up and gone); goes downtown in dishabille; writes a check in response to every mail and phone solicitation. Someone takes away her car; she is furious. Uncle Jack, a colonel and fighter pilot who flew two tours in Vietnam, weeps. In "Never Been," Huddle dreams of a family reunion, when his father and mother are young and his brothers are boys; he is there with his wife and daughters in "a green and sunlit valley" (p. 168) but out of reach; he confesses his failures. He promises his daughters the same place, "the green meadow shining / in the sunlight" (p. 169). The *Virginia Quarterly Review* noted "a sense of a man who writes poems to come to terms with his life." Frank Allen in *Library Journal* found "these candid, delicate poems become a base line for comprehending 'ordinary life.'"

In *Grayscale: Poems* (2004), the three Huddle brothers pose for a photograph in 1963. Writing from Vermont years later, Huddle now understands "time's optical illusion: we think // we stand in the vivid color of the here and now / and view the past as drab black and white, / whereas the truth is—it's our future / that's the off-center, badly-focused grayscale" (p. 2). In "Crossing New River" he sees young friends "pulled up by hooks / and flopped into rescue squad boats" (p. 12). In "April Saturday 1960," he and a girl are dancing decorously while another couple is making out; the next minute they are "a public // display of live pornography" (p. 16), which they handle with "astonishing kindness and grace" (p. 18). In "Deathlight," he thinks about death, unsure about what he wants to know: do you fall "to darkness or burst into light"? (p. 29). In "The Poem, the Snow, Jane Goodall, the Vase of Daffodils," he sees "morning sunlight on new snow" (p. 32). In "Circus," he is not sure whether his family ever went to one: "We were all good at dreaming" (p. 56). In *Booklist*, Donna Seaman

called Huddle "a source of light in an often gray world."

Glory River (2007) is a "remake" of his first book of poems, *Paper Boy*. In the first version, says Huddle, he tried to stick more or less to what really happened; here, "I'm lying and exaggerating at every possible opportunity" (Hudgens et al., p. 2). In "Courting," the boys are rough, ugly, and uncouth with girls. In "Metamorphosis," Sarah Jean is a good crawdad hunter. One day she picks up a tadpole, which she adores; when she opens her hands, a green frog springs away. Everyone reveres or despises her. One boy she goes out with is sent to prison, another is crippled in an auto accident, her father runs away with another woman. Sarah Jean and her mother live in a trailer, which is consumed by flames. No evidence remains of her existence. In "Screech Owl," a scientist comes to Glory River. Monkey's boy, Deetum, who is not quite right in the head, gives an owl to the visitor. In "Pity," the reader is exhorted not to feel sorry for Glory River: it has "this fiddle, banjo, & stand-up bass, this / steel guitar" (p. 29). "The Mayor of Glory River" is a dog. The narrator, researching Glory River for an Appalachian case study, finds murder, incest, theft, paranoia, and prejudice. The dog brings good luck to everyone who tries to adopt him. The narrator's dissertation is published and leads to employment, but he realizes his interviewees lied to him—there was no black dog, although he sometimes dreams of him.

"No End" is a sonnet for a majorette in the marching band in high school who is still "Almost unbearably alive" (p. 48), an allusion to Valerie in the short story "Playing" (*High Spirits*). In "The Hardest Thing," Huddle remembers the terrible diseases, emphysema and Alzheimer's, that destroyed his parents; his experience in Vietnam; the danger to his marriage; his fears for his daughters; his anger and disappointment. He still cannot name the hardest thing but thinks it miraculous to be alive. "In the Boston Children's Hospital" tells of his daughter, Bess, near death, who survives, apologizing to him for causing trouble; he keeps from weeping and is "pierced" with "joy" (p. 64). Writing in the *Southern Review*, Philip F. Deaver hails Huddle's "priority"

which "is telling the story in plain language and in dialect that signals superstition and primitive wonder" (p. 786).

In *Blacksnake at the Family Reunion: Poems* (2012), Huddle again imagines his parents' courtship. Between their childhood houses was a stile, which his father passed more and more frequently to meet his mother. In "1953 Dodge Coronet," the three boys go to the fair with their parents. Excited, then exhausted, by the amusements, they are "sleepy and quiet … the ride home takes us / the rest of our lives" (p. 5). "This Morning" relates his being hit by a car, first told in "Only the Little Bone." When he regains his confidence, his mother "acted like it'd never been lost" (p. 6). In "Mother Song," he cries when he hears her sing in church. Huddle repeats her symptoms ("Episodes," *Summer Lake*, p. 145): once he thought her crazy actions were *"embarrassing"*; now he finds them *"glorious"* (p. 10). "Burned Man" retells the story of the worker maimed in his father's factory: his father is the only one who will look at his "scarred, fire bubbled face" and talk to the man, who can barely rasp out words (p. 11). In "What the Stone Says," the gravestone for his sister who died immediately after birth reads "Born & Died": "the ampersand / tells the whole truth" (p. 14).

In "Boy Story," he hopes for intimate contact with Melva but has parked too near her grandmother's grave. In "Hard Drive," the narrator is in love with his friend's wife; they have changed from their younger lives and become "like actors cast in another show" (p. 33). "In My Other Life" tells of a man and his sweetie in this "brain-dead town" where everything's "out of sync" (p. 36). "The Husband's Tale" concerns a man married for forty years to a mute woman who writes books. "If she looked straight at you, / it could make you shiver" (p. 39), evoking another familiar theme in Huddle's work: looking at people's faces, looking away, trying for the best light to read people's secrets, as in "The Deacon" (*High Spirits*), and *La Tour*. Because the woman is mute, he is afraid she will get hurt and spies on her, echoing another motif found in "The Proofreader" (*A Dream with No Stump Roots*), *Tenorman*, and *Nothing Can Make Me*

Do This. In "Weather Report," "the vultures of this landscape came to call." Depressed, he invites them in and turns off the lights: "I know you like the dark" (p. 47). "Linguistics 101" is about marriage—some couples suffer; some make it through, "like old friends in love" (p. 52). Keenan Walsh of *Seven Days* wrote that while Huddle's "colloquial tone, though generally a virtue, can occasionally distract," he found the collection "a deceptively simple, slithering and fluid meditation" that "gathers emotional momentum as it proceeds and deserves to be read from beginning to end."

SHORT FICTION

"Eudora Welty and Flannery O'Connor are probably my instructors in the short story," Huddle said in a *Willow Springs* interview (p. 5); "I have a lust for a good sentence, as a reader and a writer" (p. 3). His work is drawn from his life: "Autobiographical fiction is the highest form of narrative art," he asserted in 1992's *Writing Habit* (p. 39).

A Dream with No Stump Roots in It (1975) contains two stories about Vietnam. "The Interrogation of the Prisoner Bung by Mister Hawkins and Sergeant Tree" is a grim, cynical story of an indifferent, bored American presiding over an interrogation with the help of his duplicitous interpreter. The venue is the local police station. Using a rubber club, the interpreter casually beats up the prisoner until the police chief arrives with documents showing the prisoner was falsely accused. Released, the latter reports to his cell what American intelligence he has gleaned. In "Rosie Baby," an American corporal named Kramer, friendly with the locals, is in charge of the army dump, where villagers scavenge. Because of possible classified information in the landfill, his instructions are to keep them out, using a truncheon but not his weapon. Rosie, accompanied by her baby girl, sells beer and Coca-Cola to the truck drivers. When she becomes violent, Kramer loses control of the situation and accidentally stomps on the child's leg, breaking its "baby bone" (p. 56). He is appalled and ashamed.

In "Luther," the church sends the title character to Africa with his wife and baby to bring the word of the Lord to the black people. Luther learns from the local deacon that his predecessor recruited nuns from the female population. Luther attends a pseudo-religious sex orgy, temporarily loses his senses, confesses his sins to a priest, and returns to America a Catholic. In "The Proofreader," Carson Moore, an aspiring poet, looks at his aging, overweight wife, who does not resemble the slender Virginia girl he married, and decides love only exists in books. His habit of "pretending to keep his eyes closed so that he could watch what Mrs. Moore was doing without her know he was doing it" introduces the spying theme (p. 75). After many rejection slips, he blames his wife for his failure and spends his time at peep-show joints and pornography shops, foreshadowing the pornography concept in *Million Years*. In the park, he meets Leslie, who asks what he thinks about love; he confesses he wants to die. Leslie takes him home to his wife, who defends Carson's good, gentle, quiet traits, which, she explains, he is unable to see in himself. Leslie reconnects the couple. In "A Dream with No Stump Roots in It," the narrator takes an ax to an oak tree, but he cannot stop worrying about the roots. They should not be as bothersome as car payments and dentists' bills, but they harass him. He sets fire to the stump, but the flame dies. His wife tells the story to amuse friends; he is "ashamed" (p. 108). He yearns for a "plain of freshly mown grass" (p. 108) with "warm rich sunlight all around us" (p. 109). John Engels wrote in the *Carleton Miscellany*, "Everybody sins in this book, and knows it, and is humiliated by it. The word shame crops up over and over" (p. 132).

The stories in *Only the Little Bone* (1986), linked by the narrator, Reed Bryant, tell about his life in Rosemary. In "Poison Oak," Reed goes outside after supper, although he fears the dark; the "side yard held shafts of light" from a bedroom (p. 3). When he comes in, his father, he says, looks "at my face, trying to guess what I was thinking" (p. 4). Their mother takes Reed and his older brother Duncan to the river for swimming lessons, because she fears their drown-

ing; the drowning death of twin boys is a recurring motif in the poems and stories. Walking through the fields daily, she is troubled by blisters from poison ivy. In "The Undesirable," in the "bright haze of sunlight," Reed's father, as a joke, drives his car directly at his son and stops in the nick of time. Reed is used to being called a "hick" in high school, which prefigures Bill Hyatt's feelings of social inferiority when he goes to Charlottesville ("Brothers," *High Spirits*). Reed, going on fifteen and taking driving lessons, has an accident in his father's new car. His father is disappointed but understanding; Reed reacts badly, smoking and roughhousing on the bus. He starts playing tenor sax, anticipating *Tenorman*. "If the light was right, I could see my reflection in the windows of the band room, and I looked exactly the way I wanted to look" (p. 74). A terrible fire in the factory maims one man, which affects his father profoundly. Reed and his friend are hired to play with some older musicians in a combo, the Mellowtones, which plays for dances in the region. Like Bill Hyatt, he travels with the older musicians. His father hires a pretty young woman, Darcy. When she comes to a club dance in Madison, she and Reed dance and walk outside. He confides, "I don't think my father knows anything about my life" (p. 91); she comments that he would be surprised what his father knows. Darcy rejects his sexual overtures and stops communicating with him. He behaves dishonorably, encouraging his father to fire her. In the parking lot, in a scene that mimics the earlier one, he drives straight at his father as though he were going to hit him: "His face was a way I had never seen it before" (p. 115). In "Save One for Mainz," Reed, six months out of Fort Benning, has been overseas in Germany for five months. He teaches his girlfriend Hilda the nine jump commands, which Huddle refers to in his poem "Military Parachuting Exercise" (*Summer Lake*). He volunteers for Vietnam. Before he leaves, Hilda asks him to recover some provocative pictures of her. He does—and looks at them. He goes home, taking one with him.

"Dirge Notes" consists of a series of sketches about Huddle's childhood: he is a little boy breaking milkweed pods with his brother; his grandparents sit on the concrete water tank cursing at each other; his grandfather kills a starling by mistake; and he spends a whole day threshing with the men. Here, Huddle celebrates work; as he told George Garrett, "I liked the texture of work, and I liked the notion of that low activity, that kind of enlisted man approach to literature" (p. 251). This remark reinforces his seeing himself as a "local, down-in-the-dirt kind of writer" (Hudgens et al., p. 7). In "Sharing," Reed is home from overseas, wearing his jump boots, starched khaki uniform, and overseas cap. When his grandfather enters, Reed stands to attention. About this visit, Huddle writes, "they needed to see me at least giving the appearance of an adult almost as much as I needed to see myself that way" ("Got to Go to that War," p. 194). In "The Flatted Third," Reed is married to Janie. They go with his brother Duncan and his wife to their grandfather's funeral. Reed catches his wife's eye and recognizes "the space between us" (p. 200). In "Only the Little Bone," a polio epidemic quarantines the boys to their backyard. Freed, they go for a drive with their mother. When Reed jumps out to collect something, another car tries to pass and hits him, breaking a little bone in his leg. This time it is a real accident and not feigned, as in the two previous driving duels between Reed and his father. Assessing his family, Reed says, its trait is "flawed competence." The Bryants are "industrious, intelligent, determined, and of good will…. But we usually do something wrong" (p. 212). In the *New York Times*, Meredith Willis mentioned the recurring theme of men's "watching, coveting, spying on" women. *Magill Book Reviews* wrote, "These stories reveal subtleties of feeling among apparently simple, working-class people."

The High Spirits: Stories of Men and Women (1989) begins with "Underwater Spring," in which ten-year-old Frank lives with his great aunts in his mother's family house. She takes him for a farewell swim in a muddy swimming hole before joining her lover. In "The Deacon," George, an artist, is attracted to a woman training for priesthood. He sees her officiating at a baptism, where her face has the "radiance" with which old painters imbue the visages of religious

figures (p. 28). He asks permission to sketch her. At his studio, she undresses without being asked; sketching, he tells her, "does nothing to register how your skin takes this light" (p. 40). She returns for him to paint her. He casts her rosy-white figure against the light coming through the skylight. Together, they look at her face: he has captured a woman with a vocation. Their burgeoning intimacy vanishes.

Three stories concern Billy Hyatt, a saxophone player. In "Playing," Billy, in high school, plays gigs in a band with some older men. He becomes entangled in situations too adult for him—hiring and firing players for the band and becoming sexually entangled with a young majorette who fears for a few days she is pregnant. When he returns to the high school marching band, he feels "so free he can hardly stand it" (p. 104). In "Brothers," Billy is in his second year at the University of Virginia. Geoffrey Slade, Billy's fraternity brother, is a snob who looks down on Billy as a country boy; Huddle has written that some students considered him a "hick" at Charlottesville and made fun of his accent ("Out of Ivanhoe," p. 182). Billy too is class-conscious: he does not take the small-town nursing student he dates to weekend fraternity events. She invites herself one weekend; Slade is contemptuous of her public-school voice. As events steam up, Billy almost strikes her. In his essay "Ingrained Reflexes" (Reader), Huddle comments on his fraternity brothers' behavior toward women. In the story "The High Spirits," Billy plays in a band managed by Richard, a married French teacher and seducer of young women in his high school. Billy admires Louise, one of the girls at a high school prom where they play; Richard procures her for him. Purportedly a tight social unit, the band is filled with conflicted members; Jack, the gay pianist, is in love with Richard. By the tragic end, Billy stares at Louise without recognition: he cannot "call up *her* face" (p. 185).

A sequence of stories takes place in Vermont. In "The Gorge," Braxton, a musician and music teacher, lives in Burlington with his wife and daughter. He realizes he has "closed down a considerable part of himself" and is capable of only "minor accomplishment," while his trumpet student, Monica, has "powerful forces within herself" (p. 193). She persuades him to go to Pennington Gorge and, once there, frightens him by walking too close to the steep edge; this tempting fate is another motif, seen in "Little Sawtooth" (*Intimates*). Perhaps jealous of her talent and alarmed at his strange attraction to her, he comes to the horrifying conclusion that Monica's death would keep him and his wife safe. Frank Berry, a southern middle-aged English professor at the University of Vermont, narrates three stories. The first is "In the Mean Mud Season," where he insists he is still nostalgic for Virginia's weather and its manners and feigns annoyance with his eighth-grader, Victoria, who spends hours on the telephone with a boy he dislikes. The snow falls another foot. He trudges out to clear the snow from the driveway and finds the boy has come to help, bringing his own shovel. "He had the face of an altar boy" (p. 216). Later, the sun comes out. Victoria calls him upstairs to his studio. Squeezed together, they peer out of the alcove. They can see Lake Champlain and the Adirondack Mountains. They are happy together, "bumping shoulders" (p. 219). In "The Crossing," Frank travels to Virginia to pick up his recently widowed mother. They are companionable on the ferry trip across Lake Champlain, although his mother is exhausted. She finally smiles at her son. "I wonder if I'm entitled to all this" (p. 229). "The gesture she made with her hand was up ahead, where the water took the reflection of the Vermont shore and held it like a treasure" (p. 229). In "The Beautiful Gestures," a former student, Susan, invites Frank to give a paper at her university. He thinks back sixteen years, when it seemed acceptable to flirt with women students. He and a colleague injudiciously attended a Halloween party in the women's dorm. Susan asked him to her apartment. Looking at her books and artifacts, he realized his influence on her life and has the painful insight that he assigned her the wrong kinds of poems to read. He wishes he could relive the experience. In *Prairie Schooner*, Judith Kitchen wrote, "Running through these stories is the theme of dishonesty, or, at the very least, a

lack of honesty." She summed up by saying, "He is a master of prose so clean you can see it shine."

Intimates (1993) pursues Huddle's familiar themes of lack of communication, jealousy, snobbery, and betrayal. In "Night," Angela, age eleven, sees her drunkard father through a panic attack until he finally passes out. She turns off the lights. In "Scotland," two years later, she is in London with her mother, who is divorcing her father. Their lawyer sends them on a trip to Scotland with a team shooting advertising spots. Sitting on the bus with a black male model from New York, Angela feels intensely connected to him. "Henry Lagoon" features another teenager, Henry Lague, whose grandfather came from Quebec City to work in the quarry. When the other children start calling him Henry "Lagoon," he doesn't know what it means, although he rather likes the sound. He starts spending time with Lisa Yancey, another freshman. They hitchhike to Montpelier to look into the legalities of changing his name. She invites him to her house to make a video. They mug for the camera and exchange a kiss before Lisa's father sends him home. When Henry leaves, after another more considered kiss, he has changed. He knows he will leave Barre when he graduates; he doesn't know what his future holds, but he has time to decide.

The narrator of "Little Sawtooth" is in thrall to the twenty-year-old memory of a fellow graduate student, Michelle, who describes meeting a new professor at Boise State. One morning the professor, who is married, looks "straight into Michelle's eyes" (p. 54), and soon the two decide to slip quietly out of town for an excursion to Little Sawtooth Falls. Walking dangerously close to the edge after dark, he tumbles down a cliff; she never finds his body nor tells anyone her secret. The narrator learns that "people carry out their lives with their stories locked inside themselves" (p. 68). When he is lost in his writing that night, "light makes its way" into his living room (p. 69).

Four stories feature Professor Eugene Riggins, who also lives in Vermont. In "The Page," Riggins, a poet, and his family drive from Vermont to Tucson, Arizona, to attend a writers'

conference. His workshop is a triumph. During the cocktail reception, an unknown woman invites him to her room. He is intrigued and sorely tempted. In "Collision," he and his wife crash in their separate cars and are furious with each other. In "The Meeting of the Tisdale Fellows," Riggins reminisces about Rosa, a brilliant woman at Columbia with whom he shared honors. He sends her a note because he is feeling depressed. Rosa, who is now blind but has found God, appears with her husband to help him. Talking to her, he remembers the exhilaration of parachute training in the army; he wonders what his life holds. In "The Hearing," Riggins testifies in his own defense before the dean's proceeding. He has been teaching for forty years; he has tenure; he has nothing to worry about. After all, he only spent a couple of hours alone in the company of his student, Honorée. He considers himself unusually sensitive to issues of student-faculty relationships, though he is not unaware of his students' charms. As he tells the story, Honorée came to a conference in his office. When she revealed she was unhappy, he naturally responded with a comforting hug. She followed up by coming to his office over the weekend with a bottle of wine. He had settled himself with some reading and music. When she entered his office, he closed the door, as he always does when he is listening to music. Before Riggins knew what was happening, Honorée undressed; soon she lay across his desk, naked. He did not say, "Stop" (p. 150). The custodian heard noises and unlocked the door. Riggins confides that he had no remorse; rather, he felt, during that time with Honorée, "immortal" (p. 155).

The narrator in "The Side Effects of Lucille" is a professor who runs a poetry-writing workshop and is the winner of the Yale Prize for his book of poems. He is immediately aware of Lucille in his class; she has come down from Montreal, where her husband Carly is a thug. She easily seduces him. After one of these encounters, he challenges her to be as bold in her poetry as she is in person. She responds with a breakthrough in her work and offers a way of thanking him—a getaway in the country. At the hotel she collapses in a seizure but is able to give

him a doctor's number to call. Carly's people arrive and deliver him, terrified, home. His pleasure in life dies. All he can look forward to is a life of "neutral sensation" (p. 179). In "Trouble at the Home Office," Peter is having an affair with Julie, and his wife, Susan, presents him with an ultimatum: in or out. Under the circumstances, he and his boss decide he should work from home. From his office on the third floor, he hears someone sneaking through the house. It is Julie, who undresses him as though he were a helpless invalid, and seduces him. Then she tells him she never liked him.

In "The Short Flight," the narrator engages in a flirtation aboard a commuter flight. He and his seatmate do not speak, but he is aware of their "sneaking looks at each other" and of "the catch of our eyes" (p. 195). He realizes "how intimate" it is being on an airplane (p. 197). He finds the woman's face "as full of meaning as a Tolstoy novel" (p. 200). The pilot loses control of the airplane: they cling to each other. They connect; the crisis is over. Later, at the airport, his third wife has not yet arrived to meet him. In "The Reunion Joke," Francine and Randall meet every five years. They have been flirting for thirty years, since high school. She is divorced once; he, thrice. They finally chance a sexual encounter; ironically, he is unable to perform.

In *Library Journal*, Paul E. Hutchinson reported that this collection "strikes gold when it focuses on people 'with their stories locked inside themselves'" (p. 120), though he found "less successful … the lapses into campus fiction." *Publishers Weekly* wrote, "The stories come to life because of Huddle's clear, unpretentious style." *Kirkus Reviews* thought the stories "occasionally chew over more than they've bitten off, but generally satisfy by exploring the nooks and crannies of everyday emotional crises."

In the novella *Tenorman* (1995), which "started as a poem" (Hudgens et al., p. 8), the National Endowment rediscovers Carnes, a fifty-nine-year-old African American musician near death in Stockholm, brings him to America, and sets him up in a fancy studio in Chevy Chase, Maryland, to record his every sound and to capture his creative process. They install tiny mobile microphones in his jacket pocket. The project director is thirty-year-old Henry, who plays the piano and lives in Fairfax, Virginia. Carnes requests the company of an intelligent woman; his arranged meeting with Thelma Watkins at a party has "*dramatic content*" (p. 29). She had been married to a white man who treated her badly; she finds Carnes's music a "mating signal" (p. 34). Henry and his wife Marianne realize that "almost every human couple we know has its difficulties; almost every individual of our acquaintance seems to us … painfully isolated" (pp. 20–21). Fascinated with Carnes and Thelma, they listen to the tapes; their voyeurism stems from their hope that the couple's flirtation will revive their faltering sex life. They are out of sync. "Did one person ever get to see what really mattered about another person?" Henry wonders (p. 54). He decides, "Timing is the secret to most issues of human relations" (p. 57).

In the *Harvard Review*, Rod Kessler described *Tenorman* as a "thoughtful and appreciative book" about "the nature of jazz, of artistic creation." Abby Frucht in the *New York Times* called it "terse and disturbing," portrayed in "subtle tones." *Kirkus Reviews* pronounced it "gear-grinding work from an often very fine story-crafter."

Not: A Trio (2000), two short stories and a novella set in Bennington, Vermont, presents three interrelated characters. In "The Village," Danny runs a small business and has a bad reputation regarding women. He sees Claire, a psychiatrist, once a week, ostensibly for a therapy session but actually for a sexual encounter on her office rug. Though she craves sex with him, she does not like him and fears the villagers' disapproval. In "Wherever I Am Not," Ben, a professor-turned-administrator at Bennington, is Claire's second husband; he too has been married before. He finds himself uttering little prayers to himself, believing that "some kind of a pattern-maker is or was 'out there,' *anywhere I am not*" (p. 20). He is obsessing about where he went wrong with Julie, his first wife, and succumbs to a compulsion to telephone her while Claire is sleeping. Although Ben hasn't spoken to her in over a year, Julie knows all about him from

small-town gossip. Their conversation again exemplifies how little married couples understand each other. Julie thinks he should talk out his problems about intimacy with Claire "in broad daylight" (p. 34). She calls him an "emotional mole" (p. 36), all by himself in the dark, afraid of the daylight. On his way to the grocery store, he meets Danny, who appears to recognize him. He wonders what the village grocer has been telling Danny about him. Margaret Allen, who really should not be driving, crashes her car up over the curb and kills Ben.

In "Not," a novella, Claire, nearing forty, owns the deed to land near Lincoln once owned by her grandfather. She decides to leave the life she has "so carefully constructed" (p. 47), the town, her clients, and her lover. She has a choice: "There is this distant light, as if I am soon to be released into a meadow of sunlit green" (p. 47). She asks herself, "Who knows me?" (p. 53). A "displaced person" (p. 54), what she wants more than anything is "to be still on a sunny day" (p. 67). Sexual intimacy with her husband was like "trying to dance with someone clumsy" (p. 74), imagery that recurs in other stories with couples whose sexual selves are out of tune. She has saved medication to kill herself. She believes she has never been able to help any of her patients or herself. When the moment comes, she is unable to act.

The *Virginia Quarterly Review* admired Huddle's "lapidary technique," saying, "*Not: A Trio* treats its characters as gems do light." *Publishers Weekly* noted that while it "lacks the ambition of his novel" [*The Story of a Million Years*], the collection still exhibits Huddle's strengths." He "remains an accomplished observer of the pangs of middle age."

NOVELS

George Garrett states that Huddle is one of only a few who "write both fiction and poetry simultaneously," that he has "found a way to use the poetry and fiction to play off against each other" (p. 248). Huddle's first novel, *The Story of a Million Years* (1999), features seven linked narrators, each with a secret. Like other stories, it is

aglow with light, shining on characters' faces, for example, to fathom their thoughts. In "Past My Future," Marcy's secret is that when she was fifteen, Robert, an acquaintance and contemporary of her parents, propositioned her. Marcy was in charge of the "commerce," as Robert called their relationship (p. 10): "Robert harmed me no more than I harmed him" (p. 3). After their affair, Marcy sees Robert with his wife in a restaurant: "My sight seemed to soar across the room and cast light on him" (p. 19). In "Past Perfect," Allen meets and marries Marcy, but harbors the idea that their marriage is a mistake. In "The Lesson," Allen suspects Marcy of an affair and follows her; he discovers she is taking piano lessons, looking "*radiant*" (p. 115) with her "shining face" (p. 116). In "ABC," Jimmy, who lives in Allen's dorm in Charlottesville, has never liked him, although he has always desired Marcy. He marries her best friend, Uta, who secretly lusts after Allen. The title story gives Uta's perspective on the relations among the four friends and the single time that circumstances find her alone with Allen.

In "Girly-Man Recapitulates," Jimmy suspects something between Uta and Allen; he believes, "I was missing what they call a center" (p. 127). (In the introduction to his *Reader*, Huddle discusses finding a center as an important "truth" [p. 4]). Jimmy enters the bedroom he shares with Uta, trying "to see how her [Uta's] face looked" (p. 138). In "Goodness," Robert Gordon feels suicidal about his former relationship with Marcy. He comforts himself that she made a rational decision and carefully differentiates his situation from Humbert's attraction to Lolita. In "Summer Afternoon," Robert's wife, Suzanne, encourages his passion for Marcy; she and Robert are like secret agents "posing as a married couple" (p. 154). Marcy's daughter sees her mother in "Silk Dress" not as a victim, but as a woman in charge of her life. When Marcy realizes Robert's effect on her, she says, "I have no desire to turn on the lights in the living room. My life has caved in on me" (p. 172).

Publishers Weekly called *The Story of a Million Years* "a shimmering debut novel." The *New Yorker* reported: "the characters inevitably sniff

out the truth about one another even as they believe their own secrets to be inviolable." Polly Shulman in the *New York Times* found "a yearning for the ideals of love and an elegiac vision of the passage of time." In the *Boston Globe*, Gail Caldwell admired "a place of light and shadow and endless possibility, where things are never, merely, as they seem," though she noted that occasionally the novel "veers toward metaphorical overkill."

La Tour Dreams of the Wolf Girl (2001) takes place in contemporary Burlington, where Suzanne and Jack live, and, in Suzanne's imagination, in seventeenth-century Lunéville, where the artist Georges de La Tour resides. He discovers a technique for using light to convey spirituality, "to make his work appear divinely inspired" (p. 35), one of several instances in Huddle's work of the way painters respond to faces, as in "Deacon" (*High Spirits*) and *The Faulkes Chronicle*. Suzanne is a professor of art history at the University of Vermont; Jack is in public relations. Jack is unable to tell the truth to himself, to his wife, or to his lover, Elly. When he decides to divorce Suzanne, he cannot "bring to mind the face of his wife" (p. 69). Suzanne grew up in the sticks of the Blue Mountains, sitting on the school bus next to a mute boy, Elijah, who both attracted her sympathy and revolted her. She often thinks with shame of her behavior. Jack was raised in a privileged household on the Upper East Side, attended Choate, and worked as a counselor at a camp where he discovered that a little girl, who threatened to drown another child, had a brain tumor. He told her about seeing two boys drown, another recurrence of this motif.

Early in their marriage, Suzanne understands they are trying to escape who they are. Jack feels he is nobody, "a series of masks, a pretender even to himself," and knows not "what was at the center" (p. 122), another reference to Huddle's belief in finding "the center" (*Reader*, p. 2). The scenes switch rapidly from the present to the past and back again. La Tour is a feeble, almost blind old man who invites Vivienne, the daughter of the village shoemaker, to sit for him. Once she disrobes, he discovers a coarse patch of hair on her shoulder and back, which is unbeknownst to her. He paints her; his purpose is "to demonstrate light becoming flesh" (p. 63). Jack and Suzanne divorce; he and Elly move to California. While Elly is out, Jack calls Suzanne in the middle of the night. La Tour desires Vivienne, who hates his meddling in her life. When he is dying, she returns to his studio to answer questions about her life.

Donna Seaman in *Booklist* found that Huddle "brilliantly conveys ... the transforming heat of an intimate's gaze." Patrick Sullivan in *Library Journal* admired Huddle's "vividly imagined world" where characters "struggle to identify truth from fiction." Jane Mendelsohn wrote in the *New York Times*, "His characters don't come to life in the conventional way.... Like light, they seem always on the verge of changing." Jeff Zaleski in *Publishers Weekly* wrote, "Huddle's talent still shines through here, but this book is a step down from his successful debut."

In *Nothing Can Make Me Do This* (2011), the characters are linked through Horace Housman's family in Burlington; many chapters are self-contained. In "The Way of the Blue-Winged Wangdoodle," Horace's granddaughter, Eve, introduces the reverberating fact that her grandfather stored pornographic videos in a wooden crate. Clara, her grandmother, shows Eve a picture of herself and Horace as young people, saying, "You have to protect that part of your mind that might become visible if you let someone get a good look in there" (pp. 5–6). Horace, provost of the University of Vermont, reveals in "Doubt Administration" his interest in the new dean; he sits in meetings "to watch her face" (p. 38). He wonders if she has a "sexual secret" (p. 39); he kisses her. In "A Thousand Wives," Eve's father, Bill, is a morning person: "my relationship with my black & chrome machine is so intimate it makes me high every day" (p. 49). Huddle told Christina Arregoces, "I also claim that I owe a great deal of my writing success to coffee." When Eve was a newborn, Bill saw her as a "baby who glowed in the dark" and "floated in a nimbus of light" (p. 49). While secretly watching Horace's pornography, he recognizes his wife Hannah's coolness: their sex life has diminished. Sometimes she looks him

"straight in the eye" (p. 57), and her searching his face makes him uncomfortable—"Something out of whack" (p. 57). This incompatibility echoes the married couple in *Tenorman*: when he is aroused, she isn't. Bill buys more pornography.

Clara and Eve alternate their stories in "Wages of Love." Clara reviews her courtship, studying the picture of herself with Horace. She cannot forgive him the pornographic films; he tells her truthfully that they are Sonny's and make him sick. "His eyes did not move away from her face" (p. 91). Eve meets an older boy, Sylvester, who teaches her, with sexual undertones, about art and photography. Eve observes, "There is something naked about his face" as he looks at women nudes (p. 88). She does not trust him: "He won't look at her" (p. 92). After she photographs him nude, it is her turn to remove her clothes. Like Marcy in *Million Years*, she is free to choose: *"I don't have to do this.... Nothing can make me"* (p. 100). In "Half Man," when Bill is thirteen, he goes out with his brother Robert and some girls. They prowl around, watching women undress. Bill watches one dancing alone. "He saw himself in her face" (p. 109). This voyeurism echoes Sonny's watching pornography and the couple in *Tenorman*.

Hannah, Bill's wife, feels as though she wears a mask in "Hannah Outside In." Like Jack in *La Tour,* no one can see her real self. At Skidmore, she has an affair with a professor. If what they do "came to light at the college," they would have to tell the truth (p. 135). In "Helga After Midnight," Bill, engaged to Hannah—he fell for her "within minutes of entering his sight" (p. 137)—keeps a previous date with an actress. He and Caroline aren't "exactly on the same page," but they are close enough (p. 141). He wakes in the night and spies on Caroline standing at the window: "Every now and then somebody gets a glimpse of what it's like to be somebody else" (p. 144). Horace describes in "Snowy Day" a sexual adventure in high school. He is slow to develop; the more experienced girl is in charge of the seduction. "Sunlight was washing over them" (p. 155). She is disgusted by his hairy body; "Illumination was how he thought of it" (p. 160). In "High on a Hill," Horace and Sonny

are on the faculty at Hollins College in the 1960s. Sonny, confident and good-looking, flirts with Clara. Horace tries to look directly into the face of each student; he notes the "squares of sunlight" (p. 170). Sonny receives "flashes of insight" into Clara's thoughts (p. 173); he tries not to stare at her face.

In "Volunteer," Sonny, sixty-one, is a professor of computer science and married to wife number three. He volunteers at a youth center, where he helps a little boy learn to read. His two troubling childhood secrets are that his grandmother exposed herself to him and the parish priest evinced sexual interest in him, both secrets intimating an explanation for his later preoccupation with pornography. In "Two Lives," Eve's family wants her to marry Joseph, but she is cautious: "Intuition tells you the only worthwhile truth" (p. 240), an idea Huddle discusses in *Reader* (p. 1). Joseph wins a prize for poems that may have exploited his father's death in Vietnam when he was ten. Eve divorces him and moves home, where her parents are separating, and Horace is dying. Eve thinks about Sylvester, who returns. She says, "I'm reading your face" (p. 287), knowing he is happy to see her.

Publishers Weekly called Huddle's novel "ravishing, charged with both desire and emotional turmoil." Reba Leiding in *Library Journal* pinpointed the characters' "secret episodes of impropriety and shame that have shaped their lives." *Booklist*'s Carol Haggas found "crisply textured characters, an assured style, and seductive pacing."

The Faulkes Chronicle (2014), narrated in the first-person plural, records the way a family of ten children ranging in age from one to twenty, along with their taciturn father, respond to the dying of their mother, in the last stages of cancer. A glowing personality who becomes more beautiful as her disease progresses, the mother exhorts them to participate in her death. She bathes them with pride for the family. *"A Faulkes will maybe flinch, but a Faulkes persists"* (p. 16), she reassures them. The drowning motif recurs when the mother and father describe seeing twin fifth-graders pulled out of the water. The children follow the family rules for a Faulkes, who "does

what he's supposed to do, doesn't shirk his chores, doesn't make a fuss, and steps up when asked to carry out a task" (p. 56). The children feel conflicted about their mother's courage: "All she does is make us love her more" (p. 65). The morning sun makes her bald head "pearl-like, milky, luminescent" (p. 70). Their task, she says, is to "witness her," to "absorb her" (p. 71): "her face rises into the light like that of an angel" (p. 80). When she talks, "her face is bathed in gold" (p. 108).

Dr. Lawson, the oncologist, raises funds to take the family on a farewell tour that will allow him to scientifically study both the patient's and her family's reactions. Their goals are Cape May, New Jersey, and Washington, D.C. A big bus serves the family and the hospice worker; a smaller van carries Lawson and another doctor. In a hotel on the Jersey Shore, the children ask their father for stories about their parents' courtship. In Washington, their mother yearns to see Johannes Vermeer's *Girl with the Red Hat*. In the painting, "the intensity of life in that girl's face is so tangible that it almost pushes you backward" (p. 231), executed with "those dots of light" (p. 232). Toward the end, their mother sleeps frequently. Awake, her eyes "shine with awareness" (p. 269). The children behold her as "a flare, one of those phosphorescent rockets an army patrol will send up at night to illuminate a landscape" (p. 270). One day, "Our mother's light begins to fade" (p. 274). Finally, "Each Faulkes face lightens in the presence of our mother" (p. 278). Carol Haggas wrote in *Booklist*, "Huddle is a master at mining the depths of a discomfiting situation. A marvel."

ESSAYS

The title essay in *The Writing Habit* (1992) lays out in clear, readable prose lessons from Huddle's experience: "The first project for a writer is that of constructing a writer's life" (p. 1). As a house-husband, like many of his male characters, he is absorbed in his daily schedule: "My writing time is when I set my life in order. I examine my life through the act of writing" (p. 8). He is dependent upon his writer friends: "the help of peers is es-

sential to most writers I know" (p. 10). Having spelled out a plan for a writing day, he quotes Hemingway on when to stop—at a point where "you knew what you were going to do next" (p. 12). For a writer, he says, "The only valuable possession is the ongoing work" (p. 12). "Memory's Power" discusses writing autobiography, which means writing about family, friends, and enemies: "Diplomatic relations can be strained" (p. 25). He stresses that the writer must avoid "hurting feelings" (p. 25). He believes that "we write for the work itself ... [then] for ourselves ... [then] for others" (p. 27). In *Library Journal*, Cathy Sabol described the book as "an open, honest examination of some of the principles of successful writing."

In Huddle's introduction to *A David Huddle Reader: Selected Prose and Poetry* (1994), titled "Confessions of a Multi-Genre Writer: What It Feels Like from the Inside," he describes his work as "all of a piece," trying to achieve "something true and interesting about human experience" (p. 1). In his art, whether poetry or prose, what matters to Huddle is the truth in his art, asking the question, "Am I journeying toward 'the very Center'"? (p. 4). At least half the various pieces he has written "were conceived of in drastically different forms than what they actually turned out to be" (p. 3). Rochelle Ratner observed in *Library Journal* that, "though insightful, his reflective essays on the writing process ... lack a necessary frame of reference."

About These Stories: Fiction for Fiction Writers and Readers (1995) is a collection of classic short stories, edited by Huddle and two colleagues. Their premise is that a writer learns to write by reading. They present stories, followed by essays about the "fiction-writing possibilities" the stories may reveal (p. 1). These essays are "natural responses" to the stories they analyze, "a discussion that can go on indefinitely" (p. 4).

CONCLUSION

In his analysis of Huddle's career, Philip F. Deaver evokes the sunlight imagery that is one of the key elements running through Huddle's

work. He points out that his poem "Vermont," his "current homeland, is about Vietnam; forever, he shows us they will shed light on one another" (p. 790). Overall, he thinks Huddle has created a body of work that is, in its own "beautifully human way, luminous and majestic" (p. 792). Sunlight for Huddle is emblematic of goodness, clarity, communication, dreams, and happiness. His large and sympathetic body of work is tinged with love, regret, loyalty, and wonder; it shines with curiosity, acuity, and cogent revelations about human interaction.

Selected Bibliography

WORKS OF DAVID HUDDLE

Novels
The Story of a Million Years. Boston: Houghton Mifflin, 1999.

La Tour Dreams of the Wolf Girl. Boston: Houghton Mifflin, 2001.

Nothing Can Make Me Do This. North Adams, Mass.: Tupelo Press, 2011.

The Faulkes Chronicle. North Adams, Mass.: Tupelo Press, 2014.

Short Fiction
A Dream with No Stump Roots in It. Columbia: University of Missouri Press, 1975.

Only the Little Bone: Stories. Boston: David Godine, 1986.

The High Sprits: Stories of Men and Women. Boston: David Godine, 1989.

Intimates: A Book of Stories. Boston: David Godine, 1993.

Tenorman: A Novella. San Francisco: Chronicle Books, 1995.

Not: A Trio; Two Stories and a Novella. South Bend, Ind.: University of Notre Dame Press, 2000.

Poetry
Paper Boy. Pittsburgh, Pa.: University of Pittsburgh Press, 1979.

Stopping by Home. Salt Lake City: Peregrine Smith, 1988.

The Nature of Yearning. Salt Lake City: Peregrine Smith, 1992.

Summer Lake: New and Selected Poems. Baton Rouge: Louisiana State University Press, 1999.

Grayscale: Poems. Baton Rouge: Louisiana State University Press, 2004.

Glory River: Poems. Baton Rouge: Louisiana State University Press, 2007.

Blacksnake at the Family Reunion: Poems. Baton Rouge: Louisiana State University Press, 2012.

Essays
The Writing Habit. Salt Lake City: Peregrine Smith, 1992.

Afterword to *Montana 1948*, by Larry Watson. New York: Washington Square Press, 1993.

A David Huddle Reader: Selected Prose and Poetry. Middlebury, Vt.: Middlebury College Press, 1994.

"Out of Ivanhoe." In *Contemporary Authors Autobiography Series*. Vol. 20. Detroit: Gale Research, 1994.

"Got to Go to That War: How the Army Made a Man Out of Me." *Contemporary Authors*. Vol. 261. Detroit: Gale, Cengage Learning, 2008.

As Editor
About These Stories: Fiction for Fiction Writers and Readers. With Ghita Orth and Allen Shepherd. New York: McGraw-Hill, 1995.

CRITICAL AND BIOGRAPHICAL STUDIES
Brosi, George. "David Huddle: A Versatile Author with Deep Roots in the New River Valley." *Appalachian Heritage* 41, no. 3:15–20 (summer 2013).

Clabough, Casey. "Here, There, Where: The Shifting Nature of David Huddle's Appalachia." *Hollins Critic* 47, no. 3:1 (June 2010).

Daley, Yvonne. *Vermont Writers: A State of Mind*. Hanover, N.H.: University Press of New England, 2005.

Deaver, Philip F. "Writing to the Center: Glory River and Other Works by David Hubble." *Southern Review* 44, no. 4:785–792 (autumn 2008).

Gilman, Owen W., Jr. *Vietnam and the Southern Imagination*. Jackson: University Press of Mississippi, 1992.

———. "David Huddle." In *Southern Writers: A New Biographical Dictionary*. Edited by Joseph M. Flora, Amber Vogel, and Bryan Alban Giemza. Baton Rouge: Louisiana State University Press, 2006.

Lampe, David. "David Huddle." In *Dictionary of Literary Biography*. Vol. 130, *American Short-Story Writers Since World War II*. Edited by Patrick Meanor. Detroit: Gale, 1993.

REVIEWS
Allen, Frank. Review of *Summer Lake*. *Library Journal*

124, no. 12:94 (July 1999).

Balitas, Vincent D. "Stopping by Home." *Library Journal* 114 no. 4:73 (March 1989).

Caldwell, Gail. "Voices Carry." *Boston Globe,* October 10, 1999. (Review of *The Story of a Million Years.*)

Engels, John. "Of Sin, Damnation, and Salvation." *Carleton Miscellany* 15, no. 2:132–134 (spring–summer, 1975–1976). (Review of *A Dream with No Stump Roots in It.*)

Frucht, Abby. Review of *Tenorman. New York Times,* October 22, 1995.

Haggas, Carol. Review of *Nothing Can Make Me Do This. Booklist* 108, no. 4:18 (October 15, 2011).

———. Review of *The Faulkes Chronicle. Booklist* 110, no. 22:33 (August 2014).

Hutchinson, Paul E. Review of *Intimates. Library Journal* 117, no. 18:20 (November 1992).

Kessler, Rod. Review of *Tenorman. Harvard Review* 10:30 (spring 1996).

Kirkus Reviews. Review of *Intimates.* February 1, 1993. https://www.kirkusreviews.com/book-reviews/david -huddle/intimates/

———. Review of *Tenorman.* October 1, 1995. https://www .kirkusreviews.com/book-reviews/david-huddle-3/ tenorman-2/

Kitchen, Judith. "The High Spirits." *Prairie Schooner* 64, no. 3:126–128 (fall 1990).

Leiding, Reba. Review of *Nothing Can Make Me Do This. Library Journal* 136, no. 19:67 (November 15, 2011).

Magill Book Reviews. Review of *Only the Little Bone.* January 1986, p. 1.

Mendelsohn, Jane. "Paints with Wolves: A Novel Involves the 17th-Century Artist Georges de La Tour and an Art Historian Studying Him." *New York Times Book Review,* February 17, 2002, p. 7.

New Yorker. Review of *The Story of a Million Years.* September 27, 1999, p. 96.

Portis, Rowe. Review of *A Dream with No Stump Roots in It. Library Journal* 100, no. 12:1240 (June 1975).

Publishers Weekly. Review of *Intimates.* November 23, 1992, p. 53.

———. Review of *The Story of a Million Years.* August 2, 1999, p. 71.

———. Review of *Not: A Trio.* September 4, 2000, p. 84.

———. Review of *Nothing Can Make Me Do This.* January 21, 2011. http://www.publishersweekly.com/978-1 -936797-11-0

Ratner, Rochelle. Review of *A David Huddle Reader. Library Journal* 118, no. 21:126 (December 15, 1993).

Sabol, Cathy. Review of *The Writing Habit: Essays. Library Journal* 117, no. 6:118 (April 1, 1992).

Seaman, Donna. *La Tour Dreams of the Wolf Girl. Booklist* 98, no. 11:1417 (February 1, 2002).

———. *Grayscale: Poems. Booklist* 100, no. 16 (April 15, 2004).

Shulman, Polly. "Lost Loves." *New York Times,* October 24, 1999. (Review of *The Story of a Million Years.*)

Sullivan, Patrick. *La Tour Dreams of the Wolf Girl. Library Journal* 127, no. 2:130 (February 1, 2002).

Virginia Quarterly Review. Review of *The Nature of Yearning.* Vol. 68, no. 4:136 (autumn 1992).

———. Review of *Summer Lake.* Vol. 76, no. 1:27 (winter 2000).

———. Review of *Not: A Trio.* Vol. 77, no. 4:137–138 (autumn 2001).

Walsh, Keenan. Review of *Blacksnake at the Family Reunion. Seven Days,* February 13, 2013. http://www .sevendaysvt.com/vermont/book-review-blacksnake-at-the -family-reunion-by-david-huddle-and-vermont-exit-ramps -by-neil-shepard/Content?oid=2242840

Washburn, Keith E. Review of *Paper Boy. Library Journal* 104, no. 3:406 (February 1, 1979).

Willis, Meredith Sue. "A Gene for Flawed Competence." *New York Times,* September 14, 1986. (Review of *Only the Little Bone.*)

Zaleski, Jeff. Review of *La Tour Dreams of the Wolf Girl. Publishers Weekly,* December 10, 2001, p. 48.

INTERVIEWS

Arregoces, Christina. "David Huddle." *Superstition Review* 8 (fall 2011). http://superstitionreview.asu.edu/issue8/ interviews/davidhuddle

Brodeur, Brian. "David Huddle." *How a Poem Happens: Contemporary Poets Discuss the Making of Poems.* September 16, 2010. http://howapoemhappens.blogspot .com/2010/09/david-huddle.html

Eder, Clair, and Andrew Donovan. "David Huddle." *Subtropics,* 2013. http://www.english.ufl.edu/subtropics/ Huddle_interview.html

Garrett, George. *Southern Excursions: Views on Southern Letters in My Time.* Edited by James Conrad McKinley. Baton Rouge: Louisiana State University Press, 2003.

Hallenbeck, Brent. "David Huddle: The Life on the Inside." *Burlington Free Press*, October 29, 2011. http://www .english.ufl.edu/subtropics/Huddle_interview.html

Hudgens, Sarah, Thomas King, and J. Duncan Wiley. "A Conversation with David Huddle." *Willow Springs,* October 14, 2005. http://willowsprings.ewu.edu/ interviews/huddle.pdf

HELENE JOHNSON

(1906—1995)

Eleanor Wakefield

THE HARLEM RENAISSANCE poet Helene Johnson guarded her privacy closely, published no books of her poems, and disappeared from public life after only eight years as a part of the vibrant community of black writers in New York (1927–1935). Though she had been a part of the literary community in Boston for two years prior to her move to New York, she is associated with her community of artists in Harlem. As a result of her short career, compounded by her lack of self-promotion, readers and editors scarcely remember her today.

Despite her small publication record, her legacy of poems, both those published in magazines in the 1920s and 1930s and those she never submitted that have been published more recently (Mitchell, ed., *This Waiting for Love,* 2000), are colorful, political, hopeful, and haunting. Her role in the Harlem Renaissance community and her network of relationships with other writers too provide current readers and scholars with additional means of understanding that literary landscape. Nearly all the scholarship about her begs for further study: "Because much of her poetry is both innovative and thematically relevant beyond her time, she is one of the movement's most important poets despite her short time in the public eye" (Patton and Honey, p. 599).

Johnson's sense of herself as a member of a community of black people was vividly present in her poetry, exemplified in her 1925 poem "My Race":

Ah my race,
Hungry race,
Throbbing and young—
Ah, my race,
Wonder race,
Sobbing with song—

Ah, my race,
Laughing race,
Careless in mirth—
Ah, my veiled race,
Unformed race,
Fumbling in birth.

(*Opportunity*, July 1925, qtd. in Mitchell, p. 24)

Here, without offering commentary, Johnson captures both pride and pain; her race, a group the poem asserts the speaker's membership in every three lines, is "hungry" and "throbbing," yearning for something yet to come, but also "unformed" and "fumbling," young and learning in the American context. Though Johnson does not explain her own poetry or her theories of blackness, as did so many of her contemporaries and influences in the Harlem Renaissance, these few poems illuminate the tensions inherent in black arts at the time and offer some new themes perhaps less evident in other Harlem Renaissance work. Taking her previously published work along with the new poems first made available to the public in 2000, this overview gives a sense of the scope and themes of Johnson's poetic work, as well as her life and legacy.

BIOGRAPHY

Born July 7, 1906 (though some texts give the year as 1907), in Boston, to George William and Ella Benson Johnson, Helen Virginia Johnson was an only child raised in a large extended family. (The spelling "Helene" came from a family nickname.) Her father left her mother and her shortly after her birth, and she and her mother lived with an uncle, two aunts, two cousins, and sometimes other family members in Boston. Johnson was of the impression that her father was of Greek origin, from Tennessee, and lived

later in Chicago. Her father's possibly Greek origins explain her coloring; she was light skinned—"a golden-skin kid," according to her cousin, the writer Dorothy West (Mitchell, p. 5). The cousins spent most of their childhood, beginning in 1914, in a four-story house on Brookline Avenue in Boston. Helene and her mother, Ella, along with Ella's sisters Minnie and Rachel and their daughters Jean and Dorothy (respectively), lived together, the girls taking piano lessons and going to schools in Boston.

While the house was large, and they vacationed in the summers at Martha's Vineyard, the family's wealth was a combination of money and pooled resources. Helene Johnson's daughter, Abigail McGrath, notes, "there can be no question that for a while we were a family of substance, but by the time I came around [1940] we were shabby gentility at best. Helen never aspired to be rich, that was Dorothy's thing" (Mitchell, p. 123). Though Johnson biographical material is scarce, Dorothy West biographies, according to McGrath, portray the family, inaccurately, as "Boston Brahmins," their wealth supplied by West's father, Isaac, "the Banana King of Boston." However, McGrath explains that the children were spoiled by people devoted to giving them the best, as opposed to just money. Their childhood together, with "several aunts" and a shared value in arts and culture, sounds idyllic:

> The girls had a Finnish governess and did not go to school with other children until they were "molded." They knew their Goethe, Schiller, and Shakespeare. At night, they would write pieces and read them aloud at the end of the evening as entertainment.... They went to the theater, joined writing clubs, and did all of the cultural things that young ladies of privilege did, except they did it with the resources pooled together by all three mothers and several aunts.... They were a kibbutz, a commune, and the big house in Boston and the beach house at Martha's Vineyard were part of the large family collective.
>
> (p. 124)

The maternal side of Johnson's family, the Bensons, originated in South Carolina: daughters Ella, Minnie, and Rachel (three of eighteen children born to their parents) moved north along with their widowed father, Benjamin Benson, who had been born into slavery in South Carolina. They came to Massachusetts after the death of Benjamin's wife Helen Pease Benson, followed by other siblings; according to McGrath, other aunts lived with the family throughout Helene's childhood as well. The family spent their summers in Oak Bluffs, an African American community on Martha's Vineyard, in a house that cousin Dorothy West would eventually live in full time. Johnson, West, and their cousin Jean were educated at several Boston schools, and Johnson and West would eventually study journalism at Columbia University in New York. Johnson also took courses at Boston University, where she and West joined the Saturday Evening Quill Club, the African American literary organization behind the journal of the same name.

Johnson began her publishing career as the winner of a contest by the magazine *Opportunity* in 1925, which resulted in the 1926 publication of six of her poems; one of the judges of this contest was the poet Robert Frost (Mitchell, p. 16). Her poems "Fulfillment," "Magula" (sometimes written "Magalu"), and "The Road" were awarded honorable mentions—first, fourth, and seventh, respectively. She was also published in *Fire!!*, the avant-garde magazine of the "younger negro artists" (1926). The following year her poem "Bottled," probably the most written-about of her poems, appeared in *Vanity Fair*.

Also in 1927, she and Dorothy West moved to Harlem. They stayed for a time at the YWCA but were able to stay in a friend's apartment for a time thereafter as they settled in. (McGrath claims that they continued getting mail at the YWCA so their mothers would not find out they were living unchaperoned in Harlem.) That generous friend, the writer Zora Neale Hurston, had befriended the cousins at a literary banquet for the *Opportunity* awards, where she and West had tied for second place in the short-story division, West for "The Typewriter" and Hurston for "Muttsy." West recalled later, "At first she [Hurston] had mixed feelings about sharing a prize with an unknown teenager. But in time I became her little sister, and my affection for her has never

diminished. In time I was to play my part in the Harlem Renaissance. I was nineteen and its youngest member" (Mitchell, p. 7). Only ten months West's senior, Johnson was among the youngest group of writers to join the artistic movement in Harlem, ushered into the fold by Hurston. (Hurston was researching in the South while Johnson and West used her apartment.)

Johnson's poetry appeared in magazines of the period, including her cousin's endeavor *Challenge*. She is perhaps best known by students today for her poem "A Southern Road," which was included in *Fire!!* (1926), or for her several poems in the collections *Caroling Dusk* (1927) and *The Book of American Negro Poetry* (1931). "Bottled" (*Vanity Fair*, 1927; *Caroling Dusk*, 1927), seems to be her most studied poem, though scholarly work on both is lacking. She was also published frequently in the African American literary magazine the *Saturday Evening Quill*, which originated in Boston in 1928, and contributed poems that same year to the short-lived literary magazine *Harlem*. In all, Johnson's promise and power as a poet is represented by thirty-four poems originally published in magazines between 1925 and 1935, along with twenty-two collected by the editor Werner Mitchell (2000).

She continued publishing in magazines, primarily those aimed at African American audiences, until 1935 and continued writing every day nearly until her death in 1995, but she remained little known or studied. According to her daughter, Abigail McGrath, Johnson continued working on her poetry "for herself because she enjoyed writing," and, until she was crippled by osteoporosis, "she wrote a poem every single day, sometimes tossing out yesterday's piece, sometimes rewriting" (Pace). McGrath remembers her as an eccentric and good mother: "She worked hard at being a good mother, and succeeded at being one of the best. She was a marvel" (Mitchell, p. 125). McGrath recalls her mother hiding their poverty from her by taking free Christmas trees as an act of so-called humanitarianism ("Helen had convinced me that if we didn't take these trees home, they would never know the joys of being trimmed and bring-

ing happiness to families") and by taking standing-room-only tickets to the ballet and opera as an opportunity to dance along (p. 127). Though relatively quiet politically in her poems, Johnson evidently engaged in at least one political action later in life, making a one-woman picket line to protest the firing of her daughter's schoolteacher—for being a Communist—in the late 1940s.

Johnson so assiduously guarded her privacy that though she married William Warner Hubbell in 1933, her married name and location remained unknown to the public for most of the rest of her life. She sought no fame or recognition, and in fact actively avoided curating her legacy. In her foreword to *This Waiting for Love*, Cheryl Wall recounts seeing a notice in the *New York Times* for a reading by Johnson in 1987, which had happened the day prior; Wall later learned that Johnson had not read in person, but rather had sent a tape of herself reading some poems. Wall did manage to contact Abigail McGrath, through whom Wall was able to mail some written questions, as Johnson was unwilling to conduct an interview in any other manner. At this point Johnson was eighty and had been out of the spotlight for fifty years, during which time she had married, had a child, divorced, and evidently written hundreds of poems without the public knowing about any of it. Wall concludes her anecdote about the elderly Johnson by reinforcing the poet's commitment to privacy: "Many months later, Johnson returned my questionnaire. The handwritten answers were too brief not to seem grudging. Everything about the exchange made me feel that my inquiries were invasive" (Mitchell, p. xii). McGrath notes that Johnson always wanted "attention to the work and not the person" (p. 126), which her posthumous republication perhaps provided.

CRITICISM

Most writers who choose to study Johnson write positively about her work and influence, though the dearth of scholarship might suggest a general neutrality or negativity about her contribution to the Harlem Renaissance. In an entry on Johnson

for *The Oxford Companion to African American Literature*, though, SallyAnn H. Ferguson offers a scathing commentary: "But Helene Johnson never fulfilled early expectations, probably because her poetry replicates to a greater degree than most the aesthetic confusion that beset Harlem Renaissance literature generally" (p. 404). She goes on to argue that in poems like "Remember Not" (1929) and "Invocation" (1929) her "sentimentalism at once reveals Johnson's mastery of outdated poetic forms and her alienation from the aesthetic spirit of those Harlem Renaissance artists who tried to focus concretely and candidly on African American experience." Finally, in her descriptions of black characters, particularly men and boys, "the primitivism and racial condescension expose the conflicted nature of Harlem Renaissance writers, whose middle-class upbringings and poetic visions apparently limited their abilities to capture the lives of the African American masses. Furthermore, Johnson's poetry all too often displays the self-rejection characteristic of many Harlem Renaissance writings." Certainly Ferguson's criticisms are worth noting; in "Sonnet to a Negro in Harlem" (see below), such a reading might be as valid as Katherine R. Lynes's ethnographic take. This entry, though, is both brief and somewhat outside the published consensus.

To add context to Ferguson's argument without seeking to dismantle her critique, one can point to an ongoing discussion about the role of primitivism in African American art during the Harlem Renaissance—a smaller, more complicated version of a discussion about primitivism and cultural exchange taking place more broadly during the first four decades of the twentieth century. In an article discussing Harlem Renaissance primitivism, Tracy McCabe points out that "primitivism—the promotion of the 'not-civilized'—is not … a monolithic discourse that can be simply labeled as either subversive or supportive of dominant ideology…. It takes on diverse and often contradictory meanings in its various social, historical, and literary contexts" (p. 475).

It is certainly possible to take the instances cited here by Ferguson as subversive in various ways; however, this critique being in a reference book has no doubt colored many first impressions of Johnson as a writer. Ferguson criticizes Johnson's use of the primitive and positioning of the observer as potentially racist, or at least influenced by white racist stereotypes of black subjects. Such a view, combined with criticism that West and, by extension, Johnson, were perhaps too wealthy to participate in a particular black experience, may contribute to Johnson's critical neglect.

POETRY

In style, Helene Johnson's poems vary widely; in the debate about creating a unique black poetics or mastering the conventions of white writers, Johnson chooses both. She has several masterful, technically sound sonnets, along with free-verse poems evocative of jazz rhythms. In general, Johnson's poetry celebrates the life and energy of African American life in Boston and Harlem. Its figuring of the human body is physical and feeling, and love is frequently associated with eating good food. "Chromatic words," a phrase from "Magula" especially admired by Cheryl Wall, paint Johnson's poems in colorful, evocative language. Her major themes include age and aging (about which she is generally very positive), love, faith, race, and the intersections thereof, often irreverently. Venetra K. Patton and Maureen Honey note her boldness: she was "experimenting with erotic themes and the use of street vernacular, a new form mastered by Langston Hughes but eschewed, for a variety of reasons, by women poets" (p. 599). She refused to be restrained by what was common or even what she had done successfully before; in both theme and practice, her joy at being different was evident.

Unlike Langston Hughes, and many of their Harlem Renaissance contemporaries, Johnson did not publish essays or manifestos about her political stances. The best readings of her poems (for which there is a want) acknowledge her network of social engagement through participation in black magazines and salons, while also noting the generally celebratory nature of her poems

about the black experience. If she comes down negatively about anything in particular, it is propriety for propriety's sake, which she gently criticizes in poems like "Cui Bono" (*Harlem*, 1928) and "Futility" (*Opportunity*, 1926). Her most extreme negative feelings, as expressed in the poems available to us, are for Christian faith that does not acknowledge the humanity of black people, most evident in poems like "A Missionary Brings a Young Native to America" (*Harlem*, 1928) and "A Southern Road" (*Fire!!*, 1926). Her political affiliations can be read in her choice of publication venues—nearly always black magazines, some explicitly political editorially—more than in the texts of most of her poems.

Johnson's celebration of blackness and black culture in Boston and Harlem is evident in most of her poems; her approach is not to project political or social preferences on her subject but to observe and comment. When her commentary is critical it is generally of outside forces that limit or damage black subjects. Her association with Hurston perhaps sparked an anthropological interest in people and culture, but whatever the genesis, her work is characterized by "attention to collection and collecting of culture (in its varied meanings); by [her] attempt to *represent* and preserve a voice of a culture; and by [her] attempt in her work to resist audience assumptions and expectations about her and her work" (Lynes, p. 525). Though many of Johnson's poems are deeply personal—her various takes on age, in particular, seem very specific to her outlook—another large group do indeed observe and collect people and culture(s), not shying away from difficulty but not attempting to solve it, either.

Johnson's poems also vary widely in diction, often within the same poem. Colloquial words like "golly" and "gee" intermingle with obscure or multisyllabic, Latinate words with ease. Some poems, particularly those about African American men, use African American dialect. Like her use of primitive imagery, her use of dialect can be read either as stereotyping or poetic experimentation. The wide variety at the level of language mirrors the diversity of poem forms, rhyme schemes, layouts, and subject matter. A

common comment on Johnson's career is that it showed promise (some would say unrealized), and perhaps her interest and ability in so many registers best speaks to that promise.

"SONNET TO A NEGRO IN HARLEM"

The poem "Sonnet to a Negro in Harlem" helps to illustrate Johnson's ethnographic eye along with her deft straddling of different political stances, engaging with racial and artistic debates of the early twentieth century without explicitly arguing in one particular direction. It is one of her most famous poems, though most critical readings available are glosses for students, not articles aimed at scholars.

George S. Schuyler's 1926 essay "The Negro-Art Hokum" outlines one side of the Harlem Renaissance debate—about whether African Americans had or ought to have had their own distinct culture and arts. Schuyler acknowledges that certain artistic genres originated in particular black populations, but argues that the distinctions among different groups of African Americans are exactly as stark as those between groups of white Americans: "[these art forms] are no more expressive or characteristic of the Negro race than the music and dancing of the Appalachian highlanders or the Dalmatian peasantry are expressive or characteristic of the Caucasian race" (p. 36). That is, Schuyler is not opposed to black arts inherently but thinks that "African American" is an artificial category, not united culturally per se. This argument in part mourns the loss of specific heritages and cultures, but does not acknowledge the vital community—and, indeed, culture—blossoming among African Americans in cities throughout America. For black writers in Boston, Harlem, Chicago, and elsewhere, who collaborated about their experiences as simultaneously of two (or more) cultures, the sameness of their experiences was as important as their differences. So Schuyler's insistence that black arts and white arts are not categorically distinct is worth noting, particularly when reading a Petrarchan sonnet.

On the other side of the black arts debate (though both views can coexist, and did,

certainly) is W. E. B. Du Bois' famous statement in *Crisis* that "all Art is propaganda and ever must be, despite the wailing of the purists. I stand in utter shamelessness and say that whatever art I have for writing has been used always for propaganda for gaining the right of black folk to love and enjoy" (Johnson and Johnson, p. 364). That is, black art is always, inherently, making the case for itself, for black artists, and for opportunity. Whether black poetry emulates the white masters or innovates by making use of black cultural traditions (jazz music and black vernacular language in particular), it always shows the variety of talents of black artists. Johnson's engagement in black literary groups and publication almost exclusively in black journals points to some affinity, whether deliberate or incidental, with Du Bois's take here. Her career, though of course bolstered by the enthusiasm of white readers as well, took place almost exclusively in black publications, some politically radical (most notably *Fire!!*).

These multiple contexts come to bear on the description of the "Negro in Harlem" walking proudly down the street, not fitting in with those around him. The sonnet's first sentence, which comprises the entire octave, describes the man as "disdainful and magnificent," "dark eyes flashing solemnly with hate" but also with his "head thrown back in rich, barbaric song," and later "laughter" (Mitchell, p. 40; ll. 1, 3, 7, 13). These contradictions demonstrate the precarious psychological position of African Americans, existing as insiders and outsiders, able to participate in society (particularly in places like Harlem, northern cities with large African American populations and neighborhoods) and also apart from it. However, the man's inability to blend in is curious, given that Harlem was a haven for black people at the time. The poem demonstrates his difference both in his behavior—the song and laughter, his eyes flashing—and in his physical being, describing his "shoulders towering high above the throng" (l. 6). The images he calls to the speaker's mind, too, separate him from the street on which he walks: "Palm trees and mangoes stretched before your eyes" as if he is oriented toward the tropics, not the urban landscape that surrounds him. Literally, the poem describes the speaker apprehending a tall black man, who is singing and laughing, walking down the streets of Harlem, but his attitude and bearing separate him from the workaday folks around him, the ones content to see the urban landscape, go to work—"toil and sweat for labor's sake" (l. 9)—and lose the elements of their identities that keep them separate. An aside in the octave, four lines separated by dashes, shows the character's position in the debate about fitting in with the larger culture: "Small wonder that you are incompetent / To imitate those whom you so despise" (ll. 4–5). Here, though the character obviously refuses to participate in the charade that he is the same as white America, he also refuses to fit in with Harlem's black culture, bringing Schuyler's arguments to mind. His memories of Africa, whether ancestral or personal, remind him that the community of Harlem is a world removed from his origins. The description of his song as "barbaric" suggests that the speaker, while admiring, also has internalized a view of Africa as primitive, and the man's refusal to hew to urban social conventions prompts consideration of this contrast. Though the speaker claims to "love" his laughter, his way of being, and says in the final line that he is "too splendid" for the city street, this admiration is removed; the speaker remains apart, observational, not changing her behavior even while enjoying his.

Even in descriptions that sound judgmental, Johnson's speaker complicates her view; what she sees—and thus what the reader sees—is nuanced, open to various interpretations. The man of the poem's title is "disdainful," his gait is "pompous," his feet are "supercilious," his laughter is "arrogant and bold," and finally he is "too splendid" (ll. 1, 2, 11, 13, 14); the first four of these adjectives read initially as negative, but in the context of the poem seem to be celebrated by the speaker. The speaker provides little context for herself, only using the first-person "I" once, in line 13: "I love your laughter arrogant and bold." This line and the intrusion of a first-person viewer complicates the perspective of the poem; suddenly our observation is embodied, by an "I" who is watching this man quite closely; the

reader, like the speaker, is also on the street, watching a stranger and drawing conjecture about his life. The conclusions of the speaker are called into question; is he or only the speaker looking out at images of the tropics? Is he arrogant? If the images stretched before his eyes are our conjecture, what details are literally true?

Here, Schuyler's note that African American cultures vary is useful, because like the speaker we are tempted to take the subject character as synecdochic for all African Americans attempting to fit into a broader American culture, whereas the poem does not quite allow that reading to stand. Because the character refuses to fit in in Harlem, because he's too supercilious to work like those around him, because his own scorn will erase the traces of his existence (l. 12), the Negro character can here be read as skeptical of the project of trying at all. And because the speaker might well be hypothesizing about his intentions and attitudes, we can read her as projecting her doubts onto him. Thus one possible reading of the poem is that the speaker, a Johnson-like person in Harlem, wonders if the enterprise of creating an African American community in a white society is ultimately worthwhile. Here, though the speaker avoids putting these views into her own voice, aside from "I love," the poem invites readers to interpret the attitudes as the speaker's, or at least attitudes admired by the speaker. This is perhaps the clearest didactic message Johnson is willing to provide, skepticism projected onto an anonymous character on the city street. However, her participation in the community and the poem's oblique questioning combine to suggest that Johnson's politics were not naively positive, even as she avoided taking an explicit stance. The careful collection of details, ethnographic observation of people and contexts, allows Johnson to be both neutral and celebratory.

Formally, of course, it is important that Johnson chose the sonnet to memorialize this image; long associated with unrequited love, the sonnet is also a form of memorial, and here it operates on both levels. For African American writers, the connotations of the sonnet were slightly different from those of their white counterparts, explaining—in part—the relative dearth of modern-period sonnets by white poets as compared to the flourishing of the genre among black ones. While white writers had embraced the sonnet for long enough that, by the early twentieth century, it carried elite, memorial connotations, black writers in Harlem took up other of Dante's early purposes of the genre: its ability to speak for and to a particular group, its possibilities for vernacular and highly targeted in-group speech. As Antonella Francini writes, "Much like its medieval archetype, it appears to be a vehicle of communication rather than a mere display of a poet's technical skills or a conventional replica of European aesthetic manners, as were the majority of sonnets produced in the 19th-century in America" (p. 37). Because so many African American writers embraced the form, put violence and politics and dialect into fourteen lines often associated with love, its function was reclaimed: "In making it one of their chosen modes of expression, these [black] poets succeeded in recovering the sonnet's original function centuries after its birth and within a very different cultural setting. In their hands, the fourteen-line structure turns into an ideal forum, a public space for dynamic argumentation of social and political themes directed to a specific category of readers" (Francini, p. 38). Here, then, we begin to see the role of the speaker as ethnographer for her people, a collective voice entering a communal discussion of how they see themselves, in person and in representation. The single "Negro in Harlem" and the "I" observing him is transformed, through the history of the African American sonnet, into a representation of a group's struggle to reconcile the streets of Harlem with the mangoes and palm trees of a mythical home.

Putting the description of the man in the second person—"You are disdainful and magnificent" (l. 1)—puts the reader in the position of the man. This puts a community of readers in a position of understanding themselves as the man and the observer, seeing through the poem's perspective both views. Normally the "I" of a poem invites the reader's empathy, acting as the reader's "eyes" to the vision the poem presents,

but here, because the "I" is so delayed, the "you" comes also to be a source of empathy. For readers whose experiences are similar to Johnson's, people reading *Caroling Dusk* and *Ebony and Topaz* (both 1927, both aimed at African American audiences), both of these positions are likely familiar. The sonnet thus invites people to empathize, to see from multiple sides someone like themselves and vividly distinct. Through ethnographic observation of her environment, Johnson's speaker creates a shared experience among her readers.

"MAGULA" ("MAGALU") AND POEMS ABOUT RELIGION AND RESTRAINT

This free-verse poem, alternately written as "Magula" and "Magalu" in different collections, imagines a tropical African setting and a scene of missionary work, positioning the speaker against the religious missionary. This poem, like Edna St. Vincent Millay's "To a Calvinist in Bali" (*Harper's*, October 1938), figures the lush tropical setting as a kind of antireligious temptation; in Millay's version, the speaker takes the position of the religious traveler, who "sense[s]" the nature of Bali "with delight but not with ease," because the majesty and danger of the flora and fauna there inspire "solemn envy kin to shame" (ll. 5, 8). Johnson's lush descriptions of Magula's environment are similar, but the perspective seeks to both suggest familiarity and impress with the American reader's (likely) *un*familiarity with the African landscape:

> Summer comes.
> The ziczac hovers
> Round the greedy-mouthed crocodile.
> A vulture bears away a foolish jackal.
> The flamingo is a dash of pink
> Against dark green mangroves,
> Her slender legs rivalling her slim neck.
>
> (Mitchell, p. 34; ll. 1–7)

Beginning in the present tense, "Summer comes," the speaker suggests that she, and perhaps we, have been in this place prior to this moment, and are observing something in flux. The list of animals foreign to most American readers serves to make each one normal, another in a list of items on the landscape, both fantastic and typical. Operating on both registers, the poem puts the reader in the position of someone else, perhaps their own African ancestors, observing "this pulsing, riotous gasp of color" (l. 12). Commenting on the pastoral setting here, Lynes notes that though the description of the scenery is heightened, it "is not without conflict, ... and not entirely idealized—nature here is not wholly nurturing but rather reveals both the warm comforts of early summer and the (implied) bloody realities of living and dying" (pp. 532–533). Mitchell concurs, pointing out further subtle points of conflict throughout this description: "In drawing our attention to the flamingo's fragility and vulnerability—her slender legs and slim neck— the poem ... suggests an extended analogy between the devoured or soon-to-be devoured animals and vulnerable Magula" (Mitchell, pp. 13–14). The rich, unhurried interplay between these images of beauty and danger set the scene for the subject of the poem to face temptation.

The speaker, heretofore unspecified, intrudes in line 13—"I met Magula, ... / ... listening to a man with a white collar / And a small black book with a cross on it" (ll. 13–15). The "I" of these lines looks at a common natural scene and remembers a time in the past ("I met") when Magula and the priest were there too. This moment replays a common pastoral trope, as noted by Lynes, of "a maiden waiting for love in an idealized setting," though the extent to which she is actively waiting is not made clear (p. 533). However, Magula's "Eager-lipped" countenance as she listens to the man suggests that she is susceptible to him. Religion, on this model, separates people—in this case specifically black Africans, but elsewhere in Johnson's work everyone else too—from their natures, their preferences, and their bodies. The pastoral scene here and the music and poetry the speaker can offer are at risk if Magula chooses to "let him lure" her "from [her] laughing waters" (l. 20). The waters are Magula's, her own laughing landscape, perhaps personified as the speaker, who could "Fill up [her] throat with laughter and [her] heart with song" (l. 19). The close associa-

tion of laughter with the lake and waters suggests that the speaker, who can provide laughter, might be the landscape.

This conflict between the pastoral scene, with its "chromatic words" of poetry, and the offer of faith, is nearly the same dilemma offered in Millay's poem, but here the speaker takes a firm stance. (Millay's speaker is detached, knowingly observing the moral conflict of the titular Calvinist, reassuring him that his strong faith can rationalize away the tempting majesty of the natural world.) The conflict in "Magula" is heightened by the historical context of missionary colonization of Africa and of slaves in the Americas: "Slavery is not directly mentioned but the western religion that was a part of slavery's tenets is explicitly present in the man with a 'white collar' and a Bible" (Lynes, p. 533). Though the man with the Bible is talking directly to Magula (or at least within her hearing), the speaker of the poem talks only to the reader; her plea is voiceless, without quotation marks, suggesting that Magula does not literally hear it:

Oh Magula, come! Take my hand and I'll read you poetry,
Chromatic words,
Seraphic symphonies,
Fill up your throat with laughter and your heart with song.

(ll. 16–19)

The laughter and music previously associated with the lake (l. 8) are now at risk for Magula; the speaker's offer to give them to her again figures the speaker as the landscape itself. (Though the speaker's use of the idiom "take my hand" might suggest otherwise.) The multicolored words, the music and rhythms of nature, contrast starkly with the priest, who is figured with a white collar and a black book, offering a creed that is similarly black-and-white in its proscriptions. The speaker asks an unanswered (and, for Magula, unheard) question, contrasting Magula's landscape, bodily autonomy, and sensuality with the superficial comforts of religion as offered by the missionary:

Would you sell the colors of your sunset and the fragrance

Of your flowers, and the passionate wonder of your forest
For a creed that will not let you dance?

(ll. 22–24)

As in other of Johnson's poems, the restrictions associated with organized religion seem to be more problematic than faith per se. The "creed that will not let you dance" represents all the religious losses, present in culture more generally too, that confine and restrain people, women in particular, just for the sake of doing so. Just as the priest's appearance denies the chromatic colors of the landscape around him, his faith denies the music and laughter Magula enjoys now. The dance Magula would lose is part of her current culture, one that readings of Africans as primitive (and the missionary endeavor, perhaps) often ignore. The speaker suggests that her poetry, which might or might not be a part of Magula's existing culture, is an acceptable substitute for organized religion, not merely superficial fun, because the natural setting can fill not only her "throat with laughter" but also her "heart with song." That song, or poetry, could also fill someone's heart, for its own sake instead of in the service of worship, is a potentially subversive claim for the speaker of the poem to make.

Additionally, and complicating our reading of the poem, is the unresolved question of who the speaker is. Though it was suggested earlier that the speaker could be the landscape itself (or someone closely associated with the landscape, that is, a local person), Lynes notes that actually, aside from the words linking the speaker to the landscape, the verb tenses suggesting the speaker has been in and remains in the landscape, and the speaker's celebration of poetry, we learn nothing about her. Actually, as Mitchell and Lynes both note, the poem does not reveal Magula's gender, either; we assume she is a woman because of the tropes of the pastoral and the scene of temptation, but perhaps our willingness to make assumptions about Magula is a deliberate iteration by Johnson of the way people do the same toward African Americans more generally. Reading Magula as a woman seems to make the most sense; but it is worth noting Mitchell's praise of

Johnson's poetry more generally, that "exploring possible answers to this question will show the boldness and beauty of Johnson's artistic vision" (p. 16). Though Mitchell is talking about a different question—where the speaker will lead Magula—he points to the gaps she leaves in many poems as the very source of their pleasure.

"Magula" offers a rare opportunity to synthesize critical commentary, but many less-discussed poems deal with religion and social constraint in different registers. The poem "A Missionary Brings a Young Native to America" (*Harlem*, 1928, qtd. in Mitchell, p. 43) suggests what Magula has to look forward to if she chooses to go with the priest. This violent, painful sonnet, loosely Petrarchan in form, narrates the arrival of a native woman in America. The experience of being forcibly brought to a new place and into a new faith is figured as physical pain: "A belt / Of alien tenets choked the songs that surged / Within her when alone each night she knelt / At prayer" (ll. 7–10). The physical pain of being choked by a belt is equated to the psychological pain of being repressed by "alien tenets," or the dogma of a religion that is not hers. The "songs" she would express are "choked," and thus silenced, supplanted by Christian prayer. In the sonnet's final lines the superficial recitations of religion are contrasted with the truer expression of the woman's feelings:

afraid that she would scream
Aloud her young abandon to the night,
She mumbled Latin litanies and dreamed
Unholy dreams while waiting for the light.

(ll. 11–14)

Her dreams and "abandon" are internal and external manifestations of something deeper within her than the foreign, "alien," Latin litanies; it is unclear, though, if either is leading her toward the "light" of the poem's end. Earlier in the poem the word "light" appears in a violent image—"She felt / A steel-spiked wave of brick and light submerge / Her mind in cold immensity" (ll. 5–7)—suggesting that the light she waits for in the end might not be a refuge, but just a way of bearing the pain differently. In this and several other poems, Johnson links organized

religion to the violent repression of culture. See also "A Southern Road," "Fiat Lux," "Regalia," and "Worship," the last of which presents organized religion as desirable, if complicated.

Religion is not the only institution repressing Johnson's speakers, though; social mores limit others, often more humorously. The brief poem "Futility" pokes fun at conventions while alluding to the symbols of religion only briefly:

It is silly—
This waiting for love
In a parlor.
When love is singing up and down the alley
Without a collar.

(*Opportunity*, August 1926, qtd. in Mitchell, p. 31)

This is one of her earliest poems, and the sense of being stifled by convention runs throughout her career. In this instance, the freedom of running is mimicked in the fourth line's length, punctuated by the final, brief observation of the last line. A reader can imagine the speaker chafing in her collared dress, looking longingly out a window; the moment is perfectly distilled, the mood disgruntled but light.

Some of Johnson's later, unpublished poems echo the sentiments of "Futility," contrasting the self of public expectation and the irreverent, unrepressed self inside. In "Foraging" (not dated), a very small deviation is a cause for joy:

I cannot go on living in this very little way—
This tea, this bread and butter set so neatly on a tray.
If I close the door behind me, careful not to let it slam
I might sneak out and get myself a little bit of jam.

(Mitchell, p. 69)

For this speaker, order is "little," limiting, but not something one can completely abandon. Even in her escape for jam, she is "careful" to close the door softly. The connection of "little" with limiting recalls Abigail McGrath's memories of her mother teaching her to cease "ghetto thinking," by which she meant "thinking [that] was controlled by boundaries, that I was encircled by limitations in the same manner that a geographical ghetto is within boundaries" (Mitchell, p. 127). Of course it is hard not to read some class

critique into Johnson's word choice, but it also reinforces the theme she returns to so often in her collected poems.

The 1928 poem "Cui Bono," the title of which translates to "for whose benefit" or "of what good," is a ballad of a young woman, perhaps the same one chafing at expectations as in "Futility" and "Foraging," dreaming of finding love. When Fate finally intervenes to send her a "passionate / Young knight" (ll. 7–8) she is intimidated by his ardor, and turns him down. The poem ends with the girl conflicted about what she ought to have done:

"I wish I'd let him kiss me tho.
Oh just the merest peck.
I wish—I wish—I wish—but no,
I'd lose my self-respect."

(*Harlem*, ll. 17–20, qtd. in Mitchell, p. 44)

The final stanza has her regretting, dreaming of love, "anaemic." Though she has done the "right" thing, since the man had not offered marriage, she is not comforted. The ballad stanzas of this poem make it almost into a parable, a common story about the perils of convention. For whose benefit, these dictates about women's sexuality? Certainly not the girl's, in this case; she is left with no love and no kiss, just anemic dreams.

The conflict between restraint and passionate, sensual freedom is embodied by the sea, at once both and neither, in the poem "Metamorphism" (*Opportunity*, 1926); it is also a theme in "Night" (*Opportunity*, 1926) and "The Little Love" (*Messenger*, 1926), among others.

Many poems dispense with the apologies for propriety entirely, and joyously celebrate sensuality. Poems like "Fulfillment" (*Opportunity*, 1926) and "What Do I Care for Morning" (*Caroling Dusk*, 1927) capture the pleasures of the human body, only complicated briefly by images of convention and religion that should suppress the joy they celebrate.

OTHER THEMES

Interestingly, among the unpublished poems Mitchell collects in *This Waiting for Love* are two poems about war, violent and experimental. Because Mitchell does not date them, their exact context is not clear. The first, "War," begins:

War is delectable
the blood
the shredded limb
the belly, yielding grace
guts funnily displace.

(Mitchell, pp. 77–78, ll.1–5)

Though Johnson is violent in her racial poems, this blazon of horror still sticks out. The contrast of "delectable" with the images thereafter is troubling, in a way somewhat similar to Stephen Crane's 1899 "War Is Kind." Johnson was not active in the civil rights movement or, to the best of anyone's knowledge, in other political activism (with the exception of her one-woman picket line for a fired teacher), and as far as research has revealed she spent no time in any war zones, but these two poems impress the violence and destruction of war nonetheless.

One poem explicitly addresses the class question hovering over her and Dorothy West's biographies, not answering any questions but putting voice to a perhaps universal feeling. The humorous poem laments the speaker's lack of pedigree, noting that her actions would be read differently if people knew she were noble: "I could wear my last year's hat. / Or the chapeau prior to that / And still inspire gallantry, / Were I a dame of pedigree" ("Plea of a Plebeian," Mitchell, p. 61, ll. 21–24). The speaker longs to be noble, not necessarily to behave so differently than she does now, but to have the freedom to behave as she chooses: "The middle class has quite a pull, / But they are so respectable" (ll. 17–18). As is usual in Johnson's poems, "respectable" is a negative word. In rhyming couplets, Johnson plays with unusual words and rhymes, pairing "salon" and "liaisons," and later "palisade" and "escapade." The form is distinct from her other poems, bouncing along the iambic tetrameter, drawing the reader along on a daydream. The theme of class does not recur throughout the published poems, but more speculation and commentary on its role in her life and career is in her biography, above.

It would not be practical to attempt to outline every theme Johnson returns to in the few published poems available to readers, but in addition to race, which is not covered here in its own section because it appears throughout, Johnson writes with some frequency about age and aging. Perhaps surprisingly, Johnson's approach to aging and even death seems quite positive; even as early as 1929, Johnson celebrated the future in her poems.

"Invocation" (*Saturday Evening Quill,* 1929), a fourteen-line poem that is not quite a sonnet, revels in the messiness of life by asking for an untended grave. By looking forward to what happens after life, Johnson, like Dickinson before her, subverts tropes of time and loss. The poem begins, "Let me be buried in the rain," suggestive of a burial in spring, traditionally the season of new life (particularly in poetic parlance). The end of the poem requests a benevolent lack of care:

And do not keep my plot mowed smooth
And clean as a spinster's bed,
But let the weed, the flower, the tree,
Riotous, rampant, wild and free,
Grow high above my head.

(Mitchell, p. 46, ll. 10–14)

As is often the case, restraint and tidiness are linked with repression, a lack of physical or sexual expression; wild nature better matches the speaker's character, as was the case in "Magula" and in "Trees at Night" (Johnson's first published poem; *Opportunity,* 1925). Death does not end the wild, embodied soul of the speaker, but merely provides another site of the same conflict she has discussed before.

The short poem "Why Do They Prate?" encapsulates Johnson's broader attitude about aging:

Why do they prate of youth so much?
'Tis too near the root.
A budding, yes, but I prefer
The ripening of the fruit.

(*Saturday Evening Quill,* 1929, qtd. in Mitchell, p. 53)

The unpublished poem "He's About 22. I'm 63." deals with aging in a humorous way, expanding

on the joys of ripened age. The experimental poem narrates the speaker's thought process as she takes an interest in and eventually engages in an affair with her younger neighbor. The poem is often funny—it is one of her longest poems, multiple pages in length, in free verse—and characterizes the couple's flirtation and sex in elided dialog, jumbled thoughts that are at once unclear and easy to follow. When the speaker has the young man in her apartment, she observes: "He seems a little scattered. / How does it really matter? At 22, at 63, / any eccentricity?" (Mitchell, p. 72, ll. 49–51). Unexpected rhymes pepper the uneven lines, with irregular spacing separating lines and ideas visually as well as in content. Parenthetical asides insert self-deprecating jokes, like this one, from the end of their sexual encounter:

Whisper triumphantly,
"Merci, Merci."
(Or less jubilantly,
"Mercy!")

(Michell, p. 73, ll. 82–85)

The formal experimentation, bawdy subject matter, and self-aware (and amused) speaker all contrast with the Johnson of violent, painful racial poems like "A Southern Road" and "A Missionary Brings a Young Native to America," and to a lesser extent to the passionate intensity of the sensuality in "Magula" and "Summer Matures" (*Opportunity,* 1927). The variety evident in the small collection of work Mitchell gathered for publication is astounding, and compounds the sense that this is a writer who did too little with her generous talents.

LEGACY

Until Mitchell's 2000 volume, Johnson's later poetry had not been collected for publication; it is not known how many of her daily poems exist today. Mitchell's volume includes twenty-two poems from the 1960s through the 1980s. Johnson died on July 6, 1995. In that same year, her cousin Dorothy West reentered the literary public eye with her novel *The Wedding*; Mitchell claims

that the protagonist of West's novel is modeled on Abigail McGrath. West's renewed popularity in the 1990s provided some of the latest first-person recollections of the Harlem Renaissance and of Helene Johnson.

Johnson's obituary makes the only reference to a planned 1996 poetry collection, to be titled "Inklings and Trinkets." This book was evidently never published, nor written about elsewhere.

More recently, a manuscript of later Johnson poems edited by Emily Rosamund Claman was published as part of the Graduate Center at City University of New York's archival research series, *Lost & Found: The CUNY Poetics Document Initiative*. This 2014 chapbook contains an unpublished, but evidently arranged by Johnson herself, manuscript called "'The Boat Is Tethered to the Floor': After the Harlem Renaissance." The poems are in free verse, without titles; it is not entirely clear where poems are meant to begin and end. Claman presents these poems with a note about coming into possession of the manuscript, but without any critical analysis. This latest publication provides new opportunities in Johnson scholarship, particularly in seeing the evolution of her poetic style.

Despite her lack of further publication after 1935, Helene Johnson leaves much to study and analyze, and many poems rich for analysis. Scholars like Lynes have applied other fields (ecocriticism) to Johnson's poetry to enrich both fields. As more work is done on modernist and Harlem Renaissance magazines, women writers, and perhaps ecopoetry, it is likely that more work on Johnson will be published and more about her later life discovered.

Selected Bibliography

WORKS OF HELENE JOHNSON

Claman, Emily Rosamund. "'The Boat Is Tethered to the Floor': After the Harlem Renaissance." In *Lost & Found: The CUNY Poetics Document Initiative*. Series 4. New York: SPD Books, 2014. (Chapbook.)

Honey, Maureen. *Shadowed Dreams: Woman's Poetry of the Harlem Renaissance*. New Brunswick, N.J.: Rutgers University Press, 1989. (There are two editions of this text, the 1989 being more expansive, with newer biographical notes.)

Mitchell, Varner D., ed. *This Waiting for Love: Helene Johnson, Poet of the Harlem Renaissance*. Amherst: University of Massachusetts Press, 2000. (This text offers the most comprehensive collection of Johnson's poetry available, along with some excerpted letters and a biographical introduction.)

Patton, Venetria K., and Maureen Honey. *Double-Take: A Revisionist Harlem Renaissance Anthology*. New Brunswick, N.J.: Rutgers University Press, 2001. Pp. 599–605. (This, too, includes a biography, and slightly different editions of some poems than the previous text.)

Thurman, Wallace. *FIRE!! A Quarterly Devoted to the Younger Negro Artists*. New York: Kraus-Thomson, 1926.

CRITICAL AND BIOGRAPHICAL STUDIES

Dove, Rita. "Poet's Choice: Helene Johnson." *Washington Post*, February 27, 2000, p X12.

Esparza, Crystal, Caroline Klohs, and Camille Cyprian. "Helene Johnson." *VG: Voices from the Gaps*. University of Minnesota. December 16, 2005. http://voices.cla.umn.edu/artistpages/johnsonHelene.php

Ferguson, SallyAnn H. "Helene Johnson." *The Oxford Companion to African American Literature*. Edited by William L. Andrews et al. New York: Oxford University Press, 1997. P. 404.

Francini, Antonella. "Sonnet vs. Sonnet: The Fourteen Lines in African American Poetry." *RSA Journal* 14:37–66 (2003).

Johnson, Abby Ann Arthur, and Ronald M. Johnson. "Forgotten Pages: Black Literary Magazines in the 1920s." *Journal of American Studies* 8, no. 3:363–382 (December 1974).

Lynes, Katherine R. "'Sprung from American Soil': The 'Nature' of Africa in the Poetry of Helene Johnson." *Interdisciplinary Studies in Literature & Environment* 16, no. 3:525–549 (2009).

McCabe, Tracy. "The Multifaceted Politics of Primitivism in Harlem Renaissance Writing." *Soundings: An Interdisciplinary Journal* 80, no. 4:475–497 (1997).

Miller, Nina. *Making Love Modern: The Intimate Public Worlds of New York's Literary Women*. New York: Oxford University Press, 1999.

Pace, Eric. "Helene Johnson, Poet of Harlem, 89, Dies." *New York Times*, July 11, 1995. http://www.nytimes.com/1995/07/11/obituaries/helene-johnson-poet-of-harlem-89-dies.html

Roses, Lorraine Elena, and Ruth Elizabeth Randolph. *Harlem's Glory: Black Women Writing 1900–1950*. Cambridge, Mass.: Harvard University Press, 1996.

Schuyler, George S. "The Negro Art Hokum." *Nation,* June 16, 1926. Reprinted in *Double-Take: A Revisionist Harlem Renaissance Anthology*. Edited by Venetria K. Patton and Maureen Honey. New Brunswick, N.J.: Rutgers University Press, 2001. Pp. 36–39.

Wall, Cheryl A. *Women of the Harlem Renaissance*. Bloomington: Indiana University Press, 1995.

Watson, Steven. *The Harlem Renaissance: Hub of African-American Culture, 1920–1930*. New York: Pantheon, 1996.

Wheeler, Lesley. "This Waiting for Love." *African American Review* 36, no. 2:340–343 (2002).

WILLIAM KITTREDGE

(1932—)

Susan Carol Hauser

WILLIAM KITTREDGE'S WRITING career is largely defined by a personal mission: to expose the old, dominating American myths of individualism and ownership that he sees as dangerous and ruinous to land and people, and to provide examples of new myths to replace the old. He had grown up with the old myths, and they informed his work as the farming boss on the family ranch. The new myths, based on appreciation and community rather than competition and commercial development, are demonstrated in his stories and essays. These writings recommend examination of the personal values that guide one's decision-making and identifying values that are positive not just for personal benefit but for the benefit of the land and all of its inhabitants, animals and humans alike. Kittredge is best known for *Hole in the Sky: A Memoir* (1992) and for personal essays. He also writes short stories and has collaborated on movie scripts. He is the recipient of many literary and humanitarian awards.

LIFE

William Alfred "Bill" Kittredge was born on August 14, 1932, in Portland, Oregon, to Josephine Miessner and Oscar Franklin Kittredge. In 1937 his grandfather and namesake, William Kittredge (1875–1958), purchased the MC Ranch in Warner Valley in southeastern Oregon. The family, including grandparents, parents, Kittredge, and his brother Pat and sister Roberta, moved there from Portland to work the ranch.

In the spring of 1938, when Kittredge was five going on six, he contracted polio and spent much of a year in hospitals. Although he recovered fully, the endless hours of solitude and inactivity led him to contemplate life with a seriousness that was extraordinary and coura-

geous for such a young person: he wondered why it was better to be alive than not. In *Hole in the Sky*, he identifies this period as an "end-of-innocence time" (p. 3), though he would be in his thirties before he stood back and assessed the life of the ranch from a new perspective. Until then, he mostly embraced the values handed to him, in part by his father but in greater part by his grandfather, who saw the earth and its animals as property and who believed it was his responsibility to tame and utilize both for his own benefit, the benefit of his family, and, therefore, the benefit of society. The elder Kittredge may have believed his actions over the next several decades to be altruistic, but in fact, says Kittredge, they destroyed much of the ecosystem of the ranch, including wild bird habitat, water resources, and the very soil itself, and contributed to the despair and dissolution of the family and its members.

An understanding of the effect of the ranch on the land came much later in Kittredge's life. As a boy, from the age of about nine, he, his brother, and a cousin started working with the ranch hands. They rode out with them to tend cattle, camping out and learning how to live in that rugged community. The ranch hands ("buckaroos") generally lived and raised their families on the ranch, and there were men among them whom Kittredge knew into his adult life.

These men, who understood hard work and loyalty, and who lived communally with nature and its elements, remained strong in Kittredge's memory and were the subject of some of his first writing. He also remembers, in *Hole in the Sky*, the ranch work itself, but much of the memory concerns place, the still-natural environment of the ranch at the time he was growing up:

Around May 10 the homesteader's row of Lombardy poplars in front of our house would crack

their heart-shaped buds. The translucent lime-green leaves would emerge, and cast their tiny flittering shadows over my mother's face as she studied the morning. I thought the world was alive like a creature, and it was.

(p. 3)

Kittredge attended elementary school in nearby Adel, Oregon, and junior high in northern California, where he and his siblings and his mother lived for several years. The move was ostensibly made necessary by his sister's asthma, but Kittredge suspected later that it had more to do with his parents' marriage. By his late teens, the family was back together in Oregon and he graduated from high school in Klamath Falls.

Summers were spent at the ranch, riding and working with the buckaroos. It was assumed that young Bill would follow in the footsteps of his father and grandfather, although his father, Oscar, had not done so willingly. After graduating from Oregon Agricultural College in Corvallis, Oscar had wanted to study law. When he returned home for the interim between school years, his own father had a long, persuasive talk with him, and in the end he yielded and committed himself to the ranch. It was a decision he regretted, and when Kittredge, at age thirty-five, told Oscar that he was going away to study writing, his father, instead of chastising him, encouraged him: "'Do what you want,' he said. 'I've done things I hated all my life and I sure as hell wouldn't recommend that'" (*Taking Care*, p. 31).

Kittredge's mother also had interests that she was not able to fulfill on the ranch. She had studied music, loved opera, and was an avid reader. When her children were young, she took them frequently to San Francisco where they sometimes stayed for weeks at a time, living in grand hotels. Although these extended outings provided new experiences for the children, they did not break the isolation of ranch life. For Kittredge, the MC Ranch and Warner Valley were the real world. The road that was the driveway into the ranch was twenty-five miles long. Although they eventually had television, the rest of the world was something that happened very far away and had little to do with the Kittredge family.

Beginning in the fall of 1949, Kittredge attended his father's alma mater in Corvallis, by then called Oregon State College, where he studied general agriculture. In his freshman year he met Janet O'Connor. They married in 1951, both of them age nineteen. He graduated with a bachelor's degree in 1953. His status as a college student had exempted him from the draft for the Korean War (June 1950–July 1953), and he knew that when he graduated he would eventually, if not immediately, be called up for military service. He and Janet chose instead for him to enlist in the U.S. Air Force, a four-year tour. On January 14, 1954, he boarded a train for Lackland Air Force Base in Texas, where he would undergo basic training.

In the air force, Kittredge was trained in photo interpretation, reading aerial maps. But he also made plans to begin writing seriously. The act of writing, however, did not come easily to him. While stationed in Colorado, he had tried to write daily, but failed. He decided to read instead, and also was unable to concentrate on that. Between his posting in Colorado and a new one in California, he worked back at the ranch. He thought then that he would never be a writer, that the wheat fields that choked him with dust as he worked would be his posting after the air force.

Still, he did not quit trying to become a writer. At Travis Air Force Base near San Francisco, he wrote almost daily. He started with short stories, but when his first submission to a magazine was rejected, he set the stories aside and started a novel about ranching. At the time, he did not recognize the story behind the story, of a country boy trying to ferret out the values— the mythologies—that underpinned his home culture that he loved, nor did he know those mythologies would become a theme in his mature writing. The novel was never published, but later Kittredge revised it into a short story, "Society of Eros," which became his first published story (*Northwest Review*, fall–winter 1965–1966).

When Kittredge was not satisfied with his writing, he turned to books to fill the lonely gaps. As with the writing, at this point his reading was driven by an intuitive sense that it was the right thing to do. Later, he came to understand that

stories can drive our lives, that they inform our lives and that the values expressed in them can become manifest in our deeds and our behaviors. But during the years in the service, he tried to use ideas, rather than stories, to contemplate his life, without much success. His parents and grandparents had little, if any, experience with such thinking and so gave him no background in it, although his mother believed in his abilities and his intelligence and told him so, engendering in him a confidence that he could be whatever he chose to be.

Kittredge's last military posting was in Guam. He and Janet now had two children—Karen, born in March 1954, and Bradley, born in March 1956—and they joined him at all of his military posts. In 1957, at the end of his tour, the family returned to the United States. Kittredge's parents were living apart and would soon divorce. His father was no longer working at the ranch, after a falling out with his own father. In the spring of 1958 Kittredge was back on the ranch, this time as a husband and father, and working as an adult, no longer as the boss's kid. His grandfather's vision still drove all ranch decisions: work well done—God's work—will see you through. As was typical for the mid-twentieth century, this driving mythology was not identified or discussed. Even Kittredge was still mostly unaware of the forces that shaped the ranch and its people, although soon enough it would surface for him and everything would change.

Reentry into the ranch's life was not seamless for Kittredge. He had been away for eight years, attending college and serving in the military. Farming operations and processes had changed. In May, not long after he and Janet were settled at the ranch, his grandfather died and Kittredge became the farm boss, another significant change for him. Alcohol was already a factor in his personal struggle to understand/avoid the realities of life, marriage, and parenthood, and now, with new tensions, it became pivotal for him. In *Hole in the Sky*, he writes about severe depression, about living emotionally and mentally apart from others, as though in a bubble. Along with the loneliness that came with the depression, he suffered from a dire fear "that

nothing you do connects to any other particular thing in your daily life," that all of one's actions were meaningless (p. 177). Alcohol, he quickly discovered, alleviated the symptoms, though it did not neutralize the fears and terrors. It also eroded his marriage, just as his father's drinking had contributed to the dissolution of his parents' marriage.

Working the ranch full-time, deeply connected by his own actions to the ongoing decimation of the land and animals, the work horses gone that had once been part of their community and were now replaced by heavy machinery, his old cowhand friends dying and for the most part unmourned, Kittredge became more and more anxious and frantic. In an effort to save himself, he turned again to writing. Beginning on the day after Thanksgiving in 1964, he pledged to himself that he would write every day, and he honored that pledge. He was not writing to get published but to forge coherencies in his life.

By the mid-1960s the MC Ranch, now more than 15,000 acres, was no longer a viable family operation. Unconstrained by the single-minded will of the first William Kittredge and freed from isolation by the opening of roads, communities, and media, the children and grandchildren left Warner Valley for other interests. All agreed it was time to let go of the ranch, and it was sold in 1967. Kittredge and Janet also got divorced that year, and Janet and the children moved to California. Kittredge met Patricia Hauser and they were married before the end of the year. Kittredge gathered his strength and determined that he would, at last, study writing. He entered a graduate program at the University of Oregon, Eugene, for one semester, and in late summer 1968, having been accepted in the Iowa Writers' Workshop, he and Patty packed up and drove to the University of Iowa in Iowa City, fueled by his father's blessing to leave all that he had known and to become what he could.

"I WAS GOING TO BE A WRITER"

Although Kittredge had been a lifelong reader, he did not study the craft of writing with a men-

tor until he took a workshop with Bernard Malamud at the University of Oregon. Malamud had just published his novel *The Natural*, but he was from the East Coast and Kittredge had no faith in this easterner's understanding of the stories Kittredge had to tell, stories of the ranch and the men—they were mostly men—who worked it. Theirs was work he understood. He recorded the stories faithfully and saw them as precious. Malamud talked to him about the arc of a story, and about the point of recognition where something meaningful changes for a character. Kittredge had no time for what he considered then to be academic nonsense. He earned one F after another from Malamud. Finally he gave in and, though disgusted with himself, wrote a story to Malamud's specifications. He received an A.

In spite of that success, the point of the elements of story was still incipient for Kittredge. When he left the ranch, he was aware that he wanted a life with more meaning, but at the time that just meant a writing life. He had not yet understood, could not even ask the question about, how writing changed things in the world— how it might change people or a culture or a country. At the behest of his father-in-law he had read Ernest Hemingway and found his first model for writing accurately about real life, including war. Kittredge was still keenly aware of the Korean War and how close he had come to experiencing it firsthand. He felt that Hemingway's work was of consequence, that it mattered. Kittredge had not yet identified what he had to say that might be of consequence, but he did recognize it in Hemingway.

In the end, he also recognized what Malamud had to say to him about writing. Malamud pushed him away from his limited understanding of ranch life and toward a more raw and honest look at the harsh realities behind it. Malamud talked about the differences between mere narratives and stories that were revelatory to readers, stories that gave them a new way to see the world.

Kittredge still did not accept the notion that a story could be about change in the reader more than about the characters and plot of the story, although that understanding is what would eventually drive his work. He was, however, with Hemingway and Malamud in his kit, on his way to the M.F.A. writing program at the University of Iowa. It was there that the roads of reading and writing, which had been parallel for him, merged into one. At Iowa he continued to write, but he also studied literature and came to a new understanding of mythology and of the role of cultural and personal mythologies in one's life. He also began to understand how to use his writing to reveal the mythologies of his own upbringing, to identify their failures, and to propose new mythologies that could be of consequence to the world.

At Iowa, the vision that would later be clear to him began to take shape. At the time, the late 1960s, the creative nonfiction genre was in flux, segueing from a more intellectual essay form about ideas to a revised form that drew heavily on the traditions of storytelling, relying on the personal voice and drawing from the personal experience of the narrator. This reinvented form offered him means to contemplate and comment on the stories and mythologies of Warner Valley and, in part, illuminated for him the possibility and necessity of writing about responsibilities inherent in the human experience, including responsibility for personal decisions and for caring about—and taking care of—the communities and land that sustain us.

Kittredge completed his studies at Iowa, and in the fall of 1969, thirty-seven years old, he accepted a position in the M.F.A. creative writing program at the University of Montana, Missoula, where he would teach for nearly thirty years. The Montana landscape felt like home to him, but he was also embraced by the writing community at the university, where he made lifelong friends who were also writers, among them Richard Hugo, Raymond Carver, and Madeline DeFrees.

In 1973–1974 he lived in Berkeley, California, on a prestigious one-year Stegner Fellowship at Stanford University, where he continued to develop his writing in an effort, he said in *Hole in the Sky*, to become someone of consequence. His subject matter was still mostly about Warner Valley and his childhood life on the ranch. The material was running thin and so was his energy for writing. At Stanford, he says in his memoir,

he did not accomplish much and lived on the mercy and graciousness of friends. When he returned to Missoula in 1974, his marriage to Patty, which was in disrepair before he left for Stanford, had ended.

Kittredge describes the subsequent several years in *Hole in the Sky*: "Our man, he was weeping, running the roads, on his own" (p. 223). He still had not discovered the mission that would inform the writing that was to come, as he describes in an essay in his 1999 collection *Taking Care*:

> I was as far adrift as ever. I'd gone back to writing with the intention of celebrating people and places I loved. But by 1976 that intention was running dry. I'd published a number of short stories, and felt like I'd said what I had to say. Nostalgic stories were already seeming repetitive and self-imitative (it was probably a mistaken way to think—artists often spend their careers working specific emotional terrain, witness Faulkner and Virginia Woolf, and my friends Dick Hugo and Ray Carver).

> But I wanted to claim new territory, and couldn't find any.

> (pp. 32–33)

He found that new territory during the summer of 1976 when he attended a conference on western movies in Sun Valley, Idaho. It was to be a lark, in the company of his brother Pat and two of his colleagues at Montana, Steven M. Krauzer and James Crumley. But at the conference Kittredge's long training and reading in philosophy and literature converged with the idea of the West as an intellectual topic. He found himself taking notes and thinking about politics and mythologies. In "Learning to Think," in *Taking Care*, he describes the experience of opening his mind to broader social contexts as leaving the ranch one more time. The life he had been describing and evoking in stories for ten years took on a new glow: those stories would eventually become the illustrations of the ideas he was beginning to formulate. With a new sense of purpose, he engaged the notion of being a citizen of the American West, and the responsibilities that came with that citizenship.

A MISSION AND A PURPOSE

At the time of the Sun Valley conference, Kittredge was already a successful author in the mind of the public, the publishers, and the critics. In addition to his teaching post at one of the most prestigious graduate writing programs in the country and his Stegner Fellowship at Stanford, Kittredge had published more than twenty-five short stories and some essays. In 1978 his first book, *The Van Gogh Field and Other Stories*, won the University of Missouri Breakthrough Fiction Contest and was published by the university's press. His writing was controlled and evocative, and engendered in his readers an understanding that a way of life in the American West was passing. He brought to life the buckaroos who knew that no one could control everything and who lived within the rhythms of the land. He also exposed the agri-ranchers he himself had worked with, for whom the land was mere commodity. It did not matter to them that the bird habitat at the ranch had been destroyed or that flocks of birds no longer rested there, or that the very soil itself came to be lost.

It was his own grandfather Kittredge who instigated the ecological destruction at Warner Ranch. Because it was God's work, he said, more was better. By the time he died, the ranch had swallowed up hundreds of acres of wilderness and altered it profoundly in order to convert it for profit. Kittredge did not blame his grandfather and others like him for their flawed values. He felt that they believed in what they did, that their intentions, though shallowly based, were good ones: to provide for their families and the country. They worked hard; they were good citizens; they prevailed over the raw land. They did not question either their values or their actions.

Kittredge's largesse in accepting the past did not prevent him from trying to improve the present and the future. To do this, he started by evaluating his own experience: he faced some frightening truths, including his participation in the decimation of the land that he, his father, and grandfather all loved, though in different ways. He was able to move forward by embracing responsibility not just for his past actions, but by

accepting responsibility for the present and for addressing the future. Through his own writing efforts, his study of literature and mythology, and the revelations at the conference, he created for himself a mission: to offer readers a way to recognize that they make choices based on values and mythologies that are often, perhaps usually, invisible to them; to learn to see, recognize, and articulate those philosophies; to assess them for validity; and to create new mythologies as a basis for change. This precise path gave Kittredge hope, enabling him to hold the past without living in it.

His mission was educational: to let people know that they acted on values, whether they were aware of them of not, and that values can be adjusted, thereby changing actions. The purpose was to improve the human relationship to land and animals, so that humans might once again live within the community of nature, to draw sustenance from it. Kittredge knew that his proposal, his willingness to say that the original purpose of the ranch had been destructive, that much ranching today is destructive, would challenge his relationships with many people who would be, at the least, hurt and insulted by his position. But the courageous six-year-old boy with polio, who asked why it is better to live than to not live, was still present in the forty-four year old man, and he proceeded to investigate and conjure and create a literature for change.

Kittredge returned to the western literature conference for several years, and along the way he and his colleague Steven M. Krauzer edited several anthologies: *Great Action Stories* (1977), *The Great American Detective* (1978), and *Stories into Film* (1979). He also taught literature of the West at Montana. Influenced by the idea of the American West and already an accomplished storyteller, Kittredge's writing took an unexpected turn: with Krauzer, he embarked on the pseudonymous writing of old-fashioned western novels, published from 1982 to 1986. They wrote under the pen name "Owen Rountree" about a protagonist named Cord. The formula novels in many ways portrayed the very lifestyle and values that Kittredge was now rethinking and rejecting. In *Taking Care*, he describes the process of writing

them as educational, a means to discovering and understanding the political implications of personal actions: "We cowrote nine formula Western novels, the Cord Series. All that work, for me, was a start toward rethinking my own purposes. It was the beginning of an education in political implications, one more way of leaving the ranch" (p. 33).

At the same time that Kittredge was writing the Cord novels with Krauzer, he was completing a second short-story collection, *We Are Not in This Together*, which was published in 1984. It included three stories from *The Van Gogh Field*. This reuse of his work, both stories and essays, would become a pattern for Kittredge, and he also used many reminiscences and memories in more than one or even two or three later works. For example, the story about his father encouraging him to go away to study writing is told in both *Hole in the Sky* and *Taking Care*, though with slightly different dialogue.

For Kittredge, the important thing is to know that life experiences overlap, that they run forward and back and, perhaps most important, that we revisit them as we ourselves move forward. In Kittredge's work, revision of the understanding of one's life is critical to change, and change is critical to moving forward in positive ways so that we do not merely relive our past or the past of our families. In *Taking Care* he notes that this book, like much of his writing, "is made of fragmentary explorations, told and retold in an attempt to get closer to what I mean to say (occasionally these were sorted into a books). This text is a continuation of that process, work reassembled and often rewritten" (p. 39).

The writing is a process, a reassembling, and the stories and essays are handed to readers not as a way to end a discussion, but as a way to start one. They are gifts that can be used for reassembling and re-understanding the reader's own life.

THE PERSONAL ESSAY

Between 1976 and 1986 Kittredge's writing life greatly expanded. In addition to the publication

of the short-story collection *We Are Not in This Together* and the Cord novels, he started writing the personal essays that came to exemplify his writing career.

Although Kittredge had published a couple of nonfiction pieces in 1972 and 1973, the genre had not engaged him. When the editor Terry Mc-Donnel asked him to write a personal essay for *Rocky Mountain Magazine*'s premier issue, he said he did not know how. McDonnel, he said in *Taking Care*, gave him a quick course in the process:

> "I'll tell you," Terry said, and he did, on the phone, in a few minutes. What he wanted was a series of scenes in what constituted an emotional progression, witnessed by a figure (the author) who is trying to fathom their meaning. Sort of like a detective story, he said, a learning and teaching story leading to a recognition and implication of the consequences, for both witness, maybe those involved in the acting out, and certainly the reader (this is my language).
>
> (p. 38)

Kittredge wrote the essay and found it both fun and invigorating to tell true stories about things that had actually happened. Many, perhaps most, of his short stories were based on real incidents, mostly at the ranch, but they were fictionalized to suit the intent of the story. In the personal essay, he could tell a story directly and could also directly spell out its significance.

Writing the facts of an incident is, of course, different from writing the story of an incident, including its mood and tones and import: the voice and trustworthiness of the writer become part of the story. As he was developing his own voice in the genre, Kittredge taught the personal essay in workshops in the Montana writing program. One of the goals he talked about was learning how to transcend the facts of a personal experience, thus making it useful to the reader.

For Kittredge, this meant parsing the story itself for mythologies, for its meaning to community and society. In *Taking Care*, he describes our everyday actions as stories that we live in, and he recognizes us as characters. Each of us is a character, as in a story, who is motivated by personal characteristics. Our stories are maps for

our lives, guiding us in decisions and actions. The stories we tell ourselves help us see who we are. When the stories fail us, we can invent new ones.

It is when we fail to see that the old story no longer works that we get in trouble, at all levels, from the personal to the public, from the neighborhood to the country. Kittredge believes this is what happened at Warner Ranch. Stories that outlived their usefulness were tightly adhered to even as they caused the crumbling of that small community and the land it held in trust. Stories, he says, are not meant to be rigid plans. They are meant to help us see ourselves and to reinvent ourselves.

In 1977, as he was grappling in his writing with the implications of his new understanding of the potential of the personal essay, another change happened in his life. As with his epiphany at the western conference, this personal change was not planned: he met the writer and film producer Annick Smith (b. 1932), with whom he embarked on a relationship that he calls a lifelong love affair. She taught him, he says in *Taking Care*, how to step out of his philosophizing self and to experience the world before him:

> The shallow lakes in North Warner were brimming with spring run-off, shimmering in the morning, edged with green and populated by rafts of white pelicans and snow geese, like a dream of what the world could be if we let it, alive and significant without us. With Annick I began trying to shut down my incessant self-preoccupied puzzling, and experience what is. I felt like the lost piece falling into a puzzle.
>
> (p. 36)

She noticed details that he did not—when touring his old home country together one time, she noticed small flowers that he had never noticed when he lived there—and she encouraged him to deepen his relationships with his now-adult children rather than to back away from them.

Smith and Kittredge were also partners in writing projects. When they met she was beginning to work, with Beth Ferris, on the script for the movie *Heartland*, based on the book *Letters of a Woman Homesteader* (1919), written by Elinore Pruitt Stewart about her homesteading

experiences in Wyoming. In 1979, with the movie in production and because of his ranching background and his writing credentials, Kittredge was invited to contribute to the script. His efforts failed at first, he said, but eventually he paid attention to the story itself, and scenes he wrote or reworked were included in the movie. He learned through that experience to reconsider his notion of perfection. When he was working on the seventh iteration of a particular scene, he was told that the second iteration would be filmed that day. Kittredge would again acquire film credentials in 1992, when he and Smith were two of the coproducers of Robert Redford's *A River Runs Through It*, based on the novella by Montana writer Norman Maclean.

In 1987 Kittredge published *Owning It All*, his first collection of personal essays. They are autobiographical and relentless in their effort to delineate the contradictions of his experiences on the ranch, of immersion in a wilderness that turned sour with its commercialization, of the roles of women and men, of the fate of the buckaroos and their way of life. The stories are framed in direct explications of their meaning, the values expressed in them, and their political and social context.

FICTION AND NONFICTION

Kittredge's first writing and his first publications were fiction. When he was in the air force in the 1950s, he wrote a novel that he later dismissed as frivolous. However, in 1965, he dug out the manuscript and revised it into the short story "Society of Eros," which appeared in the *Northwest Review*. He published short stories steadily after that into the 1990s, placing more than fifty stories in magazines, journals, and anthologies. His first two books, *The Van Gogh Field and Other Stories* (1978) and *We Are Not in This Together* (1984), are short-story collections that draw from the periodical publications, and *We Are Not in This Together* includes three stories from *The Van Gogh Field*, presaging Kittredge's later practice of reassembling his essays and their components into new pieces and collections. His next fiction book, the novel *The Willow Field*, a

western saga, would not be published until 2007. There are few short-story publications in the interim.

The failures of romance and sexuality, the quest for justice, and contemplation of mortality are frequent themes in Kittredge's short stories. Many of the stories clearly derive from Kittredge's experiences growing up in the near-wilderness of Warner Ranch: vividly detailed and often violent images permeate many of them. However, they are not essentially autobiographical and, for the most part, do not state the intentional message, as in his later nonfiction work. Instead, they demonstrate by example the dangers of living out myths that are no longer morally right or that are not generous to people, animals, or the land, and the dangers of not being aware of the myths that drive one's decisions.

After the crash course from Terry McDonnel in writing the personal essay, Kittredge began regularly writing essays, which came together in his first nonfiction collection, *Owning It All*. About half of the fourteen stand-alone pieces had been previously published in eight periodicals and, according to a note in the acknowledgements, had been "considerably revised," once again demonstrating Kittredge's belief and practice that our understanding and interpretation of life is not static, and that it does not merely move forward. The essays are autobiographical. They depict life on the ranch before overmanagement of water resources and before tractors, and life after, when the new capabilities for using the land overwhelmed its natural functioning.

Owning It All introduced Kittredge's writing to a larger audience than the short-story readers who already admired him and sought the company of his voice. His fourth book, *Hole in the Sky: A Memoir* (1992), increased that audience once again. Published by Knopf and then Random House, it received broader distribution and new attention from reviewers. The narrative runs from his childhood to the present. It is a confessional of his unaware past, and a reconciliation with it. In the process of telling his story, he contemplates the actions and values of his parents and grandparents all the while trying to not judge them.

They did what they knew how to do and they did it as well as they could. For them, the twenty-five-mile driveway between the road and the ranch was the only way in and the only way out. But Kittredge found another way out, through writing and through understanding experience in a context beyond the driveway, through consideration of myth and social and political context, which he explores in *Hole in the Sky*.

In 1996, sixty-four years old and one year from retirement from the University of Montana, Kittredge published *Who Owns the West?*, the second of his five essay collections. The essays build, as in previous works, on his life experiences, still including those at the ranch but reaching sometimes now into his recent past, relationships and experiences closer to the moment in which he is writing, and concerned, more than before, with how to approach the future. The book ends with an epilogue, "Doing Good Work Together: The Politics of Storytelling," where he parses the notion of stories in our lives, how they affect us, how we use them, and how we could use them. His hope is for change, not just in our actions but in understanding our actions and our motivations for them.

His next book, *Taking Care: Thoughts on Storytelling and Belief* (1999), also focuses on the notion of storytelling and brings forward an idea that has been with him through all of the books, though less in the foreground than the notion of change itself. Kittredge elaborates on the value of our approach to change: there is no point in anger, he says. Anger only looks backward and offers no guidance. Worse, anger is sentimental. The appropriate, the desired approach is one of taking care, of compassion, understanding, and generosity. He does not ask that we excuse past behavior, but that we understand it in context, as he did with the behavior of his grandfather at the ranch, and turn away from it in order to move forward. He makes these recommendations in the context of his own life, telling the stories of his gradual awakening to his own values, their conflict with his actions, and the grief that came with his emergent awareness.

The Next Rodeo: New and Selected Essays (2007) sacred forms a bridge between Kittredge's earlier essays and the ones to come. The new essay in the collection is the title essay, which is frankly didactic. It starts with an anecdote from the ranch days, summarizes the American West's history of exploitation of the land and of its original peoples, points out the contradictions of the past (ranchers who loved the land that they ruthlessly exploited) and their echo in the present (tourists who love the land that they swarm over). But he also recognizes that new traditions are being established by the many groups and associations that work to protect the land and its animals and birds.

Throughout the essay he asks questions that no one can answer, perhaps in hopes that by framing the question he will help instigate discussions and actions that will lead to eventual resolutions. He asks what we might want from the future, where we are going with our desires, how we will pursue our ends. He wonders if we can provide for, or share, or care for each other. The answers, he says, might lie in our ability to accept responsibility for working out the problems. This will require flexibility—a skill lacking at the Warner Valley MC Ranch—and cooperation within diverse demographics, rich and poor, high-minded and not.

In the closing words of the essay he does not return to the notions of myth that permeate so much of his writing. Instead, he offers a quiet encouragement that embodies recognition of the difficulty of the task he has set forth. He does not threaten disaster, nor does he promise a utopia. He recommends, and thus recognizes the need for, patience, endurance, and generosity. It is not a call to arms, he says in "The Next Rodeo," but to community:

> Citizens who base ethical judgments on rigid political, economic, or religious doctrines, however commonly accepted or deplored those emotions may be, are at least partly dysfunctional in democratic societies because they have essentially abandoned their responsibility to work out problems for themselves. We hope future liberals and conservatives aren't blinded by concepts and precepts and don't turn into just another set of rigid, dogmatic "true believers." The quandaries westerners face will have to be flexibly resolved by the raggedy and the rich, up-country and downtown. Love life;

maintain patience and strength of will while attempting generosity.

(p. 240)

Kittredge continues that call in *The Nature of Generosity* (2000). It is more memoir than essay collection, a sort of continuation of *Hole in the Sky*, certainly a continuation of Kittredge's ongoing effort to confront himself, to identify who he is and what he should be doing during his lifetime. But, unlike *Hole in the Sky*, it is not a chronological story of a given period of time. Rather it moves through four stated ideas: part 1, "The Old Animal"; part 2, "Agriculture"; part 3, "Commodification"; and part 4, "Generosity." The four parts are bracketed by an introduction, "The Imperishable World," and an epilogue, "Jitterbugging at Parties."

As with much of Kittredge's work, the four parts are essentially personal essays that arise from his specific life experiences. However, in this book the experiences take place not just in the American West or even just in America. He and his partner Annick Smith travel the world, where he seeks out and experiences and recognizes some of the universal habits and hopes of human beings. He acknowledges sorrows and tragedies, but he focuses on the human desire to "take care," a positive trait that he says is more powerful than any of the negative ones (an idea he first explored in his 1999 collection). It is taking care, he says, not war or meanness, that has brought us this far as a species, and to continue forward, we must re-embrace it. It brings us solace, brings us back to ourselves. In his very earliest considerations about what it means to be alive, he wondered what it would take to find or build paradise on earth. He does not speak of that here. The youthful desire for perfection has waned, has given way to the power and beauty of process and change. It could be called a new myth, one that can be lived by.

THE AMERICAN WEST

The American West is both a place and an idea, a literal geography and an abstract concept. William Kittredge was born into the place. His parents and grandparents and other people in his life generally did not think about the meanings of their lives or their actions, at least not beyond a simplified notion of what was good (God's work). If you worked hard, you would be rewarded. This fundamental notion was supported by the acquisition of land, money, and other material goods.

The conversation at the MC Warner Valley Ranch was about ranching, about cows and pastures and water flow. There was no discussion about how the Kittredge family came to be on the land, land that had previously been home to American Indian tribes, who lived within its rhythms. There was no consideration of the detrimental effects that agricultural practices could have on the land and its wild creatures. The balance sheet showed progress and profit. There was no problem.

The early literature of the American West was similarly blinkered and simplified, especially in western novels such as those by Zane Grey and Louis L'Amour: men were men; women were used and tolerated; American Indians were of no consequence; control was the ideal; ownership was all. But by the middle of the twentieth century, the myth of the early West was eroding. Writers such as Kittredge were beginning to speak another truth. The myth of the Lone Ranger, he explained to Stephen Hirst and Shawn Vestal in *Willow Springs*, was a lie: there was no one person in the West who could right the wrongs and fix the injustices:

> The mythology of the West is artificial. Those kinds of cowboy conflicts did exist, but those silly, truth-and-righteousness stories never, ever happened— there were no Lone Rangers riding around. Years ago someone pointed out that there were more gunshot killings in a trailer village on the outskirts of Missoula in the last ten years than Dodge City had in ten years of its gun-fighting heyday.

(p. 4)

That fantasy is based on the notion of individualism and conquest, says Kittredge. It was community, cooperation and generosity that allowed the survival of individuals and towns from the nineteenth century into the twentieth.

The new literature of the American West as written by Kittredge, Annie Proulx, James Welch,

Rick Bass, Gretel Ehrlich, Richard Hugo, Marilynne Robinson and others offers, first, a revised understanding of the history of the West that includes the vital and vibrant roles of American Indians and of women, and portrays the land as a sacred resource. Second, the new literature proposes another way for humans to be part of the land: environmentalism emerged and has thrived, although the outcome of its efforts is sometimes slow to take hold. Land and water are still held in contention and treated as commodities.

As Kittredge and other writers helped raise the American consciousness about the vulnerability and value of the American West, the question became—and still is—what to do. How can a population be convinced to give up its quest for commodities and enter into a quest for community, cooperation, and generosity? This question is at the crux of Kittredge's writing. Through his reading and his study of philosophy, literature, and mythology, he came to recognize that his own actions as a rancher, a life he lived into his mid-thirties, had arisen out of the unexamined mythology that was handed to him in his childhood. If he changed his mythology, changed his understanding of what he valued, the decisions he made could also change.

In much of his work, Kittredge describes this as a process of discovering and creating a coherent self. He examines his behavior, tries to identify the values behind it; he examines his desires—for community, trustworthiness, generosity, purpose—and chooses his actions in support of those values. His writing has offended some of his neighbors at Warner Valley and he is often asked how he responds to being criticized for his perceptions, for being called a traitor. The situation provides an example of how changing the myths we subscribe to can change our behavior: if the prevailing mythology is to be loyal to neighbors and to the old ways, then his speaking out would be traitorous; but if the appropriate mythology is to recognize and tell the truth about the consequences of agribusiness, then to be silent would be the traitorous act. Kittredge has shifted from the mythology of his youth to one of his own choosing and construction.

Kittredge's eloquence in portraying his American West and his proposal for change have been widely recognized in literary and academic communities. It is, in part, the style of his writing that encourages readers to take his side. It is "Meditative, eloquent prose from a modern master," says Bill Ott in *Booklist* (p. 34). His language has also been described as powerful, earthy, rich, and strong. The writing process he learned for nonfiction writing became the methodology for his personal essays. Writing in *Fourth Genre: Explorations in Nonfiction*, Daniel Minock summarizes the process: "He tells his story, and then he tells the story behind his story, and makes us think hard and well about both" (p. 259).

With the story and the story behind the story, Kittredge provides both an example of the point he wants to make and the reason for the point, as he does in the essay "Grizzly" in *Owning It All:*

> As the sky broke light over the peaks of Glacier, I found myself deeply moved by the view from our elevation, off west the lights of Montana, Hungry Horse, and Columbia Falls, and farmsteads along the northern edge of Flathead Lake, and back in the direction of sunrise the soft and misted valleys of the parklands, not an electric light showing: little enough to preserve the wanderings of a great and sacred animal who can teach us, if nothing else, by his power and his dilemma, a little common humility.
>
> (p. 137)

It is passages such as this, with their evocative language and direct comment, says Lisa Gerber in "Standing Humbly Before Nature," that make Kittredge's point: "Humility is the proper response to the power and dilemma of the grizzly" (p. 44).

For Kittredge, it is necessary that we Americans change our approach to the land and its animals. This world, he says, cannot be replicated. We have just this one chance. He is heartened by changes that have occurred, such as the environmental movement. He is not daunted by the flaws in these efforts—that is the nature of human endeavor. It is not an excuse, he says in *The Nature of Generosity*, to quit trying to reimagine the future, to replace myths of conquest with

myths of community: "We are not entirely programmed by drives coded into our genetic makeup and doomed to selfishness. We can turn our lives into gifts. Many have. We can live in accord with our desire to take care—if we want to" (p. 36).

OTHER WORK

When he was in his thirties, still working on the ranch where he grew up, William Kittredge began to question the value and meaning of his life and his actions. He realized he wanted to be a writer and he has accomplished that goal, with ten books published and scores of publications in magazines, journals and anthologies. He also yearned for a life of purpose. While his writing is the core of his influence on matters of the American West and on environmentalism, his work has not been limited to the written word. In addition to twenty-nine years of teaching and influencing emerging writers at the University of Montana and in public writing seminars and workshops, he has edited anthologies, written introductions to the books of others, spoken at conferences, been interviewed in print and on radio and television, interviewed other writers, and made video and sound recordings.

His first anthologies, edited with Steven M. Krauzer, coauthor of the Cord western novels, focused on popular literature. In 1980, again with Krauzer, he edited a special fiction edition of the literary periodical *Triquarterly*. In 1984 he and Annick Smith attended a history conference, "Montana Myths: Sacred Stories, Sacred Cows," in Helena. On the way home, they decided to do an anthology of writing about Montana. Consulting with Montanan James Welch and other writers, they gathered nearly 1,200 pages of work for *The Last Best Place: A Montana Anthology* (1988), which includes Native American stories, journals of exploration, memoirs, fiction and poetry.

In interviews, Kittredge is frequently asked how he feels about the state of environmental affairs in the West. He notes the profusion of environmental organizations and other efforts to protect the land and its animals. The citizens of Missoula, for example, voted to purchase the hillsides surrounding the city to protect them from further development. They are paying attention to their commons. At the same time, other residents of the state—especially, perhaps, in small towns—fear the loss of their own communities and their cultures to the environmental movement. The task, says Kittredge, is not to eliminate agriculture, but to make it work in synchrony with the protection of the land. It is possible, he believes, to do both. But for that to happen, both sides have to consider options.

Kittredge notes that there is still a perception that the West is primarily rural. However, based on 2006 census numbers, 80 percent of the region's sixty million people live in cities. The old myths persist, even as they become less relevant. There is a movement of sorts toward a new, a second colonization of the West, at least in Montana. The first colonization was the wave of European explorers and settlers who co-opted the land for themselves. The new wave is of urban residents who are moving into Montana, but not to run ranches, not to live in isolation, as Kittredge's family did. When asked what the land offers to them, Kittredge replies in an interview in *Ranch & Reata* magazine, "Same thing it's always offered: a promise that you can start over."

Kittredge is not particularly bothered by this new incursion. It is his hope that this time we'll get things right, that the land will be tended to, as with the Missoula hillside purchases.

Although throughout his teaching career he had mostly stayed close to home in Montana, Kittredge also ventured into the American Southwest, sometimes residing there. His 2002 book *Southwestern Homelands* contemplates what he found there, including contradictions and complexities similar to those in the northern Mountain West: poverty and privilege, agribusiness and craft fairs. Without predicting the future for the area, he portrays in words the richness and strength of the land and how those attributes are echoed in its people. He also meditates on the meaning of home and a homeland. Travel, he says, is not a mere diversion, but is a responsibility we have to ourselves for staying in touch with

the world. What we see and experience can jog us out of complacency and turn us toward new understandings and actions.

In 2010 he took abroad his quest to understand the universality of home and concepts of community and care. He and Smith traveled the globe with visits, sometimes extended, to Europe, Japan, and New York City. He found in all of them confirmation of his belief and hope for a better future: the human impetus toward care and generosity is alive all over the world. Often it exists within terrible realities of war, greed, and deprivation, but still it is present, especially at the level of family and community. It can be, he says, our salvation. Resolution will not come quickly or easily or wholly, he says in *The Nature of Generosity*: "Generosity is the endless project" (p. 276).

CONCLUSION

The elder William Kittredge, Bill's grandfather, started his modest cattle ranch in Warner Valley, Oregon, in 1937. When the ranch was sold in 1967, it comprised more than twenty-one thousand irrigated acres, plus more than fifty thousand acres extending into Nevada and California and close to one million acres of U.S. Bureau of Land Management grazing land. Kittredge is sometimes asked if he misses the ranch, if he would like to return to it. Although he has been back to visit on rare occasions, he reminded the Willow Springs interviewers what it is like to work on a ranch:

> There's a lot of romance connected to ranching. People forget. I remember the first thing I did when I got out of the Air Force and went back to the Warner Valley. We had to collect 6,200 mother cows for brucellosis testing. These big bang-headed mothers. And it was January. It was sleeting, the mud about five inches deep, the cow shit about three inches on top of it. After couple of weeks of that, the romance kind of goes out of it.
>
> (p. 9)

Although he and his brother worked side by side with the buckaroos when they were boys, and although he himself had managed much of the

ranch until he was in his thirties, and although he loved the land in its early state, rife with waterfowl and natural beauty, it had never been the right world for him, as writing has become. A buckaroo once said that he and his brother weren't of use for anything more than reading.

It was reading, also his mother's passion, that eventually led to writing and to the place that Bill Kittredge does belong. His writing is deemed to be trustworthy, a quality he sought to develop in himself. It is also eloquent. He is recognized as an accomplished storyteller. These and other qualities of the writing and of his expressive and generous personality have led not only to his many publications, but to awards and other acknowledgments for both his writing and for lifetime achievement. He retired in 1997 from the University of Montana as Regents Professor of English and Creative Writing. Other awards include National Endowment for the Arts, PEN West Award, Pacific Northwest Bookseller Award for Excellence, Montana Governor's Award for the Arts, and the Neil Simon Award–American Playhouse. In addition to his contributions to many literary journals, he has been published in national media including the *Atlantic*, *Harper's*, *Esquire*, *Time*, *Newsweek*, the *Washington Post*, and the *New York Times*. *The Best Short Stories of William Kittredge* was published in 2003. These and other honors are testimony to his standing as an iconic writer of the American West.

Selected Bibliography

WORKS OF WILLIAM KITTREDGE

NOVEL AND SHORT-STORY COLLECTIONS
The Van Gogh Field and Other Stories. Columbia: University of Missouri Press, 1978.

We Are Not in This Together. St. Paul, Minn.: Graywolf Press, 1984. (Short stories; foreword by Raymond Carver.)

Phantom Silver. Missoula, Mont.: Kutenai Press, 1987. (Short stories.)

The Willow Field. New York: Knopf, 2006. (Novel.)

The Best Short Stories of William Kittredge. St. Paul, Minn.: Graywolf Press, 2003.

THE "CORD" NOVEL SERIES

With Steven M. Krauzer under joint pseudonym Owen Rountree.

Cord. New York: Ballantine, 1982.

The Nevada War. New York: Ballantine, 1982.

The Black Hills Duel. New York: Ballantine, 1983.

Gunman Winter. New York: Ballantine, 1983.

Hunt the Man Down. New York: Ballantine, 1984.

King of Colorado. New York: Ballantine, 1984.

Gunsmoke River. New York: Ballantine, 1985.

Paradise Valley. New York: Ballantine, 1986.

Brimstone Basin. New York: Ballantine, 1986.

MEMOIR AND ESSAY COLLECTIONS

Owning It All. Saint Paul, Minn.: Graywolf Press, 1987. (Essays.)

Hole in the Sky: A Memoir. New York: Knopf, 1992.

Taking Care: Thoughts on Storytelling and Belief. Minneapolis, Minn.: Milkweed Editions, 1999. (Essays.)

The Nature of Generosity. New York: Knopf, 2000. (Memoir.)

Southwestern Homelands. Washington, D.C.: National Geographic, 2002. (Essays.)

The Next Rodeo: New and Selected Essays. Saint Paul, Minn.: Graywolf Press, 2007.

AS EDITOR

Great Action Stories. With Steven M. Krauzer. New American Library, 1977.

The Great American Detective. With Steven M. Krauzer. New York: New American Library, 1978. (Short stories; introduction by Kittredge.)

Stories into Film. With Steven M. Krauzer. New York: Harper and Row, 1979.

Montana Spaces: Essays and Photographs in Celebration of Montana. New York: Nick Lyons Books, 1988. (Introduction by Kittredge; photographs by John Smart.)

The Last Best Place: A Montana Anthology. With Annick Smith. Helena: Montana Historical Society Press, 1988.

The Portable Western Reader. New York: Penguin, 1997.

The Best of Montana's Short Fiction. With Allen Morris Jones. Guilford, Conn: Lyons Press, 2004.

PAPERS

William Kittredge Papers, 1954–2000 and undated. Southwest Collection/Special Collections Library, Texas Tech University, Lubbock.

CRITICAL AND BIOGRAPHICAL STUDIES

Cates, David Allen. "The Author of *Owning It All* and *Hole in the Sky* Shares His Thoughts on Writing and the American West." *Ranch & Reata*, December–January 2012. http://www.ranchandreata.com/in-the-magazine/decemberjanuary-2012/qa-william-kittredge/

Gerber, Lisa. "Standing Humbly Before Nature." *Ethics & the Environment* 7, no. 1:39–53 (spring 2002).

Hirst, Stephen, and Shawn Vestal. "A Conversation with William Kittredge." *Willow Springs*, September 30, 2006. http://willowsprings.ewu.edu/interviews/kittredge.pdf

McFarland, Ronald E. *William Kittredge.* Boise, Id.: Boise State University Western Writers Series 152, 2002.

Minock, Daniel. "*Taking Care: Thoughts on Storytelling and Belief,* and: *Writing the Sacred into the Real.*" *Fourth Genre: Explorations in Nonfiction* 3, no. 2:258–259 (fall 2001).

Ott, Bill. "*The Next Rodeo: New and Selected Essays.*" *Booklist* 104, nos. 9–10:34 (2008).

JAMES McBRIDE

(1957—)

Allen Guy Wilcox

JAMES MCBRIDE IS an American author and musician who has written fiction, memoir, and screenplays and whose novel *The Good Lord Bird* won the National Book Award in 2013. Born on September 4, 1957, he was raised in a large family in Brooklyn and Queens in New York City; his memoir of his upbringing, *The Color of Water* (1996), became a best seller. His work as a musician has been fruitful and ongoing since his boyhood. His main instrument is the tenor saxophone, and his main musical genre is jazz. After earning a bachelor of music degree from Oberlin College in 1979, he went on to work with artists including Anita Baker, Grover Washington, Jr., Jimmy Scott, and Rachelle Ferrell; for his work in musical theater he received the Stephen Sondheim Award in 1993. As a writer, he earned a master's degree in journalism from Columbia University in 1980 and worked for many years as a journalist, notably on the staffs of the *Washington Post, Boston Globe,* and *People*. Since 2006 he has been a distinguished writer in residence at the Arthur L. Carter Journalism Institute at New York University.

THE COLOR OF WATER

McBride's first book, *The Color of Water,* was much heralded by critics and much loved by readers at the time of its debut. Eventually it was included in the curricula of many American high schools and colleges. While the book calls itself a "tribute to his white mother," its form is readily identifiable as memoir, with a few important innovations.

The book is composed in alternating chapters, the first set written in the author's own voice, the other in the italicized voice of his mother, Ruth McBride Jordan, who was born in 1921 into an Orthodox Jewish family as Rachel Deborah Shilsky and raised in rural Virginia. Fleeing an abusive father, after high school she moved to Harlem, New York City, where in 1942 she married a black Baptist minister, Andrew McBride. They had eight children, James being the youngest. After Andrew's death, Ruth married Hunter Jordan, with whom she had four more children before his death in 1972.

While *The Color of Water* reads like a memoir, engaging and informative, it is built from the same cognitive music that makes up novels: there is a causal logic to the images he shares about his mother's life, which are bound up in the construction of the drama as a whole. McBride's opening salvo cuts to the quick:

> As a boy, I never knew where my mother was from—where she was born, who her parents were. When I asked she'd say, "God made me." When I asked if she was white, she'd say, "I'm light-skinned," and change the subject. She raised twelve black children and sent us all to college and in most cases graduate school. Her children became doctors, professors, chemists, teachers—yet none of us even knew her maiden name until we were grown. It took me fourteen years to unearth her remarkable story—the daughter of an Orthodox Jewish rabbi, she married a black man in 1942—and she revealed it more as a favor to me than out of any desire to revisit her past.
>
> (p. xvii)

A scene of life among the siblings in Brooklyn's Red Hook projects, before the family moved to St. Albans, Queens:

> All the boys slept in one room, girls slept in another, but the labels "boys' room" and "girls' room" meant nothing. We snuck into each other's rooms by night to trade secrets, argue, commiserate, spy, and continue chess games and monopoly games that had begun days earlier. Four of us played the same

clarinet, handing it off to one another in the hallway at school like halfbacks on a football field. Same with coats, hats, sneakers, clean socks, and gym uniforms. One washcloth was used by all. A solitary toothbrush would cover five sets of teeth and gums. We all swore it belonged to us personally. Our furniture consisted of two beautiful rocking chairs that Ma bought from Macy's because on television she saw her hero President John F. Kennedy use one to rock his kids, a living room couch, and an assortment of chairs, tables, dressers, and beds. The old black-and-white TV set worked—sometimes. It wasn't high on Mommy's list of things to fix. She called it "the boob tube" and rarely allowed us to watch it.

(p. 68)

McBride's composition is relatively irony-free, scrubbed clean of dark humor or satire. The narrative voice favors and honors received wisdom, such as Ruth's straightforward Protestant interpretation of Christian faith, as much as the fruits of the family's peculiar experience. The overarching sentiment of the book is one of human warmth—that is its primary charisma.

The details on display are razor sharp in their rendering and often harrowing in their emotional import, yet the fact that McBride's memoir has been rendered in two voices lends the book a dreamlike quality. One voice is always beckoning in from the past, an italicized message coming through the ages. This split-narrative technique comes to us primarily from the novel, though McBride makes it central to the telling of his own, and his mother's, life stories. *The Color of Water* gains in symbolic weight, in large part resulting from this split-apart, then rebraided narrative, a style familiar to readers of literary fiction, employed here in biographical "tribute."

McBride's mother's story employs a great variety of Yiddish and Hebrew terms, which are woven into a tapestry of lower-class English. This in turn features slang and linguistic tropes from Suffolk, Virginia, where McBride's mother lived as a girl. In a way, the richness and complexity of the linguistic background is an important clue to the mother's background, and testament to the difficult, complex early life she struggled through before she left her family and Judaism behind her, an act for which she was excommunicated from her nuclear family life.

In the chapter "Boys," McBride adopts his mother's voice to describe her reflections on her first boyfriend, Peter, a black youth in Suffolk, Virginia, who took walks with her in secret, on pain of death. Her picture of the American South of the 1930s is chilling:

He was the first man other than my grandfather who ever showed me any kindness in my life, and he did it at the risk of his own because they would've strung him up faster than you can blink if they'd have found out. Not just the Ku Klux Klan but the regular white folks in town would've killed him. Half of them were probably the Klan anyway, so it was all the same. You know death was always around Suffolk, always around. It was always so hot, and everyone was so polite, and everything was all surface but underneath it was like a bomb waiting to go off. I always felt that way about the South, that beneath the smiles and southern hospitality and politeness were a lot of guns and liquor and secrets. A lot of those secrets ended up floating down the Nansemond River just down the road from us. Folks would go down to the wharf and throw out nets for crabs and turtles and haul in human bodies. I remember one of our customers, Mrs. Mayfield, they found her son out there, he wasn't more than seventeen or so. He'd been killed and tied to a wagon wheel and tossed into the water until he drowned or the crabs ate him. You know a crab will eat anything. You have never seen me eat a crab to this day and you never will.

(p. 111)

In terms of style, the author conjures an atmosphere of exuberance, chaos, and zaniness in the household in which he was raised, mainly by using a technique of visual listing, combined with a range of similes appropriate to the scene at hand:

Over the years we assembled a stable of pets that resembled a veritable petting zoo: gerbils, mice, dogs, cats, rabbits, fish, birds, turtles, and frogs that would alternatively lick and bite us and spread mysterious diseases that zipped through our house as if it were a Third World country, prompting health clinic visits chaperoned by Ma where bored doctors slammed needles into our butts like we were on a GMC assembly line.

(pp. 68–69)

The "orchestrated chaos" of domestic life in McBride's youth had been arranged by his mother in order to stave off questions of race and identity, to which she would reply in clipped fashion:

The question of race was like the power of the moon in my house. It's what made the river flow, the ocean swell, and the tide rise, but it was a silent power, intractable, indomitable, indisputable, and thus completely ignorable. Mommy kept us at a frantic living pace that left no time for the problem. We thrived on thought, books, music, and art, which she fed to us instead of food.

(p. 94)

As the children progressed through school, McBride experienced a growing feeling that Jews were different from other whites, and that his mother, who could speak Yiddish and haggled with Hasidic store owners over the price of back-to-school clothing, had a deep, if still mysterious, relation with Jewish people.

She invariably chose predominantly Jewish public schools: P.S. 138 in Rosedale, J.H.S. 231 in Springfield Gardens.... Every morning we hit the door at six-thirty, fanning out across the city like soldiers.... We grew accustomed to being the only black, or "Negro," in school and were standout students, neat and well-mannered, despite the racist attitudes of many of our teachers, who were happy to knock our 95 test scores down to 85's and 80's over the most trivial mistakes.

(pp. 88–89)

The chapters that center on Ruth are told in a folksy style, employing the repetition of certain phrases, images, and themes to give the reader the sense of a person sitting in a rocking chair, recounting her life off the top of her head. About three-quarters of the way through the book, Ruth's interiority, which he glimpses in the chapters penned in her voice, converge with the seemingly impenetrable, frenetic, force-of-nature woman that the author knew her to be as he grew up. The portrait of the mother begins to fuse with the portrait of a young girl, coming of age in interesting times.

As part of his research for the memoir, in 1992 McBride traveled to Suffolk, Virginia, to complete a round of interviews with those who knew the Shilskys. After a day spent sitting on the steps of the Shilskys' old synagogue in the August heat, with no one to open the door to him, he retreats to his hotel room; in the middle of the night he is stirred from a dream, and leaves the hotel to walk the predawn wharf of the Nansemond River:

The loneliness and agony that [his grandmother] Hudis Shilsky felt as a Jew in this lonely southern town—far from her mother and sisters in New York, unable to speak English, a disabled Polish immigrant whose husband had no love for her and whose dreams of seeing her children grow up in America vanished as her life drained out of her at the age of forty-six—suddenly rose up in my blood and washed over me in waves.

(p. 229)

In this scene we find the sacred heart of McBride's memoir, the moment of human understanding he was searching for in setting out to write the book. As he stands on the wharf and considers the trajectory of his mother's life, the author is overcome with a moral revelation:

My own humanity was awakened, rising up to greet me with a handshake as I watched the first glimmers of sunlight peek over the horizon. There's such a big difference between being dead and alive, I told myself, and the greatest gift that anyone can give anyone else is life. And the greatest sin a person can do to another is to take away that life. Next to that, all the rules and religions in the world are secondary; mere words and beliefs that people choose to believe and kill and hate by. My life won't be lived that way, and neither, I hope, will my children's. I left for New York happy in the knowledge that my grandmother had not suffered and died for nothing.

(p. 229)

McBride's first book initiates a set of thematic motifs which remain consistent in his oeuvre, even as his genre changes from memoir to fiction. Among the most important of these thematic concerns are faith and literacy. For McBride, these are life-saving enterprises, the first of which is inscribed in the title of his memoir and elaborated in a dialogue between mother and son:

A deep sigh. "Oh boy ... God's not black. He's not white. He's a spirit."

"Does he like black or white people better?"

"He loves all people. He's a spirit."

"What's a spirit?"

"A spirit's a spirit."

"What color is God's spirit?"

"It doesn't have a color," she said. "God is the color of water. Water doesn't have a color."

(pp. 50–51)

MIRACLE AT ST. ANNA

McBride's first novel opens on a cold winter day in 1983, at the Thirty-Fourth Street post office in midtown Manhattan. Hector Negron, a dark-skinned Puerto Rican American just nearing retirement age, who has been working for the post office for thirty-odd years, looks up at a customer who asks him for a twenty-cent stamp. Negron, without explanation, pulls a handgun out of his pocket and shoots the man at point-blank range.

Who is this man? And why would Hector Negron kill him? The scene is as startling as it is improbable, and as readers we are thrown into a maelstrom of confusion. Appearing on the scene, a late-arriving rookie journalist, Tim Boyle, misses most of the dramatic action but manages to charm his way uptown, riding in a squad car with the police investigation unit that is heading toward Negron's apartment in Harlem.

What they discover in Negron's apartment is the first clue in unlocking this violent puzzle. Amid the items in Hector's "ramshackle" apartment on 145th Street, the officers discover what appears to be the marble head of an old statue. Upon further investigation it turns out that it is the missing head of the *Primavera* from the Santa Trinità, a bridge in Florence, Italy, destroyed by the Germans in World War II.

The scene then shifts to Tuscany, Italy, during World War II, where Sam Train, an American soldier in the 92nd Infantry Division, is fighting in mountainous territory. Train had salvaged the marble head his first day in Florence, and carries it strapped to his belt in a net bag. It is his good luck charm. With it, Train experiences a kind of quickening experience, a connectedness and invulnerability, which will be shared by different McBride characters in later novels, notably, by Liz Spocott in *Song Yet Sung*. Here is a look at Train, in the middle of battle, as he experiences what he believes to be invisibility:

It came on him again. True and real. Invisibility. He could've walked over there with an ice cream cone like it was Sunday morning after church. Nothing would touch him. He could see better, hear better, smell better. There was no noise, no pain, no fear. He felt the rush of fresh Tuscan morning air on his face, heard every bush, every tree, every rock, which seemed to speak to him, shake his hand, saying, Hello, Sam Train. Good morning, Sam Train. We love you, Sam Train. What can we do to help you out today, Mr. Sam Train?

This, he thought as he leaped over rocks and gullies, is what it must feel like to be white.

(pp. 27–28)

As in his subsequent novels, McBride's first major fiction features a varied cast of black Americans, thrown into a context beyond their control. In this case, the context is wartime Italy. We meet Train and the troops of the 92nd Division during the Cinquale Canal attack, which ends up being a disastrous loss. Joining Train is Bishop Cummings, a coal-black minister from Kansas, who fights alongside him. Cummings is a wry character who repeatedly insists that Train owes him "fourteen hundred dollars!" from card playing, and who sneeringly prompts Train to embark on what amounts to a suicide mission across the river to rescue a young Italian boy they see hiding in a barn. To do this, Train must cross the canal and run behind the German line of defense. Once Train recovers the boy, an episode that highlights their racial differences, Train is forced to retreat higher into the mountains to avoid the Germans. When Cummings, the white second lieutenant Aubrey Stamps, and the third remaining member of Train's squad, Hector Negron, notice Train receding into the distance with the boy over his shoulder, they break after him, splintering off from the rest of their company.

The 92nd Infantry Division is overwhelmingly made up of African American troops known as "Buffalo Soldiers," a name preserved from the Plains Wars of the nineteenth century, when Native Americans "saw the first black cavalry as having hair akin to that of their beloved buffalo" (p. 37). In McBride's novel, as in life, they are forced to confront their social, class, and racial boundaries while being summoned to acts of valor, chain-of-command discipline, and spur-of-

the-moment decision-making on the front lines of the greatest war American troops had yet faced abroad. All of the men's qualities and defects are on display in this milieu, and as they fight through the craggy mountains and rivers of Tuscany, which McBride depicts as haunted territory, we find the shortcomings of the systems in which these characters operate—in particular, the U.S. military—also on display. Experienced black soldiers bridle at the orders of incompetent, fickle white commanders, and face the kind of verbal brutality typical of racist minds. The context is a perfect testing ground for character and mettle, and McBride thrusts his characters into danger straight away.

Part of the dynamic between whites and blacks emerges from the interiority of the character Colonel Jack Driscoll. We are introduced to Driscoll in a moment of quiet consternation, as he considers his company's next steps in the wake of the disastrous battle that separates Train, Cummings, Stamps, and Negron from the rest of G Company:

> There was a time when ten Negroes staring at him would have made him nervous, but that was long ago. Driscoll smoked, ignoring them. He didn't hate them like a lot of white commanders did. He didn't even dislike them. He hated their trust in him. He turned his head back to the report, smoking silently and looking at the photo one more time…. He had to pass this on to the old man, General Allman, commander of the 92nd Division. Allman had been under a lot of pressure lately, and even though he was a tough old geezer, Driscoll was worried about him. A graduate of Virginia Military Institute, … Allman didn't think coloreds were qualified to command, and he said it. He didn't think many of the whites assigned to the division were up to the task either, and he said that too. The coloreds hated him….
>
> (p. 39)

But what of the statue head that Train carried along with him? The statue that, almost forty years later, will be found in Negron's apartment after he shoots a customer in the Thirty-Fourth Street post office at point-blank range? McBride informs us that the stone was quarried in Italy in the year 1590, in a disastrous cliffside episode that saw a marble worker, Filippo Guanio, lose an arm due to a falling boulder. The hurtling rock

ripped the arm off at the shoulder; it fell many feet and was never recovered.

The marble was then carted away by twelve mules and shipped to France, where the impecunious sculptor, Pierre Tranqueville, had been "commissioned by a duchess de' Medici, wife of the Duke of Florence, to carve one of the four statues that would sit atop each corner of the Ponte Santa Trinità, the most beautiful bridge in Florence, whose looping curved arches conform to no line or figure in geometry and are believed to have been drawn free hand by a linear genius, rumored to be Michelangelo. The duchess," McBride adds, "wanted each statue to represent a season. She assigned the 'summer,' 'winter,' and 'fall' statues to Italian sculptors. Tranqueville, who was commissioned to do spring—*primavera* in Italian—was the only Frenchman" (p. 53).

Though the four years that Tranqueville worked on the sculpture were years of immense hardship, financial difficulty, personal turmoil, and family calamity, he eventually finished the *Primavera* sculpture and sent it back to the duchess, where it became, as McBride assures us, "the toast of Florence." Nevertheless, Tranqueville perished before receiving remuneration for his work. Despite the glory of the statue itself, an air of calamity surrounds it, as when Hitler bombed the Santa Trinità in 1944, and the calamity persists through the opening of the novel, when it is found in the Harlem apartment of Hector Negron.

Once Train's three compatriots, Bishop, Stamps, and Negron, catch up to him and the ailing Italian child—who had been kept alive because for a few days an old man had set a thin soup out for him—the main action of the novel begins. Negron, the only member of the group trained as a medic, is asked to look over the boy, and we are given insight into Negron's response to the situation:

> He felt like he wanted to throw up, he was so scared. He was a draftee, a Puerto Rican. He had no part in this war. He was stuck between colored and white in the division. His cousin Felix had been drafted the same day as he had and had been sent with the all-white 65th Division to France. Felix had written him and told him he was frigging all

the French girls he could find. And here he was stuck with these guys, following Diesel the dope [a nickname for Train], because he looked more colored than Felix. It had been bad luck from the first day.

(p. 62)

Stamps is confounded by Train's refusal to move. Train's obsession with the statue head is beginning to bring forth a sort of sickness in him. He is possessed by it and it is weakening his resolve. Stamps gathers his thoughts, riffing on the roles of different black Americans:

The Negro draftees from the South like Train were a puzzle to Stamps. He could not understand their lack of pride, their standing low, accepting the punishment that whites doled out, never trying to take the extra step. Yet in battle they were often tenacious fighters, smart, fierce soldiers who reacted to stress with calm and deliberateness. Why didn't they save a little of that fight for the white man back home? Instead, they walked around like idiots, superstitious of every damn thing, carrying cats' bones and Bibles and wearing little black bags filled with potions around their necks, with names like Jeepers and Pig and Bobo, kowtowing to the white man at every step. He didn't understand it and he didn't want to. To him, they were everything he did not want to be: dumb niggers, spooks, moolies.

(pp. 67–68)

A personal breakthrough comes for Train when the young Italian boy, curious about his large size and dark skin, touches his face and hair:

The boy raised himself on his elbows and gently ran a hand across Train's face, then through the rough texture of Train's wooly hair.... A white person had never touched his face before. Never reached out and stroked him with love, and the force of it, the force of the child's innocence, trust, and purity drew tears to his eyes. He expected to feel nothing when the boy touched him, but instead he felt mercy, he felt humanity, he felt love, harmony, longing, thirst for kindness, yearnings for peace—qualities he'd never known existed in the white man.

(pp. 73–74)

The four soldiers' first true encounter with Italian people occurs on a rainy night in the small hill town of Bornacchi, with a prominent if predictably eerie church, St. Anna, at its center. We encounter a widower, Ludovico, hiding twenty-odd rabbits beneath the floorboards, for fear the Germans will take them. With him is his daughter Renata, a classic beauty, who has taken to wearing a soldier's costume as mourning for her husband, missing in action. Also joining the cast is a witch-healer, as she is known in the village, the blunt, enchanting, and distinguished Ettora, who had been Ludovico's lover when they were teenagers. Once in town, the soldiers deposit the sick and wounded Italian boy with Ludovico and his guests, and make for an abandoned house in the village where they can sleep and recharge their dead radio. Train, who is increasingly detached from conventional reality and believes the boy to be one of God's angels, stays with Ludovico and the Italians, wishing to remain near the boy, whose name, we eventually learn, is Angelo Tornacelli.

In Bornacchi the four errant Buffalo Soldiers encounter the legendary partisan fighter and poet Peppi Grotta, known as the Black Butterfly. Wise for his twenty-six years, and deeply committed to strategic victory against the Germans, the Black Butterfly and his closest band of partisans live in hiding, near starvation, in the hills and mountains near Bornacchi. One of these partisans is a close childhood friend of Peppi's named Rodolfo. Early in the action Rodolfo, dressed as a priest, had met Captain Driscoll and told him of the German regiments assembling in the mountains. Rodolfo and Bishop Cummings both represent false priests in the novel: one loses his faith, the other has to find it. War divides friendships as well as nations, and ultimately Rodolfo betrays both Peppi and his faith in fighting for the true Italy.

Suspense and foreboding build across the novel, especially in regard to Hector Negron. We know he has committed murder at the beginning of the novel, yet during most of the narrative, he is the most affable, interesting, and indeed, centered, fellow in the group. Properly skeptical of foolish actions and absurd situations, he is also the only Italian speaker in the group, and the only one trained as a medic. These are crucial qualities, and Hector is an indispensable member of the foursome. As readers, we await whatever calamity must be in store for him to turn him into a disgruntled postal employee who carries a

handgun to work. While the men are arguing about how to leave Bornacchi, we have another glimpse of Hector's inner life:

> A wave of shame suddenly made Hector blanch. He was glad he didn't love anybody. It was easier, safer, not to love somebody, not to have children and raise kids in this crummy world where a Puerto Rican wants to kill an innocent woman for nothing more than trying to help him. He was sick in his heart, sick of translating, sick of her, sick of all of them. He wanted to get out of the middle of it and go home.
>
> (p. 156)

This reflection, along with many anecdotes featured in the text, evokes the brutalizing effect of war on all parties involved: soldiers, partisans, and the innocent. Despite the strongly delivered portrait of black soldiers in the U.S. military confronted with white leadership, fighting in what Bishop Cummings often refers to as "a white man's war," the truest message of the book is its most universal: war might bring one's best individual qualities to the forefront, but its total effect is deeply dehumanizing and brutal.

While McBride's novel depicts the horrors of war and disgusting realities of racism, it also initiates the author's ongoing fascination with dreams, surreality, and fantasy. It is a novel filled with miraculously regenerating rabbits under floorboards, witches that heal the sick, and a soldier who believes a statue head can make him invisible. Perhaps this is testament to the fact that conditions of war can produce conditions of insanity. As the boy Angelo's condition improves and he begins to show loving affection for all of the soldiers, the brutalization and insanity begin to melt away. Cummings, the preacher who never believed in God, the hustler who only cared for money and women, now cares for the child, and questions the very doubt which had been his bedrock and source of self-reliance:

> After months of savage fighting, with the white man at their backs whipping them and the white man at their fronts shooting at them, the boy restored their humanity, and for that they loved him. He was their hero. They called him Santa Claus, in honor of the Christmas that was coming in four days, and they fought over what kinds of gifts to get him.
>
> (p. 185)

Though for most of the novel Angelo is convinced that Sam Train is what he calls a "Chocolate Giant"—a feeling reinforced by delirious dreaming and the words of his imaginary friend, Arturo—the human connection between Train and the boy is real, and it affects those around them. They develop a shared language, tapping out messages to each other on their arms. Train is generally considered dimwitted and gullible, but he is better described as shy, with a strong undercurrent of charisma. He is a wonderful singer and possesses immense physical strength and size. He believes the boy is more than an angel of God: he is a miracle, meant to bring him luck and to share with him human affection Train had never before experienced with white folk. He considers adopting the boy and raising him in his hometown of Mt. Gilead, North Carolina.

The curmudgeonly, greedy, truculent, seductive Bishop Cummings cooks up the rabbits "Kansas City–style" for the starving populace of Bornacchi. One miracle at St. Anna, then, is the human connection forged between white Italians and the black Buffalo Soldiers in the days leading up to Christmas 1944. When they had every reason to snap under indignity and starvation, the thirty-odd townspeople of Bornacchi came together and cooked what food they had, shared what wine they had, bartered with the four men of G Company who had become separated from their division, played guitar, sang, and danced, at least for one day.

This reprieve from torment does not last. The partisans capture a German soldier, a youth who we learn had encouraged Angelo to run away, thus saving his life. The American soldiers and the Italian partisans, both wary of one another, agree to keep the German soldier alive. When Hector and Rodolfo march off with the soldier, Rodolfo pulls a knife out, and, attempting to kill Hector, wounds him and kills the soldier. Before learning this, Peppi considers his old friend, Rodolfo, and how war had changed him for the worse: "Rodolfo had killed the two Germans in Ruosina and enjoyed it, stabbing one in the chest and watching him gurgle in his own blood and choke helplessly till Peppi had shot him to put

him out of his misery. Rodolfo had enjoyed the killing" (p. 244).

Once the German soldier is killed and Peppi and Rodolfo part ways, Angelo, who has long been delirious, dreaming, and delusional, remembers what happened to him and his parents and wails in a paroxysm of grief and torment.

Angelo's story is bound up with a real-life event during the war, when the Nazi SS perpetrated a massacre at a different St. Anna, the small Tuscan village of St. Anna di Stazzema. Here the Nazis killed 560 men, women, and children, committing rape and abuse and finally exterminating the livestock and setting fire to the village. This event took place on August 12, 1944. One hundred and thirty of the victims were children. In the novel, Angelo narrowly escapes but loses his parents in the massacre. And it is Rodolfo, the false priest, who had given them up to the Germans. When Angelo finally snaps back into reality, he gives an account of that fateful day:

> They marched his mother and his grandfather to the square. There was a big fire there. People were burning. A little baby was burning in the fire with his arms out like this—he demonstrated—and had a long stick stuck through him. Some Germans were eating lunch and listening to accordion music as the fire burned. A soldier—that one, he said, pointing to the dead German who lay in Ludovico's bedroom—he took my mother and several others to the side of the church. He told us to turn around. He fired his gun in the air and said, "Run! Run as fast as you can." My mother ran, but I was afraid to run because of the fire. My mother came back to get me. A second German came around the side of the church and saw the people running. He shot my mother. The other German, that one—he pointed to the dead German again—he shot the German who shot my mother. Then he picked me up and ran into the mountains. Then he was gone and there was the old man. That is all I remember.
>
> (p. 256)

A chaotic situation occurs when the 92nd Division sends men to recover the four soldiers from G Company. Yet old Ludovico, seeing this awful confusion, remembers the prophecy of the nearby Mountain of the Sleeping Man (where the German Army was bunkered down), and in so doing, he witnesses the true miracle at St. Anna. When the white-skinned Captain Nokes sends Lieutenant Birdsong in to separate the colossal Train from Angelo, Train lifts Birdsong in the air by his neck.

> Ludovico knew then that he'd seen a miracle, that Ettora's spell had worked, that the Mountain of the Sleeping Man had awakened to wreak vengeance and to claim his true love, except his true love wasn't a fair damsel after all; it was this child of innocence, a child who had survived a massacre, a miracle boy who represented everything that every Italian held dear, the power to love, unconditionally, forever, to forgive, to live after the worst of atrocities, and, most of all, the power to believe in God's miracles.
>
> (p. 276)

After this violent episode, the German artillery shelling reaches Bornacchi. The rescue team flees, and the four soldiers are left without having been recovered. Nokes's jeep, fleeing the scene, erupts into flames as a German eighty-eight shell strikes it dead on. Ettora, the good witch, dies from a shrapnel wound to the stomach. Ludovico is with her, and Hector recovers him.

In a final, horrific firefight, Train, Stamps, and Bishop Cummings are killed. McBride conveys the bishop's final moment of conversion and understanding as solace to the dying soul, but the effect is altogether unsettling, and without apparent rhyme or reason. What's worse is that the boy Angelo too falls victim to the violence, and we are privy to his dying thoughts: he knows that the massacre at St. Anna will become "a dry fig in the wind tunnel of history, the place forgotten, a museum perhaps, the 560 victims never truly revealed to the world, lost even to the Italians who would take up residence in the village just months after the war.... It would be gone, they would all be gone, and he was glad" (pp. 291–292).

Of course, Rodolfo is the man in the post office Hector kills years later. And after Hector is released on bail money supplied by an Italian who saw the news story in the papers, McBride ends Hector's story on a beach in South Africa where he encounters ... by some miracle ... a grown Angelo Tornacelli.

A lesson of McBride's novel is that there are moral actors of every race, age, and milieu, and

the opposite is true as well. Certain systems, like the military, may work to institutionalize immorality; as much as they may bring out the best in people, they may also bring out the worst. The antidote to this quandary is faith, which can reveal personal dishonesty and provide a roadmap to righteous living. With McBride's first novel he ventures into a career that makes him not merely a soulful novelist, but a deeply religious one too.

Miracle at St. Anna was made into a film of the same name by the American director Spike Lee, whom McBride had referenced glowingly in his memoir. McBride himself was responsible for the book's adaptation into screenplay. The film was released in 2008.

SONG YET SUNG

McBride's second novel, *Song Yet Sung* (2008), takes placed in 1850s coastal Maryland. It is the most visceral, heart-rending, and phantasmagoric of the author's novels. The magic of this littoral landscape—swampy, mystical, and practically impenetrable—provides an opportunity for the novel's plot to move from slave-escape story, which is its primary plot concern, into the realm of allegory, where it makes bold statements about race and class in the United States. The narrative focus centers on Liz Spocott, a beautiful, twice-wounded, escaped slave on the run and in hiding in the woods and swamps of the Chesapeake Bay.

Liz is described variously as a conjurer, a witch, and a shape-shifter, though her most common designation in the novel is the Dreamer. We learn that her visions of the future arise in part from her head wounds, caused both by slave owners and by those charged with apprehending her. The reader is given to understand that special vision comes through special hardship. In this case: Liz's ability to see the future is a consequence of her inhumane treatment. But the visions offer a mixed blessing, and it takes the whole of the novel to clarify the importance and meaning of the dreams, of the "song yet sung." In the book's opening lines we are given Liz's first vision:

She dreamed of Negroes driving horseless carriages on shiny rubber wheels with music booming throughout, and fat black children who smoked odd-smelling cigars and walked around with pistols in their pockets and murder in their eyes. She dreamed of Negro women appearing as flickering images in powerfully lighted boxes that could be seen in sitting rooms far distant, and colored men dressed in garish costumes like children, playing odd sporting games and bragging like drunkards—every bit of pride, decency and morality squeezed clean out of them.

(p. 1)

Part of the marvel of the book is its explanation of how the Underground Railroad, led by Harriet Tubman ("Moses") and referred to as the "gospel train," actually functioned, and the code language that was employed to keep information and movements secreted from the white power structure. The "code," as described in the novel and explained to Liz by the Woman with No Name in the attic of Patty Cannon's house, is based in a series of five signs. Insofar as these five signs are emblematic, they represent "north, south, east, west, and free."

Patty Cannon is a historical figure who has been fictionalized by McBride and transported some forty years into the future from the time in which she actually lived. She was notorious, as McBride alludes to in his novel, for kidnapping slaves and selling them south to slave traders for a profit. She is a veritable black widow in McBride's novel, dangerously attractive and seductive but merciless and without religion or remorse. She represents the worst of white culture and capitalism. Here is a fleeting glimpse of Patty's thinking, painted with McBride's typical free, indirect discourse.

Long experience running slaves taught Patty Cannon the true secret of success. Know your prey from within. She actually liked the colored. She trusted them more than she did the white man. They were predictable. They gravitated towards kindness. She could tell when they thought or did wrong, could read it in their faces. They were like dogs, loyal, easy to train, unless of course they learned to read, which made them useless.

(pp. 23–24)

While few black characters learn to read standard English in the pages of *Song Yet Sung*, there is a thriving language among slaves, one which is as exclusive and guarded as it is complicated and versatile. This is the code. Any apparatus of daily life, be it a rope with five knots, a quilt with five stars, or series of rings caused by a blacksmith's hammer, helps communicate to the network of black folk how to stay safe and steer clear from trouble. In McBride's fictional representation of this world, any level of detail can be expressed through the different arrangement of five signs. In his afterward to the book, the author references a text that was illuminating to him in this regard, *Hidden in Plain View*, by Jacqueline L. Tobin and Raymond G. Dobard. An example of the code in action, as McBride represents it:

> Five knots, wrapped with a collar at the bottom looped towards the setting sun. That meant go. If wrapped the other way, against the setting sun, it meant the coast wasn't clear and to hold tight. Left leg trousers rolled up. Everything to the left, left, left, and in fives. And not to kill, for to do so was to raise your hand against God and to become a sheep of the Devil.
>
> (p. 56)

Liz Spocott herself crosses this line early in the book, killing Patty Cannon's loyal head slave, Little George, a handsome, muscular, violent Negro who perpetuates Patty's system of control by the rape and abuse of fellow slaves. In this way, Liz's person is doomed from the book's beginning, but her actions throughout the course of the novel lead toward the fulfillment of the book's title, the prophecy that a dream of the future will produce a dreamer. The strong echo of the book is that the young black boy who is saved by Liz after her escape, and who moves north with Liz's star-crossed love, Amber, into Philadelphia, will begin a line that culminates in the Reverend Dr. Martin Luther King, Jr.

In the novel, the music of Maryland speech and storytelling is wrought into a style that must be termed Chesapeake Gothic. The natural world comes alive in Liz's consciousness, in part as a reaction to the brutality (the head wounds) she received, first as a child and again as a nineteen-year-old. She developed headaches that brought about hallucinations, visions. One such dream gets at the heart of the book's message:

> *I dreamed of thousands of Negroes,* she said, *and thousands of white people with them, folks stretching as far as the eye could see. They were at a great camp meeting, and one after another various preachers spoke out. Finally the best of them rose up to speak. He was a colored preacher. He was dressed in the oddest suit of clothing you can imagine; I reckon it's the finery of his time. He stood before these thousands of people and spoke to a magic thing that carried his voice for miles. And Lord, he preached. As Jesus is at His resting place, that man preached. He opened up the heavens. On and on he went, in the most proper voice, using the most proper words. He used words so powerful, so righteous, I can't describe them—words that seemed to lift him into the air above the others, words that came from God Himself.… A song not yet sung.*
>
> (p. 280)

McBride is working on a broad moral canvas here, with images that span two centuries of black experience in the United States. The dream of future conditions in America is the center of this adventurous story, and the disruption that this dreaming brings to the status quo of slavery in eastern Maryland, precipitating the escape of fourteen slaves from Patty Cannon's property, is summarized in the book's title, *Song Yet Sung*. In his author's note to the hardcover edition, McBride discusses how the life of the legendary Maryland-born abolitionist Harriet Tubman inspired him to write the novel:

> In a society that loves to mythologize its heroes and make them larger than life, her life is treated as a sort of Aesop's fable. With the exception of a couple of excellent biographies, Mrs. Tubman's story is a children's tale, a moral, polite, good-girl story taught to elementary school kids, when in fact the depth, meaning, and purpose of her extraordinary journey were anything but fable. Rather, her life was an adventure that should ring up any writer's imagination.… I got in my car and went to work. This book is the result.
>
> (p. 356)

Unlike McBride's subsequent novel, *The Good Lord Bird*, which addresses the legend of the white abolitionist John Brown, *Song Yet Sung* deals directly with the legends, tall tales, supersti-

tions, and stories of magic related to slaver and escape in the Chesapeake area.

We meet Amber later in the novel, and his character speaks to the aspirations of a young man for, on the one hand, personal love, a family, and self-respect; and on the other, confrontation with the existential crisis posed by slavery and the desire to escape by any means necessary—taking the Underground Railroad to freedom—even if it means relinquishing every relationship he has ever known.

For several years, Amber, a slave belonging to the Boyd family, has wished to get on the gospel train and head north from Maryland's eastern coast toward Philadelphia. However, those who know him understand he is of marrying age, and he is encouraged to woo and wed. Only when circumstances compel him to try to hold together his tenuous life is Amber actually forced to decide one way or another. Whereas Liz Spocott's role in the novel appears to be to reflect the concerns and future prospects of an entire populace enslaved, Amber's psychological bent represents the individual drama: one person against a sea of troubles:

> He'd seen it happen too often. A Negro man meets a woman. He falls in love, follows nature's course, starts a family, then the moment his master needs money, he bears the crushing hurt of watching his wife whipped, his children sold, his family separated, all for the price of a horse or the cost of putting on a new roof.
>
> (p. 125)

The character known as the Woolman is crucial not only to the unfolding plot but to the mosaic of character types McBride wishes to represent in the novel, and ultimately in American society. The Woolman has no given name. He represents an extreme of the Negro experience during the period of historical slavery in America; he is an archetypal figure of fierce strength and independence, representing a total rejection of society in his age. With wild, tangled hair, and an odor of the swamps and woods in which he lives, the Woolman is often referred to by other characters as a devil.

Indeed, the Woolman takes on legendary status at the beginning of the novel, due in large part to his intransigence but also to the fact that very few people in the area can actually confirm his existence. He is an outlier, and a source of fear for both blacks and whites in the novel. He lives in a hut, on a far outcropping of land, deeply removed from slave society and thus fully estranged from white society. Abandoned to the wild as a young boy, he is emblematic of all that is pure and wild. Not only is he an immense, perhaps unparalleled physical specimen, he also represents natural consciousness and physical connectedness to nature. He is also the father of a child, a boy as wild as he, and his devotion to his child's cause is complete and unimpeded by a concern for self.

The Woolman's philosophy, insofar as it might be articulated, is present in the following passage:

> Standing frozen was more than second nature to him. It was a way of life. He always trusted the notion of patience. It was how he believed the world worked. Everything, he was sure, had already been decided, so moving against it was like moving against the tide of the Chesapeake, or against the dark swirling waters of the Sinking Creek, which surrendered its treasures to him regularly and naturally. Be silent. Wait. Waiting was how he had saved himself when he first found himself alone in the wild nineteen years ago.
>
> (p. 116)

The "song" in the title *Song Yet Sung* is a reference to Martin Luther King, Jr.'s famous "I Have a Dream" speech, given during the 1963 civil rights march on Washington, D.C. The Woolman's son, referred to only as "boy," moves to Philadelphia with Amber as his adoptive father at the end of the novel, after the death of Woolman himself. The boy is understood by Liz as continuing the line that will include Dr. King. While this is depicted in the novel as a hereditary lineage, part of the power of Liz's dream is in demonstrating the Woolman's death as an allegorical striving for a freedom that all black Americans may enjoy. That is to say, Liz's vision is part of a shared continuum, linked directly to the civil rights movement, which gained international prominence one hundred years after the events of the novel.

THE GOOD LORD BIRD

The prologue of McBride's third novel, *The Good Lord Bird* (2013), places the book in a tradition of novels, none perhaps surpassing Cervantes' masterpiece, *Don Quixote*, which take as their premise the recovery of lost papers. While it is a trope to which the author never truly returns after the initial pages, the motif of the author as mere "editor" presenting a story, which he in turn discovered from a previous source, works to give the story a sense of deep groundedness and authenticity. Simultaneously, it gives the tale the feeling of a fable, with the moral implications that fables can produce. It is like reading the words "Once upon a time." The prologue to the book opens with the following newspaper account:

Rare Negro Papers Found

by A. J. Watson

Wilmington, Del. (AP) June 14, 1966—*A fire that destroyed the city's oldest Negro church has led to the discovery of a wild slave narrative that highlights a little-known era of American history.*

(p. 1)

Like *Song Yet Sung, The Good Lord Bird* is a historical novel that deals primarily with slavery in the United States in the 1850s. Curiously, the novel's main character is a young black slave named Henry Shackleford who, after having been liberated from his slave owner, lives as a member of the female sex—a hoax put on by accident, and perpetuated by Henry, for considerations of his safety. The episode in which this gender switch occurs introduces an element of slapstick into what is otherwise an adventure novel with a grave backdrop: the years of historical slavery in the United States directly preceding the Civil War. John Brown, a historical abolitionist, is often referred to in the narrative as the Old Man, chiefly characterized by his grizzled beard, tattered clothes, marathon prayers, and preference for outdoor living and eating. This vivid rendering helps nourish the cult of personality around John Brown which develops in the novel; it feeds both his legend and the backlash surrounding his

character, motivation, and strategy. The institution of American slavery was widespread and deeply entrenched, after all. Slave owners not only sought to secure their own financial advancement, but looked to their neighbors, to tradition, and to religious representations for the moral justification for their dominion over other human lives. At the same time, McBride depicts slave owners as people who lived in fear of reversal or retribution for turning human beings into chattel.

John Brown is characterized not merely as deeply religious, but as superstitious. This becomes evident early in the book, when he effectively takes Henry Shackleford, living under the haphazard guise "Henrietta" and known as "Onion," as his good luck charm.

Old Man heard Pa say "Henry ain't a," and took it to be "Henrietta," which is how the Old Man's mind worked. Whatever he believed, he believed. It didn't matter to him whether it was really true or not. He just changed the truth till it fit him. He was a real white man.

(p. 19)

McBride's work, on one level, appears to trace John Brown's failures up to his crucial failure to heed Harriet Tubman's repeated warnings on holding to the day of his attack on the Armory at Harpers Ferry, Virginia. Timing was everything, since so many supporters had to travel so far in a coordinated way, and from such a diverse kitty of individual motives. As Tubman's character says: "Remember, Captain [as Brown is known], whatever your plan, be on time. Don't deviate the time. Compromise life before you compromise time. Time is the only thing you can't compromise" (p. 252).

Yet John Brown's persona in this novel, for all his righteousness, betrays a fatal flaw: the man clings to his beliefs and is willing to swing from one tactic to the next in service to the conviction that drives him. As he says to Onion, in stoic fashion: "Is it the white man upon whom the Negro can depend to fight his war, Little Onion? No. It is the Negro himself. We are 'bout to unleash the true gladiators in this hellion against the infernal wickedness. The leaders of the Negro people themselves. Onward" (p. 242).

JAMES McBRIDE

But delivering on time would have been the only way to ensure that "the leaders of the Negro people" attended and fought in the attack of the armory at Harpers Ferry. Brown's judgment is flawed from the beginning, and yet that flaw is related to his power and charisma. As McBride writes: "Nobody in America could outdo John Brown when it came to tooting his own whistle" (p. 245). He consistently refers to his program in light of other revolutionaries. From Spartacus to Toussaint-Louverture, John Brown sees himself as an insurrectionist and a revolutionary working with righteousness and divine cause. Unlike those other revolutionary figures, whose lives were intimately tied up with their revolts, Brown, a white man, chooses to side with the cause of abolition not because it affects him directly but because of his personal identity, which has been shaped by a deep religious conviction. Brown's political and temporal motivations are eternal or transcendent in character. His work is born out of scripture and personal faith in God:

He was strict as the devil on the matter of religion when it come to his own self, but if your spiritual purpose took you a different way, why, he'd lecture you a bit, then let you move to your own purpose. So long as you didn't cuss, drink, or chew tobacco, and was against slavery, he was all for you.

(p. 275)

However well-intentioned the Old Man John Brown might have been in his desire to overturn the institution of slavery, his characterization in the novel shows a deeply charismatic, deeply faithful man, who is yet at odds with many facts, at odds with political reality, and driven to violence as recourse to achieve his goals. He is plainly figured as an outlaw who is willing to behead and kill ruthlessly for his faithful purposes. In light of today's struggles with faith and lawlessness, such convictions not only play badly, but are downright frightening to learn about.

John Brown's relentless rejection of the historic institution of slavery in the United States is configured in the novel as, if not entirely beyond reproach, then representative of a voice given to the black masses who had been wronged. It is important in McBride's fiction that the

justification for the rejection of slavery is found and sourced in religious discourse.

As for the novel's title, *The Good Lord Bird* takes its name from the woodpecker, a feather of which is discovered in the fireproof box under the floorboards of the First United Negro Baptist Church of the Abyssinia, along with Onion Shackleford's history, written by Mr. Charles D. Higgins. As John Brown's son, Fred, tells us about the Good Lord Bird: "It's so pretty that when man sees it, he says, 'Good Lord'" (p. 30).

A moment as mysterious as it is revelatory appears in chapter 12, "Sibonia," when "Old Man" John Brown has ventured to different battles, and Onion has been recaptured. Named for an "outdoor" slave, Sibonia introduces herself to Onion, who has been working in the relatively privileged comfort of Miss Abby's whorehouse and tavern, an "indoor" slave, by throwing a mud ball in her face. We are given to understand that Sibonia is "soft in the head." She is described as "clucking like a chicken" and speaking gibberish. As background before the scene begins, McBride writes from Onion's perspective. We see a degree of myopia in Onion's reflexive analysis, combined with certain truths, relative to her power and position:

I was right at home in [Miss Abby's] place, living 'round gamblers and pickpockets who drank rotgut and pounded each other's brains out over card games. I was back in bondage, true, but slavery ain't too troublesome when you're in the doing of it and growed used to it. Your meals is free. Your roof is paid for. Somebody else got to bother themselves about you.... But you could see the slave pen from Pie's window.

(p. 146)

Pie is an immensely beautiful slave who works for Miss Abby as a "respected" and exalted whore. While sympathetic to Onion (she knows the secret that Onion, though dressed in a bonnet and dress, is truly a boy), it becomes clear that oversharing with Pie could lead Onion to certain trouble. Pie's power is contingent, to an extent, on compromising possible insurrections and conniving among the other slaves in Miss Abby's

business: "'Leave them niggers in the yard alone,' [Pie] said, 'They're trouble'" (p. 147).

Included in the set of "outside" slaves, Pie warns against is the mesmerizing figure of Sibonia. In the subsequent chapter, "Insurrection," Sibonia and her sister are the leaders of a plot to execute many of the townspeople, if not precisely for their freedom, then as retribution for their enslavement and the enslavement of their families. This plot is betrayed, however, and Sibonia is apprehended as their leader. When confronted by the Judge and threatened with torture if she refuses to divulge the other conspirators, Sibonia remains "calm as a blade of grass." Her "talking straight" to the Judge discomfits and confounds all the white slave owners around her. Finally she is taken to jail (p. 162).

In a harrowing scene at the end of this chapter, the local minister, who is antislavery, is brought to the jail cell where Sibonia is kept, in order to get her to confess her coconspirators. Sibonia's response floors the minister, who returns to the tavern hours later, despondent, and relinquishing his ministerial duties to the community:

"I said, 'Sibonia, I come to find out everything you know about the wicked'—and she cut me off."

"She said, 'Reverend, you come for no such purpose. Maybe you was persuaded to come or forced to come. But would you, who taught me the word of Jesus; you, the man who taught me that Jesus suffered and died in truth; would you tell me to betray confidence secretly entrusted to me? Would you, who taught me that Jesus's sacrifice was for me and me only, would you now ask me to forfeit the lives of others who would help me? Reverend, you know me!'"

(p. 165)

Sibonia has become a moral exemplar for the blacks themselves. This is counterpoised beautifully with Old Man John Brown, who takes the gospels as part of his justification for abolition. Her character is in part an elaboration of the character Ducky, who appears in the earlier novel *Song Yet Sung*. Ducky, though outwardly a lunatic, is able to convey a message to the old man Clarence, precisely because no one is suspi-cious of him. Sibonia, a more fully realized moral actor, demonstrates the ingenuity, inventiveness, and moral courage of those working to end slavery from inside the system itself.

The Old Man and his crew eventually recover Onion, and they go on to meet the abolitionist Frederick Douglass at his home in Rochester, New York. Douglass, depicted as much as a self-preservationist as an abolitionist, is at odds with John Brown regarding style and approach to ending slavery. In the end it is a great disappointment for Brown, but he lets any and all personal distractions fall away from his main purpose: attacking the Federal Armory at Harpers Ferry, Virginia, with an eye to arming the slaves and leading them in a revolt.

Near the end of the book, Onion himself takes stock:

Being a Negro means showing your best face to the white man every day. You know his wants, his needs, and watch him proper. But he don't know your wants. He don't know your needs or feelings or what's inside you, for you ain't equal to him in no measure. You just a nigger to him. A thing: like a dog or a shovel or a horse. Your needs and wants got no track, whether you is a girl or a boy, a woman or a man, or shy, or fat, or don't eat biscuits, or can't suffer the change of weather easily.... A body can't prosper if a person don't know who they are.

(p. 343)

Onion's survival in the fighting and his passage north, his abandonment of his female garb for his truer male self, are timed with his finding of faith. This is both a hetero-normative narrative device and classically McBridian in its equation of faith with rightness and goodness. Because of this, *The Good Lord Bird* reads like a romance or a comedy, rather than a tragedy or a slapstick farce about slavery, of which it partakes at various points. The presiding sentiment of the book is that slavery is emasculating, that slaves should be forgiven for whatever unmanly things they may have needed to do in order to survive. Onion's final move toward his maleness indicates his move toward freedom and faith, twin lodestars of McBride's art.

Selected Bibliography

WORKS OF JAMES MCBRIDE

MEMOIR
The Color of Water: A Black Man's Tribute to His White Mother. New York: Riverhead Books, 1996.

FICTION
Miracle at St. Anna. New York: Riverhead Books, 2002.
Song Yet Sung. New York: Riverhead Books, 2008.
The Good Lord Bird. New York: Riverhead Books, 2013.

INTERVIEWS AND FEATURES

Bosman, Julie. "Traveling with John Brown Along the Road to Literary Celebrity." *New York Times*, November 24, 2013. http://www.nytimes.com/2013/11/25/books/james -mcbride-on-his-novel-the-good-lord-bird.html?_r=0

Charney, Noah. "How I Write: James McBride, the New National Book Award Winner for Fiction." *Daily Beast*, December 4, 2013. http://www.thedailybeast.com/articles/ 2013/12/04/how-i-write-james-mcbride-the-new-national -book-award-winner-for-fiction.html

Carlozo, Louis R. "My Other Passion / James McBride." *Chicago Tribune*, February 26, 2008. http://articles .chicagotribune.com/2008-02-26/features/0802220485 _1_james-mcbride-music-passion

Hesse, Monica. "Novelist James McBride on Bringing John Brown to Life." *Washington Post*, December 3, 2013. http://www.washingtonpost.com/lifestyle/style/novelist -james-mcbride-on-bringing-john-brown-to-life/2013/12/ 03/61d48ca2-5c22-11e3-be07-006c776266ed_story.html

James McBride website. http://www.jamesmcbride.com/

Trachtenberg, Jeffrey A. "James McBride on 'Song Yet Sung.'" *Wall Street Journal*, February 9, 2008. http:// online.wsj.com/articles/SB120222661678044327

FILMS BY OR BASED ON THE WORK OF JAMES MCBRIDE

Miracle at St. Anna. Directed by Spike Lee. Screenplay by James McBride. Forty Acres & A Mule Filmworks, On My Own, Rai Cinema, Touchstone Pictures, 2008.

Red Hook Summer. Directed by Spike Lee. Screenplay by Spike Lee and James McBride. Forty Acres & A Mule Filmworks, 2012.

BICH MINH NGUYEN

(1974—)

Kathleen Pfeiffer

BICH MINH NGUYEN (whose name is pronounced "Bic Min New-ín," and who often goes by the name Beth) recalls her childhood as a time of uncertainty and questioning, filled with a sense of wondering that she once described as a "missingness" (*Stealing Buddha's Dinner*, p. 12). Born in Saigon, she spent the first decade of her life without knowing her biological mother—neither where she was, nor why she was separated from the family—and while Nguyen celebrates her birthday on August 31, this date is just a guess. In fact, she has no specific knowledge of her own true birthday, a lacuna resulting from the chaos of her family's hasty departure in the midst of Saigon's capture by the Viet Cong. Nguyen arrived in the United States under the most harrowing of conditions along with her father Dung, Grandmother Toan Thi (known as Noi), sister Anh, and uncles Chu Anh, Chu Cuong, and Chu Dai. "We had left Vietnam in the spring of 1975," she explains in the memoir of her childhood, *Stealing Buddha's Dinner* (2007), "when my sister was two and I was eight months old" (p. 4). In the early chaos of Saigon's fall, the group snuck aboard a departing ship. This pivotal moment of exodus, described with spare prose in the book's opening pages, seems both magical and terrifying:

> How this happened—quickly, almost easily—my father doesn't understand.... As we ran to the docks a guard grabbed my father and swung him around, pushing the barrel of an M-16 at his stomach. *What are you doing here? Go back,* he ordered.

> My father just looked at him. Chu Anh and Noi were moving ahead with me and Anh. *Shoot me if you have to,* he said. *But my family is going.* He backed away, turning to run. The guard didn't shoot.
>
> (p. 6)

From the Saigon River to the Philippines to refugee camps in Guam and then in Fort Chafee,

Arkansas, the family waited months for sponsorship. Nguyen explains how, under desperately grueling circumstances, her father's ability to charm (the ship's crew members, the refugee camp guards) gave the family precious, if few, comforts (an apple, chocolate, some powdered milk). When the family finally accepted a placement in Grand Rapids, Michigan, the Nguyen adults pooled their money to host a farewell party for their friends in the refugee camp, still waiting in limbo. "*We are a people without a country,* someone in the camp said. *Until we walk out of that gate,* my father replied. *And then we are American*" (p. 10).

During the first few years of her childhood, Nguyen and her family lived in "a house of splintery wooden floors" on Baldwin Street in Grand Rapids, aided by their sponsor, Mr. Heidenga. Yet at the initiation of Rosa Fraga, the woman who became Nguyen's stepmother in 1979, they moved to a ranch on Florence Street, in a noticeably better part of town. "It was clear we had moved up a little," Nguyen writes, "into a neighborhood where people mowed their lawns" (p. 28). The family grew: not only in the addition of Rosa and her daughter, Crissy, but a new brother Vinh, born a few months after the couple married in January. Nguyen's father worked at the North American Feather Company for many years before leaving that job to pursue independent contracting work in construction. Rosa, the second-generation daughter of Mexican American migrant farmworkers, developed a multifaceted career in education, citizen activism, and political organization. She helped support the family through her work at the Hispanic Institute teaching GED and ESL classes, while pursuing graduate work in education at Grand Valley State University.

While *Stealing Buddha's Dinner* depicts the marriage as tense, it also provides context for that tension, details that illustrate the peculiar challenges faced by a blended, economically struggling family of differing ethnic traditions. The young Nguyen's narrative persona experiences (and depicts) her childhood as anxious and stressful, a home life where her parents "glared at each other, fighting about the parties, the drinking, and most of all, the money he kept pulling from their account to finance his nights out" (p. 201). Yet the adult writer understands, compassionately, her parents' struggle to both raise and protect their children. While she objects to the invasion of privacy when Rosa reads her and her sisters' diaries, for instance, she also notes that Rosa "was worried that if she didn't monitor us, we would become wayward and bad" (p. 161). As a child, she fears and hides from her father's moodiness and unpredictable temper; as an adult, she recognizes and appreciates the impossible choices he had to make to save his family, the enormity of his sacrifices and disappointments.

Family life became even more crowded and hectic when the Nguyens took in several foster children. While the news of these additions sent young Bich "into a tailspin" (p. 204), Rosa insisted that the family commit themselves to community outreach. "'It's time to give back,' she said, looking straight at me" (p. 206). Huynh, a teenaged Vietnamese refugee, stayed a short time; Saigon-born brothers Phuong and Vu remained with the family for many years; Pina and Thien, orphaned Cambodian refugees, stayed only a few months.

When Nguyen was in the fifth grade, her father and Rosa mentioned to her and her sister Anh that they had received a letter from their birth mother. They were told that she had recently arrived in the United States—via Saigon, Singapore, and Los Angeles—and was then residing in Swarthmore, Pennsylvania. "I never read or saw the actual letter," she explains. "They presented me and Anh with the news almost casually" (p. 221). The sisters wrote back, but received no reply, and her mother faded back into an elusive absence for the next eight years. "How could we miss her," Nguyen wonders, "if we did not know her?"

In 1986 the family moved to the eastern Grand Rapids suburb of Ada, Michigan, into a larger house with an enclosed swimming pool. Rosa also initiated this move, believing as she did "that isolating us in Ada would keep us safe and keep us together" (p. 213). While it was true that moving to Ada kept the family together logistically, they remained emotionally disconnected: during Nguyen's fourteenth summer, she learned that Rosa and her father had divorced. Yet after that abrupt and unexpected announcement, "no one mentioned the divorce again." She writes,

> My father, in fact, never once spoke the word. I don't recall him ever moving out of the house. He and Rosa went on living the way they always had, except my father slept on the worn black leather sectional in the living room. After a few months we almost forgot that they were ever divorced at all.
>
> (pp. 218–219)

Nguyen attended the University of Michigan as an undergraduate, earning her degree summa cum laude. Midway through her college career, Nguyen met her birth mother for the first time, spending an afternoon at her mother's Somerville apartment during a visit to Boston. She also met her half-sister Nho—whose existence, along with that of a half-brother named Huy, Nguyen had only learned about the year before—as well as Nho's husband and children. In *Stealing Buddha's Dinner*, she describes their reunion:

> She leaned forward and hugged me, a quick kiss hello as if we had only seen each other a few months ago. "Look at you," she said, holding me at arm's length. She made a clicking noise with her tongue. "You're late. Almost twenty years I wait, and you're late."
>
> (p. 227)

In 1997, while she was studying poetry at the M.F.A. program at the University of Michigan, she traveled to Vietnam with her grandmother and uncle Chu Anh, supported by a University of Michigan travel grant. During the four weeks that she stayed in Saigon, meeting relatives and retracing the steps of a life she might have had,

Nguyen encountered the thick heat and humidity of the region, the confusing labyrinth of Saigon's streets and alleyways, and the evocative and resonant food of her native land. "Chu Anh walked around," she explains, "shaking his head. 'I can't believe we lived like this,' he said" (p. 243).

Following graduate school, Nguyen taught as a lecturer in the English Department at the University of North Carolina at Greensboro, then as an assistant professor of writing at Purdue University. She currently serves as academic director of the M.F.A. program at the University of San Francisco, where she is associate professor. She married the novelist Porter Shreve in 2002; they have two sons, Henry and Julian.

Nguyen's published writing includes fiction, personal essay, memoir, and food writing, categories that often merge; she embraces a variety of platforms, thereby appealing to a wide-ranging audience. Her food writing, for example, has appeared as a personal essay in *Gourmet* magazine and as a recipe/essay addressing the "Family Traditions" of her stepmother's Mexican culinary history on the Foodfit.com website. Likewise, on November 23, 2006, she presented an essay on Thanksgiving on the PBS News Hour:

> As a kid, I imagined a big buffet, with cornucopias, and pies, and dried corn, everyone sitting around the same table.... For immigrants, it can be hard to figure out how much of that Thanksgiving story is myth.... Thanksgiving is about the hopeful ideal of America: cultures converging, always evolving and changing, bringing an abundant and ever-richer variety to the national table.

In writing for a general reading public, she brings the messages of her fiction and creative nonfiction into popular culture, often in unexpected ways. When the Hostess company reported that it was going out of business in 2012, for example, her *New York Times* op-ed piece "Goodbye to My Twinkie Days" offered a clever, playful, yet politically shrewd meditation on the iconoclastic junk food. While the essay does note the stereotype that associates "Twinkie" with "sellout" for Asian Americans, she complicates any easy equivocation by focusing instead on the sensual details of her own memory. "For me, a child of Vietnamese immigrants growing up in Michigan in the 1980s," she explains, "Twinkies were a ticket to assimilation: the golden cake, more golden than the hair I wished I had, filled with sweet white cream." Such rhetorical versatility bespeaks a writer who is deeply committed to the socially transformative potential of creative production.

STEALING BUDDHA'S DINNER

Nguyen's first book has received considerable attention, both in complimentary reviews upon its publication in 2007 and in subsequent scholarly analysis. Winner of the PEN/Jerard Award, Nguyen's memoir of her childhood was named the *Chicago Tribune* Best Book of the Year, a Kiriyama Notable Book, and was selected for numerous all-community and all-university reads, including the Great Michigan Read. Many reviewers agree with Marjorie Kehe's observation in the *Christian Science Monitor* that "Nguyen is a gifted storyteller who doles out humor and hurt in equal portions as she fleshes out the plight of the immigrant." Ben Fong Torres' *New York Times* review makes note of a prose style that is "engaging, precise, compact," an observation that is shared by many reviewers. And in *USA Today*, Carol Memmott praises Nguyen for being "a brave writer who is willing to share intimate family memories many of us would choose to keep secret."

As the title makes clear, *Stealing Buddha's Dinner* cares a lot about food. The cover image from the first hardback edition depicts an array of junk food treats artfully arranged in an offering plate: Pringles, a candy necklace, a Hostess Sno Ball and orange cupcake, Skittles, a Sundae cone. The paperback version's cover shows an Asian girl sitting cross-legged, gazing down at her two cupped hands: she holds a pink Sno Ball, the confection is more brightly lit than the face of the girl herself. Each chapter names a food ("Pringles," "Salt Pork," "Moon Cakes") or a meal ("School Lunch," "Stealing Buddha's Dinner"); in one instance, it names a restaurant: "Ponderosa." In each chapter, food offers passage

to a deeper meditation on some aspect of desire, nourishment, hunger, or longing. Many of the connections are startling: she associates "the mustache grin on Mr. Pringles' broad, pale face" (p. 3) as being akin to "Santa Claus or Mr. Heidenga—a big white man, gentle of manner, whose face signaled a bounty of provisions" (p. 14). And while the chapter on Ponderosa ostensibly begins as a series of recollections of the restaurants of her childhood, it makes an elegant and unexpected turn into a meditation on her stepmother. "It wasn't until after we stopped going to Ponderosa that the name of the restaurant struck me, a signpost instruction in my mind: Ponder Rosa" (p. 212). The subtlety of this transition, together with the myriad resonant layers of insight about Rosa's complex role in her family—and by extension, in Bich Nguyen's life— unify the chapter. "Ponderosa" thus illustrates Timothy K. August's celebration of "the literariness of Nguyen's memoir and in particular the techniques used to construct her language so that it stands as an aesthetic intervention" (p. 106).

Scholars of ethnic American identity have found in the memoir's complex references to food a nuanced examination of assimilation, immigrant identity, and selfhood. Nguyen's preoccupation with the processed American foods of her childhood becomes the means through which she seeks authenticity as an American. In so doing, she participates in a broad and rich conversation, not only with food writers generally, but more specifically with a community of contemporary literary memoirs by Asian American women. The anthropologist Jane Dusselier examines the phenomenon in "Understandings of Food as Culture," where she notes that "Asian American food memoirs are a flourishing new area of food studies" (p. 334). In examining how food participates in the cultural construction of identity, Dusselier offers a helpful paradigm for understanding some of the strategies at work in Nguyen's book.

> Connections between food and identity development ... are central to studying Asian American foodways. Debates about this notion occur on several levels with some practitioners in the field arguing that foodways offer a path to cultural preservation while others lean more toward the idea

that food serves assimilationist purposes. Food as encompassing agency, power, and subjectivity is yet another approach that Asian Americanists employ when studying food.

(p. 336)

Throughout the memoir, Nguyen positions food in metaphorical terms, as the pathway to inclusion, to belonging, to Americanness. "I wanted to savor new food, different food, white food," she writes. "I was convinced I was falling far behind on becoming American, and then what would happen to me? I would be an outcast the rest of my days" (p. 52). In *Stealing Buddha's Dinner*, memories of food and longing for food are closely connected to identity formation, both in Nguyen's desire to fit in and in the shame created by her ethnic otherness. Her stepmother's overarching frugality, as well as her own preferences, often left young Nguyen feeling wholly out of sync with her classmates. When Rosa's preferences—"like olive loaf instead of bologna, orange Faygo instead of crush, raisin cookies instead of chocolate chip"—take Nguyen out of step with her blond American classmates, her sense of otherness intensifies. "These small differences accumulated within my growing stockpile of shame and resentment" she writes, "as if Rosa herself were preventing me from fitting in and being like everyone else" (p. 52).

In such scenes, Nguyen's tale connects with the broader immigrant experience of assimilation. "Food is one space," Dusselier argues, "where people reposition themselves and become rooted in unfamiliar and often hostile environments" (p. 337). Nguyen herself has agreed on this point, in interviews where she notes that "one thing immigrants keep is their food heritage" (Kalb 2012). *Stealing Buddha's Dinner* makes it clear how complicated and painful such a heritage can be— particularly for someone like Nguyen, who hungered for more than food. "In my mind," she writes, "I used that term: real people. Real people did not eat *cha gio*. Real people ate hamburgers and casseroles and brownies. And I wanted to be a real person, or at least make others believe that I was one" (p. 56). Longing for authenticity as an American, young Nguyen attached herself to American food as if eating it would fill that deeper, ontological hunger.

When the memoir opens with a declaration that "we arrived in Grand Rapids with five dollars and a knapsack of clothes," Nguyen positions herself as a figure of mediation, a narrator interested in transition. The opening chapter describes the violent upheaval that led her to be carried away not only from her motherland, but also from her mother. Framing her story with images of departure and arrival, Nguyen aligns herself with other members of the so-called "1.5 generation," a term employed by the scholar Bunkong Tuon to describe the experiences of particularly young Vietnamese refugees. Tuon explains that members of this in-between generation "are caught in this liminal space between being and understanding, where they have both fragmented memories of Asia and partial understanding of America" (p. 4). Understood in terms of the 1.5 generation, Nguyen demonstrates all of the characteristics of this generation's writers, where we see "young narrators haunted by memories of war in Viet Nam, grappling with issues of identity and belonging, and struggling to find a sense of 'home' in the United States" (p. 4). The memoir makes clear that the infant Nguyen had no conscious memory of the wartime violence that fueled her family's escape and immigration, yet her story remains saturated in trauma, as she is haunted by the ghosts of her lost mother and of her lost life. "Every girl I passed on the street was my theoretical double," she writes, reflecting on her first return to Vietnam as a young adult, "a person I might have been, a life I might have had" (p. 245).

In an author's note, Nguyen discusses the "immigrant's dilemma to blend in or remain apart," and her self-consciousness about her generational identity appears clear. Yet as this postscript indicates, she resists becoming the voice of a generation; indeed, she asserts her individuality throughout the narrative. Among the decisions she made in writing the memoir, the author's note explains, is "owning up to my memories rather than others'." Lest readers misunderstand her intended emphasis on "my memories" in that sentence, Nguyen explains, "I generally tried to avoid turning my family into collaborators" (p. 255). Timothy K. August examines the implications of such a politically loaded term as "collaborator" in this context, arguing that Nguyen's use of that word circumvents a politicized reading of her life, insisting instead on an individualized, autonomous subjectivity. August explains:

> In this memoir she does not allow for a unified, representative Vietnamese American experience to be held up and judged under the unforgiving scale of aesthetic worth, which will then decide if it is authentically native enough. Indeed, she recognizes that her artistic performance could stand in for the achievements of the US and/or Vietnam. Instead, she short-circuits this authorized reading with her author's note and writes a book firmly in the trenches of popular culture, gesturing to her own subjective experience, and bypasses the headiness of high literary objects, preferring a diffuse general audience to a single, withering, objective gaze.
>
> (p. 112)

Such a strategy offers an aesthetic mediation of what would otherwise appear as social, racial, and cultural marginalization; Nguyen celebrates the pop culture of her youth in a carefully crafted and highly individualized narrative of selfhood.

In memoir workshops, Nguyen teaches creative-writing students that memoir writing requires a serious commitment to honesty, and this belief is evident throughout *Stealing Buddha's Dinner*. Nguyen tells her students that the question they must ask is "Am I willing to admit the trouble, put it on the page, court more trouble?" Her own writerly response to such questions appears, for example, in a chapter titled "Toll House Cookies," where she examines the "embarrassment and shame" revealed in the contrast between her own foreign family and her next door neighbor's Christian, blond, wholly American home. She confesses to the day when she and her sister Ahn broke into the Vander Wals' house to vandalize the "Jennifer Zone," the gleaming, color-coordinated, elegant princess bedroom of her neighbor and putative best friend. "As we moved in swift silence," she writes, "I felt a heady, dizzying rush, the thrill of the trespass" (p. 69). Yet what begins as a childish prank—the sisters' most damaging act of vandalism involves sprinkling baby powder throughout the room—ends with an unexpected, and deeply

painful admission. After their "crime" is detected and the sisters "mumble apologies" to Jennifer and her parents, Nguyen reflects on the moment of encounter. "Jennifer had looked indignant the night of the apology, but there was something more: pity," she writes. "I saw then that she had always pitied me and my unsaved soul" (p. 71). Moments of such recognition, of seeing pity in the eyes of others, run through the memoir and sabotage young Nguyen when she least expects the assault.

In a psychoanalytic reading of the memoir, Wenying Xu views "food as a stage where ontological drama is acted out, where desire, appetite, hunger, rejection of food, and disgust are symptomatic of tensions of a higher order" (p. 9). Xu calls attention to the "obsessive cataloging of and insistent craving for American foods and snacks" (p. 13) that runs throughout the memoir, suggesting that in such lists of the foods she so desired, the writer reveals a deep melancholia, as well as "tumultuous emotions that border on rage" (p. 14). By examining the food imagery through the lens of psychoanalytic theory, Xu calls attention to aesthetic strategies whereby Nguyen addresses the primal alienation of childhood. In this case, a longing for the symbolic other becomes painfully entangled with the complete absence of her biological mother.

While the memoir begins with young Nguyen's escape from her motherland and separation from her mother, it ends with two moments of reimagining that scene. In the first, she concludes the story of meeting her mother by visualizing the day of her family's escape from her mother's point of view, thinking of her mother "opening the door and feeling, instantly, the emptiness." Such emptiness both parallels and recalls the "missingness" of young Nguyen's own childhood. "I couldn't comprehend the loss," she writes, "the nearly twenty years' absence, the silence and unknowing, the physical distance literally impossible to break" (p. 237). In the second, more deeply evocative transport, she wonders "what it must have been like for [her] father, taking Anh and [her] into his arms, pursuing a boat, a way out, knowing all the while that [their] mother would not know where [they]

were." These moments of intervention, of deeply compassionate sympathy, stand as the memoir's emotional center. "That I cannot imagine that moment," she writes, "the panic and fear, the push to leave his country and aim for an unknown land, is perhaps his gift. It is my Americanness.... I am grateful for his unimaginable choice" (p. 251).

SHORT GIRLS

Nguyen's first novel, *Short Girls*, appeared in 2009. Dedicated to her beloved grandmother Noi, the novel won the 2010 American Book Award and was selected as one of *Library Journal*'s Best Books of 2009. Marion Winik, reviewing the novel for the *Los Angeles Times,* rightly remarks that the novel is "more sad than funny, more real than lightweight." Andrea Kempf describes the book as a "lovely first novel ... a depiction of immigrant culture in which everyone is a short person trying to measure up to the United States" (p. 92). Writing in the *Independent*, Emma Hagestadt finds "this gentle comedy of intergenerational strife [to be] a polished and poised affair," and praises Nguyen as an "amusing observer of assimilation angst." While entertaining and emotionally satisfying, this fiction is driven by a deep sense of purpose, an aesthetically rich understanding of the intersection between the personal and the political.

Biographical influences are clear throughout Nguyen's fiction, as she transforms the immigrant experience into an insightful commentary on several central themes in American identity: self-invention, invisibility, naming, food, family. Echoes of Nguyen's family run throughout *Short Girls*; she has remarked that the book was "partly inspired by [her] own relationship with [her] two older sisters and partly by Jane Austen's *Sense and Sensibility*" (Davidson). Thus, when *Short Girls* describes the complex rivalry between Van and Linny Luong, readers are reminded of the intense familial tension that runs throughout *Stealing Buddha's Dinner.* Van and Linny are haunted by the death of their mother, much as questions about Nguyen's own absent mother run

throughout the memoir. Even in the book's prefatory "About the Author" material, Nguyen invites an autobiographical reading when she notes that she herself "is just under five feet." The author explains her approach to genre and the differences and overlaps between fiction and memory:

> Though *Short Girls* is about a Vietnamese American family, the characters and conflicts are all fiction. At the same time, nonfiction provides the great freedom of *not* having to make things up—of getting to tell the truth. So to me it's beneficial to work in two genres, because when you get exhausted with one the other one feels liberating. It's also helped me figure out which ideas and images should belong in which genre. Some things feel too true for fiction; some memories are too hazy for nonfiction.

> (Kalb 2012)

Short Girls has been identified by Quan Manh Ha as one of several contemporary Vietnamese American novels that create new literary themes, eschewing "the traditional war-related issues treated by their Vietnamese American literary forbears" (p. 63). Moreover, the novel also deals quite progressively with this broad range of themes. Ha writes that "*Short Girls* is an intergenerational novel about contrasting personalities and lifestyles, the fragility of human relationships, dysfunctional communication, generational gaps within a family, and the collapse of the American dream" (p. 73). In Ha's reading of the novel, Nguyen dismantles the mechanism by which ethnic stereotypes are automatically assigned. The title characters both are and are not typically Vietnamese; they both are and are not typically American. By developing characters who experience "post- rather than pre- assimilationist situations ... the novel moves Vietnamese American literature into new, and potentially very fruitful, thematic areas" (p. 77).

Short Girls traces the ambitions, insecurities, desires, and challenges of the parents and two daughters who make up the Luong family, first- and second-generation immigrants from Vietnam. Dinh and Thuy Luong fled Saigon in 1975, and Thuy gave birth to Van three months later in a California refugee camp. A sense of Christian charity led a Michigan couple named Dirk and Paula Oortsema to sponsor the family, which came to include a second daughter named Linny, born a year after Van. While the Oortsemas did provide practical support for the family's relocation to a Grand Rapids suburb, their sponsorship came with a cost, particularly for the daughters. "In Linny's first memory of the Oortsemas," we learn, "she and Van were given matching white leatherette Bibles.... The Oortsemas wouldn't force the issue [of Sunday school attendance], though every once in a while Paula would say, 'I just want what's best for my girls'" (p. 129). The sisters recoil from the Oortsemas' condescending sense of proprietorship, refusing to share their parents' self-effacing and never-ending gratitude. "*You didn't sponsor me,* Linny wanted to say" (p. 158), just one of many deep-seated generational differences between the parents and their children.

Mr. Luong is a vivid presence throughout the novel, an ambitious but disappointed man who spends his happiest hours in a basement workshop crafting inventions designed to improve the lives of short people. Shortness, he believes—not his Vietnamese heritage but shortness—is the reason why he hasn't been able to achieve success in America. In an amusing but deeply resonant linguistic misunderstanding, Mr. Luong believes that Randy Newman's song declares "Short People Are No Reason to Live"; appalled at the sentiment, he utterly rejects any suggestion that it is meant to be ironic, humorous. His hopes for professional achievement and recognition—"he had studied civil engineering in Vietnam" (p. 121), he often reminds his daughters—have long since been disappointed. He works odd jobs, mostly in construction, to support the family. His financial contributions, however, fall far short of his wife's ambitions for her two daughters, and so Mrs. Luong accepts a full-time job sewing for Roger's Department Store, leaving the six- and seven-year-old sisters home alone "in an apartment complex near a freeway and a construction site that turned out to be a correctional facility" (p. 121).

If these childhood days establish a pattern in which Van bears a great deal more responsibility than an older sister typically assumes, they also create some of the girls' most intimate moments. "Those early evening hours between Linny and

Van," Nguyen notes, "made up the closest years of their sisterhood, when they pretended to live in the apartment by themselves" (p. 122). Those afternoons of television and snacking, the evenings of sharing dreams and secrets in their cramped bedroom, are days that leave indelible marks on each girl. But their intimacy disintegrates when the cramped isolation disappears: Mrs. Luong's earnings provide the down payment for a ranch house in a leafy suburban neighborhood. Each girl gets her own bedroom; thus separated, each also develops her own fraught identity. When their mother dies suddenly of a massive stroke at age forty-two, the sisters are left without any maternal presence to guide and support them.

This family history emerges through flashbacks, as the sisters are called home by their father who has decided (after "twenty-eight years of stubbornness," according to Van) to take the oath of citizenship. Returning thus, both women embark on metaphorical journeys home as well, each viewing their father's citizenship as an occasion to examine her own life's path, her choices, ambitions, sense of self. The novel is structured as a conversation between parallel chapters, following Linny and Van's lives in an alternating sequence that is narrated by an omniscient voice offering access to each sister's point of view. These are parallel chapters, but separate lives: Linny and Van have grown to negotiate their Vietnamese American identities from opposite ends of the spectrum. "By portraying her characters with contrasting values, personalities, and perspectives," Quan Manh Ha notes, "Nguyen effectively demystifies the 'model minority' image that prevails in American ethnic mythology, and which too often is perpetuated in Asian American writing" (p. 77). Sadly, and ironically, neither sister is aware of the pain they have in common, nor that the other also mourns the loss of their childhood intimacy. Van, the industrious older sister, is the ideal daughter—a dutiful and successful lawyer who is drawn to work on immigration cases at the International Center in Detroit. Yet as the novel opens in 2003, her husband has just left her for another woman, forcing her to reconsider the horrible marriage that she had deluded herself into thinking had been happy. Linny, the beautiful, rebellious younger daughter, has spent her life floating between jobs and men, and the novel's opening finds her enmeshed in a toxic affair with a married man.

In the childhood home to which they return, a sense of division has already been in place for years:

> After Van left for college her parents decided to live on separate floors of the house they'd had for twenty years…. They'd fallen into the arrangement after yet another petty argument…. But this time when Thuy Luong told her husband to go sleep in the basement "like a dog," he stayed there instead of slinking back upstairs.
>
> (p. 4)

Dinh Luong reconfigures the basement into a bachelor pad, complete with a big screen television, a George Foreman grill and a mini-refrigerator; Thuy had collected her husband's belongings from the upstairs part of the house "and left them on the basement steps"; claiming the upstairs for herself, she "painted their bedroom lavender" (p. 6). As the story unfolds, we see how multifaceted this sense of division becomes. The architectural partition between upstairs and downstairs offers a metaphor for many of the family's other disjunctions: between female space and male space, between citizen and permanent alien, between American and Vietnamese, between belonging and isolation.

Short Girls links the sisters through several interlocking parallels that underscore the fundamental differences between each woman's personal identity. Linny, for example, is as compulsively drawn to domesticity as Van is disengaged from it; Linny conjures glorious meals while Van eats leftover frozen pizza; Linny crafts exquisite clothing on her mother's old sewing machine while Van wears a uniform of turtlenecks, boxy cardigans, and khaki pants from Talbots. Yet the critic Quan Manh Ha warns against a politicized reading of these differences, arguing that "the characters' individualized perceptions of themselves in American culture are not determined so much by external racial prejudice as by internal aspirations and abilities, and the characters'

personal struggle to realize them" (p. 77). Rather, *Short Girls* suggests, the oppositions by which they are defined—between single and married, urban and suburban, elegant and plain, studious and rebellious, domestic and professional—enact the division of their childhood home life.

The ostensibly straightforward title contains a wealth of complexity, for shortness is revealed to be a multifaceted, complicated state of affairs. The diminutive stature of the Luong family both reflects and informs their social marginalization, as they find themselves just as easily overlooked in crowds as in life. For Mr. Luong, shortness becomes a deeply problematic philosophical challenge, one that is directly connected to his identity as an American.

> Whenever Linny complained about wanting to be taller he would reprimand her. "Not about being tall," he said. "It's about being just as equal as tall people."
>
> "Well, that problem would be solved if we were just taller."
>
> "No, Linh. It means we want to be *smarter*. If you not seen as equal you do whatever you can to make equalness happen. Why you think I invent things?"

And when Linny bemoans her shortness, her father tells her, "It's not your fault. It's your family" (p. 61).

Mr. Luong's inventions—the Luong Arm, designed to allow a short person to reach items from high shelves, and the Luong Eye, a sort of periscope, giving short people vision over and above a crowd of taller heads, and the Luong Wall, an automated system of shelves that rotate so that the high shelves move down to lower positions—also speak to the quintessentially American notion of self-invention. Yet the novel is haunted by the metaphorical implications of these gadgets, for they continually evoke blindness, limited vision, a lack of agency. "*Short girls have to take care of themselves*," Mr. Luong tells Van when he presents her with a prototype Luong Arm as a college graduation gift (p. 5). Van's father seeks to compensate for a corporeal inadequacy that cannot be so easily overcome, however.

Indeed, throughout the novel, the Luong family's shortness repeatedly evokes the sort of invisibility that Ralph Ellison rendered so metaphorically rich in examining the complex fate of his novel's eponymous narrator. Whether intentionally or not, *Short Girls'* attention to invisibility offers respectful homage to *Invisible Man*. "I am invisible," Ellison's protagonist tells us in the opening paragraph, "simply because people refuse to see me" (p. 3). Van and Linny's father experiences a similar alienation from the American dream. "On the day of his citizenship ceremony, Dinh Luong sat alone in the ivory-paneled auditorium of the Gerald R. Ford Museum.… to Linny, he seemed to be set apart, nearly invisible" (p. 124). Ellison's protagonist regards his own social marginalization as the result of the blindness of others, and this is precisely the sort of invisibility that Dinh Luong seeks to countermand with his inventions. Convinced that his failures result from shortness, and shortness alone, Dinh is equally convinced that his creations offer him the key to success, wealth, and especially to an authentically American identity. He becomes enraged when he (mistakenly) believes that his patent application for the Luong Arm was rejected because of his citizenship status. "He does not so much demand recognition as exceptional within the society," Quan Manh Ha argues, "so much as acknowledgement by the society of his worthwhile existence within it" (p. 12). "Your ba was different then," Linny's mother tells her, reflecting on her husband's bitter disappointments. "What he expected from America is not what he got" (p. 205). His inventions seek to mitigate the disadvantage of shortness, but the disadvantages of his ethnicity always loom in the background of these discussions about height.

When Van and Linny are called home to celebrate their father's naturalization, they are drawn back into the familial and social intimacy with their Vietnamese heritage that each had ostensibly been trying to avoid for nearly a decade. As they clean their father's house, prepare traditional Vietnamese food for his guests, and reconnect with the family friends they'd left behind in search of adult selfhood,

they also share conversations and reminiscences that both recall and evoke the intimacy of their childhood. It becomes clear that neither sister has truly separated from her Vietnamese heritage. We learn that Van has been offering legal counsel to members of this community, and "over the years she'd filed dozens of applications for her father's friends" (p. 188), often without pay. Meanwhile, Linny has become the repository of her culture's culinary legacy, having learned from her mother how to cook numerous traditional Vietnamese dishes. Her boss at You Did It Dinners encourages Linny to develop new recipes for the business to develop:

> Linny's recipe notes had expanded, reaching toward questions beyond her job.... [she] realized she was writing notes toward another anniversary of her mother's death and it became a comfort, as though she were calling forth her mother, bringing back the hours they had spent in the kitchen together when Linny was a girl.

(p. 14)

In Linny's messy apartment, her mother's sewing machine sits in a corner, a modern-day altar to the dead.

The sisters' long-established patterns and habits break apart in the wake of their father's naturalization ceremony. They come to recognize the shifts in their own lives, and they begin confronting the fears they'd been running from for years. "Look at how Van had already changed," Linny thinks, wondering with awe about "what else might change for" Linny herself (p. 237). Having been drawn back home by their father's quest for authentic Americanness, the sisters find themselves drawn into an authenticity that had previously eluded them as well. "It gave Linny a strange sense of having changed places, of having become the older sister" when Van shares the shame and pain of having been abandoned by her husband (p. 250). For the first time in their lives, the two exchange roles, and when Van challenges Linny, "Why don't *you* take care of things for a change?" the younger sister accepts the challenge. These changes move both women into a state of visibility—multifaceted and substantive—that had previously eluded them. Linny notices the acknowledgment of a stranger on the sidewalk; Van refuses to capitulate to Miles's self-serving narrative about their marriage; Linny treats an ugly confrontation with her ex-lover's wife with dignity and poise; Van frees herself of the role of responsible older sister. In the end, the futures predicted for each member of the Luong family prove magically rich with potential, previously unimagined possibilities that can never be diminished by their shortness.

PIONEER GIRL

Nguyen's 2014 novel *Pioneer Girl* has elicited an enthusiastic critical and popular response that underscores her significance in contemporary American literary history. *Pioneer Girl* was honored, for example, as the inaugural selection of BookDragon, the book club of the Smithsonian Asian Pacific American Center, which held an interactive online discussion on August 26, 2014. In a review explaining the novel's selection, the critic Terry Hong offered a strong endorsement, writing, "Mark my words: if nothing else, the ingenious layers are going to prove dissertation-worthy and beyond." Many critics agreed. Anthony Marra's review, for example, suggests the potentially broad resonance of the novel: "a surprising synthesis of the personal and the public, the intimate and the epic, the historical and the fictional. Nguyen takes two disparate strands of our national mythology and weaves them into a powerful and wholly original American saga." In the months following its appearance, many reviewers critically engaged the novel in fairly specific detail, suggesting that more sustained literary criticism would be forthcoming. "Nguyen crafts a truly imaginative novel," Sharon Tran notes, "that links Vietnam, the war, and the private history of one Vietnamese immigrant family with the Wilders, America's beloved pioneer family" (p. 116).

Lee Lien, the novel's first person narrator, is the only daughter of Vietnamese immigrants who have spent their lives moving about the Midwest. Lee and her older brother Sam have been raised by their mercurial, frugal mother and their gentle, kindhearted grandfather, Ong Hai, Vietnamese

refugees who fled their native land in 1975. Their father died when Lee was six, having drowned during a fishing trip with his best friend Hieu on the St. Joseph River; Hieu survived and went on to live a financially prosperous life. As the novel opens, the Liens are settled in a Chicago suburb, though much of the family's life has been spent on the move, "tracing a wide arc from Wisconsin to Illinois to Indiana, often near colleges, where the public schools were decent and the buffet business a sure thing" (p. 30). Lee has just returned home after a failed academic job search put her professorial aspirations on hold, and she joins her mother and grandfather in working at the family business, the Lotus Leaf Café. While she knows she should be spending this time revising her Edith Wharton dissertation into publishable articles that will help her land an academic job, she finds herself drawn instead to a literary mystery connecting her family with that of Laura Ingalls Wilder.

The novel's prologue sets up the mystery, explaining that in August of 1965, an American woman named Rose had been a customer at Ong Hai's Saigon Café 88 (so named because of the lucky number), and she left behind a small, distinctive gold pin, "engraved with a picture of a house" (p. 3); that pin was one of the few items Lee's mother and Ong Hai brought with them out of Vietnam. Lee had grown up hearing her grandfather's story about Rose, and when she encountered the *Little House* books as a girl, she immediately recognized the pin as a gift presented to Laura Ingalls by her fiancé Almanzo Wilder in the years before they married and gave birth to their daughter, Rose. Lee quotes the description of the pin in *These Happy Golden Years*: "There in a nest of [soft] white cotton lay a gold bar pin. On its flat surface was etched a little house, and before it along the bar lay a tiny lake, and a spray of grasses and leaves" (p. 4); she recalls how she would idly fantasize about a connection between the two pins as a child. As *Pioneer Girl* opens, Sam steals the pin from his mother's bedroom in a fit of angry rebellion and leaves it for Lee. "And it was then that I considered what had never seemed significant before," she realizes. "Hadn't Ong Hai always said that Rose was a reporter

working on an article about Vietnam?" (p. 42). This is the question that sets both Lee and *Pioneer Girl* in motion.

Lee applies her skills and credentials as a literary scholar to the task of tracking down Ingalls and Wilder family history—considering whether Rose Wilder, a woman who had, in fact, served as a reporter in Vietnam, might have been the same Rose who left the gold bar pin in her grandfather's café; and considering whether the pin left behind might have been the same pin as the one described in the *Little House* books. As Nguyen explains in an interview, the plot of Lee's research serves an important ideological function in the novel: "the real story of our family is never known to us because so much of it happens before us. We're researchers picking up clues, trying to understand our parents and family members who are no longer with us. We're wondering, guessing and coming to conclusions that may not be 100 percent accurate" (Mudge). Indeed, in the process of trying to understand her own family's history, Lee stumbles onto another family mystery entirely when she discovers evidence suggesting that Rose may have had a child out of wedlock and given him up for adoption. In this way, the mysteries of the past reach forward into the present and beyond into the future.

Pioneer Girl expands and develops the fascination with Laura Ingalls Wilder that first received voice in the "Salt Pork" chapter of *Stealing Buddha's Dinner*. Nguyen chronicles each meal in "Salt Pork," each delicacy, each hunger that runs throughout the *Little House* series, noting that "for the Ingalls family, out on the plains and prairies, every harvest means a year of leanness or a year of fullness" (p. 153). She is attracted to the like-minded Laura Ingalls because they are both small and dark-haired, because they share ravenous appetites, a questioning disposition, and a sense of displacement. "In many ways, their pioneer life reminded me of immigrant life," she writes. "As they search for new homesteads, they, too, experience isolation and the scramble for shelter, food, work, and a place to call home" (p. 159). Yet the memoir makes clear that Nguyen sees the limits of what she and Laura can share,

and this is a deeply painful realization. Belén Martín-Lucas' essay "Burning Down the Little House on the Prairie: Asian Pioneers in Contemporary North America" offers detailed and penetrating insights into this connection. "Although Laura's story coincides with both girls' displacement," she argues, "there are obvious and irreconcilable differences in their racialized experiences of resettlement" (p. 33). In ruminating on the Ingalls family's sense of American identity, for example, Nguyen grapples with the racism running throughout the *Little House* books. "Not just Ma Ingalls's hatred of Indians, which would have persisted no matter what Pa said," she writes. "I knew that people like me would also have been considered outcasts, heathens, and strangers; we didn't even count" (p. 160). By writing *Stealing Buddha's Dinner*, Nguyen writes her own racialized immigrant story into the mythology of pioneer settlement; she writes her way into American history.

In both families' histories, an ineffable restlessness drives the pioneers as well as the immigrants. In *Pioneer Girl*, Lee points out that "Pa Ingalls is anxious to keep looking for a better homestead" because he seeks more fertile land, a better farm yield, a foothold on financial security—a white family heading out into Indian territory (p. 84). So too the Liens move from job to job, running one Oriental buffet-style restaurant after another, usually "relying on friends of friends who were trusted, even if unknown, simply for being Vietnamese" because they all shared the alienation of being Asians in the white Midwest (p. 53). The problematic legacy of westward expansion complicates this parallel, however, as Anca Szilagyi's review of the novel makes clear. As she notes, we might view "the ubiquitous mid-American Chinese buffet ... as a modern Manifest Destiny." Nguyen's lengthy, voluptuous description of the "all you can eat" buffet certainly recalls the elaborate catalogs of "food porn" that ran throughout *Stealing Buddha's Dinner*, with detailed explication of the buffet's unending delights. Nguyen concludes, "You find yourself getting caught up in the allure, the expanse, dizzied by the promise, the challenge of all you can eat, all you can get, all

you can demand.... Eat now, forget tomorrow" (p. 52). The present-day all-you-can-eat Chinese buffet thus illustrates and reinforces the quintessentially American itch for unrestricted acquisition. As Sharon Tran perceptively notes, in *Pioneer Girl*, Nguyen "foregrounds troubling incongruencies between the pioneer and immigrant mentality and experiences. The settler colonial privilege, the presumed right to claim homesteads which underlies and drives the Wilders' pioneer adventures, runs in stark contrast to the history of alien land laws that prohibited Asian immigrants from owning land" (p. 117). The juxtaposition of past and present repeatedly illustrates the advantages and the limits of Ingalls' white privilege, and by extension, its counterpoint—the Liens' racial marginalization.

Pioneer Girl expands and develops the twinned themes of pioneer and immigrant experience with far more complexity and invention than the memoir form allows. "The great joy of this genre," Nguyen comments about her approach to fiction, "is the imaginative freedom to stray from, change, and subvert whatever it is that the mind calls truth or reality" (Malandrinos). *Pioneer Girl* employs the trope of a detective story, merging fictional characters with historical facts about Laura Ingalls Wilder and her daughter, Rose; occasionally, Nguyen invents historical details. Yet she also weaves numerous carefully chosen literary references throughout the story. While Lee recognizes that her choice of Edith Wharton for a dissertation topic may well be "identity avoidance," her scholarly interest in "Reifying the Aesthetics of Place" bears directly on her own family's history of immigration, resettlement, their frustrated search for a homeland (pp. 227, 173). Through Lee, Nguyen thus offers numerous subtle insights about how the American literary tradition has participated in constructing a myth of American identity. "Basically I'm drawing a kind of parallel between the pioneer's westward search and the immigrant's westward search," Nguyen explained in an interview as the novel was in process (Kalb 2012). Yet the anchoring presence of Edith Wharton makes it clear that a broader, more deliberate and self-conscious

understanding of American space is at work in the novel.

Nguyen has remarked that she is "not fond of the title *Pioneer Girl*. For years, it was called *Little Gray House in the West*, but [she] was told that wasn't a good title" (Kalb 2014). Nevertheless, the title serves a valuable organizing function in the novel, calling attention to the resonant parallels between protagonist Lee Lien and her research prey. *Pioneer Girl*, we learn, was the title of Laura Ingalls Wilder's original memoir, which drew together recollections about her childhood in the 1880s. When the manuscript was rejected by publishers, mother and daughter collaborated in reworking and expanding the memoir into the series of stories that became the *Little House* books. Nguyen invites us to see the parallels between Lee's life and those of the Wilder women through the ostensible disagreements between Lee and her mother. Yet the mother-daughter conflict also operates silently in the background references to Edith Wharton, a writer who also sustained a deeply conflicted relationship with her mother. In Wharton's memoir *A Backward Glance*, the writer reflects ruefully on her mother's coldness and rigidity, recalling the cutting remarks that crushed her early creative impulses as a young writer. Thus, while Lee "worried that [her] decision to stick with Wharton for [her] dissertation might seem like identity avoidance" (p. 227), readers familiar with American literary history recognize the parallels between Edith Wharton, Rose Wilder, and Lee Lien. In the end, Lee understands this as well, realizing she "had returned to the *Little House*, wanting escape from the escape of Edith Wharton—as if the literature of childhood wouldn't be so fettered with critical complications" (p. 252). *Pioneer Girl* repeatedly demonstrates how ineluctably fettered all literature is with critical complications.

The parallel is ultimately multifaceted and deeply resonant: Lee's fraught relationship with her own mother unfolds alongside of—and in thematic relation to—Rose Wilder's relationship with her mother, Laura Ingalls Wilder. In each narrative trajectory, the writer-daughter struggles to control the story of her own life in a vexed and complex effort to understand her mother's history. Both Lee and Rose return home to their mothers in moments of financial, personal, and professional uncertainty: for both, this return is at once a comfort and a prison. "I looked back all the time, too much, too often," Lee remarks. "Like Rose, I would be circling my mother the rest of my life" (p. 282). Both daughters seek independent lives as writers, and each woman recognizes the challenges to convention involved in her professional aspirations. "I wanted Lee and her mother to be a kind of indirect parallel to Rose and Laura," Nguyen explains in an interview with Cheryl C. Malandrinos:

> Both relationships are marked by back and forth squabbling, passive-aggressiveness, and a sense of obligation mixed up with guilt and resentment. Both Lee and Rose owe so much to their mothers yet at the same time often feel trapped by them, bound by expectations. They have benefited from their mothers' (im)migrations. At the same time, they don't want to fit the roles their mothers want them to have. I drafted this novel for a good long while before I realized that I was trying to say something about power dynamics in a family. Who gets to shape and set the narrative of a family history?

The novel openly moves between fiction and biography as Lee's storytelling neatly summarizes the Ingalls and Wilder family histories, reinforcing the relationship between the fictional Lee Lien and the historical (if occasionally fictionalized) Rose Wilder. While Laura Ingalls had never wanted to become a schoolteacher and did so only from financial necessity, Lee craves a teaching job and is daunted by her inability to find one. Laura Ingalls sought security in marriage and family, but Lee's pursuit of an academic career is motivated by her desire to escape from her family, an independence that her brother Sam craves as well. "Like Rose, we thought ourselves suited to bigger lives," she notes (p. 165). Both Lee and Sam are able to move on to bigger lives in the novel's conclusion, and several dramatic turns move the plot rapidly forward.

"If memory is a shifting mirror," Nguyen writes in the author's note that concludes *Stealing Buddha's Dinner*, "then writing is an effort to keep it stilled, if only for a while, to try to find a point of focus, some sense of understanding" (p.

256). Lee Lien realizes the truth of this statement in the denouement of *Pioneer Girl*, as she comes to a new understanding about her own life and experience—and she does this through an act of writing. When she returns home to report to her mother and Ong Hai the results of her research, their interest in her discoveries makes her giddy and proud for a moment; she shows them a photograph that Rose had taken in Saigon, suggesting to them the strong likelihood that the man in the photograph was Ong Hai. While her grandfather regards Lee's work with appreciation and respect, her mother's skepticism proves deflating. "But even as I focused on the page," Lee notes, "I could feel the moment slipping from my grasp" (p. 247). The imaginary world that had fueled Lee's research—a fictional space in which past merges with present, fiction with history, the Lien family with the Ingalls—falls apart at the very moment that Lee had hoped to merge them. The realization enervates Lee, as she realizes that "the past had never been [hers] to challenge" (p. 249). Years of training as a researcher have left her ill equipped to fully or properly understand her own immediate family.

Later, as she reflects on her distance from history, the questions Lee asks herself offer a striking commentary on Bich Minh Nguyen's own relationship to her familial and literary history. "I knew that the story I'd tracked down was only slightly, peripherally, mine," Lee realizes.

> Me, I was a bystander. A finder. Was this to be the rest of my future, trailing other people's lives, whether they were real or fiction, then turning them inside out, looking for critical nodes to explore and exploit? Was I always going to be the go-between, the one translating one text to another, one person to another, conveying interpretation?
>
> (p. 251)

This passage evokes Bunkong Tuon's depiction of the 1.5 generation of Vietnamese writers with uncanny accuracy. Lee understands her role as a witness to her family's history, both a part of it and apart from it. Significantly, however, once she is equipped with this understanding, Lee becomes unstuck. Her career thrives; she moves forward—first to a postdoctoral fellowship in

Philadelphia, then to a visiting professor position in Colorado. Her relationship with her mother progresses as well, so that when her mother offers her a gift of money to help with her move, Lee comes to understand the gesture of rapprochement as something "if not of love, exactly, then something in its general vicinity, something having to do with protecting and, equally, relenting" (p. 282).

Yet perhaps the most resonant manifestation of Lee's forward movement comes through the image of her writing: "I pressed command-N: new window. New blankness. I closed my eyes for a moment, and started writing" (p. 253). Leaving behind her dissertation analysis of *The Age of Innocence*, Lee directs her energy toward the telling of her own story rather than the critical engagement with Edith Wharton's. The metaphor of writing reconfigures Lee as a new kind of pioneer, not as a traveler moving from east to west into the country's past, but rather as a creator, writing from the left margin to the right, projecting herself across the page into her own future. Lee learns a new kind of discipline, the kind that keeps her locked in her chair, listening to hear, and watching to see, where the writing will take her. "In this way I could imagine the future washing to past," she realizes, "not negating it exactly but nonetheless polishing it, wearing down the stones" (p. 291).

In the "Salt Pork" chapter of *Stealing Buddha's Dinner*—the section dedicated to ruminations of the Ingalls family—Nguyen concludes by detailing many fictional heroines who, along with Laura Ingalls, helped alleviate her childhood loneliness and alienation. As a child, she believed that through immersion in fictional worlds, "drawn to what [she] could not have," she might find escape. Young and hungry, she believed that she might model herself on fictional characters and thereby become them. "I could read my way out of Grand Rapids," she explained. Yet as an adult, she has found empowerment and a clear path to selfhood not by imbibing another writer's work but by creating her own. She has, in effect, written her way out. This much is manifestly clear about this talented and

perceptive writer's extraordinarily promising early career.

Selected Bibliography

WORKS OF BICH MINH NGUYEN

FICTION AND MEMOIR

Stealing Buddha's Dinner: A Memoir. New York: Viking Penguin, 2007.

Short Girls. New York: Viking Penguin, 2009.

Pioneer Girl. New York: Viking Penguin, 2014.

NONFICTION

"The Good Immigrant Student." In *Tales Out of School: Contemporary Writers on Their Student Years.* Edited by Susan Richards Shreve and Porter Shreve. Boston: Beacon Press, 2000.

"Toadstools." In *Dream Me Home Safely: Writers on Growing Up in America.* Edited by Susan Richards Shreve. New York: Houghton Mifflin, 2003.

"Family Traditions." FoodFit.com. http://www.foodfit.com/cooking/archive/foodFamily_jun03.asp

"A World Without Measurements." *Gourmet* 64:190 (December 2004).

"The Plum's Eye." In *Bread, Body, Spirit: Finding the Sacred in Food.* Edited by Alice Peck. Woodstock, Vt.: SkyLight Paths, 2008.

"Finding Allies in Books." *eJournal USA* 14, no. 2:34 (February 2009). (Bureau of International Information Programs, U.S. Department of State.) http://iipdigital.usembassy.gov/media/pdf/ejs/0209.pdf

"Laverne and Shirley Days." In *An Angle of Vision: Women Writers on Their Poor and Working-Class Roots.* Edited by Lorraine López. Ann Arbor: University of Michigan Press, 2009.

"Goodbye to My Twinkie Days." *New York Times,* November 16, 2012. http://www.nytimes.com/2012/11/17/opinion/goodbye-to-my-twinkie-days.html

AS EDITOR

The Contemporary American Short Story. With Porter Shreve. New York: Pearson Longman, 2003.

Contemporary Creative Nonfiction: I & Eye. With Porter Shreve. New York: Pearson Longman, 2004.

30/30: Thirty American Stories from the Last Thirty Years. With Porter Shreve. New York: Pearson Longman, 2005.

CRITICAL STUDIES

August, Timothy K. "The Contradictions in Culinary Collaboration: Vietnamese American Bodies in *Top Chef* and *Stealing Buddha's Dinner.*" *MELUS* 37, no. 3:97–115 (2012).

Dusselier, Jane. "Understandings of Food as Culture." *Environmental History* 14, no. 2:331–338 (April 2009).

Ha, Quan Manh. "Thematic Shifts in Contemporary Vietnamese American Novels." *Ethnic Studies Review* 33, no. 2:36–81 (winter 2010).

Martín-Lucas, Belén. "Burning Down the Little House on the Prairie: Asian Pioneers in Contemporary North America." *Atlantis* 33, no. 2:27–41 (2011).

Tuon, Bunkong. "'An Outsider with Inside Information:' The 1.5 Generation in Lan Cao's *Monkey Bridge.*" *Postcolonial Text* 7, no. 1:1–16 (2012).

Xu, Wenying. "A Psychoanalytical Approach to Bich Minh Nguyen's *Stealing Buddha's Dinner.*" *Asian American Literature: Discourses & Pedagogies* 2:8–21 (2011).

REVIEWS

Fong-Torres, Ben. "Hungry Heart." *New York Times Book Review,* February 4, 2007, p. 11. (Review of *Stealing Buddha's Dinner.*)

Hagestadt, Emma. "*Short Girls,* by Bich Minh Nguyen." *Independent,* September 25, 2009. http://www.independent.co.uk/arts-entertainment/books/reviews/short-girls-by-bich-minh-nguyen-1792704.html

Hong, Terry. "*Pioneer Girl* by Bich Minh Nguyen." Book Dragon, Smithsonian Asian Pacific American Center, 2014. http://smithsonianapa.org/bookdragon/pioneer-girl-by-bich-minh-nguyen

Kehe, Marjorie. "Oh, How She Longed for SpaghettiOs!" *Christian Science Monitor,* February 6, 2007. (Review of *Stealing Buddha's Dinner.*) http://www.csmonitor.com/2007/0206/p15s01-bogn.html

Kempf, Andrea. "*Short Girls.*" *Library Journal* 134, no. 12:86–92 (2009).

Marra, Anthony. "*Pioneer Girl.*" *SFGate,* February 7, 2014. http://www.sfgate.com/books/article/Pioneer-Girl-by-Bich-Minh-Nguyen-5215355.php

Memmott, Carol. "An Asian Child Finds America in 'Dinner.'" *USA Today,* February 8, 2007, p. 5D.

Szilagyi, Anca. "*Pioneer Girl.*" *Ploughshares,* February 5, 2014. http://blog.pshares.org/index.php/pioneer-girl/

Tran, Sharon. "*Pioneer Girl: A Novel.* By Bich Minh Nguyen." *Amerasia Journal* 40, no. 1:116–118 (2014).

Winik, Marion. "*Short Girls.*" *Los Angeles Times,* July 24, 2009. http://articles.latimes.com/2009/jul/24/entertainment/et-book24

INTERVIEWS/BROADCAST

Davidson, Karin C. "Points of Connection: A Conversation

with Bich Minh Nguyen." http://www.karincdavidson .com/2014/04/points-of-connection-conversation-with .html

Kalb, Deborah. "Q&A with Writer Bich Minh Nguyen." *Haunting Legacy*, August 1, 2012. http://www .hauntinglegacy.com/qas-with-experts/2012/8/1/qa-with -writer-bich-minh-nguyen.html

————. "Q&A with Author Bich Minh Nguyen." Book Q&As with Deborah Kalb, May 10, 2014. http:// deborahkalbbooks.blogspot.com/2014/05/q-with-author -bich-minh-nguyen.html

Malandrinos, Cheryl C. "Q&A with Bich Minh Nguyen, Author of *Pioneer Girl*." *Busy Moms Daily,* March 5, 2014. http://www.thebusymomsdaily.com/2014/03/q-with -bich-minh-nguyen-author-of.html

Mudge, Alden. "Bich Minh Nguyen: From Vietnam to Wilder's Little House." *Book Page*, February 2014. http:// bookpage.com/interviews/16071-bich-minh-nguyen# .VFZMxUugn1q

"Thanksgiving About Gathering of Traditions, Essayist Says." Transcript, *PBS News Hour*, November 23, 2006. http://www.pbs.org/newshour/bb/social_issues-july-dec06 -thanksgiving_11-23/

OTHER SOURCES

Ellison, Ralph. *Invisible Man*. New York: Vintage, 1980.

Wharton, Edith. *A Backward Glance*. New York: Simon & Schuster, 1998.

GEORGE OPPEN

(1908—1984)

Anton Vander Zee

No SINGLE SET of lines can fully capture the evolving complexities and intensities of a remarkable poetic career. But the opening lines of George Oppen's Pulitzer Prize–winning book of poems *Of Being Numerous* (1968) come very close. "There are things / We live among 'and to see them / Is to know ourselves.'" (*New Collected Poems [NCP]*, p. 163). These lines arrive as both an admonition and a challenge to readers. Published in the wake of John F. Kennedy's assassination and in the midst of the Vietnam War, the poem that unfolds from these opening lines is full of things that Oppen thought his mid-1960s audience must see, even if they are reluctant to do so. The poet draws attention to "A plume of smoke," for example, "visible at a distance / In which people burn" (p. 173). This act of seeing quickly merges with an uncompromising sense of the complicity: "If it is true we must do these things," Oppen continues, "We must cut our throats."

Although these charged words about truly *seeing* the things that we live among speak to their wartime context, much of what distinguishes Oppen's poetry in general resides in these lines as well: an intense focus on the meaning of existence; a deeply ethical scrutiny of the self in relation to other; and the promise of some deepening knowledge, at once mysteriously charged and utterly matter-of-fact. Indeed, it is a hallmark of Oppen's poetry that he can seem most profound when expressing himself in the simplest terms.

Oppen's dedication to clarity and sincerity, to conviction and truth—these are totemic words in his poetic imagination—might at times have seemed almost naive in the era following World War II. It can certainly seem so today. Oppen's readers now are familiar with a postmodern

poetry that traffics in knowing irony and skepticism, having moved beyond such illusory hopes for truth or knowledge. Yet, for reasons that are quite clear once one grasps the shape of Oppen's career and the constellating moments of conviction that comprise it, poets and critics alike tend to accept his strong and grounded ethical stance and his commitment to truth on its own terms: so earnestly it is expressed in his poetry, and so authentically it is reflected in his life.

FROM MODERN TO CONTEMPORARY

Before considering Oppen's extraordinary life work and life, it is important to note more broadly the unique position he occupies in relation to both modern and contemporary poetry. Critics and anthologists alike tend to divide twentieth-century poetry neatly between poetry before and after World War II. On the one side, one finds the modernist greats such Robert Frost, Wallace Stevens, Marianne Moore, Ezra Pound, T. S. Eliot, Jean Toomer, William Carlos Williams, and Hart Crane. On the other, one finds the emerging contemporary voices that filled out Donald Allen's landmark *New American Poetry* (1960) anthology—poets such as Allen Ginsberg, Robert Creeley, Robert Duncan, Frank O'Hara, John Ashbery, Denise Levertov, Amiri Baraka, and Barbara Guest. The modernist poets, the story goes, were heavily invested in the restorative power of form and myth. They tended toward an achieved impersonality in their poetry while maintaining a strong ambition for a totalizing, coherent poetic vision that might adequately contain the world, if not make it new. Postmodern poets, however, were skeptical of any such totalizing vision and tended, instead, toward a free verse that would more closely reflect and scrutinize the intimate rhythms of life and mind.

It is a clarifying, if reductive, story—and it is not a story in which Oppen fits in any neat or sensible way. Figures that fit uneasily within received critical narratives often reveal overlooked intensities in the poetic mainstream. They therefore help one tell new stories about how and why poetry might matter beyond convenient accounts of schools and movements, of influence and inheritance. Oppen is certainly one such figure.

Though he would achieve poetic success much later in life after earning the Pulitzer Prize in 1969 for his fourth collection, *Of Being Numerous*, Oppen's literary career had its moorings in the 1930s, when he emerged as a promising young modernist upstart. By the time he published his first book, *Discrete Series,* in 1934 at the age of twenty-six, he had already brought out key works by Ezra Pound, William Carlos Williams, and Louis Zukofsky through two different publishing ventures—one based in France, one in the United States. He visited Pound in Italy and the sculptor Constantine Brancusi in Paris. A portfolio of his poems had appeared in a special 1931 issue of *Poetry Magazine* dedicated to the so-called objectivist school, which appeared to be a calculated response to, and extension of, the imagist movement of early modernism. He published additional poems in *Poetry* in 1932 and was anthologized in Pound's *Active Anthology* in 1933. Furthermore, his first book was introduced by Pound himself and reviewed generously by Williams, offering an enviable modernist pedigree. Given Oppen's accelerated entry into the modernist mainstream, he would seem to have quickly assumed the role of a cosmopolitan figure in touch with the transnational literary currents of the day.

Oppen, however, could not square his early poetic success with the political realities of the times. After *Discrete Series*, Oppen did not publish another book until 1962, a period of silence without parallel in American poetry. Behind this silence lay many pressing political concerns and personal matters. Oppen and his wife, Mary, joined the Communist Party in 1935 and were heavily involved in community organizing and advocacy. The couple later had a daughter, Linda, and Oppen departed to fight in World War II shortly thereafter, unable to remain on the sidelines in light of the clear Fascist threat. After the war, despite Oppen's heroic service in the European theater, where he was gravely injured, the Oppens were forced into political exile in light of the Smith Act and the aggressive prosecutions and inquisitions of the House Un-American Activities Committee. They remained in Mexico for nearly a decade, raising their daughter and accomplishing the necessary work of survival among the expatriate community. Understandably, when Oppen returned to America and to the poetry scene in the late 1950s, he felt as though he was beginning again.

Oppen, then, is one of the rare figures in twentieth-century poetry who, despite arriving late to the formative moments of both modern and contemporary poetry, still casts a profound shadow over both. Indeed, Oppen's early poetry offers a powerful critique of the modernism that seemed to inspire it, just as his later poetry admonishes, variously, the cult of personality, the mannerism, the lyric reserve, and the inward confessional turn that dominated so much postwar poetry. After making a strong initial impression on the modernist literary scene, Oppen quickly assumed a role as a sort of "elder statesmen," as Michael Davidson notes in the introduction to the *New Collected Poems* (2002), for the host of young poets emerging in the decades after World War II (p. xxii).

THE LONG FOREGROUND: SUCCESS, SILENCE, AND EXILE

George Oppen was born in 1908 into an upper-class Jewish family in New Rochelle, New York, an upbringing of financial privilege against which he would define himself for the rest of his life. His father, George Oppenheimer, was a wealthy diamond merchant who in 1927 changed the family name to Oppen. Alongside the material comforts of these early years, however, was a deep sense of personal tragedy. Oppen's mother, Elsie Rothfeld Oppenheimer, killed herself when he was just four years old, and the record of his reflection on these years suggest a strained,

abusive relationship with the woman who became his father's second wife, Seville Shainwald. This led to a turbulent high school career at Warren Military Academy that was cut short when Oppen was behind the wheel in a fatal car accident, resulting in his expulsion (he had been suspected of drinking). After traveling through Europe, Oppen returned to take his high school diploma and, almost on a whim, accompanied a friend to attend what is now Oregon State University at Corvallis.

There, Oppen experienced two momentous and nearly simultaneous events that impacted his future in both life and letters: a poetry instructor named Jack Lyons introduced him both to Mary Colby, with whom he would share a most intimate and remarkable married life, and to modern poetry, via Conrad Aiken's anthology *Modern American Poets* (1922). Like his high school career, however, Oppen's time in higher education would end prematurely—and abruptly. But while his high school years ended tragically after years of personal and psychological hardship, his college career ended almost before it started in a pact of love that would illuminate his life until the end.

In Mary Oppen's autobiography, *Meaning a Life* (1978), she describes this coincidence of love and letters that they both felt so profoundly: "I found George Oppen and poetry at one moment," she writes (p. 63). After Lyons introduced the two, Oppen asked Mary out. "He came for me in his roommate's Model T Ford," Mary recalls, "and we drove out into the country, sat and talked, made love, and talked until morning" (p. 61). A lake of fog descended on the field where they had camped, a moment that would attain an iconic quality of mystery and wonder in Oppen's poetry. Nearly forty years later, in a poem called "The Forms of Love" from *This in Which* (1965), Oppen would dramatize this formative moment. As they talked away the evening hours, the car perched on a hill, a lake seemed magically to emerge below them as the moon rose. The car in which they camped became "ancient" as they emerged into a strange new world. By the poem's end, their "heads / Ringing under the stars" (*NCP*, p. 106), Mary

and Oppen descended into a thick patch of illuminated fog, a place of surreal mystery and ephemeral beauty that nevertheless marked the entrance to their very real and enduring love.

That Oppen returns to this formative moment forty years later speaks to the intensity of his relationship with Mary, who was a near constant presence both in his poetry and as an interlocutor in so many of his later interviews (she is nearly always present and contributing, often completing Oppen's own sentences). It is Mary's love—and, by extension, the domestic space of home and fatherhood—that gives Oppen's poetry, which can so often seem spare and ascetic, a sustaining softness. It also offers a grounding model for the kind of human connection that would be such a crucial part of Oppen's broader political vision.

Oppen and Mary's illicit night out resulted in Mary's expulsion and George's suspension. Both chose to leave school rather than appeal the charges despite the unevenness of the punishment; they had, after all, found each other. By the next summer, they were living together in San Francisco, and by summer's end they had scrapped more sensible plans—nursing training for Mary, matriculation at Berkeley for George—and abandoned relative stability and family support for deeper ties to the American landscape. Mary, in her memoir, describes their search in a way that shows how closely wed art and life were for the two: "We were in search of an esthetic within which to live," she writes, "and we were looking for it in our own American roots, in our own country" (p. 68). They went to seek the poetry that was living now, and the life that might give rise to that poetry. "Hitchhiking became more than a flight from a powerful family," she continues. "Our discoveries themselves became an esthetic and a disclosure" (p. 68).

Their travels took them to Texas, where they married, and then back to San Francisco, where tensions with family emerged once more. In 1928—Oppen was just twenty, and Mary slightly younger—they decided to make their way east, hitchhiking once again, this time as far as Detroit, where they purchased a small sailboat and charted a path toward New York City. There they

mingled with key modernist figures and formed lasting connections with two in particular who would figure prominently in George's poetic development—Louis Zukofsky and Charles Reznikoff. Still unsettled, by 1929 they were back in San Francisco and then off to Europe. Settling in the south of France, they launched a more formal literary venture, starting the small press To Publishers, which published important work by major modernist figures such as William Carlos Williams and Ezra Pound as well as Louis Zukofsky's *An Objectivist's Anthology* (1932), which featured early work from Oppen. As noted above, they also visited Pound in Rappalo, Italy, where they glimpsed warily the aesthetic and political disposition that would turn sharply toward fascism and anti-Semitism as World War II approached. By 1933 the couple had moved back to New York and launched the Objectivist Press, which continued to bring out key works by modernist poets, and which would also publish Oppen's first book, *Discrete Series*, in 1934.

Oppen's first book was deeply informed by the general atmosphere of the 1930s: economic collapse, widespread suffering, and the surging force of political organization on the Left. The book's unassuming title suggests its governing organizational strategies, strategies that also reflect Oppen's emerging politics. In a 1968 interview with the literary critic L. S. Dembo, Oppen explains that "discrete series" refers to a "phrase in mathematics. A pure mathematical series would be one in which each term is derived from the preceding term by a rule. A discrete series is a series of terms each of which is empirically derived, each of which is empirically true" (*Speaking with George Oppen [SWGO]*, p. 10). A specific kind of lyric series, the serial poem suggests a movement motivated not by some overarching structure, but by the negotiation between—and often chance encounter with—distinct particulars. Put simply, the serial poem, as Oppen deployed it, allowed him formally to dramatize the relationship between the one and the many, between part and whole, without subsuming one into the other. William Carlos Williams, in his review of the book, offers his own gloss on the title that captures the key con-

nection between poetic experiment and literal experience: "I feel that he is justified in so using the term," Williams writes. "It has something of the implications about it of work in a laboratory when one is following what he believes to be a profitable lead along some one line of possible investigation" (Hatlan, p. 268).

These poetic experiments, for Oppen, were also experiential, and many of the poems in *Discrete Series* track the poem's speaker as he moves through urban space, settling now upon a man selling postcards, now a parked car, now a ship's mast, now the inside of an elevator. Such poems seek to give a glimpse into the world, but their idiosyncratic syntax blocks easy access to that world, which is very much the point: to make it new often entailed making it strange. In the poem that places us inside an elevator, for example, the initial image—"White. From the / Under arm of T // The red globe"—resists any easy association with the poem's place, focusing initially not on the mode of locomotion itself, but on the buttons and their embellishments, what Oppen later in the poem calls the "shiny fixed / Alternatives" that constrain one's action in this place (*NCP*, p. 6).

In such poems, we are not quite sure what we are looking at, nor how we are supposed to feel about it. The reference in this poem might have been more familiar to a reader in the early 1930s, describing, as it does, the controls in an elevator of that era. But even then, the poem's intense focus on the particular speaks to a certain difficulty of relating the part to the whole. This difficulty has less to do with literary or cultural posturing than it does with a certain difficulty of experience itself. In this poem's case, the fine period detail ironically reflects what seem to be shiny alternatives of economic class: you are either going up or going down. As with life itself, where some hoped-for ascent is balanced against the certainties of death, the economic choice seems "fixed" in advance.

Another poem—one of the many poems in *Discrete Series* that serve as aesthetic self-reflections—depicts, with only slightly less obscurity, a car, "closed in glass... / Unapplied and empty: A thing among others" (*NCP*, p. 13). Even as the

poem is about a certain exclusive waste and luxury as the car sits closed, vacant, "unapplied," it also speaks to a certain detachment from experience. The car, like so many workers, is just one thing among others, and the poem's syntactic difficulty and vague references at times force readers' own sense of detachment as they struggle to relate and connect the poem's particular references. The poem, then, is a comment on the luxurious safety from which one might view the urban environment, but also a cautionary comment on the luxurious safety of poetry itself—its gaze safely ensconced in its own "unapplied and empty" gestures safely positioned behind glass.

In poems such as these, one can see the relationship of Oppen's early work to the "objectivism" with which it was initially aligned. Objectivism was never intended to name a coherent poetic movement or even to define a set of shared poetic strategies. Instead, Louis Zukofsky invented the moniker under some pressure from the editor of *Poetry*. In an essay accompanying the special issue, Zukofsy broadly positions this cohort of poets in relation to the imagists that preceded them: "Writing occurs which is the detail, not mirage, of seeing," he writes, "of thinking with things as they exist, and of directing them along a line of melody" (p. 273). While Oppen's poems are not always melodious—indeed, their jarring syntax often resists the easy accommodations of melody—the emphasis on detail, direction, and thinking with things as they exist captures something crucial about Oppen's poetry, both at this early stage and throughout his career. In "The Mind's Own Place," Oppen's most significant (and one of his very few) prose publications, Oppen writes that "modern American poetry begins with the determination to find the image, the thing encountered, the things seen each day whose meaning has become the meaning and the color of our lives. Verse, which had become a rhetoric of exaggeration, of inflation, was to the modernist a skill of accuracy, of precision, a test of truth" (*Selected Prose*, p. 30). That insight has more to do with his work and that of his fellow objectivists than it does with modernism proper, a movement that he would as often

define himself *against*, whether explicitly or implicitly.

Indeed, Oppen also sought to distinguish his poetic project from the insular sentimentalism into which imagism had devolved. "The weakness of Imagism," Oppen writes in his daybooks, is that "a man writes of the moon rising over a pier who knows nothing about piers and is disregarding all that he knows about the moon" (*Selected Prose*, p. 82). Oppen, in this early work, sought something less contrived, something simpler: to make knowledge of accrued experience, and to make poems of that accrued knowledge. His early poems are objects of experience and perception, loosely bound "moments of conviction," as he would later describe them (*SWGO,* p. 10).

Oppen's primary concern in his early poetry was not unlike the one Whitman announces in the first inscription poem to the Deathbed edition of *Leaves of Grass*. What does it mean to sing the self, a single separate person, yet also utter what Whitman famously called the word "democratic," the word of the people? In *Discrete Series,* this tension between the singular self and the multiplying others is consistently modeled on the level of both form and content. And while Oppen would later return with confidence, or at least considered conviction, to utter something like Whitman's democratic word, it was his investment in the people, in the suffering of those myriad others, that led to a poetic silence that would last nearly twenty-six years.

The charged confluence of poetry and politics that informed Oppen's first literary efforts buckled under the weight of the times. Oppen no longer found in poetry a viable response to the unfolding crisis of the Depression, and in 1935 he and Mary joined the Communist Party. Compelled by Socialist ideals and the Marxist view of history, the couple devoted themselves to work as community activists and organizers, experiencing a political awakening that seemed a world apart from the poetry scene they had joined so eagerly.

Why politics instead of poetry? Why did Oppen see the two as such distinct endeavors? In his 1968 interview with Dembo, Oppen reflects

on the necessity of choosing political engagement. Faced with millions of families visibly suffering on the streets, Oppen describes how, for people like himself and Mary who had precisely *chosen* a certain class existence, turning their back on privilege, political engagement and fellow-feeling with the masses was the most obvious choice. And at this time for Oppen, poetry and political engagement were simply not compatible: "If you decide to do something politically, you do something that has political efficacy," he reasoned. "And if you decide to write poetry, then you write poetry, not something that you hope, or deceive yourself into believing, can save people who are suffering" (*SWGO*, p. 20). But even as the Depression caused Oppen to abandon poetry as an act of political conscience, there were other more personal factors as well: "there were some things I had to live through," Oppen continues, "some things I had to think my way through, some things I had to try out—and it was more than politics, really; it was the whole experience of working in factories, of having a child, and so on."

The reasons for Oppen's literary silence, then, are complex. Thus it makes some sense that Oppen, when asked about his long departure from the literary world, most often gave a rather curt answer—one supplied for him by the conservative critic Hugh Kenner during one such conversation. Kenner, who perhaps did not want to hear about the leftist backdrop to Oppen's charged choice, interrupted the poet mid-story: "In brief, it took twenty-five years to write the next poem" (*SWGO*, p. 20). Oppen appreciated the shorthand explanation and would trot this line out in nearly every interview he gave for the rest of his life.

As the Depression deepened, Oppen and Mary's choice to involve themselves more directly in social and political matters might seem an abandonment of poetry and of the aesthetic more generally. Yet in retrospect, Oppen would frame even this abandonment of his literary ambitions precisely as a poetic endeavor, not unlike how Mary frames their early travels in which they sought an "esthetic" in which to live. "And when the crisis occurred," Oppen explains in an interview later in life, "we knew we didn't know what the world was and we knew we had to find out so it was a poetic exploration at the same time that it was an action of conscience, of feeling that one was worth something or other" (*SWGO*, p. 218). For Oppen, seeking knowledge—not propositional knowledge or knowledge of mere facts, but knowledge of deeper truths rooted in personal and communal experience—was a fundamentally poetic endeavor. Poetry, for Oppen, was a preconceptual activity, an activity that must precede argument and concrete knowledge. It represents an openness to experience and ideas: a "making," to recall the roots of the Greek *poiesis*, in the deepest sense. The prominent Oppen critic Peter Nicholls, in his major study *George Oppen and the Fate of Modernism* (2007), cites a passage from Oppen's papers that aptly captures this sense of poetry: "For me," Oppen writes, "the writing of the poem is the process of finding out what I mean, discovering what I mean" (p. 39). Thus, although Kenner's interpretation of Oppen's silence is a bit reductive, obscuring, as it does, the political reasons behind the silence, it does aptly frame the choice as an extended aesthetic pause—a sort of epic caesura allowing space for experience and reflection.

Just as Oppen's literary record thins out during this period to the point of vanishing, so too does the biographical record. With few extant letters and notebooks, what one knows of this time must be gleaned from Oppen's later letters and interviews that briefly address this period; from Mary Oppen's autobiography *Meaning a Life*; and from the FBI files kept on the Oppens for twenty-five years—a record that Rachel Blau DuPlessis makes excellent use of in her introduction to the *Selected Letters* (1990).

Concurrently with joining the Communist Party in 1935, the Oppens joined the Workers Alliance of America (WAA). This latter group sought to create a unified political platform for the masses of unemployed. While the organization counted its members in the millions, its organization was driven by local engagements, with neighborhoods divided into separate councils. Working on this level, the Oppens were

directly engaged in the struggles of their neighbors. As a result of their organizational work, the Oppens were arrested on multiple occasions. With the birth of their daughter, Linda, in 1940 and the looming crisis of World War II—the signing of the Nazi-Soviet Pact caused them to doubt their commitment to the Communist Party—Oppen increasingly felt called to engage this global conflict. In 1942 Oppen was exempted from military service not due to his age—he still qualified in that regard—but because he had work at Grumman Aircraft in Long Island. As Oppen was aware, his choice to leave that job and move to Detroit to take another job amounted to a direct enlistment into the U.S. Army. Oppen's military service took him to Europe, where he was engaged in some of the key battles of World War II, including the Battle of the Bulge. Just weeks before the war ended, Oppen was badly wounded after taking cover in a foxhole under heavy bombardment. All of his companions died in the attack, and Oppen was helplessly pinned under their weight in addition to shrapnel. This experience of horror and survival would haunt him for his remaining decades. Indeed, the foxhole and the blasted landscape of the war-torn front became, for Oppen, indelible images of ruin, apocalypse, and a rending of the human fabric, images that would challenge and temper his future attempts to ground his poetics in enduring faith in the human community.

Having recovered from his injuries, Oppen returned from the war with a Purple Heart, among other commendations. The Oppens moved shortly after his return to Redondo Beach, California, where Oppen took on various construction and carpentry jobs. Though they technically remained members of the Communist Party, the Oppens had no close ties with the organization or its leadership at this time. This didn't stop the harassment by authorities in the midst of the increasingly hostile environment of the Second Red Scare. Authorities had launched a witch hunt for subversives with connections to radical politics; they wanted names. In 1950, unwilling to name names, and fearing backlash and possible arrest due to their past political affiliations from the thirties, the Oppens decided to exile

themselves in Mexico. They made this choice to protect those with whom they worked, but also to protect their young daughter, fearing that they could be taken away from her.

The Oppens remained in Mexico for eight years. As an American, Oppen was barred from undertaking any kind of manual labor, so the family found its options restricted to a life of bourgeois ease among the expatriate crowd. Thus the Oppens were forced to live a life they had abandoned in a place in which they had no inclination to remain. Given the heavy scrutiny of their leftist affiliations, political conversation, much less action of any kind, was simply impossible. And even as foreigners, they were still subject to frequent harassment and suspicion on behalf of the Mexican government as well as the CIA and FBI. Their years in exile were marked by stress, depression, and struggle.

Finally in 1958—Oppen was then fifty years old, Linda just entering college—the Oppens were able to renew their passports; after visiting the states and returning for brief periods to Mexico, the Oppens moved back to the United States permanently in 1960. They settled once more in New York—Brooklyn, to be more precise, not far from Louis Zukofsky, their old colleague from their early publishing ventures. This urban location—along with the vast experiences Oppen had accrued during his long silence—would form the backdrop of his next three books. Once back in the States, Oppen worked tirelessly to reenter the literary world, resuming friendships with his fellow objectivist poets from the 1930s, contacting editors of key literary journals and presses, and working diligently on what would be his first collection since *Discrete Series* in 1934.

A RETURN TO POETRY: THE MATERIALS, THIS IN WHICH, *AND* OF BEING NUMEROUS

Oppen had made a deliberate and forward-looking decision to abandon his literary efforts in the mid-1930s. His return to writing after a long absence was marked by a similar clarity of purpose and vision. "I knew that there would be three books when I started *The Materials*," he

explains in an interview from the early 1970s, even noting a "vague outline" for how he hoped to proceed (*SWGO*, p. 39).

The first book, *The Materials* (1962), would think through what he called his noumenalism, which we see in this book's intense phenomenological focus on humankind's relationship to the physical universe, and how an awareness of the self is inextricably tied to an often difficult recognition of arbitrary, intractable, and sometimes violent forces. Oppen saw the second book, *This in Which* (1965), as drawing these disparate materials into a more coherent vision, one that makes room for a sense of wonder—even sublime wonder. The final book in his projected three-book series—*Of Being Numerous* (1968)—is Oppen's best known and justly considered his masterpiece. There, the concerns with the things of the world and history, along with his finely tuned capacity for wonder, find a firmer middle ground in the social. The book, as Oppen put it, would lay out "the fact that one does live historically ... that one must live in some relation to history" (*SWGO*, p. 39). To live historically, for Oppen, is not to live in the past, but to live one's life in conscious connection with an unfolding social history—the story of the people—and to see one's life as inextricably bound to those of others, for better or worse. What Oppen would often call the necessary concept of humanity, then, became a necessary and grounding force in his work and life.

This clear shift of attention from an alien and often violent world in *The Materials*, to a sense of wonder in relation to nature in *This in Which*, and finally to an accommodation with the social fact of existence in *Of Being Numerous*, provides a useful, though obviously reductive, shorthand for understanding this important middle period of Oppen's career.

Oppen would often speak of his second book, *The Materials*—the first after that momentous silence—in matter-of-fact terms. In a 1970 interview Oppen describes the book as "just gathering again the way to begin this" (*SWGO*, p. 39). That simplicity masks two guiding inquiries that motivate this book and suggest the contours of his evolving literary career: the first

inquiry is aesthetic, and hinges on the compatibility of poetry and politics, or art and life; the second inquiry is existential, and hinges on the meaning of human existence more generally. If the first inquiry asks what it means authentically to make art, given the political crises of the times, the second asks what it means *to be* at all.

Frequently in *The Materials*, ideals of family and love form a protective reserve that frame these two guiding inquiries: these ideals model his sense of broader human interconnection, and also serve as a barrier from harsher existential realities. The first poem he wrote after his long silence—"Blood from the Stone"—embodies these inter-animating tendencies. The poem consists of four numbered sections, a formal echo of the loosely linked lyric series that Oppen had also deployed in *Discrete Series*. The first section opens upon a domestic interior, his wife returning home with a bundle of groceries, catching his eye as she stands framed by the entryway. The familiar simplicity of this initial scene leads, as often happens in Oppen's poetry, to a more momentous realization: "Everything I am is / Us. Come home" (*NCP*, p. 52). This is what one might call a threshold poem in the broad, generic sense: think of Walt Whitman's "There Was a Child Went Forth," or other poems pitched between inside and outside, safety and risk. But Oppen's threshold poem unfolds on a much smaller, domestic scale, and it is less a poem of setting out than of returning—returning home to the United States after nearly a decade in exile, returning to writing, returning to a literary community. Oppen captures the momentousness of that return in a way that invites the reader to see the domestic sphere as an essential link to, and metaphor for, broader ideals of community.

Section 2 of the poem shifts radically from the domestic interior and its easy ethic of connection to memories of the past and the political struggles of the 1930s, memories that appear as a "spectre" as Oppen struggles to grasp the "inexplicable crowds" (*NCP*, p. 52). After the clear homecoming in section 1, section 2 seems more difficult to parse. Why are the thirties—which invite the poet to imagine the "spectre" of these "inexplicable" crowds—so obscure and inacces-

sible? And to whom? Oppen, here, reflects on how the passing of time causes historical particulars to become fuzzy—a process in which he is perhaps also complicit. In response to historical forgetfulness, which is a forgetfulness of the social itself, Oppen pushes against the modernist aesthetic of invention—one senses Pound's dictum, make it new, echoing in the background—with an ethic of answerability, of response to crisis. After asking himself and the reader to square belief and action, to square one's sense of how the world *might* be with the way it is, Oppen responds by presenting what we might call an ethic of answerability:

Not invent—just answer—all
That verse attempts.

The ethic of love that drives the first poem in this series, then, is harnessed here to drive a broader social cohesion, even if that cohesion is cast in the form of a question: "That we can somehow add each to each other?", the section concludes: "Still our lives" (*NCP*, p. 52)

The ethic of "answerability" and response requires an understanding of history that seeks to address the "inexplicable," and to clarify the "spectral," by drawing a line of connection between past and present. Driving this effort is the simple word "still," which suggests both imagistic clarity (a "still" image), and a continuity or endurance that signals a commitment to ideals of communality. The difference between answering and inventing, then, is the difference between an aesthetic that leads outward toward ethical and communitarian concerns, and one that folds in on itself and its own aesthetic ambitions.

The third section shifts abruptly as well, showing a deepening sense of crisis moving from the Depression to the global conflict of World War II. This section strains against the opening epigraph from Jacques Maritain and its easy equation of personal awareness and human connection: "We wake in the same moment to ourselves and to things" (*NCP*, p. 38). Against this easy identification, Oppen writes that "There is a simple ego in a lyric, / A strange one in war" (*NCP*, p. 53). Deeply rooted in Oppen's war experience, this section looks with horror on the ways in which war reduces bodies to mere matter.

In the final section, the poem shifts from the domestic space of section 1, to dueling visions of historical memories of the Depression and war in the following two sections, to a concluding cosmic scale beyond history. Here, Oppen poses more profound existential questions, where the human life span and all the tragedies that unfold therein are pitched against a cosmic backdrop of space and time. Near the end of the final section, however, Oppen attempts to hold the generational and cosmic registers together at once:

Mother
Nature! because we find the others
Deserted like ourselves and therefore brothers.

(*NCP*, p. 54)

Blood and stone, human time and the planet's time. These pitched oppositions of scope and scale are beautifully held together in that broken exclamation: "Mother / Nature!" How distant these two poles can seem; how difficult to draw blood from the stone, life from nothingness; how dire the need to grasp the significance of the *now* in relation to the vastness of geological time. And yet, how necessary. For Oppen, though we are divided from nature and alienated from the earth's raw materials, we also find compatriots in desertion. And this is the root of Oppen's ethic of community—a community, as Oppen makes clear in the poem's final lines, that must be *chosen*: "So we lived," Oppen concludes. "And chose to live."

The patterns that emerge in "Blood from a Stone" repeat throughout *The Materials*. Reflecting on his own childhood in "Birthplace: New Rochelle," the force of survival is found, once more, in family: "My child, / Not now a child, our child / Not altogether lone in a lone universe" (*NCP*, p. 55). Oppen, here, invests so much in some ethic of hope for the future, as he would also do in "Return" from the same collection: "Mary, we turn to the children … / Wanting so much to have created happiness" (*NCP*, p. 48). Once again, this family ethic leads to a broader sense of connection with the people—what Op-

pen calls "that crowd, the living, that other / Marvel among the mineral" (*NCP*, p. 65).

In "Time of the Missile," encountering the nuclear threat, Oppen returns once more to what threatens the ethic of love, that marvel among the mineral: "My love, my love," he writes, "We are endangered / Totally at last" (*NCP*, p. 70). An openness to the world entails an openness to inhumanity as well—an inhumanity evident in the war, and magnified by the threat of nuclear annihilation. This anxiety hovers over many of the poems in *The Materials*. Such a threat leads to a dangerous inwardness, a falling back within the shelter of the self. "What is the name of that place / We have entered," Oppen asks in "The Crowded Countries of the Bomb." "Despair? Ourselves?" (*NCP*, p. 78). The world has grown utterly precarious, a sense signaled by Oppen's reflection on the cold doctrine of mutually assured destruction, which for him amounts to an assault on human bonds. This realization calls forth a false ethic of inward shelter and self-concern. The poem ends with a dark vision of retreat: "Walking in the shelter, / The young and the old ... // Entering the country that is / impenetrably ours" (*NCP*, p. 78).

In "Survival, Infantry," later in the collection, Oppen returns again to the devastated landscape of war. "Where did all the rocks come from?" Oppen asks. "And the smell of explosives / Iron standing in mud?" (*NCP*, p. 81). Driving this blasted landscape to a postapocalyptic future threatened by nuclear war, Oppen writes in this poem of being "ashamed of our half life and our misery." The nuclear pun could not be clearer.

This in Which, while it shares much with the earlier book, seems, as Peter Nicholls notes, to mark a shift: "The voice is now less anxious," he writes, "the social criticism drier and more assured, and here it is coupled with a determined effort to 'grasp the world' ... in all its actuality" (p. 63). It is that latter aspect that most distinguishes this volume from what comes directly before and after. In *The Materials*, Oppen struggled to locate a sense of affirmation in domestic particulars and in the broader structures of generational continuity; in *This in Which*, Oppen works ambitiously to develop a broader

relationship to the ineffable core of being itself, returning more earnestly and intentionally to that earlier collection's epigraph from Maritain: "We awake in the same moment to ourselves and to things."

No single poem embodies this strategy more fully than "Psalm," one of Oppen's most widely known poems next to his sprawling serial poem "Of Being Numerous."

In "Psalm," the poet attempts to bring the reader face-to-face with ordinary experience—here, an encounter with a deer. But rather than lead the reader to see the familiar as strange, as was his strategy in *Discrete Series*, he invites the reader to grasp the familiar's charged, elemental presence. The poem begins:

> In the small beauty of the forest
> The wild deer bedding down—
> That they are there!
>
> (*NCP*, p. 99)

Though Oppen had attempted a similar epiphanic vision in his "Eclogue," the first poem of *The Materials*, his efforts there seemed ironic, shadowed by "men talking / Near the room's center" plotting "[a]n assault / On the quiet continent" (*NCP*, p. 39). This mysterious seat of power—one isn't sure what these men are discussing or planning, but it seems to have nefarious implications—leads to a bucolic vision through the window where "Flesh and rock and hunger" persist. Amidst what seems a degraded landscape, Oppen's glimpse of some pastoral resurgence cannot fully answer the mysterious machinations of power, the threat of assault, and the bare sense of hunger that shroud the poem in despair. In "Psalm," however, Oppen is able to isolate the charged sense of recognition and emergence—it seems a moment outside, beyond, or perhaps beneath history. The small beauty here is not shrouded by impending historical crises but lifted out of that morass into a realm of rare natural beauty. "That they are there!" he exclaims, urging us to sense the immensity of a scene that seems constructed of the small and diminutive: "the small beauty of the forest," the "eyes / effortless" the "soft lips," the "small teeth," and, of

course, those "small nouns / crying faith" with which the poem concludes.

With this final gesture Oppen connects the same restorative powers of nature to the potential of language itself. Poetry, Oppen suggests in "Five Poems About Poetry," is only of use insofar as it might rescue humanity—rescue us, he writes, "As only the true // Might rescue us, gathered // In the smallest corners // Of man's triumph" (*NCP*, p. 104). *This in Which*, as a collection, emphasizes these smallest corners: as in that scene of deer bedding down, as in a simple and direct language that might bring this familiar scene to life.

This in Which has a core tendency toward metaphysical, sometimes abstract speculation as Oppen engages a certain kind of romantic sublime, but if one takes the collection as a whole, one notices how Oppen often catches himself at times in the excesses of reverie. At the end of a longer serial poem near the conclusion of *This in Which*, for example, Oppen draws the reader out to a certain extremity of sublime feeling. Seeking to define a certain experience of pure presence, of *being-there*, Oppen describes an ideal world offering a clarity of experience and truth: "thought leaped on us in that sea / For in that sea we breathe the open / Miracle // Of place, and speak / If we would rescue / Love to the ice-lit // Upper World, a substantial language / Of clarity, and of respect" (*NCP*, p. 156).

But that upper world of crystalline clarity, so distant from crisis on the ground, is also a siren song portending danger. Oppen was always cautious of his power as a poet. It is fitting, then, that the poems that conclude *This in Which* seem to beat a path away from these "northerly" abstractions of the "ice-lit / Upper world" as they realize that any substantial language must be found much closer to everyday experience rather then natural reveries. The final poem in the collection, "World, World—," speaks directly to the dangers of a false "northerly" vision: "Failure, worse failure, nothing seen / From prominence, / Too much seen in the ditch." The northerly vantage obscures real vision, however damaged and damaging. Quoting that earlier poem, Oppen writes that "'Thought leaps on us' because we

are here. That is the fact of the matter." Those moments of intense reverie, he notes, are too often taken as an inward escape, a false shelter. The poem turns, in the end, to a sense of self once more oriented toward the social: not only "the act of being," but the "act of being / More than oneself" (*NCP*, p. 159). The existential drive to grasp "being" is grounded once more in the social—a grounding that would deeply inform Oppen's next book.

Oppen's reputation as a poet rests largely on his accomplishment in *Of Being Numerous*—particularly in the eponymous title poem of that collection. Oppen's great serial poem suggestively collates the social and existential anxieties that persisted in his earlier work, as well as its small triumphs of vision and love that might redress those anxieties. In this poem, he revels in a sense of the ordinary that is both beneath and yet above art: "I too am in love down there with the streets," he writes. "To talk of the house and the neighborhood and the docks // And it is not 'art'" (*NCP*, p. 169). He rails against war and power: "It is the air of atrocity, / An event as ordinary / As a President. // A plume of smoke, visible at a distance, / In which people burn" (*NCP*, p. 173). And he turns to love as a matter of final importance: "Not truth but each other // The bright bright skin, her hands wavering / In her incredible need // Which is ours, which is ourselves" (*NCP*, pp. 183–184). And yet beneath these resonant intensities, the poem's energies are directed clearly toward a more muted social ethic that in many ways speaks for itself.

Oppen's sense of communion with humanity is precisely not ecstatic, and it is not always particularly inspiring; it is simply necessary. When asked in a 1973 interview to talk about how Whitman's more ecstatic and emphatic sense of union with others might relate to his own, Oppen admits that "[*Of Being Numerous*] didn't come out entirely optimistically on those grounds. What I was saying there is that we're absolutely dependent on some concept of a thing called 'humanity' in which we participate, that we cannot really live without it. I wasn't saying that because I think it's a good moral. I was saying it because it seems true" (*SWGO*, p. 50). This

response captures something that critics rarely say about Oppen: that his masterpiece "Of Being Numerous" is not a confident or final statement on that ethic of connection, but a finely tempered, attenuated, and cautious one.

Along these lines, Oppen famously ends his poem with an excerpt from a letter Whitman wrote to his mother in which the bard meditates on the newly installed statue atop the Capitol Building: "The capital grows upon one in time," Whitman writes in the excerpt, "especially as they have got the great figure on top of it now, and you can see it very well.... The sun when it is nearly down shines on the headpiece and it dazzles and glistens like a big star: it looks quite"—and here, Oppen breaks the prose paragraph, suspending the final word on its own line a few hard breaks below—"curious …" (*NCP*, p. 188).

This ending, Oppen notes in an earlier interview, was "partly a joke on Whitman, but also because men are curious, and at the end of a very long poem, I couldn't find anything more positive to say than that" (*SWGO*, p. 12). "Of Being Numerous," then, is not so much a confident statement of interpersonal connection but an honest reflection of how fragile that connection could be. The recognition that emerges near the end of *This in Which* as it cautiously balances transcendent vision and apocalyptic anxiety precipitates this crucial choice in "Of Being Numerous." It is not a natural choice for Oppen. Admitting this difficulty explicitly into the poem, Oppen excerpts words shared with him in correspondence with the poet Rachel Blau DuPlessis, who was trying to help Oppen describe the tenuous position a poet occupies: "'Whether, as the intensity of seeing increases,' she wonders, 'one's distance from Them, the people, does not also increase'" (*NCP*, p. 167). Even as Oppen crafted a poetics of vision that would be sincere and honest, he understands here that the space an artist carves out is necessarily removed, necessarily apart from the crowd. Art risks singularity, risks what he calls "the bright light of shipwreck." But it is precisely that shipwreck that precipitates the poem's grounding ideal in numerousness:

Obsessed, bewildered

By the shipwreck
Of the singular

We have chosen the meaning
of being numerous.

(*NCP*, p. 166)

And it is, precisely, a *choice*.

Thus, Oppen leaves us in this crucial collection with a vision not of singularity but of numerousness; not of clarity but of conflicted curiosity; not of confident knowledge but of careful self-scrutiny; not of ecstatic connection but of simply choosing to be with and among others.

POETIC LATENESS: METAPHYSICS AND MORTALITY FROM SEASCAPE: NEEDLE'S EYE TO PRIMITIVE

Oppen's final collections mark a striking change in his evolving poetics that were in some ways anticipated by his and Mary's relocation in the mid-1960s, after the bulk of *Of Being Numerous* had been written, from Brooklyn to San Francisco, where he would live for the rest of his life. More than a merely geographical shift, this was a move from the polis to the periphery, from the urban center to the edge of the republic. With the move, Oppen's poetry focused increasingly on the concept of the horizon—the horizon of empire, the horizon of life, the horizon of being itself. The poems emerging from this move tend to be more abstract and more philosophical; while earlier work used an honest (albeit idiosyncratic) syntax in the service of clarity, these new poems seem to embody and enact Oppen's admission, in *Of Being Numerous*, that "Words cannot be wholly transparent. And that is the 'heartlessness' of words" (*NCP*, p. 194).

These poems meditate on the sea, on mortality, and, increasingly, on memories of the past and childhood. Oppen's earlier poems had coincided with an investment in existential and continental philosophy—Martin Heidegger and Georg Wilhelm Friedrich Hegel were both key figures for him, as were the works of Simone Weil. The late work, by contrast, returns to more

specifically literary currents, with William Blake figuring prominently—his "Tyger," brightly burning, being a prime example of those small nouns Oppen favored—and also to religious themes, particularly related to his Jewish identity (the Oppens took an extended trip to Israel in these later years, and the experience, though difficult, furnished ample materials for Oppen's late poetry). The new poems abandon punctuation and, eventually, capitalization—cues that would typically help the reader decipher or parse the difficult syntax. This makes the poems feel less familiar, less immediate, and therefore more strange and estranging. To substitute for the more prosaic forms of writerly control that have been stretched to the point of vanishing in the late work, the reader relies on visual cues unique to poetry: generous use of white space, pronounced caesurae, and line breaks that seem, like the sea, to wash over one another offering wave upon wave of mingled meanings.

This resistance to grammars that could be more easily parsed marked, for Oppen, a resistance to the grammatical tyranny of predication. In an interview with Dembo, Oppen clarifies what might seem a strange grammatical hang-up: "I'm really concerned with the substantive," he writes, "with the subject of the sentence, with what we are talking about, and not rushing over the subject-matter in order to make a comment about it. It is still a principle with me, of more than poetry, to notice, to state, to lay down the substantive for its own sake" (*SWGO*, p. 10).

To resist predication, of course, is to resist the basic structures of grammatical sense. But the ultimate goal was not obscurity, but rather clarity: to let the thing speak for itself. In one of his daybook entries, Oppen tries to define this sense of clarity with reference to what he calls the "object" (here "object" should be understood as any substantive): "The OBJECT in the poem: its function is to burst the boundaries of the poem" (*Selected Prose*, p. 214). In many ways, Oppen's late work operates via precisely this logic: the individual words, individual objects, of a poem are framed in such a way that easy sense and predication are held at bay as Oppen seeks to recover the initial power and force of substan-

tives themselves. In that sense, the late works emerge from that shift we witnessed near the end of "Psalm" where Oppen moves from a more familiar tradition of wonder in his recognition of the "small beauty of the forest" and to those "wild deer" to a sense of wonder grounded in language itself that is the primary instrument of this wonder: "The small nouns / Crying faith / In this in which the wild deer / Startle, and stare out" (*NCP*, p. 99). The poem, here, its small nouns, is precisely the thing—the *this in which*.

This is also a primary meaning of objectivism as Oppen understood it. It had less to do with some objective point of view, or some strict observational stance; rather, it meant, as he writes in a letter to Mary Ellen Scott, "to objectify the poem, to make the poem an object. Meant form" (*Selected Letters*, p. 47). While Oppen still remained very much committed to seeing those things we live among, to recall the opening lines of "Of Being Numerous," the emphasis on poetic form in his earlier work was more of a means to an end. In the late work, however, the tortuous grammars are not merely a test of some broader sincerity or social commitment; rather, they can often seem an end in themselves as Oppen seeks the real in the aesthetic itself: "What is seen in the window is 'realism' what is seen in the mirror is beauty," Oppen writes in a daybook entry around the time he composed his final books (*Selected Prose*, p. 221).

One might think that the opposition here would favor the former—a vision of reality over mere beauty. This, as we have seen, is the tendency of Oppen's early work, and the window was a crucial metaphor for outward-looking vision from the very first poem in *Discrete Series,* where Maude Blessingbourne—a literary borrowing from Henry James and a stand-in for Oppen's own emergence from class privilege to political activism—moves to look out the window "'as if to see / what really was going on'" and sees clearly past rain and road toward a vision of "the world, weather-swept, with which one shares the century" (*NCP*, p. 5).

As many critics have noted, Oppen would come to see this as a crucial gesture in his mature poetry. But in the late work this essential gesture,

this ethic of seeing, comes into question. Oppen had already come to second-guess this metaphor near the end of "Of Being Numerous." It seemed to presume a sheltered access to that external view, when one really only sees "the motes / In the air, the dust" that obscure rather than enable vision (*NCP*, p. 186). In this late daybook entry, however, over that typed language about mirrors and windows, Oppen writes in script: "*But beauty does appear to reflect / to shine: to reflect* to shimmer / *the world: to reflect!*" (*Selected Prose*, p. 221). This "shimmer" of beauty, which frees the poet from mere conceptual domination, allows the poet, as he would write in a 1974 letter to Martin Rosenblum, to "[learn] from the poem, his poem: the poem's structure, image, language: he also does not write what he already knows" (*Selected Letters*, p. 285).

In an interview from the winter of 1973, Oppen's interlocutor asks about what distinguishes these new poems, about what has changed in the years since the publication of *Of Being Numerous*. Oppen, at first, demurs: "No … I think the books all led here. I think my life led here. It's about a further time of life. It's about the horizon, the needle's eye, somewhere near as far as one's going to get" (*SWGO*, p. 46). Even as Oppen denies any sharp change, he signals the shift toward metaphysical concerns, toward a contemplation of mortality as he approaches the ultimate horizon of his own life: "The earlier poems dealt with some concentration on the fact of the actual. All of them were about that—the actual as miracle, the common places, the most, 'that which one cannot / Not see,' I wrote, over and over again in the poems." Oppen notes that his newer poems have the same intentional vision, but what comes into view has simply changed: "They seem different," he continues, "because it's a different kind of actualness which seems more lucent, less solid, less chunky" (*SWGO*, p. 46). Whereas Oppen would often discuss his early work through metaphors of physical materials and substance—he would describe shaking a line to make sure nothing jangled, or note his intricate composition process in which words were continually cut and pasted over one another or physically nailed to a wall—

these later works threaten to rise off the page, the syntax breaking off into abstraction and shot through with lucent jolts of sense. This shift in Oppen's poetics, perhaps, achieves what Oppen talks about when he notes that sense of reflective shimmer: the way beauty might capture the real, the thing itself—or at least capture the difficulty of the attempt.

The first poem in Oppen's *Seascape: Needle's Eye* (1972) embodies some of these qualities associated with the late work. And like most of the late poems, it is nearly impossible simply to extract quotes from, so imbricated and uncertain are the connections between words and phrases. The poem, titled "From a Phrase of Simone Weil's and Some Words of Hegel's," seems to regress rather than progress, to move deeper into the mysterious significance of the poem's object rather than outward toward a simpler explanation. We are far from those iconic opening lines from "Of Being Numerous" and their readily available sense. As the poem opens, its tempo carefully paced by white space, Oppen tries to bring the reader to something elemental, something essential: "In back deep the jewel" (*NCP*, p. 211). Seeking that treasure, nature's pride, the poem continually folds back on itself like a wave presenting a series of substantives that comprise a series of repetitions: liquid, pride, birds, beaks, place, glass, water. But to what end? In a sense, the poem dramatizes a search for meaning, for that gleaming treasure which is too often obscured by the ego and its presumptions. Pitched between that elemental treasure and the pride of the living, the poem enacts the foundational struggle of the late work: how to get past the ego and back to language itself, and therefore back to reality, to the thing itself.

In the end, this particular poem's answer to that struggle is to bring the reader to the "shimmer" of beauty that concludes the poem: "glass of the glass sea shadow of water / On the open water no other way / To come here the outer / Limit of the ego." No longer able to dissolve his ego into the populous, into the ideal of numerousness, Oppen undertakes a solitary venture to that horizon, the limit of life and knowledge and sense. The late work struggles with this outer

limit—a limit that threatens ideals of social commitment and continuity while risking a radical openness to interpretation.

If there is a force that works against this dissolution, it is through language and through love. Oppen is most easily understood in these late poems when he imagines language as something solid, something one might grasp:

> so poor the words
> *would with and* take on substantial
> meaning handholds footholds
>
> (*NCP*, p. 220)

And when he does speak with clarity in these late works, the effect is often devastating. "Anniversary Poem," a section from a longer series, begins with ruminations on the abstractions of time and depth as the poem threatens to drift from sense. But life's attachments—here, his life with Mary—so precious, return in the end to give the poem a final, grounding sadness: "We have begun to say good bye / To each other / And cannot say it" (*NCP*, p. 227).

Oppen struggled throughout his career to balance the poetic self against the other, the solitary singer against the crowd, the shipwreck of the singular against the meaning of being numerous. Indeed, this is the generative tension that gives his oeuvre such dynamic tension. If the late work tends toward extreme abstraction at times, if its meaning can be difficult to grasp much less parse grammatically, Oppen maintained, in the end, an absolute commitment to sociality, to the voices and lives of others. Nowhere is this more clear than in the final poem in his final book, *Primitive* (1978). There, Oppen returns to a certain comfort—comfort in memory, comfort in the idea of the continuity of generations as offering a sense of permanence beyond one's life, and comfort in the presence of others. Returning to the themes of his early work, he describes the social and material world he lived through as a "music more powerful / than music," for mere art can only sustain one for so long until, as the poem's conclusion reminds us, "other voices wake / us or we drown" (*NCP*, p. 286).

These lines, in many critical accounts of the poem, are often interpreted with reference to their revision of the final lines of T. S. Eliot's "Love Song of J. Alfred Prufrock," with the subtle substitution of "or" for "and" signaling a shift from a certain antisocial high modernism out of touch with the people to an engaged objectivist politics. This is true enough, but more fundamentally, where "and" obviates choice, "or" demands it. "Or" reminds us that Oppen's work is driven not only by a commitment to those other voices but by a commitment to commitment itself, a commitment to sincerity and truth, and to those moments of conviction, each one a choice, that constitute the broader web of Oppen's evolving poetics.

The choice of being numerous, of being open to other voices, underscores how important it is to attend to the many registers, the many voices, of Oppen's own work—its anxieties and self-examinations, its broad historical and philosophical references, its shifting formal strategies, and, of course, its commitment to those literal other voices that ground Oppen's work from beginning to end.

What Oppen admired about his contemporary William Bronk might be said of his own work:

> that clarity & honesty can produce so piercing a
> music
> a poet who fits no school whose work justifies no
> one's poetry but his own
>
> (*Selected Prose*, p. 183)

Unlike William Bronk, however, who remains the more obscure figure, George Oppen has had a remarkable and enduring impact on poets at least since the publication of *Of Being Numerous*. Part of this has to do with his association with fellow objectivists, many of whom coincidentally returned to the literary scene with important publications in the sixties and seventies, and who themselves continue to animate contemporary poetry in remarkable ways.

Rather than register Oppen's importance in relation to this or that school, or this or that poetic tendency, one can finally say that his achievement was fundamental in both the sense of the questions it sought to explore and in the formal and ethical model this inquiry offered for later poets. As the critic Rachel Blau DuPlessis

has noted, "the impact of Oppen's poetry is not aesthetic only, but a kind of ontological arousal to thinking itself—not to knowledge as such, but to the way thought feels emotionally and morally and processually in time" (Shoemaker, p. 212). Perhaps because Oppen spoke not so much beyond but beneath the primary movements of the day, he continues to speak to us today. Oppen offers a fundamental, grounding poetic orientation, and poets continue to look where he points.

Selected Bibliography

WORKS OF GEORGE OPPEN

POETRY
Discrete Series. New York: Objectivist Press, 1934.
The Materials. New York: New Directions, 1962.
This in Which. New York: New Directions, 1965.
Of Being Numerous. New York: New Directions, 1968.
Alpine: Poems. Mount Horeb, Wis.: Perishable Press, 1969.
Seascape: Needle's Eye. Freemont, Mich.: Sumac Press, 1972.
Collected Poems. London: Fulcrum Press, 1972.
The Collected Poems of George Oppen. New York: New Directions, 1975.
Primitive. Santa Barbara, Calif.: Black Sparrow Press, 1978.
New Collected Poems. Edited by Michael Davidson. New York: New Directions, 2002.
Selected Poems. Edited by Robert Creeley. New York: New Directions, 2003.

PROSE, INTERVIEWS, AND LETTERS
Selected Prose, Daybooks, and Papers. Edited by Stephen Cope. Berkeley: University of California Press, 2007.
Speaking with George Oppen: Interviews with the Poet and Mary Oppen, 1968–1987. Edited by Richard Swigg. London: McFarland, 2012.
The Selected Letters of George Oppen. Edited by Rachel Blau DuPlessis. Durham, N.C.: Duke University Press, 1990.

PAPERS
George Oppen Papers, 1958–1984. MSS 16, Mandeville Special Collections Library, University of California at San Diego.

CRITICAL AND BIOGRAPHICAL STUDIES
Baker, Robert. *In Dark Again in Wonder: The Poetry of René Char and George Oppen*. South Bend, Ind.: University of Notre Dame Press, 2012.
Barzilai, Lyn Graham. *George Oppen: A Critical Study*. London: McFarland, 2006.
Cuddihy, Michael, ed. "George Oppen: A Special Issue." *Ironwood* 5 (1975).
———. "George Oppen: A Special Issue." *Ironwood* 26 (1985).
Duplessis, Rachel Blau, and Peter Quartermain, eds. *The Objectivist Nexus: Essays in Cultural Poetics*. Tuscaloosa: University of Alabama Press, 1999.
"Feature: George Oppen." Edited by Thomas Devaney. *Jacket* 36 (2008).
Freeman, John. *Not Comforts, but Vision: Essays on the Poetry of George Oppen*. Devon, U.K.: Interim, 1985.
Hatlen, Burton, ed. *George Oppen, Man and Poet*. Orono: National Poetry Foundation/University of Maine at Orono, 1981.
Heller, Michael, ed. *Speaking the Estranged: Essays on the Works of George Oppen*. Exp. ed. Bristol, U.K.: Shearsman Books, 2012.
Izenberg, Oren. *Being Numerous: Poetry and the Ground of Social Life*. Princeton, N.J.: Princeton University Press, 2011.
Jenkins, Grant Matthew. *Poetic Obligation: Ethics in Experimental American Poetry After 1945*. Iowa City: University of Iowa Press, 2008.
Jennison, Ruth. *The Zukofsky Era: Modernity, Margins, and the Avant-Garde*. Baltimore: Johns Hopkins University Press, 2012.
Nicholls, Peter. *George Oppen and the Fate of Modernism*. Oxford: Oxford University Press, 2007.
Oppen, Mary. *Meaning a Life: An Autobiography*. Santa Barbara, Calif.: Black Sparrow Press, 1978.
Shoemaker, Steve, ed. *Thinking Poetics: Essays on George Oppen*. Tuscaloosa: University of Alabama Press, 2009.
"Special Issue: George Oppen." *Paiduma* 10, no. 1 (1981).
Weinfield, Henry. *The Music of Thought in the Poetry of George Oppen and William Bronk*. Iowa City: University of Iowa Press, 2009.
Williams, William Carlos. "The New Poetical Economy." In *George Oppen, Man and Poet*. Edited by Burton Hatlen. Orono: National Poetry Foundation/University of Maine at Orono, 1981. Pp. 267–270.
Zukofsky, Louis. "Sincerity and Objectification: With Special Reference to the Work of Charles Reznikoff." *Poetry* 37, no. 5:272–283 (1931).

JOHN KENNEDY TOOLE
(1937—1969)

Jeffrey Bickerstaff

JOHN KENNEDY TOOLE's life and death left enough unanswered questions to generate several competing narratives intended to explain their most perplexing elements. These interpretations spring from an array of motives, some more self-serving than others. A telling characteristic is the definitiveness with which one version or another handles enigmatic aspects of Toole's sexuality and suicide. Those motivated by ulterior agendas tend toward conclusive pronouncements, while others have made a humble peace with the ambiguous and unknowable.

The meaning of his work (published years after his death) has also proved bewildering. *The Neon Bible* (1989) has been dismissed as a work of juvenilia and praised as a remarkable achievement. *A Confederacy of Dunces* (1980) has been critiqued as funny but pointless and recognized as a complex study of worldviews intermixed with broad humor and pointed satire. Each has been mined for clues about its inscrutable author. The story of these books' path to publication is itself fascinating, with extraordinary characters, plot twists, and triumph snatched from the jaws of death. The fact that they were published posthumously, that they were created by a person who ended his life when he was only thirty-one, ensures that the success of *Confederacy*, along with the laughter in its pages, will always have an undercurrent of melancholy. These books mean more than just one thing. As is the case with so many aspects of John Kennedy Toole's life, they're complicated.

LIFE

John Kennedy Toole (known as "Ken" to friends and family) was born on December 17, 1937, in New Orleans, Louisiana, to John Dewey Toole, Jr., and Thelma Toole (née Ducoing). Thelma and John had, by all accounts, an unhappy marriage. John earned high marks in school and received a full scholarship to Louisiana State University. He declined the offer and, to Thelma's chagrin, settled into a job selling cars. Touting her son's legal, oratorical, and mathematical abilities, Thelma surmised that John could have been a professor but never realized his full potential. Late in life, with the dramatic flair for which she was known, Mrs. Toole declared that her husband "never honorably supported his multitalented wife and multitalented son" (MacLauchlin, p. 12).

Thelma Toole's theatrical inclinations were obvious early in life. She was considered a natural actress and received piano and violin lessons as a child. She claimed to have started training for the stage at the age of three, and she received a degree from the Southern College of Music and emerged from the Normal School of New Orleans as a certified kindergarten teacher. Although she dreamed of making her mark in New York, she opted to teach music and theater in the New Orleans public school system. But even these modest ambitions were compromised when she married John Toole. New Orleans public schools prohibited married women from holding full-time teaching positions, so the resilient Thelma earned her income by offering private lessons.

According to Robert Byrne, one of Ken Toole's colleagues at Southwestern Louisiana Institute, Thelma was actually "a professional mother" (Palumbo, p. 63). Byrne was the inspiration for Ignatius J. Reilly, the protagonist of *A Confederacy of Dunces*, and his Aunt May was the young Toole's second-grade teacher. Byrne recalls that May liked the boy very much; "it

was the mother who was the problem" (qtd. in Palumbo, p. 63). This problem stemmed from a couple of interrelated sources. The first was John Toole, whom Byrne describes as a pleasant but unsuccessful man. Because her husband failed to amount to anything, Thelma Toole redirected her ambitions toward her son, Ken, and the outcome, Byrne concludes, "was pretty disastrous" (p. 69).

The second was what Professor Jane Bethune describes—in the 2013 documentary film *John Kennedy Toole: The Omega Point* (directed by Joe Sanford)—as Thelma's narcissism, which led her to treat her son as her "project." Joel Fletcher, a friend of Ken and Thelma, adds that Thelma "considered her son an extension of herself" and regarded his accomplishments as personal validation (Sanford). Such observations explain why Thelma's tales of her wunderkind begin in the nursery. Her newborn had "an aura of distinction," a six-month-old's charm, and the liveliest facial expressions the nurses had ever seen. He was also a born leader; when he cried, all of the other babies cried too (MacLauchlin, p. 15). After a toddlerhood marked by precocious verbal and descriptive abilities, Kenny entered kindergarten when he was four. When he was not promoted to first grade due to the age requirement, Thelma complained to the superintendent, who waived the rule. After a month, Thelma decided her son should skip ahead to the second grade. To accomplish this, Thelma had the school psychologist administer a Stanford-Binet IQ test, which yielded a score of 133. This impressive outcome enabled Toole to join the second grade at the age of five. It did not, however, certify Kenny's genius, the criterion being a score of 160. Mrs. Toole rationalized that her prodigy had grown bored and stopped talking to the psychologist, opting instead to observe her. But Byrne's estimation of his former colleague corroborates the Stanford-Binet findings. He appears to mock Thelma's proclamation that her son was a genius, adding, "He wasn't. Ken was bright" (Palumbo, p. 69).

Byrne also relates a story about a visit he'd had with Ken Toole toward the end of the latter's life, during the dark period between Simon & Schuster's rejection of *Confederacy* and Toole's

suicide. Byrne had told Ken Toole that his Aunt May had bumped into Thelma, who had once again referred to her son as a genius. Ken expressed surprise at hearing that because "my mother spends all her time telling me how stupid I am" (Palumbo, p. 69). On the one hand, given Thelma's hagiographic recollections of her son, such a statement might be baffling. On the other, those very hagiographic recollections indicate that, as Toole's biographer Cory MacLauchlin puts it, "From the moment he was born, his mother deemed he was destined for greatness" (p. 15). By any normal standards, Ken Toole had achieved a great deal: he had finished his master of arts degree from Columbia University with high honors, his novel had caught and kept the attention of one of the industry's top publishing houses, and he was an admired and well-liked assistant professor of English. But in Thelma's world, these accomplishments appear to have constituted failure. Perhaps Jane Bethune puts it best when she concludes, in *The Omega Point*, "There'd be nothing that you could do to please that woman." Except, it seems, to garner (posthumously) the commercial rewards and critical accolades, including the Pulitzer Prize, for which you were said to be destined. Joel Fletcher, in the same documentary, speaks of how Thelma basked in the glory of *Confederacy*'s success and accepted it as validation and vindication of herself. To this Bethune adds, "The book reflected her more than anything else, her talent. The son kind of gets lost." This is followed in the film by a clip of Thelma proclaiming, "The Pulitzer Prize was not given for the comedy. The Pulitzer Prize was given for my son's erudition, his scholarly genius." Since Thelma Toole seemed unable or unwilling to recognize her son as an entity distinct from herself, she was essentially engaging in self-aggrandizing; indeed, when she speaks of "my genius" in another part of the film, one has to wonder to what extent she means "my son."

Thelma steadfastly steered Ken toward literature and the stage. He joined a youth theater group, the Traveling Theatre Troupers, in 1948. Unhappy with how the troupe's directors failed to appreciate Ken's gifts, Thelma founded her

own group, the Junior Varsity Performers, with the intention of putting Ken front and center. In addition to the stage, Ken's picture appeared in the newspaper to promote performances, and he could be seen on a television show titled *Tele-Kids* and heard as a guest newscaster on New Orleans radio (p. 18). Despite Thelma's reluctance to give Ken his own space, she came to accept that his interest in performing dwindled as his time in grade school drew to a close.

In 1950 Toole entered Alcee Fortier High as a twelve-year-old freshman. His focus shifted from acting to writing as he won essay contests and joined the newspaper and yearbook staffs. He also befriended Cary Laird, another freshman who had skipped two grades. When the boys were seniors, in 1954, Ken Toole joined the Laird family on a trip to visit relatives in Mississippi. He was taken by the novelty of rural life and inspired by the ubiquity of conservative religious dogma. Toole declared his intention to write a novel, and he started work on what would become *The Neon Bible* when he got home. The fact that Toole decided on an ambitious literary undertaking while far from his mother's scrutiny suggests that he wanted to establish a realm that was entirely his. He never told her about his project, and he made sure she remained unaware that he had unsuccessfully submitted it to a writing contest.

Toole had less luck escaping his mother's surveillance when it came to dating, however. Laird recounts that Thelma Toole sometimes trailed her son on dates. Late in life Thelma said that women were attracted to her son, but "he only had eyes for her" (MacLauchlin, p. 31). While an undergraduate at Tulane, Toole began dating his classmate Ruth Lafrantz, whom he took home and introduced to a disapproving Thelma. Lafrantz attended Columbia's graduate school at the same time as Ken, and their relationship continued in New York. Although Joel Fletcher reports that Toole proposed and Lafrantz hedged, Byrne states that they were actually engaged but Lafrantz grew tired of waiting and married somebody else (Palumbo, p. 71). Toole also dated Emilie Dietrich, a childhood friend who was working for a New York advertis-ing agency while he was studying at Columbia. Although she was quoted as saying "It would be easy to fall in love with a man that could dance like John Kennedy Toole" (MacLauchlin, p. 58), she ultimately described their relationship as "never exactly a romance" (Fletcher, p. 132). Fletcher relates this statement to Lafrantz's description of her time with Toole as "light, not heavy—light, but profound," and wonders if readers should take that to mean "platonic" (p. 131).

The issue of Toole's sexuality is cloaked in mystery and has led writers down dark alleys of speculation and sensationalism. Fletcher felt betrayed by René Pol Nevils and Deborah Hardy, the authors of the biography *Ignatius Rising*, for being, among other things, "over-eager to depict Ken as a homosexual, which he may or may not have been" (Fletcher, p. 187). Hardy wrote Fletcher asking for his assistance in 1994, and he obliged because her correspondence included a letter from Les Phillabaum, the director of Louisiana State University Press, which indicated the authors were under contract with him. From Fletcher's perspective this gave the authors and their project credibility, so he sent them his unpublished essay about Toole along with copies of letters Toole had sent to him. But follow-up communications shook his confidence that the authors were developing a serious and scholarly work. In the spring of 2000, LSU Press gave the galleys of *Ignatius Rising* to Carmine Palumbo, whose interview with Robert Byrne is cited throughout this essay, and Palumbo shared them with Fletcher. Both were appalled, as was Nicholas Polites, a mutual friend of Toole and Fletcher. Polites wrote to LSU Press's editor in chief, Maureen Hewitt, complaining that the authors "embellished, distorted, and outright fabricated" the information he provided them. He argues that because the book was being published by a respected university press, "these factoids will be footnoted in subsequent scholarly publica-tions and cited as facts. It will take a long time if ever to eradicate them" (Fletcher, pp. 185–186).

Ignatius Rising, MacLauchlin's *Butterfly in the Typewriter*, and *The Omega Point* are largely in agreement when it comes to the basic facts of

Toole's life. The issues arise, as MacLauchlin implies, when Hardy and Nevils aim to diagnose their subject and fit him into the archetype of the tortured artist. Their main diagnosis is, of course, that Toole was a tormented, closeted homosexual. They build their case largely upon the testimony of Chuck Layton, who claims to have known Toole during the summer of 1967. Layton admits that his days and nights revolved around drinking scotch, and much of the sixties and seventies are a blur. Despite the conspicuous unreliability of his account, the authors uncritically present Layton's tale of seeing Toole's picture on the back of *Confederacy* and recognizing him as a man he had picked up at a gay bar twelve years before. This is the most sensational section of *Ignatius Rising*, replete as it is with phrases such as "hit-and-run promiscuity" and increasingly tawdry descriptions of Toole's lifestyle (Hardy and Nevils, pp. 150–151).

Hardy and Nevils have not been the only authors mining Toole's sexuality for material. MacLauchlin points out that since Ken and Thelma Toole are both dead, and Thelma presented only the most idealizing details of her son's life, Toole scholars often resort to combing his works for biographical clues. This has led, he argues, "to grave missteps in biographical and literary interpretations of Toole" (p. 253). He cites Michael Hardin's 2007 article "Between Queer Performances" as an example. Hardin, MacLauchlin asserts, bases his readings of *The Neon Bible* and *A Confederacy of Dunces* on the idea that Toole was a latent homosexual, and when read through the lens of queer theory, both novels contain clues indicating their function as declarations of Toole's sexuality. MacLauchlin also cites the entry Raymond-Jean Frontain wrote about Toole for *GLBTQ*, an online encyclopedia of gay, lesbian, bisexual, transgender, and queer culture. Troubled that Frontain would "drag a dead man out of the proverbial closet," MacLauchlin argues that Frontain could have made his point about Toole's depictions of homosexuality without unequivocally declaring that the author was gay (p. 254).

Scholarly works making such declarations call to mind the concerns Nicholas Polites

expressed in his letter to Maureen Hewitt. The ambiguities of Toole's sexuality might be treated as definitive because *Ignatius Rising*, which enjoyed the credibility that comes with publication by a university press, treated it as such. Still, Fletcher states that Polites recalls Toole telling him that his relationship with a high school friend named Doonie Guibet had a sexual component to it. Although, as Fletcher points out, this may merely have been adolescent experimentation, MacLauchlin writes that Polites sometimes sensed gay tendencies in Toole. Both MacLauchlin and Fletcher follow up these speculations with stories of Toole showing sexual interest in women. The story of a woman known only as "Ellen" is the most noteworthy because it is tinged with mystery and suggests a side of Toole he would have had difficulty showing while living with his mother. A letter from this woman, whom Toole apparently knew while in New York, indicates he had met and positively impressed her mother. Ellen also repeatedly expresses her love for Toole and, as Fletcher puts it, their relationship seems "much less platonic" than the ones he had with the other women (p. 134). There is no known response from Toole to shed any more light on who Ellen was or how he felt toward her. As with the rest of Toole's sexual identity, it is likely that the enigma itself will stand as the story. For those without agendas to forward or any other ulterior motives, this does not seem to be a problem. Fletcher accepts "the fact that I will never know for sure whether Ken was gay or straight or something in between" (p. 136), and MacLauchlin states that "Toole's sexuality remains his own" (p. 215).

While Ellen and the clandestine composition of *The Neon Bible* suggest Toole's desire to establish a life beyond his mother's sweeping dominion, Fletcher stresses the positive impact Thelma Toole had on her son's development as a writer, particularly his ability to observe and mimic. When Toole was a boy, he and his mother would entertain themselves by making up dialogues of what they considered to be the typical lower-class of New Orleans He adds that Thelma Toole provided her son "the ore that he refined and made into literature" (p. 66). Ken Toole

ventured into writing in dialect when he created a Russian ring-toss athlete for his high school paper's satire issue. Entering Tulane University in 1954, he continued his development as a satirist by contributing cartoons to *Hullabaloo*, the student newspaper, and *Carnival*, the student literary magazine. Early in his undergraduate career Toole also showed himself capable of using his observational gifts to explore spiritual matters. The president of the Newman Club, a Catholic student organization, remembered Toole as "a gifted observer of the human condition" with "superior writing talent" (MacLauchlin, p. 44).

Toole was also lauded for his academic gifts, which led to his being conflicted about pursuing a career as a professor or taking his chance at becoming a novelist. During his senior year, the scales tipped toward academia as he quit the *Hullabaloo* and *Carnival* to focus on his honors program and procuring funding for graduate school. Toole won a Woodrow Wilson National Fellowship and moved to New York in 1958 to being his graduate work at Columbia. With money tight, Toole completed his degree in just two semesters, and he graduated with high honors the following spring. With this distinction, he could have continued into the Ph.D. program, but he needed a way to support himself. A mentor tried to persuade Hunter College to hire Toole, but the administration refused to bend their rule of only hiring teachers with classroom experience. These events seem to have suited Toole, however, because in between his two semesters at Columbia he came to question the field of literary criticism. In "The Arbiter," a poem composed during this time of uncertainty, Toole describes a critic more intent on crushing than interpreting poetry. MacLauchlin, who developed the title of his biography, *Butterfly*, from his reading of the poem, speculates that Toole seemed to have been questioning the relationship of the critic to the artist; and if it were indeed an adversarial relationship, then it seemed that he had to stand with one side against the other, a dilemma made all the more poignant by his own literary ambitions.

After Columbia, Toole accepted an offer to teach freshman writing at Southwestern Louisiana Institute. The importance of Toole's year at SLI cannot be overestimated. This is where he met Nicholas Polites, Joel Fletcher, and, of course, Robert Byrne. Toole also became close with his colleague Patricia Rickels and her family. They stayed in touch until the end of Toole's life, when the Rickels family bore sorrowful witness to Toole's disturbing decline. During the 1959–1960 school year, however, when Toole turned twenty-two and his promise shined luminously, he earned a reputation as a skilled and dedicated educator. In *The Omega Point*, Fletcher states that he never met one of Toole's students "who didn't think he was just a marvelous, marvelous teacher."

The next year Toole secured a teaching position at Hunter College and headed back to Columbia. Fletcher describes Toole as unhappy with his studies, but enjoying teaching at Hunter "because the aggressive, pseudo-intellectual, 'liberal' girl students are continuously amusing" (p. 26). Just as Toole found his inspiration for the fictional character Ignatius Reilly at SLI, at Hunter it was Myrna Minkoff who was "under observation" (p. 26). And just as Toole had lost his élan for literary criticism two years before, he came to question whether a doctorate was worth the "financial scrimping, stultifying research, and meaningless seminars" he would have to endure to get it (MacLauchlin, p. 108). Those feelings coincided with Toole redirecting his energy from scholarly to creative projects during the winter of 1961. He began sketching an Ignatius J. Reilly prototype named Humphrey Wildblood, and seemed to have been in the process of quitting graduate school when he was drafted by the army.

Toole was fluent in Spanish and an experienced English teacher, so the army assigned him to Fort Buchanan in Puerto Rico. There Toole taught elementary English to Puerto Rican recruits. He was well liked and quickly promoted to sergeant. Of all the perks his rank granted him, a private room proved the most consequential. During the late winter of 1963, Toole borrowed a typewriter from his friend David Kubach and began work on what would become *A Confederacy of Dunces*. When Kubach was transferred

that spring, Toole's manuscript was proceeding well enough to warrant an investment in a typewriter of his own. In the same letter home that introduces his new machine, Toole asks his parents to send him a list of private colleges and high schools in New Orleans. Because his focus had turned completely from academia to creative writing, he planned to drop out of Columbia, return home to an undemanding teaching job, and polish his manuscript. His next letter home states his ambition: "You both know that my greatest desire is to be a writer and I finally feel that I am doing something that is more than barely readable.... If this thing can be worked upon, I am almost certain that a publisher would accept it and so do one or two others to whom I have shown excerpts" (Hardy and Nevils, p. 113). Fletcher contends that although Toole probably believed that it would be easier to finish his novel in New Orleans than in what Toole called "the Columbia-Hunter axis," by returning home he was yielding to pressure from his parents and making "what must have been the worst decision of his life" (p. 75).

This was a consensus opinion within Ken Toole's circle. Citing John Toole's declining mental health and "that overbearing mother," Byrne describes the home to which Ken returned as "a bad situation" (Palumbo, pp. 69–70). Although Toole complained about the grind of teaching, in the classroom at St. Mary's Dominican College he enjoyed his work, his students enjoyed his classes, and he was eventually promoted to assistant professor. The situation at home, by contrast, was as bad as his friends feared, and Toole came to be increasingly under his mother's thumb. Byrne believes that Toole's ultimate plan was to make enough money to support his parents and move back to New York (Palumbo, p. 70), a feat he could only have accomplished by publishing a best seller.

To that end, Toole finished the manuscript in early 1964 and sent it off to Simon & Schuster in New York. Within just four months the senior editor Robert Gottlieb had read the work and was impressed enough to make contact and begin the long process of getting the novel ready for publication. Copies of much of the correspon-

dence between Gottlieb and Toole still exist, and the editor's critiques focus on the same basic issues. In mid-June, Gottlieb explained the story lines "must be strong and meaningful all the way through," rather than "wittily pulled together to make everything look as if it's come out right" (Fletcher, p. 110). Gottlieb also advised that "there must be a point to everything you have in the book, a real point, not just amusingness that's forced to figure itself out" (Fletcher, p. 110). Toole made revisions and sent a new version to New York. Still dissatisfied, Gottlieb asked the renowned literary agent Candida Donadio to give it a read. In December, Gottlieb reported that they both found Toole "wildly funny, funnier than anyone around, and our kind of funny" (MacLauchlin, pp. 173–174). While praising all of the characters except for Myrna and the Levys, Gottlieb bluntly stated that Ignatius "is not as good as you think he is. There is much too much of him" (p. 174). He and Donadio also thought the book was too long; worse, he argued that "it isn't really about anything. And that's something no one can do anything about" (Fletcher, p. 111). Ultimately, "The book could be improved and published. But it wouldn't succeed; we could never say that it was anything" (p. 111). A month later Toole wrote Gottlieb and asked for his manuscript back.

Perhaps the most puzzling part of Toole's story is the fact that he submitted his manuscript only to Simon & Schuster, even after that working relationship fizzled. After Gottlieb returned the manuscript, Toole flew unannounced to New York to speak with the editor in person. But Gottlieb was out of town, so Toole had what he described as an "an apprehensive, incoherent meeting" with Gottlieb's assistant (Fletcher, p. 112). MacLauchlin states that Toole blacked out and actually had a nervous breakdown in the office, an early indication of the mental illness that would claim his life. Toole wrote to Gottlieb expressing humiliation over the encounter. In that letter, the one in which he mentioned his "incoherent meeting," Toole described his "confusion and depression" and provided a long history of the book's origins (Fletcher, p. 116). Gottlieb's reply included an acknowledgment of his own

insecurities and neurosis to put Toole at ease about his behavior. He also stated that he and Toole "have a connection," expressed a "possibility of friendship," and encouraged him to write him "short or long at any time" (pp. 117–118). Toole's response, the last one from Toole to Gottlieb in existence, indicated that he was working but still struggling with what *Confederacy* does and could mean. In Gottlieb's final letter, written during the winter of 1966, the editor stated that "My interest in the book remains what it was" (p. 120). But as Bethune puts it, Toole knew he had a masterpiece, and to edit it as Gottlieb wanted "would have destroyed it" (Sanford). Unable to revise his manuscript without spoiling its essence, and unwilling to consider any publishing house than the one he considered the best, Toole put it away and tried to move on with his life.

Toole's lectures at Dominican, however, suggest he may have been working through issues from his childhood. According to MacLauchlin, one student remembers him returning consistently to the topic of the Mother, a generalized caricature intent on living vicariously through her child. Polites, frustrated by failed attempts to contact Toole, complained that Thelma Toole was "building a wall around him" (Fletcher, p. 34). When Polites did see him during a trip to New Orleans in early 1968, the palpable depression of the Toole household spurred him to make excuses to avoid returning. He subsequently told Fletcher that "Ken's not with us anymore" (MacLauchlin, p. 195). In the classroom, the once affable Professor Toole became irritable and even scary. His increasingly disheveled appearance reflected this change. Worst of all was Toole's descent into paranoia.

Many of Toole's friends and colleagues can recall the moment they realized something was seriously wrong. Kubach remembers seeing a friend of his approach and Toole diving into a store to avoid meeting him (MacLauchlin, p. 192). A classmate at Tulane, where Toole had reconvened his Ph.D. work, recounts that Toole stood up in the middle of a class and declared that there was a plot against him. His professor diffused the situation, and Toole never returned

(pp. 197–198). Pat Rickels recalls that during his last visit, Toole refused to get out of his car because he was convinced she did not want him there. During dinner, their guest explained how Simon & Schuster had stolen *Confederacy of Dunces*, given it to another author, and published it under a different title. Recognizing telltale signs of paranoia, her husband later broke it to Rickels that her friend was going insane. Byrne also describes Toole's disturbing final visit to his home, a "dreadful session" during which Toole explained that there was a plot against him (Palumbo, pp. 74, 71).

Both Byrne and Rickels discuss how Toole had hoped that *Confederacy* would liberate him from the pressure of supporting and living with his parents. Byrne even compared Toole's situation to that of *The Glass Menagerie*, in which the character Tom Wingfield "finally opts out" (Palumbo, p. 71). A key difference, of course, is that Tom escaped to preserve himself, whereas Toole escaped by destroying himself. On January 19, 1969, Toole had a cataclysmic fight with his mother. The next day, while Thelma was out, he returned home to pack some things, withdrew his money from the bank, got in his car, and took off. Toole traveled for sixty-six days on a journey that, according to receipts found in his car, took him west to California and back east again to Milledgeville, Georgia, the home of Flannery O'Connor. From there he drove to an unremarkable wooded spot in Biloxi, Mississippi, and ran a garden hose from the exhaust to the inside of the car. He left a suicide note that, according to Thelma Toole, begged his parents and God to forgive him for what he had done. Later, with her guard down, she said it contained "insane ravings" (Fletcher, p. 39). Thelma ultimately burned the letter and took its contents to her grave, while the rest of the documents found in Ken's car, which by some accounts included notes, manuscripts, and possibly the beginnings of a third novel, were stored in the basement of the Biloxi police department until later that year, when Hurricane Camille flooded the coast and washed them out to sea.

As with most suicides, the question of why lingered. Thelma Toole, being of a generation

that stigmatized mental illness, tried to hide its prevalence within her family. Ken Toole's father suffered from neuroses that sometimes took the form of "slight paranoia" (MacLauchlin, p. 28). Before Ken was born, one of Thelma's uncles committed suicide, as did the grief-stricken husband of her deceased sister. She also had a brother with severe mental illness. After the publication and success of *Confederacy*, Thelma Toole attained a degree of celebrity that she used to promote her version of why her son killed himself, says Fletcher. In Thelma's mythic version, Robert Gottlieb is the villain who drove her son into despair. Thelma must have chosen to ignore the mixture of professionalism and human decency with which Gottlieb treated Ken. There were also plenty of people who blamed Thelma. In *The Omega Point*, Pat Rickels bluntly states that when she was asked about why Toole ended his life, she would reply, "Well, you should have met his mother and you wouldn't have to ask." In the same film Kubach refers to Thelma Toole as a "splendid monster," and even Joel Fletcher, who emphasized the intricacies of Ken Toole's story while regarding Thelma Toole with sympathy and gentlemanly respect, said she was Ken Toole's "best friend, and also his worst enemy," adding "she helped create him, and I think she helped destroy him in a way." Add to that the psychosexual motive concocted by Nevils and Hardy, and we have a set of competing narratives designed to explain the inexplicable. But Cory MacLauchlin, in a beautifully written passage, stresses that "suicide is not simple," and "it cannot be explained by a series of events like some kind of formula" (p. 216). He cites the work of the suicidologist Edwin Shneidman, who underscores that suicide is a purposeful, complex act performed by a person attempting to gain control of his or her excruciating pain. As with the other mysterious elements of Toole's life, his death will forever remain his own.

THE NEON BIBLE

In one of his last letters to Robert Gottlieb, Toole described *The Neon Bible* as "a grim, adolescent sociological attack upon the hatreds spawned by the various Calvinist religions of the South." He also conclusively dismissed it as "bad" (Fletcher, pp. 118–119). Echoing Toole's assessment of the novel as "adolescent," MacLauchlin asserts that it now rests "in its rightful place as a work of juvenilia" (p. 250). On the other hand, the *New York Times* literary critic Michiko Kakutani found *The Neon Bible* to be not only "a remarkable achievement for a 16-year old writer," but "more organic and satisfying" than *Confederacy* because its "heartfelt emotion" affects the reader more profoundly than the latter's "willful manipulation."

Toole's coming-of-age story earnestly explores conformity and individualism, sexuality, religious fundamentalism, and loss. The novel reads "young,"—that is, it has an authenticity stemming from the youthful voice of its creator. David, a sixteen-year-old who is riding a train for the first time in his life, tells his story via flashback, and it isn't until the very end that the reader learns why he's there. The narration segues smoothly from the rhythm of the train he's riding to the toy train he received for Christmas when he was three years old. During this time his father, Frank, works in the factory in town; Frank and David's mother, Sarah, are both dues-paying members of the church, and their house is full of guests. The following spring his mother's Aunt Mae comes to live with them. Toole uses a scrapbook of Mae's "notices" to illustrate the downward trajectory of her career as a nightclub singer.

David is drawn to his aunt because of the attention she pays him and the way her animated presence contrasts with the monochromatic fundamentalism of his small town. Her flashy, knee-length skirts and feather boa draw scrutiny as she takes long walks through town with her young nephew. Toole contrasts profound human decency with facile religiosity, and he uses the Aunt Mae character to highlight the difference. By the conclusion, the teenage David has grown tired of the preacher and his flock calling whatever he does "Christian," and he argues with one of the town's "church people" that Mae is just as Christian as the schoolteacher Mrs. Watkins. Although dismissed as "a babe who

[doesn't] know the true word," David knows of what he speaks (p. 140). When David was in the first grade, Mrs. Watkins hated him because of his relation to "the hussy," and she took a sadistic delight in physically abusing the boy (pp. 24, 26). Her husband, a deacon in the church, worked to keep the county dry and "colored people" disenfranchised. When the library refused to remove its copy of *Gone with the Wind* (objectionable to Mr. Watkins because of its "licentious" qualities), a group from the church donned black masks, grabbed the book off the shelves, and set fire to it on the sidewalk (pp. 24–25).

Aunt Mae, on the other hand, functions as a salvation figure for David until the very end of the novel. Just after starting school, David witnesses a harrowing scene of domestic violence between his parents. Laid off from the factory, Frank takes his meager wages from pumping gas and buys seeds and farming equipment. Furious that her husband has spent all of their food money on what she dismisses as a foolish endeavor, Sarah confronts him, and he basically knocks her out. That night, with his mother injured and his father gone, David comes to perceive his aunt in a different light.

> She made me lose some of the frightened feeling I had. Behind her the moonlight was shining into the room so that it made her look all silvery around the edges. Her hair was down on her shoulders, and the light made every separate hair shine like a spider's web in the sun. Aunt Mae looked big and strong.... She was the only one in the house that could help me, the only strong person older than I was.
>
> (p. 34)

Outlined in silver, Mae stands hallowed and robust, an angelic source of comfort and assurance. She also shows vulnerability by confessing to David that she never was really good as a singer, but got by on her looks. Men took advantage of her, and as her beauty faded, she played increasingly rough joints until a sailor beaned her on the head with a beer bottle. By being honest about her travails, Mae teaches her nephew spiritual resilience and perseverance. Then, as they pray a humble prayer before going to sleep, David is interrupted by the philistine

gaudiness of the neon Bible radiating from the center of town, but he is able to reconnect after witnessing "the stars in the heaven shining like the beautiful prayer" (p. 38).

Sadly, though, Aunt Mae weakens as the plight of her family worsens. With Frank buried in Italy as a casualty of World War II and Sarah insane from grief, Mae cuts her losses and moves to Nashville. Feeling abandoned, teenaged David waits for the bus with his aunt, who is wearing "clothes like anybody in the valley now, and not the different things she wore at first" (p. 147). Mae's attire acts as an outward indication of an internal change. By failing to help those close to her in their greatest time of need, she has finally conformed to the "Christianity" espoused by the town's most prominent church people.

As Mae's story line suggests, the themes of religion and conformity are inextricably linked in *The Neon Bible*, and each factor plays into the formation of David's identity. He's disgusted by the sanctimonious busybodies who always "had some time left over from their life to bother about other people and what they did" (p. 138). He adds with scathing irony that they felt compelled "to get together to help other people out," and cites as examples the time they descended on "the woman who let a colored man borrow her car and told her the best place for her was up north with all the other nigger lovers, and the time they got the veterans with overseas wives out" (p. 138). Anybody different was ostracized or banished because if "the right person" hated something, everybody else had to fall in line or they themselves would become the focus of hate.

Besides his aunt, the only other individuals in town who live unconventionally are his mother and Mr. Farney, a schoolteacher Toole indicates is a homosexual. Mr. Farney is intelligent, cultured, and "a very nice person" (p. 100). In other words, he represents the opposite of the local norm. He works quixotically to introduce his students to literature and classical music, and manages to reach David with Henry Wadsworth Longfellow's "The Day Is Done." David describes the poem as "the only beautiful thing I ever heard," but doesn't acknowledge that he likes it for fear that his classmates will think he

is crazy. But Aunt Mae understands, which underscores the point that David feels a kinship with the town's outsiders. Mr. Farney and his aunt are the only people he knows who appreciate creativity and aren't hypocrites. Mr. Watkins burns books, Mrs. Watkins is a deranged child abuser, and the preacher divorces his wife and marries a woman half his age. David is a sensitive nonconformist longing to create his own path, a desire he expresses through symbolic gestures:

> The stairs were all worn so that you had to put your feet where everybody else put theirs when they went up. Every step had two spots, both along the side, where the wood was about an inch lower than it was in the middle and at the end of the steps. Sometimes to be different I'd walk right up the center of the steps where nobody ever did. I did that now. I walked right in the middle where the wood looked like it was new.
>
> (p. 151)

The significance of the stairs is enhanced by the fact that there are sixteen, which is how old David is at this point in the story. Each step represents a year of his life, years during which he desires to eschew the well-worn path for one of his own.

The innuendo swirling around Aunt Mae and Mr. Farney and the aftermath of Frank's demise enable Toole to explore how his protagonist comes to terms with sex and death. When Mae first moves in, David hears women calling her names that he does not understand the meaning of until he is nearly ten. He also remembers walking to school and seeing bed sheets, black lace lingerie, and net stockings drying on the balcony above the barroom in town. He will not learn that it is a brothel until he is in seventh grade. David also hears about sex from older boys at school, but when he is younger he does not understand what they are talking about.

Unlike a lot of coming-of-age novels, the protagonist doesn't lose his virginity. At the point in the story where such a climactic scene might occur, David kills somebody instead. This, along with book burning and child abusing, suggest a link between sexual repression and violence. David does have a close call, though, with a woman who always answers the door in her robe when he delivers her order from the pharmacy, but the fifteen-year-old decisively rejects her advances. This is not to say David shows no interest in girls. On the night he graduates from eighth grade, he begins to think about whether girls would go out with him. He asks Aunt Mae to assess his looks, and she tells him that his face is beginning to look like a man's and that he would be good-looking in about a year. He eventually goes on a date and kisses Jo Lynne, a pretty out-of-towner who is there to nurse her ailing grandfather.

It is difficult not to think about Ken and Thelma Toole as David apprehensively dips his toe into the dating pool. When David tells Aunt Mae about Jo Lynne, he wonders if she is angry. She is not, but without even knowing about David's love interest, his mother laments to Aunt Mae that her son "didn't care about her anymore and cried and laid her head on the kitchen table" (p. 122). When one considers that *The Neon Bible* was written by a sixteen-year-old whose mother trailed him on dates and insisted that he only had eyes for her, such passages stand out. So too does the image Toole creates to express David's frustration at being unable to free himself from his mother and create an independent life for himself. With Jo Lynne and Aunt Mae gone, David walks into the kitchen and contemplates the light, an "old greasy bulb" hanging uncovered from the ceiling: "And I thought that I was really alone with Mother like that bulb hanging from a cord it couldn't get off of" (p. 150). The bulb represents David, who longs to cut the cord and break free from his familial obligation. The passage reads as an eerily prescient description of the turn Toole's life took when he moved back home after the army to take care of his parents. David has the same realization that Toole had a decade later when he was unable to liberate himself by publishing *Confederacy*. As his friend David Kubach describes it, Toole "had felt that life was going to get long" (Sanford). That also perfectly describes how David feels while pondering the bulb, and it is telling that both escape through acts of violence.

For the citizens not indulging in violence or the brothel, religion provides an outlet. Toole dedicates a chapter to a traveling tent show revival featuring the young, renowned preacher Bobbie Lee Taylor. David points out that Taylor stays on the top floor of the hotel in a fifteen-dollar-a-night room available to only the rich and powerful, and that the traveling preacher's last words to his temporary flock remind them of the donation box (p. 73). David also picks up on the fact that Taylor looks twenty-five but is conspicuously not fighting in the war. Toole implies throughout the chapter that Taylor is running a racket, a point he underscores with a description of one of the preacher's oratorical techniques: David recalls that as Taylor took the podium, he said nothing as he tried to find a specific page in his Bible. After finding it, "he coughed and then looked at the people for another minute. It made everyone uneasy around me. You could hear the wooden chairs squeaking where people were moving" (p. 67). Not only is Bobbie Lee Taylor a draft dodger living lavishly off of poor country Christians; he manipulates his audience as Adolph Hitler did, glaring silently until the whole of the room is unnerved and off balance. Then, feeling his opening, Taylor generates guilt by asking women if they are being faithful to their husbands who are fighting overseas. After one woman cries contritely, others fall in line, including a sixty-five-year-old who David knew "couldn't have done anything wrong" (p. 69). By the end, Taylor has convinced even the youth, save for David, of their depravity. One of his classmates, Billy Sunday Thompson—a winking allusion to Billy Sunday, the famous fundamentalist who earned millions and hobnobbed with the elite of his time—testifies that he has "needed Jesus for a long time" (p. 73). And even though the town preacher denounces the revival and excommunicates members of his flock who attend it instead of attending his competing Bible conference, Toole criticizes fundamentalism by noting what the clashing clergymen share in common, including their fostering of censoriousness and guilt and their xenophobia and racism. Both rail against soldiers marrying overseas women and tainting the valley with foreign and heathen blood. Toole pointedly attacks organized religion, particularly clergy who exploit faith to enrich themselves and sanctify their own prejudices.

Toole's least subtle statement about religion comes at the conclusion when David kills the town preacher and escapes on a train. He had barged in to take David's mother to an insane asylum and was halfway up the stairs before David took out a gun and shot him dead. Although killing the representative of a noxious worldview is a compelling way for an author to express his disdain, David's capacity for such brutality comes out of nowhere. Another problem is that the gun was introduced only two pages before, casting the shadow of a deus ex machina over the scene.

The most artful aspect of the ending, however, is the way Toole had layered levels of foreshadowing in the second chapter. At school, Mrs. Watkins knees little David in the chin and knocks out a loose tooth, an action that will mirror his father kneeing his mother and knocking her unconscious as well as knocking out one of her teeth during their fight over seeds. Frank storms out and is gone the entire night. His absence later hovers over the scene in which David finds his mother with blood gushing from her mouth at the end of the novel. She utters the name of her husband before she dies during the night, hours before the preacher enters to take her away. Toole even insinuates the preacher's death during the second chapter. When the neon Bible intrudes upon David's prayer, he speculates that the church keeps it aglow "even if the preacher isn't there" (p. 32).

Toole explores death and feelings of loss, particularly the way the protagonist learns to deal with them, throughout *The Neon Bible*. He uses the patch of land where Frank tried to grow crops to illustrate David's struggle to make sense of his father's death in the war. After receiving the news, he goes outside and notices grass covering the area his father had cleared, weather wearing down the high places where rows of crops once were, and seedling pines taking root. The following spring he observes saplings growing tall and babies from the postwar boom learning to walk. David sees life going on, despite the fact that his

father is dead and his mother cannot function as his mother anymore. Sarah too recognizes the significance of the patch of land, and later in the novel when David comes home from work to find her sitting there, he notes that "the seedling pines were big now, and you never would think the land was ever cleared" (p. 111). These passages, which articulate a longing for meaning in the face of an indifferent nature, strike a distinctly existential tone.

Indeed, *The Neon Bible* indicates Toole's deep interest in how people make meaning of experience, a theme he would pick up with *Confederacy*'s articulation of competing worldviews. It also hints at his love of language and his appreciation of the power of the written word. Looking at the telegram bearing the news of his father's death, David "thought of how funny it was that a few black letters on some yellow paper could make people feel the way it made Mother feel. I thought what it would do if the black letters were just changed around a little to read something else, anything" (p. 91).

One cannot help but picture a young John Kennedy Toole writing those sentences, exhilarated to be creating a novel, putting down black letters on a page, imagining the feelings they will conjure. He clearly regards words with love and awe, and he recognizes that they are the medium through which he can touch people and leave his mark on the world. It would take a while, but he would do just that with *A Confederacy of Dunces*.

A CONFEDERACY OF DUNCES

The correspondence between Toole and Gottlieb concerning the meaning of *A Confederacy of Dunces* haunts any reading of it. In one of the earliest academic considerations of the novel, Robert Coles recognized a real point in its pages, not just amusing narrative strands cleverly tied together at the end. Coles's interpretation hinges on a perception of Toole as "a dialectician in the Augustinian tradition, able to envision the devil as a prodding if not provocative ally" (p. 125). In other words, Toole puts forth two polar opposite worldviews, and progress results when they provoke and prod each other into a progressive synthesis. On the one hand there stands Ignatius J. Reilly, not just "a representation of the Catholic Church itself" but specifically the Church of the 1950s. The bloated, pre–Vatican II medievalist carries an antagonistic torch for Myrna Minkoff, his antithetical former girlfriend, embodiment of "the avowed enemy, secular humanism" (p. 125). According to Coles, this setup yields two possible interpretations of the conclusion, when Myrna saves Ignatius from being institutionalized and they ride off together into the night. In the first, twentieth-century secular humanism rescues the Church from its own corruptions, contradictions, and blind spots; in the second, Toole is questioning what will result from the Church's early-sixties turn toward Myrna's humanist worldview. Although its ultimate significance remains indeterminate, Myrna does in fact rescue Ignatius in the end, a touching ending to what is, in essence, a bizarre romantic comedy.

Boethius' *Consolation of Philosophy* serves as the foundation of Ignatius' worldview, which he inscribes on the pages of several Big Chief tablets. According to Ignatius, after a period of order, peace, and oneness with God and the Trinity, "merchants and charlatans gained control of Europe, calling their insidious gospel 'The Enlightenment'" (p. 28). This is the point in history when Western culture went awry, when focus shifted from the soul to the sale. Not only did death, destruction, and anarchy loom ominously on the horizon, so too did progress, ambition, self-improvement, and democracy. Optimism nauseates Ignatius, he rails against modern Catholicism's lapse into relativism, and he considers having to go to work a perversion. New Orleans is his home by birth and choice, for he finds it has a "certain apathy and stagnation" that he finds inoffensive (p. 119). For his utter rejection of bourgeois values, Ignatius could stand as the ultimate countercultural figure; but in the American 1960s, his privileging of sloth over activism and hierarchy over egalitarianism ensures his vehement estrangement from even the ardent dissidents of his era.

Myrna Minkoff functions as a caricature of a leftist dissident and an unconventional love interest for Ignatius. Through his journals and her let-

ters emerges the figure of a "loud, offensive maiden from the Bronx," whose bourgeois father funds her activism (p. 124). They had met in a campus coffeehouse and started attacking one another's worldviews; the intensity of their clashing perspectives led to an affair "of sorts," which Ignatius takes pains to point out was platonic (p. 125). Ignatius and Myrna did share a dislike of WASP culture; but while Myrna was "terribly *engaged* in her society," Ignatius, "older and wiser, was terribly *dis-engaged*" (p. 125). After several semesters, Myrna left college and "the black leotards, the matted mane of hair, the monstrous valise" (stuffed with sundry manifestos and pamphlets) were gone from Ignatius' life, save for letters and Myrna's occasional "inspection tours" of the South (p. 126). Her letters detail her politicized artistic endeavors, and they implore Ignatius to commit himself "to the crucial problems of the times" (p. 79). Her worldview is based in Freudian theory, and she beseeches Ignatius to free himself of the "great Oedipus bonds" tethering him to the "womb-house" in which he is mired (pp. 181, 215). Myrna prescribes carnal release as a crucial first step Ignatius must take to revitalize himself. He feigns offense, but the sexually charged punishments he imagines for his liberal adversary belie his prudery.

The correspondence between Myrna and Ignatius reads like a peculiar mating ritual. Ignatius' sexual fantasy about a nude woman (who turns out to be Lana Lee) "reading" a copy of *The Consolation of Philosophy* in a pornographic photograph suggests the extent to which Myrna's unabashed sexuality causes him great trepidation. Unlike Myrna, who "probably attacked sex with the vehemence and seriousness that she brought to social protest," Ignatius imagines the learned mystery woman taking "a very stoic and fatalistic view of whatever sexual gaucheries and blunders he committed. She would be understanding" (p. 292). More than the act itself, Ignatius relishes the thought of an anguished Myrna gnawing "at her espresso cup rim in envy" as he describes "every lush moment" of his "tender pleasures" (pp. 291–292). The inclusion of Myrna in this erotic reverie indicates that he actually longs to

be with her, but wants to learn how to make love from a patient, philosophical woman so he does not humiliate himself when they finally consummate their relationship.

As funny as *Confederacy* can be, descriptions of the effects of Ignatius' repressed sexuality tend toward the disturbing. His "hobby" having grown stale, Ignatius sets aside his onanistic accoutrements and conjures an image of his former dog to successfully complete the act (p. 31). Toole underscores Ignatius' warped sexuality throughout the novel, and even suggests that his eroticized fascination with movies is at the core of his very existence. Ignatius' parents had gone to see *Red Dust*, and the sight of Jean Harlow taking a bath got Mr. Reilly so worked up that he and Irene conceived Ignatius later that night. Contemplating why it is he "*must*" be at the cinema on opening night to see a movie starring his favorite actress, Ignatius parenthetically writes that he does "not understand this compulsion of mine for seeing movies; it almost seems as if movies are 'in my blood'" (p. 271). During the screening, Ignatius reacts to his arousal by yelling "Filth!" "Rape her!" "That woman must be lashed until she drops" (pp. 290–291).

Ignatius also expresses his attraction to Myrna through violent outbursts and ghastly images. In one racially charged scene, Myrna describes her new Kenyan friend as "virile and aggressive" while suggesting Ignatius is impotent. Ignatius exclaims that "the minx has been raped by a Mau-Mau," and imagines her "impaled on a particularly large stallion" for punishment (p. 215). Later in his journal he proclaims his desire to have her lashed "about her erogenous zones" (p. 227). After failing to best Myrna at her own game, political activism, by organizing New Orleans' gay community into a political party, Ignatius concludes he and Myrna would have to "joust" on "the field of sex" (p. 327). This scene follows the same basic pattern of Ignatius' earlier attempt to marshal Levy Pants's black factory workers into an uprising against their middle-management oppressors. Ignatius planned to film the riot with meaningful cinematic flourishes that would, in an unconscious expression of lust, cause envy to "gnaw at Myrna's musky vitals"

(p. 139). Finally, after his plan for a romantic rendezvous with the enigmatic woman in the photograph goes spectacularly wrong, he curses Myrna while he "frantically abuse[s] the glove" (p. 379), the glove being one of the aforementioned "accoutrements."

As the virile Kenyan and aborted factory riot suggest, race plays a significant role in *A Confederacy of Dunces*. Robert Coles reads Burma Jones—a young, chain-smoking black man in dark shades who has been railroaded, under threat of being jailed for vagrancy, into performing janitorial work at Lana Lee's Night of Joy club—as the possessor of "a curious and winning grace" (p. 122). Coles references Flannery O'Connor in relation to Jones, who indeed delivers grace to each of the novel's (good) characters by sabotaging Lana's pornography and prostitution racket and setting off a chain of events that cleverly tie together each of *Confederacy*'s narrative strands. The grace afforded some characters is more gentle than others; for Ignatius, his is of the awful-grace-of-God variety that leaves him unconscious in a Bourbon Street gutter, soon to be whisked away reborn in Myrna's Renault.

Jones and Ignatius cross paths before the pinnacle of the story, when Ignatius is selling hot dogs. His job baffles Jones, who asks him, "How come a white cat like you, talkin so good, sellin weenies?" (p. 295). Jones also wonders why Ignatius, a college man, doesn't have "a good job, big Buick, all that shit. Whoa! Air condition, color TV ..." (p. 296). Ignatius, appalled, accuses Jones and all American blacks of wanting "to become totally bourgeois. You people have all been brainwashed. I imagine that you'd like to become a success or something equally vile" (p. 296). Ignatius does not know the half of it. Jones peruses *Life* magazine for the advertisements, believing that insurance ads featuring young couples in lovely new homes and cool and rich men hawking shaving lotion could help him to improve himself. "He wanted to look just like those men" (p. 54). Scolding Jones for having ambition, Ignatius lectures him about the virtues of (Ignatius' ignorant, romanticized version of) "Negro" life, a life lived contentedly "in some hovel," free from ulcers and badgering Caucasian

parents, emerging only monthly to retrieve a "relief check" from the mailbox (p. 298).

MacLauchlin notes Toole's admiration for Jack Kerouac multiple times throughout *Butterfly in the Typewriter*, which leads one to wonder if Toole might be using Ignatius to poke fun at the racial perspective of the "king of the Beats." A depressive episode of *On the Road* finds Sal Paradise wandering around the "colored section" of Denver, longing to be black or "anything but what I was so drearily, a 'white man' disillusioned," and wishing he "could exchange worlds with the happy, true-hearted, ecstatic Negroes of America" (New York: Penguin, 1976, p. 180). In the twenty-first century, these passages are cringe-inducing. Toole's are too, but coming as they do from a belching, virginal buffoon, it is easier to read them as satirical. In his journal, Ignatius expresses "something of a kinship with the colored race because its position is the same as mine: we both exist outside the realm of American society"; stressing that his alienation is voluntary, he laments "that many of the Negroes wish to become active members of the American middle class" (p. 122). In a passage that precedes the lecture he bestows upon Jones, Ignatius—echoing Kerouac—muses, "Perhaps I should have been a Negro.... I would not be pressured by my mother to find a good job, for no good jobs would be available." He imagines himself and his mother living "pleasantly in some moldy shack in the slums in a state of ambitionless peace, realizing contentedly that we were unwanted, that striving was meaningless" (p. 123).

The racial politics of *A Confederacy of Dunces* remain murky. Coles correctly sums up Jones as "down-to-earth, clear-headed, and above all, attentive," everything his white counterparts are not (p. 122). And ultimately Jones's role in thwarting Lana Lee earns him a generous reward and a solid, middle-class job. But while this reads like a happy ending, there remains an undercurrent of doubt. Toole by no means even hints that Jones is better off living in squalor, but he does not present Jones's desire to model himself after the people he admires in print advertisements as an admirable alternative. Toole does not endorse

Ignatius' unambitious lethargy either, but his protagonist's diatribes against television, frozen food, hair sprays, plastic, and subdivisions have the ring of an authentic animosity toward consumer culture. As for the synthesis of old-school Catholicism and secular humanism, it is difficult to say whether the latter saves the former from itself, or if the latter takes the former in a perilously questionable direction. As is the case with Jones's entry into the realm of middle-class consumerism, the meaning remains difficult to discern. It does mean something, though. And we are left wishing that Toole had sent his manuscript out to other publishing houses, that he had persisted in his quest to find an editor who recognized that it did.

CONCLUSION

The meaning of *A Confederacy of Dunces* would be a lot clearer if it existed in the context of an extensive body of work. Toole's untimely death in 1969, however, ensured that such an oeuvre was not to be. Even *Confederacy*, and by extension *The Neon Bible*, would have vanished into the ether of time had it not been for Thelma Toole's tenacity. In the spring of 1973, just months after the passing of her husband, she opened the box containing the manuscript and began the long, discouraging process of sending it to publishers for their consideration. Over the course of three years she sent it to eight publishers and received eight rejection notices. Her fortunes spun upward in 1976 when she discovered that the novelist Walker Percy was teaching at nearby Loyola University. In his foreword to the novel, Percy tells the tale of how the eccentric, persistent Mrs. Toole tracked him down and enlisted him in her campaign to publish the manuscript. They succeeded, but even with Percy's prestige and clout it took another four years.

Thelma Toole herself actually became a bit of a celebrity. She appeared on Tom Snyder's *Tomorrow* show and performed readings that she interspersed with songs. *The Omega Point* includes a clip of her singing and playing the piano under a big banner reading "THELMA." A cynic, or at least anybody who has dealt with narcissistic, spotlight-craving parents, might point out that Thelma had finally succeeded in using her son to become a star. As true as that is, there is a more sympathetic, and soul-satisfying, way of looking at it. In *The Neon Bible*, after learning of his father's death, David retreats to the land his father had cleared for farming and laments that "besides me, that was the only thing Poppa did while he was living you could see now." Worse, David realizes that in just a few years "the whole little place would look just like any other place in the hills and you'd never know anyone spent almost all of one week's pay on it and put in a lot of time too" (p. 92). Frank had only two things to show for his time on earth, and one of them was already disappearing. That passage comes to mind when picturing Thelma Toole reaching for the box containing her deceased son's brilliant manuscript. Yes, as a teacher he had touched the lives of innumerable students, but *A Confederacy of Dunces* was the only thing Ken Toole had done that his mother could see, and she wanted to ensure that the time and energy he devoted to creating his dazzling story would not be lost to an indifferent world. She engaged in an existential struggle to make meaning of her son's life, and she won. We all did.

Selected Bibliography

WORKS OF JOHN KENNEDY TOOLE

NOVELS

A Confederacy of Dunces. Baton Rouge: Louisiana State University Press, 1980. New York: Grove Press, 1981.

The Neon Bible. New York: Grove Press, 1989.

PAPERS

John Kennedy Toole Papers. Manuscripts Collection 740, Manuscripts Department, Howard-Tilton Memorial Library, Tulane University, New Orleans.

CRITICAL AND BIOGRAPHICAL STUDIES

Coles, Robert. "Gravity and Grace in the Novel *A Confed-*

eracy of Dunces." In his *Times of Surrender: Selected Essays*. Iowa City: University of Iowa, 1988. Pp. 119–125.

Fletcher, Joel L. *Ken and Thelma: The Story of* Confederacy of Dunces. Gretna, La.: Pelican, 2005.

Frontain, Raymond-Jean. "John Kennedy Toole." In *GLBTQ: An Encyclopedia of Gay, Lesbian, Bisexual, Transgender, and Queer Culture*. Edited by Claude J. Summers. Chicago: Glbtq, Inc., 2004. www.glbtq.com/literature/toole_jk.html

Hardin, Michael. "Between Queer Performances: John Kennedy Toole's *The Neon Bible* and *A Confederacy of Dunces*." *Southern Literary Journal* 39, no. 2:58–77 (spring 2007).

Sanford, Joe, dir. *John Kennedy Toole: The Omega Point*. Pelican Pictures, 2013. http://jktoole.com/ (Documentary film.)

Kakutani, Michiko. "A Novelist's Story of Love, Pain and (Neon) Signs of Life." *New York Times*, May 12, 1989. http://www.nytimes.com/1989/05/12/books/books-of-the-times-a-novelist-s-story-of-love-pain-and-neon-signs-of-life.html

MacLauchlin, Cory. *Butterfly in the Typewriter: The Tragic Life of John Kennedy Toole and the Remarkable Story of A Confederacy of Dunces*. New York: Da Capo Press, 2012.

Nevils, René Pol, and Deborah George Hardy. *Ignatius Rising: The Life of John Kennedy Toole*. Baton Rouge: Louisiana State University Press, 2001.

Palumbo, Carmine D. "John Kennedy Toole and His *Confederacy of Dunces*." *Louisiana Folklore Miscellany* 10:59–77 (1995).

FILM BASED ON THE WORK OF JOHN KENNEDY TOOLE

The Neon Bible. Directed and adapted by Terence Davies, 1995.

KATHERINE VAZ

(1955—)

Nancy Bunge

KATHERINE VAZ BELIEVES that successful literature conveys realities too large for language to capture. This ambitious goal not only makes Vaz's job as a fiction writer difficult, it demands engaged, imaginative readers for its fulfillment. Vaz believes her mother's love of stories and her father's background as a native of the island of Terceira in the Azores have supplied her with much of the creative equipment she requires for the challenging task she has undertaken. She especially credits her father's expertise in Portuguese culture with giving her not only a deep understanding and appreciation of it, but also an enthusiasm for losing herself in mystery. And Vaz repeatedly calls upon this background to distance her subject matter enough from ordinary life to lift her readers into a world that encourages sufficient faith in miracles to set aside common sense, however briefly, and risk surrendering to their emotional and spiritual lives.

Katherine Vaz was born August 26, 1955, at Castro Valley, California, to Elizabeth Sullivan and August Mark Vaz. One of six children in the family, she graduated from the University of California at Santa Barbara in 1977, receiving her bachelor's degree in English. Her early publications often focused on sports, especially swimming and triathlons. Although these interests seem remote from the mythic fiction Vaz would eventually produce, her writings about these subjects suggest some affinities with the imaginative work that followed. For instance, Vaz believes that when things go well for the swimmer, she lets go and loses herself in the process, propelled by something larger than her will. Similarly, she explains that she first became fascinated by writing when, as a schoolgirl, the words seemed to just happen when she produced a sentence for Sister Delfina's vocabulary

exercise. When Vaz recommends to her readers that they train for a triathlon, she argues that shifting from one sport to another will reward them with a vitality that will enrich the whole of their lives. And her fiction, above all, exposes the reader to a multidimensional, life-enhancing vision. Writing about sports also develops an acute awareness of the body. And despite the abstract perspective central to her work, all Vaz's writing has a rich physicality that calls upon a variety of senses, luring readers into losing themselves in an experience so rich it carries them beyond the mundane.

In the 1980s Vaz lost a number of people close to her, including both grandmothers, a man she dated, and her best friend, Lee. Some of these deaths involved significant spiritual events. One of her grandmothers sent everyone except one aunt off to her nephew's wedding, dressed herself for burial, and quietly passed away, sparing all but one person the burden of dealing directly with her death. The parents of her best friend, Lee, found their meal in the hospital cafeteria interrupted by the sudden realization that they had to join their daughter. They arrived at her bedside just in time to share her death with her. When discussing her friend, Vaz focuses on the way Lee's impending death caused her to live more fully, underlining the ways life and death resist making simple distinctions between them. The shock of Lee's death also encouraged Vaz to live more compassionately; the realization that everyone feels the kind of intense pain she endured helped her feel close to others. Whether or not Vaz consciously sought an M.F.A. in creative writing (received from the University of California at Irvine in 1991) because she felt she needed a way to express these complicated new insights, the impact of death, the ways life and

death enhance each other, and the importance of compassion to living well all play important roles in the fiction Vaz would go on to publish.

SAUDADE

Vaz's first novel, *Saudade* (1994), like all her books, draws heavily on her Portuguese background. The title is a Portuguese word for longing, especially for beloved people and places that have vanished from one's present life. The central character, Clara, who lives in the Azores, cannot speak or hear from birth, so she learns to communicate by using sugar to signify her thoughts and feelings (a sprinkle on someone's head, for example, means "Kiss me"). Her father also encourages her to listen to the ocean sounds coming from conch shells, and she seems to respond. Having a central character with such an extraordinary way of handling communication underlines from the start Vaz's unstated argument that life's most significant events transcend language and that the most important realities of life must be encountered and understood with more than the mind.

Clara deals with one loss after another, even earlier than Vaz herself did. Her father dies in the sea he loves as the result of an accident, and her mother passes away soon after. Concerned about abandoning her child, her mother signs over California land she owns to a priest, Father Eiras, who promises to take care of Clara. Clara and the priest move to California, where he gives little indication of recalling his pledge to her mother. (A priest played a similar stunt on one of Vaz's great aunts, so here she draws upon a family story.) When her mother dies, Clara calls out, and at that moment, bereft of her parents, she acquires the ability to hear and speak, so that she can engage with the world. This event, however, which in the work of other writers might signal a huge step forward, does not improve Clara's lonely, empty life. This seems consistent with the narrator's repeated affirmations that dreams matter more than reality, suggesting that the ability to function efficiently in the conventional world offers relatively slight benefit compared to engaging the imaginative one.

Determined to get back her land, Clara begins to work at seducing Father Eiras. She pretends to be submissive and touches him as she teaches him how to swim. Presumably because their physical contact makes him uncomfortable, the priest wants to stop the lessons. So she crawls onto his lap and he melts. They begin having sex, but this activity does not engage either one of them emotionally: the priest's narcissism allows him to believe that whatever gives him pleasure makes her happy, and Clara's determination to win back her land causes her to see their affair simply as something she cleverly uses to get control of the priest. Clara shares her plans with Tio Vitor, the former owner of the land and her ancestor, whom she has conjured up imaginatively. He warns her, fruitlessly, that seeking revenge will harm rather than redeem her life. Her sexual involvement with the priest results in her giving birth to a badly damaged boy. The child's arrival exposes the priest for breaking his vows of celibacy, and he is removed from his parish. But Clara does not win back her land; another priest takes control of it.

Clara's intense love for her afflicted child overshadows everything else, a development she failed to anticipate when she plotted revenge on Father Eiras. This affection makes the world bloom for her; she enjoys colors, light, and music. The boy's chest has a huge opening which Clara believes exists to expose his large heart. Despite her care and concern, the boy clearly will die. Clara thinks she must find a way to make colors sing, because "then the baby can be a song of pink dreams flying up to heaven" (p. 103). She also embraces the view that an injured heart has more value and purity than one that has stayed remote and safe.

Despite Clara's scorn for emotional safety, she tries to numb herself after the child dies. But the kind gestures of a friend named Glória keep her tied to life. Clara's quiet demeanor masks her sadness, making it possible for others to assume that she has achieved peace. Then she meets Helio Gabriel, a man brokenhearted over the deaths of his wife and daughter. He knows that he has

retreated from life too long and must find his way back toward the light. Clara comes to understand that Helio's fine manners show that he has both suffered and retained a love for life. The two of them rescue a girl named Marina, who has been surviving in a chicken coop. And then they save each other. Their lives, like Marina's, will not be redeemed merely by recovering physically; they also must reclaim their responsiveness to the world. This will involve discomfort: Clara wants to protect Marina from pain, but Helio reminds her that people cannot save themselves without also losing part of themselves to others. When Helio and Clara give themselves completely to each other, Vaz calls upon multiple senses to render their exaltation: sounds, sights, light, and music. They communicate principally with language that consists of colors because it has more vibrancy than ordinary speech. (Here Vaz undoubtedly calls upon her memory of a family friend who thought in colors; Vaz's father painted bracelets of colors for her, corresponding to colors he put on her telephone dial so that she could dial the right numbers.) Helio also uses colors to record music that Clara plays on the piano. Helio proclaims that it sounds as though nature has come to inhabit the room where she plays, presumably because her work involves so many senses. Helio sees books, music, and paintings as interchangeable and interconnected manifestations of the same reality, which makes him wonder, "Could a book be presented to an orchestra and, upon hearing how it was played, might artists ply their brushes so that anyone seeing only the canvases could recite the words of the original book?" (p. 229). He believes that those who grasp that all art emerges from one foundation could sing celestial songs as they faced death, like swans.

Despite Helio's warnings of its futility, Clara seeks revenge, and confronts Father Eiras in Eureka. Although he writes a contract giving back her land, it turns out to be unenforceable, so once more, the pursuit of revenge wins her nothing. Clara decides that she needs to travel on her own to clarify her sense of herself. After she leaves, although he has no idea where she has gone, Helio writes her color letters every Friday and sends them to the Azores, trusting that she will find her way there some day. When Clara visits there and a friend gives her the letters, Clara understands that she always carries the past with her. She declares that the world she and Helio created together with their words, colors, and music was the foundation of reality: "it was not *a* world but *the* world when we made words and colors sing and when I had you." And she still carries her child with her, "for she had never lost what she had carried close to her heart" (p. 289). Both Helio and Clara understand that even if they never see each other again, the ecstatic moments they shared bind them together forever; what matters is not the past or the future, but those periods of time, however brief, when one fully engages multiple dimensions of the present.

The book concludes with Clara affirming ecstatic moments that integrate the present and the past, all varieties of art, and love: "Do not plan or worry beyond this present instant in which I am with you. In which I am art and music and words with you. Let us sculpt this moment to be everlasting like no other" (p. 297). *Saudade* moves toward grand moments that Vaz evokes not only with large philosophic statements about life but also with vivid imagery, trusting readers to lose themselves in the text completely enough to experience intuitively the happy fusion of art, life, and love it suggests. This fusion is something Vaz herself has experienced. During the nine years she played the piano, for example, Vaz sometimes got the sense that the notes carried her away, just as the words sometimes do as she writes. In an interview, she told Nancy Bunge: "That exhilaration made me want to be a writer. It was that simple" (p. 229). To understand the novel, then, the reader must also surrender to the text of *Saudade* and experience it without trying to give it sharp conceptual shape, sampling the exhilaration Vaz enjoys when she writes.

Vaz's awareness of Portuguese culture saturates this book, which helps explain why it was praised as the first novel about Portuguese Americans published by a major New York press. Originally printed by Barnes & Noble as part of its Discover Great New Writers series, it subsequently appeared in Portugal, where it became a

best seller. Critics have praised the book's magical lyricism; Sybil Steinberg, writing for *Publishers Weekly,* described it as a novel that invites the suspension of disbelief, allowing the reader to enter into an original and captivating world. Although a few critics had trouble giving themselves over to the novel, most lauded the book's poetry and inventiveness.

MARIANA

Vaz's second novel, *Mariana* (1997), is a stylistic departure from the first. In contrast to Clara's picaresque travels, this book focuses on a woman who spends her whole life in one location, the town of Beja in Portugal, and lives in a convent for the majority of her existence, practicing penance there for thirty years. Vaz has stressed the importance of her own Catholicism; this novel's characterization of the nun, Mariana, as a woman with an extraordinarily intense inner life hints at the value Vaz sees in her religion. But while Mariana possesses and enjoys overwhelming passion, Vaz's novel conveys this with more direct and quieter language than she used in *Saudade,* and with far more conventional and muted imagery. This stylistic understatement serves to highlight rather than obscure the emotional intensity of its central character. And despite its external differences from *Saudade, Mariana* also centers upon and moves toward moments of exaltation.

As the novel opens, Mariana, a passionate and confident young woman, decides that she will love a man named Rui forever. But her father declares that Rui will marry her more docile sister Ana Maria and then puts Mariana in a convent to limit the number of sons-in-law who can make claims on his land. In the convent, Mariana misses her family intensely, even pretending that the sound she makes shaking a box of buttons is her mother singing, but she reconciles herself to life there. She keeps accurate accounts under the guidance of a nun who assures her that even numbers relate to life and death and that Mariana needs to bring her emotional life to bear on this work to do it well.

Mariana then falls in love and has an affair with a French soldier named Noel Bouton. She feels as though this relationship re-creates her; daily life in the convent becomes something she must endure until he arrives in the evening. She brings such overwhelming passion to the relationship that it scares him away. Bouton believes that so much emotional intensity can lead only to trouble, so he abandons her. Mariana writes him a series of letters talking of her undying love and berating him for leaving her. The letters' bluntness both frightens and flatters Bouton, who publishes them anonymously in France. Eventually they get reprinted in many other countries. Mariana learns of the letters' publication and chooses to see it as testimony that Bouton has not forgotten her.

Because, like Clara, Mariana believes that her sorrow connects her to love, she refuses to renounce either one, even after thirty years of penance. Her tiny convent room remains saturated with the love she enjoyed there, and the connection she felt for Bouton becomes extended to others. She becomes particularly close to her sister, Peregrina, who also lives in the convent. Mariana serves as a surrogate mother to her younger sister, and the pleasure she finds in this role surprises her. When she dies, Mariana savors the fullness of her love not only for Bouton but for everyone she has known, both alive and dead; like *Saudade,* this novel asserts that love allows those who have passed from this life to continue to live through their influence on others. Mariana experiences such enormous joy that as she dies, she catches fire and becomes a star that comforts young lovers: "The greatest miracle open to anyone is to love madly. Therefore I defy everything in order to stand thus joyfully undone before you" (p. 299).

Meanwhile, Bouton enjoys a conventional, placid marital life. Given his dullness, people doubt rumors that the passionate love letters in the collection he published, *Letters of the Portuguese,* were addressed to him. And as he spends another torpid night sitting with his wife, he dreams of Mariana and the love they shared. Even though he has moved dramatically through the world while Mariana passed away her life in

a convent, she seems far more intensely alive than he, precisely because she refuses to disown her love for him or anyone else. The novel suggests that Bouton could not take the risk of living out his emotions completely, and for this he pays with a relatively desolate life. Mariana, on the other hand, welcomes discomforts and challenges, claiming that "any thought or action that did not entertain risk was merely a point of rest before the challenge of some other risk arrived" (p. 242).

In the novel, other nuns share Mariana's enthusiasm for exaltation and love. One dying nun explains to Mariana the French word *mouvement*, which she considers the finest in the world because it represents being carried away by emotion, "ecstasy unplanned for" (p. 95). Another nun tells Mariana that the greatest source of evil is lack of imagination. Yet another speaks of the joy of spending her life singing about mystery. The nuns even recognize the value of Mariana's passion, greedily absorbing it: "The sick nuns wanted to bathe in the almost supernatural love pouring from her like sunlight" (p. 241). And Catarina, another of Mariana's sisters who joins her in the convent, admires Saint Teresa's description of the four levels of water: the higher the level, the more the individual submits to larger powers until achieving "the searing ecstasy of actual heaven" (p. 113). So in this book, the exhilaration of love comes not only from human relationships but also from losing oneself in God.

Like *Saudade*, then, *Mariana* primarily values giving over the self to larger forces. To some extent this also describes the way Vaz shaped this book. Just as Mariana's father sits before his easel waiting patiently for God to send him a picture, Vaz lived with these materials a long time before they coalesced into a novel that she liked. A friend gave her the letters of Mariana Alcoforado, a seventeenth-century Portuguese nun who had an affair with a French solider. The letters have attracted the attention of other authors, including Rainer Maria Rilke, who translated them into German. Georges Braque, Amedeo Modigliani, and Henri Matisse attempted to render Mariana's image. Vaz translated the letters into English and began writing a book that used them to combine Mariana's story with a contemporary one. But after swimming one day, Vaz got a splitting headache and realized that Mariana wanted her own story. So she began the novel again and completed it in nine months, after working on the material for years. But all that patience paid off: the pieces came together into a compelling narrative.

The Library of Congress selected *Mariana* as one of the top thirty international books of 1998, and it has been published in six languages. Critics from other countries have praised the novel, including those reviewing for the *Times Literary Supplement* and the magazines *La Vanguardia* in Spain and *Activa* in Portugal. Vaz's two novels about American-Portuguese culture have made her something of a celebrity in Portugal: recognizing her from television interviews, people would send Vaz drinks in bars. She has also received recognition from the Portuguese community in the United States. *Luso-Americano* named her one of the top fifty Luso-Americans of the twentieth century; the Portuguese American Women's Association named her 2003 Woman of the Year, and she was appointed to a six-person delegation to attend the 1998 World's Fair in Portugal and meet with the president of Portugal, Jorge Sampaio. Vaz is also the first Portuguese American to have her work recorded for the Library of Congress.

FADO AND OTHER STORIES

Her next book, the short-story collection *Fado and Other Stories* (1997), perhaps can be most clearly understood with the backdrop provided by her two novels celebrating transcendent experiences, whether through love, art, or God. The Portuguese word *fado* refers to a genre of music characterized by *saudade*, or melancholy and longing, and in most of these stories characters fail to achieve the ecstasy that Clara and Mariana enjoy, so collectively, the book explores why most people fall short of these experiences. The first story, "Original Sin," uses some of the same material as *Saudade* but arrives at an entirely different conclusion because the unnamed

protagonist lacks Clara's courage. The central character, like Clara, has sex with a priest in an attempt to get revenge and, as a result, gives birth to a child—in this case a healthy girl who lives, but from whom she is alienated. She has a conventional marriage to a good man, with the accoutrements of a comfortable life, but she experiences misery rather than the intense happiness Clara enjoys: "The burning in me will not wash clean. I slip ice onto my tongue and into my clothes to fight the valley heat, but even many drops of water bring me no relief" (p. 8). She draws from her situation the lesson that seeking revenge is fruitless, but judging from *Saudade*, a more complete principle would be that bravely following the heart wherever it leads is the course to true joy. This protagonist lacks the backbone even to imagine Clara's courage as a possibility.

The next story, "The Birth of Water Stories," focuses on the connection between love and the discovery of this courage. The protagonist fears that the death of her love will cause her to become cowardly once more, but by the end of the story she believes that having known him is enough to sustain her. The tale begins with a woman frantically having sex with her fatally injured lover so that she can have his child. He has taught her, she claims, to trust herself enough to open herself to the world, having faith that what she encounters will enrich her: "To leap in and not be afraid of swimming in the open water. To carry my yearning into the unpredictable ocean" (p. 13). Her frantic attempt to have his child seems to grow from her fear that, without him, she will lose the nerve to expose herself to events she cannot control. Then her lover dies and she feels herself getting her period: there will be no child. But as bats appear while she eats her dinner, she believes they carry her a message from her lover, telling her to persist in living bravely despite his death: "You were telling me *enclose what is invisible, and then go on.* And I do, here now, so full of the water of you I am a prayer to bursting" (p. 15). The tale ends before the reader knows whether the protagonist fulfills this vow, but she at least knows the way to happiness.

The next story, "My Hunt for King Sebastião," similarly suggests that the courage to live fully also requires having enough optimism to trust in what life will bring rather than attempting to control it. It focuses on a purposeful American named David who goes to the Azores to resolve a property dispute for his father. But, instead, he discovers things about himself. First, he learns that he will not put his life at risk to save another man, or even to save a child. Then he discovers that he had a brother. While visiting a church, he has an epiphany, realizing that he and his contemporaries have substituted achievements and travel for transcendent ecstasy. He finally discovers life's magical possibilities with the help of people who gather along the shoreline to await the visit of the legendary hero King Sebastião, a young king who apparently died in battle, but whose missing body became the basis for a myth that some misty evening, he would return and restore Portugal to its triumphant past. These people do not believe King Sebastião really will appear and save them, but entertaining the hope that he might makes them happy. David concludes the story by addressing the reader, saying that this faith makes him brave enough to risk connecting with the reader and hearing his or her deepest yearnings, fears, and satisfactions: "You could tell me who you are and what glories you've seen, and if you are alone, you can impart to me truthfully how you feel to be abandoned; and if you would do me the exquisite kindness, then, of allowing me to read your face, and all that is borne in your eyes" (p. 41).

In "Math Bending unto Angels," Vaz once more returns to ecstatic experience, stressing that it cannot be constrained by the material world. In this story Clara's husband, a man obsessed with mathematics, knows that because of her angelic nature, he must lose her because he remains earthbound, even though she has brought him to life: "She made his geometry ... real and alive, and *singing*" (p. 45). Her intense spirituality means she must leave him, but her impact on his soul remains.

In the following story, "Undressing the Vanity Dolls," that spiritual sense is passed not between husband and wife but between student

and teacher. The former student, Reginald, goes to visit his dying professor, Eduardo Dias, suspecting that the professor may have had an affair with Reginald's wife, Alicia. Although he wants to ask about this, he falls back into the connection with nature the professor taught him; while admiring a glowing ocean and listening to the sounds of flowers talking, realities the professor introduced him to, he finds himself uninterested in asking about Eduardo's relationship with Alicia. An astronomer, Reginald begins talking about the stars in a way that seems compulsive, but eventually he presents the stars to the dying Eduardo as ways of approaching the spirit. He realizes that Eduardo has not always behaved well, but he brushes this reality aside to urge Eduardo to put his hand on his own heart to grasp the center of the galaxy. He acknowledges that Eduardo taught him about the infinitude of the spirit and urges him to continue to teach others this lesson and to allow Reginald's companionship to bring him peace: "*If you hear this language from someone who esteems you deeply, speak the stellar words with him, and say: I shall remember you, and how this grasp of what we learned together sings me to my rest*" (p. 74). Reginald wisely puts aside his anger and his confusion in order to treat Dias with compassion, and thus, they both reenter the rich spiritual world that Dias had initially exposed him to, a world in which Reginald must treat Eduardo with kindness.

The very short story "Island Fever" seems to summarize these tales by featuring a painter, ridiculed for his eccentricity, who realizes that those with imagination enjoy fuller lives than those who lack it. Although sorrow certainly enters into all these stories, they also present a variety of factors that enhance the ability to experience the joy that is central to Vaz's novels: courage, optimism, imagination, compassion, and love.

Still, many of the remaining stories in the collection stress that most people's lives remain closed to this larger dimension. "The Journey of an Eyeball" follows an eyeball that becomes detached from its owner and goes on a painful trip by itself. For instance, a woman mistakes it for an egg and tries to crack it open, an example of the utilitarian stance that dominates the world. It seeks the home of its owner's lover, and with this goal in mind, the eye has a moment when it perceives the rich colors of its environment. But the lover has little interest in the eye disconnected from its owner. After bouncing from place to place and getting damaged, the eye becomes discouraged because, without a brain, it can see no depth in objects. A doctor undertakes to cure it and, as a result, it can see only black and white. When it is cut to pieces and disintegrates, the eye has few regrets because its life has become so dull. The tale seems to be an allegory on the emptiness of living only in the physical world.

In "Still Life," a grandmother, like Vaz's, arranges to die while most of her relatives attend a wedding; she thinks she spares them discomfort. But, as Vaz's other work shows, even though losing someone one loves inevitably causes discomfort, that sorrow testifies to the depth of the love, and grief becomes a celebration of the departed person and the relationship. Ultimately the young woman in the story realizes that her grandmother had wanted no deathbed scenes because they would too painfully evoke her own love for those she was leaving behind. Rather than sparing them, she was saving herself from a full realization of her attachment to her relatives, a realization that would have enriched rather than diminished her life. This story suggests that fear of emotional turmoil also can prevent one from living fully.

The story "Fado" presents one disappointment after another. The young woman who narrates has spent time with her older neighbor Donna Xica, at the encouragement of her parents, because she has no grandmother. But Xica has a house full of melancholy. She left the Azores to find happiness in America, but her husband died at sea and now she tends to her son, Manuel, whose automobile accident has left him too injured to speak. Xica teaches the narrator some positive things, such as how to get honey from the stamen of an azalea and how to get over her fear of wild beasts, but, principally, the girl learns sadness in Xica's house. Sorrow pervades even the narrator's own home. When she enjoys time

with her father, she realizes that she misses him even when he sits beside her because she knows they will eventually be separate from one another. And the narrator's mother is spiteful: when the plumber cannot make adequate repairs, the mother hangs her mildewed towels over his windows.

Xica tries futilely to teach her son words so that he will speak again. Manuel's wife, Marina, betrays him, and an angry Xica begins to record the offenses she has endured from everyone she knows, along with her plans for retaliation. She pledges to call up a local gossip five times on the telephone and say nothing. She even includes God on her list of parties deserving retribution. Despite Manuel's intense love for Marina, Xica throws her out. A priest takes Xica, Manuel, and the narrator out on a boat in an attempt to help them find some peace. But Manuel, seeing a couple making love, jumps toward them and drowns. Shortly thereafter, his mother prepares to die. The narrator takes revenge on Marina, letting her birds loose in her house and hiding eggs there that she hopes will rot before Marina can find them.

Meanwhile, the narrator begins a romantic relationship with a boy named Michael, who acts as though he does not know her after they have sex. Then, the rotting eggs and the birds flying around Marina's house drive her mad. Presumably because the narrator's own pain over being jilted helps her develop compassion, she realizes the inappropriateness of her behavior. She remembers that when Xica washed the mute Manuel, she looked radiant because she acted out of love. And that when Xica turned to revenge, she destroyed herself. After acknowledging this, the narrator drops her own pursuit of revenge and finds peace taking care of Marina. She realizes that the best way to live is not seeking vengeance, but holding others close: "We must create Pietás in order to live. Flesh that is torn, flesh that is dead or dying, even as it is rotting through your fingers—hold it next to your heart.... Hold it for as long as you can, and ask for its blessing" (p. 110). Once again, Vaz affirms that joy necessarily comes interlaced with sorrow and that the wisest choice consists not in trying to

shape a world free of pain but in accepting the world, complete with its sorrow, and caring for others who also suffer.

Nineteenth-century Hawaii is the setting for "The Remains of Princess Kaiulani's Garden," which interweaves real historical figures—prominently the short-lived Kaiulani (1875–1899), heir to the Hawaiian throne—with a fictional young protagonist named Elena. Elena has a father full of joy and a mother too frightened to express her emotions. The family has emigrated to Hawaii from Portugal, and her father enchants the Hawaiians, including King Kalakaua, with his ukulele playing. Her mother, on the other hand, worries too much about what others think to enjoy herself. While her husband plays, she sits rigid. Elena believes that since she herself cannot make ukuleles, she has no music in her. Her father asks what she loves to do and she confesses that she enjoys ironing, so she and her mother open a laundry. The story represents ironing as a kind of art form, since it exposes the hidden beauty in washed clothes, just as, say, a sculptor reveals the aesthetic potential of a piece of marble. Elena decides to be different from her cranky mother, so she tries to make music as she washes the laundry, even though her mother reprimands her for splashing water. And the garments Elena handles with her embarrassingly large hands have magical powers. A man struggling with a chest cold loses it after wearing a shirt Elena has washed; after donning something Elena ironed, an old lady turns cartwheels; after inhaling the clean clothes Elena has produced, a man's sinuses clear. The streets of Hawaii fill with people singing and dancing because they wear clothes Elena has prepared for them by doing what she loves.

The sickly Princess Kaiulani sends clothes for Elena and her mother to clean, but when her mother claims it is she who has the magical touch, Elena remains silent. The mother, not Elena, washes and irons the clothes the princess has sent, and when the princess wears them, they make her anxious, like the mother. Their laundry stops doing well; her father stops spending time at home, and the royal family of Hawaii loses its power. Elena believes this happens because when

the princess expressed unhappiness with her clothes, Elena cursed her. Elena reverses herself, praying for the princess and feeling a connection with her. But everything continues to deteriorate. Elena's mother eventually sustains a head injury and becomes docile, so Elena finds it easy to care for her. As the tale concludes, Elena draws the moral that there is no point in planting gardens because everything passes away. But the reader sadly notes that Elena, who never trusted herself, did possess powers but threw them away when she deferred to her anxious, competitive mother instead of asserting herself. So the story's true moral is to have enough confidence in oneself and one's abilities to do what one loves.

In "Add Blue to Make White Whiter," Vaz explores the danger of seeking too much purity. Vas opens the story with a discussion of the need to modulate the amount of blue one adds to make white whiter by talking about an aunt who had to stay home because she added too much blue to her white hair. The tale then shifts to a woman listening to her friend advise her that she needs to break off an affair with a married man. The woman listens, hears this judgment, stops talking about him, and moves, convincing her friends that she has left him behind. She has fooled them, but she still feels compelled to cleanse herself. She keeps trying to purify herself with various substances, finally losing patches of her skin. As the story ends, she resorts to bleach: "All that was remaining of me was concentrated into poisonous fumes, a cleanser that would cause skin rashes" (p. 137). This story metaphorically illustrates yet another path that leads away from the kind of joy Vaz writes about in *Saudade* and *Mariana*: disowning all inappropriate impulses in an attempt to achieve perfection. Here, perfection means emotional death.

"How to Grow Orchids Without Grounds: A Manual" focuses on a man named Alfonso, who, as a soldier in Africa, had discovered that he could not find the courage to aid an African woman while his commanding officer and then another soldier raped her. Realizing his cowardice has left him shattered. His sense of unworthiness keeps him inside, raising orchids that he sneaks into people's houses, expecting that they will enjoy making corsages with them. One person actually does this: a nun named Sister Angela. Others react according to their own obsessions. A policeman and the nun who runs the convent resent the intrusion. Maria hopes that her husband or some other man gives them to her to declare his admiration. And George, Maria's husband, knows that the man who has left the orchids must be a soldier, because the hairs on George's arm—which had been wounded in battle—stand on end. George wants to talk with Alonso to discover why he delivers orchids to people's houses. The war has left George as rudderless as it has Alonso; he hopes that in understanding Alonso, he will achieve some clarity about himself. The story focuses on these two men frozen by war, but most of the tale's other characters also seem lost to themselves and disconnected from others. The two possible exceptions consist of the nun who happily pins an orchid to her habit and the son of George and Marie who first draws a picture of his father as a blank. Although the boy understands his father's emptiness, his own hunger for fighting and confrontation may well lead him into the haunted existence shared by Alonso and his father. This tale implies that war, confrontation, or an intense need to protect one's territory all obstruct happiness.

In *Fado and Other Stories,* then, many characters yearn for the kind of passionate abandon Clara and Mariana enjoyed in Vaz's first two novels, but this requires courage, compassion, imagination, and optimism that these characters may lack. It also requires more than a purely physical view of reality and the ability to tolerate emotional turbulence, resist obsession with protecting one's territory, develop self-trust, and shun revenge.

Fado and Other Stories won the 1997 Drue Heinz Literature Prize. The collection won praise for its magic and for its ties to Portuguese culture, but appropriately, since Vaz had begun to explore not only these moments of exaltation but the psychological issues that encourage or obstruct them, reviewers also started to note the depth of Vaz's psychological depictions. In the *Washington Post Book Review,* Angie Cruz praised Vaz for

bravely writing about the emptiness in her characters' lives.

Vaz comments that when she was fifty, she left California, where she had lived all her life, for the East Coast. This meant walking away from a well-established life including a teaching job at the University of California at Davis. Once she arrived she started to apply for work and was offered a position as Briggs-Copeland Lecturer in Fiction at Harvard University. This brave shift is consistent with Vaz's claim that writers need to remain open to the world's influence, giving themselves a chance to see where events take them.

OUR LADY OF THE ARTICHOKES AND OTHER PORTUGUESE-AMERICAN STORIES

In her next collection, *Our Lady of the Artichokes and Other Portuguese-American Stories* (2008), Vaz continues studying what it takes to facilitate the emotional surrender that represents the highest good in her writing. "Taking a Stitch in a Dead Man's Arm" again stresses the value of courage and self-trust, this time through the narrator, Isabel Dias, as she looks back on her relationship with her father. As a boy, her father once took a stitch in a dead man's arm to in order to conquer fear, as the mythology of his childhood had promised. But as he dies, he says it is not fear, but waiting, that causes the most harm.

As a teenager, Isabel makes larger and larger gestures toward following her father's advice and attempting to seize what she wants. She considers herself in love with James, a boy who once threw a live cigarette butt at a Hell's Angel and survived. She writes him a speech that wins a contest for him, but he has a girlfriend. On the school bus, Isabel tells Charles Mayer, who everyone agrees has a future as a professional basketball player, that he has misspelled "receive." After that he gives her other work to correct. One of Charles' essays argues for the importance of every moment; Isabel believes that this validates her significance to him, and that notion thrills her. When she writes this story as an adult, however, Isabel comes to the conclu-

sion that she must break off her relationship with a married man—a relationship that, on its face, might suggest that she has been following her father's advice to seize what she wants. What she realizes, however, is that her involvement with him shuts out the rest of her world, leaving her reduced to nothing but waiting. She ends the story declaring that she will spend the rest of her days learning how to follow her father's advice not to wait for life to come to her.

"All Riptides Roar with Sand from Opposing Shores," written in epistolary form, traces another woman's life from childhood to adulthood. This protagonist, Lara Pereira, and her friends write an extremely sweet and naive letter to a nun named Lucia who has had a vision of Mary, asking what secret Mary shared with her. When no reply arrives, Lara herself writes again in a manner that makes clear she had become sharply focused on her appearance during the intervening year. Six years later, at fifteen, she sets out to write an angry letter to the still silent Lucia, reprimanding her for her rudeness, but what the letter ends up revealing is that Lara's father's death has depressed and upset her. She concludes it by asking Lucia to use her influence to help her father's case in the afterlife. The letters seem to offer wildly different versions of Lara, but, in fact, they all manifest her passionate commitment to whatever seizes her attention at the moment.

By the time she writes Lucia again at twenty-four, Lara is focusing on relationships with men and her child. Although she has the nerve and emotional fervor that Isabel Dias seems to lack, Lara has also come to understand and expect that she will spend her life learning to conquer fear. She sees that even the human tendency to demand finished results from God reflects our terror: "Our fear of learning how to love the world's mystery" (p. 22).

At thirty, Lara writes to a friend about Lucia and guesses that the nun's visions resulted from her repressed sexuality. But no matter what their basis, those visions afforded her the ecstatic insight that, again and again, redeems the lives of Vaz's protagonists. Lara asks her friend, "Who can blame her for having enormous desires?

Whatever was operating, she spilled it out, created a story, a refigured sky, an event that history will retain." Lara believes this gave Lucia the few moments of transcendence for which everyone longs: "I see her as a woman alone who pierced herself with a few stunning, life-cracking hours. Isn't that what we all want?" (p. 24).

Then Lara receives a letter from Helen Dodd, a journalist assigned to do a story on Lucia. Helen tells Lara that she sobbed when she saw Lucia's pathetic condition, so she has taken on Lucia's care. Cynical about the religious aspects of the world she has entered, she finds the activities at Fatima so appalling that she faints there. But she claims she discovered "the music I needed" (p. 26) when she read the letter Lara had sent about her boyfriend's death; Helen has lost her son and husband. Unable to connect to nature, Helen turns down an offer to go look at a river, but enjoys the sounds made by green bottles on a pear tree. Lara responds with a letter full of love and rich associations between powerful images, unintentionally demonstrating to Helen the vivid world her detachment has cost her. Helen tells Lara that someone tied green bottles around the pear blossoms on a pear tree behind the house and, at night, she listens to the music made by the leaves on grown pears brushing against the bottles. She sends Lara a picture and Lara concludes her response by telling Helen that she had pressed it against her chest. First, she smelled the pears and, eventually, "I heard the music of which you spoke" (p. 32). Lara's letters reveal her as a person who gives herself to strong emotions and, as a result, lives in a vibrant world.

In "Our Lady of the Artichokes," a seventeen-year-old named Isabel Serpa moves from cynicism to hope. Isabel's difficulty with trust makes sense in terms of her background: she lives with her aunt because her father committed suicide and her mother abandoned her. As the story begins, her aunt, Tia Connie, attempts to derail their landlord's plan to raise their rent by claiming to have a vision of the Virgin Mary in the artichoke grove outside their apartment. Although Isabel reveals some commitment to imagination's power when she consoles herself with fantasies of a banker boyfriend she names Noland, her

experiences have left her deeply cynical about religious matters, so her aunt decides that the report of seeing the Virgin would have more credibility if it came from Isabel. But Isabel's aunt recruits elderly widows for this task, and Isabel regards the widows with contempt as they fervently pray at the place where the visitation supposedly happened. Then miracles actually do begin to occur. Isabel kicks a lame girl out of jealousy and cures her; her aunt breaks her neck and survives. These events attract religious fanatics to their home and the landlord lowers the rent. But when no third miracle occurs, everyone turns on them, including the landlord; their rent goes up again. Isabel and her aunt take the bus after a failed attempt to win the money they need at bingo, and they recognize their kind bus driver, Rui, who comes from the Azores, as the man who saved Isabel from a mob of fanatics. He brushes off this generous act by claiming that the Virgin rescued her, even after Tia Connie has told him she invented the vision. Rui and Connie marry, Rui pays the rent, and the three of them enjoy a happy, eccentric existence.

But then Rui gets sick. After he is diagnosed with leukemia, he asks Isabel to look at him, and she notes that death forces people to resign their defenses and honestly confront one another: "Death runs a scalpel through the gel surrounding us and says, Come out" (p. 50). She knows Rui has saved them all with his faith and hopefulness, and Isabel wonders if living well means loving each other so intensely that the world becomes richer than any fantasy: "Oh, what if prayer is really surrender? What if it is up to each of us to love in a way that gives birth into the dreamed-up realm of the world?" (p. 50). When Rui asks her the sex and name of the baby she will have someday, Isabel says, "Clara," the name of the passionate protagonist of *Saudade*. Isabel explains to Rui that the name means "light, gap or opening, egg white, clarity" (p. 51). So, through experiencing the pleasures love and faith has introduced into her life through the kind, generous Rui, Isabel embraces the potential of hope.

In "My Bones Here Are Waiting for Yours," a woman achieves some acceptance of her

daughter's death by experiencing unreciprocated love: even resigning oneself to passion that results in failure has benefits. The protagonist has had her picture taken every year at the place her daughter's body was found seventeen years before the story begins. At the story's start, the woman appears rigid, posing always in a stiff turquoise suit. Then she falls in love with a man who reciprocates sexual attraction, but not love; still, the affair awakens her emotionally, and her new vitality helps her understand that her daughter killed herself because of an affair with her swimming coach. She gives the coach a token, not out of vengeance, but because she hopes it will help him remember her daughter and their time together. She now poses in an aqua shift, showing that while she still continues to mourn her daughter, a process that will persist for all her life, she has progressed beyond rigidity.

"The Man Who Was Made of Netting" tells of Manny Cruz, a supposedly recovered gambler who helps himself to money from his brother-in-law's business in order to buy his daughter a stunning cape for her to wear at the Portuguese Holy Ghost Festival in Monterey, which a talent scout is expected to attend. Manny thinks that his daughter's appearance in the cape will win over the talent scout, guaranteeing her a lucrative movie career. Manny calls the event a "Hollywood lottery" (p. 68), which makes it clear that he is stealing the money as a kind of bet. But Manny cannot allow himself to admit that what he has done is gambling because he has promised his daughter to stop.

His daughter, Gemma, looks magnificent in her cape, but Manny realizes that his niece, Daisy, has a beauty that comes not from expensive adornments but from an easy self-acceptance. Manny promises the Holy Ghost that if his daughter Gemma becomes a star, he will feed everyone. When his brother-in-law, Frank, reminds Manny that an auditor will review the books at their firm the following week, Manny's concerns escalate. When the talent scout sees the girls, he wants Daisy to wear Gemma's cape in the movie, a decision that delights Gemma, who says that, unlike Daisy, she gets stage fright. Even after this news tosses Manny into misery, he ap-

preciates his daughter's kindness: "What had he ever done, to be rewarded with such a generous girl?" (p. 84). But the talent scout's decision leaves Manny vulnerable to both poverty and jail.

That night Gemma has a nightmare that makes her feel suffocated. Her father reassures her that people learn compassion when they begin to understand that everyone experiences such feelings of suffocation. The story ends with Manny reflecting on the painfully temporary nature of love. The tale leaves open what disappeared or disappointing love makes Gemma panic; the nightmare might concern her recently deceased grandfather, with whom she developed a close tie when her mother abandoned the family and her father struggled with his gambling; or it might be her intuitive realization that she has already lost her father to prison. In either case, the tale provides ample evidence that even though Gemma's empathy will guarantee that the loss of any relationship will pain her, she will also enjoy many more connections with others. Ultimately the tale validates the force of self-confidence and empathy as well as the fruitlessness of competitiveness.

"The Knife Longs for the Ruby" links loving someone and creating a work of art; Vaz not only highlights the tie between them, but also suggests that the artwork has superior power. The tale centers on the relationship between a nineteenth-century priest in Brazil, Father Jaime, and Tónio, whom he had adopted after the boy's mother died in childbirth. When the story opens, Tónio, now thirty, is recovering from a late evening with a prostitute and tending to the inebriated priest, who drinks himself into oblivion every Friday to forget the deaths of his wife and child. The priest gives a piece of rosewood to Tónio, who begins to carve with blunt knives because, the priest suspects, he understands that difficulty makes completing a task more satisfying. Tónio sees his job as giving himself over to the rosewood and helping it to realize itself. At the start, Tónio's relationship with a woman named Teresa helps inspire him, but when she moves on, he keeps working. After eight years, he produces a crucifix that does not satisfy him. Father Jaime gives

KATHERINE VAZ

Tónio a sack of rubies so he can establish a free and independent life for himself. But instead, he smashes the rubies with a hammer and uses the fragments to represent Christ's blood on his crucifix, finally completing his statue in a way that pleases him: "He fell deeply in love with this living thing given to him, this beautiful sorrowing creation, and death came for him hardly a heartbeat after he closed his eyes" (p. 101).

Father Jaime, expelled by the Jesuits for objecting to their use of slaves, also attempts to make art, writing stories about medieval Lisbon. After Tónio starts carving the rosewood, Father Jaime begins writing stories about his wife that immerse him in the realities of their life together and the pain of her passing. He realizes that Tónio had given himself up while carving his rosewood: "Perhaps there comes a moment when one's own wants give way toward the inspiration of God's will" (p. 95). One could argue that Father Jaime has the same experience when he composes stories that force him to engage his own difficult history. Once he begins writing about his wife, his respect for her forces him to stop drinking: "He would die before sullying the writing of her name with an unsteady hand" (p. 98). Father Jaime envies a writer whose work comes more easily to him, but the tale's narrator suggests that this author's wife paid for his fluency: "The scars of her marriage had sliced into her in a way that no one else should fathom" (p. 100). Father Jaime and Tónio both struggle to produce art because at the heart of their creation rests the same kind of profound giving over that undergirds the best relationships.

"The Mandarin Question" has as its protagonist a woman named Faye, whose father shot and killed her mother the day she was born two months premature. She attributes her survival to the constant care of her aunt, Tia Clara, who raises her. Faye passes on this caring to others, playing her violin to soothe the cows on the way to slaughter and lying next to Evan Redken, a man dying alone of cancer, so she can hold him: three weeks later, no sign of his cancer remains. At the story's end, she meets Henry Dunne, whose tour in Iraq has left him with dead-looking eyes. She makes love with him and plays her violin and believes that her love for him, like her aunt's affection for her, leads him back into life: "Out of his insides there came a glowing, light as the touch of a newborn, come back to life to love me" (p. 113). So the love Faye extends to both animals and people also redeems her.

"Lisbon Story," the last tale in this collection, validates the central importance of love and empathy for everyone. It follows an American woman, Catarina, whose father wants her to sell his Lisbon apartment before he dies. She arrives to discover a young man in the apartment: named Mateus, he is dying of AIDS and living there courtesy of her friend Tónio, who once loved him. Catarina and Tónio too love each other: they sleep together and often embrace each other, but given his homosexuality, they have no sexual relationship. Though all three care deeply about each other, Catarina wants Mateus out so that she can settle her dying father's affairs and allow him to pass away in peace.

When her father hears about Mateus, he instructs her to go out and buy two cherry liqueurs: one for Mateus and another for Catarina and Tónio to share. They enjoy them with a meal of fruit and fish so beautiful that "the pause of beholding it all was our grace" (p. 138). They call Catarina's father to report the event, and Mateus gets a fish bone caught in his throat. Tónio and Catarina struggle to remove it as Catarina's father, a former hospital worker, guides them. The episode leaves Mateus exhausted, so Catarina's father blesses him as he falls asleep. These characters have all become a family as loving as it is unconventional.

Vaz's descriptions of Lisbon, especially of all the activity in the streets, complement the story's emotional richness. As Catarina carries the cherry liqueurs toward the apartment, she toasts her surroundings: "Here's to the gargoyles on cornices; here's to you, funiculars and iron Juliet balconies, and to you, azulejos—tiles of griffins, bears, and explorers in the hues of sky and ocean, cloud and whitecap" (p. 137). Vaz's description suggests a city that appeals to every sense, populated by people as easily kind to one another as those settled in her father's apartment. Catarina's father tells Mateus, who is reluctant to die at home

because his parents disapprove of his homosexuality, that parents push away children because the intensity of their desire to keep their children close frightens them. Catarina uses this truth to justify rushing home to care for her father; Mateus returns to his parents the day her father dies and passes away himself a month later. As her father's end nears, Catarina takes him to the children's hospital where he worked and dresses him in pajamas covered with whales and dolphins. She is certain these animals will take him across the sea to Lisbon and then "from there to lift as fallen rain does in an exaltation of quiet back to the wide blue sky" (p. 151). As the story ends, Catarina concludes that it is never too late to save yourself by rescuing someone else. The tale's gorgeous imagery and language underline its theme that kindness restores us all, both the giver and the receiver, both parents and child.

Our Lady of the Artichokes and Other Portuguese-American Stories won the Prairie Schooner Book Prize in Fiction. Vaz undoubtedly worked on it during her year as a fellow at the Radcliffe Institute for Advanced Study. Critics once again praised her sensual, vivid writing and psychological insight, as well as the wisdom of these tales and their portrayals of people struggling toward grace.

Vaz has sometimes worried about writing so many short stories, but it made sense that after her two novels she turn to shorter work. The ecstatic experiences central to her work are necessarily intermittent and brief. In her two short-story collections, she clarifies why. The tales in *Fado and Other Stories* set out obstructions to these moments of elation: a lack of courage, an obsession with purity, a desire for revenge, a passion for protecting one's private space. *Our Lady of the Artichokes* concentrates more on the ways one can increase those moments, through bravery, love, art, and compassion. Vaz dedicates this book to "my Christopher," her partner Christopher Cerf. But allusions to fathers surface frequently in the stories and in epigraphs between the tales. The book appeared in 2008, five years before her eighty-seven-year-old father passed away on September 12, 2013. So the collection also seems a testimony to her father's

impact on her life and work. The love of Portuguese culture her father introduced her to has blessed Vaz with a readiness to welcome imagination, and her fiction generously makes this world available to all her readers. Perhaps because she first experienced this magic while listening to her father as a child, Vaz has also produced a number of wildly fanciful stories for children that undoubtedly pass on to the very young the bewitching domain her father presented to her. Vaz believes that nurturing the ability to entertain the supernatural could enrich everyone's life: "This cultivation of the miraculous is open to us all if we believe that our memories and imaginations provide unlimited visions" ("My Hunt for King Sebastião," p. 54). Near the end of her essay about her father's final illness, "Gone to Feed the Roses," Vaz writes, "My father is my home forever." Then she concludes by acknowledging the reverence for marvels that has shaped her life and her work: "I must be tender toward mystery."

Selected Bibliography

WORKS OF KATHERINE VAZ

NOVELS

Saudade. New York: St. Martin's Press, 1994.

Mariana. London: Flamingo, 1997; Minneapolis, Minn.: Aliform, 2004.

SHORT STORIES

Fado and Other Stories. Pittsburgh, Pa.: University of Pittsburgh Press, 1997. (Contains "Original Sin," "The Birth of Water Stories," "My Hunt for King Sebastião," "Math Bending Unto Angels," "Undressing the Vanity Dolls," "Island Fever," "The Journey of the Eyeball," "Still Life," "Fado," "The Remains of Princess Kaiulani's Garden," "Add Blue to Make White Whiter," "How to Grow Orchids Without Grounds: A Manual.")

Our Lady of the Artichokes and Other Portuguese-American Stories. Lincoln and London: University of Nebraska Press, 2008. (Contains "Taking a Stitch in a Dead Man's Arm," "All Riptides Roar with Sand from Opposing Shores," "Our Lady of the Artichokes," "My Bones Here Are Waiting for Yours," "The Man Who Was Made of Netting," "The Knife Longs for the Ruby," "The Mandarin

Question," "Lisbon Story.")

OTHER WORKS

Cross-Training: The Complete Book of the Triathlon. New York: Avon, 1984.

The High-Performance Triathlete. Chicago: Contemporary Books, 1985.

Swim, Swim: A Complete Handbook for Fitness Swimmers. Chicago: Contemporary Books, 1986.

"Songs of the Soul." *New York Times Magazine,* September 18, 1994. Pp. 44–46, 54–57.

"Baptism." In *Signatures of Grace.* Edited by Thomas Grady, Paula Huston, and Murray Bodo. New York: Dutton, 2000. Pp. 1–33.

"My Hunt for King Sebastião: How We Invite Miracles into Art and Everyday Life." In *Global Impact of the Portuguese Language.* Edited by Asela Rodríguez de Laguna. New Brunswick, N.J., and London: Transaction, 2001. Pp. 51–60.

Introduction to *My World Is Not of This Kingdom,* by João De Melo. Translated by Gregory Rabassa. Minneapolis, Minn.: Aliform, 2003. Pp. ii–ix.

"A Tabula Rasa Experiment." In *Now Write! Fiction Writing Exercises from Today's Best Writers.* Edited by Sherry Ellis. New York: Tarcher/Penguin, 2006. Pp. 39–42.

"Gone to Feed the Roses." *Narrative,* winter 2014. http://www.narrativemagazine.com/issues/winter-2014/gone-feed-roses-katherine-vaz

CRITICAL AND BIOGRAPHICAL STUDIES

Bunge, Nancy. "Katherine Vaz." In her *Master Class: Lessons from Leading Writers.* Iowa City: University of Iowa Press, 2005. Pp. 228–237. (Interview.)

Cruz, Angie. "Portuguese Blues." *Washington Post Book Review,* December 28, 1997. P. 8.

Silva, Reinaldo Francisco. "Madly in Love Outside the Church and the Nunnery." In *Expanding Latinidad: An Inter-American Perspective.* Trier, Germany: Wissenschaftlicher Verlag Trier, 2012. Pp. 71–86.

Steinberg, Sybil. "*Saudade.*" *Publishers Weekly,* April 11, 1954, p. 53.

CAROLYN WELLS

(1862—1942)

Windy Counsell Petrie

CAROLYN WELLS WAS that now rarely seen type of author who openly defied the twentieth-century trend toward specialization. Equally notable as a sharp-witted American humorist, a purveyor of sentimental children's stories, and a prolific murder-mystery novelist, the indefatigable Carolyn Wells published an average of three books a year for her entire adult life. When she was not writing limericks, idylls, or detective fiction, she worked first as a town librarian, and then privately to amass the most comprehensive collection of Walt Whitman's works, correspondence, and ephemera in existence. The Whitman material now resides in Rare and Special Collections in the U.S. Library of Congress, the juvenile fiction has a cult following and continues to sell in reprinted paperback facsimiles, and the mysteries still circulate through libraries, used bookstores, and ninety-nine-cent downloadable files. To this day, one reader's or collector's Carolyn Wells may bear no resemblance to another's. Only an exploration of her endless energies, determinedly good-natured outlook, and love for a challenging puzzle can bring the seemingly disparate aspects of her oeuvre into a coherent whole.

LIFE

Wells was born on June 18, 1862, in Rahway, New Jersey, to indulgent middle-class parents, William and Anna Wells. She traces her "stern and rockbound ancestors" from New England, where the first Welles to arrive in America (the spelling was later changed in the American branch of the family) became an early governor of Connecticut, all the way back to Old England in 1299, paying attention to the roles played by the Welles family in the war of Gascony and the

"restoration of King Henry VI" (*The Rest of My Life*, pp. 75–78). Aside from that, she merely notes in her autobiography that both her parents were great natural spellers, avid chess players whose regular family tournaments ranged from fifty to one hundred games each, and devout but loving Presbyterians who prayed with her to receive God's grace when she erred. Her depiction of her childhood in *The Rest of My Life* (1937) reads as an idyllic exploration of her inherent attraction to words and games. Claiming to have debunked Alexander Pope's popular lines from *An Essay on Criticism*, "True ease in writing come from art, not chance / As those move easiest who have learned to dance," she declares that "writing is not an art, it is nature. It cannot be learned, it is inborn" (*My Maiden Effort*, p. 255). To her, "writing never seemed like work" (*The Rest of My Life*, p. 170). Establishing herself as hailing from a line of scribblers, Wells's memoir quotes lines from a poem her mother's mother wrote to amuse her children. Like the toddler Edith Wharton described in that author's autobiography, *A Backward Glance*, Wells explains that she also wrote her first poems at the age of three (with "perfect meter"), and her first book at the age of six (*The Rest of My Life*, p. 30). Her precociousness was noted and cherished by her parents, who encouraged her preschool efforts in literature; in fact, Anna Wells saved bits of her daughter's literary juvenilia all her life.

When she was six years old, Wells contracted scarlet fever along with her younger sister, Allie. While her sister died, Wells eventually recovered, but lost most of her hearing. She underwent many painful and unsuccessful operations throughout her life trying to restore it, and declared her deafness to be "the one cherry in my bowl that ought to be thrown out." (p. 54). Because of it, she

declared in her 1937 autobiography, "I have lost one proposal of marriage, two invitations for trips abroad, three or four worth-while gifts, an airplane ride and a few requests for autographs" (p. 56). She relates a number of amusing stories about it, including an awkward conversation with President Theodore Roosevelt, and publically concluded that her handicap "hurt [her] most through [her] pride and vanity" (p. 57). Though she joked about it, she and others have speculated on the strong role it may have played in the course of her life and career as an author. Having discussed their mutual deafness several times with her good friend Thomas Edison, she quoted him as saying "it let him shut out all noises and concentrate on his work" (p. 56). Perhaps his advice influenced her own ability to cope: "I have many resources within myself," she mused, "and it is these that help me bear my deafness with equanimity" (p. 56). The isolation it caused her (and the occasional misunderstandings with others) could be temporarily ameliorated and perhaps even forgotten in the world of reading and writing books, and in her copious lifelong correspondence with her many friends.

Though she graduated Rahway High School as valedictorian, Wells refused to be sent to college to learn what other people thought was important in a manner that she considered wasted a great deal of time. She wished instead to stay in "the home [she] loved so much" and learn what she wished on her own schedule (*The Rest of My Life,* p. 36). Although her parents had already picked out a college for her, they acquiesced to her request to stay home, and there, she declared, "I began my education" (p. 36). For the next few years, Wells simply corralled or corresponded with people whom she thought expert in the areas she wanted to master. In the small social world of the late-nineteenth-century Northeast, Wells made great use of her self-designed education, going to Amherst to attend the Sauveur Summer School of Languages and studying Shakespeare with the noted scholar William J. Rolfe. On such educational jaunts as these, her family's network of acquaintances came in handy: she found herself taking tea with Emily Dickinson's sister Lavinia one afternoon,

and lunching with Rudyard Kipling at a mutual friend's party, quizzing him about his Jungle Books, on another occasion.

Since she was living at home, hoped never to leave (in fact, she never lived anywhere else until her move to New York City after she married at age fifty-six), and adored books, the town of Rahway put their library in her charge. For Wells, it was the perfect occupation, and though she was only eighteen, she already felt it had been a long time in coming. The first time she saw a library, in the home of the family's Presbyterian minister, she was "awed beyond words at the sight of books that ran up to the ceiling" (p. 189). Young Carolyn had soon started seeking out other libraries, befriending a local "Quaker gentleman" in order to visit his book room and slipping out of town meetings to explore the library next to her church. Soon she was volunteering at the semiannual ladies' association library, cleaning, wiping dust from the volumes on the top shelf until she found one she wanted to read, and then settling down on top of a stepladder for the rest of the day. When she was appointed librarian, she promptly and aggressively built the Rahway Library Association an impressive and eclectic collection, establishing some new contacts with publishers and authors in the process. The position also afforded her opportunities to travel around New England and to Europe to visit the world's best libraries, including the Bodleian, which she loved, the British Museum library, which she loathed, and the Boston Athenaeum, which she ranked the highest for its "coziness" (p. 194). Back in Rahway, she had all the publishers' catalogs sent to her, with "no restrictions of expense or judgment" as to what she ordered (p. 193). Since the town library was only open to patrons two days a week, her work there became her primary means of self-education: "every book worth having we bought; every periodical worth reading we subscribed to, and the librarian sat in the middle and read her way out," she recalled in her memoirs (p. 193). Having read everything she ordered for the library, Wells's next career began. With "a good memory," as well as "time, and the liberty to publish" (p. 48), she began writing nearly as

quickly she could read. Her body of work provides continual proof of her voracious reading and her memory for words, for she and her characters quote freely and extensively from Plutarch, Francis Bacon, Henry Fielding, Alexander Pope, Nathaniel Hawthorne, Jonathan Swift, Alexandre Dumas, Kipling, Leo Tolstoy, and P. T. Barnum, among many others.

Wells's ability to appreciate the work of others led to extensive literary friendships, both in person and via correspondence. Her autographed collection of poems, drawings, notes, and other ephemera was kept in her "Mermaid" book, which began as the ubiquitous autograph album possessed by every high school girl from 1870 to 1920. Hers was named for the picture of a tavern emblem called *At the Sign of the Mermaid* on the cover, and featured a collection of quotes from poems and stories about mermaids in its pages. Unlike most high school girls, however, Wells kept adding to the album all her life and by the 1930s it was as eclectic and impressive in its own way as was the Whitman collection she assembled in her sixties. Many pages from the album were reproduced as plates in her autobiography, and they alone would make the book worth the purchase. All of them are original sketches, poems, notes, quips, and cartoons from the celebrities of her day, which can be found in no other book, magazine, or collection. They include a self-portrait of G. K. Chesterton, an original poem Rudyard Kipling handwrote for Wells and autographed, and a get-well note with a private joke from Mark Twain, among many others. Wells was clearly a born collector, with the eye and the energy that entails, and also a woman who immediately put people from all walks of life at their ease, as evidenced by a cartoon in her possession that was drawn and dedicated to her by a famous military man, Rear Admiral Charles D. Sigsbee. The only literary celebrity Wells met but apparently did not impress was Theodore Dreiser, when she was a young woman trying to get an assignment as a society reporter for the *Delineator*. Wells reported that Dreiser took one look at her, her hat and coat bedraggled by a rainstorm, and declared her not right for the job. Despite that minor setback, she never lost

her optimism that people were always ready for some good company and witty repartee, and she rarely left home without her Mermaid Book in which to collect drawings, signatures, limericks, and the nonsense she so treasured from any noteworthy person whom she met.

Though she was always surrounded by congenial company, Wells did not marry until her mid-fifties. On April 2, 1918, Wells wed Hadwin Houghton—not the Henry Oscar Houghton of the famed publishing house Houghton Mifflin, nor a son, as Henry Houghton had no children, but his cousin from another branch of the family. The Houghton whom Wells married was the superintendent of a varnish manufacturing company. She explains in her autobiography that, because of her husband's last name, the public impression was that she had married into her own publishing house. The misunderstanding was so pervasive that she even received letters wrongly directed to "Mrs. Mifflin" (*The Rest of My Life*, p. 225). Unfortunately, the error was cemented in the public's perception after her death when the common error about which Houghton she had married was reprinted as a headline for her obituary in the *New York Times*. Sadly, this misstatement has been taken as fact and cited repeatedly on e-text sites, publishers' blurbs, and internet biographies ever since. Despite the public's confusion, she and Hadwin appear to have been immensely happy for the less than two years that elapsed between the wedding and his death. In her autobiography, she calls him "a counsel of perfection," their union "crammed with joyful interest," and their brief time together her "most blessed memory" (pp. 223–225).

The marriage also marked a new epoch in her life as it "gratified a lifelong longing" to live in New York City (p. 233). As a single woman, she had kept her primary residence in Rahway but had belonged to a woman's club called the Town and Country in New York in order to have a city pied-à-terre, and she had often traveled to the city by train. With her husband, she found the New York apartment of her dreams: on West Sixty-Seventh Street, it offered an expansive sense of space with its twenty-foot-high ceilings and a fourteen-foot-wide north window for light.

Wells never moved again, proudly cluttering it up with four desks, bookcases along every wall, and knickknacks of any kind that suited her current whim, including silver toys, wooden penguins, Chinese bowls, tiger claws, and carved reliquaries. Books, of course, dominated the place, from which Wells, refusing the common wisdom not to deface a book, freely cut out pages or illustrations, no matter how expensive or rare the volume, for any friend or acquaintance she thought might like them.

After Hadwin's death, Wells's general habit of random book collecting focused itself on the famous Walt Whitman collection, apparently on yet another whim, but also possibly as a response to the grief she was too private a person to express. She started the legendary collection at the urging of friends who wished to help her find a new outlet for her energies. Her New York friend Edward Norton recalled encountering Wells in a restless moment when she was looking to start a new collector's quest to use up her "surplus energy." According to him, when he recommended Whitman, whom he felt was destined to "take an important place" in literary history, she replied, "Comics are more in my line, but I believe you are right" (*The Rest of My Life*, p. 248). Norton wasn't the only one who set her on the trail of what may now be her biggest literary legacy. Wells also stated that an unnamed female friend pressed a copy of *Leaves of Grass* into her hand in a bookshop one day and ordered her to make it the first book in a new collection. After the incident, Wells recalled that Norton had said the same thing to her and so she "began to collect Whitman with both hands" (p. 256). Having always flouted the traditional method of doing anything expected of her, she "adopted the absurdly simple plan of writing to all the dealers I could hear of and asking for lists of their Whitman items," ignoring all the unwritten rules of "diplomacy and canny bartering" and simply paying anyone exactly what they asked (pp. 256–257). Once she had every book, edition, and autographed copy of Whitman imaginable, she began collecting ephemera, photographs, cancelled checks, contracts, and letters. The collection would have brought an astronomical price if she had followed through on her declared intention to sell it, but instead she bequeathed it to the Library of Congress in her will.

Wells died on March 26, 1942, at the Flower–Fifth Avenue hospital in New York City, having lived nearly her last decade with heart disease. At the time of her death, she was still enough of a personage to merit obituaries in the *New York Times* and *Washington Post*, along with other smaller newspapers and magazines nationwide. All the notices of her death emphasize the breadth of her popularity in multiple genres and the remarkable output of her four-decade writing career. The *New York Times* recalled her as quite a personage in the literati of the city, noting that "her teas attracted a select but wide circle of the figures in New York literary life." The *Milwaukee Journal* claimed she had been "the most prolific of living writers" in her time ("Carolyn Wells Turns a Candid Camera...").

METRICAL NONSENSE

The first phase of Wells's public career as a writer began in the 1890s, when she was in her early thirties. Drawn to the clever wordplay of Lewis Carroll and Edward Lear since her early youth, Wells's first publications were in the field of poetic nonsense. Humor, which she called "the great gift of the 90s" (*The Rest of My Life*, p. 118) was extremely popular at that time. It was also widely saleable in the form of puns, parodies, jingles, and limericks, collected and distributed in journals and magazines like the *Lark*, a journal established in 1895, with Wells as one of the original subscribers. Purportedly, when the British guest of a neighbor told her she could get $1 for a four-line jingle for the magazine *Puck*, Wells started writing them. When *Puck* took her first submission, she doggedly sent joke after rejected joke for a year to all the other humor magazines until one was published in the *Lark* in 1896. That same year, her first collection of literary puzzles, *At the Sign of the Sphinx*, came out as a book. Through her growing correspondence with Gelett Burgess, editor in chief of the *Lark*, Wells declared that she learned "to distinguish silliness

and nonsense" (Dresner, p. 557). Nonsense, she learned from Burgess, "is organic, well-ordered, and ... almost mathematical in its precision, and its certainty to hit the reader or listener straight between the eyes" (p. 557). Working for Burgess, she affirms, "I passed through an experience that might be known as *The Wit's Awakening*" (*The Rest of My Life*, p. 147). She also began writing jingles for *St. Nicholas* magazine at that time, and thus began her friendship with Oliver Herford, then known as the American version of Oscar Wilde, who did the drawings to accompany her metrical nonsense and whom she instantly recognized as a "kindred spirit," devoting an entire chapter to him in her autobiography (p. 130). These connections led to her ongoing collaboration and friendship with the two men, first to establish a new humor journal called *Enfant Terrible* with Burgess in 1898, and then to jointly create and publish a book of jingles for children with Herford in 1899. The new journal failed, but Wells was launched, and her first solo project, *Idle Idylls,* a book of humorous poetry for adults, came out in 1900.

After the turn of the century, Wells was "considered the chief woman humorist" in America, a reputation which lasted until after the First World War (Fishinger, p. 206). Her works of nonsense, including rollicking send-ups of cultural trends like bridge and the motorcar, both written in parodic imitation of *The Rubáiyát of Omar Khayyám*, were best sellers. Her volume *A Phenomenal Fauna* (1902) showed her facility as a wordsmith as she created and versified on such animals as the "Clothes Horse," "The Cream Puffin," and the "Wall-Street Bull." By 1908 she was such a household name that a yearbook of Carolyn Wells's *Old Favorites and New Fancies for 1909* was a sure bet for the Henry Holt company. She was also a regular contributor to the *Bookman* and *Punch* in the first decade of the twentieth century, writing book reviews or contributing tongue-in-cheek verse on things she found silly or pretentious, such as a poem titled "An Illusion," mocking the notion of "the Literary Spirit in the Modern Magazine" in the March 1909 issue. She soon became famous for her witty dissections and commentaries on the mad-

ness of the Christmas season, famously declaring "forgive us our Christmases as we forgive those who Christmas against us" (Dresner, p. 559), and was sought by publishers to collect her Christmas material, including her few plays, into three books: *Christmas Carollin'* (1913), *Jolly Plays for Holidays* (1914), and *Queen Christmas* (1922).

In addition to the jingles and witticisms, Wells had begun writing comical short stories, and her often breathtakingly paced send-ups of the frivolous feminine trends of the time (such as the Gibson Girl, the Suffragette, or the Sport) were always in demand. Her 1913 collection of short stories titled *The Eternal Feminine*, written almost entirely in dialogue and stream-of-feminine-consciousness, peeks into the seemingly fluffy minds of women who nonetheless seem to outwit everyone around them. Many of these Wells characters talk and act like precursors to the feminine archetype made famous decades later by the radio and television comedian Gracie Allen.

In 1922 Carolyn Wells was one of only three women to be included in Thomas Masson's book-length study *Our American Humorists*, the other two being Dorothy Parker and Beatrice Herford, Oliver Herford's sister. By 1925 she had enough pull to spearhead the composition and publication of a collaboratively written satiric novel about the flapper era, *Bobbed Hair*, with chapters by Dorothy Parker, Alexander Woolcott, Edward Streeter, and Rube Goldberg, among many others, and to publically satirize Sinclair Lewis' bleak and serious novel *Main Street* in a parody Wells titled *Ptomaine Street* (1921). Her collections of parody, satire, whimsy, limericks, and charades are composed of not only her work but also of witty contributions from many other humorists. Wells's work as an editor of humor anthologies doubtlessly owed some of its brilliance and popularity to the years spent with her beloved Rahway Library Association building the collection, reading everything she ordered, and practically memorizing the works she loved best. She was consistently praised for her ability to collect the best of all-things-nonsense, and to surprise and delight the reading public with her

selections. Always ready to bring funny people together, she started the Re-Echo Club as a loose literary association of parodists of popular verse of the day, and published a volume named for the club in 1913, collecting the parodies of her fellow club members along with her own.

After the 1917 publication of *Baubles*, which featured many of her older poems alongside new send-ups of trends like Cubist art and the American cowboy, her brand of nonsense was considered dull and dated, and she turned to other literary avenues and outlets when she wrote new material, only compiling, rather than composing, humorous verse for publication until the last years of her life. Or perhaps she herself was considered dated by the new literary voices of modernism; when the rising modernist literati relegated her to the old ladies of literature gone by, she was in good company. Edith Wharton, Ellen Glasgow, Gertrude Atherton, and Mary Roberts Rinehart received similar treatment throughout the 1920s and all had to fight to maintain their careers and reestablish their reputations against the twin tides of cultural cynicism and literary modernism. Wells refused to change her work to conform to those powerful influences, and her lighthearted nonsense was still in demand for loyal readers until the year of her death, 1942, in which she wrote a farcical tale of a society girl's endeavors to do something for the war effort, titled "Flossy Frills Helps Out," for the *American Weekly* Sunday magazine.

IDYLLS FOR YOUNG READERS

A few years after her career as a literary humorist began, Wells had also started publishing chapter books for children and young adults. Most of them revolved around the adventures of happy, boisterous families, or of sweet, though not saccharine, young ladies and their coming of age. They can all be considered escape fiction for children, in a way, because the main characters all lead various sorts of dream lives, though not unpunctuated by common crises of the day, such as scarlet fever or facing the loss of a family homestead, as well as smaller ones, such as another girl trying out for the same part in a lo-

cal pageant. The children in a Wells book are resourceful, good-natured, and fun-loving, and always manage to have access to upper-class amenities and experiences, even though they are rarely wealthy themselves. Readers became so comfortable in the worlds which these characters inhabit (with their predictably happy endings) that Wells rarely wrote a stand-alone book in the genre. The adventures of Marjorie, one of the four jolly Maynard children, extend into six volumes just like the Anne of Green Gables series so popular in the same era. However, Marjorie, not an orphan, is always accompanied by her gray Persian kitten, Puff, and her harmless adventures include a summer at her grandmother's farm. Wells's Patty Fairfield series ran much longer: Patty's escapades are told over the course of seventeen books and include such indulgences as *Patty in Paris* (1907) and *Patty's Motor Car* (1911). Today, collectors of the series can be found online writing, reading, and responding to reviews of the works and their reprints on blogs such as *Redeeming Qualities*, review wikis like Goodreads.com, and on eBay and Amazon. Patty fans today refer to her as "much more fun" than Pollyanna, more self-reflective than Nancy Drew, and confess that they envy Patty the constant stream of parties she attends ("Patty Fairfield," *Redeeming Qualities*). One reviewer places the Patty books "midway between classics like *Little Women* and girls' series books like the Stratemeyers; accessible yet with Carolyn Wells' trademark witty touch" (manybooks.net). Another contemporary Patty fan reflects on the escapism and nostalgia the books provide, writing "Whenever I want to get away from the craziness in this world—I sit down and read [the Patty books]" (manybooks.net). The lead blogger on the *Redeeming Qualities* website explains Patty's cult following, saying, "They never really lose their appeal ... I tend to think it's because Wells conveys a clear sense of her characters' enjoyment. They genuinely seem to be having fun when you read about them, so, so do you." Wells's other fun-loving child heroes and heroines can be found in the "Folly" books, such as *Folly in the Forest* (1902); and the escapades of Dick and Dolly, Pete and Polly,

CAROLYN WELLS

Doris of Dobbs Ferry (1917), and the *Two Little Women on a Holiday* (1917). The Dorrance children, featured in *The Dorrance Domain* (1905) and *Dorrance Doings* (1906), though they do not range too far from Wells's general atmosphere and formula, provide an interesting example of a family of orphaned children who must make their way in the world and strategize to maintain their independence and togetherness, first by running their family's seaside hotel on their own, and then by running a candy-making business out of a ramshackle, abandoned Victorian home. Fortunately, since Wells believed that reading should be a harmless diversion (her customarily mild reply to those who accused her of writing to a formula), the children find hidden treasure in the house at the end of the second book, and thereby do not have to struggle to make their own living any more. Though the Dorrance children face catastrophe and the dissolution of their family over and over, one knows as one reads the books that tragedy will never really strike within the pages of a Carolyn Wells young-adult novel.

A FORMULA FOR MURDER

Tragedy, however, became the basis of Wells's ongoing popularity from 1910 until nearly the middle of the twentieth century, by which time she had published nearly eighty murder mysteries. In her autobiography, she remarks, "about 1910, Detective stories came into high vogue, and at once appealed to me" (p. 171). Her initial encounter with detective fiction, in the form of Anna Katharine Green's *That Affair Next Door* (1897), she explained in her autobiography, was love at first sight, and she declares "I had not read more than a hundred detective stories before I began to write them" (p. 50). Her first mystery, *The Clue*, came out in 1909. When World War I began, sentiment, nostalgia, and an assurance of happily-ever-after were considered inadequate literature, even for children, and Wells ceased publishing young adult fiction and focused instead on murder. With the time she had spent creating Patty's and Marjorie's worlds now available to her new career in literary crime, Wells's

output of mystery books grew from an average of one per year before 1917 to three per year from 1917 to 1940.

By the 1930s Wells was publishing a new mystery on three predetermined dates every year; while this may be seen as a shrewd marketing ploy, it also denotes a rare energy and drive. However, says Jon L. Breen in his introduction to a 2011 edition of Wells's *The Technique of the Mystery Story*, she was often criticized for publishing so quickly, and of sacrificing art to expedience: because of her haste, Bill Pronzini declares her work to be the equivalent of any "dime novel" of its time, (qtd. in Breen, p. 13). In 1927, though her sales were still extremely strong, Dashiell Hammett panned her work in the *Saturday Review of Literature*, referring to her mysteries as not just formula, but bad formula (Breen, p. 12). Despite Hammett's criticism, the always gracious Wells included his work in two of her popular *Best Mystery Stories* anthologies. Other writers, who perhaps were not competing with her for market share, were kinder than Hammett. Howard Haycroft defended her in 1941, declaring the "harmless pleasure" she gave her faithful readers for more than three decades was justification enough for her books, though they would likely not be considered "immortal" works (Breen, p. 13). Wells herself, having had vast experience in creating fancies and fantasies in her career writing for children, linked the two this way: "the detective story must *seem* real in the same way a fairy tale must *seem* real to children" (Breen, p. 13). In his essay, Breen agreed with both Wells and Haycroft that a "pure detective story" is always a "fantasy" anyway (p. 13).

Most, although not all, of Wells's mystery novels feature her most famous fictional professional detective, Fleming Stone. He was so widely known that every book with him in it was marketed using his name. Premiering in 1909's *The Clue,* Stone was probably, after Sir Arthur Conan Doyle's Sherlock Holmes, the first celebrity detective of mystery fiction. Certainly he predates the publication of Agatha Christie's first Hercule Poirot novel by more than a decade, and yet, like Poirot, whenever there is a baffling

problem in society, some character remembers hearing of Stone's prowess in solving unsolvable problems and hires him to assist, or resist, the ineffective local police. The tall, dark, handsome Stone is difficult to picture, or to define, being almost utterly nondescript otherwise. Sometimes the man-of-the-world Stone just knows more than anyone else, such as when he solves a murder by deducing that a lady must have lived in China because her clothes were well tailored but she had spent very little money on them (*The Master Murderer*, 1933), or when he solves a killing by recalling a book that described the same method of murder and searching for it in the perpetrator's attic (*Crime Tears On*, 1939). At other times, he just seems more detail-oriented—no one else thought of measuring the marks on a victim's neck against the fangs of the cobra in his room, as Stone does in *The Visiting Villain* (1934). A man of the world, Stone is also more willing to believe in evil where others believe it could not be hiding—no one else could believe the lovely, delicate, and dignified society matron could have stuffed her husband into a barrel of potash, but Stone proves it to be true (*Fuller's Earth*, 1932). In some books, Stone is accompanied by his assistant, Fibsy McGuire, a "fresh," wisecracking youngster who investigates the houses of the rich below stairs while Stone is interviewing the residents upstairs.

Kenneth Carlisle, a fictional detective that Wells used in several books, looks and talks a lot like Fleming Stone but is different because he bases his success as a detective on his previous career in acting. He perhaps embodied best Wells's personal belief that "detection is an art, and all arts go hand in hand" (*The Doorstep Murders*, 1930; p. 143). According to Carlisle, however, detection is the most intellectual of all the arts, for "his real self could find expression only in some pursuit that called for a busier brain and a more active and analytic mind" (p. 143). Acting has given him a broad knowledge of human nature, a knack for getting people off their guard, and an ability not to let suspects know they are in his sights. In *The Skeleton at the Feast* (1931), the handsome, smiling Carlisle solves the case because, "being gifted in social speech and manner, the detective said just the right things at just the right way and cautiously watched the faces of his hearers for reactions" (pp. 83–84). Having practiced registering every emotion himself in Hollywood, Kenneth Carlisle can read other people's faces like books.

Pennington Wise, another Wells artist-detective (this time he is a visual artist and does illustrations for the magazines), stands out not for himself so much as for his impish girl Friday, Zizi, who is also one of his artist's models. Featured in eight Wells books, Pennington is described as "eccentric, of course but what worthwhile detective is not?" (*The Room with the Tassels*, 1917; p. 192). Like Stone and Carlisle, he is "tall," well-built, "clean-cut," "fine-featured," although his hair tends toward "chestnut" (p. 194). In fact, in his 1982 study *Gun in Cheek*, Pronzini declares "under all but the closest scrutiny, he appears indistinguishable from Fleming Stone" (p. 44). Like the others, Wise is highly efficient, but he likes to joke around a bit more than Stone or Carlisle, though these two are also witty conversationalists. Wise often brings lighthearted humor to the somber group of suspects and seems to be distracted by irrelevant details of architecture or fashion while his brain is honing in on the killer behind his jovial distractions. However, the single most interesting thing about the Pennington Wise books is Zizi, who, like Kenneth Carlisle, has worked in Hollywood and draws on her acting experience to detect when people are lying. Tiny as an elf, black-haired and sleek as a kitten, Zizi has a habit of entering and leaving rooms without anyone noticing, often catching suspects off guard and causing many other characters to declare that she must be a witch. However, Wise refers to her as a "property—in the theatrical sense" (*The Room with the Tassels*, 1917; p. 196). Zizi uses emotion to ferret out the criminals in the case, either by being so empathetic that characters confide in her, as in *The Vanishing of Betty Varian* (1922), or by annoying them with her sharp, flippant speeches. When Wise scolds her for her sauciness, she retorts, "I've got to get her real mad at me, to find out her secret" (*The Room with the Tassels*, p. 227). She provides Wise with the

information all his deductions and superior knowledge cannot glean.

Finally, Alan Ford served as the celebrity detective in two of Wells's mysteries, to be called in when people are "willing to have the matter probed to the utmost" (*The Bride of a Moment,* 1916; p. 155). Ford is tall, with a strong jaw and piercing gray eyes to match his silver hair, and a gentle smile to offset the forcefulness of his physical presence. Like the others, he solves crime for the pure pleasure of exercising his faculties, and while he could charge the astronomical fees that they do, he investigates for free, if he is sufficiently interested by the case. An impeccable dresser, with the "always correct and never conspicuous" ensembles one also imagines on Stone, Carlisle, and Wise, he, like them, is "a gentleman in the best and finest sense of the much misused word" (p. 162). Ford judges the majority of police detectives as too vulgar, too focused on obvious motives and clues, to solve the most difficult cases. His strength is a combination of "psychology and ratiocination" (p. 306). Besides Stone, Carlisle, and Wise, a handful of Wells's mysteries have no professional detective in them at all and rely on a character's deductions; others, such as *The Moss Mystery* (1925) feature detectives like Owen Prall, whom Wells abandoned after the book was finished.

Despite the different names and backstories, Wells's detectives all tend to blend together in the way they operate. Even when she published a novel without one of these paragons of deduction, the acting detective in the text feels nearly indistinguishable from the others. Upon perusal of her work, her detectives do seem nondescript, except for their uncanny ability to always be correct, usually because they have either found or correctly interpreted a single, baffling clue. In one novel it is the metal from a bridge of false teeth; in another, an eyelash. It is worth noting that the critic William Deeck has speculated whether Wells, who began her career as a humorist, was really parodying the normal devices and characters of the popular murder mysteries of her time, particularly the unbelievably arrogant, preternaturally wise detective. Whether or not Deeck's assessment is accurate, Wells's detec-

tives do not hesitate to openly, sometimes rudely, contradict those they think foolish. They are indeed certain of their own superiority. And they are all detached from the emotions and passions of those around them. As a voracious reader of mystery stories, Wells may in fact have known too much about fictional detectives to try to create a truly original one. "Superhuman Logic," she had decided in her study of the genre, was the one and only essential characteristic of the fictional detective; all others were mere gimmicks (*The Technique of the Mystery Story,* p. 61). She makes fun of the concept of an original fictional detective, remarking through the protagonist of one book: "There are two kinds of fictional detectives, my dear girl … the detective of fiction and the storybook sleuth who declares that he is not the detective of fiction" (*The Deep-Lake Mystery,* 1928; p. 171).

Wells's opinion can be difficult to pin down on the subject of clues. Despite the fact that many plots hinge on details such as a purple flower versus a red one left behind at a deadly cocktail party (*Sleeping Dogs,* 1929) or a gunpowder stain on a sheet of music (*The Bride of a Moment*), her fictional detectives repeatedly forswear the importance of clues at all, laughing at their friends' earnest pursuit of them. Kenneth Carlisle openly declares that he seldom believes in clues dropped at a murder scene (*The Doorstep Murders,* p. 262). However, Fleming Stone prefers "nice, fat clues" to "immaterial analysis," rejecting the trend of psychoanalysis in 1933's *The Clue of the Eyelash* (p. 74). The distinction seems to be that obvious clues, objects that scream "clue" to the observer, are not worth investigating. Rather, in a Wells book, the only useful clues are the ones that seem to have nothing to contribute to the solution until interpreted correctly by the detective.

Several critics have rightly noted that the concept of many of Wells's mystery novels was originally brilliant, but the works faltered in the execution. It is true that the writing itself, as well as the denouement, often fails to live up to the riddle generally presented in the first chapter of each book, most of which were standard "locked door" mysteries. It is astounding, really, that she

came up with so many different seemingly impossible puzzles, which include a dead automobile passenger's arrival at a country club (*Triple Murder*, 1929), a murder committed in a sealed radio studio (*The Radio Studio Murder*, 1937), two men found dead on a derelict boat in such a way that neither could have killed the other (*The Beautiful Derelict*, 1935), or a household of servants waking up to find four members of the family dead, by different methods in different rooms, killed at what were obviously different times of the night and early morning (*The Master Murderer*). Never averse to little self-deprecating irony, Wells has Fleming Stone remark to another character, "You don't read many detective stories, do you? ... One of the favorite plots of the detective story writers is the so-called 'hermetically sealed room.' This has been used over and over again and I confess it always has a charm for me" (*The Broken O*, 1933; p. 245). The ingenious or unusual murder clearly had a similar fascination for Wells herself, as the same book is dedicated to a Dr. Otto, who had explained to Wells how someone could be killed with a mystifying delay by the hypodermic injection of radium capsules into the heart, thus offering her and her readers a never-before-heard-of method of murder. Readers, then and now, most likely keep reading just to find out who did it, and, even more importantly, how it was done, or to see if they can outwit Wells and figure it out before her detective does. Indeed, Wells herself believed the primary reason to read mysteries was as a sort of brain exercise (*Technique*, p. 21).

Some of Wells's solutions are less worthwhile as an exercise than others, however, and among her nearly eighty mysteries one is not terribly surprised to find several evil twins or siblings (*Triple Murder*; *The Deep-Lake Mystery*) or siblings who were separated or stolen at birth (*The Daughter of the House*, 1925). In one case, a man hires his double to impersonate him so he will have an alibi for murder, but the double, not coming from the highest echelons of society, wears a wristwatch with his evening clothes, a sure giveaway to Fleming Stone in *The Luminous Face* (1921). Hidden doorways and passages that the reader believed had been eliminated as pos-

sibilities earlier in the book also occur (*The Vanishing of Betty Varian*, *The Room with the Tassels*, *The Daughter of the House*). In *Vicky Van* (1918), both hard-to-swallow premises are used at one time: the protagonist is her own double, leading a double life in a home around the corner connected by secret passages she had built when her husband was out of town. In *The Clue of the Eyelash*, the plot revolves around the ridiculous premise that the murderer had held two lifelong dreams: to work for and to murder a man who was his doppelgänger.

This undeniable gap between planning and execution may be best attributed to Wells's lifelong fascination with puzzles and games of all kinds. It seems likely that once she had invented a seemingly impossible crime, about which she alone knew the truth, she became bored and hurried through the process in order to get on to the next puzzle. Perhaps knowing this about herself, she claims in chapter 2 of *The Technique of the Mystery Story:* "what makes for worthwhileness in mystery fiction of any kind is the puzzle and its answer—not the gruesomeness of a setting or the personality of a hero or the delineation of a character" (p. 28). Puzzling was her strong suit, she knew, and in fact, one of her works, *The Visiting Villain* (1934), maintains interest better than the average Wells simply because the dead man has left an intricate literary puzzle in lieu of a traditional will, which the reader must try to solve along with the characters. In another baffling story a bride collapses at the altar, shot through the head, although no one saw or heard a thing, and a series of ciphers made out of musical compositions sustains the time between the death in chapter one and the denouement on the final page. In between those events, most of her books tend to lead the reader in circles in a maze of clues and suspects.

Reading the novels in order, one might conclude that the works between 1929 and 1935 marked a high point in Wells's craft, with the decade 1910–1920 being an apprenticeship during which she honed and strengthened her technique. *Sleeping Dogs* (1929), for instance, maintains interest throughout because of the psychological depth of the characters and rela-

tionships, as well as some fascinating developments in the subplots. The book features a female-impersonating male private detective who masquerades as the suspicious victim-to-be's private secretary until his ingenious but horrible murder. Both the method of the murder—the killer had entwined "her" scarf in the spokes of an automobile's front wheel with one hand, while embracing "her" with the other just before the car took off—and the shock waves that ripple through the book when the truth about the victim is discovered could keep any reader of thrillers engaged. The books after 1935, sadly, sometimes feel like hack work done to the market's unrelenting demand, with a few exceptions, such as *Gilt Edged Guilt* (1938) or *The Missing Link* (1938). Wells's increasing heart problems may possibly have made keeping up with her rigorous work schedule more of a challenge after 1935.

What, then, is Wells's place among the crafters of mysteries, ancient and modern? Modern bloggers and mystery mavens agree that her work is formulaic, usually well set up but often disappointing in its development, and uneven in quality, recommending a few specific texts as superior examples of her work that are still worth reading. Unfortunately, no one agrees on which are the best, each holding to his or her own personal favorites. In 2011, the *Pretty Sinister Books* blog published a comparison of Wells's works to the premises she laid out in *The Technique of the Mystery Story*, concluding her work to be "a mess" of inconsistencies and repetition. "But," it goes on, "a loveable mess if you have an appreciation for her mastery of the early American alternative classic mystery."

Overall, Wells's mystery fiction stands solidly in between those "dime novels" whose authors are now completely forgotten and the enduring, sharply outlined characters and narrative voices of writers like Agatha Christie, Dashiell Hammett, and Rex Stout. Wells does not fit into our traditional picture of the classic "hard-boiled" school of her era, because she deliberately did not follow the trends that dominated 1920s and 1930s crime fiction—refusing, she said, to write "the goriest, most horrifying type" of murder, or to depict the criminal underworld (*Crime Tears*

On, p. 233). In a Wells book, the main characters, except when they are servants, are solidly middle class or above, and they generally mind their manners. Her work does not often offer the intricate, expert subplotting or sustained suspense and humor of her contemporary Mary Roberts Rinehart. But Wells did have a flare for witty dialogue to relieve the tedium in between her presentation of a fascinating initial puzzle and its hasty, counter-climatic unraveling in the last chapter. In her books, almost everyone is the same sort of sparkling conversationalist that she herself was.

LASTING CONTRIBUTIONS

Most scholars agree that Wells's most significant book is her study of the composition and history of the literary mystery, *The Technique of the Mystery Story*, first published as a manual for would-be mystery writers in 1913, reprinted in 1929, and reissued in 2011 with a new introduction by Jon Breen. Reading *The Technique of the Mystery Story*, one begins to feel that if there has ever been anyone who had read every mystery ever written before 1929, that person would be Carolyn Wells. In his introduction to the original 1913 edition, J. Berg Esenwein praises the work as "a labor of distinction … the first exhaustive study of the genre" (p. xiii). The book is astonishingly comprehensive in its research and extensive list of examples of the genre; it would be a rare mystery buff indeed who did not garner the name of at least one author or work from its pages of which he or she was previously unaware. Wells's earliest cited and analyzed example of the genre dates back over a thousand years, a Buddhist tale titled "The Clever Thief" (p. 37). Again, her early career as a librarian must have played a role in the making of this book, whose twenty-six chapters include commentary on plot, structure, clues, characters, motives, evidence, devices, deductive ratiocination, and subdivisions of the genre such as ghost stories, robberies, riddles, and romantic subplots. These categories are then divided into subcategories, as minute as "detectives who make lists," and a section cataloging times when apples, bitten or unbitten, have served

as convenient clues. She tells aspiring writers to use their own judgment when plotting their work, that even "hackneyed devices" can work if used in an original way (p. 201). Other direct advice includes using a "secondary detective" or assistant—such as Sherlock Holmes's Watson, or Wells's flirtatious Fibsy or uncanny Zizi—as a device, and to avoid dwelling on the physical details of the corpse (p. 231).

In her chapter on the history of the detective, Wells points out the necessary differences between the sleuth of fiction and that of real life. In early mystery fiction, she observes, the detective is often a person of aristocratic mind and manners and characterized by strong and simple-to-recognize idiosyncrasies, rather than a delicately delineated individual character. The essential quality for any fictional detective is "superhuman reasoning." The "Transcendent Detective," as she calls him, appears superhuman because he is helped along by an omniscient author (p. 61). "No," she admits, "the fiction detective is not a real person, any more than the fairy godmother is a real person; but both are honored and popular celebrities in the realm of fiction" (p. 62). Wells's belief that there is no such thing as a realistic detective may reflect, more than anything else, the timing of her career: Pronzini observes that it was not until the 1920s that Dashiell Hammett, because of his personal experience working for the Pinkerton detective agency, "gave the American fictional investigator the one vital element he had been lacking: realism" (p. 45). Since Hammett started publishing in the pages of *Black Mask* and his works delved into the criminal underworld, Wells would likely not have been interested in this new realism, anyway, since she scorned writing anything about "gangsters" throughout her career. Back in 1913 Wells argued that even characters who are drawn from real-life models, such as Conan Doyle's Sherlock Holmes, who was drawn from a Dr. Bell he knew at the University of Edinburgh, must be embellished and helped along by the conveniences of fiction and authorial omniscience.

Aside from Conan Doyle, Wells's other favorite touchstone in *The Technique of the Mystery Story* is Edgar Allen Poe. Wells not only cites much of his work in that volume, but paid literary tribute to Edgar Allen Poe on several occasions in her fiction. In *The Tapestry Room Murder* (1929), the killer turns out to be Poe's "*monstrum horrendum*" (p. 314), an unprincipled genius who copies Poe's technique in "The Purloined Letter" by hiding his victim's will in plain sight. A similarly deranged murderer operates in *The Skeleton at the Feast* (1931), a Kenneth Carlisle book in which the killer had years building an alibi for the crime he had been planning. Wells also acknowledges the contributions of the female mystery writers who preceded her, like Anna Katharine Green, and those whose career paralleled hers, like Mary Roberts Rinehart. She pronounces these two women to be among the best writers in the genre.

CRITICAL REPUTATION

The Technique of the Mystery Story serves as a defense of detective fiction as literature, a cause Wells also took up in her autobiography and other publications as well. Wells, like many other mystery novelists of her time, was quick to point out that the genre was particularly popular as the chosen leisure reading of intellectuals. Wells knew that her devoted followers and collectors included notable mystery writers as well as several U.S. presidents, and she dedicated *The Tapestry Room Murder* to her loyal reader Herbert Hoover. Further, in 1923's *Feathers Left Around*, the entire house party is discussing the merits of method versus motive during a dinner party that occurs before the murder, and one guest flippantly observes that "detective fiction is no longer read solely by statesmen and college professors" (p. 22). In *Technique*, she quotes a literature professor, Harry Thurston Peck, who responds to popular accusations that mysteries are not "serious" fiction by claiming they are "acutely analytical" and result in a "battle of wits, a mental duel" that require an ingenious mind to create them. This, Peck concludes, "justif[ies] the acceptance of such stories as literature" (pp. 28–29). Wells adds to Peck's asseverations that there is nothing lowbrow about mysteries, and claims that if that genre is to be dismissed from serious

consideration, then so must all genre fiction, including works dealing with history, love, or adventure. She proceeds to offer a list of eminent mystery lovers, including presidents, professors, and British members of Parliament, and to quote extensively from Thomas De Quincey's "On Murder Considered as One of the Fine Arts," an essay that can only be sketched properly by a "connoisseur" (p. 217).

For nearly the first half of the twentieth century, Wells was a household name who was broadly published in journals and magazines of her time, including the *Bookman, Harper's, Scribner's, Century, Delineator, Saturday Evening Post, Ladies' Home Journal, Good Housekeeping, Putnam's,* and *Collier's.* Most critics agree, however, that the breakneck speed at which Wells wrote was detrimental to her critical standing in her time and in ours. By 1937, she had written an astounding 166 books. Some critics have accused her—perhaps not entirely inaccurately—of "never having had an unpublished thought" (Hayne, p. 1036). She herself was known to have sent manuscripts to the publishers in an empty chocolate box, declaring, "When the chocolate and paper are gone, the book is done" (p. 69). Such prolific output had several consequences, both for the quality of the writing and for the quality of her reputation. She took pride in her speed, though all her critics agree it may have been her biggest weakness, boasting, "I can produce more copy in less time than any other writer in my class," without actually explaining what class that is (*The Rest of My Life,* p. 69). She repeatedly asserts in her memoir that speed was an intrinsic part of her personality, claiming she penned detective stories "as fast as I could, because I had to" (*The Rest of My Life,* p. 52), also referring to herself as "a jack-in-the-box brain" (p. 75). This is quite evident in her works, especially in the numerous places where she makes a statement that seems to open up ambiguity in the plot, and then immediately shuts it down in the next sentence. It is almost as if she had no patience to explore the inadvertent avenue to which she had pointed, nor to go back and retype the page to omit the statement itself. In fact, her autobiography declares her two most powerful traits to be impatience and perseverance (p. 94). Beyond her confessed impatience, however, some of her incredible prolificacy may have come from her intrinsic desire to be obliging. Contemplating her diverse, fast-paced publishing history in *The Rest of My Life,* Wells muses, "Why I had so many publishers I don't know, except that they asked me for books and I was too good-natured to refuse" (pp. 170–171). The same statement could be applied to her relationship with her readers. If they wanted three Fleming Stone books per year, she was willing to oblige them, too.

Clearly aware that her hastily published works were considered frivolous reading by the critics, Wells waxes flippant in her autobiography when she mocks "ideals, standards, and aspirations" as "chameleon words [which] take color from their speakers—often false tints" (p. 70). She has the last laugh at the critics who chastise her for lack of seriousness, joking that "I've long wanted to do a book on the Deeper Issues [caps hers] of life. But I don't know what they are and I can't find out. I've asked a dozen of my friends, the wisest ones, but they either reply with some bit of foolishness or say frankly that they don't know" (p. 171). To add to her image as a literary freethinker, an enfant terrible of literature, she vehemently defends the right of any reader, high, low, or middlebrow, to select his or her own favorite reading material free of the judgments of others. She lauds the person who can disregard pride in assembling his or her library and think only of personal taste, declaring that she herself has discarded "perfectly good sets of Dickens and Thackeray" because they "left a soul-satisfying space for books that interest me more" in her own personal library (p. 201). She mocks pretension, laughing that she had seen too many libraries that "had everything in them except something to read" (*The Rest of My Life,* p. 205).

But she must have undertaken some serious consideration of her reputation, particularly the repeated criticism of her pace and its detrimental effect on her powers of characterization, as she goes out of her way to quote S. S. Van Dine's defense of her in the *Bookman* in 1930: "Carolyn Wells has done for the mystery story what Planck

did for physics, what Copernicus did for Astronomy, what Freud did for Psychology" (p. 160). Anecdote after anecdote in her autobiography seems to be directed, under the surface of a lot of joking around, at responding to the continual complaint that she did not take her art seriously enough. To this end, she also quotes the editor of the *Bookman*, Harry Thurston Peck, who calls her writing "plenty of fun ... giv[ing] the effect of being written for the pure pleasure of expressing herself.... One should always judge a writer by his or her own standards. If you set out to compose an epic poem, that is one thing. If you merely wish to have some fun with your muse, why that is quite another" (p. 163). In this point, both Peck and Wells are adhering to Alexander Pope's dictum in *An Essay on Criticism*: "A perfect judge will read each work of wit / with the same spirit its author writ." She turns again to her favorite essayist, De Quincey, to defend her own genius from its twentieth-century detractors, quoting his adage, "None but a man of extraordinary talent can write first-rate nonsense" (*The Rest of My Life*, p. 176).

All in all, Wells's legions of fans seemed to be more fond of her, the person they imagined behind the wit, than of the works she wrote. One fan letter defends Wells against a somber reviewer who, he claims, "has a fit because Carolyn didn't write an Epic with current fiction for inspiration. I never saw Miss Wells ... but I am happy to think of her as cheery, full of good humour, and with a most deft and delicate touch" (*The Rest of My Life,* p. 166). In the turmoil of a darkening twentieth century, with a hard-boiled quality taking over more than detective fiction, readers in search of good cheer and reassurance seemed to find Wells's work a cozy port in the gathering storm. Other fan letters, some of which she reproduced in *Bookman* articles, others of which she reprinted in her autobiography, show that many of her readers found in her a kindred spirit of sorts; they sent her their own little bits of nonsensical verse, or shared their nicknames for her, such as "Princess Perilla, mistress of epigram" (p. 182). Her cleverness was so prized that, reportedly, at any dinner party, "to begin a sentence sharply with 'Carolyn Wells says' is to

attract the attention of a whole tableful and silence any spasmodic, needless chatter that may be going on elsewhere around the board" (Dresner, p. 556). When all is said and done, the keen wit, engaging puzzles, and jolly camaraderie for which Wells was famous both in person and in print are clearly the trump cards she held for her readers, then and now.

Selected Bibliography

WORKS OF CAROLYN WELLS

Humor
At the Sign of the Sphinx. New York: Stone & Kimball, 1896.

Idle Idylls. New York: Dodd, Mead, 1900.

Abeniki Caldwell: A Burlesque Historical Novel. New York: R. H. Russell, 1902.

A Phenomenal Fauna. New York: R. H. Russell, 1902.

Folly for the Wise. Indianapolis, Ind.: Bobbs-Merrill, 1904.

A Parody Anthology. New York: Scribners, 1904.

The Matrimonial Bureau. With Harry Persons Taber. London: J. B. Lippincott, 1905.

A Satire Anthology. New York: Scribners, 1905.

A Whimsey Anthology. New York: Scribners, 1906.

The Carolyn Wells Year Book of Old Favorites and New Fancies for 1909. New York: Holt, 1908.

Christmas Carollin'. New York: Bigelow, 1913.

The Eternal Feminine. New York: Bigelow, 1913.

Girls and Gayety. New York: Bigelow, 1913.

The Re-Echo Club. New York: Bigelow, 1913.

Baubles. New York: Dodd, Mead, 1917.

Ptomaine Street: The Tale of Warble Petticoat. Philadelphia and London: J. B. Lippincott, 1921.

Bobbed Hair. New York: Putnam, 1925. (With chapters by Dorothy Parker, Alexander Woolcott, Edward Streeter, Rube Goldberg, and others.)

Juvenile Fiction
Folly in Fairyland. Philadelphia: Henry Altemus, 1901.

Mother Goose's Menagerie. Boston: Noyes, Platt, 1901.

Patty Fairfield. New York: Grosset & Dunlap, 1901.

The Story of Betty. New York: Century, 1901.

Eight Girls and a Dog. New York: Century, 1902.

Folly in the Forest. Philadelphia: Altemus, 1902.

The Pete and Polly Stories. Chicago: A. C. McClurg, 1902.

Trotty's Trip. Philadelphia: Biddle, 1902.

The Bumblepuppy Book. London: Ibister, 1903.

In the Reign of Queen Dick. New York: D. Appleton, 1904.

Patty at Home. New York: Dodd, Mead, 1904.

The Dorrance Domain. New York: Grosset & Dunlap, 1905.

Patty in the City. New York: Dodd, Mead, 1905.

Dorrance Doings. New York: Grosset & Dunlap, 1906.

Patty's Summer Days. New York: Dodd, Mead, 1906.

The Emily Emmins Papers. New York and London: Putnam, 1907.

Fluffy Ruffles. New York: D. Appleton, 1907.

Marjorie's Vacation. New York: Grosset & Dunlap, 1907.

Patty in Paris. New York: Dodd, Mead 1907.

Rainy Day Diversions. New York: Moffat, Yard, 1907.

Marjorie's Busy Days. New York: Grosset & Dunlap, 1908.

Patty's Friends. New York: Grosset & Dunlap, 1908.

The Happy Chaps. New York: Century, 1909.

Marjorie's New Friend. New York: Grosset & Dunlap, 1909.

Patty's Pleasure Trip. New York: Dodd, Mead, 1909.

Pleasant Day Diversions. New York: Moffat Yard, 1909.

Betty's Happy Year. New York: Century, 1910.

Dick and Dolly's Adventures. New York: Grosset & Dunlap, 1910.

Marjorie in Command. New York: Grosset & Dunlap, 1910.

Patty's Success. New York: Grosset & Dunlap, 1910.

Marjorie's Maytime. New York: Grosset & Dunlap, 1911.

Patty's Motor Car. New York: Grosset & Dunlap, 1911.

Marjorie at Seacote. New York: Grosset & Dunlap, 1912.

Patty's Butterfly Days. New York: Dodd, Mead, 1912.

Patty's Social Season. New York: Dodd, Mead, 1913.

Patty's Suitors. New York: Grosset & Dunlap, 1914.

Patty's Romance. New York: Grosset & Dunlap, 1915.

Two Little Women. New York: Grosset & Dunlap, 1915.

Patty's Fortune. New York: Grosset & Dunlap, 1916.

Two Little Women and Treasure House. New York: Grosset and Dunlap, 1916.

Doris of Dobbs Ferry. New York: Doran, 1917.

Patty Blossom. New York: Grosset & Dunlap, 1917.

Two Little Women on a Holiday. New York: Grosset & Dunlap, 1917.

Patty-Bride. New York: Grosset & Dunlap, 1918.

Patty and Azalea. New York: Grosset & Dunlap, 1919.

A Book of Charades. New York: Doran, 1927.

Carolyn Wells Edition of Mother Goose. Garden City, N.Y.: Garden City Publishing, 1946.

MYSTERY FICTION

The Clue. Philadelphia and London: J. B. Lippincott, 1909.

The Gold Bag. Philadelphia and London: J. B. Lippincott, 1911.

A Chain of Evidence. Philadelphia and London: J. B. Lippincott, 1912.

The Maxwell Mystery. Philadelphia and London: J. B. Lippincott, 1913.

Anybody but Anne. Philadelphia and London: J. B. Lippincott, 1914.

The White Alley. Philadelphia and London: J. B. Lippincott, 1915.

The Bride of a Moment. New York: Doran, 1916.

The Curved Blades. Philadelphia and London: J. B. Lippincott, 1916.

Faulkner's Folly. New York: George H. Doran, 1917.

The Mark of Cain. Philadelphia and London: J. B. Lippincott, 1917.

The Room with the Tassels. New York: George H. Doran, 1917.

Vicky Van. Philadelphia and London: J. B. Lippincott, 1918.

The Diamond Pin. Philadelphia and London: J. B. Lippincott, 1919.

In the Onyx Lobby. Philadelphia and London: J. B. Lippincott, 1920.

Raspberry Jam. Philadelphia and London: J. B. Lippincott, 1920.

The Come Back. Philadelphia and London: J. B. Lippincott, 1921.

The Luminous Face. New York: George H. Doran, 1921.

The Mystery of the Sycamore. Philadelphia and London: J. B. Lippincott, 1921.

The Mystery Girl. Philadelphia and London: J. B. Lippincott, 1922.

The Vanishing of Betty Varian. Philadelphia and London: J. B. Lippincott, 1922.

The Affair at Flower Acres. New York: George H. Doran, 1923.

Feathers Left Around. Philadelphia: J. B. Lippincott, 1923.

Spooky Hollow. Philadelphia and London: J. B. Lippincott, 1923.

Wheels Within Wheels. New York: George H. Doran, 1923.

The Fourteenth Key. New York: Putnam, 1924.

The Furthest Fury. Philadelphia and London: J. B. Lippincott, 1924.

The Man Who Fell Through the Earth. Philadelphia and London: J. B. Lippincott, 1924.

Prilligirl. Philadelphia and London: J. B. Lippincott, 1924.

Anything but the Truth. Philadelphia and London: J. B. Lippincott, 1925.

The Daughter of the House. Philadelphia and London: J. B. Lippincott, 1925.

Face Cards. New York and London: Putnam, 1925.

The Bronze Hand. Philadelphia and London: J. B. Lippincott, 1926.

The Red-Haired Girl. Philadelphia and London: J. B. Lippincott, 1926.

The Vanity Case. New York and London: Putnam, 1926.

All at Sea. Philadelphia and London: J. B. Lippincott, 1927.

Where's Emily? New York: A. L. Burt, 1927.

The Crime in the Crypt. Philadelphia and London: J. B. Lippincott, 1928.

The Deep-Lake Mystery. New York: Doubleday, Doran, 1928.

The Tannahill Tangle. Philadelphia and London: J. B. Lippincott, 1928.

Sleeping Dogs. New York: Doubleday, Doran, 1929.

The Tapestry Room Murder. Philadelphia and London: J. B. Lippincott, 1929.

Triple Murder. Philadelphia and London: J. B. Lippincott, 1929.

The Doomed Five. Philadelphia and London: J. B. Lippincott, 1930.

The Doorstep Murders. New York: Doubleday, Doran, 1930.

The Ghosts' High Noon. Philadelphia and London, 1930.

Horror House. Philadelphia and London: J. B. Lippincott, 1931.

The Skeleton at the Feast. New York: Doubleday, Doran, 1931.

The Umbrella Murder. Philadelphia and London: J. B. Lippincott, 1931.

Fuller's Earth. Philadelphia and London: J. B. Lippincott, 1932.

The Roll-Top Desk Mystery. London: J. B. Lippincott, 1932.

The Broken O. Philadelphia and London: J. B. Lippincott, 1933.

The Clue of the Eyelash. Philadelphia and London: J. B. Lippincott, 1933.

The Master Murderer. Philadelphia and London: J. B. Lippincott, 1933.

Eyes in the Wall. Philadelphia and London: J. B. Lippincott, 1934.

In the Tiger's Cage. Philadelphia and London: J. B. Lippincott, 1934.

The Visiting Villain. Philadelphia and London: J. B. Lippincott, 1934.

The Beautiful Derelict. Philadelphia and London: J. B. Lippincott, 1935.

The Wooden Indian. Philadelphia and London: J. B. Lippincott, 1935.

For Goodness' Sake. Philadelphia and London: J. B. Lippincott, 1936.

The Huddle. Philadelphia and London: J. B. Lippincott, 1936.

Money Musk. Philadelphia and London: J. B. Lippincott, 1936.

Murder in the Bookshop. Philadelphia and London: J. B. Lippincott, 1936.

The Mystery of the Tarn. Philadelphia and London: J. B. Lippincott, 1937.

The Radio Studio Murder. Philadelphia and London: J. B. Lippincott, 1937.

Gilt Edged Guilt. Philadelphia and London: J. B. Lippincott, 1938.

The Killer. Philadelphia and London: J. B. Lippincott, 1938.

The Missing Link. Philadelphia and London. J. B. Lippincott, 1938.

Calling All Suspects. Philadelphia and London: J. B. Lippincott, 1939.

Crime Tears On. Philadelphia and London: J. B. Lippincott, 1939.

The Importance of Being Murdered. Philadelphia and London: J. B. Lippincott, 1939.

Crime Incarnate. Philadelphia and London: J. B. Lippincott, 1940.

Devil's Work. Philadelphia and London: J. B. Lippincott, 1940.

Murder on Parade. Philadelphia and London: J. B. Lippincott, 1940.

Murder Plus. Philadelphia and London: J. B. Lippincott, 1940.

The Black Night Murders. Philadelphia and London: J. B. Lippincott, 1941.

Murder at the Casino. Philadelphia and London: J. B. Lippincott, 1941.

Murder Will In. Philadelphia and London: J. B. Lippincott, 1942.

Who Killed Caldwell? Philadelphia and London: J. B. Lippincott, 1942.

NONFICTION

"Flossy Frills Helps Out." *American Weekly Magazine,* May 16, 1942.

The Technique of the Mystery Story, Etc. Springfield, Mass: Writer's Library, 1913.

A Concise Bibliography of the Works of Walt Whitman: With a Supplement of Fifty Books About Whitman. With Alfred F. Goldsmith and Bruce Rogers. Boston: Houghton Mifflin, 1922.

The Rest of My Life. Philadelphia and London: J. B. Lippincott, 1937.

POETRY

The Jingle Book. With Oliver Herford and Lewis Carroll. New York: Macmillan, 1899.

A Phenomenal Fauna. With Oliver Herford and Robert H. Russell. New York: R. H. Russell, 1902.

Children of Our Town. New York: R. H. Russell, 1902.

Rubáiyát of a Motor Car. New York: Dodd, Mead, 1906.

"An Illusion." *Bookman,* March 1909, p. 21.

The Ruba'iya't of Bridge [in Verse]. New York and London: Harper, 1909.

The Re-Echo Club. New York: Franklin Bigelow, 1913.

The Book of Humorous Verse. New York: Doran, 1920.

Carolyn Wells' Book of American Limericks. New York: Putnam, 1925.

Ballade of Baker Street. New York: Simon & Schuster, 1936.

PLAYS

Maid of Athens. Produced in New York, 1914.

Jolly Plays for Holidays. Boston: Baker, 1914.

The Meaning of Thanksgiving. Philadelphia: Penn Publishing, 1922.

Queen Christmas. Philadelphia: Penn Publishing, 1922.

The Sweet Girl Graduate. Philadelphia: Penn Publishing, 1922.

AS EDITOR

A Nonsense Anthology. New York: Scribners, 1902.

Such Nonsense! New York: Doran, 1918.

The Book of Humorous Verse. New York: Doran, 1920.

An Outline of Humor. New York: Putnam, 1923.

Ask Me A Question. Philadelphia: Winston, 1927.

American Detective Stories. New York: Oxford University Press, 1927.

Best American Mystery Stories of the Year. 2 vols. New York: Day, 1931, 1932.

The World's Best Humor. New York: Boni, 1933.

The Cat in Verse. Boston: Little, Brown, 1935.

CRITICAL AND BIOGRAPHICAL STUDIES

Breen, Jon L. *What About Murder? A Guide to Books About Mystery and Detective Fiction.* Metuchen, N. J.: Scarecrow Press, 1981.

———. Introduction to *The Technique of the Mystery Story,* by Carolyn Wells. Vancleave, Miss.: Ramble House, 2011.

"The Carolyn Wells Technique; or, How I Learned to Stop Thinking and Love the Mess." *Pretty Sinister Books: Crime, Supernatural, and Adventure Fiction: Obscure, Forgotten, and Well-Worth Reading,* December 10, 2011. http://prettysinister.blogspot.com

"Carolyn Wells Turns a Candid Camera on the Frailties of Fellow Celebrities." *Milwaukee Journal,* November 10, 1937, pp. 12–13. http://news.google.com/newspapers?nid=1499&dat=19371110&id=_XYxAAAAIBAJ&sjid=DilEAAAAIBAJ&pg=7079,4813362

Deeck, William. "The Backward Reviewer." *Mystery File.* Mysteryfile.com/blog

Dresner, Zita Zatkin. "Carolyn Wells." In *American Humorists, 1800–1950.* Edited by Stanley Trachtenbert. *Dictionary of Literary Biography.* Vol. 11. Detroit: Gale, 1982.

Esenwein, J. Berg. Introduction to *The Technique of the Mystery Story,* by Carolyn Wells. New York: Writer's Library, 1913. Reprinted, Vancleave, Miss.: Ramble House, 2011. (Quotes in the essay refer to the reprinted edition.)

Fishinger, Sondra. "Carolyn Wells." In *Past and Promise: Lives of New Jersey Women.* Edited by Joan N. Bursytn. Syracuse, N.Y.: Syracuse University Press, 1997.

Hayne, Barrie. "Carolyn Wells." In *St. James Guide to Crime and Mystery Writers.* 4th ed. Edited by Jay P. Pederson. Detroit: St. James Press, 1996.

Masson, Thomas. *Our American Humorists.* New York: Moffat, Yard, 1922.

My Maiden Effort: Being the Personal Confessions of Well-Known American Authors as to Their Literary Beginnings. Edited by Gelett Burgess. New York: Doubleday, Page, 1921.

"Patty Fairfield." *Redeeming Qualities,* May 19, 2007. Redeemingqualities@wordpress.com

Pronzini, Bill. *Gun in Cheek: A Study of "Alternative" Crime Fiction.* Toronto: Coward, McCann & Geoghegan, 1982.

Cumulative Index

All references include volume numbers in boldface roman numerals followed by page numbers within that volume. Subjects of articles are indicated by boldface type.

A

"A" (Zukofsky), **Supp. III Part 2:** 611, 612, 614, 617, 619, 620, 621, 622, 623, 624, 626, 627, 628, 629, 630, 631; **Supp. IV Part 1:** 154; **Supp. XVI:** 287, 287

Aal, Katharyn Machan, **Supp. IV Part 1:** 332; **Supp. XXIII:** 54

Aaron, Daniel, **IV:** 429; **Supp. I Part 2:** 647, 650

Aaron's Rod (Lawrence), **Supp. I Part 1:** 255

Abacus (Karr), **Supp. XI:** 240–242, 248, 254

Abádi-Nagy, Zoltán, **Supp. IV Part 1:** 280, 289, 291

"Abandoned Farmhouse" (Kooser), **Supp. XIX:** 117, 119

"Abandoned House, The" (L. Michaels), **Supp. XVI:** 214

"Abandoned Newborn, The" (Olds), **Supp. X:** 207

"Abandoned Stone Schoolhouse in the Nebraska Sandhills, An" (Kooser), **Supp. XIX:** 124–125

"Abba Jacob" (Nelson), **Supp. XVIII:** 177

"Abbé François Picquet"(Kenny), **Supp. XXIII:** 153

Abbey, Edward, **Supp. VIII:** 42; **Supp. X:** 24, 29, 30, 31, 36; **Supp. XIII:** 1–18; **Supp. XIV:** 179; **Supp. XXV:** 208; **Supp. XXVI:** 31, 37

Abbey's Road (Abbey), **Supp. XIII:** 12

Abbott, Carl, **Supp. XVIII:** 142

Abbott, Clifford F., **Supp. XXVI:** 89

Abbott, Edith, **Supp. I Part 1:** 5

Abbott, Jack Henry, **Retro. Supp. II:** 210

Abbott, Jacob, **Supp. I Part 1:** 38, 39

Abbott, Lyman, **III:** 293

Abbott, Sean, **Retro. Supp. II:** 213

ABC of Color, An: Selections from Over a Half Century of Writings (Du Bois), **Supp. II Part 1:** 186

ABC of Reading (Pound), **III:** 468, 474–475

"Abdication, An" (Merrill), **Supp. III Part 1:** 326

'Abdu'l-Bahá, **Supp. XX:** 117, 122

Abel, Lionel, **Supp. XIII:** 98

Abel, Sam, **Supp. XIII:** 199

Abelard, Peter, **I:** 14, 22

Abeles, Sigmund, **Supp. VIII:** 272

Abeng (Cliff), **Supp. XXII:** 66, 69–71

Abercrombie, Joe, **Supp. XXV:** 74

Abercrombie, Lascelles, **III:** 471; **Retro. Supp. I:** 127, 128

Abernathy, Milton, **Supp. III Part 2:** 616

Abernon, Edgar Vincent, Viscount d', **Supp. XVI:** 191

Aberration of Starlight (Sorrentino), **Supp. XXI:** 234–235

Abhau, Anna. *See* Mencken, Mrs. August (Anna Abhau)

"Abide with Me" (Hoffman), **Supp. XVIII:** 86

Abide with Me (Strout), **Supp. XXIII:** 273, 275, **278–280,** 285

"Ability" (Emerson), **II:** 6

Abingdon, Alexander, **Supp. XVI:** 99

Abish, Walter, **Supp. V:** 44

"Abishag" (Glück), **Supp. V:** 82

"Abnegation, The" (Bronk), **Supp. XXI:** 32

Abney, Lisa, **Supp. XXII:** 9

Abood, Maureen, **Supp. XXII:** 90

"Abortion, The" (Sexton), **Supp. II Part 2:** 682

"Abortions" (Dixon), **Supp. XII:** 153

"About C. D. Wright" (Colburn), **Supp. XV:** 341

"About Effie" (Findley), **Supp. XX:** 50

"About Hospitality" (Jewett), **Retro. Supp. II:** 131

"About Kathryn" (Dubus), **Supp. VII:** 91

"About Language" (Wrigley), **Supp. XVIII:** 300–301

"About Looking Alone at a Place: Arles" (M. F. K. Fisher), **Supp. XVII:** 89, 91

About the House (Auden), **Supp. II Part 1:** 24

About These Stories: Fiction for Fiction Writers and Readers (Huddle, ed.), **Supp. XXVI:** 160

About Town: "The New Yorker" and the World It Made (Yagoda), **Supp. VIII:** 151

"About Zhivago and His Poems"(O'Hara), **Supp. XXIII:** 214

"Above Pate Valley" (Snyder), **Supp. VIII:** 293

Above the River (Wright), **Supp. III Part 2:** 589, 606

"Abraham" (Schwartz), **Supp. II Part 2:** 663

Abraham, Nelson Algren. *See* Algren, Nelson

Abraham, Pearl, **Supp. XVII:** 49; **Supp. XX:** 177; **Supp. XXIV:** 1–15

"Abraham Davenport" (Whittier), **Supp. I Part 2:** 699

"Abraham Lincoln" (Emerson), **II:** 13

Abraham Lincoln: The Prairie Years (Sandburg), **III:** 580, 587–589, 590

Abraham Lincoln: The Prairie Years and the War Years (Sandburg), **III:** 588, 590

Abraham Lincoln: The War Years (Sandburg), **III:** 588, 589–590; **Supp. XVII:** 105

"Abraham Lincoln Walks at Midnight" (Lindsay), **Supp. I Part 2:** 390–391

"Abram Morrison" (Whittier), **Supp. I Part 2:** 699

Abramovich, Alex, **Supp. X:** 302, 309

Abrams, David, **Supp. XXII:** 61

Abrams, M. H., **Supp. XVI:** 19; **Supp. XXIII:** 42

Abridgment of Universal Geography, An: Together with Sketches of History (Rowson), **Supp. XV:** 243

"Absalom" (Rukeyser), **Supp. VI:** 278–279

Absalom, Absalom! (Faulkner), **II:** 64, 65–67, 72, 223; **IV:** 207; **Retro. Supp. I:** 75, 81, 82, 84, 85, 86, 87, 88, 89, 90, 92, 382; **Supp. V:** 261; **Supp. X:** 51; **Supp. XIV:** 12–13; **Supp. XXVI:** 8, 12

"Absence"(J. Schoolcraft), **Supp. XXIII:** 228, 231

"Absence of Mercy" (Stone), **Supp. V:** 295

"Absentee, The" (Levertov), **Supp. III Part 1:** 284

Absentee Ownership (Veblen), **Supp. I Part 2:** 642

"Absent-Minded Bartender" (X. J. Kennedy), **Supp. XV:** 159

"Absent Thee from Felicity Awhile" (Wylie), **Supp. I Part 2:** 727, 729

Absolutely True Diary of a Part-Time Indian, The (Alexie), **Supp. XXVI:** 108

"Absolution" (Fitzgerald), **Retro. Supp. I:** 108

"Absolution" (Sobin), **Supp. XVI:** 289

"Abuelita's Ache" (Mora), **Supp. XIII:** 218

Abysmal Brute, The (London), **II:** 467

Abyssinia and the Imperialists (C. L. R. James), **Supp. XXI:** 166

Abyss of Human Illusion, The (Sorrentino), **Supp. XXI:** 225, 227, 237–238

"Academic Story, An" (Simpson), **Supp. IX:** 279–280

"Academic Zoo, The: Theory—in Practice" (Epstein), **Supp. XIV:** 107–108, 109

"A Capella" (Wrigley), **Supp. XVIII:** 300

"Accident" (Minot), **Supp. VI: 208–209**

"Accident, The" (Southern), **Supp. XI:** 295

"Accident, The" (Strand), **Supp. IV Part 2:** 624

Accident/A Day's News (Wolf), **Supp. IV Part 1:** 310

Accidental Tourist, The (Tyler), **Supp. IV Part 2:** 657, 668–669; **Supp. V:** 227

Accordion Crimes (Proulx), **Supp. VII:** 259–261

"Accountability" (Dunbar), **Supp. II Part 1:** 197, 204

"Account of the Method of Drawing Birds" (Audubon), **Supp. XVI:** 12

"Accusation, The" (Wright), **Supp. III Part 2:** 595

"Accusation of the Inward Man, The" (Taylor), **IV:** 156

"Accusing Message from Dead Father" (Karr), **Supp. XI:** 244

Ace, Goodman, **Supp. IV Part 2:** 574

Ache of Appetite, The (Hadas), **Supp. XXIII: 120–121**

Achievement in American Poetry (Bogan), **Supp. III Part 1:** 63–64

Acker, Kathy, **Supp. XII:1–20; Supp. XXI:** 236

Ackerley, J. R., **Supp. XX: 237**

Ackerman, Diane, **Supp. XIII:** 154

"Acknowledgment" (Lanier), **Supp. I Part 1:** 364

Ackroyd, Peter, **Supp. V:** 233; **Supp. XVII:** 180

"Acquaintance in the Heavens, An" (Dillard), **Supp. VI:** 34

"Acquainted with the Night" (Frost), **II:** 155; **Retro. Supp. I:** 137; **Supp. XXI:** 26

Across Spoon River (Masters), **Supp. I Part 2:** 455, 457, 459, 460, 466, 474–475, 476

Across the Layers: Poems Old and New (Goldbarth), **Supp. XII:** 181, **187–189**

Across the River and into the Trees (Hemingway), **I:** 491; **II:** 255–256, 261; **Retro. Supp. I:** 172, **184–185; Supp. XIX:** 248

"Acteon" (Stallings), **Supp. XXV:** 231–232

"Actfive" (MacLeish), **III:** 18–19, 22

Actfive and Other Poems (MacLeish), **III:** 3, 17–19, 21

Action (Shepard), **Supp. III Part 2:** 446

Active Anthology (Pound, ed.), **Supp. III Part 2:** 617; **Supp. XXVI:** 224

Active Service (Crane), **I:** 409

"Act of Creation and Its Artifact, The" (Sorrentino), **Supp. XXI:** 229, 235

Act of Love (film), **Supp. XXVI:** 136

Act of Love, An (Wolfert), **Supp. XXI:** 270, **275–277**

Act of Love, An: A Completely Retold Version of the Novel (Wolfert), **Supp. XXI:** 276

Acton, Patricia Nassif, **Supp. X:** 233

Actor's Nightmare, The (Durang), **Supp. XXIV:** 116, 119

Acts and Monuments of These Latter and Perilous Days (Fox), **Supp. XXII:** 36

Acts of Faith (Caputo), **Supp. XIX: 29–30**

"Acts of the Apostles, The" (Bronk), **Supp. XXI:** 28

Actual, The (Bellow), **Retro. Supp. II:** 33

"Actual Experience, Preferred Narratives" (Julier), **Supp. IV Part 1:** 211

Acuff, Roy, **Supp. V:** 335

Ada (Nabokov), **Retro. Supp. I:** 265, 266, 270, 276–277, 278, 279

"Ada" (Stein), **IV:** 43

"Adagia" (Stevens), **IV:** 78, 80, 88, 92

"Adagio" (Hull), **Supp. XXI:** 136–137

"Adam" (Hecht), **Supp. X:** 62

"Adam" (W. C. Williams), **Retro. Supp. I:** 422, 423

"Adam and Eve" (Eugene), **Supp. X:** 204

"Adam and Eve" (Shapiro), **Supp. II Part 2:** 708, 712

"Adamantine Practice of Poetry, The" (Wright), **Supp. XV:** 341–342, 343–344

Adam Bede (G. Eliot), **II:** 181

Adamé, Leonard, **Supp. XIII:** 316

Adam & Eve & the City (W. C. Williams), **Retro. Supp. I:** 423

Adamic, Louis, **Supp. XXIII:** 166

"Adamic Purity as Double Agent" (Whalen-Bridge), **Retro. Supp. II:** 211–212

"Adam Robinson Acquires Grandparents and a Little Sister" (P. E. Jones), **Supp. XXII:** 151

"Adams" (Saunders), **Supp. XIX:** 232

Adams, Althea. *See* Thurber, Mrs. James (Althea Adams)

Adams, Annie. *See* Fields, Annie Adams

Adams, Brooks, **Supp. I Part 2:** 484

Adams, Charles, **Supp. I Part 2:** 644

Adams, Charles Francis, **I:** 1, 4; **Supp. I Part 2:** 484

Adams, Franklin P., **Supp. I Part 2:** 653; **Supp. IX:** 190; **Supp. XV:** 294, 297

Adams, Henry, **I: 1–24**, 111, 243, 258; **II:** 278, 542; **III:** 396, 504; **IV:** 191, 349; **Retro. Supp. I:** 53, 59; **Retro. Supp. II:** 207; **Supp. I Part 1:** 299–300, 301, 314; **Supp. I Part 2:** 417, 492, 543, 644; **Supp. II Part 1:** 93–94, 105; **Supp. III Part 2:** 613; **Supp. IV Part 1:** 31, 208; **Supp. XXIV:** 224

Adams, Mrs. Henry (Marian Hooper), **I:** 1, 5, 10, 17–18

Adams, Henry B., **Supp. I Part 1:** 369

Adams, James Truslow, **Supp. I Part 2:** 481, 484, 486

Adams, J. Donald, **IV:** 438

Adams, John, **I:** 1; **II:** 103, 301; **III:** 17, 473; **Supp. I Part 2:** 483, 506, 507, 509, 510, 511, 517, 518, 520, 524

Adams, John Luther, **Supp. XII:** 209

Adams, John Quincy, **I:** 1, 3, 16–17; **Supp. I Part 2:** 685, 686

Adams, Léonie, **Supp. I Part 2:** 707; **Supp. IX:** 229; **Supp. V:** 79; **Supp. XVII:** 75

Adams, Luella, **Supp. I Part 2:** 652

Adams, Noah, **Supp. XVII:** 218

Adams, Phineas, **Supp. XXV:** 37

Adams, Phoebe, **Supp. IV Part 1:** 203; **Supp. VIII:** 124

Adams, Samuel, **Supp. I Part 2:** 516, 525

Adams, Timothy Dow, **Supp. XVI:** 67, 69

Ada; or Ardor (Nabokov), **III:** 247

Adaptation (film), **Supp. XXV:** 160

"Ad Castitatem" (Bogan), **Supp. III Part 1:** 50

Adcock, Betty, **Supp. XVIII:** 181–182, 182

Addams, Jane, **Supp. I Part 1: 1–26; Supp. XI:** 200, 202

Addams, John Huy, **Supp. I Part 1:** 2

"Add Blue to Make White Whiter" (Vaz), **Supp. XXVI:** 263

"Addendum" (Wright), **Supp. V:** 339

Addiego, John, **Supp. XII:** 182

Adding Machine, The (Rice), **I:** 479

Adding Machine, The: Selected Essays (Burroughs), **Supp. III Part 1:** 93, 97

"Adding to the Unhappiness: Those Poems You Are Writing" (Gallagher), **Supp. XXIV:** 172

Addison, Joseph, **I:** 8, 105, 106–107, 108, 114, 131, 300, 304; **III:** 430

"Address Delivered at Lenox, An" (Channing), **Supp. XXIV: 79–80**

"Addressed to a Political Shrimp, or, Fly upon the Wheel" (Freneau), **Supp. II Part 1:** 267

"Address to My Soul" (Wylie), **Supp. I Part 2:** 729

"Address to the Deist, An" (Wheatley), **Supp. XX: 287**

"Address to the Devil" (Jarman), **Supp. XVII:** 114

Address to the Government of the United States on the Cession of Louisiana to the French, An (Brown), **Supp. I Part 1:** 146

"Address to the Scholars of New England" (Ransom), **III:** 491

"Address with Exclamation Points, A" (Simic), **Supp. VIII:** 283

"Adieu to Norman, Bon Jour to Joan and Jean-Paul" (O'Hara), **Supp. XXIII:** 219

Adisa, Opal Palmer, **Supp. XXII:** 66, 74, 78

"Adjutant Bird, The" (Banks), **Supp. V:** 5

Adkins, Nelson F., **II:** 20

Adler, Alfred, **I:** 248

Adler, Betty, **III:** 103

Adler, George J., **III:** 81

Adler, Renata, **Supp. X:** 171

Admiral of the Ocean Sea: A Life of Christopher Columbus (Morison), **Supp. I Part 2:** 486–488

"Admirals" (Chabon), **Supp. XI:** 72

"Admonition, An" (Brodsky), **Supp. VIII:** 33

"Adolescence" (Bidart), **Supp. XV:** 32
"Adolescence" (Dove), **Supp. IV Part 1:** 245
"Adolescence" (Olds), **Supp. X:** 211
"Adolescence II" (Dove), **Supp. IV Part 1:** 242, 244–245
Adolescent's Christmas, An: 1944 (C. Bly), **Supp. XVI:** 31–32
"Adolf Eichmann" (Carruth), **Supp. XVI:** 47
"Adonais" (Shelley), **II:** 516, 540
Adonai: The Pilgrim of Eternity (Lippard), **Supp. XXIII:** 180, 189, 190
Adorno, Theodor, **Supp. I Part 2:** 645, 650; **Supp. IV Part 1:** 301
"Adrienne Rich: The Poetics of Change" (Gelpi), **Supp. I Part 2:** 554
Adrift in Macao (Durang), **Supp. XXIV:** 125
"Adultery" (Banks), **Supp. V:** 15
"Adultery" (Dubus), **Supp. VII:** 85
Adultery and Other Choices (Dubus), **Supp. VII:** 83–85
Adulthood Rites (O. Butler), **Supp. XIII:** 63, **64–65**
Adult Life of Toulouse Lautrec by Henri Toulouse Lautrec, The (Acker), **Supp. XII:** 5, 6, **8–9**
Adventure (London), **II:** 466
Adventures in Ancient Egypt (Goldbarth), **Supp. XII:** 191
Adventures in Value (Cummings), **I:** 430
"Adventures of a Book Reviewer" (Cowley), **Supp. II Part 1:** 137, 142
Adventures of a Novelist (Atherton), **Supp. XXIV:** 17–18, 19–20, 21
Adventures of Augie March, The (Bellow), **I:** 144, 147, 149, 150, 151, 152–153, 154, 155, 157, 158–159, 164; **Retro. Supp. II:** 19, 20, **22–23**, 24, 30; **Supp. VIII:** 234, 236–237; **Supp. XXIV:** 220
Adventures of a Young Man (Dos Passos), **I:** 488, 489, 492
Adventures of Captain Bonneville (Irving), **II:** 312
Adventures of Harry Franco, The: A Tale of the Great Panic (Briggs), **Supp. XVIII:** 1, 2, 5–8
Adventures of Harry Richmond, The (Meredith), **Supp. XX: 234**
Adventures of Huckleberry Finn, The (Twain), **I:** 307, 506; **II:** 26, 72, 262, 266–268, 290, 418, 430; **III:** 101, 112–113, 357, 554, 558, 577; **IV:** 198, 201–204, 207; **Retro. Supp. I:** 188; **Retro. Supp. II:** 121; **Supp. I Part 1:** 247; **Supp. IV Part 1:** 247, 257; **Supp. IV Part 2:** 502; **Supp. V:** 131; **Supp. VIII:** 198; **Supp. X:** 230; **Supp. XII:** 16; **Supp. XVI:** 222; **Supp. XX: 171; Supp. XXII:** 81
Adventures of Jimmy (Broughton), **Supp. XV:** 146
Adventures of Roderick Random, The (Smollett), **I:** 134
Adventures of the Letter I (Simpson), **Supp. IX:** 266, **273–274**
Adventures of Tom Sawyer, The (Twain), **II:** 26; **III:** 223, 572, 577; **IV:** 199–

200, 203, 204; **Supp. I Part 2:** 456, 470; **Supp. XVI:** 66
Adventures While Preaching the Gospel of Beauty (Lindsay), **Supp. I Part 2:** 374, 376, 381, 382–384, 389, 399
Adventures with Ed (Loeffler), **Supp. XIII:** 1
Advertisements for Myself (Mailer), **III:** 27, 35–38, 41–42, 45, 46; **Retro. Supp. II:** 196, 199, 200, 202, 203, 212; **Supp. IV Part 1:** 90, 284; **Supp. XIV:** 157; **Supp. XXIV:** 281
"Advertisements for Myself on the Way Out" (Mailer), **III:** 37
Advice (Bodenheim), **Supp. XXV:** 22
"Advice to a Prophet" (Wilbur), **Supp. III Part 2:** 555–557
Advice to a Prophet and Other Poems (Wilbur), **Supp. III Part 2:** 554–558
"Advice to a Raven in Russia" (Barlow), **Supp. II Part 1:** 65, 74, 80, 83
"Advice to Players" (Bidart), **Supp. XV:** 35
Advice to the Lovelorn (film), **Retro. Supp. II:** 328
Advice to the Privileged Orders, Part I (Barlow), **Supp. II Part 1:** 80
Aegerter, Lindsay Pentolfe, **Supp. XXII:** 69
"Aeneas and Dido" (Brodsky), **Supp. VIII:** 24–25
"Aeneas at Washington" (Tate), **IV:** 129
Aeneid (Virgil), **I:** 396; **II:** 542; **III:** 124; **Supp. XV:** 23; **Supp. XXIV:** 162–163
Aeneus Tacticus, **I:** 136
Aerial View (Barabtarlo), **Retro. Supp. I:** 278
"Aeria the Evanescent" (Sobin), **Supp. XVI:** 292
Aeschylus, **I:** 274, 433; **III:** 398; **IV:** 358, 368, 370; **Retro. Supp. I:** 65; **Supp. I Part 2:** 458, 494
Aesop, **I:** 387; **II:** 154, 169, 302; **III:** 587
Aesthetic (Croce), **III:** 610
"Aesthetics" (Mumford), **Supp. II Part 2:** 476
"Aesthetics of Silence, The" (Sontag), **Supp. III Part 2:** 459
"Aesthetics of the Shah" (Olds), **Supp. X:** 205
"Affair at Coulter's Notch, The" (Bierce), **I:** 202
Affaire de viol, Une (C. Himes). *See Case of Rape, A* (C. Himes)
"Affair of Outposts, An" (Bierce), **I:** 202
Affliction (Banks), **Supp. V:** 15, 16
Affluent Society, The (Galbraith), **Supp. I Part 2:** 648
Afghanistan Picture Show, An: or, How I Saved the World (Vollmann), **Supp. XVII:** 226, **228–229**, 233
"Aficionados, The" (Carver), **Supp. III Part 1:** 137
"Afloat" (Beattie), **Supp. V:** 29
Afloat and Ashore (Cooper), **I:** 351, 355
"Afoot" (P. N. Warren as Kilina), **Supp. XX: 261–262**
Africa, Its Geography, People, and Products (Du Bois), **Supp. II Part 1:** 179

Africa, Its Place in Modern History (Du Bois), **Supp. II Part 1:** 179
"Africa, to My Mother" (D. Diop), **Supp. IV Part 1:** 16
Africana (H. L. Gates, ed.), **Supp. XX: 99**
African American Century, The : How Black Americans Have Shaped Our Country (H. L. Gates), **Supp. XX: 102**
African American Lives (television production), **Supp. XX:** 99
African American Lives 2 (television production), **Supp. XX:** 99
African American National Biography (H. L. Gates, ed.), **Supp. XX:** 99
African American Writers (Smith, ed.), **Supp. XIII:** 115, 127
"African Book" (Hemingway), **II:** 259
"African Chief, The" (Bryant), **Supp. I Part 1:** 168
"African Fragment" (Brooks), **Supp. III Part 1:** 85
African Queen, The (film), **Supp. XI:** 17
"African Roots of War, The" (Du Bois), **Supp. II Part 1:** 174
African Silences (Matthiessen), **Supp. V:** 203
African Treasury, An (Hughes, ed.), **Supp. I Part 1:** 344
"Afrika Revolution" (Baraka), **Supp. II Part 1:** 53
"AFRO-AMERICAN LYRIC" (Baraka), **Supp. II Part 1:** 59
After (Bukiet), **Supp. XVII:** 43, **44–45**
After (Hirshfield), **Supp. XXIII:** 133–135, 139
"After a Greek Proverb" (Stallings), **Supp. XXV:** 225
After All: Last Poems (Matthews), **Supp. IX:** 155, **167–169**
After and Before the Lightning (Ortiz), **Supp. IV Part 2:** 513
"After a Nightmare" (Davison), **Supp. XXVI:** 69
"After a Party" (Salinas), **Supp. XIII:** 327
"After Apple-Picking" (Frost), **Retro. Supp. I:** 126, 128
"After Arguing against the Contention That Art Must Come from Discontent" (Stafford), **Supp. XI:** 327
After Confession: Poetry as Autobiography (Harris), **Supp. XIV:** 269
After Confession: Poetry as Autobiography (K. Sontag and D. Graham), **Supp. XV:** 104
"After Cowboy Chicken Came to Town" (Jin), **Supp. XVIII:** 97–98
"After Disappointment" (Jarman), **Supp. XVII:** 118–119
After Disillusion: Poems (Wolf), **Supp. XXII:** 275
"After Edward Hopper: Somebody in a Bar" (Ferry), **Supp. XXIV:** 162
After Experience (Snodgrass), **Supp. VI:** 314–316, 317
"After great pain, a formal feeling comes" (Dickinson), **Retro. Supp. I:** 37
"After Hearing a Waltz by Bartók" (Lowell), **II:** 522

After Henry (Didion), **Supp. IV Part 1:** 195, 196, 199, 207, 208, 211

"After Henry" (Didion), **Supp. IV Part 1:** 211

After Holbein" (Wharton), **IV:** 325; **Retro. Supp. I:** 382

After House, The (Rinehart), **Supp. XXV:** 193

After Ikkyu and Other Poems (Harrison), **Supp. VIII:** 42

"After-Image" (Bierds), **Supp. XVII:** 31–32

"After-Image" (Caldwell), **I:** 309

After-Images: Autobiographical Sketches (Snodgrass), **Supp. VI:** 314, **319–323,** 324, 326–327

After I's (Zukofsky), **Supp. III Part 2:** 628, 629

Afterlife (Monette), **Supp. X:** 153

Afterlife (Updike), **Retro. Supp. I:** 322

Afterlife, The (Levis), **Supp. XI:** 259, **260–264**

"After Magritte" (McClatchy), **Supp. XII:** 264

"After Making Love" (Dunn), **Supp. XI:** 153

Aftermath (Longfellow), **II:** 490

"Aftermath" (Longfellow), **II:** 498

After New Formalism (A. Finch, ed.), **Supp. XVII:** 74

"Afternoon" (Ellison), **Supp. II Part 1:** 238

"Afternoon at MacDowell" (Kenyon), **Supp. VII:** 159

"Afternoon Miracle, An" (O. Henry), **Supp. II Part 1:** 390

Afternoon of a Faun (Hearon), **Supp. VIII: 63–64**

Afternoon of an Author: A Selection of Uncollected Stories and Essays (Fitzgerald), **II:** 94

"Afternoon of a Playwright" (Thurber), **Supp. I Part 2:** 620

Afternoon of the Unreal (Salinas), **Supp. XIII:** 311, **316–318**

"Afternoon with the Old Man, An" (Dubus), **Supp. VII:** 84

"After Punishment Was Done with Me" (Olds), **Supp. X:** 213

"After Reading *Barely and Widely,*" (Zukofsky), **Supp. III Part 2:** 625, 631

"After Reading 'In the Clearing' for the Author, Robert Frost" (Corso), **Supp. XII:** 130

"After Reading *Mickey in the Night Kitchen* for the Third Time before Bed" (Dove), **Supp. IV Part 1:** 249

"After Reading the Greek Poet"(Kenny), **Supp. XXIII:** 150

"After Reading Tu Fu, I Go Outside to the Dwarf Orchard" (Wright), **Supp. V:** 343

"After Reading Wang Wei, I Go Outside to the Full Moon" (Wright), **Supp. V:** 343

Aftershocks (Stallings), **Supp. XXV:** 222

"Aftershocks" (Stallings), **Supp. XXV:** 222, 231

After Shocks, Near Escapes (Dobyns), **Supp. XIII: 80–82**

"After Song, An" (W. C. Williams), **Retro. Supp. I:** 413

After Strange Gods (T. S. Eliot), **I:** 588

After Such Knowledge: Memory, History, and the Legacy of the Holocaust (E. Hoffman), **Supp. XVI:** 152–153, **158–161**

"After the Alphabets" (Merwin), **Supp. III Part 1:** 356

"After the Argument" (Dunn), **Supp. XI:** 149

"After the Baptism" (C. Bly), **Supp. XVI:** 40

"After the Burial" (Lowell), **Supp. I Part 2:** 409

"After the Curfew" (Holmes), **Supp. I Part 1:** 308

"After the Death of John Brown" (Thoreau), **IV:** 185

"After the Denim" (Carver), **Supp. III Part 1:** 144

"After the Dentist" (Swenson), **Supp. IV Part 2:** 645

After the Fall (A. Miller), **III:** 148, 149, 156, 161, 162, 163–165, 166

"After the Fire" (Merrill), **Supp. III Part 1:** 328

"After the Flood" (Sanders), **Supp. XVI:** 274–275

After the Fox (film), **Supp. IV Part 2:** 575

After the Genteel Tradition (Cowley), **Supp. II Part 1:** 143

"After the Heart's Interrogation" (Komunyakaa), **Supp. XIII:** 120

After the Lost Generation: A Critical Study of the Writers of Two Wars (Aldridge), **Supp. IV Part 2:** 680; **Supp. XIX:** 250

"After the Night Office—Gethsemani Abbey" (Merton), **Supp. VIII:** 195–196

After the Others (Weigl), **Supp. XIX:** 282, 283–284

"After the Persian" (Bogan), **Supp. III Part 1:** 64

After the Plague (Boyle), **Supp. XX: 20**

"After the Plague" (Boyle), **Supp. XX: 20**

"After the Pleasure Party" (Melville), **III:** 93

"After the Rain" (Halliday), **Supp. XIX:** 91

"After the Resolution" (Dunn), **Supp. XI:** 151

After the Stroke (Sarton), **Supp. VIII:** 264

"After the Surprising Conversions" (Lowell), **I:** 544, 545; **II:** 550; **Retro. Supp. II:** 187

"After 37 Years My Mother Apologizes for My Childhood" (Olds), **Supp. X:** 208

After This (McDermott), **Supp. XVIII:** 155, **166–167**

Afterthoughts (L. P. Smith), **Supp. XIV:** 339, 345

"Afterthoughts on the Rosenbergs" (Fiedler), **Supp. XIII:** 99

"After Twenty Years" (Rich), **Supp. I Part 2:** 559–560

"Afterwake, The" (Rich), **Supp. I Part 2:** 553

"Afterward" (Wharton), **Retro. Supp. I:** 372

"Afterword"(Hadas), **Supp. XXIII:** 113

"After Working Long" (Kenyon), **Supp. VII:** 170

"After Yitzl" (Goldbarth), **Supp. XII:** 186

"After You, My Dear Alphonse" (Jackson), **Supp. IX:** 119

"After Your Death" (Trethewey), **Supp. XXI:** 255

"After Your Nap" (B. Kelly), **Supp. XVII:** 124

"Again" (Dixon), **Supp. XII:** 157

"Again, Kapowsin" (Hugo), **Supp. VI:** 141

"Again Just Now" (Budbill), **Supp. XIX:** 11

"Against" (Goldbarth), **Supp. XII:** 193

"Against Decoration" (Karr), **Supp. XI:** 248

"Against Epiphanies" (C. Baxter), **Supp. XVII:** 20

Against Interpretation (Sontag), **Supp. III Part 2:** 451, 455; **Supp. XIV:** 15

"Against Interpretation" (Sontag), **Supp. III Part 2:** 456–458, 463

"Against Modernity" (Ozick), **Supp. V:** 272

"Against Nature" (Karr), **Supp. XI:** 243

Against Nature (Updike), **Retro. Supp. I:** 323

Against Our Vanishing: Winter Conversations with Allen Grossman on the Theory and Practice of Poetry (Halliday), **Supp. XIX: 82–84,** 88

"Against Realism" (Halliday), **Supp. XIX:** 93

Against the Cold (Bynner), **Supp. XV:** 51

"Against the Crusades" (Stern), **Supp. IX:** 300

Against the Current: As I Remember F. Scott Fitzgerald (Kroll Ring), **Supp. IX:** 63

Agamben, Giorgio, **Supp. XVI:** 289

Agapida, Fray Antonio (pseudonym). *See* Irving, Washington

"Agassiz" (Lowell), **Supp. I Part 2:** 414, 416

Agassiz, Louis, **II:** 343; **Supp. I Part 1:** 312; **Supp. IX:** 180

Âge cassant, L' (Char; Sobin, trans.), **Supp. XVI:** 282

"Aged Wino's Counsel to a Young Man on the Brink of Marriage, The" (X. J. Kennedy), **Supp. XV:** 156

Agee, Emma, **I:** 26

Agee, James, **I: 25–47,** 293; **IV:** 215; **Supp. IX:** 109; **Supp. XIV:** 92; **Supp. XV:** 143

"Agency Without Mastery: Chronic Pain and Posthuman Life Writing" (Gilmore), **Supp. XXVI:** 53

"Agent, The" (Wilbur), **Supp. III Part 2:** 557–561

Age of Anxiety, The (Auden), **Supp. II Part 1:** 2, 19, 21
"Age of Conformity, The" (Howe), **Supp. VI:** 117
Age of Grief, The: A Novella and Stories (Smiley), **Supp. VI:** 292, **299–301**
Age of Innocence, The (Wharton), **IV:** 320–322, 327–328; **Retro. Supp. I:** 372, 374, **380–381; Supp. IV Part 1:** 23
Age of Longing, The (Koestler), **I:** 258
Age of Reason, The (Paine), **Supp. I Part 2:** 503, 515–517, 520
"Age of Strolling, The" (Stern), **Supp. IX:** 297
"Ages, The" (Bryant), **Supp. I Part 1:** 152, 155, 166, 167
"Ages of the Women, The" (Gibran), **Supp. XX: 115**
"Aggrandizement, The" (Bronk), **Supp. XXI:** 32
"Aging" (Jarrell), **II:** 388
Aging and Gender in Literature (George), **Supp. IV Part 2:** 450
"Agio Neró" (Mora), **Supp. XIII:** 224
"Agitato ma non Troppo" (Ransom), **III:** 493
"Agnes of Iowa" (Moore), **Supp. X:** 165, 178
Agnes of Sorrento (Stowe), **Supp. I Part 2:** 592, 595–596
Agnon, S. Y., **Supp. V:** 266; **Supp. XXV:** 267
Agony & the Agony, The (Silver), **Supp. XXIV:** 265, **274–275**
"Agosta the Winged Man and Rasha the Black Dove" (Dove), **Supp. IV Part 1:** 246–247
Agrarian Justice (Paine), **Supp. I Part 2:** 517–518
"Agricultural Show, The" (McKay), **Supp. X:** 139
Agrippa: A Book of the Dead (W. Gibson), **Supp. XVI:** 125
Agua de dos ríos/Water from Two Rivers (Espaillat), **Supp. XXI:** 104, 112–113
Agua Fresca: An Anthology of Raza Poetry (Rodríguez, ed.), **Supp. IV Part 2:** 540
Agua Santa/Holy Water (Mora), **Supp. XIII: 222–225**
Agüero Sisters, The (García), **Supp. XI: 185–190**
Aguiar, Marian, **Supp. XXII:** 68
Aguiar, Sarah Appleton, **Supp. XIII:** 30
Aguilar, Carmen, **Supp. XXIII:** 200
Ah, Wilderness! (O'Neill), **III:** 400–401; **Supp. IV Part 2:** 587
Ah, Wilderness!: The Frontier in American Literature (Humphrey), **Supp. IX:** 104
Ahearn, Barry, **Retro. Supp. I:** 415
Ahearn, Frederick L., Jr., **Supp. XI:** 184
Ahearn, Kerry, **Supp. IV Part 2:** 604
Ahmed Arabi Pasha, **I:** 453
Ahnebrink, Lars, **III:** 328
Ahrens, Sylvia, **Supp. XX: 162**
Ah Sin (Harte), **Supp. II Part 1:** 354–355
"Ah! Sun-flower" (Blake), **III:** 19

Ai, **Supp. XXVI:** 66
Aida (rock musical), **Supp. XXI:** 148
Aidoo, Ama Ato, **Supp. XXII:** 68
AIDS and Its Metaphors (Sontag), **Supp. III Part 2:** 452, 466–468
Aids to Reflection (Coleridge), **II:** 10
Aiieeeee! An Anthology of Asian-American Writers (The Combined Asian Resources Project), **Supp. X:** 292
Aiken, Conrad, **I: 48–70,** 190, 211, 243; **II:** 55, 530, 542; **III:** 458, 460; **Retro. Supp. I:** 55, 56, 57, 58, 60, 62; **Supp. X:** 50, 115; **Supp. XV:** 144, 297, 298, 302, 306, 309; **Supp. XVII:** 135; **Supp. XXIV:** 36; **Supp. XXV:** 19; **Supp. XXVI:** 225
"Aimless Love" (Collins), **Supp. XXI:** 61
"Aim Was Song, The" (Frost), **Retro. Supp. I:** 133
Ainger, Arthur Campbell, **Supp. XX: 230**
Ainsworth, Linda, **Supp. IV Part 1:** 274
Ainsworth, William, **III:** 423
Air-Conditioned Nightmare, The (H. Miller), **III:** 186
Airing Dirty Laundry (Reed), **Supp. X:** 241
"Air Is Full of Little Holes, The" (Brockmeier), **Supp. XXII:** 60
"Airmail from Mother" (Kooser), **Supp. XIX:** 120
"Air Plant, The" (Crane), **I:** 401
Air Raid: A Verse Play for Radio (MacLeish), **III:** 21
"Airs above the Ground" (Sarton), **Supp. VIII:** 261
Air Tight: A Novel of Red Russia. See We the Living (Rand)
Air Up There, The (film, Glaser), **Supp. XVII:** 9
"Airwaves" (Mason), **Supp. VIII:** 146
Airways, Inc. (Dos Passos), **I:** 482
A Is for Anne: Mistress Hutchinson Disturbs the Commonwealth (Schott), **Supp. XXIII:** 240, **246–247**
"A is for Dining Alone" (M. F. K. Fisher), **Supp. XVII:** 86
Aitken, Robert, **Supp. I Part 2:** 504
Aizenberg, Susan, **Supp. XXI:** 131
Akhmadulina, Bella, **Supp. III Part 1:** 268
Akhmatova, Anna, **Supp. III Part 1:** 268, 269; **Supp. VIII:** 20, 21, 25, 27, 30; **Supp. XXI:** 132
Akhmatova Translations, The (Kenyon), **Supp. VII:** 160
"Akhnilo" (Salter), **Supp. IX:** 260
Akins, Zoë, **Supp. XVI:** 187
Aksenev, Vasily P., **Retro. Supp. I:** 278
"Al Aaraaf" (Poe), **III:** 426–427
Al Aaraaf, Tamerlane, and Minor Poems (Poe), **III:** 410
"Alabama Jones" (Mosher), **Supp. XXII:** 204, 211
"Alain Locke and Cultural Pluralism" (Kallen), **Supp. XIV:** 197
"Alain Locke: Bahá'í Philosopher" (Buck), **Supp. XIV:** 199

Alain Locke: Faith and Philosophy (Buck), **Supp. XIV:** 200
Alarçon, **Supp. XVII:** 74
Alarcón, Justo, **Supp. IV Part 2:** 538, 539, 540
Alarcón, Norma, **Supp. XXIII:** 194, 204–205
À la Recherche du Temps Perdu (Proust), **IV:** 428
"Alarm" (X. J. Kennedy), **Supp. XV:** 163
"Alastor" (Shelley), **Supp. I Part 2:** 728
"Alatus" (Wilbur), **Supp. III Part 2:** 563
Alaya (Hirshfield), **Supp. XXIII:** 131
"Alba" (Creeley), **Supp. IV Part 1:** 150
Alba, Richard D., **Supp. XX: 43**
Albee, Edward, **I: 71–96,** 113; **II:** 558, 591; **III:** 281, 387; **IV:** 4, 230; **Retro. Supp. II:** 104; **Supp. VIII:** 331; **Supp. XIII:** 196, 197; **Supp. XXIV:** 113, 263, 270
Albers, Joseph, **Supp. IV Part 2:** 621
Alberti, Rafael, **Supp. XV:** 75
Albright, Margery, **Supp. I Part 2:** 613
"Album, The" (Morris), **III:** 220
Album, The (Rinehart), **Supp. XXV:** 197, 200
Alcestiad, The (Wilder), **IV:** 357, 374
"Alchemist, The" (Bogan), **Supp. III Part 1:** 50
"Alchemist in the City, The" (Hopkins), **Supp. IV Part 2:** 639
Alchymist's Journal, The (Connell), **Supp. XIV:** 80
"Alcmena" (Winters), **Supp. II Part 2:** 801
Alcott, Abba. *See* Alcott, Mrs. Amos Bronson (Abigail May)
Alcott, Amos Bronson, **II:** 7, 225; **IV:** 172, 173, 184; **Retro. Supp. I:** 217; **Supp. I Part 1:** 28, 29–32, 35, 39, 41, 45; **Supp. II Part 1:** 290; **Supp. XVI:** 84, 89; **Supp. XXV:** 250
Alcott, Mrs. Amos Bronson (Abigail May), **IV:** 184; **Supp. I Part 1:** 29, 30, 31, 32, 35
Alcott, Anna. *See* Pratt, Anna
Alcott, Louisa May, **IV:** 172; **Supp. I Part 1: 28–46; Supp. IX:** 128; **Supp. XV:** 338; **Supp. XVI:** 84
Alcott, May, **Supp. I Part 1:** 41
Alcuin: A Dialogue (Brown), **Supp. I Part 1:** 126–127, 133
Alden, Hortense. *See* Farrell, Mrs. James T. (Hortense Alden)
Alden, John, **I:** 471; **II:** 502–503
"Alder Fork, The" (Leopold), **Supp. XIV:** 186
Aldington, Perdita, **Supp. I Part 1:** 258
Aldington, Richard, **II:** 517; **III:** 458, 459, 465, 472; **Retro. Supp. I:** 63, 127; **Supp. I Part 1:** 257–262, 270
Aldington, Mrs. Richard. *See* Doolittle, Hilda
Aldo Leopold: His Life and Work (Meine), **Supp. XIV:** 179
"Aldo Leopold's Intellectual Heritage" (Nash), **Supp. XIV:** 191–192
Aldon, Raymond, **Supp. XV:** 297

Aldrich, Thomas Bailey, **II:** 400; **Supp. II Part 1:** 192; **Supp. XIV:** 45; **Supp. XVIII:** 4

Aldrich, Tom, **Supp. I Part 2:** 415

Aldridge, John W., **Supp. I Part 1:** 196; **Supp. IV Part 1:** 286; **Supp. IV Part 2:** 680, 681; **Supp. VIII:** 189; **Supp. XI:** 228; **Supp. XIX:** 250

Aleck Maury Sportsman (Gordon), **II:** 197, 200, 203–204

Alegría, Claribel, **Supp. IV Part 1:** 208

Aleichem, Sholem, **Supp. XXIII:** 4, 7

Aleichem, Sholom, **IV:** 3, 10; **Supp. IV Part 2:** 585

"Alert Lovers, Hidden Sides, and Ice Travelers: Notes on Poetic Form and Energy" (Dunn), **Supp. XI:** 153

"Ale&sacaron; Debeljak" (Simic), **Supp. VIII:** 279

"Alex" (Oliver), **Supp. VII:** 232

Alexander, Doris, **Supp. XVII:** 99

Alexander, Elizabeth, **Supp. XVIII:** 171, 185, 186; **Supp. XXI:** 246, 257

Alexander, George, **II:** 331

Alexander, Michael, **Retro. Supp. I:** 293

Alexander, Paul, **Supp. XXV:** 84

"Alexander Crummell Dead" (Dunbar), **Supp. II Part 1:** 207, 208–209

Alexander's Bridge (Cather), **I:** 313, 314, 316–317, 326; **Retro. Supp. I:** 1, 6, 7, 8

Alexander the Great, **IV:** 322

"Alexandra" (Cather), **Retro. Supp. I:** 7, 9, 17

Alexandrov, V. E., **Retro. Supp. I:** 270

Alexie, Sherman, **Supp. XVIII:** 58; **Supp. XXVI:** 103, 108

Algic Researches (H. Schoolcraft), **Supp. XXIII:** 227

Algonquin Round Table, **Supp. IX:** 190, 191, 197

Algren, Nelson, **I:** 211; **Supp. IX:** 1–18; **Supp. V:** 4; **Supp. XII:** 126; **Supp. XIII:** 173; **Supp. XIV:** 3; **Supp. XVII:** 161; **Supp. XXI:** 264; **Supp. XXIII:** 165; **Supp. XXV:** 185

Alhambra, The (Irving), **II:** 310–311

Ali, Agha Shahid, **Supp. XVII:** 74

Ali, Ayaan Hirsi, **Supp. XXIV:** 15

Alias Grace (Atwood), **Supp. XIII:** 20, 31–32

Alice (film; Allen), **Supp. XV:** 2, 11

"Alice Doane's Appeal" (Hawthorne), **II:** 227

"Alice Drops Her Cigarette on the Floor ..." (Findley), **Supp. XX: 50–51**

"Alice in the Looking Glass" (Stallings), **Supp. XXV:** 234

Alice in Wonderland (Carroll), **Supp. I Part 2:** 622

Alice Ordered Me to Be Made (Notley), **Supp. XXII:** 224, 227, 228

"Alice Ordered Me to Be Made" (Notley), **Supp. XXII:** 227

Alice's Adventures in Wonderland (Carroll), **Supp. XVI:** 261

"Alicia and I Talking on Edna's Steps" (Cisneros), **Supp. VII:** 64

"Alicia Who Sees Mice" (Cisneros), **Supp. VII:** 60

Alien 3 (screenplay, W. Gibson), **Supp. XVI:** 120, 124

"Ali in Havana" (Talese), **Supp. XVII:** 207, 208

Alison, Archibald, **Supp. I Part 1:** 151, 159

Alison's House (Glaspell), **Supp. III Part 1:** 182, 188, 189

Alive (screenplay, Shanley), **Supp. XIV:** 316

Alive and Writing: Interviews with American Authors of the 1980s (McCaffery and Gregory), **Supp. X:** 260

"Alki Beach" (Hugo), **Supp. VI:** 135

Alla Breve Loving (Wright), **Supp. XV:** 339, 340

"Alla Breve Loving" (Wright), **Supp. XV:** 340

"All Apologies" (Biss), **Supp. XXVI:** 56

"All Around the Town" (Benét), **Supp. XI:** 48, 58

"All Around the Town" (Taggard), **Supp. XXVI:** 144

All at Sea (Lardner), **II:** 427

All Aunt Hagar's Children (E. P. Jones), **Supp. XXII:** 140, 143, **150–153**

"All Aunt Hagar's Children" (E. P. Jones), **Supp. XXII:** 151

"All Boy" (Rawlings), **Supp. X:** 222

Allegiances (Stafford), **Supp. XI: 322– 323,** 329

"Allegory of the Cave" (Dunn), **Supp. XI:** 150

"Allegory Unlimited" (Cassill), **Supp. XIX:** 266

Allegro, Johnny (film, Tetzloff), **Supp. XVII:** 62

"Allegro, L' " (Milton), **Supp. XIV:** 8

Allen, Brooke, **Supp. VIII:** 153

Allen, Bruce, **Supp. XXII:** 205, 212; **Supp. XXIII:** 106, 300

Allen, Claudia, **Supp. XXIII:** 79

Allen, Dick, **Supp. IX:** 279

Allen, Donald, **Supp. VIII:** 291; **Supp. XIII:** 112; **Supp. XXIII:** 215, 220; **Supp. XXVI:** 223

Allen, Frank, **Supp. XI:** 126; **Supp. XII:** 186; **Supp. XXVI:** 150

Allen, Fred, **Supp. XXV:** 255

Allen, Frederick Lewis, **Supp. I Part 2:** 655

Allen, Gay Wilson, **IV:** 352; **Supp. I Part 2:** 418

Allen, Ivan, **Supp. XXII:** 245

Allen, Paula Gunn. *See* Gunn Allen, Paula

Allen, Robert Moore, **Supp. XX: 164**

Allen, Walter, **I:** 505; **III:** 352; **Supp. IV Part 2:** 685; **Supp. IX:** 231

Allen, Woody, **Supp. I Part 2:** 607, 623; **Supp. IV Part 1:** 205; **Supp. X:** 164; **Supp. XI:** 307; **Supp. XV:** 1–18; **Supp. XVII:** 48

"Aller et Retour" (Barnes), *Supp. III Part 1:* 36

Aller Retour New York (H. Miller), **III:** 178, 182, 183

Allerton, Isaac, **Supp. XXII:** 44

Allessandrini, Goffredo, **Supp. IV Part 2:** 520

Alleys of Eden, The (R. O. Butler), **Supp. XII:** 62, **62–64,** 68

All God's Children Need Traveling Shoes (Angelou), **Supp. IV Part 1:** 2, 9–10, 12–13, 17

All God's Chillun Got Wings (O'Neill), **III:** 387, 391, 393–394

All Gone (Dixon), **Supp. XII:** 148, 149

"All Hallows" (Glück), **Supp. V:** 82

"All I Can Remember" (Jackson), **Supp. IX:** 115

"Alligators, The" (Updike), **IV:** 219

Allingham, John Till, **Supp. XV:** 243

All in the Family (Boyce), **Supp. XXI:** 8

"ALL IN THE STREET" (Baraka), **Supp. II Part 1:** 53

Allison, Dorothy, **Supp. XVIII:** 195

"All I Want" (Tapahonso), **Supp. IV Part 2:** 508

"All Little Colored Children Should Play the Harmonica" (Patchett), **Supp. XII:** 309

"All Mountains" (Doolittle), **Supp. I Part 1:** 271

All My Friends Are Going to Be Strangers (McMurtry), **Supp. V:** 224, 228, 229

All My Pretty Ones (Sexton), **Supp. II Part 2:** 678, 679–683

"All My Pretty Ones" (Sexton), **Supp. II Part 2:** 681–682

"All My Sad Captains" (Jewett), **Retro. Supp. II:** 134

All My Sons (A. Miller), **III:** 148, 149, 150, 151–153, 154, 155, 156, 158, 159, 160, 164, 166

All New People (Lamott), **Supp. XX: 135–136**

"All Night, All Night" (Schwartz), **Supp. II Part 2:** 665

All Night Long (Caldwell), **I:** 297

"All-Night Melodies" (Nelson), **Supp. XVIII:** 185

All-Night Visitors (Major), **Supp. XXII: 173–174**

"All of Us" (Major), **Supp. XXII:** 185

All of Us: The Collected Poems (Carver), **Supp. XXIV:** 167

All of What We Loved (Bronk), **Supp. XXI:** 32

"All Our Lost Children: Trauma and Testimony in the Performance of Childhood" (Pace), **Supp. XI:** 245

All Our Yesterdays (Parker), **Supp. XIX: 187–188**

"All Out" (Hecht), **Supp. X:** 72

All Over (Albee), **I:** 91–94

"Allowance" (Minot), **Supp. VI:** 206, 207–208

"Alloy" (Rukeyser), **Supp. VI:** 279

"All Parrots Speak" (Bowles), **Supp. IV Part 1:** 89

Allport, Gordon, **II:** 363–364

All Quiet on the Western Front (Remarque), **Supp. IV Part 1:** 380, 381

"ALL REACTION IS DOOMED-!-!-!" (Baraka), **Supp. II Part 1:** 59

"All Revelation" (Frost), **II:** 160–162

"All Riptides Roar with Sand from Opposing Shores" (Vaz), **Supp. XXVI:** 264–265

Allsburg, Christ Van, **Supp. XXV:** 83, 87

"All Shall Love Me and Despair"(Thompson), **Supp. XXIII:** 295

All Shot Up (C. Himes), **Supp. XVI:** 143, 144

"All Souls" (Gioia), **Supp. XV:** 117

"All Souls" (Wharton), **IV:** 315–316; **Retro. Supp. I:** 382

"All Souls' Night" (Yeats), **Supp. X:** 69

All Souls' Rising (Bell), **Supp. X:** 12, **13–16,** 17

"All-Star Literary Vaudeville" (Wilson), **IV:** 434–435

Allston, Washington, **II:** 298

All Stories Are True (Wideman), **Supp. X:** 320

"All That Is" (Wilbur), **Supp. III Part 2:** 563

All That Was Possible (Sturgis), **Supp. XX: 227, 232, 235–237**

"All the Bearded Irises of Life: Confessions of a Homospiritual" (Walker), **Supp. III Part 2:** 527

"All the Beautiful Are Blameless" (Wright), **Supp. III Part 2:** 597

ALL: The Collected Poems, 1956–1964 (Zukofsky), **Supp. III Part 2:** 630

ALL: The Collected Short Poems, 1923–1958 (Zukofsky), **Supp. III Part 2:** 629

All the Conspirators (Isherwood), **Supp. XIV:** 156, 159, 160

All the Dark and Beautiful Warriors (Hansberry), **Supp. IV Part 1:** 360, 374

All the Days and Nights: The Collected Stories (Maxwell), **Supp. VIII:** 151, 158, 169

"All the Dead Dears" (Plath), **Retro. Supp. II:** 246; **Supp. I Part 2:** 537

"All the Dead"(P. Benedict), **Supp. XXIII:** 37

All the Good People I've Left Behind (Oates), **Supp. II Part 2:** 510, 522, 523

"All the Hippos Were Boiled in Their Tanks" (Burroughs and Kerouac), **Supp. III Part 1:** 94

All the King's Men (Warren), **I:** 489; **IV:** 243, 248–249, 252; **Supp. V:** 261; **Supp. VIII:** 126; **Supp. X:** 1; **Supp. XVIII:** 77, 79; **Supp. XXIV:** 226

All the Little Live Things (Stegner), **Supp. IV Part 2:** 599, 604, 605, 606, 609–610, 611, 613

All the Pretty Horses (film), **Supp. VIII:** 175

All the Pretty Horses (McCarthy), **Supp. VIII:** 175, **182–183,** 188

All the Sad Young Men (Fitzgerald), **II:** 94; **Retro. Supp. I:** 108

"All the Time in the World" (Dubus), **Supp. VII:** 91

"All the Way to Flagstaff, Arizona" (Bausch), **Supp. VII:** 47, 49

"All This and More" (Karr), **Supp. XI:** 243

All Thy Conquests (Hayes), **Supp. XXVI:** 134,135–136

All Tomorrow's Parties (W. Gibson), **Supp. XVI:** 119, 121, 123, 124, **130**

"All Too Real" (Vendler), **Supp. V:** 189

All Trivia: Triva, More Trivia, Afterthoughts, Last Words (L. P. Smith), **Supp. XIV:** 339

All-True Travels and Adventures of Lidie Newton (Smiley), **Supp. VI:** 292, **305–307**

All We Need of Hell (Crews), **Supp. XI: 114**

Almack, Edward, **Supp. IV Part 2:** 435

al-Maghut, Muhammad, **Supp. XIII:** 278

"Almanac" (Swenson), **Supp. IV Part 2:** 641

Almanac of the Dead (Silko), **Supp. IV Part 2:** 558–559, 560, 561, 570–571

Alma: or, The Dead Women (Notley), **Supp. XXII:** 223, 224, 231, 236

Almon, Bert, **Supp. IX:** 93

"Almost" (Untermeyer), **Supp. XV:** 304

Almost Learning to Live in This World (Schott), **Supp. XXIII: 247–248**

Almost Revolution, The (Priaulx and Ungar), **Supp. XI:** 228

Alnilam (Dickey), **Supp. IV Part 1:** 176, 186, 188–189

"Alone" (Caputo), **Supp. XIX:** 29

"Alone" (Levine), **Supp. V:** 184, 185, 186

"Alone" (Pickering), **Supp. XXI:** 204

"Alone" (Poe), **Retro. Supp. II:** 266

"Alone" (Singer), **IV:** 15

"Alone" (Winters), **Supp. II Part 2:** 786, 811

"Alone and Lonely" (Budbill), **Supp. XIX:** 10

Aloneness (Brooks), **Supp. III Part 1:** 85, 86

Alone with America (Corso), **Supp. XII:** 131

Alone with America (Howard), **Supp. IX:** 326

"Along America's Edges" (Sobin), **Supp. XVI:** 288

"Along the Color Line" (Du Bois), **Supp. II Part 1:** 173

Along the Illinois (Masters), **Supp. I Part 2:** 472

Alouette, L' (Anouilh), **Supp. I Part 1:** 286–288

"Alphabet" (Nye), **Supp. XIII:** 283

Alphabet, An (Doty), **Supp. XI:** 120

Alphabet for Gourmets, An (M. F. K. Fisher), **Supp. XVII:** 86, 87, 92

Alphabet of Grace, The (Buechner), **Supp. XII:** 52

"Alphabet of My Dead, An" (Pinsky), **Supp. VI:** 235, 250

"Alphabet of Subjects, An" (Zukofsky), **Supp. III Part 2:** 624

"Alpine Christ, The" (Jeffers), **Supp. II Part 2:** 415, 419

Alpine Christ and Other Poems, The (Jeffers), **Supp. II Part 2:** 419

"Alpine Idyll, An" (Hemingway), **II:** 249; **Retro. Supp. I:** 176

Al Que Quiere! (W. C. Williams), **Retro. Supp. I:** 414, 416, **417,** 428

Alraune (Ewers; Endore, trans.), **Supp. XVII:** 54

Alsop, Joseph, **II:** 579

"Altar, The" (Herbert), **Supp. IV Part 2:** 646

"Altar, The" (MacLeish), **III:** 4

"Altar Boy" (Fante), **Supp. XI:** 160, 164

"Altar of the Dead, The" (James), **Retro. Supp. I:** 229

"Altars in the Street, The" (Levertov), **Supp. III Part 1:** 280

Alter, Robert, **Supp. XII:** 167

Altgeld, John Peter, **Supp. I Part 2:** 382, 455

Althea (Masters), **Supp. I Part 2:** 455, 459

Altick, Richard, **Supp. I Part 2:** 423

Altieri, Charles, **Supp. VIII:** 297, 303; **Supp. XXIII:** 220

Altman, Robert, **Supp. IX:** 143; **Supp. XXIV:** 166, 172

"Alto" (C. Frost), **Supp. XV:** 101

"Altra Ego" (Brodsky), **Supp. VIII:** 31–32

Altruists, The (Silver), **Supp. XXIV: 273**

A Lume Spento (Pound), **Retro. Supp. I:** 283, 285

"Aluminum House" (F. Barthelme), **Supp. XI:** 26

Alvares, Mosseh, **Supp. V:** 11

Alvarez, A., **Supp. I Part 2:** 526, 527; **Supp. II Part 1:** 99; **Supp. IX:** 248

Alvarez, Joseph A., **Supp. XXII:** 13–14

Alvarez, Julia, **Supp. VII: 1–21; Supp. XI:** 177; **Supp. XVII:** 71, 112; **Supp. XXIV:** 86, 89

"Always a Rose" (L.-Y. Lee), **Supp. XV:** 215, 216

"Always in Good Humor" (Adams), **Supp. XV:** 294

Always Outnumbered, Always Outgunned (Mosley), **Supp. XIII:** 242

"Always the Stories" (Ortiz), **Supp. IV Part 2:** 499, 500, 502, 504, 512

Always the Young Strangers (Sandburg), **III:** 577–578, 579

Always Young and Fair (Richter), **Supp. XVIII: 215–216**

Amadeus (Shaffer), **Supp. XIV:** 330

"Amahl and the Night Visitors: A Guide to the Tenor of Love" (Moore), **Supp. X:** 167

"Am and Am Not" (Olds), **Supp. X:** 212

"Amanita, The" (Francis), **Supp. IX:** 81

Amaranth (Robinson), **III:** 509, 510, 512, 513, 522, 523

"Amateur Iconography: Resurrection" (Stallings), **Supp. XXV:** 233

"Amateurs, The" (Swados), **Supp. XIX:** 256

Amazing Adele, The (Barillet and Grédy; Loos, trans.), **Supp. XVI:** 194

Amazing Adventures of Kavalier and Clay, The (Chabon), **Supp. XI:** 68, 76, **77–80; Supp. XXII:** 49

Amazing Adventures of Leticia Carberry (Rinehart), **Supp. XXV:** 194

Amazing Adventures of the Escapist, The (Chabon, ed.), **Supp. XIX:** 174

Amazing Interlude, The (Rinehart), **Supp. XXV:** 194

Amazing Science Fiction Stories, **Supp. XVI:** 121

Amazons: An Intimate Memoir by the First Woman to Play in the National Hockey League (DeLillo), **Supp. VI:** 2

Ambassador Morgenthau's Story (Morgenthau), **Supp. XXIII:** 21, 22

Ambassador of Peace, An (Abernon), **Supp. XVI:** 191

Ambassadors, The (H. James), **II:** 320, 333–334, 600; **III:** 517; **IV:** 322; **Retro. Supp. I:** 215, 218, 219, 220, 221, **232–233**

Ambelain, Robert, **Supp. I Part 1:** 260, 273, 274

"Amber" (Gansworth), **Supp. XXVI:** 114

"Ambition Bird, The" (Sexton), **Supp. II Part 2:** 693

Ambition: The Secret Passion (Epstein), **Supp. XIV:** 113–114

Ambler, Eric, **III:** 57

Ambrose Holt and Family (Glaspell), **Supp. III Part 1:** 175, 181, 184, 187, 188

"Ambrose Seyffert" (Masters), **Supp. I Part 2:** 464

"Ambush" (Komunyakaa), **Supp. XIII:** 122

Amen Corner, The (Baldwin), **Retro. Supp. II:** 5, 7; **Supp. I Part 1:** 48, 51, 54, 55, 56

America (Benét), **Supp. XI:** 46, 47, 51

"America" (Ginsberg), **Supp. II Part 1:** 58–59, 317

"America" (song), **IV:** 410

"America, America!" (poem) (Schwartz), **Supp. II Part 2:** 665

"America, Commerce, and Freedom" (Rowson and Reinagle), **Supp. XV:** 240

"America, Home of the Red Man" (Zitkala-Ša), **Supp. XXV:** 281

"America, Seen Through Photographs, Darkly" (Sontag), **Supp. III Part 2:** 464

"America! America!" (story) (Schwartz), **Supp. II Part 2:** 640, 658–659, 660

America and Americans (Steinbeck), **IV:** 52

"America and the Vidal Chronicles" (Pease), **Supp. IV Part 2:** 687

America as a Civilization (Lerner), **III:** 60

America Behind the Color Line (H. L. Gates), **Supp. XX:** 102, 105

America Beyond the Color Line (television program), **Supp. XX:** 99

America Hispana: A Portrait and a Prospect (W. Frank), **Supp. XX:** 76

"America Independent" (Freneau), **Supp. II Part 1:** 261

America Is Worth Saving (Dreiser), **Retro. Supp. II:** 96

American, The (James), **I:** 226; **II:** 326–327, 328, 331, 334; **IV:** 318; **Retro.**

Supp. I: 220, **221,** 228, 376, 381

Americana (DeLillo), **Supp. VI:** 2, **3,** 5, 6, 8, 13, 14

American Adam, The (R. W. B. Lewis), **II:** 457–458; **Supp. XIII:** 93

American Almanac (Leeds), **II:** 110

American Anthem (Doctorow and Suares), **Supp. IV Part 1:** 234

"American Apocalypse" (Gunn Allen), **Supp. IV Part 1:** 325

American Aristocracy (film), **Supp. XVI:** 185–186

American Blood, (Nichols), **Supp. XIII:** 268

American Blues (T. Williams), **IV:** 381, 383

American Buffalo (Mamet), **Supp. XIV:** 239, 241, 242, 244–245, 246, 254, 255

American Caravan: A Yearbook of American Literature (Mumford, ed.), **Supp. II Part 2:** 482

American Cause, The (MacLeish), **III:** 3

American Childhood, An (Dillard), **Supp. VI:** **19–21,** 23, 24, 25, 26, 30, 31

"American Childhood in the Dominican Republic, An" (Alvarez), **Supp. VII:** 2, 5

American Child Supreme, An: The Education of a Liberation Ecologist (Nichols), **Supp. XIII:** 256, 257, 258, 264, 265, 266, 267, 268, 269

American Civilization (C. L. R. James), **Supp. XXI:** 169

American Claimant, The (Twain), **IV:** 194, 198–199

American Crisis I (Paine), **Supp. I Part 2:** 508

American Crisis II (Paine), **Supp. I Part 2:** 508

American Crisis XIII (Paine), **Supp. I Part 2:** 509

"American Critic, The" (J. Spingarn), **I:** 266

American Culture, Canons, and the Case of Elizabeth Stoddard (Smith and Weinauer), **Supp. XV:** 270

American Daughter, An (Wasserstein), **Supp. XV:** **330–332,** 333

American Democrat, The (Cooper), **I:** 343, 346, 347, 353

American Desert (Everett), **Supp. XVIII:** **62–63**

American Diary (Webb), **Supp. I Part 1:** 5

American Drama since World War II (Weales), **IV:** 385

American Dream, An (Mailer), **III:** 27, 33–34, 35, 39, 41, 43, 44; **Retro. Supp. II:** 203, **204–205**

American Dream, The (Albee), **I:** 74–76, 77, 89, 94; **Supp. XXIV:** 113

"American Dreams" (Simpson), **Supp. IX:** 274

American Earth (Caldwell), **I:** 290, 308

"American Emperors" (Poirier), **Supp. IV Part 2:** 690

American English (Marckwardt), **Supp. XXIV:** 255

American Exodus, An (Lange and Taylor), **I:** 293

American Experience, The (Parkes), **Supp. I Part 2:** 617–618

American Express (Corso), **Supp. XII:** 129

"American Express" (Salter), **Supp. IX:** 260–261

"American Fear of Literature, The" (Lewis), **II:** 451

American Female Patriotism (S. Warner as Wetherell), **Supp. XVIII: 260–261,** 262, **263**

American Fictions (Hardwick), **Supp. X:** 171

American Fictions, 1940–1980 (Karl), **Supp. IV Part 1:** 384; **Supp. XXI:** 234

"American Financier, The" (Dreiser), **II:** 428

American Folkways (book series), **I:** 290

American Guerilla in the Philippines (Wolfert), **Supp. XXI:** 267

"American Heart of Darkness: The Moral Vision of Five Novels of the Vietnam War" (Palm), **Supp. XXII:** 103

"American Heritage" (Gansworth), **Supp. XXVI:** 114

American Heroine: The Life and Legend of Jane Addams (A. F. Davis), **Supp. I Part 1:** 1

American Historical Novel, The (Leisy), **Supp. II Part 1:** 125

"American Horse" (Erdrich), **Supp. IV Part 1:** 333

American Humor: A Study of the National Character (Rourke), **IV:** 339, 352; **Supp. XIX:** 147

American Hunger (Wright), **Supp. IV Part 1:** 11

"American Husband, The" (Atherton), **Supp. XXIV:** 24

American Indian Anthology, An (Tvedten, ed.), **Supp. IV Part 2:** 505

American Indian Stories (Zitkala-Ša), **Supp. XXV:** 272–273, 282–283, 284–285

"American Indian Women: At the Center of Indigenous Resistance in Contemporary North America" (Jaimes and Halsey), **Supp. IV Part 1:** 331

"American in England, An" (Wylie), **Supp. I Part 2:** 707

Americanize the First American (Zitkala-Ša), **Supp. XXV:** 283

American Jitters, The: A Year of the Slump (Wilson), **IV:** 427, 428

American Journal (Hayden), **Supp. II Part 1:** 367

American Journey: The Times of Robert F. Kennedy (Plimpton, ed.), **Supp. XVI:** 245

"American Land Ethic, An" (Momaday), **Supp. IV Part 2:** 488

American Landscape, The, **Supp. I Part 1:** 157

American Language, The (Mencken), **II:** 289, 430; **III:** 100, 104, 105, 108, 111, 119–120

American Language, The: Supplement One (Mencken), **III:** 111

American Language, The: Supplement Two (Mencken), **III:** 111

"American Letter" (MacLeish), **III:** 13

"American Liberty" (Freneau), **Supp. II Part 1:** 257

"American Life in Poetry" (column, Kooser), **Supp. XIX:** 116, 127

American Linden (Zapruder), **Supp. XXVI:** 54

American Literary History (Harrison), **Supp. VIII:** 37

American Mercury, **Supp. XI:** 163, 164

American Mind, The (Commager), **Supp. I Part 2:** 650

American Moderns: Bohemian New York and the Creation of a New Century (Stansell), **Supp. XVII:** 106

American Moderns: From Rebellion to Conformity (Geismar), **Supp. IX:** 15; **Supp. XI:** 223

"American Names" (Benét), **Supp. XI:** 47

American Nature Writers (Elder, ed.), **Supp. IX:** 25

American Nature Writers (Winter), **Supp. X:** 104

American Negro, The (W. H. Thomas), **Supp. II Part 1:** 168

American Notebooks, The (Hawthorne), **II:** 226

American Novel Since World War II, The (Klein, ed.), **Supp. XI:** 233

Americano, The (film), **Supp. XVI:** 185

"American Original, An: Learning from a Literary Master" (Wilkinson), **Supp. VIII:** 164, 165, 168

American Ornithology (Wilson), **Supp. XVI:** 4, 6

American Pastoral (P. Roth), **Retro. Supp. II:** 279, 289, **292–293; Supp. XI:** 68

American Pictures: A Personal Journey Through the American Underclass (Holdt), **Supp. XXVI:** 26

American Places (Porter, Stegner and Stegner), **Supp. IV Part 2:** 599

"American Poet" (Shapiro), **Supp. II Part 2:** 701

"American Poetry" (Simpson), **Supp. IX:** 272

American Poetry, 1922: A Miscellany (Untermeyer, ed.), **Supp. XV:** 306

"American Poetry and American Life" (Pinsky), **Supp. VI:** 239–240

American Poetry from the Beginning to Whitman (Untermeyer, ed.), **Supp. XV:** 310

American Poetry since 1900 (Untermeyer, ed.), **Supp. XV:** 306

American Poetry since 1945: A Critical Survey (Stepanchev), **Supp. XI:** 312

American Poetry since 1960 (Mesic), **Supp. IV Part 1:** 175

American Poets since World War II Dictionary of Literary Biography (Gwynn, ed.), **Supp. XV:** 343

American Primer, An (Boorstin), **I:** 253

American Primer, An (Whitman), **IV:** 348

"American Primitive" (W. J. Smith), **Supp. XIII:** 333

American Primitive: Poems (Oliver), **Supp. VII:** 234–237, 238

American Procession, An: The Major American Writers from 1830–1930—the Crucial Century (Kazin), **Supp. VIII: 105–106,** 108

"American Prose Writers" articles (Briggs), **Supp. XVIII:** 11

American Radio Company, The (radio show, Keillor), **Supp. XVI:** 176–177

"American Realist Playwrights, The" (McCarthy), **II:** 562

American Register, or General Repository of History, Politics, and Science, The (Brown, ed.), **Supp. I Part 1:** 146

American Renaissance (Matthiessen), **I:** 259–260; **III:** 310; **Supp. XIII:** 93

"American Rendezvous, An" (Beauvoir), **Supp. IX:** 4

American Scene, The (James), **II:** 336; **III:** 460; **Retro. Supp. I:** 232, 235

American Scenes (Kozlenko, ed.), **IV:** 378

"American Scholar, The" (Emerson), **I:** 239; **II:** 8, 12–13; **Retro. Supp. I:** 62, 74–75, 149, 298; **Retro. Supp. II:** 155; **Supp. I Part 2:** 420; **Supp. IX:** 227, 271; **Supp. XIV:** 104

"American Scholar, The" (Pickering), **Supp. XXI:** 196

Americans in England; or, Lessons for Daughters (Rowson), **Supp. XV:** 240

"American Soldier, The" (Freneau), **Supp. II Part 1:** 269

American Songbag, The (Sandburg), **III:** 583

"American Student in Paris, An" (Farrell), **II:** 45

"American Sublime, The" (Stevens), **IV:** 74

American Taliban (Abraham), **Supp. XXIV:** 2, **12–14**

"American Tar, The; or, The Press Gang Defeated" (Rowson and Taylor), **Supp. XV:** 238

"American Temperament, The" (Locke), **Supp. XIV:** 211

American Tragedy, An (Dreiser), **I:** 497, 498, 499, 501, 502, 503, 511–515, 517, 518, 519; **III:** 251; **IV:** 35, 484; **Retro. Supp. II:** 93, 95, **104–108; Supp. XVII:** 155

"American Triptych" (Kenyon), **Supp. VII:** 165

"American Use for German Ideals" (Bourne), **I:** 228

American Village, The (Freneau), **Supp. II Part 1:** 256, 257

"American Village, The" (Freneau), **Supp. II Part 1:** 256

American Wives and English Husbands (Atherton), **Supp. XXIV:** 18, 22

America's Coming-of-Age (Brooks), **I:** 228, 230, 240, 245, 258; **IV:** 427

America's Humor: From Poor Richard to Doonesbury (Blair and Hill), **Retro. Supp. II:** 286

"America's Indian Problem" (Zitkala-Ša), **Supp. XXV:** 282

"America's Part in World Peace" (Locke), **Supp. XIV:** 208

America's Rome (Vance), **Supp. IV Part 2:** 684

America: The Story of a Free People (Commager and Nevins), **I:** 253

America Was Promises (MacLeish), **III:** 16, 17

"Amerika" (Snyder), **Supp. VIII:** 301

Ames, Christopher, **Supp. XVIII:** 242–243

Ames, Fisher, **Supp. I Part 2:** 486

Ames, Lois, **Supp. I Part 2:** 541, 547

Ames, William, **IV:** 158

Ames Stewart, Beatrice, **Supp. IX:** 200

Amichai, Yehuda, **Supp. XI:** 267

Amick, Steve, **Supp. XXII:** 205, 216

Amidon, Stephen, **Supp. XI:** 333

Amiel, Henri F., **I:** 241, 243, 250

Amis, Kingsley, **IV:** 430; **Supp. IV Part 2:** 688; **Supp. VIII:** 167; **Supp. XIII:** 93; **Supp. XV:** 117

Amis, Martin, **Retro. Supp. I:** 278

"Amish, The"(Thompson), **Supp. XXIII:** 295–296

"Amity Hills" (Skloot), **Supp. XX: 204**

Ammons, A. R., **Supp. III Part 2:** 541; **Supp. IX:** 41, 42, 46; **Supp. VII: 23–38; Supp. XII:** 121; **Supp. XIX:** 83; **Supp. XV:** 115; **Supp. XVII:** 242; **Supp. XXVI:** 67

Ammons, Elizabeth, **Retro. Supp. I:** 364, 369; **Retro. Supp. II:** 140

Amnesia Moon (Lethem), **Supp. XVIII:** 136, **138–139**

"Among Children" (Levine), **Supp. V:** 192

Among Friends (M. F. Fisher), **Supp. XVII:** 89, 90–91, 92

Among My Books (Lowell), **Supp. I Part 2:** 407

"Among School Children" (Yeats), **III:** 249; **Supp. IX:** 52; **Supp. XIV:** 8

"Among the Hills" (Whittier), **Supp. I Part 2:** 703

Among the Isles of Shoals (Thaxter), **Supp. XIII:** 152

"Among Those Present" (Benét), **Supp. XI:** 53

"Amoral Moralist" (White), **Supp. I Part 2:** 648

Amory, Cleveland, **Supp. I Part 1:** 316

Amory, Fred, **Supp. III Part 1:** 2

Amos (biblical book), **II:** 166

Amos and Andy (television program), **Supp. XX: 103**

Amplitude (Gallagher), **Supp. XXIV:** 166, 170

Amran, David, **Supp. XIV:** 150

"Am Strand von Tanger" (Salter), **Supp. IX:** 257

"AMTRAK" (Baraka), **Supp. II Part 1:** 60

"Amulet, The" (Antin), **Supp. XX: 10**

"Amulets" (Hull), **Supp. XXI:** 139

Amy and Isabelle (film), **Supp. XXIII:** 275–276

Amy and Isabelle (Strout), **Supp. X:** 86; **Supp. XXIII:** 273, 274–275, **276–278,** 285

"Amy Lowell of Brookline, Mass." (Scott), **II:** 512

Amy Lowell: Portrait of the Poet in Her Time (Gregory), **II:** 512

"Amy Wentworth" (Whittier), **Supp. I Part 2:** 694, 696

Anabase (Perse), **III:** 12

"Anabasis (I)" (Merwin), **Supp. III Part 1:** 342, 346

"Anabasis (II)" (Merwin), **Supp. III Part 1:** 342, 346

Anagrams: A Novel (Moore), **Supp. X:** 163, 164, 167, **169–171,** 172

Analects (Confucius), **Supp. IV Part 1:** 14

Analects, The (Pound, trans.), **III:** 472

Analogy (J. Butler), **II:** 8

"Analysis of a Theme" (Stevens), **IV:** 81

Anarchiad, The, A Poem on the Restoration of Chaos and Substantial Night, in Twenty Four Books (Barlow), **Supp. II Part 1:** 70

Anarchist Woman, An (Hapgood), **Supp. XVII:** 102–103; **Supp. XXI:** 5

Anatomy Lesson, and Other Stories, The (Connell), **Supp. XIV:** 84, 87, 89

"Anatomy Lesson, The" (Connell), **Supp. XIV:** 84, 86, 87

Anatomy Lesson, The (P. Roth), **Retro. Supp. II:** 286, 290; **Supp. III Part 2:** 422–423, 425

"Anatomy Lesson of Dr. Nicholaas Tulp, Amsterdam, 1632, The" (Bierds), **Supp. XVII:** 27–28

Anatomy of Criticism (Frye), **Supp. XIII:** 19; **Supp. XIV:** 15

Anatomy of Melancholy (Burton), **III:** 78; **Supp. XVII:** 229

Anatomy of Nonsense, The (Winters), **Supp. II Part 2:** 811, 812

Anaya, Rudolfo A., **Supp. IV Part 2:** 502; **Supp. XIII:** 213, 220; **Supp. XIX:** 97

"Ancestor" (A. Finch), **Supp. XVII:** 72

Ancestors (Atherton), **Supp. XXIV:** 23, 25

Ancestors (Maxwell), **Supp. VIII:** 152, 168

"Ancestors, The" (Tate), **IV:** 128

Ancestral Voice: Conversations with N. Scott Momaday (Woodard), **Supp. IV Part 2:** 484, 485, 486, 489, 493

"Anchorage" (Harjo), **Supp. XII:** 220–221

Ancient Child, The: A Novel (Momaday), **Supp. IV Part 2:** 488, 489–491, 492, 493

"Ancient Dog Grave, Unearthed During Construction of the Athens Metro, An" (Stallings), **Supp. XXV:** 232

"Ancient Egypt/Fannie Goldbarth" (Goldbarth), **Supp. XII:** 191–192

Ancient Evenings (Mailer), **Retro. Supp. II:** 206, 210, 213

Ancient Law, The (Glasgow), **II:** 179–180, 192

Ancient Musics (Goldbarth), **Supp. XII:** 191–192

"Ancient Semitic Rituals for the Dead" (Goldbarth), **Supp. XII:** 191–192

Ancient Track, The (Lovecraft), **Supp. XXV:** 120

"Ancient World, The" (Doty), **Supp. XI:** 122

& (And) (Cummings), **I:** 429, 431, 432, 437, 445, 446, 448

Andersen, Hans Christian, **I:** 441; **Supp. I Part 2:** 622

Andersen, Hendrik Christian, **Supp. XX:** **232**

Anderson, Charles R., **Supp. I Part 1:** 356, 360, 368, 371, 372

Anderson, Frances, **I:** 231

Anderson, Guy, **Supp. X:** 264, 265

Anderson, Henry J., **Supp. I Part 1:** 156

Anderson, Irwin M., **I:** 98–99

Anderson, Mrs. Irwin M., **I:** 98–99

Anderson, Jon, **Supp. V:** 338

Anderson, Judith, **III:** 399

Anderson, Karl, **I:** 99, 103

Anderson, Lorraine, **Supp. XVIII:** 189

Anderson, Margaret, **I:** 103; **III:** 471; **Supp. XXV:** 18

Anderson, Margaret Bartlett, **III:** 171

Anderson, Marian, **Supp. XXII:** 283

Anderson, Mary Jane. *See* Lanier, Mrs. Robert Sampson (Mary Jane Anderson)

Anderson, Maxwell, **III:** 159

Anderson, Quentin, **Retro. Supp. I:** 392

Anderson, Robert, **Supp. I Part 1:** 277; **Supp. V:** 108

Anderson, Sally, **Supp. XIII:** 95

Anderson, Sherwood, **I:** **97–120,** 211, 374, 375, 384, 405, 423, 445, 480, 487, 495, 506, 518; **II:** 27, 38, 44, 55, 56, 68, 250–251, 263, 271, 289, 451, 456–457; **III:** 220, 224, 382–383, 453, 483, 545, 576, 579; **IV:** 27, 40, 46, 190, 207, 433, 451, 482; **Retro. Supp. I:** 79, 80, 177; **Supp. I Part 2:** 378, 430, 459, 472, 613; **Supp. IV Part 2:** 502; **Supp. IX:** 14, 309; **Supp. V:** 12, 250; **Supp. VIII:** 39, 152; **Supp. XI:** 159, 164; **Supp. XII:** 343; **Supp. XV:** 298; **Supp. XVI:** 17, 20; **Supp. XVII:** 105; **Supp. XX: 69, 75; Supp. XXIII:** 68, 162, 164; **Supp. XXIV:** 136; **Supp. XXV:** 18

Anderson, Mrs. Sherwood (Tennessee Mitchell), **I:** 100; **Supp. I Part 2:** 459, 460

Anderson, T. J., **Supp. XIII:** 132

Anderson, Wendy, **Supp. XXI:** 255

Andersson, A., **III:** 252

"And Hickman Arrives" (Ellison), **Retro. Supp. II:** 118, 126; **Supp. II Part 1:** 248

And in the Hanging Gardens (Aiken), **I:** 63

"And It Came to Pass" (Wright), **Supp. XV:** 348

And I Worked at the Writer's Trade (Cowley), **Supp. II Part 1:** 137, 139, 141, 143, 147, 148

"...And Ladies of the Club" (J. W. Miller), **Supp. XX: 161**

And Live Apart (Peacock), **Supp. XIX: 196–197**

Andorra (Cameron), **Supp. XII:** 79, 81, **88–91**

"—and Other Poets" (column; Untermeyer), **Supp. XV:** 294

"—and Other Poets" (Untermeyer), *Supp. XV:* 297

Andracki, Thaddeus, **Supp. XXVI:** 108

Andral, Gabriel, **Supp. I Part 1:** 302

Andre, Michael, **Supp. XII:** 117–118, 129, 132, 133–134

"Andrea Is Changing Her Name" (Brockmeier), **Supp. XXII:** 61

Andre's Mother (McNally), **Supp. XIII:** 206

Andress, Ursula, **Supp. XI:** 307

"Andrew Jackson" (Masters), **Supp. I Part 2:** 472

Andrews, Bruce, **Supp. IV Part 2:** 426

Andrews, Peter, **Supp. XX: 87**

Andrews, Raymond, **Supp. XXVI: 1–16**

Andrews, Roy Chapman, **Supp. X:** 172

Andrews, Tom, **Supp. XI:** 317

Andrews, Wayne, **IV:** 310

Andrews, William L., **Supp. IV Part 1:** 13; **Supp. XIX:** 72; **Supp. XX: 105**

Andrews, William P., **Supp. XXV:** 250

Andreyev, Leonid Nikolaevich, **I:** 53; **II:** 425

Andria (Terence), **IV:** 363

"Androgynous Kiss" (Gallagher), **Supp. XXIV:** 170

"Andromache" (Dubus), **Supp. VII:** 84

"And Summer Will Not Come Again" (Plath), **Retro. Supp. II:** 242

"And That Night Clifford Died" (Levine), **Supp. V:** 195

And the Band Played On (Shilts), **Supp. X:** 145

"And the Moon Be Still as Bright" (Bradbury), **Supp. IV Part 1:** 106

"And the Sea Shall Give up Its Dead" (Wilder), **IV:** 358

And Things That Go Bump in the Night (McNally), **Supp. XIII: 196–197,** 205, 208

And to Think That I Saw It on Mulberry Street (Geisel), **Supp. XVI:** 100, 101, 104

"And Ut Pictura Poesis Is Her Name" (Ashbery), **Supp. III Part 1:** 19

And We Are Millions (Ryan), **Supp. XVIII:** 225

"And Winter" (Boyle), **Supp. XXIV:** 63

"Anecdote and Storyteller" (Howe), **Supp. VI:** 127

"Anecdote of the Jar" (Stevens), **IV:** 83–84

"Anemone" (Rukeyser), **Supp. VI:** 281, 285

"Angel, The" (Buck), **Supp. II Part 1:** 127

"Angel and Unicorn and Butterfly" (Everwine), **Supp. XV:** 76

Angela's Ashes (McCourt), **Supp. XII: 271–279,** 283, 285; **Supp. XXII:** 94

"Angel at the Grave, The" (Wharton), **IV:** 310; **Retro. Supp. I:** 365

"Angel Butcher" (Levine), **Supp. V:** 181

Angel City (Shepard), **Supp. III Part 2:** 432, 445

Angelica (Holding), **Supp. XXII: 120–121**

"Angel Is My Watermark!, The" (H. Miller), **III:** 180

Angell, Carol, **Supp. I Part 2:** 655

Angell, Katharine Sergeant. *See* White, Katharine

Angell, Roger, **Supp. I Part 2:** 655; **Supp. V:** 22; **Supp. VIII:** 139

Angel Landing (Hoffman), **Supp. X:** 82–83

"Angel Levine" (Malamud), **Supp. I Part 2:** 431, 432, 433–434, 437

Angel of Bethesda, The (Mather), **Supp. II Part 2:** 464

"Angel of the Bridge, The" (Cheever), **Supp. I Part 1:** 186–187

"Angel of the Odd, The" (Poe), **III:** 425

Angelo Herndon Jones (Hughes), **Retro. Supp. I:** 203

"Angel on the Porch, An" (Wolfe), **IV:** 451

Angelou, Maya, **Supp. IV Part 1: 1–19; Supp. XI:** 20, 245; **Supp. XIII:** 185; **Supp. XVI:** 259; **Supp. XXI:** 172

"Angel Poem, The" (Stern), **Supp. IX:** 292

Angels and Earthly Creatures (Wylie), **Supp. I Part 2:** 709, 713, 724–730

Angels Flight (Connelly), **Supp. XXI:** 72, **72–73,** 75, 80

"Angels for Djuna Barnes" (Boyle), **Supp. XXIV:** 63

Angels in America: A Gay Fantasia on National Themes (Kushner), **Supp. IX:** 131, 134, **141–146; Supp. XXIV:** 272

"Angels of the Love Affair" (Sexton), **Supp. II Part 2:** 692

"Angel's Trumpet, The"(P. Benedict), **Supp. XXIII:** 48

"Angel Surrounded by Paysans" (Stevens), **IV:** 93

Angel That Troubled the Waters, The (Wilder), **IV:** 356, 357–358

"Anger" (Creeley), **Supp. IV Part 1:** 150–152

Anger (Sarton), **Supp. VIII: 256**

"Anger against Children" (R. Bly), **Supp. IV Part 1:** 73

Angle of Ascent (Hayden), **Supp. II Part 1:** 363, 367, 370

"Angle of Geese" (Momaday), **Supp. IV Part 2:** 485

Angle of Geese and Other Poems (Momaday), **Supp. IV Part 2:** 487, 491

Angle of Repose (Stegner), **Supp. IV Part 2:** 599, 605, 606, 610–611

"*Angle of Repose* and the Writings of Mary Hallock Foote: A Source Study" (Williams-Walsh), **Supp. IV Part 2:** 611

"Anglo-Mongrels and the Rose" (Loy), **Supp. XXII:** 156, 159, 166–167

Anglo-Saxon Century, The (Dos Passos), **I:** 474–475, 483

Angoff, Charles, **III:** 107

"Angola Question Mark" (Hughes), **Supp. I Part 1:** 344

Angry Hills, The (Uris), **Supp. XX: 246, 250**

Angry Wife, The (Sedges), **Supp. II Part 1:** 125

"Angry Women Are Building: Issues and Struggles Facing American Indian Women Today" (Gunn Allen), **Supp. IV Part 1:** 324

"Animal, Vegetable, and Mineral" (Bogan), **Supp. III Part 1:** 66

"Animal Acts" (Simic), **Supp. VIII:** 278

Animal and Vegetable Physiology Considered with Reference to Natural Theology (Roget), **Supp. I Part 1:** 312

"Animal Bodies: Corporeality, Class, and Subject Formation in *The Wide, Wide World*" (Mason), **Supp. XVIII:** 263

Animal Dreams (Kingsolver), **Supp. VII:** 199, 204–207

Animal Magnetism (Prose), **Supp. XVI:** 251, 260

"Animals, The" (Merwin), **Supp. III Part 1:** 348

"Animals Are Passing from Our Lives" (Levine), **Supp. V:** 181, 182

Animals in That Country, The (Atwood), **Supp. XIII:** 20, 33

Animals of the Soul: Sacred Animals of the Oglala Sioux (Brown), **Supp. IV Part 2:** 487

"Animals You Eat, The" (X. J. Kennedy), **Supp. XV:** 169

"Animula" (Eliot), **Retro. Supp. I:** 64

Anita Loos Rediscovered (M. A. Loos), **Supp. XVI:** 196

Ankor Wat (Ginsberg), **Supp. II Part 1:** 323

Ann, Leslee, **Supp. XXIV:** 264

"Annabelle" (Komunyakaa), **Supp. XIII:** 117

"Annabel Lee" (Poe), **Retro. Supp. I:** 273; **Retro. Supp. II:** 266

Anna Christie (O'Neill), **III:** 386, 389, 390; **Supp. XXII:** 24

"Anna Grasa" (Weigl), **Supp. XIX:** 278

"Anna in Mourning" (Weigl), **Supp. XIX:** 288

Anna Karenina (Tolstoy), **I:** 10; **II:** 290; **Retro. Supp. I:** 225; **Supp. V:** 323

"*Anna Karenina*" (Trilling), **Supp. III Part 2:** 508

Annan, Noel, **Supp. XX: 240**

"Anna's Grace" (Weigl), **Supp. XIX:** 282–283

"Anna Who Was Mad" (Sexton), **Supp. II Part 2:** 692

"Ann Burlak" (Rukeyser), **Supp. VI:** 280

"Anne" (Oliver), **Supp. VII:** 232

"Anne" (R. H. Davis), **Supp. XVI:** 91, 92

"Anne at the Symphony" (Shields), **Supp. VII:** 310

"Anne Bradstreet's Poetic Voices" (Requa), **Supp. I Part 1:** 107

Anne of Geierstein: or, The Maiden of the Mist (Scott), **Supp. XX: 234**

Anne Sexton: The Artist and Her Critics (McClatchy), **Supp. XII:** 253

"Ann from the Street" (Dixon), **Supp. XII:** 146–147

"Ann Garner" (Agee), **I:** 27

"Anniad, The" (Brooks), **Supp. III Part 1:** 77, 78

Annie (musical), **Supp. IV Part 2:** 577

Annie Allen (Brooks), **Supp. III Part 1:** 76–79

Annie Dillard Reader, The (Dillard), **Supp. VI:** 23

Annie Hall (film; Allen), **Supp. IV Part 1:** 205; **Supp. XV:** 1, 2, 4, 5, **6–7,** 14

Annie John (Kincaid), **Supp. VII:** 184–186, 193

Annie Kilburn, a Novel (Howells), **II:** 275, 286, 287

"Annihilation" (X. J. Kennedy), **Supp. XV:** 168

"Annihilation of Matter, The" (Bronk), **Supp. XXI:** 30

Anniversary (Shields), **Supp. VII:** 320, 322, 323, 324

"Anniversary Poem" (Oppen), **Supp. XXVI:** 237

"Annunciation" (Nelson), **Supp. XVIII:** 174

"Annunciation, The" (Le Sueur), **Supp. V:** 130

Ann Vickers (Lewis), **II:** 453

"A No-Account Creole, A" (Chopin), **Retro. Supp. II:** 64

"Anodyne" (Komunyakaa), **Supp. XIII:** 130

Another America/Otra America (Kingsolver), **Supp. VII:** 207–209

"Another Animal" (Swenson), **Supp. IV Part 2:** 639

Another Animal: Poems (Swenson), **Supp. IV Part 2:** 639–641, 649

Another Antigone (Gurney), **Supp. V:** 97, 98, 100, 101, 102, 105

"Another August" (Merrill), **Supp. III Part 1:** 326

"Another Beer" (Matthews), **Supp. IX:** 158

Another Country (Baldwin), **Retro. Supp. II:** 9–11, 14; **Supp. I Part 1:** 51, 52, 56–58, 63, 67, 337; **Supp. II Part 1:** 40; **Supp. VIII:** 349

"Another Language" (Jong), **Supp. V:** 131

Another Mother Tongue: Gay Words, Gay Worlds (Grahn), **Supp. IV Part 1:** 330

"Another Night in the Ruins" (Kinnell), **Supp. III Part 1:** 239, 251

"Another Night with Snow" (W. V. Davis), **Supp. XXI:** 90, 91

"Another Old Woman" (W. C. Williams), **Retro. Supp. I:** 423

Another Part of the Forest (Hellman), **Supp. I Part 1:** 282–283, 297

Another Republic: 17 European and South American Writers (Strand, trans.), **Supp. IV Part 2:** 630

Another Roadside Attraction (Robbins), **Supp. X:** 259, 261, 262, 263, 264, 265–266, **267–269,** 274, 275, 277, 284

Another Side of Bob Dylan (album, Dylan), **Supp. XVIII:** 25

"Another Spring Uncovered" (Swenson), **Supp. IV Part 2:** 644

Another Thin Man (film), **Supp. IV Part 1:** 355

Another Time (Auden), **Supp. II Part 1:** 15

Another Turn of the Crank (Berry), **Supp. X:** 25, 35

"Another upon the Same" (Taylor), **IV:** 161

"Another Voice" (Wilbur), **Supp. III Part 2:** 557

"Another Wife" (Anderson), **I:** 114

"Another Winter Night" (Budbill), **Supp. XIX:** 10

Another Woman (film; Allen), **Supp. XV:** 11

Another You (Beattie), **Supp. V:** 29, 31, 33–34

Anouilh, Jean, **Supp. I Part 1:** 286–288, 297

Ansa, Tina McElroy, **Supp. XVIII:** 195

Ansay, A. Manette, **Supp. XXV:** 142

"Anselm" (Berrigan), **Supp. XXIV:** 43

Ansen, Alan, **Supp. XXIII:** 112, 122, 123

Ansky, S., **IV:** 6

Ansky, Shloime, **Supp. IX:** 131, 138

"Answer, The" (Jeffers), **Supp. III Part 2:** 423

Answered Prayers: The Unfinished Novel (Capote), **Supp. III Part 1:** 113, 125, 131–132; **Supp. XVI:** 245

"Answering the Deer: Genocide and Continuance in the Poetry of American Indian Women" (Gunn Allen), **Supp. IV Part 1:** 322, 325

"Answer of Minerva, The: Pacifism and Resistance in Simone Weil" (Merton), **Supp. VIII:** 204

Antaeus (Wolfe), **IV:** 461

"Ante-Bellum Sermon, An" (Dunbar), **Supp. II Part 1:** 203–204

Antheil, George, **III:** 471, 472; **IV:** 404

Anthem (Rand), **Supp. IV Part 2:** 523

Anthology of Holocaust Literature (Glatstein, Knox, and Margoshes, eds.), **Supp. X:** 70

Anthology of Modern American Poetry (Nelson, ed.), **Supp. XXII:** 271

Anthology of Twentieth-Century Brazilian Poetry, An (Bishop and Brasil, eds.), **Retro. Supp. II:** 50; **Supp. I Part 1:** 94

Anthon, Kate, **I:** 452

Anthony, Adelina, **Supp. XXIII:** 197

Anthony, Andrew, **Supp. XVI:** 235, 245, 246

Anthony, Saint, **III:** 395

Anthony, Susan B., **Supp. XI:** 200

"Anthropologist as Hero, The" (Sontag), **Supp. III Part 2:** 451

"Anthropology of Water, The" (Carson), **Supp. XII:** 102–103

Anthropos: The Future of Art (Cummings), **I:** 430

Antichrist (Nietzsche), **III:** 176

"Anti-Father" (Dove), **Supp. IV Part 1:** 246

"Anti-Feminist Woman, The" (Rich), **Supp. I Part 2:** 550

Antigone (Sophocles), **Supp. I Part 1:** 284; **Supp. X:** 249

"Anti-Memoir"(Dybek), **Supp. XXIII:** 78

Antin, David, **Supp. VIII:** 292; **Supp. XII:** 2, 8

Antin, Mary, **Supp. IX:** 227; **Supp. XVI:** 148, 149; **Supp. XX:** 1–16

Anti-Oedipus: Capitalism and Schizophrenia (Deleuze and Guattari), **Supp. XII:** 4

Antiphon, The (Barnes), **Supp. III Part 1:** 43–44

"Antiquities" (Mather), **Supp. II Part 2:** 452

"Antiquity of Freedom, The" (Bryant), **Supp. I Part 1:** 168

"Antislavery Tocsin, An" (Douglass), **Supp. III Part 1:** 171

Antoine, Andre, **III:** 387

Antonioni, Michelangelo, **Supp. IV Part 1:** 46, 47, 48

Antony and Cleopatra (Shakespeare), **I:** 285

"Antony on Behalf of the Play" (Burke), **I:** 284

"An trentiesme de mon Eage, L" (MacLeish), **III:** 9

Antrim, Donald, **Supp. XX:** 90

"Ants" (R. Bly), **Supp. IV Part 1:** 71

Anxiety of Influence, The (Bloom), **Supp. XIII:** 46

"Any City" (Untermeyer), **Supp. XV:** 296

"Any Object" (Swenson), **Supp. IV Part 2:** 640

Anyplace but Here (Bontemps and Conroy), **Supp. XXII:** 11

"Any Porch" (Parker), **Supp. IX:** 194

Anything Else (film; Allen), **Supp. XV:** 2, 11

"Anywhere Out of This World" (Baudelaire), **II:** 552

Any Woman Can't (Wasserstein), **Supp. XV:** 322

Any Woman's Blues (Jong), **Supp. V:** 115, 123, 126

Anzaldúa, Gloria, **Supp. IV Part 1:** 330; **Supp. XIII:** 223; **Supp. XXIII:** 193, 194, 205

"Apache Tears" (Cliff), **Supp. XXII:** 76

"Aphorisms on Futurism" (Loy), **Supp. XXII:** 159

"Aphorisms on Society" (Stevens), **Retro. Supp. I:** 303

"Apiary IX" (C. Frost), **Supp. XV:** 106

"Apisculptures" (Bierds), **Supp. XVII:** 29

"Apocalypse: What Disaster Reveals" (Díaz), **Supp. XXIV:** 94–95

Apollinaire, Guillaume, **I:** 432; **II:** 529; **III:** 196; **IV:** 80; **Retro. Supp. II:** 326; **Supp. XV:** 182; **Supp. XXIII:** 208

"Apollo Takes Charge of His Muses" (Stallings), **Supp. XXV:** 229

Apologies to the Iroquois (Wilson), **IV:** 429

"Apology" (C. Frost), **Supp. XV:** 103

"Apology, An" (Malamud), **Supp. I Part 2:** 435, 437

"Apology for Bad Dreams" (Jeffers), **Supp. II Part 2:** 427, 438; **Supp. XVII:** 112

"Apology for Crudity, An" (Anderson), **I:** 109

Apology for Poetry (Sidney), **Supp. II Part 1:** 105

Apostle, The (Asch), **Supp. XXIII:** 2, 4, 9, **13–14**

"Apostle of the Tules, An" (Harte), **Supp. II Part 1:** 356

"Apostrophe to a Dead Friend" (Kumin), **Supp. IV Part 2:** 442, 451, 452

"Apostrophe to a Pram Rider" (White), **Supp. I Part 2:** 678

"Apostrophe to Man (on reflecting that the world is ready to go to war again)" (Millay), **III:** 127

"Apostrophe to Vincentine, The" (Stevens), **IV:** 90

"Apotheosis" (Kingsolver), **Supp. VII:** 208

"Apotheosis of Martin Luther King, The" (Hardwick), **Supp. III Part 1:** 203–204

Appalachee Red (Andrews), **Supp. XXVI:** 5–6, 7, 14

Appalachia (Wright), **Supp. V:** 333, 345

Appalachia Inside Out (Miller, Higgs, and Manning, eds.), **Supp. XX:** 166

"Appalachian Book of the Dead III" (Wright), **Supp. V:** 345

"Appalachian Education: A Critique and Suggestions for Reform" (J. W. Miller), **Supp. XX:** 165

"Appalachian Literature: At Home in This World" (J. W. Miller), **Supp. XX:** 165

"Appalachian Values/American Values" (J. W. Miller), **Supp. XX:** 165

Appaloosa (Parker), **Supp. XIX:** 187

"Appeal to H. G. Wells" (Sturgis), **Supp. XX: 233, 240**

"Appeal to Progressives, An" (Wilson), **IV:** 429

Appeal to Reason (Paine), **I:** 490

Appeal to the World, An (Du Bois), **Supp. II Part 1:** 184

Appearance and Reality (Bradley), **I:** 572

"Appendix to 'The Anniad' " (Brooks), **Supp. III Part 1:** 77

"Applause, Applause"(Thompson), **Supp. XXIII:** 289, 291, 301

Apple, Max, **Supp. VIII:** 14; **Supp. XVII: 1–11,** 49–50

Apple, Sam, **Supp. XVII:** 8

"Apple, The" (Kinnell), **Supp. III Part 1:** 250

Applebaum, Anne, **Supp. XVI:** 153

Applebome, Peter, **Supp. XXI:** 38

Applegarth, Mabel, **II:** 465, 478

"Apple-Maggot Fly, The" (Major), **Supp. XXII:** 182

"Apple of Discord, The" (Humphrey), **Supp. IX:** 109

"Apple Peeler" (Francis), **Supp. IX:** 82

"Apple Rind" (C. Frost), **Supp. XV:** 102

"Apples" (Brockmeier), **Supp. XXII:** 51, 53

"Apples, The" (Di Piero), **Supp. XIX:** 46

Appleseed, Johnny (pseudonym). *See* Chapman, John (Johnny Appleseed)

Apple That Astonished Paris, The (Collins), **Supp. XXI:** 53, 57

Appleton, Nathan, **II:** 488

Appleton, Thomas Gold, **Supp. I Part 1:** 306; **Supp. I Part 2:** 415

"Apple Tree, The" (McCarriston), **Supp. XIV:** 263, 268

"Applicant, The" (Plath), **Retro. Supp. II:** 252; **Supp. I Part 2:** 535, 544, 545

"Application, The" (Neugeboren), **Supp. XVI:** 219, 220, 225

"Applications of the Doctrine" (Hass), **Supp. VI: 100–101**

Appointment, The (film), **Supp. IX:** 253

Appointment in Samarra (O'Hara), **III:** 361, 363–364, 365–367, 371, 374, 375, 383

Appreciation of Sarah Orne Jewett (Cary), **Retro. Supp. II:** 132

"Apprentice, The"(Dybek), **Supp. XXIII:** 71

"Approaches, The" (Merwin), **Supp. III Part 1:** 350

"Approaching Artaud" (Sontag), **Supp. III Part 2:** 470–471

"Approaching Prayer" (Dickey), **Supp. IV Part 1:** 175

"Approaching the Mohawk Village: Jogues' Journal"(Kenny), **Supp. XXIII:** 152

Approach to Literature, An: A Collection of Prose and Verse with Analyses and Discussions (Brooks, Warren, and Purser), **Su pp. XIV:**4

"Approach to Thebes, The" (Kunitz), **Supp. III Part 1:** 265–267

Approach to Vedanta, An (Isherwood), **Supp. XIV:** 157, 163, 164

"Appropriation of Cultures, The" (Everett), **Supp. XVIII:** 66

Approximately Paradise (Skloot), **Supp. XX: 196, 202, 203–204**

"Après-midi d'un faune, L' " (Mallarmé), **III:** 8

"April" (Bierds), **Supp. XVII:** 29

"April" (W. C. Williams), **Retro. Supp. I:** 422

"April" (Winters), **Supp. II Part 2:** 788

April, Steve. *See* Lacy, Ed

April Galleons (Ashbery), **Supp. III Part 1:** 26

"April Galleons" (Ashbery), **Supp. III Part 1:** 26

April Hopes (Howells), **II:** 285, 289

"April Lovers" (Ransom), **III:** 489–490

"April Saturday 1960" (Huddle), **Supp. XXVI:** 150

"April Showers" (Wharton), **Retro. Supp. I:** 361

"April Today Main Street" (Olson), **Supp. II Part 2:** 581

April Twilights (Cather), **I:** 313; **Retro. Supp. I:** 5

"Apt Pupil" (King), **Supp. V:** 152

Arabian Nights, **I:** 204; **II:** 8; **Supp. I Part 2:** 584, 599; **Supp. IV Part 1:** 1

"Arabic Coffee" (Nye), **Supp. XIII:** 276

"Araby" (Joyce), **I:** 174; **Supp. VIII:** 15

Aragon, Louis, **I:** 429; **III:** 471; **Retro. Supp. II:** 85, 321

Arana-Ward, Marie, **Supp. VIII:** 84

Ararat (Glück), **Supp. V:** 79, 86–87

Aratani, Mariko, **Supp. XXIII:** 136

"Arbiter, The" (Toole), **Supp. XXVI:** 243

Arbre du voyageur, L' (W. J. Smith; Haussmann, trans.), *Supp. XIII:* 347

Arbus, Diane, **Supp. XII:** 188

Arbuthnott, John (pseudonym). *See* Henry, O.

"Arc, The" (Bidart), **Supp. XV:** 25–26, 27

Archaeologist of Morning (Olson), **Supp. II Part 2:** 557

Archaeology of the Circle: New and Selected Poems (Weigl), **Supp. XIX:** 282

"Archaic Maker, The" (Merwin), **Supp. III Part 1:** 357

Archaic Smile (Stallings), **Supp. XXV:** 221, 222, 223, 224, 228–231, 233

"Archaic Torso of Apollo" (Rilke), **Supp. XV:** 148

"Archaischer Torso Apollos" (Rilke), **Supp. XVII:** 244

"Archbishop, The" (Gioia), **Supp. XV:** 126, 127

Archer (television show), **Supp. IV Part 2:** 474

Archer, William, **IV:** 131; **Retro. Supp. I:** 228

Archer at Large (Macdonald), **Supp. IV Part 2:** 473

Archer in Hollywood (Macdonald), **Supp. IV Part 2:** 474

"Archetype and Signature: The Relationship of Poet and Poem" (Fiedler), **Supp. XIII:** 101

"Archibald Higbie" (Masters), **Supp. I Part 2:** 461

"Architect, The" (Bourne), **I:** 223

Architect, The (Briggs and Ranlett), **Supp. XVIII:** 3

Archuleta, Elizabeth, **Supp. XXVI:** 106

Arctic Dreams (Lopez), **Supp. V:** 211

Arctic Refuge: A Circle of Testimony (Haines), **Supp. XII:** 205

"Arcturus" (Connell), **Supp. XIV:** 88

À rebours (Huysmans), **Supp. XX: 239**

Arendt, Hannah, **II:** 544; **Retro. Supp. I:** 87; **Retro. Supp. II:** 28, 117; **Supp. I Part 2:** 570; **Supp. IV Part 1:** 386; **Supp. VIII:** 98, 99, 100, 243; **Supp. XII:** 166–167

Arensberg, Louise, **Supp. XXII:** 162

Arensberg, Walter, **IV:** 408; **Retro. Supp. I:** 416; **Supp. XXII:** 162

Aren't You Happy for Me? (Bausch), **Supp. VII:** 42, 51, 54

Areopagitica (Milton), **Supp. I Part 2:** 422

"Are You a Doctor?" (Carver), **Supp. III Part 1:** 139–141

"Are You Mr. William Stafford?" (Stafford), **Supp. XI:** 317

Are You My Mother? A Comic Drama (Bechdel), **Supp. XXV:** 1, 2, 9–14

Argall: The True Story of Pocahontas and Captain John Smith (Vollmann), **Supp. XVII:** 225, 226, 231, 232, 233

"Argonauts of 49, California's Golden Age" (Harte), **Supp. II Part 1:** 353, 355

"Arguantando" (Díaz), **Supp. XXIV:** 88–89

"Arguments of Everlasting" (B. Kelly), **Supp. XVII:** 129

"Arguments with the Gestapo Continued: II" (Wright), **Supp. XV:** 344

"Arguments with the Gestapo Continued: Literary Resistance" (Wright), **Supp. XV:** 344

Ari (musical, Uris), **Supp. XX: 247**

Aria da Capo (Millay), **III:** 137–138

"Ariadne and the Rest" (Stallings), **Supp. XXV:** 223, 229

Ariadne's Thread: A Collection of Contemporary Women's Journals (Lifshin, ed.), **Supp. XVI:** 37–38

"Arias, 1971" (Hull), **Supp. XXI:** 135

Ariel (Plath), **Retro. Supp. II: 250–255; Supp. I Part 2:** 526, 539, 541; **Supp. V:** 79; **Supp. XXI:** 58; **Supp. XXII:** 93

"Ariel" (Plath), **Supp. I Part 2:** 542, 546

"Ariel Poems" (Eliot), **I:** 579

Ariosto, Ludovico, **Supp. XV:** 175

"Ariosto: Critical Notice of His Life and Genius" (Hunt), **Supp. XV:** 175

Arise, Arise (Zukofsky), **Supp. III Part 2:** 619, 629

Aristides. *See* Epstein, Joseph

"Aristocracy" (Emerson), **II:** 6

Aristocracy and Justice (More), **I:** 223

Aristocrat, The (Richter), **Supp. XVIII:** 220

Aristophanes, **I:** 436; **II:** 577; **Supp. I Part 2:** 406

Aristotle, **I:** 58, 265, 280, 527; **II:** 9, 12, 198, 536; **III:** 20, 115, 145, 157, 362, 422, 423; **IV:** 10, 18, 74–75, 89; **Supp. I Part 1:** 104, 296; **Supp. I Part 2:** 423; **Supp. IV Part 1:** 391; **Supp. IV Part 2:** 526, 530; **Supp. X:** 78; **Supp. XI:** 249; **Supp. XII:** 106; **Supp. XIV:** 242–243

Aristotle Contemplating the Bust of Homer (Rembrandt), **Supp. IV Part 1:** 390, 391

"Arkansas Traveller" (Wright), **Supp. V:** 334

Arlen, Harold, **Supp. XXII:** 6

"Arm, The" (X. J. Kennedy), **Supp. XV:** 169

"Armadillo, The" (Bishop), **Supp. I Part 1:** 93

Armadillo in the Grass (Hearon), **Supp. VIII: 58–59**

"Armageddon" (Ransom), **III:** 489, 492

Armageddon (Uris), **Supp. XX: 243, 247, 248, 252–253**

Armah, Aiy Kwei, **Supp. IV Part 1:** 373

Armenian Golgotha: A Memoir of the Armenian Genocide, 1915– 1918 (Grigoris Balakian; trans. Peter Balakian and Sevag), **Supp. XXIII: 28, 29–32**

Armies of the Night, The (Mailer), **III:** 39–40, 41, 42, 44, 45, 46; **Retro. Supp. II:** 205, 206–207, 208; **Supp. IV Part 1:** 207; **Supp. XIV:** 49, 162

"Arm in Arm" (Simpson), **Supp. IX:** 267–268

Arminius, Jacobus, **I:** 557

Armitage, Shelley, **Supp. IV Part 2:** 439

Arm of Flesh, The (Salter), **Supp. IX:** 251

"Armor" (Dickey), **Supp. IV Part 1:** 179

Armored Attack (film), **Supp. I Part 1:** 281

Arms, George W., **Supp. I Part 2:** 416–417

Armstrong, George, **Supp. I Part 2:** 386

Armstrong, Louis, **Retro. Supp. II:** 114

"'Arm the Paper Arm': Kenneth Koch's Postmodern Comedy" (Chinitz), **Supp. XV:** 180, 185

"Army" (Corso), **Supp. XII:** 117, 127

Army Brat (W. J. Smith), **Supp. XIII:** 331, 347

"Army Recruiting Methods" (Bodenheim), **Supp. XXV:** 19

Arna Bontemps Langston Hughes: Letters 1925–1967 (Nichols), **Retro. Supp. I:** 194

"Arna Bontemps Talks About the Renaissance" (Collins), **Supp. XXII:** 7

Arner, Robert D., **Retro. Supp. II:** 62

"Arnie" (Budbill), **Supp. XIX:** 6

Arnold, Edwin T., **Supp. VIII:** 189

Arnold, George W., **Supp. I Part 2:** 411

Arnold, Marilyn, **Supp. IV Part 1:** 220

Arnold, Matthew, **I:** 222, 228, 275; **II:** 20, 110, 338, 541; **III:** 604; **IV:** 349; **Retro. Supp. I:** 56, 325; **Supp. I Part 2:** 416, 417, 419, 529, 552, 602; **Supp. IX:** 298; **Supp. XIV:** 11, 335; **Supp. XIX:** 41; **Supp. XXI:** 90

Arnold, Thurman, **Supp. I Part 2:** 645

Aronson, Steven M. L., **Supp. V:** 4

Around about America (Caldwell), **I:** 290

"Arrangement in Black and White" (Parker), **Supp. IX:** 198

Arregoces, Christina, **Supp. XXVI:** 148, 158

"Arrival at Santos" (Bishop), **Retro. Supp. II:** 46; **Supp. IX:** 45–46

"Arrival of the Bee Box, The" (Plath), **Retro. Supp. II:** 255

Arrivistes, The: Poem 1940–1949 (Simpson), **Supp. IX:** 265, **267–268**

Arrogance (J. Scott), **Supp. XVII: 186–188,** 189, **191,** 192, **194**

"Arrow" (Dove), **Supp. IV Part 1:** 250

"Arrowhead Hunting" (Stallings), **Supp. XXV:** 232

Arrowsmith (Lewis), **I:** 362; **II:** 445–446, 449

"Arsenal at Springfield, The" (Longfellow), **Retro. Supp. II:** 168

"Arson at Midnight" (Nelson), **Supp. XVIII:** 186

"Arson Plus" (Hammett), **Supp. IV Part 1:** 343; **Supp. XXI:** 68

"Ars Poetica" (Dove), **Supp. IV Part 1:** 250

"Ars Poetica" (Dunn), **Supp. XI:** 154

"Ars Poetica" (MacLeish), **III:** 9–10

"Ars Poetica" (X. J. Kennedy), **Supp. XV:** 154

"Ars Poetica: A Found Poem" (Kumin), **Supp. IV Part 2:** 455

"Ars Poetica; or, Who Lives in the Ivory Tower" (McGrath), **Supp. X:** 117

"Ars Poetica: Some Recent Criticism" (Wright), **Supp. III Part 2:** 603

"Art" (Emerson), **II:** 13

Art (Reza), **Supp. XXI:** 148

"Art and Architecture of the Double Ending, The"(Painter), **Supp. XXIII:** 295

"Art and Neurosis" (Trilling), **Supp. III Part 2:** 502

Art and Technics (Mumford), **Supp. II Part 2:** 483

Art & Ardor: Essays (Ozick), **Supp. V:** 258, 272

Art as Experience (Dewey), **I:** 266

Art by Subtraction (Reid), **IV:** 41

Art Chronicles 1954–1966 (O'Hara), **Supp. XXIII:** 220

Art de toucher le clavecin, L' (Couperin), *III:* 464

"Artemis" (Davison), **Supp. XXVI:** 69

Artemis to Actaeon and Other Verse (Wharton), **Retro. Supp. I:** 372

Arte of English Poesie (Puttenham), **Supp. I Part 1:** 113

"Art"(Hadas), **Supp. XXIII:** 115–116

"Art History" (Cliff), **Supp. XXII:** 75–76

Arthur, Anthony, **Supp. IV Part 2:** 606

Arthur Mervyn; or, Memoirs of the Year 1793 (Brown), **Supp. I Part 1:** 137–140, 144

"Article of Faith" (Sobin), **Supp. XVI:** 291

Articles of Light & Elation (Sobin), **Supp. XVI:** 291

Articulation of Sound Forms in Time (Howe), **Supp. IV Part 2:** 419, 431–433

"Artificer" (X. J. Kennedy), **Supp. XV:** 160

"Artificial Nigger, The" (O'Connor), **III:** 343, 351, 356, 358; **Retro. Supp. II:** 229, 232

Artist, The: A Drama without Words (Mencken), **III:** 104

Artist as Revolutionary, The (Buhle), **Supp. XXI:** 172

"Artist of the Beautiful, The" (Hawthorne), **Retro. Supp. I:** 149

Artistry of Grief (Torsney), **Retro. Supp. I:** 224

Artists and Concubines (Silver), **Supp. XXIV:** 265

"Artists' and Models' Ball, The" (Brooks), **Supp. III Part 1:** 72

Art of Detective Fiction, The (Swales), **Supp. XIX:** 183

"Art of Disappearing, The" (Nye), **Supp. XIII:** 287

Art of Drowning, The (Collins), **Supp. XXI:** 54, 60, 64

Art of Eating, The (M. F. K. Fisher), **Supp. XVII:** 87, 90, 91

Art of Fiction, The (Gardner), **Supp. VI:** 73

"Art of Fiction, The" (H. James), **Retro. Supp. I:** 226; **Retro. Supp. II:** 223

Art of Hunger, The (Auster), **Supp. XII:** 22

"Art of Keeping Your Mouth Shut, The" (Heller), **Supp. IV Part 1:** 383

"Art of Literature and Commonsense, The" (Nabokov), **Retro. Supp. I:** 271

Art of Living and Other Stories, The (Gardner), **Supp. VI:** 72

Art of Love, The (Koch), **Supp. XV:** 182

"Art of Love, The" (Koch), **Supp. XV:** 182

Art of Poetry, The (Koch), **Supp. XV:** 175–176, 178, 188

"Art of Poetry, The" (Koch), **Supp. XV:** 182

"Art of Poetry, The" (McClatchy), **Supp. XII:** 262

Art of Political Murder, The (Goldman), **Supp. XXV:** 49, 57–59

"Art of Romare Bearden, The" (Ellison), **Retro. Supp. II:** 123

"Art of Storytelling, The" (Simpson), **Supp. IX:** 277

Art of Sylvia Plath, The (Newman), **Supp. I Part 2:** 527

Art of the Moving Picture, The (Lindsay), **Supp. I Part 2:** 376, 391–392, 394; **Supp. XVI:** 185

Art of the Novel (H. James), **Retro. Supp. I:** 227

"Art of Theodore Dreiser, The" (Bourne), **I:** 235

Art of the Personal Essay, The (Lopate, comp.), **Supp. XIII:** 280–281; **Supp. XVI:** 266

Art of the Self, The: Essays a Propos "Steps" (Kosinski), *Supp. VII:* 222

Art of the Wasted Day, The (Hampl), **Supp. XXII:** 85

Arts and Sciences (Goldbarth), **Supp. XII: 184–186**

Arts and Sciences: A Seventies Seduction (Mallon), **Supp. XIX:** 132, 135

"Art's Bread and Butter" (Benét), **Retro. Supp. I:** 108

Artsybashev, Mikhail, **Supp. XXIII:** 1

Arvin, Newton, **I:** 259; **II:** 508; **Retro. Supp. I:** 19, 137

Asali, Muna, **Supp. XIII:** 121, 126

"As a Little Child" (Taggard), **Supp. XXII:** 272

"As a Young Man" (Hayes), **Supp. XXVI:** 134–135

Asbury, Herbert, **Supp. IV Part 1:** 353

Ascent of F6, The (Auden), **Supp. II Part 1:** 11, 13

Ascent to Truth, The (Merton), **Supp. VIII:** 208

Asch, Nathan, **Supp. XV:** 133, 134; **Supp. XXIII:** 4; **Supp. XXVI: 17–29**

Asch, Sholem, **IV:** 1, 9, 11, 14; **Retro. Supp. II:** 299; **Supp. XXIII: 1–18; Supp. XXVI:** 18

Ascherson, Neal, **Supp. XII:** 167

Ascher-Walsh, Rebecca, **Supp. XIX:** 54

"As Close as Breathing" (Jarman), **Supp. XVII:** 120

As David Danced (Bronk), **Supp. XXI:** 24

"As David Danced" (Bronk), **Supp. XXI:** 26

As Does New Hampshire and Other Poems (Sarton), **Supp. VIII:** 259
"As Evening Lays Dying" (Salinas), **Supp. XIII:** 319
"As Flowers Are" (Kunitz), **Supp. III Part 1:** 265
"Ash" (Sobin), **Supp. XVI:** 284–285
Ash, Nathan, **Supp. XXII:** 277
Ashbery, John, **Retro. Supp. I:** 313; **Supp. I Part 1:** 96; **Supp. III Part 1:** 1–29; **Supp. III Part 2:** 541; **Supp. IV Part 2:** 620; **Supp. IX:** 52; **Supp. VIII:** 272; **Supp. XI:** 139; **Supp. XIII:** 85; **Supp. XIX:** 40, 83; **Supp. XV:** 176, 177, 178, 188, 250; **Supp. XXI:** 227; **Supp. XXIII:** 207, 209, 210, 211, 215, 217, 220; **Supp. XXIV:** 33, 37, 44; **Supp. XXVI:** 70
"Ashes" (Lamott), **Supp. XX: 141**
"Ashes" (Levine), **Supp. V:** 188
"Ashes of the Beacon" (Bierce), **I:** 209
Ashes: Poems Old and New (Levine), **Supp. V:** 178, 188–189
Ashford, Margaret Mary (Daisy), **II:** 426
Ashman, Angela, **Supp. XXIV:** 200
"Ash Wednesday" (Garrett), **Supp. VII:** 109–110
"Ash Wednesday" (Merton), **Supp. VIII:** 199
Ash Wednesday (T. S. Eliot), **I:** 570, 574–575, 578–579, 580, 582, 584, 585; **Retro. Supp. I:** 64
"Ash Wednesday" (T. S. Eliot), **Supp. IV Part 2:** 436
Asian American Authors (Hsu and Palubinskas, eds.), **Supp. X:** 292
Asian American Heritage: An Anthology of Prose and Poetry (Wand), **Supp. X:** 292
Asian Figures (Mervin), **Supp. III Part 1:** 341
Asian Journal of Thomas Merton, The (Merton), **Supp. VIII:** 196, 206, 208
"Asian Peace Offers Rejected without Publication" (R. Bly), **Supp. IV Part 1:** 61
"Asides on the Oboe" (Stevens), **Retro. Supp. I:** 305
"As I Ebb'd with the Ocean of Life" (Whitman), **IV:** 342, 345–346; **Retro. Supp. I:** 404, 405
As I Lay Dying (Faulkner), **II:** 60–61, 69, 73, 74; **IV:** 100; **Retro. Supp. I:** 75, 82, 84, 85, 86, 88, 89, 91, 92; **Supp. IV Part 1:** 47; **Supp. IX:** 99, 103, 251; **Supp. VIII:** 37, 178; **Supp. XIV:** 24
"As I Lay with My Head in Your Lap, Camerado" (Whitman), **IV:** 347
Asimov, Isaac, **Supp. IV Part 1:** 116; **Supp. XVI:** 122
Asinof, Eliot, **II:** 424
As I Remember It (PBS documentary), **Supp. XVIII:** 277
Asirvatham, Sandy, **Supp. XVI:** 249
"As Is the Daughter, So Is Her Mother" (Patchett), **Supp. XII:** 310
"As It Was in the Beginning" (Benét), **Supp. XI:** 56

"As I Walked Out One Evening" (Auden), **Supp. II Part 1:** 13; **Supp. XV:** 126; **Supp. XX: 138**
"As I Went Down by Havre de Grace" (Wylie), **Supp. I Part 2:** 723
Ask a Policeman (Hinojosa), **Supp. XIX: 110–111**
"Ask Me" (Stafford), **Supp. XI:** 326–327
Ask Me Tomorrow (Cozzens), **I:** 365–367, 379
Ask the Dust (Fante), **Supp. XI:** 159, 160, 166, **167–169**, 172, 173, 174
"Ask the Optimist!" (Saunders), **Supp. XIX:** 235
Ask Your Mama (Hughes), **Supp. I Part 1:** 339, 341–342
Ask Your Mama: 12 Moods for Jazz (Hughes), **Retro. Supp. I:** 210, 211
As Little Children (R. P. Smith), **Supp. XIV:** 333
"As One Put Drunk into the Packet Boat" (Ashbery), **Supp. III Part 1:** 18
"Asparagus" (Nelson), **Supp. XVIII:** 178
"Aspects of Robinson" (Kees), **Supp. XV:** 134
Aspects of the Novel (Forster), **Retro. Supp. I:** 232; **Supp. VIII:** 155; **Supp. XXI:** 233
"Aspen and the Stream, The" (Wilbur), **Supp. III Part 2:** 555, 556
Aspern Papers, The (James), **Supp. V:** 101, 102
"Aspern Papers, The" (James), **Retro. Supp. I:** 219, 227, 228
Asphalt Georgics (Carruth), **Supp. XVI:** 54
Asphalt Jungle (film, Huston), **Supp. XIII:** 174
"Asphodel" (Welty), **IV:** 265, 271
"Asphodel, That Greeny Flower" (W. C. Williams), **Retro. Supp. I:** 429
"Aspic and Buttermilk" (Olds), **Supp. X:** 213
Asquith, Herbert Henry, **Retro. Supp. I:** 59
"Ass" (Cisneros), **Supp. VII:** 67
Assante, Armand, **Supp. VIII:** 74
Assassin, The: A Play in Three Acts (Shaw), **Supp. XIX:** 248
Assassins, The (Oates), **Supp. II Part 2:** 512, 517–519
"Assault" (Millay), **III:** 130–131
"Assemblage of Husbands and Wives, An" (Lewis), **II:** 455–456
"Assembloir" (Monson), **Supp. XXIV:** 237
Assembly (O'Hara), **III:** 361
As She Climbed Across the Table (Lethem), **Supp. XVIII: 140–141,** 148
Assignment, Wildlife (LaBastille), **Supp. X: 99,** 104
"Assimiliation in Recent American Jewish Autobiographies" (Krupnick), **Supp. XVI:** 153
Assistant, The (Malamud), **Supp. I Part 2:** 427, 428, 429, 431, 435, 441–445, 451; **Supp. XVI:** 220
Assommoir, L' (Zola), **II:** 291; **III:** 318
Assorted Prose (Updike), **IV:** 215–216, 218; **Retro. Supp. I:** 317, 319, 327

Astaire, Adele, **Supp. XVI:** 187
As They Were (M. F. K. Fisher), **Supp. XVII:** 88, 89, 91
Astor, Mary, **Supp. IV Part 1:** 356; **Supp. XII:** 173
Astoria, or, Anecdotes of an Enterprise beyond the Rocky Mountains (Irving), **II:** 312
"Astounding News by Electric Express via Norfolk! The Atlantic Crossed in Three Days Signal Triumph of Mr. Monck's Flying-Machine . . ." (Poe), **III:** 413, 420
Astraea (Holmes), **III:** 82
Astro, Richard, **Supp. I Part 2:** 429, 445
"Astrological Fricassee" (H. Miller), **III:** 187
"Astronomer's Wife" (Boyle), **Supp. XXIV:** 58
Astrophil and Stella (Sidney), **Supp. XIV:** 128
Asturias, Miguel Ángel, **Supp. XXIV:** 89
"As Weary Pilgrim" (Bradstreet), **Supp. I Part 1:** 103, 109, 122
As We Know (Ashbery), **Supp. III Part 1:** 9, 21–25
"As We Know" (Ashbery), **Supp. III Part 1:** 21–22
Aswell, Edward C., **IV:** 458, 459, 461
"Asylum, The" (Carruth), **Supp. XVI:** 48–49
"As You Like It" (Chopin), **Supp. I Part 1:** 217
As You Like It (Shakespeare), **Supp. I Part 1:** 308
"At a Bar" (Ferry), **Supp. XXIV:** 162
"At a Bar in Charlotte Amalie" (Updike), **IV:** 214
"At a Lecture" (Brodsky), **Supp. VIII:** 33
"At a Low Bar" (Ferry), **Supp. XXIV:** 149
"At a March against the Vietnam War" (R. Bly), **Supp. IV Part 1:** 61
"At a Reading" (McClatchy), **Supp. XII:** 256–257
"Atavism of John Tom Little Bear, The" (O. Henry), **Supp. II Part 1:** 410
"At Chênière Caminada" (Chopin), **Supp. I Part 1:** 220
"At Chinese Checkers" (Berryman), **I:** 182
Atchity, Kenneth John, **Supp. XI:** 227
"At Death's Window" (Lamott), **Supp. XX: 144**
At Eighty-Two (Sarton), **Supp. VIII:** 264
"At Every Gas Station There Are Mechanics" (Dunn), **Supp. XI:** 144
At Fault (Chopin), **Retro. Supp. II:** 57, 60, **62–63; Supp. I Part 1:** 207, 209–211, 220
"At Fifty" (Bronk), **Supp. XXI:** 31
At Heaven's Gate (Warren), **IV:** 243, 247–248, 251
Atheism Refuted: in a Discourse to Prove the Existence of God (Paine), **Supp. I Part 2:** 517
"Athénaïse" (Chopin), **Retro. Supp. II:** 66, 67; **Supp. I Part 1:** 219–220

Atherton, Gertrude, **I:** 199, 207–208; **Supp. XXIV: 17–32; Supp. XXVI:** 276

Athey, Jean L., **Supp. XI:** 184

At Home: Essays, 1982–1988 (Vidal), **Supp. IV Part 2:** 682, 687, 688

"At Home With" (column; Leland), **Supp. XV:** 69

"At Kino Viejo, Mexico" (Ríos), **Supp. IV Part 2:** 541

Atkinson, Brooks, **IV:** 288; **Supp. IV Part 2:** 683; **Supp. XIX:** 244

Atlanta (film, July), **Supp. XXIV:** 201, 209–210

Atlantis (Doty), **Supp. XI:** 121, **126–129**

"Atlantis" (Doty), **Supp. XI:** 127–128

Atlas, James, **Supp. V:** 233; **Supp. XV:** 25; **Supp. XXIV:** 172

Atlas, The (Vollmann), **Supp. XVII:** 226, 227

Atlas Shrugged (Rand), **Supp. IV Part 2:** 517, 521, 523, 524–526, 528, 531

At Liberty (T. Williams), **IV:** 378

"At Melville's Tomb" (H. Crane), **I:** 393; **Retro. Supp. II:** 76, 78, 80, 82

"At Mother Teresa's" (Nye), **Supp. XIII:** 276

"At Nightfall" (Kooser), **Supp. XIX:** 122–123

At Night the Salmon Move (Carver), **Supp. III Part 1:** 142

At Night the States (Notley), **Supp. XXII:** 224, 231–232

"At night the states" (Notley), **Supp. XXII:** 232

"At North Farm" (Ashbery), **Supp. III Part 1:** 1–2

At Paradise Gate (Smiley), **Supp. VI:** 292, **293–294**

"At Paso Rojo" (Bowles), **Supp. IV Part 1:** 87

At Play in the Fields of the Lord (Matthiessen), **Supp. V:** 199, 202, 204–206, 212

"At Play in the Paradise of Bombs" (Sanders), **Supp. XVI:** 272–273, 274, 277

"At Pleasure By" (Pinsky), **Supp. VI:** 245

"A-Train / Ziggurat / Elegy"(Balakian), **Supp. XXIII:** 32

At Risk (Hoffman), **Supp. X:** 87

"At Sea" (Hemingway), **II:** 258

"At Shaft 11" (Dunbar), **Supp. II Part 1:** 212

"At Sixty" (Davison), **Supp. XXVI:** 77

"At Slim's River" (Haines), **Supp. XII:** 208–209

"At St. Croix" (Dubus), **Supp. VII:** 83, 87

At Sundown (Whittier), **Supp. I Part 2:** 704

"At Sunset" (Simic), **Supp. VIII:** 282

At Swim-Two-Birds (O'Brien), **Supp. XXV:** 65

Attaway, William, **Supp. XXI:** 264

Attebery, Brian, **Supp. IV Part 1:** 101

Attendant, The (Bronk), **Supp. XXI:** 24

"Attendant, The" (Bronk), **Supp. XXI:** 26

"Attention"(Hadas), **Supp. XXIII:** 121

"At That Time, or The History of a Joke" (Paley), **Supp. VI:** 229–230

"At the Alhambra"(P. Benedict), **Supp. XXIII:** 40

At the Back of the North Wind (Macdonald), **Supp. XIII:** 75

"At the Birth of an Age" (Jeffers), **Supp. II Part 2:** 432

"At the Bomb Testing Site" (Stafford), **Supp. XI:** 317–318, 321, 323

At the Bottom of the River (Kincaid), **Supp. VII:** 182–184, 185

"At the 'Cadian Ball" (Chopin), **Retro. Supp. II:** 64, 65, 68

"At the Cancer Clinic" (Kooser), **Supp. XIX:** 127

"At the Chelton-Pulver Game" (Auchincloss), **Supp. IV Part 1:** 27

"At the Drugstore" (Taylor), **Supp. V:** 323

At the Edge of the Body (Jong), **Supp. V:** 115, 130

"At the End of the Curse, a Blessing" (Verducci), **Supp. XXII:** 209

At the End of the Open Road (Simpson), **Supp. IX:** 265, 269, **271–273,** 277

At the End of This Summer: Poems 1948–1954, **Supp. XII:** 211

"At the End of War" (Eberhart), **I:** 522–523

"At the Executed Murderer's Grave" (Wright), **Supp. III Part 2:** 595, 597

"At the Fishhouses" (Bishop), **Retro. Supp. II:** 45; **Supp. I Part 1:** 90, 92

At the Gates of the Animal Kingdom (Hempel), **Supp. XXI:** 115, **122–124**

"At the Grave of My Guardian Angel: St. Louis Cemetery, New Orleans" (Levis), **Supp. XI:** 268–269

"At the Gym" (Doty), **Supp. XI:** 135

"At the Indian Store" (McCarriston), **Supp. XIV:** 271

"At the Lake" (Oliver), **Supp. VII:** 244

"At the Landing" (Welty), **IV:** 265–266; **Retro. Supp. I:** 348

"At the Last" (Bynner), **Supp. XV:** 44

"At the Last Rites for Two Hot Rodders" (X. J. Kennedy), **Supp. XV:** 166

At the Mountains of Madness (Lovecraft), **Supp. XXII:** 58; **Supp. XXV:** 109, 111, 114

"At the Owl Club, North Gulfport, Mississippi, 1950" (Trethewey), **Supp. XXI:** 249

At the Owl Woman Saloon (Gallagher), **Supp. XXIV:** 166, 172, 173, 174, 175–177

"At the Premiere" (Keillor), **Supp. XVI:** 167

At the Rendezvous of Victory (C. L. R. James), **Supp. XXI:** 172

At the Root of Stars (Barnes), **Supp. III Part 1:** 34

At the Sign of the Sphinx (Wells), **Supp. XXVI:** 274

"At the Site of Last Night's Fire" (Davison), **Supp. XXVI:** 69

"At the Slackening of the Tide" (Wright), **Supp. III Part 2:** 597

"At the Street Corner" (Ferry), **Supp. XXIV:** 162

"At the Tomb of Walt Whitman" (Kunitz), **Supp. III Part 1:** 262

"At the Tourist Centre in Boston" (Atwood), **Supp. XIII:** 33

"At the Town Dump" (Kenyon), **Supp. VII:** 167

"At the Worcester Museum" (Pinsky), **Supp. VI:** 251

"At the Zoo in Spain" (Major), **Supp. XXII:** 182

"Atticus Finch and the Mad Dog: Harper Lee's *To Kill a Mockingbird*" (Jones), **Supp. VIII:** 128

"Atticus Finch—Right and Wrong" (Freedman), **Supp. VIII:** 127–128

"Attic Which Is Desire, The" (W. C. Williams), **Retro. Supp. I:** 422

"At Tikal" (Bronk), **Supp. XXI: 28–29**

"At Times in Flight: A Parable" (H. Roth), **Supp. IX:** 234

Attitudes toward History (Burke), **I:** 274

Atwan, Robert, **Supp. XVI:** 273, 277

At Weddings and Wakes (McDermott), **Supp. XVIII:** 155, **160–162,** 166

"At White River" (Haines), **Supp. XII:** 208–209

Atwood, Margaret, **Supp. IV Part 1:** 252; **Supp. V:** 119; **Supp. XI:** 317; **Supp. XIII: 19–39,** 291, 306; **Supp. XXI:** 39, 42

"Atwood's Gorgon Touch" (Davey), **Supp. XIII:** 33

"Aubade" (McCarriston), **Supp. XIV:** 271

"Aubade: November" (McCarriston), **Supp. XIV:** 261–262

"Aubade of an Early Homo Sapiens" (C. Frost), **Supp. XV:** 97–98

"Aubade: Opal and Silver" (Doty), **Supp. XI:** 129

"Au Bal Musette" (Van Vechten), **Supp. II Part 2:** 735

Auchincloss, Hugh D., **Supp. IV Part 2:** 679

Auchincloss, Louis, **I:** 375; **III:** 66; **Retro. Supp. I:** 370, 373; **Supp. IV Part 1: 21–38**

"Auction" (Simic), **Supp. VIII:** 278

"Auction, The" (Crane), **I:** 411

"Auction Model 1934" (Z. Fitzgerald), **Supp. IX:** 61

Auden, W. H., **I:** 71, 381, 539; **II:** 367, 368, 371, 376, 586; **III:** 17, 134, 269, 271, 292, 476–477, 504, 527, 530, 542, 615; **IV:** 136, 138, 240, 430; **Retro. Supp. I:** 430; **Retro. Supp. II:** 183, 242, 244, 323; **Supp. I Part 1:** 270; **Supp. I Part 2:** 552, 610; **Supp. II Part 1: 1–28; Supp. III Part 1:** 2, 3, 14, 26, 60, 61, 64, 341; **Supp. III Part 2:** 591, 595; **Supp. IV Part 1:** 79, 84, 136, 225, 302, 313; **Supp. IV Part 2:** 440, 465; **Supp. IX:** 94, 287, 288; **Supp. V:** 337; **Supp. VIII:** 19, 21, 22, 23, 30, 32, 155, 190; **Supp. X:** 35, 57, 59, 115–116, 117, 118–119; **Supp. XI:** 243, 244; **Supp. XII:** 253, 264–265, 266, 269–270; **Supp. XIV:**

156, 158, 160, 162, 163; **Supp. XIX:** 147, 151; **Supp. XV:** 74, 117–118, 139, 144, 186; **Supp. XX: 138; Supp. XXI:** 60, 98; **Supp. XXIII:** 117, 207

"Auden's OED" (McClatchy), **Supp. XII:** 264–265

"Audition" (Alvarez), **Supp. VII:** 10

Audubon, John James, **III:** 210; **IV:** 265; **Supp. IX:** 171; **Supp. XVI:** 1–14

Audubon, John Woodhouse, **Supp. XVI:** 10

Audubon, Maria Rebecca, **Supp. XVI:** 11

Audubon, Victor Gifford, **Supp. XVI:** 10

Audubon and His Journals (M. Audubon, ed.), **Supp. XVI:** 11, 12

Audubon Reader, The: The Best Writings of John James Audubon (Sanders, ed.), **Supp. XVI:** 269

Auer, Jane. *See* Bowles, Jane

Auerbach, Eric, **III:** 453

Auerbach, Nina, **Supp. I Part 1:** 40

"August" (Oliver), **Supp. VII:** 235

"August" (Rich), **Supp. I Part 2:** 564

August, Timothy K., **Supp. XXVI:** 210, 211

"August 1968" (Auden), **Supp. II Part 1:** 25

"August Darks, The" (Clampitt), **Supp. IX:** 43, **50–51,** 52

Augustine, Saint, **I:** 279, 290; **II:** 537; **III:** 259, 270, 292, 300; **IV:** 69, 126; **Retro. Supp. I:** 247; **Supp. VIII:** 203; **Supp. XI:** 245; **Supp. XIII:** 89; **Supp. XXI:** 83; **Supp. XXII:** 92–93

August Snow (Price), **Supp. VI:** 264

"Au Jardin" (Pound), **III:** 465–466

Aunt Carmen's Book of Practical Saints (Mora), **Supp. XIII: 227–229**

"Aunt Cynthy Dallett" (Jewett), **II:** 393

"Aunt Gladys" (Karr), **Supp. XI:** 241

"Aunt Granny Lith" (Offutt), **Supp. XIX:** 165, 166

"Aunties, The" (Lamott), **Supp. XX: 141**

"Aunt Imogen" (Robinson), **III:** 521

"Aunt Jemima of the Ocean Waves" (Hayden), **Supp. II Part 1:** 368, 379

"Aunt Jennifer's Tigers" (Rich), **Supp. XV:** 252

Aunt Jo's Scrapbooks (Alcott), **Supp. I Part 1:** 43

"Aunt Mary" (Oliver), **Supp. VII:** 232

"Aunt Mary" (Stowe), **Supp. I Part 2:** 587

"Aunt Moon's Young Man" (Hogan), **Supp. IV Part 1:** 400

"Aunt Rectita's Good Friday" (X. J. Kennedy), **Supp. XV:** 166

"Aunt Sarah" (Lowell), **II:** 554

"Aunt Sue's Stories" (Hughes), **Retro. Supp. I:** 197, 199

"Aunt Violet's Canadian Honeymoon/ 1932" (Shields), **Supp. VII:** 311

"Aunt Violet's Things" (Shields), **Supp. VII:** 311–312

"Aurelia: Moon Jellies" (Mora), **Supp. XIII:** 224

"Aurelio" (Di Piero), **Supp. XIX:** 38

Au revoir les enfants (film, Malle), **Supp. XXIII:** 122

Aurora 7 (Mallon), **Supp. XIX:** 132, **135–136**

Aurora Dawn (Wouk), **Supp. XXV:** 255, 258

Aurora Leigh (E. Browning), **Retro. Supp. I:** 33; **Supp. XI:** 197

Aurora Means Dawn (Sanders), **Supp. XVI:** 268

Auroras of Autumn, The (Stevens), **Retro. Supp. I:** 297, 300, **309–312**

"Auroras of Autumn, The" (Stevens), **Retro. Supp. I:** 311, 312; **Supp. III Part 1:** 12

Auschwitz: the Nazis and the "Final Solution" (television documentary), *Supp. XVII:* 40

Auslander, Joseph, **Supp. XIV:** 120

"Auspex" (Frost), **Retro. Supp. I:** 122

"Auspex" (Lowell), **Supp. I Part 2:** 424

Austen, Jane, **I:** 130, 339, 375, 378; **II:** 272, 278, 287, 568–569, 577; **IV:** 8; **Retro. Supp. I:** 354; **Supp. I Part 1:** 267; **Supp. I Part 2:** 656, 715; **Supp. IV Part 1:** 300; **Supp. IX:** 128; **Supp. VIII:** 125, 167; **Supp. XII:** 310; **Supp. XV:** 338; **Supp. XX: 108; Supp. XXII:** 206; **Supp. XXVI:** 130

Austenfeld, Thomas, **Supp. XXIV:** 64

Auster, Paul, **Supp. XII: 21–39; Supp. XIV:** 292; **Supp. XXI:** 20

Austerities (Simic), **Supp. VIII: 276– 278,** 283

"Austerities" (Simic), **Supp. VIII:** 277

"Austerity Measures" (Stallings), **Supp. XXV:** 221

"Austerity Measures: A Letter from Greece" (Stallings), **Supp. XXV:** 221, 224, 225

Austin, Mary, **Supp. XXVI:** 31

Austin, Mary Hunter, **Retro. Supp. I:** 7; **Supp. IV Part 2:** 503; **Supp. X:** 29; **Supp. XIII:** 154

"Authentic Unconscious, The" (Trilling), **Supp. III Part 2:** 512

Author and Agent: Eudora Welty and Diarmuid Russell (Kreyling), **Retro. Supp. I:** 342, 345, 347, 349–350

"Author at Sixty, The" (Wilson), **IV:** 426

"Author of 'Beltraffio,' The" (James), **Retro. Supp. I:** 227

"Author's Explanation, The" (Larsen), **Supp. XVIII:** 131

"Author's House" (Fitzgerald), **Retro. Supp. I:** 98

"Author's Reflections, An: Willie Loman, Walter Younger, and He Who Must Live" (Hansberry), **Supp. IV Part 1:** 370

"Author to Her Book, The" (Bradstreet), **Supp. I Part 1:** 119; **Supp. V:** 117– 118; **Supp. XV:** 125–126

"Autism Poem #20: The Knot Garden"(Crooker), **Supp. XXIII:** 56–57

"Autobiographical Note" (H. Miller), **III:** 174–175

"Autobiographical Notes" (Baldwin), **Supp. I Part 1:** 54

"Autobiographical Notes" (Holmes), **Supp. I Part 1:** 301

"Autobiographic Chapter, An" (Bourne), **I:** 236

Autobiography (Franklin), **II:** 102, 103, 108, 121–122, 302

Autobiography (James), **I:** 462

"Autobiography" (MacLeish), **III:** 20

Autobiography (Van Buren), **III:** 473

Autobiography (W. C. Williams), **Supp. I Part 1:** 254

Autobiography (Zukofsky), **Supp. III Part 2:** 627

Autobiography by Jesus of Nazareth (Pettis), **Supp. XXIII:** 189

"Autobiography"(Dybek), **Supp. XXIII:** 78

"Autobiography in the Shape of a Book Review" (Bynner), **Supp. XV:** 40

"Autobiography of a Confluence, The" (Gunn Allen), **Supp. IV Part 1:** 321

Autobiography of Alice B. Toklas, The (Stein), **IV:** 26, 30, 35, 43; **Supp. IV Part 1:** 11, 81

Autobiography of an Ex-Colored Man, The (J. W. Johnson), **Supp. II Part 1:** 33, 194; **Supp. XVIII:** 127; **Supp. XXII:** 7

Autobiography of a Schizophrenic Girl (Renée), **Supp. XVI:** 64, 66

Autobiography of a Thief, The (Hapgood), **Supp. XVII:** 96, 101–102

Autobiography of Benjamin Franklin (Franklin), **Supp. IV Part 1:** 5

Autobiography of LeRoi Jones, The (Baraka), **Retro. Supp. I:** 411

Autobiography of Malcolm X (Little), **Supp. I Part 1:** 66; **Supp. X:** 27; **Supp. XIII:** 264; **Supp. XXII:** 95

Autobiography of Mark Twain, The (Twain), **IV:** 209

Autobiography of My Mother, The (Kincaid), **Supp. VII:** 182, 188–190, 191, 192, 193

Autobiography of Red: A Novel in Verse (Carson), **Supp. XII:** 97, **106–110**

Autobiography of Upton Sinclair, The (Sinclair), **Supp. V:** 276, 282

Autobiography of W. E. B. Du Bois, The (Du Bois), **Supp. II Part 1:** 159, 186

Autobiography of William Carlos Williams, The (W. C. Williams), **Retro. Supp. I:** 51, 428

Autocrat of the Breakfast-Table, The (Holmes), **Supp. I Part 1:** 306–307

"Autographic Disclosures and Genealogies of Desire in Alison Bechdel's *Fun Home*" (Watson), **Supp. XXV:** 8

"Automatic Gate, The" (Southern), **Supp. XI:** 294

"Automotive Passacaglia" (H. Miller), **III:** 186

"Autopsy Room, The" (Carver), **Supp. III Part 1:** 137

"Auto Wreck" (Shapiro), **Supp. II Part 2:** 706

"Autre Temps" (Wharton), **IV:** 320, 324

"Autumn" (Berrigan), **Supp. XXIV:** 37

"Autumn, Mist" (Hull), **Supp. XXI:** 133

"Autumn Afternoon" (Farrell), **II:** 45

"Autumnal" (Eberhart), **I:** 540–541

"Autumn Begins in Martins Ferry, Ohio" (Wright), **Supp. III Part 2:** 599

"Autumn Courtship, An" (Caldwell), **I:** 309

"Autumn Equinox" (Skloot), **Supp. XX: 202**

Autumn Garden, The (Hellman), **Supp. I Part 1:** 285–286, 290

"Autumn Garden, The: Mechanics and Dialectics" (Felheim), **Supp. I Part 1:** 297

"Autumn Holiday, An" (Jewett), **II:** 391; **Retro. Supp. II:** 140–141

"Autumn Musings" (Harte), **Supp. II Part 1:** 336

"Autumn of the Revolutionary, The" (Goldman), **Supp. XXV:** 54–55

"Autumn's Day" (Rilke; Berrigan, trans.), **Supp. XXIV:** 37

Autumn Spring (Pickering), **Supp. XXI:** 204–205, 206

"Autumn Within" (Longfellow), **II:** 499

"Autumn Woods" (Bryant), **Supp. I Part 1:** 164

Autum of the Patriarch, The (García Márquez), **Supp. XXIV:** 89

"Au Vieux Jardin" (Aldington), **Supp. I Part 1:** 257

"Aux Imagistes" (W. C. Williams), **Supp. I Part 1:** 266

Available World, The (Monson), **Supp. XXIV:** 230, **239–240,** 241

Avakian, Aram, **Supp. XI:** 294, 295, 309

Avalanche (Boyle), **Supp. XXIV:** 62

Avalanche, The (Atherton), **Supp. XXIV:** 24–25

"Ave Atque Vale" (Bynner), *Supp. XV:* 49

Avedon, Richard, **Supp. I Part 1:** 58; **Supp. V:** 194; **Supp. X:** 15

Aveling, Edward, **Supp. XVI:** 85

"Avenue" (Pinsky), **Supp. VI:** 248

Avenue Bearing the Initial of Christ into the New World: Poems 1946–1964 (Kinnell), **Supp. III Part 1:** 235, 239–241

"Avenue of the Americas" (Simic), **Supp. VIII:** 278

"Average Torture" (Karr), **Supp. XI:** 243

Avery, George C., **Supp. XX: 84**

Avery, John, **Supp. I Part 1:** 153

"Avey" (Toomer), **Supp. IX:** 317

Avon's Harvest (Robinson), **III:** 510

Awake and Sing! (Odets), **Supp. II Part 2:** 530, 531, 536–538, 550; **Supp. IV Part 2:** 587

"Awake at Midnight"(Schott), **Supp. XXIII:** 246

Awake in Spain (O'Hara), **Supp. XXIII:** 216

Awakening, The (Chopin), **Retro. Supp. I:** 10; **Retro. Supp. II:** 57, 59, 60, 67, **68–71,** 73; **Supp. I Part 1:** 200, 201, 202, 211, 220–225; **Supp. V:** 304; **Supp. VIII:** 198; **Supp. XII:** 170

Awakening Land, The (Richter), **Supp. XVIII:** 207, 215

Awful Rowing Toward God, The (Sexton), **Supp. II Part 2:** 694–696

Awiakta, Marilou, **Supp. IV Part 1:** 319, 335

Awkward Age, The (James), **II:** 332; **Retro. Supp. I:** 229, **230–231**

Axe Handles (Snyder), **Supp. VIII: 303–305**

Axel's Castle: A Study in the Imaginative Literature of 1870 to 1930 (Wilson), **I:** 185; **II:** 577; **IV:** 428, 431, 438, 439, 443; **Supp. VIII:** 101

"Ax-Helve, The" (Frost), **Retro. Supp. I:** 133

Azikewe, Nnamdi, **Supp. IV Part 1:** 361

"Aztec Angel" (Salinas), **Supp. XIII:** 314

Aztec Treasure House, The: New and Selected Essays (Connell), **Supp. XIV:** 80, 97

B

"Bab, the Sub-Deb" (Rinehart), **Supp. XXV:** 195

Babbitt (Lewis), **II:** 442, 443–445, 446, 447, 449; **III:** 63–64, 394; **IV:** 326

Babbitt, Irving, **I:** 247; **II:** 456; **III:** 315, 461, 613; **IV:** 439; **Retro. Supp. I:** 55; **Supp. I Part 2:** 423

Babcock, Elisha, **Supp. II Part 1:** 69

Babel, Isaac, **IV:** 1; **Supp. IX:** 260; **Supp. XII:** 308–309; **Supp. XVII:** 41; **Supp. XXIII:** 68

Babel, Isaak, **Supp. XIV:** 83, 84

Babel to Byzantium (Dickey), **Supp. IV Part 1:** 177, 185

Baber, Asa, **Supp. XXIII:** 52

Baber, Bob Henry, **Supp. XXIII:** 39

Babeuf, François, **Supp. I Part 2:** 518

"Babies, The" (Strand), **Supp. IV Part 2:** 625

Babouk (Endore), **Supp. XVII: 56–57, 61, 64**

Baby, Come on Inside (Wagoner), **Supp. IX: 335**

"Baby, The" (Barthelme), **Supp. IV Part 1:** 49

Baby Doll (T. Williams), **IV:** 383, 386, 387, 389, 395

"Baby Face" (Sandburg), **III:** 584

"Babylon Revisited" (Fitzgerald), **II:** 95; **Retro. Supp. I:** 109

"Baby or the Botticelli, The" (Gass), **Supp. VI:** 92

"Baby Pictures of Famous Dictators" (Simic), **Supp. VIII:** 276

"Baby's Breath" (Bambara), **Supp. XI:** 15, 16

"Babysitter, The" (Coover), **Supp. V:** 43–44

Baby Sweet's (Andrews), **Supp. XXVI:** 7–9, 12, 14

"Baby Villon" (Levine), **Supp. V:** 182

Baby with the Bathwater (Durang), **Supp. XXIV: 121–122**

Bacall, Lauren, **Supp. IV Part 1:** 130

"Baccalaureate" (MacLeish), **III:** 4

Bacchae, The (Euripides), **Supp. VIII:** 182

Bach, Caleb, **Supp. XXV:** 53

Bach, Johann Sebastian, **Supp. I Part 1:** 363; **Supp. III Part 2:** 611, 612, 619

Bachardy, Don, **Supp. XIV:** 166, 170, 172, 173

Bache, Richard, **Supp. I Part 2:** 504

Bachelard, Gaston, **Supp. XIII:** 225; **Supp. XVI:** 292

"Bachelor Girl, The" (Boyce), **Supp. XXI:** 3

Bachelor Girls (Wasserstein), **Supp. XV: 327–328,** 332

Bachman, John, **Supp. XVI:** 10, 11

Bachmann, Ingeborg, **Supp. IV Part 1:** 310; **Supp. VIII:** 272

Bachofen, J. J., **Supp. I Part 2:** 560, 567

Back Bog Beast Bait (Shepard), **Supp. III Part 2:** 437, 438

Backbone (C. Bly), **Supp. XVI: 34–36,** 37, 40, 41

Back Country, The (Snyder), **Supp. VIII: 296–299**

"Back from the Argentine" (Leopold), **Supp. XIV:** 186

"Background with Revolutionaries" (MacLeish), **III:** 14–15

"Back in the Saddle Again" (Swados), **Supp. XIX:** 259

Back in the World (Wolff), **Supp. VII:** 344, 345

Backis, Charles, **Supp. XXI:** 195

"Backlash Blues, The" (Hughes), **Supp. I Part 1:** 343

"Backlash of Kindness, A" (Nye), **Supp. XIII:** 285, 286

"Backslider, The" (R. Fisher), **Supp. XIX:** 70, 71

"Back Street Guy" (Halliday), **Supp. XIX:** 88

Back to China (Fiedler), **Supp. XIII: 102–103**

Back to Methuselah (Shaw), **IV:** 64

"Backwacking: A Plea to the Senator" (Ellison), **Retro. Supp. II:** 126; **Supp. II Part 1:** 248

Backward Glance, A (Wharton), **Retro. Supp. I:** 360, 363, 366, 378, 380, 382; **Supp. XX: 229; Supp. XXVI:** 271

"Backward Glance o'er Travel'd Roads, A" (Whitman), **IV:** 348

Bacon, Francis, **II:** 1, 8, 11, 15–16, 111; **III:** 284; **Retro. Supp. I:** 247; **Supp. I Part 1:** 310; **Supp. I Part 2:** 388; **Supp. IX:** 104; **Supp. XIV:** 22, 210

Bacon, Helen, **Supp. X:** 57

Bacon, Katie, **Supp. XXII:** 207; **Supp. XXIII:** 275

Bacon, Leonard, **II:** 530; **Supp. XXII:** 273

Bacon, Roger, **IV:** 69

"Bacterial War, The" (Nemerov), **III:** 272

Bad and the Beautiful, The (film), **Supp. XVIII:** 250

Bad Boy Brawly Brown (Mosley), **Supp. XIII:** 237, 239, 240–241

Bad Boys (Cisneros), **Supp. VII:** 58

"Bad Company" (Gallagher), **Supp. XXIV:** 174, 176

"Bad Dream" (Taylor), **Supp. V:** 320

Badè, William Frederic, **Supp. IX:** 178

"Bad Fisherman, The" (Wagoner), **Supp. IX:** 328

Bad for Each Other (film), **Supp. XIII:** 174

"Badger" (Clare), **II:** 387

Badger, A. G., **Supp. I Part 1:** 356

"Badger and the Bear, The" (Zitkala-Ša), **Supp. XXV:** 275

Bad Government and Silly Literature (C. Bly), **Supp. XVI:** 37, 38, 40

Badlands (film; Malick), **Supp. XV:** 351

"Bad Lay" (McCarriston), **Supp. XIV:** 267

Badley, Linda, **Supp. V:** 148

Bad Man, A (Elkin), **Supp. VI:** 47

Bad Man Ballad (Sanders), **Supp. XVI:** 268

Bad Man Blues: A Portable George Garrett (Garrett), **Supp. VII:** 111

"Bad Music, The" (Jarrell), **II:** 369

"Bad People" (Halliday), **Supp. XIX:** 90, 91

"Bad Summer on K2, A" (Krakauer and Child), **Supp. XVIII:** 107, 108

"Bad Woman, A" (Fante), **Supp. XI:** 165

Baeck, Leo, **Supp. V:** 260

Baecker, Diann L., **Supp. VIII:** 128

Baer, William, **Supp. XIII:** 112, 118, 129; **Supp. XXIII:** 124

Baez, Joan, **Supp. IV Part 1:** 200; **Supp. VIII:** 200, 202; **Supp. XVIII:** 24, 25–26, 27

Bag of Bones (King), **Supp. V:** 139, 148, 151

"Bagpipe Music" (MacNeice), **Supp. X:** 117

"Bahá'í Faith: Only Church in World That Does Not Discriminate" (Locke), **Supp. XIV:** 200

Bahá'u'lláh, **Supp. XX: 117, 121, 122**

"Bahá'u'lláh in the Garden of Ridwan" (Hayden), **Supp. II Part 1:** 370, 378

Bahr, David, **Supp. XV:** 66

Bahr, Thomas, **Supp. XXII:** 206, 214

"Bailbondsman, The" (Elkin), **Supp. VI:** 49, **50,** 58

Bailey, Gamaliel, **Supp. I Part 2:** 587, 590

Bailey, Peter, **Supp. XVI:** 69

Bailey, William, **Supp. IV Part 2:** 631, 634

Bailey's Café (Naylor), **Supp. VIII: 226–228**

Bailyn, Bernard, **Supp. I Part 2:** 484, 506

Bair, Deirdre, **Supp. X:** 181, 186, 187, 188, 192, 194, 195, 196, 197

Baird, Linnett, **Supp. XII:** 299

Baird, Peggy, **I:** 385, 401

Baiting the Void (Schott), **Supp. XXIII: 247–248**

Bakan, David, **I:** 59

Baker, Carlos, **II:** 259

Baker, Chet, **Supp. XXI:** 131

Baker, David, **Supp. IX:** 298; **Supp. XI:** 121, 142, 153; **Supp. XII:** 175, 191–192; **Supp. XIX:** 115

Baker, George Pierce, **III:** 387; **IV:** 453, 455

Baker, Gladys, **Supp. XIV:** 121

Baker, Houston, **Supp. XXII:** 6

Baker, Houston A., Jr., **Retro. Supp. II:** 121; **Supp. IV Part 1:** 365; **Supp. X:** 324

Baker, Jeff, **Supp. XXIV:** 166, 178

Baker, Katherine, **Supp. XX: 69**

Baker, Kevin, **Supp. XIV:** 96

Baker, Mabel, **Supp. XVIII:** 259, 263, 266–267, 269

Baker, Nicholson, **Supp. XIII: 41–57**

Baker, Robert, **Supp. XVI:** 288, 290

Bakerman, Jane S., **Supp. IV Part 2:** 468

Bakhtin, Mikhail, **Retro. Supp. II:** 273; **Supp. IV Part 1:** 301; **Supp. X:** 120, 239; **Supp. XXII:** 259

Bakst, Léon, **Supp. IX:** 66

Bakunin, Mikhail Aleksandrovich, **IV:** 429

Balaban, John, **Supp. XIX:** 281

Balakian, Anna, **Supp. XXIII:** 20

Balakian, Diran, **Supp. XXIII:** 28

Balakian, Grigoris, **Supp. XXIII:** 28, 29–32

Balakian, Jan, **Supp. XV:** 327

Balakian, Nona, **Supp. XXIII:** 20

Balakian, Peter, **Supp. XXIII: 19–34**

"Balance" (Bierds), **Supp. XVII:** 31

"Balance" (Nelson), **Supp. XVIII:** 174–175

Balbo, Ned, **Supp. XIX:** 161; **Supp. XVII:** 120

Balbuena, Bernado de, **Supp. V:** 11

Balch, Emily Greene, **Supp. I Part 1:** 25

Balcony, The (Genet), **I:** 84

Bald Soprano, The (Ionesco), **I:** 74

Baldwin, David, **Supp. I Part 1:** 47, 48, 49, 50, 51, 54, 65, 66

Baldwin, James, **Retro. Supp. II: 1–17; Supp. I Part 1: 47–71,** 337, 341; **Supp. II Part 1:** 40; **Supp. III Part 1:** 125; **Supp. IV Part 1:** 1, 10, 11, 163, 369; **Supp. V:** 201; **Supp. VIII:** 88, 198, 235, 349; **Supp. X:** 136, 324; **Supp. XI:** 288, 294; **Supp. XIII:** 46, 111, 181, 186, 294; **Supp. XIV:** 54, 71, 73, 306; **Supp. XVI:** 135, 141, 143; **Supp. XVIII:** 25; **Supp. XX: 147; Supp. XXI:** 245; **Supp. XXIV:** 185

Baldwin, Samuel, **Supp. I Part 1:** 48

Balitas, Vincent D., **Supp. XVI:** 222; **Supp. XXVI:** 149

Balkian, Nona, **Supp. XI:** 230

Balkun, Mary McAleer, **Supp. XX: 281**

Ball, Gordon, **Supp. XIV:** 148

Ball, John, **Supp. XV:** 202

"Ballad: Between the Box Cars" (Warren), **IV:** 245

"Ballade" (MacLeish), **III:** 4

"Ballade at Thirty-Five" (Parker), **Supp. IX:** 192

"Ballade for the Duke of Orléans" (Wilbur), **Supp. III Part 2:** 556

"Ballade of Broken Flutes, The" (Robinson), **III:** 505

"Ballade of Meaty Inversions" (White), **Supp. I Part 2:** 676

"Ballad of a Thin Man" (song, Dylan), **Supp. XVIII:** 30, 31

"Ballad of Aunt Geneva, The" (Nelson), **Supp. XVIII:** 175

"Ballad of Billie Potts, The" (Warren), **IV:** 241–242, 243, 253

"Ballad of Carmilhan, The" (Longfellow), **II:** 505

"ballad of chocolate Mabbie, the" (Brooks), **Supp. IV Part 1:** 15

"Ballad of Dead Ladies, The" (Villon), **Retro. Supp. I:** 286

Ballad of Dingus Magee, The (Markson), **Supp. XVII:** 139, 141

"Ballad of East and West, The" (Kipling), **Supp. IX:** 246; **Supp. XX: 23**

"Ballad of Jesse Neighbours, The" (Humphrey), **Supp. IX:** 100

"Ballad of Jesus of Nazareth, A" (Masters), **Supp. I Part 2:** 459

"Ballad of John Cable and Three Gentlemen" (Merwin), **Supp. III Part 1:** 342

"Ballad of Larry and Club" (Jarman), **Supp. XVII:** 115

"Ballad of Nat Turner, The" (Hayden), **Supp. II Part 1:** 378

"Ballad of Pearl May Lee, The" (Brooks), **Supp. III Part 1:** 74, 75

"Ballad of Plastic Fred, The" (Gansworth), **Supp. XXVI:** 104

Ballad of Remembrance, A (Hayden), **Supp. II Part 1:** 367

"Ballad of Remembrance, A" (Hayden), **Supp. II Part 1:** 368, 372, 373

"Ballad of Ruby, The" (Sarton), **Supp. VIII:** 259–260

"Ballad of San Isidro, The" (Espaillat), **Supp. XXI:** 108

"Ballad of Sue Ellen Westerfield, The" (Hayden), **Supp. II Part 1:** 364

Ballad of the Brown Girl, The (Cullen), **Supp. IV Part 1:** 167, 168, 169–170, 173

"Ballad of the Brown Girl, The" (Cullen), **Supp. IV Part 1:** 168

"Ballad of the Children of the Czar, The" (Schwartz), **Supp. II Part 2:** 649

"Ballad of the Girl Whose Name Is Mud" (Hughes), **Retro. Supp. I:** 205

"Ballad of the Goodly Fere", **III:** 458

"Ballad of the Harp-Weaver" (Millay), **III:** 135

"Ballad of the Sad Cafe, The" (McCullers), **II:** 586, 587, 588, 592, 595, 596–600, 604, 605, 606

"Ballad of the Sixties" (Sarton), **Supp. VIII:** 259

"Ballad of Trees and the Master, A" (Lanier), **Supp. I Part 1:** 370

"Ballad of Typical Lovers" (Taggard), **Supp. XXII:** 277

"Ballad of William Sycamore, The" (Benét), **Supp. XI:** 44, 47

Ballads and Other Poems (Longfellow), **II:** 489; **III:** 412, 422; **Retro. Supp. II:** 157, 168

Ballads for Sale (Lowell), **II:** 527

"Ballads of Lenin" (Hughes), **Supp. I Part 1:** 331

Ballantyne, Sheila, **Supp. V:** 70

Ballard, J. G., **Supp. XVI:** 123, 124; **Supp. XVIII:** 136

Ballard, Josephine. *See* McMurtry, Josephine

"Ballena" (Mora), **Supp. XIII:** 224

"Ballet in Numbers for Mary Ellen, A" (Karr), **Supp. XI:** 241

"Ballet of a Buffoon, The" (Sexton), **Supp. II Part 2:** 693

"Ballet of Central Park, The" (Boyle), **Supp. XXIV:** 59

"Ballet of the Fifth Year, The" (Schwartz), **Supp. II Part 2:** 650

Ball Four (Bouton), **Supp. XX: 274**

"Ball Game, The" (Creeley), **Supp. IV Part 1:** 140

Ballistics (Collins), **Supp. XXI:** 57, 65

"Ballistics" (Collins), **Supp. XXI:** 65

"Balloon Hoax, The" (Poe), **III:** 413, 420

Balloonists, The (Biss), **Supp. XXVI:** 45, 48–50

"Balm of Recognition, The: Rectifying Wrongs through Generations" (E. Hoffman, lecture), **Supp. XVI:** 155

Balo (Toomer), **Supp. III Part 2:** 484

Balsan, Consuelo, **IV:** 313–314

Balthus, **Supp. IV Part 2:** 623

Balthus Poems, The (Dobyns), **Supp. XIII:** 87

Baltimore, Lord, **I:** 132

Balzac, Honoré de, **I:** 103, 123, 339, 376, 474, 485, 499, 509, 518; **II:** 307, 322, 324, 328, 336, 337; **III:** 61, 174, 184, 320, 382; **IV:** 192; **Retro. Supp. I:** 91, 217, 218, 235; **Retro. Supp. II:** 93; **Supp. I Part 2:** 647; **Supp. XVI:** 72

Bambara, Toni Cade, **Supp. XI: 1–23**

Bam opgrunt (At the abyss) (Asch), **Supp. XXIII:** 6

Banana Bottom (McKay), **Supp. X:** 132, **139–140**

Bananas (film; Allen), **Supp. XV:** 3, 4

Bancal, Jean, **Supp. I Part 2:** 514

Bancroft, George, **I:** 544; **Supp. I Part 2:** 479; **Supp. XXII:** 33

Band, Millen, **Supp. XVIII:** 238

Bandaged Nude, The (Ryan as Finnegan), **Supp. XVIII:** 233, **235–236**

"Bandages" (Davison), **Supp. XXVI:** 72

Bandbox (Mallon), **Supp. XIX:** 132, 143

Band of Angels (Warren), **IV:** 245, 254–255

Bandung Files (television series), **Supp. XXI:** 170

Bang the Drum Slowly (Harris), **II:** 424–425

Banjo: A Story without a Plot (McKay), **Supp. X:** 132, **138–139**

"Banjo Song, A" (Dunbar), **Supp. II Part 1:** 197

Bank Director's Son, The: A Real and Intensely Interesting Revelation of City Life (Lippard), **Supp. XXIII:** 184

Bankhead, Tallulah, **IV:** 357; **Supp. IV Part 2:** 574

"Banking Potatoes" (Komunyakaa), **Supp. XIII:** 126

"Bank of England Restriction, The" (Adams), **I:** 4

Banks, Carolyn, **Supp. XXVI:** 9

Banks, Joanne Trautmann, **Supp. XIII:** 297

Banks, Russell, **Supp. IX:** 153; **Supp. V: 1–19,** 227; **Supp. X:** 85; **Supp. XI:** 178; **Supp. XII:** 295, 309, 343; **Supp. XX: 90; Supp. XXIV:** 97

"Banned Poem" (Nye), **Supp. XIII:** 282

Bannon, Barbara, **Supp. XI:** 228

"Banyan" (Swenson), **Supp. IV Part 2:** 651, 652

"Baptism" (Olsen). *See* "O Yes" (Olsen)

"Baptism" (Trethewey), **Supp. XXI:** 246

Baptism, The (Baraka), **Supp. II Part 1:** 40, 41–42, 43

Baptism of Desire (Erdrich), **Supp. IV Part 1:** 259

Barabtarlo, Gennady, **Retro. Supp. I:** 278

Baraka, Imamu Amiri (LeRoi Jones), **Retro. Supp. I:** 411; **Retro. Supp. II:** 280; **Supp. I Part 1:** 63; **Supp. II Part 1: 29–63,** 247, 250; **Supp. III Part 1:** 83; **Supp. IV Part 1:** 169, 244, 369; **Supp. VIII:** 295, 329, 330, 332; **Supp. X:** 324, 328; **Supp. XIII:** 94; **Supp. XIV:** 125, 144; **Supp. XXI:** 172, 227, 228; **Supp. XXIII:** 215; **Supp. XXIV:** 34, 183

"Bar at the Andover Inn, The" (Matthews), **Supp. IX:** 168

"Barbados" (Marshall), **Supp. XI:** 281

"Barbara Frietchie" (Whittier), **Supp. I Part 2:** 695–696

Barbarella (film), **Supp. XI:** 293, **307–308**

"Barbarian Status of Women, The" (Veblen), **Supp. I Part 2:** 636–637

Barbarous Coast, The (Macdonald), **Supp. IV Part 2:** 472, 474

Barbary Shore (Mailer), **III:** 27, 28, 30–31, 33, 35, 36, 40, 44; **Retro. Supp. II: 199–200,** 207; **Supp. XIV:** 162

Barber, Charles, **Supp. XXIII:** 125

Barber, David, **Supp. IV Part 2:** 550; **Supp. XII:** 188–189

Barber, Rowland, **Supp. IV Part 2:** 581

Barber, Samuel, **Supp. IV Part 1:** 84

"Barber's Unhappiness, The" (Saunders), **Supp. XIX:** 229

"Barclay of Ury" (Whittier), **Supp. I Part 2:** 693

Barcott, Bruce, **Supp. XVII:** 32

Bard of Savagery, The: Thorstein Veblen and Modern Social Theory (Diggins), **Supp. I Part 2:** 650

"Barefoot Boy, The" (Whittier), **Supp. I Part 2:** 691, 699–700

Barefoot in the Park (Simon), **Supp. IV Part 2:** 575, 578–579, 586, 590

Bare Hills, The (Winters), **Supp. II Part 2:** 786, 788

"Bare Hills, The" (Winters), **Supp. II Part 2:** 790

Barely and Widely (Zukofsky), **Supp. III Part 2:** 627, 628, 635

Barenblat, Rachel, **Supp. XIII:** 274

Barfield, Owen, **III:** 274, 279

"Bargain Lost, The" (Poe), **III:** 411

Barillas, William, **Supp. XIV:** 177

Barillet, Pierre, **Supp. XVI:** 194

Barker, Arthur, **Supp. XIII:** 167

Barker, Clive, **Supp. V:** 142

Barking Dog (Budbill), **Supp. XIX:** 1, 5

"Barking Man" (Bell), **Supp. X:** 9

Barking Man and Other Stories (Bell), **Supp. X:** 9

Barksdale, Richard, **Retro. Supp. I:** 202, 205; **Supp. I Part 1:** 341, 346

Barlow, Joel, **Supp. I Part 1:** 124; **Supp. I Part 2:** 511, 515, 521; **Supp. II Part 1: 65–86,** 268

Barlow, Judith, **Supp. XXI:** 6

Barlow, R. H., **Supp. XXV:** 122

Barlow, Ruth Baldwin (Mrs. Joel Barlow), **Supp. II Part 1:** 69

"B.A.R. Man, The" (Yates), **Supp. XI:** 341

Barnaby Rudge (Dickens), **III:** 421

Barnacle Soup and Other Stories of the West of Ireland (Gallagher and Gray), **Supp. XXIV:** 166, 172, 178

Barnard, Frederick, **Supp. I Part 2:** 684

Barnard, Rita, **Retro. Supp. II:** 324

Barn Blind (Smiley), **Supp. VI: 292–293**

"Barn Burning" (Faulkner), **II:** 72, 73; **Supp. IV Part 2:** 682; **Supp. XX: 174**

Barnes, Djuna, **Supp. III Part 1: 31–46; Supp. IV Part 1:** 79, 80; **Supp. XVI:** 282; **Supp. XXII:** 165, 167

Barnes, Kate, **Supp. XXVI:** 36

Barnes, Kim, **Supp. XVIII:** 293

Barnet, Andrea, **Supp. XXII:** 159, 164

Barnett, Claudia, **Supp. XV:** 323, 330, 334

Barnett, Samuel, **Supp. I Part 1:** 2

Barn Fever (Davison), **Supp. XXVI:** 66, 75–76, 77

"Barn Fever" (Davison), **Supp. XXVI:** 75, 77

Barnhardt, Wilton, **Supp. XXII:** 266

"Barn Owl" (Kooser), **Supp. XIX:** 123

Barnstone, Tony, **Supp. XIII:** 115, 126

Barnstone, Willis, **Supp. I Part 2:** 458

Barnum, P. T., **Supp. I Part 2:** 703

Baroja, Pío, **I:** 478

Baron, Zach, **Supp. XVIII:** 150

"Baroque Comment" (Bogan), **Supp. III Part 1:** 56, 58

"Baroque Sunburst, A" (Clampitt), **Supp. IX:** 49

"Baroque Wall-Fountain in the Villa Sciarra, A" (Wilbur), **Supp. III Part 2:** 553

Barr, Robert, **I:** 409, 424

Barracks Thief, The (Wolff), **Supp. VII:** 344–345

"Barred Owl" (Offutt), **Supp. XIX:** 170

Barren Ground (Glasgow), **II:** 174, 175, 178, 179, 184–185, 186, 187, 188, 189, 191, 192, 193, 194; **Supp. X:** 228

Barrés, Auguste M., **I:** 228

Barresi, Dorothy, **Supp. XV:** 100, 102

Barrett, Amy, **Supp. XVIII:** 136

Barrett, E. B., **Supp. XV:** 309

Barrett, Elizabeth, **Supp. IV Part 2:** 430

Barrett, George, **Supp. IX:** 250

Barrett, Ralph, **Supp. I Part 2:** 462

Barrie, J. M., **Supp. XX: 234**

"Barrie Cooke Painting" (Gallagher), **Supp. XXIV:** 171

Barrier, Rober G., **Supp. XXI:** 48–49

Barrier of a Common Language: An American Looks at Contemporary British Poetry (Gioia), **Supp. XV:** 112, **116–117**

"Barroco: An Essay" (Sobin), **Supp. XVI:** 291

Barron, Jonathan, **Supp. IX:** 299

Barrow, John, **II:** 18

Barrus, Clara, **I:** 220

"Barry" (Biss), **Supp. XXVI:** 47

Barry, Iris, **Supp. XIII:** 170

Barry, Philip, **Retro. Supp. I:** 104; **Supp. IV Part 1:** 83; **Supp. V:** 95

Barstow, Elizabeth Drew. *See* Stoddard, Elizabeth

Bartas, Seigneur du, **IV:** 157

Barth, John, **I: 121–143; Supp. I Part 1:** 100; **Supp. III Part 1:** 217; **Supp. IV Part 1:** 48, 379; **Supp. IX:** 208; **Supp. V:** 39, 40; **Supp. X:** 263, 301, 302, 307; **Supp. XI:** 309; **Supp. XII:** 29, 289, 316; **Supp. XIII:** 41, 101, 104; **Supp. XVII:** 183; **Supp. XVIII:** 136, 140, 141; **Supp. XX: 21; Supp. XXII:** 259, 261; **Supp. XXIII:** 42

Barth, Karl, **III:** 40, 258, 291, 303, 309; **IV:** 225; **Retro. Supp. I:** 325, 326, 327

Barth, Robert C., **Supp. XV:** 169

Barthé, Richmond, **Retro. Supp. II:** 115

Barthelme, Donald, **Supp. IV Part 1: 39–58,** 227; **Supp. V:** 2, 39, 44; **Supp. VIII:** 75, 138; **Supp. X:** 263; **Supp. XI:** 25; **Supp. XII:** 29; **Supp. XIII:** 41, 46; **Supp. XIX:** 235; **Supp. XVI:** 206

Barthelme, Frederick, **Supp. XI: 25–41; Supp. XXI:** 38

Barthelme, Peter, **Supp. XI:** 25

Barthelme, Steven, **Supp. XI:** 25, 27, 37

Barthes, Roland, **Supp. IV Part 1:** 39, 119, 126; **Supp. XIII:** 83; **Supp. XVI:** 285, 294; **Supp. XVII:** 244

Bartholomew and the Oobleck (Geisel), **Supp. XVI:** 104

"Bar Time" (B. Collins), **Supp. XVII:** 245

"Bartleby, the Scrivener; A Story of Wall-Street" (Melville), **III:** 88–89; **Retro. Supp. I:** 255

Bartleby in Manhattan and Other Essays (Hardwick), **Supp. III Part 1:** 204, 210

"Bartleby the Scrivener" (Melville), **Supp. XVIII:** 4

Bartlet, Phebe, **I:** 562

Bartlett, Lee, **Supp. VIII:** 291

Bartlett, Mary Dougherty, **Supp. IV Part 1:** 335

Bartlett, William Irving, **Supp. XXV:** 250–251

Barton, Bruce, **III:** 14; **Retro. Supp. I:** 179

Barton, Priscilla. *See* Morison, Mrs. Samuel Eliot (Priscilla Barton)

Barton, Ralph, **Supp. XVI:** 195

Barton, Rev. William E., **Retro. Supp. I:** 179

Bartov, Omer, **Supp. XVI:** 153–154

Bartram, John, **Supp. I Part 1:** 244

Bartram, William, **II:** 313; **Supp. IX:** 171; **Supp. X:** 223

Barzun, Jacques, **Supp. XIV:** 54

"Basement" (Bambara), **Supp. XI:** 5

Basement Tapes, The (album, Dylan), **Supp. XVIII:** 27, 30, 32

"Base of All Metaphysics, The" (Whitman), **IV:** 348

"Base Stealer, The" (Francis), **Supp. IX:** 82

Bashevis, Isaac. *See* Singer, Isaac Bashevis

Bashir, Antonious, **Supp. XX: 116, 120**

Basil Stories, The (Fitzgerald), **Retro. Supp. I:** 109

Basin and Range (McPhee), **Supp. III Part 1:** 309

"Basin of Eggs, A" (Swenson), **Supp. IV Part 2:** 645

"Basket" (Huddle), **Supp. XXVI:** 150

"Basket, The" (Lowell), **II:** 522

"Basketball and Beefeaters" (McPhee), **Supp. III Part 1:** 296

"Basketball and Poetry: The Two Richies" (Dunn), **Supp. XI:** 140

"Basketball Player" (L. Michaels), **Supp. XVI:** 209

"Basket of Trips"(Strout), **Supp. XXIII:** 283, 285

Baskin, Leonard, **Supp. X:** 58, 71; **Supp. XV:** 348

Bass, George, **Supp. XXII:** 6

Bass, Rick, **Supp. XIV:** 227; **Supp. XVI: 15–29; Supp. XXI:** 40, 45; **Supp. XXVI:** 31, 187

Bassard, Katherine Clay, **Supp. XXII:** 148

Basso, Hamilton, **Retro. Supp. I:** 80

Bastard, The (Caldwell), **I:** 291, 292, 308

"Bastille Day" (Lamott), **Supp. XX: 143**

"Bat, The" (Kenyon), **Supp. VII:** 168

Bat, The (Rinehart and Hopwood), **Supp. XXV:** 195, 200

Bataille, Georges, **Supp. VIII:** 4; **Supp. XII:** 1

"Batard" (London), **II:** 468–469

Batchelor, John Calvin, **Supp. XIX:** 142

Bate, Walter Jackson, **II:** 531; **Supp. XXVI:** 63

"Bateau ivre, Le" (Rimbaud; Berrigan, trans.), **Supp. XXIV:** 40

Bates, Arlo, **Retro. Supp. I:** 35

Bates, Blanche, **Supp. XVI:** 182

Bates, Kathy, **Supp. XIII:** 207

Bates, Lee, **Retro. Supp. II:** 46

Bates, Milton J., **Supp. XII:** 62

Bates, Sylvia Chatfield, **II:** 586

Bateson, Gregory, **Supp. XV:** 146

"Bath, The" (Carver), **Supp. III Part 1:** 144, 145

"Bath, The" (Snyder), **Supp. VIII:** 302

Bathwater Wine (Coleman), **Supp. XI:** 83, 90, **91**

"Batter my heart, three person'd God" (Donne), **Supp. I Part 2:** 726; **Supp. XVII:** 119

"Battle, The" (Simpson), **Supp. IX:** 268–269

Battle Cry (film), **Supp. XX: 246**

Battle Cry (Uris), **Supp. XX: 243, 246, 248–250, 255, 256**

Battlefield Where the Moon Says I Love You, The (Stanford), **Supp. XV:** 345

Battle for the Solomons (Wolfert), **Supp. XXI:** 267

Battle-Ground, The (Glasgow), **II:** 175, 176, 177, 178, 193

"Battle Hymn of the Republic" (Sandburg), **III:** 585

"Battle Hymn of the Republic, The" (Howe), **III:** 505

"Battle Hymn of the Republic, The" (Updike), **Retro. Supp. I:** 324

Battle of Angels (T. Williams), **IV:** 380, 381, 383, 385, 386, 387

"Battle of Aspen, The" (Thompson), **Supp. XXIV:** 286–287

"Battle of Lovell's Pond, The" (Longfellow), **II:** 493

Battle of the Atlantic, The (Morison), **Supp. I Part 2:** 490

"Battle of the Baltic, The" (Campbell), **Supp. I Part 1:** 309

"Battle of the Bunker, The" (Snodgrass), **Supp. VI:** 319–320

"***Battle of the Century!!!, The***" (Goldbarth), **Supp. XII:** 193

Battle of the Little Big Horn, The (Sandoz), **Supp. XXIII:** 146

Battle-Pieces and Aspects of the War (Melville), **II:** 538–539; **III:** 92; **IV:** 350; **Retro. Supp. I:** 257

"Battler, The" (Hemingway), **II:** 248; **Retro. Supp. I:** 175

"Battle That Ended the Century, The" (Lovecraft and Barlow), **Supp. XXV:** 122

Baubles (Wells), **Supp. XXVI:** 275

"Baubles after Bombs" (Peacock), **Supp. XIX:** 200

"Baudelaire" (Schwartz), **Supp. II Part 2:** 663

Baudelaire, Charles, **I:** 58, 63, 384, 389, 420, 569; **II:** 543, 544–545, 552; **III:** 137, 141–142, 143, 409, 417, 418, 421, 428, 448, 466, 474; **IV:** 74, 79, 80, 87, 211, 286; **Retro. Supp. I:** 56, 90; **Retro. Supp. II:** 261, 262, 322, 326; **Supp. I Part 1:** 271; **Supp. III Part 1:** 4, 6, 105; **Supp. XIII:** 77, 284; **Supp. XV:** 165; **Supp. XXI:** 228; **Supp. XXIV:** 152; **Supp. XXVI:** 39

Baudrillard, Jean, **Supp. IV Part 1:** 45

Bauer, Dale, **Retro. Supp. I:** 381

Bauer, Douglas, **Supp. XII:** 290

Baum, L. Frank, **Supp. I Part 2:** 621; **Supp. IV Part 1:** 101, 113; **Supp. XII:** 42

Baumann, Walter, **III:** 478

Bausch, Richard, **Supp. VII: 39–56; Supp. XVII:** 21; **Supp. XXVI:** 13

Bawer, Bruce, **Supp. IX:** 135; **Supp. VIII:** 153; **Supp. X:** 187

Baxter, Charles, **Supp. XII:** 22; **Supp. XIV:** 89, 92; **Supp. XVII: 13–24; Supp. XXIII:** 289

Baxter, John, **Supp. XI:** 302

Baxter, Richard, **III:** 199; **IV:** 151, 153; **Supp. I Part 2:** 683

"Baxter's Procrustes" (Chesnutt), **Supp. XIV:** 76

"Bay City Blues" (Chandler), **Supp. IV Part 1:** 129

Baylies, William, **Supp. I Part 1:** 153

Baym, Nina, **Supp. IV Part 2:** 463; **Supp. X:** 229; **Supp. XVI:** 92; **Supp. XVIII:** 258, 259; **Supp. XXIV:** 28

"Bayou" (Di Piero), **Supp. XIX:** 37

Bayou Folk (Chopin), **Retro. Supp. II:** **64–65**, 73; **Supp. I Part 1:** 200, 216, 218

Baziotes, William, **Supp. XV:** 144

"B.C." (Taggard), **Supp. XXII:** 278

Beach, Anna Hampstead, **Supp. XVII:** 75

Beach, Joseph Warren, **I:** 309, 500; **II:** 27; **III:** 319

Beach, Sylvia, **IV:** 404; **Retro. Supp. I:** 109, 422; **Supp. XXII:** 165

"Beaches in Winter" (Kriegel), **Supp. XXIV:** 220, 225

"Beach Women, The" (Pinsky), **Supp. VI:** 241

"Beaded Pear, The" (Simpson), **Supp. IX:** 276

Beagle, Peter, **Supp. X:** 24

Beam, Jeffrey, **Supp. XII:** 98

Beaman, E. O., **Supp. IV Part 2:** 604

Bean, Michael, **Supp. V:** 203

Bean, Robert Bennett, **Supp. II Part 1:** 170

Bean Eaters, The (Brooks), **Supp. III Part 1:** **79–81**

Be Angry at the Sun (Jeffers), **Supp. II Part 2:** 434

Bean Spasms (Berrigan, Padgett, and Brainard), **Supp. XXIV:** 41–42

"Beanstalk Country, The" (T. Williams), **IV:** 383

Bean Trees, The (Kingsolver), **Supp. VII:** 197, 199–201, 202, 207, 209

"Bear" (Hogan), **Supp. IV Part 1:** 412

Bear, The (Faulkner), **Supp. VIII:** 184

"Bear, The" (Faulkner), **II:** 71–72, 73, 228; **IV:** 203; **Supp. IV Part 2:** 434; **Supp. IX:** 95; **Supp. X:** 30; **Supp. XIV:** 32; **Supp. XXI:** 37

"Bear, The" (Kinnell), **Supp. III Part 1:** 244

"Bear, The" (Momaday), **Supp. IV Part 2:** 480, 487

Bear and His Daughter: Stories (Stone), **Supp. V:** 295, 308

Beard, Charles, **I:** 214; **IV:** 429; **Supp. I Part 2:** 481, 490, 492, 632, 640, 643, 647

Beard, James, **I:** 341; **Supp. XVII:** 89, 90

Beard, Mary, **Supp. I Part 2:** 481

"Bearded Oaks" (Warren), **IV:** 240

Bearden, Romare, **Retro. Supp. I:** 209; **Supp. VIII:** 337, 342; **Supp. XXI:** 249

"Beard of Bees, A" (X. J. Kennedy), **Supp. XV:** 171

Beardon, Romare, **Supp. XV:** 144

"Beards, The" (Lethem), **Supp. XVIII:** 148

Beardsley, Aubrey, **II:** 56; **IV:** 77

Beaser, Robert, **Supp. XV:** 259

"Beast" (Swenson), **Supp. IV Part 2:** 639

"Beast & Burden, The: Seven Improvisations" (Komunyakaa), **Supp. XIII:** 120, 121

Beast God Forgot to Invent, The (Harrison), **Supp. VIII:** 37, 46, **51–52**

Beast in Me, The (Thurber), **Supp. I Part 2:** 615

"Beast in the Jungle, The" (H. James), **I:** 570; **II:** 335; **Retro. Supp. I:** 235; **Supp. V:** 103–104; **Supp. XXVI:** 141

Beast in View (Rukeyser), **Supp. VI:** 272, 273, 279, 280

Beasts of Bethlehem, The (X. J. Kennedy), **Supp. XV:** 163

"Beat! Beat! Drums!" (Whitman), **III:** 585

Beat Down to Your Soul: What Was the Beat Generation? (Charters, ed.), **Supp. XIV:** 152

"Beatific Effigies" (Bronk), **Supp. XXI:** 31

Beaton, Cecil, **Supp. XVI:** 191

"Beatrice Palmato" (Wharton), **Retro. Supp. I:** 379

Beats, The (Krim, ed.), **Supp. XV:** 338

Beattie, Ann, **Supp. V: 21–37; Supp. XI:** 26; **Supp. XII:** 80, 139, 294; **Supp. XXI:** 118; **Supp. XXIII:** 289

Beattie, L. Elisabeth, **Supp. XX: 164, 165**

Beatty, General Sam, **I:** 193

Beaty, Jerome, **Supp. IV Part 1:** 331

"Beau Monde of Mrs. Bridge, The" (Connell), **Supp. XIV:** 88, 89

Beaumont, Francis, **Supp. I Part 2:** 422

"Beauties of Santa Cruz, The" (Freneau), **Supp. II Part 1:** 260

Beautiful and Damned, The (Fitzgerald), **II:** 88, 89–91, 93, 263; **Retro. Supp. I: 103–105**, 105, 106, 110; **Supp. IX:** 56, 57

Beautiful Changes, The (Wilbur), **Supp. III Part 2:** 544–550

"Beautiful Changes, The" (Wilbur), **Supp. III Part 2:** 549, 550

Beautiful Child (Silver), **Supp. XXIV: 273–274**

"Beautiful Child, A" (Capote), **Supp. III Part 1:** 113, 125

"Beautiful & Cruel" (Cisneros), **Supp. VII:** 63, 67

"Beautiful Gestures, The" (Huddle), **Supp. XXVI:** 154

"Beautiful Wall, Machu Picchu, The" (Bronk), **Supp. XXI:** 31, 32

"Beautiful Woman Who Sings, The" (Gunn Allen), **Supp. IV Part 1:** 326

"Beauty" (Emerson), **II:** 2, 5

"Beauty" (Sanders), **Supp. XVI:** 277

"Beauty" (Wylie), **Supp. I Part 2:** 710

"Beauty and the Beast" (Dove), **Supp. IV Part 1:** 245

"Beauty and the Beast" (fairy tale), **IV:** 266; **Supp. X:** 88

"Beauty and the Shoe Sluts" (Karr), **Supp. XI:** 250

Beauty of the Husband, The: A Fictional Essay in Twenty-Nine Tangos (Carson), **Supp. XII: 113–114**

Beauty Queen, The (P. N. Warren), **Supp. XX: 268–269**

Beauty's Punishment (Rice), **Supp. VII:** 301

Beauty's Release: The Continued Erotic Adventures of Sleeping Beauty (Rice), **Supp. VII:** 301

Beauvoir, Simone de, **IV:** 477; **Supp. I Part 1:** 51; **Supp. III Part 1:** 200–201, 208; **Supp. IV Part 1:** 360; **Supp. IX:** 4

Beaver Men: Spearheads of Empire (Sandoz), **Supp. XXIV:** 244, **246–247**

"Be Careful" (Zach; Everwine, trans.), **Supp. XV:** 86

Be Careful How You Live (Lacy), **Supp. XV:** 203–204

"Because I could not stop for Death—" (Dickinson), **Retro. Supp. I: 38–40**, 41, 43, 44

"Because It Happened" (Goldbarth), **Supp. XII:** 192

"Because of Libraries We Can Say These Things" (Nye), **Supp. XIII:** 283

"Because of the Waters of the Flood" (Helprin), **Supp. XXV:** 85

"Because the Body Is a Flower"(Crooker), **Supp. XXIII:** 55

"Because You Mentioned the Spiritual Life" (Dunn), **Supp. XI:** 154

Bech: A Book (Updike), **IV:** 214; **Retro. Supp. I:** 329, 335

Bechdel, Alison, **Supp. XXV: 1–15**

Beck, Dave, **I:** 493

Beck, Ervin, **Supp. XXIII:** 94, 95

Beck, Jack, **Supp. IV Part 2:** 560

Beck, Nicholas, **Supp. XVIII:** 252

Beck, Stefan, **Supp. XXII:** 268

Becker, Carl, **Supp. I Part 2:** 492, 493

Becker, Paula. *See* Modersohn, Mrs. Otto (Paula Becker)

Beckett, Samuel, **I:** 71, 91, 142, 298, 461; **III:** 387; **IV:** 95; **Retro. Supp. I:** 206; **Supp. IV Part 1:** 297, 368–369; **Supp. IV Part 2:** 424; **Supp. V:** 23, 53; **Supp. XI:** 104; **Supp. XII:** 21, 150–151; **Supp. XIII:** 74; **Supp. XIV:** 239; **Supp. XVII:** 185; **Supp. XX:** 17; **Supp. XXI:** 18; **Supp. XXII:** 263

Beckett, Tom, **Supp. IV Part 2:** 419

Beckford, William, **I:** 204

Beckonings (Brooks), **Supp. III Part 1:** 85

"Becky" (Toomer), **Supp. III Part 2:** 481, 483; **Supp. IX:** 312

Becky and Her Friends (Hinojosa), **Supp. XIX: 108–109**

Becoming a Man: Half a Life Story (Monette), **Supp. X:** 146, 147, 149, 151, 152, **155–157**

"Becoming a Meadow" (Doty), **Supp. XI:** 124–125

"Becoming and Breaking: Poet and Poem" (Ríos), **Supp. IV Part 2:** 539

Becoming Canonical in American Poetry (Morris), **Retro. Supp. I:** 40

Becoming Light: New and Selected Poems (Jong), **Supp. V:** 115

Bécquer, Gustavo Adolfo, **Supp. XIII:** 312

"Bed, The" (Dixon), **Supp. XII:** 154

Beddoes, Thomas Lovell, **III:** 469; **Retro. Supp. I:** 285
Bedichek, Roy, **Supp. V:** 225
Bedient, Calvin, **Supp. IX:** 298; **Supp. XII:** 98
"Bed in the Sky, The" (Snyder), **Supp. VIII:** 300
Bednarik, Joseph, **Supp. VIII:** 39
"Bedrock" (Proulx), **Supp. VII:** 253
"Bed Time" (Davison), **Supp. XXVI:** 72
"Bee, The" (Lanier), **Supp. I Part 1:** 364
Beecher, Catharine, **Supp. I Part 2:** 581, 582–583, 584, 586, 588, 589, 591, 599; **Supp. X:** 103; **Supp. XI:** 193
Beecher, Charles, **Supp. I Part 2:** 588, 589
Beecher, Edward, **Supp. I Part 2:** 581, 582, 583, 584, 588, 591
Beecher, Harriet. *See* Stowe, Harriet Beecher
Beecher, Henry Ward, **II:** 275; **Supp. I Part 2:** 581; **Supp. XI:** 193; **Supp. XVIII:** 4
Beecher, Lyman, **Supp. I Part 2:** 580–581, 582, 583, 587, 588, 599; **Supp. XI:** 193
Beecher, Mrs. Lyman (Roxanna Foote), **Supp. I Part 2:** 580–581, 582, 588, 599
Beeching, Jack, **Supp. X:** 114, 117, 118, 123, 125, 126
"Beehive" (Toomer), **Supp. IX:** 317
"Bee Hunt, The" (Irving), **II:** 313
"Beekeeper's Daughter, The" (Plath), **Retro. Supp. II:** 246–247
"Bee Meeting, The" (Plath), **Retro. Supp. II:** 254–255
Bee Poems (Plath), **Retro. Supp. II:** 254–255
Beer, John, **Supp. XVII:** 239
Beer, Thomas, **I:** 405
Beerbohm, Max, **III:** 472; **IV:** 436; **Supp. I Part 2:** 714
"Beer Bottle" (Kooser), **Supp. XIX:** 117
"Beer in the Sergeant Major's Hat, or The Sun Also Sneezes" (Chandler), **Supp. IV Part 1:** 121
Beers, Henry A., **Supp. XX: 68**
"Bees Bees Bees" (J. Scott), **Supp. XVII:** 188, 190
Beethoven, Ludwig van, **II:** 536; **III:** 118; **IV:** 274, 358; **Supp. I Part 1:** 363; **Supp. VIII:** 103
Beet Queen, The (Erdrich), **Supp. IV Part 1:** 259, 260, 264–265, 266, 273, 274, 275
Befo' de War: Echoes in Negro Dialect (Gordon), **Supp. II Part 1:** 201
"Before" (Goldbarth), **Supp. XII:** 175
"Before" (Snyder), **Supp. VIII:** 301
Before Adam (London), **II:** 466
Before Breakfast (O'Neill), **Supp. XXII:** 22
Before Disaster (Winters), **Supp. II Part 2:** 786, 800
"Before Disaster" (Winters), **Supp. II Part 2:** 801, 815
"Before I Knocked" (D. Thomas), **III:** 534

Beforelife, The (F. Wright), **Supp. XVII:** 240, 245–246
"Before March" (MacLeish), **III:** 15
Before My Life Began (Neugeboren), **Supp. XVI: 224–225**
"Before the Altar" (Lowell), **II:** 516
"Before the Birth of one of her children" (Bradstreet), **Supp. I Part 1:** 118
Before the Gringo Came (Atherton), **Supp. XXIV:** 22
"Before the Sky Darkens" (Dunn), **Supp. XI:** 155
"Begat" (Sexton), **Supp. II Part 2: 693**
Beget, Philippe, **Supp. XXIII:** 74
Beggarman, Thief (Shaw), **Supp. XIX:** 251–252
Beggar on Horseback (Kaufman and Connelly), **III:** 394
"Beggar Said So, The" (Singer), **IV:** 12
Beggars in the House of Plenty (Shanley), **Supp. XIV:** 316, **327–328**
Beggar's Opera, The (Gay), **Supp. I Part 2:** 523
Begiebing, Robert, **Retro. Supp. II:** 210
Begin Again (Paley), **Supp. VI:** 221
Beginners (Carver), **Supp. XXIV:** 177
"Beginning and the End, The" (Jeffers), **Supp. II Part 2:** 420–421, 424
"Beginning of Decadence, The" (Jeffers), **Supp. II Part 2:** 420
"Beginning of Enthusiasm, The" (Salinas), **Supp. XIII:** 327–328
Beginning of Wisdom, The (Benét), **I:** 358; **Supp. XI:** 44
"Beginnings of Sorrow, The"(P. Benedict), **Supp. XXIII:** 48
Be Glad You're Neurotic (Bisch), **Supp. I Part 2:** 608
"Begotten of the Spleen" (Simic), **Supp. VIII:** 277
"Behaving Like a Jew" (Stern), **Supp. IX: 290–291,** 294
"Behavior" (Emerson), **II:** 2, 4
Behavior of Titans, The (Merton), **Supp. VIII:** 201
Behind a Mask (Alcott), **Supp. I Part 1:** 36–37, 43–44
"Behind a Wall" (Lowell), **II:** 516
Behind the Movie Camera (radio show), **Supp. XV:** 147
"Behold the Key" (Malamud), **Supp. I Part 2:** 437
Behrendt, Stephen, **Supp. X:** 204
Behrman, S. N., **Supp. V:** 95
Beichman, Arnold, **Supp. XXV:** 254, 258, 264
Beidler, Peter G., **Supp. IV Part 2:** 557
Beidler, Philip D., **Supp. XII:** 69
Beige Dolorosa (Harrison), **Supp. VIII:** 40, 51
Beiles, Sinclair, **Supp. XII:** 129
Beiliss, Mendel, **Supp. I Part 2:** 427, 446, 447, 448
"Being a Constellation" (A. Finch), **Supp. XVII:** 72
"Being a Lutheran Boy-God in Minnesota" (R. Bly), **Supp. IV Part 1:** 59, 67
Being and Race (C. Johnson), **Supp. VI:** 193, 199

Being and Time (Heidegger), **Supp. VIII:** 9
Being Busted (Fiedler), **Supp. XIII:** 95, 102, 104
Being Geniuses Together: 1920–1930 (Boyle), **Supp. XXIV:** 63, 64
Being John Malkovich (Kaufman), **Supp. XV:** 16
Being Perfect (Quindlen), **Supp. XVII:** 167, 179
Being There (Kosinski), **Supp. VII:** 215, 216, 222–223
Beiswanger, George, **Retro. Supp. II:** 220
Beka Lamb (Edgell), **Supp. XXIII:** 83, 85, **86–88,** 93–94, 95
Belasco, David, **Supp. XVI:** 182; **Supp. XXI:** 151
Bel Canto (Patchett), **Supp. XII:** 307, 310, **320–322**
Belchamber (Sturgis), **Supp. XX: 227, 233, 238–240**
"Beleaguered City, The" (Longfellow), **II:** 498
Belfry of Bruges, The, and Other Poems (Longfellow), **II:** 489; **Retro. Supp. II:** 157, 168
"Belief" (Levine), **Supp. V:** 186, 190
"Belief in the Self Abandoned, The" (Bronk), **Supp. XXI:** 30
"Beliefs of Writers, The" (Doctorow), **Supp. IV Part 1:** 235–236
Believeniks! (Lethem and Sorrentino), **Supp. XVIII:** 148–149
Believers (C. Baxter), **Supp. XVII:** 20–21, 22
"Believers" (C. Baxter), **Supp. XVII:** 21
"Believers, The/Los Creyentes" (Kingsolver), **Supp. VII:** 208
Belinda (Rice), **Supp. VII:** 301–302
"Belinda's Petition" (Dove), **Supp. IV Part 1:** 245
"Belita" (Ríos), **Supp. IV Part 2:** 541
Belitt, Ben, **Supp. XII:** 260
Bell, Archibald, **Supp. XX: 284, 285**
Bell, Bernard, **Supp. XXII:** 182
Bell, Clive, **IV:** 87
Bell, Daniel, **Supp. I Part 2:** 648
Bell, George Kennedy Allen, **Retro. Supp. I:** 65
Bell, Madison Smartt, **Supp. X: 1–20; Supp. XIX:** 58–59, 60–61; **Supp. XVII:** 236; **Supp. XXI:** 48; **Supp. XXIII:** 43
Bell, Marvin, **Supp. IX:** 152; **Supp. V:** 337, 339; **Supp. XI:** 316; **Supp. XXIV:** 165
Bell, Michael, **Retro. Supp. II:** 139
Bell, Pearl K., **Supp. XI:** 233; **Supp. XXV:** 253
Bell, Quentin, **Supp. I Part 2:** 636
Bell, Whitfield J., Jr., **II:** 123
Bellafante, Gina, **Supp. VIII:** 85
Bellamy, Edward, **II:** 276; **Supp. I Part 2:** 641; **Supp. XI:** 200, 203
Bellarosa Connection, The (Bellow), **Retro. Supp. II:** 31, 32
"Belle Dollinger" (Masters), **Supp. I Part 2:** 463
Belleforest, François de, **IV:** 370

"Belle Zoraïde, La" (Chopin), **Supp. I Part 1:** 215–216

Bell in the Fog and Other Stories, The (Atherton), **Supp. XXIV:** 23

Bell Jar, The (Plath), **Retro. Supp. II:** 242, **249–250; Supp. I Part 2:** 526, 527, 529, 531–536, 539, 540, 541, 542, 544

Belloc, Hilary, **III:** 176; **IV:** 432

"Bellocq" (Trethewey), **Supp. XXI:** 253

Bellocq, E. J., **Supp. XXI:** 246, 251

Bellocq's Ophelia (Trethewey), **Supp. XXI:** 243, 246, **251–254**

"Bellocq's Ophelia" (Trethewey), **Supp. XXI:** 254

Bellow, Saul, **I:** 113, 138–139, **144–166,** 375, 517; **III:** 579; **III:** 40; **IV:** 3, 19, 217, 340; **Retro. Supp. II: 19–36,** 118, 279, 307, 324; **Supp. I Part 2:** 428, 451; **Supp. II Part 1:** 109; **Supp. IV Part 1:** 30; **Supp. IX:** 212, 227; **Supp. V:** 258; **Supp. VIII:** 98, 176, 234, 236–237, 245; **Supp. XI:** 64, 233; **Supp. XII:** 159, 165, 170, 310; **Supp. XIII:** 106; **Supp. XIX:** 157, 158, 261; **Supp. XV:** 143; **Supp. XVI:** 208; **Supp. XVIII:** 90; **Supp. XX: 244; Supp. XXII:** 268; **Supp. XXIII:** 166; **Supp. XXV:** 79

Bellows, George, **Supp. XV:** 295

"Bells, The" (Poe), **III:** 593; **Retro. Supp. II:** 266; **Supp. I Part 2:** 388

"Bells, The" (Sexton), **Supp. II Part 2:** 673

"Bells for John Whiteside's Daughter" (Ransom), **III:** 490

"Bells of Lynn, The" (Longfellow), **II:** 498

"Bells of San Blas, The" (Longfellow), **II:** 490–491, 493, 498

"Bell Tower, The" (Melville), **III:** 91

"Belly, The" (Dobyns), **Supp. XIII:** 87

'Bel of Prairie Eden (Lippard), **Supp. XXIII:** 178, 186

"Belonging" (Pickering), **Supp. XXI:** 202

"Belonging Kind, The" (W. Gibson and J. Shirley), **Supp. XVI:** 123

Beloved (Morrison), **Supp. III Part 1:** 364, 372–379; **Supp. IV Part 1:** 13–14; **Supp. V:** 259; **Supp. VIII:** 343; **Supp. XIII:** 60; **Supp. XXII:** 78, 109; **Supp. XXIV:** 186

Beloved, The (Gibran), **Supp. XX: 125**

"Beloved, The" (Halliday), **Supp. XIX:** 92

Beloved Lady: A History of Jane Addams' Ideas on Reform and Peace (Farrell), **Supp. I Part 1:** 24

Beloved Stranger, The (Bynner), **Supp. XV:** 44, 50

Bemorse, John, **Supp. XX: 62**

Benchley, Robert, **I:** 48, 482; **II:** 435; **III:** 53; **Supp. IX:** 190, 195, 204

Benda, W. T., **Retro. Supp. I:** 13

Bender, Aimee, **Supp. XXII:** 49

Bending of a Twig, The (Coke), **Supp. XX: 235**

Bend Sinister (Nabokov), **III:** 253–254; **Retro. Supp. I:** 265, 266, 270

"Beneath the Sidewalk" (Dunn), **Supp. XI:** 145

"Beneath the Smooth Skin of America" (Sanders), **Supp. XVI:** 275

Benedict, Elizabeth, **Supp. XVIII:** 289

Benedict, Laura, **Supp. XXIII:** 35, 36, 49

Benedict, Pinckney, **Supp. XXIII: 35–50**

Benedict, Ruth, **Supp. IX:** 229

Benefactor, The (Sontag), **Supp. III Part 2:** 451, 455, 468, 469

"Benefit Performance" (Malamud), **Supp. I Part 2:** 431

Benét, Laura, **Supp. XI:** 44

Benét, Rosemary, **Supp. XI:** 44, 51; **Supp. XXV:** 201

Benét, Stephen Vincent, **I:** 358; **II:** 177; **III:** 22; **IV:** 129; **Supp. XI: 43–61**

Benét, William Rose, **II:** 530; **Retro. Supp. I:** 108; **Supp. I Part 2:** 709; **Supp. XI:** 43, 44; **Supp. XIV:** 119, 122, 129

Ben Franklin's Wit and Wisdom (Franklin), **II:** 111

Ben-Gurion, David, **Supp. XX: 243**

Ben-Hur (film), **Supp. IV Part 2:** 683

Benigna Machiavelli (Gilman), **Supp. XI:** 201, 208

Benitez, R. Michael, **Retro. Supp. II:** 264

Benito Cereno (Lowell), **II:** 546; **Retro. Supp. II:** 181

"Benito Cereno" (Melville), **III:** 91; **Retro. Supp. I:** 255; **Retro. Supp. II:** 188; **Supp. XVII:** 185

Benito's Dream Bottle (Nye), **Supp. XIII:** 278

"Bénitou's Slave, The" (Chopin), **Retro. Supp. II:** 64

Benjamin, Walter, **Supp. IX:** 133; **Supp. XVI:** 290, 291; **Supp. XXIII:** 28, 29, 30, 31

Benjamin Franklin (Van Doren), **Supp. I Part 2:** 486

"Benjamin Pantier" (Masters), **Supp. I Part 2:** 461

Bennett, Anne Virginia, **II:** 184

Bennett, Arnold, **I:** 103; **II:** 337; **Supp. XVI:** 190

Bennett, Elizabeth, **Supp. VIII:** 58

Bennett, Patrick, **Supp. V:** 225

Bennett, Paula, **Retro. Supp. I:** 29, 33, 42; **Supp. XX: 286**

Bennett, Reginald, **Supp. XXII:** 218

Bennett, William, **Supp. VIII:** 245

Benson, A. C., **Supp. XX: 238**

Benson, Arthur, **Supp. XX: 233**

Benson, E. F., **Supp. XX: 229**

Benson, Heidi, **Supp. XVIII:** 136

Benson, Jackson J., **Supp. IV Part 2:** 613

Benson, Martin, **Supp. XVIII:** 38

Benstock, Shari, **Retro. Supp. I:** 361, 368, 371, 382; **Supp. XX: 240**

Bentham, Jeremy, **I:** 279; **Supp. I Part 2:** 635

Bentley, Anna, **Supp. XXI:** 5

Bentley, Arthur, **Supp. XXI:** 4, 5

Bentley, Eric R., **IV:** 396

Bentley, Nelson, **Supp. IX:** 324

Bentley, Richard, **III:** 79, 86

Benton, Robert, **Supp. IV Part 1:** 236

"Bent Tones" (Wright), **Supp. XV:** 346

Benveniste, Emile, **Supp. XVI:** 292

Benzel, Jan, **Supp. XVI:** 112

Beowulf, **Supp. II Part 1:** 6; **Supp. XVII:** 70, 73

Beran, Carol, **Supp. XIII:** 25

"Berck-Plage" (Plath), **Retro. Supp. II:** 253–254

Bercovitch, Sacvan, **Retro. Supp. I:** 408; **Retro. Supp. II:** 325, 330; **Supp. I Part 1:** 99; **Supp. I Part 2:** 659

Berdyaev, Nikolai, **I:** 494; **III:** 292

"Bereaved Apartments" (Kingsolver), **Supp. VII:** 203

"Bereavement in their death to feel" (Dickinson), **Retro. Supp. I:** 43, 44

"Berenice" (Poe), **III:** 415, 416, 425; **Retro. Supp. II:** 270

Bérénice (Racine), **II:** 573

Berenson, Bernard, **Retro. Supp. I:** 381; **Supp. IV Part 1:** 314; **Supp. XIV:** 335, 336, 337; **Supp. XVII:** 99; **Supp. XXI:** 5

Berenson, Mary Smith, **Supp. XXI:** 4, 5, 6

Berg, James, **Supp. XIV:** 157, 159

Berg, Stephen, **Supp. IV Part 1:** 60

Berger, Alan, **Supp. XVII:** 39

Berger, Charles, **Retro. Supp. I:** 311

Berger, John, **Supp. XVI:** 284; **Supp. XXIII:** 167, 168–169; **Supp. XXIV:** 94

Berger, Roger, **Supp. XIII:** 237

Berger, Thomas, **III:** 258; **Supp. XII:** 171

Berghash, Rachel, **Supp. XXIV:** 172

Bergman, Ingmar, **I:** 291; **Supp. XV:** 7, 8, 12

Bergson, Henri, **I:** 224; **II:** 163, 165, 166, 359; **III:** 8, 9, 488, 619; **IV:** 86, 122, 466, 467; **Retro. Supp. I:** 55, 57, 80; **Supp. IV Part 1:** 42; **Supp. XXII:** 158

Berkeley, Anthony, **Supp. IV Part 1:** 341

Berkeley, George, **II:** 10, 349, 357, 480, 554

Berkman, Alexander, **Supp. XXIII:** 161; **Supp. XXV:** 19

Berkman, Leonard, **Supp. XV:** 321

Berkowitz, Gerald, **Supp. IV Part 2:** 590

Berkson, Bill, **Supp. XXIII:** 217, 218

Berlin, Isaiah, **Supp. XXII:** 258

Berlin Alexanderplatz (Döblin), **Supp. XV:** 137

Berlin Stories (Isherwood), **Supp. IV Part 1:** 82; **Supp. XIV:** 155, 156, 161, 162, 164, 165

Berlioz, Hector, **Supp. XV:** 33

Berlyne, Daniel E., **Supp. I Part 2:** 672

Berman, Alexander, **Supp. XVII:** 103

Berman, Carolyn Vellenga, **Supp. XXII:** 147

Bernard Clare (Farrell), **II:** 38, 39

Bernardin, Susan, **Supp. XXVI:** 111

Bernard of Clairvaux, Saint, **I:** 22; **II:** 538

Bernays, Thekla, **Retro. Supp. II:** 65

Berne, Suzanne, **Supp. XII:** 320

Berne, Victoria (pseudonym). *See* Fisher, M. F. K.

Berneis, Peter, **IV:** 383
Bernhard, Brendan, **Supp. XIV:** 163
Bernhard, Thomas, **Supp. XX: 91**
Bernhardt, Sarah, **I:** 484; **Retro. Supp. I:** 377
Bernice (Glaspell), **Supp. III Part 1:** 179
"Bernice Bobs Her Hair" (Fitzgerald), **II:** 88; **Retro. Supp. I:** 103
Bernstein, Aline, **IV:** 455, 456
Bernstein, Andrea, **Supp. IX:** 146
Bernstein, Carl, **Supp. XXIV:** 293
Bernstein, Charles, **Supp. IV Part 2:** 421, 426; **Supp. XXIV:** 40, 41, 45–46
Bernstein, Elizabeth, **Supp. XII:** 318
Bernstein, Leonard, **I:** 28; **Supp. I Part 1:** 288, 289; **Supp. IV Part 1:** 83, 84
Bernstein, Melvin, **Supp. XIV:** 41, 46
Bernstein, Michael André, **Retro. Supp. I:** 427
Bernstein, Richard, **Supp. IX:** 253, 262; **Supp. XII:** 113; **Supp. XIV:** 33; **Supp. XXII:** 261
Berrett, Jesse, **Supp. XIII:** 241, 242
Berrigan, Ted, **Supp. XIV:** 150; **Supp. XXII:** 224, 225, 228, 231; **Supp. XXIII:** 218, 221; **Supp. XXIV: 33–47**
Berroa y Canelo, Quiterio, **Supp. XXI:** 104
"Berry" (Hughes), **Supp. I Part 1:** 329, 330
Berry, Eleanor, **Supp. XXIII:** 246
Berry, Faith, **Retro. Supp. I:** 194, 201
Berry, Walter, **IV:** 313–314, 326
Berry, Wendell, **Supp. VIII:** 304; **Supp. X: 21–39; Supp. XII:** 202; **Supp. XIII:** 1–2; **Supp. XIV:** 179; **Supp. XVI:** 39, 56; **Supp. XVIII:** 192; **Supp. XXI:** 90
"Berry Feast, A" (Snyder), **Supp. VIII:** 289, 297
Berryman, John, **I: 167–189,** 405, 441–442, 521; **II:** 554; **III:** 273; **IV:** 138, 430; **Retro. Supp. I:** 430; **Retro. Supp. II:** 175, 178; **Supp. I Part 2:** 546; **Supp. II Part 1:** 109; **Supp. III Part 2:** 541, 561, 595, 596, 603; **Supp. IV Part 2:** 620, 639; **Supp. IX:** 152; **Supp. V:** 179–180, 337; **Supp. XI:** 240; **Supp. XV:** 93; **Supp. XVII:** 111; **Supp. XXII:** 83
Berryman, Mrs. John, **I:** 168–169
Berryman's Sonnets (Berryman), **I:** 168, 175–178
"Berry Territory" (Snyder), **Supp. VIII:** 304
Berthoff, Warner, **Supp. I Part 1:** 133
Berthoff, Werner, **Supp. XXVI:** 23
Bertolucci, Bernardo, **Supp. IV Part 1:** 94
"Bertrand Hume" (Masters), **Supp. I Part 2:** 463–464
Besco, Glenn, **Supp. XXIII:** 125
Bessie, Alvah C., **Supp. XXVI:** 28
"Best, the Most, The" (Carruth), **Supp. XVI:** 59
Best American Essays 1987, The (G. Talese and R. Atwan, eds.), **Supp. XVI:** 273
Best American Essays 1988, The (Dillard, ed.), **Supp. VIII:** 272

Best American Essays 1989, The (Wolff, ed.), **Supp. XVII:** 208
Best American Essays 1993, The (J. Epstein, ed.), **Supp. XVI:** 275
Best American Essays 1997, The (Frazier, ed.), **Supp. VIII:** 272; **Supp. XVII:** 207
Best American Essays 1999, The (E. Hoagland and R. Atwan, eds.), **Supp. XVI:** 277
Best American Essays 2008, The, **Supp. XXIV:** 230
Best American Essays 2009, The, **Supp. XXIV:** 230
Best American Essays for College Students, The (R. Atwan, ed.), **Supp. XVI:** 273
Best American Fantasy, 2010 (Brockmeier, ed.), **Supp. XXII:** 49–50
Best American New Voices 2001 (C. Baxter, ed.), **Supp. XVII:** 22
Best American Poetry, The: 1988 (Ashbery, ed.), **Supp. III Part 1:** 26
Best American Poetry 2000, The (Dove and Lehman, eds.), **Supp. XXI:** 246
Best American Poetry 2006, The (Collins, ed.), **Supp. XXI:** 54
Best American Short Stories, **I:**174; **II:** 587; **III:** 443; **Supp. IV Part 1:** 102, 315; **Supp. IX:** 114; **Supp. X:** 301
Best American Short Stories, 1915–1050, The, **Supp. IX:** 4
Best American Short Stories 1965, The (Foley, ed.), **Supp. XVI:** 225
Best American Short Stories 1979, The, **Supp. XXIII:** 290
Best American Short Stories 1982, The (Gardner, ed.), **Supp. XVII:** 16
Best American Short Stories 1983, The (A. Tyler, ed.), **Supp. XVI:** 37
Best American Short Stories 1986, The (Carver, ed.), **Supp. XVII:** 17
Best American Short Stories 1988, The (Helprin, ed.), **Supp. XVI:** 16
Best American Short Stories 1989, The (Atwood, ed.), **Supp. XVII:** 18; **Supp. XXI:** 39, 42
Best American Short Stories 1991, The (Adams and Kenison, eds.), **Supp. XVI:** 256
Best American Short Stories 1996, The, **Supp. XXIII:** 295
Best American Short Stories 1997, **Supp. XXII:** 75
Best American Short Stories 2001, The (Kenison and Kingsover, eds.), **Supp. XVI:** 24
Best American Short Stories 2007, The, **Supp. XXIII:** 290
Best American Short Stories of 1942, The, **Supp. V:** 316
Best American Short Stories of 1944, The, **Supp. IX:** 119
Best American Short Stories of the Century (Updike, ed.), **Supp. X:** 163
Best American Short Stories of the Eighties, The (Ravenal, ed.), **Supp. IV Part 1:** 93
Best American Sports Writing of the Century, The (Halberstam, ed.), **Supp.**

XVII: 204
"Best China Saucer, The" (Jewett), **Retro. Supp. II:** 145–146
Best Creative Nonfiction, Vol. 1, The (Gutkind, ed.), **Supp. XXVI:** 53
Best Creative Nonfiction, Vol. 2, The (Gutkind, ed.), **Supp. XXIV:** 230
Bester, Alfred, **Supp. XVI:** 123
Best Hour of the Night, The (Simpson), **Supp. IX: 277–279**
Bestiaire, Le (Apollinaire), **IV:** 80
Bestiary, A (Wilbur), **Supp. III Part 2:** 552
"Bestiary for the Fingers of My Right Hand" (Simic), **Supp. VIII:** 274, 275
Best Man, The: A Play About Politics (Vidal), **Supp. IV Part 2:** 683
Best Mystery Stories (Wells, ed.), **Supp. XXVI:** 277
"Best of Everything, The" (Yates), **Supp. XI:** 341
Best of Pickering, The (Pickering), **Supp. XXI:** 192, 198
Best of Plimpton (Plimpton), **Supp. XVI:** 238, 239, 240
Beston, Henry, **Supp. XXVI: 31–44**
Best Short Plays, The (Mayorga), **IV:** 381
Best Short Stories, The (O'Brien, ed.), **I:** 289
Best Short Stories by Negro Writers, The (Hughes, ed.), **Supp. I Part 1:** 345
Best Short Stories of 1926, The (O'Brien, ed.), **Supp. XVIII:** 279
Best Short Stories of 1934 (O'Brien, ed.), **Supp. XVIII:** 227
Best Short Stories of 1938 (O'Brien, ed.), **Supp. XIX:** 256; **Supp. XX:** 34
Best That Ever Did It, The (Lacy), **Supp. XV:** 201–202
Best Times, The: An Informal Memoir (Dos Passos), **I:** 475, 482
Best Words, Best Order: Essays on Poetry (Dobyns), **Supp. XIII:** 74, **76–78,** 87
Best Years of Our Lives, The (film; Wyler), **Supp. XV:** 195
"BETANCOURT" (Baraka), **Supp. II Part 1:** 33, 34
Bête humaine, La (Zola), **III:** 316, 318
"Bethe" (Hellman), **Supp. I Part 1:** 293
Bethea, David, **Supp. VIII:** 27
Bethel Merriday (Lewis), **II:** 455
Bethke, Bruce, **Supp. XVI:** 121
Bethlehem in Broad Daylight (Doty), **Supp. XI:** 121, **122–123**
Bethune, Jane, **Supp. XXVI:** 240, 245
Bethune, Mary McLeod, **Retro. Supp. I:** 197; **Supp. I Part 1:** 333
Bethurum, Dorothy, **IV:** 121
"Betrayal" (Lanier), **Supp. I Part 1:** 364
"Betrothed" (Bogan), **Supp. III Part 1:** 49–51
Bettelheim, Bruno, **Supp. I Part 2:** 622; **Supp. X:** 77, 84; **Supp. XIV:** 126; **Supp. XVI:** 33
Better Days (Price), **Supp. VI:** 264
Better Sort, The (James), **II:** 335
Better Than Sex (Thompson), **Supp. XXIV:** 283
"Better Things in Life, The" (Loos), **Supp. XVI:** 194

Betty Leicester (Jewett), **II:** 406
Betty Leicester's Christmas (Jewett), **II:** 406; **Retro. Supp. II:** 145
Betty's Summer Vacation (Durang), **Supp. XXIV: 125–126**
Between Angels (Dunn), **Supp. XI: 149–159**
"Between Angels" (Dunn), **Supp. XI:** 150
Between Fantoine and Agapa (Pinget), **Supp. V:** 39
"Between Memory and History: A Writer's Voice" (Kreisler), **Supp. XVI:** 155
"Between Queer Performances" (Hardin), **Supp. XXVI:** 242
Between Silences: A Voice from China (Jin), **Supp. XVIII:** 91, 92, 93
"Between the Porch and the Altar" (Lowell), **II:** 540–541
"Between the World and Me" (Wright), **Supp. II Part 1:** 228
Between Time and Timbuktu (Vonnegut), **Supp. II Part 2:** 753, 759
Between Two Rivers (Kenny), **Supp. XXIII:** 143
Beuka, Robert A., **Supp. XIX:** 263; **Supp. XXI:** 47
"Be Very Afraid—Of Loss of Liberty at Home" (P. N. Warren), **Supp. XX: 272–273**
Bevis, Howard L., **Supp. I Part 2:** 611
Bevis, John, **Supp. I Part 2:** 503
Bewilderment: New Poems and Translations (Ferry), **Supp. XXIV: 160–161**
"Bewitched" (Wharton), **IV:** 316
Bewley, Marius, **I:** 336
Beyer, Werner, **Supp. XXIII:** 145
Beyle, Marie Henri. *See* Stendhal
Beyond (Goldbarth), **Supp. XII:** 192
Beyond a Boundary (C. L. R. James), **Supp. XXI:** 159, 170–171
Beyond Black Bear Lake (LaBastille), **Supp. X:** 95, **99–102,** 108
"Beyond Charles River to the Acheron" (Lowell), **II:** 541
Beyond Criticism (Shapiro), **Supp. II Part 2:** 703, 711
Beyond Culture (Trilling), **Supp. III Part 2:** 508–512
Beyond Desire (Anderson), **I:** 111
Beyond Document: The Art of Nonfiction Film (Warren, ed.), **Supp. IV Part 2:** 434
Beyond Forgetting (Hughes, ed.; foreword by Gallagher), **Supp. XXIV:** 167, 171
Beyond Good and Evil (Nietzsche), **Supp. IV Part 2:** 519
"Beyond Harm" (Olds), **Supp. X:** 210
Beyond Katrina: A Meditation on the Mississippi Gulf Coast (Trethewey), **Supp. XXI:** 248
"Beyond My Solitude" (Gibran), **Supp. XX:** 119
"Beyond the Alps" (Lowell), **II:** 547, 550
"Beyond the Bayou" (Chopin), **Supp. I Part 1:** 215
Beyond the Boom: New Voices on American Life, Culture and Politics (Teachout), **Supp. XIX:** 137

Beyond the Horizon (O'Neill), **III:** 389; **Supp. XXI:** 13; **Supp. XXII:** 22
Beyond the Hundredth Meridian: John Wesley Powell and the Second Opening of the West (Stegner), **Supp. IV Part 2:** 599, 603–604, 611
"Beyond the Kittery Bridge" (Hatlen), **Supp. V:** 138
Beyond the Law (film) (Mailer), **Retro. Supp. II:** 205
Beyond Therapy (Durang), **Supp. XXIV: 119–120**
"Beyond the Sea (at the sanatorium)" (Salinas), **Supp. XIII:** 325
Beyond the Wall: Essays from the Outside (Abbey), **Supp. XIII:** 13
Beyond the Wall of Sleep (Lovecraft), **Supp. XXV:** 113
Beyond the Writers' Workshop: New Ways to Write Creative Nonfiction (C. Bly), **Supp. XVI:** 41
Beyond Tragedy (Niebuhr), **III:** 300–303
Bezner, Kevin, **Supp. XII:** 202
B. F.'s Daughter (Marquand), **III:** 59, 65, 68, 69
Bhagavad Gita, **III:** 566; **IV:** 183
"Biafra: A People Betrayed" (Vonnegut), **Supp. II Part 2:** 760
Bianchi, Martha Dickinson, **I:** 470; **Retro. Supp. I:** 35, 37, 38
Bible, **I:** 191, 280, 414, 421, 490, 506; **II:** 6, 12, 15, 17, 108, 231, 237, 238, 252, 267, 302; **III:** 28, 199, 308–309, 341, 343, 350, 356, 402, 492, 519, 565, 577; **IV:** 11, 13, 42, 57, 60, 67, 152, 153, 154, 155, 164, 165, 296, 337, 341, 367, 369, 370, 371, 438; **Retro. Supp. I:** 91; **Supp. I Part 1:** 4, 6, 63, 101, 104, 105, 113, 193, 369; **Supp. I Part 2:** 388, 433, 494, 515, 516, 517, 583, 584, 587, 589, 653, 689, 690, 691; **Supp. IV Part 1:** 284; **Supp. IX:** 246; **Supp. VIII:** 20; **Supp. XIV:** 225. *See also* names of biblical books; New Testament; Old Testament
Biblia Americana (Mather), **Supp. II Part 2:** 442
Biblical Dialogues between a Father and His Family (Rowson), **Supp. XV:** 245–246
"Bibliography of the King's Book, A, or, Eikon Basilike" (Howe), **Supp. IV Part 2:** 435
Bibliography of the King's Book, A; or, Eikon Basilike (Almack), **Supp. IV Part 2:** 435
"Bicentennial" (Davison), **Supp. XXVI:** 73, 77
Bickel, Freddy. *See* March, Fredric
Bicycle Thieves (film, De Sica), **Supp. XXVI:** 134
Bidart, Frank, **Retro. Supp. II:** 48, 50, 52, 182, 183, 184; **Supp. XIX:** 82; **Supp. XV: 19–37; Supp. XVIII:** 91,92
Bid Me to Live (Doolittle), **Supp. I Part 1:** 258, 260, 268, 269, 270
"Bien Pretty" (Cisneros), **Supp. VII:** 70
"Bienvenidos" (Mora), **Supp. XIII:** 220
Bierce, Albert, **I:** 191, 209

Bierce, Ambrose, **I: 190–213,** 419; **II:** 74, 264, 271; **IV:** 350; **Retro. Supp. II:** 72; **Supp. XXV:** 26
Bierce, Mrs. Ambrose, **I:** 194–195, 199
Bierce, Day, **I:** 195, 199
Bierce, Helen, **I:** 210
Bierce, Leigh, **I:** 195, 198, 208
Bierce, General Lucius Verus, **I:** 191
Bierce, Marcus, **I:** 190, 191
Bierce, Mrs. Marcus, **I:** 190, 191
Bierds, Linda, **Supp. XVII: 25–37**
Biffle, Kent, **Supp. V:** 225
"Bi-Focal" (Stafford), **Supp. XI:** 318, 321
Bigamist's Daughter, A (McDermott), **Supp. XVIII:** 155, **156–158,** 160, 166
Big as Life (Doctorow), **Supp. IV Part 1:** 231, 234
Big Bad Love (film, Howard), **Supp. XXI:** 39
Big Bad Love (L. Brown), **Supp. XXI:** 40, 42, **44–45**
"Big Bite" (Mailer), **Retro. Supp. II:** 204
"Big Blonde" (Parker), **Supp. IX:** 189, 192, 193, 195, 196, 203
Big Bozo, The (Glaspell), **Supp. III Part 1:** 182
Bigelow, Gordon, **Supp. X:** 222, 227, 229
Bigelow, Jacob, **Supp. I Part 1:** 302
Bigelow Papers, Second Series, The (Lowell), **Supp. I Part 2:** 406, 415–416
Bigelow Papers, The (Lowell), **Supp. I Part 2:** 406, 407, 408, 410, 411–412, 415, 417, 424
"Big Fiddle" (Boyle), **Supp. XXIV:** 54
Big Fix, The (Lacy), **Supp. XV:** 204–205
Bigfoot Dreams (Prose), **Supp. XVI:** 253–254
Big Funk, The: A Casual Play (Shanley), **Supp. XIV:** 316, **327**
"Big Game" (Boyle), **Supp. XX: 20**
Big Game, The (film), **Supp. XIX:** 244
Big Gold Dream, The (C. Himes), **Supp. XVI:** 143, 144
"Bight, The" (Bishop), **Retro. Supp. II:** 38, 45
Big Hunger: Stories 1932–1959 (Fante), **Supp. XI:** 160
Big Knife, The (Odets), **Supp. II Part 2:** 546, 547, 548
Big Knockover, The (Hammett), **Supp. I Part 1:** 292; **Supp. IV Part 1:** 344, 345, 356
Big Laugh, The (O'Hara), **III:** 362, 373–375
Big Man (Neugeboren), **Supp. XVI:** 219, **220,** 221, 225
Big Money, The (Dos Passos), **I:** 482, 483, 486–487, 489; **Supp. I Part 2:** 646, 647
Big Picture (Everett), **Supp. XVIII:** 54, 66
"Big Picture" (Everett), **Supp. XVIII:** 66
"Big Picture" (Halliday), **Supp. XIX:** 93
"Big Rock Candy Figgy Pudding Pitfall, The" (Didion), **Supp. IV Part 1:** 195
Big Rock Candy Mountain, The (Stegner), **Supp. IV Part 2:** 596, 597, 598, 599, 600, 603, 604, 605, 606–607, 608, 610–611

Bigsby, C. W. E. (Christopher), **Supp. IX:** 137, 140; **Supp. XV:** 332

Big Sea, The (Hughes), **Retro. Supp. I:** 195, 197, 199, 201, 204; **Supp. I Part 1:** 322, 332, 333; **Supp. II Part 1:** 233–234; **Supp. XIX:** 77; **Supp. XXII:** 3

Big Sky, The (Mora), **Supp. XIII:** 221

Big Sleep, The (Chandler), **Supp. IV Part 1:** 122–125, 127, 128, 134

Big Sleep, The (film), **Supp. IV Part 1:** 130; **Supp. XVIII:** 148

Big Strike, The (Ryan as Quin), **Supp. XVIII:** 226,**232–233**

Big Sur (Kerouac), **Supp. III Part 1:** 230

Big Sur and the Oranges of Hieronymous Bosch (H. Miller), **III:** 189–190

Big Time, The (Hayes), **Supp. XXVI:** 144

Big Town, The (Lardner), **II:** 426, 429

"Big Two-Hearted River" (Hemingway), **II:** 249; **Retro. Supp. I:** 170–171; **Supp. IX:** 106; **Supp. XIV:** 227, 235

"Big Wind" (Roethke), **III:** 531

"Big Winner Rises Late, The" (Dunn), **Supp. XI:** 146

"Bilingual/*Bilingüe*" (essay; Espaillat), *Supp. XXI:* 103

"Bilingual/*Bilingüe*" (poem; Espaillat), *Supp. XXI:* 104

"Bilingual Christmas" (Mora), **Supp. XIII:** 216–217

"Bilingual Sestina" (Alvarez), **Supp. VII:** 10

"Bill" (Winters), **Supp. II Part 2:** 792

"Bill, The" (Malamud), **Supp. I Part 2:** 427, 430, 434

"Bill Collector's Vacation, The" (Hampl), **Supp. XXII:** 83

"Billie Holiday" (Carruth), **Supp. XVI:** 50

Billings, Gladys. *See* Brooks, Mrs. Van Wyck

Billings, Josh, **Supp. XVIII:** 1, 4

Bill of Rites, a Bill of Wrongs, a Bill of Goods, A (Morris), **III:** 237

"Bill's Beans" (Nye), **Supp. XIII:** 283

"Billy" (Gordon), **Supp. IV Part 1:** 306

"Billy" (McCarriston), **Supp. XIV:** 265

Billy Bathgate (Doctorow), **Supp. IV Part 1:** 217, 219, 222, 224, 227, 229–231, 231, 232, 233, 238

Billy Bathgate (film), **Supp. IV Part 1:** 236

Billy Budd, Sailor (Melville), **III:** 40, 93–95; **IV:** 105; **Retro. Supp. I:** 249, **258–260**

Billy Collins Live: A Performance at the Peter Norton Symphony Space April 20, 2005 (CD, Collins), **Supp. XXI:** 51

"Billy Gardner's Ground Out" (Skloot), **Supp. XX: 205, 207**

Billy Phelan's Greatest Game (W. Kennedy), **Supp. VII:** 131, 132, 134, 135, 142–147, 149, 151, 153, 155

Billy Ray's Farm: Essays from a Place Called Tula (L. Brown), **Supp. XXI:** 48, 49

Billy's Boy (P. N. Warren), **Supp. XX: 261, 265–267**

Billy the Kid, **Supp. IV Part 2:** 489, 490, 492

Biloxi Blues (Simon), **Supp. IV Part 2:** 576, 577, 584, 586–587, 590

"Bimini" (Hemingway), **II:** 258

Bingham, Anne, **Supp. XV:** 239

Bingham, Millicent Todd, **I:** 470; **Retro. Supp. I:** 36

Bingham, Remica L., **Supp. XXI:** 256

Bingo Palace, The (Erdrich), **Supp. IV Part 1:** 259, 260, 261, 263–264, 265, 266–267, 268–269, 270, 271–273, 274, 275

"Binsey Poplars" (Hopkins), **Supp. I Part 1:** 94; **Supp. IV Part 2:** 639

Binswanger, Ludwig, **Supp. XV:** 26

Biographia Literaria (Coleridge), **II:** 10; **Retro. Supp. I:** 308

"Biography" (Francis), **Supp. IX:** 77

"Biography" (Pinsky), **Supp. VI:** 235, 236, 239, 241, **243**, 249, 250

Biography and Poetical Remains of the Late Margaret Miller Davidson (Irving), **II:** 314

"Biography in the First Person" (Dunn), **Supp. XI:** 144

"Biography of an Armenian Schoolgirl" (Nye), **Supp. XIII:** 275, 280

"Biography of a Story" (Jackson), **Supp. IX:** 113

Biondi, Joann, **Supp. XI:** 103

"Biopoetics Sketch for *Greenfield Review*" (Harjo), **Supp. XII:** 216

"Biotherm"(O'Hara), **Supp. XXIII:** 208, 218–219

"Birchbrook Mill" (Whittier), **Supp. I Part 2:** 699

"Birches" (Frost), **II:** 154; **Retro. Supp. I:** 132; **Supp. XIII:** 147

Bird, Alan, **Supp. I Part 1:** 260

Bird, Gloria, **Supp. XII:** 216

Bird, Isabella, **Supp. X:** 103

Bird, Robert M., **III:** 423

"Bird, The" (Simpson), **Supp. IX:** 269–270

"Bird, the Bird, the Bird, The" (Creeley), **Supp. IV Part 1:** 149

"Bird, The"(Le Sueur), **Supp. XXIII:** 167

"Bird Banding with the Biologists" (Ray), **Supp. XVIII:** 194

Bird by Bird: Some Instructions on Writing and Life (Lamott), **Supp. XX: 132, 137–138**

"Bird came down the Walk, A" (Dickinson), **Retro. Supp. I:** 37

"Bird Frau, The" (Dove), **Supp. IV Part 1:** 245

"Bird in Hand" (screen story) (West and Ingster), **Retro. Supp. II:** 330

Bird Kingdom of the Mayas (LaBastille), **Supp. X:** 96

Birds and Beasts (W. J. Smith), **Supp. XIII:** 346

"Birds for Christmas, The" (Richard), **Supp. XIX:** 221

Bird's Nest, The (Jackson), **Supp. IX: 124–125**

Birds of America (McCarthy), **II:** 579–583; **Supp. X:** 177

Birds of America (Moore), **Supp. X:** 163, 165, 167, 168, 171, **177–179**

Birds of America, The (Audubon), **Supp. XVI: 5–6,** 7, 9, 10, 12, 13

"Birds of Killingsworth, The" (Longfellow), **Retro. Supp. II:** 164

Birds of North America (Audubon Society), **Supp. X:** 177

"Birds of Vietnam, The" (Carruth), **Supp. XVI:** 55

"Bird-Window-Flying" (Gallagher), **Supp. XXIV:** 169

"Bird-Witted" (Moore), **III:** 214

Birkelo, Cheryl, **Supp. XX: 220–221**

Birkerts, Sven, **Supp. IV Part 2:** 650; **Supp. V:** 212; **Supp. VIII:** 85; **Supp. X:** 311; **Supp. XX:** 92

Birkhead, L. M., **III:** 116

"Birmingham Sunday" (Hughes), **Supp. I Part 1:** 343

Birnbaum, Henry, **Supp. XII:** 128

Birnbaum, Robert, **Supp. X:** 13; **Supp. XVI:** 75; **Supp. XXIII:** 73, 75, 275

Birney, James G., **Supp. I Part 2:** 587, 588

Birstein, Ann, **Supp. VIII:** 100

"Birthday, A" (Untermeyer), **Supp. XV:** 296

Birthday Basket for Tía, A (Mora), **Supp. XIII:** 221

"Birthday Cake" (Carruth), **Supp. XVI:** 59

"Birthday Cake for Lionel, A" (Wylie), **Supp. I Part 2:** 721

"Birthday Girl: 1950" (McCarriston), **Supp. XIV:** 261

"Birthday of Mrs. Pineda, The" (Ríos), **Supp. IV Part 2:** 542, 546

"Birthday Poem, A" (Hecht), **Supp. X:** 64

"Birthday Present, A" (Plath), **Supp. I Part 2:** 531

"Birthmark" (July), **Supp. XXIV:** 206

"Birthmark, The" (Ellison), **Retro. Supp. II:** 116; **Supp. II Part 1:** 237–238

"Birth-mark, The" (Hawthorne), **Retro. Supp. I:** 152

Birth-mark, The: Unsettling the Wilderness in American Literary History (Howe), **Supp. IV Part 2:** 422, 431, 434

Birth of a Nation, The (film), **Supp. I Part 1:** 66

Birth of a World: Bolívar in Terms of His Peoples (W. Frank), **Supp. XX:** 80

Birth of the Poet, The (Gordon), **Supp. XII:** 7

Birth of Tragedy, The (Nietzsche), **Supp. IV Part 1:** 105, 110; **Supp. IV Part 2:** 519; **Supp. VIII:** 182

"Birth of Venus, The" (Botticelli), **IV:** 410

"Birth of Venus, The" (Rukeyser), **Supp. VI:** 281

"Birth of Water Stories, The" (Vaz), **Supp. XXVI:** 260

"Birthplace: New Rochelle" (Oppen), **Supp. XXVI:** 231

"Birthplace Revisited" (Corso), **Supp. XII:** 123

"Birthright" (McKay), **Supp. X:** 136
Bisch, Louis E., **Supp. I Part 2:** 608
Bisco, John, **Supp. XVIII:** 11
"B is for Bachelors" (M. F. K. Fisher), **Supp. XVII:** 86
Bishop, Elizabeth, **Retro. Supp. I:** 140, 296, 303; **Retro. Supp. II: 37–56,** 175, 178, 189, 233, 234, 235; **Supp. I Part 1: 72–97,** 239, 320, 326; **Supp. III Part 1:** 6, 7, 10, 18, 64, 239, 320, 326; **Supp. III Part 2:** 541, 561; **Supp. IV Part 1:** 249, 257; **Supp. IV Part 2:** 439, 626, 639, 641, 644, 647, 651, 653; **Supp. IX:** 40, 41, 45, 47, 48; **Supp. V:** 337; **Supp. X:** 58; **Supp. XI:** 123, 136; **Supp. XIII:** 115, 348; **Supp. XV:** 20–21, 100, 101, 112, 119, 249, 251; **Supp. XVII:** 36, 76; **Supp. XXI:** 58, 84, 131; **Supp. XXIII:** 117; **Supp. XXV:** 222; **Supp. XXVI:** 67, 78
Bishop, James, Jr., **Supp. XIII:** 1, 5, 6, 7, 9, 11, 15
Bishop, John Peale, **I:** 432, 440; **II:** 81, 85, 86–87, 91, 209; **IV:** 35, 140, 427; **Retro. Supp. I:** 109; **Supp. I Part 2:** 709
Bishop, John W., **Supp. I Part 1:** 83
Bishop, Judith, **Supp. XVI:** 295
Bishop, Morris, **Supp. I Part 2:** 676
Bishop, William Thomas, **Supp. I Part 1:** 83
"Bishop Orders His Tomb at St. Praxed's Church, The" (R. Browning), **Supp. XV:** 127
"Bishop's Beggar, The" (Benét), **Supp. XI:** 56
"Bismarck" (Chapman), **Supp. XIV:** 52, 53
Bismark, Otto von, **Supp. I Part 2:** 643
Biss, Eula, **Supp. XXVI: 45–60**
"Bistro Styx, The" (Dove), **Supp. IV Part 1:** 250–251
Bitov, Andrei, **Retro. Supp. I:** 278
Bits of Gossip (R. H. Davis), **Supp. XVI:** 82–83, 84, 85, 89
"Bitte Nehmen Sie Die Blumen" (Boyle), **Supp. XXIV:** 57
"Bitter Drink, The" (Dos Passos), **Supp. I Part 2:** 647
"Bitter Farce, A" (Schwartz), **Supp. II Part 2:** 640, 657–658
Bitter Medicine (Paretsky), **Supp. XXV:** 174, 179, 183
"Bitter Pills for the Dark Ladies" (Jong), **Supp. V:** 118
Bitterroot (Burke), **Supp. XIV:** 34, 35
"Bittersweet Nightshade" (Skloot), **Supp. XX: 202**
Bitter Victory (Hardy; Kinnell, trans.), **Supp. III Part 1:** 235
Bittner, William, **Supp. XX: 74,Supp. XX: 77, 76, 78, 80**
Bitzer, G. W. "Billy", **Supp. XVI:** 183
Bixby, Horace, **IV:** 194
Bjerre, Thomas Aervold, **Supp. XXI:** 41, 47
Bjorkman, Frances Maule, **Supp. V:** 285
Bjorkman, Stig, **Supp. XV:** 6
Björnson, Björnstjerne, **II:** 275

Black, Cheryl, **Supp. XXI:** 6
Black 100, The (Salley), **Supp. XIV:** 195
Blackamerican Literature, 1760-Present (R. Miller), **Supp. X:** 324
Black American Literature Forum, **Supp. XI:** 86, 92, 93
Black and Blue (Quindlen), **Supp. XVII:** 166, **176–178**
"Black and Tan" (Bell), **Supp. X:** 9
Black and White (Sorrentino), **Supp. XXI:** 228
Black Armour (Wylie), **Supp. I Part 2:** 708, 709, 712–714, 729
"Black Art" (Baraka), **Supp. II Part 1:** 49, 50–51, 59, 60
"Black Art, The" (Sexton), **Supp. II Part 2:** 682
Black Aspen, The (Davison), **Supp. XXVI:** 78
"Black Ball, The" (Ellison), **Retro. Supp. II:** 124
Black Bart and the Sacred Hills (Wilson), **Supp. VIII:** 330, 331
Black Beetles in Amber (Bierce), **I:** 204, 209
"Blackberries" (Komunyakaa), **Supp. XIII:** 126
"Blackberry Eating" (Kinnell), **Supp. III Part 1:** 250
"Blackberrying" (D. West), **Supp. XVIII:** 283
Blackberry Winter (Warren), **IV:** 243, 251, 252
Black Betty (Mosley), **Supp. XIII:** 237, **Supp. XIII:** 240, 243
"Black Birch in Winter, A" (Wilbur), **Supp. III Part 2:** 561
"Black Boy" (Boyle), **Supp. XXIV:** 59
Black Boy (Wright), **IV:** 477, 478, 479, 480–482, 488, 489, 494; **Retro. Supp. II:** 117; **Supp. II Part 1:** 235–236; **Supp. IV Part 1:** 11; **Supp. XVIII:** 286
"Black Boys and Native Sons" (Howe), **Retro. Supp. II:** 112
Blackburn, Alex, **Supp. XIII:** 112
Blackburn, Paul, **Supp. XXII:** 164, 169; **Supp. XXIV:** 34, 37
Blackburn, William, **IV:** 100
"Black Buttercups" (Clampitt), **Supp. IX:** 42
Black Cargo, The (Marquand), **III:** 55, 60
Black Cargoes: A History of the Atlantic Slave Trade (Cowley), **Supp. II Part 1:** 140
"Black Cat, The" (Poe), **III:** 413, 414, 415; **Retro. Supp. II:** 264, 267, 269, 270; **Supp. XXV:** 112
Black Cherry Blues (Burke), **Supp. XIV:** 30
"Black Christ, The" (Cullen), **Supp. IV Part 1:** 170, 171–172
Black Christ and Other Poems, The (Cullen), **Supp. IV Part 1:** 166, 170
"Black Clay Fish from Oaxaca, A" (Bronk), **Supp. XXI:** 31

"BLACK DADA NIHILISMUS" (Baraka), **Supp. II Part 1:** 39, 41
"Black Death" (Hurston), **Supp. VI:** 153
Black Dog, Red Dog (Dobyns), **Supp. XIII:** 87, **88–89**
"Black Dog, Red Dog" (Dobyns), **Supp. XIII:** 89
Black Dog of Fate: A Memoir (Balakian), **Supp. XXIII:** 19, **20–24,** 24, 25
"Black Earth" (Moore), **III:** 197, 212
Black Echo, The (Connelly), **Supp. XXI:** 67, 68, 75, 80
Black Fire (Jones and Neal, eds.), **Supp. X:** 324, 328
Black Fire: An Anthology of Afro American Writing (Baraka, ed.), **Supp. II Part 1:** 53
Black Flame, The (Du Bois), **Supp. II Part 1:** 159, 185–186
Black Folk, Then and Now: An Essay in the History and Sociology of the Negro Race (Du Bois), **Supp. II Part 1:** 159, 178, 183, 185
Blackford, Holly, **Supp. XXII:** 300
"Black Fox, The" (Whittier), **Supp. I Part 2:** 692
Black Freckles (Levis), **Supp. XI:** 257, 271
"Black Gang", **IV:** 406, 407
Black Genius (Mosley, ed.), **Supp. XIII:** 246
Blackguard (Bodenheim), **Supp. XXV:** 17, 18, 22, 23–24
"Black Hood, The" (Francis), **Supp. IX:** 83, 91
Black House, The (Theroux), **Supp. VIII:** 319
Black Humor (C. Johnson), **Supp. VI:** 187, 199
Black Ice, The (Connelly), **Supp. XXI:** **70,** 75
Black Image in the White Mind, The (Fredrickson), **Supp. I Part 2:** 589
"Black Is My Favorite Color" (Malamud), **Supp. I Part 2:** 437
Black Jacobins, The (C. L. R. James), **Supp. XXI:** 159, 166–167
"Black Jewel, The" (Merwin), **Supp. III Part 1:** 355
Black Lamb and Grey Falcon (R. West), **Supp. XVI:** 152
"Black Laughter" (Taggard), **Supp. XXII:** 274
"Blacklegs" (B. Kelly), **Supp. XVII:** 131
Black Light (Kinnell), **Supp. III Part 1:** 235, 243
Black Like Me (Griffin), **Supp. XXV:** 51
Blacklist (Paretsky), **Supp. XXV:** 182, 184
"Blacklist and the Cold War, The" (Kramer), **Supp. I Part 1:** 295
Black Literature in America (Baker), **Supp. X:** 324
Black Magic, A Pictorial History of the Negro in American Entertainment (Hughes), **Supp. I Part 1:** 345
Black Magic: Collected Poetry 1961–1967 (Baraka), **Supp. II Part 1:** 45, 49–50

"Blackmailers Don't Shoot" (Chandler), **Supp. IV Part 1:** 121–122

Black Manhattan (J. W. Johnson), **Supp. IV Part 1:** 169

Black Mass, A (Baraka), **Supp. II Part 1:** 46, 48–49, 56, 57

"Black Mesa, The" (Merrill), **Supp. III Part 1:** 328

Black Metropolis (Cayton and Drake), **IV:** 475, 486, 488

Black Misery (Hughes), **Supp. I Part 1:** 336

Blackmur, Helen Dickson (Mrs. R. P. Blackmur), **Supp. II Part 1:** 90

Blackmur, Richard P., **I:** 50, 63, 67, 280, 282, 386, 455, 472; **II:** 320, 537; **III:** 194, 208, 462, 478, 497; **Supp. II Part 1:** 87–112, 136; **Supp. II Part 2:** 543, 643; **Supp. XII:** 45

Black Music (Baraka), **Supp. II Part 1:** 47, 51

Black Nativity (Hughes), **Retro. Supp. I:** 196

"Black News" (Biss), **Supp. XXVI:** 56

Black No More (Schuyler), **Supp. XIX:** 73; **Supp. XVI:** 142

Black on Black: "Baby Sister" and Selected Writings (C. Himes), **Supp. XVI:** 145

"Black or White" (Major), **Supp. XXII:** 185

"Blackout" (Hay), **Supp. XIV:** 121

Black Oxen (Atherton), **Supp. XXIV:** 25–26

Black Oxen (Atherton, Dawson, ed.), **Supp. XXIV:** 31

"Black Panther" (Hughes), **Retro. Supp. I:** 211

"Black Petal" (L.-Y. Lee), **Supp. XV:** 224–225

Black Power (Wright), **IV:** 478, 488, 494

"Black Rainbow, A: Modern Afro-American Poetry" (Dove and Waniek), **Supp. IV Part 1:** 244

Black Reconstruction (Du Bois), **Supp. II Part 1:** 159, 162, 171, 182

Black Riders and Other Lines, The (Crane), **I:** 406, 419

Black Riviera, The (Jarman), **Supp. XVII:** 109, 110, 115–116

Blackrobe: Isaac Jogues (Kenny), **Supp. XXIII:** 143, 147, 151–152, 153, 154

"Black Rook in Rainy Weather" (Plath), **Supp. I Part 2:** 543, 544; **Supp. XXIII:** 63

Blacks (Brooks), **Supp. III Part 1:** 69, 72, 86, 87

Blacks, The (Genet), **Supp. IV Part 1:** 8

Black Skin, White Masks (Fanon), **Retro. Supp. II:** 118

Black Sleuth, The (J. Bruce), **Supp. XVI:** 143

Blacksnake at the Family Reunion (Huddle), **Supp. XXVI:** 147, 151

Black Spear, The (Hayden), **Supp. II Part 1:** 375

Black Spring (H. Miller), **III:** 170, 175, 178, 180–182, 183, 184; **Supp. X:** 187

"Black Stone Lying on a White Stone" (Vallejo), **Supp. XIII:** 324

Black Sun (Abbey), **Supp. XIII:** 4, **8–9,** 17

"Black Swan" (B. Kelly), **Supp. XVII:** 130–131

"Black Swan, The" (Jarrell), **II:** 382

Black Swan, The (Merrill), **Supp. III Part 1:** 319, 320

"Black Tambourine" (Crane), **I:** 387–388; **II:** 371

Black Thunder (Bontemps), **Supp. XXII:** 4, 9

"Black Tuesday" (Swenson), **Supp. IV Part 2:** 646

Black Virgin Mountain (Heinemann), **Supp. XXII:** 103, **114–116**

Black Voices (Chapman), **IV:** 485

"Blackwater Mountain" (Wright), **Supp. V:** 335, 340

"Black Wedding, The" (Singer), **IV:** 12–13

Blackwell, Alice Stone, **Supp. XI:** 195, 197

Blackwell, Elizabeth, **Retro. Supp. II:** 146

Black Woman, The (Bambara, ed.), **Supp. XI:** 1

"Black Workers" (Hughes), **Retro. Supp. I:** 202

"Black Writer and the Southern Experience, The" (Walker), **Supp. III Part 2:** 521

Black Zodiac (Wright), **Supp. V:** 333, 344, 345

Blade Runner (film), **Supp. XI:** 84

Blades, John, **Supp. XX:** 87

"Blades of Steel" (R. Fisher), **Supp. XIX:** 72

Blaine, Anita McCormick, **Supp. I Part 1:** 5

Blaine, Nell, **Supp. XV:** 179; **Supp. XXIII:** 217

Blair, Hugh, **II:** 8, 17; **Supp. I Part 2:** 422

Blair, Robert, **Supp. I Part 1:** 150

Blair, Walter, **II:** 20; **Retro. Supp. II:** 286

Blaisdell, Gus, **Supp. XIV:** 87

Blake, Casey Nelson, **Supp. XX: 69, 70, 78**

Blake, William, **I:** 381, 383, 389, 390, 398, 447, 476, 525, 526, 533; **II:** 321; **III:** 5, 19, 22, 195, 196, 197, 205, 485, 528, 540, 544–545, 567, 572; **IV:** 129; **Retro. Supp. II:** 76, 300; **Supp. I Part 1:** 80; **Supp. I Part 2:** 385, 514, 517, 539, 552, 708; **Supp. V:** 208, 257, 258; **Supp. VIII:** 26, 99, 103; **Supp. X:** 120; **Supp. XII:** 45; **Supp. XIV:** 344; **Supp. XVI:** 282; **Supp. XVII:** 119; **Supp. XX: 115, 116; Supp. XXII:** 225, 257; **Supp. XXIV:** 159; **Supp. XXV:** 248; **Supp. XXVI:** 235

Blakely, Barbara, **Supp. XIII:** 32

Blanc, Marie Thérèse, **Retro. Supp. II:** 135

Blanc-Bentzon, Mme. Thérèse, **II:** 405

Blanchard, Paula, **Retro. Supp. II:** 131, 133–134, 135

Blanche, Jacques-Émile, **Supp. XX: 232**

Blanche of Brandywine (Lippard), **Supp. XXIII:** 178, 185

Blanchot, Maurice, **Supp. XVI:** 288; **Supp. XXIV:** 40

Blancs, Les (Hansberry), **Supp. IV Part 1:** 359, 364, 365, 369, 372–374

Blancs, Les: The Collected Last Plays of Lorraine Hansberry (Nemiroff, ed.), **Supp. IV Part 1:** 365, 368, 374

"'Blandula, Tenulla, Vagula' " (Pound), **III:** 463; **Supp. V:** 336, 337, 345

Blankenship, Tom, **IV:** 193

"Blank Paper" (Peacock), **Supp. XIX:** 198–199

Blank Wall, The (Holding), **Supp. XXII:** 119, 120, 121, 130, **131–133,** 134

Blanshard, Rufus A., **I:** 67

Blassingame, John, **Supp. XX: 106**

Blauvelt, William Satake, **Supp. V:** 171, 173

Blavatsky, Elena Petrovna, **III:** 176

"Blazing in Gold and Quenching in Purple" (Dickinson), **Retro. Supp. I:** 30

Bleak House (Dickens), **II:** 291; **Supp. IV Part 1:** 293

Blechman, Burt, **Supp. I Part 1:** 290

"Bleeder" (Dobyns), **Supp. XIII:** 88

"Bleeding" (Swenson), **Supp. IV Part 2:** 646–647

Bleeding Kansas (Paretsky), **Supp. XXV:** 183

"Blessed Is the Man" (Moore), **III:** 215

"Blessed Man of Boston, My Grandmother's Thimble, and Fanning Island, The" (Updike), **IV:** 219

"Blessing, A" (Wright), **Supp. III Part 2:** 600, 606

Blessing on the Moon, A (Skibell), **Supp. XVII:** 48

Blessings (Quindlen), **Supp. XVII:** 167, **178–179**

"Blessing the Animals" (Komunyakaa), **Supp. XIII:** 129–130

"Blessing the Children" (Hogan), **Supp. IV Part 1:** 401

Bless Me, Ultima (Anya), **Supp. XIII:** 220

Blew, Mary Clearman, **Supp. XIV:** 227

Bligh, S. M., **I:** 226

"Blight"(Dybek), **Supp. XXIII:** 72

Blind Alleys (film), **Supp. XXI:** 146

Blind Assassin, The (Atwood), **Supp. XIII:** 20, **32**

Blind Bow-Boy, The (Van Vechten), **Supp. II Part 2:** 737, 740–742

"Blind Date" (Halliday), **Supp. XIX:** 85

Blind Date (Kosinski), **Supp. VII:** 215, 224–225

"Blinded by the Light" (Boyle), **Supp. XX: 20**

Blind Lion, The (Gunn Allen), **Supp. IV Part 1:** 324

"Blind Man's Holiday" (O. Henry), **Supp. II Part 1:** 401

Blind Man with a Pistol (C. Himes), **Supp. XVI:** 143, 144

Blindness and Insight (de Man), **Retro. Supp. I:** 67

"Blind Poet, The: Sidney Lanier" (Warren), **Supp. I Part 1:** 371, 373

"Blindsided" (E. P. Jones), **Supp. XXII:** 151–152

"Blind Tom" (R. H. Davis), **Supp. XVI:** 89, 90

Blithedale Romance, The (Hawthorne), **II:** 225, 231, 239, 241–242, 271, 282, 290; **IV:** 194; **Retro. Supp. I:** 63, 149, 152, 156–157, **162–163; Supp. I Part 2:** 579; **Supp. II Part 1:** 280; **Supp. VIII:** 153, 201

Blitzstein, Marc, **Supp. I Part 1:** 277

Blix (Norris), **III:** 314, 322, 327, 328, 333

Blixen, Karen Denisen Baroness. *See* Dinesen, Isak

"Blizzard in Cambridge" (Lowell), **II:** 554

Blizzard Voices, The (Kooser), **Supp. XIX: 123**

Bloch, Ernest, **Supp. XX: 75**

Bloch, Robert, **Supp. XXV:** 111, 145

Block, Lawrence, **Supp. XXI:** 67

"Blocks"(O'Hara), **Supp. XXIII:** 214

Blok, Aleksandr Aleksandrovich, **IV:** 443; **Supp. XXVI:** 144

"Blond" (Trethewey), **Supp. XXI:** 244

Blonde Bait (Lacy), **Supp. XV:** 204

Blonde on Blonde (album, Dylan), **Supp. XVIII:** 20, 27, 30

Blondin, Antoine, **Supp. XVI:** 230

"Blood" (Hoffman), **Supp. XVIII:** 86

"Blood" (Singer), **IV:** 15, 19

Blood, Tin, Straw (Olds), **Supp. X: 212–215**

Blood and Guile (Hoffman), **Supp. XVIII: 83–84**

Blood and Guts in High School (Acker), **Supp. XII:** 5, 6, **11–12**

"Blood Bay, The" (Proulx), **Supp. VII:** 262–263

"Blood-Burning Moon" (Toomer), **Supp. III Part 2:** 483; **Supp. IX:** 314–315

"Bloodchild" (O. Butler), **Supp. XIII:** 61, **69–70**

Bloodchild and Other Stories (O. Butler), **Supp. XIII:** 69

"Blood Donor" (Hay), **Supp. XIV:** 121

Blood for a Stranger (Jarrell), **II:** 367, 368–369, 370–371, 375, 377

"Blood from the Stone" (Oppen), **Supp. XXVI:** 230–231

Blood Issue (Crews), **Supp. XI:** 103

Bloodlines (Wright), **Supp. V:** 332, 335, 340

Blood Meridian (McCarthy), **Supp. XXIII:** 42

Blood Meridian; or, The Evening Redness in the West (McCarthy), **Supp. VIII:** 175, 177, **180–182,** 188, 190

Blood of My Blood (Gambino), **Supp. XX:** 35

"Blood of the Conquistadores, The" (Alvarez), **Supp. VII:** 7

"Blood of the Lamb, The" (hymn), **Supp. I Part 2:** 385

Blood of the Martyr (Crane), **I:** 422

"Blood of the Martyrs, The" (Benét), **Supp. XI:** 56, 58

Blood of the Prophets, The (Masters), **Supp. I Part 2:** 458, 459, 461

Blood on the Forge (Attaway), **Supp. II Part 1:** 234–235

Blood on the Tracks (album, Dylan), **Supp. XVIII:** 20, 27, 30

"Blood Relatives" (Apple), **Supp. XVII:** 6

"Blood Returns, The" (Kingsolver), **Supp. VII:** 209

"Bloodshed" (C. Ozick), **Supp. XVII:** 43

Bloodshed and Three Novellas (Ozick), **Supp. V:** 259–260, 261, 266–268

"Blood Soup"(Dybek), **Supp. XXIII:** 71

"Blood Stains" (Francis), **Supp. IX:** 86

Blood Work (Connelly), **Supp. XXI:** 72

Blood Work (film, Eastwood), **Supp. XXI:** 74

Bloody Crossroads, The: Where Literature and Politics Meet (Podhoretz), **Supp. VIII: 241–242**

Bloody News from My Friend (Samianto, trans. Balakian), **Supp. XXIII:** 28

Bloom, Alice, **Supp. IV Part 1:** 308

Bloom, Allan, **Retro. Supp. II:** 19, 30, 31, 33–34

Bloom, Claire, **Retro. Supp. II:** 281; **Supp. IX:** 125

Bloom, Harold, **Retro. Supp. I:** 67, 193, 299; **Retro. Supp. II:** 81, 210, 262; **Supp. IV Part 2:** 620, 689; **Supp. IX:** 146, 259; **Supp. V:** 178, 272; **Supp. VIII:** 180; **Supp. XII:** 261; **Supp. XIII:** 46, 47; **Supp. XIV:** 14; **Supp. XV:** 134; **Supp. XVII:** 70, 141; **Supp. XXIII:** 42; **Supp. XXV:** 251

Bloom, Larry, **Supp. XIII:** 133

Bloom, Leopold, **I:** 27, 150; **III:** 10

Bloom, Lynn Z., **Supp. IV Part 1:** 6

Bloomfield, Leonard, **I:** 64

Bloomingdale Papers, The (Carruth), **Supp. XVI:** 48–50

"Blossom and Fruit" (Benét), **Supp. XI:** 52–53

Blotner, Joseph, **Retro. Supp. I:** 88

Blouin, Lenora, **Supp. VIII:** 266

"Blouse, The"(Rudman), **Supp. XXIII:** 124

"Blowing Soap Bubbles"(Crooker), **Supp. XXIII:** 56

"Blowin' in the Wind" (song, Dylan), **Supp. XVIII:** 24, 25, 26, 29

Bluckled Bag, The (Rinehart), **Supp. XXV:** 197

Blue Angel (Prose), **Supp. XVI:** 249, 259–260

Blue Angel, The (film), **Supp. XVIII:** 243

Blue Arabesque: A Search for the Sublime (Hampl), **Supp. XXII:** 86, 98–99

"Blue Battalions, The" (Crane), **I:** 419–420

"Blue Bead, The"(Hadas), **Supp. XXIII:** 118, 119

"Bluebeard" (Barthelme), **Supp. IV Part 1:** 47

"Bluebeard" (Millay), **III:** 130

"Blueberries" (Frost), **Retro. Supp. I:** 121, 128

"Blue Boy"(Dybek), **Supp. XXIII:** 76

Blue Calhoun (Price), **Supp. VI:** 265–266

Blue Caterpillar, The (Pickering), **Supp. XXI:** 202–203

Blue City (Macdonald, as Millar), **Supp. IV Part 2:** 466–467

Blue Devils of Nada, The: A Contemporary American Approach to Aesthetics (Murray), **Supp. XIX: 159–160**

Blue Estuaries, The: Poems, 1923–1968 (Bogan), **Supp. III Part 1:** 48, 57, 66

Blue Hammer, The (Macdonald), **Supp. IV Part 2:** 462

"Blue Hour, The" (Komunyakaa), **Supp. XIII:** 130

Blue in the Face (Auster), **Supp. XII:** 21

Blue Jay's Dance, The: A Birth Year (Erdrich), **Supp. IV Part 1:** 259–260, 265, 270, 272

"Blue Juniata" (Cowley), **Supp. II Part 1:** 144

Blue Juniata: Collected Poems (Cowley), **Supp. II Part 1:** 140

"Blue Lick" (Offutt), **Supp. XIX:** 164, 165

Blue Light (Mosley), **Supp. XIII: 245–247,** 248, 249

"Blue Light Lounge Sutra for the Performance Poets at Harold Park Hotel" (Komunyakaa), **Supp. XIII:** 125

"Blue Meridian" (Toomer), **Supp. III Part 2:** 476, 487; **Supp. IX:** 320

"Blue Moles" (Plath), **Supp. I Part 2:** 539

Blue Mountain Ballads (music) (Bowles), **Supp. IV Part 1:** 84

Blue Movie (Southern), **Supp. XI:** 309

"Blue Notes" (Matthews), **Supp. IX:** 169

Blue Pastoral (Sorrentino), **Supp. XXI:** 226, 235–236

Blue Pastures (Oliver), **Supp. VII:** 229–230, 245

"Blueprint for Negro Writing" (Wright), **Supp. XVIII:** 282–283

"Blueprints" (Kingsolver), **Supp. VII:** 203

Blue Religion, The (Connelly, ed.), **Supp. XXI:** 74–75, 79

Blue Rhine, Black Forest (Untermeyer), **Supp. XV:** 310

"Blue Ribbon at Amesbury, A" (Frost), **Retro. Supp. I:** 138

"Blues Ain't No Mockin Bird" (Bambara), **Supp. XI:** 3

"Blues and the Fable in the Flesh, The" (lecture, Murray), **Supp. XIX:** 153

"Blues Chant Hoodoo Rival" (Komunyakaa), **Supp. XIII:** 117, 118

Blue Screen (Parker), **Supp. XIX:** 186

"Blues for Another Time" (Dunn), **Supp. XI:** 148

"Blues for Jimmy" (McGrath), **Supp. X:** 116

"Blues for John Coltraine, Dead at 41" (Matthews), **Supp. IX:** 157

Blues for Mister Charlie (Baldwin), **Retro. Supp. II:** 8; **Supp. I Part 1:** 48, 61–62, 63

"Blues for Warren" (McGrath), **Supp. X:** 116

Blue Shoe (Lamott), **Supp. XX:** 138–140

Blues If You Want (Matthews), **Supp. IX:** 155, **163–165**

"Blues I'm Playing, The" (Hughes), **Retro. Supp. I:** 204; **Supp. XIX:** 75

"Blue Sky, The" (Snyder), **Supp. VIII:** 306

Blues Legacies and Black Feminism (A. Davis), **Supp. XXVI:** 50

Bluesman (Dubus III), **Supp. XXIV: 102–104**

"Blues on a Box" (Hughes), **Retro. Supp. I:** 208

"Blues People" (Ellison), **Retro. Supp. II:** 124

Blues People: Negro Music in White America (Baraka), **Retro. Supp. II:** 124; **Supp. II Part 1:** 30, 31, 33–35, 37, 41, 42, 53

"Blue Spruces in Pairs, a Bird Bath Between" (Bronk), **Supp. XXI:** 30

Bluest Eye, The (Morrison), **Supp. III Part 1:** 362, 363–367, 379; **Supp. IV Part 1:** 2, 253; **Supp. VIII:** 213, 214, 227; **Supp. XI:** 4, 91

Bluestone, George, **Supp. IX:** 7, 15

Blue Swallows, The (Nemerov), **III:** 269, 270, 271, 274–275, 278, 284, 286–288

"Blue Tattoo" (Nelson and Espeland), **Supp. XVIII:** 181

Blue Voyage (Aiken), **I:** 53, 56

Bluhm, Norman, **Supp. XXIII:** 217

Blum, Gustav, **Supp. XV:** 194

Blum, Morgan, **I:** 169

Blum, W. C (pseudonym). *See* Watson, James Sibley, Jr.

Blumenthal, Nathaniel. *See* Branden, Nathaniel

Blumenthal, Sidney, **Supp. VIII:** 241

Blunden, Edmund, **Supp. XIX:** 133

Blunt, Wilfrid Scawen, **III:** 459

Bly, Carol, **Supp. XVI: 31–43**

Bly, Robert, **I:** 291; **Supp. III Part 2:** 599; **Supp. IV Part 1: 59–77,** 177; **Supp. IV Part 2:** 623; **Supp. IX:** 152, 155, 265, 271, 290; **Supp. V:** 332; **Supp. VIII:** 279; **Supp. X:** 127; **Supp. XI:** 142; **Supp. XIII:** 284; **Supp. XV:** 74, 176; **Supp. XVI:** 32, 36, 39, 177, 212, 230; **Supp. XVII:** 243, 244; **Supp. XXI:** 83, 84–86, 87, 91, 93, 94, 95; **Supp. XXII:** 83; **Supp. XXIII:** 136; **Supp. XXIV:** 219

"B Negative" (X. J. Kennedy), **Supp. XV: 156–157**

"Boarder, The" (Simpson), **Supp. IX:** 269

Boarding House Blues (Farrell), **II:** 30, 43, 45

Boarding School, The (Foster), **Supp. XXV:** 35, 36, 37, 45–47

Boas, Franz, **I:** 214; **Supp. I Part 2:** 641; **Supp. IX:** 329; **Supp. VIII:** 295; **Supp. XIV:** 199, 209, 210

"Boat, The" (Oliver), **Supp. VII:** 247

"Boat, The" (Sexton), **Supp. II Part 2:** 692

Boating Party, The (Renoir), **Supp. XII:** 188

"Boat Is Tethered to the Floor,' The: After the Harlem Renaissance" (H. Johnson), **Supp. XXVI:** 175

Boat of Quiet Hours, The (Kenyon), **Supp. VII:** 167–169, 171

"Boat of Quiet Hours, The" (Kenyon), **Supp. VII:** 168

"Boat Ride" (Gallagher), **Supp. XXIV:** 169

"Bob and Spike" (Wolfe), **Supp. III Part 2:** 580

Bobbed Hair (Wells, et al), **Supp. XXVI:** 275

"Bobby Shafter's Gone to Sea" (Swados), **Supp. XIX:** 267

"Bob Dylan's 115th Dream" (song, Dylan), **Supp. XVIII:** 25

Bobrowski, Johannes, **Supp. XV:** 78

Bob the Gambler (F. Barthelme), **Supp. XI:** 30, 31, 32, 34–35, 36–37

Boccaccio, Giovanni, **III:** 283, 411; **IV:** 230

"Bocca della Verità, La" (Davison), **Supp. XXVI:** 74

Bocock, Maclin, **Supp. X:** 79

Boddy, Kasia, **Supp. XXII:** 261

Bodelson, Anders, **Supp. XVI:** 33

Bodenheim, Maxwell, **II:** 42, 530; **Retro. Supp. I:** 417; **Supp. I Part 1:** 257; **Supp. XXV: 17–33**

"Bodies" (Oates), **Supp. II Part 2:** 520

"Bodies and Souls: The Haitian Revolution and Madison Smartt Bell's *All Souls' Rising*" (Trouillot), **Supp. X:** 14

Bodies of Water (Cliff), **Supp. XXII:** 66–67, 74–75

Bodies of Work: Essays (Acker), **Supp. XII:** 7

Bodily Harm (Atwood), **Supp. XIII: 25–27**

Bodley Head Jack London (London), **II:** 483

Body (Crews), **Supp. XI: 108–109**

"Body, The" (Heldreth), **Supp. V:** 151

Body and Soul (Conroy), **Supp. XVI:** 63, **72–74,** 77

"Body and Soul: A Meditation" (Kumin), **Supp. IV Part 2:** 442, 452

Body and Soul: Essays on Poetry (Jarman), **Supp. XVII:** 110, **111–112**

"Body and Soul: Parts of a Life" (Jarman), **Supp. XVII:** 112, 113

Body and the Song, The (Bishop), **Retro. Supp. II:** 40

"Body Bright" (Sanders), **Supp. XVI:** 276

Body of Martin Aquilera, The (Everett), **Supp. XVIII:** 57

Body of Poetry, The: Essays on Women, Form, and the Poetic Self (A. Finch), **Supp. XVII:** 69–70, **77–78**

Body of This Death: Poems (Bogan), **Supp. III Part 1:** 47, 49–52, 58

Body of Waking (Rukeyser), **Supp. VI:** 274, 281

"Body of Waking" (Rukeyser), **Supp. VI:** 279

"Body on Fire, the Soul in Flight, The" (Jarman), **Supp. XVII:** 111, 112

Body Rags (Kinnell), **Supp. III Part 1:** 235, 236, 243–245, 250, 253, 254

"Body's Curse, The" (Dobyns), **Supp. XIII:** 87

"Body's Weight" (Espaillat), **Supp. XXI:** 111

"Body's Weight, The" (Dobyns), **Supp. XIII:** 89

Body Traffic (Dobyns), **Supp. XIII:** 87, 89

"'Body with the Lamp Lit Inside, The'" (Mills), **Supp. IV Part 1:** 64

Body Work (Paretsky), **Supp. XXV:** 177, 178, 179, 181, 184–185

Boehm, David, **Supp. XVII:** 58

Boehme, Jakob, **I:** 10

Bogan, Louise, **I:** 169, 185; **Retro. Supp. I:** 36; **Supp. I Part 2:** 707, 726; **Supp. III Part 1: 47–68; Supp. IX:** 229; **Supp. VIII:** 171, 265; **Supp. X:** 58, 102; **Supp. XIII:** 347; **Supp. XIV:** 129; **Supp. XVII:** 75; **Supp. XXIII:** 145

Bogan, Major Benjamin Lewis, **IV:** 120

Bogart, Humphrey, **Supp. I Part 2:** 623; **Supp. IV Part 1:** 130, 356

Bogdanovich, Peter, **Supp. V:** 226

Bogey Man, The (Plimpton), **Supp. XVI:** 241

Boggs, Francis W., **Supp. XVI:** 182

"Bogs" (Pickering), **Supp. XXI:** 198

"Bohemian, The" (Hapgood), **Supp. XVII:** 103

"Bohemian, The" (Harte), **Supp. II Part 1:** 339

"Bohemian Girl, The" (Cather), **Retro. Supp. I:** 7

"Bohemian Hymn, The" (Emerson), **II:** 19

"Bohemians" (Saunders), **Supp. XIX:** 234

"Boids and Beasties" (Geisel), **Supp. XVI:** 100

Boissevain, Eugen, **III:** 124

Boissière, Ralph de, **Supp. XXI:** 160

Boit, Edward, **Retro. Supp. I:** 366

Bojorquez, Jennifer, **Supp. XII:** 318

"Boke, A" (Berrigan), **Supp. XXIV:** 42

Boker, George, **Supp. XV:** 269

Bolaño, Roberto, **Supp. XXV:** 49

"Bold Words at the Bridge" (Jewett), **II:** 394

Boleslavsky, Richard, **Supp. XIV:** 240, 243

Boleyn, Anne, **Supp. I Part 2:** 461

Bolick, Katie, **Supp. XVI:** 167; **Supp. XXIII:** 135, 137, 138; **Supp. XXIV:** 167, 173, 177

Bolivar, Simon, **Supp. I Part 1:** 283, 284, 285

Bolonik, Kera, **Supp. XVIII:** 60

Bolton, Guy, **Supp. I Part 1:** 281

Bolts of Melody: New Poems of Emily Dickinson (Todd and Bingham, eds.), **I:** 470; **Retro. Supp. I:** 36

"Bomb" (Corso), **Supp. XII:** 117, 124, 125–126, 127

Bombeck, Erma, **Supp. XVII:** 168

Bombs Away (Steinbeck), **IV:** 51–52

"Bona and Paul" (Toomer), **Supp. IX:** 307, 318–319

Bonaparte, Darren, **Supp. XXVI:** 88

Bonaparte, Marie, **III:** 418; **Retro. Supp. II:** 264, 266

"Bon-Bon" (Poe), **III:** 425

Bond, The (Boyce), **Supp. XXI:** 5, 11–12

Bond, The (N. Boyce), **Supp. XVII:** 99, 100

Bondage (Hwang), **Supp. XXI:** 147

Bondsman, The (Massinger), **Supp. XV:** 238

Bondwoman's Narrative, by Hannah Crafts, a Fugitive Slave, Recently Escaped from North Carolina, The, **Supp. XX:** 105

Bone, Martyn, **Supp. XXII:** 247

Bone, Robert, **Supp. IX:** 318–319; **Supp. XI:** 283; **Supp. XVIII:** 285

Bone by Bone (Matthiessen), **Supp. V:** 199, 212, 213, 214

"Bone Deposit" (Ray), **Supp. XVIII:** 194

Boners (Abingdon). *See Schoolboy Howlers* (Abingdon)

"Bones" (Goldbarth), **Supp. XII: 173–174**

"Bones and Jewels" (Monette), **Supp. X:** 159

"Bones and Shells" (Sanders), **Supp. XVI:** 271–272

"Bones of a House" (Cowley). *See* "Blue Juniata"

Bones on Black Spruce Mountain, The (Budbill), **Supp. XIX: 11–12**

Bonetti, Kay, **Supp. VIII:** 47, 152, 159, 160, 165, 168, 170, 223; **Supp. XII:** 61; **Supp. XIV:** 232, 234; **Supp. XXI:** 36

"Bonfire" (Gallagher), **Supp. XXIV:** 170

Bonfire of the Vanities, The (Wolfe), **Supp. III Part 2:** 584–586

Bonheur, Rosa, **Supp. XV:** 276

Bonhoeffer, Dietrich, **Supp. VIII:** 198

Boni, Charles, **Supp. XIV:** 288

Boni and Liveright, **Retro. Supp. I:** 59, 80, 178

Bonicelli, Vittorio, **Supp. XI:** 307

Bonifacius (Mather), **Supp. II Part 2:** 461, 464

Bonnefoy, Yves, **Supp. III Part 1:** 235, 243

Bonner, Robert, **Retro. Supp. I:** 246

Bonneville, Mme. Marguerite, **Supp. I Part 2:** 520, 521

Bonneville, Nicolas de, **Supp. I Part 2:** 511, 518, 519

Bonney, William. *See* Billy the Kid

Bontemps, Arna, **Retro. Supp. I:** 194, 196, 203; **Supp. I Part 1:** 325; **Supp. IV Part 1:** 170; **Supp. IX:** 306, 309; **Supp. XVIII:** 282; **Supp. XXII: 1–16**

Book, A (Barnes), **Supp. III Part 1:** 36, 39, 44

Book about Myself, A (Dreiser), **I:** 515; **Retro. Supp. II:** 104

"Book as a Container of Consciousness, The" (Gass), **Supp. VI:** 92

Booker, Keith, **Supp. XV:** 197

"Bookies, Beware!" (Heller), **Supp. IV Part 1:** 383

"Book Notes and News" (column, Boyce), **Supp. XXI:** 2

Book of American Negro Poetry, The (J. W. Johnson, ed.), **Supp. IV Part 1:** 165, 166; **Supp. XXII:** 11; **Supp. XXVI:** 165

Book of Americans, A (Benét), **Supp. XI:** 46, 47, 51

Book of Beb, The (Buechner), **Supp. XII:** 53

Book of Breeething, The (Burroughs), **Supp. III Part 1:** 97, 103

Book of Burlesques, A (Mencken), **III:** 104

Book of Common Prayer, A (Didion), **Supp. IV Part 1:** 196, 198, 203–205, 207, 208

Book of Daniel, The (Doctorow), **Supp. IV Part 1:** 218, 219, 220–222, 227, 231, 237–238, 238; **Supp. V:** 45

Book of Dreams (Kerouac), **Supp. III Part 1:** 225

"Book of Ephraim, The" (Merrill), **Supp. III Part 1:** 330–334

Book of Folly, The (Sexton), **Supp. II Part 2:** 691, 692–694

Book of Gallant Vagabonds, The (Beston), **Supp. XXVI:** 33

Book of Gods and Devils, The (Simic), **Supp. VIII: 281**

Book of Guys, The (Keillor), **Supp. XVI:** 177

"Book of Hours of Sister Clotilde, The" (Lowell), **II:** 522

Book of Jamaica, The (Banks), **Supp. V:** 11, 12, 16

"Book of Life" (Bidart), **Supp. XV:** 23

Book of Living Verse, The; English and American Poetry from the Thirteenth Century to the Present Day (Untermeyer, ed.), **Supp. XV:** 310

Book of Love, A (Vildrac; Bynner, trans.), **Supp. XV:** 50

Book of Lyrics (Bynner), **Supp. XV:** 51

Book of Martyrs (Fox). *See Acts and Monuments of These Latter and Perilous Days* (Fox)

Book of Medicines, The (Hogan), **Supp. IV Part 1:** 397, 410, 411–414

"Book of Medicines, The" (Hogan), **Supp. IV Part 1:** 412, 413

"Book of Memory, The" (Auster), **Supp. XII:** 21–22

Book of My Nights (L.-Y. Lee), **Supp. XV:** 215, **223–226**

Book of Negro Folklore, The (Hughes, ed.), **Supp. I Part 1:** 345; **Supp. XXII:** 11–12

Book of Nightmares, The (Kinnell), **Supp. III Part 1:** 235, 236, 243, 244, 246–254

Book of One's Own, A: People and Their Diaries (Mallon), **Supp. XIX:** 134

Book of Prefaces, A (Mencken), **III:** 99–100, 105

Book of Repulsive Women, The (Barnes), **Supp. III Part 1:** 33

Book of Revelation, **Supp. XXIII:** 44

Book of Roses, The (Parkman), **Supp. II Part 2:** 597, 598

Book of the Body, The (Bidart), **Supp. XV:** 21, **25–27**

"Book of the Dead, The" (Rukeyser), **Supp. VI:** 272, 278, 279; **Supp. XV:** 349

"Book of the Grotesque, The" (Anderson), **I:** 106

Book of the Homeless, The (Wharton), **Retro. Supp. I:** 377

Book of the Hopi (Waters), **Supp. X:** 124

Book of Tobit (Bible), **Supp. XII:** 54

Book of Verses, A (Masters), **Supp. I Part 2:** 458

Book of Wonder (Dunsany), **Supp. XXV:** 113

Book of Yaak, The (Bass), **Supp. XVI: 18–19**

"Book of Yolek, The" (Hecht), **Supp. X:** 69, **70–71**

"Books" (Collins), **Supp. XXI:** 55

"Books Considered" (Bloom), **Supp. I Part 1:** 96

"Books I Left Behind, The" (Pickering), **Supp. XXI:** 196

Books in My Life, The (H. Miller), **II:** 176, 189

"Books/P,L,E, The" (Goldbarth), **Supp. XII:** 190

Bookviews, **Supp. XI:** 216

"Book World Live", **Supp. XVIII:** 143–144

"Boolean Algebra: X2=X" (Bronk), **Supp. XXI:** 30

"Boom" (Nemerov), **III:** 278

Boom! (T. Williams), **IV:** 383

Boomer Girls: Poems by Women of the Baby Boom Generation (Gemin and Sergi, eds.), **Supp. XXI:** 246

Boom Town (Wolfe), **IV:** 456

"Boom Town" (Wolfe), **IV:** 469

Boone, Daniel, **II:** 207; **III:** 444; **IV:** 192, 193

Boorstin, Daniel, **I:** 253

Booth, Charles, **Supp. I Part 1:** 13

Booth, John Wilkes, **III:** 588

Booth, Philip, **I:** 522; **Supp. IX:** 269; **Supp. XI:** 141; **Supp. XIII:** 277; **Supp. XV:** 92; **Supp. XXVI:** 68

Booth, General William, **Supp. I Part 2:** 384, 386

"Booze" (P. Benedict), **Supp. XXIII:** 36

Borah, William, **III:** 475

Borden, Lizzie, **II:** 5

Border and the Buffalo, The (J. Cook), **Supp. XXIV:** 248

"Border Crossings: An Interview with Eric Gansworth" (de la Paz and Purdy), **Supp. XXVI:** 101

Borderlands/La Frontera: The New Mestiza (Anzaldúa), **Supp. XIII:** 223

Border Matters (Saldívar), **Supp. XIX:** 112–113

Borders (Mora), **Supp. XIII:** 213, **215–217**

Border Trilogy (McCarthy), **Supp. VIII:** 175, 182

"Border View, Hot Springs, Texas" (W. V. Davis), **Supp. XXI:** 95

Borel, Pétrus, **III:** 320

Borges, Jorge Luis, **I:** 123, 135, 138, 140, 142; **Supp. III Part 2:** 560; **Supp. IV Part 2:** 623, 626, 630; **Supp. V:** 238; **Supp. VIII:** 15, 348, 349; **Supp. XII:** 21, 147; **Supp. XIX:** 131; **Supp. XV:** 34; **Supp. XVI:** 201, 206; **Supp. XVII:** 47; **Supp. XXIII:** 68; **Supp. XXV:** 50, 69

"Borges and I" (Bidart), **Supp. XV:** 34, 35

"Borinken Blues" (Komunyakaa), **Supp. XIII:** 117

"Born, The" (Lamott), **Supp. XX: 143–144**

"Born a Square: The Westerner's Dilemma" (Stegner), **Supp. IV Part 2:** 595; **Supp. V:** 224

"Born Bad" (Cisneros), **Supp. VII:** 62

Born on the Fourth of July (Kovic), **Supp. XIX:** 17

"Borough of Cemeteries" (Shaw), **Supp. XIX:** 246

Borrowed Time: An AIDS Memoir (Monette), **Supp. X:** 145, 146, 147, 152, 154, 155

Bose, Sudip, **Supp. XXII:** 205, 206, 214

Bosmajian, Hamida, **Supp. XXII:** 290

"Bosque del Apache Wildlife Refuge" (Mora), **Supp. XIII:** 218

Boss Dog, The: A Story of Provence (M. F. K. Fisher), **Supp. XVII:** 91

Bost, Suzanne, **Supp. XXII:** 66, 70, 75, 78

"Boston" (Hardwick), **Supp. III Part 1:** 201

Boston (Sinclair), **Supp. V:** 282, 288–289

Boston, B. H., **Supp. XIII:** 312

Boston Adventure (Stafford), **Retro. Supp. II:** 177, 178

"Boston Common" (Berryman), **I:** 172

"Boston Hymn" (Emerson), **II:** 13, 19

Bostonians, The (H. James), **I:** 9; **II:** 282; **IV:** 202; **Retro. Supp. I:** 216, 225

Boston Marriage (Mamet), **Supp. XIV:** 247

"Boston Nativity, The" (Lowell), **II:** 538

Boswell, James, **IV:** 431; **Supp. I Part 2:** 656

Boswell: A Modern Comedy (Elkin), **Supp. VI:** 42, **44–45,** 57

Bosworth, Patricia, **Supp. IV Part 2:** 573, 591

"Bothersome Sex and O'Brien, The" (Ryan as Quin), **Supp. XVIII:** 238

Botticelli (McNally), **Supp. XIII:** 197

Botticelli, Sandro, **IV:** 410; **Retro. Supp. I:** 422

"Botticellian Trees, The" (W. C. Williams), **Retro. Supp. I:** 422

"Bottled" (H. Johnson), **Supp. XXVI:** 164, 165

"Bottle of Milk for Mother, A" (Algren), **Supp. IX:** 3

"Bottle of Perrier, A" (Wharton), **IV:** 316

"Bottles" (Kenyon), **Supp. VII:** 171

"Bottom Line, The" (Elkin), **Supp. VI:** 52, **53**

Bottom: On Shakespeare (Zukofsky), **Supp. III Part 2:** 622, 624, 625, 626, 627, 629

Boublil, Alain, **Supp. XXI:** 155

Boucher, Anthony, **Supp. IV Part 2:** 473; **Supp. XV:** 203, 205

Boucicault, Dion, **Supp. XXII:** 70

Boughton, Henrietta Breckenridge. *See* Young, Barbara

Boukreev, Anatoli, **Supp. XVIII:** 112

Boulanger, Nadia, **Supp. IV Part 1:** 81

"Boulot and Boulette" (Chopin), **Supp. I Part 1:** 211

Boulton, Agnes, **III:** 403; **Supp. XXII: 17–31**

Bound East for Cardiff (O'Neill), **III:** 388

Bound for Glory (Guthrie), **Supp. XVIII:** 23

"Bounty" (Saunders), **Supp. XIX:** 226, 227

"Bounty"(P. Benedict), **Supp. XXIII:** 41

"Bouquet, The" (Stevens), **IV:** 90

"Bouquet of Dark Red Mums, The" (Notley), **Supp. XXII:** 230

"Bouquet of Roses in Sunlight" (Stevens), **IV:** 93

Bourdin, Henri L., **Supp. I Part 1:** 251

Bourgeois, Monique, **Supp. XXII:** 99–100

Bourgeois Poet, The (Shapiro), **Supp. II Part 2:** 701, 703, 704, 713, 714–716

Bourget, James, **IV:** 319

Bourget, Paul, **II:** 325, 338; **IV:** 311, 315; **Retro. Supp. I:** 224, 359, 373; **Supp. XX: 232; Supp. XXIV:** 23

Bourjaily, Vance, **III:** 43; **Supp. IX:** 260; **Supp. XXIV:** 225

Bourke-White, Margaret, **I:** 290, 293, 295, 297

Bourne, Charles Rogers, **I:** 215

Bourne, Mrs. Charles Rogers, **I:** 215

Bourne, Randolph, **I: 214–238,** 243, 245, 246–247, 251, 259; **Supp. I Part 2:** 524; **Supp. XV:** 141, 298, 301

Boursicot, Bernard, **Supp. XXI:** 152, 153, 154

Bouton, Jim "Bulldog", **Supp. XX: 274**

Bouton, John Bell, **Supp. XXIII:** 188, 189

Bowden, Charles, **Supp. XIII:** 17

Bowditch, Nathaniel, **Supp. I Part 2:** 482

Bowen, Barbara, **Supp. IX:** 311

Bowen, Elizabeth, **Retro. Supp. I:** 351; **Supp. IV Part 1:** 299; **Supp. IX:** 128; **Supp. VIII:** 65, 165, 251, 265

Bowen, Francis, **Supp. I Part 2:** 413

Bowen, Henry, **Supp. XVIII:** 4

Bowen, Louise de Koven, **Supp. I Part 1:** 5

Bowen, Michael, **Supp. VIII:** 73

Bowers, John, **Supp. XI:** 217–218

"Bowlers Anonymous" (Dobyns), **Supp. XIII:** 86

Bowles, Emily, **Supp. XVIII:** 200, 202

Bowles, Jane (Jane Auer), **II:** 586; **Supp. IV Part 1:** 89, 92

Bowles, Paul, **I:** 211; **II:** 586; **Supp. II Part 1:** 17; **Supp. IV Part 1: 79–99**

Bowles, Samuel, **I:** 454, 457; **Retro. Supp. I:** 30, 32, 33

"Bowl of Blood, The" (Jeffers), **Supp. II Part 2:** 434

"Bowls" (Moore), **III:** 196

Bowman, James, **I:** 193

"Bows to Drouth" (Snyder), **Supp. VIII:** 303

Box, Edgar (pseudonym). *See* Vidal, Gore

Box and Quotations from Chairman Mao Tse-tung (Albee), **I:** 89–91, 94

Boxer and the Spy, The (Parker), **Supp. XIX:** 190

Box Garden, The (Shields), **Supp. VII:** 314–315, 320

"Box of Pastels, A" (Kooser), **Supp. XIX:** 128

"Box of Rocks, A" (Gallagher), **Supp. XXIV:** 175

"Box Seat" (Toomer), **Supp. III Part 2:** 484; **Supp. IX:** 316, 318

Boy, A (Ashbery), **Supp. III Part 1:** 5

"Boy and Dog" (L. Brown), **Supp. XXI:** 38, 42, **43–44**

Boyce, Horace, **II:** 136

Boyce, Neith, **Supp. XVII:** 96, 97, 98–99, 100, 106; **Supp. XXI: 1–16**

Boyd, Brian, **Retro. Supp. I:** 270, 275

Boyd, Janet L., **Supp. X:** 229

Boyd, Kristen, **Supp. XXIII:** 246

Boyd, Nancy (pseudonym). *See* Millay, Edna St. Vincent

Boyd, Thomas, **I:** 99; **IV:** 427

Boyesen, H. H., **II:** 289

"Boy from Lam Kien, The" (July), **Supp. XXIV:** 200, 204

"Boyhood" (Collins), **Supp. XXI:** 64

"Boyhood" (Farrell), **II:** 28

"Boy in France, A" (Salinger), **III:** 552–553

"Boy in the Basement, The" (Inge), **Supp. XXV:** 105, 106

Boy in the Water (Dobyns), **Supp. XIII:** 75, **84**

Boyle, Kay, **IV:** 404; **Supp. XXIV: 49–66**

Boyle, T. Coraghessan, **Supp. VIII: 1–17; Supp. XX: 17–32; Supp. XXI:** 226; **Supp. XXII:** 262

Boyle, Thomas John. *See* Boyle, T. C.

Boynton, H. W., **Supp. IX:** 7

Boynton, Percy Holmes, **Supp. I Part 2:** 415

Boynton, Robert, **Supp. XVII:** 209; **Supp. XVIII:** 105, 107, 116

Boynton, Robert S., **Supp. XXV:** 158

"Boy on a Train" (Ellison), **Retro. Supp. II:** 124

"Boy Riding Forward Backward" (Francis), **Supp. IX:** 82

"Boys and Girls" (Cisneros), **Supp. VII:** 59–60

"Boy's Dream Ballad, The" (Very), **Supp. XXV:** 244

Boy's Froissart, The (Lanier), **Supp. I Part 1:** 361

"Boys"(Kenny), **Supp. XXIII:** 149

Boy's King Arthur, The (Lanier), **Supp. I Part 1:** 361

Boy's Mabinogion, The (Lanier), **Supp. I Part 1:** 361

"Boys of '29, The" (Holmes), **Supp. I Part 1:** 308

Boys of '76, The (Coffin), **III:** 577

Boy's Percy, The (Lanier), **Supp. I Part 1:** 361

"Boy Story" (Huddle), **Supp. XXVI:** 151

Boy's Town (Howells), **I:** 418

Boy's Will, A (Frost), **II:** 152, 153, 155–156, 159, 164, 166; **Retro. Supp. I:** 124, 127, 128, 131; **Retro. Supp. II:** 168

"Boy Up a Tree" (Hoffman), **Supp. XVIII:** 86

"Boy Who Wrestled with Angels, The" (Hoffman), **Supp. X:** 90

"Boy with One Shoe, The" (Jewett), **Retro. Supp. II:** 132

"Brace, The" (Bausch), **Supp. VII:** 48

Bracebridge Hall, or, The Humorists (Irving), **I:** 339, 341; **II:** 308–309, 313

Bracher, Frederick, **I:** 378, 380; **Supp. I Part 1:** 185

Brackenridge, Hugh Henry, **Supp. I Part 1:** 124, 127, 145; **Supp. II Part 1:** 65

Brackett, Leigh, **Supp. IV Part 1:** 130

Bradbury, John M., **I:** 288–289; **IV:** 130, 135

Bradbury, Malcolm, **Supp. VIII:** 124; **Supp. XVIII:** 140

Bradbury, Ray, **Supp. I Part 2:** 621–622; **Supp. IV Part 1: 101–118; Supp. XVI:** 122; **Supp. XVII:** 41; **Supp. XXIII:** 290; **Supp. XXV:** 141

"Brad Carrigan, American" (Saunders), **Supp. XIX:** 233

Braddon, Mary E., **Supp. I Part 1:** 35, 36

Bradfield, Scott, **Supp. VIII:** 88

Bradford, Gamaliel, **I:** 248, 250

Bradford, Roark, **Retro. Supp. I:** 80

Bradford, William, **Retro. Supp. II:** 161, 162; **Supp. I Part 1:** 110, 112; **Supp. I Part 2:** 486, 494; **Supp. XXII: 33–47**

Bradlee, Ben, **Supp. V:** 201

Bradley, Bill, **Supp. VIII:** 47

Bradley, F. H., **Retro. Supp. I:** 57, 58

Bradley, Francis Herbert, **I:** 59, 567–568, 572, 573

Bradshaw, Barbara, **Supp. XIII:** 313

Bradstreet, Anne, **I:** 178–179, 180, 181, 182, 184; **III:** 505; **Retro. Supp. I:** 40; **Supp. I Part 1: 98–123,** 300; **Supp. I Part 2:** 484, 485, 496, 546, 705; **Supp. V:** 113, 117–118; **Supp. XIII:** 152; **Supp. XIV:** 128; **Supp. XVIII:** 304; **Supp. XXII:** 46

Bradstreet, Elizabeth, **Supp. I Part 1:** 108, 122

Bradstreet, Simon, **I:** 178; **Supp. I Part 1:** 103, 110, 116

Bradstreet, Mrs. Simon. *See* Bradstreet, Anne

Brady, Alice, **III:** 399

Brady, Catherine, **Supp. XXIII:** 301

Brady, Matthew, **Supp. XVIII:** 4

Bragdon, Claude, **Supp. XX: 117**

"Bragdowdy and the Busybody, The" (Thurber), **Supp. I Part 2:** 617

Bragg, Rick, **Supp. XVIII:** 195

"Brahma" (Emerson), **II:** 19, 20

Brahms, Johannes, **III:** 118, 448

"Brahms in Delirium" (Skloot), **Supp. XX: 203**

Braided Creek (Kooser and Harrison), **Supp. XIX:** 126

"Braiding" (L.-Y. Lee), **Supp. XV:** 214

"Brain and the Mind, The" (James), **II:** 346

Brainard, Joe, **Supp. XV:** 33; **Supp. XXIII:** 217; **Supp. XXIV:** 33, 34, 35, 39, 41, 42, 43

"Brain Damage" (Barthelme), **Supp. IV Part 1:** 44

"Braindead Megaphone, The" (Saunders), **Supp. XIX:** 235

Braindead Megaphone, The: Essays (Saunders), **Supp. XIX: 234–236**

"Brain Scan" (Skloot), **Supp. XX: 200**

"Brain to the Heart, The" (Komunyakaa), **Supp. XIII:** 120

Braithwaite, Chris, **Supp. XXII:** 212

Braithwaite, William Stanley, **Retro. Supp. I:** 131; **Supp. IX:** 309; **Supp. XV:** 296–297, 301–302, 305, 306

Brakhage, Stan, **Supp. XII:** 2

Braly, Malcolm, **Supp. XVIII:** 147

"Bramble, The" (Wrigley), **Supp. XVIII:** 301

Brame, Gloria, **Supp. XV:** 113; **Supp. XXIII:** 122

Bramen, Carrie Tirado, **Supp. XXIV:** 192

Bramer, Monte, **Supp. X:** 152

Branch Will Not Break, The (Wright), **Supp. III Part 2:** 596, 598–601; **Supp. IV Part 1:** 60; **Supp. IX:** 159

Brancusi, Constantin, **III:** 201; **Retro. Supp. I:** 292

Brancusi, Constantine, **Supp. XXVI:** 224

Brande, Dorothea, **Supp. I Part 2:** 608

Brandel, Marc, **Supp. XXI:** 276

Branden, Nathaniel, **Supp. IV Part 2:** 526, 528

"Branding Cities" (Greenberg), **Supp. XXII:** 244

"Brand-Name Blues" (Kaufmann), **Supp. XI:** 39

Brand New Life, A (Farrell), **II:** 46, 48

Brando, Marlon, **II:** 588; **Supp. IV Part 2:** 560; **Supp. XVIII:** 251

Brandon, Henry, **Supp. I Part 2:** 604, 612, 618

Brandt, Alice, **Supp. I Part 1:** 92

Brandt, Carl, **Supp. XI:** 45

Brant, Sebastian, **III:** 447, 448

Brantley, Ben, **Supp. XXIV:** 268, 269–270, 271, 272, 274

Braque, Georges, **III:** 197; **Supp. IX:** 66; **Supp. XXVI:** 259

Brashford, Jake, **Supp. X:** 252

Brasil, Emanuel, **Supp. I Part 1:** 94

"Brasília" (Plath), **Supp. I Part 2:** 544, 545

"Brass Buttons" (McCoy), **Supp. XIII:** 161

"Brass Candlestick, The" (Francis), **Supp. IX:** 89

Brass Check, The (Sinclair), **Supp. V:** 276, 281, 282, 284–285

Brass Knuckles (Dybek), **Supp. XXIII: 68–69**

"Brass Ring, The" (Carver), **Supp. III Part 1:** 137

"Brass Spittoons" (Hughes), **Supp. I Part 1:** 326–327

Brass Verdict, The (Connelly), **Supp. XXI: 78–79**

Brats (X. J. Kennedy), **Supp. XV:** 163

Brautigan, Richard, **III:** 174; **Supp. VIII:** 42, 43; **Supp. XII:** 139; **Supp. XVI:** 172; **Supp. XXI:** 53

Brave Cowboy, The (Abbey), **Supp. XIII:** 4–5

Brave Men (Pyle), **Supp. XVII:** 61

Brave New World (Huxley), **II:** 454; **Supp. XIII:** 29; **Supp. XVIII:** 137

"Brave New World" (MacLeish), **III:** 18

Bravery of Earth, A (Eberhart), **I:** 522, 524, 525, 526, 530

"Brave Tailors of Maida, The" (Talese), **Supp. XVII:** 208

"Brave Words for a Startling Occasion" (Ellison), **Retro. Supp. II:** 118

Braving the Elements (Merrill), **Supp. III Part 1:** 320, 323, 325–327, 329

Bravo, The (Cooper), **I:** 345–346, 348

"Bravura" (Francis), **Supp. IX:** 90

Brawley, Benjamin, **Supp. I Part 1:** 327, 332

Brawl in a Tavern, A (Shaw), **Supp. XIX:** 241

Brawne, Fanny, **I:** 284; **II:** 531

Braxton, Joanne, **Supp. IV Part 1:** 12, 15

Brazil (Bishop), **Retro. Supp. II:** 45; **Supp. I Part 1:** 92

"Brazil" (Marshall), **Supp. XI:** 281

Brazil (Updike), **Retro. Supp. I:** 329, 330, 334

"Brazil, January 1, 1502" (Bishop), **Retro. Supp. II:** 47

Braziller, George, **Supp. X:** 24; **Supp. XXIII:** 214

Brazzi, Rossano, **Supp. IV Part 2:** 520

"Bread" (Dickey), **Supp. IV Part 1:** 182

"Bread" (Olds), **Supp. X:** 206

"Bread Alone" (Wylie), **Supp. I Part 2:** 727

Bread in the Wilderness (Merton), **Supp. VIII:** 197, 208

"Bread of Desire, The" (Nelson), **Supp. XVIII:** 177

Bread of Idleness, The (Masters), **Supp. I Part 2:** 460

"Bread of This World, The" (McGrath), **Supp. X:** 119, 127

Bread of Time, The (Levine), **Supp. V:** 180

Bread without Sugar (Stern), **Supp. IX: 297–298**

"Break, The" (Sexton), **Supp. II Part 2:** 689

"Breakaways, The" (Siddons), **Supp. XXII:** 244

Breakdown (Paretsky), **Supp. XXV:** 185

Breakfast at Tiffany's (Capote), **Supp. III Part 1:** 113, 117, 119–121, 124, 126

Breakfast of Champions (Vonnegut), **Supp. II Part 2:** 755, 759, 769, 770, 777–778

Breaking and a Death, A (Kees), **Supp. XV:** 145

Breaking and Entering (X. J. Kennedy), **Supp. XV:** 153, **160–162**

Breaking Hard Ground (D. Hunter), **Supp. XVI:** 38

Breaking Ice (McMillan, ed.), **Supp. XIII:** 182–183

Breaking of the Day, The (Davison), **Supp. XXVI:** 65, 68–70

"Breaking of the Day, The" (Davison), **Supp. XXVI:** 68, 69

Breaking Open (Rukeyser), **Supp. VI:** 274, 281

"Breaking Open" (Rukeyser), **Supp. VI:** 286

Breaking Point, The (Rinehart), **Supp. XXV:** 196

Breaking Ranks: A Political Memoir (Podhoretz), **Supp. VIII: 239–241,** 245

"Breaking the Code of Silence: Ideology and Women's Confessional Poetry" (Harris), **Supp. XIV:** 269

"Breaking Up of the Winships, The" (Thurber), **Supp. I Part 2:** 616

Brearton, Fran, **Supp. XXIV:** 167

Breast, The (P. Roth), **Retro. Supp. II:** 287–288; **Supp. III Part 2:** 416, 418

"Breast, The" (Sexton), **Supp. II Part 2:** 687

"Breasts" (Gallagher), **Supp. XXIV:** 168, 174

"Breasts" (Simic), **Supp. VIII:** 275

"Breasts" (Dybek), **Supp. XXIII:** 77

"Breath" (Espaillat), **Supp. XXI:** 109

"Breath" (Levine), **Supp. V:** 185

Breathe No More, My Lady (Lacy), **Supp. XV:** 203

Breathing Lessons (Tyler), **Supp. IV Part 2:** 669–670

Breathing Room (Davison), **Supp. XXVI:** 66, 78–79

"Breathing Room" (Davison), **Supp. XXVI:** 79

Breathing the Monster Alive (Gansworth), **Supp. XXVI:** 112–113

Breathing the Water (Levertov), **Supp. III Part 1:** 274, 283, 284

"Breath of Life, The" (C. Baxter), **Supp. XVII:** 23

Breath's Burials (Sobin), **Supp. XVI: 288–289**

Breaux, Zelia, **Retro. Supp. II:** 114

Brecht, Bertolt, **I:** 60, 301; **III:** 161, 162; **IV:** 394; **Supp. I Part 1:** 292; **Supp. II Part 1:** 10, 26, 56; **Supp. IV Part 1:** 359; **Supp. IX:** 131, 133, 140; **Supp. X:** 112; **Supp. XIII:** 206, 286; **Supp. XIV:** 162; **Supp. XVIII:** 33; **Supp. XXIV:** 267

Breen, Jon L., **Supp. XXVI:** 277, 281

Breen, Joseph I., **IV:** 390

Breines, Ron, **Supp. XVIII:** 97

Breit, Harvey, **I:** 433; **III:** 575; **Retro. Supp. II:** 230; **Supp. XVIII:** 254; **Supp. XXI:** 277

Breman, Paul, **Supp. XXII:** 8

Bremer, Anne, **Supp. XXII:** 277

Bremer, Fredrika, **Supp. I Part 1:** 407

Bremer, Richard, **Supp. XXIII:** 236

Brendan: A Novel (Buechner), **Supp. XII:** 53

Brennan, Matthew C., **Supp. XIX:** 121; **Supp. XV:** 113, 125

Brent, David, **Supp. XXII:** 259

Brent, Linda, **Supp. IV Part 1:** 12, 13

Brentano, Franz, **II:** 350; **Supp. XIV:** 198, 199

Brer Rabbit (tales), **Supp. IV Part 1:** 11, 13; **Supp. XIV:** 88

Breslin, James E. B., **Retro. Supp. I:** 430

Breslin, John B., **Supp. IV Part 1:** 308

Breslin, Paul, **Supp. VIII:** 283

Bresson, Robert, **Supp. IV Part 1:** 156

"Bresson's Movies" (Creeley), **Supp. IV Part 1:** 156–157

Breton, André, **III:** 425; **Supp. XIII:** 114; **Supp. XVII:** 244

Brett, George, **II:** 466; **Supp. V:** 286

Brett, Reginald Baliol, **Supp. XX: 230**

Brevoort, Henry, **II:** 298

Brew, Kwesi, **Supp. IV Part 1:** 10, 16

Brewer, Gaylord, **Supp. XV:** 330

"Brewing of Soma, The" (Whittier), **Supp. I Part 2:** 704

Brewsie and Willie (Stein), **IV:** 27

Brewster, Martha, **Supp. I Part 1:** 114

"Brewsterville Croesus, A" (Briggs), **Supp. XVIII:** 16

Brewsterville letters (Briggs), **Supp. XVIII:** 1, 5, **15–16**

"Brian Age 7" (Doty), **Supp. XI:** 136

Briand, Paul, **Supp. XVIII:** 155

"Briar Patch, The" (Warren), **IV:** 237

Briar Rose (Coover), **Supp. V:** 52

"Briar Rose (Sleeping Beauty)" (Sexton), **Supp. II Part 2:** 690

Brice, Fanny, **II:** 427

"Brick, The" (Nye), **Supp. XIII:** 276

"Bricklayer in the Snow" (Fante), **Supp. XI:** 164–165

"Brick Layer's Lunch Hour, The" (Ginsberg), **Supp. II Part 1:** 318

Brickman, Marshall, **Supp. XV:** 5

"Bricks, The" (Hogan), **Supp. IV Part 1:** 413

"Bridal Ballad, The" (Poe), **III:** 428

"Bridal Bed, The" (Gibran), **Supp. XX: 124**

Bridal Dinner, The (Gurney), **Supp. V:** 109, 110

Bridal Hunt (Silver), **Supp. XXIV:** 264

"Bride Comes to Yellow Sky, The" (Crane), **I:** 34, 415, 416, 423

Bridegroom, The (Jin), **Supp. XVIII: 97–98**

"Bridegroom, The" (Jin), **Supp. XVIII:** 98

Bridegroom Cometh, The (W. Frank), **Supp. XX: 77**

"Bridegroom's Body, The" (Boyle), **Supp. XXIV:** 54, **55–56**

"Bride in the 30's, A" (Auden), **Supp. II Part 1:** 9

Bride of Lammermoor (Scott), **II:** 291

Bride of Samoa (film), **Supp. IV Part 1:** 82

"Bride of the Innisfallen, The" (Welty), **IV:** 278–279; **Retro. Supp. I:** 353

Bride of the Innisfallen, The, and Other Stories (Welty), **IV:** 261, 275–279; **Retro. Supp. I:** 352–353, 355

Brides of the South Wind: Poems 1917–1922 (Jeffers), **Supp. II Part 2:** 419

Bridge, Horatio, **II:** 226

"BRIDGE, THE" (Baraka), **Supp. II Part 1:** 32, 36

Bridge, The (H. Crane), **I:** 62, 109, 266, 385, 386, 387, 395–399, 400, 402; **IV:** 123, 341, 418, 419, 420; **Retro. Supp. I:** 427; **Retro. Supp. II:** 76, 77, 81, 83, **84–87; Supp. IX:** 306; **Supp. V:** 342; **Supp. XXIII:** 146; **Supp. XXVI:** 21, 25, 28

Bridge, The (Talese), **Supp. XVII:** 202, 203, 208

Bridge at Remagen, The (film), **Supp. XI:** 343

"Bridge Burners, The" (Van Vechten), **Supp. II Part 2:** 733

Bridgehead: The Drama of Israel (W. Frank), **Supp. XX: 80**

Bridge of San Luis Rey, The (Wilder), **I:** 360; **IV:** 356, 357, 360–363, 365, 366

"Bridge of Sighs" (P. Benedict), **Supp. XXIII:** 47–48

Bridge of Years, The (Sarton), **Supp. VIII:** 253

"Bridges" (Kingsolver), **Supp. VII:** 208

Bridges, Harry, **I:** 493; **Supp. XIX:** 264; **Supp. XVIII:** 238

Bridges, Lloyd, **Supp. XV:** 202

Bridges, Robert, **II:** 537; **III:** 527; **Supp. I Part 2:** 721; **Supp. II Part 1:** 21; **Supp. XIV:** 336, 341, 342, 343

"Bridging" (Apple), **Supp. XVII:** 5

Bridgman, P. W., **I:** 278

"Bridle, The" (Carver), **Supp. III Part 1:** 138

"Brief and Blameless Outline of the Ontogeny of Crow, A" (Wright), **Supp. XV:** 347

Brief and Frightening Reign of Phil, The (Saunders), **Supp. XIX: 230–231,** 233

"Brief Début of Tildy, The" (O. Henry), **Supp. II Part 1:** 408

"Brief Encounters on the Inland Waterway" (Vonnegut), **Supp. II Part 2:** 760

"Brief History of My Mother's Temper, A" (Huddle), **Supp. XXVI:** 150

Brief History of the Dead, The (Brockmeier), **Supp. XXII:** 57–59, 61

Briefings (Ammons), **Supp. VII:** 29

Brief Interviews with Hideous Men (Wallace), **Supp. X: 308–310**

"Brief Interviews with Hideous Men" (Wallace), **Supp. X:** 309

"Briefly It Enters, and Briefly Speaks" (Kenyon), **Supp. VII:** 174

"Brief Study of the British, A" (Saunders), **Supp. XIX:** 235

Brief Wondrous Life of Oscar Wao, The (Díaz), **Supp. XXIV:** 83, 84, 85, 87, **89–92,** 93

Brier, His Book (J. W. Miller), **Supp. XX: 165, 168, 170**

"Brier Grows Wild, The" (J. W. Miller), **Supp. XX: 170**

"Brier Losing Touch with His Traditions, The" (J. W. Miller), **Supp. XX: 165, 169**

Brier Poems, The (J. W. Miller), **Supp. XX: 168**

"Brier Sermon, The—You Must Be Born Again" (J. W. Miller), **Supp. XX: 165, 169–170**

Briffault, Robert, **Supp. I Part 2:** 560, 567

"Brigade de Cuisine" (McPhee), **Supp. III Part 1:** 307–308

Brigadier and the Golf Widow, The (Cheever), **Supp. I Part 1:** 184–185, 192

Briggs, Charles Frederick, **Supp. I Part 2:** 411; **Supp. XVIII: 1–18**

brigham, besmilr, **Supp. XV:** 349

"Bright and Morning Star" (Wright), **IV:** 488

Bright Book of Life: American Novelists and Storytellers from Hemingway to Mailer (Kazin), **Supp. VIII:** 102, 104

Bright Center of Heaven (Maxwell), **Supp. VIII: 153–155,** 164

"Brightness from the North" (B. Kelly), **Supp. XVII:** 131

Brighton Beach Memoirs (Simon), **Supp. IV Part 2:** 576, 577, 584, 586–587, 590

Bright Procession (Sedges), **Supp. II Part 1:** 125

Bright Room Called Day, A (Kushner), **Supp. IX:** 133, **138–141,** 142

Brillat-Savarin, Jean Anthelme, **Supp. XVII:** 82, 86, 87

"Brilliance" (Doty), **Supp. XI:** 124, 128

"Brilliant California Novelist, A" (Forman), **Supp. XXIV:** 30

"Brilliant Leaves" (Gordon), **II:** 199

"Brilliant Sad Sun" (W. C. Williams), **Retro. Supp. I:** 422

"Bring Brang Brung" (Muñoz), **Supp. XXV:** 135–136

"Bringing Back the Trumpeter Swan" (Kumin), **Supp. IV Part 2:** 454

Bringing It All Back Home (album, Dylan), **Supp. XVIII:** 20, 25, 26, 30

Bringing It All Back Home (McNally), **Supp. XIII:** 197–198

Bringing the Devil to His Knees (C. Baxter), **Supp. XVII:** 22

"Bringing the Strange Home" (Dunn), **Supp. XI:** 141

"Bring the Day!" (Roethke), **III:** 536

Brinkley, Douglas, **Supp. XIII:** 9; **Supp. XXIV:** 281, 293

Brinkmeyer, Robert H., Jr., **Supp. XI:** 38

Brinnin, John Malcolm, **IV:** 26, 27, 28, 42, 46; **Supp. XV:** 139

Brissot, Jacques Pierre, **Supp. I Part 2:** 511

"Britain's Negro Problem in Sierra Leone" (Du Bois), **Supp. I Part 1:** 176

"British Guiana" (Marshall), **Supp. XI:** 281–282

"British Poets, The" (Holmes), **Supp. I Part 1:** 306

"British Prison Ship, The" (Freneau), **Supp. II Part 1:** 261

Brittan, Gordon G., Jr., **Supp. XIV:** 234

Britten, Benjamin, **II:** 586; **Supp. II Part 1:** 17; **Supp. IV Part 1:** 84

Broadwater, Bowden, **II:** 562

Broadway, Broadway (McNally). *See It's Only a Play* (McNally)

Broadway, J. William, **Supp. V:** 316

Broadway Bound (Simon), **Supp. IV Part 2:** 576, 577, 584, 586–587, 590

Broadway Danny Rose (film; Allen), **Supp. XV:** 9

"Broadway Sights" (Whitman), **IV:** 350

Broccoli, Albert R. "Cubby", **Supp. XI:** 307

Brock

Bröck, Sabine, **Supp. XI:** 275, 277, 278

Brockmeier, Kevin, **Supp. XXII: 49–63**

Brodeur, Brian, **Supp. XXVI:** 150

Brodhead, Richard, **Retro. Supp. II:** 139; **Supp. XIV:** 61

Brodkey, Harold, **Supp. VIII:** 151; **Supp. X:** 160

Brodkin, Joel, **Supp. XXV:** 261

Brodskii, Iosif Alexsandrovich. *See* Brodsky, Joseph

Brodsky, Joseph, **Supp. VIII: 19–35; Supp. X:** 65, 73; **Supp. XV:** 134, 135, 256; **Supp. XXIII:** 122

Brody, Alter, **Supp. XV:** 302, 307

Brodyar, Anatole, **Supp. XIV:** 106

Brokeback Mountain (film), **Supp. XX: 273**

"Brokeback Mountain" (Proulx), **Supp. VII:** 264–265

"Broken Balance, The" (Jeffers), **Supp. II Part 2:** 426

"Broken Field Running" (Bambara), **Supp. XI:** 10, 11

Broken Frieze, The (Everwine), **Supp. XV:** 74, 75, 89

Broken Ground, The (Berry), **Supp. X:** 30

"Broken Home, The" (Merrill), **Supp. III Part 1:** 319, 325

"Broken Oar, The" (Longfellow), **Retro. Supp. II:** 169

"Broken Promise" (MacLeish), **III:** 15

Broken Span, The (W. C. Williams), **IV:** 419; **Retro. Supp. I:** 424

"Broken Tower, The" (H. Crane), **I:** 385, 386, 400, 401–402; **Retro. Supp. II:** 89, 90

Broken Vessels (Dubus), **Supp. VII:** 90–91; **Supp. XI:** 347

"Broken Vessels" (Dubus), **Supp. VII:** 90

Broken Wings, The (al-Ajni&hudot;a al-Mutakassirah) (Gibran), **Supp. XX: 115, 124, 125**

"Broker" (H. Roth), **Supp. IX:** 234

Bromfield, Louis, **IV:** 380

"Brompton Cocktail" (Mamet), **Supp. XIV:** 252

Bromwich, David, **Retro. Supp. I:** 305; **Supp. XII:** 162

"Broncho That Would Not Be Broken, The" (Lindsay), **Supp. I Part 2:** 383

Bronk, William, **Supp. XV:** 115; **Supp. XXI: 17–34; Supp. XXVI:** 237

Brontë, Anne, **Supp. IV Part 2:** 430

Brontë, Branwell, **I:** 462

Brontë, Charlotte, **I:** 458; **II:** 175; **Supp. IV Part 2:** 430; **Supp. IX:** 128; **Supp. XII:** 104, 303; **Supp. XV:** 338; **Supp. XVI:** 158; **Supp. XX: 108**

Brontë, Emily, **I:** 458; **Retro. Supp. I:** 43; **Supp. IV Part 2:** 430; **Supp. IX:** 128; **Supp. X:** 78, 89; **Supp. XV:** 338

"Bronze" (Francis), **Supp. IX:** 76

"Bronze" (Merrill), **Supp. III Part 1:** 336

Bronze Booklets on the History, Problems, and Cultural Contributions of the Negro series, **Supp. XIV:** 202

"Bronze Buckaroo, The" (Baraka), **Supp. II Part 1:** 49

"Bronze Horses, The" (Lowell), **II:** 524

"Bronze Tablets" (Lowell), **II:** 523

Bronzeville Boys and Girls (Brooks), **Supp. III Part 1:** 79

"Bronzeville Mother Loiters in Mississippi, A. Meanwhile, a Mississippi Mother Burns Bacon" (Brooks), **Supp. III Part 1:** 80

"Brooch, The" (Singer), **IV:** 20

Brook, Peter, **Retro. Supp. II:** 182

Brooke, Rupert, **II:** 82; **III:** 3

Brook Evans (Glaspell), **Supp. III Part 1:** 182–185

"Brooking Likeness" (Glück), **Supp. V:** 85

"Brooklyn" (Marshall), **Supp. XI:** 281, 282

"Brooklyn" (Shaw), **Supp. XIX:** 239, 240

Brooklyn Noir (McLoughlin, ed.), **Supp. XXIV:** 14

Brooks, Albert (Al Pew), **Supp. XXI:** 22

Brooks, Carrellin, **Supp. XXV:** 8

Brooks, Cleanth, **I:** 280, 282; **III:** 517; **IV:** 236, 279; **Retro. Supp. I:** 40, 41, 90; **Retro. Supp. II:** 235; **Supp. I Part 2:** 423; **Supp. III Part 2:** 542; **Supp. IX:** 153, 155; **Supp. V:** 316; **Supp. X:** 115, 123; **Supp. XIV: 1–20; Supp. XIX:** 246

Brooks, David, **Supp. IV Part 2:** 623, 626, 630; **Supp. VIII:** 232

Brooks, Gwendolyn, **Retro. Supp. I:** 208; **Supp. III Part 1: 69–90; Supp. IV Part 1:** 2, 15, 244, 251, 257; **Supp. XI:** 1, 278; **Supp. XIII:** 111, 112, 296; **Supp. XIV:** 73; **Supp. XVIII:** 175, 181, 185; **Supp. XXI:** 230

Brooks, Mel, **Supp. IV Part 1:** 390; **Supp. IV Part 2:** 591

Brooks, Paul, **Supp. IX:** 26, 31, 32

Brooks, Phillips, **II:** 542; **Retro. Supp. II:** 134; **Supp. XIII:** 142

Brooks, Van Wyck, **I:** 106, 117, 215, 222, 228, 230, 231, 233, 236, **239–263,** 266, 480; **II:** 30, 271, 285, 309, 337, 482; **III:** 394, 606; **IV:** 171, 312, 427, 433; **Retro. Supp. II:** 46, 137; **Supp. I Part 2:** 423, 424, 650; **Supp. II Part 1:** 137; **Supp. VIII:** 98, 101; **Supp. XIV:** 11; **Supp. XV:** 298, 301; **Supp. XX: 68**

Brooks, Mrs. Van Wyck (Eleanor Kenyon Stimson), **I:** 240, 245, 250, 252

Brooks, Mrs. Van Wyck (Gladys Billings), **I:** 258

Broom of the System, The (Wallace), **Supp. X:** 301, **302–305,** 310

"Brooms" (Simic), **Supp. VIII:** 275

Brosi, George, **Supp. XX: 166; Supp. XXIII:** 39

Brosnan, Jim, **II:** 424–425; **Supp. XX: 195**

Brossard, Chandler, **Supp. XXII:** 258

Brother Carl (Sontag), **Supp. III Part 2:** 452

"Brother Death" (Anderson), **I:** 114

Brother Fire (Di Piero), **Supp. XIX:** 35, 38, 45–47

Brotherhood of the Grape, The (Fante), **Supp. XI:** 160, **171–172**

Brother in Elysium, The: Ideas of Friendship and Society in the United States (Bronk), **Supp. XXI:** 21, 22, 25, 31

"Brothers" (Anderson), **I:** 114

"Brothers" (Huddle), **Supp. XXVI:** 154

Brothers, The (F. Barthelme), **Supp. XI:** 25, 28, 29, 30, 32–33

Brothers and Keepers (Wideman), **Supp. X:** 320, 321–322, 323, **325–327,** 328, 329–330, 331, 332

Brothers Ashkenazi, The (Singer), **IV:** 2

Brothers Karamazov, The (Dostoevsky), **II:** 60; **III:** 146, 150, 283; **Supp. IX:** 102, 106; **Supp. XI:** 172; **Supp. XII:** 322

Brothers of No Kin (Richter), **Supp. XVIII:** 209

"Brothers of No Kin" (Richter), **Supp. XVIII:** 208

Brother to Dragons: A Tale in Verse and Voices (Warren), **IV:** 243–244, 245, 246, 251, 252, 254, 257

Broughton, James, **Supp. XV:** 146

Broughton, Rhoda, **II:** 174; **IV:** 309, 310; **Supp. XX: 232**

Broun, Heywood, **I:** 478; **II:** 417; **IV:** 432; **Supp. IX:** 190; **Supp. XXII:** 277

Broussais, François, **Supp. I Part 1:** 302

Brouwer, Joel, **Supp. XXII:** 223, 237

Browder, Earl, **I:** 515; **Supp. XX: 76, 77**

Brower, David, **Supp. X:** 29

Brower, Reuben, **Supp. XV:** 20

Brown, Alice, **II:** 523; **Retro. Supp. II:** 136

Brown, Andrew, **Supp. XVI:** 150

Brown, Ashley, **Retro. Supp. II:** 48; **Supp. I Part 1:** 79, 80, 82, 84, 92

Brown, Charles Brockden, **I:** 54, 211, 335; **II:** 74, 267, 298; **III:** 415; **Supp. I Part 1: 124–149; Supp. II Part 1:** 65, 292; **Supp. XXIII:** 178

Brown, Mrs. Charles Brockden (Elizabeth Linn), **Supp. I Part 1:** 145, 146

Brown, Clifford, **Supp. V:** 195

Brown, Deborah, **Supp. XVII:** 75

Brown, Dee, **Supp. IV Part 2:** 504

Brown, Elijah, **Supp. I Part 1:** 125

Brown, Fleda, **Supp. XXIII:** 59

Brown, George Douglas, **III:** 473

Brown, Harry, **Supp. IV Part 2:** 560

Brown, Harvey, **Supp. XIV:** 148

Brown, Himan, **Supp. XIX:** 241, 242

Brown, H. Rap, **Supp. XXI:** 171

Brown, John, **II:** 13; **IV:** 125, 126, 172, 237, 249, 254; **Supp. I Part 1:** 345;

Supp. VIII: 204

Brown, Joseph Epes, **Supp. IV Part 2:** 487

Brown, Larry, **Supp. XVIII:** 195; **Supp. XXI: 35–50**

Brown, Leonard, **Supp. IX:** 117

Brown, Mary Armitt, **Supp. I Part 1:** 125

Brown, Nell Porter, **Supp. XXV:** 130, 131, 138

Brown, Percy, **II:** 20

Brown, Robert (Anahalihs), **Supp. XXVI:** 89, 95

Brown, Robert E., **Supp. X:** 12

Brown, Scott, **Supp. XI:** 178

Brown, Slater, **IV:** 123; **Retro. Supp. II:** 79

Brown, Solyman, **Supp. I Part 1:** 156

Brown, Sterling, **Retro. Supp. I:** 198; **Supp. IV Part 1:** 169; **Supp. XIV:** 202; **Supp. XXII:** 1, 8, 12

Brown, Tina, **Supp. XVI:** 176–177

Brown, Wesley, **Supp. V:** 6

Brown, William Hill, **Supp. XXV:** 38

Brown, William Wells, **Supp. XXIII:** 184

Brown Decades, The (Mumford), **Supp. II Part 2:** 475, 478, 491–492

Brown Dog (Harrison), **Supp. VIII:** 51

Brown Dog of the Yaak: Essays on Art and Activism (Bass), **Supp. XVI:** 22

"Brown Dwarf of Rügen, The" (Whittier), **Supp. I Part 2:** 696

Browne, Charles Farrar, **II:** 289; **IV:** 193, 196; **Supp. XVIII:** 1, 4

Browne, Roscoe Lee, **Supp. VIII:** 345

Browne, Thomas, **II:** 15–16, 304; **III:** 77, 78, 198, 487; **IV:** 147; **Supp. IX:** 136; **Supp. XII:** 45; **Supp. XVI:** 292

Browne, William, **Supp. I Part 1:** 98

Brownell, W. C., **II:** 14

Brownell, William Crary, **Retro. Supp. I:** 365, 366

Browner, Stephanie P., **Supp. XVIII:** 17

Brown Girl, Brownstones (Marshall), **Supp. XI:** 275, 276, **278–280,** 282

Brownies' Book, The (Hughes), **Supp. I Part 1:** 321

Browning, Dominique, **Supp. XXVI:** 131

Browning, Elizabeth Barrett, **I:** 458, 459; **Retro. Supp. I:** 33, 43; **Supp. XVIII:** 175–176; **Supp. XX: 108**

Browning, Oscar, **Supp. XX: 231**

Browning, Robert, **I:** 50, 66, 103, 458, 460, 468; **II:** 338, 478, 522; **III:** 5, 8, 467, 469, 484, 511, 521, 524, 606, 609; **IV:** 135, 245, 366, 416; **Retro. Supp. I:** 43, 55, 217; **Retro. Supp. II:** 188, 190; **Supp. I Part 1:** 2, 6, 79, 311; **Supp. I Part 2:** 416, 468, 622; **Supp. III Part 1:** 5, 6; **Supp. IV Part 2:** 430; **Supp. X:** 65; **Supp. XV:** 92, 250, 275

Brownmiller, Susan, **Supp. X:** 252

Brownrigg, Sylvia, **Supp. XXV:** 59–60

"Brown River, Smile" (Toomer), **Supp. IV Part 1:** 16

Brownstone Eclogues and Other Poems (Aiken), **I:** 65, 67

Brown: The Last Discovery of America (Rodriguez), **Supp. XIV:** 297, 298, 300, **305–309,** 310, 311–312

Broyard, Anatole, **Supp. IV Part 1:** 39; **Supp. VIII:** 140; **Supp. X:** 186; **Supp. XI:** 348; **Supp. XVI:** 213

Broyles, Yolanda Julia, **Supp. XIX:** 112

Bruccoli, Matthew, **Retro. Supp. I:** 98, 102, 105, 114, 115, 359; **Supp. IV Part 2:** 468, 470

Bruce, John Edward, **Supp. XVI:** 143

Bruce, Lenny, **Supp. VIII:** 198

Bruce, Virginia, **Supp. XII:** 173

Bruce-Novoa, Juan, **Supp. VIII:** 73, 74

Bruchac, Joseph, **Supp. IV Part 1:** 261, 319, 320, 321, 322, 323, 325, 328, 398, 399, 403, 408, 414; **Supp. IV Part 2:** 502, 506

Brueghel, Pieter, **I:** 174; **Supp. I Part 2:** 475

Brueghel, Pieter, the Elder, **Retro. Supp. I:** 430

Bruell, Edwin, **Supp. VIII:** 126

Brugh, Spangler Arlington. *See* Taylor, Robert

"Bruja: Witch" (Mora), **Supp. XIII:** 214, 220, 221, **Supp. XIII:** 222

Brulé, Claude, **Supp. XI:** 307

Brumer, Andy, **Supp. XIII:** 88

Brummels, J. V., **Supp. XIX:** 119

Brunner, Emil, **III:** 291, 303

"Brush Fire" (J. Wright), **Supp. XVII:** 241

Brustein, Robert, **Supp. VIII:** 331; **Supp. XXIV:** 116

Brutus, **IV:** 373, 374; **Supp. I Part 2:** 471

"Brutus and Antony" (Masters), **Supp. I Part 2:** 472

"Bryan, Bryan, Bryan, Bryan" (Lindsay), **Supp. I Part 2:** 394, 395, 398

Bryan, George, **Retro. Supp. II:** 76

Bryan, Sharon, **Supp. IX:** 154

Bryan, William Jennings, **I:** 483; **IV:** 124; **Supp. I Part 2:** 385, 395–396, 455, 456

Bryant, Austin, **Supp. I Part 1:** 152, 153

Bryant, Frances, **Supp. I Part 1:** 153

Bryant, Louise, **Supp. X:** 136

Bryant, Peter, **Supp. I Part 1:** 150, 151, 152, 153. *See also* George, Peter

Bryant, William Cullen, **I:** 335, 458; **II:** 311; **III:** 81; **IV:** 309; **Retro. Supp. I:** 217; **Retro. Supp. II:** 155; **Supp. I Part 1: 150–173,** 312, 362; **Supp. I Part 2:** 413, 416, 420; **Supp. IV Part 1:** 165; **Supp. XIII:** 145; **Supp. XIX:** 4; **Supp. XXV:** 250

Bryant, Mrs. William Cullen (Frances Fairchild), **Supp. I Part 1:** 153, 169

Bryer, Jackson R., **Supp. IV Part 2:** 575, 583, 585, 586, 589, 591; **Supp. XIII:** 200, **Supp. XIII:** 205

Bryher, Jackson R. (pseudonym). *See* Ellerman, Winifred

Brynner, Witter, **Supp. XXII:** 273

Bubber Goes to Heaven (Bontemps), **Supp. XXII:** 4

"Bubbs Creek Haircut" (Snyder), **Supp. VIII:** 306

Buber, Martin, **II:** 228; **III:** 45, 308, 528; **IV:** 11; **Supp. I Part 1:** 83, 88; **Supp. XVI:** 291

Buccaneers, The (Wharton), **IV**: 327; **Retro. Supp. I**: 382

Buchanan Dying (Updike), **Retro. Supp. I**: 331, 335

Buchbinder, David, **Supp. XIII**: 32

Buchwald, Art, **Supp. XII**: 124–125; **Supp. XVI**: 110–111

Buchwald, Emilie, **Supp. XVI**: 35, 36

Buck, Dudley, **Supp. I Part 1**: 362

Buck, Gene, **II**: 427

Buck, John, Sr., **Supp. XXVI**: 89

Buck, Pearl S., **Supp. II Part 1**: 113–134; **Supp. XIV**: 274

Buckdancer's Choice (Dickey), **Supp. IV Part 1**: 176, 177, 178, 180

"Buckdancer's Choice" (Dickey), **Supp. IV Part 1**: 191

Bucke, Richard Maurice, **Retro. Supp. I**: 407

"Buckeyes"(P. Benedict), **Supp. XXIII**: 46

"Buck Fever" (Humphrey), **Supp. IX**: 109

"Buck in the Snow, The" (Millay), **III**: 135

Buckley, Christopher, **Supp. IX**: 169; **Supp. XI**: 257, 329; **Supp. XV**: 76–77, 86

Buckley, James, Jr., **Supp. XVII**: 220

Buckminster, Joseph, **Supp. II Part 1**: 66–67, 69

Bucknell, Katherine, **Supp. XIV**: 170

Bucolics (Auden), **Supp. II Part 1**: 21, 24

Budbill, David, **Supp. XIX**: 1–16

Budd, Louis J., **IV**: 210

Buddha, **I**: 136; **II**: 1; **III**: 173, 179, 239, 567; **Supp. I Part 1**: 363; **Supp. I Part 2**: 397

Buddha, The: The Story of Siddhartha (film, Grubin), **Supp. XXIII**: 138, 140

"Buddha Boy" (Saunders), **Supp. XIX**: 235

"Buddha's Last Instruction, The" (Oliver), **Supp. VII**: 239

"Buddies"(Kenny), **Supp. XXIII**: 150

Budding Prospects (Boyle), **Supp. VIII**: 8–9; **Supp. XX**: 27–28

Buechner, Frederick, **III**: 310; **Supp. XII**: 41–59

Buell, Lawrence, **Supp. IX**: 29; **Supp. V**: 209; **Supp. XV**: 269, 282

"Buffalo" (Peacock), **Supp. XIX**: 198

"Buffalo, The" (Moore), **III**: 215

"Buffalo Bill". *See* Cody, William

Buffalo Girls (McMurtry), **Supp. V**: 229

Buffalo Girls (screenplay) (McMurtry), **Supp. V**: 232

Buffalo Hunters, The: The Story of the Hide Men (Sandoz), **Supp. XXIV**: 244, **247–249**, 256

Buffett, Jimmy, **Supp. VIII**: 42

Buffon, Comte de, **II**: 101

Buford, Fanny McConnell, **Retro. Supp. II**: 117

Bugeja, Michael, **Supp. X**: 201

Bugged for Murder (Lacy), **Supp. XV**: 205

"Buglesong" (Stegner), **Supp. IV Part 2**: 606

Buhle, Paul, **Supp. XXI**: 172

"Buick" (Shapiro), **Supp. II Part 2**: 705

"Builders" (Yates), **Supp. XI**: **342–343**

Builders, The (Glasgow), **II**: 183–184, 193

"Builders, The" (Hay), **Supp. XIV**: 125

Builders in Sand (W. Frank), **Supp. XX**: **68**

Builders of the Bay Colony (Morison), **Supp. I Part 2**: 484–485

"Builders of the Bridge, The" (Mumford), **Supp. II Part 2**: 475

"Building" (Snyder), **Supp. VIII**: 305

"Building, Dwelling, Thinking" (Heidegger), **Retro. Supp. II**: 87

Building a Character (Stanislavsky), **Supp. XIV**: 243

" 'Building' Larry Brown(s) at Algonquin Books of Chapel Hill" (Perry), **Supp. XXI**: 42

"Building of the Ship, The" (Longfellow), **II**: 498; **Retro. Supp. II**: 159, 167, 168

"Build Soil" (Frost), **Retro. Supp. I**: 138, 139

"Build Soil" (Snyder), **Supp. VIII**: 304

Build-Up, The (W. C. Williams), **Retro. Supp. I**: 423

Bukiet, Melvin Jules, **Supp. XVII**: **39–51**

Bukowski, Charles, **Supp. III Part 1**: 147; **Supp. XI**: 159, 161, 172, 173; **Supp. XVII**: 245

Bulgakov, Mikhail, **Supp. XIV**: 97

"Bulgarian Poetess, The" (Updike), **IV**: 215, 227; **Retro. Supp. I**: 329

Bull, Ole, **II**: 504

"Bulldozer, The" (Francis), **Supp. IX**: 87

"Bullet in the Brain" (Wolff), **Supp. VII**: 342–343

Bullet Park (Cheever), **Supp. I Part 1**: 185, 187–193, 194, 195

Bullets over Broadway (film; Allen), **Supp. XV**: 12, **12–13**

Bullfight, The (Mailer), **Retro. Supp. II**: 205

Bullfighter Checks Her Makeup, The: My Encounters with Extraordinary People (Orlean), **Supp. XXV**: 159, 163–164

Bullins, Ed, **Supp. II Part 1**: 34, 42

Bullock, Sandra, **Supp. X**: 80

"Bull-Roarer, The" (Stern), **Supp. IX**: 297

"Bully, The" (Dubus), **Supp. VII**: 84

"Bulsh" (X. J. Kennedy), **Supp. XV**: 161

Bultmann, Rudolf, **III**: 309

Bulwark, The (Dreiser), **I**: 497, 506, 516–517; **Retro. Supp. II**: 95, 96, 105, 108

Bulwer-Lytton, Edward George, **IV**: 350

"Bums in the Attic" (Cisneros), **Supp. VII**: 62

Bunche, Ralph, **Supp. I Part 1**: 343; **Supp. XIV**: 202; **Supp. XXII**: 12

"Bunchgrass Edge of the World, The" (Proulx), **Supp. VII**: 263

Bunge, Nancy, **Supp. XVII**: 218; **Supp. XXII**: 175, 177, 178, 180, 183; **Supp. XXVI**: 257

"Bunner Sisters, The" (Wharton), **IV**: 317

Bunting, Basil, **Retro. Supp. I**: 422; **Supp. III Part 2**: 616, 620, 624;

Supp. XIV: 286

Buntline, Ned, **Supp. XXIII**: 182

Buñuel, Luis, **III**: 184; **Retro. Supp. II**: 337

Bunyan, John, **I**: 445; **II**: 15, 104, 228; **IV**: 80, 84, 156, 437; **Supp. I Part 1**: 32

Bunyan, Paul, **Supp. XXII**: 203

Burana, Lily, **Supp. XI**: 253

Burbank, Luther, **I**: 483

Burbank, Rex, **IV**: 363

Burch, Michael, **Supp. XXI**: 99

Burchfield, Alice, **Supp. I Part 2**: 652, 660

Burden of Proof, The (Turow), **Supp. XVII**: **216–217**, 218

Burden of Southern History, The (Woodward), **Retro. Supp. I**: 75

Burdens of Formality, The (Lea, ed.), **Supp. X**: 58

Burger, Gottfried August, **II**: 306

Burgess, Anthony, **Supp. IV Part 1**: 227; **Supp. IV Part 2**: 685; **Supp. V**: 128; **Supp. XXIII**: 42

Burgh, James, **Supp. I Part 2**: 522

"Burglar of Babylon, The" (Bishop), **Retro. Supp. II**: 47; **Supp. I Part 1**: 93

Burgum, E. B., **IV**: 469, 470

Burham, Philip, **Supp. XX**: **44**

"Burial of Jonathan Brown, The"(Hadas), **Supp. XXIII**: 115

Buried Child (Shepard), **Supp. III Part 2**: 433, 447, 448; **Supp. XIV**: 327

"Buried Lake, The" (Tate), **IV**: 136

Burkard, Michael, **Supp. XXIV**: 165

Burke, Carolyn, **Supp. XXII**: 156, 158, 162, 166, 167, 168

Burke, Edmund, **I**: 9; **III**: 310; **Supp. I Part 2**: 496, 511, 512, 513, 523; **Supp. II Part 1**: 80; **Supp. XVII**: 236

Burke, James Lee, **Supp. XIV**: **21–38**; **Supp. XXI**: 67, 72, 80

Burke, Kenneth, **I**: **264–287**, 291; **III**: 497, 499, 546; **IV**: 123, 408; **Retro. Supp. I**: 297; **Retro. Supp. II**: 117, 120; **Supp. I Part 2**: 630; **Supp. II Part 1**: 136; **Supp. IX**: 229; **Supp. VIII**: 105; **Supp. XIV**: 3; **Supp. XXI**: 89

Burke, William, **Supp. XXI**: 215

"Burl" (Mosher), **Supp. XXII**: 204, 211

Burley, Justin, **Supp. XVI**: 158

"Burly Fading One, The" (Hayden), **Supp. II Part 1**: 366

Burn, Stephen J., **Supp. XX**: **85**; **Supp. XXII**: 266, 268

"Burned" (Levine), **Supp. V**: 186, 192

"Burned" (Stallings), **Supp. XXV**: 233

"Burned Diary, The" (Olds), **Supp. X**: 215

"Burned Man" (Huddle), **Supp. XXVI**: 148, 151

Burne-Jones, Edward, **Supp. XXII**: 156

Burnett, Allison, **Supp. XVII**: 22

Burnett, David, **Supp. XI**: 299

Burnett, Frances Hodgson, **Supp. I Part 1**: 44

Burnett, Whit, **III**: 551; **Supp. XI**: 294

Burney, Fanny, **Supp. XV:** 232; **Supp. XX: 108**

Burnham, James, **Supp. I Part 2:** 648

Burnham, John Chynoweth, **I:** 59

"Burning, The" (Welty), **IV:** 277–278; **Retro. Supp. I:** 353

Burning Angel (Burke), **Supp. XIV:** 30, 32

Burning Bright (Steinbeck), **IV:** 51, 61–62

Burning Bright: An Anthology of Sacred Poetry (Hampl, ed.), **Supp. XXII:** 87

"Burning Bush" (Cliff), **Supp. XXII:** 75

Burning Bush (Untermeyer), **Supp. XV: 309**

"Burning Bush" (Untermeyer), **Supp. XV:** 309

Burning Bush, The (Asch), **Supp. XXIII:** 7

Burning Bush, The (H. and G. Herczeg), **Supp. XVII:** 62

Burning Chrome (W. Gibson), **Supp. XVI:** 118, 122, **128**

"Burning Chrome" (W. Gibson), **Supp. XVI:** 117, 120, 123, 124, 128

Burning City (Benét), **Supp. XI:** 46, 58

Burning Daylight (London), **II:** 474, 481

Burning Down the House: Essays on Fiction (C. Baxter), **Supp. XVII:** 13, 20, 21

"Burning Down the Little House on the Prairie: Asian Pioneers in Contemporary North America" (Martín-Lucas), **Supp. XXVI:** 218

Burning House, The (Beattie), **Supp. V:** 29

"Burning Ladder, The" (Gioia), **Supp. XV:** 118

Burning Mystery of Anna in 1951, The (Koch), **Supp. XV:** 182–183

"Burning of Paper Instead of Children, The" (Rich), **Supp. I Part 2:** 558

"Burning Shit at An Khe" (Weigl), **Supp. XIX:** 279–280

Burning the Days (Salter), **Supp. XIX:** 252

Burning the Days: Recollections (Salter), **Supp. IX:** 245, 246, 248, 260, **261–262**

"Burning the Small Dead" (Snyder), **Supp. VIII:** 298

Burning Tigris, The: The Armenian Genocide and America's Response (Balakian), **Supp. XXIII:** 19, 21, 22, **25–28,** 30

"Burning Tobacco Beds" (J. W. Miller), **Supp. XX: 167**

Burn Marks (Paretsky), **Supp. XXV:** 174–175, 178, 180

Burns, Carol, **Supp. XVIII:** 162

Burns, David, **III:** 165–166

Burns, Ken, **Supp. XIV:** 14

Burns, Michael, **Supp. XV:** 339

Burns, Robert, **II:** 150, 306; **III:** 592; **IV:** 453; **Supp. I Part 1:** 158; **Supp. I Part 2:** 410, 455, 683, 685, 691, 692; **Supp. IX:** 173; **Supp. XII:** 171; **Supp. XIII:** 3; **Supp. XVIII:** 82

Burnshaw, Stanley, **Retro. Supp. I:** 298, 303; **Supp. III Part 2:** 615

"Burn the Cities" (West), **Retro. Supp. II:** 338

Burnt Mountain (Siddons), **Supp. XXII:** 253

Burnt Norton (T. S. Eliot), **I:** 575, 580–581, 582, 584, 585; **III:** 10

"Burnt Norton" (T. S. Eliot), **Retro. Supp. I:** 66; **Supp. XV:** 216

Burnt-Out Case, A (Greene), **Supp. VIII:** 4

"Burnt-out Spa, The" (Plath), **Retro. Supp. II:** 246

Burn Witch Burn (A. Merritt), **Supp. XVII:** 58

Burr, Aaron, **I:** 7, 549, 550; **II:** 300; **IV:** 264; **Supp. I Part 2:** 461, 483

Burr: A Novel (Vidal), **Supp. IV Part 2:** 677, 682, 684, 685, 687, 688, 689, 691

Burr Oaks (Eberhart), **I:** 533, 535

Burroughs, Edgar Rice, **Supp. IV Part 1:** 101

Burroughs, John, **I:** 220, 236, 506; **IV:** 346; **Supp. IX:** 171; **Supp. XXVI:** 37

Burroughs, William S., **III:** 45, 174, 258; **Supp. II Part 1:** 320, 328; **Supp. III Part 1: 91–110,** 217, 226; **Supp. IV Part 1:** 79, 87, 90; **Supp. XI:** 297, 308; **Supp. XII:** 1, 3, 118, 121, 124, 129, 131, 136; **Supp. XIV:** 137, 140–141, 143–144, 150; **Supp. XVI:** 123, 135; **Supp. XVII:** 225; **Supp. XVIII:** 137; **Supp. XXIII:** 213; **Supp. XXIV:** 42

Burrow, Trigant, **Supp. II Part 1:** 6

Burrows, Ken, **Supp. V:** 115

Bursey, Jeff, **Supp. XXII:** 257

Burson, Claudia, **Supp. XV:** 343

Burstein, Janet, **Supp. XVII:** 41, 44, 48

"Bursts of Light" (Bronk), **Supp. XXI:** 33

Burt, Stephen, **Supp. XV:** 341, 342, 345, 347, 351; **Supp. XVII:** 18, 246

Burt, Steve, **Supp. V:** 83

Burtis, Thomson, **Supp. XIII:** 163

Burton, Robert, **II:** 535; **III:** 77, 78; **Supp. I Part 1:** 349

Burton, Sue D., **Supp. XIX:** 90

Burton, William Evans, **III:** 412

"Burying Ground by the Ties" (MacLeish), **III:** 14

Bury My Heart at Wounded Knee (Brown), **Supp. IV Part 2:** 504

Bury the Dead (Shaw), **IV:** 381; **Supp. XIX:** 242–244, 249, 252

"Bus Along St. Clair: December, A" (Atwood), **Supp. XIII:** 33

Busch, Frederick, **Supp. X:** 78; **Supp. XII:** 343; **Supp. XVII:** 175; **Supp. XXVI:** 9

Bush, Barney, **Supp. XII:** 218, 222

Bush, Douglas, **Supp. I Part 1:** 268; **Supp. XIV:** 10

"Busher Comes Back, The" (Lardner), **II:** 422

"Busher's Letters Home, A" (Lardner), **II:** 418–419, 421

Bushrui, Suheil, **Supp. XX: 113, 117, 120, 122, 126–127**

"Business and Poetry" (Gioia), **Supp. XV:** 113, 115

"Business Deal" (West), **IV:** 287

"Business Man, A" (Jewett), **Retro. Supp. II:** 132

Business of Memory, The: The Art of Remembering in an Age of Forgetting (C. Baxter, ed.), **Supp. XVII:** 21

"Business Trip" (Hoffman), **Supp. XVIII:** 86

"Bus Riley's Back in Town" (Inge), **Supp. XXV:** 95

Buss, Helen M., **Supp. IV Part 1:** 12

Bus Stop (Inge), **Supp. XXV:** 93, 99–100

Butcher, Fanny, **Supp. XXV:** 199

Butcher, Margaret Just, **Supp. XIV:** 203

"Butcher, The" (Southern), **Supp. XI:** 294

"Butcher Cock, The"(P. Benedict), **Supp. XXIII:** 46–47

"Butcher Shop" (Simic), **Supp. VIII:** 273

But Gentlemen Marry Brunettes (Loos), **Supp. XVI:** 190–191

"But He Says I Misunderstood" (Notley), **Supp. XXII:** 227

Butler, Benjamin, **I:** 457

Butler, Dorothy. *See* Farrell, Mrs. James T. (Dorothy Butler)

Butler, Elizabeth, **Supp. I Part 1:** 260

Butler, Ethel, **Supp. XIV:** 125

Butler, Hugo, **Supp. XVII:** 63

Butler, James D., **Supp. IX:** 175

Butler, Joseph, **II:** 8, 9

Butler, Judith, **Supp. XII:** 6

Butler, Maud. *See* Falkner, Mrs. Murray C. (Maud Butler)

Butler, Nicholas Murray, **I:** 223; **Supp. I Part 1:** 23; **Supp. III Part 2:** 499

Butler, Octavia, **Supp. XIII: 59–72**

Butler, Robert Olen, **Supp. XII: 61–78,** 319

Butler, Samuel, **II:** 82, 86; **IV:** 121, 440; **Supp. VIII:** 171

Butler-Evans, Elliot, **Retro. Supp. II:** 121

"But Only Mine" (Wright), **Supp. III Part 2:** 595

Butscher, Edward, **Supp. I Part 2:** 526

Butter Battle Book, The (Geisel), **Supp. XVI:** 110

"Buttercups" (Lowell), **Retro. Supp. II:** 187

Butterfield, R. W., **I:** 386

Butterfield, Stephen, **Supp. IV Part 1:** 3, 11

Butterfield 8 (O'Hara), **III:** 361

"Butterflies Under Persimmon" (Jarman), **Supp. XVII:** 120

Butterfly (Harvey), **Supp. XIII:** 184

"Butterfly, The" (Brodksy), **Supp. VIII:** 26

"Butterfly and the Traffic Light, The" (Ozick), **Supp. V:** 263, 265

Butterfly in the Typewriter (MacLaughlin), **Supp. XXVI:** 241, 243, 252

Butterfly Plague, The (Findley), **Supp. XX: 50, 52, 53**

Butterfly Stories (Vollmann), **Supp. XVII:** 226

"Butterfly-toed Shoes" (Komunyakaa), **Supp. XIII:** 126

Butter Hill and Other Poems (Francis), **Supp. IX:** 88, 89

"Button-Down Builders, The" (Siddons), **Supp. XXII:** 243–244

Buttons, Red, **Supp. IV Part 2:** 574

Buttrick, George, **III:** 301; **Supp. XII:** 47–48

"But What Is the Reader to Make of This?" (Ashbery), **Supp. III Part 1:** 25

Butz, Earl, **Supp. X:** 35

"Buz" (Alcott), **Supp. I Part 1:** 43

Buzinski, Jim, **Supp. XX:** 273

"By an *Objibwa Female* Pen: Invitation to sisters to a walk in the Garden, after a shower"(J. Schoolcraft), **Supp. XXIII:** 230

Byatt, A. S., **Supp. XXI:** 147

By Avon River (Doolittle), **Supp. I Part 1:** 272

"By Blue Ontario's Shore" (Whitman), **Retro. Supp. I:** 399, 400

"By Candlelight" (Major), **Supp. XXII:** 185

"By Disposition of Angels" (Moore), **III:** 214

"By Earth" (Olds), **Supp. X:** 214

"Bye for Now, Broadway, My New Friend" (Silver), **Supp. XXIV:** 276

"By Fire" (Olds), **Supp. X:** 214

Bygones (Untermeyer), **Supp. XV:** 304, **308–309**, 312, 313

By Land, By Sea (Hoffman), **Supp. XVIII:** 86

By Land and by Sea (Morison), **Supp. I Part 2:** 492

Byles, Mather, **Supp. XX:** 279, 282

By-Line: Ernest Hemingway (Hemingway), **II:** 257–258

By Love Possessed (Cozens), **I:** 358, 365, 372–374, 375, 376, 377, 378, 379

"By Morning" (Swenson), **Supp. IV Part 2:** 642

"By Night" (Francis), **Supp. IX:** 76

Bynner, Witter, **II:** 513, 527; **Supp. XIII:** 347; **Supp. XV:** 39–54

Byrd, William, **Supp. IV Part 2:** 425; **Supp. XXI:** 35; **Supp. XXII:** 193

Byrne, Donn, **IV:** 67

Byrne, Edward, **Supp. XXV:** 226, 227

Byron, George Gordon, Lord, **I:** 343, 568, 577; **II:** 135, 193, 296, 301, 303, 310, 315, 331, 566; **III:** 82, 137, 170, 409, 410, 412, 469; **IV:** 245, 435; **Supp. I Part 1:** 150, 312, 349; **Supp. I Part 2:** 580, 591, 683, 685, 719; **Supp. XIII:** 139; **Supp. XVI:** 188, 203, 206, 210

"Byron's Cain" (L. Michaels), **Supp. XVI:** 203

"Bystanders" (Matthews), **Supp. IX:** 160

By the Bias of Sound (Sobin), **Supp. XVI:** 281

By the North Gate (Oates), **Supp. II Part 2:** 504

"By the People" (Stratton-Porter), **Supp. XX:** 221

By the Shores of Silver Lake (L. I. Wilder), **Supp. XXII:** 294, 295, 299

"By the Time You Get There, by the Time You Get Back" (Muñoz), **Supp. XXV:** 134

"By the Waters of Babylon" (Benét), **Supp. XI:** 56, 58

By the Waters of Manhattan (Reznikoff), **Supp. XIV:** 288, 293, 294

By the Waters of Manhattan: An Annual (Reznikoff), **Supp. XIV:** 277, 280, 289

By the Waters of Manhattan: Selected Verse (Reznikoff), **Supp. XIV:** 281, 291

By the Well of Living and Seeing and the Fifth Book of the Maccabees (Reznikoff), **Supp. XIV:** 281

By the Well of Living and Seeing: New and Selected Poems 1918–1973 (Reznikoff), **Supp. XIV:** 281, 287–288, 295

By Way of Orbit (O'Neill), **III:** 405

Byzantine Parables (Notley), **Supp. XXII:** 235, 237

C

"C 33" (H. Crane), **I:** 384; **Retro. Supp. II:** 76

Cabala, The (Wilder), **IV:** 356, 358–360, 369, 374

"Cabaret" (Boyle), **Supp. XXIV:** 61

Cabaret (film), **Supp. XIV:** 155, 162

Cabaret (play), **Supp. XIV:** 162; **Supp. XVII:** 45

Cabbages and Kings (O. Henry), **Supp. II Part 1:** 394, 409

Cabell, James Branch, **II:** 42; **III:** 394; **IV:** 67, 359, 360; **Retro. Supp. I:** 80; **Supp. I Part 2:** 613, 714, 718, 721; **Supp. X:** 223

"Cabin, The" (Carver), **Supp. III Part 1:** 137, 146

Cabin, The: Reminiscence and Diversions (Mamet), **Supp. XIV:** 240

Cabinet of Dr. Caligari, The (film), **Retro. Supp. I:** 268

Cable, George Washington, **II:** 289; **Retro. Supp. II:** 65; **Supp. I Part 1:** 200; **Supp. II Part 1:** 198; **Supp. XIV:** 63

Cables to the Ace; or, Familiar Liturgies of Misunderstanding (Merton), **Supp. VIII:** 208

Cabot, James, **II:** 14; **IV:** 173

Cabot, John, **Supp. I Part 2:** 496, 497

Cachoeira Tales and Other Poems, The (Nelson), **Supp. XVIII:** 178–179

"Cachoiera Tales, The" (Nelson), **Supp. XVIII:** 179

Cactus Flower (Barillet and Grédy), **Supp. XVI:** 194

"Caddy's Diary, A" (Lardner), **II:** 421–422

"Cadence" (Dubus), **Supp. VII:** 84–85

Cadieux, Isabelle, **Supp. XIII:** 127

"Cadillac Flambé" (Ellison), **Retro. Supp. II:** 119, 126; **Supp. II Part 1:** 248

Cadillac Jack (McMurtry), **Supp. V:** 225

Cadillac Jukebox (Burke), **Supp. XIV:** 32

Cadle, Dean, **Supp. I Part 2:** 429

Cady, Edwin H., **II:** 272

"Caedmon" (Garrett), **Supp. VII:** 96–97

Caesar, Julius, **II:** 12, 502, 561–562; **IV:** 372, 373

Caesar, Sid, **Supp. IV Part 2:** 574, 591

"Cafeteria, The" (Singer), **Retro. Supp. II:** 316

Cage, John, **Supp. IV Part 1:** 84; **Supp. V:** 337, 341; **Supp. XXIII:** 211

"Cage and the Prairie: Two Notes on Symbolism, The" (Bewley), **Supp. I Part 1:** 251

Cage Keeper, The (Dubus III), **Supp. XXIV: 99–102**

"Cage Keeper, The" (Dubus III), **Supp. XXIV:** 101–102, 104

Cage of Age, The (Bronk), **Supp. XXI:** 32

Cage of Spines, A (Swenson), **Supp. IV Part 2:** 641–642, 647

"Cage of the Body, The"(Schott), **Supp. XXIII:** 243–244

Cagney, James, **Supp. IV Part 1:** 236; **Supp. XIII:** 174

Cagney, William, **Supp. XIII:** 174

Cahalan, James, **Supp. XIII:** 1, 2, 3, 4, 12

Cahan, Abraham, **Supp. IX:** 227; **Supp. XIII:** 106; **Supp. XXI:** 3, 14; **Supp. XXIII:** 1, 2, 9, 16; **Supp. XXVI:** 123

Cahill, Tim, **Supp. XIII:** 13

Cain, James M., **III:** 99; **Supp. IV Part 1:** 130; **Supp. XI:** 160; **Supp. XIII:** 159, 165

Cain, Kathleen Shine, **Supp. XX: 247, 248**

Caine Mutiny, The (film), **Supp. XXV:** 260, 261

Caine Mutiny, The (Wouk), **Supp. XXV:** 253, 255, 256, 259–261

Caine Mutiny Court-Martial, The (Wouk), **Supp. XXV:** 253, 256

Caird, G. B., **Supp. XXI:** 91–92

Cairns, Huntington, **III:** 103, 108, 114, 119

Cairo! Shanghai! Bombay! (Williams and Shapiro), **IV:** 380

Cake (Bynner), **Supp. XV:** 50

Cakes and Ale (Maugham), **III:** 64

Calabria, Frank, **Supp. XIII:** 164

Calamity Jane (Martha Jane Canary), **Supp. V:** 229–230; **Supp. X:** 103

"Calamus" (Whitman), **IV:** 342–343; **Retro. Supp. I:** 52, 403, 404, 407

Calasso, Roberto, **Supp. IV Part 1:** 301

Calavito, Jason, **Supp. XXV:** 123

Calder, William M., III, **Supp. XXIII:** 112

Calderón, Hector, **Supp. IV Part 2:** 544

Caldwell, Christopher, **Supp. IV Part 1:** 211

Caldwell, Erskine, **I:** 97, 211, **288–311;** **IV:** 286; **Supp. IV Part 2:** 601; **Supp. XXI:** 35; **Supp. XXII:** 196

Caldwell, Mrs. Erskine (Helen Lannegan), **I:** 289

Caldwell, Mrs. Erskine (Margaret Bourke-White), **I:** 290, 293–295, 297

Caldwell, Mrs. Erskine (Virginia Fletcher), **I:** 290

Caldwell, Gail, **Supp. XXVI:** 158

Caldwell, Reverend Ira Sylvester, **I:** 289, 305

Caldwell, Zoe, **Supp. XIII:** 207

Caleb Williams (Godwin), **III:** 415

"Calendar" (Creeley), **Supp. IV Part 1:** 158

Calendar of Saints for Unbelievers, A (Wescott), **Supp. XIV:** 342

Calendars (A. Finch), **Supp. XVII:** **76–77**

Calhoun, John C., **I:** 8; **III:** 309

"Caliban in the Coal Mines" (Untermeyer), **Supp. XV:** 296

"California" (Carruth), **Supp. XVI:** 56

"California" (Didion), **Supp. IV Part 1:** 195

"California, This Is Minnesota Speaking" (Dunn), **Supp. XI:** 146

California and Oregon Trail, The (Parkman), **Supp. I Part 2:** 486

California: An Intimate History (Atherton), **Supp. XXIV:** 27

California Daughter (Leider), **Supp. XXIV:** 30

"California Hills in August" (Gioia), **Supp. XV:** 118–119

"California Indians of Today, The" (Zitkala-Ša), **Supp. XXV:** 284

"California Indian Trails and Prayer Trees" (Zitkala-Ša), **Supp. XXV:** 284

Californians (Jeffers), **Supp. II Part 2:** 415, 418, 420

Californians, The (Atherton), **Supp. XXIV:** 18, 21, 22

"California Oaks, The" (Winters), **Supp. II Part 2:** 798

"California Plush" (Bidart), **Supp. XV:** 23

"California Republic" (Didion), **Supp. IV Part 1:** 205

"California Requiem, A" (Gioia), **Supp. XV:** 126

California Suite (film), **Supp. IV Part 2:** 589

California Suite (Simon), **Supp. IV Part 2:** 581, 582

"Caligula" (Lowell), **II:** 554

Callahan, John F., **Retro. Supp. II:** 119, 126, 127

"Call at Corazón" (Bowles), **Supp. IV Part 1:** 82, 87

Calle, Sophia, **Supp. XII:** 22

"Called Back" (Kazin), **Supp. VIII:** 104

Calley, Captain William, **II:** 579

Calley, John, **Supp. XI:** 305

Callicott, J. Baird, **Supp. XIV:** 184

Calligrammes (Apollinaire), **I:** 432

"Calling Jesus" (Toomer), **Supp. III Part 2:** 484

Calling Myself Home (Hogan), **Supp. IV Part 1:** 397, 399, 400, 401, 413

Calling the Wind: Twentieth Century African-American Short Stories (Major, ed.), **Supp. XXII:** 172

Calling Western Union (Taggard), **Supp. XXII:** 271–272, **281–283**

Call It Experience (Caldwell), **I:** 290–291, 297

"Call It Fear" (Harjo), **Supp. XII:** 220

Call It Sleep (H. Roth), **Supp. IX:** 227, 228, **229–231; Supp. VIII:** 233; **Supp. XIII:** 106

"Call Letters: Mrs. V. B." (Angelou), **Supp. IV Part 1:** 15

Call Me Ishmael (Olson), **Supp. II Part 2:** 556; **Supp. XXI:** 21

Call Me Shakespeare (Endore), **Supp. XVII:** 65

"Call of Cthulhu, The" (Lovecraft), **Supp. XXV:** 109, 114, 116–117, 118

Call of the Gospel, The (Mather), **Supp. II Part 2:** 448

Call of the Wild, The (London), **II:** 466, 470–471, 472, 481

"Call of the Wild, The" (Snyder), **Supp. VIII:** 301

"Calloway's Code" (O. Henry), **Supp. II Part 1:** 404

"Call to Arms" (Mumford), **Supp. II Part 2:** 479

Call to Arms, The (film), **Retro. Supp. I:** 325

Calmer, Ned, **Supp. XI:** 219

Calvert, George H., **Supp. I Part 1:** 361

Calverton, V. F., **Supp. VIII:** 96

Calvin, John, **II:** 342; **IV:** 160, 490

Calvino, Italo, **Supp. IV Part 2:** 623, 678; **Supp. XIX:** 34; **Supp. XXI:** 225; **Supp. XXII:** 263

Cambridge Companion to Native American Literature, The (Porter and Roemer, eds.), **Supp. XX:** **270**

Cambridge Edition of the Works of F. Scott Fitzgerald, The (Bruccoli, ed.), **Retro. Supp. I:** 115

Cambridge Film Handbook for *On the Waterfront* (Rapf), **Supp. XVIII:** 251

"Cambridge"(O'Hara), **Supp. XXIII:** 219

"Cambridge Thirty Years Ago" (Lowell), **Supp. I Part 2:** 419

Cambridge University Press, **Retro. Supp. I:** 115

"Camellia Sabina" (Moore), **III:** 208, 215

"Cameo" (Trethewey), **Supp. XXI:** 250

"Cameo Appearance" (Simic), **Supp. VIII:** 283

"Camera Notes" (column, Stratton-Porter), **Supp. XX:** **217**

Camera Obscura (Nabokov), **III:** 255

Cameron, Angus, **Supp. XXI:** 268, 269, 275, 278

Cameron, Elizabeth, **I:** 10, 17

Cameron, Kenneth W., **II:** 16

Cameron, Peter, **Supp. XII:** **79–95**

Cameron, Sharon, **Retro. Supp. I:** 43; **Retro. Supp. II:** 40

Camerson, Don, **I:** 10, 17

Camino, Léon Felipe, **Retro. Supp. II:** 89

Camino Real (T. Williams), **IV:** 382, 385, 386, 387, 388, 391, 392, 395, 398

Camões, Luiz Vaz de, **II:** 133; **Supp. I Part 1:** 94

"Camouflaging the Chimera" (Komunyakaa), **Supp. XIII:** **122–123**

Camp, James, **Supp. XV:** 165

Camp, Walter, **II:** 423

Campana, Dino, **Supp. V:** 337

Campbell, Alan, **Supp. IV Part 1:** 353; **Supp. IX:** 196, 198, 201

Campbell, Alexander, **Supp. I Part 2:** 381, 395

Campbell, Donna, **Retro. Supp. II:** 139

Campbell, E. Simms, **Supp. XXII:** 12

Campbell, Helen, **Supp. XI:** 200, 206

Campbell, James, **Supp. XII:** 127

Campbell, James Edwin, **Supp. II Part 1:** 202

Campbell, Joanna (pseudonym). *See* Bly, Carol

Campbell, Joseph, **I:** 135; **IV:** 369, 370; **Supp. IX:** 245; **Supp. XXV:** 74

Campbell, Lewis, **III:** 476

Campbell, Thomas, **II:** 8, 303, 314; **III:** 410; **Supp. I Part 1:** 309, 310

Campbell, Virginia, **Supp. XIII:** 114

Campbell, Will D., **Supp. XXI:** 247

Campbell (Hale), Janet, **Supp. IV Part 2:** 503

"Campers Leaving: Summer 1981" (Kenyon), **Supp. VII:** 169

"Camp Evergreen" (Kenyon), **Supp. VII:** 168

"Camping in Madera Canyon" (Swenson), **Supp. IV Part 2:** 649

Campion, Jane, **Supp. XXIV:** 172

Campion, Peter, **Supp. XXV:** 227, 233

Campion, Thomas, **I:** 439; **Supp. VIII:** 272

"Campo" (Muñoz), **Supp. XXV:** 130

Campo, Rafael, **Supp. XVII:** 112

Camus, Albert, **I:** 53, 61, 292, 294, 494; **II:** 57, 244; **III:** 292, 306, 453; **IV:** 6, 211, 236, 442, 487; **Retro. Supp. I:** 73; **Retro. Supp. II:** 20; **Supp. I Part 2:** 621; **Supp. VIII:** 11, 195, 241; **Supp. XI:** 96; **Supp. XIII:** 74, 165, 233, 247; **Supp. XVII:** 137

Camuto, Christopher, **Supp. V:** 212–213

"Canada" (Di Piero), **Supp. XIX:** 39

Canada Fragrant with Resin, **Supp. XVI:** 149

Canadé, Eugene, **Supp. XXI:** 22, 23

"Canadian Mosaic, The" (Beran), **Supp. XIII:** 25

"Canadians and Pottawatomies" (Sandburg), **III:** 592–593

"Can a Good Wife Be a Good Sport?" (T. Williams), **IV:** 380

"Canal, The: A Poem on the Application of Physical Science to Political Economy" (Barlow), **Supp. II Part 1:** 73

Canan, Peter, **Supp. XXV:** 123

Canary, Martha Jane. *See* Calamity Jane (Martha Jane Canary)

"Canary for One, A" (Hemingway), **Retro. Supp. I:** 170, 189

Canary in a Cat House (Vonnegut), **Supp. II Part 2:** 758

"Canary in Bloom" (Dove), **Supp. IV Part 1:** 248

Canby, Henry Seidel, **IV:** 65, 363

"Cancer" (McClatchy), **Supp. XII:** 266

"Cancer Match, The" (Dickey), **Supp. IV Part 1:** 182

"Canción y Glosa" (Merwin), **Supp. III Part 1:** 342

Candide (Hellman), **I:** 28; **Supp. I Part 1:** 288–289, 292

Candide (Voltaire), **Supp. I Part 1:** 288–289; **Supp. XI:** 297; **Supp. XVI:** 189

Candide (Voltaire; Wilbur, trans.), **Supp. III Part 2:** 560

"Candle Hat" (Collins), **Supp. XXI:** 60

Candle in the Cabin, The (Lindsay), **Supp. I Part 2:** 398, 400

"Candles" (Plath), **Retro. Supp. II:** 248, 257

Candles in Babylon (Levertov), **Supp. III Part 1:** 283

Candles in the Sun (T. Williams), **IV:** 381

Candles of Your Eyes, The (Purdy), **Supp. VII:** 278

Candy (Southern), **Supp. XI:** 297, **298–299,** 305

"Candy-Man Beechum" (Caldwell), **I:** 309

Cane (Toomer), **Supp. III Part 2:** 475, 481–486, 488; **Supp. IV Part 1:** 164, 168; **Supp. IX:** 305, 306, 307, **308–320; Supp. XIX:** 73; **Supp. XX:** 73

"Cane in the Corridor, The" (Thurber), **Supp. I Part 2:** 616

Canfield, Cass, **Supp. I Part 2:** 668

Canfield, Dorothy, **Retro. Supp. I:** 4, 11, 14, 18; **Supp. XX: 39.** *See also* Fisher, Dorothy Canfield

Canfield, William W., **Supp. XXVI:** 86

Can Grande's Castle (Lowell), **II:** 518, 524

"Canicula di Anna" (Carson), **Supp. XII: 101–102**

"Can I Get You Anything?" (Carver and Gallagher), **Supp. XXIV:** 178

"Canis Major" (Frost), **Retro. Supp. I:** 137

"Canned Stuff" (Pickering), **Supp. XXI:** 198

Cannery Row (Steinbeck), **IV:** 50, 51, 64–65, 66, 68

Cannibal Galaxy, The (Ozick), **Supp. V:** 270

Cannibals and Christians (Mailer), **III:** 38–39, 40, 42; **Retro. Supp. II:** 203, 204, 205; **Supp. XXIV:** 281

Canning, George, **I:** 7, 8

Canning, Richard, **Supp. X:** 147

Cannon, Jimmy, **II:** 424

Cannon, Steve, **Retro. Supp. II:** 111

Cannon between My Knees, A (Gunn Allen), **Supp. IV Part 1:** 324

Canolle, Jean, **Supp. XVI:** 194

"Canonization, The" (Donne), **Supp. XIV:** 8

"Can Poetry Matter?" (Gioia), **Supp. XV:** 113, 114

Can Poetry Matter?: Essays on Poetry and American Culture (Gioia), **Supp. XV:** 112, **113–115**

"Canso" (Merwin), **Supp. III Part 1:** 344

Can Such Things Be? (Bierce), **I:** 203, 204, 205, 209

Canterbury Tales (Chaucer), **II:** 504; **III:** 411; **IV:** 65

Canterbury Tales, The (Chaucer), **Supp. XIX:** 4

"Canticle of Her Coming and Going" (Espaillat), **Supp. XXI:** 106

"Canto Amor" (Berryman), **I:** 173

Canto I (Pound), **III:** 469, 470; **Retro. Supp. I:** 286

Canto II (Pound), **III:** 470

Canto III (Pound), **III:** 470

Canto IV (Pound), **III:** 470

Canto VIII (Pound), **III:** 472

Canto IX (Pound), **III:** 472

Canto X (Pound), **III:** 472

Canto XIII (Pound), **III:** 472

Canto XXXIX (Pound), **III:** 468

Canto LXV (Pound), **Retro. Supp. I:** 292

Canto LXXXI (Pound), **III:** 459; **Retro. Supp. I:** 293

Cantor, Lois, **Supp. IV Part 1:** 285

Cantos (Pound), **I:** 482; **III:** 13–14, 17, 457, 462, 463, 466, 467, 469–470, 472–473, 474, 475, 476, 492; **Retro. Supp. I:** 284, 292, **292–293,** 293, 427; **Supp. I Part 1:** 272; **Supp. II Part 1:** 5; **Supp. II Part 2:** 420, 557, 564, 644; **Supp. III Part 1:** 153; **Supp. V:** 343, 345; **Supp. VIII:** 305; **Supp. XIV:** 55, 96; **Supp. XV:** 349

"Cantus Planis" (Pound), **III:** 466

Cantwell, Robert, **Retro. Supp. I:** 85; **Supp. VIII:** 96; **Supp. XIII:** 292

Can Women Be Gentlemen? (Atherton), **Supp. XXIV:** 20–21, 30

"Canyon de Chelly, Return, 1978"(Kenny), **Supp. XXIII:** 155

"Can You Carry Me" (O'Hara), **III:** 369

Can You See Me Yet? (Findley), **Supp. XX:** 52–53

Canzoneri, Robert, **IV:** 114, 116

Canzoni (Pound), **Retro. Supp. I:** 286, 288, 413

"Cap" (Shaw), **Supp. IV Part 1:** 345

"Cape Breton" (Bishop), **Supp. I Part 1:** 92; **Supp. IX:** 45

Cape Cod (Thoreau), **II:** 540

"Cape Cod, Rome, and Jerusalem" (Chapman), **Supp. XIV:** 55

Capital City (Sandoz), **Supp. XXIV:** 244, **252–253,** 255

Capitalism: The Unknown Ideal (Rand), **Supp. IV Part 2:** 518, 527, 531, 532

Caponi, Gena Dagel, **Supp. IV Part 1:** 95

Capote, Truman, **Supp. I Part 1:** 291, 292; **Supp. III Part 1:** 111–133; **Supp. III Part 2:** 574; **Supp. IV Part 1:** 198, 220; **Supp. VIII:** 105; **Supp. XII:** 43, 249; **Supp. XV:** 146; **Supp. XVI:** 245–246; **Supp. XVII:** 236

Capouya, Emile, **Supp. I Part 1:** 50

Cappetti, Carla, **Supp. IX:** 4, 8

Capra, Frank, **Supp. XVI:** 102

Capra, Fritjof, **Supp. X:** 261

"Capricious Gardens" (Eugenides), **Supp. XXIV:** 133–134

Capron, Marion, **Supp. IX:** 193

"Capsule History of Conservation, A" (Stegner), **Supp. IV Part 2:** 600

"Captain Carpenter" (Ransom), **III:** 491

Captain Craig (Robinson), **III:** 508, 523; **Supp. II Part 1:** 192

"Captain Jim's Friend" (Harte), **Supp. II Part 1:** 337

"Captain Jones's Invitation" (Freneau), **Supp. II Part 1:** 261

"Captain's Son, The" (Taylor), **Supp. V:** 314, 325, 327

"Captain's Wife, The" (Salter), **Supp. IX:** 261

"Capt Christopher Levett (of York)" (Olson), **Supp. II Part 2:** 576, 577

Captive Israel (Reznikoff), **Supp. XIV:** 283

"Captivity and Restoration of Mrs. Mary Rowlandson, The" (Howe), **Supp. IV Part 2:** 419, 431, 434

"Captivity of the Fly" (MacLeish), **III:** 19

"Captured Goddess, The" (Lowell), **II:** 520

Caputi, Jane, **Supp. IV Part 1:** 334, 335

Caputo, Philip, **Supp. XI:** 234; **Supp. XIX: 17–31; Supp. XXII:** 104; **Supp. XXV:** 153

Capuzzo, Michael, **Supp. XIII:** 254

Car (Crews), **Supp. XI: 110–111**

Carabi, Angels, **Supp. VIII:** 223; **Supp. XII:** 215

"Caramels" (Zinberg), **Supp. XV:** 195

"Caravaggio: Swirl & Vortex" (Levis), **Supp. XI:** 258, 269

Caravan (Bynner), **Supp. XV:** 50

Carby, Hazel B., **Supp. IV Part 1:** 13; **Supp. XXI:** 171

"Carcassonne" (Faulkner), **Retro. Supp. I:** 81

Card, Antha E., **Supp. I Part 2:** 496

Cárdenas, Lupe, **Supp. IV Part 2:** 538, 539, 540

Cardinale, Anthony, **Supp. XVII:** 239

Cardinale, Ernesto, **Supp. XII:** 225

"Cardinal Ideograms" (Swenson), **Supp. IV Part 2:** 645

"Cards" (Beattie), **Supp. V:** 31

"Career Woman" (Hay), **Supp. XIV:** 131

Carefree (film, Sandrich), **Supp. XVII:** 59

"Careful" (Carver), **Supp. III Part 1:** 138

Careful and Strict Enquiry into the Modern Prevailing Notions of That Freedom of Will, Which Is Supposed to be Essential to Moral Agency, Vertue and Vice, Reward and Punishment, Praise and Blame, A (Edwards), **I:** 549, 557, 558, 562

Carel: A Poem and Pilgrimage in the Holy Land (Melville), **III:** 92–93

Careless Love and Its Apostrophes (Bronk), **Supp. XXI:** 32

"Carentan O Carentan" (Simpson), **Supp. IX:** 267

Carew, Thomas, **IV:** 453

Carey, Gary, **Supp. XVI:** 186

Carey, Lynn, **Supp. XXIII:** 273

Carey, Mathew, **Supp. XV:** 238

"Car Games" (Conroy), **Supp. XVI:** 72

Cargill, Oscar, **Supp. II Part 1:** 117

Caribbean as Columbus Saw It (Morison and Obregon), **Supp. I Part 2:** 488

"Caribou Kitchen" (A. Finch), **Supp. XVII:** 76–77

Caribou Rising: Defending the Porcupine Herd, Gwich-'in Culture, and the Arctic National Wildlife Refuge (Bass), **Supp. XVI:** 27–28, 28

"Caring for the World"(Schott), **Supp. XXIII:** 249–250

Carl, K. A., **III:** 475

Carleton, George W., **Supp. XVIII:** 4

Carlin, George, **Supp. XXI:** 51

Carlin, Terry, **Supp. XXI:** 4, 5, 14

Carlisle, Harry, **Supp. XVIII:** 223, 233

Carl Krinken: His Christmas Stocking (S. and A. Warner), **Supp. XVIII:** 264

"Carlos Who Died, and Left Only This, The" (Ríos), **Supp. IV Part 2:** 547

Carlotta (empress of Mexico), **Supp. I Part 2:** 457

Carl Sandburg (Golden), **III:** 579

Carlson, Susan L., **Supp. XV:** 323

Carlyle, Thomas, **I:** 103, 279; **II:** 5, 7, 11, 15–16, 17, 20, 145, 315; **III:** 82, 84, 85, 87; **IV:** 169, 182, 338, 350; **Retro. Supp. I:** 360, 408; **Supp. I Part 1:** 2, 349; **Supp. I Part 2:** 410, 422, 482, 485, 552; **Supp. XXV:** 242

"Carma" (Toomer), **Supp. III Part 2:** 481–483; **Supp. IX:** 312–313

"Carmen de Boheme" (Crane), **I:** 384

Carmen Jones (film), **Supp. I Part 1:** 66

Carmina Burana, **Supp. X:** 63

Carmon, Walt, **Supp. XXII:** 277

Carnegie, Andrew, **I:** 483; **IV:** 192; **Supp. I Part 2:** 639, 644; **Supp. V:** 285

Carnegie, Dale, **Supp. I Part 2:** 608

"Carnegie Hall: Rescued" (Moore), **III:** 215

Carne-Ross, Donald S., **Supp. I Part 1:** 268, 269; **Supp. XXIV:** 153

Carnes, Mark C., **Supp. X:** 14

"Carnets" poems (Sobin), **Supp. XVI:** 286–287

Carnovsky, Morris, **III:** 154

"Carol for Carolyn, A" (A. Finch), **Supp. XVII:** 74, 75

Caroling Dusk: An Anthology of Verse by Negro Poets (Cullen, ed.), **Supp. IV Part 1:** 166, 169; **Supp. XXVI:** 165, 170

"Carol of Occupations" (Whitman), **I:** 486

"Carolyn Kizer and the Chain of Women" (A. Finch), **Supp. XVII:** 74–75

Carolyn Kizer: Perspectives on Her Life and Work (A. Finch), **Supp. XVII: 74–75**

"Carpe Diem" (Frost), **Supp. XII:** 303

"Carpe Noctem, if You Can" (Thurber), **Supp. I Part 2:** 620

Carpenter, Dan, **Supp. V:** 250

Carpenter, David, **Supp. VIII:** 297

Carpenter, Edward, **Supp. XX: 230**

Carpenter, Frederic I., **II:** 20

"Carpenter Bee" (Trethewey), **Supp. XXI:** 250

Carpentered Hen and Other Tame Creatures, The (Updike), **IV:** 214; **Retro. Supp. I:** 320

Carpenter's Gothic (Gaddis), **Supp. IV Part 1:** 288, 289–291, 293, 294

Carr, Dennis W., **Supp. IV Part 2:** 560

Carr, Elias, **Supp. XIV:** 57

Carr, Rosemary. *See* Benét, Rosemary

Carrall, Aaron, **Supp. IV Part 2:** 499

Carrel, Alexis, **IV:** 240

"Carrell/Klee/and Cosmos's Groom" (Goldbarth), **Supp. XII:** 183

"Carriage from Sweden, A" (Moore), **III:** 212

Carrie (King), **Supp. V:** 137

Carried Away (Harrison), **Supp. VIII:** 39

Carrier of Ladders (Merwin), **Supp. III Part 1:** 339, 346, 350–352, 356, 357

"Carriers of the Dream Wheel" (Momaday), **Supp. IV Part 2:** 481

Carriers of the Dream Wheel: Contemporary Native American Poetry (Niatum, ed.), **Supp. IV Part 2:** 484, 505

Carrington, Carroll, **I:** 199

"Carrion Spring" (Stegner), **Supp. IV Part 2:** 604

Carroll, Bart, **Supp. XXV:** 71

Carroll, Charles, **Supp. I Part 2:** 525

Carroll, Lewis, **I:** 432; **II:** 431; **III:** 181; **Supp. I Part 1:** 44; **Supp. I Part 2:** 622, 656; **Supp. XVI:** 103; **Supp. XXV:** 87; **Supp. XXVI:** 274

Carroll, Maureen P., **Supp. XXIV:** 177

"Carrots, Noses, Snow, Rose, Roses" (Gass), **Supp. VI:** 87

Carrouges, Michel, **Supp. IV Part 1:** 104

"Carrousel, The" (Rilke), **III:** 558

Carruth, Hayden, **Supp. IV Part 1:** 66; **Supp. IX:** 291; **Supp. VIII:** 39; **Supp. XIII:** 112; **Supp. XIV:** 273–274; **Supp. XIX:** 1; **Supp. XVI: 45–61;** **Supp. XXI:** 31; **Supp. XXIV:** 167

Carruth, Joe-Anne McLaughlin, **Supp. XVI:** 47

"Carry" (Hogan), **Supp. IV Part 1:** 412

"Carrying On" (Dunn), **Supp. XI:** 145

Cars of Cuba (García), **Supp. XI:** 190

Carson, Anne, **Supp. XII: 97–116; Supp. XV:** 252; **Supp. XXV:** 222

Carson, Johnny, **Supp. IV Part 2:** 526

Carson, Rachel, **Supp. IX: 19–36; Supp. V:** 202; **Supp. X:** 99; **Supp. XVI:** 36; **Supp. XXVI:** 31

Carson, Tom, **Supp. XI:** 227

Cart, Michael, **Supp. X:** 12

Carter, Elliott, **Supp. III Part 1:** 21

Carter, Hodding, **Supp. XIV:** 2

Carter, Jared, **Supp. XVII:** 110

Carter, Jimmy, **Supp. I Part 2:** 638; **Supp. XIV:** 107

Carter, Marcia, **Supp. V:** 223

Carter, Mary, **Supp. IV Part 2:** 444

Carter, Paul, **Supp. XX: 77, 78**

Carter, Peter, **Supp. XVIII:** 267

Carter, Stephen, **Supp. XI:** 220

Cartesian Sonata and Other Novellas (Gass), **Supp. VI: 92–93**

Cartier, Jacques, **Supp. I Part 2:** 496, 497

Cartier-Bresson, Henri, **Supp. VIII:** 98

"Cartographies of Silence" (Rich), **Supp. I Part 2:** 571–572

"Cartography" (Espaillat), **Supp. XXI:** 107

Cartwright, Louis, **Supp. XIV:** 147, 149, 151

Carver, Raymond, **Supp. III Part 1: 135–151; Supp. IV Part 1:** 342; **Supp. V:** 22, 23, 220, 326; **Supp. VIII:** 15; **Supp. X:** 85, 167; **Supp. XI:** 26, 65, 116, 153; **Supp. XII:** 79, 139, 289, 294; **Supp. XIX:** 209; **Supp. XXI:** 36, 115, 116, 118, 119; **Supp. XXIII:** 289, 296; **Supp. XXIV:** 97, 166, 167, 173, 177–178; **Supp. XXVI:** 147, 180

Carver: A Life in Poems (Nelson), **Supp. XVIII:** 171, 172, **181–182,** 183

Carville, James, **Supp. XXIV:** 282

Carving Hawk (Kenny), **Supp. XXIII:** 143, 150

Cary, Alice, **Retro. Supp. II:** 145; **Supp. XV:** 273; **Supp. XXII:** 206

Cary, Phoebe, **Supp. XV:** 273

Cary, Richard, **Retro. Supp. II:** 132, 137

"Casabianca" (Bishop), **Retro. Supp. II:** 42; **Supp. I Part 1:** 86

Casablanca (film), **Supp. VIII:** 61; **Supp. XV:** 14

Casanova: His Known and Unknown Life (Endore), **Supp. XVII:** 54

"Casa solariega, La" ("The Family Mansion") (Espaillat), **Supp. XXI:** 107

"Case Against Mist, The" (Halliday), **Supp. XIX:** 91

Case for West-Indian Self-Government, The (C. L. R. James), **Supp. XXI:** 159, 161

Case of Jennie Brice, The (Rinehart), **Supp. XXV:** 193, 200

Case of Rape, A (C. Himes), **Supp. XVI:** 143

Case of the Crushed Petunias, The (T. Williams), **IV:** 381

Case of the Officers of Excise (Paine), **Supp. I Part 2:** 503–504

Casey, Helen Marie, **Supp. XXIII:** 246

Casey, John, **Supp. X:** 164

Cash, Arthur, **Supp. IV Part 1:** 299

Cashman, Nellie, **Supp. X:** 103

Casiero, Robert, **Supp. XIV:** 167

Casino Royale (film), **Supp. XI: 306–307**

Caskey, William, **Supp. XIV:** 166

"Cask of Amontillado, The" (Poe), **II:** 475; **III:** 413; **Retro. Supp. II:** 268, 269, 270, 273

Caso, Frank, **Supp. XVIII:** 95

Caspary, Vera, **Supp. XIX:** 78

Casper, Robert N., **Supp. XV:** 339, 347

Casper and His Friends (S. and A. Warner), **Supp. XVIII:** 264

Cassada (Salter), **Supp. IX: 251–252**

Cassada, Jackie, **Supp. XXIII:** 291

Cassady, Carolyn, **Supp. XIV:** 150

Cassady, Neal, **Supp. II Part 1:** 309, 311; **Supp. XIV:** 137, 144

"Cassandra" (Stallings), **Supp. XXV:** 233

"Cassandra Southwick" (Whittier), **Supp. I Part 2:** 693

Cassell, Verlin, **Supp. XI:** 315

Cassill, Ronald Verlin, **Supp. V:** 323; **Supp. XIX:** 266; **Supp. XVIII:** 72

Cassirer, Ernst, **I:** 265; **IV:** 87, 89

Cass Timberlane (Lewis), **II:** 455–456

Cast a Cold Eye (McCarthy), **II:** 566

Castaway (Cozzens), **I:** 363, 370, 374, 375, 379
"Caste in America" (Du Bois), **Supp. II Part 1:** 169
Castiglione, Baldassare, **I:** 279; **III:** 282
"Castilian" (Wylie), **Supp. I Part 2:** 714
Castillo, Ana, **Supp. XI:** 177; **Supp. XXIII:** 194
"Castle in Lynn, A" (McCarriston), **Supp. XIV:** 265, 268
"Castles and Distances" (Wilbur), **Supp. III Part 2:** 550
Castle Sinister (Marquand), **III:** 58
Cast of Thousands (Loos), **Supp. XVI:** 192, 193, 195
Castro, Fidel, **II:** 261, 434; **Supp. XX:** **80**
Cast the First Stone (C. Himes), **Supp. XVI:** 135, 137–138
"Casual Incident, A" (Hemingway), **II:** 44
"Casualty Report" (Halliday), **Supp. XIX:** 85
Caswell, Michelle, **Supp. XXII:** 262
"Cat, The" (Matthews), **Supp. IX:** 157–**158**
Cat, You Better Come Home (Keillor), **Supp. XVI:** 177
"Catbird Seat, The" (Thurber), **Supp. I Part 2:** 623
"Catch" (Francis), **Supp. IX:** 82
Catch-22 (Heller), **III:** 558; **Supp. IV Part 1:** 379, 380, 381–382, 383, 384–386, 387, 390, 391, 392, 393, 394; **Supp. V:** 244, 248; **Supp. XII:** 167–168; **Supp. XXIII:** 100
Catcher in the Rye, The (Salinger), **I:** 493; **III:** 551, 552, 553–558, 567, 571; **Retro. Supp. I:** 102; **Retro. Supp. II:** 222, 249; **Supp. I Part 2:** 535; **Supp. V:** 119; **Supp. VIII:** 242; **Supp. XI:** 65; **Supp. XVII:** 2; **Supp. XXIII:** 100; **Supp. XXIV:** 133
"Catching Frogs" (Kenyon), **Supp. VII:** 170
Catching the Mermother (A. Finch), **Supp. XVII:** 72
catechism of d neoamerican hoodoo church (Reed), **Supp. X:** 240, 241
Catered Affair, The (film), **Supp. IV Part 2:** 683
"Cathay" (Goldbarth), **Supp. XII:** 185, 186
Cathay (Pound), **II:** 527; **Retro. Supp. I:** 289
Cathedral (Carver), **Supp. III Part 1:** 144–146; **Supp. XII:** 139
"Cathedral" (Carver), **Supp. III Part 1:** 144–145; **Supp. XXIV:** 177
Cathedral, The (Lowell), **Supp. I Part 2:** 407, 416–417
Cather, Willa, **I:** 312–334, 405; **II:** 51, 96, 177, 404, 412; **III:** 453; **IV:** 190; **Retro. Supp. I:** 1–23, 355, 382; **Retro. Supp. II:** 71, 136; **Supp. I Part 2:** 609, 719; **Supp. IV Part 1:** 31; **Supp. VIII:** 101, 102, 263; **Supp. X:** 103; **Supp. XIII:** 253; **Supp. XIV:** 112; **Supp. XIX:** 131; **Supp. XV:** 40, 51; **Supp. XVI:** 226; **Supp. XVIII:**

207; **Supp. XXIII:** 290; **Supp. XXIV:** 29, 30, 244; **Supp. XXV:** 201
Catherine, Saint, **II:** 211
Catherine II, **Supp. I Part 2:** 433
Catholic Art and Culture (Watkin), **Retro. Supp. II:** 187
"Catholic Novelist in the Protestant South, The" (O'Connor), **Retro. Supp. II:** 223, 224
"Cathy Queen of Cats" (Cisneros), **Supp. VII:** 59
Cat Inside, The (Burroughs), **Supp. III Part 1:** 105
Cat in the Hat, The (Geisel), **Supp. XVI:** 106–107, 112
Cat in the Hat Come Back, The (Geisel), **Supp. XVI:** 107
"Cat in the Hat for President, The" (Coover), **Supp. V:** 44, 46–47
Cat in The Hat Songbook, The (Geisel), **Supp. XVI:** 104
Cato, **II:** 114, 117
Cat on a Hot Tin Roof (T. Williams), **II:** 190; **IV:** 380, 382, 383, 386, 387, 389, 390, 391, 394, 395, 397–398; **Supp. XXV:** 93
"Cat People: What Dr. Seuss Really Taught Us" (Menand), **Supp. XVI:** 106
Cats and Dogs (Silver), **Supp. XXIV:** 265, 274
Cat's Cradle (Vonnegut), **Supp. II Part 2:** 758, 759, 767–768, 770, 771, 772; **Supp. V:** 1
Cat's Eye (Atwood), **Supp. XIII:** **29–30**
Catskill Eagle, A (Parker), **Supp. XIX:** 185
"Cat's Meow, A" (Brodsky), **Supp. VIII:** 31
"Cats of Ulthar, The" (Lovecraft), **Supp. XXV:** 114
Cat's Quizzer, The (Geisel), **Supp. XVI:** 111
"Catterskill Falls" (Bryant), **Supp. I Part 1:** 160
"Cattle Car Complex" (T. Rosenbaum), **Supp. XVII:** 48
Cattlemen from the Rio Grande Across the Far Marias (Sandoz), **Supp. XXIV:** 244, **249–251**, 256
Catullus, **Supp. XII:** 2, 13, **112; Supp. XV:** 23, 27, 35, 36
Catullus, Gaius Valerius, **I:** 381; **Supp. I Part 1:** 261; **Supp. I Part 2:** 728
Catullus (Gai Catulli Veronensis Liber) (Zukofsky), **Supp. III Part 2:** 625, 627, 628, 629
"Catullus: *Carmina*" (Carson), **Supp. XII:** **112**
"Catullus: Excrucior" (Bidart), **Supp. XV:** 32, 35
"Cat Walked Through the Casserole, The" (Nelson and Espeland), **Supp. XVIII:** **181**
Cat Walked Through the Casserole and Other Poems for Children (Nelson and Espeland), **Supp. XVIII:** 181
"Cat Who Aspired to Higher Things, The" (X. J. Kennedy), **Supp. XV:** 163

Cat Who Went to Heaven, The (Coatsworth), **Supp. XXVI:** 33
"Caucasian Storms Harlem, The" (R. Fisher), **Supp. XIX:** 78
Caudwell, Christopher, **Supp. X:** 112; **Supp. XXII:** 284
"Caul, The" (Banks), **Supp. V:** 10–11
Cause for Wonder (Morris), **III:** 232–233
"Causerie" (Tate), **IV:** 129
Causes and Consequences (Chapman), **Supp. XIV:** 41, 49, 51
"Causes of American Discontents before 1768, The" (Franklin), **II:** 120
Causley, Charles, **Supp. XV:** 117
Cavafy, Constantine P., **Supp. IX:** 275; **Supp. XI:** 119, 123; **Supp. XXI:** 131; **Supp. XXIII:** 150; **Supp. XXV:** 225, 233
Cavalcade of America, The (radio program), **III:** 146
Cavalcanti (Pound, opera), **Retro. Supp. I:** 287
Cavalcanti, Guido, **I:** 579; **III:** 467; **Supp. III Part 2:** 620, 621, 622, 623
Cavalieri, Grace, **Supp. IV Part 2:** 630, 631
"Cavalry Crossing the Ford" (Whitman), **IV:** 347
"Cave, The" (Bass), **Supp. XVI:** 23
Cave, The (Warren), **IV:** 255–256
Cavelieri, Grace, **Supp. XXIII:** 135
Cavell, Stanley, **Retro. Supp. I:** 306–307, 309
Cavender's House (Robinson), **III:** 510
Caver, Christine, **Supp. XXI:** 215
Caves of Death, The (Atherton; Joshi, ed.), **Supp. XXIV:** 23
"Caviar" (Boyle), **Supp. XX:** **19**
Caviare at the Funeral (Simpson), **Supp. IX:** 266, **276–277**
"Cawdor" (Jeffers), **Supp. II Part 2:** 431
Caxton, William, **III:** 486
Cayton, Horace, **IV:** 475, 488
Cazamian, Louis, **II:** 529
"Ceiling, The" (Brockmeier), **Supp. XXII:** 52–53
Celan, Paul, **Supp. X:** 149; **Supp. XII:** 21, 110–111; **Supp. XVI:** 284–285, 288; **Supp. XVII:** 241
"Celebrated Jumping Frog of Calaveras County, The" (Twain), **IV:** 196
Celebrated Jumping Frog of Calaveras County, The, and Other Sketches (Twain), **IV:** 197
Celebration (Crews), **Supp. XI:** 103, **108**
Celebration (Swados), **Supp. XIX:** **269– 270**
Celebration at Dark (W. J. Smith), **Supp. XIII:** 332
"Celebration for June 24th" (McGrath), **Supp. X:** 116
Celebration of the Sound Through (Sobin), **Supp. XVI:** 284–285
Celebrations after the Death of John Brennan (X. J. Kennedy), **Supp. XV:** 165
Celebrity (film; Allen), **Supp. XV:** 11
"Celebrity" (Pickering), **Supp. XXI:** 198
"Celery" (Stein), **IV:** 43

"Celestial Games" (Conroy), **Supp. XVI:** 72

"Celestial Globe" (Nemerov), **III:** 288

Celestial Navigation (Tyler), **Supp. IV Part 2:** 662–663, 671

"Celestial Railroad, The" (Hawthorne), **Retro. Supp. I:** 152; **Supp. I Part 1:** 188

Celibate Season, A (Shields), **Supp. VII:** 323, 324

Cellini (Shanley), **Supp. XIV:** 316, **329–330**

"Cemetery at Academy, California" (Levine), **Supp. V:** 182

Cemetery Nights (Dobyns), **Supp. XIII:** 85, 87, 89

"Cenotaph, The" (Stallings), **Supp. XXV:** 225, 234

"Censors As Critics: *To Kill a Mockingbird* As a Case Study" (May), **Supp. VIII:** 126

"Census-Taker, The" (Frost), **Retro. Supp. I:** 129

"Centaur, The" (Swenson), **Supp. IV Part 2:** 641

Centaur, The (Updike), **IV:** 214, 216, 217, 218, 219–221, 222; **Retro. Supp. I:** 318, 322, 324, 331, 336

"Centennial Meditation of Columbia, The" (Lanier), **Supp. I Part 1:** 362

Centeno, Agusto, **IV:** 375

"Centipede" (Dove), **Supp. IV Part 1:** 246

"Cento: A Note on Philosophy" (Berrigan), **Supp. XXIV:** 42–43

"Central Man, The" (Bloom), **Supp. IV Part 2:** 689

"Central Park" (Lowell), **II:** 552

Central Park (Wasserstein and Drattel), **Supp. XV:** 333

Central Park West (Allen), **Supp. XV:** 13

Century of Dishonor, A (Jackson), **Retro. Supp. I:** 31

"Cerebral Snapshot, The" (Theroux), **Supp. VIII:** 313

"Ceremonies" (Rukeyser), **Supp. VI:** 279

"Ceremony" (Monson), **Supp. XXIV:** 230

Ceremony (Silko), **Supp. IV Part 1:** 274, 333; **Supp. IV Part 2:** 557–558, 558–559, 559, 561–566, 570; **Supp. XVIII:** 59

Ceremony (Wilbur), **Supp. III Part 2:** 550–551

"Ceremony, The" (Harjo), **Supp. XII:** 230

"Ceremony, The—Anatomy of a Massacre" (E. Hoffman, play), **Supp. XVI:** 160

Ceremony in Lone Tree (Morris), **III:** 229–230, 232, 238, 558

Ceremony of Brotherhood, A (Anaya and Ortiz, eds.), **Supp. IV Part 2:** 502

Cerf, Bennett, **III:** 405; **IV:** 288; **Retro. Supp. II:** 330; **Supp. XIII:** 172; **Supp. XIX:** 244

"Certain Attention to the World, A" (Haines), **Supp. XII:** 201

"Certain Beasts, Like Cats" (Bronk), **Supp. XXI:** 30

Certain Distance, A (Francis), **Supp. IX:** 85

"Certain Music, A" (Rukeyser), **Supp. VI:** 273

Certain Noble Plays of Japan (Pound), **III:** 458

Certain People (Wharton), **Retro. Supp. I:** 382

"Certain Poets" (MacLeish), **III:** 4

Certain Slant of Sunlight, A (Berrigan), **Supp. XXIV:** 43

"Certain Testimony" (Bausch), **Supp. VII:** 48

Certificate, The (Singer), **IV:** 1; **Retro. Supp. II:** **314–315**

"Cerulean" (Everett), **Supp. XVIII:** 66

Cervantes, Lorna Dee, **Supp. IV Part 2:** 545

Cervantes, Miguel de, **I:** 130, 134; **II:** 8, 272, 273, 276, 289, 302, 310, 315; **III:** 113, 614; **IV:** 367; **Retro. Supp. I:** 91; **Supp. I Part 2:** 406; **Supp. V:** 277; **Supp. XIII:** 17; **Supp. XXIII:** 4

Césaire, Aimé, **Supp. X:** 132, 139; **Supp. XIII:** 114

"Cesarean" (Kenyon), **Supp. VII:** 173

Cézanne, Paul, **II:** 576; **III:** 210; **IV:** 26, 31, 407; **Supp. V:** 333, 341–342; **Supp. XIX:** 36

Chabon, Michael, **Supp. XI:** **63–81**; **Supp. XIX:** 135, 138, 174, 223; **Supp. XVI:** 259; **Supp. XX:** **177**; **Supp. XXII:** 49; **Supp. XXIV:** 131

Chaboseau, Jean, **Supp. I Part 1:** 260

Chace, Bill, **Supp. XXI:** 256

Chagall, Marc, **Supp. XXIII:** 6

Chaikin, Joseph, **Supp. III Part 2:** 433, 436–437

"Chain, The" (Kumin), **Supp. IV Part 2:** 452

Chainbearer, The (Cooper), **I:** 351, 352–353

"Chain of Love, A" (Price), **Supp. VI:** **258–259,** 260

Chain Saw Dance, The (Budbill), **Supp. XIX:** **5–6**

Chains of Dew (Glaspell), **Supp. III Part 1:** 181

Chalk Face (W. Frank), **Supp. XX:** **73–74**

Challacombe, Robert Hamilton, **III:** 176

Challenge (Untermeyer), **Supp. XV:** 296, 303

"Challenge" (Untermeyer), **Supp. XV:** 296

"Challenge from Beyond, The" (Lovecraft, Howard, Long, Merritt, and Moore), **Supp. XXV:** 122

Chalmers, George, **Supp. I Part 2:** 514, 521

"Chambered Nautilus, The" (Holmes), **Supp. I Part 1:** 254, 307, 312–313, 314

Chamberlain, John, **Supp. I Part 2:** 647; **Supp. IV Part 2:** 525

Chamberlain, Neville, **II:** 589; **Supp. I Part 2:** 664

Chamber Music (Joyce), **III:** 16

Chambers, Richard, **Supp. III Part 2:** 610, 611, 612

Chambers, Whittaker, **Supp. III Part 2:** 610; **Supp. IV Part 2:** 526; **Supp. XV:** 143

Chameleon (C. Baxter), **Supp. XVII:** 14–15

"Champ, The" (Zinberg), **Supp. XV:** 193

"Champagne Regions" (Ríos), **Supp. IV Part 2:** 553

"Champion" (Lardner), **II:** 420–421, 428, 430

Champion, Laurie, **Supp. VIII:** 128

Champollion-Figeac, Jean Jacques, **IV:** 426

"Chance" (Doolittle), **Supp. I Part 1:** 271

Chance, Frank, **II:** 418

Chance Acquaintance, A (Howells), **II:** 278

"Chance Encounter, A" (Swados), **Supp. XIX:** 261, 262

"Chanclas" (Cisneros), **Supp. VII:** 61

Chandler, Raymond, **Supp. III Part 1:** 91; **Supp. IV Part 1: 119–138,** 341, 344, 345; **Supp. IV Part 2:** 461, 464, 469, 470, 471, 472, 473; **Supp. XI:** 160, 228; **Supp. XII:** 307; **Supp. XIII:** 159, 233; **Supp. XIV:** 21; **Supp. XIX:** 178, 189; **Supp. XV:** 119; **Supp. XVI:** 122; **Supp. XVII:** 137; **Supp. XVIII:** 136,137, 137–138; **Supp. XXI:** 67; **Supp. XXII:** 119; **Supp. XXIV:** 284; **Supp. XXV:** 180

Chandler, Sherry, **Supp. XXIII:** 247

Chaney, "Professor" W. H., **II:** 463–464

Chang, Leslie C., **Supp. IV Part 1:** 72

"Change, The: Kyoto-Tokyo Express" (Ginsberg), **Supp. II Part 1:** 313, 329

Changed Man, A (Prose), **Supp. XVI:** 261–262

"Changeling" (Espaillat), **Supp. XXI:** 100

Changeling (Middleton), **Retro. Supp. I:** 62

"Changeling, The" (Lowell), **Supp. I Part 2:** 409

"Changeling, The" (Whittier), **Supp. I Part 2:** 697

Change of World, A (Rich), **Supp. I Part 2:** 551, 552

"Changes of Mind" (Baker), **Supp. XIII:** 52

"Changes of the Soul" (Taggard), **Supp. XXII:** 280

"Change the Joke and Slip the Yoke" (Ellison), **Retro. Supp. II:** 118

Change Your Bedding! (O'Hara), **Supp. XXIII:** 210

Changing Light at Sandover, The (Merrill), **Supp. III Part 1:** 318, 319, 323, 327, 332, 335–336; **Supp. XII:** 269–270; **Supp. XV:** 264

"Changing Same, The" (Baraka), **Supp. II Part 1:** 47, 51, 53

Changing the Bully Who Rules the World: Reading and Thinking about Ethics (C. Bly), **Supp. XVI:** 32, **39–40,** 41

Chanler, Mrs. Winthrop, **I:** 22; **IV:** 325

Channing, Carol, **IV:** 357

Channing, Edward, **Supp. I Part 2:** 479–480

Channing, Edward Tyrrel, **Supp. I Part 1**: 155; **Supp. I Part 2**: 422; **Supp. XXV**: 240

Channing, William Ellery, **I**: 336; **II**: 224, 495; **IV**: 172, 173, 176, 177; **Retro. Supp. I**: 54; **Supp. I Part 1**: 103; **Supp. I Part 2**: 589; **Supp. XXIV**: 67–81; **Supp. XXV**: 250

Channing, William Henry, **IV**: 178; **Supp. II Part 1**: 280, 285; **Supp. XXIV**: 68

Channing: The Reluctant Radical (Mendelsohn), **Supp. XXIV**: 72

Chanson de Roland, La, **I**: 13

"Chanson un Peu Naïve" (Bogan), **Supp. III Part 1**: 50–51

"Chanteuse" (Doty), **Supp. XI**: 119

"Chant for May Day" (Hughes), **Supp. I Part 1**: 331

Chants (Mora), **Supp. XIII**: 214–215

Chaos (Dove), **Supp. IV Part 1**: 243

Chapelle, Howard I., **Supp. XXV**: 217

"Chaperone, The" (Van Vechten), **Supp. II Part 2**: 728

Chaplin, Charles Spencer "Charlie," **I**: 27, 32, 43, 386, 447; **III**: 403; **Supp. I Part 2**: 607; **Supp. IV Part 1**: 146; **Supp. IV Part 2**: 574; **Supp. XX**: 75; **Supp. XXI**: 170; **Supp. XXII**: 25, 26

"Chaplinesque" (H. Crane), **Retro. Supp. II**: 79

"Chapman" (Rukeyser), **Supp. VI**: 273

Chapman, Abraham, **IV**: 485

Chapman, George, **Supp. I Part 2**: 422

Chapman, John, **Supp. XXV**: 105

Chapman, John (Johnny Appleseed), **Supp. I Part 2**: 397

Chapman, John Jay, **IV**: 436; **Supp. XIV**: 39–56

Chapman, Stephen, **Supp. XIII**: 12

Chappell, Fred, **Supp. IV Part 1**: 69; **Supp. XI**: 317; **Supp. XVIII**: 87

Chapters in a Mythology: The Poetry of Sylvia Plath (Kroll), **Supp. I Part 2**: 541–543

Chapters on Erie (Adams and Adams), **Supp. I Part 2**: 644

Chapter Two (Simon), **Supp. IV Part 2**: 575, 586

"Chapter VI" (Hemingway), **II**: 252

Char, René, **Supp. XVI**: 282; **Supp. XVII**: 244

"Character" (Emerson), **II**: 6

"Character of Aboriginal Historical Tradition"(J. Schoolcraft), **Supp. XXIII**: 228–229

"Character of Presidents, The" (Doctorow), **Supp. IV Part 1**: 224

"Character of Socrates, The" (Emerson), **II**: 8–9

Character of the Poet, The (Simpson), **Supp. IX**: 273, 275, 278

"Characters in Fiction" (McCarthy), **II**: 562

"Charades" (Moore), **Supp. X**: 178

"Charge It" (Fante), **Supp. XI**: 164–165

"Charioteer, The" (Stallings), **Supp. XXV**: 233

Chariot in the Sky: A Story of the Jubilee Singers (Bontemps), **Supp. XXII**: 6, 13

"Charity" (Peacock), **Supp. XIX**: 221–222

Charity (Richard), **Supp. XIX**: 220–222

Charlatan, The (Singer), **IV**: 1

"Charles" (Jackson), **Supp. IX**: 125

Charles, Abram, **Supp. XXVI**: 87

Charles, Larry, **Supp. XVIII**: 21

"Charles Baxter, August Kleinzahler, Adrienne Rich: Contemporary Stevensians and the Problem of 'Other Lives' " (S. Burt), **Supp. XVII**: 18–19

Charles Goodnight: Cowman and Plainsman (Haley), **Supp. V**: 226

Charles Simic: Essays on the Poetry (Weigl), **Supp. VIII**: 269

Charles the Bold, Duke of Burgundy, **III**: 487

Charleville, Victoria Verdon, **Supp. I Part 1**: 200–201, 205, 206, 210

Charley's Aunt (B. Thomas), **II**: 138

Charlie Chan Is Dead: An Anthology of Contemporary Asian American Fiction (Hagedorn), **Supp. X**: 292

"Charlie Christian Story, The" (Ellison), **Retro. Supp. II**: 121

"Charlie Howard's Descent" (Doty), **Supp. XI**: 122

Charlotte: A Tale of Truth (Rowson), **Supp. I Part 1**: 128; **Supp. XV**: 234–235, 238. *See also Charlotte Temple* (Rowson)

Charlotte's Daughter; or, The Three Orphans (Rowson), **Supp. XV**: 246

Charlotte's Web (White), **Supp. I Part 2**: 655, 656, 658, 667, 670

Charlotte Temple (Rowson), **Supp. XV**: 229, 238–239; **Supp. XXV**: 35, 36. *See also Charlotte: A Tale of Truth* (Rowson)

Charm, The (Creeley), **Supp. IV Part 1**: 139, 141, 144, 149–150

Charmed Life, A (McCarthy), **II**: 571–574

Charming Billy (McDermott), **Supp. XVIII**: 155, 162–164, 166

Charms for the Easy Life (Gibbons), **Supp. X**: 45, 47–48

Charnel Rose, The (Aiken), **I**: 50, 57, 62

Charney, Samuel, **Supp. XXIII**: 6

Charon's Cosmology (Simic), **Supp. VIII**: 276–278

Charterhouse, The (Percy), **Supp. III Part 1**: 388

Chart for Rough Water (W. Frank), **Supp. XX**: 78

Charvat, William, **II**: 244

Charyn, Jerome, **Supp. XVII**: 5

Chase, Mary Ellen, **Retro. Supp. II**: 243, 245; **Supp. XXIV**: 30

Chase, Richard, **IV**: 202, 443; **Retro. Supp. I**: 40, 395

Chase, Salmon P., **Supp. I Part 2**: 584

Chase, Stuart, **Supp. I Part 2**: 609

Chase, The (Foote), **Supp. I Part 1**: 281

Chasing the Dime (Connelly), **Supp. XXI**: 74

"Chaste Land, The" (Tate), **IV**: 122

Château, The (Maxwell), **Supp. VIII**: 152, 160, 165–167, 168, 169

Chatham, Russell, **Supp. VIII**: 40

"Chattanooga Nights" (L. Brown), **Supp. XXI**: 39

Chatterdon, The Black Death, and Meriwether Lewis (Reznikoff), **Supp. XIV**: 288

Chatterton, Thomas, **Supp. I Part 1**: 349; **Supp. I Part 2**: 410, 716

Chatterton, Wayne, **Supp. IX**: 2, 4, 11–12

"Chatty Letters During a Journey from Aruba to Rio" (Thompson), **Supp. XXIV**: 282

Chatwin, Bruce, **Supp. VIII**: 322

Chaucer, Geoffrey, **I**: 131; **II**: 11, 504, 516, 542, 543; **III**: 283, 411, 473, 492, 521; **Retro. Supp. I**: 135, 426; **Supp. I Part 1**: 356, 363; **Supp. I Part 2**: 422, 617; **Supp. V**: 259; **Supp. XII**: 197; **Supp. XIX**: 4; **Supp. XVII**: 70

Chauncy, Charles, **I**: 546–547; **IV**: 147

Chavez, César, **Supp. V**: 199

Chávez, Denise, **Supp. IV Part 2**: 544; **Supp. XI**: 316

Chavez, Lydia, **Supp. VIII**: 75

Chavkin, Allan, **Supp. IV Part 1**: 259

Chavkin, Nancy Feyl, **Supp. IV Part 1**: 259

Chawla, Louise, **Supp. XXI**: 24

Chayefsky, Paddy, **Supp. XI**: 306

Cheang, Shu Lea, **Supp. XI**: 20

"Cheater's Guide To Love, The" (Díaz), **Supp. XXIV**: 84, 92, 93

"Cheat Takes Over" (Leopold), **Supp. XIV**: 189

"Cheers" (Carver), **Supp. III Part 1**: 138

Cheetham, James, **Supp. I Part 2**: 521

Cheever, Benjamin Hale, **Supp. I Part 1**: 175; **Supp. XXIV**: 97

Cheever, David W., **Supp. I Part 1**: 304

Cheever, Ezekiel, **Supp. I Part 1**: 174, 193

Cheever, Federico, **Supp. I Part 1**: 175

Cheever, Fred, **Supp. I Part 1**: 174

Cheever, Frederick L., **Supp. I Part 1**: 174

Cheever, John, **Retro. Supp. I**: 116, 333, 335; **Supp. I Part 1**: 174–199; **Supp. IX**: 114, 208; **Supp. V**: 23, 95; **Supp. VIII**: 151; **Supp. XI**: 65, 66, 99; **Supp. XII**: 140; **Supp. XIV**: 93; **Supp. XV**: 119, 142; **Supp. XXIII**: 104, 109, 275; **Supp. XXV**: 79, 142; **Supp. XXVI**: 147

Cheever, Mrs. John (Mary Winternitz), **Supp. I Part 1**: 175

Cheever, Mary Liley, **Supp. I Part 1**: 174

Cheever, Susan. *See* Cowley, Susan Cheever (Susan Cheever)

Cheever Evening, A (Gurney), **Supp. V**: 95

Chekhov, Anton, **I**: 52, 90; **II**: 27, 38, 44, 49, 198, 542; **III**: 362, 467; **IV**: 17, 53, 359, 446; **Retro. Supp. I**: 5, 355; **Retro. Supp. II**: 299; **Supp. I Part 1**: 196; **Supp. II Part 1**: 6; **Supp. IV Part 2**: 585; **Supp. IX**: 260, 265, 274; **Supp. V**: 265; **Supp. VIII**: 153, 332; **Supp. XI**: 66; **Supp. XII**: 94, 307; **Supp. XIII**: 79; **Supp. XIV**: 87, 242; **Supp. XIX**: 172, 241; **Supp. XV**: 320, 329; **Supp. XVIII**: 102; **Supp. XXII**:

60; **Supp. XXIII:** 162, 290

"Chekhov's Sense of Writing as Seen Through His Letters" (Dobyns), **Supp. XIII:** 77–78

"Chemin de Fer" (Bishop), **Retro. Supp. II:** 41; **Supp. I Part 1:** 80, 85, 86

Cheney, Brainard, **Retro. Supp. II:** 229

Cheney, Matthew, **Supp. XXII:** 50

Chenzira, Ayoka, **Supp. XI:** 19

Chéri (Colette; stage adaptation, Loos), **Supp. XVI:** 194

Cherkovski, Neeli, **Supp. XII:** 118, 132, 134

Chernyshevski, Nikolai, **III:** 261, 262, 263; **Retro. Supp. I:** 269

Cherokee Lottery, The: A Sequence of Poems (W. J. Smith), **Supp. XIII: 340–344**

"Cherríe Moraga's Radical Revision of *Death of a Salesman*"(Wiley), **Supp. XXIII:** 199

Cherry (Karr), **Supp. XI:** 239, **251–254**

"Cherrylog Road" (Dickey), **Supp. XVIII:** 191

Cherry Orchard, The (Chekhov), **IV:** 359, 426; **Supp. VIII:** 153

Cheslock, Louis, **III:** 99, 118, 119

Chesnutt, Charles Waddell, **Supp. II Part 1:** 174, 193, 211; **Supp. IV Part 1:** 257; **Supp. XIV: 57–78**

"Chess House, The" (Dixon), **Supp. XII:** 139

Chessman, Caryl, **Supp. I Part 2:** 446

Chester, Alfred, **Retro. Supp. II:** 111, 112; **Supp. X:** 192

Chesterfield, Lord, **II:** 36

Chesterton, Gilbert Keith, **I:** 226; **IV:** 432

Cheuse, Alan, **Supp. IV Part 2:** 570

Chevigny, Bell Gale, **Supp. XI:** 283

Cheyenne Autumn (Sandoz), **Supp. XXIII:** 146; **Supp. XXIV:** 244, 248, 256, **258–260**

"Chicago" (Sandburg), **III:** 581, 592, 596; **Supp. III Part 1:** 71

Chicago (Shepard), **Supp. III Part 2:** 439

Chicago: City on the Make (Algren), **Supp. IX:** 1, 3

"*Chicago Defender* Sends a Man to Little Rock, The" (Brooks), **Supp. III Part 1:** 80–81

"Chicago Hamlet, A" (Anderson), **I:** 112

Chicago Loop (Theroux), **Supp. VIII:** 324

"Chicago Picasso, The" (Brooks), **Supp. III Part 1:** 70–71, 84

Chicago Poems (Sandburg), **III:** 579, 581–583, 586

"Chicano/Borderlands Literature and Poetry" (Ríos), **Supp. IV Part 2:** 537, 538, 542, 545

Chicano! The History of the Mexican American Civil Rights Movement (Rosales), **Supp. XXV:** 133

Chick, Nancy, **Supp. IV Part 1:** 1

"Chickamauga" (Bierce), **I:** 201

"Chickamauga" (Wolfe), **IV:** 460

Chickamauga (Wright), **Supp. V:** 333, 343–344

"Chickamauga" (Wright), **Supp. V:** 334

"Chicken Market" (Skloot), **Supp. XX: 198, 200**

"Chiefly about War Matters" (Hawthorne), **II:** 227; **Retro. Supp. I:** 165

"Chiffon" (Hull), **Supp. XXI:** 138

"Child" (Plath), **Supp. I Part 2:** 544

Child, Greg, **Supp. XVIII:** 107

Child, Julia, **Supp. XVII:** 89, 90

Child, Lydia Maria, **Supp. XIII:** 141; **Supp. XVIII:** 11

"Child, The" (Ríos), **Supp. IV Part 2:** 543

"Child by Tiger, The" (Wolfe), **IV:** 451

"Childhood" (Wright), **Supp. V:** 341

Childhood, A: The Biography of a Place (Crews), **Supp. XI:** 102–103, 245

"Childhood, When You Are in It . . ." (Kenyon), **Supp. VII:** 160, 170

Childhood and Other Neighborhoods (Dybek), **Supp. XXIII:** 68, **69–70**

"Childhood Sketch" (Wright), **Supp. III Part 2:** 589

"Child Is Born, A" (Benét), **Supp. XI:** 46

"Child Is the Meaning of This Life, The" (Schwartz), **Supp. II Part 2:** 659–660

"Childlessness" (Merrill), **Supp. III Part 1:** 323

"Childless Woman" (Plath), **Supp. I Part 2:** 544

Child-Life (Whittier and Larcom, eds.), **Supp. XIII:** 142

Child-Life in Prose (Whittier and Larcom, eds.), **Supp. XIII:** 142

Childlike Life of the Black Tarantula, The (Acker), **Supp. XII:** 4, 6, **7–8**

"Child Margaret" (Sandburg), **III:** 584

"Child of Courts, The" (Jarrell), **II:** 378, 379, 381

Child of God (McCarthy), **Supp. VIII: 177–178**

Child of My Heart (McDermott), **Supp. XVIII:** 155, **164–166**

Child of the Century, A (Hecht), **Supp. XXV:** 29

"CHILD OF THE THIRTIES" (Baraka), **Supp. II Part 1:** 60

"Child on Top of a Greenhouse" (Roethke), **III:** 531

Children (Gurney), **Supp. V:** 95, 96

"Children" (Stowe), **Supp. I Part 2:** 587

"Children, The" (Jarman), **Supp. XVII:** 116

Children, The (Wharton), **IV:** 321, 326; **Retro. Supp. I:** 381

"Children, the Sandbar, That Summer" (Rukeyser), **Supp. VI:** 274

Children and Others (Cozzens), **I:** 374

Children Is All (Purdy), **Supp. VII:** 277, 278, 282

"Children of Adam" (Whitman), **IV:** 342; **Retro. Supp. I:** 403, 405

Children of Job, The: American Second-Generation Witnesses to the Holocaust (A. Berger), **Supp. XVII:** 39

Children of Light (Stone), **Supp. V:** 304–306

Children of Light and the Children of Darkness, The (Niebuhr), **III:** 292, 306, 310

"Children of the Dirty War" (Goldman), **Supp. XXV:** 52

Children of the Frost (London), **II:** 469, 483

Children of the Holocaust (H. Epstein), **Supp. XVII:** 48; **Supp. XXII:** 95

"Children of the Lord's Supper, The" (Tegnér), **Retro. Supp. II:** 155, 157

Children of the Market Place (Masters), **Supp. I Part 2:** 471

"Children on Their Birthdays" (Capote), **Supp. III Part 1:** 114, 115

Children Playing Before a Statue of Hercules (Sedaris, ed.), **Supp. XXIII:** 289

"Children Selecting Books in a Library" (Jarrell), **II:** 371

Children's Hour, The (Hellman), **Supp. I Part 1:** 276–277, 281, 286, 297

"Children's Rhymes" (Hughes), **Supp. I Part 1:** 340

Childress, Mark, **Supp. X:** 89

Child's Garden of Verses, A (Stevenson), **Supp. IV Part 1:** 298, 314; **Supp. XIII:** 75

"Child's Nature, A" (Jin), **Supp. XVIII:** 93

"Child's Reminiscence, A" (Whitman), **IV:** 344

Childwold (Oates), **Supp. II Part 2:** 519–520

Chile Woman (G. Jones), **Supp. XXIV:** 185

Chill, The (Macdonald), **Supp. IV Part 2:** 473

Chills and Fever (Ransom), **III:** 490, 491–492, 493

Chilly Scenes of Winter (Beattie), **Supp. V:** 21, 22, 23, 24, 26, 27

Chime of Words, A: The Letters of Logan Pearsall Smith (Tribble, ed.), **Supp. XIV:** 348–349

Chimera (C. Frost), **Supp. XV:** 94, 95, 100

"Chimes for Yahya" (Merrill), **Supp. III Part 1:** 329

Chin, Frank, **Supp. V:** 164, 172

Chin, Mei, **Supp. XVIII:** 95

"China" (C. Johnson), **Supp. VI: 193–194**

Chinaberry Tree, The (Fauset), **Supp. XIX:** 73

"Chinaman's Hat" (Kingston), **Supp. V:** 169

China Men (Kingston), **Supp. V:** 157, 158, 159, 160, 161, 164–169; **Supp. X:** 292; **Supp. XV:** 220

"China Poet, The" (Sturgis), **Supp. XX: 233, 240**

China Trace (Wright), **Supp. V:** 332, 340, 341, 342

"Chinese Apples" (Di Piero), **Supp. XIX:** 40

Chinese Apples: New and Selected Poems (Di Piero), **Supp. XIX:** 33, 36, 37, 38, 39, 40, 44, 45, 46, 47–48

Chinese Classics (Legge), **III:** 472

Chinese Materia Medica (P. Smith), **III:** 572

"Chinese New Year" (Hull), **Supp. XXI:** 135

"Chinese Nightingale, The" (Lindsay), **Supp. I Part 2:** 392–393, 394

Chinese Nightingale and Other Poems, The (Lindsay), **Supp. I Part 2:** 392

Chinese Siamese Cat, The (Tan), **Supp. X:** 289

Chinese Translations, The (Bynner), **Supp. XV:** 47, 52

Chinitz, David, **Supp. XV:** 180, 185

"Chinoiseries" (Lowell), **II:** 524–525

Chip (Untermeyer), **Supp. XV:** 310

"Chipeta, Widow of Chief Ouray with a Word About a Deal in Blankets" (Zitkala-Ša), **Supp. XXV:** 281

Chirico, Giorgio de, **Supp. III Part 1:** 14

Chirico, Miriam M., **Supp. XV:** 323

"Chiron" (Winters), **Supp. II Part 2:** 801

"Chitlins at the Waldorf" (Crouch), **Supp. XIX:** 158

"Chloroform Jags" (J. Scott), **Supp. XVII:** 189

"Chocklit Geography: Raymond Andrews's Mythical South" (Harris), **Supp. XXVI:** 14

Chodorov, Jerome, **IV:** 274

"Choice, The" (Karr), **Supp. XI:** 251

"Choice of Accommodations, A" (Lahiri), **Supp. XXI:** 183

"Choice of Profession, A" (Malamud), **Supp. I Part 2:** 437

Choice of Wars, A (Shaw), **Supp. XIX:** 245

"Choices" (Gallagher), **Supp. XXIV:** 171

Chomei, Kamo No, **IV:** 170, 171, 184

Chomsky, Noam, **Supp. IV Part 2:** 679

Choosing not Choosing (Cameron), **Retro. Supp. I:** 43

Chopin, Felix, **Supp. I Part 1:** 202

Chopin, Frédéric, **Supp. I Part 1:** 363

Chopin, Jean, **Supp. I Part 1:** 206

Chopin, Kate, **II:** 276; **Retro. Supp. I:** 10, 215; **Retro. Supp. II: 57–74;** **Supp. I Part 1: 200–226;** **Supp. V:** 304; **Supp. X:** 227; **Supp. XVIII:** 194

"Chopin in Winter"(Dybek), **Supp. XXIII:** 72

"Choral: The Pink Church" (W. C. Williams), **Retro. Supp. I:** 428

"Chord" (Merwin), **Supp. III Part 1:** 356

"Chord"(Dybek), **Supp. XXIII:** 78

"Chords and Dischords" (column; Untermeyer), **Supp. XV:** 294

"Chorus, The"(Hadas), **Supp. XXIII:** 119–120

Choruses from Iphigenia in Aulis (Doolittle, trans.), **Supp. I Part 1:** 257, 268, 269

Chosen, The (Potok), **Supp. XXVI:** 125

"Chosen Blindness" (Karr), **Supp. XI:** 251

Chosen Country (Dos Passos), **I:** 475, 490–491

Chosen Place, The Timeless People, The (Marshall), **Supp. XI:** 275, 276, **282–284**

Chosön (Lowell), **II:** 513

Choukri, Mohamed, **Supp. IV Part 1:** 92

Chovteau, Mane Thérèse, **Supp. I Part 1:** 205

Chris Durang and Dawne (Durang), **Supp. XXIV:** 113, 124

"ChrisEaster" (Peacock), **Supp. XIX:** 198, 199

Chrisman, Robert, **Supp. IV Part 1:** 1

Christabel (Coleridge), **Supp. IV Part 2:** 465

"Christ for Sale" (Lowell), **II:** 538

Christian, Graham, **Supp. XII:** 193

Christian Dictionary, A (Wilson), **IV:** 153

"Christian in World Crisis, The" (Merton), **Supp. VIII:** 203

Christianity and Power Politics (Niebuhr), **III:** 292, 303

"Christianity and the Survival of Creation" (Berry), **Supp. X:** 30

Christianity of Sholem Asch, The: An Appraisal from the Jewish Viewpoint (Lieberman), **Supp. XXIII:** 3, 7

"Christian Minister, The" (Emerson), **II:** 10

Christian Philosopher, The (Mather), **Supp. II Part 2:** 463–464

Christian Realism and Practical Problems (Niebuhr), **III:** 292, 308

"Christian Roommates, The" (Updike), **IV:** 226–227; **Retro. Supp. I:** 319, 323

Christiansen, Carrie, **I:** 210

Christian's Secret of a Happy Life, The (H. W. Smith), **Supp. XIV:** 333–334

Christie, Agatha, **Supp. IV Part 1:** 341; **Supp. IV Part 2:** 469

Christ in Concrete (di Donato), **Supp. XX:** 33, 34–40, 42, 43, 46

"Christ in Concrete" (di Donato), **Supp. XX:** 34

Christine (King), **Supp. V:** 139, 148

"Christ Light, The" (Chopin), **Retro. Supp. II:** 61

"Christmas" (Saunders), **Supp. XIX:** 232

"Christmas, or the Good Fairy" (Stowe), **Supp. I Part 2:** 586

"Christmas 1944" (Levertov), **Supp. III Part 1:** 274

"Christmas Banquet, The" (Hawthorne), **II:** 227

Christmas Card, A (Theroux), **Supp. VIII:** 322

Christmas Carol, A (Dickens), **Retro. Supp. I:** 196; **Supp. I Part 2:** 409–410; **Supp. X:** 252, 253; **Supp. XXV:** 149, 152

Christmas Carollin' (Wells), **Supp. XXVI:** 275

"Christmas Eve at Johnson's Drugs N Goods" (Bambara), **Supp. XI:** 11–12

"Christmas Eve in the Time of War: A Capitalist Meditates by a Civil War Monument" (Lowell), **II:** 538

"Christmas Eve under Hooker's Statue" (Lowell), **II:** 539–540

"Christmas Gift" (Warren), **IV:** 252–253

"Christmas Greeting, A" (Wright), **Supp. III Part 2:** 601

"Christmas Hymn, A" (Wilbur), **Supp. III Part 2:** 557

Christmas Memory, A (Capote), **Supp. III Part 1:** 118, 119, 129

"Christmass Poem" (West), **Retro. Supp. II:** 338

Christmas Story (Mencken), **III:** 111

"Christmas to Me" (Lee), **Supp. VIII:** 113

Christographia (Taylor), **IV:** 164–165

Christ on a Clothesline (Loy), **Supp. XXII:** 168

"*Christ on the Cross*/Nuestro Señor Crucificado" (Mora), **Supp. XIII:** 229

Christopher, Mary (pseudonym). *See* West, Dorothy

Christopher and His Kind: 1929–1939 (Isherwood), **Supp. XIV:** 157, 163, 164, 171

"Christopher Cat" (Cullen), **Supp. IV Part 1:** 173

Christopher Columbus, Mariner (Morison), **Supp. I Part 2:** 488

Christopher Isherwood: A Critical Biography (Finney), **Supp. XIV:** 158

Christophersen, Bill, **Supp. IX:** 159, 167; **Supp. XI:** 155; **Supp. XIII:** 87; **Supp. XXI:** 103

"Christ's Passion" (Karr), **Supp. XI:** 251

Christus: A Mystery (Longfellow), **II:** 490, 493, 495, 505–507; **Retro. Supp. II:** 161, 165, 166

Chroma (F. Barthelme), **Supp. XI:** 30, 33, 34

"Chroma" (F. Barthelme), **Supp. XI:** 31

"Chronicle of Race Relations, A" (Du Bois), **Supp. II Part 1:** 182

Chronicle of the Conquest of Granada (Irving), **II:** 310

Chronicles: Volume One (Dylan), **Supp. XVIII:** 20, 21, 23, 24, 28, **32–33**

"Chronologues" (Goldbarth), **Supp. XII:** 183, 184

"Chrysanthemums, The" (Steinbeck), **IV:** 53

"Chrysaor" (Longfellow), **II:** 498

Chu, Louis, **Supp. X:** 291

Chuang, Hua, **Supp. X:** 291

Chuang-Tzu, **Supp. VIII:** 206

"Chunk of Amethyst, A" (R. Bly), **Supp. IV Part 1:** 72

Church, Margaret, **IV:** 466

"Church and the Fiction Writer, The" (O'Connor), **Retro. Supp. II:** 223, 233; **Supp. XVIII:** 161

"Church Going" (Larkin), **Supp. XXI:** 93

"Churchgoing" (Nelson), **Supp. XVIII:** 173

Churchill, Charles, **Supp. XV:** 232

Churchill, Winston, **I:** 9, 490; **Supp. I Part 2:** 491

Church of Dead Girls, The (Dobyns), **Supp. XIII:** 75, **83–84**

"Church of Omnivorous Light, The" (Wrigley), **Supp. XVIII:** 306–307

"Church of the Latter Day Saints, The" (Mosher), **Supp. XXII:** 208

"Church Porch, The" (Herbert), **IV:** 153

Church Psalmody, Selected from Dr. Watts and Other Authors (Mason and Greene, ed.), **I:** 458

Ciannic, Saint, **II:** 215

Ciano, Edda, **IV:** 249

Ciardi, John, **I:** 169, 179, 535; **III:** 268; **Supp. IV Part 1:** 243; **Supp. IV Part 2:** 639; **Supp. IX:** 269, 324; **Supp. XII:** 119

Cicada (Haines), **Supp. XII: 206–207**

"Cicadas" (Wilbur), **Supp. III Part 2:** 549

Cicero, **I:** 279; **II:** 8, 14–15; **III:** 23; **Supp. I Part 2:** 405

Cider House Rules, The (Irving), **Supp. VI:** 164, **173–175**

"Cigales" (Wilbur), **Supp. III Part 2:** 549

"Cigarette" (L. Michaels), **Supp. XVI:** 214

Cimarron, Rose (Burke), **Supp. XIV:** 22, 35

"Cimetière Marin, Le" (Valéry), **IV:** 91–92

Cimino, Michael, **Supp. X:** 126

Cincinnati Kid, The (film), **Supp. XI: 306**

"Cinderella" (Jarrell), **II:** 386

"Cinderella" (Perrault), **IV:** 266, 267

"Cinderella" (Sexton), **Supp. II Part 2:** 691

"Cinema, The" (Salter), **Supp. IX:** 257

Cinema of Tony Richardson, The: Essays and Interviews (Phillips), **Supp. XI:** 306

Cinthio, **IV:** 370

Ciolkowski, Laura, **Supp. XVI:** 24

CIOPW (Cummings), **I:** 429

"Circe" (Welty), **Retro. Supp. I:** 353

Circle Game, The (Atwood), **Supp. XIII:** 20, 33

Circle in the Dirt (Moraga), **Supp. XXIII:** 195, 202

"Circle in the Fire, A" (O'Connor), **III:** 344–345, 349–350, 351, 353, 354; **Retro. Supp. II:** 229, 232

"Circle of Breath" (Stafford), **Supp. XI:** 318, 322

Circle of Hanh, The (Weigl), **Supp. XIX:** 273, 275, 282, **284–286**

"Circles" (Emerson), **I:** 455, 460

"Circles" (Lowell), **II:** 554

Circular Staircase, The (Rinehart), **Supp. XXV:** 189, 192, 200

Circumference: Varieties of Metaphysical Verse 1456–1928 (Taggard, ed.), **Supp. XXII:** 279

"Circus" (Huddle), **Supp. XXVI:** 150

"Circus, The" (Porter), **III:** 443, 445

"Circus Animals' Desertion" (Yeats), **I:** 389

Circus Fire, The (O'Nan), **Supp. XXV:** 153

"Circus in the Attic" (Warren), **IV:** 253

Circus in the Attic, The (Warren), **IV:** 243, 251–253

"Circus in Three Rings" (Plath), **Retro. Supp. II:** 243; **Supp. I Part 2:** 536

Circus of Needs, A (Dunn), **Supp. XI: 147–148**

"Cirque d'Hiver" (Bishop), **Supp. I Part 1:** 85

Cisneros, Sandra, **Supp. IV Part 2:** 544; **Supp. VII: 57–73; Supp. XI:** 177;

Supp. XVII: 71; **Supp. XXII:** 177; **Supp. XXV:** 133

Cities of the Interior (Nin), **Supp. X:** 182

Cities of the Plain (McCarthy), **Supp. VIII:** 175, **186–187**

Cities of the Red Night (Burroughs), **Supp. III Part 1:** 106

"Citizen Cain" (Baraka), **Supp. II Part 1:** 49

Citizen Kane (film), **Retro. Supp. I:** 115; **Supp. V:** 251; **Supp. XI:** 169

"Citizen of the World" (Goldsmith), **II:** 299

Citro, Joseph, **Supp. XXII:** 208, 218

"City" (Francis), **Supp. IX:** 87

"City, The" (Stallings), **Supp. XXV:** 233

"City and Country"(Hadas), **Supp. XXIII:** 115, 116

City and the Island, The (Davison), **Supp. XXVI:** 65, 70–71

City and the Pillar, The (Vidal), **Supp. IV Part 2:** 677, 680–681; **Supp. XIV:** 170

"*City and the Pillar, The, as Gay Fiction*" (Summers), **Supp. IV Part 2:** 680–681

"City Articles" series (Briggs), **Supp. XVIII:** 12

City Block (W. Frank), **Supp. XX: 71, 72, 76**

City Boy (L. Michaels), **Supp. XVI:** 212

"City Boy" (L. Michaels), **Supp. XVI:** 203–204

City Boy (Thompson), **Supp. XXIII:** 294, **298–299**

City Boy, The (Wouk), **Supp. XXV:** 256, 259

City Dog (Di Piero), **Supp. XIX:** 33–34, 35, 38, 46, 48

"City Dog" (Di Piero), **Supp. XIX:** 47

City in History, The (Mumford), **Supp. II Part 2:** 495

"City in the Sea, The" (Poe), **III:** 411; **Retro. Supp. II:** 274

City in Which I Love You, The (L.-Y. Lee), **Supp. XV:** 212, **215–220**

"City in Which I Love You, The" (L.-Y. Lee), **Supp. XV:** 215, **217–218**

City in Winter, A (Helprin), **Supp. XXV:** 84, 87

City Life (Barthelme), **Supp. IV Part 1:** 44, 47

City of Bones (Connelly), **Supp. XXI: 74–75,** 77

"City of Change, A" (Bynner), **Supp. XV:** 45

City of Dreadful Night (Siegel), **Supp. XXII:** 258

City of Glass (Auster), **Supp. XII:** 22, **24–26**

City of God, The (St. Augustine), **IV:** 126

City of Names (Brockmeier), **Supp. XXII:** 55–56, 57

"City of Refuge, The" (R. Fisher), **Supp. XIX:** 65, 66, **67–68**

City of Refuge, The: The Collected Stories of Rudolph Fisher (McCluskey, ed.), **Supp. XIX:** 68–69

City of the Living and Other Stories, The (Stegner), **Supp. IV Part 2:** 599, 609, 613

City of Words: American Fiction 1950-1970 (T. Tanner), **Supp. XVI:** 69

City of Your Final Destination, The (Cameron), **Supp. XII:** 79, 82, **91–94**

"City on a Hill" (Lowell), **II: 552**

City on a Hill: Testing the American Dream at City College (Traub), **Supp. XXIV:** 221

"City Person Encountering Nature, A" (Kingston), **Supp. V:** 170

"City Planners, The" (Atwood), **Supp. XIII:** 33

"City Winter, A"(O'Hara), **Supp. XXIII:** 210

City Winter and Other Poems, A (O'Hara), **Supp. XXIII:** 210, 214

City Without Men (film), **Supp. XVIII:** 247

City Without Walls (Auden), **Supp. II Part 1:** 24

Civil Disobedience (Thoreau), **IV:** 185; **Supp. I Part 2:** 507

Civilization in the United States (Stearns), **I:** 245

"Civil Rights" (Lanier), **Supp. I Part 1:** 357

CivilWarLand in Bad Decline (Saunders), **Supp. XIX: 224–227**

"CivilWarLand in Bad Decline" (Saunders), **Supp. XIX:** 224–225, 227

Civitatis Anthology of African American Slave Narratives, The (H. L. Gates and Andrews, eds.), **Supp. XX: 105**

Cixous, Hélène, **Supp. X:** 102; **Supp. XIII:** 297; **Supp. XV:** 347

Clabough, Casey, **Supp. XXIV:** 194

Claiborne, Craig, **Supp. XVII:** 89

Claiborne, William, **I:** 132

"Claim, The"(Balakian), **Supp. XXIII:** 20

Claiming an Identity They Taught Me to Despise (Cliff), **Supp. XXII:** 66, 67–68, 70

Claiming of Sleeping Beauty, The (Rice), **Supp. VII:** 301

Claman, Emily Rosamund, **Supp. XXVI:** 175

Clampitt, Amy, **Supp. IX: 37–54; Supp. X:** 120; **Supp. XI:** 249; **Supp. XV:** 251, 256

Clancy's Wake, At (Crane), **I:** 422

"Clandeboye" (Leopold), **Supp. XIV:** 189

Clara Howard; or, The Enthusiasm of Love (Brown), **Supp. I Part 1:** 145

Clara's Ole Man (Bullins), **Supp. II Part 1:** 42

Clara Wharton (Hayden), **Supp. XXV:** 38

Clare, John, **II:** 387; **III:** 528; **Supp. XVI:** 295

Clarel: A Poem and Pilgrimage in the Holy Land (Melville), **Retro. Supp. I:** 257

Clarence Major and His Art (Bell), **Supp. XXII:** 182

Clarissa (Richardson), **II:** 111; **Supp. I Part 2:** 714; **Supp. V:** 127; **Supp. XV:**

231; **Supp. XX: 236**

Clarissa Harlow (Richardson), **Supp. XXV:** 39

Clark, Alex, **Supp. XII:** 307

Clark, Charles, **I:** 470

Clark, Eleanor. *See* Warren, Mrs. Robert Penn (Eleanor Clark)

Clark, Francis Edward, **II:** 9

Clark, Geoffrey, **Supp. XI:** 342

Clark, Harry Hayden, **Supp. I Part 2:** 423

Clark, John Bates, **Supp. I Part 2:** 633

Clark, Kenneth, **Supp. XIV:** 342, 348; **Supp. XIX:** 151

Clark, Lewis Gaylord, **Supp. XVIII:** 4, 7, 8

Clark, Shirley, **Supp. XXI:** 22

Clark, Thomas, **Supp. III Part 2:** 629; **Supp. IV Part 1:** 140, 145, 147

Clark, Tom, **Supp. XXIV:** 36, 37, 41, 44

Clark, Walter, **Supp. XI:** 315

Clark, William, **III:** 14; **IV:** 179, 283

Clark, Willis Gaylord, **Supp. I Part 2:** 684

Clarke, Brock, **Supp. XXIII:** 109

Clarke, James Freeman, **Supp. II Part 1:** 280; **Supp. XXV:** 250

Clarke, John, **Supp. IV Part 1:** 8

Clarke, John J., **III:** 356

Clarke, Samuel, **II:** 108

Clark Lectures, **Retro. Supp. I:** 65

Claros varones de Belken (Hinojosa). *See Fair Gentlemen of Belken County* (Hinojosa)

Clash by Night (film), **Supp. XXVI:** 134

Clash by Night (Odets), **Supp. II Part 2:** 531, 538, 544–546, 550, 551

Classical Tradition, The (Highet), **Supp. I Part 1:** 268

Classic Ballroom Dances (Simic), **Supp. VIII:** 271, **276–278,** 283

Classics (Hadas), **Supp. XXIII: 124**

Classics and Commercials: A Literary Chronicle of the Forties (Wilson), **IV:** 433

"Classics"(Hadas), **Supp. XXIII:** 124

"CLASS STRUGGLE" (Baraka), **Supp. III Part 1:** 55

"Claude Glass, The: 1890" (Bierds), **Supp. XVII:** 27

Claudel, Paul, **I:** 60

Claudelle Inglish (Caldwell), **I:** 304

Clavel, Marcel, **I:** 343

"CLAY" (Baraka), **Supp. II Part 1:** 54

Clay, Henry, **I:** 8; **Supp. I Part 2:** 684, 686

Clay's Ark (O. Butler), **Supp. XIII:** 63

Clayton, John J., **Supp. IV Part 1:** 238

Clayton, Sarah Turner, **Supp. XXV:** 251

"Clean, Well Lighted Place, A" (Hemingway), **Retro. Supp. I:** 181

"Clear, with Light Variable Winds" (Lowell), **II:** 522

"Clear Days" (White), **Supp. I Part 2:** 664, 665

Clearing (Berry), **Supp. X:** 22

"Clearing, A" (Simpson), **Supp. IX:** 280

"Clearing, The" (Kenyon), **Supp. VII:** 174

"Clearing the Title" (Merrill), **Supp. III Part 1:** 336

"Clearing Up the Question of Stesichoros' Blinding by Helen" (Carson), **Supp. XII:** 107–108

"Clear Morning" (Glück), **Supp. V:** 88

"Clearness" (Wilbur), **Supp. III Part 2:** 544, 550

"Clear Night" (Wright), **Supp. V:** 341

Clear Pictures: First Loves, First Guides (Price), **Supp. VI:** 253, 254, 255, 256, 265

Clear Springs (Mason), **Supp. VIII:** 134–136, 137–138, 139, 147

Cleary, Rebecca Lauck, **Supp. XVIII:** 195

Cleaver, Eldridge, **Retro. Supp. II:** 12; **Supp. IV Part 1:** 206; **Supp. X:** 249

"Cleaving, The" (L.-Y. Lee), **Supp. XV:** 215, **218–220**

Cleland, John, **Supp. V:** 48, 127

Clemenceau, Georges, **I:** 490

"Clemency" (Wrigley), **Supp. XVIII:** 307–308

Clemens, Jane, **I:** 247

Clemens, Orion, **IV:** 193, 195

Clemens, Samuel Langhorne. *See* Twain, Mark

Clemens, Mrs. Samuel Langhorne (Olivia Langdon), **I:** 197, 208, 247; **Supp. I Part 2:** 457

Clemens, Susie, **IV:** 208

Clementine Recognitions (novel), **Supp. IV Part 1:** 280

Clements, Colin Campbell, **Supp. XVI:** 190

Clemons, Walter, **Supp. IV Part 1:** 305, 307

Cleopatra, **III:** 44; **IV:** 373; **Supp. I Part 1:** 114

"Clepsydra" (Ashbery), **Supp. III Part 1:** 10–15

"Clerks, The" (Robinson), **III:** 517–518

"Cleveland" (Halliday), **Supp. XIX:** 90

Cleveland, Carol, **Supp. IX:** 120, 125

Cleveland, Ceil, **Supp. V:** 222

Cleveland, Grover, **II:** 126, 128, 129, 130, 137, 138; **Supp. I Part 2:** 486

"Clever Magician Carrying My Heart, A" (Salinas), **Supp. XIII:** 323

Cliff, Michelle, **Supp. XXII: 65–80**

"Cliff, The" (C. Baxter), **Supp. XVII:** 16–17

Clifford, Craig, **Supp. IX:** 99

Clift, Montgomery, **III:** 161

Clifton, Lucille, **Supp. XVIII:** 177

Climate of Monastic Prayer, The (Merton), **Supp. VIII:** 205, 207

Climb, The (Boukreev), **Supp. XVIII:** 112

"Climber, The" (Mason), **Supp. VIII:** 140–141

Climbing High: A Woman's Account of Surviving the Everest Tragedy (Gammelgaard), **Supp. XVIII:** 112

"Climbing the Tower" (Crews), **Supp. XI:** 102

Clinton, De Witt, **I:** 338

"Clipped Wings" (H. Miller), **III:** 176–177

Clippinger, David, **Supp. XXI:** 24

Clive, Robert, **Supp. I Part 2:** 505

Clock Winder, The (Tyler), **Supp. IV Part 2:** 661–662, 670

Clock Without Hands (McCullers), **II:** 587–588, 604–606

Clockwork Orange, A (Burgess), **Supp. XIII:** 29

Clorindy (Cook), **Supp. II Part 1:** 199

"Close, The" (Jarman), **Supp. XVII:** 113

"Close Calls" (Wolff), **Supp. VII:** 332–333

"Closed Book, A" (Mosley), **Supp. XIII:** 237

Close Quarters (Heinemann), **Supp. XXII:** 103, **104–109,** 111, 115

Close Range: Wyoming Stories (Proulx), **Supp. VII:** 261–265

"Close Reading: Windows"(Hirshfield), **Supp. XXIII:** 131

Closers, The (Connelly), **Supp. XXI: 76–77**

Closest Possible Union, The (J. Scott), **Supp. XVII: 185–186,** 188, 191

"Closet, The" (Goodman), **Supp. XXVI:** 121

Close the Book (Glaspell), **Supp. III Part 1:** 179

"Close the Book" (Lowell), **II:** 554

Close to Me & Closer ... (The Language of Heaven) and Désamère (Notley), **Supp. XXII:** 234

Close to Shore: A True Story of Terror in an Age of Innocence (Capuzzo), **Supp. XIII:** 254

Closet Writing & Gay Reading: The Case of Melville's Pierre (Creech), **Retro. Supp. I:** 254

Closing Circle, The (Commoner), **Supp. XIII:** 264

Closing of the American Mind, The (Bloom), **Retro. Supp. II:** 19, 30, 31

"Closing of the Rodeo, The" (W. J. Smith), **Supp. XIII:** 332

Closing Time (Heller), **Supp. IV Part 1:** 382, 386, 391–394

Closset, Marie, **Supp. VIII:** 251, 265

Clotel (Brown), **Supp. XXIII:** 184

"Cloud, The" (Shelley), **Supp. I Part 2:** 720

"Cloud and Fame" (Berryman), **I:** 173

Cloud Atlas (D. Mitchell), **Supp. XXIV:** 86

Cloud Forest, The: A Chronicle of the South American Wilderness (Matthiessen), **Supp. V:** 202, 204

"Cloud on the Way, The" (Bryant), **Supp. I Part 1:** 171

"Cloud River" (Wright), **Supp. V:** 341

"Clouds" (Levine), **Supp. V:** 184

Cloudsplitter (Banks), **Supp. V:** 16

"Clover" (Lanier), **Supp. I Part 1:** 362–364

Clover and Other Poems (Lanier), **Supp. I Part 1:** 362

"Clown" (Corso), **Supp. XII:** 127

Clown in the Belfry, The: Writings on Faith and Fiction (Buechner), **Supp. XII:** 53

Cluck, Julia, **Supp. I Part 2:** 728

Clue, The (Wells), **Supp. XXVI:** 277
Clue of the Eyelash, The (Wells), **Supp. XXVI:** 280
Clum, John M., **Supp. XIII: 200,** 201, 209
Cluny, Hugo, **IV:** 290
Clurman, Harold, **I:** 93; **IV:** 381, 385
Clytus, Radiclani, **Supp. XIII:** 128, **Supp. XIII:** 129, 132
"C.O." (Wrigley), **Supp. XVIII:** 298
"Coal: Beginning and End" (Winters), **Supp. II Part 2:** 791
Coale, Howard, **Supp. XIII:** 15
"Coals" (Hoffman), **Supp. XVIII:** 86
"Coast, The" (column), **Supp. IV Part 1:** 198
"Coast Guard's Cottage, The" (Wylie), **Supp. I Part 2:** 723
Coast of Chicago, The (Dybek), **Supp. XXIII: 72–74,** 75
Coast of Trees, A (Ammons), **Supp. VII:** 24, 34
"Coast-Range Christ, The" (Jeffers), **Supp. II Part 2:** 414, 419
"Coast-Road, The" (Jeffers), **Supp. II Part 2:** 425
"Coat, The" (Everwine), **Supp. XV:** 80
Coates, Joseph, **Supp. VIII:** 80; **Supp. XXII:** 205
Coates, Robert, **I:** 54; **IV:** 298
"Coatlicue's Rules: Advice from an Aztec Goddess" (Mora), **Supp. XIII:** 223
"Coats" (Kenyon), **Supp. VII:** 172
Coatsworth, Elizabeth Jane, **Supp. XXVI:** 33
Cobb, Lee J., **III:** 153
Cobb, Ty, **III:** 227, 229
Cobbett, William, **Supp. I Part 2:** 517; **Supp. XV:** 237
"Cobbler Keezar's Vision" (Whittier), **Supp. I Part 2:** 699
"Cobweb, The" (Carver), **Supp. III Part 1:** 148
Cobwebs From an Empty Skull (Bierce), **I:** 195
Coccimiglio, Vic, **Supp. XIII:** 114
"Cock-a-Doodle-Doo!" (Melville), **III:** 89
"Cockayne" (Emerson), **II:** 6
"Cock-Crow" (Gordon), **II:** 219
Cock Pit (Cozzens), **I:** 359, 378, 379
Cockpit (Kosinski), **Supp. XII:** 21
Cockpit: A Novel (Kosinski), **Supp. VII:** 215, 223–224, 225
"Cock Robin Takes Refuge in the Storm House" (Snodgrass), **Supp. VI:** 319
Cocktail Hour, The (Gurney), **Supp. V:** 95, 96, 100, 101, 103, 105, 108
Cocktail Hour and Two Other Plays: Another Antigone and *The Perfect Party* (Gurney), **Supp. V:** 100
Cocktail Party, The (Eliot), **I:** 571, 582–583; **III:** 21; **Retro. Supp. I:** 65; **Supp. V:** 101, 103
Cocteau, Jean, **III:** 471; **Retro. Supp. I:** 82, 378; **Supp. IV Part 1:** 82; **Supp. XVI:** 135; **Supp. XX:** 236
"Coda: Wilderness Letter" (Stegner), **Supp. IV Part 2:** 595

"Code, The" (Frost), **Retro. Supp. I:** 121, 128
Codex (Grossman), **Supp. XXV:** 64, 66–68
Codman, Florence, **Supp. II Part 1:** 92, 93
Codman, Ogden, Jr., **Retro. Supp. I:** 362, 363
Codrescu, Andrei, **Supp. XXII:** 155
Cody, William ("Buffalo Bill"), **I:** 440; **III:** 584; **Supp. V:** 230
"Coffee Lips" (Ferry), **Supp. XXIV:** 153, 162
Coffey, Michael, **Supp. V:** 243; **Supp. XV:** 65; **Supp. XX: 88**
Coffey, Warren, **III:** 358
Coffin, Charles, **III:** 577
Cogan, David J., **Supp. IV Part 1:** 362
Cogan, Joshua, **Supp. XXI:** 247
Cogewea the Half-Blood: A Depiction of the Great Montana Cattle Range (Mourning Dove (Christal Quintasket)), **Supp. XXV:** 285
Coghill, Nevill, **Supp. II Part 1:** 4; **Supp. XIV:** 13
Cohan, George M., **II:** 427; **III:** 401
Cohen, Edward M., **Supp. XVI:** 212
Cohen, Esther, **Supp. XV:** 323
Cohen, Hettie, **Supp. II Part 1:** 30
Cohen, Joshua, **Supp. XXII:** 268
Cohen, Marty, **Supp. X:** 112
Cohen, Norman J., **Supp. IX:** 132, 143
Cohen, Rosetta, **Supp. XV:** 257
Cohen, Sarah Blacher, **Supp. V:** 273
Cohen, Victor, **Supp. XVIII:** 235, 236
"Coherent Decentering: Towards a New Model of the Poetic Self" (A. Finch), **Supp. XVII:** 76
Cohn, Jan, **Supp. XXV:** 192, 200
"Coin" (Goldbarth), **Supp. XII:** 187
Coindreau, Maurice, **III:** 339
Coiner, Constance, **Supp. XIII:** 297, 302
Coit, Lille Hitchcock, **Supp. X:** 103
"Coitus" (Pound), **III:** 466
Coke, Desmond, **Supp. XX: 235**
Colburn, Nadia Herman, **Supp. XV:** 339, 341, 347
"Cold, The" (Kenyon), **Supp. VII:** 164
"Cold, The" (Winters), **Supp. II Part 2:** 790–791, 809, 811
"Cold-blooded Creatures" (Wylie), **Supp. I Part 2:** 729
Colden, Cadwallader, **Supp. I Part 1:** 250
"Colder the Air, The" (Bishop), **Supp. I Part 1:** 86
Cold Feet (Harrison), **Supp. VIII:** 39
Cold Frame (C. Frost), **Supp. XV:** 93, 96
Cold Ground Was My Bed Last Night (Garrett), **Supp. VII:** 98
"Cold Ground Was My Bed Last Night" (Garrett), **Supp. VII:** 100
"Cold Hill Side, The"(Hadas), **Supp. XXIII:** 121
"Cold Night, The" (W. C. Williams), **Retro. Supp. I:** 418
"Cold Plunge into Skin Diving, A" (Knowles), **Supp. XII:** 241

Cold Spring, A (Bishop), **Retro. Supp. II:** 45
Cold Springs Harbor (Yates), **Supp. XI:** 348
Cold War American Poetry, **Supp. V:** 182
Cold War and the Income Tax, The (Wilson), **IV:** 430
Cole, Bruce, **Supp. XX: 106**
Cole, Goody, **Supp. I Part 2:** 696–697
Cole, Lester, **Retro. Supp. II:** 329
Cole, Nat King, **Retro. Supp. I:** 334; **Supp. X:** 255
Cole, Thomas, **Supp. I Part 1:** 156, 158, 171
Cole, William, **Supp. XIX:** 120
"Coleman" (Karr), **Supp. XI:** 244
Coleman, Wanda, **Supp. XI: 83–98**
Coleridge, Samuel Taylor, **I:** 283, 284, 447, 522; **II:** 7, 10, 11, 19, 71, 169, 273, 301, 502, 516, 549; **III:** 77, 83–84, 424, 461, 488, 523; **IV:** 74, 173, 250, 349, 453; **Retro. Supp. I:** 65, 308; **Supp. I Part 1:** 31, 311, 349; **Supp. I Part 2:** 376, 393, 422; **Supp. IV Part 2:** 422, 465; **Supp. IX:** 38, 50; **Supp. V:** 258; **Supp. XIII:** 139; **Supp. XIV:** 21–22; **Supp. XV:** 250; **Supp. XXI:** 52, 55; **Supp. XXIII:** 231; **Supp. XXIV:** 74
Coles, Katharine, **Supp. IV Part 2:** 630
Coles, Robert, **Supp. XXIV:** 172, 265; **Supp. XXVI:** 250, 252
Colette, Sidonie-Gabrielle, **Supp. VIII:** 40, 171; **Supp. XVI:** 193–194
"Coliseum, The" (Poe), **III:** 411
Collage of Dreams (Spencer), **Supp. X:** 196
"Collapse of Tomorrow, The" (Mumford), **Supp. II Part 2:** 482
"Collected by a Valetudinarian" (E. Stoddard), **Supp. XV:** 286–287
Collected Earlier Poems (Hecht), **Supp. X:** 58, 59
Collected Earlier Poems (W. C. Williams), **Retro. Supp. I:** 414, 428
Collected Earlier Poems 1940–1960 (Levertov), **Supp. III Part 1:** 273, 275
Collected Essays (Tate), **IV:** 133–134
Collected Essays, Volume 2: Literary Criticism (Lovecraft), **Supp. XXV:** 121
Collected Essays of Ralph Ellison, The (Ellison), **Retro. Supp. II:** 119
Collected Essays of Robert Creeley, The (Creeley), **Supp. IV Part 1:** 153, 154
Collected Later Poems (W. C. Williams), **Retro. Supp. I:** 428
Collected Plays (A. Miller), **III:** 158
Collected Plays, 1974–1983 (Gurney), **Supp. V:** 99
Collected Poems (Aiken), **I:** 50
Collected Poems (Berrigan), **Supp. XXIV:** 39, 45, 46
Collected Poems (Burke), **I:** 269
Collected Poems (Cummings), **I:** 430, 439, 441
Collected Poems (Doolittle), **Supp. I Part 1:** 264–267, 269
Collected Poems (Frost), **Retro. Supp. I:** 136

Collected Poems (Hull), **Supp. XXI:** 141

Collected Poems (Kees; Justice, ed.), **Supp. XV:** 134

Collected Poems (Lindsay), **Supp. I Part 2:** 380, 387, 392, 396–397, 400

Collected Poems (Lowell), **Supp. XV:** 20

Collected Poems (Markson), **Supp. XVII:** 143

Collected Poems (Moore), **III:** 194, 215

Collected Poems (O'Hara), **Supp. XXIII:** 207, 211, 220

Collected Poems (Price), **Supp. VI:** 267

Collected Poems (Simpson), **Supp. IX:** 279

Collected Poems (W. C. Williams), **IV:** 415; **Retro. Supp. I:** 430

Collected Poems (Winters), **Supp. II Part 2:** 791, 810

Collected Poems (Wright), **Supp. III Part 2:** 602

Collected Poems (Yeats), **Supp. XV:** 152

Collected Poems, 1918–1938 (Taggard), **Supp. XXII:** 283

Collected Poems, 1923–1953 (Bogan), **Supp. III Part 1:** 64

Collected Poems, 1936–1976 (Francis), **Supp. IX:** 77, 80, **87**

Collected Poems, The (Stevens), **III:** 273; **IV:** 75, 76, 87, 93; **Retro. Supp. I:** 296, 309

Collected Poems 1909–1935 (Eliot), **I:** 580; **Retro. Supp. I:** 66

Collected Poems 1909–1962 (Eliot), **I:** 583

Collected Poems 1917–1952 (MacLeish), **III:** 3, 4, 19

Collected Poems 1921–1931 (W. C. Williams), **Retro. Supp. I:** 422; **Supp. XIV:** 285

Collected Poems 1930–1960 (Eberhart), **I:** 522, 525–526, 540, 541

Collected Poems: 1939–1989 (W. J. Smith), **Supp. XIII:** 332, 340, 343, 345

Collected Poems: 1940–1978 (Shapiro), **Supp. II Part 2:** 703, 717

Collected Poems: 1951–1971 (Ammons), **Supp. VII:** 24, 26–29, 32, 33

Collected Poems: 1956–1976 (Wagoner), **Supp. IX:** 323, **328–329**

Collected Poems of Amy Clampitt, The (Clampitt), **Supp. IX:** 37, 44, 53

Collected Poems of George Garrett (Garrett), **Supp. VII:** 109

Collected Poems of Hart Crane, The (Crane), **I:** 399–402

Collected Poems of James Agee, The (Fitzgerald, ed.), **I:** 27–28

Collected Poems of James T. Farrell, The (Farrell), **II:** 45

Collected Poems of Kay Boyle (Boyle), **Supp. XXIV:** 63

Collected Poems of Langston Hughes, The (Rampersad and Roessel, ed.), **Retro. Supp. I:** 194, 196, 212

Collected Poems of Muriel Rukeyser, The (Rukeyser), **Supp. VI:** 274

Collected Poems of Thomas Merton, The, **Supp. VIII:** 207, 208

Collected Poetry (Auden), **Supp. II Part 1:** 18

Collected Prose (Wright), **Supp. III Part 2:** 596

Collected Prose, The (Bishop), **Retro. Supp. II:** 51

Collected Recordings (W. C. Williams), **Retro. Supp. I:** 431

Collected Shorter Poems, 1946-1991 (Carruth), **Supp. XVI:** 47

Collected Short Stories, The (Wharton), **Retro. Supp. I:** 362, 363, 366

Collected Sonnets (Millay), **III:** 136–137

Collected Stories (Carver), **Supp. XXIV:** 177

Collected Stories, 1939–1976 (Bowles), **Supp. IV Part 1:** 92

Collected Stories, The (Paley), **Supp. VI:** 218

Collected Stories, The (Price), **Supp. VI:** 266

Collected Stories, The (Theroux), **Supp. VIII:** 318

Collected Stories, The (Wharton), **Retro. Supp. I:** 361

Collected Stories of Amy Hempel, The (Hempel), **Supp. XXI:** 115, 117

Collected Stories of Eudora Welty, The (Welty), **Retro. Supp. I:** 355

Collected Stories of Isaac Bashevis Singer (Singer), **Retro. Supp. II:** 307–308

Collected Stories of Katherine Anne Porter (Porter), **III:** 454

Collected Stories of Peter Taylor (Taylor), **Supp. V:** 314, 320, 323–324, 325, 326

Collected Stories of Richard Yates, The, **Supp. XI:** 349

Collected Stories of Wallace Stegner (Stegner), **Supp. IV Part 2:** 599, 605

Collected Stories of William Faulkner (Faulkner), **II:** 72; **Retro. Supp. I:** 75

Collected Stories of William Humphrey, The (Humphrey), **Supp. IX:** 106

Collected Works (Bierce), **I:** 204, 208–210

Collected Works of Buck Rogers in the 25th Century, The (Bradbury), **Supp. IV Part 1:** 101

Collected Writings, The (Z. Fitzgerald; Bruccoli, ed.), **Supp. IX:** 65, 68

Collecting the Animals (Everwine), **Supp. XV:** 73, 75, **78–81,** 85, 88

Collection of Epigrams, **II:** 111

Collection of Poems, on American Affairs, and a Variety of Other Subjects . . . (Freneau), **Supp. II Part 1:** 274

Collection of Select Aphorisms and Maxims (Palmer), **II:** 111

"Collectors" (Carver), **Supp. III Part 1:** 141–142

Collette, **Supp. XVII:** 86

Collier, John, **Supp. XXI:** 8

Collier, Lucy Wood, **Supp. XXI:** 8

Collier, Michael, **Supp. XVII:** 23, 110

Collingwood, R. G., **I:** 278

Collins, Billy, **Supp. XI:** 143; **Supp. XIV:** 123; **Supp. XVII:** 245; **Supp. XXI:** 51–66; **Supp. XXIII:** 138

Collins, Brennan, **Supp. XXVI:** 12, 13

Collins, Doug, **Supp. V:** 5

Collins, Eddie, **II:** 416

Collins, L. M., **Supp. XXII:** 7

Collins, Richard, **Supp. XI:** 171

Collins, Ronald, **Supp. XXI:** 24

Collins, Wilkie, **Supp. I Part 1:** 35, 36; **Supp. IV Part 1:** 341; **Supp. XX:** 236

Collins, William, **Supp. I Part 2:** 714

Collinson, Peter , **II:** 114

Collinson, Peter (pseudonym). *See* Hammett, Dashiell

"Collision" (Huddle), **Supp. XXVI:** 155

Colloff, Pamela, **Supp. XIII:** 281

Colloque Sentimental (ballet), **Supp. IV Part 1:** 83

"Colloquy" (Kees), **Supp. XV:** 133

"Colloquy in Black Rock" (Lowell), **II:** 535; **Retro. Supp. II:** 178

"Colloquy of Monos and Una, The" (Poe), **III:** 412

"Colloquy on a Bed" (Bronk), **Supp. XXI:** 31

Colonel's Dream, The (Chesnutt), **Supp. XIV:** 63, 75–76

Colônia, Regina, **Retro. Supp. II:** 53

Colony (Siddons), **Supp. XXII:** 239

Color (Cullen), **Supp. IV Part 1:** 164, 166, 167, 168

"Colorado" (Beattie), **Supp. V:** 27

Color and Democracy: Colonies and Peace (Du Bois), **Supp. II Part 1:** 184, 185

"Color-Blind Raspberry Picker, The"(Hadas), **Supp. XXIII:** 113

Color Curtain, The (Wright), **IV:** 478, 488

"Colored Americans" (Dunbar), **Supp. II Part 1:** 197

Colored People (H. L. Gates), **Supp. XX: 101, 103, 104–105, 109, 111**

"Color Line, The" (Douglass), **Supp. III Part 1:** 163–165

Color Line, The (W. B. Smith), **Supp. II Part 1:** 168

Color of a Great City, The (Dreiser), **Retro. Supp. II:** 104

Color of Darkness (Purdy), **Supp. VII:** 271

Color of Water, The (McBride), **Supp. XXVI:** 191

Color Purple, The (Walker), **Supp. III Part 2:** 517, 518, 520, 525–529, 532–537; **Supp. VIII:** 141; **Supp. X:** 252, 330; **Supp. XX: 107**

Color Schemes (Cheang; film), **Supp. XI:** 20

"Colors of Night, The" (Momaday), **Supp. IV Part 2:** 490

"Colors without Objects" (Swenson), **Supp. IV Part 2:** 645

"Color: The Unfinished Business of Democracy" (Locke), **Supp. XIV:** 202, 207

Colossus, The (Plath), **Retro. Supp. II: 245–247; Supp. I Part 2:** 529, 531, 536, 538, 540; **Supp. V:** 79; **Supp. XI:** 317

"Colossus, The" (Plath), **Retro. Supp. II:** 250; **Supp. XXIII:** 113

Colossus of Maroussi, The (H. Miller), **III:** 178, 185–186

"Colour out of Space, The" (Lovecraft), **Supp. XXV:** 109, 111, 114–116, 118, 121

"Colt, The" (Stegner), **Supp. IV Part 2:** 600

Coltelli, Laura, **Supp. IV Part 1:** 323, 330, 335, 409; **Supp. IV Part 2:** 493, 497, 559

Colter: The True Story of the Best Dog I Ever Had (Bass), **Supp. XVI:** 23

Coltrane, John, **Supp. VIII:** 197; **Supp. XXII:** 172

Coltrane, John (pseud.). *See* O'Nan, Stewart

Colum, Mary, **I:** 246, 252, 256; **Supp. I Part 2:** 708, 709

"Columba" (Cliff), **Supp. XXII:** 74, 76

Columbia Anthology of American Poetry (Parini, ed.), **Supp. XXV:** 251

Columbiad, The (Barlow), **Supp. II Part 1:** 67, 72, 73, 74, 75–77, 79

Columbia History of the American Novel, **Supp. XV:** 270

Columbia Literary History of the United States, **Supp. XV:** 270

"Columbian Ode" (Dunbar), **Supp. II Part 1:** 199

"Columbia U Poesy Reading—1975" (Corso), **Supp. XII:** 134

"Columbine, The" (Very), **Supp. XXV:** 242, 244

Columbus, Christopher, **I:** 253; **II:** 6, 310; **III:** 8; **Supp. I Part 2:** 397, 479, 480, 483, 486–488, 491, 495, 497, 498

"Columbus to Ferdinand" (Freneau), **Supp. II Part 1:** 255

Comanche Moon (McMurtry), **Supp. V:** 232

"Come, Break With Time" (Bogan), **Supp. III Part 1:** 52

Come, Thief (Hirshfield), **Supp. XXIII:** 134, 138

Come Along with Me (Jackson), **Supp. IX:** 117, 118, 122

Come Back, Charleston Blue (film), **Supp. XVI:** 144

Come Back, Little Sheba (film), **Supp. XXV:** 95

Come Back, Little Sheba (Inge), **Supp. XXV:** 94–95, 96–97

Comeback, The (Gurney), **Supp. V:** 97

"Come Back to the Raft Ag'in, Huck Honey!" (Fiedler), **Supp. XIII:** 93, **96–97,** 101

Come Blow Your Horn (Simon), **Supp. IV Part 2:** 574, 575, 577, 578, 586, 587, 591

Come By Here (Major), **Supp. XXII:** 171, 182

"Come Dance with Me in Ireland" (Jackson), **Supp. IX:** 119

"Comedian as the Letter C, The" (Stevens), **IV:** 84–85, 88; **Retro. Supp. I:** 297, 301, 302

"Comedy Cop" (Farrell), **II:** 45

Comedy of a Country House (J. Sturgis), **Supp. XX: 238**

"Comedy's Greatest Era" (Agee), **I:** 31

"Come In" (Frost), **Retro. Supp. I:** 139

"Come On, Baby" (Zinberg), **Supp. XV:** 195

Come On All You Ghosts (Zapruder), **Supp. XXVI:** 54

"Come on Back" (Gardner), **Supp. VI:** 73

"Come Out into the Sun" (Francis), **Supp. IX:** 82

Come Out into the Sun: Poems New and Selected (Francis), **Supp. IX:** 82–83

"Come out the Wilderness" (Baldwin), **Supp. I Part 1:** 63

Comer, Anjanette, **Supp. XI:** 305

Comer, Cornelia, **I:** 214

"Come Rain or Come Shine" (song), **Supp. XXII:** 6

"Come Shining: The Spiritual South" (exhibition; Luster), **Supp. XV:** 350

Come with Me: Poems for a Journey (Nye), **Supp. XIII:** 279

"Comforts of Home, The" (O'Connor), **III:** 349, 351, 355; **Retro. Supp. II:** 237

Comic Artist, The (Glaspell and Matson), **Supp. III Part 1:** 182

"Comic Imagination of the Young Dickens, The" (Wright), **Supp. III Part 2:** 591

"Comic Textures and Female Communities 1937 and 1977: Clare Boothe and Wendy Wasserstein" (Carlson), **Supp. XV:** 323

Comic Tragedies (Alcott), **Supp. I Part 1:** 33

Coming After (Notley), **Supp. XXII:** 223, 227, 230, 232, 236

"Coming and Going" (Gallagher), **Supp. XXIV:** 175, 176–177

"Coming Close" (Levine), **Supp. V:** 192

Coming Forth by Day of Osiris Jones, The (Aiken), **I:** 59

"Coming Home" (Gordon), **Supp. IV Part 1:** 309

"Coming Home to Vermont" (McCarriston), **Supp. XIV:** 269

"Coming in From the Cold" (Walker), **Supp. III Part 2:** 526

Coming into Eighty (Sarton), **Supp. VIII:** 262

"Coming into Eighty" (Sarton), **Supp. VIII:** 262

Coming into the Country (McPhee), **Supp. III Part 1:** 298, 301–306, 309, 310

Coming Into Writing (Cixous), **Supp. X:** 102

Coming of Age in Mississippi (Moody), **Supp. IV Part 1:** 11

Comings Back (Goldbarth), **Supp. XII:** 180

"Coming to Canada--Age Twenty Two" (Shields), **Supp. VII:** 311

Coming to Canada: Poems (Shields), **Supp. VII:** 311–312

"Coming to Memoir as a Journalist" (Epstein), **Supp. XXII:** 95

"Coming to the Morning" (Merwin), **Supp. III Part 1:** 356

"Coming to This" (Strand), **Supp. IV Part 2:** 627

Comiskey, Charles, **II:** 422

Commager, Henry Steele, **I:** 253; **Supp. I Part 1:** 372; **Supp. I Part 2:** 484, 647, 650

Command the Morning (Buck), **Supp. II Part 1:** 125

"CommComm" (Saunders), **Supp. XIX:** 234

"Commencement Address, A" (Brodsky), **Supp. VIII:** 31

"Commencement Day Address, The" (Schwartz), **Supp. II Part 2:** 660

Commentaries (Caesar), **II:** 502, 561

"Commentary" (Auden), **Supp. II Part 1:** 13

"Comment on Curb" (Hughes), **Supp. I Part 1:** 340

"Comments/Questions" (Nelson), **Supp. XVIII:** 172

"Commerce" (Nye), **Supp. XIII:** 281

Commins, Saxe, **Retro. Supp. I:** 73; **Retro. Supp. II:** 337

Commodity of Dreams & Other Stories, A (Nemerov), **III:** 268–269, 285

Common Carnage (Dobyns), **Supp. XIII:** 87

"Common Ground, A" (Levertov), **Supp. III Part 1:** 277

"Common Life, The" (Auden), **Supp. IV Part 1:** 302, 313

"Common Meter" (R. Fisher), **Supp. XIX:** 71

Common Room, A: Essays 1954–1987 (Price), **Supp. VI:** 264–265, 267

Commons, John, **Supp. I Part 2:** 645

Common Sense (Paine), **II:** 117; **Supp. I Part 1:** 231; **Supp. I Part 2:** 505, 506–508, 509, 513, 516, 517, 521

Communal Cot (Loy), **Supp. XXII:** 168

"Communication" (Dobyns), **Supp. XIII:** 91

"Communion" (Dubus), **Supp. VII:** 91

Communion (Mora), **Supp. XIII: 217–219**

Communist Manifesto, The (Marx and Engels), **II:** 463; **Supp. XXI:** 162–163

"Community Life" (Moore), **Supp. X:** 178

"Community of Glaciers, The" (Bass), **Supp. XVI:** 23

Comnes, Gregory, **Supp. IV Part 1:** 283, 284, 291

"Companions, The" (Nemerov), **III:** 269, 278, 287

Company of Poets, A (Simpson), **Supp. IX:** 265, 275

Company of Women, The (Gordon), **Supp. IV Part 1:** 302–304, 304, 306, 313

Company She Keeps, The (McCarthy), **II:** 562, 563–566

"Comparisons of Wonder" (Jarman), **Supp. XVII:** 114

Compass Flower, The (Merwin), **Supp. III Part 1:** 353, 357

"Compassionate Friendship" (Doolittle), **Supp. I Part 1:** 257, 258, 259, 260, 271

"Compatibility" (C. Frost), **Supp. XV:** 103

"Compendium" (Dove), **Supp. IV Part 1:** 248

"Complaint" (W. C. Williams), **Retro. Supp. I:** 418

"Complete Birth of the Cool, The" (Wright), **Supp. XV:** 343, 344

Complete Collected Poems of William Carlos Williams, 1906–1938, The (W. C. Williams), **Retro. Supp. I:** 424

"Complete Destruction" (W. C. Williams), **IV:** 413

"Complete Life of John Hopkins, The" (O. Henry), **Supp. II Part 1:** 405

Complete Poems (Frost), **II:** 155, 164

Complete Poems (Reznikoff), **Supp. XIV:** 281

Complete Poems (Sandburg), **III:** 590–592, 594, 596

Complete Poems, The (Bishop), **Retro. Supp. II:** 49; **Supp. I Part 1:** 72, 82, 94

Complete Poems, The (Bradbury), **Supp. IV Part 1:** 105

Complete Poems, The: 1927–1979 (Bishop), **Retro. Supp. II:** 51

Complete Poems of Emily Dickinson, The (Bianchi and Hampson, eds.), **Retro. Supp. I:** 35

Complete Poems of Emily Dickinson, The (T. H. Johnson, ed.), **I:** 470

Complete Poems of Frederick Goddard Tuckerman, The (Momaday), **Supp. IV Part 2:** 480

Complete Poems of Hart Crane, **Retro. Supp. II:** 81

Complete Poems to Solve, The (Swenson), **Supp. IV Part 2:** 652

Complete Poetical Works (Hulme), **III:** 464

Complete Poetical Works (Longfellow), **Retro. Supp. II:** 154

Complete Poetical Works (Lowell), **II:** 512, 516–517

Complete Poetical Works of Amy Lowell, The, **Supp. XV:** 295–296

Complete Stories (O'Connor), **Supp. X:** 1

Complete Tragedies, The: Euripedes II, **Supp. XV:** 50

"Complete with Starry Night and Bourbon Shots" (Goldbarth), **Supp. XII:** 192–193

Complete Works of Kate Chopin, The (Seyersted, ed.), **Supp. I Part 1:** 212, 225

Complete Works of the Gawain-Poet (Gardner), **Supp. VI:** 64, 65

"Complex Histories, Contested Memories: Some Reflections on Remembering Difficult Pasts" (E. Hoffman, lecture), **Supp. XVI:** 155

"Complicated Thoughts About a Small Son" (White), **Supp. I Part 2:** 678

"Compliments of the Season" (O. Henry), **Supp. II Part 1:** 392, 399

"Compline" (Auden), **Supp. II Part 1:** 23

"Composing a Life" (Pickering), **Supp. XXI:** 191, 196

Composition as Explanation (Stein), **IV:** 32, 33, 38

"Composition as Explanation" (Stein), **IV:** 27, 28

"Compound Eye, The" (Davison), **Supp. XXVI:** 74

"Compounding *of* Consciousness" (James), **II:** 358–359

Comprehensive Bibliography (Hanneman), **II:** 259

Compton-Burnett, Ivy, **I:** 93; **II:** 580; **Supp. XXIII:** 209

"Comrade Laski, C.P.U.S.A. \[M.L.\]" (Didion), **Supp. IV Part 1:** 200

"Comrade Poets" (Hayes), **Supp. XXVI:** 144

Comstock, Anthony, **Retro. Supp. II:** 95

Comus (Milton), **II:** 12; **Supp. I Part 2:** 622

Conan Doyle, Arthur. *See* Doyle, Arthur Conan

Conceptions of Reality in Modern American Poetry (Dembo), **Supp. I Part 1:** 272

"Concept of Character in Fiction, The" (Gass), **Supp. VI:** 85, **86**

Concept of Dread, The (Kierkegaard), **III:** 305

Concerning Children (Gilman), **Supp. XI:** 206

"Concerning Mold upon the Skin, Etc." (J. Scott), **Supp. XVII:** 188

"Concerning Necessity" (Carruth), **Supp. XVI:** 57

"Concerning Some Recent Criticism of His Work" (Doty), **Supp. XI:** 131

Concerning the End for Which God Created the World (Edwards), **I:** 549, 557, 559

Concerning the League (Woodbury, Henry, and Webster, trans.), **Supp. XXVI:** 81, 82, 87, 90

"Concerning Things That Can Be Doubled"(Crooker), **Supp. XXIII:** 64

Concerto for Two Pianos, Winds, and Percussion (Bowles), **Supp. IV Part 1:** 83

"Concert of Tenses, A" (Gallagher), **Supp. XXIV:** 172

Concert of Tenses, A: Essays on Poetry (Gallagher), **Supp. XXIV:** 166, 167, 171–172

Conchologist's First Book, The (Poe), **III:** 412

Conclusive Evidence (Nabokov), **III:** 247–250, 252

"Concord Hymn" (Emerson), **II:** 19

Concrete Blonde, The (Connelly), **Supp. XXI:** **70–71,** 78, 80

"Concrete Universal, The: Observations on the Understanding of Poetry" (Ransom), **III:** 480

Concurring Beasts (Dobyns), **Supp. XIII:** 76

Condé, Maryse, **Supp. XXIII:** 94

Condensed Novels and Other Papers (Harte), **Supp. II Part 1:** 342

"Condition, The" (Karmi; Everwine, trans.), **Supp. XV:** 78

Condition of Man, The (Mumford), **Supp. II Part 2:** 483, 484, 486, 495–496, 498

"Condolence" (Parker), **Supp. IX:** 191

"Condominium, The" (Elkin), **Supp. VI:** 49, **50–51,** 55, 56

Condon, Charles R., **Supp. XIII:** 163

Condor and the Cows, The: A South American Travel Diary (Isherwood and Caskey), **Supp. XIV:** 166

"Condor and the Guests, The" (Connell), **Supp. XIV:** 86

Condorcet, Marquis de, **Supp. I Part 2:** 511

Conduct of Life, The (Emerson), **II:** 1–5, 8

Conduct of Life, The (Mumford), **Supp. II Part 2:** 485, 496–497

"Conductor of Nothing, The" (Levine), **Supp. V:** 189

Coney Island of the Mind, A (Ferlinghetti), **Supp. XIX:** 4; **Supp. XXI:** 53

Confederacy of Dunces, A (Toole), **Supp. XXVI:** 239, 240, 242, 243–244, 246, 250–253

"Conference Male, The" (Mora), **Supp. XIII:** 218

"Confession" (Peacock), **Supp. XIX:** 206

Confession, The (Rinehart), **Supp. XXV:** 200

"Confessional" (Bidart), **Supp. XV:** 29–30, 31

"Confessional Poem" (Nelson), **Supp. XVIII:** 174

Confession de Claude, La (Zola), **I:** 411

"Confession of a House-Breaker, The" (Jewett), **Retro. Supp. II:** 146–147

Confession of Jereboam O. Beauchamp, The (pamphlet), **IV:** 253

Confessions (Augustine), **I:** 279; **Supp. XVI:** 288; **Supp. XXII:** 93

"Confessions" (Huddle), **Supp. XXVI:** 150

Confessions (Rousseau), **I:** 226

Confessions of a Barbarian: Selections from the Journals of Edward Abbey, 1951–1989 (Abbey; Petersen, ed.), **Supp. XIII:** 2, 4

"Confessions of a Latina Author" (Mora), **Supp. XIII:** 221

"Confessions of a Wannabe Negro" (McKnight), **Supp. XX: 152–153, 158**

Confessions of Nat Turner, The (Styron), **IV:** 98, 99, 105, 113–117; **Supp. X:** 16, 250

Confetti (Mora), **Supp. XIII:** 221

Confidence (James), **II:** 327, 328

Confidence-Man, The (Melville), **III:** 91; **Retro. Supp. I:** 255–256, 257; **Retro. Supp. II:** 121; **Supp. XIV:** 49

Confidence Man, The (Van Vechten), **Supp. II Part 2:** 737

Confidential Clerk, The (Eliot), **I:** 570, 571–572, 583, 584; **Retro. Supp. I:** 65

Confident Years, 1885–1915, The (Brooks), **I:** 257, 259; **Supp. I Part 2:** 650

"Configurations" (Ammons), **Supp. VII:** 28

Configurations: New and Selected Poems, 1958–1998 (Major), **Supp. XXII: 182**

Confronting the Horror: The Novels of Nelson Algren (Giles), **Supp. IX:** 11, 15

Confucius, **II:** 1; **III:** 456, 475; **Supp. IV Part 1:** 14

Confusion (Cozzens), **I:** 358, 359, 377, 378

"Confusion of Planes We Must Wander in Sleep, The" (Weigl), **Supp. XIX:** 283

Congdon, Don, **Supp. XXII:** 204

Congo (film), **Supp. IV Part 1:** 83

Congo (screenplay, Shanley), **Supp. XIV:** 316

"Congo, The" (Lindsay), **Supp. I Part 2:** 388–389, 392, 395

Congo and Other Poems, The (Lindsay), **Supp. I Part 2:** 379, 382, 389, 390, 391; **Supp. XXV:** 18

"Congregation" (Trethewey), **Supp. XXI:** 245, 247

"Congregation of Grackles, A"(Crooker), **Supp. XXIII:** 63

"Congress of the Insomniacs, The" (Simic), **Supp. VIII:** 281–282

Congreve, William, **III:** 195; **Supp. V:** 101; **Supp. XVIII:** 12

Coningsby (Disraeli), **II:** 127

"Conjectural Reading" (Bronk), **Supp. XXI:** 31

Conjectures of a Guilty Bystander (Merton), **Supp. VIII:** 197, 206, 207

Conjugal Bliss: A Comedy of Marital Arts (Nichols), **Supp. XIII:** 269

"Conjugation of the Paramecium, The" (Rukeyser), **Supp. VI:** 271

Conjugations and Reiterations (Murray), **Supp. XIX:** 161

"Conjuration" (Wilbur), **Supp. III Part 2:** 551

Conjure (recording), **Supp. X:** 241

Conjure (Reed), **Supp. X:** 240, 242

Conjure-Man Dies, The: A Mystery Tale of Dark Harlem (R. Fisher), **Supp. XIX:** 65, 71, **77–78**; **Supp. XVI:** 143

Conjure Woman, The (Chesnutt), **Supp. II Part 1:** 193; **Supp. XIV:** 57, **58–61**, 62, 63

Conklin, Grof, **Supp. I Part 2:** 672

Conklin, Peggy, **Supp. XXII:** 27

Conkling, Hilda, **II:** 530

Conkling, Roscoe, **III:** 506

Conley, Robert J., **Supp. V:** 232

Conley, Susan, **Supp. XIII:** 111, 112

Connaroe, Joel, **Supp. IV Part 2:** 690

"Connecticut Lad, A" (White), **Supp. I Part 2:** 677

"Connecticut Valley" (Cowley), **Supp. II Part 1:** 141–142

Connecticut Yankee in King Arthur's Court, A (Twain), **I:** 209; **II:** 276; **IV:** 205

Connell, Evan S., **Supp. XIV: 79–100**; **Supp. XXIII:** 302

Connell, Norreys (pseudonym). *See* O'Riordan, Conal Holmes O'Connell

Connelly, Marc, **III:** 394; **Supp. I Part 2:** 679; **Supp. IX:** 190

Connelly, Michael, **Supp. XXI: 67–82**

Conner, Dan, **Supp. XXIII:** 125

Connery, Thomas B., **Supp. XVII:** 106

Connoisseur, The (Connell), **Supp. XIV:** 87

"Connoisseur of Chaos" (Stevens), **IV:** 89; **Retro. Supp. I:** 306

Connolly, Cyril, **Supp. XIV:** 158, 343, 348

Connors, Elizabeth. *See* Lindsay, Mrs. Vachel (Elizabeth Connors)

Connotations (Kenny), **Supp. XXIII:** 143, 144, 146, 150, 155

Conover, Roger, **Supp. I Part 1:** 95

Conover, Roger L., **Supp. XXII:** 155, 162

Conquering Horse (Manfred), **Supp. X:** 126

Conqueror, The (Atherton), **Supp. XXIV:** 23

"Conqueror Worm, The" (Poe), **Retro. Supp. II:** 261

Conquest of Canaan (Dwight), **Supp. I Part 1:** 124

Conquistador (MacLeish), **III:** 2, 3, 13–14, 15

Conrad, Alfred, **Retro. Supp. II:** 245

Conrad, Alfred H., **Supp. I Part 2:** 552

Conrad, C. A., **Supp. XXII:** 155

Conrad, David, **Supp. I Part 2:** 552

Conrad, Jacob, **Supp. I Part 2:** 552

Conrad, Joseph, **I:** 123, 343, 394, 405, 409, 415, 421, 485, 506, 575–576, 578; **II:** 58, 73, 74, 91, 92, 144, 263, 320, 338, 595; **III:** 28, 102, 106, 328, 464, 467, 491, 512; **IV:** 476; **Retro. Supp. I:** 80, 91, 106, 108, 231, 274, 377; **Retro. Supp. II:** 222; **Supp. I Part 1:** 292; **Supp. I Part 2:** 621, 622; **Supp. IV Part 1:** 197, 341; **Supp. IV Part 2:** 680; **Supp. V:** 249, 251, 262, 298, 307, 311; **Supp. VIII:** 4, 310; **Supp. XIV:** 112; **Supp. XIX:** 27; **Supp. XVI:** 158, 212; **Supp. XVIII:** 98, 102; **Supp. XX: 195; Supp. XXIV:** 286; **Supp. XXV:** 208

Conrad, Paul, **Supp. I Part 2:** 552

Conrad, Peter, **Supp. IV Part 2:** 688

"Conrad Aiken: From Savannah to Emerson" (Cowley), **Supp. II Part 1:** 43

Conrad Richter's Ohio Trilogy (Edwards), **Supp. XVIII:** 220

Conroy, Frank, **Supp. VIII:** 145; **Supp. XI:** 245; **Supp. XVI: 63–78**; **Supp. XXII:** 50

Conroy, Jack, **Supp. XXII:** 1, 5, 10

Conroy, Pat, **Supp. XVIII:** 193; **Supp. XXII:** 239

Cons, Scams, and Grifts (Gores), **Supp. XXI:** 70

Conscience with the Power and Cases thereof (Ames), **IV:** 158

"Conscientious Objector, The" (Shapiro), **Supp. II Part 2:** 710

"Consciousness and Dining" (Harrison), **Supp. VIII:** 46

"Conscript, The" (Lovecraft), **Supp. XXV:** 119

"Conscription Camp" (Shapiro), **Supp. II Part 2:** 705

"Consejos de Nuestra Señora de Guadalupe: Counsel from the Brown Virgin" (Mora), **Supp. XIII:** 224

"Conservation Esthetic" (Leopold), **Supp. XIV:** 179, 181, 186, 189–190

"Conserving Natural and Cultural Diversity: The Prose and Poetry of Pat Mora" (Murphy), **Supp. XIII:** 214

Considerable Town, A (M. F. K. Fisher), **Supp. XVII:** 90

"Considerations by the Way" (Emerson), **II:** 2, 5

Consider the Oyster (M. F. K. Fisher), **Supp. XVII:** 84, 87

Considine, Bob, **II:** 424

"Consolation" (Bausch), **Supp. VII:** 48

"Consolation for Tamar" (Stallings), **Supp. XXV:** 228

Consolation of Philosophy, The (Boethius), **Supp. XXVI:** 250

"Consolations" (Stafford), **Supp. XI:** 329

"Conspiracy of History, The: E. L. Doctorow's *The Book of Daniel*" (Levine), **Supp. IV Part 1:** 221

Conspiracy of Kings, The (Barlow), **Supp. II Part 1:** 80

Conspiracy of Pontiac, The (Parkman), **Supp. II Part 2:** 590, 595, 596, 599–600

Constab Ballads (McKay), **Supp. X:** 131, 133

Constance (Kenyon), **Supp. VII:** 170–172

Constancy (Boyce), **Supp. XVII:** 100; **Supp. XXI:** 6, 7, 12

"Constellation Orion, The" (Kooser), **Supp. XIX:** 120

Constitution of the Confederacy by Dekanawidah: Collected and Translated from \[the\] Mohawk Text by Chief Seth Newhouse, **Supp. XXVI:** 90

Constitution of the Five Nations, The (Parker), **Supp. XXVI:** 87

Construction of Boston, The (Koch), **Supp. XV:** 187

"Constructive Work" (Du Bois), **Supp. II Part 1:** 172

"Consumer's Report" (X. J. Kennedy), **Supp. XV:** 161–162

"Consumption" (Bryant), **Supp. I Part 1:** 169–170

Contact Collection of Contemporary Writers (McAlmon), **Supp. XXII:** 166

"Contagiousness of Puerperal Fever, The" (Holmes), **Supp. I Part 1:** 303–304

"Contemplation in a World of Action" (Merton), **Supp. VIII:** 204

"Contemplation of Poussin" (Sarton), **Supp. VIII:** 261

"Contemplations" (Bradstreet), **Supp. I Part 1:** 112, 113, 119–122

Contemporaries (Kazin), **Supp. VIII:** 102, **103–104**

Contemporary American Playwrights (Bigsby), **Supp. XV:** 332

Contemporary American Poetry (Poulin, ed.), **Supp. IX:** 272; **Supp. XI:** 259

Contemporary Authors Autobiography, **Supp. XXII:** 225

Contending Forces (Hopkins), **Supp. XVIII:** 284

"Contentment" (Holmes), **Supp. I Part 1:** 307

"Contents" (Halliday), **Supp. XIX:** 92

"Contest, The" (Paley), **Supp. VI:** 223, 230, 231

"Contest for Aaron Gold, The" (P. Roth), **Supp. III Part 2:** 403

Continental Drift (Banks), **Supp. V:** 13–14, 16, 227

Continental Op, The (Hammett), **Supp. IV Part 1:** 344

Continent's End: An Anthology of Contemporary California Poets (Taggard, Sterling, and Rorty, eds.), **Supp. XXII:** 276

Continuing Education, A (Pickering), **Supp. XXI:** 194, 195–196

Continuity of American Poetry, The (Pearce), **Supp. I Part 1:** 111; **Supp. I Part 2:** 475

Continuous Harmony, A: Essays Cultural and Agricultural (Berry), **Supp. X:** 33

Continuous Life, The (Strand), **Supp. IV Part 2:** 630, 631–633

Contoski, Victor, **Supp. XII:** 181

"Contract" (Lardner), **II:** 432

"Contraption, The" (Swenson), **Supp. IV Part 2:** 643

"Contrariness of the Mad Farmer, The" (Berry), **Supp. X:** 35

"Contrast, a Spenetic Effusion, The" (J. Schoolcraft), **Supp. XXIII:** 231–232

"Contrition" (Dubus), **Supp. VII:** 84

"Control Burn" (Snyder), **Supp. VIII:** 301

"Control Is the Mainspring" (Komunyakaa), **Supp. XIII:** 122, 124

"Controlling the 'Sloppiness of Things' in Frank Conroy's *Stop-Time*" (Strychacz), **Supp. XVI:** 69–70

Control of Nature, The (McPhee), **Supp. III Part 1:** 310–313

Controversial Sholem Asch, The (Siegel), **Supp. XXIII:** 3

"Conventional Wisdom, The" (Elkin), **Supp. VI:** 52–53

"Convergence" (Ammons), **Supp. VII:** 28

"Convergence of the Twain, The" (Hardy), **Supp. VIII:** 31, 32

Conversation (Aiken), **I:** 54

Conversation at Midnight (Millay), **III:** 138

"Conversation of Eiros and Charmion, The" (Poe), **III:** 412

"Conversation on Conversation" (Stowe), **Supp. I Part 2:** 587

"Conversations in Moscow" (Levertov), **Supp. III Part 1:** 282

Conversations on Some of the Old Poets (Lowell), **Supp. I Part 2:** 405

Conversations with Albert Murray (Maguire, ed.), **Supp. XIX:** 160–161

Conversations with Byron (Blessington), **Retro. Supp. II:** 58

Conversations with Eudora Welty (Prenshaw, ed.), **Retro. Supp. I:** 339, 340, 341, 342, 343, 352, 354

"Conversations with Helmholtz" (Allen), **Supp. XV:** 15

Conversations with Ishmael Reed (Dick and Singh, eds.), **Supp. X:** 244

Conversations with James Baldwin (Standley and Pratt, eds.), **Retro. Supp. II:** 6

Conversations with Richard Wilbur (Wilbur), **Supp. III Part 2:** 542–543

"Conversation with a Fireman from Brooklyn" (Gallagher), **Supp. XXIV:** 169–170

"Conversation with My Father, A" (Paley), **Supp. VI:** 220

"Conversion of the Jews, The" (P. Roth), **Retro. Supp. II:** 281; **Supp. III Part 2:** 404, 406; **Supp. XXVI:** 119

Convict, The: Stories (Burke), **Supp. XIV:** 25

"Convicta et Combusta" (J. Scott), **Supp. XVII:** 189

"Convolvulus" (Schott), **Supp. XXIII:** 248

"Convoy" (Weigl), **Supp. XIX:** 278

Conway, Jill, **Supp. I Part 1:** 19

Coode, John, **I:** 132

Cook, Bruce, **Supp. XII:** 130, 131, 133–134

Cook, Captain James, **I:** 2

Cook, Eleanor, **Retro. Supp. I:** 311

Cook, Elisha, **Supp. IV Part 1:** 356

Cook, Elizabeth Christine, **II:** 106

Cook, George Cram "Jig", **Supp. XXI:** 5, 6

Cook, Jessie W., **Supp. XXV:** 278

Cook, Johnny, **Supp. XXIV:** 248

Cook, Mercer, **Supp. IV Part 1:** 368

Cook, Richard, **Supp. XXII:** 158

Cookbook Collector, The (Goodman), **Supp. XXVI:** 130–131

Cooke, Alistair, **III:** 113, 119, 120

Cooke, Delmar G., **II:** 271

Cooke, Grace MacGowan, **Supp. V:** 285

Cooke, Philip Pendleton, **III:** 420

Cooke, Rose Terry, **II:** 401; **Retro. Supp. II:** 51, 136, 138; **Supp. XIII:** 152

"Cookie" (Taylor), **Supp. V:** 320

"Cookies, The" (Nye), **Supp. XIII:** 281

Cooking of Provincial France, The (M. F. K. Fisher), **Supp. XVII:** 89

Cook-Lynn, Elizabeth, **Supp. IV Part 1:** 325

"Cool Air" (Lovecraft), **Supp. XXV:** 110

Coolbrith, Ina, **I:** 193, 196

"Coole Park" (Yeats), **Supp. VIII:** 155, 159

"Coole Park and Ballylee" (Yeats), **Supp. VIII:** 156

Cooler by the Lake (Heinemann), **Supp. XXII:** 103, **114**

Cooley, John, **Supp. V:** 214

Cooley, Peter, **Supp. XIII:** 76

Coolidge, Calvin, **I:** 498; **II:** 95; **Supp. I Part 2:** 647

Cooling Time: An American Poetry Vigil (Wright), **Supp. XV:** 353

Cool Million, A (West), **III:** 425; **IV:** 287, 288, 297–299, 300; **Retro. Supp. II:** 321, 322–323, 328, **335–337**

"Cool Million, A" (screen story) (West and Ingster), **Retro. Supp. II:** 330

"Cool Tombs" (Sandburg), **III:** 554

Coon, Ross, **IV:** 196

Cooney, Seamus, **Supp. XIV:** 289

"Coon Hunt" (White), **Supp. I Part 2:** 669

Co-op (Sinclair), **Supp. V:** 290

Cooper, Bernard, **Supp. XI:** 129

Cooper, Frederic Taber, **Supp. XX: 219–220; Supp. XXIV:** 28–29

Cooper, Gary, **Supp. IV Part 2:** 524

Cooper, James Fenimore, **I:** 211, 257, **335–357; II:** 74, 277, 295–296, 302, 306, 309, 313, 314; **III:** 51; **IV:** 205, 333; **Retro. Supp. I:** 246; **Retro. Supp. II:** 160; **Supp. I Part 1:** 141, 155, 156, 158, 171, 372; **Supp. I Part 2:** 413, 495, 579, 585, 652, 660; **Supp. IV Part 1:** 80; **Supp. IV Part 2:** 463, 469; **Supp. V:** 209–210; **Supp. VIII:** 189; **Supp. XIV:** 227; **Supp. XVIII:** 4; **Supp. XXIII:** 178

Cooper, Mrs. James Fenimore (Susan A. De Lancey), **I:** 338, 351, 354

Cooper, Jane, **Supp. XV:** 259

Cooper, Rand Richards, **Supp. XVI:** 74

Cooper, Susan Fenimore, **I:** 337, 354

Cooper, William, **I:** 337–338, 351

Cooper, Mrs. William, **I:** 337

Cooperman, Robert, **Supp. XXIII:** 247

Coover, Robert, **Supp. IV Part 1:** 388; **Supp. V: 39–55; Supp. XII:** 152; **Supp. XIV:** 96; **Supp. XVII:** 6; **Supp. XXI:** 236; **Supp. XXII:** 259

Copacetic (Komunyakaa), **Supp. XIII: 116–118,** 126

Cope, Wendy, **Supp. XV:** 117

Copelin, David, **Supp. XXIV:** 264

Copland, Aaron, **II:** 586; **Supp. I Part 1:** 281; **Supp. III Part 2:** 619; **Supp. IV Part 1:** 79, 80–81, 84; **Supp. XXII:** 283; **Supp. XXVI:** 134

Coplas de Don Jorge Manrique (Longfellow, trans.), **II:** 488, 492

Coppée, François Edouard Joachim, **II:** 325

Copperhead, The (Frederic), **II:** 134–135

Copperhead Cane (J. W. Miller), **Supp. XX: 163, 164, 166–167**

Copper Sun (Cullen), **Supp. IV Part 1:** 167, 168

Coppola, Francis Ford, **Supp. XI:** 171, 172; **Supp. XII:** 75

Coprolites (Goldbarth), **Supp. XII: 177–178,** 180, 183

Coquette, The (Foster), **Supp. XXV:** 35, 36, 38–45

Coral and Captive Israel (Reznikoff), **Supp. XIV:** 288

"Coral Ring, The" (Stowe), **Supp. I Part 2:** 586

"Cora Unashamed" (Hughes), **Supp. I Part 1:** 329, 330

"Corazón del Corrido" (Mora), **Supp. XIII:** 225

Corban Ephphata (Li Lin Lee), **Supp. XV:** 225
Corbett, Gentlemen Jim, **II:** 416
Corbett, William, **Supp. XI:** 248; **Supp. XVI:** 286, 295; **Supp. XXIV:** 45
Corbière, Jean Antoine, **II:** 354–355, 528
Cordiall Water, A: A garland of Odd & Old Receipts to Assuage the Ills of Man and Beast (M. F. K. Fisher), **Supp. XVII:** 88, 90
Cording, Robert, **Supp. IX:** 328; **Supp. XII:** 184
Core, George, **Supp. XVIII:** 86; **Supp. XXI:** 193
Corelli, Marie, **III:** 579
Corey, Lewis, **Supp. I Part 2:** 645
"Corinna's Going a-Maying" (Herrick), **Supp. XIV:** 8, 9
"Coriolan" (Eliot), **I:** 580
"Coriolanus and His Mother" (Schwartz), **Supp. II Part 2:** 643, 644–645
"Corkscrew" (Hammett), **Supp. IV Part 1:** 345, 347
Corkum, Gerald, **I:** 37
Corky's Brother (Neugeboren), **Supp. XVI:** 225
"Corky's Brother" (Neugeboren), **Supp. XVI:** 225
Corliss, Richard, **Supp. VIII:** 73
Corman, Cid, **Supp. III Part 2:** 624, 625, 626, 627, 628; **Supp. IV Part 1:** 144; **Supp. VIII:** 292; **Supp. XV:** 74, 153; **Supp. XXI:** 23, 27
Corman, Roger, **Supp. XXV:** 154
"Corn" (Lanier), **Supp. I Part 1:** 352, 353, 354, 356–361, 364, 366
Corn, Alfred, **Supp. IX:** 156; **Supp. XV:** 250
Corneille, Pierre, **Supp. I Part 2:** 716; **Supp. IX:** 131
Cornelius, Randy, **Supp. XXVI:** 89
Cornell, Esther, **I:** 231
Cornell, Joseph, **Supp. XXI:** 131; **Supp. XXII:** 167, 168
Cornell, Katherine, **IV:** 356
Cornell, Valerie, **Supp. XX: 94–95**
"Corners" (Dunn), **Supp. XI:** 148
Cornhuskers (Sandburg), **III:** 583–585
"Corn-Planting, The" (Anderson), **I:** 114
"Corn story (or the origin of corn)"(J. Schoolcraft), **Supp. XXIII:** 234–235
Cornucopia: New and Selected Poems, 1975–2002 (Peacock), **Supp. XIX: 203–204**
Corn Village (Le Sueur), **Supp. XXIII:** 167
Coronation Murder-Mystery, The (O'Hara, Ashbery, and Koch), **Supp. XXIII:** 217
"Coroner's Report" (Wrigley), **Supp. XVIII:** 295
"Corporal of Artillery" (Dubus), **Supp. VII:** 84, 85
"Corpse Plant, The" (Rich), **Supp. I Part 2:** 555
Corpus Christi (McNally), **Supp. XIII: 205–206,** 209
Corradi, Juan, **Supp. IV Part 1:** 208

Corrections, The (Franzen), **Supp. XIX:** 54; **Supp. XX: 83, 84, 85, 90, 91, 91–93, 95**
Corregidora (G. Jones), **Supp. XXIV:** 183–184, **185–187,** 190, 193, 194, 195
"Correspondences" (Baudelaire), **I:** 63
"Corrido de Gregorio Cortez" (Mora), **Supp. XIII:** 225
"Corrigenda" (Komunyakaa), **Supp. XIII:** 115, 116
Corrosive Sublimate (Sorrentino), **Supp. XXI:** 226, 228
Corruption City (McCoy), **Supp. XIII:** 175
Corso, Gregory, **Supp. II Part 1:** 30; **Supp. IV Part 1:** 90; **Supp. XII: 117–138; Supp. XIV:** 150; **Supp. XVI:** 135; **Supp. XXI:** 53; **Supp. XXIII:** 215
Corsons Inlet (Ammons), **Supp. VII:** 25–26, 28–29, 36
"Corsons Inlet" (Ammons), **Supp. VII:** 25–26
Cortázar, Julio, **Retro. Supp. I:** 278; **Supp. XXII:** 265
"Cortège for Rosenbloom" (Stevens), **IV:** 81
Cortez, Hernando, **III:** 2
" 'Coruscating Glamour': Lynda Hull and the Movies" (Goldstein), **Supp. XXI:** 134
Cory, William Johnson, **Supp. XX: 230, 231**
Coser, Lewis, **Supp. I Part 2:** 650
Cosgrave, Patrick, **Retro. Supp. II:** 185
Cosmic Optimism: A Study of the Interpretation of Evolution by American Poets from Emerson to Robinson (Conner), **Supp. I Part 1:** 73
Cosmogony of the Iroquois Confederacy (Newhouse), **Supp. XXVI:** 87
Cosmological Eye, The (H. Miller), **III:** 174, 184
"Cosmological Eye, The" (H. Miller), **III:** 183
"Cosmos" (Beattie), **Supp. V:** 35
"Cost, The" (Hecht), **Supp. X:** 62–63
Costello, Bonnie, **Retro. Supp. II:** 40
Costello, Mark, **Supp. XXIII:** 290
Costner, Kevin, **Supp. VIII:** 45
"Cost of Living, The" (Malamud), **Supp. I Part 2:** 429, 437
"Costume as Metaphor" (Bronk), **Supp. XXI:** 26
Cott, Jonathan, **Supp. XVI:** 104, 106
"Cottagers' Corner" column (D. West), **Supp. XVIII:** 286
"Cottage Street, 1953" (Wilbur), **Supp. III Part 2:** 543, 561
"Cottagette, The" (Gilman), **Supp. XI:** 207
Cotten, Joseph, **Supp. IV Part 2:** 524
Cotter, James Finn, **Supp. X:** 202
Cotton, John, **Supp. I Part 1:** 98, 101, 110, 111, 116
Cotton, Joseph, **Supp. XII:** 160
Cotton, Seaborn, **Supp. I Part 1:** 101
Cotton Club, The (Major), **Supp. XXII:** 174

"Cotton Club Classics" (Halliday), **Supp. XIX:** 92, 93
Cotton Comes to Harlem (C. Himes), **Supp. XVI:** 143, 144
Cotton Comes to Harlem (film, O. Davis), **Supp. XVI:** 144
"Cotton Song" (Toomer), **Supp. IX:** 312
Couch, W. T., **Supp. X:** 46
Coughlin, Ruth Pollack, **Supp. VIII:** 45
Coulette, Henri, **Supp. V:** 180; **Supp. XIII:** 312; **Supp. XV:** 74, 75
Coultrap-McQuin, Susan, **Supp. XVI:** 85, 92
"Council of State, A" (Dunbar), **Supp. II Part 1:** 211, 213
Count Bruga (Hecht), **Supp. XXV:** 27
"Count Dracula" (Allen), **Supp. XV:** 15
"Countee Cullen at 'The Heights' " (Tuttleton), **Supp. IV Part 1:** 166
Counterfeiters, The (Gide), **Supp. IV Part 1:** 80; **Supp. IV Part 2:** 681
"Countering" (Ammons), **Supp. VII:** 28
Counterlife, The (P. Roth), **Retro. Supp. II:** 279, 280, 291; **Supp. III Part 2:** 424–426
Counter-Statement (Burke), **I:** 270–272; **IV:** 431
"Countess, The" (Whittier), **Supp. I Part 2:** 691, 694
Count Frontenac and New France Under Louis XIV (Parkman), **Supp. II Part 2:** 607, 609–610
"Counting Small-Boned Bodies" (R. Bly), **Supp. IV Part 1:** 62
"Counting the Body"(Schott), **Supp. XXIII:** 251–252
"Counting the Children" (Gioia), **Supp. XV: 122–123**
"Counting the Mad" (Justice), **Supp. VII:** 117
"Count Lothar's Heart" (Boyle), **Supp. XXIV:** 58
Count of Monte Cristo, The (Dumas), **III:** 386, 396; **Supp. XVII:** 64, 216
"Countries We Live In, The" (Zach; Everwine, trans.), **Supp. XV:** 87
"Country Boy in Boston, The" (Howells), **II:** 255
Country By-Ways (Jewett), **II:** 402
Country Doctor, A (Jewett), **II:** 391, 392, 396, 404–405; **Retro. Supp. II:** 131, 141, 146
"Country Full of Swedes" (Caldwell), **I:** 297, 309
Country Girl, The (Odets), **Supp. II Part 2:** 546, 547, 548–549
"Country House" (Kumin), **Supp. IV Part 2:** 446
"Country Husband, The" (Cheever), **Supp. I Part 1:** 184, 189
"Country Life" (Pickering), **Supp. XXI:** 197
"Country Marriage" (C. Frost), **Supp. XV:** 99
Countrymen of Bones (R. O. Butler), **Supp. XII:** 62, **65–66**
"Country Mouse, The" (Bishop), **Retro. Supp. II:** 37, 38, 51
Country Music: Selected Early Poems (Wright), **Supp. V:** 332, 335, 338, 342

Country of a Thousand Years of Peace, The (Merrill), **Supp. III Part 1:** 321, 322, 331

"Country of Elusion, The" (O. Henry), **Supp. II Part 1:** 407

Country Of Language, The (Sanders), **Supp. XVI:** 277

Country of Marriage, The (Berry), **Supp. X:** 33

Country of Strangers, A (Richter), **Supp. XVIII:** 217

Country of Survivors (Di Piero), **Supp. XIX:** 36

Country of the Pointed Firs, The (Jewett), **II:** 392, 399, 405, 409–411; **Retro. Supp. I:** 6; **Retro. Supp. II:** 134, 136, 139, 140, 141, 145, 146, 147; **Supp. VIII:** 126; **Supp. XIII:** 152; **Supp. XXIII:** 275, 278

"Country Printer, The" (Freneau), **Supp. II Part 1:** 269

"Country Song" (Stallings), **Supp. XXV:** 222, 234

"Country Wife, The" (Gioia), **Supp. XV:** 120

Count Your Bullets (film), **Supp. XVII:** 141

Count Zero (W. Gibson), **Supp. XVI:** 19, **126–127,** 129

Coup, The (Updike), **Retro. Supp. I:** 331, 334, 335

"Coup de Grâce, The" (Bierce), **I:** 202

Couperin, François, **III:** 464

"Couple, The" (Olds), **Supp. X:** 206

"Couple of Hamburgers, A" (Thurber), **Supp. I Part 2:** 616

"Couple of Nuts, A" (Z. Fitzgerald), **Supp. IX:** 58, 71, 72

"Couples" (Halliday), **Supp. XIX:** 89

Couples (Updike), **IV:** 214, 215, 216, 217, 227, 229–230; **Retro. Supp. I:** 320, 327, 330; **Supp. XII:** 296

Cournos, John, **III:** 465; **Supp. I Part 1:** 258

"Course in Creative Writing, A" (Stafford), **Supp. XI:** 327

"Course of a Particular, The" (Stevens), **Retro. Supp. I:** 312

"Coursier de Jeanne d'Arc, Le" (McCarriston), **Supp. XIV:** 267–268

Courtier, The (Castiglione), **III:** 282

" 'Courtin,' The" (Lowell), **Supp. I Part 2:** 415

"Courting" (Huddle), **Supp. XXVI:** 151

"Courting of Sister Wisby, The" (Jewett), **Retro. Supp. II:** 134, 135, 146

"Courting the Famous Figures at the Grotto of Improbable Thought" (B. Kelly), **Supp. XVII:** 127–128

Courtney, W. L., **Supp. XXIV:** 29

"Courtship" (Dove), **Supp. IV Part 1:** 248

"Courtship, A" (Thompson), **Supp. XXIII:** 293

"Courtship, Diligence" (Dove), **Supp. IV Part 1:** 248

Courtship of Miles Standish, The (Longfellow), **II:** 489, 502–503; **Retro. Supp. II:** 155, **161–162,** 163, 166, 168

"Cousin Aubrey" (Taylor), **Supp. V:** 328

"Cousin Claire" (Andrews), **Supp. XXVI:** 11

Cousine Bette (Balzac), **Retro. Supp. II:** 98

Couturier, Maurice, **Supp. IV Part 1:** 44

Covarrubias, Miguel, **Supp. XVI:** 187

"Covered Bridges" (Kingsolver), **Supp. VII:** 203

"Cover Photograph" (Nelson), **Supp. XVIII:** 173

"Cover Stories" (Skloot), **Supp. XX: 195, 207**

"Cover Versions" (Halliday), **Supp. XIX:** 84

Cowan, Lester, **III:** 148

Cowan, Louise, **IV:** 120, 125

Coward, Noel, **Retro. Supp. I:** 65; **Supp. I Part 1:** 332; **Supp. V:** 101; **Supp. XV:** 329; **Supp. XXIV:** 267

"Cowardice" (Theroux), **Supp. VIII:** 313

Cowboy Mouth (Shepard), **Supp. III Part 2:** 441–442

"Cowboys" (Salter). *See* "Dirt" (Salter)

Cowboys (Shepard), **Supp. III Part 2:** 432

Cowboys #2 (Shepard), **Supp. III Part 2:** 437, 438

Cowell, Henry, **Supp. IV Part 1:** 80, 82

Cowen, Philip, **Supp. XX:** 2

Cowen, Wilson Walker, **Supp. IV Part 2:** 435

Cowie, Alexander, **IV:** 70

"Cow in Apple Time, The" (Frost), **II:** 154; **Retro. Supp. I:** 131

Cowl, Jane, **IV:** 357

Cowley, Abraham, **III:** 508; **IV:** 158; **Supp. I Part 1:** 357

Cowley, Malcolm, **I:** 246, 253, 254, 255, 256, 257, 283, 385; **II:** 26, 57, 94, 456; **IV:** 123; **Retro. Supp. I:** 73, 91, 97; **Retro. Supp. II:** 77, 83, 89, 221, 330; **Supp. I Part 1:** 174; **Supp. I Part 2:** 609, 610, 620, 647, 654, 678; **Supp. II Part 1:** 103, **135–156; Supp. VIII:** 96; **Supp. XV:** 142; **Supp. XX: 76; Supp. XXVI:** 17

Cowley, Marguerite Frances Baird (Mrs. Malcolm Cowley), **Supp. I Part 2:** 615; **Supp. II Part 1:** 138, 139

Cowley, Muriel Maurer (Mrs. Malcolm Cowley), **Supp. II Part 1:** 139

Cowley, Susan Cheever (Susan Cheever), **Supp. I Part 1:** 175; **Supp. IX:** 133; **Supp. XXIV:** 97

Cowper, William, **II:** 17, 304; **III:** 508, 511; **Supp. I Part 1:** 150, 151, 152; **Supp. I Part 2:** 539

"Cow Wandering in the Bare Field, The" (Jarrell), **II:** 371, 388

Cox, Martha Heasley, **Supp. IX:** 2, 4, 11–12

Cox, Sidney, **Retro. Supp. I:** 131; **Supp. XXI:** 19, 21

Cox, Stephen, **Supp. IV Part 2:** 523, 524

Cox, Steve, **Supp. XIX:** 116, 128

Coxey, Jacob, **II:** 464

"Coxon Fund, The" (James), **Retro. Supp. I:** 228

"Coy Mistress" (A. Finch), **Supp. XVII:** 72

Coyne, Patricia, **Supp. V:** 123

"Coyote Ortiz: *Canis latrans latrans* in the Poetry of Simon Ortiz" (P. C. Smith), **Supp. IV Part 2:** 509

Coyote's Daylight Trip (Gunn Allen), **Supp. IV Part 1:** 320, 324

Coyote Was Here (Ortiz), **Supp. IV Part 2:** 499

Cozzens, James Gould, **I: 358–380; II:** 459

Crabbe, George, **II:** 304; **III:** 469, 508, 511, 521; **Supp. XXIV:** 159

"Crab-Boil" (Dove), **Supp. IV Part 1:** 249

"Cracked Looking-Glass, The" (Porter), **III:** 434, 435, 446

"Cracker Chidlings" (Rawlings), **Supp. X:** 224, 228

Cracks (Purdy), **Supp. VII:** 277–278

"Cracks in the Universe" (Davison), **Supp. XXVI:** 78

Crack-Up, The (Fitzgerald), **II:** 80; **III:** 35, 45; **Retro. Supp. I:** 113, 115; **Supp. IX:** 61; **Supp. V:** 276

"Crack-Up, The" (Fitzgerald), **I:** 509; **Retro. Supp. I:** 113, 114

"Crack-up of American Optimism, The: Vachel Lindsay, the Dante of the Fundamentalists" (Viereck), **Supp. I Part 2:** 403

"Cradle and the Bookcase, The"(Hadas), **Supp. XXIII:** 122

"Cradle Me" (Biss), **Supp. XXVI:** 48

Cradle Will Rock, The (Blitzstein), **Supp. I Part 1:** 277, 278

Craft of Fiction, The (Lubbock), **I:** 504; **Supp. VIII:** 165

Craft of Peter Taylor, The (McAlexander, ed.), **Supp. V:** 314

Craig, David M., **Supp. XXII:** 187, 191, 192

Craig, Gordon, **III:** 394; **Supp. XXI:** 6

Crain, Jane Larkin, **Supp. V:** 123; **Supp. XII:** 167, 168

Crais, Robert, **Supp. XXI:** 70

Cram, Ralph Adams, **I:** 19

Cramer, Steven, **Supp. XI:** 139; **Supp. XV:** 26

"Cramped Quarters" (Davison), **Supp. XXVI:** 77

"Cranbrook Schools: Adventures in Bourgeois Topologies" (Monson), **Supp. XXIV:** 235

Crandall, Reuben, **Supp. I Part 2:** 686

Crane, Agnes, **I:** 406

Crane, Edmund, **I:** 407

Crane, Hart, **I:** 61, 62, 97, 109, 116, 266, **381–404; II:** 133, 215, 306, 368, 371, 536, 542; **III:** 260, 276, 453, 485, 521; **IV:** 122, 123–124, 127, 128, 129, 135, 139, 140, 141, 341, 380, 418, 419; **Retro. Supp. I:** 427; **Retro. Supp. II: 75–91; Supp. I Part 1:** 86; **Supp. II Part 1:** 89, 152; **Supp. III Part 1:** 20, 63, 350; **Supp. IX:** 38, 229, 320; **Supp. V:** 342; **Supp. VIII:** 39; **Supp. X:** 115, 116, 120; **Supp. XI:** 123, 131; **Supp. XII:** 198; **Supp. XIX:** 35;

Supp. XV: 138; **Supp. XX: 80; Supp. XXI:** 131, 132, 136, 230; **Supp. XXII:** 274; **Supp. XXIII:** 146, 174, 207; **Supp. XXV:** 19; **Supp. XXVI:** 21, 23–24, 25, 28, 143

Crane, Jonathan, Jr., **I:** 407

Crane, Jonathan Townley, **I:** 406

Crane, Mrs. Jonathan Townley, **I:** 406

Crane, Luther, **I:** 406

Crane, Milton, **Supp. XV:** 144

Crane, Nellie, **I:** 407

Crane, R. S., **Supp. I Part 2:** 423

Crane, Stephen, **I:** 34, 169–170, 201, 207, 211, **405–427,** 477, 506, 519; **II:** 58, 144, 198, 262, 263, 264, 276, 289, 290, 291; **III:** 314, 317, 334, 335, 454, 505, 585; **IV:** 207, 208, 256, 350, 475; **Retro. Supp. I:** 231, 325; **Retro. Supp. II:** 97, 123; **Supp. I Part 1:** 314; **Supp. III Part 2:** 412; **Supp. IV Part 1:** 350, 380; **Supp. IV Part 2:** 680, 689, 692; **Supp. IX:** 1, 14; **Supp. VIII:** 98, 105; **Supp. X:** 223; **Supp. XI:** 95; **Supp. XII:** 50; **Supp. XIV:** 21, 50, 51, 227; **Supp. XVII:** 71, 228; **Supp. XVIII:** 74, 75; **Supp. XXIII:** 26

Crane, William, **I:** 407

Cranford (Gaskell), **Supp. IX:** 79

Crash (film, Cronenberg), **Supp. XXVI:** 28

Crashaw, William, **IV:** 145, 150, 151, 165

"Crash Report" (McGrath), **Supp. X:** 116

Crater, The (Cooper), **I:** 354, 355

Cratylus (Plato), **II:** 10

Cravan, Arthur, **Supp. XXII:** 164, 169

"Craven Street Gazette" (Franklin), **II:** 119

"Crawdad, The" (F. Wright), **Supp. XVII:** 244

Crawdad Creek (Sanders), **Supp. XVI:** 269

Crawford, Brad, **Supp. XI:** 133

Crawford, Eva, **I:** 199

Crawford, F. Marion, **III:** 320

Crawford, Joan, **Supp. I Part 1:** 67

Crawford, John E., **Supp. XXIII:** 165

Crawford, Kathleen, **I:** 289

Crawford, Neta C., **Supp. XXVI:** 85

"Crayon House" (Rukeyser), **Supp. VI:** 273

Crayon Miscellany, The (Irving), **II:** 312–313

Crazed, The (Jin), **Supp. XVIII: 99–100**

"Crazy about her Shrimp" (Simic), **Supp. VIII:** 282

"Crazy Cock" (H. Miller), **III:** 177

Crazy Gypsy (Salinas), **Supp. XIII:** 311, **313–315,** 316

"Crazy Gypsy" (Salinas), **Supp. XIII:** 313–314

Crazy Horse, **Supp. IV Part 2:** 488, 489

Crazy Horse (McMurtry), **Supp. V:** 233

Crazy Horse in Stillness (Heyen), **Supp. XIII:** 344

Crazy Horse: The Strange Man of the Oglaglas (Sandoz), **Supp. XXIV:** 244, 256, **257–258**

"Crazy Hunter, The" (Boyle), **Supp. XXIV: 54–55**

Crazy Hunter, The: Three Short Novels (Boyle), **Supp. XXIV: 54–56**

"Crazy in the Stir" (C. Himes), **Supp. XVI:** 137

Crazy Kill, The (C. Himes), **Supp. XVI:** 143

Crazy Man (Bodenheim), **Supp. XXV:** 22, 24

Creating a Role (Stanislavsky), **Supp. XIV:** 243

"Creation, According to Coyote, The" (Ortiz), **Supp. IV Part 2:** 505

Creation: A Novel (Vidal), **Supp. IV Part 2:** 677, 685, 688

"Creation of Anguish" (Nemerov), **III:** 269

"Creation Story" (Gunn Allen), **Supp. IV Part 1:** 325

"Creative and Cultural Lag" (Ellison), **Retro. Supp. II:** 116; **Supp. II Part 1:** 229; **Supp. XVIII:** 283

Creative Criticism (Spingarn), **I:** 266

"Creative Democracy" (Locke), **Supp. XIV:** 208

Creative Present, The (Balkian and Simmons, eds.), **Supp. XI:** 230

"Creatures" (Gallagher), **Supp. XXIV:** 176, 177

Creatures in an Alphabet (illus. Barnes), **Supp. III Part 1:** 43

"Creatures of the Genitive" (Davison), **Supp. XXVI:** 74

"Credences of Summer" (Stevens), **IV:** 93–94

"Credentials" (Halliday), **Supp. XIX:** 90

"Credo" (Bynner), **Supp. XV:** 50

"Credo" (Du Bois), **Supp. II Part 1:** 169

"Credo" (Jeffers), **Supp. II Part 2:** 424

"Credos and Curios" (Thurber), **Supp. I Part 2:** 606, 613

Creech, James, **Retro. Supp. I:** 254

"Creed for Americans, A" (Benét), **Supp. XI:** 52

"Creed of a Beggar, The" (Lindsay), **Supp. I Part 2:** 379

Creegan, Andy, **Supp. XIX:** 205

Creekmore, Hubert, **II:** 586

Creeley, Robert, **Retro. Supp. I:** 411; **Supp. II Part 1:** 30; **Supp. III Part 1:** 2; **Supp. III Part 2:** 622, 626, 629; **Supp. IV Part 1: 139–161,** 322, 325; **Supp. XI:** 317; **Supp. XIII:** 104, 112; **Supp. XIV:** 150; **Supp. XVI:** 283; **Supp. XXI:** 23, 27, 227, 230; **Supp. XXII:** 227; **Supp. XXIV:** 35, 37

Creelman, James Ashmore, **Supp. XVI:** 186–187

"Cremona Violin, The" (Lowell), **II:** 523

"Crêpe de Chine" (Doty), **Supp. XI:** 128

"Crêpes Flambeau" (Gallagher), **Supp. XXIV:** 170

"Cressy" (Harte), **Supp. II Part 1:** 354, 356

"Cretan Woman, The" (Jeffers), **Supp. II Part 2:** 435

Crèvecoeur, Michel-Guillaume Jean de, **I:** 229; **Supp. I Part 1: 227–252**

Crèvecoeur's Eighteenth-Century Travels in Pennsylvania and New York (Adams), **Supp. I Part 1:** 251

Crevel, René, **Supp. XIV:** 343

Crewe-Jones, Florence, **Supp. XVII:** 58

Crewe Train (Macaulay), **Supp. XII:** 88

Crews, Harry, **Supp. X:** 11, 12; **Supp. XI: 99–117,** 245; **Supp. XVIII:** 195; **Supp. XXI:** 35, 38, 40, 44

Crews, James, **Supp. XXIII:** 134–135

Crichton, Michael, **Supp. XIV:** 316

Crick, Philip, **Supp. XVI:** 289

Cricket (C. L. R. James; Grimshaw, ed.), **Supp. XXI:** 172

"Cricket" (C. Miller), **Supp. XXII:** 199

"Crickets" (R. O. Butler), **Supp. XII:** 71

Criers and Kibitzers, Kibitzers and Criers (Elkin), **Supp. VI: 45–46,** 57

Crime and Punishment (Dostoevsky), **II:** 60, 130; **IV:** 484; **Supp. IV Part 2:** 525; **Supp. VIII:** 282; **Supp. XII:** 281; **Supp. XIX:** 276; **Supp. XVII:** 155; **Supp. XVIII:** 278

Crime at Scottsboro, The (Endore), **Supp. XVII:** 59

Crime Beat (Connelly), **Supp. XXI:** 67, 79

Crimes and Misdemeanors (film; Allen), **Supp. XV:** 1, 2, **11,** 12

"Criminal"(Strout), **Supp. XXIII:** 283, 285

Crisis papers (Paine), **Supp. I Part 2:** 508–509, 510

"Criteria of Negro Art" (Du Bois), **Supp. II Part 1:** 181; **Supp. XIX:** 66–67

"Critiad, The" (Winters), **Supp. II Part 2:** 794, 799

Critical Anthology A (Untermeyer), **Supp. XV:** 310

Critical Essays on Charlotte Perkins Gilman (Karpinski, ed.), **Supp. XI:** 201

Critical Essays on Kay Boyle (Elkins, ed.), **Supp. XXIV:** 64

Critical Essays on Peter Taylor (McAlexander), **Supp. V:** 319, 320, 323–324

Critical Essays on Robert Bly (W. V. Davis), **Supp. IV Part 1:** 64, 69

Critical Essays on Wallace Stegner (Arthur), **Supp. IV Part 2:** 606

Critical Fable, A (Lowell), **II:** 511–512, 527, 529–530

Critical Guide to Leaves of Grass, A (J. Miller), **IV:** 352

Critical Mass (Paretsky), **Supp. XXV:** 185

Critical Response to Joan Didion, The (Felton), **Supp. IV Part 1:** 210

Critical Temper of Alain Locke, The: A Selection of His Essays on Art and Culture (Stewart, ed.), **Supp. XIV:** 196, **210–211,** 213

"Critic as Artist, The" (Wilde), **Supp. X:** 189

Criticism and Fiction (Howells), **II:** 288

Criticism and Ideology (Eagleton), **Retro. Supp. I:** 67

Criticism in the Borderlands (Calderón and Saldívar, eds.), **Supp. IV Part 2:** 544

"Critics, The" (Jong), **Supp. V:** 119

"Critics and Connoisseurs" (Moore), **III:** 209

Critic's Notebook, A (Howe), **Supp. VI:** 126–128

"Critic's Task, The" (Kazin), **Supp. VIII:** 103

"Critic Who Does Not Exist, The" (Wilson), **IV:** 431

"Critique de la Vie Quotidienne" (Barthelme), **Supp. IV Part 1:** 50

Critique of Pure Reason (Kant), **Supp. XVI:** 184

Croce, Benedetto, **I:** 58, 255, 265, 273, 281; **III:** 610

Crockett, Davy, **II:** 307; **III:** 227; **IV:** 266; **Supp. I Part 2:** 411

"Crocodilopolis" (Cliff), **Supp. XXII:** 76

Crofter and the Laird, The (McPhee), **Supp. III Part 1:** 301–302, 307

Croly, Herbert, **I:** 229, 231, 235; **IV:** 436

Cromwell, Oliver, **IV:** 145, 146, 156; **Supp. I Part 1:** 111

Cronenberg, David, **Supp. XXI:** 152, 154

Cronin, A. J., **Supp. XVII:** 59

Cronin, Dr. Archibald, **III:** 578

Cronin, Gloria, **Supp. XXVI:** 123

Cronin, Justin, **Supp. X:** 10

Crooke, Dr. Helkiah, **Supp. I Part 1:** 98, 104

Crooked Little Heart (Lamott), **Supp. XX:** 138

Crooker, Barbara, **Supp. XXIII: 51–66,** 245, **246,** 251

Crooks, Alan, **Supp. V:** 226

Crooks, Robert, **Supp. XIII:** 237

"Crop, The" (O'Connor), **Retro. Supp. II:** 223–225

Crosby, Caresse, **I:** 385; **III:** 473; **Retro. Supp. II:** 85; **Supp. XII:** 198

Crosby, Harry, **I:** 385; **Retro. Supp. II:** 85

"Cross" (Hughes), **Supp. I Part 1:** 325; **Supp. XVIII:** 124

Cross, Charles, **Supp. XXIV:** 173

Crossan, John Dominic, **Supp. V:** 251

"Cross Country Snow" (Hemingway), **II:** 249

Cross Creek (Rawlings), **Supp. X:** 223, 226, 228, **231–232,** 233, 234, 235

Cross Creek Cookery (Rawlings), **Supp. X:** 233

"Cross Cut" (Davison), **Supp. XXVI:** 74

"Crossing, The" (Huddle), **Supp. XXVI:** 154

Crossing, The (McCarthy), **Supp. VIII:** 175, **184–186**

"Crossing, The" (Swenson), **Supp. IV Part 2:** 644

"Crossing Brooklyn Ferry" (Whitman), **IV:** 333, 340, 341; **Retro. Supp. I:** 389, 396, 397, 400–401; **Supp. XXIII:** 109

"Crossing into Poland" (Babel), **Supp. XIV:** 84

"Crossing New River" (Huddle), **Supp. XXVI:** 148, 150

Crossings (Chuang), **Supp. X:** 291

"Crossings" (Hogan), **Supp. IV Part 1:** 412

"Crossing the Void" (Davison), **Supp. XXVI:** 76

Crossing the Water (Plath), **Retro. Supp. II:** 248; **Supp. I Part 2:** 526, 538

Crossing to Safety (Stegner), **Supp. IV Part 2:** 599, 606, 612, 613–614

"Cross of Snow, The" (Longfellow), **II:** 490; **Retro. Supp. II:** 169–170

"Crossover" (O. Butler), **Supp. XIII:** 61

"Cross-PolliNation" (Gansworth), **Supp. XXVI:** 111

"Cross-Roads, The" (Lowell), **II:** 523

"Crossroads of the World Etc." (Merwin), **Supp. III Part 1:** 347, 348

Cross-Section (Seaver), **IV:** 485

Cross the Border, Close the Gap (Fiedler), **Supp. XIII:** 104

Cross Ties (X. J. Kennedy), **Supp. XV:** 165, **166–167**

"Cross Ties" (X. J. Kennedy), **Supp. XV:** 158

Crouch, Stanley, **Supp. XIX:** 158

"Croup" (Karr), **Supp. XI:** 243

Crouse, Russel, **III:** 284

"Crow" (Hogan), **Supp. IV Part 1:** 405

Crow (Hughes), **Supp. XV:** 347, 348

"Crow, The" (Creeley), **Supp. IV Part 1:** 148–149

Crow and the Heart, The (Carruth), **Supp. XVI:** 47–48

"Crowded Countries of the Bomb, The" (Oppen), **Supp. XXVI:** 232

"Crowded Street, The" (Bryant), **Supp. I Part 1:** 168

Crowder, A. B., **Supp. XI:** 107

"Crow Jane" (Baraka), **Supp. II Part 1:** 38

Crow Mercies (Schott), **Supp. XXIII: 252–254**

"Crow Mercies" (Schott), **Supp. XXIII:** 253

Crowninshield, Frank, **III:** 123; **Supp. IX:** 201

Crown of Columbus (Erdrich and Dorris), **Supp. IV Part 1:** 260

"Crows, The" (Bogan), **Supp. III Part 1:** 50, 51

Crucial Instances (Wharton), **Retro. Supp. I:** 365, 367

Crucible, The (A. Miller), **III:** 147, 148, 155, 156–158, 159, 166; **Supp. XIII:** 206; **Supp. XXV:** 93

"Crucified" (Gibran), **Supp. XX: 119**

"Crucifix in the Filing Cabinet" (Shapiro), **Supp. II Part 2:** 712

"Crude Foyer" (Stevens), **Retro. Supp. I:** 310

"Cruel and Barbarous Treatment" (McCarthy), **II:** 562, 563

"Cruel Mother, The" (B. Kelly), **Supp. XVII:** 126

Cruise of the Dazzler, The (London), **II:** 465

Cruise of the Snark, The (London), **II:** 476–477; **Supp. XXV:** 217

"Cruising with the Beach Boys" (Gioia), **Supp. XV:** 118

" 'Crumbling Idols' by Hamlin Garland" (Chopin), **Supp. I Part 1:** 217

"Crusade of the Excelsior, The" (Harte), **Supp. II Part 1:** 336, 354

"Crusoe in England" (Bishop), **Retro. Supp. II:** 50; **Supp. I Part 1:** 93, 95, 96; **Supp. III Part 1:** 10, 18

Cruz, Angie, **Supp. XXVI:** 263–264

Cruz-Hacker, Alba, **Supp. XXI:** 107

Cry, the Beloved Country (Paton), **Supp. VIII:** 126

Cryer, Dan, **Supp. VIII:** 86, 88; **Supp. XII:** 164

Crying of Lot 49, The (Pynchon), **Supp. II Part 2:** 618, 619, 621, 630–633

"Crying Sisters, The" (Rand), **Supp. IV Part 2:** 524

"Crying Wolf" (C. Frost), **Supp. XV:** 101

"Cry of the Graves, The" (Gibran), **Supp. XX: 124**

Cryptogram, The (Mamet), **Supp. XIV:** 240, 247, 255

"Crystal, The" (Aiken), **I:** 60

"Crystal, The" (Lanier), **Supp. I Part 1:** 364, 370

"Crystal Cage, The" (Kunitz), **Supp. III Part 1:** 258

Crystal Cup, The (Atherton), **Supp. XXIV:** 26

Crystal Vision (Sorrentino), **Supp. XXI:** 235, 236

"Crytal" (Sobin), **Supp. XVI:** 283

Cry to Heaven (Rice), **Supp. VII:** 300–301

"Cuba" (Hemingway), **II:** 258

"Cuba Libre" (Baraka), **Supp. II Part 1:** 33

Cuba: Prophetic Island (W. Frank), **Supp. XX: 80, 81**

"Cubism, Barcelona" (Hull), **Supp. XXI:** 137

Cudjoe, Selwyn, **Supp. IV Part 1:** 6

"Cudjo's Own Story of the Last American Slaver" (Hurston), **Supp. VI:** 153

Cudlipp, Thelma, **I:** 501

Cudworth, Ralph, **II:** 9, 10

"Cuentista" (Mora), **Supp. XIII:** 224

"Cuento de agua santa, Un" (Mora), **Supp. XIII:** 224

"Cui Bono" (H. Johnson), **Supp. XXVI:** 167, 173

Cujo (King), **Supp. V:** 138–139, 143, 149, 152

Cukor, George, **Supp. XVI:** 192

Cullen, Countee, **Retro. Supp. I:** 207; **Retro. Supp. II:** 114; **Supp. I Part 1:** 49, 325; **Supp. III Part 1:** 73, 75, 76; **Supp. IV Part 1: 163–174; Supp. IX:** 306, 309; **Supp. X:** 136, 140; **Supp. XIII:** 186; **Supp. XIX:** 78; **Supp. XVIII:** 122,131, 185, 279, 280, 282, 284; **Supp. XXII:** 3, 6, 7, 8

"Cultivation of Christmas Trees, The" (Eliot), **I:** 579

Cult of Alien Gods, The: H. P. Lovecraft and Extraterrestrial Pop Culture (Calavito), **Supp. XXV:** 123

"Cult of Personality in American Letters, The" (Swados), **Supp. XIX:** 265

"Cult of the Best, The" (Arnold), **I:** 223

"Cultural Exchange" (Hughes), **Supp. I Part 1:** 341

"Cultural Pluralism: A New Americanism" (Locke), **Supp. XIV:** 195

"Cultural Relativism and Ideological Peace" (Locke), **Supp. XIV:** 202, 212
"Culture" (Emerson), **III:** 2, 4
"Culture, Self, and Style" (Gass), **Supp. VI:** 88
"Culture and Religion" (Olds), **Supp. X:** 214
Culture of Cities, The (Mumford), **Supp. II Part 2:** 492, 494–495
Cummings, E. E., **I:** 44, 48, 64, 105, 176, **428–450,** 475, 477, 482, 526; **III:** 20, 196, 476; **IV:** 384, 402, 415, 427, 433; **Retro. Supp. II:** 178, 328; **Supp. I Part 2:** 622, 678; **Supp. III Part 1:** 73; **Supp. IV Part 2:** 637, 641; **Supp. IX:** 20; **Supp. XV:** 312, 338; **Supp. XXVI:** 32
Cummings, Robert, **Supp. IV Part 2:** 524
Cummins, Ann, **Supp. XXIII:** 280
Cummins, James, **Supp. XVII:** 74
Cunard, Lady, **III:** 459
Cunningham, J. V., **Supp. XV:** 169
Cunningham, Merce, **Supp. IV Part 1:** 83; **Supp. XV:** 187
Cunningham, Michael, **Supp. XII:** 80; **Supp. XV: 55–71**
Cunningham, Rodger, **Supp. XXIII:** 38–39
Cup of Gold (Steinbeck), **IV:** 51, 53, 61–64, 67
"Cupola, The" (Bogan), **Supp. III Part 1:** 53
"Curandera" (Mora), **Supp. XIII:** 214, 222
Curé de Tours, Le (Balzac), **I:** 509
Cure for Dreams, A: A Novel (Gibbons), **Supp. X: 45–47,** 48, 50
Curie, Marie, **IV:** 420, 421; **Supp. I Part 2:** 569
Curie, Pierre, **IV:** 420
Curiosa Americana (Mather), **Supp. II Part 2:** 463
Curiosities (Matthews), **Supp. IX:** 151, 152
"Curious Case of Sidd Finch, The" (Plimpton), **Supp. XVI:** 244
"Curious Shifts of the Poor" (Dreiser), **Retro. Supp. II:** 97
"Current" (Espaillat), **Supp. XXI:** 106
"Currents and Counter-Currents in Medical Science" (Holmes), **Supp. I Part 1:** 305
"Curried Cow" (Bierce), **I:** 200
Curry, Professor W. C., **IV:** 122
Curse of the Jade Scorpion, The (film; Allen), **Supp. XV:** 11
Curse of the Starving Class (Shepard), **Supp. III Part 2:** 433, 447–448
Curse of the Werewolf, The (film), **Supp. XVII:** 56
"Curse of Yig, The" (Lovecraft and Bishop), **Supp. XXV:** 122
"Curse on a Thief, A" (X. J. Kennedy), **Supp. XV:** 171
"Curtain, The" (Chandler), **Supp. IV Part 1:** 122
Curtain Calls: British and American Women and the Theater, 1660–1820 (Saar), **Supp. XV:** 237

Curtain of Green, A (Welty), **IV:** 261–264, 268, 283
"Curtain of Green, A" (Welty), **IV:** 263–264
Curtain of Green and Other Stories, A (Welty), **Retro. Supp. I:** 343, 344, 345, 346, 347, 355
Curtain of Trees (opera), **Supp. IV Part 2:** 552
"Curtain Raiser, A" (Stein), **IV:** 43, 44
"Curtains" (Cisneros), **Supp. VII:** 66
Curtin, John, **Supp. IX:** 184
Curtis, George William, **Supp. I Part 1:** 307; **Supp. XVIII:** 3, 14
Curve (Goldbarth), **Supp. XII:** 181
Curve of Binding Energy, The (McPhee), **Supp. III Part 1:** 301
Curzon, Mary, **III:** 52
Cushing, Caleb, **Supp. I Part 2:** 684, 686
Cushman, Howard, **Supp. I Part 2:** 652
Cushman, Stephen, **Retro. Supp. I:** 430
Cusick, Albert, **Supp. XXVI:** 87
"Custard Heart, The" (Parker), **Supp. IX:** 201
Custer, General George, **I:** 489, 491
Custer Died for Your Sins (Deloria), **Supp. IV Part 1:** 323; **Supp. IV Part 2:** 504
"Custody"(Schott), **Supp. XXIII:** 241
"Custom House, The" (Hawthorne), **II:** 223; **Retro. Supp. I:** 147–148, 157; **Supp. XXI:** 181
Custom of the Country, The (Wharton), **IV:** 318; **Retro. Supp. I:** 374, **375–376; Supp. XXIV:** 23
"Cut" (Plath), **Retro. Supp. II:** 253
"Cut-Glass Bowl, The" (Fitzgerald), **II:** 88
Cutting, Bronson, **III:** 600
Cutting Lisa (Everett), **Supp. XVIII: 56**
"Cuttings, *later*" (Roethke), **III:** 532
"Cyberpunk" (Bethke), **Supp. XVI:** 121
Cyberspace trilogy (W. Gibson). *See* Sprawl trilogy (W. Gibson)
"Cycles, The" (Pinsky), **Supp. VI:** 250–252
Cyclopedia of American Literature (Duyckinck and Duyckinck), **Supp. XXV:** 250
Cynic's Word Book, The (Bierce), **I:** 197, 205, 208, 209, 210
Cynthia Ozick (Lowin), **Supp. V:** 273
Cynthia Ozick's Comic Art (Cohen), **Supp. V:** 273
Cynthia Ozick's Fiction (Kauvar), **Supp. V:** 273
"Czeslaw Milosz and Memory" (Hampl), **Supp. XXII:** 92

D

Da Capo: Best Music Writing 2002 (Lethem, ed.), **Supp. XVIII:** 148
Dacey, Philip, **Supp. IV Part 1:** 70
Dacier, André, **II:** 10
"Dad" (Cullen), **Supp. IV Part 1:** 167
"Daddy" (Plath), **Retro. Supp. II:** 250–251; **Supp. I Part 2:** 529, 542, 545, 546; **Supp. II Part 2:** 688; **Supp. XXII:** 30; **Supp. XXIII:** 112, 113

"Daddy"(Hadas), **Supp. XXIII:** 112, 113
Daddy's Little Boy (Collins), **Supp. XXI:** 54
"Daemon, The" (Bogan), **Supp. III Part 1:** 58, 61
"Daemon Lover, The" (Jackson), **Supp. IX:** 116–117
"Daffodils" (Nelson and Espeland), **Supp. XVIII:** 181
"Daffodils" (Wordsworth), **Supp. XIII:** 284
"Daffy Duck in Hollywood" (Ashbery), **Supp. III Part 1:** 18
D'Agata, John, **Supp. XII:** 97, 98
"Dagon" (Lovecraft), **Supp. XXV:** 111, 121
Dago Red (Fante), **Supp. XI:** 160, 169
Dahl, Roald, **Supp. IX:** 114
Dahlberg, Edward, **I:** 231; **Retro. Supp. I:** 426; **Supp. III Part 2:** 624; **Supp. XIV:** 148; **Supp. XVIII:** 148; **Supp. XXII:** 257
Dahlberg, R'lene, **Supp. XIV:** 148
Daiches, David, **Retro. Supp. II:** 243; **Supp. I Part 2:** 536
Daily Horoscope (Gioia), **Supp. XV:** 112, **118–121,** 126
"Daily Horoscope" (Gioia), **Supp. XV:** 119
Daily Modernism (Podnieks), **Supp. X:** 189
Dain Curse, The (Hammett), **Supp. IV Part 1:** 348
"Daisies" (Glück), **Supp. V:** 88
"Daisy" (Oates), **Supp. II Part 2:** 523
Daisy (S. and A. Warner), **Supp. XVIII:** 268
Daisy-Head Mayzie (Geisel), **Supp. XVI:** 112
Daisy Miller (H. James), **Retro. Supp. I:** 216, 220, 222, 223, 228, 231; **Supp. XVIII:** 165; **Supp. XXIV:** 23
"Daisy Miller" (H. James), **II:** 325, 326, 327, 329; **IV:** 316
"Dakota (IV)" (Gansworth), **Supp. XXVI:** 111
Dale, Charlie, **Supp. IV Part 2:** 584
Daley, Yvonne, **Supp. XXII:** 216
Dali, Salvador, **II:** 586; **Supp. IV Part 1:** 83; **Supp. XIII:** 317
Dalibard, Thomas-François, **II:** 117
"Dallas-Fort Worth: Redband and Mistletoe" (Clampitt), **Supp. IX:** 45
"Dalliance of Eagles, The" (Whitman), **IV:** 348
Dalva (Harrison), **Supp. VIII:** 37, 45, 46, **48–49**
Daly, Carroll John, **Supp. IV Part 1:** 343, 345
Daly, John, **II:** 25, 26
Daly, Julia Brown, **II:** 25, 26
"Dalyrimple Goes Wrong" (Fitzgerald), **II:** 88
"Dam, The" (Rukeyser), **Supp. VI:** 283
Damas, Leon, **Supp. X:** 139
Damascus Gate (Stone), **Supp. V:** 308–311
Damballah (Wideman), **Supp. X:** 319, 320, 321, 322, 323, 326, 327, 331, 333–334

Dameshek, Brandon, **Supp. XIX:** 273, 277, 287

Damnation of Theron Ware, The (Frederic), **II:** 140–143, 144, 146, 147; **Retro. Supp. I:** 325

Damned If I Do (Everett), **Supp. XVIII:** 66

"Damned Thing, The" (Bierce), **I:** 206

Damon, Matt, **Supp. VIII:** 175

Damon, S. Foster, **I:** 26; **II:** 512, 514, 515

"Damon and Vandalia" (Dove), **Supp. IV Part 1:** 252

Dana, H. W. L., **I:** 225

Dana, Richard Henry, Jr., **III:** 81; **Supp. XX:** 227; **Supp. XXV:** 208

Dana, Richard Henry, Sr., **I:** 339, 351; **Supp. I Part 1:** 103, 154, 155; **Supp. I Part 2:** 414, 420; **Supp. XXV:** 250

Dana, Robert, **Supp. V:** 178, 180

"Dana Gioia and Fine Press Printing" (Peich), **Supp. XV:** 117

"Dance" (Kenny), **Supp. XXIII:** 148

"Dance, The" (Crane), **I:** 109

"Dance, The" (Roethke), **III:** 541

"Dance, The" (W. C. Williams), **Supp. XVII:** 113

Dance and the Railroad, The (Hwang), **Supp. XXI:** 145, 146

"Dance in a Buffalo Skull" (Zitkala-Ša), **Supp. XXV:** 276

Dance of Death, The (Auden), **Supp. II Part 1:** 10

Dance of Death, The (Bierce and Harcourt), **I:** 196

Dance of Life, The (Ellis), **Supp. XX:** 117

Dance of the Sleepwalkers (Calabria), **Supp. XIII:** 164

"Dance of the Solids, The" (Updike), **Retro. Supp. I:** 323

"Dancer" (Hoffman), **Supp. XVIII:** 86

"Dancer, The" (Swados), **Supp. XIX:** 261, 263–264

"Dancers Work by Forgetting" (Espaillat), **Supp. XXI:** 102

"Dances of Madness" (Schott), **Supp. XXIII:** 245

Dances with Wolves (film), **Supp. X:** 124

Dance to the Music of Time, A (Powell), **Supp. XVIII:** 146

Dancing After Hours (Dubus), **Supp. VII:** 91

Dancing Back Strong the Nation (Kenny), **Supp. XXIII:** 144, **148**

Dancing Bears, The (Merwin), **Supp. III Part 1:** 343–344

Dancing on the Stones (Nichols), **Supp. XIII:** 256, 257, 259, 267, 269

"Dancing the Jig" (Sexton), **Supp. II Part 2:** 692

Dandelion Wine (Bradbury), **Supp. IV Part 1:** 101, 109–110

Dandurand, Karen, **Retro. Supp. I:** 30

"Dandy Frightening the Squatters, The" (Twain), **IV:** 193–194

Dangel, Mary Jo, **Supp. XVIII:** 156

Dangerous Crossroads (film), **Supp. XIII:** 163

Dangerous Day (Rinehart), **Supp. XXV:** 195

Dangerous Moonlight (Purdy), **Supp. VII:** 278

"Dangerous Road Before Martin Luther King" (Baldwin), **Supp. I Part 1:** 52

"Dangerous Summer, The" (Hemingway), **II:** 261

Dangerous Thoughts (Ryan as Quin), **Supp. XVIII:** 226

"Dangers of Authorship, The" (Blackmur), **Supp. II Part 1:** 147

Dangling Man (Bellow), **I:** 144, 145, 147, 148, 150–151, 153–154, 158, 160, 161, 162, 163; **Retro. Supp. II:** 19, 20–21, 22, 23; **Supp. VIII:** 234; **Supp. XIX:** 157

"Dang Little Squirt" (Bontemps), **Supp. XXII:** 4

Daniel (biblical book), **Supp. I Part 1:** 105

Daniel (film), **Supp. IV Part 1:** 236

Daniel, Arnaut, **III:** 467

Daniel, Robert W., **III:** 76

Daniel, Samuel, **Supp. I Part 1:** 369

Daniel Deronda (G. Eliot), **I:** 458

Daniels, Frank, **Supp. XXII:** 196

Daniels, Kate, **Supp. XVII:** 112

Danielson, Linda, **Supp. IV Part 2:** 569

D'Annunzio, Gabriele, **II:** 515

Danny and the Deep Blue Sea: An Apache Dance (Shanley), **Supp. XIV:** 315, **318–319,** 320, 321, 323, 324

Danny O'Neill pentalogy (Farrell), **II:** 35–41

Danse Macabre (King), **Supp. IV Part 1:** 102; **Supp. V:** 144; **Supp. XXV:** 123

"Danse Russe" (W. C. Williams), **IV:** 412–413

"Dans le Restaurant" (Eliot), **I:** 554, 578

Dans l'ombre des cathédrales (Ambelain), **Supp. I Part 1:** 273

Dante Alighieri, **I:** 103, 136, 138, 250, 384, 433, 445; **II:** 8, 274, 278, 289, 490, 492, 493, 494, 495, 504, 508, 524, 552; **III:** 13, 77, 124, 182, 259, 278, 448, 453, 467, 533, 607, 609, 610–612, 613; **IV:** 50, 134, 137, 138, 139, 247, 437, 438; **Retro. Supp. I:** 62, 63, 64, 66, 360; **Retro. Supp. II:** 330; **Supp. I Part 1:** 256, 363; **Supp. I Part 2:** 422, 454; **Supp. III Part 2:** 611, 618, 621; **Supp. IV Part 2:** 634; **Supp. V:** 277, 283, 331, 338, 345; **Supp. VIII:** 27, 219–221; **Supp. X:** 120, 121, 125; **Supp. XII:** 98; **Supp. XV:** 254; **Supp. XVII:** 227, 241

Danvis Tales: Selected Stories (Robinson; Budbill, ed.), **Supp. XIX:** 6

Danziger, Adolphe, **I:** 199–200

Danziger, Jeff, **Supp. XXII:** 208

Dar (Nabokov), **III:** 246, 255

D'Arcy, Randall, **Supp. XVII:** 76

Dardis, Tom, **Supp. XVIII:** 249

"Dare's Gift" (Glasgow), **II:** 190

Dark and Feeling, The: Black American Writers and Their Work (Major), **Supp. XXII:** 180

Dark Angel, The (Bolton), **Supp. I Part 1:** 281

"Dark Angel Travels With Us to Canada and Blesses Our Vacation, The" (Dunn), **Supp. XI:** 146

Dark at the Top of the Stairs, The (film), **Supp. XXV:** 102

Dark at the Top of the Stairs, The (Inge), **Supp. XXV:** 93, 95, 100–102

Dark Carnival (Bradbury), **Supp. IV Part 1:** 102

Darker (Strand), **Supp. IV Part 2:** 619, 626–628

Darker Face of the Earth, The (Dove), **Supp. IV Part 1:** 255–257

"Dark Fire" (Hadas), **Supp. XXIII:** 126

Dark Green, Bright Red (Vidal), **Supp. IV Part 2:** 677

Dark Half, The (King), **Supp. V:** 141

Dark Harbor: A Poem (Strand), **Supp. IV Part 2:** 633–634

"Dark Hills, The" (Robinson), **III:** 523

Dark Horses (X. J. Kennedy), **Supp. XV:** **167–170**

Dark Hours, The (W. V. Davis), **Supp. XXI:** **91–92,** 93

"Dark Houses" (Davison), **Supp. XXVI:** 72

Dark Laughter (Anderson), **I:** 111, 116; **II:** 250–251

"Darkling Alphabet, A" (Snodgrass), **Supp. VI:** 323

Darkling Child (Merwin and Milroy), **Supp. III Part 1:** 346

"Darkling Summer, Ominous Dusk, Rumorous Rain" (Schwartz), **Supp. II Part 2:** 661

"Darkling Thrush" (Hardy), **Supp. IX:** 40

"Dark Men, The" (Dubus), **Supp. VII:** 86

Dark Mirrors (Sobin), **Supp. XVI:** 295

Dark Mother, The (W. Frank), **Supp. XX:** **70–71**

Dark Mountains, The (Hoffman), **Supp. XVIII:** **76–77**

Darkness and the Light, The (Hecht), **Supp. X:** 58

Darkness at Noon (Koestler), **Supp. XXIII:** 1

Darkness More Than Night, A (Connelly), **Supp. XXI:** **73–74,** 80

"Darkness on the Edge of Town" (O'Brien), **Supp. V:** 246

Darkness Surrounding Us, The (Sorrentino), **Supp. XXI:** 227, 228

Darkness under the Trees/Walking behind the Spanish (Salinas), **Supp. XIII:** 311, **319–324**

"Dark Night" (St. John of the Cross), **Supp. XV:** 30

Dark Night of the Soul, The (St. John of the Cross), **I:** 1, 585

"Dark Ones" (Dickey), **Supp. IV Part 1:** 182

Dark Power (Holding), **Supp. XXII:** **122–123,** 124

Dark Princess: A Romance (Du Bois), **Supp. II Part 1:** 179, 181–182

Dark Room, The (T. Williams), **IV:** 381

Dark Sacred Night (CD), **Supp. XXI:** 75
Dark Shadows (television show), **Supp. XIX:** 57
"Dark Summer" (Bogan), **Supp. III Part 1:** 51, 53
Dark Summer: Poems (Bogan), **Supp. III Part 1:** 52–53, 57
"Dark Tower, The" (column), **Supp. IV Part 1:** 168, 170
Dark Tower, The: The Gunslinger (King), **Supp. V:** 152
Dark Tower IV, The: Wizard and Glass (King), **Supp. V:** 139
Dark Tunnel, The (Macdonald as Millar), **Supp. IV Part 2:** 465, 466
"Dark TV Screen" (Simic), **Supp. VIII:** 282
"Dark Voyage, The" (McLay), **Supp. XIII:** 21
"Dark Walk, The" (Taylor), **Supp. V:** 320–321, 322, 326
Darkwater: Voices from Within the Veil (Du Bois), **Supp. II Part 1:** 178, 180, 183
Dark Waves and Light Matter (Goldbarth), **Supp. XII:** 176, 193
Dark World (Carruth), **Supp. XVI:** 55
"Darling" (Nye), **Supp. XIII:** 283–284
"Darling, The" (Chekhov), **Supp. IX:** 202
Darling-Darling (Barillet and Grédy; Loos, trans.), **Supp. XVI:** 194
Darnell, Linda, **Supp. XII:** 173
Darragh, Tina, **Supp. IV Part 2:** 427
Darreu, Robert Donaldson, **Supp. II Part 1:** 89, 98, 102
Darrow, Clarence, **Supp. I Part 1:** 5; **Supp. I Part 2:** 455
Dartmouth, Earl of, **Supp. XX:** 284
Darwin, Charles, **I:** 457; **II:** 323, 462, 481; **III:** 226, 231; **IV:** 69, 304; **Retro. Supp. I:** 254; **Retro. Supp. II:** 60, 65; **Supp. I Part 1:** 368; **Supp. IX:** 180; **Supp. XI:** 203; **Supp. XVI:** 13; **Supp. XX:** 18
"Darwin in 1881" (Schnackenberg), **Supp. XV:** 253, 254, 258
Daryush, Elizabeth, **Supp. V:** 180
Dasburg, Andrew, **Supp. XXI:** 6
Dash, Julie, **Supp. XI:** 17, 18, 20
Dashell, Alfred, **Supp. X:** 224
"DAS KAPITAL" (Baraka), **Supp. II Part 1:** 55
Datlow, Ellen, **Supp. XVI:** 123
"Datum Centurio" (Wallace), **Supp. X:** 309
Daudet, Alphonse, **II:** 325, 338
"Daughter" (Caldwell), **I:** 309
"Daughter in the House" (X. J. Kennedy), **Supp. XV:** 160
Daughter of Earth (Smedly), **Supp. XIII:** 295
Daughter of the Land, A (Stratton-Porter), **Supp. XX:** 222
Daughter of the Snows, A (London), **II:** 465, 469–470
Daughter of the Vine, A (Atherton), **Supp. XXIV:** 18, 22
"Daughters" (Anderson), **I:** 114
Daughters (Marshall), **Supp. XI:** 275, 276, 277, **286–288**, 289, 290

"Daughters, 1900" (Nelson), **Supp. XVIII:** 175
Daughters, I Love You (Hogan), **Supp. IV Part 1:** 397, 399, 401
"Daughters of Invention" (Alvarez), **Supp. VII:** 9
Daughters of the Dust (Dash; film), **Supp. XI:** 17, 18; **Supp. XX:** **154**
Daughters of Valor: Contemporary Jewish American Women Writers (Halio and Siegel, eds.), **Supp. XXVI:** 123
Daumier, Honoré, **IV:** 412
Dave, R. A., **Supp. VIII:** 126
Davenport, Abraham, **Supp. I Part 2:** 699
Davenport, Basil, **Supp. XXV:** 27
Davenport, Gary, **Supp. IX:** 98
Davenport, Guy, **Supp. XIV:** 96; **Supp. XXI:** 235
Davenport, Herbert J., **Supp. I Part 2:** 642
Davenport, James, **I:** 546
Daves, E. G., **Supp. I Part 1:** 369
Davey, Frank, **Supp. XIII:** 33
"David" (Garrett), **Supp. VII:** 109–110
"David" (Gordon), **Supp. IV Part 1:** 298–299
David, Gray, **Supp. XX:** **260**
"David and Agnes, a Romance" (Keillor), **Supp. XVI:** 175
David Blaize (Benson), **Supp. XX:** **234**
David Copperfield (Dickens), **I:** 458; **II:** 290; **Retro. Supp. I:** 33; **Supp. XVI:** 65, 72; **Supp. XX:** 234
"David Crockett's Other Life" (Nye), **Supp. XIII:** 282
Davideis (Cowley), **IV:** 158
David Harum (Westcott), **I:** 216
David Huddle Reader, A: Selected Prose and Poetry (Huddle), **Supp. XXVI:** 160
"David Lynch Keeps His Head" (Wallace), **Supp. X:** 314
David Show, The (Gurney), **Supp. V:** 97
Davidson, Cathy, **Supp. XV:** 238
Davidson, Donald, **I:** 294; **III:** 495, 496; **IV:** 121, 122, 124, 125, 236; **Supp. II Part 1:** 139; **Supp. XIV:** 2; **Supp. XX:** **164**
Davidson, James West, **Supp. XXII:** 218
Davidson, Jo, **Supp. XXI:** 7
Davidson, John, **Retro. Supp. I:** 55
Davidson, Michael, **Supp. VIII:** 290, 293, 294, 302–303; **Supp. XXVI:** 224
Davidson, Phebe, **Supp. XXIII:** 252
Davidson, Sara, **Supp. IV Part 1:** 196, 198, 203
Davidson, Sue, **Supp. XIX:** 260
Davidsz de Heem, Jan, **Supp. XI:** 133
Davie, Donald, **III:** 478; **Supp. IV Part 2:** 474; **Supp. V:** 331; **Supp. X:** 55, 59; **Supp. XVII:** 111, 112, 121
Davies, Arthur, **III:** 273
Davies, Sir John, **III:** 541
Davies, Marion, **Supp. XVI:** 186
Da Vinci, Leonardo, **I:** 274; **II:** 536; **III:** 210
Davis, Allen F., **Supp. I Part 1:** 1, 7
Davis, Allison, **Supp. I Part 1:** 327
Davis, Angela, **Supp. I Part 1:** 66; **Supp. X:** 249; **Supp. XXVI:** 50

Davis, Arthur B., **Supp. XVIII:** 119
Davis, Bette, **I:** 78; **Supp. I Part 1:** 67
Davis, Bill, **Supp. XIII:** 267
Davis, Christina, **Supp. XV:** 264
Davis, Cynthia, **Supp. XVIII:** 281, 286
Davis, Donald, **Supp. XIII:** 93
Davis, Elizabeth Gould, **Supp. I Part 2:** 567
Davis, George, **II:** 586
Davis, Glover, **Supp. V:** 180, 182, 186
Davis, Jefferson, **II:** 206; **IV:** 122, 125, 126
Davis, Jordan, **Supp. XV:** 178, 181, 186, 188
Davis, Katie, **Supp. VIII:** 83
Davis, L. J., **Supp. XI:** 234
Davis, Lydia, **Supp. XII:** 24; **Supp. XVII:** 21
Davis, Marcia, **Supp. XVIII:** 91, 100
Davis, Mary H., **Supp. XVIII:** 77
Davis, Miles, **Supp. XV:** 346; **Supp. XXII:** 172
Davis, Ossie, Jr., **Supp. IV Part 1:** 362; **Supp. XVI:** 144
Davis, Rebecca Harding, **Supp. I Part 1:** 45; **Supp. XIII:** 292, 295, 305; **Supp. XVI:** **79–96**
Davis, Richard Harding, **III:** 328; **Supp. II Part 1:** 393; **Supp. XVI:** 85
Davis, Robert Gorham, **II:** 51; **IV:** 108
Davis, Stuart, **IV:** 409; **Supp. XV:** 295; **Supp. XXI:** 6
Davis, Thadious, **Supp. XVIII:** 120, 121, 123, 127, 129
Davis, Thulani, **Supp. XI:** 179; **Supp. XIII:** 233, 234, 239
Davis, William Virgil, **Supp. IV Part 1:** 63, 64, 68, 69, 70; **Supp. XXI:** **83–96**
Davison, Jane, **Supp. XXVI:** 64, 65
Davison, Peter, **Supp. XXI:** 91; **Supp. XXVI:** **61–80**
Davy's Lake (M. Finch), **Supp. XVII:** 69
Dawn (Dreiser), **I:** 498, 499, 503, 509, 515, 519
Dawn (O. Butler), **Supp. XIII:** 63, **64**
"Dawnbreaker" (Hayden), **Supp. II Part 1:** 370
Dawn in Russia (W. Frank), **Supp. XX:** **76**
Dawn Patrol, The (film), **Supp. XIV:** 81
"Dawn Patrol: A Review of the Literature of the Negro for 1948" (Locke), **Supp. XIV:** 211
Dawson, Edward, **IV:** 151
Dawson, Emma, **I:** 199
Dawson, Melanie, **Supp. XXIV:** 25, 31
Dawson, Ruth, **Supp. XI:** 120
Day, Dorothy, **II:** 215; **Supp. I Part 2:** 524; **Supp. X:** 142; **Supp. XXV:** 19, 30
Day, Fred Holland, **Supp. XX:** **114, 115**
Day, Georgiana, **Supp. I Part 2:** 585
Day, Richard, **Supp. XVIII:** 251
Dayan, Joan, **Retro. Supp. II:** 270
"Day Book" (Notley), **Supp. XXII:** 230
Day Book, A (Creeley), **Supp. IV Part 1:** 155
"Daybreak" (Kinnell), **Supp. III Part 1:** 250
"Daybreak Blues" (Kees), **Supp. XV:** 133

"Day-Breakers, The" (Bontemps), **Supp. XXII:** 8

"Daybreak in Alabama" (Hughes), **Retro. Supp. I:** 211; **Supp. I Part 1:** 344

Day by Day (Lowell), **Retro. Supp. II:** 184, 186, 191

"Day-Care Field Trip: Aquarium" (Karr), **Supp. XI:** 243

"Day-Dream, A" (Bryant), **Supp. I Part 1:** 160

"Day-Dream of a Grocer, The" (Twain), **Supp. XVIII:** 9

"Day for Poetry and Song, A" (Douglass), **Supp. III Part 1:** 172

"Day in the Life of Half of Rumpel-stiltskin, A" (Brockmeier), **Supp. XXII:** 50, 52, 53

"Day Lady Died, The" (O'Hara), **Supp. XIX:** 85; **Supp. XXIII:** 216, 219

Day Late and a Dollar Short, A (McMillan), **Supp. XIII:** 184, **Supp. XIII:** 185, **191–192**

"Day longs for the evening, The" (Levertov), **Supp. III Part 1:** 274

Daynard, Jodi, **Supp. XVIII:** 97

Day of a Stranger (Merton), **Supp. VIII:** 203

"Day of Days, A" (James), **II:** 322

Day of Doom (Wigglesworth), **IV:** 147, 155, 156

Day of the Body (C. Frost), **Supp. XV:** 93, **98–100,** 106

Day of the Locust, The (West), **I:** 298; **IV:** 288, 299–306; **Retro. Supp. II:** 321, 323, 324, 329, **337–338; Supp. II Part 2:** 626; **Supp. XI:** 296; **Supp. XII:** 173; **Supp. XIII:** 170; **Supp. XIV:** 328; **Supp. XVIII:** 246

"Day of Wrath" (Davison), **Supp. XXVI:** 74

"Day on the Big Branch, A" (Nemerov), **III:** 275–276

"Day on the Connecticut River, A" (Merrill), **Supp. III Part 1:** 336

Day Room, The (DeLillo), **Supp. VI:** 4

"Days" (Emerson), **II:** 19, 20

"Days and Nights" (Koch), **Supp. XV:** 179, 180

"Days and Nights: A Journal" (Price), **Supp. VI:** 265

Days Before, The (Porter), **III:** 433, 453

Days in the Yellow Leaf (Hoffman), **Supp. XVIII:** 75

"Days of 1935" (Merrill), **Supp. III Part 1:** 325, 328

"Days of 1941 and '44" (Merrill), **Supp. III Part 1:** 336

"Days of 1964" (Merrill), **Supp. III Part 1:** 328, 352

"Days of 1971" (Merrill), **Supp. III Part 1:** 328

"Days of 1981" (Doty), **Supp. XI:** 123

"Days of Awe: The Birth of Lucy Jane" (Wasserstein), **Supp. XV:** 332

"Days of Edward Hopper" (Haines), **Supp. XII:** 210

"Days of Heaven" (Bass), **Supp. XVI:** 20

Days of Obligation: An Argument with My Mexican Father (Rodriguez),

Supp. XIV: 298, 300, **302–305,** 307, 310

Days of Our Lives (soap opera), **Supp. XI:** 83

Days of Our Lives Lie in Fragments: New and Old Poems (Garrett), **Supp. VII:** 109–110, 111

Days of the Phoenix (Brooks), **I:** 266

Days of Wine and Roses (J. P. Miller), **Supp. XIII:** 262

Days: Tangier Journal, 1987–1989 (Bowles), **Supp. IV Part 1:** 94

Days to Come (Hellman), **Supp. I Part 1:** 276, 277–278

Days without End (O'Neill), **III:** 385, 391, 397

"Day's Work, A" (Capote), **Supp. III Part 1:** 120

"Day's Work, A" (Porter), **III:** 443, 446

"Day the Presidential Candidate Came to Ciudad Tamaulipas, The" (Caldwell), **I:** 309

"Day the Singer Fell, The" (Swados), **Supp. XIX:** 258

Day the World ended, The (Coover), **Supp. V:** 1

"Day with Conrad Green, A" (Lardner), **II:** 428–429, 430

"Deacon, The" (Huddle), **Supp. XXVI:** 151, 153–154, 158

"Deacon's Masterpiece, The" (Holmes), **Supp. I Part 1:** 302, 307

"Dead, The" (Collins), **Supp. XXI:** 64

"Dead, The" (Joyce), **I:** 285; **III:** 343; **Supp. XXIII:** 71

"Dead, The" (Very), **Supp. XXV:** 249

Dead and the Living, The (Olds), **Supp. X:** 201, **204–206,** 207

"Dead Body, The" (Olds), **Supp. X:** 210

"Dead by the Side of the Road, The" (Snyder), **Supp. VIII:** 301

"Dead Doe" (B. Kelly), **Supp. XVII:** 128–129

Dead End (Kingsley), **Supp. I Part 1:** 277, 281

Dead Father, The (Barthelme), **Supp. IV Part 1:** 43, 47, 50–51

"Dead Fiddler, The" (Singer), **IV:** 20

Dead Fingers Talk (Burroughs), **Supp. III Part 1:** 103

"Dead Hand" series (Sinclair), **Supp. V:** 276, 277, 281

"Dead Language Lessons" (Stallings), **Supp. XXV:** 233

"Dead Languages, The" (Humphrey), **Supp. IX:** 109

Dead Lecturer, The (Baraka), **Supp. II Part 1:** 31, 33, 35–37, 49

Dead Letters Sent (Kenny), **Supp. XXIII:** 143, 145

"Dead Letters Sent (By the Ontario Shores)"(Kenny), **Supp. XXIII:** 145

Deadline at Dawn (Odets), **Supp. II Part 2:** 546

Deadlock (Paretsky), **Supp. XXV:** 173, 176, 178–179

"Dead-Lock and Its Key, A" (E. Stoddard), **Supp. XV:** 286

"Dead Loon, The" (Bynner), **Supp. XV:** **44–45**

Deadly Affair, A (Lacy), **Supp. XV:** 205–206

Deadly is the Female (film), **Supp. XVII:** 62

Dead Man's Walk (McMurtry), **Supp. V:** 231, 232

Dead Man's Walk (screenplay; McMurtry and Ossana), **Supp. V:** 231

Dead Man Walking (opera libretto, McNally), **Supp. XIII:** 207

Dead Poets Society (film), **Supp. XXI:** 192, 193, 194, 199

"Dead Reckoning" (Jarman), **Supp. XVII:** 113

"Dead Soldier's Talk, The" (Jin), **Supp. XVIII:** 92

Dead Souls (Gogol), **I:** 296

"Dead Souls on Campus" (Kosinski), **Supp. VII:** 222

"Dead Wingman, The" (Jarrell), **II:** 374

"Dead Wood, Green Wood" (Hadas), **Supp. XXIII:** 120

"Dead Yellow Women" (Hammett), **Supp. IV Part 1:** 345

Dead Zone, The (King), **Supp. V:** 139, 143, 144, 148, 152

Dean, James, **I:** 493

Dean, Man Mountain, **II:** 589

Deane, Silas, **Supp. I Part 2:** 509, 524

"Dean of Men" (Taylor), **Supp. V:** 314, 323

Dean's December, The (Bellow), **Retro. Supp. II:** 30–31

"Dear Adolph" (Benét), **Supp. XI:** 46

"Dear America" (Ortiz), **Supp. IV Part 2:** 503

"Dear Dark Continent" (Notley), **Supp. XXII:** 223

"Dearest M—" (Carruth), **Supp. XVI:** 59

Dear Ghosts (Gallagher), **Supp. XXIV:** 166, 167, 170–171, 176

"Dear Judas" (Jeffers), **Supp. II Part 2:** 431–432, 433

Dear Juliette (Sarton), **Supp. VIII:** 265

Dear Lovely Death (Hughes), **Retro. Supp. I:** 203; **Supp. I Part 1:** 328

"Dear Mr. Walrus" (Boyle), **Supp. XXIV:** 58–59

Dear Rafe (Hinojosa), **Supp. XIX:** 98, **105–106**

"Dear Smoker" (Biss), **Supp. XXVI:** 51

"Dear Villon" (Corso), **Supp. XII:** 135

"Dear World" (Gunn Allen), **Supp. IV Part 1:** 321

Deasy, Philip, **Supp. XX: 42**

Death (Allen), **Supp. XV:** 3

"Death" (Corso), **Supp. XII:** 127

"Death" (Lowell), **II:** 536

"Death" (Mailer), **III:** 38

"Death" (W. C. Williams), **Retro. Supp. I:** 422

"Death" (West), **IV:** 286

"Death, Decay and Change" (Very), **Supp. XXV:** 243

"Death and Absence" (Glück), **Supp. V:** 82

Death and Birth of David Markand, The (W. Frank), **Supp. XX: 76–77**

Death and Taxes (Parker), **Supp. IX:** 192

"Death and the Child" (Crane), **I:** 414

"Death as a Society Lady" (Hecht), **Supp. X:** 71–72

Death before Bedtime (Vidal as Box), **Supp. IV Part 2:** 682

"Death Be Not Proud" (Donne), **Supp. XVI:** 158

"Death by Water" (Eliot), **I:** 395, 578

Death Comes for the Archbishop (Cather), **I:** 314, 327, 328–330; **Retro. Supp. I:** 16–18, 21; **Supp. XIII:** 253; **Supp. XXIV:** 253

Death in Paradise (Parker), **Supp. XIX:** 186

Death in the Afternoon (Hemingway), **II:** 253; **IV:** 35; **Retro. Supp. I:** 182; **Supp. VIII:** 182; **Supp. XIX:** 246; **Supp. XVI:** 205; **Supp. XX: 76**

"Death in the Country, A" (Benét), **Supp. XI:** 53–54

Death in the Family, A (Agee), **I:** 25, 29, 42, 45

Death in the Fifth Position (Vidal as Box), **Supp. IV Part 2:** 682

"Death in the Woods" (Anderson), **I:** 114, 115; **Supp. XXIV:** 136

Death in the Woods and Other Stories (Anderson), **I:** 112, 114, 115

Death in Venice (Mann), **III:** 231; **Supp. IV Part 1:** 392; **Supp. V:** 51

"Death in Viet Nam" (Salinas), **Supp. XIII:** 315

"Death in Winter" (C. Frost), **Supp. XV:** 98

Death Is a Lonely Business (Bradbury), **Supp. IV Part 1:** 102, 103, 111–112, 115

"Death Is Not the End" (Wallace), **Supp. X:** 309

Death Is the Place (Bronk), **Supp. XXI:** 32

Death Kit (Sontag), **Supp. III Part 2:** 451, 468–469

"Deathlight" (Huddle), **Supp. XXVI:** 150

Death Likes It Hot (Vidal as Box), **Supp. IV Part 2:** 682

"*Death*/Muerta" (Mora), **Supp. XIII:** 228

Death Notebooks, The (Sexton), **Supp. II Part 2:** 691, 694, 695

"Death of a Columnist" (Siddons), **Supp. XXII:** 241–242

Death of Adam, The: Essays on Modern Thought (Robinson), **Supp. XXI:** 212

"Death of a Jazz Musician" (W. J. Smith), **Supp. XIII:** 334

Death of a Kinsman, The (Taylor), **Supp. V:** 324, 326

Death of a Man (Boyle), **Supp. XXIV:** 60

"Death of an Old Seaman" (Hughes), **Retro. Supp. I:** 199

"Death of a Pig" (White), **Supp. I Part 2:** 665–668

Death of a Salesman (A. Miller), **I:** 81; **III:** 148, 149, 150, 153–154, 156, 157, 158, 159, 160, 163, 164, 166; **IV:** 389; **Supp. IV Part 1:** 359; **Supp. XIV:** 102, 239, 254, 255; **Supp. XV:** 205; **Supp. XX: 27; Supp. XXIII:** 199

"Death of a Soldier, The" (Stevens), **Retro. Supp. I:** 299, 312. *see also*

"Lettres d'un Soldat" (Stevens)

"Death of a Soldier, The" (Wilson), **IV:** 427, 445

"Death of a Toad" (Wilbur), **Supp. III Part 2:** 550

"Death of a Traveling Salesman" (Welty), **IV:** 261; **Retro. Supp. I:** 344

"Death of a Young Son by Drowning" (Atwood), **Supp. XIII:** 33

Death of Bessie Smith, The (Albee), **I:** 76–77, 92

Death of Billy the Kid, The (Vidal), **Supp. IV Part 2:** 683

Death of Cock Robin, The (Snodgrass), **Supp. VI:** 315, **317–319,** 324

Death of Dreams, A (Hoffman), **Supp. XVIII:** 79

"Death of General Wolfe, The" (Paine), **Supp. I Part 2:** 504

"Death of Halpin Frayser, The" (Bierce), **I:** 205

"Death of Justina, The" (Cheever), **Supp. I Part 1:** 184–185

Death of Life, The (Barnes), **Supp. III Part 1:** 34

Death of Malcolm X, The (Baraka), **Supp. II Part 1:** 47

"Death of Marilyn Monroe, The" (Olds), **Supp. X:** 205

"Death of Me, The" (Malamud), **Supp. I Part 2:** 437

"Death of Slavery, The" (Bryant), **Supp. I Part 1:** 168–169

"Death of St. Narcissus, The" (Eliot), **Retro. Supp. I:** 291

"Death of the Ball Turret Gunner, The" (Jarrell), **II:** 369–370, 372, 374, 375, 376, 378

"Death of the Fathers, The" (Sexton), **Supp. II Part 2:** 692

"Death of the Flowers, The" (Bryant), **Supp. I Part 1:** 170

Death of the Fox (Garrett), **Supp. VII:** 99, 101–104, 108

"Death of the Hat, The" (Collins), **Supp. XXI:** 59

"Death of the Hired Man, The" (Frost), **III:** 523; **Retro. Supp. I:** 121, 128; **Supp. IX:** 261

Death of the Kapowsin Tavern (Hugo), **Supp. VI:** 133–135

"Death of the Kapowsin Tavern" (Hugo), **Supp. VI:** 137, 141

"Death of the Lyric, The: The Achievement of Louis Simpson" (Jarman and McDowell), **Supp. IX:** 266, 270, 276

"Death of the Virgin, The (Rembrandt)" (Davison), **Supp. XXVI:** 70

"Death of Venus, The" (Creeley), **Supp. IV Part 1:** 143, 144–145

"Death on All Fronts" (Ginsberg), **Supp. II Part 1:** 326

"Deaths" (Dunn), **Supp. XI:** 147

"Death Sauntering About" (Hecht), **Supp. X:** 72

Deaths for the Ladies (and Other Disasters) (Mailer), **Retro. Supp. II:** 203

Death's Jest-Book (Beddoes), **Retro. Supp. I:** 285

Death Song (McGrath), **Supp. X:** 127

"Death the Carnival Barker" (Hecht), **Supp. X:** 72

"Death the Film Director" (Hecht), **Supp. X:** 72

"Death the Judge" (Hecht), **Supp. X:** 72

"Death the Mexican Revolutionary" (Hecht), **Supp. X:** 72

"Death the Oxford Don" (Hecht), **Supp. X:** 72

"Death the Painter" (Hecht), **Supp. X:** 72

Death the Proud Brother (Wolfe), **IV:** 456

"Death to Van Gogh's Ear!" (Ginsberg), **Supp. II Part 1:** 320, 322, 323

"Death Warmed Over!" (Bradbury), **Supp. IV Part 1:** 104–105, 112

Death Wish, The (Holding), **Supp. XXII:** 120, **123,** 134, 135

Deaver, Philip F., **Supp. XXVI:** 151, 160–161

Débâcle, La (Zola), **III:** 316

"Debate with the Rabbi" (Nemerov), **III:** 272

Debeljak, Ale&sacaron;, **Supp. VIII:** 272

De Bellis, Jack, **Supp. I Part 1:** 366, 368, 372

Debo, Annette, **Supp. XXI:** 254

DeBoer-Langworthy, Carol, **Supp. XVII:** 98, 99, 100

DeBold, Kathleen, **Supp. XXV:** 4

De Bosis, Lauro, **IV:** 372

"Debriefing" (Sontag), **Supp. III Part 2:** 468–470

Debs, Eugene, **I:** 483, 493; **III:** 580, 581; **Supp. I Part 2:** 524; **Supp. IX:** 1, 15; **Supp. XXIII:** 161, 162

Debt to Pleasure, The (Lanchester), **Retro. Supp. I:** 278

Debussy, Claude, **Retro. Supp. II:** 266; **Supp. XIII:** 44

"Decades" (Sorrentino), **Supp. XXI:** 229

Decameron (Boccaccio), **III:** 283, 411; **Supp. IX:** 215

"Deceased" (Hughes), **Retro. Supp. I:** 208

"December" (Oliver), **Supp. VII:** 245

"December 1, 1994" (Stern), **Supp. IX:** 299

December 7 (film, Ford), **Supp. XVIII:** 247

"December 24" (Di Piero), **Supp. XIX:** 39

"December 28: Returning to Chicago" (Di Piero), **Supp. XIX:** 39

"December Dawn" (Skloot), **Supp. XX: 202**

"December Eclogue" (Winters), **Supp. II Part 2:** 794

"Decent Woman, A" (Boulton), **Supp. XXII:** 22–23

De Cenzo, Giorgia, **Supp. XXI:** 256

Deception (P. Roth), **Retro. Supp. II:** 291; **Supp. III Part 2:** 426–427

"Deceptions" (Dobyns), **Supp. XIII:** 77

De Chiara, Ann. *See* Malamud, Mrs. Bernard (Ann de Chiara)

De Chirico, Giorgio, **Supp. XIII:** 317

"Decided Loss, A" (Poe), **II:** 411

"Decision" (Boyle), **Supp. XXIV:** 54

"Decisions to Disappear" (Dunn), **Supp. XI:** 144

"Decisive Moment, The" (Auster), **Supp. XIV:** 292

Decker, James A., **Supp. III Part 2:** 621

Declaration of Gentlemen and Merchants and Inhabitants of Boston, and the Country Adjacent, A (Mather), **Supp. II Part 2:** 450

"Declaration of Paris, The" (Adams), **I:** 4

Declaration of the Rights of Man and the Citizen, **Supp. I Part 2:** 513, 519

Declaration of Universal Peace and Liberty (Paine), **Supp. I Part 2:** 512

Declension in the Village of Chung Luong (Weigl), **Supp. XIX:** 287, 288

Decline and Fall (Waugh), **Supp. I Part 2:** 607; **Supp. XV:** 142

Decline and Fall of the English System of Finance, The (Paine), **Supp. I Part 2:** 518

Decline and Fall of the Roman Empire, The (Gibbons), **Supp. III Part 2:** 629

"Decline of Book Reviewing, The" (Hardwick), **Supp. III Part 1:** 201–202

Decline of the West, The (Spengler), **I:** 270; **IV:** 125

"Decolonizing the Tongue: Reading Speech and Aphasia in the Work of Michelle Cliff" (Aguiar), **Supp. XXII:** 68

Deconstructing Harry (film; Allen), **Supp. XV:** 12, **13**

"Décor" (X. J. Kennedy), **Supp. XV:** 171

"Decoration Day" (Jewett), **II:** 412; **Retro. Supp. II:** 138

Decoration of Houses, The (Wharton and Codman), **IV:** 308; **Retro. Supp. I:** 362, 363–364, 366

"Decoy" (Ashbery), **Supp. III Part 1:** 13–14

Decter, Midge, **Supp. XX: 248**

Dedalus, Stephen, **Supp. XIX:** 47

"De Daumier-Smith's Blue Period" (Salinger), **III:** 560–561

"Dedication" (Nelson), **Supp. XVIII:** 173, 180

"Dedication and Household Map" (Erdrich), **Supp. IV Part 1:** 272

"Dedication Day" (Agee), **I:** 34

"Dedication for a Book" (Hay), **Supp. XIV:** 125

"Dedication for a Book of Criticism" (Winters), **Supp. II Part 2:** 801

"Dedication in Postscript, A" (Winters), **Supp. II Part 2:** 801

Dedications and Other Darkhorses (Komunyakaa), **Supp. XIII:** 112, **113–114**

"Dedication to Hunger" (Glück), **Supp. V:** 83

"Dedication to My Wife, A" (Eliot), **I:** 583

Dee, Jonathan, **Supp. XXIII:** 302

Dee, Ruby, **Supp. IV Part 1:** 362

Deeck, William, **Supp. XXVI:** 278

Deeds of Utmost Kindness (Gander), **Supp. XV:** 340

Deegan, Thomas, **Supp. XXIII:** 100, 107–108

"Deep Breath at Dawn, A" (Hecht), **Supp. X:** 58

Deep End, The (film), **Supp. XXII:** 120, 131, 133

Deeper into Movies: The Essential Kael Collection from '69 to '72 (Kael), **Supp. IX:** 253

"Deeper Wisdom, The" (Hay), **Supp. XIV:** 129

Deep Green Sea (R. O. Butler), **Supp. XII:** 62, **74**

Deephaven (Jewett), **II:** 398–399, 400, 401, 410, 411; **Retro. Supp. II:** 133, 134, 135, 136, 137, 138, 140, 141, 143, 144

"Deep Sight and Rescue Missions" (Bambara), **Supp. XI:** 18–19

Deep Sightings and Rescue Missions: Fiction, Essays, and Conversations (Bambara), **Supp. XI:** 1, 3, **14–20**

Deep Sleep, The (Morris), **III:** 224–225

"Deep Song" (G. Jones), **Supp. XXIV:** 194

Deep South (Caldwell), **I:** 305, 309, 310

Deepstep Come Shining (Wright), **Supp. XV:** 337, 341, 344, **349–350,** 351, 353

"Deep Water" (Marquand), **III:** 56

"Deep Woods" (Nemerov), **III:** 272–273, 275

"Deer at Providencia, The" (Dillard), **Supp. VI:** 28, 32

Deer Camp: Last Light in the Northeast Kingdom (Ostrum, ed.), **Supp. XXII:** 218

"Deer Dancer" (Harjo), **Supp. XII:** 224–225

"Deer Ghost" (Harjo), **Supp. XII:** 225

Deer Park, The (Mailer), **I:** 292; **III:** 27, 31–33, 35–36, 37, 39, 40, 42, 43, 44; **Retro. Supp. II: 200–202,** 205, 207, 211

Deer Park, The: A Play (Mailer), **Retro. Supp. II:** 205

Deer Pasture, The (Bass), **Supp. XVI:** 15, 16, 23

Deerslayer, The (Cooper), **I:** 341, 349, 350, 355; **Supp. I Part 1:** 251

Deese, Helen, **Supp. XXV:** 251

"Defeat" (Boyle), **Supp. XXIV: 60–61**

Defence, The (Nabokov), **Supp. XXII:** 263

"Defence of Poesie, The" (Bronk), **Supp. XXI:** 32

"Defence of Poesy, The" (Sidney), **Supp. V:** 250

"Defence of Poetry" (Longfellow), **II:** 493–494

"Defender of the Faith" (P. Roth), **Retro. Supp. II:** 281; **Supp. III Part 2:** 404, 407, 420

"Defending *The Searchers* (Scenes in the Life of an Obsession)" (Lethem), *Supp. XVIII:* 136,141

"Defenestration in Prague" (Matthews), **Supp. IX:** 168

Defenestration of Prague (Howe), **Supp. IV Part 2:** 419, 426, 429–430

Defense, The (Nabokov), **III:** 251–252; **Retro. Supp. I:** 266, 268, **270–272**

"Defense of Poetry" (Francis), **Supp. IX:** 83–84

DeFeo, Ronald, **Supp. XXIII:** 106

Defiant Ones, The (film), **Supp. I Part 1:** 67

"Defining the Age" (W. V. Davis), **Supp. IV Part 1:** 64

"Definition" (Ammons), **Supp. VII:** 28

Defoe, Daniel, **I:** 204; **II:** 104, 105, 159, 304–305; **III:** 113, 423; **IV:** 180; **Supp. I Part 2:** 523; **Supp. V:** 127

De Forest, John William, **II:** 275, 280, 288, 289; **IV:** 350

DeFrees, Madeline, **Supp. XVIII:** 293; **Supp. XXVI:** 180

Deganawida, the Peacemaker, **Supp. XXVI: 81–100**

"Deganawidah: The Peacemaker"(Kenny), **Supp. XXIII:** 151

Degas, Brian, **Supp. XI:** 307

Degler, Carl, **Supp. I Part 2:** 496

"Degrees of Fidelity" (Dunn), **Supp. XI:** 148, 156

Deguy, Michel, **Supp. XV:** 178

De Haven, Tom, **Supp. XI:** 39; **Supp. XII:** 338–339

Deitch, Joseph, **Supp. VIII:** 125

"Dejection" (Coleridge), **II:** 97

DeJong, Constance, **Supp. XII:** 4

DeJong, David Cornel, **I:** 35

Dekker,Thomas, **Supp. XVII:** 232

de Kooning, Elaine de, **Supp. XXIII:** 210, 217

de Kooning, Willem, **Supp. XII:** 198; **Supp. XV:** 177, 178

de Kooning, Willem de, **Supp. XXIII:** 208, 210, 211, 217, 220

Delacroix, Henri, **I:** 227

De La Mare, Walter, **III:** 429; **Supp. II Part 1:** 4; **Supp. XVII:** 69

Delamotte, Eugenia C., **Supp. XI:** 279

De Lancey, James, **I:** 338

De Lancey, Mrs. James (Anne Heathcote), **I:** 338

De Lancey, Susan A. *See* Cooper, Mrs. James Fenimore

De Lancey, William Heathcote, **I:** 338, 353

Delano, Amasa, **III:** 90

De la Paz, Oliver, **Supp. XXVI:** 101, 103, 111

Delattre, Roland A., **I:** 558

De Laurentiis, Dino, **Supp. XI:** 170, 307

De la Valdéne, Guy, **Supp. VIII:** 40, 42

Delbanco, Andrew, **Supp. XXIV:** 69

Delbanco, Nicholas, **Supp. XXII:** 204

Del Cabral, Manuel, **Supp. XXI:** 104

DelCorso's Gallery (Caputo), **Supp. XIX:** 22–23

Delectorskaya, Lydia, **Supp. XXII:** 99

De l'éducation d'un homme sauvage (Itard), **Supp. I Part 2:** 564

Deleuze, Gilles, **Supp. XXV:** 123

"Delft" (Goldbarth), **Supp. XII:** 189

Delft: An Essay-Poem (Goldbarth), **Supp. XII:** 187

Delicate Balance, A (Albee), **I:** 86–89, 91, 93, 94

Delicate Balance, The (Hay), **Supp. XIV:** 121, 122, 124, 129, 133–134

"Delicate Balance, The" (Hay), **Supp. XIV:** 122

"Delicate Prey, The" (Bowles), **Supp. IV Part 1:** 86

Delicate Prey and Other Stories, The (Bowles), **Supp. IV Part 1:** 86–87

Délie (Scève), **Supp. III Part 1:** 11

Delights & Shadows (Kooser), **Supp. XIX:** 115, 116, 117, 121, **127–128**

DeLillo, Don, **Retro. Supp. I:** 278; **Retro. Supp. II:** 279; **Supp. IX:** 212; **Supp. VI: 1–18; Supp. XI:** 68; **Supp. XII:** 21, 152; **Supp. XIX:** 54; **Supp. XVII:** 183; **Supp. XVIII:** 136, 140; **Supp. XX: 83, 87, 91; Supp. XXIII:** 109

De Lint, Charles, **Supp. XXII:** 59

DeLisle, Anne, **Supp. VIII:** 175

Deliverance (Dickey), **Supp. IV Part 1:** 176, 186–188, 190; **Supp. X:** 30; **Supp. XX: 173–174; Supp. XXIII:** 43, 50

Deliverance, The (Glasgow), **II:** 175, 176, 177–178, 181

"Delivering" (Dubus), **Supp. VII:** 87

Dell, Floyd, **I:** 103, 105; **Supp. I Part 2:** 379; **Supp. XV:** 295; **Supp. XVII:** 96; **Supp. XXI:** 6; **Supp. XXII:** 275; **Supp. XXV:** 18

Della Francesca, Piero, **Supp. XV:** 262

"Della Primavera Trasportata al Morale" (W. C. Williams), **Retro. Supp. I:** 419, 422

DeLoria, Philip J., **Supp. XIV:** 306

Deloria, Vine, Jr., **Supp. IV Part 1:** 323; **Supp. IV Part 2:** 504; **Supp. XXVI:** 98

"Delta Autumn" (Faulkner), **II:** 71

"Delta Factor, The" (Percy), **Supp. III Part 1:** 386

Delta of Venus: Erotica (Nin), **Supp. X:** 192, 195

Delta Wedding (Welty), **IV:** 261, 268–271, 273, 281; **Retro. Supp. I:** 349–350, 351

Delusions (Berryman), **I:** 170

De Man, Paul, **Retro. Supp. I:** 67; **Supp. XVII:** 70

DeMarinis, Rick, **Supp. XIV:** 22

DeMars, James, **Supp. IV Part 2:** 552

Dembo, L. S., **I:** 386, 391, 396, 397, 398, 402; **III:** 478; **Supp. I Part 1:** 272; **Supp. XIV:** 277, 282, 288, 290; **Supp. XXVI:** 226, 226–227, 235

"Dementia Translucida" (Bierds), **Supp. XVII:** 33

"Demeter"(Crooker), **Supp. XXIII:** 61

"Demeters"(Hadas), **Supp. XXIII:** 113

Demetrakopoulous, Stephanie A., **Supp. IV Part 1:** 12

De Mille, Agnes, **Supp. XXVI:** 66

DeMille, Cecil B., **Supp. IV Part 2:** 520; **Supp. XV:** 42

Demme, Jonathan, **Supp. V:** 14

Democracy (Adams), **I:** 9–10, 20; **Supp. IV Part 1:** 208; **Supp. XIX:** 139

Democracy (Didion), **Supp. IV Part 1:** 198, 208–210

"Democracy" (Lowell), **Supp. I Part 2:** 419

Democracy and Education (Dewey), **I:** 232

Democracy and Other Addresses (Lowell), **Supp. I Part 2:** 407

Democracy and Social Ethics (Addams), **Supp. I Part 1:** 8–11

Democracy in America (Tocqueville), **Retro. Supp. I:** 235; **Supp. XIV:** 306

Democratic Vistas (Whitman), **IV:** 333, 336, 348–349, 351, 469; **Retro. Supp. I:** 408; **Supp. I Part 2:** 456

Democritus, **I:** 480–481; **II:** 157; **III:** 606; **Retro. Supp. I:** 247

"Demon Lover, The" (Rich), **Supp. I Part 2:** 556

"Demonstrators, The" (Welty), **IV:** 280; **Retro. Supp. I:** 355

DeMott, Benjamin, **Supp. IV Part 1:** 35; **Supp. V:** 123; **Supp. XIII:** 95; **Supp. XIV:** 106; **Supp. XXV:** 86

DeMott, Robert, **Supp. VIII:** 40, 41

Demuth, Charles, **IV:** 404; **Retro. Supp. I:** 412, 430; **Supp. XXI:** 6

"Demystified Zone" (Paley), **Supp. VI:** 227

Denby, Edwin, **Supp. XXIV:** 36, 45

Denmark Vesey (opera) (Bowles), **Supp. IV Part 1:** 83

Dennett, Daniel, **Supp. XXII:** 265

Denney, Joseph Villiers, **Supp. I Part 2:** 605

Denney, Reuel, **Supp. XII:** 121; **Supp. XXI:** 19

Dennie, Joseph, **II:** 298; **Supp. I Part 1:** 125

Denning, Michael, **Supp. XXVI:** 28

Denniston, Dorothy Hamer, **Supp. XI:** 276, 277

"Den of Lions" (Plath), **Retro. Supp. II:** 242

"Dental Assistant, The" (Simpson), **Supp. IX:** 280

Den Uyl, Douglas, **Supp. IV Part 2:** 528, 530

"Deodand, The" (Hecht), **Supp. X:** 65

"Departing" (Cameron), **Supp. XII:** 81

"Departure" (Glück), **Supp. V:** 89

"Departure" (Plath), **Supp. I Part 2:** 537

"Departure, The" (Freneau), **Supp. II Part 1:** 264

"Departure from Hydra, The" (Koch), **Supp. XV:** 180–181

Departures (Justice), **Supp. VII:** 124–127

Departures and Arrivals (Shields), **Supp. VII:** 320, 322

"Depressed by a Book of Bad Poetry, I Walk Toward an Unused Pasture and Invite the Insects to Join Me" (Wright), **Supp. III Part 2:** 600

"Depressed Person, The" (Wallace), **Supp. X:** 309

"Depression Days" (Mora), **Supp. XIII:** 224–225

"Deprived of Unhappiness" (Pickering), **Supp. XXI:** 203

De Puy, John, **Supp. XIII:** 12

De Quincey, Thomas, **Supp. XXVI:** 283

D'Erasmo, Stacey, **Supp. IX:** 121

Derby, J. C., **Supp. XVIII:** 4

De Reilhe, Catherine, **Supp. I Part 1:** 202

De Rerum Natura (Lucretius), **II:** 162

"De Rerum Virtute" (Jeffers), **Supp. II Part 2:** 424

De Rioja, Francisco, **Supp. I Part 1:** 166

"Derivative Sport in Tornado Alley" (Wallace), **Supp. X:** 314

Derleth, August, **Supp. I Part 2:** 465, 472; **Supp. XXV:** 111, 122

Deronda, Daniel, **II:** 179

Derricotte, Toi, **Supp. XVIII:** 177

Derrida, Jacques, **Supp. IV Part 1:** 45; **Supp. XV:** 215, 224; **Supp. XVI:** 285, 288

Deruddere, Dominique, **Supp. XI:** 173

Der Wilde Jäger (Bürger), **II:** 306

Derzhavin, Gavrila Romanovich, **Supp. VIII:** 27

Desai, Anita, **Supp. XVI:** 156, 157, 158

Désamère (Notley), **Supp. XXII:** 226

De Santis, Christopher, **Retro. Supp. I:** 194

Descartes, René, **I:** 255; **III:** 618–619; **IV:** 133

"Descendant of Solomon and the Queen of Sheba" (Major), **Supp. XXII:** 182

Descendents, The (Glasgow), **II:** 173, 174–175, 176

Descending Figure (Glück), **Supp. V:** 83–84

"Descending Theology: Christ Human" (Karr), **Supp. XI:** 251

"Descending Theology: The Garden" (Karr), **Supp. XI:** 251

"Descent, The" (W. C. Williams), **Retro. Supp. I:** 428, 429

"Descent from the Cross" (Eliot), **Retro. Supp. I:** 57, 58

"Descent in the Maelström, A" (Poe), **Retro. Supp. II:** 274

"Descent into Proselito" (Knowles), **Supp. XII:** 237

"Descent into the Maelström, A" (Poe), **III:** 411, 414, 416, 424

Descent of Alette, The (Notley), **Supp. XXII:** 223, 224, 226, 227, 233–234

Descent of Man (Boyle), **Supp. VIII:** 1, 12–13; **Supp. XX: 17, 18, 20**

"Descent of Man" (Boyle), **Supp. VIII:** 14; **Supp. XX: 18**

Descent of Man, The (Darwin), **Supp. XIV:** 192

Descent of Man, The (Wharton), **IV:** 311; **Retro. Supp. I:** 367

Descent of Man and Other Stories, The (Wharton), **Retro. Supp. I:** 367

Descent of Winter, The (W. C. Williams), **Retro. Supp. I:** 419, 428

De Schloezer, Doris, **III:** 474

"Describers" (Halliday), **Supp. XIX:** 85

"Description" (Doty), **Supp. XI:** 126

"Description of the great Bones dug up at Clavarack on the Banks of Hudsons River A.D. 1705, The" (Taylor), **IV:** 163, 164

"Description without Place" (Stevens), **Retro. Supp. I:** 422

"Desert" (Hughes), **Retro. Supp. I:** 207

"Deserted Cabin" (Haines), **Supp. XII:** 203

Deserted Village, The (Goldsmith), **II:** 304

Desert Is My Mother, The/El desierto es mi madre (Mora), **Supp. XIII:** 214, 221

Desert Music, The (W. C. Williams), **IV:** 422; **Retro. Supp. I:** 428, 429

"Desert Music, The" (W. C. Williams), **Retro. Supp. I:** 428, 429

"Desert Places" (Frost), **II:** 159; **Retro. Supp. I:** 121, 123, 129, 138, 299; **Supp. XIV:** 229

Desert Rose, The (McMurtry), **Supp. V:** 225, 231

Desert Solitaire (Abbey), **Supp. X:** 30; **Supp. XIII: 7–8,** 12; **Supp. XIV:** 177, 179

Desert Solitaire: A Season in the Wilderness (Abbey), **Supp. XXV:** 208

"Design" (Frost), **II:** 158, 163; **Retro. Supp. I:** 121, 126, 138, 139; **Supp. IX:** 81; **Supp. XVII:** 132; **Supp. XVIII:** 298

"Designated National Park, A" (Ortiz), **Supp. IV Part 2:** 509

"Designs on a Point of View" (Everwine), **Supp. XV:** 76

DeSilva, Bruce, **Supp. XXII:** 205, 206, 217

Des Imagistes (Pound), **II:** 513; **Supp. I Part 1:** 257, 261, 262

Desire (album, Dylan), **Supp. XVIII:** 28

"Desire" (Beattie), **Supp. V:** 29

Desire (Bidart), **Supp. XV: 32–34,** 35

"Desire" (Everwine), **Supp. XV:** 85

Desire, Desire, Desire (Durang), **Supp. XXIV:** 113

"Desire and Denial" (Bronk), **Supp. XXI:** 26

"Désirée's Baby" (Chopin), **Retro. Supp. II:** 64, 65; **Supp. I Part 1:** 213–215

"Desire"(Hadas), **Supp. XXIII:** 117

Desire under the Elms (O'Neill), **III:** 387, 390

"Desolate Field, The" (W. C. Williams), **Retro. Supp. I:** 418

"Desolation, A" (Ginsberg), **Supp. II Part 1:** 313

Desolation Angels (Kerouac), **Supp. III Part 1:** 218, 225, 230

"Desolation Is a Delicate Thing" (Wylie), Supp. I Part 2: 729

"Desolation Row" (song, Dylan), **Supp. XVIII:** 30

Despair (Nabokov), **Retro. Supp. I:** 270, 274

Desperate Characters (Fox), **Supp. XX: 91**

"Despisals" (Rukeyser), **Supp. VI:** 282

Des Pres, Terrence, **Supp. X:** 113, 120, 124

"Destiny and the Lieutenant" (McCoy), **Supp. XIII:** 171

"Destroyer, The" (Davison), **Supp. XXVI:** 71

"Destruction of Kreshev, The" (Singer), **IV:** 13; **Retro. Supp. II:** 307

Destruction of the European Jews, The (Hilberg), **Supp. V:** 267

"Destruction of the Goetheanum, The" (Salter), **Supp. IX:** 257

"Destruction of the Long Branch, The" (Pinsky), **Supp. VI:** 239, 240, 243–244, 245, 247, 250

Destructive Element, The (Spender), **Retro. Supp. I:** 216

"Detail & Parody for the poem 'Paterson' " (W. C. Williams), **Retro. Supp. I:** 424

Detmold, John, **Supp. I Part 2:** 670

De Tolnay, Charles, **Supp. XXII:** 255

Detour at Night (Endore), **Supp. XVII:** 64

Deuce, The (R. O. Butler), **Supp. XII:** 62, **69–70,** 72

Deus Lo Volt! (Connell), **Supp. XIV:** 80, 81, 95

Deuteronomy (biblical book), **II:** 166

Deutsch, Andre, **Supp. XI:** 297, 301

Deutsch, Babette, **Supp. I Part 1:** 328, 341; **Supp. XV:** 305; **Supp. XXV:** 21

Deutsch, Michel, **Supp. IV Part 1:** 104

"Devaluation Blues: Ruminations on Black Families in Crisis" (Coleman), **Supp. XI:** 87

Devane, William, **Supp. XI:** 234

Devasahayam, Madona, **Supp. XXII:** 260

"Development of My Mind and Character, The" (Notley), **Supp. XXII:** 227

"Development of the Literary West" (Chopin), **Retro. Supp. II:** 72

"Development of the Modern English Novel, The" (Lanier), **Supp. I Part 1:** 370–371

DeVeriante (Herbert of Cherbury), **II:** 108

"Devil and Daniel Webster, The" (Benét), **III:** 22; **Supp. XI:** 45–46, 47, 50–51, 52

Devil and Daniel Webster and Other Writings, The (Benét), **Supp. XI:** 48

"Devil and Tom Walker, The" (Irving), **II:** 309–310

Devil At Large, The: Erica Jong on Henry Miller (Jong), **Supp. V:** 115, 131

Devil-Doll, The (film, Browning), **Supp. XVII:** 58–59

Devil Finds Work, The (Baldwin), **Retro. Supp. II:** 14; **Supp. I Part 1:** 48, 52, 66–67

Devil in a Blue Dress (Mosley), **Supp. XIII:** 237, 239

"Devil in Manuscript, The" (Hawthorne), **II:** 226; **Retro. Supp. I:** 150–151

Devil in Paradise, A (H. Miller), **III:** 190

"Devil in the Belfry, The" (Poe), **III:** 425; **Retro. Supp. II:** 273

"Devil Is a Busy Man, The" (Wallace), **Supp. X:** 309

Devil's Dictionary, The (Bierce), **I:** 196, 197, 205, 208, 209, 210

Devil's Stocking, The (Algren), **Supp. IX:** 5, 16

"Devil's Thumb, The" (Krakauer), **Supp. XVIII:** 107

Devil's Tour, The (Karr), **Supp. XI:** 240, **242–244**

Devil Tree, The (Kosinski), **Supp. VII:** 215, 222, 223

"Devising" (Ammons), **Supp. VII:** 28

Devlin, Paul, **Supp. XIX:** 159

De Voe, Edward Thomas, **Supp. XXV:** 23, 29

De Voto, Bernard, **I:** 247, 248; **II:** 446; **Supp. IV Part 2:** 599, 601

"Devout Meditation in Memory of Adolph Eichmann, A" (Merton), **Supp. VIII:** 198, 203

De Vries, Peter, **Supp. I Part 2:** 604

Dewberry, Elizabeth, **Supp. XII:** 62, 72

Dewey, John, **I:** 214, 224, 228, 232, 233, 266, 267; **II:** 20, 27, 34, 229, 361; **III:** 112, 294–295, 296, 303, 309–310, 599, 605; **IV:** 27, 429; **Supp. I Part 1:** 3, 5, 7, 10, 11, 12, 24; **Supp. I Part 2:** 493, 641, 647, 677; **Supp. IX:** 179; **Supp. V:** 290; **Supp. XIV:** 3; **Supp. XV:** 41

Dewey, Joseph, **Supp. IX:** 210

Dewey, Thomas, **IV:** 161

Dewey Defeats Truman (Mallon), **Supp. XIX:** 132, 137, **138**

Dexter, Peter, **Supp. XIV:** 221

De Young, Charles, **I:** 194

Dhairyam, Sagari, **Supp. IV Part 1:** 329, 330

Dharma Bums, The (Kerouac), **Supp. III Part 1:** 230, 231; **Supp. VIII:** 289, 305

"D. H. Lawrence" (Bynner), **Supp. XV:** 46

D. H. Lawrence: An Unprofessional Study (Nin), **Supp. X:** 182–183

D. H. Lawrence: The World of the Major Novels (Sanders), **Supp. XVI:** 267

D'Houdetot, Madame, **Supp. I Part 1:** 250

"Diabetes" (Dickey), **Supp. IV Part 1:** 182

Diaghilev, Sergei, **Supp. I Part 1:** 257

Dial (publication), **I:** 58, 109, 115, 116, 215, 231, 233, 245, 261, 384, 429; **II:** 8, 430; **III:** 194, 470, 471, 485; **IV:** 122, 171, 427; **Retro. Supp. I:** 58; **Retro. Supp. II:** 78; **Supp. I Part 2:** 642, 643, 647; **Supp. II Part 1:** 168, 279, 291; **Supp. II Part 2:** 474; **Supp. III Part 2:** 611

"Dialectical Materialism" (Weigl), **Supp. XIX:** 281

Dialectical Materialism and the Fate of Humanity (C. L. R. James), **Supp. XXI:** 169

"Dialectics of Love, The" (McGrath), **Supp. X:** 116

"Dialogue" (Rich), **Supp. I Part 2:** 560

Dialogue, A (Baldwin and Giovanni), **Supp. I Part 1:** 66

"Dialogue Between Franklin and the Gout" (Franklin), **II:** 121

"Dialogue Between General Wolfe and General Gage in a Wood near Boston, A" (Paine), **Supp. I Part 2:** 504

"Dialogue between Old England and New" (Bradstreet), **Supp. I Part 1:**

105–106, 110–111, 116

"Dialogue between the Writer and a Maypole Dresser, A" (Taylor), **IV:** 155

Dialogues (Bush, ed.), **III:** 4

Dialogues in Limbo (Santayana), **III:** 606

"Dialogue: William Harvey; Joan of Arc" (Goldbarth), **Supp. XII:** 178

Dialogue with a Dead Man (J. W. Miller), **Supp. XX:** 163, 164, 167

"Diamond as Big as the Ritz, The" (Fitzgerald), **II:** 88–89

Diamond Cutters and Other Poems, The (Rich), **Supp. I Part 2:** 551, 552, 553

"Diamond Guitar, A" (Capote), **Supp. III Part 1:** 124

Diamond Necklace, A (Notley), **Supp. XXII:** 228

"Diana and Persis" (Alcott), **Supp. I Part 1:** 32, 41

"Diaper Brigade, The" (Ryan as Quin), **Supp. XVIII:** 230

Diaries of Charlotte Perkins Gilman (Knight, ed.), **Supp. XI:** 201

"Diary–1903" (Boyce), **Supp. XXI:** 8

Diary of a Chambermaid, The (film; Renoir), **Supp. XVI:** 193

*Diary of Anaïs Nin, The (1931–1974), **Supp. X:** 181, 185–189, 191, 192, 193, 195

Diary of Anne Frank, The, **Supp. XXI:** 245

Diary of a Rapist, The: A Novel (Connell), **Supp. XIV:** 80, 82, 94

Diary of a Yuppie (Auchincloss), **Supp. IV Part 1:** 31, 32–33

Diary of "Helena Morley", The (Bishop, trans.), **Retro. Supp. II:** 45, 51; **Supp. I Part 1:** 92

Dias, Robert Vas, **Supp. XXII:** 164, 169

Díaz, Junot, **Supp. XXIV: 83–95; Supp. XXV:** 49, 61

Díaz del Castillo, Bernál, **III:** 13, 14

Dick, Philip K., **Supp. XVI:** 123; **Supp. XVIII:** 136, 137, 138, 139, 142; **Supp. XXII:** 49

Dickens, Charles, **I:** 152, 198, 505; **II:** 98, 179, 186, 192, 271, 273–274, 288, 290, 297, 301, 307, 316, 322, 559, 561, 563, 577, 582; **III:** 146, 247, 325, 368, 411, 421, 426, 572, 577, 613–614, 616; **IV:** 21, 192, 194, 211, 429; **Retro. Supp. I:** 33, 91, 218; **Retro. Supp. II:** 204; **Supp. I Part 1:** 13, 34, 35, 36, 41, 49; **Supp. I Part 2:** 409, 523, 579, 590, 622, 675; **Supp. IV Part 1:** 293, 300, 341; **Supp. IV Part 2:** 464; **Supp. IX:** 246; **Supp. VIII:** 180; **Supp. XI:** 277; **Supp. XII:** 335, 337; **Supp. XIII:** 233; **Supp. XV:** 62; **Supp. XVI:** 63, 65–66, 72–73, 202; **Supp. XVIII:** 7, 136, 146; **Supp. XX: 21, 87, 195; Supp. XXII:** 206; **Supp. XXIII:** 4, 85, 290; **Supp. XXIV:** 87; **Supp. XXV:** 258

Dickey, James, **I:** 29, 535; **III:** 268; **Retro. Supp. II:** 233; **Supp. III Part 1:** 354; **Supp. III Part 2:** 541, 597; **Supp. IV Part 1: 175–194; Supp. V:** 333; **Supp. X:** 30; **Supp. XI:** 312, 317; **Supp. XIX:** 282; **Supp. XV:** 115,

348; **Supp. XVIII:** 191, 299; **Supp. XXI:** 35; **Supp. XXIII:** 43, 50; **Supp. XXIV:** 42; **Supp. XXVI:** 67

Dick Gibson Show, The (Elkin), **Supp. VI:** 42, **48–49**

Dickie, Margaret, **Retro. Supp. II:** 53, 84

Dickinson, Donald, **Retro. Supp. I:** 206, 212

Dickinson, Edward, **I:** 451–452, 453

Dickinson, Mrs. Edward, **I:** 451, 453

Dickinson, Emily, **I:** 384, 419, 433, **451–473; II:** 272, 276, 277, 530; **III:** 19, 194, 196, 214, 493, 505, 508, 556, 572, 576; **IV:** 134, 135, 331, 444; **Retro. Supp. I: 25–50; Retro. Supp. II:** 39, 40, 43, 45, 50, 76, 134, 155, 170; **Supp. I Part 1:** 29, 79, 188, 372; **Supp. I Part 2:** 375, 546, 609, 682, 691; **Supp. II Part 1:** 4; **Supp. III Part 1:** 63; **Supp. III Part 2:** 600, 622; **Supp. IV Part 1:** 31, 257; **Supp. IV Part 2:** 434, 637, 641, 643; **Supp. IX:** 37, 38, 53, 87, 90; **Supp. V:** 79, 140, 332, 335; **Supp. VIII:** 95, 104, 106, 108, 198, 205, 272; **Supp. XII:** 226; **Supp. XIII:** 153, 339; **Supp. XIV:** 45, 127–128, 133, 261, 284; **Supp. XIX:** 86; **Supp. XV:** 287, 303, 309; **Supp. XVI:** 288; **Supp. XVII:** 71, 73, 74, 75, 132; **Supp. XVIII:** 301; **Supp. XX: 106, 108; Supp. XXI:** 52, 61, 64, 132, 214; **Supp. XXII:** 81, 82, 225, 277–278; **Supp. XXIII:** 19, 165

Dickinson, Gilbert, **I:** 469

Dickinson, Goldsworthy Lowes, **Supp. XIV:** 336

Dickinson, Lavinia Norcross, **I:** 451, 453, 462, 470

Dickinson, Stephanie, **Supp. XXIII:** 250

Dickinson, Mrs. William A. (Susan Gilbert), **I:** 452, 453, 456, 469, 470

Dickinson, William Austin, **I:** 451, 453, 469

Dickinson and the Strategies of Reticence (Dobson), **Retro. Supp. I:** 29, 42

Dickson, Helen. *See* Blackmur, Helen Dickson

Dickstein, Morris, **Supp. XIII:** 106; **Supp. XXIV:** 222, 223

"Dick Whittington and His Cat", **Supp. I Part 2:** 656

"DICTATORSHIP OF THE PROLE-TARIAT, THE" (Baraka), **Supp. II Part 1:** 54

Dictionary of Afro-American Slang (Major), **Supp. XXII:** 172, 174, 180

Dictionary of Literary Biography (Barron and Meyer, eds.), **Supp. XIX:** 195; **Supp. XVIII:** 173

Dictionary of Literary Biography (Gwynn, ed.), **Supp. XIX:** 121; **Supp. XVIII:** 173

Dictionary of Literary Biography (Kibler, ed.), **Supp. IX:** 94, 109; **Supp. XI:** 297

Dictionary of Literary Biography (Knight, ed.), **Supp. XIV:** 144

Dictionary of Literary Biography (Martine, ed.), **Supp. XXII:** 187

Dictionary of Literary Biography (Sicher, ed.), **Supp. XVII:** 41

Dictionary of Literary Biography (Twentieth-Century American Nature Poets, Bryson and Thompson, eds.), **Supp. XXIII:** 129

Dictionary of Modern English Usage, A (Fowler), **Supp. I Part 2:** 660

Dictionary of the Mohawk Language, A (Pyrlaeus), **Supp. XXVI:** 86

"Dictum: For a Masque of Deluge" (Merwin), **Supp. III Part 1:** 342–343

"Didactic Poem" (Levertov), **Supp. III Part 1:** 280

Diderot, Denis, **II:** 535; **IV:** 440; **Supp. XVI:** 293; **Supp. XVII:** 145

Did I Ever Tell You How Lucky You Are? (Geisel), **Supp. XVI:** 109

Didion, Joan, **Retro. Supp. I:** 116; **Retro. Supp. II:** 209; **Supp. I Part 1:** 196, 197; **Supp. III Part 1:** 302; **Supp. IV Part 1: 195–216; Supp. XI:** 221; **Supp. XII:** 307; **Supp. XXV:** 208; **Supp. XXVI:** 45, 49, 53

Dido, **I:** 81

Dido, Queen of Hearts (Atherton), **Supp. XXIV:** 26

Di Donato, Peter, **Supp. XX: 34**

Di Donato, Pietro, **Supp. XX: 33–47**

"Did 'Paco's Story' Deserve Its Award" (Kakutani), **Supp. XXII:** 109

"Did You Ever Dream Lucky?" (Ellison), **Supp. II Part 1:** 246

Dieckmann, Katherine, **Supp. XXIII:** 295, 296

"Die-Hard, The" (Benét), **Supp. XI:** 54–55, 56

Diehl, Digby, **Supp. IV Part 1:** 204

Dien Cai Dau (Komunyakaa), **Supp. XIII:** 121, **122–124,** 125, 131, 132

Dies, Martin, **Supp. XVIII:** 229

"Dies Irae" (Lowell), **II:** 553

Die Zeit Ohne Beispiel, (Goebbels), **III:** 560

Difference Engine, The (W. Gibson and B. Sterling), **Supp. XVI:** 121, 124, **128–129**

Different Drummer, A (Larkin; film), **Supp. XI:** 20

Different Fleshes (Goldbarth), **Supp. XII:** 181–182, 188

Different Hours (Dunn), **Supp. XI:** 139, 142, 143, 155

"Different Road, A" (Strout), **Supp. XXIII:** 282–283

Different Seasons (King), **Supp. V:** 148, 152

Different Ways to Pray (Nye), **Supp. XIII:** 274, 275, 277, 285, 287

"Different Ways to Pray" (Nye), **Supp. XIII:** 275

"Difficulties of a Statesman" (Eliot), **I:** 580

"Difficulties of Modernism and the Modernism of Difficulty" (Poirier), **Supp. II Part 1:** 136

Diff'rent (O'Neill), **III:** 389; **Supp. XXII:** 22

Di Filippo, Paul, **Supp. XXII:** 260, 261

DiGaetani, John L., **Supp. XIII:** 200

Digges, Deborah, **Supp. XXIII:** 57

"Digging" (Sanders), **Supp. XVI:** 272

"Digging in the Garden of Age I Uncover a Live Root" (Swenson), **Supp. IV Part 2:** 649

Digging Up the Dirt (Moraga), **Supp. XXIII:** 197

Diggins, John P., **Supp. I Part 2:** 650

Digital Barbarism: A Writer's Manifesto (Helprin), **Supp. XXV:** 81, 84, 88–89

"Dignity of Life, The" (C. Bly), **Supp. XVI:** 34, 36–37

Digregorio, Charles, **Supp. XI:** 326

"Digression on *Number 1, 1948*" (O'Hara), **Supp. XXIII:** 214

"Dilemma" (Budbill), **Supp. XIX:** 2

"Dilemma of Determinism, The" (James), **II:** 347–348, 352

"Dilemma of the Negro Writer, The" (speech, C. Himes), **Supp. XVI:** 140

"Dilettante, The" (Wharton), **IV:** 311, 313

"Dilettante, The: A Modern Type" (Dunbar), **Supp. II Part 1:** 199

Dillard, Annie, **Supp. VI: 19–39; Supp. VIII:** 272; **Supp. X:** 31; **Supp. XIII:** 154; **Supp. XXVI:** 31, 37

Dillard, R. H. W., **Supp. XII:** 16

Dillman, Bradford, **III:** 403; **Supp. XII:** 241

Dillon, Brian, **Supp. X:** 209

Dillon, George, **III:** 141; **Supp. III Part 2:** 621

Dillon, Millicent, **Supp. IV Part 1:** 95

Dilsaver, Paul, **Supp. XIII:** 112

Dilthey, Wilhelm, **I:** 58

Dime-Store Alchemy: The Art of Joseph Cornell, **Supp. VIII:** 272

"Diminuendo" (Dunn), **Supp. XI:** 152–153

"Dimout in Harlem" (Hughes), **Supp. I Part 1:** 333

"Dinah's Lament" (Nelson), **Supp. XVIII:** 183

Dinesen, Isak, **IV:** 279; **Supp. VIII:** 171; **Supp. XVI:** 250

Dining Room, The (Gurney), **Supp. V:** 105–106

"Dinner at ------, A" (O. Henry), **Supp. II Part 1:** 402

"Dinner at Sir Nigel's" (Bowles), **Supp. IV Part 1:** 94

Dinner at the Homesick Restaurant (Tyler), **Supp. IV Part 2:** 657, 667–668

"Dinner at Uncle Borris's" (Simic), **Supp. VIII:** 272

Dinner Bridge (Lardner), **II:** 435

Dinosaur Tales (Bradbury), **Supp. IV Part 1:** 103

"Diogenes Invents a Game" (Karr), **Supp. XI:** 240–241

"Diogenes Tries to Forget" (Karr), **Supp. XI:** 241

Diomede, Matthew, **Supp. XX:** 46

Dionysis in Doubt (Robinson), **III:** 510

Dionysus in 69 (Schechner), **Supp. XXIV:** 116

Diop, Birago, **Supp. IV Part 1:** 16

Diop, David, **Supp. IV Part 1:** 16

Di Piero, W. S., **Supp. XIX: 33–48; Supp. XVII:** 241

Di Prima, Diane, **Supp. III Part 1:** 30; **Supp. XIV:** 125, 144, 148, 150

Dirda, Michael, **Supp. XXI:** 233

Direction of Poetry, The: An Anthology of Rhymed and Metered Verse Written in the English Language since 1975 (Richman, ed.), **Supp. XV:** 250, 251

Direction of Poetry, The: Rhymed and Metered Verse Written in the English Language since 1975 (Richman), **Supp. XI:** 249

"Directive" (Bishop), **Retro. Supp. II:** 42

"Directive" (Frost), **III:** 287; **Retro. Supp. I:** 140; **Supp. VIII:** 32, 33; **Supp. XXVI:** 77

"Dire Cure" (Matthews), **Supp. IX:** 168

"Dirge" (Dunbar), **Supp. II Part 1:** 199

"Dirge Notes" (Huddle), **Supp. XXVI:** 148, 153

"Dirge without Music" (Millay), **III:** 126

"Dirt" (Salter), **Supp. IX:** 257, 260, 261

"Dirt and Desire: Essay on the Phenomenology of Female Pollution in Antiquity" (Carson), **Supp. XII: 111**

Dirty Bird Blues (Major), **Supp. XXII: 180–181**

Dirty Dingus Magee (film), **Supp. XVII:** 139

"Dirty English Potatoes" (X. J. Kennedy), **Supp. XV:** 165

"Dirty Memories" (Olds), **Supp. X:** 211

Dirty Story (Shanley), **Supp. XIV:** 316, 331

"Dirty Word, The" (Shapiro), **Supp. II Part 2:** 710

Dirty Work (L. Brown), **Supp. XXI:** 37, 39, 40, 42, **45**

"'Disabled Imagination' and the Masculine Metaphor in the Works of Leonard Kriegel, The" (Haugen), **Supp. XXIV:** 215

Disappearance of the Jews, The (Mamet), **Supp. XIV:** 249–250, 250–251, 252, 254

Disappearances (Auster), **Supp. XII:** 23

"Disappearances" (Hogan), **Supp. IV Part 1:** 401

Disappearances (Mosher), **Supp. XXII:** 204, 205, 206, 207, 208, 209, **210**

"Disappeared, The " (C. Baxter), **Supp. XVII:** 19

Disappearing Acts (McMillan), **Supp. XIII:** 182, 183, **188–189,** 192

Disappearing Ink: Poetry at the End of Print Culture (Gioia), **Supp. XV:** 112

"Disappointment, The" (Creeley), **Supp. IV Part 1:** 143

"Disappointment and Desire" (R. Bly), **Supp. IV Part 1:** 71

Disappointment Artist, The (Lethem), **Supp. XVIII:** 135, 141, **148**

"Discards" (Baker), **Supp. XIII:** 53, 55–56

Discerning the Signs of the Times (Niebuhr), **III:** 300–301, 307–308

Disch, Thomas M., **Supp. XIX:** 1

"Disciple of Bacon, The" (Epstein), **Supp. XII:** 163–164

"Discipline" (L. Brown), **Supp. XXI:** 44

Discomfort, Zone, The: A Personal History (Franzen), **Supp. XX: 83, 84, 95**

"Discordants" (Aiken), **I:** 65

Discourse on Method (Descartes), **I:** 255

"Discourtesies" (Kirsch), **Supp. XV:** 341

"Discovering Theme and Structure in the Novel" (Schuster), **Supp. VIII:** 126

"Discovery" (Freneau), **Supp. II Part 1:** 258

"Discovery of the Madeiras, The" (Frost), **Retro. Supp. I:** 139

"Discovery of What It Means to Be an American, The" (Baldwin), **Supp. I Part 1:** 54–55

Discovery! The Search for Arabian Oil (Stegner), **Supp. IV Part 2:** 599

"Discrete Series" (Oppen), **Supp. XXVI:** 224, 226–227, 230, 235

"Discrete Series" (Zukofsky), **Supp. III Part 2:** 616

"Discretions of Alcibiades" (Pinsky), **Supp. VI:** 241

"Disease, The" (Rukeyser), **Supp. VI:** 279

Disenchanted, The (play, Schulberg and Breit), **Supp. XVIII:** 254

Disenchanted, The (Schulberg), **II:** 98; **Retro. Supp. I:** 113; **Supp. XVIII: 247–250,** 253

Disenchantments: An Anthology of Modern Fairy Tale Poetry (Mieder), **Supp. XIV:** 126

"Dish of Green Pears, A" (Ríos), **Supp. IV Part 2:** 552

"Disillusion and Dogma" (Untermeyer), **Supp. XV:** 306

Dismantling the Silence (Simic), **Supp. VIII: 273–274,** 275, 276

Disney, Walt, **III:** 275, 426

"Disney of My Mind" (Chabon), **Supp. XI:** 63

Disobedience (Notley), **Supp. XXII:** 235, 236

Dispatches (Herr), **Supp. XI:** 245; **Supp. XIX:** 17

"Displaced Person, The" (O'Connor), **III:** 343–344, 350, 352, 356; **Retro. Supp. II:** 229, 232, 236

"Disposal" (Snodgrass), **Supp. VI:** 314

Dispossessed, The (Berryman), **I:** 170, 172, 173, 174, 175, 176, 178

"Disquieting Muses, The" (Plath), **Supp. I Part 2:** 538

Disraeli, Benjamin, **II:** 127

Dissent (Didion), **Supp. IV Part 1:** 208

"Dissent in Ashcroft's America" (P. N. Warren), **Supp. XX: 273**

"Dissenting Opinion on Kafka, A" (Wilson), **IV:** 437–438

Dissent in Three American Wars (Morison, Merk, and Freidel), **Supp. I Part 2:** 495

Dissertation on Liberty and Necessity, Pleasure and Pain, A (Franklin), **II:** 108

Dissertations on Government; the Affairs of the Bank: and Paper Money (Paine),

Supp. I Part 2: 510
"Distance" (Carver), **Supp. III Part 1:** 146
"Distance" (Everwine), **Supp. XV:** 85
"Distance" (Paley), **Supp. VI:** 222
"Distance, The" (Karr), **Supp. XI:** 241
"Distance from the Sea, A" (Kees), **Supp. XV:** 147
"Distance Nowhere" (Hughes), **Retro. Supp. I:** 207
"Distance Up Close, The" (Peacock), **Supp. XIX:** 196–197, 198
"Distant Episode, A" (Bowles), **Supp. IV Part 1:** 84–85, 86, 90
Distant Episode, A: The Selected Stories (Bowles), **Supp. IV Part 1:** 79
Distant Rain: A Conversation Between Jakuch\[omacron\] Setouchi & Tess Gallagher (Setouchi and Gallagher), **Supp. XXIV:** 166, 178
Distinguished Guest, The (Miller), **Supp. XII:** 299–301
Distortions (Beattie), **Supp. V:** 21, 23, 24, 25, 27
"Distrest Shepherdess, The" (Freneau), **Supp. II Part 1:** 258
District of Columbia (Dos Passos), **I:** 478, 489–490, 492
Disturber of the Peace (Manchester), **III:** 103
Disturbing the Peace (Yates), **Supp. XI:** 345, 346
"Diver, The" (Hayden), **Supp. II Part 1:** 368, 372, 373
"Divided Life of Jean Toomer, The" (Toomer), **Supp. III Part 2:** 488
Divided Self, The (Laing), **Supp. XX: 95**
Divina Commedia (Longfellow, trans.), **II:** 490, 492, 493
"Divina Pastora, La" (C. L. R. James), **Supp. XXI:** 160
"Divine, The" (Di Piero), **Supp. XIX:** 41
"Divine Collaborator" (Simic), **Supp. VIII:** 282
Divine Comedies (Merrill), **Supp. III Part 1:** 324, 329–332
Divine Comedy (Dante), **I:** 137, 265, 400, 446; **II:** 215, 335, 490, 492, 493; **III:** 13, 448, 453; **Supp. V:** 283, 331, 338, 345; **Supp. X:** 253; **Supp. XIV:** 6; **Supp. XIX:** 36, 39
Divine Husband, The (Goldman), **Supp. XXV:** 49–50, 55–57
"Divine Image, The" (Blake), **Supp. V:** 257
Divine Pilgrim, The (Aiken), **I:** 50, 55
Divine Right's Trip (Norman), **Supp. XXIII:** 42
Divine Tragedy, The (Longfellow), **II:** 490, 500, 505, 506, 507; **Retro. Supp. II:** 165, 166
Divine Weekes and Workes (Sylvester, trans.), **Supp. I Part 1:** 104
Divine Weeks (Du Bartas), **IV:** 157–158
Diving into the Wreck: Poems 1971–1972 (Rich), **Supp. I Part 2:** 550, 559–565, 569; **Supp. XV:** 252
"Diving Past African Violets" (A. Finch), **Supp. XVII:** 72

Diving Rock on the Hudson, A (H. Roth), **Supp. IX:** 236, **237–238**
"Divinity in Its Fraying Fact, A" (Levis), **Supp. XI:** 271
"Divinity School Address" (Emerson), **II:** 12–13
"Divinity School or Trusting the Act of Writing" (Abraham), **Supp. XXIV:** 1, 3–4
"Divisions upon a Ground" (Hecht), **Supp. X:** 58
"Divorce" (Karr), **Supp. XI:** 244
"Divorced Fathers and Pizza Crusts" (Halliday), **Supp. XIX:** 93
Divorced in America: Marriage in an Age of Possibility (Epstein), **Supp. XIV:** 113
"Divorce Dream" (Halliday), **Supp. XIX:** 90
"Divorce in the United States" (Atherton), **Supp. XXIV:** 24
Dix, Douglas Shields, **Supp. XII:** 14
Dixie City Jam (Burke), **Supp. XIV:** 32
Dixon, Ivan, **Supp. IV Part 1:** 362
Dixon, Stephen, **Supp. XII: 139–158**
Dixon, Terrell F., **Supp. XVI:** 21
Dixon, Thomas, Jr., **Supp. II Part 1:** 169, 171, 177
Djinn (Robbe-Grillet), **Supp. V:** 48
D'Lugoff, Burt, **Supp. IV Part 1:** 362, 370
Dmytryk, Edward, **Supp. XX: 41**
Do, Lord, Remember Me (Garrett), **Supp. VII:** 98–100, 110
"Doaksology, The" (Wolfe), **IV:** 459
Do Androids Dream of Electric Sheep? (Dick), **Supp. XVIII:** 137
Dobard, Raymond G., **Supp. XXVI:** 200
Dobie, J. Frank, **Supp. V:** 225; **Supp. XIII:** 227
Döblin, Alfred, **Supp. XV:** 137
Dobriansky, Lev, **Supp. I Part 2:** 648, 650
Dobrin, Sidney I., **Supp. XVIII:** 192, 195
Dobson, Joanne, **Retro. Supp. I:** 29, 31, 42; **Supp. XVIII:** 259
Dobyns, Stephen, **Supp. XIII: 73–92**
"Docking at Palermo" (Hugo), **Supp. VI:** 137–138
"Dock Rats" (Moore), **III:** 213
"Dock-Witch, The" (Ozick), **Supp. V:** 262, 264
"Doc Mellhorn and the Pearly Gates" (Benét), **Supp. XI:** 55
"Doctor, The" (Dubus), **Supp. VII:** 80–81
"Doctor and the Doctor's Wife, The" (Hemingway), **II:** 248; **Retro. Supp. I:** 174, 175
Doctor Breen's Practice, a Novel (Howells), **I:** 282
Doctor Faustus (Mann), **III:** 283
Doctor Jazz (Carruth), **Supp. XVI:** 47, 59
"Doctor Jekyll" (Sontag), **Supp. III Part 2:** 469
"Doctor Leavis and the Moral Tradition" (Trilling), **Supp. III Part 2:** 512–513
Doctor Martino and Other Stories (Faulkner), **II:** 72; **Retro. Supp. I:** 84

"Doctor of the Heart, The" (Sexton), **Supp. II Part 2:** 692
Doctorow, E. L., **Retro. Supp. I:** 97; **Supp. III Part 2:** 590, 591; **Supp. IV Part 1: 217–240; Supp. V:** 45; **Supp. XVI:** 73; **Supp. XVII:** 183; **Supp. XX: 84, 90; Supp. XXI:** 18–19; **Supp. XXII:** 268
Doctor Sax (Kerouac), **Supp. III Part 1:** 220–222, 224–227
Doctor Sleep (Bell), **Supp. X: 9–11**
"Doctors' Row" (Aiken), **I:** 67
Doctor's Son and Other Stories, The (O'Hara), **III:** 361
Doctor Stories, The (W. C. Williams), **Retro. Supp. I:** 424
"Doctor's Wife, The" (Ozick), **Supp. V:** 262, 265
Doctor Zhivago (Pasternak), **IV:** 434, 438, 443
"Documentary" (Simic), **Supp. VIII:** 282
Dodd, Elizabeth, **Supp. V:** 77
Dodd, Susan, **Supp. XXV:** 129
Dodd, Wayne, **Supp. IV Part 2:** 625
Dodge, Mabel, **Supp. XX: 69; Supp. XXI:** 5, 6, 8, 12; **Supp. XXII:** 158, 161. *See also* Luhan, Mabel Dodge
Dodson, Owen, **Supp. I Part 1:** 54
Dodsworth (Lewis), **II:** 442, 449–450, 453, 456
Doenitz, Karl, **Supp. I Part 2:** 491
Does Civilization Need Religion? (Niebuhr), **III:** 293–294
"Does 'Consciousness' Exist?" (James), **II:** 356
"Does Education Pay?" (Du Bois), **Supp. II Part 1:** 159
"Dog" (B. Kelly), **Supp. XVII:** 126
Dog (Shepard), **Supp. III Part 2:** 434
"Dog Act, The" (Komunyakaa), **Supp. XIII:** 114–115
"Dog and the Playlet, The" (O. Henry), **Supp. II Part 1:** 399
Dog Beneath the Skin, The (Auden), **Supp. II Part 1:** 10
"Dog Creek Mainline" (Wright), **Supp. V:** 340
"Dogdom of the Dead, The" (Stallings), **Supp. XXV:** 228
"Dogfight" (W. Gibson and Swanwick), **Supp. XVI:** 128
Dog in the Manger, The (Vega; Merwin, trans.), **Supp. III Part 1:** 341, 347
Dog of the Marriage, The (Hempel), **Supp. XXI:** 115, 116, 117, 118, **126–127**
"Dog"(P. Benedict), **Supp. XXIII:** 36–37, 39
Dogs Bark, but the Caravan Rolls On (Conroy), **Supp. XVI:** 63, 70, 74, **75–76**
Dogs Bark, The: Public People and Private Places (Capote), **Supp. III Part 1:** 120, 132
"Dog's Eye" (J. W. Miller), **Supp. XX: 167**
"Dogs of Bucharest, The" (Gallagher), **Supp. XXIV:** 171
Dogs of God (Benedict), **Supp. XXIII:** 35, **41–45**, 49–50

Dog Soldiers (Stone), **Supp. V:** 298, 299–301

Dog Star, The (Di Piero), **Supp. XIX:** 38, **40–41,** 43

"Dog Stories" (Prose), **Supp. XVI:** 256

Dog & the Fever, The (Quevedo), **Retro. Supp. I:** 423

"Dogtown Letters, The" (Jarman and R. McDowell), **Supp. XVII:** 111

"Dogwood, The" (Levertov), **Supp. III Part 1:** 276

"Dogwood Tree, The: A Boyhood" (Updike), **IV:** 218; **Retro. Supp. I:** 318, 319

Doig, Ivan, **Supp. XIV:** 227

"Doing Battle with the Wolf" (Coleman), **Supp. XI:** 87–88

"Doing Jigsaw Puzzles" (Crooker), **Supp. XXIII:** 56

Doing Literary Business: American Women Writers in the Nineteenth Century (Coultrap-McQuin), **Supp. XVI:** 85

Doings and Undoings (Podhoretz), **Supp. VIII:** **236–237**

"Do-It-Yourself" (C. Baxter), **Supp. XVII:** 14–15

Dolan, Jill, **Supp. XV:** 327

Dolben, Digby Mackworth, **Supp. XX:** **230**

"Dolce Far' Niente" (Humphrey), **Supp. IX:** 106

Dolci, Carlo, **III:** 474–475

Dollars and Cents (A. Warner), **Supp. XVIII:** 264

"Dollhouse, The" (Haines), **Supp. XII:** 204

"Dollhouse, The" (Stallings), **Supp. XXV:** 231, 232

Dollmaker's Ghost, The (Levis), **Supp. XI:** 259, 260, **264–268**

Doll's House, A (Ibsen), **III:** 523; **IV:** 357; **Supp. XVI:** 182

Dolmetsch, Arnold, **III:** 464

Dolores Claiborne (King), **Supp. V:** 138, 141, 147, 148, 149–150, 152

"Dolph Heyliger" (Irving), **II:** 309

Dolphin, The (Lowell), **Retro. Supp. II:** 183, 186, 188, **190–191; Supp. XII:** 253–254

"Dolphins" (Francis), **Supp. IX:** 83

Dome of Many-Coloured Class, A (Lowell), **II:** 515, 516–517

Domesday Book (Masters), **Supp. I Part 2:** 465, 466–469, 471, 473, 476

"Domestic Economy" (Gilman), **Supp. XI:** 206

"Domestic Manners" (Hardwick), **Supp. III Part 1:** 211

Domestic Work (Trethewey), **Supp. XXI:** 243, 244, **248–251,** 254

"Domestic Work, 1937" (Trethewey), **Supp. XXI:** 248

"Dominant White, The" (McKay), **Supp. X:** 134

Dominguez, Robert, **Supp. VIII:** 83

Domini, John, **Supp. XIX:** 45; **Supp. XXI:** 235

Dominique, Jean. *See* Closset, Marie

Donahoe, Edward, **Supp. XVIII:** 132

Donahue, Deirdre, **Supp. XXV:** 9

Donahue, Phil, **Supp. IV Part 2:** 526; **Supp. X:** 311

Donaldson, Susan, **Supp. XXII:** 148

Doña Perfecta (Galdós), **II:** 290

Dong, Stella, **Supp. XVI:** 222

Don Juan (Byron), **Supp. XV:** 259

"DON JUAN IN HELL" (Baraka), **Supp. II Part 1:** 33

Donkey of God, The (Untermeyer), **Supp. XV:** 310

"Donna mi Prega" (Cavalcanti), **Supp. III Part 2:** 620, 621, 622

Donn-Byrne, Brian Oswald. *See* Byrne, Donn

Donne, John, **I:** 358–359, 384, 389, 522, 586; **II:** 254; **III:** 493; **IV:** 83, 88, 135, 141, 144, 145, 151, 156, 165, 331, 333; **Retro. Supp. II:** 76; **Supp. I Part 1:** 80, 364, 367; **Supp. I Part 2:** 421, 424, 467, 725, 726; **Supp. III Part 2:** 614, 619; **Supp. IX:** 44; **Supp. VIII:** 26, 33, 164; **Supp. XII:** 45, 159; **Supp. XIII:** 94, 130; **Supp. XIV:** 122; **Supp. XV:** 92, 251; **Supp. XVI:** 158, 204; **Supp. XVIII:** 35, 39, 50–51, 307; **Supp. XXIV:** 167

Donne's Sermons: Selected Passages (L. P. Smith, ed.), **Supp. XIV:** 342

Donoghue, Denis, **I:** 537; **Supp. IV Part 1:** 39; **Supp. VIII:** 105, 189

Donohue, H. E. F., **Supp. IX:** 2, 3, 15, 16

Donoso, José, **Supp. XXIV:** 86

Do Not Deny Me (Thompson), **Supp. XXIII:** **300–301**

"Do Not Weep Maiden, For War Is Kind" (Crane), **Supp. XVIII:** 75

Donovan, Josephine, **Retro. Supp. II:** 138, 139, 147

Don Quixote (Cervantes), **I:** 134; **II:** 291, 434; **III:** 113, 614; **Supp. I Part 2:** 422; **Supp. IX:** 94; **Supp. XXIV:** 87

Don Quixote: Which Was a Dream (Acker), **Supp. XII:** 5, **12–14**

Don't Ask (Levine), **Supp. V:** 178

Don't Ask Questions (Marquand), **III:** 58

Don't Bet on the Prince: Contemporary Feminist Fairy Tales in North America and England (Zipes), **Supp. XIV:** 126

Don't Drink the Water (Allen), **Supp. XV:** 3, **14**

Don't Look Back (film, Pennebaker), **Supp. XVIII:** 19

"Don't Neglect Your Wife" (script, Atherton), **Supp. XXIV:** 25

"Don't Shoot the Warthog" (Corso), **Supp. XII:** 123

Don't Stop the Carnival (Wouk), **Supp. XXV:** 257, 263–264

"Don't Tell Mother" (Wasserstein), **Supp. XV:** 319

"Don't Think Twice, It's All Right" (song, Dylan), **Supp. XVIII:** 24

Don't Worry About the Kids (Neugeboren), **Supp. XVI:** 226

"Don't Worry About the Kids" (Neugeboren), **Supp. XVI:** 226

Don't You Want to Be Free? (Hughes), **Retro. Supp. I:** 203; **Supp. I Part 1:** 339

"Doodler, The" (Merrill), **Supp. III Part 1:** 321

Doolan, Moira, **Retro. Supp. II:** 247

Doolittle, Hilda (H. D.), **II:** 517, 520–521; **III:** 194, 195–196, 457, 465; **IV:** 404, 406; **Retro. Supp. I:** 288, 412, 413, 414, 415, 417; **Supp. I Part 1:** **253–275; Supp. I Part 2:** 707; **Supp. III Part 1:** 48; **Supp. III Part 2:** 610; **Supp. IV Part 1:** 257; **Supp. V:** 79; **Supp. XV:** 43, 249, 301, 302; **Supp. XVII:** 77; **Supp. XXII:** 88; **Supp. XXIV:** 64

Doolittle, Thomas, **IV:** 150

"Doomed by Our Blood to Care" (Orfalea), **Supp. XIII:** 278

"Doomsday" (Plath), **Retro. Supp. II:** 242

Doomsters, The (Macdonald), **Supp. IV Part 2:** 462, 463, 472, 473

Doomswoman, The (Atherton), **Supp. XXIV:** 22

Doonesbury (Trudeau), **Supp. XXIV:** 283

"Door, The" (Creeley), **Supp. IV Part 1:** 145, 146, 156–157

Door, The (Rinehart), **Supp. XXV:** 197, 200

"Door, The" (White), **Supp. I Part 2:** 651, 675–676

"Door in the Dark, The" (Frost), **II:** 156

Door in the Hive, A (Levertov), **Supp. III Part 1:** 283, 284

"Door of the Trap, The" (Anderson), **I:** 112

"Doors" (Dybek), **Supp. XXIII:** 69

Doors (Hoffman), **Supp. XVIII:** 86–87

"Doors" (Hoffman), **Supp. XVIII:** 86–87

"Doors, Doors, Doors" (Sexton), **Supp. II Part 2:** 681

Doors, The, **Supp. X:** 186

"Doorways into the Depths" (Sanders), **Supp. XVI:** 272

Doreski, William, **Retro. Supp. II:** 185

Dorfman, Ariel, **Supp. IX:** 131, 138

Dorfman, Joseph, **Supp. I Part 2:** 631, 647, 650

Doris of Dobbs Ferry (Wells), **Supp. XXVI:** 277

Dorman, Jen, **Supp. XI:** 240

Dorn, Edward, **Supp. IV Part 1:** 154; **Supp. XXIV:** 33, 44

Dorn, Sarah, **Supp. XXI:** 243

"Dorothea Dix, Samaritan" (J. Scott), **Supp. XVII:** 189

Dorr, Julia, **Supp. XV:** 286

Dorrance Doings (Wells), **Supp. XXVI:** 277

Dorrance Domain, The (Wells), **Supp. XXVI:** 277

Dorris, Michael, **Supp. IV Part 1:** 260, 272

Dos Passos, John, **I:** 99, 288, 374, 379, **474–496,** 517, 519; **II:** 74, 77, 89, 98; **III:** 2, 28, 29, 70, 172, 382–383; **IV:** 340, 427, 433; **Retro. Supp. I:** 105, 113, 187; **Retro. Supp. II:** 95, 196; **Supp. I Part 2:** 646; **Supp. III Part**

1: 104, 105; **Supp. V:** 277; **Supp. VIII:** 101, 105; **Supp. XIV:** 24; **Supp. XV:** 135, 137, 182; **Supp. XVII:** 105, 107; **Supp. XXI:** 8; **Supp. XXIII:** 68; **Supp. XXVI:** 17, 32, 133, 135

"Dos Passos: Poet Against the World" (Cowley), **Supp. II Part 1:** 143, 145

Dostoesvsky: A Screenplay (Carver and Gallagher), **Supp. XXIV:** 178

Dostoevsky, Fyodor, **I:** 53, 103, 211, 468; **II:** 60, 130, 275, 320, 587; **III:** 37, 61, 155, 174, 176, 188, 189, 267, 272, 283, 286, 354, 357, 358, 359, 467, 571, 572; **IV:** 1, 7, 8, 17, 21, 50, 59, 106, 110, 128, 134, 285, 289, 476, 485, 491; **Retro. Supp. II:** 20, 204, 299; **Supp. I Part 1:** 49; **Supp. I Part 2:** 445, 466; **Supp. IV Part 2:** 519, 525; **Supp. VIII:** 175; **Supp. X:** 4–5; **Supp. XI:** 161; **Supp. XII:** 322; **Supp. XVI:** 63; **Supp. XVII:** 225; **Supp. XVIII:** 278, 280; **Supp. XX:** 45; **Supp. XXIII:** 4; **Supp. XXIV:** 132

Doty, Mark, **Supp. IX:** 42, 300; **Supp. XI:** 119–138; **Supp. XXI:** 129, 130, 131, 139, 141; **Supp. XXIII:** 126, 221

Doty, M. R. *See* Dawson, Ruth; Doty, Mark

Double, The (Dostoevsky), **Supp. IX:** 105

"Double, The" (Levis), **Supp. XI:** 260, **261–263**

Double, The (Rank), **Supp. IX:** 105

Double Agent, The (Blackmur), **Supp. II Part 1:** 90, 108, 146

Double Axe, The (Jeffers), **Supp. II Part 2:** 416, 434

"Double Blind" (Skloot), **Supp. XX: 194, 208**

Doubleday, Frank, **I:** 500, 502, 515, 517; **III:** 327

Doubleday, Mrs. Frank, **I:** 500

Double Deuce (Parker), **Supp. XIX:** 183

Double Down (F. and S. Barthelme), **Supp. XI:** 27, 34, 35, 36–38

Double Dream of Spring, The (Ashbery), **Supp. III Part 1:** 11–13

Double Fold: Libraries and the Assault on Paper (Baker), **Supp. XIII:** 52, 56

Double Game (Calle), **Supp. XII:** 22

"Double Gap, The" (Auchincloss), **Supp. IV Part 1:** 33

"Double-Headed Snake of Newbury, The" (Whittier), **Supp. I Part 2:** 698

Double Honeymoon (Connell), **Supp. XIV:** 80, 87

Double Image, The (Levertov), **Supp. III Part 1:** 274, 276

"Double Image, The" (Sexton), **Supp. II Part 2:** 671, 677–678

Double Indemnity (film), **Supp. IV Part 1:** 130

Double Legacy: Reflections on a Pair of Deaths (Hadas), **Supp. XXIII:** 123, **126–127**

"Double Limbo" (Komunyakaa), **Supp. XIII:** 132

Double Man, The (Auden), **Supp. III Part 1:** 16; **Supp. X:** 118

"Double Ode" (Rukeyser), **Supp. VI:** 282–283, 286

Double Persephone (Atwood), **Supp. XIII:** 19

Double Play (Parker), **Supp. XIX: 189– 190**

Doubles in Literary Psychology (Tymms), **Supp. IX:** 105

Double Vision: American Thoughts Abroad (Knowles), **Supp. XII:** 249

"Doubt on the Great Divide" (Stafford), **Supp. XI:** 322

Dougherty, Robin, **Supp. XXII:** 205

Dougherty, Steve, **Supp. X:** 262

Douglas, Aaron, **Supp. I Part 1:** 326

Douglas, Alfred, **Supp. X:** 151

Douglas, Ann, **Supp. XII:** 136; **Supp. XVIII:** 258; **Supp. XX: 69**

Douglas, Claire, **III:** 552

Douglas, Ellen, **Supp. XXI:** 38

Douglas, George (pseudonym). *See* Brown, George Douglas

Douglas, Kirk, **Supp. XIII:** 5–6

Douglas, Lloyd, **IV:** 434

Douglas, Marjory Stoneman, **Supp. XVIII:** 195

Douglas, Melvyn, **Supp. V:** 223

Douglas, Michael, **Supp. XI:** 67

Douglas, Paul, **III:** 294

Douglas, Stephen A., **III:** 577, 588–589; **Supp. I Part 2:** 456, 471

Douglas, William O., **III:** 581

Douglass, Frederick, **Supp. I Part 1:** 51, 345; **Supp. I Part 2:** 591; **Supp. II Part 1:** 157, 195, 196, 292, 378; **Supp. III Part 1: 153–174; Supp. IV Part 1:** 1, 2, 13, 15, 256; **Supp. VIII:** 202; **Supp. XVIII:** 16; **Supp. XX: 109, 281; Supp. XXIII:** 167

Douglass, Thomas E., **Supp. XXIII:** 36

Douglass Pilot, The (Baldwin, ed.), **Supp. I Part 1:** 49

Dove, Belle, **I:** 451

Dove, Rita, **Supp. IV Part 1: 241–258; Supp. XVII:** 71, 110; **Supp. XVIII:** 172, 174; **Supp. XXI:** 243, 246, 247, 249, 251

Dove of the East and Other Stories, A (Helprin), **Supp. XXV:** 79, 83, 84–85

"Dover Beach" (Arnold), **Retro. Supp. I:** 325; **Supp. XIX:** 41

Dow, Lorenzo, **IV:** 265

Dowd, Douglas, **Supp. I Part 2:** 645, 650

"Do We Understand Each Other?" (Ginsberg), **Supp. II Part 1:** 311

Dowie, William, **Supp. V:** 199

Do with Me What You Will (Oates), **Supp. II Part 2:** 506, 515–517

Dowling, Eddie, **IV:** 394

Down and Out (Shanley), **Supp. XIV:** 317

"Down at City Hall" (Didion), **Supp. IV Part 1:** 211

"Down at the Cross" (Baldwin), **Retro. Supp. II:** 1, 2, 7, 12, 13, 15; **Supp. I Part 1:** 60, 61

"Down at the Dinghy" (Salinger), **III:** 559, 563

"Down by the Station, Early in the Morning" (Ashbery), **Supp. III Part 1:** 25

Downey, Sharon D., **Supp. XX: 244**

Downhill Racer (film), **Supp. IX:** 253

"Down Home" (J. W. Miller), **Supp. XX: 169**

"Down in Alabam" (Bierce), **I:** 193

Downing, Ben, **Supp. XII:** 175, 189, 190–191

Downing, Major Jack (pseudonym). *See* Smith, Seba

Down in My Heart (Stafford), **Supp. XI:** 313, 315

Down Mailer's Way (Solotaroff), **Retro. Supp. II:** 203

"Down the Highway" (song, Dylan), **Supp. XVIII:** 24

Down the Rabbit Hole: Adventures and Misadventures in the Realm of Children's Literature (Lanes), **Supp. XVI:** 104

Down There on a Visit (Isherwood), **Supp. XIV:** 159, 161, 164, **168–169**, 170, 171

Down the River (Abbey), **Supp. XIII:** 12–13

"Down the River with Henry Thoreau" (Abbey), **Supp. XIII:** 12–13

Down These Mean Streets (P. Thomas), **Supp. XIII:** 264

Down the Starry River (Purdy), **Supp. VII:** 278

Down to the River: Portraits of Iowa Musicians (Dyas), **Supp. XIX:** 174

Downtown (Siddons), **Supp. XXII:** 239, 240, 242, **247–249, 251–252,** 253

"Downtrodden Mary's Failed Campaign of Terror" (Saunders), **Supp. XIX:** 226

"Downward Path to Wisdom, The" (Porter), **III:** 442, 443, 446

"Down Where I Am" (Hughes), **Supp. I Part 1:** 344

Down with Starvation Wages in Southeast Missouri (C. L. R. James), **Supp. XXI:** 169

"Dowsing for Joy" (Skloot), **Supp. XX: 203**

Dowson, Ernest C., **I:** 384

Doyle, Arthur Conan, **Retro. Supp. I:** 270; **Supp. IV Part 1:** 128, 341; **Supp. IV Part 2:** 464, 469; **Supp. XI:** 63; **Supp. XXVI:** 282

Doyle, C. W., **I:** 199

"Draba" (Leopold), **Supp. XIV:** 186

Drabble, Margaret, **Supp. IV Part 1:** 297, 299, 305

Drabelle, Dennis, **Supp. XIII:** 13

Drach, Ivan, **Supp. III Part 1:** 268

Dracula (film), **Supp. IV Part 1:** 104; **Supp. XVII:** 57

Dracula (Stoker), **Supp. XXVI:** 58

"Draft Horse, The" (Frost), **Retro. Supp. I:** 141

"Draft Lyrics for *Candide*" (Agee), **I:** 28

Draft of XVI Cantos, A (Pound), **III:** 472; **Retro. Supp. I:** 292

Draft of XXX Cantos, A (Pound), **III:** 196; **Retro. Supp. I:** 292

Drafts &Fragments (Pound), **Retro. Supp. I:** 293

"Dragon" (Lovecraft), **Supp. XXV:** 111

Dragon Country (T. Williams), **IV:** 383

Dragone, Nichole, **Supp. XXIII:** 157

Dragon Seed (Buck), **Supp. II Part 1:** 124

Dragon's Teeth (Sinclair), **Supp. V:** 290

Drake, Benjamin, **Supp. I Part 2:** 584

Drake, Daniel, **Supp. I Part 2:** 584

Drake, Sir Francis, **Supp. I Part 2:** 497

Drake, Robert, **Supp. XX: 274**

Drake, St. Clair, **IV:** 475

Drake, Sylvia, **Supp. XXI:** 155

Drake, William, **Supp. XV:** 295

Dramatic Duologues (Masters), **Supp. I Part 2:** 461

"Drapery Factory, Gulfport. Mississippi, 1956" (Trethewey), **Supp. XXI:** 246

Drattel, Deborah, **Supp. XV:** 333

Drat These Brats (X. J. Kennedy), **Supp. XV:** 163

"Draught" (Cowley), **Supp. II Part 1:** 141, 142

Drayton, Michael, **IV:** 135; **Retro. Supp. II:** 76

"Dr. Bergen's Belief" (Schwartz), **Supp. II Part 2:** 650

Dr. Bloodmoney (Dick), **Supp. XVIII:** 138

"Dreadful Has Already Happened, The" (Strand), **Supp. IV Part 2:** 627

Dread Road, The (Le Sueur), **Supp. XXIII:** 168, 169, **169–170,** 173

"Dream, A" (Ginsberg), **Supp. II Part 1:** 312

"Dream, A" (Tate), **IV:** 129

"Dream, The" (Hayden), **Supp. II Part 1:** 368, 377

Dream at the End of the World, The: Paul Bowles and the Literary Renegades in Tangier (Green), **Supp. IV Part 1:** 95

"Dream Avenue" (Simic), **Supp. VIII:** 282

"Dream Boogie" (Hughes), **Retro. Supp. I:** 208; **Supp. I Part 1:** 339–340

"Dreambook Bestiary" (Komunyakaa), **Supp. XIII:** 120

Dreamer (C. Johnson), **Supp. VI:** 186, **196–199**

dreamer examines his pillow, the (Shanley), **Supp. XIV:** 315, **327**

"Dreamer in a Dead Language" (Paley), **Supp. VI:** 217

Dreaming in Cuban (García), **Supp. XI:** 178, **179–185,** 190

"Dreaming of Hair" (L.-Y. Lee), **Supp. XV:** 214

"Dreaming the Breasts" (Sexton), **Supp. II Part 2:** 692

"Dreaming Water" (Espaillat), **Supp. XXI:** 102

"Dream Interpretation" (Hadas), **Supp. XXIII:** 113, 121

"Dream Interpreted, The" (Paine), **Supp. I Part 2:** 505

Dream Jumbo (Longo), **Supp. XVI:** 124

Dream Keeper, The (Hughes), **Supp. I Part 1:** 328, 332, 333, 334

Dream Keeper and Other Poems, The (Hughes), **Retro. Supp. I:** 201, 202

Dreamland (Baker), **Supp. XIV:** 96

"Dream-Land" (Poe), **Retro. Supp. II:** 274

Dream Life of Balso Snell, The (West), **IV:** 286, 287, 288–290, 291, 297; **Retro. Supp. II:** 321, 322, 327, 328, **330–332**

"Dream Machine, The" (Hadas), **Supp. XXIII:** 122–123

Dream Me Home Safely: Writers on Growing up in America (Shreve, ed.), **Supp. XXIII:** 284

Dream of a Common Language, The: Poems, 1974–1977 (Rich), **Supp. I Part 2:** 551, 554, 569–576

Dream of Arcadia: American Writers and Artists in Italy (Brooks), **I:** 254

Dream of Governors, A (Simpson), **Supp. IX:** 265, **269–270**

"Dream of Her Grandfather, A" (Zitkala-Ša), **Supp. XXV:** 282, 283

"Dream of Italy, A" (Masters), **Supp. I Part 2:** 458

"Dream of Mourning, The" (Glück), **Supp. V:** 84

"Dream of the Blacksmith's Room, A" (R. Bly), **Supp. IV Part 1:** 73

"Dream of the Cardboard Lover" (Haines), **Supp. XII:** 204

Dream of the Golden Mountains, The (Cowley), **Supp. II Part 1:** 139, 141, 142, 144

"Dream Pang, A" (Frost), **II:** 153

Dream-Quest of Unkown Kadath, The (Lovecraft), **Supp. XXV:** 113–114

"Dreams About Clothes" (Merrill), **Supp. III Part 1:** 328–329

"Dreams"(Dybek), **Supp. XXIII:** 73

Dreams from Bunker Hill (Fante), **Supp. XI:** 160, 166, **172–173**

"Dreams in the Witch House, The" (Lovecraft), **Supp. XXV:** 111, 123

"Dreams"(Kenny), **Supp. XXIII:** 153

"Dreams of Adulthood" (Ashbery), **Supp. III Part 1:** 26

"Dreams of Glory on the Mound" (Plimpton), **Supp. XVI:** 238–239

"Dreams of Math" (Kenyon), **Supp. VII:** 160–161

"Dreams of the Animals" (Atwood), **Supp. XIII:** 33

"Dream Variations" (Hughes), **Retro. Supp. I:** 198; **Supp. I Part 1:** 323

"Dream Vision" (Olsen), **Supp. XIII:** 295–296

Dream with No Stump Roots in It, A (Huddle), **Supp. XXVI:** 152

"Dream with No Stumps in It, A" (Huddle), **Supp. XXVI:** 152

Dream Work (Oliver), **Supp. VII:** 234–235, 236–238, 240

Dred: A Tale of the Great Dismal Swamp (Stowe), **Supp. I Part 2:** 592

Dreiser, Theodore, **I:** 59, 97, 109, 116, 355, 374, 375, 475, 482, **497–520; II:** 26, 27, 29, 34, 38, 44, 74, 89, 93, 180, 276, 283, 428, 444, 451, 456–457, 467–468; **III:** 40, 103, 106, 251, 314, 319, 327, 335, 453, 576, 582; **IV:** 29, 35, 40, 135, 208, 237, 475, 482, 484; **Retro. Supp. I:** 325, 376; **Retro. Supp. II: 93–110,** 114, 322; **Supp. I Part 1:** 320; **Supp. I Part 2:** 461, 468;

Supp. III Part 2: 412; **Supp. IV Part 1:** 31, 236, 350; **Supp. IV Part 2:** 689; **Supp. IX:** 1, 14, 15, 308; **Supp. V:** 113, 120; **Supp. VIII:** 98, 101, 102; **Supp. XI:** 207; **Supp. XIV:** 111; **Supp. XVII:** 95, 96–97, 105, 155; **Supp. XVIII:** 1, 6, 76, 226; **Supp. XXI:** 275; **Supp. XXIII:** 161, 164; **Supp. XXV:** 18; **Supp. XXVI:** 133, 273

"Drenched in Light" (Hurston), **Supp. VI:** 150–151

Drennen, Eileen M., **Supp. XXII:** 241, 243

Dresser, Paul, **Retro. Supp. II:** 94, 103

Dress Gray (teleplay), **Supp. IV Part 2:** 683

Dress Gray (Truscott), **Supp. IV Part 2:** 683

"Dressing for Dinner" (Ríos), **Supp. IV Part 2:** 548

Dressing Up for the Carnival (Shields), **Supp. VII:** 328

"Dress of One Occasion" (Stallings), **Supp. XXV:** 233

"Dress Rehearsal" (Skloot), **Supp. XX: 204**

Drew, Bettina, **Supp. IX:** 2, 4

Drew, Elizabeth, **Retro. Supp. II:** 242, 243

Drexler, Eric, **Supp. XVI:** 121

Dreyfus, Alfred, **Supp. I Part 2:** 446

"Dr. Hanray's Second Chance" (Richter), **Supp. XVIII:** 218

Drift and Mastery (Lippmann), **I:** 222–223

"Driftwood" (C. Frost), **Supp. XV:** 106–107

"Drinker, The" (Lowell), **II:** 535, 550

"Drinking Cold Water" (Everwine), **Supp. XV:** 80–81

"Drinking from a Helmet" (Dickey), **Supp. IV Part 1:** 180

Drinking Gourd, The (Hansberry), **Supp. IV Part 1:** 359, 365–367, 374

Drinks before Dinner (Doctorow), **Supp. IV Part 1:** 231, 234–235

Driscoll, David, **Supp. XIX:** 241, 242

Driskill, Qwo-Li, **Supp. XXIII:** 147, 148, 149

Drive, He Said (Larner), **Supp. XVI:** 220

"Drive Home, The" (Banks), **Supp. V:** 7

"Driver" (Merrill), **Supp. III Part 1:** 331

"Driving Alone in Winter" (W. V. Davis), **Supp. XXI:** 89, 90, 94

"Driving Through Minnesota During the Hanoi Bombings" (R. Bly), **Supp. IV Part 1:** 61; **Supp. XVII:** 243

"Driving through Oregon" (Haines), **Supp. XII:** 207

"Driving to Oregon"(Thompson), **Supp. XXIII:** 291

"Driving toward the Lac Qui Parle River" (R. Bly), **Supp. IV Part 1:** 61

"Dr. Jack-o'-Lantern" (Yates), **Supp. XI:** 340–341

Dr. Jekyll and Mr. Hyde (film), **Supp. XVII:** 57

"Drone" (Coleman), **Supp. XI:** 85–86

Drop City (Boyle), **Supp. XX: 30–31**

Drown (Díaz), **Supp. XXIV:** 83, 84, 85, 86, **88–89,** 90, 93
"Drowned Man, The: Death between Two Rivers" (McGrath), **Supp. X:** 116
"Drowning" (Boyle), **Supp. XX:** 18
"Drowning 1954" (Keillor), **Supp. XVI:** 172
Drowning Pool, The (film), **Supp. IV Part 2:** 474
Drowning Pool, The (Macdonald), **Supp. IV Part 2:** 470, 471
Drowning Season, The (Hoffman), **Supp. X:** 82
Drowning with Others (Dickey), **Supp. IV Part 1:** 176, 178, 179
"Drowsy Day, A" (Dunbar), **Supp. II Part 1:** 198
Dr. Seuss. *See* Geisel, Theodor Seuss (Dr. Seuss)
Dr. Seuss and Mr. Geisel (J. and N. Morgan), **Supp. XVI:** 103
Dr. Seuss Goes to War: The World War II Editorial Cartoons of Theodor Seuss Geisel (Minear), **Supp. XVI:** 101
Dr. Seuss's ABC (Geisel), **Supp. XVI:** 99
Dr. Strangelove; or, How I Learned to Stop Worrying and Love the Bomb (film), **Supp. XI:** 293, **301–305**
Drugiye Berega (Nabokov), **III:** 247–250, 252
"Drug Shop, The, or Endymion in Edmonstoun" (Benét), **Supp. XI:** 43
"Drug Store" (Shapiro), **Supp. II Part 2:** 705
"Drugstore in Winter, A" (Ozick), **Supp. V:** 272
Drukman, Steven, **Supp. XIII:** 195, 197, 202
"Drum" (Hogan), **Supp. IV Part 1:** 413
"Drum, The" (Alvarez), **Supp. VII:** 7
"Drumlin Woodchuck, A" (Frost), **II:** 159–160; **Retro. Supp. I:** 138
Drummond, William, **Supp. I Part 1:** 369
Drummond de Andrade, Carlos, **Supp. IV Part 2:** 626, 629, 630
Drums at Dusk (Bontemps), **Supp. XXII:** 5, 9–10
Drum-Taps (Whitman), **IV:** 346, 347, 444; **Retro. Supp. I:** 406
"Drunken Fisherman, The" (Lowell), **II:** 534, 550
"Drunken Sisters, The" (Wilder), **IV:** 374
Drunk in the Furnace, The (Merwin), **Supp. III Part 1:** 345–346
"Drunk in the Furnace, The" (Merwin), **Supp. III Part 1:** 346
Druten, John van, **Supp. XIV:** 162
"Dr. Williams' Position" (Pound), **Supp. XVII:** 226–227
Dryden, John, **II:** 111, 542, 556; **III:** 15; **IV:** 145; **Retro. Supp. I:** 56; **Supp. I Part 1:** 150; **Supp. I Part 2:** 422; **Supp. IX:** 68; **Supp. XIV:** 5; **Supp. XV:** 258; **Supp. XX: 280; Supp. XXIV:** 158; **Supp. XXV:** 119
Drye, Captain Frank, **Retro. Supp. II:** 115
Dry Salvages, The (Eliot), **I:** 581
"Dry Salvages, The" (Eliot), **Retro. Supp. I:** 66

"Dry September" (Faulkner), **II:** 72, 73
"Dry Spring"(Thompson), **Supp. XXIII:** 291
Dry Sun, Dry Wind (Wagoner), **Supp. IX:** 323, 324
D'Souza, Dinesh, **Supp. X:** 255
"Dual" (Goldbarth), **Supp. XII:** 188
"Dual Curriculum" (Ozick), **Supp. V:** 270
"Dualism" (Reed), **Supp. X:** 242
Duane's Depressed (McMurtry), **Supp. V:** 233
Du Bartas, Guillaume, **Supp. I Part 1:** 98, 104, 111, 118, 119
Duberman, Martin, **Supp. I Part 2:** 408, 409
Dubie, Norman, **Supp. XXIV:** 165
"Dubin's Lives" (Malamud), **Supp. I Part 2:** 451
Dubious Honors (M. F. K. Fisher), **Supp. XVII:** 91
"Dubliners" (J. Joyce), **Supp. XVI:** 41
Dubliners (Joyce), **I:** 130, 480; **III:** 471; **Supp. VIII:** 146
Dublin's Lives (Malamud), **Supp. XIX:** 142
Du Bois, Nina Gomer (Mrs. W. E. B. Du Bois), **Supp. II P art 1:** 158; **Supp. XIV:** 200
Du Bois, Shirley Graham, **Supp. II Part 1:** 186; **Supp. XXI:** 171. *See also* Graham, Shirley
Du Bois, W. E. B., **I:** 260; **Supp. I Part 1:** 5, 345; **Supp. II Part 1:** 33, 56, 61, **157–189,** 195; **Supp. IV Part 1:** 9, 164, 170, 362; **Supp. X:** 133, 134, 137, 139, 242; **Supp. XIII:** 185, **Supp. XIII:** 186, 233, 238, 243, 244, 247; **Supp. XIV:** 54, 69, 72, 201, 202; **Supp. XIX:** 67, 69, 77; **Supp. XVI:** 135; **Supp. XVIII:** 119, 122, 126, 130; **Supp. XX: 102, 105, 106; Supp. XXI:** 166, 277; **Supp. XXII:** 3; **Supp. XXVI:** 88, 168
DuBose, Martha Hailey, **Supp. XXV:** 192, 199, 200
Dubreuil, Jean, **Supp. IV Part 2:** 425
Dubus, Andre, **Supp. VII: 75–93; Supp. XI:** 347,**Supp. XI:** 349; **Supp. XIV:** 21; **Supp. XXIV:** 97
Dubus, Andre, III, **Supp. XXIV: 97–112**
Duchamp, Marcel, **IV:** 408; **Retro. Supp. I:** 416, 417, 418, 430; **Supp. IV Part 2:** 423, 424; **Supp. XII:** 124; **Supp. XV:** 157; **Supp. XXII:** 162, 163, 168
"Duchess at Prayer, The" (Wharton), **Retro. Supp. I:** 365
Duchess of Malfi, The (Webster), **IV:** 131
"Duckling Girl" (Dubus III), **Supp. XXIV:** 100–101, 105
Duck Soup (film), **Supp. IV Part 1:** 384
Duck Variations, The (Mamet), **Supp. XIV:** 239, 240, 249
Ducornet, Rikki, **Supp. XXII:** 261
Dudley, Anne. *See* Bradstreet, Anne
Dudley, Joseph, **III:** 52
Dudley, Thomas, **III:** 52; **Supp. I Part 1:** 98, 99, 110, 116
"Duenna"(Schott), **Supp. XXIII:** 249
"Duet, With Muffled Brake Drums" (Updike), **Retro. Supp. I:** 319

Duet for Cannibals (Sontag), **Supp. III Part 2:** 452, 456
Duffey, Bernard, **Supp. I Part 2:** 458, 471
Duffield, Pitts, **Supp. XXI:** 3
Duffus, R. L., **Supp. I Part 2:** 650
Duffy, Martha, **Supp. IV Part 1:** 207; **Supp. XX: 244**
Duffy, William, **Supp. XVI:** 32
Du Fu (Tu Fu), **Supp. XV:** 217
Dufy, Raoul, **I:** 115; **IV:** 80
Dugan, Alan, **Supp. XIII:** 76
Dugan, James, **Supp. XV:** 197
"Dugout"(Kenny), **Supp. XXIII:** 155
Duhamel, Marcel, **Supp. XVI:** 135, 143
Dujardin, Edouard, **I:** 53
"Duke de l'Omelette, The" (Poe), **III:** 411, 425
Duke Herring (Bodenheim), **Supp. XXV:** 27
"Duke in His Domain, The" (Capote), **Supp. III Part 1:** 113, 126
Duke of Deception, The (G. Wolff), **Supp. II Part 1:** 97; **Supp. XI:** 246
"Duke's Child, The" (Maxwell), **Supp. VIII:** 172
"Dulce et Decorum Est" (Owen), **Supp. XVIII:** 92
"Dulham Ladies, The" (Jewett), **II:** 407, 408; **Retro. Supp. II:** 143
Duluth (Vidal), **Supp. IV Part 2:** 677, 685, 689, 691–692
Dumas, Alexandre, **III:** 386; **Supp. XVII:** 64
"Dumb Oax, The" (Lewis), **Retro. Supp. I:** 170
"Dummy, The" (Sontag), **Supp. III Part 2:** 469
"Dump Ground, The" (Stegner), **Supp. IV Part 2:** 601
Dunant, Sarah, **Supp. XIX:** 186
Dunayevskaya, Raya, **Supp. XXI:** 169
Dunbar, Alice Moore (Mrs. Paul Laurence Dunbar), **Supp. II Part 1:** 195, 200, 217
Dunbar, Paul Laurence, **Supp. I Part 1:** 320; **Supp. II Part 1:** 174, **191–219; Supp. III Part 1:** 73; **Supp. IV Part 1:** 15, 165, 170; **Supp. X:** 136; **Supp. XI:** 277; **Supp. XIII:** 111; **Supp. XXII:** 11
Duncan, Harry, **Supp. XV:** 75
Duncan, Isadora, **I:** 483; **Supp. XV:** 42, 50
Duncan, Robert, **Retro. Supp. II:** 49; **Supp. III Part 2:** 625, 626, 630, 631; **Supp. VIII:** 304; **Supp. XVI:** 282–283; **Supp. XXIII:** 213
Dunciad, The (Pope), **I:** 204
Dunford, Judith, **Supp. VIII:** 107
Dunlap, William, **Supp. I Part 1:** 126, 130, 137, 141, 145
Dunn, Stephen, **Supp. XI: 139–158; Supp. XIX:** 85
Dunne, Finley Peter, **II:** 432
Dunne, John Gregory, **Supp. IV Part 1:** 197, 198, 201, 203, 207
"Dunnet Shepherdess, A" (Jewett), **II:** 392–393; **Retro. Supp. II:** 139
Dunning, Stephen, **Supp. XIV:** 126

Dunning, William Archibald, **Supp. II Part 1:** 170; **Supp. XIV:** 48

Dunnock, Mildred, **III:** 153

Dunster, Henry, **Supp. I Part 2:** 485

"Dunwich Horror, The" (Lovecraft), **Supp. XXV:** 111, 120

"Duo Tried Killing Man with Bacon" (Goldbarth), **Supp. XII:** 176

Dupee, F. W., **I:** 254; **II:** 548; **Supp. IX:** 93, 96; **Supp. VIII:** 231

DuPlessis, Rachel Blau, **Supp. IV Part 2:** 421, 426, 432; **Supp. XVI:** 284; **Supp. XXVI:** 228, 234, 237–238

Duplicate Keys (Smiley), **Supp. VI:** 292, **294–296**

Duplications, The (Koch), **Supp. XV:** 181, 183, 186

Durable Fire, A (Sarton), **Supp. VIII:** 260

Durand, Asher, B., **Supp. I Part 1:** 156, 157

Durand, Régis, **Supp. IV Part 1:** 44

Durang, Christopher, **Supp. XXIV:** 113–130, 263

"Durango Suite" (Gunn Allen), **Supp. IV Part 1:** 326

Durant, Kenneth, **Supp. XXII:** 278, 281

"Durations" (Matthews), **Supp. IX:** 152–153, 154

Dürer, Albrecht, **III:** 212; **Supp. XII:** 44

Durham, David Anthony, **Supp. XVIII:** 100

"During Fever" (Lowell), **II:** 547

Durkheim, Émile, **I:** 227; **Retro. Supp. I:** 55, 57; **Supp. I Part 2:** 637, 638

Durrell, Lawrence, **III:** 184, 190; **IV:** 430; **Supp. X:** 108, 187; **Supp. XVI:** 294

Dürrenmatt, Friedrich, **Supp. IV Part 2:** 683

Duse, Eleonora, **II:** 515, 528

Dusk and Other Stories (Salter), **Supp. IX:** 260–261

Dusk of Dawn: An Essay Toward an Autobiography of a Race Concept (Du Bois), **Supp. II Part 1:** 159, 183, 186

Dusselier, Jane, **Supp. XXVI:** 210

"Dust" (R. Fisher), **Supp. XIX:** 71

"Dusting" (Alvarez), **Supp. VII:** 4

"Dusting" (Dove), **Supp. IV Part 1:** 247, 248

"Dusting" (Schnackenberg), **Supp. XV:** 256

"Dust of Snow" (Frost), **II:** 154

Dust Tracks on a Road (Hurston), **Supp. IV Part 1:** 5, 11; **Supp. VI:** 149, 151, 158–159

"Dusty Braces" (Snyder), **Supp. VIII:** 302

Dutchman (Baraka), **Supp. II Part 1:** 38, 40, 42–44, 54, 55

"Dutch Nick Massacre, The" (Twain), **IV:** 195

"Dutch Picture, A" (Longfellow), **Retro. Supp. II:** 171

Dutton, Charles S., **Supp. VIII:** 332, 342

Dutton, Clarence Earl, **Supp. IV Part 2:** 598

Duvall, Robert, **Supp. V:** 227

"Duwamish" (Hugo), **Supp. VI:** 136

"Duwamish, Skagit, Hoh" (Hugo), **Supp. VI:** 136–137

"Duwamish No. 2" (Hugo), **Supp. VI:** 137

Duyckinck, Evert, **III:** 77, 81, 83, 85; **Retro. Supp. I:** 155, 247, 248; **Supp. I Part 1:** 122, 317; **Supp. XXV:** 250

Duyckinck, George, **Supp. I Part 1:** 122; **Supp. XXV:** 250

"Dvonya" (Simpson), **Supp. IX:** 274

Dwelling Places: Poems and Translations (Ferry), **Supp. XXIV: 152–153**

Dwellings: A Spiritual History of the Living World (Hogan), **Supp. IV Part 1:** 397, 410, 415–416, 417

Dwight, Sereno E., **I:** 547

Dwight, Timothy, **Supp. I Part 1:** 124; **Supp. I Part 2:** 516, 580; **Supp. II Part 1:** 65, 69

Dworkin, Andrea, **Supp. XII:** 6

Dwyer, Jim, **Supp. XVI:** 16, 19

Dyas, Sandra, **Supp. XIX:** 174

Dybbuk, A, or Between Two Worlds: Dramatic Legend in Four Acts (Kushner), **Supp. IX:** 138

Dybbuk, The (Ansky), **IV:** 6

Dybek, Stuart, **Supp. XXIII: 67–81**

Dybuk, The (Ansky), **Supp. XXIII:** 8

Dyer, Geoff, **Supp. X:** 169

Dyer, Joyce, **Supp. XX: 166**

Dyer, R. C., **Supp. XIII:** 162

Dyer, Richard, **Supp. XXII:** 261

Dyer's Thistle (Balakian), **Supp. XXIII:** 25

Dying Animal, The (P. Roth), **Retro. Supp. II:** 288

"Dying Elm, The" (Freneau), **Supp. II Part 1:** 258

"Dying Indian, The" (Freneau), **Supp. II Part 1:** 262

"Dying Man, The" (Roethke), **III:** 540, 542, 543–545

Dykeman, Wilma, **Supp. XX: 163**

Dykes to Watch Out For (Bechdel), **Supp. XXV:** 1, 3–4

Dylan, Bob, **Supp. VIII:** 202; **Supp. XIII:** 114, 119; **Supp. XV:** 349, 350; **Supp. XVIII: 19–34; Supp. XXII:** 83

Dylan's Visions of Sin (Ricks), **Supp. XVIII:** 20

"Dynamics of Heroic Action, The" (lecture, Murray), **Supp. XIX:** 153

Dynamo (O'Neill), **III:** 396

"Dynasties" (Gibran), **Supp. XX: 118**

"Dysfunctional Narratives: Or, 'Mistakes Were Made'" (C. Baxter), **Supp. XVII:** 20

"Dysfunctional Nation" (Karr), **Supp. XI:** 245

Dyson, A. E., **Retro. Supp. II:** 247

Dyson, Freeman, **Supp. XVII:** 42

E

"Each and All" (Emerson), **II:** 19

Each Happiness Ringer by Lions (Hirshfield), **Supp. XXIII:** 135

Each in His Season (Snodgrass), **Supp. VI:** 324, 327

"Each Like a Leaf" (Swenson), **Supp. IV Part 2:** 644

Eads, Martha Greene, **Supp. XVIII:** 49

Eady, Cornelius, **Supp. XXI:** 246

Eager, Allen, **Supp. XI:** 294

"Eagle, The" (Tate), **IV:** 128

"Eagle and the Mole, The" (Wylie), **Supp. I Part 2:** 710, 711, 713, 714, 729

"Eagle and the Skylark, The" (Gibran), **Supp. XX:** 124

Eagle as Wide as the World, The (X. J. Kennedy), **Supp. XV:** 162, 164

"Eagle Poem" (Harjo), **Supp. XII:** 224, 226

"Eagles" (Dickey), **Supp. IV Part 1:** 186

Eagle's Mile, The (Dickey), **Supp. IV Part 1:** 178, 185–186

"Eagle That Is Forgotten, The" (Lindsay), **Supp. I Part 2:** 382, 387

Eagleton, Terry, **Retro. Supp. I:** 67

Eakin, Paul John, **Supp. VIII:** 167, 168; **Supp. XIII:** 225; **Supp. XVI:** 70

Eakins, Thomas, **Supp. XIV:** 338; **Supp. XXII:** 18–19

Eames, Emma, **Supp. XX: 232, 240**

Eames, Roscoe, **II:** 476

"Earl: My Life with a Louse" (Keillor), **Supp. XVI:** 176

"Earl Painter" (Banks), **Supp. V:** 14–15

"Early Adventures of Ralph Ringwood, The" (Irving), **II:** 314

Early Americana (Richter), **Supp. XVIII:** 208, 210, 211, 220

Early Autumn (Parker), **Supp. XIX:** 184–185

Early Ayn Rand, The: A Selection of Her Unpublished Fiction (Rand), **Supp. IV Part 2:** 520

Early Dark (Price), **Supp. VI:** 262

Early Diary of Anaïs Nin, The, **Supp. X:** 184, 192

Early Elkin (Elkin), **Supp. VI: 42–43,** 45

"Early Evenin' Blues" (Hughes), **Retro. Supp. I:** 205

"Early Evening, Frankfort, Kentucky" (Trethewey), **Supp. XXI:** 243, 250

"Early History of a Seamstress" (Reznikoff), **Supp. XIV:** 277, 289

Early History of a Sewing-Machine Operator (Reznikoff), **Supp. XIV:** 289

"Early History of a Sewing-Machine Operator" (Reznikoff), **Supp. XIV:** 277

"Early History of a Writer" (Reznikoff), **Supp. XIV:** 278, 290

"Early in the Morning" (L.-Y. Lee), **Supp. XV:** 214

Early Lectures of Ralph Waldo Emerson, The (Emerson), **II:** 11

Early Light (Di Piero), **Supp. XIX:** 38, **38–40**

Early Lives of Melville, The (Sealts), **Retro. Supp. I:** 257

"Early Marriage" (Richter), **Supp. XVIII:** 209

Early Martyr and Other Poems, An (W. C. Williams), **Retro. Supp. I:** 423

"Early Morning: Cape Cod" (Swenson), **Supp. IV Part 2:** 641

"Early Rooms"(Hirshfield), **Supp. XXIII:** 130

"Early Spring between Madison and Bellingham" (R. Bly), **Supp. IV Part 1:** 71

Early Writing (O'Hara), **Supp. XXIII:** 220

Earnhardt, Dale, **Supp. XII:** 310

Earnshaw, Doris, **Supp. IV Part 1:** 310

"Earth" (Bryant), **Supp. I Part 1:** 157, 164, 167

"Earth, The" (Sexton), **Supp. II Part 2:** 696

Earth Abides (Stewart), **Supp. XVIII:** 138

"Earth and Fire" (Berry), **Supp. X:** 27

Earth as Air, The: An Ars Poetica (Sobin), **Supp. XVI: 285–286**

"Earth Being" (Toomer), **Supp. IX:** 320

Earth Goat (online), **Supp. XXII:** 61

Earth Gods, The (Gibran), **Supp. XX: 116, 123**

"Earth is parched with heat, The" (Very), **Supp. XXV:** 239

"Earthly Care a Heavenly Discipline" (Stowe), **Supp. I Part 2:** 586

"Earthly City of the Jews, The" (Kazin), **Retro. Supp. II:** 286

Earthly Meditations (Wrigley), **Supp. XVIII:** 304–305

"Earthly Meditations" (Wrigley), **Supp. XVIII:** 304–306

Earthly Possessions (Tyler), **Supp. IV Part 2:** 665–666, 671

Earth Power Coming (Ortiz, ed.), **Supp. IV Part 2:** 502

"Earth's Holocaust" (Hawthorne), **II:** 226, 231, 232, 242; **III:** 82; **Retro. Supp. I:** 152

Earth Without You, The (F. Wright), **Supp. XVII:** 243

Eason, Laura, **Supp. XXIII:** 79

East Coker (Eliot), **I:** 580, 581, 582, 585, 587

"East Coker" (Eliot), **Retro. Supp. I:** 66; **Supp. VIII:** 195, 196

"Easter" (Toomer), **Supp. III Part 2:** 486

"Easter, an Ode" (Lowell), **II:** 536

"Easter 1916" (Yeats), **Supp. XXI:** 61

"Easter Island: The Statues Speak" (Davison), **Supp. XXVI:** 71

"Easter Morning" (Ammons), **Supp. VII:** 34

"Easter Morning" (Clampitt), **Supp. IX:** 45

"Eastern Standard" (Huddle), **Supp. XXVI:** 149

"Easter Ode, An" (Dunbar), **Supp. II Part 1:** 196

"Easter"(O'Hara), **Supp. XXIII:** 211

Easter Parade, The (Yates), **Supp. XI:** 346, 349

"Easter Sermon, 1866" (Nelson), **Supp. XVIII:** 177

"Easter Service" (Di Piero), **Supp. XIX:** 39–40

"Easter Sunday: Recollection" (Gunn Allen), **Supp. IV Part 1:** 322

"Easter Wings" (Herbert), **Supp. IV Part 2:** 646

"East European Cooking" (Simic), **Supp. VIII:** 277

East Is East (Boyle), **Supp. VIII:** 1–3; **Supp. XX: 23–24, 25, 28**

Eastlake, William, **Supp. XIII:** 12

East Lynne (Wood), **Supp. I Part 1:** 35, 36; **Supp. I Part 2:** 459, 462; **Supp. XVI:** 182

Eastman, Elaine Goodale, **Supp. X:** 103

Eastman, Max, **Supp. III Part 2:** 620; **Supp. X:** 131, 134, 135, 137; **Supp. XV:** 295; **Supp. XVI:** 185; **Supp. XVII:** 96; **Supp. XXI:** 6; **Supp. XXII:** 274, 275, 277

Eastman, P. D., **Supp. XXV:** 1

East of Eden (Steinbeck), **IV:** 51, 56–57, 59

"East of the Sun and West of the Moon" (Merwin), **Supp. III Part 1:** 344

Easton, Alison, **Retro. Supp. II:** 143, 144, 145

Easton, Bret Ellis, **Supp. XI:** 65

Easton, Nina J., **Supp. XIX:** 137

Easton, Robert, **Supp. IV Part 2:** 461, 474

East River (Asch), **Supp. XXIII:** 1, 3, 7, **14–15**

"East-Side: New York" (Bodenheim), **Supp. XXV:** 22

East Wind (Lowell), **II:** 527

East Wind: West Wind (Buck), **Supp. II Part 1:** 114–115

Easy Rawlins mysteries, **Supp. XIII:** 236, **237–241,** 242

Easy Rider (film), **Supp. XI:** 293, **308,** 309

Easy Rider (Hopper), **Supp. XXVI:** 26

Eat a Bowl of Tea (Chu), **Supp. X:** 291

"Eating " (Bass), **Supp. XVI:** 23–24

"Eating Alone" (L.-Y. Lee), **Supp. XV:** 214

"Eating Barley Sugar and Waiting to Be Ninety"(Hadas), **Supp. XXIII:** 120–121

Eating Naked (Dobyns), **Supp. XIII: 78–79**

"Eating Out" (L. Michaels), **Supp. XVI:** 209

"Eating Poetry" (Strand), **Supp. IV Part 2:** 626

"Eating the Whole" (C. Frost), **Supp. XV:** 101

"Eating Together" (L.-Y. Lee), **Supp. XV:** 214

"Eating with My Fingers" (C. Frost), **Supp. XV:** 97

Eaton, Edith, **Supp. X:** 291

Eaton, Mark A., **Supp. XXIII:** 129, 130, 136

Eaton, Peggy, **Supp. I Part 2:** 461

Eaton, Winnifred, **Supp. X:** 291

"Eatonville Anthology, The" (Hurston), **Supp. VI:** 152

Eat Pray Love (Gilbert), **Supp. XXII:** 83, 90

Eat the Document (film, Pennebaker), **Supp. XVIII:** 19, 26, 27, 28

"Ebb and Flow, The" (Taylor), **IV:** 161

"Ebenezer Marsh, 1725" (Schnackenberg), **Supp. XV:** 256

Eben Holden (Bacheller), **I:** 216

Eberhardt, Isabelle, **Supp. IV Part 1:** 92

Eberhart, Mrs., **I:** 521–522, 530

Eberhart, Richard, **I: 521–543; II:** 535–536; **III:** 527; **IV:** 416; **Retro. Supp. II:** 176, 178; **Supp. I Part 1:** 83; **Supp. XII:** 119; **Supp. XXVI:** 68

Eble, Kenneth E., **Supp. I Part 1:** 201

Ebony and Topaz (C. S. Johnson, ed.), **Supp. XXVI:** 170

"Ecce Homo" (Cliff), **Supp. XXII:** 76

Eccentricities of a Nightingale (T. Williams), **IV:** 382, 385, 397, 398

Ecclesiastica Historia Integram Ecclesiae (Taylor), **IV:** 163

"Echart" (Sobin), **Supp. XVI:** 289

"Echo, The" (Bowles), **Supp. IV Part 1:** 84, 86, 87

Echo, Thomas William, **Supp. XXVI:** 87

Echoes inside the Labyrinth (McGrath), **Supp. X:** 127

Echo Park (Connelly), **Supp. XXI: 77–78**

Eckehart, Meister, **Supp. XV:** 225

Eckhart, Maria, **Supp. V:** 212

Eclipse (Hogan), **Supp. IV Part 1:** 397, 400, 402

Eclipse, a Nightmare (Montalembert), **Supp. XV:** 349

"Eclipse"(Schott), **Supp. XXIII:** 252

"Eclogue" (Oppen), **Supp. XXVI:** 232

Eclogues (Virgil), **Supp. VIII:** 31; **Supp. XXIV:** 156

Eclogues of Virgil, The (Ferry, trans.), **Supp. XXIV: 156–157**

"Ecologue" (Ginsberg), **Supp. II Part 1:** 326

"Ecologues of These States 1969–1971" (Ginsberg), **Supp. II Part 1:** 325

Ecology of a Cracker Childhood (Ray), **Supp. XVIII:** 189, 191, 192, 193, **195–199,** 201, 202, 204

"Economics of Negro Emancipation in the United States, The" (Du Bois), **Supp. II Part 1:** 174

"Economics of the Cracker Landscape: Poverty as an Environmental Issue in Larry Brown's *Joe*" (Watson), *Supp. XXI:* 46

"Economic Theory of Women's Dress, The" (Veblen), **Supp. I Part 2:** 636

Economy of the Unlost: Reading Simonides of Keos with Paul Celan (Carson), **Supp. XII:** 110–111

Ecotactics: The Sierra Club Handbook for Environmental Activists (Mitchell and Stallings, eds.), **Supp. IV Part 2:** 488

"Ecstasy" (Bierds), **Supp. XVII:** 34

"Ecstasy" (Olds), **Supp. X:** 206

"Ecstasy of Influence, The" (Lethem), **Supp. XVIII:** 150

"Ecstatic" (Komunyakaa), **Supp. XIII:** 131

Edda, **Supp. X:** 114

Eddy, Mary Baker, **I:** 583; **III:** 506

Edel, Leon, **I:** 20; **II:** 338–339; **Retro. Supp. I:** 218, 224, 231

Edelberg, Cynthia, **Supp. IV Part 1:** 155

"Eden and My Generation" (Levis), **Supp. XI:** 270

Edenbaum, Robert, **Supp. IV Part 1:** 352
Eden Tree (Bynner), **Supp. XV:** 42, 51
Edenville Owls (Parker), **Supp. XIX:** 190
Eder, Richard, **Supp. XII:** 189; **Supp. XV:** 62, 187, 259, 261
Edgar Huntly; or, Memoirs of a Sleep-Walker (Brown), **Supp. I Part 1:** 140–144, 145
"Edge" (Plath), **Retro. Supp. II:** 256; **Supp. I Part 2:** 527, 547
Edge, Mary E., **II:** 316
Edgell, David, **Supp. XXIV:** 71
Edgell, Zee, **Supp. XXIII: 83–96**
"Edge of Possibility, The: Susan Warner and the World of Sunday School Fiction" (S. Gates), **Supp. XVIII:** 267
"Edge of the Great Rift, The" (Theroux), **Supp. VIII:** 325
Edge of the Sea, The (Carson), **Supp. IX:** 19, **25–31,** 32
Edge of the Woods, The: Iroquoia, 1534–1701 (Parmenter), **Supp. XXVI:** 85
Edgers, Geoff, **Supp. XV:** 113
Edgeworth, Maria, **II:** 8; **Supp. XV:** 231; **Supp. XX: 108**
Edible Woman, The (Atwood), **Supp. XIII:** 19, 20, **20–21**
"Edict by the King of Prussia, An" (Franklin), **II:** 120
Edie: An American Biography (Stein), **Supp. XVI:** 245
Edinburgh Days: or, Doing What I Want to Do (Pickering), **Supp. XXI:** 200–201
Edison, Thomas A., **I:** 483; **Supp. I Part 2:** 392
Edith Wharton (Joslin), **Retro. Supp. I:** 376
Edith Wharton: A Biography (Lewis), **Retro. Supp. I:** 362
Edith Wharton: A Woman in Her Time (Auchincloss), **Retro. Supp. I:** 370
Edith Wharton: Matters of Mind and Spirit (Singley), **Retro. Supp. I:** 373
Edith Wharton's Argument with America (Ammons), **Retro. Supp. I:** 364
Edith Wharton's Brave New Politics (Bauer), **Retro. Supp. I:** 381
Edith Wharton's Letters from the Underworld (Waid), **Retro. Supp. I:** 360
Edith Wharton: Traveller in the Land of Letters (Goodwyn), **Retro. Supp. I:** 370
"Editing and Glosses" (Reznikoff), **Supp. XIV:** 283
Editing of Emily Dickinson, The (Franklin), **Retro. Supp. I:** 41
"Editor and the Schoolma'am, The" (Frederic), **II:** 130
"Editor's Easy Chair" (Howells), **II:** 276
"Editor's Study, The" (Howells), **II:** 275, 276, 285
"Editor Whedon" (Masters), **Supp. I Part 2:** 463
Edlin, Mari, **Supp. X:** 266
Edman, Irwin, **III:** 605; **Supp. XXV:** 255, 258
Edmond (Mamet), **Supp. XIV:** 241, 248, 249, 250
Edmonds, Dale, **Supp. XXIII:** 291

Edmondson, Belinda, **Supp. XXII:** 70
Edmundson, Mark, **Retro. Supp. II:** 262
Edmund Wilson (Kriegel), **Supp. XXIV: 216–217**
Edsel (Shapiro), **Supp. II Part 2:** 703, 704, 717–719
Edson, Margaret, **Supp. XVIII: 35–52**
Edson, Russell, **Supp. VIII:** 279
"Educated American Woman, An" (Cheever), **Supp. I Part 1:** 194
"Education, An" (Ozick), **Supp. V:** 267
Education and Living (Bourne), **I:** 252
"Education by Poetry" (Frost), **Supp. XV:** 215
"Education of a Storyteller, The" (Bambara), **Supp. XI:** 20
Education of Black People, The (Du Bois), **Supp. II Part 1:** 186
Education of Harriet Hatfield, The (Sarton), **Supp. VIII: 257–258**
Education of Henry Adams, The (Adams), **I:** 1, 5, 6, 11, 14, 15–18, 19, 20–21, 111; **II:** 276; **III:** 504; **Retro. Supp. I:** 53, 59; **Supp. IX:** 19; **Supp. XIV:** 299
Education of H*y*m*a*n K*a*p*l*a*n, The (Rosten), **Supp. XVII:** 9
"Education of Mingo, The" (C. Johnson), **Supp. VI:** 193, 194
"Education of Norman Podhoretz, The" (Goldberg), **Supp. VIII:** 238
Education of Oscar Fairfax, The (Auchincloss), **Supp. IV Part 1:** 25, 36
"Education of the Poet" (Glück), **Supp. V:** 78, 80
Education sentimentale (Flaubert), **III:** 315
"Education the Imagination" (Koch), **Supp. XV:** 175–176, 177
Edwards, Clifford, **Supp. XVIII:** 220
Edwards, Eli. *See* McKay, Claude
Edwards, Esther, **I:** 545
Edwards, Harry Stillwell, **Supp. XXII:** 193
Edwards, John, **I:** 478
Edwards, Jonathan, **I: 544–566; II:** 432; **Retro. Supp. II:** 187; **Supp. I Part 1:** 301, 302; **Supp. I Part 2:** 552, 594, 700; **Supp. IV Part 2:** 430; **Supp. VIII:** 205; **Supp. XXIV:** 72
Edwards, Sarah, **I:** 545
Edwards, Thomas, **Supp. XV:** 20
Edwards, Thomas R., **Supp. XVI:** 207
Edwards, Timothy, **I:** 545
Edwards-Yearwood, Grace, **Supp. VIII:** 81; **Supp. XXII:** 213
"Edwin Arlington Robinson" (Cowley), **Supp. II Part 1:** 144
Edwin Arlington Robinson (Winters), **Supp. II Part 2:** 812
Edwin Booth (play), **Supp. IV Part 1:** 89
E. E. Cummings (Marks), **I:** 438
E. E. Cummings: A Miscellany (Cummings), **I:** 429, 441
E. E. Cummings: A Miscellany, Revised (Cummings), **I:** 429
"Effects of Analogy" (Stevens), **Retro. Supp. I:** 297

Effluences from the Sacred Caves; More Selected Essays and Reviews (Carruth), **Supp. XVI:** 46
"Effort at Speech between Two People" (Rukeyser), **Supp. VI:** 276, 284
"Efforts of Affection" (Moore), **III:** 214
"Efforts of Affection: A Memoir of Marianne Moore" (Bishop), **Retro. Supp. II:** 52
Egan, Jennifer, **Supp. XIX: 49–63; Supp. XXIII:** 299, 300
Egan, Leona, **Supp. XXI:** 6
"Egg, The" (Anderson), **I:** 113, 114
"Egg, The" (Snyder), **Supp. VIII:** 302
Eggers, David, **Supp. XXIV:** 131, 200
Eggleston, George Cary, **Supp. XVIII:** 15
"Eggplant Epithalamion, The" (Jong), **Supp. V:** 119
"Eggs" (Olds), **Supp. X:** 206
"Eggshell" (Stern), **Supp. IX:** 299
Egoist, The (Meredith), **II:** 186
Egorova, Lubov, **Supp. IX:** 58
"Egotism, or the Bosom Sergent" (Hawthorne), **II:** 227, 239
"Egyptian Pulled Glass Bottle in the Shape of a Fish, An" (Moore), **III:** 195, 213
Ehrenfels, Christian von, **Supp. XIV:** 198
Ehrenpreis, Irvin, **Supp. XII:** 128
Ehrenreich, Barbara, **Supp. XVII:** 210
Ehrhart, W. D., **Supp. XIX:** 281
Ehrlich, Gretel, **Supp. XIV:** 227; **Supp. XVIII:** 189; **Supp. XXVI:** 31, 187
"Ehue! fugaces, Posthume, Posthume, Labuntur anni" (Very), **Supp. XXV:** 243, 247
Eichmann, Adolf, **Supp. XII:** 166
Eichmann in Jerusalem (Arendt), **Retro. Supp. II:** 28; **Supp. VIII:** 243; **Supp. XII:** 166
"Eichmann in New York: The New York Intellectuals and the Hannah Arendt Controversy" (Rabinbach), **Supp. XII:** 166
"Eidolon" (Warren), **IV:** 239
"Eiger Dreams" (Krakauer), **Supp. XVIII:** 107
Eiger Dreams: Ventures Among Men and Mountains (Krakauer), **Supp. XVIII:** 105, 106, 107
Eight Cousins (Alcott), **Supp. I Part 1:** 29, 38, 42, 43
18 Poems from the Quechua (Strand, trans.), **Supp. IV Part 2:** 630
"18 West 11th Street" (Merrill), **Supp. III Part 1:** 323, 328
1876: A Novel (Vidal), **Supp. IV Part 2:** 677, 684, 688, 689, 691, 692; **Supp. XIX:** 141
"18,000 CDs" (Halliday), **Supp. XIX:** 92
"Eighth Air Force" (Jarrell), **II:** 373–374, 377
Eight Harvard Poets, **I:** 429, 475
"Eighth Avenue Incident" (Halliday), **Supp. XIX:** 89–90
"Eighth Day, The" (Apple), **Supp. XVII:** 6, 50
"Eighth Ditch, The" (Baraka), **Supp. II Part 1:** 40

"'80s Pastoral: Frederick Barthelme's *Moon Deluxe* Ten Years On" (Peters), **Supp. XI:** 39

Eight Men (Wright), **IV:** 478, 488, 494

80 Flowers (Zukofsky), **Supp. III Part 2:** 631

Eikon Basilike, The, **Supp. IV Part 2:** 435

Eileen (Masters), **Supp. I Part 2:** 460

Eimi (Cummings), **I:** 429, 433, 434, 439–440

"Einstein" (MacLeish), **III:** 5, 8, 10–11, 18–19

Einstein, Albert, **I:** 493; **III:** 8, 10, 21, 161; **IV:** 69, 375, 410, 411, 421; **Retro. Supp. I:** 63; **Supp. I Part 2:** 609, 643; **Supp. III Part 2:** 621; **Supp. V:** 290; **Supp. XII:** 45

Eiseley, Loren, **III:** 227–228

Eisenberg, Deborah, **Supp. XXIII:** 290

Eisenhower, Dwight D., **I:** 136, 376; **II:** 548; **III:** 215; **IV:** 75; **Supp. I Part 1:** 291; **Supp. III Part 2:** 624; **Supp. V:** 45

Eisenstadt, Jill, **Supp. XVIII:** 135

Eisenstein, Sergei, **I:** 481; **Supp. XXI:** 170

Eisinger, Chester E., **I:** 302; **II:** 604; **Supp. IX:** 15

Eisner, Douglas, **Supp. X:** 155

Elam, Angela, **Supp. XI:** 290

El Bernardo (Balbuena), **Supp. V:** 11

Elbert, Sarah, **Supp. I Part 1:** 34, 41

Elder, Donald, **II:** 417, 426, 435, 437; **Supp. XV:** 137

Elder, John, **Supp. IX:** 25; **Supp. XXVI:** 38

Elder, Lonne, III, **Supp. IV Part 1:** 362

Elder, Richard, **Supp. XII:** 172

"Elder Sister, The" (Olds), **Supp. X:** 205–206

Elder Statesman, The (Eliot), **I:** 572, 573, 583; **Retro. Supp. I:** 53, 65

"Eldest Sister to Psyche, The" (Stallings), **Supp. XXV:** 234

E. L. Doctorow (Harter and Thompson), **Supp. IV Part 1:** 217

Eldredge, Kay, **Supp. IX:** 254, 259

Eldridge, Florence, **III:** 154, 403; **IV:** 357

Eleanor of Aquitaine, **III:** 470

Eleanor of Guienne, **I:** 14

Eleanor: or, Slave Catching in the Quaker City (Lippard), **Supp. XXIII:** 180, 185

"Elect, The" (Taylor), **Supp. V:** 323

"Elections, Nicaragua, 1984" (Kingsolver), **Supp. VII:** 208

Elective Affinities (Goethe; Bogan and Mayer, trans.), **Supp. III Part 1:** 63

Electra (Euripides), **III:** 398

Electra (Sophocles), **III:** 398; **IV:** 370; **Supp. IX:** 102

"Electra on Azalea Path" (Plath), **Supp. I Part 2:** 538

"Electrical Storm" (Bishop), **Supp. I Part 1:** 93

"Electrical Storm" (Hayden), **Supp. II Part 1:** 370

"Electric Arrows" (Proulx), **Supp. VII:** 256

"Electric Girl, The" (P. Benedict), **Supp. XXIII:** 40

"Electricity Saviour" (Olds), **Supp. X:** 215

Electric Kool-Aid Acid Test, The (Wolfe), **Supp. III Part 2:** 575–577, 582–584; **Supp. XI:** 239

Electric Lady, The (film), **Supp. XI:** 309

Electronic Book Review, **Supp. XXII:** 256, 257, 261

Elegant Extracts (Knox), **II:** 8

"Elegant Tom Dillar" (Briggs), **Supp. XVIII:** 17

"Elegiac" (Ferry), **Supp. XXIV:** 148–149

Elegiac Feelings American (Corso), **Supp. XII: 131–134**

"Elegiac Fragments" (Everwine), **Supp. XV:** 89

Elegies (Rukeyser), **Supp. VI:** 273

"Elegies" (Rukeyser), **Supp. VI:** 272

"Elegies for Paradise Valley" (Hayden), **Supp. II Part 1:** 363

"Elegy" (Bidart), **Supp. XV:** 25, 29

Elegy (Levis), **Supp. XI:** 257, 259, 261, **271–272**

"Elegy" (Merwin), **Supp. III Part 1:** 351

"Elegy" (Stafford), **Supp. XI:** 322

"Elegy" (Tate), **IV:** 128

"Elegy, for the U.S.N. Dirigible, Macon, An" (Winters), **Supp. II Part 2:** 810

"Elegy Ending in the Sound of a Skipping Rope" (Levis), **Supp. XI:** 271–272

"Elegy for 41 Whales Beached in Florence, Oregon, June 1979" (Bierds), **Supp. XVII:** 27

"Elegy for D. H. Lawrence, An" (W. C. Williams), **Retro. Supp. I:** 421

"Elegy for My Father" (Strand), **Supp. IV Part 2:** 628

"Elegy for My Mother" (Wagoner), **Supp. IX:** 330

"Elegy for Redondo Beach" (Jarman), **Supp. XVII:** 112, 113

Elegy for September, An (Nichols), **Supp. XIII:** 268

"Elegy for Thelonious" (Komunyakaa), **Supp. XIII:** 118

"Elegy for the Lost Umbrella" (Stallings), **Supp. XXIII:** 124; **Supp. XXV:** 231, 232

"Elegy for the Native Guards" (Trethewey), **Supp. XXI:** 255

"Elegy for the U.S.N. Dirigible, Macon, A" (Winters), **Supp. II Part 2:** 810

"Elegy in Dialogue" (Taggard), **Supp. XXII:** 276

"Elegy"(J. Schoolcraft), **Supp. XXIII:** 231

"Elegy of Last Resort" (Nemerov), **III:** 271

"Elegy with a Thimbleful of Water in the Cage" (Levis), **Supp. XI:** 272

Elegy Written in a Country Churchyard (Gray), **I:** 68

"Elegy Written in a Country Churchyard" (Gray), **Supp. XIV:** 8

"Elementary Scene, The" (Jarrell), **II:** 387, 388, 389

"Elements" (M. Frank), **Supp. X:** 213

Elements of Style, The (Strunk), **Supp. I Part 2:** 670

"Elenita, Cards, Palm, Water" (Cisneros), **Supp. VII:** 64

"Eleonora" (Poe), **III:** 412

Eleothriambos (Lee), **IV:** 158

"Elephant & Ocean" (Notley), **Supp. XXII:** 230

"Elephants" (Moore), **III:** 203

"Elephant's Dance, The" (D. West), **Supp. XVIII:** 281

"Elevator, The" (Dixon), **Supp. XII:** 154

"Elevator Boy" (Hughes), **Retro. Supp. I:** 200; **Supp. I Part 1:** 326

"Eleven" (Cisneros), **Supp. VII:** 69

Eleven Essays in the European Novel (Blackmur), **Supp. II Part 1:** 91, 111

Eleven Heavy Things (installation, July), **Supp. XXIV:** 200

Eleven Kinds of Loneliness (Yates), **Supp. XI: 340–343,** 349

Eleven Poems on the Same Theme (Warren), **IV:** 239–241

"Eleven Times a Poem" (Corso), **Supp. XII:** 132, 133

El Greco (Doménikos Theotokópoulos), **I:** 387; **III:** 212

El-Hage, George N., **Supp. XX: 116**

"El-Hajj Malik El-Shabazz" (Hayden), **Supp. II Part 1:** 379

"Eli, the Fanatic" (P. Roth), **Supp. III Part 2:** 407–408

Elia, Nada, **Supp. XXII:** 73

Eliade, Mircea, **Supp. XVI:** 292

Elie, Paul, **Supp. XXII:** 91–92

Eliot, Charles William, **I:** 5; **II:** 345; **Retro. Supp. I:** 55; **Supp. I Part 2:** 479; **Supp. IX:** 94

Eliot, George, **I:** 375, 458, 459, 461, 467; **II:** 179, 181, 191–192, 275, 319, 324, 338, 577; **IV:** 311, 322; **Retro. Supp. I:** 218, 220, 225; **Supp. I Part 1:** 370; **Supp. I Part 2:** 559, 579; **Supp. IV Part 1:** 31, 297; **Supp. IV Part 2:** 677; **Supp. IX:** 38, 43, 51; **Supp. V:** 258; **Supp. XI:** 68; **Supp. XII:** 335; **Supp. XIV:** 344; **Supp. XX: 108**

Eliot, T. S., **I:** 48, 49, 52, 59, 60, 64, 66, 68, 105, 107, 215–216, 236, 243, 256, 259, 261, 266, 384, 386, 395, 396, 399, 403, 430, 433, 441, 446, 475, 478, 479, 482, 521, 522, 527, **567–591; II:** 65, 96, 158, 168, 316, 331, 376, 386, 529, 530, 532, 537, 542, 545; **III:** 1, 4, 5, 6, 7–8, 9, 10, 11, 14, 17, 20, 21, 23, 26, 34, 174, 194, 195–196, 205–206, 220, 236, 239, 269, 270–271, 277–278, 301, 409, 428, 435, 436, 453, 456–457, 459–460, 461–462, 464, 466, 471, 476, 478, 485, 488, 492, 493, 498, 504, 509, 511, 517, 524, 527, 539, 572, 575, 586, 591, 594, 600, 613; **IV:** 27, 74, 82, 83, 95, 122, 123, 127, 129, 134, 138, 140, 141, 191, 201, 237, 331, 379, 402, 403, 418, 419, 420, 430, 431, 439, 442, 491; **Retro. Supp. I: 51–71,** 74, 80, 89, 91, 171, 198, 210, 283, 289, 290, 292, 296, 298, 299, 311, 324, 359, 411, 413, 414, 416,

417, 420, 428; **Retro. Supp. II:** 79, 178, 189, 262, 326; **Supp. I Part 1:** 257, 264, 268, 270, 274, 299; **Supp. I Part 2:** 387, 423, 455, 536, 554, 624, 659, 721; **Supp. II Part 1:** 1, 4, 8, 20, 30, 91, 98, 103, 136, 314; **Supp. III Part 1:** 9, 10, 26, 31, 37, 41, 43, 44, 48, 62–64, 73, 91, 99–100, 105–106, 273; **Supp. III Part 2:** 541, 611, 612, 617, 624; **Supp. IV Part 1:** 40, 47, 284, 380, 404; **Supp. IV Part 2:** 436; **Supp. IX:** 158–159, 229; **Supp. V:** 79, 97, 101, 338, 343, 344; **Supp. VIII:** 19, 21, 93, 102, 105, 182, 195, 205, 290, 292; **Supp. X:** 59, 115, 119, 124, 187, 324; **Supp. XI:** 242; **Supp. XII:** 45, 159, 198, 308; **Supp. XIII:** 77, 104, 115, 332, 341–342, 344, 346; **Supp. XIV:** 5, 13, 107, 287, 290, 306, 347; **Supp. XIX:** 12; **Supp. XV:** 20, 51, 139, 177, 181, 186, 216, 218, 250, 251, 258, 298, 302, 303, 306, 307; **Supp. XVI:** 158–159, 204, 207, 282; **Supp. XVII:** 36, 71, 75, 111, 240; **Supp. XVIII:** 136; **Supp. XX: 86, 108, 199; Supp. XXIII:** 25, 60, 166; **Supp. XXVI:** 143

Eliot's Early Years (Gordon), **Retro. Supp. I:** 55

"Elizabeth" (Longfellow), **I:** 502

"Elizabeth, 1905" (Schnackenberg), **Supp. XV:** 253, 256

Elizabeth Appleton (O'Hara), **III:** 362, 364, 375–377

"Elizabeth Bishop (1911–1979)" (Merrill), **Retro. Supp. II:** 53

"Elizabeth Bishop in Brazil" (Brown), **Supp. I Part 1:** 96

"Elizabeth Bishop's *North & South*" (Lowell), *Retro. Supp. II:* 40–41

"Elizabeth Gone" (Sexton), **Supp. II Part 2:** 674, 681

Elizabeth Rex (Findley), **Supp. XX:** 62–63

Elizabeth Stoddard and the Boundaries of Bourgeois Culture (Mahoney), **Supp. XV:** 270

Elk Heads on the Wall (Ríos), **Supp. IV Part 2:** 540

Elkin, Stanley, **Supp. VI: 41–59**

Elkins, Andrew, **Supp. XXIII:** 131, 135

Elkins, Marilyn, **Supp. XXIV:** 64

"Elk Song" (Hogan), **Supp. IV Part 1:** 406

Ella in Bloom (Hearon), **Supp. VIII: 70–71**

Elledge, Jim, **Supp. XIII:** 88

Ellen Foster: A Novel (Gibbons), **Supp. X:** 41, **42–44,** 46, 47, 49, 50

Ellen Montgomery's Bookshelf (S. and A. Warner), **Supp. XVIII:** 264

Ellen Rogers (Farrell), **II:** 42–43

"Ellen's Dream" (Gioia), **Supp. XV:** 128

"Ellen West" (Bidart), **Supp. XV: 26–27**

Eller, Ernest, **Supp. I Part 2:** 497

Ellerman, Winifred, **Supp. I Part 1:** 258–259. *See also* McAlmon, Mrs. Robert (Winifred Ellerman)

"El libro de la sexualidad" (Simic), *Supp. VIII:* 283

Ellington, Duke, **Retro. Supp. II:** 115; **Supp. IV Part 1:** 360; **Supp. IX:** 164

Elliot, Charles, **Supp. V:** 161

Elliot, George P., **Supp. XV:** 92

Elliott, George B., **III:** 478

Elliott, J. W. M., **Supp. XXVI:** 87, 88

Ellipse, The: Selected Poems of Leonardo Sinisgalli (Di Piero, trans.), **Supp. XIX:** 34

"Ellipsis" (C. Frost), **Supp. XV:** 107

Ellis, Albert, **Supp. IV Part 2:** 527

Ellis, Anne, **Supp. XVI:** 38

Ellis, Bret Easton, **Supp. XII:** 81; **Supp. XVIII:** 135

Ellis, Brett Easton, **Supp. X:** 7

Ellis, Charles, **Supp. I Part 1:** 99

Ellis, Havelock, **II:** 276; **Supp. XX: 117, 235; Supp. XXII:** 198

Ellis, John Harvard, **Supp. I Part 1:** 103

Ellis, Katherine, **IV:** 114

Ellis, Kelly, **Supp. XXI:** 249

Ellis, Ron, **Supp. XXII:** 209

Ellis, Thomas Sayers, **Supp. XXI:** 246

"Ellis Island" (Helprin), **Supp. XXV:** 85

Ellis Island and Other Stories (Helprin), **Supp. XXV:** 82, 83, 85

Ellison, Harlan, **Supp. XIII:** 61

Ellison, Ralph, **IV:** 250, 493; **Retro. Supp. II:** 3, **111–130; Supp. II Part 1:** 33, **221–252; Supp. IV, Part 1:** 374; **Supp. IX:** 114, 316; **Supp. VIII:** 105, 245; **Supp. X:** 324; **Supp. XI:** 18, 92, 275; **Supp. XIII:** 186, 233, 305; **Supp. XIV:** 306; **Supp. XIX:** 148, 149, 155; **Supp. XV:** 194; **Supp. XVI:** 135, 139; **Supp. XVIII:** 59, 61, 62, 277, 283

Ellmann, Maud, **Supp. IV Part 1:** 302

Ellmann, Richard, **Supp. VIII:** 105; **Supp. XV:** 74

Ellroy, James, **Supp. XIV:** 26; **Supp. XXI:** 71

Elm, Damas, **Supp. XXVI:** 89

Elman, Richard, **Supp. V:** 40

"Elmer" (Faulkner), **Retro. Supp. I:** 79, 80

Elmer Gantry (Lewis), **I:** 26, 364; **II:** 447–449, 450, 455

Elmer the Great (Lardner), **II:** 427

"Elms" (Glück), **Supp. V:** 85

"Elms Dying, The—And My Friend, Lew Stillwell, Dead" (Bronk), **Supp. XXI:** 31

Eloges (Perse), **Supp. XIII:** 344

"Eloquence of Grief, An" (Crane), **I:** 411

"El Paso Del Norte"(Kenny), **Supp. XXIII:** 150

"El Río Grande" (Mora), **Supp. XIII:** 224

"*El* Round up" (Alvarez), **Supp. VII:** 11

"El Salvador: Requiem and Invocation" (Levertov), **Supp. III Part 1:** 284

Elsasser, Henry, **I:** 226

"Elsa Wertman" (Masters), **Supp. I Part 2:** 462–463

Elsie John and Joey Martinez: Two Stories (Huncke), **Supp. XIV:** 148

Elsie Venner (Holmes), **Supp. I Part 1:** 243, 315–316

Elton, Charles, **Supp. XIV:** 192

Éluard, Paul, **III:** 528; **Supp. IV Part 1:** 80; **Supp. XVII:** 244

Elvins, Kells, **Supp. III Part 1:** 93, 101

Ely, Richard T., **Supp. I Part 1:** 5; **Supp. I Part 2:** 640, 645

"Emancipation. A Life Fable" (Chopin), **Retro. Supp. II:** 59; **Supp. I Part 1:** 207–208

"Emancipation in the British West Indies" (Emerson), **II:** 13

"Emancipation Proclamation, The" (Emerson), **II:** 13

Emanuel, James, **Supp. I Part 1:** 346

Embargo, The (Bryant), **Supp. I Part 1:** 152–153

"Embarkation for Cythera, The" (Ferry), **Supp. XXIV:** 149

Embarrassments (James), **Retro. Supp. I:** 229

Embezzler, The (Auchincloss), **Supp. IV Part 1:** 24, 30–31

"Embraces" (Davison), **Supp. XXVI:** 72

"Embroidery, The" (C. Frost), **Supp. XV:** 97

"Emerald" (Doty), **Supp. XI:** 131

"Emerald, The" (Merrill), **Supp. III Part 1:** 328

Emerald City (Egan), **Supp. XIX:** 49, **52–53**

"Emerald City" (Egan), **Supp. XIX:** 52

"Emergence of Flight from Aristotle's Mud, The" (Goldbarth), **Supp. XII:** 190

Emergency Exit (Major), **Supp. XXII:** 174, **175,** 182

"Emergency Haying" (Carruth), **Supp. XVI:** 55

"Emergency Room" (Mora), **Supp. XIII:** 218

"Emerging Voices: The Teaching of Writing" (Mora), **Supp. XIII:** 220

Emerson, and Other Essays (Chapman), **Supp. XIV:** 41–44

Emerson, Ellen, **Supp. I Part 1:** 33

Emerson, John, **Supp. XVI:** 185, 186, 190, 192

Emerson, Ralph Waldo, **I:** 98, 217, 220, 222, 224, 228, 239, 246, 251, 252, 253, 257, 260, 261, 283, 386, 397, 402, 424, 433, 444, 447, 455, 458, 460–461, 463, 464, 485, 561; **II: 1–24,** 49, 92, 127–128, 169, 170, 226, 233, 237, 273–274, 275, 278, 289, 295, 301, 313, 315, 336, 338, 344, 402, 491, 503; **III:** 53, 82, 171, 174, 260, 277, 409, 424, 428, 453, 454, 507, 576–577, 606, 614; **IV:** 60, 167, 169, 170, 171, 172, 173–174, 176, 178, 183, 186, 187, 192, 201, 202, 211, 335, 338, 340, 342, 350; **Retro. Supp. I:** 34, 53, 54, 57, 62, 74–75, 76, 125, 148–149, 152–153, 159, 217, 250, 298, 392, 400, 403; **Retro. Supp. II:** 96, 113, 135, 142, 155, 207, 262; **Supp. I Part 1:** 2, 28–29, 31, 33, 188, 299, 308–309, 317, 358, 365, 366, 368; **Supp. I Part 2:** 374, 383, 393, 407, 413, 416, 420, 422, 474, 482, 580, 582, 602, 659, 679; **Supp. II Part 1:** 280, 288; **Supp. III Part 1:**

387; **Supp. IV Part 2:** 439, 597, 619; **Supp. IX:** 38, 90, 175, 176, 181; **Supp. V:** 118; **Supp. VIII:** 42, 105, 106, 108, 198, 201, 204, 205, 292; **Supp. X:** 42, 45, 121, 223; **Supp. XI:** 203; **Supp. XIII:** 141, 145, 233, 246, **Supp. XIII:** 247; **Supp. XIV:** 41–44, 46, 54, 104, 177; **Supp. XV:** 219, 224; **Supp. XVI:** 84; **Supp. XVII:** 42, 236; **Supp. XX: 115, 116; Supp. XXI:** 217; **Supp. XXIII:** 161, 190; **Supp. XXIV:** 4, 67, 74, 77; **Supp. XXV:** 241, 250; **Supp. XXVI:** 37

"Emerson and the Essay" (Gass), **Supp. VI:** 88

"Emerson the Lecturer" (Lowell), **Supp. I Part 2:** 420, 422

Emerson-Thoreau Award, **Retro. Supp. I:** 67

Emery, Clark, **III:** 478

Emery, Mary Lou, **Supp. XXII:** 73

E. M. Forster (Trilling), **Supp. III Part 2:** 496, 501, 504

"Emigre in Autumn, An" (Gioia), **Supp. XV:** 120

Emily, Alone (O'Nan), **Supp. XXV:** 145, 149, 150–151

"Emily Dickinson and Class" (Erkkila), **Retro. Supp. I:** 42–43

Emily Dickinson Editorial Collective, **Retro. Supp. I:** 47

Emily Dickinson in Southern California (X. J. Kennedy), **Supp. XV: 164–165**

"Emily Dickinson's Defunct" (Nelson), **Supp. XVIII:** 173

Emily Dickinson: Woman Poet (Bennett), **Retro. Supp. I:** 42

Eminent Victorians (Strachey), **Supp. I Part 2:** 485

Emma (Austen), **Supp. XVIII:** 149

"Emma and Eginhard" (Longfellow), **III:** 505

"Emma Enters a Sentence of Elizabeth Bishop's" (Gass), **Supp. VI:** 93

Emmanuel Appodocca: or, A Blighted Life (Philip), **Supp. XXI:** 160

"Emmaus" (Di Piero), **Supp. XIX:** 42, 43

Emperor Jones, The (O'Neill), **II:** 278; **III:** 391, 392

Emperor of Haiti (Hughes), **Supp. I Part 1:** 339

"Emperor of Ice Cream, The" (Stevens), **IV:** 76, 80–81

"Emperors" (Dunn), **Supp. XI:** 155

"Emperor's New Clothes, The" (Anderson), **I:** 441

"Empire" (Ford), **Supp. V:** 69

Empire: A Novel (Vidal), **Supp. IV Part 2:** 677, 684, 686, 690; **Supp. XIX:** 132

"Empire Builders" (MacLeish), **III:** 14

Empire City, The: or, New York by Night and Day (Lippard), **Supp. XXIII:** 178, 180, 183, 184, 185

Empire Falls (Russo), **Supp. XII: 339–343**

Empire of Summer, The (Doty), **Supp. XI:** 120

Empire of the Senseless (Acker), **Supp. XII:** 5, **6, 14–16**

"Empires" (Simic), **Supp. VIII:** 282

"Emporium" (Shapiro), **Supp. II Part 2:** 705

Empress of the Splendid Season (Hijuelos), **Supp. VIII: 86–89**

Empson, William, **I:** 522, 533; **II:** 536; **III:** 286, 497, 498, 499; **IV:** 136, 431; **Retro. Supp. I:** 263; **Retro. Supp. II:** 253; **Supp. XVI:** 190

Empty Bed, The (Hadas), **Supp. XXIII: 117–118**

Empty Hands, The (Bronk), **Supp. XXI:** 31

"Empty Hills, The" (Winters), **Supp. II Part 2:** 792, 793, 796

"Empty Icon Frame" (Stallings), **Supp. XXV:** 233

Empty Mirror, Early Poems (Ginsberg), **Supp. II Part 1:** 308, 311, 313–314, 319, 329

"Empty Room" (Hughes), **Supp. I Part 1:** 337

"Empty Threat, An" (Frost), **II:** 159

Emshwiller, Ed, **Supp. XVIII:** 145

"Encantadas, The" (Melville), **III:** 89; **Supp. XVIII:** 4

Enchanter, The (Nabokov), **Retro. Supp. I:** 266

"Enclosed Dreams, Highways and Labyrinths: Jonathan Lethem's *Amnesia Moon*" (Rossi), *Supp. XVIII:* 139

"Encomium Twenty Years Later" (Tate), **I:** 381

"Encounter" (Espaillat), **Supp. XXI:** 107

"Encounter, The" (Pound), **III:** 466

Encounter in April (Sarton), **Supp. VIII:** 259

"Encounter in April" (Sarton), **Supp. VIII:** 259

"Encountering the Sublime" (McClatchy), **Supp. XII:** 261

"Encounter in Vindija Cave, Present-Day Croatia: Late October"(Schott), **Supp. XXIII:** 254

"Encounter on the Seine: Black Meets Brown" (Baldwin), **Retro. Supp. II:** 2

Encounters with Chinese Writers (Dillard), **Supp. VI:** 19, 23, 31

Encounters with the Archdruid (McPhee), **Supp. III Part 1:** 292–294, 301; **Supp. X:** 30

Encyclopedia of Arkansas History and Culture, The (online), **Supp. XXII:** 50

Encyclopedia of Scotland, The (A. Finch), **Supp. XVII: 70–71**

Encyclopedia of World Biography, The, **Supp. XXI:** 74

"End, The" (Olds), **Supp. X:** 205

"Endangered Species" (Mora), **Supp. XIII:** 219–220

Endecott and the Red Cross (Lowell), **II:** 545

Endgame (Beckett), **Supp. XIII:** 196; **Supp. XXII:** 263

"Endgame" (Tan), **Supp. X:** 290

"Endicott and the Red Cross" (Hawthorne), **Retro. Supp. II:** 181, 187–188

"End of Books, The" (Coover), **Supp. V:** 53

End of Books, The" (Coover), **Supp. XXII:** 259

End of Dreams, The (Skloot), **Supp. XX: 196, 202–203**

End of Education, The (Postman), **Supp. XI:** 275

"End of FIRPO in the World, The" (Saunders), **Supp. XIX:** 229

End of Me, The (Hayes), **Supp. XXVI:** 142–143

"End of Season" (Warren), **IV:** 239–240

"End of Something, The" (Hemingway), **II:** 248

End of the Affair, The (Greene), **Supp. XI:** 99

End of the Age of Innocence, The (Price), **Retro. Supp. I:** 377

"End of the Line, The" (Helprin), **Supp. XXV:** 81

"End of the Line, The" (Jarrell), **III:** 527

"End of the Rainbow, The" (Jarrell), **II:** 386

End of the Road (film), **Supp. XI:** 309

End of the Road, The (Barth), **I:** 121, 122, 126–131; **Supp. XI:** 309; **Supp. XVIII:** 140, 141

"End of the World, The" (Gioia), **Supp. XV:** 126

"End of the World, The" (MacLeish), **III:** 8

Endor (Nemerov), **III:** 269, 270, 279

Endore, Guy, **Supp. XVII: 53–67**

"Ends" (Dixon), **Supp. XII:** 153

End to Innocence, An: Essays on Culture and Politics (Fiedler), **Supp. XIII: 98–99**

Endure: The Diaries of Charles Walter Stetson (Stetson), **Supp. XI:** 196

"Enduring Chill, The" (O'Connor), **III:** 349, 351, 357; **Retro. Supp. II:** 236

Enduring Vision of Norman Mailer, The (Leeds), **Retro. Supp. II:** 204

Endymion (Keats), **IV:** 405; **Retro. Supp. I:** 412

End Zone (DeLillo), **Supp. VI:** 2, 3, 4, 10, 11, 12

Enemies (Boyce and Hapgood), **Supp. XVII:** 100; **Supp. XXI:** 7, 13

Enemies: A Love Story (Singer), **IV:** 1; **Retro. Supp. II: 310–311**

Enemy, The: Time (T. Williams), **IV:** 391

Enemy of the People, An (adapt. Miller), **III:** 154–156

"Energy Vampire" (Ginsberg), **Supp. II Part 1:** 326

"Enforcement of the Slave Trade Laws, The" (Du Bois), **Supp. II Part 1:** 161

"Engaging the Past" (Bell), **Supp. X:** 17

Engel, Bernard F., **I:** 532

Engels, Friedrich, **IV:** 429, 443–444; **Supp. I Part 1:** 13; **Supp. XXI:** 162

Engels, John, **Supp. XXVI:** 152

Engineer of Beasts, The (Sanders), **Supp. XVI:** 270

Engineer of Moonlight (DeLillo), **Supp. VI:** 4

Engineers and the Price System, The (Veblen), **I:** 475–476; **Supp. I Part 2:**

638, 642, 648

Engines of Creation: the Coming Era of Nanotechnology (Drexler), **Supp. XVI:** 121

"England" (Moore), **III:** 203, 207, 214

Englander, Nathan, **Supp. XX: 177, 179; Supp. XXIV:** 131; **Supp. XXV:** 268

Engle, Paul, **III:** 542; **Retro. Supp. II:** 220, 221; **Supp. V:** 337; **Supp. XI:** 315; **Supp. XIII:** 76; **Supp. XVIII:** 72

English, Zoë, **Supp. XVI:** 293

English Elegy, The: Studies in the Genre from Spenser to Yeats (Sacks), **Supp. IV Part 2:** 450

English Hours (James), **II:** 337; **Retro. Supp. I:** 235

English Language, The (L. P. Smith), **Supp. XIV:** 341

English-Latin Gradus or Verse Dictionary, An (Ainger), **Supp. XX: 230**

"English Lesson"(Strout), **Supp. XXIII:** 273–274, 284

Englishmen of Letters (James), **II:** 327

English Notebooks, The (Hawthorne), **II:** 226, 227–228

English Novel, The (Lanier), **Supp. I Part 1:** 371

English Poets, The: Lessing, Rousseau (Lowell), **Supp. I Part 2:** 407

English Prosody and Modern Poetry (Shapiro), **Supp. II Part 2:** 710

English Traits (Emerson), **II:** 1, 5, 6–7, 8

"English Writers on America" (Irving), **II:** 308

Engstrand, Stuart, **Supp. I Part 1:** 51

"Enigma Variations" (Nelson), **Supp. XVIII:** 177

"Enoch" (Very), **Supp. XXV:** 246, 247

"Enoch and the Gorilla" (O'Connor), **Retro. Supp. II:** 225

Enormous Changes at the Last Minute (Paley), **Supp. VI:** 218

"Enormous Changes at the Last Minute" (Paley), **Supp. VI:** 226, 232

"Enormous Radio, The" (Cheever), **Supp. I Part 1:** 175–177, 195

Enormous Radio and Other Stories, The (Cheever), **Supp. I Part 1:** 175–177

Enormous Room, The (Cummings), **I:** 429, 434, 440, 445, 477; **Supp. XXI:** 277

"Enough for a Lifetime" (Buck), **Supp. II Part 1:** 127

Enough Rope (Parker), **Supp. IX:** 189, 192

Enquiry Concerning Political Justice (Godwin), **Supp. I Part 1:** 126, 146

"En Route" (Boulton), **Supp. XXII:** 25

Entered From the Sun (Garrett), **Supp. VII:** 105–106, 107–109

"Entering the Building" (Notley), **Supp. XXII:** 237

"Entering the Kingdom" (Oliver), **Supp. VII:** 234

Entertaining Strangers (Gurney), **Supp. V:** 98, 99

Enter without Desire (Lacy), **Supp. XV:** 201

Entranced, The (Lippard), **Supp. XXIII:** 178, 180, 190

Entrance: Four Chicano Poets, **Supp. XIII:** 316

Entrance to Porlock, The (Buechner), **Supp. XII:** 52

Entries (Berry), **Supp. X:** 23

"Entropy" (Pynchon), **Supp. II Part 2:** 619, 621

"Entry" (Huddle), **Supp. XXVI:** 149

Entry in an Unknown Hand (F. Wright), **Supp. XVII:** 240, 244, 245

Environmental Imagination, The (Buell), **Supp. IX:** 29; **Supp. V:** 209

"Envoy" (Collins), **Supp. XXI:** 57

"Envoys, The" (Merrill), **Supp. III Part 1:** 326

"Envy; or, Yiddish in America" (Ozick), **Supp. V:** 263, 265–266

"Eolian Harp, The" (Coleridge), **I:** 284

"Eolian Harp, The"(Coleridge), **Supp. XXIII:** 231

"Eototo" (Sobin), **Supp. XVI:** 283–284

"Ephemera, The" (Franklin), **II:** 121

Ephesians (biblical book), **Supp. I Part 1:** 117

"Epic Poetry" (Very), **Supp. XXV:** 241

Epictetus, **III:** 566

"Epicurean, The" (Auchincloss), **Supp. IV Part 1:** 25

Epicurus, **I:** 59

Epidemic of Genius, An (Wolfert), **Supp. XXI:** 278

"Epigram" (Lowell), **II:** 550

"Epilogue" (Lowell), **Retro. Supp. II:** 191

"Epimanes" (Poe), **III:** 411

"Epimetheus" (Longfellow), **II:** 494

"Epiphany" (X. J. Kennedy), **Supp. XV:** 166, 167

"Epipsychidion" (Shelley), **Supp. I Part 2:** 718

"Episode, The" (Huddle), **Supp. XXVI:** 150

Episode in Palmetto (Caldwell), **I:** 297, 307

"Episode in the Life of an Ancestor" (Boyle), **Supp. XXIV:** 56

Episode of the Wandering Knife, The (Rinehart), **Supp. XXV:** 198, 200

"Epistle" (L.-Y. Lee), **Supp. XV:** 212

Epistles (Horace), **Supp. XXIV:** 156

Epistles of Horace, The (Ferry, trans.), **Supp. XXIV: 157–158**

Epistle to a Godson (Auden), **Supp. II Part 1:** 24

"Epistle to Be Left in the Earth" (MacLeish), **III:** 13

"Epistle to George William Curtis" (Lowell), **Supp. I Part 2:** 416

"Epistle to Léon-Paul Fargue" (MacLeish), **III:** 15

"Epitaph Ending in And, The" (Stafford), **Supp. XI:** 321–322

Epitaph for a Dead Beat (Markson), 139; **Supp. XVII: 136–138,** 141

Epitaph for a Desert Anarchist (Bishop), **Supp. XIII:** 1

Epitaph for a Tramp (Markson), **Supp. XVII:** 136, 137, 139 142

"Epitaph for Fire and Flower" (Plath), **Supp. I Part 2:** 537

"Epitaph for S.P." (Davison), **Supp. XXVI:** 71

"Epitaph for the Race of Man" (Millay), **III:** 127–128

"Epithalamium" (Auden), **Supp. II Part 1:** 15

"Epstein" (P. Roth), **Retro. Supp. II:** 281; **Supp. III Part 2:** 404, 406–407, 412, 422

Epstein, Barbara, **Supp. XIX:** 268

Epstein, Helen, **Supp. XVII:** 47; **Supp. XXII:** 95

Epstein, Jacob, **Supp. XXIII:** 6

Epstein, Jason, **Supp. VIII:** 233

Epstein, Joseph, **Supp. IV Part 2:** 692; **Supp. VIII:** 236, 238; **Supp. XIV: 101–117; Supp. XVI:** 230, 275

Epstein, Leslie, **Supp. XII: 159–174; Supp. XVIII:** 92, 99

Epstein, Philip, **Supp. XII:** 159

"Equal in Paris" (Baldwin), **Retro. Supp. II:** 3; **Supp. I Part 1:** 52

"Equals" (Untermeyer), **Supp. XV:** 304

Equation for Evil (Caputo), **Supp. XIX:** 25–26

"Equations of the Light" (Gioia), **Supp. XV:** 125

"Equilibrists, The" (Ransom), **III:** 490, 494

"Equinox 1980" (Davison), **Supp. XXVI:** 77

"Equinox"(Crooker), **Supp. XXIII:** 55

"Equipment for Pennies" (H. Roth), **Supp. IX:** 233

Erasmus, Desiderius, **Supp. XV:** 258

Erasure (Everett), **Supp. XVIII:** 54, 60, **61–62**

"Erat Hora" (Pound), **III:** 463; **Retro. Supp. I:** 413

Erdrich, Louise, **Supp. IV Part 1: 259–278,** 333, 404; **Supp. X:** 290; **Supp. XVIII:** 189; **Supp. XXIV:** 245; **Supp. XXVI:** 102

"Erectus" (Karr), **Supp. XI:** 243

"Ere Sleep Comes Down to Soothe the Weary Eyes" (Dunbar), **Supp. II Part 1:** 199, 207–208

"Ergo Non Sum. Est." (Bronk), **Supp. XXI:** 31

"Ergotism"(Schott), **Supp. XXIII:** 245

Erikson, Erik, **I:** 58, 214, 218

Erisman, Fred, **Supp. VIII:** 126

Erkkila, Betsy, **Retro. Supp. I:** 42; **Supp. XX: 281, 287, 287–288**

Ernest, John, **Supp. XXI:** 24

"Ernest: or Parent for a Day" (Bourne), **I:** 232

Ernst, Max, **Retro. Supp. II:** 321

"Eros" (Komunyakaa), **Supp. XIII:** 130

"Eros and Anteros" (E. Stoddard), **Supp. XV:** 283

Eros and Civilization (Marcuse), **Supp. XII:** 2

"Eros at Temple Stream" (Levertov), **Supp. III Part 1:** 278–279

Eros the Bittersweet (Carson), **Supp. XII:** 97, **98–99**

Eros Trilogy, The (Silver), **Supp. XXIV:** 264, 267

"Eros Turannos" (Robinson), **III:** 510, 512, 513–516, 517, 518

"Eroticism in Women" (Nin), **Supp. X:** 195

"Errand" (Carver), **Supp. III Part 1:** 149

Erskine, Albert, **IV:** 261; **Retro. Supp. II:** 117

Erskine, John, **I:** 223; **Supp. X:** 183; **Supp. XIV:** 120

Erstein, Hap, **Supp. IV Part 2:** 589, 590

"Escape" (MacLeish), **III:** 4

Escape Artist, The (Wagoner), **Supp. IX:** 324, **334–335**

"Escape"(Thompson), **Supp. XXIII:** 301

Escher, M. C., **Supp. XII:** 26; **Supp. XVI:** 102

"Escudilla" (Leopold), **Supp. XIV:** 188

Esenwein, J. Berg, **Supp. XXVI:** 281

Eshleman, Clayton, **Supp. XVI:** 284

"Eskimo Love" (Apple), **Supp. XVII:** 5

Espaillat, Rhina P., **Supp. XXI: 97–114**

Esparza, Laura, **Supp. XXIII:** 197

Especially Maine (Beston), **Supp. XXVI:** 32

Espeland, Pamela, **Supp. XVIII:** 180, 181

Espen, Hal, **Supp. X:** 15

Espey, John, **III:** 463, 468, 478

Esposito, Michael, **Supp. XX: 34, 40**

Esposito, Scott, **Supp. XVII:** 234

Esquibel, Catrióna Rueda, **Supp. XXIII:** 202

Essais (Renouvier), **II:** 344–345

Essay Concerning Human Understanding, An (Locke), **I:** 554; **II:** 8, 348–349

Essay on American Poetry (Brown), **Supp. I Part 1:** 156

"Essay on Aristocracy" (Paine), **Supp. I Part 2:** 515

Essay on Criticism, An (Pope), **Supp. XXVI:** 271, 284

"Essay on Friendship, An" (McClatchy), **Supp. XII:** 258–259

"Essay on Love" (Carruth), **Supp. XVI:** 56

Essay on Man (Pope), **II:** 111; **Supp. I Part 2:** 516

"Essay on Marriage" (Carruth), **Supp. XVI:** 48

Essay on Our Changing Order (Veblen), **Supp. I Part 2:** 629, 642

"Essay on Poetics" (Ammons), **Supp. VII:** 29–31

Essay on Projects (Defoe), **II:** 104

"Essay on Psychiatrists" (Pinsky), **Supp. VI:** 237, 238, 241, 242, 249, 250

Essay on Rime (Shapiro), **I:** 430; **Supp. II Part 2:** 702, 703, 708–711

"Essay on Sanity" (Dunn), **Supp. XI:** 147

"Essay on the Character of Robespierre" (Paine), **Supp. I Part 2:** 515

Essay on the Chinese Written Character (Fenollosa), **III:** 474

"Essay on What I Think About Most" (Carson), **Supp. XII: 111–112**

Essays (Emerson), **II:** 1, 7, 8, 12–13, 15, 21

Essays (Montaigne), **Supp. XXVI:** 39

Essays, Speeches, and Public Letters by William Faulkner (Meriweather, ed.), **Retro. Supp. I:** 77

Essays and Poems (Very), **Supp. XXV:** 247, 249–250

Essays in Anglo-Saxon Law (Adams), **I:** 5

Essays in London (James), **II:** 336

Essays in Radical Empiricism (James), **II:** 355, 356–357

Essays on Norman Mailer (Lucid), **Retro. Supp. II:** 195

Essays on the Nature and Principles of Taste (Alison), **Supp. I Part 1:** 151

Essays to Do Good (Mather), **II:** 104; **Supp. II Part 2:** 461, 467

"Essay: The Love of Old Houses" (Doty), **Supp. XI:** 136

"Essay Toward a Point of View, An" (Brooks), **I:** 244

"Essay Vanishes, The" (Monson), **Supp. XXIV:** 238

"Essence, Absence, and Sobin's *Venus Blue*" (English), **Supp. XVI:** 293

Essential Dykes to Watch Out For, The (Bechdel), **Supp. XXV:** 2

Essential Haiku, The (Hass), **Supp. VI:** 102

Essential Keats (Levine, ed.), **Supp. V:** 179

"Essential Oils—are wrung" (Dickinson), **I:** 471; **Retro. Supp. I:** 43, 46

"Essentials" (Toomer), **Supp. III Part 2:** 486

Essentials: A Philosophy of Life in Three Hundred Definitions and Aphorisms (Toomer), **Supp. III Part 2:** 486

Essentials: Definitions and Aphorisms (Toomer), **Supp. IX:** 320

"Essentials of Spontaneous Prose" (Kerouac), **Supp. III Part 1:** 227–228

Essential Works of the Founding Fathers, The (Kriegel, ed.), **Supp. XXIV:** 214

Estampas del valle y otras obras (Hinojosa). *See Valley, The* (Hinojosa)

Esta puente, mi espalda: Voces de mujeres tercermundistas en los Estados Unidos (Moraga, Castillo, and Alarcón, eds.), **Supp. XXIII:** 194

"Estate Sale" (Nye), **Supp. XIII:** 283

Estess, Sybil, **Supp. IV Part 2:** 449, 452

Esther (Adams), **I:** 9–10, 20

"Esther" (Toomer), **Supp. IX:** 313–314

"Esther Kahn" (Symons), **Supp. XX: 239**

"Esthétique du Mal" (Stevens), **IV:** 79; **Retro. Supp. I:** 300, 311, 312

"Estoy-eh-muut and the Kunideeyahs (Arrowboy and the Destroyers)" (film), **Supp. IV Part 2:** 560

Estrada, Genaro, **Retro. Supp. II:** 89

Estray, The (Longfellow, ed.), **Retro. Supp. II:** 155

Esty, William, **III:** 358

"Etching, An" (Masters), **Supp. I Part 2:** 458

Eternal Feminine, The (Wells), **Supp. XXVI:** 275

"Eternal Goodness, The" (Whittier), **Supp. I Part 2:** 704

Eternal Spring, The (Boyce), **Supp. XVII:** 100; **Supp. XXI:** 4, 5, 11

"Eternity, An" (W. C. Williams), **Retro. Supp. I:** 423

"Eternity Is Now" (Roethke), **III:** 544–545

"Ethan Brand" (Hawthorne), **II:** 227

Ethan Frome (Wharton), **IV:** 316–317, 327; **Retro. Supp. I:** 372–373; **Supp. IX:** 108; **Supp. XVIII:** 216; **Supp. XXIII:** 275, 281

"Ethical Turn in Postcolonial Theory and Narrative, The: Michelle Cliff's *No Telephone to Heaven*" (Moynagh), **Supp. XXII:** 73

Ethics (Spinoza), **IV:** 12; **Retro. Supp. II:** 300

"Ethics of Culture, The" (Locke), **Supp. XIV:** 211

"Ethnics of Frank Costello, The" (Talese), **Supp. XVII:** 202

Etiquette and Vitriol: The Food Chain and Other Plays (Silver), **Supp. XXIV:** 263, 264

"Étiquettes Jaunes, Les"(O'Hara), **Supp. XXIII:** 214

"Etude" (Kooser), **Supp. XIX:** 115

Etulain, Richard, **Supp. IV Part 2:** 597, 601, 604, 606, 607, 608, 610, 611

"Etymology" (Nelson), **Supp. XVIII:** 185

Euclid, **III:** 6, 620

"Euclid Alone Has Looked on Beauty Bare" (Millay), **III:** 133

"Euclidean Spaces: Linear Time" (Bronk), **Supp. XXI:** 31

Eugene, Frank, **Supp. X:** 204

Eugene Onegin (Pushkin), **III:** 246, 263

Eugene Onegin (Pushkin; Nabokov, trans.), **Retro. Supp. I:** 266, 267, 272

Eugenides, Jeffrey, **Supp. XIX:** 138; **Supp. XXI:** 229; **Supp. XXIV: 131–146**

Eugénie, Empress, **IV:** 309

Eugénie Grandet (Balzac), **II:** 328

"Eugénie Grandet" (Barthelme), **Supp. IV Part 1:** 47

"Eulogy for Richard Hugo (1923–1982)" (Wagoner), **Supp. IX:** 330–331

"Eulogy on the Flapper" (Z. Fitzgerald), **Supp. IX:** 71

Eumenides (Aeschylus), **Retro. Supp. I:** 65

"E Unibus Pluram: Television and U.S. Fiction" (Wallace), **Supp. X:** 315–316

"Euphemisms" (Matthews), **Supp. IX: 167–168**

Eureka (Poe), **III:** 409, 424, 428–429

Eurekas (Goldbarth), **Supp. XII:** 181

Euripides, **I:** 325; **II:** 8, 282, 543; **III:** 22, 145, 398; **IV:** 370; **Supp. I Part 1:** 268, 269, 270; **Supp. I Part 2:** 482; **Supp. V:** 277

"Euripides and Professor Murray" (Eliot), **Supp. I Part 1:** 268

"Euripides—A Playwright" (West), **IV:** 286; **Retro. Supp. II:** 326

"Europe" (Ashbery), **Supp. III Part 1:** 7–10, 13, 18

European Discovery of America, The: The Northern Voyages (Morison),

Supp. I Part 2: 496–497

Europeans, The (H. James), **I:** 452; **II:** 327, 328; **Retro. Supp. I:** 216, 220

Europe Central (Vollmann), **Supp. XVII:** 225, 226, 227, 229, 231, **233–235,** 236

"Europe! Europe!" (Ginsberg), **Supp. II Part 1:** 320, 322

Europe of Trusts, The: Selected Poems (Howe), **Supp. IV Part 2:** 420, 422, 426

Europe without Baedeker (Wilson), **IV:** 429

"Eurydice in Darkness" (Davison), **Supp. XXVI:** 71

Eurydice in the Underworld (Acker), **Supp. XII:** 7

"Eurydice Reveals Her Strength" (Stallings), **Supp. XXV:** 230

"Eurydice's Footnote" (Stallings), **Supp. XXV:** 230

Eustace, Saint, **II:** 215

Eustace Chisholm and the Works (Purdy), **Supp. VII:** 273–274, 279–280

"Euthanasia" (Tate), **IV:** 122

"Evaluation" (Bronk), **Supp. XXI:** 32

Eva-Mary (McCarriston), **Supp. XIV:** 259, 260, **263–268**

"Evangeline" (Dixon), **Supp. XII:** 153

Evangeline (Longfellow), **II:** 489, 501–502; **Retro. Supp. II:** 155, **156–159,** 162, 164; **Supp. I Part 2:** 586

Evanier, David, **Supp. XVI:** 212

Evans, Alice, **Supp. XVII:** 71, 72

Evans, Mary Ann. *See* Eliot, George

Evans, Oliver, **Supp. IV Part 1:** 85, 91

Evans, Sandy, **Supp. XIII:** 129

Evans, Walker, **I:** 36, 38, 293; **Retro. Supp. II:** 85

Eva's Man (G. Jones), **Supp. XXIV:** 183, 184, 185, **188–190,** 193

Eve (A. Finch), **Supp. XVII: 72–74**

"Eve" (W. C. Williams), **Retro. Supp. I:** 423

Even Cowgirls Get the Blues (Robbins), **Supp. X:** 259, 260, 261, 262–263, 264, 266, **269–271,** 272, 274, 277, 284; **Supp. XIII:** 11

"Evening" (Carver), **Supp. III Part 1:** 148

Evening (Minot), **Supp. VI:** 204–205, 208, **213–215**

"Evening at a Country Inn" (Kenyon), **Supp. VII:** 167

"Evening in Advent, An" (W. V. Davis), **Supp. XXI:** 92

"Evening in a Lumber Yard"(Le Sueur), **Supp. XXIII:** 165

"Evening in a Sugar Orchard" (Frost), **Retro. Supp. I:** 133

"Evening in Nuevo Leon, An" (Caldwell), **I:** 309

"Evening in the Sanitarium" (Bogan), **Supp. III Part 1:** 61

Evening Light, The (Skloot), **Supp. XX: 196, 201–202**

"Evening Love-of-Self" (Taggard), **Supp. XXII:** 280–281

"Evening of the 4th of July, The" (Kees), **Supp. XV:** 140, 142

"Evening on the Cote d'Azur" (Yates), **Supp. XI:** 349

Evening Performance, An: New and Selected Short Stories (Garrett), **Supp. VII:** 109

"Evenings at Home" (Hardwick), **Supp. III Part 1:** 195–196

"Evening's at Seven, The" (Thurber), **Supp. I Part 2:** 616

"Evening Star" (Bogan), **Supp. III Part 1:** 56

Evening Star, The (McMurtry), **Supp. V:** 230

Evening Star, The (screenplay, McMurtry), **Supp. V:** 232

"Evening Sun" (Kenyon), **Supp. VII:** 168

Evening Sun Turned Crimson, The (Huncke), **Supp. XIV:** 140, 149–150

"Evening Sun Turned Crimson, The" (Huncke), **Supp. XIV:** 137–138, 139

"Evening Wind, The" (Bryant), **Supp. I Part 1:** 164

"Evening without Angels" (Stevens), **Retro. Supp. I:** 302

Evening with Richard Nixon, An (Vidal), **Supp. IV Part 2:** 683

"Even Sea, The" (Swenson), **Supp. IV Part 2:** 641

Even Stephen (Perelman and West), **Retro. Supp. II:** 328

"Event, An" (Wilbur), **Supp. III Part 2:** 547, 554

"Event, The" (Dove), **Supp. IV Part 1:** 242, 247–248

"Even the Vanishing Housed"(Hirshfield), **Supp. XXIII:** 132

"Eventide" (Brooks), **Supp. III Part 1:** 73

"Eventide" (Purdy), **Supp. VII:** 270

"Event Itself, The" (Carruth), **Supp. XVI:** 47

Eve of Saint Agnes, The (Keats), **II:** 82, 531

"Eve of St. Agnes, The" (Clampitt), **Supp. IX:** 40

"Ever a Bridegroom: Reflections on the Failure of Texas Literature" (McMurtry), **Supp. V:** 225

Everett, Alexander Hill, **Supp. I Part 1:** 152

Everett, Percival, **Supp. XVIII: 53–67**

Everlasting Story of Nory, The (Baker), **Supp. XIII:** 52; **Supp. XIII: 53–55**

"Everly Brothers, The" (Skloot), **Supp. XX: 199**

Ever-Present Past, The (Hamilton), **Supp. XVI:** 196

Evers, Medgar, **IV:** 280; **Retro. Supp. II:** 13; **Supp. I Part 1:** 52, 65

Everson, William, **Supp. XXII:** 276

Everwine, Peter, **Supp. V:** 180; **Supp. XIII:** 312; **Supp. XV: 73–90**

"Everybody's Protest Novel" (Baldwin), **Retro. Supp. II:** 4; **Supp. I Part 1:** 50, 51

"Everybody's Reading Li Po' Silk-screened on a Purple T-Shirt" (Komunyakaa), **Supp. XIII:** 120

Everybody's Story: Writing by Older Minnesotans (C. Bly, ed.), **Supp. XVI:** 38

"Everybody Was Very Nice" (Benét), **Supp. XI:** 53

"Everyday Alchemy" (Taggard), **Supp. XXII:** 274–275, 276, 279

"Every-Day Girl, A" (Jewett), **Retro. Supp. II:** 132

Everyday People (O'Nan), **Supp. XXV:** 142, 146–147, 150

"Everyday Use" (Walker), **Supp. III Part 2:** 534

"Every-Day Work" (Jewett), **Retro. Supp. II:** 132

Everyman (Ashbery), **Supp. XXIII:** 210

Everyone Says I Love You (film; Allen), **Supp. XV:** 11

Every Pleasure (Goldbarth), **Supp. XII:** 181

Every Soul Is a Circus (Lindsay), **Supp. I Part 2:** 384, 394, 399

"Everything Is a Human Being" (Walker), **Supp. III Part 2:** 527

Everything Is Illuminated (Foer), **Supp. XII:** 169

Everything Is Now (Cliff), **Supp. XXII:** 67, 74, 76

"Everything Stuck to Him" (Carver), **Supp. III Part 1:** 143

Everything That Moves (Schulberg), **Supp. XVIII:** 254

Everything That Rises Must Converge (O'Connor), **III:** 339, 348–349, 350–351; **Retro. Supp. II:** 235, **236–237**

"Everything That Rises Must Converge" (O'Connor), **III:** 349, 352, 357; **Retro. Supp. II:** 236

Everything You Always Wanted to Know about Sex (film; Allen), **Supp. XV:** 4–5, 13

Eve's Diary (Twain), **IV:** 208–209

"Eve Speaks" (Untermeyer), **Supp. XV:** 300

"Eve the Fox" (Gunn Allen), **Supp. IV Part 1:** 331

"Evidence" (Harjo), **Supp. XII:** 219

"Evidence-cum-Witness: Subaltern History, Violence, and the (De)formation of a Nation in Michelle Cliff's *No Telephone to Heaven*" (Sethuraman), **Supp. XXII:** 73

Evidence of the Senses, The (Kelley), **Supp. IV Part 2:** 529

Evidence of Things Not Seen, The (Baldwin), **Retro. Supp. II:** 15

"Evidences of Revealed Religion, The" (Channing), **Supp. XXIV:** 74

"Evil Seekers, The" (Sexton), **Supp. II Part 2:** 696

"Evolution" (Swenson), **Supp. IV Part 2:** 639

Evolving the Idol: The Poetry of Gustaf Sobin (Crick), **Supp. XVI:** 289

Ewing, Jon, **Supp. X:** 253

Ewings, The (O'Hara), **III:** 383

"Examination at the Womb Door" (Hughes), **Supp. XV:** 347

"Examination of the Hero in a Time of War" (Stevens), **Retro. Supp. I:** 305–306, 308

"Excavation of Troy" (MacLeish), **III:** 18

Excellent Becomes the Permanent, The (Addams), **Supp. I Part 1:** 25

"Excelsior" (Longfellow), **Retro. Supp. II:** 169

"Excerpts from Swan Lake" (Cameron), **Supp. XII:** 80, **84**

"Excerpts from the Epistemology Workshops" (Rand), **Supp. IV Part 2:** 529

"Excess of Charity" (Wylie), **Supp. I Part 2:** 720

"Exchange, The" (Swenson), **Supp. IV Part 2:** 644

"Excitement, The " (Jarman), **Supp. XVII:** 120–121

"Exclusive" (Olds), **Supp. X:** 206

"Excrement Poem, The" (Kumin), **Supp. IV Part 2:** 448

"Excursion" (Garrett), **Supp. VII:** 100

Excursions (Thoreau), **IV:** 188

"Excursion to Canada, An" (Thoreau), **Supp. XVIII:** 4

"Excursus of Reassurance in Begonia Time, An" (Carruth), **Supp. XVI:** 58

Executioner (Weigl), **Supp. XIX:** 277

Executioner's Song, The (Mailer), **Retro. Supp. II:** 108, 209

Exekiel, **Supp. XXI:** 91

Exemplar of Liberty: Native America and the Evolution of Democracy (Grinde and Johansen), **Supp. XXVI:** 98

"Exercise and Abstinence" (Swados), **Supp. XIX:** 265

Exercises in History, Chronology, and Biography, in Question and Answer (Rowson), **Supp. XV:** 245

Ex-Friends: Falling Out with Allen Ginsberg, Lionel and Diana Trilling, Lillian Hellman, Hannah Arendt, and Norman Mailer (Podhoretz), **Supp. VIII:** 239, **242–244**

"Exhausted Bug, The" (R. Bly), **Supp. IV Part 1:** 73

"Exhortation" (Bogan), **Supp. III Part 1:** 58

"Exhortation" (McKay), **Supp. X:** 135

"Ex-husband"(Schott), **Supp. XXIII:** 249

"Exile" (Gass), **Supp. VI:** 92

"Exile" (Oates), **Supp. II Part 2:** 523

Exile, The (Buck), **Supp. II Part 1:** 119, 131

"Exiles, The" (Bradbury), **Supp. IV Part 1:** 113

"Exiles, The" (Whittier), **Supp. I Part 2:** 692–693

Exiles and Fabrications (Scott), **II:** 512

Exile's Daughter, The (Spencer), **Supp. II Part 1:** 121

"Exile's Departure, The" (Whittier), **Supp. I Part 2:** 683

Exiles from Paradise: Zelda and Scott Fitzgerald (Mayfield), **Supp. IX:** 65

"Exile's Letter" (Karr), **Supp. XI:** 241

Exile's Return (Cowley), **Supp. III Part 1:** 136, 138, 140, 141, 144, 147, 148

"Exile's Return, The" (Lowell), **II:** 539; **Retro. Supp. II:** 187

Exiles: Three Short Novels (Caputo), **Supp. XIX:** 25, **26–27**

"Existences" (Stafford), **Supp. XI:** 324

Existentialism from Dostoevsky to Sartre (W. Kaufmann), **Supp. XVII:** 137

Exit into History (Hoffman), **Supp. XVI:** 148, 150, **151–153**

Exit to Eden (Rampling), **Supp. VII:** 301–302

Exley (Clarke), **Supp. XXIII:** 109

Exley, Frederick, **Supp. XVI:** 69; **Supp. XVII:** 135; **Supp. XXIII:** 78, **97–110**

Exodus (biblical book), **IV:** 300

Exodus (film), **Supp. XX:** 246

Exodus (Uris), **Supp. IV Part 1:** 379; **Supp. XX: 243–244, 244, 245, 247, 248, 250–251, 257**

Exodus Revisited (Uris), **Supp. XX:** 247

"Exorcism" (Snodgrass), **Supp. VI:** 314

"Exorcism, An" (Malamud), **Supp. I Part 2:** 435

Exorcist, The (film), **Supp. I Part 1:** 66

"Expanded Composition, The" (Major), **Supp. XXII:** 174

"Expanding Rooms" (Notley), **Supp. XXII:** 229

"Expanses" (Dickey), **Supp. IV Part 1:** 186

"Ex Parte" (Lardner), **II:** 432

"Expatiation on the Combining of Weathers at Thirty-seventh and Indiana Where the Southern More or Less Crosses the Dog, The" (Carruth), **Supp. XVI:**51–52

"Expectant Father Compares His Wife to a Rabbit, An" (White), **Supp. I Part 2:** 678

"Expedition to the Pole, An" (Dillard), **Supp. VI:** 32, 34

"Expelled" (Cheever), **Supp. I Part 1:** 174, 186

Expense of Greatness, The (Blackmur), **Supp. II Part 1:** 90, 107

Expense of Vision, The (Holland), **Retro. Supp. I:** 216

"Expensive Gifts" (Miller), **Supp. XII:** 294

"Expensive Moment, The" (Paley), **Supp. VI:** 222, **227–228,** 230

Expensive People (Oates), **Supp. II Part 2:** 509, 510–511

"Experience" (Emerson), **Supp. XIV:** 42

"Experience and Fiction" (Jackson), **Supp. IX:** 121

"Experience and the Objects of Knowledge in the Philosophy of F. H. Bradley" (Eliot), **I:** 572; **Retro. Supp. I:** 59

Experience of Literature, The (Trilling), **Supp. III Part 2:** 493

"Experiences and Principles of an Historian" (Morison), **Supp. I Part 2:** 492

Experimental Death Unit # 1 (Baraka), **Supp. II Part 1:** 46

"Experimental Life, The" (Bourne), **I:** 217, 220

"Experiment in Misery, An" (S. Crane), **I:** 411; **Retro. Supp. II:** 97

Experiments and Observations on Electricity (Franklin), **II:** 102, 114–115

Experiments in Survival (Kriegel and Henrich, eds.), **Supp. XXIV:** 214

"Expiation" (Hoffman), **Supp. XVIII:** 86

"Expiation" (Wharton), **Retro. Supp. I:** 367

"Explaining an Affinity for Bats" (Stallings), **Supp. XXV:** 227, 233

"Explaining Evil" (Gordon), **Supp. IV Part 1:** 310

"Explaining Ted Kooser" (Gioia), **Supp. XIX:** 121

"Explanation" (Stevens), **IV:** 79

Explanation of America, An (Pinsky), **Supp. VI:** 237, **241–243**

Exploding Gravy (X. J. Kennedy), **Supp. XV:** 163

"Exploit" (Wharton), **IV:** 324

"Exploration in the Great Tuolumne Cañon" (Muir), **Supp. IX:** 181

"Explorer, The" (Brooks), **Supp. III Part 1:** 79–80

"Exploring the Magalloway" (Parkman), **Supp. II Part 2:** 591

"Exposed Nest, The" (Frost), **Supp. XXVI:** 74

Expositor's Bible, The (G. A. Smith), **III:** 199

Expressions of Sea Level (Ammons), **Supp. VII:** 24, 28, 36

"Exteriority" (Monson), **Supp. XXIV:** 230, 238

"Extinction of Silence, The" (Stallings), **Supp. XXV:** 234

Extract from Captain Stormfeld's Visit to Heaven (Twain), **IV:** 209–210

Extracts from Adam's Diary (Twain), **IV:** 208–209

Extra Indians (Gansworth), **Supp. XXVI:** 104, 107–108

"*Extraño, Un*" (Gallagher), *Supp. XXIV:* 170

"Exulting, The" (Roethke), **III:** 544

"Eye, The" (Bowles), **Supp. IV Part 1:** 93

Eye, The (Nabokov), **III:** 251

Eye-Beaters, Blood, Victory, Madness, Buckhead and Mercy, The (Dickey), **Supp. IV Part 1:** 178, 182–183

"Eye for an Eye, An" (Humphrey), **Supp. IX:** 108

"Eye in the Rock, The" (Haines), **Supp. XII:** 208, 209

Eye in the Sky (Dick), **Supp. XVIII:** 138

"Eye-Mote, The" (Plath), **Retro. Supp. II:** 246, 247

"Eye of Paris, The" (H. Miller), **III:** 183–184

Eye of the Poet, The: Six Views of the Art and Craft of Poetry (Citino, ed.), **Supp. XIII:** 115; **Supp. XXI:** 54

"Eye of the Rock, The" (Haines), **Supp. XII:** 208

"Eye of the Story, The" (Porter), **IV:** 279

Eye of the Story, The: Selected Essays and Reviews (Welty), **Retro. Supp. I:** 339, 342, 344, 345, 346, 351, 354, 355, 356

"Eyes, The" (Wharton), **IV:** 315

"Eyes like They Say the Devil Has" (Ríos), **Supp. IV Part 2:** 543, 544

Eyes of the Dragon, The (King), **Supp. V:** 139, 152

Eyes of the Heart: A Memoir of the Lost and Found (Buechner), **Supp. XII:** 53
"Eyes of Zapata" (Cisneros), **Supp. VII:** 70
"Eyes to See" (Cozzens), **I:** 374
Eye-to-Eye (Nye), **Supp. XIII:** 274
Eysturoy, Annie O., **Supp. IV Part 1:** 321, 322, 323, 328
Ezekiel (biblical book), **II:** 541
"Ezekiel" (R. Fisher), **Supp. XIX:** 71
Ezekiel, Mordecai, **Supp. I Part 2:** 645
"Ezekiel Learns" (R. Fisher), **Supp. XIX:** 71
"Ezra Pound" (Bynner), **Supp. XV:** 49
"Ezra Pound: His Cantos" (Zukofsky), **Supp. III Part 2:** 612, 619, 622
Ezra Pound's Mauberley (Espey), **III:** 463
"Ezra Pound's Very Useful Labors" (Schwartz), **Supp. II Part 2:** 644

F

Faas, Ekbert, **Supp. VIII:** 292
"Fabbri Tape, The" (Auchincloss), **Supp. IV Part 1:** 21–22
Fabens, Charles, **Supp. XXV:** 283
Faber, Geoffrey, **Retro. Supp. I:** 63
Faber Book of Movie Verse, The (French and Wlaschin, eds.), **Supp. XVI:** 294
"Fable" (Merwin), **Supp. III Part 1:** 343
"Fable" (Wylie), **Supp. I Part 2:** 714
Fable, A (Faulkner), **II:** 55, 73; **Retro. Supp. I:** 74
"Fable, A" (Glück), **Supp. V:** 86
"Fable, The" (Winters), **Supp. II Part 2:** 792, 793, 796
"Fable Containing a Reflection the Size of a Match Head in Its Pupil, A" (Brockmeier), **Supp. XXII:** 59
"Fable Ending in the Sound of a Thousand Parakeets, A" (Brockmeier), **Supp. XXII:** 59
Fable for Critics, A (Lowell), **Supp. I Part 2:** 406, 407–408, 409, 412–413, 416, 420, 422
"Fable for Critics, A" (Lowell), **Supp. XVIII:** 3, 8
"Fable of the War, A" (Nemerov), **III:** 272
Fables (Gay), **II:** 111
Fables and Distances: New and Selected Essays (Haines), **Supp. XII:** 197, 199, 207–208, 211
Fables for Our Time (Thurber), **Supp. I Part 2:** 610
Fables of Identity: Studies in Poetic Mythology (Frye), **Supp. X:** 80
Fables of La Fontaine, The (Moore), **III:** 194, 215
"Fables of Representation: Poetry of the New York School" (Hoover), **Supp. XV:** 179
"Fables of the Fallen Guy" (Rosaldo), **Supp. IV Part 2:** 544
"Fables of the Moscow Subway" (Nemerov), **III:** 271
"Fable with a Photograph of a Glass Mobile on the Wall, A" (Brockmeier), **Supp. XXII:** 59

"Fable with Slips of White Paper Spilling from the Pockets, A" (Brockmeier), **Supp. XXII:** 59
Fabulators, The (Scholes), **Supp. V:** 40
Fabulous Small Jews (Epstein), **Supp. XIV:** 112
Face against the Glass, The (Francis), **Supp. IX: 80–81**
Face in the Crowd, A (film, Kazan), **Supp. XVIII:** 252–253
Face in the Crowd, A (O'Nan and King), **Supp. XXV:** 150, 152
Face of Time, The (Farrell), **II:** 28, 34, 35, 39
Faces of Jesus, The (Buechner), **Supp. XII:** 53
Face to the Wind (film), **Supp. XVII:** 141
Face Value (Hwang), **Supp. XXI:** 148, 154, 155
Fachinger, Petra, **Supp. XVI:** 153
"Facing It" (Komunyakaa), **Supp. XIII:** 117, 124, 125
Facing Shadows (Jin), **Supp. XVIII:** 92, **93**
"Facing the Music" (L. Brown), **Supp. XXI:** 39, 42, **42–44**
"Facing the Music" (L. Brown), **Supp. XXI: 38–39,** 41, 42, 43
"*Facing the Music:* What's Wrong with All Those Happy Endings" (Neal), **Supp. XXI:** 41
"Facing West from California's Shores" (Jeffers), **Supp. II Part 2:** 437–438
Fact, Fiction, and Representation: Four Novels by Gilbert Sorrentino (Mackey), **Supp. XXI:** 236
"Fact in Fiction, The" (McCarthy), **II:** 562
"Fact of Blackness, The" (Fanon), **Supp. XX: 152**
"Facts" (Franzen), **Supp. XX: 85**
"Facts" (Levine), **Supp. V:** 193
"Facts" (Oliver), **Supp. VII:** 231–232
"Facts" (Snyder), **Supp. VIII:** 301
"Facts, The" (Lardner), **II:** 431
Facts, The: A Novelist's Autobiography (P. Roth), **Retro. Supp. II:** 280, 291; **Supp. III Part 2:** 401, 405, 417, 426
"Facts and Traditions Respecting the Existence of Indigenous Intermittent Fever in New England" (Holmes), **Supp. I Part 1:** 303
"Facts in the Case of M. Valdemar, The" (Poe), **III:** 416
Faderman, Lillian, **Retro. Supp. II:** 135; **Supp. XIII:** 313
Fadiman, Clifton, **II:** 430, 431, 443, 591–592; **Supp. IX:** 8; **Supp. XVI:** 100, 106; **Supp. XVII:** 87, 90; **Supp. XXIII:** 2
Fading, My Parmacheene Belle (J. Scott), **Supp. XVII: 184–185,** 188
Fading Smile, The (Davison), **Supp. XXVI:** 61, 66, 68
"Fado" (McClatchy), **Supp. XII:** 265–266
"Fado" (Vaz), **Supp. XXVI:** 261–262
Fado and Other Stories (Vaz), **Supp. XXVI:** 259–264, 268

Faerie Queene, The (Spenser), **III:** 487; **IV:** 253; **Supp. XIV:** 6; **Supp. XV:** 181
Faery, Rebecca Blevins, **Retro. Supp. I:** 374
Fagan, Kathy, **Supp. V:** 180; **Supp. XV:** 73
Fagan, Louise, **Supp. XIX:** 204, 205
Fahrenheit 451 (Bradbury), **Supp. IV Part 1:** 101, 102, 104, 107–109, 110, 113; **Supp. XIII:** 29
"Failure" (Gioia), **Supp. XV:** 125
"Failure" (Zach; Everwine, trans.), **Supp. XV:** 86
"Failure: A Meditation" (Monson), **Supp. XXIV:** 236
"Failure of David Barry, The" (Jewett), **Retro. Supp. II:** 132
Fainlight, Ruth, **Supp. XV:** 261, 264
Faint Perfume (Gale), **Supp. I Part 2:** 613
Fair, Bryan K., **Supp. VIII:** 128
Fairbanks, Douglas, **Supp. XVI:** 185, 186
Fairchild, Frances. *See* Bryant, Mrs. William Cullen (Frances Fairchild)
Fairchild, Hoxie, **Supp. XIV:** 120
Fairfield, Flora (pseudonym). *See* Alcott, Louisa May
Fair Gentlemen of Belken County (Hinojosa), **Supp. XIX: 105**
Fairly Conventional Woman, A (Shields), **Supp. VII:** 312, 316, 318
"Fairly Sad Tale, A" (Parker), **Supp. IX:** 192
Fair Warning (R. O. Butler), **Supp. XII:** 62, **75–76**
"Fairy-Tale Logic" (Stallings), **Supp. XXV:** 223, 234
Faith (Goldbarth), **Supp. XII:** 181, **182–183**
Faith and History (Niebuhr), **III:** 308
Faith and the Good Thing (C. Johnson), **Supp. VI:** 187, **188–190,** 191, 193, 194, 196
Faith for Living (Mumford), **Supp. II Part 2:** 479–480
Faithful Narrative of the Surprising Works of God in the Conversion of Many Hundred Souls in Northampton, and the Neighboring Towns and Villages of New-Hampshire in New-England, A (Edwards), **I:** 545, 562
Faithful: Two Diehard Boston Red Sox Fans Chronicle the Historic 2004 Season (O'Nan and King), **Supp. XXV:** 153
"Faith Healer" (Komunyakaa), **Supp. XIII:** 117
Faith Healer of Olive Avenue, The (Muñoz), **Supp. XXV:** 127, 131, 135–137
"Faith in a Tree" (Paley), **Supp. VI:** 217–218, 224, 230
"Faith in Search of Understanding" (Updike), **Retro. Supp. I:** 327
"Faith of an Historian" (Morison), **Supp. I Part 2:** 492
"Faith of Fishermen, The" (J. W. Miller), **Supp. XX: 170**

Faker's Dozen, A (Bukiet), **Supp. XVII:** 47

Falcoff, Mark, **Supp. VIII:** 88

Falcon (Hammett), **Supp. IV Part 1:** 351

Falconer (Cheever), **Supp. I Part 1:** 176, 193–195, 196

Falconer, A. F., **Supp. XIV:** 2

"Falcon of Ser Federigo, The" (Longfellow), **II:** 505

Falcon: Poems on Soviet Themes (Taggard), **Supp. XXII:** 284

Falk, Peter, **Supp. XI:** 174

Falkner, Dean, **II:** 55

Falkner, John, **II:** 55

Falkner, Murray, **II:** 55

Falkner, Murray C., **II:** 55

Falkner, Mrs. Murray C. (Maud Butler), **II:** 55

Falkner, William C., **II:** 55

"Fall" (Francis), **Supp. IX:** 76

"Fall, The" (Bass), **Supp. XVI:** 25

"Fall 1961" (Lowell), **II:** 550

"Fallen Western Star: The Decline of San Francisco as a Literary Region" (Gioia), **Supp. XV:** 112, **115–116**

"Fallen Western Star" Wars, The: A Debate about Literary California (Foley, ed.), **Supp. XV:** 112, 116

"Fall in Corrales" (Wilbur), **Supp. III Part 2:** 556

Falling (Dickey), **Supp. IV Part 1:** 178, 181–182

"Falling" (Dickey), **Supp. IV Part 1:** 182

"Falling Asleep over the Aeneid" (Lowell), **II:** 542; **Retro. Supp. II:** 188

Falling in Place (Beattie), **Supp. V:** 28–29

"Falling into Holes in Our Sentences" (R. Bly), **Supp. IV Part 1:** 71

Falling into Life (Kriegel), **Supp. XXIV:** **217–219**

"Falling Water" (Davison), **Supp. XXVI:** 79

"Fall Journey" (Stafford), **Supp. XI:** 322

Fall of a Doll's House, The (J. Davison), **Supp. XXVI:** 65

Fall of America, The: 1965–1971 (Ginsberg), **Supp. II Part 1:** 323, 325, 327; **Supp. XV:** 264

Fall of Eve, The (Loos), **Supp. XVI:** 187

Fall of the City, The: A Verse Play for Radio (MacLeish), **III:** 20

"Fall of the Dolls' House, The" (Davison), **Supp. XXVI:** 73–74

"Fall of the House of Usher, The" (Poe), **III:** 412, 414, 415, 419; **Retro. Supp. II:** 270; **Supp. XXV:** 112

Fall of the Magicians, The (Kees), **Supp. XV:** 144

Fall of the Year, The (Mosher), **Supp. XXII:** 205, 206, 208, 209, **214**

"Fall of Troy, Teh"(Hadas), **Supp. XXIII:** 113

Fallows, James, **Supp. VIII:** 241

Fall Quarter (Kees), **Supp. XV:** 141

Fall & Rise (Dixon), **Supp. XII:** 147–148, 148, 153, 157

Falls, Robert, **Supp. XXI:** 148; **Supp. XXIV:** 270

"Falls, The" (Olds), **Supp. X:** 215

"Falls, The" (Saunders), **Supp. XIX:** 229

"Falls Fight, The" (Howe), **Supp. IV Part 2:** 431–432

Falon, Janet Ruth, **Supp. IV Part 2:** 422

False Coin (Swados), **Supp. XIX: 260–261,** 263

"False Dawn" (Wharton), **Retro. Supp. I:** 381

"False Documents" (Doctorow), **Supp. IV Part 1:** 220, 236

"False Leads" (Komunyakaa), **Supp. XIII:** 116

Falwell, Jerry, **Supp. XX: 273**

Fame and Obscurity: Portraits by Gay Talese (Talese), **Supp. XVII:** 202, 203, 204

Fame & Folly: Essays (Ozick), **Supp. V:** 272

"Familiar Epistle to a Friend, A" (Lowell), **Supp. I Part 2:** 416

Familiar Territory: Observations on American Life (Epstein), **Supp. XIV:** **106**

"Familiar Things" (Pickering), **Supp. XXI:** 204

"Family" (Sanders), **Supp. XVI:** 276

"Family" (Wilson), **IV:** 426

Family, Kinship, and Sympanthy in Nineteenth-Century America (Weinstein), **Supp. XVIII:** 261

"Family, The" (Taggard), **Supp. XXII:** 284

"Family Affair, A" (Chopin), **Retro. Supp. II:** 71

"Family and Socialism, The" (Ryan as Quin), **Supp. XVIII:** 238

Family Arsenal, The (Theroux), **Supp. VIII:** 322

"Family Barcus, The"(Thompson), **Supp. XXIII:** 299

Family Chronicle: An Odyssey from Russia to America (Reznikoff), **Supp. XIV:** 277, 288, 289

Family Devotions (Hwang), **Supp. XXI:** 145, 146

"Family History" (Mora), **Supp. XIII:** 217

"Family History, A" (R. H. Davis), **Supp. XVI:** 82

Family Honor (Parker), **Supp. XIX:** 186

Family Life (Banks), **Supp. V:** 7

Family Markowitz, The (Goodman), **Supp. XXVI:** 119, 121–123

"Family Matters" (Alvarez), **Supp. VII:** 10

Family Moskat, The (Singer), **IV:** 1, 17, 20, 46; **Retro. Supp. II:** 304

"Family of Little Feet, The" (Cisneros), **Supp. VII:** 61

Family Party, A (O'Hara), **III:** 362

Family Pictures (Brooks), **Supp. III Part 1:** 69, 85, 86

Family Pictures (Miller), **Supp. XII:** 291, **295–297,** 299

"Family Portrait" (Trethewey), **Supp. XXI:** 250

"Family Reunion" (J. W. Miller), **Supp. XX: 167**

"Family Reunion" (X. J. Kennedy), **Supp. XV:** 169

Family Reunion, The (Eliot), **I:** 570–571, 572, 581, 584, 588; **Retro. Supp. I:** 62, 65

"Family Secrets" (Kingsolver), **Supp. VII:** 208

"Family Sideshow, The" (Karr), **Supp. XI:** 245

"Family Story, The" (Skloot), **Supp. XX: 195**

"Family Ties" (Mora), **Supp. XIII:** 215

"Family Tree" (Komunyakaa), **Supp. XIII:** 117–118, 126

"Family Wasserstein, The" (Hoban), **Supp. XV:** 319, 325

Famous American Negroes (Hughes), **Supp. I Part 1:** 345

"Famous Gilson Bequest, The" (Bierce), **I:** 204

Famous Last Words (Findley), **Supp. XX: 49, 55–56**

Famous Negro Athletes (Bontemps), **Supp. XXII:** 6

Famous Negro Music Makers (Hughes), **Supp. I Part 1:** 345

"Famous New York Trials" (Ellison), **Supp. II Part 1:** 230

Fanatics, The (Dunbar), **Supp. II Part 1:** 213–214

Fancher, Edwin, **Retro. Supp. II:** 202

Fancher, Lou, **Supp. XVI:** 177

"Fancy and Imagination" (Poe), **III:** 421

Fancy Dancer, The (P. N. Warren), **Supp. XX: 267–268**

"Fancy Flights" (Beattie), **Supp. V:** 25

"Fancy's Show Box" (Hawthorne), **II:** 238

"Fancy Woman, The" (Taylor), **Supp. V:** 316–317, 319, 323

"Fang" (Goldbarth), **Supp. XII:** 190

Fanny: Being the True History of the Adventures of Fanny Hackabout-Jones (Jong), **Supp. V:** 115, 127

Fanny Hill (Cleland), **Supp. V:** 48, 127

Fan of Swords, The (al-Maghut), **Supp. XIII:** 278

Fanon, Frantz, **Retro. Supp. II:** 118; **Supp. X:** 131, 141; **Supp. XX: 152**

"Fan's Further Notes, A"(Exley), **Supp. XXIII:** 108

Fanshawe (Hawthorne), **II:** 223–224; **Retro. Supp. I:** 149, 151

Fan's Notes, A: A Fictional Memoir (Exley), **Supp. XVI:** 69; **Supp. XXIII:** 78, 97, 98, **99–103,** 106, 109

"Fantasia on 'The Nut-Brown Maid' " (Ashbery), **Supp. III Part 1:** 19

"Fantasia on the Relations between Poetry and Photography" (Strand), **Supp. IV Part 2:** 631

"Fantastic Fables" (Bierce), **I:** 209

"Fantasy"(O'Hara), **Supp. XXIII:** 220

Fante, John, **Supp. XI: 159–176**

Faraday, Michael, **I:** 480–481

Far and Away (Jarman), **Supp. XVII:** 110, 115

"Far and Away" (Jarman), **Supp. XVII:** 115

"Farewell" (Emerson), **II:** 13

"Farewell" (Ryan as Quin), **Supp. XVIII:** 229

Farewell, My Lovely (Chandler), **Supp. IV Part 1:** 122, 125–126, 127, 128, 130

"Farewell, My Lovely!" (White), **Supp. I Part 2:** 661–663, 665

Farewell, The (Gibran), **Supp. XX:** 121

"Farewell Performance" (Merrill), **Supp. III Part 1:** 336–337

Farewell-Sermon Preached at the First Precinct in Northampton, after the People's Publick Rejection of their Minister, A (Edwards), **I:** 548, 562

"Farewell Sweet Dust" (Wylie), **Supp. I Part 2:** 727–728

"Farewell to America, A" (Wheatley), **Supp. XX: 283**

Farewell to Arms, A (Hemingway), **I:** 212, 421, 476, 477; **II:** 68–69, 248–249, 252–253, 254, 255, 262, 265; **Retro. Supp. I:** 171, 178, **180–182,** 187, 189; **Retro. Supp. II:** 108; **Supp. IV Part 1:** 380–381, 381; **Supp. VIII:** 179; **Supp. XII:** 241–242; **Supp. XXI:** 277

"Farewell to Miles" (Berryman), **I:** 173

"Farewell to My Union Brothers" (Ryan as Quin), **Supp. XVIII:** 238

Farewell to Reform (Chamberlain), **Supp. I Part 2:** 647

Farewell to Sport (Gallico), **Supp. XVI:** 238

"Farewell to the Middle Class" (Updike), **Retro. Supp. I:** 321

Far Field, The (Roethke), **III:** 528, 529, 539, 545, 547–548

"Far Field, The" (Roethke), **III:** 537, 540

Far-Flung (Cameron), **Supp. XII:** 81

Far from the Madding Crowd (Hardy), **II:** 291

Faríd, 'Umar ibn al-, **Supp. XX:** 117

Faris, Athénaíse Charleville, **Supp. I Part 1:** 204

Farley, Abbie, **I:** 458

Farley, Harriet, **Supp. XIII:** 140

"Farm, The" (Creeley), **Supp. IV Part 1:** 155

Farmer (Harrison), **Supp. VIII:** 39, **44–45**

Farmer, Frances, **Supp. XV:** 196–197

Farmer, Richard, **Supp. XIV:** 2

"Farmer and the Fox, The" (Leopold), **Supp. XIV:** 188

Farmer Boy (L. I. Wilder), **Supp. XXII:** 294, 297, 299

"Farmers' Daughters, The" (W. C. Williams), **Retro. Supp. I:** 423

Farmers Hotel, The (O'Hara), **III:** 361

"Farmer's Sorrow, A" (Jewett), **Retro. Supp. II:** 132

"Farmer's Wife, The" (Sexton), **Supp. II Part 2:** 676

"Farmer & Wife" (Davison), **Supp. XXVI:** 79

"Farm Garden" (Nelson), **Supp. XVIII:** 186

"Farm Implements and Rutabagas in a Landscape" (Ashbery), **Supp. III Part 1:** 13

Farming: A Hand Book (Berry), **Supp. X:** 31, 35

"Farmlights in Iowa" (Kooser), **Supp. XIX:** 120

"Farm on the Great Plains, The" (Stafford), **Supp. XI:** 322

Farnol, Jeffrey, **Supp. I Part 2:** 653

Far North (Shepard), **Supp. III Part 2:** 433, 435

"Far Northern Birch, The" (Francis), **Supp. IX:** 90

Farnsworth, Elizabeth, **Supp. XI:** 139

"Farrago" (Kees), **Supp. XV:** 145

Farrand, Max, **II:** 122

Farrar, Geraldine, **Retro. Supp. I:** 10

Farrar, John, **II:** 191; **Supp. XI:** 47

Farrell, Barry, **Supp. XIV:** 142

Farrell, James Francis, **II:** 25, 26

Farrell, James T., **I:** 97, 288, 475, 508, 517, 519; **II: 25–53,** 416, 424; **III:** 28, 114, 116, 118, 119, 317, 382; **IV:** 211, 286; **Retro. Supp. II:** 196, 327; **Supp. I Part 2:** 679; **Supp. VIII:** 96, 97; **Supp. IX:** 3; **Supp. XV:** 141; **Supp. XXVI:** 18

Farrell, Mrs. James T. (Dorothy Butler), **II:** 26

Farrell, Mrs. James T. (Hortense Alden), **II:** 26, 27, 45, 48

Farrell, John, **II:** 26

Farrell, John C., **Supp. I Part 1:** 24

Farrell, Kate, **Supp. XV:** 187–188,**Supp. XV:** 190

Farrell, Kevin, **II:** 26

Farrell, Mary, **II:** 25

"Far Rockaway" (Schwartz), **Supp. II Part 2:** 649

Farrow, Mia, **Supp. XV:** 8, 10

Far Side of the Dollar, The (Macdonald), **Supp. IV Part 2:** 473

Farther Off from Heaven (Humphrey), **Supp. IX:** 93, 96, 101, **103–104,** 105, 109

Farther Off from Heaven (Inge), **Supp. XXV:** 94, 100

Far Tortuga (Matthiessen), **Supp. V:** 201, 206–207

"Fascinating Fascism" (Sontag), **Supp. III Part 2:** 465

"Fascination of Cities, The" (Hughes), **Supp. I Part 1:** 325

Fashion, Power, Guilt and the Charity of Families (Shields), **Supp. VII:** 323

Fasman, Jonathan, **Supp. V:** 253

Fast, Howard, **Supp. I Part 1:** 295; **Supp. XXI:** 277; **Supp. XXIII:** 165

Fast, Jonathan, **Supp. V:** 115

Fast and Loose (Wharton), **Retro. Supp. I:** 361

"Faster than Light" (Nelson), **Supp. XVIII:** 178–179

"Fastest Runner on Sixty-first Street, The" (Farrell), **II:** 45

Fast Lane on a Dirt Road (Sherman), **Supp. XXII:** 205

Fast Sooner Hound, The (Bontemps and Conroy), **Supp. XXII:** 5, 10–11

"Fat" (Carver), **Supp. III Part 1:** 141

Fatal Interview (Millay), **III:** 128–129, 130

"Fatality" (Bausch), **Supp. VII:** 54

Fatal Lady (film), **Supp. XIII:** 166

"Fate" (Emerson), **II:** 2–3, 4, 16; **Supp. XIV:** 42

"Fate" (Koch), **Supp. XV:** 183

"Fate" (Mailer), **Retro. Supp. II:** 207

"Fate of Pleasure, The" (Trilling), **Supp. III Part 2:** 510

Fate of the Jury, The (Masters), **Supp. I Part 2:** 466, 468, 469

"Fat Girl, The" (Dubus), **Supp. VII:** 84, 85

"Father" (Kooser), **Supp. XIX:** 117, 127

"Father" (Levine), **Supp. V:** 188

"Father" (Sanders), **Supp. XVI:** 277

"Father" (Trethewey), **Supp. XXI:** 253

"Father" (Walker), **Supp. III Part 2:** 522

"Father, The" (Carver), **Supp. III Part 1:** 137, 140

Father, The (Olds), **Supp. X: 209–211**

"Father Abraham" (Faulkner), **Retro. Supp. I:** 81, 82

Fatheralong: A Meditation on Fathers and Sons, Race and Society (Wideman), **Supp. X:** 320, 332–333, 334, 335

"Father and Daughter" (Eberhart), **I:** 539

Father and Glorious Descendant (Lowe), **Supp. X:** 291

"Father and Son" (Eberhart), **I:** 539

Father and Son (Farrell), **II:** 34, 35, 290, 291

Father and Son (Gosse), **Supp. VIII:** 157

"Father and Son" (Hughes), **Retro. Supp. I:** 204; **Supp. I Part 1:** 329, 339

"Father and Son" (Kunitz), **Supp. III Part 1:** 262

Father and Son (L. Brown), **Supp. XXI:** 36, 40, 41, **46–47**

"Father and Son" (Schwartz), **Supp. II Part 2:** 650

Father Bombo's Pilgrimage to Mecca (Freneau), **Supp. II Part 1:** 254

Father Fisheye (Balakian), **Supp. XXIII:** 19

"Father Fisheye"(Balakian), **Supp. XXIII:** 19

"Father Fitzgerald" (Nelson and Espeland), **Supp. XVIII:** 181

"Father Guzman" (Stern), **Supp. IX: 293,** 296

"Father John Melby and the Ghost of Amy Elizabeth" (Brockmeier), **Supp. XXII:** 60

Father of the Blues (Bontemps as Handy), **Supp. XXII:** 5

"Father out Walking on the Lawn, A" (Dove), **Supp. IV Part 1:** 246

"Fathers" (Creeley), **Supp. IV Part 1:** 157–158

Fathers, The (Tate), **IV:** 120, 127, 130, 131–133, 134, 141; **Supp. X:** 52

Fathers and Crows (Vollmann), **Supp. XVII:** 226, 231–232

"Fathers and Daughters, Mothers and Sons"(Hadas), **Supp. XXIII:** 119

"Fathers and Sons" (Hemingway), **II:** 249, 265–266; **Retro. Supp. I:** 175

"Father's Body, The" (Dickey), **Supp. IV Part 1:** 176

"Father's Day" (Connelly), **Supp. XXI:** 79–80

"Father's Story, A" (Dubus), **Supp. VII:** 88

"Father's Voice" (Stafford), **Supp. XI:** 322

"Fat Lady, The" (Carruth), **Supp. XVI:** 48

"Fat Man, Floating" (Dunn), **Supp. XI:** 144

Fat Men in Skirts (Silver), **Supp. XXIV: 265–267,** 275

"Fat Tuesday"(P. Benedict), **Supp. XXIII:** 38

Faulkes Chronicle, The (Huddle), **Supp. XXVI:** 148, 158, 159–160

Faulkner, Barry, **Supp. XV:** 41

Faulkner, William, **I:** 54, 97, 99, 105, 106, 115, 117, 118, 123, 190, 204–205, 211, 288, 289, 291, 292, 297, 305, 324, 374, 378, 423, 480, 517; **II:** 28, 51, **54–76,** 131, 174, 194, 217, 223, 228, 230, 259, 301, 306, 431, 458–459, 542, 594, 606; **III:** 45, 70, 108, 164, 218, 220, 222, 236–237, 244, 292, 334, 350, 382, 418, 453, 454, 482, 483; **IV:** 2, 4, 33, 49, 97, 98, 100, 101, 120, 131, 203, 207, 211, 217, 237, 257, 260, 261, 279, 280, 352, 461, 463; **Retro. Supp. I: 73–95,** 215, 339, 347, 356, 379, 382; **Retro. Supp. II:** 19, 221, 326; **Supp. I Part 1:** 196, 197, 242, 372; **Supp. I Part 2:** 450, 621; **Supp. III Part 1:** 384–385, 396; **Supp. IV Part 1:** 47, 130, 257, 342; **Supp. IV Part 2:** 434, 463, 468, 502, 677, 682; **Supp. IX:** 20, 95; **Supp. V:** 58, 59, 138, 210, 226, 237, 261, 262, 334–336; **Supp. VIII:** 37, 39, 40, 104, 105, 108, 175, 176, 180, 181, 183, 184, 188, 189, 215; **Supp. X:** 44, 228; **Supp. XI:** 92, 247; **Supp. XII:** 16, 289, 310, 313; **Supp. XIII:** 100, 169; **Supp. XIV:** 1, 12–13, 21, 24, 93, 306; **Supp. XIX:** 97, 154, 166; **Supp. XV:** 92, 135, 338; **Supp. XVI:** 148, 189; **Supp. XVII:** 225; **Supp. XVIII:** 76, 84, 90, 148, 249; **Supp. XX: 137, 162, 185, 195; Supp. XXI:** 36, 38, 256; **Supp. XXII:** 193, 203, 205; **Supp. XXIII:** 166; **Supp. XXIV:** 54, 64, 132, 136, 215; **Supp. XXV:** 49; **Supp. XXVI:** 1, 9, 45, 144, 147

Faulkner: A Collection of Critical Essays (Warren), **Retro. Supp. I:** 73

Faulkner at Nagano (Jelliffe, ed.), **I:** 289; **II:** 63, 65

Faulkner-Cowley File, The: Letters and Memories 1944–1962 (Cowley, ed.), **Retro. Supp. I:** 73, 92; **Supp. II Part 1:** 140, 141

"Faultlines"(Hadas), **Supp. XXIII:** 117–118

"Faun" (Plath), **Supp. I Part 2:** 537

"Fauna" (Jeffers), **Supp. II Part 2:** 415

Fauset, Arthur Huff, **Supp. XVIII:** 126

Fauset, Jessie, **Supp. I Part 1:** 321, 325; **Supp. IV Part 1:** 164

Fauset, Jessie Redmon, **Supp. XIX:** 69, 78; **Supp. XVIII:** 122,127

Faust (Goethe), **I:** 396; **II:** 489; **III:** 395; **Supp. II Part 1:** 16; **Supp. IX:** 141

Faust, Beatrix Hapgood, **Supp. XXI:** 8

Faust, Clarence H., **II:** 20

Faute de l'Abbé Mouret, La (Zola), **III:** 322

"Favor, The" (Carver and Gallagher), **Supp. XXIV:** 178

Favor Island (Merwin), **Supp. III Part 1:** 346, 347

"Favor of Love, A" (Peacock), **Supp. XIX:** 203

"Favrile" (Doty), **Supp. XI:** 131

"Fawn" (Davison), **Supp. XXVI:** 75

"Fawn, with a Bit of Green" (Swados), **Supp. XIX:** 258

Fay (L. Brown), **Supp. XXI:** 40, 41, 47

Fay, Bernard, **IV:** 41

"Fear, The" (Frost), **Retro. Supp. I:** 128

Fear and Loathing in Las Vegas (Thompson), **Supp. XXIV:** 280, 282, 283, 287, **288–292,** 293

Fear and Loathing on the Campaign Trail '72 (Thompson), **Supp. XXIV:** 279, 281, 282, 289, **292–293**

Fear and Trembling (Kierkegaard), **Supp. XX: 132**

"Fear & Fame" (Levine), **Supp. V:** 192

Fearful Child, The (C. Frost), **Supp. XV:** 96, 97, 106

"Fearful Child, The" (C. Frost), **Supp. XV:** 96

Fearing, Kenneth, **Supp. XV:** 138; **Supp. XXVI:** 134, 143

"Fearless" (Mosley), **Supp. XIII:** 241

Fearless Jones (Mosley), **Supp. XIII: 241–242**

"Fear of Concrete" (Halliday), **Supp. XIX:** 91

Fear of Fifty: A Midlife Memoir (Jong), **Supp. V:** 114, 115, 116, 131

Fear of Flying (Jong), **Supp. V:** 113, 115, 116, 119–123, 124, 129

"Feast, The" (Kinnell), **Supp. III Part 1:** 239, 250

Feast of All Saints, The (Rice), **Supp. VII:** 299–301

Feast of Love, The (C. Baxter), **Supp. XVII:** 13, 21–22

Feast of Love, The (film, R. Benton), **Supp. XVII:** 22

Feast of Snakes, A (Crews), **Supp. XI:** 102, **107–108; Supp. XXI:** 40

"Feast of Stephen, The" (Hecht), **Supp. X:** 63–64

Feast of the Goat, The (Llosa), **Supp. XXIV:** 89

"Featherbed for Critics, A" (Blackmur), **Supp. II Part 1:** 93, 151

Feather Crowns (Mason), **Supp. VIII: 146–147**

"Feathers" (Carver), **Supp. III Part 1:** 145

Feathers (Van Vechten), **Supp. II Part 2:** 736, 749

"Feathers, The" (Hogan), **Supp. IV Part 1:** 416

Feathers Left Around (Wells), **Supp. XXVI:** 282

"February" (Ellison), **Supp. II Part 1:** 229

"February 14th" (Levine), **Supp. V:** 194

February in Sydney (Komunyakaa), **Supp. XIII: 124–125,** 129

"February in Sydney" (Komunyakaa), **Supp. XIII:** 125

"February: Thinking of Flowers" (Kenyon), **Supp. VII:** 171

"Feces" (McClatchy), **Supp. XII:** 266, 267–268

Fechner, Gustav, **II:** 344, 355, 358, 359, 363

Feder, Lillian, **IV:** 136; **Supp. XVI:** 49, 50

Federal Arts Project, **Supp. III Part 2:** 618

Federigo, or, The Power of Love (Nemerov), **III:** 268, 276, 282, 283–284, 285

"Fedge, The" (Halliday), **Supp. XIX:** 93

"Fedora" (Chopin), **Supp. I Part 1:** 220

Fedorko, Kathy A., **Retro. Supp. I:** 361, 374

"Feeling and Precision" (Moore), **III:** 206

Feeling Italian: The Art of Ethnicity in America (Ferraro), **Supp. XX: 43**

"Feeling of Effort, The" (James), **II:** 349

Feeling Very Strange: The Slipstream Anthology (Kelly and Kessel, eds.), **Supp. XIX:** 231

"Feel Like a Bird" (Swenson), **Supp. IV Part 2:** 639

"Feel Me" (Swenson), **Supp. IV Part 2:** 647

Feeney, Mary, **Supp. IX:** 152, 154

Feinsilver, Pamela, **Supp. XX: 135**

Feinstein, Herbert, **Supp. XIX:** 260

Feinstein, Sascha, **Supp. XIII:** 125

Feldman, Charles K., **Supp. XI:** 307

Feldman, Morton, **Supp. XXIII:** 211

Fellini, Federico, **Supp. XII:** 172; **Supp. XV:** 8

"Fellini the Cat" (Peacock), **Supp. XIX:** 206

"Fellow Citizens" (Sandburg), **III:** 553

Fellows, John, **Supp. I Part 2:** 520

Fellow Travelers (Mallon), **Supp. XIX:** 132, **143–144**

"Felo de Se" (Wylie), **Supp. I Part 2:** 727, 729

Felton, Sharon, **Supp. IV Part 1:** 210

"Female Author" (Plath), **Retro. Supp. II:** 243

"Female Frailty" (Freneau), **Supp. II Part 1:** 258

"Female Laughter and Comic Possibilities: *Uncommon Women and Others*" (Chirico), **Supp. XV:** 323

Female Patriot, The; or, Nature's Rights (Rowson), **Supp. XV:** 237–238

Female Prose Writers of America (Hart), **Supp. XVIII:** 257, 264

"Female Voice in *To Kill a Mockingbird,* The: Narrative Strategies in Film and Novel" (Shakelford), **Supp. VIII:** 129

" 'Feminine' Epic, The" (Notley), **Supp. XXII:** 232, 234, 236

"Feminine Landscape of Leslie Marmon Silko's *Ceremony,* The" (Gunn Allen),

Supp. IV Part 1: 324

Feminine Note in Fiction, The (Courtney), **Supp. XXIV:** 29

Feminism and the Politics of Literary Reputation: The Example of Erica Jong (Templin), **Supp. V:** 116

"Feminismo" (Robbins), **Supp. X:** 272

"Feminist Criticism in the Wilderness" (Showalter), **Supp. X:** 97

"Feminist Manifesto" (Loy), **Supp. XXII:** 160

Feminization of American Culture, The (Douglas), **Supp. XVIII:** 258

"Fence, The" (Oliver), **Supp. VII:** 232

"Fence Posts" (Snyder), **Supp. VIII:** 304

Fences (Wilson), **Supp. VIII:** 329, 330, 331, **334–337,** 350

Fenick, Elizabeth, **Retro. Supp. II:** 221

"Fenimore Cooper's Literary Offenses" (Twain), **IV:** 204–205

Fennell, Frank L., **Supp. XVII:** 177–178

Fenollosa, Ernest, **III:** 458, 465, 466, 474, 475, 477; **Retro. Supp. I:** 289; **Supp. IV Part 1:** 154

Fenollosa, Mrs. Ernest, **III:** 458

"Fenstad's Mother" (C. Baxter), **Supp. XVII:** 18

Fenton, Charles, **Supp. XI:** 43

Fenton, James, **Supp. XV:** 117

Fenton, William, **Supp. XXVI:** 96

Ferdinand: Including "It Was" (Zukofsky), **Supp. III Part 2:** 630

"Fergus" (Bourne), **I:** 229

Ferguson, James, **Supp. I Part 2:** 503

Ferguson, Otis, **Supp. IX:** 7

Ferguson, SallyAnn H., **Supp. XXVI:** 166

Ferguson, William, **Supp. XII:** 189

Ferguson Affair, The (Macdonald), **Supp. IV Part 2:** 473

Fergusson, Francis, **I:** 265, 440; **Supp. XV:** 20

Ferlinghetti, Lawrence, **Supp. IV Part 1:** 90; **Supp. VIII:** 290, 292; **Supp. XII:** 121, 125; **Supp. XIII:** 275; **Supp. XIX:** 4; **Supp. XXI:** 53; **Supp. XXIII:** 219

Fermata, The (Baker), **Supp. XIII: 49–52,** 54

"Fern" (Toomer), **Supp. III Part 2:** 481; **Supp. IX:** 313

Fern, Fanny, **Retro. Supp. I:** 246; **Supp. V:** 122

Fernández, Enrique, **Supp. VIII:** 73

Fernandez, Ramon, **Retro. Supp. I:** 302, 303; **Supp. XVI:** 214

"Fern-Beds in Hampshire Country" (Wilbur), **Supp. III Part 2:** 558

"Fern Hill" (D. Thomas), **IV:** 93; **Supp. XX: 204**

"Fern-Life" (Larcom), **Supp. XIII:** 143

Ferragammo, Salvatore, **Supp. XVI:** 192

Ferraro, Thomas J., **Supp. XX: 34, 43**

Ferreo, Guglielmo, **Supp. I Part 2:** 481

Ferris, Anthony, **Supp. XX: 124**

Ferris, Beth, **Supp. XXVI:** 183

Ferry, David, **Supp. XXIV: 147–164; Supp. XXV:** 222

"Ferry, The" (Cliff), **Supp. XXII:** 74

Fessenden, Thomas Green, **II:** 300

Fessier, Michael, **Supp. XIII:** 164

"Festival Aspect, The" (Olson), **Supp. II Part 2:** 585

"Festival of Regrets, The" (Wasserstein), **Supp. XV:** 333

Festival of San Joaquin, The (Edgell), **Supp. XXIII:** 84, 85, **90–91,** 94

Fetching the Dead (Sanders), **Supp. XVI:** 269

Fêtes galantes (Verlaine), **IV:** 79

Fetid Itch (Silver), **Supp. XXIV:** 265

"Fetish" (McClatchy), **Supp. XII:** 256

Fetterley, Judith, **Retro. Supp. II:** 139; **Supp. XXIV:** 28

Fetterly, Judith, **Supp. XXV:** 285

"Feud" (Zinberg), **Supp. XV:** 195

"Fever" (Carver), **Supp. III Part 1:** 145

"Fever 103°" (Plath), **Supp. I Part 2:** 541

Fever Pitch (Hornby), **Supp. XII:** 286; **Supp. XXIII:** 109

Fever: Twelve Stories (Wideman), **Supp. X:** 320

"Few Don'ts by an Imagiste, A" (Pound), **III:** 465; **Retro. Supp. I:** 288; **Supp. I Part 1:** 261–262

"Few Kind Words for Anger, A" (Kriegel), **Supp. XXIV:** 220

"Few Stray Comments on the Cultivation of the Lyric, A" (Sobin), **Supp. XVI:** 285

"Few Words of Introduction, A" (McNally), **Supp. XIII:** 198–199

Feydeau, Georges, **Supp. XXIV:** 271

Feynman, Richard, **Supp. XXV:** 267

Fiamengo, Janice, **Supp. XIII:** 35

"Fiat Lux" (H. Johnson), **Supp. XXVI:** 172

Fiber (Bass), **Supp. XVI:** 22

"*Fiber:* A Post-Pastoral Georgic" (Gifford), **Supp. XVI:** 22

Ficke, Arthur Davison, **Supp. XIII:** 347; **Supp. XV:** 40, 42, 43, 46, 48, 49

"Fiction" (Stafford), **Supp. XI:** 327

"Fiction: A Lens on Life" (Stegner), **Supp. IV Part 2:** 595, 596, 600

Fictional World of William Hoffman, The (Frank, ed.), **Supp. XVIII:** 74, 79, 80, 87

Fiction and the Figures of Life (Gass), **Supp. VI:** 85

Fiction of Joseph Heller, The (Seed), **Supp. IV Part 1:** 391

Fiction of Paule Marshall, The (Denniston), **Supp. XI:** 276

Fiction of the Forties (Eisinger), **I:** 302; **II:** 604

Fictions in Autobiography: Studies in the Art of Self-Invention (Eakin), **Supp. XVI:** 70

"Fiction Writer and His Country, The" (O'Connor), **III:** 342; **Retro. Supp. II:** 223, 225; **Supp. II Part 1:** 148

Fiddler's Trance, The (Skloot), **Supp. XX: 196, 202**

Fidelity (Glaspell), **Supp. III Part 1:** 177

Fiedler, Leslie A., **II:** 27; **III:** 218; **Retro. Supp. II:** 280, 324; **Supp. II Part 1:** 87; **Supp. IV Part 1:** 42, 86; **Supp. IX:** 3, 227; **Supp. X:** 80; **Supp. XIII: 93–110; Supp. XIV:** 11; **Supp. XIX:**

251; **Supp. XVIII:** 146; **Supp. XXIII:** 42; **Supp. XXV:** 268

Fiedler on the Roof: Essays on Literature and Jewish Identity (Fiedler), **Supp. XIII:** 106–107

"Fie! Fie! Fi-Fi!" (Fitzgerald), **Retro. Supp. I:** 100

Field, Eugene, **Supp. II Part 1:** 197

Field, John, **IV:** 179

"Field Events" (Bass), **Supp. XVI:** 19

"Field Full of Black Cats, A" (C. Frost), **Supp. XV:** 101

Field Guide, (Hass), **Supp. VI:** 97–98, **99–101,** 102, 103, 106

Field Guide to Contemporary Poetry and Poetics (Friebert and Young, eds.), **Supp. XI:** 270

"Field Guide to the Western Birds" (Stegner), **Supp. IV Part 2:** 609

Fielding, Henry, **I:** 134; **II:** 302, 304–305; **III:** 61; **Supp. I Part 2:** 421, 422, 656; **Supp. IV Part 2:** 688; **Supp. IX:** 128; **Supp. V:** 127; **Supp. XI:** 277; **Supp. XVIII:** 2, 7; **Supp. XXV:** 258

Fielding, Richard, **Supp. XV:** 232

"Field-larks and Blackbirds" (Lanier), **Supp. I Part 1:** 355

Field of Honor (Hay), **Supp. XIV:** 120–121, 125, 130

"Field of Honor" (Hay), **Supp. XIV:** 120–121, 129–130

Field of Vision, The (Morris), **III:** 226–228, 229, 232, 233, 238

"Field Report" (Corso), **Supp. XII:** 124, **136**

"Fields" (Wright), **Supp. XV:** 342

Fields, Annie Adams, **II:** 401, 402, 403–404, 406, 412; **IV:** 177; **Retro. Supp. II:** 134, 135, 142; **Supp. I Part 1:** 317; **Supp. XVI:** 84, 88

Fields, James T., **II:** 274, 279, 402–403; **Retro. Supp. II:** 135; **Supp. I Part 1:** 317; **Supp. XIII:** 150; **Supp. XVI:** 84, 88

Fields, Mrs. James T., **Supp. XIV:** 44, 46. *See* Fields, Annie Adams

Fields, Jerry, **Supp. XXVI:** 86

Fields, Joseph, **IV:** 274

Fields, The (Richter), **Supp. XVIII: 213–214,** 220

Fields, W. C., **II:** 427; **IV:** 335

"Fields at Dusk, The" (Salter), **Supp. IX:** 260

Fields of Fire (Webb), **Supp. XXII:** 115

Fields of Praise, The (Nelson), **Supp. XVIII:** 171, 173, **177–178**

Fields of Wonder (Hughes), **Retro. Supp. I:** 206, 207; **Supp. I Part 1:** 333–334

Fierce Invalids Home from Hot Climates (Robbins), **Supp. X:** 267, 276–277, **282–285**

Fiery, Marion, **Supp. XXII:** 293

Fiery Chariot, The (Hurston), **Supp. VI:** 155–156

"Fiesta, 1980" (Díaz), **Supp. XXIV:** 88

15 Poems (Banks), **Supp. V:** 5

"Fifteenth Farewell" (Bogan), **Supp. III Part 1:** 51, 58

"Fifth Avenue, Uptown" (Baldwin), **Supp. I Part 1:** 52

"Fifth Avenue—Spring Afternoon" (Untermeyer), **Supp. XV:** 296

Fifth Book of Peace, The (Kingston), **Supp. V:** 173

Fifth Chinese Daughter (Wong), **Supp. X:** 291

Fifth Column, The (Hemingway), **II:** 254, 258; **Retro. Supp. I:** 184

"Fifth Column of the Fencerow" (Leopold), **Supp. XIV:** 185

Fifth Decad of Cantos, The (Pound), **Retro. Supp. I:** 292

"Fifth Movement: *Autobiography*" (Zukofsky), **Supp. III Part 2:** 611

Fifth Sunday (Dove), **Supp. IV Part 1:** 251, 252–253

"Fifth Sunday" (Dove), **Supp. IV Part 1:** 252

50 Poems (Cummings), **I:** 430, 440, 442–443, 444–445, 446

Fifty Best American Short Stories (O'Brien), **III:** 56

"Fifty Dollars" (Elkin), **Supp. VI:** 43–44

"55 Miles to the Gas Pump" (Proulx), **Supp. VII:** 264

55 Poems (Zukofsky), **Supp. III Part 2:** 611, 621

"Fifty Grand" (Hemingway), **II:** 250, 424; **Retro. Supp. I:** 177

Fifty Stories (Boyle), **Supp. XXIV:** 58

"Fifty Suggestions" (Poe), **Retro. Supp. II:** 266

"52 Oswald Street" (Kinnell), **Supp. III Part 1:** 251

Fifty Years Among Authors, Editors, and Publishers (Derby), **Supp. XVIII:** 4

"Fifty Years Among the Black Folk" (Du Bois), **Supp. II Part 1:** 169

"Fifty Years of American Poetry" (Jarrell), **Retro. Supp. I:** 52

Fig Connection, The (Franzen and Siebert), **Supp. XX:** 84

Fight, The (Mailer), **Retro. Supp. II:** 207, 208

Fight Back: For the Sake of the People, For the Sake of the Land (Ortiz), **Supp. IV Part 2:** 497, 498, 499, 503, 510–512, 514

"Fighters, The" (Zinberg), **Supp. XV:** 193

Fight for Freedom (Hughes), **Supp. I Part 1:** 345

Fighting Angel (Buck), **Supp. II Part 1:** 119, 131

Fighting France; From Dunkerque to Belfort (Wharton), **Retro. Supp. I:** 377, 378

Fightin': New and Collected Stories (Ortiz), **Supp. IV Part 2:** 513

"Figlia che Piange, La" (Eliot), **I:** 570, 584; **III:** 9

Figliola, Samantha, **Supp. V:** 143

"Figure a Poem Makes, The" (Frost), **Retro. Supp. I:** 139

"Figured Wheel, The" (Pinsky), **Supp. VI:** 243, 244, 245, 246

Figured Wheel, The: New and Collected Poems (Pinsky), **Supp. VI:** 247–248

"Figure in the Carpet, The" (James), **Retro. Supp. I:** 228, 229

"Figure in the Doorway, The" (Frost), **Retro. Supp. I:** 138

Figure of Fulfillment, The (Lerperger; Miller, trans.), **Supp. XX:** 165, 167–168

Figures from the Double World (McGrath), **Supp. X:** 118–119

Figures in Black: Words, Signs, and the "Racial" Self (H. L. Gates), **Supp. XX:** 99, 100, 106, 107

"Figures in the Clock, The" (McCarthy), **II:** 561–562

Figures Made Visible in the Sadness of Time (Everwine), **Supp. XV:** 75, 88

Figures of Time (Hayden), **Supp. II Part 1:** 367

Filbin, Thomas, **Supp. XXIII:** 299

"Filling Out a Blank" (Wagoner), **Supp. IX:** 324

Fillmore, Millard, **III:** 101

Film Flam: Essays on Hollywood (McMurtry), **Supp. V:** 228

Films of Ayn Rand, The (Cox), **Supp. IV Part 2:** 524

Filo, John, **Supp. XII:** 211

Filreis, Alan, **Supp. XXI:** 262, 267, 268, 269, 271, 273, 275, 277, 278

Filson, John, **Retro. Supp. I:** 421

Final Beast, The (Buechner), **Supp. XII:** 49–51

"Finale" (Longfellow), **II:** 505, 506–507

"Finale: Presto" (Davison), **Supp. XXVI:** 70

"Final Fear" (Hughes), **Supp. I Part 1:** 338

Final Harvest: Emily Dickinson's Poems (T. H. Johnson, ed.), **I:** 470, 471

"Finally Harriet" (Wolfert), **Supp. XXI:** 265–267

Final Payments (Gordon), **Supp. IV Part 1:** 297, 299, 300–302, 304, 306, 314

"Final Report, A" (Maxwell), **Supp. VIII:** 169

"Final Soliloquy of the Interior Paramour" (Stevens), **Retro. Supp. I:** 312

Final Solution, The (Reitlinger), **Supp. XII:** 161

Financier, The (Dreiser), **I:** 497, 501, 507, 509; **Retro. Supp. II:** 94, 101–102, 105; **Supp. XVIII:** 246

Finch, Annie, **Supp. XVII:** 69–79

Finch, Henry Leroy, **Supp. XVII:** 69

Finch, Margaret Rockwell, **Supp. XVII:** 69

Finch, Robert, **Supp. XIV:** 186–187; **Supp. XXVI:** 38

"Finches, Little Pats of Butter on the Wing"(Crooker), **Supp. XXIII:** 62

Find a Victim (Macdonald), **Supp. IV Part 2:** 467, 472, 473

Fin de Chéri, La (Colette; stage adaptation, Loos), **Supp. XVI:** 194

Finder, Henry, **Supp. XX:** 90

"Fin de Saison Palm Beach" (White), **Supp. I Part 2:** 673

"Finding a Bible in an Abandoned Cabin" (Wrigley), **Supp. XVIII:** 293–294, 296, 297, 300, 301, 303

Finding a Form (Gass), **Supp. VI:** 91–92, 93

Finding a Girl in America (Dubus), **Supp. VII:** 85–88

"Finding a Girl in America" (Dubus), **Supp. VII:** 87

"Finding Amy" (O'Nan), **Supp. XXV:** 143, 150

"Finding Beads" (Hogan), **Supp. IV Part 1:** 400

Finding Losses (Bronk), **Supp. XXI:** 31, 32

"Finding of Zach, The" (Dunbar), **Supp. II Part 1:** 212

Findings and Keepings: Analects for an Autobiography (Mumford), **Supp. II Part 2:** 483

Finding the Center: Narrative Poetry of the Zuni Indians (Tedlock), **Supp. IV Part 2:** 509

Finding the Islands (Merwin), **Supp. III Part 1:** 353, 357

"Finding the Place: A Migrant Childhood" (Stegner), **Supp. IV Part 2:** 597

Findley, Timothy, **Supp. XX:** 49–65

"Find the Woman" (Macdonald, as Millar), **Supp. IV Part 2:** 466

Fine, David, **Supp. XI:** 160

Fine, Richard, **Supp. XVIII:** 248

Fine Clothes to the Jew (Hughes), **Retro. Supp. I:** 200, 201, 203, 205; **Supp. I Part 1:** 326–328

"Fine Old Firm, A" (Jackson), **Supp. IX:** 120

Fine Preserving (Plagemann), **Supp. XVII:** 91

Fine Preserving: M. F. K. Fisher's Annotated Edition of Catherine Plagemann's Cookbook (Plagemann; M. F. K. Fisher, ed.), **Supp. XVII:** 91

Finer Grain, The (James), **II:** 335

Fine Writing (L. P. Smith), **Supp. XIV:** 347

"Finis" (X. J. Kennedy), **Supp. XV:** 169

"Finished Basement" (Di Piero), **Supp. XIX:** 47

Finished Man, The (Garrett), **Supp. VII:** 96, 97–98

Fink, Jonathan, **Supp. XXI:** 244, 245, 248, 255, 256

Fink, Mike, **IV:** 266

Finkelstein, Norman, **Supp. XXI:** 24, 33

Finkle, David, **Supp. XXI:** 47

Finley, John H., **II:** 418

Finn, David, **Supp. VIII:** 106–107

Finnegan, Robert (pseudonym). *See* Ryan, Paul William

Finnegans Wake (Joyce), **III:** 7, 12, 14, 261; **IV:** 182, 369–370, 418, 421; **Supp. I Part 2:** 620; **Supp. II Part 1:** 2; **Supp. XIII:** 191; **Supp. XVIII:** 32

Finney, Brian, **Supp. XIV:** 158, 160, 161, 165, 166, 167, 169

"Finnish Rhapsody" (Ashbery), **Supp. III Part 1:** 26

Finster, Howard, **Supp. XV:** 349

Firbank, Ronald, **IV:** 77, 436; **Supp. XXIII:** 209

"Fire" (Hughes), **Supp. I Part 1:** 327

"Fire and Cloud" (Wright), **IV:** 488

"Fire and Ice" (Frost), **II:** 154; **Retro. Supp. I:** 133; **Supp. XIX:** 122

Fire and Ice (Stegner), **Supp. IV Part 2:** 598, 607–608

"Fire and the Cloud, The" (Hurston), **Supp. VI:** 158

"Fire and the Hearth, The" (Faulkner), **II:** 71

Firebird (Doty), **Supp. XI:** 119–120, 121, **132–133,** 134

"Firebombing, The" (Dickey), **Supp. IV Part 1:** 180–181, 187, 189–190

"Fireborn Are at Home in Fire, The" (Sandburg), **III:** 591

"Fire by Night" (R. Fisher), **Supp. XIX:** 70–71

"Fire Chaconne" (Francis), **Supp. IX:** 87

Firecrackers (Van Vechten), **Supp. II Part 2:** 740, 742–744, 749

"Fire Dreams"(Thompson), **Supp. XXIII:** 296

Fire: From "A Journal of Love," the Unexpurgated Diary of Anaïs Nin, 1934–1937, **Supp. X:** 184, 185, 189, 194, 195

"Fire in the House, The" (Davison), **Supp. XXVI:** 71

Firelight Fairy Book, The (Beston), **Supp. XXVI:** 33

"Fireman, The " (Bass), **Supp. XVI:** 24

Fireman's Wife and Other Stories, The (Bausch), **Supp. VII:** 48, 54

Fire Next Time, The (Baldwin), **Retro. Supp. II:** 5, 8, 9; **Supp. I Part 1:** 48, 49, 52, 60–61

"Fire Next Time, The" (Baldwin). *See* "Down at the Cross" (Baldwin)

"Fire of Driftwood, The" (Longfellow), **II:** 499; **Retro. Supp. II:** 159, 168

"Fire of Life" (McCullers), **II:** 585

Fire on the Mountain (Abbey), **Supp. XIII:** 6

"Fire Poem" (Merrill), **Supp. III Part 1:** 321

"Fires" (Bass), **Supp. XVI:** 20

"Fires" (Carver), **Supp. III Part 1:** 136–139, 147

Fire Sale (Paretsky), **Supp. XXV:** 175–176, 178

Fire Screen, The (Merrill), **Supp. III Part 1:** 319, 325–329

"Fire Season" (Didion), **Supp. IV Part 1:** 199

"Fire Sequence" (Winters), **Supp. II Part 2:** 791, 796, 800

Fire Sermon (Morris), **III:** 238–239

"Fire Sermon, The" (Eliot), **Retro. Supp. I:** 60–61

Fires: Essays, Poems, Stories (Carver), **Supp. III Part 1:** 136, 140, 142, 146–147

Fireside Travels (Lowell), **Supp. I Part 2:** 407, 419–420

Firestarter (King), **Supp. IX:** 114; **Supp. V:** 140, 141, 144

"fire the bastards" (Green), **Supp. IV Part 1:** 285

"Fire-Truck, A" (Wilbur), **Supp. III Part 2:** 556

"Fireweed" (Clampitt), **Supp. IX: 44–45**

"Firewood" (Banks), **Supp. V:** 15

"Fireworks" (Ford), **Supp. V:** 69

"Fireworks" (Shapiro), **Supp. II Part 2:** 707

Fireworks: A History and Celebration (Plimpton), **Supp. XVI:** 245

Fir-Flower Tablets (Lowell), **II:** 512, 526–527

Firger, Jessica, **Supp. XIX:** 51, 58, 59, 62

Firkins, Oscar W., **II:** 271; **Supp. XV:** 297, 309

"Firmament, The" (Bryant), **Supp. I Part 1:** 162

Firmat, Gustavo Pérez, **Supp. VIII:** 76, 77, 79; **Supp. XI:** 184

"First American, The" (Toomer), **Supp. III Part 2:** 480, 487

"First Birth" (Olds), **Supp. X:** 212

First Book of Africa, The (Hughes), **Supp. I Part 1:** 344–345

First Book of Jazz, The (Hughes), **Supp. I Part 1:** 345

First Book of Negroes, The (Hughes), **Supp. I Part 1:** 345

First Book of Rhythms, The (Hughes), **Supp. I Part 1:** 345

First Book of the West Indies, The (Hughes), **Supp. I Part 1:** 345

Firstborn (Glück), **Supp. V:** 80, 81, 82, 84

"Firstborn" (Wright), **Supp. V:** 340

"First Chaldaic Oracle" (Carson), **Supp. XII: 111**

"First Communion" (Fante), **Supp. XI:** 160

"First Confession" (X. J. Kennedy), **Supp. XV: 154–155**

"First Day of School, The" (Gibbons), **Supp. X:** 41, 42

"First Death in Nova Scotia" (Bishop), **Supp. I Part 1:** 73

"First Formal" (Olds), **Supp. X:** 212

First Four Books of Poems, The (Glück), **Supp. V:** 81, 83

First Four Years, The (L. I. Wilder), **Supp. XXII:** 296, 298, 299–300

"First Grade" (Stafford), **Supp. XI:** 328

First Hand (Bierds), **Supp. XVII:** 32, 34–36

"First Hawaiian Bank" (Nye), **Supp. XIII:** 278

"First Heat" (Taylor), **Supp. V:** 323

First Hour, The (Di Piero), **Supp. XIX:** 36–37, 40

"First Hour of the Night, The" (Bidart), **Supp. XV: 30–32**

"First Hunters and the Last, The" (Sobin), **Supp. XVI:** 292

First Indian on the Moon (Alexie), **Supp. XXVI:** 103

"First Job, The" (Cisneros), **Supp. VII:** 62

"1st Letter on Georges" (Olson), **Supp. II Part 2:** 578

First Light (C. Baxter), **Supp. XVII:** 15, **17–18,** 19, 22

First Light (Preston), **Supp. XVII:** 18

First Light (Wagoner), **Supp. IX:** 330

"Firstling, The" (Davison), **Supp. XXVI:** 69

"First Love" (Welty), **IV:** 264; **Retro. Supp. I:** 347

First Love: A Lyric Sequence (Untermeyer), **Supp. XV:** 295

"First Love: A Quiz" (Stallings), **Supp. XXV:** 221, 233

First Lover and Other Stories, The (Boyle), **Supp. XXIV: 57–58**

First Man, The (O'Neill), **III:** 390

First Manifesto (McGrath), **Supp. X:** 115

"First Meditation" (Roethke), **III:** 545–546

"First Noni Daylight, The" (Harjo), **Supp. XII:** 219

"First Passover" (Longfellow), **II:** 500–501

"First Person Female" (Harrison), **Supp. VIII:** 40, 41, 48

"First Place, The" (Wagoner), **Supp. IX:** 328

First Poems (Buechner), **Supp. XII:** 45

First Poems (Merrill), **Supp. III Part 1:** 318–321, 323

First Poems 1946–1954 (Kinnell), **Supp. III Part 1:** 235, 238–239

"First Praise" (W. C. Williams), **Retro. Supp. I:** 413

First Principles (Spencer), **Supp. I Part 1:** 368

"First Reader" (Collins), **Supp. XXI:** 55–56

"First Ride and First Walk" (Goldbarth), **Supp. XII:** 182–183

"First Seeing the St. Lawrence River"(Kenny), **Supp. XXIII:** 152

"First Seven Years, The" (Malamud), **Supp. I Part 2:** 431

"First Sex" (Olds), **Supp. X:** 208

"First Snow" (Mosher), **Supp. XXII:** 211

"First Snow in Alsace" (Wilbur), **Supp. III Part 2:** 545, 546, 559

"First Song" (Kinnell), **Supp. III Part 1:** 239

"First Spade in the West, The" (Fiedler), **Supp. XIII:** 103

"First Steps" (McClatchy), **Supp. XII:** 256

First There Is the Need (Reznikoff), **Supp. XIV:** 291

"First Things First" (Auden), **Supp. II Part 1:** 13

"First Thought, Best Thought" (Ginsberg), **Supp. II Part 1:** 327

"First Time I Saw Paris, The" (Fante), **Supp. XI:** 174

"First Travels of Max" (Ransom), **III:** 490–491

"First Tycoon of Teen, The" (Wolfe), **Supp. III Part 2:** 572

"First Views of the Enemy" (Oates), **Supp. II Part 2:** 508

"First Wife, The" (Buck), **Supp. II Part 1:** 127

First Words before Spring (Untermeyer), **Supp. XV:** 310

"First World War" (White), **Supp. I Part 2:** 665

"Fish" (F. Barthelme), **Supp. XI:** 26

"Fish" (Levis), **Supp. XI:** 259–260

Fish, Stanley, **Supp. IV Part 1:** 48; **Supp. XIV:** 14, 15

"Fish, The" (Bishop), **Supp. XV:** 100, 102

"Fish, The" (Moore), **III:** 195, 197, 209, 211, 213–214; **Supp. XXI:** 26

"Fish, The" (Oliver), **Supp. VII:** 236

"Fish, The/Lago Chapala" (Everwine), **Supp. XV:** 82–83

"Fish and Shadow" (Pound), **III:** 466

"Fishboy" (Richard), **Supp. XIX:** 212–213

Fishboy: A Ghost's Story (Richard), **Supp. XIX:** 209, **213–220,** 221

Fishburne, Laurence, **Supp. VIII:** 345

"Fish Cannery" (Fante), **Supp. XI:** 167

Fisher, Alexander Metcalf, **Supp. I Part 2:** 582

Fisher, Alfred, **Retro. Supp. II:** 243

Fisher, Barbara, **Supp. XXII:** 206

Fisher, Craig, **Supp. V:** 125

Fisher, Dorothy Canfield, **Retro. Supp. I:** 21, 133; **Supp. II Part 1:** 117. *See also* Canfield, Dorothy

Fisher, Mary, **Supp. I Part 2:** 455

Fisher, M. F. K., **Supp. XVII:** 81–93

Fisher, Phillip, **Retro. Supp. I:** 39

Fisher, Rudolph, **Retro. Supp. I:** 200; **Supp. I Part 1:** 325; **Supp. X:** 139; **Supp. XIX:** 65–80; **Supp. XVI:** 143

Fisher, Vardis, **Supp. IV Part 2:** 598

Fisher King, The (Marshall), **Supp. XI:** 275–276, **288–290**

"Fisherman, The" (Merwin), **Supp. II Part 1:** 346

"Fisherman and His Wife, The" (Welty), **IV:** 266

"Fisherman from Chihuahua, The" (Connell), **Supp. XIV:** 86

"Fishing" (Harjo), **Supp. XII:** 227–228

"Fishing Idyll, A" (Mosher), **Supp. XXII:** 209

"Fish in the Stone, The" (Dove), **Supp. IV Part 1:** 245, 257

"Fish in the unruffled lakes" (Auden), **Supp. II Part 1:** 8–9

"Fish R Us" (Doty), **Supp. XI:** 135

Fisk, James, **I:** 4, 474

Fiske, John, **Supp. I Part 1:** 314; **Supp. I Part 2:** 493

Fisketjon, Gary, **Supp. XXIV:** 178

"Fit Against the Country, A" (Wright), **Supp. III Part 2:** 591–592, 601

Fitch, Clyde, **Supp. IV Part 2:** 573

Fitch, Elizabeth. *See* Taylor, Mrs. Edward (Elizabeth Fitch)

Fitch, James, **IV:** 147

Fitch, Noël Riley, **Supp. X:** 186, 187

"Fitting, The" (Hull), **Supp. XXI:** 134, 135

Fit to Be Tied (Silver), **Supp. XXIV: 271–272**

Fitts, Dudley, **I:** 169, 173; **Supp. I Part 1:** 342, 345; **Supp. XIII:** 346; **Supp. XXII:** 281; **Supp. XXVI:** 65

FitzGerald, Edward, **Supp. I Part 2:** 416; **Supp. III Part 2:** 610

Fitzgerald, Ella, **Supp. XIII:** 132

Fitzgerald, F. Scott, **I:** 107, 117, 118, 123, 188, 221, 288, 289, 358, 367, 374–375, 382, 423, 476, 482, 487, 495, 509, 511; **II:** 77–100, 257, 263, 272, 283, 415, 416, 417–418, 420, 425, 427, 430, 431, 432, 433, 434, 436, 437, 450, 458–459, 482, 560; **III:** 2, 26, 35, 36, 37, 40, 44, 45, 69, 106, 244, 284, 334, 350–351, 453, 454, 471, 551, 552, 572; **IV:** 27, 49, 97, 101, 126, 140, 191, 222, 223, 287, 297, 427, 471; **Retro. Supp. I:** 1, 74, **97–120,** 178, 180, 186, 215, 359, 381; **Retro. Supp. II:** 257, 321, 326, 328; **Supp. I Part 1:** 196, 197; **Supp. I Part 2:** 622; **Supp. III Part 2:** 409, 411, 585; **Supp. IV Part 1:** 123, 197, 200, 203, 341; **Supp. IV Part 2:** 463, 468, 607, 689; **Supp. IX:** 15, 20, 55, 57–63, 199; **Supp. V:** 23, 95, 226, 251, 262, 276, 313; **Supp. VIII:** 101, 103, 106, 137; **Supp. X:** 225; **Supp. XI:** 65, 221, 334; **Supp. XII:** 42, 173, 295; **Supp. XIII:** 170, 263; **Supp. XV:** 135; **Supp. XVI:** 64, 75, 191, 192, 294; **Supp. XVIII:** 148, 246, 248, 251, 254; **Supp. XX: 74; Supp. XXI:** 262; **Supp. XXII:** 82, 92; **Supp. XXIII:** 68, 101, 174

Fitzgerald, Robert, **I:** 27–28; **III:** 338, 348; **Retro. Supp. II:** 179, 221, 222, 223, 228, 229; **Supp. IV Part 2:** 631; **Supp. XV:** 112, 249; **Supp. XXII:** 281; **Supp. XXIII:** 112

Fitzgerald, Zelda (Zelda Sayre), **I:** 482; **II:** 77, 79, 82–85, 88, 90–91, 93, 95; **Supp. IV Part 1:** 310; **Supp. IX:** 55–73; **Supp. X:** 172. *See also* Sayre, Zelda

"Fitzgerald's Tragic Sense" (Schorer), **Retro. Supp. I:** 115

"Fitzgerald: The Romance of Money" (Cowley), **Supp. II Part 1:** 143

5 Detroits (Levine), **Supp. V:** 178

Five Came Back (West), **IV:** 287

Five Corners (screenplay, Shanley), **Supp. XIV:** 316

"Five-Dollar Bill, The" (D. West as Mary Christopher), **Supp. XVIII:** 282

"Five Dollar Guy, The" (W. C. Williams), **Retro. Supp. I:** 423

Five Easy Pieces (film), **Supp. V:** 26

"Five Elephants" (Dove), **Supp. IV Part 1:** 244–245

"Five Fucks" (Lethem), **Supp. XVIII:** 139

Five Groups of Verse (Reznikoff), **Supp. XIV:** 279, 282

Five Hundred Hats of Bartholomew Cubbins, The (Geisel), **Supp. XVI:** 100

Five Hundred Scorpions (Hearon), **Supp. VIII:** 57, 65, **66**

Five Indiscretions (Ríos), **Supp. IV Part 2:** 545–547

Five Men and Pompey (Benét), **Supp. XI:** 43, 44

Five Plays (Hughes), **Retro. Supp. I:** 197, 209

"Five Poems About Poetry" (Oppen), **Supp. XXVI:** 233

"Five Psalms" (Jarman), **Supp. XVII:** 120

Five Temperaments (Kalstone), **Retro. Supp. II:** 40

5,000 Fingers of Dr. T, The (film), **Supp. XVI:** 103

Five Young American Poets, **I:** 170; **II:** 367

Fixer, The (Malamud), **Supp. I Part 2:** 428, 435, 445, 446–448, 450, 451

"Fixin' Road" (Boulton), **Supp. XXII:** 23

"Fix It (Winter)"(Hadas), **Supp. XXIII:** 115

Fjellestad, Danuta Zadworna, **Supp. XVI:** 150

Flaccus, Kimball, **Retro. Supp. I:** 136

Flacius, Matthias, **IV:** 163

"Flagellant's Song" (X. J. Kennedy), **Supp. XV:** 165

Flag for Sunrise, A (Stone), **Supp. V:** 301–304

Flagg, Fannie, **Supp. XXII:** 213–214

Flag of Childhood, The: Poems from the Middle East (Nye, ed.), **Supp. XIII:** 280

"Flag of Summer" (Swenson), **Supp. IV Part 2:** 645

Flagons and Apples (Jeffers), **Supp. II Part 2:** 413, 414, 417–418

Flags in the Dust (Faulkner), **Retro. Supp. I:** 81, 82, 83, 86, 88

Flamel, Nicolas, **Supp. XII:** 178

Flaming Corsage, The (W. Kennedy), **Supp. VII:** 133, 153–156

Flammarion, Camille, **Supp. I Part 1:** 260

Flanagan, John T., **Supp. I Part 2:** 464, 465, 468

Flanner, Janet, **Supp. XVI:** 195

"Flannery O'Connor: Poet to the Outcast" (Sister Rose Alice), **III:** 348

Flappers and Philosophers (Fitzgerald), **II:** 88; **Retro. Supp. I:** 103; **Supp. IX:** 56

"Flappers Were Her Daughters, The: The Liberated, Literary World of Gertrude Atherton" (Richey), **Supp. XXIV:** 30

Flash and Filigree (Southern), **Supp. XI:** 295, **296–297**

"Flashcards" (Dove), **Supp. IV Part 1:** 250

Flash Fiction: Seventy-two Very Short Stories (J. Thomas, ed.), **Supp. XVI:** 268

"Flash in the Pan" (Shaw), **Supp. XIX:** 245

Flats (Wurlitzer), **Supp. XXVI:** 26

"Flat Sky of Summer"(Balakian), **Supp. XXIII:** 25

Flatt, Lester, **Supp. V:** 335

"Flatted Third, The" (Huddle), **Supp. XXVI:** 153

Flaubert, Gustave, **I:** 66, 123, 130, 272, 312, 314, 315, 477, 504, 506, 513, 514; **II:** 182, 185, 194, 198–199, 205, 209, 230, 289, 311, 316, 319, 325, 337, 392, 401, 577, 594; **III:** 196, 207, 251, 315, 461, 467, 511, 564; **IV:** 4, 29, 31, 37, 40, 134, 285, 428; **Retro.**

Supp. I: 5, 215, 218, 222, 225, 235, 287; **Supp. III Part 2:** 411, 412; **Supp. XI:** 334; **Supp. XIV:** 87, 336; **Supp. XXIII:** 254

"Flavia and Her Artists" (Cather), **Retro. Supp. I:** 5

Flavoring of New England, The (Brooks), **I:** 253, 256

Flavor of Man, The (Toomer), **Supp. III Part 2:** 487

"Flaw, The" (Peacock), **Supp. XIX:** 206

Flaxman, Josiah, **Supp. I Part 2:** 716

"Flea, The" (Donne), **Supp. XVIII:** 307

"Flèche d'Or" (Merrill), **Supp. III Part 1:** 328

Flecker, James Elroy, **Supp. I Part 1:** 257

"Flee on Your Donkey" (Sexton), **Supp. II Part 2:** 683, 685

Fleming, Ian, **Supp. XI:** 307; **Supp. XX:** 195; **Supp. XXVI:** 126

Fleming, Rene, **Supp. XII:** 321

Fleming, Robert E., **Supp. XVII:** 155; **Supp. XXII:** 184

Flesch, Rudolf, **Supp. XVI:** 105, 106

Flesh and Blood (Cunningham), **Supp. XV:** 63–65

Flesh and Blood (play; Cunningham and Gaitens), **Supp. XV:** 65

"Fleshbody" (Ammons), **Supp. VII:** 27

Fletcher, H. D., **II:** 517, 529

Fletcher, John, **Supp. IV Part 2:** 621

Fletcher, John Gould, **I:** 243; **II:** 517, 529; **III:** 458; **Supp. I Part 1:** 263; **Supp. I Part 2:** 422; **Supp. XV:** 298, 302, 306, 307, 308

Fletcher, Phineas, **Supp. I Part 1:** 369

Fletcher, Virginia. *See* Caldwell, Mrs. Erskine (Virginia Fletcher)

Fleurs du mal, Les (Beaudelaire; Millay and Dillon, trans.), **III:** 141–142

"Flight" (Bierds), **Supp. XVII:** 36

"Flight" (Updike), **IV:** 218, 222, 224; **Retro. Supp. I:** 318

Flight (White), **Supp. XVIII:** 127

"Flight, The" (Haines), **Supp. XII:** 204–205

"Flight, The" (Roethke), **III:** 537–538

Flight 115; or, Pas de Fumer sur la Piste (O'Hara and Berkson), **Supp. XXIII:** 217, 218

Flight among the Tombs (Hecht), **Supp. X:** 58, 71–74

"Flight for Freedom" (McCoy), **Supp. XIII:** 170

"Flight from Byzantium" (Brodsky), **Supp. VIII:** 30–31

"Flight of Besey Lane, The" (Jewett), **Retro. Supp. II:** 139

Flight of the Rocket, The (Fitzgerald), **II:** 89

Flights of the Harvest-Mare (Bierds), **Supp. XVII:** 26–27

Flight to Canada (Reed), **Supp. X:** 240, 249–252

Flinn, Mary, **Supp. XVII:** 110

Flint, F. S., **II:** 517; **III:** 459, 464, 465; **Retro. Supp. I:** 127; **Supp. I Part 1:** 261, 262

Flint, Helen, **Supp. XXII:** 278

Flint, R. W., **Supp. XVI:** 47, 49, 57

"Flitting Flies" (X. J. Kennedy), **Supp. XV:** 166, **167**

Flivver King, The (Sinclair), **Supp. V:** 290

Floating House, The (Sanders), **Supp. XVI:** 269

Floating Light Bulb, The (Allen), **Supp. XV:** 2, 3, 13

Floating Opera, The (Barth), **I:** 121, 122–126, 127, 129, 130, 131

"Floating Poem, Unnumbered, The" (Rich), **Supp. I Part 2:** 572–573

"Floating Trees" (Wright), **Supp. XV:** 348

Flood (Matthews), **Supp. IX:** 154, **160–161**

Flood (Warren), **IV:** 252, 256–257

"Flood of Years, The" (Bryant), **Supp. I Part 1:** 159, 170, 171; **Supp. I Part 2:** 416

"Floor and the Ceiling, The" (W. J. Smith), **Supp. XIII:** 345, 346

"Floor Plans" (Komunyakaa), **Supp. XIII:** 114

"Floral Conversation" (Peacock), **Supp. XIX:** 200

"Floral Decorations for Bananas" (Stevens), **IV:** 8

Florida (Acker), **Supp. XII:** 5

"Florida" (Bishop), **Retro. Supp. II:** 43

"Florida Road Workers" (Hughes), **Retro. Supp. I:** 203

"Florida Sunday, A" (Lanier), **Supp. I Part 1:** 364, 366

Florist's Daughter, The (Hampl), **Supp. XXII:** 84, 85, 94, **95–98**

"Flossie Cabanis" (Masters), **Supp. I Part 2:** 461–462

"Flossy Frills Helps Out" (Wells), **Supp. XXVI:** 276

"Flounder" (Trethewey), **Supp. XXI:** 244, 245, 246, 251

Flow Chart (Ashbery), **Supp. VIII:** 275

"Flowchart" (Ashbery), **Supp. III Part 1:** 26

Flower, Dean, **Supp. XXII:** 205, 212

Flower, Fruit, and Thorn Pieces (Richter), **Supp. XVI:** 182

Flower-de-Luce (Longfellow), **II:** 490

Flower Drum Song (Rodgers and Hammerstein), **Supp. XXI:** 148

Flower Drum Song, The (Lee), **Supp. XXI:** 148

Flower Fables (Alcott), **Supp. I Part 1:** 33

"Flower-Fed Buffaloes, The" (Lindsay), **Supp. I Part 2:** 398

"Flower Garden" (Jackson), **Supp. IX:** 119

"Flower-gathering" (Frost), **II:** 153

Flower Herding on Mount Monadnock (Kinnell), **Supp. III Part 1:** 235, 239, 241–244

"Flower Herding on Mount Monadnock" (Kinnell), **Supp. III Part 1:** 242

"Flowering Death" (Ashbery), **Supp. III Part 1:** 22

"Flowering Dream, The" (McCullers), **II:** 591

"Flowering Judas" (Porter), **III:** 434, 435–436, 438, 441, 445, 446, 450–451

Flowering Judas and Other Stories (Porter), **III:** 433, 434

Flowering of New England, The (Brooks), **IV:** 171–172; **Supp. VIII:** 101

Flowering of the Rod (Doolittle), **Supp. I Part 1:** 272

Flowering Peach, The (Odets), **Supp. II Part 2:** 533, 547, 549–550

"Flowering Plum" (Glück), **Supp. V:** 82

Flowers, The (Gilb), **Supp. XXV:** 138

"Flowers for Marjorie" (Welty), **IV:** 262

"Flowers of the Fallow" (Larcom), **Supp. XIII:** 143, 145–146

"Flowers Well if anybody" (Dickinson), **Retro. Supp. I:** 30

"Fluff and Mr. Ripley" (D. West), **Supp. XVIII:** 284

"Fly, The" (Kinnell), **Supp. III Part 1:** 249

"Fly, The" (Shapiro), **Supp. II Part 2:** 705

"Fly, The" (Simic), **Supp. VIII:** 278

Flye, Father James Harold, **I:** 25, 26, 35–36, 37, 42, 46; **IV:** 215

"Fly in Buttermilk, A" (Baldwin), **Retro. Supp. II:** 8

Flying at Night: Poems 1965–1985 (Kooser), **Supp. XIX:** 128

"Flying High" (Levertov), **Supp. III Part 1:** 284

"Flying Home" (Ellison), **Retro. Supp. II:** 117, **125–126;** **Supp. II Part 1:** 235, 238–239

"Flying Home" (Kinnell), **Supp. III Part 1:** 250

"Flying Home" and Other Stories (Ellison), **Retro. Supp. II:** 119, 124

"Flying Home from Utah" (Swenson), **Supp. IV Part 2:** 645

"Flying over Clouds" (Gioia), **Supp. XV:** 118

Flying Solo (Kriegel), **Supp. XXIV: 219–221**

"Flying to Hanoi" (Rukeyser), **Supp. VI:** 279

Flynn, Elizabeth Gurley, **Supp. XVIII:** 225

Flynn, Richard, **Supp. XVII:** 115; **Supp. XVIII:** 183

Fly-Truffler, The (Sobin), **Supp. XVI: 294–295,** 296

Foata, Anne, **Supp. XI:** 104

FOB (Hwang), **Supp. XXI:** 143, 144, 145, 146, **148–150**

Focillon, Henri, **IV:** 90

Focus (A. Miller), **III:** 150–151, 156

Foer, Jonathan Safran, **Supp. XII:** 169; **Supp. XX: 177; Supp. XXIV:** 131; **Supp. XXV:** 268

Foerster, Norman, **I:** 222; **Supp. I Part 2:** 423, 424; **Supp. IV Part 2:** 598

"Fog" (Sandburg), **III:** 586

"Fog Galleon" (Komunyakaa), **Supp. XIII:** 127

"Foggy and dripping" (Kooser), **Supp. XIX:** 125

"Foggy Lane, The" (Simpson), **Supp. IX:** 274

"Fog Man, The" (Boyle), **Supp. XX: 20**
Folded Leaf, The (Maxwell), **Supp. III Part 1:** 62; **Supp. VIII: 159–162**
Folding Star, The (Hollinghurst), **Supp. XIII:** 52
Foley, Barbara, **Supp. XXVI:** 28
Foley, Jack, **Supp. X:** 125; **Supp. XV:** 112, 116; **Supp. XVII:** 77
Foley, Martha, **II:** 587; **Supp. XVI:** 225
Folk-Lore in the Old Testament (Frazer), **Supp. XX: 116–117**
Folks, Jeffrey, **Supp. XXVI:** 15
Folks from Dixie (Dunbar), **Supp. II Part 1:** 211–212
Folkways (Sumner), **III:** 102
Follain, Jean, **Supp. IX:** 152, 154
Follett, Wilson, **I:** 405; **Supp. XIII:** 173
Follower of Dusk (Salinas), **Supp. XIII:** 326
"Following the Bones" (W. V. Davis), **Supp. XXI:** 96
Following the Equator (Twain), **II:** 434; **IV:** 208
Follow Me Home (Hoffman), **Supp. XVIII:** 86
Folly (Minot), **Supp. VI:** 205, 208, **210–213**
Folly in the Forest (Wells), **Supp. XXVI:** 276
Folly of Others, The (Boyce), **Supp. XVII:** 100; **Supp. XXI:** 10
Folsom, Charles, **Supp. I Part 1:** 156
Folsom, Ed, **Retro. Supp. I:** 392
Folson, Marcia McClintock, **Retro. Supp. II:** 139
Fonda, Henry, **Supp. I Part 1:** 67; **Supp. IV Part 1:** 236
Fonda, Jane, **III:** 284; **Supp. XI:** 307
Fonda, Peter, **Supp. VIII:** 42; **Supp. XI:** 293, 308
"Fondled Memories" (Molesworth), **Supp. XIX:** 121–122
"Fond Memories of a Black Childhood" (D. West), **Supp. XVIII:** 289
Foner, Eric, **Supp. I Part 2:** 523
Fong and the Indians (Theroux), **Supp. VIII:** 314, 315, **316–317**
Fontanne, Lynn, **III:** 397
Food and Drink (Untermeyer), **Supp. XV:** 310
Food Chain, The (Silver), **Supp. XXIV:** 265, **270–271**, 274
Fool for Love (Shepard), **Supp. III Part 2:** 433, 447, 448
Fooling with Words (PBS special, Moyers), **Supp. XXIII:** 139
"Foolishness" (Pickering), **Supp. XXI:** 197
Fools (Simon), **Supp. IV Part 2:** 584–585
Fools Crow (Welch), **Supp. XXIV:** 257
Fool's Progress, The: An Honest Novel (Abbey), **Supp. XIII:** 52
"Football Rebellion in Backwoods Georgia, A" (Andrews), **Supp. XXVI:** 3, 4
Foot Book, The (Geisel), **Supp. XVI:** 108
Foote, Bud, **Supp. XXVI:** 5
Foote, Horton, **Supp. I Part 1:** 281; **Supp. VIII:** 128, 129

Foote, Mary Hallock, **Retro. Supp. II:** 72; **Supp. IV Part 2:** 611
Foote, Roxanna. *See* Beecher, Mrs. Lyman (Roxanna Foote)
Foote, Samuel, **Supp. I Part 2:** 584
Foote, Stephanie, **Retro. Supp. II:** 139
"Foot Fault" (pseudonym). *See* Thurber, James
Footing on This Earth, A (Hay), **Supp. XIV:** 125, 126, 130
"Footing up a Total" (Lowell), **II:** 528
"Footnote to Howl" (Ginsberg), **Supp. II Part 1:** 316–317
"Footnote to Weather Forecasts, A" (Brodsky), **Supp. VIII:** 32
Footprints (Hearon), **Supp. VIII: 69–70**
Footprints (Levertov), **Supp. III Part 1:** 272, 281
"Footsteps of Angels" (Longfellow), **II:** 496
"For A, at Fourteen" (Weigl), **Supp. XIX:** 287
For a Bitter Season: New and Selected Poems (Garrett), **Supp. VII:** 99–100
"For a Dead Kitten" (Hay), **Supp. XIV:** 119–120
"For a Dead Lady" (Robinson), **III:** 508, 513, 517
"For a Ghost Who Once Placed Bets in the Park" (Levis), **Supp. XI:** 265
"Foraging" (H. Johnson), **Supp. XXVI:** 172
"For a Lamb" (Eberhart), **I:** 523, 530, 531
"For All" (Snyder), **Supp. VIII:** 304
"For All Tuesday Travelers" (Cisneros), **Supp. VII:** 67–68
"For a Lost Child" (Stafford), **Supp. XI:** 329
"For a Marriage" (Bogan), **Supp. III Part 1:** 52
"For an Emigrant" (Jarrell), **II:** 371
"For Anna Akmatova" (Lowell), **II:** 544
"For Anna Mae Pictou Aquash, Whose Spirit Is Present Here and in the Dappled Stars" (Harjo), **Supp. XII:** 225
"For Anne, at a Little Distance" (Haines), **Supp. XII:** 207
"For Annie" (Poe), **III:** 427; **Retro. Supp. II:** 263
"For an Old Friend Encountered Unexpectedly" (Espaillat), **Supp. XXI:** 111–112
"For a Southern Man" (Cisneros), **Supp. VII:** 67
"For Bailey" (Angelou), **Supp. IV Part 1:** 15
Forbes, Genevieve, **Supp. XXV:** 196
Forbes, Malcolm, **Supp. IV Part 1:** 94
"Forbidden, The" (Glück), **Supp. XIV:** 269
"For Bill Nestrick (1940–96)" (Bidart), **Supp. XV:** 35
For Bread Alone (Choukri), **Supp. IV Part 1:** 92
"Force" (Di Piero), **Supp. XIX:** 35–36, 42, 44
Force of Desire, The (Bronk), **Supp. XXI:** 31, 32

Force of Evil (film, Polonsky), **Supp. XXI:** 261, 272, 275
Force of Spirit, The (Sanders), **Supp. XVI:** 277–278
Forché, Carolyn, **Supp. IV Part 1:** 208; **Supp. XIX:** 193
Ford, Arthur, **Supp. IV Part 1:** 140
Ford, Ford Madox, **I:** 288, 405, 409, 417, 421, 423; **II:** 58, 144, 198, 257, 263, 265, 517, 536; **III:** 458, 464–465, 470–471, 472, 476; **IV:** 27, 126, 261; **Retro. Supp. I:** 127, 177, 178, 186, 231, 286–287, 418; **Supp. II Part 1:** 107; **Supp. III Part 2:** 617; **Supp. VIII:** 107; **Supp. XIV:** 3
Ford, Harrison, **Supp. VIII:** 323
Ford, Harry, **Supp. V:** 179; **Supp. XIII:** 76
Ford, Henry, **I:** 295, 480–481; **III:** 292, 293; **Supp. I Part 1:** 21; **Supp. I Part 2:** 644; **Supp. III Part 2:** 612, 613; **Supp. IV Part 1:** 223; **Supp. V:** 290
Ford, John, **Supp. I Part 2:** 422; **Supp. III Part 2:** 619; **Supp. XVIII:** 247
Ford, Mark, **Supp. XXIII:** 220
Ford, Mary K., **Supp. XX: 239**
Ford, Richard, **Supp. IV Part 1:** 342; **Supp. V:** 22, **57–75; Supp. XXIV:** 97
Ford, Webster (pseudonym). *See* Masters, Edgar Lee
"Fording and Dread" (Harrison), **Supp. VIII:** 41
"Ford Madox Ford" (Lowell), **II:** 547; **Retro. Supp. II:** 188
"For Dudley" (Wilbur), **Supp. III Part 2:** 558
Fordyce, David, **II:** 113
For Eager Lovers (Taggard), **Supp. XXII: 274–275**
Foregone Conclusion, A (Howells), **II:** 278–279, 282
"Foreign Affairs" (Kunitz), **Supp. III Part 1:** 265
"Foreigner, A" (Bynner), **Supp. XV:** 46
"Foreigner, The" (Jewett), **II:** 409–410; **Retro. Supp. II:** 133, 142
"Foreigners" (Jarman), **Supp. XVII:** 113
"Foreign Language, The" (Franzen), **Supp. XX: 84**
"Foreign Shores" (Salter), **Supp. IX:** 260
Forensic and the Navigators (Shepard), **Supp. III Part 2:** 439
Forerunner, The (Boyce), **Supp. XXI:** 2, 4, **10–11**
Forerunner, The: His Parables and Poems (Gibran), **Supp. XX: 115, 118–119, 119**
Foreseeable Future, The (Price), **Supp. VI:** 265
Foreseeable Futures (Matthews), **Supp. IX:** 155, **163**, 169
Foresman, Rebecca, **Supp. XXIV:** 171
"For Esmé with Love and Squalor" (Salinger), **III:** 560
"Forest" (Simic), **Supp. VIII:** 273
Forest, Jean-Claude, **Supp. XI:** 307
Forester's Letters (Paine), **Supp. I Part 2:** 508
"Forest Hymn, A" (Bryant), **Supp. I Part 1:** 156, 162, 163, 164, 165, 170

"Forest in the Seeds, The" (Kingsolver), **Supp. VII:** 203

Forest of the South, The (Gordon), **II:** 197

"Forest of the South, The" (Gordon), **II:** 199, 201

Forest without Leaves (Adams and Haines), **Supp. XII:** 209

"Forever, Said the Duck" (Lethem), **Supp. XVIII:** 139

"Forever and the Earth" (Bradbury), **Supp. IV Part 1:** 102

"Forever in That Year" (Carruth), **Supp. XVI:** 51

"Forever"(Thompson), **Supp. XXIII:** 296

"Forever Young" (Jarman and R. McDowell), **Supp. XVII:** 111

"For Fathers of Girls" (Dunn), **Supp. XI:** 146

For Frank O'Hara's Birthday (Notley), **Supp. XXII:** 224, 227

"For/From Lew" (Snyder), **Supp. VIII:** 303

"For Garrison Keillor, Fantasy Is a Lot More Fun then Reality" (Letofsky), **Supp. XVI:** 167

"For George Santayana" (Lowell), **II:** 547

"Forgetfulness" (Collins), **Supp. XXI:** 58

"Forgiveness" (Peacock), **Supp. XIX:** 200

Forgotten Helper, The: A Story for Children (Moore), **Supp. X:** 175

"Forgotten in an Old Notebook" (F. Wright), **Supp. XVII:** 244

Forgotten Village, The (Steinbeck), **IV:** 51

"For Grace, After a party"(O'Hara), **Supp. XXIII:** 214

"For Grizzel McNaught (1709–1792)" (A. Finch), **Supp. XVII:** 72

Forgue, Guy J., **III:** 118, 119

For Her Dark Skin (Everett), **Supp. XVIII:** 56, 60

"FOR HETTIE" (Baraka), **Supp. II Part 1:** 32

"FOR HETTIE IN HER FIFTH MONTH" (Baraka), **Supp. II Part 1:** 32, 38

"For Homer" (Corso), **Supp. XII:** 135

"For I'm the Boy" (Barthelme), **Supp. IV Part 1:** 47

"For James Dean"(O'Hara), **Supp. XXIII:** 214

"For Janice and Kenneth to Voyage"(O'Hara), **Supp. XXIII:** 214

"For Jeff" (Kooser), **Supp. XIX:** 125

"For Jessica, My Daughter" (Strand), **Supp. IV Part 2:** 629

"For John, Who Begs Me not to Enquire Further" (Sexton), **Supp. II Part 2:** 676

"For Johnny Pole on the Forgotten Beach" (Sexton), **Supp. II Part 2:** 675

"For Joy to Leave Upon" (Ortiz), **Supp. IV Part 2:** 508

"For Judy, Whose Husband Is Undergoing Surgery"(Crooker), **Supp. XXIII:** 61

"Fork" (Simic), **Supp. VIII:** 275

"For Karl Shapiro, Having Gone Back to the Sonnet" (Kooser), **Supp. XIX:** 118

"Forked Tongue" (Davison), **Supp. XXVI:** 71

"Forky" (Dubus III), **Supp. XXIV:** 99, 101

"For Lack of a Treaty" (Davison), **Supp. XXVI:** 79

For Lancelot Andrewes (Eliot), **Retro. Supp. I:** 64

For Lizzie and Harriet (Lowell), **Retro. Supp. II:** 183, 186, 190

"Forlorn Hope of Sidney Lanier, The" (Leary), **Supp. I Part 1:** 373

For Love (Creeley), **Supp. IV Part 1:** 139, 140, 142–145, 147–149, 150, 154

"For Love" (Creeley), **Supp. IV Part 1:** 145

For Love (Miller), **Supp. XII: 297–299,** 299

For Love of Imabelle (C. Himes), **Supp. XVI:** 135, 143, 144

Form, Cycle, Infinity: Landscape Imagery in the Poetry of Robert Frost and George Seferis (Hadas), **Supp. XXIII: 121–122**

"Formal Elegy" (Berryman), **I:** 170

Formal Feeling Comes, A (A. Finch, ed.), **Supp. XVII: 71–72**

"Formalist Criticism: Its Principles and Limits" (Burke), **I:** 282

Forman, Henry James, **Supp. XXIV:** 29, 30

Forman, Milos, **Supp. IV Part 1:** 236

"Form and Function of the Novel, The" (Goldbarth), **Supp. XII:** 183

"For Marse Chouchoute" (Chopin), **Retro. Supp. II:** 60

"For Mary Ann Youngren" (Bidart), **Supp. XV:** 29

"Format and Form" (A. Rich), **Supp. XVII:** 74

"Formation of a Separatist, I" (Howe), **Supp. IV Part 2:** 427

"Form Is Emptiness" (Baraka), **Supp. II Part 1:** 51

"For Mr. Death Who Stands with His Door Open" (Sexton), **Supp. II Part 2:** 695

Forms of Discovery (Winters), **Supp. II Part 2:** 812, 813

Forms of Fiction, The (Gardner and Dunlap), **Supp. VI:** 64

"Forms of Love, The" (Oppen), **Supp. XXVI:** 225

"For My Children" (Karr), **Supp. XI:** 254

"For My Daughter" (Kees), **Supp. XV:** 141, 147

"For My Daughter" (Olds), **Supp. X:** 206

"For My Former Wife, Watching TV, in the Past" (Kooser), **Supp. XIX:** 120

"For My Lover, Returning to His Wife" (Sexton), **Supp. II Part 2:** 688

Fornés, Maria Irene, **Supp. XXI:** 144; **Supp. XXIII:** 194, 200

"For Night to Come" (Stern), **Supp. IX:** 292

"For Once, Then, Something" (Frost), **II:** 156–157; **Retro. Supp. I:** 126, 133, 134

"For Peg: A Remnant of Song Still Distantly Sounding" (Carruth), **Supp. XVI:** 54

"For Pot-Boiling" (Hay), **Supp. XIV:** 128

"For Radicals" (Bourne), **I:** 221

"For Rainer Gerhardt" (Creeley), **Supp. IV Part 1:** 142–143, 147

Forrestal, James, **I:** 491; **Supp. I Part 2:** 489

Forrester, Fanny, **Supp. XVIII:** 13

Forrey, Carolyn, **Supp. XXIV:** 30

"For Richard After All" (Kingsolver), **Supp. VII:** 208

"For Sacco and Vanzetti" (Kingsolver), **Supp. VII:** 208

"Forsaken Brother, The"(J. Schoolcraft), **Supp. XXIII:** 235

"Forsaken Merman" (Arnold), **Supp. I Part 2:** 529

"Forsaking the Promised Land" (diss. Collins), **Supp. XXVI:** 12

"For S.F.S. 1875–1962" (J. W. Miller), **Supp. XX: 166**

For Spacious Skies (Buck), **Supp. II Part 1:** 131

Forster, E. M., **I:** 292; **IV:** 201; **Retro. Supp. I:** 59, 232; **Supp. III Part 2:** 503; **Supp. IX:** 128; **Supp. V:** 258; **Supp. VIII:** 155, 171; **Supp. XII:** 79, 81; **Supp. XIV:** 159, 160, 163; **Supp. XV:** 62; **Supp. XVI:** 236; **Supp. XVIII:** 143; **Supp. XX: 229, 235, 239, 240; Supp. XXI:** 233

Forster, John, **II:** 315

Fort, Paul, **II:** 518, 528, 529; **Retro. Supp. I:** 55

"For the Ahkoond" (Bierce), **I:** 209

For the Body (Nelson), **Supp. XVIII:** 173

For the Century's End: Poems 1990–1999 (Haines), **Supp. XII: 211–213**

"For the Chinese New Year and Bill Berkson"(O'Hara), **Supp. XXIII:** 218

"For the Dedication of the New City Library, Boston" (Holmes), **Supp. I Part 1:** 308

"For the Fallen" (Levine), **Supp. V:** 188

For the Health of the Land: Previously Unpublished Essays and Other Writings (Leopold), **Supp. XIV:** 183

"For the Lady in the Black Raincoat Who Slept Through an Entire Poetry Reading" (Espaillat), **Supp. XXI:** 108

"For the Last Wolverine" (Dickey), **Supp. IV Part 1:** 182

"For the Losers of Things" (Stallings), **Supp. XXV:** 222

"For the Lovers of the Absolute" (Simic), **Supp. VIII:** 278–279

"For the Man Cutting the Grass" (Oliver), **Supp. VII:** 235

"For the Marriage of Faustus and Helen" (H. Crane), **I:** 395–396, 399, 402; **Retro. Supp. II:** 78–79, 82

"For the Meeting of the National Sanitary Association, 1860" (Holmes), **Supp. I Part 1:** 307

For the New Intellectual (Rand), **Supp. IV Part 2:** 521, 526–527, 527, 532

"For the New Railway Station in Rome" (Wilbur), **Supp. III Part 2:** 554

"For the Night" (Kenyon), **Supp. VII:** 163

"For Theodore Roethke: 1908–1963" (Lowell), **II:** 554

"For the Poem *Patterson*" (W. C. Williams), **Retro. Supp. I:** 424

"For the Poets of Chile" (Levine), **Supp. V:** 188

"FOR THE REVOLUTIONARY OUTBURST BY BLACK PEOPLE" (Baraka), **Supp. II Part 1:** 55

"For the Sleepless" (Dunn), **Supp. XI:** 145

For the Time Being (Auden), **Supp. II Part 1:** 2, 17, 18

For the Time Being (Dillard), **Supp. VI:** 23, 27, 29, 32, **34–35**

"For the Twentieth Century" (Bidart), **Supp. XV:** 35

For the Union Dead (Lowell), **II:** 543, 550–551, 554, 555; **Retro. Supp. II:** 181, 182, 186, 189; **Supp. X:** 53

"For the Union Dead" (Lowell), **II:** 551; **Retro. Supp. II:** 189

"For the Walking Dead" (Komunyakaa), **Supp. XIII:** 121

"For the West" (Snyder), **Supp. VIII:** 299

"For the Word Is Flesh" (Kunitz), **Supp. III Part 1:** 262–264

"Fortress, The" (Glück), **Supp. V:** 82

"Fortress, The" (Sexton), **Supp. II Part 2:** 682

Fortress of Solitude, The (Lethem), **Supp. XVIII:** 135, 136, **145–148,** 150

"Fort Robinson" (Kooser), **Supp. XIX:** 120

"Fortunate Traveler" (Hull), **Supp. XXI:** 140

Fortune, T. Thomas, **Supp. II Part 1:** 159

Fortune's Bones: The Manumission Requiem (Nelson), **Supp. XVIII:** 171, 172–173, 182–183

Fortune's Daughter (Hoffman), **Supp. X:** 77, 85

"Fortune Spill, The" (Nelson), **Supp. XVIII:** 175

45 Mercy Street (Sexton), **Supp. II Part 2:** 694, 695, 697

Forty Poems Touching on Recent American History (Bly, ed.), **Supp. IV Part 1:** 61

42nd Parallel, The (Dos Passos), **I:** 482, 484–485

Forty Stories (Barthelme), **Supp. IV Part 1:** 47, 49, 53, 54

For Whom the Bell Tolls (Hemingway), **II:** 249, 254–255, 261; **III:** 18, 363; **Retro. Supp. I:** 115, 176–177, 178, **184,** 187; **Supp. XVII:** 229; **Supp. XXV:** 146

For Whom the Southern Belle Tolls (Durang), **Supp. XXIV:** 113, 118, 125

Foscolo, Ugo, **II:** 543

Foss, Sam Walter, **Supp. II Part 1:** 197

"Fossils, The" (Kinnell), **Supp. III Part 1:** 244

Foster, Edward, **Supp. IV Part 2:** 431, 434; **Supp. XVI:** 281, 293; **Supp. XXI:** 33

Foster, Edward Halsey, **Supp. XII:** 120, 129, 130, 135; **Supp. XVIII:** 265, 268

Foster, Emily, **II:** 309

Foster, Frances Smith, **Supp. XX: 287**

Foster, Hannah Webster, **Supp. XV:** 234; **Supp. XXV: 35–48**

Foster, John Wilson, **Supp. XIII:** 32–33

Foster, Michael K., **Supp. XXVI:** 83

Foster, Phil, **Supp. IV Part 2:** 574

Foster, Richard, **Supp. XV:** 269

Foster, Stephen, **Supp. I Part 1:** 100–101; **Supp. I Part 2:** 699

Foucault, Michel, **Supp. VIII:** 5; **Supp. XII:** 98; **Supp. XV:** 344; **Supp. XVI:** 285

Foulke, Robert, **Supp. XXV:** 217

"Founder, The" (Stern), **Supp. IX:** 297

Founding of Harvard College, The (Morison), **Supp. I Part 2:** 485

"Foundry Workers" (Bodenheim), **Supp. XXV:** 22

"Fountain, The" (Bryant), **Supp. I Part 1:** 157, 165, 166, 168

Fountain, The (O'Neill), **III:** 391

Fountain and Other Poems, The (Bryant), **Supp. I Part 1:** 157

Fountainhead, The (film), **Supp. IV Part 2:** 524

Fountainhead, The (Rand), **Supp. IV Part 2:** 517, 521–523, 525, 531; **Supp. XXIV:** 281

Fountainhead, The: A Fiftieth Anniversary Celebration (Cox), **Supp. IV Part 2:** 523

"Fountain Piece" (Swenson), **Supp. IV Part 2:** 641

4-H Club (Shepard), **Supp. III Part 2:** 439

"Four Ages of Man, The" (Bradstreet), **Supp. I Part 1:** 111, 115

Four American Indian Literary Masters (Velie), **Supp. IV Part 2:** 486

"Four Angers"(Hadas), **Supp. XXIII:** 115

"Four Beasts in One; the Homo Cameleopard" (Poe), **III:** 425

Four Black Revolutionary Plays (Baraka), **Supp. II Part 1:** 45; **Supp. VIII:** 330

"Four Brothers" (Di Piero), **Supp. XIX:** 37

"Four Brothers, The" (Sandburg), **III:** 585

"Four Dancers at an Irish Wedding" (Gallagher), **Supp. XXIV:** 168, 170

Four Days (screenplay, P. Benedict), **Supp. XXIII:** 35

Four Dogs and a Bone and the Wild Goose (Shanley), **Supp. XIV:** 316, **328–329**

"Four Evangelists, The" (Komunyakaa), **Supp. XIII:** 131

"Four for Sir John Davies" (Roethke), **III:** 540, 541

"Four Girls, The" (Alvarez), **Supp. VII:** 7

"Four Horse Songs" (Harjo), **Supp. XII:** 220

"400-Meter Free Style" (Kumin), **Supp. IV Part 2:** 442

"400-Pound CEO, The" (Saunders), **Supp. XIX:** 225

Fourier, Charles, **II:** 342

"Four in a Family" (Rukeyser), **Supp. VI:** 272

Four in Hand: A Quartet of Novels (Warner), **Supp. VIII:** 164

"Four Lakes' Days" (Eberhart), **I:** 525

"Four Mad Studies" (Di Piero), **Supp. XIX:** 37

"Four Meetings" (James), **II:** 327

Four Million, The (O. Henry), **Supp. II Part 1:** 394, 408

"Four Monarchyes" (Bradstreet), **Supp. I Part 1:** 105, 106, 116

"Four Mountain Wolves" (Silko), **Supp. IV Part 2:** 561

Four of a Kind (Marquand), **III:** 54, 55

"Four of the Horsemen (Hypertense and Stroke, Coronary Occlusion and Cerebral Insult)" (Karr), **Supp. XI:** 250

"Four Poems" (Bishop), **Supp. I Part 1:** 92

"Four Poems at the End of Summer"(Hadas), **Supp. XXIII:** 117

"Four Preludes on Playthings of the Wind" (Sandburg), **III:** 586

Four Quartets (T. S. Eliot), **I:** 570, 576, 580–582, 585, 587; **II:** 537; **III:** 539; **Retro. Supp. I:** 66, 67; **Supp. II Part 1:** 1; **Supp. IV Part 1:** 284; **Supp. V:** 343, 344; **Supp. VIII:** 182, 195; **Supp. XIII:** 344; **Supp. XIV:** 167; **Supp. XV:** 216, 260, 266

Four Saints in Three Acts (Stein), **IV:** 30, 31, 33, 43, 44–45

"Four Seasons" (Bradstreet), **Supp. I Part 1:** 112–113

Four Seasons of Success, The (Schulberg), **Supp. XVIII:** 254

"Four Sides of One Story" (Updike), **Retro. Supp. I:** 328

"Four Skinny Trees" (Cisneros), **Supp. VII:** 64

"14: In A Dark Wood: Wood Thrushes" (Oliver), **Supp. VII:** 244

"14 Men Stage Head Winter 1624/ 25" (Olson), **Supp. II Part 2:** 574

14 Stories (Dixon), **Supp. XII:** 141, **145–147**

Fourteen Hundred Thousand (Shepard), **Supp. III Part 2:** 439

Fourteen Sisters of Emilio Montez O'Brien, The (Hijuelos), **Supp. VIII: 82–85**

Fourteen Stories (Buck), **Supp. II Part 1:** 126

"Fourteenth Ward, The" (H. Miller), **III:** 175

Fourth Book of Peace, The (Kingston), **Supp. V:** 173

"Fourth Down" (Marquand), **III:** 56

Fourth Group of Verse, A (Reznikoff), **Supp. XIV:** 282, 284

"Fourth of July in Maine" (Lowell), **II:** 535, 552–553

Fourth Wall, The (Gurney), **Supp. V:** 109–110

Fowler, Douglas, **Supp. IV Part 1:** 226, 227

Fowler, Gene, **Supp. VIII:** 290

Fowler, Henry Watson, **Supp. I Part 2:** 660

Fowler, Karen Joy, **Supp. XXII:** 49

Fowler, Singrid, **Supp. VIII:** 249, 258

Fowler, Virginia C., **Supp. VIII:** 224

Fox, Alan, **Supp. XIII:** 120

Fox, Dixon Ryan, **I:** 337

Fox, Joe, **Supp. IX:** 259, 261

Fox, John, **Supp. XIII:** 166; **Supp. XXII:** 36

Fox, Linda C., **Supp. XIII:** 217–218

Fox, Paula, **Supp. XX:** 91

Fox, Ruth, **Supp. I Part 2:** 619

"Fox, The" (Levine), **Supp. V:** 181, 189

Fox-Genovese, Elizabeth, **Supp. IV Part 1:** 286; **Supp. XXII:** 190, 192, 200

Fox in Socks (Geisel), **Supp. XVI:** 108, 112

"Fox Night" (Jarman), **Supp. XVII:** 120

Fox of Peapack, The (White), **Supp. I Part 2:** 676, 677–678

"Fox of Peapack, The" (White), **Supp. I Part 2:** 677

"Fox Point Health Clinic, 1974" (Halliday), **Supp. XIX:** 89, 93

Fox's Earth (Siddons), **Supp. XXII:** 239

Foye, Raymond, **Supp. XIV:** 150

Fradkin, Lori, **Supp. XIX:** 52

Fraenkel, Michael, **III:** 178, 183

"Fragging" (Komunyakaa), **Supp. XIII:** 123

Fragile Beauty, A: John Nichols' Milagro Country: Text and Photographs from His Life and Work (Nichols), **Supp. XIII:** 268

"Fragility" (Shields), **Supp. VII:** 318

"Fragment" (Ashbery), **Supp. III Part 1:** 11, 13, 14, 19, 20

"Fragment" (Lowell), **II:** 516

"Fragment" (Ortiz), **Supp. IV Part 2:** 507

"Fragment of a Meditation" (Tate), **IV:** 129

"Fragment of an Agon" (Eliot), **I:** 579–580

"Fragment of a Prologue" (Eliot), **I:** 579–580

"Fragment of New York, 1929" (Eberhart), **I:** 536–537

"Fragments" (Emerson), **II:** 19

"Fragments for Fall" (Salinas), **Supp. XIII:** 320–321

"Fragments of a Hologram Rose" (W. Gibson), **Supp. XVI:** 122, 123, 128

"Fragments of a Liquidation" (Howe), **Supp. IV Part 2:** 426

"Fragments: On Dentistry" (Monson), **Supp. XXIV:** 236

Fragonard, Jean Honoré, **III:** 275; **IV:** 79

Fraiman, Susan, **Supp. IV Part 1:** 324

"Frame for Poetry, A" (W. J. Smith), **Supp. XIII:** 333

France, Anatole, **IV:** 444; **Supp. I Part 2:** 631; **Supp. XIV:** 79

France and England in North America (Parkman), **Supp. II Part 2:** 596, 600–605, 607, 613–614

Franchere, Hoyt C., **II:** 131

Franchiser, The (Elkin), **Supp. VI:** 51–52, 58

Francini, Antonella, **Supp. XXVI:** 169

Franciosi, Robert, **Supp. XIV:** 283

Francis, Lee, **Supp. IV Part 2:** 499

Francis, Richard, **Supp. XV:** 121

Francis, Robert, **Supp. IX:** 75–92

Francis of Assisi, Saint, **III:** 543; **IV:** 69, 375, 410; **Supp. I Part 2:** 394, 397, 441, 442, 443

Franco, Francisco, **II:** 261

Franco, Harry (pseudonym). *See* Briggs, Charles Frederick

Franconia (Fraser), **Retro. Supp. I:** 136

"Franconia" tales (Abbott), **Supp. I Part 1:** 38

Frank, Anne, **Supp. X:** 149; **Supp. XVII:** 39

Frank, Frederick S., **Retro. Supp. II:** 273

Frank, Harriet, Jr., **Supp. XXV:** 102

Frank, James M., **Supp. XIV:** 1

Frank, Jerome, **Supp. I Part 2:** 645

Frank, Joseph, **II:** 587

Frank, Mary, **Supp. X:** 213

Frank, Robert, **Supp. XI:** 295; **Supp. XII:** 127; **Supp. XIV:** 150

Frank, Sheldon, **Supp. XXII:** 210

Frank, Waldo, **I:** 106, 109, 117, 229, 236, 245, 259, 400; **Retro. Supp. II:** 77, 79, 83; **Supp. IX:** 308, 309, 311, 320; **Supp. XV:** 298; **Supp. XX:** 67–82

Frank, W. L., Jr., **Supp. XVIII:** 77

Frankel, Charles, **III:** 291

Frankel, Haskel, **Supp. I Part 2:** 448

Frankenberg, Lloyd, **I:** 436, 437, 445, 446; **III:** 194

Frankenheimer, John, **Supp. XI:** 343

Frankenstein (film), **Supp. IV Part 1:** 104; **Supp. XVII:** 57

Frankenstein (Gardner), **Supp. VI:** 72

Frankenstein (Shelley), **Supp. XII:** 79

Frankfurter, Felix, **I:** 489

"Frankie" (Keillor), **Supp. XVI:** 167

Frankie and Johnny (film), **Supp. XIII:** 206

Frankie and Johnny in the Clair de Lune (McNally), **Supp. XIII:** 200, 201

Franklin, Benjamin, **II:** 6, 8, 92, 101–125, 127, 295, 296, 302, 306; **III:** 74, 90; **IV:** 73, 193; **Supp. I Part 1:** 306; **Supp. I Part 2:** 411, 503, 504, 506, 507, 510, 516, 518, 522, 524, 579, 639; **Supp. VIII:** 202, 205; **Supp. XIII:** 150; **Supp. XIV:** 306; **Supp. XVIII:** 12; **Supp. XX:** 284; **Supp. XXIV:** 224; **Supp. XXVI:** 83, 84

Franklin, Cynthia, **Supp. IV Part 1:** 332

Franklin, Ruth, **Supp. XVI:** 160

Franklin, R. W., **Retro. Supp. I:** 29, 41, 43, 47

Franklin, Sarah, **II:** 122

Franklin, Temple, **II:** 122

Franklin, Walt, **Supp. XXIII:** 54

Franklin, Wayne, **Supp. XXII:** 205

Franklin, William, **II:** 122; **Supp. I Part 2:** 504

Franklin Evans (Whitman), **Retro. Supp. I:** 393

"Frank O'Connor and *The New Yorker*" (Maxwell), **Supp. VIII:** 172

Frank O'Hara: Poet Among Painters (Perloff), **Supp. XXIII:** 210

Franks, Lucinda, **Supp. XIII:** 12

"Frank Sinatra Has a Cold" (Talese), **Supp. XVII:** 203

"Frank Stanford of the Mulberry Family: An Arkansas Epilogue" (Wright), **Supp. XV:** 339–340

"Franny" (Salinger), **III:** 564, 565–566

Franny and Zooey (Salinger), **III:** 552, 564–567; **IV:** 216; **Supp. XIII:** 263

Franscell, Ron, **Supp. XXII:** 206, 216

Franzen, Jonathan, **Retro. Supp. II:** 279; **Supp. XIX:** 54; **Supp. XX:** 83–97; **Supp. XXII:** 255; **Supp. XXIV:** 131

Fraser, G. S., **Supp. XII:** 128; **Supp. XIV:** 162

Fraser, Joe, **III:** 46

Fraser, Marjorie Frost, **Retro. Supp. I:** 136

Frayn, Michael, **Supp. IV Part 2:** 582

Frazee, E. S., **Supp. I Part 2:** 381

Frazee, Esther Catherine. *See* Lindsay, Mrs. Vachel Thomas (Esther Catherine Frazee)

Frazer, Sir James G., **I:** 135; **II:** 204; **III:** 6–7; **IV:** 70; **Retro. Supp. I:** 80; **Supp. I Part 1:** 18; **Supp. I Part 2:** 541; **Supp. XX:** 117

Frazier, Ian, **Supp. VIII:** 272

Frazier, Kathleen, **Supp. XXI:** 22

"Freak Power in the Rockies" (Thompson), **Supp. XXIV:** 286–287, 292, 293

"Freak Show, The" (Sexton), **Supp. II Part 2:** 695

Freaks: Myths and Images of the Secret Self (Fiedler), **Supp. XIII:** 106, 107

Freckles (film), **Supp. XX:** 223

Freckles (Stratton-Porter), **Supp. XX:** 211, 218, 218–219, 222

Fred Allen Show, **Supp. XXV:** 254

Freddy and Fredericka (Helprin), **Supp. XXV:** 81, 84, 87–88

Freddy's Book (Gardner), **Supp. VI:** 72

Frederic, Harold, **I:** 409; **II:** 126–149, 175, 276, 289; **Retro. Supp. I:** 325; **Supp. XXIV:** 30

"Frederick Douglass" (Dunbar), **Supp. II Part 1:** 197, 199

"Frederick Douglass" (Hayden), **Supp. II Part 1:** 363

Frederick Douglass: Slave, Fighter, Freeman (Bontemps), **Supp. XXII:** 13

Frederick the Great, **II:** 103; **Supp. I Part 2:** 433

Fredrickson, George M., **Supp. I Part 2:** 589

"Free" (O'Hara), **III:** 369

Free, and Other Stories (Dreiser), **Retro. Supp. II:** 104

Free Agents (Apple), **Supp. XVII:** 5–6

Free Air (Lewis), **II:** 441

Freedman, David, **Supp. XXV:** 255

Freedman, Monroe H., **Supp. VIII:** 127

Freedman, Richard, **Supp. V:** 244

Freedom (Franzen), **Supp. XXII:** 255

"Freedom" (Larsen), **Supp. XVIII:** 124

"Freedom" (White), **Supp. I Part 2:** 659

"Freedom, New Hampshire" (Kinnell), **Supp. III Part 1:** 238, 239, 251

"Freedom and Discipline" (Carruth), **Supp. XVI:** 50

Freedom Business, The (Nelson), **Supp. XVIII:** 186

Freedom Is the Right to Choose: An Inquiry into the Battle for the American Future (MacLeish), **III:** 3

"Freedom's a Hard-Bought Thing" (Benét), **Supp. XI:** 47, 48

"Freedom's Plow" (Hughes), **Supp. I Part 1:** 346

Free Enterprise (Cliff), **Supp. XXII:** 66–67, **77–78**

"Free Everything" (July), **Supp. XXIV:** 210

"Free Fantasia: Tiger Flowers" (Hayden), **Supp. II Part 1:** 363, 366

Freeing of the Dust, The (Levertov), **Supp. III Part 1:** 281–282

"Free Lance, The" (Mencken), **III:** 104, 105

Free-Lance Pallbearers, The (Reed), **Supp. X:** 240, **242–243,** 244

Freeland (Lane), **Supp. XXII:** 297

Free Life, A (Jin), **Supp. XVIII: 101–102**

Freeloaders, The (Lacy), **Supp. XV:** 204

"Free Man" (Hughes), **Supp. I Part 1:** 333

Freeman, Chris, **Supp. XIV:** 157, 159

Freeman, Douglas Southall, **Supp. I Part 2:** 486, 493

Freeman, Jesse, **Supp. XXVI:** 11

Freeman, John, **Supp. XVIII:** 90

Freeman, Joseph, **II:** 26; **Supp. I Part 2:** 610; **Supp. XXII:** 274, 277

Freeman, Mary E. Wilkins, **II:** 401; **Retro. Supp. II:** 51, 136, 138; **Supp. IX:** 79

Freeman, Morgan, **Supp. XII:** 317

Freeman, Suzanne, **Supp. X:** 83

Free Man, The (Richter), **Supp. XVIII:** 215

"Free Man's Worship, A" (Russell), **Supp. I Part 2:** 522

Freewheelin' Bob Dylan, The (album, Dylan), **Supp. XVIII:** 20, 24, 29

Free Will & Wanton Lust (Silver), **Supp. XXIV:** 265, **267–268,** 270

Freier, Mary, **Supp. XXV:** 197

Freilicher, Jane, **Supp. XV:** 178; **Supp. XXIII:** 209, 210, 212, 217

Freinman, Dorothy, **Supp. IX:** 94

Frémont, John Charles, **Supp. I Part 2:** 486

Fremont-Smith, Eliot, **Supp. XIII:** 263

Fremstad, Olive, **I:** 319; **Retro. Supp. I:** 10

French, Warren, **Supp. XII:** 118–119

French Chef, The (television program), **Supp. XVII:** 89

French Connection, The (film), **Supp. V:** 226

"French Informal Report, The"(Kenny), **Supp. XXIII:** 152

French Leave (X. J. Kennedy), **Supp. XV:** 165

Frenchman Must Die, A (Boyle), **Supp. XXIV:** 62

French Poets and Novelists (James), **II:** 336; **Retro. Supp. I:** 220

"French Scarecrow, The" (Maxwell), **Supp. VIII:** 169, 170

French Ways and Their Meaning (Wharton), **IV:** 319; **Retro. Supp. I:** 378

Freneau, Eleanor Forman (Mrs. Philip Freneau), **Supp. II Part 1:** 266

Freneau, Philip M., **I:** 335; **II:** 295; **Supp. I Part 1:** 124, 125, 127, 145; **Supp. II Part 1:** 65, **253–277**

Frenzy (Everett), **Supp. XVIII: 59–60**

Frescoes for Mr. Rockefeller's City (MacLeish), **III:** 14–15

"Fresh Air" (Koch), **Supp. XV:** 181, 185

Fresh Air Fiend: Travel Writings, 1985–2000 (Theroux), **Supp. VIII:** 325

Fresh Brats (X. J. Kennedy), **Supp. XV:** 163

"Freshman" (Sanders), **Supp. XVI:** 277

Freud, Sigmund, **I:** 55, 58, 59, 66, 67, 135, 241, 242, 244, 247, 248, 283; **II:** 27, 370, 546–547; **III:** 134, 390, 400, 418, 488; **IV:** 7, 70, 138, 295; **Retro. Supp. I:** 80, 176, 253; **Retro. Supp. II:** 104; **Supp. I Part 1:** 13, 43, 253, 254, 259, 260, 265, 270, 315; **Supp. I Part 2:** 493, 527, 616, 643, 647, 649; **Supp. IV Part 2:** 450; **Supp. IX:** 102, 155, 161, 308; **Supp. VIII:** 103, 196; **Supp. X:** 193, 194; **Supp. XII:** 14–15; **Supp. XIII:** 75; **Supp. XIV:** 83; **Supp. XV:** 219; **Supp. XVI:** 157–158, 161, 292; **Supp. XXII:** 165, 198

"Freud and Literature" (Trilling), **Supp. III Part 2:** 502–503

Freudenberger, Nell, **Supp. XXV:** 149

Freudian Psychology and Veblen's Social Theory, The (Schneider), **Supp. I Part 2:** 650

Freudian Wish and Its Place in Ethics, The (Holt), **I:** 59

"Freud's Room" (Ozick), **Supp. V:** 268

Freud: The Mind of the Moralist (Sontag and Rieff), **Supp. III Part 2:** 455

"Freud: Within and Beyond Culture" (Trilling), **Supp. III Part 2:** 508

Frey, Charles, **Supp. XXII:** 301

Frey, Hillary, **Supp. XIX:** 55; **Supp. XXII:** 53

Frey, James, **Supp. XXII:** 95; **Supp. XXIII:** 109; **Supp. XXIV:** 230, 236

"Friday Morning Trial of Mrs. Solano, The" (Ríos), **Supp. IV Part 2:** 538, 548

Friebert, Stuart, **Supp. XIX:** 276

Frieburger, William, **Supp. XIII:** 239

Friede, Donald, **Supp. XVII:** 85, 86, 87, 90

Friedenberg, Edgar Z., **Supp. VIII:** 240

Friedman, Bruce Jay, **I:** 161; **Supp. IV Part 1:** 379

Friedman, Lawrence S., **Supp. V:** 273

Friedman, Milton, **Supp. I Part 2:** 648

Friedman, Norman, **I:** 431–432, 435, 439

Friedman, Stan, **Supp. XII:** 186

Friedmann, Georges, **Supp. I Part 2:** 645

"Fried Sausage" (Simic), **Supp. VIII:** 270

Friend, Julius, **Retro. Supp. I:** 80

Friend, The (Coleridge), **II:** 10

"Friend Husband's Latest" (Sayre), **Retro. Supp. I:** 104

"Friendly Debate between a Conformist and a Non-Conformist, A" (Wild), **IV:** 155

"Friendly Neighbor" (Keillor), **Supp. XVI:** 172

Friend of the Earth, A (Boyle), **Supp. VIII:** 12, 16; **Supp. XX: 29–30**

"Friend of the Fourth Decade, The" (Merrill), **Supp. III Part 1:** 327

"Friends" (Beattie), **Supp. V:** 23, 27

"Friends" (Paley), **Supp. VI:** 219, 226

"Friends" (Sexton), **Supp. II Part 2:** 693

Friend's Delight, The (Bierce), **I:** 195

"Friends from Philadelphia" (Updike), **Retro. Supp. I:** 319

"Friendship" (Emerson), **Supp. II Part 1:** 290; **Supp. XXV:** 250

Friends: More Will and Magna Stories (Dixon), **Supp. XII:** 148, 149

"Friends of Heraclitus, The" (Simic), **Supp. VIII:** 284

"Friends of Kafka, The" (Singer), **Retro. Supp. II:** 308

"Friends of the Family, The" (McCarthy), **II:** 566

"Friend to Alexander, A" (Thurber), **Supp. I Part 2:** 616

"Frigate Pelican, The" (Moore), **III:** 208, 210–211, 215

Frightened Wife, The (Rinehart), **Supp. XXV:** 198, 200

"Frill, The" (Buck), **Supp. XIV:** 274

"Fringe, The" (Bass), **Supp. XVI:** 19

Frings, Ketti, **Supp. XXV:** 95

Frobenius, Leo, **III:** 475; **Supp. III Part 2:** 620

Froebel, Friedrich, **Supp. XIV:** 52–53

Frog (Dixon), **Supp. XII:** 151

"Frog Dances" (Dixon), **Supp. XII:** 151

"Frog Pond, The" (Kinnell), **Supp. III Part 1:** 254

"Frogs" (Nelson), **Supp. XVIII:** 176

"Frog Takes a Swim" (Dixon), **Supp. XII:** 152

Frohock, W. M., **I:** 34, 42

Frolic of His Own, A (Gaddis), **Supp. IV Part 1:** 279, 291, 292–294; **Supp. XX:** 91

"From a Mournful Village" (Jewett), **Retro. Supp. II:** 146

"From an Alabama Farm" (Nelson), **Supp. XVIII:** 182

"From an Old House in America" (Rich), **Supp. I Part 2:** 551, 565–567

From Another World (Untermeyer), **Supp. XV:** 293, 303, 310–311, 313

"From a Phrase of Simone Weil's and Some Words of Hegel's" (Oppen), **Supp. XXVI:** 236

"From a Roadside Motel" (F. Wright), **Supp. XVII:** 245

"From a Survivor" (Rich), **Supp. I Part 2:** 563

From A to Z (musical review; Allen), **Supp. XV:** 3, 13

From a Work in Progress (Notley), **Supp. XXII:** 232

"From a Work in Progress" (Notley), **Supp. XXII:** 232

From a Writer's Notebook (Brooks), **I:** 254

From Bauhaus to Our House (Wolfe), **Supp. III Part 2:** 580, 581, 584

From Bondage (H. Roth), **Supp. IX:** 236, **238–240**

"From *Chants* to *Borders* to *Communion*" (Fox), *Supp. XIII:* 217, 217–218

"From Chicago" (Anderson), **I:** 108–109

From Colony to Nation: Women Activists and the Gendering of Politics in Belize, 1912–1982 (Macpherson), **Supp. XXIII:** 84

From Death to Morning (Wolfe), **IV:** 450, 456, 458

"From Dick to Lethem: The Dickian Legacy, Postmodernism, and Avant-Pop in Jonathan Lethem's *Amnesia Moon*" (Rossi), *Supp. XVIII:* 137, 138–139

"From Discord, a Wife Makes a Nice New Life—Too Nice" (Linfield), **Supp. XVII:** 177

From Down to the Village (Budbill), **Supp. XIX:** 6–7

"From Feathers to Iron" (Kunitz), **Supp. III Part 1:** 261

"From Fifth Avenue Up" (Barnes), **Supp. III Part 1:** 33, 44

"From Gorbunov and Gorchakov" (Brodsky), **Supp. VIII:** 26

"From Grand Canyon to Burbank" (H. Miller), **III:** 186

"From Hell to Breakfast", **Supp. IX:** 326–327

From Here to Eternity (film), **Supp. XI:** 221

From Here to Eternity (J. Jones), **I:** 477; **Supp. XI:** 215, 216, 217, 218, **219–221**, 223, 224, 226, 229, 230, 231, 232, 234; **Supp. XIX:** 248; **Supp. XX:** 248; **Supp. XXII:** 140

From Here to Eternity (miniseries), **Supp. XI:** 234

From Jordan's Delight (Blackmur), **Supp. II Part 1:** 91

"From Lumaghi Mine" (Wrigley), **Supp. XVIII:** 295

Fromm, Erich, **I:** 58; **Supp. VIII:** 196

From Morn to Midnight (Kaiser), **I:** 479

"From Native Son to Invisible Man" (Locke), **Supp. IX:** 306

"From Pico, the Women: A Life" (Creeley), **Supp. IV Part 1:** 149

From Plotzk to Boston (Antin), **Supp. XX:** 2

From Ritual to Romance (Weston), **II:** 540; **III:** 12; **Supp. I Part 2:** 439

From Room to Room (Kenyon), **Supp. VII:** 163–165, 166, 167

"From Room to Room" (Kenyon), **Supp. VII:** 159, 163–165

From Sand Creek: Rising in this Heart Which Is Our America (Ortiz), **Supp. IV Part 2:** 512–513

"From Sea Cliff, March" (Swenson), **Supp. IV Part 2:** 649

From Stone Orchard: A Collection of Memories (Findley), **Supp. XX: 57**

"From the Antigone" (Yeats), **III:** 459

From the Ashes: Voices of Watts (Schulberg, ed.), **Supp. XVIII:** 254

From the Barrio: A Chicano Anthology (Salinas and Faderman, eds.), **Supp. XIII:** 313

From the Beginning (Notley), **Supp. XXII:** 226, 235–236

From the Briarpatch File: On Context, Procedure, and American Identity (Murray), **Supp. XIX:** 161

"From the Childhood of Jesus" (Pinsky), **Supp. VI:** 244–245, 247

"From the Corpse Woodpiles, From the Ashes" (Hayden), **Supp. II Part 1:** 370

"From the Country to the City" (Bishop), **Supp. I Part 1:** 85, 86

"From the Cupola" (Merrill), **Supp. III Part 1:** 324–325, 331

"From the Dark Side of the Earth" (Oates), **Supp. II Part 2:** 510

"From the Diary of a New York Lady" (Parker), **Supp. IX:** 201

"From the Diary of One Not Born" (Singer), **IV:** 9

"From the Dreams" (Notley), **Supp. XXII:** 224

"From the East, Light" (Carver), **Supp. III Part 1:** 138

From the First Nine: Poems 1946–1976 (Merrill), **Supp. III Part 1:** 336

"From the Flats" (Lanier), **Supp. I Part 1:** 364

From the Flower Courtyard (Everwine), **Supp. XV:** 75

From the Heart of Europe (Matthiessen), **III:** 310

From the Meadow: Selected and New Poems (Everwine), **Supp. XV:** 75, **88–89**

"From the Memoirs of a Private Detective" (Hammett), **Supp. IV Part 1:** 343

"From the Nursery" (Kenyon), **Supp. VII:** 171

"From the Poets in the Kitchen" (Marshall), **Supp. XI:** 277

"From the Reservation to *Dawn of the Dead* to James Dickey and Back Again" (Gansworth), **Supp. XXVI:** 113

From the Terrace (O'Hara), **III:** 362

"From the Thirties: Tillie Olsen and the Radical Tradition" (Rosenfelt), **Supp. XIII:** 296, 304

From the Western Door to the Lower West Side (Gansworth and Rogovin), **Supp. XXVI:** 112

"From Trollope's Journal" (Bishop), **Retro. Supp. II:** 47

"Front, A" (Jarrell), **II:** 374

Front, The (film), **Supp. I Part 1:** 295

Frontain, Raymond-Jean, **Supp. XXVI:** 242

"Front and the Back Parts of the House, The" (Maxwell), **Supp. VIII:** 169

Frontier Eden (Bigelow), **Supp. X:** 227

"Frontiers of Culture" (Locke), **Supp. XIV:** 213

"Front Lines" (Snyder), **Supp. VIII:** 301

Front Porch (Inge), **Supp. XXV:** 94

Front Runner, The (P. N. Warren), **Supp. XX: 259, 262–264**

Frost, A. B., **Retro. Supp. II:** 72

Frost, Carol, **Supp. XV: 91–109**

Frost, Isabelle Moodie, **II:** 150, 151

Frost, Jeanie, **II:** 151

Frost, Richard, **Supp. XV:** 92

Frost, Robert, **I:** 26, 27, 60, 63, 64, 171, 229, 303, 326, 418; **II:** 55, 58, **150–172**, 276, 289, 388, 391, 471, 523, 527, 529, 535; **III:** 5, 23, 67, 269, 271, 272, 275, 287, 453, 510, 523, 536, 575, 581, 591; **IV:** 140, 190, 415; **Retro. Supp. I:** 67, **121–144**, 276, 287, 292, 298, 299, 311, 413; **Retro. Supp. II:** 40, 47, 50, 146, 178, 181; **Supp. I Part 1:** 80, 242, 263, 264; **Supp. I Part 2:** 387, 461, 699; **Supp. II Part 1:** 4, 19, 26, 103; **Supp. III Part 1:** 63, 74–75, 239, 253; **Supp. III Part 2:** 546, 592, 593; **Supp. IV Part 1:** 15; **Supp. IV Part 2:** 439, 445, 447, 448, 599, 601; **Supp. IX:** 41, 42, 75, 76, 80, 87, 90, 266, 308; **Supp. VIII:** 20, 30, 32, 98, 100, 104, 259, 292; **Supp. X:** 64, 65, 66, 74, 120, 172; **Supp. XI:** 43, 123, 150, 153, 312; **Supp. XII:** 130, 241, 303, 307; **Supp. XIII:** 143, 147, 334–335; **Supp. XIV:** 42, 122, 222, 229; **Supp. XIX:** 1, 123; **Supp. XV:** 21, 51, 65, 96, 212, 215, 250, 256, 293, 296, 299, 301, 302, 306, 348; **Supp. XVII:** 36, 110, 115–116; **Supp. XVIII:** 298, 300; **Supp. XX: 69, 199; Supp. XXI:** 19, 28, 51, 99, 104, 107, 205; **Supp. XXII:** 206; **Supp. XXIII:** 79, 145; **Supp. XXIV:** 159; **Supp. XXV:** 222; **Supp. XXVI:** 61, 62, 63, 65, 67, 164

Frost, William Prescott, **II:** 150–151

"Frost: A Dissenting Opinion" (Cowley), **Supp. II Part 1:** 143

Frost: A Time to Talk (Francis), **Supp. IX:** 76, **85–86**

"Frost at Midnight" (Coleridge), **Supp. X:** 71

"Frost Flowers" (Kenyon), **Supp. VII:** 168

"Frost: He Is Sometimes a Poet and Sometimes a Stump-Speaker" (NewsWeek), **Retro. Supp. I:** 137

Frothingham, Nathaniel, **I:** 3

Frothingham, Octavius B., **IV:** 173

"Frozen City, The" (Nemerov), **III:** 270

"Frozen Fields, The" (Bowles), **Supp. IV Part 1:** 80

"Frozen Ship, The" (Very), **Supp. XXV:** 243

Frucht, Abby, **Supp. XXVI:** 156

"Fructifying a Cycle: Homage to Alan Ansen"(Hadas), **Supp. XXIII:** 123

"Fruit Garden Path, The" (Lowell), **II:** 516

"Fruit of the Flower" (Cullen), **Supp. IV Part 1:** 167

Fruit of the Tree, The (Wharton), **IV:** 314–315; **Retro. Supp. I:** 367, **370–371,** 373

"Fruit of Travel Long Ago" (Melville), **III:** 93

Fruits and Vegetables (Jong), **Supp. V:** 113, 115, 117, 118, 119

"Fruits of the Sea, The" (Di Piero), **Supp. XIX:** 47

Frumkes, Lewis Burke, **Supp. XII:** 335–336

Fry, Christopher, **Supp. I Part 1:** 270

Fry, Roger, **Supp. XIV:** 336

Fry, Stephen M., **Supp. XIX:** 159

Frye, Joanne, **Supp. XIII:** 292, 296, 298, 302

Frye, Northrop, **Supp. I Part 2:** 530; **Supp. II Part 1:** 101; **Supp. X:** 80; **Supp. XIII:** 19; **Supp. XIV:** 11, 15; **Supp. XVI:** 149, 156; **Supp. XX: 50; Supp. XXIII:** 42

Fryer, Judith, **Retro. Supp. I:** 379

F. Scott Fitzgerald: A Critical Portrait (Piper), **Supp. IX:** 65

"F. S. F., 1896–1996, R.I.P." (Doctorow), **Retro. Supp. I:** 97

Fuchs, Daniel, **Supp. XIII:** 106

Fuchs, Miriam, **Supp. IV Part 1:** 284

Fuehrer Bunker, The (Snodgrass), **Supp. VI:** 314, 315–317, 319–321

Fuel (Nye), **Supp. XIII:** 277, **282–284**

"Fuel" (Nye), **Supp. XIII:** 283

Fuertes, Gloria, **Supp. V:** 178

Fugard, Athol, **Supp. VIII:** 330; **Supp. XIII:** 205

Fugitive Group, The (Cowan), **IV:** 120

Fugitive Kind, The (T. Williams), **IV:** 381, 383

Fugitives, The (group), **IV:** 122, 124, 125, 131, 237, 238

Fugitives, The: A Critical Account (Bradbury), **IV:** 130

"Fugitive Slave Law, The" (Emerson), **II:** 13

Fugitive's Return (Glaspell), **Supp. III Part 1:** 182–184

"Fulfillment" (H. Johnson), **Supp. XXVI:** 164, 173

Fuller, B. A. G., **III:** 605

Fuller, Edmund, **Supp. XXII:** 211, 212

Fuller, Hiram, **Supp. XVIII:** 12,14

Fuller, Jesse "Lonecat", **Supp. XV:** 147

Fuller, Margaret, **I:** 261; **II:** 7, 276; **IV:** 172; **Retro. Supp. I:** 155–156, 163; **Retro. Supp. II:** 46; **Supp. I Part 2:** 524; **Supp. II Part 1: 279–306; Supp. IX:** 37; **Supp. XVIII:** 3, 11, 12, 16; **Supp. XXV:** 249

Fuller, Thomas, **II:** 111, 112

Fullerton, Morton, **Supp. XX: 231**

Fullerton Street (Wilson), **Supp. VIII:** 331

"Full Fathom Five" (Plath), **Supp. I Part 2:** 538

Full Measure: Modern Short Stories on Aging (D. Sennett, ed.), **Supp. XVI:** 37

Full Monty, The (musical, McNally), **Supp. XIII:** 207

"Full Moon" (Hayden), **Supp. II Part 1:** 370

Full Moon and Other Plays (Price), **Supp. VI:** 266

"Full Moon and You're Not Here" (Cisneros), **Supp. VII:** 71–72

"Full Moon: New Guinea" (Shapiro), **Supp. II Part 2:** 707

"Fullness of Life, The" (Wharton), **Retro. Supp. I:** 363

Full of Life (Fante), **Supp. XI:** 160

Full of Life (film), **Supp. XI:** 170

Full of Lust and Good Usage (Dunn), **Supp. XI: 145–147**

Full Speed Ahead: Tales from the Log of a Correspondent with Our Navy (Beston), **Supp. XXVI:** 33

"Full Summer" (Olds), **Supp. X:** 212

Fulton, Ben, **Supp. XXII:** 207

Fulton, Robert, **Supp. I Part 2:** 519; **Supp. II Part 1:** 73

Fun and Games (Major), **Supp. XXII:** 180

Funaroff, Sol, **Supp. XXVI:** 143

"Functional Poem" (Halliday), **Supp. XIX:** 85

Function of Criticism, The (Winters), **Supp. II Part 2:** 812, 813

"Fundamentalism" (Tate), **IV:** 125

"Fundamental Project of Technology, The" (Kinnell), **Supp. III Part 1:** 253

"Funeral of Bobò, The" (Brodsky), **Supp. VIII:** 27, 28

Fungi from Yuggoth (Lovecraft), **Supp. XXV:** 119–120

Fun Home: A Family Tragicomic (Bechdel), **Supp. XXV:** 1, 4–9

Funiculi-Funicula (Wellman), **Supp. XXV:** 20

"Funnel" (Sexton), **Supp. II Part 2:** 675

"Furious Seasons, The" (Carver), **Supp. III Part 1:** 137

Furious Seasons and Other Stories (Carver), **Supp. III Part 1:** 142, 143, 146

"Furious Versions" (L.-Y. Lee), **Supp. XV:** 215–217, 218, 220

"Furnished Room, The" (Hayden), **Supp. II Part 1:** 386–387, 394, 397, 399, 406, 408

"Furor Scribendi" (O. Butler), **Supp. XIII:** 70

Furors Die (Hoffman), **Supp. XVIII: 80–81**

Fur Person, The (Sarton), **Supp. VIII: 264–265**

Further Adventures with You (Wright), **Supp. XV:** 339, 342, **343–345**

Further Fables for Our Time (Thurber), **Supp. I Part 2:** 612

"Further in Summer than the Birds" (Dickinson), **I:** 471

Further Poems of Emily Dickinson (Bianchi and Hampson, ed.), **Retro. Supp. I:** 35

Further Range, A (Frost), **II:** 155; **Retro. Supp. I:** 132, 136, 137, 138, 139

"Fury, The (Skloot), **Supp. XX: 197**

"Fury of Aerial Bombardment, The" (Eberhart), **I:** 535–536

"Fury of Flowers and Worms, The" (Sexton), **Supp. II Part 2:** 694

"Fury of Rain Storms, The" (Sexton), **Supp. II Part 2:** 695

Fury of the Jungle (film), **Supp. XIII:** 163

Fussell, Paul, **Supp. V:** 241

Fussell, Paul K., **Supp. XXV:** 253

"Futility" (H. Johnson), **Supp. XXVI:** 167, 172

"Future, if Any, of Comedy, The" (Thurber), **Supp. I Part 2:** 620

Future, The (film, July), **Supp. XXIV:** 199, 200, 202, **209,** 210

Future in the Present, The (C. L. R. James), **Supp. XXI:** 172

Future is Ours, Comrade, The: Conversations with the Russians (Kosinski), **Supp. VII:** 215

Futureland: Nine Stories of an Imminent World (Mosley), **Supp. XIII: 247–249**

"Future Life, The" (Bryant), **Supp. I Part 1:** 170

Future of Southern Letters, The (J. W. Miller), **Supp. XX: 161**

Future of the Race, The (H. L. Gates), **Supp. XX: 101, 104, 111**

Future Punishment of the Wicked, The (Edwards), **I:** 546

G

"Gabriel" (Rich), **Supp. I Part 2:** 557

Gabriel, Ralph H., **Supp. I Part 1:** 251

Gabriel, Trip, **Supp. V:** 212

Gabriel Conroy (Harte), **Supp. II Part 1:** 354

"Gabriel's Truth" (Kenyon), **Supp. VII:** 166

Gaddis, William, **Supp. IV Part 1: 279–296; Supp. IV Part 2:** 484; **Supp. IX:** 208; **Supp. V:** 52; **Supp. X:** 301, 302; **Supp. XX: 83, 91; Supp. XXI:** 226; **Supp. XXIII:** 107

Gadiot, Pud, **Supp. XI:** 295

Gain (Powers), **Supp. IX:** 212, **220–221**

Gaines, Ernest J., **Supp. X:** 24, 250

Gaines, James R., **Supp. IX:** 190

Gainor, J. Ellen, **Supp. XXI:** 6

Gaitens, Peter, **Supp. XV:** 65

Gajarsa, Arthur, **Supp. XXVI:** 83

Galamain, Ivan, **Supp. III Part 2:** 624

Galassi, Jonathan, **Supp. XIX:** 34; **Supp. XVIII:** 92; **Supp. XXII:** 177

Galatea 2.2 (Powers), **Supp. IX:** 212, **219–220**

"Galatea Encore" (Brodsky), **Supp. VIII:** 31

Galbraith, John Kenneth, **Supp. I Part 2:** 645, 650

Galdós, Benito Pérez. *See* Pérez Galdós, Benito

Gale, Zona, **Supp. I Part 2:** 613; **Supp. VIII:** 155

Galehouse, Maggie, **Supp. XXI:** 215

"Gale in April" (Jeffers), **Supp. II Part 2:** 423

Galignani, Giovanni Antonio, **II:** 315

Galileo Galilei, **I:** 480–481; **Supp. XII:** 180; **Supp. XIII:** 75

Gallagher, Tess, **Supp. XVI:** 36; **Supp. XVII:** 110; **Supp. XXI:** 246; **Supp. XXIV: 165–181**

Gallant, Mavis, **Supp. VIII:** 151

Gallatin, Albert, **I:** 5

"Gallery" (Goldbarth), **Supp. XII:** 188

"Gallery of Real Creatures, A" (Thurber), **Supp. I Part 2:** 619

Gallico, Paul, **Supp. XVI:** 238

Gallows Songs (Snodgrass), **Supp. VI:** 317

Gallup, Dick, **Supp. XXIV:** 34, 35, 39, 44

Gallup, Donald, **III:** 404, 478

"Galop" (Davison), **Supp. XXVI:** 71

Galsworthy, John, **III:** 70, 153, 382

Galton Case, The (Macdonald), **Supp. IV Part 2:** 463, 473, 474

Galvin, Frances, **Supp. XXI:** 5

"Gal Young 'Un" (Rawlings), **Supp. X:** 228

Gambino, Richard, **Supp. XX: 35**

"Gambler, the Nun, and the Radio, The" (Hemingway), **II:** 250

"Gambler's Wife, The" (Dunbar), **Supp. II Part 1:** 196

Gambone, Philip, **Supp. XII:** 81

"Gambrel Roof, A" (Larcom), **Supp. XIII:** 144

"Game at Salzburg, A" (Jarrell), **II:** 384, 389

Game Management (Leopold), **Supp. XIV:** 182

"Game of Catch, A" (Wilbur), **Supp. III Part 2:** 552

Game Players of Titan, The (Dick), **Supp. XVIII:** 138

"Games in Frank Conroy's *Stop-Time*" (T. Adams), **Supp. XVI:** 67

"Games Two" (Wilbur), **Supp. III Part 2:** 550

Gammelgaard, Lene, **Supp. XVIII:** 112

"Gamut, The" (Angelou), **Supp. IV Part 1:** 15

Gander, Forrest, **Supp. XV:** 339, 340, 342

Gandhi, Indira, **Supp. X:** 108

Gandhi, Mahatma, **III:** 179, 296–297; **IV:** 170, 185, 367; **Supp. VIII:** 203, 204; **Supp. X:** 27

Gandhi on Non-Violence (Merton, ed.), **Supp. VIII:** 204–205

Gangemi, Merry, **Supp. XXV:** 6

Gang of Five: Leaders at the Center of the Conservative Crusade (Easton), **Supp. XIX:** 137

"Gang of Mirrors, The" (Simic), **Supp. VIII:** 283

Gannett, Ezra Stiles, **Supp. XXIV:** 74

Gansevoort, Guert, **III:** 94

Gansevoort, Peter, **III:** 92

Gansworth, Eric, **Supp. XXVI: 101–116**

"Gap" (Bierds), **Supp. XVII:** 35–36

Garabedian, Michael, **Supp. XIII:** 115

Garbage (Ammons), **Supp. VII:** 24, 35–36

Garbage (Dixon), **Supp. XII:** 147, 148

Garbage Man, The (Dos Passos), **I:** 478, 479, 481, 493

Garber, Frederick, **Supp. IX:** 294–295

Garbo, Greta, **Supp. I Part 2:** 616

García, Cristina, **Supp. VIII:** 74; **Supp. XI: 177–192**

García Lorca, Federico. *See* Lorca, Federico García

"García Lorca: A Photograph of the Granada Cemetery, 1966" (Levis), **Supp. XI:** 264

García Márquez, Gabriel, **Supp. V:** 244; **Supp. VIII:** 81, 82, 84, 85; **Supp. XII:** 147, 310, 316, 322; **Supp. XIII:** 226; **Supp. XVII:** 45; **Supp. XXIV:** 86, 89, 190; **Supp. XXV:** 49, 69

Gard, Claire, **Supp. XXIII:** 94

Gardaphe, Fred, **Supp. XX: 38, 41**

"Garden" (Marvell), **IV:** 161; **Supp. XVI:** 204

"Garden, The" (Glück), **Supp. V:** 83

"Garden, The" (Strand), **Supp. IV Part 2:** 629

"Garden, The" (Very), **Supp. XXV:** 248

"Garden Among Tombs" (B. Kelly), **Supp. XVII:** 126

"Garden by Moonlight, The" (Lowell), **II:** 524

"Gardener Delivers a Fawn, The" (C. Frost), **Supp. XV:** 99

Gardener's Son, The (McCarthy), **Supp. VIII:** 187

Garden God, The: A Tale of Two Boys (Reid), **Supp. XX: 235**

"Gardenias" (Doty), **Supp. XI:** 122

"Gardenias" (Monette), **Supp. X:** 159

"Garden Lodge, The" (Cather), **I:** 316, 317

Garden of Adonis, The (Gordon), **II:** 196, 204–205, 209

Garden of Earthly Delights, A (Oates), **Supp. II Part 2:** 504, 507–509

Garden of Earthly Delights, The (Bosch), **Supp. XXII:** 255, 261

"Garden of Eden" (Hemingway), **II:** 259

Garden of Eden, The (Hemingway), **Retro. Supp. I:** 186, **187–188**

"Garden of Flesh, Garden of Stone" (B. Kelly), **Supp. XVII:** 128

Garden of Last Days, The (Dubus III), **Supp. XXIV:** 101, **107–108**

"Garden of the Moon, The" (Doty), **Supp. XI:** 122

Garden of the Prophet, The (Gibran), **Supp. XX: 119, 122**

"Garden of the Trumpet Tree, The" (B. Kelly), **Supp. XVII:** 131

"Gardens, The" (Oliver), **Supp. VII:** 236

"Gardens of Mont-Saint-Michel, The" (Maxwell), **Supp. VIII:** 169

"Gardens of the Villa D'Este, The" (Hecht), **Supp. X:** 59

"Gardens of Zuñi, The" (Merwin), **Supp. III Part 1:** 351

Garden Thieves, The: Twentieth Century African-American Poetry (Major, ed.), **Supp. XXII:** 172

Gardiner, Judith Kegan, **Supp. IV Part 1:** 205

Gardner, Erle Stanley, **Supp. IV Part 1:** 121, 345

Gardner, Isabella, **IV:** 127

Gardner, John, **Supp. I Part 1:** 193, 195, 196; **Supp. III Part 1:** 136, 142, 146; **Supp. VI: 61–76; Supp. XXV:** 152

Gardner, Thomas, **Supp. XXI:** 214

Gardons, S. S. *See* Snodgrass, W. D.

"Gare de Lyon" (M. F. K. Fisher), **Supp. XVII:** 91

Garfield, John, **Supp. XII:** 160

Garibaldi, Giuseppe, **I:** 4; **II:** 284

Garibay, Angel M., **Supp. XV:** 77

Garland, Hamlin, **I:** 407; **II:** 276, 289; **III:** 576; **Retro. Supp. I:** 133; **Retro. Supp. II:** 72; **Supp. I Part 1:** 217; **Supp. IV Part 2:** 502; **Supp. XVIII:** 6

Garland Companion, The (Zverev), **Retro. Supp. I:** 278

"Garments" (Gibran), **Supp. XX: 124**

Garments the Living Wear (Purdy), **Supp. VII:** 278–279, 280–281

Garner, Dwight, **Supp. X:** 202; **Supp. XVIII:** 89; **Supp. XXV:** 9

Garnett, Edward, **I:** 405, 409, 417; **III:** 27

Garrett, George P., **Supp. I Part 1:** 196; **Supp. VII: 95–113; Supp. X:** 3, 7; **Supp. XI:** 218; **Supp. XVIII:** 74, 75; **Supp. XXVI:** 153, 157

Garrigue, Jean, **Supp. XII:** 260

Garrison, Deborah, **Supp. IX:** 299

Garrison, Fielding, **III:** 105

Garrison, William Lloyd, **Supp. I Part 2:** 524, 588, 683, 685, 686, 687; **Supp. XIV:** 54; **Supp. XXIV:** 77

"Garrison of Cape Ann, The" (Whittier), **Supp. I Part 2:** 691, 694

Garry Moore Show (television show), **Supp. IV Part 2:** 575

"Garter Motif" (White), **Supp. I Part 2:** 673

Gartner, Zsuzsi, **Supp. X:** 276

Garvey, Marcus, **Supp. III Part 1:** 175, 180; **Supp. IV Part 1:** 168; **Supp. X:** 135, 136; **Supp. XXI:** 166, 168; **Supp. XXII:** 7

Gas (Kaiser), **I:** 479

Gas-House McGinty (Farrell), **II:** 41–42

Gaskell, Elizabeth, A., **Supp. I Part 2:** 580

Gasoline (Corso), **Supp. XII:** 118, **121–123,** 134

Gasoline Wars, The (Thompson), **Supp. XXIII:** 290

"Gasoline Wars, The"(Thompson), **Supp. XXIII:** 291

Gass, William H., **Supp. IX:** 208; **Supp. V:** 44, 52, 238; **Supp. VI: 77–96; Supp. XII:** 152; **Supp. XIV:** 305; **Supp. XVII:** 183

Gassner, John, **IV:** 381; **Supp. I Part 1:** 284, 292

"Gas Stations" (Apple), **Supp. XVII:** 4

Gastronomical Me, The (M. F. K. Fisher), **Supp. XVII:** 84, 85, 87, 91, 92

Gates, David, **Supp. V:** 24; **Supp. XIII:** 93; **Supp. XVI:** 73, 74; **Supp. XX: 92**

Gates, Elmer, **I:** 515–516

Gates, Henry Louis, Jr., **Retro. Supp. I:** 194, 195, 203; **Supp. X:** 242, 243, 245, 247; **Supp. XIX:** 147, 149; **Supp. XVIII:** 287; **Supp. XX: 99–112, 279, 286; Supp. XXIV:** 192; **Supp. XXVI:** 13

Gates, Lewis E., **III:** 315, 330

Gates, Sondra Smith, **Supp. XVIII:** 267, 269

Gates, The (Rukeyser), **Supp. VI:** 271, 274, 281

"Gates, The" (Rukeyser), **Supp. VI:** 286

Gates, Tudor, **Supp. XI:** 307

Gates of Ivory, the Gates of Horn, The (McGrath), **Supp. X:** 118

Gates of Wrath, The; Rhymed Poems (Ginsberg), **Supp. II Part 1:** 311, 319

"Gathering" (Trethewey), **Supp. XXI:** 249

Gathering Forces, The (C. L. R. James), **Supp. XXI:** 171

"Gathering of Dissidents, A" (Applebaum), **Supp. XVI:** 153

Gathering of Fugitives, A (Trilling), **Supp. III Part 2:** 506, 512

Gathering of Zion, The: The Story of the Mormon Trail (Stegner), **Supp. IV Part 2:** 599, 602–603

Gather Together in My Name (Angelou), **Supp. IV Part 1:** 2, 3, 4–6, 11

Gathorne-Hardy, Robert, **Supp. XIV:** 344, 347, 348, 349

Gaudier-Brzeska, Henri, **III:** 459, 464, 465, 477

Gaughran, Richard, **Supp. XXI:** 47–48

Gauguin, Paul, **I:** 34; **IV:** 290; **Supp. IV Part 1:** 81; **Supp. XII:** 128

"Gauguin in Oregon" (Skloot), **Supp. XX: 203**

"Gauley Bridge" (Rukeyser), **Supp. VI:** 278

Gauss, Christian, **II:** 82; **IV:** 427, 439–440, 444

Gauthier, Jacquie, **Supp. XIX:** 204

Gautier, Théophile, **II:** 543; **III:** 466, 467; **Supp. I Part 1:** 277

Gay, John, **II:** 111; **Supp. I Part 2:** 523; **Supp. XIV:** 337

Gay, Peter, **I:** 560

Gay, Sydney Howard, **Supp. I Part 1:** 158; **Supp. XVIII:** 3

Gay, Walter, **IV:** 317

Gayatri Prayer, The, **III:** 572

Gay Canon, The (Drake), **Supp. XX: 274**

"Gay Chaps at the Bar" (Brooks), **Supp. III Part 1:** 74, 75

" 'Gay Culture': Still of the Wild Frontier" (P. N. Warren), **Supp. XX: 272**

Gaylord, Winfield R., **III:** 579–580

Gay Talese Reader, The: Portraits & Encounters (Talese), **Supp. XVII:** 202, 208

"Gaze, The"(Hadas), **Supp. XXIII:** 120

"Gazebo" (Carver), **Supp. III Part 1:** 138, 144, 145

Gazer's Spirit, The (Hollander), **Supp. XIX:** 121

Gazer Within, The, and Other Essays by Larry Levis, **Supp. XI:** 270

Gazzara, Ben, **Supp. VIII:** 319

Gazzo, Michael V., **III:** 155

"Geas" (Monson), **Supp. XXIV:** 238–239

Geddes, Virgil, **Supp. XXV:** 23

"Geese Flying over Hamilton, New York"(Balakian), **Supp. XXIII:** 24

"Geese Gone Beyond" (Snyder), **Supp. VIII:** 304

Geffen, David, **Supp. XXI:** 154

"Gegenwart" (Goethe), **Supp. II Part 1:** 26

Geisel, Theodor Seuss (Dr. Seuss), **Supp. X:** 56; **Supp. XVI:** 97–115

Geismar, Maxwell, **II:** 178, 431; **III:** 71; **Supp. IX:** 15; **Supp. XI:** 223

Geist, Bill, **Supp. XXIII:** 298

Gelb, Arthur, **IV:** 380; **Supp. XXI:** 12

Gelb, Barbara, **Supp. XXI:** 12

Gelbart, Larry, **Supp. IV Part 2:** 591

Gelder, Robert Van, **Supp. XIII:** 166

Gelfant, Blanche H., **II:** 27, 41; **Supp. XVII:** 161

Gelfman, Jean, **Supp. X:** 3

Gellert, Hugo, **Supp. XXII:** 277

Gellhorn, Martha. *See* Hemingway, Mrs. Ernest (Martha Gellhorn)

Gelpi, Albert, **Supp. I Part 2:** 552, 554, 560

Gelpi, Barbara, **Supp. I Part 2:** 560

Gemin, Pamela, **Supp. XXI:** 246

Gemini (Innaurato), **Supp. XXIV:** 117

Gemini: an extended autobiographical statement on my first twenty-five years of being a black poet (Giovanni), **Supp. IV Part 1:** 11

"Gen" (Snyder), **Supp. VIII:** 302

"Gender Norms" (Radinovsky), **Supp. XV:** 285

"Gender of Sound, The" (Carson), **Supp. XII: 106**

"Genealogies"(Hadas), **Supp. XXIII:** 116

"Genealogy" (Komunyakaa), **Supp. XIII:** 129

"General Aims and Theories" (Crane), **I:** 389

General Died at Dawn, The (Odets), **Supp. II Part 2:** 546

"General Gage's Confession" (Freneau), **Supp. II Part 1:** 257

"General Gage's Soliloquy" (Freneau), **Supp. II Part 1:** 257

General History of the Robberies and Murders of the Most Notorious Pyrates from Their First Rise and Settlement in the Island of New Providence to the Present Year, A (C. Johnson), **Supp. V:** 128

General in His Labyrinth, The (García Márquez), **Supp. XXIV:** 89

"General Returns from One Place to Another, The"(O'Hara), **Supp. XXIII:** 216–217

"General William Booth Enters into Heaven" (Lindsay), **Supp. I Part 2:** 374, 382, 384, 385–388, 389, 392, 399

General William Booth Enters into Heaven and Other Poems (Lindsay), **Supp. I Part 2:** 379, 381, 382, 387–388, 391

"Generation of the Dispossessed" (P. N. Warren), **Supp. XX: 272**

"Generations"(Kenny), **Supp. XXIII:** 154

"Generations of Men, The" (Frost), **Retro. Supp. I:** 128; **Supp. XIII:** 147

Generation Without Farewell (Boyle), **Supp. XXIV:** 60, 62

Generous Man, A (Price), **Supp. VI:** 259, 260, 261

Genesis (biblical book), **I:** 279; **II:** 540; **Retro. Supp. I:** 250, 256; **Supp. XII:** 54

"Genesis" (Stegner), **Supp. IV Part 2:** 604

Genesis: Book One (Schwartz), **Supp. II Part 2:** 640, 651–655

Gene Stratton-Porter (Richards), **Supp. XX: 217–218**

Gene Stratton-Porter, Naturalist and Novelist (Long), **Supp. XX: 212**

"Gene Stratton-Porter: Women's Advocate" (Obuchowski), **Supp. XX: 222**

Genet, Jean, **I:** 71, 82, 83, 84; **Supp. IV Part 1:** 8; **Supp. XI:** 308; **Supp. XII:** 1; **Supp. XIII:** 74; **Supp. XVII:** 95; **Supp. XXIII:** 213; **Supp. XXIV:** 210

"Genetic Coding" (Sorrentino), **Supp. XXI:** 227

"Genetic Expedition" (Dove), **Supp. IV Part 1:** 249, 257

"Genetics of Justice" (Alvarez), **Supp. VII:** 19

"Genial Host, The" (McCarthy), **II:** 564

"Genie in the Bottle, The" (Davison), **Supp. XXVI:** 74

"Genie in the Bottle, The" (Wilbur), **Supp. III Part 2:** 542

"Genius, The" (MacLeish), **III:** 19

Genius and Lust: A Journey through the Major Writings of Henry Miller (Mailer), **Retro. Supp. II:** 208

"Genius Child" (Hughes), **Retro. Supp. I:** 203

"Genius of Bob Dylan, The" (Lethem), **Supp. XVIII:** 146

"Genius," The (Dreiser), **I:** 497, 501, 509–511, 519; **Retro. Supp. II:** 94–95, 102–103, 104, 105

Genocide of the Mind: New Native America Writing (Moore, ed.), **Supp. XXVI:** 113

Genova, Lisa, **Supp. XXIII:** 127

"Genteel Tradition in American Philosophy, The" (Santayana), **I:** 222

"Gentle Communion" (Mora), **Supp. XIII:** 218–219

Gentle Crafter, The (O. Henry), **Supp. II Part 1:** 410

Gentle Furniture-Shop, The (Bodenheim), **Supp. XXV:** 20

"Gentle Lena, The" (Stein), **IV:** 37, 40

Gentleman Caller, The (T. Williams), **IV:** 383

"Gentleman from Cracow, The" (Singer), **IV:** 9

"Gentleman of Bayou Têche, A" (Chopin), **Supp. I Part 1:** 211–212

"Gentleman of Shalott, The" (Bishop), **Supp. I Part 1:** 85, 86

Gentleman's Agreement (Hobson), **III:** 151

"Gentleman's Agreement" (Richard), **Supp. XIX:** 220–221

Gentlemen I Address You Privately (Boyle), **Supp. XXIV:** 53–54

Gentlemen Prefer Blondes (Loos; musical adaptation), **Supp. XVI:** 193

Gentlemen Prefer Blondes: The Illuminating Diary of a Professional Lady

(Loos), **Supp. XVI:** 181, 183, 186, **188–189**

Gentlemen Prefer "Books" (J. Yeats), Supp. XVI: 190

Gentle People, The: A Brooklyn Fable (Shaw), **Supp. XIX:** 244–245, 249

Gentry, Marshall Bruce, **Supp. IV Part 1:** 236

"Genuine Man, The" (Emerson), **II:** 10

"Genus Narcissus" (Trethewey), **Supp. XXI:** 256

Geo-Bestiary (Harrison), **Supp. VIII:** 53

"Geode" (Frost), **II:** 161

Geographical History of America, The (Stein), **IV:** 31, 45; **Supp. XVIII:** 148

Geography and Plays (Stein), **IV:** 29–30, 32, 43, 44

Geography III (Bishop), **Retro. Supp. II:** 50; **Supp. I Part 1:** 72, 73, 76, 82, 93, 94, 95

Geography of a Horse Dreamer (Shepard), **Supp. III Part 2:** 432

Geography of Home, The: California's Poetry of Place (Bluckey and Young, eds.), **Supp. XIII:** 313

Geography of Lograire, The (Merton), **Supp. VIII:** 208

Geography of the Heart (F. Johnson), **Supp. XI:** 129

"Geometric Poem, The" (Corso), **Supp. XII:** 132, 133–134

George, Diana Hume, **Supp. IV Part 2:** 447, 449, 450

George, Henry, **II:** 276; **Supp. I Part 2:** 518

George, Jan, **Supp. IV Part 1:** 268

George, Lynell, **Supp. XIII:** 234–235, 237, 249

George, Peter, **Supp. XI:** 302, 303, 304

George and the Dragon (Shanley), **Supp. XIV:** 315

George Bernard Shaw: His Plays (Mencken), **III:** 102

George Mills (Elkin), **Supp. VI: 53–54**

George Oppen and the Fate of Modernism (Nicholls), **Supp. XXVI:** 228

George Palmer Putnam: Representative American Publisher (Greenspan), **Supp. XVIII:** 257

"George Robinson: Blues" (Rukeyser), **Supp. VI:** 279

George's Mother (Crane), **I:** 408

"George Thurston" (Bierce), **I:** 202

George Washington Crossing the Delaware (Koch), **Supp. XV:** 186

"George Washington"(Kenny), **Supp. XXIII:** 154

Georgia Boy (Caldwell), **I:** 288, 305–306, 308, 309, 310

"Georgia Dusk" (Toomer), **Supp. IX:** 309

"Georgia: Invisible Empire State" (Du Bois), **Supp. II Part 1:** 179

"Georgia Night" (Toomer), **Supp. III Part 2:** 481

Georgia Scenes (Longstreet), **II:** 70, 313; **Supp. I Part 1:** 352

Georgics (Virgil), **Retro. Supp. I:** 135; **Supp. XVI:** 22; **Supp. XXIV:** 153

Georgics of Virgil, The (Ferry. trans.), **Supp. XXIV: 158–160**

Georgie May (Bodenheim), **Supp. XXV:** 25

Georgoudaki, Ekaterini, **Supp. IV Part 1:** 12

Gerald McBoing-Boing (film), **Supp. XVI:** 102

"Geraldo No Last Name" (Cisneros), **Supp. VII:** 60–61

Gerald's Game (King), **Supp. V:** 141, 148–150, 151, 152

Gerald's Party (Coover), **Supp. V:** 49–50, 51, 52

Gérando, Joseph Marie de, **II:** 10

"Geranium" (O'Connor), **Retro. Supp. II:** 221, 236

Gerard, Jeremy, **Supp. XXI:** 147

Gerber, Dan, **Supp. VIII:** 39

Gerber, Lisa, **Supp. XXVI:** 187

Gerhardt, Rainer, **Supp. IV Part 1:** 142

"German Girls! The German Girls!, The" (MacLeish), **III:** 16

"German Refugee, The" (Malamud), **Supp. I Part 2:** 436, 437

"Germany's Reichswehr" (Agee), **I:** 35

Germinal (Zola), **III:** 318, 322

Gernsback, Hugo, **Supp. IV Part 1:** 101

"Gernsback Continuum, The" (W. Gibson), **Supp. XVI:** 123, 128

"Gerontion" (Eliot), **I:** 569, 574, 577, 578, 585, 588; **III:** 9, 435, 436; **Retro. Supp. I:** 290; **Supp. XV:** 341; **Supp. XVI:** 158–159

Gerry, Elbridge, **Supp. I Part 2:** 486

"Gerry's Jazz" (Komunyakaa), **Supp. XIII:** 125

Gershwin, Ira, **Supp. I Part 1:** 281

"Gert" (Monette), **Supp. X:** 158

"Gertrude Atherton and the New Woman" (Forrey), **Supp. XXIV:** 30

Gertrude of Stony Island Avenue (Purdy), **Supp. VII:** 281–282

Gertrude Stein (Sprigge), **IV:** 31

Gertrude Stein: A Biography of Her Work (Sutherland), **IV:** 38

"Gertrude Stein and the Geography of the Sentence" (Gass), **Supp. VI:** 87

Gesell, Silvio, **III:** 473

"Gestalt at Sixty" (Sarton), **Supp. VIII:** 260

"Gesture of a Woman-in-Process" (Trethewey), **Supp. XXI:** 249–250

"Gesture toward an Unfound Renaissance, A" (Stafford), **Supp. XI:** 323

"Get It Again" (Halliday), **Supp. XIX:** 85

Getlin, Josh, **Supp. V:** 22; **Supp. VIII:** 75, 76, 78, 79

"Getting Along" (Larcom), **Supp. XIII:** 144

"Getting Along with Nature" (Berry), **Supp. X:** 31–32

"Getting Away from Already Pretty Much Being Away from It All" (Wallace), **Supp. X:** 314–315

"Getting Born" (Shields), **Supp. VII:** 311

Getting Even (Allen), **Supp. XV:** 3, 14, 15

"Getting Lucky" (L. Michaels), **Supp. XVI:** 205, 209

"Getting Out of Jail on Monday" (Wagoner), **Supp. IX:** 327

"Getting Over Arnette"(P. Benedict), **Supp. XXIII:** 39

"Getting over Robert Frost" (Davison), **Supp. XXVI:** 79

"Getting There" (Plath), **Supp. I Part 2:** 539, 542

"Getting to the Poem" (Corso), **Supp. XII:** 135

Getty, J. Paul, **Supp. X:** 108

Getty, Norris, **Supp. XV:** 136–137, 138, 139, 142, 143, 145, 146

Gettysburg, Manila, Acoma (Masters), **Supp. I Part 2:** 471

"Gettysburg: July 1, 1863" (Kenyon), **Supp. VII:** 172

Gevers, Nick, **Supp. XXII:** 59

Geyer, Bernadette, **Supp. XXIII:** 251

Ghachem, Malick, **Supp. X:** 17

Ghazálí, al-, **Supp. XX: 117**

"Ghazals: Homage to Ghalib" (Rich), **Supp. I Part 2:** 557

Ghost, The (Crane), **I:** 409, 421

"Ghost, The" (Peacock), **Supp. XIX:** 199

"Ghost Cat" (Peacock), **Supp. XIX:** 206

"Ghost Chant, et alii" (Komunyakaa), **Supp. XIII:** 114

Ghost Country (Paretsky), **Supp. XXV:** 183

Ghost in the Music, A (Nichols), **Supp. XIII:** 267

"Ghost Jam"(Hadas), **Supp. XXIII:** 119

"Ghostlier Demarcations, Keener Sounds" (Vendler), **Supp. I Part 2:** 565

"Ghostly Father, I Confess" (McCarthy), **II:** 565–566

Ghostly Lover, The (Hardwick), **Supp. III Part 1:** 194–196, 208, 209

Ghost Money (Hull), **Supp. XXI:** 129, **132–135,** 136

Ghost of Meter, The (A. Finch), **Supp. XVII:** 71, 73

"Ghost of the Buffaloes, The" (Lindsay), **Supp. I Part 2:** 393

Ghost of Tradition, The (Walzer), **Supp. XVIII:** 174

Ghosts (Auster), **Supp. XII:** 22, **24, 26–27**

Ghosts (Ibsen), **III:** 152

Ghosts (Wharton), **IV:** 316, 327

Ghosts of Tsavo: Stalking the Mystery Lions of East Africa (Caputo), **Supp. XIX:** 28

Ghost Town (Coover), **Supp. V:** 52–53

Ghost Trio, The (Bierds), **Supp. XVII:** 29, **30**

Ghost Writer, The (P. Roth), **Retro. Supp. II:** 22, 290, 291; **Supp. III Part 2:** 420–421; **Supp. XVII:** 43

Giachetti, Fosco, **Supp. IV Part 2:** 520

"Giacometti" (Wilbur), **Supp. III Part 2:** 551

Giacometti, Alberto, **Supp. VIII:** 168, 169

Giacomo, Padre, **II:** 278–279

Giant's House, The: A Romance (McCracken), **Supp. X:** 86

"Giant Snail" (Bishop), **Retro. Supp. II:** 49

Giant Weapon, The (Winters), **Supp. II Part 2:** 810

"Giant Woman, The" (Oates), **Supp. II Part 2:** 523

Gibbon, Edward, **I:** 4, 378; **IV:** 126; **Supp. I Part 2:** 503; **Supp. III Part 2:** 629; **Supp. XIII:** 75; **Supp. XIV:** 97

Gibbons, James, **Supp. XVII:** 228

Gibbons, Kaye, **Supp. X: 41–54; Supp. XII:** 311

Gibbons, Reginald, **Supp. X:** 113, 124, 127; **Supp. XIX:** 40, 41–42, 281; **Supp. XV:** 105

Gibbons, Richard, **Supp. I Part 1:** 107

"Gibbs" (Rukeyser), **Supp. VI:** 273

Gibbs, Barbara, **Supp. IV Part 2:** 644

Gibbs, Wolcott, **Supp. I Part 2:** 604, 618; **Supp. VIII:** 151

Gibran, Kahlil, **Supp. XX: 69, 113–129**

"GIBSON" (Baraka), **Supp. II Part 1:** 54

Gibson, Charles Dana, **Supp. X:** 184

Gibson, Graeme, **Supp. XIII:** 20

Gibson, John Arthur, **Supp. XXVI:** 83, 84, 87, 89

Gibson, Simeon, **Supp. XXVI:** 96

Gibson, Wilfrid W., **Retro. Supp. I:** 128

Gibson, William, **Supp. XVI: 117–133; Supp. XXII:** 49

Giddins, Gary, **Supp. XIII:** 245

Gide, André, **I:** 271, 290; **II:** 581; **III:** 210; **IV:** 53, 289; **Supp. I Part 1:** 51; **Supp. IV Part 1:** 80, 284, 347; **Supp. IV Part 2:** 681, 682; **Supp. VIII:** 40; **Supp. X:** 187; **Supp. XIV:** 24, 348; **Supp. XVII:** 242

Gideon Planish (Lewis), **II:** 455

Gielgud, John, **I:** 82; **Supp. XI:** 305

Gierow, Dr. Karl Ragnar, **III:** 404

Gifford, Barry, **Supp. XXV:** 29

Gifford, Bill, **Supp. XI:** 38

Gifford, Terry, **Supp. XVI:** 22

"Gift, The" (Creeley), **Supp. IV Part 1:** 153

"Gift, The" (Doolittle), **Supp. I Part 1:** 267

Gift, The (Hyde), **Supp. XVIII:** 150

"Gift, The" (Jarman), **Supp. XVII:** 116

"Gift, The" (L.-Y. Lee), **Supp. XV:** 213, 214

Gift, The (Nabokov), **III:** 246, 255, 261–263; **Retro. Supp. I:** 264, 266, **268–270,** 273, 274–275, 278

"Gift from the City, A" (Updike), **Retro. Supp. I:** 320

"Gift of God, The" (Robinson), **III:** 512, 517, 518–521, 524

Gift of the Black Folk, The: The Negroes in the Making of America (Du Bois), **Supp. II Part 1:** 179

"Gift of the Magi, The" (O. Henry), **Supp. II Part 1:** 394, 406, 408

"Gift of the *Osuo,* The" (C. Johnson), **Supp. VI:** 194

"Gift of the Prodigal, The" (Taylor), **Supp. V:** 314, 326

"Gift Outright, The" (Frost), **II:** 152; **Supp. IV Part 1:** 15

"Gifts" (Davison), **Supp. XXVI:** 71

"Gifts of Our Fathers, The" (Gansworth), **Supp. XXVI:** 110

Gigi (Colette; stage adaptation, Loos), **Supp. XVI:** 193

"Gigolo" (Plath), **Retro. Supp. II:** 257

"G.I. Graves in Tuscany" (Hugo), **Supp. VI:** 138

"Gila Bend" (Dickey), **Supp. IV Part 1:** 185–186

Gilb, Dagoberto, **Supp. XXV:** 138

Gilbert, Elizabeth, **Supp. XXII:** 83, 90

Gilbert, Jack, **Supp. IX:** 287

Gilbert, Peter, **Supp. IX:** 291, 300

Gilbert, Roger, **Supp. XI:** 124

Gilbert, Sandra M., **Retro. Supp. I:** 42; **Retro. Supp. II:** 324; **Supp. IX:** 66; **Supp. XV:** 270; **Supp. XXIV:** 28

Gilbert, Susan. *See* Dickinson, Mrs. William A.

Gilbert and Sullivan, **Supp. IV Part 1:** 389

"Gilbert Stuart Portrait of Washington, The" (Kooser), **Supp. XIX:** 124

Gil Blas (Le Sage), **II:** 290

Gilded Age, The (Twain), **III:** 504; **IV:** 198

Gilded Lapse of Time, A (Schnackenberg), **Supp. XV:** 258, **260–263**

"Gilded Lapse of Time, A" (Schnackenberg), **Supp. XV:** 257

"Gilded Six-Bits, The" (Hurston), **Supp. VI:** 154–155

Gilder, R. W., **Retro. Supp. II:** 66; **Supp. I Part 2:** 418

Gildersleeve, Basil, **Supp. I Part 1:** 369

Gildner, Gary, **Supp. XXVI:** 4

Gilead (Robinson), **Supp. XXI:** 212, **216–220,** 223

Giles, H. A., **Retro. Supp. I:** 289

Giles, James R., **Supp. IX:** 11, 15; **Supp. XI:** 219, 223–224, 228, 234

"Giles Corey of the Salem Farms" (Longfellow), **II:** 505, 506; **Retro. Supp. II:** 166, 167

Giles Goat-Boy (Barth), **I:** 121, 122–123, 129, 130, 134, 135–138; **Supp. V:** 39

Gilgamesh: A New Rendering in English Verse (Ferry), **Supp. XXIV:** 147, **150–151**

Gill, Brendan, **Supp. I Part 2:** 659, 660

Gillespie, Nick, **Supp. XIV:** 298, 311

Gillette, Chester, **I:** 512

Gillian, Maria Mazziotti, **Supp. XXIII:** 248

Gilligan, Carol, **Supp. XIII:** 216; **Supp. XXII:** 18

Gillis, Jim, **IV:** 196

Gillis, Steve, **IV:** 195

Gilman, Charlotte Perkins, **Supp. I Part 2:** 637; **Supp. V:** 121, 284, 285; **Supp. XI: 193–211; Supp. XIII:** 295, 306; **Supp. XVI:** 84; **Supp. XXIII:** 26

Gilman, Daniel Coit, **Supp. I Part 1:** 361, 368, 370

Gilman, Owen W., Jr., **Supp. XXVI:** 148

Gilman, Richard, **IV:** 115; **Supp. IV Part 2:** 577; **Supp. XIII:** 100; **Supp. XIX:** 251

Gilmore, Eddy, **Supp. I Part 2:** 618

Gilmore, Leigh, **Supp. XXVI:** 53

Gilmore, Lyman, **Supp. XXI:** 20, 22, 24

Gilmore, Mikal, **Supp. XVI:** 123, 124

Gilpin, Charles, **III:** 392

Gilpin, Dewitt, **Supp. XV:** 197

Gilpin, Laura, **Retro. Supp. I:** 7

Gilpin, Sam, **Supp. V:** 213

Gilpin, William, **Supp. IV Part 2:** 603

"Gil's Furniture Bought & Sold" (Cisneros), **Supp. VII:** 61–62, 64

Gilt Edged Guilt (Wells), **Supp. XXVI:** 281

Gilyard, Keith, **Supp. XXI:** 246

"Gimcrackery" articles (Briggs), **Supp. XVIII:** 8–9

"Gimpel the Fool" (Singer), **IV:** 14; **Retro. Supp. II:** 22, 307

Gimpel the Fool and Other Stories (Singer), **IV:** 1, 7–9, 10, 12

"Gin" (Levine), **Supp. V:** 193

"Gingerbread House, The" (Coover), **Supp. V:** 42–43

Gingerbread Lady, The (Simon), **Supp. IV Part 2:** 580, 583–584, 588

Gingerich, Willard, **Supp. IV Part 2:** 510

Gingertown (McKay), **Supp. X:** 132, 139

Gingold, Hermione, **Supp. XV:** 13

Gingrich, Arnold, **Retro. Supp. I:** 113; **Supp. XVII:** 88; **Supp. XX: 34**

Ginna, Robert, **Supp. IX:** 259

Ginsberg, Allen, **I:** 183; **Retro. Supp. I:** 411, 426, 427; **Retro. Supp. II:** 280; **Supp. II Part 1:** 30, 32, 58, **307–333; Supp. III Part 1:** 2, 91, 96, 98, 100, 222, 226; **Supp. III Part 2:** 541, 627; **Supp. IV Part 1:** 79, 90, 322; **Supp. IV Part 2:** 502; **Supp. IX:** 299; **Supp. V:** 168, 336; **Supp. VIII:** 239, 242–243, 289; **Supp. X:** 120, 204; **Supp. XI:** 135, 297; **Supp. XII:** 118–119, 121–122, 124, 126, 130–131, 136, 182; **Supp. XIV:** 15, 53, 54, 125, 137, 141, 142, 143–144, 148, 150, 269, 280, 283; **Supp. XV:** 134, 177, 263; **Supp. XVI:** 123, 135; **Supp. XVII:** 138, 243; **Supp. XVIII:** 20, 27, 29, 30; **Supp. XXI:** 53; **Supp. XXII:** 172, 225; **Supp. XXIII:** 211, 213, 215; **Supp. XXIV:** 34, 36, 37; **Supp. XXV:** 29; **Supp. XXVI:** 70

Gioia, Dana, **Supp. IX:** 279; **Supp. XII:** 209; **Supp. XIII:** 337; **Supp. XIX:** 117, 144; **Supp. XV: 111–131,** 251; **Supp. XVII:** 69, 72, 112; **Supp. XXI:** 99; **Supp. XXIII:** 112; **Supp. XXV:** 222

Giono, Jean, **Supp. XVI:** 135

Giordano, Tony J., **Supp. XXIII:** 125

Giotto di Bondone, **Supp. I Part 2:** 438; **Supp. XI:** 126

Giovani, Regula, **Supp. XV:** 270

Giovanni, Nikki, **Supp. I Part 1:** 66; **Supp. II Part 1:** 54; **Supp. IV Part 1:** 11; **Supp. VIII:** 214; **Supp. XXII:** 11

Giovanni's Room (Baldwin), **Retro. Supp. II:** 5, 6, **6–7,** 8, 10; **Supp. I Part 1:** 51, 52, 55–56, 57, 60, 63, 67; **Supp. III Part 1:** 125

Giovannitti, Arturo, **I:** 476; **Supp. XV:** 299, 301, 302, 307

"Giraffe" (Swenson), **Supp. IV Part 2:** 651

Giraldi, Giovanni Battista. *See* Cinthio

"Girl" (Kincaid), **Supp. VII:** 182–183

Girl, The (Le Sueur), **Supp. XXIII: 172–174**

"Girl, The" (Olds), **Supp. X:** 207

"Girl Friend Poems" (Wright), **Supp. XV:** 349

"Girl from Lynn Bathes Horse!!" (McCarriston), **Supp. XIV:** 266

"Girl from Red Lion, P.A., A" (Mencken), **III:** 111

Girl in Glass, The: Love Poems (W. J. Smith), **Supp. XIII:** 335

Girl in Landscape (Lethem), **Supp. XVIII: 136, 141–143**

"Girl in the Grave, The" (McCoy), **Supp. XIII:** 170

Girl Like I, A (Loos), **Supp. XVI:** 181, 183, 184, 187, 194, 196

"Girl of the Golden West" (Didion), **Supp. IV Part 1:** 195, 208, 211

Girl of the Golden West, The (Puccini), **III:** 139

Girl of the Limberlost (film), **Supp. XX: 223**

Girl of the Limberlost (Stratton-Porter), **Supp. XX: 211, 221–222**

"Girl on a Scaffold" (C. Frost), **Supp. XV:** 98

"Girl on the Baggage Truck, The" (O'Hara), **III:** 371–372

Girl on the Via Flaminia, The (Hayes), **Supp. XXVI:** 135, 136–137, 144

"Girls" (Gallagher), **Supp. XXIV:** 174–175, 177

Girls at Play (Theroux), **Supp. VIII:** 314, 315, 316, **317**

"Girls at the Sphinx, The" (Farrell), **II:** 45

"Girls in Their Summer Dresses, The" (Shaw), **Supp. XIX:** 246

Girl Sleuth, The: A Feminist Guide (Mason), **Supp. VIII:** 133, 135, **139,** 142

"Girl's Story, A" (Bambara), **Supp. XI:** 10–11

"Girl the Prince Liked, The" (Z. Fitzgerald), **Supp. IX:** 71

Girl Who Had to Die, The (Holding), **Supp. XXII: 126–127**

Girl Who Loved Tom Gordon, The (King), **Supp. V:** 138, 152

"Girl Who Raised Pigeons, The" (E. P. Jones), **Supp. XXII:** 143

Girl with Curious Hair (Wallace), **Supp. X: 301, 305–308**

"Girl with Curious Hair" (Wallace), **Supp. X:** 306

"Girl with Silver Eyes, The" (Hammett), **Supp. IV Part 1:** 344, 345

"Girl with Talent, The" (Z. Fitzgerald), **Supp. IX:** 71

Girodias, Maurice, **III:** 171; **Supp. XI:** 297

Giroux, Robert, **Retro. Supp. II:** 177, 229, 235; **Supp. IV Part 1:** 280; **Supp. VIII:** 195; **Supp. XV:** 146

Gish, Dorothy, **Retro. Supp. I:** 103

Gish, Lillian, **Supp. XVI:** 184

Gissing, George, **II:** 138, 144

Gitagovinda, **Supp. XXII:** 258

Gita-govínda: Love Songs of Radha and Krishna (Jayadeva; Siegel, trans.), **Supp. XXII:** 258

Gittings, Robert, **II:** 531

Gittleman, Edwin, **Supp. XXV:** 237, 251

"Given" (C. Frost), **Supp. XV:** 96

Given Sugar, Given Salt (Hirshfield), **Supp. XXIII:** 133

"Give Us Back Our Country" (Masters), **Supp. I Part 2:** 472

Give Us This Day (film, Dmytryk), **Supp. XX: 40–41**

"Give Way, Ye Gates" (Roethke), **III:** 536

"Give Your Heart to the Hawks" (Jeffers), **Supp. II Part 2:** 433

"Giving Blood" (Updike), **IV:** 226; **Retro. Supp. I:** 332

Giving Good Weight (McPhee), **Supp. III Part 1:** 307

"Giving in to You" (X. J. Kennedy), **Supp. XV:** 160

"Giving Myself Up" (Strand), **Supp. IV Part 2:** 627

Giving Up America (Abraham), **Supp. XXIV:** 2, 3, **7–9**

Giving Up the Ghost (Moraga), **Supp. XXIII: 197–199**

G. K. the DJ (Keillor), **Supp. XVI:** 171

Glackens, William, **Retro. Supp. II:** 103

Gladden, Washington, **III:** 293; **Supp. I Part 1:** 5

Gladstone, William Ewart, **Supp. I Part 2:** 419

"Gladys Poem, The" (Alvarez), **Supp. VII:** 10

"Glance at German 'Kultur,' A" (Bourne), **I:** 228

Glance Away, A (Wideman), **Supp. X:** 320

"Glance from the Bridge, A" (Wilbur), **Supp. III Part 2:** 551

"Glance in the Mirror, A" (Swados), **Supp. XIX:** 261–262

Glance toward Shakespeare, A (Chapman), **Supp. XIV:** 44

Glancy, Diane, **Supp. XXI:** 246

Glanville-Hicks, Peggy, **Supp. IV Part 1:** 84

Glare (Ammons), **Supp. VII:** 35–36

Glasgow, Cary, **II:** 173, 182

Glasgow, Ellen, **II:** 173–195; **IV:** 328; **Supp. X:** 228, 234; **Supp. XXIV:** 30; **Supp. XXV:** 201; **Supp. XXVI:** 276

Glasmon, Kubec, **Supp. XIII:** 166

Glaspell, Susan, **Supp. III Part 1:** 175–191; **Supp. X:** 46; **Supp. XVII:** 99; **Supp. XXI:** 5

"Glass" (Francis), **Supp. IX:** 80

Glass, Irony, and God (Carson), **Supp. XII:** 97, **104–106**

Glass, Philip, **Supp. XXI:** 146, 147

"Glass Ark, The" (Komunyakaa), **Supp. XIII:** 129

Glass Bees, The (Jünger; Bogan and Mayer, trans.), **Supp. III Part 1:** 63

"Glass Blower of Venice" (Malamud), **Supp. I Part 2:** 450

"Glass Essay, The" (Carson), **Supp. XII: 104–105**

Glass Face in the Rain, A: New Poems (Stafford), **Supp. XI: 327–328**

Glass Key, The (Hammett), **Supp. IV Part 1:** 351–353

"Glass Meadows" (Bausch), **Supp. VII:** 53–54

Glass Menagerie, The (T. Williams), **I:** 81; **IV:** 378, 379, 380, 382, 383, 385, 386, 387, 388, 389, 390, 391, 392, 393–394, 395, 398; **Supp. IV Part 1:** 84; **Supp. XXV:** 101

"Glass Mountain, The" (Barthelme), **Supp. IV Part 1:** 47

"Glass Tent, The" (Everwine), **Supp. XV:** 76

Glatstein, Jacob, **Supp. X:** 70

Glazer, Nathan, **Supp. VIII:** 93, 243

"Gleaners, The" (Merwin), **Supp. III Part 1:** 346

Gleanings in Europe (Cooper), **I:** 346

Gleason, Ralph J., **Supp. IX:** 16

Glenday, Michael, **Retro. Supp. II:** 210

Glengarry Glen Ross (film), **Supp. XIV:** 242

Glengarry Glen Ross (Mamet), **Supp. XIV:** 239, 240, 242, 245, 246, 250, 254, 255

Glimcher, Arne, **Supp. VIII:** 73

"Glimpses" (Jones), **Supp. XI:** 218

Glimpses of the Moon, The (Wharton), **II:** 189–190; **IV:** 322–323; **Retro. Supp. I:** 381

"Glimpses of Vietnamese Life" (Levertov), **Supp. III Part 1:** 282

Glisson, J. T., **Supp. X:** 234

"Glittering Trout" (Davison), **Supp. XXVI:** 79

Gloria Mundi (Frederic), **II:** 144–145

Gloria Naylor (Fowler), **Supp. VIII:** 224

"Glorious Fourth, The" (Ryan as Quin), **Supp. XVIII:** 229

Glorious Ones, The (Prose), **Supp. XVI:** 251

Glory, The (Wouk), **Supp. XXV:** 254, 257, 265–266

Glory of Hera, The (Gordon), **II:** 196–197, 198, 199, 217–220

Glory of the Conquered, The (Glaspell), **Supp. III Part 1:** 176

Glory River (Huddle), **Supp. XXVI:** 151

Gloss, Molly, **Supp. XXIII:** 280

Glossary of Literary Terms (Abrams), **Supp. XVI:** 19

Glotfelty, Cheryll, **Supp. IX:** 25

Glover, Joyce Lee, **Supp. XIX:** 112

Glover, Michael, **Supp. XXIV:** 168

Glow, The (Wrigley), **Supp. XVIII:** 295

"Glow, The" (Wrigley), **Supp. XVIII:** 296–297, 307

Gluck, Christoph Willibald, **II:** 210, 211

Glück, Louise, **Supp. V: 77–94; Supp. VIII:** 272; **Supp. X:** 209; **Supp. XIV:** 269; **Supp. XV:** 19, 252; **Supp. XVII:** 241; **Supp. XXV:** 222

"Glutton, The" (Shapiro), **Supp. II Part 2:** 705

"Glutton for Punishment, A" (Yates), **Supp. XI:** 341

Glyph (Everett), **Supp. XVIII: 60–61**

Gnädiges Fräulein, The (T. Williams), **IV:** 382, 395, 398

Gnomes and Occasions (Nemerov), **III:** 269

Gnomologia (Fuller), **II:** 111

"Gnothis Seauton" (Emerson), **II:** 11, 18–19

Go (Holmes), **Supp. XIV:** 144

"Go Ahead; Goodbye; Good Luck; and Watch Out" (Bronk), **Supp. XXI:** 31

"Goal of Intellectual Men, The" (Eberhart), **I:** 529–530

Go-Between, The (Hartley), **Supp. I Part 1:** 293

Gobineau, Joseph Arthur de, **Supp. XIV:** 209

God (Allen), **Supp. XV:** 3

God and the American Writer (Kazin), **Supp. VIII: 108–109**

Godard, Jean-Luc, **Supp. I Part 2:** 558

Godbey (Masters), **Supp. I Part 2:** 472

God Bless You, Mr. Rosewater (Vonnegut), **Supp. II Part 2:** 758, 767, 768–769, 771, 772

Goddess Abides, The (Buck), **Supp. II Part 1:** 129, 131–132

Gödel, Kurt, **Supp. IV Part 1:** 43

Godfather (Puzo), **Supp. IV Part 1:** 390

Godfires (Hoffman), **Supp. XVIII: 81–82**

God in Ruins, A (Uris), **Supp. XX: 247, 256**

"God in the Doorway" (Dillard), **Supp. VI:** 28

"God is a distant-stately Lover" (Dickinson), **I:** 471

Godkin, E. L., **II:** 274

God Knows (Heller), **Supp. IV Part 1:** 386, 388–389

God Made Alaska for the Indians (Reed), **Supp. X:** 241

God of His Fathers, The (London), **II:** 469

God of Vengeance, The (Asch), **IV:** 11; **Supp. XXIII: 5, 8–9**

Go Down, Moses (Faulkner), **Retro. Supp. I:** 75, 82, 85, 86, 88, 89, 90, 92; **Supp. XVIII:** 203

"Go Down, Moses" (Faulkner), **II:** 71–72

Go Down, Moses (Hayden), **Supp. II Part 1:** 365

Go Down, Moses and Other Stories (Faulkner), **II:** 71; **Supp. X:** 52

"Go Down Death A Funeral Sermon" (J. W. Johnson), **Supp. IV Part 1:** 7

"God Rest Ye Merry, Gentlemen" (Hemingway), **IV:** 122

Godric (Buechner), **Supp. XII:** 53

Gods, The (Goldbarth), **Supp. XII:** 189, 190

Gods Arrive, The (Wharton), **IV:** 326–327; **Retro. Supp. I:** 382

God Save the Child (Parker), **Supp. XIX:** 183–184

"God Save the Rights of Man" (Freneau), **Supp. II Part 1:** 268

"Gods|Children" (Swenson), **Supp. IV Part 2:** 645

"God's Christ Theory" (Carson), **Supp. XII: 106**

God's Country (Everett), **Supp. XVIII: 57–58,** 64, 65

God's Country and My People (Morris), **III:** 238

Gods Determinations touching his Elect: and the Elects Combat in their Conversion, and Coming up to God in Christ together with the Comfortable Effects thereof (Taylor), **IV:** 155–160, 165

God-Seeker, The (Lewis), **II:** 456

God Sends Sunday (Bontemps), **Supp. XXII:** 2, 3, 9

God's Favorite (Simon), **Supp. IV Part 2:** 575, 586, 588, 590

"God's Fool" (Gibran), **Supp. XX: 118**

God's Little Acre (Caldwell), **I:** 288, 289, 290, 297, 298–302, 305–306, 309, 310; **Supp. XXII:** 196

God's Man: A Novel in Wood Cuts (Ward), **I:** 31

Gods of Peg¿na, The (Dunsany), **Supp. XXV:** 113

Gods of Winter, The (Gioia), **Supp. XV:** 112, **121–125**

"Gods of Winter, The" (Gioia), **Supp. XV:** 117

"God's Peace in November" (Jeffers), **Supp. II Part 2:** 420

God's Silence (F. Wright), **Supp. XVII:** 240, 246–247

"God Stiff" (Carson), **Supp. XII: 106**

God's Trombones (J. W. Johnson), **Supp. II Part 1:** 201

"God's Youth" (Untermeyer), **Supp. XV:** 296

"God the Father and the Empty House" (McCarriston), **Supp. XIV:** 273

Godwin, William, **II:** 304; **III:** 415; **Supp. I Part 1:** 126, 146; **Supp. I Part 2:** 512, 513–514, 522, 709, 719

God without Thunder (Ransom), **III:** 495–496, 499

Godwulf Manuscript, The (Parker), **Supp. XIX: 178–182**

Goebbels, Josef, **III:** 560

Goebel, Irma, **Supp. X:** 95

Goen, C. C., **I:** 560

Goethe, Johann Wolfgang von, **I:** 181, 396, 587–588; **II:** 5, 6, 320, 344, 488, 489, 492, 502, 556; **III:** 395, 453, 607, 612, 616; **IV:** 50, 64, 173, 326; **Retro. Supp. I:** 360; **Retro. Supp. II:** 94; **Supp. I Part 2:** 423, 457; **Supp. II Part 1:** 26; **Supp. III Part 1:** 63; **Supp. IX:** 131, 308; **Supp. X:** 60; **Supp. XI:** 169; **Supp. XVIII:** 278; **Supp. XX: 84; Supp. XXIV:** 152

Go for the Body (Lacy), **Supp. XV:** 201, 204

Gogan, Robert, **Supp. XXI:** 24

Gogol, Nikolai, **I:** 296; **IV:** 1, 4; **Retro. Supp. I:** 266, 269; **Supp. VIII:** 14; **Supp. XVII:** 45; **Supp. XVIII:** 102; **Supp. XXII:** 59

Goia, Dana, **Supp. XIX:** 121

Goines, Donald, **Supp. XXIII:** 174

"Going, Going, Gone" (Skloot), **Supp. XX: 207**

Going, William T., **Supp. VIII:** 126

"Going 1960–1970" (Huddle), **Supp. XXVI:** 148

Going After Cacciato (O'Brien), **Supp. V:** 237, 238, 239, 244–246, 248, 249

Going All the Way (Wakefield), **Supp. VIII:** 43

Going Away (Sigal), **Supp. XXVI:** 26

"Going Critical" (Bambara), **Supp. XI:** 14

Going Down (Markson), **Supp. XVII:** 136, 138, **139–140,** 141, 142–143, 144, 145

Going for the Rain (Ortiz), **Supp. IV Part 2:** 499, 505–508, 509, 514

"Going Home by Last Night" (Kinnell), **Supp. III Part 1:** 244

"Going Home in America" (Hardwick), **Supp. III Part 1:** 205

"Going Home"(Kenny), **Supp. XXIII:** 144, 148

"Going North" (Salinas), **Supp. XIII:** 316

Going Places (L. Michaels), **Supp. XVI:** 201, **203–206**

"Going Places" (L. Michaels), **Supp. XVI:** 203

"Going South" (J. W. Miller), **Supp. XX: 169**

Going South (Lardner and Buck), **II:** 427

Going To and Fro and Walking Up and Down (Reznikoff), **Supp. XIV:** 280, 282, 284, 285

Going to Meet the Man (Baldwin), **Supp. I Part 1:** 60, 62–63; **Supp. XX: 147**

"Going to Meet the Man" (Baldwin), **Retro. Supp. II:** 8, 9; **Supp. I Part 1:** 62–63

"Going to Naples" (Welty), **IV:** 278; **Retro. Supp. I:** 352, 353

"Going to Shrewsbury" (Jewett), **II:** 393

"Going to the Bakery" (Bishop), **Supp. I Part 1:** 93

Going-to-the-Stars (Lindsay), **Supp. I Part 2:** 398

Going-to-the-Sun (Lindsay), **Supp. I Part 2:** 397–398

Going to the Territory (Ellison), **Retro. Supp. II:** 119, 123–124

"Going towards Pojoaque, A December Full Moon/72" (Harjo), **Supp. XII:** 218

"Going Under" (Dubus), **Supp. VII:** 83

"Gold" (Francis), **Supp. IX:** 82

Gold (O'Neill), **III:** 391

Gold, Arthur, **Supp. XXIV:** 160, 161

Gold, Charles H., **Supp. XXVI:** 6

Gold, Don, **Supp. XXII:** 258

Gold, Michael, **II:** 26; **IV:** 363, 364, 365; **Retro. Supp. II:** 323; **Supp. I Part 1:** 331; **Supp. I Part 2:** 609; **Supp. XIV:** 288; **Supp. XXII:** 277

Goldbarth, Albert, **Supp. XII: 175–195**

Goldbarth's Book of Occult Phenomena (Goldbarth), **Supp. XII:** 181

Goldberg, Carole, **Supp. XXII:** 207

Goldberg, Michael, **Supp. XXIII:** 210, 216, 217

Goldberg, S. L., **Supp. VIII:** 238

"Gold Bug, The" (Poe), **III:** 410, 413, 419, 420

Gold Bug Variations, The (Powers), **Supp. IX:** 210, 212, **216–217,** 219

Gold Cell, The (Olds), **Supp. X: 206–209**

Gold Diggers, The (Monette), **Supp. X:** 153

Golde, Miss (Mencken's Secretary), **III:** 104, 107

Golden, Harry, **III:** 579, 581; **Supp. VIII:** 244

Golden, Mike, **Supp. XI:** 294, 295, 297, 299, 303

Golden Age, The (Gurney), **Supp. V:** 101–103

Golden Apples (Rawlings), **Supp. X: 228–229,** 230, 234

Golden Apples, The (Welty), **IV:** 261, 271–274, 281, 293; **Retro. Supp. I:** 341, 342, 343, **350–351,** 352, 355

Golden Apples of the Sun, The (Bradbury), **Supp. IV Part 1:** 102, 103

Golden Book of Springfield, The (Lindsay), **Supp. I Part 2:** 376, 379, 395, 396

Golden Bough, The (Frazer), **II:** 204, 549; **III:** 6–7; **Supp. I Part 1:** 18; **Supp. IX:** 123; **Supp. X:** 124

Golden Bowl, The (James), **II:** 320, 333, 335; **Retro. Supp. I:** 215, 216, 218–219, 232, **234–235,** 374

Golden Boy (Odets), **Supp. II Part 2:** 538, 539, 540–541, 546, 551

Golden Calves, The (Auchincloss), **Supp. IV Part 1:** 35

Golden Child (Hwang), **Supp. XXI:** 147–148

Golden Day, The (Mumford), **Supp. II Part 2:** 471, 475, 477, 483, 484, 488–489, 493

Golden Fleece, The (Gurney), **Supp. V:** 97

Golden Gate (film, Madden), **Supp. XXI:** 147

Golden Gate, The (Seth), **Supp. XVII:** 117

Golden Gate Country (Atherton), **Supp. XXIV:** 27

Golden Grove, The: Selected Passages from the Sermons and Writings of Jeremy Taylor (L. P. Smith), **Supp. XIV:** 345

"Golden Heifer, The" (Wylie), **Supp. I Part 2:** 707

"Golden Honeymoon, The" (Lardner), **II:** 429–430, 431

Golden Journey, The (W. J. Smith and Bogan, comps.), **Supp. XIII:** 347

Golden Ladder series (S. and A. Warner), **Supp. XVIII:** 267

"Golden Lads" (Marquand), **III:** 56

Golden Legend, The (Longfellow), **II:** 489, 490, 495, 505, 506, 507; **Retro. Supp. II:** 159, 165, 166

Golden Mean and Other Poems, The (Tate and Wills), **IV:** 122

Golden Peacock (Atherton), **Supp. XXIV:** 26

"Golden Retrievals" (Doty), **Supp. XI:** 132

Golden Shakespeare, The: An Anthology (L. P. Smith), **Supp. XIV:** 349

Golden Slippers: An Anthology of Negro Poetry for Young Readers (Bontemps, ed.), **Supp. XXII:** 5, 11

Goldensohn, Lorrie, **Retro. Supp. II:** 51

Golden State (Bidart), **Supp. XV:** 21, **23–25**

"Golden State" (Bidart), **Supp. XV:** 23, 24, 25

Golden States (Cunningham), **Supp. XV:** 55, **56–59,** 63

Golden Treasury of Best Songs and Lyrical Poems in the English Language (Palgrave), **Retro. Supp. I:** 124

Golden Treasury of the Best Songs and Lyrical Poems in the English Language (Palgrave), **Supp. XIV:** 340

Goldenweiser, Alexander Aleksandrovich, **Supp. XXVI:** 89

Golden Whales of California and Other Rhymes in the American Language, The (Lindsay), **Supp. I Part 2:** 394–395, 396

"Goldfish Bowl, The" (Francis), **Supp. IX:** 78

Gold Fools (Sorrentino), **Supp. XXI:** 237

Goldin Boys, The (Epstein), **Supp. XIV:** 112

Golding, Arthur, **III:** 467, 468

Golding, William, **Supp. IV Part 1:** 297

Goldini, Carlo, **II:** 274

Goldkorn Tales (Epstein), **Supp. XII: 163–164**

Goldman, Albert, **Supp. XI:** 299

Goldman, Arnold, **Supp. XXI:** 13

Goldman, Emma, **III:** 176, 177; **Supp. I Part 2:** 524; **Supp. XVII:** 96, 103, 104; **Supp. XXIII:** 162

Goldman, Francisco, **Supp. XXV: 49–62**

Goldman, William, **Supp. IV Part 2:** 474

"Gold Mountain Stories" project (Kingston), **Supp. V:** 164

Gold of Chickaree, The (S. and A. Warner), **Supp. XVIII:** 267, 268, 269

Goldring, Douglas, **III:** 458

Goldsmith, Oliver, **II:** 273, 282, 299, 304, 308, 314, 315, 514; **Retro. Supp. I:** 335; **Supp. I Part 1:** 310; **Supp. I Part 2:** 503, 714, 716; **Supp. XVIII:** 12

Gold Standard and the Logic of Naturalism, The (W. B. Michaels), **Retro. Supp. I:** 369

Goldstein, Laurence, **Supp. XXI:** 134

Goldstein, Rebecca, **Supp. XVII:** 44

Goldthwaite, Melissa, **Supp. XXVI:** 56

Goldwater, Barry, **I:** 376; **III:** 38

Goldwyn, Samuel, **Retro. Supp. II:** 199; **Supp. I Part 1:** 281; **Supp. XXIV:** 28; **Supp. XXV:** 195

Golem, The (Leivick), **IV:** 6; **Supp. XXIII:** 8

"Golgotha Is a Mountain" (Bontemps), **Supp. XXII:** 3, 8

"Goliardic Song" (Hecht), **Supp. X:** 63

"Go Like This" (Moore), **Supp. X:** 165

Goll, Ivan, **Supp. III Part 1:** 235, 243–244; **Supp. III Part 2:** 621

Gomes, Albert, **Supp. XXI:** 160

Goncharova, Natalya, **Supp. IX:** 66

Goncourt, Edmond de, **II:** 325, 328; **III:** 315, 317–318, 321; **Retro. Supp. I:** 226

Goncourt, Jules de, **II:** 328; **III:** 315, 317–318, 321

Gone Fishin' (Mosley), **Supp. XIII:** 235–236, 240

"Gone to Feed the Roses" (Vaz), **Supp. XXVI:** 268

"Gone to War" (E. Stoddard), **Supp. XV:** 282

"Gone West" (Rodriguez), **Supp. XIV:** 308

Gone with the Wind (film), **Retro. Supp. I:** 113

Gone with the Wind (Mitchell), **II:** 177; **Retro. Supp. I:** 340; **Supp. XX: 243; Supp. XXII:** 190, 195

Gongora y Argote, Luis de, **II:** 552

Gonzalez, David, **Supp. VIII:** 85

González, Jovita, **Supp. XIX:** 99

Gonzo: The Life of Hunter S. Thompson (Wenner and Seymour), **Supp. XXIV:** 280, 281, 282, 288

Gooch, Brad, **Supp. XII:** 121; **Supp. XXIII:** 218, 220

Good, George, **Supp. XI:** 306

"Good, the Plaid, and the Ugly, The" (Wasserstein), **Supp. XV:** 327

"Good and Not So Good, The" (Dunn), **Supp. XI:** 141

"Good Anna, The" (Stein), **IV:** 37, 40, 43

Good As Gold (Heller), **Supp. IV Part 1:** 386, 388, 394

Good as I Been to You (album, Dylan), **Supp. XVIII:** 28

"Good As Yesterday" (Muñoz), **Supp. XXV:** 134, 135

Good Boys and Dead Girls and Other Essays (Gordon), **Supp. IV Part 1:** 309–310

"Good Brother" (Muñoz), **Supp. XXV:** 135

Good Brother, The (Offutt), **Supp. XIX:** 163, **168–169**

"Good-by and Keep Cold" (Frost), **Retro. Supp. I:** 135

"Goodbye" (Davison), **Supp. XXVI:** 69

"Good-bye" (Emerson), **II:** 19

"Goodbye, Christ" (Hughes), **Retro. Supp. I:** 202, 203

Goodbye, Columbus (P. Roth), **Retro. Supp. II:** 280, 281, 290; **Supp. III Part 2:** 403–406; **Supp. XIV:** 112; **Supp. XX: 177; Supp. XXVI:** 123

"Goodbye, Columbus" (P. Roth), **Supp. III Part 2:** 401, 404, 408–409, 411

Goodbye, Columbus and Five Short Stories (P. Roth), **Retro. Supp. II:** 279

"Goodbye, Goldeneye" (Swenson), **Supp. IV Part 2:** 651

"Goodbye, Mr. Chipstein" (Epstein), **Supp. XIV:** 103, 108

"Goodbye, My Brother" (Cheever), **Supp. I Part 1:** 175, 177, 193

"Goodbye and Good Luck" (Paley), **Supp. VI:** 219, 223

Goodbye Girl, The (film), **Supp. IV Part 2:** 589

Goodbye Girl, The (musical), **Supp. IV Part 2:** 576, 588

Goodbye Girl, The (Simon), **Supp. IV Part 2:** 575

Goodbye Look, The (Macdonald), **Supp. IV Part 2:** 473, 474

"Good-Bye My Fancy" (Whitman), **IV:** 348

"Goodbye to All That" (Biss), **Supp. XXVI:** 46, 47, 53

"Goodbye to All That" (Didion), **Supp. IV Part 1:** 197

Goodbye to All That (Graves), **I:** 477; **Supp. XXVI:** 53

Goodbye to Berlin (Isherwood), **Supp. XIV:** 159, 161, 162, 169

"Goodbye to My Twinkle Days" (Nguyen), **Supp. XXVI:** 209

"Good-Bye to the Mezzogiorno" (Auden), **Supp. II Part 1:** 19

"Goodbye to the Poetry of Calcium" (Wright), **Supp. III Part 2:** 599

"Good Company" (Matthews), **Supp. IX:** 160

"Good Country People" (O'Connor), **III:** 343, 350, 351, 352, 358; **Retro. Supp. II:** 229, 232

Good Day to Die, A (Harrison), **Supp. VIII:** 42–44, 45, 47

Good Day to Die, A (O'Nan as James Coltrane), **Supp. XXV:** 146

Good Doctor, The (Simon), **Supp. IV Part 2:** 575, 585

Good Earth, The (Buck), **Supp. I Part 1:** 49; **Supp. II Part 1:** 115–175, 118, 125, 132

Good European, The (Blackmur), **Supp. II Part 1:** 91

Good Evening Mr. & Mrs. America, and All the Ships at Sea (Bausch), **Supp. VII:** 41, 47, 52

"Good Friday" (Jarman), **Supp. XVII:** 116

"Good Girl" (Peacock), **Supp. XIX:** 199

Good Gray Poet, The (O'Connor), **Retro. Supp. I:** 407

Good Health and How We Won It (Sinclair), **Supp. V:** 285–286

Good Hearts (Price), **Supp. VI:** 259, 265

"Good Job Gone, A" (Hughes), **Retro. Supp. I:** 204

Good Journey, A (Ortiz), **Supp. IV Part 2:** 497, 499, 503, 505, 509–510, 514

Good Life, The (Nearing and Nearing), **Supp. XXVI:** 35

Good Lord Bird, The (McBride), **Supp. XXVI:** 191, 200, 202–204

Good Luck, Miss Wyckoff (Inge), **Supp. XXV:** 93, 95, 106–107

Good Luck in Cracked Italian (Hugo), **Supp. VI:** 133, 137–138

Goodman, Allegra, **Supp. XII:** 159; **Supp. XVI:** 205; **Supp. XX: 177; Supp. XXVI: 117–132**

Goodman, Ellen, **Supp. XVI:** 103

Goodman, Jack, **Supp. XXI:** 277

Goodman, Jenny, **Supp. XV:** 343, 344

Goodman, Paul, **I:** 218, 261; **III:** 39; **Supp. I Part 2:** 524; **Supp. VIII:** 239–240

Goodman, Philip, **III:** 105, 108

Goodman, Walter, **Supp. IV Part 2:** 532

Good Man Is Hard to Find, A (O'Connor), **III:** 339, 343–345

"Good Man Is Hard to Find, A" (O'Connor), **III:** 339, 344, 353; **Retro. Supp. II:** 230–231

Good Man Is Hard to Find and Other Stories, A (O'Connor), **Retro. Supp. II:** 229, **230–232**

Good Morning, America (Sandburg), **III:** 592–593

"Good Morning, Major" (Marquand), **III:** 56

Good Morning, Midnight (Rhys), **Supp. III Part 1:** 43

"Good Morning, Revolution" (Hughes), **Retro. Supp. I:** 201, 203

Good Morning Blues: The Autobiography of Count Basie (Murray), **Supp. XIX:** 159

Good Morning Revolution: Uncollected Writings of Social Protest (Hughes), **Retro. Supp. I:** 194, 201, 202, 209

Good Mother, The (Miller), **Supp. XII:** 289, **290–294**, 299, 301

Good News (Abbey), **Supp. XIII: 11–12**

"Good News from New-England" (E. Johnson), **Supp. I Part 1:** 115

Good News of Death and Other Poems (Simpson), **Supp. IX:** 265, **268–269**

"Goodnight, Saigon" (lecture, Caputo), **Supp. XIX:** 17, 30

Good Night, Willie Lee, I'll See You in the Morning (Walker), **Supp. III Part 2:** 520, 531

"Good Oak" (Leopold), **Supp. XIV:** 185, 187, 191

"Good Old Times, The: New York Fifty Years Ago" (Briggs), **Supp. XVIII:** 15

"Good Pine, A" (Offutt), **Supp. XIX:** 174

Goodrich, Chris, **Supp. XXII:** 206, 214

Goodrich, Samuel G., **Supp. I Part 1:** 38

Good Scent from a Strange Mountain, A (R. O. Butler), **Supp. XII:** 62, **70–72**

Good School, A (Yates), **Supp. XI:** 334, **346–347**, 348, 349

"Good Shepherdess, The/La Buena Pastora" (Mora), **Supp. XIII:** 228–229

Good Wife, The (O'Nan), **Supp. XXV:** 145, 149

Good Will (Smiley), **Supp. VI:** 292, **299–300**

Goodwin, K. L., **III:** 478

Goodwin, Stephen, **Supp. V:** 314, 316, 322, 323, 325

"Good Word for Winter, A" (Lowell), **Supp. I Part 2:** 420

Goodwyn, Janet, **Retro. Supp. I:** 370

Goody, Alex, **Supp. XXII:** 160

"Goophered Grapevine, The" (Chesnutt), **Supp. XIV:** 57, **58–61**

"Goose Fish, The" (Nemerov), **III:** 272, 284

"Goose Pond" (Kunitz), **Supp. III Part 1:** 262

Goose-Step, The (Sinclair), **Supp. V:** 276

Gordimer, Nadine, **Supp. XV:** 251

Gordon, Ambrose, **Supp. XV:** 144

Gordon, A. R., **III:** 199

Gordon, Caroline, **II: 196–222,** 536, 537; **III:** 454, 482; **IV:** 123, 126–127, 139, 282; **Retro. Supp. II:** 177, 222, 229, 233, 235; **Supp. II Part 1:** 139

Gordon, Charles G., **I:** 454

Gordon, Don, **Supp. X:** 119

Gordon, Eugene, **Supp. II Part 1:** 170; **Supp. XVIII:** 280

Gordon, Fran, **Supp. XIII:** 111

Gordon, James Morris, **II:** 197

Gordon, Lois, **Supp. IV Part 1:** 48; **Supp. V:** 46

Gordon, Lyndall, **Retro. Supp. I:** 55

Gordon, Mary, **Supp. IV Part 1: 297–317**

Gordon, Neil, **Supp. XVI:** 156

Gordon, Peter, **Supp. XII:** 3–4, 4–5, 8

Gordon, Ruth, **IV:** 357; **Supp. XX: 50**

Gore, Thomas Pryor, **Supp. IV Part 2:** 679

Gores, Joe, **Supp. XXI:** 70

Gorey, Edward, **IV:** 430, 436; **Supp. XXIII:** 209

"Gorge, The" (Huddle), **Supp. XXVI:** 154

Gorilla, My Love (Bambara), **Supp. XI:** 1, **2–7**

"Gorilla, My Love" (Bambara), **Supp. XI:** 2, 3–4

Gorki, Maxim, **I:** 478; **II:** 49; **III:** 402; **IV:** 299; **Supp. I Part 1:** 5, 51; **Supp. XIX:** 241

Gorky, Maxim, **Supp. XXIII:** 1, 4

Gorman, Herbert, **Supp. XXV:** 25

Gorney, Cynthia, **Supp. XVI:** 112

Gorra, Michael, **Supp. V:** 71

Goslings, The (Sinclair), **Supp. V:** 276, 281

Go South to Sorrow (Rowan), **Supp. XIV:** 306

Gospel According to Joe, The (Gurney), **Supp. V:** 99

"Gospel According to Saint Mark, The" (Gordon), **Supp. IV Part 1:** 310

Gospel according to the Son (Mailer), **Retro. Supp. II:** 213

"Gospel for the Twentieth Century, The" (Locke), **Supp. XIV:** 206

"Gospel of Beauty, The" (Lindsay), **Supp. I Part 2:** 380, 382, 384, 385, 391, 396

Gospels, The (di Donato), **Supp. XX: 45–46**

Gospel Singer, The (Crews), **Supp. XI:** 102, **109**

Gosse, Edmund, **II:** 538; **IV:** 350; **Supp. VIII:** 157

"Gossip" (Conroy), **Supp. XVI:** 71–72

Gossips, Gorgons, and Crones: The Fates of the Earth (Caputi), **Supp. IV Part 1:** 335

Go Tell It on the Mountain (Baldwin), **Retro. Supp. II:** 1, 2, 3, **4–5**, 7, 14; **Supp. I Part 1:** 48, 49, 50, 51, 52, 53–54, 55, 56, 57, 59, 61, 63, 64, 67; **Supp. II Part 1:** 170

Gotera, Vince, **Supp. XIII:** 115, 116, 119, 121, 127

Gothic Revival, The: An Essay on the History of Taste (Clark), **Supp. XIV:** 348

Gothic Writers (Thomson, Voller, and Frank, eds.), **Retro. Supp. II:** 273

"Go to the Devil and Shake Yourself" (song), **Supp. I Part 2:** 580

"Go to the Shine That's on a Tree" (Eberhart), **I:** 523

Go to the Widow-Maker (Jones), **Supp. XI:** 214, **225–226,** 227, 229, 233

"Gots Is What You Got" (Di Piero), **Supp. XIX:** 35, 36, 38, 41, 42, 45–46

Gottfried, Alex, **Supp. XIX:** 260

Gottfried, Martin, **Supp. IV Part 2:** 584

Gotthelf, Allan, **Supp. IV Part 2:** 528

Gottlieb, Adolph, **Supp. XV:** 144

Gottlieb, Edward, **Supp. XX: 250**

Gottlieb, Leopold, **Supp. XXIII:** 6

Gottlieb, Morton, **Supp. XVI:** 196

Gottlieb, Robert, **Supp. IV Part 2:** 474; **Supp. XXVI:** 244, 246, 250

Gottschalk and the Grande Tarantelle (Brooks), **Supp. III Part 1:** 86

"Gottschalk and the Grande Tarantelle" (Brooks), **Supp. III Part 1:** 86–87

Gould (Dixon), **Supp. XII:** 152, **153**

Gould, Edward Sherman, **I:** 346

Gould, Janice, **Supp. IV Part 1:** 322, 327; **Supp. XII:** 229

Gould, Jay, **I:** 4

Gould, Joe, **Supp. XV:** 143

Gourd Dancer, The (Momaday), **Supp. IV Part 2:** 481, 487, 491, 493

Gourmont, Remy de, **I:** 270, 272; **II:** 528, 529; **III:** 457, 467–468, 477; **Retro. Supp. I:** 55

Gouverneurs de la Rosée (Roumain), **Supp. IV Part 1:** 360, 367

Government Girl (film, Nichols), **Supp. XVIII:** 247

"Governors of Wyoming, The" (Proulx), **Supp. VII:** 264

"Gowane"(Kenny), **Supp. XXIII:** 147–148

Goyen, William, **Supp. V:** 220

Grabhorn, Janet, **Supp. XV:** 142

"Grace" (Budbill), **Supp. XIX:** 2

"Grace" (Dubus), **Supp. VII:** 91

"Grace" (Harjo), **Supp. XII:** 224

Grace Notes (Dove), **Supp. IV Part 1:** 248–250, 252

Grace (Eventually): Thoughts on Faith (Lamott), **Supp. XX: 143–145**

Grade, Chaim, **Supp. XVII:** 41

"Graduation" (Dubus), **Supp. VII:** 84

Grady, Henry W., **Supp. I Part 1:** 370

Graeber, Laurel, **Supp. V:** 15

Graham, Billy, **I:** 308

Graham, David, **Supp. XIX:** 81; **Supp. XV:** 104

Graham, Don, **Supp. XI:** 252, 254

Graham, Jorie, **Supp. IX:** 38, 52; **Supp. X:** 73; **Supp. XII:** 209; **Supp. XIII:** 85; **Supp. XVII:** 110, 111, 133, 240, 241, 242

Graham, Martha, **Supp. XI:** 152

Graham, Maryemma, **Retro. Supp. I:** 201, 204

Graham, Nan, **Supp. XII:** 272

Graham, Sheilah, **II:** 94; **Retro. Supp. I:** 97, 113–114, 115; **Supp. IX:** 63

Graham, Shirley, **Supp. I Part 1:** 51; **Supp. XXI:** 277. *See also* Du Bois, Shirley Graham

Graham, Stephen, **Supp. I Part 2:** 397

Graham, Tom (pseudonym). *See* Lewis, Sinclair

"Graham House, April '76"(Balakian), **Supp. XXIII:** 24

Grahn, Judy, **Supp. IV Part 1:** 325, 330; **Supp. XXIII:** 195

"Grain Field" (Crapsey), **Supp. XVII:** 77

Grainger, Percy, **Supp. I Part 2:** 386

Grain of Mustard Seed, A (Sarton), **Supp. VIII: 259–260,** 263

Gramar (Lowth), **II:** 8

Grammar of Motives, A (Burke), **I:** 272, 275, 276–278, 283, 284

Gramsci, Antonio, **Supp. XX: 35–36**

Granados, Gabriel Bernal, **Supp. XV:** 350

Granath, Jack, **Supp. XVIII:** 93

Granberry, Edwin, **I:** 288

Grand Canyon, Inc. (Everett), **Supp. XVIII:** 66

Grand Design, The (Dos Passos), **I:** 489–490

"Grande Malade, The" (Barnes), **Supp. III Part 1:** 36

"Grandfather" (Dunn), **Supp. XI:** 147

"Grandfather and Grandson" (Singer), **Retro. Supp. II:** 307

Grandfathers, The (Richter), **Supp. XVIII: 219–220**

"Grandfather's Blessing" (Alvarez), **Supp. VII:** 2

"Grand Forks" (Bierds), **Supp. XVII:** 34

"Grand Forks" (Simpson), **Supp. IX:** 280–281

"Grand Inquisitor" (Dostoevsky), **IV:** 106

Grandissimes (Cable), **II:** 291

"Grand-Master Nabokov" (Updike), **Retro. Supp. I:** 317

"Grand Miracle, The" (Karr), **Supp. XI:** 251

"Grandmother" (Gunn Allen), **Supp. IV Part 1:** 320, 325

"Grandmother in Heaven" (Levine), **Supp. V:** 186

"Grandmother of the Sun: Ritual Gynocracy in Native America" (Gunn Allen), **Supp. IV Part 1:** 328

Grandmothers of the Light: A Medicine Woman's Sourcebook (Gunn Allen, ed.), **Supp. IV Part 1:** 332, 333–334

"Grandmother Songs, The" (Hogan), **Supp. IV Part 1:** 413

"Grandpa and the Statue" (A. Miller), **III:** 147

"Grandparents" (Lowell), **II:** 550

"Grandsire Bells, The" (Bierds), **Supp. XVII:** 28–29

"Grandstand Complex, The" (McCoy), **Supp. XIII:** 166

Grange, Red, **II:** 416

Granger's Index to Poetry (anthology), **Retro. Supp. I:** 37, 39

Granite & Cedar (Miller), **Supp. XXII:** 214

Grant, Gavin, **Supp. XIX:** 175

Grant, Lee, **Supp. XIII:** 295

Grant, Madison, **Supp. II Part 1:** 170

Grant, Richard, **Supp. X:** 282

Grant, Ulysses S., **I:** 4, 15; **II:** 542; **III:** 506, 584; **IV:** 348, 446; **Supp. I Part 2:** 418; **Supp. XXIV:** 224

Grantwood, **Retro. Supp. I:** 416, 417

"Grapes, The" (Hecht), **Supp. X:** 65–66

"Grape Sherbet" (Dove), **Supp. IV Part 1:** 246

Grapes of Wrath, The (Steinbeck), **I:** 301; **III:** 589; **IV:** 51, 53–55, 59, 63, 65, 67, 68, 69; **Supp. V:** 290; **Supp. XI:** 169; **Supp. XIV:** 181; **Supp. XV:** 351; **Supp. XX: 28**

"Grapevine, The" (Ashbery), **Supp. III Part 1:** 4

"Grass" (Sandburg), **III:** 584

Grass, Günter, **Supp. VIII:** 40

Grass County (Kooser), **Supp. XIX:** 119

"Grasse: The Olive Trees" (Wilbur), **Supp. III Part 2:** 550

Grass Harp, The (Capote), **Supp. III Part 1:** 114–117, 123

Grass Still Grows, The (A. Miller), **III:** 146

"Gratified Desire" (Davison), **Supp. XXVI:** 74

"Grating Parmesan"(Crooker), **Supp. XXIII:** 56

Gratitude to Old Teachers (R. Bly), **Supp. IV Part 1:** 73

Grattan, Bill, **Supp. XXIII:** 273, 274, 275, 276, 279, 280

Graupner, Gottlieb, **Supp. XV:** 240, 244

"Grave, A" (Moore), **III:** 195, 202, 208, 213

Grave, The (Blair), **Supp. I Part 1:** 150

"Grave, The" (Porter), **III:** 433, 443, 445–446

"Grave, The" (Winters), **Supp. II Part 2:** 795, 796

"Graven Image" (O'Hara), **III:** 320

Grave of Light: New and Selected Poems, 1970–2005 (Notley), **Supp. XXII:** 226, 235, 236

Grave of the Right Hand, The (Wright), **Supp. V:** 332, 338, 339

"Grave Piece" (Eberhart), **I:** 533

Graves, Billy, **Supp. I Part 2:** 607

Graves, John, **Supp. V:** 220

Graves, Morris, **Supp. X:** 264

Graves, Peter, **Supp. IV Part 2:** 474

Graves, Rean, **Supp. I Part 1:** 326

Graves, Robert, **I:** 437, 477, 523; **Supp. I Part 2:** 541; **Supp. IV Part 1:** 280, 348; **Supp. IV Part 2:** 685; **Supp. XXVI:** 53

"Graveyard, The" (Very), **Supp. XXV:** 249

"Graveyard Blues" (Trethewey), **Supp. XXI:** 245, 255, 256

Graveyard for Lunatics, A (Bradbury), **Supp. IV Part 1:** 102, 114–116

Gravity's Rainbow (Pynchon), **Supp. II Part 2:** 617, 618–619, 621–625, 627, 630, 633–636; **Supp. IV Part 1:** 279; **Supp. V:** 44; **Supp. XIV:** 49; **Supp. XVII:** 236; **Supp. XXII:** 255; **Supp. XXIV:** 140

Gray, Cecil, **Supp. I Part 1:** 258
Gray, Francine Du Plessix, **Supp. V:** 169
Gray, James, **III:** 207; **Supp. I Part 2:** 410
Gray, Jeffrey, **Supp. XV:** 27
Gray, Josie, **Supp. XXIV:** 166, 167, 172, 178
Gray, Paul, **Supp. IV Part 1:** 305; **Supp. IV Part 2:** 639; **Supp. XVI:** 74; **Supp. XVIII:** 94
Gray, Thomas, **I:** 68; **Supp. I Part 1:** 150; **Supp. I Part 2:** 422, 716
Gray, Thomas A., **Supp. I Part 2:** 710
"Gray Heron, The" (Kinnell), **Supp. III Part 1:** 250
"Gray Mills of Farley, The" (Jewett), **Retro. Supp. II:** 132, 144
"Gray Poem" (Everwine), **Supp. XV:** 81
Grayscale: Poems (Huddle), **Supp. XXVI:** 150
Grayson, Charles, **Supp. XIII:** 171
"Gray Squirrel" (Francis), **Supp. IX:** 90
"Gray Wolf's H 'ant, The" (Chesnutt), **Supp. XIV:** 60
Grealy, Lucy, **Supp. XII:** 310
Greasy Lake (Boyle), **Supp. VIII: 14–15**
"Greasy Lake" (Boyle), **Supp. VIII:** 15; **Supp. XX: 18–19**
Greasy Lake & Other Stories (Boyle), **Supp. XX:** 17, 18–19
Great Action Stories (Kittredge and Krauzer), **Supp. XXVI:** 182
"Great Adventure of Max Breuck, The" (Lowell), **II:** 522
Great American Detective, The (Kittredge and Krauzer), **Supp. XXVI:** 182
Great American Novel, The (P. Roth), **Retro. Supp. II:** 283, 288–289; **Supp. III Part 2:** 414–416
Great American Short Novels (Phillips, ed.), **Supp. VIII:** 156
Great Battles of the World (Crane), **I:** 415
"Great Carousel, The" (Untermeyer), **Supp. XV:** 296
Great Christian Doctrine of Original Sin Defended, The . . . (Edwards), **I:** 549, 557, 559
Great Circle (Aiken), **I:** 53, 55, 57
"Great Class-Reunion Bazaar, The" (Theroux), **Supp. VIII:** 312
Great Day, The (Hurston), **Supp. VI:** 154
Great Days (Barthelme), **Supp. IV Part 1:** 39
Great Days, The (Dos Passos), **I:** 491
Great Digest (Pound, trans.), **III:** 472
"Great Divider, The" (Saunders), **Supp. XIX:** 235
"Great Elegy for John Donne" (Brodsky), **Supp. VIII:** 21, 23
"Greater Good, A" (Di Piero), **Supp. XIX:** 39
Greater Inclination, The (Wharton), **Retro. Supp. I:** 363, **364–365,** 366
Greater Sea, The (Gibran), **Supp. XX:** 118
"Greater Self, The" (Gibran), **Supp. XX:** 118
"Greater Torment, The" (Blackmur), **Supp. II Part 1:** 92

Greatest Hits 1969–1996 (Salinas), **Supp. XIII:** 311
"Greatest of These, The" (C. Miller), **Supp. XXII:** 188, 196
"Greatest Thing in the World, The" (Mailer), **Retro. Supp. II:** 196
Great Expectations (Acker), **Supp. XII:** 5, **9–11**
Great Expectations (Dickens), **III:** 247; **Supp. I Part 1:** 35; **Supp. XVI:** 73; **Supp. XVIII:** 146
"Great Expectations, No Satisfaction" (D. Gates), **Supp. XVI:** 73
"Great Figure, The" (W. C. Williams), **IV:** 414
"Great Fillmore Street Buffalo Drive, The" (Momaday), **Supp. IV Part 2:** 493
Great Gatsby, The (Fitzgerald), **I:** 107, 375, 514; **II:** 77, 79, 83, 84, 85, 87, 91–93, 94, 96, 98; **III:** 244, 260, 372, 572; **IV:** 124, 297; **Retro. Supp. I:** 98, 105, **105–108,** 110, 114, 115, 335, 359; **Retro. Supp. II:** 107, 201; **Supp. II Part 2:** 626; **Supp. III Part 2:** 585; **Supp. IV Part 2:** 468, 475; **Supp. IX:** 57, 58; **Supp. X:** 175; **Supp. XI:** 65, 69, 334; **Supp. XVI:** 64, 75; **Supp. XVIII:** 76, 148, 165; **Supp. XX: 59, 60, 61, 72; Supp. XXII:** 81, 82, 88; **Supp. XXIII:** 101
Great Gatsby, The (Fitzgerald) (Modern Library), **Retro. Supp. I:** 113
Great God Brown, The (O'Neill), **III:** 165, 391, 394–395
Great Goodness of Life: A Coon Show (Baraka), **Supp. II Part 1:** 47
Great Heart: The History of a Labrador Adventure (Davidson and Rugge), **Supp. XXII:** 218
"Great Idea Lives Forever, A: Shouldn't Its Copyright?" (Helprin), **Supp. XXV:** 84, 88
Great Inclination, The (Wharton), **IV:** 310
"Great Infirmities" (Simic), **Supp. VIII:** 277
Great Jones Street (DeLillo), **Supp. VI:** 2, 3, 8–9, 11, 12
"Great Lawsuit, The: Man *versus* Men: Woman *versus* Women" (Fuller), **Retro. Supp. I:** 156; **Supp. II Part 1:** 292
Great Ledge, The (Davison), **Supp. XXVI:** 66, 77–78
"Great Ledge, The" (Davison), **Supp. XXVI:** 77, 78
"Great Men and Their Environment" (James), **II:** 347
"Great Mississippi Bubble, The" (Irving), **II:** 314
Great Mistake, The (Rinehart), **Supp. XXV:** 198, 200
Great Railway Bazaar, The: By Train through Asia (Theroux), **Supp. VIII:** 318, 319, **320–321,** 322
"Great Scott" (Conroy), **Supp. XVI:** 75, 77
Great Shark Hunt, The (Thompson), **Supp. XXIV:** 286

"Great Sleigh-Ride of Brewsterville, The" (Briggs), **Supp. XVIII:** 16
"Great Spirit, The" (Zitkala-Ša), **Supp. XXV:** 276, 282
Great Stories of Suspense (Millar, ed.), **Supp. IV Part 2:** 474
Great Topics of the World (Goldbarth), **Supp. XII:** 187, 189, 191
Great Valley, The (Masters), **Supp. I Part 2:** 465
Great World and Timothy Colt, The (Auchincloss), **Supp. IV Part 1:** 25, 31, 32
Grédy, Jean-Pierre, **Supp. XVI:** 194
"Greek Boy, The" (Bryant), **Supp. I Part 1:** 168
Greek Mind/Jewish Soul: The Conflicted Art of Cynthia Ozick (Strandberg), **Supp. V:** 273
"Greek Partisan, The" (Bryant), **Supp. I Part 1:** 168
"Greeks, The" (McCarriston), **Supp. XIV:** 271
"Greeks, the Chines, or Say the Mayans, The" (Bronk), **Supp. XXI:** 31
Greeley, Horace, **II:** 7; **IV:** 197, 286–287
Green, Anna Katharine, **Supp. XXV:** 199; **Supp. XXVI:** 277, 282
Green, Archie, **Supp. XXVI:** 134
Green, Ashbel, **Supp. IV Part 2:** 474
Green, David Gordon, **Supp. XXV:** 153
Green, Henry, **IV:** 279; **Retro. Supp. I:** 354; **Supp. III Part 1:** 3; **Supp. XI:** 294–295, 296, 297; **Supp. XII:** 315
Green, Jack, **Supp. IV Part 1:** 284–285
Green, Martin, **Supp. I Part 1:** 299
Green, Michelle, **Supp. IV Part 1:** 95
Green, Rose Basile, **Supp. XX:** 33, 41
"Green Automobile, The" (Ginsberg), **Supp. II Part 1:** 322
Greenberg, Clement, **Supp. XV:** 141, 143, 144, 145
Greenberg, Eliezer, **Supp. I Part 2:** 432; **Supp. XXIII:** 7
Greenberg, Hayim, **Supp. XXIII:** 3
Greenberg, Jonathan, **Supp. XII:** 285
Greenberg, Miriam, **Supp. XXII:** 244
Greenberg, Samuel, **I:** 393
Green Bough, A (Faulkner), **Retro. Supp. I:** 84
"Green Canoe" (Halliday), **Supp. XIX:** 88
Green Centuries (Gordon), **II:** 196, 197–207, 209
"Green Crab's Shell, A" (Doty), **Supp. XI:** 126
"Green Door, The" (O. Henry), **Supp. II Part 1:** 395
Greene, A. C., **Supp. V:** 223, 225
Greene, Graham, **I:** 480; **II:** 62, 320; **III:** 57, 556; **Retro. Supp. I:** 215; **Supp. I Part 1:** 280; **Supp. IV Part 1:** 341; **Supp. IX:** 261; **Supp. V:** 298; **Supp. XI:** 99, **Supp. XI:** 104; **Supp. XIII:** 233; **Supp. XIX:** 29–30; **Supp. XVIII:** 79
Greene, Helga, **Supp. IV Part 1:** 134, 135
Greene, J. Lee, **Retro. Supp. II:** 121
Greene, Nathanael, **Supp. I Part 2:** 508

Greene, Richard Tobias, **III:** 76
Greene, Robert, **Supp. XVII:** 232
Green Eggs and Ham (Geisel), **Supp. XVI:** 108, 109
"Greene-ing of the Portables, The" (Cowley), **Supp. II Part 1:** 140
"Greenest Continent, The" (Stevens), **Retro. Supp. I:** 304
Greenfeld, Josh, **III:** 364
Greenfield, Josh, **Supp. XIX:** 269
"Green Hell" (Boyle), **Supp. XX:** 18
Green Hills of Africa (Hemingway), **II:** 253; **Retro. Supp. I:** 182, 186
Greening of America, The (C. Reich), **Supp. XVII:** 3
"Green Lagoons, The" (Leopold), **Supp. XIV:** 188
"Green Lampshade" (Simic), **Supp. VIII:** 283
Greenlanders, The (Smiley), **Supp. VI:** 292, **296–298,** 299, 305, 307
Greenlaw, Edwin A., **IV:** 453
"Greenleaf" (O'Connor), **III:** 350, 351; **Retro. Supp. II:** 233, 237
Greenman, Walter F., **I:** 217, 222
Green Memories (Mumford), **Supp. II Part 2:** 474, 475, 479, 480–481
Green Mountain Ghosts, Ghouls, and Unsolved Mysteries (Citro), **Supp. XXII:** 208, 218
"Green Pasture, The" (Leopold), **Supp. XIV:** 184
Green Pastures, The (Connelly), **Supp. II Part 1:** 223
"Green Red Brown and White" (Swenson), **Supp. IV Part 2:** 639
"Green River" (Bryant), **Supp. I Part 1:** 155, 164
Green Shadows, White Whale (Bradbury), **Supp. IV Part 1:** 102, 103, 116
"Green Shirt, The" (Olds), **Supp. X:** 209
"Greensleeves" (Jarman), **Supp. XVII:** 113
"Greensleeves" (Notley), **Supp. XXII:** 228
Greenslet, Ferris, **I:** 19; **Retro. Supp. I:** 9, 10, 11, 13; **Retro. Supp. II:** 41
Greenspan, Alan, **Supp. IV Part 2:** 526
Greenspan, Ezra, **Supp. XVIII:** 257
Greenstreet, Sydney, **Supp. IV Part 1:** 356
"Green Thought, A" (L. Michaels), **Supp. XVI:** 204
"Green-Thumb Boy" (Nelson), **Supp. XVIII:** 182
Greenwald, Ted, **Supp. IV Part 2:** 423
Green Wall, The (Wright), **Supp. III Part 2:** 591, 593, 595
Green Wave, The (Rukeyser), **Supp. VI:** 273, 280
"Green Ways" (Kunitz), **Supp. III Part 1:** 265
Green with Beasts (Merwin), **Supp. III Part 1:** 340, 344–346
Greenwood, Grace, **Supp. XIII:** 141
"Greeting Card Verse" (Peacock), **Supp. XIX:** 200
Greetings from Ice Country (Muñoz), **Supp. XXV:** 130

Gregerson, Linda, **Supp. IV Part 2:** 651; **Supp. X:** 204–205; **Supp. XI:** 142
"Gregorio Valdes" (Bishop), **Retro. Supp. II:** 51
Gregory, Alyse, **I:** 221, 226, 227, 231
Gregory, Horace, **II:** 512; **Supp. III Part 2:** 614, 615; **Supp. IX:** 229; **Supp. XV:** 143
Gregory, Lady Isabella Augusta, **III:** 458
Gregory, Sinda, **Supp. X:** 260, 268
Grendel (Gardner), **Supp. VI:** 63, **67,** 68, 74
Grenstone Poems (Bynner), **Supp. XV:** 44
"Gretel in Darkness" (Glück), **Supp. V:** 82
Gretta (Caldwell), **I:** 301, 302
Greuze, Jean Baptiste, **Supp. I Part 2:** 714
Grey, Zane, **Supp. XIII:** 5; **Supp. XXVI:** 186
Greyhounding This America (Kenny), **Supp. XXIII:** 155
Gridley Firing (Hayford), **Supp. XXII:** 204
"Grief Has Stamped" (Pedersen; Nelson, trans.), **Supp. XVIII:** 180
Grieg, Michael, **Supp. XV:** 133, 148
Griffin, Bartholomew, **Supp. I Part 1:** 369
Griffin, John Howard, **Supp. VIII:** 208; **Supp. XXI:** 74; **Supp. XXV:** 51
Griffin, Merv, **Supp. IV Part 2:** 526
Griffith, Albert J., **Supp. V:** 325
Griffith, D. W., **I:** 31, 481–482; **Retro. Supp. I:** 103, 325; **Supp. XI:** 45; **Supp. XVI:** 183, 184; **Supp. XXI:** 170
Griffith, Paul, **Supp. XVIII:** 173, 175
Griffiths, Clyde, **I:** 511
Grile, Dod (pseudonym). *See* Bierce, Ambrose
Grimm, Herman, **II:** 17
Grimm brothers, **II:** 378; **III:** 101, 491, 492; **IV:** 266; **Supp. I Part 2:** 596, 622; **Supp. X:** 78, 84, 86
Grimshaw, Anna, **Supp. XXI:** 172
Grinde, Donald A., Jr., **Supp. XXVI:** 98
Grinnell, George Bird, **Supp. XVI:** 13
Gris, Juan, **I:** 442; **Retro. Supp. I:** 430
Griswold, Rufus Wilmot, **III:** 409, 429; **Retro. Supp. II:** 261, 262; **Supp. XV:** 277, 278; **Supp. XVI:** 8, 10–11; **Supp. XXV:** 250
"Grizzly" (Kittredge), **Supp. XXVI:** 187
Grogg, Sam, Jr., **Supp. IV Part 2:** 468, 471
Gromer, Crystal, **Supp. XII:** 297
Gronlund, Laurence, **II:** 276
Grooms, Red, **Supp. XV:** 178
Grooves: A Kind of Mystery (Brockmeier), **Supp. XXII:** 55, 56, 59
"Groping for Trouts" (Gass), **Supp. VI:** 87
Grosholz, Emily, **Supp. XII:** 185; **Supp. XIX:** 37–38, 278
Grosman un zun (Grosman and Son) (Asch), **Supp. XXIII:** 7
Gross, Robert A., **Supp. XIX:** 151

Gross, Terry, **Supp. XVI:** 167; **Supp. XXI:** 247, 255
"Grosse Fuge" (Doty), **Supp. XI:** 126–127
Grossman, Allen, **Retro. Supp. II:** 83; **Supp. XIX:** 82, 86, 94; **Supp. XVIII:** 91
Grossman, Lev, **Supp. XXV:** 4, **63–78**
Grosz, George, **III:** 172; **IV:** 438; **Retro. Supp. II:** 321; **Supp. X:** 137
"Grotesque in Modern Fiction, The" (E. Hoffman, Ph.D. dissertation), **Supp. XVI:** 147
"Groundhog, The" (Eberhart), **I:** 523, 530–532, 533
"Ground on Which I Stand, The" (Wilson), **Supp. VIII:** 331
"Ground Swell" (Jarman), **Supp. XVII:** 118
Group, The (McCarthy), **II:** 570, 574–578
"Group of Two, A" (Jarrell), **II:** 368
Group Therapy (Hearon), **Supp. VIII:** **64–65**
"Grove" (Goldbarth), **Supp. XII:** 176
Groves of Academe, The (McCarthy), **II:** 568–571
Growing into Love (X. J. Kennedy), **Supp. XV:** 153, **158–160**
Growing Pains (J. S. Untermeyer), **Supp. XV:** 303
"Growing Season, The" (Caldwell), **I:** 309
Growing Up Gay: A Literary Anthology (Singer, ed.), **Supp. IV Part 1:** 330
"Growing Up Good in Maycomb" (Shaffer), **Supp. VIII:** 128
Growing Up Native American (Riley, ed.), **Supp. XXVI:** 104
"Grown-Up" (Jewett), **Retro. Supp. II:** 134
"Growth" (Lowell), **II:** 554
"Growth and Decay in Recent Verse" (Untermeyer), **Supp. XV:** 299
Growth of the American Republic, The (Morison and Commager), **Supp. I Part 2:** 484
"Growtown Buggle, The" (Jewett), **Retro. Supp. II:** 132
Grubin, David, **Supp. XXIII:** 138
Gruenberg, Louis, **III:** 392
Grumbach, Doris, **II:** 560
"Gryphon" (C. Baxter), **Supp. XVII:** 14, 17
"Guacamaja" (Leopold), **Supp. XIV:** 188–189
Guardian Angel (Paretsky), **Supp. XXV:** 178, 179
Guardian Angel, The (Holmes), **Supp. I Part 1:** 315–316
"Guardian of the Law" (R. Fisher), **Supp. XIX:** 71
Guard of Honor (Cozzens), **I:** 370–372, 375, 376–377, 378, 379
Guardsman, The (Molnar), **Supp. XVI:** 187
Guare, John, **Supp. XIII:** 196, 207
Guattari, Félix, **Supp. XXV:** 123
Gubar, Susan, **Retro. Supp. I:** 42; **Retro. Supp. II:** 324; **Supp. IX:** 66; **Supp.**

XV: 270; **Supp. XXIV:** 28
Guerard, Albert, Jr., **Supp. X:** 79; **Supp. XIII:** 172
Guérin, Maurice de, **I:** 241
"Guerrilla Handbook, A" (Baraka), **Supp. II Part 1:** 36
Guess and Spell Coloring Book, The (Swenson), **Supp. IV Part 2:** 648
Guess Who's Coming to Dinner (film), **Supp. I Part 1:** 67
Guest, Barbara, **Supp. XXIII:** 215
Guest, Judith, **Supp. XVI:** 36
Guest, Val, **Supp. XI:** 307
Guest Book (Bynner), **Supp. XV:** 51
"Guest Ellen at the Supper for Street People, The" (Ferry), **Supp. XXIV:** 152–153, 162
"Guests of Mrs. Timms, The" (Jewett), **II:** 408; **Retro. Supp. II:** 135
Guevara, Martha, **Supp. VIII:** 74
Guevara, Fray Miguel de, **Supp. XXI:** 104
"Guevara . . .Guevara" (Salinas), **Supp. XIII:** 312–313, 315
Guggenheim, Peggy, **Supp. XXII:** 165
Guided Tours of Hell (Prose), **Supp. XVI:** 257, 261
"Guided Tours of Hell" (Prose), **Supp. XVI:** 257
Guide for the Perplexed (Maimonides), **Supp. XVII:** 46
Guide in the Wilderness, A (Cooper), **I:** 337
"Guidelines" (Espaillat), **Supp. XXI:** 99
"Guide to Dungeness Spit, A" (Wagoner), **Supp. IX:** 325–326, 329
Guide to Ezra Pound's Selected Cantos' (Kearns), **Retro. Supp. I:** 292
Guide to Kulchur (Pound), **III:** 475
Guide to the Ruins (Nemerov), **III:** 269, 270–271, 272
Guillén, Jorge, **Supp. XXIV:** 152
Guillén, Nicolás, **Retro. Supp. I:** 202; **Supp. I Part 1:** 345
Guillevic, Eugene, **Supp. III Part 1:** 283
"Guilt, The" (Peacock), **Supp. XIX:** 200
"Guilty Man, The" (Kunitz), **Supp. II Part 1:** 263
Guilty of Everything: The Autobiography of Herbert Huncke (Huncke), **Supp. XIV:** 138, 140, 141, 150
Guilty Pleasures (Barthelme), **Supp. IV Part 1:** 44, 45, 53
Guimond, James, **Supp. XXI:** 228
Guinness, Alec, **Retro. Supp. I:** 65; **Supp. XX: 50**
Gulag Archipelago, The (Solzhenitsyn), **Supp. XVII:** 229
"Gulf, The" (Dunn), **Supp. XI:** 149
Gulistan (Saadi), **II:** 19
Gullible's Travels (Lardner), **II:** 426, 427
Gulliver, Adelaide Cromwell, **Supp. XVIII:** 286
"Gulliver Found" (Bronk), **Supp. XXI:** 33
Gulliver's Travels (Swift), **I:** 209, 348, 366; **II:** 301; **Supp. I Part 2:** 656; **Supp. XI:** 209; **Supp. XVI:** 110
"Gulls" (Hayden), **Supp. II Part 1:** 367
"Gulls, The" (Nemerov), **III:** 272

"Gulls on Dumps" (Di Piero), **Supp. XIX:** 41
"Gun, The" (Dobyns), **Supp. XIII:** 88
Gun, with Occasional Music (Lethem), **Supp. XVIII: 137–138**
Günderode: A Translation from the German (Fuller), **Supp. II Part 1:** 293
Gunderson, Gwen, **Supp. XXVI:** 134
Gundy, Jeff, **Supp. XI:** 315; **Supp. XVI:** 46, 265, 275
Gunfight at the O.K. Corral (film), **Supp. XX: 246**
"Gun Hand, The" (Davison), **Supp. XXVI:** 71
Gun in Cheek (Pronzini), **Supp. XXVI:** 278
Gunman's Rhapsody (Parker), **Supp. XIX:** 187
Gunn, Robin Wright, **Supp. XXI:** 243, 244
Gunn, Thom, **Supp. IX:** 269
Gunn, Thomas, **Supp. V:** 178
Gunn Allen, Paula, **Supp. IV Part 1: 319–340,** 404; **Supp. IV Part 2:** 499, 502, 557, 568; **Supp. XII:** 218
"Gunnar's Sword" (C. Bly), **Supp. XVI:** 34, 35, 37, 42
"Guns as Keys; and the Great Gate Swings" (Lowell), **II:** 524
Gurdjieff, Georges, **Supp. IX:** 320; **Supp. V:** 199
Gurganus, Allan, **Supp. XII:** 308–309, 310
Gurko, Leo, **III:** 62
Gurney, A. R., **Supp. IX:** 261; **Supp. V: 95–112**
Gurney, Mary (Molly) Goodyear, **Supp. V:** 95
Gussow, Mel, **Supp. IX:** 93; **Supp. XII:** 325, 328, 341
Gustavus Vassa, the African (Vassa), **Supp. IV Part 1:** 11
Gusto, Thy Name Was Mrs. Hopkins: A Prose Rhapsody (Francis), **Supp. IX:** 89
Guston, Philip, **Supp. XXIII:** 210
Gute Mensch von Sezuan, Der (Brecht), **Supp. IX:** 138
Gutenberg, Johann, **Supp. I Part 2:** 392
Guthrie, A. B., **Supp. X:** 103
Guthrie, Woody, **Supp. XVIII:** 23
Gutman, Herbert, **Supp. I Part 1:** 47
Guttenplan, D. D., **Supp. XI:** 38
"Gutting of Couffignal, The" (Hammett), **Supp. IV Part 1:** 345
Guy, David, **Supp. XXVI:** 9
Guy Domville (James), **II:** 331; **Retro. Supp. I:** 228
"Gwendolyn" (Bishop), **Retro. Supp. II:** 51
Gwynn, R. S., **Supp. XVIII:** 184
Gypsy Ballads (Hughes, trans.), **Supp. I Part 1:** 345
Gypsy's Curse, The (Crews), **Supp. XI: 110**
"Gyroscope, The" (Rukeyser), **Supp. VI:** 271
Gysin, Brion, **Supp. XII:** 129

H

Ha, Quan Manh, **Supp. XXVI:** 213, 214, 215
Haardt, Sara. *See* Mencken, Mrs. H. L. (Sara Haardt)
Haas, Robert, **Supp. XXII:** 177
Habakkuk (biblical book), **III:** 200, 347
Habibi (Nye), **Supp. XIII:** 273, **279**
"Habit" (James), **II:** 351
Habitations of the Word (Gass), **Supp. VI:** 88
"Hack, The" (Swados), **Supp. XIX:** 267
"Hackberry"(P. Benedict), **Supp. XXIII:** 37–38, 39
Hacker, Marilyn, **Supp. XV:** 250; **Supp. XVII:** 71, 76, 112; **Supp. XVIII:** 177, 178
Hacker, Randi, **Supp. XXVI:** 121
Hackett, David, **Supp. XII:** 236
Hadas, Rachel, **Supp. XXIII: 111–128; Supp. XXIV:** 157
Hadda, Janet, **Retro. Supp. II:** 317
Haddád, 'Abd al-Masíh, **Supp. XX:** 116
"Hades Welcomes His Bride" (Stallings), **Supp. XXV:** 229–230
Haeckel, Ernst Heinrich, **II:** 480
Haegert, John, **Supp. XVI:** 69
Hafen, P. Jane, **Supp. XXV:** 280
Hafif, Marcia, **Supp. IV Part 2:** 423
Hagar's Daughter (P. Hopkins), **Supp. XVI:** 143
Hagedorn, Jessica, **Supp. X:** 292
Hagen, Beulah, **Supp. I Part 2:** 679
Hager, Kelly, **Supp. XVIII:** 183
Hagestadt, Emma, **Supp. XXVI:** 212
Haggard, Rider, **III:** 189
Haggas, Carol, **Supp. XXVI:** 159, 160
Hagoromo (play), **III:** 466
Hagstrum, Jean, **Supp. XV:** 74
"Hail Mary" (Fante), **Supp. XI:** 160, 164
Haines, George, IV, **I:** 444
Haines, John, **Supp. XII: 197–214**
"Hair" (Corso), **Supp. XII:** 117, 126, 127
"Hair, The" (Carver), **Supp. III Part 1:** 137
"Haircut" (Lardner), **II:** 430, 436
"Hair Dressing" (Untermeyer), **Supp. XV:** 304, 305
Hairpiece: A Film for Nappy-Headed People (Chenzira; film), **Supp. XI:** 19–20
"Hairs" (Cisneros), **Supp. VII:** 59
Hairs/Pelitos (Cisneros), **Supp. VII:** 58
Hairy Ape, The (O'Neill), **III:** 391, 392, 393
"Haïta the Shepherd" (Bierce), **I:** 203
Haj, The (Uris), **Supp. XX: 244, 245, 247, 255–256**
Haldeman, Anna, **Supp. I Part 1:** 2
Hale, Edward Everett, **Supp. I Part 2:** 584; **Supp. XI:** 193, 200
Hale, John Parker, **Supp. I Part 2:** 685
Hale, Nancy, **Supp. VIII:** 151, 171
Haley, Alex, **Supp. I Part 1:** 47, 66
Haley, J. Evetts, **Supp. V:** 226
"Half a Century Gone" (Lowell), **II:** 554
Half-a-Hundred: Tales by Great American Writers (Grayson, ed.), **Supp. XIII:** 171
Half and Half:Writers on Growing Up Biracial and Bicultural (Hearn, ed.),

Supp. XXV: 51
Half Asleep in Frog Pajamas (Robbins), **Supp. X:** 259, **279–282**
Half Breed, The (film), **Supp. XVI:** 185
Half-Century of Conflict, A (Parkman), **Supp. II Part 2:** 600, 607, 610
"Half Deity" (Moore), **III:** 210, 214, 215
"Half Hour of August" (Ríos), **Supp. IV Part 2:** 552
"Half-Life of Cardio-Pulmonary Function, A" (Gansworth), **Supp. XXVI:** 111
Half-Life of Cardio-Pulmonary Function, A: Poems and Paintings (Gansworth), **Supp. XXVI:** 110–111
Half-Lives (Jong), **Supp. V:** 115, 119
Half Moon Street: Two Short Novels (Theroux), **Supp. VIII:** 322, 323
Half of Paradise (Burke), **Supp. XIV:** 22, 24
Half-Past Nation Time (C. Johnson), **Supp. VI:** 187
Half Remembered (Davison), **Supp. XXVI:** 61, 63, 65, 66–67, 70, 71
"Half-Skinned Steer, The" (Proulx), **Supp. VII:** 261–262
"Half Sonnets" (Jarman), **Supp. XVII:** 115
Half Sun Half Sleep (Swenson), **Supp. IV Part 2:** 645–646
Halfway (Kumin), **Supp. IV Part 2:** 441–442
"Halfway" (Rich), **Supp. I Part 2:** 553
Halfway Down the Hall: New and Selected Poems (Hadas), **Supp. XXIII:** **118–119**
Halfway Home (Monette), **Supp. X:** 154
Halfway to Silence (Sarton), **Supp. VIII:** 261
Half You Don't Know, The: Selected Stories (Cameron), **Supp. XII:** 79, 80, 81
Haliburton, Thomas Chandler, **II:** 301; **IV:** 193; **Supp. I Part 2:** 411
Halifax, Lord, **II:** 111
Hall, Daniel, **Supp. XII:** 258
Hall, Donald, **I:** 567; **III:** 194; **Supp. IV Part 1:** 63, 72; **Supp. IV Part 2:** 621; **Supp. IX:** 269; **Supp. XIV:** 82, 126; **Supp. XV:** 21, 153, 176; **Supp. XVI:** 39, 230, 235; **Supp. XX: 194; Supp. XXI:** 86; **Supp. XXIII:** 209; **Supp. XXVI:** 68
Hall, Hazel, **Supp. XXII:** 275
Hall, James, **II:** 313; **Supp. I Part 2:** 584, 585
Hall, James Baker, **Supp. X:** 24
Hall, Rachel, **Supp. XXIII:** 301
Hall, Timothy L., **Supp. VIII:** 127, 128
Halleck, Fitz-Greene, **Supp. I Part 1:** 156, 158
"Hallelujah: A Sestina" (Francis), **Supp. IX:** 82
"Hallelujah on the Bum" (Abbey), **Supp. XIII:** 2
"Haller's Second Home" (Maxwell), **Supp. VIII:** 169
Halliday, Mark, **Supp. XIX:** **81–95; Supp. XV:** 19, 20, 21, 23, 25, 27, 30
Hallock, Rev. Moses, **Supp. I Part 1:** 153

Hall of Mirrors, A (Stone), **Supp. V:** 295, 296–299, 300, 301
"Hallowe'en" (Huncke), **Supp. XIV:** 145
"Halloween Party, The" (Chabon), **Supp. XI:** 72
Halloween Tree, The (Bradbury), **Supp. IV Part 1:** 102, 112–113
"Halls, The" (Halliday), **Supp. XIX:** 90
Hallwas, John E., **Supp. I Part 2:** 454
Halpern, Daniel, **Supp. IV Part 1:** 94–95, 95
Halpern, Paul, **Supp. XXV:** 123
Halpern, Sue, **Supp. XXVI:** 128
Halsey, Theresa, **Supp. IV Part 1:** 330, 331
"Halt in the Desert, A" (Brodsky), **Supp. VIII:** 24
"Halves" (Dunn), **Supp. XI:** 149
Hamburg, Victoria, **Supp. XVI:** 126
Hamerik, Asger, **Supp. I Part 1:** 356
Hamill, Pete, **Supp. XX: 244, 255**
Hamill, Sam, **Supp. X:** 112, 125, 126, 127
Hamilton, Alexander, **I:** 485; **Supp. I Part 2:** 456, 483, 509
Hamilton, Alice, **Supp. I Part 1:** 5
Hamilton, David, **Supp. IX:** 296
Hamilton, Edith, **Supp. XVI:** 196
Hamilton, Lady Emma, **II:** 524
Hamilton, Hamish, **Supp. I Part 2:** 617
Hamilton, Walton, **Supp. I Part 2:** 632
Hamilton Stark (Banks), **Supp. V:** 8, 9–10, 11
"Hamlen Brook" (Wilbur), **Supp. III Part 2:** 564
"Hamlet" (Laforgue), **I:** 573; **III:** 11
Hamlet (Miller and Fraenkel), **III:** 178, 183
Hamlet (Shakespeare), **I:** 53, 183, 205, 377, 586–587; **II:** 158, 531; **III:** 7, 11, 12, 183; **IV:** 116, 131, 227; **Supp. I Part 1:** 369; **Supp. I Part 2:** 422, 457, 471; **Supp. IV Part 2:** 612; **Supp. IX:** 14
Hamlet, The (Faulkner), **II:** 69–71, 73, 74; **IV:** 131; **Retro. Supp. I:** 82, 91, 92; **Supp. IX:** 103; **Supp. VIII:** 178; **Supp. XI:** 247
"Hamlet and His Problems" (Eliot), **I:** 586–587
Hamlet of A. MacLeish, The (MacLeish), **III:** 11–12, 14, 15, 18
Hamlin, Eva, **Retro. Supp. II:** 115
"Hammer" (Bidart), **Supp. XV:** 35
Hammer, Adam, **Supp. XIII:** 112
Hammer, Langdon, **Retro. Supp. II:** 45, 53; **Supp. X:** 65
"Hammer Man, The" (Bambara), **Supp. XI:** 4–5
Hammett, Dashiell, **IV:** 286; **Retro. Supp. II:** 327; **Supp. I Part 1:** 286, 289, 291, 292, 293, 294, 295; **Supp. III Part 1:** 91; **Supp. IV Part 1:** 120, 121, **341–357; Supp. IV Part 2:** 461, 464, 468, 469, 472, 473; **Supp. IX:** 200; **Supp. XI:** 228; **Supp. XIII:** 159; **Supp. XIV:** 21; **Supp. XIX:** 178; **Supp. XVII:** 137; **Supp. XXI:** 68; **Supp. XXVI:** 277, 282
Hammon, Jupiter, **Supp. XXII:** 11

Hammond, John, **Supp. XVIII:** 24
Hammond, Karla, **Supp. IV Part 2:** 439, 442, 448, 637, 640, 644, 648
Hampl, Patricia, **Supp. IX:** 291; **Supp. XI:** 126; **Supp. XVII:** 21; **Supp. XXII: 81–101**
Hampson, Alfred Leete, **Retro. Supp. I:** 35–36, 38
"Hamrick's Polar Bear" (Caldwell), **I:** 309–310
Hamsun, Knut, **Supp. VIII:** 40; **Supp. XI:** 161, 167; **Supp. XII:** 21, 128
Hancock, John, **Supp. I Part 2:** 524; **Supp. XX: 282**
Hancock, Wade, **Supp. XVI:** 34
Handbook of North American Indians (Sando), **Supp. IV Part 2:** 510
Handcarved Coffins: A Nonfiction Account of an American Crime (Capote), **Supp. III Part 1:** 131
Handel, Georg Friedrich, **III:** 210; **IV:** 369
"Handfasting" (Wright), **Supp. XV:** 343
"Handfuls" (Sandburg), **III:** 584
"Handle with Care" (Fitzgerald), **Retro. Supp. I:** 114
Handley, William R., **Supp. XVIII:** 58
Handmaid's Tale, The (Atwood), **Supp. XIII:** 19, 20, **27–29**
"Hand of Casino, 1954, A" (Skloot), **Supp. XX: 194, 202**
"Hand of Emmagene, The" (Taylor), **Supp. V:** 314, 325–326
Hand of the Potter, The: A Tragedy in Four Acts (Dreiser), **Retro. Supp. II:** 104; **Supp. XVII:** 96
"Hands" (Anderson), **I:** 106, 107
"Hands" (Mora), **Supp. XIII:** 215
Hands of Orlac, The (M. Renard; Crewe-Jones, trans.), **Supp. XVII:** 58
Hand to Mouth (Auster), **Supp. XII:** 21
"Hand to Mouth" (Auster), **Supp. XII:** 31
Handy, Lowney, **Supp. XI:** 217, 220, 221, 225
Handy, W. C., **Supp. VIII:** 337
Handy Guide for Beggars, A (Lindsay), **Supp. I Part 2:** 376–378, 380, 382, 399
Haney, David, **Supp. XXI:** 253
"Hanged Man, A" (Cliff), **Supp. XXII:** 74
"Hanging Burley" (J. W. Miller), **Supp. XX: 167**
Hanging Garden, The (Wagoner), **Supp. IX: 338–339**
"Hanging Gardens of Tyburn, The" (Hecht), **Supp. X:** 58
"Hanging Man, The" (Davison), **Supp. XXVI:** 74
"Hanging of the Crane, The" (Longfellow), **Retro. Supp. II:** 169, 171
Hanging On (Conroy), **Supp. XVI:** 69
"Hanging Pictures in Nanny's Room" (Kenyon), **Supp. VII:** 164
"Hanging the Wash" (Alvarez), **Supp. VII:** 4
"Hangman, The" (Sexton), **Supp. II Part 2:** 680, 691

Hangover Mass (X. J. Kennedy), **Supp. XV:** 165
Hangsaman (Jackson), **Supp. IX:** 116, 123, **124**
Hanh, Thich Nhat, **Supp. V:** 199
Hanks, Lucy, **III:** 587
Hanks, Nancy. *See* Lincoln, Mrs. Thomas (Nancy Hanks)
Hanley, Lynne T., **Supp. IV Part 1:** 208
"Hanlon Mountain in Mist" (J. W. Miller), **Supp. XX: 164, 166–167**
Hanna, Mark, **Supp. I Part 2:** 395
Hannah, Barry, **Supp. X:** 285; **Supp. XIX:** 209; **Supp. XXI:** 38, 118
Hannah and Her Sisters (film; Allen), **Supp. XV: 9, 10–11**
"Hannah Armstrong" (Masters), **Supp. I Part 2:** 461
"Hannah Binding Shoes" (Larcom), **Supp. XIII:** 141, 143
"Hannah Byde" (D. West), **Supp. XVIII:** 280
Hannah's House (Hearon), **Supp. VIII:** 58, **60–61**
Hanneman, Audre, **II:** 259
Hannibal Lecter, My Father (Acker), **Supp. XII:** 6
Hanoi (McCarthy), **II:** 579
"Hanoi Drifting, January 2003" (Weigl), **Supp. XIX:** 288
Hansberry, Lorraine, **Supp. IV Part 1: 359–377; Supp. VIII:** 329
Hanscom, Leslie, **Supp. XI:** 229
"Hansel and Gretel" (Prose), **Supp. XVI:** 256, 258
Hansen, Erik, **Supp. V:** 241
Hansen, Harry, **IV:** 366; **Supp. XXII:** 194, 277
Han-shan, **Supp. VIII:** 292
Hanson, Curtis, **Supp. XI:** 67
Hanson, Elizabeth, **Supp. XXIV:** 220
Hanson, William F., **Supp. XXV:** 279, 280
Han Suyin, **Supp. X:** 291
Hanzlicek, C. G., **Supp. XV:** 73
Hapax (Stallings), **Supp. XXV:** 221, 222, 224, 231–233
Hapgood, Charles H., II, **Supp. XXI:** 6
Hapgood, Hutchins, **Supp. XVII: 95–108; Supp. XXI:** 1, 3, 9, 10
Hapgood, Norman, **Supp. XXI:** 2
Hapgoods, The: Three Earnest Brothers (Marcaccio), **Supp. XVII:** 106
"Happenings: An Art of Radical Juxtaposition" (Sontag), **Supp. III Part 2:** 456
"Happenstance" (Komunyakaa), **Supp. XIII:** 130
Happenstance (Shields), **Supp. VII:** 315–318, 320, 323, 324, 326
Happersberger, Lucien, **Supp. I Part 1:** 51
"Happiest Girl in the Whole U.S.A., The" (Muñoz), **Supp. XXV:** 131, 132
"Happiest I've Been, The" (Updike), **IV:** 219
Happily Ever After (Quindlen), **Supp. XVII:** 167
"Happiness" (Oliver), **Supp. VII:** 236
"Happiness" (Sandburg), **III:** 582–583
"Happiness"(Hadas), **Supp. XXIII:** 117

Happiness of Getting It Down Right, The (Steinman, ed.), **Supp. VIII:** 172
"Happiness of the Garden Variety" (Richard), **Supp. XIX:** 212
"Happy Birthday" (Bambara), **Supp. XI:** 4
Happy Birthday (Loos), **Supp. XVI:** 193
Happy Birthday, Wanda June (Vonnegut), **Supp. II Part 2:** 759, 776–777
Happy Birthday of Death, The (Corso), **Supp. XII: 127–129**
Happy Childhood, A (Matthews), **Supp. IX:** 155, 160, **161–163**
Happy Days (Beckett), **Retro. Supp. I:** 206; **Supp. XXIV:** 123
Happy Days, 1880–1892 (Mencken), **III:** 100, 111, 120
"Happy End" (Simic), **Supp. VIII:** 276–277
"Happy Failure, The" (Melville), **III:** 90
Happy Families Are All Alike (Taylor), **Supp. V:** 322–323, 325
Happy Isles of Oceania, The: Paddling the Pacific (Theroux), **Supp. VIII:** 324
"Happy Journey to Trenton and Camden, The" (Wilder), **IV:** 366
"Happy Man, The" (Lethem), **Supp. XVIII:** 139
"Happy Marriage, The" (MacLeish), **III:** 15–16
Happy Marriage and Other Poems, The (MacLeish), **III:** 4
Happy to Be Here (Keillor), **Supp. XVI:** 165, 171
"Happy To Be Here" (Keillor), **Supp. XVI:** 168
"Hapworth 16, 1924" (Salinger), **III:** 552, 571–572
Haram, Karen, **Supp. XXIII:** 276
"Harbor Dawn, The" (H. Crane), **Supp. XXI:** 132, 136
"Harbor Lights" (Doty), **Supp. XI:** 122
Harcourt, Alfred, **II:** 191, 451–452; **III:** 587; **Retro. Supp. I:** 131; **Supp. XV:** 308
Harcourt, Lewis, **Supp. XX: 232–233**
Harcourt, T. A., **I:** 196
Hardball (Paretsky), **Supp. XXV:** 177, 182, 184
Hard Candy, a Book of Stories (T. Williams), **IV:** 383
"Hardcastle Crags" (Plath), **Supp. I Part 2:** 537
"Hard Daddy" (Hughes), **Retro. Supp. I:** 200
"Hard Drive" (Huddle), **Supp. XXVI:** 151
"Hardened Criminals, The" (Lethem), **Supp. XVIII:** 139
Harder They Fall, The (Schulberg), **Supp. XV:** 194, 201
"Hardest Thing, The" (Huddle), **Supp. XXVI:** 151
Hard Facts (Baraka), **Supp. II Part 1:** 54, 55, 58
Hard Freight (Wright), **Supp. V:** 332, 339–340
Hard Hours, The (Hecht), **Supp. X:** 57, **59–62,** 63, 64
Hardie, Kier, **Supp. I Part 1:** 5

Hardin, Michael, **Supp. XXVI:** 242
Harding, Walter, **IV:** 177, 178
Harding, Warren G., **I:** 486; **II:** 253, 433; **Supp. I Part 1:** 24
"Hard Kind of Courage, The" (Baldwin), **Supp. I Part 1:** 52
Hard Laughter (Lamott), **Supp. XX: 132–133**
Hard Maple (S. and A. Warner), **Supp. XVIII:** 264
"Hard Rain's A-Gonna Fall, A" (song, Dylan), **Supp. XVIII:** 26, 29
Hard Time (Paretsky), **Supp. XXV:** 176, 177, 179, 182, 183
"Hard Time Keeping Up, A" (Ellison), **Retro. Supp. II:** 124
Hard Times (Dickens), **Supp. I Part 2:** 675
"Hard Times in Elfland, The" (Lanier), **Supp. I Part 1:** 365
"Hard Traveling: *Fay's* Deep South Landscape of Violence" (Beuka), **Supp. XXI:** 47
Hard Way Around, The: The Passages of Joshua Slocum (Wolff), **Supp. XXV:** 217
Hardwick, Elizabeth, **II:** 543, 554, 566; **Retro. Supp. II:** 179, 180, 183, 184, 190, 221, 228–229, 245; **Supp. I Part 1:** 196; **Supp. III Part 1: 193–215; Supp. IV Part 1:** 299; **Supp. V,** 319; **Supp. X,** 171; **Supp. XII:** 209; **Supp. XIV:** 89
"Hard Work 1956" (Dunn), **Supp. XI:** 147
Hardy, Barbara, **Supp. I Part 2:** 527
Hardy, Deborah, **Supp. XXVI:** 241, 242, 246
Hardy, Oliver, **Supp. I Part 2:** 607; **Supp. IV Part 2:** 574
Hardy, René, **Supp. III Part 1:** 235
Hardy, Thomas, **I:** 59, 103, 292, 317, 377; **II:** 181, 184–185, 186, 191–192, 271, 275, 372, 523, 542; **III:** 32, 453, 485, 508, 524; **IV:** 83, 135, 136; **Retro. Supp. I:** 141, 377–378; **Supp. I Part 1:** 217; **Supp. I Part 2:** 429, 512; **Supp. II Part 1:** 4, 26; **Supp. IX:** 40, 78, 85, 108, 211; **Supp. VIII:** 32; **Supp. X:** 228; **Supp. XI:** 311; **Supp. XIII:** 294, **Supp. XIII:** 130; **Supp. XIV:** 24; **Supp. XIX:** 86, 87; **Supp. XV:** 170; **Supp. XVIII:** 74; **Supp. XX: 195; Supp. XXI:** 109; **Supp. XXVI:** 67, 78
Hardy and the Poetry of Truth-Seeking (Halliday), **Supp. XIX:** 82
Harjo, Joy, **Supp. IV Part 1:** 325, 404; **Supp. IV Part 2:** 499, 507; **Supp. XII: 215–234; Supp. XVIII:** 189
Harlan's Race (P. N. Warren), **Supp. XX: 264–265**
"Harlem" (Hughes), **Retro. Supp. I:** 194, 204; **Supp. I Part 1:** 340; **Supp. VIII:** 213
Harlem, Mecca of the New Negro (Locke), **Supp. XIV:** 201
"Harlem Dancer, The" (McKay), **Supp. X:** 134

Harlem Gallery (Tolson), **Retro. Supp. I:** 208, 209, 210

Harlem Glory: A Fragment of Aframerican Life (McKay), **Supp. X:** 132, **141–142**

Harlem: Negro Metropolis (McKay), **Supp. X:** 132, 141, 142

Harlem Renaissance Remembered, The (Bontemps, ed.), **Supp. XXII:** 7

"Harlem Runs Wild" (McKay), **Supp. X:** 140

Harlem Shadows (McKay), **Supp. X:** 131–132, 136

Harlem Underground (Lacy), **Supp. XV:** 206

"Harlequin of Dreams, The" (Lanier), **Supp. I Part 1:** 365

Harlot's Ghost (Mailer), **Retro. Supp. II:** 211–212

Harlow, Jean, **IV:** 256; **Retro. Supp. I:** 110

"Harm" (C. Frost), **Supp. XV:** 101

Harmon, William, **Retro. Supp. I:** 37; **Supp. XI:** 248

"Harmonic" (F. Barthelme), **Supp. XI:** 26

Harmonium (Stevens), **III:** 196; **IV:** 76, 77, 78, 82, 87, 89, 92; **Retro. Supp. I:** 296, 297, 299, **300–302,** 301, 302

"Harmony of the Gospels" (Taylor), **IV:** 149

Harmony of the World (C. Baxter), **Supp. XVII:** 16–17

"Harmony of the World" (C. Baxter), **Supp. XVII:** 16

Harnett, Vincent, **Supp. XV:** 198

"Harp, The" (Weigl), **Supp. XIX:** 278

Harper (film), **Supp. IV Part 2:** 473

Harper, Donna, **Retro. Supp. I:** 194, 195, 209

Harper, Frances E. Watkins, **Supp. II Part 1:** 201–202; **Supp. XVIII:** 284; **Supp. XXII:** 11

Harper, Gordon Lloyd, **Retro. Supp. II:** 23

Harper, Michael S., **Retro. Supp. II:** 116, 123; **Supp. XV:** 74; **Supp. XXIV:** 184

Harper, William Rainey, **Supp. I Part 2:** 631

Harper's Anthology of 20th Century Native American Poetry (Niatum, ed.), **Supp. IV Part 1:** 331

"Harriet" (Lowell), **II:** 554

Harrigan, Edward, **II:** 276; **III:** 14

Harriman, Margaret, **Supp. XXIV:** 19

Harrington, Michael, **I:** 306

Harrington, Ollie, **Supp. XVI:** 142–143

Harris, Celia, **Retro. Supp. I:** 9

Harris, Corra, **Supp. XXII:** 190, 193, 196

Harris, George, **II:** 70

Harris, George Washington, **Supp. XXII:** 193

Harris, Joel Chandler, **III:** 338; **Supp. I Part 1:** 352; **Supp. II Part 1:** 192, 201; **Supp. XIV:** 61; **Supp. XX: 103**

Harris, Judith, **Supp. XIV:** 269

Harris, Julie, **II:** 587, 601; **Supp. IX:** 125

Harris, Leonard, **Supp. XIV:** 196, 211–212

Harris, MacDonald, **Supp. XI:** 65

Harris, Marie, **Supp. IX:** 153

Harris, Peter, **Supp. X:** 206, 207

Harris, Susan K., **Supp. XV:** 269

Harris, Thomas, **Supp. XIV:** 26; **Supp. XXI:** 67, 78

Harris, Trudier, **Supp. XXVI:** 13–14

Harris, Victoria Frenkel, **Supp. IV Part 1:** 68, 69

Harris, Violet J., **Supp. XXII:** 10, 13

Harris, William E., **Supp. XXIV:** 26

Harris, Wilson, **Supp. XXI:** 170

Harrison, Colin, **Supp. XIV:** 26

Harrison, Hazel, **Retro. Supp. II:** 115

Harrison, Jim, **Supp. VIII: 37–56; Supp. XIX:** 125, 126

Harrison, Judy, **Supp. XXIII:** 278

Harrison, Kathryn, **Supp. X:** 191

Harrison, Ken, **Supp. IX:** 101

Harrison, Oliver (pseudonym). *See* Smith, Harrison

Harrod, Lois Marie, **Supp. XXIII:** 131–132

Harry: A Portrait (Boyce), **Supp. XVII:** 104; **Supp. XXI:** 7, **13–14**

Harryhausen, Ray, **Supp. IV Part 1:** 115

Harryman, Carla, **Supp. XV:** 344

"Harry of Nothingham" (Hugo), **Supp. VI:** 146–147

"Harry's Death" (Carver), **Supp. III Part 1:** 146

"Harsh Judgment, The" (Kunitz), **Supp. III Part 1:** 264

Hart, Albert Bushnell, **Supp. I Part 2:** 479, 480, 481

Hart, Bernard, **I:** 241, 242, 248–250, 256

Hart, Henry, **Retro. Supp. II:** 187; **Supp. XIV:** 97

Hart, James D., **Supp. XVIII:** 257

Hart, John Seely, **Supp. XVIII:** 257, 258, 264

Hart, Lorenz, **III:** 361

Hart, Moss, **Supp. IV Part 2:** 574; **Supp. XV:** 329

Hart, Pearl, **Supp. X:** 103

"Hart Crane" (Tate), **I:** 381

"Hart Crane and Poetry: A Consideration of Crane's Intense Poetics with Reference to 'The Return' " (Grossman), **Retro. Supp. II:** 83

Harte, Anna Griswold, **Supp. II Part 1:** 341

Harte, Bret, **I:** 193, 195, 203; **II:** 289; **IV:** 196; **Retro. Supp. II:** 72; **Supp. II Part 1: 335–359,** 399; **Supp. XV:** 115

Harte, Walter Blackburn, **I:** 199

Harter, Carol C., **Supp. IV Part 1:** 217

Hartigan, Grace, **Supp. XXIII:** 210, 212, 217

Hartley, David, **III:** 77

Hartley, Lois, **Supp. I Part 2:** 459, 464–465

Hartley, L. P., **Supp. I Part 1:** 293

Hartley, Marsden, **IV:** 409, 413; **Retro. Supp. I:** 430; **Supp. X:** 137; **Supp. XV:** 298

Hartman, Geoffrey, **Supp. IV Part 1:** 119; **Supp. XII:** 130, 253

Hartman, Saidiya, **Supp. XX:** 154

Harum, David, **II:** 102

"Harvard" (Lowell), **II:** 554

Harvard College in the Seventeenth Century (Morison), **Supp. I Part 2:** 485

"Harvest" (E. P. Jones), **Supp. XXII:** 141

"Harvest, The" (Hempel), **Supp. XXI:** 115, **122–123**

Harvester, The (Stratton-Porter), **Supp. XX: 211, 212, 218, 221**

"*Harvester, The:* The Natural Bounty of Gene Stratton-Porter" (Birkelo), **Supp. XX: 220–221**

"Harvesters of Night and Water" (Hogan), **Supp. IV Part 1:** 412

"Harvest Song" (Toomer), **Supp. III Part 2:** 483

Harvill Book of 20th Century Poetry in English, **Supp. X:** 55

Harvin, Emily, **Supp. XXIII:** 174

"Harv Is Plowing Now" (Updike), **Retro. Supp. I:** 318

Haselden, Elizabeth Lee, **Supp. VIII:** 125

"Hasidic Noir" (Abraham), **Supp. XXIV: 14–15**

Haskell, Mary, **Supp. XX: 115, 117**

"Haskell's Mill" (Davison), **Supp. XXVI:** 73, 75, 76

Hass, Robert, **Supp. VI: 97–111; Supp. VIII:** 24, 28; **Supp. XI:** 142, 270; **Supp. XIV:** 83, 84; **Supp. XXI:** 60; **Supp. XXVI:** 61, 68

Hassam, Childe, **Retro. Supp. II:** 136

Hassan, Ihab, **IV:** 99–100, 115; **Supp. XI:** 221

Hasse, Henry, **Supp. IV Part 1:** 102

Hasty-Pudding, The (Barlow), **Supp. II Part 1:** 74, 77–80

"Hater of Mediocrity, The" (Boulton), **Supp. XXII:** 23

Hate That Hate Produced, The (CBS documentary), **Supp. XX: 102**

Hatful of Rain, A (film), **Supp. XXVI:** 134

Hatful of Rain, A (Gazzo), **III:** 155

Hatlen, Burton, **Supp. V:** 138, 139–140; **Supp. XXI:** 24

"Hatred"(O'Hara), **Supp. XXIII:** 212

"Hattie Bloom" (Oliver), **Supp. VII:** 232

Haugen, Hayley Mitchell, **Supp. XXIV:** 215

Haunch, Paunch, and Jowl (Ornitz), **Supp. IX:** 227

Haunted Lady, The (Rinehart), **Supp. XXV:** 198, 200

"Haunted Landscape" (Ashbery), **Supp. III Part 1:** 22

Haunted Merchant, The (Briggs), **Supp. XVIII:** 2, 8

"Haunted Mind" (Simic), **Supp. VIII:** 282

"Haunted Mind, The" (Hawthorne), **II:** 230–231

"Haunted Oak, The" (Dunbar), **Supp. II Part 1:** 207, 208

"Haunted Palace, The" (Poe), **III:** 421

"Haunted Valley, The" (Bierce), **I:** 200

Haunting, The (film), **Supp. IX:** 125

Haunting of Hill House, The (Jackson), **Supp. IX:** 117, 121, 126

Hauptmann, Gerhart, **III:** 472

Haussmann, Sonja, **Supp. XIII:** 331, **Supp. XIII:** 347
"Havanna vanities come to dust in Miami" (Didion), **Supp. IV Part 1:** 210
Havel, Hippolyte, **Supp. XXI:** 4, 6
Haven, Cynthia, **Supp. XV:** 252, 264; **Supp. XXIII:** 134, 138, 139
Haven's End (Marquand), **III:** 55, 56, 63, 68
"Have You Ever Faked an Orgasm" (Peacock), **Supp. XIX:** 199
"Have You Ever Tried to Enter the Long Black Branches" (Oliver), **Supp. VII:** 247
"Having a Coke with You"(O'Hara), **Supp. XXIII:** 219
"Having Been Interstellar" (Ammons), **Supp. VII:** 25
"Having It Out With Melancholy" (Kenyon), **Supp. VII:** 171
"Having Lost My Sons, I Confront the Wreckage of the Moon: Christmas, 1960" (Wright), **Supp. III Part 2:** 600
"Having Saints" (Davison), **Supp. XXVI:** 71
"Having Snow" (Schwartz), **Supp. II Part 2:** 652
"Having Words"(Thompson), **Supp. XXIII:** 293–294
"Hawaii, Washington, Vermont: A Frame for the Verse" (Taggard), **Supp. XXII:** 281–282
Hawaiian Hilltop (Taggard), **Supp. XXII:** 275
Hawai'i One Summer (Kingston), **Supp. V:** 157, 160, 166, 169–170
Haweis, Stephen, **Supp. XXII:** 157, 158, 159, 161, 163, 165
"Hawk, The" (Francis), **Supp. IX:** 81
Hawke, David Freeman, **Supp. I Part 2:** 511, 516
Hawkes, John, **I:** 113; **Retro. Supp. II:** 234; **Supp. III Part 1:** 2; **Supp. IX:** 212; **Supp. V:** 40; **Supp. XVII:** 183; **Supp. XXI:** 210
Hawkins, Gary, **Supp. XXI:** 35, 39
Hawkins, William, **II:** 587
Hawk in the Rain, The (Hughes), **Retro. Supp. II:** 244; **Supp. I Part 2:** 537, 540
Hawk Is Dying, The (Crews), **Supp. XI:** 111
Hawk Moon (Shepard), **Supp. III Part 2:** 445
Hawks, Howard, **Supp. IV Part 1:** 130; **Supp. XVIII:** 148
"Hawk's Cry in Autumn, The" (Brodsky), **Supp. VIII:** 29
"Hawk's Shadow" (Glück), **Supp. V:** 85
Hawk's Well, The (Yeats), **III:** 459–460
Hawley, Adelaide, **Supp. XIV:** 207
Hawley, Joseph, **I:** 546
Hawthorne (James), **II:** 372–378; **Retro. Supp. I:** 220, **223–224**
"Hawthorne" (Longfellow), **Retro. Supp. II:** 169
"Hawthorne" (Lowell), **II:** 550
Hawthorne, Julian, **II:** 225; **Supp. I Part 1:** 38; **Supp. XV:** 274

Hawthorne, Nathaniel, **I:** 106, 204, 211, 340, 355, 363, 384, 413, 458, 561–562; **II:** 7, 8, 40, 60, 63, 74, 89, 127–128, 138, 142, 198, **223–246**, 255, 259, 264, 267, 272, 274, 277, 281, 282, 295, 307, 309, 311, 313, 322, 324, 326, 402, 408, 446, 501, 545; **III:** 51, 81–82, 83, 84, 85, 87, 88, 91, 92, 113, 316, 359, 412, 415, 421, 438, 453, 454, 507, 565, 572; **IV:** 2, 4, 167, 172, 179, 194, 333, 345, 453; **Retro. Supp. I:** 1, 53, 59, 62, 63, 91, **145–167**, 215, 218, 220, 223, 248–249, 252, 257, 258, 330, 331, 365; **Retro. Supp. II:** 136, 142, 153, 156–157, 158, 159, 187, 221; **Supp. I Part 1:** 38, 188, 197, 317, 372; **Supp. I Part 2:** 420, 421, 545, 579, 580, 582, 587, 595, 596; **Supp. III Part 2:** 501; **Supp. IV Part 1:** 80, 127, 297; **Supp. IV Part 2:** 463, 596; **Supp. IX:** 114; **Supp. V:** 152; **Supp. VIII:** 103, 105, 108, 153, 201; **Supp. X:** 78; **Supp. XI:** 51, 78; **Supp. XII:** 26; **Supp. XIII:** 102; **Supp. XIV:** 48; **Supp. XV:** 269, 272, 282; **Supp. XVI:** 83, 84, 157; **Supp. XVII:** 42; **Supp. XVIII:** 258, 260; **Supp. XXI:** 201; **Supp. XXIII:** 161, 190, 290; **Supp. XXV:** 242, 249
Hawthorne, Mrs. Nathaniel (Sophia Peabody), **II:** 224, 244; **III:** 75, 86
Hawthorne, Rose, **II:** 225
Hawthorne, Una, **II:** 225
"Hawthorne and His Mosses" (Melville), **Retro. Supp. I:** 254; **Supp. XIV:** 48
"Hawthorne Aspect \[of Henry James\], The" (Eliot), **Retro. Supp. I:** 63
"Hawthorne in Solitude" (Cowley), **Supp. II Part 1:** 143
Hay, John, **I:** 1, 10, 12, 14–15; **Supp. I Part 1:** 352
Hay, Mrs. John, **I:** 14
Hay, Sara Henderson, **Supp. XIV:** 119–135
Hayakawa, S. I., **I:** 448; **Supp. I Part 1:** 315; **Supp. XV:** 176
Haycroft, Howard, **Supp. XXV:** 199; **Supp. XXVI:** 277
Hayden, Robert, **Supp. II Part 1:** 361–383; **Supp. IV Part 1:** 169; **Supp. XIII:** 115, 127; **Supp. XIV:** 119, 123
Hayden, Sterling, **Supp. XI:** 304
Hayden, William R., **Supp. XXV:** 38
Haydn, Hiram, **IV:** 100, 358
Hayduke Lives! (Abbey), **Supp. XIII:** 16
Hayek, Friedrich A. von, **Supp. IV Part 2:** 524
Hayes, Alfred, **Supp. XXVI:** 133–146
Hayes, Helen, **Supp. XVI:** 193, 195
Hayes, Ira, **Supp. IV Part 1:** 326
Hayes, Richard, **Supp. V:** 320
Hayes, Rutherford B., **Supp. I Part 2:** 419
Hayford, James, **Supp. XXII:** 204, 218
Haygood, Wil, **Supp. VIII:** 79
"Haying While the Sun Shines" (L. I. Wilder), **Supp. XXII:** 290
Hayne, Paul Hamilton, **Supp. I Part 1:** 352, 354, 355, 360, 372

Haynes, Todd, **Supp. XVIII:** 23
Haynes-Smith, William, **Supp. XX: 231, 232, 233**
Hayward, Florence, **Retro. Supp. II:** 65
Hayward, John, **Retro. Supp. I:** 67
Hayward, Leland, **Supp. XIX:** 250
Haywood, "Big" Bill, **I:** 483; **Supp. V:** 286; **Supp. XXIII:** 162
Hazan, Joe, **Supp. XXIII:** 212
Hazard, Grace, **II:** 530
Hazard of Fortunes, A (Howells), **Retro. Supp. II:** 288
Hazard of New Fortunes, A (Howells), **II:** 275, 276, 286–297, 290
Hazel, Robert, **Supp. VIII:** 137, 138
Hazen, General W. B., **I:** 192, 193
Hazlitt, Henry, **Supp. IV Part 2:** 524
Hazlitt, William, **I:** 58, 378; **II:** 315; **Supp. XXI:** 205
Hazmat (McClatchy), **Supp. XII:** 265–270
Hazo, Samuel, **I:** 386; **Supp. XIV:** 123, 124
Hazzard, Shirley, **Supp. VIII:** 151
H.D. *See* Doolittle, Hilda
"He" (Porter), **III:** 434, 435
"Head and Shoulders" (Fitzgerald), **Retro. Supp. I:** 101
Headhunter (Findley), **Supp. XX: 57–59, 60, 61**
"Head-Hunter, The" (O. Henry), **Supp. II Part 1:** 403
"Headless Hawk, The" (Capote), **Supp. III Part 1:** 124
Headlines (T. Williams), **IV:** 381
Headlong Hall (Peacock), **Supp. I Part 1:** 307
Headmaster, The (McPhee), **Supp. III Part 1:** 291, 294, 298
"Head of Joaquín Murrieta, The" (Rodriguez), **Supp. XIV:** 303
Headsman, The (Cooper), **I:** 345–346
Heads of Grain (al-Sanábil) (Gibran), **Supp. XX: 124**
"Headwaters" (Momaday), **Supp. IV Part 2:** 486
"Head Wound" (Halliday), **Supp. XIX:** 92
Healing, The (G. Jones), **Supp. XXIV:** 183, 185, **190–192,** 195
Healy, Eloise Klein, **Supp. XI:** 121, 124, 126, 127, 129, 137
Healy, Tim, **II:** 129, 137
Heaney, Sally, **Supp. XVII:** 241
Heaney, Seamus, **Retro. Supp. II:** 245; **Supp. IX:** 41, 42; **Supp. X:** 67, 122; **Supp. XI:** 249; **Supp. XV:** 256; **Supp. XXI:** 54, 243
"Heard through the Walls of the Racetrack Glen Motel" (X. J. Kennedy), **Supp. XV:** 170
"Hearing, The" (Huddle), **Supp. XXVI:** 155
Hearn, Lafcadio, **I:** 211; **II:** 311
Hearon, Shelby, **Supp. VIII:** 57–72
Hearst, Patty, **Supp. IV Part 1:** 195
Hearst, William Randolph, **I:** 198, 207, 208; **IV:** 298
Heart and Perimeter (Bierds), **Supp. XVII: 28–29**

"Heart and the Lyre, The" (Bogan), **Supp. III Part 1:** 65

"Heart as Origami, The" (Hirshfield), **Supp. XXIII:** 132

"Heartbeat" (Harjo), **Supp. XII:** 221–222

Heartbreak Hotel (Siddons), **Supp. XXII:** 239, 241, 242

Heartbreak Kid, The (film), **Supp. IV Part 2:** 575, 589

"Heart Failure"(Schott), **Supp. XXIII:** 252

"Heart Finds Its Own Conclusion, The" (Muñoz), **Supp. XXV:** 136

Heart for the Gods of Mexico, A (Aiken), **I:** 54

"Hear the Nightingale Sing" (Gordon), **II:** 200

Hear the Wind Blow (Sanders), **Supp. XVI:** 268

Heart is a Lonely Hunter, The (McCullers), **II:** 586, 588–593, 604, 605

Heartland (film), **Supp. XXVI:** 183–184

Heart of a Woman, The (Angelou), **Supp. IV Part 1:** 2, 5, 7–9, 9, 14, 17

Heart of Darkness (Conrad), **Retro. Supp. II:** 292; **Supp. V:** 249, 311; **Supp. VIII:** 4, 316; **Supp. XIX:** 28; **Supp. XX:** 18, 57–58; **Supp. XXIV:** 286

"Heart of Darkness" (Conrad), **I:** 575, 578; **II:** 595; **Supp. XVI:** 212

Heart of Darkness (Didion), **Supp. IV Part 1:** 207

Heart of Dixie (film), **Supp. XXII:** 239, 241

Heart of Haiku, The (Hirshfield), **Supp. XXIII:** 137–138

Heart of Happy Hollow, The (Dunbar), **Supp. II Part 1:** 214

Heart of Knowledge, The: American Indians on the Bomb (Gunn Allen and Caputi, eds.), **Supp. IV Part 1:** 334–335

"Heart of Knowledge, The: Nuclear Themes in Native American Thought and Literature" (Caputi), **Supp. IV Part 1:** 335

Heart of the Earth (Moraga), **Supp. XXIII:** 196

"Heart of the Park, The " (O'Connor), **Retro. Supp. II:** 225

Heart of the West (O. Henry), **Supp. II Part 1:** 410

"Hearts, The" (Pinsky), **Supp. VI:** 245–247, 248

"'Hearts and Flowers' " (MacLeish), **III:** 8

"Hearts and Heads" (Ransom), **Supp. I Part 1:** 373

"Heart's Graveyard Shift, The" (Komunyakaa), **Supp. XIII:** 120

Heart-Shape in the Dust (Hayden), **Supp. II Part 1:** 365, 366

Heart's Needle (Snodgrass), **I:** 400

"Heart's Needle" (Snodgrass), **Supp. VI:** 311–313, 320

"Hearts of Oak" (Rowson), **Supp. XV:** 243

"Heart Songs" (Proulx), **Supp. VII:** 254

Heart Songs and Other Stories (Proulx), **Supp. VII:** 252–256, 261

Heart to Artemis, The (Bryher), **Supp. I Part 1:** 259

"Heart to Heart" (Zitkala-Ša), **Supp. XXV:** 284

Heartwood (Burke), **Supp. XIV:** 35

Heath, Shirley, **Supp. XX: 90**

Heath Anthology of American Literature, The, **Supp. IX:** 4; **Supp. XV:** 270, 313

Heathcote, Anne. *See* De Lancey, Mrs. James

"Heathen Chinee, The" (Harte), **Supp. II Part 1:** 350–351, 352

Heathen Days, 1890–1936 (Mencken), **III:** 100, 111

Heath-Stubbs, John, **Supp. XV:** 153

Heaton, David, **Supp. XXVI:** 7

Heat's On, The (C. Himes), **Supp. XVI:** 143, 144

"Heaven" (Dunn), **Supp. XI:** 154

"Heaven" (Levine), **Supp. V:** 182

"Heaven" (Patchett), **Supp. XII:** 309

Heaven and Earth: A Cosmology (Goldbarth), **Supp. XII: 187**

"Heaven and Earth in Jest" (Dillard), **Supp. VI:** 24, 28

"Heaven as Anus" (Kumin), **Supp. IV Part 2:** 448

Heavenly Conversation, The (Mather), **Supp. II Part 2:** 460

"Heavenly Feast, The" (Schnackenberg), **Supp. XV:** 257, 259

Heavens (Untermeyer), **Supp. XV:** 306

Heavens and Earth (Benét), **Supp. XI:** 44

Heaven's Coast (Doty), **Supp. XI:** 119, 121, **129–130,** 134; **Supp. XXIII:** 126

Heaven's Prisoners (Burke), **Supp. XIV:** 23, 29

"Heavy Angel, The" (Everwine), **Supp. XV:** 80

"Heavy Bear Who Goes with Me, The" (Schwartz), **Supp. II Part 2:** 646

"Heavy Trash" (Halliday), **Supp. XIX:** 92, 93

Hebert, Ernest, **Supp. XXII:** 207

"He Came Also Still" (Zukofsky), **Supp. III Part 2:** 612

Hecht, Anthony, **IV:** 138; **Supp. III Part 2:** 541, 561; **Supp. X: 55–75; Supp. XII:** 269–270; **Supp. XV:** 251, 256

Hecht, Ben, **I:** 103; **II:** 42; **Supp. I Part 2:** 646; **Supp. XI:** 307; **Supp. XIII:** 106; **Supp. XXV:** 18, 19, 22, 27, 29

Hecht, S. Theodore, **Supp. III Part 2:** 614

Heckewelder, John, **II:** 503

"Hedge Island" (Lowell), **II:** 524

Hedges, William I., **II:** 311–312

"He 'Digesteth Harde Yron' " (Moore), **Supp. IV Part 2:** 454

Hedin, Robert, **Supp. XII:** 200, 202

Hedylus (Doolittle), **Supp. I Part 1:** 259, 270

"Heel & Toe To the End" (W. C. Williams), **Retro. Supp. I:** 430

Heffernan, Michael, **Supp. XII:** 177

"HEGEL" (Baraka), **Supp. II Part 1:** 53

Hegel, Georg Wilhelm Friedrich, **I:** 265; **II:** 358; **III:** 262, 308–309, 480, 481, 487, 607; **IV:** 86, 333, 453; **Supp. I Part 2:** 633, 635, 640, 645; **Supp. XVI:** 289; **Supp. XXVI:** 234

"Hegemony of Race, The" (Du Bois), **Supp. II Part 1:** 181

Hegger, Grace Livingston. *See* Lewis, Mrs. Sinclair (Grace Livingston Hegger)

"He Had Spent His Youth Dreaming" (Dobyns), **Supp. XIII:** 90

Heidegger, Martin, **II:** 362, 363; **III:** 292; **IV:** 491; **Retro. Supp. II:** 87; **Supp. V:** 267; **Supp. VIII:** 9; **Supp. XVI:** 283, 288; **Supp. XXVI:** 234

Heidenmauer, The (Cooper), **I:** 345–346

Heidi Chronicles, The (Wasserstein), **Supp. IV Part 1:** 309; **Supp. XV:** 319, **325–327**

"Height of the Ridiculous, The" (Holmes), **Supp. I Part 1:** 302

Heilbroner, Robert, **Supp. I Part 2:** 644, 648, 650

Heilbrun, Carolyn G., **Supp. IX:** 66; **Supp. XI:** 208; **Supp. XIV:** 161, 163; **Supp. XX: 108**

Heilman, Robert Bechtold, **Supp. XIV:** 11, 12

Heilpern, John, **Supp. XIV:** 242

Heim, Michael, **Supp. V:** 209

Heine, Heinrich, **II:** 272, 273, 277, 281, 282, 387, 544; **IV:** 5; **Supp. XV:** 293, 299; **Supp. XVI:** 188

Heineman, Frank, **Supp. III Part 2:** 619

Heinemann, Larry, **Supp. XXII: 103–117**

Heinlein, Robert, **Supp. IV Part 1:** 102; **Supp. XVI:** 122; **Supp. XVIII:** 149

Heinz, Helen. *See* Tate, Mrs. Allen (Helen Heinz)

Heiress, The (film), **Retro. Supp. I:** 222

"Heirs" (Nye), **Supp. XIII:** 284

"He Is Not Worth the Trouble" (Rowson), **Supp. XV:** 240

"He Knew" (C. Himes), **Supp. XVI:** 137

"Helas" (Creeley), **Supp. IV Part 1:** 150, 158

Helburn, Theresa, **IV:** 381

Heldreth, Leonard, **Supp. V:** 151

"Helen" (Lowell), **II:** 544

"Helen, Thy Beauty Is to Me" (Fante), **Supp. XI:** 169

"Helen: A Courtship" (Faulkner), **Retro. Supp. I:** 81

"Helen I Love You" (Farrell), **II:** 28, 45

Helen in Egypt (Doolittle), **Supp. I Part 1:** 260, 272, 273, 274; **Supp. XV:** 264

Helen Keller: Sketch for a Portrait (Brooks), **I:** 254

"Helen of Tyre" (Longfellow), **II:** 496

Heliodora (Doolittle), **Supp. I Part 1:** 266

"He Lives On the Landing" (Espaillat), **Supp. XXI:** 108

"Helix" (Sobin), **Supp. XVI:** 283

Hellbox (O'Hara), **III:** 361

Helle, Anita, **Supp. XXIII:** 117

Heller, Joseph, **III:** 2, 258; **IV:** 98; **Retro. Supp. II:** 324; **Supp. I Part 1:** 196; **Supp. IV Part 1: 379–396; Supp. V:**

244; **Supp. VIII:** 245; **Supp. XI:** 307; **Supp. XII:** 167–168; **Supp. XV:** 322; **Supp. XVII:** 139; **Supp. XXIII:** 100
"Hell-Heaven" (Lahiri), **Supp. XXI: 181–183,** 183, 184–186, 188
Hellman, Lillian, **I:** 28; **III:** 28; **Supp. I Part 1: 276–298; Supp. IV Part 1:** 1, 12, 83, 353, 355, 356; **Supp. IX:** 196, 198, 200–201, 204; **Supp. VIII:** 243
Hellmann, Lillian, **Retro. Supp. II:** 327
Hello (Creeley), **Supp. IV Part 1:** 155, 157
"Hello, Hello Henry" (Kumin), **Supp. IV Part 2:** 446
"Hello, Stranger" (Capote), **Supp. III Part 1:** 120
Hello Dolly! (musical play), **IV:** 357
Hell's Angels: A Strange and Terrible Saga (Thompson), **Supp. XXIV:** 282, 283, 288, 290–291
Hellyer, John, **Supp. I Part 2:** 468
Helm, Bob, **Supp. XV:** 147
Helm, Levon, **Supp. XVIII:** 26
Helmets (Dickey), **Supp. IV Part 1:** 175, 178, 180
"Helmsman, The" (Doolittle), **Supp. I Part 1:** 266
"Help" (Barth), **I:** 139
"Help Her to Believe" (Olsen). *See* "I Stand There Ironing" (Olsen)
Helprin, Mark, **Supp. XIX:** 142; **Supp. XXV: 79–91**
Helsel, Philip Browning, **Supp. XXVI:** 53
"Helsinki Window" (Creeley), **Supp. IV Part 1:** 158
"Hema and Kaushik" (Lahiri), **Supp. XXI:** 183, 188
Hemenway, Robert E., **Supp. IV Part 1:** 6
Hemingway, Dr. Clarence Edwards, **II:** 248, 259
Hemingway, Ernest, **I:** 28, 64, 97, 99, 105, 107, 117, 150, 162, 190, 211, 221, 288, 289, 295, 367, 374, 378, 421, 423, 445, 476, 477, 478, 482, 484–485, 487, 488, 489, 491, 495, 504, 517; **II:** 27, 44, 51, 58, 68–69, 78, 90, 97, 127, 206, **247–270,** 289, 424, 431, 456, 457, 458–459, 482, 560, 600; **III:** 2, 18, 20, 35, 36, 37, 40, 61, 108, 220, 334, 363, 364, 382, 453, 454, 471–472, 476, 551, 575, 576, 584; **IV:** 27, 28, 33, 34, 35, 42, 49, 97, 108, 122, 126, 138, 190, 191, 201, 216, 217, 257, 297, 363, 404, 427, 433, 451; **Retro. Supp. I:** 74, 98, 108, 111, 112, 113, 115, **169–191,** 215, 292, 359, 418; **Retro. Supp. II:** 19, 24, 30, 68, 115, 123; **Supp. I Part 2:** 621, 658, 678; **Supp. II Part 1:** 221; **Supp. III Part 1:** 146; **Supp. III Part 2:** 617; **Supp. IV Part 1:** 48, 102, 123, 197, 236, 342, 343, 344, 348, 350, 352, 380–381, 383; **Supp. IV Part 2:** 463, 468, 502, 607, 679, 680, 681, 689, 692; **Supp. IX:** 16, 57, 58, 94, 106, 260, 262; **Supp. V:** 237, 240, 244, 250, 336; **Supp. VIII:** 40, 101, 105, 179, 182, 183, 188, 189, 196;
Supp. X: 137, 167, 223, 225; **Supp. XI:** 214, 221; **Supp. XIII:** 96, 255, 270; **Supp. XIV:** 24, 83; **Supp. XIX:** 131, 154, 157, 246; **Supp. XV:** 69, 135; **Supp. XVI:** 203, 205–206, 208, 210, 233, 236–237, 281–282; **Supp. XVII:** 4, 105, 107, 137, 228, 229; **Supp. XVIII:** 74, 90, 102; **Supp. XX: 45, 74, 76; Supp. XXI:** 7, 8, 36, 262; **Supp. XXIII:** 4, 68, 166, 174, 275, 299; **Supp. XXIV:** 54, 64, 97, 284; **Supp. XXVI:** 17, 32, 135, 147, 180
Hemingway, Mrs. Ernest (Hadley Richardson), **II:** 257, 260, 263
Hemingway, Mrs. Ernest (Martha Gellhorn), **II:** 260
Hemingway, Mrs. Ernest (Mary Welsh), **II:** 257, 260
Hemingway, Mrs. Ernest (Pauline Pfeiffer), **II:** 260
"Hemingway in Paris" (Cowley), **Supp. II Part 1:** 144
"Hemingway Story, A" (Dubus), **Supp. VII:** 91
"Hemingway: The Old Lion" (Cowley), **Supp. II Part 1:** 143
"Hemp, The" (Benét), **Supp. XI:** 44
Hempel, Amy, **Supp. XIX:** 209; **Supp. XXI: 115–128**
"Henchman, The" (Whittier), **Supp. I Part 2:** 696
Henderson, Alice Corbin, **Supp. I Part 2:** 387; **Supp. XV:** 302–303
Henderson, Darwin L., **Supp. XIII:** 213, 221–222
Henderson, Jane, **Supp. VIII:** 87; **Supp. XX: 84**
Henderson, Katherine, **Supp. IV Part 1:** 203, 207
Henderson, Linda. *See* Hogan, Linda
Henderson, Robert W., **Supp. VIII:** 124
Henderson, Stephen, **Supp. IV Part 1:** 365
Henderson, the Rain King (Bellow), **I:** 144, 147, 148, 152, 153, 154, 155, 158, 160, 161, 162–163; **Retro. Supp. II:** 19, **24–25,** 30
"Hen Flower, The" (Kinnell), **Supp. III Part 1:** 247–248
Henie, Sonja, **Supp. XII:** 165
Henkin, Joshua, **Supp. XXII:** 216
Henle, James, **II:** 26, 30, 38, 41; **Supp. IX:** 2
Henley, Beth, **Supp. XXI:** 145
Hennesy, Dale, **Supp. XV:** 5
Henninger, Katherine, **Supp. XXI:** 253
Henri, Robert, **IV:** 411; **Supp. I Part 2:** 376
Henrich, Edith, **Supp. XXIV:** 214
Henry, Arthur, **I:** 515; **Retro. Supp. II:** 97
Henry, DeWitt, **Supp. XI:** 342
Henry, O., **I:** 201; **III:** 5; **Supp. I Part 2:** 390, 462; **Supp. II Part 1: 385–412; Supp. XV:** 40
Henry, Robert, **Retro. Supp. II:** 103
Henry, William A., III, **Supp. IV Part 2:** 574
Henry and Clara (Mallon), **Supp. XIX:** 132, **136–137,** 139, 141
Henry and June (film), **Supp. X:** 186
Henry and June: From the Unexpurgated Diary of Anaïs Nin, **Supp. X:** 184, 185, 187, 194
Henry Holt and Company, **Retro. Supp. I:** 121, 131, 133, 136
Henry IV (Shakespeare), **III:** 166; **Supp. VIII:** 164
"Henry James, Jr." (Howells), **II:** 289; **Retro. Supp. I:** 220
"Henry James and the Art of Teaching" (Rowe), **Retro. Supp. I:** 216
"Henry Lagoon" (Huddle), **Supp. XXVI:** 155
"Henry Manley, Living Alone, Keeps Time" (Kumin), **Supp. IV Part 2:** 451
"Henry Manley Looks Back" (Kumin), **Supp. IV Part 2:** 451
"Henry Manley" poems (Kumin), **Supp. IV Part 2:** 446
Henry Miller Reader, The (Durrell, ed.), **III:** 175, 190
"Henry's Confession" (Berryman), **I:** 186
Henry VIII (Shakespeare), **Supp. IX:** 235
Henslee, **Supp. IV Part 1:** 217
Henson, Josiah, **Supp. I Part 2:** 589
Hentoff, Margot, **Supp. IV Part 1:** 205
Hentz, Caroline Lee, **Supp. I Part 2:** 584
Henze, Hans Werner, **Supp. II Part 1:** 24
"He of the Assembly" (Bowles), **Supp. IV Part 1:** 90
Hepburn, Katharine, **Supp. IX:** 189; **Supp. XI:** 17
Heraclitus, **II:** 1, 163; **IV:** 86
Herakles: A Play in Verse (MacLeish), **III:** 21, 22
Herald of the Autochthonic Spirit (Corso), **Supp. XII:** 134–136
He Ran All the Way (film), **Supp. XVII:** 63
Herberg, Will, **III:** 291
Herbert, Edward, **II:** 11
Herbert, Francis (pseudonym). *See* Bryant, William Cullen
Herbert, George, **II:** 12; **IV:** 141, 145, 146, 151, 153, 156, 165; **Retro. Supp. II:** 40; **Supp. I Part 1:** 80, 107, 108, 122; **Supp. IV Part 2:** 646; **Supp. XV:** 92, 212, 251; **Supp. XXI:** 109
Herbert, Zbigniew, **Supp. VIII:** 20
Herbert Huncke Reader, The (Schafer, ed.), **Supp. XIV:** 137, 138, 139, 140, 145, 147, 150, 151–152
Herbert of Cherbury, Lord, **II:** 108
"Herbert West—Reanimator" (Lovecraft), **Supp. XXV:** 112
"Herbert White" (Bidart), **Supp. XV:** 24, 27
Herbs and the Earth (Beston), **Supp. XXVI:** 35–36
Herbst, Josephine, **Retro. Supp. II:** 325, 328; **Supp. XIII:** 295; **Supp. XXVI:** 18, 26, 28
"Her Choice" (Larcom), **Supp. XIII:** 144
"Her Dead Brother" (Lowell), **Retro. Supp. II:** 188
"Her Dream Is of the Sea" (Ríos), **Supp. IV Part 2:** 546
"Here" (Kenyon), **Supp. VII:** 164

Here and Beyond (Wharton), **Retro. Supp. I:** 382

Here and Now (Levertov), **Supp. III Part 1:** 275, 276

"Here and There" (Wallace), **Supp. X:** 305–306

Here Comes the Mystery Man (Sanders), **Supp. XVI:** 269

"Here Comes Winston, Full of the Holy Spirit" (Eugenides), **Supp. XXIV:** 133

Heredia, Juanita, **Supp. XI:** 185, 190

Heredity and Variation (Lock), **Retro. Supp. I:** 375

Heredity: A Psychological Study of Its Phenomena, Laws, Causes, and Consequences (Ribot), **Supp. XX:** 238

"Here Inside My Forehead" (Rasmussen; Nelson and Espeland, trans.), **Supp. XVIII:** 180

Here is Your War (Pyle), **Supp. XVII:** 61

Here Let Us Feast (M. F. K. Fisher), **Supp. XVII:** 86, 87

Here Lies (Parker), **Supp. IX:** 192

Herendeen, Anne, **Supp. XXII:** 275

Here on Earth (Hoffman), **Supp. X:** 77, 89

Heresy and the Ideal: On Contemporary Poetry (Baker), **Supp. XI:** 142

"Here to Learn" (Bowles), **Supp. IV Part 1:** 93

"Here to Yonder" (Hughes), **Retro. Supp. I:** 205

"Her Father's Letters" (Milburn), **Supp. XI:** 242

"Her Favorite Story" (Richard), **Supp. XIX:** 211, 212

Herford, Beatrice, **Supp. XXVI:** 275

Herford, Oliver, **Supp. XXVI:** 275

Herford, Reverend Brooke, **I:** 471

Herford, Will, **Supp. XXII:** 275

"Her Game" (Skloot), **Supp. XX: 196, 202**

Hergesheimer, Joseph, **Supp. I Part 2:** 620; **Supp. XVI:** 187

"Heritage" (Cullen), **Supp. IV Part 1:** 164–165, 168, 170, 171

"Heritage" (Hogan), **Supp. IV Part 1:** 413

"Her Kind" (Sexton), **Supp. II Part 2:** 687

Herland (Gilman), **Supp. XI:** 208–209

Herman, Florence. *See* Williams, Mrs. William Carlos (Florence Herman)

Herman, Jan, **Supp. XIV:** 150–151

Herman, William (pseudonym). *See* Bierce, Ambrose

"Her Management" (Swenson), **Supp. IV Part 2:** 642

"Herman Melville" (Auden), **Supp. II Part 1:** 14

Herman Melville (Mumford), **Supp. II Part 2:** 471, 476, 489–491

"Hermes of the Ways" (Doolittle), **Supp. I Part 1:** 266

"Hermes: Port Authority: His Song" (Di Piero), **Supp. XIX:** 47

Hermetic Definition (Doolittle), **Supp. I Part 1:** 271, 272, 273, 274

Hermia Suydam (Atherton), **Supp. XXIV:** 21, 28

"Hermitage, The" (Haines), **Supp. XII:** 205–206

Hermit and the Wild Woman, The (Wharton), **IV:** 315; **Retro. Supp. I:** 371

"Hermit and the Wild Woman, The" (Wharton), **Retro. Supp. I:** 372

"Hermit Meets the Skunk, The" (Kumin), **Supp. IV Part 2:** 447

Hermit of 69th Street, The: The Working Papers or Norbert Kosky (Kosinski), **Supp. VII:** 215, 216, 223, 226–227

"Hermit of Saba, The" (Freneau), **Supp. II Part 1:** 259

"Hermit Picks Berries, The" (Kumin), **Supp. IV Part 2:** 447

Hermit's Story, The (Bass), **Supp. XVI:** 23–24

"Hermit Thrush, A" (Clampitt), **Supp. IX:** 40

Hermit-Woman, The (G. Jones), **Supp. XXIV:** 185, 194

Hernández, Miguel, **Supp. V:** 194; **Supp. XIII:** 315, 323; **Supp. XXI:** 104

Herne, James A., **II:** 276; **Supp. II Part 1:** 198

Hernton, Calvin, **Supp. X:** 240

"Hero, The" (Moore), **III:** 200, 211, 212

Hero, The: A Study in Tradition, Myth, and Drama (Raglan), **I:** 135; **Supp. XIX:** 147

Hero and the Blues, The (Murray), **Supp. XIX:** 153, 154

Hérodiade (Mallarmé), **I:** 66

Herodotus, **Supp. I Part 2:** 405

Heroes, The (Ashbery), **Supp. III Part 1:** 3

Heroes and Saints (Moraga), **Supp. XXIII:** 195, 196, 197, **203–204**

Heroes and Saints and Other Plays (Moraga), **Supp. XXIII:** 197

Hero in America, The (Van Doren), **II:** 103

"Heroines of Nature: Four Women Respond to the American Landscape" (Norwood), **Supp. IX:** 24

"Heron, The" (Roethke), **III:** 540–541

"Her One Bad Eye" (Karr), **Supp. XI:** 244

"Her Own People" (Warren), **IV:** 253

Her Place in These Designs (Espaillat), **Supp. XXI:** 99, 104

"Her Quaint Honour" (Gordon), **II:** 196, 199, 200

Herr, Michael, **Supp. XI:** 245; **Supp. XIX:** 17

Herreshoff, David, **Supp. XIX:** 265

Herrick, Robert, **II:** 11, 18, 444; **III:** 463, 592; **IV:** 453; **Retro. Supp. I:** 319; **Retro. Supp. II:** 101; **Supp. I Part 2:** 646; **Supp. XIII:** 334; **Supp. XIV:** 8, 9; **Supp. XV:** 155; **Supp. XXI:** 14

Herrmann, John, **Retro. Supp. II:** 328; **Supp. XXII:** 277

Herron, George, **Supp. I Part 1:** 7

"Hers" (column, Prose), **Supp. XVI:** 254

Herschdorfer, Helen, **Supp. XXI:** 262

Herschel, Sir John, **Supp. I Part 1:** 314

"Her Sense of Timing" (Elkin), **Supp. VI:** 56, 58

Hersey, John, **IV:** 4; **Supp. I Part 1:** 196; **Supp. XVI:** 105–106; **Supp. XX: 251**

"Her Sweet turn to leave the Homestead" (Dickinson), **Retro. Supp. I:** 44

"Her Untold Story"(Thompson), **Supp. XXIII:** 301

Herzog (Bellow), **I:** 144, 147, 149, 150, 152, 153, 154, 155, 156, 157, 158, 159–160; **Retro. Supp. II:** 19, **26–27**; **Supp. IV Part 1:** 30; **Supp. XIX:** 157

Herzog, Tobey C., **Supp. XXII:** 116

"He's About 22. I'm 63" (H. Johnson), **Supp. XXVI:** 174

Heschel, Abraham, **Supp. XXI:** 110, 112

Hesford, Walter A., **Supp. XV:** 215, 217, 218

"He/She" (Dunn), **Supp. XI:** 149

"Hesitation Blues" (Hughes), **Retro. Supp. I:** 211

He Sleeps (McKnight), **Supp. XX: 151, 152–155, 158**

"He Sleeps" (McKnight), **Supp. XX:** 152, 155

Hesse, Hermann, **Supp. V:** 208

Hester, Carolyn, **Supp. XVIII:** 24

"Hetch Hetchy Valley" (Muir), **Supp. IX:** 185

He Who Gets Slapped (Andreyev), **II:** 425

"He Who Spits at the Sky" (Stegner), **Supp. IV Part 2:** 605

"He Will Not Leave a Note" (Ríos), **Supp. IV Part 2:** 548

Hewitt, James, **Supp. XV:** 240

Hewitt, J. N. B., **Supp. XXVI:** 81, 89, 90, 96, 97

Hewlett, Maurice, **I:** 359

Heyen, William, **Supp. XIII:** 285, 344; **Supp. XV:** 212

"Hey! Hey!" (Hughes), **Supp. I Part 1:** 327–328

Heyman, Stanley, **Supp. XXV:** 253

Hey Rub-a-Dub-Dub (Dreiser), **I:** 515; **II:** 26; **Retro. Supp. II:** 104, 105, 108

"Hey Sailor, What Ship?" (Olsen), **Supp. XIII:** 293, 294, 298, **299**

Heyward, DuBose, **Supp. XIX:** 78; **Supp. XVIII:** 281

Hiawatha, **Supp. XXVI:** 81, 82, 83, 86

Hiawatha (Longfellow), **Supp. I Part 1:** 79; **Supp. III Part 2:** 609, 610; **Supp. XXI:** 53

"Hibernaculum" (Ammons), **Supp. VII:** 26–27

Hichborn, Philip, **Supp. I Part 2:** 707, 708

Hichborn, Mrs. Philip. *See* Wylie, Elinor

"Hic Jacet" (W. C. Williams), **Retro. Supp. I:** 414

Hickok, Guy, **Supp. XXI:** 7

Hickok, James Butler ("Wild Bill"), **Supp. V:** 229, 230

Hicks, Granville, **I:** 254, 259, 374; **II:** 26; **III:** 342, 355, 452; **Supp. I Part 1:** 361; **Supp. I Part 2:** 609; **Supp. IV Part 1:** 22; **Supp. IV Part 2:** 526; **Supp. VIII:** 96, 124; **Supp. XII:** 250; **Supp. XIII:** 263; **Supp. XXI:** 276; **Supp. XXII:** 279; **Supp. XXVI:** 144

Hicks, Sally, **Supp. XXI:** 255

Hicok, Bethany, **Retro. Supp. II:** 39

"Hidden" (Nye), **Supp. XIII:** 283

"Hidden Gardens" (Capote), **Supp. III Part 1:** 125

Hidden in Plain View (Tobin and Dobard), **Supp. XXVI:** 200

Hidden Law, The (Hecht), **Supp. X:** 58

"Hidden Name and Complex Fate" (Ellison), **Supp. II Part 1:** 245

Hiddenness, Uncertainty, Surprise: Three Generative Energies of Poetry (Hirshfield), **Supp. XXIII:** 137

Hidden Wound, The (Berry), **Supp. X:** 23, 25, 26–27, 29, 34, 35

"Hide-and-Seek" (Francis), **Supp. IX:** 81

"Hiding" (Minot), **Supp. VI:** 203, 206

Hiding Place (Wideman), **Supp. X:** 320, 321, 327, 329, 331–332, 333

"Hidin' Out in Honky Heaven: On Race Relations in Vermont" (Budbill), **Supp. XIX:** 5

Hienger, Jorg, **Supp. IV Part 1:** 106

Hieronymus Bosch (De Tolnay), **Supp. XXII:** 255

Higgins, George, **Supp. IV Part 1:** 356

Higginson, Thomas Wentworth, **I:** 451–452, 453, 454, 456, 458, 459, 463, 464, 465, 470; **Retro. Supp. I:** 26, 31, 33, 35, 39, 40; **Supp. I Part 1:** 307, 371; **Supp. IV Part 2:** 430

Higgs, Robert, **Supp. XX:** 166

"High Bridge above the Tagus River at Toledo, The" (W. C. Williams), **Retro. Supp. I:** 429

"High Dive: A Variant" (Kumin), **Supp. IV Part 2:** 442

"High Diver" (Francis), **Supp. IX:** 82

"Higher Keys, The" (Merrill), **Supp. III Part 1:** 335–336

Higher Learning in America, The (Veblen), **Supp. I Part 2:** 630, 631, 641, 642

Highet, Gilbert, **Supp. I Part 1:** 268

"High Heav'd my breast"(J. Schoolcraft), **Supp. XXIII:** 235

High Noon (film), **Supp. V:** 46

"High on Sadness" (Komunyakaa), **Supp. XIII:** 114

"High School Senior" (Olds), **Supp. X:** 212

Highsmith, Patricia, **Supp. IV Part 1:** 79, 94, 132; **Supp. XXII:** 136

"High Spirits, The" (Huddle), **Supp. XXVI:** 154

High Spirits, The: Stories of Men and Women (Huddle), **Supp. XXVI:** 153–154

"High Tide" (Marquand), **III:** 56

High Tide in Tucson: Essays from Now or Never (Kingsolver), **Supp. VII:** 198, 201, 209

"High-Toned Old Christian Woman, A" (Stevens), **Retro. Supp. I:** 301

"High Water" (Mosher), **Supp. XXII:** 205, 211

"Highway, The" (Merwin), **Supp. III Part 1:** 346

Highway 61 Revisited (album, Dylan), **Supp. XVIII:** 20, 27, 30, 32

"Highway 61 Revisited" (song, Dylan), **Supp. XVIII:** 30

"Highway 99E from Chico" (Carver), **Supp. III Part 1:** 136

"Highway Apple Trees" (Espaillat), **Supp. XXI: 100–102**

High Window, The (Chandler), **Supp. IV Part 1:** 127–129, 130, 131

"High Yaller" (R. Fisher), **Supp. XIX:** 72

Hijuelos, Oscar, **Supp. IV Part 1:** 54; **Supp. VIII: 73–91**

Hike and the Aeroplane (Lewis), **II:** 440–441

Hilberg, Raul, **Supp. V:** 267

Hildebrand, Al, **III:** 118

Hiler, Hilaire (Retro. **Supp. II:** 327; **Supp. III Part 2:** 617

"Hill, A" (Hecht), **Supp. X:** 59–60, 63

Hill, Abram, **Supp. XV:** 194

Hill, Anita, **Supp. XX: 110**

Hill, Geoffrey, **Supp. XXVI:** 67

Hill, Hamlin, **Retro. Supp. II:** 286

Hill, James J., **Supp. I Part 2:** 644

Hill, Joe, **I:** 493; **Supp. XVIII:** 224; **Supp. XXIII:** 162

Hill, Josiah, **Supp. XXVI:** 87, 88

Hill, Lee, **Supp. XI:** 293, 294, 297, 299, 301, 305, 307

Hill, Pamela Smith, **Supp. XXII:** 295

Hill, Patti, **I:** 289

Hill, Peggy, **Supp. XIII:** 163

"Hill, The" (Strand), **Supp. IV Part 2:** 627

"Hill, The" (Toomer), **Supp. III Part 2:** 486

Hill, Vernon, **Supp. I Part 2:** 397

"Hillcrest" (Robinson), **III:** 504

Hill-Lubin, Mildred A., **Supp. IV Part 1:** 13

Hillman, Sidney, **Supp. I Part 1:** 5

Hillringhouse, Mark, **Supp. IX:** 286, 288, 299

Hills Beyond, The (Wolfe), **IV:** 450, 451, 460, 461

"Hills Beyond, The" (Wolfe), **IV:** 460

Hillside and Seaside in Poetry (Larcom, ed.), **Supp. XIII:** 142

"Hillside Thaw, A" (Frost), **Retro. Supp. I:** 133

"Hills Like White Elephants" (Hemingway), **Retro. Supp. I:** 170

Hills of the Shatemuc, The (S. Warner), **Supp. XVIII:** 266

"Hill-Top View, A" (Jeffers), **Supp. II Part 2:** 417

Hill Towns (Siddons), **Supp. XXII:** 239, 253

"Hill Wife, The" (Frost), **II:** 154; **Retro. Supp. I:** 131

Hillyer, Catherine, **Supp. XV:** 244

Hillyer, Robert, **I:** 475; **Supp. IX:** 75; **Supp. XIV:** 11

Hilton, James, **Supp. XIII:** 166

"Hiltons' Holiday, The" (Jewett), **II:** 391; **Retro. Supp. II:** 134

Him (Cummings), **I:** 429, 434–435

Himes, Chester Bomar, **Retro. Supp. II:** 117; **Supp. I Part 1:** 51, 325; **Supp. XIII:** 233; **Supp. XVI: 135–146**

Himes, Norman, **Supp. V:** 128

"Him on a Bicycle" (Weigl), **Supp. XIX:** 276

"Him with His Foot in His Mouth" (Bellow), **Retro. Supp. II:** 34

Him with His Foot in His Mouth and Other Stories (Bellow), **Retro. Supp. II:** 31

Hinchman, Sandra K., **Supp. IV Part 1:** 210

Hinckley, David, **Supp. XXII:** 215

Hindemith, Paul, **IV:** 357; **Supp. IV Part 1:** 81

Hindsell, Oliver, **Supp. XIII:** 162

Hindus, Milton, **Supp. XIV:** 288, 291, 292, 293; **Supp. XXIII:** 16

Hines, Suzanne, **Supp. XIV:** 151

Hinge Picture (Howe), **Supp. IV Part 2:** 423–424

Hinojosa, Rolando, **Supp. XIX: 97–114**

"Hinterlands" (W. Gibson), **Supp. XVI:** 123, 128

"Hippies: Slouching towards Bethlehem" (Didion), **Supp. IV Part 1:** 200

Hippolytus (Euripides), **II:** 543; **Supp. I Part 1:** 270

Hippolytus Temporizes (Doolittle), **Supp. I Part 1:** 270

"Hips" (Cisneros), **Supp. VII:** 61, 62

"Hipster's Hipster" (Ginsberg), **Supp. XIV:** 141

Hirsch, Edward D., **Supp. IX:** 262; **Supp. V:** 177; **Supp. XIV:** 15; **Supp. XIX:** 202; **Supp. XV:** 78, 225; **Supp. XVII:** 23; **Supp. XXIII:** 124

Hirsch, Sidney, **Supp. XIV:** 1. *See* Mttron-Hirsch, Sidney

Hirschfeld, Jane, **Supp. XVII:** 241

Hirschorn, Clive, **Supp. IV Part 2:** 577, 579

Hirshfield, Jane, **Supp. XXIII: 129–141**

Hirson, Roger, **Supp. XI:** 343

"His Bride of the Tomb" (Dunbar), **Supp. II Part 1:** 196

"His Chest of Drawers" (Anderson), **I:** 113, 114

"His Daily Journal"(Kenny), **Supp. XXIII:** 153

"His Father's Whistle" (Wrigley), **Supp. XVIII:** 299

His First, Best Country (J. W. Miller), **Supp. XX: 163, 166, 172–175**

His Fortunate Grace (Atherton), **Supp. XXIV:** 22

His Human Majesty (Boyle), **Supp. XXIV:** 62

"His Last Day" (C. Himes), **Supp. XVI:** 137

"His Lover" (Dubus), **Supp. VII:** 86

"His Music" (Dunn), **Supp. XI:** 149

"His Own Key" (Ríos), **Supp. IV Part 2:** 543

His Picture in the Papers (film; Emerson), **Supp. XVI:** 185

His Religion and Hers (Gilman), **Supp. XI:** 209

Hiss, Alger, **Supp. XV:** 143

"Hiss, Chambers, and the Age of Innocence" (Fiedler), **Supp. XIII:** 99

"His Shield" (Moore), **III:** 211

"His Story" (Cisneros), **Supp. VII:** 67

His Thought Made Pockets & the Plane Buckt (Berryman), **I:** 170

"His Three Women" (Gioia), **Supp. XV:** 119–120

Histoire comparée des systèmes de philosophie (Gérando), **II:** 10

Histoire de la brume, L' (Dybek; trans. Beget), **Supp. XXIII:** 74

Historical and Moral View of the Origin and Progress of the French Revolution (Wollstonecraft), **Supp. I Part 1:** 126

"Historical Conceptualization" (Huizinga), **I:** 255

Historical Evidence and the Reading of Seventeenth-Century Poetry (Brooks), **Supp. XIV:** 11

"Historical Interpretation of Literature, The" (Wilson), **IV:** 431, 433, 445

Historical Jesus, The: The Life of a Mediterranean Jewish Peasant (Crossan), **Supp. V:** 251

Historical Life of Jesus, The (Pettis), **Supp. XXIII:** 189

"Historical Value of Crèvecoeur's *Voyage . . .,*" (Adams), **Supp. I Part 1:** 251

"History" (Emerson), **II:** 13, 15

"History" (Hughes), **Supp. I Part 1:** 344

History (Lowell), **Retro. Supp. II:** 183, 190

"History" (Simic), **Supp. VIII:** 279

"History, Myth, and the Western Writer" (Stegner), **Supp. IV Part 2:** 596, 601

"History among the Rocks" (Warren), **IV:** 252

History as a Literary Art (Morison), **Supp. I Part 2:** 493

"History as Fate in E. L. Doctorow's Tale of a Western Town" (Arnold), **Supp. IV Part 1:** 220

"History Is the Memory of Time" (Olson), **Supp. II Part 2:** 574

"History Lesson" (Trethewey), **Supp. XXI:** 248, 249

"History Lessons" (Komunyakaa), **Supp. XIII:** 126

History Man, The (Bradbury), **Supp. XVIII:** 140

"History of a Literary Movement" (Nemerov), **III:** 270

"History of a Literary Radical, The" (Bourne), **I:** 215, 235, 236

History of a Radical: Essays by Randolph Bourne (Brooks), **I:** 245

"History of Armenia, The"(Balakian), **Supp. XXIII:** 23, 24

"History of Buttons, The" (Goldbarth), **Supp. XII:** 187

History of English Literature (Taine), **III:** 323

History of English Prosody (Saintsbury), **Supp. XV:** 181

History of Fortus, The (Emerson), **II:** 8

History of Henry Esmond, The (Thackeray), **II:** 91, 130

History of Modern Poetry, A (Perkins), **Supp. I Part 2:** 475; **Supp. XV:** 185

History of My Heart (Pinsky), **Supp. VI:** 243, 244, 245

History of New York, from the Beginning of the World to the End of the Dutch Dynasty, A (Irving), **II:** 300–303, 304, 310

History of Pendennis, The (Thackeray), **II:** 291

"History of Red, The" (Hogan), **Supp. IV Part 1:** 411

"History of Rodney, The" (Bass), **Supp. XVI:** 77

History of Roxbury Town (Ellis), **Supp. I Part 1:** 99

History of Southern Literature, The (Rubin), **Supp. XX: 161**

History of the African-American People (Proposed) by Strom Thurmond, The (Everett and Kincaid), **Supp. XVIII:** 62, **63–64**

History of the American Film, A (Durang), **Supp. XXIV:** 113, 117, **118–119**

"History of the Blues, A" (Biss), **Supp. XXVI:** 50

History of the Conquest of Mexico (Prescott), **Retro. Supp. I:** 123

History of the Conquest of Peru (Morison, ed.), **Supp. I Part 2:** 494

History of the Dividing Line betwixt Virginia and North Carolina (Byrd), **Supp. IV Part 2:** 425

History of the Life and Voyages of Christopher Columbus, A (Irving), **II:** 310, 314

History of the Navy of the United States of America (Cooper), **I:** 347

History of the Rise and Fall of the Slavepower in America (Wilson), **Supp. XIV:** 48, 49

History of the Russian Revolution, A (Trotsky), **Supp. XXI:** 161

History of the United States (Bancroft), **Supp. XXII:** 33

History of the United States of America during the Administrations of Thomas Jefferson and James Madison (Adams), **I:** 6–9, 10, 20, 21

History of the Work of Redemption, A (Edwards), **I:** 560

History of United States Naval Operations in World War II (Morison), **Supp. I Part 2:** 490–492

History of Womankind in Western Europe, The, **Supp. XI:** 197

"History Teacher, The" (Collins), **Supp. XXI:** 57

"History Through a Beard" (Morison), **Supp. I Part 2:** 490

His Toy, His Dream, His Rest (Berryman), **I:** 169, 170, 183, 184–186

"His Words" (Roethke), **III:** 544

Hitchcock, Ada. *See* MacLeish, Mrs. Archibald (Ada Hitchcock)

Hitchcock, Alfred, **IV:** 357; **Supp. IV Part 1:** 132; **Supp. VIII:** 177; **Supp. XX:** 253; **Supp. XXIII:** 119

Hitchcock, George, **Supp. X:** 127; **Supp. XVII:** 110

"Hitch Haiku" (Snyder), **Supp. VIII:** 297

"Hitch-Hikers, The" (Welty), **IV:** 262

"Hitchhiking Is Illegal in Nevada" (Lethem), **Supp. XVIII:** 136

Hitchins, Christopher, **Supp. VIII:** 241

Hitler, Adolf, **I:** 261, 290, 492; **II:** 146, 454, 561, 565, 592; **III:** 2, 3, 110, 115, 140, 156, 246, 298, 446; **IV:** 5, 17, 18, 298, 372; **Supp. I Part 2:** 431, 436, 446, 664; **Supp. V:** 290

Hitler, Wendy, **III:** 404

Hitler Lives ? (film), **Supp. XVI:** 102

Hix, H. L., **Supp. XV:** 114

H. L. Mencken, a Portrait from Memory (Angoff), **III:** 107

"H. L. Mencken Meets a Poet in the West Side Y.M.C.A." (White), **Supp. I Part 2:** 677

H. L. Mencken: The American Scene (Cairns), **III:** 119

H. M. Pulham, Esquire (Marquand), **II:** 482–483; **III:** 58, 59, 65, 68–69

Hnizdovsky, Jacques, **Supp. XIII:** 346

"Hoadley's Test Case in Indiana" (Neugeboren), **Supp. XVI:** 219

Hoagland, Edward, **Supp. XIV:** 80; **Supp. XVI:** 277; **Supp. XXII:** 204, 206

Hoagland, Tony, **Supp. XIX:** 81, 89

"Hoarder, The" (Sexton), **Supp. II Part 2:** 692

"Hoarfrost" (C. Baxter), **Supp. XVII:** 15

Hoban, Phoebe, **Supp. XV:** 319, 325

Hoban, Russell, **Supp. XXIII:** 42

Hobb, Gormley, **I:** 203

Hobbes, Thomas, **I:** 277; **II:** 9, 10, 540; **III:** 306; **IV:** 88; **Supp. XII:** 33; **Supp. XIV:** 5, 7

Hobson, Geary, **Supp. IV Part 1:** 321; **Supp. IV Part 2:** 502

Hobson, J. A., **I:** 232

Hobson, John A., **Supp. I Part 2:** 650

Hobson, Laura Z., **III:** 151

Hocking, Agnes, **Supp. VIII:** 251

Hocking, William Ernest, **III:** 303

Hodge, Merle, **Supp. XXIII:** 94

Hodges, Campbell B., **Supp. XIV:** 8

Hodgson, Captain Joseph, **III:** 328

Hoffa, Jimmy, **I:** 493

Hoffenberg, Mason, **Supp. XI:** 294, 297, 299, 305

Hoffer, Eric, **Supp. VIII:** 188; **Supp. XIX:** 264

Hoffman, Abbie, **Supp. XIV:** 150

Hoffman, Alice, **Supp. X: 77–94; Supp. XIII:** 13

Hoffman, Allen, **Supp. XVII:** 42, 44

Hoffman, Daniel, **Retro. Supp. II:** 265

Hoffman, Daniel G., **I:** 405; **II:** 307; **Supp. XI:** 152

Hoffman, Dustin, **Supp. IV Part 1:** 236

Hoffman, E. T. A., **Supp. XVI:** 157

Hoffman, Eva, **Supp. XVI: 147–164**

Hoffman, Frederick J., **I:** 60, 67; **II:** 443; **IV:** 113

Hoffman, Josiah Ogden, **II:** 297, 300

Hoffman, Matilda, **II:** 300, 314

Hoffman, Paul, **Supp. XV:** 141–142

Hoffman, Roy, **Supp. XX: 177**

Hoffman, Todd, **Supp. XVIII:** 101

Hoffman, William, **Supp. XVIII: 69–88**

Hoffman, William M., **Supp. X:** 153

Hoffmann, E. T. A., **III:** 415
Hofmann, Hans, **Supp. XV:** 144
Hofmeister, Tim, **Supp. XIX:** 115
Ho for a Hat (W. J. Smith), **Supp. XIII:** 346
Hofstadter, Richard, **Supp. VIII:** 98, 99, 108
Hogan, Linda, **Supp. IV Part 1:** 324, 325, **397–418; Supp. XVIII:** 189
Hogan, Randolph, **Supp. XVI:** 252–253
Hogan, Ron, **Supp. XVIII:** 138, 139
Hogarth, William, **Supp. XII:** 44
Hogg, James, **I:** 53; **Supp. I Part 1:** 349; **Supp. IX:** 275
Hoggart, Richard, **Supp. XIV:** 299
"Hog-Nosed Snake, The" (Kooser), **Supp. XIX:** 128
Hogue, W. Lawrence, **Supp. XXII:** 175–176
Hohne, Karen, **Supp. V:** 147
Hojoki (Chomei), **IV:** 170
Holbrook, David, **Supp. I Part 2:** 526–527, 546
Holcroft, Thomas, **Supp. I Part 2:** 514
Holden, Jonathan, **Supp. XI:** 143
Holden, Raymond, **Supp. XIV:** 121–122
Holden, William, **Supp. XI:** 307
Hölderlin, Friedrich, **Supp. XVI:** 48; **Supp. XXIV:** 152
Holding, Elisabeth Sanxay, **Supp. XXII: 119–137**
"Holding On" (Levine), **Supp. V:** 184
Holding the Line: Women in the Great Arizona Mine Strike of 1983 (Kingsolver), **Supp. VII:** 197, 201–202, 204
"Holding the Mirror Up to Nature" (Nemerov), **III:** 275, 276
"Hold Me" (Levine), **Supp. V:** 186
Holdt, Jacob, **Supp. XXVI:** 26
Hold the Press (film), **Supp. XIII:** 163
Hold with the Hares (Zinberg), **Supp. XV:** 197–198,**Supp. XV:** 203
Hole in Texas, A (Wouk), **Supp. XXV:** 257, 266–267
"Hole in the Floor, A" (Wilbur), **Supp. III Part 2:** 556–557
Hole in the Sky: A Memoir (Kittredge), **Supp. XXVI:** 177, 179, 180–181, 182, 184–185
Holiday (Barry), **Retro. Supp. I:** 104
"Holiday" (Porter), **III:** 454
Holiday (W. Frank), **Supp. XX: 72–73**
Holiday, Billie, **Supp. I Part 1:** 80; **Supp. IV Part 1:** 2, 7; **Supp. XIX:** 147
Holiday Song for Four-Part Chorus of Mixed Voices with Piano Accompaniment (Taggard and Schuman), **Supp. XXII:** 283
Holinshed, Raphael, **IV:** 370
Holladay, Polly, **Supp. XXI:** 6
Holland, Josiah, **Supp. I Part 2:** 420
Holland, Laurence Bedwell, **Retro. Supp. I:** 216
Holland, Theodore, **I:** 453
Holland, Mrs. Theodore, **I:** 453, 455, 465
Holland, William, **IV:** 381
Hollander, John, **Supp. III Part 2:** 541; **Supp. IV Part 2:** 642; **Supp. IX:** 50, 153, 155; **Supp. XII:** 254, 255, 260;

Supp. XIX: 121; **Supp. XV:** 256; **Supp. XVII:** 112; **Supp. XXIII:** 112
Hollenberg, Donna, **Supp. XXIV:** 64
Holley, Marietta, **Supp. XIII:** 152
Holliday, Billie, **Supp. XXI:** 131
Hollinghurst, Alan, **Supp. XIII:** 52
Hollins Critic (Nelson), **Supp. XIX:** 3
Hollis, Thomas Brand, **Supp. I Part 2:** 514
Hollow Men, The (T. S. Eliot), **I:** 574, 575, 578–579, 580, 585; **III:** 586; **Retro. Supp. I:** 63, 64
"Hollow Tree, A" (R. Bly), **Supp. IV Part 1:** 64, 66
Hollyberrys at the Shore, The, **Supp. X:** 42
"Hollywood!" (Vidal), **Supp. IV Part 2:** 688
Hollywood: American Movie-City (Rand, unauthorized), **Supp. IV Part 2:** 519
Hollywood: A Novel of America in the 1920s (Vidal), **Supp. IV Part 2:** 677, 684, 686, 688, 690, 691
Hollywood Ending (film; Allen), **Supp. XV:** 11
Hollywood on Trial (film), **Supp. I Part 1:** 295
Holmes, Abiel, **Supp. I Part 1:** 300, 301, 302, 310
Holmes, Mrs. Abiel (Sarah Wendell), **Supp. I Part 1:** 300
Holmes, John, **I:** 169; **Supp. II Part 1:** 87; **Supp. IV Part 2:** 440–441; **Supp. XIV:** 119; **Supp. XXVI:** 68
Holmes, John Clellon, **Supp. XII:** 118; **Supp. XIV:** 144, 150
Holmes, Martha Stoddard, **Supp. XX: 205, 207**
Holmes, Oliver Wendell, **I:** 487; **II:** 225, 273–274, 402, 403; **III:** 81–82, 590, 591–592; **IV:** 429, 436; **Retro. Supp. II:** 155; **Supp. I Part 1:** 103, 243, 254, **299–319; Supp. I Part 2:** 405, 414, 415, 420, 593, 704, 705; **Supp. XI:** 194; **Supp. XXIV:** 77
Holmes, Oliver Wendell, Jr., **I:** 3, 19; **Supp. IV Part 2:** 422
Holmes, Mrs. Oliver Wendell (Amelia Jackson), **Supp. I Part 1:** 303
Holmes, Steven J., **Supp. IX:** 172, 177
Holmes, Ted, **Supp. V:** 180
Holmes, William Henry, **Supp. IV Part 2:** 603–604
Holocaust (Reznikoff), **Supp. XIV:** 281, **291–293**
Holocaust in American Life, The (Novick), **Supp. XVI:** 154
Holt, Edwin E., **I:** 59
Holt, Felix, **II:** 179
Holt, Henry, **II:** 348; **III:** 587
Holt, Patricia, **Supp. XIV:** 89
Holtby, Winifred, **Supp. I Part 2:** 720
Holy Ghostly, The (Shepard), **Supp. III Part 2:** 437–438, 447
"Holy Innocents, The" (Lowell), **II:** 539
Holy Sonnets (Donne), **IV:** 145; **Supp. I Part 1:** 367; **Supp. III Part 2:** 619; **Supp. XIII:** 130–131; **Supp. XVIII:** 50–51
"Holy Terror, A" (Bierce), **I:** 203

"Holy Terror, The" (Maxwell), **Supp. VIII:** 169
Holy the Firm (Dillard), **Supp. VI:** 23, **29,** 30, 31, 32
Holy War, The (Bunyan), **IV:** 156
"Holy Week"(Thompson), **Supp. XXIII:** 300
"Homage to Arthur Rimbaud" (Wright), **Supp. V:** 339
Homage to Baudelaire (Duncan, ed.), **Supp. XV:** 75
Homage to Catalonia (Orwell), **Supp. XVII:** 229
"Homage to Che Guevara" (Banks), **Supp. V:** 5
Homage to Clio (Auden), **Supp. II Part 1:** 24
"Homage to Elizabeth Bishop" (Ivask, ed.), **Supp. I Part 1:** 96
"Homage to Ezra Pound" (Wright), **Supp. V:** 339
Homage to Frank O'Hara (Ashbery), **Supp. III Part 1:** 2–3
"Homage to Franz Joseph Haydn" (Hecht), **Supp. X:** 69
"Homage to Hemingway" (Bishop), **IV:** 35
Homage to Mistress Bradstreet (Berryman), **I:** 168, 169, 170–171, 172, 174, 175, 178–183, 184, 186
"Homage to Paul Cézanne" (Wright), **Supp. V:** 341–342
Homage to Sextus Propertius (Pound), **Retro. Supp. I:** 290
"Homage to Sextus Propertius" (Pound), **III:** 462, 476; **Supp. III Part 2:** 622
"Homage to Shakespeare" (Cheever), **Supp. I Part 1:** 180
"Homage to the Empress of the Blues" (Hayden), **Supp. II Part 1:** 379
"Homage to the Memory of Wallace Stevens" (Justice), **Supp. VII:** 126
Homage to Theodore Dreiser (Warren), **I:** 517
Homans, Margaret, **Supp. X:** 229
"Home" (Hughes), **Supp. I Part 1:** 329, 330
"Home" (Mora), **Supp. XIII:** 217
Home (Robinson), **Supp. XXI:** 212, **220–223**
Home (Updike), **Retro. Supp. I:** 320
"Home" (Weigl), **Supp. XIX:** 287
"Home, Home on the Strange" (J. D. Reed), **Supp. XVI:** 174
"Home, Sweet Home" (Fante), **Supp. XI:** 164, 165
Home, The (Gilman), **Supp. XI: 206–207**
"Home, The" (Jarman), **Supp. XVII:** 116
"Home Address" (Bronk), **Supp. XXI:** 27
"Home after Three Months Away" (Lowell), **II:** 547
Home and Colonial Library (Murray), **Retro. Supp. I:** 246
"Home and the Open Road: The Nonfiction of Larry Brown" (Barrier), **Supp. XXI:** 48–49
Home as Found (Cooper), **I:** 348, 349, 350, 351

Home at the End of the World, A (Cunningham), **Supp. XV: 59–62,** 63

"Home Away from Home, A" (Humphrey), **Supp. IX:** 101

Home Book of Shakespeare Quotations (Stevenson), **Supp. XIV:** 120

"Home Burial" (Frost), **Retro. Supp. I:** 124, 125, 128, **129–130; Supp. VIII:** 31; **Supp. XIX:** 9; **Supp. XV:** 159

Homecoming (Alvarez), **Supp. VII:** 1, 3–5, 9

"Homecoming" (Carruth), **Supp. XVI:** 55

"Homecoming" (McGrath), **Supp. X:** 116

"Homecoming, The" (Gioia), **Supp. XV:** 123, 124

Homecoming, The (Wilson), **Supp. VIII:** 330

Homecoming Game, The (Nemerov), **III:** 268, 282, 284–285

"Home during a Tropical Snowstorm I Feed My Father Lunch" (Karr), **Supp. XI:** 241–242, 248

Home Economics (Berry), **Supp. X:** 28, 31–32, 35, 36, 37

"Home Economics for Halfbacks" (Skloot), **Supp. XX: 195, 207**

Home Fires and Reservation Roads (Gansworth), **Supp. XXVI:** 114

Home from the Hill (film), **Supp. IX:** 95

Home from the Hill (Humphrey), **Supp. IX:** 93, 95, **96–98,** 104, 106, 109

"Home Grown" (Vital), **Supp. XVI:** 160

"Homeland" (Merwin), **Supp. III Part 1:** 351

Homeland and Other Stories (Kingsolver), **Supp. VII:** 199, 202–204, 207

Home on the Range (Baraka), **Supp. II Part 1:** 47

Homeplace (Siddons), **Supp. XXII:** 253

Home Place, The (Morris), **III:** 221, 222, 232

Homeplace, The (Nelson), **Supp. XVIII: 174–175**

Homer, **I:** 312, 433; **II:** 6, 8, 133, 302, 543, 544, 552; **III:** 14, 21, 278, 453, 457, 473, 567; **IV:** 54, 371; **Retro. Supp. I:** 59; **Supp. I Part 1:** 158, 283; **Supp. I Part 2:** 494; **Supp. X:** 36, 120, 122; **Supp. XIV:** 21; **Supp. XVII:** 70, 227

Homer, Louise, **Retro. Supp. I:** 10

Homer, Winslow, **Supp. XXI:** 243

"Home Range" (Leopold), **Supp. XIV:** 184, 185

"Home Repairs" (Skloot), **Supp. XX: 204**

Homer's Art (Notley), **Supp. XXII:** 232

"Homer's Art" (Notley), **Supp. XXII:** 232–233

"Homesick Blues" (Hughes), **Supp. I Part 1:** 327

Home: Social Essays (Baraka), **Supp. II Part 1:** 45, 61

"Homesteading on the Extraterrestrial Frontier" (Abbott), **Supp. XVIII:** 142

Home to Harlem (McKay), **Supp. X:** 132, 137–138, **138–139; Supp. XVIII:** 127

"Home Videos" (Brockmeier), **Supp. XXII:** 60

Homeward Bound (Cooper), **I:** 348

"Homeward Star, The" (Palmer), **Supp. XV:** 81–82

Homewood trilogy (Wideman), **Supp. X:** 319

"Homework" (Cameron), **Supp. XII:** 80, **83,** 84

"Homily" (Tate), **IV:** 121–122

Homing with the Birds (Stratton-Porter), **Supp. XX: 212, 216, 222**

"Homme Moyen Sensuel, L' " (Pound), **III:** 462

Homme révolté, L' (Camus), III: 306

"Homoeopathy and Its Kindred Delusions" (Holmes), **Supp. I Part 1:** 303–304, 305

Homo Ludens (Huizinga), **II:** 416–417, 425

"Homosexuality: Is It Disgusting, or Is It Delightful?" (Durang), **Supp. XXIV:** 114

"Homosexuality"(O'Hara), **Supp. XXIII:** 212

"Homosexual Villain, The" (Mailer), **III:** 36

"Homo Will Not Inherit" (Doty), **Supp. XI:** 128

"Homunculus, The: A Novel in One Chapter" (McKnight), **Supp. XX: 152**

Hone and Strong Diaries of Old Manhattan, The (Auchincloss, ed.), **Supp. IV Part 1:** 23

"Honey" (Beattie), **Supp. V:** 33

"Honey" (Wright), **Supp. III Part 2:** 589

Honey, Maureen, **Supp. XXVI:** 166

"Honey, We'll Be Brave" (Farrell), **II:** 45

Honey and Salt (Sandburg), **III:** 594–596

"Honey and Salt" (Sandburg), **III:** 594

"Honey Babe" (Hughes), **Supp. I Part 1:** 334

"Honey Tree, The" (Oliver), **Supp. VII:** 236

Hong, Maxine. *See* Kingston, Maxine Hong

Hong, Terry, **Supp. XXVI:** 216

Hongo, Garrett, **Supp. X:** 292; **Supp. XIII:** 114; **Supp. XVII:** 112

"Honkytonk" (Shapiro), **Supp. II Part 2:** 705

"Honky Tonk in Cleveland, Ohio" (Sandburg), **III:** 585

Honorable Men (Auchincloss), **Supp. IV Part 1:** 23

Honor Thy Father (Talese), **Supp. XVII:** 204–205, 210

Hood, Mary, **Supp. XXVI:** 15

Hood, Tom, **I:** 195

"Hoodoo in America" (Hurston), **Supp. VI:** 153–154

"Hook" (Wright), **Supp. III Part 2:** 604

Hook, Sidney, **I:** 265; **Supp. IV Part 2:** 527; **Supp. VIII:** 96, 100; **Supp. XIV:** 3

Hooker, Adelaide. *See* Marquand, Mrs. John P. (Adelaide Hooker)

Hooker, Isabella Beecher, **Supp. XI:** 193

Hooker, Samuel, **IV:** 162, 165

Hooker, Thomas, **II:** 15–16; **IV:** 162

Hooper, Marian. *See* Adams, Mrs. Henry (Marian Hooper)

Hoosier Holiday, A (Dreiser), **Retro. Supp. II:** 104

Hoover, Herbert, **Supp. I Part 2:** 638

Hoover, J. Edgar, **Supp. XIII:** 170

Hoover, Paul, **Supp. XV:** 179

"Hope" (Bontemps), **Supp. XXII:** 2

"Hope" (Jarrell), **II:** 389

"Hope" (Matthews), **Supp. IX:** 163

Hope, A. D., **Supp. XIII:** 347

Hope, Lynn, **Supp. II Part 1:** 38

Hope, The (Wouk), **Supp. XXV:** 254, 257, 265–266

"Hope Atherton's Wanderings" (Howe), **Supp. IV Part 2:** 432

"Hopeless Kill, The"(Kenny), **Supp. XXIII:** 145

Hope of Heaven (O'Hara), **III:** 361

"Hopes Rise" (Boyle), **Supp. XX: 20**

"Hop-Frog" (Poe), **Retro. Supp. II:** 264, 268, 269

"Hop Frog" (Poe), **Supp. XXV:** 112

Hopkin, Pauline, **Supp. XVI:** 143

Hopkins, Anne Yale, **Supp. I Part 1:** 100, 102, 113

Hopkins, Gerard Manley, **I:** 171, 179, 397, 401, 522, 525, 533; **II:** 537; **III:** 197, 209, 523; **IV:** 129, 135, 141, 421; **Retro. Supp. II:** 40; **Supp. I Part 1:** 79, 81, 94; **Supp. III Part 2:** 551; **Supp. IV Part 1:** 178; **Supp. IV Part 2:** 637, 638, 639, 641, 643; **Supp. IX:** 39, 42; **Supp. V:** 337; **Supp. X:** 61, 115; **Supp. XIII:** 294; **Supp. XIV:** 83; **Supp. XV:** 250, 347; **Supp. XVI:** 282; **Supp. XVII:** 241; **Supp. XVIII:** 78, 79; **Supp. XX: 230; Supp. XXIII:** 121

Hopkins, Gerard Walter Sturgis, **Supp. XX: 229, 233, 240**

Hopkins, L. A., **I:** 502

Hopkins, Lemuel, **Supp. II Part 1:** 70

Hopkins, Miriam, **IV:** 381; **Supp. I Part 1:** 281

Hopkins, Pauline, **Supp. XVIII:** 284

Hopkins, Samuel, **I:** 547, 549; **Supp. XXIV:** 68

Hopkins, Vivian, **II:** 20

Hopkinson, Francis, **Supp. I Part 2:** 504

Hopler, Jay, **Supp. XXIII:** 132

Hopper (Strand), **Supp. IV Part 2:** 632

Hopper, Dennis, **Supp. XI:** 293, 308; **Supp. XXVI:** 26

Hopper, Edward, **IV:** 411, 413; **Supp. IV Part 2:** 619, 623, 631, 634; **Supp. XIX:** 117

Hopwood, Avery, **Supp. IV Part 2:** 573; **Supp. XXV:** 195

Horace, **II:** 8, 154, 169, 543, 552, 568; **III:** 15; **IV:** 89; **Supp. I Part 2:** 423; **Supp. IX:** 152; **Supp. X:** 65; **Supp. XII:** 258, 260, 262

Horae Canonicae (Auden), **Supp. II Part 1:** 21

"Horatian Ode" (Marvell), **IV:** 135

"Horatian Ode upon Cromwell's Return from Ireland" (Marvell), **Supp. XIV:** 10

Horgan, Paul, **Supp. XV:** 46, 49, 52

Horkheimer, Max, **Supp. I Part 2:** 645; **Supp. IV Part 1:** 301
Horn, Dara, **Supp. XVII:** 50; **Supp. XX: 177**
Horn, Mother, **Supp. I Part 1:** 49, 54
Hornby, Nick, **Supp. XII:** 286; **Supp. XXIII:** 109
Horn of Africa (Caputo), **Supp. XIX:** 21–23
Horn of Life, The (Atherton), **Supp. XXIV:** 26, 27
"Horn of Plenty" (Hughes), **Retro. Supp. I:** 210; **Supp. I Part 1:** 342
Horovitz, Israel, **Supp. XV:** 321
Horowitz, James. *See* Salter, James
Horowitz, Mark, **Supp. V:** 219, 231
"Horrible" (Halliday), **Supp. XIX:** 91
"Horror at Martin's Beach, The" (Lovecraft and Greene), **Supp. XXV:** 122
"Horror at Red Hook, The" (Lovecraft), **Supp. XXV:** 110
"Horse, The" (Levine), **Supp. V:** 182
"Horse, The" (Wright), **Supp. III Part 2:** 592, 601
"Horse, The"(Le Sueur), **Supp. XXIII:** 168
Horse Eats Hay (play), **Supp. IV Part 1:** 82
Horse Feathers (film), **Supp. IV Part 1:** 384
"Horseflies" (Wrigley), **Supp. XVIII:** 307
Horse Has Six Legs, The (Simic), **Supp. VIII:** 272
"Horselaugh on Dibber Lannon" (Fante), **Supp. XI:** 164
Horseman, Pass By (McMurtry), **Supp. V:** 220–221, 224
"Horses" (Doty), **Supp. XI:** 122
Horses and Men (Anderson), **I:** 112–113, 114
"Horses and Men in Rain" (Sandburg), **III:** 584
"Horse Show, The" (W. C. Williams), **Retro. Supp. I:** 423
Horses Make a Landscape More Beautiful (Walker), **Supp. III Part 2:** 521, 533
"Horse Thief" (Caldwell), **I:** 310
"Horseweed" (Offutt), **Supp. XIX:** 166, 167
Horse With a Green Vinyl Mane (P. N. Warren), **Supp. XX: 261**
"Horsie" (Parker), **Supp. IX:** 193
Horstmann, Steffen, **Supp. XXV:** 226
Horton, George Moses, **Supp. XXII:** 11
Horton, Philip, **I:** 383, 386, 387, 393, 441; **Supp. XV:** 138
Horton Hatches the Egg (Geisel), **Supp. XVI:** 100, 112
Horton Hears a Who! (Geisel), **Supp. XVI:** 102
"Horton's Ape"(P. Benedict), **Supp. XXIII:** 41
Horwitz, Tony, **Supp. XVIII:** 195–196
Hosea (biblical book), **II:** 166
Hospers, John, **Supp. IV Part 2:** 528
"Hospice" (Hull), **Supp. XXI:** 138

Hospital, Janette Turner, **Supp. IV Part 1:** 311–302
Hospital Sketches (Alcott), **Supp. I Part 1:** 34, 35
Hostages to Fortune (Humphrey), **Supp. IX:** 96, **104–106**, 109
Hostess to Murder (Holding), **Supp. XXII:** 126, **127**
"Hot Combs" (Trethewey), **Supp. XXI:** 249
"Hot Cross Bum" (Loy), **Supp. XXII:** 168
"Hot Dog" (Stern), **Supp. IX: 298–299**
"Hotel, The"(Hadas), **Supp. XXIII:** 121
"Hotel Bar" (McClatchy), **Supp. XII:** 269
Hotel Dwellers, The (Lacy), **Supp. XV:** 205
Hotel Insomnia (Simic), **Supp. VIII:** 280, **281–282**
Hotel Lambosa and Other Stories (Koch), **Supp. XV:** 186
Hotel New Hampshire, The (Irving), **Supp. VI:** 163, 164, **172–173**, 177, 179; **Supp. XIX:** 164
"Hot-Foot Hannibal" (Chesnutt), **Supp. XIV:** 60
"Hot Ice"(Dybek), **Supp. XXIII:** 72–73
"Hot Night on Water Street" (Simpson), **Supp. IX:** 269, 270
"Hot Time, A" (Gunn Allen), **Supp. IV Part 1:** 333
Houdini, Harry, **IV:** 437; **Supp. XXV:** 121
"Hound of Heaven" (Thompson), **Retro. Supp. I:** 55
"Hourglass, The" (Kees), **Supp. XV:** 147
"Hour in Chartres, An" (Bourne), **I:** 228
"Hour of Peonies, The"(Crooker), **Supp. XXIII:** 58
Hours, The (Cunningham), **Supp. XII:** 80; **Supp. XV: 65–68**
"Hours before Eternity" (Caldwell), **I:** 291
House, Bridge, Fountain, Gate (Kumin), **Supp. IV Part 2:** 448, 449, 451, 454
House, Edward, **Supp. I Part 2:** 643
"House, The" (Merrill), **Supp. III Part 1:** 323
House at Pooh Corner, The (Milne), **Supp. IX:** 189
"House at the End of the World, The" (Brockmeier), **Supp. XXII:** 52, 53
House Behind the Cedars, The (Chesnutt), **Supp. XIV: 69–71**
Houseboat Days (Ashbery), **Supp. III Part 1:** 18–20
Housebreaker of Shady Hill and Other Stories, The (Cheever), **Supp. I Part 1:** 184
"House by the Sea, The" (E. Stoddard), **Supp. XV:** 277
House by the Sea, The (Sarton), **Supp. VIII:** 264
House Divided, A (Buck), **Supp. II Part 1:** 118
"House Divided, The/La Casa Divida" (Kingsolver), **Supp. VII:** 207
"House Guest" (Bishop), **Retro. Supp. II:** 49; **Supp. I Part 1:** 93

"House Holding" (Davison), **Supp. XXVI:** 73, 74
Household Saints (film), **Supp. XVI:** 256
Household Saints (Prose), **Supp. XVI:** 252–253, 254, 261
"House in Athens, The" (Merrill), **Supp. III Part 1:** 323
House in the Uplands, A (Caldwell), **I:** 297, 301, 306
"House in Turk Street, The" (Hammett), **Supp. IV Part 1:** 344
"House in Winter, The" (Sarton), **Supp. VIII:** 259
"House in Winter, The"(Hirshfield), **Supp. XXIII:** 132
"Housekeeping" (Alvarez), **Supp. VII:** 3–5, 10
Housekeeping (Robinson), **Supp. XXI:** 210–211, **212–216**, 218, 223
"Housekeeping" (Trethewey), **Supp. XXI:** 249
"Housekeeping for Men" (Bourne), **I:** 231
House Made of Dawn (Momaday), **Supp. IV Part 1:** 274, 323, 326; **Supp. IV Part 2:** 479, 480, 481–484, 485, 486, 504, 562
Houseman, John, **Supp. IV Part 1:** 173
House Next Door, The (Siddons), **Supp. XXII:** 239
House Next Door, The (television movie), **Supp. XXII:** 239
House of Dust, The: A Symphony (Aiken), **I:** 50
House of Earth trilogy (Buck), **Supp. II Part 1:** 118, 123
House of Five Talents, The (Auchincloss), **Supp. IV Part 1:** 21, 25–27
"House of Flowers" (Capote), **Supp. III Part 1:** 123
House of Games (Mamet), **Supp. XIV:** 243
House of Houses (Mora), **Supp. XIII:** 213, 215, 218, 219, 223–224, **225–227**, 228, 229
House of Incest (Nin), **Supp. III Part 1:** 43; **Supp. X:** 187, 190, 193
House of Lee, The (Atherton), **Supp. XXIV:** 26–27
House of Life, The: Rachel Carson at Work (Brooks), **Supp. IX:** 26
House of Light (Oliver), **Supp. VII:** 238–240
House of Mirth, The (Wharton), **II:** 180, 193; **IV:** 311–313, 314, 316, 318, 323, 327; **Retro. Supp. I:** 360, 366, 367, **367–370**, 373, 380; **Supp. XX: 239, 240**
"House of Mist, The" (Rand), **Supp. IV Part 2:** 524
"House of My Own, A" (Cisneros), **Supp. VII:** 64
"House of Night, The" (Freneau), **Supp. II Part 1:** 259, 260
"House of Representatives and Me, The" (Conroy), **Supp. XVI:** 75
House of Sand and Fog (Dubus III), **Supp. XXIV:** 97, **104–107**
House of Sleeping Beauties, The (Hwang), **Supp. XXI:** 146

House of the Far and Lost, The (Wolfe), **IV:** 456

"House of the Injured, The" (Haines), **Supp. XII:** 203

"House of the One Father" (Antin), **Supp. XX: 3, 13**

House of the Prophet, The (Auchincloss), **Supp. IV Part 1:** 31

House of the Seven Gables (Hawthorne), **I:** 106; **II:** 60, 224, 225, 231, 237, 239, 240–241, 243, 244; **Retro. Supp. I:** 63, 149, **160–162**, 163, 164; **Supp. I Part 2:** 579

House of the Solitary Maggot, The (Purdy), **Supp. VII:** 274–275

"House on 15th S.W., The" (Hugo), **Supp. VI:** 140

"House on Main Street, The" (B. Kelly), **Supp. XVII:** 127

House on Mango Street, The (Cisneros), **Supp. VII:** 58, 59–64, 65, 66, 67, 68, 72; **Supp. XXV:** 133

"House on Mango Street, The" (Cisneros), **Supp. VII:** 59

House on Marshland, The (Glück), **Supp. V:** 81–83, 84

"House on Moscow Street, The" (Nelson), **Supp. XVIII:** 174

"House on the Heights, A" (Capote), **Supp. II Part 1:** 120

"House on the Hill, The" (Robinson), **III:** 505, 524

"House Raising" (Offutt), **Supp. XIX:** 166

"Houses" (Hogan), **Supp. IV Part 1:** 402

"Houses, The" (Merwin), **Supp. III Part 1:** 354

"Houses of the Spirit" (Karr), **Supp. XI:** 250

"House Sparrows" (Hecht), **Supp. X: 68**

"House That Doesn't House, The" (Bronk), **Supp. XXI:** 34

House That Tai Maing Built, The (Lee), **Supp. X:** 291

"House Unroofed by the Gale" (Tu Fu), **II:** 526

"House Where Mark Twain Was Born, The" (Masters), **Supp. I Part 2:** 472

"Housewife" (Hempel), **Supp. XXI:** 124

"Housewife" (Sexton), **Supp. II Part 2:** 682

"Housewife's Paradise, The" (Davison), **Supp. XXVI:** 76

" 'Housing the Deliberations': New York, War, and Frank O'Hara"(Ward), **Supp. XXIII:** 218

Housman, A. E., **III:** 15, 136, 606; **Supp. II Part 1:** 4; **Supp. IV Part 1:** 165; **Supp. XV:** 40–41

Houston, Robert, **Supp. XXV:** 54

Houston Trilogy (McMurtry), **Supp. V:** 223–225

How" (Ginsberg), **Supp. XIV:** 142, 143

"How" (Moore), **Supp. X:** 167

"How About This?" (Carver), **Supp. III Part 1:** 141

"How America Came to the Mountains" (J. W. Miller), **Supp. XX: 169**

"How Annandale Went Out" (Robinson), **III:** 513

Howard, Arliss, **Supp. XXI:** 39

Howard, Ben, **Supp. XVI:** 54

Howard, Gerald, **Supp. XII:** 21

Howard, Jane, **Retro. Supp. I:** 334

Howard, June, **Retro. Supp. II:** 139

Howard, Leon, **Supp. I Part 2:** 408, 422, 423

Howard, Maureen, **Supp. XII:** 285; **Supp. XVII:** 183

Howard, Richard, **Retro. Supp. II:** 43; **Supp. IV Part 2:** 624, 626, 640; **Supp. IX:** 324, 326; **Supp. VIII:** 273; **Supp. X:** 152; **Supp. XI:** 317; **Supp. XII:** 254; **Supp. XIII:** 76; **Supp. XV:** 23, 24; **Supp. XXIV:** 155

Howard, Robert E., **Supp. XXV:** 122

Howard, Vilma, **Retro. Supp. II:** 111, 112

Howards, J. Z., **Supp. VIII:** 178

Howards End (Forster), **Supp. XII:** 87

Howarth, Cora, **I:** 408, 409

Howbah Indians (Ortiz), **Supp. IV Part 2:** 513

"How Black Sees Green and Red" (McKay), **Supp. X:** 136

How Britain Rules Africa (Padmore), **Supp. XXI:** 166

"How David Did Not Care" (R. Bly), **Supp. IV Part 1:** 73

"How Did I Love Him?" (Nelson), **Supp. XVIII:** 176

"How Do I Love Thee?" (Browning), **Supp. XVIII:** 176

Howe, Daniel Walker, **Supp. XXIV:** 79

Howe, Darcus, **Supp. XXI:** 170

Howe, E.W., **I:** 106

Howe, Florence, **Supp. XIII:** 295, 306

Howe, Harriet, **Supp. XI:** 200, 201

Howe, Irving, **IV:** 10; **Retro. Supp. I:** 369; **Retro. Supp. II:** 112, 286; **Supp. I Part 2:** 432; **Supp. II Part 1:** 99; **Supp. IX:** 227; **Supp. VI: 113–129;** **Supp. VIII:** 93, 232; **Supp. X:** 203, 245; **Supp. XIII:** 160; **Supp. XIII:** 98; **Supp. XIV:** 103–104, 104; **Supp. XIX:** 257, 265; **Supp. XVII:** 50; **Supp. XXIII:** 3, 7; **Supp. XXIV:** 220–221, 222

Howe, James Wong, **Supp. I Part 1:** 281; **Supp. V:** 223

Howe, Julia Ward, **III:** 505; **Retro. Supp. II:** 135

Howe, LeAnne, **Supp. XXVI:** 84, 98

Howe, M. A. DeWolfe, **I:** 258; **II:** 406; **Supp. XIV:** 54

Howe, Mary Manning, **Supp. IV Part 2:** 422

Howe, Samuel, **Supp. I Part 1:** 153

Howe, Susan, **Retro. Supp. I:** 33, 43; **Supp. IV Part 2: 419–438;** **Supp. XVI:** 284

Howell, Chris, **Supp. XIII:** 112

Howell, James, **II:** 111

Howells, Margaret, **II:** 271

Howells, William C., **II:** 273

Howells, William Dean, **I:** 109, 192, 204, 210, 211, 254, 355, 407, 411, 418, 459, 469; **II:** 127–128, 130, 131, 136, 137, 138, 140, **271–294**, 322, 331–332, 338, 397–398, 400, 415, 444, 451, 556; **III:** 51, 118, 314, 327–328, 461, 576, 607; **IV:** 192, 202, 342, 349; **Retro. Supp. I:** 220, 334, 362, 378; **Retro. Supp. II:** 93, 101, 135, 288; **Supp. I Part 1:** 306, 318, 357, 360, 368; **Supp. I Part 2:** 414, 420, 645–646; **Supp. II Part 1:** 198, 352; **Supp. IV Part 2:** 678; **Supp. VIII:** 98, 101, 102; **Supp. XI:** 198, 200; **Supp. XIV:** 45–46; **Supp. XV:** 269, 274, 285, 287; **Supp. XVIII:** 6; **Supp. XXIV:** 24

Howells, Mrs. William Dean (Elinor Mead), **II:** 273

Howells, Winifred, **II:** 271

"Howells as Anti-Novelist" (Updike), **Retro. Supp. I:** 334

Howells: His Life and World (Brooks), **I:** 254

Hower, Edward, **Supp. XII:** 330, 343

Howes, Barbara, **Supp. XIII:** 331

How Good Is David Mamet, Anyway? (Heilpern), **Supp. XIV:** 242

"How I Became a Shadow" (Purdy), **Supp. VII:** 269

"How I Came to Vedanta" (Isherwood), **Supp. XIV:** 164

"How I Come to You" (Peacock), **Supp. XIX:** 198

"How I Learned to Sweep" (Alvarez), **Supp. VII:** 4

"How I Spent My Forties" (Wasserstein), **Supp. XV:** 325, 330, 332

"How It Began" (Stafford), **Supp. XI:** 327

"How It Feels to Be Colored Me" (Hurston), **Supp. VI:** 152

"How It Is" (Budbill), **Supp. XIX:** 10

"How It Is" (Everwine), **Supp. XV:** 79, 86

"How I Told My Child About Race" (Brooks), **Supp. III Part 1:** 78

"How I Went to the Mines" (Harte), **Supp. II Part 1:** 336

"How I Write" (Franzen), **Supp. XX: 84**

"How I Write" (Welty), **IV:** 279, 280

"How I Wrote *The Promised Land*" (Antin), **Supp. XX: 3**

"How Jonah Did Not Care" (R. Bly), **Supp. IV Part 1:** 73

Howl (Ginsberg), **Retro. Supp. I:** 426; **Supp. II Part 1:** 92; **Supp. IV Part 1:** 90; **Supp. V:** 336; **Supp. VIII:** 290; **Supp. XIV:** 15, 126, 157; **Supp. XVIII:** 20, 29

"How Laddie and the Princess Spelled Down at the Christmas Bee" (Stratton-Porter), **Supp. XX: 216**

Howl and Other Poems (Ginsberg), **Supp. II Part 1:** 308, 317–318, 319; **Supp. X:** 123

Howlett, William, **Retro. Supp. I:** 17

Howl: Original Draft Facsimile, Transcript and Variant Versions (Gimsberg), **Supp. XIV:** 142

"How Many Midnights" (Bowles), **Supp. IV Part 1:** 86–87

"How Many Nights" (Kinnell), **Supp. III Part 1:** 245–246

How Much? (Blechman), **Supp. I Part 1:** 290

"How Much Are You Worth" (Salinas), **Supp. XIII:** 325–326

"How Much Earth" (Levine), **Supp. V:** 184

How Much Earth: The Fresno Poets (Buckley, Oliveira, and Williams, eds.), **Supp. XIII:** 313

"How Not to Forget" (Bartov), **Supp. XVI:** 153–154

"How Poetry Comes to Me" (Corso), **Supp. XII:** 122

"How Poetry Comes to Me" (Snyder), **Supp. VIII:** 305

How Reading Changed My Life (Quindlen), **Supp. XVII:** 167, 179–180

"How She Came By Her Name: An Interview with Louis Massiah" (Bambara), **Supp. XI:** 20

"How Soon Hath Time" (Ransom), **IV:** 123

How Spring Comes (Notley), **Supp. XXII:** 226, 229

How Stella Got Her Groove Back (McMillan), **Supp. XIII:** 185, **190–191**

How the Alligator Missed Breakfast (Kinney), **Supp. III Part 1:** 235, 253

"How the Devil Came Down Division Street" (Algren), **Supp. IX:** 3

How the García Girls Lost Their Accents (Alvarez), **Supp. VII:** 3, 5–9, 11, 15, 17, 18

How the Grinch Stole Christmas! (Geisel), **Supp. XVI:** 102

How the Other Half Lives (Riis), **I:** 293

"How the Saint Did Not Care" (R. Bly), **Supp. IV Part 1:** 73

"How the Women Went from Dover" (Whittier), **Supp. I Part 2:** 694, 696, 697

"How This Magazine Wronged Herman Wouk" (Lewis), **Supp. XXV:** 253

"How To" (Carruth), **Supp. XVI:** 51

"How-To" (Monson), **Supp. XXIV:** 237

How To Be Alone: Essays (Franzen), **Supp. XX: 83, 90, 93–94**

"How to Be an Other Woman" (Moore), **Supp. X:** 165, 167, 168

"How to Become a Writer" (Moore), **Supp. X:** 167, 168

"How to Be Happy: Another Memo to Myself" (Dunn), **Supp. XI:** 145

How To Cook a Wolf (M. F. K. Fisher), **Supp. XVII:** 84–85, 87

"How to Date a Browngirl, Blackgirl, Whitegirl, or Halfie" (Díaz), **Supp. XXIV:** 88

How to Develop Your Personality (Shellow), **Supp. I Part 2:** 608

"How to Grow Orchids Without Grounds: A Manual" (Vaz), **Supp. XXVI:** 263

How to Know God: The Yoga Aphorisms of Patanjali (Isherwood and Prabhavananda)), **Supp. XIV:** 164

"How To Like It" (Dobyns), **Supp. XIII: 85–86**

"How to Live on $36,000 a Year" (Fitzgerald), **Retro. Supp. I:** 105

"How to Live. What to Do" (Stevens), **Retro. Supp. I:** 302

"How to Love a Bicycle" (Biss), **Supp. XXVI:** 48

"How Tom is Doin' " (Kees), **Supp. XV:** 143

How to Read (Pound), **Supp. VIII:** 291

How to Read a Novel (Gordon), **II:** 198

How to Read a Poem and Fall in Love with Poetry (Hirsch), **Supp. XIX:** 202

How to Read a Poem: And Fall in Love with Poetry (Hirsch), **Supp. XXIII:** 124

How to Read a Poem . . . and Start a Poetry Circle (Peacock), **Supp. XIX:** 194, 202–203, 205

How to Save Your Own Life (Jong), **Supp. V:** 115, 123–125, 130

"How to Study Poetry" (Pound), **III:** 474

"How to Talk to Your Mother" (Moore), **Supp. X:** 167, 172

"How to Tell Stories to Children" (July), **Supp. XXIV:** 206–207

How to Win Friends and Influence People (Carnegie), **Supp. I Part 2:** 608

How to Worry Successfully (Seabury), **Supp. I Part 2:** 608

How to Write (Stein), **IV:** 32, 34, 35

"How to Write a Blackwood Article" (Poe), **III:** 425; **Retro. Supp. II:** 273

"How to Write a Memoir Like This" (Oates), **Supp. III Part 2:** 509

"How to Write Like Somebody Else" (Roethke), **III:** 540

How to Write Short Stories (Lardner), **II:** 430, 431

"How Vincentine Did Not Care" (R. Bly), **Supp. IV Part 1:** 73

How We Became Human: New and Selected Poems (Harjo), **Supp. XII: 230–232**

"How We Danced" (Sexton), **Supp. II Part 2:** 692

How We Got Insipid (Lethem), **Supp. XVIII:** 149

"How We Got in Town and Out Again" (Lethem), **Supp. XVIII:** 149

"How You Sound??" (Baraka), **Supp. II Part 1:** 30

Hoy, Philip, **Supp. X:** 56, 58

Hoyer, Linda Grace (pseudonym). *See* Updike, Mrs. Wesley

Hoyt, Constance, **Supp. I Part 2:** 707

Hoyt, Elinor Morton. *See* Wylie, Elinor

Hoyt, Helen, **Supp. XXII:** 275

Hoyt, Henry (father), **Supp. I Part 2:** 707

Hoyt, Henry (son), **Supp. I Part 2:** 708

Hoyt, Henry Martyn, **Supp. I Part 2:** 707

H. P. Lovecraft (Canan), **Supp. XXV:** 123

Hsu, Kai-yu, **Supp. X:** 292

Hsu, Ruth Y., **Supp. XV:** 212

Hubba City (Reed), **Supp. X:** 241

Hubbard, Elbert, **I:** 98, 383

Hubbell, Jay B., **Supp. I Part 1:** 372

"Hubbub, The" (Ammons), **Supp. VII:** 35

Huber, François, **II:** 6

Huckins, Olga, **Supp. IX:** 32

Huckleberry Finn (Twain). *See Adventures of Huckleberry Finn, The* (Twain)

Hucksters, The (Wakeman), **Supp. XXV:** 258

Hud (film), **Supp. V:** 223, 226

Huddle, David, **Supp. XXVI: 147–162**

Hudgins, Andrew, **Supp. X:** 206; **Supp. XVII:** 111, 112; **Supp. XVIII:** 176

Hudson, Henry, **I:** 230; **Supp. XXVI:** 86

"Hudsonian Curlew, The" (Snyder), **Supp. VIII:** 302

Hudson River Bracketed (Wharton), **IV:** 326–327; **Retro. Supp. I:** 382

Huebsch, B. W., **III:** 110

Hueffer, Ford Madox, **Supp. I Part 1:** 257, 262. *See also* Ford, Ford Madox

Huene-Greenberg, Dorothee von, **Supp. XX:** 46

Huff (television series), **Supp. XIX:** 222

"Hug, The" (Gallagher), **Supp. XXIV:** 168

Hug Dancing (Hearon), **Supp. VIII: 67–68**

Huge Season, The (Morris), **III:** 225–226, 227, 230, 232, 233, 238

Hugging the Jukebox (Nye), **Supp. XIII: 275–276, 277**

"Hugging the Jukebox" (Nye), **Supp. XIII:** 276

Hughes, Brigid, **Supp. XVI:** 247

Hughes, Carolyn, **Supp. XII:** 272, 285

Hughes, Frieda, **Supp. I Part 2:** 540, 541

Hughes, Glenn, **Supp. I Part 1:** 255

Hughes, H. Stuart, **Supp. VIII:** 240

Hughes, James Nathaniel, **Supp. I Part 1:** 321, 332

Hughes, Ken, **Supp. XI:** 307

Hughes, Langston, **Retro. Supp. I: 193–214; Retro. Supp. II:** 114, 115, 117, 120; **Supp. I Part 1: 320–348; Supp. II Part 1:** 31, 33, 61, 170, 173, 181, 227, 228, 233, 361; **Supp. III Part 1:** 72–77; **Supp. IV Part 1:** 15, 16, 164, 168, 169, 173, 243, 368; **Supp. IX:** 306, 316; **Supp. VIII:** 213; **Supp. X:** 131, 136, 139, 324; **Supp. XI:** 1; **Supp. XIII:** 75, 111, 132, 233; **Supp. XIX:** 72, 75, 77; **Supp. XVI:** 135, 138; **Supp. XVIII:** 90, 277, 279, 280, 281, 282; **Supp. XXI:** 243; **Supp. XXII:** 3, 4, 5, 6, 8, 13–14; **Supp. XXIV:** 183; **Supp. XXVI:** 166

Hughes, Nicholas, **Supp. I Part 2:** 541

Hughes, Robert, **Supp. X:** 73

Hughes, Ted, **IV:** 3; **Retro. Supp. II:** 244, 245, 247, 257; **Supp. I Part 2:** 536, 537, 538, 539, 540, 541; **Supp. XV:** 117, 347, 348; **Supp. XXII:** 30

Hughes, Thomas, **Supp. I Part 2:** 406

"Hugh Harper" (Bowles), **Supp. IV Part 1:** 94

Hughie (O'Neill), **III:** 385, 401, 405

Hugh Selwyn Mauberley (Pound), **I:** 66, 476; **III:** 9, 462–463, 465, 468; **Retro. Supp. I: 289–290,** 291, 299; **Supp. XIV:** 272

Hugo, Richard, **Supp. IX:** 296, 323, 324, 330; **Supp. VI: 131–148; Supp. XI:** 315, 317; **Supp. XII:** 178; **Supp.**

XIII: 112, 113, 133; **Supp. XVIII:** 293, 299; **Supp. XXI:** 243; **Supp. XXVI:** 180, 187

Hugo, Victor, **II:** 290, 490, 543; **Supp. IV Part 2:** 518; **Supp. IX:** 308

Hui-neng, **III:** 567

Huis Clos (Sartre), **Supp. IV Part 1:** 84

Huizinga, Johan, **I:** 225; **II:** 416–417, 418, 425

Hulbert, Ann, **Supp. XI:** 38–39

Hull, Lynda, **Supp. XI:** 131; **Supp. XXI:** **129–142**

Hull, Thomas, **Supp. XXV:** 123

Hulme, Thomas E., **I:** 68, 69, 475; **III:** 196, 209, 463–464, 465; **IV:** 122; **Supp. I Part 1:** 261, 262; **Supp. XV:** 43

Human, All Too Human (Nietzsche), **Supp. X:** 48

"Human Culture" (Emerson), **II:** 11–12

Human Desire (film), **Supp. XXVI:** 134

Human Factor, The (Greene), **Supp. V:** 298

"Human Figures" (Doty), **Supp. XI:** 123–124

"Human Fly, The" (Boyle), **Supp. XX:** **19**

"Human Geography" (Jarman), **Supp. XVII:** 116

"Human Immortality" (James), **II:** 353–354

"Human Life" (Emerson), **II:** 11–12

"Human Pig" (Jin), **Supp. XVIII:** 99

Human Rights, Human Wrongs: The Oxford Amnesty Lectures, 2001, **Supp. XVI:** 155

"Human Soul as a Rube Goldberg Device, The: A Choose-Your-Own-Adventure-Story" (Brockmeier), **Supp. XXII:** 60–61

Human Stain, The (P. Roth), **Retro. Supp. II:** 279, 289, 294–295

"Human Things" (Nemerov), **III:** 279

Human Universe (Olson), **Supp. II Part 2:** 571

"Human Universe" (Olson), **Supp. II Part 2:** 565, 567

Human Vibration (Richter), **Supp. XVIII:** 209

Human Wishes (Hass), **Supp. VI:** 105–106, 107

Human Work (Gilman), **Supp. XI:** 206

Humbert, Humbert, **Supp. X:** 283

Humble Inquiry into the Rules of the Word of God, An, Concerning the Qualifications Requisite to a Complete Standing and Full Communion in the Visible Christian Church (Edwards), **I:** 548

Humboldt, Alexander von, **III:** 428

Humboldt's Gift (Bellow), **Retro. Supp. II:** 19, 28–29, 34; **Supp. XIII:** 320

Hume, David, **I:** 125; **II:** 349, 357, 480; **III:** 618

Humes, Harold, **Supp. V:** 201; **Supp. XIV:** 82

Humes, Harry, **Supp. XIX:** 281; **Supp. XXIII:** 54

Humes, H. L. "Doc", **Supp. XI:** 294

"Humility" (Hoffman), **Supp. XVIII:** 86

Hummer, T. R., **Supp. XIX:** 278; **Supp. XXI:** 91

"Hummingbirds, The" (Welty), **IV:** 273

Humors and/or Not So Humorous (Kenny), **Supp. XXIII:** 155

Humphrey, William, **Supp. IX: 93–112; Supp. XV:** 353

Humphreys, Christmas, **Supp. V:** 267

Humphreys, David, **Supp. II Part 1:** 65, 69, 70, 268

Humphreys, Josephine, **Supp. XII:** 311

Humphries, Rolfe, **III:** 124; **Retro. Supp. I:** 137

Hunchback of Notre Dame, The (film), **Supp. IV Part 1:** 101

Hunches in Bunches (Geisel), **Supp. XVI:** 111

Huncke, Herbert, **Supp. XII:** 118; **Supp. XIV: 137–153**

Huncke's Journal (Huncke), **Supp. XIV:** 139, 144, 145, 146

Hundred Camels in the Courtyard, A (Bowles), **Supp. IV Part 1:** 90

"Hundred Collars, A" (Frost), **Retro. Supp. I:** 128; **Supp. XIII:** 147

Hundred Secret Senses, The (Tan), **Supp. X:** 289, 293, 295, 297, 298, 299

Hundreds of Hens and Other Poems for Children by Halfdan Rasmussen (Nelson and Espeland, trans.), **Supp. XVIII:** 180

Hundred White Daffodils, A: Essays, Interviews, Newspaper Columns, and One Poem (Kenyon), **Supp. VII:** 160–162, 165, 166, 167, 174

Huneker, James, **III:** 102

"Hunger" (Davison), **Supp. XXVI:** 69

Hunger (Hamsun), **Supp. XI:** 167

"Hunger" (Hogan), **Supp. IV Part 1:** 411

"Hunger . . ." (Rich), **Supp. I Part 2:** 571

"Hungerfield" (Jeffers), **Supp. II Part 2:** 416–417, 436

Hungerfield and Other Poems (Jeffers), **Supp. II Part 2:** 422

Hunger of Memory: The Education of Richard Rodriguez (Rodriguez), **Supp. XIV:** 297, 298, **298–302,** 310

Hungry Ghosts, The (Oates), **Supp. II Part 2:** 504, 510

Hungry Hearts (Prose), **Supp. XVI:** 253

"Hungry Intellectual, A" (Le Sueur), **Supp. XXIII:** 164

Hungry Woman, The: A Mexican Medea (Moraga), **Supp. XXIII:** 196

Hunnewell, Susannah, **Supp. VIII:** 83

Hunt, Harriot K., **Retro. Supp. II:** 146

Hunt, Leigh, **II:** 515–516; **Supp. XV:** 175

Hunt, Richard Morris, **IV:** 312

Hunt, Robert, **Supp. XV:** 42, 49, 52

Hunt, William, **II:** 343

"Hunter" (Bierds), **Supp. XVII:** 30

Hunter, Dianna, **Supp. XVI:** 38

Hunter, Dr. Joseph, **II:** 217

Hunter, J. Paul, **Supp. IV Part 1:** 332

Hunter, Kim, **Supp. I Part 1:** 286

"Hunter of Doves" (Herbst), **Retro. Supp. II:** 325

"Hunter of the West, The" (Bryant), **Supp. I Part 1:** 155

Hunters, The (film), **Supp. IX:** 250

Hunters, The (Salter), **Supp. IX:** 246, **249–250**

Hunters and Gatherers (Prose), **Supp. XVI:** 257

"Hunters in the Snow" (Brueghel), **I:** 174; **Retro. Supp. I:** 430

"Hunters in the Snow" (Wolff), **Supp. VII:** 339–340

"Hunter's Moon—Eating the Bear" (Oliver), **Supp. VII:** 234

"Hunter's Vision, The" (Bryant), **Supp. I Part 1:** 160

Hunting for Hope: A Father's Journey (Sanders), **Supp. XVI:** 276–277, 278

"Hunting Is Not Those Heads on the Wall" (Baraka), **Supp. II Part 1:** 45

Huntington, Collis P., **I:** 198, 207

"Hunt in the Black Forest, The" (Jarrell), **II:** 379–380

Huntley, Jobe, **Supp. I Part 1:** 339

"Hurrah, Hurrah" (Nelson), **Supp. XVIII:** 175

Hurray Home (Wideman), **Supp. X:** 320

Hurricane (radio play, Boyce), **Supp. XXI:** 13

"Hurricane, The" (Crane), **I:** 401

"Hurricane, The" (Freneau), **Supp. II Part 1:** 262

"Hurricane Belle" (Notley), **Supp. XXII:** 228

"Hurry Kane" (Lardner), **II:** 425, 426, 427

"Hurry up Please It's Time" (Sexton), **Supp. II Part 2:** 694, 695

Hurst, Fannie, **Supp. XVIII:** 278, 279

Hurston, Zora Neale, **Retro. Supp. I:** 194, 198, 200, 201, 203; **Supp. I Part 1:** 325, 326, 332; **Supp. II Part 1:** 33; **Supp. IV Part 1:** 5, 11, 12, 164, 257; **Supp. VI: 149–161; Supp. VIII:** 214; **Supp. X:** 131, 139, 232, 242; **Supp. XI:** 85; **Supp. XIII:** 185, 233, 236, 295, 306; **Supp. XIX:** 72, 75; **Supp. XVIII:** 122, 279, 280, 282; **Supp. XX: 107; Supp. XXII:** 12; **Supp. XXVI:** 1, 12, 164, 167

Hurt, John, **Supp. XIII:** 132

"Hurt Hawks" (Jeffers), **Supp. XXIII:** 145

Hurwitt, Robert, **Supp. XXIII:** 281

Husbands and Wives (film; Allen), **Supp. XV:** 12

"Husband's Song, The" (Di Piero), **Supp. XIX:** 39

Husband's Story, The (Shields), **Supp. VII:** 316. *See also* "Happenstance" (Shields)

"Husband's Tale, The" (Huddle), **Supp. XXVI:** 151

Husserl, Edmund, **II:** 362, 363; **IV:** 491; **Supp. IV Part 1:** 42, 43

Hussey, Jo Ella, **Supp. XII:** 201

Hustler, The (film), **Supp. XI:** 306

Huston, John, **I:** 30, 31, 33, 35; **II:** 588; **III:** 161; **Supp. IV Part 1:** 102, 116, 355; **Supp. XI:** 307; **Supp. XIII:** 174

"Huswifery" (Taylor), **IV:** 161; **Supp. I Part 2:** 386

"Hut, The" (Sobin), **Supp. XVI:** 284–285

Ickes, Harold, **Supp. I Part 1:** 5

Iconographs (Swenson), **Supp. IV Part 2:** 638, 646–648, 651

"Icosphere, The" (Moore), **III:** 213

"I Could Believe" (Levine), **Supp. V:** 189

"I Could Take" (Carruth), **Supp. XVI:** 56

I Could Tell You Stories: Sojourns in the Land of Memory (Hampl), **Supp. XXII:** 84, **92–94**

"I Cry, Love! Love!" (Roethke), **III:** 539–540

Ida (Stein), **IV:** 43, 45

"Ida y Vuelta" (Muñoz), **Supp. XXV:** 136

"Idea, The" (Carver), **Supp. III Part 1:** 143

"Idea, The" (Strand), **Supp. IV Part 2:** 631

Ideal Husband (Wilde), **II:** 515

Idea of Florida in the American Literary Imagination, The (Rowe), **Supp. X:** 223

"Idea of Form at Spruce Creek, The" (Weigl), **Supp. XIX:** 283–284

"Idea of Ice, The" (C. Baxter), **Supp. XVII:** 15

"Idea of Order, An" (Wiman), **Supp. XVIII:** 173

"Idea of Order at Key West, The" (Stevens), **IV:** 89–90; **Retro. Supp. I:** 302, 303, 313

Ideas of Order (Stevens), **Retro. Supp. I:** 296, 298, **302–303**, 303, 305

"Identification Pleas" (Gansworth), **Supp. XXVI:** 114

"Identity Theft: True Memory, False Memory, and the Holocaust" (R. Franklin), **Supp. XVI:** 160

Ideograms in China (Michaux; Sobin, trans.), **Supp. XVI:** 288

"Ideographs" (Olds), **Supp. X:** 205

Ides of March, The (Wilder), **IV:** 357, 372

"I Did Not Learn Their Names" (Ellison), **Retro. Supp. II:** 124

"I Died with the First Blow & Was Reborn Wrong" (Coleman), **Supp. XI:** 91

"Idiom of a Self, The" (Pinsky), **Supp. VI:** 240

"Idiot, The" (Crane), **I:** 401

Idiot, The (Dostoevsky), **I:** 468

"Idiots First" (Malamud), **Supp. I Part 2:** 434–435, 437, 440–441

Idiots Karamazov, The (Durand and Innaurato), **Supp. XXIV:** 113, 116

"Idiot Wind" (song, Dylan), **Supp. XVIII:** 30

Idle Idylls (Wells), **Supp. XXVI:** 275

I Don't Need You Any More (A. Miller), **III:** 165

Idoru (W. Gibson), **Supp. XVI:** 119, 124, **129–130**

"I Dream I'm the Death of Orpheus" (Rich), **Supp. I Part 2:** 557–558

I Dreamt I Became a Nymphomaniac! Imagining (Acker), **Supp. XII:** 4, 6, **8**, 11

"I Dreamt You Young" (Espaillat), **Supp. XXI:** 107

"Idyll" (Shaw), **Supp. XIX:** 241

Idylls of the King (Tennyson), **III:** 487; **Supp. I Part 2:** 410; **Supp. XIII:** 146

Idyl of Work, An (Larcom), **Supp. XIII:** 139, 142, 146–147, 150

"If" (Creeley), **Supp. IV Part 1:** 158

If Beale Street Could Talk (Baldwin), **Retro. Supp. II:** 13–14; **Supp. I Part 1:** 48, 59–60, 67

"If Biblical Law Ruled Modern Society . . ." (P. N. Warren), **Supp. XX:** 272

If Blessing Comes (Bambara), **Supp. XI:** 1

I Feel a Little Jumpy around You (Nye and Janeczko, eds.), **Supp. XIII:** 280

"I felt a Funeral, in my Brain" (Dickinson), **Retro. Supp. I:** 38

"If Grown-Ups Were Smart" (Nelson and Espeland), **Supp. XVIII:** 181

If He Hollers Let Him Go (C. Himes), **Supp. XVI:** 135, 138–139, 142

"If I Could Be Like Wallace Stevens" (Stafford), **Supp. XI:** 327

"If I Could Do Whatever I Wanted" (Nelson and Espeland), **Supp. XVIII:** 181

"If I Could Only Live at the Pitch That Is Near Madness" (Eberhart), **I:** 523, 526–527

If I Could Write This in Fire (Cliff), **Supp. XXII:** 67, 69

"If I Could Write This in Fire, I Would Write This in Fire" (Cliff), **Supp. XXII:** 65–66, 68–69

If I Die in a Combat Zone (O'Brien), **Supp. V:** 238, 239, 240, 245

If I Ever Get Out of Here (Gansworth), **Supp. XXVI:** 102, 108–109

"If I Had My Way" (Creeley), **Supp. IV Part 1:** 157

"If I Might Be" (Chopin), **Retro. Supp. II:** 61

"I Find the Real American Tragedy" (Dreiser), **Retro. Supp. II:** 105

If I Ran the Circus (Geisel), **Supp. XVI:** 105

If I Ran the Zoo (Geisel), **Supp. XVI:** 104–105

If It Die (Gide), **I:** 290

"If It Were Not for You" (Carruth), **Supp. XVI:** 57

"If I Were a Man" (Gilman), **Supp. XI:** 207

"If I Were the Wind" (Leopold), **Supp. XIV:** 184

If Morning Ever Comes (Tyler), **Supp. IV Part 2:** 658–659

If Mountains Die: A New Mexico Memoir (Nichols), **Supp. XIII:** 255, 257, 267

I Forgot to Go to Spain (Harrison), **Supp. VIII:** 39, **52–53**

"If Poetry Were Not a Morality" (Gallagher), **Supp. XXIV:** 170

If the River Was Whiskey (Boyle), **Supp. VIII:** 15–16; **Supp. XX:** 17, 19

"If They Knew Yvonne" (Dubus), **Supp. VII:** 81

"If We Had Bacon" (H. Roth), **Supp. IX:** 232, 234

"If We Had Known" (Francis), **Supp. IX:** 78

"If We Must Die" (McKay), **Supp. IV Part 1:** 3; **Supp. X:** 132, 134

"If We Take All Gold" (Bogan), **Supp. III Part 1:** 52

If You Call This a Cry Song (Carruth), **Supp. XVI:** 56

If You Want to Write (Ueland), **Supp. XVII:** 13

I Gaspiri (Lardner), **II:** 435

"I Gather the Limbs of Osiris" (Pound), **Retro. Supp. I:** 287

I Get on the Bus (McKnight), **Supp. XX:** **148–150, 152**

"I Give You Back" (Harjo), **Supp. XII:** 223

Ignatius of Loyola, **IV:** 151; **Supp. XI:** 162

Ignatius Rising (Nevils and Hardy), **Supp. XXVI:** 241

Ignatow, David, **Supp. XIII:** 275

"Ignis Fatuus" (Tate), **IV:** 128

"Ignorant Lust after Knowledge, The" (Bronk), **Supp. XXI:** 31

"I Go Back to May 1937" (Olds), **Supp. X:** 207

I Go Dreaming Serenades (Salinas), **Supp. XIII:** 316

"I Got a Guy Once" (Gallagher), **Supp. XXIV:** 176

I Got the Blues (Odets), **Supp. II Part 2:** 530

Iguana Killer, The (Ríos), **Supp. IV Part 2:** 542–544

"I Had Eight Birds Hatcht in One Nest" (Bradstreet), **Supp. I Part 1:** 102, 115, 117, 119

"I had no time to Hate" (Dickinson), **Retro. Supp. I:** 44–45, 46

I Had Trouble in Getting to Solla Sollew (Geisel), **Supp. XVI:** 108, 109

I Hate Miranda July (blog), **Supp. XXIV:** 200

"I Have a Rendezvous with Life" (Cullen), **Supp. IV Part 1:** 168

"I Have Been Thinking About Snow" (Monson), **Supp. XXIV:** 235

"I Have Increased Power" (Ginsberg), **Supp. II Part 1:** 313

"I Have Moved West" (Taggard), **Supp. XXII:** 274

"I Have Seen Black Hands" (Wright), **Supp. II Part 1:** 228

"I Hear an Army" (Joyce), **Supp. I Part 1:** 262

"I heard a Fly buzz when I died" (Dickinson), **Retro. Supp. I:** 38

"I Heard Immanuel Singing" (Lindsay), **Supp. I Part 2:** 379

I Heard It Through the Grapevine (Turner), **Supp. XX:** **110**

"I Hear It Was Charged against Me" (Whitman), **IV:** 343

I Hear Men Talking (Le Sueur), **Supp. XXIII:** 162, 167, **171–172**

"I Held a Shelley Manuscript" (Corso), **Supp. XII:** 128

"I Held His Name" (Ríos), **Supp. IV Part 2:** 547

"Ike and Nina" (Boyle), **Supp. XX:** 19

"I Kiss a Door" (July), **Supp. XXIV:** 204

I Knew a Phoenix (Sarton), **Supp. VIII:** 249, 251–252

"I Know a Man" (Creeley), **Supp. IV Part 1:** 147–148, 149

I Know Some Things: Stories about Childhood by Contemporary Writers (Moore, ed.), **Supp. X:** 175

"I Know Why the Caged Bird Cannot Read" (Prose), **Supp. XVI:** 259

I Know Why the Caged Bird Sings (Angelou), **Supp. IV Part 1:** 2–4, 5, 7, 11, 12, 13, 14, 15, 17; **Supp. XVI:** 259

"Ikon: The Harrowing of Hell" (Levertov), **Supp. III Part 1:** 284

"Iktomi and the Ducks" (Zitkala-Ša), **Supp. XXV:** 275–276

Ile (O'Neill), **III:** 388; **Supp. XXV:** 20

"I Led Three Lives" (television program), **Supp. XX:** 195

"I Let Him Take Me" (Cisneros), **Supp. VII:** 71

Iliad (Bryant, trans.), **Supp. I Part 1:** 158

Iliad (Chapman, trans.), **Supp. XXV:** 226

Iliad (Homer), **II:** 470; **Supp. IV Part 2:** 631; **Supp. IX:** 211; **Supp. X:** 114; **Supp. XVII:** 117; **Supp. XXI:** 36

Iliad (Pope, trans.), **Supp. I Part 1:** 152

"I like to see it lap the Miles" (Dickinson), **Retro. Supp. I:** 37

"I Live Up Here" (Merwin), **Supp. III Part 1:** 349

"I'll Be Doing More of Same" (Franzen), **Supp. XX:** 89

"Illegal Alien" (Mora), **Supp. XIII:** 215

"Illegal Days, The" (Paley), **Supp. VI:** 222

"Illegibility" (F. Wright), **Supp. XVII:** 244

Illig, Joyce, **Retro. Supp. II:** 20

"Illinois" (Masters), **Supp. I Part 2:** 458

"Illinois Bus Ride" (Leopold), **Supp. XIV:** 189

Illinois Poems (Masters), **Supp. I Part 2:** 472

"Illinois Village, The" (Lindsay), **Supp. I Part 2:** 381

"Ill-Lit" (F. Wright), **Supp. XVII:** 245

Ill-Lit: Selected & New Poems (F. Wright), **Supp. XVII:** 245

Illness as Metaphor (Sontag), **Supp. III Part 2:** 452, 461, 466

I'll Take My Stand ("Twelve Southerners"), **II:** 196; **III:** 496; **IV:** 125, 237; **Supp. X:** 25, 52–53; **Supp. XIV:** 3

"I'll Take You to Tennessee" (Connell), **Supp. XIV:** 82

Illumination (Frederic), **II:** 141

Illumination, The (Brockmeier), **Supp. XXII:** 61

Illumination Night (Hoffman), **Supp. X:** 85, **86,** 88, 89

Illuminations (Rimbaud), **Supp. XXI:** 233

"Illusion, An" (Wells), **Supp. XXVI:** 275

Illusion and Reality (Caudwell), **Supp. XXII:** 284

Illusion comique, L' (Corneille), **Supp. IX:** 138

"Illusion of Eternity, The" (Eberhart), **I:** 541

"Illusion of Fiction in Frank Conroy's *Stop-Time,* The" (R. Ramsey), **Supp. XVI:** 69

Illusions (Dash; film), **Supp. XI:** 20

"Illusions" (Emerson), **II:** 2, 5, 14, 16

Illustrated Man, The (Bradbury), **Supp. IV Part 1:** 102, 103, 113

Illustrations of China and Its People (Thompson), **Supp. XXI:** 151

Illustrations of Political Economy (Martineau), **Supp. II Part 1:** 288

"I Look at My Hand" (Swenson), **Supp. IV Part 2:** 638, 647

I Love Gootie: My Grandmother's Story (Apple), **Supp. XVII:** 9–10

I Love Myself When I Am Laughing . . . : A Zora Neale Hurston Reader (Walker), **Supp. III Part 2:** 531, 532

"I Love the Way It Goes"(O'Hara), **Supp. XXIII:** 220

"I'm a Fool" (Anderson), **I:** 113, 114, 116; **Supp. I Part 2:** 430

Image and Idea (Rahv), **Supp. II Part 1:** 146

Image and the Law, The (Nemerov), **III:** 268, 269–271, 272

"Image in the Mirror, The" (Swados), **Supp. XIX:** 265

"Images" (Hass), **Supp. VI:** 103

"Images and 'Images' " (Simic), **Supp. VIII:** 274

"Images for Godard" (Rich), **Supp. I Part 2:** 558

"Images of Walt Whitman" (Fiedler), **IV:** 352

"Imaginary Dialogue, An" (Espaillat), **Supp. XXI:** 103

"Imaginary Friendships of Tom McGrath, The" (Cohen), **Supp. X:** 112

"Imaginary Iceberg, The" (Bishop), **Retro. Supp. II:** 42; **Supp. I Part 1:** 86, 88

"Imaginary Jew, The" (Berryman), **I:** 174–175

Imaginary Letters (Pound), **III:** 473–474

Imaginary Paintings (C. Baxter), **Supp. XVII:** 18–19

"Imaginary Prisons" (Schnackenberg), **Supp. XV:** 257, 258

Imagination and Fancy; or, Selections from the English Poets, illustrative of those first requisites of their art; with markings of the best passages, critical notices of the writers, and an essay in answer to the question'What is Poetry?' (Hunt), **II:** 515–516

"Imagination as Value" (Stevens), **Retro. Supp. I:** 298

"Imagination of Disaster, The" (Gordon), **Supp. IV Part 1:** 306

Imaginative Qualities of Actual Things (Sorrentino), **Supp. XXI:** 226, 230, 231–232, 234

"Imagine a Day at the End of Your Life" (Beattie), **Supp. V:** 33

Imagined London: A Tour of the World's Greatest Fictional City (Quindlen), **Supp. XVII:** 167, 180

Imagineering Atlanta (Rutheiser), **Supp. XXII:** 244

"Imagine Kissing Pete" (O'Hara), **III:** 372; **Supp. VIII:** 156

Imaging Robert: My Brother, Madness, and Survival (Neugeboren), **Supp. XVI:** 225, **226–229**

"Imagining How It Would Be to Be Dead" (Eberhart), **I:** 533

Imagining Los Angeles: A City in Fiction (Fine), **Supp. XI:** 160

"Imagining Their Own Hymns" (B. Kelly), **Supp. XVII:** 126–127

"Imagining the Midwest" (Sanders), **Supp. XVI:** 275–276

Imagining the Worst: Stephen King and the Representations of Women (Lant and Thompson), **Supp. V:** 141

"Imagisme" (Pound), **Retro. Supp. I:** 288

Imagistes, Des: An Anthology of the Imagists (Pound, ed.), **III:** 465, 471; **Retro. Supp. I:** 288

Imago (O. Butler), **Supp. XIII:** 63, **65–66**

"Imago" (Stevens), **IV:** 74, 89

Imagoes (Coleman), **Supp. XI:** 89–90

I Married a Communist (P. Roth), **Retro. Supp. II:** 289, 293–294

I Married an Angel (film), **Supp. XVI:** 193

"I May, I Might, I Must" (Moore), **III:** 215

Imbusch, Kevin, **Supp. XXIII:** 125

"I'm Crazy" (Salinger), **III:** 553

"I'm Here" (Roethke), **III:** 547

Imitations (Lowell), **II:** 543, 544–545, 550, 555; **Retro. Supp. II:** 181, 187

"Imitations of Drowning" (Sexton), **Supp. II Part 2:** 684, 686

"Immaculate Man" (Gordon), **Supp. IV Part 1:** 311

"Immanence of Dostoevsky, The" (Bourne), **I:** 235

"Immigrants" (Mora), **Supp. XIII:** 216

Immigrant Saint: The Life of Mother Cabrini (di Donato), **Supp. XX: 44**

"Immigrant Story, The" (Paley), **Supp. VI:** 230

Immobile Wind, The (Winters), **Supp. II Part 2:** 786

"Immobile Wind, The" (Winters), **Supp. II Part 2:** 788, 811

"Immolatus" (Komunyakaa), **Supp. XIII:** 126

"Immoral Proposition, The" (Creeley), **Supp. IV Part 1:** 144

"Immortal Autumn" (MacLeish), **III:** 13

"Immortality Ode" (Nemerov), **III:** 87

Immortality Ode (Wordsworth), **II:** 17; **Supp. I Part 2:** 673

Immortal Marriage, The (Atherton), **Supp. XXIV:** 26

"Immortal Woman, The" (Tate), **IV:** 130, 131, 137

"I'm Not Ready to Die Yet" (Harjo), **Supp. XII:** 231

I'm Not There (film, Haynes), **Supp. XVIII:** 23

"I'm on My Way" (Salinas), **Supp. XIII:** 320

"Impasse" (Hughes), **Supp. I Part 1:** 343

"Impatient Mary" (Taggard), **Supp. XXII:** 278

Imperative Duty, An, a Novel (Howells), **II:** 286

Imperial Eyes: Travel Writing and Transculturation (Pratt), **Retro. Supp. II:** 48

Imperial Germany and the Industrial Revolution (Veblen), **Supp. I Part 2:** 642, 643

Imperial Way, The: By Rail from Peshawar to Chittagong (Theroux), **Supp. VIII:** 323

"Implements from the 'Tomb of the Poet' " (Stallings), **Supp. XXV:** 232

"Implosions" (Rich), **Supp. I Part 2:** 556

"Imp of the Perverse, The" (Poe), **III:** 414–415; **Retro. Supp. II:** 267

Impolite Interviews, **Supp. XI:** 293

"Importance of Artists' Biographies, The" (Goldbarth), **Supp. XII:** 183, 184, 191

Importance of Being Earnest, The (Wilde), **Supp. XIV:** 324, 339

Importance of Gaining and Preserving the Friendship of the Indians to the British Interest Considered (Kennedy and Parker), **Supp. XXVI:** 84

"Important Houses, The" (Gordon), **Supp. IV Part 1:** 315

"Impossible Indispensability of the Ars Poetica, The" (Carruth), **Supp. XVI:** 57

"Impossible to Tell" (Pinsky), **Supp. VI:** 247, 248

"Imposter, The" (West), **Retro. Supp. II:** 322, 327

"Impressionism and Symbolism in *Heart of Darkness*" (Watt), **Supp. VIII:** 4

"Impressionism"(Crooker), **Supp. XXIII:** 57

"Impressions of a European Tour" (Bourne), **I:** 225

"Impressions of an Indian Childhood" (Zitkala-Ša), **Supp. XXV:** 272

"Impressions of a Plumber" (H. Roth), **Supp. IX:** 228, 234

"Impressions of Europe, 1913–1914" (Bourne), **I:** 225

"I Must Have Called and So He Comes" (Notley), **Supp. XXII:** 224

"I'm Walking behind the Spanish" (Salinas), **Supp. XIII:** 323–324

"I/Myself" (Shields), **Supp. VII:** 311

"In a (Low) Bar" (Ferry), **Supp. XXIV:** 153

"In Absence" (Lanier), **Supp. I Part 1:** 364

"In Absentia" (Bowles), **Supp. IV Part 1:** 94

"In a Cab" (Untermeyer), **Supp. XV:** 296

"In a Coffee Pot" (Hayes), **Supp. XXVI:** 133–134, 144

"In a Country Cemetery" (Kooser), **Supp. XIX:** 120

Inada, Lawson Fusao, **Supp. V:** 180

"In a Dark Room, Furniture" (Nye), **Supp. XIII:** 274

"In a Dark Time" (Roethke), **III:** 539, 547, 548

In a Different Voice (Gilligan), **Supp. XXII:** 18

"In a Disused Graveyard" (Frost), **Retro. Supp. I:** 126, 133

In a Dusty Light (Haines), **Supp. XII:** 207

"In a Garden" (Lowell), **II:** 513

"In a Hard Intellectual Light" (Eberhart), **I:** 523

"In a Hollow of the Hills" (Harte), **Supp. II Part 1:** 354

In America (Sontag), **Supp. XIV:** 95–96

"In Amicitia" (Ransom), **IV:** 141

In a Narrow Grave: Essays on Texas (McMurtry), **Supp. V:** 220, 223

"Inanna" (A. Finch), **Supp. XVII:** 72

"In Another Country" (Hemingway), **I:** 484–485; **II:** 249

In April Once (Percy), **Retro. Supp. I:** 341

"In a Prominent Bar in Secaucus One Day" (X. J. Kennedy), **Supp. XV:** 154, 155–156

"In Armenia, 1987"(Balakian), **Supp. XXIII:** 25

In A Shallow Grave (Purdy), **Supp. VII:** 272

In a shlekhter tsayt (In a bad time) (Asch), **Supp. XXIII:** 4

"In a Station of the Metro" (Pound), **Retro. Supp. I:** 288; **Supp. I Part 1:** 265; **Supp. XIV:** 284–285

"In a Strange Town" (Anderson), **I:** 114, 115

"In Athens Once" (Rodriguez), **Supp. XIV:** 303

"In a Tub" (Hempel), **Supp. XXI:** 119

In Battle for Peace: The Story of My 83rd Birthday (Du Bois), **Supp. II Part 1:** 185

In Bed One Night & Other Brief Encounters (Coover), **Supp. V:** 49, 50

"In Bertram's Garden" (Justice), **Supp. VII:** 117

"In Blackwater Woods" (Oliver), **Supp. VII:** 244, 246

In Black & Whitey (Lacy), **Supp. XV:** 206–207

"In Broad Daylight" (Jin), **Supp. XVIII:** 94

In Broken Country (Wagoner), **Supp. IX:** 330

"In California" (Simpson), **Supp. IX:** 271

"In Camp" (Stafford), **Supp. XI:** 329

"Incant against Suicide" (Karr), **Supp. XI:** 249

"In Celebration of My Uterus" (Sexton), **Supp. II Part 2:** 689

"Incendiary, The" (Rowson), **Supp. XV:** 234

"In Certain Places and Certain Times There Can Be More of You" (Dunn), **Supp. XI:** 144

Incest: From "A Journal of Love," the Unexpurgated Diary of Anaïs Nin, 1932–1934 (Nin), **Supp. X:** 182, 184, 185, 187, 191

"In Chandler Country" (Gioia), **Supp. XV:** 119

Inchbald, Elizabeth, **II:** 8

"In Cheever Country" (Gioia), **Supp. XV:** 119

Inchiquin, the Jesuit's Letters (Ingersoll), **I:** 344

"Incident" (Cullen), **Supp. IV Part 1:** 165, 166

Incidental Numbers (Wylie), **Supp. I Part 2:** 708

Incidentals (Sandburg), **III:** 579

Incidentals in the Day World (Notley), **Supp. XXII:** 223, 226, 227

Incident at Vichy (A. Miller), **III:** 165, 166

Incidents in the Life of a Slave Girl (Brent), **Supp. IV Part 1:** 13

Incidents in the Life of a Slavegirl (Jacobs), **Supp. XVI:** 85

"Incipience" (Rich), **Supp. I Part 2:** 559

"In Clare" (McCarriston), **Supp. XIV:** 270–271

Including Horace (Untermeyer), **Supp. XV:** 301, 303–304

In Cold Blood: A True Account of a Multiple Murder and Its Consequences (Capote), **Retro. Supp. II:** 107–108; **Supp. I Part 1:** 292; **Supp. III Part 1:** 111, 117, 119, 122, 123, 125–131; **Supp. III Part 2:** 574; **Supp. IV Part 1:** 220; **Supp. XIV:** 162; **Supp. XXV:** 57

In Cold Hell, in Thicket (Olson), **Supp. II Part 2:** 571

"In Cold Hell, in Thicket" (Olson), **Supp. II Part 2:** 558, 563–564, 566, 572, 580

"Incoming Tide"(Strout), **Supp. XXIII:** 282, 285

"Incomparable Light, The" (Eberhart), **I:** 541

Incorporative Consciousness of Robert Bly, The (Harris), **Supp. IV Part 1:** 68

In Country (Mason), **Supp. VIII:** 133, **142–143,** 146

"In Country of Conscience" (J. W. Miller), **Supp. XX: 165**

"Incredible Survival of Coyote, The" (Snyder), **Supp. VIII:** 297

"Increment" (Ammons), **Supp. VII:** 28

In Defense of Ignorance (Shapiro), **Supp. II Part 2:** 703, 704, 713–714

In Defense of Reason (Winters), **Supp. I Part 1:** 268

In Defense of Women (Mencken), **III:** 109

Indelible (Hadas), **Supp. XXIII: 119**

Indelible Alison Bechdel, The (Bechdel), **Supp. XXV:** 4

Indemnity Only (Paretsky), **Supp. XXV:** 172–173, 176, 178

Independence Day (film), **Supp. X:** 80

Independence Day (Ford), **Supp. V:** 57, 62–63, 67–68

"Independent Candidate, The, a Story of Today" (Howells), **II:** 277

"Indestructible Mr. Gore, The" (Vidal), **Supp. IV Part 2:** 679

Index of American Design, **Supp. III Part 2:** 618

"India" (Rodriguez), **Supp. XIV:** 302

"Indian at the Burial-Place of His Fathers, An" (Bryant), **Supp. I Part 1:** 155–156, 167–168

"Indian Burying Ground, The" (Freneau), **Supp. II Part 1:** 264, 266

"Indian Camp" (Hemingway), **II:** 247–248, 263; **Retro. Supp. I:** 174–175, 176, 177, 181; **Supp. XVI:** 208

Indian Country (Caputo), **Supp. XIX:** 22–25

Indian Country (Matthiessen), **Supp. V:** 211

"Indian Country" (McCarriston), **Supp. XIV:** 271

"Indian Country" (Simpson), **Supp. IX:** 274

Indian Earth (Bynner), **Supp. XV:** 46

"Indian Gifts to Civilized Man" (Zitkala-Ša), **Supp. XXV:** 281

"Indian Girls" (McCarriston), **Supp. XIV:** 272–273

"Indian Manifesto" (Deloria), **Supp. IV Part 1:** 323

"Indian Names" (Sigourney), **Retro. Supp. II:** 47

"Indian's Awakening, The" (Zitkala-Ša), **Supp. XXV:** 281

"Indian Student, The" (Freneau), **Supp. II Part 1:** 264

"Indian Student, The" (Simpson), **Supp. IX:** 280

Indian Summer (Howells), **II:** 275, 279–281, 282

Indian Summer (Knowles), **Supp. XII:** 249, 250

Indian Summer: Musings on the Gift of Life (Pickering), **Supp. XXI:** 204

Indian Summers (Gansworth), **Supp. XXVI:** 104

"Indian Teacher Among Indians, An" (Zitkala-Ša), **Supp. XXV:** 272

"Indian Uprising, The" (Barthelme), **Supp. IV Part 1:** 44

"Indian Wooing" (C. Miller), **Supp. XXII:** 197–198

Indifferent Children, The (Auchincloss), **Supp. IV Part 1:** 25

Indirections (Cox), **Supp. XXI:** 21

Indiscretions (Pound), **Retro. Supp. I:** 284

"Indispensability of the Eyes, The" (Olds), **Supp. X:** 202

"In Distrust of Merits" (Moore), **III:** 201, 214

"Individual and the State, The" (Emerson), **II:** 10

Individualism, Old and New (Dewey), **Supp. I Part 2:** 677

"Indolence" (Pickering), **Supp. XXI:** 203

In Dreams Begin Responsibilities (Schwartz), **Supp. II Part 2:** 642, 645–650

"In Dreams Begin Responsibilities" (Schwartz), **Supp. II Part 2:** 641, 649, 654

In Dubious Battle (Steinbeck), **IV:** 51, 55–56, 59, 63

"In Durance" (Pound), **Retro. Supp. I:** 285

"Industry of Hard Kissing, The" (Ríos), **Supp. IV Part 2:** 547

"In Duty Bound" (Gilman), **Supp. XI:** 196–197

"I Need, I Need" (Roethke), **III:** 535–536

"I Need Help" (Stern), **Supp. IX:** 290

"Ineffectual Marriage" (Loy), **Supp. XXII:** 165

"Inés in the Kitchen" (García), **Supp. XI:** 190

"I never saw a Moor" (Dickinson), **Retro. Supp. I:** 37

I Never Told Anybody: Teaching Poetry Writing in a Nursing Home (Koch), **Supp. XV:** 190

"I Never Will Be Married, I'd Rather Be Excus'd" (Rowson), **Supp. XV:** 240

Inevitable Exiles (Kielsky), **Supp. V:** 273

"Inevitable Trial, The" (Holmes), **Supp. I Part 1:** 318

"Inexhaustible Hat, The" (Wagoner), **Supp. IX:** 327

"In Extremis" (Berry), **Supp. X:** 23

Incz, Colette, **Supp. XXIII:** 54, 245

"Infancy" (Wilder), **IV:** 375

"Infant Boy at Midcentury" (Warren), **IV:** 244–245, 252

Infante, Guillermo Cabrera, **Retro. Supp. I:** 278

"Infant Sea Turtles" (F. Wright), **Supp. XVII:** 245

Infants of the Spring (Thurman), **Supp. XIX:** 73; **Supp. XVIII:** 281

Inferno (Dante), **IV:** 139; **Supp. V:** 338; **Supp. VIII:** 219–221

Inferno of Dante, The (Pinsky), **Supp. VI:** 235, 248

Infidel (Ali), **Supp. XXIV:** 15

"Infidelity" (Komunyakaa), **Supp. XIII:** 130

Infidels (album, Dylan), **Supp. XVIII:** 28

"Infiltration of the Universe" (MacLeish), **III:** 19

Infinite Jest: A Novel (Wallace), **Supp. X:** 301, **310–314; Supp. XX:** 91

"Infinite Reason, The" (MacLeish), **III:** 19

"Infirmity" (Lowell), **II:** 554

"Infirmity" (Roethke), **III:** 548

In Five Years Time (Haines), **Supp. XII:** 206

"In Flower" (Snodgrass), **Supp. VI:** 325

"Influence of Landscape upon the Poet, The" (Eliot), **Retro. Supp. I:** 67

"In Football Season" (Updike), **IV:** 219

Informer, The (film), **Supp. III Part 2:** 619

Inge, William, **Supp. XXV: 93–108**

Ingersoll, Charles J., **I:** 344

Ingersoll, Robert Green, **Supp. II Part 1:** 198

Ingmundson, Kris, **Supp. XXIV:** 230, 234

Ingraham, Lloyd, **Supp. XVI:** 184

"Ingrained Reflexes" (Huddle), **Supp. XXVI:** 154

Ingster, Boris, **Retro. Supp. II:** 330

"In Guatemala, All Is Forgotten" (Goldman), **Supp. XXV:** 58

Inhabitants, The (Morris), **III:** 221–222

"Inheritance and Invention in Li-Young Lee's Poetry" (Xiaojing), **Supp. XV:** 214

"Inheritance"(Kenny), **Supp. XXIII:** 154

"Inheritance of Tools, The" (Sanders), **Supp. XVI:** 273

Inheritors (Glaspell), **Supp. III Part 1:** 175, 179–181, 186, 189

"In him we live, & move, & have our being" (Very), **Supp. XXV:** 246

"In Hollywood with the Zuni God of War" (Major), **Supp. XXII:** 180

"In Honor of David Anderson Brooks, My Father" (Brooks), **Supp. III Part 1:** 79

"Inhumanist, The" (Jeffers), **Supp. II Part 2:** 423, 426

"In Illo Tempore" (Karr), **Supp. XI:** 242

"In Interims: Outlyer" (Harrison), **Supp. VIII:** 38

"Initial" (F. Wright), **Supp. XVII:** 243

"Injudicious Gardening" (Moore), **III:** 198

"Injustice" (Paley), **Supp. VI:** 220

Injustice Collectors, The (Auchincloss), **Supp. IV Part 1:** 25

Ink, Blood, Semen (Goldbarth), **Supp. XII:** 181, 183

Ink Dark Moon, The: Love Poems by Ono no Komachi and Izumi Shikibu (Aratani and Hirshfield, trans.), **Supp. XXIII:** 136

Ink Truck, The (W. Kennedy), **Supp. VII:** 132, 133–138, 140, 141, 149, 152

In Life Sentences: Literary Essays (Epstein), **Supp. XIV:** 112

"In Limbo" (Wilbur), **Supp. III Part 2:** 544, 561

In Limestone Country (Sanders), **Supp. XVI:** 272

"In Line" (Major), **Supp. XXII:** 185

In Love (Hayes), **Supp. XXVI:** 133, 139, 140–141

In Love and Trouble: Stories of Black Women (Walker), **Supp. III Part 2:** 520, 521, 530, 531, 532

In Mad Love and War (Harjo), **Supp. XII: 224–226**

"In Memoriam" (Emerson), **II:** 13

"In Memoriam" (Hay), **Supp. XIV:** 122, 127

"In Memoriam" (Tennyson), **Retro. Supp. I:** 325; **Supp. I Part 2:** 416

In Memoriam: 1933 (Reznikoff), **Supp. XIV:** 280, 285

In Memoriam to Identity (Acker), **Supp. XII: 5, 16–18**

"In Memory of Arthur Winslow" (Lowell), **II:** 541, 547, 550; **Retro. Supp. II:** 187

"In Memory of Congresswoman Barbara Jordan" (Pinsky), **Supp. VI:** 250

"In Memory of Joe Brainard" (Bidart), **Supp. XV:** 33

"In Memory of My Feelings" (O'Hara), **Supp. XV:** 215–216

In Memory of My Feelings (O'Hara; Berkson, ed.), **Supp. XXIII:** 220

"In Memory of My Feelings"(O'Hara), **Supp. XXIII:** 208, 215–216

"In Memory of W. B. Yeats" (Auden), **Supp. VIII:** 19, 30; **Supp. XI:** 243, 244; **Supp. XIX:** 85

"In Memory of W. H. Auden" (Stern), **Supp. IX:** 288

"In Memory"(Schott), **Supp. XXIII:** 254

"In Mercy on Broadway" (Doty), **Supp. XI:** 132

In Morocco (Wharton), **Retro. Supp. I:** 380; **Supp. IV Part 1:** 81

Inmost Leaf, The: A Selection of Essays (Kazin), **Supp. VIII:** 102, 103

In Motley (Bierce), **I:** 209

In My Father's Court (Singer), **IV:** 16–17; **Retro. Supp. II:** 301–302

"In My Life" (Dubus), **Supp. VII:** 81

"In My Other Life" (Huddle), **Supp. XXVI:** 151

Innaurato, Albert, **Supp. XXIV:** 113, 116, 117

"In Navaho Country" (Bronk), **Supp. XXI:** 30

Inner Circle, The (Boyle), **Supp. XX: 24, 26**

Inner Landscape (Sarton), **Supp. VIII:** 259

Inner Room, The (Merrill), **Supp. III Part 1:** 336

"In Nine Sleep Valley" (Merrill), **Supp. III Part 1:** 328

Innocent Mrs. Duff, The (Holding), **Supp. XXII:** 119, 120, 123, **130–131,** 135, 136

Innocents, The: A Story for Lovers (Lewis), **II:** 441

Innocents Abroad, The; or, The New Pilgrim's Progress (Twain), **II:** 275, 434; **IV:** 191, 196, 197–198

Innocents at Cedro, The: A Memoir of Thorstein Veblen and Some Others (Duffus), **Supp. I Part 2:** 650

"In Off the Cliffs of Moher" (McCarriston), **Supp. XIV:** 270

In Old Plantation Days (Dunbar), **Supp. II Part 1:** 214

In Ole Virginia (Page), **Supp. II Part 1:** 201

In Orbit (Morris), **III:** 236

In Other Words (Swenson), **Supp. IV Part 2:** 650–652

In Other Words: Literature by Latinas of the United States (Fernandez, ed.), **Supp. XXI:** 104

In Our Terribleness (Some elements and meaning in black style) (Baraka), **Supp. II Part 1:** 52, 53

In Our Time (Hemingway), **I:** 117; **II:** 68, 247, 252, 263; **IV:** 42; **Retro. Supp. I:** 170, 173, 174, 178, 180; **Supp. IX:** 106

"In Our Time" (Wolfe), **Supp. III Part 2:** 584

"Inpatient" (Kenyon), **Supp. VII:** 169

In Persuasion Nation (Saunders), **Supp. XIX: 231–234**

"In Persuasion Nation" (Saunders), **Supp. XIX:** 233–234

In Pharaoh's Army: Memories of the Lost War (Wolff), **Supp. VII:** 331–334, 335, 338

"In Plaster" (Plath), **Supp. I Part 2:** 540

"In Prague, in Montmartre" (Bierds), **Supp. XVII:** 27

"In Praise of Johnny Appleseed" (Lindsay), **Supp. I Part 2:** 397

"In Praise of Limestone" (Auden), **Supp. II Part 1:** 20–21; **Supp. VIII:** 23

In Pursuit of a Vanishing Star (Sobin), **Supp. XVI: 294**

"In Quercy, 1993" (Davison), **Supp. XXVI:** 78

In Quest of the Ordinary (Cavell), **Retro. Supp. I:** 307

Inquiry into the Moral and Religious Character of the American Government, An (H. Warner), **Supp. XVIII:** 259

Inquiry into the Nature of Peace, An (Veblen), **Supp. I Part 2:** 642

Inquisitor, The (Rowson), **Supp. XV: 232, 238**

In Radical Pursuit (Snodgrass), **Supp. VI:** 312, 316, 318

In Reckless Ecstasy (Sandburg), **III:** 579

In Recognition of William Gaddis (Kuehl and Moore), **Supp. IV Part 1:** 279

"In Retirement" (Malamud), **Supp. I Part 2:** 437

"In Retrospect" (Angelou), **Supp. IV Part 1:** 15

"In Right" (Wolfert), **Supp. XXI:** 263, 264, 272

"Inroads of Time, The" (D. West), **Supp. XVIII:** 286–287

In Russia (A. Miller), **III:** 165

"In Sabine" (Chopin), **Supp. I Part 1:** 213

"In School-Days" (Whittier), **Supp. I Part 2:** 699–700

"Inscription for the Entrance to a Wood" (Bryant), **Supp. I Part 1:** 154, 155, 161–162

Inscriptions, 1944–1956 (Reznikoff), **Supp. XIV:** 281

In Search of America: The Image of the United States in Travel Writing of the 1980s and 1990s (Rutkowska), **Supp. XXII:** 208

"In Search of a Motif for Expressive Female Figuration" (Major), **Supp. XXII:** 184

In Search of Bisco (Caldwell), **I:** 296

In Search of Lost Time (Proust), **Supp. XXV:** 71

In Search of Nella Larsen: A Biography of the Color Line (Hutchinson), **Supp. XVIII:** 120

"In Search of Our Mothers' Gardens" (Walker), **Supp. III Part 2:** 520–532, 524, 525, 527, 529, 532–533, 535, 536; **Supp. IX:** 306; **Supp. XVIII:** 200, 283

"In Search of Thomas Merton" (Griffin), **Supp. VIII:** 208

"In Search of Yage" (Burroughs), **Supp. III Part 1:** 98

"Insect Life in Florida" (Hull), **Supp. XXI:** 133

Insel (Loy), **Supp. XXII:** 167

"Insertion of Self into a Space of Borderless Possibilities, The" (Fjellestad), **Supp. XVI:** 150

"In Shadow" (Crane), **I:** 386

"In Sickness and in Health" (Auden), **Supp. II Part 1:** 15

"In Sickness and in Health" (Humphrey), **Supp. IX:** 94

Inside, Outside (Wouk), **Supp. XXV:** 254, 255, 257, 265

Inside Diameter: The France Poems (Major), **Supp. XXII:** 182

Inside His Mind (A. Miller), **III:** 154

Inside Memory (Findley), **Supp. XX: 51, 63**

"Inside Norman Mailer" (Apple), **Supp. XVII:** 3, 4

"Insider Baseball" (Didion), **Supp. IV Part 1:** 211

Inside Sports magazine, **Supp. V:** 58, 61

"Insipid Profession of Jonathan Horneboom, The" (Lethem), **Supp. XVIII:** 149

"In So Many Dark Rooms" (Hogan), **Supp. IV Part 1:** 400

"Insomnia" (Bishop), **Supp. I Part 1:** 92

"Insomniac" (Plath), **Supp. I Part 2:** 539

"In Spain, Throwing Carnations" (P. N. Warren), **Supp. XX: 272**

"Inspiration for Greatness" (Caldwell), **I:** 291

"Instability of Race Types, The" (Boas), **Supp. XIV:** 209

"Installation #6" (Beattie), **Supp. V:** 33

"Instead of Dying" (Gallagher), **Supp. XXIV:** 171

"Interstices" (Berrigan), **Supp. XXIV:** 36

Instinct of Workmanship and the State of the Industrial Arts, The (Veblen), **Supp. I Part 2:** 642

Instincts of the Herd in Peace and War, The (Trotter), **I:** 249

Institute (Calvin), **IV:** 158, 160

"Instruction Manual, The" (Ashbery), **Supp. III Part 1:** 6–7, 10, 12

Instructions, The (Levin), **Supp. XXII:** 268

"Instructions for the Afternoon" (Gioia), **Supp. XV:** 120

Instructions to the Double (Gallagher), **Supp. XXIV:** 165, 167, 168, 169, 174

"Instructions to the Double" (Gallagher), **Supp. XXIV:** 168

"Instruction to Myself" (Brooks), **Supp. III Part 1:** 87

Instrument, The (O'Hara), **III:** 362, 364

"In Such Times, Ties Must Bind" (Nye), **Supp. XIII:** 286

In Sunlight and in Shadow (Helprin), **Supp. XXV:** 81, 88

"Insurance and Social Change" (Stevens), **Retro. Supp. I:** 297

Insurgent Mexico (Reed), **I:** 476

In Suspect Terrain (McPhee), **Supp. III Part 1:** 309, 310

"In Tall Grass" (Sandburg), **III:** 585

"Integer Vitae" (Horace), **Supp. XV:** 304

Intellectual History, An (Senghor), **Supp. X:** 139

"Intellectual Pre-Eminence of Jews in Modern Europe, The" (Veblen), **Supp. I Part 2:** 643–644

Intellectual Things (Kunitz), **Supp. III Part 1:** 260, 262–264

Intellectual versus the City, The (White), **I:** 258

"In Temporary Pain" (Bynner), **Supp. XV:** 41–42

Intentions (Wilde), **Retro. Supp. I:** 56

"Interest in Life, An" (Paley), **Supp. VI:** 222, 224–225

Interest of Great Britain Considered, with Regard to Her Colonies and the Acquisition of Canada and Guadeloupe, The (Franklin), **II:** 119

Interior Landscapes (Vizenor), **Supp. IV Part 1:** 262

Interiors (film; Allen), **Supp. IV Part 1:** 205; **Supp. XV:** 1, **7**, 10

Interlocking Lives (Koch), **Supp. XV:** 185

"Interlude" (A. Lowell), **Retro. Supp. II:** 46

Interlunar (Atwood), **Supp. XIII:** 35

"Intermezzo" (Schnackenberg), **Supp. XV:** 254

"In Terms of the Toenail: Fiction and the Figures of Life" (Gass), **Supp. VI:** 85

"International Episode, An" (James), **II:** 327

International Workers Order, **Retro. Supp. I:** 202

Interpretation of Christian Ethics, An (Niebuhr), **III:** 298–300, 301, 302

"Interpretation of Dreams, The" (Matthews), **Supp. IX:** 162–163

Interpretation of Music of the XVIIth and XVIIIth Centuries, The (Dolmetsch), **III:** 464

Interpretations and Forecasts: 1922–1972 (Mumford), **Supp. II Part 2:** 481

Interpretations of Poetry and Religion (Santayana), **III:** 611

Interpreter of Maladies (Lahiri), **Supp. XXI:** 175–176, **177–180**, 183

"Interpreter of Maladies" (Lahiri), **Supp. XXI:** 183, 184

Interpreters and Interpretations (Van Vechten), **Supp. II Part 2:** 729, 733–734

"Interrogate the Stones" (MacLeish), **III:** 9

"Interrogation of the Prisoner Bung By Mister Hawkins and Sergeant Tree, The" (Huddle), **Supp. XXVI:** 147, 149, 152

Interrogations at Noon (Gioia), **Supp. XV:** 112, **125–127**, 128, 129

"Interrupted Conversation, An" (Van Vechten), **Supp. II Part 2:** 735

"Interrupted Elegy" (Peacock), **Supp. XIX:** 200

Intersect: Poems (Shields), **Supp. VII:** 310–311

Intersexes, The (Prime-Stevenson as Mayne), **Supp. XX: 235**

Interstate (Dixon), **Supp. XII:** 140, 152–153, 153, 156

"Interview" (Hay), **Supp. XIV:** 132

"Interview, The" (Thurber), **Supp. I Part 2:** 616

"Interview With a Lemming" (Thurber), **Supp. I Part 2:** 603

"Interview with Larry Rivers, An"(O'Hara), **Supp. XXIII:** 214

"Interview with Peter Everwine, An" (Veinberg and Buckley), **Supp. XV:** 76–77

"Interview with the Crab" (Lethem), **Supp. XVIII:** 148

Interview with the Vampire (Rice), **Supp. VII:** 287, 288–291, 297–298, 303

"Interview with the Vampire" (Rice), **Supp. VII:** 288

Interzone (Burroughs), **Supp. IV Part 1:** 90

"In the Absence of Bliss" (Kumin), **Supp. IV Part 2:** 453

"In the Afternoon" (Dunn), **Supp. XI:** 146

"In the Alley" (Elkin), **Supp. VI: 46–47**

In the American Grain (W. C. Williams), **Retro. Supp. I:** 420–421

In the American Jungle (W. Frank), **Supp. XX: 76**

In the American Tree (Silliman), **Supp. IV Part 2:** 426

In the Bank of Beautiful Sins (Wrigley), **Supp. XVIII: 300–302**

In the Bar of a Tokyo Hotel (T. Williams), **IV:** 382, 386, 387, 391, 393

In the Beauty of the Lilies (Updike), **Retro. Supp. I:** 322, 325, 326, 327, 333

"In the Beeyard" (Bierds), **Supp. XVII:** 29

"In the Beginning" (Quindlen), **Supp. XVII:** 166

"In the Beginning . . ." (Simic), **Supp. VIII:** 270, 271

In the Belly of the Beast: Letters from Prison (Abbott), **Retro. Supp. II:** 210

"In the Black Morning" (Wolfert), **Supp. XXI:** 265

"In the Black Museum" (Nemerov), **III:** 275

"In the Blink of God's Eye" (E. P. Jones), **Supp. XXII:** 150

"In the Bodies of Words" (Swenson), **Supp. IV Part 2:** 651

"In the Boston Children's Hospital" (Huddle), **Supp. XXVI:** 151

"In the Box"(Kenny), **Supp. XXIII:** 155

"In the Cage" (Gass), **Supp. VI:** 85

In the Cage (James), **Retro. Supp. I:** 229

"In the Cage" (James), **II:** 332; **Retro. Supp. I:** 231

"In the Cage" (Lowell), **Retro. Supp. II:** 187

"In the Cave at Lone Tree Meadow" (Haines), **Supp. XII:** 212

"In the Cemetery Where Al Jolson Is Buried" (Hempel), **Supp. XXI:** 115, **121–122**

"In the City Ringed with Giants" (Kingsolver), **Supp. VII:** 209

"In the Clearing" (Brodsky), **Supp. VIII:** 32

In the Clearing (Frost), **II:** 153, 155, 164; **Retro. Supp. I:** 121, 122, 141

"In the Closet of the Soul" (Walker), **Supp. III Part 2:** 526

"In the Cold Air Register" (W. V. Davis), **Supp. XXI:** 94

"In the Confidence of a Story-Writer" (Chopin), **Retro. Supp. II:** 66–67; **Supp. I Part 1:** 217

In the Country of Last Things (Auster), **Supp. XII:** 23, **29–30**, 31, 32

"In the Courtyard of the Isleta Missions" (R. Bly), **Supp. IV Part 1:** 71

"In the Dark" (Levine), **Supp. V:** 194

"In the Dark New England Days" (Jewett), **Retro. Supp. II:** 139

"In the Days of Prismatic Colour" (Moore), **III:** 205, 213

In the Days of the Comet (Wells), **Supp. XX: 233, 240**

In the Electric Mist with Confederate Dead (Burke), **Supp. XIV:** 30, 31–32

"In the Field" (Wilbur), **Supp. III Part 2:** 558

"In the 51st State" (Berrigan), **Supp. XXIV:** 35

"In the First Stanza" (C. Kizer), **Supp. XVII:** 75

"In the Fleeting Hand of Time" (Corso), **Supp. XII:** 122–123

"In the Footsteps of Gutenberg" (Mencken), **III:** 101

"In the Forest" (Simpson), **Supp. IX:** 270

"In the Forest of the Laughing Elephant" (Caputo), **Supp. XIX:** 27

"In the Forties" (Lowell), **II:** 554

"In the Garden" (Ferry), **Supp. XXIV:** 153

In the Garden of the North American Martyrs (Wolff), **Supp. VII:** 341–342

In the Garret (Van Vechten), **Supp. II Part 2:** 735

"In the Grove: The Poet at Ten" (Kenyon), **Supp. VII:** 160

"In the Hall of Mirrors" (Merrill), **Supp. III Part 1:** 322

In the Harbor (Longfellow), **II:** 491

In the Heart of the Heart of the Country (Gass), **Supp. VI: 82–83**, 84, 85, 93

In the Heat of the Night (Ball), **Supp. XV:** 202

In the Heat of the Night (film), **Supp. I Part 1:** 67

In the Hollow of His Hand (Purdy), **Supp. VII:** 278–280

In the House of Light (Everwine, trans.), **Supp. XV:** 73, 75, **76–78**, 82

"In the Laboratory of Kisses" (Gallagher), **Supp. XXIV:** 170

In the Lake of the Woods (O'Brien), **Supp. V:** 240, 243, 250–252

In the Land of the White Death: A Epic Story of Survival in the Siberian Arctic (Albanov), **Supp. XVIII:** 114

"In the Last Days" (Everwine), **Supp. XV:** 88, 89

"In the Late Summer Garden"(Crooker), **Supp. XXIII:** 55

In the Loyal Mountains (Bass), **Supp. XVI: 19–20**

"In the Loyal Mountains" (Bass), **Supp. XVI:** 20

"In the Mean Mud Season" (Huddle), **Supp. XXVI:** 154

In the Mecca (Brooks), **Supp. III Part 1:** 74

"In the Mecca" (Brooks), **Supp. III Part 1:** 70, 83–84

In the Midst of Life (Bierce), **I:** 200–203, 204, 206, 208, 212

"In the Miro District" (Taylor), **Supp. V:** 323

In the Miro District and Other Stories (Taylor), **Supp. V:** 325–326

In the Money (W. C. Williams), **Retro. Supp. I:** 423

"In the Motel" (X. J. Kennedy), **Supp. XV:** 163

"In the Naked Bed, in Plato's Cave" (Schwartz), **Supp. II Part 2:** 646–649

In the Name of the Neither (Sobin), **Supp. XVI:** 291

"In the Night" (Kincaid), **Supp. VII:** 183

In the Night Season: A Novel (Bausch), **Supp. VII:** 52–53

"In the Old Neighborhood" (Dove), **Supp. IV Part 1:** 241, 257

"In the Old World" (Oates), **Supp. II Part 2:** 503, 504

"In the Park" (Biss), **Supp. XXVI:** 48

"In the Park" (Huncke), **Supp. XIV:** 139

In the Pines (Notley), **Supp. XXII:** 236–237

"In the Pit" (Proulx), **Supp. VII:** 255, 261

In the Pond (Jin), **Supp. XVIII: 95–96**

In the Presence of the Sun (Momaday), **Supp. IV Part 2:** 489, 490, 491–493, 493

"In the Quiet Night" (Li Po), **Supp. XV:** 47

"In the Realm of the Fisher King" (Didion), **Supp. IV Part 1:** 211

"In the Red Room" (Bowles), **Supp. IV Part 1:** 93

"In the Region of Ice" (Oates), **Supp. II Part 2:** 520

In the Room We Share (Simpson), **Supp. IX:** 279

"In These Dissenting Times" (Walker), **Supp. III Part 2:** 522

"In the Shadow of Gabriel, A.D.1550" (Frederic), **II:** 139

In the Shadow of Memory (Skloot), **Supp. XX:** 193, 196, 205, 205–206

"In the Shadow of Memory" (Skloot), **Supp. XX: 206**

In the Shadow of the Morning: Essays on Wild Lands, Wild Waters, and a Few Untamed People (Caputo), **Supp. XIX:** 28–29

In the Spirit of Crazy Horse (Matthiessen), **Supp. V:** 211

"In the Subway" (Untermeyer), **Supp. XV:** 296

In the Summer House (Jane Bowles), **Supp. IV Part 1:** 83, 89

"In the Syntax: Rewriting Joan Didion's 'Goodbye to All That' " (Biss), **Supp. XXVI:** 54

In the Tennessee Country (Taylor), **Supp. V:** 328

"In the Thick of Darkness" (Salinas), **Supp. XIII:** 325

In the Time of Butterflies (Alvarez), **Supp. XXIV:** 89

"In the Time of the Blossoms" (Mervin), **Supp. III Part 1:** 352

In the Time of the Butterflies (Alvarez), **Supp. VII:** 1, 12–15, 18

In the Time of the Present (Kenny), **Supp. XXIII:** 146, **156**

"In the Tube" (Jarman), **Supp. XVII:** 121

"In the Tunnel Bone of Cambridge" (Corso), **Supp. XII:** 120–121

"In the Upper Pastures" (Kumin), **Supp. IV Part 2:** 453

In the Valley (Frederic), **II:** 133–134, 136, 137

"In the Village" (Bishop), **Retro. Supp. II:** 38; **Supp. I Part 1:** 73, 74–75, 76, 77, 78, 88

"In the Waiting Room" (Bishop), **Retro. Supp. II:** 50; **Supp. I Part 1:** 81, 94, 95; **Supp. IV Part 1:** 249

In the Walled City (O'Nan), **Supp. XXV:** 142

"In the Ward: The Sacred Wood" (Jarrell), **II:** 376, 377

In the Western Night: Collected Poems 1965–90 (Bidart), **Supp. XV:** 19, **30–32**

"In the White Night" (Beattie), **Supp. V:** 30–31

"In the Wind My Rescue Is" (Ammons), **Supp. VII:** 25

"In the Winter Dark" (Peacock), **Supp. XIX:** 206

In the Winter of Cities (T. Williams), **IV:** 383

"In the X-Ray of the Sarcophagus of Tapero" (Goldbarth), **Supp. XII:** 191

"In the Yard" (Swenson), **Supp. IV Part 2:** 647

In the Zone (O'Neill), **III:** 388

In This, Our Life (film), **Supp. I Part 1:** 67

"In This Country, but in Another Language, My Aunt Refuses to Marry the Men Everyone Wants Her To" (Paley), **Supp. VI:** 225

"In This Dream" (J. W. Miller), **Supp. XX: 170**

In This Hung-up Age (Corso), **Supp. XII: 119–120,** 129

In This Our Life (Glasgow), **II:** 175, 178, 189

In This Our World (Gilman), **Supp. XI:** 196, 200, 202

"In Those Days" (Jarrell), **II:** 387–388

"Intimately Connected to the Zeitgeist" (Franzen), **Supp. XX: 94**

Intimates (Huddle), **Supp. XXVI:** 155–156

"In Time of War" (Auden), **Supp. II Part 1:** 8, 13

In Times Like These (Edgell), **Supp. XXIII:** 84, **89–90,** 94

"Into Egypt" (Benét), **Supp. XI:** 56, 57–58

Intolerance (film; Griffith), **Supp. XVI:** 184

"Into My Own" (Frost), **II:** 153; **Retro. Supp. I:** 127

"Into Night" (McKnight), **Supp. XX: 151–152**

Into the Interior (Cliff), **Supp. XXII:** 67, 78–79

"Into the Night Life . . ." (H. Miller), **III:** 180, 184

"Into the Nowhere" (Rawlings), **Supp. X:** 220

"Into the Stone" (Dickey), **Supp. IV Part 1:** 178

"Into the Stone" (Dickey), **Supp. IV Part 1:** 179

Into the Stone and Other Poems (Dickey), **Supp. IV Part 1:** 176

"Into the Streets May First" (Hayes), **Supp. XXVI:** 134, 144

Into the Wild (Krakauer), **Supp. XVIII:** 106, **107–108,** 116, 117

Into Thin Air: A Personal Account of the Mount Everest Disaster (Krakauer), **Supp. XVII:** 210; **Supp. XVIII:** 105, **109–113,** 117

In Touch: The Letters of Paul Bowles (J. Miller, ed.), **Supp. IV Part 1:** 95

"Intoxicated, The" (Jackson), **Supp. IX:** 116

"Intrigue" (Crane), **I:** 419

Introducing Irony: A Book of Poetic Short Stories and Poems (Bodenheim), **Supp. XXV:** 22–23

"Introducing the Fathers" (Kumin), **Supp. IV Part 2:** 452

Introductio ad Prudentiam (Fuller), **II:** 111

"Introduction"(Strout; *Ploughshares* spring 2010), **Supp. XXIII:** 284

"Introduction to a Haggadah" (Paley), **Supp. VI:** 219

Introduction to Objectivist Epistemology (Rand), **Supp. IV Part 2:** 527, 528–529

Introduction to Objectivist Epistemology 2nd ed. (Rand), **Supp. IV Part 2:** 529

"Introduction to Poetry" (Collins), **Supp. XXI:** 57

Introduction to Poetry, An (Gioia and X. J. Kennedy), **Supp. XV:** 113, 153

"Introduction to Some Poems, An" (Stafford), **Supp. XI:** 311, 324

Introduction to the Geography of Iowa, The (Doty), **Supp. XI:** 120

"Introduction to the Hoh" (Hugo), **Supp. VI:** 136–137

"Introduction to *The New Writing in the USA*" (Creeley), **Supp. IV Part 1:** 153–154

"Introduction to William Blake, An" (Kazin), **Supp. VIII:** 103

Introitus (Longfellow), **II:** 505, 506–507

"Intruder, The" (Dubus), **Supp. VII:** 76–78, 91

Intruder, The (Maeterlinck), **I:** 91

Intruder in the Dust (Faulkner), **II:** 71, 72; **Supp. XVI:** 148

Intuition (Goodman), **Supp. XXVI:** 128–130

"Invaders, The" (Haines), **Supp. XII:** 205

Invaders, The (W. Frank), **Supp. XX:** **79–80**

Invasion of Privacy: The Cross Creek Trial of Marjorie Kinnan Rawlings (Acton), **Supp. X:** 233

Inventing Memory: A Novel of Mothers and Daughters (Jong), **Supp. V:** 115, 129

Inventing the Abbotts (Miller), **Supp. XII:** **294–295**

"Invention of Autobiography. The" (Hampl), **Supp. XXII:** 93–94

"Invention of God in a Mouthful of Milk, The" (Karr), **Supp. XI:** 250

Invention of Solitude, The (Auster), **Supp. XII:** 21–22

Inventions of the March Hare (Eliot), **Retro. Supp. I:** 55–56, 58

"Inventions of the March Hare" (Eliot), **Retro. Supp. I:** 55

"Inventory" (Parker), **Supp. IX:** 192

"Inverted Forest, The" (Salinger), **III:** 552, 572

"Investigation" (Ryan as Quin), **Supp. XVIII:** 227–228

"Investigations of a Dog" (Kafka), **IV:** 438

"Investiture, The" (Banks), **Supp. V:** 7

"Investiture at Cecconi's" (Merrill), **Supp. III Part 1:** 336

"Invicibility"(O'Hara), **Supp. XXIII:** 214

"Invisible" (Pickering), **Supp. XXI:** 201

Invisible Circus, The (Egan), **Supp. XIX:** 49, **50–52**

Invisible Company, The (Sanders), **Supp. XVI:** 270–271

Invisible Man (Ellison), **IV:** 493; **Retro. Supp. II:** 3, 12, 111, 112, 113, 117, 119, **120–123**, 125; **Supp. II Part 1:** 40, 170, 221, 224, 226, 227, 230, 231–232, 235, 236, 241–245; **Supp. IX:** 306; **Supp. X:** 242; **Supp. XI:** 18, 92; **Supp. XIX:** 154, 155; **Supp. XVIII:** 59; **Supp. XXVI:** 215

Invisible: Poems (Nye), **Supp. XIII:** 277

Invisible Spectator, An (Sawyer-Lauçanno), **Supp. IV Part 1:** 95

Invisible Swords (Farrell), **II:** 27, 46, 48–49

Invisible Worm, The (Millar), **Supp. IV Part 2:** 465

Invitation to a Beheading (Nabokov), **III:** 252–253, 254, 257–258; **Retro. Supp. I:** 265, 270, 273

"Invitation to the Country, An" (Bryant), **Supp. I Part 1:** 160

"Invocation" (H. Johnson), **Supp. XXVI:** 166, 174

"Invocation" (McKay), **Supp. X:** 134

"Invocation" (Untermeyer), **Supp. XV:** 296

"Invocation to Kali" (Sarton), **Supp. VIII:** 260

"Invocation: *To my Maternal Grand-father on hearing his descent from Chippewa ancestors misrepresented"(J. Schoolcraft), Supp. XXIII:* 232

"Invocation to the Social Muse" (MacLeish), **III:** 15

"In Weather" (Hass), **Supp. VI:** **102–103**

"In Your Fugitive Dream" (Hugo), **Supp. VI:** 143

"In Your Good Dream" (Hugo), **Supp. VI:** 143–144

"Iola, Kansas" (Clampitt), **Supp. IX:** 45–46

Iola Leroy (Harper), **Supp. XVIII:** 284

Ion (Doolittle, trans.), **Supp. I Part 1:** 269, 274

Ion (Plato), **I:** 523

"Ione" (Dunbar), **Supp. II Part 1:** 199

Ionesco, Eugène, **I:** 71, 74, 75, 84, 295; **II:** 435; **Supp. VIII:** 201; **Supp. XIX:** 131; **Supp. XXIV:** 113

Ionica (Cory), **Supp. XX:** **230**

Ionica II (Cory), **Supp. XX:** **230**

"I Only Am Escaped Alone to Tell Thee" (Nemerov), **III:** 272, 273–274

"I Opened All the Portals Wide" (Chopin), **Retro. Supp. II:** 71

I Ought to Be in Pictures (Simon), **Supp. IV Part 2:** 584

Iphigenia (Notley), **Supp. XXII:** 226, 235

Iphigenia in Tauris (Euripedes), **Supp. XV:** 42, 50

I Promessi Sposi (Manzoni), **II:** 291

"I Put My Hand on My Son's Head" (Kooser), **Supp. XIX:** 120

Iram, Dhát al-'Imád (Gibran), **Supp. XX:** **116**

"Iraq Drifting, July 2003" (Weigl), **Supp. XIX:** 288

"Irascibles, The" (Kees), **Supp. XV:** 145–146

Ireland: A Terrible Beauty (Uris), **Supp. XX: 244, 245–246, 246, 254**

"I Remember" (Sexton), **Supp. II Part 2:** 680

"Irenicon" (Shapiro), **Supp. II Part 2:** 704

Irigaray, Luce, **Supp. XII:** 6

Iris (Jarman), **Supp. XVII:** 110, **116–117**

"Iris by Night" (Frost), **Retro. Supp. I:** 132

"Irises" (L.-Y. Lee), **Supp. XV:** 214–215

Irish in America, The (Coffey, ed.), **Supp. XIX:** 133

Irish Stories of Sarah Orne Jewett, The (Jewett), **Retro. Supp. II:** 142

Irish Triangle, An (Barnes), **Supp. III Part 1:** 34

"Iron Characters, The" (Nemerov), **III:** 279, 282

"Iron Hans" (Sexton), **Supp. II Part 2:** 691

Iron Heel, The (London), **II:** 466, 480

Iron John: A Book about Men (R. Bly), **Supp. IV Part 1:** 59, 67; **Supp. XVI:** 177

"Iron Table, The" (Jane Bowles), **Supp. IV Part 1:** 82–83

"Iron Throat, The" (Olsen), **Supp. XIII:** 292, 297, 299

Ironweed (W. Kennedy), **Supp. VII:** 132, 133, 134, 135, 142, 144, 145–147, 148, 150, 153

"Irony as Art: The Short Fiction of William Humphrey" (Tebeaux), **Supp. IX:** 109

"Irony Is Not Enough: Essay on My Life as Catherine Deneuve" (Carson), **Supp. XII:** **112–113**

Irony of American History, The (Niebuhr), **III:** 292, 306–307, 308

"Irrational Element in Poetry, The" (Stevens), **Retro. Supp. I:** 298, 301

"Irrevocable Diameter, An" (Paley), **Supp. VI:** 231–232

Irvine, Lorna, **Supp. XIII:** 26

Irving, Ebenezer, **II:** 296

Irving, Sir Henry, **IV:** 350

Irving, John, **Supp. VI:** **163–183**; **Supp. X:** 77, 85

Irving, John Treat, **II:** 296

Irving, Peter, **II:** 296, 297, 298, 299, 300, 303

Irving, Washington, **I:** 211, 335, 336, 339, 343; **II:** **295–318,** 488, 495; **III:** 113; **IV:** 309; **Retro. Supp. I:** 246; **Supp. I Part 1:** 155, 157, 158, 317; **Supp. I Part 2:** 377, 487, 585; **Supp. II Part 1:** 335; **Supp. IV Part 1:** 380; **Supp. XVIII:** 12; **Supp. XXIII:** 178

Irving, William, **II:** 296

Irving, William, Jr., **II:** 296, 297, 298, 299, 303

Irwin, Mark, **Supp. XII:** 21, 22, 24, 29

Irwin, Robert, **Supp. XX:** **120**

Irwin, William Henry, **Supp. II Part 1:** 192

Is 5 (Cummings), **I:** 429, 430, 434, 435, 440, 445, 446, 447

"Isaac and Abraham" (Brodsky), **Supp. VIII:** 21

"Isaac and Archibald" (Robinson), **III:** 511, 521, 523

Isaacs, Neil D., **Supp. XIX:** 255

"Isabelle" (Saunders), **Supp. XIX:** 225

"Isabel Sparrow" (Oliver), **Supp. VII:** 232

Isaiah (biblical book), **Supp. I Part 1:** 236; **Supp. I Part 2:** 516; **Supp. XXI:** 107

"Isaiah Beethoven" (Masters), **Supp. I Part 2:** 461

I Sailed with Magellan (Dybek), **Supp. XXIII: 75–78,** 79

"I Saw in Louisiana a Live-Oak Growing" (Whitman), **I:** 220

"I Shall Be Released" (Dylan), **Supp. XV:** 349

I Shall Spit on Your Graves (film), **Supp. I Part 1:** 67

Isháq, Adib, **Supp. XX:** 117

Isherwood, Christopher, **II:** 586; **Supp. II Part 1:** 10, 11, 13; **Supp. IV Part 1:** 79, 82, 102; **Supp. XI:** 305; **Supp. XIV: 155–175; Supp. XVI:** 194

Isherwood Century, The (Berg and Freeman), **Supp. XIV:** 157, 159

Isherwood's Fiction (Schwerdt), **Supp. XIV:** 155

Ishiguro, Kazuo, **Supp. VIII:** 15

Ishi Means Man (Merton), **Supp. VIII:** 208

"Ishmael's Dream" (Stern), **Supp. IX:** 287

I Should Have Stayed Home (McCoy), **Supp. XIII:** 167, **168–170,** 171

"I Should Worry" (Kees), **Supp. XV:** 140

"I Sigh in the Afternoon" (Salinas), **Supp. XIII:** 318

"I Sing the Body Electric" (Whitman), **Retro. Supp. I:** 394, 395

"Isis: Dorothy Eady, 1924" (Doty), **Supp. XI:** 122

"Is It O.K. to Be a Luddite?" (Pynchon), **Supp. XVI:** 128

"Is It True?" (Hughes), **Supp. I Part 1:** 342

I: Six Nonlectures (Cummings), **I:** 430, 433, 434

"Island" (Hughes), **Supp. I Part 1:** 340

"Island Fever" (Vaz), **Supp. XXVI:** 261

Island Garden, An (Thaxter), **Retro. Supp. II:** 136; **Supp. XIII:** 152

Island Holiday, An (Henry), **I:** 515

Island in the Atlantic (W. Frank), **Supp. XX:** 79

Island in the Sun (film), **Supp. XXVI:** 134

"Island of the Fay, The" (Poe), **III:** 412, 417

Islands (Siddons), **Supp. XXII:** 239

"Islands, The" (Hayden), **Supp. II Part 1:** 373

"Island Sheaf, An" (Doty), **Supp. XI:** 136

Islands in the Stream (Hemingway), **II:** 258; **Retro. Supp. I:** 186

Isn't It Romantic (Wasserstein), **Supp. XV:** 323–325, 327

Is Objectivism a Religion? (Ellis), **Supp. IV Part 2:** 527

"Isolation of Modern Poetry, The" (Schwartz), **Supp. II Part 2:** 644

"Israel" (Reznikoff), **Supp. XIV:** 283

Israel Potter, or Fifty Years of Exile (Melville), **III:** 90; **Supp. XVIII:** 4

"Israfel" (Poe), **III:** 411

Is Sex Necessary? (Thurber and White), **Supp. I Part 2:** 607, 612, 614, 653

"Issues, The" (Olds), **Supp. X:** 205

"Istanbul" (Collins), **Supp. XXI:** 60

"I Stand Here Ironing" (Olsen), **Supp. XIII:** 292, 294, 296, 298, 300, 305

I Stole a Million (West), **IV:** 287

"Is Verse a Dying Technique?" (Wilson), **IV:** 431

It (Creeley), **Supp. IV Part 1:** 157, 158

IT (King), **Supp. V:** 139, 140, 141, 146–147, 151, 152

"It" (Olds), **Supp. X:** 208

Italian American Reconciliation: A Folktale (Shanley), **Supp. XIV:** 315, **324–326,** 328, 330

Italian Backgrounds (Wharton), **Retro. Supp. I:** 370

Italian Hours (James), **I:** 12; **II:** 337; **Retro. Supp. I:** 235

Italian Journeys (Howells), **II:** 274

"Italian Morning" (Bogan), **Supp. III Part 1:** 58

Italian Villas and Their Gardens (Wharton), **IV:** 308; **Retro. Supp. I:** 361, 367

Italie, Hillel, **Supp. XV:** 128

It All Adds Up: From the Dim Past to the Uncertain Future (Bellow), **Retro. Supp. II:** 32

"It Always Breaks Out" (Ellison), **Retro. Supp. II:** 126; **Supp. II Part 1:** 248

Itard, Jean-Marc Gaspard, **Supp. I Part 2:** 564

"I taste a liquor never brewed" (Dickinson), **Retro. Supp. I:** 30, 37

It Came from Outer Space (film), **Supp. IV Part 1:** 102

It Can't Happen Here (Lewis), **II:** 454

It Chooses You (July), **Supp. XXIV:** 199, 209, 210

"It Don't Mean a Thing If It Ain't Got That Swing" (Matthews), **Supp. IX:** **164–165**

I Tell You Now (Ortiz), **Supp. IV Part 2:** 500

"It Goes Something Like This" (Gansworth), **Supp. XXVI:** 110

"Ithaca" (Glück), **Supp. V:** 89

It Happened One Night (Capra), **Supp. XV:** 197

It Has Come to Pass (Farrell), **II:** 26

"I think to live May be a Bliss" (Dickinson), **Retro. Supp. I:** 44

"I Thought It Was Harry" (Bronk), **Supp. XXI:** 31

I Thought of Daisy (Wilson), **IV:** 428, 434, 435

"Itinerary of an Obsession" (Kumin), **Supp. IV Part 2:** 450

"It Is a Strange Country" (Ellison), **Supp. II Part 1:** 238

"It Is Dangerous to Read Newspapers" (Atwood), **Supp. XIII:** 33

"It Must Be Abstract" (Stevens), **IV:** 95; **Retro. Supp. I:** 307

"It Must Change" (Stevens), **Retro. Supp. I:** 300, 307, 308

"It Must Give Pleasure" (Stevens), **Retro. Supp. I:** 307, 308, 309

"'It Out-Herods Herod. Pray You, Avoid It'" (Hecht), **Supp. X:** 62, 64

"It's All Over Now, Baby Blue" (song, Dylan), **Supp. XVIII:** 30

It's Loaded, Mr. Bauer (Marquand), **III:** 59

It's Nation Time (Baraka), **Supp. II Part 1:** 52, 53

"It's Nation Time" (Baraka), **Supp. II Part 1:** 53

It's Only a Play (McNally), **Supp. XIII:** 198

It Was (Zukofsky), **Supp. III Part 2:** 630

"It Was Romance" (July), **Supp. XXIV:** 202–203

It Was the Nightingale (Ford), **III:** 470–471

"It Was When" (Snyder), **Supp. VIII:** 300

Ivanhoe (Scott), **I:** 216; **Supp. I Part 2:** 410

Ivens, Bryna, **Supp. XV:** 311, 312

Ivens, Joris, **I:** 488; **Retro. Supp. I:** 184

"Iverson Boy, The" (Simpson), **Supp. IX:** 280

"Ives" (Rukeyser), **Supp. VI:** 273, 283

Ives, George H., **Supp. I Part 1:** 153

Ivory Grin, The (Macdonald), **Supp. IV Part 2:** 471, 472

"Ivory Novel, The" (Halliday), **Supp. XIX:** 90

Ivory Tower, The (James), **II:** 337–338

"Ivory Tower, The: Louis Untermeyer as Critic" (Aiken), **Supp. XV:** 298

Ivry, Sara, **Supp. XX:** 179

"Ivy Winding" (Ammons), **Supp. VII:** 33

Iwamatsu, Mako, **Supp. XXI:** 150

"I Wandered Lonely as a Cloud" (Wordsworth), **Retro. Supp. I:** 121–122; **Supp. X:** 73; **Supp. XIV:** 184

"I want, I want" (Plath), **Retro. Supp. II:** 246

"I Wanted to Be There When My Father Died" (Olds), **Supp. X:** 210

"I Want to Be a Father Like the Men" (Cisneros), **Supp. VII:** 71

"I Want to Be Miss America" (Alvarez), **Supp. VII:** 18

"I Want to Know Why" (Anderson), **I:** 114, 115, 116; **II:** 263

"I Want You Women Up North To Know" (Olsen), **Supp. XIII:** 292, 297

"I Was Born in Lucerne" (Levine), **Supp. V:** 181, 189

"I Was Marching" (Le Sueur), **Supp. XXIII:** 167

"I Was Really Very Hungry" (M. F. K. Fisher), **Supp. XVII:** 91

"I Went into the Maverick Bar" (Snyder), **Supp. VIII:** 301

"I Will Lie Down" (Swenson), **Supp. IV Part 2:** 640

I Will Say Beauty (C. Frost), **Supp. XV:** 96, **105–107**

I Wonder As I Wander (Hughes), **Retro. Supp. I:** 196, 203; **Supp. I Part 1:** 329, 332–333

I Would Have Saved Them If I Could (L. Michaels), **Supp. XVI:** 203, 205, **206–210**

"Iya, the Camp-Eater" (Zitkala-Ša), **Supp. XXV:** 276

"Iyani: It goes this Way" (Gunn Allen), **Supp. IV Part 1:** 321

"I years had been from home" (Dickinson), **I:** 471

Iyer, Pico, **Supp. V:** 215

Izzo, David Garrett, **Supp. XIV:** 155, 156, 159, 160, 161, 163, 169, 171

J

Jab (Halliday), **Supp. XIX:** 91–94

"Jachid and Jechidah" (Singer), **IV:** 15

Jack and Jill (Alcott), **Supp. I Part 1:** 42

"Jack and the Beanstalk" (Hay), **Supp. XIV:** 124

"Jack in the Pot" (D. West), **Supp. XVIII:** 283

Jack Kelso (Masters), **Supp. I Part 2:** 456, 471–472

Jacklight (Erdrich), **Supp. IV Part 1:** 259, 270

Jack London, Hemingway, and the Constitution (Doctorow), **Supp. IV Part 1:** 220, 222, 224, 232, 235

Jackman, Harold, **Supp. XVIII:** 131

Jackpot (Caldwell), **I:** 304

"Jack Schmidt, Arts Administrator" (Keillor), **Supp. XVI:** 171

"Jack Schmidt on the Burning Sands" (Keillor), **Supp. XVI:** 171

Jackson, Amelia. *See* Holmes, Mrs. Oliver Wendell (Amelia Jackson)

Jackson, Andrew, **I:** 7, 20; **III:** 473; **IV:** 192, 248, 298, 334, 348; **Supp. I Part 2:** 456, 461, 473, 474, 493, 695

Jackson, Blyden, **Supp. I Part 1:** 337

Jackson, Charles, **Supp. I Part 1:** 303

Jackson, George, **Supp. I Part 1:** 66

Jackson, Helen Hunt, **I:** 459, 470; **Retro. Supp. I:** 26, 27, 30–31, 32, 33

Jackson, James, **Supp. I Part 1:** 302, 303

Jackson, J. O., **III:** 213

Jackson, Joe, **Supp. I Part 2:** 441

Jackson, Katherine Gauss, **Supp. VIII:** 124

Jackson, Lawrence, **Retro. Supp. II:** 113, 115

Jackson, Lawrence P., **Supp. XXII:** 140

Jackson, Melanie, **Supp. X:** 166

Jackson, Michael, **Supp. VIII:** 146

Jackson, Richard, **II:** 119; **Supp. IX:** 165

Jackson, Shelley, **Supp. XVIII:** 136

Jackson, Shirley, **Supp. IX: 113–130**

Jackson, Thomas J. ("Stonewall"), **IV:** 125, 126

"Jackson Hotel" (Hull), **Supp. XXI:** 134, 135

Jackson Pollock (O'Hara), **Supp. XXIII:** 214–215

"Jackson Square" (Levertov), **Supp. III Part 1:** 276

Jackstraws (Simic), **Supp. VIII:** 280, 282–283

"Jackstraws" (Simic), **Supp. VIII: 283**

Jack Tier (Cooper), **I:** 354, 355

"Jacob" (Garrett), **Supp. VII:** 109–110

"Jacob" (Schwartz), **Supp. II Part 2:** 663

Jacob, Max, **Supp. XV:** 178, 182

"Jacob and the Indians" (Benét), **Supp. XI:** 47–48

"Jacob Bayer and the Telephone" (Helprin), **Supp. XXV:** 81

Jacobs, Catherine Haydon, **Supp. XXI:** 98

Jacobs, Harriet, **Supp. XVI:** 85

Jacobs, Jill Suzanne, **Supp. XX: 178, 186**

Jacobs, Rita D., **Supp. XII:** 339

Jacobsen, Josephine, **Supp. XIII:** 346; **Supp. XIV:** 260

"Jacob's Ladder" (Rawlings), **Supp. X:** 224, 228

Jacob's Ladder, The (Levertov), **Supp. III Part 1:** 272, 276–278, 281

"Jacob's Ladder, The" (Levertov), **Supp. III Part 1:** 278

Jacobson, Dale, **Supp. X:** 112

Jacobson, Kristin, **Supp. XVIII:** 113

Jacobson, Leslie, **Supp. XV:** 323

Jacoby, Russell, **Supp. IV Part 2:** 692

"Jacquerie, The" (Lanier), **Supp. I Part 1:** 355, 356, 360, 364, 370

Jacques le fataliste (D. Diderot), **Supp. XVII:** 145

Jade Mountain, The: A Chinese Anthology, Being Three Hundred Poems of the T'ang Dynasty (Bynner, trans.), **II:** 527; **Supp. XV:** 46, 47, 48

Jafsie and John Henry: Essays on Hollywood, Bad Boys, and Six Hours of Perfect Poker (Mamet), **Supp. XIV:** 252

Jaggi, Maya, **Supp. XXV:** 50, 56, 57

Jaguar Totem (LaBastille), **Supp. X:** 99, 106, **107–109**

Jailbird (Vonnegut), **Supp. II Part 2:** 760, 779–780

Jaimes, M. Annette, **Supp. IV Part 1:** 330, 331

Jain, Manju, **Retro. Supp. I:** 53, 58

"Jake Flower, The" (Major), **Supp. XXII:** 182

Jake's Women (Simon), **Supp. IV Part 2:** 576, 588

"Jakie's Mother" (Fante), **Supp. XI:** 164

Jakobson, Roman, **Supp. IV Part 1:** 155

"Jamaica Kincaid's New York" (Kincaid), **Supp. VII:** 181

James, Alice, **I:** 454; **Retro. Supp. I:** 228, 235

James, A. Lloyd, **Supp. XIV:** 343

James, Caryn, **Supp. X:** 302, 303

James, C. L. R. (Cyril Lionel Robert), **Supp. XXI: 159–173**

James, Etta, **Supp. X:** 242

James, Henry, **I:** 4, 5, 9, 10, 12, 15, 16, 20, 52, 93, 109, 211, 226, 228, 244, 246, 251, 255, 258, 259, 336, 363, 374, 375, 379, 384, 409, 429, 436, 439, 452, 454, 459, 461–462, 463, 464, 485, 500, 504, 513, 514, 517–518, 571; **II:** 38, 58, 60, 73, 74, 95, 138, 140, 144, 147, 196, 198, 199, 228, 230, 234, 243, 259, 267, 271, 272, 275, 276, 278, 281, 282, 283, 284, 285, 286, 287, 288, 290, 306, 309, 316, **319–341**, 398, 404, 410, 415, 427, 444, 542, 544, 547–548, 556, 600; **III:** 44, 51, 136, 194–195, 199, 206, 208, 218, 228–229, 237, 281, 319, 325, 326, 334, 409, 453, 454, 457, 460, 461, 464, 511, 522, 576, 607; **IV:** 8, 27, 34, 37, 40, 53, 58, 73, 74, 134, 168, 172, 182, 198, 202, 285, 308, 309, 310, 311, 314, 316, 317, 318, 319, 321, 322, 323, 324, 328, 347, 352, 359, 433, 439, 476; **Retro. Supp. I:** 1, 8, 53, 56, 59, 108, 112, **215–242**, 272, 283, 284, 362, 366, 367, 368, 371, 373, 374, 375, 376, 377, 378, 379; **Retro. Supp. II:** 93, 135, 136, 203, 223; **Supp. I Part 1:** 35, 38, 43; **Supp. I Part 2:** 414, 454, 608, 609, 612–613, 618, 620, 646; **Supp. II Part 1:** 94–95; **Supp. III Part 1:** 14, 200; **Supp. III Part 2:** 410, 412; **Supp. IV Part 1:** 31, 35, 80, 127, 197, 349, 353; **Supp. IV Part 2:** 613, 677, 678, 682, 689, 693; **Supp. IX:** 121; **Supp. V:** 97, 101, 103, 258, 261, 263, 313; **Supp. VIII:** 98, 102, 156, 166, 168; **Supp. XI:** 153; **Supp. XIII:** 102; **Supp. XIV:** 40, 110, 112, 335, 336, 348, 349; **Supp. XV:** 41; **Supp. XVII:** 5, 47; **Supp. XVIII:** 160, 258; **Supp. XX: 227, 228, 232, 233, 238, 240; Supp. XXI:** 225; **Supp. XXII:** 89; **Supp. XXIV:** 132, 224; **Supp. XXVI:** 141, 145

James, Henry (father), **II:** 7, 275, 321, 337, 342–344, 364; **IV:** 174; **Supp. I Part 1:** 300

James, Henry (nephew), **II:** 360

James, Horace, **Supp. XIV:** 57

James, P. D., **Supp. XIX:** 131

James, William, **I:** 104, 220, 224, 227, 228, 255, 454; **II:** 20, 27, 165, 166, 276, 321, 337, **342–366**, 411; **III:** 303, 309, 509, 599, 600, 605, 606, 612; **IV:** 26, 27, 28–29, 31, 32, 34, 36, 37, 43, 46, 291, 486; **Retro. Supp. I:** 57, 216, 227, 228, 235, 295, 300, 306; **Supp. I Part 1:** 3, 7, 11, 20; **Supp. XIV:** 40, 50, 197, 199, 212, 335; **Supp. XVII:** 97

James, William (grandfather), **II:** 342

James Baldwin: The Legacy (Troupe, ed.), **Retro. Supp. II:** 15

James Baldwin—The Price of the Ticket (film), **Retro. Supp. II:** 2

James Dickey and the Politics of Canon (Suarez), **Supp. IV Part 1:** 175

"James Dickey on Yeats: An Interview" (Dickey), **Supp. IV Part 1:** 177

James Hogg: A Critical Study (Simpson), **Supp. IX:** 269, 276

"James Is a Girl" (Egan), **Supp. XIX:** 61

James Jones: A Friendship (Morris), **Supp. XI:** 234

James Jones: An American Literary Orientalist Master (Carter), **Supp. XI:** 220

"James Jones and Jack Kerouac: Novelists of Disjunction" (Stevenson), **Supp. XI:** 230

James Jones: Reveille to Taps (television documentary), **Supp. XI:** 234

Jameson, Anna Brownell, **Supp. XXIII:** 225, 226, 232, 235

Jameson, F. R., **Supp. IV Part 1:** 119

Jameson, Sir Leander Starr, **III:** 327

James Shore's Daughter (Benét), **Supp. XI:** 48

"James Thurber" (Pollard), **Supp. I Part 2:** 468

"James Whitcomb Riley (From a Westerner's Point of View)" (Dunbar), **Supp. II Part 1:** 198

Jammes, Francis, **II:** 528; **Retro. Supp. I:** 55

"Jan, the Son of Thomas" (Sandburg), **III:** 593–594

Jan. 31 (Goldbarth), **Supp. XII:** 177, **178–179,** 180

"Jane Awake"(O'Hara), **Supp. XXIII:** 210

Janeczko, Paul, **Supp. XIII:** 280

Jane Eyre (Brontë), **Supp. XVI:** 158; **Supp. XXII:** 120

Janet, Pierre, **I:** 248, 249, 252; **Retro. Supp. I:** 55, 57

Jane Talbot: A Novel (Brown), **Supp. I Part 1:** 145–146

"Janet Waking" (Ransom), **III:** 490, 491

"Janice" (Jackson), **Supp. IX:** 117

Janowitz, Tama, **Supp. X:** 7

Jantz, Harold S., **Supp. I Part 1:** 112

"January" (Barthelme), **Supp. IV Part 1:** 54

"January" (W. V. Davis), **Supp. XXI:** 89, 90

January Man, The (screenplay, Shanley), **Supp. XIV:** 316

"January Thaw" (Leopold), **Supp. XIV:** 183–184

"Janus" (Beattie), **Supp. V:** 31

Janzen, Jean, **Supp. V:** 180

"Japan" (Collins), **Supp. XXI:** 56

Japanese Americans: The Formation and Transformations of an Ethnic Group (Spickard), **Supp. XXI:** 149

"Japanese Beetles" (X. J. Kennedy), **Supp. XV:** 161, 165

Japanese by Spring (Reed), **Supp. X:** 241, **253–255**

Japanese Cooking: A Simple Art (Tsuji), **Supp. XVII:** 90

"Japan's Young Dreams" (Geisel), **Supp. XVI:** 102

Jara, Victor, **Supp. IV Part 2:** 549

Jarecki, Dave, **Supp. XXIII:** 239

Jarman, Mark, **Supp. IV Part 1:** 68; **Supp. IX:** 266, 270, 276; **Supp. XII:** 209; **Supp. XV:** 251; **Supp. XVIII:** 178; **Supp. XXV:** 221–222

Jarmon, Mark, **Supp. XVII: 109–122**

Jarrell, Randall, **I:** 167, 169, 173, 180; **II: 367–390,** 539–540; **III:** 134, 194, 213, 268, 527; **IV:** 352, 411, 422; **Retro. Supp. I:** 52, 121, 135, 140; **Retro. Supp. II:** 44, 177, 178, 182; **Supp. I Part 1:** 89; **Supp. I Part 2:** 552; **Supp. II Part 1:** 109, 135; **Supp. III Part 1:** 64; **Supp. III Part 2:** 541, 550; **Supp. IV Part 2:** 440; **Supp. IX:** 94, 268; **Supp. V:** 315, 318, 323; **Supp. VIII:** 31, 100, 271; **Supp. XI:** 311, 315; **Supp. XII:** 121, 260, 297; **Supp. XV:** 93, 153; **Supp. XVII:** 111; **Supp. XXVI:** 67

Jarrell, Mrs. Randall (Mary von Schrader), **II:** 368, 385

Jarry, Alfred, **Retro. Supp. II:** 326; **Supp. XV:** 177–178, 182, 188

Jarvis, John Wesley, **Supp. I Part 2:** 501, 520

Jaskoski, Helen, **Supp. IV Part 1:** 325; **Supp. XXII:** 166

"Jasmine" (Komunyakaa), **Supp. XIII:** 132

"Jason" (Hecht), **Supp. X:** 62

"Jason" (MacLeish), **III:** 4

Jason and Medeia (Gardner), **Supp. VI:** 63, **68–69**

"Jasper Notes" (G. Jones), **Supp. XXIV:** 194

Jaspers, Karl, **III:** 292; **IV:** 491

Jauss, David, **Supp. XXI:** 129, 132, 133, 134, 139

Jay, William, **I:** 338

Jayber Crow (Berry), **Supp. X:** 28, 34

"Jaz Fantasia" (Sandburg), **III:** 585

"Jazz Age Clerk, A" (Farrell), **II:** 45

Jazz Country: Ralph Ellison in America (Porter), **Retro. Supp. II:** 127

"Jazzonia" (Hughes), **Supp. I Part 1:** 324

Jazz Poetry Anthology, The (Komunyakaa and Feinstein, eds.), **Supp. XIII:** 125

"Jazztet Muted" (Hughes), **Supp. I Part 1:** 342

J. B.: A Play in Verse (MacLeish), **II:** 163, 228; **III:** 3, 21–22, 23; **Supp. IV Part 2:** 586

"Jealous" (Ford), **Supp. V:** 71

Jealous Gods, The (Atherton), **Supp. XXIV:** 26

Jealousies, The: A Faery Tale, by Lucy Vaughan Lloyd of China Walk, Lambeth (Keats), **Supp. XII:** 113

Jean-Christophe (Rolland), **Supp. XX: 70**

"Jean Harlow's Wedding Night" (Wasserstein), **Supp. XV:** 328

Jean Huguenot (Benét), **Supp. XI:** 44

"Jeff Briggs's Love Story" (Harte), **Supp. II Part 1:** 355

Jeffers, Robinson, **I:** 66; **III:** 134; **Retro. Supp. I:** 202; **Supp. II Part 2: 413– 440; Supp. IX:** 77; **Supp. VIII:** 33, 292; **Supp. X:** 112; **Supp. XI:** 312; **Supp. XV:** 113, 114, 115; **Supp. XVII:** 111, 112, 117; **Supp. XXI:** 87; **Supp. XXIII:** 145

Jeffers, Una Call Kuster (Mrs. Robinson Jeffers), **Supp. II Part 2:** 414

Jefferson, Blind Lemon, **Supp. VIII:** 349

Jefferson, Margo, **Supp. XX: 87; Supp. XXIV:** 271

Jefferson, Thomas, **I:** 1, 2, 5, 6–8, 14, 485; **II:** 5, 6, 34, 217, 300, 301, 437; **III:** 3, 17, 18, 294–295, 306, 310, 473, 608; **IV:** 133, 243, 249, 334, 348; **Supp. I Part 1:** 146, 152, 153, 229, 230, 234, 235; **Supp. I Part 2:** 389, 399, 456, 474, 475, 482, 507, 509, 510, 511, 516, 518–519, 520, 522; **Supp. X:** 26; **Supp. XIV:** 191; **Supp. XX:** 285; **Supp. XXIV:** 85, 281

Jefferson and/or Mussolini (Pound), **Retro. Supp. I:** 292

"Jefferson Davis as a Representative American" (Du Bois), **Supp. II Part 1:** 161

J-E-L-L-O (Baraka), **Supp. II Part 1:** 47

"Jelly-Bean, The" (Fitzgerald), **II:** 88

"Jellyfish, A" (Moore), **III:** 215

Jemie, Onwuchekwa, **Supp. I Part 1:** 343

Jenkins, J. L., **I:** 456

Jenkins, Joe, **Supp. XX: 117, 120, 122**

Jenkins, Kathleen, **III:** 403

Jenkins, Susan, **IV:** 123

Jenks, Deneen, **Supp. IV Part 2:** 550, 554

Jenks, Tom, **Supp. XIX:** 51

Jenkyns, Richard, **Supp. XXV:** 223

Jennie Gerhardt (Dreiser), **I:** 497, 499, 500, 501, 504–505, 506, 507, 519; **Retro. Supp. II:** 94, **99–101**

"Jennie M'Grew" (Masters), **Supp. I Part 2:** 468

Jennifer Lorn (Wylie), **Supp. I Part 2:** 709, 714–717, 718, 721, 724

Jennison, Peter S., **Supp. XIX:** 268

"Jenny Garrow's Lover" (Jewett), **II:** 397

"Jerboa, The" (Moore), **III:** 203, 207, 209, 211–212

Jeremiah, **Supp. X:** 35

Jeremy's Version (Purdy), **Supp. VII:** 274

"Je Reviens"(Dybek), **Supp. XXIII:** 78

"Jericho" (Lowell), **II:** 536

Jerome, Judson, **Supp. XXIII:** 54

"Jerry's Garage" (Budbill), **Supp. XIX:** 7

"Jersey City Gendarmerie, Je T'aime" (Lardner), **II:** 433

Jersey Rain (Pinsky), **Supp. VI:** 235, **247–250**

"Jerusalem" (Nye), **Supp. XIII:** 287

Jerusalem: Song of Songs (Uris), **Supp. XX: 244–245, 246, 255**

Jerusalem the Golden (Reznikoff), **Supp. XIV:** 280, 285, 286

"Jessie and Jesus" (Andrews), **Supp. XXVI:** 11

Jessie and Jesus and Cousin Claire (Andrews), **Supp. XXVI:** 2, 10, 11–12

Jessup, Richard, **Supp. XI:** 306

"Je Suis Perdu" (Taylor), *Supp. V:* 314, 321–322

Jesuits in North America in the Seventeenth Century, The (Parkman), **Supp. II Part 2:** 597, 603–605

Jesus, **I:** 27, 34, 68, 89, 136, 552, 560; **II:** 1, 16, 197, 198, 214, 215, 216, 218, 219, 239, 373, 377, 379, 537, 538, 539, 549, 569, 585, 591, 592; **III:** 39, 173, 179, 270, 291, 296–297, 300, 303, 305, 307, 311, 339, 340, 341, 342, 344, 345, 346, 347, 348, 352, 353, 354, 355, 436, 451, 489, 534, 564, 566, 567, 582; **IV:** 51, 69, 86, 107, 109, 117, 137, 138, 141, 144, 147, 149, 150, 151, 152, 155, 156, 157, 158, 159, 163, 164, 232, 241, 289, 293, 294, 296, 331, 364, 392, 396, 418, 430; **Supp. I Part 1:** 2, 54, 104, 107, 108, 109, 121, 267, 371; **Supp. I Part 2:** 379, 386, 458, 515, 580, 582, 583, 587, 588, 683; **Supp. V:** 280

Jesus, the Son of Man (Gibran), **Supp. XX: 115–116, 117, 122–123**

"Jesus Asleep" (Sexton), **Supp. II Part 2:** 693

"Jesus of Nazareth, Then and Now" (Price), **Supp. VI:** 268

"Jesus Papers, The" (Sexton), **Supp. II Part 2:** 693

"Jesus Raises Up the Harlot" (Sexton), **Supp. II Part 2:** 693

"Jesus Shaves" (Davison), **Supp. XXVI:** 74

"Jesus Stories, The" (Brockmeier), **Supp. XXII:** 52

Jetée, La (film), **Supp. IV Part 2:** 436

"Jeune Parque, La" (Valéry), **IV**: 92

"Jew as Writer/The Writer as Jew, The: Reflections on Literature and Identity" (Apple), **Supp. XVII**: 1, 9

"Jewbird, The" (Malamud), **Supp. I Part 2**: 435

"Jewboy, The" (P. Roth), **Supp. III Part 2**: 412

Jewett, Caroline, **II**: 396

Jewett, Katharine, **Retro. Supp. II**: 46

Jewett, Mary, **II**: 396, 403

Jewett, Rutger, **Retro. Supp. I**: 381

Jewett, Sarah Orne, **I**: 313; **II**: **391–414**; **Retro. Supp. I**: 6, 7, 19; **Retro. Supp. II**: 51, 52, **131–151**, 156; **Supp. I Part 2**: 495; **Supp. IX**: 79; **Supp. VIII**: 126; **Supp. XIII**: 153; **Supp. XXIII**: 275, 278

Jewett, Theodore Furber, **II**: 395

Jewett, Dr. Theodore Herman, **II**: 396–397, 402

"Jew for Export, The" (Mamet), **Supp. XIV**: 251–252

Jew in Our Day, The (W. Frank), **Supp. XX**: **79**

Jew in the American Novel, The (Fiedler), **Supp. XIII**: 106

"Jewish Graveyards, Italy" (Levine), **Supp. V**: 190

"Jewish Hunter, The" (Moore), **Supp. X**: 163, 165, **174**

Jewison, Norman, **Supp. XI**: 306; **Supp. XIV**: 316

"Jew of Persia, A" (Helprin), **Supp. XXV**: 80, 85

Jews of Shklov (Schneour), **IV**: 11

Jews without Money (Gold), **Supp. XIV**: 288–289

JFK (film), **Supp. XIV**: 48

Jig of Forslin, The: A Symphony (Aiken), **I**: 50, 51, 57, 62, 66

Jigonsaseh, **Supp. XXVI**: 81, 82, 83, 86

"Jig Tune: Not for Love" (McGrath), **Supp. X**: 116

"Jihad" (McClatchy), **Supp. XII**: 266

"Jilting of Granny Weatherall, The" (Porter), **III**: 434, 435, 438

Jim Crow's Last Stand (Hughes), **Retro. Supp. I**: 205

Jiménez, Juan Ramón, **Supp. XIII**: 315, 323

Jimmie Higgins (Sinclair), **Supp. V**: 288

"Jimmy Harlow" (X. J. Kennedy), **Supp. XV**: 170

Jimmy's Blues (Baldwin), **Retro. Supp. II**: 8, 9, 15

Jim's Book: A Collection of Poems and Short Stories (Merrill), **Supp. III Part 1**: 319

Jin, Ha, **Supp. XVIII**: **89–104**

Jitney (Wilson), **Supp. VIII**: 330, 331, 351

Jitterbug Perfume (Robbins), **Supp. X**: 273, **274–276**, 279

Joachim, Harold, **Retro. Supp. I**: 58

Joan, Pope, **IV**: 165

Joanna and Ulysses (Sarton), **Supp. VIII**: **254–255**

Joan of Arc, **IV**: 241; **Supp. I Part 1**: 286–288; **Supp. I Part 2**: 469

Joans, Ted, **Supp. IV Part 1**: 169

Job (biblical book), **II**: 165, 166–167, 168; **III**: 21, 199, 512; **IV**: 13, 158; **Supp. I Part 1**: 125

Job, The (Burroughs and Odier), **Supp. III Part 1**: 97, 103

Job, The: An American Novel (Lewis), **II**: 441

"Job History" (Proulx), **Supp. VII**: 262

Jobim, Antonio Carlos, **Supp. IV Part 2**: 549

Jobim, Antônio Carlos, **Supp. XXI**: 100

"Job of the Plains, A" (Humphrey), **Supp. IX**: 101

Jocks, Christopher, **Supp. XXVI**: 97

"Jody Rolled the Bones" (Yates), **Supp. XI**: 335, 341

"Joe" (Alvarez), **Supp. VII**: 7–8

Joe (Brown), **Supp. XVIII**: 195

Joe (L. Brown), **Supp. XXI**: 41, **45–46**, 47

"Joe, the Vanishing American" (Swados), **Supp. XIX**: 258–259

"Joe Hill" (Hayes), **Supp. XXVI**: 134

Joe Hill: A Biographical Novel (Stegner), **Supp. IV Part 2**: 599

Joe Jones (Lamott), **Supp. XX**: **134–135**

"Joe Louis: The King as a Middle-Aged Man" (Talese), **Supp. XVII**: 202

"Joe Messenger Is Dreaming"(P. Benedict), **Supp. XXIII**: 47

"Joe's Jitters" (Bronk), **Supp. XXI**: 27

Joe Turner's Come and Gone (Wilson), **Supp. VIII**: 334, **337–342**, 345

Joe versus the Volcano (screenplay, Shanley), **Supp. XIV**: 316

"Joey Martiney" (Huncke), **Supp. XIV**: 149

Johannes in Eremo (Mather), **Supp. II Part 2**: 453

Johansen, Bruce E., **Supp. XXVI**: 98

John XXIII, Pope, **Supp. I Part 2**: 492

John (biblical book), **I**: 68; **Supp. XV**: 222, 224

"John" (Shields), **Supp. VII**: 310–311

John, Augustus, **Supp. XXII**: 157

John, Elton, **Supp. XXI**: 148

"John, John Chinaman" (Buck), **Supp. II Part 1**: 128

John, Orrick, **Supp. XXVI**: 134

John Addington Symonds: A Biographical Study (Brooks), **I**: 240, 241

John-a Dreams: A Tale (J. Sturgis), **Supp. XX**: **233**

"John Archer's Nose" (R. Fisher), **Supp. XIX**: 71–72, 78

John Barleycorn (London), **II**: 467, 481

John Brown (Du Bois), **Supp. II Part 1**: 171–172

"John Brown" (Emerson), **II**: 13

"John Brown" (Lindsay), **Supp. I Part 2**: 393

John Brown's Body (Benét), **II**: 177; **Supp. XI**: 45, 46, 47, **56–57**

John Brown: The Making of a Martyr (Warren), **IV**: 236

John Bull in America; or, The New Munchausen (Paulding), **I**: 344

"John Burke" (Olson), **Supp. II Part 2**: 579, 580

"John Burns of Gettysburg" (Harte), **Supp. II Part 1**: 343

"John Carter" (Agee), **I**: 27

John Chancellor Makes Me Cry (Siddons), **Supp. XXII**: 245

"John Coltrane: Where Does Art Come From?" (Baraka), **Supp. II Part 1**: 60

John Deth: A Metaphysical Legend and Other Poems (Aiken), **I**: 61

"John Endicott" (Longfellow), **II**: 505, 506; **Retro. Supp. II**: 165–166, 167

"John Evereldown" (Robinson), **III**: 524

John Fante Reader, The (Cooper, ed.), **Supp. XI**: 174

John Fante: Selected Letters, 1932–1981 (Cooney, ed.), **Supp. XI**: 170

"John Gardner: The Writer As Teacher" (Carver), **Supp. III Part 1**: 136, 146–147

John Gaunt (R. H. Davis), **Supp. XVI**: 89

John Jay Chapman and His Letters (Howe), **Supp. XIV**: 54

John Keats (Lowell), **II**: 530–531

John Kennedy Toole: The Omega Point (film, Sandord), **Supp. XXVI**: 240, 241, 243, 246, 253

"John Kinsella's Lament for Mrs. Mary Moore" (Yeats), **Supp. XVII**: 144

"John Lamar" (R. H. Davis), **Supp. XVI**: 89–90

John Lane, **Retro. Supp. I**: 59

"John L. Sullivan" (Lindsay), **Supp. I Part 2**: 394, 395

"John Marr" (Melville), **III**: 93

John Marr and Other Sailors (Melville), **III**: 93; **Retro. Supp. I**: 257

John Muir: A Reading Bibliography (Kimes and Kimes), **Supp. IX**: 178

Johnny Appleseed and Other Poems (Lindsay), **Supp. I Part 2**: 397

"Johnny Bear" (Steinbeck), **IV**: 67

Johnny Got His Gun (Trumbo), **Supp. XXI**: 45

"Johnny Mnemonic" (W. Gibson), **Supp. XVI**: 122, 123–125, 128, 131

"Johnny Panic and the Bible of Dreams" (Plath), **Retro. Supp. II**: 245

"Johnny Ray" (Ríos), **Supp. IV Part 2**: 543

Johnny Tremain (Forbes), **Supp. XIX**: 235

John of the Cross (Saint), **I**: 585; **Supp. IV Part 1**: 284; **Supp. XV**: 223; **Supp. XVII**: 112

John Paul Jones: A Sailor's Biography (Morison), **Supp. I Part 2**: 494–495

"John Redding Goes to Sea" (Hurston), **Supp. VI**: 150

Johns, George Sibley, **Retro. Supp. II**: 65

Johns, Jasper, **Supp. XXIII**: 217

Johns, Orrick, **Retro. Supp. II**: 71

John Sloan: A Painter's Life (Brooks), **I**: 254

"John Smith Liberator" (Bierce), **I**: 209

Johnson, Alexandra, **Supp. X**: 86

Johnson, Alvin, **I**: 236; **Supp. XV**: 304

Johnson, Ben, **Retro. Supp. I**: 56

Johnson, Buffie, **Supp. IV Part 1**: 94

Johnson, Caitlin, **Supp. XXIII:** 281

Johnson, Carol Siri, **Supp. XXIII:** 257, 258, 264, 269

Johnson, Charles, **Supp. I Part 1:** 325; **Supp. V:** 128; **Supp. VI: 185–201;** **Supp. X:** 239; **Supp. XIII:** 182; **Supp. XIX:** 160

Johnson, Charles S., **Supp. IX:** 309; **Supp. XXII:** 6, 7

Johnson, Claudia Durst, **Supp. VIII:** 126–127

Johnson, Clifton, **Supp. XXI:** 248, 250

Johnson, Denis, **Supp. XIX:** 209; **Supp. XXI:** 118, 131

Johnson, Diane, **Retro. Supp. I:** 196; **Supp. XIII:** 127

Johnson, Eastman, **IV:** 321

Johnson, Edward, **IV:** 157; **Supp. I Part 1:** 110, 115

Johnson, Fenton, **Supp. XI:** 129

Johnson, Georgia Douglas, **Supp. IV Part 1:** 164

Johnson, Helene, **Supp. XVIII:** 282; **Supp. XXVI: 163–176**

Johnson, James Weldon, **Retro. Supp. II:** 114; **Supp. I Part 1:** 324, 325; **Supp. II Part 1:** 33, 194, 200, 202–203, 206–207; **Supp. III Part 1:** 73; **Supp. IV Part 1:** 7, 11, 15, 16, 164, 165, 166, 169; **Supp. X:** 42, 136, **246;** **Supp. XIX:** 73; **Supp. XVIII:** 122, 127, 282

Johnson, Jeff, **Supp. XXV:** 98

Johnson, Joyce, **Supp. XIV:** 150

Johnson, Kent, **Supp. XV:** 347

Johnson, Lady Bird, **Supp. IV Part 1:** 22

Johnson, Lyndon B., **I:** 254; **II:** 553, 582; **Retro. Supp. II:** 27

Johnson, Marguerite. *See* Angelou, Maya

Johnson, Maurice, **Supp. XV:** 136, 137, 138

Johnson, Michael K., **Supp. XVIII:** 59, 64

Johnson, Mordecai, **Supp. XIV:** 202

Johnson, Nunnally, **Supp. IV Part 1:** 355

Johnson, Pamela Hansford, **IV:** 469

Johnson, Rafer, **Supp. I Part 1:** 271

Johnson, Reed, **Supp. IV Part 2:** 589

Johnson, Richard, **Supp. XIII:** 132

Johnson, Robert, **Supp. IV Part 1:** 146; **Supp. VIII:** 15, 134

Johnson, Robert K., **Supp. IV Part 2:** 573, 584

Johnson, Robert Underwood, **Supp. IX:** 182, 184, 185

Johnson, Samuel, **II:** 295; **III:** 491, 503; **IV:** 452; **Retro. Supp. I:** 56, 65; **Supp. I Part 1:** 33; **Supp. I Part 2:** 422, 498, 503, 523, 656; **Supp. IV Part 1:** 34, 124; **Supp. XI:** 209; **Supp. XII:** 159; **Supp. XIII:** 55, 347; **Supp. XVI:** 204; **Supp. XVII:** 1; **Supp. XXIV:** 152

Johnson, Samuel, Jr., **Supp. XXV:** 241, 250

Johnson, Sarah Anne, **Supp. XIX:** 49, 50, 52, 54, 55, 56, 58, 59, 60, 61; **Supp. XVIII:** 145

Johnson, Steve, **Supp. XVI:** 177

Johnson, Thomas H., **I:** 470–471; **IV:** 144, 158; **Retro. Supp. I:** 26, 28, 36, 39, 40, 41, 43

Johnson, Walter, **II:** 422

Johnson, Willard "Spud", **Supp. XV:** 42, 46

"Johnson Girls, The" (Bambara), **Supp. XI:** 7

Johnsrud, Harold, **II:** 562

Johnston, Basil, **Supp. IV Part 1:** 269

Johnston, Jill, **Supp. XXV:** 5

Johnston, Mary, **II:** 194

Johnston, Robert M., **Supp. I Part 1:** 369

"John Sutter" (Winters), **Supp. II Part 2:** 810

John's Wife (Coover), **Supp. V:** 51–52

John the Baptist, **I:** 389; **II:** 537, 591

John Wesley Harding (album, Dylan), **Supp. XVIII:** 27

Jolas, Eugène, **Retro. Supp. II:** 85, 328; **Supp. IV Part 1:** 80

Jolie Blon's Bounce (Burke), **Supp. XIV:** 26, 33–34

Jolly (Mamet), **Supp. XIV:** 240, 254

"Jolly Corner, The" (James), **I:** 571; **Retro. Supp. I:** 235

Jolly Plays for Holidays (Wells), **Supp. XXVI:** 275

"Jon" (Saunders), **Supp. XIX:** 232, 234

"Jonah" (Lowell), **II:** 536

Jonah's Gourd Vine (Hurston), **Supp. VI:** 149, 155

"Jonathan Edwards" (Holmes), **Supp. I Part 1:** 302, 315

"Jonathan Edwards in Western Massachusetts" (Lowell), **II:** 550

Jonathan Franzen at the End of Postmodernism (Burns), **Supp. XX:** 85

Jonathan Troy (Abbey), **Supp. XIII:** 4, 13

Jones, Anne, **Supp. X:** 8

Jones, Anne Goodwyn, **Supp. XXII:** 252

Jones, Carolyn M., **Supp. VIII:** 128; **Supp. XIX:** 160

Jones, Chuck, **Supp. XVI:** 102

Jones, David, **Supp. XVII:** 241

Jones, Dennis, **Supp. XXIII:** 228, 233

Jones, Derek Anson, **Supp. XVIII:** 38, 39

Jones, Edith Newbold. *See* Wharton, Edith

Jones, Edward P., **Supp. XXI:** 247; **Supp. XXII: 139–153**

Jones, E. Stanley, **III:** 297

Jones, Everett LeRoi. *See* Baraka, Imamu Amiri

Jones, Gayl, **Supp. XXIV: 183–197**

Jones, George Frederic, **IV:** 309

Jones, Grover, **Supp. XIII:** 166

Jones, Harry, **Supp. I Part 1:** 337

Jones, Harry L., **Supp. XXV:** 251

Jones, Howard Mumford, **I:** 353; **Supp. IV Part 2:** 606; **Supp. XIV:** 11; **Supp. XXVI:** 63

Jones, James, **III:** 40; **IV:** 98; **Supp. XI: 213–237;** **Supp. XIX:** 248, 252; **Supp. XX:** 248; **Supp. XXV:** 145

Jones, James Earl, **Supp. VIII:** 334; **Supp. XI:** 309

Jones, Jennifer, **Supp. IV Part 2:** 524

Jones, John Paul, **II:** 405–406; **Supp. I Part 2:** 479, 480, 494–495

Jones, Kirkland C., **Supp. XVIII:** 173, 174, 175; **Supp. XXII:** 9

Jones, LeRoi. *See* Baraka, Imamu Amiri

Jones, Louis B., **Supp. XVI:** 41

Jones, Loyal, **Supp. XX: 170**

Jones, Lucretia Stevens Rhinelander, **IV:** 309

Jones, Madison, **Retro. Supp. II:** 235; **Supp. X:** 1

Jones, Major (pseudonym). *See* Thompson, William T.

Jones, Malcolm, **Supp. V:** 219; **Supp. XX: 93, 138**

Jones, Mildred, **Supp. XVIII:** 281

Jones, Robert Edmond, **III:** 387, 391, 394, 399; **Supp. XXI:** 6, 12

Jones, Rodney, **Supp. XXVI:** 66

Jones, Sharon L., **Supp. XVIII:** 280, 285, 286

Jones, Tommy Lee, **Supp. V:** 227

"Jones's Private Argyment" (Lanier), **Supp. I Part 1:** 352

"Jones's *The Thin Red Line:* The End of Innocence" (Michel-Michot), **Supp. XI:** 224–225

Jong, Allan, **Supp. V:** 115

Jong, Erica, **Supp. V: 113–135**

Jong-Fast, Molly Miranda, **Supp. V:** 115

Jonson, Ben, **I:** 58, 358; **II:** 11, 16, 17, 18, 436, 556; **III:** 3, 463, 575–576; **IV:** 395, 453; **Retro. Supp. II:** 76; **Supp. I Part 2:** 423; **Supp. IV Part 2:** 585; **Supp. XX: 197; Supp. XXIV:** 159

Jonsson, Thorsten, **Retro. Supp. I:** 73

Joplin, Janis, **Supp. IV Part 1:** 206; **Supp. XI:** 239

Joplin, Scott, **Supp. IV Part 1:** 223

Jordan, A. Van, **Supp. XVIII:** 172

Jordan, Barbara, **Supp. VIII:** 63; **Supp. XI:** 249

Jordan, David, **Supp. XIX:** 141

Jordan, June, **Supp. XII:** 217; **Supp. XXII:** 172; **Supp. XXIV:** 188

Jordan, Marie, **Supp. XV:** 224

Jo's Boys (Alcott), **Supp. I Part 1:** 32, 35, 40–41, 42

Joseph Heller (Ruderman), **Supp. IV Part 1:** 380

"Josephine Has Her Day" (Thurber), **Supp. I Part 2:** 606

Josephine Stories, The (Fitzgerald), **Retro. Supp. I:** 109

"Joseph Martinez" (Huncke), **Supp. XIV:** 149

"Joseph Pockets" (Stern), **Supp. IX:** 292

Josephson, Matthew, **I:** 259

"José's Country" (Winters), **Supp. II Part 2:** 789, 790

Joshi, S. T., **Supp. XXIV:** 23; **Supp. XXV:** 111, 118, 123

Joshua (biblical book), **Supp. I Part 2:** 515

"Joshua Clark"(Kenny), **Supp. XXIII:** 154

Joslin, Katherine, **Retro. Supp. I:** 376

Journal (Emerson), **Supp. I Part 1:** 309

"Journal" (L. Michaels), **Supp. XVI:** 213

Journal (Thoreau), **IV:** 175

Journal (Woolman), **Supp. VIII:** 202

"Journal for My Daughter" (Kunitz), **Supp. III Part 1:** 268

"Journal of an Airman" (Auden), **Supp. XIX:** 151

Journal of Arthur Stirling, The (Sinclair), **Supp. V:** 280

"Journal of a Solitary Man, The" (Hawthorne), **II:** 226

Journal of a Solitude (Sarton), **Supp. VIII:** 256, 262–263

Journal of My Other Self (Rilke), **Retro. Supp. II:** 20

Journal of the Fictive Life (Nemerov), **III:** 267, 268, 269, 272, 273, 274, 280–281, 284–285, 286, 287

Journal of the Plague Year, A (Defoe), **III:** 423

"Journal of the Year of the Ox, A" (Wright), **Supp. V:** 343

Journals (Thoreau), **Supp. I Part 1:** 299

Journals and Other Documents on the Life and Voyages of Christopher Columbus (Morison, ed.), **Supp. I Part 2:** 494

Journals of Ralph Waldo Emerson, The (Emerson), **II:** 8, 17, 21

Journals of Susanna Moodie, The: Poems (Atwood), **Supp. XIII:** 33

"Journey, A" (Wharton), **Retro. Supp. I:** 364

"Journey, The" (Winters), **Supp. II Part 2:** 795

"Journey, The" (Wright), **Supp. III Part 2:** 605–606

"Journey, the Arrival and the Dream, The" (Gioia), **Supp. XV:** 120

"Journey, The: For Jane at Thirteen" (Kumin), **Supp. IV Part 2:** 442

Journey and Other Poems, The (Winters), **Supp. II Part 2:** 786, 794, 795, 796, 799, 800, 801

Journey Around My Room: The Autobiography of Louise Bogan—A Mosaic (Bogan), **Supp. III Part 1:** 47, 48, 52, 53

Journey Down, The (Bernstein), **IV:** 455

Journey Home, The (Abbey), **Supp. XIII:** 2, 12

"Journey into Speech, A" (Cliff), **Supp. XXII:** 69

Journeyman (Caldwell), **I:** 297, 302–304, 307, 309; **Supp. XXVI:** 134

Journeyman: Travels of a Writer (Findley), **Supp. XX:** 50

"Journey of an Eyeball, The" (Vaz), **Supp. XXVI:** 261

Journey of Tai-me, The (Momaday), **Supp. IV Part 2:** 485

"Journey of the Magi" (Eliot), **Retro. Supp. I:** 64

Journey to a War (Auden and Isherwood), **Supp. II Part 1:** 13; **Supp. XIV:** 156, 158, 162

Journey to Love (W. C. Williams), **IV:** 422; **Retro. Supp. I:** 429

Journey to My Father; Isaac Bashevis Singer (Zamir), **Retro. Supp. II:** 317

"Journey to Nine Miles" (Walker), **Supp. III Part 2:** 527

"Journey to the Interior" (W. J. Smith), **Supp. XIII:** 339, 340

Journey with Genius: Recollections and Reflections Concerning the D. H. Lawrences (Bynner), **Supp. XV:** 46

Jowett, Benjamin, **Supp. XIV:** 335

"Joy" (Moore), **Supp. X:** 174

"Joy" (Singer), **IV:** 9; **Retro. Supp. II:** 307

Joyce, Cynthia, **Supp. X:** 194, 195, 196

Joyce, James, **I:** 53, 105, 108, 130, 174, 256, 285, 377, 395, 475–476, 478, 480, 483, 576; **II:** 27, 42, 58, 73, 74, 198, 209, 264, 320, 569; **III:** 7, 16, 26–27, 45, 174, 181, 184, 261, 273, 277, 343, 396, 398, 465, 471, 474; **IV:** 32, 73, 85, 95, 103, 171, 182, 211, 286, 370, 412, 418, 419, 428, 434, 456; **Retro. Supp. I:** 59, 63, 75, 80, 89, 91, 108, 109, 127, 287, 290, 292, 334, 335, 420; **Retro. Supp. II:** 221, 326; **Supp. I Part 1:** 257, 262, 270; **Supp. I Part 2:** 437, 546, 613, 620; **Supp. II Part 1:** 136; **Supp. III Part 1:** 35, 36, 65, 225, 229; **Supp. III Part 2:** 611, 617, 618; **Supp. IV Part 1:** 40, 47, 80, 227, 300, 310; **Supp. IV Part 2:** 424, 677; **Supp. IX:** 211, 229, 235, 308; **Supp. V:** 261, 331; **Supp. VIII:** 14, 40, 103; **Supp. X:** 115, 137, 194, 324; **Supp. XI:** 66; **Supp. XII:** 139, 151, 165, 191, 289; **Supp. XIV:** 83; **Supp. XIX:** 151, 172; **Supp. XVI:** 41, 189, 282; **Supp. XVII:** 44; **Supp. XXI:** 7; **Supp. XXII:** 141, 143–144; **Supp. XXIII:** 162; **Supp. XXVI:** 17, 135

Joy Comes in the Morning (J. Rosen), **Supp. XVII:** 50

Joy in the Morning (B. Smith), **Supp. XXIII:** 257, 258, **269–270**

Joy Luck Club, The (Tan), **Supp. X:** 289, 291, 293, 294, 296, 297, 298, 299

"Joy of Sales Resistance, The" (Berry), **Supp. X:** 36

J R (Gaddis), **Supp. IV Part 1:** 279, 280, 285–289, 291, 294; **Supp. IV Part 2:** 484; **Supp. XXI:** 226

Juana Inés de la Cruz, Sor, **Supp. XXI:** 94, 104

Juan de la Cruz (John of the Cross), **Supp. XXI:** 99, 104

"Juan's Song" (Bogan), **Supp. III Part 1:** 50

Juba to Jive: A Dictionary of African-American Slang (Major), **Supp. XXII:** 172, 180

Jubilate Agno (Smart), **Supp. IV Part 2:** 626

Judah, Hettie, **Supp. XIII:** 246

Judah the Pious (Prose), **Supp. XVI:** 249, 250, 262

"Judas Maccabaeus" (Longfellow), **II:** 506; **Retro. Supp. II:** 165, 167

Judd, Sylvester, **II:** 290; **Supp. I Part 2:** 420

Judd Rankin's Daughter (Glaspell), **Supp. III Part 1:** 186–188

Jude the Obscure (Hardy), **Supp. I Part 1:** 217

Judevine (Budbill), **Supp. XIX:** 4, **8–9,** 12

Judevine: A Play in Three Acts/Two Acts (Budbill), **Supp. XIX:** **12–13**

Judge, Jane, **Supp. XXII:** 191

"Judgement Day" (O'Connor), **III:** 349, 350; **Retro. Supp. II:** 236

Judgment Day (Farrell), **II:** 29, 31, 32, 34, 39

"Judgment of Paris, The" (Merwin), **Supp. III Part 1:** 350

Judgment of Paris, The (Vidal), **Supp. IV Part 2:** 680, 682

"Judgment of the Sage, The" (Crane), **I:** 420

Judith (Farrell), **II:** 46, 48

"Judith" (Garrett), **Supp. VII:** 109–110

"Juggernaut" (Bass), **Supp. XVI:** 16–17

"Jug of Sirup, A" (Bierce), **I:** 206

"Jugurtha" (Longfellow), **II:** 499

"Juice or Gravy" (P. Roth), **Retro. Supp. II:** 279

"Juke Box Love Song" (Hughes), **Retro. Supp. I:** 209

"Julia" (Hellman), **Supp. I Part 1:** 280, 293

Julia France and Her Times (Atherton), **Supp. XXIV:** 24, 27

"Julia Miller" (Masters), **Supp. I Part 2:** 461

Julian (Vidal), **Supp. IV Part 2:** 677, 684–685, 685, 689

Julian the Apostate, **Retro. Supp. I:** 247

"Julian Vreden" (Bowles), **Supp. IV Part 1:** 94

Julie and Romeo (Ray), **Supp. XII:** 308, 310

Julien, Isaac, **Supp. XI:** 19

Julie; ou, La nouvelle Héloïse (Rousseau), **Supp. XVI:** 184

Julier, Laura, **Supp. IV Part 1:** 211

Julip (Harrison), **Supp. VIII:** 51

Julius Caesar (Shakespeare), **I:** 284; **Supp. XXVI:** 40

July, Miranda, **Supp. XXIV:** **199–211**

"July Midnight" (Lowell), **II:** 521

Jumel, Madame, **Supp. I Part 2:** 461

Jumping Out of Bed (R. Bly), **Supp. IV Part 1:** 71

"Jump-Up Day" (Kingsolver), **Supp. VII:** 203

"Junctions" (Lamott), **Supp. XX:** **143**

"June 1940" (Kees), **Supp. XV:** 141

"June Light" (Wilbur), **Supp. III Part 2:** 545

June Moon (Lardner and Kaufman), **II:** 427

"June Recital" (Welty), **IV:** 272–273

Juneteenth (Ellison), **Retro. Supp. II:** 119, 124, **126–128**

"Juneteenth" (Ellison), **Retro. Supp. II:** 119, 126; **Supp. II Part 1:** 248

"June the Third" (Gander), **Supp. XV:** 340

June-Tree: New and Selected Poems, 1974–2000 (Balakian), **Supp. XXIII:** 19, **24–25,** 32

Jung, Carl, **I:** 58, 135, 241, 248, 252, 402; **III:** 400, 534, 543; **Supp. I Part 2:** 439; **Supp. IV Part 1:** 68, 69; **Supp. VIII:** 45; **Supp. X:** 193; **Supp. XV:** 214; **Supp. XX:** 63, 117

Junger, Ernst, **Supp. III Part 1:** 63

Jungle, The (Sinclair), **III:** 580; **Supp. V:** 281–284, 285, 289

Jungle Lovers (Theroux), **Supp. VIII:** 314, 315, 316, 317

"Junior Addict" (Hughes), **Supp. I Part 1:** 343

"Juniper" (Francis), **Supp. IX:** 79

"Junk" (Wilbur), **Supp. III Part 2:** 556

Junker, Howard, **Supp. XV:** 116

Junkie: Confessions of an Unredeemed Drug Addict (Burroughs), **Supp. III Part 1:** 92, 94–96, 101

Junky (Burroughs), **Supp. XIV:** 143

Juno and the Paycock (O'Casey), **Supp. IV Part 1:** 361

"Jupiter Doke, Brigadier General" (Bierce), **I:** 204

Jupiter Laughs (A. Cronin), **Supp. XVII:** 59

Jurgen (Cabell), **III:** 394; **IV:** 286; **Retro. Supp. I:** 80; **Supp. I Part 2:** 718

Jury of Her Peers, A: American Women Writers from Anne Bradstreet to Annie Proulx (Showalter), **Supp. XX:** 274

Jusserand, Jules, **II:** 338

Just above My Head (Baldwin), **Retro. Supp. II:** 14–15

"Just a Little One" (Parker), **Supp. IX:** 191

Just and the Unjust, The (Cozzens), **I:** 367–370, 372, 375, 377, 378, 379

Just an Ordinary Day (Jackson), **Supp. IX:** 120

Just Before Dark: Collected Nonfiction (Harrison), **Supp. VIII:** 41, 45, 46, 53

Just Before the Divorce (Hayes), **Supp. XXVI:** 144

"Just Before the War with the Eskimos" (Salinger), **III:** 559

"Just Boys" (Farrell), **II:** 45

"Just for the Thrill: An Essay on the Difference between Women and Men" (Carson), **Supp. XII:** 103–104

"Justice" (Hughes), **Supp. I Part 1:** 331

"Justice, A" (Faulkner), **Retro. Supp. I:** 83

Justice, Donald, **Retro. Supp. I:** 313; **Supp. III Part 2:** 541; **Supp. V:** 180, 337, 338, 341; **Supp. VII:** 115–130; **Supp. XI:** 141, 315; **Supp. XIII:** 76, 312; **Supp. XV:** 74, 93, 118, 119, 134; **Supp. XVII:** 110, 120, 246; **Supp. XX:** 199; **Supp. XXIV:** 165

Justice and Expediency (Whitter), **Supp. I Part 2:** 686

"Justice Denied in Massachusetts" (Millay), **III:** 140

Justice for Salcido (Endore), **Supp. XVII:** 63

Justice of Gold in the Damnation of Sinners, The (Edwards), **I:** 559

"Justice to Feminism" (Ozick), **Supp. V:** 272

"Just Introduced" (Taggard), **Supp. XXII:** 274

Just Kids (Smith), **Supp. XXII:** 94

"Just Like a Woman" (Dylan), **Supp. XV:** 350

"Just Like Job" (Angelou), **Supp. IV Part 1:** 15

"Just One of the Boys" (Swados), **Supp. XIX:** 259

Just Whistle: A Valentine (Wright), **Supp. XV:** 346–348

Just Wild About Harry (H. Miller), **III:** 190

Juvenal, **II:** 8, 169, 552

K

K (Rinehart), **Supp. XXV:** 193–194, 200

"K, The" (Olson), **Supp. II Part 2:** 558, 563, 569

Kaaterskill Falls (Goodman), **Supp. XXVI:** 123–125

Kabir, **Supp. IV Part 1:** 74

"Kabnis" (Toomer), **Supp. III Part 2:** 481, 484; **Supp. IX:** 309, 310, 319–320

Kachel, Elsie. *See* Stevens, Mrs. Wallace (Elsie Kachel)

"Kaddish" (Ginsberg), **Supp. II Part 1:** 319, 327

Kaddish and Other Poems, 1958–1960 (Ginsberg), **Supp. II Part 1:** 309, 319–320; **Supp. XIV:** 269

Kael, Pauline, **Supp. IX:** 253; **Supp. XV:** 147, 148

Kafka, Franz, **II:** 244, 565, 569; **III:** 51, 253, 418, 566, 572; **IV:** 2, 113, 218, 437–439, 442; **Retro. Supp. II:** 20, 221, 282; **Supp. I Part 1:** 197; **Supp. III Part 1:** 105; **Supp. III Part 2:** 413; **Supp. IV Part 1:** 379; **Supp. IV Part 2:** 623; **Supp. VIII:** 14, 15, 103; **Supp. XII:** 21, 37, 98, 168; **Supp. XIII:** 305; **Supp. XVI:** 17, 201, 206, 209; **Supp. XVII:** 244; **Supp. XX:** 18, 21, 85, 87; **Supp. XXII:** 89, 90, 94; **Supp. XXIII:** 68

Kafka Americana (Lethem and Scholtz), **Supp. XVIII:** 144–145

Kaganoff, Penny, **Supp. XI:** 122

Kagan's Superfecta (A. Hoffman), **Supp. XVII:** 42

Kahane, Jack, **III:** 171, 178

Kahn, Otto, **I:** 385; **IV:** 123; **Retro. Supp. II:** 81, 84, 85; **Supp. XX:** 75

Kahn, R. T., **Supp. XI:** 216

"Kai, Today" (Snyder), **Supp. VIII:** 300

Kaiser, Georg, **I:** 479

Kaiser, Henry, **Supp. I Part 2:** 644

Kakutani, Michiko, **Supp. IV Part 1:** 196, 201, 205, 211, 212; **Supp. V:** 63; **Supp. VIII:** 81, 84, 86, 88, 141; **Supp. X:** 171, 301, 302, 310, 314; **Supp. XI:** 38, 179; **Supp. XII:** 165, 171, 172, 299; **Supp. XIX:** 142; **Supp. XVI:** 71; **Supp. XVII:** 6; **Supp. XX:** 92, 94; **Supp. XXII:** 109; **Supp. XXVI:** 246

Kalem, T. E., **Supp. IV Part 2:** 585

Kalevala (Finnish epic), **II:** 503, 504; **Retro. Supp. II:** 155

Kalevala (Lönnrot), **Retro. Supp. II:** 159, 160

Kalfus, Ken, **Supp. XVII:** 50

Kalki: A Novel (Vidal), **Supp. IV Part 2:** 677, 682, 685, 691, 692

Kallan, Richard A., **Supp. XX:** 244

Kallen, Horace, **I:** 229; **Supp. I Part 2:** 643; **Supp. XIV:** 195, 197, 198

Kallman, Chester, **II:** 586; **Supp. II Part 1:** 15, 17, 24, 26

"Kallundborg Church" (Whittier), **Supp. I Part 2:** 696

Kalstone, David, **Retro. Supp. II:** 40

Kamel, Rose, **Supp. XIII:** 306

Kamenev, Lev, **Supp. XXI:** 167

Kamera Obskura (Nabokov), **III:** 255

Kamhi, Michelle Moarder, **Supp. IV Part 2:** 529, 530

Kaminsky, Wally, **Supp. XVIII:** 72

Kamp, David, **Supp. XVIII:** 150

Kandy-Kolored Tangerine-Flake Streamline Baby, The (Wolfe), **Supp. III Part 2:** 569, 573–576, 580, 581

Kane, Daniel, **Supp. XXIV:** 37

Kane, Julie, **Supp. XVII:** 78

Kane, Lesley, **Supp. XIV:** 250

Kanellos, Nicolás, **Supp. VIII:** 82; **Supp. XIII:** 213

Kanin, Garson, **Supp. IV Part 2:** 574

"Kansas City Coyote" (Harjo), **Supp. XII:** 219, 222

"Kansas Emigrants, The" (Whittier), **Supp. I Part 2:** 687

Kant, Immanuel, **I:** 61, 277, 278; **II:** 10–11, 362, 480, 580–581, 582, 583; **III:** 300, 480, 481, 488, 612; **IV:** 90; **Supp. I Part 2:** 640; **Supp. IV Part 2:** 527; **Supp. XIV:** 198, 199; **Supp. XVI:** 184

Kanter, Hal, **IV:** 383

Kapital, Das (Marx), **III:** 580; **Supp. XXI:** 161, 162, 163

Kaplan, Abraham, **I:** 277

Kaplan, Justin, **I:** 247–248; **Retro. Supp. I:** 392

Kaplan, Mary Jo, **Supp. XIX:** 266

Kaplan, Steven, **Supp. V:** 238, 241, 243, 248

Karate Is a Thing of the Spirit (Crews), **Supp. XI:** 112–113

Karbo, Karen, **Supp. X:** 259, 262

"Karintha" (Toomer), **Supp. IX:** 311

Karl, Frederick R., **Supp. IV Part 1:** 384; **Supp. XXI:** 234

"Karloff and the Rock" (Di Piero), **Supp. XIX:** 44

Karl Shapiro's America (film), **Supp. II Part 2:** 703

Karmi, T., **Supp. XV:** 78, 88

Karr, Mary, **Supp. XI:** 239–256; **Supp. XIII:** 285; **Supp. XV:** 223; **Supp. XVI:** 63, 70, 77; **Supp. XVII:** 242

Karyotakis, Konstantine, **Supp. XXIII:** 125

Kasabian, Linda, **Supp. IV Part 1:** 206

Kasper, Catherine, **Supp. XVI:** 294–295

Kate Chopin (Toth), **Retro. Supp. II:** 71

Kate Chopin: A Critical Biography (Seyersted), **Retro. Supp. II:** 65; **Supp. I Part 1:** 225

Kate Chopin and Edith Wharton: An Annotated Bibliographical Guide to Secondary Sources (Springer), **Supp. I Part 1:** 225

Kate Chopin and Her Creole Stories (Rankin), **Retro. Supp. II:** 57; **Supp. I Part 1:** 200, 225

"Kate Chopin's *The Awakening* in the Perspective of Her Literary Career" (Arms), **Supp. I Part 1:** 225

Kate Vaiden (Price), **Supp. VI:** 264, 265

"Käthe Kollwitz" (Rukeyser), **Supp. VI:** 283, 284

Katherine and Jean (Rice), **Supp. VII:** 288

"Kathleen" (Whittier), **Supp. I Part 2:** 693

Kathleen and Frank: The Autobiography of a Family (Isherwood), **Supp. XIV:** 158, 171

Kathy Goes to Haiti (Acker), **Supp. XII:** 5

Katz, Alan, **Supp. XXII:** 177

Katz, Alex, **Supp. XV:** 185

Katz, Jonathan, **Supp. XII:** 179

Katz, Steve, **Supp. V:** 44

Katz, Steven T., **Supp. XVI:** 154

Katzenberg, Jffrey, **Supp. XXI:** 154

Kauffman, Carol, **Supp. XI:** 295

Kauffmann, Stanley, **III:** 452; **Supp. I Part 2:** 391; **Supp. XVI:** 74

Kaufman, Boris, **Supp. XVIII:** 251

Kaufman, Charlie, **Supp. XV:** 16

Kaufman, Ellen, **Supp. XXIII:** 132, 133

Kaufman, George S., **II:** 427, 435, 437; **III:** 62, 71–72, 394; **Retro. Supp. II:** 327; **Supp. IV Part 2:** 574; **Supp. IX:** 190; **Supp. XV:** 329

Kaufmann, James, **Supp. XI:** 39

Kaufmann, Walter, **Supp. XVII:** 137

Kauvar, Elaine M., **Supp. V:** 273

Kavanaugh (Longfellow), **I:** 458; **II:** 489, 491; **Retro. Supp. II:** 156; **Supp. I Part 2:** 420

Kaveney, Roz, **Supp. XI:** 39

Kawabata, Yasunari, **Supp. XV:** 186; **Supp. XXI:** 146

Kay Boyle: Artist and Activist (Spanier), **Supp. XXIV:** 64

Kay Boyle: Author of Herself (Mellen), **Supp. XXIV:** 64

Kay Boyle for the Twenty-First Century (Austenfeld, ed.), **Supp. XXIV:** 64

Kaye-Smith, Sheila, **Supp. XVIII:** 130–131

Kazan, Elia, **III:** 153, 163; **IV:** 383; **Supp. I Part 1:** 66, 295; **Supp. XVI:** 193; **Supp. XVIII:** 250–251, 252; **Supp. XXV:** 95, 102

Kazin, Alfred, **I:** 248, 417, 419, 517; **II:** 177, 459; **IV:** 236; **Retro. Supp. II:** 206, 243, 246, 286; **Supp. I Part 1:** 195, 196, 294, 295, 296; **Supp. I Part 2:** 536, 631, 647, 650, 678, 679, 719; **Supp. II Part 1:** 143; **Supp. IV Part 1:** 200, 382; **Supp. IX:** 3, 227; **Supp. V:** 122; **Supp. VIII: 93–111; Supp. XIII:** 98, 106; **Supp. XIV:** 11; **Supp. XV:** 142; **Supp. XXIII:** 2, 106; **Supp. XXIV:** 222

Keach, Stacey, **Supp. XI:** 309

Kean, Danuta, **Supp. XXI:** 80

Keane, Sarah, **Supp. I Part 1:** 100

Kearns, Cleo McNelly, **Retro. Supp. I:** 57

Kearns, George, **Retro. Supp. I:** 292

Keating, AnnLouise, **Supp. IV Part 1:** 330

Keaton, Buster, **I:** 31; **Supp. I Part 2:** 607; **Supp. IV Part 2:** 574

Keaton, Diane, **Supp. XV:** 5

Keats, John, **I:** 34, 103, 284, 314, 317–318, 385, 401, 448; **II:** 82, 88, 97, 214, 368, 512, 516, 530–531, 540, 593; **III:** 4, 10, 45, 122, 133–134, 179, 214, 237, 272, 275, 469, 485, 523; **IV:** 360, 405, 416; **Retro. Supp. I:** 91, 301, 313, 360, 395, 412; **Supp. I Part 1:** 82, 183, 266, 267, 312, 349, 362, 363, 365; **Supp. I Part 2:** 410, 422, 424, 539, 552, 675, 719, 720; **Supp. III Part 1:** 73; **Supp. IV Part 1:** 123, 168, 325; **Supp. IV Part 2:** 455; **Supp. IX:** 38, 39, 45; **Supp. VIII:** 41, 273; **Supp. XI:** 43, 320; **Supp. XII:** 9, 113, 255; **Supp. XIII:** 131, 281; **Supp. XIV:** 274; **Supp. XIX:** 33, 276; **Supp. XV:** 92; **Supp. XVII:** 76, 112; **Supp. XX: 115, 116; Supp. XXI:** 131; **Supp. XXIII:** 159

Keats, John (other), **Supp. IX:** 190, 195, 200

Keegan, Abigail, **Supp. XXIII:** 129, 130, 136

"Keela, the Outcast Indian Maiden" (Welty), **IV:** 263

Keeley, Mary Paxton, **Supp. XV:** 136

"Keen Scalpel on Racial Ills" (Bruell), **Supp. VIII:** 126

Keep, The (Egan), **Supp. XIX:** 49, **56–61**

"*Keep A-Inchin' Along*" (Van Vechten), *Supp. III Part 2:* 744

Keeping (Goldbarth), **Supp. XII:** 179–180, 180

"Keeping Accounts" (Davison), **Supp. XXVI:** 77

"Keeping Informed in D.C." (Nemerov), **III:** 287

Keeping Slug Woman Alive: A Holistic Approach to American Indian Texts (Sarris), **Supp. IV Part 1:** 329

"'Keeping Their World Large'" (Moore), **III:** 201–202

Keeping the Night (Everwine), **Supp. XV:** 75, **81–85,** 86

"Keeping Things Whole" (Strand), **Supp. IV Part 2:** 624

Keep It Simple: A Defense of the Earth (Nichols), **Supp. XIII:** 268

"Keep the Saving Habit" (L. I. Wilder), **Supp. XXII:** 290

"Keep Your Pity" (Boyle), **Supp. XXIV:** 58, 59

Kees, Weldon, **Supp. X:** 118; **Supp. XII:** 198; **Supp. XV:** 113, 114, 115, **133–149**

Kehe, Marjorie, **Supp. XXVI:** 209

Keillor, Garrison, **Supp. XII:** 343; **Supp. XIII:** 274; **Supp. XVI: 165–179; Supp. XXI:** 53, 62; **Supp. XXII:** 83; **Supp. XXIII:** 57, 58, 138

Keillor, Gary Edward. *See* Keillor, Garrison

Keith, Brian, **Supp. IV Part 2:** 474

Keith, Minor C., **I:** 483

Kelleghan, Fiona, **Supp. XVIII:** 136, 139, 140

Keller, A. G., **III:** 108

Keller, Christopher J., **Supp. XVIII:** 192, 195

Keller, Helen, **I:** 254, 258; **Supp. XXIII:** 161

Keller, Lynn, **Supp. IV Part 2:** 423; **Supp. V:** 78, 80

Kelley, David, **Supp. IV Part 2:** 528, 529

Kelley, Florence, **Supp. I Part 1:** 5, 7

Kelley, Mary, **Supp. XVIII:** 257, 260

Kelley, Robin, **Supp. XVIII:** 231

Kellogg, Reverend Edwin H., **III:** 200

Kellogg, Paul U., **Supp. I Part 1:** 5, 7, 12

Kelly, **II:** 464

Kelly, Brigit Pegeen, **Supp. XVII: 123–134; Supp. XXIII:** 54

Kelly, Emmett, **Supp. XI:** 99, 106

Kelly, Gene, **Supp. XXI:** 148

Kelly, James Patrick, **Supp. XIX:** 231; **Supp. XVIII:** 145

Kelly, Walt, **Supp. XI:** 105

Kelly, William, **Supp. XV:** 75, 88

Kelsey, Penelope Myrtle, **Supp. XXIII:** 143, 153–164

Kelsh, Nick, **Supp. XVII:** 167, 179

Kemble, Fanny, **Retro. Supp. I:** 228

Kemble, Gouverneur, **II:** 298

Kemble, Peter, **II:** 298

Kempf, Andrea, **Supp. XXVI:** 212

Kempton, Murray, **Supp. VIII:** 104

Kempton-Wace Letters, The (London and Strunsky), **II:** 465

Kendall, Elaine, **Supp. XXVI:** 121

Kennan, George F., **Supp. VIII:** 241

Kennedy, Albert J., **Supp. I Part 1:** 19

Kennedy, Archibald, **Supp. XXVI:** 84

Kennedy, Arthur, **III:** 153

Kennedy, Burt, **Supp. IV Part 1:** 236

Kennedy, Jeffery, **Supp. XXI:** 6; **Supp. XXV:** 20

Kennedy, J. Gerald, **Retro. Supp. II:** 271

Kennedy, John F., **I:** 136, 170; **II:** 49, 152–153; **III:** 38, 41, 42, 234, 411, 415, 581; **IV:** 229; **Supp. I Part 1:** 291; **Supp. I Part 2:** 496; **Supp. VIII:** 98, 104, 203; **Supp. XII:** 132; **Supp. XXVI:** 43

Kennedy, Mrs. John F., **I:** 136

Kennedy, John Pendleton, **II:** 313; **Supp. XXII:** 193

Kennedy, Robert, **Supp. V:** 291

Kennedy, Robert F., **I:** 294; **Supp. I Part 1:** 52; **Supp. XI:** 343

Kennedy, Sarah, **Supp. XVIII:** 293, 299, 301

Kennedy, William, **Supp. VII: 131–157; Supp. XIX:** 141; **Supp. XVII:** 135; **Supp. XX: 90; Supp. XXIV:** 281, 282, 283

Kennedy, X. J., **Supp. V:** 178, 182; **Supp. XV:** 113, **151–173**

Kenner, Hugh, **III:** 475, 478; **IV:** 412; **Supp. I Part 1:** 255; **Supp. IV Part 2:** 474; **Supp. XV:** 147; **Supp. XXI:** 235; **Supp. XXVI:** 228

Kenneth Koch, a Tragedy (O'Hara and Rivers), **Supp. XXIII:** 217

"Kenneth Koch's 'Serious Moment' " (Spurr), **Supp. XV:** 183

Kenneth Millar/Ross Macdonald: A Checklist (Bruccoli), **Supp. IV Part 2:** 464, 469, 471

Kenney, Michael, **Supp. XIX:** 51, 52–53

Kenney, Susan, **Supp. XVIII:** 288, 289

Kenny, Maurice, **Supp. IV Part 2:** 502; **Supp. XXIII: 143–159**

Kent, George, **Supp. IV Part 1:** 11

Kent, Rockwell, **Supp. XV:** 41; **Supp. XXII:** 281

Kenton, Edna, **Supp. XXI:** 6; **Supp. XXV:** 21

Kenton, Maxwell. *See* Burnett, David; Hoffenberg, Mason; Southern, Terry

"Kent State, May 1970" (Haines), **Supp. XII:** 211

"Kentucky Derby Is Decadent and Depraved, The" (Thompson), **Supp. XXIV:** 282, **287–288**

Kentucky Straight (Offutt), **Supp. XIX: 163–167,** 171, 172

Kenya, the Land of Conflict (Kenyatta), **Supp. XXI:** 166

Kenyatta, Jomo, **Supp. X:** 135; **Supp. XXI:** 166

Kenyon, Jane, **Supp. VII: 159–177; Supp. VIII:** 272

Keogh, Tom, **Supp. XVI:** 230

Kepler, Johannes, **III:** 484; **IV:** 18

Keplinger, David, **Supp. XIX:** 273

Keppel, Frederick P., **I:** 214

"Kéramos" (Longfellow), **II:** 494; **Retro. Supp. II:** 167, 169

Kéramos and Other Poems (Longfellow), **II:** 490

Kerber, Linda K., **Supp. XXV:** 44

Kercheval, Jesse Lee, **Supp. XIX:** 51

Kerim, Ussin, **Supp. IX:** 152

Kermode, Frank, **IV:** 133; **Retro. Supp. I:** 301

Kern, Jerome, **II:** 427

Kerouac, Jack, **III:** 174; **Retro. Supp. I:** 102; **Supp. II Part 1:** 31, 307, 309, 318, 328; **Supp. III Part 1:** 91–94, 96, 100, **217–234; Supp. IV Part 1:** 90, 146; **Supp. IX:** 246; **Supp. V:** 336; **Supp. VIII:** 42, 138, 289, 305; **Supp. XII:** 118, 121, 122, 123, 126, 131, 132; **Supp. XIII:** 275, 284; **Supp. XIV:** 137, 138, 141, 142, 143–144; **Supp. XV:** 134, 221; **Supp. XVI:** 123; **Supp. XVII:** 135, 138; **Supp. XX:** 17; **Supp. XXIII:** 100, 213; **Supp. XXIV:** 34, 44; **Supp. XXV:** 29; **Supp. XXVI:** 252

Kerr, Deborah, **Supp. XI:** 307

Kerr, Orpheus C. (pseudonym). *See* Newell, Henry

Kerr, Walter, **Supp. IV Part 2:** 575, 579

Kerridge, Richard, **Supp. XVI:** 26

Kesey, Ken, **III:** 558; **Supp. III Part 1:** 217; **Supp. V:** 220, 295; **Supp. X:** 24,

265; **Supp. XI:** 104; **Supp. XXIII:** 100

Kessel, John, **Supp. XIX:** 231; **Supp. XVIII:** 145

Kessler, Milton, **Supp. XIX:** 195

Kessler, Rod, **Supp. XXVI:** 156

Kesten, Stephen, **Supp. XI:** 309

Ketchum, Liza, **Supp. XIX:** 266

Ketchup (Shanley), **Supp. XIV:** 315

Kevane, Bridget, **Supp. XI:** 185, 190

"Key, The" (Welty), **IV:** 262

"Keys" (Nye), **Supp. XIII:** 281

"Key to the Highway" (Halliday), **Supp. XIX:** 84

Key to Uncle Tom's Cabin, A (Stowe), **Supp. I Part 2:** 580

Key West (H. Crane), **Retro. Supp. II:** 84

"Key West" (H. Crane), **I:** 400

Key West: An Island Sheaf (Crane), **I:** 385, 399–402

"Khalil the Heretic" (Gibran), **Supp. XX:** 124

Khrushchev, Nikita, **I:** 136

Kiang Kang-hu, **Supp. XV:** 45, 47

Kick for a Bite, A (Cobbett), **Supp. XV:** 237

"Kicking the Candles Out" (Jarman), **Supp. XVII:** 113

Kid, The (Aiken), **I:** 61

Kid, The (Chaplin), **I:** 386

Kidder, Tracy, **Supp. III Part 1:** 302; **Supp. XVIII:** 106, 114

Kiddush Ha-Shem: An Epic of 1648 (Asch), **Supp. XXIII:** 3, 6, **10,** 11, 12, 16

Kidesh ha-Shem (Sanctification of the name) (Asch), **Supp. XXIII:** 6

Kidman, Nicole, **Supp. X:** 80

"Kidnaper" (Gallagher), **Supp. XXIV:** 168, 174

"Kidnapping in the Family, A" (Fante), **Supp. XI:** 164

"Kid's Guide to Divorce, The" (Moore), **Supp. X:** 167, 172

Kidwell, Clara Sue, **Supp. IV Part 1:** 333

Kielsky, Vera Emuna, **Supp. V:** 273

Kiely, Brendan, **Supp. XVII:** 75

Kieran, John, **II:** 417

Kierkegaard, Søren Aabye, **II:** 229; **III:** 292, 305, 309, 572; **IV:** 438, 491; **Retro. Supp. I:** 326; **Retro. Supp. II:** 222; **Supp. V:** 9; **Supp. VIII:** 7–8; **Supp. XX:** 132

Kiernan, Robert F., **Supp. IV Part 2:** 684

Kieseritsky, L., **III:** 252

Kilgo, Jim, **Supp. XVIII:** 192

"Kilim" (McClatchy), **Supp. XII:** 258

Kilina, Patricia (pseudonym). *See* Warren, Patricia Nell

"Killed at Resaca" (Bierce), **I:** 202

"Killed at the Ford" (Longfellow), **Retro. Supp. II:** 170–171

Killens, John Oliver, **Supp. IV Part 1:** 8, 369

"Killer in the Rain" (Chandler), **Supp. IV Part 1:** 122

"Killers, The" (Hemingway), **II:** 249; **Retro. Supp. I:** 188, 189

Killers, The: A Narrative of Real Life in Philadelphia (Lippard), **Supp. XXIII:** 178, 184

Killing Mister Watson (Matthiessen), **Supp. V:** 212, 214

"Killing of a State Cop, The" (Ortiz), **Supp. IV Part 2:** 499

Killing of Sister George, The (Marcus), **Supp. I Part 1:** 277

Killing Orders (Paretsky), **Supp. XXV:** 176, 177, 179, 182–813

"Killings" (Dubus), **Supp. VII:** 85–86

"Killing the Ghost of Ripton" (Carruth), **Supp. XIX:** 1

"Killing the Plants" (Kenyon), **Supp. VII:** 167, 168

Kilmer, Joyce, **Supp. I Part 2:** 387; **Supp. XV:** 294

Kilpatrick, James K., **Supp. X:** 145

Kilvert, Francis, **Supp. VIII:** 172

Kim (Kipling), **Supp. X:** 230

Kim, Alfred, **Supp. XI:** 140

Kim, Sharon, **Supp. XVIII:** 267

Kimball, Frederic, **Supp. XXI:** 146

Kimball, J. Golden, **Supp. IV Part 2:** 602

Kimbrough, Mary Craig. *See* Sinclair, Mary Craig (Mary Craig Kimbrough)

Kimes, Maymie B., **Supp. IX:** 178

Kimes, William F., **Supp. IX:** 178

Kimmelman, Bert, **Supp. XXI:** 24

Kimura, Takeshi, **Supp. XXVI:** 88

"Kin" (Welty), **IV:** 277; **Retro. Supp. I:** 353

Kinard, Agnes Dodds, **Supp. XIV:** 122, 123, 127

Kincaid, Jamaica, **Supp. VII: 179–196**

Kincaid, James, **Supp. XVIII:** 62, 63

"Kindness" (Dunn), **Supp. XI:** 149, 150

"Kindness" (Nye), **Supp. XIII:** 285

"Kindness" (Plath), **Retro. Supp. II:** 256

Kind of Light that Shines on Texas, The (McKnight), **Supp. XX: 151–152**

"Kind of Light that Shines on Texas, The" (McKnight), **Supp. XX: 151**

Kind of Order, A Kind of Folly, A: Essays and Conversations (Kunitz), **Supp. III Part 1:** 262, 268

Kindred (O. Butler), **Supp. XIII: 59–60,** 69

"Kind Sir: These Woods" (Sexton), **Supp. II Part 2:** 673

Kinds of Love (Sarton), **Supp. VIII: 253– 254,** 256

Kinfolk (Buck), **Supp. II Part 1:** 126

King, Alexander, **IV:** 287

King, Carole, **Supp. XII:** 308

King, Clarence, **I:** 1

King, Ernest, **Supp. I Part 2:** 491

King, Fisher, **II:** 425

King, Francis, **Supp. XIV:** 155, 156, 166, 169

King, Grace, **Retro. Supp. II:** 136

King, Martin Luther, Jr., **Retro. Supp. II:** 12, 13; **Supp. XVIII:** 24; **Supp. XX: 281**

King, Michael, **Supp. XII:** 182

King, Queen, Knave (Nabokov), **III:** 251; **Retro. Supp. I:** 270

King, Starr, **Supp. II Part 1:** 341, 342

King, Stephen, **Supp. IV Part 1:** 102, 104; **Supp. IV Part 2:** 467; **Supp. IX:** 114; **Supp. V:** 137–155; **Supp. XIII:** 53; **Supp. XXIII:** 290; **Supp. XXV:** 123, 152, 153

King, Tabitha (Mrs. Stephen King), **Supp. V:** 137

King, The (Barthelme), **Supp. IV Part 1:** 47, 52

"King, The" (Gibran), **Supp. XX: 123–124**

King Coffin (Aiken), **I:** 53–54, 57

"King David" (Benét), **Supp. XI:** 44

"King David" (Reznikoff), **Supp. XIV:** 283

Kingdom and the Power, The (Talese), **Supp. XVII:** 202, 203, 204, 210

Kingdom by the Sea, The: A Journey around Great Britain (Theroux), **Supp. VIII:** 323

"Kingdom County Come" (Mosher), **Supp. XXII:** 211–212

Kingdom Far and Clear, A: The Complete Swan Lake Trilogy (Helprin), **Supp. XXV:** 87

Kingdom of Earth (T. Williams), **IV:** 382, 386, 387, 388, 391, 393, 398

"Kingdom of Earth, The" (T. Williams), **IV:** 384

Kingdom of Fear (Thompson), **Supp. XXIV:** 283

"Kingdom of God Is Within You, The" (Very), **Supp. XXV:** 249

Kingfisher, The (Clampitt), **Supp. IX:** 38

"Kingfishers, The" (Olson), **Supp. II Part 2:** 557, 558–563, 582

King Jasper (Robinson), **III:** 523

King Kong (film), **Supp. IV Part 1:** 104; **Supp. XVII:** 58

King Lear (Shakespeare), **I:** 538; **II:** 540, 551; **Retro. Supp. I:** 248; **Supp. IV Part 1:** 31, 36; **Supp. IX:** 14; **Supp. XI:** 172; **Supp. XV:** 349

King Leopold's Soliloquy (Twain), **IV:** 208

King My Father's Wreck, The (Simpson), **Supp. IX:** 266, 267, 270, 275, 276

King of Babylon Shall Not Come Against You, The (Garrett), **Supp. VII:** 110–111; **Supp. X:** 3

"King of Beasts" (P. N. Warren), **Supp. XX: 272**

"King of Folly Island, The" (Jewett), **II:** 394; **Retro. Supp. II:** 132, 133

King of Kings (film), **Supp. IV Part 2:** 520

King of Paris (Endore), **Supp. XVII:** 64

King of Spain, The (Bodenheim), **Supp. XXV:** 26

"King of the Bingo Game" (Ellison), **Retro. Supp. II:** 117, 125; **Supp. II Part 1:** 235, 238, 240–241

"King of the Cats, The" (Benét), **Supp. XI:** 49–50

"King of the Clock Tower" (Yeats), **III:** 473

"King of the Desert, The" (O'Hara), **III:** 369

King of the Fields, The (Singer), **Retro. Supp. II:** 317

King of the Jews (Epstein), **Supp. XII:** 161, **166–170**, 172

King of the Mountain (Garrett), **Supp. VII:** 96, 97

"King of the River" (Kunitz), **Supp. III Part 1:** 263, 267–268

"King of the Sea" (Marquand), **III:** 60

"King over the Water" (Blackmur), **Supp. II Part 1:** 107

"King Pandar" (Blackmur), **Supp. II Part 1:** 92, 102

"King Pest" (Poe), **Retro. Supp. II:** 273

Kingsblood Royal (Lewis), **II:** 456

Kingsbury, John, **Supp. I Part 1:** 8

"King's Daughters, Home for Unwed Mothers, 1948" (Stanford), **Supp. XV:** 345

King's Henchman, The (Millay), **III:** 138–139

Kingsley, Sidney, **Supp. I Part 1:** 277, 281

King's Mare, The (Canolle; Loos, trans.), **Supp. XVI:** 194

"King's Missive, The" (Whittier), **Supp. I Part 2:** 694

Kingsolver, Barbara, **Supp. VII: 197–214; Supp. XIII:** 16; **Supp. XVIII:** 189

King's Stilts, The (Geisel), **Supp. XVI:** 100, 104

Kingston, Earll, **Supp. V:** 160

Kingston, Maxine Hong, **Supp. IV Part 1:** 1, 12; **Supp. V: 157–175,** 250; **Supp. X:** 291–292; **Supp. XI:** 18, 245; **Supp. XV:** 220, 223

"King Volmer and Elsie" (Whittier), **Supp. I Part 2:** 696

Kinkaid, Jamaica, **Supp. XXII:** 65

Kinmont, Alexander, **Supp. I Part 2:** 588–589

Kinnaird, John, **Retro. Supp. I:** 399

Kinnell, Galway, **Supp. III Part 1: 235–256; Supp. III Part 2:** 541; **Supp. IV Part 2:** 623; **Supp. V:** 332; **Supp. VIII:** 39; **Supp. XI:** 139; **Supp. XII:** 241; **Supp. XV:** 212; **Supp. XVI:** 53; **Supp. XXII:** 83; **Supp. XXVI:** 67

Kinsella, Thomas, **Supp. XX: 195–196, 197, 207**

Kinsey, Alfred, **IV:** 230; **Supp. XIV:** 140

Kinzie, Mary, **Supp. XII:** 181; **Supp. XXIII:** 124

"Kipling" (Trilling), **Supp. III Part 2:** 495

Kipling, Rudyard, **I:** 421, 587–588; **II:** 271, 338, 404, 439; **III:** 55, 328, 508, 511, 521, 524, 579; **IV:** 429; **Supp. IV Part 2:** 603; **Supp. X:** 255; **Supp. XX: 23**

Kirby, David, **Supp. XIII:** 89; **Supp. XIX:** 81

Kirkland, Caroline, **Supp. XVIII:** 258

Kirkland, David, **Supp. XVI:** 186

Kirkland, Jack, **I:** 297

Kirkland, John, **Supp. XXIV:** 70

Kirkpatrick, Jeane, **Supp. VIII:** 241

Kirkus, Virginia, **Supp. XV:** 198

Kirkwood, Cynthia A., **Supp. XI:** 177, 178, 179

Kirp, David L., **Supp. XI:** 129

Kirsch, Adam, **Supp. XV:** 251, 260, 264, 266, 341, 347, 350–351; **Supp. XXV:** 222, 233, 253, 262, 268

Kirstein, Lincoln, **Supp. II Part 1:** 90, 97; **Supp. IV Part 1:** 82, 83; **Supp. XXII:** 281

Kishef-makherin fun Kastilye, Di (The witch of Castle) (Asch), **Supp. XXIII:** 6

"Kiss, The" (Di Piero), **Supp. XIX:** 45, 47

Kiss, The (Harrison), **Supp. X:** 191

"Kiss, The" (Sexton), **Supp. II Part 2:** 687

"Kiss Away" (C. Baxter), **Supp. XVII:** 20

Kissel, Howard, **Supp. IV Part 2:** 580

Kiss Hollywood Good-by (Loos), **Supp. XVI:** 190, 195

Kissinger, Henry, **Supp. IV Part 1:** 388; **Supp. XII:** 9, 14; **Supp. XXV:** 264

Kiss of the Spider Woman, the Musical (McNally), **Supp. XIII:** 207, **Supp. XIII:** 208

Kiss Tomorrow Good-bye (McCoy), **Supp. XIII:** 170, **172–173,** 174

"Kit and Caboodle" (Komunyakaa), **Supp. XIII:** 115

Kit Brandon: A Portrait (Anderson), **I:** 111

Kitchen, Judith, **Supp. IV Part 1:** 242, 245, 252; **Supp. IX:** 163; **Supp. XI:** 312, 313, 315, 317, 319, 320, 326, 329; **Supp. XV:** 215, 219; **Supp. XXVI:** 154–155

"Kitchenette" (Brooks), **Retro. Supp. I:** 208

Kitchen God's Wife, The (Tan), **Supp. X:** 289, 292, 293, 294–295, 296–297, 298–299

"Kitchen Terrarium: 1983" (McCarriston), **Supp. XIV:** 270

Kit O'Brien (Masters), **Supp. I Part 2:** 471

Kittel, Frederick August. *See* Wilson, August

Kittredge, Charmian. *See* London, Mrs. Jack (Charmian Kittredge)

Kittredge, William, **Supp. VIII:** 39; **Supp. XI:** 316; **Supp. XII:** 209; **Supp. XIII:** 16; **Supp. XXVI: 177–190**

"Kitty Hawk" (Frost), **II:** 164; **Retro. Supp. I:** 124, 141

Kizer, Carolyn, **Supp. XVII:** 71, 72, 73, 74

Klaidman, Stephen, **Supp. XIX:** 269

Klail City (Hinojosa), **Supp. XIX: 97, 101–103**

Klail City Death Trip (Hinojosa). *See Ask a Policeman* (Hinojosa); *Becky and Her Friends* (Hinojosa); *Dear Rafe* (Hinojosa); *Fair Gentlemen of Belken County* (Hinojosa); *Klail City* (Hinojosa); *Korean Love Songs from Klail City Death Trip* (Hinojosa); *Partners in Crime: A Rafe Buenrostro Mystery* (Hinojosa); *Rites and Witnesses: A Comedy* (Hinojosa); *Useless Servants, The* (Hinojosa); *Valley, The* (Hinojosa)

"Klassikal Lymnaeryx" (Stallings), **Supp. XXV:** 233

Klein, Joe, **Supp. XII:** 67–68

Klein, Marcus, **Supp. I Part 2:** 432; **Supp. XI:** 233

Kleist, Heinrich von, **Supp. IV Part 1:** 224

Kline, Franz, **Supp. XII:** 198; **Supp. XXIII:** 210, 211, 217

Kline, George, **Supp. VIII:** 22, 28

Klinghoffer, David, **Supp. XVI:** 74

Klinkowitz, Jerome, **Supp. IV Part 1:** 40; **Supp. X:** 263; **Supp. XI:** 347; **Supp. XXI:** 233

Klise, James, **Supp. XXII:** 53

Kloefkorn, Bill, **Supp. XIX:** 119

Knapp, Adeline, **Supp. XI:** 200

Knapp, Friedrich, **III:** 100

Knapp, Samuel, **I:** 336

Knapp, Samuel Lorenzo, **Supp. XV:** 246

"Kneeling Down to Look into a Culvert" (R. Bly), **Supp. XXI:** 88

Kneel to the Rising Sun (Caldwell), **I:** 304, 309

"Knees/Dura-Europos" (Goldbarth), **Supp. XII:** 185

"Knife" (Simic), **Supp. VIII:** 275

"Knife Longs for the Ruby, The" (Vaz), **Supp. XXVI:** 266–267

Knight, Arthur, **Supp. XIV:** 144

Knight, Etheridge, **Supp. XI:** 239; **Supp. XXIII:** 174

Knight, Lania, **Supp. XXIII:** 273, 274, 275, 276, 279, 280

"Knight in Disguise, The" (Lindsay), **Supp. I Part 2:** 390

Knightly Quest, The (T. Williams), **IV:** 383

Knight's Gambit (Faulkner), **II:** 72

Knish, Anne. *See* Ficke, Arthur Davison

"Knit One, Purl Two" (K. Snodgrass), **Supp. XVI:** 42

"Knock" (Dickey), **Supp. IV Part 1:** 182

Knocked Out Loaded (album, Dylan), **Supp. XVIII:** 28

"Knocking Around" (Ashbery), **Supp. III Part 1:** 22

"Knocking on Heaven's Door" (Lamott), **Supp. XX:** 140–141

"Knocking on Three, Winston" (Epstein), **Supp. XIV:** 109

Knock on Any Door (film, Ray), **Supp. XVII:** 150

Knock on Any Door (W. Motley), 158; **Supp. XVII: 150–155,** 159, 160

Knockout Artist, The (Crews), **Supp. XI: 113–114**

Knoll, Robert E., **Supp. XV:** 118

Knopf, Alfred A., **III:** 99, 105, 106, 107; **Retro. Supp. I:** 13, 19, 317; **Supp. I Part 1:** 324, 325, 327; **Supp. IV Part 1:** 125, 354; **Supp. XIII:** 172

Knopf, Blanche, **Supp. I Part 1:** 324, 325, 327, 328, 332, 341; **Supp. IV Part 1:** 128, 346, 348; **Supp. XIII:** 169

"Knot, The" (Rich), **Supp. I Part 2:** 555

Knot-Holes (Bodenheim and Saphier), **Supp. XXV:** 20

Knotts, Kristina, **Supp. XIII:** 238

"Knowing, The" (Olds), **Supp. X:** 215

"Knowledge Forwards and Backwards" (Stern), **Supp. IX:** 296

"Knowledge of Plates" (Bronk), **Supp. XXI:** 33

Knowles, John, **Supp. IV Part 2:** 679; **Supp. XII: 235–250; Supp. XX:** 84

Known World, The (E. P. Jones), **Supp. XXII:** 139, 140, 142, **146–150,** 150

Knox, Bernard, **Supp. XXIV:** 153

Knox, Frank, **Supp. I Part 2:** 488, 489

Knox, Israel, **Supp. X:** 70

Knox, Vicesimus, **II:** 8

Knoxville: Summer of 1915 (Agee), **I:** 42–46

Knudson, R. Rozanne, **Supp. IV Part 2:** 648

Kober, Arthur, **Supp. I Part 1:** 292

Koch, Frederick, **IV:** 453

Koch, John, **Supp. VIII:** 88

Koch, Kenneth, **Supp. XIX:** 81; **Supp. XV: 175–192; Supp. XXIII:** 124, 207, 209, 210, 211, 215, 217, 220; **Supp. XXIV:** 33, 36, 42, 44

Koch, Vivienne, **III:** 194; **IV:** 136, 140; **Retro. Supp. I:** 428, 430

"Kochinnenako in Academe: Three Approaches to Interpreting a Keres Indian Tale" (Gunn Allen), **Supp. IV Part 1:** 329

"Kodachromes of the Island" (Hayden), **Supp. II Part 1:** 367, 380

Koestler, Arthur, **I:** 258; **Supp. I Part 2:** 671; **Supp. XXIII:** 1

Kokkinen, Eila, **Supp. XIV:** 146, 148

"Kola Street"(Asch), **Supp. XXIII:** 7

Kolba, Ellen D., **Supp. XVIII:** 257

Kolbenheyer, Dr. Frederick, **Supp. I Part 1:** 207

Kolodny, Annette, **Supp. X:** 97, 103, 229

Komisarjevsky, W. P., **Supp. XXIII:** 5

"Komodo" (C. Frost), **Supp. XV:** 95

Komunyakaa, Yusef, **Supp. XIII: 111–136; Supp. XXI:** 129, 139; **Supp. XXIII:** 254

Konigsberg, Allan Stewart. *See* Allen, Woody

Kon-Tiki (Heyerdahl), **II:** 477

Koopman, Harry Lyman, **Retro. Supp. I:** 40

Ko; or, A Season on Earth (Koch), **Supp. XV:** 175, 180, 181, 183, 186

Kooser, Ted, **Supp. XIX: 115–130; Supp. XV:** 113, 115; **Supp. XXI:** 243

Kootz, Samuel, **Supp. XV:** 144

Kora and Ka (Doolittle), **Supp. I Part 1:** 270

Kora in Hell (W. C. Williams), **Retro. Supp. I:** 416, **417–418,** 419, 430, 431; **Supp. XXI:** 232

Korb, Rena, **Supp. XI:** 2

Korczak, Janosz, **Supp. X:** 70

Korean Love Songs from Klail City Death Trip (Hinojosa), **Supp. XIX:** 98, **103–104**

Kornblatt, Joyce Reiser, **Supp. XV:** 62

Kornfield, Jack, **Supp. XX: 142; Supp. XXIII:** 138

Korrektur (Bernhard), **Supp. XX:** 91

Kort, Amy, **Supp. XIII:** 148

Korwin, Yala, **Supp. XXI:** 99

Kosinski, Jerzy, **Supp. VII: 215–228; Supp. XII:** 21

"Kostas Tympakianakis" (Merrill), **Supp. III Part 1:** 326

Koteliansky, S. S., **Supp. VIII:** 251, 265

Kouidis, Virginia M., **Supp. XXII:** 161, 162, 166, 167, 169

Kovic, Ron, **Supp. XIX:** 17; **Supp. XXII:** 104

Kowloon Tong (Theroux), **Supp. VIII:** 325

Kozlenko, William, **IV:** 378, 381

Krabbenhoft, Ken, **Supp. XVII:** 112

Kraft, James, **Supp. XV:** 40, 41, 42, 43, 52

Krakauer, Jon, **Supp. XVII:** 210; **Supp. XVIII: 105–118**

Kramer, Dale, **Supp. I Part 2:** 669

Kramer, Glenn Philip, **Supp. XXIII:** 125

Kramer, Hilton, **III:** 537; **Supp. I Part 1:** 295, 296; **Supp. VIII:** 239; **Supp. XIX:** 269; **Supp. XV:** 113

Kramer, Lawrence, **Supp. IV Part 1:** 61, 65, 66; **Supp. IX:** 291

Kramer, Peter D., **Supp. XVI:** 229

Kramer, Robert, **Supp. XXVI:** 26

Kramer, Stanley, **II:** 421, 587

Krapp's Last Tape (Beckett), **I:** 71; **III:** 387; **Retro. Supp. I:** 206

Krassner, Paul, **Supp. IV Part 1:** 385; **Supp. XI:** 293

Kraus, Karl, **Supp. XX: 84**

Krauth, Leland, **Supp. XVIII:** 58

Krauzer, Steven M., **Supp. XXVI:** 181, 182, 188

Kreisler, Harry, **Supp. XVI:** 155

Kreitman, Esther, **IV:** 2

Krementz, Jill, **Supp. XXV:** 263

"Kremlin of Smoke" (Schnackenberg), **Supp. XV:** 257–258

Kreyling, Michael, **Supp. XXVI:** 14

Kreymborg, Alfred, **II:** 530; **III:** 465; **IV:** 76; **Retro. Supp. I:** 417; **Supp. XV:** 301, 306; **Supp. XXII:** 161–162; **Supp. XXV:** 18, 19, 21

Kriegel, Leonard, **Supp. XXIV: 213–228**

Krim, Seymour, **Supp. XV:** 338; **Supp. XVI:** 217; **Supp. XVIII:** 285

Krisak, Len, **Supp. XXI:** 99, 104

Kristeva, Julia, **Supp. XII:** 6

Kristofferson, Kris, **Supp. XIII:** 119

Kristol, Irving, **Supp. VIII:** 93, 244; **Supp. XIII:** 98

Kristwald, Elfriede, **Supp. XXVI:** 4, 7

Krivak, Andrew, **Supp. XVII:** 242

Kroll, Jack, **Supp. IV Part 2:** 590; **Supp. XXIII:** 103

Kroll, Judith, **Supp. I Part 2:** 541–543, 544, 546

Kroll Ring, Frances. *See* Ring, Frances Kroll

Krondorfer, Björn, **Supp. XVI:** 160

Kronenberger, Louis, **Supp. XXII:** 191, 192

Krook, Dorothea, **Retro. Supp. II:** 243

Kropotkin, Peter, **I:** 493; **Supp. I Part 1:** 5; **Supp. IV Part 2:** 521

Kruif, Paul de, **II:** 446

Krupat, Arnold, **Supp. IV Part 2:** 500

Krupnick, Mark, **Supp. XVI:** 153
Krutch, Joseph Wood, **II:** 459; **III:** 425; **IV:** 70, 175
Krutikov, Mikhail, **Supp. XXIII:** 11
Kubach, David, **Supp. XXVI:** 243, 245, 246, 248
Kublai Khan, **III:** 395
"Kubla Khan" (Coleridge), **Supp. XIII:** 131, 283
Kubrick, Stanley, **Supp. IV Part 1:** 392; **Supp. XI:** 293,**Supp. XI:** 301, 302–303
"Kubuku Rides (This Is It) " (L. Brown), **Supp. XXI:** 39, 42–43
Kuehl, John, **Supp. IV Part 1:** 279, 284, 285, 287
Kuehl, Linda, **Supp. IV Part 1:** 199
"Kugelmass Episode, The" (Allen), **Supp. XV:** 15, 16
Kukachin, Princess, **III:** 395
"Ku Klux" (Hughes), **Retro. Supp. I:** 205
Kulshrestha, Chirantan, **Retro. Supp. II:** 21
Kumin, Maxine, **Supp. IV Part 2: 439–457; Supp. XIII:** 294; **Supp. XVII:** 71, 75–76; **Supp. XX: 164; Supp. XXVI:** 68
Kundera, Milan, **Supp. VIII:** 241
Kunerth, Jeff, **Supp. XXI:** 47
Kunitz, Stanley, **I:** 179, 180, 181, 182, 521; **II:** 545; **Supp. III Part 1: 257–270; Supp. V:** 79; **Supp. XI:** 259; **Supp. XIII:** 341; **Supp. XXVI:** 64, 67, 68
Kuo, Helena, **Supp. X:** 291
Kuropatkin, General Aleksei Nikolaevich, **III:** 247–248
Kurth, Peter, **Supp. XVIII:** 145
Kurzy of the Sea (Barnes), **Supp. III Part 1:** 34
Kushner, Tony, **Supp. IX: 131–149; Supp. XX: 177; Supp. XXI:** 145; **Supp. XXIV:** 263
Kussy, Bella, **IV:** 468
Kutnik, Jerzy, **Supp. XXII:** 177
Kuttner, Henry, **Supp. IV Part 1:** 102
Kuzma, Greg, **Supp. XV:** 118
Kyger, Joanne, **Supp. XXIV:** 37

L

LaBastille, Anne, **Supp. X: 95–110; Supp. XXVI:** 34
"Labor's Cultural Degradation" (Swados), **Supp. XIX:** 264–265
"Labours of Hercules, The" (Moore), **III:** 201
La Bruyère, Jean de, **I:** 58
La Bufera e Altro (Montale), **Supp. V:** 337
LaBute, Neil, **Supp. XXI:** 147
Labyrinth of Love (Untermeyer), **Supp. XV:** 312
Labyrinth of Solitude, The (Paz), **Supp. XIII:** 223
Lacan, Jacques, **Supp. IV Part 1:** 45; **Supp. VIII:** 5; **Supp. XII:** 98
La Casa en Mango Street (Cisneros), **Supp. VII:** 58–59
Lacayo, Richard, **Supp. XXV:** 4

Lachaise, Gaston, **I:** 434
"Lackawanna" (Merwin), **Supp. III Part 1:** 350
Lackawanna Elegy (Goll; Kinnell, trans.), **Supp. III Part 1:** 235, 243–244
Laclède, Pierre, **Supp. I Part 1:** 205
"Lacquer Prints" (Lowell), **II:** 524–525
Lacy, Ed, **Supp. XV: 193–210**
Ladder, The (Rasmussen; Nelson, trans.), **Supp. XVIII:** 180–181
Ladder of Years (Tyler), **Supp. IV Part 2:** 657, 671–672
Ladders to Fire (Nin), **Supp. X:** 185
Laddie (Stratton-Porter), **Supp. XX: 211, 213**
"Laddie, the Princess and the Pie" (Stratton-Porter), **Supp. XX:** 216
"Ladies" (Coleman), **Supp. XI:** 93
Ladies Almanack (Barnes), **Supp. III Part 1:** 37–39, 42; **Supp. XXII:** 167
Ladies Auxiliary, The (Mirvis), **Supp. XX: 177, 179–185**
"Ladies in Spring" (Welty), **IV:** 276–277; **Retro. Supp. I:** 353
Lady, The (Richter), **Supp. XVIII: 211–212,** 220
Lady Audley's Secret (Braddon), **Supp. I Part 1:** 35, 36
"Lady Barberina" (James), **Retro. Supp. I:** 227
"Lady Bates" (Jarrell), **II:** 380–381
Lady Chatterley's Lover (Lawrence), **III:** 170; **IV:** 434; **Supp. XVI:** 267
Ladye Annabel (Lippard), **Supp. XXIII:** 178
Lady from Louisiana (film, Vorhaus), **Supp. XVII:** 59
"Lady from Redhorse, A" (Bierce), **I:** 203
Lady in Kicking Horse Reservoir, The (Hugo), **Supp. VI:** 134, **138–139**
Lady in the Lake, The (Chandler), **Supp. IV Part 1:** 127, 129–130
"Lady in the Lake, The" (Chandler), **Supp. IV Part 1:** 129
Lady in the Lake, The (film), **Supp. IV Part 1:** 130
"Lady in the Pink Mustang, The" (Erdrich), **Supp. IV Part 1:** 270
"Lady Is Civilized, The" (Taylor), **Supp. V:** 315
Lady Is Cold, The (White), **Supp. I Part 2:** 653
Lady Killer (Holding), **Supp. XXII: 126, 127,** 130
"Lady Lazarus" (Plath), **Retro. Supp. II:** 250, 251, 255; **Supp. I Part 2:** 529, 535, 542, 545
Lady of Aroostook, The (Howells), **II:** 280
"Lady of Bayou St. John, A" (Chopin), **Retro. Supp. II:** 58
"Lady of the Lake, The" (Malamud), **Supp. I Part 2:** 437
Lady Oracle (Atwood), **Supp. XIII:** 21, **23–24**
"Lady Poverty" (Notley), **Supp. XXII:** 234–235
Lady Sings the Blues (film), **Supp. I Part 1:** 67
"Lady's Maid's Tale, The" (Wharton), **IV:** 316

"Lady Wentworth" (Longfellow), **II:** 505
"Lady with a Lamp" (Parker), **Supp. IX:** 193
"Lady with the Heron, The" (Merwin), **Supp. III Part 1:** 343
"Lady with the Pet Dog, The" (Chekov), **Supp. XXII:** 60
"Lady with the Pet Tribble, The" (Brockmeier), **Supp. XXII:** 60
La Farge, John, **I:** 1, 2, 20; **II:** 322, 338; **Retro. Supp. I:** 217
La Farge, Oliver, **Supp. IV Part 2:** 503
Lafayette, Marquis de, **I:** 344, 345; **II:** 405–406; **Supp. I Part 2:** 510, 511, 683
"La Figlia che Piange" (Eliot), **Retro. Supp. I:** 63
La Follette, Robert, **I:** 483, 485, 492; **III:** 580
La Fontaine, Jean de, **II:** 154; **III:** 194; **IV:** 80
Laforgue, Jules, **I:** 386, 569, 570, 572–573, 575, 576; **II:** 528; **III:** 8, 11, 466; **IV:** 37, 79, 80, 122; **Retro. Supp. I:** 55, 56; **Supp. XIII:** 332, 335, 346; **Supp. XV:** 165
La Gallienne, Eva, **Supp. VIII:** 251
"Lager Beer" (Dunbar), **Supp. II Part 1:** 193
"La Gringuita: On Losing a Native Language" (Alvarez), **Supp. VII:** 18
Laguna Woman (Silko), **Supp. IV Part 2:** 557, 560–561
Lahiri, Jhumpa, **Supp. XXI: 175–189; Supp. XXIII:** 289
Lahr, John, **Supp. XXI:** 18
Laing, R. D., **Supp. I Part 2:** 527; **Supp. XX:** 94
La kabbale pratique (Ambelain), **Supp. I Part 1:** 273
"Lake, The" (Bradbury), **Supp. IV Part 1:** 101
Lake, The (play), **Supp. IX:** 189
Lakeboat (Mamet), **Supp. XIV:** 240–241
"Lake Chelan" (Stafford), **Supp. XI:** 321
Lake Effect Country (Ammons), **Supp. VII:** 34, 35
"Lake Isle of Innisfree, The" (Yeats), **Retro. Supp. I:** 413; **Supp. XIX:** 92
"Lake Return" (Wright), **Supp. XV:** 345
Lake Wobegon Days (Keillor), **Supp. XVI:** 165, 166, **173–174**
Lake Wobegon Summer 1956 (Keillor), **Supp. XVI:** 178
Lalic, Ivan V., **Supp. VIII:** 272
Lamantia, Philip, **Supp. VIII:** 289
Lamb, Brian, **Supp. XIX:** 156; **Supp. XX:** 101
Lamb, Charles, **III:** 111, 207; **Supp. VIII:** 125
Lamb, Wendy, **Supp. IV Part 2:** 658
Lambardi, Marilyn May, **Retro. Supp. II:** 45–46
Lamb in His Bosom (C. Miller), **Supp. XXII:** 187, **189–191,** 193–194, 195, 197, 198, 199, 200
"Lambkill" (Davison), **Supp. XXVI:** 75
"Lame Feet of Salvation, The" (W. V. Davis), **Supp. XXI:** 87–88

"Lament" (Wilbur), **Supp. III Part 2:** 550

Lament and Chastisement (O'Hara), **Supp. XXIII:** 209

"Lamentation in Winter"(Schott), **Supp. XXIII:** 243

"Lamentations" (Glück), **Supp. V:** 83, 84

"Lament for Dark Peoples" (Hughes), **Retro. Supp. I:** 199

"Lament for Saul and Jonathan" (Bradstreet), **Supp. I Part 1:** 111

"Lament-Heaven" (Doty), **Supp. XI:** 125

"Lament of a New England Mother, The" (Eberhart), **I:** 539

Laments for the Living (Parker), **Supp. IX:** 192

"Lame Shall Enter First, The" (O'Connor), **III:** 348, 351, 352, 355, 356–357, 358; **Retro. Supp. II:** 237

"Lamia" (Davison), **Supp. XXVI:** 74

Lamia (Keats), **II:** 512; **III:** 523

Lamming, George, **Supp. XXI:** 170

Lamott, Anne, **Supp. XX: 131–146**

La Motte-Fouqué, Friedrich Heinrich Karl, **III:** 77, 78

L'Amour, Louis, **Supp. XIII:** 5; **Supp. XXVI:** 186

Lamp for Nightfall, A (Caldwell), **I:** 297

Lamplit Answer, The (Schnackenberg), **Supp. XV:** 251, 254, **256–260**

"Lana Turner Has Collapsed!"(O'Hara), **Supp. XXIII:** 220

"Lance" (Nabokov), **Retro. Supp. I:** 266

Lancelot (Percy), **Supp. III Part 1:** 384, 395–396

Lancelot (Robinson), **III:** 513, 522

Lanchester, John, **Retro. Supp. I:** 278

"Land" (Emerson), **II:** 6

"Land Aesthetic, The" (Callicott), **Supp. XIV:** 184

Land and Freedom (film, Loach), **Supp. XXIII:** 163

"Land and Language" (J. W. Miller), **Supp. XX: 170**

Landau, Deborah, **Supp. XI:** 122, 123

"Land beyond the Blow, The" (Bierce), **I:** 209

"Land Ethic, The" (Leopold), **Supp. XIV:** 179, 180, 183, 191, 192

Landfall (Wagoner), **Supp. IX:** 330

"Landing in Luck" (Faulkner), **Retro. Supp. I:** 85

"Landing on the Moon" (Swenson), **Supp. IV Part 2:** 643

"Landings" (Hoffman), **Supp. XVIII:** 86

"Landing Under Water, I See Roots" (A. Finch), **Supp. XVII:** 76

"Land"(Kenny), **Supp. XXIII:** 147

Landlord at Lion's Head, The (Howells), **II:** 276, 287–288

Landmarks of Healing: A Study of House Made of Dawn (Scarberry-García), **Supp. IV Part 2:** 486

Land of Little Rain, The (Dillard), **Supp. VI:** 27–28

Land of Look Behind, The (Cliff), **Supp. XXII:** 65–66, 68–69

Land of the Free U.S.A. (MacLeish), **I:** 293; **III:** 16–17

Land of Unlikeness (Lowell), **II:** 537–538, 539, 547; **Retro. Supp. II:** 177, 178, **184–185**

Landor, Walter Savage, **III:** 15, 469; **Supp. I Part 2:** 422

"Landscape" (Sarton), **Supp. VIII:** 259

"Landscape #11" (Halliday), **Supp. XIX:** 93

Landscape and Journey (W. V. Davis), **Supp. XXI:** 83, 88, 90, **92–93**, 95

"Landscape as a Nude" (MacLeish), **III:** 14

Landscape at the End of the Century (Dunn), **Supp. XI:** 139, 143, **150–151**

"Landscape Chamber, The" (Jewett), **II:** 408–409

"Landscape for the Disappeared" (Komunyakaa), **Supp. XIII:** 120, 126

Landscape in American Poetry (Larcom), **Supp. XIII:** 142

"Landscape Painter, A" (James), **II:** 322; **Retro. Supp. I:** 219

"Landscape Symbolism in Kate Chopin's *At Fault*" (Arner), **Retro. Supp. II:** 62

"Landscape: The Eastern Shore" (Barth), **I:** 122

"Landscape with Boat" (Stevens), **Retro. Supp. I:** 306

"Landscape with Bottles"(Schott), **Supp. XXIII:** 242

"Landscape with the Fall of Icarus" (Brueghel), **Retro. Supp. I:** 430

Land's End: A Walk through Provincetown (Cunningham), **Supp. XV:** 69

Land That Drank the Rain, The (Hoffman), **Supp. XVIII:** 76, 80, 81, 82

"Land Where There Is No Death, The" (Benét), **Supp. XI:** 56

Lane, Ann, **Supp. XI:** 195, 208

Lane, Cornelia. *See* Anderson, Mrs. Sherwood

Lane, Homer, **Supp. II Part 1:** 6; **Supp. XIV:** 160

Lane, John, **Supp. XXIV:** 22

Lane, Nathan, **Supp. XIII:** 207

Lane, Rose Wilder, **Supp. IV Part 2:** 524; **Supp. XXII:** 293–294, 295, 296, 297, 301

Lanes, Selma G., **Supp. XVI:** 104, 107

Lang, Andrew, **Retro. Supp. I:** 127; **Supp. XXVI:** 33

Lang, Violet, **Supp. XII:** 119

Lang, V. R. "Bunny", **Supp. XXIII:** 209

Langdon, Olivia. *See* Clemens, Mrs. Samuel Langhorne (Olivia Langdon)

Lange, Carl Georg, **II:** 350

Lange, Dorothea, **I:** 293; **Supp. XIV:** 181

Langland, Joseph, **III:** 542

Langston Hughes, American Poet (Walker), **Supp. III Part 2:** 530–531

Langston Hughes and the "Chicago Defender": Essays on Race, Politics, and Culture (De Santis, ed.), **Retro. Supp. I:** 194

Langston Hughes: Modern Critical Views (Bloom, ed.), **Retro. Supp. I:** 193

Langston Hughes Reader, The (Hughes), **Retro. Supp. I:** 202; **Supp. I Part 1:** 345

Langston Hughes: The Poet and His Critics (Barksdale), **Retro. Supp. I:** 202

"Language, Visualization and the Inner Library" (Shepard), **Supp. III Part 2:** 436, 438, 449

Language and Imagery of the Bible, The (Caird), **Supp. XXI:** 91–92

"Language and the Writer" (Bambara), **Supp. XI:** 18

Language As Gesture (Blackmur), **Supp. II Part 1:** 108

Language as Symbolic Action (Burke), **I:** 275, 282, 285

Language Book, The (Andrews and Bernstein), **Supp. IV Part 2:** 426

"Language Divine!"(J. Schoolcraft), **Supp. XXIII:** 225

Language God Talks, The: On Science and Religion (Wouk), **Supp. XXV:** 257, 267

Language in Thought and Action (Hayakawa), **I:** 448

"Language of Being and Dying, The" (Gass), **Supp. VI:** 91

"Language of Home, The" (Wideman), **Supp. X:** 320, 323–324

Language of Life, The (Moyers, television series), **Supp. XIII:** 274, 276

Language of the American South, The (Brooks), **Supp. XIV:** 14

"Language of the Brag, The" (Olds), **Supp. X:** 204

"Language We Know, The" (Ortiz), **Supp. IV Part 2:** 500

Lanier, Clifford, **Supp. I Part 1:** 349, 350, 353, 355, 356, 371

Lanier, James F. D., **Supp. I Part 1:** 350

Lanier, Lyle H., **Supp. X:** 25

Lanier, Robert Sampson, **Supp. I Part 1:** 349, 351, 355, 356, 361

Lanier, Mrs. Robert Sampson (Mary Jane Anderson), **Supp. I Part 1:** 349

Lanier, Sidney, **IV:** 444; **Supp. I Part 1: 349–373; Supp. I Part 2:** 416; **Supp. IV Part 1:** 165

Lanier, Mrs. Sidney (Mary Day), **Supp. I Part 1:** 351, 355, 357, 361, 362, 364, 370, 371

"Lanier as Poet" (Parks), **Supp. I Part 1:** 373

"Lanier's Reading" (P. Graham), **Supp. I Part 1:** 373

"Lanier's Use of Science for Poetic Imagery" (Beaver), **Supp. I Part 1:** 373

Lankes, J. J., **Supp. XXII:** 275

Lannegan, Helen. *See* Caldwell, Mrs. Erskine

Lannin, Paul, **II:** 427

Lanny Budd novels (Sinclair), **Supp. V:** 290

Lansdale, Joe R., **Supp. XXV:** 145

Lant, Kathleen Margaret, **Supp. V:** 141

Lanterns on the Levee (Percy), **Supp. XXII:** 193

Lanthenas, François, **Supp. I Part 2:** 515

"Lanyard, The" (Collins), **Supp. XXI:** 56, **62–64**

Laotzu, **III:** 173, 189, 567; **Supp. XV:** 39, 46, 48

Lapine, James, **Supp. XXI:** 147–148

"Lapis Lazuli" (Yeats), **I:** 532; **III:** 40

Laplace, Pierre Simon de, **III:** 428

Lapouge, M. G., **Supp. I Part 2:** 633

Lappa, Katherine, **Supp. XV:** 176

Lapsing to Grace (Espaillat), **Supp. XXI:** 99, 100

Lapsley, Gaillard, **Supp. XX: 231**

Laqueur, Thomas, **Supp. XVI:** 154

Larbaud, Valery, **IV:** 404; **Supp. XIII:** 332; **Supp. XIV:** 338

Larcom, Lucy, **Retro. Supp. II:** 145; **Supp. XIII: 137–157**

Larcom's Poetical Works (Larcom), **Supp. XIII:** 142

Lardner, John, **II:** 437

Lardner, Ring, **I:** 487; **II:** 44, 91, 259, 263, **415–438; III:** 566, 572; **IV:** 433; **Retro. Supp. I:** 105; **Retro. Supp. II:** 222; **Supp. I Part 2:** 609; **Supp. IX:** 200; **Supp. XVI:** 189

Lardner, Ring, Jr., **Supp. XI:** 306

"Lardner, Shakespeare and Chekhov" (Matthews), **II:** 430

"Large Bad Picture" (Bishop), **Retro. Supp. II:** 43; **Supp. I Part 1:** 73, 80–82, 85, 86, 89, 90

"Large Coffee" (Lardner), **II:** 437

Large Glass, or The Bride Stripped Bare by Her Bachelors, Even (Duchamp), **Supp. IV Part 2:** 423, 424

Largo (Handel), **IV:** 369

"Lark" (Taggard), **Supp. XXII:** 280

Lark, The (Hellman), **Supp. I Part 1:** 286–288, 297

Lark: Four-Part Chorus for Mixed Voices (A Capella) with Baritone Solo (Taggard and Copland), **Supp. XXII:** 283

Larkin, Philip, **Supp. I Part 2:** 536; **Supp. XI:** 243, 249; **Supp. XIII:** 76, 85; **Supp. XV:** 117, 251; **Supp. XVII:** 110; **Supp. XVIII:** 173; **Supp. XX: 199; Supp. XXI:** 84, 93; **Supp. XXVI:** 67

Larkin, Sharon Alile, **Supp. XI:** 20

Larmore, Phoebe, **Supp. X:** 266

Larner, Jeremy, **Supp. XVI:** 220

La Rochefoucauld, François de, **I:** 279; **II:** 111; **Supp. XIV:** 130

"La Rose des Vents" (Wilbur), **Supp. III Part 2:** 550

"Larry Brown's *Dirty Work*: A Study of Man's Responsibility for Suffering" (Prevost), **Supp. XXI:** 45

"Larry"(O'Hara), **Supp. XXIII:** 212

Larry's Party (Shields), **Supp. VII:** 324, 326–327

Larsen, Nella, **Supp. I Part 1:** 325, 326; **Supp. IV Part 1:** 164; **Supp. XVIII: 119–134**

Larson, Charles, **Supp. IV Part 1:** 331

Larson, Clinton, **Supp. XI:** 328

Larson, Kelli, **Supp. XVIII:** 131

LaRue, Dorie, **Supp. XXI:** 43

"Larval Stage of a Bookworm" (Mencken), **III:** 101

La Salle and the Discovery of the Great West (Parkman), **Supp. II Part 2:** 595, 598, 605–607; **Supp. XVIII:** 114

Las Casas, Bartolomé de, **Supp. XXIV:** 87

Lasch, Christopher, **I:** 259

Lasdun, James, **Supp. XXIV:** 154

Lasher (Rice), **Supp. VII:** 299–300

Lask, Thomas, **III:** 576; **Supp. XVI:** 250

Laski, Harold, **Supp. I Part 2:** 632, 643

Lass, Abraham H., **Supp. XXIV:** 214

Lassalle, Ferdinand, **IV:** 429

Lasser, Louise, **Supp. XV:** 4

"Last Acts" (Olds), **Supp. X:** 210

Last Adam, The (Cozzens), **I:** 362–363, 364, 368, 375, 377, 378, 379

Last Analysis, The (Bellow), **I:** 152, 160, 161; **Retro. Supp. II:** 26

Last and Lost Poems of Delmore Schwartz (Phillips, ed.), **Supp. II Part 2:** 661, 665

Last Avant-Garde, The: The Making of the New York School of Poets (Lehman), **Supp. XV:** 178–179, 187

Last Beautiful Days of Autumn, The (Nichols), **Supp. XIII:** 254, 255, 267, 269

Last Best Place, The: A Montana Anthology (Kittredge and Smith, eds.), **Supp. XXVI:** 188

Last Blue (Stern), **Supp. IX: 299–300**

Last Book, The (Pickering), **Supp. XXI:** 203–204

Last Carousel, The (Algren), **Supp. IX:** 16

Last Centennial, The (P. N. Warren as Kilina), **Supp. XX: 261–262**

"Last Child" (X. J. Kennedy), **Supp. XV:** 162, 165

"Last Class with Roethke" (Gallagher), **Supp. XXIV:** 171

Last Clean Shirt, The (film, Leslie and O'Hara), **Supp. XXIII:** 217

Last Coyote, The (Connelly), **Supp. XXI:** 71

"Last Dance" (Dubus III), **Supp. XXIV:** 100

"Last Day in the Field, The" (Gordon), **II:** 200

"Last Day of the Last Furlough" (Salinger), **III:** 552–553

"Last Days of Alice" (Tate), **IV:** 129

"Last Days of August, The" (Nye), **Supp. XIII:** 284

"Last Days of John Brown, The" (Thoreau), **IV:** 185

Last Days of Louisiana Red, The (Reed), **Supp. X:** 240, **248–249**

Last Decade, The (Trilling), **Supp. III Part 2:** 493, 499

"Last Demon, The" (Singer), **IV:** 15, 21

Last Detective, The (Crais), **Supp. XXI:** 70

Last Exit to Brooklyn (Selby), **Supp. III Part 1:** 125; **Supp. XXI:** 227, 231

Last Flower, The (Thurber), **Supp. I Part 2:** 610

"Last Frontier" (McCarriston), **Supp. XIV:** 272

Last Generation, The (Moraga), **Supp. XXIII:** 201

Last Gentleman, The (Percy), **Supp. III Part 1:** 383–388, 392–393

"Last Good Country, The" (Hemingway), **II:** 258–259

Last Good Time, The (Bausch), **Supp. VII:** 45–46

"Last Great Saloon, The"(Exley), **Supp. XXIII:** 103

"Last Hiding Places of Snow, The" (Kinnell), **Supp. III Part 1:** 252

"Last Hours, The" (Dunn), **Supp. XI:** 141

Last House: Reflections, Dreams, and Observations, 1943–1991 (M. F. K. Fisher), **Supp. XVII:** 92

Last Husband and Other Stories, The (Humphrey), **Supp. IX:** 94

Last Jew in America, The (Fiedler), **Supp. XIII:** 103

"Last Jew in America, The" (Fiedler), **Supp. XIII:** 103

Last Laugh, Mr. Moto (Marquand), **III:** 57

"Last Leaf, The" (Holmes), **Supp. I Part 1:** 302, 309

"Last Leaf, The" (Porter), **III:** 444

"Last Lie, The" (Weigl), **Supp. XIX:** 279

"Last Light" (Major), **Supp. XXII:** 185

"Last Look at the Lilacs" (Stevens), **IV:** 74

Last Man, The (Kees), **Supp. XV:** 142, 143, 145

"Last May" (Dixon), **Supp. XII: 143**

"Last Mermother, The" (A. Finch), **Supp. XVII:** 72

"Last Mohican, The" (Malamud), **Supp. I Part 2:** 437–438, 450, 451

"Lastness" (Kinnell), **Supp. III Part 1:** 248–249

"Last Night" (Olds), **Supp. X:** 212

Last Night at the Lobster (O'Nan), **Supp. XXV:** 149–150, 151

"Last Night at Tía's" (Alvarez), **Supp. VII:** 5

Last Night of Summer, The (Caldwell), **I:** 292–293

Last Notes from Home (Exley), **Supp. XXIII:** 97, 98, **106–108**

Last of Mr. Norris, The (Isherwood), **Supp. XIV:** 161

"Last of the Brooding Miserables, The" (Karr), **Supp. XI:** 250

"Last of the Caddoes, The" (Humphrey), **Supp. IX:** 101

Last of the Crazy People, The (Findley), **Supp. XX: 51–52**

"Last of the Gold Star Mothers, The" (C. Bly), **Supp. XVI:** 34, 35, 36

"Last of the Legions, The" (Benét), **Supp. XI:** 56, 57

Last of the Mohicans, The (Cooper), **I:** 341, 342, 349

Last of the Red Hot Lovers (Simon), **Supp. IV Part 2:** 575, 583, 589

"Last of the Valerii, The" (James), **II:** 327; **Retro. Supp. I:** 218

"Last One, The" (Merwin), **Supp. III Part 1:** 355

Last Picture Show, The (film), **Supp. V:** 223, 226

Last Picture Show, The (McMurtry), **Supp. V:** 220, 222–223, 233

Last Place on Earth, The: Scott and Amundsen's Race to the South Pole (Huntford), **Supp. XVIII:** 114

Last Puritan, The (Santayana), **III:** 64, 600, 604, 607, 612, 615–617

Last Radio Baby, The (Andrews), **Supp. XXVI:** 2–3, 7, 10

"Last Ride Together, The" (Browning), **I:** 468

"Last River, The" (Kinnell), **Supp. III Part 1:** 236

Last Song, The (Harjo), **Supp. XII:** 218

"Last Song for the Mend-It Shop" (Nye), **Supp. XIII:** 283

"Last Tango in Fresno" (Salinas), **Supp. XIII:** 318

"Last Trip to Greece"(Hadas), **Supp. XXIII:** 118–119

Last Tycoon, The: An Unfinished Novel (Fitzgerald), **II:** 84, 98; **Retro. Supp. I:** 109, 114, **114–115; Retro. Supp. II:** 337; **Supp. IV Part 1:** 203; **Supp. IX:** 63; **Supp. XII:** 173; **Supp. XIII:** 170; **Supp. XVIII:** 248, 250

"Last WASP in the World, The" (Fiedler), **Supp. XIII:** 103

"Last Watch, The" (Gibran), **Supp. XX:** **119**

Last Watch of the Night: Essays Too Personal and Otherwise (Monette), **Supp. X:** 147, 148, 153, **157–159**

"Last Will" (Stallings), **Supp. XXV:** 232

"Last Word, The" (column, Quindlen), **Supp. XVII:** 165, 167, 170

Last Word, The: Letters between Marcia Nardi and William Carlos Williams (O'Neil, ed.), **Retro. Supp. I:** 427

"Last Words" (Levine), **Supp. V:** 190

"Last Words" (Olds), **Supp. X:** 210

Last Worthless Evening, The (Dubus), **Supp. VII:** 87–88

"Las Vegas (What?) Las Vegas (Can't Hear You! Too Noisy) Las Vegas! ! !" (Wolfe), **Supp. III Part 2:** 572

"Late" (Bogan), **Supp. III Part 1:** 53

"Late Air" (Bishop), **Supp. I Part 1:** 89

"Late Autumn" (Sarton), **Supp. VIII:** 261

"Late Bronze, Early Iron: A Journey Book" (Sobin), **Supp. XVI:** 290

Late Child, The (McMurtry), **Supp. V:** 231

"Late Conversation" (Doty), **Supp. XI:** 122

"Late Elegy for John Berryman, A" (W. V. Davis), **Supp. XXI:** 91

"Late Encounter with the Enemy, A" (O'Connor), **III:** 345; **Retro. Supp. II:** 232

Late Fire, Late Snow (Francis), **Supp. IX:** **89–90**

"Late Fragment" (Gallagher), **Supp. XXIV:** 172

Late George Apley, The (Marquand), **II:** 482–483; **III:** 50, 51, 52, 56–57, 58,

62–64, 65, 66

Late George Apley, The (Marquand and Kaufman), **III:** 62

"Late Hour" (Everwine), **Supp. XV:** 85

Late Hour, The (Strand), **Supp. IV Part 2:** 620, 629–630

"Lately, at Night" (Kumin), **Supp. IV Part 2:** 442

"Late Moon" (Levine), **Supp. V:** 186

"Late Night Ode" (McClatchy), **Supp. XII:** 262–263

Later (Creeley), **Supp. IV Part 1:** 153, 156, 157

Later Life (Gurney), **Supp. V:** 103, 105

La Terre (Zola), **III:** 316, 322

Later the Same Day (Paley), **Supp. VI:** 218

"Late September in Nebraska" (Kooser), **Supp. XIX:** 120

Late Settings (Merrill), **Supp. III Part 1:** 336

"Late Sidney Lanier, The" (Stedman), **Supp. I Part 1:** 373

"Late Snow & Lumber Strike of the Summer of Fifty-Four, The" (Snyder), **Supp. VIII:** 294

"Late Start, A" (L. Brown), **Supp. XXI:** 40–41

"Latest Freed Man, The" (Stevens), **Retro. Supp. I:** 306

"Latest Injury, The" (Olds), **Supp. X:** 209

Latest Literary Essays and Addresses (Lowell), **Supp. I Part 2:** 407

"Late Subterfuge" (Warren), **IV:** 257

"Late Summer Lilies" (Weigl), **Supp. XIX:** 288

"Late Summer Love Song" (Davison), **Supp. XXVI:** 69

"Late Supper, A" (Jewett), **Retro. Supp. II:** 137

"Late Victorians" (Rodriguez), **Supp. XIV:** 303–304

"Late Walk, A" (Frost), **II:** 153; **Retro. Supp. I:** 127

Latham, Edyth, **I:** 289

Lathrop, George Parsons, **Supp. I Part 1:** 365

Lathrop, H. B., **Supp. III Part 2:** 612

Lathrop, Julia, **Supp. I Part 1:** 5

Latière de Trianon, La (Wekerlin), **II:** 515

"La Tigresse" (Van Vechten), **Supp. II Part 2:** 735, 738

Latimer, Hugh, **II:** 15

Latimer, Margery, **Supp. IX:** 320

La Tour Dreams of the Wolf Girl (Huddle), **Supp. XXVI:** 148, 151, 158, 159

La Traviata (Verdi), **III:** 139

"Latter-Day Warnings" (Holmes), **Supp. I Part 1:** 307

"Latter Rain, The" (Very), **Supp. XXV:** 249

La Turista (Shepard), **Supp. III Part 2:** 440

Lauber, John, **Supp. XIII:** 21

Laud, Archbishop, **II:** 158

"Lauds" (Auden), **Supp. II Part 1:** 23

"Laughing Man, The" (Salinger), **III:** 559

Laughing Matters (Siegel), **Supp. XXII:** 260

Laughing to Keep From Crying (Hughes), **Supp. I Part 1:** 329–330

Laughing Wild (Durang), **Supp. XXIV:** 114, **124**

"Laughing with One Eye" (Schnackenberg), **Supp. XV:** 253

Laughlin, James, **III:** 171; **Retro. Supp. I:** 423, 424, 428, 430, 431; **Supp. VIII:** 195; **Supp. XV:** 140; **Supp. XVI:** 284; **Supp. XXI:** 29

Laughlin, Jay, **Supp. II Part 1:** 94

Laughlin, J. Laurence, **Supp. I Part 2:** 641

Laughter in the Dark (Nabokov), **III:** 255–258; **Retro. Supp. I:** 270

"Laughter of Women, The" (Davison), **Supp. XXVI:** 75

Laughter on the 23rd Floor (Simon), **Supp. IV Part 2:** 575, 576, 588, 591–592

"Launcelot" (Lewis), **II:** 439–440

"Laura Dailey's Story" (Bogan), **Supp. III Part 1:** 52

Laurel, Stan, **Supp. I Part 2:** 607; **Supp. IV Part 2:** 574

Laurel and Hardy Go to Heaven (Auster), **Supp. XII:** 21

Laurence, Alexander, **Supp. XVIII:** 138

Laurence, Dan H., **II:** 338–339

Laurens, John, **Supp. I Part 2:** 509

Lauter, Paul, **Supp. XV:** 313

Lautréamont, Comte de, **III:** 174

Lavender Locker Room, The (P. N. Warren), **Supp. XX: 261, 273–274**

Law, John, **Supp. XI:** 307

Law and Order (television), **Supp. XVII:** 153

Law and the Testimony, The (S. and A. Warner), **Supp. XVIII:** 264

Lawd Today (Wright), **IV:** 478, 492

Law for the Lion, A (Auchincloss), **Supp. IV Part 1:** 25

Lawgiver, The (Wouk), **Supp. XXV:** 253, 256, 257, 267–268

"Law Lane" (Jewett), **II:** 407

"Lawns of June, The" (Peacock), **Supp. XIX:** 196

"Law of Nature and the Dream of Man, The: Ruminations of the Art of Fiction" (Stegner), **Supp. IV Part 2:** 604

Lawrence, D. H., **I:** 291, 336, 377, 522, 523; **II:** 78, 84, 98, 102, 264, 517, 523, 532, 594, 595; **III:** 27, 33, 40, 44, 46, 172, 173, 174, 178, 184, 229, 261, 423, 429, 458, 546–547; **IV:** 138, 339, 342, 351, 380; **Retro. Supp. I:** 7, 18, 203, 204, 421; **Retro. Supp. II:** 68; **Supp. I Part 1:** 227, 230, 243, 255, 257, 258, 263, 329; **Supp. I Part 2:** 546, 613, 728; **Supp. II Part 1:** 1, 9, 20, 89; **Supp. IV Part 1:** 81; **Supp. VIII:** 237; **Supp. X:** 137, 193, 194; **Supp. XII:** 172; **Supp. XIV:** 310; **Supp. XV:** 45, 46, 158, 254; **Supp. XVI:** 267; **Supp. XX: 69; Supp. XXII:** 198; **Supp. XXIII:** 166, 275; **Supp. XXIV:** 51, 52, 57, 58, 64; **Supp. XXVI:** 144

Lawrence, Elizabeth, **Supp. XXIII:** 259, 264

Lawrence, Frieda, **Supp. XV:** 46

Lawrence, Rhoda, **Supp. I Part 1:** 45

Lawrence, Seymour, **Supp. IX:** 107; **Supp. XI:** 335, 346, 348

Lawrence, T. E., **Supp. XIV:** 159

Lawrence of Arabia (Aldington), **Supp. I Part 1:** 259

Lawrence of Arabia (film), **Supp. I Part 1:** 67

Laws (Hadas), **Supp. XXIII:** 119–120, 124

Laws (Plato), **Supp. IV Part 1:** 391

Laws of Ice, The (Price), **Supp. VI:** 264

Laws of Our Fathers, The (Turow), **Supp. XVII: 218–219**

Lawson, John Howard, **I:** 479, 482

Lawton Girl, The (Frederic), **II:** 132–133, 144

Layachi, Larbi (Driss ben Hamed Charhadi), **Supp. IV Part 1:** 92, 93

Layard, John, **Supp. XIV:** 160

Lay Down My Sword and Shield (Burke), **Supp. XIV:** 22, 25, 34

"Layers, The" (Kunitz), **Supp. III Part 1:** 260, 266–267

"Layers, The: Some Notes on 'The Abduction' " (Kunitz), **Supp. III Part 1:** 266

"Lay-mans Lamentation, The" (Taylor), **IV:** 162–163

Lay of the Land, The: Metaphor as Experience and History in American Life and Letters (Kolodny), **Supp. X:** 97

"Layover" (Hass), **Supp. VI:** 109

"Lay Preacher" (Dennie), **Supp. I Part 1:** 125

Layton, Irving, **Supp. XII:** 121

Lazar, Irving "Swifty", **Supp. XIX:** 250

Lazarillo de Tormes (Mendoza), **III:** 182

Lazar Malkin Enters Heaven (S. Stern), **Supp. XVII:** 42; **Supp. XX: 178**

Lazarus Laughed (O'Neill), **III:** 391, 395–396

Lazer, Hank, **Supp. IX:** 265

Lea, Luke, **IV:** 248

Leachman, Cloris, **Supp. XXI:** 146

Leacock, Stephen, **Supp. IV Part 2:** 464

"LEADBELLY GIVES AN AUTOGRAPH" (Baraka), **Supp. II Part 1:** 49

Leaflets: Poems, 1965–1968 (Rich), **Supp. I Part 2:** 551, 556–557

"League of American Writers, The: Communist Organizational Activity among American Writers 1929–1942" (Wolfe), **Supp. II Part 2:** 568

League of Brightened Philistines and Other Papers, The (Farrell), **II:** 49

Leahy, Anna, **Supp. XXI:** 246

"Leakage" (Skloot), **Supp. XX: 202**

Leal, Luis, **Supp. XIX:** 98, 112

"Leaning" (Webb), **Supp. XX: 56**

Leaning Forward (Paley), **Supp. VI:** 221

"Leaning Tower, The" (Porter), **III:** 442, 443, 446–447

Leaning Tower and Other Stories, The (Porter), **III:** 433, 442, 443–447

"Leap, The" (Dickey), **Supp. IV Part 1:** 182

"Leaping Up into Political Poetry" (R. Bly), **Supp. IV Part 1:** 61, 63

Leap Year (Cameron), **Supp. XII:** 79–80, 81, **85–86**, 88

Lear, Edward, **III:** 428, 536; **Supp. XVI:** 103; **Supp. XXVI:** 274

Lear, Linda, **Supp. IX:** 19, 22, 25, 26

Learned Ladies, The (Molière; Wilbur, trans.), **Supp. III Part 2:** 560

"Learning a Dead Language" (Merwin), **Supp. III Part 1:** 345

Learning a Trade: A Craftsman's Notebooks, 1955–1997 (Price), **Supp. VI:** 254, 255, 267

"Learning Bones" (Espaillat), **Supp. XXI:** 107

Learning to Live in This World (Schott), **Supp. XXIII:** 248

Learning to Love: Exploring Solitude and Freedom (Merton), **Supp. VIII:** 200

Learning to Love You More (website), **Supp. XXIV:** 200

"Learning to Read" (Harper), **Supp. II Part 1:** 201–202

"Learning to Speak" (Everwine), **Supp. XV:** 79

"Learning to Speak" (Gansworth), **Supp. XXVI:** 111

"Learning to Think" (Kittredge), **Supp. XXVI:** 181

"Learning to Work Together" (L. I. Wilder), **Supp. XXII:** 290

Learning Tree, The (Park), **Supp. XIX:** 154

Leary, Lewis, **III:** 478

Leary, Paris, **Supp. IV Part 1:** 176

Leary, Timothy, **Supp. X:** 265; **Supp. XIV:** 150

Lease, Joseph, **Supp. XXI:** 246

Least Heat Moon, William, **Supp. V:** 169

Leather-Stocking Tales, The (Cooper), **I:** 335

Leatherwood God, The (Howells), **II:** 276, 277, 288

Leave It to Beaver (television show), **Supp. XX: 103**

"Leave Me Alone a Little" (Taggard), **Supp. XXII:** 274

"Leaves" (Updike), **Retro. Supp. I:** 323, 329, 335

Leaves and Ashes (Haines), **Supp. XII:** 206

Leaves from the Notebook of a Tamed Cynic (Niebuhr), **III:** 293

Leaves of Grass (Whitman), **II:** 8; **IV:** 331, 332, 333, 334, 335, 336, 340, 341–342, 348, 350, 405, 464; **Retro. Supp. I:** 387, 388, 389, 390, **392–395,** 406, 407, 408; **Retro. Supp. II:** 93; **Supp. I Part 1:** 365; **Supp. I Part 2:** 416, 579; **Supp. III Part 1:** 156; **Supp. IX:** 265; **Supp. V:** 170; **Supp. VIII:** 275; **Supp. X:** 120; **Supp. XIV:** 334; **Supp. XIX:** 276; **Supp. XV:** 218; **Supp. XVIII:** 4; **Supp. XXI:** 205; **Supp. XXII:** 92; **Supp. XXIII:** 165; **Supp. XXIV:** 85

"Leaves of Grass" (Whitman), **IV:** 463

Leaves of Grass (1856) (Whitman), **Retro. Supp. I:** 399–402

Leaves of Grass (1860) (Whitman), **Retro. Supp. I:** 402–405

Leaves of the Tree, The (Masters), **Supp. I Part 2:** 460

"Leaving" (Hogan), **Supp. IV Part 1:** 400

"Leaving" (Wilbur), **Supp. III Part 2:** 563

"Leaving, The" (B. Kelly), **Supp. XVII:** 127, 132

Leaving a Doll's House: A Memoir (C. Bloom), **Retro. Supp. II:** 281

Leaving Another Kingdom: Selected Poems (Stern), **Supp. IX:** 296

"Leaving Bartram's Garden in Southwest Philadelphia" (Di Piero), **Supp. XIX:** 46

"Leaving Brooklyn" (Neugeboren), **Supp. XVI:** 226

Leaving Cheyenne (McMurtry), **Supp. V:** 220, 221–222, 224, 229

Leaving Home (Keillor), **Supp. XVI:** 175

"Leaving One, The" (Offutt), **Supp. XIX:** 165–166

"Leaving the Island" (Olds), **Supp. X:** 214

"Leaving the Yellow House" (Bellow), **Retro. Supp. II:** 27, 32

"Leaving Town" (Kenyon), **Supp. VII:** 163

Leavis, F. R., **I:** 522; **III:** 462–463, 475, 478; **Retro. Supp. I:** 67; **Retro. Supp. II:** 243; **Supp. I Part 2:** 536; **Supp. VIII:** 234, 236, 245

Leavis, Queenie, **Supp. XX: 232**

"Leavis-Snow Controversy, The" (Trilling), **Supp. III Part 2:** 512

Leavitt, Caroline, **Supp. XX: 186**

Leavitt, David, **Supp. VIII:** 88

Lebanon (C. Miller), **Supp. XXII:** 198–199

Le Braz, Anatole, **Supp. XIII:** 253

Le Carre, John, **Supp. XX: 195**

Lecker, Robert, **Supp. XIII:** 21

LeClair, Thomas (Tom), **Supp. IV Part 1:** 286; **Supp. V:** 53; **Supp. XII:** 152; **Supp. XX: 93; Supp. XXII:** 206, 210, 261, 264

Le Conte, Joseph, **II:** 479; **III:** 227–228

"Lecture, The" (Singer), **IV:** 21

"LECTURE PAST DEAD CATS" (Baraka), **Supp. II Part 1:** 52

Lectures in America (Stein), **IV:** 27, 32, 33, 35, 36, 41, 42

"Lectures on Poetry" (Bryant), **Supp. I Part 1:** 159, 161

Lectures on Rhetoric (Blair), **II:** 8

"Leda and the Swan" (Yeats), **III:** 347; **Supp. IX:** 52

Ledger (Fitzgerald), **Retro. Supp. I:** 109, 110

Lee (Masters), **Supp. I Part 2:** 471

Lee, Baayork, **Supp. XXI:** 148

Lee, C. Y., **Supp. XXI:** 148

Lee, Don, **Supp. XII:** 295; **Supp. XVII:** 13, 14, 15, 16

Lee, Don L. *See* Madhubuti, Haki R.

Lee, Gypsy Rose, **II:** 586; **III:** 161; **Supp. IV Part 1:** 84
Lee, Harper, **Supp. VIII:** 113–131
Lee, Harriett, **Supp. XV:** 230
Lee, James Kyun-Jin, **Supp. XV:** 213
Lee, James W., **Supp. IX:** 94, 97, 109
Lee, James Ward, **Supp. VIII:** 57
Lee, Lawrence, **Supp. XXV:** 29
Lee, Li Lin, **Supp. XV:** 211, 212
Lee, Li-Young, **Supp. XV:** 211–228; **Supp. XVII:** 241
Lee, Richard E., **Supp. XIX:** 226, 227
Lee, Robert E., **II:** 150, 206; **IV:** 126; **Supp. I Part 2:** 471, 486
Lee, Samuel, **IV:** 158
Lee, Spike, **Retro. Supp. II:** 12; **Supp. XI:** 19; **Supp. XIII:** 179, 186; **Supp. XVI:** 144; **Supp. XX:** 110; **Supp. XXVI:** 199
Lee, Virginia Chin-lan, **Supp. X:** 291
Leeds, Barry, **Retro. Supp. II:** 204
Leeds, Daniel, **II:** 110
Leeds, Titan, **II:** 110, 111
Leeming, David, **Retro. Supp. II:** 4, 10
"Lees of Happiness, The" (Fitzgerald), **II:** 88
"Le Filme" (Weigl), **Supp. XIX:** 288
Left Hand of God, The (film), **Supp. XXVI:** 134
Left Out in the Rain: New Poems 1947–1985 (Snyder), **Supp. VIII:** 305
"Legacy" (Dunn), **Supp. XI:** 148
"Legacy" (Komunyakaa), **Supp. XIII:** 132
"Legacy" (W. V. Davis), **Supp. XXI:** 93–94
"Legacy of Aldo Leopold, The" (Stegner), **Supp. XIV:** 193
"Legacy of Channing, The" (Robinson), **Supp. XXIV:** 79
Legacy of Fear, A (Farrell), **II:** 39
"Legacy of the Ancestral Arts, The" (Locke), **Supp. XIV:** 201
Legacy of the Civil War, The: Meditations on the Centennial (Warren), **IV:** 236
"Legal Alien" (Mora), **Supp. XIII:** 215
"Legal Tender Act, The" (Adams), **I:** 5
Légende de la mort, La (Le Braz), **Supp. XIII:** 253
"Legend of Duluoz, The" (Kerouac), **Supp. III Part 1:** 218, 226, 227, 229
"Legend of Lillian Hellman, The" (Kazin), **Supp. I Part 1:** 297
"Legend of Monte del Diablo, The" (Harte), **Supp. II Part 1:** 339
"Legend of Paper Plates, The" (Haines), **Supp. XII:** 204
"Legend of Sammtstadt, A" (Harte), **Supp. II Part 1:** 355
"Legend of Sleepy Hollow, The" (Irving), **II:** 306–308
Legends (Lowell), **II:** 525–526
Legends and Dreams (P. N. Warren), **Supp. XX:** 261
Legends of Mexico (Lippard), **Supp. XXIII:** 178, 186
Legends of New England (Whittier), **Supp. I Part 2:** 684, 692
Legends of the Fall (Harrison), **Supp. VIII:** 38, 39, 45–46, 48

"Legends of the Revolution"(series, Lippard), **Supp. XXIII:** 178
Legends of the West (Hall), **II:** 313
Léger, Fernand, **Retro. Supp. I:** 292
Legge, James, **III:** 472
Leggett, William, **Supp. I Part 1:** 157
"Legion, The" (Karr), **Supp. XI:** 243
"Legs" (Halliday), **Supp. XIX:** 90
Legs (W. Kennedy), **Supp. VII:** 133, 134, 138–142, 143, 151
Le Guin, Ursula K., **Supp. IV Part 1:** 333; **Supp. XXII:** 49
Lehan, Richard, **Retro. Supp. II:** 104
Lehman, David, **Supp. IX:** 161; **Supp. XIII:** 130; **Supp. XV:** 178–179, 180, 187, 190; **Supp. XXI:** 246; **Supp. XXVI:** 50
Lehmann, John, **Retro. Supp. II:** 243; **Supp. XIV:** 158, 159
Lehmann, Paul, **III:** 311
Lehmann-Haupt, Christopher, **Retro. Supp. II:** 291; **Supp. IV Part 1:** 205, 209, 306; **Supp. IX:** 95, 103; **Supp. XVI:** 73, 210, 294, 295; **Supp. XXII:** 205, 213; **Supp. XXIII:** 103
Lehrer, Jim, **Supp. XVIII:** 39
Leiber, Fritz, **Supp. XVI:** 123
Leibling, A. J., **Supp. XIV:** 112
Leibniz, Gottfried Wilhelm von, **II:** 103; **III:** 428
Leibowitz, Herbert A., **I:** 386; **Supp. XV:** 78
Leich, Roland, **Supp. XIV:** 123
Leichum, Laura, **Supp. XIX:** 197
Leider, Emily Wortis, **Supp. XXIV:** 19, 20, 22, 26, 27, 30
Leiding, Reba, **Supp. XXVI:** 159
Leighton, Betty, **Supp. XXI:** 42
Leimbach, Laura, **Supp. XXIII:** 54
Leithauser, Brad, **Retro. Supp. I:** 133; **Supp. XV:** 250; **Supp. XVII:** 112; **Supp. XXII:** 207
Leitz, Robert, **Supp. XIV:** 62
Leivick, H., **IV:** 6
Lekachman, Robert, **Supp. I Part 2:** 648
Leland, Charles, **Supp. II Part 1:** 193
Leland, Charles Godfrey, **I:** 257
Leland, John, **Supp. XIX:** 157; **Supp. XV:** 202
Lem, Stanislaw, **Supp. IV Part 1:** 103
"Le marais du cygne" (Whittier), **Supp. I Part 2:** 687
Lemay, Harding, **Supp. IX:** 98; **Supp. VIII:** 125
Lemercier, Eugène, **Retro. Supp. I:** 299
Lemkin, Raphael, **Supp. XXIII:** 31
"Lemorne *versus* Huell" (E. Stoddard), **Supp. XV:** 270, 273, 283
Le Morte D'Arthur Notes (Gardner), **Supp. VI:** 65, 66
Lenin, V. I., **I:** 366, 439, 440; **III:** 14–15, 262, 475; **IV:** 429, 436, 443–444; **Supp. I Part 2:** 647; **Supp. XXI:** 164
Lennon, J. Robert, **Supp. XXV:** 151
"Lenny Dying, Pacific Standard Time"(Thompson), **Supp. XXIII:** 294
"Lenore" (Poe), **III:** 411
"Lenox Avenue: Midnight" (Hughes), **Retro. Supp. I:** 198

"Lens of Poetry, The" (Bronk). *See Attendant, The* (Bronk)
Leonard, Elmore, **Supp. IV Part 1:** 356; **Supp. X:** 5; **Supp. XIV:** 26
Leonard, John, **Supp. IV Part 1:** 24; **Supp. IV Part 2:** 474; **Supp. V:** 164, 223–224; **Supp. XI:** 13; **Supp. XIX:** 269; **Supp. XVIII:** 147, 148; **Supp. XXI:** 233, 239
Leonardo da Vinci, **Supp. XII:** 44; **Supp. XXII:** 171
León-Portilla, Miguel, **Supp. XV:** 77
Leontiev, Constantine, **Supp. XIV:** 98
Leopard, The (Lampedusa), **Supp. XII:** 13–14
Leopardi, Giacomo, **II:** 543; **Supp. XIX:** 33, 43
"Leopard Man's Story, The" (London), **II:** 475
Leopard's Mouth Is Dry and Cold Inside, The (Levis), **Supp. XI:** 258
Leopold, Aldo, **Supp. V:** 202; **Supp. X:** 108; **Supp. XIV:** 177–194; **Supp. XXI:** 203; **Supp. XXVI:** 31
"Leper's Bell, the" (Komunyakaa), **Supp. XIII:** 118
Lerman, Leo, **Supp. X:** 188; **Supp. XVI:** 194
Lerner, Ben, **Supp. XXIV:** 45
Lerner, Max, **III:** 60; **Supp. I Part 2:** 629, 630, 631, 647, 650, 654
Lerperger, Emil, **Supp. XX:** 165, 167
Lesbian Nation: The Feminist Solution (Johnston), **Supp. XXV:** 5
"Lesbos" (Plath), **Retro. Supp. II:** 254
Lesesne, Teri, **Supp. XIII:** 277
LeSieg, Theo (pseudonym). *See* Geisel, Theodor Seuss (Dr. Seuss)
Leskov, Nikolai, **IV:** 299
Leslie, Alfred, **Supp. XII:** 127; **Supp. XXIII:** 217
"Less and Less Human, O Savage Spirit" (W. Stevens), **Supp. XVI:** 64
Lesser, Wendy, **Supp. IV Part 2:** 453; **Supp. XII:** 297; **Supp. XVI:** 201
Lessing, Gotthold, **Supp. I Part 2:** 422
"Lesson, The" (Bambara), **Supp. XI:** 5–6
"Lesson, The" (Dunbar), **Supp. II Part 1:** 199
"Lesson, The" (Olsen), **Supp. XIII:** 297
"Lesson, The"(Schott), **Supp. XXIII:** 254
"Lesson for the Ill Clothed and Ill Fed, A" (Ryan as Quin), **Supp. XVIII:** 230–231
Lesson of the Master, The (James), **Supp. XVIII:** 248
"Lesson of the Master, The" (James), **Retro. Supp. I:** 227
Lesson of the Masters: An Anthology of the Novel from Cervantes to Hemingway (Cowley-Hugo, ed.), **Supp. II Part 1:** 140
"Lesson on Concealment, A" (Brown), **Supp. I Part 1:** 133
"Lessons" (Epstein), **Supp. XII:** 163
"Lessons from an Older Man"(Thompson), **Supp. XXIII:** 293
"Lessons of the Body" (Simpson), **Supp. IX:** 267

Less than One (Brodsky), **Supp. VIII:** 22, 29–31

Lester, Jerry, **Supp. IV Part 2:** 574

Lester, Ketty, **Supp. XV:** 133, 147

Le Style Apollinaire (Zukofsky), **Supp. III Part 2:** 616

Le Sueur, Arthur, **Supp. XXIII:** 161, 162

LeSueur, Joe, **Supp. XXIII:** 212, 216, 218, 220

Le Sueur, Meridel, **Supp. V:** 113, 130; **Supp. XII:** 217; **Supp. XXIII: 161–176; Supp. XXVI:** 28

Lesy, Michael, **Supp. XXV:** 146

"Let America Be America Again" (Hughes), **Retro. Supp. I:** 202; **Supp. I Part 1:** 331

Let Evening Come (Kenyon), **Supp. VII:** 160, 169–171

Lethem, Jonathan, **Supp. IX:** 122; **Supp. XVIII: 135–153; Supp. XXII:** 49

Let It Come Down (Bowles), **Supp. IV Part 1:** 87

Let It Ride (Pickering), **Supp. XXI:** 198–199

"Let Me Be" (Levine), **Supp. V:** 181, 189

"Let Me Begin Again" (Levine), **Supp. V:** 181, 189

"Let No Charitable Hope" (Wylie), **Supp. I Part 2:** 713–714, 729

Let No Man Write My Epitaph (film, Leacock), **Supp. XVII:** 150, 158

Let No Man Write My Epitaph (W. Motley), **Supp. XVII:** 150, **158–160**

Let Noon Be Fair (W. Motley), **Supp. XVII:** 161

Letofsky, Irv, **Supp. XVI:** 167

"Let one Eye his watches keep/While the Other Eye doth sleep" (Fletcher), **Supp. IV Part 2:** 621

Let's Balance the Books (radio show; Untermeyer), **Supp. XV:** 311

"Letter . . ." (Whittier), **Supp. I Part 2:** 687

"Letter, A" (Bogan), **Supp. III Part 1:** 54

"Letter, May 2, 1959" (Olson), **Supp. II Part 2:** 579, 580

"Letter, Much Too Late" (Stegner), **Supp. IV Part 2:** 613

"Letter, The" (Boulton), **Supp. XXII:** 22

"Letter, The" (Gioia), **Supp. XV:** 120

"Letter, The" (Malamud), **Supp. I Part 2:** 435–436

"Letter about Money, Love, or Other Comfort, If Any, The" (Warren), **IV:** 245

Letter Addressed to the People of Piedmont, on the Advantages of the French Revolution, and the Necessity of Adopting Its Principles in Italy, A (Barlow), **Supp. II Part 1:** 80, 81

"Letter for Marion, A" (McGrath), **Supp. X:** 116

"Letter from Aldermaston" (Merwin), **Supp. III Part 1:** 347

"Letter from a London Attic" (Pickering), **Supp. XXI:** 194

"Letter from a Region in My Mind" (Baldwin). *See* "Down at the Cross"

"Letter from Aunt Belle, A" (Kooser), **Supp. XIX:** 117

Letter from Li Po, A (Aiken), **I:** 68

"Letter from 'Manhattan' " (Didion), **Supp. IV Part 1:** 205

"Letter from the Country" (column, C. Bly), **Supp. XVI:** 33

Letter from the End of the Twentieth Century (Harjo), **Supp. XII:** 223

"Letter from the End of the Twentieth Century" (Harjo), **Supp. XII:** 227

"Letter Home" (Trethewey), **Supp. XXI:** 254

"Letter on Céline" (Kerouac), **Supp. III Part 1:** 232

Letters (Cato), **II:** 114

Letters (Landor), **Supp. I Part 2:** 422

Letters (White), **Supp. I Part 2:** 651, 653, 675, 680

Letters (Wolfe), **IV:** 462

"Letters, The" (Swados), **Supp. XIX:** 261, 262

Letters and Leadership (Brooks), **I:** 228, 240, 245, 246

"Letters for the Dead" (Levine), **Supp. V:** 186

Letters from an American Farmer (Crèvecoeur), **Supp. I Part 1:** 227–251

Letters from Maine (Sarton), **Supp. VIII: 261**

"Letters from Maine" (Sarton), **Supp. VIII:** 261

"Letters from My Father" (R. O. Butler), **Supp. XII:** 71

Letters from the Country (C. Bly), **Supp. XVI: 33–34,** 35, 37

Letters from the East (Bryant), **Supp. I Part 1:** 158

"Letters from the Ming Dynasty" (Brodsky), **Supp. VIII:** 28

"Letters from the *Samantha*" (Helprin), **Supp. XXV:** 85

Letters of Angelicus and Fidelio Fobb (O'Hara and Berkson), **Supp. XXIII:** 218

Letters of a Traveller (Bryant), **Supp. I Part 1:** 158

Letters of a Traveller, Second Series (Bryant), **Supp. I Part 1:** 158

Letters of a Woman Homesteader (Stewart), **Supp. XXVI:** 183

Letters of Emily Dickinson, The (T. H. Johnson and Ward, eds.), **I:** 470; **Retro. Supp. I:** 28

Letters of William James (Henry James, ed.), **II:** 362

Letters on Various Interesting and Important Subjects . . . (Freneau), **Supp. II Part 1:** 272

Letters to a Niece (Adams), **I:** 22

Letters to a Teacher (Pickering), **Supp. XXI:** 195, 201–202

Letters to a Young Poet (Rilke), **Supp. XIII:** 74; **Supp. XV:** 93

"Letters to Dead Imagists" (Sandburg), **I:** 421

"Letters Written on a Ferry While Crossing Long Island Sound" (Sexton), **Supp. II Part 2:** 683

"Letter to Abbé Raynal" (Paine), **Supp. I Part 2:** 510

"Letter to a Kiss That Died for Us" (Gallagher), **Supp. XXIV:** 170

Letter to a Man in the Fire: Does God Exist or Does He Care? (Price), **Supp. VI:** 267–268

"Letter to American Teachers of History, A" (Adams), **I:** 19

Letter to an Imaginary Friend (McGrath), **Supp. X:** 111, 112–113, 116, **119–125**

"Letter to a Reader" (Sanders), **Supp. XVI:** 266, 267, 268, 269, 275

"Letter to a Young Author" (P. N. Warren), **Supp. XX: 272**

"Letter to a Young Contributor" (Higginson), **Retro. Supp. I:** 31

"Letter to a Young Writer" (Price), **Supp. VI:** 267

"Letter to Bell from Missoula" (Hugo), **Supp. VI:** 142–143

"Letter to E. Franklin Frazier" (Baraka), **Supp. II Part 1:** 49

"Letter to Elaine Feinstein" (Olson), **Supp. II Part 2:** 561

"Letter to Francis Picabia, A" (Boyle), **Supp. XXIV:** 63

"Letter to Freddy" (music) (Bowles), **Supp. IV Part 1:** 82

"Letter to Garber from Skye" (Hugo), **Supp. VI:** 146

"Letter to George Washington" (Paine), **Supp. I Part 2:** 517

"Letter to His Brother" (Berryman), **I:** 172, 173

Letter to His Countrymen, A (Cooper), **I:** 346, 347, 349

"Letter to Kizer from Seattle" (Hugo), **Supp. VI:** 142

Letter to Lord Byron (Auden), **Supp. II Part 1:** 11

"Letter to Lord Byron" (Mumford), **Supp. II Part 2:** 494

"Letter to Matthews from Barton Street Flats" (Hugo), **Supp. VI:** 133

"Letter to Mexico" (Biss), **Supp. XXVI:** 48

"Letter to Minnesota" (Dunn), **Supp. XI:** 146

"Letter to Mr." (Poe), **III:** 411

"Letter Too Late to Vallejo" (Salinas), **Supp. XIII:** 313, 324

"Letter to Sister Madeline from Iowa City" (Hugo), **Supp. VI:** 142–143

"Letter to Soto" (Salinas), **Supp. XIII:** 325

"Letter to the Lady of the House" (Bausch), **Supp. VII:** 48

"Letter to the Rising Generation, A" (Comer), **I:** 214

"Letter to Walt Whitman" (Doty), **Supp. XI:** 135–136

"Letter to Wendell Berry, A" (Stegner), **Supp. IV Part 2:** 600

"Letter Writer, The" (Singer), **IV:** 20–21

"Let the Air Circulate" (Clampitt), **Supp. IX:** 45

Let the Hurricane Roar (Lane), **Supp. XXII:** 297

"Letting Down of the Hair, The" (Sexton), **Supp. II Part 2:** 692

Letting Go (P. Roth), **Retro. Supp. II:** 282, 283; **Supp. III Part 2:** 403, 404, 409–412

"Letting the Puma Go" (Dunn), **Supp. XI:** 149

"Lettres d'un Soldat" (Stevens), **Retro. Supp. I:** 299

Let Us Go into the Starry Night (Shanley), **Supp. XIV:** 317

Let Us Highly Resolve (Stratton-Porter), **Supp. XX: 223**

Let Us Now Praise Famous Men (Agee and Evans), **I:** 25, 27, 35, 36–39, 42, 45, 293

Let Your Mind Alone! (Thurber), **Supp. I Part 2:** 608

Leutze, Emanuel, **Supp. X:** 307

Levels of the Game (McPhee), **Supp. III Part 1:** 292, 294, 301

Levertov, Denise, **Retro. Supp. I:** 411; **Supp. III Part 1: 271–287; Supp. III Part 2:** 541; **Supp. IV Part 1:** 325; **Supp. VIII:** 38, 39; **Supp. XIX:** 282; **Supp. XVI:** 39, 40; **Supp. XXI:** 228; **Supp. XXII:** 83, 168, 177

Levi, Primo, **Supp. X:** 149; **Supp. XVII:** 48

Leviathan (Auster), **Supp. XII:** 27, **33–34**

"Leviathan" (Lowell), **II:** 537, 538

"Leviathan" (Merwin), **Supp. III Part 1:** 345

Levin, Adam, **Supp. XXII:** 268

Levin, Harry, **Supp. I Part 2:** 647

Levin, Jennifer, **Supp. X:** 305

Levin, Meyer, **Supp. XX: 34**

Lévinas, Emmanuel, **Supp. XVI:** 290, 291

Levine, Ellen, **Supp. V:** 4; **Supp. XI:** 178

Levine, Paul, **Supp. IV Part 1:** 221, 224

Levine, Philip, **Supp. III Part 2:** 541; **Supp. IX:** 293; **Supp. V: 177–197,** 337; **Supp. XI:** 123, 257, 259, 267, 271, 315; **Supp. XIII:** 312; **Supp. XIX:** 45; **Supp. XV:** 73, 74, 212

Levine, Rosalind, **Supp. XII:** 123

Levine, Sherry, **Supp. XII:** 4

Levis, Larry, **Supp. IX:** 299; **Supp. V:** 180; **Supp. XI: 257–274; Supp. XIII:** 312; **Supp. XV:** 73; **Supp. XVII:** 110

Lévi-Strauss, Claude, **Supp. I Part 2:** 636; **Supp. IV Part 1:** 45; **Supp. IV Part 2:** 490; **Supp. XVIII:** 190

Levitation: Five Fictions (Ozick), **Supp. V:** 268–270

"Levitation with Baby" (Nelson), **Supp. XVIII:** 173

Levitt, Saul, **Supp. XV:** 197

Levy, Alan, **Supp. IV Part 2:** 574, 589

Levy, D. A., **Supp. XXIII:** 174

Levy, G. Rachel, **Supp. I Part 2:** 567

Levy, Julien, **Supp. XXII:** 167, 168

Lévy-Bruhl, Lucien, **Retro. Supp. I:** 57

Levy Mayer and the New Industrial Era (Masters), **Supp. I Part 2:** 473

Lewes, George Henry, **II:** 569

Lewin, Albert, **Supp. XIV:** 279, 293

Lewis, C. Day, **III:** 527

Lewis, Dr. Claude, **II:** 442

Lewis, C. S., **Supp. XXV:** 73

Lewis, David Levering, **Supp. XIX:** 74, 75; **Supp. XVIII:** 127; **Supp. XXII:** 13

Lewis, Edith, **I:** 313; **Retro. Supp. I:** 19, 21, 22

Lewis, Edwin, J., **II:** 439, 442

Lewis, Jerry, **Supp. IV Part 2:** 575; **Supp. X:** 172

Lewis, John L., **I:** 493

Lewis, Lilburn, **IV:** 243

Lewis, Lorene, **Supp. IV Part 2:** 596, 597

Lewis, Lucy, **IV:** 243

Lewis, Maggie, **Supp. V:** 23

Lewis, Meriwether, **II:** 217; **III:** 14; **IV:** 179, 243, 283

Lewis, Merrill, **Supp. IV Part 2:** 596, 597

Lewis, Michael, **II:** 451, 452; **Supp. XVII:** 210

Lewis, Michael J., **Supp. XXV:** 253

Lewis, Robert Q., **Supp. IV Part 2:** 574

Lewis, R. W. B., **I:** 386, 561; **II:** 457–458; **Retro. Supp. I:** 362, 367; **Supp. I Part 1:** 233; **Supp. XIII:** 93; **Supp. XXIII:** 42

Lewis, Sinclair, **I:** 116, 212, 348, 355, 362, 374, 378, 487, 495; **II:** 27, 34, 74, 79, 271, 277, 306, **439–461,** 474; **III:** 28, 40, 51, 60, 61, 63–64, 66, 70, 71, 106, 394, 462, 572, 606; **IV:** 53, 326, 366, 455, 468, 475, 482; **Retro. Supp. I:** 332; **Retro. Supp. II:** 95, 108, 197, 322; **Supp. I Part 2:** 378, 613, 709; **Supp. IV Part 2:** 678; **Supp. IX:** 308; **Supp. V:** 278; **Supp. X:** 137; **Supp. XVII:** 41; **Supp. XVIII:** 278; **Supp. XXII:** 190; **Supp. XXIII:** 165, 166; **Supp. XXIV:** 29

Lewis, Mrs. Sinclair (Dorothy Thompson), **II:** 449–450, 451, 453

Lewis, Mrs. Sinclair (Grace Livingston Hegger), **II:** 441

Lewis, Wyndham, **III:** 458, 462, 465, 470; **Retro. Supp. I:** 59, 170, 292; **Supp. III Part 2:** 617; **Supp. XXVI:** 144

Lewisohn, Ludwig, **Supp. XXIII:** 1

Lexicon Tetraglotton (Howell), **II:** 111

"Lexington Avenue Musedog" (Peacock), **Supp. XIX:** 204

"Leyenda" (Mora), **Supp. XIII:** 214

Leyner, Mark, **Supp. XIX:** 223

Leyte (Morison), **Supp. I Part 2:** 491

"Liar, The" (Baraka), **Supp. II Part 1:** 36

"Liars, The" (Sandburg), **III:** 586

Liars' Club, The: A Memoir (Karr), **Supp. XI:** 239, 240, 241, 242, **244–248,** 252, 254; **Supp. XVI:** 70

Liar's Dice (C. Frost), **Supp. XV:** 93, 96

"Liar's Dice" (C. Frost), **Supp. XV:** 94, 107

Liars in Love (Yates), **Supp. XI:** 348, 349

Libation Bearers, The (Aeschylus), **III:** 398; **Supp. IX:** 103

Li Bay. *See* Li Po

Libby, Anthony, **Supp. XIII:** 87

Libera, Padre, **II:** 278

Liberal Imagination, The (Trilling), **III:** 308; **Retro. Supp. I:** 97, 216; **Supp. II Part 1:** 146; **Supp. III Part 2:** 495, 498, 501–504

Liberating Voices: Oral Tradition in African American Literature (G. Jones), **Supp. XXIV:** 185

Liberation (J. Scott), **Supp. XVII:** 192, **194–196**

"Liberation" (Winters), **Supp. II Part 2:** 791

Liber Brunenesis (yearbook), **IV:** 286

Liberties, The (Howe), **Supp. IV Part 2:** 426–428, 430, 432

Liberties of America, The (H. Warner), **Supp. XVIII:** 259

Liberty Jones (play), **Supp. IV Part 1:** 83

"Liberty Tree" (Paine), **Supp. I Part 2:** 505

Libra (DeLillo), **Supp. VI:** 2, **4, 5,** 6, **7,** 9, 10, 12, 13, 14, 16

Library for Juana, A (Mora), **Supp. XIII:** 218

Library of America, **Retro. Supp. I:** 2

"Library of Babel, The" (J. Borges), **Supp. XVII:** 47

"Library of Law, A" (MacLeish), **III:** 4

"Library of Moloch, The" (Bukiet), **Supp. XVII:** 47, 49

"Librettos for Eros" (Gander), **Supp. XV:** 340

Lice, The (Merwin), **Supp. III Part 1:** 339, 341–342, 346, 348, 349, 355

"License Plate, The" (Ferry), **Supp. XXIV:** 157

Lichtenberg, Georg Christoph, **Supp. XIV:** 339

Lichtenstein, Roy, **Supp. I Part 2:** 665; **Supp. XV:** 186

"Liddy's Orange" (Olds), **Supp. X:** 209

"Lie, The" (Antin), **Supp. XX: 7, 9–10**

Lieberman, Herman (Chaim), **Supp. XXIII:** 3, 7

Lieberman, Laurence, **Supp. XI:** 323–324

Liebestod (Wagner), **I:** 284, 395

Liebling, A. J., **IV:** 290; **Supp. VIII:** 151; **Supp. XVI:** 167

Lie Down in Darkness (Styron), **IV:** 98, 99, 100–104, 105, 111; **Supp. XI:** 343

"Lie Down with the Lamb" (Gallagher), **Supp. XXIV:** 171

Lie of the Mind, A (Shepard), **Supp. III Part 2:** 433, 435, 441, 447–449

"Lies" (Haines), **Supp. XII:** 204

Lies (Hoffman), **Supp. XVIII: 78–79**

"Lies and Consequences" (Pickering), **Supp. XXI:** 204

Lies Like Truth (Clurman), **IV:** 385

Lieutenant, The (Dubus), **Supp. VII:** 78

"Life" (Wharton), **Retro. Supp. I:** 372

Life along the Passaic River (W. C. Williams), **Retro. Supp. I:** 423

Life Among the Savages (Jackson), **Supp. IX:** 115, **125**

Life and Adventures of Charles Anderson Chester, The (Lippard), **Supp. XXIII:** 184

"Life and Death Kisses, The" (Grossman), **Supp. XIX:** 87

Life and Gabriella (Glasgow), **II:** 175, 176, 182–183, 184, 189

"Life and I" (Wharton), **Retro. Supp. I:** 360, 361, 362

"Life and Letters" (Epstein), **Supp. XIV:** 104–105

"Life and Letters in New England" (Emerson), **Supp. XXIV:** 67

Life and Letters of Harrison Gray Otis, Federalist, 1765–1848, The (Morison), **Supp. I Part 2:** 480–481

Life and Letters of Sir Henry Wotton (L. P. Smith), **Supp. XIV:** 340–341

Life and Mind of Emily Dickinson, The (Taggard), **Supp. XXII:** 279

Life and Times of Frederick Douglass, Written by Himself, The (Douglass), **Supp. III Part 1:** 155, 159–163

Life and Writings of Horace McCoy, The (Wolfson), **Supp. XIII:** 172, 174

"Life as a Visionary Spirit" (Eberhart), **I:** 540, 541

"Life at Angelo's, A" (Benét), **Supp. XI:** 53

Life at Happy Knoll (Marquand), **III:** 50, 61

Life Before Man (Atwood), **Supp. XIII: 24–25**

"Life Cycle of Common Man" (Nemerov), **III:** 278

"Lifecycle Stairmaster" (Karr), **Supp. XI:** 250

Life Estates (Hearon), **Supp. VIII: 68–69**

Life for Life's Sake (Aldington), **Supp. I Part 1:** 256

Life Full of Holes, A (Layachi), **Supp. IV Part 1:** 92

"Lifeguard" (Updike), **IV:** 226; **Retro. Supp. I:** 325

"Lifeguard, The" (Dickey), **Supp. IV Part 1:** 179–180

"Life in the 30s" (column, Quindlen), **Supp. XVII:** 165, 167–169

Life in the Clearings (Shields), **Supp. VII:** 313

"Life in the Country: A City Friend Asks, 'Is It Boring?' " (Paley), **Supp. VI:** 231

Life in the Forest (Levertov), **Supp. III Part 1:** 282–283

Life in the Iron Mills (R. H. Davis), **Supp. XIII:** 292, 295, 299, 305; **Supp. XVI:** 79–82, **85–88,** 91

Life in the Iron Mills and Other Stories (T. Olson, ed.), **Supp. XVI:** 83

Life in the Theatre, A (Mamet), **Supp. XIV:** 241, 255

Life in the War Zone (Atherton), **Supp. XXIV:** 24

Life Is a Miracle: An Essay Against Modern Superstition (Berry), **Supp. X:** 35

"Life Is Fine" (Hughes), **Supp. I Part 1:** 334, 338

"Life Is Motion" (Stevens), **IV:** 74

Life & Letters of Gene Stratton-Porter (Meehan), **Supp. XX: 213**

Life of Albert Gallatin, The (Adams), **I:** 6, 14

"Life of a Man of the World, The"(Lippard), **Supp. XXIII:** 189

Life of an Ordinary Woman, The: Anne Ellis (A. Ellis), **Supp. XVI:** 38

Life of Captain Cipriani, The: An Account of British Government in the West Indies (C. L. R. James), **Supp. XXI:** 161

Life of Dryden (S. Johnson), **Retro. Supp. II:** 223

Life of Emily Dickinson, The (Sewall), **Retro. Supp. I:** 25

Life of Forms, The (Focillon), **IV:** 90

Life of Franklin Pierce (Hawthorne), **Retro. Supp. I:** 163

Life of George Cabot Lodge, The (Adams), **I:** 21

Life of George Washington (Irving), **II:** 314, 315–316

Life of Henry James (Edel), **Retro. Supp. I:** 224

"Life of Irony, The" (Bourne), **I:** 219

Life of Jesus (Renan), **Supp. XX:** 122

"Life of Lincoln West, The" (Brooks), **Supp. III Part 1:** 86

Life of Mary, The (Rilke; F. Wright, trans.), **Supp. XVII:** 244

Life of Michelangelo (Grimm), **II:** 17

"Life of Nancy, The" (Jewett), **Retro. Supp. II:** 133, 144

Life of Oliver Goldsmith, The, with Selections from His Writings (Irving), **II:** 315

Life of Phips (Mather), **Supp. II Part 2:** 451, 452, 459

Life of Poetry, The (Rukeyser), **Supp. VI:** 271, 273, 275–276, 282, 283, 286

Life of Samuel Johnson (Boswell), **Supp. I Part 2:** 656

Life of Savage (S. Johnson), **Supp. I Part 2:** 523

Life of the Drama, The (Bentley), **IV:** 396

"Life of the Mind, The" (Kees), **Supp. XV:** 140

Life of the Right Reverend Joseph P. Machebeuf, The (Howlett), **Retro. Supp. I:** 17

Life of Thomas Paine, author of Rights of Men, With a Defence of his Writings (Chalmers), **Supp. I Part 2:** 514

Life of Thomas Paine, The (Cobbett), **Supp. I Part 2:** 517

"Life of Towne, The" (Carson), **Supp. XII: 102**

Life of William Ellery Channing (W. H. Channing), **Supp. XXIV:** 68

"Life on Beekman Place, A" (Naylor), **Supp. VIII:** 214

"Life on the Black List" (Endore), **Supp. XVII:** 63

Life on the Hyphen: The Cuban-American Way (Firmat), **Supp. VIII:** 76; **Supp. XI:** 184

Life on the Mississippi (Twain), **I:** 209; **IV:** 198, 199; **Supp. I Part 2:** 440

"Life on the Rocks: The Galápagos" (Dillard), **Supp. VI:** 32

"Life Stories, East and West" (E. Hoffman), **Supp. XVI:** 157

Life Story (Baker), **II:** 259

Life Studies (Lowell), **I:** 400; **II:** 384, 386, 543, 546–550, 551, 555; **Retro. Supp. II:** 180, 185, 186, 188, 189, 191; **Supp. I Part 2:** 543; **Supp. XI:** 240, 244, 250, 317; **Supp. XII:** 255; **Supp. XIV:** 15; **Supp. XV:** 252

"Life Studies" (Lowell), **Retro. Supp. II:** 188

"Life Styles in the Golden Land" (Didion), **Supp. IV Part 1:** 200

Life Supports: New and Collected Poems (Bronk), **Supp. XXI:** 19, 31, 32

"Life That Is, The" (Bryant), **Supp. I Part 1:** 169

"Life Work" (Stafford), **Supp. XI:** 329–330

"Life You Save May Be Your Own, The" (O'Connor), **III:** 344, 350, 354; **Retro. Supp. II:** 229, 230, 233

Lifshin, Lyn, **Supp. XVI:** 37

"Lifting, The" (Olds), **Supp. X:** 210

"Ligeia" (Poe), **III:** 412, 414; **Retro. Supp. II:** 261, 270, 271, 275

Liggett, Walter W., **Supp. XIII:** 168

Light, James F., **IV:** 290; **Retro. Supp. II:** 325

Light, Kate, **Supp. XVII:** 109

Light and Dark (Bronk), **Supp. XXI: 27–29,** 31

"Light and the Sufferer" (Lethem), **Supp. XVIII:** 139–140

Light around the Body, The (R. Bly), **Supp. IV Part 1:** 61–62, 62; **Supp. XVII:** 243; **Supp. XXI:** 84–85

"Light Comes Brighter, The" (Roethke), **III:** 529–530

"Light from Above" (Eberhart), **I:** 541

Light in August (Faulkner), **II:** 63–64, 65, 74; **IV:** 207; **Retro. Supp. I:** 82, 84, 85, 86, 89, 92; **Supp. XIV:** 12

Light in the Forest, The (Richter), **Supp. XVIII: 216–217**

Light in the Morning (Baker), **Supp. XVIII:** 263, 269

Light in the Window, A (Rinehart), **Supp. XXV:** 198–199, 202

"Light Man, A" (James), **II:** 322; **Retro. Supp. I:** 219

"Lightning" (Barthelme), **Supp. IV Part 1:** 53

"Lightning" (Bynner), **Supp. XV:** 44

"Lightning" (Oliver), **Supp. VII:** 235

"Lightning, The" (Swenson), **Supp. IV Part 2:** 645

"Lightning Flash, The" (Gibran), **Supp. XX: 123**

"Lightning Rod Man, The" (Melville), **III:** 90; **Supp. XVIII:** 4

"Light of the Body, The" (Davison), **Supp. XXVI:** 71

"Light of the World, The" (Hemingway), **II:** 249

"Lights"(Dybek), **Supp. XXIII:** 72

Lights in the Valley (Bodenheim), **Supp. XXV:** 29

"Lights in the Windows" (Nye), **Supp. XIII:** 280

"Lights Must Never Go Out, The"(Hadas), **Supp. XXIII:** 125

"Light Through the Window, The" (Brockmeier), **Supp. XXII:** 52, 59

Light Verse and Satires (Bynner), **Supp. XV:** 52

Light Years (Salter), **Supp. IX: 257–259**

"LIKE, THIS IS WHAT I MEANT!" (Baraka), **Supp. II Part 1:** 59

"Like All the Other Nations" (Paley), **Supp. VI:** 220

"Like a Rolling Stone" (song, Dylan), **Supp. XVIII:** 20, 30

"Like Decorations in a Nigger Cemetery" (Stevens), **IV:** 74, 79; **Retro. Supp. I:** 305

Like Ghosts of Eagles (Francis), **Supp. IX:** 86

"Like Life" (Moore), **Supp. X:** 163, 165, **172–173**

Like Life: Stories (Moore), **Supp. X:** 163, **171–175,** 177, 178

"Likeness to God" (Channing), **Supp. XXIV: 75–76,** 77, 78

"Like Talk" (Mills), **Supp. XI:** 311

"Like the New Moon I Will Live My Life" (R. Bly), **Supp. IV Part 1:** 71

Li'l Abner (Capp), **IV:** 198

"Lilacs" (Lowell), **II:** 527

"Lilacs, The" (Wilbur), **Supp. III Part 2:** 557–558

"Lilacs for Ginsberg" (Stern), **Supp. IX:** 299

Liliom (Molnar), **Supp. XVI:** 187

Lilith's Brood (O. Butler), **Supp. XIII:** 63

Lillabulero Press, **Supp. V:** 4, 5

Lillian Hellman (Adler), **Supp. I Part 1:** 297

Lillian Hellman (Falk), **Supp. I Part 1:** 297

Lillian Hellman: Playwright (Moody), **Supp. I Part 1:** 280

Lillo, George, **II:** 111, 112

"Lily Daw and the Three Ladies" (Welty), **IV:** 262

Lily for My Love, A (Berrigan), **Supp. XXIV:** 35

Lima, Agnes de, **I:** 231, 232

Lima, Frank, **Supp. XXIII:** 217, 221

Lima, Maria Helena, **Supp. XXII:** 73

Lima Beans (Kreymborg), **Supp. XXII:** 163

"Limbo: Altered States" (Karr), **Supp. XI:** 249–250

"Limen" (Trethewey), **Supp. XXI:** 250

Lime Orchard Woman, The (Ríos), **Supp. IV Part 2:** 538, 547–550, 553

"Lime Orchard Woman, The" (Ríos), **Supp. IV Part 2:** 548

Limitations (Turow), **Supp. XVII: 222–223**

"Limits" (Emerson), **II:** 19

Limits of Mortality, The: An Essay on Wordsworth's Major Poems (Ferry), **Supp. XXIV:** 147, 148

Lincoln, Abraham, **I:** 1, 4, 30; **II:** 8, 13, 135, 273, 555, 576; **III:** 576, 577, 580, 584, 587–590, 591; **IV:** 192, 195, 298, 347, 350, 444; **Supp. I Part 1:** 2, 8, 26, 309, 321; **Supp. I Part 2:** 379, 380, 382, 385, 390, 397, 399, 418, 424, 454, 456, 471, 472, 473, 474, 483, 579, 687; **Supp. IX:** 15; **Supp. VIII:** 108; **Supp. XIV:** 73

Lincoln, Kenneth, **Supp. IV Part 1:** 329; **Supp. IV Part 2:** 507

Lincoln, Thomas, **III:** 587

Lincoln, Mrs. Thomas (Nancy Hanks), **III:** 587

Lincoln: A Novel (Vidal), **Supp. IV Part 2:** 677, 684, 685, 688, 689–690, 691, 692

Lincoln Lawyer, The (Connelly), **Supp. XXI: 77,** 78

Lincoln on Race and Slavery (H. L. Gates), **Supp. XX: 108–109**

"Lincoln Relics, The" (Kunitz), **Supp. III Part 1:** 269

Lincoln: The Man (Masters), **Supp. I Part 2:** 471, 473–474

Lindbergh, Charles A., **I:** 482

"Linden Branch, The" (MacLeish), **III:** 19, 20

Linden Hills (Naylor), **Supp. VIII:** 214, 218, **219–223**

Linderman, Lawrence, **Supp. IV Part 2:** 579, 583, 585, 589

Lindner, April, **Supp. XV:** 111, 119

"Lindo y Querido" (Muñoz), **Supp. XXV:** 135

Lindsay, Howard, **III:** 284

Lindsay, John, **Supp. I Part 2:** 374

Lindsay, Olive, **Supp. I Part 2:** 374, 375, 392

Lindsay, Vachel, **I:** 384; **II:** 263, 276, 530; **III:** 5, 505; **Retro. Supp. I:** 133; **Supp. I Part 1:** 324; **Supp. I Part 2: 374–403,** 454, 473, 474; **Supp. III Part 1:** 63, 71; **Supp. XV:** 293, 297, 299, 301, 306; **Supp. XVI:** 184–185; **Supp. XXV:** 18

Lindsay, Mrs. Vachel (Elizabeth Connors), **Supp. I Part 2:** 398, 399, 473

Lindsay, Vachel Thomas, **Supp. I Part 2:** 374, 375

Lindsay, Mrs. Vachel Thomas (Esther Catherine Frazee), **Supp. I Part 2:** 374, 375, 384–385, 398

Lindsey, David, **Supp. XIV:** 26

"Line, The" (Olds), **Supp. X:** 206

Lineage of Ragpickers, Songpluckers, Elegiasts, and Jewelers, A (Goldbarth), **Supp. XII:** 191

"Line"(Crooker), **Supp. XXIII:** 58

Line Dance (Crooker), **Supp. XXIII:** 56, **58–60**

"Line Dance"(Crooker), **Supp. XXIII:** 59

"Line of Least Resistance, The" (Wharton), **Retro. Supp. I:** 366

Line Out for a Walk, A: Familiar Essays (Epstein), **Supp. XIV: 107**

"Liner Notes for the Poetically Unhep" (Hughes), **Retro. Supp. I:** 210

"Lines, Written on Reading Stuart's Account of the Treatment of Slaves in Charleston" (Very), **Supp. XXV:** 239

"Lines After Rereading T. S. Eliot" (Wright), **Supp. V:** 343

"Lines Composed a Few Miles Above Tintern Abbey" (Wordsworth), **Supp. III Part 1:** 12

"Lines Composed Over Three Thousand Miles from Tintern Abbey" (Collins), **Supp. XXI:** 57–58

"Lines for an Interment" (MacLeish), **III:** 15

"Lines for My Father" (Cullen), **Supp. IV Part 1:** 167

"Lines from Israel" (Lowell), **II:** 554

"Lines from Pietro Longhi" (Sobin), **Supp. XVI:** 289

"Lines on Revisiting the Country" (Bryant), **Supp. I Part 1:** 164

"Lines Suggested by a Tennessee Song" (Agee), **I:** 28

"Lines to a Friend Asleep"(J. Schoolcraft), **Supp. XXIII:** 228, 230

"Line-Storm Song, A" (Frost), **Retro. Supp. I:** 127

"Lines written at Castle Island, Lake Superior"(J. Schoolcraft), **Supp. XXIII:** 229, 232, 233

"Lines Written at Port Royal" (Freneau), **Supp. II Part 1:** 264

"Lines Written in an Asylum" (Carruth), **Supp. XVI:** 48

"Lines Written in Manassas", **Supp. XV:** 99–100

Lineup, The (Connelly), **Supp. XXI:** 67, 68–69

"Line Written in the Dark Illegible Next Day" (F. Wright), **Supp. XVII:** 242

Linfield, Susie, **Supp. XVII:** 169, 177

Lingeman, Richard, **Supp. X:** 82; **Supp. XXII:** 104

"Linguistics 101" (Huddle), **Supp. XXVI:** 152

Linn, Elizabeth. *See* Brown, Mrs. Charles Brockden (Elizabeth Linn)

Linn, John Blair, **Supp. I Part 1:** 145

Linnaeus, Carolus, **II:** 6; **Supp. I Part 1:** 245

"Linnets" (Levis), **Supp. XI:** 260, 261

"Linoleum" (Gallagher), **Supp. XXIV:** 170

"Linoleum Roses" (Cisneros), **Supp. VII:** 63, 66

Linotte: 1914–1920 (Nin), **Supp. X:** 193, 196, 197

Linschoten, Hans, **II:** 362, 363, 364

"Lion" (B. Kelly), **Supp. XVII:** 133

"Lion and Honeycomb" (Nemerov), **III:** 275, 278, 280

Lion and the Archer, The (Hayden), **Supp. II Part 1:** 366, 367

Lion and the Honeycomb, The (Blackmur), **Supp. II Part 1:** 91

Lion Country (Buechner), **Supp. XII:** 52, 53

Lionel Lincoln (Cooper), **I:** 339, 342

"Lion for Real, The" (Ginsberg), **Supp. II Part 1:** 320

Lionhearted, The: A Story about the Jews of Medieval England (Reznikoff), **Supp. XIV:** 280, 289

Lion in the Garden (Meriweather and Millgate), **Retro. Supp. I:** 91

"Lionizing" (Poe), **III:** 411, 425

"Lions, Harts, and Leaping Does" (Powers), **III:** 356

Lions and Shadows: An Education in the Twenties (Isherwood), **Supp. XIV:** 158, 159, 160, 162

"Lions in Sweden" (Stevens), **IV:** 79–80

Lipman, William R., **Supp. XIII:** 170

Li Po, **Supp. XI:** 241; **Supp. XII:** 218; **Supp. XV:** 47, 217

Lippard, George, **Supp. XXIII: 177–192**

Lippmann, Walter, **I:** 48, 222–223, 225; **III:** 291, 600; **IV:** 429; **Supp. I Part 2:** 609, 643; **Supp. VIII:** 104

Lipschitz, Moryce, **Supp. XXIII:** 6

Lips Together, Teeth Apart (McNally), **Supp. XIII: 201–202,** 208, 209

Lipsyte, Robert, **Supp. XVI:** 220

Lipton, James, **Supp. IV Part 2:** 576, 577, 579, 583, 586, 588

Lipton, Lawrence, **Supp. IX:** 3

"Lisbon Story" (Vaz), **Supp. XXVI:** 267–268

Lisbon Traviata, The (McNally), **Supp. XIII:** 198, **199–200,** 201, 204, 208

Lish, Gordon, **Supp. XIX:** 209; **Supp. XXI:** 115, 121; **Supp. XXIII:** 274; **Supp. XXIV:** 166, 177

Lisicky,Paul, **Supp. XI:** 120, 131, 135

Lisk, Thomas, **Supp. XXI:** 24

"Lisp, The" (Olds), **Supp. X:** 211

Listen, Ruben Fontanez (Neugeboren), **Supp. XVI: 220–221**

"Listeners, The" (de la Mare), **Supp. XVII:** 69

"Listeners and Readers: The Unforgetting of Vachel Lindsay" (Trombly), **Supp. I Part 2:** 403

"Listening" (J. W. Miller), **Supp. XX: 167**

"Listening" (Paley), **Supp. VI:** 218, 231, 232

"Listening" (Stafford), **Supp. XI:** 321, 322

Listening to Prozac (P. Kramer), **Supp. XVI:** 229

"Listening to the Desert" (Henderson), **Supp. XIII:** 221–222

"Listening to the Mockingbird" (Woodard), **Supp. VIII:** 128

Listening to Your Life: Daily Meditations with Frederick Buechner (Buechner), **Supp. XII:** 53

Listen to the Desert/Oye al desierto (Mora), **Supp. XIII:** 221

"Listen to the People" (Benét), **Supp. XI:** 51–52

Liston, Sonny, **III:** 38, 42

Li T'ai-po, **II:** 526

"Litany" (Ashbery), **Supp. III Part 1:** 21–22, 25, 26

"Litany" (Collins), **Supp. XXI:** 56–57

"Litany" (Sandburg), **III:** 593

"Litany, The" (Gioia), **Supp. XV:** 125, 126

"Litany for Dictatorships" (Benét), **Supp. XI:** 46, 58

"Litany for Survival, A" (Lorde), **Supp. XII:** 220

"Litany of the Dark People, The" (Cullen), **Supp. IV Part 1:** 170, 171

"Litany of the Heroes" (Lindsay), **Supp. I Part 2:** 397

"Litany of Washington Street, The" (Lindsay), **Supp. I Part 2:** 376, 398–399

Literary Anthropology (Trumpener and Nyce), **Retro. Supp. I:** 380

Literary Art and Activism of Rick Bass, The (Weltzien), **Supp. XVI:** 20–21

"Literary Blacks and Jews" (Ozick), **Supp. V:** 272

"Literary Career of Elizabeth Barstow Stoddard, The" (Matlack), **Supp. XV:** 269

Literary Criticism: A Short History (Brooks and Wimsatt), **Supp. XIV:** 12

"Literary Criticism of Georg Lukács, The" (Sontag), **Supp. III Part 2:** 453

"Literary Development or California, The" (Atherton), **Supp. XXIV:** 22

Literary Disruptions (Klinkowitz), **Supp. XXI:** 233

Literary Essays of Thomas Merton, The, **Supp. VIII:** 207

"Literary Folk As They Came and Went with Ourselves" (E. Stoddard), **Supp. XV:** 274

Literary Friends and Acquaintance (Howells), **Supp. I Part 1:** 318; **Supp. XV:** 287

"Literary Heritage of Tennyson, The" (Locke), **Supp. XIV:** 197

Literary History of the United States (Spiller et al., ed.), **Supp. I Part 1:** 104; **Supp. II Part 1:** 95

"Literary Importation" (Freneau), **Supp. II Part 1:** 264

"Literary Life of America, The" (Brooks), **I:** 245

"Literary London" (Atherton), **Supp. XXIV:** 24

Literary Outlaw: The Life and Times of William S. Burroughs (Morgan), **Supp. XIV:** 141

Literary Situation, The (Cowley), **Supp. II Part 1:** 135, 140, 144, 146, 147, 148

"Literary Worker's Polonius, The" (Wilson), **IV:** 431, 432

"Literature" (Emerson), **II:** 6

Literature (X. J. Kennedy), **Supp. XV:** 153

Literature and American Life (Boynton), **Supp. I Part 2:** 415

Literature and Insurgency: Ten Studies in Racial Evolution (Underwood), **Supp. XXIV:** 29

Literature and Life (Howells), **Supp. XIV:** 45–46

Literature and Morality (Farrell), **II:** 49

"Literature and Place: Varieties of Regional Experience" (Erisman), **Supp. VIII:** 126

"Literature as a Symptom" (Warren), **IV:** 237

"Literature in Low Life" (Hapgood), **Supp. XVII:** 103

"Literature of Exhaustion, The" (Barth), **Supp. IV Part 1:** 48

"Lithuanian Nocturne" (Brodsky), **Supp. VIII:** 29

"Lit Instructor" (Stafford), **Supp. XI:** 321

Littauer, Kenneth, **Retro. Supp. I:** 114

Little Acts of Kindness (Budbill), **Supp. XIX:** 3, **14–15**

"Little Bernhardt" (Shaw), **Supp. XIX:** 246

Little Big Man (Berger), **Supp. XII:** 171

Little Big Man (film), **Supp. X:** 124

Littlebird, Harold, **Supp. IV Part 2:** 499

Littlebird, Larry, **Supp. IV Part 2:** 499, 505

Little Birds: Erotica (Nin), **Supp. X:** 192, 195

"Little Brown Baby" (Dunbar), **Supp. II Part 1:** 206

"Little Brown Jug" (Baraka), **Supp. II Part 1:** 51

"Little Burst, A"(Strout), **Supp. XXIII:** 282

"Little by Little"(Hadas), **Supp. XXIII:** 115

Little Casino (Sorrentino), **Supp. XXI:** 237, 238

"Little Clown, My Heart" (Cisneros), **Supp. VII:** 71

"Little Cosmic Dust Poem" (Haines), **Supp. XII:** 209–210

"Little Country Girl, A" (Chopin), **Retro. Supp. I:** 71

"Little Curtis" (Parker), **Supp. IX:** 193

Little Disturbances of Man, The (Paley), **Supp. VI:** 218

"Little Dog" (Hughes), **Supp. I Part 1:** 329

Little Dorrit (Dickens), **Supp. I Part 1:** 35

"Little Edward" (Stowe), **Supp. I Part 2:** 587

"Little Elegy" (X. J. Kennedy), **Supp. XV:** 155

"Little Elegy for Antonio Machado"(O'Hara), **Supp. XXIII:** 220

Little Essays Drawn from the Writings of George Santayana (L. P. Smith), **Supp. XIV:** 342

"Little Expressionless Animals" (Wallace), **Supp. X:** 305

"Little Fable" (Hay), **Supp. XIV:** 131

Little Face and Other Stories (Thompson), **Supp. XXIII: 293–294**

"Little Face"(Thompson), **Supp. XXIII:** 293

Littlefield, Catherine, **Supp. IX:** 58

Little Fling, A (Pickering), **Supp. XXI:** 203

Little Foxes, The (Hellman), **Supp. I Part 1:** 276, 278–279, 281, 283, 297

"Little Fred, the Canal Boy" (Stowe), **Supp. I Part 2:** 587

"Little French Mary" (Jewett), **II:** 400

Little Friend, Little Friend (Jarrell), **II:** 367, 372, 375–376

"Little Gidding" (Eliot), **I:** 582, 588; **II:** 539; **Retro. Supp. I:** 66

"Little Girl, My Stringbean, My Lovely Woman" (Sexton), **Supp. II Part 2:** 686

"Little Girl, The" (Paley), **Supp. VI:** 222, **228–229**

"Little Girl Tells a Story to a Lady, A" (Barnes), **Supp. III Part 1:** 36

"Little Goose Girl, The" (Grimm), **IV:** 266

Little Ham (Hughes), **Retro. Supp. I:** 203; **Supp. I Part 1:** 328, 339

Little House in the Big Woods (L. I. Wilder), **Supp. XXII:** 294, 295, 296, 297, 298–299, 300

Little House on the Prairie (L. I. Wilder), **Supp. XXII:** 294, 295–296, 297, 299, 301

Little House on the Prairie (television series), **Supp. XXII:** 289

"Little House" series (L. A. Wilder), **Supp. XXII:** 289

"Little House" series (L. I. Wilder), **Supp. XXVI:** 217–218

Little House Traveler, A (L. I. Wilder), **Supp. XXII:** 301

Little Ignorance, A (Schott), **Supp. XXIII:** 239, 241

Little King, The (Bynner), **Supp. XV:** 42, 50

Little Lady of the Big House, The (London), **II:** 481–482

Little Liar, The (film; Ingraham), **Supp. XVI:** 184–185

"Little Lion Face" (Swenson), **Supp. IV Part 2:** 651

"Little Lobelia's Song" (Bogan), **Supp. III Part 1:** 66

"Little Local Color, A" (Henry), **Supp. II Part 1:** 399

Little Lord Fauntleroy (Burnett), **Retro. Supp. I:** 188; **Supp. XVI:** 182

"Little Love, The" (H. Johnson), **Supp. XXVI:** 173

"Little Lyric" (Hughes), **Supp. I Part 1:** 334

Little Man, Little Man (Baldwin), **Supp. I Part 1:** 67

"Little Man at Chehaw Station, The" (Ellison), **Retro. Supp. II:** 123

Little Me (musical), **Supp. IV Part 2:** 575

Little Men (Alcott), **Supp. I Part 1:** 32, 39, 40

"Little Morning Music, A" (Schwartz), **Supp. II Part 2:** 662–663

Little Ocean (Shepard), **Supp. III Part 2:** 447

"Little Old Girl, A" (Larcom), **Supp. XIII:** 144

"Little Old Spy" (Hughes), **Supp. I Part 1:** 329

Little Orphan Annie (film), **Supp. XVIII:** 244

"Little Owl Who Lives in the Orchard" (Oliver), **Supp. VII:** 239

"Little Peasant, The" (Sexton), **Supp. II Part 2:** 690

"Little People"(Kenny), **Supp. XXIII:** 151

"Little Rapids, The" (Swenson), **Supp. IV Part 2:** 645

Little Red Song Book (Hill), **Supp. XVIII:** 224

Little Regiment and Other Episodes of the American Civil War, The (Crane), **I:** 408

Little River: New and Selected Poems (McCarriston), **Supp. XIV:** 269–272

"Little Road not made of Man , A" (Dickinson), **Retro. Supp. I:** 44

"Little Sawtooth" (Huddle), **Supp. XXVI:** 154, 155

Little Sister, The (Chandler), **Supp. IV Part 1:** 122, 130, 131–132

"Little Sleep's-Head Sprouting Hair in the Moonlight" (Kinnell), **Supp. III Part 1:** 247

"Little Snow White" (Grimm), **IV:** 266

"Little Spirit, or Boy-Man, The: An Odjibwa Tale"(J. Schoolcraft), **Supp. XXIII:** 234

Little Star (Halliday), **Supp. XIX:** 82, **84–85,** 87

"Little Star" (Halliday), **Supp. XIX:** 83, 84, 93

"Little Testament of Bernard Martin, Aet. 30" (Mumford), **Supp. II Part 2:** 472, 473, 474

"Little Things" (Olds), **Supp. X:** 208

Little Tour in France (James), **II:** 337

Little Town, The (Asch), **Supp. XXIII:** 4, 5, **7–8**

"Little Travel Diary, A"(O'Hara), **Supp. XXIII:** 220

Little Women (Alcott), **Supp. I Part 1:** 28, 29, 32, 35, 37, 38, 39–40, 41, 43, 44; **Supp. IX:** 128

Little Yellow Dog, A (Mosley), **Supp. XIII:** 237, 241

"Liturgy and Spiritual Personalism" (Merton), **Supp. VIII:** 199

Litz, A. Walton, **Retro. Supp. I:** 306

"Liu Ch'e" (Pound), **III:** 466

"Live" (Sexton), **Supp. II Part 2:** 684, 686

Live from Baghdad (screenplay, Shanley), **Supp. XIV:** 316

Live from Golgotha (Vidal), **Supp. IV Part 2:** 677, 682, 691, 692

Live Now and Pay Later (Garrett), **Supp. VII:** 111

"Live-Oak with Moss" (Whitman), **Retro. Supp. I:** 403

Live or Die (Sexton), **Supp. II Part 2:** 670, 683–687

Liveright, Horace, **Retro. Supp. I:** 80, 81, 83; **Supp. I Part 2:** 464; **Supp. XX: 71, 75; Supp. XXII:** 25; **Supp. XXIV:** 28; **Supp. XXV:** 24

Livermore, Elizabeth, **Supp. XXII:** 70

Lives (Plutarch), **II:** 5, 104

Lives of a Cell, The (L. Thomas), **Retro. Supp. I:** 322, 323

Lives of Distinguished American Naval Officers (Cooper), **I:** 347

"Lives of Gulls and Children, The" (Nemerov), **III:** 271, 272

Lives of the Animals (Wrigley), **Supp. XVIII:** 306–308

Lives of the Artists (Vasari), **Supp. I Part 2:** 450

"Lives of the Bohemians" (Lethem), **Supp. XVIII:** 135

Lives of the Heart, The (Hirshfield), **Supp. XXIII:** 132–133, 135

Lives of the Muses, The: Nine Women and the Artists They Inspired (Prose), **Supp. XVI:** 250, 260

"Lives of the Philosophers, The" (Brockmeier), **Supp. XXII:** 59, 61

Lives of the Poets (Doctorow), **Supp. IV Part 1:** 234

"Lives of the Poets" (Doctorow), **Supp. IV Part 1:** 234

"Lives of the—Wha'?, The" (Goldbarth), **Supp. XII:** 191

"Living" (Wright), **Supp. XV:** 345

Living, The (Dillard), **Supp. VI:** 23

"Living at Home" (Gordon), **Supp. IV Part 1:** 311

Living by Fiction (Dillard), **Supp. VI:** 23, 31, **32,** 33

Living by the Word (Walker), **Supp. III Part 2:** 521, 522, 526, 527, 535

Living End, The (Elkin), **Supp. VI: 54,** 58

Living Instead (Bronk), **Supp. XXI:** 32

"Living in the Flatlands" (Carruth), **Supp. XVI:** 54

Living in Time (Hadas), **Supp. XXIII:** 120, **122–123**

Living Is Easy, The (D. West), **Supp. XVIII:** 277, 280, **284–286,** 287

"Living Like Weasels" (Dillard), **Supp. VI:** 26, 33

Living Novel, The (Hicks), **III:** 342

Living of Charlotte Perkins Gilman, The (Gilman), **Supp. XI:** 193, 209

Living off the Country: Essays on Poetry and Place (Haines), **Supp. XII:** 199, 203, 207

"Living on a Giant" (X. J. Kennedy), **Supp. XV:** 163

Living Out Loud (Quindlen), **Supp. XVII:** 166, **167–169**

Living Present, The (Atherton), **Supp. XXIV:** 24

Living Reed, The (Buck), **Supp. II Part 1:** 129–130

Livingston, Myra Cohn, **Supp. XV:** 153, 162

Living Theater, **Retro. Supp. I:** 424

"Living There" (Dickey), **Supp. IV Part 1:** 182–183

Living the Spirit: A Gay American Indian Anthology (Roscoe, ed.), **Supp. IV Part 1:** 330

"Living Together: A Letter" (Biss), **Supp. XXVI:** 51

Living to Prowl (Pickering), **Supp. XXI:** 203

"Living with a Peacock" (O'Connor), **III:** 350

"Living Words and Cartoon Translations" (Jocks), **Supp. XXVI:** 97

"Livvie" (Welty), **IV:** 265; **Retro. Supp. I:** 348–349

"Livvie Is Back" (Welty), **Retro. Supp. I:** 351

Livy, **II:** 8

Lizzie (film), **Supp. IX:** 125

"Llantos de La Llorona: Warnings from the Wailer" (Mora), **Supp. XIII:** 217, 224

"L'Lapse" (Barthelme), **Supp. IV Part 1:** 45–47, 48

Llosa, Mario Vargas, **Supp. XIX:** 131; **Supp. XXIV:** 89

Lloyd, Fabien. *See* Cravan, Arthur

Lloyd, Henry Demarest, **Supp. I Part 1:** 5

Lloyd George, Harold, **I:** 490

"LMFBR" (Snyder), **Supp. VIII:** 302

Loach, Ken, **Supp. XXIII:** 163

"Loaded Inflections" (Halliday), **Supp. XIX:** 90, 91

"Loam" (Sandburg), **III:** 584–585

"Loan, The" (Malamud), **Supp. I Part 2:** 427, 428, 431, 437

Loberer, Eric, **Supp. XV:** 339

"Local" (McCarriston), **Supp. XIV:** 270

Local Color (Capote), **Supp. III Part 1:** 120

"Local Color" (London), **II:** 475

"Local Family Keeps Son Happy" (Keillor), **Supp. XVI:** 168, 169

Local Girls (Hoffman), **Supp. X:** 77, **90–91,** 92

"Local Girls" (Hoffman), **Supp. X:** 90

Local Habitation & A Name, A (Kooser), **Supp. XIX:** 116, 118, **119–120**

Local Men (Whitehead), **Supp. XV:** 339

"Local Metaphysics" (Huddle), **Supp. XXVI:** 149

Local Time (Dunn), **Supp. XI:** 143, **148–149**

Local Wonders: Seasons in the Bohemian Alps (Kooser), **Supp. XIX:** 115, **126**

"Location" (Halliday), **Supp. XIX:** 87

Lock, Helen, **Supp. XIII:** 233, 237–238

Lock, Robert H., **IV:** 319; **Retro. Supp. I:** 375

Locke, Alain, **Retro. Supp. II:** 115; **Supp. I Part 1:** 323, 325, 341; **Supp. II Part 1:** 53, 176, 182, 228, 247; **Supp. IV Part 1:** 170; **Supp. IX:** 306, 309; **Supp. X:** 134, 137, 139; **Supp. XIV:** **195–219; Supp. XIX:** 69, 75; **Supp. XVIII:** 122; **Supp. XXII:** 7, 13

Locke, Duane, **Supp. IX:** 273

Locke, Jane Ermine, **Supp. XXV:** 38

Locke, John, **I:** 554–555, 557; **II:** 15–16, 113–114, 348–349, 480; **III:** 294–295; **IV:** 149; **Supp. I Part 1:** 130, 229, 230; **Supp. I Part 2:** 523

Locke, Sondra, **II:** 588

"Locked House, A" (Snodgrass), **Supp. VI:** 323

Locked Room, The (Auster), **Supp. XII:** 22, 24, **27–28**

Locket, The (Masters), **Supp. I Part 2:** 460

Lockridge, Ross, Jr., **Supp. XIX:** 263

"Locksley Hall" (Tennyson), **Supp. IX:** 19

Lockwood Concern, The (O'Hara), **III:** 362, 364, 377–382

"Locus" (Ammons), **Supp. VII:** 28

"Locus" (Hayden), **Supp. II Part 1:** 361–362, 381

"Locusts, the Plaza, the Room, The" (Kees), **Supp. XV:** 141

Loden, Barbara, **III:** 163

Lodge, Henry Cabot, **I:** 11–12, 21

Lodge, Mrs. Henry Cabot, **I:** 11–12, 19

Lodge, Thomas, **IV:** 370

Loeb, Gerald, **Supp. IV Part 2:** 523

Loeb, Harold, **Supp. XXIV:** 49

Loeb, Jacques, **I:** 513; **Retro. Supp. II:** 104; **Supp. I Part 2:** 641

Loeffler, Jack, **Supp. XIII:** 1, 3, 12, 14, 16

Loft, William D., **Supp. XXVI:** 96

Loftus, Mary J., **Supp. XXI:** 245

Lofty Dogmas (A. Finch, M. Kumin and D. Brown, eds.), **Supp. XVII:** 75–76

"Log" (Merrlll), **Supp. III Part 1:** 328

Logan, Joshua, **Supp. XXV:** 95

Logan, Rayford W., **Supp. II Part 1:** 171, 194; **Supp. XIV:** 73

Logan, William, **Supp. X:** 201, 213; **Supp. XI:** 131, 132; **Supp. XII:** 98, 107, 113, 184; **Supp. XV:** 212, 226, 251, 257, 260–261, 262,**Supp. XV:** 263, 266

Log Book of "The Loved One," The, **Supp. XI:** 306

Logenbach, James, **Supp. XVII:** 183

"Logging and Pimping and 'Your Pal, Jim' " (Maclean), **Supp. XIV:** 229

Logue, Christopher, **Supp. XIV:** 82

Lohengrin (Wagner), **I:** 216

Lohrfinck, Rosalind, **III:** 107, 117

Lolita (Nabokov), **III:** 246, 247, 255, 258–261; **Retro. Supp. I:** 263, 264, 265, 266, 269, 270, **272–274,** 275; **Supp. V:** 127, 252; **Supp. VIII:** 133; **Supp. XVI:** 294; **Supp. XXII:** 260

"Lolita" (Parker), **Supp. IX:** 193

Lolly Dinks' Doings (E. Stoddard), **Supp. XV:** 273,**Supp. XV:** 286

Lombardi, Marilyn May, **Retro. Supp. II:** 40

Lomokome Papers, The (Wouk), **Supp. XXV:** 256, 262

London, Eliza, **II:** 465

London, Jack, **I:** 209; **II:** 264, 440, 444, 451, 462, **462–485; III:** 314, 580; **Supp. IV Part 1:** 236; **Supp. IX:** 1, 14; **Supp. V:** 281; **Supp. XIII:** 312; **Supp. XIV:** 227; **Supp. XV:** 115; **Supp. XVI:** 181; **Supp. XVIII:** 90; **Supp. XXII:** 203

London, Mrs. Jack (Bessie Maddern), **II:** 465, 466, 473, 478

London, Mrs. Jack (Charmian Kittredge), **II:** 466, 468, 473, 476, 478, 481

London, John, **II:** 464, 465

London, Scott, **Supp. XIV:** 301, 307, 311

"London 1972: Silent Zone" (Davison), **Supp. XXVI:** 72

London Embassy, The (Theroux), **Supp. VIII:** 323

London Fields (Amis), **Retro. Supp. I:** 278

"London Letter" (column; Eliot), **Supp. XV:** 306

London Magazine (Plath), **Supp. I Part 2:** 541

London Snow: A Christmas Story (Theroux), **Supp. VIII:** 322

London Suite (Simon), **Supp. IV Part 2:** 576, 581, 582, 588

London: The Biography (Ackroyd), **Supp. XVII:** 180

Loneliness of the Long Distance Runner, The (Sillitoe), **Supp. XX: 195**

Lonely Are the Brave (film), **Supp. XIII:** 6

"Lonely Coast, A" (Proulx), **Supp. VII:** 264

Lonely Crusade (C. Himes), **Supp. XVI:** 135, 139–140

Lonely for the Future (Farrell), **II:** 46, 47

"Lonely Gay Teen Seeking Same" (Egan), **Supp. XIX:** 61

Lonely Impulse of Delight, A (Shanley), **Supp. XIV:** 317–318

"Lonely Street, The" (W. C. Williams), **IV:** 413

"Lonely Worker, A" (Jewett), **Retro. Supp. II:** 132

Lonergan, Wayne, **Supp. I Part 1:** 51

Lonesome Boy (Bontemps), **Supp. XXII:** 6, 13–14

Lonesome Dove (McMurtry), **Supp. V:** 226–228, 231, 232, 233

Lonesome Traveler (Kerouac), **Supp. III Part 1:** 219, 225

"Lonesome Whistle Blowing" (Skow), **Supp. XVI:** 174

"Lone Striker, A" (Frost), **Retro. Supp. I:** 136, 137

Long, Ada, **Supp. V:** 178

Long, Frank Belknap, **Supp. XXV:** 111, 122

Long, Haniel, **Supp. XV:** 46, 49

Long, Huey, **I:** 489; **II:** 454; **IV:** 249; **Supp. IV Part 2:** 679; **Supp. XIV:** 14

Long, John Luther, **Supp. XXI:** 150

Long, Judith Reick, **Supp. XX: 212, 215, 217, 223**

Long, Ray, **II:** 430; **III:** 54

Long after Midnight (Bradbury), **Supp. IV Part 1:** 102

Long Ago in France: The Years in Dijon (M. F. K. Fisher), **Supp. XVII:** 91

Long and Happy Life, A (Price), **Supp. VI:** 258, **259–260,** 262, 264, 265

Long Approach, The (Kumin), **Supp. IV Part 2:** 452–453, 453

Longbottom, Robert, **Supp. XXI:** 148

Long Christmas Dinner, The (Wilder), **IV:** 357, 365; **Supp. V:** 105

Long Christmas Dinner and Other Plays (Wilder), **IV:** 365–366

Long Day's Dying, A (Buechner), **Supp. XII: 45–47**

Long Day's Journey into Night (O'Neill), **III:** 385, 401, 403–404; **Supp. IV Part 1:** 359; **Supp. XIV:** 327; **Supp. XXI:** 13; **Supp. XXII:** 27, 29, 30

Long Desire, A (Connell), **Supp. XIV:** 79, 80, 97

"Long Distance" (Stafford), **Supp. XI:** 329

"Long-Distance Runner, The" (Paley), **Supp. VI:** 221–222, 228, 230

Long Dream, The (Wright), **IV:** 478, 488, 494

"Long Embrace, The" (Levine), **Supp. V:** 187

"Long Enough" (Rukeyser), **Supp. VI:** 274

"Longest Night of My Life, The " (Nichols), **Supp. XIII:** 269

Longfellow, Henry Wadsworth, **I:** 458, 471; **II:** 274, 277, 295–296, 310, 313, 402, **486–510; III:** 269, 412, 421, 422, 577; **IV:** 309, 371; **Retro. Supp. I:** 54, 123, 150, 155, 362; **Retro. Supp. II: 153–174; Supp. I Part 1:** 158, 299, 306, 317, 362, 368; **Supp. I Part 2:** 405, 406, 408, 409, 414, 416, 420, 586, 587, 602, 699, 704; **Supp. II Part 1:** 291, 353; **Supp. III Part 2:** 609; **Supp. IV Part 1:** 165; **Supp. IV Part 2:** 503; **Supp. XII:** 260; **Supp. XIII:** 141; **Supp. XIV:** 120; **Supp. XVIII:** 4; **Supp. XXI:** 51; **Supp. XXIII:** 223

"Long Feud" (Untermeyer), **Supp. XV:** 309

Long Feud: Selected Poems (Untermeyer), **Supp. XV:** 312

"Long Fourth, A" (Taylor), **Supp. V:** 313

Long Fourth and Other Stories, A (Taylor), **Supp. V:** 318–319

Long Gay Book, A (Stein), **IV:** 42

Long Goodbye, The (Chandler), **Supp. IV Part 1:** 120, 122, 132–134, 135

Long Goodbye, The (T. Williams), **IV:** 381

"Long Hair" (Snyder), **Supp. VIII:** 300

Longing for Home, The: Recollections and Reflections (Buechner), **Supp. XII:** 53

Longinus, Dionysius Cassius, **I:** 279

"Long-Legged House, The" (Berry), **Supp. X:** 21, 24–25, 27, 31

Long Live Man (Corso), **Supp. XII:** 129–130, 132

Long Love, The (Sedges), **Supp. II Part 1:** 125

Long Made Short (Dixon), **Supp. XII:** 152

Long March, The (Styron), **IV:** 97, 99, 104–107, 111, 113, 117

"Long Night, The" (Bambara), **Supp. XI:** 9

Long Night of White Chickens, The (Goldman), **Supp. XXV:** 49, 51–53

"Long Novel, A" (Ashbery), **Supp. III Part 1:** 6

Longo, Robert, **Supp. XVI:** 124

Long Patrol, The (Mailer), **III:** 46

"Long Peace Among Iroquois Nations, The" (Crawford), **Supp. XXVI:** 85

"Long Point Light" (Doty), **Supp. XI:** 127

Long Road of Woman's Memory, The (Addams), **Supp. I Part 1:** 17–18

"Long Run, The" (Wharton), **IV:** 314

Long Season, The (Brosnan), **II:** 424, 425; **Supp. XX: 195**

"Long Shadow of Lincoln, The: A Litany" (Sandburg), **III:** 591, 593

Longshot O'Leary (McGrath), **Supp. X:** 117

"Long Shower, The" (Francis), **Supp. IX:** 90

"Long Stemmed Roses" (Jarman), **Supp. XVII:** 115

Longstreet, Augustus B., **II:** 70, 313; **Supp. I Part 1:** 352; **Supp. V:** 44; **Supp. X:** 227

"Long Summer" (Lowell), **II:** 553–554

"Long Term" (Dunn), **Supp. XI:** 149

"Long Thoughts, The"(Dybek), **Supp. XXIII:** 71

Longtime Companion (film), **Supp. X:** 146, 152

Long Valley, The (Steinbeck), **IV:** 51

Long View (Taggard), **Supp. XXII: 283–284**

Long Voyage Home, The (O'Neill), **III:** 388

"Long Wail, A" (Crews), **Supp. XI:** 101

"Long Walk, The" (Bogan), **Supp. III Part 1:** 61

Long Walk Home, The (Kriegel), **Supp. XXIV:** 214–216

Long Walks and Intimate Talks (Paley), **Supp. VI:** 221

Long Way from Home, A (McKay), **Supp. X:** 132, 140

Long Winter, The (L. I. Wilder), **Supp. XXII:** 291, 294, 295

Lönnrot, Elias, **Retro. Supp. II:** 159

Looby, Christopher, **Supp. XIII:** 96

Look, Dan, **Supp. XXV:** 123

Look, Stranger! (Auden), **Supp. II Part 1:** 11

"Look, The" (Olds), **Supp. X:** 210

Look at Me (Egan), **Supp. XIX:** 49, **53–56,** 60, 61

Look at the Harlequins (Nabokov), **Retro. Supp. I:** 266, 270

"Look for My White Self" (Ammons), **Supp. VII:** 25

"Look Fred, You're a Doctor, My Problem Is Something Like This" (Berrigan), **Supp. XXIV:** 37

Look Homeward, Angel (Wolfe), **II:** 457; **IV:** 450, 452, 453, 454, 455–456, 461, 462, 463, 464, 468, 471; **Supp. XI:** 216

"Looking" (Sanders), **Supp. XVI:** 277

"Looking a Mad Dog Dead in the Eyes" (Komunyakaa), **Supp. XIII:** 114

"Looking at Each Other" (Rukeyser), **Supp. VI:** 280, 285–286

"Looking at Kafka" (P. Roth), **Supp. III Part 2:** 402

"Looking at Women" (Sanders), **Supp. XVI:** 274

"Looking Back" (Harjo), **Supp. XII:** 218

"Looking Back" (Merwin), **Supp. III Part 1:** 352

"Looking Back at Girlhood" (Jewett), **Retro. Supp. II:** 131, 133

Looking Backward (Bellamy), **II:** 276; **Supp. I Part 2:** 641; **Supp. XI:** 200

"Looking for a Ship" (McPhee), **Supp. III Part 1:** 312–313

"Looking for Dragon Smoke" (R. Bly), **Supp. IV Part 1:** 60

Looking for Holes in the Ceiling (Dunn), **Supp. XI:** 139, **143–145**

Looking for Langston (Julien; film), **Supp. XI:** 19, 20

Looking for Lincoln (television production), **Supp. XX: 99**

Looking for Luck (Kumin), **Supp. IV Part 2:** 453, 454–455

"Looking for Mr. Green" (Bellow), **Retro. Supp. II:** 27

"Looking for the Buckhead Boys" (Dickey), **Supp. IV Part 1:** 182, 183

"Looking Forward to Age" (Harrison), **Supp. VIII:** 49

"Looking from Inside My Body" (R. Bly), **Supp. IV Part 1:** 71

"Looking Glass, The" (Wharton), **Retro. Supp. I:** 382

"Lookout's Journal" (Snyder), **Supp. VIII:** 291

"Looks Like They'll Never Learn" (McCoy), **Supp. XIII:** 166

"Look to the Woods" (P. N. Warren), **Supp. XX: 272**

"Look to Thy Heart . . ." (Hay), **Supp. XIV:** 130

Loon, Hendrik Willem van, **Supp. XVI:** 185

Loon Lake (Doctorow), **Supp. IV Part 1:** 219, 222, 224–227, 230, 231, 232, 233

"Loon Point" (O'Brien), **Supp. V:** 237

Loos, Adolf, **Supp. XVI:** 187

Loos, Anita, **Supp. XVI: 181–199**

Loos, Mary Anita, **Supp. XVI:** 196

Loose Canons (H. L. Gates), **Supp. XX: 101, 108, 109–110, 111**

Loosestrife (Dunn), **Supp. XI: 152–154**

"Loosestrife" (Dunn), **Supp. XI:** 154

"Loose Woman" (X. J. Kennedy), **Supp. XV:** 159

Loose Woman: Poems (Cisneros), **Supp. VII:** 58, 71–72

Lopate, Edward, **Supp. XVI:** 266

Lopate, Philip, **Supp. XII:** 184; **Supp. XIII:** 280–281; **Supp. XVI:** 230

Lopatnikoff, Nikolai, **Supp. XIV:** 123

Lopez, Barry, **Supp. IV Part 1:** 416; **Supp. V:** 211; **Supp. X:** 29, 31; **Supp. XIII:** 16; **Supp. XIV:** 227

Lopez, Rafael, **Supp. IV Part 2:** 602

Lorax, The (Geisel), **Supp. XVI:** 109–110

Lorca, Federico García, **IV:** 380; **Supp. I Part 1:** 345; **Supp. IV Part 1:** 83; **Supp. VIII:** 38, 39; **Supp. XIII:** 315, 323, 324; **Supp. XV:** 186; **Supp. XXI:** 100

Lord, Judge Otis P., **I:** 454, 457, 458, 470

Lorde, Audre, **Supp. I Part 2:** 550, 571; **Supp. IV Part 1:** 325; **Supp. XI:** 20; **Supp. XII:** 217, 220; **Supp. XIII:** 295; **Supp. XVII:** 71; **Supp. XXIII:** 194

Lord Jim (Conrad), **I:** 422; **II:** 26; **Retro. Supp. II:** 292; **Supp. I Part 2:** 623; **Supp. IV Part 2:** 680; **Supp. V:** 251

"Lord of Hosts" (Pinsky), **Supp. VI:** 244

Lord of the Flies (W. Golding), **Supp. XVI:** 65

Lord of the Rings (Tolkien), **Supp. V:** 140

Lords of Misrule, The (X. J. Kennedy), **Supp. XV:** 154, **170–171**

Lords of the Housetops (Van Vechten), **Supp. II Part 2:** 736

Lord's Prayer, **I:** 579

Lord Timothy Dexter of Newburyport, Mass. (Marquand), **III:** 55

Lord Weary's Castle (Lowell), **II:** 538, 542–551; **Retro. Supp. II:** 178, **186– 187,** 188; **Supp. XV:** 252

"Lorelei" (Plath), **Retro. Supp. II:** 246; **Supp. I Part 2:** 538

"Lorenzo" (Bynner), **Supp. XV:** 46, 50

Lorimer, George Horace, **II:** 430; **Retro. Supp. I:** 101, 113

Lorre, Peter, **Supp. IV Part 1:** 356

"Los Alamos" (Momaday), **Supp. IV Part 2:** 482

Los Amigos de Becky (Hinojosa). *See Becky and Her Friends* (Hinojosa)

"Los Angeles, 1980" (Gunn Allen), **Supp. IV Part 1:** 325

"Los Angeles Days" (Didion), **Supp. IV Part 1:** 211

Los Cerritos (Atherton), **Supp. XXIV:** 22

"Lo! School in Poetry, The" (Taggard), **Supp. XXII:** 276

"Loser, The" (Talese), **Supp. XVII:** 202, 208

Loser and Still Champion: Muhammad Ali (Schulberg), **Supp. XVIII:** 254

Losey, Joseph, **IV:** 383

Lose Your Mother: A Journey Along the Atlantic Slave Route (Hartman), **Supp. XX:** 154

"Losing a Language" (Merwin), **Supp. III Part 1:** 356

Losing Battles (Welty), **IV:** 261, 281–282; **Retro. Supp. I:** 341, 352, **353–354**

"Losing the Marbles" (Merrill), **Supp. III Part 1:** 337

"Losing Track of Language" (Clampitt), **Supp. IX:** 38, 40

Losses (Jarrell), **II:** 367, 372, 373–375, 376, 377, 380–381

"Losses" (Jarrell), **II:** 375–376

Lossky, N. O., **Supp. IV Part 2:** 519

"Loss of Breath" (Poe), **III:** 425–426

"Loss of My Arms and Legs, The" (Kingsolver), **Supp. VII:** 208

Loss of Roses, A (Inge), **Supp. XXV:** 95, 103–104, 106

"Loss of the Creature, The" (Percy), **Supp. III Part 1:** 387

"Lost" (Wagoner), **Supp. IX:** 328

"Lost, The" (Boyle), **Supp. XXIV:** 59

"Lost, The/Los Perdidos" (Kingsolver), **Supp. VII:** 208

"Lost and Found" (Levine), **Supp. V:** 188

"Lost and Found" (Nelson), **Supp. XVIII:** 176

"Lost Bodies" (Wright), **Supp. V:** 342

"Lost Boy, The" (Wolfe), **IV:** 451, 460, 466–467

"Lost Children, The"(Crooker), **Supp. XXIII:** 54

"Lost Decade, The" (Fitzgerald), **II:** 98

"Lost Dogs of Phnom Penh, The" (Boyle), **Supp. XXIV:** 64

Lost Ecstasy (Rinehart), **Supp. XXV:** 196

"Lost Fugue for Chet" (Hull), **Supp. XXI:** 137–138, 141

Lost Galleon and Other Tales, The (Harte), **Supp. II Part 1:** 344

Lost Get-Back Boogie, The (Burke), **Supp. XIV:** 22, 25

"Lost Girls, The" (Hogan), **Supp. IV Part 1:** 406–407

Lost Grizzlies, The: A Search for Survivors in the Wilderness of Colorado (Bass), **Supp. XVI:** 25, 26

Lost Highway (film), **Supp. X:** 314

Lost Illusions (Balzac), **I:** 500

"Lost in Nostalgia: The Autobiographies of Eva Hoffman and Richard Rodriguez" (Fachinger), **Supp. XVI:** 153

Lost in the Bonewheel Factory (Komunyakaa), **Supp. XIII:** **114–115,** 116

Lost in the City (E. P. Jones), **Supp. XXII:** 140, 142, **143–146,** 148, 149

Lost in the Cosmos: The Last Self-Help Book (Percy), **Supp. III Part 1:** 397

Lost in the Funhouse (Barth), **I:** 122, 135, 139; **Supp. X:** 307

"Lost in the Whichy Thicket" (Wolfe), **Supp. III Part 2:** 573, 574

Lost in Translation (E. Hoffman), **Supp. XVI:** 147, **148–151,** 153, 154, 159

"Lost in Translation" (Hass), **Supp. VIII:** 28

"Lost in Translation" (Merrill), **Supp. III Part 1:** 324, 329–330

Lost in Yonkers (film), **Supp. IV Part 2:** 588

Lost in Yonkers (Simon), **Supp. IV Part 2:** 576, 577, 584, 587–588, 590–591

"Lost Jerusalem" (Untermeyer), **Supp. XV:** 307

Lost Lady, A (Cather), **I:** 323–325, 327; **Retro. Supp. I:** 15–16, 20, 21, 382

Lost Light (Connelly), **Supp. XXI:** 72, **75–76**

"Lost Lives" (Sorrentino), **Supp. XXI:** 226

"Lost Lover, A" (Jewett), **II:** 400–401, 402; **Retro. Supp. II:** 137

"Lost Loves" (Kinnell), **Supp. III Part 1:** 237, 245

Lost Man's River (Matthiessen), **Supp. V:** 212, 213, 214, 215

"Lost on September Trail, 1967" (Ríos), **Supp. IV Part 2:** 540

Lost Puritan (Mariani), **Retro. Supp. II:** 189

Lost Roads Project, The: A Walk-In Book of Arkansas (exhibition; Wright and Luster), **Supp. XV:** 337, 348

"Lost Sailor, The" (Freneau), **Supp. II Part 1:** 264

Lost Son, The (Roethke), **III:** 529, 530–532, 533

"Lost Son, The" (Roethke), **III:** 536, 537–539, 542

"Lost Sons" (Salter), **Supp. IX:** 260

Lost Souls (Singer). *See* Meshugah (Singer)

"Lost"(Thompson), **Supp. XXIII:** 299, 300

"Lost Treaties of the California Indians" (Zitkala-Ša), **Supp. XXV:** 284

Lost Weekend, The (Jackson), **Supp. XIII:** 262

"Lost World, A" (Ashbery), **Supp. III Part 1:** 9

"Lost World, The" (Chabon), **Supp. XI:** 72–73

Lost World, The (Jarrell), **II:** 367, 368, 371, 379–380, 386, 387

"Lost World, The" cycle (Chabon), **Supp. XI: 71–73**

"Lost World of Richard Yates, The: How the Great Writer of the Age of Anxiety Disappeared from Print" (O'Nan), **Supp. XI:** 348

"Lost Young Intellectual, The" (Howe), **Supp. VI:** 113, **115–116**

Lost Zoo, The: (A Rhyme for the Young, But Not Too Young) (Cullen), **Supp. IV Part 1:** 173

Loti, Pierre, **II:** 311, 325; **Supp. IV Part 1:** 81

"Lot of People Bathing in a Stream, A" (Stevens), **IV:** 93

Lotringer, Sylvère, **Supp. XII:** 4

"Lot's Wife" (Nemerov), **III:** 270

"Lottery, The" (Jackson), **Supp. IX:** 113, 114, 118, 120, **122–123**

Lottery, The; or, The Adventures of James Harris (Jackson), **Supp. IX:** 113, 115, 116, 124, 125

Lotze, Hermann, **III:** 600

Loud and Clear (Quindlen), **Supp. XVII:** 167, **170–172**

Louganis, Greg, **Supp. XX: 264**

"Louie, His Cousin & His Other Cousin" (Cisneros), **Supp. VII:** 60

Louis, Joe, **II:** 589; **Supp. IV Part 1:** 360

Louis, Pierre Charles Alexandre, **Supp. I Part 1:** 302, 303

"Louisa, Please Come Home" (Jackson), **Supp. IX:** 122

Louis Lambert (Balzac), **I:** 499

"Louis Simpson and Walt Whitman: Destroying the Teacher" (Lazer), **Supp. IX:** 265

"Louis Zukofsky: *All: The Collected Short Poems, 1923–1958*" (Creeley), **Supp. IV Part 1:** 154

"Lounge" (Francis), **Supp. IX:** 83

Lounsberry, Barbara, **Supp. XVII:** 208

Lounsbury, Floyd G., **Supp. XXVI:** 89

Lounsbury, Thomas R., **I:** 335

Louter, Jan, **Supp. XI:** 173

"Love" (Collins), **Supp. XXI:** 61

"Love," (Gibran), **Supp. XX: 119**

"Love" (Olson), **Supp. II Part 2:** 571

"Love" (Paley), **Supp. VI:** 219, 222, 230

Love, Deborah, **Supp. V:** 208, 210

Love Alone: 18 Elegies for Rog (Monette), **Supp. X:** 146, 154

Love Always (Beattie), **Supp. V:** 29, 30, 35

Love among the Cannibals (Morris), **III:** 228, 230–231

"Love Among the Ruins" (Mosley), **Supp. XIII:** 247

"Love and Art" (Huddle), **Supp. XXVI:** 150

Love and Death (film; Allen), **Supp. XV:** 2, **5–6,** 7, 11

Love and Death in the American Novel (Fiedler), **Supp. XIII:** 93, 96, **99–101,** 104

Love and Exile (Singer), **Retro. Supp. II:** 302–304, 315

Love and Fame (Berryman), **I:** 170

Love and Friendship (Bloom), **Retro. Supp. II:** 31, 33–34

Love and Glory (Parker), **Supp. XIX:** 189

"Love and How to Cure It" (Wilder), **IV:** 365

Love and Other Games of Chance (Siegel), **Supp. XXII:** 255, 256, **261–265,** 266, 267

Love and Scorn: New and Selected Poems (C. Frost), **Supp. XV:** 95, 96, 100, 103–105, 106

Love and Theft (album, Dylan), **Supp. XVIII:** 28, 31

"Love and the Hate, The" (Jeffers), **Supp. II Part 2:** 434–435

Love and the Incredibly Old Man (Siegel), **Supp. XXII:** 267–268

Love and Will (Dixon), **Supp. XII:** 148, 149

Love and Work (Price), **Supp. VI:** 261

"Love as a Great Power" (Bronk), **Supp. XXI:** 31

"Love Calls Us to the Things of This World" (Wilbur), **Supp. III Part 2:** 544, 552–553

Love Course, The (Gurney), **Supp. V:** 98

Lovecraft, H. P., **Supp. XXII:** 49; **Supp. XXV:** 109–126

Lovecraft and Influence (R. H. Waugh, ed.), **Supp. XXV:** 123

Loved One, The (film), **Supp. XI:** 305–306, 307

Loved One, The (Waugh), **Supp. XI:** 305

Love Expert, The (film; Kirkland), **Supp. XVI:** 186

Love Feast (Buechner), **Supp. XII:** 52

Love for Love (Congreve), **Supp. XVIII:** 12

"Love Fossil" (Olds), **Supp. X:** 203

"Love"(Hadas), **Supp. XXIII:** 117

Love in a Dead Language (Siegel), **Supp. XXII:** 255, **258–261,** 265–266, 267

Love in Buffalo (Gurney), **Supp. V:** 96

Love in Chartres (Asch), **Supp. XXVI:** 18, 19, 20–21, 25

"Love—In Other Words" (Lee), **Supp. VIII:** 113

"Love in the Air" (Jin), **Supp. XVIII:** 93–94

"Love in the Morning" (Dubus), **Supp. VII:** 91

Love in the Ruins: The Adventures of a Bad Catholic at a Time near the End of the World (Percy), **Supp. III Part 1:** 385, 387, 393–394, 397–398

Love in the Western World (de Rougemont), **Retro. Supp. I:** 328

"Love Is a Deep and a Dark and a Lonely" (Sandburg), **III:** 595

Lovejoy, Elijah P., **Supp. I Part 2:** 588; **Supp. XXIV:** 78

Lovejoy, Owen R., **Supp. I Part 1:** 8

Lovejoy, Thomas, **Supp. X:** 108

"Lovejoy Street" (Stallings), **Supp. XXV:** 224

Lovelace, Richard, **II:** 590

"Love Letter (Schnackenberg), **Supp. XV:** 258–259

Love Letters (film), **Supp. IV Part 2:** 524

Love Letters (Gurney), **Supp. V:** 105, 108–109

Love Letters, The (Massie), **Supp. IV Part 2:** 524

Love Letters and Two Other Plays: The Golden Age and What I Did Last Summer (Gurney), **Supp. V:** 100

"Love Lies Sleeping" (Bishop), **Retro. Supp. II:** 42

Love Life (Mason), **Supp. VIII:** 145–146

"Love Life" (Mason), **Supp. VIII:** 145–146

Lovell, Julia, **Supp. XVIII:** 101

Lovely Bones, The (Sebold), **Supp. XXII:** 55

Lovely Lady, The (Lawrence), **Retro. Supp. I:** 203

"Lovely Lady, The" (Lawrence), **Supp. I Part 1:** 329

Love Me (Keillor), **Supp. XVI:** 178

Love Medicine (Erdrich), **Supp. IV Part 1:** 259, 260, 261, 263, 265, 266, 267–268, 270, 271, 274–275; **Supp. X:** 290

Love Medicine (expanded version) (Erdrich), **Supp. IV Part 1:** 263, 273, 274, 275

"Love Minus Zero/No Limit" (song, Dylan), **Supp. XVIII:** 31

"Love Nest, The" (Lardner), **II:** 427, 429

Love Nest, The, and Other Stories (Lardner), **II:** 430–431, 436

Lovenheim, Barbara, **Supp. X:** 169

"Love of Annunziata, The" (di Donato), **Supp. XX:** 40

"Love of Elsie Barton: A Chronicle, The" (Warren), **IV:** 253

Love of Landry, The (Dunbar), **Supp. II Part 1:** 212

"Love of Morning, The" (Levertov), **Supp. III Part 1:** 284

Love of the Last Tycoon, The: A Western. See Last Tycoon, The

"Love on the Bon Dieu" (Chopin), **Supp. I Part 1:** 213

Love on the Hoof (O'Hara and Lima), **Supp. XXIII:** 217

Love Poems (Sexton), **Supp. II Part 2:** 687–689

Love Poems (Tentative Title) (O'Hara), **Supp. XXIII:** 219

Love Poems of May Swenson, The (Swenson), **Supp. IV Part 2:** 652, 653

"Love Poet" (Agee), **I:** 28

"Lover" (Hoffman), **Supp. XVIII:** 87

"Love Ritual" (Mora), **Supp. XIII:** 215

Lover of Horses, The (Gallagher), **Supp. XXIV:** 166, 172, 173–174, 176

"Lover of Horses, The" (Gallagher), **Supp. XXIV:** 173–174, 176

Loveroot (Jong), **Supp. V:** 115, 130

"Lovers, The" (Berryman), **I:** 174

"Lovers, The" (Buck), **Supp. II Part 1:** 128

"Lover's Garden, A" (Ginsberg), **Supp. II Part 1:** 311

"Lovers of the Poor, The" (Brooks), **Supp. III Part 1:** 81, 85

Lovers Should Marry (Martin), **Supp. IV Part 1:** 351

"Lover's Song" (Yeats), **Supp. I Part 1:** 80

"Love Rushes By" (Salinas), **Supp. XIII:** 326–327

"Love's Ghost" (Nelson), **Supp. XVIII:** 176

Lovesick (Stern), **Supp. IX:** 295–296

Love's Labour's Lost (Shakespeare), **III:** 263

Love's Old Sweet Song (Saroyan), **Supp. IV Part 1:** 83

"Love Song During Riot with Many Voices" (Hull), **Supp. XXI:** 136

"Love Song of J. Alfred Prufrock, The" (T. S. Eliot), **I:** 52, 66, 569–570; **III:** 460; **Retro. Supp. I:** 55, 56, 57, 60; **Supp. II Part 1:** 5; **Supp. XIII:** 346; **Supp. XVI:** 150; **Supp. XXV:** 22; **Supp. XXVI:** 237

"Love Song of St. Sebastian" (Eliot), **Retro. Supp. I:** 57

"Love Songs" (Loy), **Supp. XXII:** 161

"Love Songs to Joannes" (Loy), **Supp. XXII:** 161, 163

Love's Pilgrimage (Sinclair), **Supp. V:** 286

"Love the Wild Swan" (Jeffers), **Supp. VIII:** 33

Love to Mamá: A Tribute to Mothers (Mora, ed.), **Supp. XIII:** 221

Lovett, Robert Morss, **II:** 43

Lovett-Graff, Bennett, **Supp. XXV:** 123

"Love-Unknown" (Herbert), **Supp. I Part 1:** 80

Love! Valor! Compassion! (film), **Supp. XIII:** 206

Love! Valour! Compassion! (McNally), **Supp. XIII:** 199, **203–204,** 208, 209

"Love *versus* Law" (Stowe), **Supp. I Part 2:** 585–586

"Love Wall" (Peacock), **Supp. XIX:** 200

Love with a Few Hairs (Mrabet), **Supp. IV Part 1:** 92

Loving a Woman in Two Worlds (R. Bly), **Supp. IV Part 1:** 66, 67, 68–69, 71, 72

Loving in the War Years: Lo que nunca pasó por sus labios (Moraga), **Supp. XXIII:** 194, 195

"Loving on Borrowed Time" (J. W. Miller), **Supp. XX:** 164

"Loving Shepherdess, The" (Jeffers), **Supp. II Part 2:** 432

"Loving the Killer" (Sexton), **Supp. II Part 2:** 688

"Loving Wife" (C. Miller), **Supp. XXII:** 196–197, 199

Lovin' Molly (film), **Supp. V:** 223, 226

Low Country (Siddons), **Supp. XXII:** 239

Lowe, John, **Supp. XIII:** 238

Lowe, Pardee, **Supp. X:** 291

Lowell, Abbott Lawrence, **I:** 487; **II:** 513; **Supp. I Part 2:** 483

Lowell, Amy, **I:** 231, 384, 405, 475, 487; **II:** 174, **511–533,** 534; **III:** 465, 581, 586; **Retro. Supp. I:** 131, 133, 288; **Retro. Supp. II:** 46, 175; **Supp. I Part 1:** 257–259, 261–263, 265, 266; **Supp. I Part 2:** 465, 466, 707, 714, 729; **Supp. XIV:** 128; **Supp. XV:** 43, 293, 295, 297, 298, 299, 300, 301, 303, 306; **Supp. XX: 69; Supp. XXII:** 161

Lowell, Blanche, **Supp. I Part 2:** 409

Lowell, Harriet, **II:** 553, 554

Lowell, James Russell, **I:** 216, 458; **II:** 273, 274, 289, 302, 320, 402, 529, 530, 532, 534, 551; **III:** 409; **IV:** 129, 171, 175, 180, 182–183, 186; **Retro. Supp. I:** 228; **Retro. Supp. II:** 155, 175, 326; **Supp. I Part 1:** 168, 299, 300, 303, 306, 311, 312, 317, 318, 362; **Supp. I Part 2: 404–426; Supp. II Part 1:** 197, 291, 352; **Supp. XV:** 278, 279; **Supp. XVI:** 84; **Supp. XVIII:** 2–3, 4, 8, 12

Lowell, Mrs. James Russell (Maria White), **Supp. I Part 2:** 405, 406, 414, 424

Lowell, Percival, **II:** 513, 525, 534

Lowell, Robert, **I:** 172, 381, 382, 400, 442, 521, 544–545, 550; **II:** 371, 376, 377, 384, 386–387, 532, **534–557; III:** 39, 44, 142, 508, 527, 528–529, 606; **IV:** 120, 138, 402, 430; **Retro. Supp. I:** 67, 140, 411; **Retro. Supp. II:** 27, 40, 44, 46, 48, 50, **175–193,** 221, 228– 229, 235, 245; **Supp. I Part 1:** 89; **Supp. I Part 2:** 538, 543, 554; **Supp. III Part 1:** 6, 64, 84, 138, 147, 193, 194, 197–202, 205–208; **Supp. III Part 2:** 541, 543, 555, 561, 599; **Supp. IV Part 2:** 439, 620, 637; **Supp. IX:** 325; **Supp. V:** 81, 179, 180, 315–316, 337, 344; **Supp. VIII:** 27, 100, 271; **Supp. X:** 53, 58; **Supp. XI:** 146, 240, 244, 250, 317; **Supp. XII:** 253–254, 255; **Supp. XIII:** 76; **Supp. XIV:** 15, 126, 269; **Supp. XIX:** 197; **Supp. XV:** 20, 22, 93, 184, 249, 251, 253, 340; **Supp. XVII:** 239; **Supp. XX: 199, 203;** **Supp. XXI:** 131; **Supp. XXIII:** 211, 220; **Supp. XXIV:** 153; **Supp. XXVI:** 67, 68

Lowell, Rose, **Supp. I Part 2:** 409

"Lowell in the Classroom" (Vendler), **Retro. Supp. II:** 191

Lowenthal, Michael, **Supp. XII:** 82

Lower Depths, The (Gorki), **III:** 402

"Lower the Standard" (Shapiro), **Supp. II Part 2:** 715

Lowes, John Livingston, **II:** 512, 516, 532; **IV:** 453, 455

Lowin, Joseph, **Supp. V:** 273

"Low Lands" (Davison), **Supp. XXVI:** 76

"Low-Lands" (Pynchon), **Supp. II Part 2:** 620, 624

Lowle, Percival, **Supp. I Part 2:** 404

Lownsbrough, John, **Supp. IV Part 1:** 209, 211

Lowry, Beverly, **Supp. XXI:** 48

Lowry, Malcolm, **Supp. XVII:** 135, 136; **Supp. XXVI:** 28

Lowth, Richard, **II:** 8

Loy, Mina, **III:** 194; **Supp. XXII: 155– 170**

Loy, Myrna, **Supp. IV Part 1:** 355

"Loyal Woman's No, A" (Larcom), **Supp. XIII:** 142, 143–144

"Luani of the Jungle" (Hughes), **Supp. I Part 1:** 328

Lubbock, Percy, **I:** 504; **II:** 337; **IV:** 308, 314, 319, 322; **Retro. Supp. I:** 366, 367, 373; **Supp. VIII:** 165; **Supp. XX: 231**

Lubin, Isidor, **Supp. I Part 2:** 632

Lubow, Arthur, **Supp. VIII:** 310

Lucas, Craig, **Supp. XXIV:** 263

Lucas, Victoria (pseudonym). *See* Plath, Sylvia

Luce, Dianne C., **Supp. VIII:** 189

Lucid, Robert F., **Retro. Supp. II:** 195, 204

"Lucid Eye in Silver Town, The" (Updike), **IV:** 218

"Lucid Walking" (A. Finch), **Supp. XVII:** 72

"Lucinda Matlock" (Masters), **Supp. I Part 2:** 461, 465

"Luck" (Dunn), **Supp. XI:** 149

Luck of Barry Lyndon, The (Thackeray), **II:** 290

"Luck of Roaring Camp, The" (Harte), **Supp. II Part 1:** 335, 344, 345–347

"Luck of the Bogans, The" (Jewett), **Retro. Supp. II:** 142

Lucky Life (Stern), **Supp. IX: 290–291**

"Lucky Lucy's Daily Dream Book" (Di Piero), **Supp. XIX:** 38–39

Lucretius, **I:** 59; **II:** 162, 163; **III:** 600, 610–611, 612; **Supp. I Part 1:** 363

Lucy (Kincaid), **Supp. VII:** 180, 185, 186, 187–188, 194

Lucy, Saint, **II:** 211

Lucy Crown (Shaw), **Supp. XIX:** 251

Lucy Gayheart (Cather), **I:** 331; **Retro. Supp. I:** 19

"Lucy Tavish's Journey" (E. Stoddard), **Supp. XV:** 286

Lucy Temple (Rowson). *See Charlotte's Daughter; or, The Three Orphans*

Ludlow, Andrea, **Supp. XVIII:** 90

Ludvigson, Susan, **Supp. IV Part 2:** 442, 446, 447, 448, 451

Lueders, Edward, **Supp. XVI:** 265

"Luggage" (Bidart), **Supp. XV:** 35

Luhan, Mabel Dodge, **Retro. Supp. I:** 7; **Supp. XV:** 46, 50; **Supp. XXIV:** 30. *See also* Dodge, Mabel

Lu Ji, **Supp. VIII:** 303

Lukas, Michael, **Supp. XXVI:** 56

Luke (biblical book), **III:** 606

"Luke Havergal" (E. A. Robinson), **Supp. XVII:** 69

"Luke Havergal" (Robinson), **III:** 524

Lukeman, Gary, **Supp. XV:** 221

Luks, George, **IV:** 411; **Retro. Supp. II:** 103

"Lullaby" (Auden), **Supp. II Part 1:** 9

"Lullaby" (Bishop), **Supp. I Part 1:** 85

"Lullaby" (Everwine), **Supp. XV:** 89

"Lullaby" (Silko), **Supp. IV Part 2:** 560, 568–569

"Lullaby for Amy" (Jarman), **Supp. XVII:** 113, 121

"Lullaby of Cape Cod" (Brodsky), **Supp. VIII:** 27–28

Lullaby Raft (Nye), **Supp. XIII:** 278

Lullaby Raft (Nye, album), **Supp. XIII:** 274

Lullaby: The Comforting of Cock Robin (Snodgrass), **Supp. VI:** 324

"Lulls" (Walker), **Supp. III Part 2:** 525

"Lulu" (Wedekind), **Supp. XII:** 14

Lulu on the Bridge (film), **Supp. XII:** 21

Lulu's Library (Alcott), **Supp. I Part 1:** 43

"Lumber" (Baker), **Supp. XIII:** 55, 56

"Lumens, The" (Olds), **Supp. X:** 209

Lume Spento, A (Pound), **III:** 470

Lumet, Sidney, **Supp. IV Part 1:** 236; **Supp. IX:** 253

Luminous Debris: Reflecting on Vestige in Provence and Languedoc (Sobin), **Supp. XVI: 291–293,** 293–294

Luminous Face, The (Wells), **Supp. XXVI:** 280

"Lumumba's Grave" (Hughes), **Supp. I Part 1:** 344

"Luna, Luna" (Mora), **Supp. XIII:** 217

Lunar Baedecker (Loy), **Supp. XXII:** 165,**Supp. XXII:** 167, 166, 168

Lunar Baedecker and Time-Tables (Loy), **Supp. XXII:** 168

Lunar Follies (Sorrentino), **Supp. XXI:** 226, 237, 238–239

Lunch Poems (O'Hara), **Supp. XXIII:** 219–220, 220

Lunsford, Bascom Lamar, **Supp. XX: 163**

Lupercal (Hughes), **Retro. Supp. II:** 245; **Supp. I Part 2:** 540

Lupton, Mary Jane, **Supp. IV Part 1:** 7

Lure of the Labrador Wild, The (Wallace), **Supp. XXII:** 218

Luria, Isaac, **IV:** 7

Lurie, Alison, **Supp. X:** 166; **Supp. XVI:** 103, 111–112

Lusitania Songspiel, Das (Durang), **Supp. XXIV:** 113, 116

Lust and Other Stories (Minot), **Supp. VI:** 205

Luster, Deborah, **Supp. XV:** 337,**Supp. XV:** 353, 348, 349, 350

Lustgarten, Edith, **III:** 107

Lustra (Pound), **Retro. Supp. I:** 289, 290

"Luther" (Huddle), **Supp. XXVI:** 152

Luther, Martin, **II:** 11–12, 506; **III:** 306, 607; **IV:** 490

"Luther on Sweet Auburn" (Bambara), **Supp. XI:** 16–17

Lux, Thomas, **Supp. XI:** 270; **Supp. XIX:** 276

Luxury Girl, The (McCoy), **Supp. XIII:** 163

Lyall, Sarah, **Supp. XIII:** 247

Lycidas (Milton), **II:** 540; **IV:** 347; **Retro. Supp. I:** 60; **Retro. Supp. II:** 186; **Supp. I Part 1:** 370; **Supp. IX:** 41

Lycographia (Paullini), **Supp. XVII:** 55

"Lydia and Marian" (Rowson), **Supp. XV:** 234

Lydon, Meghan, **Supp. XXVI:** 14–15

Lydon, Susan, **Supp. XII:** 170

Lyell, Charles, **Supp. IX:** 180

Lyell, Frank H., **Supp. VIII:** 125

Lyford, Harry, **Supp. I Part 2:** 679

"Lying" (Wilbur), **Supp. III Part 2:** 547, 562

"Lying and Looking" (Swenson), **Supp. IV Part 2:** 652

"Lying in a Hammock at William Duffy's Farm in Pine Island, Minnesota" (Wright), **Supp. III Part 2:** 589, 599, 600

"Lying in the Pollen and Water" (C. Frost), **Supp. XV:** 96

Lying Ladies, The (Ryan as Finnegan), **Supp. XVIII: 233–235,** 237

"Lying Next to the Knife" (McElwee), **Supp. XXIV:** 167, 173

Lyles, Lois F., **Supp. XI:** 7, 8

Lyly, John, **III:** 536; **Supp. I Part 1:** 369

Lynch, Anne, **Supp. XV:** 273

Lynch, Doris, **Supp. XVI:** 294

Lynchburg (Gander), **Supp. XV:** 340

"Lynched Man, The" (Karr), **Supp. XI:** 241

Lynchers, The (Wideman), **Supp. X:** 320

"Lynching, The" (McKay), **Supp. I Part 1:** 63

"Lynching of Jube Benson, The" (Dunbar), **Supp. II Part 1:** 214

"Lynching Song" (Hughes), **Supp. I Part 1:** 331

Lynd, Staughton, **Supp. VIII:** 240

Lynda Hull: Collected Poems (Hull), **Supp. XXI:** 129

Lynes, Katherine R., **Supp. XXVI:** 166, 170, 171, 175

Lynn, Kenneth, **Supp. XIII:** 96–97

Lynn, Kenneth S., **Supp. XIV:** 103

Lynn, Vera, **Supp. XI:** 304

Lyon, George Ella, **Supp. XX: 161–162**

Lyon, Kate, **I:** 409; **II:** 138, 143, 144

Lyon, Thomas, **Supp. IX:** 175

"Lyonnesse" (Plath), **Supp. I Part 2:** 541

Lyons, Bonnie, **Supp. V:** 58; **Supp. VIII:** 138

Lyons, Donald, **Supp. XXIV:** 274

Lyons, Nathan, **Supp. XXV:** 251

Lyons, The (Silver), **Supp. XXIV:** 263, **276**

Lyotard, Jean-François, **Supp. IV Part 1:** 54

Lyrical Ballads (Wordsworth), **III:** 583; **IV:** 120; **Supp. IX:** 274; **Supp. XI:** 243; **Supp. XIX:** 1; **Supp. XV:** 21

Lyrics of Love and Laughter (Dunbar), **Supp. II Part 1:** 207

Lyrics of Lowly Life (Dunbar), **Supp. II Part 1:** 197, 199, 200, 207

Lyrics of the Hearthside (Dunbar), **Supp. II Part 1:** 206

Lytal, Tammy, **Supp. XI:** 102

Lytle, Andrew, **IV:** 125; **Retro. Supp. II:** 220, 221, 235; **Supp. II Part 1:** 139; **Supp. X:** 1, 25; **Supp. XI:** 101

Lyttelton, Alfred, **Supp. XX:** 230

Lytton of Knebworth. *See* Bulwer-Lytton, Edward George

M

Mabie, Hamilton W., **Supp. XVIII:** 257

MCabe, Susan, **Supp. XXII:** 234

McAlexander, Hubert H., **Supp. V:** 314, 319, 320, 323

McAlmon, Robert, **IV:** 404; **Retro. Supp. I:** 418, 419, 420; **Retro. Supp. II:** 328; **Supp. I Part 1:** 259; **Supp. III Part 2:** 614; **Supp. XXII:** 166, 215; **Supp. XXIV:** 62, 63

McAlmon, Mrs. Robert (Winifred Ellerman), **III:** 194. *See also* Ellerman, Winifred

McAlpine, Erica, **Supp. XXV:** 222, 233, 234

McAninch, Jerry, **Supp. XI:** 297, 298

Macaulay, Catherine, **Supp. I Part 2:** 522

Macaulay, Rose, **Supp. XII:** 88; **Supp. XIV:** 348

Macaulay, Thomas, **II:** 15–16; **III:** 113, 591–592

Macaulay, Robie, **Retro. Supp. II:** 228; **Supp. X:** 56

Macbeth (Shakespeare), **I:** 271; **IV:** 227; **Retro. Supp. I:** 131; **Supp. I Part 1:** 67; **Supp. I Part 2:** 457; **Supp. IV Part 1:** 87; **Supp. XIV:** 8

Macbeth (silent film), **Supp. XVI:** 184

MacBeth, George, **Retro. Supp. II:** 250

McBride, James, **Supp. XXVI: 191–205**

MacBride, Roger, **Supp. XXII:** 297, 301

McCabe, Tracy, **Supp. XXVI:** 166

McCafferty, Larry, **Supp. XVII:** 227

McCaffery, Larry, **Supp. IV Part 1:** 217, 227, 234; **Supp. V:** 53, 238; **Supp. VIII:** 13, 14; **Supp. X:** 260, 268, 301, 303, 307; **Supp. XVI:** 117; **Supp. XXII:** 177

McCann, Janet, **Supp. XXIII:** 51, 53, 54, 64

McCann, Jannet, **Supp. XXI:** 92

McCarriston, Linda, **Supp. X:** 204; **Supp. XIV: 259–275**

McCarthy, Charles Joseph, Jr. *See* McCarthy, Cormac

McCarthy, Cormac, **Supp. VIII: 175–192; Supp. XII:** 310; **Supp. XVII:** 185; **Supp. XXI:** 38, 40; **Supp. XXII:** 49; **Supp. XXIII:** 42, 44

McCarthy, Eugene, **Retro. Supp. II:** 182

McCarthy, Joseph, **I:** 31, 492; **II:** 562, 568; **Supp. I Part 1:** 294, 295; **Supp. I Part 2:** 444, 611, 612, 620; **Supp. XV:** 198, 311–312; **Supp. XXIII:** 7

McCarthy, Mary, **II: 558–584; Supp. I Part 1:** 84; **Supp. IV Part 1:** 209, 297, 310; **Supp. VIII:** 96, 99, 100; **Supp. X:** 177; **Supp. XI:** 246; **Supp. XIV:** 3; **Supp. XV:** 142; **Supp. XVI:** 64, 70; **Supp. XVII:** 43

McCay, Maura, **Supp. XII:** 271, 276

McClanahan, Ed, **Supp. X:** 24

McClanahan, Thomas, **Supp. XII:** 125–126

McClatchy, J. D., **Supp. XII: 253–270; Supp. XV:** 185, 257, 258

McClaurin, Irma, **Supp. XXIII:** 84, 86, 93, 94

McClellan, John L., **I:** 493

McClung, Isabelle, **Retro. Supp. I:** 5

McClure, Charlotte, **Supp. XXIV:** 29

McClure, John, **Retro. Supp. I:** 80

McClure, Michael, **Supp. II Part 1:** 32; **Supp. VIII:** 289; **Supp. XVI:** 283

McClure, S. S., **I:** 313; **II:** 465; **III:** 327; **Retro. Supp. I:** 5, 6, 9; **Supp. XV:** 40

McCluskey, John, Jr., **Supp. XIX:** 65, 68, 71, 72, 78

McCombs, Judith, **Supp. XIII:** 33

McConagha, Alan, **Supp. XVI:** 166

McConnell, Frank, **Supp. X:** 260, 274

McCorkle, Jill, **Supp. X:** 6; **Supp. XVIII:** 195; **Supp. XXV:** 129, 130

McCourt, Frank, **Supp. XII: 271–287**

McCoy, Horace, **Supp. XIII: 159–177; Supp. XXV:** 26

McCracken, Elizabeth, **Supp. X:** 86; **Supp. XII:** 310, 315–316, 321

McCrae, Fiona, **Supp. XVIII:** 60, 62

McCullers, Carson, **I:** 113, 190, 211; **II: 585–608; IV:** 282, 384, 385, 386; **Retro. Supp. II:** 324; **Supp. II Part 1:** 17; **Supp. IV Part 1:** 31, 84; **Supp. IV Part 2:** 502; **Supp. VIII:** 124; **Supp. XII:** 309; **Supp. XIV:** 120; **Supp. XV:** 338

McCullers, Reeves, **III:** 585, 586, 587

McDavid, Raven I., **III:** 120; **Supp. XIV:** 14

McDermott, Alice, **Supp. XII:** 311; **Supp. XVIII: 155–169**

McDermott, John J., **II:** 364

MacDiarmid, Hugh, **Supp. X:** 112

Macdonald, C. G., **Supp. XVII:** 73–74

MacDonald, Dwight, **Supp. XXV:** 268

Macdonald, Dwight, **I:** 233, 372, 379; **III:** 39; **Supp. V:** 265; **Supp. XIV:** 340; **Supp. XV:** 140

McDonald, E. J., **Supp. I Part 2:** 670

Macdonald, George, **Supp. XIII:** 75

MacDonald, Jeanette, **II:** 589

Macdonald, Ross, **Supp. IV Part 1:** 116, 136; **Supp. IV Part 2: 459–477; Supp. XIII:** 233; **Supp. XVIII:** 137,136; **Supp. XXI:** 67

MacDonald, Ruth K., **Supp. XVI:** 102

McDonnell, Thomas P., **Supp. XX: 45**

MacDougall, Ruth Doan, **Supp. XV:** 58; **Supp. XVI:** 174

MacDowell, Edward, **I:** 228; **III:** 504, 508, 524

McDowell, Frederick P. W., **II:** 194

McDowell, Mary, **Supp. I Part 1:** 5

McDowell, Robert, **Supp. IX:** 266, 270, 276, 279

McDowell, Robert, **Supp. XI:** 249

McDowell, Robert, **Supp. XVII:** 109, 110, 111

McDowell. Deborah, **Supp. XVIII:** 125, 129

McElderry, Margaret K., **Supp. XV:** 162

McElligot's Pool (Geisel), **Supp. XVI:** 104

McElrath, Joseph, **Supp. XIV:** 62

McElroy, Joseph, **Supp. IV Part 1:** 279, 285

McElwee, Caroline, **Supp. XXIV:** 167, 173

McEuen, Kathryn, **II:** 20

McEwen, Arthur, **I:** 206

McFarland, Ron, **Supp. IX:** 323, 327, 328, 333

McGann, Jerome, **Retro. Supp. I:** 47

McGill, Meredith, **Supp. XVIII:** 17

McGillis, Ian, **Supp. XVIII:** 150

MacGillivray, William, **Supp. XVI:** 8

McGinity, Keren, **Supp. XX: 9**

McGovern, Edythe M., **Supp. IV Part 2:** 573, 582, 585

McGovern, George, **III:** 46

MacGowan, Christopher, **Retro. Supp. I:** 430

MacGowan, Kenneth, **III:** 387, 391

McGrath, Abigail, **Supp. XXVI:** 164, 165, 172

McGrath, Douglas, **Supp. XV:** 12

McGrath, Joseph, **Supp. XI:** 307, 309

McGrath, Patrick, **Supp. IX:** 113; **Supp. XXII:** 58

McGrath, Thomas, **Supp. X: 111–130**

"McGrath on McGrath" (McGrath), **Supp. X:** 119, 120

McGuane, Thomas, **Supp. V:** 53, 220; **Supp. VIII:** 39, 40, 42, 43

MacGuffin, The (Elkin), **Supp. VI: 55–56**

McGuiness, Daniel, **Supp. XV:** 261

Machado y Ruiz, Antonio, **Supp. XIII:** 315, 323

Machan, Tibor, **Supp. IV Part 2:** 528

McHaney, Pearl, **Supp. XXI:** 244, 255, 256, 257

McHaney, Thomas, **Supp. XVIII:** 199,203

Machen, Arthur, **IV:** 286

McHenry, Tim, **Supp. XXV:** 161

Machiavelli, Niccolò, **I:** 485; **Supp. XIX:** 34

"Machine-Gun, The" (Jarrell), **II:** 371

"Machines Mourn the Passing of People, The" (Stallings), **Supp. XXV:** 228

"Machine Song" (Anderson), **I:** 114

McHugh, Heather, **Supp. XIX:** 84; **Supp. XXIV:** 154

McHugh, Vincent, **Supp. XV:** 147

McInerney, Jay, **Supp. X:** 7, 166; **Supp. XI:** 65; **Supp. XII:** 81; **Supp. XVIII:** 148

"Mac in Love" (Dixon), **Supp. XII: 142**

McIntire, Holly, **Supp. V:** 338

McIntosh, Maria, **Retro. Supp. I:** 246

Mack, Maynard, **Supp. XIV:** 12

Mackail, John William, **Supp. I Part 1:** 268; **Supp. I Part 2:** 461

McKay, Claude, **Supp. I Part 1:** 63; **Supp. III Part 1:** 75, 76; **Supp. IV Part 1:** 3, 79, 164; **Supp. IX:** 306; **Supp. X: 131–144; Supp. XI:** 91; **Supp. XIX:** 73; **Supp. XVII:** 74; **Supp. XVIII:** 122, 127, 280, 282; **Supp. XX: 69; Supp. XXII:** 275

McKay, Donald, **Supp. I Part 2:** 482

McKay, Nellie Y., **Supp. XX: 105**

McKee, Elizabeth, **Retro. Supp. II:** 221, 222

McKee, Ellen, **Retro. Supp. II:** 67

McKeen, William, **Supp. XXIV:** 279, 280, 281, 282, 288

McKenney, Eileen, **IV:** 288; **Retro. Supp. II:** 321, 330

McKenney, Ruth, **IV:** 288; **Retro. Supp. II:** 321; **Supp. XVIII:** 238

MacKenzie, Agnes, **I:** 199

Mackenzie, Captain Alexander, **III:** 94

Mackenzie, Compton, **II:** 82; **Retro. Supp. I:** 100, 102

McKenzie, Geraldine, **Supp. XII:** 107

MacKenzie, Margaret, **I:** 199

Mackey, Louis, **Supp. XXI:** 236, 237

McKibben, Bill, **Supp. XVIII:** 192

McKinley, William, **I:** 474; **III:** 506; **Supp. I Part 2:** 395–396, 707

MacKinnon, Catharine, **Supp. XII:** 6

McKnight, Reginald, **Supp. XX: 147–159**

MacLachlan, Suzanne L., **Supp. XII:** 300,**Supp. XII:** 299

MacLauchlin, Cory, **Supp. XXVI:** 240, 241, 242, 243, 244, 246, 252

McLaverty, Michael, **Supp. X:** 67

McLay, Catherine, **Supp. XIII:** 21

Maclean, Alasdair, **Supp. V:** 244

McLean, Carolyn (pseudonym). *See* Bly, Carol

Maclean, Norman, **Supp. XIV: 221–237; Supp. XVI:** 98; **Supp. XXVI:** 184

MacLeish, Archibald, **I:** 283, 293, 429; **II:** 165, 228; **III: 1–25,** 427; **Supp. I Part 1:** 261; **Supp. I Part 2:** 654; **Supp. IV Part 1:** 359; **Supp. IV Part 2:** 586; **Supp. X:** 120; **Supp. XIV:** 11

MacLeish, Mrs. Archibald (Ada Hitchcock), **III:** 1

MacLeish, Kenneth, **III:** 1

McLellan, Joseph, **Supp. XXIV:** 226

McLennan, Gordon Lawson, **Supp. IX:** 89

McLeod, A. W., **Supp. I Part 1:** 257

MacLeod, Charlotte, **Supp. XXV:** 192

McLuhan, Marshall, **Supp. IV Part 2:** 474

McLure, Michael, **Supp. XIV:** 150

Macmahon, Arthur, **I:** 226

McMahon, Helen, **Supp. IV Part 2:** 579

McMichael, Barbara Lloyd, **Supp. XXII:** 206, 207, 215, 216

McMichael, George, **Supp. VIII:** 124

McMichael, Morton, **Supp. I Part 2:** 707

McMichaels, James, **Supp. XIII:** 114

McMillan, James B., **Supp. VIII:** 124

McMillan, Terry, **Supp. XIII: 179–193**

McMullan, Jim, **Supp. XIV:** 124

McMurtry, Josephine, **Supp. V:** 220

McMurtry, Larry, **Supp. V: 219–235; Supp. X:** 24; **Supp. XI:** 172

McNally, Terrence, **Supp. XIII: 195–211**

McNally, T. M., **Supp. XX: 92**

McNamee, Thomas, **Supp. XXII:** 218

McNamer, Deirdre, **Supp. XI:** 190

McNeese, Gretchen, **Supp. V:** 123

MacNeice, Louis, **II:** 586; **III:** 527; **Supp. II Part 1:** 17, 24; **Supp. II Part 2:** 440; **Supp. X:** 116; **Supp. XIII:** 347

McNeil, Claudia, **Supp. IV Part 1:** 360, 362

M-a-c-n-o-l-i-a (Jordan), **Supp. XVIII:** 172

McPhee, John, **Supp. III Part 1: 289–316; Supp. X:** 29, 30; **Supp. XVIII:** 106–107, 114

MacPherson, Aimee Semple, **Supp. V:** 278

Macpherson, Anne, **Supp. XXIII:** 84

McPherson, Dolly, **Supp. IV Part 1:** 2, 3, 4, 6, 8, 11, 12

McPherson, James Alan, **Supp. XXII:** 141

McPherson, James Allen, **Retro. Supp. II:** 126

Macpherson, Jay, **Supp. XIII:** 19

MacPherson, Jennifer, **Supp. XXIII:** 248

MacPherson, Kenneth, **Supp. I Part 1:** 259

McPherson, Sandra, **Supp. XXIII:** 57

McPhillips, Robert, **Supp. XV:** 119, 250, 251, 252, 264, 266; **Supp. XXIII:** 111, 112, 114, 127

McQuade, Molly, **Supp. IX:** 151, 163; **Supp. VIII:** 277, 281; **Supp. XX: 90**

McQueen, Steve, **Supp. XI:** 306

Macrae, John, **I:** 252–253

McRobbie, Angela, **Supp. IV Part 2:** 691

MacShane, Frank, **Supp. IV Part 2:** 557; **Supp. XI:** 214, 216

"MacSwiggen" (Freneau), **Supp. II Part 1:** 259

McTaggart, John, **I:** 59

McTeague (Norris), **III:** 314, 315, 316–320, 322, 325, 327–328, 330, 331, 333, 335; **Retro. Supp. II:** 96; **Supp. IX:** 332

McWhorter, Dianne, **Supp. XXIII:** 38

McWilliams, Carey, **Supp. XI:** 169; **Supp. XXIV:** 282

Madama Butterfly (opera, Puccini), **III:** 139; **Supp. XXI:** 150, 155

"Madam and the Minister" (Hughes), **Supp. I Part 1:** 335

"Madam and the Wrong Visitor" (Hughes), **Supp. I Part 1:** 335

"Madame and Ahmad" (Bowles), **Supp. IV Part 1:** 93

"Madame Bai and the Taking of Stone Mountain" (Bambara), **Supp. XI:** 14–15

Madame Bovary (Flaubert), **II:** 185; **Retro. Supp. I:** 225; **Retro. Supp. II:** 70; **Supp. XI:** 334; **Supp. XX: 58**

"Madame Célestin's Divorce" (Chopin), **Supp. I Part 1:** 213

Madame Curie (film), **Retro. Supp. I:** 113

"Madame de Mauves" (James), **II:** 327; **Retro. Supp. I:** 218, 220

Madame de Treymes (Wharton), **IV:** 314, 323; **Retro. Supp. I:** 376

"Madame Rose Hanie" (Gibran), **Supp. XX: 124**

"Madame Swann at Home"(Hadas), **Supp. XXIII:** 113

"Madam's Calling Cards" (Hughes), **Retro. Supp. I:** 206

Madden, David, **Supp. IV Part 1:** 285

Maddern, Bessie. *See* London, Mrs. Jack (Bessie Maddern)

Mad Dog Black Lady (Coleman), **Supp. XI: 85–89,** 90

Mad Dog Blues (Shepard), **Supp. III Part 2:** 437, 438, 441

Maddox, Lucy, **Supp. IV Part 1:** 323, 325

Mad Ducks and Bears: Football Revisited (Plimpton), **Supp. XVI:** 243

Mademoiselle Coeur-Brisé (Sibon, trans.), **IV:** 288

Mademoiselle de Maupin (Gautier), **Supp. I Part 1:** 277

"Mad Farmer, Flying the Flag of Rough Branch, Secedes from the Union, The" (Berry), **Supp. X:** 35

"Mad Farmer Manifesto, The: The First Amendment" (Berry), **Supp. X:** 35

"Mad Farmer's Love Song, The" (Berry), **Supp. X:** 35

Madheart (Baraka), **Supp. II Part 1:** 47

Madhouse, The (Farrell), **II:** 41

Madhubuti, Haki R. (Don L. Lee), **Supp. II Part 1:** 34, 247; **Supp. IV Part 1:** 244

Madison, Charles, **Supp. XXIII:** 6, 13

Madison, Dolley, **II:** 303

Madison, James, **I:** 1, 2, 6–9; **II:** 301; **Supp. I Part 2:** 509, 524

"Madison Smartt Bell: *The Year of Silence*" (Garrett), **Supp. X:** 7

Mad Love (film, Freund), **Supp. XVII:** 58

"Madman, A" (Updike), **Retro. Supp. I:** 320

Madman, The: His Parables and Poems (Gibran), **Supp. XX: 115, 118, 125**

"Madman's Song" (Wylie), **Supp. I Part 2:** 711, 729

Madonick, Michael, **Supp. XVII:** 123

"Madonna" (Lowell), **II:** 535–536

"Madonna of the Evening Flowers" (Lowell), **II:** 524

"Madonna of the Future, The" (James), **Retro. Supp. I:** 219

"Mad Song" (Gioia), **Supp. XV:** 128

Madwoman in the Attic, The (Gilbert and Gubar), **Retro. Supp. I:** 42; **Supp. IX:** 66

"Maelzel's Chess-Player" (Poe), **III:** 419, 420

"Maestria" (Nemerov), **III:** 275, 278–279

Maeterlinck, Maurice, **I:** 91, 220; **Supp. XX: 115, 116**

"Magalu" (H. Johnson). *See* "Magula" (H. Johnson)

"Magazine-Writing Peter Snook" (Poe), **III:** 421

Magdeburg Centuries (Flacius), **IV:** 163

Magellan, Ferdinand, **Supp. I Part 2:** 497

Maggie: A Girl of the Streets (S. Crane), **I:** 407, 408, 410–411, 416; **IV:** 208; **Retro. Supp. II:** 97, 107; **Supp. XVII:** 228; **Supp. XXIII:** 165

Maggie Cassidy (Kerouac), **Supp. III Part 1:** 220–221, 225, 227, 229, 232

Maggie-Now (B. Smith), **Supp. XXIII:** 258, **267–269**

"Maggie of the Green Bottles" (Bambara), **Supp. XI:** 2–3

"Maggie's Farm" (song, Dylan), **Supp. XVIII:** 25, 26

"Magi" (Plath), **Supp. I Part 2:** 544–545

"Magi, The" (Garrett), **Supp. VII:** 97

"Magic" (Pickering), **Supp. XXI:** 202

"Magic" (Porter), **III:** 434, 435

"Magical Thinking" (Hull), **Supp. XXI:** 137, 139

Magic Barrel, The (Malamud), **Supp. I Part 2:** 427, 428, 430–434

"Magic Barrel, The" (Malamud), **Supp. I Part 2:** 427, 428, 431, 432–433

Magic Christian, The (film), **Supp. XI:** 309

Magic Christian, The (Southern), **Supp. XI:** 297, **299–301,** 309

Magic City (Komunyakaa), **Supp. XIII: 125–127,** 128, 131

"Magic Flute, The" (Epstein), **Supp. XII:** 165

Magic Flute, The (Mozart), **III:** 164

Magician King, The (Grossman), **Supp. XXV:** 74–77

Magician of Lublin, The (Singer), **IV:** 6, 9–10; **Retro. Supp. II: 308–309**

Magicians, The (Grossman), **Supp. XXV:** 64, 68–74

Magician's Assistant, The (Patchett), **Supp. XII:** 307, 310, **317–320,** 322

Magician's Land, The (Grossman), **Supp. XXV:** 77

"Magician's Wife, The" (Gordon), **Supp. IV Part 1:** 306

Magic Journey, The (Nichols), **Supp. XIII:** 266–267

Magic Keys, The (Murray), **Supp. XIX:** 157–158

Magic Kingdom, The (Elkin), **Supp. VI:** 42, **54–55,** 56, 58

"Magic Mirror, The: A Study of the Double in Two of Doestoevsky's Novels" (Plath), **Supp. I Part 2:** 536

Magic Mountain, The (Mann), **III:** 281–282; **Supp. IV Part 2:** 522; **Supp. XII:** 321; **Supp. XVII:** 137

Magic Tower, The (Willams), **IV:** 380

Magnaghi, Ambrogio, **Supp. XVI:** 286

Magnalia Christi Americana (Mather), **II:** 302; **Supp. I Part 1:** 102; **Supp. I Part 2:** 584; **Supp. II Part 2:** 441, 442, 452–455, 460, 467, 468; **Supp. IV Part 2:** 434

Magnes, Judah, **Supp. XXIII:** 6

Magnificat (Nelson), **Supp. XVIII: 176–177**

"Magnificent Little Gift" (Salinas), **Supp. XIII:** 318

"Magnifying Mirror" (Karr), **Supp. XI:** 240

Magpie, The (Baldwin, ed.), **Supp. I Part 1:** 49

"Magpie Exhorts"(Schott), **Supp. XXIII:** 250

Magpie's Shadow, The (Winters), **Supp. II Part 2:** 786, 788

"Magpie's Song" (Snyder), **Supp. VIII:** 302

Magritte, René, **Supp. IV Part 2:** 623

Maguire, Roberta S., **Supp. XIX:** 160–161

"Magula" (H. Johnson), **Supp. XXVI:** 164, 166, 170–172, 174

Magus, The (Fowles), **Supp. XIX:** 58

Mahan, Albert Thayer, **Supp. I Part 2:** 491

Mahan, David C., **Supp. XXI:** 86

"Mahatma Joe" (Bass), **Supp. XVI:** 19

Mahlis, Kristen, **Supp. XXIII:** 90, 94

"Mahogany Tree, The" (M. F. K. Fisher), **Supp. XVII:** 88

Mahomet and His Successors (Irving), **II:** 314

Mahoney, Jeremiah, **IV:** 285

Mahoney, Lynn, **Supp. XV:** 270

"Maiden, Maiden" (Boyle), **Supp. XXIV:** 58

"Maiden in a Tower" (Stegner), **Supp. IV Part 2:** 613

Maiden's Prayer, The (Silver), **Supp. XXIV:** 275–276

"Maiden Without Hands" (Sexton), **Supp. II Part 2:** 691

"Maid of St. Philippe, The" (Chopin), **Retro. Supp. II:** 63

"Maid's Shoes, The" (Malamud), **Supp. I Part 2:** 437

Mailer, Fanny, **III:** 28

Mailer, Isaac, **III:** 28

Mailer, Norman, **I:** 261, 292, 477; **III: 26–49,** 174; **IV:** 98, 216; **Retro. Supp. II:** 182, **195–217,** 279; **Supp. I Part 1:** 291, 294; **Supp. III Part 1:** 302; **Supp. IV Part 1:** 90, 198, 207, 236, 284, 381; **Supp. IV Part 2:** 689; **Supp. VIII:** 236; **Supp. XI:** 104, 218, 222, 229; **Supp. XIV:** 49, 53, 54, 111, 162; **Supp. XVII:** 225, 228, 236; **Supp. XVIII:** 19–20; **Supp. XX: 90; Supp. XXIII:** 105, 106; **Supp. XXIV:** 281; **Supp. XXV:** 145

"Maimed Man, The" (Tate), **IV:** 136

Maimonides, Moses, **Supp. XVII:** 46–47

Main Currents in American Thought: The Colonial Mind, 1625–1800 (Parrington), **I:** 517; **Supp. I Part 2:** 484

"Maine Roustabout, A" (Eberhart), **I:** 539

"Maine Speech" (White), **Supp. I Part 2:** 669–670

Maine Woods, The (Thoreau), **IV:** 188

Mains d'Orlac, Les (M. Renard), **Supp. XVII:** 58

Main Street (Lewis), **I:** 362; **II:** 271, 440, 441–442, 447, 449, 453; **III:** 394; **Supp. XIX:** 142; **Supp. XXII:** 282

"Maintenance" (Pickering), **Supp. XXI:** 204

Maitland, Margaret Todd, **Supp. XVI:** 292

Majdoubeh, Ahmad, **Supp. XX:** 116

"Majesty" (July), **Supp. XXIV:** 201–202, 203

Major, Clarence, **Supp. XXII: 171–186**

"Majorat, Das" (Hoffman), **III:** 415

Major Barbara (Shaw), **III:** 69

"Major Chord, The" (Bourne), **I:** 221

Majors and Minors (Dunbar), **Supp. II Part 1:** 197, 198

"Major's Tale, The" (Bierce), **I:** 205

Make Believe (J. Scott), **Supp. XVII: 191–192,** 193, **194,** 195

Make-Believe Town: Essays and Remembrances (Mamet), **Supp. XIV:** 240, 251

Make It New (Pound), **III:** 470

Makers and Finders (Brooks), **I:** 253, 254, 255, 257, 258

Makers of the Modern World (Untermeyer), **Supp. XV:** 312

"Making a Change" (Gilman), **Supp. XI:** 207

"Making a Living" (Sexton), **Supp. II Part 2:** 695

"Making Changes" (L. Michaels), **Supp. XVI:** 204

"Making Do" (Hogan), **Supp. IV Part 1:** 406

Making Face, Making Soul: Haciendo Caras, Creative and Critical Perspectives by Feminists of Color (Anzaldúa, ed.), **Supp. IV Part 1:** 330

Making It (Podhoretz), **Supp. VIII:** 231, 232, 233, **237–238,** 239, 244

"Making Light of Auntie" (X. J. Kennedy), **Supp. XV:** 163

"Making Love in 2003" (July), **Supp. XXIV:** 204–205, 210

"Making Marks" (Davison), **Supp. XXVI:** 72

"Making Much of Orioles" (Davison), **Supp. XXVI:** 74, 75

"Making of a Marginal Farm, The" (Berry), **Supp. X:** 22

Making of Americans, The (Stein), **IV:** 35, 37, 40–42, 45, 46; **Supp. III Part 1:** 37

"Making of Ashenden, The" (Elkin), **Supp. VI:** 49, 50

"Making of a Soldier USA, The" (Simpson), **Supp. IX:** 270

"Making of Garrison Keillor, The" (McConagha), **Supp. XVI:** 166"

Making of Modern Atlanta, The (documentary), **Supp. XXII:** 251

"Making of Paths, The" (Stegner), **Supp. IV Part 2:** 614

"Making of Poems, The" (W. J. Smith), **Supp. XIII:** 348

Making of the Modern Mind (Randall), **III:** 605

Making the Light Come: The Poetry of Gerald Stern (Somerville), **Supp. IX:** 296–297

"Making Up Stories" (Didion), **Supp. IV Part 1:** 196, 203, 205

Making Your Own Days: The Pleasures of Reading and Writing Poetry (Koch), **Supp. XV:** 188; **Supp. XXIII:** 124

Maladies de la volonté, Les (Ribot), **Supp. XX: 238**

Malady of the Ideal, The: Oberman, Maurice de Guérin, and Amiel (Brooks), **I:** 240, 241, 242

Malamud, Bernard, **I:** 144, 375; **II:** 424, 425; **III:** 40, 272; **IV:** 216; **Retro. Supp. II:** 22, 279, 281; **Supp. I Part 2: 427–453; Supp. IV Part 1:** 297, 382; **Supp. IX:** 114, 227; **Supp. V:** 257, 266; **Supp. XIII:** 106, 264, 265,

294; **Supp. XVI:** 220; **Supp. XXVI:** 180

Malamud, Mrs. Bernard (Ann de Chiara), **Supp. I Part 2:** 451

Malandrinos, Cheryl C., **Supp. XXVI:** 219

Malanga, Gerard, **Supp. III Part 2:** 629; **Supp. XXIII:** 221

Malaquais, Jean, **Retro. Supp. II:** 199

Malatesta, Sigismondo de, **III:** 472, 473

Malcolm (Purdy), **Supp. VII:** 270–273, 277

"Malcolm Cowley and the American Writer" (Simpson), **Supp. II Part 1:** 147

Malcolm Lowry's "Volcano": Myth Symbol Meaning (Markson), **Supp. XVII:** 142, 144

"MALCOLM REMEMBERED (FEB. 77)" (Baraka), **Supp. II Part 1:** 60

Malcolm X, **Retro. Supp. II:** 12, 13; **Supp. I Part 1:** 52, 63, 65, 66; **Supp. IV Part 1:** 2, 10; **Supp. VIII:** 330, 345; **Supp. X:** 240; **Supp. XIV:** 306

Malcolm X (film), **Retro. Supp. II:** 12

"Maldrove" (Jeffers), **Supp. II Part 2:** 418

Male, Roy, **II:** 239

Male Animal, The (Thurber), **Supp. I Part 2:** 605, 606, 610–611

"Malediction upon Myself" (Wylie), **Supp. I Part 2:** 722

Malefactors, The (Gordon), **II:** 186, 199, 213–216; **IV:** 139

"Malest Cornifici Tuo Catullo" (Ginsberg), **Supp. II Part 1:** 315

Malick, Terrence, **Supp. XI:** 234; **Supp. XV:** 351

Malin, Irving, **I:** 147; **Supp. XVI:** 71–72

"Malinche's Tips: Pique from Mexico's Mother" (Mora), **Supp. XIII:** 223

"Malinke's Atonement" (Antin), **Supp. XX: 10**

"Mallard" (C. Frost), **Supp. XV:** 98, 99

Mallarmé, Stéphane, **I:** 66, 569; **II:** 529, 543; **III:** 8, 409, 428; **IV:** 80, 86; **Retro. Supp. I:** 56; **Supp. I Part 1:** 261; **Supp. II Part 1:** 1; **Supp. III Part 1:** 319–320; **Supp. III Part 2:** 630; **Supp. XIII:** 114; **Supp. XV:** 158; **Supp. XVI:** 282, 285

Malle, Louis, **Supp. XXIII:** 122

Mallia, Joseph, **Supp. XII:** 26, 29, 37

Mallon, Anne-Marie, **Supp. XXI:** 215

Mallon, Thomas, **Supp. IV Part 1:** 200, 209; **Supp. XIX: 131–145**

Maloff, Saul, **Supp. VIII:** 238

Malory, Thomas, **II:** 302; **III:** 486; **IV:** 50, 61; **Supp. IV Part 1:** 47

"Mal Paso Bridge" (Jeffers), **Supp. II Part 2:** 415, 420

Malraux, André, **I:** 33–34, 127, 509; **II:** 57, 376; **III:** 35, 310; **IV:** 236, 247, 434; **Retro. Supp. I:** 73; **Retro. Supp. II:** 115–116, 119; **Supp. II Part 1:** 221, 232; **Supp. XIX:** 157

Maltese Falcon, The (film), **Supp. IV Part 1:** 342, 353, 355

Maltese Falcon, The (Hammett), **IV:** 286; **Supp. IV Part 1:** 345, 348–351

Mama (McMillan), **Supp. XIII:** 182, **187–188**

"Mama and Daughter" (Hughes), **Supp. I Part 1:** 334

Mama Day (Naylor), **Supp. VIII: 223–226,** 230

"Mama I Remember" (Nelson), **Supp. XVIII:** 173

Mama Poc: An Ecologist's Account of the Extinction of a Species (LaBastille), **Supp. X:** 99, **104–105,** 106

Mama Poems, The (Kenny), **Supp. XXIII:** 143, **154**

Mama's Bank Account (K. Forbes), **Supp. XVII:** 9

Mama's Promises (Nelson), **Supp. XVIII:** **173–174**

"Mama Still Loves You" (Naylor), **Supp. VIII:** 214

Mambo Hips and Make Believe (Coleman), **Supp. XI: 94–96**

Mambo Kings, The (film), **Supp. VIII:** 73, 74

Mambo Kings Play Songs of Love, The (Hijuelos), **Supp. VIII:** 73–74, **79–82**

"Ma'me Pélagie" (Chopin), **Retro. Supp. II:** 64

Mamet, David, **Supp. XIV: 239–258,** 315

"Mamie" (Sandburg), **III:** 582

Mammedaty, Novarro Scott. *See* Momaday, N. Scott

"Mammon and the Archer" (O. Henry), **Supp. II Part 1:** 394, 408

Mammonart (Sinclair), **Supp. V:** 276–277

"Mammy" (D. West), **Supp. XVIII:** 283

"Mamouche" (Chopin), **Retro. Supp. II:** 66

Mamoulian, Rouben, **Supp. XVIII:** 281

"Man" (Corso), **Supp. XII:** 130

"Man" (Herbert), **II:** 12

"Man Against the Sky, The" (Robinson), **III:** 509, 523

"Man and a Woman Sit Near Each Other, A" (R. Bly), **Supp. IV Part 1:** 71

Man and Boy (Morris), **III:** 223, 224, 225

"Man and the Snake, The" (Bierce), **I:** 203

"Man and Woman" (Caldwell), **I:** 310

Manassas (Sinclair), **Supp. V:** 280, 281, 285

"Man Bring This Up Road" (T. Williams), **IV:** 383–384

"Man Carrying Thing" (Stevens), **IV:** 90

Manchester, William, **III:** 103

"Man Child, The" (Baldwin), **Supp. I Part 1:** 63

Man Could Stand Up, A (Ford), **I:** 423

"Mandarin's Jade" (Chandler), **Supp. IV Part 1:** 125

Mandel, Charlotte, **Supp. XVI:** 57

Mandelbaum, Maurice, **I:** 61

Mandelbaum, Michael, **Supp. XXV:** 264

Mandelstam, Osip, **Retro. Supp. I:** 278; **Supp. III Part 1:** 268; **Supp. VIII:** 21, 22, 23, 27; **Supp. XIII:** 77; **Supp. XV:** 254, 261, 263

"Mandelstam: The Poem as Event" (Dobyns), **Supp. XIII:** 78

"Mandolin" (Dove), **Supp. IV Part 1:** 247

"Mandoline" (Verlaine), **IV:** 79

"Mandrin Question, The" (Vaz), **Supp. XXVI:** 267

"Man Eating" (Kenyon), **Supp. VII:** 173

"Manet in Late Summer" (Skloot), **Supp. XX: 201**

"Man Feeding Pigeons" (Clampitt), **Supp. IX: 49–50,** 52

Manfred, Frederick, **Supp. X:** 126

Man from Kinvara, The (Gallagher), **Supp. XXIV:** 166, 172, 173

Man From Limbo, The (Endore), **Supp. XVII:** 55

Man fun natseres, Der (Asch), **Supp. XXIII:** 6

Mangione, Jerre, **Supp. XXV:** 28

"Mango Says Goodbye Sometimes" (Cisneros), **Supp. VII:** 64

Manhattan (film; Allen), **Supp. IV Part 1:** 205; **Supp. XV:** 5, **7–8,** 13

"Manhattan Dawn" (Justice), **Supp. VII:** 117

"Manhattan: Luminism" (Doty), **Supp. XI:** 135

Manhattan Murder Mystery (film; Allen), **Supp. XV:** 5, 11

Manhattan Transfer (Dos Passos), **I:** 26, 475, 478, 479, 480, 481, 482–484, 487; **II:** 286; **Supp. I Part 1:** 57; **Supp. XXVI:** 18

"Mania" (Lowell), **II:** 554

"Manic in the Moon, The" (Thurber), **Supp. I Part 2:** 620

Manifest; and Furthermore (Bronk), **Supp. XXI:** 32

"Manifesto: A Press Release from PRKA" (Saunders), **Supp. XIX:** 235

Manikin, The (J. Scott), **Supp. XVII: 189–191,** 192, **194**

"Man in Black" (Plath), **Supp. I Part 2:** 538

Man in Lower Ten, The (Rinehart), **Supp. XXV:** 192, 200

Man in Prehistory (Chard), **Supp. XII:** 177–178

Man in the Black Coat Turns, The (R. Bly), **Supp. IV Part 1:** 66–68, 71, 73

"Man in the Brooks Brothers Shirt, The" (McCarthy), **II:** 563–564

"Man in the Drawer, The" (Malamud), **Supp. I Part 2:** 437

Man in the Flying Lawn Chair and Other Excursions and Observations, The (Plimpton), **Supp. XVI:** 234

Man in the Gray Flannel Suit, The (Wilson), **Supp. IV Part 1:** 387

Man in the High Castle, The (Dick), **Supp. XVIII:** 138

Man in the Middle, The (Wagoner), **Supp. IX:** 324, **332–333**

"Man in the Rain, The" (Ryan as Quin), **Supp. XVIII:** 226

"Man in the Toolhouse, The" (Swados), **Supp. XIX:** 263

Mankiewicz, Frank, **Supp. XXIV:** 279

Mankiewicz, Herman, **Supp. XVI:** 189

Mankiewicz, Joseph, **Retro. Supp. I:** 113

Mankowitz, Wolf, **Supp. XI:** 307

"Man Made of Words, The" (Momaday), **Supp. IV Part 2:** 481, 484–485, 486, 487, 488

Man-Made World, The (Gilman), **Supp. XI:** 207

"Man-Moth, The" (Bishop), **Retro. Supp. II:** 42; **Supp. I Part 1:** 85–87, 88

Mann, Barbara Alice, **Supp. XXVI:** 81, 85, 86, 88, 90, 92, 95

Mann, Charles, **Retro. Supp. II:** 40

Mann, Erika, **Supp. II Part 1:** 11

Mann, Seymour (Samuel Weisman), **Supp. V:** 113

Mann, Thomas, **I:** 271, 490; **II:** 42, 539; **III:** 231, 281–282, 283; **IV:** 70, 73, 85; **Supp. IV Part 1:** 392; **Supp. IV Part 2:** 522; **Supp. IX:** 21; **Supp. V:** 51; **Supp. XI:** 275; **Supp. XII:** 173, 310, 321; **Supp. XIV:** 87; **Supp. XIX:** 147, 151, 157; **Supp. XVII:** 137; **Supp. XX: 85; Supp. XXIII:** 4

Mannequins' Demise: A Play in Eight Scenes (Budbill), **Supp. XIX:** 12

Mannerhouse (Wolfe), **IV:** 460

Manner Music, The (Reznikoff), **Supp. XIV: 293–295**

"Manners" (Bishop), **Supp. I Part 1:** 73

"Manners" (Emerson), **II:** 4, 6

"Manners, Morals, and the Novel" (Trilling), **Supp. III Part 2:** 502, 503

Mannheim, Karl, **I:** 279; **Supp. I Part 2:** 644

Manning, Ambrose, **Supp. XX: 166**

Manning, Frederic, **III:** 459

Manning, Robert, **Supp. IX:** 236

Mannix, Daniel P., **Supp. II Part 1:** 140

Man Nobody Knows, The (B. Barton), **Retro. Supp. I:** 179

Mano, D. Keith, **Supp. XVI:** 250

Mano, Guy Levis, **Supp. XVI:** 282

"Man of Indeterminate Age on a Subway Grate, A" (DI Piero), **Supp. XIX:** 47

"Man of Letters" (Pickering), **Supp. XXI:** 192, 195–196

"Man of Letters as a Man of Business, The" (Howells), **Supp. XIV:** 45–46

"Man of No Account, The" (Harte), **Supp. II Part 1:** 339

"Man of the Crowd, The" (Poe), **III:** 412, 417; **Retro. Supp. I:** 154

Man on Spikes (Asinof), **II:** 424

Man on Stage (Dixon), **Supp. XII:** 141, **154–155**

"Man on the Dump, The" (Stevens), **IV:** 74; **Retro. Supp. I:** 306

"Man on the Stairs, The" (July), **Supp. XXIV:** 202

"Man on the Train, The" (Percy), **Supp. III Part 1:** 387

Manor, The (Singer), **IV:** 6, 17–19

Manrique, Jorge, **Retro. Supp. II:** 154

Mansart Builds a School (Du Bois), **Supp. II Part 1:** 185–186

Man's Fate (Malraux), **I:** 127; **Retro. Supp. II:** 121

"Man's Fate A Film Treatment of the Malraux Novel" (Agee), **I:** 33–34

Mansfield, June, **Supp. X:** 183, 194

Mansfield, Katherine, **III:** 362, 453

Mansfield, Stephanie, **Supp. IV Part 1:** 227

Man's Hope (Malraux), **IV:** 247

Mansion, The (Faulkner), **II:** 73; **Retro. Supp. I:** 74, 82

Man's Nature and His Communities (Niebuhr), **III:** 308

Manson, Charles, **Supp. IV Part 1:** 205

"Man Splitting Wood in the Daybreak, The" (Kinnell), **Supp. III Part 1:** 254

"Man's Pride" (Jeffers), **Supp. II Part 2:** 417

"Man's Story, The" (Anderson), **I:** 114

Man's Woman, A (Norris), **III:** 314, 322, 328, 329, 330, 332, 333

Man That Corrupted Hadleyburg, The (Twain), **I:** 204; **IV:** 208

"Man That Was Used Up, The" (Poe), **III:** 412, 425

"Mantis" (Zukofsky), **Supp. III Part 2:** 617

"'Mantis': An Interpretation" (Zukofsky), **Supp. III Part 2:** 617–618

"Man to Know in the Restaurants, The" (Siddons), **Supp. XXII:** 244

Man to Send Rain Clouds, The (Rosen, ed.), **Supp. IV Part 2:** 499, 505, 513

"Man to Send Rain Clouds, The" (Silko), **Supp. IV Part 2:** 559

Mantrap (Lewis), **II:** 447

Manuductio Ad Ministerium (Mather), **Supp. II Part 2:** 465–467

"Manuelzinho" (Bishop), **Retro. Supp. II:** 47–48

Manuscript Books of Emily Dickinson, The (Franklin, ed.), **Retro. Supp. I:** 29, 41

"Man Waiting for It to Stop, A" (Dunn), **Supp. XI:** 144

"Man Who Became a Woman, The" (Anderson), **I:** 114

"Man Who Carries the Desert Around Inside Himself, The: For Wally" (Komunyakaa), **Supp. XIII:** 125

"Man Who Closed Shop, The" (Dunn), **Supp. XI:** 149

Man Who Gave Up His Name, The (Harrison), **Supp. VIII:** 45, 52

Man Who Had All the Luck, The (A. Miller), **III:** 148, 149, 164, 166

"Man Who Knew Belle Star, The" (Bausch), **Supp. VII:** 46

"Man Who Knew Coolidge, The" (Lewis), **II:** 449

Man Who Knew Coolidge, The: Being the Soul of Lowell Schmaltz, Constructive and Nordic Citizen (Lewis), **II:** 450

Man Who Lived Underground, The (Wright), **Supp. II Part 1:** 40

"Man Who Lived Underground, The" (Wright), **IV:** 479, 485–487, 492; **Retro. Supp. II:** 121

"Man Who Made Me Love Him, The" (Weigl), **Supp. XIX:** 278

"Man Who Makes Brooms, The" (Nye), **Supp. XIII:** 276

"Man Who Studied Yoga, The" (Mailer), **III:** 35–36; **Retro. Supp. II:** 200

"Man Who Wanted to Win, The" (McCoy), **Supp. XIII:** 161

"Man Who Was Made of Netting, The" (Vaz), **Supp. XXVI:** 266

Man Who Was There, The (Morris), **III:** 220–221

"Man Who Writes Ants, The" (Merwin), **Supp. III Part 1:** 348

"Man with a Family" (Humphrey), **Supp. IX:** 94

Man without a Country, The (Hale), **I:** 488

"Man with the Blue Guitar, The" (Stevens), **I:** 266; **IV:** 85–87; **Retro. Supp. I:** 303–305, 306, 307, 309

Man with the Blue Guitar and Other Poems, The (Stevens), **IV:** 76; **Retro. Supp. I:** 303, 422

Man with the Golden Arm, The (Algren), **Supp. IX:** 1, 3, 9–11, 14, 15; **Supp. V:** 4

Man with the Golden Arm, The (film), **Supp. IX:** 3

"Man with the Golden Beef, The" (Podhoretz), **Supp. IX:** 3

"Man with the Hoe, The" (Markham), **Supp. XV:** 115

Man with the Mask, The (Lippard), **Supp. XXIII:** 178, 183–184, 188

Many a Monster (Ryan as Finnegan), **Supp. XVIII:** 233, 236–238

Manyan Letters (Olson), **Supp. II Part 2:** 571

Many Circles (Goldbarth), **Supp. XII:** 193

"Many Handles" (Sandburg), **III:** 594

"Many Happy Returns" (Auden), **Supp. II Part 1:** 15

Many Happy Returns (Berrigan), **Supp. XXII:** 224; **Supp. XXIV:** 37, 41

Many Loves (W. C. Williams), **Retro. Supp. I:** 424

"Many Mansions" (H. Roth), **Supp. IX:** 233, 234

Many Marriages (Anderson), **I:** 104, 111, 113

"Many of Our Waters: Variations on a Poem by a Black Child" (Wright), **Supp. III Part 2:** 602

"Many Swans" (Lowell), **II:** 526

"Many Thousands Gone" (Baldwin), **Retro. Supp. II:** 4; **Supp. I Part 1:** 51

"Many Wagons Ago" (Ashbery), **Supp. III Part 1:** 22

Many-Windowed House, A (Cowley), **Supp. II Part 1:** 141, 143

"Many-Windowed House, A" (Cowley), **Supp. II Part 1:** 137

Mao II (DeLillo), **Supp. VI:** 2, 4, 5, 6, 7, 8, 9, 14, 16

"Map, The" (Bishop), **Retro. Supp. II:** 41; **Supp. I Part 1:** 72, 82, 85–88, 93

"Map, The" (Strand), **Supp. IV Part 2:** 623–624

"Maple Leaf, The" (Joplin), **Supp. IV Part 1:** 223

"Maple Tree, The" (D. West), **Supp. XVIII:** 284

Map of Another Town: A Memoir of Provence (M. F. K. Fisher), **Supp. XVII:** 88, 89, 92

"Map of Montana in Italy, A" (Hugo), **Supp. VI:** 139

Mapp and Lucia (Benson), **Supp. XX:** 229

Mapping American Culture (Franklin and Steiner), **Supp. XXII:** 205

"Maps" (Hass), **Supp. VI:** 103–104

Mapson, Jo-Ann, **Supp. IV Part 2:** 440, 454

Map to the Next World, A: Poems and Tales (Harjo), **Supp. XII:** 228–230

"Maquillage" (Hull), **Supp. XXI:** 133

"Mara" (Jeffers), **Supp. II Part 2:** 434

Ma Rainey's Black Bottom (Wilson), **Supp. VIII:** 331, 332–334, 346, 349, 350

Maranen (Asch), **Supp. XXIII:** 10

Marat, Jean Paul, **IV:** 117; **Supp. I Part 2:** 514, 515, 521

"Marathon" (Glück), **Supp. V:** 85

Marble Faun, The (Faulkner), **II:** 55, 56; **Retro. Supp. I:** 79

Marble Faun, The; or, The Romance of Monte Beni (Hawthorne), **II:** 225, 239, 242–243, 290, 324; **IV:** 167; **Retro. Supp. I:** 63, 149, 163, 164–165; **Supp. I Part 1:** 38; **Supp. I Part 2:** 421, 596; **Supp. XIII:** 102

Marbles (Brodsky), **Supp. VIII:** 26–27

Marburg, Anita, **Supp. XXII:** 281

Marcaccio, Michael, **Supp. XVII:** 97, 106

"March" (W. C. Williams), **Retro. Supp. I:** 418

March, Alan, **Supp. XVI:** 242

March, Fredric, **III:** 154, 403; **IV:** 357; **Supp. X:** 220

"March, March on Down the Field" (Shaw), **Supp. XIX:** 246

Marchalonis, Shirley, **Supp. XIII:** 138, 140, 141, 143, 147–148

"Marché aux Oiseaux" (Wilbur), **Supp. III Part 2:** 550

"Märchen, The" (Jarrell), **II:** 378–379

March Hares (Frederic), **II:** 143–144

Marching Men (Anderson), **I:** 99, 101, 103–105, 111

"Marching Music" (Simic), **Supp. VIII:** 281

"Marcia" (R. H. Davis), **Supp. XVI:** 91–92

Marcks, Greg, **Supp. XVIII:** 150

Marckwardt, Albert H., **Supp. XXIV:** 255

Marco Millions (O'Neill), **III:** 391, 395

Marcosson, Isaac, **III:** 322

Marcus, Greil, **Supp. XVIII:** 30, 53; **Supp. XXVI:** 142

Marcus, Steven, **Retro. Supp. II:** 196, 200

Marcus Aurelius, **II:** 1; **III:** 566; **Supp. XVIII:** 304

Marcuse, Herbert, **Supp. I Part 2:** 645; **Supp. VIII:** 196; **Supp. XII:** 2

Mardi and a Voyage Thither (Melville), **I:** 384; **II:** 281; **III:** 77–79, 84, 87, 89; **Retro. Supp. I:** 247, 254, 256

Margaret (Judd), **II:** 290

Margaret & Dusty (Notley), **Supp. XXII:** 231

"Margaret Fuller, 1847" (Clampitt), **Supp. IX:** 43

"Marginalia" (Wilbur), **Supp. III Part 2:** 544

Margin of Hope, A: An Intellectual Autobiography (Howe), **Supp. VI:** 113–114, 117, 125, 128

"Margins of Maycomb, The: A Rereading of *To Kill a Mockingbird*" (Phelps), **Supp. VIII:** 128

Margoshes, Samuel, **Supp. X:** 70

"Margrave" (Jeffers), **Supp. II Part 2:** 426

Margret Howth (R. H. Davis), **Supp. XVI:** 81, 83, 84, 88–89

Margret Howth: A Story of Today (J. Yellin, ed.), **Supp. XVI:** 88

Margulies, Donald, **Supp. XXI:** 145

"Maria Concepción" (Porter), **III:** 434–435, 451

Mariana (Vaz), **Supp. XXVI:** 258–259, 263

Mariani, Paul L., **Retro. Supp. I:** 412, 419; **Retro. Supp. II:** 189

Marianne Moore Reader, (Moore), **III:** 199

Marie Antoinette (film), **Retro. Supp. I:** 113

Marie Blythe (Mosher), **Supp. XXII:** 206, 209, 212

Marie Laveau (Prose), **Supp. XVI:** 251

Mariella Gable, Sister, **III:** 339, 355

"Marijuana and a Pistol" (C. Himes), **Supp. XVI:** 137

"Marijuana Notation" (Ginsberg), **Supp. II Part 1:** 313

Maril, Herman, **Supp. XXI:** 22, 23

Marilyn: A Biography (Mailer), **Retro. Supp. II:** 208

"Marin" (Cisneros), **Supp. VII:** 60, 61

Marin, Jay, **Retro. Supp. II:** 325

"Marina" (Eliot), **I:** 584, 585; **Retro. Supp. I:** 64

Mariners, Renegades, and Castaways (C. L. R. James), **Supp. XXI:** 159, 169–170

"Marine Surface, Low Overcast" (Clampitt), **Supp. IX:** 47–48

Marinetti, F. T., **Supp. XXII:** 159, 160, 161, 163

Marinetti, Tommaso, **Retro. Supp. I:** 59

Marionettes, The (Faulkner), **Retro. Supp. I:** 79

"Mari Sandoz's *Slogum House:* Greed as a Woman" (Riley), **Supp. XXIV:** 252

Maritain, Jacques, **I:** 402; **Supp. XXVI:** 231, 232

Maritime Compact (Paine), **Supp. I Part 2:** 519

Maritime History of Massachusetts, 1783–1860, The (Morison), **Supp. I Part 2:** 481–483

Marjolin, Jean-Nicolas, **Supp. I Part 1:** 302

Marjorie Kinnan Rawlings: Sojourner at Cross Creek (Silverthorne), **Supp. X:** 220, 234

Marjorie Morningstar (film), **Supp. XXV:** 262

Marjorie Morningstar (Wouk), **Supp. XXV:** 253, 254, 256, 258, 261–262, 268

"Mark, The" (Bogan), **Supp. III Part 1:** 52

Marker, Chris, **Supp. IV Part 2:** 434, 436

"Market" (Hayden), **Supp. II Part 1:** 368, 369

Marketplace, The (Frederic), **II:** 145–146

Markham, Edwin, **I:** 199, 207; **Supp. XV:** 115

Markings (Hammarskjold), **Supp. II Part 1:** 26

Mark of the Vampire (film, Browning), **Supp. XVII:** 58

Markopoulos, Gregory, **Supp. XII:** 2

Markowick-Olczakova, Hanna, **Supp. X:** 70

Marks, Alison, **Supp. I Part 2:** 660

Marks, Barry A., **I:** 435, 438, 442, 446

Markson, David, **Supp. XVII: 135–147**

Mark Twain in Eruption (Twain), **IV:** 209

Mark Twain's America (De Voto), **I:** 248

Mark Twain's Autobiography (Twain), **IV:** 209

Marley, Bob, **Supp. IX:** 152

Marlowe, Christopher, **I:** 68, 368, 384; **II:** 590; **III:** 259, 491; **Retro. Supp. I:** 127; **Retro. Supp. II:** 76; **Supp. I Part 2:** 422; **Supp. XXI:** 227

Marlowe, Kimberly B., **Supp. XXII:** 214

"Marlowe Takes on the Syndicate" (Chandler), **Supp. IV Part 1:** 135

Marne, The (Wharton), **IV:** 319, 320; **Retro. Supp. I:** 378

Marquand, John, **Supp. XI:** 301

Marquand, Mrs. John P. (Adelaide Hooker), **III:** 57, 61

Marquand, Mrs. John P. (Christina Sedgwick), **III:** 54, 57

Marquand, J. P., **I:** 362, 375; **II:** 459, 482–483; **III: 50–73**, 383; **Supp. I Part 1:** 196; **Supp. IV Part 1:** 31; **Supp. V:** 95

Marquand, Philip, **III:** 52

Marquis, Don, **Supp. I Part 2:** 668

Marra, Anthony, **Supp. XXVI:** 216

Marrásh, Francis al-, **Supp. XX: 117**

"Marriage" (Corso), **Supp. XII:** 117, 124, **127–128**

Marriage (Moore), **III:** 194

"Marriage" (Moore), **III:** 198–199, 213

"Marriage, A" (Untermeyer), **Supp. XV:** 305

Marriage A-la-Mode (Dryden), **Supp. IX:** 68

Marriage and Other Science Fiction (Goldbarth), **Supp. XII:** 189, 190

"Marriage in the Sixties, A" (Rich), **Supp. I Part 2:** 554

Marriage of Bette and Boo, The (Durang), **Supp. XXIV:** 114, 121, **122–123**

Marriage of Heaven and Hell (Blake), **Supp. XXII:** 257

"Marriage of Heaven and Hell, The" (Blake), **III:** 544–545; **Supp. VIII:** 99

"Marriage of Phaedra, The" (Cather), **Retro. Supp. I:** 5

Marriage Plot, The (Eugenides), **Supp. XXIV:** 135, **143–145**

"Marriage Rhapsody"(Hadas), **Supp. XXIII:** 114

Married (Strindberg), **Supp. XXII:** 23

"Married" (Taggard), **Supp. XXII:** 274

Married Men (Wolfert), **Supp. XXI:** 277

Married People (Rinehart), **Supp. XXV:** 201

Marrow of Tradition, The (Chesnutt), **Supp. XIV:** 63, **71–75**, 76

Marryat, Captain Frederick, **III:** 423

"Marrying Absurd" (Didion), **Supp. IV Part 1:** 200

"Marrying Iseult?" (Updike), **Retro. Supp. I:** 329

Marrying Man (Simon), **Supp. IV Part 2:** 588

"Marrying the Hangman" (Atwood), **Supp. XIII:** 34

Marry Me: A Romance (Updike), **Retro. Supp. I:** 329, 330, 332

"Mars and Hymen" (Freneau), **Supp. II Part 1:** 258

Marsden, Dora, **III:** 471; **Retro. Supp. I:** 416

Marsena (Frederic), **II:** 135, 136–137

Marsh, Edward, **Supp. I Part 1:** 257, 263

Marsh, Frederick T., **Supp. XX: 39, 46**

Marsh, Fred T., **Supp. IX:** 232

Marsh, John R., **Supp. XIX:** 187

Marsh, Mae, **Supp. I Part 2:** 391

Marshall, George, **III:** 3

Marshall, John, **Supp. I Part 2:** 455; **Supp. XIX:** 62; **Supp. XVI:** 117; **Supp. XXIII:** 275, 276

Marshall, Paule, **Supp. IV Part 1:** 8, 14, 369; **Supp. XI:** 18, **275–292**; **Supp. XIII:** 295; **Supp. XX:** 154

Marshall, Tod, **Supp. XV:** 224; **Supp. XVII:** 25, 26, 29, 32

"Marshall Carpenter" (Masters), **Supp. I Part 2:** 463

"Marshes of Glynn, The" (Lanier), **Supp. I Part 1:** 364, 365–368, 370, 373

"'Marshes of Glynn, The': A Study in Symbolic Obscurity" (Ross), **Supp. I Part 1:** 373

Marsh Island, A (Jewett), **II:** 405; **Retro. Supp. II:** 134

"Marshland Elegy" (Leopold), **Supp. XIV:** 187, 189

"Mars Is Heaven!" (Bradbury), **Supp. IV Part 1:** 103, 106

Mars-Jones, Adam, **Supp. XXI:** 116

Marsman, Henrik, **Supp. IV Part 1:** 183

Marston, Ed, **Supp. IV Part 2:** 492

Marston, Elsa, **Supp. XXIII:** 241

Marta y Maria (Valdes), **II:** 290

"Martha's Lady" (Jewett), **Retro. Supp. II:** 140, 143

Marthe, Saint, **II:** 213

Martial, **II:** 1, 169; **Supp. IX:** 152

Martian Chronicles, The (Bradbury), **Supp. IV Part 1:** 102, 103, 106–107

Martian Time-Slip (Dick), **Supp. XVIII:** 142

Martin, Benjamin, **Supp. I Part 2:** 503

Martin, Charles, **Supp. XVII:** 112

Martin, Dick, **Supp. XII:** 44

Martin, Jay, **I:** 55, 58, 60, 61, 67; **III:** 307; **Retro. Supp. II:** 326, 327, 329;

Supp. XI: 162

Martin, John, **Supp. XI:** 172

Martin, Judith, **Supp. V:** 128

Martin, Nell, **Supp. IV Part 1:** 351, 353

Martin, Reginald, **Supp. X:** 247, 249

Martin, Robert, **Supp. XX: 165**

Martin, Stephen-Paul, **Supp. IV Part 2:** 430

Martin, Tom, **Supp. X:** 79

Martin du Gard, Roger, **Supp. I Part 1:** 51

Martineau, Harriet, **Supp. II Part 1:** 282, 288, 294; **Supp. XVIII:** 7; **Supp. XXIV:** 78

Martin Eden (London), **II:** 466, 477–481

Martinelli, Sheri, **Supp. IV Part 1:** 280

Martínez, Guillermo, **Supp. XIII:** 313

Martinez-Avila, Raul, **Supp. XXIII:** 125

Martini, Adrienne, **Supp. XVIII:** 35

Martín-Lucas, Belén, **Supp. XXVI:** 218

Mart'nez, Rafael, **Retro. Supp. I:** 423

Martone, John, **Supp. V:** 179

Marty (Chayefsky), **Supp. XV:** 205

"Martyr, The" (Porter), **III:** 454

Martz, Louis L., **IV:** 151, 156, 165; **Supp. I Part 1:** 107; **Supp. XIV:** 12; **Supp. XXI:** 85

Marvell, Andrew, **IV:** 135, 151, 156, 161, 253; **Retro. Supp. I:** 62, 127; **Retro. Supp. II:** 186, 189; **Supp. I Part 1:** 80; **Supp. XII:** 159; **Supp. XIV:** 10; **Supp. XVI:** 204; **Supp. XXI:** 227; **Supp. XXIII:** 62

"Marvella, for Borrowing" (Ríos), **Supp. IV Part 2:** 551

"Marvelous Sauce, The", **Supp. XVII:** 189

Marvels and Masterpieces (al-Badá'i' wa'l-Tará'if) (Gibran), **Supp. XX: 116, 124**

Marx, Eleanor, **Supp. XVI:** 85

Marx, Karl, **I:** 60, 267, 279, 283, 588; **II:** 376, 462, 463, 483, 577; **IV:** 429, 436, 443–444, 469; **Retro. Supp. I:** 254; **Supp. I Part 2:** 518, 628, 632, 633, 634, 635, 639, 643, 645, 646; **Supp. III Part 2:** 619; **Supp. IV Part 1:** 355; **Supp. IX:** 133; **Supp. VIII:** 196; **Supp. X:** 119, 134; **Supp. XIII:** 75; **Supp. XXI:** 162, 263

Marx, Leo, **Supp. I Part 1:** 233

"Marxism and Monastic Perpectives" (Merton), **Supp. VIII:** 196

Mary (Asch), **Supp. XXIII:** 2, 7, **14**

Mary (Nabokov), **Retro. Supp. I: 267– 268,** 270, 277

"Mary" (Trethewey), **Supp. XXI:** 246

"Mary in Old Age" (Ferry), **Supp. XXIV:** 162

"Mary Karr, Mary Karr, Mary Karr, Mary Karr" (Harmon), **Supp. XI:** 248

Maryles, Daisy, **Supp. XII:** 271

Mary Magdalene, **I:** 303

"Mary Magdalene at Easter" (Davison), **Supp. XXVI:** 71

Mary; or, The Test of Honour (Rowson), **Supp. XV: 233,** 236

"Mary O'Reilly" (Anderson), **II:** 44

"Mary Osaka , I Love You" (Fante), **Supp. XI:** 169

Mary Roberts Rinehart Crime Book, The (Rinehart), **Supp. XXV:** 199

"Mary Snorak the Cook, Skermo the Gardener, and Jack the Parts Man Provide Dinner for a Wandering Stranger" (Grossman), **Supp. XIX:** 87

"Mary's Song" (Plath), **Supp. I Part 2:** 541

"Mary Winslow" (Lowell), **Retro. Supp. II:** 187

Marzynski, Marian, **Supp. XVI:** 153

Masefield, John, **II:** 552; **III:** 523

Masked and Anonymous (film, Dylan and Charles), **Supp. XVIII:** 21, 28

Mask for Janus, A (Merwin), **Supp. III Part 1:** 339, 341, 342

Maslin, Janet, **Supp. XVI:** 213; **Supp. XXI:** 79

Maslow, Abraham, **Supp. I Part 2:** 540

Maso, Carole, **Supp. XXII:** 261

Mason, Bobbie Ann, **Supp. VIII: 133–149; Supp. XI:** 26; **Supp. XII:** 294, 298, 311; **Supp. XX: 162; Supp. XXV:** 153

Mason, Charlotte, **Supp. XIV:** 201

Mason, David, **Supp. V:** 344; **Supp. XV:** 116, 251; **Supp. XVII:** 109, 110, 112, 121; **Supp. XVIII:** 182, 183

Mason, Jennifer, **Supp. XVIII:** 263

Mason, Lowell, **I:** 458

Mason, Margaret, **Supp. XXIII:** 209

Mason, Marsha, **Supp. IV Part 2:** 575, 586

Mason, Otis Tufton, **Supp. I Part 1:** 18

Mason, Walt, **Supp. XV:** 298

Mason & Dixon (Pynchon), **Supp. XVII:** 232

"Mason Jars by the Window" (Ríos), **Supp. IV Part 2:** 548

"Masque in Green and Black"(Hadas), **Supp. XXIII:** 121

Masque of Mercy, A (Frost), **II:** 155, 165, 167–168; **Retro. Supp. I:** 131, 140

"Masque of Mummers, The" (MacLeish), **III:** 18

"Masque of Pandora, The" (Longfellow), **Retro. Supp. II:** 167

Masque of Pandora, The, and Other Poems (Longfellow), **II:** 490, 494, 506; **Retro. Supp. II:** 169

Masque of Poets, A (Lathrop, ed.), **Retro. Supp. I:** 31; **Supp. I Part 1:** 365, 368

Masque of Reason, A (Frost), **II:** 155, 162, 165–167; **Retro. Supp. I:** 131, 140; **Retro. Supp. II:** 42

"Masque of the Red Death, The" (Poe), **III:** 412, 419, 424; **Retro. Supp. II:** 262, 268–269

"Masquerade" (Banks), **Supp. V:** 7

Massachusetts, Its Historians and Its History (Adams), **Supp. I Part 2:** 484

"Massachusetts 1932" (Bowles), **Supp. IV Part 1:** 94

"Massachusetts to Virginia" (Whittier), **Supp. I Part 2:** 688–689

"Massacre and the Mastermind, The" (Bausch), **Supp. VII:** 49

"Massacre at Scio, The" (Bryant), **Supp. I Part 1:** 168

"Massacre of the Innocents, The" (Davison), **Supp. XXVI:** 70

"Massacre of the Innocents, The" (Simic), **Supp. VIII:** 282

Masses and Man (Toller), **I:** 479

"Masseur de Ma Soeur, Le" (Hecht), **Supp. X:** 58

Massey, Raymond, **Supp. IV Part 2:** 524

"Mass Eye and Ear: The Ward" (Karr), **Supp. XI:** 244

"Mass for the Day of St. Thomas Didymus" (Levertov), **Supp. III Part 1:** 283

Massie, Chris, **Supp. IV Part 2:** 524

Massing, Michael, **Supp. IV Part 1:** 208

Massinger, Philip, **Supp. I Part 2:** 422; **Supp. XV:** 238

Master Builder, The (Ibsen), **Supp. IV Part 2:** 522

Master Class (McNally), **Supp. XIII: 204–205,** 208

"Masterful" (Matthews), **Supp. IX: 161–162**

Mastering the Art of French Cooking (Child), **Supp. XVII:** 89

"Master Misery" (Capote), **Supp. III Part 1:** 117

Master of Dreams: A Memoir of Isaac Bashevis Singer (Telushkin), **Retro. Supp. II:** 317

Master of Secret Revenges, The (Gass), **Supp. VI:** 93

Master of the Crossroads (Bell), **Supp. X: 16–17**

"'Masterpiece of Filth, A': Portrait of Knoxville Forgets to Be Fair" (Howards), **Supp. VIII:** 178

Masterpieces of American Fiction, **Supp. XI:** 198

"Master Player, The" (Dunbar), **Supp. II Part 1:** 200

Masters, Edgar Lee, **I:** 106, 384, 475, 480, 518; **II:** 276, 529; **III:** 505, 576, 579; **IV:** 352; **Retro. Supp. I:** 131; **Supp. I Part 2:** 378, 386, 387, **454–478; Supp. III Part 1:** 63, 71, 73, 75; **Supp. IV Part 2:** 502; **Supp. IX:** 308; **Supp. XIV:** 282–283; **Supp. XV:** 256, 293, 297, 301, 306; **Supp. XXV:** 18

Masters, Hardin W., **Supp. I Part 2:** 468

Masters, Hilary, **Supp. IX:** 96

Masters of Sociological Thought (Coser), **Supp. I Part 2:** 650

Masters of the Dew (Roumain), **Supp. IV Part 1:** 367

Masters of the Short Story (Kriegel and Lass, eds.), **Supp. XXIV:** 214

"Masters of War" (song, Dylan), **Supp. XVIII:** 24

"Master's Pieces, The" (H. L. Gates), **Supp. XX: 109**

Matchmaker, The (Wilder), **IV:** 357, 369, 370, 374; **Supp. XX: 50**

Mate of the Daylight, The, and Friends Ashore (Jewett), **II:** 404; **Retro. Supp. II:** 146–147

Materassi, Mario, **Supp. IX:** 233

Materials, The (Oppen), **Supp. XXVI:** 229–232

"Math Bending unto Angels" (Vaz), **Supp. XXVI:** 260

Mather, Cotton, **II:** 10, 104, 302, 506, 536; **III:** 442; **IV:** 144, 152–153, 157; **Supp. I Part 1:** 102, 117, 174, 271; **Supp. I Part 2:** 584, 599, 698; **Supp. II Part 2: 441–470; Supp. IV Part 2:** 430, 434

Mather, Increase, **II:** 10; **IV:** 147, 157; **Supp. I Part 1:** 100

Mathews, Cornelius, **III:** 81; **Supp. I Part 1:** 317

Mathews, Shailer, **III:** 293

"Matinees" (Merrill), **Supp. III Part 1:** 319, 327

"Matins" (C. Frost), **Supp. XV:** 105

"Matins" (Glück), **Supp. V:** 88

"Matins" (Nelson), **Supp. XVIII:** 177

Matisse, Henri, **III:** 180; **IV:** 90, 407; **Supp. I Part 2:** 619; **Supp. IX:** 66; **Supp. VIII:** 168; **Supp. X:** 73, 74; **Supp. XXII:** 98, 99; **Supp. XXVI:** 259

"Matisse: Blue Interior with Two Girls–1947" (Hecht), **Supp. X: 73–74**

"Matisse: The Red Studio" (Snodgrass), **Supp. VI:** 316–317

Matlack, James, **Supp. XV:** 269, 271, 286

Matlock, Lucinda, **Supp. I Part 2:** 462

Matos, Juan, **Supp. XXI:** 104

Matrimaniac, The (film), **Supp. XVI:** 185, 186

Matrix Trilogy, The (film), **Supp. XVI:** 271

Matson, Harold, **Supp. XIII:** 164, 166, 167, 169, 172

Matson, Peter, **Supp. IV Part 1:** 299

Matson, Suzanne, **Supp. VIII:** 281

Matters of Fact and Fiction: Essays 1973–1976 (Vidal), **Supp. IV Part 2:** 687

Matters of Life and Death: New American Stories (Wolff, ed.), **Supp. XXIII:** 289

Matthew (biblical book), **IV:** 164; **Supp. XV:** 222

Matthew Arnold (Trilling), **Supp. III Part 2:** 500–501

Matthews, Jackson, **Supp. XVI:** 282

Matthews, T. S., **II:** 430; **Supp. XV:** 142

Matthews, William, **Supp. IX: 151–170; Supp. V:** 4, 5; **Supp. XIII:** 112; **Supp. XXI:** 87; **Supp. XXVI:** 66

Matthiessen, F. O., **I:** 254, 259–260, 517; **II:** 41, 554; **III:** 310, 453; **IV:** 181; **Retro. Supp. I:** 40, 217; **Retro. Supp. II:** 137; **Supp. IV Part 2:** 422; **Supp. XIII:** 93; **Supp. XIV:** 3; **Supp. XXI:** 277; **Supp. XXV:** 251

Matthiessen, Peter, **Supp. V: 199–217,** 332; **Supp. XI:** 231, 294; **Supp. XIV:** 82; **Supp. XIX:** 268; **Supp. XVI:** 230

Mattingly, Garrett, **Supp. IV Part 2:** 601

Mattos, Anita, **Supp. XXIII:** 197

Mattu, Ravi, **Supp. XVI:** 124

"Maud Island" (Caldwell), **I:** 310

Maud Martha (Brooks), **Supp. III Part 1:** 74, 78–79, 87; **Supp. XI:** 278

"Maud Muller" (Whittier), **Supp. I Part 2:** 698

Maugham, W. Somerset, **III:** 57, 64; **Supp. IV Part 1:** 209; **Supp. X:** 58; **Supp. XIV:** 161

Maule's Curse: Seven Studies in the History of American Obscurantism (Winters), **Supp. II Part 2:** 807–808, 812

"Mau-mauing the Flak Catchers" (Wolfe), **Supp. III Part 2:** 577

Maupassant, Guy de, **I:** 309, 421; **II:** 191–192, 291, 325, 591; **IV:** 17; **Retro. Supp. II:** 65, 66, 67, 299; **Supp. I Part 1:** 207, 217, 223, 320; **Supp. XIV:** 336

"Maurice Barrès and the Youth of France" (Bourne), **I:** 228

Maurice Kenny: Celebrations of a Mohawk Writer (Kelsey, ed.), **Supp. XXIII:** 143

Maurier, George du, **II:** 338

Maurras, Charles, **Retro. Supp. I:** 55

Maus II: And Here My Troubles Began (A. Speigelman), **Supp. XVII:** 48

Mauve Gloves & Madmen, Clutter & Vine (Wolfe), **Supp. III Part 2:** 581

Maverick, Augustus, **Supp. XVIII:** 4

Maverick in Mauve (Auchincloss), **Supp. IV Part 1:** 26

"Mavericks, The" (play) (Auchincloss), **Supp. IV Part 1:** 34

"Mavericks, The" (story) (Auchincloss), **Supp. IV Part 1:** 32

"Max" (H. Miller), **III:** 183

Max, D. T., **Supp. XXI:** 117

Max and the White Phagocytes (H. Miller), **III:** 178, 183–184

Maximilian (emperor of Mexico), **Supp. I Part 2:** 457–458

Maximilian: A Play in Five Acts (Masters), **Supp. I Part 2:** 456, 457–458

"Maximus, to Gloucester" (Olson), **Supp. II Part 2:** 574

"Maximus, to himself" (Olson), **Supp. II Part 2:** 565, 566, 567, 569, 570, 572

Maximus Poems, The (Olson), **Retro. Supp. I:** 209; **Supp. II Part 2:** 555, 556, 563, 564–580, 584; **Supp. VIII:** 305; **Supp. XV:** 170, 264, 349; **Supp. XVI:** 287

Maximus Poems 1–10, The (Olson), **Supp. II Part 2:** 571

Maximus Poems IV, V, VI (Olson), **Supp. II Part 2:** 555, 580, 582–584

Maximus Poems Volume Three, The (Olson), **Supp. II Part 2:** 555, 582, 584–585

"Maximus to Gloucester, Letter 19 (A Pastoral Letter)" (Olson), **Supp. II Part 2:** 567

"Maximus to Gloucester, Sunday July 19" (Olson), **Supp. II Part 2:** 580

"Maximus to himself June 1964" (Olson), **Supp. II Part 2:** 584

Maxwell, Glyn, **Supp. XV:** 252, 253, 260, 261, 263, 264

Maxwell, William, **Supp. I Part 1:** 175; **Supp. III Part 1:** 62; **Supp. VIII:** 151–174; **Supp. XVII:** 23

May, Abigail (Abba). *See* Alcott, Mrs. Amos Bronson (Abigail May)

May, Elaine Tyler, **Supp. XXII:** 81, 95

May, Jill, **Supp. VIII:** 126

"May 24, 1980" (Brodsky), **Supp. VIII:** 28

"May 1968" (Olds), **Supp. X:** 211–212

Mayakovsky, Vladimir, **Supp. XXIII:** 207; **Supp. XXVI:** 144

"Mayakovsky" (O'Hara), **Supp. XXIII:** 212, 214

"Mayan Glyphs Unread, The" (Bronk), **Supp. XXI:** 31

"Mayan Warning" (Mora), **Supp. XIII:** 214

Maybe (Hellman), **Supp. IV Part 1:** 12

"Maybe" (Oliver), **Supp. VII:** 239

"Maybe, Someday" (Ritsos), **Supp. XIII:** 78

May Blossom (Belasco), **Supp. XVI:** 182

"Mayday" (Faulkner), **Retro. Supp. I:** 80

"May Day" (Fitzgerald), **II:** 88–89; **Retro. Supp. I:** 103

"May Day Dancing, The" (Nemerov), **III:** 275

May Days (Pickering), **Supp. XXI:** 197–198

May Days: An Anthology of Verse from Masses-Liberator (Taggard, ed.), **Supp. XXII:** 275–276

"May Day Sermon to the Women of Gilmer County, Georgia, by a Woman Preacher Leaving the Baptist Church" (Dickey), **Supp. IV Part 1:** 182

Mayer, Bernadette, **Supp. XXIV:** 41

Mayer, Elizabeth, **Supp. II Part 1:** 16; **Supp. III Part 1:** 63

Mayer, John, **Retro. Supp. I:** 58

Mayer, Louis B., **Supp. XII:** 160; **Supp. XVIII:** 250

Mayes, Wendell, **Supp. IX:** 250

Mayfield, Sara, **Supp. IX:** 65

"May First" (Hayes), **Supp. XXVI:** 144

Mayflower, The (Stowe), **Supp. I Part 2:** 585, 586

Mayle, Peter, **Supp. XVI:** 295

Maynard, Joyce, **Supp. V:** 23

Maynard, Tony, **Supp. I Part 1:** 65

Mayne, Xavier. *See* Prime-Stevenson, Edward Irenaeus

Mayo, Robert, **III:** 478

Mayor (Allen), **Supp. XXII:** 245

Mayorga, Margaret, **IV:** 381

"Mayor of Glory River, The" (Huddle), **Supp. XXVI:** 151

"May-Pole of Merry Mount, The" (Hawthorne), **Supp. XXII:** 44

"Maypole of Merrymount, The" (Hawthorne), **II:** 229

"May Queen" (Di Piero), **Supp. XIX:** 41

May Sarton: Selected Letters 1916–1954, **Supp. VIII:** 265

"May Sun Sheds an Amber Light, The" (Bryant), **Supp. I Part 1:** 170

"May Swenson: The Art of Perceiving" (Stanford), **Supp. IV Part 2:** 637

May the Generations Die in the Right Order (Schott), **Supp. XXIII:** 248–250

"Maze" (Eberhart), **I:** 523, 525–526, 527

Mazel (R. Goldstein), **Supp. XVII:** 44

Mazower, David, **Supp. XXIII:** 4, 5

Mazur, Gail, **Supp. XVIII:** 92

Mazurkiewicz, Margaret, **Supp. XI:** 2

Mazzeno, Laurence W., **Supp. XXV:** 253, 256, 258, 259, 263

Mazzini, Giuseppe, **Supp. I Part 1:** 2, 8; **Supp. II Part 1:** 299

M. Butterfly (Hwang), **Supp. X:** 292; **Supp. XXI:** 143, 147, 150–154

Mc. Names starting with Mc are alphabetized as if spelled Mac.

"M. Degas Teaches Art & Science at Durfee Intermediate School, Detroit, 1942" (Levine), **Supp. V:** 181, 193

"Me, Boy Scout" (Lardner), **II:** 433

Me, Vashya! (T. Williams), **IV:** 381

Mead, Elinor. *See* Howells, Mrs. William Dean (Elinor Mead)

Mead, George Herbert, **II:** 27, 34; **Supp. I Part 1:** 5; **Supp. I Part 2:** 641

Mead, Margaret, **Supp. I Part 1:** 49, 52, 66; **Supp. IX:** 229

Mead, Taylor, **Supp. XV:** 187

Meade, Frank, **Retro. Supp. II:** 114

Meade, Marion, **Supp. IX:** 191, 193, 194, 195

Meadow, Lynne, **Supp. XIII:** 198

"Meadow House" (Carruth), **Supp. XVI:** 48

Meadowlands (Glück), **Supp. V:** 88–90

"Mean, Mrs." (Gass), **Supp. VI:** 83

"Me and the Mule" (Hughes), **Supp. I Part 1:** 334

Me and You and Everyone We Know (film, July), **Supp. XXIV:** 199, 200, 201, 203, 206, 207–209

Mean Free Path (Lerner), **Supp. XXIV:** 45

Meaning a Life (M. Oppen), **Supp. XXVI:** 225, 228

"Meaningless Institution, A" (Ginsberg), **Supp. II Part 1:** 313

"Meaning of a Literary Idea, The" (Trilling), **Supp. III Part 2:** 498

"Meaning of Birds, The" (C. Smith), **Supp. X:** 177

"Meaning of Death, The, An After Dinner Speech" (Tate), **IV:** 128, 129

"Meaning of Life, The" (Tate), **IV:** 137

"Meaning of Simplicity, The" (Ritsos), **Supp. XIII:** 78

"Mean Mud Season, The" (Huddle), **Supp. XXVI:** 149

Means of Escape (Caputo), **Supp. XIX:** 18, 21, 25

Mean Spirit (Hogan), **Supp. IV Part 1:** 397, 404, 407–410, 415, 416–417

Meantime, The (Bronk), **Supp. XXI:** 31

Mearns, Hughes, **III:** 220

"Measure" (Hass), **Supp. VI:** 99–100, 101

Measure for Measure (Shakespeare), **Supp. XXVI:** 78

"Measuring My Blood" (Vizenor), **Supp. IV Part 1:** 262

Meatyard, Gene, **Supp. X:** 30

Me: By Jimmy (Big Boy) Valente (Keillor), **Supp. XVI:** 177

Mechan, Dennis B., **Supp. XVI:** 267–268

Mechanic, The (Bynner and DeMille), **Supp. XV:** 42, 50

"Mechanism" (Ammons), **Supp. VII:** 28

"Mechanism in Thought and Morals" (Holmes), **Supp. I Part 1:** 314

Mecom, Mrs. Jane, **II:** 122

"Meddlesome Jack" (Caldwell), **I:** 309

Medea (Jeffers), **Supp. II Part 2:** 435

Medea and Some Poems, The (Cullen), **Supp. IV Part 1:** 169, 173

"Me Decade and the Third Great Awakening, The" (Wolfe), **Supp. III Part 2:** 581

"Médecin Malgré Lui, Le" (W. C. Williams), **IV:** 407–408

"Medfield" (Bryant), **Supp. I Part 1:** 157

Medical History of Contraception, A (Himes), **Supp. V:** 128

"Medicine Song" (Gunn Allen), **Supp. IV Part 1:** 326

Médicis, Marie de, **II:** 548

Medina (McCarthy), **II:** 579

"Meditation, A" (Eberhart), **I:** 533–535

"Meditation 1.6" (Taylor), **IV:** 165

"Meditation 1.20" (Taylor), **IV:** 165

"Meditation 2.68A" (Taylor), **IV:** 165

"Meditation 2.102" (Taylor), **IV:** 150

"Meditation 2.112" (Taylor), **IV:** 165

"Meditation 20" (Taylor), **IV:** 154–155

"Meditation 40" (Second Series) (Taylor), **IV:** 147

"Meditation at Lagunitas" (Hass), **Supp. VI:** 104–105; **Supp. XXI:** 60; **Supp. XXVI:** 61

"Meditation at Oyster River" (Roethke), **III:** 537, 549

Meditations (Descartes), **III:** 618

Meditations (Marcus Aurelius), **Supp. XVIII:** 304

"Meditations for a Savage Child" (Rich), **Supp. I Part 2:** 564–565

Meditations from a Movable Chair (Dubus), **Supp. VII:** 91

Meditations in an Emergency (O'Hara), **Supp. XXIII:** 213–214, 219, 220

"Meditations in an Emergency"(O'Hara), **Supp. XXIII:** 212, 214

"Meditations in a Swine Yard" (Komunyakaa), **Supp. XIII:** 131

"Meditations of an Old Woman" (Roethke), **III:** 529, 540, 542, 543, 545–547, 548

"Meditations on Grass"(Crooker), **Supp. XXIII:** 55

Meditations on the Insatiable Soul (R. Bly), **Supp. IV Part 1:** 72–73

Meditative Poems, The (Martz), **IV:** 151

"Mediterranean, The" (Tate), **IV:** 129

"Medium of Fiction, The" (Gass), **Supp. VI:** 85–86

"Medley" (Bambara), **Supp. XI:** 9

"Medusa" (Bogan), **Supp. III Part 1:** 50, 51

Meehan, Jeannette Porter, **Supp. XX: 213, 214, 217, 220, 224**

Meehan, Thomas, **Supp. IV Part 2:** 577–578, 586, 590

Meek, Martha, **Supp. IV Part 2:** 439, 440, 441, 442, 445, 447, 448

Meeker, Richard K., **II:** 190

Meese, Elizabeth, **Supp. XIII:** 297

"Meeting" (J. W. Miller), **Supp. XX: 167**

"Meeting, The" (F. Wright), **Supp. XVII:** 245

"Meeting and Greeting Area, The" (Cameron), **Supp. XII: 84–85**

Meeting by the River, A (Isherwood), **Supp. XIV:** 164, **170–171,** 172

"Meeting-House Hill" (Lowell), **II:** 522, 527

"Meeting in the Kitchen, The" (Schnackenberg), **Supp. XV:** 256

"Meeting of the Tisdale Fellows, The" (Huddle), **Supp. XXVI:** 155

"Meeting South, A" (Anderson), **I:** 115

"Meeting the Mountains" (Snyder), **Supp. VIII:** 300

Meeting Trees (Sanders), **Supp. XVI:** 269

Meet Me at the Morgue (Macdonald), **Supp. IV Part 2:** 472

Mehta, Sonny, **Supp. XI:** 178

Mehta, Ved, **Supp. XX: 87**

Meine, Curt, **Supp. XIV:** 179

Meiners, R. K., **IV:** 136, 137, 138, 140

Meinong, Alexius, **Supp. XIV:** 198, 199

Meisner, Sanford, **Supp. XIV:** 240, 242

Meister, Charles W., **II:** 112

Mejia, Jaime, **Supp. XIX:** 97

"Melancholia" (Dunbar), **Supp. II Part 1:** 194

Melancholy Baby (Parker), **Supp. XIX:** 186

"Melanctha" (Stein), **IV:** 30, 34, 35, 37, 38–40, 45

"Melancthon" (Moore), **III:** 212, 215

Melbourne House (S. and A. Warner), **Supp. XVIII:** 268

Meliboeus Hipponax (Lowell). *See Bigelow Papers, The* (Lowell)

Melinda and Melinda (Allen), **Supp. XV:** 16

Mellaart, James, **Supp. I Part 2:** 567

Mellard, James, **Supp. IV Part 1:** 387

Mellen, Joan, **Supp. XXIV:** 51, 52, 56, 64

Mellon, Andrew, **III:** 14

Mellor, W. M., **Supp. XX: 56**

Melnick, Jeffrey, **Supp. X:** 252

Melnyczuk, Askold, **Supp. IV Part 1:** 70

Melodrama Play (Shepard), **Supp. III Part 2:** 440–441, 443, 445

Melodramatists, The (Nemerov), **III:** 268, 281–283, 284

Melopoeia (Espaillat and Tavano), **Supp. XXI:** 99–100

Melting-Pot, The (Zangwill), **I:** 229

"Melungeons" (Offutt), **Supp. XIX:** 171

Melville, Allan, **III:** 74, 77

Melville, Gansevoort, **III:** 76

Melville, Herman, **I:** 104, 106, 211, 288, 340, 343, 348, 354, 355, 561–562; **II:** 27, 74, 224–225, 228, 230, 232, 236, 255, 259, 271, 272, 277, 281, 295, 307, 311, 319, 320, 321, 418, 477, 497, 539–540, 545; **III:** 29, 45, 70, **74–98,** 359, 438, 453, 454, 507, 562–563, 572, 576; **IV:** 57, 105, 194, 199, 202, 250, 309, 333, 345, 350, 380, 444, 453; **Retro. Supp. I:** 54, 91, 160, 215, 220, **243–262; Retro. Supp. II:** 76; **Supp. I Part 1:** 147, 238, 242, 249, 309, 317, 372; **Supp. I Part 2:** 383, 495, 579, 580, 582, 602; **Supp. IV Part 2:** 463, 613; **Supp. V:** 279, 281, 298, 308; **Supp. VIII:** 48, 103, 104, 105, 106, 108, 156, 175, 181, 188; **Supp. XI:** 83; **Supp. XII:** 282; **Supp. XIII:** 294, 305; **Supp. XIV:** 48, 227; **Supp. XV:** 287; **Supp. XVII:** 42, 185; **Supp. XVIII:** 1, 4, 6, 7, 9; **Supp. XXI:** 169; **Supp. XXII:** 174, 262; **Supp. XXIII:** 164, 165, 174, 190; **Supp. XXIV:** 88

Melville, Mrs. Herman (Elizabeth Shaw), **III:** 77, 91, 92

Melville, Maria Gansevoort, **III:** 74, 77, 85

Melville, Thomas, **III:** 77, 79, 92; **Supp. I Part 1:** 309

Melville, Whyte, **IV:** 309

Melville Goodwin, USA (Marquand), **III:** 60, 65–66

Melville's Marginalia (Cowen), **Supp. IV Part 2:** 435

"Melville's Marginalia" (Howe), **Supp. IV Part 2:** 435

Member of the Wedding, The (McCullers), **II:** 587, 592, 600–604, 605, 606; **Supp. VIII:** 124

"Meme Ortiz" (Cisneros), **Supp. VII:** 60

Memmon (song cycle) (Bowles), **Supp. IV Part 1:** 82

Memmott, Carol, **Supp. XXVI:** 209

Memnoch the Devil (Rice), **Supp. VII:** 289, 290, 294, 296–299

"Memoir" (Hempel), **Supp. XXI:** 118

"Memoir" (Untermeyer), **II:** 516–517

"Memoir, A" (Koch), **Supp. XV:** 184

Memoir from Antproof Case (Helprin), **Supp. XXV:** 84, 87

"Memoirist's Apology, A" (Karr), **Supp. XI:** 245, 246

Memoir of Mary Ann, A (O'Connor), **III:** 357

Memoir of Thomas McGrath, A (Beeching), **Supp. X:** 114, 118

Memoirs (W. Frank), **Supp. XX: 67, 69, 70, 81**

Memoirs of a Preacher, a Revelation of the Church and the Home, The (Lippard), **Supp. XXIII:** 178, 183–184, 188, 190

Memoirs of Arii Taimai (Adams), **I:** 2–3

"Memoirs of Carwin, the Biloquist" (Brown), **Supp. I Part 1:** 132

Memoirs of Hecate County (Wilson), **IV:** 429

Memoirs of Margaret Fuller Ossoli (Fuller), **Supp. II Part 1:** 280, 283, 285

"Memoirs of Stephen Calvert" (Brown), **Supp. I Part 1:** 133, 144

Memorabilia (Xenophon), **II:** 105

Memorable Providences (Mather), **Supp. II Part 2:** 458

Memorial, The: Portrait of a Family (Isherwood), **Supp. XIV:** 156, 159, 160–161

"Memorial Day" (Cameron), **Supp. XII:** 80, **82–83**

"Memorial for the City" (Auden), **Supp. II Part 1:** 20

"Memorial Rain" (MacLeish), **III:** 15

"Memorial to Ed Bland" (Brooks), **Supp. III Part 1:** 77

"Memorial Tribute" (Wilbur), **Supp. IV Part 2:** 642

"Memories" (Whittier), **Supp. I Part 2:** 699

Memories of a Catholic Girlhood (McCarthy), **II:** 560–561, 566; **Supp. XI:** 246; **Supp. XVI:** 64, 70

"Memories of East Texas" (Karr), **Supp. XI:** 239

"Memories of Uncle Neddy" (Bishop), **Retro. Supp. II:** 38; **Supp. I Part 1:** 73, 93

"Memories of West Street and Lepke" (Lowell), **II:** 550

"Memory" (Epstein), **Supp. XII:** 163

"Memory" (Everwine), **Supp. XV:** 82

"Memory, A" (Welty), **IV:** 261–262; **Retro. Supp. I:** 344–345

"Memory, Narrative, and the Discourses of Identity in *Abeng* and *No Telephone to Heaven*" (Smith), **Supp. XXII:** 70

"Memory, The" (Gioia), **Supp. XV:** 119

Memory and Enthusiasm: Essays, 1975–1985 (Di Piero), **Supp. XIX:** 34, 41, 42

"Memory and Imagination" (Hampl), **Supp. XXII:** 94

Memory Gardens (Creeley), **Supp. IV Part 1:** 141, 157

"Memory Harbor" (Skloot), **Supp. XX:** **201**

Memory of Murder, A (Bradbury), **Supp. IV Part 1:** 103

Memory of Old Jack, The (Berry), **Supp. X:** 34

Memory of Two Mondays, A (A. Miller), **III:** 153, 156, 158–159, 160, 166

"Memory's Power" (Huddle), **Supp. XXVI:** 160

"Memo to Non-White Peoples" (Hughes), **Retro. Supp. I:** 209

"Men" (Boyle), **Supp. XXIV:** 61

Men, Women and Ghosts (Lowell), **II:** 523–524

"Menace of the Peyote, The" (Zitkala-Ša), **Supp. XXV:** 281

Menaker, Charlotte, **Supp. XIX:** 266

Menaker, Daniel, **Supp. VIII:** 151; **Supp. XXIII:** 276

Menand, Louis, **Supp. XIV:** 40, 197; **Supp. XVI:** 106, 107; **Supp. XXIII:** 104–105

Men and Angels (Gordon), **Supp. IV Part 1:** 304–305, 306, 308

Men and Brethen (Cozzens), **I:** 363–365, 368, 375, 378, 379

Men and Cartoons (Lethem), **Supp. XVIII:** 145, **148**

"Men and Women" (R. Bly), **Supp. IV Part 1:** 72

"Men at Forty" (Justice), **Supp. VII:** 126–127

Mencius (Meng-tzu), **IV:** 183

Mencken, August, **III:** 100, 108

Mencken, August, Jr., **III:** 99, 109, 118–119

Mencken, Mrs. August (Anna Abhau), **III:** 100, 109

Mencken, Burkhardt, **III:** 100, 108

Mencken, Charles, **III:** 99

Mencken, Gertrude, **III:** 99

Mencken, H. L., **I:** 199, 210, 212, 235, 245, 261, 405, 514, 515, 517; **II:** 25, 27, 42, 89, 90, 91, 271, 289, 430, 443, 449; **III: 99–121,** 394, 482; **IV:** 76, 432, 440, 475, 482; **Retro. Supp. I:** 1, 101; **Retro. Supp. II:** 97, 98, 102, 265; **Supp. I Part 2:** 484, 629–630, 631, 647, 651, 653, 659, 673; **Supp. II Part 1:** 136; **Supp. IV Part 1:** 201, 314, 343; **Supp. IV Part 2:** 521, 692, 693; **Supp. XI:** 163–164, 166; **Supp. XIII:** 161; **Supp. XIV:** 111; **Supp. XV:** 297, 301, 303; **Supp. XVI:** 187–188, 189; **Supp. XVII:** 106; **Supp. XXII:** 23, 187, 277; **Supp. XXIV:** 26, 281

Mencken, Mrs. H. L. (Sara Haardt), **III:** 109, 111

"Men Deified Because of Their Cruelty" (Simic), **Supp. VIII:** 282

Mendelbaum, Paul, **Supp. V:** 159

Mendele, **IV:** 3, 10

Mendelief, Dmitri Ivanovich, **IV:** 421

Mendelsohn, Daniel, **Supp. X:** 153, 154; **Supp. XV:** 257, 258, 261, 266

Mendelsohn, Jack, **Supp. XXIV:** 72, 77

Mendelsohn, Jane, **Supp. XXVI:** 158

Mendelssohn, Moses, **Supp. XXIII:** 4

Mendes, Alfred, **Supp. XXI:** 160

Mending Skins (Gansworth), **Supp. XXVI:** 103, 104, 106

"Mending Wall" (Frost), **II:** 153–154; **Retro. Supp. I:** 128, 130; **Supp. X:** 64

Men from the Boys, The (Lacy), **Supp. XV:** 202, 205

"Menielle" (Stallings), **Supp. XXV:** 223

Men in the Off Hours (Carson), **Supp. XII: 111–113**

"Men in the Storm, The" (Crane), **I:** 411

"Men Loved Wholly Beyond Wisdom" (Bogan), **Supp. III Part 1:** 50

"Men Made Out of Words" (Stevens), **IV:** 88

Men Must Act (Mumford), **Supp. II Part 2:** 479

Mennes, John, **II:** 111

Mennoti, Gian Carlo, **Supp. IV Part 1:** 84

Men of Brewster Place, The (Naylor), **Supp. VIII:** 213, **228–230**

"Men of Color, to Arms!" (Douglass), **Supp. III Part 1:** 171

Men of Good Hope: A Story of American Progressives (Aaron), **Supp. I Part 2:** 650

Mens' Club, The (film), **Supp. XVI:** 212–213

Men's Club, The (L. Michaels), **Supp. XVI:** 206, **210–212**

"Men's Sauna" (Huddle), **Supp. XXVI:** 150

"Menstruation at Forty" (Sexton), **Supp. II Part 2:** 686

"Mental Hospital Garden, The" (W. C. Williams), **Retro. Supp. I:** 428

Mental Radio (Sinclair), **Supp. V:** 289

Mentoria; or, The Young Lady's Friend (Rowson), **Supp. XV: 233–234,** 238

"Men We Carry in Our Minds, The" (Sanders), **Supp. XVI:** 273

Men Who Made the Nation, The (Dos Passos), **I:** 485

Men Without Women (Hemingway), **II:** 249; **Retro. Supp. I:** 170, 176; **Supp. IX:** 202

"Merced" (Rich), **Supp. I Part 2:** 563

"Mercedes" (E. Stoddard), **Supp. XV:** 278

"Mercedes Hospital" (Bishop), **Retro. Supp. II:** 51

"Mercenary, A" (Ozick), **Supp. V:** 267

Mercer, Johnny, **Supp. XXII:** 6

Merchandising (Hwang), **Supp. XXI:** 147

Merchant of Venice, The (Shakespeare), **IV:** 227; **Supp. XIV:** 325

Mercury Theatre, **Retro. Supp. I:** 65

Mercy, Pity, Peace, and Love (Ozick), **Supp. V:** 257, 258

Mercy, The (Levine), **Supp. V:** 194–195

Mercy of a Rude Stream (H. Roth), **Supp. IX:** 231, 234, **235–242**

"Mercy"(P. Benedict), **Supp. XXIII:** 49

Mercy Philbrick's Choice (Jackson), **Retro. Supp. I:** 26, 27, 33

Mercy Street (Sexton), **Supp. II Part 2:** 683, 689

"Mercy"(Thompson), **Supp. XXIII:** 295, 296

Meredith, George, **II:** 175, 186; **Supp. IV Part 1:** 300

Meredith, Mary. *See* Webb, Mary

Meredith, William, **II:** 545; **Retro. Supp. II:** 181

"Merely by Wilderness" (Peacock), **Supp. XIX:** 199

"Merely to Know" (Rich), **Supp. I Part 2:** 554

"Mère Pochette" (Jewett), **II:** 400

"Merger II, The" (Auchincloss), **Supp. IV Part 1:** 34

Meri (Asch), **Supp. XXIII:** 5, 11

"Mericans" (Cisneros), **Supp. VII:** 69

"Merida, 1969" (Matthews), **Supp. IX:** 151

"Meridian" (Clampitt), **Supp. IX: 48–49**

Meridian (Walker), **Supp. III Part 2:** 520, 524, 527, 528, 531–537

Mérimée, Prosper, **II:** 322

Meriwether, James B., **Retro Supp. I:** 77, 91

"Meriwether Connection, The" (Cowley), **Supp. II Part 1:** 142

Merker, Kim K., **Supp. XI:** 261; **Supp. XV:** 75, 77

"Merlin" (Emerson), **II:** 19, 20

Merlin (Robinson), **III:** 522

"Merlin Enthralled" (Wilbur), **Supp. III Part 2:** 544, 554

"Mermother" (A. Finch), **Supp. XVII:** 72

Merril, Judith, **Supp. XVI:** 123

Merrill, Cavafy, Poems, and Dreams (Hadas), **Supp. XXIII: 123–124**

Merrill, Christopher, **Supp. XI:** 329

Merrill, James, **Retro. Supp. I:** 296; **Retro. Supp. II:** 53; **Supp. III Part 1: 317–338; Supp. III Part 2:** 541, 561; **Supp. IX:** 40, 42, 48, 52; **Supp. X:** 73; **Supp. XI:** 123, 131, 249; **Supp. XII:** 44, 254, 255, 256, 261–262, 269–270; **Supp. XIII:** 76, 85; **Supp. XV:** 249, 250, 253; **Supp. XVII:** 123; **Supp. XXIII:** 112, 122, 123; **Supp. XXV:** 222, 227–228; **Supp. XXVI:** 67

Merrill, Mark (pseudonym). *See* Markson, David

Merrill, Robert, **Retro. Supp. II:** 201

Merrill, Ronald, **Supp. IV Part 2:** 521

Merritt, A., **Supp. XXV:** 122

Merritt, Abraham, **Supp. XVII:** 58

Merritt, Theresa, **Supp. VIII:** 332

Merritt, Vernon, **Supp. XXII:** 245

"Merry-Go-Round" (Hughes), **Retro. Supp. I:** 194, 205; **Supp. I Part 1:** 333

Merry-Go-Round, The (Van Vechten), **Supp. II Part 2:** 734, 735

Merry Month of May, The (Jones), **Supp. XI: 227–228**

Merry Widow, The (Lehar), **III:** 183

Merton, Thomas, **III:** 357; **Supp. VIII: 193–212; Supp. XXII:** 83, 90; **Supp. XXIV:** 133

Merwin, W. S., **Supp. III Part 1: 339–360; Supp. III Part 2:** 541; **Supp. IV Part 2:** 620, 623, 626; **Supp. IX:** 152, 155, 290; **Supp. V:** 332; **Supp. XIII:** 274, 277; **Supp. XIX:** 82; **Supp. XV:** 222, 342; **Supp. XXI:** 95; **Supp. XXVI:** 67, 68

Meryman, Richard, **Supp. IV Part 2:** 579, 583

Meshiekhs tsaytn (Times of the Messiah) (Asch), **Supp. XXIII:** 5

Meshugah (Singer), **Retro. Supp. II: 315–316**

Mesic, Michael, **Supp. IV Part 1:** 175

Mesic, Penelope, **Supp. X:** 15

Message in the Bottle, The (Percy), **Supp. III Part 1:** 387–388, 393, 397

"Message in the Bottle, The" (Percy), **Supp. III Part 1:** 388

"Message of Flowers and Fire and Flowers, The" (Brooks), **Supp. III Part 1:** 69

Messengers Will Come No More, The (Fiedler), **Supp. XIII:** 103

Messerli, Douglas, **Supp. XVI:** 293

Messiah (Vidal), **Supp. IV Part 2:** 677, 680, 681–682, 685, 691, 692

"Messiah, The" (Wasserstein), **Supp. XV:** 328

Messiah of Stockholm, The (Ozick), **Supp. V:** 270–271; **Supp. XVII:** 42

Messud, Claire, **Supp. XVIII:** 98

Metamorphic Tradition in Modern Poetry (Quinn), **IV:** 421

Metamorphoses (Golding, trans.), **Supp. XXV:** 226

Metamorphoses (Ovid), **II:** 542–543; **III:** 467, 468; **Supp. XV:** 33; **Supp. XVI:** 20; **Supp. XX: 280; Supp. XXIV:** 132

Metamorphoses (Pound, trans.), **III:** 468–469

"Metamorphosis" (Huddle), **Supp. XXVI:** 151

Metamorphosis, The (Kafka), **IV:** 438; **Retro. Supp. II:** 287–288; **Supp. VIII:** 3; **Supp. XXI:** 89

"Metamorphosis and Survival" (Woodcock), **Supp. XIII:** 33

"Metaphor as Mistake" (Percy), **Supp. III Part 1:** 387–388

"Metaphor for Guatemala, A: The Long Night of White Chickens" (Perera), **Supp. XXV:** 50

Metaphor & Memory: Essays (Ozick), **Supp. V:** 272

Metaphor of Trees and Last Poems (Bronk), **Supp. XXI:** 32

"Metaphors of a Magnifico" (Stevens), **IV:** 92

Metaphysical Club, The (Menand), **Supp. XIV:** 40, 197

"Metaphysical Poets, The" (Eliot), **I:** 527, 586

"Metaphysics" (Ginsberg), **Supp. II Part 1:** 313

Metcalf, Paul, **Supp. XIV:** 96; **Supp. XXIII:** 163, 174

"Meteor, The" (Bradbury), **Supp. IV Part 1:** 102

Methinks the Lady...(Endore), **Supp. XVII:** 61–62

"Metonymy as an Approach to the Real World" (Bronk), **Supp. XXI:** 30

Metress, Christopher P., **Supp. V:** 314

Metrical History of Christianity, The (Taylor), **IV:** 163

"Metrical Regularity" (Lovecraft), **Supp. XXV:** 120

Metropolis, The (Sinclair), **Supp. V:** 285

"Metterling Lists, The" (Allen), **Supp. XV:** 15

"Metzengerstein" (Poe), **III:** 411, 417

Mew, Charlotte, **Retro. Supp. II:** 247

Mewshaw, Michael, **Supp. V:** 57; **Supp. X:** 82

"Mexican Hands" (Ryan as Quin), **Supp. XVIII:** 227

"Mexico" (Lowell), **II:** 553, 554

"Mexico, Age Four" (Salinas), **Supp. XIII:** 315

Mexico City Blues (Kerouac), **Supp. III Part 1:** 225, 229

"Mexico Is a Foreign Country: Five Studies in Naturalism" (Warren), **IV:** 241, 252

"Mexico's Children" (Rodriguez), **Supp. XIV:** 302

Meyer, Carolyn, **Supp. XIX:** 194–195, 197

Meyer, Donald B., **III:** 298

Meyer, Ellen Hope, **Supp. V:** 123

Meyer, Robert, **Supp. XXI:** 23

Meyers, Jeffrey, **Retro. Supp. I:** 124, 138; **Retro. Supp. II:** 191

Meynell, Alice, **Supp. I Part 1:** 220

Mezey, Robert, **Supp. IV Part 1:** 60; **Supp. V:** 180; **Supp. XIII:** 312; **Supp. XV:** 74

Mezzanine, The (Baker), **Supp. XIII: 41–43,** 44, 45, 48, 55

"Mezzo Cammin" (Longfellow), **II:** 490

"Mi Abuelo" (Ríos), **Supp. IV Part 2:** 541

Miami (Didion), **Supp. IV Part 1:** 199, 210

Miami and the Siege of Chicago (Mailer), **Retro. Supp. II:** 206

Miasma (Holding), **Supp. XXII: 121–122**

"Michael" (Wordsworth), **III:** 523

Michael, Magali Cornier, **Supp. XIII:** 32

"Michael Angelo: A Fragment" (Longfellow), **II:** 490, 494, 495, 506; **Retro. Supp. II:** 167

"Michael Egerton" (Price), **Supp. VI:** 257–258, 260

Michael Kohlhaas (Kleist), **Supp. IV Part 1:** 224

Michael O'Halloran (Stratton-Porter), **Supp. XX: 222**

Michaels, Leonard, **Supp. XVI: 201–215**

Michaels, Walter Benn, **Retro. Supp. I:** 115, 369, 379

Michael Scarlett (Cozens), **I:** 358–359, 378

"Michael's Veterans Remember" (Espaillat), **Supp. XXI:** 110

Michaux, Henri, **Supp. XVI:** 288

Michelangelo, **I:** 18; **II:** 11–12; **III:** 124; **Supp. I Part 1:** 363; **Supp. XVII:** 112

Michel-Michot, Paulette, **Supp. XI:** 224–225

Michelson, Albert, **IV:** 27

Mickelsson's Ghosts (Gardner), **Supp. VI:** 63, **73–74**

Mickiewicz, Adam, **Supp. II Part 1:** 299

"Microscope" (Trethewey), **Supp. XXI:** 251

Midair (Conroy), **Supp. XVI:** 63, **71–72**

"Mid-Air" (Conroy), **Supp. XVI:** 69, 71

Mid-American Chants (Anderson), **I:** 109, 114

"Midas" (Winters), **Supp. II Part 2:** 801

"Mid-August at Sourdough Mountain Lookout" (Snyder), **Supp. VIII:** 292–293

Midcentury (Dos Passos), **I:** 474, 475, 478, 490, 492–494; **Supp. I Part 2:** 646

Mid-Century American Poets, **III:** 532

"Mid-Day" (Doolittle), **Supp. I Part 1:** 266–267

"Middle Age" (Lowell), **II:** 550

"Middle-Aged, Middle-Class Woman at Midnight, A" (Taggard), **Supp. XXII:** 282–283

"Middleaged Man, The" (Simpson), **Supp. IX:** 274–275

Middle Ages, The (Gurney), **Supp. V:** 96, 105, 108

Middlebrook, Diane Wood, **Supp. IV Part 2:** 444, 451; **Supp. XXVI:** 66

"Middle Daughter, The" (Kingsolver), **Supp. VII:** 209

Middlemarch (G. Eliot), **I:** 457, 459; **II:** 290, 291; **Retro. Supp. I:** 225; **Supp. I Part 1:** 174; **Supp. IX:** 43; **Supp. XI:** 68; **Supp. XII:** 335

Middle of My Tether, The: Familiar Essays (Epstein), **Supp. XIV: 106–107**

"Middle of Nowhere, The" (Wagoner), **Supp. IX:** 327–328

Middle of the Journey, The (Trilling), **Supp. III Part 2:** 495, 504–506

"Middle of the Way" (Kinnell), **Supp. III Part 1:** 242

Middle Passage (C. Johnson), **Supp. VI: 194–196,** 198, 199; **Supp. XIII:** 182

"Middle Passage" (Hayden), **Supp. II Part 1:** 363, 375–376

Middlesex (Eugenides), **Supp. XXIV:** 131, 134–135, **138–142**

"Middle Toe of the Right Foot, The" (Bierce), **I:** 203

Middleton, Thomas, **Retro. Supp. I:** 62

"Middle Way, The"(Hadas), **Supp. XXIII:** 121

Middle Years, The (James), **II:** 337–338; **Retro. Supp. I:** 235

"Middle Years, The" (James), **Retro. Supp. I:** 228, 272

"Midnight" (Dunn), **Supp. XI:** 147

"Midnight Consultations, The" (Freneau), **Supp. II Part 1:** 257

Midnight Cry, A (Mather), **Supp. II Part 2:** 460

"Midnight Gladness" (Levertov), **Supp. III Part 1:** 284–285

Midnight Lantern (Gallagher), **Supp. XXIV:** 167, 171

"Midnight Lantern" (Gallagher), **Supp. XXIV:** 171

"Midnight Magic" (Mason), **Supp. VIII:** 146

Midnight Magic: Selected Stories of Bobbie Ann Mason (Mason), **Supp. VIII:** 148

Midnight Mass (Bowles), **Supp. IV Part 1:** 93

"Midnight Postscript" (F. Wright), **Supp. XVII:** 245, 246

Midnight Queen, The (Lippard), **Supp. XXIII:** 180

"Midnight Show" (Shapiro), **Supp. II Part 2:** 705

"Midpoint" (Updike), **Retro. Supp. I:** 321, 323, 327, 330, 335

Midpoint and Other Poems (Updike), **IV:** 214

"Midrash on Happiness" (Paley), **Supp. VI:** 217

"Midsummer" (Bronk), **Supp. XXI:** 30

"Midsummer in the Blueberry Barrens" (Clampitt), **Supp. IX:** 40–41

"Midsummer Letter" (Carruth), **Supp. XVI:** 47

Midsummer Night's Dream, A (Shakespeare), **Supp. I Part 1:** 369–370; **Supp. X:** 69

Midsummer Night's Sex Comedy, A (film; Allen), **Supp. XV:** 8

"Midwest" (Stafford), **Supp. XI:** 317

"Midwest Poetics" (C. Baxter), **Supp. XVII:** 18

Mieder, Wolfgang, **Supp. XIV:** 126

Mies van der Rohe, Ludwig, **Supp. IV Part 1:** 40

Mighty Aphrodite (film; Allen), **Supp. XV:** 11

"Mighty Fortress, A" (Leopold), **Supp. XIV:** 185

"Mighty Lord, The" (Rowson), **Supp. XV:** 243

"Migration, The" (Tate), **IV:** 130

Mihailovitch, Bata, **Supp. VIII:** 272

Mikado, The (Gilbert and Sullivan), **Supp. XXI:** 151

Miklitsch, Robert, **Supp. IV Part 2:** 628, 629

Mikolowski, Ken and Ann, **Supp. XXIV:** 43

Mila 18 (Uris), **Supp. IV Part 1:** 379; **Supp. XX: 244, 247, 248, 251–252, 253**

Milagro Beanfield War, The (film), **Supp. XIII:** 267

Milagro Beanfield War, The (Nichols), **Supp. XIII:** 253, **265–266**

Milburn, Michael, **Supp. XI:** 239, 242

Milch, David, **Supp. XI:** 348

Mild Day, The (Bronk), **Supp. XXI:** 32

Miles, Barry, **Supp. XII:** 123

Miles, Jack, **Supp. VIII:** 86

Miles, Josephine, **Supp. XIII:** 275

Miles, Julie, **I:** 199

Miles, Kitty, **I:** 199

"Miles of Night, The" (Halliday), **Supp. XIX:** 91

Milestone, Lewis, **Supp. I Part 1:** 281

Milestones (Kramer), **Supp. XXVI:** 26

Miles Wallingford (Cooper). *See Afloat and Ashore* (Cooper)

Milford, Kate, **Supp. XVIII:** 150

Milford, Nancy, **II:** 83; **Supp. IX:** 60

Milhaud, Darius, **Supp. IV Part 1:** 81

Miligate, Michael, **IV:** 123, 130, 132

"Militant Nudes" (Hardwick), **Supp. III Part 1:** 210–211

"Military Parachuting Exercise" (Huddle), **Supp. XXVI:** 150, 153

Milk (film), **Supp. XX: 269**

"Milk Bottles" (Anderson), **I:** 114

"Milk Prose" (Weigl), **Supp. XIX:** 278

Milk Train Doesn't Stop Here Anymore, The (T. Williams), **IV:** 382, 383, 384, 386, 390, 391, 392, 393, 394, 395, 398

Mill, James, **II:** 357

Mill, John Stuart, **III:** 294–295; **Supp. XI:** 196; **Supp. XIV:** 22

Millar, Kenneth. *See* Macdonald, Ross

Millar, Margaret (Margaret Sturm), **Supp. IV Part 2:** 464, 465

Millay, Cora, **III:** 123, 133–134, 135–136

Millay, Edna St. Vincent, **I:** 482; **II:** 530; **III: 122–144; IV:** 433, 436; **Retro. Supp. II:** 48; **Supp. I Part 2:** 707, 714, 726; **Supp. IV Part 1:** 168; **Supp. IV Part 2:** 607; **Supp. IX:** 20; **Supp. V:** 113; **Supp. XIV:** 120, 121, 122, 127; **Supp. XV:** 42, 46, 51, 250, 293, 307; **Supp. XVII:** 69, 75, 96;

Supp. XXII: 273; **Supp. XXIII:** 164; **Supp. XXVI:** 170, 171

Millennium Approaches (Kushner), **Supp. IX:** 141, 142, 145

Miller, Arthur, **I:** 81, 94; **III: 145–169; Supp. IV Part 1:** 359; **Supp. IV Part 2:** 574; **Supp. VIII:** 334; **Supp. XIII:** 127; **Supp. XIV:** 102, 239; **Supp. XVI:** 194

Miller, Mrs. Arthur (Ingeborg Morath), **III:** 162–163

Miller, Mrs. Arthur (Marilyn Monroe), **III:** 161, 162–163

Miller, Mrs. Arthur (Mary Grace Slattery), **III:** 146, 161

Miller, Brown, **Supp. IV Part 1:** 67

Miller, Carol, **Supp. IV Part 1:** 400, 405, 409, 410, 411

Miller, Caroline, **Supp. XXII: 187–201**

Miller, Henry, **I:** 97, 157; **III:** 40, **170–192; IV:** 138; **Retro. Supp. II:** 327; **Supp. I Part 2:** 546; **Supp. V:** 119, 131; **Supp. X:** 183, 185, 187, 194, 195; **Supp. XIII:** 1, 17; **Supp. XXII:** 88, 256, 257, 258; **Supp. XXIII:** 100; **Supp. XXIV:** 52, 281

Miller, Henry (actor), **Supp. XVI:** 182

Miller, Herman, **Supp. I Part 2:** 614, 617

Miller, James E., Jr., **IV:** 352

Miller, Jean Baker, **Supp. XXII:** 18

Miller, Jeffrey, **Supp. IV Part 1:** 95

Miller, J. Hillis, **Supp. IV Part 1:** 387

Miller, Jim Wayne, **Supp. XX: 161–176; Supp. XXIII:** 39

Miller, Joaquin, **I:** 193, 195, 459; **Supp. II Part 1:** 351

Miller, John Duncan, **Supp. I Part 2:** 604

Miller, John E., **Supp. XXII:** 295

Miller, John M., **Supp. XXII:** 214, 218

Miller, Jonathan, **Retro. Supp. II:** 181

Miller, Laura, **Supp. XIII:** 48; **Supp. XIX:** 53, 54, 56; **Supp. XXII:** 239; **Supp. XXV:** 12, 13

Miller, Marilyn, **Supp. XVI:** 187

Miller, Matt, **Supp. XV:** 211

Miller, Matthew, **Supp. XVI:** 47, 51

Miller, Orilla, **Supp. I Part 1:** 48

Miller, Perry, **I:** 546, 547, 549, 550, 560; **IV:** 186; **Supp. I Part 1:** 31, 104; **Supp. I Part 2:** 484; **Supp. IV Part 2:** 422; **Supp. VIII:** 101; **Supp. XXV:** 251

Miller, R. Baxter, **Retro. Supp. I:** 195, 207

Miller, Robert Ellis, **II:** 588

Miller, Ruth, **Supp. X:** 324

Miller, Stuart, **Supp. XVI:** 242

Miller, Sue, **Supp. X:** 77, 85; **Supp. XI:** 190; **Supp. XII: 289–305**

Miller of Old Church, The (Glasgow), **II:** 175, 181

"Miller's Tale" (Chaucer), **III:** 283

Miller Williams and the Poetry of the Particular (Burns), **Supp. XV:** 339

Millett, Kate, **Supp. X:** 193, 196

Millgate, Michael, **Retro. Supp. I:** 91

Mill Hand's Lunch Bucket (Bearden), **Supp. VIII:** 337

Millhauser, Steven, **Supp. XXII:** 49

Millier, Brett C., **Retro. Supp. II:** 39

Milligan, Bryce, **Supp. XIII:** 274, 275, 277

Million Little Pieces, A (Frey), **Supp. XXII:** 95; **Supp. XXIII:** 109; **Supp. XXIV:** 230, 236

Millions of Strange Shadows (Hecht), **Supp. X:** 57, **62–65**

"Million Young Workmen, 1915, A" (Sandburg), **III:** 585

Millroy the Magician (Theroux), **Supp. VIII:** 325

Mills, Alice, **Supp. XIII:** 233

Mills, Benjamin Fay, **III:** 176

Mills, C. Wright, **Supp. I Part 2:** 648, 650

Mills, Florence, **Supp. I Part 1:** 322

Mills, Ralph J., Jr., **III:** 530; **Supp. IV Part 1:** 64; **Supp. XI:** 311

Mills, Tedi López, **Supp. XVI:** 281

Mills of the Kavanaughs, The (Lowell), **II:** 542–543, 546, 550; **III:** 508; **Retro. Supp. II:** 178, 179, 188; **Supp. XXIII:** 211

"Mills of the Kavanaughs, The" (Lowell), **II:** 542–543

Milne, A. A., **Supp. IX:** 189; **Supp. XXIV:** 132, 133

Milne, A. J. M., **I:** 278

Milosz, Czeslaw, **Supp. III Part 2:** 630; **Supp. VIII:** 20, 22; **Supp. XI:** 267, 312; **Supp. XVII:** 241; **Supp. XX: 165; Supp. XXI:** 132; **Supp. XXII:** 92; **Supp. XXIII:** 134, 140

Miltner, Robert, **Supp. XI:** 142

Milton, Edith, **Supp. VIII:** 79; **Supp. X:** 82

Milton, John, **I:** 6, 138, 273, 587–588; **II:** 11, 15, 113, 130, 411, 540, 542; **III:** 40, 124, 201, 225, 274, 468, 471, 486, 487, 503, 511; **IV:** 50, 82, 126, 137, 155, 157, 241, 279, 347, 422, 461, 494; **Retro. Supp. I:** 60, 67, 127, 360; **Retro. Supp. II:** 161, 295; **Supp. I Part 1:** 124, 150, 370; **Supp. I Part 2:** 412, 422, 491, 501, 522, 622, 722, 724; **Supp. IV Part 2:** 430, 634; **Supp. VIII:** 294; **Supp. X:** 22, 23, 36; **Supp. XII:** 180; **Supp. XIV:** 5, 7; **Supp. XX: 108; Supp. XXIII:** 122; **Supp. XXIV:** 159

Milton, John R., **Supp. IV Part 2:** 503

Milton and His Modern Critics (L. P. Smith), **Supp. XIV:** 347

"Milton by Firelight" (Snyder), **Supp. II Part 1:** 314; **Supp. VIII:** 294

"Miltonic Sonnet, A" (Wilbur), **Supp. III Part 2:** 558

Mimesis (Auerbach), **III:** 453

"Mimnermos and the Motions of Hedonism" (Carson), **Supp. XII: 99–100**

"Mimnermos Interviews, The" (Carson), **Supp. XII: 100–101**

Mims, Edwin, **Supp. I Part 1:** 362, 364, 365, 371

"Mind" (Wilbur), **Supp. III Part 2:** 554

"Mind, The" (Kinnell), **Supp. III Part 1:** 245

Mind Breaths: Poems 1972–1977 (Ginsberg), **Supp. II Part 1:** 326

Mindfield: New and Selected Poems (Corso), **Supp. XII: 136**

"Mind in the Modern World" (Trilling), **Supp. III Part 2:** 512

"Mind Is Shapely, Art Is Shapely" (Ginsberg), **Supp. II Part 1:** 327

Mindlin, Henrique, **Supp. I Part 1:** 92

Mind of My Mind (O. Butler), **Supp. XIII:** 62, 63

Mind of Primitive Man, The (Boas), **Supp. XIV:** 209

Mind-Reader, The (Wilbur), **Supp. III Part 2:** 560–562

"Mind-Reader, The" (Wilbur), **Supp. III Part 2:** 561–562

"Mind's Landscape on an Early Winter Day, The" (Bronk), **Supp. XXI:** 28

"Mind's Own Place, The" (Oppen), **Supp. XXVI:** 227

Mindwheel (Pinsky), **Supp. VI:** 235

Minear, Richard H., **Supp. XVI:** 101, 102

"Mined Country" (Wilbur), **Supp. III Part 2:** 546–548

"Minefields" (Espaillat), **Supp. XXI:** 106

"Mine Own John Berryman" (Levine), **Supp. V:** 179–180

Miner, Bob, **Supp. V:** 23

Miner, Earl, **III:** 466, 479

Miner, Madonne, **Supp. XIII:** 29

Miner, Valerie, **Supp. XXIII:** 295, 296

"Minerva Writes Poems" (Cisneros), **Supp. VII:** 63–64, 66

Mingus, Charles, **Supp. IX:** 152

"Mingus in Diaspora" (Matthews), **Supp. IX:** 166

"Mingus in Shadow" (Matthews), **Supp. IX:** 168–169

Ming Yellow (Marquand), **III:** 56

"Minimal, The" (Roethke), **III:** 531–532

Minimus Poems, The (X. J. Kennedy), **Supp. XV:** 169–170

"Mini-novela: *Rosa y sus espinas*" *(Mora), Supp. XIII:* 218

"Minions of Midas, The" (London), **II:** 474–475

Minister's Charge, The, or The Apprenticeship of Lemuel Barber (Howells), **II:** 285–286, 287

Minister's Wooing, The (Stowe), **II:** 541

"Minister's Wooing, The" (Stowe), **Supp. I Part 2:** 592–595

"Ministration of Our Departed Friends, The" (Stowe), **Supp. I Part 2:** 586–587

Minna and Myself (Bodenheim), **Supp. XXV:** 21

"Minneapolis Poem, The" (Wright), **Supp. III Part 2:** 601–602

Minnesota Grain Show, The (radio, Keillor), **Supp. XVI:** 170

"Minnesota Transcendentalist" (Peseroff), **Supp. IV Part 1:** 71

Minnie, Temple, **II:** 344

Minock, Daniel, **Supp. XXVI:** 187

Minority Report: H. L. Mencken's Notebooks (Mencken), **III:** 112

Minor Pleasures of Life, The (Macaulay), **Supp. XIV:** 348

"Minor Poems" (Eliot), **I:** 579

"Minor Poet" (Hay), **Supp. XIV:** 127

"Minor Topics" (Howells), **II:** 274

Minot, Stephen, **Supp. XXIII:** 290

Minot, Susan, **Supp. VI: 203–215**

"Minotaur Loves His Labyrinth, The" (Simic), **Supp. VIII:** 270, 279, 281

"Minstrel Man" (Hughes), **Supp. I Part 1:** 325

Mint (Nye), **Supp. XIII:** 277

"Minting Time" (Sarton), **Supp. VIII:** 259

Mint Snowball (Nye), **Supp. XIII:** 277–278, **284–285**

"Mint Snowball" (Nye), **Supp. XIII:** 278, 284

"Mint Snowball II" (Nye), **Supp. XIII:** 284, 285

Minty Alley (C. L. R. James), **Supp. XXI:** 159, 161

Mintz, Susannah B., **Supp. XXVI:** 52

Mintzlaff, Dorothy, **Supp. XV:** 153

Minus, Marian, **Supp. XVIII:** 282

Minutes to Go (Corso, Gysin, Beiles and Burroughs), **Supp. XII:** 129

Mi querido Rafa (Hinojosa). *See Dear Rafe* (Hinojosa)

Mirabai: Ecstatic Poems (Hirshfield and Bly, trans.), **Supp. XXIII:** 136

Mirabell: Books of Number (Merrill), **Supp. III Part 1:** 332–334

"Miracle" (Carver), **Supp. III Part 1:** 139–140

Miracle at St. Anna (film, Lee), **Supp. XXVI:** 199

Miracle at St. Anna (McBride), **Supp. XXVI:** 194–199

Miracle at Verdun (Chlumberg), **Supp. XIX:** 242

Miracle Boy and Other Stories (P. Benedict), **Supp. XXIII:** 35, **45–50**

"Miracle Boy"(P. Benedict), **Supp. XXIII:** 45–46, 50

"Miracle for Breakfast, A" (Bishop), **Retro. Supp. II:** 43

Miracle of Catfish, A (L. Brown), **Supp. XXI:** 39–40, 47, **48**

"Miracle of Lava Canyon, The" (Henry), **Supp. II Part 1:** 389, 390

Miracle of Mindfulness, The: A Manual on Meditation (Thich Nhat Hanh), **Supp. V:** 199–200

Mirage (Masters), **Supp. I Part 2:** 459, 470, 471

"Mirages, The" (Hayden), **Supp. II Part 1:** 373

"Miranda" (Buck), **Supp. II Part 1:** 128

Miranda, Carmen, **Supp. XII:** 165

Miranda, Francisco de, **Supp. I Part 2:** 522

"Miranda Over the Valley" (Dubus), **Supp. VII:** 81–83

"Miriam" (Capote), **Supp. III Part 1:** 117, 120, 122

"Miriam" (Whittier), **Supp. I Part 2:** 691, 703

"Miriam Tazewell" (Ransom), **Supp. X:** 58

"Mirror" (Merrill), **Supp. III Part 1:** 322

"Mirror" (Plath), **Retro. Supp. II:** 248–249, 257

"Mirror, The" (Glück), **Supp. V:** 83

"Mirror, The"(Hadas), **Supp. XXIII:** 116

"Mirroring Evil: Nazi Images/Recent Art" (Epstein), **Supp. XII:** 166

"Mirror of Leopold Leopoldovitch Siegelevsky, The" (Siegel), **Supp. XXII:** 257–258

Mirrors (Creeley), **Supp. IV Part 1:** 156

Mirrors and Windows (Nemerov), **III:** 269, 275–277

Mirrors of Astonishment (Hadas), **Supp. XXIII: 115–116**

"Mirrors of Chartres Street" (Faulkner), **II:** 56

Mirsky, Norman, **Supp. XX: 244**

Mirvis, Tova, **Supp. XX: 177–191**

Misanthrope, The (Molière; Wilbur, trans.), **Supp. III Part 2:** 552, 560

Miscellaneous Poems (Rowson), **Supp. XV:** 243

Miscellaneous Works of Mr. Philip Freneau, Containing His Essays and Additional Poems (Freneau), **Supp. II Part 1:** 263, 264, 266

Miscellany of American Poetry, A (Untermeyer, ed.), **Supp. XV:** 305, 310

Misérables, Les (Hugo), **II:** 179; **Supp. I Part 1:** 280

Misery (King), **Supp. V:** 140, 141, 142, 147–148, 151, 152

Mises, Ludwig von, **Supp. IV Part 2:** 524

Misfits, The (A. Miller), **III:** 147, 149, 156, 161–162, 163

Misfit: The Strange Life of Frederick Exley (Yardley), **Supp. XXIII:** 97

Mish, Jeanetta Calhoun, **Supp. XXVI:** 112

"Mishōsha, or the Magician and his daughters: A Chippewa Tale"(J. Schoolcraft), **Supp. XXIII:** 234, 235

"Misogamist, The" (Dubus), **Supp. VII:** 86–87

Misread City, The: New Literary Los Angeles (Gioia and Timberg, eds.), **Supp. XV:** 116

Misrepresentations Corrected, and Truth Vindicated, in a Reply to the Rev. Mr. Solomon Williams's Book (Edwards), **I:** 549

Miss Crandall's School for Young Ladies & Little Misses of Color (Nelson and Alexander), **Supp. XVIII:** 171, 175, 181, **185–186**

"Miss Cynthie" (R. Fisher), **Supp. XIX:** 65, 69

Miss Doll, Go Home (Markson), **Supp. XVII:** 138

"Miss Ella" (Z. Fitzgerald), **Supp. IX:** 57, 59, **71–72**

"Miss Emily and the Bibliographer" (Tate), **Supp. II Part 1:** 103

"Miss Furr and Miss Skeene" (Stein), **IV:** 29–30

"Missing Child" (Simic), **Supp. VIII:** 282

"Missing in Action" (Komunyakaa), **Supp. XIII:** 123, 124

Missing/Kissing: Missing Marisa, Kissing Christine (Shanley), **Supp. XIV:** 316

Missing Link (X. J. Kennedy), **Supp. XV:** 165

Missing Link, The (Wells), **Supp. XXVI:** 281

"Missing Poem, The" (Halliday), **Supp. XIX:** 93–94

"Missionary Brings a Young Native to America, A" (H. Johnson), **Supp. XXVI:** 167, 173, 174

"Mission of Jane, The" (Wharton), **Retro. Supp. I:** 367

"Missions, The" (Rodriguez), **Supp. XIV:** 303

Mission to Moscow (film), **Supp. I Part 1:** 281

"Mississippi" (Bass), **Supp. XVI:** 17

"Mississippi" (Faulkner), **Retro. Supp. I:** 77

"Mississippi" (Simpson), **Supp. IX:** 271

"Miss Kate in H-1" (Twain), **IV:** 193

Miss Kelly (Holding), **Supp. XXII: 133–134**

Miss Leonora When Last Seen (Taylor), **Supp. V:** 323

Miss Lonelyhearts (West), **I:** 107; **II:** 436; **III:** 357; **IV:** 287, 288, 290–297, 300, 301, 305, 306; **Retro. Supp. II:** 321, 322, 325, 328, **332–335**

"Miss Lora" (Díaz), **Supp. XXIV:** 86

Miss Mamma Aimee (Caldwell), **I:** 308, 309, 310

"Miss Mary Pask" (Wharton), **IV:** 316; **Retro. Supp. I:** 382

"Miss McEnders" (Chopin), **Retro. Supp. II:** 67

Miss Morissa: Doctor of the Gold Trail (Sandoz), **Supp. XXIV:** 244, **255–256**

"Missoula Softball Tournament" (Hugo), **Supp. VI:** 132

Miss Pinkerton (Rinehart), **Supp. XXV:** 197

Miss Ravenel's Conversion from Secession to Loyalty (De Forest), **IV:** 350

Miss Saigon (musical), **Supp. XXI:** 155

"Miss Tempy's Watchers" (Jewett), **II:** 401; **Retro. Supp. II:** 139

"Miss Terriberry to Wed in Suburbs" (Updike), **Retro. Supp. I:** 335

"Miss Urquhart's Tiara" (Jarman), **Supp. XVII:** 116

Miss Witherspoon (Durang), **Supp. XXIV:** 113, **126**

"Mist, The" (King), **Supp. V:** 144

"Mistaken Charity, A" (Freeman), **Retro. Supp. II:** 138

"Mister Brother" (Cunningham), **Supp. XV:** 68

Misterioso (Sorrentino), **Supp. XXI:** 236, 237

"Mister Toussan" (Ellison), **Retro. Supp. II:** 124–125; **Supp. II Part 1:** 238

"Mistress of Sydenham Plantation, The" (Jewett), **Retro. Supp. II:** 141

Mitcham, Matthew, **Supp. XX: 264**

Mitchell, Burroughs, **Supp. XI:** 218, 222, 227

Mitchell, David, **Supp. XXIV:** 86

Mitchell, Don, **Supp. XXII:** 207, 211, 212

Mitchell, Joan, **Supp. XXIII:** 210

Mitchell, Margaret, **II:** 177; **Supp. XX: 243; Supp. XXII:** 195

Mitchell, Pat, **Supp. XXIV:** 35, 42

Mitchell, Roger, **Supp. IV Part 1:** 70; **Supp. XV:** 213, 215

Mitchell, Dr. S. Weir, **IV:** 310

Mitchell, Tennessee. *See* Anderson, Mrs. Sherwood (Tennessee Mitchell)

Mitchell, Verner, **Supp. XVIII:** 281, 286

Mitchell, Werner, **Supp. XXVI:** 165, 170, 171–172, 174

Mitchell, Wesley C., **Supp. I Part 2:** 632, 643

"Mitchie-Gawa" (Taggard), **Supp. XXII:** 272

Mitch Miller (Masters), **Supp. I Part 2:** 456, 466, 469–471, 474, 475, 476

Mitchum, Robert, **Supp. IX:** 95, 250

Mitgang, Herbert, **Supp. IV Part 1:** 220, 226, 307; **Supp. VIII:** 124; **Supp. XIX:** 251; **Supp. XX: 243**

Mitla Pass (Uris), **Supp. XX: 244, 247, 248, 256**

Mixed Company: Collected Short Stories (Shaw), **Supp. XIX:** 251

"Mixed Sequence" (Roethke), **III:** 547

Miyazawa Kenji, **Supp. VIII:** 292

Mizener, Arthur, **II:** 77, 81, 84, 94; **IV:** 132; **Supp. XVIII:** 249

Mizner, Addison, **Supp. XVI:** 191

Mizner, Wilson, **Supp. XVI:** 191, 195

Mladenoff, Nancy, **Supp. X:** 176

"M'liss: An Idyl of Red Mountain" (Harte), **Supp. II Part 1:** 339

"Mnemonic Devices" (Goldbarth), **Supp. XII:** 183

"Mnemosyne" (Hölderlin), **Supp. XXIV:** 152

"Mobile in Back of the Smithsonian, The" (Swenson), **Supp. IV Part 2:** 646

Mobilio, Albert, **Supp. VIII:** 3; **Supp. XIX:** 45; **Supp. XVIII:** 144

Moby Dick (film), **Supp. IV Part 1:** 102, 116

Moby Dick; or, The Whale (Melville), **I:** 106, 354; **II:** 33, 224–225, 236, 539–540; **III:** 28–29, 74, 75, 77, 81, 82, 83–86, 87, 89, 90, 91, 93, 94, 95, 359, 453, 556; **IV:** 57, 199, 201, 202; **Retro. Supp. I:** 160, 220, 243, 244, 248, **249–253**, 254, 256, 257, 335; **Retro. Supp. II:** 121, 186, 275; **Supp. I Part 1:** 249; **Supp. I Part 2:** 579; **Supp. IV Part 2:** 613; **Supp. V:** 281; **Supp. VIII:** 106, 188, 198; **Supp. XXI:** 159; **Supp. XXII:** 81, 268; **Supp. XXIV:** 88

Mock, John, **Supp. XIII:** 174

"Mocking-Bird, The" (Bierce), **I:** 202

"Mock Orange" (Glück), **Supp. V:** 84–85

Modarressi, Mitra, **Supp. IV Part 2:** 657

"Model Father" (Huddle), **Supp. XXVI:** 150

Models of Misrepresentation: On the Fiction of E. L. Doctorow (Morris), **Supp. IV Part 1:** 231

Model World and Other Stories, A (Chabon), **Supp. XI:** 66

Modern American and British Poetry (Untermeyer, ed.), **Supp. XV:** 306

Modern American Poetry (Untermeyer, ed.), **Supp. XV:** 293, 303, 306, 312

Modern American Poets (Aiken, ed.), **Supp. XXVI:** 225

Modern American Verse (Untermeyer, ed.), **Supp. XV:** 301

Modern Brazilian Architecture (Bishop, trans.), **Supp. I Part 1:** 92

Modern British Poetry (Untermeyer, ed.), **Supp. XV:** 305, 308, 312

Modern Fiction Studies, **Supp. V:** 238

Modern Fiction Studies (Haegert), **Supp. XVI:** 69

"Modern Greek for 'Nightmare' Is *Ephialtes,* The" (Stallings), **Supp. XXV:** 233

Modern Instance a Novel, A (Howells), **II:** 275, 279, 282–283, 285

Modern Library, The, **Retro. Supp. I:** 112, 113

Modern Mephistopheles, A (Alcott), **Supp. I Part 1:** 37–38

Modern Poetic Sequence, The (Rosenthal), **Supp. V:** 333

"Modern Poetry" (Crane), **I:** 390

Modern Poetry and the Tradition (Brooks), **Supp. XIV:** 5–7

"Modern Primer: Helpful Hints to Tell Appearances from Truth" (Taubman), **Supp. XXV:** 106

"Modern Race Creeds and Their Fallacies" (Locke), **Supp. XIV:** 210

Modern Rhetoric, with Readings (Brooks and Warren), **Supp. XIV:** 11

"Modern Sorcery" (Simic), **Supp. VIII:** 283

Modern Times (album, Dylan), **Supp. XVIII:** 28, 31, 33

"Modern Times" (Zukofsky), **Supp. III Part 2:** 624

Modern Writer, The (Anderson), **I:** 117

Modersohn, Otto, **Supp. I Part 2:** 573

Modersohn, Mrs. Otto (Paula Becker), **Supp. I Part 2:** 573–574

"Modes of Being" (Levertov), **Supp. III Part 1:** 282

Modest Enquiry into the Nature and Necessity of a Paper-Currency, A (Franklin), **II:** 108–109

"Modest Proposal, A" (Swift), **I:** 295; **Retro. Supp. II:** 287

"Modest Proposal with Feline Feeling, A" (Neugeboren), **Supp. XVI:** 219

"Modest Self-Tribute, A" (Wilson), **IV:** 431, 432

Modigliani, Amedeo, **Supp. XXVI:** 259

Moeller, Philip, **III:** 398, 399

"Moench von Berchtesgaden, Der" (Voss), **I:** 199–200

Moers, Ellen, **Retro. Supp. II:** 99

Moe's Villa and Other Stories (Purdy), **Supp. VII:** 270, 280

Moffat, Juan, **Supp. XX:** 52

Moffet, Penelope, **Supp. XXIV:** 165, 167

Mogen, David, **Supp. IV Part 1:** 106

Mohammed, **I:** 480; **II:** 1

Mohawk (Russo), **Supp. XII: 326–328**

Moir, William Wilmerding, **Supp. V:** 279

Mojo Hand (Phillips), **Supp. XXIII:** 174

Moldaw, Carol, **Supp. XV:** 264; **Supp. XVII:** 127, 130

"Moles" (Oliver), **Supp. VII:** 235

Molesworth, Charles, **Supp. IV Part 1:** 39; **Supp. VIII:** 292, 306; **Supp. XIX:** 121–122

Molière (Jean-Baptiste Poquelin), **III:** 113; **Supp. I Part 2:** 406; **Supp. III Part 2:** 552, 560; **Supp. IV Part 2:** 585; **Supp. V:** 101

"Molino Rojo, El" (Ríos), **Supp. IV Part 2:** 544

Moll Flanders (Defoe), **Supp. V:** 127; **Supp. XIII:** 43

"Molloch in State Street" (Whittier), **Supp. I Part 2:** 687

"Moll Pitcher" (Whittier), **Supp. I Part 2:** 684

"Molly Brant, Iroquois Matron" (Gunn Allen), **Supp. IV Part 1:** 331

"Molly Brant to Willie"(Kenny), **Supp. XXIII:** 153

Molnar, Ferenc, **Supp. XVI:** 187

"Moloch" (H. Miller), **III:** 177

Momaday, N. Scott, **Supp. IV Part 1:** 274, 323, 324, 404; **Supp. IV Part 2: 479–496,** 504, 557, 562; **Supp. XII:** 209; **Supp. XVIII:** 58

" 'Momentary Stay against Confusion,' A: Frank Conroy's *Stop-Time*" (T. Adams), **Supp. XVI:** 69

Moment of Untruth (Lacy), **Supp. XV:** 206, 207

Moments of the Italian Summer (Wright), **Supp. III Part 2:** 602

Moment to Moment: Poems of a Mountain Recluse (Budbill), **Supp. XIX:** 2, 7, **9–10**

"Momus" (Robinson), **III:** 508

Monaghan, Charles, **Supp. XIX:** 155

Monaghan, Pat, **Supp. XI:** 121

Monaghan, Patricia, **Supp. XVII:** 76, 123, 127, 129

Mona Lisa Overdrive (W. Gibson), **Supp. XVI:** 119, 120, **127–128**

"Mon Ami" (Bourne), **I:** 227

Monday Night (Boyle), **Supp. XXIV:** 54

Monet, Claude, **Retro. Supp. I:** 378

"Monet's 'Waterlilies' " (Hayden), **Supp. II Part 1:** 361–362

Monette, Paul, **Supp. X: 145–161**

Money (Amis), **Retro. Supp. I:** 278

"Money" (Matthews), **Supp. IX:** 166

"Money" (Nemerov), **III:** 287

Money, Money, Money (Wagoner), **Supp. IX:** 324, **333–334**

Moneyball: The Art of Winning an Unfair Game (M. Lewis), **Supp. XVII:** 210

Moneychangers, The (Sinclair), **Supp. V:** 285

Money Writes! (Sinclair), **Supp. V:** 277

Monica, Saint, **IV:** 140

Monikins, The (Cooper), **I:** 348, 354

Monk, Craig, **Supp. XXIV:** 64

Monk, Thelonious, **Supp. XVIII:** 62

Monk and the Hangman's Daughter, The (Bierce), **I:** 199–200, 209

"Monkey" (Weigl), **Supp. XIX:** 278

"Monkey Garden, The" (Cisneros), **Supp. VII:** 63

"Monkey Puzzle, The" (Moore), **III:** 194, 207, 211

Monkeys (Minot), **Supp. VI:** 203–205, **206–210**

"Monkeys, The" (Moore), **III:** 201, 202

Monkey Wars, The (Weigl), **Supp. XIX:** 276, 278–280

Monkey Wrench Gang, The (Abbey), **Supp. VIII:** 42; **Supp. XIII: 9–11,** 16

"Monk of Casal-Maggiore, The" (Longfellow), **II:** 505

"Monocle de Mon Oncle, Le" (Stevens), **IV:** 78, 84; **Retro. Supp. I:** 301; **Supp. III Part 1:** 20; **Supp. X:** 58

"Monody to the Sound of Zithers" (Boyle), **Supp. XXIV:** 63

"Monolog from a Mattress" (Untermeyer), **Supp. XV:** 307

"Monologue for Mothers" (Taggard), **Supp. XXII:** 279

"Mon Plaisir" (July), **Supp. XXIV:** 205–206

Monro, Harold, **III:** 465; **Retro. Supp. I:** 127; **Supp. XV:** 296

Monroe, Harriet, **I:** 235, 384, 390, 393; **III:** 458, 581, 586; **IV:** 74; **Retro. Supp. I:** 58, 131; **Retro. Supp. II:** 82, 83; **Supp. I Part 1:** 256, 257, 258, 262, 263, 267; **Supp. I Part 2:** 374, 387, 388, 464, 610, 611, 613, 614, 615, 616; **Supp. XIV:** 286; **Supp. XV:** 43, 299, 302; **Supp. XXV:** 18

Monroe, James, **Supp. I Part 2:** 515, 517

Monroe, Lucy, **Retro. Supp. II:** 70

Monroe, Marilyn, **III:** 161, 162–163

Monroe's Embassy; or, the Conduct of the Government in Relation to Our Claims to the Navigation of the Mississippi (Brown), **Supp. I Part 1:** 146

Monson, Ander, **Supp. XXIV: 229–242**

"Monsoon Season" (Komunyakaa), **Supp. XIII:** 122

Monsour, Leslie, **Supp. XV:** 125

"Monster, The" (Crane), **I:** 418

Monster, The, and Other Stories (Crane), **I:** 409

"Monstro" (Díaz), **Supp. XXIV:** 86

Montage of a Dream Deferred (Hughes), **Retro. Supp. I:** 194, **208–209; Supp. I Part 1:** 333, 339–341

Montagu, Ashley, **Supp. I Part 1:** 314

"Montaigne" (Emerson), **II:** 6

Montaigne, Michel de, **II:** 1, 5, 6, 8, 14–15, 16, 535; **III:** 600; **Retro. Supp. I:** 247; **Supp. XIV:** 105; **Supp. XXI:** 111, 205; **Supp. XXVI:** 39

Montale, Eugenio, **Supp. III Part 1:** 320; **Supp. V:** 337–338; **Supp. VIII:** 30; **Supp. XV:** 112

Montalembert, Hughes de, **Supp. XV:** 349

"Montana Memory" (Maclean), **Supp. XIV:** 221

"Montana; or the End of Jean-Jacques Rousseau" (Fiedler), **Supp. XIII: 97–98**

"Montana Ranch Abandoned" (Hugo), **Supp. VI:** 139

"Mont Blanc" (Shelley), **Supp. IX:** 52

Montcalm, Louis Joseph de, **Supp. I Part 2:** 498

Montcalm and Wolfe (Parkman), **Supp. II Part 2:** 596, 609, 610, 611–613

Montemarano, Nicholas, **Supp. XVI:** 227

Montgomery, Benilde, **Supp. XIII:** 202

Montgomery, George, **Supp. XXIII:** 209

Montgomery, Robert, **Supp. I Part 2:** 611; **Supp. IV Part 1:** 130

Month of Sundays, A (Updike), **Retro. Supp. I:** 325, 327, 329, 330, 331, 333, 335

Monti, Luigi, **II:** 504

Montoya, José, **Supp. IV Part 2:** 545

"Montrachet-le-Jardin" (Stevens), **IV:** 82

Mont-Saint-Michel and Chartres (Adams), **I:** 1, 9, 12–14, 18, 19, 21; **Supp. I Part 2:** 417

Montserrat (Hellman), **Supp. I Part 1:** 283–285

Montserrat (Robles), **Supp. I Part 1:** 283–285

"Monument, The" (Bishop), **Supp. I Part 1:** 89

Monument, The (Strand), **Supp. IV Part 2:** 629, 630

"Monument in Utopia, A" (Schnackenberg), **Supp. XV:** 261, 263

"Monument Mountain" (Bryant), **Supp. I Part 1:** 156, 162

"Monument to After-Thought Unveiled, A" (Frost), **Retro. Supp. I:** 124

Moo (Smiley), **Supp. VI:** 292, **303–305**

Moods (Alcott), **Supp. I Part 1:** 33, 34–35, 43

Moody, Anne, **Supp. IV Part 1:** 11

Moody, Richard, **Supp. I Part 1:** 280

Moody, Rick, **Supp. XXI:** 117; **Supp. XXIV:** 131

Moody, Ron, **Supp. XXII:** 49

Moody, William Vaughn, **III:** 507; **IV:** 26

Moody, Mrs. William Vaughn, **I:** 384; **Supp. I Part 2:** 394

Moody-Freeman, Julie, **Supp. XXIII:** 91, 94, 95

"Moon" (A. Finch), **Supp. XVII:** 77

Moon, Henry Lee, **Supp. XVIII:** 281, 285

"Moon and the Night and the Men, The" (Berryman), **I:** 172

Moon Crossing Bridge (Gallagher), **Supp. XXIV:** 166, 170

"Moon Deluxe" (F. Barthelme), **Supp. XI:** 26, 27, 33, 36

Mooney, Tom, **I:** 505

"Moon-Face" (London), **II:** 475

Moon-Face and Other Stories (London), **II:** 483

"Moon Flock" (Dickey), **Supp. IV Part 1:** 186

Moon for the Misbegotten, A (O'Neill), **III:** 385, 401, 403, 404

Moon in a Mason Jar (Wrigley), **Supp. XVIII: 295–298**

Moon in Its Flight, The (Sorrentino), **Supp. XXI:** 226

"Moon in Its Flight, The" (Sorrentino), **Supp. XXI:** 229

Moon Is a Gong, The (Dos Passos). *See Garbage Man, The* (Dos Passos)

Moon Is Down, The (Steinbeck), **IV:** 51

Moon Lady, The (Tan), **Supp. X:** 289

"Moonlight Alert" (Winters), **Supp. II Part 2:** 801, 811, 815

"Moonlight: Chickens on a Road" (Wrigley), **Supp. XVIII:** 295–296, 297

"Moonlit Night" (Reznikoff), **Supp. XIV:** 285–286

Moon of the Caribbees, The (O'Neill), **III:** 388

Moon Palace (Auster), **Supp. XII:** 22, 27, **30–32**

"Moonshine" (Komunyakaa), **Supp. XIII:** 127, 128

"Moon Solo" (Laforgue), **Supp. XIII:** 346

Moonstone, The (Collins), **Supp. XX: 236**

Moonstruck (screenplay, Shanley), **Supp. XIV:** 315, 316, **321–324**

"Moon upon her fluent Route, The" (Dickinson), **I:** 471

Moony's Kid Don't Cry (T. Williams), **IV:** 381

Moore, Arthur, **Supp. I Part 1:** 49

Moore, C. L., **Supp. XXV:** 122

Moore, Deborah Dash, **Supp. XX: 246**

Moore, George, **I:** 103

Moore, Hannah, **Supp. XV:** 231

Moore, Jack B., **Supp. XXV:** 24, 26, 27

Moore, John Milton, **III:** 193

Moore, Julie L., **Supp. XXIII:** 252

Moore, Lorrie, **Supp. VIII:** 145; **Supp. X: 163–180; Supp. XXV:** 142

Moore, Marianne, **I:** 58, 285, 401, 428; **III: 193–217,** 514, 592–593; **IV:** 74, 75, 76, 91, 402; **Retro. Supp. I:** 416, 417; **Retro. Supp. II:** 39, 44, 48, 50, 82, 178, 179, 243, 244; **Supp. I Part 1:** 84, 89, 255, 257; **Supp. I Part 2:** 707; **Supp. II Part 1:** 21; **Supp. III Part 1:** 58, 60, 63; **Supp. III Part 2:** 612, 626, 627; **Supp. IV Part 1:** 242, 246, 257; **Supp. IV Part 2:** 454, 640, 641; **Supp. XIV:** 124, 130; **Supp. XV:** 306, 307; **Supp. XVII:** 131; **Supp. XXI:** 98; **Supp. XXII:** 273–274

Moore, Marie Lorena. *See* Moore, Lorrie

Moore, MariJo, **Supp. XXVI:** 113

Moore, Mary Tyler, **Supp. V:** 107

Moore, Mary Warner, **III:** 193

Moore, Dr. Merrill, **III:** 506

Moore, Steven, **Supp. IV Part 1:** 279, 283, 284, 285, 287; **Supp. XII:** 151; **Supp. XVII:** 230, 231, 232; **Supp. XXII:** 261, 265

Moore, Sturge, **III:** 459

Moore, Thomas, **II:** 296, 299, 303; **Supp. IX:** 104; **Supp. X:** 114; **Supp. XXIII:** 138

Moore, Virginia, **Supp. XV:** 308

Moorehead, Caroline, **Supp. XIV:** 337

Moorepack, Howard, **Supp. XV:** 199

"Moorings" (Hoffman), **Supp. XVIII:** 87

Moos, Malcolm, **III:** 116, 119

"Moose, The" (Bishop), **Retro. Supp. II:** 50; **Supp. I Part 1:** 73, 93, 94, 95; **Supp. IX:** 45, 46

"Moose Wallow, The" (Hayden), **Supp. II Part 1:** 367

"Moowis, The Indian Coquette"(J. Schoolcraft), **Supp. XXIII:** 234

"Moquihuitzin's Answer" (Everwine), **Supp. XV:** 78

Mora, Pat, **Supp. XIII: 213–232**

Moraga, Cherríe, **Supp. XXIII: 193–206**

"Moral Argument Against Calvinism, The" (Channing), **Supp. XXIV: 73–74,** 75

"Moral Bully, The" (Holmes), **Supp. I Part 1:** 302

"Moral Character, the Practice of Law, and Legal Education" (Hall), **Supp. VIII:** 127

"Moral Equivalent for Military Service, A" (Bourne), **I:** 230

"Moral Equivalent of War, The" (James), **II:** 361; **Supp. I Part 1:** 20

"Moral Imperatives for World Order" (Locke), **Supp. XIV:** 207, 213

Moralités Légendaires (Laforgue), **I:** 573

"Morality and Mercy in Vienna" (Pynchon), **Supp. II Part 2:** 620, 624

"Morality of Indian Hating, The" (Momaday), **Supp. IV Part 2:** 484

"Morality of Poetry, The" (Wright), **Supp. III Part 2:** 596–597, 599

Moral Man and Immoral Society (Niebuhr), **III:** 292, 295–297

"Morals Is Her Middle Name" (Hughes), **Supp. I Part 1:** 338

"Morals of Chess, The" (Franklin), **II:** 121

"Moral Substitute for War, A" (Addams), **Supp. I Part 1:** 20

"Moral Theology of Atticus Finch, The" (Shaffer), **Supp. VIII:** 127

"Moral Thought, A" (Freneau), **Supp. II Part 1:** 262

Moran, Thomas, **Supp. IV Part 2:** 603–604

Moran, William L., **Supp. XXIV:** 150–151, 152

Moran of the Lady Letty (Norris), **II:** 264; **III:** 314, 322, 327, 328, 329, 330, 331, 332, 333

Morath, Ingeborg. *See* Miller, Mrs. Arthur (Ingeborg Morath)

Moravec, Paul, **Supp. XIX:** 123

Moravia, Alberto, **I:** 301

More (Crooker), **Supp. XXIII: 60–62**

Moré, Gonzalo, **Supp. X:** 185

More, Henry, **I:** 132

More, Paul Elmer, **I:** 223–224, 247; **Supp. I Part 2:** 423

Moreau, Gustave, **I:** 66

"More Blues and the Abstract Truth" (Wright), **Supp. XV:** 345

More Boners (Abingdon), **Supp. XVI:** 99

More Conversations with Eudora Welty (Prenshaw, ed.), **Retro. Supp. I:** 340, 341, 342, 343, 344, 352, 353, 354

More Dangerous Thoughts (Ryan as Quin), **Supp. XVIII:** 226, **229–230,** 231, 238

More Die of Heartbreak (Bellow), **Retro. Supp. II:** 31, 33, 34

"More Girl Than Boy" (Komunyakaa), **Supp. XIII:** 117
"More Light! More Light! (Hecht), **Supp. X:** 60
"More Like an Extension of the Spirit: Clothing in Lyric Poems"(Hadas), **Supp. XXIII:** 124
"Morella" (Poe), **III:** 412; **Retro. Supp. II:** 270
"More Love in the Western World" (Updike), **Retro. Supp. I:** 327–328, 329
"Morels" (W. J. Smith), **Supp. XIII: 336–339**
Moreno, Gary, **Supp. XV:** 5
"More Observations Now" (Conroy), **Supp. XVI:** 75
"More of a Corpse Than a Woman" (Rukeyser), **Supp. VI:** 280
"More Pleasant Adventures" (Ashbery), **Supp. III Part 1:** 1
More Poems to Solve (Swenson), **Supp. IV Part 2:** 640, 642, 648
More Stately Mansions (O'Neill), **III:** 385, 401, 404–405
"More Than Human" (Chabon), **Supp. XI:** 71–72
More Things Change The More They Stay the Same, The (J. W. Miller), **Supp. XX: 164**
More Tish (Rinehart), **Supp. XXV:** 194
More Triva (L. P. Smith), **Supp. XIV:** 339
Morgan, Edmund S., **IV:** 149; **Supp. I Part 1:** 101, 102; **Supp. I Part 2:** 484
Morgan, Edwin, **Supp. IV Part 2:** 688
Morgan, Emanuel. *See* Bynner, Witter
Morgan, Henry, **II:** 432; **IV:** 63; **Supp. XXV:** 255
Morgan, Jack, **Retro. Supp. II:** 142
Morgan, J. P., **I:** 494; **III:** 14, 15
Morgan, Judith, **Supp. XVI:** 103
Morgan, Neil, **Supp. XVI:** 103
Morgan, Robert, **Supp. V:** 5; **Supp. XX: 161, 162**
Morgan, Robin, **Supp. I Part 2:** 569
Morgan, Ted, **Supp. XIV:** 141
Morgan's Passing (Tyler), **Supp. IV Part 2:** 666–667, 668, 669
Morgenstern, Dan, **Supp. XIX:** 159
Morgenthau, Hans, **III:** 291, 309
Morgenthau, Henry, Sr., **Supp. XXIII:** 21, 22, 26, 30
Morgesons, The (E. Stoddard), **Supp. XV:** 270, 273, 274, 278, **279–282,** 283
Morgesons and Other Writings, Published and Unpublished, The (Buell and Zagarell), **Supp. XV:** 269
Moricand, Conrad, **III:** 190
Morison, Samuel Eliot, **Supp. I Part 2: 479–500; Supp. XXII:** 35
Morison, Mrs. Samuel Eliot (Elizabeth Shaw Greene), **Supp. I Part 2:** 483
Morison, Mrs. Samuel Eliot (Priscilla Barton), **Supp. I Part 2:** 493, 496, 497
Morita, Pat, **Supp. XXI:** 146
"Morituri Salutamus" (Longfellow), **II:** 499, 500; **Retro. Supp. II:** 169; **Supp. I Part 2:** 416
"Moriturus" (Millay), **III:** 126, 131–132

Morley, Christopher, **III:** 481, 483, 484; **Supp. I Part 2:** 653; **Supp. IX:** 124
Morley, Edward, **IV:** 27
Morley, Lord John, **I:** 7
Mormon Country (Stegner), **Supp. IV Part 2:** 598, 601–602
"Morning, The" (Updike), **Retro. Supp. I:** 329
"Morning after My Death, The" (Levis), **Supp. XI:** 260, 263–264
"Morning Arrives" (F. Wright), **Supp. XVII:** 244
Morning Face (Stratton-Porter), **Supp. XX: 223**
Morning for Flamingos, A (Burke), **Supp. XIV:** 30, 31, 32
"Morning Glory" (Merrill), **Supp. III Part 1:** 337
Morning Glory, The (R. Bly), **Supp. IV Part 1:** 63–65, 66, 71
"Morning Imagination of Russia, A" (W. C. Williams), **Retro. Supp. I:** 428
Morning in Antibes (Knowles), **Supp. XII:** 249
Morning in the Burned House (Atwood), **Supp. XIII:** 20, 35
Morning Is Near Us, The (Glaspell), **Supp. III Part 1:** 184–185
Morning Noon and Night (Cozzens), **I:** 374, 375, 376, 377, 379, 380
"Morning of the Day They Did It, The" (White), **Supp. I Part 2:** 663
"Morning Prayers" (Harjo), **Supp. XII:** 231
"Morning Roll Call" (Anderson), **I:** 116
"Morning Roundup" (Sorrentino), **Supp. XXI:** 228
"Mornings, I Walk Past the First Cemetery of Athens" (Stallings), **Supp. XXV:** 225
"Morning Shadows" (Skloot), **Supp. XX: 199**
"Mornings in a New House" (Merrill), **Supp. III Part 1:** 327
"Mornings in Ormos"(Hadas), **Supp. XXIII:** 112, 113, 123
Mornings Like This (Dillard), **Supp. VI:** 23, 34
"Morning Song" (Plath), **Retro. Supp. II:** 252; **Supp. XXIII:** 115
Morning Watch, The (Agee), **I:** 25, 39–42
"Morning with Broken Window" (Hogan), **Supp. IV Part 1:** 405
"Moro Like Me" (Goldman), **Supp. XXV:** 51
Morrell, Ottoline, **Retro. Supp. I:** 60
Morris, Bernard E., **Supp. XV:** 154, 169
Morris, Christopher D., **Supp. IV Part 1:** 231, 236
Morris, Gary, **Supp. XXII:** 262
Morris, George Sylvester, **Supp. I Part 2:** 640
Morris, Gouverneur, **Supp. I Part 2:** 512, 517, 518
Morris, Lloyd, **III:** 458
Morris, Robert, **Supp. I Part 2:** 510
Morris, Timothy, **Retro. Supp. I:** 40
Morris, William, **II:** 323, 338, 523; **IV:** 349; **Supp. I Part 1:** 260, 356; **Supp. XI:** 202

Morris, Willie, **Supp. XI:** 216, 231, 234; **Supp. XIX:** 151, 252
Morris, Wright, **I:** 305; **III: 218–243,** 558, 572; **IV:** 211
Morrison, Charles Clayton, **III:** 297
Morrison, Jim, **Supp. IV Part 1:** 206
Morrison, Toni, **Retro. Supp. II:** 15, 118; **Supp. III Part 1: 361–381; Supp. IV Part 1:** 2, 13, 14, 250, 253, 257; **Supp. V:** 169, 259; **Supp. VIII:** 213, 214; **Supp. X:** 85, 239, 250, 325; **Supp. XI:** 4, 14, 20, 91; **Supp. XII:** 289, 310; **Supp. XIII:** 60, 185; **Supp. XVI:** 143; **Supp. XVII:** 183; **Supp. XX: 108; Supp. XXI:** 172, 243; **Supp. XXII:** 65, 78; **Supp. XXIV:** 183, 184, 185; **Supp. XXV:** 142
Morrison, Tony, **Supp. XXVI:** 14
"Morro Bay" (Jeffers), **Supp. II Part 2:** 422
Morrow, W. C., **I:** 199
Morse, Jedidiah, **Supp. XV:** 243
Morse, Robert, **Supp. XI:** 305
Morse, Samuel F. B., **Supp. I Part 1:** 156
Morse, Samuel French, **Supp. XXI:** 17, 19, 23, 27
Mortal Acts, Mortal Words (Kinnell), **Supp. III Part 1:** 235, 236, 237, 249–254
Mortal Antipathy, A (Holmes), **Supp. I Part 1:** 315–316
"Mortal Enemies" (Humphrey), **Supp. IX:** 109
"Mortal Eternal" (Olds), **Supp. X:** 214
Mortal No, The (Hoffman), **IV:** 113
Mortal Stakes (Parker), **Supp. XIX:** 183–184
Morte D'Arthur, Le (Malory), **Supp. IV Part 1:** 47
Mortmere Stories, The (Isherwood and Upward), **Supp. XIV:** 159
Morton, David, **Supp. IX:** 76
Morton, Jelly Roll, **Supp. X:** 242
Morton, Thomas, **Supp. XXII:** 44, 45, 46
"Mosaic of the Nativity: Serbia, Winter 1993" (Kenyon), **Supp. VII:** 173
Mosby's Memoirs and Other Stories (Bellow), **Retro. Supp. II:** 27
"Moscow, Idaho" (Offutt), **Supp. XIX:** 170
Moscow under Fire (Caldwell), **I:** 296
Moser, Barry, **Supp. XIV:** 223
Moses (Asch), **Supp. XXIII:** 7
Moses (Untermeyer), **Supp. XV: 309**
Moses, Man of the Mountain (Hurston), **Supp. VI:** 149, 158, 160
"Moses on Sinai" (Untermeyer), **Supp. XV:** 300
Mosher, Howard Frank, **Supp. XXII: 203–221**
Moskowitz, Alfred, **Supp. XXI:** 98, 106
Mosle, Sara, **Supp. XI:** 254
Mosley, Walter, **Supp. XIII: 233–252; Supp. XVI:** 143
Mosquito (G. Jones), **Supp. XXIV:** 183, 184, 185, 190, **192–194,** 195
Mosquito Coast, The (film), **Supp. VIII:** 323

Mosquito Coast, The (Theroux), **Supp. VIII:** 321, **322–323**

Mosquitos (Faulkner), **II:** 56; **Retro. Supp. I:** 79, 81

Moss, Howard, **III:** 452; **Supp. IV Part 2:** 642; **Supp. IX:** 39; **Supp. XIII:** 114; **Supp. XV:** 143, 152

Moss, Stanley, **Supp. XI:** 321

Moss, Thylias, **Supp. XI:** 248

Mosses from an Old Manse (Hawthorne), **I:** 562; **II:** 224; **III:** 82, 83; **Retro. Supp. I:** 157, 248

Moss Mystery, The (Wells), **Supp. XXVI:** 278

"Moss of His Skin" (Sexton), **Supp. II Part 2:** 676

Most, Doug, **Supp. XVIII:** 101

"Most Extraordinary Case, A" (James), **II:** 322; **Retro. Supp. I:** 218

"Most Girl Part of You, The" (Hempel), **Supp. XXI:** 116

Most Likely to Succeed (Dos Passos), **I:** 491

"Most of It, The" (Frost), **Retro. Supp. I:** 121, 125, 129, 139; **Supp. XVIII:** 300

"Most Popular Novels in America, The" (Mabie), **Supp. XVIII:** 257

Motel Chronicles (Shepard), **Supp. III Part 2:** 445

"Mother" (Kooser), **Supp. XIX:** 117, 126, 127

"Mother" (Paley), **Supp. VI: 222–223**

Mother (Schjeldahl), **Supp. XXIV:** 44

"Mother" (Snyder), **Supp. VIII:** 298

Mother (Whistler), **IV:** 369

Mother, The (Buck), **Supp. II Part 1:** 118–119

"Mother and Child #3" (Davison), **Supp. XXVI:** 77

"Mother and Jack and the Rain" (Sexton), **Supp. II Part 2:** 686

"Mother and Son" (Tate), **IV:** 128, 137–138

Mother Country: Britain, the Welfare State and Nuclear Pollution (Robinson), **Supp. XXI:** 211

Mother Courage and Her Children (Brecht), **III:** 160; **Supp. IX:** 140; **Supp. XII:** 249

"Mother Earth: Her Whales" (Snyder), **Supp. VIII:** 302

"Motherhood" (Swenson), **Supp. IV Part 2:** 645

Mother Hubbard (Reed), **Supp. X:** 241

Motherless Brooklyn (Lethem), **Supp. XXII:** 49

Motherless in Brooklyn (Lethem), **Supp. XVIII:** 135, **143–144**

Mother Love (Dove), **Supp. IV Part 1:** 250–251, 254

"Mother Marie Therese" (Lowell), **Retro. Supp. II:** 188

Mother Night (Vonnegut), **Supp. II Part 2:** 757, 758, 767, 770, 771

"Mother Rosarine" (Kumin), **Supp. IV Part 2:** 442

"Mothers and Daughters in the Fiction of the New Republic" (Davidson), **Supp. XV:** 238

"Mother's lament for the absence of a child, A"(J. Schoolcraft), **Supp. XXIII:** 236

"Mother Song" (Huddle), **Supp. XXVI:** 151

Mother's Recompense, The (Wharton), **IV:** 321, 324; **Retro. Supp. I:** 382

"Mother's Tale, A" (Agee), **I:** 29–30

"Mother's Things" (Creeley), **Supp. IV Part 1:** 141

"Mother Suite, The"(Crooker), **Supp. XXIII:** 61

"Mother's Voice" (Creeley), **Supp. IV Part 1:** 156

Mother to Daughter, Daughter to Mother (Olsen, ed.), **Supp. XIII:** 295

"Mother Tongue" (Simic), **Supp. VIII:** 283

"Mother to Son" (Hughes), **Retro. Supp. I:** 199, 203; **Supp. I Part 1:** 321–322, 323

Motherwell, Robert, **Supp. XV:** 145; **Supp. XXI:** 125

"Mother Writes to the Murderer, The: A Letter" (Nye), **Supp. XIII:** 276

Moths of the Limberlost (Stratton-Porter), **Supp. XX: 218**

"Motion, The" (Olson), **Supp. II Part 2:** 571

Motion of History, The (Baraka), **Supp. II Part 1:** 55, 56

"Motive for Metaphor, The" (Stevens), **IV:** 89; **Retro. Supp. I:** 310

Motiveless Malignity (Auchincloss), **Supp. IV Part 1:** 31

Motke ganef (Asch), **Supp. XXIII:** 5

Motley, John Lothrop, **Supp. I Part 1:** 299; **Supp. I Part 2:** 479; **Supp. XX: 228, 231**

Motley, Willard, **Supp. XVII: 149–163;** **Supp. XXIII:** 145

"Motor Car, The" (White), **Supp. I Part 2:** 661

Motor-Flight Through France (Wharton), **I:** 12; **Retro. Supp. I:** 372

Mott, Michael, **Supp. VIII:** 204, 208

Motta, Gustavo, **Supp. XXIII:** 125

Mottetti: Poems of Love: The Motets of Eugenio Montale (Montale; Gioia, trans.), **Supp. XV:** 112, **127–128**

Mottke, the Thief (Asch), **Supp. XXIII: 9,** 12

Mottke, the Thief (Asch; tr. Willa and Edwin Muir), **Supp. XXIII:** 5

Mouawad, Nelly, **Supp. XX: 126**

"Mound, The" (Lovecraft and Bishop), **Supp. XXV:** 122

"Mountain, The" (Frost), **Retro. Supp. I:** 121

"Mountain Hermitage, The: Pages from a Japanese Notebook" (Passin), **Supp. XIII:** 337

Mountain Interval (Frost), **II:** 154; **Retro. Supp. I:** 131, 132, 133

"Mountain Lion" (Hogan), **Supp. IV Part 1:** 412

"Mountain Music" essays (Sanders), **Supp. XVI:** 276–277

Mountain on the Desert, The (Richter), **Supp. XVIII:** 216, 219

Mountainous Journey, A (Tuqan), **Supp. XIII:** 278

"Mountains" (Dubus III), **Supp. XXIV:** 101

Mountains, The (Wolfe), **IV:** 461

Mountains and Rivers without End (Snyder), **Supp. VIII:** 295, **305–306**

"Mountains grow unnoticed, The" (Dickinson), **Retro. Supp. I:** 46

Mountains Have Come Closer, The (J. W. Miller), **Supp. XX: 165, 168, 169–170**

Mountains Look Down, The: A History of Chichester, a Company Town in the Catskills (Bennett), **Supp. XXII:** 218

Mountains of California, The (Muir), **Supp. IX:** 183

"Mountain Whippoorwill, The" (Benét), **Supp. XI:** 44–45, 46, 47

"Mount-Joy: or Some Passages Out of the Life of a Castle-Builder" (Irving), **II:** 314

"Mount Venus" (Wright), **Supp. XV:** 346

"Mourners" (Kooser), **Supp. XIX:** 127

"Mourners, The" (Malamud), **Supp. I Part 2:** 431, 435, 436–437

Mourners Below (Purdy), **Supp. VII:** 274, 280

"Mourning and Melancholia" (Freud), **Supp. IV Part 2:** 450; **Supp. XVI:** 161

Mourning Becomes Electra (O'Neill), **III:** 391, 394, 398–400

"Mourning Doves" (Pedersen; Nelson, trans.), **Supp. XVIII:** 180

"Mourning Poem for the Queen of Sunday" (Hayden), **Supp. II Part 1:** 379–380

"Mouse Elegy" (Olds), **Supp. X:** 209

Mouse Is Born, A (Loos), **Supp. XVI:** 193

"Mouse Roulette Wheel, The" (C. Bly), **Supp. XVI:** 34

Moustapha's Eclipse (McKnight), **Supp. XX: 147, 150**

"Mouth of Brass" (Humphrey), **Supp. IX:** 101

Moveable Feast, A (Hemingway), **II:** 257; **Retro. Supp. I:** 108, 171, **186–187**

Movement, The: Documentary of a Struggle for Equality (Student Nonviolent Coordinating Committee), **Supp. IV Part 1:** 369

"Move over Macho, Here Comes Feminismo" (Robbins), **Supp. X:** 272

Movers and Shakers (Sochen), **Supp. XXI:** 1

"Moves, The" (July), **Supp. XXIV:** 205

"Move to California, The" (Stafford), **Supp. XI:** 318, 321

"Movie" (Shapiro), **Supp. II Part 2:** 707

Movie at the End of the World, The (McGrath), **Supp. X:** 127

Moviegoer, The (Percy), **Supp. III Part 1:** 383–385, 387, 389–392, 394, 397

"Movie Magazine, The: A Low 'Slick' " (Percy), **Supp. III Part 1:** 385

Movies (Dixon), **Supp. XII:** 147

Movies About the Movies (Ames), **Supp. XVIII:** 242–243

"Movie Star Peter at the Supper for Street People" (Ferry), **Supp. XXIV:** 153

"Moving Around" (Matthews), **Supp. IX:** 155

"Moving Finger, The" (Wharton), **Retro. Supp. I:** 365

"Moving Inward at Last" (Bly), **Supp. XXI:** 84–85

Moving On (McMurtry), **Supp. V:** 223–224

"Moving On" (Pickering), **Supp. XXI:** 197

Moving Pictures: Memoirs of a Hollywood Prince (Schulberg), **Supp. XVIII:** 242, 243, 254

"Moving Sale" (Stallings), **Supp. XXV:** 228

Moving Target, The (Macdonald), **Supp. IV Part 2:** 462, 463, 467, 470, 471, 473, 474

Moving Target, The (Merwin), **Supp. III Part 1:** 346, 347–348, 352, 357

Mowat, Farley, **Supp. XXVI:** 61

"Mowbray Family, The" (Farrell and Alden), **II:** 45

"Mowing" (Frost), **II:** 169–170; **Retro. Supp. I:** 127, 128

"Moxan's Master" (Bierce), **I:** 206

Moxley, Jennifer, **Supp. XVII:** 70

Moyers, Bill, **Supp. IV Part 1:** 267; **Supp. VIII:** 331; **Supp. XI:** 126, 132; **Supp. XII:** 217; **Supp. XIII:** 274, 276; **Supp. XV:** 212; **Supp. XXIII:** 129, 130, 131, 139

Moynagh, Maureen, **Supp. XXII:** 73

Moynihan, Daniel Patrick, **Retro. Supp. II:** 123; **Supp. VIII:** 241; **Supp. XIX:** 150–151

"Moyshele"(Asch), **Supp. XXIII:** 4

"Mozart" (C. Frost), **Supp. XV:** 94

Mozart, Wolfgang Amadeus, **I:** 479, 588; **IV:** 74, 358; **Supp. IV Part 1:** 284

"Mozart and the Gray Steward" (Wilder), **IV:** 358

Mrabet, Mohammed, **Supp. IV Part 1:** 92, 93

Mr. and Mrs. Baby and Other Stories (Strand), **Supp. IV Part 2:** 631

"Mr. and Mrs. Fix-It" (Lardner), **II:** 431

Mr. Arcularis (Aiken), **I:** 54, 56

"Mr. Big" (Allen), **Supp. XV:** 15

Mr. Bridge (Connell), **Supp. XIV:** 80, 82, 93; **Supp. XXIII:** 302

Mr. Brown Can Moo! Can You? (Geisel), **Supp. XVI:** 104

"Mr. Bruce" (Jewett), **II:** 397; **Retro. Supp. II:** 134, 143

"Mr. Burnshaw and the Statue" (Stevens), **Retro. Supp. I:** 298, 303

"Mr. Carson Death on His Nights Out" (McGrath), **Supp. X:** 118

Mr. Clemens and Mark Twain (Kaplan), **I:** 247–248

"Mr. Coffee and Mr. Fixit" (Carver), **Supp. III Part 1:** 145

"Mr. Cornelius Johnson, Office-Seeker" (Dunbar), **Supp. II Part 1:** 211, 213

"Mr. Costyve Duditch" (Toomer), **Supp. III Part 2:** 486

"Mr. Dajani, Calling from Jericho" (Nye), **Supp. XIII:** 286–287

"Mr. Edwards and the Spider" (Lowell), **I:** 544; **II:** 550; **Retro. Supp. II:** 187

Mr. Field's Daughter (Bausch), **Supp. VII:** 47–48, 51–52

"Mr. Flood's Party" (Robinson), **III:** 512

"Mr. Forster's Pageant" (Maxwell), **Supp. VIII:** 172

"Mr. Frost's Chickens" (Oliver), **Supp. VII:** 232–233

Mr. Hodge and Mr. Hazard (Wylie), **Supp. I Part 2:** 708, 709, 714, 721–724

"Mr. Hueffer and the Prose Tradition" (Pound), **III:** 465

Mr. Ives' Christmas (Hijuelos), **Supp. VIII:** 85–86

Mr. Kelso's Lion (Bontemps), **Supp. XXII:** 7

"Mr. Longfellow and His Boy" (Sandburg), **III:** 591

"Mr. Luna and History" (Ríos), **Supp. IV Part 2:** 551

"Mr. Mitochondria" (Stollman), **Supp. XVII:** 50

Mr. Moto Is So Sorry (Marquand), **III:** 57, 58

Mr. Norris Changes Trains (Isherwood), **Supp. XIV:** 161

"Mr. Preble Gets Rid of His Wife" (Thurber), **Supp. I Part 2:** 615

"Mr. Rat"(Thompson), **Supp. XXIII:** 301–302

"Mr. Rolfe" (Wilson), **IV:** 436

Mr. Rutherford's Children (S. and A. Warner), **Supp. XVIII:** 264

"Mrs. Adis" (Kaye-Smith), **Supp. XVIII:** 130–131

Mrs. Albert Grundy: Observations in Philistia (Frederic), **II:** 138–139

Mr. Sammler's Planet (Bellow), **I:** 144, 147, 150, 151, 152, 158; **Retro. Supp. II:** 19, 28, 30

Mrs. Balfame (Atherton), **Supp. XXIV:** 20

"Mrs. Bilingsby's Wine" (Taylor), **Supp. V:** 323

Mrs. Bob Cratchit's Wild Christmas Binge (Durang), **Supp. XXIV:** 113, 125

Mrs. Bridge: A Novel (Connell), **Supp. XIV:** 79, 80, 81, 82, 89–94, 95; **Supp. XXIII:** 302

"Mrs. Cassidy's Last Year" (Gordon), **Supp. IV Part 1:** 306

Mrs. Dalloway (Woolf), **Supp. IV Part 1:** 299; **Supp. VIII:** 5; **Supp. XV:** 55, 65–66

"Mrs. Green" (Huddle), **Supp. XXVI:** 148

"Mr. Shelley Speaking" (Wylie), **Supp. I Part 2:** 719

"Mrs. Jellison" (Hay), **Supp. XIV:** 123

"Mrs. Krikorian" (Olds), **Supp. X:** 211

"Mrs. Maecenas" (Burke), **I:** 271

"Mrs. Mandrill" (Nemerov), **III:** 278

"Mrs. Manstey's View" (Wharton), **Retro. Supp. I:** 362, 363

"Mrs. Mobry's Reason" (Chopin), **Retro. Supp. II:** 61

Mr. Spaceman (R. O. Butler), **Supp. XII:** 62, 74–75

Mrs. Reynolds (Stein), **IV:** 43

"Mrs. Sen's" (Lahiri), **Supp. XXI:** 177–178, 180–181

Mrs. Stevens Hears the Mermaids Singing (Sarton), **Supp. VIII:** 252–253, 256–257

Mrs. Ted Bliss (Elkin), **Supp. VI: 56,** 58

"Mrs. Turner Cutting the Grass" (Shields), **Supp. VII:** 319–320

"Mrs. Walpurga" (Rukeyser), **Supp. VI:** 273

"Mr. Thompson's Prodigal" (Harte), **Supp. II Part 1:** 354

"Mr. Trumm's Eyes"(Schott), **Supp. XXIII:** 243

Mr. Vertigo (Auster), **Supp. XII: 34–35,** 36

"Mr. Vonnegut in Sumatra" (Saunders), **Supp. XIX:** 235

"Mr. Whittier" (Scott), **Supp. I Part 2:** 705

Mr. Wilson's War (Dos Passos), **I:** 485

"Mr. Woodriff's Neckties" (Gallagher), **Supp. XXIV:** 175–176

"MS. Found in a Bottle" (Poe), **III:** 411, 416; **Retro. Supp. II:** 274

"Ms. Lot" (Rukeyser), **Supp. VI:** 281

Ms. Magazine, **Supp. V:** 259

Mttron-Hirsch, Sidney, **III:** 484–485

"Muchas Gracias Por Todo" (Nye), **Supp. XIII:** 282–283

"Much Madness is divinest Sense" (Dickinson), **Retro. Supp. I:** 37–38

"Muck-A-Muck" (Harte), **Supp. II Part 1:** 342

"Mud Below, The" (Proulx), **Supp. VII:** 262

Mudge, Alden, **Supp. XIV:** 35

"Mudman"(P. Benedict), **Supp. XXIII:** 47

Mudrick, Marvin, **Retro. Supp. II:** 289

"Mud Season" (Kenyon), **Supp. VII:** 167–168

Mueller, Lisel, **Supp. I Part 1:** 83, 88; **Supp. XIV:** 268

Muggli, Mark, **Supp. IV Part 1:** 207

Muhammad, Elijah, **Supp. I Part 1:** 60

Muir, Edwin, **I:** 527; **II:** 368; **III:** 20; **Supp. XXII:** 166; **Supp. XXIII:** 1; **Supp. XXVI:** 67

Muir, John, **Supp. IX:** 33, 171–188; **Supp. VIII:** 296; **Supp. X:** 29; **Supp. XIV:** 177, 178, 181; **Supp. XXVI:** 34, 37, 43

Muir, Willa, **Supp. XXIII:** 1

Muirhead, Deborah, **Supp. XVIII:** 186

Mujica, Barbara, **Supp. VIII:** 89

Mulas, Franco, **Supp. XX: 38**

Mulatto (Hughes), **Retro. Supp. I:** 197, 203; **Supp. I Part 1:** 328, 339

Mulching of America, The (Crews), **Supp. XI:** 107

Muldoon, William, **I:** 500–501

Mule Bone (Hughes and Hurston), **Retro. Supp. I:** 194, 203; **Supp. VI:** 154

Mules and Men (Hurston), **Supp. VI:** 149, 153, 154, 160

Mulford, Prentice, **I:** 193

Mullennix, Joel, **Supp. XXIII:** 281

Muller, Kathryn, **Supp. XXVI:** 95

Mulligan, Robert, **Supp. VIII:** 128, 129

Mulligan Stew (Sorrentino), **Supp. XII:** 139; **Supp. XXI:** 233

Mullins, Eustace, **III:** 479

Mullins, Priscilla, **II:** 502–503

"Multiplication of Wool, The" (Sanders), **Supp. XVI:** 268

Multitudes, Multitudes (Clampitt), **Supp. IX:** 39

Mumbo Jumbo (Reed), **Supp. X:** 240, 242, **245–248,** 251

Mumford, Lewis, **I:** 245, 250, 251, 252, 259, 261; **II:** 271, 473–474; **Supp. I Part 2:** 632, 638; **Supp. II Part 2: 471–501**

Mumford, Sophia Wittenberg (Mrs. Lewis Mumford), **Supp. II Part 2:** 474, 475

"Mummers, The" (Di Piero), **Supp. XIX:** 44

Mummy, The (film), **Supp. IV Part 1:** 104; **Supp. XVII:** 57

Mundo y Palabra (Espaillat), **Supp. XXI:** 104

"Mundus et Infans" (Auden), **Supp. II Part 1:** 15

"Munich, 1938" (Lowell), **II:** 554

"Munich Mannequins, The" (Plath), **Retro. Supp. II:** 256

"Municipal Report, A" (Henry), **Supp. II Part 1:** 406–407

Muñoz, Manuel, **Supp. XXV: 127–139**

Munro, Alice, **Supp. IX:** 212; **Supp. X:** 290; **Supp. XII:** 289–290, 310; **Supp. XXIII:** 289, 296

Munsey, Frank, **I:** 501

Munson, Gorham, **I:** 252, 388, 432; **Retro. Supp. II:** 77, 78, 79, 82, 83; **Supp. I Part 2:** 454; **Supp. XX: 70, 74**

Münsterberg, Hugo, **Supp. XIV:** 197

Murakami, Haruki, **Supp. XVI:** 124

"Murano" (Doty), **Supp. XI:** 131

Murasaki, Lady, **II:** 577

Muratori, Fred, **Supp. XVI:** 281

Muray, Nicholas, **Supp. I Part 2:** 708

Murchison, Ginger, **Supp. XXV:** 222, 223, 226

Murder, My Sweet (film), **Supp. IV Part 1:** 130

"Murder Comes for the Bishop" (Goldman), **Supp. XXV:** 57

"Murderer Guest, The" (Gordon), **Supp. IV Part 1:** 306

"Murderers" (L. Michaels), **Supp. XVI:** 207–208

Murder in Mount Holly (Theroux), **Supp. VIII:** 315–316

Murder in the Cathedral (T. S. Eliot), **I:** 571, 573, 580, 581; **II:** 20; **Retro. Supp. I:** 65; **Retro. Supp. II:** 222

Murder of Lidice, The (Millay), **III:** 140

"Murders in the Rue Morgue, The" (Poe), **III:** 412, 416, 419–420; **Retro. Supp. II:** 271, 272; **Supp. XIX:** 77

Murdoch, Iris, **Supp. VIII:** 167; **Supp. XVIII:** 136,149

Murnau, F. W., **Supp. XV:** 128

Murphy, Brenda, **Supp. XXI:** 6

Murphy, Cullen, **Supp. XXVI:** 61

Murphy, Jacqueline Shea, **Retro. Supp. II:** 143

Murphy, Patrick, **Supp. XIII:** 214

Murphy, Richard, **Retro. Supp. II:** 250; **Supp. XXIII:** 75

Murray, Albert, **Retro. Supp. II:** 119, 120; **Supp. XIX: 147–162**

Murray, Bill, **Supp. XXI:** 51

Murray, Edward, **I:** 229

Murray, G. E., **Supp. X:** 201; **Supp. XI:** 143, 155

Murray, Gilbert, **III:** 468–469

Murray, Jan, **Supp. IV Part 2:** 574

Murray, John, **II:** 304; **III:** 76, 79; **Retro. Supp. I:** 246

Murray, Judith Sargent, **Supp. XV:** 236–237

Murray, Les, **Supp. XIX:** 131

Murray, Margaret A., **Supp. V:** 128

Murrell, John A., **IV:** 265

Mursell, James L., **Supp. I Part 2:** 608

"Muse" (Ammons), **Supp. VII:** 29

"Muse, Postmodern and Homeless, The" (Ozick), **Supp. V:** 272

"Musée des Beaux Arts" (Auden), **Retro. Supp. I:** 430; **Supp. II Part 1:** 14

"Musée des Beaux Arts Revisited" (Collins), **Supp. XXI:** 60

"Muse of Aboutness, The" (Baker), **Supp. XVI:** 288

Muses Are Heard, The (Capote), **Supp. III Part 1:** 126

"Muses of Terrence McNally, The" (Zinman), **Supp. XIII:** 207–208

"Muse's Tragedy, The" (Wharton), **Retro. Supp. I:** 364

Museum (Dove), **Supp. IV Part 1:** 245–247, 248

"Museum" (Hass), **Supp. VI:** 107

Museums and Women (Updike), **Retro. Supp. I:** 321

"Museum Vase" (Francis), **Supp. IX:** 83

"Mushrooms" (Plath), **Retro. Supp. II:** 246; **Supp. I Part 2:** 539

"Music" (Huddle), **Supp. XXVI:** 150

"Music" (Oliver), **Supp. VII:** 236

Music (al-Músíqá) (Gibran), **Supp. XX: 115, 124**

Music After the Great War (Van Vechten), **Supp. II Part 2:** 732

Music and Bad Manners (Van Vechten), **Supp. II Part 2:** 733

Music Appreciation (Skloot), **Supp. XX: 196, 197–201**

"Music for a Farce" (Bowles), **Supp. IV Part 1:** 83

Music for Chameleons (Capote), **Supp. III Part 1:** 120, 125–127, 131, 132

"Music for Museums?" (Van Vechten), **Supp. II Part 2:** 732

"Music for the Movies" (Van Vechten), **Supp. II Part 2:** 733

"Music from Spain" (Welty), **IV:** 272

Music Like Dirt (Bidart), **Supp. XV:** 35

"Music Like Dirt" (Bidart), **Supp. XV:** 35

Music of Chance, The (Auster), **Supp. XII:** 21, 23, **32–33**

"Music of My Own Kind Too, The" (Budbill), **Supp. XIX:** 10

"Music of Prose, The" (Gass), **Supp. VI:** 92

Music of Spain, The (Van Vechten), **Supp. II Part 2:** 734, 735

"Music of the Spheres" (Epstein), **Supp. XII:** 165

"Music School" (B. Kelly), **Supp. XVII:** 124

Music School, The (Updike), **IV:** 214, 215, 219, 226, 227; **Retro. Supp. I:** 320, 328, 329, 330

"Music School, The" (Updike), **Retro. Supp. I:** 326, 329, 335

"Music Swims Back to Me" (Sexton), **Supp. II Part 2:** 673

Muske, Carol, **Supp. IV Part 2:** 453–454

"Mussel Hunter at Rock Harbor" (Plath), **Supp. I Part 2:** 529, 537

Musset, Alfred de, **I:** 474; **II:** 543

Mussolini, Benito, **III:** 115, 473, 608; **IV:** 372, 373; **Supp. I Part 1:** 281, 282; **Supp. I Part 2:** 618; **Supp. V:** 290; **Supp. XVI:** 191

"Mustafa Ferrari" (X. J. Kennedy), **Supp. XV:** 170–171

Mustich, James, **Supp. XXI:** 52

"Must the Novelist Crusade?" (Welty), **IV:** 280

"Mutability of Literature, The" (Irving), **II:** 308

"Mutation of the Spirit" (Corso), **Supp. XII:** 132, 133

Mute, The (McCullers), **II:** 586

Mutilated, The (T. Williams), **IV:** 382, 386, 393

Mutiny of the Elsinore, The (London), **II:** 467

"Muttsy" (Hurston), **Supp. XVIII:** 279; **Supp. XXVI:** 164

Muyumba, Walton, **Supp. XIX:** 158

"My Adventures as a Social Poet" (Hughes), **Retro. Supp. I:** 194, 207

"My Alba" (Ginsberg), **Supp. II Part 1:** 320, 321

My Alexandria (Doty), **Supp. XI:** 119, 120, 121, **123–125,** 130

"My Amendment" (Saunders), **Supp. XIX:** 232

My Amputations (Major), **Supp. XXII:** 174, **175–176**

My Ántonia (Cather), **I:** 321–322; **Retro. Supp. I:** 1, 3, 4, **11–13,** 14, 17, 18, 22; **Supp. IV Part 2:** 608; **Supp. XVI:** 226

"My Appearance" (Wallace), **Supp. X:** 306–307

My Argument with the Gestapo: A Macaronic Journal (Merton), **Supp. VIII:** 207; **Supp. XV:** 344

"My Arkansas" (Angelou), **Supp. IV Part 1:** 15

"My Aunt" (Holmes), **Supp. I Part 1:** 302, 310

"My Beginnings" (Simpson), **Supp. IX:** 273

"My Bird Problem" (Franzen), **Supp. XX: 94**

My Black Horse (Gallagher), **Supp. XXIV:** 170

"My Bodyguard" (Notley), **Supp. XXII:** 230

My Bondage and My Freedom (Douglass), **Supp. III Part 1:** 155, 173

"My Bones Here Are Waiting for Yours" (Vaz), **Supp. XXVI:** 265–266

My Brother (Kincaid), **Supp. VII:** 191–193

"My Brother Paul" (Dreiser), **Retro. Supp. II:** 94

"My Brothers the Silent" (Merwin), **Supp. III Part 1:** 349–350

"My Brother's Work" (Dunn), **Supp. XI:** 147

"My Brother Takes a Hammer to the Mirror" (F. Wright), **Supp. XVII:** 244

"My Butterfly" (Frost), **II:** 151; **Retro. Supp. I:** 124

"My Children, and a Prayer for Us" (Ortiz), **Supp. IV Part 2:** 507

My Children! My Africa! (Fugard), **Supp. XXIV:** 267

"My College Sex Group" (Peacock), **Supp. XIX:** 199

"My Coney Island Uncle" (Swados), **Supp. XIX:** 267–268

"My Confession" (McCarthy), **II:** 562

"My Confessional Sestina" (Gioia), **Supp. XV:** 123

"My Corner" (Major), **Supp. XXII:** 184

My Country and My People (Yutang), **Supp. X:** 291

"My Country Tish of Thee" (Rinehart), **Supp. XXV:** 194

"My Country 'Tis of Thee" (Reznikoff), **Supp. III Part 2:** 616

"My Daughter Considers Her Body" (Skloot), **Supp. XX: 197–198, 200**

My Days of Anger (Farrell), **II:** 34, 35–36, 43

"My Dear Niece" (Boyce), **Supp. XXI:** 10

"My Dear Republican Mother" (C. Bly), **Supp. XVI:** 31–32

My Death My Life by Pier Paolo Pasolini (Acker), **Supp. XII:** 7

My Dog Stupid (Fante), **Supp. XI:** 160, **170–171**

My Dog Tulip (Ackerley), **Supp. XX: 237**

"My Ear-Rings"(J. Schoolcraft), **Supp. XXIII:** 226

My Emily Dickinson (Howe), **Retro. Supp. I:** 33, 43; **Supp. IV Part 2:** 430–431

"My English" (Alvarez), **Supp. VII:** 2

Myers, John Bernard, **Supp. XXIII:** 210, 219

Myers, Linda A., **Supp. IV Part 1:** 10

"My Extended Family" (Theroux), **Supp. VIII:** 311

My Face for the World to See (Hayes), **Supp. XXVI:** 139, 141–142

"My Father" (Biss), **Supp. XXVI:** 47

"My Father" (Budbill), **Supp. XIX:** 5

"My Father" (L. Michaels), **Supp. XVI:** 214

"My Father" (Sterne), **IV:** 466

"My Father at Eighty-Five" (R. Bly), **Supp. IV Part 1:** 73

"My Father Is a Simple Man" (Salinas), **Supp. XIII:** 324

"My Father Is with Me" (Budbill), **Supp. XIX:** 15

"My Father: October 1942" (Stafford), **Supp. XI:** 323

My Father Photographed with Friends (Bronk), **Supp. XXI:** 26–27,**Supp. XXI:** 31

"My Father Photographed with Friends" (Bronk), **Supp. XXI:** 23, 27

"My Fathers Came From Kentucky" (Lindsay), **Supp. I Part 2:** 395

"My Father's Employment"(Schott), **Supp. XXIII:** 247

"My Father's Friends" (Maxwell), **Supp. VIII:** 171

"My Father's Ghost" (Wagoner), **Supp. IX:** 330

"My Father's God" (Fante), **Supp. XI:** 160, 174

"My Father's House" (L.-Y. Lee), **Supp. XV:** 225

"My Father's Love Letters" (Gallagher), **Supp. XXIV:** 171–172

"My Father's Love Letters" (Komunyakaa), **Supp. XIII:** 127

"My Father Speaks to me from the Dead" (Olds), **Supp. X:** 210

"My Father's Telescope" (Dove), **Supp. IV Part 1:** 246, 248

"My Father with Cigarette Twelve Years Before the Nazis Could Break His Heart" (Levine), **Supp. V:** 194

"My Favorite Murder" (Bierce), **I:** 205

My Favorite Plant: Writers and Gardeners on the Plants They Love (Kincaid), **Supp. VII:** 193–194

My Favorites in Suspense (Hitchcock, ed.), **Supp. XXII:** 119

"My Fifty-Plus Years Celebrate Spring" (Salinas), **Supp. XIII:** 327

"My First Book" (Harte), **Supp. II Part 1:** 343

My First Summer in the Sierra (Muir), **Supp. IX:** 172, 173, **178–181,** 183, 185; **Supp. XIV:** 177

"My Flamboyant Grandson" (Saunders), **Supp. XIX:** 231–232

"My Fountain Pen" (McClatchy), **Supp. XII:** 254, 260

My Friend, Henry Miller (Perlès), **III:** 189

My Friend, Julia Lathrop (Addams), **Supp. I Part 1:** 25

"My Friend, Walt Whitman" (Oliver), **Supp. VII:** 245

"My Garden Acquaintance" (Lowell), **Supp. I Part 2:** 420

My Garden \[Book\]: (Kincaid), **Supp. VII:** 193–194

"My Good-bye" (Weigl), **Supp. XIX:** 288

"My Good Man" (Gansworth), **Supp. XXVI:** 114

"My Grandfather" (Lowell), **II:** 554

"My Grandmother's Love Letters" (H. Crane), **Retro. Supp. II:** 78

My Grandparents Were Married for Sixty-five Years (Schott), **Supp. XXIII:** 240–241

"My Grandson, Home at Last" (Angelou), **Supp. IV Part 1:** 13

My Green Hills of Jamaica (McKay), **Supp. X:** 132, 142

"My Gun" (Gallagher), **Supp. XXIV:** 175

My Guru and His Disciple (Isherwood), **Supp. XIV:** 157, 164, 172

"My Heart" (Collins), **Supp. XXI:** 58

My Heart's in the Highlands (Saroyan), **Supp. IV Part 1:** 83

"My High School Reunion" (Kingston), **Supp. V:** 169

"My House New-Painted" (Bronk), **Supp. XXI:** 30

"My Hunt for King Sebastião" (Vaz), **Supp. XXVI:** 260

"My Ideal Home" (Stratton-Porter), **Supp. XX: 222**

"My Indigo" (L.-Y. Lee), **Supp. XV:** 214

My Kind of Place: Travel Stories from a Woman Who's Been Everywhere (Orlean), **Supp. XXV:** 160, 164–165

"My Kinsman, Major Molineux" (Hawthorne), **II:** 228, 229, 237–239, 243; **Retro. Supp. I:** 153–154, 158, 160, 161; **Retro. Supp. II:** 181, 187; **Supp. XVI:** 157

My Kinsman, Major Molineux (Lowell), **II:** 545–546

"My Last Afternoon with Uncle Devereux Winslow" (Lowell), **II:** 547–548; **Retro. Supp. II:** 189

"My Last Drive" (Hardy), **Supp. VIII:** 32

"My Last Duchess" (Browning), **Supp. XV:** 121; **Supp. XXV:** 229

Myles, Eileen, **Supp. XXIV:** 45

"My Life" (Strand), **Supp. IV Part 2:** 627

My Life, Starring Dara Falcon (Beattie), **Supp. V:** 31, 34–35

My Life a Loaded Gun: Dickinson, Plath, Rich, and Female Creativity (Bennett), **Retro. Supp. I:** 29

My Life and Hard Times (Thurber), **Supp. I Part 2:** 607, 609

My Life and Loves in Greenwich Village (attr. Bodenheim), **Supp. XXV:** 30

My Life as a Man (P. Roth), **Retro. Supp. II:** 281, 286, 289; **Supp. III Part 2:** 401, 404, 405, 417–418

"My Life as a P.I.G., or the True Adventures of Smokey the Cop" (Abbey), **Supp. XIII:** 3

"My life closed twice before its close" (Dickinson), **Retro. Supp. I:** 38

"My Life had stood a Loaded Gun" (Dickinson), **Retro. Supp. I:** 42, 43, 45, 46; **Supp. IV Part 2:** 430

My Life of Absurdity (C. Himes), **Supp. XVI:** 145

"My Life with Medicine" (Nye), **Supp. XIII:** 282

"My Life with *Playboy*" (Plimpton), **Supp. XVI:** 246

"My Life with R. H. Macy" (Jackson), **Supp. IX:** 118

"My Little Utopia" (Simic), **Supp. VIII:** 283

My Lives and How I Lost Them (Cullen), **Supp. IV Part 1:** 173

"My Lord Bag of Rice" (C. Bly), **Supp. XVI:** 40

My Lord Bag of Rice: New and Selected Stories (C. Bly), **Supp. XVI:** 41

"My Lost City" (Fitzgerald), **Retro. Supp. I:** 102

"My Lost Youth" (Longfellow), **II:** 487, 499; **Retro. Supp. II:** 168

My Love Affair with America: The Cautionary Tale of a Cheerful Conservative (Podhoretz), **Supp. VIII:** 232, 233, 237, **244–246**

"My Lover Has Dirty Fingernails" (Updike), **Retro. Supp. I:** 332, 333

"My lover is tall and handsome"(J. Schoolcraft), **Supp. XXIII:** 235

"My Lucy Friend Who Smells Like Corn" (Cisneros), **Supp. VII:** 68–69

"My Mammogram" (McClatchy), **Supp. XII:** 263–264

"My Man Bovanne" (Bambara), **Supp. XI:** 2

"My Mariner" (Larcom), **Supp. XIII:** 147

My Mark Twain (Howells), **II:** 276

"My Metamorphosis" (Harte), **Supp. II Part 1:** 339

My Mistress's Sparrow Is Dead (Eugenides, ed.), **Supp. XXIV:** 135

"My Moby Dick" (Humphrey), **Supp. IX:** 95

"My Monkey" (Nelson), **Supp. XVIII:** 178

"My Moral Life" (Halliday), **Supp. XIX:** 89

My Mortal Enemy (Cather), **I:** 327–328; **Retro. Supp. I:** 16–17; **Supp. I Part 2:** 719

"My Mother" (Biss), **Supp. XXVI:** 47

My Mother, My Father and Me (Hellman), **Supp. I Part 1:** 290–291

"My Mother and My Sisters" (Ortiz), **Supp. IV Part 2:** 499

My Mother: Demonology (Acker), **Supp. XII:** 6

"My Mother Is Speaking from the Desert" (Gordon), **Supp. IV Part 1:** 309, 314

"My Mother Remembers That She Was Beautiful" (Gallagher), **Supp. XXIV:** 169

"My Mother's Goofy Song" (Fante), **Supp. XI:** 164

"My Mother's Memoirs, My Father's Lie, and Other True Stories" (Banks), **Supp. V:** 15

"My Mother's Nipples" (Hass), **Supp. VI:** 109

"My Mother's Story" (Kunitz), **Supp. III Part 1:** 259

"My Mother's Voice" (Very), **Supp. XXV:** 244

"My Mother"(Taylor), **Supp. XXIII:** 231

"My Mother Then and Now" (Wasserstein), **Supp. XV:** 327

"My Mother with Purse the Summer They Murdered the Spanish Poet" (Levine), **Supp. V:** 194

My Movie Business: A Memoir (Irving), **Supp. VI:** 164

"My Name" (Cisneros), **Supp. VII:** 60

"My Negro Problem—And Ours" (Podhoretz), **Supp. VIII: 234–236**

"My Neighborhood"(Dybek), **Supp. XXIII:** 69

"My New Diet" (Karr), **Supp. XI:** 241

My Next Bride (Boyle), **Supp. XXIV: 53,** 59

"My Number" (Collins), **Supp. XXI:** 64

"My Old Man" (Hemingway), **II:** 263

My Other Life (Theroux), **Supp. VIII:** 310, 324

"My Own Story" (E. Stoddard), **Supp. XV:** 273, 279, 283

My Own True Name: New and Selected Poems for Young Adults, 1984–1999 (Mora), **Supp. XIII:** 222

"My Parents Have Come Home Laughing" (Jarman), **Supp. XVII:** 113

"My Passion for Ferries" (Whitman), **IV:** 350

"My People" (Hughes), **Retro. Supp. I:** 197; **Supp. I Part 1:** 321–322, 323

"My Philosophy" (Allen), **Supp. XV:** 15

"My Playmate" (Whittier), **Supp. I Part 2:** 699–700

"My Priests" (Monette), **Supp. X:** 159

"My Public" (Rinehart), **Supp. XXV:** 201

Myra Breckinridge (Vidal), **Supp. IV Part 2:** 677, 685–686, 689, 691

"My Race" (H. Johnson), **Supp. XXVI:** 163

"My Raptor" (A. Finch), **Supp. XVII:** 72

"My Recollections of S. B. Fairchild" (Jackson), **Supp. IX:** 118–119

"My Religion" (Carson), **Supp. XII: 105–106**

Myrer, Anton, **Supp. XXV:** 145

"My Road to Hell Was Paved" (Patchett), **Supp. XII:** 310–311

Myron (Vidal), **Supp. IV Part 2:** 677, 685, 686, 691

"My Roomy" (Lardner), **II:** 420, 421, 428, 430

"My Sad Self" (Ginsberg), **Supp. II Part 1:** 320

My San Francisco (Atherton), **Supp. XXIV:** 27

My Secret History (Theroux), **Supp. VIII:** 310, 324

"Myself" (Audubon), **Supp. XVI:** 1–2, 5, 12

Myself Painting (Major), **Supp. XXII: 184–185**

"My Shoes" (Simic), **Supp. VIII:** 275

"My Side of the Matter" (Capote), **Supp. III Part 1:** 114, 115

My Silk Purse and Yours: The Publishing Scene and American Literary Art (Garrett), **Supp. VII:** 111; **Supp. X:** 7

My Sister Eileen (McKenney), **IV:** 288; **Retro. Supp. II:** 321

My Sister's Hand in Mine: The Collected Works of Jane Bowles, **Supp. IV Part 1:** 82–83

"My Son" (Strand), **Supp. IV Part 2:** 629

My Son, John (film), **Supp. I Part 1:** 67

"My Son, the Murderer" (Malamud), **Supp. I Part 2:** 437

My Son Is a Splendid Driver (Inge), **Supp. XXV:** 93, 95, 107

"My Son the Man" (Olds), **Supp. X:** 212

"My Speech to the Graduates" (Allen), **Supp. XV:** 16

"Mysteries of Caesar, The" (Hecht), **Supp. X:** 73

"Mysteries of Eleusis, The" (Hardwick), **Supp. III Part 1:** 195

Mysteries of Paris, The (Sue), **Supp. XXIII:** 182

Mysteries of Pittsburgh, The (Chabon), **Supp. XI:** 65, 68, **69–71; Supp. XIX:** 135

Mysteries of Small Houses (Notley), **Supp. XXII:** 223, 224, 226, 234–235

"Mysterious Case of R, The" (Conroy), **Supp. XVI:** 72

Mysterious Stranger, The (Twain), **IV:** 190–191, 210

Mystery, A (Shields). *See Swann* (Shields)

"Mystery, The" (Dunbar), **Supp. II Part 1:** 199, 210

"Mystery, The" (Glück), **Supp. V:** 91

Mystery and Manners (O'Connor), **Retro. Supp. II:** 230

"'Mystery Boy' Looks for Kin in Nashville" (Hayden), **Supp. II Part 1:** 366, 372

"Mystery of Coincidence, The" (Conroy), **Supp. XVI:** 74

"Mystery of Heroism, A" (Crane), **I:** 414

"Mystery of Marie Rogêt, The" (Poe), **III:** 413, 419; **Retro. Supp. II:** 271

"Mystic" (Plath), **Retro. Supp. II:** 257; **Supp. I Part 2:** 539, 541

"Mystical Poet, A" (Bogan), **Retro. Supp. I:** 36

"Mystic of Sex, The—A First Look at D. H. Lawrence" (Nin), **Supp. X:** 188

"Mystic Vision in 'The Marshes of Glynn' " (Warfel), **Supp. I Part 1:** 366, 373

"Mystification" (Poe), **III:** 425

"My Strange New Poetry" (Halliday), **Supp. XIX:** 88, 94

My Study Windows (Lowell), **Supp. I Part 2:** 407

"My Teacher" (Conroy), **Supp. XVI:** 75

"Myth" (Rukeyser), **Supp. VI:** 281–282

"Myth" (Trethewey), **Supp. XXI:** 245, 255, 256

"Myth"(Hadas), **Supp. XXIII:** 119

"Mythmaker" (Trethewey), **Supp. XXI:** 243

Myth of American Manhood, The (Kriegel, ed.), **Supp. XXIV:** 214

Myth of Sisyphus, The (Camus), **I:** 294; **Supp. XIII:** 165

"Myth of the Happy Worker, The" (Swados), **Supp. XIX:** 265

"Myth of the Isolated Artist, The" (Oates), **Supp. II Part 2:** 520

Myth of the Machine, The (Mumford), **Supp. II Part 2:** 476, 478, 482, 483, 493, 497

"Myth of the Powerful Worker, The" (Swados), **Supp. XIX:** 265

Mythology and the Romantic Tradition in English Poetry (Bush), **Supp. I Part 1:** 268

Myths and Texts (Snyder), **Supp. VIII: 295–296**

"Myths of Bears, The" (Bass), **Supp. XVI:** 19, 20

My Tocaya (Cisneros), **Supp. VII:** 69

My Uncle Dudley (Morris), **I:** 305; **III:** 219–220

"My Uncle's Favorite Coffee Shop" (Nye), **Supp. XIII:** 283

"My Unopened Life" (Gallagher), **Supp. XXIV:** 171

"My Weariness of Epic Proportions" (Simic), **Supp. VIII:** 276

My Wicked Wicked Ways (Cisneros), **Supp. VII:** 58, 64–68, 71

"My Wicked Wicked Ways" (Cisneros), **Supp. VII:** 58, 64–66

My Wisdom (Thompson), **Supp. XXIII: 291–293**

"My Word-house" (Mora), **Supp. XIII:** 219, 225

My Works and Days (Mumford), **Supp. II Part 2:** 475, 477, 481

"My World and My Critics" (Stratton-Porter), **Supp. XX: 220**

My World and Welcome to It (Thurber), **Supp. I Part 2:** 610

N

Nabokov, Peter, **Supp. IV Part 2:** 490

Nabokov, Véra, **Retro. Supp. I:** 266, 270

Nabokov, Vladimir, **I:** 135; **III: 244–266,** 283, 286; **Retro. Supp. I: 263–281,** 317, 335; **Supp. I Part 1:** 196; **Supp. II Part 1:** 2; **Supp. IV Part 1:** 135; **Supp. IX:** 152, 212, 261; **Supp. V:** 127, 237, 251, 252, 253; **Supp. VIII:** 105, 133, 138; **Supp. X:** 283; **Supp. XI:** 66; **Supp. XII:** 310; **Supp. XIII:** 46, 52; **Supp. XVI:** 148, 294; **Supp. XVIII:** 98, 102; **Supp. XXII:** 263; **Supp. XXIV:** 133

Nabokov's Dozen (Nabokov), **Retro. Supp. I:** 266

Nabokov's Garden: A Guide to Ada (Mason), **Supp. VIII:** 138

Naca, Kristin, **Supp. XIII:** 133

Nadeau, Robert, **Supp. X:** 261, 270

Nadel, Alan, **Supp. IV Part 1:** 209

Naimy, Mikhail, **Supp. XX: 116, 119, 120**

Naipaul, V. S., **Supp. IV Part 1:** 297; **Supp. VIII:** 314; **Supp. X:** 131; **Supp. XIV:** 111; **Supp. XX: 87; Supp. XXI:** 170; **Supp. XXII:** 240, 241, 242, 246, 253

Naison, Mark, **Supp. XVIII:** 231

Naked and the Dead, The (Mailer), **I:** 477; **III:** 26, 27, 28–30, 31, 33, 35, 36, 44; **Retro. Supp. II: 197–199; Supp. IV Part 1:** 381; **Supp. XI:** 218; **Supp. XIX:** 248; **Supp. XX:** 248; **Supp. XXI:** 277

Naked Author (di Donato), **Supp. XX:** 45

Naked Babies (Quindlen and Kelsh), **Supp. XVII:** 167, 179

Naked in Garden Hills (Crews), **Supp. XI:** 102, **110**

Naked Lunch (Burroughs), **Supp. III Part 1:** 92–95, 97–105; **Supp. IV Part 1:** 90

"Naked Nude" (Malamud), **Supp. I Part 2:** 450

Naked on Roller Skates (Bodenheim), **Supp. XXV:** 27

Naked Poetry (Berg and Mezey, eds.), **Supp. IV Part 1:** 60

Naked Poetry (Levine), **Supp. V:** 180

Naked Revenge (film), **Supp. XVII:** 141

Nall, Gus, **Supp. XXII:** 172, 184

Namedropping: Mostly Literary Memoirs (Coover), **Supp. V:** 40

"Name in the Papers" (Hughes), **Supp. I Part 1:** 330

Name Is Archer, The (Macdonald, under Millar), **Supp. IV Part 2:** 466

"Name Is Burroughs, The" (Burroughs), **Supp. III Part 1:** 93

Name Is Fogarty, The: Private Papers on Public Matters (Farrell), **II:** 49

"Names" (Carruth), **Supp. XVI:** 54, 56

"Names, The" (Collins), **Supp. XXI:** 54, 61–62

Names, The (DeLillo), **Supp. VI:** 3, 10, 13, 14

Names, The (Momaday), **Supp. IV Part 2:** 479, 480, 483, 486, 487, 488, 489

Namesake, The (Lahiri), **Supp. XXI:** 176, 184, **186–188**

Names and Faces of Heroes, The (Price), **Supp. VI:** 258, 260

Names of the Dead, The (O'Nan), **Supp. XXV:** 142, 143–144, 149, 151

Names of the Lost, The (Levine), **Supp. V:** 177–178, 179, 187–188

"Naming for Love" (Carruth), **Supp. XVI:** 48

"Naming Myself" (Kingsolver), **Supp. VII:** 208

"Naming of Names, The" (Sanders), **Supp. XVI:** 268

Naming of the Beasts, The (Stern). *See Rejoicings: Selected Poems, 1966–1972* (Stern)

Naming the Unseen (Ray), **Supp. XVIII:** 192, **193–195**

"Naming the Unseen" (Ray), **Supp. XVIII:** 203

Nana (Zola), **III:** 321

Nance, Kevin, **Supp. XXVI:** 58

"Nancy Culpepper" (Mason), **Supp. VIII:** 141

Nancy Drew stories, **Supp. VIII:** 133, 135, 137, 142

"Nancy Knapp" (Masters), **Supp. I Part 2:** 461

"Naola Beauty Academy, New Orleans, 1943" (Trethewey), **Supp. XXI:** 246

"Naomi Counting Time"(Thompson), **Supp. XXIII:** 293

"Naomi Shihab Nye: U.S. Mideast-History a Harbinger of 9-11?" (Nye), **Supp. XIII:** 286

"Naomi Trimmer" (X. J. Kennedy), **Supp. XV:** 170

"Nap, The" (Banks), **Supp. V:** 7

"Napoleon" (Emerson), **II:** 6

Napoleon I, **I:** 6, 7, 8, 474; **II:** 5, 309, 315, 321, 523; **Supp. I Part 1:** 153; **Supp. I Part 2:** 518, 519

Napolitano, Louise, **Supp. XX: 35, 45, 46–47**

Narcissa and Other Fables (Auchincloss), **Supp. IV Part 1:** 21, 34

"Narcissus as Narcissus" (Tate), **IV:** 124

"Narcissus Leaves the Pool" (Epstein), **Supp. XIV:** 110

Narcissus Leaves the Pool: Familiar Essays (Epstein), **Supp. XIV:** 110

Nardal, Paulette, **Supp. X:** 139

Nardi, Marcia, **Retro. Supp. I:** 426, 427

"Narragansett Boulevard" (Halliday), **Supp. XIX:** 91

Narration (Stein), **IV:** 27, 30, 32, 33, 36

Narrative of a Four Months' Residence among the Natives of a Valley of the Marquesas Islands (Melville), **III:** 76

Narrative of Arthur Gordon Pym, The (Poe), **III:** 412, 416; **Retro. Supp. II:** 265, **273–275; Supp. XI:** 293

"Narrative of Arthur Gordon Pym, The" (Poe), **Supp. XXII:** 58

Narrative of the Life of Frederick Douglass, an American Slave, Written by Himself (Douglass), **Supp. III Part 1:** 154–159, 162, 165; **Supp. IV Part 1:** 13; **Supp. VIII:** 202

"Narrativity Scenes" (Wright), **Supp. XV:** 345

Narrenschiff, Das (Brant), **III:** 447

"Narrow Fellow in the Grass, A" (Dickinson), **Retro. Supp. I:** 30, 37

Narrow Heart, A: Portrait of a Woman (Gordon), **II:** 197, 217

Narrow Rooms (Purdy), **Supp. VII:** 274

Narrows, The (Connelly), **Supp. XXI:** 71, **76**

Nasby, Petroleum, **Supp. XVIII:** 1

Nash, Noreen, **Supp. XXII:** 256

Nash, Ogden, **Supp. XXI:** 51; **Supp. XXIV:** 45

Nash, Roderick, **Supp. IX:** 185; **Supp. XIV:** 191–192

Nash, Susan Smith, **Supp. XVI:** 274

Nash, Thomas, **Supp. III Part 1:** 387–388

Nashe, Thomas, **I:** 358; **Supp. XVII:** 232

Nashville (film), **Supp. IX:** 143

"Nashville Gone to Ashes" (Hempel), **Supp. XXI:** 115, 118, **120–121**

Nashville Skyline (album, Dylan), **Supp. XVIII:** 27

Nason, Elias, **Supp. XV:** 242

Nasser, Gamal Abdel, **IV:** 490

Nasty Bits (Silver), **Supp. XXIV:** 265

Natalie Mann (Toomer), **Supp. III Part 2:** 484–486

Nathan, George Jean, **II:** 91; **III:** 103, 104, 106, 107; **IV:** 432; **Supp. IV Part 1:** 343; **Supp. IX:** 56–57; **Supp. XIII:** 161; **Supp. XXII:** 23

"Nathanael West" (Herbst), **Retro. Supp. II:** 325

Nathanael West: The Art of His Life (Martin), **Retro. Supp. II:** 325
Nathan Coulter (Berry), **Supp. X:** 24, 33
National Dream, The: Building the Impossible Railway (Findley and Whitehead), **Supp. XX: 51**
"Nationalist, The" (Anderson), **I:** 115
"Nation Is Like Ourselves, The" (Baraka), **Supp. II Part 1:** 53
"Native, The" (Olds), **Supp. X:** 215
"Native American Attitudes to the Environment" (Momaday), **Supp. IV Part 2:** 481, 491
Native American Renaissance (Lincoln), **Supp. IV Part 2:** 507
Native American Testimony (Nabokov, ed.), **Supp. IV Part 2:** 490
"Native Blessing" (Ray), **Supp. XVIII:** 202
Native Guard (Trethewey), **Supp. XXI:** 243, 244, 247, **254–257**
"Native Guard" (Trethewey), **Supp. XXI:** 256
"Native Hill, A" (Berry), **Supp. X:** 21
Native in a Strange Land: Trials & Tremors (Coleman), **Supp. XI: 84–85,** 87
Native of Winby and Other Tales, A (Jewett), **II:** 396; **Retro. Supp. II:** 138
"Natives Don't Cry" (Boyle), **Supp. XXIV:** 57–58
Native Son (Wright), **IV:** 476, 477, 478, 479, 481, 482–484, 485, 487, 488, 491, 495; **Retro. Supp. II:** 107, 116; **Supp. I Part 1:** 51, 64, 67, 337; **Supp. II Part 1:** 170, 235–236; **Supp. IX:** 306; **Supp. XIV:** 73; **Supp. XVII:** 155; **Supp. XVIII:** 283, 286; **Supp. XXI:** 169
"Native Trees" (Merwin), **Supp. III Part 1:** 355
Natorp, Paul, **Supp. XIV:** 198
Natural, The (Malamud), **II:** 424, 425; **Retro. Supp. II:** 288; **Supp. I Part 2:** 438–441, 443; **Supp. XXVI:** 180
"*Natural, The:* Malamud's World Ceres" (Wasserman), **Supp. I Part 2:** 439
Natural Affection (Inge), **Supp. XXV:** 95, 103, 104–105, 106
"Natural History" (Olds), **Supp. X:** 210
"Natural History Note" (Hay), **Supp. XIV:** 124, 130
"Natural History of Some Poems, A" (Harrison), **Supp. VIII:** 53
"Natural History of the Dead" (Hemingway), **II:** 206; **Retro. Supp. I:** 176
Natural Laws of Good Luck, The (Graf), **Supp. XXVI:** 46
"Naturally Superior School, A" (Knowles), **Supp. XII:** 235, 240–241
"Natural Method of Mental Philosophy" (Emerson), **II:** 14
"Natural Resources" (Rich), **Supp. I Part 2:** 575
Natural Selection (F. Barthelme), **Supp. XI:** 2, 28, 32, 33
Nature (Emerson), **I:** 463; **II:** 1, 8, 12, 16; **IV:** 171, 172–173; **Supp. XXIV:** 75, 79; **Supp. XXV:** 241

"Nature" (Emerson), **Retro. Supp. I:** 250; **Supp. I Part 2:** 383; **Supp. III Part 1:** 387; **Supp. IX:** 178
"Nature" (Very), **Supp. XXV:** 242
"Nature, Inc." (Lewis), **II:** 441
Nature and Destiny of Man, The (Niebuhr), **III:** 292, 303–306, 310
"Nature and Life" (Emerson), **II:** 19
"Nature and New America Painting" (O'Hara), **Supp. XXIII:** 212
"Nature and Nurture: When It Comes to Twins, Sometimes It's Hard to Tell the Two Apart" (Bausch), **Supp. VII:** 40
Nature and Purpose of the Universe, The (Durang), **Supp. XXIV: 115–116**
"Nature-Metaphors" (Lanier), **Supp. I Part 1:** 352
Nature Morte (Brodsky), **Supp. VIII:** 25
Nature of Evil, The (James), **II:** 343
Nature of Generosity, The (Kittredge), **Supp. XXVI:** 186, 187–188, 189
Nature of Peace, The (Veblen), **Supp. I Part 2:** 642
Nature of Things, The (Lucretius; Stallings, trans.), **Supp. XXV:** 221, 226–227
Nature of Things, The (television show), **Supp. XX: 51**
Nature of True Virtue, The (Edwards), **I:** 549, 557–558, 559
Nature of Yearning, The (Huddle), **Supp. XXVI:** 149–150
Nature: Poems Old and New (Swenson), **Supp. IV Part 2:** 652
Nature's Economy: A History of Ecological Ideas (Worster), **Supp. IX:** 19
Nature's Way (Wouk), **Supp. XXV:** 253
Naumburg, Margaret, **Supp. XX: 68, 74–75**
Nausea (Sartre), **Supp. VIII:** 7
"Navajo Blanket, A" (Swenson), **Supp. IV Part 2:** 649
Navarette, Don Martín de, **II:** 310
Navarro, Ramon, **Supp. IV Part 1:** 206
Navigator, The (film), **I:** 31
Navratilova, Martina, **Supp. XX: 264**
Naylor, Gloria, **Supp. VIII: 213–230; Supp. XX: 108**
Naylor, Paul Kenneth, **Supp. IV Part 2:** 420
Nazarene, The (Asch), **Supp. XXIII:** 2, 3, 4, 6, 9, **12–13,** 14, 15, 16
Nazarene, The: or, The Last of the Washingtons (Lippard), **Supp. XXIII:** 183, 184, 187, 190
Nazimova, **III:** 399
Neal, Darlin', **Supp. XXI:** 41
Neal, Larry, **Retro. Supp. II:** 112, 128; **Supp. X:** 324, 328
Neal, Lawrence P., **Supp. II Part 1:** 53
Neal, Patricia, **Supp. I Part 1:** 286; **Supp. IV Part 2:** 524; **Supp. V:** 223
Neale, Walter, **I:** 192, 208
"Near Damascus" (Di Piero), **Supp. XIX:** 43
Nearer the Moon: From "A Journal of Love," the Unexpurgated Diary of Anaïs Nin, 1937–1939, **Supp. X:** 184, 185

Nearing, Helen and Scott, **Supp. XXVI:** 35
Near-Johannesburg Boy and Other Poems, The (Brooks), **Supp. III Part 1:** 86
Near Klamath (Carver), **Supp. III Part 1:** 137
"Near Perigord" (Pound), **Retro. Supp. I:** 289, 290
"Near Spring" (Pickering), **Supp. XXI:** 198
Near the Ocean (Lowell), **II:** 543, 550, 551–553, 554, 555; **Retro. Supp. II:** 182, 186, 189–190
"Near View of the High Sierra, A" (Muir), **Supp. IX:** 183
Nebeker, Helen, **Supp. IX:** 122
"Nebraska Blizzard" (F. Wright), **Supp. XVII:** 247
Necessary Angel, The (Stevens), **IV:** 76, 79, 89, 90
Necessities of Life: Poems, 1962–1965 (Rich), **Supp. I Part 2:** 553, 555
"Necessity of Blacks' Writing Fiction About the South, The" (Andrews), **Supp. XXVI:** 1, 13
"Necessity of Lemons, The" (Schott), **Supp. XXIII:** 247, 248
Nechayev, Sergey, **Supp. XXI:** 164
Neck Deep and Other Predicaments (Monson), **Supp. XXIV:** 230, **234–236,** 241
"Necrological" (Ransom), **III:** 486–489, 490, 492
Ned Christie's War (Conley), **Supp. V:** 232
"Need for a Cultural Base to Civil Rites & Bpower Mooments, The" (Baraka), **Supp. II Part 1:** 48
"Need for Christian Preaching, The" (Buechner), **Supp. XII:** 49
Needful Things (King), **Supp. V:** 139, 146
"Needle" (Simic), **Supp. VIII:** 275
"Needle Trade" (Reznikoff), **Supp. XIV:** 277, 289
"Need of Being Versed in Country Things, The" (Frost), **II:** 154; **Retro. Supp. I:** 133, 135
"Need to Say It, The" (Hampl), **Supp. XXII:** 94
Neel, Philippe, **Supp. XIV:** 338
Neelakantappa, Tara, **Supp. XV:** 104–105
Neeley, Barbara, **Supp. XVI:** 143
"Negative Capability" (Komunyakaa), **Supp. XIII:** 131
Negligible Tales (Bierce), **I:** 209
"Negotiating the Darkness, Fortified by Poets' Strength" (Karr), **Supp. XI:** 254; **Supp. XIII:** 285
Negotiating with the Dead (Atwood), **Supp. XIII:** 20, 35
Negritude movement, **Supp. X:** 131, 139
"Negro" (Hughes), **Supp. I Part 1:** 321–322
Negro, The (Du Bois), **Supp. II Part 1:** 178, 179, 185
Negro, The: The Southerner's Problem (Page), **Supp. II Part 1:** 168
Negro and His Music, The (Locke), **Supp. XIV:** 202

"Negro-Art Hokum, The" (Schuyler), **Supp. XXVI:** 167

"Negro Artisan, The" (Du Bois), **Supp. II Part 1:** 166

"Negro Artist and the Racial Mountain, The" (Hughes), **Retro. Supp. I:** 200, 207; **Supp. I Part 1:** 323, 325; **Supp. IV Part 1:** 169

Negro Art: Past and Present (Locke), **Supp. XIV:** 202

"Negro Assays the Negro Mood, A" (Baldwin), **Supp. I Part 1:** 52

"Negro Citizen, The" (Du Bois), **Supp. II Part 1:** 179

"Negro Dancers" (Hughes), **Retro. Supp. I:** 199; **Supp. I Part 1:** 324

"Negroes" (Bodenheim), **Supp. XXV:** 22

Negroes in America, The (McKay), **Supp. X:** 132, 136

"Negroes of Farmville, Virginia, The: A Social Study" (Du Bois), **Supp. II Part 1:** 166

Negro Family, The: The Case for National Action (Moynihan), **Retro. Supp. II:** 123

"Negro Farmer, The" (Du Bois), **Supp. II Part 1:** 167

"Negro Fight, The" (column, C. L. R. James), **Supp. XXI:** 169

"Negro Ghetto" (Hughes), **Supp. I Part 1:** 331

Negro in America, The (Locke), **Supp. XIV:** 208

Negro in American Civilization, The (Du Bois), **Supp. II Part 1:** 179

Negro in American Culture, The (Locke and Butcher), **Supp. XIV:** 202–203

Negro in Art, The: A Pictorial Record of the Negro Artist and of the Negro Theme in Art (Locke), **Supp. XIV:** 202

"Negro in Large Cities, The" (Du Bois), **Supp. II Part 1:** 169

"Negro in Literature and Art, The" (Du Bois), **Supp. II Part 1:** 174

Negro in New York, The (Ellison), **Supp. II Part 1:** 230

"Negro in the Black Belt, The: Some Social Sketches" (Du Bois), **Supp. II Part 1:** 166

Negro in the Caribbean, The (Williams), **Supp. XXI:** 166

"Negro in the Three Americas, The" (Locke), **Supp. XIV:** 211

"Negro in the Well, The" (Caldwell), **I:** 309

"Negro Love Song, A" (Dunbar), **Supp. II Part 1:** 204

"Negro Martyrs Are Needed" (C. Himes), **Supp. XVI:** 138

Negro Mother, The (Hughes), **Supp. I Part 1:** 328

Negro Mother and Other Dramatic Recitations, The (Hughes), **Retro. Supp. I:** 203

Negro Novel in America, The (Bone), **Supp. IX:** 318–319; **Supp. XVIII:** 285

Negro Publication Society of America, **Retro. Supp. I:** 205

"Negro Renaissance, The: Jean Toomer and the Harlem of the 1920s" (Bontemps), **Supp. IX:** 306

"Negro Schoolmaster in the New South, A" (Du Bois), **Supp. II Part 1:** 168

"Negro's Contribution to American Culture, The" (Locke), **Supp. XIV:** 210, 211

"Negro Sermon, A: Simon Legree" (Lindsay), **Supp. I Part 2:** 393

"Negro Sings of Rivers, The" (Hughes), **Supp. IV Part 1:** 16

"Negro Speaks of Rivers, The" (Hughes), **Retro. Supp. I:** 199; **Supp. I Part 1:** 321

"Negro Spirituals, The (Locke), **Supp. XIV:** 201

"Negro Takes Stock, The" (Du Bois), **Supp. II Part 1:** 180

"Negro Theatre, The" (Van Vechten), **Supp. II Part 2:** 735

"Negro Voter Sizes Up Taft, A" (Hurston), **Supp. VI:** 160

"Negro Writer and His Roots, The: Toward a New Romanticism" (Hansberry), **Supp. IV Part 1:** 364

"Negro Youth Speaks" (Locke), **Supp. XIV:** 201

"Nehemias Americanus" (Mather), **Supp. II Part 2:** 453

Nehru, Jawaharlal, **IV:** 490

"Neighbor" (Hugo), **Supp. VI:** 135–136

"Neighborhood Drunk"(Dybek), **Supp. XXIII:** 71

"Neighbors" (Carver), **Supp. III Part 1:** 135, 139, 141; **Supp. XI:** 153

"Neighbors" (Hogan), **Supp. IV Part 1:** 405

"Neighbors, The" (Hay), **Supp. XIV:** 126

"Neighbour Rosicky" (Cather), **I:** 331–332

Neil Simon (R. K. Johnson), **Supp. IV Part 2:** 573

"Neil Simon's Jewish-Style Comedies" (Walden), **Supp. IV Part 2:** 584, 591

"Neil Simon: Toward Act III?" (Walden), **Supp. IV Part 2:** 591

Neilson, Heather, **Supp. IV Part 2:** 681

Neiman, Gilbert, **Supp. XV:** 140

"Neither Out Far Nor In Deep" (Frost), **I:** 303; **Retro. Supp. I:** 121, 138

"Nellie Clark" (Masters), **Supp. I Part 2:** 461

Nelson, Alice Dunbar, **Supp. XVII:** 75

Nelson, Cary, **Supp. XVIII:** 226, 227, 230, 231; **Supp. XXII:** 271

Nelson, Ernest, **I:** 388

Nelson, Howard, **Supp. IV Part 1:** 66, 68; **Supp. XIX:** 3; **Supp. XXI:** 95

Nelson, Lord Horatio, **II:** 524

Nelson, Lynn (pseudonym). *See* Nelson, Marilyn

Nelson, Marilyn, **Supp. XVII:** 74, 112; **Supp. XVIII: 171–188**

Nelson, Shirley, **Supp. XII:** 293

Nelson, Steve, **Supp. XVIII:** 226

Nelson Algren (Cox and Chatterton), **Supp. IX:** 11–12

Nelson Algren: A Life on the Wild Side (Drew), **Supp. IX:** 2

Nemerov, David, **II:** 268

Nemerov, Howard, **III: 267–289; IV:** 137, 140; **Supp. III Part 2:** 541; **Supp. IV Part 2:** 455, 650; **Supp. IX:** 114

"Nemesis" (Lovecraft), **Supp. XXV:** 119

Nemesis (P. Roth), **Supp. XXIV:** 214

Nemiroff, Robert Barron, **Supp. IV Part 1:** 360, 361, 365, 369, 370, 374

Neoconservative Criticism: Norman Podhoretz, Kenneth S. Lynn, and Joseph Epstein (Winchell), **Supp. VIII:** 241; **Supp. XIV:** 103

"Neo-Formalism: A Dangerous Nostalgia" (Sadoff), **Supp. XXI:** 100

"Neo-Hoodoo Manifesto, The" (Reed), **Supp. X:** 242

Neon Bible, The (Toole), **Supp. XXVI:** 239, 241, 242, 246–250, 253

Neon Rain, The (Burke), **Supp. XIV:** 22, 24, 26–27, 28–29, 30

Neon Vernacular (Komunyakaa), **Supp. XIII:** 121, **127–128,** 131

Neon Wilderness, The (Algren), **Supp. IX:** 3, 4

Neo-Slave Narratives (Rushdy), **Supp. X:** 250

Nepantla: Essays from the Land in the Middle (Mora), **Supp. XIII:** 213, **219–221,** 227

Nephew, The (Purdy), **Supp. VII:** 271, 273, 282

"Nereids of Seriphos, The" (Clampitt), **Supp. IX:** 41

Nericcio, William, **Supp. XIV:** 304–305

Neruda, Pablo, **Supp. I Part 1:** 89; **Supp. IV Part 2:** 537; **Supp. IX:** 157, 271; **Supp. V:** 332; **Supp. VIII:** 272, 274; **Supp. X:** 112; **Supp. XI:** 191; **Supp. XII:** 217; **Supp. XIII:** 114, 315, 323; **Supp. XXI:** 61, 100; **Supp. XXIV:** 170

"Nerves" (Huddle), **Supp. XXVI:** 149

Nesbit, Edith, **Supp. VIII:** 171

Nesbit, Lynn, **Supp. XXIII:** 100

Nesbitt, Robin, **Supp. VIII:** 89

Nessmuk (George Washington Sears), **Supp. XIX:** 10

Nesting Ground, The (Wagoner), **Supp. IX:** 324, **325–326**

Nest of Ninnies, A (Ashbery and Schuyler), **Supp. III Part 1:** 3; **Supp. XV:** 178

"Nests"(Le Sueur), **Supp. XXIII:** 165

Net of Cobwebs (Holding), **Supp. XXII:** 126, **129–130,** 134

Net of Magic: Wonders and Deceptions in India (Siegel), **Supp. XXII:** 262

Nets to Catch the Wind (Wylie), **Supp. I Part 2:** 709, 710–712, 714

Nettleton, Asahel, **I:** 458

"Net to Snare the Moonlight, A" (Lindsay), **Supp. I Part 2:** 387

Neubauer, Carol E., **Supp. IV Part 1:** 9

Neugeboren, Jacob Mordecai. *See* Neugeboren, Jay

Neugeboren, Jay, **Supp. XVI: 217–231**

Neugroschel, Joachim, **Supp. IX:** 138

Neuhaus, Richard John, **Supp. VIII:** 245; **Supp. XIX:** 144

Neumann, Erich, **Supp. I Part 2:** 567; **Supp. IV Part 1:** 68, 69

Neuromancer (W. Gibson), **Supp. XII:** 15; **Supp. XVI:** 117, 119–120, 122, 124, **125–126,** 127, 129, 131

Neurotica: Jewish Writers on Sex (Bukiet, ed.), **Supp. XVII:** 48

"Neurotic America and the Sex Impulse" (Dreiser), **Retro. Supp. II:** 105

Neutra, Richard, **Supp. XVI:** 192

"Never Been" (Huddle), **Supp. XXVI:** 150

"Never Bet the Devil Your Head" (Poe), **III:** 425; **Retro. Supp. II:** 273

Never Come Morning (Algren), **Supp. IX:** 3, **7–9**

Never in a Hurry: Essays on People and Places (Nye), **Supp. XIII:** 273, **280–282,** 286

"Never Marry a Mexican" (Cisneros), **Supp. VII:** 70

"Never Room with a Couple" (Hughes), **Supp. I Part 1:** 330

"Nevertheless" (Moore), **III:** 214

Nevils, René Pol, **Supp. XXVI:** 241, 242, 246

Nevins, Allan, **I:** 253; **Supp. I Part 2:** 486, 493

"Nevsky Prospekt" (Olds), **Supp. X:** 205

New Adam, The (Untermeyer), **Supp. XV:** 304, 305

New Addresses (Koch), **Supp. XV:** 177, 184

"New Age of the Rhetoricians, The" (Cowley), **Supp. II Part 1:** 135

New American Cyclopedia, **Supp. XVIII:** 4

New American Literature, The (Pattee), **II:** 456

New American Novel of Manners, The (Klinkowitz), **Supp. XI:** 347

"New American Ode, The" (Wright), **Supp. XV:** 346

New American Poetry (Allen, ed.), **Supp. XXVI:** 223

New American Poetry, 1945–1960, The (Allen, ed.), **Supp. VIII:** 291, 292; **Supp. XIII:** 112; **Supp. XXIII:** 215–216

"New American Writer, A" (W. C. Williams), **Retro. Supp. II:** 335

New and Collected Poems (Reed), **Supp. X:** 241

New and Collected Poems (Wilbur), **Supp. III Part 2:** 562–564

New and Selected Poems (Nemerov), **III:** 269, 275, 277–279

New and Selected Poems (Oliver), **Supp. VII:** 240–241, 245

New and Selected Poems (W. J. Smith), **Supp. XIII:** 332

New and Selected Poems (Wagoner), **Supp. IX:** **326–327**

New and Selected Poems, 1958–1998 (Sorrentino), **Supp. XXI:** 229

New and Selected Poems: 1974–1994 (Dunn), **Supp. XI:** **151–152**

New and Selected Things Taking Place (Swenson), **Supp. IV Part 2:** 648–650, 651

"New Aristocracy, The" (Atherton), **Supp. XXIV:** 24

"New Art Gallery Society, The" (Wolfe), **Supp. III Part 2:** 580

Newberger, Julee, **Supp. XVIII:** 168

"New Birth, The" (Very), **Supp. XXV:** 246, 247, 248

New Black Poetry, The (Major, ed.), **Supp. XXII:** 172, 174, 176, 180

"New Capitalist Tool, The" (Wasserstein), **Supp. XV:** 328

New Collected Poems (Oppen), **Supp. XXVI:** 224

Newcomb, Ralph, **Supp. XIII:** 12

Newcomb, Robert, **II:** 111

New Conscience and an Ancient Evil, A (Addams), **Supp. I Part 1:** 14–15, 16

"New Conservatism in American Poetry, The" (Wakoski), **Supp. XVII:** 112

"New Conservatives, The: Intellectuals in Retreat" (Epstein), **Supp. XIV:** 103

New Critical Essays on H. P. Lovecraft (Simmons, ed.), **Supp. XXV:** 123

New Criticism, The (Ransom), **III:** 497–498, 499, 501

"New Day, A" (Levine), **Supp. V:** 182

Newdick, Robert Spangler, **Retro. Supp. I:** 138

Newdick's Season of Frost (Newdick), **Retro. Supp. I:** 138

New Dictionary of Quotations, A (Mencken), **III:** 111

New Directions Anthology in Prose and Poetry (Laughlin, ed.), **Supp. XVI:** 284

"New Directions in Poetry" (D. Locke), **Supp. IX:** 273

"New Dog, The: Variations on a Text by Jules Laforgue" (C. Frost), **Supp. XV:** 98

Newell, Henry, **IV:** 193

"New England" (Lowell), **II:** 536

"New England" (Robinson), **III:** 510, 524

"New England Bachelor, A" (Eberhart), **I:** 539

"New Englander, The" (Anderson), **I:** 114

New England Girlhood, A (Larcom), **Supp. XIII:** 137, 142, 143, 144, **147–154**

New England Gothic Literature (Ringel), **Supp. XXII:** 205

New England: Indian Summer (Brooks), **I:** 253, 256

New England Local Color Literature (Donovan), **Retro. Supp. II:** 138

"New England Sabbath-Day Chace, The" (Freneau), **Supp. II Part 1:** 273

New-England Tale, A (Sedgwick), **I:** 341

New England Tragedies, The (Longfellow), **II:** 490, 505, 506; **Retro. Supp. II:** 165, 167

New English Canaan (Morton), **Supp. XXII:** 45

New Era in American Poetry, The (Untermeyer, ed.), **Supp. XV:** 301, 303, 306

Newer Ideals of Peace (Addams), **Supp. I Part 1:** 11–12, 15, 16–17, 19, 20–21

"New Experience in Millinery, A" (Stratton-Porter), **Supp. XX: 216**

New Feminist Criticism, The: Essays on Women, Literature, and Theory (Showalter), **Supp. X:** 97

New Fire: To Put Things Right Again (Moraga), **Supp. XXIII:** 197

"New Folsom Prison" (Matthews), **Supp. IX:** 165

New Formalism, The: A Critical Introduction (McPhillips), **Supp. XV:** 250, 251, 252, 264

Newfound (J. W. Miller), **Supp. XX: 163, 166, 170–172**

New Found Land: Fourteen Poems (MacLeish), **III:** 12–13

"New Hampshire" (Frost), **Supp. XXVI:** 78

"New Hampshire, February" (Eberhart), **I:** 536

New Hampshire: A Poem with Notes and Grace Notes (Frost), **II:** 154–155; **Retro. Supp. I:** 132, 133, 135

New Hard-Boiled Writers (Panek), **Supp. XIV:** 27

"New Home" (Richter), **Supp. XVIII:** 209

Newhouse, Seth, **Supp. XXVI:** 87, 89, 90

New Industrial State, The (Galbraith), **Supp. I Part 2:** 648

"New Journalism, The" (Wolfe), **Supp. III Part 2:** 571

New Journalism, The (Wolfe and E. W. Johnson, eds.), **Supp. III Part 2:** 570, 579–581, 583, 586; **Supp. XXIV:** 282

New Left, The: The Anti-Industrial Revolution (Rand), **Supp. IV Part 2:** 527

"New Letters from Thomas Jefferson" (Stafford), **Supp. XI:** 324

New Letters on the Air: Contemporary Writers on Radio, **Supp. X:** 165, 169, 173

"New Life" (Glück), **Supp. V:** 90

New Life, A (Malamud), **Supp. I Part 2:** 429–466

"New Life, The" (Bynner), **Supp. XV:** 44

"New Life, The" (Schott), **Supp. XXIII:** 242

"New Life at Kyerefaso" (Sutherland), **Supp. IV Part 1:** 9

"New Light on Veblen" (Dorfman), **Supp. I Part 2:** 650

"New Man, A" (E. P. Jones), **Supp. XXII:** 144

Newman, Charles, **Supp. I Part 2:** 527, 546–548

Newman, Edwin, **Supp. IV Part 2:** 526

Newman, Frances, **Supp. XXII:** 198

Newman, Judie, **Supp. IV Part 1:** 304, 305

Newman, Paul, **Supp. IV Part 2:** 473, 474

New Man, The (Merton), **Supp. VIII:** 208

"New Mecca, The" (Saunders), **Supp. XIX:** 235, 236

"New Medea, The" (Howells), **II:** 282

New Mexico trilogy (Nichols), **Supp. XIII:** 269

New Morning (album, Dylan), **Supp. XVIII:** 27, 33

"New Mother" (Olds), **Supp. X:** 206
"New Mothers, The" (Shields), **Supp. VII:** 310
New Music (Price), **Supp. VI:** 264, 265
"New Mutants, The" (Fiedler), **Supp. XIII:** 104
"New Name for Some Old Ways of Thinking, A" (James), **II:** 353
New Native American Novel, The: Works in Progress (Bartlett), **Supp. IV Part 1:** 335
"New Natural History, A" (Thurber), **Supp. I Part 2:** 619
New Negro, The (Locke), **Supp. XIX:** 69
"New Negro, The" (Locke), **Supp. XIV:** 201
New Negro, The (Locke, ed.), **Supp. II Part 1:** 176; **Supp. IX:** 309; **Supp. X:** 137; **Supp. XXII:** 8
New Negro, The: An Interpretation (Locke, ed.), **Retro. Supp. I:** 199; **Supp. IV Part 1:** 170; **Supp. XIV:** 195, 201–202
New Negro for a New Century, A (Washington, Wood, and Williams), **Supp. XIV:** 201
New New Journalism, The (R. Boynton), **Supp. XVII:** 209
"New Nomads, The" (E. Hoffman), **Supp. XVI:** 161
"New Orleans" (Carruth), **Supp. XVI:** 50
New Orleans Sketches (Faulkner), **Retro. Supp. I:** 80
New Path to the Waterfall, A (Carver), **Supp. III Part 1:** 138–140, 147, 149; **Supp. XXIV:** 172
"New Poem, The" (Wright), **Supp. V:** 339, 340
"New Poems" (MacLeish), **III:** 19
"New Poems" (Oliver), **Supp. VII:** 240
New Poems 1960 (Bynner), **Supp. XV:** 51
New Poems: 1980–88 (Haines), **Supp. XII:** 209–210
New Poetry, The (Monroe and Henderson, eds.), **Supp. I Part 2:** 387
"New Poetry Handbook, The" (Strand), **Supp. IV Part 2:** 626
New Poetry of Mexico (Strand, trans.), **Supp. IV Part 2:** 630
New Poets of England and America (Hall, Pack, and Simpson, eds.), **Supp. IV Part 2:** 621
"Newport of Anchuria" (Henry), **Supp. II Part 1:** 409
New Princeton Encyclopedia of Poetry and Poetics (Preminger and Brogan, eds.), **Supp. XV:** 250
"*New Republic* Moves Uptown, The" (Cowley), **Supp. II Part 1:** 142
"New Rose Hotel" (W. Gibson), **Supp. XVI:** 120, 122, 124
"News, The" (McClatchy), **Supp. XII:** 269
"New Season" (Levine), **Supp. V:** 188
New Seeds of Contemplation (Merton), **Supp. VIII:** 200, 208
News from the Glacier: Selected Poems 1960–1980 (Haines), **Supp. XII:** 207, 208–209

"News Item" (Parker), **Supp. IX:** 190
News of a Kidnapping (García Márquez), **Supp. XXV:** 57
New Song, A (Hughes), **Retro. Supp. I:** 202; **Supp. I Part 1:** 328, 331–332
"New Song"(Kenny), **Supp. XXIII:** 156
Newson-Horst, Adele, **Supp. XXIII:** 95
"New South, The" (Lanier), **Supp. I Part 1:** 352, 354, 370
New Southern Girl, The: Female Adolescence in the Works of 12 Women Authors (Town), **Supp. XVIII:** 195
Newspaper Days, 1899–1906 (Mencken), **III:** 100, 102, 120
"New Spirit, The" (Ashbery), **Supp. III Part 1:** 14, 15
New Spoon River, The (Masters), **Supp. I Part 2:** 461–465, 473
New Star Chamber and Other Essays, The (Masters), **Supp. I Part 2:** 455–456, 459
New Tales of the Vampires (Rice), **Supp. VII:** 290
New Tenant, The (Ionesco), **Supp. XXIV:** 113
New Testament, **I:** 303, 457, 458; **II:** 167; **III:** 305; **IV:** 114, 134, 152; **Retro. Supp. I:** 58, 140, 360; **Supp. I Part 1:** 104, 106; **Supp. I Part 2:** 516; **Supp. XVII:** 155; **Supp. XXIII:** 13. *See also* names of New Testament books
New Testament, A (Anderson), **I:** 101, 114
"New Theory of Thorstein Veblen, A" (Galbraith), **Supp. I Part 2:** 650
Newton, Benjamin Franklin, **I:** 454
Newton, Huey P., **Supp. I Part 1:** 66; **Supp. IV Part 1:** 206
Newton, Isaac, **I:** 132, 557; **II:** 6, 103, 348–349; **III:** 428; **IV:** 18, 149
Newton, Maud, **Supp. XXIII:** 290
Newton, Sarah Emily, **Supp. XV:** 234
"New-Wave Format, A" (Mason), **Supp. VIII:** 141, 143, 147
New West of Edward Abbey, The (Ronald), **Supp. XIII:** 4
"New Wife" (Halliday), **Supp. XIX:** 89
New Wolves, The: The Return of the Mexican Wolf to the American Southwest (Bass), **Supp. XVI:** 26–27
New Woman's Survival Sourcebook, The (Rennie and Grimstead, eds.), **Supp. I Part 2:** 569
New World, The (Bronk), **Supp. XXI:** 25–26, 31
New World, The (Bynner), **Supp. XV:** 41, 42
"New World, The" (Very), **Supp. XXV:** 248
New World, The: Tales (Banks), **Supp. V:** 8, 9, 10
New World Naked, A (Mariani), **Retro. Supp. I:** 419
New Worlds of Literature (Beaty and Hunter, eds.), **Supp. IV Part 1:** 331
New World Writing (Updike), **IV:** 217
"New Year, The" (Very), **Supp. XXV:** 240, 244
New Year Letter (Auden), **Supp. II Part 1:** 14, 16

"New Year's Day" (Wharton), **Retro. Supp. I:** 381
"New Year's Eve" (Schwartz), **Supp. II Part 2:** 640, 656–657
New Year's Eve/1929 (Farrell), **II:** 43
"New Year's Eve 1968" (Lowell), **II:** 554
New Year's Eve: A Play (W. Frank), **Supp. XX: 75**
"New Year's Gift, The" (Stowe), **Supp. I Part 2:** 587
"New Year Two Thousand, The" (Weigl), **Supp. XIX:** 287–288
"New York" (Capote), **Supp. III Part 1:** 122
"New York" (Moore), **III:** 196, 198, 202, 206
"New York 1965" (Bowles), **Supp. IV Part 1:** 94
New York: A Serendipiter's Journey (Talese), **Supp. XVII:** 202, 203
"New York Breeze" (Halliday), **Supp. XIX:** 85
New York City Arts Project, **Supp. III Part 2:** 618
"New York City in 1979"(Acker), **Supp. XII:** 5
New York Edition, **Retro. Supp. I:** 235
"New York Edition" (James), **II:** 336, 337
"New York Gold Conspiracy, The" (Adams), **I:** 4
New York Hat, The (film; Griffith), **Supp. XVI:** 183
New York Intellectuals, **Supp. VIII:** 93
"New York Intellectuals, The" (Howe), **Supp. VI:** 120
"New York Is a City of Things Unnoticed" (Talese), **Supp. XVII:** 202, 209
New York: Its Upper Ten and Lower Million (Lippard), **Supp. XXIII:** 180, 183, 184
New York Jew (Kazin), **Supp. VIII:** 95, **97–100**
New York Madness (Bodenheim), **Supp. XXV:** 28
"New York Theater: Isn't It Romantic" (Wasserstein), **Supp. XV:** 320
New York Trilogy, The (Auster), **Supp. XII:** 21, **24–28**
Next (McNally), **Supp. XIII:** 197
"Next in Line, The" (Bradbury), **Supp. IV Part 1:** 102
"Next Rodeo, The" (Kittredge), **Supp. XXVI:** 185–186
Next Rodeo, The: New and Selected Essays (Kittredge), **Supp. XXVI:** 185–186
Next Room of the Dream, The (Nemerov), **III:** 269, 275, 278, 279–280, 284
"Next Time I Crossed the Line into Oklahoma, The" (Wright), **Supp. XV:** 345
Next-to-Last Things: New Poems and Essays (Kunitz), **Supp. III Part 1:** 257–259, 261, 262, 265, 266, 268
"'Next to Reading Matter' " (Henry), **Supp. II Part 1:** 399
Nexus (H. Miller), **III:** 170, 187, 188, 189

Nguyen, Bich Minh, **Supp. XXVI: 207–222**

Niatum, Duane, **Supp. IV Part 1:** 331; **Supp. IV Part 2:** 505

Nice and Noir (Schwartz), **Supp. XIV:** 23

"Nice Girl" (Nelson), **Supp. XVIII:** 178

Nice Jewish Boy, The (P. Roth), **Supp. III Part 2:** 412

"Nice Part f Town, A" (Hayes), **Supp. XXVI:** 144

Nicholas II, Tsar, **Supp. I Part 2:** 447

"Nicholas in the Park" (Halliday), **Supp. XIX:** 88

Nicholls, Peter, **Supp. XIX:** 232; **Supp. XXVI:** 228, 232

Nichols, Charles, **Retro. Supp. I:** 194

Nichols, Dudley, **Supp. XVIII:** 247

Nichols, John Treadwell, **Supp. XIII: 253–272**

Nichols, Luther, **Supp. X:** 265

Nichols, Mike, **Supp. IV Part 1:** 234; **Supp. IV Part 2:** 577

Nicholson, Colin, **Supp. VIII:** 129

Nicholson, Harold, **Supp. XIV:** 163

Nicholson, Jack, **Supp. V:** 26; **Supp. VIII:** 45; **Supp. XI:** 308

Nicholson, John, **Supp. XVI:** 293

Nick Adams Stories, The (Hemingway), **II:** 258; **Retro. Supp. I:** 174

"Nick and the Candlestick" (Plath), **Supp. I Part 2:** 544

Nickel and Dimed: On (Not) Getting By in America (Ehrenreich), **Supp. XVII:** 210

Nickel Eclipse: Iroquois Moon (Gansworth), **Supp. XXVI:** 110

Nickel Mountain: A Pastoral Novel (Gardner), **Supp. VI:** 63, 64, 68, **69**

Nickerson, Catherine Ross, **Supp. XXV:** 192, 200, 202

"Nicodemus" (Keillor), **Supp. XVI:** 167

Nicoll, Allardyce, **III:** 400

Nicoloff, Philip, **II:** 7

Niebuhr, Gustav, **III:** 292

Niebuhr, H. Richard, **I:** 494

Niebuhr, Lydia, **III:** 292

Niebuhr, Reinhold, **III: 290–313; Supp. I Part 2:** 654; **Supp. XX:** 79

Niedecker, Lorine, **Supp. III Part 2:** 616, 623; **Supp. XIV:** 287; **Supp. XXIII:** 174

Nielsen, Ed, **Supp. IX:** 254

Nielson, Dorothy, **Supp. I Part 2:** 659

Nietzsche, Friedrich Wilhelm, **I:** 227, 283, 383, 389, 396, 397, 402, 509; **II:** 7, 20, 27, 42, 90, 145, 262, 462, 463, 577, 583, 585; **III:** 102–103, 113, 156, 176; **IV:** 286, 491; **Supp. I Part 1:** 254, 299, 320; **Supp. I Part 2:** 646; **Supp. IV Part 1:** 104, 105–106, 107, 110, 284; **Supp. IV Part 2:** 519; **Supp. V:** 277, 280; **Supp. VIII:** 11, 181, 189; **Supp. X:** 48; **Supp. XII:** 98; **Supp. XIV:** 339; **Supp. XX:** 117

Nieves, Felipe, **Supp. XVIII:** 90

Niflis, N. Michael, **Supp. IV Part 1:** 175

Niger, S. *See* Charney, Samuel

Nigger Heaven (Van Vechten), **Supp. II Part 2:** 739, 744–746; **Supp. XIX:** 76; **Supp. XVIII:** 123, 127

"Nigger Jeff" (Dreiser), **Retro. Supp. II:** 97

Nigger of the "Narcissus," The (Conrad), **II:** 91; **Retro. Supp. I:** 106; **Supp. XVIII:** 224; **Supp. XXIV:** 286

"NIGGY THE HO" (Baraka), **Supp. II Part 1:** 54

"Night" (H. Johnson), **Supp. XXVI:** 173

"Night" (Huddle), **Supp. XXVI:** 155

"Night, Death, Mississippi" (Hayden), **Supp. II Part 1:** 369

'*Night, Mother* (Norman), **Supp. VIII:** 141

"Night above the Avenue" (Merwin), **Supp. III Part 1:** 355

"Night among the Horses, A" (Barnes), **Supp. III Part 1:** 33–34, 39, 44

"Night and the Madman" (Gibran), **Supp. XX: 118**

Night at the Movies, A, or, You Must Remember This: Fictions (Coover), **Supp. V:** 50–51

"Night at the Opera, A" (Matthews), **Supp. IX:** 167

"Night before the Sentence Is Carried Out, The" (Wright), **Supp. XV:** 341

"Nightbird" (Komunyakaa), **Supp. XIII:** 132

Night-Blooming Cereus, The (Hayden), **Supp. II Part 1:** 367, 373

"Night-Blooming Cereus, The" (Hayden), **Supp. II Part 1:** 367

Night-Born, The (London), **II:** 467

"Nightbreak" (Rich), **Supp. I Part 2:** 556

"Nightclub" (Collins), **Supp. XXI:** 60

Night Country, The (O'Nan), **Supp. XXV:** 141, 148–149, 150

Night Dance (Price), **Supp. VI:** 264

"Night Dances, The" (Plath), **Supp. I Part 2:** 544

"Night Dream, The" (MacLeish), **III:** 15

"Night Ferry" (Doty), **Supp. XI:** 124

"Nightfishing" (Schnackenberg), **Supp. XV:** 254

"Nighthawks"(Dybek), **Supp. XXIII:** 73, 74

"Night I Met Little Floyd, The" (Wright), **Supp. XV:** 345–346

Night in Acadie, A (Chopin), **Retro. Supp. I: 66–67,** 73; **Supp. I Part 1:** 200, 219, 220, 224

"Night in Acadie, A" (Chopin), **Retro. Supp. II:** 66

"Night in June, A" (W. C. Williams), **Retro. Supp. I:** 424

"Night in New Arabia, A" (Henry), **Supp. II Part 1:** 402

Night in Question, The: Stories (Wolff), **Supp. VII:** 342–344

"Night Journey" (Roethke), **Supp. III Part 1:** 260

"Night Letter to the Reader" (Collins), **Supp. XXI:** 55

Night Light (Justice), **Supp. VII:** 126–127

"Nightmare" (Kumin), **Supp. IV Part 2:** 442

Nightmare Factory, The (Kumin), **Supp. IV Part 2:** 444–447, 451

"Nightmare Factory, The" (Kumin), **Supp. IV Part 2:** 445, 453

Nightmare on Main Street (Poe), **Retro. Supp. II:** 262

"Nightmare" poems (Benét), **Supp. XI:** 46, 58

"Night Mirror" (L.-Y. Lee), **Supp. XV:** 225

Night Music (Odets), **Supp. II Part 2:** 541, 543, 544

"Night of First Snow" (R. Bly), **Supp. IV Part 1:** 71

Night of January 16th (Rand), **Supp. IV Part 2:** 527

Night of the Iguana, The (T. Williams), **IV:** 382, 383, 384, 385, 386, 387, 388, 391, 392, 393, 394, 395, 397, 398

"Night of the Iguana, The" (T. Williams), **IV:** 384

"Night of the Living Beanfield: How an Unsuccessful Cult Novel Became an Unsuccessful Cult Film in Only Fourteen Years, Eleven Nervous Breakdowns, and $20 Million" (Nichols), **Supp. XIII:** 267

Night Passage (Parker), **Supp. XIX:** 185–186

Night Rider (Warren), **IV:** 243, 246–247

Nights (Doolittle), **Supp. I Part 1:** 270, 271

Nights and Days (Merrill), **Supp. III Part 1:** 319, 320, 322–325

"Nights and Days" (Rich), **Supp. I Part 2:** 574

"Night's for Cryin,' The" (C. Himes), **Supp. XVI:** 137

"Night Shift" (Plath), **Supp. I Part 2:** 538

"Nightshine Beyond Memory, A: Ten More Years with Ray" (Gallagher), **Supp. XXIV:** 167, 172

Night-Side (Oates), **Supp. II Part 2:** 522

"Night-Side" (Oates), **Supp. II Part 2:** 523

Night-Side, The (Skloot), **Supp. XX: 193, 196, 205, 208**

Nights in the Gardens of Brooklyn (Swados), **Supp. XIX: 261–264**

"Nights in the Gardens of Brooklyn" (Swados), **Supp. XIX:** 261

"Night Sketches: Beneath an Umbrella" (Hawthorne), **II:** 235–237, 238, 239, 242; **Supp. XXI:** 201

"Night Sport" (Hoffman), **Supp. XVIII:** 86, 87

"Night-Sweat" (Lowell), **II:** 554

"Night-Talk" (Ellison), **Retro. Supp. II:** 126; **Supp. II Part 1:** 248

Night Thoughts (Young), **III:** 415

"Night-Time River Road, A" (Ferry), **Supp. XXIV:** 150

Night Traveler, The (Oliver), **Supp. VII:** 233

"Night Watch" (Gioia), **Supp. XV:** 117

"Night Watch, The" (Wright), **Supp. V:** 339

"Night We All Had Grippe, The" (Jackson), **Supp. IX:** 118

Nightwood (Barnes), **Supp. III Part 1:** 31, 32, 35–37, 39–43

Night World and the Word Night, The (F. Wright), **Supp. XVII:** 240, 244–245
"Nihilist as Hero, The" (Lowell), **II:** 554; **Retro. Supp. II:** 190
Nijinsky, Vaslav, **Supp. XV:** 28–29
Nikolai Gogol (Nabokov), **Retro. Supp. I:** 266
"Nilda" (Díaz), **Supp. XXIV:** 92
Niles, Thomas, **Retro. Supp. I:** 35
Niles, Thomas, Jr., **Supp. I Part 1:** 39
Nilsson, Christine, **Supp. I Part 1:** 355
Nilsson, Harry, **Supp. XI:** 309
Nilsson, Jenny Lind, **Supp. XVI:** 177
Nimitz, Chester, **Supp. I Part 2:** 491
"Nimram" (Gardner), **Supp. VI:** 73
Nims, John Frederick, **III:** 527; **Supp. XVII:** 112
Nin, Anaïs, **III:** 182, 184, 190; **Supp. III Part 1:** 43; **Supp. IV Part 2:** 680; **Supp. X: 181–200; Supp. XIX:** 134
"9" (Oliver), **Supp. VII:** 244
"9 Failures of the Imagination" (Lethem), **Supp. XVIII:** 148
"Nine-Ball" (Offutt), **Supp. XIX:** 166, 167
Nine Dragons (Connelly), **Supp. XXI:** 74, **79–80**
"Nine from Eight" (Lanier), **Supp. I Part 1:** 352–354
Nine Gates: Entering the Mind of Poetry (Hirshfield), **Supp. XXIII:** 136, 137
Nine Headed Dragon River: Zen Journals 1969–1982 (Matthiessen), **Supp. V:** 199
Nine Horses (Collins), **Supp. XXI:** 55, 60, 61, 62, 65
"Nine Horses" (Collins), **Supp. XXI:** 61
Ninemile Wolves,The (Bass), **Supp. XVI:** 24–25, 26
"Nine Nectarines" (Moore), **III:** 203, 209, 215
Nine Plays (Reznikoff), **Supp. XIV:** 288
"Nine Poems for the Unborn Child" (Rukeyser), **Supp. VI:** 280–281, 284
Nine Stories (Nabokov), **Retro. Supp. I:** 266
Nine Stories (Salinger), **III:** 552, 558–564
"19 Hadley Street" (Schnackenberg), **Supp. XV:** 253
19 Necromancers from Now (Reed), **Supp. X:** 240
19 Varieties of Gazelle (Nye), **Supp. XIII:** 275, **286–288**
"19 Varieties of Gazelle" (Nye), **Supp. XIII:** 286
1984 (Orwell), **Supp. XIII:** 29; **Supp. XVIII:** 137, 138
"1953 Dodge Coronet" (Huddle), **Supp. XXVI:** 151
"1940" (Stafford), **Supp. XI:** 328–329
"1945–1985: Poem for the Anniversary" (Oliver), **Supp. VII:** 237
1919 (Dos Passos), **I:** 482, 485–486, 487, 489, 490, 492
"1975" (Wright), **Supp. V:** 341
"1973"(Hirshfield), **Supp. XXIII:** 130
"1910" (Mora), **Supp. XIII:** 215
Nineteenth-Century Minor Poets (Auden), **Supp. XXV:** 237

"1938" (Komunyakaa), **Supp. XIII:** 114
1939 (Boyle), **Supp. XXIV:** 62
"1939" (Taylor), **Supp. V:** 316
1933 (Levine), **Supp. V:** 185–187
"1933" (Levine), **Supp. V:** 188
"Nineteenth New York, The" (Doctorow), **Supp. IV Part 1:** 232
"1929" (Auden), **Supp. II Part 1:** 6
"1926" (Kees), **Supp. XV:** 135
"93990" (Saunders), **Supp. XIX:** 233
"90 North" (Jarrell), **II:** 370, 371
90 Trees (Zukofsky), **Supp. III Part 2:** 631
95 Poems (Cummings), **I:** 430, 433, 435, 439, 446, 447
"91 Revere Street" (Lowell), **II:** 547; **Retro. Supp. II:** 188; **Supp. XI:** 240
Ninety Percent of Everything (Lethem, Kelly and Kessel), **Supp. XVIII:** 145
"92 Days" (L. Brown), **Supp. XXI:** 44–45
"Nine Years Later" (Brodsky), **Supp. VIII:** 32
Ninth Avenue (Bodenheim), **Supp. XXV:** 24–25
"Nirvana" (Lanier), **Supp. I Part 1:** 352
Nirvana Blues, The (Nichols), **Supp. XIII:** 266, 267
Nishikigi (play), **III:** 466
Niven, David, **Supp. XI:** 307
Nixon (film), **Supp. XIV:** 48
Nixon, Richard M., **I:** 376; **III:** 38, 46; **Supp. I Part 1:** 294, 295; **Supp. V:** 45, 46, 51; **Supp. XII:** 14; **Supp. XIV:** 306
"NJ Transit" (Komunyakaa), **Supp. XIII:** 132
Nketia, J. H., **Supp. IV Part 1:** 10
Nketsia, Nana, **Supp. IV Part 1:** 2, 10
Nkize, Julius, **Supp. IV Part 1:** 361
Nkrumah, Kwame, **I:** 490, 494; **Supp. IV Part 1:** 361; **Supp. X:** 135
Nkrumah and the Ghana Revolution (C. L. R. James), **Supp. XXI:** 159, 171–172
NO (Major), **Supp. XXII:** 174
"Noah" (Biss), **Supp. XXVI:** 48
Noailles, Anna de, **IV:** 328
Noa Noa (Gauguin), **I:** 34
Nobel Lecture (Singer), **Retro. Supp. II:** 300
"No Better Than a 'Withered Daffodil' " (Moore), **III:** 216
Noble, David W., **Supp. I Part 2:** 650
Noble, Marianne, **Supp. XVIII:** 267
"Noble Rider and the Sound of Words, The" (Stevens), **Retro. Supp. I:** 299
Noble Savage, The (Coover), **Supp. V:** 40
"No Bobolink reverse His Singing" (Dickinson), **Retro. Supp. I:** 45
Nobodaddy (MacLeish), **III:** 5–6, 8, 10, 11, 18, 19, 20
"Nobodaddy" (W. Blake), **Supp. XVII:** 245
"Nobody in Hollywood" (Bausch), **Supp. VII:** 54
Nobody Knows My Name (Baldwin), **Supp. XIII:** 111

"Nobody Knows My Name" (Baldwin), **Retro. Supp. II:** 8; **Supp. I Part 1:** 52
Nobody Knows My Name: More Notes of a Native Son (Baldwin), **Retro. Supp. II:** 6, 8; **Supp. I Part 1:** 47, 52, 55
"Nobody knows this little Rose" (Dickinson), **Retro. Supp. I:** 30
"Nobody Said Anything" (Carver), **Supp. III Part 1:** 141
"Nobody's Business" (Lahiri), **Supp. XXI:** 183
Nobody's Fool (Russo), **Supp. XII:** 326, **331–335**, 340
"No Change of Place" (Auden), **Supp. II Part 1:** 5
"Noche Triste, La" (Frost), **Retro. Supp. I:** 123
Nock, Albert Jay, **I:** 245; **Supp. IV Part 2:** 521, 524
"No Coward Soul Is Mine" (Brontë), **I:** 458
"No Crime in the Mountains" (Chandler), **Supp. IV Part 1:** 129
"Nocturne" (Komunyakaa), **Supp. XIII:** 126
"Nocturne" (MacLeish), **III:** 8
"Nocturne at Bethesda" (Bontemps), **Supp. XXII:** 3, 8
"Nocturne in a Deserted Brickyard" (Sandburg), **III:** 586
Nocturne of Remembered Spring (Aiken), **I:** 50
No Direction Home (documentary film, Scorsese), **Supp. XVIII:** 22, 23, 29
No Direction Home (Shelton), **Supp. XVIII:** 21
No Door (Wolfe), **IV:** 451–452, 456
"No Door" (Wolfe), **IV:** 456
"No End" (Huddle), **Supp. XXVI:** 151
"No Epitaph" (Carson), **Supp. XII:** 111
No Exit (Sartre), **I:** 82, 130; **Supp. XIV:** 320
No Exit (Sartre; Bowles, trans.), **Supp. IV Part 1:** 84
No Gifts from Chance (Benstock), **Retro. Supp. I:** 361
"No-Good Blues" (Komunyakaa), **Supp. XIII:** 130
No Hero (Marquand), **III:** 57
No Heroes: A Memoir of Coming Home (Offutt), **Supp. XIX:** 163, **172–174**, 175
No! In Thunder (Fiedler), **Supp. XIII:** 101
"Noir" (Stallings), **Supp. XXV:** 232
"Noiseless Patient Spider" (Whitman), **III:** 555; **IV:** 348; **Supp. IV Part 1:** 325
Noises Off (Frayn), **Supp. IV Part 2:** 582
Noi vivi. See We the Living (film)
"No Jury Would Convict" (Shaw), **Supp. XIX:** 245
"No Lamp Has Ever Shown Us Where to Look" (MacLeish), **III:** 9
Nolan, Sidney, **Retro. Supp. II:** 189
No Laughing Matter (Heller and Vogel), **Supp. IV Part 1:** 384, 389
No Love Lost, a Romance of Travel (Howells), **II:** 277

Nomad (Ali), **Supp. XXIV:** 15
Nomad's Land (Rinehart), **Supp. XXV:** 195
No Man Is an Island (Merton), **Supp. VIII:** 207
"No Man's Land" (Biss), **Supp. XXVI:** 47, 56
"No More This Home" (Taggard), **Supp. XXII:** 277, 280
No Mother to Guide Her (Loos), **Supp. XVI:** 194
No Name in the Street (Baldwin), **Retro. Supp. II:** 13, 14; **Supp. I Part 1:** 47, 48, 52, 65–66, 67
No Nature: New and Selected Poems (Snyder), **Supp. VIII: 305**
Nonconformist's Memorial, The (Howe), **Supp. IV Part 2:** 434, 435–436
Nonconformity (Algren), **Supp. IX:** 15
None but the Lonely Heart (film), **Supp. II Part 2:** 546
Nones (Auden), **Supp. II Part 1:** 21
"Nones" (Auden), **Supp. II Part 1:** 22–23
None Shall Look Back (Gordon), **II:** 205–207, 208
"No No, Bad Daddy" (Nelson), **Supp. XVIII:** 177, 178
"Non-Tenured" (Halliday), **Supp. XIX:** 90, 91
Nonverbal Communication: Notes on the Visual Perception of Human Relations (Kees and Ruesch), **Supp. XV:** 147
"Noon" (Bryant), **Supp. I Part 1:** 157
No One Belongs Here More Than You (July), **Supp. XXIV:** 199, **200–207**
"No One Remembers" (Levine), **Supp. V:** 187
"Noon Walk on the Asylum Lawn" (Sexton), **Supp. II Part 2:** 673
"Noon Wine" (Porter), **III:** 436, 437–438, 442, 446
"No Pain Whatsoever" (Yates), **Supp. XI:** 341
"No Place for You, My Love" (Welty), **IV:** 278, 279; **Retro. Supp. I:** 353
No Plays of Japan, The (Waley), **III:** 466
No Pockets in a Shroud (McCoy), **Supp. XIII: 166–168,** 171, 172, 173, 174
"No Poem So Fine" (Francis), **Supp. IX:** 83
Norcross, Frances, **I:** 456, 462
Norcross, Louise, **I:** 456, 462
Nordfeldt, B. J. O., **Supp. XXI:** 6
Nordfeldt, Margaret, **Supp. XXI:** 6
Nordyke, Lewis, **Supp. XIII:** 5
No Relief (Dixon), **Supp. XII:** 139, **142–143**
No Resting Place (Humphrey), **Supp. IX:** 94, **106–108**
Norfolk Poems, The (Carruth), **Supp. XVI:** 47, 48
Norma (Bellini), **IV:** 309
Norma Ashe (Glaspell), **Supp. III Part 1:** 175, 186–187
"Normal Life, A"(Thompson), **Supp. XXIII:** 300
"Normal Motor Adjustments" (Stein and Solomons), **IV:** 26
Norman, Charles, **III:** 479

Norman, Gurney, **Supp. X:** 24; **Supp. XXIII:** 42
Norman, Jessye, **Supp. XX: 110**
Norman, Marsha, **Supp. VIII:** 141; **Supp. XXI:** 145; **Supp. XXIV:** 124
Norman Mailer (Poirier), **Retro. Supp. II:** 207–208
Norman Mailer: Modern Critical Views (Bloom), **Retro. Supp. II:** 205
Norman Mailer Revisited (Merrill), **Retro. Supp. II:** 201
Norna; or, The Witch's Curse (Alcott), **Supp. I Part 1:** 33
Norris, Charles, **III:** 320; **Retro. Supp. I:** 100; **Supp. XVIII:** 226
Norris, Frank, **I:** 211, 355, 500, 506, 517, 518, 519; **II:** 89, 264, 276, 289, 307; **III:** 227, **314–336,** 596; **IV:** 29; **Retro. Supp. I:** 100, 325; **Retro. Supp. II:** 96, 101; **Supp. III Part 2:** 412; **Supp. IX:** 14, 15; **Supp. VIII:** 101, 102; **Supp. XV:** 115
"North" (Budbill), **Supp. XIX:** 7–8
"North" (Hugo), **Supp. VI:** 135
North, Milou (pseudonym), **Supp. IV Part 1:** 260. *See also* Dorris, Michael; Erdrich, Louise
North, Sir Thomas, **IV:** 370
"North American Sequence" (Roethke), **I:** 171–172, 183; **III:** 529, 545, 547, 548
"North Beach" (Snyder), **Supp. VIII:** 289
North Country: A Personal Journey Through the Borderland (Mosher), **Supp. XXII: 203–204,** 206, 212, **217–218**
"North Country Sketches" (McClatchy), **Supp. XII:** 256
"Northeast Playground" (Paley), **Supp. VI:** 226–227, 229
Northern Borders (Mosher), **Supp. XXII:** 203, 204, 206, 207, 208, 209, **213–214**
Northern Lights (O'Brien), **Supp. V:** 237, 239, 241–244, 250
"Northern Motive" (Levine), **Supp. V:** 195
Northfield Poems (Ammons), **Supp. VII:** 29
"Northhanger Ridge" (Wright), **Supp. V:** 335, 340
"North Haven" (Bishop), **Retro. Supp. II:** 50
"North Labrador" (Crane), **I:** 386
North of Boston (Frost), **II:** 152, 153–154, 527; **Retro. Supp. I:** 121, 125, 127, **128–130,** 131; **Supp. I Part 1:** 263; **Supp. XIII:** 146
North of Jamaica (Simpson), **Supp. IV Part 2:** 448; **Supp. IX:** 275, 276
North of the Danube (Caldwell), **I:** 288, 290, 293, 294, 309, 310
North: Poems of Home (Kenny), **Supp. XXIII: 147–148**
Northrup, Cyrus, **Supp. I Part 1:** 350
North Sea (Jarman), **Supp. XVII:** 110, 113
"North Sea Undertaker's Complaint, The" (Lowell), **II:** 550

North & South (Bishop), **Retro. Supp. II: 41–43; Supp. I Part 1:** 72, 84, 85, 89
North Star, The (Hellman), **Supp. I Part 1:** 281
Northup, Solomon, **Supp. XIV:** 32
"Northwest Writers at Work" (Baker), **Supp. XXIV:** 178
"North Winter" (Carruth), **Supp. XVI:** 53
Norton, Charles Eliot, **I:** 223, 568; **II:** 279, 322–323, 338; **Retro. Supp. I:** 371; **Retro. Supp. II:** 135; **Supp. I Part 1:** 103; **Supp. I Part 2:** 406, 479
Norton, Jody, **Supp. VIII:** 297
Norton, John, **Supp. I Part 1:** 99, 110, 112, 114
Norton Anthology of African American Literature, The (H. L. Gates and McKay, eds.), **Supp. X:** 325; **Supp. XX: 105**
Norton Anthology of American Literature, **Supp. X:** 325; **Supp. XV:** 270
Norton Anthology of Literature by Women (Gilbert and Gubar, eds.), **Supp. XV:** 270
Norton Anthology of Modern Poetry, The, **Supp. XI:** 259; **Supp. XV:** 258; **Supp. XXIV:** 35, 39
Norton Anthology of Poetry, The, **Supp. XVIII:** 20
Norton Anthology of Short Fiction, The, **Supp. IX:** 4
Norton Book of Personal Essays, The, **Supp. XIV:** 105
Norton Lectures, **Retro. Supp. I:** 65
Norwood, Vera, **Supp. IX:** 24
No Safe Harbour (Porter), **III:** 447
Nosferatu: An Opera Libretto (Gioia), **Supp. XV:** 112, **128**
"Nosferatu's Serenade" (Gioia), **Supp. XV:** 128
No Siege Is Absolute (Char; version of F. Wright), **Supp. XVII:** 244
"No Snake" (A. Finch), **Supp. XVII:** 72
"No Speak English" (Cisneros), **Supp. VII:** 63
"Nostalgia" (Collins), **Supp. XXI:** 57
"Nostalgia" (Saunders), **Supp. XIX:** 235
Nostalgia for 70 (J. W. Miller), **Supp. XX: 165**
"Nostalgia of the Lakefronts" (Justice), **Supp. VII:** 118, 119, 120
"Nostalgic Mood" (Farrell), **II:** 45
No Star Is Lost (Farrell), **II:** 34, 35, 44
Nostrandt, Jeanne, **Supp. XVIII:** 80–81
Nostromo (Conrad), **II:** 600; **IV:** 245
"Nosty Fright, A" (Swenson), **Supp. IV Part 2:** 651
"Not" (Huddle), **Supp. XXVI:** 157
Not about Nightingales (T. Williams), **IV:** 381
"Not a Sparrow" (Gallagher), **Supp. XXIV:** 171
Not: A Trio (Huddle), **Supp. XXVI:** 150, 156–157
"Not a Womb in the House" (Quindlen), **Supp. XVII:** 166, 171
"(Not) Born in he U.S.A." (Gansworth), **Supp. XXVI:** 111

Not Coming to Be Barked At (Kooser), **Supp. XIX:** 116, **120**

Not Dancing (Dunn), **Supp. XI:** 143, **148**

"Note about *Iconographs*, A" (Swenson), **Supp. IV Part 2:** 646

Notebook (Lowell), **Retro. Supp. II:** 186, 190; **Supp. V:** 343

Notebook 1967–68 (Lowell), **II:** 553–555; **Retro. Supp. II:** 182, 186, 190

Notebook of Malte Laurids Brigge, The (Rilke), **III:** 571

Notebooks (Fitzgerald), **Retro. Supp. I:** 110

Notebooks of Captain George, The (Renoir), **Supp. XXII:** 257

No Telephone to Heaven (Cliff), **Supp. XXII:** 66, 69, 71–72

"Note on Abraham Lincoln" (Vidal), **Supp. IV Part 2:** 688

"Note on Commercial Theatre" (Hughes), **Retro. Supp. I:** 207

"Note on Ezra Pound, A" (Eliot), **Retro. Supp. I:** 290

"Note on Lanier's Music, A" (P. Graham), **Supp. I Part 1:** 373

Note on Literary Criticism, A (Farrell), **II:** 26, 49

"Note on Poetry, A" (Doolittle), **Supp. I Part 1:** 254, 267–268

"Note on Realism, A" (Anderson), **I:** 110

"Note on the Limits of 'History' and the Limits of 'Criticism,' A" (Brooks), **Supp. XIV:** 11

"Note on the Poetry of Love, A" (Untermeyer), **Supp. XV:** 304

"Note on the Truth of the Tales, A" (Vollmann), **Supp. XVII:** 230

"Notes" (Dove), **Supp. IV Part 1:** 246

"Notes for a Moving Picture: The House" (Agee), **I:** 33, 34

"Notes for an Autobiography" (Van Vechten), **Supp. II Part 2:** 749

"Notes for a Novel About the End of the World" (Percy), **Supp. III Part 1:** 393

"Notes for a Preface" (Sandburg), **III:** 591, 596–597

"NOTES FOR A SPEECH" (Baraka), **Supp. II Part 1:** 33

Notes for the Green Box (Duchamp), **Supp. IV Part 2:** 423

Notes for the Two-Dollar Window: Portraits from an American Neighborhood (Kriegel), **Supp. XXIV:** 223–224

Notes from a Bottle Found on the Beach at Carmel (Connell), **Supp. XIV:** 80, 87, 96, 97

Notes from a Sea Diary: Hemingway All the Way (Algren), **Supp. IX:** 16

Notes from No Man's Land (Biss), **Supp. XXVI:** 45, 46, 47, 48, 50, 53, 55–57

"Notes from the Childhood and Girlhood" (Brooks), **Supp. III Part 1:** 77

"Notes from the River" (Stern), **Supp. IX:** 285, 287, 294, 295

Notes from Underground (Dostoevsky), **III:** 571; **IV:** 485; **Retro. Supp. II:** 121

Notes Left Behind: Last and Selected Poems (Hayford), **Supp. XXII:** 218

"Notes of a Faculty Wife" (Jackson), **Supp. IX:** 126

"Notes of a Native Daughter" (Didion), **Supp. IV Part 1:** 196, 197, 200, 201

Notes of a Native Son (Baldwin), **Retro. Supp. II:** 1, 2, 3, 5, 6; **Supp. I Part 1:** 50, 52, 54; **Supp. IV Part 1:** 163

"Notes of a Native Son" (Baldwin), **Supp. I Part 1:** 50, 54

Notes of a Son and Brother (James), **II:** 337; **Retro. Supp. I:** 235

"Notes on a Departure" (Trilling), **Supp. III Part 2:** 498

"Notes on Babbitt and More" (Wilson), **IV:** 435

"Notes on 'Camp' " (Sontag), **Supp. III Part 2:** 455–456; **Supp. XIV:** 167

Notes on Democracy (Mencken), **III:** 104, 107–108, 109, 116, 119

Notes on Dialectics (C. L. R. James), **Supp. XXI:** 169

"Notes on Free Verse" (Dobyns), **Supp. XIII:** 77

"Notes on 'Layover' " (Hass), **Supp. VI:** 109

"Notes on Memory and Enthusiasm" (Di Piero), **Supp. XIX:** 42

Notes on Novelists (James), **II:** 336, 337; **Retro. Supp. I:** 235

"Notes on Nukes, Nookie, and Neo-Romanticism" (Robbins), **Supp. X:** 272

"Notes on Poetry" (Eberhart), **I:** 524, 527–528, 529

"Notes on Teaching" (Hadas), **Supp. XXIII:** 122

"Notes on the Craft of Poetry" (Strand), **Supp. IV Part 2:** 626

"Notes on the Decline of Outrage" (Dickey), **Supp. IV Part 1:** 181

"Notes on the New Formalism" (Gioia), **Supp. XV:** 113, 114–115

"Notes on the Novel-as-Autobiography" (P. Bailey), **Supp. XVI:** 69

"Notes on 'The Poetry of Everday Life' " (Notley), **Supp. XXII:** 232

Notes on the State of Virginia (1781–1782) (Jefferson), **Supp. XIV:** 191

"Notes on Writing Weird Fiction" (Lovecraft), **Supp. XXV:** 120–121

"Notes to Be Left in a Cornerstone" (Benét), **Supp. XI:** 46, 58

"Notes toward a Supreme Fiction" (Stevens), **IV:** 87–89; **Retro. Supp. I:** 300, 306, **306–309**, 311; **Supp. I Part 1:** 80

"Notes towards a Poem That Can Never Be Written" (Atwood), **Supp. XIII:** 34–35

"Not Exactly for Talia" (Halliday), **Supp. XIX:** 94

"Not Forgotten" (Davison), **Supp. XXVI:** 70

No Thanks (Cummings), **I:** 430, 431, 432, 436, 437, 441, 443, 446

Not Heaven: A Novel in the Form of Prelude, Variations, and Theme (W. Frank), **Supp. XX:** 80

"Nothing" (C. Frost), **Supp. XV:** 94

"Nothing Big" (Komunyakaa), **Supp. XIII:** 121

Nothing Can Make Me Do This (Huddle), **Supp. XXVI:** 147, 151–152, 158–159

Nothing Ever Breaks Except the Heart (Boyle), **Supp. XXIV:** 59

Nothing for Tigers (Carruth), **Supp. XVI:** 47, 48, 50

"Nothing Gold Can Stay" (Frost), **Retro. Supp. I:** 133

"Nothing in Heaven Functions as It Ought" (X. J. Kennedy), **Supp. XV:** 158–159

Nothing Makes You Free: Writings by Descendants of Jewish Holocaust Survivors (Bukiet, ed.), **Supp. XVII: 39–40,** 48–49

"Nothing Missing" (O'Hara), **III:** 369

Nothing Personal (Baldwin), **Supp. I Part 1:** 58, 60

Nothing Sacred (film), **Supp. XVIII:** 243

"Nothing Song, The" (Snodgrass), **Supp. VI:** 326

"Nothing Stays Put" (Clampitt), **Supp. IX:** 42

"Nothing Sudden" (Davison), **Supp. XXVI:** 76

"Nothing Will Yield" (Nemerov), **III:** 279

No Third Path (Kosinski), **Supp. VII:** 215

"Not Ideas About the Thing but the Thing Itself" (Stevens), **IV:** 87

"No Time" (Collins), **Supp. XXI:** 61

Notions of the Americans: Picked up by a Travelling Bachelor (Cooper), **I:** 343–345, 346

"Not-Knowing" (Barthelme), **Supp. IV Part 1:** 48

"Not Leaving the House" (Snyder), **Supp. VIII:** 300

Notley, Alice, **Supp. XXII: 223–238; Supp. XXIII:** 221; **Supp. XXIV:** 35, 37, 39, 41, 43, 45

" 'Not Marble nor the Gilded Monument' " (MacLeish), **III:** 12

Not Mine to Finish: Poems, 1928–1934 (Taggard), **Supp. XXII:** 280

"Not My Bones" (Nelson), **Supp. XVIII:** 183

Not Now But Now (M. F. K. Fisher), **Supp. XVII:** 86, 90

"Not Quite Social" (Frost), **II:** 156

"Not Sappho, Sacco" (Rukeyser), **Supp. VI:** 277

"Not Sixteen" (Anderson), **I:** 114

"Not Slightly" (Stein), **IV:** 44

Not So Deep as a Well (Parker), **Supp. IX:** 192

"Not Somewhere Else, but Here" (Rich), **Supp. I Part 2:** 552, 573

Not-So-Simple Neil Simon (McGovern), **Supp. IV Part 2:** 573

Not So Simple: The "Simple" Stories by Langston Hughes (Harper), **Retro. Supp. I:** 194, 209

"Not the Point" (Cameron), **Supp. XII: 83**

"Not They Who Soar" (Dunbar), **Supp. II Part 1:** 199

Not This Pig (Levine), **Supp. V:** 178, 181, 182–183

"Not to Be Satan nor to Deal with Him" (Bronk), **Supp. XXI:** 32

Not to Eat; Not for Love (Weller), **III:** 322

Not Wanted on the Voyage (Findley), **Supp. XX: 50, 56–57, 59**

Not Without Laughter (Hughes), **Retro. Supp. I:** 197, 198, 201; **Supp. I Part 1:** 328, 332; **Supp. XIX:** 73, 154

Nouvelle Héloïse, La (Rousseau), **Supp. XV:** 232

Nova Express (Burroughs), **Supp. III Part 1:** 93, 103, 104; **Supp. XVIII:** 137

Novel, The (Bulwer), **Retro. Supp. II:** 58

Novel, The: An Alternative History (Moore), **Supp. XXII:** 261

"Novel as a Function of American Democracy, The" (Ellison), **Retro. Supp. II:** 124

"Novel Démeublé, The" (Cather), **Retro. Supp. I:** 15

Novel History: Historians and Novelists Confront America's Past (and Each Other) (Carnes), **Supp. X:** 14

"Novelists of 2007" (Halliday), **Supp. XIX:** 90

Novella (Goethe; Bogan and Mayer, trans.), **Supp. III Part 1:** 63

Novellas and Other Writings (Wharton), **Retro. Supp. I:** 360

"Novel of the Thirties, A" (Trilling), **Supp. III Part 2:** 499

Novels and Other Writings (Bercovitch), **Retro. Supp. II:** 325

Novels and Tales of Henry James, The (James), **Retro. Supp. I:** 232

"Novel-Writing and Novel-Reading" (Howells), **II:** 276, 290

"November" (Larcom), **Supp. XIII:** 143

"November Cotton Flower" (Toomer), **Supp. IX:** 312

November Twenty Six Nineteen Sixty Three (Berry), **Supp. X:** 24

"Novices" (Moore), **III:** 200–201, 202, 213

Novick, Peter, **Supp. XVI:** 154–155

"Novogodnee" ("New Year's Greetings") (Tsvetaeva), **Supp. VIII:** 30

"Novotny's Pain" (P. Roth), **Supp. III Part 2:** 403

"No Voyage" (Oliver), **Supp. VII:** 231

No Voyage and Other Poems (Oliver), **Supp. VII:** 230–231, 232

Now and Another Time (Hearon), **Supp. VIII:** 58, **61–62**

Now and Then (Buechner), **Supp. XII:** 49, 53

"Now and Then, America" (Mora), **Supp. XIII:** 217

"Nowhere" (J. Scott), **Supp. XVII:** 189

Nowhere Is a Place: Travels in Patagonia (Theroux and Chatwin), **Supp. VIII:** 322

"Now I Am Married" (Gordon), **Supp. IV Part 1:** 299

"Now I Lay Me" (Hemingway), **II:** 249; **Retro. Supp. I:** 175

"Now I Lay Me" (Olds), **Supp. X:** 208

"Now Is the Air Made of Chiming Balls" (Eberhart), **I:** 523

"No Word" (Kunitz), **Supp. III Part 1:** 263

"No Worst" (Nelson), **Supp. XVIII:** 177, 178

Now Sheba Sings the Song (Angelou), **Supp. IV Part 1:** 16

"Now That We Live" (Kenyon), **Supp. VII:** 165

"Now the Servant's Name Was Malchus" (Wilder), **IV:** 358

"Now We Know" (O'Hara), **III:** 368–369

NOW with Bill Moyers (television), **Supp. XIII:** 286

Noyes, Alfred, **IV:** 434

Nuamah, Grace, **Supp. IV Part 1:** 10

"Nuances of a Theme by Williams" (Stevens), **Retro. Supp. I:** 422

Nuclear Age, The (O'Brien), **Supp. V:** 238, 243, 244, 246–248, 249, 251

"Nuclear Arms and Morality" (Sanders), **Supp. XVI:** 266

"Nude at a Dressing Table" (Peacock), **Supp. XIX:** 204

Nude Croquet (Fiedler), **Supp. XIII:** 103

"Nude Descendig a Staircase" (X. J. Kennedy), **Supp. XV:** 168

Nude Descending a Staircase (Duchamp), **IV:** 408; **Retro. Supp. I:** 416; **Supp. XXII:** 162

Nude Descending a Staircase (X. J. Kennedy), **Supp. XV:** 153, **154–157**

Nugent, Bruce, **Retro. Supp. I:** 200

Nugent, Elliot, **Supp. I Part 2:** 606, 611, 613

Nuggets and Dust (Bierce), **I:** 195

"Nullipara" (Olds), **Supp. X:** 209

Number One (Dos Passos), **I:** 489

"Numbers" (Skloot), **Supp. XX: 196, 207**

"Numbers, Letters" (Baraka), **Supp. II Part 1:** 50

"Numbers Trouble" (Stallings), **Supp. XXV:** 224

Nunc Dimittis (Brodsky), **Supp. VIII:** 25–26, 28

"Nun No More, A" (Fante), **Supp. XI:** 160

"Nun's Priest's Tale" (Chaucer), **III:** 492

Nunzio, Nanzia, **IV:** 89

Nuptial Flight, The (Masters), **Supp. I Part 2:** 460, 471

"Nuptials" (Tate), **IV:** 122

"Nurse Whitman" (Olds), **Supp. X:** 203

Nurture (Kumin), **Supp. IV Part 2:** 453–454, 455

Nussbaum, Emily, **Supp. XI:** 143

Nussbaum, Felicity A., **Supp. X:** 189

Nutcracker, The (Tchaikovsky), **Retro. Supp. I:** 196

"Nux Postcoenatica" (Holmes), **Supp. I Part 1:** 303

Nyce, James M., **Retro. Supp. I:** 380

Nye, Naomi Shihab, **Supp. XI:** 316; **Supp. XIII: 273–290; Supp. XXIII:** 253

Nyerere, Julius, **Supp. X:** 135

"Nympholepsy" (Faulkner), **Retro. Supp. I:** 81

Nymphs of the Valley ('Ará'is al-Murúj) (Gibran), **Supp. XX: 115, 124, 125**

O

"Ö" (Dove), **Supp. IV Part 1:** 245

Oak and Ivy (Dunbar), **Supp. II Part 1:** 98

"Oak Bluffs" column (D. West), **Supp. XVIII:** 286

Oak Openings, The (Cooper), **I:** 354, 355

Oandasan, Bill, **Supp. IV Part 2:** 499

Oasis, The (McCarthy), **II:** 566–568

Oates, Joyce Carol, **Supp. II Part 2: 503–527; Supp. IV Part 1:** 205; **Supp. IV Part 2:** 447, 689; **Supp. V:** 323; **Supp. XI:** 239; **Supp. XII:** 343; **Supp. XIII:** 306; **Supp. XIV:** 26, 109; **Supp. XXIII:** 35; **Supp. XXV:** 86, 123; **Supp. XXVI:** 126

"Oath, The" (Tate), **IV:** 127

Obbligati (Hecht), **Supp. X:** 57

Ober, Harold, **Retro. Supp. I:** 101, 103, 105, 110, 113

Oberndorf, Clarence P., **Supp. I Part 1:** 315

Obey, André, **IV:** 356, 375

"Obit" (Lowell), **II:** 554

"Obituaries" (Collins), **Supp. XXI:** 65

"Obituary Writer, The" (Davison), **Supp. XXVI:** 72

"Objective Value of a Social Settlement, The" (Addams), **Supp. I Part 1:** 4

"Objective Woman, The" (Jong), **Supp. V:** 119

Objectivist Anthology, An, **Supp. XIV:** 287

"Objectivist Ethics, The" (Rand), **Supp. IV Part 2:** 530–532

"Objectivists" Anthology, An (Zukofsky), **Supp. III Part 2:** 613, 615

Objectivist's Anthology, An (Zukofsky, ed.), **Supp. XXVI:** 226

Object Lessons (Quindlen), **Supp. XVII: 173–174**

"Objects" (Wilbur), **Supp. III Part 2:** 545–547

Oblique Prayers (Levertov), **Supp. III Part 1:** 283

"Oblivion" (Justice), **Supp. VII:** 121

Oblivion Seekers, The (Eberhardt), **Supp. IV Part 1:** 92

"Oblong Box, The" (Poe), **III:** 416

"Obnoxious Truth, The" (Notley), **Supp. XXII:** 234

Obregon, Maurice, **Supp. I Part 2:** 488

O'Briant, Don, **Supp. X:** 8

O'Brien, Edward, **Supp. XV:** 140

O'Brien, Edward J., **I:** 289; **III:** 56; **Supp. XIX:** 256; **Supp. XVIII:** 227; **Supp. XX: 34**

O'Brien, Edwin, **Supp. XVIII:** 208

O'Brien, Fitzjames, **I:** 211

O'Brien, Geoffrey, **Supp. IV Part 2:** 471, 473

O'Brien, Joe, **Supp. XXI:** 5, 6

O'Brien, John, **Supp. V:** 48, 49; **Supp. X:** 239, 244; **Supp. XXI:** 228, 229, 233

O'Brien, Tim, **Supp. V: 237–255; Supp. XI:** 234; **Supp. XVII:** 14; **Supp. XXI:** 122; **Supp. XXV:** 142, 143, 153

"Obscene Poem, An" (Creeley), **Supp. IV Part 1:** 150

Obscure Destinies (Cather), **I:** 331–332; **Retro. Supp. I:** 19

"Observation Relative to the Intentions of the Original Founders of the Academy in Philadelphia" (Franklin), **II:** 114

"Observations" (Dillard), **Supp. VI:** 34

Observations (Moore), **III:** 194, 195–196, 197, 199, 203, 205, 215

"Observations Now" (Conroy), **Supp. XVI:** 75

Observations: Photographs by Richard Avedon: Comments by Truman Capote, **Supp. III Part 1:** 125–126

Obuchowski, Mary DeJong, **Supp. XX:** 222

O Canada: An American's Notes on Canadian Culture (Wilson), **IV:** 429–430

"O Carib Isle!" (Crane), **I:** 400–401

O'Casey, Sean, **III:** 145; **Supp. IV Part 1:** 359, 361, 364

"Occidentals" (Ford), **Supp. V:** 71–72

Occom, Samuel, **Supp. XX:** 288

"Occultation of Orion, The" (Longfellow), **Retro. Supp. II:** 168

"Occurrence at Owl Creek Bridge, An" (Bierce), **I:** 200–201; **II:** 264; **Supp. XXV:** 26

"Ocean 1212-W" (Plath), **Supp. I Part 2:** 528

"Ocean of Words" (Jin), **Supp. XVIII:** 94

Ocean of Words: Army Stories (Jin), **Supp. XVIII:** 89, 92, **93–94**

O'Connell, Nicholas, **Supp. IX:** 323, 325, 334

O'Connell, Shaun, **Supp. XXI:** 231

O'Connor, Edward F., Jr., **III:** 337

O'Connor, Flannery, **I:** 113, 190, 211, 298; **II:** 606; **III: 337–360; IV:** 4, 217, 282; **Retro. Supp. II:** 179, **219–239,** 272, 324; **Supp. I Part 1:** 290; **Supp. III Part 1:** 146; **Supp. V:** 59, 337; **Supp. VIII:** 13, 14, 158; **Supp. X:** 1, 26, 69, 228, 290; **Supp. XI:** 104; **Supp. XIII:** 294; **Supp. XIV:** 93; **Supp. XIX:** 166, 209, 223; **Supp. XV:** 338; **Supp. XVI:** 219; **Supp. XVII:** 43, 114; **Supp. XVIII:** 156, 161, 194; **Supp. XXI:** 197; **Supp. XXIII:** 289; **Supp. XXV:** 142; **Supp. XXVI:** 152, 252

O'Connor, Frank, **III:** 158; **Retro. Supp. II:** 242; **Supp. I Part 2:** 531; **Supp. VIII:** 151, 157, 165, 167, 171; **Supp. XV:** 74

O'Connor, Philip F., **Supp. XXIII:** 290

O'Connor, Richard, **II:** 467

O'Connor, T. P., **II:** 129

O'Connor, William, **IV:** 346; **Retro. Supp. I:** 392, 407

O'Connor, William Van, **III:** 479; **Supp. I Part 1:** 195

"Octascope" (Beattie), **Supp. V:** 27, 28

"Octaves" (Robinson), **Supp. III Part 2:** 593

"Octet" (Wallace), **Supp. X:** 309

October (Isherwood), **Supp. XIV:** 157, 164

"October" (Oliver), **Supp. VII:** 241

"October" (Swenson), **Supp. IV Part 2:** 649

"October, 1866" (Bryant), **Supp. I Part 1:** 169

"October 1913" (McCarriston), **Supp. XIV:** 266

"October and November" (Lowell), **II:** 554

"October in the Railroad Earth" (Kerouac), **Supp. III Part 1:** 225, 227, 229

October Light (Gardner), **Supp. VI:** 63, **69–71,** 72

"October Maples, Portland" (Wilbur), **Supp. III Part 2:** 556

October Palace, The (Hirshfield), **Supp. XXIII:** 131

"October: With Rain" (W. V. Davis), **Supp. XXI:** 94

"Octopus, An" (Moore), **III:** 202, 207–208, 214

"Octopus, The" (Merrill), **Supp. III Part 1:** 321

Octopus, The (Norris), **I:** 518; **III:** 314, 316, 322–326, 327, 331–333, 334, 335

"O Daedalus, Fly Away Home" (Hayden), **Supp. II Part 1:** 377–378

"OD and Hepatitis Railroad or Bust, The" (Boyle), **Supp. VIII:** 1

Odd Couple, The (1985 version, Simon), **Supp. IV Part 2:** 580

Odd Couple, The (film), **Supp. IV Part 2:** 589

Odd Couple, The (Simon), **Supp. IV Part 2:** 575, 579–580, 585, 586; **Supp. XVII:** 8

Odd Jobs (Updike), **Retro. Supp. I:** 334

Odd Mercy (Stern), **Supp. IX: 298–299**

Odd Number (Sorrentino), **Supp. XXI:** 236

"Odds, The" (Hecht), **Supp. X:** 64–65

Odds, The (O'Nan), **Supp. XXV:** 150, 151–152

"Odds, The" (Salinas), **Supp. XIII:** 321

"Ode" (Emerson), **II:** 13

"Ode" (Sobin), **Supp. XVI:** 284–285

"Ode" (X. J. Kennedy), **Supp. XV:** 160

"Ode (Intimations of Immortality)" (Matthews), **Supp. IX:** 162

"Ode for Memorial Day" (Dunbar), **Supp. II Part 1:** 199

"Ode for the American Dead in Asia" (McGrath), **Supp. X:** 119

"Ode: For the Budding of Islands" (Sobin), **Supp. XVI:** 287

"Ode Inscribed to W. H. Channing" (Emerson), **Supp. XIV:** 46

"Ode: Intimations of Immortality" (Wordsworth), **Supp. I Part 2:** 729; **Supp. III Part 1:** 12; **Supp. XIV:** 8

"Ode in Time of Crisis" (Taggard), **Supp. XXII:** 271

Odell, Margaretta Matilda, **Supp. XX: 278, 284, 288**

"Ode: My 24th Year" (Ginsberg), **Supp. II Part 1:** 312

"Ode on a Grecian Urn" (Keats), **I:** 284; **III:** 472; **Supp. XII:** 113; **Supp. XIV:** 8, 9–10; **Supp. XV:** 100; **Supp. XXI:** 64

"Ode on Human Destinies" (Jeffers), **Supp. II Part 2:** 419

"Ode on Indolence" (Keats), **Supp. XII:** 113

"Ode on Melancholy" (Keats), **Retro. Supp. I:** 301

Ode Recited at the Harvard Commemoration (Lowell), **Supp. I Part 2:** 416–418, 424

"Ode Recited at the Harvard Commemoration" (Lowell), **II:** 551

Odes (Horace), **Supp. XXIV:** 153

Odes (O'Hara), **Supp. XXIII:** 216

"Ode: Salute to the French Negro Poets" (O'Hara), **Supp. XXIII:** 216

"Ode Secrète" (Valéry), **III:** 609

"Odes of Estrangement" (Sobin), **Supp. XVI:** 289

Odes of Horace, The (Ferry, trans.), **Supp. XXIV: 153–156**

"Odes to Natural Processes" (Updike), **Retro. Supp. I:** 323

"Ode: The Capris" (Halliday), **Supp. XIX:** 88

"Ode to a Nightingale" (Keats), **II:** 368; **Retro. Supp. II:** 261; **Supp. IX:** 52

"Ode to Autumn" (Masters), **Supp. I Part 2:** 458

"Ode to Cervantes" (Salinas), **Supp. XIII:** 324

"Ode to Coit Tower" (Corso), **Supp. XII:** 122

"Ode to Ethiopia" (Dunbar), **Supp. II Part 1:** 199, 207, 208, 209

"Ode to Fear" (Tate), **IV:** 128

Ode to Harvard and Other Poems, An (Bynner), **Supp. XV:** 41, 44

"Ode to Joy" (O'Hara), **Supp. XXIII:** 208, 216

"Ode to Meaning" (Pinsky), **Supp. VI: 249–250,** 251

"Ode to Michael Goldberg ('s Birth and Other Births)" (O'Hara), **Supp. XXIII:** 209, 216, 218

"Ode to Night" (Masters), **Supp. I Part 2:** 458

"Ode to Our Young Pro-Consuls of the Air" (Tate), **IV:** 135

"Ode to the Austrian Socialists" (Benét), **Supp. XI:** 46, 58

"Ode to the Confederate Dead" (Tate), **II:** 551; **IV:** 124, 133, 137; **Supp. X:** 52

"Ode to the Johns Hopkins University" (Lanier), **Supp. I Part 1:** 370

"Ode to the Maggot" (Komunyakaa), **Supp. XIII:** 130

"Ode to the Mexican Experience" (Salinas), **Supp. XIII:** 316–317

"Ode to the Virginian Voyage" (Drayton), **IV:** 135

"Ode to the West Wind" (Shelley), **Retro. Supp. I:** 308; **Supp. I Part 2:** 728; **Supp. IX:** 52; **Supp. XII:** 117; **Supp.**

XIV: 271–272; **Supp. XV:** 221

"Ode to Walt Whitman" (Benét), **Supp. XI:** 52

"Ode to Willem de Kooning"(O'Hara), **Supp. XXIII:** 208, 216

Odets, Clifford, **Supp. I Part 1:** 277, 295; **Supp. I Part 2:** 679; **Supp. II Part 2: 529–554; Supp. IV Part 2:** 587; **Supp. V:** 109; **Supp. VIII:** 96; **Supp. XVIII:** 238; **Supp. XX: 34**

Odier, Daniel, **Supp. III Part 1:** 97

"Odi et Amo" (Catullus), **Supp. XV:** 27, 32, 35

"Odom"(P. Benedict), **Supp. XXIII:** 41

O'Donnell, George Marion, **II:** 67

O'Donnell, Mary King, **Supp. XVIII:** 232

O'Donnell, Thomas F., **II:** 131

"Odor of Verbena" (Faulkner), **II:** 66

O'Doul, Lefty, **II:** 425

Odysseus (Homer), **Supp. XXVI:** 79

"Odysseus to Telemachus" (Brodsky), **Supp. VIII:** 25

Odyssey (Bryant, trans.), **Supp. I Part 1:** 158

Odyssey (Homer), **III:** 14, 470; **Retro. Supp. I:** 286, 290; **Retro. Supp. II:** 121; **Supp. I Part 1:** 185; **Supp. IV Part 2:** 631; **Supp. IX:** 211; **Supp. X:** 114; **Supp. XIV:** 191; **Supp. XVII:** 117; **Supp. XXI:** 36

"Odyssey of a Wop, The" (Fante), **Supp. XI:** 164, 165

Oedipus Rex (Sophocles), **I:** 137; **III:** 145, 151, 152, 332; **Supp. I Part 2:** 428

Oedipus Tyrannus (Sophocles), **II:** 203; **Supp. XV:** 265

Oehlschlaeger, Fritz, **Supp. IX:** 123

Oelze, Richard, **Supp. XXII:** 167

"Of Alexander Crummell" (Du Bois), **Supp. II Part 1:** 170

O'Faoláin, Seán, **Supp. II Part 1:** 101

Of a World That Is No More (Singer), **IV:** 16

Of Being Numerous (Oppen), **Supp. XXVI:** 223, 230, 233–234, 237

"Of Being Numerous" (Oppen), **Supp. XXVI:** 232, 233–234, 236

"Of Booker T. Washington and Others" (Du Bois), **Supp. II Part 1:** 168

"Of Bright & Blue Birds & the Gala Sun" (Stevens), **IV:** 93

"Of Christian Heroism" (Ozick), **Supp. V:** 272

"Of Dying Beauty" (Zukofsky), **Supp. III Part 2:** 610

"Of Epiphanies and Poets" (Phillips), **Supp. XX: 221**

"Of 'Father and Son' " (Kunitz), **Supp. III Part 1:** 262

Offenbach, Jacques, **II:** 427

"Offering for Mr. Bluehart, An" (Wright), **Supp. III Part 2:** 596, 601

"Offerings" (Mason), **Supp. VIII:** 141

"Offertory" (Hempel), **Supp. XXI: 126– 127**

Office, The (Asch), **Supp. XXVI:** 18–20, 21, 25

Official Entry Blank (Kooser), **Supp. XIX:** 116, **117–118**

"Official Entry Form" (Kooser), **Supp. XIX:** 117

"Official Piety" (Whittier), **Supp. I Part 2:** 687

"Offloading for Mrs. Schwartz" (Saunders), **Supp. XIX:** 225–226

"Of Freemasons, Kings, and Constitutions" (P. N. Warren), **Supp. XX: 273**

"Off-Shore Pirates, The" (Fitzgerald), **II:** 88

Off the Beaten Path (Proulx), **Supp. VII:** 261

Off the Beaten Path: Stories of Place, **Supp. XVI:** 22

"Off the Cuff" (Simpson), **Supp. IX:** 278

"Off the Highway" (Wolfert), **Supp. XXI:** 265

Off the Map (Levine), **Supp. V:** 178

Offut, Chris, **Supp. XIX: 163–176**

Of Gravity and Angels (Hirshfield), **Supp. XXIII:** 131

O'Flaherty, George, **Supp. I Part 1:** 202, 205–206

O'Flaherty, Kate. *See* Chopin, Kate

O'Flaherty, Thomas, **Supp. I Part 1:** 202, 203–204, 205

O'Flaherty, Thomas, Jr., **Supp. I Part 1:** 202

"Of Maids and Other Muses" (Alvarez), **Supp. VII:** 11

"Of Margaret" (Ransom), **III:** 491

Of Mice and Men (Steinbeck), **IV:** 51, 57–58

"Of Modern Poetry" (Stevens), **IV:** 92

Of No Country I Know: New and Selected Poems and Translations (Ferry), **Supp. XXIV: 157**

Of Plymouth Plantation (Bradford), **Retro. Supp. II:** 161, 162; **Supp. XXII:** 33, **35–47**

Of Plymouth Plantation (Morison, ed.), **Supp. I Part 2:** 494

"Ofrenda for Lobo" (Mora), **Supp. XIII:** 224

"Often" (Kenyon), **Supp. VII:** 171

"Often, in Dreams, He Moved through a City" (Dobyns), **Supp. XIII:** 90

"Of the Coming of John" (Du Bois), **Supp. II Part 1:** 170

"Of the Culture of White Folk" (Du Bois), **Supp. II Part 1:** 175

Of the Farm (Updike), **IV:** 214, 217, 223–225, 233; **Retro. Supp. I:** 318, 329, 332

"Of the Four-Winged Cherubim as Signature" (Sobin), **Supp. XVI:** 287

"Of 'The Frill' " (McCarriston), **Supp. XIV:** 274

"Of the Passing of the First-Born" (Du Bois), **Supp. II Part 1:** 170

"Of the Sorrow Songs" (Du Bois), **Supp. II Part 1:** 170

"Of the Wings of Atlanta" (Du Bois), **Supp. II Part 1:** 170

Of This Time, Of This Place (Trilling), **Supp. III Part 2:** 498, 504

Of Time and the River (Wolfe), **IV:** 450, 451, 452, 455, 456, 457, 458, 459, 462, 464–465, 467, 468, 469

Of Woman Born: Motherhood as Experience and Institution (Rich), **Supp. I Part 2:** 554, 567–569

Of Women and Their Elegance (Mailer), **Retro. Supp. II:** 209

Ogden, Archie, **Supp. XIII:** 174

Ogden, Henry, **II:** 298

Ogden, Uzal, **Supp. I Part 2:** 516

Ogle, Connie, **Supp. XXIII:** 300, 301

"Oh, Atonement" (Weigl), **Supp. XIX:** 287

"Oh, Fairest of the Rural Maids" (Bryant), **Supp. I Part 1:** 169

"Oh, Immobility, Death's Vast Associate" (Dobyns), **Supp. XIII:** 89

"Oh, Joseph, I'm So Tired" (Yates), **Supp. XI:** 348

Oh, the Places You'll Go! (Geisel), **Supp. XVI:** 111

Oh, the Thinks You can Think! (Geisel), **Supp. XVI:** 111

"O'Halloran's Luck" (Benét), **Supp. XI:** 47

O'Hara, Frank, **Supp. XII:** 121; **Supp. XIX:** 81, 85; **Supp. XV:** 93, 176, 177, 178, 179–180, 182, 186, 187, 215– 216; **Supp. XXII:** 226, 236; **Supp. XXIII: 207–222; Supp. XXIV:** 33, 34, 36, 42, 43, 44

O'Hara, J. D., **Supp. IV Part 1:** 43; **Supp. V:** 22; **Supp. XVI:** 221; **Supp. XXI:** 228

O'Hara, John, **I:** 375, 495; **II:** 444, 459; **III:** 66, **361–384; IV:** 59; **Retro. Supp. I:** 99, 112; **Supp. I Part 1:** 196; **Supp. II Part 1:** 109; **Supp. IV Part 1:** 31, 383; **Supp. IV Part 2:** 678; **Supp. IX:** 208; **Supp. V:** 95; **Supp. VIII:** 151, 156; **Supp. XIX:** 209

O'Hara's Choice (Uris), **Supp. XX: 247, 256–257**

"O Heaven born muse! inspire my humble lay" (Very), **Supp. XXV:** 239

O'Hehir, Andrew, **Supp. XII:** 280

O. Henry Biography (C. A. Smith), **Supp. II Part 1:** 395

"Ohio Pagan, An" (Anderson), **I:** 112, 113

Ohio trilogy (Richter), **Supp. XVIII:** 212–215

Oh Mercy (album, Dylan), **Supp. XVIII:** 28, 33

Oh Say Can You Say? (Geisel), **Supp. XVI:** 111

Oil! (Sinclair), **Supp. V:** 276, 277–279, 282, 288, 289

Oil Notes (Bass), **Supp. XVI:** 17

"Oil Painting of the Artist as the Artist" (MacLeish), **III:** 14

"O-jib-way Maid, The"(J. Schoolcraft), **Supp. XXIII:** 235

O'Keeffe, Georgia, **Supp. IX:** 62, 66; **Supp. XX: 75**

"Oklahoma" (Levis), **Supp. XI:** 267

Oklahoma's Poor Rich Indians: An Orgy of Graft and Exploitation of the Five Civilized Tribes—Legalized Robbery (Zitkala-Ša, Sniffen, and Fabens), **Supp. XXV:** 283

Oktenberg, Adrian, **Supp. XVII:** 76; **Supp. XXI:** 253; **Supp. XXIII:** 133

"Old, Old, Old, Old Andrew Jackson" (Lindsay), **Supp. I Part 2:** 398

"Old Amusement Park, An" (Moore), **III:** 216

"Old Angel Midnight" (Kerouac), **Supp. III Part 1:** 229–230

"Old Apple Dealer, The" (Hawthorne), **II:** 227, 233–235, 237, 238

"Old Apple-Tree, The" (Dunbar), **Supp. II Part 1:** 198

"Old Army Game, The" (Garrett), **Supp. VII:** 100–101

"Old Aunt Peggy" (Chopin), **Retro. Supp. II:** 64

"Old Barn at the Bottom of the Fogs, The" (Frost), **Retro. Supp. I:** 138

Old Battle-Ax, The (Holding), **Supp. XXII: 128–129**

Old Beauty and Others, The (Cather), **I:** 331

"Old Boys, Old Girls" (E. P. Jones), **Supp. XXII:** 151

Old Bruin: Commodore Matthew C. Perry, 1794–1858 (Morison), **Supp. I Part 2:** 494–495

"Old Cracked Tune, An" (Kunitz), **Supp. III Part 1:** 264

Old Curiosity Shop, The (Dickens), **I:** 458; **Supp. I Part 2:** 409

Oldest Killed Lake in North America, The (Carruth), **Supp. XVI:** 51

"Oldest Man, The" (M. F. K. Fisher), **Supp. XVII:** 91

"Old Farmer, The" (Jeffers), **Supp. II Part 2:** 418

Old-Fashioned Girl, An (Alcott), **Supp. I Part 1:** 29, 41, 42

"Old Father Morris" (Stowe), **Supp. I Part 2:** 586

Old Favorites and New Fancies for 1909 (Wells), **Supp. XXVI:** 275

"Old Flame, The" (Lowell), **II:** 550

"Old Florist" (Roethke), **III:** 531

"Old Folsom Prison" (Matthews), **Supp. IX:** 165

Old Forest, The (Taylor), **Supp. V:** 320, 321, 326, 327

"Old Forest, The" (Taylor), **Supp. V:** 313, 321, 323, 326

Old Forest and Other Stories (Taylor), **Supp. V:** 326

Old Friends and New (Jewett), **II:** 402; **Retro. Supp. II:** 137, 140

Old Glory, The (Lowell), **II:** 543, 545–546, 555; **Retro. Supp. II:** 188

Old Helmet, The (S. and A. Warner), **Supp. XVIII:** 267

"Old Homestead, The" (Dunbar), **Supp. II Part 1:** 198

"Old House" (Espaillat), **Supp. XXI:** 112, 113

Old Indian Legends (Zitkala-Ša), **Supp. XXV:** 275, 278, 285

"Old Iron" (Nye), **Supp. XIII:** 276

"Old Ironsides" (Holmes), **Supp. I Part 1:** 302

Old Jules (Sandoz), **Supp. XXIV:** 243, 244, **245–246,** 249, 251, 255, 257

"Old Lady We Saw, An" (Shields), **Supp. VII:** 310–311

"Old Love" (Singer), **Retro. Supp. II:** 307

"Old McGrath Place, The" (McGrath), **Supp. X:** 114

"Old Maid, The" (Wharton), **Retro. Supp. I:** 381, 382

"Old Man" (Faulkner), **II:** 68, 69

Old Man and the Sea, The (Hemingway), **II:** 250, 256–257, 258, 265; **III:** 40; **Retro. Supp. I:** 180, **185,** 186

"Old Man Drunk" (Wright), **Supp. III Part 2:** 595

"Old Man Feeding Hens" (Francis), **Supp. IX:** 78

"Old Man on the Hospital Porch" (Ríos), **Supp. IV Part 2:** 546–547

Old Man Rubbing His Eyes (R. Bly), **Supp. IV Part 1:** 65

"Old Manse, The" (Hawthorne), **II:** 224

"Old Man's Winter Night, An" (Frost), **Retro. Supp. I:** 126, 131

Old Man Who Love Cheese, The (Keillor), **Supp. XVI:** 177

"Old Man with a Dog" (Wright), **Supp. XV:** 346

Old Marriage and New (Kooser), **Supp. XIX: 120–121**

"Old Meeting House, The" (Stowe), **Supp. I Part 2:** 586

"Old Memory, An" (Dunbar), **Supp. II Part 1:** 198

"Old Men, Old Horses" (P. N. Warren as Kilina), **Supp. XX: 262**

"Old Men, The" (McCarthy), **II:** 566

"Old Men Pitching Horseshoes" (X. J. Kennedy), **Supp. XV:** 166

Old Money (Wasserstein), **Supp. XV: 333–334**

"Old Morgue, The" (Prose), **Supp. XVI:** 250

Old Morning Program, The (radio show, Keillor). *See* Prairie Home Companion, A (radio show, Keillor)

"Old Mortality" (Porter), **III:** 436, 438–441, 442, 445, 446

"Old Mrs. Harris" (Cather), **I:** 332; **Retro. Supp. I:** 19

Old Neighborhood, The (Mamet), **Supp. XIV:** 240, 241, 242, 249–250, 251, 252, 254

Old New York (Wharton), **IV:** 322; **Retro. Supp. I:** 381

"Ol' Doc Hyar" (Campbell), **Supp. II Part 1:** 202

"Old of the Moon" (Offutt), **Supp. XIX:** 165, 166

Old One-Two, The (Gurney), **Supp. V:** 98

"Old Order, The" (Porter), **III:** 443, 444–445, 451

"Old Osawatomie" (Sandburg), **III:** 584

Old Patagonia Express, The: By Train through the Americas (Theroux), **Supp. VIII:** 322

"Old People" (Ferry), **Supp. XXIV:** 162

"Old People, The" (Faulkner), **II:** 71–72

"Old Photograph" (Davison), **Supp. XXVI:** 72

"Old Photograph, An" (Kooser), **Supp. XIX:** 121

"Old Poet Moves to a New Apartment 14 Times, The" (Zukofsky), **Supp. III Part 2:** 628

Old Possum's Book of Practical Cats (T. S. Eliot), **Supp. XIII:** 228, 344

"Old Red" (Gordon), **II:** 199, 200, 203

Old Red and Other Stories (Gordon), **II:** 157

Old Régime in Canada, The (Parkman), **Supp. II Part 2:** 600, 607, 608–609, 612

Old Religion, The (Mamet), **Supp. XIV:** 253

Olds, Sharon, **Supp. X: 201–217; Supp. XI:** 139, 142, 244; **Supp. XII:** 229; **Supp. XIV:** 265; **Supp. XVII:** 114, 240; **Supp. XXI:** 249

"Old Saws" (Garrett), **Supp. VII:** 96–97

Old South, The: "A Summer Tragedy" and Other Stories (Bontemps), **Supp. XXII:** 7

"Old Stories" (Skloot), **Supp. XX: 200**

Old Testament, **I:** 109, 181, 300, 328, 401, 410, 419, 431, 457, 458; **II:** 166, 167, 219; **III:** 270, 272, 348, 390, 396; **IV:** 41, 114, 152, 309; **Retro. Supp. I:** 122, 140, 249, 311, 360; **Retro. Supp. II:** 299; **Supp. I Part 1:** 60, 104, 106, 151; **Supp. I Part 2:** 427, 515, 516; **Supp. IX:** 14. *See also* names of Old Testament books

"Old Things, The" (James), **Retro. Supp. I:** 229

"Old Times on the Mississippi" (Twain), **IV:** 199

Oldtown Folks (Stowe), **Supp. I Part 2:** 587, 596–598

"Old Town of Berwick, The" (Jewett), **Retro. Supp. II:** 132

"Old Trails" (Robinson), **III:** 513, 517

"Old Tyrannies" (Bourne), **I:** 233

"Old West" (Bausch), **Supp. VII:** 48

"Old Whorehouse, An" (Oliver), **Supp. VII:** 235

"Old Woman" (Pinsky), **Supp. VI:** 238

"Old Woman of Beare, The" (X. J. Kennedy), **Supp. XV:** 156

"Old Word, The" (Simic), **Supp. VIII:** 282

"Old-World Landowners" (Gogol), **Supp. XV:** 262

Oldys, Francis. *See* Chalmers, George

Oleanna (Mamet), **Supp. XIV:** 239, 241, 245, 248, 250

Olendorf, Donna, **Supp. IV Part 1:** 196

"Olga Poems, The" (Levertov), **Supp. III Part 1:** 279–281

"Olive Groves of Thasos, The" (Clampitt), **Supp. IX: 51–52**

Olive Kitteridge (Strout), **Supp. XXIII:** 273, 275, **280–284,** 285

Oliver, Bill, **Supp. VIII:** 138

Oliver, Douglas, **Supp. XXII:** 225, 226, 233, 235

Oliver, Mary, **Supp. VII: 229–248; Supp. X:** 31; **Supp. XVI:** 39; **Supp. XVII:** 111, 240; **Supp. XXIII:** 51

Oliver, Sydney, **I:** 409

Oliver Goldsmith: A Biography (Irving), **II:** 315

Oliver Twist (Dickens), **I:** 354; **Supp. IV Part 2:** 464

Olives (Stallings), **Supp. XXV:** 221, 223, 224, 233–234

"Olivia" (Salinas), **Supp. XIII:** 316

"Olivier Bergmann" (Halliday), **Supp. XIX:** 93–94

Olivieri, David (pseudonym), **Retro. Supp. I:** 361. *See also* Wharton, Edith

Ollive, Samuel, **Supp. I Part 2:** 503

Olmsted, Frederick Law, **Supp. I Part 1:** 355

Olor de la memoria, El/The Scent of Memory (Espaillat), **Supp. XXI:** 104

Olsen, Lance, **Supp. IV Part 1:** 54; **Supp. IV Part 2:** 623

Olsen, Tillie, **Supp. V:** 114, 220; **Supp. XIII: 291–309; Supp. XVI:** 83, 90

Olshan, Joseph, **Supp. XIX:** 52

Olson, Charles, **Retro. Supp. I:** 209; **Supp. II Part 1:** 30, 328; **Supp. II Part 2: 555–587; Supp. III Part 1:** 9, 271; **Supp. III Part 2:** 542, 624; **Supp. IV Part 1:** 139, 144, 146, 153, 154, 322; **Supp. IV Part 2:** 420, 421, 423, 426; **Supp. VIII:** 290, 291; **Supp. XII:** 2, 198; **Supp. XIII:** 104; **Supp. XIV:** 96; **Supp. XV:** 177; **Supp. XXI:** 19, 21, 23; **Supp. XXIV:** 42

Olson, Clarence, **Supp. XX: 84, 85, 86**

Olson, Ray, **Supp. XVII:** 111, 112, 119

"Ol' Tunes, The" (Dunbar), **Supp. II Part 1:** 197

"O Lull Me, Lull Me" (Roethke), **III:** 536–537

O'Malley, Anne, **Supp. XXII:** 56

Omar Khayyam, **Supp. I Part 1:** 363

O'Meally, Robert, **Retro. Supp. II:** 112

Omega the Unknown (comic book series), **Supp. XVIII:** 149

"Omen" (Komunyakaa), **Supp. XIII:** 126, 127

Omensetter's Luck (Gass), **Supp. VI: 80–82,** 87

Omeros (Walcott), **Supp. XV:** 264

"Ominous Baby, An" (Crane), **I:** 411

Ommateum, with Doxology (Ammons), **Supp. VII:** 24–26, 27, 28, 36

Omni-Americans, The: New Perspectives on Black Experience and American Culture (Murray), **Supp. XIX:** 147, **149–151,** 154

"Omnibus Jaunts and Drivers" (Whitman), **IV:** 350

Omoo: A Narrative of Adventures in the South Seas (Melville), **III:** 76–77, 79, 84; **Retro. Supp. I:** 247

O My Land, My Friends (H. Crane), **Retro. Supp. II:** 76

"On Abrigador Hill" (Nelson), **Supp. XVIII:** 183

"On a Certain Condescension in Foreigners" (Lowell), **Supp. I Part 2:** 419

"On a Certain Engagement South of Seoul" (Carruth), **Supp. XVI:** 47

"On a Child Who Lived One Minute" (X. J. Kennedy), **Supp. XV:** 152, 155

"On Acquiring Riches" (Banks), **Supp. V:** 5

On a Darkling Plain (Stegner), **Supp. IV Part 2:** 598, 607

On a Fire on the Moon (Mailer), **Retro. Supp. II:** 206

"On a Hill Far Away" (Dillard), **Supp. VI:** 28

"On a Honey Bee, Drinking from a Glass and Drowned Therein" (Freneau), **Supp. II Part 1:** 273

"On a Monument to a Pigeon" (Leopold), **Supp. XIV:** 187–188

"On a Mountainside" (Wagoner), **Supp. IX:** 332

O'Nan, Stewart, **Supp. XI:** 348; **Supp. XXV: 141–155**

"On an Old Photograph of My Son" (Carver), **Supp. III Part 1:** 140

"Onan's Soliloquy" (X. J. Kennedy), **Supp. XV:** 165

"On a Proposed Trip South" (W. C. Williams), **Retro. Supp. I:** 413

"On a Scale of 1 to 10: Life Writing and Lyrical Pain" (Mintz), **Supp. XXVI:** 52–53

Onassis, Jacqueline Kennedy, **Supp. XVIII:** 287

"On a Tree Fallen across the Road" (Frost), **Retro. Supp. I:** 134

"On a View of Pasadena from the Hills" (Winters), **Supp. II Part 2:** 795, 796–799, 814

"On a Visit to a Halfway House after a Long Absence" (Salinas), **Supp. XIII:** 325

"On a Windy Night" (Dixon), **Supp. XII:** 155

On Becoming a Novelist (Gardner), **Supp. VI:** 64

"On Being an American" (Toomer), **Supp. III Part 2:** 479

"On Being Asked to Write a Poem against the War in Vietnam" (Carruth), **Supp. XVI:** 55–56

"On Being a Woman" (Parker), **Supp. IX:** 201

On Being Blue (Gass), **Supp. VI:** 77, 78, 86, 94; **Supp. XIV:** 305

"On Being Brought from Africa to America" (Wheatley), **Supp. XX: 280–281, 286–287**

"On Being Too Inhibited" (Hay), **Supp. XIV:** 130

"On Being Unable to Read" (Cornell), **Supp. XX: 94–95**

On Beyond Zebra! (Geisel), **Supp. XVI:** 105

"On Burroughs' Work" (Ginsberg), **Supp. II Part 1:** 320

Once (Walker), **Supp. III Part 2:** 519, 522, 530

Once at Antietam (Gaddis), **Supp. IV Part 1:** 285

"Once by the Pacific" (Frost), **II:** 155; **Retro. Supp. I:** 122, 137

"Once More, the Round" (Roethke), **III:** 529

Once More around the Block: Familiar Essays (Epstein), **Supp. XIV: 107**

"Once More to the Lake" (White), **Supp. I Part 2:** 658, 668, 673–675

"On Certain Political Measures Proposed to Their Consideration" (Barlow), **Supp. II Part 1:** 82

"Once There Was Light" (Kenyon), **Supp. VII:** 171–172

Once Upon a Time in Atlanta (Andrews), **Supp. XXVI:** 3, 11

"On *Credo Ut Intelligam*" (Bronk), **Supp. XXI:** 31

Ondaatje, Michael, **Supp. IV Part 1:** 252

"On Dining Alone" (M. F. K. Fisher), **Supp. XVII:** 83

On Distant Ground (R. O. Butler), **Supp. XII:** 62, **66–68,** 69, 74

"On Divers Geometries" (Bronk), **Supp. XXI:** 31

"On Dreams"(Hadas), **Supp. XXIII:** 117

"One, The" (Weigl), **Supp. XIX:** 282–283

"1 January 1965" (Brodsky), **Supp. VIII:** 23–24

O'Neale, Sondra, **Supp. IV Part 1:** 2

"One A.M. with Voices" (X. J. Kennedy), **Supp. XV:** 157

"One Arm" (T. Williams), **IV:** 383

One Arm, and Other Stories (T. Williams), **IV:** 383

"One Art" (Bell), **Supp. X:** 2

One Art (Bishop), **Retro. Supp. II:** 51

"One Art" (Bishop), **Retro. Supp. II:** 50; **Supp. I Part 1:** 72, 73, 82, 93, 94–95, 96; **Supp. XV:** 126; **Supp. XXI:** 58; **Supp. XXIII:** 117; **Supp. XXV:** 222

"One Art: The Poetry of Elizabeth Bishop, 1971–1976" (Schwartz), **Supp. I Part 1:** 81

One Big Self: Prisoners of Louisiana (Wright and Luster), **Supp. XV:** 337, 344, 350, **351–353**

"One Blessing had I than the rest" (Dickinson), **Retro. Supp. I:** 45

"One Body" (Hass), **Supp. VI:** 106

One Boy's Boston, 1887–1901 (Morison), **Supp. I Part 2:** 494

"One Coat of Paint" (Ashbery), **Supp. III Part 1:** 26

"One Dash-Horses" (Crane), **I:** 416

One Day (Morris), **III:** 233–236

One Day, When I Was Lost (Baldwin), **Retro. Supp. II:** 13; **Supp. I Part 1:** 48, 66, 67

"One Dead Friend" (Kumin), **Supp. IV Part 2:** 441

One Destiny: An Epistle to the Christians (Asch), **Supp. XXIII:** 2, 7

"One Down" (Goodman), **Supp. XXVI:** 122–123

One Fish Two Fish Red Fish Blue Fish (Geisel), **Supp. XVI:** 108

One Flesh (Major), **Supp. XXII: 183–184**

One Flew Over the Cuckoo's Nest (Kesey), **III:** 558

One Flew Over the Cuckoo's Nest (Kesey), **Supp. XXIII:** 100

"One for the Road" (Swados), **Supp. XIX:** 259

One for the Rose (Levine), **Supp. V:** 178, 179, 181, 187, 189–191

"One for the Rose" (Levine), **Supp. V:** 181, 190

"One Friday Morning" (Hughes), **Supp. I Part 1:** 330

"One Holy Night" (Cisneros), **Supp. VII:** 69–70

"One Home" (Stafford), **Supp. XI:** 321

100 Faces of Death, The, Part IV (Boyle), **Supp. VIII:** 16

100 Great Poets of the English Language (Gioia, ed.), **Supp. XXI:** 99

100 Years of Negro Freedom (Bontemps), **Supp. XXII:** 6

$106,000 Blood Money (Hammett), **Supp. IV Part 1:** 345

"$106,000 Blood Money" (Hammett), **Supp. IV Part 1:** 345, 346

One Hundred Days in Europe (Holmes), **Supp. I Part 1:** 317

180 More: Extraordinary Poems for Every Day (Collins, ed.), **Supp. XXI:** 54

158-Pound Marriage, The (Irving), **Supp. VI:** 163, 164, **167–170**

O'Neil, Elizabeth Murrie, **Retro. Supp. I:** 427

O'Neill, Brendan, **Supp. XII:** 286

O'Neill, Eugene, **I:** 66, 71, 81, 94, 393, 445; **II:** 278, 391, 427, 585; **III:** 151, 165, **385–408**; **IV:** 61, 383; **Retro. Supp. II:** 82, 104; **Supp. III Part 1:** 177–180, 189; **Supp. IV Part 1:** 359; **Supp. IV Part 2:** 587, 607; **Supp. V:** 277; **Supp. VIII:** 332, 334; **Supp. XIV:** 239, 320, 328; **Supp. XVI:** 193; **Supp. XVII:** 96, 99–100, 103, 105, 107; **Supp. XX: 69; Supp. XXI:** 6, 13; **Supp. XXII:** 17, 18, 22, 28; **Supp. XXV:** 19

O'Neill, Oona, **Supp. XXII:** 25, 26

"One Is a Wanderer" (Thurber), **Supp. I Part 2:** 616

One Is the Sun (P. N. Warren), **Supp. XX: 269–270**

One L (Turow), **Supp. XVII: 214,** 215, 217

"One Last Look at the Adige: Verona in the Rain" (Wright), **Supp. III Part 2:** 603

One Life (Rukeyser), **Supp. VI:** 273, 281, 283

One Life at a Time, Please (Abbey), **Supp. XIII:** 13

One Man in His Time (Glasgow), **II:** 178, 184

"One Man's Fortunes" (Dunbar), **Supp. II Part 1:** 211, 212–213

One Man's Initiation (Dos Passos), **I:** 476–477, 479, 488

One Man's Meat (White), **Supp. I Part 2:** 654, 669, 676

"One Man's Meat" (White), **Supp. I Part 2:** 655

One Matchless Time: A Life of William Faulkner (Parini), **Supp. XXII:** 205

"One Moment on Top of the Earth" (Nye), **Supp. XIII:** 282

One More July: A Football Dialogue with Bill Curry (Plimpton), **Supp. XVI:** 243

"One More"(Kenny), **Supp. XXIII:** 156

"One More Song" (Lindsay), **Supp. I Part 2:** 400–401

"One More Thing" (Carver), **Supp. III Part 1:** 138, 144

"One More Time" (Gordon), **II:** 200

One Nation (Stegner), **Supp. IV Part 2:** 599, 608

"One-Night Homecoming" (X. J. Kennedy), **Supp. XV:** 167

"ONE NIGHT STAND" (Baraka), **Supp. II Part 1:** 32

"One of Our Conquerors" (Bourne), **I:** 223

One of Ours (Cather), **I:** 322–323; **Retro. Supp. I:** 1, 3, **13–15,** 20

One of the Dangerous Trades (Davison), **Supp. XXVI:** 61, 67–68

"One of the Missing" (Bierce), **I:** 201–202

"One of the Rooming Houses of Heaven" (Doty), **Supp. XI:** 131

"One of the Smallest" (Stern), **Supp. IX:** 299–300

"One of Us" (Fante), **Supp. XI:** 165

Oneóta: or, The Red Race of America (H. Schoolcraft), **Supp. XXIII:** 232

"One Out of Twelve: Writers Who Are Women in Our Century" (Olsen), **Supp. XIII:** 294

"One Part Humor, 2 Parts Whining" (Kakutani), **Supp. XI:** 38

"One Person" (Wylie), **Supp. I Part 2:** 709, 724–727

"One Sister have I in our house" (Dickinson), **Retro. Supp. I:** 34

165 Meeting House Lane (Notley), **Supp. XXII:** 224, 225, 226

"One Song, The" (Strand), **Supp. IV Part 2:** 619

"One Summer in Spain" (Coover), **Supp. V:** 40

One That Got Away, The (Everett), **Supp. XVIII:** 54

1000 Airplanes on the Roof (Glass, Hwang, and Sirlin), **Supp. XXI:** 147

One Thousand Avant-Garde Plays (Koch), **Supp. XV:** 187

"One Thousandth, The" (Weigl), **Supp. XIX:** 288

One Time, One Place: Mississippi in the Depression, a Snapshot Album (Welty), **Retro. Supp. I:** 339, 343, 344

1 x 1 (One Times One) (Cummings), **I:** 430, 436, 438–439, 441, 446, 447, 448

"One Touch of Nature" (McCarthy), **II:** 580

One Train (Koch), **Supp. XV:** 177, 184

"One Trip Abroad" (Fitzgerald), **II:** 95

One True Thing (film), **Supp. XVII:** 176

One True Thing (Quindlen), **Supp. XVII:** 166, **174–176**

"One Way" (Creeley), **Supp. IV Part 1:** 150–151

One Way or Another (Cameron), **Supp. XII:** 81

One-Way Ticket (Hughes), **Retro. Supp. I:** 206, 207, 208; **Supp. I Part 1:** 333–334

One Way to Heaven (Cullen), **Supp. IV Part 1:** 170, 172

One Way to Reconstruct the Scene (W. V. Davis), **Supp. XXI:** 83, **88–91**

"One Way to Reconstruct the Scene" (W. V. Davis), **Supp. XXI: 88–89,** 90, **91,** 92, **93**

One Way to Spell Man (Stegner), **Supp. IV Part 2:** 595, 598, 601, 609

"One Way to Spell Man" (Stegner), **Supp. IV Part 2:** 601

One Whose Eyes Open When You Close Your Eyes, The (F. Wright), **Supp. XVII:** 240, 243

"One Who Skins Cats, The" (Gunn Allen), **Supp. IV Part 1:** 331

"One Who Went Forth to Feel Fear" (Grimms), **Supp. X:** 86

"One Winter I Devise a Plan of My Own" (Ríos), **Supp. IV Part 2:** 549

One Winter Night in August (X. J. Kennedy), **Supp. XV:** 154, 162

One World at a Time (Kooser), **Supp. XIX:** 116, **122–123**

"One Year" (Olds), **Supp. X:** 210

On Fire (L. Brown), **Supp. XXI:** 41, **48–49**

On Fire (Silver), **Supp. XXIV:** 264

"On First Looking Into Chapman's Homer" (Keats), **Supp. XXI:** 64; **Supp. XXV:** 226

"On First Looking Out through Juan de la Cosa's Eyes" (Olson), **Supp. II Part 2:** 565, 566, 570, 579

"On First Opening *The Lyric Year*" (W. C. Williams), **Retro. Supp. I:** 414

"On Freedom's Ground" (Wilbur), **Supp. III Part 2:** 562

On Glory's Course (Purdy), **Supp. VII:** 275–276, 279, 280

On Grief and Reason (Brodsky), **Supp. VIII:** 31–32

"On Hearing a Symphony of Beethoven" (Millay), **III:** 132–133

"On Hearing the Airlines Will Use a Psychological Profile to Catch Potential Skyjackers" (Dunn), **Supp. XI:** 144–145

On Human Finery (Bell), **Supp. I Part 2:** 636

"On *Imagerie*: Esther Williams, 1944" (Sobin), **Supp. XVI:** 294

"On Imagination" (Wheatley), **Supp. XX:** 281

"On Imminence: An Essay" (Sobin), **Supp. XVI:** 291

On Immunity: An Inoculation (Biss), **Supp. XXVI:** 45, 57–58, 59

"Onionskin" (Goodman), **Supp. XXVI:** 121, 125

"On Ithaka" (Davison), **Supp. XXVI:** 79

On Kingdom Mountain (Mosher), **Supp. XXII:** 203, 205, 206, 207, 208, 209, 212, 214, **216**

Onkl Mozes (Uncle Moses) (Asch), **Supp. XXIII:** 5

"On leaving my children John and Jane at School, in the Atlantic states, and preparing to return to the interior"(J. Schoolcraft), **Supp. XXIII:** 227, 228, 232, 233, 235, 236

On Liberty (Mill), **Supp. XI:** 196

"On Looking Alone at a Place" (M. F. K. Fisher), **Supp. XVII:** 91

"On Looking at a Copy of Alice Meynell's Poems, Given Me, Years Ago, by a Friend" (Lowell), **II:** 527–528

"On Lookout Mountain" (Hayden), **Supp. II Part 1:** 380

Only a Few of Us Left (Marquand), **III:** 55

"Only Animal, The" (F. Wright), **Supp. XVII:** 245

"Only a Pawn in Their Game" (song, Dylan), **Supp. XVIII:** 24

Only as Far as Brooklyn (Kenny), **Supp. XXIII: 148–151,** 152

"Only Bar in Dixon, The" (Hugo), **Supp. VI:** 140, 141

Only Dangerous Thing, The (Di Piero), **Supp. XIX: 37–38**

Only Dark Spot in the Sky, The (Dove), **Supp. IV Part 1:** 244

"Only Good Indian, The" (Humphrey), **Supp. IX:** 101

"Only Goodness" (Lahiri), **Supp. XXI:** 186, 188

Only in America (Golden), **Supp. VIII:** 244

"Only in the Dream" (Eberhart), **I:** 523

"Only Path to Tomorrow, The" (Rand), **Supp. IV Part 2:** 524

"Only Professional Player of the Toy Piano, Margaret Leng Tan, The" (Biss), **Supp. XXVI:** 51

"Only Rose, The" (Jewett), **II:** 408

"Only Son of the Doctor, The" (Gordon), **Supp. IV Part 1:** 305, 306

"Only the Cat Escapes", **Supp. XII:** 150–151

"Only the Dead Know Brooklyn" (Wolfe), **IV:** 451

Only the Little Bone (Huddle), **Supp. XXVI:** 152–153

"Only the Little Bone" (Huddle), **Supp. XXVI:** 151, 153

"Only When I Am Quiet and Do Not Speak"(Hirshfield), **Supp. XXIII:** 133

Only When I Laugh (Simon), **Supp. IV Part 2:** 575

Only World, The (Hull), **Supp. XXI:** 129, **138–141**

On Man and Manhood (Kriegel), **Supp. XXIV: 224–225**

"On Manhood, Disease, and the Authentic Self" (Kriegel), **Supp. XXIV:** 215

"On Meditation"(J. Schoolcraft), **Supp. XXIII:** 229

"On Meeting My Father in a Bar for the First Time" (Gansworth), **Supp. XXVI:** 110

"On Messrs. Hussey and Coffin" (Wheatley), **Supp. XX:** 280

On Moral Fiction (Gardner), **Supp. VI:** 61, **71,** 72, 73

"On Morality" (Didion), **Supp. IV Part 1:** 196

"On Mt. Philo in November" (Di Piero), **Supp. XIX:** 37, 39

"On Murder Considered as One of the Fine Arts" (De Quincey), **Supp. XXVI:** 283

"On My Own" (Levine), **Supp. V:** 181, 189–190

"On My Own Work" (Wilbur), **Supp. III Part 2:** 541–542

On Native Grounds: An Interpretation of Modern American Prose Literature (Kazin), **I:** 517; **Supp. I Part 2:** 650; **Supp. VIII:** 93, 96–97, 98, **100–102**

"On Not Being a Dove" (Updike), **Retro. Supp. I:** 323

"On Open Form" (Merwin), **Supp. III Part 1:** 347–348, 353

On Photography (Sontag), **Supp. III Part 2:** 451, 458, 462–465

"On Poetry"(Hadas), **Supp. XXIII:** 115, 116

"On Political Poetry" (R. Bly), **Supp. IV Part 1:** 61

On Politics: A Carnival of Buncombe (Moos, ed.), **III:** 116

"On Pretentiousness" (Kushner), **Supp. IX:** 131–132

"On Quitting a Little College" (Stafford), **Supp. XI:** 321

"On Reading Eckerman's Conversations with Goethe" (Masters), **Supp. I Part 2:** 458

On Reading Shakespeare (L. P. Smith), **Supp. XIV:** 345–346

"On Reading to Oneself" (Gass), **Supp. VI:** 88, 89

"On Recollection" (Wheatley), **Supp. XX:** 287

On Revolution (Arendt), **Retro. Supp. I:** 87

On Second Thought (Kenny), **Supp. XXIII:** 144

"On Seeing Larry Rivers's *Washington Crossing the Delaware* at the Museum of Modern Art" (O'Hara), **Supp. XV:** 186; **Supp. XXIII:** 208, 214

"On Seeing Red" (Walker), **Supp. III Part 2:** 527

"On Social Plays" (A. Miller), **III:** 147, 148, 159

Onstad, Katrina, **Supp. XXIV:** 209

"On Steinbeck's Story 'Flight' " (Stegner), **Supp. IV Part 2:** 596

"On Style" (Sontag), **Supp. III Part 2:** 456–459, 465–466

"On Suicide" (Hay), **Supp. XIV:** 130, 132

"On Teaching the Young Laurel to Shoot" (Bynner), **Supp. XV:** 50

"On the Antler" (Proulx), **Supp. VII:** 252–253

"On the Avenue" (Espaillat), **Supp. XXI:** 112

On the Banks of Plum Creek (L. I. Wilder), **Supp. XXII:** 294, 299

"On the Banks of the Wabash" (Paul Dresser), **Retro. Supp. II:** 94

"On the Beach, at Night" (Whitman), **IV:** 348

"On the Bosom of This Grave and Wasted Land I Will Lay My Head" (Ray), **Supp. XVIII:** 189

On the Boundary (Tillich), **Retro. Supp. I:** 326

"On the Building of Springfield" (Lindsay), **Supp. I Part 2:** 381

"On the Coast of Maine" (Hayden), **Supp. II Part 1:** 381

On the Contrary: Articles of Belief (McCarthy), **II:** 559, 562

"On the Death of a Friend's Child" (Lowell), **Supp. I Part 2:** 409

"On the Death of Cardinal Tisserant" (Bronk), **Supp. XXI:** 32

"On the Death of General Wooster" (Wheatley), **Supp. XX: 287**

"On the Death of Rev. Mr. George White-field—1770" (Wheatley), **Supp. XX: 280,Supp. XX: 282–283**

"On the Death of Senator Thomas J. Walsh" (Winters), **Supp. II Part 2:** 802, 806

"On the Death of Yeats" (Bogan), **Supp. III Part 1:** 59

"On the Death of Zhukov" (Brodsky), **Supp. VIII:** 27

"On the Disadvantages of Central Heating" (Clampitt), **Supp. IX:** 41, 47, 52

"On the Doric Rock, Lake Superior"(J. Schoolcraft), **Supp. XXIII:** 232

On the Drumhead: A Selection from the Writing of Mike Quin (Carlisle, ed.), **Supp. XVIII:** 223, 226

"On the Edge" (Levine), **Supp. V:** 181–182

On the Edge and Over (Levine), **Supp. V:** 178, 180–182, 186

On the Edge of the Great Rift: Three Novels of Africa (Theroux), **Supp. VIII:** 316

"On the Edge of Visible Light"(Schott), **Supp. XXIII:** 242

"On the Eve of the Feast of the Im-maculate Conception, 1942" (Lowell), **II:** 538; **Retro. Supp. II:** 185

"On the Eyes of an SS Officer" (Wilbur), **Supp. III Part 2:** 548

"On the Failure of Meaning in the Ab-sence of Objective Analogs" (Bronk), **Supp. XXI:** 31

"On the Fall of General Earl Cornwallis" (Freneau), **Supp. II Part 1:** 261

"On the Folly of Writing Poetry" (Freneau), **Supp. II Part 1:** 263

On the Frontier (Auden and Isherwood), **Supp. II Part 1:** 13; **Supp. XIV:** 163

On the Great Atlantic Rainway: Selected Poems, 1950–1988 (Koch), **Supp. XV:** 177

"On the History of Poetry" (Halliday), **Supp. XIX:** 88, 89

"On the Hysterical Playground" (Watman), **Supp. XX: 93**

"On the Island" (Stern), **Supp. IX:** 290

"On the Late Eclipse" (Bryant), **Supp. I Part 1:** 152

On the Laws of the Poetic Art (Hecht), **Supp. X:** 58

On the Line (Swados), **Supp. XIX: 258–260**

"On the Line" (Swados), **Supp. XIX:** 259

"On the Marginal Way" (Wilbur), **Supp. III Part 2:** 558, 559

On the Mesa (Nichols), **Supp. XIII:** 268

"On the Moon and Matriarchal Consciousness" (Neumann), **Supp. IV Part 1:** 68

"On the Morning after the Sixties" (Didion), **Supp. IV Part 1:** 205, 206

On the Motion and Immobility of Douve (Bonnefoy; Kinnell, trans.), **Supp. III Part 1:** 235

"On the Mullica"(Schott), **Supp. XXIII:** 253

"On the Murder of Lieutenant José del Castillo by the Falangist Bravo Martinez, July 12, 1936" (Levine), **Supp. V:** 187

"On the Night of a Friend's Wedding" (Robinson), **III:** 524

"On the Occasion of a Poem: Richard Hugo" (Wright), **Supp. III Part 2:** 596

On the Occasion of My Last Afternoon (Gibbons), **Supp. X:** 46, **50–53**

On the Origin of Species (Darwin), **Supp. XIV:** 192

"On the Parapet" (Tanner), **Retro. Supp. II:** 205

"On the Platform" (Nemerov), **III:** 287

On the Poetry of Philip Levine: Stranger to Nothing (Levis), **Supp. XI:** 257

"On the Pottlecombe Cornice" (Sturgis), **Supp. XX: 233, 240**

"On the Powers of the Human Understanding" (Freneau), **Supp. II Part 1:** 274

On the Prejudices, Predilections, and Firm Beliefs of William Faulkner (Brooks), **Supp. XIV:** 13

"On the Pulse of Morning" (Angelou), **Supp. IV Part 1: 15–17**

"On the Railway Platform" (Jarrell), **II:** 370

"On the Rainy River" (O'Brien), **Supp. V:** 250

On the Rebound: A Story and Nine Poems (Purdy), **Supp. VII:** 276–277

"On the Religion of Nature" (Freneau), **Supp. II Part 1:** 275

"On the River" (Dunbar), **Supp. II Part 1:** 193

"On the River" (Levine), **Supp. V:** 193

On the River Styx and Other Stories (Matthiessen), **Supp. V:** 212

On the Road (Kerouac), **Retro. Supp. I:** 102; **Supp. III Part 1:** 92, 218, 222–224, 226, 230–231; **Supp. V:** 336; **Supp. X:** 269; **Supp. XIII:** 275; **Supp. XIV:** 138, 150; **Supp. XV:** 221; **Supp. XVIII:** 20, 138; **Supp. XXI:** 53; **Supp. XXIV:** 281; **Supp. XXVI:** 26, 252

"On the Road Home" (Stevens), **Retro. Supp. I:** 306

On the Road with the Archangel (Buechner), **Supp. XII:** 54

"On the Rope" (Richard), **Supp. XIX:** 211–212

"On the Run" (Boyle), **Supp. XXIV:** 52

On These I Stand: An Anthology of the Best Poems of Countee Cullen (Cullen), **Supp. IV Part 1:** 173

"On the Skeleton of a Hound" (Wright), **Supp. III Part 2:** 593

"On the Staten Island Ferry"(Kenny), **Supp. XXIII:** 154

"On the Street" (Peacock), **Supp. XIX:** 199

"On the Street: Monument" (Gunn Allen), **Supp. IV Part 1:** 326

"On the Subway" (Olds), **Supp. X:** 207

"On the System of Policy Hitherto Pursued by Their Government" (Barlow), **Supp. II Part 1:** 82

"On the Teaching of Modern Literature" (Trilling), **Supp. III Part 2:** 509–510

"On the Uniformity and Perfection of Nature" (Freneau), **Supp. II Part 1:** 275

"On the Universality and Other Attributes of the God of Nature" (Freneau), **Supp. II Part 1:** 275

"On the Use of Trisyllabic Feet in Iambic Verse" (Bryant), **Supp. I Part 1:** 156

On the Verge: Emerging Poets (Ellis and Lease, eds.), **Supp. XXI:** 246

On the Waterfront (film, Kazan), **Supp. XVIII: 250–251,** 252, 253

"On the Way Home" (L. I. Wilder), **Supp. XXII:** 292

On the Way to the Island (Ferry), **Supp. XXIV:** 147, **148–149,** 150

"On the Way to the San Remo"(O'Hara), **Supp. XXIII:** 212, 219

On the Way toward a Phenomenological Psychology: The Psychology of William James (Linschoten), **II:** 362

"On the Way to Work" (Dunn), **Supp. XI:** 149–150

"On the Wide Heath" (Millay), **III:** 130

"On the Writing of Novels" (Buck), **Supp. II Part 1:** 121

On the Yard (Braly), **Supp. XVIII:** 147

On This Island (Auden), **Supp. II Part 1:** 11

On This Side of the River (Ferry), **Supp. XXIV: 161–162**

"On Time" (O'Hara), **III:** 369–370

"Ontological Episode of the Asylum" (Carruth), **Supp. XVI:** 48, 50

"Ontology of the Sentence, The" (Gass), **Supp. VI:** 77

"On Top" (Leopold), **Supp. XIV:** 188

"On Top" (Snyder), **Supp. VIII:** 304

"On Translating Akhmatova" (Kunitz), **Supp. III Part 1:** 268

"On Turning Ten" (Collins), **Supp. XXI:** 64

"On Visiting a Borrowed Country House in Arcadia" (Stallings), **Supp. XXV:** 233–234

"On Waking to Old Debts" (Keillor), **Supp. XVI:** 167

On William Stafford: The Worth of Local Things (Andrews, ed.), **Supp. XI:** 311, 312, 317, 321, 324, 326

On Writers and Writing (O'Nan, ed.), **Supp. XXV:** 152–153

"On Writing" (Carver), **Supp. III Part 1:** 142–143

"On Writing" (Nin), **Supp. X:** 182

On Your Own (Gallagher), **Supp. XXIV:** 166

Opatoshu, Joseph, **IV:** 9

"Open Boat, The" (Crane), **I:** 408, 415, 416–417, 423; **Retro. Supp. I:** 325; **Supp. XIV:** 51

Open Boat and Other Stories (Crane), **I:** 408

Open Door, The (Skloot), **Supp. XX: 194, 196, 208**

Open Heart: A Patient's Story of Life-Saving Medicine and Life-Giving Friendship (Neugeboren), **Supp. XVI:** 217, **229–230**

Open House (Roethke), **III:** 529–530, 540

"Open House" (Roethke), **III:** 529

"Opening, An" (Swenson), **Supp. IV Part 2:** 639

Opening of the Field, The (Duncan), **Supp. III Part 2:** 625

Opening the Hand (Merwin), **Supp. III Part 1:** 341, 353, 355

"Open Letter" (Roethke), **III:** 532, 534

"Open Letter to Surrealists Everywhere, An" (H. Miller), **III:** 184

Open Meeting, The (Gurney), **Supp. V:** 98

Open Net (Plimpton), **Supp. XVI:** 241

"Open Road, The" (Dreiser), **II:** 44

Open Sea, The (Masters), **Supp. I Part 2:** 471

Open Season: Sporting Adventures (Humphrey), **Supp. IX:** 95

"Open Secret" (Nelson), **Supp. XVIII:** 185

"Open the Gates" (Kunitz), **Supp. III Part 1:** 264–265, 267

"Opera Company, The" (Merrill), **Supp. III Part 1:** 326

Operating Instructions: A Journal of My Son's First Year (Lamott), **Supp. XX: 136–137, 142**

"Operation, The" (Sanders), **Supp. XVI:** 266

"Operation, The" (Sexton), **Supp. II Part 2:** 675, 679

Operation Shylock: A Confession (P. Roth), **Retro. Supp. II:** 279, 280, 291

Operation Sidewinder (Shepard), **Supp. III Part 2:** 434–435, 439, 446–447

Operations in North African Waters (Morison), **Supp. I Part 2:** 490

Operation Wandering Soul (Powers), **Supp. IX:** 212, **217–219**

Opffer, Emil, **Retro. Supp. II:** 80

"Opinion" (Du Bois), **Supp. II Part 1:** 173

Opinionator, The (Bierce), **I:** 209

Opinions of Oliver Allston (Brooks), **I:** 254, 255, 256

O Pioneers! (Cather), **I:** 314, 317–319, 320; **Retro. Supp. I:** 1, 5, 6, **7–9,** 10, 13, 20; **Retro. Supp. II:** 136

Oppen, George, **IV:** 415; **Supp. III Part 2:** 614, 615, 616, 626, 628; **Supp.**

XIV: 285, 286, 287; **Supp. XVI:** 282, 283; **Supp. XVII:** 243; **Supp. XXI:** 19,**Supp. XXI:** 29, 23; **Supp. XXIII:** 165–166, 168; **Supp. XXVI: 223–238**

Oppen, Mary, **Supp. XXVI:** 225

Oppenheim, James, **I:** 106, 109, 239, 245; **Supp. XV:** 294, 296, 298, 299, 301, 302, 307, 313; **Supp. XX:** 68

Oppenheimer, J. Robert, **I:** 137, 492

Oppenheimer, Judy, **Supp. IX:** 115, 116, 118, 120, 126

"Opportunity for American Fiction, An" (Howells), **Supp. I Part 2:** 645–646

Opposing Self, The (Trilling), **Supp. III Part 2:** 506–507

"Opposition" (Lanier), **Supp. I Part 1:** 368, 373

Oprah's Roots: An African American Lives Special (television production), **Supp. XX:** 99

Opticks: A Poem in Seven Sections (Goldbarth), **Supp. XII:** 177, **178**

Optimist's Daughter, The (Welty), **IV:** 261, 280; **Retro. Supp. I:** 339, 355

"Optimist's Daughter, The" (Welty), **IV:** 280–281

Options (O. Henry), **Supp. II Part 1:** 410

Opus Posthumous (Stevens), **IV:** 76, 78

Opus Posthumous (W. Stevens), **Supp. XVII:** 241

Oracle at Stoneleigh Court, The (Taylor), **Supp. V:** 328

Orage, Alfred, **III:** 473

"O/Rain-in-the-Face"(Kenny), **Supp. XXIII:** 156

"Oral History" (Goodman), **Supp. XXVI:** 118, 119

Orange, Max (pseudonym). *See* Heller, Joseph

Orange Fish, The (Shields), **Supp. VII:** 318, 320, 323, 328

Orangery, The (Sorrentino), **Supp. XXI:** 228

Oranges (exhibition, Hartigan), **Supp. XXIII:** 210

Oranges (McPhee), **Supp. III Part 1:** 298–299, 301, 309

Oranges: 12 Pastorals (O'Hara), **Supp. XXIII:** 210

"Oranging of America, The" (Apple), **Supp. XVII:** 3–4, 6

Oranging of America and Other Short Stories, The (Apple), **Supp. XVII:** 1–2, **3–4**, 7, 8

Oration Delivered at Washington, July Fourth, 1809 (Barlow), **Supp. II Part 1:** 80, 83

Orations and Addresses (Bryant), **Supp. I Part 1:** 158

Orators, The (Auden), **Supp. II Part 1:** 6, 7, 11, 18–19

Orbach, Jerry, **Supp. XXIII:** 103

Orb Weaver, The (Francis), **Supp. IX: 81–82**

"Orchard" (Doolittle), **Supp. I Part 1:** 263–264, 265, 266

"Orchard" (Eberhart), **I:** 539

Orchard, The (B. Kelly), **Supp. XVII:** 123, 127, **130–133**

"Orchard, The" (B. Kelly), **Supp. XVII:** 133

Orchard Keeper, The (McCarthy), **Supp. VIII: 175–176**

Orchestra (Davies), **III:** 541

"Orchid Fever" (Orlean), **Supp. XXV:** 160

"Orchids" (Roethke), **III:** 530–531

Orchid Thief, The: A True Story of Beauty and Obsession (Orlean), **Supp. XXV:** 160, 161–162

"Or Consider Prometheus" (Clampitt), **Supp. IX:** 44

Ordeal of Mansart, The (Du Bois), **Supp. II Part 1:** 185–186

Ordeal of Mark Twain, The (Brooks), **I:** 240, 247, 248; **II:** 482

Ordering the Façade: Photography and Contemporary Southern Women's Writing (Henninger), **Supp. XXI:** 253

"Order of Insects" (Gass), **Supp. VI:** 83

Order Out of Chaos (McPherson), **Supp. IV Part 1:** 2, 12

"Ordinary Afternoon in Charlottesville, An" (Wright), **Supp. V:** 344

"Ordinary Days" (Dunn), **Supp. XI:** 151

"Ordinary Evening in New Haven, An" (Stevens), **IV:** 91–92; **Retro. Supp. I:** 297, 300, 311, 312

Ordinary Heroes (Turow), **Supp. XVII: 221–222,** 223

Ordinary Life (Crooker), **Supp. XXIII: 56**

Ordinary Love (Smiley), **Supp. VI:** 292, **299–300**

Ordinary Love; and Good Will: Two Novellas (Smiley), **Supp. VI:** 292, **299–300**

Ordinary Miracles (Jong), **Supp. V:** 115, 130–131

Ordinary Seaman, The (Goldman), **Supp. XXV:** 49, 50, 53–54

"Ordinary Time: Virginia Woolf and Thucydides on War" (Carson), **Supp. XII:** 111

"Ordinary Women, The" (Stevens), **IV:** 81

Ordways, The (Humphrey), **Supp. IX:** 95, **98–100,** 109; **Supp. XV:** 353

"Oread" (Doolittle), **II:** 520–521; **Supp. I Part 1:** 265–266

Oregon Message, An (Stafford), **Supp. XI: 328–329**

Oregon Trail, The (Parkman), **II:** 312; **Supp. II Part 2:** 592, 595–596, 598, 606

Oresteia (Aeschylus), **Supp. IX:** 103

"Orestes at Tauris" (Jarrell), **II:** 376, 377

Orfalea, Gregory, **Supp. XIII:** 278

Orfeo ed Euridice (Gluck), **II:** 210, 211

Orff, Carl, **Supp. X:** 63

"Organizer's Wife, The" (Bambara), **Supp. XI:** 8–9

"Organmeister: Hasse After Marienkirche" (Bierds), **Supp. XVII:** 34

"Orgy" (Rukeyser), **Supp. VI:** 280

Orgy, The (Rukeyser), **Supp. VI:** 274, 283

"Orgy of Southerness, An" (Pickering), **Supp. XXI:** 203

"Oriental Rug"(Balakian), **Supp. XXIII:** 23, 24–25

"Orientation of Hope, The" (Locke), **Supp. XIV:** 212–213

Orient Express (Dos Passos), **I:** 480

"Orient Express, The" (Jarrell), **II:** 382, 383–384

Origen, Adamantius, **IV:** 153

"Origin" (Harjo), **Supp. XII:** 219

Original Child Bomb: Points for Meditation to Be Scratched on the Walls of a Cave (Merton), **Supp. VIII:** 203

Original Essays on the Poetry of Anne Sexton (George), **Supp. IV Part 2:** 450

"Original Follies Girl, The" (Z. Fitzgerald), **Supp. IX:** 71

Original Light (Goldbarth), **Supp. XII:** 181, **183–184,** 188

Original Love (Peacock), **Supp. XIX: 199–201,** 206

Original of Laura, The (Nabokov), **Retro. Supp. I:** 266

"Original Sin" (Jeffers), **Supp. II Part 2:** 426

"Original Sin" (Vaz), **Supp. XXVI:** 259–260

"Original Sin" (Warren), **IV:** 245

"Original Story" (Gansworth), **Supp. XXVI:** 114

Origin: Hawaii (Taggard), **Supp. XXII:** 272, 284

"Origin of Extermination in the Imagination, The" (Gass), **Supp. VI:** 89

Origin of Species, The (Darwin), **II:** 173, 462; **Supp. XVI:** 13

Origin of the Brunists, The (Coover), **Supp. V:** 39, 41, 52

"Origin of the Miscodeed, or the Maid of Taquimenon"(J. Schoolcraft), **Supp. XXIII:** 235

"Origin of the Robin, The"(J. Schoolcraft), **Supp. XXIII:** 234, 235

"Origins and History of Consciousness" (Rich), **Supp. I Part 2:** 570

"Origins of a Nonfiction Writer" (Talese), **Supp. XVII:** 208

"Origins of a Poem" (Levertov), **Supp. III Part 1:** 273

"Origins of the Beat Generation, The" (Kerouac), **Supp. III Part 1:** 231

Origo, Iris, **IV:** 328

"O'Riley's Late-Bloomed Little Son" (X. J. Kennedy), **Supp. XV:** 159

"Orion" (Rich), **Supp. I Part 2:** 557

O'Riordan, Conal Holmes O'Connell, **III:** 465

Orlacs Hände (film, Weine), **Supp. XVII:** 58

Orlando (V. Woolf), **Supp. XVII:** 86

Orlando (Woolf), **Supp. I Part 2:** 718; **Supp. VIII:** 263; **Supp. XII:** 9

Orlando Furioso (Ariosto), **Supp. XV:** 175

Orlean, Susan, **Supp. XXV: 157–167**

Orlik, Emil, **Supp. XXIII:** 6

Orloff, Chana, **Supp. XXIII:** 6

Orlovsky, Peter, **Supp. XII:** 121, 126; **Supp. XIV:** 150; **Supp. XVIII:** 27

Ormonde, Czenzi, **Supp. IV Part 1:** 132

Ormond; or, The Secret Witness (Brown), **Supp. I Part 1:** 133–137

Ornament and Crime (Loos), **Supp. XVI:** 187

Orne, Sarah. *See* Jewett, Sarah Orne

Ornithological Biography; or, An Account of the Habits of the Birds of the United States of America, and Interspersed with Delineations of American Scenery and Manners (Audubon), **7–10; Supp. XVI:** 13

"Ornithology" (Hull), **Supp. XXI:** 138–139

Ornitz, Samuel, **Supp. IX:** 227; **Supp. XIII:** 166

Ornstein, Leo, **Supp. XX: 75**

O'Rourke, Meghan, **Supp. XXV:** 10

O'Rourke, William, **Supp. XXII:** 213

Orphan Angel, The (Wylie), **Supp. I Part 2:** 707, 709, 714, 717, 719–721, 722, 724

Orphan's Tale, An (Neugeboren), **Supp. XVI:** 222, 223

Orpheus (Rukeyser), **Supp. VI:** 273

"Orpheus" (Winters), **Supp. II Part 2:** 801

"Orpheus, Eurydice, Hermes" (Rilke), **Supp. VIII:** 31, 32

"Orpheus (1)" (Atwood), **Supp. XIII:** 35

"Orpheus (2)" (Atwood), **Supp. XIII:** 35

"Orpheus Alone" (Strand), **Supp. IV Part 2:** 632

Orpheus Descending (T. Williams), **IV:** 380, 381, 382, 385, 386, 387, 389, 391–392, 395, 396, 398

Orr, David, **Supp. XXI:** 62

Orr, Peter, **Supp. I Part 2:** 538, 540, 543

Orse, Brian, **Supp. XX: 264**

Ortega y Gasset, José, **I:** 218, 222; **Supp. IV Part 2:** 521; **Supp. XXIII:** 165

Ortiz, Simon J., **Supp. IV Part 1:** 319, 404; **Supp. IV Part 2: 497–515,** 557; **Supp. XII:** 217, 218

"Ortlieb's Uptown Taproom" (Di Piero), **Supp. XIX:** 46, 47

Orton, Joe, **Supp. XXIV:** 113, 126, 263

O'Ruddy, The (Crane), **I:** 409, 424

Orwell, George, **I:** 489; **II:** 454, 580; **Supp. I Part 2:** 523, 620; **Supp. II Part 1:** 143; **Supp. IV Part 1:** 236; **Supp. V:** 250; **Supp. VIII:** 241; **Supp. XIV:** 112, 158; **Supp. XVII:** 228, 229; **Supp. XVIII:** 137, 138; **Supp. XX: 86**

Osborn, Dwight, **III:** 218–219, 223

"Osborn Look, The" (Morris), **III:** 221

Osgood, Frances, **Supp. XVII:** 75

Osgood, J. R., **II:** 283

O'Shea, Kitty, **II:** 137

O'Shea, Milo, **Supp. XI:** 308

"Oshkikwe's Baby" (traditional Chippewa story), **Supp. IV Part 1:** 333

Oshogay, Delia, **Supp. IV Part 1:** 333

Ossana, Diana, **Supp. V:** 230–231, 232

Ossian, **Supp. I Part 2:** 491

Ossip, Kathleen, **Supp. X:** 201

"Osso Bucco" (Collins), **Supp. XXI:** 60

Ostanovka v Pustyne (A halt in the wilderness) (Brodsky), **Supp. VIII:** 21

Oster, Judith, **Supp. XVI:** 151

Ostriker, Alicia, **Supp. I Part 2:** 540; **Supp. IV Part 2:** 439, 447, 449; **Supp. X:** 207, 208; **Supp. XI:** 143; **Supp. XV:** 251

Ostrom, Hans, **Retro. Supp. I:** 195

Oswald, Lee Harvey, **III:** 234, 235

Oswald II (DeLillo), **Supp. VI:** 16

Oswald's Tale (Mailer), **Retro. Supp. II:** 212–213

"Otagamiad, The"(J. Schoolcraft), **Supp. XXIII:** 223

O Taste and See (Levertov), **Supp. III Part 1:** 278–279, 281

Othello (Shakespeare), **I:** 284–285

"Other, The" (Sexton), **Supp. II Part 2:** 692

Other America, The (Harrington), **I:** 306

"Other American Renaissance, The" (Tompkins), **Supp. XVIII:** 258

Other Destinies: Understanding the American Indian Novel (Owens), **Supp. IV Part 1:** 404

otherelectricities.com, **Supp. XXIV:** 240–241

Other Electricities: Stories (Monson), **Supp. XXIV:** 230, **231–234,** 235–236, 238, 241

"Other Frost, The" (Jarrell), **Retro. Supp. I:** 121

"Other Gods, The" (Lovecraft), **Supp. XXV:** 114

Other Gods: An American Legend (Buck), **Supp. II Part 1:** 123, 130–131

Other House, The (James), **Retro. Supp. I:** 229

"Other League of Nations, The" (Ríos), **Supp. IV Part 2:** 552

"Other Margaret, The" (Trilling), **Supp. III Part 2:** 504–505

"Other Miller, The" (Wolff), **Supp. VII:** 343–344

"Other Mothers" (Paley), **Supp. VI:** 225

"Other Night at Columbia, The" (Trilling), **Supp. XII:** 126

"Other People's Secrets" (Hampl), **Supp. XXII:** 94

"Other Robert Frost, The" (Jarrell), **Retro. Supp. I:** 135

Others (Shields), **Supp. VII:** 310

Other Side, The (Gordon), **Supp. IV Part 1:** 299, 306, 307–309, 310–311

Other Side, The/El Otro Lado (Alvarez), **Supp. VII:** 9–12

"Other Side, The"(Hadas), **Supp. XXIII:** 120

Other Side of the River, The (Wright), **Supp. V:** 332–333, 342

"Other Side of the River, The" (Wright), **Supp. V:** 335

"Other Tradition, The" (Ashbery), **Supp. III Part 1:** 15, 18

"Other Two, The" (Wharton), **Retro. Supp. I:** 367

Other Voices, Other Rooms (Capote), **Supp. III Part 1:** 113–118, 121, 123–124

"Other Wanderer, The" (Gibran), **Supp. XX: 124**

"Other War, The" (Cowley), **Supp. II Part 1:** 144

"Otherwise" (Kenyon), **Supp. VII:** 172, 174

Otherwise: New and Selected Poems (Kenyon), **Supp. VII:** 167, 172–174

Otherwise Than Being; or, Beyond Essence (Lévinas), **Supp. XVI:** 290, 291

"Other Woman, The" (Anderson), **I:** 114

"Other World, The" (Wrigley), **Supp. XVIII:** 307

Other Worlds Than This (Hadas), **Supp. XXIII:** 118, **124–125**

Otho the Great: A Tragedy in Five Acts (Keats), **Supp. XII:** 113

Otis, Harrison Gray, **Supp. I Part 2:** 479–481, 483, 486, 488

Otis, James, **III:** 577; **Supp. I Part 2:** 486; **Supp. XV:** 229

O to Be a Dragon (Moore), **III:** 215

"Otravida, Otravez" (Díaz), **Supp. XXIV:** 93

Ott, Bill, **Supp. XXVI:** 187

Otto, Rudolf, **Supp. XVII:** 243

"Ouija" (McClatchy), **Supp. XII:** 269–270

Oupensky, Peter, **Supp. XIV:** 188

Our America (Michaels), **Retro. Supp. I:** 379

Our America (W. Frank), **I:** 229; **Supp. IX:** 308; **Supp. XX: 69–70,** 75

Our American Humorists (Masson), **Supp. XXVI:** 275

Our Aperture (Monson), **Supp. XXIV:** 230, 239

"Our Assistant's Column" (Twain), **IV:** 193

"Our Bourgeois Literature" (Sinclair), **Supp. V:** 281

Our Brains and What Ails Them (Gilman), **Supp. XI:** 207

Our Century (Wilder), **IV:** 374

"Our Christmas Party" (E. Stoddard), **Supp. XV:** 273, 278

Our Country (Strong), **Supp. XIV:** 64

"Our Countrymen in Chains!" (Whittier), **Supp. I Part 2:** 688

"Our Cultural Humility" (Bourne), **I:** 223, 228

Our Depleted Society (Seymour), **Supp. XIII:** 264

"Our Dust" (Wright), **Supp. XV:** 345, 346

"Our Eyes" (Davison), **Supp. XXVI:** 78

"Our Father Who Drowns the Birds" (Kingsolver), **Supp. VII:** 208–209

"Our First House" (Kingston), **Supp. V:** 169

Our Gang (P. Roth), **Retro. Supp. II:** 287; **Supp. III Part 2:** 414; **Supp. IV Part 1:** 388

"Our Good Day" (Cisneros), **Supp. VII:** 60

Our Ground Time Here Will Be Brief (Kumin), **Supp. IV Part 2:** 450–452

Our House in the Last World (Hijuelos), **Supp. VIII:** 73, **76–79,** 87, 88

"Our Lady" (A. Finch), **Supp. XVII:** 77

"*Our Lady of the Annunciation*/Nuestra Señora de Anunciación" (Mora), **Supp. XIII:** 217, 224, 228

"Our Lady of the Artichokes" (Vaz), **Supp. XXVI:** 265

Our Lady of the Artichokes and Other Portuguese-American Stories (Vaz), **Supp. XXVI:** 264–268

"Our Lady of Troy" (MacLeish), **III:** 3, 20

"Our Limitations" (Holmes), **Supp. I Part 1:** 314

"Our Martyred Soldiers" (Dunbar), **Supp. II Part 1:** 193

"Our Master" (Whittier), **Supp. I Part 2:** 704

"Our Mother Pocahontas" (Lindsay), **Supp. I Part 2:** 393

Our Mr. Wrenn: The Romantic Adventures of a Gentle Man (Lewis), **II:** 441

Our National Parks (Muir), **Supp. IX:** 181, 184

Our New York: A Personal Vision in Words and Photographs (Kazin), **Supp. VIII:** 106–107

Our Nig (Wilson), **Supp. XX:** 105

"Our Old Aunt Who Is Now in a Retirement Home" (Shields), **Supp. VII:** 310

Our Old Home: A Series of English Sketches (Hawthorne), **II:** 225; **Retro. Supp. I:** 163

"Our Own Movie Queen" (Z. Fitzgerald), **Supp. IX:** 71

"Our River Now" (L.-Y. Lee), **Supp. XV:** 224, 225

Our Selves (Bronk), **Supp. XXI:** 32

Ourselves to Know (O'Hara), **III:** 362, 365

Our Sister Killjoy: or, Reflections from a Black-Eyed Squint (Aidoo), **Supp. XXII:** 68

"Our Story Begins" (Wolff), **Supp. VII:** 345

"Our Sweating Selves" (Di Piero), **Supp. XIX:** 36

Our Town (Wilder), **IV:** 357, 364, 365, 366, 368–369

"Our Unplanned Cities" (Bourne), **I:** 229, 230

Our Wonder World, **Retro. Supp. I:** 341

Ouspensky, P. D., **I:** 383; **Supp. XX:** 116

"Out" (Harjo), **Supp. XII:** 219

"'Out, Out'" (Frost), **Retro. Supp. I:** 131

"Outcast" (McKay), **Supp. X:** 135

"Outcasts of Poker Flats, The" (Harte), **Supp. II Part 1:** 345, 347–348

Outcroppings (Harte), **Supp. II Part 1:** 343

Out Cry (T. Williams), **IV:** 383, 393

Outcry, The (James), **Retro. Supp. I:** 235

"Outdoor Shower" (Olds), **Supp. X:** 214

Outer Banks (Siddons), **Supp. XXII:** 239

Outerbridge Reach (Stone), **Supp. V:** 306–308

Outer Dark (McCarthy), **Supp. VIII:** 176–177

Outermost Dream, The: Essays and Reviews (Maxwell), **Supp. VIII:** 171–172

Outermost House, The (Beston), **Supp. XXVI:** 31, 34, 37–43

"Outing, The" (Baldwin), **Supp. I Part 1:** 63

Outlaw Journalist (McKeen), **Supp. XXIV:** 279, 288

"Out Like a Lamb" (Dubus), **Supp. VII:** 91

"Outline of an Autobiography" (Toomer), **Supp. III Part 2:** 478

"Outline Toward a Theory of the Mine Versus the Mind and the Harvard Outline" (Monson), **Supp. XXIV:** 235

Outlyer and Ghazals (Harrison), **Supp. VIII:** 41

"Out of Business" (Mora), **Supp. XIII:** 217

Out of Eden: Essays on Modern Art (Di Piero), **Supp. XIX:** 41, 42

"Out of My Deeper Heart" (Gibran), **Supp. XX:** 118

Out of My League (Plimpton), **Supp. XVI:** 233, 239

"Out of Nowhere into Nothing" (Anderson), **I:** 113

"Out of Season" (Hemingway), **II:** 263

"Out of the Cradle Endlessly Rocking" (Whitman), **IV:** 342, 343–345, 346, 351; **Retro. Supp. I:** 404, 406

"Out of the Deeps" (E. Stoddard), **Supp. XV:** 286

"Out of the Hospital and Under the Bar" (Ellison), **Retro. Supp. II:** 118–119; **Supp. II Part 1:** 246

"Out of the Rainbow End" (Sandburg), **III:** 594–595

"Out of the Sea, Early" (Swenson), **Supp. IV Part 2:** 645

"Out of the Snow" (Dubus), **Supp. VII:** 91

Out of the Stars (Purdy), **Supp. VII:** 281–282

"Out of the Woods" (Offutt), **Supp. XIX:** 169–170

Out of the Woods: Stories (Offutt), **Supp. XIX:** 163, 167, **169–172,** 175

"Out of Your Nakedness, Out of My Nakedness"(Hadas), **Supp. XXIII:** 125

"Outrageous" (Pickering), **Supp. XXI:** 202

Outre-Mer: A Pilgrimage beyond the Sea (Longfellow), **II:** 313, 491; **Retro. Supp. II:** 155, 165

"Outside" (Stafford), **Supp. XI:** 318

Outside, The (Glaspell), **Supp. III Part 1:** 179, 187

"Outside In" (Pickering), **Supp. XXI:** 197

Outsider, The (Wright), **IV:** 478, 481, 488, 491–494, 495

Outside World, The (Mirvis), **Supp. XX:** 177, 178, 185–190

Out Went the Candle (Swados), **Supp. XIX:** 257

Out West (Shanley), **Supp. XIV:** 317

"Out with the Old" (Yates), **Supp. XI:** 342

"Ouzo for Robin" (Merrill), **Supp. III Part 1:** 326

"Oval Portrait, The" (Poe), **III:** 412, 415; **Retro. Supp. II:** 270

"Oven Bird, The" (Frost), **Retro. Supp. I:** 131; **Supp. XI:** 153; **Supp. XIX:** 15

"Over 2,000 Illustrations and a Complete Concordance" (Bishop), **Retro. Supp. II:** 45; **Supp. I Part 1:** 90–91

"Over by the River" (Maxwell), **Supp. VIII:** 169, 170

"Overcoat, The" (Gogol), **Supp. XXII:** 59

"Overgrown Pasture, The" (Lowell), **II:** 523

"Overheard through the Walls of the Invisible City" (Bidart), **Supp. XV:** 32

"Over Kansas" (Ginsberg), **Supp. II Part 1:** 320

Overland to the Islands (Levertov), **Supp. III Part 1:** 275, 276

Overlook, The (Connelly), **Supp. XXI:** 78

"Overlooking Lake Champlain" (Di Piero), **Supp. XIX:** 47

"Overnight Pass" (X. J. Kennedy), **Supp. XV:** 168

Overreachers, The (Talese), **Supp. XVII:** 202

"Over-Soul, The" (Emerson), **II:** 7

Over the Blue Mountain (Richter), **Supp. XVIII:** 220

"Over the Edge"(Hadas), **Supp. XXIII:** 115

"Over the Hill" (Dubus), **Supp. VII:** 76, 79–80

Overtime (Gurney), **Supp. V:** 104

Overton, Grant, **Supp. XXV:** 200

"Overwhelming Question, An" (Taylor), **Supp. V:** 323

Ovid, **I:** 62; **II:** 542–543; **III:** 457, 467, 468, 470; **Retro. Supp. I:** 63; **Supp. IV Part 2:** 634; **Supp. XII:** 264

"Ovid in Exile" (Di Piero), **Supp. XIX:** 44

"Ovid's Farewell" (McClatchy), **Supp. XII:** 257–258

Owen, David, **II:** 34

Owen, Maureen, **Supp. IV Part 2:** 423

Owen, Wilfred, **II:** 367, 372; **III:** 524; **Supp. X:** 146; **Supp. XIX:** 17; **Supp. XVII:** 245; **Supp. XVIII:** 92

Owens, Hamilton, **III:** 99, 109

Owens, Louis, **Supp. IV Part 1:** 404

"O Where Are You Going?" (Auden), **Supp. X:** 116

"Owl, The" (Wrigley), **Supp. XVIII:** 297–298, 301

Owl in the Attic, The (Thurber), **Supp. I Part 2:** 614

Owl in the Mask of the Dreamer, The: Collected Poems (Haines), **Supp. XII:** 211

"Owl in the Sarcophagus, The" (Stevens), **Retro. Supp. I:** 300

Owl's Clover (Stevens), **Retro. Supp. I:** 298, **303–304**

"Owl's Clover" (Stevens), **IV:** 75

Owl's Insomnia, Poems by Rafael Alberti, The (Strand, trans.), **Supp. IV Part 2:** 630

Owl Spirit Dwelling (Gallagher), **Supp. XXIV:** 170

Owlstone Crown, The (X. J. Kennedy), **Supp. XV:** 162, **164**

"Owl Who Was God, The" (Thurber), **Supp. I Part 2:** 610

Owning It All (Kittredge), **Supp. XXVI:** 184, 187

Owning Jolene (Hearon), **Supp. VIII:** **66–67**

"Owning the Masters" (Nelson), **Supp. XVIII:** 171

Oxford Anthology of American Literature, The, **III:** 197; **Supp. I Part 1:** 254

Oxford Book of American Verse (Matthiessen, ed.), **Retro. Supp. I:** 40

Oxford Book of Children's Verse in America, The (Hall, ed.), **Supp. XIV:** 126

Oxford Companion to African American Literature, The (Andrews et al., eds), **Supp. XXVI:** 166

Oxford Companion to Twentieth-Century Poetry (Hamilton, ed.), **Supp. XVII:** 243

Oxford History of the American People, The (Morison), **Supp. I Part 2:** 495–496

Oxford History of the United States, 1783–1917, The (Morison), **Supp. I Part 2:** 483–484

"Oxford Town" (song, Dylan), **Supp. XVIII:** 24

Oxherding Tale (C. Johnson), **Supp. VI:** **190–192,** 193, 194, 196

Oxley, William, **Supp. XV:** 125

"O Yes" (Olsen), **Supp. XIII:** 294, 298, **299–300,** 301

"O Youth and Beauty!" (Cheever), **Retro. Supp. I:** 335

"Oysters" (Sexton), **Supp. II Part 2:** 692

"Ozark Odes" (Wright), **Supp. XV:** 346

Ozick, Cynthia, **Supp. V:** **257–274;** **Supp. VIII:** 141; **Supp. X:** 192; **Supp. XVII:** 42, 43, 49, 50

O-Zone (Theroux), **Supp. VIII:** 323–324

P

Pace, Patricia, **Supp. XI:** 245

Pacernik, Gary, **Supp. IX:** 287, 291

Pacific and Other Stories, The (Helprin), **Supp. XXV:** 84, 85

"Pacific Distances" (Didion), **Supp. IV Part 1:** 211

"Pacific Village" (M. F. K. Fisher), **Supp. XVII:** 83

"Pacifist War Song" (Lovecraft), **Supp. XXV:** 119

Pack, Robert, **Supp. IV Part 2:** 621

"Packed Dirt, Churchgoing, a Dying Cat, a Traded Cat" (Updike), **IV:** 219

Packer, Nancy Huddleston, **Supp. XXIII:** 290

"Packing Mother's Things" (C. Frost), **Supp. XV:** 97

Pack of Lies (Sorrentino), **Supp. XXI:** 236, 237

Paco's Story (Heinemann), **Supp. XXII:** 103, **109–114,** 115

Paddock, Joe, **Supp. XVI:** 36

Paddock, Nancy, **Supp. XVI:** 36

Padel, Ruth, **Supp. XII:** 107

Padgett, Ron, **Supp. XV:** 190; **Supp. XXIII:** 218, 221; **Supp. XXIV:** 33, 34, 35, 37, 38, 39, 41, 42, 43, 44

Padmore, Dorothy, **Supp. XXI:** 166

Padmore, George, **Supp. XXI:** 166

"Paesano with a Trowel" *(Time),* **Supp. XX:** **46**

Pafko at the Wall (DeLillo), **Supp. VI:** 4

"Paganini and the Powers of Darkness" (Skloot), **Supp. XX:** **201**

"Pagan Prayer" (Cullen), **Supp. IV Part 1:** 170

"Pagan Rabbi, The" (Ozick), **Supp. V:** 262, 264, 265; **Supp. XVII:** 43

Pagan Rabbi and Other Stories, The (Ozick), **Supp. V:** 260, 261, 263–265

Pagan Spain (Wright), **IV:** 478, 488, 495

Page, Geraldine, **Supp. XV:** 7

Page, Kirby, **III:** 297

Page, Myra, **Supp. XXIII:** 166

"Page, The" (Huddle), **Supp. XXVI:** 155

Page, Thomas Nelson, **II:** 174, 176, 194; **Supp. XIV:** 61; **Supp. XXII:** 193

Page, Walter Hines, **II:** 174, 175; **Supp. I Part 1:** 370

Page, William, **Supp. XVIII:** 2, 11

Pages from a Cold Island (Exley), **Supp. XXIII:** 97, **103–106,** 108

"Pages from Cold Point" (Bowles), **Supp. IV Part 1:** 85, 86, 87

Paid on Both Sides: A Charade (Auden), **Supp. II Part 1:** 6, 18–19

Paige, Satchel, **Supp. I Part 1:** 234

Paige, T. D. D., **III:** 475

"Pail, The" (R. Bly), **Supp. XXI:** 85

Pain, Joseph, **Supp. I Part 2:** 502

Paine, Albert Bigelow, **I:** 249

Paine, Thomas, **I:** 490; **II:** 117, 302; **III:** 17, 148, 219; **Retro. Supp. I:** 390; **Supp. I Part 1:** 231; **Supp. I Part 2:** **501–525; Supp. XI:** 55

"Pain has an Element of Blank" (Dickinson), **Retro. Supp. I:** 44

"Pain Scale, The" (Biss), **Supp. XXVI:** 51–53

"Painstaking Historian, The" (Skloot), **Supp. XX:** **205–206**

"Paint and Powder" (Z. Fitzgerald), **Supp. IX:** 71

Painted Bird, The (Kosinski), **Supp. VII:** 215–217, 219–221, 222, 227

Painted Desert (F. Barthelme), **Supp. XI:** 28–29, 32

Painted Dresses (Hearon), **Supp. VIII:** **63**

"Painted Head" (Ransom), **III:** 491, 494; **Supp. II Part 1:** 103, 314

Painted Turtle: Woman with Guitar (Major), **Supp. XXII: 178–180,** 182

Painted Word, The (Wolfe), **Supp. III Part 2:** 580–581, 584; **Supp. XV:** 143

Painter, Pamela, **Supp. XXIII:** 295

"Painter, The" (Ashbery), **Supp. III Part 1:** 5–6, 13

Painter Dreaming in the Scholar's House, The (Nemerov), **III:** 269

"Painters" (Rukeyser), **Supp. VI:** 281

"Painting a Mountain Stream" (Nemerov), **III:** 275

"Pair a Spurs" (Proulx), **Supp. VII:** 263–264

"Pair of Bright Blue Eyes, A" (Taylor), **Supp. V:** 321

"Pair of Glasses, A" (Gallagher), **Supp. XXIV:** 174, 176

Paisan (film, Rossellini), **Supp. XXVI:** 134

"Pajamas" (Olds), **Supp. X:** 206

Pakula, Alan, **Supp. XIII:** 264

Palace at 4 A.M. (Giacometti), **Supp. VIII:** 169

Palahniuk, Chuck, **Supp. XXI:** 116

"Palantine, The" (Whittier), **Supp. I Part 2:** 694, 696

Palatella, John, **Retro. Supp. II:** 48; **Supp. XXIV:** 39

"Palatski Man, The"(Dybek), **Supp. XXIII:** 70

Pale Fire (Nabokov), **III:** 244, 246, 252, 263–265; **Retro. Supp. I:** 264, 265, 266, 270, 271, 272, 276, 278, 335; **Supp. V:** 251, 253; **Supp. XXII:** 260

"Pale Horse, Pale Rider" (Porter), **III:** 436, 437, 441–442, 445, 446, 449

Pale Horse, Pale Rider: Three Short Novels (Porter), **III:** 433, 436–442; **Supp. VIII:** 157

"Pale Pink Roast, The" (Paley), **Supp. VI:** 217

"Pale Rider" (B. Kelly), **Supp. XVII:** 132–133

Paley, Grace, **Supp. IX:** 212; **Supp. VI: 217–233; Supp. X:** 79, 164; **Supp. XII:** 309; **Supp. XXI:** 118; **Supp. XXII:** 172

Paley, William, **II:** 9

Palgrave, Francis Turner, **Retro. Supp. I:** 124; **Supp. XIV:** 340

Palgrave's Golden Treasury (Palgrave), **IV:** 405

Palimpsest (Doolittle), **Supp. I Part 1:** 259, 268, 269, 270–271

Palimpsest (Vidal), **Supp. X:** 186

"Palingenesis" (Longfellow), **II:** 498

Pal Joey (O'Hara), **III:** 361, 367–368

"Pal Joey" stories (O'Hara), **III:** 361

Pallbearers Envying the One Who Rides (Dobyns), **Supp. XIII:** 89

Palm, Edward Frederick, **Supp. XXII:** 103

"Palm, The" (Merwin), **Supp. III Part 1:** 355

Palmer, Charles, **II:** 111

Palmer, Elihu, **Supp. I Part 2:** 520

Palmer, George Herbert, **Supp. XIV:** 197

Palmer, Michael, **Supp. IV Part 2:** 421; **Supp. XVI:** 284; **Supp. XVII:** 240

Palmer, Samuel, **Supp. XV:** 81

Palmerston, Lord, **I:** 15

Palm-of-the-Hand-Stories (Kawabata), **Supp. XV:** 186

"Palm Wine" (McKnight), **Supp. XX:** **155**

"Palo Alto: The Marshes" (Hass), **Supp. VI:** 100

Palpable God, A: Thirty Stories Translated from the Bible with an Essay on the Origins and Life of Narrative (Price), **Supp. VI:** 262, 267

Palubinskas, Helen, **Supp. X:** 292

Palumbo, Carmine, **Supp. XXVI:** 241

Pamela (Richardson), **Supp. V:** 127; **Supp. XX: 236; Supp. XXII:** 120

Pamela's First Musical (Wasserstein), **Supp. XV:** 333

Panache de bouquets (Komunyakaa; Cadieux, trans.), **Supp. XIII:** 127

Pan-African movement, **Supp. II Part 1:** 172, 175

Pancake, Breece D'J, **Supp. XXIII:** 35

Pandaemonium (Epstein), **Supp. XII:** 161, **172–173**

"Pandora" (Adams), **I:** 5

Pandora: New Tales of Vampires (Rice), **Supp. VII:** 295

Panek, LeRoy, **Supp. XIV:** 27

"Pangolin, The" (Moore), **III:** 210

Panic: A Play in Verse (MacLeish), **III:** 2, 20

Panic in Needle Park (film), **Supp. IV Part 1:** 198

Pankey, Eric, **Supp. XIX:** 44

Pantagruel (Rabelais), **II:** 112

"Pantaloon in Black" (Faulkner), **II:** 71

"Panther, The: A Bedtime Story"(P. Benedict), **Supp. XXIII:** 40

Panther and the Lash, The (Hughes), **Retro. Supp. I:** 204, 211; **Supp. I Part 1:** 342–344, 345–346

"Panthers, The" (Southern), **Supp. XI:** 295

"Panties and the Buddha" (Peacock), **Supp. XIX:** 199

"Pan *versus* Moses" (Ozick), **Supp. V:** 262

"Paolo Castelnuovo" (Everwine), **Supp. XV:** 83–84

"Papa and Mama Dance, The" (Sexton), **Supp. II Part 2:** 688

"Papago II"(Kenny), **Supp. XXIII:** 149–150

"Papago I"(Kenny), **Supp. XXIII:** 149–150

"Papa Who Wakes Up Tired in the Dark" (Cisneros), **Supp. VII:** 62

Pape, Greg, **Supp. V:** 180; **Supp. XIII:** 312; **Supp. XV:** 73

Paper Boy (Huddle), **Supp. XXVI:** 148, 150, 151

"Paper Covers Rock"(Thompson), **Supp. XXIII:** 291

Paper Doll (Parker), **Supp. XIX:** 184

"Paper Dolls Cut Out of a Newspaper" (Simic), **Supp. VIII:** 282

"Paper House, The" (Mailer), **III:** 42–43

Paper Lion (film, March), **Supp. XVI:** 242

Paper Lion: Confessions of a Last-String Quarterback (Plimpton), **Supp. XVI: 242–243**

Papernick, Jon, **Supp. XVII:** 50

Papers on Literature and Art (Fuller), **Supp. II Part 1:** 292, 299

Papini, Giovanni, **Supp. XVI:** 195; **Supp. XXII:** 159, 161, 163

Papp, Joseph, **Supp. IV Part 1:** 234; **Supp. XXI:** 145

"Paprika Johnson" (Barnes), **Supp. III Part 1:** 33

"Par" (Bausch), **Supp. VII:** 54

"Parable from a Christian" (Notley), **Supp. XXII:** 235

"Parable in the Later Novels of Henry James" (Ozick), **Supp. V:** 257

"Parable of the Gift" (Glück), **Supp. V:** 89

"Parable of the Hostages" (Glück), **Supp. V:** 89

"Parable of the King" (Glück), **Supp. V:** 89

Parable of the Sower (O. Butler), **Supp. XIII: 66–67,** 69

Parable of the Talents (O. Butler), **Supp. XIII:** 61,Supp. XIII: 66, **67–69**

"Parable of the Trellis" (Glück), **Supp. V:** 89

Parachutes & Kisses (Jong), **Supp. V:** 115, 123, 125–126, 129

"Paradelle for Susan" (Collins), **Supp. XXI:** 58

"Parade of Painters" (Swenson), **Supp. IV Part 2:** 645

"Paradigm, The" (Tate), **IV:** 128

Paradise (Barthelme), **Supp. IV Part 1:** 52

"Paradise" (Caputo), **Supp. XIX:** 26–27

"Paradise" (Doty), **Supp. XI:** 123

Paradise, Piece by Piece (Peacock), **Supp. XIX:** 193, 194–195, 195–196, **201–202**

Paradise Lost (Milton), **I:** 137; **II:** 168, 549; **IV:** 126; **Supp. XII:** 173, 297; **Supp. XV:** 181; **Supp. XX: 280**

Paradise Lost (Odets), **Supp. II Part 2:** 530, 531, 538–539, 550

Paradise Now (Living Theater), **Supp. XXIV:** 116

"Paradise of Bachelors and the Tartarus of Maids, The" (Melville), **III:** 91

Paradise of Bombs, The (Sanders), **Supp. XVI:** 265, 272–273

Paradise Park (Goodman), **Supp. XXVI:** 126–128

Paradise Poems (Stern), **Supp. IX: 293–294,** 295

Paradiso (Dante), **Supp. IX:** 50

"Paradoxes and Oxymorons" (Ashbery), **Supp. III Part 1:** 23–24

Paradox of Progressive Thought, The (Noble), **Supp. I Part 2:** 650

Paragon, The (Knowles), **Supp. XII:** 249

"Paragraphs" (Carruth), **Supp. XVI:** 52–53

"Parameters" (Dunn), **Supp. XI:** 154

"Para Mi Tataranieto El Astropionero" (Espaillat), **Supp. XXI:** 104

"Paraphrase" (Crane), **I:** 391–392, 393

"Pardon, The" (Wilbur), **Supp. III Part 2:** 544, 550

Paredes, Américo, **Supp. XIII:** 225; **Supp. XIX:** 97, 98, 100

Paredes, Raymund A., **Supp. XIII:** 320, 321

"Parentage" (Stafford), **Supp. XI:** 321, 322

Parentheses: An Autobiographical Journey (Neugeboren), **Supp. XVI:** 217, 218, 219, 221, 226

"Parents" (F. Barthelme), **Supp. XI:** 34

"Parents Taking Shape" (Karr), **Supp. XI:** 243

"Parents' Weekend: Camp Kenwood" (Kenyon), **Supp. VII:** 169

Pareto, Vilfredo, **II:** 577

Paretsky, Sara, **Supp. IV Part 2:** 462; **Supp. XIV:** 26; **Supp. XXV: 169–187**

Parini, Jay, **Supp. X:** 17; **Supp. XIX:** 120, 129; **Supp. XX: 243; Supp. XXI:** 192; **Supp. XXII:** 205; **Supp. XXV:** 251

"Paris" (Collins), **Supp. XXI:** 60

"Paris" (Stern), **Supp. IX:** 300

"Paris, 7 A.M." (Bishop), **Retro. Supp. II:** 41, 42; **Supp. I Part 1:** 85, 89

Paris, Bob, **Supp. XX: 264**

Paris, Paris (Shaw), **Supp. XIX:** 240

Paris France (Stein), **IV:** 45

Park, Ed, **Supp. XXII:** 255

Park, Robert, **IV:** 475

"Park Bench" (Hughes), **Supp. I Part 1:** 331–332

Park City (Beattie), **Supp. V:** 24, 35–36

"Park City" (Beattie), **Supp. V:** 35

Parker, Arthur C., **Supp. XXVI:** 87, 88

Parker, Charlie, **Supp. I Part 1:** 59; **Supp. X:** 240, 242, 246; **Supp. XIII:** 129

Parker, Dorothy, **Retro. Supp. II:** 327; **Supp. IV Part 1:** 353; **Supp. IX:** 62, 114, **189–206; Supp. X:** 164; **Supp. XI:** 28; **Supp. XVIII:** 242, 246, 252; **Supp. XXVI:** 275

Parker, Emily, **Supp. XVIII:** 102

Parker, Idella, **Supp. X:** 232, 234–235

Parker, James, **Supp. XXVI:** 84

Parker, Joan, **Supp. XIX:** 187

Parker, Lonnae O'Neal, **Supp. XXIII:** 276

Parker, Muriel, **Supp. IX:** 232

Parker, Patricia, **Supp. XV:** 242

Parker, Robert B., **Supp. IV Part 1:** 135, 136; **Supp. XIX: 177–192**

Parker, Robert Dale, **Supp. XXIII:** 223, 228, 229

Parker, Theodore, **Supp. I Part 1:** 38; **Supp. I Part 2:** 518; **Supp. XXIV:** 70

Parker, Thomas, **Supp. I Part 1:** 102

"Parker's Back" (O'Connor), **III:** 348, 352, 358

"Parkersburg" (Halliday), **Supp. XIX:** 92

Parkes, Henry Bamford, **Supp. I Part 2:** 617

Park-Fuller, Linda, **Supp. XIII:** 297

Parkman, Francis, **II:** 278, 310, 312; **IV:** 179, 309; **Supp. I Part 2:** 420, 479, 481–482, 486, 487, 493, 498; **Supp. II Part 2: 589–616**

Parkman Reader, The (Morison, ed.), **Supp. I Part 2:** 494

Parks, Gordon, Sr., **Supp. XI:** 17

Parks, Larry, **Supp. I Part 1:** 295

Parks, Rosa, **Supp. I Part 1:** 342

"Park Street Cemetery, The" (Lowell), **II:** 537, 538

Par le Détroit (cantata) (Bowles), **Supp. IV Part 1:** 82

Parliament of Fowls, The (Chaucer), **III:** 492

Parmenides (Plato), **II:** 10

Parmenter, Jon, **Supp. XXVI:** 85
Parnassus (Emerson), **II:** 8, 18
Parnell, Charles Stewart, **II:** 129, 137
Parole (film), **Supp. XIII:** 166
Parole Fixer (film), **Supp. XIII:** 170
Parrington, Vernon Louis, **I:** 254, 517, 561; **III:** 335, 606; **IV:** 173; **Supp. I Part 2:** 484, 640
Parrish, Dillwyn, **Supp. XVII:** 83–84, 90
Parrish, Robert, **Supp. XI:** 307
"Parrot, The" (Merrill), **Supp. III Part 1:** 320
"Parsley" (Dove), **Supp. IV Part 1:** 245, 246
Parson, Annie, **Supp. I Part 2:** 655
Parsons, Elsie Clews, **I:** 231, 235
Parsons, Ian, **Supp. IX:** 95
Parsons, Louella, **Supp. XII:** 173
Parsons, Talcott, **Supp. I Part 2:** 648
Parsons, Theophilus, **II:** 396, 504; **Retro. Supp. II:** 134; **Supp. I Part 1:** 155
"Parthian Shot, The" (Hammett), **Supp. IV Part 1:** 343
Partial Glossary, A (Bronk), **Supp. XXI:** 26
Partial Payments: Essays on Writers and Their Lives (Epstein), **Supp. XIV:** 111
Partial Portraits (James), **II:** 336
"Partial Relief" (Halliday), **Supp. XIX:** 91
Partial Truth (Nelson), **Supp. XVIII:** 175–176, 178
"Particulars" (Pickering), **Supp. XXI:** 197
Parties (Van Vechten), **Supp. II Part 2:** 739, 747–749
"Parting" (Kunitz), **Supp. III Part 1:** 263
"Parting Gift" (Wylie), **Supp. I Part 2:** 714
"Parting Glass, The" (Freneau), **Supp. II Part 1:** 273
"Partings" (Hogan), **Supp. IV Part 1:** 413
Partington, Blanche, **I:** 199
Partisans (Matthiessen), **Supp. V:** 201
"Partner, The" (Roethke), **III:** 541–542
Partners, The (Auchincloss), **Supp. IV Part 1:** 31, 34
Partners in Crime: A Rafe Buenrostro Mystery (Hinojosa), **Supp. XIX:** 107–108
"Part of a Letter" (Wilbur), **Supp. III Part 2:** 551
Part of a Long Story: Eugene O'Neill as a Young Man in Love (Boulton), **Supp. XXII:** 18, 21, 27–30
Part of Speech, A (Brodsky), **Supp. VIII:** 22
"Part of the Bee's Body Embedded in the Flesh, The" (C. Frost), **Supp. XV:** 105, 107
"Part of the Story" (Dobyns), **Supp. XIII:** 79
Part of Vermont, A (Taggard), **Supp. XXII:** 284
Parton, Sara, **Retro. Supp. I:** 246
Partridge, Jeffrey F., **Supp. XV:** 219
Partridge, John, **II:** 110, 111
"Parts of a Journal" (Gordon), **Supp. IV Part 1:** 310

Parts of a World (Stevens), **Retro. Supp. I: 305–306,** 307, 309, 313
"Parturition" (Loy), **Supp. XXII:** 159, 160–161
"Party, The" (Dunbar), **Supp. II Part 1:** 198, 205–206
"Party, The" (Taylor), **Supp. V:** 315
Party at Jack's, The (Wolfe), **IV:** 451–452, 469
"Party Down at the Square, A" (Ellison), **Retro. Supp. II:** 124
Party of Five (television series), **Supp. XIX:** 222
"Party Poem" (Huddle), **Supp. XXVI:** 149
Pascal, Blaise, **II:** 8, 159; **III:** 292, 301, 304, 428; **Retro. Supp. I:** 326, 330
"Paskudnyak" (Pilcer), **Supp. XVII:** 50
"Pass, The" (Neugeboren), **Supp. XVI:** 225
"Passage" (Crane), **I:** 391
"Passage in the Life of Mr. John Oakhurst, A" (Harte), **Supp. II Part 1:** 353–354
Passage in the Night, A (Asch), **Supp. XXIII:** 7
"Passages" (Duncan), **Supp. XVI:** 287
"Passages for Puritans" (Davison), **Supp. XXVI:** 62
"Passages from a Relinquished Work" (Hawthorne), **Retro. Supp. I:** 150
Passages toward the Dark (McGrath), **Supp. X:** 126, 127
"Passage to India" (Whitman), **IV:** 348
Passage to India, A (Forster), **II:** 600; **Supp. XVIII:** 143
Passaro, Vince, **Supp. X:** 167, 302, 309, 310
"Passenger, The" (Brockmeier), **Supp. XXII:** 52
"Passenger Pigeons" (Jeffers), **Supp. II Part 2:** 437
Passin, Herbert, **Supp. XIII:** 337
Passing (Larsen), **Supp. XVIII:** 119, 123, **127–130**
"Passing Beauty" (C. Frost), **Supp. XV:** 97
"Passing of Grandison, The" (Chesnutt), **Supp. XIV:** 62, **66–69**
"Passing of Sister Barsett, The" (Jewett), **Retro. Supp. II:** 138–139, 143
"Passing Ports and Crossing Walks" (Gansworth), **Supp. XXVI:** 114
"Passing Show, The" (Bierce), **I:** 208
"Passing Through" (Kunitz), **Supp. III Part 1:** 265
"Passion, The" (Barnes), **Supp. III Part 1:** 36
"Passion, The" (Merwin), **Supp. III Part 1:** 343
Passionate, Accurate Story, The: Making Your Heart's Truth into Literature (C. Bly), **Supp. XVI:** 41–42
Passionate Pilgrim, A (James), **II:** 324; **Retro. Supp. I:** 219
"Passionate Pilgrim, A" (James), **II:** 322, 323–324; **Retro. Supp. I:** 218
Passion Play (Kosinski), **Supp. VII:** 215, 225–226

Passions of Uxport, The (Kumin), **Supp. IV Part 2:** 444
Pass It On (Hadas), **Supp. XXIII: 115,** 123
"Pass It On, I" (Hadas), **Supp. XXIII:** 115
"Pass It On, II" (Hadas), **Supp. XXIII:** 115
"Passive Resistance" (McKay), **Supp. X:** 133
Passport to the War (Kunitz), **Supp. III Part 1:** 261–264
Passwords (Stafford), **Supp. XI: 329–330**
"Past, The" (Bryant), **Supp. I Part 1:** 157, 170
Past, The (Kinnell), **Supp. III Part 1:** 235, 253–254
"Past, The" (Kinnell), **Supp. III Part 1:** 254
Past and Present (Carlyle), **Supp. I Part 2:** 410
Pasternak, Boris, **II:** 544; **Supp. XXIII:** 209
"Pastiches et Pistaches" (Van Vechten), **Supp. II Part 2:** 732
"Past Is the Present, The" (Moore), **III:** 199–200
"Pastoral" (Carver), **Supp. III Part 1:** 137, 146
"Pastoral" (Dove), **Supp. IV Part 1:** 249
"Pastoral" (Trethewey), **Supp. XXI:** 257
"Pastoral Hat, A" (Stevens), **IV:** 91
Pastoralia (Saunders), **Supp. XIX: 227–229**
"Pastoralia" (Saunders), **Supp. XIX:** 227, 229
"Pastor Dowe at Tacaté" (Bowles), **Supp. IV Part 1:** 87
Pastorela (ballet) (Kirstein), **Supp. IV Part 1:** 83
Pastorius, Francis Daniel, **Supp. I Part 2:** 700
"Pasture Poems" (Kumin), **Supp. IV Part 2:** 446
Pastures of Heaven, The (Steinbeck), **IV:** 51
Patch, Jerry, **Supp. XVIII:** 38
Patchen, Kenneth, **Supp. III Part 2:** 625
Patchett, Ann, **Supp. XII: 307–324**
Patchwork Planet (Lethem), **Supp. XVIII:** 150
Pater, Walter, **I:** 51, 272, 476; **II:** 27, 338; **III:** 604; **IV:** 74; **Retro. Supp. I:** 56, 79; **Retro. Supp. II:** 326; **Supp. I Part 2:** 552; **Supp. IX:** 66
Paterna (Mather), **Supp. II Part 2:** 451
Paternostro, Silvana, **Supp. XXV:** 55, 58
"Paterson" (Ginsberg), **Supp. II Part 1:** 314–315, 321, 329
Paterson (W. C. Williams), **I:** 62, 446; **IV:** 418–423; **Retro. Supp. I:** 209, 284, 413, 419, 421, **424–428,** 428, 429, 430; **Retro. Supp. II:** 321, 328; **Supp. II Part 2:** 557, 564, 625; **Supp. VIII:** 275, 305; **Supp. XIV:** 96; **Supp. XV:** 264, 349
Paterson, Book Five (W. C. Williams), **IV:** 422–423
Paterson, Book One (W. C. Williams), **IV:** 421–422
Paterson, Isabel, **Supp. IV Part 2:** 524

Paterson, Part Three (W. C. Williams), **IV:** 420–421

Pat Garrett and Billy the Kid (film, Peckinpah), **Supp. XVIII:** 27

"Path, The" (Bryant), **Supp. I Part 1:** 169

Pathfinder, The (Cooper), **I:** 349, 350, 355

Pat Hobby Stories, The (Fitzgerald), **Retro. Supp. I:** 114

"Pathos of Low Life, The" (Hapgood), **Supp. XVII:** 103

"Patience of a Saint, The" (Humphrey), **Supp. IX:** 106

Patience Sparhawk and Her Times (Atherton), **Supp. XXIV:** 18, 20, 22, 27

Patient 002 (Skloot), **Supp. XX: 194, 208**

Patinkin, Mandy, **Supp. IV Part 1:** 236

Paton, Alan, **Supp. VIII:** 126

Patria Mia (Pound), **III:** 460–461; **Retro. Supp. I:** 284

"Patria Mia" (Pound), **Retro. Supp. I:** 284

"Patriarch, The" (Alvares), **Supp. V:** 11

"Patrick Kavanagh at First Light" (Skloot), **Supp. XX: 204**

Patrimony: A True Story (P. Roth), **Retro. Supp. II:** 279, 280, 291; **Supp. III Part 2:** 427

Patriot, The (Buck), **Supp. II Part 1:** 122–123

Patriot, The (Connell), **Supp. XIV:** 94–95

Patriot Act (Gansworth), **Supp. XXVI:** 114

Patriotic Gore: Studies in the Literature of the American Civil War (Wilson), **III:** 588; **IV:** 430, 438, 443, 445–445, 446; **Supp. VIII:** 100

"Patriotic Thing, The" (Ryan as Quin), **Supp. XVIII:** 229

"Patriots, The/Los Patriotas" (Kingsolver), **Supp. VII:** 209

Patron Saint of Liars, The (Patchett), **Supp. XII:** 307, 310, **311–314,** 317

Pattee, Fred L., **II:** 456

Patten, Gilbert, **II:** 423

Patten, Simon, **Supp. I Part 2:** 640

Patternmaster (O. Butler), **Supp. XIII:** 61, 62, 63

Patternmaster Series (O. Butler), **Supp. XIII: 62–63**

Pattern Recognition (W. Gibson), **Supp. XVI:** 124, **130–131**

"Patterns" (Lowell), **II:** 524

Patterson, Floyd, **III:** 38

Patterson, Margot, **Supp. XXII:** 85

Patterson, William M., **Supp. I Part 1:** 265

Patton, General George, **III:** 575; **Supp. I Part 2:** 664

Patton, Venetra K., **Supp. XXVI:** 166

"Patty-Cake, Patty-Cake...A Memoir" (Apple), **Supp. XVII:** 7

Patty Fairfield series (Wells), **Supp. XXVI:** 276

Paul, Saint, **I:** 365; **II:** 15, 494; **IV:** 122, 154, 164, 335; **Retro. Supp. I:** 247; **Supp. I Part 1:** 188

Paul, Sherman, **I:** 244; **IV:** 179

"Paula Becker to Clara Westhoff" (Rich), **Supp. I Part 2:** 573–574

"Paula Gunn Allen" (Ruppert), **Supp. IV Part 1:** 321

Paul Ardenheim, the Monk of Wissahikon (Lippard), **Supp. XXIII:** 178, 186, 187, 189, 190

Paul Bowles: Romantic Savage (Caponi), **Supp. IV Part 1:** 95

Paulding, James Kirke, **I:** 344; **II:** 298, 299, 303; **Supp. I Part 1:** 157

Pauley, Jane, **Supp. XXI:** 39

Paul Jones (Hapgood), **Supp. XVII:** 100–101

Paul Marchand, F.M.C. (Chesnutt), **Supp. XIV:** 76

"Paul Monette: The Brink of Summer's End" (film), **Supp. X:** 152

"Paul Revere" (Longfellow), **II:** 489, 501

"Paul Revere's Ride" (Longfellow), **Retro. Supp. II:** 163

"Paul's Case" (Cather), **I:** 314–315; **Retro. Supp. I:** 3, 5

Paulsen, Friedrich, **III:** 600

"Pauper Witch of Grafton, The" (Frost), **Retro. Supp. II:** 42

"Pause by the Water, A" (Merwin), **Supp. III Part 1:** 354

"Pavane for the Nursery, A" (W. J. Smith), **Supp. XIII:** 335

"Pavement, The" (Olson), **Supp. II Part 2:** 571

Pavese, Cesare, **Supp. XXI:** 132

Pavic, Milorad, **Supp. XXII:** 265

Pavilion of Women (Buck), **Supp. II Part 1:** 125–126

"Pawnbroker, The" (Kumin), **Supp. IV Part 2:** 442, 443–444, 451

Pawnbroker, The (Wallant), **Supp. XVI:** 220

Pay Day (Asch), **Supp. XXVI:** 19, 21–23

"Paying Dues" (Bass), **Supp. XVI:** 16

Payne, Daniel, **Supp. V:** 202; **Supp. XXVI:** 33, 35, 37, 40

Payne, John Howard, **II:** 309

Payne Tom, **Supp. XXII:** 266

Paz, Octavio, **Supp. III Part 2:** 630; **Supp. VIII:** 272; **Supp. XI:** 191; **Supp. XIII:** 223

P. D. Kimerakov (Epstein), **Supp. XII:** 160, **162**

Peabody, Elizabeth Palmer, **Retro. Supp. I:** 155–156, 225; **Supp. XXIV:** 75; **Supp. XXV:** 242, 246, 250

Peabody, Francis G., **III:** 293; **Supp. I Part 1:** 5

Peabody, Josephine Preston, **III:** 507; **Supp. XX: 115**

Peaceable Kingdom, The (Prose), **Supp. XVI:** 256–257

Peace and Bread in Time of War (Addams), **Supp. I Part 1:** 21, 22–23

"Peace Between Black and White in the United States" (Locke), **Supp. XIV:** 205

Peace Breaks Out (Knowles), **Supp. XII:** 249

"Peacemaker"(Kenny), **Supp. XXIII:** 151

"Peace March, The" (Simpson), **Supp. IX:** 279

"Peace of Cities, The" (Wilbur), **Supp. III Part 2:** 545

"Peace of Mind" (Boyle), **Supp. XX:** 19

"Peaches" (Davison), **Supp. XXVI:** 77

"Peaches—Six in a Tin Box, Sarajevo" (Cisneros), **Supp. VII:** 67

Peachtree Road (Siddons), **Supp. XXII:** 239, 240, 242, **246–247, 248–251,** 252

Peaco, Ed, **Supp. XXIV:** 221

Peacock, Doug, **Supp. VIII:** 38; **Supp. XIII:** 12

Peacock, Gibson, **Supp. I Part 1:** 360

Peacock, Molly, **Supp. XIX: 193–207; Supp. XVII:** 74

"Peacock, The" (Merrill), **Supp. III Part 1:** 320

"Peacock, The" (Mosher), **Supp. XXII:** 211

Peacock, Thomas Love, **Supp. I Part 1:** 307; **Supp. VIII:** 125

"Peacock Room, The" (Hayden), **Supp. II Part 1:** 374–375

"Peacocks of Avignon, The" (Swados), **Supp. XIX:** 263

Pearce, Richard, **Supp. IX:** 254

Pearce, Roy Harvey, **II:** 244; **Supp. I Part 1:** 111, 114; **Supp. I Part 2:** 475

"Pearl" (Kooser), **Supp. XIX:** 127–128

Pearl, The (Steinbeck), **IV:** 51, 62–63

Pearlman, Daniel, **III:** 479

Pearlman, Mickey, **Supp. XIII:** 293, 306

Pearl of Orr's Island, The (Stowe), **Supp. I Part 2:** 592–593, 595

"Pearls" (A. Finch), **Supp. XVII:** 72

Pears, Peter, **II:** 586; **Supp. IV Part 1:** 84

Pearson, Drew, **Supp. XIV:** 126

Pearson, Norman Holmes, **Supp. I Part 1:** 259, 260, 273

Pearson, Tom, **Supp. XXVI:** 113

"Pear Tree" (C. Frost), **Supp. XV:** 105

"Peasants' Way O' Thinkin' " (McKay), **Supp. X:** 133

Pease, Donald E., **Supp. IV Part 2:** 687

"Peboan and Seegwun (Winter and Spring): A Chippewa Allegory"(J. Schoolcraft), **Supp. XXIII:** 235

Peck, Gregory, **Supp. VIII:** 128, 129; **Supp. XII:** 160, 173

Peckinpah, Sam, **Supp. XI:** 306; **Supp. XVIII:** 27

"Peck of Gold, A" (Frost), **II:** 155

Peculiar Treasures: A Biblical Who's Who (Buechner), **Supp. XII:** 53

Pedagogy of the Oppressed (Freire), **Supp. XXV:** 133

"Pedal Point" (Francis), **Supp. IX:** 87

Pedersen, Inge, **Supp. XVIII:** 179

"Pedersen Kid, The" (Gass), **Supp. VI:** 83

"Pedigree, The" (Creeley), **Supp. IV Part 1:** 150

Peebles, Melvin Van, **Supp. XI:** 17; **Supp. XVI:** 144

"Peed Onk" (Moore). *See* "People Like That Are the Only People Here: Canonical Babbling in Peed Onk" (Moore)

"Peeler, The" (O'Connor), **Retro. Supp. II:** 225

"Peeper, The" (Davison), **Supp. XXVI:** 69

Peich, Michael, **Supp. XV:** 113, 117; **Supp. XXV:** 222

Peikoff, Leonard, **Supp. IV Part 2:** 520, 526, 529

Peirce, Charles Sanders, **II:** 20, 352–353; **III:** 599; **Supp. I Part 2:** 640; **Supp. III Part 2:** 626

Pelagius, **III:** 295

"Pelican, The" (Merrill), **Supp. III Part 1:** 320

"Pelican, The" (Wharton), **IV:** 310; **Retro. Supp. I:** 364

Pellacchia, Michael, **Supp. XIII:** 16

Pelley, Denise, **Supp. XIX:** 205

Pelonero, Michael, **Supp. XXIII:** 125

Peltier, Leonard, **Supp. V:** 212

"Penance"(Dybek), **Supp. XXIII:** 69

"Pen and Paper and a Breath of Air" (Oliver), **Supp. VII:** 245

Pence, Amy, **Supp. XV:** 211, 223

"Pencil, The" (Chandler), **Supp. IV Part 1:** 135

Pencillings by the Way (Willis), **II:** 313; **Supp. XVIII:** 12

"Pencils" (Sandburg), **III:** 592

Pendleton, Devon, **Supp. XVIII:** 151

"Pendulum" (Bradbury and Hasse), **Supp. IV Part 1:** 102

"Penelope's Song" (Glück), **Supp. V:** 89

Penelope: The Story of the Half-Scalped Woman (Schott), **Supp. XXIII:** 240, **244–245**

Penhally (Gordon), **II:** 197, 199, 201–203, 204

"Penis" (McClatchy), **Supp. XII:** 266–267

Penitent, The (di Donato), **Supp. XX: 44, 45**

Penitent, The (Singer), **Retro. Supp. II: 309–310,** 313

Penland, Nell Bates, **Supp. XXII:** 188

Penn, Robert, **I:** 489

Penn, Sean, **Supp. XI:** 107

Penn, Thomas, **II:** 118

Penn, William, **Supp. I Part 2:** 683

Penna, Sandro, **Supp. XIX:** 34

Pennebaker, D. A., **Supp. XVIII:** 19, 26

"Pennsylvania Pilgrim, The" (Whittier), **Supp. I Part 2:** 700

"Pennsylvania Planter, The" (Freneau), **Supp. II Part 1:** 268

Penny, Rob, **Supp. VIII:** 330

"Penny, The" (D. West), **Supp. XVIII:** 283–284

Penrod (Tarkington), **III:** 223

"Penseroso, Il" (Milton), **Supp. XIV:** 8

Pensieri (Leopardi; Di Piero, trans.), **Supp. XIX:** 34

"Pensive Hours"(J. Schoolcraft), **Supp. XXIII:** 230–231

Pentagon of Power, The (Mumford), **Supp. II Part 2:** 498

Pentimento (Hellman), **Supp. I Part 1:** 280, 292–294, 296; **Supp. IV Part 1:** 12; **Supp. VIII:** 243

"Peonies at Dusk" (Kenyon), **Supp. VII:** 171

People, The (Glaspell), **Supp. III Part 1:** 179

People, Yes, The (Sandburg), **III:** 575, 589, 590, 591

"PEOPLE BURNING, THE" (Baraka), **Supp. II Part 1:** 49

"People in Hell Just Want a Drink of Water" (Proulx), **Supp. VII:** 263

"People Like That Are the Only People Here: Canonical Babbling in Peed Onk" (Moore), **Supp. X:** 168, **178–179**

People Live Here: Selected Poems 1949–1983 (Simpson), **Supp. IX:** 269, 277

"People Next Door, The" (Simpson), **Supp. IX:** 279

People of the Abyss, The (London), **II:** 465–466

"People on the Roller Coaster, The" (Hardwick), **Supp. III Part 1:** 196

People Shall Continue, The (Ortiz), **Supp. IV Part 2:** 510

People's History of the United States, A (Zinn), **Supp. XXIV:** 87

"People's Surroundings" (Moore), **III:** 201, 202, 203

"People v. Abe Lathan, Colored, The" (Caldwell), **I:** 309

"Peppermint Lounge Revisited, The" (Wolfe), **Supp. III Part 2:** 571

Peppis, Paul, **Supp. XXII:** 160

Pepys, Samuel, **Supp. I Part 2:** 653

"Perchance to Dream" (Franzen), **Supp. XX: 90, 93**

Perchance to Dream: Robert B. Parker's Sequel to Raymond Chandler's "Big Sleep" (Parker), Supp. XIX: 189

"Perch'io non spero di tornar giammai" (Cavalcanti), **Supp. III Part 2:** 623

Perch of the Devil (Atherton), **Supp. XXIV:** 24, 29

Percy, Thomas, **Supp. XIV:** 2

Percy, Walker, **Supp. III Part 1: 383–400; Supp. IV Part 1:** 297; **Supp. V:** 334; **Supp. X:** 42; **Supp. XIV:** 21; **Supp. XIX:** 209; **Supp. XXVI:** 253

Percy, William, **Supp. V:** 334

Percy, William Alexander, **Retro. Supp. I:** 341; **Supp. XXII:** 193

Peregrin, Tony, **Supp. XV:** 69

"Peregrine" (Wylie), **Supp. I Part 2:** 712–713, 714

Perelman, Bob, **Supp. XII:** 23

Perelman, S. J., **IV:** 286; **Retro. Supp. I:** 342; **Retro. Supp. II:** 321, 322, 325, 326, 327, 336; **Supp. IV Part 1:** 353; **Supp. XI:** 66

Perera, Victor, **Supp. XXV:** 50, 52

Perestroika (Kushner), **Supp. IX:** 141, 142, 145

Péret, Benjamin, **Supp. VIII:** 272

Peretz, Isaac Leib, **IV:** 1, 3; **Retro. Supp. II:** 299; **Supp. XXIII:** 4, 7, 8–9

Pérez Galdós, Benito, **II:** 275

Perfect Analysis Given by a Parrot, A (T. Williams), **IV:** 395

"Perfect Couple, The" (Nelson), **Supp. XVIII:** 173

"Perfect Day for Bananafish, A" (Salinger), **III:** 563–564, 571

Perfect Fiction, The (Sorrentino), **Supp. XXI:** 228

Perfect Ganesh, A (McNally), **Supp. XIII: 202–203,** 208, 209

"Perfect Gerbil, The: Reading Barthelme's 'The School' " (Saunders), **Supp. XIX:** 235

"Perfection" (Helprin), **Supp. XXV:** 80

"Perfect Knight, The" (Chandler), **Supp. IV Part 1:** 120

Perfect Mother, The (Schott), **Supp. XXIII: 241–242**

Perfect Party, The (Gurney), **Supp. V:** 100, 105, 106–107

"Perfect Things" (F. Barthelme), **Supp. XI:** 30, 33–34

"Performance, The" (Dickey), **Supp. IV Part 1:** 178–179, 181

"Perfume" (Mora), **Supp. XIII:** 218

"Perhaps the World Ends Here" (Harjo), **Supp. XII:** 228, 231

Perhaps Women (Anderson), **I:** 114

Pericles (Shakespeare), **I:** 585; **Supp. III Part 2:** 624, 627, 629

Perillo, Lucia, **Supp. XXVI:** 68

"Period Metaphor" (Bronk), **Supp. XXI:** 33

Period of Adjustment (T. Williams), **IV:** 382, 386, 387, 388, 389, 390, 392, 393, 394, 397

"Period Pieces from the Mid-Thirties" (Agee), **I:** 28

"Peripheral Vision" (Davison), **Supp. XXVI:** 69–70

"Periphery" (Ammons), **Supp. VII:** 28

Perkins, David, **Supp. I Part 2:** 459, 475; **Supp. XV:** 185

Perkins, Maxwell, **I:** 252, 289, 290; **II:** 87, 93, 95, 252; **IV:** 452, 455, 457, 458, 461, 462, 463, 469; **Retro. Supp. I:** 101, 105, 108, 109, 110, 113, 114, 178; **Supp. IX:** 57, 58, 60, 232; **Supp. X:** 219, 224, 225, 229, 230, 233; **Supp. XI:** 218, 227

Perlès, Alfred, **III:** 177, 183, 187, 189

Perloff, Marjorie, **Supp. I Part 2:** 539, 542; **Supp. IV Part 1:** 68; **Supp. IV Part 2:** 420, 424, 432; **Supp. XXII:** 161, 271; **Supp. XXIII:** 210, 220

Permanence and Change (Burke), **I:** 274

Permanent Errors (Price), **Supp. VI:** 261

"Permanent Traits of the English National Genius" (Emerson), **II:** 18

Permit Me Voyage (Agee), **I:** 25, 27

"Perosa Canavese" (Everwine), **Supp. XV:** 84

Perrault, Charles, **IV:** 266; **Supp. I Part 2:** 622

Perrin, Noel, **Supp. XVI:** 34; **Supp. XXII:** 205, 207, 211, 218

Perrins, Carol. *See* Frost, Carol

Perry, Anne, **Supp. V:** 335

Perry, Bliss, **I:** 243

Perry, Donna, **Supp. IV Part 1:** 322, 327, 335

Perry, Edgar A., **III:** 410

Perry, Keith Ronald, **Supp. XXI:** 42

Perry, Lincoln, **Supp. V:** 24, 33

Perry, Matthew C., **Supp. I Part 2:** 494–495

Perry, Pam, **Supp. XXVI:** 12
Perry, Patsy Brewington, **Supp. I Part 1:** 66
Perry, Phyllis Alesia, **Supp. XVIII:** 96
Perry, Ralph Barton, **I:** 224; **II:** 356, 362, 364; **Supp. XIV:** 197
Perry, Dr. William, **II:** 395, 396
Perse, St.-John, **III:** 12, 13, 14, 17; **Supp. III Part 1:** 14; **Supp. IV Part 1:** 82; **Supp. XIII:** 344; **Supp. XV:** 178
"Persephone in Hell" (Dove), **Supp. IV Part 1:** 250, 251
"Persephone"(Le Sueur), **Supp. XXIII:** 162, 165, **170–171**
"Persephone to Psyche" (Stallings), **Supp. XXV:** 234
"Persephone Writes a Letter to Her Mother" (Stallings), **Supp. XXV:** 228
"Persimmons" (L.-Y. Lee), **Supp. XV:** 211, 213
"Persistence of Desire, The" (Updike), **IV:** 222–223, 228
"Persistence of Poetry, The" (Bynner), **Supp. XV:** 49
"Persistences" (Hecht), **Supp. X: 68–69**
Person, Place, and Thing (Shapiro), **Supp. II Part 2:** 702, 705
Personae of Ezra Pound (Pound), **III:** 458
Personae: The Collected Poems (Pound), **Retro. Supp. I:** 285, 286; **Supp. I Part 1:** 255; **Supp. XVII:** 32
"Personal" (Stern), **Supp. IX:** 299
"Personal and Occasional Pieces" (Welty), **Retro. Supp. I:** 355
"Personal and the Individual, The" (L. Michaels), **Supp. XVI:** 201
Personal Injuries (Turow), **Supp. XVII: 219–220**, 221, 223
"Personalities" (column, Briggs), **Supp. XVIII:** 15
Personal Narrative (Edwards), **I:** 545, 552, 553, 561, 562; **Supp. I Part 2:** 700
"Personal Poem #9" (Berrigan), **Supp. XXIV:** 34, 35
"Personal Poem"(O'Hara), **Supp. XXIII:** 219
Personal Recollection of Joan of Arc (Twain), **IV:** 208
Personals (Bontemps), **Supp. XXII:** 7, 8
"Personals" (Didion), **Supp. IV Part 1:** 200
"Personism" (O'Hara), **Supp. XV:** 181
"Personism: A Manifesto" (O'Hara), **Supp. XXIII:** 212, 215; **Supp. XXIV:** 43
Persons and Places (Santayana), **III:** 615
Persons in Hiding (film), **Supp. XIII:** 170
Persons in Hiding (Hoover), **Supp. XIII:** 170
Person Sitting in Darkness, A (Twain), **IV:** 208
"Persons Who Interest Us" (*Harper's Bazaar),* **Supp. XXV:** 277–278
"Perspective" (Francis), **Supp. IX:** 78
"Perspective: Anniversary D-Day" (Karr), **Supp. XI:** 241

Perspectives by Incongruity (Burke), **I:** 284–285
"Perspectives: Is It Out of Control?" (Gleason), **Supp. IX:** 16
Perspectives on Cormac McCarthy (Arnold and Luce, eds.), **Supp. VIII:** 189
Persse, Dudley Jocelyn, **Supp. XX: 232**
Pertes et Fracas (McCoy), **Supp. XIII:** 175
"Peruvian Child" (Mora), **Supp. XIII:** 218
Peseroff, Joyce, **Supp. IV Part 1:** 71
Pesetsky, Bette, **Supp. XXIV:** 173
"Pestilence" (Nelson), **Supp. XVIII:** 186
Pest Maiden, The (Schott), **Supp. XXIII: 245–246**
"Peter" (Cather), **Retro. Supp. I:** 4
"Peter" (Moore), **III:** 210, 212
Peter, Saint, **III:** 341, 346; **IV:** 86, 294
Peterkin, Julia, **Supp. I Part 1:** 328; **Supp. XXII:** 12, 189
"Peter Klaus" (German tale), **II:** 306
Peter Pan (Barrie), **Supp. XV:** 319
"Peter Parley" works (Goodrich), **Supp. I Part 1:** 38
"Peter Pendulum" (Poe), **III:** 425
"Peter Quince at the Clavier" (Stevens), **IV:** 81, 82
Peter Rabbit tales, **Retro. Supp. I:** 335
Peters, Cora, **Supp. I Part 2:** 468
Peters, Jacqueline, **Supp. XII:** 225
Peters, Margot, **Supp. VIII:** 252
Peters, Robert, **Supp. XIII:** 114
Peters, S. H. (pseudonym). *See* Henry, O.
Peters, Timothy, **Supp. XI:** 39
"Peter's Avocado" (Rodriguez), **Supp. XIV:** 308–309
Petersen, David, **Supp. XIII:** 2
Petersen, Donald, **Supp. V:** 180; **Supp. XV:** 74, 92
Peterson, Dorothy, **Supp. XVIII:** 131, 132
Peterson, George, **Supp. XXII:** 250
Peterson, Houston, **I:** 60
Peterson, Roger Tory, **Supp. V:** 202
Peterson, Virgilia, **Supp. IV Part 1:** 30
Peter Whiffle: His Life and Works (Van Vechten), **Supp. II Part 2:** 728–729, 731, 735, 738–741, 749
"Petey and Yotsee and Mario" (H. Roth), **Supp. IX:** 234
"Petition, A" (Winters), **Supp. II Part 2:** 785
"Pet Milk"(Dybek), **Supp. XXIII:** 74
"'Pet Negro' System, The" (Hurston), **Supp. VI:** 159
"Petra and Its Surroundings" (Frost), **Retro. Supp. I:** 124
Petrarch, **I:** 176; **II:** 590; **III:** 4
"Petrarch, Shakespeare, and the Blues" (C. Frost), **Supp. XV:** 92, 104, 105
"Petrified Man" (Welty), **IV:** 262; **Retro. Supp. I:** 345, 351
"Petrified Man, The" (Twain), **IV:** 195
"Petrified Woman, The" (Gordon), **II:** 199
Petronius, **III:** 174, 179
Petry, Ann, **Supp. VIII:** 214; **Supp. XI:** 6, 85; **Supp. XVIII:** 286

Pet Sematary (King), **Supp. V:** 138, 143, 152
Pettengill, Claire C., **Supp. XXV:** 40
Pettengill, Richard, **Supp. VIII:** 341, 345, 348
Pettingell, Phoebe, **Supp. XV:** 251, 256–257, 262
Pettis, Joyce, **Supp. XI:** 276, 277, 278, 281
Pettis, Olive G., **Supp. XXIII:** 189
Petty, Jill, **Supp. XXI:** 244, 248, 249, 250
Pfaelzer, Jean, **Supp. XVI:** 88, 90
Pfaff, Timothy, **Supp. V:** 166
Pfeil, Fred, **Supp. XIV:** 36
Pfister, Karin, **IV:** 467, 475
Phaedo (Plato), **II:** 10
Phaedra (Lowell and Barzun, trans.), **II:** 543–544
"Phantasia for Elvira Shatayev" (Rich), **Supp. I Part 2:** 570
Phantasms of War (Lowell), **II:** 512
"Phantom of the Movie Palace, The" (Coover), **Supp. V:** 50–51
Phantom Ship, The (Marryat), **Supp. XVII:** 55
"Pharaoh, The" (Kenyon), **Supp. VII:** 172
"Pharmacy"(Strout), **Supp. XXIII:** 281
Pharr, Mary, **Supp. V:** 147
"Phases" (E. Stoddard), **Supp. XV:** 273
"Phases" (Stevens), **Retro. Supp. I:** 299
Phases of an Inferior Planet (Glasgow), **II:** 174–175
"Pheasant, The" (Carver), **Supp. III Part 1:** 146
Phelan, Alice, **Supp. XXII:** 193
Pheloung, Grant, **Supp. XI:** 39
Phelps, Donald, **Supp. XXIII:** 174
Phelps, Elizabeth Stuart, **Retro. Supp. II:** 146; **Supp. XIII:** 141; **Supp. XVI:** 80
Phelps, Teresa Godwin, **Supp. VIII:** 128
Phelps, William Lyon "Billy", **Supp. XX: 68, 75, 220**
"Phenomena and Laws of Race Contacts, The" (Locke), **Supp. XIV:** 210
Phenomenal Fauna, A (Wells), **Supp. XXVI:** 275
"Phenomenology of Anger, The" (Rich), **Supp. I Part 2:** 562–563, 571
Phenomenology of Moral Experience, The (Mandelbaum), **I:** 61
"Phenomenology of *On Moral Fiction*" (C. Johnson), **Supp. VI:** 188
Phidias, **Supp. I Part 2:** 482
Philadelphia Fire (Wideman), **Supp. X:** 320, 334
Philadelphia Negro, The (Du Bois), **Supp. II Part 1:** 158, 163–164, 166
Philbrick, Thomas, **I:** 343
"Philemon and Baucis"(Hadas), **Supp. XXIII:** 114
"Phil in the Marketplace" (Lethem), **Supp. XVIII:** 148
Philip, Jim, **Supp. XII:** 136
Philip, Maxwell, **Supp. XXI:** 160
Philip, Prince, **Supp. X:** 108
"Philip of Pokanoket" (Irving), **II:** 303
Philippians (biblical book), **IV:** 154

"Philippine Conquest, The" (Masters), **Supp. I Part 2:** 456

"Philip Roth Reconsidered" (Howe), **Retro. Supp. II:** 286

"Philistinism and the Negro Writer" (Baraka), **Supp. II Part 1:** 39, 44

Phillips, Adam, **Supp. XII:** 97–98

Phillips, Anne K., **Supp. XX: 221**

Phillips, Carl, **Supp. XXI:** 246

Phillips, David Graham, **II:** 444; **Retro. Supp. II:** 101

Phillips, Gene D., **Supp. XI:** 306

Phillips, Jayne Anne, **Supp. XIV:** 21

Phillips, J. J., **Supp. XXIII:** 174

Phillips, J. O. C., **Supp. I Part 1:** 19

Phillips, Robert, **Supp. XIII:** 335, 344

Phillips, Wendell, **Supp. I Part 1:** 103; **Supp. I Part 2:** 524

Phillips, Willard, **Supp. I Part 1:** 154, 155

Phillips, William, **Supp. VIII:** 156

Phillips, William L., **I:** 106

"Philly Babylon" (Di Piero), **Supp. XIX:** 46

"Philoctetes"(Hadas), **Supp. XXIII:** 115

"Philoctetes: The Wound and the Bow" (Wilson), **Supp. XXIV:** 217

"Philosopher, The" (Farrell), **II:** 45

Philosopher of the Forest (pseudonym). *See* Freneau, Philip

Philosophes classiques, Les (Taine), **III:** 323

"Philosophical Cobbler, The" (Sanders), **Supp. XVI:** 268

"Philosophical Concepts and Practical Results" (James), **II:** 352

"Philosophical Investigation of Metaphor, A" (Gass), **Supp. VI:** 79

Philosophical Transactions (Watson), **II:** 114

"Philosophy, Or Something Like That" (P. Roth), **Supp. III Part 2:** 403

"Philosophy and Its Critics" (James), **II:** 360

"Philosophy and the Form of Fiction" (Gass), **Supp. VI:** 85

"Philosophy for People" (Emerson), **II:** 14

"Philosophy in Warm Weather" (Kenyon), **Supp. VII:** 168

"Philosophy Lesson" (Levine), **Supp. V:** 195

Philosophy of Alain Locke, The: Harlem Renaissance and Beyond (Harris, ed.), **Supp. XIV:** 196, 211–212

"Philosophy of Composition, The" (Poe), **III:** 416, 421; **Retro. Supp. II:** 266, 267, 271; **Supp. XXV:** 120, 121

Philosophy of Friedrich Nietzsche, The (Mencken), **III:** 102–103

"Philosophy of Handicap, A" (Bourne), **I:** 216, 218

"Philosophy of History" (Emerson), **II:** 11–12

Philosophy of Literary Form, The (Burke), **I:** 275, 281, 283, 291

Philosophy of the Human Mind, The (Stewart), **II:** 8

Philosophy: Who Needs It (Rand), **Supp. IV Part 2:** 517, 518, 527, 533

Philoxenes, **Supp. VIII:** 201

"Phineas" (Knowles), **Supp. XII:** 238–240

Phineas: Six Stories (Knowles), **Supp. XII:** 249

"Phocion" (Lowell), **II:** 536

Phoebe Light (Notley), **Supp. XXII:** 227

Phoenix and the Turtle, The (Shakespeare), **I:** 284

"Phoenix Lyrics" (Schwartz), **Supp. II Part 2:** 665

"Phone Booths, The" (Jarman), **Supp. XVII:** 112–113

"Phony War Films" (Jones), **Supp. XI:** 217, 232

"Photograph: Carlisle Indian School (1879–1918)"(Kenny), **Supp. XXIII:** 156

"Photograph: Migrant Worker, Parlier, California, 1967" (Levis), **Supp. XI:** 272

"Photograph of a Bawd Drinking Raleigh Rye" (Trethewey), **Supp. XXI:** 254

"Photograph of a Child on a Vermont Hillside" (Kenyon), **Supp. VII:** 168

"Photograph of My Mother as a Young Girl" (Gioia), **Supp. XV:** 119

"Photograph of the Girl" (Olds), **Supp. X:** 205

"Photograph of the Unmade Bed" (Rich), **Supp. I Part 2:** 558

Photographs (Welty), **Retro. Supp. I:** 343

"Photographs, The" (Barthelme), **Supp. IV Part 1:** 53

"Photography" (Levine), **Supp. V:** 194

Phyrrho, **Retro. Supp. I:** 247

"Physical Universe" (Simpson), **Supp. IX:** 278

"Physicist We Know, A" (Shields), **Supp. VII:** 310

"Physics and Cosmology in the Fiction of Tom Robbins" (Nadeau), **Supp. X:** 270

Physiologie du goût (Brillat-Savarin), **Supp. XVII:** 82, 86

Physiology of Taste, The; or, Meditations on Transcendent Gastronomy (Brillat-Savarin; M. F. K. Fisher, trans.), **Supp. XVII:** 86, 87, 91

"Physiology of Versification, The: Harmonies of Organic and Animal Life" (Holmes), **Supp. I Part 1:** 311

Physique de l'Amour (Gourmont), **III:** 467–468

Piaf, Edith, **Supp. IV Part 2:** 549

Piaget, Jean, **Supp. XIII:** 75

"Piano" (Lawrence), **Supp. XV:** 254

"Piano Fingers" (Mason), **Supp. VIII:** 146

Piano Lesson, The (Bearden), **Supp. VIII:** 342

Piano Lesson, The (Wilson), **Supp. VIII:** 342–345

Piano Man's Daughter, The (Findley), **Supp. XX: 59–61**

"Piano Player, The"(Strout), **Supp. XXIII:** 283, 285

Piatt, James, **Supp. I Part 2:** 420

Piatt, John J., **II:** 273

Piazza, Ben, **Supp. XIII:** 163

Piazza, Paul, **Supp. XIV:** 157, 160, 171

"Piazza de Spagna, Early Morning" (Wilbur), **Supp. III Part 2:** 553

Piazza Tales (Melville), **III:** 91

Picabia, Francis, **Retro. Supp. I:** 416; **Retro. Supp. II:** 331; **Supp. XXII:** 162

Picasso (Stein), **IV:** 28, 32, 45

Picasso, Pablo, **I:** 429, 432, 440, 442, 445; **II:** 602; **III:** 197, 201, 470; **IV:** 26, 31, 32, 46, 87, 407, 436; **Retro. Supp. I:** 55, 63; **Supp. IV Part 1:** 81; **Supp. IX:** 66

Piccione, Anthony, **Supp. XV:** 212

"Piccola Comedia" (Wilbur), **Supp. III Part 2:** 561

Pickard, Samuel T., **Supp. I Part 2:** 682

Picked-Up Pieces (Updike), **Retro. Supp. I:** 320, 322, 323, 335

Picker, Lauren, **Supp. VIII:** 78, 83

Picker, Tobias, **Supp. XII:** 253

Pickering, Sam, **Supp. XXI: 191–207**

Pickford, Mary, **Retro. Supp. I:** 325; **Supp. I Part 2:** 391

"Picking and Choosing" (Moore), **III:** 205

"Pickman's Model" (Lovecraft), **Supp. XXV:** 113, 114

Picnic (film), **Supp. XXV:** 95

Picnic (Inge), **Supp. XXV:** 93, 95, 97–99

"Picnic" (Peacock), **Supp. XIX:** 206

Picnic, Lightning (Collins), **Supp. XXI:** 54, 60

"Picnic, Lightning" (Collins), **Supp. XXI:** 64–65

Picnic Cantata (music) (Bowles), **Supp. IV Part 1:** 89

"Picnic Remembered" (Warren), **IV:** 240

Pictorial History of the Negro in America, A (Hughes), **Supp. I Part 1:** 345

"Picture" (Huddle), **Supp. XXVI:** 150

"Picture, The" (Olson), **Supp. II Part 2:** 574

Picture Bride (Son), **Supp. X:** 292

"Picture I Want, The" (Olds), **Supp. X:** 209

Picture of Dorian Gray, The (Wilde), **Supp. IX:** 105

"Picture of Little J. A. in a Prospect of Flowers, A" (Ashbery), **Supp. III Part 1:** 3

Picture Palace (Theroux), **Supp. VIII:** 322

"Pictures" (Pickering), **Supp. XXI:** 197

"Pictures at an Extermination" (Epstein), **Supp. XII:** 161

"Pictures from an Expedition" (Duffy), **Supp. IV Part 1:** 207

Pictures from an Institution (Jarrell), **II:** 367, 385

Pictures from Brueghel (W. C. Williams), **Retro. Supp. I:** 429–431

"Pictures from Brueghel" (W. C. Williams), **Retro. Supp. I:** 419

"Pictures of Columbus, the Genoese, The" (Freneau), **Supp. II Part 1:** 258

Pictures of Fidelman: An Exhibition (Malamud), **Supp. I Part 2:** 450–451

"Pictures of the Artist" (Malamud), **Supp. I Part 2:** 450

Pictures of the Floating World (Lowell), **II:** 521, 524–525

Pictures of Travel (Heine), **II:** 281

Picturesque America; or, the Land We Live In (Bryant, ed.), **Supp. I Part 1:** 158

"Picturesque Ghetto, The" (Hapgood), **Supp. XVII:** 101

"Picturesque: San Cristóbal de las Casas" (Mora), **Supp. XIII:** 218

Picture This (Heller), **Supp. IV Part 1:** 386, 388, 390–391

Picturing Will (Beattie), **Supp. V:** 29, 31–32, 34

"Pie" (X. J. Kennedy), **Supp. XV:** 170

"Piece, A" (Creeley), **Supp. IV Part 1:** 155, 156

"Piece of Moon, A" (Hogan), **Supp. IV Part 1:** 407

Piece of My Heart, A (Ford), **Supp. V:** 57, 58–61, 62

Piece of My Mind, A: Reflections at Sixty (Wilson), **IV:** 426, 430, 438, 441

"Piece of News, A" (Welty), **IV:** 263; **Retro. Supp. I:** 345, 346

Pieces (Creeley), **Supp. IV Part 1:** 155

Pieces and Pontifications (Mailer), **Retro. Supp. I:** 209–210

Pieces of the Frame (McPhee), **Supp. III Part 1:** 293

"Pie of the Month"(Thompson), **Supp. XXIII:** 300

Pierce, Franklin, **II:** 225, 226, 227; **III:** 88; **Retro. Supp. I:** 150, 163, 164, 165

Pierce, Frederick, **Retro. Supp. I:** 136

Piercy, Josephine K., **Supp. I Part 1:** 103

"Pierian Handsprings" (column, Untermeyer), **Supp. XV:** 294

Pierpont, Claudia Roth, **Supp. X:** 192, 193, 196

Pierre et Jean (Maupassant), **I:** 421

Pierre: or The Ambiguities (Melville), **III:** 86–88, 89; **IV:** 194; **Retro. Supp. I:** 249, 253–254, 256; **Supp. I Part 2:** 579

Pierrepont, Sarah. *See* Edwards, Sarah

Pierrot qui pleure et Pierrot qui rit (Rostand), **II:** 515

Pierson, George W, **Supp. XXII:** 289

Pig Cookies (Ríos), **Supp. IV Part 2:** 537, 550, 552–554

Pigeon Feathers (Updike), **IV:** 214, 218, 219, 221–223, 226

"Pigeon Feathers" (Updike), **Retro. Supp. I:** 318, 322, 323

"Pigeons" (Rilke), **II:** 544

"Pigeons, The" (Espaillat), **Supp. XXI:** 98

"Pigeon Woman" (Swenson), **Supp. IV Part 2:** 644

"Pig Helmet and the Wall of Life"(P. Benedict), **Supp. XXIII:** 48–49

Pigs in Heaven (Kingsolver), **Supp. VII:** 197, 199, 209–210

Pike County Ballads, The (Hay), **Supp. I Part 1:** 352

Piket, Vincent, **Supp. IV Part 1:** 24

Pilar San-Mallafre, Maria del, **Supp. V:** 40

Pilcer, Sonya, **Supp. XVII:** 50

Pilgrim (Findley), **Supp. XX:** 61–62

"Pilgrim" (Freneau), **Supp. I Part 1:** 125

"Pilgrimage" (Ray), **Supp. XVIII:** 193

"Pilgrimage" (Sontag), **Supp. III Part 2:** 454–455

"Pilgrimage" (Trethewey), **Supp. XXI:** 255

"Pilgrimage, The" (Maxwell), **Supp. VIII:** 169, 171

Pilgrimage of Festus, The (Aiken), **I:** 50, 55, 57

Pilgrimage of Henry James, The (Brooks), **I:** 240, 248, 250; **IV:** 433

Pilgrim at Tinker Creek (Dillard), **Supp. VI:** 22, **23–26,** 28, 29, **30–31,** 34; **Supp. XVIII:** 189

"Pilgrim Makers" (Lowell), **II:** 541

Pilgrim's Harbor (Skloot), **Supp. XX: 196, 207**

Pilgrim's Progress (Bunyan), **I:** 92; **II:** 15, 168, 572; **Supp. I Part 1:** 32, 38; **Supp. I Part 2:** 599

Pili's Wall (Levine), **Supp. V:** 178, 183–184

"Pillar of Fire" (Bradbury), **Supp. IV Part 1:** 113–114

Pillars of Hercules, The: A Grand Tour of the Mediterranean (Theroux), **Supp. VIII:** 325

"Pillow" (L.-Y. Lee), **Supp. XV:** 224

Pilot, The (Cooper), **I:** 335, 337, 339, 342–343, 350

"Pilot from the Carrier, A" (Jarrell), **II:** 374

"Pilots, Man Your Planes" (Jarrell), **II:** 374–375

"Pilots, The" (Levertov), **Supp. III Part 1:** 282

Pilsudski, Joseph, **Supp. XXIII:** 6

"Pimp's Revenge, A" (Malamud), **Supp. I Part 2:** 435, 450, 451

Pinball (Kosinski), **Supp. VII:** 215, 226

Pinchot, Gifford, **Supp. IX:** 184; **Supp. XIV:** 178

Pindar, **I:** 381; **II:** 543; **III:** 610

"Pine" (Dickey), **Supp. IV Part 1:** 183

Pine Barrens, The (McPhee), **Supp. III Part 1:** 298–301, 309

"Pineys, The" (Stern), **Supp. IX:** 288, 296

Pinget, Robert, **Supp. V:** 39

Pinhook: Finding Wholeness in a Fragmented Land (Ray), **Supp. XVIII:** 189, 192, 202–204

"Pink Dog" (Bishop), **Retro. Supp. II:** 48

"Pink Dress, The" (Boulton), **Supp. XXII:** 19

Pinker, James B., **I:** 409; **Retro. Supp. I:** 231

Pinkerton, Jan, **Supp. V:** 323–324

"Pink Moon—The Pond" (Oliver), **Supp. VII:** 234

Pinktoes (C. Himes), **Supp. XVI: 142**

Pinocchio in Venice (Coover), **Supp. V:** 40, 51

Pinsker, Sanford, **Retro. Supp. II:** 23; **Supp. IX:** 293, 327; **Supp. V:** 272; **Supp. XI:** 251, 254, 317

Pinsky, Robert, **Retro. Supp. II:** 50; **Supp. IX:** 155, 158; **Supp. VI: 235–251; Supp. XIII:** 277, 285; **Supp. XXI:** 243; **Supp. XXIII:** 111, 124

Pinter, Harold, **I:** 71; **Supp. XIII:** 20, 196; **Supp. XIV:** 239; **Supp. XVI:** 207

Pinto, Ferdinand Mendes (pseudonym). *See* Briggs, Charles Frederick

Pinto and Sons (Epstein), **Supp. XII:** 170, **171–172**

Pinto letters (Briggs), **Supp. XVIII:** 3, **12–13**

"Pinup" (Collins), **Supp. XXI:** 59

"Pioneer Girl" (L. I. Wilder), **Supp. XXII:** 290, 293, 294, 295

Pioneer Girl (Nguyen), **Supp. XXVI:** 216–220

Pioneers, The (Cooper), **I:** 336, 337, 339, 340–341, 342, 348; **II:** 313

Pioneers of France in the New World (Parkman), **Supp. III Part 2:** 599, 602

"Pioneers! O Pioneers!" (Whitman), **Retro. Supp. I:** 8

"Pioneer's Vision, The" (Larcom), **Supp. XIII:** 140

Pious and Secular America (Niebuhr), **III:** 308

Pipe Night (O'Hara), **III:** 361, 368

Piper, Dan, **Supp. IX:** 65

Pipers at the Gates of Dawn: The Wisdom of Children's Literature (Cott), **Supp. XVI:** 104

"Piper's Rocks" (Olson), **Supp. IV Part 1:** 153

"Pipistrelles" (B. Kelly), **Supp. XVII:** 129–130

Pipkin, Charles W., **Supp. XIV:** 3

Pippa Passes (Browning), **IV:** 128

Piquion, René, **Supp. I Part 1:** 346

Pirandello, Luigi, **Supp. IV Part 2:** 576, 588

Piranesi, Giovanni Battista, **Supp. XV:** 258

Pirate, The (Robbins), **Supp. XII:** 6

Pirate, The (Scott), **I:** 339

Pirates of Penzance, The (Gilbert and Sullivan), **IV:** 386

Pisan Cantos, The (Pound), **III:** 476; **Retro. Supp. I:** 140, 283, 285, 293; **Supp. III Part 1:** 63; **Supp. V:** 331, 337; **Supp. XIV:** 11; **Supp. XV:** 351

Pisarev, Dimitri, **Supp. XXI:** 164

Piscator, Erwin, **IV:** 394

"Pissaro: Tropical Impressions"(Kenny), **Supp. XXIII:** 146

Pissarro, Camille, **I:** 478

"Pissing off the Back of the Boat into the Nevernais Canal" (Matthews), **Supp. IX:** 160–161

Pistol, The (Jones), **Supp. XI:** 219, **223–224,** 227, 234

Pit, The (Norris), **III:** 314, 322, 326–327, 333, 334

"Pit, The" (Roethke), **III:** 538

"Pit and the Pendulum, The" (Poe), **III:** 413, 416; **Retro. Supp. II:** 264, 269–270, 273

"Pitcher" (Francis), **Supp. IX:** 82

"Pitcher, The" (Dubus), **Supp. VII:** 87

Pitchford, Nicola, **Supp. XII:** 13

"Pits, The" (D. Graham), **Supp. XI:** 252, 254

Pitt, William, **Supp. I Part 2:** 510, 518

Pitts, Rebecca, **Supp. XXII:** 280, 281

"Pittsburgh" (Carruth), **Supp. XVI:** 58

"Pity" (Huddle), **Supp. XXVI:** 151

"Pity Me" (Wylie), **Supp. I Part 2:** 729

Pity the Monsters (Williamson), **Retro. Supp. II:** 185

Pius II, Pope, **III:** 472

Pius IX, Pope, **II:** 79

"Piute Creek" (Snyder), **Supp. VIII:** 293

Pixley, Frank, **I:** 196

Pizer, Donald, **III:** 321; **Retro. Supp. II:** 100, 199

"Place" (Hoffman), **Supp. XVIII:** 86

"Place at the Outskirts" (Simic), **Supp. VIII:** 282

Place Called Estherville, A (Caldwell), **I:** 297, 307

Place Called Freedom, A (Sanders), **Supp. XVI:** 269

Place for My Head, A (Hoffman), **Supp. XVIII:** 76

"Place in Fiction" (Welty), **IV:** 260, 279

Place of Dead Roads, The (Burroughs), **Supp. III Part 1:** 196

Place of Love, The (Shapiro), **Supp. II Part 2:** 702, 706

"Place of Poetry, The" (Stevens), **Retro. Supp. I:** 304

Place of Science in Modern Civilization and Other Essays, The (Veblen), **Supp. I Part 2:** 629, 642

"Place of Trumpets, The" (B. Kelly), **Supp. XVII:** 127

Place on Earth, A (Berry), **Supp. X:** 33–34, 36

Places Left Unfinished at the Time of Creation (Santos), **Supp. XIII:** 274

"Places to Look for Your Mind" (Moore), **Supp. X:** 174–175

"Place They'd Never Seen, A: The Theater" (Wasserstein), **Supp. XV:** 332

"Place to Live, A" (Levertov), **Supp. III Part 1:** 281

"Place to Stand, A" (Price), **Supp. VI:** 258

Place to Stand, A (Wagoner), **Supp. IX:** 324

"Place (Any Place) to Transcend All Places, A" (W. C. Williams), **Retro. Supp. I:** 422

"Place Where My Poems Are Coming From, The"(Crooker), **Supp. XXIII:** 64

Placi, Carlo, **IV:** 328

Plagemann, Catherine, **Supp. XVII:** 91

"Plagiarist, The" (Singer), **IV:** 19

Plagued by the Nightingale (Boyle), **Supp. XXIV:** 51–52, 53, 56

Plague of Dreamers, A (Stern), **Supp. XX:** 178

Plainest Narrative, The (Bronk), **Supp. XXI:** 31

"Plain Language from Truthful James" (Harte). *See* "Heathen Chinee, The"

"Plain Sense of Things, The" (Stevens), **Retro. Supp. I:** 298, 299, 307, 312

"Plain Song" (Carruth), **Supp. XVI:** 54

Plain Song (Harrison), **Supp. VIII:** 38–39

"Plain Song" (Kooser), **Supp. XIX:** 120

"Plain Song for Comadre, A" (Wilbur), **Supp. III Part 2:** 554

"Plain Talk". *See Common Sense* (Paine)

Plaint of a Rose, The (Sandburg), **III:** 579

Plain Truth: Or, Serious Considerations on the Present State of the City of Philadelphia, and Province of Pennsylvania (Franklin), **II:** 117–119

Plainwater: Essays and Poetry (Carson), **Supp. XII:** 97, 99–104

Plan B (C. Himes), **Supp. XVI:** 143, 144

Plan B: Further Thoughts on Faith (Lamott), **Supp. XX:** 142–143

"Planchette" (London), **II:** 475–476

"Planetarium" (Rich), **Supp. I Part 2:** 557

Planet News: 1961–1967 (Ginsberg), **Supp. II Part 1:** 321

Planet Waves (album, Dylan), **Supp. XVIII:** 27

"Plantation a beginning, a" (Olson), **Supp. II Part 2:** 573

Plant Dreaming Deep (Sarton), **Supp. VIII:** 250, 263

Plante, David, **Supp. IV Part 1:** 310

Planting a Sequoia (Gioia), **Supp. XV:** 117

"Planting a Sequoia" (Gioia), **Supp. XV:** 111, 112, 117, **121–122**

"Plants Fed On By Fawns" (B. Kelly), **Supp. XVII:** 133

Plarr, Victor, **III:** 459, 477

Plath, James, **Retro. Supp. I:** 334; **Supp. XXIII:** 73, 74, 80

Plath, Sylvia, **Retro. Supp. II:** 181, **241–260; Supp. I Part 2:** 526–549, 554, 571; **Supp. III Part 2:** 543, 561; **Supp. IV Part 2:** 439; **Supp. V:** 79, 81, 113, 117, 118, 119, 344; **Supp. X:** 201, 202, **203,** 215; **Supp. XI:** 146, 240, 241, 317; **Supp. XII:** 217, 308; **Supp. XIII:** 35, 76, 312; **Supp. XIV:** 269; **Supp. XV:** 123, 148, 184, 252, 253, 340; **Supp. XVII:** 239; **Supp. XXI:** 58; **Supp. XXII:** 30, 92, 93; **Supp. XXIII:** 63, 64, 112, 113, 254; **Supp. XXV:** 222; **Supp. XXVI:** 45, 64, 67, 68, 77

Plath, Warren, **Supp. I Part 2:** 528

Plato, **I:** 224, 279, 383, 389, 485, 523; **II:** 5, 8, 10, 15, 233, 346, 391–392, 591; **III:** 115, 480, 600, 606, 609, 619–620; **IV:** 74, 140, 333, 363, 364; **Retro. Supp. I:** 247; **Retro. Supp. II:** 31; **Supp. I Part 2:** 595, 631; **Supp. IV Part 1:** 391; **Supp. IV Part 2:** 526; **Supp. X:** 78

"Plato" (Emerson), **II:** 6

"Platonic Relationship, A" (Beattie), **Supp. V:** 22

Platonic Scripts (Justice), **Supp. VII:** 115

Platonov, Dmitri, **Supp. VIII:** 30

Platt, Anthony M., **Supp. I Part 1:** 13–14

Platt, Edward, **Supp. XXIII:** 97

Platte River (Bass), **Supp. XVI:** 19

"Platte River" (Bass), **Supp. XVI:** 20

"Plausible Man" (Davison), **Supp. XXVI:** 71

Plausible Prejudices: Essays on American Writing (Epstein), **Supp. XIV:** 111

Plautus, Titus Maccius, **IV:** 155; **Supp. III Part 2:** 630

Play and Other Stories, The (Dixon), **Supp. XII:** 148, 149

Playback (Chandler), **Supp. IV Part 1:** 134–135; **Supp. XVIII:** 138

Playback (script) (Chandler), **Supp. IV Part 1:** 131

"Play Ball!" (Francis), **Supp. IX:** 89

Playboy of the Western World, The (Synge), **Supp. III Part 1:** 34

Play Days (Jewett), **Retro. Supp. II:** 135

Play Days: A Book of Stories for Children (Jewett), **II:** 401–402

Player Piano (Vonnegut), **Supp. II Part 2:** 756, 757, 760–765

Players (DeLillo), **Supp. VI:** 3, 6, 8, 14

"Players, The" (W. J. Smith), **Supp. XIII:** 340, 343

"Playground, The" (Bradbury), **Supp. IV Part 1:** 104

"Playing" (Huddle), **Supp. XXVI:** 151, 154

Playing at Stillness (Espaillat), **Supp. XXI:** 112

Playing in the Dark (Morrison), **Retro. Supp. II:** 118; **Supp. XIII:** 185–186

"Playing the Bawd at Twenty" (Skloot), **Supp. XX:** **204–205**

Play in Poetry (Untermeyer), **Supp. XV:** 310

"Playin with Punjab" (Bambara), **Supp. XI:** 6

Play It Again Sam (Allen), **Supp. XV:** 2, 3, 14

Play It as It Lays (Didion), **Supp. IV Part 1:** 198, 201–203, 203, 211

Play It as It Lays (film), **Supp. IV Part 1:** 198

"Plays and Operas Too" (Whitman), **IV:** 350

Plays of Negro Life: A Source-Book of Native American Drama (Locke and Gregory), **Supp. XIV:** 202

Plays: Winesburg and Others (Anderson), **I:** 113

"Playthings" (Komunyakaa), **Supp. XIII:** 126

"Playtime: Danish Fun" (Larsen), **Supp. XVIII:** 120, 122–123

"Playtime: Three Scandinavian Stories" (Larsen), **Supp. XVIII:** 122–123

Playwright's Voice, The (Savran), **Supp. XIII:** 209; **Supp. XV:** 321; **Supp. XXIV:** 263

Plaza Suite (Simon), **Supp. IV Part 2:** 575, 581–582, 583, 589

"Pleaders, The" (Davison), **Supp. XXVI:** 71

Pleading Guilty (Turow), **Supp. XVII:** **218,** 219

"Plea for Captain Brown, A" (Thoreau), **IV:** 185

"Plea of a Plebeian" (H. Johnson), **Supp. XXVI:** 173

"Please" (Komunyakaa), **Supp. XIII:** 122

"Please Don't Kill Anything" (A. Miller), **III:** 161

"Please Don't Take My Sunshine Away" (Conroy), **Supp. XVI:** 69

"Pleasure" (Very), **Supp. XXV:** 242, 244

Pleasure Dome (Frankenberg), **I:** 436

Pleasure Dome (Komunyakaa), **Supp. XIII:** 113, 121, **131–133**

Pleasure of Hope, The (Emerson), **II:** 8

"Pleasure of Ruins, The" (McClatchy), **Supp. XII:** 256

"Pleasures of Formal Poetry, The" (Bogan), **Supp. III Part 1:** 51

"Pleasures of Peace, The" (Koch), **Supp. XV:** 180

"Plea to the Protestant Churches, A" (Brooks), **Supp. XIV:** 4

Plimpton, George, **Supp. IV Part 1:** 386; **Supp. IX:** 256; **Supp. V:** 201; **Supp. VIII:** 82, 157; **Supp. XI:** 294; **Supp. XIV:** 82; **Supp. XVI: 233–248**

Pliny the Elder, **Supp. XVI:** 292

Pliny the Younger, **II:** 113

"Ploesti Isn't Long Island" (Zinberg), **Supp. XV:** 195

"Plot against the Giant, The" (Stevens), **IV:** 81

Plotinus, **Supp. XV:** 33; **Supp. XVI:** 291

Plough and the Stars, The (O'Casey), **III:** 159

"Ploughing on Sunday" (Stevens), **IV:** 74

Plowing the Dark (Powers), **Supp. IX:** 212–213, **221–224**

Plum Bun (Fauset), **Supp. XIX:** 73; **Supp. XVIII:** 127

Plumed Serpent, The (Lawrence), **Supp. XV:** 46

"Plumet Basilisk, The" (Moore), **III:** 203, 208, 215

Plumly, Stanley, **Supp. IV Part 2:** 625

Plummer, Amanda, **Supp. IV Part 1:** 236

Plunder (serial movie), **Supp. IV Part 2:** 464

Plunket, Robert, **Supp. XV:** 68

Plunkett, Edward (Lord Dunsany), **Supp. XXV:** 113

"Plunkville Patriot" (O'Henry), **Supp. II Part 1:** 389

"Pluralism and Ideological Peace" (Locke), **Supp. XIV:** 202, 212

"Pluralism and Intellectual Democracy" (Locke), **Supp. XIV:** 202, 208, 212

Pluralistic Universe, A (James), **II:** 342, 348, 357–358

Plutarch, **II:** 5, 8, 16, 555; **Retro. Supp. I:** 360; **Supp. XVI:** 292

Plymell, Charles, **Supp. XIV:** 149

Plymell, Pam, **Supp. XIV:** 149

Pnin (Nabokov), **III:** 246; **Retro. Supp. I:** 263, 265, 266, 275, 335

"Po' Boy Blues" (Hughes), **Supp. I Part 1:** 327

Pocahontas, **I:** 4; **II:** 296; **III:** 584

"Pocahontas to Her English Husband, John Rolfe" (Gunn Allen), **Supp. IV Part 1:** 331

"Pocketbook and Sauerkraut" (Di Piero), **Supp. XIX:** 35, 36, 41, 42, 45

"Pocket Poem" (Kooser), **Supp. XIX:** 128

Podhoretz, Norman, **IV:** 441; **Retro. Supp. II:** 323; **Supp. IV Part 1:** 382; **Supp. IX:** 3; **Supp. VIII:** 93, **231–247**; **Supp. XIV:** 103; **Supp. XXV:** 253, 268

Podnieks, Elizabeth, **Supp. X:** 189, 190, 191, 192

"Pod of the Milkweed" (Frost), **Retro. Supp. I:** 141

Podulka, Fran, **Supp. XXVI:** 6

Poe (screenplay, O'Nan), **Supp. XXV:** 154

Poe, Edgar Allan, **I:** 48, 53, 103, 190, 194, 200, 210, 211, 261, 340, 459; **II:** 74, 77, 194, 255, 273, 295, 308, 311, 313, 421, 475, 482, 530, 595; **III:** 259, **409–432**, 485, 507, 593; **IV:** 123, 129, 133, 141, 187, 261, 345, 350, 432, 438, 439, 453; **Retro. Supp. I:** 41, 273, 365, 421; **Retro. Supp. II:** 102, 104, 160, 164, 220, **261–277**, 322; **Supp. I Part 1:** 36, 309; **Supp. I Part 2:** 376, 384, 385, 388, 393, 405, 413, 421, 474, 682; **Supp. II Part 1:** 385, 410; **Supp. III Part 2:** 544, 549–550; **Supp. IV Part 1:** 80, 81, 101, 128, 341, 349; **Supp. IV Part 2:** 464, 469; **Supp. IX:** 115; **Supp. VIII:** 105; **Supp. X:** 42, 78; **Supp. XI:** 85, 293; **Supp. XIII:** 100, 111; **Supp. XVI:** 294; **Supp. XVIII:** 3, 11; **Supp. XX: 74; Supp. XXIII:** 161, 164, 169, 177, 178; **Supp. XXIV:** 54; **Supp. XXV:** 111, 119

Poe, Edgar Allen, **Supp. XV:** 275; **Supp. XXI:** 51; **Supp. XXVI:** 282

Poe Abroad: Influence, Reputation, Affinities (Vines), **Retro. Supp. II:** 261

"Poe-et's Nightmare, The" (Lovecraft), **Supp. XXV:** 119

"Poem" (Bishop), **Retro. Supp. II:** 40; **Supp. I Part 1:** 73, 76–79, 82, 95

"Poem" (Harrison), **Supp. VIII:** 38

"Poem" (Justice), **Supp. VII:** 125

"Poem" (Kunitz), **Supp. III Part 1:** 263

"Poem" (Notley), **Supp. XXII:** 228–229

"Poem" (O'Hara), **Supp. XIX:** 85

"Poem" (Wright), **Supp. III Part 2:** 590

"Poem, the Snow, Jane Goodall, the Vase of Daffodils, The" (Huddle), **Supp. XXVI:** 150

"Poem About Black Power, A" (Boyle), **Supp. XXIV:** 64

"Poem About George Doty in the Death House, A" (Wright), **Supp. III Part 2:** 594–595, 597–598

"Poem about People" (Pinsky), **Supp. VI: 240–241**, 244, 248

"Poem as Mask, The" (Rukeyser), **Supp. VI:** 281, 285

"Poem as Time Machine, The" (Gallagher), **Supp. XXIV:** 172

"Poem Beginning 'The' " (Zukofsky), **Supp. III Part 2:** 610, 611, 614

"Poem Catching Up with an Idea" (Carruth), **Supp. XVI:** 56

"Poem for a Birthday" (Plath), **Supp. I Part 2:** 539

"POEM FOR ANNA RUSS AND FANNY JONES, A" (Baraka), **Supp. II Part 1:** 58

"Poem for Black Hearts, A" (Baraka), **Supp. II Part 1:** 50

"POEM FOR DEEP THINKERS, A" (Baraka), **Supp. II Part 1:** 55

"Poem for D. H. Lawrence" (Creeley), **Supp. IV Part 1:** 141

"Poem for Dorothy, A" (Merwin), **Supp. III Part 1:** 342

"Poem for Hemingway and W. C. Williams" (Carver), **Supp. III Part 1:** 147

"Poem for my Son" (Kumin), **Supp. IV Part 2:** 442

"Poem for People Who Are Understandably Too Busy to Read Poetry" (Dunn), **Supp. XI:** 147

"Poem for Someone Killed in Spain, A" (Jarrell), **II:** 371

"Poem for the Blue Heron, A" (Oliver), **Supp. VII:** 235–236

"Poem for Two Voices" (Everwine), **Supp. XV:** 89

"Poem For Willie Best, A" (Baraka), **Supp. II Part 1:** 36

"Poem in Prose" (Bogan), **Supp. III Part 1:** 58

"Poem in the Park, The" (Davison), **Supp. XXVI:** 74

"Poem in Which I Refuse Contemplation" (Dove), **Supp. IV Part 1:** 249

"Poem Is a Walk, A" (Ammons), **Supp. VII:** 36

"Poem Like a Grenade, A" (Haines), **Supp. XII:** 204

"Poem of Flight, The" (Levine), **Supp. V:** 189

"Poem of Liberation, The" (Stern), **Supp. IX:** 292

Poem of the Cid (Merwin, trans.), **Supp. III Part 1:** 347

"Poem of the Forgotten" (Haines), **Supp. XII:** 202–203

"Poem (V (F) W)"(O'Hara), **Supp. XXIII:** 219

"Poem on a Line by Anne Sexton, 'We Are All Writing God's Poem' "(Crooker), **Supp. XXIII:** 59

"Poem on the Memorable Victory Obtained by the Gallant Captain Paul Jones" (Freneau), **Supp. II Part 1:** 261

"Poem out of Childhood" (Rukeyser), **Supp. VI:** 272, 277

Poem-Paintings (O'Hara and Bluhm), **Supp. XXIII:** 217

"Poem Read at the Dinner Given to the Author by the Medical Profession" (Holmes), **Supp. I Part 1:** 310–311

Poems (Auden), **Supp. II Part 1:** 6

Poems (Berryman), **I:** 170

Poems (Bryant), **II:** 311; **Supp. I Part 1:** 155, 157

Poems (Cummings), **I:** 430, 447

Poems (E. Stoddard), **Supp. XV:** 274

Poems (Eliot), **I:** 580, 588; **IV:** 122; **Retro. Supp. I:** 59, 291

Poems (Emerson), **II:** 7, 8, 12–13, 17

Poems (Holmes), **Supp. I Part 1:** 303

Poems (Koch), **Supp. XV:** 179

Poems (Lowell), **Supp. I Part 2:** 405

Poems (Moore), **III:** 194, 205, 215

Poems (Poe), **III:** 411

Poems (Reznikoff), **Supp. XIV:** 282, 283, 284, 285

Poems (Tate), **IV:** 121

Poems (W. C. Williams), **Retro. Supp. I:** 412–413, 416, 424

Poems (W. J. Smith), **Supp. XIII:** 332

Poems (Williams), **Supp. XXIV:** 35

Poems (Winters), **Supp. II Part 2:** 809, 810

Poems (Wordsworth), **I:** 468

Poems, 1909–1925 (Eliot), **Retro. Supp. I:** 64

Poems, 1924–1933 (MacLeish), **III:** 7, 15

Poems, 1943–1956 (Wilbur), **Supp. III Part 2:** 554

Poems, The (Freneau), **Supp. II Part 1:** 263

Poems 1918–1975 : The Complete Poems of Charles Reznikoff (Cooney, ed.), **Supp. XIV:** 289

Poems 1940–1953 (Shapiro), **Supp. II Part 2:** 703, 711

Poems 1947–1954 (Kees), **Supp. XV:** 147

Poems: 1947–1957 (W. J. Smith), **Supp. XIII:** 333

Poems 1957–1967 (Dickey), **Supp. IV Part 1:** 178, 181

Poems about God (Ransom), **III:** 484, 486, 491; **IV:** 121

"Poems about Painting" (Snodgrass), **Supp. VI:** 316

Poems and Essays (Ransom), **III:** 486, 490, 492

Poems and New Poems (Bogan), **Supp. III Part 1:** 60–62

"Poems and Places" (Haines), **Supp. XII:** 203

Poems and Poetry of Europe, The (Longfellow, ed.), **Retro. Supp. II:** 155

Poems by Emily Dickinson (Todd and Higginson, eds.), **I:** 469, 470; **Retro. Supp. I:** 35, 39

Poems by Emily Dickinson, Second Series (Todd and Higginson, eds.), **I:** 454; **Retro. Supp. I:** 35

Poems by Emily Dickinson, The (Bianchi and Hampson, eds.), **Retro. Supp. I:** 35

Poems by Emily Dickinson, Third Series (Todd, ed.), **Retro. Supp. I:** 35

Poems by James Russell Lowell, Second Series (Lowell), **Supp. I Part 2:** 406, 409

Poems by Sidney Lanier, (Lanier), **Supp. I Part 1:** 364

Poems from Black Africa (Hughes, ed.), **Supp. I Part 1:** 344

"Poems I Have Lost, The" (Ortiz), **Supp. IV Part 2:** 507

Poems: North & South–A Cold Spring, (Bishop), **Supp. I Part 1:** 83, 89

Poems of a Jew (Shapiro), **Supp. II Part 2:** 703, 712–713

"Poems of a Mountain Recluse" (Budbill), **Supp. XIX:** 9, 10

Poems of Anna Akhmatova, The (Kunitz and Hayward, trans.), **Supp. III Part 1:** 269

Poems of Emily Dickinson, The (Bianchi and Hampson, eds.), **Retro. Supp. I:** 35

Poems of Emily Dickinson, The (T. H. Johnson, ed.), **I:** 470

Poems of François Villon (Kinnell, trans.), **Supp. III Part 1:** 235, 243, 249

"Poems of Our Climate, The" (Stevens), **Retro. Supp. I:** 313

Poems of Peter Davison, The (Davison), **Supp. XXVI:** 66, 78

Poems of Philip Freneau, Written Chiefly during the Late War (Freneau), **Supp. II Part 1:** 261

Poems of Places (Longfellow, ed.), **II:** 490; **Retro. Supp. II:** 155; **Supp. I Part 1:** 368

Poems of Stanley Kunitz, The (Kunitz), **Supp. III Part 1:** 258, 263, 264, 266, 268

"Poems of These States" (Ginsberg), **Supp. II Part 1:** 323, 325

Poems of Two Friends (Howells and Piatt), **II:** 273, 277

"POEM SOME PEOPLE WILL HAVE TO UNDERSTAND, A" (Baraka), **Supp. II Part 1:** 49

Poems on Slavery (Longfellow), **II:** 489; **Retro. Supp. II:** 157, 168; **Supp. I Part 2:** 406

Poems on Various Subjects (Rowson), **Supp. XV:** 232

Poems on Various Subjects, Religious and Moral (Wheatley), **Supp. XX: 277, 282, 284, 285, 289**

Poem Spoken at the Public Commencement at Yale College, in New Haven; September 1, 1781, A (Barlow), **Supp. II Part 1:** 67–68, 74, 75

Poems Retrieved (O'Hara), **Supp. XXIII:** 220

Poems to Solve (Swenson), **Supp. IV Part 2:** 642

Poems Written and Published during the American Revolutionary War (Freneau), **Supp. II Part 1:** 273, 274

Poems Written between the Years 1768 and 1794 (Freneau), **Supp. II Part 1:** 269

"Poem That Took the Place of a Mountain" (Olson), **Supp. II Part 2:** 582

"Poem to My First Lover" (Olds), **Supp. X:** 206

"Poem to the Reader" (Olds), **Supp. X:** 213

"Poem with No Ending, A" (Levine), **Supp. V:** 186, 190

"Poem You Asked For, The" (Levis), **Supp. XI:** 259–260

Poe Poe Poe Poe Poe Poe Poe (Hoffman), **Retro. Supp. II:** 265

Poesía Náhuatl, **Supp. XV:** 77

Poésies 1917–1920 (Cocteau), **Retro. Supp. I:** 82

"Poesis: A Conceit" (Sobin), **Supp. XVI:** 288

"Poet" (Taggard), **Supp. XXII:** 284

Poet, The (Connelly), **Supp. XXI: 71,** 78

"Poet, The" (Dunbar), **Supp. II Part 1:** 207, 209–210

"Poet, The" (Emerson), **II:** 13, 19, 20, 170

"Poet, The" (Ortiz), **Supp. IV Part 2:** 505

"Poet and His Book, The" (Millay), **III:** 126, 138

"Poet and His Public, The" (Jarrell), **Supp. I Part 1:** 96

"Poet and His Song, The" (Dunbar), **Supp. II Part 1:** 199

"Poet and the Person, The" (Kinard), **Supp. XIV:** 127

"Poet and the Queen, The" (Shaw), **Supp. XIX:** 241

"Poet and the World, The" (Cowley), **Supp. II Part 1:** 145

"Poet as Anti-Specialist, The" (Swenson), **Supp. IV Part 2:** 638, 643

"Poet as *Curandera*" (Mora), **Supp. XIII:** 214, 220

"Poet as Hero, The: Keats in His Letters" (Trilling), **Supp. III Part 2:** 506–507

"Poet as Religious Moralist, The" (Larson), **Supp. XI:** 328

"Poet at Seven, The" (Rimbaud), **II:** 545

Poet at the Breakfast-Table, The (Holmes), **Supp. I Part 1:** 313–314

"Poète contumace, Le" (Corbiere), **II:** 384–385

"Poet for President, A" (Mora), **Supp. XIII:** 220–221

Poetic Achievement of Ezra Pound, The (Alexander), **Retro. Supp. I:** 293

Poetic Diction: A Study in Meaning (Barfield), **III:** 274, 279

"Poetic Principle, The" (Poe), **III:** 421, 426; **Retro. Supp. II:** 266

"Poetics" (Ammons), **Supp. VII:** 29–30

Poetics (Aristotle), **III:** 422; **Supp. XI:** 249; **Supp. XIII:** 75; **Supp. XIV:** 243; **Supp. XV:** 265

Poetics of Space, The (Bachelard), **Supp. XIII:** 225; **Supp. XVI:** 292

"Poetics of the Periphery: Literary Experimentalism in Kathy Acker's *In Memoriam to Identity*" (Acker), **Supp. XII:** 17

"Poetics of the Physical World, The" (Kinnell), **Supp. III Part 1:** 239

"Poetics of Tourette Syndrome, The: Language, Neurobiology, and Poetry" (Schleifer), **Supp. XVIII:** 144

Poet in the World, The (Levertov), **Supp. III Part 1:** 271, 273, 278, 282

"Poet or the Growth of a Lit'ry Figure" (White), **Supp. I Part 2:** 676

Poetry (Barber), **Supp. IV Part 2:** 550

"Poetry" (Moore), **III:** 204–205, 215

"Poetry" (Nye), **Supp. XIII:** 282

"Poetry" (Wrigley), **Supp. XVIII:** 301–302

"Poetry, Community and Climax" (Snyder), **Supp. VIII:** 290

"Poetry, Pleasure, and the Hedonist Reader" (Collins), **Supp. XXI:** 54

"Poetry: A Metrical Essay" (Holmes), **Supp. I Part 1:** 310

"Poetry and Belief in Thomas Hardy" (Schwartz), **Supp. II Part 2:** 666

Poetry and Criticism (Nemerov, ed.), **III:** 269

"Poetry and Drama" (Eliot), **I:** 588

Poetry and Fiction: Essays (Nemerov), **III:** 269, 281

"Poetry and Place" (Berry), **Supp. X:** 22, 28, 31, 32

Poetry and Poets (Lowell), **II:** 512

"Poetry and Religion" (Jarman), **Supp. XVII:** 111

Poetry and the Age (Jarrell), **IV:** 352; **Retro. Supp. I:** 121; **Supp. II Part 1:** 135

"Poetry and the Primitive: Notes on Poetry as an Ecological Survival Technique" (Snyder), **Supp. VIII:** 291, 292, 299, 300

"Poetry and the Public World" (MacLeish), **III:** 11

Poetry and the World (Pinsky), **Supp. VI:** 236, 239, 244, 247

Poetry and Truth (Olson), **Supp. II Part 2:** 583

"Poetry and Uncertainty"(Hirshfield), **Supp. XXIII:** 137

"Poetry As a Way of Life" (Bishop interview), **Retro. Supp. II:** 53

"Poetry as Survival" (Harrison), **Supp. VIII:** 45

"Poetry Baron, The" (Gallagher), **Supp. XXIV:** 166, 177

"Poetry Failure" (Halliday), **Supp. XIX:** 92

Poetry for Students (Taibl), **Supp. XV:** 255

"Poetry for the Advanced" (Baraka), **Supp. II Part 1:** 58

"Poetry Friendship on Earth" (Halliday), **Supp. XIX:** 90, 91

Poetry Handbook, A (Oliver), **Supp. VII:** 229, 245

Poetry Home Repair Manual, The (Kooser), **Supp. XIX:** 116, 128

Poetry in Motion (film), **Supp. XXIV:** 33

Poetry in Motion: 100 Poems from the Subways and Buses (Peacock, ed.), **Supp. XIX:** 195

"Poetry in Translation: Literary Imperialism or, Defending the Musk Ox" (Gallagher), **Supp. XXIV:** 172

"Poetry of Barbarism, The" (Santayana), **IV:** 353

Poetry of Chaucer, The (Gardner), **Supp. VI:** 63

Poetry of Meditation, The (Martz), **IV:** 151; **Supp. I Part 1:** 107

Poetry of Mourning: The Modern Elegy from Hardy to Heaney (Ramazani), **Supp. IV Part 2:** 450

Poetry of Stephen Crane, The (Hoffman), **I:** 405

Poetry of the Negro, 1746–1949, The (Hughes and Bontemps), **Supp. I Part 1:** 345; **Supp. XXII:** 11

Poetry 180: A Turning Back to Poetry (Collins, ed.), **Supp. XXI:** 54

Poetry Reading against the Vietnam War, A (Bly and Ray, eds.), **Supp. IV Part 1:** 61, 63

"Poetry Workshop, The" (column, Kumin), **Supp. XX: 164**

"Poetry Wreck, The" (Shapiro), **Supp. II Part 2:** 717

Poetry Wreck, The: Selected Essays (Shapiro), **Supp. II Part 2:** 703, 704, 717

"Poets" (X. J. Kennedy), **Supp. XV:** 158

Poet's Alphabet, A: Reflections on the Literary Art and Vocation (Bogan), **Supp. III Part 1:** 55, 64

Poets and Poetry of America (Griswold), **Supp. XV:** 277; **Supp. XXV:** 250

Poet's Choice (Engle and Langland, eds.), **III:** 277, 542

Poet's Guide to Poetry, A (Kinzie), **Supp. XXIII:** 124

"Poet's Husband Engages in Gourmet Cooking, The" (Espaillat), **Supp. XXI:** 99

Poets of the Old Testament, The (Gordon), **III:** 199

Poets of Today (Wheelock, ed.), **Supp. IV Part 2:** 639

Poets on Poetry (Nemerov, ed.), **III:** 269

"Poet's Tact, and a Necessary Tactlessness, The" (C. Frost), **Supp. XV:** 94–95

"Poet's View, A" (Levertov), **Supp. III Part 1:** 284

"Poet's Voice, The" (Oliver), **Supp. VII:** 245

"Poets with History and Poets Without History"(Tsvetaeva), **Supp. XXIII:** 168

"Poet Turns on Himself, The" (Dickey), **Supp. IV Part 1:** 177, 181, 185

Poganuc People (Stowe), **Supp. I Part 2:** 581, 596, 599–600

Pogo (comic strip), **Supp. XI:** 105

Pohl, R. D., **Supp. XXVI:** 102

Pohrt, Tom, **Supp. XIX:** 123

Poincaré, Raymond, **IV:** 320

"Point, The" (Hayden), **Supp. II Part 1:** 373

"Point at Issue!, A" (Chopin), **Retro. Supp. II:** 61; **Supp. I Part 1:** 208

"Point of Age, A" (Berryman), **I:** 173

Point of No Return (Marquand), **III:** 56, 59–60, 65, 67, 69

Point Reyes Poems (R. Bly), **Supp. IV Part 1:** 71

"Points" (Hoffman), **Supp. XVIII:** 86

Points for a Compass Rose (Connell), **Supp. XIV:** 79, 80, 96

"Point Shirley" (Plath), **Supp. I Part 2:** 529, 538

Points in Time (Bowles), **Supp. IV Part 1:** 93

"Points West" (column), **Supp. IV Part 1:** 198

Poirier, Richard, **I:** 136, 239; **III:** 34; **Retro. Supp. I:** 134; **Retro. Supp. II:** 207–208; **Supp. I Part 2:** 660, 665; **Supp. IV Part 2:** 690

"Poison Oak" (Huddle), **Supp. XXVI:** 148, 152

Poison Pen (Garrett), **Supp. VII:** 111

Poisonwood Bible, The (Kingsolver), **Supp. VII:** 197–198, 202, 210–213

Poitier, Sidney, **Supp. IV Part 1:** 360, 362

Pokerface (Collins), **Supp. XXI:** 53

"Polack Reverie" (Halliday), **Supp. XIX:** 88

Polanco, Richard, **Supp. XX: 260**

"Polar Bear" (Heller), **Supp. IV Part 1:** 383

"Polar Bears and Others" (Boyle), **Supp. XXIV:** 57

"Polar Seas and Sir John Franklin, The" (Briggs), **Supp. XVIII:** 14

Pole, Rupert, **Supp. X:** 185

"Pole Star" (MacLeish), **III:** 16

Po Li, **Supp. I Part 1:** 262

Police (Baraka), **Supp. II Part 1:** 47

"Police" (Corso), **Supp. XII:** 117, 127

"Police Court Saturday Morning" (X. J. Kennedy), **Supp. XV:** 170

"Police Dreams" (Bausch), **Supp. VII:** 47

Politian (Poe), **III:** 412

"Political and Practical Conceptions of Race, The" (Locke), **Supp. XIV:** 209–210

Political Essays (Lowell), **Supp. I Part 2:** 407

Political Fable, A (Coover), **Supp. V:** 44, 46, 47, 49, 51

"Political Fables" (Mather), **Supp. II Part 2:** 450

"Political Interests" (Stevens), **Retro. Supp. I:** 295

"Political Litany, A" (Freneau), **Supp. II Part 1:** 257

"Political Migrations: A Family Story" (Mallon), **Supp. XIX:** 141–142

"Political Pastoral" (Frost), **Retro. Supp. I:** 139

"Political Poem" (Baraka), **Supp. II Part 1:** 36

Politics (Acker), **Supp. XII:** 3, 4

Politics (Macdonald), **I:** 233–234

"Politics" (Paley), **Supp. VI:** 217

"Politics, Structure, and Poetic Development" (McCombs), **Supp. XIII:** 33

"Politics and the English Language" (Orwell), **Retro. Supp. II:** 287; **Supp. I Part 2:** 620

Politics and the Novel (Howe), **Supp. VI:** 113

"Politics and the Personal Lyric in the Poetry of Joy Harjo and C. D. Wright" (Goodman), **Supp. XV:** 344

"Politics of Ethnic Authorship, The: Li-Young Lee, Emerson, and Whitman at the Banquet Table" (Partridge), **Supp. XV:** 219

"Politics of Silence, The" (Monette), **Supp. X:** 148

Polito, Robert, **Supp. XVIII:** 33; **Supp. XXIV:** 234; **Supp. XXVI:** 55

Politt, Katha, **Supp. XII:** 159

Poliziano (Angelo Ambrogini), **Supp. XXIV:** 152

Polk, James, **Supp. XIII:** 20

Polk, James K., **I:** 17; **II:** 433–434

Pollack, Sydney, **Supp. XIII:** 159

"Pollen" (Nye), **Supp. XIII:** 284

Pollitt, Katha, **Supp. X:** 186, 191, 193; **Supp. XVI:** 39

Pollock, Jackson, **IV:** 411, 420; **Supp. XIX:** 33; **Supp. XV:** 145, 177, 178; **Supp. XXIII:** 208, 210, 211

"Polly" (Chopin), **Retro. Supp. II:** 72

Polo, Marco, **III:** 395

Polonsky, Abraham, **Supp. XXI:** 261, 275

Polybius, **Supp. I Part 2:** 491

"Polydore" (Chopin), **Retro. Supp. II:** 66

"Pomegranate" (Glück), **Supp. V:** 82

"Pomegranate Seed" (Wharton), **IV:** 316; **Retro. Supp. I:** 382

Ponce de Leon, Luis, **III:** 391

"Pond, The" (Nemerov), **III:** 272

"Pond at Dusk, The" (Kenyon), **Supp. VII:** 168

Ponder Heart, The (Welty), **IV:** 261, 274–275, 281; **Retro. Supp. I:** 351–352

"Ponderosa Pine" (Huncke), **Supp. XIV:** 146

Ponsot, Margaret, **Supp. XVII:** 241

"Pony" (Sanders), **Supp. XVI:** 277

"Pony Car"(P. Benedict), **Supp. XXIII:** 47

Poodle Springs (Parker and Chandler), **Supp. IV Part 1:** 135; **Supp. XIX:** 189

Poodle Springs Story, The (Chandler), **Supp. IV Part 1:** 135

"Pool, The" (Doolittle), **Supp. I Part 1:** 264–265

Poole, Ernest, **II:** 444

"Pool Lights" (F. Barthelme), **Supp. XI:** 25, 26–27, 36

"Pool Room in the Lions Club" (Merwin), **Supp. III Part 1:** 346

"Poolside" (Skloot), **Supp. XX: 202–203**

"Poor Black Fellow" (Hughes), **Retro. Supp. I:** 204

"Poor Bustard, The" (Corso), **Supp. XII:** 134

"Poor but Happy" (Mamet), **Supp. XIV:** 252, 253

"Poor Dead Feet of My First Husband, The"(Schott), **Supp. XXIII:** 241

Poore, Charles, **III:** 364; **Supp. XIX:** 257, 264; **Supp. XX: 38**

Poor Fool (Caldwell), **I:** 291, 292, 308

Poorhouse Fair, The (Updike), **IV:** 214, 228–229, 232; **Retro. Supp. I:** 317, 320

"Poor Joanna" (Jewett), **II:** 394

"Poor Man's Pudding and Rich Man's Crumbs" (Melville), **III:** 89–90

"Poor Richard" (James), **II:** 322

Poor Richard's Almanac for 1733 (Franklin), **II:** 108, 110

Poor Richard's Almanac for 1739 (Franklin), **II:** 112

Poor Richard's Almanac for 1758 (Franklin), **II:** 101

Poor Richard's Almanac (undated) (Franklin), **II:** 112

Poor White (Anderson), **I:** 110–111

"Poor Working Girl" (Z. Fitzgerald), **Supp. IX:** 71

Popa, Vasko, **Supp. VIII:** 272

Pope, Alexander, **I:** 198, 204; **II:** 17, 114; **III:** 263, 267, 288, 517; **IV:** 145; **Retro. Supp. I:** 335; **Supp. I Part 1:** 150, 152, 310; **Supp. I Part 2:** 407, 422, 516, 714; **Supp. II Part 1:** 70, 71; **Supp. X:** 32, 36; **Supp. XII:** 260; **Supp. XV:** 258; **Supp. XX: 280; Supp. XXV:** 119; **Supp. XXVI:** 284

Pope, James, **Supp. XXII:** 196

Pope-Hennessy, James, **Supp. XIV:** 348

"Pope's Penis, The" (Olds), **Supp. X:** 207

"Poplar, Sycamore" (Wilbur), **Supp. III Part 2:** 549

Popo and Fifina: Children of Haiti (Hughes and Bontemps), **Retro. Supp. I:** 203; **Supp. XXII:** 4, 10, 12

"Poppies" (Oliver), **Supp. VII:** 240

"Poppies in July" (Plath), **Supp. I Part 2:** 544

"Poppies in July"(Crooker), **Supp. XXIII:** 61

"Poppies in October" (Plath), **Supp. I Part 2:** 544

"Poppycock" (Francis), **Supp. IX:** 87

"Poppy Juice" (Taggard), **Supp. XXII:** 276

"Poppy Seed" (Lowell), **II:** 523

"Popular Art and the Cultural Tradition" (C. L. R. James), **Supp. XXI:** 170

Popular Book, The: A History of America's Literary Taste (Hart), **Supp. XVIII:** 257, 258

Popular Culture (Goldbarth), **Supp. XII: 186**

Popular History of the United States (Gay), **Supp. I Part 1:** 158

"Popular Songs" (Ashbery), **Supp. III Part 1:** 6

"Populist Manifesto" (Ferlinghetti), **Supp. VIII:** 290

"Porcelain Bowl" (Glück), **Supp. V:** 83

Porcher, Frances, **Retro. Supp. II:** 71

Porco, Mike, **Supp. XVIII:** 24

"Porcupine, The" (Kinnell), **Supp. III Part 1:** 244

Porcupine's Kiss, The (Dobyns), **Supp. XIII: 89–90**

"Por esas coases que pasan" (Hinojosa), **Supp. XIX:** 101

Porgy and Bess (film), **Supp. I Part 1:** 66

Porgy and Bess (play), **Supp. IV Part 1:** 6

"Porn Bought my Football" (Offutt), **Supp. XIX:** 163

"Porphyria's Lover" (Browning), **II:** 522

Portable Beat Reader, The (Charters, ed.), **Supp. XIV:** 152

Portable Blake, The (Kazin, ed.), **Supp. VIII:** 103

Portable Faulkner, The (Cowley, ed.), **II:** 57, 59; **Retro. Supp. I:** 73

Portable Kisses: Love Poems (Gallagher), **Supp. XXIV:** 170

Portable Paul and Jane Bowles, The (Dillon), **Supp. IV Part 1:** 95

Portable Veblen, The (Veblen), **Supp. I Part 2:** 630, 650

"Porte-Cochere" (Taylor), **Supp. V:** 320

"Porter" (Hughes), **Supp. I Part 1:** 327

"Porter" (Nelson), **Supp. XVIII:** 175

Porter, Bern, **III:** 171

Porter, Cole, **Supp. IX:** 189

Porter, Eliot, **Supp. IV Part 2:** 599

Porter, Fairfield, **Supp. XV:** 178; **Supp. XXIII:** 209, 211, 212; **Supp. XXIV:** 41

Porter, Herman W., **Supp. I Part 1:** 49

Porter, Horace, **Retro. Supp. II:** 4, 127

Porter, Jacob, **Supp. I Part 1:** 153

Porter, Katherine Anne, **I:** 97, 385; **II:** 194, 606; **III: 433–455,** 482; **IV:** 26, 138, 246, 261, 279, 280, 282; **Retro. Supp. I:** 354; **Retro. Supp. II:** 233, 235; **Supp. IV Part 1:** 31, 310; **Supp. IX:** 93, 94, 95, 98, 128; **Supp. V:** 225; **Supp. VIII:** 156, 157; **Supp. X:** 50; **Supp. XIII:** 294; **Supp. XIV:** 3; **Supp. XV:** 338; **Supp. XXIV:** 52; **Supp. XXVI:** 23

Porter, Nicodemus, **Supp. XXVI:** 87

Porter, Noah, **Supp. I Part 2:** 640

Porter, William Sydney. *See* Henry, O.

"Porter Paints a Picture"(O'Hara), **Supp. XXIII:** 212

Porteus, Beilby, **Supp. I Part 1:** 150

Portis, Rowe, **Supp. XXVI:** 147

"Portland Going Out, The" (Merwin), **Supp. III Part 1:** 345

Portnoy's Complaint (P. Roth), **Retro. Supp. II: 282–286,** 291; **Supp. III Part 2:** 401, 404, 405, 407, 412–414, 426; **Supp. V:** 119, 122; **Supp. XI:** 140; **Supp. XVII:** 8, 43; **Supp. XX: 177**

Port of Saints (Burroughs), **Supp. III Part 1:** 106

"Portrait" (Dixon), **Supp. XII:** 154

"Portrait, A" (Parker), **Supp. IX:** 192–193

"Portrait, The" (Kunitz), **Supp. III Part 1:** 263

"Portrait, The" (Wharton), **Retro. Supp. I:** 364

"Portrait d'une Femme" (Pound), **Retro. Supp. I:** 288

Portrait in Brownstone (Auchincloss), **Supp. IV Part 1:** 21, 23, 27, 31

"Portrait in Georgia" (Toomer), **Supp. IX:** 314

"Portrait in Greys, A" (W. C. Williams), **Retro. Supp. I:** 416

"Portrait of a Girl in Glass" (T. Williams), **IV:** 383

"Portrait of a Jewelry Drummer" (Untermeyer), **Supp. XV:** 299–300

"Portrait of a Lady" (Eliot), **I:** 569, 570, 571, 584; **III:** 4; **Retro. Supp. I:** 55, 56, 62

Portrait of a Lady, The (James), **I:** 10, 258, 461–462, 464; **II:** 323, 325, 327, 328–329, 334; **Retro. Supp. I:** 215, 216, 217, 219, 220, 223, **224–225,** 232, 233, 381

"Portrait of an Artist" (P. Roth), **Supp. III Part 2:** 412

Portrait of an Eye: Three Novels (Acker), **Supp. XII:** 6, **7–9**

"Portrait of an Invisible Man" (Auster), **Supp. XII:** 21

"Portrait of a Supreme Court Judge" (Untermeyer), **Supp. XV:** 299

Portrait of Bascom Hawkes, A (Wolfe), **IV:** 451–452, 456

Portrait of Edith Wharton (Lubbock), **Retro. Supp. I:** 366

Portrait of Logan Pearsall Smith, Drawn from His Letters and Diaries, A (Russell, ed.), **Supp. XIV:** 349

Portrait of Picasso as a Young Man (Mailer), **Retro. Supp. II:** 213

"Portrait of the Artist as an Old Man, A" (Humphrey), **Supp. IX:** 109

Portrait of the Artist as a Young Man, A (Joyce), **I:** 475–476; **III:** 471, 561; **Retro. Supp. I:** 127; **Retro. Supp. II:** 4, 331; **Supp. IX:** 236; **Supp. XIII:** 53, 95

"Portrait of the Artist with Hart Crane" (Wright), **Supp. V:** 342

"Portrait of the Great White Hunter Foxhunting in the Absence of Big Game" (Major), **Supp. XXII:** 183

"Portrait of the Intellectual as a Yale Man" (McCarthy), **II:** 563, 564–565

"Portrait of the Reader with a Bowl of Cereal, A" (Collins), **Supp. XXI:** 55

"Portrait of the Self . . . , A" (Sobin), **Supp. XVI:** 288

Portraits and Elegies (Schnackenberg), **Supp. XV:** 249, **253–256**

"Portraits of Grief" *(New York Times),* **Supp. XIX:** 142

"Port Town" (Hughes), **Retro. Supp. I:** 199

Portuguese Voyages to America in the Fifteenth Century (Morison), **Supp. I Part 2:** 488

"Po' Sandy" (Chesnutt), **Supp. XIV:** 60

Poseidon Adventure, The (film), **Supp. XII:** 321

Poseidon Adventure, The (Gallico), **Supp. XVI:** 238

"Poseidon and Company" (Carver), **Supp. III Part 1:** 137

"Positive Obsession" (O. Butler), **Supp. XIII:** 70

Poss, Stanley, **Supp. XIV:** 166

Possession (Byatt), **Supp. XXI:** 147

"Possessions" (H. Crane), **I:** 392–393; **Retro. Supp. II:** 78

Possible World, A (Koch), **Supp. XV:** 184

Postal Inspector (film), **Supp. XIII:** 166

"Postcard from Greece" (Stallings), **Supp. XXV:** 229, 231

Postcards (Proulx), **Supp. VII:** 249, 256–258, 262

"Postcard to Send to Sumer, A" (Bronk), **Supp. XXI:** 31

"Postcolonialism and Autobiography" (Skinner and Waller), **Supp. XXII:** 78

"Postcolonial Tale, A" (Harjo), **Supp. XII:** 227

"Posthumous Letter to Gilbert White" (Auden), **Supp. II Part 1:** 26

"Post-Larkin Triste" (Karr), **Supp. XI:** 242–243

Postlethwaite, Diana, **Supp. XII:** 317–318; **Supp. XVI:** 176

"Postlude" (W. C. Williams), **Retro. Supp. I:** 415

Postman, Neil, **Supp. XI:** 275

Postman Always Rings Twice, The (Cain), **Supp. XIII:** 165–166

Postman Always Rings Twice, The (film), **Supp. XIV:** 241

"Postmaster and the Clerk, The" (Budbill), **Supp. XIX:** 9

"Postmortem Guide, A" (Dunn), **Supp. XI:** 155

Postrel, Virginia, **Supp. XIV:** 298, 311

"Postscript" (Du Bois), **Supp. II Part 1:** 173

"Postscript" (Nye), **Supp. XIII:** 287

Postsouthern Sense of Place, The (Bone), **Supp. XXII:** 247

"Potato" (Wilbur), **Supp. III Part 2:** 545

"Potatoes' Dance, The" (Lindsay), **Supp. I Part 2:** 394

Pot of Earth, The (MacLeish), **III:** 5, 6–8, 10, 12, 18

Potok, Chaim, **Supp. XXVI:** 124

"Pot Roast" (Strand), **Supp. IV Part 2:** 629

Potshot (Parker), **Supp. XIX:** 185

Pot Shots at Poetry (Francis), **Supp. IX:** **83–84**

Potter, Beatrix, **Supp. I Part 2:** 656; **Supp. XVI:** 100

Potter, Stephen, **IV:** 430

Potter's House, The (Stegner), **Supp. IV Part 2:** 598, 606

Poulenc, Francis, **Supp. IV Part 1:** 81

Poulin, Al, Jr., **Supp. IX:** 272; **Supp. XI:** 259

Pound, Ezra, **I:** 49, 58, 60, 66, 68, 69, 105, 236, 243, 256, 384, 403, 428, 429, 475, 476, 482, 487, 521, 578; **II:** 26, 55, 168, 263, 316, 371, 376, 513, 517, 520, 526, 528, 529, 530; **III:** 2, 5, 8, 9, 13–14, 17, 174, 194, 196, 278, 430, 453, **456–479,** 492, 504, 511, 523, 524, 527, 575–576, 586, 590; **IV:** 27, 28, 407, 415, 416, 433, 446; **Retro. Supp. I:** 51, 52, 55, 58, 59, 63, 82, 89, 127, 140, 171, 177, 178, 198, 216, **283–294,** 298, 299, 359, 411, 412, 413, 414, 417, 418, 419, 420, 423, 426, 427, 430, 431; **Retro. Supp. II:** 178, 183, 189, 326; **Supp. I Part 1:** 253, 255–258, 261–268, 272, 274; **Supp. I Part 2:** 387, 721; **Supp. II Part 1:** 1, 8, 20, 30, 91, 136; **Supp. III Part 1:** 48, 63, 64, 73, 105, 146, 225, 271; **Supp. III Part 2:** 542, **609–617,** 619, 620, 622, 625, 626, 628, 631; **Supp. IV Part 1:** 153, 314; **Supp. IX:** 291; **Supp. V:** 331, 338, 340, 343, 345; **Supp. VIII:** 39, 105, 195, 205, 271, 290, 291, 292, 303; **Supp. X:** 24, 36, 112, 120, 122; **Supp. XII:** 97; **Supp. XIV:** 11, 55, 83, 272, 284, 286, 287, 347; **Supp. XIX:** 42; **Supp. XV:** 20, 42, 43, 51, 93, 161, 181, 297, 298, 299, 301, 302, 306; **Supp. XVI:** 47, 282; **Supp. XVII:** 111, 226–227; **Supp. XXI:** 33; **Supp. XXII:** 165; **Supp. XXIII:** 26, 166, 174; **Supp. XXIV:** 37; **Supp. XXVI:** 143, 144, 224, 226

Pound, Louise, **Retro. Supp. I:** 4; **Supp. XV:** 137

Pound, T. S., **I:** 428

"Pound Reweighed" (Cowley), **Supp. II Part 1:** 143

Powell, Anthony, **Supp. XIX:** 131; **Supp. XVIII:** 136, 146

Powell, Betty, **Retro. Supp. II:** 140

Powell, D. A., **Supp. XXIII:** 221

Powell, Dawn, **Supp. IV Part 2:** 678, 682; **Supp. XIX:** 143

Powell, Dick, **Supp. IX:** 250

Powell, John Wesley, **Supp. IV Part 2:** 598, 604, 611

Powell, Lawrence Clark, **III:** 189

Powell, Margaret K., **Supp. XXIV:** 170

Powell, William, **Supp. IV Part 1:** 355

"Power" (Corso), **Supp. XII:** 117, 126, 127, **128**

"Power" (Emerson), **II:** 2, 3

"Power" (Rich), **Supp. I Part 2:** 569

Power, Samantha, **Supp. XXIII:** 25, 26, 27

"Power and Light" (Dickey), **Supp. IV Part 1:** 182

Power and the Glory, The (Greene), **III:** 556

"Powerhouse" (Welty), **Retro. Supp. I:** 343, 346

"Power Never Dominion" (Rukeyser), **Supp. VI:** 281

"Power of Fancy, The" (Freneau), **Supp. II Part 1:** 255

Power of Myth, The (Campbell), **Supp. IX:** 245

"Power of Prayer, The" (Lanier), **Supp. I Part 1:** 357

"Power of Stories, The" (Sanders), **Supp. XVI:** 278

"Power of Suggestion" (Auchincloss), **Supp. IV Part 1:** 33

Power of Sympathy, The (W. H. Brown), **Supp. II Part 1:** 74; **Supp. XXV:** 38

Power Politics (Atwood), **Supp. XIII:** 20, 33–34, 35

Powers, Catherine A., **Supp. XXII:** 217

Powers, J. F., **Supp. V:** 319; **Supp. XVII:** 43

Powers, Kim, **Supp. VIII:** 329, 340

Powers, Richard, **Supp. IX:** **207–225;** **Supp. XVII:** 183; **Supp. XX:** 93; **Supp. XXII:** 49; **Supp. XXIV:** 131

Powers of Attorney (Auchincloss), **Supp. IV Part 1:** 31, 32, 33

"Powers of Darkness" (Wharton), **Retro. Supp. I:** 379

Powless, Peter, **Supp. XXVI:** 87

Powys, John Cowper, **Supp. I Part 2:** 454, 476; **Supp. IX:** 135

Poynton, Jerome, **Supp. XIV:** 147, 150

Pozorski, Aimee L., **Supp. XXII:** 160, 166

Practical Agitation (Chapman), **Supp. XIV:** 41

"Practical Application in This Life, by Men as Social and Intellectual Beings, of the Certainty of a Future State, The" (Very), **Supp. XXV:** 240

Practical Criticism: A Study of Literary Judgment (Richards), **Supp. XIV:** 3, 16

Practical Magic (film), **Supp. X:** 80

Practical Magic (Hoffman), **Supp. X:** 78, 82, **88–89**

"Practical Methods of Meditation, The" (Dawson), **IV:** 151

Practical Navigator, The (Bowditch), **Supp. I Part 2:** 482

Practice of Perspective, The (Dubreuil), **Supp. IV Part 2:** 425

Practice of Reading, The (Donoghue), **Supp. VII:** 189

Pragmatism: A New Name for Some Old Ways of Thinking (James), **II:** 352

"Pragmatism's Conception of Truth" (James), **Supp. XIV:** 40

Prague Orgy, The (P. Roth), **Retro. Supp. II:** 280

"Praire, The" (Clampitt), **Supp. IX:** 42

"Prairie" (Sandburg), **III:** 583, 584

Prairie, The (Cooper), **I:** 339, 342

"Prairie Birthday" (Leopold), **Supp. XIV:** 185

Prairie Home Companion, A (Keillor, radio program), **Supp. XIII:** 274; **Supp. XVI:** 169–171, 173–178

Prairie Home Morning Show, A (Keillor, radio program), **Supp. XVI:** 171

"Prairie Life, A Citizen Speaks" (Dunn), **Supp. XI:** 145

"Prairies, The" (Bryant), **Supp. I Part 1:** 157, 162, 163, 166

Praise (Hass), **Supp. VI:** 104–105, 106

"Praise for an Urn" (Crane), **I:** 388

"Praise for Sick Women" (Snyder), **Supp. VIII:** 294

"Praise in Summer" (Wilbur), **Supp. III Part 2:** 546–548, 560, 562

"Praise of a Palmtree" (Levertov), **Supp. III Part 1:** 284

"Praise of the Committee" (Rukeyser), **Supp. VI:** 278

"Praises, The" (Goldbarth), **Supp. XII:** 185

"Praises, The" (Olson), **Supp. II Part 2:** 558, 560, 563, 564

Praises and Dispraises (Des Pres), **Supp. X:** 120

Praisesong for the Widow (Marshall), **Supp. IV Part 1:** 14; **Supp. XI:** 18, 276, 278, **284–286,** 287; **Supp. XX:** 154

"Praise to the End!" (Roethke), **III:** 529, 532, 539

Prajadhipok, King of Siam, **I:** 522

Prater Violet (Isherwood), **Supp. XIV:** **164–166,** 169–170, 171

Pratt, Anna (Anna Alcott), **Supp. I Part 1:** 33

Pratt, Louis H., **Retro. Supp. II:** 6

Pratt, Mary Louise, **Retro. Supp. II:** 48

Pratt, Parley, **Supp. IV Part 2:** 603

"Prattler" (newspaper column), **I:** 207

"Prattler, The" (Bierce), **I:** 196

"Prayer" (Gioia), **Supp. XV:** 117

"Prayer" (Olds), **Supp. X:** 204

"Prayer" (Peacock), **Supp. XIX:** 198, 199, 200

"Prayer" (Toomer), **Supp. IX:** 318

"Prayer, A" (Kushner), **Supp. IX: 134**

"Prayer for Columbus" (Whitman), **IV:** 348

"Prayer for My Daughter" (Yeats), **II:** 598

"Prayer for My Grandfather to Our Lady, A" (Lowell), **II:** 541–542

"Prayer for my Son" (C. Frost), **Supp. XV:** 98–99

"Prayer for Our Daughters" (Jarman), **Supp. XVII:** 120

Prayer for Owen Meany, A (Irving), **Supp. VI:** 164, 165, 166, **175–176**

"PRAYER FOR SAVING" (Baraka), **Supp. II Part 1:** 52–53

Prayer for the Dying, A (O'Nan), **Supp. XXV:** 141, 142, 144, 145–146, 148

"Prayer in Spring, A" (Frost), **II:** 153, 164

"Prayer Meeting" (Di Piero), **Supp. XIX:** 46, 47

"Prayer on All Saint's Day" (Cowley), **Supp. II Part 1:** 138, 153

Prayers for Dark People (Du Bois), **Supp. II Part 1:** 186

"Prayer to Hermes" (Creeley), **Supp. IV Part 1:** 156, 157

"Prayer to Masks" (Senghor), **Supp. IV Part 1:** 16

"Prayer to the Child of Prague" (Salinas), **Supp. XIII:** 327

"Prayer to the Good Poet" (Wright), **Supp. III Part 2:** 603

"Prayer to the Pacific" (Silko), **Supp. IV Part 2:** 560

"Prayer to the Verb" (Davison), **Supp. XXVI:** 79

Praying Wrong (Davison), **Supp. XXVI:** 66, 76–77

"Pray without Ceasing" (Emerson), **II:** 9–10

Praz, Mario, **IV:** 430

"Preacher, The" (Whittier), **Supp. I Part 2:** 698–699

Preacher and the Slave, The (Stegner), **Supp. IV Part 2:** 599, 608, 609

Precaution (Cooper), **I:** 337, 339

"Precautions" (Karyotakis, trans. Hadas), **Supp. XXIII:** 125

"Preconceptions of Economic Science, The" (Veblen), **Supp. I Part 2:** 634

Predecessors, Et Cetera (Clampitt), **Supp. IX:** 37

"Predicament, A" (Poe), **Retro. Supp. II:** 273

Predilections (Moore), **III:** 194

Prefaces and Prejudices (Mencken), **III:** 99, 104, 106, 119

Preface to a Twenty Volume Suicide Note. . . . (Baraka), **Supp. II Part 1:** 31,

33–34, 51, 61

"Preference" (Wylie), **Supp. I Part 2:** 713

"Prejudice against the Past, The" (Moore), **IV:** 91

Prejudices (Mencken), **Supp. I Part 2:** 630

Prejudices: A Selection (Farrell, ed.), **III:** 116

Prejudices: First Series (Mencken), **III:** 105

"Preliminary Remarks on the Poetry in the First Person" (Wright), **Supp. XV:** 339

Prelude, A: Landscapes, Characters and Conversations from the Earlier Years of My Life (Wilson), **IV:** 426, 427, 430, 434, 445

Prelude, The (Wordsworth), **III:** 528; **IV:** 331, 343; **Supp. I Part 2:** 416, 676; **Supp. XI:** 248

Prelude and Liebestod (McNally), **Supp. XIII:** 201

"Preludes" (Eliot), **I:** 573, 576, 577; **Retro. Supp. I:** 55; **Supp. IV Part 2:** 436

Preludes for Memnon (Aiken), **I:** 59, 65

Preludes from Memnon (Aiken), **Supp. X:** 50

"Prelude to an Evening" (Ransom), **III:** 491, 492–493

Prelude to Darkness (Salinas), **Supp. XIII:** 311, **318–319,** 320

"Prelude to the Present" (Mumford), **Supp. II Part 2:** 471

"Premature Burial, The" (Poe), **III:** 415, 416, 418; **Retro. Supp. II:** 270

"Premeditations" (Schott), **Supp. XXIII:** 247

Preminger, Otto, **Supp. IX:** 3, 9; **Supp. XX: 246–247**

"Premonition" (Hay), **Supp. XIV:** 122

"Premonitions of the Bread Line" (Komunyakaa), **Supp. XIII:** 114, 115

Prenshaw, Peggy Whitman, **Supp. X:** 229

"Preparations" (Silko), **Supp. IV Part 2:** 560

Preparatory Meditations (Taylor), **IV:** 145, 148, 149, 150, 152, 153, 154–155, 164, 165

"Prepare" (Carruth), **Supp. XVI:** 59

Prepositions: The Collected Critical Essays of Louis Zukofsky (Zukofsky), **Supp. III Part 2:** 630

Prescott, Anne, **Supp. IV Part 1:** 299

Prescott, Orville, **Supp. IV Part 2:** 680; **Supp. XI:** 340; **Supp. XXIII:** 13

Prescott, Peter, **Supp. X:** 83

Prescott, Peter S., **Supp. XVI:** 212

Prescott, William, **Retro. Supp. I:** 123

Prescott, William Hickling, **II:** 9, 310, 313–314; **IV:** 309; **Supp. I Part 2:** 414, 479, 493, 494

"Prescription of Painful Ends" (Jeffers), **Supp. II Part 2:** 424

"Presence, The" (Gordon), **II:** 199, 200

"Presence, The" (Kumin), **Supp. IV Part 2:** 445, 455

Presence and Desire: Essays on Gender, Sexuality, Performance (Dolan), **Supp. XV:** 327

"Presence of Others, The" (Kenyon), **Supp. VII:** 164

Presences (Taylor), **Supp. V:** 325

"Present Age, The" (Emerson), **II:** 11–12

Present Danger, The: Do We Have the Will to Reverse the Decline of American Power? (Podhoretz), **Supp. VIII:** 241

"Present for the Boy, A" (Swados), **Supp. XIX:** 259

Present for Young Ladies, A (Rowson), **Supp. XV:** 245

"Present Hour" (Sandburg), **III:** 593–594

Present Philosophical Tendencies (Perry), **I:** 224

"Present State of Ethical Philosophy, The" (Emerson), **II:** 9

"Present State of Poetry, The" (Schwartz), **Supp. II Part 2:** 666

"Preservation of Innocence" (Baldwin), **Supp. I Part 1:** 51

"Preserving Wildness" (Berry), **Supp. X:** 28, 29, 32

"President and Other Intellectuals, The" (Kazin), **Supp. VIII:** 104

Presidential Papers, The (Mailer), **III:** 35, 37–38, 42, 45; **Retro. Supp. II:** 203, 204, 206

"Presidents" (Merwin), **Supp. III Part 1:** 351

Presnell, Robert, Sr., **Supp. XIII:** 166

Pressley, Nelson, **Supp. XVIII:** 37–38

"PRES SPOKE IN A LANGUAGE" (Baraka), **Supp. II Part 1:** 60

"Presto Manifesto" (Stallings), **Supp. XXV:** 227

Presumed Innocent (Turow), 217; **Supp. XVII:** 214–216, 223

Pretending to Be Asleep (Davison), **Supp. XXVI:** 65, 71–72

"Pretext, The" (Wharton), **Retro. Supp. I:** 371

Pretty Baby (film), **Supp. XXI:** 252

Pretty Boy Floyd (McMurtry), **Supp. V:** 231

"Pretty Girl, The" (Dubus), **Supp. VII:** 87–88

"Pretty Mouth and Green My Eyes" (Salinger), **III:** 560

"Previous Condition" (Baldwin), **Supp. I Part 1:** 51, 55, 63

"Previous Tenant, The" (Simpson), **Supp. IX:** 278–279

Prevost, Verbie Lovorn, **Supp. XXI:** 45

Priaulx, Allan, **Supp. XI:** 228

Price, Alan, **Retro. Supp. I:** 377

Price, E. Hoffman, **Supp. XXV:** 114

Price, Reynolds, **Supp. IX:** 256, 257; **Supp. VI:** 253–270

Price, Richard, **II:** 9; **Supp. I Part 2:** 522; **Supp. XX:** 85

Price, The (A. Miller), **III:** 165–166

"Price Is Right, The" (Skloot), **Supp. XX:** 198–199

"Price of Poetry, The" (Biss), **Supp. XXVI:** 48

"Price of the Harness, The" (Crane), **I:** 414

Pricksongs & Descants; Fictions (Coover), **Supp. V:** 39, 42, 43, 49, 50

"Pride" (Hughes), **Supp. I Part 1:** 331

Pride and Prejudice (Austen), **II:** 290; **Supp. XXVI:** 117–118

Prideaux, Tom, **Supp. IV Part 2:** 574, 590

"Priesthood, The" (Winters), **Supp. II Part 2:** 786

Priestly, Joseph, **Supp. I Part 2:** 522

Primary Colors, The (A. Theroux), **Supp. VIII:** 312

"Primary Ground, A" (Rich), **Supp. I Part 2:** 563

"Prime" (Auden), **Supp. II Part 1:** 22

"Primer Class" (Bishop), **Retro. Supp. II:** 38, 51

Primer for Blacks (Brooks), **Supp. III Part 1:** 85

Primer for Combat (Boyle), **Supp. XXIV:** 62

"Primer for the Nuclear Age" (Dove), **Supp. IV Part 1:** 246

Primer mensaje a la América Hispana (W. Frank), **Supp. XX:** 76

Primer of Ignorance, A (Blackmur), **Supp. II Part 1:** 91

Prime-Stevenson, Edward Irenaeus, **Supp. XX:** 235

Primitive (Oppen), **Supp. XXVI:** 237

Primitive, The (C. Himes), **Supp. XVI:** 139, 141–142

"Primitive Black Man, The" (Du Bois), **Supp. II Part 1:** 176

"Primitive Like an Orb, A" (Stevens), **IV:** 89; **Retro. Supp. I:** 309

Primitive People (Prose), **Supp. XVI:** 255, 256, 257

"Primitive Singing" (Lindsay), **Supp. I Part 2:** 389–390

Primitivism and Decadence (Winters), **Supp. II Part 2:** 786, 803–807, 812

Primrose, Archibald Philip, **Supp. XX:** 230

Prince, F. T., **Supp. XXIV:** 45

Prince, Richard, **Supp. XII:** 4

"Prince, The" (Jarrell), **II:** 379

"Prince, The" (Winters), **Supp. II Part 2:** 802

Prince and the Pauper, The (Twain), **IV:** 200–201, 206

Prince Hagen (Sinclair), **Supp. V:** 280

Prince of a Fellow, A (Hearon), **Supp. VIII:** 58, 62–63

Princess, The (Tennyson), **Supp. I Part 2:** 410

Princess and the Goblins, The (Macdonald), **Supp. XIII:** 75

Princess Casamassima, The (James), **II:** 276, 291; **IV:** 202; **Retro. Supp. I:** 216, 221, 222, 225, 226–227

"Princess Casamassima, The" (Trilling), **Supp. III Part 2:** 502, 503

Princess of Arcady, A (Henry), **Retro. Supp. II:** 97

"Principles" (Du Bois), **Supp. II Part 1:** 172

Principles of Literary Criticism (Richards), **I:** 274; **Supp. I Part 1:** 264; **Supp. XIV:** 3

Principles of Psychology, The (James), **II:** 321, 350–352, 353, 354, 357, 362, 363–364; **IV:** 28, 29, 32, 37

Principles of Psychology, The (W. James), **Supp. XVII:** 97

Principles of Zoölogy (Agassiz), **Supp. I Part 1:** 312

Prior, Sir James, **II:** 315

Prior, Matthew, **II:** 111; **III:** 521

"Prison, The" (Malamud), **Supp. I Part 2:** 431, 437

"Prisoned Love" (Boyce), **Supp. XXI:** 9

"Prisoner of Ours, The" (Weigl), **Supp. XIX:** 288

Prisoner of Second Avenue, The (Simon), **Supp. IV Part 2:** 583, 584

Prisoner of Sex, The (Mailer), **III:** 46; **Retro. Supp. II:** 206

Prisoner of Zenda, The (film), **Supp. I Part 2:** 615

Prisoner's Dilemma (Powers), **Supp. IX:** 212, 214–216, 221

Prison Memoirs of an Anarchist (A. Berkman), **Supp. XVII:** 103–104

Pritchard, William, **Supp. XVI:** 71

Pritchard, William H., **Retro. Supp. I:** 131, 141; **Supp. IV Part 1:** 285; **Supp. IV Part 2:** 642; **Supp. XI:** 326

Pritchett, V. S., **II:** 587; **Supp. II Part 1:** 143; **Supp. VIII:** 171; **Supp. XIII:** 168

Pritikin, Renny, **Supp. XXIV:** 40

"Privatation and Publication" (Cowley), **Supp. II Part 1:** 149

Private Contentment (Price), **Supp. VI:** 263

"Private History of a Campaign That Failed" (Twain), **IV:** 195

Private I, The: Privacy in a Public World (Peacock, ed.), **Supp. XIX:** 193, 203

Private Life of Axie Reed, The (Knowles), **Supp. XII:** 249

Private Line (Major), **Supp. XXII:** 174

"Private Man Confronts His Vulgarities at Dawn, A" (Dunn), **Supp. XI:** 146

Private Memoirs and Confessions of a Justified Sinner, The (Hogg), **Supp. IX:** 276

"Private Property and the Common Wealth" (Berry), **Supp. X:** 25

Private Snafu series (Geisel), **Supp. XVI:** 102

"Private Theatricals" (Howells), **II:** 280

Private Women, Public Stage: Literary Domesticity in Nineteenth-Century America (Kelley), **Supp. XVIII:** 257

Privilege, The (Kumin), **Supp. IV Part 2:** 442–444, 451

Prize Stories 1918 : The O. Henry Awards, **Supp. XVI:** 16

"Probe" (Ryan as Quin), **Supp. XVIII:** 229

"Probing the Dark" (Komunyakaa), **Supp. XIII:** 131

"Problem from Hell, A": America and the Age of Genocide (Power), **Supp. XXIII:** 25, 27–28

"Problem from Milton, A" (Wilbur), **Supp. III Part 2:** 550

"Problem of Anxiety, The" (Koch), **Supp. XV:** 183

"Problem of Being, The" (James), **II:** 360

Problem of Classification in the Theory of Value, The (Locke), **Supp. XIV:** 199

"Problem of Evil into Cocoon" (Taggard), **Supp. XXII:** 284

"Problem of Housing the Negro, The" (Du Bois), **Supp. II Part 1:** 168

"Problem of the Religious Novel, The" (Isherwood), **Supp. XIV:** 172

Problems and Other Stories (Updike), **Retro. Supp. I:** 322, 329

Problems of Dostoevsky's Poetics (Bakhtin), **Supp. XXII:** 259

"Problem Solving" (Goldbarth), **Supp. XII:** 185

Procedures for Underground (Atwood), **Supp. XIII:** 33

"Procedures for Underground" (Atwood), **Supp. XIII:** 33

Process (Boyle), **Supp. XXIV:** 51

Procession, The (al-Mawákib) (Gibran), **Supp. XX:** 116, 124

Processional (Lawson), **I:** 479

"Procession at Candlemas, A" (Clampitt), **Supp. IX:** 41

"Proclamation" (Saunders), **Supp. XIX:** 235

Proclus, **Retro. Supp. I:** 247

"Prodigal" (Ammons), **Supp. VII:** 29

"Prodigal" (Hoffman), **Supp. XVIII:** 86

"Prodigal, The" (Bishop), **Supp. I Part 1:** 90, 92

Prodigal Parents, The (Lewis), **II:** 454–455

"Prodigy" (Simic), **Supp. VIII:** 278

Producers, The (film, M. Brooks), **Supp. XVII:** 45

"Proem" (Crane), **I:** 397

"Proem, The: By the Carpenter" (O. Henry), **Supp. II Part 1:** 409

"Professions for Women" (Woolf), **Supp. XIII:** 305

"Professor" (Hughes), **Supp. I Part 1:** 330

"Professor, The" (Bourne), **I:** 223

Professor at the Breakfast Table, The (Holmes), **Supp. I Part 1:** 313, 316

"Professor Clark's Economics" (Veblen), **Supp. I Part 2:** 634

Professor of Desire, The (P. Roth), **Retro. Supp. II:** 288; **Supp. III Part 2:** 403, 418–420

Professor's House, The (Cather), **I:** 325–336; **Retro. Supp. I:** 16

"Professor Veblen" (Mencken), **Supp. I Part 2:** 630

Proffer, Carl R., **Supp. VIII:** 22

Profile Makers, The (Bierds), **Supp. XVII:** 29, 30–32, 33

"Profile of the Tenderloin Street Prostitute, A" (Vollmann), **Supp. XVII:** 230

Profits of Religion, The (Sinclair), **Supp. V:** 276

"Prognosis" (Warren), **IV:** 245

"Progress" (F. Wright), **Supp. XVII:** 247

"Progress Report" (Simic), **Supp. VIII:** 278

"Project for a Trip to China" (Sontag), **Supp. II Part 2:** 454, 469

"Project for *The Ambassadors*" (James), **Retro. Supp. I:** 229

"Projection" (Nemerov), **III:** 275

"Projective Verse" (Olson), **Supp. III Part 1:** 30; **Supp. III Part 2:** 555, 556, 557, 624; **Supp. IV Part 1:** 139, 153; **Supp. VIII:** 290

"Projector, The" (Baker), **Supp. XIII:** 53, 55

Prokofiev, Sergey Sergeyevich, **Supp. IV Part 1:** 81

"Prolegomena, Section 1" (Pound), **Supp. III Part 2:** 615–616

"Prolegomena, Section 2" (Pound), **Supp. III Part 2:** 616

"Prolegomenon to a Biography of Mailer" (Lucid), **Retro. Supp. II:** 195

Proletarian Literature in the United States (Hicks), **Supp. I Part 2:** 609–610; **Supp. XXVI:** 134

"Prologue" (MacLeish), **III:** 8, 14

Prologue, for Full Chorus of Mixed Voices and Orchestra (Taggard and Schuman), **Supp. XXII:** 283

"Prologue to a Life" (D. West), **Supp. XVIII:** 280

"Prologue to Our Time" (Mumford), **Supp. III Part 2:** 473

"Prometheus" (Longfellow), **II:** 494

Prometheus Bound (Lowell), **II:** 543, 544, 545, 555

Promise, The (Buck), **Supp. II Part 1:** 124

"Promise, The" (Olds), **Supp. X:** 213

"Promise and Fulfillment" (D. West), **Supp. XVIII:** 278

Promised Land (Parker), **Supp. XIX:** 183, 184, 190

Promised Land, The (M. Antin), **Supp. IX:** 227; **Supp. XVI:** 148, 149; **Supp. XX:** 1, 2, 3, 4–9, 11

Promised Land, The (Porter), **III:** 447

"Promised Land, The" (R. Fisher), **Supp. XIX:** 72

Promised Lands (Sontag), **Supp. III Part 2:** 452

Promise of American Life, The (Croly), **I:** 229

"Promise of Blue Horses, The" (Harjo), **Supp. XII:** 228

Promise of Rest, The (Price), **Supp. VI:** 262, 266

Promises (Warren), **Supp. XIV:** 15

Promises, Promises (musical), **Supp. IV Part 2:** 575

Promises: Poems 1954–1956 (Warren), **IV:** 244–245, 249, 252

"Promise This When You Be Dying" (Dickinson), **Retro. Supp. I:** 44, 46

"Pronoun Variations"(Hadas), **Supp. XXIII:** 120

Pronzini, Bill, **Supp. XXVI:** 277, 278, 282

Proof, The (Winters), **Supp. II Part 2:** 786, 791, 792–794

"Proofreader, The" (Huddle), **Supp. XXVI:** 151, 152

Proofs and Theories: Essays on Poetry (Glück), **Supp. V:** 77, 79, 92; **Supp. XIV:** 269

"Propaganda of History, The" (Du Bois), **Supp. II Part 1:** 182

Propertius, Sextus, **III:** 467; **Retro. Supp. II:** 187; **Supp. XII:** 2

Property Of: A Novel (Hoffman), **Supp. X:** 77, 79, 80–82

"Property of Loss" (W. V. Davis), **Supp. XXI:** 95

"Prophecy of Samuel Sewall, The" (Whittier), **Supp. I Part 2:** 699

Prophet, The (Asch), **Supp. XXIII:** 7

Prophet, The (Gibran), **Supp. XX:** 113, 115, 119–121, 126

"Prophet, The" (Notley), **Supp. XXII:** 229

"Prophet, The" (Very), **Supp. XXV:** 248–249

"Prophet and the Child, The" (Gibran), **Supp. XX:** 123

Propheteers, The (Apple), **Supp. XVII:** 6–7

"Prophetic Pictures, The" (Hawthorne), **II:** 227

"Proportion" (Lowell), **II:** 525

"Proposal" (Carver), **Supp. III Part 1:** 149

Proposals Relating to the Education of Youth in Pensilvania (Franklin), **II:** 113

"Proposed New Version of the Bible" (Franklin), **II:** 110

Prose, Francine, **Supp. XII:** 333; **Supp. XIX:** 209; **Supp. XVI:** 249–264; **Supp. XXIII:** 300; **Supp. XXVI:** 121, 130

"Prose for Departure" (Merrill), **Supp. III Part 1:** 336

Prose Pieces (Bynner), **Supp. XV:** 52

"Prose Poem as an Evolving Form, The" (R. Bly), **Supp. IV Part 1:** 64

"Proserpina and the Devil" (Wilder), **IV:** 358

"Prosody" (Espaillat), **Supp. XXI:** 102

"Prosody" (Shapiro), **Supp. II Part 2:** 710

Prospect before Us, The (Dos Passos), **I:** 491

"Prospective Immigrants Please Note" (Rich), **Supp. I Part 2:** 555

Prospect of Peace, The (Barlow), **Supp. II Part 1:** 67, 68, 75

Prospects of Literature, The (L. P. Smith), **Supp. XIV:** 343

Prospects on the Rubicon (Paine), **Supp. I Part 2:** 510–511

Prospectus of a National Institution, to Be Established in the United States (Barlow), **Supp. II Part 1:** 80, 82

Prospice (Browning), **IV:** 366

"Protestant Easter" (Sexton), **Supp. II Part 2:** 684

"Prothalamion" (Schwartz), **Supp. II Part 2:** 649, 652

"Prothalamion" (Spenser), **Retro. Supp. I:** 62

Proud, Robert, **Supp. I Part 1:** 125
"Proud Farmer, The" (Lindsay), **Supp. I Part 2:** 381
Proud Flesh (Humphrey), **Supp. IX:** 94, 95, 96, **102–103,** 104, 105, 109
"Proud Flesh" (Warren), **IV:** 243
Proud Highway, The (Thompson), **Supp. XXIV:** 283
Proud Lady (Boyce), **Supp. XXI:** 7, 12
"Proud Lady" (Wylie), **Supp. I Part 2:** 711–712
Proulx, Annie, **Supp. VII: 249–267; Supp. XXIV:** 245, 251; **Supp. XXVI:** 186
Proust, Marcel, **I:** 89, 319, 327, 377, 461; **II:** 377, 514, 606; **III:** 174, 181, 184, 244–245, 259, 471; **IV:** 32, 201, 237, 301, 312, 328, 359, 428, 431, 434, 439, 443, 466, 467; **Retro. Supp. I:** 75, 89, 169, 335; **Supp. III Part 1:** 10, 12, 14, 15; **Supp. IV Part 2:** 600; **Supp. IX:** 211; **Supp. VIII:** 103; **Supp. X:** 193, 194; **Supp. XII:** 289; **Supp. XIV:** 24, 83, 95; **Supp. XVI:** 295; **Supp. XXI:** 231; **Supp. XXIII:** 122
Proverbs, **Supp. X:** 45
"Proverbs" (Jarman), **Supp. XVII:** 118
"Providence" (Komunyakaa), **Supp. XIII:** 132
"Provident Woman, A" (Boyce), **Supp. XXI:** 10
"Provincetown Postcards" (F. Wright), **Supp. XVII:** 244
"Provincia deserta" (Pound), **Retro. Supp. I:** 289
"Provisional Remarks on Being / A Poet / of Arkansas" (Wright), **Supp. XV:** 337
Pruette, Lorine, **Supp. IV Part 2:** 522
Prufrock and Other Observations (Eliot), **I:** 569–570, 571, 573, 574, 576–577, 583, 584, 585; **Retro. Supp. I:** 59, 62
"Prufrock's Perivigilium" (T. S. Eliot), **Retro. Supp. I:** 57
Pryor, Richard, **Supp. XIII:** 343
Pryse, Marjorie, **Retro. Supp. II:** 139, 146; **Supp. XXV:** 285
"Psalm" (Ginsberg), **Supp. II Part 1:** 312
"Psalm" (Oppen), **Supp. XXVI:** 232–233, 235
"Psalm" (Simic), **Supp. VIII:** 282
"Psalm, A, or Supplication for mercy, and confession of Sin, addressed to the Author of Life, in the Odjibway-Alqonquin tongue" (J. Schoolcraft), **Supp. XXIII:** 232
"Psalm and Lament" (Justice), **Supp. VII:** 116, 117–118, 120–122, 124
"Psalm for Pinhook" (Ray), **Supp. XVIII:** 202
"Psalm Jew, The"(Asch). *See Salvation* (Asch)
"Psalm of Life, A" (Longfellow), **II:** 489, 496; **Retro. Supp. II:** 164, 168, 169; **Supp. I Part 2:** 409
"Psalm of the West" (Lanier), **Supp. I Part 1:** 362, 364
"Psalm: Our Fathers" (Merwin), **Supp. III Part 1:** 350

Psalms (biblical book), **I:** 83; **II:** 168, 232; **Retro. Supp. I:** 62; **Supp. I Part 1:** 125
Psalms, Hymns, and Spiritual Songs of the Rev. Isaac Watts, The (Worcester, ed.), **I:** 458
Psychiatric Novels of Oliver Wendell Holmes, The (Oberndorf), **Supp. I Part 1:** 315
"Psychology and Form" (Burke), **I:** 270
Psychology: Briefer Course (James), **II:** 351–352
Psychology of Art (Malraux), **IV:** 434
Psychology of Insanity, The (Hart), **I:** 241–242, 248–250
Psychopathia Sexualis (Shanley), **Supp. XIV:** 316, **329**
Psychophysiks (Fechner), **II:** 358
Pterodactyls (Silver), **Supp. XXIV: 268–270**
Ptomaine Street (Wells), **Supp. XXVI:** 275
"Pu-239" (Kalfus), **Supp. XVII:** 50
"Publication is the Auction" (Dickinson), **Retro. Supp. I:** 31
"Public Bath, The" (Snyder), **Supp. VIII:** 298
Public Burning, The (Coover), **Supp. IV Part 1:** 388; **Supp. V:** 44, 45, 46–47, 48, 51, 52; **Supp. XVII:** 6
"Public Burning of Julius and Ethel Rosenberg, The: An Historical Romance" (Coover), **Supp. V:** 44
"Public Figure" (Hay), **Supp. XIV:** 124
"Public Garden, The" (Lowell), **II:** 550
Public Good (Paine), **Supp. I Part 2:** 509–510
Public Poetry of Robert Lowell, The (Cosgrave), **Retro. Supp. II:** 185
"Public & Private" (column, Quindlen), **Supp. XVII:** 165, 167, 169–170
Public Speech: Poems (MacLeish), **III:** 15–16
Public Spirit (Savage), **II:** 111
"Public Woman, A" (Cliff), **Supp. XXII:** 76
Puccini, Giacomo, **Supp. XXI:** 150, 151
"Puck" (Monette), **Supp. X:** 157–158
Pudd'nhead Wilson (Twain), **I:** 197
"Pudd'nhead Wilson's Calendar" (Twain), **I:** 197
"Pueblo Revolt, The" (Sando), **Supp. IV Part 2:** 510
Puella (Dickey), **Supp. IV Part 1:** 178, 185
Pulitzer, Alfred, **Retro. Supp. I:** 257
Pull Down Vanity (Fiedler), **Supp. XIII:** 103
Pullman, George, **Supp. I Part 1:** 9
"Pullman Car Hiawatha" (Wilder), **IV:** 365–366
Pull My Daisy (film), **Supp. XII:** 126–127
"Pulp Cutters' Nativity, A" (Budbill), **Supp. XIX:** 9
"Pulpit and the Pew, The" (Holmes), **Supp. I Part 1:** 302
"Pulse-Beats and Pen-Strokes" (Sandburg), **III:** 579
"Pump, The" (Humphrey), **Supp. IX:** 101

Pump House Gang, The (Wolfe), **Supp. III Part 2:** 575, 578, 580, 581
Punch, Brothers, Punch and Other Sketches (Twain), **IV:** 200
Punch: The Immortal Liar, Documents in His History (Aiken), **I:** 57, 61
Punishment Without Vengeance (Vega; Merwin, trans.), **Supp. III Part 1:** 341, 347
"Pupil" (F. Barthelme), **Supp. XI:** 26
"Pupil, The" (H. James), **Supp. XX: 233**
"Pupil, The" (James), **II:** 331; **Retro. Supp. I:** 217, 219, 228
"Purchase" (Banks), **Supp. V:** 6
"Purchase of Some Golf Clubs, A" (O'Hara), **III:** 369
"Purdah" (Plath), **Supp. I Part 2:** 602
Purdy, Charles, **Supp. VIII:** 330
Purdy, James, **Supp. VII: 269–285**
Purdy, John Lloyd, **Supp. XXVI:** 101, 103, 105, 111
Purdy, Theodore, **Supp. VIII:** 153
Pure (C. Frost), **Supp. XV:** 93, **101–102,** 104, 106
"Pure" (C. Frost), **Supp. XV:** 101–102
"Pure and the Good, The: On Baseball and Backpaking" (Maclean), **Supp. XIV:** 222
"Pure Good of Theory, The" (Stevens), **Retro. Supp. I:** 310
Purgatorio (Dante), **III:** 182
"Purim Parade" (Espaillat), **Supp. XXI:** 108
Puritan Family (Morgan), **Supp. I Part 1:** 101
"Puritanical Pleasures" (Hardwick), **Supp. III Part 1:** 213–214
Puritan Origins of the American Self, The (Bercovitch), **Supp. I Part 1:** 99
Puritan Pronaos, The: Studies in the Intellectual Life of New England in the Seventeenth Century (Morison), **Supp. I Part 2:** 485
"Puritan Realism: *The Wide, Wide World* and *Robinson Crusoe*" (Kim), **Supp. XVIII:** 267
Puritans, The (P. Miller), **Supp. VIII:** 101
"Puritan's Ballad, The" (Wylie), **Supp. I Part 2:** 723
"Purloined Letter, The" (Poe), **Retro. Supp. II:** 271, 272
Purple Cane Road (Burke), **Supp. XIV:** 32, 33
Purple Decades, The (Wolfe), **Supp. III Part 2:** 584
"Purple Hat, The" (Welty), **IV:** 264
Purple Rose of Cairo, The (film; Allen), **Supp. XV:** 1, **9–10,** 12, 14
Purser, John T., **Supp. XIV:** 4
"Pursuit of Happiness" (Simpson), **Supp. IX:** 279
"Pursuit of Happiness, The" (Ashbery), **Supp. III Part 1:** 23
Pursuit of the Prodigal, The (Auchincloss), **Supp. IV Part 1:** 25
Pushcart at the Curb, A (Dos Passos), **I:** 478, 479
"Pushcart Man" (Hughes), **Supp. I Part 1:** 330

Pushcart Prize, XIII, The (Ford), **Supp. V:** 58

Pushcart Prize VII, The (Hendeson, ed.), **Supp. XVII:** 16

Pushcart Prize XIV, The (Henderson, ed.), **Supp. XVII:** 18

Pushcart Prize XX, The (Henderson, ed.), **Supp. XVII:** 20

"Pushing 100" (Mora), **Supp. XIII:** 215

Pushkin, Aleksander, **III:** 246, 261, 262; **Retro. Supp. I:** 266, 269; **Supp. XVI:** 188

Pussy, King of the Pirates (Acker), **Supp. XII:** 6–7

"Pussycat and the Expert Plumber Who Was a Man, The" (A. Miller), **III:** 146–147

Pussycat Fever (Acker), **Supp. XII:** 6

Putnam, George Haven, **Supp. XVIII:** 257, 260

Putnam, George P., **II:** 314; **Supp. XVIII:** 3–4, 14, 260

Putnam, Phelps, **I:** 288

Putnam, Samuel, **II:** 26; **III:** 479; **Supp. III Part 2:** 615

"Put Off the Wedding Five Times and Nobody Comes to It" (Sandburg), **III:** 586–587

Puttenham, George, **Supp. I Part 1:** 113

Puttermesser Papers, The (Ozick), **Supp. V:** 269

"Putting a Burden Down" (Peacock), **Supp. XIX:** 199

Putting It Together (Sondheim), **Supp. XXIV:** 124

"Putting on *Visit to a Small Planet*" (Vidal), **Supp. IV Part 2:** 683

Put Yourself in My Shoes (Carver), **Supp. III Part 1:** 139

"Put Yourself in My Shoes" (Carver), **Supp. III Part 1:** 139, 141

Putzi, Jennifer, **Supp. XV:** 284

Puzo, Mario, **Supp. IV Part 1:** 390

"Puzzle of Modern Society, The" (Kazin), **Supp. VIII:** 103

Pygmalion (Shaw), **Supp. XII:** 14

Pyle, Ernie, **III:** 148; **Supp. V:** 240; **Supp. XVII:** 61

Pylon (Faulkner), **II:** 64–65, 73; **Retro. Supp. I:** 84, 85

Pynchon, Thomas, **III:** 258; **Retro. Supp. I:** 278; **Retro. Supp. II:** 279, 324; **Supp. II Part 2:** 557, **617–638; Supp. III Part 1:** 217; **Supp. IV Part 1:** 53, 279; **Supp. IV Part 2:** 570; **Supp. IX:** 207, 208, 212; **Supp. V:** 40, 44, 52; **Supp. VIII:** 14; **Supp. X:** 260, 301, 302; **Supp. XI:** 103; **Supp. XII:** 289; **Supp. XIV:** 49, 53, 54, 96; **Supp. XIX:** 223; **Supp. XVI:** 123, 128; **Supp. XVII:** 183, 225, 232, 236; **Supp. XX: 21, 83, 87; Supp. XXIII:** 42, 101

Pyne, John, **Supp. XXI:** 7

Pyne, Mary, **Supp. XXI:** 7

Pyrah, Gill, **Supp. V:** 126

"Pyramid Club, The" (Doctorow), **Supp. IV Part 1:** 234

Pyrlaeus, Johann Christopher, **Supp. XXVI:** 86

"Pyrography" (Ashbery), **Supp. III Part 1:** 18

Pythagoras, **I:** 332

Pythagorean Silence (Howe), **Supp. IV Part 2:** 426, 428–429

Q

QBVII (television movie), **Supp. XX: 247**

QBVII (Uris), **Supp. XX: 244, 247, 248, 251, 253–254**

"Qebehseneuf" (Goldbarth), **Supp. XII:** 186

"Quadroons, The" (Child), **Supp. XVIII:** 124

"Quai d'Orléans" (Bishop), **Supp. I Part 1:** 89

"Quail for Mr. Forester" (Humphrey), **Supp. IX:** 94

"Quail in Autumn" (W. J. Smith), **Supp. XIII:** 334–335, 339

Quaker City, The: or, The Monks of Monk Hall (Lippard), **Supp. XXIII:** 177, 178–179, **180–183,** 184, 187, 188–189, 190

"Quaker Graveyard in Nantucket, The" (Lowell), **II:** 54, 550; **Retro. Supp. II:** 178, 186–187

"Quake Theory" (Olds), **Supp. X:** 203

Qualey, Carlton C., **Supp. I Part 2:** 650

Quality of Hurt, The (C. Himes), **Supp. XVI:** 137, 145

"Quality of Wine" (Carruth), **Supp. XVI:** 59

"Quality Time" (Kingsolver), **Supp. VII:** 203

"Quandary" (F. Wright), **Supp. XVII:** 244

Quang-Ngau-chè, **III:** 473

Quarles, Francis, **I:** 178, 179

"Quarrel" (Taggard), **Supp. XXII:** 276

Quarry, The (Chesnutt), **Supp. XIV:** 76

"Quarry, The" (Nemerov), **III:** 272

Quarry, The: New Poems (Eberhart), **I:** 532, 539

Quartermain, Peter, **Supp. IV Part 2:** 423, 434

Quatermain, Peter, **Supp. XXII:** 163

"Quaternions, The" (Bradstreet), **Supp. I Part 1:** 104–106, 114, 122

"Quatrains for Ishi" (Komunyakaa), **Supp. XIII:** 129

Queechy (S. Warner as Wetherell), **Supp. XVIII:** 257, **264–266**

Queen Christmas (Wells), **Supp. XXVI:** 275

"Queen Elizabeth and the Blind Girl or Music for the Dead Children" (B. Kelly), **Supp. XVII:** 124, 125

"Queen of the Blues" (Brooks), **Supp. III Part 1:** 75

Queen of the Damned, The (Rice), **Supp. VII:** 290, 292–293, 297, 299

Queen of the Mob (film), **Supp. XIII:** 170

"Queens of France" (Wilder), **IV:** 365

"Queen's Twin, The" (Jewett), **Retro. Supp. II:** 138

Queen's Twin, The, and Other Stories (Jewett), **Retro. Supp. II:** 140

Queen Victoria (Strachey), **Supp. I Part 2:** 485, 494; **Supp. XIV:** 342

Queer (Burroughs), **Supp. III Part 1:** 93–102

"Queer Aztlán"(Moraga), **Supp. XXIII:** 201

"Queer Beer" (Hansberry), **Supp. IV Part 1:** 374

"Quelques considérations sur la méthode subjective" (James), **II:** 345–346

"Quest, The" (Gibran), **Supp. XX: 124**

"Question" (Swenson), **Supp. IV Part 2:** 640

"Question and Answer" (Hughes), **Retro. Supp. I:** 211

"Questioning Faces" (Frost), **Retro. Supp. I:** 141

"Question Mark in the Circle, The" (Stegner), **Supp. IV Part 2:** 597

"Questionnaire, The" (Snodgrass), **Supp. VI:** 318

"Question of Fidelity, A" (Beauvoir), **Supp. IX:** 4

"Question of Loneliness, A" (Swados), **Supp. XIX:** 262

"Question of Our Speech, The" (Ozick), **Supp. V:** 272

"Question of Simone de Beauvoir, The" (Algren), **Supp. IX:** 4

Questions About Angels (Collins), **Supp. XXI:** 54, 58, 59, 60, 64

Questions for Ecclesiastes (Jarman), **Supp. XVII:** 109, 110, **118–119**

"Questions of Geography" (Hollander), **Supp. I Part 1:** 96

"Questions of Swimming, 1935" (Davison), **Supp. XXVI:** 76

Questions of Travel (Bishop), **Retro. Supp. II: 46–48; Supp. I Part 1:** 72, 83, 92, 94

"Questions of Travel" (Bishop), **Retro. Supp. II:** 47

"Questions to Tourists Stopped by a Pineapple Field" (Merwin), **Supp. III Part 1:** 355

"Questions without Answers" (T. Williams), **IV:** 384

"Quest of the Purple-Fringed, The" (Frost), **Retro. Supp. I:** 139

Quest of the Silver Fleece, The (Du Bois), **Supp. II Part 1:** 176–178

Quevedo y Villegas, Francisco Gómez, **Retro. Supp. I:** 423

Quickly: A Column for Slow Readers (Mailer), **Retro. Supp. II:** 202

Quicksand (Larsen), **Supp. XVIII:** 119, 121, 122, **124–127**

Quicksand and Passing (Larsen; McDowell, ed.), **Supp. XVIII:** 125

"Quies," (Pound), **Retro. Supp. I:** 413

Quiet American, The (Greene), **Supp. XIX:** 29

"Quiet and clear" (Kooser), **Supp. XIX:** 125

Quiet City (Shaw), **Supp. XIX:** 244

Quiet Days in Clichy (H. Miller), **III:** 170, 178, 183–184, 187

"Quiet Desperation" (Simpson), **Supp. IX:** 277–278

"Quiet Hour" (Huddle), **Supp. XXVI:** 149–150

"Quiet Light, A" (Skloot), **Supp. XX: 203**

"Quiet of the Mind" (Nye), **Supp. XIII:** 284

"Quiet Woman, The" (Taggard), **Supp. XXII:** 274

"QUILLA" (Trethewey), **Supp. XXI:** 246

"Quilting" (D. West), **Supp. XVIII:** 283

Quin, Mike (pseudonym). *See* Ryan, Paul William

Quincy, Edmund, **Supp. XVIII:** 4

Quindlen, Anna, **Supp. XVI:** 108; **Supp. XVII: 165–181**

Quinlan, Kathleen, **Supp. X:** 80

Quinn, Anthony, **Supp. XXI:** 46

Quinn, John, **III:** 471

Quinn, Paul, **Supp. V:** 71

Quinn, Sister M. Bernetta, **III:** 479; **IV:** 421

Quinn, Vincent, **I:** 386, 401, 402; **Supp. I Part 1:** 270

"Quinnapoxet" (Kunitz), **Supp. III Part 1:** 263

Quinn's Book (W. Kennedy), **Supp. VII:** 133, 148–150, 153

Quintero, José, **III:** 403

Quintilian, **IV:** 123

Quinzaine for This Yule, A (Pound), **Retro. Supp. I:** 285

Quite Contrary: The Mary and Newt Story (Dixon), **Supp. XII: 144,** 153

Quitting Time (Kriegel), **Supp. XXIV: 225–227**

Quod Erat Demonstrandum (Stein), **IV:** 34

Quo Vadis? (Sienkiewicz), **Supp. IV Part 2:** 518; **Supp. XVI:** 182

R

Raab, Max, **Supp. XI:** 309

Raban, Jonathan, **Supp. XXV:** 208, 217

"Rabbi, The" (Hayden), **Supp. II Part 1:** 363, 369

Rabbit, Run (Updike), **IV:** 214, 223, 230–234; **Retro. Supp. I:** 320, 325, 326, 327, 331, 333, 335; **Supp. XI:** 140; **Supp. XII:** 298; **Supp. XVI:** 220

"Rabbit, The" (Barnes), **Supp. III Part 1:** 34

Rabbit at Rest (Updike), **Retro. Supp. I:** 334

Rabbit Dance (Gansworth), **Supp. XXVI:** 114

Rabbit Factory, The (L. Brown), **Supp. XXI:** 40, **47–48**

"*Rabbit Factory, The:* Escaping the Isolation of the Cage" (Gaughran), **Supp. XXI:** 47–48

Rabbit Is Rich (Updike), **Retro. Supp. I:** 334; **Supp. XXVI:** 142

Rabbit novels (Updike), **Supp. V:** 269

Rabbit Redux (Updike), **IV:** 214; **Retro. Supp. I:** 332, 333

Rabbit's Umbrella, The (Plimpton), **Supp. XVI:** 244

"Rabbits Who Caused All the Trouble, The" (Thurber), **Supp. I Part 2:** 610

Rabe, David, **Supp. XXIV:** 117; **Supp. XXV:** 153

Rabelais, and His World (Bakhtin), **Retro. Supp. II:** 273

Rabelais, François, **I:** 130; **II:** 111, 112, 302, 535; **III:** 77, 78, 174, 182; **IV:** 68; **Supp. I Part 2:** 461

Rabelais and His World (Bakhtin), **Supp. X:** 120

Rabinbach, Anson, **Supp. XII:** 166

Rabinowitz, Paula, **Supp. V:** 161

"Race" (Emerson), **II:** 6

"Race, Privilege, and the Politics of (Re)Writing History: An Analysis of the Novels of Michelle Cliff" (Edmondson), **Supp. XXII:** 70

"Race Contacts and Inter-Racial Relations" (Locke), **Supp. XIV:** 211

"Race Contacts and Inter-Racial Relations: A Study in the Theory and Practice of Race" (lectures, Locke), **Supp. XIV:** 199, 209

Race Contacts and Interracial Relations: Lectures on the Theory and Practice of Race (Locke, Stewart, ed.), **Supp. XIV:** 196, **209–210**

"'RACE LINE' IS A PRODUCT OF CAPITALISM, THE" (Baraka), **Supp. II Part 1:** 61

"Race of Life, The" (Thurber), **Supp. I Part 2:** 614

"Race Problems and Modern Society" (Toomer), **Supp. III Part 2:** 486

Race Questions, Provincialism, and Other American Problems (Royce), **Supp. XIV:** 199

"Race Riot, Tulsa, 1921" (Olds), **Supp. X:** 205

Race Rock (Matthiessen), **Supp. V:** 201

"Races, The" (Lowell), **II:** 554

"Rachel" (D. West), **Supp. XVIII:** 289

Rachel Carson: Witness for Nature (Lear), **Supp. IX:** 19

Rachel River (film, Smolan), **Supp. XVI:** 36

"Racial Progress and Race Adjustment" (Locke), **Supp. XIV:** 210

Racine, Jean Baptiste, **II:** 543, 573; **III:** 145, 151, 152, 160; **IV:** 317, 368, 370; **Supp. I Part 2:** 716

Radcliffe, Ann, **Supp. XX: 108**

Radiance (Crooker), **Supp. XXIII: 57–58**

"Radical" (Moore), **III:** 211

"Radical Chic" (Wolfe), **Supp. III Part 2:** 577–578, 584, 585

Radical Chic & Mau-mauing the Flak Catchers (Wolfe), **Supp. III Part 2:** 577–578

Radical Empiricism of William James, The (Wild), **II:** 362, 363–364

Radicalism in America, The (Lasch), **I:** 259

"Radical Jewish Humanism: The Vision of E. L. Doctorow" (Clayton), **Supp. IV Part 1:** 238

"Radically Condensed History of Postindustrial Life, A" (Wallace), **Supp. X:** 309

Radical's America, A (Swados), **Supp. XIX: 264–265**

Radinovsky, Lisa, **Supp. XV:** 284, 285

"Radio" (O'Hara), **III:** 369

Radio Days (film, Allen), **Supp. XV:** 9

"Radio Pope" (Goldbarth), **Supp. XII:** 188, 192

Raditzer (Matthiessen), **Supp. V:** 201

Radkin, Paul, **Supp. I Part 2:** 539

"Rafaela Who Drinks Coconut & Papaya Juice on Tuesdays" (Cisneros), **Supp. VII:** 63

Rafelson, Bob, **Supp. XIV:** 241

Raffalovich, Marc-André, **Supp. XIV:** 335

Rafferty, Terence, **Supp. XX: 87, 92**

"Raft, The" (Lindsay), **Supp. I Part 2:** 393

Rag and Bone Shop of the Heart, The: Poems for Men (Bly, Hillman, and Meade, eds.), **Supp. IV Part 1:** 67

Rage in Harlem (C. Himes). *See For Love of Imabelle* (C. Himes)

Rage to Live, A (O'Hara), **III:** 361

Raglan, Lord, **I:** 135

Rago, Henry, **Supp. III Part 2:** 624, 628, 629

"Rag Rug"(Hadas), **Supp. XXIII:** 118

Ragtime (Doctorow), **Retro. Supp. II:** 108; **Supp. IV Part 1:** 217, 222–224, 231, 232, 233, 234, 237, 238; **Supp. V:** 45; **Supp. XXIV:** 227

"Ragtime" (Doctorow), **Supp. IV Part 1:** 234

Ragtime (film), **Supp. IV Part 1:** 236

Ragtime (musical, McNally), **Supp. XIII:** 207

Rahab (W. Frank), **Supp. XX: 71–72, 76**

Rahaim, Liz, **Supp. XVII:** 2

Rahv, Philip, **Retro. Supp. I:** 112; **Supp. II Part 1:** 136; **Supp. IX:** 8; **Supp. VIII:** 96; **Supp. XIV:** 3; **Supp. XV:** 140

"Raid" (Hughes), **Retro. Supp. I:** 208

Raids on the Unspeakable (Merton), **Supp. VIII:** 201, 208

Raikin, Judith, **Supp. XXII:** 66

Rail, DeWayne, **Supp. XIII:** 312

"Rain, the Rez, and Other Things, The" (Gansworth), **Supp. XXVI:** 111

Rain and Other Fictions (Kenny), **Supp. XXIII:** 157

"Rain and the Rhinoceros" (Merton), **Supp. VIII:** 201

Rainbow (Lawrence), **III:** 27

"Rainbows" (Marquand), **III:** 56

Rainbow Stories, The (Vollmann), **Supp. XVII:** 226, 227, 230, 231, 233

Rainbow Tulip, The (Mora), **Supp. XIII:** 221

"Rain Country" (Haines), **Supp. XII:** 210

"Rain-Dream, A" (Bryant), **Supp. I Part 1:** 164

Raine, Kathleen, **I:** 522, 527

"Rain Falling Now, The" (Dunn), **Supp. XI:** 147

"Rain Flooding Your Campfire" (Gallagher), **Supp. XXIV:** 177

"Rain in the Heart" (Taylor), **Supp. V:** 317, 319

Rain in the Trees, The (Merwin), **Supp. III Part 1:** 340, 342, 345, 349, 354–356

"Rainmaker, The" (Humphrey), **Supp. IX:** 101

Raintree County (Lockridge), **Supp. XIX:** 263

Rainwater, Catherine, **Supp. V:** 272

"Rainy Day" (Longfellow), **II:** 498

"Rainy Day, The" (Buck), **Supp. II Part 1:** 127

"Rainy Mountain Cemetery" (Momaday), **Supp. IV Part 2:** 486

Rainy Mountain Christmas Doll (painting) (Momaday), **Supp. IV Part 2:** 493

"Rainy Season: Sub-Tropics" (Bishop), **Supp. I Part 1:** 93

"Rainy Sunday" (Espaillat), **Supp. XXI:** 106

Raised in Captivity (Silver), **Supp. XXIV: 271**

"Raise High the Roof Beam, Carpenters" (Salinger), **III:** 567–569, 571

Raise High the Roof Beam, Carpenters; and Seymour: An Introduction (Salinger), **III:** 552, 567–571, 572

Raise Race Rays Raze: Essays Since 1965 (Baraka), **Supp. II Part 1:** 47, 52, 55

Raisin (musical), **Supp. IV Part 1:** 374

Raising Demons (Jackson), **Supp. IX: 125–126**

Raisin in the Sun, A (film: Columbia Pictures), **Supp. IV Part 1:** 360, 367

Raisin in the Sun, A (Hansberry), **Supp. IV Part 1:** 359, 360, 361, 362–364; **Supp. VIII:** 343

Raisin in the Sun, A (television film: American Playhouse), **Supp. IV Part 1:** 367, 374

Raisin in the Sun, A (unproduced screenplay) (Hansberry), **Supp. IV Part 1:** 360

Rajan, R., **I:** 390

"Rake, The" (Mamet), **Supp. XIV:** 240

Rake's Progress, The (opera), **Supp. II Part 1:** 24

Rakosi, Carl, **Supp. III Part 2:** 614, 615, 616, 617, 618, 621, 629; **Supp. XIV:** 286, 287

Ralegh, Sir Walter, **Supp. I Part 1:** 98

Raleigh, John Henry, **IV:** 366

Ralph, Brett, **Supp. XVII:** 245

Ramakrishna, Sri, **III:** 567

Ramakrishna and His Disciples (Isherwood), **Supp. XIV:** 164

Ramazani, Jahan, **Supp. IV Part 2:** 450

"Ramble of Aphasia, A" (O. Henry), **Supp. II Part 1:** 410

Ramey, Phillip, **Supp. IV Part 1:** 94

Ramírez, Juan, **Supp. XXIII:** 203

Ramona (Jackson), **Supp. XXIV:** 27

Rampersad, Arnold, **Retro. Supp. I:** 196, 200, 201, 204; **Supp. IV Part 1:** 244, 250

Rampling, Anne, **Supp. VII:** 201. *See also* Rice, Anne

Rampling, Charlotte, **Supp. IX:** 253

Ramsey, Priscilla R., **Supp. IV Part 1:** 15

Ramsey, Roger, **Supp. XVI:** 69

Ramsey, William, **Supp. XVIII:** 66

Ramus, Petrus, **Supp. I Part 1:** 104

Rancière, Jacques, **Supp. XXVI:** 18, 135, 136, 141

Rand, Ayn, **Supp. I Part 1:** 294; **Supp. IV Part 2: 517–535**

Randall, Jarrell, 1914–1965 (Lowell, Taylor, and Warren, eds.), **II:** 368, 385

Randall, John H., **III:** 605

Randolph, John, **I:** 5–6

Randolph, Ladette, **Supp. XXIII:** 274

"Randolphs of the Redwoods, The" (Atherton), **Supp. XXIV:** 18

"Range-Finding" (Frost), **Retro. Supp. I:** 131

Range of the Possible (T. Marshall), **Supp. XVII:** 36

Rangoon (F. Barthelme), **Supp. XI:** 25

Rangus, Eric, **Supp. XXI:** 244, 254

Rank, Otto, **I:** 135; **Supp. IX:** 105; **Supp. X:** 183, 185, 193

Ranke, Leopold von, **Supp. I Part 2:** 492

Rankin, Daniel, **Retro. Supp. II:** 57, 72; **Supp. I Part 1:** 200, 203, 225

Rankin, Tom, **Supp. XXI:** 36

Rankine, Annette, **Supp. XX: 69**

Ranlett, William H., **Supp. XVIII:** 3

Ransohoff, Martin, **Supp. XI:** 305, 306

Ransom, John Crowe, **I:** 265, 301; **II:** 34, 367, 385, 389, 536–537, 542; **III:** 454, **480–502,** 549; **IV:** 121, 122, 123, 124, 125, 127, 134, 140, 141, 236, 237, 433; **Retro. Supp. I:** 90; **Retro. Supp. II:** 176, 177, 178, 183, 220, 228, 246; **Supp. I Part 1:** 80, 361; **Supp. I Part 2:** 423; **Supp. II Part 1:** 90, 91, 136, 137, 139, 318; **Supp. II Part 2:** 639; **Supp. III Part 1:** 318; **Supp. III Part 2:** 542, 591; **Supp. IV Part 1:** 217; **Supp. V:** 315, 331, 337; **Supp. X:** 25, 56, 58; **Supp. XIV:** 1; **Supp. XIX:** 123; **Supp. XXIII:** 145

Ransome, Arthur, **Supp. XXV:** 205

"Rape" (Coleman), **Supp. XI:** 89–90

"Rape, The" (Baraka), **Supp. II Part 1:** 40

Rape of Bunny Stuntz, The (Gurney), **Supp. V:** 109

"Rape of Philomel, The" (Shapiro), **Supp. II Part 2:** 720

"Rape of the Lock, The" (Pope), **Supp. XIV:** 8

Rapf, Joanna, **Supp. XVIII:** 251

Raphael, **I:** 15; **III:** 505, 521, 524; **Supp. I Part 1:** 363

"Rapist" (Dunn), **Supp. XI:** 144

Rap on Race, A (Baldwin and Mead), **Supp. I Part 1:** 66

Rapoport, Nessa, **Supp. XXVI:** 124

"Rappaccini's Daughter" (Hawthorne), **II:** 229

"Rapture of the Deep" (Hempel), **Supp. XXI: 123**

"Rapunzel" (Sexton), **Supp. II Part 2:** 691

Rare & Endangered Species: A Novella & Short Stories (Bausch), **Supp. VII:** 51, 54

"Raree Show" (MacLeish), **III:** 9

Rascoe, Burton, **III:** 106, 115

Raskin, Jonah, **Supp. XV:** 116

Raskin, Saul, **Supp. XXIII:** 6

"Raskolnikov" (Simic), **Supp. VIII:** 282

Rasmussen, Douglas, **Supp. IV Part 2:** 528, 530

Rasmussen, Halfdan, **Supp. XVIII:** 180

Rasselas (S. Johnson), **Supp. XI:** 209

Rathmann, Andrew, **Supp. XV:** 34

Ratiner, Steven, **Supp. XXIII:** 134

"Rat in the Engine" (Espaillat), **Supp. XXI:** 106

"Ration" (Baraka), **Supp. II Part 1:** 50

"Rationale of Verse, The" (Poe), **III:** 427–428; **Retro. Supp. II:** 266

Ratner, Rochelle, **Supp. XV:** 105; **Supp. XXIV:** 168; **Supp. XXVI:** 160

Ratner's Star (DeLillo), **Supp. VI:** 1, 2, 3, 4, 10, 12, 14; **Supp. XVIII:** 140

"Rat of Faith, The" (Levine), **Supp. V:** 192

"Rats in the Walls, The" (Lovecraft), **Supp. XXV:** 109, 112

Rattigan, Terence, **III:** 152

Raugh, Joseph, **Supp. I Part 1:** 286

Rauh, Ida, **Supp. XXI:** 6

Rauschenberg, Robert, **Supp. XV:** 187

Rauschenbusch, Walter, **III:** 293; **Supp. I Part 1:** 7

Ravelstein (Bellow), **Retro. Supp. II:** 19, **33–34**

Raven, Simon, **Supp. XII:** 241

Raven, The (film, Friedlander), **Supp. XVII:** 58

"Raven, The" (Poe), **III:** 413, 421–422, 426; **Retro. Supp. II:** 265, 266–267; **Supp. XVII:** 58

Raven, The, and Other Poems (Poe), **III:** 413

Ravenal, Shannon, **Supp. IV Part 1:** 93

"Raven Days, The" (Lanier), **Supp. I Part 1:** 351

Ravenel, Shannon, **Supp. XXI:** 39

Ravenna, Michael. *See* Welty, Eudora

"Ravens at Deer Creek" (Wrigley), **Supp. XVIII:** 299–300, 306

Raven's Road (Gunn Allen), **Supp. IV Part 1:** 330, 335

Raver, Anne, **Supp. XVIII:** 191

Ravetch, Irving, **Supp. XXV:** 102

"Ravine, The" (Carruth), **Supp. XVI:** 53

Ravits, Martha, **Supp. XXI:** 215

Raw Heaven (Peacock), **Supp. XIX: 196–197**

Rawlings, Marjorie Kinnan, **Supp. X: 219–237; Supp. XVIII:** 194–195

Rawlins, C. L., **Supp. XVII:** 72, 73

Ray, David, **Supp. IV Part 1:** 61

Ray, Janisse, **Supp. XVIII: 189–206**

Ray, Jeanne Wilkinson, **Supp. XII:** 308, 310

Ray, John, **II:** 111, 112

Ray, Man, **IV:** 404; **Retro. Supp. I:** 416; **Supp. XII:** 124; **Supp. XXIII:** 6

Ray, Nicholas, **Supp. XVIII:** 253

Ray Bradbury Theatre, The (television show), **Supp. IV Part 1:** 103

Raymond, Henry J., **Supp. XVIII:** 4

"Raymond and Ann" (Budbill), **Supp. XIX:** 9

"Raymond Andrews as Griot" (Collins), **Supp. XXVI:** 13

Raymond Carver: A Writer's Life (Sklenicka), **Supp. XXIV:** 166

"Raymond Carver: The Kindest Cut" (Wood), **Supp. XXIV:** 166

"Razor's Edge, The" (Wasserstein), **Supp. XV:** 328

Reactionary Essays on Poetry and Ideas (Tate), **Supp. II Part 1:** 106, 146

Read, Deborah, **II:** 122

Read, Forrest, **III:** 478

Read, Herbert, **I:** 523; **II:** 372–373, 377– 378; **Retro. Supp. I:** 54; **Supp. III Part 1:** 273; **Supp. III Part 2:** 624, 626

Read, William A., **Supp. XIV:** 4

Reade, Charles, **Supp. I Part 2:** 580

Reader, Constant. *See* Parker, Dorothy

Reader, Dennis J., **Supp. I Part 2:** 454

"Reader, The" (F. Wright), **Supp. XVII:** 246

Reader's Block (Markson), **Supp. XVII:** 143–145, 146

Reader's Encyclopedia, The: An Encyclopedia of World Literature and the Arts (W. Benét), **Supp. XI:** 44

Reader's Guide to William Gaddis's The Recognitions, A (Moore), **Supp. IV Part 1:** 283

Reader's Map of Arkansas (Wright), **Supp. XV:** 348

"Reader's Tale, A" (Doty), **Supp. XI:** 119, 120, 128, 129

"Reading" (Auden), **Supp. VIII:** 155

"Reading, The" (Di Piero), **Supp. XIX:** 41

"Reading, Writing, Region" (J. W. Miller), **Supp. XX: 165**

"Reading an Anthology of Chinese Poems of the Sung Dynasty, I Pause to Admire the Length and Clarity of Their Titles" (Collins), **Supp. XXI:** 56

"Reading at Forty" (Pickering), **Supp. XXI:** 196

"Reading Group Guide", **Supp. XI:** 244– 245

"Reading Lao Tzu Again in the New Year" (Wright), **Supp. V:** 343

"Reading Late of the Death of Keats" (Kenyon), **Supp. VII:** 169

"Reading Myself" (Lowell), **II:** 555

Reading Myself and Others (P. Roth), **Retro. Supp. II:** 282; **Supp. V:** 45

"Reading *Ode to the West Wind* 25 Years Later" (McCarriston), **Supp. XIV:** 271–272

"Reading of the Psalm, The" (Francis), **Supp. IX:** 79

"Reading Ovid" (Di Piero), **Supp. XIX:** 44

"Reading Philosophy at Night" (Simic), **Supp. VIII:** 272

Reading Rilke: Reflections on the Problems of Translation (Gass), **Supp. VI:** 92, **93–94**

"Reading Rorty and Paul Celan One Morning in Early June" (Wright), **Supp. V:** 343

"Reading Sarcophagi: An Essay" (Sobin), **Supp. XVI:** 290

"Readings of History" (Rich), **Supp. I Part 2:** 554

"Reading the Signs, Empowering the Eye" (Bambara), **Supp. XI:** 17–18

Reading the Spirit (Eberhart), **I:** 525, 527, 530

Ready, Richard M., **Supp. XIX:** 154

"Ready Or Not" (Baraka), **Supp. II Part 1:** 50

Reagan, Ronald, **Supp. IV Part 1:** 224– 225

"Real Bowery, The" (Hapgood), **Supp. XVII:** 103

"Real Class" (Vidal), **Supp. IV Part 1:** 35

Real Cool Killers, The (C. Himes), **Supp. XVI:** 143

Real Dope, The (Lardner), **II:** 422–423

"Real Estate" (Moore), **Supp. X:** 178

"Real Gone Guy, A" (McGrath), **Supp. X:** 117

"Real Horatio Alger Story, The" (Cowley), **Supp. II Part 1:** 143

"Realities" (MacLeish), **III:** 4

"Reality in America" (Trilling), **Supp. III Part 2:** 495, 502

"Reality! Reality! What Is It?" (Eberhart), **I:** 536

Reality Sandwiches, 1953–60 (Ginsberg), **Supp. II Part 1:** 315, 320

"Reality U.S.A." (Halliday), **Supp. XIX:** 89

Real Life of Sebastian Knight, The (Nabokov), **III:** 246; **Retro. Supp. I:** 266, 269, 270, 274

"Really Good Jazz Piano, A" (Yates), **Supp. XI:** 342

"Real Movie, with Stars, The" (Hull), **Supp. XXI:** 136

Real Presence: A Novel (Bausch), **Supp. VII:** 42–43, 50

"Real Revolution Is Love, The" (Harjo), **Supp. XII:** 224, 225–226

"Real Surrounding, The: On Canaletto's Venice" (Bronk), **Supp. XXI:** 32

"Real Thing, The" (H. James), **Retro. Supp. I:** 228; **Retro. Supp. II:** 223

"Real Two-Party System" (Vidal), **Supp. IV Part 2:** 679

Real West Marginal Way, The (Hugo), **Supp. VI:** 132, 134; **Supp. XVIII:** 299

"Real World around Us, The" (Carson), **Supp. IX:** 21

Reaper Essays, The (Jarman and McDowell), **Supp. IX:** 270; **Supp. XVII:** 110–111

"*Reaper* Interviews Jean Doh and Sean Dough, The" (Jarman and McDowell), **Supp. XVII:** 110

"Reapers" (Toomer), **Supp. III Part 2:** 481; **Supp. IX:** 312

Reason and Other Women (Notley), **Supp. XXII:** 224, 227, 235, 236, 237

"Reason and Race: A Review of the Literature of the Negro for 1946" (Locke), **Supp. XIV:** 206

"Reason for Moving, A" (Strand), **Supp. IV Part 2:** 624

"Reason for Stories, The: Toward a Moral Fiction" (Stone), **Supp. V:** 298, 300

Reasons for Moving (Strand), **Supp. IV Part 2:** 624–626, 626

"Reasons for Music" (MacLeish), **III:** 19

"Reasons of the Body" (Sanders), **Supp. XVI:** 274

Reasons to Live (Hempel), **Supp. XXI:** 115, 117, 118, **119–122**

Rebecca (du Maurier), **Supp. XIX:** 57– 58; **Supp. XXII:** 120

Rebecca, or, The Fille de Chambre (Rowson), **Supp. XV:** 229, **235–236**, 238

Rebecca Harding Davis Reader, A (Pfaelzer, ed.), **Supp. XVI:** 88, 90

Rebel Angels: Twenty-five Poets of the New Formalism (Jarman and Mason, eds.), **Supp. XV:** 251; **Supp. XVII:** 109, 110, 112, 121

"Rebellion" (Lowell), **Retro. Supp. II:** 187

Rebel Powers (Bausch), **Supp. VII:** 41, 45–46, 49–51

Rebel without a Cause (film), **Supp. XII:** 9

"Rebirth" (McKnight), **Supp. XX: 147, 157**

"Rebirth of God and the Death of Man, The " (Fiedler), **Supp. XIII:** 108

Rebolledo, Tey Diana, **Supp. XIII:** 214

Reb Shloyme nogid: A poeme fun yidishn leben (Shloyme the wealthy: A poem of Jewish life)(Asch), **Supp. XXIII:** 4, 5

Recapitulation (Stegner), **Supp. IV Part 2:** 598, 600, 612–613

"Recapitulation, The" (Eberhart), **I:** 522

"Recapitulations" (Shapiro), **Supp. II Part 2:** 701, 702, 708, 710–711

"Receding Horizons" (Lethem and Scholtz), **Supp. XVIII:** 145

"Recencies in Poetry" (Zukofsky), **Supp. III Part 2:** 615

Recent Killing, A (Baraka), **Supp. II Part 1:** 55

"Recent Negro Fiction" (Ellison), **Supp. II Part 1:** 233, 235

"Recessional" (A. Finch), **Supp. XVII:** 70–71

"Recital, The" (Ashbery), **Supp. III Part 1:** 14

"Recitative" (H. Crane), **I:** 390; **Retro. Supp. II:** 78

Reckless Eyeballing (Reed), **Supp. X:** 241

Reckless Moment, The (film), **Supp. XXII:** 120, 131, 132

Recognitions, The (Gaddis), **Supp. IV Part 1:** 279, 280–285, 286, 287, 288, 289, 291, 292, 294; **Supp. XX: 91; Supp. XXIV:** 140

"Recollection and Perhaps a Tribute, A" (Espaillat), **Supp. XXI:** 103–104

Recollections (R. H. Stoddard), **Supp. XV:** 271

Recollections of Logan Pearsall Smith: The Story of a Friendship (Gathorne-

Hardy), **Supp. XIV:** 344

"Reconciliation" (Whitman), **IV:** 347

"Reconstructed but Unregenerate" (Ransom), **III:** 496

"Reconstruction and Its Benefits" (Du Bois), **Supp. II Part 1:** 171

Recovering (Sarton), **Supp. VIII:** 264

Recovering the U.S. Hispanic Literary Heritage (Paredes), **Supp. XIII:** 320

"Recovery" (Dove), **Supp. IV Part 1:** 248

Re-Creation Story (Gansworth), **Supp. XXVI:** 113–114

Rector of Justin, The (Auchincloss), **Supp. IV Part 1:** 21, 23, 27–30, 36

"Recurrent Dream" (Nelson), **Supp. XVIII:** 176

"RED AUTUMN" (Baraka), **Supp. II Part 1:** 55

Red Badge of Courage, The (S. Crane), **I:** 201, 207, 212, 405, 406, 407, 408, 412–416, 419, 421, 422, 423, 477, 506; **II:** 264; **III:** 317; **IV:** 350; **Retro. Supp. II:** 108; **Supp. IV Part 1:** 380; **Supp. XIV:** 51; **Supp. XVII:** 228; **Supp. XVIII:** 75; **Supp. XXI:** 277

"Redbirds" (C. Frost), **Supp. XV:** 99

"Red Bow, The" (Saunders), **Supp. XIX:** 232–233, 234

"Redbreast in Tampa" (Lanier), **Supp. I Part 1:** 364

"Red Brocade" (Nye), **Supp. XIII:** 288

Redburn: His First Voyage (Melville), **III:** 79–80, 84; **Retro. Supp. I:** 245, 247–248, 249; **Supp. XVIII:** 6

Red Calico (Miller and Bowden), **Supp. XXII:** 188

"Red Carpet for Shelley, A" (Wylie), **Supp. I Part 2:** 724

Red Channels (Harnett), **Supp. XV:** 198

"Red Clowns" (Cisneros), **Supp. VII:** 63

Red Coal, The (Stern), **Supp. IX:** 291–292

Red Coat, The (Shanley), **Supp. XIV:** 316–317

"Red Cords" (Lamott), **Supp. XX:** 142

"Red"(Crooker), **Supp. XXIII:** 63

"Red Cross" (Hughes), **Retro. Supp. I:** 205

Red Cross (Shepard), **Supp. III Part 2:** 440, 446

Red Death, A (Mosley), **Supp. XIII:** 237, 239, 240

"Red Deer" (C. Frost), **Supp. XV:** 101

Redding, Josephine, **Supp. XXI:** 2

Redding, Saunders, **Supp. I Part 1:** 332, 333

Reddings, J. Saunders, **Supp. IV Part 1:** 164

Red Dust (Levine), **Supp. V:** 178, 183–184, 188

"Red Dust" (Levine), **Supp. V:** 184

"Redemption" (Gardner), **Supp. VI:** 72

Redemption (Uris), **Supp. XX: 244, 246, 247, 248, 254, 255**

"Red Ensign, The" (Gallagher), **Supp. XXIV:** 175, 176

"Redeployment" (Nemerov), **III:** 267, 272

Redfield, Robert, **IV:** 475

Redford, Robert, **Supp. IX:** 253, 259; **Supp. XIII:** 267; **Supp. XIV:** 223

Redgrave, Lynn, **Supp. V:** 107

Red Harvest (Hammett), **Supp. IV Part 1:** 346–348, 348; **Supp. IV Part 2:** 468; **Supp. XXI:** 272

"Red Hat, The"(Hadas), **Supp. XXIII:** 111, 113, 118, 119, 124, 128

Red-Headed Woman (film), **Retro. Supp. I:** 110; **Supp. XVI:** 191

"Red Horse Wind over Albuquerque" (Harjo), **Supp. XII:** 219

Red Hot Vacuum, The (Solotaroff), **Retro. Supp. II:** 281

Rediscovery of America, The (W. Frank), **Supp. XX:** 75

Rediscovery of Man, The (W. Frank), **Supp. XX: 67–68, 80**

"Red Leaves" (Faulkner), **II:** 72

"Red Meat: What Difference Did Stesichoros Make?" (Carson), **Supp. XII:** 107

"Red Pawn" (Rand), **Supp. IV Part 2:** 520

Red Pony, The (Steinbeck), **IV:** 50, 51, 58, 70

Redrawing the Boundaries (Fisher), **Retro. Supp. I:** 39

Red Robins, The (Koch), **Supp. XV:** 185–186, 187

Red Roses for Bronze (Doolittle), **Supp. I Part 1:** 253, 268, 271

Red Rover, The (Cooper), **I:** 342–343, 355

Reds (Beatty), **Supp. XXIV:** 227

"Red Shift" (Berrigan), **Supp. XXIV:** 46

"Red Silk Stockings" (Hughes), **Retro. Supp. I:** 200

Redskins, The (Cooper), **I:** 351, 353

Red Sox and Bluefish: And Other Things That Make New England New England (Orlean), **Supp. XXV:** 159

"Red Sox Nation, North" (Mosher), **Supp. XXII:** 209

"Red Star, Winter Orbit" (W. Gibson and B. Sterling), **Supp. XVI:** 123

Red Suitcase (Nye), **Supp. XIII:** 277, 278, 287

Red the Fiend (Sorrentino), **Supp. XXI:** 227, 231, 237

Red Wallflower, A (S. Warner), **Supp. XVIII:** 260

"Red Wheelbarrow, The" (W. C. Williams), **IV:** 411–412; **Retro. Supp. I:** 419, 430

"Red Wind" (Chandler), **Supp. IV Part 1:** 122

"Red Wing Church, The" (Kooser), **Supp. XIX:** 119

"Redwings" (Wright), **Supp. III Part 2:** 603

Reed, Edward Bliss, **Supp. XV:** 297, 298, 300

Reed, Ishmael, **Retro. Supp. II:** 111, 324–325; **Supp. II Part 1:** 34; **Supp. X:** 239–257, 331; **Supp. XIII:** 181, 182; **Supp. XVI:** 143; **Supp. XX:** 107; **Supp. XXII:** 172

Reed, J. D., **Supp. XVI:** 174

Reed, John, **I:** 48, 476, 483; **Supp. X:** 136; **Supp. XV:** 295, 299; **Supp. XVII:** 96, 99, 100; **Supp. XVIII:** 225; **Supp. XXI:** 6, 12; **Supp. XXII:** 274, 275; **Supp. XXIII:** 161, 162

Reed, Lou, **Retro. Supp. II:** 266

"Reedbeds of the Hackensack, The" (Clampitt), **Supp. IX:** 41

"Reed of Pan, A" (McCullers), **II:** 585

Reedy, Billy, **Retro. Supp. II:** 65, 67, 71, 73

Reedy, William Marion, **Supp. I Part 2:** 456, 461, 465

Reef, The (Wharton), **IV:** 317–318, 322; **Retro. Supp. I:** 372, **373–374**

Reena and Other Stories (Marshall), **Supp. XI:** 275, 277, 278

Reese, Debbie, **Supp. XXVI:** 108–109

"Reese in Evening Shadow" (Skloot), **Supp. XX: 204**

Reeve, F. D., **Supp. XV:** 344, 349

Reeve's Tale (Chaucer), **I:** 131

"Refiguring the Postcolonial Imagination: Tropes of Visuality in Writing by Rhys, Kincaid, and Cliff" (Emery), **Supp. XXII:** 73

Refiner's Fire: The Life and Adventures of Marshall Pearl, a Foundling (Helprin), **Supp. XXV:** 83, 85–86

"Reflection from Anita Loos" (Empson), **Supp. XVI:** 190

"Reflections" (Carruth), **Supp. XVI:** 54

"Reflections" (Komunyakaa), **Supp. XIII:** 117

Reflections at Fifty and Other Essays (Farrell), **II:** 49

"Reflections by a Fire" (Sarton), **Supp. VIII:** 259

Reflections in a Golden Eye (McCullers), **II:** 586, 588, 593–596, 604; **IV:** 384, 396

Reflections of a Jacobite (Auchincloss), **Supp. IV Part 1:** 31

Reflections on a Gift of Watermelon Pickle (Dunning), **Supp. XIV:** 126

Reflections on Poetry and Poetics (Nemerov), **III:** 269

"Reflections on the Constitution of Nature" (Freneau), **Supp. II Part 1:** 274

"Reflections on the Death of the Reader" (Morris), **III:** 237

Reflections on the End of an Era (Niebuhr), **III:** 297–298

"Reflections on the Life and Death of Lord Clive" (Paine), **Supp. I Part 2:** 505

Reflections on the Revolution in France (Burke), **Supp. I Part 2:** 511, 512

Reflections: Thinking Part I (Arendt), **Supp. I Part 2:** 570

"Reflex Action and Theism" (James), **II:** 345, 363

Reflex and Bone Structure (Major), **Supp. XXII: 174–175**

"Refrains/Remains/Reminders" (Goldbarth), **Supp. XII:** 180–181, 181

"Refuge" (Kingsolver), **Supp. VII:** 208

"Refuge, A" (Goldbarth), **Supp. XII:** 190

Refugee Children: Theory, Research, and Services (Ahearn and Athey, eds.), **Supp. XI:** 184

"Refugees, The" (Jarrell), **II:** 371

"Refusal" (C. Frost), **Supp. XV:** 102
"Refusal to Publish Fifth Book" (Halliday), **Supp. XIX:** 94
"Regalia" (H. Johnson), **Supp. XXVI:** 172
Regarding Wave (Snyder), **Supp. VIII: 299–300**
Regina (Epstein), **Supp. XII: 170–171**
"Regional Literature of the South" (Rawlings), **Supp. X:** 228
"Regional Writer, The" (O'Connor), **Retro. Supp. II:** 223, 225
Régnier, Henri de, **II:** 528–529
Regulators, The (King), **Supp. V:** 141
Rehder, Robert, **Supp. IV Part 1:** 69
Rehearsing Absence (Espaillat), **Supp. XXI:** 99
Reich, Tova, **Supp. XVI:** 158
Reichel, Hans, **III:** 183
Reichl, Ruth, **Supp. X:** 79, 85
Reid, B. L., **II:** 41, 47
Reid, Forrest, **Supp. XX:** 235
Reid, Thomas, **II:** 9; **Supp. I Part 1:** 151
Reign of Snakes (Wrigley), **Supp. XVIII:** 293, **302–306**
"Reign of Snakes" (Wrigley), **Supp. XVIII:** 302–304
Reign of Wonder, The (Tanner), **I:** 260
Rein, Yevgeny, **Supp. VIII:** 22
Reinagle, Alexander, **Supp. XV:** 238, 240
"Reincarnation" (Dickey), **Supp. IV Part 1:** 181–182
Reine des pommes, La (C. Himes). *See For Love of Imabelle* (C. Himes)
Reiner, Carl, **Supp. IV Part 2:** 591
Reinfeld, Linda, **Supp. IV Part 2:** 421
Reinhardt, Max, **Supp. XV:** 307
Reinventing the Enemy's Language: Contemporary Native Women's Writing of North America (Bird and Harjo, eds.), **Supp. XII:** 216, 217
Reisman, Jerry, **Supp. III Part 2:** 618
Reiter, Amy, **Supp. XIX:** 54, 56
Reitlinger, Gerald, **Supp. XII:** 161
Reivers, The: A Reminiscence (Faulkner), **I:** 305; **II:** 57, 73; **Retro. Supp. I:** 74, 82, 91
"Rejoicings" (Stern), **Supp. IX:** 289–290
Rejoicings: Selected Poems, 1966–1972 (Stern), **Supp. IX: 289–290**
Relation of My Imprisonment, The (Banks), **Supp. V:** 8, 12–13
"Relations" (Biss), **Supp. XXVI:** 56
"Relations between Poetry and Painting, The" (Stevens), **Retro. Supp. I:** 312
Relations of the Alabama-Georgia Dialect to the Provincial Dialects of Great Britain, The (Brooks), **Supp. XIV:** 3
Relative Stranger, A (C. Baxter), **Supp. XVII:** 19, 22
"Relativity of Beauty, The" (Rawlings), **Supp. X:** 226
Relearning the Alphabet (Levertov), **Supp. III Part 1:** 280, 281
"Release" (C. Baxter), **Supp. XVII:** 15
"Release, The" (MacLeish), **III:** 16
Reles, Abe ("Kid Twist"), **Supp. IV Part 1:** 382
"Relevance of an Impossible Ethical Ideal, The" (Niebuhr), **III:** 298

"Religion" (Dunbar), **Supp. II Part 1:** 199
"Religion" (Emerson), **II:** 6
Religion of Nature Delineated, The (Wollaston), **II:** 108
"Religious Instruction" (Peacock), **Supp. XIX:** 200, 201
Religious Rebel, A: The Letters of "H. W. S." (Mrs. Pearsall Smith) (L. P. Smith), **Supp. XIV:** 349
"Reluctance" (Frost), **II:** 153
Reluctantly: Autobiographical Essays (Carruth), **Supp. XVI:** 45–46, 50
Remains (Snodgrass), **Supp. VI:** 311, **313–314**
"Remains, The" (Strand), **Supp. IV Part 2:** 627
"Remains of Princess Kaiulani's Garden, The" (Vaz), **Supp. XXVI:** 262–263
"Remarks on Color" (Wright), **Supp. XV:** 346
"Remarks on National Literature" (Channing), **Supp. XXIV:** 76–77
"Remarks on Spencer's *Definition of Mind as Correspondence*" (James), **II:** 345
Remarque, Erich Maria, **Retro. Supp. I:** 113; **Supp. IV Part 1:** 380
Rembrandt, **II:** 536; **IV:** 310; **Supp. IV Part 1:** 390, 391
"Rembrandt, The" (Wharton), **IV:** 310
"Rembrandt's Hat" (Malamud), **Supp. I Part 2:** 435, 437
Rembrandt Takes a Walk (Strand), **Supp. IV Part 2:** 631
"Rembrandt to Rembrandt" (Robinson), **III:** 521–522
Remembered Earth, The: An Anthology of Contemporary Native American Literature (Hobson, ed.), **Supp. IV Part 1:** 321
Remembered Yesterdays (R. U. Johnson), **Supp. IX:** 184
"Remembering" (Angelou), **Supp. IV Part 1:** 15
"Remembering Allen Tate" (Cowley), **Supp. II Part 1:** 153
"Remembering Barthes" (Sontag), **Supp. III Part 2:** 451, 471
"Remembering Guston" (Kunitz), **Supp. III Part 1:** 257
"Remembering James Laughlin" (Karr), **Supp. XI:** 242
Remembering Laughter (Stegner), **Supp. IV Part 2:** 598, 606, 607, 608, 611, 614
"Remembering Lobo" (Mora), **Supp. XIII:** 220, 227
"Remembering My Father" (Berry), **Supp. X:** 23
"Remembering My Parents Remembering the Books They Read" (Espaillat), **Supp. XXI:** 107
"Remembering that Island" (McGrath), **Supp. X:** 116
"Remembering the Children of Auschwitz" (McGrath), **Supp. X:** 127
"Remembering the Lost World" (Jarrell), **II:** 388

"Remembering the Sixties" (Simpson), **Supp. IX:** 279
Remember Me to Tom (T. Williams), **IV:** 379–380
"Remember Not" (H. Johnson), **Supp. XXVI:** 166
"Remember the Moon Survives" (Kingsolver), **Supp. VII:** 209
Remember to Remember (H. Miller), **III:** 186
"Remembrance, A" (Gioia), **Supp. XV:** 112
Remembrance of Things Past (Proust), **Supp. IV Part 2:** 600; **Supp. XII:** 9; **Supp. XIII:** 44
Remembrance Rock (Sandburg), **III:** 590
Reminiscence, A (Ashbery), **Supp. III Part 1:** 2
Remnick, David, **Supp. XVI:** 246
"Remora" (Merrill), **Supp. III Part 1:** 326
"Removal" (White), **Supp. I Part 2:** 664–665
"Removal, The" (Merwin), **Supp. III Part 1:** 350, 351
"Removal Service Request" (Halliday), **Supp. XIX:** 90
Removed from Time (Matthews and Feeney), **Supp. IX:** 154
Remsen, Ira, **Supp. I Part 1:** 369
"Rémy de Gourmont, A Distinction" (Pound), **III:** 467
"Renaissance" (Carruth), **Supp. XVI:** 56
Renaissance in the South (Bradbury), **I:** 288–289
Renaldo and Clara (film, Dylan and Shepard), **Supp. XVIII:** 21, 28, 31
"Renaming the Kings" (Levine), **Supp. V:** 184
Renan, Ernest, **Supp. XX: 122**
Renan, Joseph Ernest, **II:** 86; **IV:** 440, 444
Renard, Jules, **IV:** 79
"Renascence" (Millay), **III:** 123, 125–126, 128; **Supp. XV:** 42
Renault, Mary, **Supp. IV Part 2:** 685
"Rendezvous, The" (Kumin), **Supp. IV Part 2:** 455
René, Norman, **Supp. X:** 146, 152
Renée (anonymous author), **Supp. XVI:** 64, 66
"Renegade, The" (Jackson), **Supp. IX:** 120
Renewal of Life series (Mumford), **Supp. II Part 2:** 476, 479, 481, 482, 485, 495, 497
"Reno Hill ... Little Bighorn"(Kenny), **Supp. XXIII:** 155
Renoir, Jean, **Supp. XII:** 259; **Supp. XXII:** 256
Renouvrier, Charles, **II:** 344–345, 346
"Renunciation" (Banks), **Supp. V:** 10
Renza, Louis A., **Retro. Supp. II:** 142
"Repair" (Peacock), **Supp. XIX:** 204
"Repeating Dream" (Gander), **Supp. XV:** 340
Repent in Haste (Marquand), **III:** 59
Reperusals and Re-Collections (L. P. Smith), **Supp. XIV:** 346–347

"Repetitive Heart, The: Eleven Poems in Imitation of the Fugue Form" (Schwartz), **Supp. II Part 2:** 645–646

"Replacing Regionalism" (Murphy), **Retro. Supp. II:** 143

Replansky, Naomi, **Supp. X:** 119

Replenishing Jessica (Bodenheim), **Supp. XXV:** 24, 25

"Reply to Mr. Wordsworth" (MacLeish), **III:** 19

"Report, A" (Jin), **Supp. XVIII:** 93

"Report from a Forest Logged by the Weyhaeuser Company" (Wagoner), **Supp. IX:** 328

"Report from North Vietnam" (Paley), **Supp. VI:** 227

Report from Part One (Brooks), **Supp. III Part 1:** 70, 72, 80, 82–85

Report from Part Two (Brooks), **Supp. III Part 1:** 87

Report on a Game Survey of the North Central States (Leopold), **Supp. XIV:** 182

"Report on the Barnhouse Effect" (Vonnegut), **Supp. II Part 2:** 756

"Report to an Academy, A" (Kafka), **Supp. XX: 18**

"Report to Crazy Horse" (Stafford), **Supp. XI: 324–325**

"Repose of Rivers" (H. Crane), **I:** 393; **Retro. Supp. II:** 78, 81

"Repossession of a Heritage, The" (Zagarell), **Supp. XV:** 270, 281

Repp, John, **Supp. XXIII:** 302

"Representation and the War for Reality" (Gass), **Supp. VI:** 88

"Representative Indian, The" *(Outlook),* **Supp. XXV:** 277, 278

Representative Men (Emerson), **II:** 1, 5–6, 8

"Representing Far Places" (Stafford), **Supp. XI:** 321

Repression and Recovery (Nelson), **Supp. XVIII:** 226

"REPRISE OF ONE OF A. G.'S BEST POEMS" (Baraka), **Supp. II Part 1:** 59

"RepRoach" (Stallings), **Supp. XXV:** 230–231

"Reproducing Ourselves Is All Very Well" (E. Hoffman), **Supp. XVI:** 155

Republic (Plato), **I:** 485

"Republican Manifesto, A" (Paine), **Supp. I Part 2:** 511

"Republican Mother, The: Woman and the Enlightenment—An American Perspective" (Kerber), **Supp. XXV:** 44

Republic of Love, The (Shields), **Supp. VII:** 323–324, 326, 327

"Requa" (Olsen), **Supp. XIII:** 294, **302– 303,** 304

Requa, Kenneth A., **Supp. I Part 1:** 107

"Requa I" (Olsen). *See* "Requa" (Olsen)

"Request for Offering" (Eberhart), **I:** 526

"Requiem" (Akhmatova), **Supp. VIII:** 20

"Requiem" (LaBastille), **Supp. X:** 105

Requiem for a Nun (Faulkner), **II:** 57, 72–73

Requiem for Harlem (H. Roth), **Supp. IX:** 235, 236, **240–242**

"Rescue, The" (Updike), **IV:** 214

Rescued Year, The (Stafford), **Supp. XI: 321–322**

"Rescued Year, The" (Stafford), **Supp. XI:** 322, 323

"Rescue with Yul Brynner" (Moore), **III:** 215

"Rescuing Moon"(P. Benedict), **Supp. XXIII:** 40

"Resemblance" (Bishop), **Supp. I Part 1:** 86

"Resemblance" (Ferry), **Supp. XXIV:** 161

"Resemblance between a Violin Case and a Coffin, A" (T. Williams), **IV:** 378– 379

"Reservations" (Taylor), **Supp. V:** 323

"Reserved Memorials" (Mather), **Supp. II Part 2:** 446, 449

"Resignación" (Espaillat), **Supp. XXI:** 104

"Resignation"(J. Schoolcraft), **Supp. XXIII:** 228, 229–230

"Resistance to Civil Government" (Thoreau), **Supp. X:** 27, 28

Resist Much, Obey Little (Berry), **Supp. XIII:** 2

"Resolution" (Parker), **Supp. XIX:** 187

"Resolution and Independence" (Wordsworth), **Supp. XV:** 346

"Resort" (Hampl), **Supp. XXII:** 86–87

Resort and Other Poems (Hampl), **Supp. XXII:** 83, 86–87

Resources of Hope (R. Williams), **Supp. IX:** 146

"Respectable Place, A" (O'Hara), **III:** 369

"Respectable Woman, A" (Chopin), **Retro. Supp. II:** 66

"Respite" (Pedersen; Nelson, trans.), **Supp. XVIII:** 180

Responses (Wilbur), **Supp. III Part 2:** 541

"Response to a Rumor that the Oldest Whorehouse in Wheeling, West Virginia, Has Been Condemned" (Wright), **Supp. III Part 2:** 602

"Rest Cure" (Boyle), **Supp. XXIV:** 57

Restif de La Bretonne, Nicolas, **III:** 175

"Rest of Life, The" (Gordon), **Supp. IV Part 1:** 311

Rest of Life, The: Three Novellas (Gordon), **Supp. IV Part 1:** 310–312

Rest of My Life, The (Wells), **Supp. XXVI:** 271, 283

Rest of the Way, The (McClatchy), **Supp. XII:** 255, **258–259**

Restoration comedy, **Supp. I Part 2:** 617

Restorers, The (Di Piero), **Supp. XIX:** 42–43, 44

"Restorers, The" (Di Piero), **Supp. XIX:** 43

"Restraint" (F. Barthelme), **Supp. XI:** 26

"Result" (Emerson), **II:** 6

"Résumé" (Parker), **Supp. IX:** 189

"Resurrecting Methuselah" (E. P. Jones), **Supp. XXII:** 151

Resurrection (Della Francesca), **Supp. XV:** 262

"Resurrection" (Harjo), **Supp. XII:** 224

"Resurrection" (Jin), **Supp. XVIII:** 94–95

Resurrection, The (Gardner), **Supp. VI:** 61, 63, **64–65,** 68, 69, 73, 74

"Resurrection, The" (Very), **Supp. XXV:** 247–248

"Retort" (Hay), **Supp. XIV:** 133

Retour amont (Char; Sobin, trans.), **Supp. XVI:** 282

Retrieval System, The (Kumin), **Supp. IV Part 2:** 449, 451, 452

"Retrievers in Translation" (Doty), **Supp. XI:** 132

"Retroduction to American History" (Tate), **IV:** 129

"Retrospects and Prospects" (Lanier), **Supp. I Part 1:** 352

"Return" (Corso), **Supp. XII:** 135

"Return" (Creeley), **Supp. IV Part 1:** 141, 145

"Return" (MacLeish), **III:** 12

"Return" (Oppen), **Supp. XXVI:** 231

"Return, The" (Bidart), **Supp. XV:** 32–33

"Return, The" (Bontemps), **Supp. XXII:** 3, 8

"Return, The" (Pound), **Retro. Supp. I:** 288

"Return, The" (Ray), **Supp. XVIII:** 194

"Return, The" (Roethke), **III:** 533

"Return, The: Orihuela, 1965" (Levine), **Supp. V:** 194

"Return: An Elegy, The" (Warren), **IV:** 239

"Return: Buffalo" (Hogan), **Supp. IV Part 1:** 411

"Returning" (Komunyakaa), **Supp. XIII:** 122

"Returning a Lost Child" (Glück), **Supp. V:** 81

"Returning from the Enemy" (Harjo), **Supp. XII:** 229–230

"Returning the Borrowed Road" (Komunyakaa), **Supp. XIII:** 113, 133

"Return of Alcibiade, The" (Chopin), **Retro. Supp. II:** 58, 64

Return of Ansel Gibbs, The (Buechner), **III:** 310; **Supp. XII: 48**

"Return of Eros to Academe, The" (Bukiet), **Supp. XVII:** 47

"Return of Spring" (Winters), **Supp. II Part 2:** 791

Return of the Native, The (Hardy), **II:** 184–185, 186

Return of the Vanishing American, The (Fiedler), **Supp. XIII:** 103

Return to a Place Lit by a Glass of Milk (Simic), **Supp. VIII:** 274, 276, 283

"Return to Lavinia" (Caldwell), **I:** 310

"Return to Thin Air: The Everest Disaster Ten Years Later" *(Outside),* **Supp. XVIII:** 113

Return to Zion, The (Asch), **Supp. XXIII:** 5

Reuben (Wideman), **Supp. X:** 320

Reuben and Rachel; or, Tales of Old Times (Rowson), **Supp. XV: 240–241**

Reunion (Mamet), **Supp. XIV:** 240, 247, 254

"Reunion in Brooklyn" (H. Miller), **III:** 175, 184

"Reunion Joke, The" (Huddle), **Supp. XXVI:** 156

Reuther brothers, **I:** 493

"Reveille" (Kingsolver), **Supp. VII:** 208

"Reveille" (Untermeyer), **Supp. XV:** 300

"Reveille, The" (Harte), **Supp. II Part 1:** 342–343

Revelation (biblical book), **II:** 541; **IV:** 104, 153, 154; **Supp. I Part 1:** 105, 273

"Revelation" (O'Connor), **III:** 349, 353–354; **Retro. Supp. II:** 237

"Revelation" (Warren), **III:** 490

Revenge (Harrison), **Supp. VIII:** 39, 45

"Revenge of Hamish, The" (Lanier), **Supp. I Part 1:** 365

"Revenge of Hannah Kemhuff, The" (Walker), **Supp. III Part 2:** 521

"Revenge of Rain-in-the-Face, The" (Longfellow), **Retro. Supp. II:** 170

"Reverberation"(Kenny), **Supp. XXIII:** 155

Reverberator, The (James), **Retro. Supp. I:** 227

"Reverdure" (Berry), **Supp. X:** 22

Reverdy, Pierre, **Supp. XV:** 178, 182; **Supp. XXIII:** 208

"Reverend Father Gilhooley" (Farrell), **II:** 45

Reverse Transcription (Kushner), **Supp. IX:** 138

Reversible Errors (Turow), **Supp. XVII:** 220–221

"Rev. Freemont Deadman" (Masters), **Supp. I Part 2:** 463

Reviewer's ABC, A (Aiken), **I:** 58

Review of Contemporary Fiction, 1990 (Tabbi, ed.), **Supp. XVII:** 143

"Revolt, against the Crepuscular Spirit in Modern Poetry" (Pound), **Retro. Supp. I:** 286

"Revolution" (C. L. R. James), **Supp. XXI:** 160

"Revolution" (Taggard), **Supp. XXII:** 275

"Revolutionary Answer to the Negro Problem in the USA, The" (statement, C. L. R. James), **Supp. XXI:** 169

Revolutionary Petunias (Walker), **Supp. III Part 2:** 520, 522, 530

Revolutionary Road (Yates), **Supp. XI:** 334, **335–340**

"Revolutionary Symbolism in America" (Burke), **I:** 272

"Revolutionary Theatre, The" (Baraka), **Supp. II Part 1:** 42

Revolution in Taste, A: Studies of Dylan Thomas, Allen Ginsberg, Sylvia Plath, and Robert Lowell (Simpson), **Supp. IX:** 276

"Revolution in the Revolution in the Revolution" (Snyder), **Supp. VIII:** 300

Revon, Marcel, **II:** 525

"Rewaking, The" (W. C. Williams), **Retro. Supp. I:** 430

"Rewrite" (Dunn), **Supp. XI:** 147

"Rewriting Tradition in the Digital Era: The Vision of Eric Gansworth" (Purdy), **Supp. XXVI:** 105

Rexroth, Kenneth, **II:** 526; **Supp. II Part 1:** 307; **Supp. II Part 2:** 436; **Supp. III Part 2:** 625, 626; **Supp. IV Part 1:** 145–146; **Supp. VIII:** 289; **Supp. XIII:** 75; **Supp. XIV:** 287; **Supp. XV:** 140, 141, 146; **Supp. XXII:** 168

Reynolds, Ann (pseudonym). *See* Bly, Carol

Reynolds, Clay, **Supp. XI:** 254

Reynolds, David, **Supp. XV:** 269; **Supp. XXIII:** 187

Reynolds, Sir Joshua, **Supp. I Part 2:** 716

Reynolds, Quentin, **IV:** 286

Reza, Yasmina, **Supp. XXI:** 148

Rezanov (Atherton), **Supp. XXIV:** 23

Reznikoff, Charles, **IV:** 415; **Retro. Supp. I:** 422; **Supp. III Part 2:** 615, 616, 617, 628; **Supp. XIV: 277–296; Supp. XXIII:** 174; **Supp. XXIV:** 36, 45; **Supp. XXVI:** 226

"Rhapsodist, The" (Brown), **Supp. I Part 1:** 125–126

"Rhapsody on a Windy Night" (Eliot), **Retro. Supp. I:** 55

Rhetoric of Motives, A (Burke), **I:** 272, 275, 278, 279

Rhetoric of Religion, The (Burke), **I:** 275, 279

"Rhobert" (Toomer), **Supp. IX:** 316–317

"Rhode Show" (Mallon), **Supp. XIX:** 137–138

"Rhododendrons" (Levis), **Supp. XI:** 260, 263

Rhubarb Show, The (radio, Keillor), **Supp. XVI:** 178

"Rhyme of Sir Christopher, The" (Longfellow), **II:** 501

Rhymes to Be Traded for Bread (Lindsay), **Supp. I Part 2:** 380, 381–382

Rhys, Ernest, **III:** 458

Rhys, Jean, **Supp. III Part 1:** 42, 43; **Supp. XVIII:** 131

"Rhythm & Blues" (Baraka), **Supp. II Part 1:** 37–38

Rhythms (Reznikoff), **Supp. XIV:** 279, 282, 283

Rhythms II (Reznikoff), **Supp. XIV:** 282, 283, 284

Ribalow, Harold, **Supp. IX:** 236

Ribbentrop, Joachim von, **IV:** 249

Ribicoff, Abraham, **Supp. IX:** 33

Ribot, Théodule Armand, **Supp. XX: 238**

Ricardo, David, **Supp. I Part 2:** 628, 634

Rice, Allen Thorndike, **Retro. Supp. I:** 362

Rice, Anne, **Supp. VII: 287–306**

Rice, Elmer, **I:** 479; **III:** 145, 160–161

Rice, Mrs. Grantland, **II:** 435

Rice, Philip Blair, **IV:** 141

Rice, Stan, **Supp. XII:** 2

Rice, Tim, **Supp. XXI:** 148

Rice, Tom, **Supp. XIV:** 125

Rich, Adrienne, **Retro. Supp. I:** 8, 36, 42, 47, 404; **Retro. Supp. II:** 43, 191, 245; **Supp. I Part 2:** 546–547, **550–578; Supp. III Part 1:** 84, 354; **Supp. III Part 2:** 541, 599; **Supp. IV Part 1:** 257, 325; **Supp. V:** 82; **Supp. VIII:** 272; **Supp. XII:** 217, 229, 255; **Supp.**

XIII: 294; **Supp. XIV:** 126, 129; **Supp. XIX:** 83, 193; **Supp. XV:** 176, 252; **Supp. XVII:** 32, 74; **Supp. XXII:** 65, 66; **Supp. XXV:** 3; **Supp. XXVI:** 45, 68

Rich, Arnold, **Supp. I Part 2:** 552

Rich, Frank, **Supp. IV Part 2:** 585, 586; **Supp. V:** 106; **Supp. XXI:** 146; **Supp. XXIV:** 121, 124

Richard, Mark, **Supp. XIX: 209–222**

Richard Cory (Gurney), **Supp. V:** 99–100, 105

"Richard Hunt's 'Arachne' " (Hayden), **Supp. II Part 1:** 374

Richard II (Shakespeare), **Supp. XVII:** 244

Richard III (Shakespeare), **Supp. I Part 2:** 422

Richards, Bertrand F., **Supp. XX: 217–218**

Richards, Constance S., **Supp. XXII:** 73

Richards, David, **Supp. IV Part 2:** 576; **Supp. XXIV:** 266, 269

Richards, Grant, **I:** 515

Richards, I. A., **I:** 26, 273–274, 279, 522; **III:** 498; **IV:** 92; **Supp. I Part 1:** 264, 265; **Supp. I Part 2:** 647; **Supp. XXVI:** 63

Richards, Ivor Armonstrong, **Supp. XIV:** 2–3, 16

Richards, Laura E., **II:** 396; **III:** 505–506, 507

Richards, Leonard, **Supp. XIV:** 48

Richards, Lloyd, **Supp. IV Part 1:** 362; **Supp. VIII:** 331

Richards, Rosalind, **III:** 506

Richards, Tad, **Supp. XVII:** 77

Richardson, Alan, **III:** 295

Richardson, Charles, **Supp. XVIII:** 14, 15

Richardson, Dorothy, **I:** 53; **II:** 320; **Supp. III Part 1:** 65

Richardson, Helen Patges, **Retro. Supp. II:** 95

Richardson, Henry Hobson, **I:** 3, 10

Richardson, Maurice, **Supp. XII:** 241

Richardson, Samuel, **I:** 134; **II:** 104, 111, 322; **Supp. IX:** 128; **Supp. V:** 127; **Supp. XV:** 232; **Supp. XX: 236**

Richardson, Tony, **Supp. XI:** 305, 306

"Richard Wright and Recent Negro Fiction" (Ellison), **Retro. Supp. II:** 116

"Richard Wright's Blues" (Ellison), **Retro. Supp. II:** 117, 124

"Richard Yates: A Requiem" (Lawrence), **Supp. XI:** 335

"Rich Boy, The" (Fitzgerald), **II:** 94; **Retro. Supp. I:** 98, 108

Richer, the Poorer, The: Sketches and Reminiscences (D. West), **Supp. XVIII:** 277, 289

"Riches" (Bausch), **Supp. VII:** 54

Richey, Elinor, **Supp. XXIV:** 30

Richler, Mordecai, **Supp. XI:** 294, 297

Rich Man, Poor Man (miniseries), **Supp. XIX:** 252

Rich Man, Poor Man (Shaw), **Supp. XIX:** 251–252

Richman, Robert, **Supp. XI:** 249; **Supp. XV:** 120–121, 251

Richman, Shira, **Supp. XXIV:** 167
Richmond (Masters), **Supp. I Part 2:** 471
Richmond, M. A., **Supp. XX: 277, 279, 282, 286, 289, 290**
Rich Relations (Hwang), **Supp. XXI:** 146–147
Richter, Conrad, **Supp. X:** 103; **Supp. XVIII: 207–222**
Richter, Jean Paul, **II:** 489, 492; **Supp. XVI:** 182
Rick Bass (Weltzien), **Supp. XVI:** 20
Rickman, Clio, **Supp. I Part 2:** 519
Ricks, Christopher, **Retro. Supp. I:** 56; **Supp. XVIII:** 20, 30, 32
Riddel, Joseph N., **IV:** 95
"Riddle, The" (Hay), **Supp. XIV:** 130
"Ride in an Omnibus, A" (Briggs), **Supp. XVIII:** 9, 16
Rideout, Walter B., **Supp. XXVI:** 28
"Riders to the Blood-Red Wrath" (Brooks), **Supp. III Part 1:** 82–83
Riders to the Sea (Synge), **III:** 157
Ridge, Lola, **Supp. IX:** 308; **Supp. XV:** 307; **Supp. XXIV:** 49, 52; **Supp. XXVI:** 23
Riding, Alan, **Supp. XVI:** 294
Riding, Laura, **I:** 437
"Riding Out at Evening" (McCarriston), **Supp. XIV:** 262–263
Riding the Iron Rooster: By Train through China (Theroux), **Supp. VIII:** 324
Ridley, Clifford, **Supp. XXIV:** 282
Riesenberg, Felix, **I:** 360, 361
Riesman, David, **Supp. I Part 2:** 649, 650
"Rif, to Music, The" (Bowles), **Supp. IV Part 1:** 89
Riffs & Reciprocities (Dunn), **Supp. XI: 154–155**
Rifkin, Libby, **Supp. XXIV:** 39, 44
Rifles, The (Vollmann), **Supp. XVII:** 226, 233
Riggs, Marlon, **Supp. XI:** 19
Right Distance, The (Pickering), **Supp. XXI:** 196–197
Right Madness on Skye, The (Hugo), **Supp. VI:** 145–147
Rights of Man (Paine), **Supp. I Part 2:** 508, 511, 512–514, 516, 519, 523
"Rights of Woman" (Rowson), **Supp. XV:** 243
"Rights of Women, The" (Brown). *See Alcuin: A Dialogue* (Brown)
Right Stuff, The (Wolfe), **Supp. III Part 2:** 581–584
Right Thoughts in Sad Hours (Mather), **IV:** 144
Rigney, Barbara Hill, **Supp. VIII:** 215
"Rigorists" (Moore), **III:** 198
Rihani, Ameen, **Supp. XX:** 115
Rihoku, **Supp. XXII:** 228
Riis, Jacob A., **I:** 293; **Supp. I Part 1:** 13; **Supp. XVII:** 101, 106
Riley, Glenda, **Supp. XXIV:** 252
Riley, James Whitcomb, **I:** 205; **Supp. II Part 1:** 192, 193, 196, 197
Rilke, Rainer Maria, **I:** 445, 523; **II:** 367, 381, 382–383, 389, 543, 544; **III:** 552, 558, 563, 571, 572; **IV:** 380, 443; **Retro. Supp. II:** 20, 187; **Supp. I**

Part 1: 264; **Supp. I Part 2:** 573; **Supp. III Part 1:** 239, 242, 246, 283, 319–320; **Supp. IV Part 1:** 284; **Supp. V:** 208, 343; **Supp. VIII:** 30, 40; **Supp. X:** 164; **Supp. XI:** 126; **Supp. XIII:** 74, 88; **Supp. XV:** 93, 212, 222,**Supp. XV:** 223, 225; **Supp. XVI:** 292; **Supp. XVII:** 244; **Supp. XXII:** 89, 90, 94; **Supp. XXIII:** 207; **Supp. XXIV:** 37, 38, 152, 162; **Supp. XXVI:** 259
Rilke on Love and Other Difficulties (Rilke), **Supp. X:** 164
"Rilke's Growth as a Poet" (Dobyns), **Supp. XIII:** 77
"Rimbaud" (Kerouac), **Supp. III Part 1:** 232
Rimbaud, Arthur, **I:** 381, 383, 389, 391, 526; **II:** 528, 543, 545; **III:** 23, 174, 189; **IV:** 286, 380, 443; **Retro. Supp. I:** 56; **Retro. Supp. II:** 187, 326; **Supp. III Part 1:** 14, 195; **Supp. IV Part 2:** 624; **Supp. VIII:** 39, 40; **Supp. XII:** 1, 16, 128, 255; **Supp. XIII:** 284; **Supp. XIV:** 338; **Supp. XVIII:** 23, 33; **Supp. XXI:** 225, 233; **Supp. XXIII:** 207; **Supp. XXIV:** 39, 40
Rindge, Debora, **Supp. XXI:** 246
Rinehart, Mary Roberts, **Supp. XXV: 189–203;** **Supp. XXVI:** 276, 281, 282
Rinehart, Stanley, **III:** 36
Ring, Frances Kroll, **Supp. IX:** 63, 64
Ring and the Book, The (Browning), **Supp. I Part 2:** 416, 468
Ring cycle (Wagner), **Supp. IV Part 1:** 392
Ringe, Donald, **I:** 339, 343; **Retro. Supp. II:** 270
Ringel, Faye, **Supp. XXII:** 205, 207
"Ringing" (Bierds), **Supp. XVII:** 28
"Ringing the Bells" (Sexton), **Supp. II Part 2:** 672, 687
Ringle, Ken, **Supp. X:** 15
Ring of Heaven: Poems (Hongo), **Supp. X:** 292
Rink, The (musical, McNally), **Supp. XIII:** 207
Rin Tin Tin: The Life and the Legend (Orlean), **Supp. XXV:** 160, 165–166
Rio Lobo (film), **Supp. XVI:** 246
Ríos, Alberto Alvaro, **Supp. IV Part 2: 537–556**
"Riot" (Brooks), **Supp. III Part 1:** 71, 84–85
Ripening (Le Sueur), **Supp. XXIII:** 165
Ripley, Ezra, **II:** 8; **IV:** 172
Rip-off Red, Girl Detective (Acker), **Supp. XII:** 3–4
Ripostes (Pound), **Retro. Supp. I:** 287–288, 413
Ripostes of Ezra Pound, The, Whereunto Are Appended the Complete Poetical Works of T. E. Hulme, with Prefatory Note (Pound), **III:** 458, 464, 465
Riprap (Snyder), **Supp. VIII: 292–294,** 295
"Riprap" (Snyder), **Supp. VIII:** 293–294
"Rip Van Winkle" (Irving), **II:** 304–306; **Supp. I Part 1:** 185

Rischin, Moses, **Supp. XVII:** 101, 103, 106
Risco-Lozado, Eliezar, **Supp. XIII:** 313
Rise and Shine (Quindlen), **Supp. XVII:** 179
Rise of David Levinsky, The (Cahan), **Supp. IX:** 227; **Supp. XIII:** 106; **Supp. XXVI:** 123
Rise of Silas Lapham, The (Howells), **II:** 275, 279, 283–285; **IV:** 202; **Retro. Supp. II:** 93, 101
"Rise of the Middle Class" (Banks), **Supp. V:** 10
Rising and Falling (Matthews), **Supp. IX:** 154, **160**
"Rising Daughter, The" (Olds), **Supp. X:** 204
Rising from the Plains (McPhee), **Supp. III Part 1:** 309–310
Rising Glory of America, The (Brackenridge and Freneau), **Supp. I Part 1:** 124; **Supp. II Part 1:** 67, 253, 256, 263
"Rising of the Storm, The" (Dunbar), **Supp. II Part 1:** 199
Rising Sun in the Pacific, The (Morison), **Supp. I Part 2:** 490
Rising Up and Rising Down (Vollmann), **Supp. XVII:** 225, 226, **229–230,** 232, 233, 235–236
Risk Pool, The (Russo), **Supp. XII: 328–331**
Ristovic, Aleksandar, **Supp. VIII:** 272
"Rita Dove: Identity Markers" (Vendler), **Supp. IV Part 1:** 247, 257
Ritchey, John, **Supp. XIV:** 122
Ritchie, Anne Thackeray, **Supp. XX: 231, 233**
"Rite of Passage" (Olds), **Supp. X:** 206
"Rites and Ceremonies" (Hecht), **Supp. X:** 61
Rites and Witnesses: A Comedy (Hinojosa), **Supp. XIX: 106–107**
"Rites of Spring, The" (Morris), **III:** 223
Ritivoi, Andreea Deciu, **Supp. XVI:** 148
Ritschl, Albrecht, **III:** 309, 604
Ritsos, Yannis, **Supp. X:** 112
"Ritsos and the Metaphysical Moment" (Dobyns), **Supp. XIII:** 78
Rittenhouse, David, **Supp. I Part 2:** 507
Rittenhouse, Jessie, **Supp. XV:** 295
"Ritual, The" (Jarman), **Supp. XVII:** 114
"Ritual and Renewal: Keres Traditions in the Short Fiction of Leslie Silko" (Ruoff), **Supp. IV Part 2:** 559
Ritz, The (film), **Supp. XIII:** 206
Ritz, The (McNally), **Supp. XIII:** 198
"Rival, The" (Plath), **Retro. Supp. II:** 254
Riven Rock (Boyle), **Supp. VIII:** 5–6; **Supp. XX: 25–26**
"River" (Ammons), **Supp. VII:** 28
"River, The" (O'Connor), **III:** 344, 352, 353, 354, 356; **Retro. Supp. II:** 229, 231–232
Rivera, Tomás, **Supp. XIII:** 216, 221; **Supp. XIX:** 97, 102
Riverbed (Wagoner), **Supp. IX:** 327–328
"River Driftwood" (Jewett), **Retro. Supp. II:** 132, 133, 147

"River Jordan, The" (DeLillo), **Supp. VI:** 3, 4

River King, The (Hoffman), **Supp. X:** 78, 85, 90, **91–92**

"River Merchant's Wife: A Letter, The" (Pound), **III:** 463

"River Now, The" (Hugo), **Supp. VI:** 144

River of Forgetfulness, The (Hadas), **Supp. XXIII: 120**

"River of Rivers in Connecticut, The" (Stevens), **Retro. Supp. I:** 313

River of the Mother of God and Other Essays by Aldo Leopold, The (Leopold), **Supp. XIV:** 180

"River"(O'Hara), **Supp. XXIII:** 212

"River Profile" (Auden), **Supp. II Part 1:** 26

"River Road" (Kunitz), **Supp. III Part 1:** 260

River Runs Through It, A (film), **Supp. XXVI:** 184

"River Runs Through It, A" (Maclean), **Supp. XIV:** 222–223, **223–229**, 233, 234, 235; **Supp. XVI:** 98

River Runs Through It and Other Stories, A (Maclean), **Supp. XIV:** 221, 223

Rivers, Allison, **Supp. XXIII:** 51

Rivers, Larry, **Supp. III Part 1:** 3; **Supp. XV:** 177, 178, 186; **Supp. XXIII:** 209, 210, 211, 212, 215, 216, 217, 220

Rivers and Mountains (Ashbery), **Supp. III Part 1:** 10, 26

Riverside Drive (Simpson), **Supp. IX: 275–276**

Riverside Poetry (Auden, Moore, and Shapiro, eds.), **Supp. XXI:** 98

Rivers to the Sea (Teasdale), **Supp. XV:** 295

"River"(Strout), **Supp. XXIII:** 283

River Styx, Ohio, and Other Poems, The (Oliver), **Supp. VII:** 231, 232

"River That Is East, The" (Kinnell), **Supp. III Part 1:** 241–242

"River"(theater performance, Strout), **Supp. XXIII:** 281

"River Towns" (Masters), **Supp. I Part 2:** 473

Rives, Amélie, **II:** 194

Rivière, Jacques, **Retro. Supp. I:** 63

"Rivington's Last Will and Testament" (Freneau), **Supp. II Part 1:** 261

"Rivulet, The" (Bryant), **Supp. I Part 1:** 155, 162

Rix, Alice, **I:** 199

RL's Dream (Mosley), **Supp. XIII:** 234, **244–245,** 249

Roach, Max, **Supp. X:** 239

"Road, Roadsides, and the Disparate Frames of a Sequence" (Sobin), **Supp. XVI:** 288

"Road, The" (H. Johnson), **Supp. XXVI:** 164

Road, The (McCarthy), **Supp. XXII:** 49

Road, The: In Search of America (Asch), **Supp. XXVI:** 17, 21, 23, 25, 26–28

Road Between, The (Farrell), **II:** 29, 38, 39–40

"Road Between Here and There, The" (Kinnell), **Supp. III Part 1:** 254

"Road Home, The" (Hammett), **Supp. IV Part 1:** 343

Road Home, The (Harrison), **Supp. VIII:** 37, 45, 48, **49–50,** 53

Road Is Before Us, The (Boulton), **Supp. XXII:** 17, 25–26

Roadless Yaak, The: Reflections and Observations about One of Our Last Great Wild Places (Bass, ed.), **Supp. XVI:** 23

"Road Not Taken, The" (R. Frost), **II:** 154; **Retro. Supp. I:** 131; **Supp. XI:** 150; **Supp. XV:** 127

"Roadside Flowers" (Collins), **Supp. XXI:** 61

Roadside Poems for Summer Travellers (Larcom, ed.), **Supp. XIII:** 142

"Roadside Resurrection, A" (L. Brown), **Supp. XXI:** 40, 42

Roads of Destiny (O. Henry), **Supp. II Part 1:** 410

Road through the Wall, The (Jackson), **Supp. IX:** 115, 118, 120, 123–124

"Road to Avignon, The" (Lowell), **II:** 516

"Road to Hell, The" (Fante), **Supp. XI:** 160

Road to Los Angeles, The (Fante), **Supp. XI:** 160, 166, 167, **168,** 172

Road to Many a Wonder, The (Wagoner), **Supp. IX:** 327, **336**

Road to the Temple, The (Glaspell), **Supp. III Part 1:** 175, 182, 186; **Supp. XXI:** 6

Road to Wellville, The (Boyle), **Supp. VIII:** 6–8; **Supp. XX: 24–25, 26, 28**

Road to Xanadu, The (Lowes), **IV:** 453

"Road Warrior" (Pickering), **Supp. XXI:** 204

"Roan Stallion" (Jeffers), **Supp. II Part 2:** 428–429

"Roast-beef" (Stein), **IV:** 43

Roast Leviatham (Untermeyer), **Supp. XV:** 307

"Roast Possum" (Dove), **Supp. IV Part 1:** 247, 248

Robards, Jason, Jr., **III:** 163, 403

Robb, Christina, **Supp. XV:** 251

Robbe-Grillet, Alain, **I:** 123; **IV:** 95; **Supp. IV Part 1:** 42; **Supp. V:** 47, 48; **Supp. XXIII:** 213

Robber Bride, The (Atwood), **Supp. XIII: 30–31**

Robber Bridegroom, The (Welty), **IV:** 261, 266–268, 271, 274; **Retro. Supp. I:** 347

Robbins, Harold, **Supp. XII:** 6

Robbins, Henry, **Supp. IV Part 1:** 198, 201, 210, 211

Robbins, Katherine Robinson, **Supp. X:** 264

Robbins, Thomas, **Supp. XV:** 271

Robbins, Tom, **Supp. IV Part 1:** 227; **Supp. VIII:** 14; **Supp. X: 259–288;** **Supp. XIII:** 11

"Robe, The" (Douglas), **IV:** 434

Robert Bly (Sugg), **Supp. IV Part 1:** 68

"Robert Bly" (W. V. Davis), **Supp. IV Part 1:** 70

"Robert Bly and the Trouble with America" (Mitchell), **Supp. IV Part 1:** 70

Robert Bly: An Introduction to the Poetry (Nelson), **Supp. IV Part 1:** 66

Robert Bly: The Poet and His Critics (W. V. Davis), **Supp. IV Part 1:** 63; **Supp. XXI:** 84, **85–86,** 87, 95

Robert Coover: The Universal Fiction-making Process (Gordon), **Supp. V:** 46

Robert Creeley (Ford), **Supp. IV Part 1:** 140

Robert Creeley and the Genius of the American Common Place (Clark), **Supp. IV Part 1:** 140

Robert Creeley's Poetry: A Critical Introduction (Edelberg), **Supp. IV Part 1:** 155

Robert Frost (Meyers), **Retro. Supp. I:** 138

Robert Lowell (Meyers), **Retro. Supp. II:** 191

Robert Lowell and the Sublime (Hart), **Retro. Supp. II:** 187

Robert Lowell's Shifting Colors (Doreski), **Retro. Supp. II:** 185

Robert Lowell: The First Twenty years (Staples), **Retro. Supp. II:** 187

Roberts, Carol, **Supp. XX: 53**

Roberts, David, **Supp. XVIII:** 106

Roberts, Diane, **Supp. X:** 15

Roberts, J. M., **IV:** 454

Roberts, Leo, **II:** 449

Roberts, Margaret, **II:** 449; **IV:** 453, 454

Roberts, Matthew, **Retro. Supp. II:** 324

Roberts, Meade, **IV:** 383

Roberts, Michael, **I:** 527, 536

Roberts, Richard, **III:** 297

Roberts, Victoria, **Supp. XIX:** 205

Roberts, Wally, **Supp. XI:** 119, 120, 126

Roberts, William, **Supp. XI:** 343

Roberts Brothers, **Retro. Supp. I:** 31, 35

Robertson, David, **Supp. VIII:** 305

Robertson, D. B., **III:** 311

Robertson, Lisa, **Supp. XXII:** 155

Robertson, Nan, **Supp. IV Part 1:** 300

Robertson, William, **II:** 8

Robert the Devil (Merwin, trans.), **Supp. III Part 1:** 341, 346

Robeson, Paul, **III:** 392; **Supp. IV Part 1:** 360, 361; **Supp. X:** 137; **Supp. XIX:** 66; **Supp. XXI:** 167

Robeson, Susan L., **Supp. XVIII:** 268

Robespierre, Maximilien, **Supp. I Part 2:** 514, 515, 517

"Robinson" (Kees), **Supp. XV:** 143–144

Robinson, Christopher L., **Supp. XII:** 13, 14

Robinson, David, **Supp. XXIV:** 70, 71, 78–79

Robinson, Dean, **III:** 506

Robinson, Edward, **III:** 505

Robinson, Edward G., **Supp. XI:** 306

Robinson, Edwin Arlington, **I:** 480; **II:** 388, 391, 529, 542; **III:** 5, **503–526,** 576; **Supp. I Part 2:** 699; **Supp. II Part 1:** 191; **Supp. III Part 1:** 63, 75; **Supp. III Part 2:** 592, 593; **Supp. IX:** 77, 266, 276, 308; **Supp. XIX:**

123; **Supp. XV:** 256, 299, 300, 301, 306; **Supp. XVII:** 69

Robinson, Forrest G., **Supp. IV Part 2:** 597, 601, 604

Robinson, Herman, **III:** 506–507

Robinson, H. M., **IV:** 369, 370

Robinson, Jackie, **Supp. I Part 1:** 338

Robinson, James Harvey, **I:** 214; **Supp. I Part 2:** 492

Robinson, James K., **Supp. IX:** 328

Robinson, Margaret G., **Supp. IV Part 2:** 597, 601, 604

Robinson, Marilynne, **Supp. XXI: 209–224; Supp. XXII:** 50; **Supp. XXVI:** 45, 187

Robinson, Mary, **Supp. XI:** 26

Robinson, Rowland E., **Supp. XIX:** 6

Robinson, Roxana, **Supp. XXV:** 60

Robinson, Sugar Ray, **Supp. IV Part 1:** 167

Robinson, Ted, **Supp. XIII:** 166

Robinson Crusoe (Defoe), **II:** 159; **III:** 113, 423; **IV:** 369; **Retro. Supp. II:** 274; **Supp. I Part 2:** 714; **Supp. IV Part 2:** 502

Robison, Mary, **Supp. V:** 22; **Supp. XXI:** 115, 116, 118

Roblès, Emmanuel, **Supp. I Part 1:** 283

"Robstown" (Salinas), **Supp. XIII:** 315

Rochefort, Christina, **Supp. XVI:** 143

Rochefoucauld, Louis Alexandre, **Supp. I Part 2:** 510

"Rock" (Nye), **Supp. XIII:** 287

Rock (Wagoner), **Supp. IX:** 324, **334,** 335

Rock, Catherine, **Supp. XII:** 17

Rock, The (Eliot), **Retro. Supp. I:** 65

Rock, The (Stevens), **Retro. Supp. I:** 309, 312

"Rock, The" (Stevens), **Retro. Supp. I:** 312

Rockaway (Shanley), **Supp. XIV:** 315

"Rock Climbers, The" (Francis), **Supp. IX:** 82

Rock-Drill (Pound), **Retro. Supp. I:** 293

Rockefeller, John D., **I:** 273; **III:** 580; **Supp. I Part 2:** 486; **Supp. V:** 286; **Supp. XXIII:** 26

Rockefeller, Nelson, **III:** 14, 15

Rockets and Rodeos and Other American Spectacles (Mallon), **Supp. XIX:** 137

Rocket to the Moon (Odets), **Supp. II Part 2:** 541–543, 544

Rock Garden, The (Shepard), **Supp. III Part 2:** 432, 447

"Rocking Horse Winner, The" (Lawrence), **Supp. I Part 1:** 329

Rocking the Boat (Vidal), **Supp. IV Part 2:** 683

"Rockpile, The" (Baldwin), **Supp. I Part 1:** 63

Rock Springs (Ford), **Supp. V:** 57, 58–59, 68–69

Rocky Mountains, The: or, Scenes, Incidents, and Adventures in the Far West; Digested from the Journal of Captain E. L. E Bonneville, of the Army of the United States, and Illustrated from Various Other Sources (Irving), **II:** 312

Rodden, John, **Supp. XVI:** 63, 69, 72

Roddenberry, Gene, **Supp. XXII:** 60

Rodefer, Stephen, **Supp. XXIV:** 38

Roderick, David, **Supp. XV:** 223

Roderick Hudson (James), **II:** 284, 290, 324, 326, 328; **Retro. Supp. I:** 219, **220–221,** 221, 226; **Supp. IX:** 142

Rodgers, Richard, **III:** 361

Rodgers, Ronald, **Supp. IV Part 2:** 503

Rodker, John, **III:** 470

Rodman, Selden, **Supp. I Part 1:** 83; **Supp. X:** 115

Rodney, Walter, **Supp. XXI:** 171

"Rodrigo Returns to the Land and Linen Celebrates" (Cisneros), **Supp. VII:** 68

Rodríguez, Diane, **Supp. XXIII:** 203

Rodriguez, Randy A., **Supp. XIV:** 312

Rodriguez, Richard, **Supp. XIV: 297–313**

Roethke, Charles, **III:** 531

Roethke, Theodore, **I:** 167, 171–172, 183, 254, 285, 521; **III:** 273, **527–550; IV:** 138, 402; **Retro. Supp. II:** 178, 181, 246; **Supp. I Part 2:** 539; **Supp. III Part 1:** 47, 54, 56, 239, 253, 260–261, 350; **Supp. IV Part 2:** 626; **Supp. IX:** 323; **Supp. XV:** 140, 145, 212; **Supp. XVIII:** 90; **Supp. XX: 199; Supp. XXIII:** 19; **Supp. XXIV:** 165, 171

"Roger Malvin's Burial" (Hawthorne), **II:** 243; **Retro. Supp. I:** 153

Rogers, Michael, **Supp. X:** 265, 266

Rogers, Pattiann, **Supp. XVIII:** 189

Rogers, Samuel, **II:** 303; **Supp. I Part 1:** 157

Rogers, Will, **I:** 261; **IV:** 388

Roger's Version (Updike), **Retro. Supp. I:** 325, 327, 330

Roget, Peter Mark, **Supp. I Part 1:** 312

"Rogue River Jet-Board Trip, Gold Beach, Oregon, July 4, 1977" (Carver), **Supp. III Part 1:** 140

"Rogue's Gallery" (McCarthy), **II:** 563

Rohr, Richard, **Supp. XX: 143**

Roiphe, Katie, **Supp. XXV:** 10

Roland de La Platière, Jean Marie, **II:** 554

Rolando Hinojosa and the American Dream (Glover), **Supp. XIX:** 112

Rolando Hinojosa: A Reader's Guide (Zilles), **Supp. XIX:** 112

Rolando Hinojosa Reader, The (Saldívar, ed.), **Supp. XIX:** 112

Rôle du Nègre dans la culture des Amériques, La (Locke), **Supp. XIV:** 202

"Role of a Lifetime, The" (Skloot), **Supp. XX: 203**

"Role of Society in the Artist, The" (Ammons), **Supp. VII:** 34

Rolfe, Alfred, **IV:** 427

Rolfe, Frederick, **Supp. XX: 235**

"Roll, Jordan, Roll" (spiritual), **Supp. IV Part 1:** 16

Rolland, Romain, **Supp. XX: 70**

"Roll Call" (Hoffman), **Supp. XVIII:** 86

"Roll Call" (Komunyakaa), **Supp. XIII:** 123

Rolle, Esther, **Supp. IV Part 1:** 367

Rollin, Charles, **II:** 113

Rolling Stones (O. Henry), **Supp. II Part 1:** 410

Rolling Thunder Logbook (Shepard), **Supp. III Part 2:** 433

Rolling Thunder Logbook, The (Shepard), **Supp. XVIII:** 31

"Rolling Up" (Simpson), **Supp. IX:** 265, 274, 280

Rollins, Howard E., Jr., **Supp. IV Part 1:** 236

Rollins, Hyder E., **Supp. IV Part 1:** 168

Rollins, Sonny, **Supp. V:** 195

"Rollo" tales (Abbott), **Supp. I Part 1:** 38

"Roma I" (Wright), **Supp. V:** 338

"Roma II" (Wright), **Supp. V:** 338

Romains, Jules, **I:** 227

Román, David, **Supp. XIII:** 208

Romance, A (Weigl), **Supp. XIX: 277–278**

"Romance, A" (Weigl), **Supp. XIX:** 278

"Romance and a Reading List" (Fitzgerald), **Retro. Supp. I:** 101

Romance of a Plain Man, The (Glasgow), **II:** 175, 180–181

"Romance of Certain Old Clothes, The" (James), **II:** 322; **Retro. Supp. I:** 218

Romance Reader, The (Abraham), **Supp. XXIV:** 1–2, 3, **4–7**

"Roman Elegies" (Brodsky), **Supp. VIII:** 29

"Roman Fever" (Wharton), **Retro. Supp. I:** 382

"Roman Fountain" (Bogan), **Supp. III Part 1:** 56

"*Romanitas* of Gore Vidal, The" (Tatum), **Supp. IV Part 2:** 684

Romaniuk, Zbigniew, **Supp. XVI:** 154

Romano, John, **Supp. XV:** 253

"Roman Sarcophagus, A" (Lowell), **II:** 544

Roman Spring of Mrs. Stone, The (T. Williams), **IV:** 383, 385

"Romantic, The" (Bogan), **Supp. III Part 1:** 50

Romantic Comedians, The (Glasgow), **II:** 175, 186, 190, 194

Romantic Education, A (Hampl), **Supp. XXII:** 82, 83, **87–90,** 91

Romantic Egoists, The (Auchincloss), **Supp. IV Part 1:** 25

Romantic Egotist, The (Fitzgerald), **II:** 82

"Romantic Egotist, The" (Fitzgerald), **Retro. Supp. I:** 100

"Romanticism and Classicism" (Hulme), **III:** 196

"Romanticism Comes Home" (Shapiro), **Supp. II Part 2:** 713

Romantic Manifesto, The: A Philosophy of Literature (Rand), **Supp. IV Part 2:** 521, 523, 527, 529–530

"Romantic Regionalism of Harper Lee, The" (Erisman), **Supp. VIII:** 126

Romantics, The (Rinehart), **Supp. XXV:** 196

"Rome" (W. C. Williams), **Retro. Supp. I:** 420

Rome Brothers, **Retro. Supp. I:** 393

Romeo and Juliet (Shakespeare), **Supp. V:** 252; **Supp. VIII:** 223

Romola (G. Eliot), **II:** 291; **IV:** 311

Romulus: A New Comedy (Vidal), **Supp. IV Part 2:** 683

Romulus der Grosse (Dürrenmatt), **Supp. IV Part 2:** 683

Ronald, Ann, **Supp. XIII:** 4, 5, 6, 7, 9, 11

"Rondel for a September Day" (White), **Supp. I Part 2:** 676

"Ron Narrative Reconstructions, The" (Coleman), **Supp. XI:** 83

"Ron Padgett's Visual Imagination" (Notley), **Supp. XXII:** 224

Ronsard, Pierre de, **Supp. X:** 65; **Supp. XV:** 165

Rood, John, **IV:** 261

"Roof, the Steeple, and the People, The" (Ellison), **Retro. Supp. II:** 118, 126; **Supp. II Part 1:** 248

"Room" (Levertov), **Supp. III Part 1:** 282

Roomates (film, P. Yates), **Supp. XVII:** 8, 9

Roomates: My Grandfather's Story (Apple), **Supp. XVII:** 2, **7–9**

"Room at the Heart of Things, A" (Merrill), **Supp. III Part 1:** 337

Room Called Remember, A: Uncollected Pieces (Buechner), **Supp. XII:** 53

"Roomful of Hovings, A" (McPhee), **Supp. III Part 1:** 291, 294

Room of One's Own, A (Woolf), **Supp. IX:** 19; **Supp. V:** 127; **Supp. XIII:** 305

Room Rented by a Single Woman (Wright), **Supp. XV:** 340–341

"Rooms" (Collins), **Supp. XXI:** 61

Room Temperature (Baker), **Supp. XIII:** 41, **43–45,** 48, 50

Room to Swing (Lacy), **Supp. XV:** 202, 203, 205, 207

"Room Upstairs, The" (Gioia), **Supp. XV:** 120–121, 124

Roosevelt, Eleanor, **IV:** 371; **Supp. IV Part 2:** 679

Roosevelt, Franklin, **Supp. V:** 290

Roosevelt, Franklin Delano, **I:** 482, 485, 490; **II:** 553, 575; **III:** 2, 18, 69, 110, 297, 321, 376, 476, 580, 581; **Supp. I Part 2:** 488, 489, 490, 491, 645, 654, 655

Roosevelt, Kermit, **III:** 508

Roosevelt, Theodore, **I:** 14, 62; **II:** 130; **III:** 508; **IV:** 321; **Retro. Supp. I:** 377; **Supp. I Part 1:** 1, 21; **Supp. I Part 2:** 455, 456, 502, 707; **Supp. IX:** 184; **Supp. V:** 280, 282; **Supp. XIX:** 29; **Supp. XX:** 221; **Supp. XXIII:** 26

Roosevelt After Inauguration And Other Atrocities (Burroughs), **Supp. III Part 1:** 98

"Roosevelt Chair, The" (Skloot), **Supp. XX:** 205

"Roosters" (Bishop), **Retro. Supp. II:** 39, 43, 250; **Supp. I Part 1:** 89

Root, Abiah, **I:** 456

Root, Elihu, **Supp. IV Part 1:** 33

Root, Simeon, **I:** 548

Root, Timothy, **I:** 548

Rootabaga Stories (Sandburg), **III:** 583, 587

"Rootedness: The Ancestor as Foundation" (Morrison), **Supp. III Part 1:** 361

"Roots" (Halliday), **Supp. XIX:** 88

Roots in the Soil (film), **Supp. IV Part 1:** 83

"Rope" (Porter), **III:** 451

Rope, The (O'Neill), **III:** 388

Ropemakers of Plymouth, The (Morison), **Supp. I Part 2:** 494

"Ropes" (Nye), **Supp. XIII:** 276

"Rope's End, The" (Nemerov), **III:** 282

Roquelaure, A. N., **Supp. VII:** 301. *See also* Rice, Anne

Rorem, Ned, **Supp. IV Part 1:** 79, 84; **Supp. XXIII:** 217

Rorschach Test (F. Wright), **Supp. XVII:** 240, 245

Rorty, James, **Supp. XXII:** 276, 277

"Rosa" (Ozick), **Supp. V:** 271

Rosa, Rodrigo Rey, **Supp. IV Part 1:** 92

Rosaldo, Renato, **Supp. IV Part 2:** 544

"Rosalia" (Simic), **Supp. VIII:** 278

Roscoe, Will, **Supp. IV Part 1:** 330

"Roscoe in Hell" (McKnight), **Supp. XX:** 151

"Rose" (Dubus), **Supp. VII:** 88

Rose (L.-Y. Lee), **Supp. XV:** 211, **212–215,** 218

Rose, Alice, Sister, **III:** 348

Rose, Charlie, **Supp. XIX:** 26, 30

Rose, Lloyd, **Supp. XXIV:** 267

Rose, Mickey, **Supp. XV:** 3

Rose, Philip, **Supp. IV Part 1:** 362

"Rose, The" (Roethke), **III:** 537

"Rose, The" (W. C. Williams), **Retro. Supp. I:** 419

Rose, Where Did You Get That Red?: Teaching Great Poetry to Children (Koch), **Supp. XV:** 189

"Rose for Emily, A" (Faulkner), **II:** 72; **Supp. IX:** 96; **Supp. XX:** 179; **Supp. XXIV:** 136

Rose-Hued Cities (P. N. Warren), **Supp. XX:** 261

Rose in Bloom (Alcott), **Supp. I Part 1:** 42

"Rose-Johnny" (Kingsolver), **Supp. VII:** 203

Rose Madder (King), **Supp. V:** 141, 148, 150, 152

"Rose-Morals" (Lanier), **Supp. I Part 1:** 364

Rosen, Jonathan, **Supp. XVII:** 50; **Supp. XX:** 179

Rosen, Kenneth, **Supp. IV Part 2:** 499, 505, 513

Rosen, Norma, **Supp. XVII:** 49, 50

Rosenbaum, Alissa Zinovievna. *See* Rand, Ayn

Rosenbaum, Thane, **Supp. XVII:** 48

Rosenberg, Bernard, **Supp. I Part 2:** 650

Rosenberg, Harold, **Supp. XIX:** 159; **Supp. XV:** 143; **Supp. XXIII:** 211

Rosenberg, Julia, **Supp. XVIII:** 136

Rosenberg, Julius and Ethel, **Supp. I Part 1:** 295; **Supp. I Part 2:** 532; **Supp. V:** 45

Rosenberg, Liz, **Supp. XV:** 251

Rosenberg, Shlomo, **Supp. XXIII:** 6

Rosenbloom, Joel, **Supp. IV Part 2:** 527

Rosenblum, Martin, **Supp. XXVI:** 236

Rosenfeld, Alvin H., **Supp. I Part 1:** 120

Rosenfeld, Isaac, **Supp. XII:** 160

Rosenfeld, Paul, **I:** 116, 117, 231, 245

Rosenfelt, Deborah, **Supp. XIII:** 296, 304

Rosenfield, Isaac, **IV:** 3

Rosengarten, Theodore, **Supp. XVIII:** 183

Rosenthal, Ira, **Supp. XIV:** 146–147

Rosenthal, Lois, **Supp. VIII:** 258

Rosenthal, M. L., **II:** 550; **III:** 276, 479; **Supp. V:** 333

Rosenthal, Peggy, **Supp. XVII:** 119

Rose of Wissahikon, The (Lippard), **Supp. XXIII:** 178

"Rose Pogonias" (Frost), **Retro. Supp. I:** 127

"Rose Red and Snow White" (Grimms), **Supp. X:** 82

"Rose Room" (Sorrentino), **Supp. XXI:** 228

"Roses" (Conroy), **Supp. XVI:** 72

"Roses" (Dove), **Supp. IV Part 1:** 246

"Roses and Skulls" (Goldbarth), **Supp. XII:** 192

"Roses for Lubbock" (Nye), **Supp. XIII:** 281

"Roses Only" (Moore), **III:** 195, 198, 200, 202, 215

Rose Tattoo, The (T. Williams), **IV:** 382, 383, 387, 388, 389, 392–393, 394, 397, 398

Rose Theatre (Sorrentino), **Supp. XXI:** 236

"Rosewood, Ohio" (Matthews), **Supp. IX:** 160

Rosie (Lamott), **Supp. XX:** **133–134**

"Rosie Baby" (Huddle), **Supp. XXVI:** 147, 152

Rosiebelle Lee Wildcat Tennessee (Andrews), **Supp. XXVI:** 6–7

Rosinante to the Road Again (Dos Passos), **I:** 478

Roskies, David, **Supp. XVII:** 39, 44, 49–50

Roskolenko, Harry, **Supp. XV:** 179

Rosmersholm (Ibsen), **III:** 152

Rosmond, Babette, **II:** 432

Ross, Eleanor. *See* Taylor, Eleanor Ross

Ross, Harold, **Supp. I Part 1:** 174; **Supp. I Part 2:** 607, 617, 653, 654, 655, 660; **Supp. IX:** 190; **Supp. VIII:** 151, 170

Ross, Herbert, **Supp. XV:** 2

Ross, Jean, **Supp. XXI:** 144, 146

Ross, John F., **II:** 110

Ross, Lillilan, **Retro. Supp. II:** 198

Ross, Mary, **Supp. XXII:** 195

Ross, Mitchell S., **Supp. IV Part 2:** 692; **Supp. X:** 260

Ross, Robert, **Supp. XXIV:** 167

Rossen, Robert, **Supp. XI:** 306

Rosset, Barney, **III:** 171

Rossetti, Christina, **Supp. XIV:** 128

Rossetti, Dante Gabriel, **I:** 433; **II:** 323; **Retro. Supp. I:** 128, 286; **Supp. I Part 2:** 552; **Supp. XXII:** 156

Rossetti, William Michael, **Retro. Supp. I:** 407

Rossi, Umberto, **Supp. XVIII:** 137, 138–139

Rossini, Clare, **Supp. XVII:** 111

Rosskam, Edwin, **IV:** 477

Ross Macdonald (Bruccoli), **Supp. IV Part 2:** 468, 470

Rostand, Edmond, **II:** 515; **Supp. IV Part 2:** 518

Rosten, Leo, **Supp. XVII:** 9

Rosy Crucifixion, The (H. Miller), **III:** 170, 187, 188–189, 190

Rote Walker, The (Jarman), **Supp. XVII:** 110, **113–115**

Roth, Henry, **Supp. IV Part 1:** 314; **Supp. IX: 227–243; Supp. VIII:** 233; **Supp. XIII:** 106

Roth, Philip, **I:** 144, 161; **II:** 591; **Retro. Supp. II:** 22, **279–297; Supp. I Part 1:** 186, 192; **Supp. I Part 2:** 431, 441, 443; **Supp. II Part 1:** 99; **Supp. III Part 2: 401–429; Supp. IV Part 1:** 236, 379, 388; **Supp. IX:** 227; **Supp. V:** 45, 119, 122, 257, 258; **Supp. VIII:** 88, 236, 245; **Supp. XI:** 64, 68, 99, 140; **Supp. XII:** 190, 310; **Supp. XIV:** 79, 93, 111, 112; **Supp. XVI:** 206; **Supp. XVII:** 43, 48, 183; **Supp. XVIII:** 89; **Supp. XXI:** 234; **Supp. XXII:** 268; **Supp. XXVI:** 119, 123

Roth, Rita, **Supp. XVI:** 112

Roth, William, **Supp. XV:** 142

Rothenberg, Jerome, **Supp. VIII:** 292; **Supp. XII:** 3; **Supp. XXIV:** 37

Rothermere, Lady Mary, **Retro. Supp. I:** 63

Rothko, Mark, **Supp. XV:** 144

Rothstein, Mervyn, **Supp. VIII:** 142

"Rouen, France"(Kenny), **Supp. XXIII:** 152

"Rouge High" (Hughes), **Supp. I Part 1:** 330

Rougemont, Denis de, **II:** 586; **IV:** 216; **Retro. Supp. I:** 328, 329, 330, 331

Rough Edges (Skloot), **Supp. XX: 196**

Roughing It (Twain), **II:** 312; **IV:** 195, 197, 198

Roughing It in the Bush (Shields), **Supp. VII:** 313

"Rough Outline" (Simic), **Supp. VIII:** 276

"Rough-Skinned Newt, The"(Schott), **Supp. XXIII:** 253–254

Rough South of Larry Brown, The (film, Hawkins), **Supp. XXI:** 39

Rougon-Macquart, Les (Zola), **II:** 175–176

Roumain, Jacques, **Retro. Supp. I:** 202; **Supp. IV Part 1:** 360, 367

"Round, The" (Kunitz), **Supp. III Part 1:** 268

"Roundelay Between Two Shepherdesses, A" (Notley), **Supp. XXII:** 229

"Round Trip" (Dunn), **Supp. XI:** 148–149

Round Up (Lardner), **II:** 426, 430, 431

Rountree, Owen (pseud.). *See* Kittredge, William; Krauzer, Steven M.

Rourke, Constance, **I:** 258; **IV:** 339, 352

Rourke, Milton, **Retro. Supp. II:** 89

Rousseau, Jean-Jacques, **I:** 226; **II:** 8, 343; **III:** 170, 178, 259; **IV:** 80, 173, 440; **Supp. I Part 1:** 126; **Supp. I Part 2:** 637, 659; **Supp. IV Part 1:** 171; **Supp. XI:** 245; **Supp. XVI:** 292; **Supp. XXI:** 83; **Supp. XXVI:** 38–39

Roussel, Raymond, **Supp. III Part 1:** 6, 7, 10, 15, 16, 21; **Supp. XV:** 182

"Route 302" (Halliday), **Supp. XIX:** 93

"Routes" (Everwine), **Supp. XV:** 82

"Route Six" (Kunitz), **Supp. III Part 1:** 258

Route Two (Erdrich and Dorris), **Supp. IV Part 1:** 260

"Routine Things Around the House, The" (Dunn), **Supp. XI:** 148

Rover Boys (Winfield), **III:** 146

Rovit, Earl, **IV:** 102

Rowan, Carl T., **Supp. XIV:** 306

Rowe, Anne E., **Supp. X:** 223

Rowe, John Carlos, **Retro. Supp. I:** 216

Rowe, Kenneth Thorpe, **Supp. XXIII:** 258

Rowell, Charles, **Supp. XXI:** 250, 254, 255; **Supp. XXIV:** 184

"Rowing" (Sexton), **Supp. II Part 2:** 696

"Rowing Endeth, The" (Sexton), **Supp. II Part 2:** 696

Rowlandson, Mary, **Supp. IV Part 2:** 430, 431

Rowling, J. K., **Supp. XXV:** 70

"Rows of Cold Trees, The" (Winters), **Supp. II Part 2:** 790–791, 800

Rowson, Susanna, **Supp. I Part 1:** 128; **Supp. XV: 229–248**

Roxanna Slade (Price), **Supp. VI:** 267

Roxie Hart (Watkins), **Supp. XVI:** 188

Royal Family, The (Vollmann), **Supp. XVII:** 226, 230, 233

"Royal Palm" (Crane), **I:** 401

Royce, Josiah, **I:** 443; **III:** 303, 600; **IV:** 26; **Retro. Supp. I:** 57; **Supp. XIV:** 197, 199; **Supp. XVII:** 97

"Roy McInnes" (Budbill), **Supp. XIX:** 6–7

"Roy Spivey" (July), **Supp. XXIV:** 210

Royster, Sarah Elmira, **III:** 410, 429

Royte, Elizabeth, **Supp. XV:** 59

Rózewicz, Tadeusz, **Supp. X:** 60

R. S. Thomas: Poetry and Theology (W. V. Davis), **Supp. XXI: 86–87**

Ruas, Charles, **Supp. IV Part 1:** 383

Ruback, Max, **Supp. XXIII:** 290

Rubáiyát (Khayyám), **I:** 568

Rubáiyát of Omar Khayyam (Fitzgerald), **Supp. I Part 2:** 416; **Supp. III Part 2:** 610; **Supp. XV:** 156

"Rubber Life" (Prose), **Supp. XVI:** 256

Rubel, Nora L., **Supp. XXIV:** 7

Rub from Snub, A (Swanwick), **Supp. XV:** 237

"Rubicon" (Cliff), **Supp. XXII:** 76

Rubin, Louis, **Supp. I Part 2:** 672, 673, 679; **Supp. X:** 42

Rubin, Louis D., Jr., **IV:** 116, 462–463

Rubin, Stan, **Supp. XIV:** 307, 310

Rubin, Stan Sanvel, **Supp. IV Part 1:** 242, 245, 252

Rubins, Josh, **Supp. XX: 89**

"Ruby Brown" (Hughes), **Supp. I Part 1:** 327

"Ruby Daggett" (Eberhart), **I:** 539

Rucker, Rudy, **Supp. X:** 302

Rudd, Hughes, **Supp. XII:** 141

"Rude Awakening, A" (Chopin), **Retro. Supp. II:** 64

Rudens (Plautus), **Supp. III Part 2:** 630

Ruderman, Judith, **Supp. IV Part 1:** 380

Rudge, Olga, **Supp. V:** 338

Rudikoff, Sonya, **Supp. XIV:** 113

Rudman, Mark, **Supp. XXIII:** 124; **Supp. XXIV:** 153

Rueckert, William, **I:** 264

Ruesch, Jurgen, **Supp. XV:** 147

Rugby Chapel (Arnold), **Supp. I Part 2:** 416

"Rugby Road" (Garrett), **Supp. VII:** 100

Rugge, John, **Supp. XXII:** 218

Ruining the New Road (Matthews), **Supp. IX:** 154, **155–157**

"Ruins of Italica, The" (Bryant, trans.), **Supp. I Part 1:** 166

Rukeyser, Muriel, **Retro. Supp. II:** 48; **Supp. VI: 271–289; Supp. XV:** 349; **Supp. XVII:** 74

"Rule of Phase Applied to History, The" (Adams), **I:** 19

Rule of the Bone (Banks), **Supp. V:** 16

Rulers of Kings (Atherton), **Supp. XXIV:** 23

"Rules by Which a Great Empire May Be Reduced to a Small One" (Franklin), **II:** 120

Rules For the Dance: A Handbook for Reading and Writing Metrical Verse (Oliver), **Supp. VII:** 229, 247

Rules of the Game, The (film), **Supp. XII:** 259

Rulfo, Juan, **Supp. IV Part 2:** 549

Rumba (film, Gering), **Supp. XVII:** 57

Rumbaut, Rubén, **Supp. XI:** 184

Rum Diary, The (Thompson), **Supp. XXIV:** 281, **283–286,** 293

Rümelin-Oesterlen, Natalie, **Supp. XX: 235**

Rumens, Carol, **Supp. XI:** 14; **Supp. XVI:** 212

Rumi, **Supp. XX:** 117

"Rumination of Rivers, The" (Bronk), **Supp. XXI:** 32

Rumkowski, Chaim, **Supp. XII:** 168

Rummel, Mary Kay, **Supp. XIII:** 280

"Rumor and a Ladder" (Bowles), **Supp. IV Part 1:** 93

Rumor of War, A (Caputo), **Supp. XIX: 17–21,** 25, **30**

Rumors (Simon), **Supp. IV Part 2:** 582–583, 591

Rumpelstiltskin (Gardner), **Supp. VI:** 72

"Rumpelstiltskin" (Grimm), **IV:** 266

"Rumpelstiltskin" (Sexton), **Supp. II Part 2:** 690

Run, Sheep, Run (Bodenheim), **Supp. XXV:** 27

"Runagate Runagate" (Hayden), **Supp. II Part 1:** 377

"Runes" (Nemerov), **III:** 267, 277–278

Run Man Run (C. Himes), **Supp. XVI:** 142, 143

"Runner, The" (Grossman), **Supp. XIX:** 83

"Running" (Wilbur), **Supp. III Part 2:** 558–559

"RUNNING-AWAY"(Strout), **Supp. XXIII:** 274

Running Dog (DeLillo), **Supp. VI:** 3, 6, 8, 14

"Running in Church" (A. Finch), **Supp. XVII:** 72

"Running the Table" Conroy), **Supp. XVI:** 75

"Run of Bad Luck, A" (Proulx), **Supp. VII:** 253–254

Run of Jacks, A (Hugo), **Supp. VI:** 131, 133, 134, 135, 136

Run River (Didion), **Supp. IV Part 1:** 197, 199–200, 201

Ruoff, A. LaVonne Brown, **Supp. IV Part 1:** 324, 327; **Supp. IV Part 2:** 559

Rupert, Jim, **Supp. XII:** 215

Ruppert, James, **Supp. IV Part 1:** 321

Rural Hours (Cooper), **Supp. XIII:** 152

"Rural Route" (Wright), **Supp. V:** 340

"Rural South, The" (Du Bois), **Supp. II Part 1:** 174

Rush, Benjamin, **Supp. I Part 2:** 505, 507

Rushdie, Salman, **Supp. IV Part 1:** 234, 297

Rushdy, Ashraf, **Supp. X:** 250

Rushing, Jimmy, **Retro. Supp. II:** 113

Rusk, Dean, **II:** 579

Ruskin, John, **II:** 323, 338; **IV:** 349; **Retro. Supp. I:** 56, 360; **Supp. I Part 1:** 2, 10, 87, 349; **Supp. I Part 2:** 410

Rusnak, Karl, **Supp. XVIII:** 149

Russell, Ada Dwyer, **II:** 513, 527

Russell, Bertrand, **II:** 27; **III:** 605, 606; **Retro. Supp. I:** 57, 58, 59, 60; **Supp. I Part 2:** 522; **Supp. V:** 290; **Supp. XII:** 45; **Supp. XIV:** 337

Russell, Diarmuid, **Retro. Supp. I:** 342, 345, 346–347, 349–350

Russell, George, **Retro. Supp. I:** 342

Russell, Herb, **Supp. I Part 2:** 465–466

Russell, John, **Supp. XIV:** 344, 347, 348

Russell, Peter, **III:** 479

Russell, Richard, **Supp. XI:** 102

Russell, Robert, **Supp. XX: 195**

Russell, Sue, **Supp. IV Part 2:** 653

Russello, Gerald, **Supp. XXIV:** 159

Russert, Margaret, **Supp. XVIII:** 62

Russert, Tim, **Supp. XII:** 272

Russia at War (Caldwell), **I:** 296

"Russia Between Myth and Reality: From *Meri* to *Three Cities*"(Krutikov), Supp. *XXIII:* 11

Russian Journal, A (Steinbeck), **IV:** 52, 63

Russo, Richard, **Supp. XI:** 349; **Supp. XII: 325–344; Supp. XXIII:** 302

"Rusty Autumn" (Swenson), **Supp. IV Part 2:** 640

Rutabaga-Roo: I've Got a Song and It's for You (Nye, album), **Supp. XIII:** 274

Ruth (biblical book), **Supp. I Part 2:** 516

Ruth, George Herman ("Babe"), **II:** 423; **Supp. I Part 2:** 438, 440

Rutheiser, Charles, **Supp. XXII:** 244

Ruth Hall (Fern), **Supp. V:** 122

Ruthven, K. K., **Supp. XXII:** 261

Rutkowska, Malgorzata, **Supp. XXII:** 208

Rutledge, Ann, **III:** 588; **Supp. I Part 2:** 471

Ruwe, Donelle R., **Supp. XII:** 215

Ryan, Alan, **Supp. XXVI:** 5

Ryan, Katy, **Supp. XXI:** 215

Ryan, Kay, **Supp. XXI:** 20; **Supp. XXV:** 222

Ryan, Maureen, **Supp. XXI:** 215

Ryan, Paul William, **Supp. XVIII: 223–239; Supp. XXI:** 264–265

Ryder (Barnes), **Supp. III Part 1:** 31, 36–38, 42, 43

"Ryder" (Rukeyser), **Supp. VI:** 273, 283

"Ry¿kan Says" (Budbill), **Supp. XIX:** 11

Ryle, Herbert Edward, **Supp. XX: 230**

Rymer, Thomas, **IV:** 122

S

S. (Updike), **Retro. Supp. I:** 330, 331, 332, 333

S-1 (Baraka), **Supp. II Part 1:** 55, 57

Saadi, **II:** 19

Saar, Doreen Alvarez, **Supp. XV:** 237

Sabbatai Zevi (Asch), **Supp. XXIII:** 12

"Sabbath, The" (Stowe), **Supp. I Part 2:** 587

"Sabbath Mom" (White), **Supp. I Part 2:** 671–672

Sabbaths (Berry), **Supp. X:** 31

Sabbath's Theater (P. Roth), **Retro. Supp. II:** 279, 288

"Sabbatical, The" (Stallings), **Supp. XXV:** 234

"Sabbioneta to Parma" (Di Piero), **Supp. XIX:** 36–37

Sabines, Jaime, **Supp. V:** 178

Sabol, Cathy, **Supp. XXVI:** 160

"Sabotage" (Baraka), **Supp. II Part 1:** 49, 53

"Saboteur" (Jin), **Supp. XVIII:** 97

Sacco, Nicola, **I:** 482, 486, 490, 494; **II:** 38–39, 426; **III:** 139–140; **Supp. I Part 2:** 446; **Supp. IX:** 199; **Supp. V:** 288–289; **Supp. XXII:** 277

Sachs, Hanns, **Supp. I Part 1:** 259; **Supp. X:** 186

Sack Full of Old Quarrels, A (Weigl), **Supp. XIX:** 277

"Sacks" (Carver), **Supp. III Part 1:** 143–144

Sacks, Oliver, **Supp. XVIII:** 143

Sacks, Peter, **Supp. IV Part 2:** 450

Sackville-West, Vita, **Supp. VIII:** 263

"Sacrament of Divorce, The" (Patchett), **Supp. XII:** 309

"Sacrament of Self: Catholic Roots of Contemporary Memoir" (lecture, Hampl), **Supp. XXII:** 81

"Sacraments" (Dubus), **Supp. VII:** 91

Sacred and Profane Memories (Van Vechten), **Supp. II Part 2:** 735, 749

"Sacred Chant for the Return of Black Spirit and Power" (Baraka), **Supp. II Part 1:** 51

"Sacred Factory, The" (Toomer), **Supp. IX:** 320

Sacred Fount, The (James), **II:** 332–333; **Retro. Supp. I:** 219, 228, 232

"Sacred Heart" (Egan), **Supp. XIX:** 52

"Sacred Hoop, The: A Contemporary Perspective" (Gunn Allen), **Supp. IV Part 1:** 324

Sacred Hoop, The: Recovering the Feminine in American Indian Traditions (Gunn Allen), **Supp. IV Part 1:** 319, 320, 322, 324, 325, 328–330, 331, 333, 334

Sacred Journey, The (Buechner), **Supp. XII:** 42, 53

"Sacred Thing, The" (Ryan as Quin), **Supp. XVIII:** 227

Sacred Wood, The (Eliot), **IV:** 431; **Retro. Supp. I:** 59, 60; **Supp. I Part 1:** 268; **Supp. II Part 1:** 136, 146

Sacrifice, The (Bidart), **Supp. XV:** 22, **27–30,** 35

"Sacrifice, The" (Bidart), **Supp. XV:** 29

"Sacrifice, The" (Oates), **Supp. II Part 2:** 523

Sacrilege of Alan Kent, The (Caldwell), **I:** 291–292

"Sad Brazil" (Hardwick), **Supp. III Part 1:** 210

Sad Days of Light (Balakian), **Supp. XXIII:** 20

"Sad Dust Glories" (Ginsberg), **Supp. II Part 1:** 376

Sad Dust Glories: Poems Written Work Summer in Sierra Woods (Ginsberg), **Supp. II Part 1:** 326

Sade, Marquis de, **III:** 259; **IV:** 437, 442; **Supp. XII:** 1, 14–15

Sad-Faced Boy (Bontemps), **Supp. XXII:** 5, 12

Sad Flower in the Sand, A (film), **Supp. XI:** 173

Sad Heart at the Supermarket, A (Jarrell), **II:** 386

"Sadie" (Matthiessen), **Supp. V:** 201

"Sadie and Maud" (Brooks), **Supp. XVIII:** 175

Sadness and Happiness (Pinsky), **Supp. VI:** 235, **237–241**

"Sadness of Brothers, The" (Kinnell), **Supp. III Part 1:** 237, 251

"Sadness of Days, The" (Salinas), **Supp. XIII:** 325

Sadness of Days, The: Selected and New Poems (Salinas), **Supp. XIII:** 311, **324–326**

"Sadness of Lemons, The" (Levine), **Supp. V:** 184

Sadoff, Ira, **Supp. XVII:** 241; **Supp. XXI:** 100

"Sad Rite" (Karr), **Supp. XI:** 243

"Sad Strains of a Gay Waltz" (Stevens), **Retro. Supp. I:** 302

"Safe" (Gordon), **Supp. IV Part 1:** 299, 306

"Safe in their Alabaster Chambers" (Dickinson), **Retro. Supp. I:** 30

Safer, Morley, **Supp. XIX:** 25

"Safe Subjects" (Komunyakaa), **Supp. XIII:** 118

Safety Features (Monson), **Supp. XXIV:** 230

"Safeway" (F. Barthelme), **Supp. XI:** 26, 27, 36

Saffin, John, **Supp. I Part 1:** 115

Saffy, Edna, **Supp. X:** 227

Sagan, Miriam, **Supp. XXIII:** 133

"Saga of an American Ranch" (P. N. Warren), **Supp. XX: 261**

"Saga of Arturo Bandini" (Fante), **Supp. XI:** 159, **166–169**

"Saga of King Olaf, The" (Longfellow), **II:** 489, 505; **Retro. Supp. II:** 154, 155, 164

"Sage of Stupidity and Wonder, The" (Goldbarth), **Supp. XII:** 191

Sahl, Mort, **II:** 435–436

"Sah Sin" (Gallagher), Supp. XXIV: 171

"Said" (Dixon), **Supp. XII:** 149–150

Said, Edward, **Supp. XXI:** 153

"Sailing after Lunch" (Stevens), **IV:** 73

Sailing Alone Around the Room: New and Selected Poems (Collins), **Supp. XXI:** 54, 56, 62

Sailing Alone Around the World (Slocum), **Supp. XXV:** 205, 206, 208, 213–216, 218

"Sailing Home from Rapallo" (Lowell), **Retro. Supp. II:** 189

Sailing through China (Theroux), **Supp. VIII:** 323

"Sailing to Byzantium" (Yeats), **III:** 263; **Supp. VIII:** 30; **Supp. X:** 74; **Supp. XI:** 281

"Sail Made of Rags, The" (Nye), **Supp. XIII:** 277

"Sailor off the Bremen" (Shaw), **Supp. XIX:** 247

"Sailors Lost at Sea" (Shields), **Supp. VII:** 318

"St Anne/Santa Ana" (Mora), **Supp. XIII:** 229

"Saint Anthony of Padua/San Antonio de Padua" (Mora), **Supp. XIII:** 228

"St. Augustine and the Bullfights" (Porter), **III:** 454

Sainte-Beuve, Charles Augustin, **IV:** 432

St. Elmo (Wilson), **Retro. Supp. I:** 351–352

"Saint Emmanuel the Good, Martyr" (Unamuno; Everwine, trans.), **Supp. XV:** 79

Sainte Vierge, La (Picabia), **Retro. Supp. II:** 331

Saint-Exupéry, Antoine de, **Supp. IX:** 247

"St. Francis Einstein of the Daffodils" (W. C. Williams), **IV:** 409–411

Saint-Gaudens, Augustus, **I:** 18, 228; **II:** 551

Saint-Gaudens, Homer, **Supp. XV:** 41

"St. George, the Dragon, and the Virgin" (R. Bly), **Supp. IV Part 1:** 73

St. George and the Godfather (Mailer), **III:** 46; **Retro. Supp. II:** 206, 208

Saint Jack (Theroux), **Supp. VIII:** 319

St. John, David, **Supp. V:** 180; **Supp. XI:** 270, 272; **Supp. XIII:** 312

St. John, Edward B., **Supp. IV Part 2:** 490

St. John, James Hector. *See* Crèvecoeur, Michel-Guillaume Jean de

"Saint John and the Back-Ache" (Stevens), **Retro. Supp. I:** 310

Saint Judas (Wright), **Supp. III Part 2: 595–599**

"Saint Judas" (Wright), **Supp. III Part 2:** 598–599

St. Louis Woman (Bontemps and Cullen), **Supp. IV Part 1:** 170

St. Mawr (Lawrence), **II:** 595

Saint Maybe (Tyler), **Supp. IV Part 2:** 670–671

"Saint Nicholas" (Moore), **III:** 215

"Saint"(O'Hara), **Supp. XXIII:** 219

St. Petersburg (Biely), **Supp. XII:** 13

Saint-Phalle, Niki de, **Supp. XV:** 187

"St. Roach" (Rukeyser), **Supp. VI:** 286

"Saint Robert" (Dacey), **Supp. IV Part 1:** 70

Saintsbury, George, **IV:** 440; **Supp. XV:** 181

Saints' Everlasting Rest, The (Baxter), **III:** 199; **IV:** 151, 153

Saint-Simon, Claude Henri, **Supp. I Part 2:** 648

"St. Thomas Aquinas" (Simic), **Supp. VIII:** 281

Saks, Gene, **Supp. IV Part 2:** 577, 588

Salamun, Tomaz, **Supp. VIII:** 272

Salazar, Dixie, **Supp. V:** 180; **Supp. XV:** 73

Saldívar, José David, **Supp. IV Part 2:** 544, 545; **Supp. XIX:** 110, 112–113

Sale, Richard, **Supp. IV Part 1:** 379

Sale, Roger, **Supp. V:** 244

Saleh, Dennis, **Supp. V:** 182, 186

"Salem" (Lowell), **II:** 550

Salemi, Joseph, **Supp. IV Part 1:** 284

Salem's Lot (King), **Supp. V:** 139, 144, 146, 151

"Sale of the Hessians, The" (Franklin), **II: 120**

Salick, Roydan, **Supp. XXIII:** 93, 94

Salinas, Luis Omar, **Supp. IV Part 2:** 545; **Supp. V:** 180; **Supp. XIII: 311–330; Supp. XV:** 73

"Salinas Is on His Way" (Salinas), **Supp. XIII:** 317

"Salinas Sends Messengers to the Stars" (Salinas), **Supp. XIII:** 317

"Salinas Summering at the Caspian and Thinking of Hamlet" (Salinas), **Supp. XIII:** 320

"Salinas Wakes Early and Goes to the Park to Lecture Sparrows" (Salinas), **Supp. XIII:** 320

Salinger, Doris, **III:** 551

Salinger, J. D., **II:** 255; **III: 551–574; IV:** 190, 216, 217; **Retro. Supp. I:** 102, 116, 335; **Supp. IV Part 2:** 502; **Supp. V:** 23, 119; **Supp. VIII:** 151; **Supp. XI:** 2, 66; **Supp. XIV:** 93; **Supp. XXIII:** 100; **Supp. XXVI:** 119

Salisbury, Harrison, **Supp. I Part 2:** 664

Salle, David, **Supp. XII:** 4

Salley, Columbus, **Supp. XIV:** 195

"Sally" (Cisneros), **Supp. VII:** 63

"Sally's Choice" (E. Stoddard), **Supp. XV:** 282

Salmagundi; or, The Whim-Whams and Opinions of Launcelot Langstaff Esq., and Others (Irving), **II:** 299, 300, 304

Salmon, Edward G., **Supp. XVIII:** 258

Salome (Strauss), **IV:** 316

Salon (online magazine), **Supp. VIII:** 310; **Supp. X:** 202

"Salt"(Crooker), **Supp. XXIII:** 62

Salt Eaters, The (Bambara), **Supp. XI:** 1, **12–14**

Salt Ecstasies, The (White), **Supp. XI:** 123

Salter, James, **Supp. IX: 245–263; Supp. XIX:** 252; **Supp. XVI:** 237, 247

Salter, Mary Jo, **Supp. IV Part 2:** 653; **Supp. IX:** 37, 292; **Supp. XV:** 251, 253; **Supp. XVII:** 112; **Supp. XXIII:** 112

Salter, Sarah, **Supp. XXVI:** 57

Salt Garden, The (Nemerov), **III:** 269, 272–275, 277

"Salt Garden, The" (Nemerov), **III:** 267–268

Salting the Ocean (Nye, ed.), **Supp. XIII:** 280

Salt Lesson, The (C. Frost), **Supp. XV:** 92, 96

"Salt Lesson, The" (C. Frost), **Supp. XV:** 99

"Salts and Oils" (Levine), **Supp. V:** 190

Salt to the Devil (film, Dmytryk), **Supp. XX: 41**

Saltzman, Arthur, **Supp. XIII:** 48

Saltzman, Harry, **Supp. XI:** 307

"Salut au Monde!" (Whitman), **Retro. Supp. I:** 387, 396, 400

"Salute" (MacLeish), **III:** 13

Salute (Shaw), **Supp. XIX:** 244

"Salute to Mister Yates, A" (Dubus), **Supp. XI:** 347, 349

Salute to Spring (Le Sueur), **Supp. XXIII:** 164, 165, 166, 172

Salvador (Didion), **Supp. IV Part 1:** 198, 207–208, 210

"Salvage" (Clampitt), **Supp. IX:** 41

"Salvage" (Rinehart), **Supp. XXV:** 194

Salvation (Asch), **Supp. XXIII:** 3, 4, **12**, 13, 15

Salvos: An Informal Book About Books and Plays (W. Frank), **Supp. XX: 75**

Samain, Albert, **II:** 528

Same Door, The (Updike), **IV:** 214, 219, 226; **Retro. Supp. I:** 320

"Same in Blues" (Hughes), **Retro. Supp. I:** 208

"Same Kiss After Many Years, The" (Gallagher), **Supp. XXIV:** 169

Same River Twice, The (Offutt), **Supp. XIX:** 163, 164, **167–168,** 175

"Samhain" (A. Finch), **Supp. XVII:** 72

Sam Lawson's Oldtown Fireside Stories (Stowe), **Supp. I Part 2:** 587, 596, 598–599

Sam Patch, the High, Wide & Handsome Jumper (Bontemps and Conroy), **Supp. XXII:** 5, 11

"Sa'm Pèdi" (Bell), **Supp. X:** 17

"Sampler, A" (MacLeish), **III:** 4

Sampoli, Maria, **Supp. V:** 338

Sampson, Edward, **Supp. I Part 2:** 664, 673

Sampson, Martin, **Supp. I Part 2:** 652

"Sam's Dad" (Lamott), **Supp. XX: 142–143**

Sam's Legacy (Neugeboren), **Supp. XVI:** 221, 222

Samson Agonistes (Milton), **III:** 274

"Samson and Delilah" (Masters), **Supp. I Part 2:** 459

Samuel, Maurice, **Supp. XXIII:** 1, 7

Samuel de Champlain: Father of New France (Morison), **Supp. I Part 2:** 496–497

Samuels, Charles Thomas, **Retro. Supp. I:** 334

"Samuel Sewall" (Hecht), **Supp. X:** 58

"Samwheel" (Lamott), **Supp. XX: 144–145**

Sanborn, Franklin B., **IV:** 171, 172, 178

Sanborn, Kate, **Supp. XIII:** 152

Sanborn, Sara, **Supp. XIV:** 113

Sanchez, Carol Anne, **Supp. IV Part 1:** 335

Sanchez, Carol Lee, **Supp. IV Part 2:** 499, 557

Sanchez, Sonia, **Supp. II Part 1:** 34

Sánchez Beras, César, **Supp. XXI:** 100, 104

Sanctified Church, The (Hurston), **Supp. VI:** 150

"Sanction of the Victims, The" (Rand), **Supp. IV Part 2:** 528

Sanctuary (Faulkner), **II:** 57, 61–63, 72, 73, 74, 174; **Retro. Supp. I:** 73, 84, 86–87, 87; **Supp. I Part 2:** 614; **Supp. XII:** 16

"Sanctuary" (Larsen), **Supp. XVIII:** 119, 130–131

Sanctuary (Wharton), **IV:** 311

"Sanctuary" (Wylie), **Supp. I Part 2:** 711

"Sanctuary, The" (Nemerov), **III:** 272, 274

Sanctuary V (Schulberg), **Supp. XVIII:** 254

"Sanctus" (Nelson), **Supp. XVIII:** 183

Sand, George, **II:** 322; **Retro. Supp. I:** 235, 372; **Supp. XV:** 275

"Sandalphon" (Longfellow), **II:** 498

Sand and Foam: A Book of Aphorisms (Gibran), **Supp. XX: 115, 121–122**

Sandbox, The (Albee), **I:** 74–75, 89

Sandburg, Carl, **I:** 103, 109, 384, 421; **II:** 529; **III:** 3, 20, **575–598; Retro. Supp. I:** 133, 194; **Supp. I Part 1:** 257, 320; **Supp. I Part 2:** 387, 389, 454, 461, 653; **Supp. III Part 1:** 63, 71, 73, 75; **Supp. IV Part 1:** 169; **Supp. IV Part 2:** 502; **Supp. IX:** 1, 15, 308; **Supp. XIII:** 274, 277; **Supp. XV:** 293, 299, 300, 301, 302, 306; **Supp. XXII:** 275; **Supp. XXIII:** 161, 165; **Supp. XXV:** 18

Sandburg, Mrs. Carl (Lillian Steichen), **III:** 580

Sandburg, Helga, **III:** 583

Sandburg, Janet, **III:** 583, 584

Sandburg, Margaret, **III:** 583, 584

Sand County Almanac and Sketches Here and There, A (Leopold), **Supp. XIV:** 177, 178, **182–192**

"Sand Creek, Colorado" (Kenny), **Supp. XXIII:** 155

"Sand Dabs" (Oliver), **Supp. VII:** 245

"Sand Dunes" (Frost), **Retro. Supp. I:** 137; **Retro. Supp. II:** 41

Sander, August, **Supp. IX:** 211

Sanders, Mark, **Supp. XIX:** 119, 121

Sanders, Scott Russell, **Supp. XVI: 265–280**

Sandlin, Tim, **Supp. XXII:** 114

"Sandman, The" (Barthelme), **Supp. IV Part 1:** 47

Sandman's Dust (Bukiet), **Supp. XVII:** 40, 41

Sando, Joe S., **Supp. IV Part 2:** 510

Sandoe, James, **Supp. IV Part 1:** 131; **Supp. IV Part 2:** 470

Sandoval, Chela, **Supp. XXIII:** 204

Sandoz, Mari, **Supp. XV:** 141; **Supp. XXIII:** 146; **Supp. XXIV: 243–261**

Sandperl, Ira, **Supp. VIII:** 200

"Sand-Quarry and Moving Figures" (Rukeyser), **Supp. VI:** 271, 278

Sand Rivers (Matthiessen), **Supp. V:** 203

"Sand Roses, The" (Hogan), **Supp. IV Part 1:** 401

Sands, Diana, **Supp. IV Part 1:** 362

Sands, Robert, **Supp. I Part 1:** 156, 157

"Sands at Seventy" (Whitman), **IV:** 348

"Sandstone Farmhouse, A" (Updike), **Retro. Supp. I:** 318

Sandy Bottom Orchestra, The (Keillor and Nilsson), **Supp. XVI:** 177

Sanford, John, **IV:** 286, 287

San Francisco (film), **Supp. XVI:** 181, 192

"San Francisco" (Hempel), **Supp. XXI:** 118

"San Francisco Blues" (Kerouac), **Supp. III Part 1:** 225

Sangamon County Peace Advocate, The (Lindsay), **Supp. I Part 2:** 379

Sanger, Margaret, **Supp. I Part 1:** 19; **Supp. XXI:** 6; **Supp. XXIII:** 161

Sankofa (film), **Supp. XX: 154**

Sansom, William, **IV:** 279

Sans Soleil (film), **Supp. IV Part 2:** 436

"Santa" (Sexton), **Supp. II Part 2:** 693

Santa Claus: A Morality (Cummings), **I:** 430, 441

"Santa Fe, New Mexico" (Kenny), **Supp. XXIII:** 150

"Santa Fé Trail, The" (Lindsay), **Supp. I Part 2:** 389

"Santa Lucia" (Hass), **Supp. VI:** 105–106

"Santa Lucia II" (Hass), **Supp. VI:** 105–106

Santayana, George, **I:** 222, 224, 236, 243, 253, 460; **II:** 20, 542; **III:** 64, **599–622; IV:** 26, 339, 351, 353, 441; **Retro. Supp. I:** 55, 57, 67, 295; **Retro. Supp. II:** 179; **Supp. I Part 2:** 428; **Supp. II Part 1:** 107; **Supp. X:** 58; **Supp. XIV:** 199, 335, 340, 342; **Supp. XVI:** 189; **Supp. XVII:** 97, 106; **Supp. XX: 228, 229, 231**

Santiago, Esmeralda, **Supp. XI:** 177

"Santorini: Stopping the Leak" (Merrill), **Supp. III Part 1:** 336

Santos, John Phillip, **Supp. XIII:** 274

Santos, Sherod, **Supp. VIII:** 270

Saphier, William, **Supp. XXV:** 19, 20

Sapir, Edward, **Supp. VIII:** 295; **Supp. XVI:** 283

"Sapphics for Patience" (A. Finch), **Supp. XVII:** 72

Sapphira and the Slave Girl (Cather), **I:** 331; **Retro. Supp. I:** 2, **19–20**

Sappho, **II:** 544; **III:** 142; **Supp. I Part 1:** 261, 269; **Supp. I Part 2:** 458; **Supp. XII:** 98, 99; **Supp. XVII:** 74; **Supp. XXV:** 222

"Sappho" (Wright), **Supp. III Part 2:** 595, 604

"Sappho, Keats" (Hadas), **Supp. XXIII:** 113

"Sara" (song, Dylan), **Supp. XVIII:** 28

"Sarah" (Schwartz), **Supp. II Part 2:** 663

Sarah; or, The Exemplary Wife (Rowson), **Supp. XV:** 242

"Saratoga" mysteries (Dobyns), **Supp. XIII:** 79–80

Sardonic Arm, The (Bodenheim), **Supp. XXV:** 22, 23

Sargent, John Singer, **II:** 337, 338; **Supp. XX: 231**

Sarlós, Robert K., **Supp. XXI:** 7, 12, 13

Saroyan, Aram, **Supp. XV:** 182

Saroyan, William, **III:** 146–147; **IV:** 393; **Supp. I Part 2:** 679; **Supp. IV Part 1:** 83; **Supp. IV Part 2:** 502; **Supp. XIII:** 280; **Supp. XXIII:** 20; **Supp. XXV:** 29

Sarris, Greg, **Supp. IV Part 1:** 329, 330

Sarton, George, **Supp. VIII:** 249

Sarton, May, **Supp. III Part 1:** 62, 63; **Supp. VIII: 249–268; Supp. XIII:** 296; **Supp. XVII:** 71

Sartoris (Faulkner), **II:** 55, 56–57, 58, 62; **Retro. Supp. I:** 77, 81, 82, 83, 88

Sartor Resartus (Carlyle), **II:** 26; **III:** 82

Sartre, Jean-Paul, **I:** 82, 494; **II:** 57, 244; **III:** 51, 204, 292, 453, 619; **IV:** 6, 223, 236, 477, 487, 493; **Retro. Supp. I:** 73; **Supp. I Part 1:** 51; **Supp. IV Part 1:** 42, 84; **Supp. IX:** 4; **Supp. VIII:** 11; **Supp. XIII:** 74, 171; **Supp. XIV:** 24; **Supp. XVII:** 137; **Supp. XXIV:** 281

Sassone, Ralph, **Supp. X:** 171

Sassoon, Siegfried, **II:** 367; **Supp. XIX:** 18; **Supp. XV:** 308

Satan in Goray (Singer), **IV:** 1, 6–7, 12; **Retro. Supp. II:** 303, **304–305**

Satan Says (Olds), **Supp. X:** 201, 202, **202–204,** 215

"Satan Says" (Olds), **Supp. X:** 202; **Supp. XVII:** 114

Satanstoe (Cooper), **I:** 351–352, 355

"Sather Gate Illumination" (Ginsberg), **Supp. II Part 1:** 329

"Satire as a Way of Seeing" (Dos Passos), **III:** 172

Satires of Persius, The (Merwin, trans.), **Supp. III Part 1:** 347

Satirical Rogue on Poetry, The (Francis). *See Pot Shots at Poetry* (Francis)

Satori in Paris (Kerouac), **Supp. III Part 1:** 231
"Saturday" (Salinas), **Supp. XIII:** 315
"Saturday Matinee" (Trethewey), **Supp. XXI:** 251
Saturday Night (Orlean), **Supp. XXV:** 159, 161
Saturday Night at the War (Shanley), **Supp. XIV:** 315
"Saturday Rain" (Kees), **Supp. XV:** 136
"Saturday Route, The" (Wolfe), **Supp. III Part 2:** 580
Satyagraha (Gandhi), **IV:** 185
"Satyr's Heart, The" (B. Kelly), **Supp. XVII:** 132
Saucedo, José Guadalupe, **Supp. XXIII:** 197
Saudade (Vaz), **Supp. XXVI:** 256–258, 263
Saul and Patsy (C. Baxter), **Supp. XVII:** 22–23
"Saul and Patsy" (C. Baxter), **Supp. XVII:** 17
"Saul and Patsy Are Getting Comfortable in Michigan" (C. Baxter), **Supp. XVII:** 22
"Saul and Patsy Are in Labor" (C. Baxter), **Supp. XVII:** 20, 22
"Saul and Patsy Are Pregnant" (C. Baxter), **Supp. XVII:** 22
Saunders, George, **Supp. XIX: 223–237; Supp. XXII:** 49; **Supp. XXIV:** 199
Saunders, Richard, **II:** 110
Savage, Augusta, **Retro. Supp. II:** 115
Savage, James, **II:** 111
Savage, Tom, **Supp. XXIV:** 45
Savage Holiday (Wright), **IV:** 478, 488
Savage in Limbo: A Concert Play (Shanley), **Supp. XIV:** 315, **319–321,** 323, 324
Savage Love (Shepard and Chaikin), **Supp. III Part 2:** 433
Savage Place, A (Parker), **Supp. XIX:** 185
Savage Wilds (Reed), **Supp. X:** 241
Save Me, Joe Louis (Bell), **Supp. X:** 7, 10, **11–12**
Save Me the Waltz (Z. Fitzgerald), **II:** 95; **Retro. Supp. I:** 110; **Supp. IX:** 58, 59, 65, **66–68**
"Save One for Mainz" (Huddle), **Supp. XXVI:** 150, 153
Savers, Michael, **Supp. XI:** 307
Saving Lives (Goldbarth), **Supp. XII:** 192
Saving Private Ryan (film), **Supp. V:** 249; **Supp. XI:** 234
Savings (Hogan), **Supp. IV Part 1:** 397, 404, 405, 406, 410
Saving Sebastian (Taylor), **Supp. XXIII:** 57
Savo, Jimmy, **I:** 440
Savran, David, **Supp. IX:** 145; **Supp. XIII:** 209; **Supp. XV:** 321; **Supp. XXIV:** 263, 264
"Sawdust" (Offutt), **Supp. XIX:** 164
Sawyer-Lauçanno, Christopher, **Supp. IV Part 1:** 95
Saxon, Lyle, **Retro. Supp. I:** 80
"Saxophone" (Di Piero), **Supp. XIX:** 38

"Sax's and Selves" (Halliday), **Supp. XIX:** 88
"Say All" (Ray), **Supp. XVIII:** 193
Say and Seal (S. and A. Warner), **Supp. XVIII:** 258, 266
Saye and Sele, Lord, **Supp. I Part 1:** 98
Sayer, Mandy, **Supp. XIII:** 118
Sayers, Dorothy, **Supp. IV Part 1:** 341; **Supp. IV Part 2:** 464
Sayers, Valerie, **Supp. XI:** 253; **Supp. XVIII:** 99
"Say Good-bye" (Weigl), **Supp. XIX:** 288
Say Her Name (Goldman), **Supp. XXV:** 50, 59–62
"Sayings/For Luck" (Goldbarth), **Supp. XII:** 176
"Saying What Needs To Be Said" (Skloot), **Supp. XX: 201**
Say! Is This the U.S.A.? (Caldwell), **I:** 293, 294–295, 304, 309, 310
Saylor, Bruce, **Supp. XII:** 253
Sayre, Joel, **Supp. XIII:** 166
Sayre, Nora, **Supp. XII:** 119
Sayre, Zelda, **Retro. Supp. I:** 101, 102–103, 104, 105, 108, 109, 110, 113, 114. *See also* Fitzgerald, Zelda (Zelda Sayre)
"Say Yes" (Wolff), **Supp. VII:** 344
"Say You Love Me" (Peacock), **Supp. XIX:** 198
Scafe, Suzanne, **Supp. XXIII:** 94, 95
"Scale" (Halliday), **Supp. XIX:** 92
"Scales of the Eyes, The" (Nemerov), **III:** 272, 273, 277
Scalpel (McCoy), **Supp. XIII: 174–175**
Scalpel (screen treatment, McCoy), **Supp. XIII:** 174
Scandalabra (Zelda Fitzgerald), **Supp. IX:** 60, 61, 65, 67, **68–70**
"Scandal Detectives, The" (Fitzgerald), **II:** 80–81; **Retro. Supp. I:** 99
Scarberry-García, Susan, **Supp. IV Part 2:** 486
Scarborough, Dorothy, **Supp. XVIII:** 279–280
Scarecrow, The (Connelly), **Supp. XXI:** 71, 74, 78, **79**
"Scarecrow, The" (Farrell), **II:** 45
"Scarf, A" (Shields), **Supp. VII:** 328
Scarlet Cabinet, The (Notley), **Supp. XXII:** 233
Scarlet Letter, The (Hawthorne), **II:** 63, 223, 224, 231, 233, 239–240, 241, 243, 244, 255, 264, 286, 290, 291, 550; **Retro. Supp. I:** 63, 145, 147, 152, **157–159,** 160, 163, 165, 220, 248, 330, 335; **Retro. Supp. II:** 100; **Supp. I Part 1:** 38; **Supp. II Part 1:** 386; **Supp. VIII:** 108, 198; **Supp. XII:** 11; **Supp. XVII:** 143; **Supp. XX: 178, 183; Supp. XXII:** 147
"Scarlet Letter Aleph, The" (Mirvis), **Supp. XX: 183**
Scarlet Plague, The (London), **II:** 467
Scarlet Sister Mary (Peterkin), **Supp. XXII:** 189
Scar Lover (Crews), **Supp. XI:** 103, 107, **114–115**

"Scarred Girl, The" (Dickey), **Supp. IV Part 1:** 180
Scates, Maxine, **Supp. XIV:** 264, 265, 274
"Scenario" (H. Miller), **III:** 184
"Scene" (Howells), **II:** 274
"Scene in Jerusalem, A" (Stowe), **Supp. I Part 2:** 587
"Scenes" (Shields), **Supp. VII:** 318
Scènes d'Anabase (chamber music) (Bowles), **Supp. IV Part 1:** 82
"Scenes from a Documentary History of Mississippi" (Trethewey), **Supp. XXI:** 255–256
Scenes from American Life (Gurney), **Supp. V:** 95, 96, 105, 108
Scenes from Another Life (McClatchy), **Supp. XII: 255–256**
"Scenes from Childhood" (W. V. Davis), **Supp. XXI:** 95
"Scenes of Childhood" (Merrill), **Supp. III Part 1:** 322, 323, 327
"Scented Herbage of My Breast" (Whitman), **IV:** 342–343
"Scent of a Woman's Ink" (Prose), **Supp. XVI:** 259
"Scent of Unbought Flowers, The" (Ríos), **Supp. IV Part 2:** 547
Scepticisms (Aiken), **I:** 58
Scève, Maurice, **Supp. III Part 1:** 11
Schad, Christian, **Supp. IV Part 1:** 247
Schafer, Benjamin G., **Supp. XIV:** 144
Schafer, William, **Supp. XIX:** 164, 172
Schaller, George, **Supp. V:** 208, 210–211
Schapiro, Meyer, **II:** 30
Scharmann, Hermann Balthazar, **Supp. XII:** 41
Scharper, Alice, **Supp. XXII:** 175
Scharper, Diane, **Supp. XXIII:** 134
Schary, Dore, **Supp. IV Part 1:** 365; **Supp. XIII:** 163
Schatz, Tom, **Supp. XVIII:** 242
Schaum, Melita, **Supp. XXII:** 166
Schaumbergh, Count de, **II:** 120
Schechner, Richard, **Supp. XXIV:** 116
Scheele, Roy, **Supp. XVI:** 54; **Supp. XXI:** 103
Scheeman, George, **Supp. XXII:** 230
Scheffauer, G. H., **I:** 199
"Scheherazade" (Ashbery), **Supp. III Part 1:** 18
Scheick, William, **Supp. V:** 272
Schelberg, Budd, **Supp. XVIII: 241–256**
Scheler, Max, **I:** 58
Schelling, Friedrich, **Supp. I Part 2:** 422
Schenck, Joseph, **Supp. XVI:** 186
Schenk, Margaret, **I:** 199
Scheponik, Peter, **Supp. X:** 210
Scherer, Loline, **Supp. XIII:** 161
"Scherzo"(Hadas), **Supp. XXIII:** 113
Schevill, James, **I:** 116
Schickel, Richard, **Supp. XV:** 1
Schifano, Mario, **Supp. XXIII:** 217
Schifino, Martin, **Supp. XXVI:** 145
Schilder, Paul, **Supp. I Part 2:** 622
Schildkraut, Rudolph, **Supp. XXIII:** 8
Schiller, Andrew, **II:** 20
Schiller, Frederick, **Supp. V:** 290
Schiller, Johann Christoph Friedrich von, **I:** 224; **Supp. IV Part 2:** 519; **Supp.**

XVI: 292

Schiller, Lawrence, **Retro. Supp. II:** 208, 212, 214

Schimmel, Harold, **Supp. V:** 336

"Schizoid Nature of the Implied Author in Twentieth-Century American Ethnic Novels, The" (Nelson), **Supp. XVIII:** 172

Schjeldahl, Peter, **Supp. XXIV:** 44

Schlegel, Augustus Wilhelm, **III:** 422, 424

Schlegell, David von, **Supp. IV Part 2:** 423

Schleiermacher, Friedrich, **III:** 290–291, 309

Schleifer, Ronald, **Supp. XVIII:** 144

Schlepping Through the Alps (S. Apple), **Supp. XVII:** 8

Schlesinger, Arthur, Jr., **III:** 291, 297–298, 309

Schleuning, Neala, **Supp. XXIII:** 165

Schmidt, Jon Zlotnik, **Supp. IV Part 1:** 2

Schmidt, Kaspar. *See* Stirner, Max

Schmidt, Michael, **Supp. X:** 55

Schmitt, Carl, **I:** 386–387

Schmitz, Neil, **Supp. X:** 243

Schnackenberg, Gjertrud, **Supp. XV: 249–268**

Schneeman, George, **Supp. XXIV:** 41

Schneider, Alan, **I:** 87

Schneider, Louis, **Supp. I Part 2:** 650

Schneider, Romy, **Supp. IV Part 2:** 549

Schneider, Steven, **Supp. IX:** 271, 274

Schnellock, Emil, **III:** 177

Schneour, Zalman, **IV:** 11

"Schnetzer Day" (Halliday), **Supp. XIX:** 93

Schnitzler, Arthur, **Supp. XV:** 307; **Supp. XVI:** 187

Schoerke, Meg, **Supp. XVII:** 110

"Scholar Gypsy, The" (Arnold), **II:** 541

"Scholastic and Bedside Teaching" (Holmes), **Supp. I Part 1:** 305

Schöler, Bo, **Supp. IV Part 1:** 399, 400, 403, 407, 409; **Supp. IV Part 2:** 499

Scholes, Robert, **Supp. V:** 40, 42

Scholtz, Carter, **Supp. XVIII:** 144

Schomburg, Arthur, **Supp. X:** 134; **Supp. XXII:** 6

Schomburg Library of Nineteenth-Century Black Women Writers (H. L. Gates, ed.), **Supp. XX:** 105

Schönberg, Claude-Michel, **Supp. XXI:** 155

Schoolboy Howlers (Abingdon), **Supp. XVI:** 99

Schoolcraft, Henry Rowe, **II:** 503; **Retro. Supp. II:** 160; **Supp. XXIII:** 223, 227, 228, 232, 233–234

Schoolcraft, Jane Johnston (Bamewawagezhikaquay), **Supp. XXIII: 223–238**

"School Days of an Indian Girl, The" (Zitkala-Ša), **Supp. XXV:** 272

"School Daze" (Bambara), **Supp. XI:** 19

School Daze (film), **Supp. XI:** 19, 20

"Schoolhouse" (Levis), **Supp. XI:** 258

"School of Giorgione, The" (Pater), **I:** 51

"School Play, The" (Merrill), **Supp. III Part 1:** 336

"Schooner Fairchild's Class" (Benét), **Supp. XI:** 55

Schopenhauer, Arthur, **III:** 600, 604; **IV:** 7; **Retro. Supp. I:** 256; **Retro. Supp. II:** 94; **Supp. I Part 1:** 320; **Supp. I Part 2:** 457; **Supp. X:** 187; **Supp. XVI:** 184

Schorer, Mark, **II:** 28; **III:** 71; **Retro. Supp. I:** 115; **Supp. IV Part 1:** 197, 203, 211; **Supp. XVI:** 206

Schott, Penelope Scambly, **Supp. XXIII: 239–256**

Schott, Webster, **Supp. IX:** 257

Schøtt-Khristensen, Lene, **Supp. XXVI:** 124, 125

Schotts, Jeffrey, **Supp. XII:** 193

Schrader, Mary von. *See* Jarrell, Mrs. Randall (Mary von Schrader)

Schreiber, Jan, **Supp. XXI:** 105, 111

Schreiner, Olive, **I:** 419; **Supp. XI:** 203

"Schreuderspitze, The" (Helprin), **Supp. XXV:** 85

Schroeder, Eric James, **Supp. V:** 238, 244

Schubert, Bernard L., **Supp. XVII:** 58

Schubert, David, **Supp. XXIV:** 45

Schubert, Franz Peter, **Supp. I Part 1:** 363

Schubnell, Matthias, **Supp. IV Part 2:** 486

Schudel, Matt, **Supp. XXII:** 205, 214

Schuessler, Jennifer, **Supp. XXVI:** 126

Schulberg, Budd, **II:** 98; **Retro. Supp. I:** 113; **Supp. XIII:** 170; **Supp. XV:** 194

Schulberg, Stuart, **Supp. XVIII:** 254

Schulman, Grace, **Supp. XXIII:** 58

Schulman, Tom, **Supp. XXI:** 193, 194

Schulz, Bruno, **Supp. IV Part 2:** 623; **Supp. XVII:** 41

Schuman, William, **Supp. XII:** 253; **Supp. XXII:** 283

Schumann, Dr. Alanson Tucker, **III:** 505

Schuster, Edgar H., **Supp. VIII:** 126

Schuyler, George S., **III:** 110; **Supp. XIX:** 78; **Supp. XVI:** 142; **Supp. XXVI:** 167

Schuyler, James, **Supp. XV:** 177, 178; **Supp. XXIII:** 207, 212, 215, 217; **Supp. XXIV:** 33

Schuyler, William, **Supp. I Part 1:** 211

"Schuylkill, The" (Halliday), **Supp. XIX:** 92

Schwartz, Delmore, **I:** 67, 168, 188, 288; **IV:** 128, 129, 437; **Retro. Supp. II:** 29, 178; **Supp. II Part 1:** 102, 109; **Supp. II Part 2: 639–668; Supp. IX:** 299; **Supp. VIII:** 98; **Supp. XIII:** 320; **Supp. XIV:** 3; **Supp. XIX:** 257; **Supp. XV:** 184

Schwartz, Leonard, **Supp. XVI:** 289

Schwartz, Lloyd, **Supp. I Part 1:** 81; **Supp. XXIV:** 160

Schwartz, Marilyn, **Supp. XII:** 126, 128, 130, 132

Schwartz, Meryl F., **Supp. XXII:** 65, 66

Schwartz, Richard B., **Supp. XIV:** 23, 27

Schwarz, A. B. Christa, **Supp. XIX:** 77, 79

Schwed, Peter, **Supp. XXII:** 119

Schweitzer, Albert, **Supp. IV Part 1:** 373

Schweitzer, Harold, **Supp. X:** 210

Schwerdt, Lisa M., **Supp. XIV:** 155, 171

Schwitters, Kurt, **III:** 197; **Retro. Supp. II:** 322, 331, 336; **Supp. IV Part 1:** 79

"Science" (Jeffers), **Supp. II Part 2:** 426

Science and Health with Key to the Scriptures (Eddy), **I:** 383

"Science Favorable to Virtue" (Freneau), **Supp. II Part 1:** 274

Science of English Verse, The (Lanier), **Supp. I Part 1:** 368, 369

"Science of the Night, The" (Kunitz), **Supp. III Part 1:** 258, 265

"Sci-Fi Floater Genius" (Halliday), **Supp. XIX:** 91

Sciolino, Martina, **Supp. XII:** 9

"Scissors" (C. Baxter), **Supp. XVII:** 19

Scofield, Sandra, **Supp. XXI:** 119

Scooter tetralogy (Murray). *See Magic Keys, The* (Murray); *Seven League Boots, The* (Murray); *Spyglass Tree, The* (Murray); *Train Whistle Guitar* (Murray)

Scopes, John T., **III:** 105, 495

"Scorched Face, The" (Hammett), **Supp. IV Part 1:** 344

"Scorn" (C. Frost), **Supp. XV:** 105

"Scorpion, The" (Bowles), **Supp. IV Part 1:** 84, 86

Scorsese, Martin, **Supp. IV Part 1:** 356; **Supp. XVIII:** 22

"Scotland" (Huddle), **Supp. XXVI:** 155

Scott, Anne Firor, **Supp. I Part 1:** 19

Scott, A. O., **Supp. X:** 301, 302; **Supp. XII:** 343

Scott, Duncan C., **Supp. XXVI:** 87

Scott, Evelyn, **Retro. Supp. I:** 73; **Supp. XXII:** 198

Scott, Gavin, **Supp. XXII:** 218

Scott, George C., **III:** 165–166; **Supp. XI:** 304

Scott, George Lewis, **Supp. I Part 2:** 503, 504

Scott, Hazel, **Supp. XXII:** 12

Scott, Herbert, **Supp. V:** 180

Scott, Howard, **Supp. I Part 2:** 645

Scott, Joanna, **Supp. XVII: 183–197**

Scott, Lizabeth, **Supp. IV Part 2:** 524

Scott, Lynn Orilla, **Retro. Supp. II:** 12

Scott, Mark, **Retro. Supp. I:** 127

Scott, Mary Ellen, **Supp. XXVI:** 235

Scott, Nathan A., Jr., **II:** 27

Scott, Paul, **Supp. IV Part 2:** 690

Scott, Ridley, **Supp. XIII:** 268

Scott, Walter, **Supp. XVI:** 7, 13

Scott, Sir Walter, **I:** 204, 339, 341, 343, 354; **II:** 8, 17, 18, 217, 296, 301, 303, 304, 308; **III:** 415, 482; **IV:** 204, 453; **Retro. Supp. I:** 99; **Supp. I Part 2:** 579, 580, 685, 692; **Supp. IV Part 2:** 690; **Supp. IX:** 175; **Supp. X:** 51, 114

Scott, Whitney, **Supp. XXVI:** 49

Scott, Winfield Townley, **II:** 512; **Supp. I Part 2:** 705; **Supp. XV:** 51

Scottsboro boys, **I:** 505; **Supp. I Part 1:** 330

Scottsboro Limited (Hughes), **Retro. Supp. I:** 203; **Supp. I Part 1:** 328,

330–331, 332

Scoundrel Time (Hellman), **Supp. I Part 1:** 294–297; **Supp. IV Part 1:** 12; **Supp. VIII:** 243

Scrambled Eggs Super! (Geisel), **Supp. XVI:** 105

Scrambled Eggs & Whiskey: Poems, 1991–1995 (Carruth), **Supp. XVI:** 47

Scratch (MacLeish), **III:** 22–23

"Scratch Music" (Wright), **Supp. XV:** 343

"Scream, The" (Lowell), **II:** 550

"Screamer, The" (Coleman), **Supp. XI:** **92–93**

"Screamers, The" (Baraka), **Supp. II Part 1:** 38

"Screech Owl" (Huddle), **Supp. XXVI:** 151

"Screen Guide for Americans" (Rand), **Supp. IV Part 2:** 524

"Screen Memory" (Cliff), **Supp. XXII:** 75

"Screeno" (Schwartz), **Supp. II Part 2:** 660

Screens, The (Genet), **Supp. XII:** 12

Screen Sirens Scream! (Parla and Mitchell), **Supp. XXII:** 256

Scribblers on the Roof: Contemporary American Jewish Fiction (Bukiet and Roskies, eds.), **Supp. XVII:** 39, 49–50

Scripts for the Pageant (Merrill), **Supp. III Part 1:** 332, 333, 335

Scrolls from the Dead Sea, The (Wilson), **IV:** 429

Scruggs, Earl, **Supp. V:** 335

Scudder, Horace Elisha, **II:** 400, 401; **Retro. Supp. II:** 67; **Supp. I Part 1:** 220; **Supp. I Part 2:** 410, 414

Scully, James, **Supp. XII:** 131

"Sculpting the Whistle" (Ríos), **Supp. IV Part 2:** 549

"Sculptor" (Plath), **Supp. I Part 2:** 538

"Sculptor's Funeral, The" (Cather), **I:** 315–316; **Retro. Supp. I:** 5, 6; **Supp. XV:** 40

Scum (Singer), **Retro. Supp. II:** 316–317

Scupoli, Lorenzo, **IV:** 156

"Scythe Song" (Lang), **Retro. Supp. I:** 128

Sea and the Mirror, The: A Commentary on Shakespeare's "The Tempest" (Auden), *Supp. II Part 1:* 2, 18

Sea around Us, The (Carson), **Supp. IX:** 19, **23–25**

Sea around Us, The (film), **Supp. IX:** 25

Sea Birds Are Still Alive, The (Bambara), **Supp. XI:** 1, 4, **7–12**

"Sea Birds Are Still Alive, The" (Bambara), **Supp. XI:** 8

"Sea-Blue and Blood-Red" (Lowell), **II:** 524

Seabrook, John, **Supp. VIII:** 157

"Sea Burial from the Cruiser Reve" (Eberhart), **I:** 532–533

Seabury, David, **Supp. I Part 2:** 608

"Sea Calm" (Hughes), **Retro. Supp. I:** 199

"Sea Chanty" (Corso), **Supp. XII:** 118

"Sea Dream, A" (Whitter), **Supp. I Part 2:** 699

"Seafarer, The" (Pound, trans.), **Retro. Supp. I:** 287

Seagall, Harry, **Supp. XIII:** 166

Sea Garden (Doolittle), **Supp. I Part 1:** 257, 259, 266, 269, 272

Seager, Allan, **IV:** 305

Seagull on the Step, The (Boyle), **Supp. XXIV:** 60, 62

"Seagulls and Children" (C. Frost), **Supp. XV:** 95

Sea Lady, The (Boyce), **Supp. XXI:** 8, 13

"Sea Lily" (Doolittle), **Supp. I Part 1:** 266

Sea Lions, The (Cooper), **I:** 354, 355

Sealts, Merton M., Jr., **Retro. Supp. I:** 257

Seaman, Benjamin, **Supp. XXIII:** 69–70, 72

Seaman, Donna, **Supp. VIII:** 86; **Supp. X:** 1, 4, 12, 16, 213; **Supp. XIX:** 53, 55, 57, 58, 59, 60, 61; **Supp. XV:** 65; **Supp. XVIII:** 102; **Supp. XXI:** 236; **Supp. XXII:** 266; **Supp. XXIII:** 71, 74, 134, 135, 298; **Supp. XXIV:** 167, 171; **Supp. XXVI:** 150–151, 158

"Seamy Side, The"(Hadas), **Supp. XXIII:** 119

"Séance, The" (Singer), **IV:** 20

Séance and Other Stories, The (Singer), **IV:** 19–21

"Sea Oak" (Saunders), **Supp. XIX:** 228, 229, 231

Sea of Cortez (Steinbeck), **IV:** 52, 54, 62, 69

Sea of Grass, The (film), **Supp. XVIII:** 211

Sea of Grass, The (Richter), **Supp. XVIII:** **210–211**, 215–216, **217**, 220

"Sea Pieces" (Melville), **III:** 93

Searchers, The (film, Ford), **Supp. XVIII:** 57, 58, 135–136, 141

Searches and Seizures (Elkin), **Supp. VI:** **49**

"Search for Southern Identity, The" (Woodward), **Retro. Supp. I:** 75; **Supp. XXII:** 194

Search for the King, A: A Twelfth-Century Legend (Vidal), **Supp. IV Part 2:** 681

Searching for Caleb (Tyler), **Supp. IV Part 2:** 663–665, 671

"Searching for Poetry: Real *vs.* Fake" (B. Miller), **Supp. IV Part 1:** 67

Searching for Survivors (Banks), **Supp. V:** 7

"Searching for Survivors (I)" (Banks), **Supp. V:** 8

"Searching for Survivors (II)" (Banks), **Supp. V:** 7, 8

Searching for the Ox (Simpson), **Supp. IX:** 266, **274–275**

"Searching for the Ox" (Simpson), **Supp. IX:** 275, 280

"Searching in the Britannia Tavern" (Wagoner), **Supp. IX:** 327

Searching Wing, The, (Hellman), **Supp. I Part 1:** 277, 278, 281–282, 283, 292, 297

Search-Light. *See* Frank, Waldo

"Search Party, The" (Matthews), **Supp. IX:** **156**

Searle, Ronald, **Supp. I Part 2:** 604, 605

Sea Road to the Indies (Hart), **Supp. XIV:** 97

"Seascape" (Bishop), **Retro. Supp. II:** 42–43

Seascape: Needle's Eye (Oppen), **Supp. XXVI:** 236–237

"Sea's Green Sameness, The" (Updike), **IV:** 217

Seaside and the Fireside, The (Longfellow), **II:** 489; **Retro. Supp. II:** 159, 168

Season in Hell, A (Rimbaud), **III:** 189

Seasons, The (Thomson), **II:** 304; **Supp. I Part 1:** 151

Seasons' Difference, The (Buechner), **Supp. XII:** 47

Seasons of Celebration (Merton), **Supp. VIII:** 199, 208

Seasons of the Heart: In Quest of Faith (Kinard, comp.), **Supp. XIV:** 127

"Seasons of the Soul" (Tate), **IV:** 136–140

Seasons on Earth (Koch), **Supp. XV:** **183–184**

"Sea Surface Full of Clouds" (Stevens), **IV:** 82

"Sea Tides" (Hoffman), **Supp. XVIII:** 87

"Sea Treader" (Hoffman), **Supp. XVIII:** 87

"Sea Unicorns and Land Unicorns" (Moore), **III:** 202–203

Seaver, Edwin, **Supp. XXV:** 28

Seaver, Richard, **Supp. XI:** 301

"Seaweed" (Longfellow), **II:** 498

Sea-Wolf, The (London), **II:** 264, 466, 472–473

Sebald, W. G., **Supp. XIV:** 96; **Supp. XXI:** 92

Sebold, Alice, **Supp. XXII:** 55

Seckler, David, **Supp. I Part 2:** 650

"2nd Air Force" (Jarrell), **II:** 375

Second American Revolution and Other Essays (1976–1982), The (Vidal), **Supp. IV Part 2:** 679, 687, 688

Secondary Colors, The (A. Theroux), **Supp. VIII:** 312

Second Avenue (O'Hara), **Supp. XXIII:** 216

"Second Avenue"(O'Hara), **Supp. XXIII:** 208, 211, 218

Second Blush, The (Peacock), **Supp. XIX:** 197, **205–206**

Second Chance (Auchincloss), **Supp. IV Part 1:** 33

"Second Chances" (Hugo), **Supp. VI:** 144, 145

Second Coming, The (Percy), **Supp. III Part 1:** 383, 384, 387, 388, 396–397

"Second Coming, The" (Yeats), **III:** 294; **Retro. Supp. I:** 290, 311; **Supp. VIII:** 24; **Supp. XIX:** 85; **Supp. XVI:** 159

Second Decade, The. See Stephen King, The Second Decade: "Danse Macabre" to "The Dark Half" (Magistrale)

Second Dune, The (Hearon), **Supp. VIII:** 58, **59–60**

Second Flowering, A: Works and Days of the Lost Generation (Cowley), **Retro. Supp. II:** 77; **Supp. II Part 1:** 135, 141, 143, 144, 147, 149

Second Growth (Stegner), **Supp. IV Part 2:** 599, 608

"Second Hour of the Night, The" (Bidart), **Supp. XV:** 32, **33–34**

Second Marriage (F. Barthelme), **Supp. XI:** 32, 33

"Second Marriage" (McCarriston), **Supp. XIV:** 262

"Second Mortgage" (Shaw), **Supp. XIX:** 245–246

Second Nature (Hoffman), **Supp. X:** 88, 89

"Second Nesting" (Davison), **Supp. XXVI:** 77

Seconds, The (Bierds), **Supp. XVII: 33–34**

Second Set, The (Komunyakaa and Feinstein, eds.), **Supp. XIII:** 125

Second Sex, The (Beauvoir), **Supp. IV Part 1:** 360

"Second Sight" (Mosher), **Supp. XXII:** 214

Second Stone, The (Fiedler), **Supp. XIII:** 102

"Second Swimming, The" (Boyle), **Supp. VIII:** 13, 14

Second Tree from the Corner (White), **Supp. I Part 2:** 654

"Second Tree from the Corner" (White), **Supp. I Part 2:** 651

Second Twenty Years at Hull-House, The: September 1909 to September 1929, with a Record of a Growing World Consciousness (Addams), **Supp. I Part 1:** 24–25

Second Voyage of Columbus, The (Morison), **Supp. I Part 2:** 488

Second Words, (Atwood), **Supp. XIII:** 35

Second World, The (Blackmur), **Supp. II Part 1:** 91

Secret, The (E. Hoffman), **Supp. XVI:** 151, **155–158,** 161

"Secret, The" (Levine), **Supp. V:** 195

Secret Agent, The (Conrad), **Supp. IV Part 1:** 341

Secret Agent X-9 (Hammett), **Supp. IV Part 1:** 355

"Secret Courts of Men's Hearts, The: Code and Law in Harper Lee's *To Kill a Mockingbird*" (C. D. Johnson), **Supp. VIII:** 126

"Secret Dog, The" (Cameron), **Supp. XII: 83–84**

Secret Garden, The (Burnett), **Supp. I Part 1:** 44

"Secret Garden, The" (Hoffman), **Supp. XVIII:** 86

"Secret Gladness, A" (C. Frost), **Supp. XV:** 91

Secret Historie (J. Smith), **I:** 131

Secret History of the Dividing Line (Howe), **Supp. IV Part 2:** 424, 425–426

"Secret Integration, The" (Pynchon), **Supp. II Part 2:** 624

"Secret Life of Musical Instruments, The" (Wright), **Supp. XV:** 343

"Secret Life of Walter Mitty, The" (Thurber), **Supp. I Part 2:** 623; **Supp. XVI:** 233

"Secret Lion, The" (Ríos), **Supp. IV Part 2:** 543, 544

"Secret Nature of the Mechanical Rabbit, The"(P. Benedict), **Supp. XXIII:** 49

"Secret Ocean, The" (Jarman), **Supp. XVII:** 120

Secret of Poetry, The: Essays (Jarman), **Supp. XVII:** 110, 111, 120

"Secret of the Russian Ballet, The" (Van Vechten), **Supp. II Part 2:** 732

"Secret Prune" (Ríos), **Supp. IV Part 2:** 549

Secret River, The (Rawlings), **Supp. X:** 233

Secrets and Surprises (Beattie), **Supp. V:** 23, 27, 29

Secrets from the Center of the World (Harjo), **Supp. XII: 223–224**

"Secret Sharer, The" (J. Conrad), **Supp. IX:** 105; **Supp. XVI:** 158; **Supp. XXV:** 217

"Secret Society, A" (Nemerov), **III:** 282

Secrets of the Heart (Gibran), **Supp. XX: 116**

Secrets of the Universe: Scenes from the Journey Home (Sanders), **Supp. XVI:** 273–274

"Secular" (Trethewey), **Supp. XXI:** 249

Secular Journal of Thomas Merton, The, **Supp. VIII:** 206

"Security" (Boyle), **Supp. XXIV:** 58

"Security" (Stafford), **Supp. XI:** 329

"Security"(Strout), **Supp. XXIII:** 283

Sedaris, David, **Supp. XXIII:** 289

Sedges, John (pseudonym). *See* Buck, Pearl S.

Sedgwick, Catherine Maria, **I:** 341; **Supp. I Part 1:** 155, 157

Sedgwick, Christina. *See* Marquand, Mrs. John P. (Christina Sedgwick)

Sedgwick, Ellery, **I:** 217, 229, 231; **III:** 54–55

Sedgwick, Eve, **Supp. XX: 267**

Sedgwick, Henry, **Supp. I Part 1:** 156

Sedgwick, Robert, **Supp. I Part 1:** 156

Sedore, Timothy, **Supp. XIV:** 312

"Seduction and Betrayal" (Hardwick), **Supp. III Part 1:** 207

Seduction and Betrayal: Women and Literature (Hardwick), **Supp. III Part 1:** 194, 204, 206–208, 212, 213; **Supp. XIV:** 89

See, Carolyn, **Supp. XXII:** 206, 217

Seed, David, **Supp. IV Part 1:** 391

"Seed Eaters, The" (Francis), **Supp. IX:** 82

"Seed Leaves" (Wilbur), **Supp. III Part 2:** 558

"Seeds" (Anderson), **I:** 106, 114

Seeds of Contemplation (Merton), **Supp. VIII:** 199, 200, 207, 208

Seeds of Destruction (Merton), **Supp. VIII:** 202, 203, 204, 208

"Seeing Red" (column, Ryan as Quin), **Supp. XVIII:** 226

Seeing through the Sun (Hogan), **Supp. IV Part 1:** 397, 400, 401–402, 402, 413

"See in the Midst of Fair Leaves" (Moore), **III:** 215

"Seekers, The" (McGrath), **Supp. X:** 117

"Seeking a Vision of Truth, Guided by a Higher Power" (Burke), **Supp. XIV:** 21, 23

"See(k)ing the Self: Mirrors and Mirroring in Bicultural Texts" (Oster), **Supp. XVI:** 151

"Seele im Raum" (Jarrell), **II:** 382–383

"Seele im Raum" (Rilke), **II:** 382–383

"See Naples and Die" (Hecht), **Supp. X:** 69, 70

"Seen from the 'L' " (Barnes), **Supp. III Part 1:** 33

"See the Moon?" (Barthelme), **Supp. IV Part 1:** 42, 49–50, 50

Sefarim, Mendele Mokher, **Supp. XXIII:** 4

Seferis, George, **Supp. XXV:** 225

Segal, D. (pseudonym). *See* Singer, Isaac Bashevis

Segal, George, **Supp. XI:** 343

Segal, Lore, **Supp. XVI:** 203

Segregation: The Inner Conflict in the South (Warren), **IV:** 237, 238, 246, 252

"*Se:* Hegel's Absolute and Heidegger's *Ereignis*" (Agamben), **Supp. XVI:** 289

Seidel, Frederick, **I:** 185

Seidman, Hugh, **Supp. XXI:** 228

Seize the Day (Bellow), **I:** 144, 147, 148, 150, 151, 152, 153, 155, 158, 162; **Retro. Supp. II:** 19, **23–24,** 27, 32, 34; **Supp. I Part 2:** 428

Selby, Hubert, **Supp. III Part 1:** 125

Selby, Hubert, Jr., **Supp. XXI:** 227

Selby, John, **Retro. Supp. II:** 221, 222

Selden, John, **Supp. XIV:** 344

Seldes, Gilbert, **II:** 437, 445; **Retro. Supp. I:** 108

Selected Criticism: Prose, Poetry (Bogan), **Supp. III Part 1:** 64

Selected Essays (Eliot), **I:** 572

Selected Essays and Reviews (Carruth), **Supp. XVI:** 46

Selected Journals and Other Writings (Audubon), **Supp. XVI:** 10, 12, 13

Selected Letters (Bynner), **Supp. XV:** 52

Selected Letters (Oppen), **Supp. XXVI:** 228

Selected Letters (W. C. Williams), **Retro. Supp. I:** 430

Selected Letters, 1940–1956 (Kerouac), **Supp. XIV:** 137, 144

Selected Letters of Robert Frost (Thompson, ed.), **Retro. Supp. I:** 125

Selected Levis, The (Levis), **Supp. XI:** 257, 272

Selected Plays (O'Hara), **Supp. XXIII:** 216

Selected Poems (Aiken), **I:** 69

Selected Poems (Ashbery), **Supp. III Part 1:** 25–26

Selected Poems (Berrigan), **Supp. XXIV:** 37

Selected Poems (Bodenheim), **Supp. XXV:** 29

Selected Poems (Brodsky), **Supp. VIII:** 22

Selected Poems (Brooks), **Supp. III Part 1:** 82–83

Selected Poems (Bynner), **Supp. XV:** 51, 52

Selected Poems (Corso), **Supp. XII:** 129

Selected Poems (Dove), **Supp. IV Part 1:** 241, 243, 250

Selected Poems (Frost), **Retro. Supp. I:** 133, 136

Selected Poems (Guillevic; Levertov, trans.), **Supp. III Part 1:** 283

Selected Poems (Hayden), **Supp. II Part 1:** 363, 364, 367

Selected Poems (Hughes), **Retro. Supp. I:** 202; **Supp. I Part 1:** 341, 345, 346

Selected Poems (Hugo), **Supp. VI:** 143

Selected Poems (Jarrell), **II:** 367, 370, 371, 374, 377, 379, 380, 381, 382, 384

Selected Poems (Justice), **Supp. VII:** 115

Selected Poems (Kinnell), **Supp. III Part 1:** 235, 253

Selected Poems (Levine, 1984), **Supp. V:** 178, 179

Selected Poems (Lowell), **II:** 512, 516; **Retro. Supp. II:** 184, 186, 188, 190

Selected Poems (Merton), **Supp. VIII:** 207, 208

Selected Poems (Moore), **III:** 193, 194, 205–206, 208, 215

Selected Poems (Notley), **Supp. XXII:** 234

Selected Poems (O'Hara; Allen, ed.), **Supp. XXIII:** 220

Selected Poems (O'Hara; Ford, ed.), **Supp. XXIII:** 220

Selected Poems (Pound), **Retro. Supp. I:** 289, 291

Selected Poems (R. Bly), **Supp. IV Part 1:** 60, 62, 65, 66, 68, 69–71

Selected Poems (Ransom), **III:** 490, 492

Selected Poems (Reznikoff), **Supp. XIV:** 288

Selected Poems (Rukeyser), **Supp. VI:** 274

Selected Poems (Sexton), **Supp. IV Part 2:** 449

Selected Poems (Sorrentino), **Supp. XXI:** 226

Selected Poems (Strand), **Supp. IV Part 2:** 630

Selected Poems, 1923–1943 (Warren), **IV:** 241–242, 243

Selected Poems, 1928–1958 (Kunitz), **Supp. III Part 1:** 261, 263–265

Selected Poems, 1938–1988 (McGrath), **Supp. X:** 127

Selected Poems, 1958–1980 (Sorrentino), **Supp. XXI:** 228

Selected Poems, 1963–1983 (Simic), **Supp. VIII:** 275

Selected Poems 1936–1965 (Eberhart), **I:** 541

Selected Poems: 1957–1987 (Snodgrass), **Supp. VI:** 314–315, 323, 324

Selected Poems 1965–1975 (Atwood), **Supp. XIII:** 32–34

Selected Poems: 1975–2005 (Skloot), **Supp. XX: 196**

Selected Poems II: Poems Selected and New, 1976–1986 (Atwood), **Supp. XIII:** 20, **34–35**

Selected Poems of Ezra Pound (Pound), **Supp. V:** 336

Selected Poems of Gabriela Mistral (Hughes, trans.), **Supp. I Part 1:** 345

Selected Poems of Stanley Kunitz, The, **Supp. XXVI:** 64

Selected Poetry of Amiri Baraka/LeRoi Jones (Baraka), **Supp. II Part 1:** 58

Selected Poetry of Hayden Carruth, The (Carruth), **Supp. XVI:** 53

Selected Stories (Dubus), **Supp. VII:** 88–89

Selected Stories of Richard Bausch, The (Bausch), **Supp. VII:** 42

Selected Translations (Snodgrass), **Supp. VI:** 318, 324, **325–326**

Selected Verse of Margaret Haskins Durber, The (Keillor), **Supp. XVI:** 171

Selected Witter Bynner, The, **Supp. XV:** 52

Selected Works of Djuna Barnes, The (Barnes), **Supp. III Part 1:** 44

Selected Writings 1950–1990 (Howe), **Supp. VI:** 116–117, 118, 120

Selected Writings of John Jay Chapman, The (Barzun), **Supp. XIV:** 54

Select Epigrams from the Greek Anthology (Mackail), **Supp. I Part 2:** 461

"Selecting a Reader" (Kooser), **Supp. XIX:** 119–120

"Selene Afterwards" (MacLeish), **III:** 8

"Self" (James), **II:** 351

Self, William, **Supp. XXII:** 172

Self and the Dramas of History, The (Niebuhr), **III:** 308

"Self-Appraisal" (Davison), **Supp. XXVI:** 68

Self-Consciousness (Updike), **Retro. Supp. I:** 318, 319, 320, 322, 323, 324

"Self-Culture" (Channing), **Supp. XXIV: 78–79**

"Self-Exposed, The" (X. J. Kennedy), **Supp. XV:** 159

Self-Help: Stories (Moore), **Supp. X:** 163, 166, **167–169**, 174, 175

"Self-Importance" (Halliday), **Supp. XIX:** 90

Self-Interviews (Dickey), **Supp. IV Part 1:** 179

"Self-Made Man, A" (Crane), **I:** 420

"Self Pity" (C. Frost), **Supp. XV:** 93, 94, 101, 102, 104

Self Portrait (album, Dylan), **Supp. XVIII:** 27

"Self-Portrait" (Creeley), **Supp. IV Part 1:** 156

"Self-Portrait" (Davison), **Supp. XXVI:** 68

"Self-Portrait" (Mumford), **Supp. II Part 2:** 471

"(Self) Portrait" (Trethewey), **Supp. XXI:** 253

"Self-Portrait" (Wylie), **Supp. I Part 2:** 729

"Self Portrait at Fifty-three" (Weigl), **Supp. XIX:** 288

Self-Portrait: Ceaselessly into the Past (Millar, ed. Sipper), **Supp. IV Part 2:** 464, 469, 472, 475

"Self-Portrait in a Convex Mirror" (Ashbery), **Supp. III Part 1:** 5, 7, 9, 16–19, 22, 24, 26

"Self-Portrait with 1911 NY Yankees Cap" (Skloot), **Supp. XX: 202**

"Self-Reliance" (Emerson), **II:** 7, 15, 17; **Retro. Supp. I:** 159; **Retro. Supp. II:** 155; **Supp. X:** 42, 45

Selfwolf (Halliday), **Supp. XIX:** 81, **89–91,** 93

Sélincourt, Ernest de, **Supp. I Part 2:** 676

Selinger, Eric, **Supp. XVI:** 47

Selinger, Eric Murphy, **Supp. XI:** 248

Sell, Henry, **Supp. XVI:** 188

Sellers, Isaiah, **IV:** 194–195

Sellers, Peter, **Supp. XI:** 301, 304, 306, 307, 309

Sellers, William, **IV:** 208

Seltzer, Mark, **Retro. Supp. I:** 227

Selznick, David O., **Retro. Supp. I:** 105, 113; **Supp. IV Part 1:** 353; **Supp. XVIII:** 242; **Supp. XXII:** 195

Semi, Allen (pseudonym). *See* Larsen, Nella

"Semi-Lunatics of Kilmuir, The" (Hugo), **Supp. VI:** 145

"Semiotics/The Doctor's Doll" (Goldbarth), **Supp. XII:** 183–184

Semmelweiss, Ignaz, **Supp. I Part 1:** 304

Senancour, Étienne Divert de, **I:** 241

Senator North (Atherton), **Supp. XXIV:** 22

Sendak, Maurice, **Supp. IX:** 207, 208, 213, 214; **Supp. XVI:** 110

Seneca, **II:** 14–15; **III:** 77

Senghor, Leopold Sédar, **Supp. IV Part 1:** 16; **Supp. X:** 132, 139

Senier, Siobhan, **Supp. IV Part 1:** 330

"Senility" (Anderson), **I:** 114

Senior, Olive, **Supp. XXIII:** 94

"Senior Partner's Ethics, The" (Auchincloss), **Supp. IV Part 1:** 33

Senlin: A Biography (Aiken), **I:** 48, 49, 50, 52, 56, 57, 64

Sennett, Dorothy, **Supp. XVI:** 43

Sennett, Mack, **III:** 442

"Señora X No More" (Mora), **Supp. XIII:** 218

"Señor Ong and Señor Ha" (Bowles), **Supp. IV Part 1:** 87

Señor Presidente, El (Asturias), **Supp. XXIV:** 89

"Señor X" (Muñoz), **Supp. XXV:** 135

Sensational Designs: The Cultural Work of American Fiction, 1790–1860 (Tompkins), **Supp. XVIII:** 258–259

Sense and Sensibility (Austen), **Supp. XXVI:** 130, 212

Sense of Beauty, The (Santayana), **III:** 600

Sense of Life in the Modern Novel, The (Mizener), **IV:** 132

"Sense of Shelter, A" (Updike), **Retro. Supp. I:** 318

"Sense of the Meeting, The" (Conroy), **Supp. XVI:** 72

Sense of the Past, The (James), **II:** 337–338

"Sense of the Past, The" (Trilling), **Supp. III Part 2:** 503

"Sense of the Present, The" (Hardwick), **Supp. III Part 1:** 210

"Sense of the Sleight-of-Hand Man, The" (Stevens), **IV:** 93

"Sense of Where You Are, A" (McPhee), **Supp. III Part 1:** 291, 296–298

"Sensibility! O La!" (Roethke), **III:** 536

"Sensible Emptiness, A" (Kramer), **Supp. IV Part 1:** 61, 66

"Sensuality Plunging Barefoot Into Thorns" (Cisneros), **Supp. VII:** 68

"Sentence" (Barthelme), **Supp. IV Part 1:** 47

Sent for You Yesterday (Wideman), **Supp. X:** 320, 321

"Sentimental Education, A" (Banks), **Supp. V:** 10

"Sentimental Journey" (Oates), **Supp. II Part 2:** 522, 523

"Sentimental Journey, A" (Anderson), **I:** 114

Sentimental Journey, A (Sterne), **Supp. I Part 2:** 714

"Sentimental Journeys" (Didion), **Supp. IV Part 1:** 211

Sentimental Journey through France and Italy, A (Sterne), **Supp. XV:** 232

"Sentiment of Rationality, The" (James), **II:** 346–347

"Separated Father" (Halliday), **Supp. XIX:** 92, 93

Separate Flights (Dubus), **Supp. VII:** 78–83

"Separate Flights" (Dubus), **Supp. VII:** 83

Separate Peace, A (Knowles), **Supp. IV Part 2:** 679; **Supp. XII: 241–249**

Separate Way (Reznikoff), **Supp. XIV:** 280

"Separating" (Updike), **Retro. Supp. I:** 321

"Separation, The" (Kunitz), **Supp. III Part 1:** 263

"Sepia High Stepper" (Hayden), **Supp. II Part 1:** 379

September (film; Allen), **Supp. XV:** 11

"September" (Komunyakaa), **Supp. XIII:** 130

"September" (Pickering), **Supp. XXI:** 198

"September 1, 1939" (Auden), **Supp. II Part 1:** 13; **Supp. IV Part 1:** 225; **Supp. VIII:** 30, 32; **Supp. XV:** 117–118

September 11, 2001: American Writers Respond (Heyen), **Supp. XIII:** 285

"September's Book" (Notley), **Supp. XXII:** 229

September Song (Humphrey), **Supp. IX:** 101, 102, **108–109**

"September Twelfth, 2001" (X. J. Kennedy), **Supp. XV:** 171

"Sept Vieillards, Les" (Millay, trans.), **III:** 142

Sequel to Drum-Taps (Whitman), **Retro. Supp. I:** 406

"Sequence, Sometimes Metaphysical" (Roethke), **III:** 547, 548

Sequence of Seven Plays with a Drawing by Ron Slaughter, A (Nemerov), **III:** 269

Sequoya, Jana, **Supp. IV Part 1:** 334

Seraglio, The (Merrill), **Supp. III Part 1:** 331

Seraphita (Balzac), **I:** 499

Seraph on the Suwanee (Hurston), **Supp. VI:** 149, 159–160

Serenissima: A Novel of Venice (Jong). See *Shylock's Daughter: A Novel of Love in Venice (Serenissima)* (Jong)

Sergeant, Elizabeth Shepley, **I:** 231, 236, 312, 319, 323, 328

Sergeant Bilko (television show), **Supp. IV Part 2:** 575

Sergi, Paula, **Supp. XXI:** 246

"Serious Talk, A" (Carver), **Supp. III Part 1:** 138, 144

Serly, Tibor, **Supp. III Part 2:** 617, 619

"Sermon, Now Encrypted" (Monson), **Supp. XXIV:** 239–240

"Sermon by Doctor Pep" (Bellow), **I:** 151

Sermones (Horace), **II:** 154

"Sermon for Our Maturity" (Baraka), **Supp. II Part 1:** 53

"Sermon in the Cotton Field" (Nelson), **Supp. XVIII:** 177

Sermons and Soda Water (O'Hara), **III:** 362, 364, 371–373, 382

"Sermons on the Warpland" (Brooks), **Supp. III Part 1:** 84

"Serpent in the Wilderness, The" (Masters), **Supp. I Part 2:** 458

Servant of the Bones (Rice), **Supp. VII:** 298, 302

"Servant to Servants, A" (Frost), **Retro. Supp. I:** 125, 128; **Supp. X:** 66

Serve It Forth (M. F. K. Fisher), **Supp. XVII:** 83, 86, 87, 89, 92

Service, Robert W., **Supp. XXI:** 51; **Supp. XXII:** 203

Seshachari, Neila, **Supp. V:** 22

"Session, The" (Adams), **I:** 5

"Sestina" (Bishop), **Supp. I Part 1:** 73, 88

Set-angya, **Supp. IV Part 2:** 493

Seth, Vikram, **Supp. XVII:** 117

Seth's Brother's Wife (Frederic), **II:** 131–132, 137, 144

Sethuraman, Ramchandran, **Supp. XXII:** 73

Setouchi, Jakuch\[omacron\], **Supp. XXIV:** 166

Set This House on Fire (Styron), **IV:** 98, 99, 105, 107–113, 114, 115, 117

Setting Free the Bears (Irving), **Supp. VI:** 163, **166–167**, 169–170

Setting the Tone (Rorem), **Supp. IV Part 1:** 79

Settle, Mary Lee, **Supp. IX:** 96

Settlement Horizon, The: A National Estimate (Woods and Kennedy), **Supp. I Part 1:** 19

"Settling the Colonel's Hash" (McCarthy), **II:** 559, 562

Setzer, Helen, **Supp. IV Part 1:** 217

"Seurat's Sunday Afternoon along the Seine" (Schwartz), **Supp. II Part 2:** 663–665

Sevag, Aris, **Supp. XXIII:** 28, 29

7 Years from Somehwere (Levine), **Supp. V:** 178, 181, 188–189

Seven against Thebes (Aeschylus; Bacon and Hecht, trans.), **Supp. X:** 57

Seven Ages of Man, The (Wilder), **IV:** 357, 374–375

Seven Deadly Sins, The (Wilder), **IV:** 357, 374–375

Seven Descents of Myrtle, The (T. Williams), **IV:** 382

"Seven Fat Brides, The" (P. Abraham), **Supp. XVII:** 50

Seven Guitars (Wilson), **Supp. VIII:** 331, **348–351**

Seven Lady Godivas, The (Geisel), **Supp. XVI:** 100, 103

Seven League Boots, The (Murray), **Supp. XIX: 156–157**

Seven-League Crutches, The (Jarrell), **II:** 367, 372, 381, 382, 383–384, 389

Seven Mountains of Thomas Merton, The (Mott), **Supp. VIII:** 208

Seven-Ounce Man, The (Harrison), **Supp. VIII:** 51

"Seven Places of the Mind" (Didion), **Supp. IV Part 1:** 200, 210

Seven Plays (Shepard), **Supp. III Part 2:** 434

"Seven Selves, The" (Gibran), **Supp. XX: 118**

"Seven Sentences"(Dybek), **Supp. XXIII:** 74

"Seven Stanzas at Easter" (Updike), **IV:** 215

Seven Storey Mountain, The (Merton), **Supp. VIII:** 193, 195, 198, 200, 207, 208

Seventeen (Berrigan and Padgett), **Supp. XXIV:** 41

Seventh Beggar, The (Abraham), **Supp. XXIV:** 2, 3, **9–12**, 13, 14

Seventh Heaven (Hoffman), **Supp. X:** 87, 89

"Seventh of March" (Webster), **Supp. I Part 2:** 687

"7000 Romaine, Los Angeles 38" (Didion), **Supp. IV Part 1:** 200

"Seventh Street" (Toomer), **Supp. IX:** 316

Seven Types of Ambiguity (Empson), **II:** 536; **IV:** 431

77 Dream Songs (Berryman), **I:** 168, 169, 170, 171, 174, 175, 183–188

73 Poems (Cummings), **I:** 430, 431, 446, 447, 448

Seven Valleys and the Four Valleys, The (Bahá'u'lláh), **Supp. XX:** 121

"Several Short Questions About Crumbs"(Schott), **Supp. XXIII:** 249

Sevier, Jack, **IV:** 378

Sévigné, Madame de, **IV:** 361

Sewall, Richard, **Retro. Supp. I:** 25

Sewall, Samuel, **IV:** 145, 146, 147, 149, 154, 164; **Supp. I Part 1:** 100, 110

Sewell, Elizabeth, **Supp. XIII:** 344

"Sex" (Carruth), **Supp. XVI:** 58

Sex, Economy, Freedom and Community (Berry), **Supp. X:** 30, 36
"Sex Camp" (Mamet), **Supp. XIV:** 240
Sex Castle, The (Lacy), **Supp. XV:** 206
Sex & Character (Weininger), **Retro. Supp. I:** 416
"Sext" (Auden), **Supp. II Part 1:** 22
Sexton, Anne, **Retro. Supp. II:** 245; **Supp. I Part 2:** 538, 543, 546; **Supp. II Part 2: 669–700; Supp. III Part 2:** 599; **Supp. IV Part 1:** 245; **Supp. IV Part 2:** 439, 440–441, 442, 444, 447, 449, 451, 620; **Supp. V:** 113, 118, 124; **Supp. X:** 201, 202, 213; **Supp. XI:** 146, 240, 317; **Supp. XII:** 217, 253, 254, 256, 260, 261; **Supp. XIII:** 35, 76, 294, 312; **Supp. XIV:** 125, 126, 132, 269; **Supp. XIX:** 82, 203; **Supp. XV:** 123, 252, 340; **Supp. XVII:** 239; **Supp. XX: 199; Supp. XXVI:** 68
Sexual Behavior in the American Male (Kinsey), **Supp. XIII:** 96–97
Sexual Perversity in Chicago (Mamet), **Supp. XIV:** 239, 240, 246–247, 249
"Sexual Revolution, The" (Dunn), **Supp. XI:** 142
Sexus (H. Miller), **III:** 170, 171, 184, 187, 188
"Sex Without Love" (Olds), **Supp. X:** 206
"Sexy" (Lahiri), **Supp. XXI:** 183–184
Seyersted, Per E., **Retro. Supp. II:** 65; **Supp. I Part 1:** 201, 204, 211, 216, 225; **Supp. IV Part 2:** 558
Seyfried, Robin, **Supp. IX:** 324
Seymour, Corey, **Supp. XXIV:** 280
Seymour, Miranda, **Supp. VIII:** 167
"Seymour: An Introduction" (Salinger), **III:** 569–571, 572
"Shack" (L. Brown), **Supp. XXI:** 49
Shacochis, Bob, **Supp. VIII:** 80
"Shadow" (Creeley), **Supp. IV Part 1:** 158
"Shadow, The" (Lowell), **II:** 522
Shadow and Act (Ellison), **Retro. Supp. II:** 119; **Supp. I Part 1:** 245–246
"Shadow and Shade" (Tate), **IV:** 128
"Shadow and the Flesh, The" (London), **II:** 475
"Shadow A Parable" (Poe), **III:** 417–418
Shadow Country (Gunn Allen), **Supp. IV Part 1:** 322, 324, 325–326
Shadow-Line, The (Conrad), **Supp. XXV:** 217
Shadow Man, The (Gordon), **Supp. IV Part 1:** 297, 298, 299, 312–314, 315
Shadow of a Dream, The, a Story (Howells), **II:** 285, 286, 290
Shadow of a Man (Moraga), **Supp. XXIII:** 195, 197, **199–203**
Shadow of Heaven (Hayes), **Supp. XXVI:** 137–139
"Shadow of the Crime, The: A Word from the Author" (Mailer), **Retro. Supp. II:** 214
Shadow on the Dial, The (Bierce), **I:** 208, 209
"Shadow out of Time, The" (Lovecraft), **Supp. XXV:** 111

Shadow over Innsmouth, The (Lovecraft), **Supp. XXV:** 111, 117–118, 120, 121
"Shadow Passing" (Merwin), **Supp. III Part 1:** 355
Shadowplay (C. Baxter), **Supp. XVII:** 15, 19–20
Shadows (Gardner), **Supp. VI:** 74
Shadows and Fog (film; Allen), **Supp. XV:** 11
Shadows Burning (Di Piero), **Supp. XIX:** 42, 43–44
Shadows by the Hudson (Singer), **IV:** 1
Shadows of Africa (Matthiessen), **Supp. V:** 203
Shadows on the Hudson (Singer), **Retro. Supp. II:** 311–313
Shadows on the Rock (Cather), **I:** 314, 330–331, 332; **Retro. Supp. I:** 18
"Shadows over Lovecraft: Reactionary Fantasy and Immigrant Eugenics" (Lovett-Graff), **Supp. XXV:** 123
Shadow Train (Ashbery), **Supp. III Part 1:** 23–24, 26
"Shad-Time" (Wilbur), **Supp. III Part 2:** 563
Shaffer, Thomas L., **Supp. VIII:** 127, 128
Shaft (Parks; film), **Supp. XI:** 17
Shaftesbury, Earl of, **I:** 559
Shahid, Irfan, **Supp. XX: 113, 127**
Shahn, Ben, **Supp. X:** 24
Shakedown for Murder (Lacy), **Supp. XV:** 203
Shakelford, Dean, **Supp. VIII:** 129
Shaker, Why Don't You Sing? (Angelou), **Supp. IV Part 1:** 16
Shakespear, Mrs. Olivia, **III:** 457; **Supp. I Part 1:** 257
"Shakespeare" (Emerson), **II:** 6
"Shakespeare" (Very), **Supp. XXV:** 244
Shakespeare, William, **I:** 103, 271, 272, 284–285, 358, 378, 433, 441, 458, 461, 573, 585, 586; **II:** 5, 8, 11, 18, 72, 273, 297, 302, 309, 320, 411, 494, 577, 590; **III:** 3, 11, 12, 82, 83, 91, 124, 130, 134, 145, 153, 159, 183, 210, 263, 286, 468, 473, 492, 503, 511, 567, 575–576, 577, 610, 612, 613, 615; **IV:** 11, 50, 66, 127, 132, 156, 309, 313, 362, 368, 370, 373, 453; **Retro. Supp. I:** 43, 64, 91, 248; **Retro. Supp. II:** 114, 299; **Supp. I Part 1:** 79, 150, 262, 310, 356, 363, 365, 368, 369, 370; **Supp. I Part 2:** 397, 421, 422, 470, 494, 622, 716, 720; **Supp. II Part 2:** 624, 626; **Supp. IV Part 1:** 31, 83, 87, 243; **Supp. IV Part 2:** 430, 463, 519, 688; **Supp. IX:** 14, 133; **Supp. V:** 252, 280, 303; **Supp. VIII:** 160, 164; **Supp. X:** 42, 62, 65, 78; **Supp. XII:** 54–57, 277, 281; **Supp. XIII:** 111, 115, 233; **Supp. XIV:** 97, 120, 225, 245, 306; **Supp. XV:** 92; **Supp. XVIII:** 278; **Supp. XXII:** 206; **Supp. XXIV:** 33, 34, 40, 87, 159
Shakespeare and His Forerunners (Lanier), **Supp. I Part 1:** 369
Shakespeare in Harlem (Hughes), **Retro. Supp. I:** 194, 202, 205, 206, 207, 208; **Supp. I Part 1:** 333, 334, 345

Shalit, Gene, **Supp. VIII:** 73
Shalit, Wendy, **Supp. XX: 179, 182, 186**
Shall We Gather at the River (Wright), **Supp. III Part 2:** 601–602; **Supp. XVII:** 241
"Shame" (Oates), **Supp. II Part 2:** 520
"Shame" (Wilbur), **Supp. III Part 2:** 556
"Shame and Forgetting in the Information Age" (C. Baxter), **Supp. XVII:** 21
"Shameful Affair, A" (Chopin), **Retro. Supp. II:** 61
Shamela (Fielding), **Supp. V:** 127
"Shampoo, The" (Bishop), **Retro. Supp. II:** 46; **Supp. I Part 1:** 92
Shange, Ntozake, **Supp. VIII:** 214; **Supp. XVII:** 70; **Supp. XVIII:** 172; **Supp. XXI:** 172
Shank, Randy, **Supp. X:** 252
Shankaracharya, **III:** 567
Shanley, John Patrick, **Supp. XIV: 315–332**
Shannon, Sandra, **Supp. VIII:** 333, 348
"Shape of Flesh and Bone, The" (MacLeish), **III:** 18–19
Shape of Me and Other Stuff, The (Geisel), **Supp. XVI:** 111
Shape of the Journey, The (Harrison), **Supp. VIII:** 53
Shapes of Clay (Bierce), **I:** 208, 209
Shaping Joy, A: Studies in the Writer's Craft (Brooks), **Supp. XIV:** 13
Shapiro, Alan, **Supp. XXIV:** 157
Shapiro, Charles, **Supp. XIX:** 257, 259–260
Shapiro, David, **Supp. XII:** 175, 185; **Supp. XXIV:** 34
Shapiro, Dorothy, **IV:** 380
Shapiro, Edward S., **Supp. XXV:** 253
Shapiro, Karl, **I:** 430, 521; **II:** 350; **III:** 527; **Supp. II Part 2: 701–724; Supp. III Part 2:** 623; **Supp. IV Part 2:** 645; **Supp. X:** 116; **Supp. XI:** 315; **Supp. XIX:** 117, 118, 119; **Supp. XXI:** 98; **Supp. XXV:** 30
Shapiro, Laura, **Supp. IX:** 120; **Supp. XX: 87, 89**
"Shared Patio, The" (July), **Supp. XXIV:** 201, 202
Sharif, Omar, **Supp. IX:** 253
"Sharing" (Huddle), **Supp. XXVI:** 153
"Shark Meat" (Snyder), **Supp. VIII:** 300
Shatayev, Elvira, **Supp. I Part 2:** 570
Shaviro, Steven, **Supp. VIII:** 189
Shaw, Chris, **Supp. XXIII:** 155–156
Shaw, Colonel Robert Gould, **II:** 551
Shaw, Elizabeth. See Melville, Mrs. Herman (Elizabeth Shaw)
Shaw, George Bernard, **I:** 226; **II:** 82, 271, 276, 581; **III:** 69, 102, 113, 145, 155, 161, 162, 163, 373, 409; **IV:** 27, 64, 397, 432, 440; **Retro. Supp. I:** 100, 228; **Supp. IV Part 1:** 36; **Supp. IV Part 2:** 585, 683; **Supp. IX:** 68, 308; **Supp. V:** 243–244, 290; **Supp. XI:** 202; **Supp. XII:** 94; **Supp. XIV:** 343; **Supp. XVII:** 100; **Supp. XXIV:** 33, 34
Shaw, Irwin, **IV:** 381; **Supp. IV Part 1:** 383; **Supp. IX:** 251; **Supp. XI:** 221,

229, 231; **Supp. XIX: 239–254**

Shaw, Joseph Thompson ("Cap"), **Supp. IV Part 1:** 121, 345, 351; **Supp. XIII:** 161

Shaw, Judge Lemuel, **III:** 77, 88, 91

Shaw, Lytle, **Supp. XXIII:** 208; **Supp. XXIV:** 44

Shaw, Peter, **Supp. XVI:** 70

Shaw, Robert B., **Supp. XXIII:** 112

Shaw, Sarah Bryant, **Supp. I Part 1:** 169

Shaw, Wilbur, Jr., **Supp. XIII:** 162

Shawl, The (Mamet), **Supp. XIV:** 245

Shawl, The (Ozick), **Supp. V:** 257, 260, 271

"Shawl, The" (Ozick), **Supp. V:** 271–272

Shawl and Prarie du Chien, The: Two Plays (Mamet), **Supp. XIV:** 243–244

Shawn, William, **Supp. VIII:** 151, 170

"Shawshank Redemption, The" (King), **Supp. V:** 148

She (Haggard), **III:** 189

Shea, Renee, **Supp. XXIII:** 85, 86, 90, 95

Sheaffer, Louis, **Supp. XXI:** 6

Shearer, Flora, **I:** 199

"Sheaves, The" (Robinson), **III:** 510, 524

"She Came and Went" (Lowell), **Supp. I Part 2:** 409

"She-Devil" (Nelson), **Supp. XVIII:** 178

She-Devil Circus (Nelson), **Supp. XVIII:** 176, **178**

Sheed, Wilfrid, **IV:** 230; **Supp. XI:** 233; **Supp. XXI:** 233

Sheeler, Charles, **IV:** 409; **Retro. Supp. I:** 430

"Sheep Child" (B. Kelly), **Supp. XVII:** 131–132

"Sheep Child, The" (Dickey), **Supp. XVII:** 131–132

Sheeper (Rosenthal), **Supp. XIV:** 147

Sheffer, Jonathan, **Supp. IV Part 1:** 95

She Had Some Horses (Harjo), **Supp. XII: 220–223,** 231

"She Had Some Horses" (Harjo), **Supp. XII:** 215, 222

"Shell, The" (Humphrey), **Supp. IX:** 94

Shelley, Mary, **Supp. XX: 108**

Shelley, Percy Bysshe, **I:** 18, 68, 381, 476, 522, 577; **II:** 331, 516, 535, 540; **III:** 412, 426, 469; **IV:** 139; **Retro. Supp. I:** 308, 360; **Supp. I Part 1:** 79, 311, 349; **Supp. I Part 2:** 709, 718, 719, 720, 721, 722, 724, 728; **Supp. IV Part 1:** 235; **Supp. IX:** 51; **Supp. V:** 258, 280; **Supp. XII:** 117, 132, 136–137, 263; **Supp. XIV:** 271–272; **Supp. XV:** 92, 175, 182; **Supp. XX: 115; Supp. XXI:** 131

Shellow, Sadie Myers, **Supp. I Part 2:** 608

Shelnut, Blevin, **Supp. XXV:** 36

"Shelter" (C. Baxter), **Supp. XVII:** 19

"Shelter" (Doty), **Supp. XI:** 132

Sheltered Life, The (Glasgow), **II:** 174, 175, 179, 186, 187–188

Sheltering Sky, The (Bowles), **Supp. IV Part 1:** 82, 84, 85–86, 87

Sheltering Sky, The (film), **Supp. IV Part 1:** 94, 95

Shelton, Frank, **Supp. IV Part 2:** 658

Shelton, Richard, **Supp. XI:** 133; **Supp. XIII:** 7

Shelton, Robert, **Supp. XVIII:** 20, 21, 22, 23, 24, 25, 26

Shelton, Mrs. Sarah. *See* Royster, Sarah Elmira

Shenandoah (Schwartz), **Supp. II Part 2:** 640, 651–652

"Shenandoah" (Shapiro), **Supp. II Part 2:** 704

Shepard, Alice, **IV:** 287

Shepard, Gregory, **Supp. XXII:** 119

Shepard, Harvey, **Supp. XVII:** 240

Shepard, Jim, **Supp. XXI:** 115

Shepard, Odell, **II:** 508; **Supp. I Part 2:** 418

Shepard, Richard F., **Supp. XXIV:** 216

Shepard, Sam, **Supp. III Part 2: 431–450; Supp. XVIII:** 21, 28, 31; **Supp. XXI:** 144, 145

Shepard, Thomas, **I:** 554; **IV:** 158

"Shepherd of Resumed Desire, The" (Wright), **Supp. XV:** 349

Sheppard Lee (Bird), **III:** 423

"She Remembers the Future" (Harjo), **Supp. XII:** 222

Sheridan, Richard Brinsley, **Retro. Supp. I:** 127

Sherlock, William, **IV:** 152

Sherman, Joe, **Supp. XXII:** 205

Sherman, Sarah Way, **Retro. Supp. II:** 145

Sherman, Stuart Pratt, **I:** 222, 246–247; **Supp. I Part 2:** 423

Sherman, Susan, **Supp. VIII:** 265

Sherman, Tom, **IV:** 446

Sherman, William T., **IV:** 445, 446

Sherry, Denver William, **Supp. XXII:** 190

Sherwood, Robert, **II:** 435; **Supp. IX:** 190

Sherwood Anderson & Other Famous Creoles (Faulkner), **I:** 117; **II:** 56

Sherwood Anderson Reader, The (Anderson), **I:** 114, 116

Sherwood Anderson's Memoirs (Anderson), **I:** 98, 101, 102, 103, 108, 112, 116

Sherwood Anderson's Notebook (Anderson), **I:** 108, 115, 117

"She Sings" (Taggard), **Supp. XXII:** 272

She Stoops to Conquer (Goldsmith), **II:** 514

Shestov, Lev, **Supp. VIII:** 20, 24

Shetley, Vernon, **Supp. IX:** 292; **Supp. XI:** 123

"She Wept, She Railed" (Kunitz), **Supp. III Part 1:** 265

"Shiddah and Kuziba" (Singer), **IV:** 13, 15

Shidyak, Paris al-, **Supp. XX: 117**

Shield of Achilles, The (Auden), **Supp. II Part 1:** 21

"Shield of Achilles, The" (Auden), **Supp. II Part 1:** 21, 25

Shields, Carol, **Supp. VII: 307–330**

Shields, John C., **Supp. XX:** 279, 280, **281, 286**

Shifting Landscape: A Composite, 1925–1987 (H. Roth), **Supp. IX: 233–235**

Shifts of Being (Eberhart), **I:** 525

Shigematsu, Soiko, **Supp. III Part 1:** 353

Shihab, Aziz, **Supp. XIII:** 273

Shih-hsiang Chen, **Supp. VIII:** 303

Shiksa Goddess; or, How I Spent My Forties (Wasserstein), **Supp. XV:** 319, 320, 325, 332, 333

"Shiloh" (Mason), **Supp. VIII:** 140

Shiloh and Other Stories (Mason), **Supp. VIII:** 133, **139–141,** 143, 145

Shilts, Randy, **Supp. X:** 145

Shimmering Verge, The (one-woman show, Peacock), **Supp. XIX:** 194, **204–205**

Shining, The (King), **Supp. V:** 139, 140, 141, 143–144, 146, 149, 151, 152

"Shining Ones, The" (P. N. Warren), **Supp. XX: 272**

Shining Victory (film, Rapper), **Supp. XVII:** 60

Shinn, Everett, **Retro. Supp. II:** 103

Shi Pei Pu, **Supp. XXI:** 152, 153, 154

"Ship in a Bottle"(Strout), **Supp. XXIII:** 283

"Ship of Death" (Lawrence), **Supp. I Part 2:** 728

Ship of Fools (Porter), **III:** 433, 447, 453, 454; **IV:** 138

"Ships" (O. Henry), **Supp. II Part 1:** 409

Ships Going into the Blue: Essays and Notes on Poetry (Simpson), **Supp. IX:** 275

Ship to America, A (Singer), **IV:** 1

"Shipwreck, The" (Merwin), **Supp. III Part 1:** 346

Shirley, John, **Supp. XVI:** 123, 128

"Shirt" (Pinsky), **Supp. VI: 236–237,** 239, 240, 241, 245, 247

"Shirt Poem, The" (Stern), **Supp. IX:** 292

"Shirts, The" (Gallagher), **Supp. XXIV:** 169

"Shirts of a Single Color" (Ryan), **Supp. XVIII:** 227

"Shiva and Parvati Hiding in the Rain" (Pinsky), **Supp. VI:** 244

Shively, Charley, **Retro. Supp. I:** 391; **Supp. XII:** 181, 182

Shnayerson, Michael, **Supp. XIX:** 248

Shneidman, Edwin, **Supp. XXVI:** 246

"Shock of Good Poetry, The"(Hirshfield), **Supp. XXIII:** 136

Shock of Recognition, The (Wilson), **II:** 530

Shock of the New, The (Hughes), **Supp. X:** 73

Shoe Bird, The (Welty), **IV:** 261; **Retro. Supp. I:** 353

Shoemaker of Dreams (Ferragammo), **Supp. XVI:** 192

"Shoes" (O. Henry), **Supp. II Part 1:** 409

"Shoes of Wandering, The" (Kinnell), **Supp. III Part 1:** 248

Sholem Asch: Zayn levn un zayne verk (Sholem Asch: His life and his work), **Supp. XXIII:** 6

Sholl, Betsy, **Supp. XXI:** 129, 131

"Shooters, Inc." (Didion), **Supp. IV Part 1:** 207, 211

"Shooting, The" (Dubus), **Supp. VII:** 84, 85

"Shooting Niagara; and After?" (Carlyle), **Retro. Supp. I:** 408

"Shooting of the Red Eagle" (Zitkala-Ša), **Supp. XXV:** 275

"Shooting Script" (Rich), **Supp. I Part 2:** 558; **Supp. IV Part 1:** 257

Shooting Star, A (Stegner), **Supp. IV Part 2:** 599, 608–609

"Shooting the Works" (Di Piero), **Supp. XIX:** 41–42

Shooting the Works: On Poetry and Pictures (Di Piero), **Supp. XIX:** 41–42

"Shooting Whales" (Strand), **Supp. IV Part 2:** 630

"Shopgirls" (F. Barthelme), **Supp. XI:** 26, 27, 33, 36

Shopping for Joe (O'Hara and Steven Rivers), **Supp. XXIII:** 217

"Shopping with Bob Berwick" (Halliday), **Supp. XIX:** 88

Shop Talk (P. Roth), **Retro. Supp. II:** 282

Shoptaw, John, **Supp. IV Part 1:** 247

Shore Acres (Herne), **Supp. II Part 1:** 198

Shorebirds of North America, The (Matthiessen), **Supp. V:** 204

"Shore House, The" (Jewett), **II:** 397

Shore Leave (Wakeman), **Supp. IX:** 247

"Shoreline Horses" (Ríos), **Supp. IV Part 2:** 553

"Shoreline Life" (Skloot), **Supp. XX: 201**

Shores of Light, The: A Literary Chronicle of the Twenties and Thirties (Wilson), **IV:** 432, 433

Shorey, Paul, **III:** 606

Short Account of the Destruction of the Indies, A (Las Casas), **Supp. XXIV:** 87

Short and the Long of It, The (Kenny), **Supp. XXIII:** 155–156

Short Cuts (film, Altman), **Supp. IX:** 143; **Supp. XXIV:** 166, 172, 178

"Short End, The" (Hecht), **Supp. X:** 65

"Shorter View, The" (X. J. Kennedy), **Supp. XV:** 160, 168

Short Fiction of Norman Mailer, The (Mailer), **Retro. Supp. II:** 205

"Short Flight, The" (Huddle), **Supp. XXVI:** 156

Short Friday and Other Stories (Singer), **IV:** 14–16

Short Girls (Nguyen), **Supp. XXVI:** 212–216

Short Guide to a Happy Life, A (Quindlen), **Supp. XVII:** 167, 179

"Short Happy Life of Francis Macomber, The" (Hemingway), **II:** 250, 263–264; **Retro. Supp. I:** 182; **Supp. IV Part 1:** 48; **Supp. IX:** 106

Short Night, The (Turner), **Supp. XV:** 201

Short Novels of Thomas Wolfe, The (Wolfe), **IV:** 456

Short Poems (Berryman), **I:** 170

"SHORT SPEECH TO MY FRIENDS" (Baraka), **Supp. II Part 1:** 35

Short Stories (Rawlings), **Supp. X:** 224

Short Stories: Five Decades (Shaw), **Supp. XIX:** 252–253

"Short Story, The" (Welty), **IV:** 279

Short Story Masterpieces, **Supp. IX:** 4

Short Studies of American Authors (Higginson), **I:** 455

"Short-timer's Calendar" (Komunyakaa), **Supp. XIII:** 125

"Short Weight" (Davison), **Supp. XXVI:** 75

Shosha (Singer), **Retro. Supp. II: 313–314**

Shostak, Debra, **Supp. XXIV:** 136

Shostakovich, Dimitri, **IV:** 75; **Supp. VIII:** 21

Shot of Love (album, Dylan), **Supp. XVIII:** 28

"Shots" (Ozick), **Supp. V:** 268

Shotts, Jeffrey, **Supp. XV:** 103, 104

"Should Wizard Hit Mommy?" (Updike), **IV:** 221, 222, 224; **Retro. Supp. I:** 335

Shoup, Barbara, **Supp. XV:** 55, 59, 62, 69

"Shoveling Snow with Buddha" (Collins), **Supp. XXI:** 60

"Shovel Man, The" (Sandburg), **III:** 553

Showalter, Elaine, **Retro. Supp. I:** 368; **Supp. IV Part 2:** 440, 441, 444; **Supp. X:** 97; **Supp. XVI:** 80, 92; **Supp. XX: 274; Supp. XXIV:** 28

"Shower of Gold" (Welty), **IV:** 271–272

Shreve, Porter, **Supp. XXVI:** 209

Shribman, David M., **Supp. XXII:** 205, 218

"Shrike and the Chipmunks, The" (Thurber), **Supp. I Part 2:** 617

Shrimp Girl (Hogarth), **Supp. XII:** 44

"Shrine and the Burning Wheel, The" (Jarman), **Supp. XVII:** 116

"Shrine with Flowers" (Di Piero), **Supp. XIX:** 43, 44

"Shriveled Meditation" (X. J. Kennedy), **Supp. XV:** 170

Shropshire Lad, A (Housman), **Supp. XV:** 41

"Shrouded Stranger, The" (Ginsberg), **Supp. II Part 1:** 312

"Shroud of Color, The" (Cullen), **Supp. IV Part 1:** 166, 168, 170, 171

Shrunken Head of Pancho Villa, The (Valdez), **Supp. XXIII:** 203

Shtetl (film; Marzynski), **Supp. XVI:** 153

Shtetl: The Life and Death of a Small Town and the World of Polish Jews (E. Hoffman), **Supp. XVI:** 152, **153–155**

Shue, Elizabeth, **Supp. XXIII:** 276

Shuffle (L. Michaels), **Supp. XVI:** 202, 203, 213

Shuffle Along (musical), **Supp. I Part 1:** 322; **Supp. X:** 136

Shulman, Polly, **Supp. XXVI:** 158

Shultz, George, **Supp. IV Part 1:** 234

Shuman, R. Baird, **Supp. XXV:** 96

Shurr, William, **Retro. Supp. I:** 43

Shuster, Joel, **Supp. XI:** 67

Shusterman, Richard, **Retro. Supp. I:** 53

"Shut a Final Door" (Capote), **Supp. III Part 1:** 117, 120, 124

Shut Up, He Explained (Lardner), **II:** 432

Shylock's Daughter: A Novel of Love in Venice (Serenissima) (Jong), **Supp. V:** 115, 127, 128–129

Siamanto (Atom Yarjanian), **Supp. XXIII:** 28

"Siasconset: How It Arose and What It Is" (Briggs), **Supp. XVIII:** 9

Siberian Village, The (Dove), **Supp. IV Part 1:** 255, 256

Sibley, Celestine, **Supp. XXII:** 194, 199

Sibley, Mulford Q., **Supp. I Part 2:** 524

"Sibling Mysteries" (Rich), **Supp. I Part 2:** 574

Siblings (Quindlen and Kelsh), **Supp. XVII:** 167, 179

Siblings in Paradise (or Moscow when It Sizzles) (Silver), **Supp. XXIV:** 265

Sibon, Marcelle, **IV:** 288

"Sicilian Emigrant's Song" (W. C. Williams), **Retro. Supp. I:** 413

Sicilian Miniatures (Sobin), **Supp. XVI:** 288

"Sick Wife, The" (Kenyon), **Supp. VII:** 173, 174

"'Sic transit gloria mundi'" (Dickinson), **Retro. Supp. I:** 30

Sid Caesar Show (television show), **Supp. IV Part 2:** 575

Siddons, Anne Rivers, **Supp. XXII: 239–254**

Siddons, Sarah, **II:** 298

Side Effects (Allen), **Supp. XV:** 3, 14, **15–16**

"Side Effects of Lucille, The" (Huddle), **Supp. XXVI:** 155–156

Side of Paradise, This (Fitgerald), **Supp. IX:** 56

"Sidewalk, The" (Biss), **Supp. XXVI:** 48

Sidnee Poet Heroical, The (Baraka), **Supp. II Part 1:** 55

Sidney, Algernon, **II:** 114

Sidney, Mary, **Supp. I Part 1:** 98

Sidney, Philip, **II:** 470; **Supp. I Part 1:** 98, 111, 117–118, 122; **Supp. I Part 2:** 658; **Supp. II Part 1:** 104–105; **Supp. V:** 250; **Supp. XII:** 264; **Supp. XIV:** 128

Sidney, Sylvia, **Supp. I Part 1:** 67

Sidney Lanier: A Bibliographical and Critical Study (Starke), **Supp. I Part 1:** 371

Sidney Lanier: A Biographical and Critical Study (Starke), **Supp. I Part 1:** 371

Siebert, Kathy, **Supp. XX: 84**

Siege (Shaw), **Supp. XIX:** 244

Siegel, Barry, **Supp. XIV:** 82

Siegel, Ben, **Supp. XXIII:** 3, 4, 10, 11, 12, 14, 16

Siegel, Catherine, **Supp. XII:** 126

Siegel, Jerry, **Supp. XI:** 67

Siegel, Lee, **Supp. XXII: 255–269; Supp. XXV:** 56

"Siege of London, The" (James), **Retro. Supp. I:** 227

Siegle, Robert, **Supp. XII:** 8

Sienkiewicz, Henryk, **Supp. IV Part 2:** 518; **Supp. XVI:** 182

"Sierra Kid" (Levine), **Supp. V:** 180–181

Sigal, Clancy, **Supp. XXI:** 44; **Supp. XXIII:** 166; **Supp. XXVI:** 26

Sigg, Eric, **Retro. Supp. I:** 53

"Sight" (Merwin), **Supp. III Part 1:** 356

Sighted Singer, The (Halliday), **Supp. XIX:** 82, **86–87**

"Sight in Camp in the Daybreak Gray and Dim, A" (Whitman), **II:** 373

Sights and Spectacles (McCarthy), **II:** 562

"Sights from a Steeple" (Hawthorne), **Retro. Supp. I:** 62; **Supp. XXI:** 201

Sights Unseen (Gibbons), **Supp. X:** **49–50**

Sight Unseen and the Confession (Rinehart), **Supp. XXV:** 195, 200

"Signals" (Carver), **Supp. III Part 1:** 143

"Signature for Tempo" (MacLeish), **III:** 8–9

"Signed Confession of Crimes against the State" (Merton), **Supp. VIII:** 201

Signifying Monkey, The (Hughes), **Retro. Supp. I:** 195

Signifying Monkey, The: A Theory of Afro-American Literary Criticism (H. L. Gates), **Supp. X:** 243; **Supp. XX:** **99, 106–107**

"Signing, The (Dixon), **Supp. XII: 146**

Sign in Sidney Brustein's Window, The (Hansberry), **Supp. IV Part 1:** 359, 365, 369, 370–372

"Sign in the Sky, A: Dating the League of the Haudenosaunee" (Mann and Fields), **Supp. XXVI:** 86

Sign of Jonas, The (Merton), **Supp. VIII:** 194–195, 195, 197, 200, 206, 207

"Sign of Saturn, The" (Olds), **Supp. X:** 206

"Signs, Oakvale, Mississippi, 1941" (Trethewey), **Supp. XXI:** 248–249

Signs and Wonders (Bukiet), **Supp. XVII:** **45–46**

Sigourney, Lydia, **Supp. I Part 2:** 684

Sikora, Malgorzata, **Retro. Supp. II:** 324

Silas Marner (G. Eliot), **II:** 26

Silberg, Richard, **Supp. XV:** 116

Silberman, James, **Supp. XXIV:** 288

"Silence" (Moore), **III:** 212

"Silence" (Poe), **III:** 416

"Silence" (Sanders), **Supp. XVI:** 278

"Silence, A" (Clampitt), **Supp. IX:** 53

"Silence—A Fable" (Poe), **III:** 416

Silence and Metaphor (Bronk), **Supp. XXI:** 31, 32

"Silence Before Harvest, The" (Merwin), **Supp. III Part 1:** 352

Silence Dogood Papers, The (Franklin), **II:** 106–107

Silence in the Snowy Fields (R. Bly), **Supp. IV Part 1:** 60–61, 62, 63, 65, 66, 72; **Supp. XXI:** 84, 85

Silence of History, The (Farrell), **II:** 46–47

Silence of the Lambs, The (T. Harris), **Supp. XXI:** 78

Silence Opens, A (Clampitt), **Supp. IX:** **53**

Silences (Olsen), **Supp. XIII:** 293, 294, 295, 296, **304–306**

"Silences: When Writers Don't Write" (Olsen), **Supp. XIII:** 294

Silencing the Past: Power and the Production of History (Trouillot), **Supp. X:** 14

"Silent in America" (Levine), **Supp. V:** 183

Silent Life, The (Merton), **Supp. VIII:** 208

Silent Partner, The (Odets), **Supp. II Part 2:** 539

"Silent Piano, The" (Davison), **Supp. XXVI:** 78

"Silent Poem" (Francis), **Supp. IX:** 86

"Silent Season of a Hero, The" (Talese), **Supp. XVII:** 203–204

"Silent Slain, The" (MacLeish), **III:** 9

"Silent Snow, Secret Snow" (Aiken), **I:** 52

Silent Spring (Carson), **Supp. IX:** 19, 24, **31–34; Supp. V:** 202; **Supp. XIV:** 177; **Supp. XVI:** 36; **Supp. XVIII:** 189

Silhouettes of American Life (R. H. Davis), **Supp. XVI:** 85

"Silken Tent, The" (Frost), **Retro. Supp. I:** 138–139; **Supp. IV Part 2:** 448

Silko, Leslie Marmon, **Supp. IV Part 1:** 274, 319, 325, 333–334, 335, 404; **Supp. IV Part 2:** 499, 505, **557–572; Supp. V:** 169; **Supp. XI:** 18; **Supp. XII:** 217; **Supp. XVIII:** 58; **Supp. XXVI:** 102

Silliman, Ron, **Supp. IV Part 2:** 426; **Supp. XV:** 344; **Supp. XVII:** 70, 77

Silliman's Blog (R. Silliman), **Supp. XVII:** 70

Silman, Roberta, **Supp. X:** 6

Silver, Nicky, **Supp. XXIV:** 128, **263–277**

Silverblatt, Michael, **Supp. XV:** 224

"Silver Crown, The" (Malamud), **Supp. I Part 2:** 434–435, 437; **Supp. V:** 266

"Silver Dish, The" (Bellow), **Retro. Supp. II:** 30

"Silver Filigree" (Wylie), **Supp. I Part 2:** 707

"Silver Key, The" (Lovecraft), **Supp. XXV:** 114

"Silver Lake" (B. Kelly), **Supp. XVII:** 130

Silverman, Joseph, **Supp. XXIII:** 8

Silvers, Phil, **Supp. IV Part 2:** 574

Silverthorne, Elizabeth, **Supp. X:** 220, 221, 222, 226, 234

"Silver To Have and to Hurl" (Didion), **Supp. IV Part 1:** 197

Simic, Charles, **Supp. V:** 5, 332; **Supp. VIII:** 39, **269–287; Supp. XI:** 317; **Supp. XIX:** 277, 282; **Supp. XV:** 179, 185

"Similar Cases" (Gilman), **Supp. XI:** 200, 202

Similitudes, from the Ocean and Prairie (Larcom), **Supp. XIII:** 141

Simmel, Georg, **Supp. I Part 2:** 644; **Supp. XVII:** 98

Simmons, Charles, **Supp. XI:** 230

Simmons, David, **Supp. XXV:** 123

Simmons, Maggie, **Retro. Supp. II:** 21

Simms, Michael, **Supp. XII:** 184

Simms, William Gilmore, **I:** 211

Simon, Greg, **Supp. XXIV:** 166

Simon, John, **Supp. IV Part 2:** 691

Simon, Neil, **Supp. IV Part 2:** 573–594; **Supp. XVII:** 8

Simone, Nina, **Supp. XXI:** 243

"Simone Weil's Passion Mysticism: The Paradox of Chronic Pain and the Transformation of the Cross" (Helsel), **Supp. XXVI:** 53

"Simon Gerty" (Wylie), **Supp. I Part 2:** 713

Simonides, **Supp. XII:** 110–111

"Simon Ortiz" (Gingerich), **Supp. IV Part 2:** 510

Simon Ortiz (Wiget), **Supp. IV Part 2:** 509

Simonson, Lee, **III:** 396; **Supp. XXI:** 6

"Simple" (Peacock), **Supp. XIX:** 200

"Simple Art of Murder, The" (Chandler), **Supp. IV Part 1:** 121, 341

"Simple Autumnal" (Bogan), **Supp. III Part 1:** 52–53

Simple Heart (Flaubert), **I:** 504

Simple Honorable Man, A (Richter), **Supp. XVIII:** 208, 218, **219**, 220

"Simple Purchase, A" (Peacock), **Supp. XIX:** 199

Simple Speaks his Mind (Hughes), **Retro. Supp. I:** 209; **Supp. I Part 1:** 337

Simple Stakes a Claim (Hughes), **Retro. Supp. I:** 209; **Supp. I Part 1:** 337

Simple's Uncle Sam (Hughes), **Retro. Supp. I:** 209; **Supp. I Part 1:** 337

Simple Takes a Wife (Hughes), **Retro. Supp. I:** 209; **Supp. I Part 1:** 337

Simple Truth, The (Hardwick), **Supp. III Part 1:** 199, 200, 208

Simple Truth, The (Levine), **Supp. V:** 178, 179, 193–194

"Simple Widsom, The" (Skloot), **Supp. XX: 207**

"Simplicity" (Sanders), **Supp. XVI:** 276

Simply, Trixi, **Supp. XXV:** 2

Simply Heavenly (Hughes), **Retro. Supp. I:** 209; **Supp. I Part 1:** 338, 339

Simpson, Louis, **Supp. III Part 2:** 541; **Supp. IV Part 2:** 448, 621; **Supp. IX: 265–283,** 290; **Supp. VIII:** 39, 279; **Supp. XI:** 317; **Supp. XII:** 130; **Supp. XIII:** 337

Simpson, Mona, **Supp. XVI:** 206

"Sin" (C. Frost), **Supp. XV:** 96

Sinatra, Frank, **Supp. IX:** 3; **Supp. X:** 119; **Supp. XI:** 213

Sincere Convert, The (Shepard), **IV:** 158

Sincerely, Willis Wayde (Marquand), **III:** 61, 63, 66, 67–68, 69

Sincerity (Rowson), **Supp. XV:** 242

Sincerity and Authenticity (Trilling), **Supp. III Part 2:** 510–512

"Sincerity and Objectification: With Special Reference to the Work of Charles Reznikoff" (Zukofsky), **Supp. XIV:** 286

Sinclair, Mary Craig (Mary Craig Kimbrough), **Supp. V:** 275, 286, 287

Sinclair, Upton, **II:** 34, 440, 444, 451; **III:** 580; **Retro. Supp. II:** 95; **Supp. V: 275–293; Supp. VIII:** 11

Sinclair Lewis: An American Life (Schorer), **II:** 459

"Sine Qua Non" (Stallings), **Supp. XXV:** 232

"Singapore" (Oliver), **Supp. VII:** 239, 240

Singer, Bennett L., **Supp. IV Part 1:** 330

Singer, Beth, **Supp. XIV:** 203

Singer, Isaac Bashevis, **I:** 144; **IV: 1–24; Retro. Supp. II:** 22, **299–320; Supp. IX:** 114; **Supp. XVIII:** 215, 220; **Supp. XXI:** 106; **Supp. XXII:** 258

Singer, Israel Joshua, **IV:** 2, 16, 17; **Retro. Supp. II:** 302; **Supp. XVII:** 41

Singer, Joshua, **IV:** 4

Singer, Rabbi Pinchos Menachem, **IV:** 16

Singin' and Swingin' and Gettin' Merry Like Christmas (Angelou), **Supp. IV Part 1:** 2, 5, 6–7, 9, 13, 14

"Singing & Doubling Together" (Ammons), **Supp. VII:** 34–35

Singing Jailbirds (Sinclair), **Supp. V:** 277

"Singing the Black Mother" (Lupton), **Supp. IV Part 1:** 7

Single Hound, The (Sarton), **Supp. VIII:** 251, 265

Single Hound, The: Poems of a Lifetime (Dickinson; Bianchi, ed.), **Retro. Supp. I:** 35

Single Man, A (Isherwood), **Supp. XIV:** 157, 164, **169–170,** 171

"Single Sonnet" (Bogan), **Supp. III Part 1:** 56–58

Singley, Carol, **Retro. Supp. I:** 373

Singular Family, A: Rosacoke and Her Kin (Price), **Supp. VI: 258–259,** 260

"Singular First Person, The" (Sanders), **Supp. XVI:** 274

Singularities (Howe), **Supp. IV Part 2:** 431

Sin in Their Blood (Lacy), **Supp. XV:** 200

"Sinister Adolescents, The" (Dos Passos), **I:** 493

Sinister Street (Mackenzie), **II:** 82

Sinking of Clay City, The (Wrigley), **Supp. XVIII: 294–295**

Sinners in the Hands of an Angry God (Edwards), **I:** 546, 552–553, 559, 562; **Supp. XXIV:** 72

Sinning with Annie, and Other Stories (Theroux), **Supp. VIII:** 318

"Sins of Kalamazoo, The" (Sandburg), **III:** 586

Sintram and His Companions (La Motte-Fouqué), **III:** 78

"Siope" (Poe), **III:** 411

"Sioux Woman's Love for Her Grand-child, A" (Zitkala-Ša), **Supp. XXV:** 281

"Sipapu: A Cultural Perspective" (Gunn Allen), **Supp. IV Part 1:** 323

Sipchen, Bob, **Supp. X:** 145

Sipper, Ralph B., **Supp. IV Part 2:** 475

"Sire" (Cisneros), **Supp. VII:** 62–63, 64

"Siren and Signal" (Zukofsky), **Supp. III Part 2:** 611, 612

Sirens of Titan, The (Vonnegut), **Supp. II Part 2:** 757, 758, 760, 765–767

"Sir Galahad" (Tennyson), **Supp. I Part 2:** 410

Sirin, V. (pseudonym), **Retro. Supp. I:** 266. *See also* Nabokov, Vladimir

Sirlin, Jerome, **Supp. XXI:** 147

Sir Vadia's Shadow: A Friendship across Five Continents (Theroux), **Supp. VIII:** 309, 314, 321, 325

"Sir William's Reply to Molly"(Kenny), **Supp. XXIII:** 153

"Sis" (F. Barthelme), **Supp. XI:** 26

"S is for Sad" (M. F. K. Fisher), **Supp. XVII:** 86

Sisley, Alfred, **I:** 478

Sissman, L. E., **Supp. X:** 69; **Supp. XXVI:** 68, 74

"Sister" (Hughes), **Retro. Supp. I:** 208

"Sister" (Lamott), **Supp. XX: 142**

"Sister, The" (July), **Supp. XXIV:** 202

Sister Age (M. F. K. Fisher), **Supp. XVII:** 88, 91

Sister Carrie (Dreiser), **I:** 482, 497, 499, 500, 501–502, 503–504, 505, 506, 515, 519; **III:** 327; **IV:** 208; **Retro. Supp. I:** 376; **Retro. Supp. II:** 93, **96–99; Supp. XVIII:** 76, 243; **Supp. XXIII:** 165; **Supp. XXV:** 129

Sister Mary Ignatius Explains It All for You (Durang), **Supp. XXIV:** 114, **119–120**

"Sister of the Minotaur" (Stevens), **IV:** 89; **Supp. IX:** 332

"Sisters" (Boulton), **Supp. XXII:** 20

"Sisters" (Nelson), **Supp. XVIII:** 176

"Sisters, The" (Whittier), **Supp. I Part 2:** 696

Sister's Choice (Showalter), **Retro. Supp. I:** 368

Sisters-in-Law, The (Atherton), **Supp. XXIV:** 25

Sisters of the Earth: Women's Prose and Poetry About Nature (Anderson, ed.), **Supp. XVIII:** 189

Sisters Rosensweig, The (Wasserstein), **Supp. XV:** 320, **328–330**

"Sisyphus" (Kumin), **Supp. IV Part 2:** 443, 444, 451

"Sitalkas" (Doolittle), **Supp. I Part 1:** 266

"Sites of Memory" (Cliff), **Supp. XXII:** 69, 74

Sitney, P. Adams, **Supp. XII:** 2

Sitting Bull, **Supp. IV Part 2:** 492

"Sitting in a Rocking Chair Going Blind" (Komunyakaa), **Supp. XIII:** 114

Sitting In: Selected Writings on Jazz, Blues, and Related Topics (Carruth), **Supp. XVI:** 46

"Sitting Up Late with My Father, 1977" (F. Wright), **Supp. XVII:** 247

Sitti's Secrets (Nye), **Supp. XIII:** 278

Situation Normal (A. Miller), **III:** 148, 149, 156, 164

Situation of Poetry, The: Contemporary Poetry and Its Traditions (Pinsky), **Supp. VI: 237–238,** 239, 241, 242

Sitwell, Edith, **IV:** 77; **Supp. I Part 1:** 271

6 A.M. (Bodenheim), **Supp. XXV:** 27

"Six Brothers" (Cisneros), **Supp. VII:** 67

Six Characters in Search of an Author (Pirandello), **Supp. IV Part 2:** 576

"Six Days: Some Rememberings" (Paley), **Supp. VI:** 226

"65290" (Leopold), **Supp. XIV:** 184–185

Six French Poets (Lowell), **II:** 528–529

"Six in All" (Bierds), **Supp. XVII:** 31

Six Lips (Schott), **Supp. XXIII: 251–252**

"Six Persons" (Baraka), **Supp. II Part 1:** 53

Six Sections from Mountains and Rivers without End (Snyder), **Supp. VIII:** 305

"Sixteen Months" (Sandburg), **III:** 584

1601, or Conversation as It Was by the Fireside in the Time of the Tudors (Twain), **IV:** 201

"Sixth-Month Song in the Foothills" (Snyder), **Supp. VIII:** 297

Sixties, The (magazine) (R. Bly), **Supp. IV Part 1:** 60; **Supp. IX:** 271

"Sixty" (Dunn), **Supp. XI:** 155

"Sixty Acres" (Carver), **Supp. III Part 1:** 141

"64 Elmgrove" (Halliday), **Supp. XIX:** 88

"69 Hidebound Opinions, Propositions, and Several Asides from a Manila Folder concerning the Stuff of Poetry" (Wright), **Supp. XV:** 344–345

Sixty Seconds (Bodenheim), **Supp. XXV:** 26

Sixty Stories (Barthelme), **Supp. IV Part 1:** 41, 42, 44, 47, 49, 50

63: Dream Palace (Purdy), **Supp. VII:** 270–271

"Six Variations" (Levertov), **Supp. III Part 1:** 277–278

"Six-Year-Old Boy" (Olds), **Supp. X:** 206

"Six Years Later" (Brodsky), **Supp. VIII:** 26, 28

"Size and Sheer Will" (Olds), **Supp. X:** 206

Size of Thoughts, The: Essays and Other Lumber (Baker), **Supp. XIII: 52–53,** 55, 56

Sizwe Bansi Is Dead (Fugard), **Supp. VIII:** 330

Sjöwall, Maj, **Supp. XX: 87**

"Skagway" (Haines), **Supp. XII:** 206

"Skaters, The" (Ashbery), **Supp. III Part 1:** 10, 12, 13, 18, 25

"Skaters, The" (Jarrell), **II:** 368–369

Skau, Michael, **Supp. XII:** 129, 130, 132, 134

Skeeters Kirby (Masters), **Supp. I Part 2:** 459, 470, 471

Skeleton at the Feast, The (Wells), **Supp. XXVI:** 278, 282

Skeleton Crew (King), **Supp. V:** 144

"Skeleton in Armor, The" (Longfellow), **Retro. Supp. II:** 168

"Skeleton's Cave, The" (Bryant), **Supp. I Part 1:** 157

Skelton, John, **III:** 521

Skepticisms (Aiken), **Supp. XV:** 298, 302

Sketch Book of Geoffrey Crayon, Gent., The (Irving), **II:** 295, 303, 304–308, 309, 311, 491; **Supp. I Part 1:** 155

Sketches of Art (Jameson), **Retro. Supp. II:** 58

Sketches of Eighteenth Century America (Crèvecoeur), **Supp. I Part 1:** 233, 240–241, 250, 251

"Sketches of Female Biography" (Rowson), **Supp. XV:** 245

Sketches of Switzerland (Cooper), **I:** 346

Sketches Old and New (Twain), **IV:** 198

"Sketch for a Job-Application Blank" (Harrison), **Supp. VIII:** 38

"Sketch"(Kenny), **Supp. XXIII:** 155

Sketch of Old England, by a New England Man (Paulding), **I:** 344

Skibell, Joseph, **Supp. XVII:** 48

"Skier and the Mountain, The" (Eberhart), **I:** 528–529

"Skiing by Moonlight" (Davison), **Supp. XXVI:** 74

"Skin-Boats: 1830, The" (Bierds), **Supp. XVII:** 28

Skinker, Mary Scott, **Supp. IX:** 20

Skinner, Ewart, **Supp. XXII:** 78

Skinny Island (Auchincloss), **Supp. IV Part 1:** 33

Skinny Legs and All (Robbins), **Supp. X:** 267, 273, **276–279**

Skin of Our Teeth, The (Wilder), **IV:** 357, 358, 369–372; **Supp. IV Part 2:** 586; **Supp. XX:** 50

"Skins" (Wright), **Supp. V:** 340

Skins and Bones: Poems 1979–1987 (Gunn Allen), **Supp. IV Part 1:** 321, 331

"Skipper Ireson's Ride" (Whittier), **Supp. I Part 2:** 691, 693–694

"Skirmish at Sartoris" (Faulkner), **II:** 67

"Skirt" (Halliday), **Supp. XIX:** 90

Skirts and Slacks (Di Piero), **Supp. XIX:** 35, 36, 38, 45–47

Sklenicka, Carol, **Supp. XXIV:** 166

Skloot, Floyd, **Supp. XX: 193–209**

Skotheim, Robert Allen, **Supp. XVII:** 104

Skow, John, **Supp. V:** 213; **Supp. XVI:** 174

Skube, Michael, **Supp. XVIII:** 96

"Skunk Cabbage" (Bronk), **Supp. XXI:** 31

"Skunk Cabbage" (Oliver), **Supp. VII:** 235, 236

"Skunk Hour" (Lowell), **II:** 548–550; **Retro. Supp. II:** 188, 189; **Supp. XIV:** 269; **Supp. XX: 203**

Skurnick, Lizzie, **Supp. XXVI:** 49

Sky, The Stars, The Wilderness, The (Bass), **Supp. XVI:** 19, 20

Sky Changes, The (Sorrentino), **Supp. XXI:** 228, 230, 231; **Supp. XXVI:** 26

"Sky Dance" (Leopold), **Supp. XIV:** 186

"Sky Line" (Taylor), **Supp. V:** 316

"Sky Line, The" (Mumford), **Supp. II Part 2:** 475

"Skyscraper" (Sandburg), **III:** 581–582

Sky's the Limit, The: A Defense of the Earth (Nichols), **Supp. XIII:** 268

"Sky Valley Rider" (Wright), **Supp. V:** 335, 340

Sky-Walk; or the Man Unknown to Himself (Brown), **Supp. I Part 1:** 127–128

"Slang in America" (Whitman), **IV:** 348

Slappy Hooper, the Wonderful Sign Painter (Bontemps and Conroy), **Supp. XXII:** 5, 11

Slapstick (Vonnegut), **Supp. II Part 2:** 753, 754, 778

Slapstick Tragedy (T. Williams), **IV:** 382, 393

Slate, Lane, **Supp. IX:** 251, 253

Slattery, Mary Grace. *See* Miller, Mrs. Arthur (Mary Grace Slattery)

Slattery's Hurricane (Wouk), **Supp. XXV:** 257, 262–263

"Slaughterer, The" (Singer), **IV:** 19

Slaughterhouse-Five (Vonnegut), **Supp. II Part 2:** 755, 758–759, 760, 770, 772–776; **Supp. V:** 41, 244; **Supp. XIX:** 235

Slaughter Rule, The (film; Alex and Andrew Smith), **Supp. XIX:** 174

Slave, The (Baraka), **Supp. II Part 1:** 42, 44, 56

Slave, The: A Novel (Singer), **IV:** 13; **Retro. Supp. II: 305–307**

"Slave Canal" (Ray), **Supp. XVIII:** 193

"Slave Coffle" (Angelou), **Supp. IV Part 1:** 16

"Slave of the Sky" (P. N. Warren), **Supp. XX: 261**

"Slave on the Block" (Hughes), **Supp. I Part 1:** 329

Slave Power, The: The Free North and Southern Domination, 1780–1860 (Richards), **Supp. XIV:** 48

"Slave Quarters" (Dickey), **Supp. IV Part 1:** 181

Slavery (Channing), **Supp. XXIV:** 77–78

"Slave's Dream, The" (Longfellow), **Supp. I Part 2:** 409

Slave Ship: A Historical Pageant (Baraka), **Supp. II Part 1:** 47–49, 53, 56–57

"Slave-Ships, The" (Whittier), **Supp. I Part 2:** 687–688

Slaves in Algiers; or, A Struggle for Freedom (Rowson), **Supp. XV: 236–237**

"Slave Trade, The: View from the Middle Passage" (Major), **Supp. XXII:** 182

Slavs! Thinking about the Longstanding Problems of Virtue and Happiness (Kushner), **Supp. IX: 146**

Sledge, Eugene, **Supp. V:** 250

Sleek for the Long Flight (Matthews), **Supp. IX:** 154, 155, **157–158**

Sleep (Dixon), **Supp. XII:** 154

"Sleep, The" (Strand), **Supp. IV Part 2:** 627

Sleeper (film; Allen), **Supp. XV:** 5

"Sleeper, The" (Poe), **III:** 411

"Sleeper 1, The" (Hay), **Supp. XIV:** 132–133

"Sleeper 2, The" (Hay), **Supp. XIV:** 132–133

"Sleepers, The" (Whitman), **IV:** 336

"Sleepers in Jaipur" (Kenyon), **Supp. VII:** 172

Sleepers in Moon-Crowned Valleys (Purdy), **Supp. VII:** 274, 275

Sleepers Joining Hands (R. Bly), **Supp. XXI:** 85

"Sleepers Joining Hands" (R. Bly), **Supp. IV Part 1:** 63, 73

Sleeping Beauty (Macdonald), **Supp. IV Part 2:** 474, 475

Sleeping Beauty, The (Carruth), **Supp. XVI:** 53, 57–58

"Sleeping Beauty Syndrome, The: The New Agony of Single Men" (Wasserstein), **Supp. XV:** 328

Sleeping Dogs (Wells), **Supp. XXVI:** 280–281

Sleeping Fires (Atherton), **Supp. XXIV:** 25

"Sleeping Fury, The" (Bogan), **Supp. III Part 1:** 58

Sleeping Fury, The: Poems (Bogan), **Supp. III Part 1:** 55–58

Sleeping Gypsy and Other Poems, The (Garrett), **Supp. VII:** 96–98

Sleeping in the Forest (Oliver), **Supp. VII:** 233

"Sleeping in the Forest" (Oliver), **Supp. VII:** 233–234

Sleeping in the Woods (Wagoner), **Supp. IX: 328**

Sleeping on Fists (Ríos), **Supp. IV Part 2:** 540

Sleeping on the Wing: An Anthology of Modern Poetry (Koch and Farrell, eds.), **Supp. XV:** 187–188

"Sleeping on the Wing"(O'Hara), **Supp. XXIII:** 214

"Sleeping Standing Up" (Bishop), **Supp. I Part 1:** 85, 89, 93

"Sleeping with Animals" (Kumin), **Supp. IV Part 2:** 454

Sleeping with One Eye Open (Strand), **Supp. IV Part 2:** 621–624, 623, 628

Sleep in Thunder (Lacy), **Supp. XV:** 206

"Sleepless, The" (L.-Y. Lee), **Supp. XV:** 224

"Sleepless at Crown Point" (Wilbur), **Supp. III Part 2:** 561

Sleepless Nights (Hardwick), **Supp. III Part 1:** 193, 208–211

"Sleepless Nights" (Nelson), **Supp. XVIII:** 174

"Sleep-Walkers, The" (Gibran), **Supp. XX: 118**

Sleepy Lagoon Mystery, The (Endore), **Supp. XVII:** 60

"Sleepy People" (Lethem), **Supp. XVIII:** 140

Sleigh, Tom, **Supp. XIX:** 38, 40

Sleight, Ken, **Supp. XIII:** 12

Slick, Sam (pseudonym). *See* Haliburton, Thomas Chandler

"Slick Gonna Learn" (Ellison), **Retro. Supp. II:** 116; **Supp. II Part 1:** 237–238

"Slight Rebellion off Madison" (Salinger), **III:** 553

"Slight Sound at Evening, A" (White), **Supp. I Part 2:** 672

"Slim Graves Show, The" (Keillor), **Supp. XVI:** 172

"Slim Greer" series (Hayden), **Supp. II Part 1:** 369

"Slim in Hell" (Hayden), **Supp. II Part 1:** 369

"Slim Man Canyon" (Silko), **Supp. IV Part 2:** 560
"Slip, Shift, and Speed Up: The Influence of Robinson Jeffers's Narrative Syntax" (Jarman), **Supp. XVII:** 111, 112
"Slippery Fingers" (Hammett), **Supp. IV Part 1:** 343
Slipping-Down Life, A (Tyler), **Supp. IV Part 2:** 660–661
Sloan, Jacob, **IV:** 3, 6
Sloan, John, **I:** 254; **IV:** 411; **Retro. Supp. II:** 103; **Supp. XXII:** 277
Sloane, John, **Supp. XV:** 295
"Slob" (Farrell), **II:** 25, 28, 31
Slocum, Joshua, **Supp. I Part 2:** 497; **Supp. XXV:** 205–219
Slogum House (Sandoz), **Supp. XXIV:** 244, **251–252,** 255
Slonim, Véra. *See* Nabokov, Véra
Slopen, Beverly, **Supp. XX:** 59
Slouching towards Bethlehem (Didion), **Supp. IV Part 1:** 196, 197, 200–201, 202, 206, 210
Slovic, Scott, **Supp. XVI:** 277
"Slow Child with a Book of Birds" (Levis), **Supp. XI:** 268
"Slow Dance with Icarus" (Monson), **Supp. XXIV:** 240
Slow Dancing Through Ether: A Fine Binding Project (Monson and Ingmundson), **Supp. XXIV:** 230, 234
"Slow Down for Poetry" (Strand), **Supp. IV Part 2:** 620
Slow Music (Taggard), **Supp. XXII:** 284
"Slow Pacific Swell, The" (Winters), **Supp. II Part 2:** 790, 793, 795, 796, 799
Slow Parade (Kees), **Supp. XV:** 137
Slow Train Coming (album, Dylan), **Supp. XVIII:** 28
Slow Transparency (Hadas), **Supp. XXIII: 113–114**
Slow Vision (Bodenheim), **Supp. XXV:** 28
"Slum Church" (Espaillat), **Supp. XXI:** 110–111
"Slumgullions" (Olsen), **Supp. IV Part 1:** 54
Slumgullion Stew: An Edward Abbey Reader (Abbey), **Supp. XIII:** 4
Slung, Michelle, **Supp. XX:** 87
"S & M" (Komunyakaa), **Supp. XIII:** 114
"Small" (C. Frost), **Supp. XV:** 102
Small, Albion, **Supp. I Part 1:** 5
"Small, Good Thing, A" (Carver), **Supp. III Part 1:** 145, 147
Small, Miriam Rossiter, **Supp. I Part 1:** 319
Small Boy and Others, A (James), **II:** 337, 547; **Retro. Supp. I:** 235
"Small but Urgent Request to the Unknowable" (Karr), **Supp. XI:** 243
Small Ceremonies (Shields), **Supp. VII:** 312–315, 320
Small Craft Warnings (T. Williams), **IV:** 382, 383, 384, 385, 386, 387, 392, 393, 396, 398
"Small Degrees" (Brockmeier), **Supp. XXII:** 52, 59

"Small Fry" (Peacock), **Supp. XIX:** 206
Small Place, A (Kincaid), **Supp. VII:** 186–187, 188, 191
"Small Rain, The" (Pynchon), **Supp. II Part 2:** 620
Small Room, The (Sarton), **Supp. VIII:** 252, **255–256**
Smalls, Bob, **II:** 128
"Small Song for Andrew" (Weigl), **Supp. XIX:** 280
Small Time Crooks (film; Allen), **Supp. XV:** 11
Small Town, A (Hearon), **Supp. VIII: 65–66**
"Small Vases from Hebron, The" (Nye), **Supp. XIII:** 283
"Small Vision, The" (Goldbarth), **Supp. XII:** 180
"Small Voice from the Wings" (Everwine), **Supp. XV:** 76
"Small Wire" (Sexton), **Supp. II Part 2:** 696
Small Worlds (A. Hoffman), **Supp. XVII:** 44
Smardz, Zofia, **Supp. XVI:** 155
Smart, Christopher, **III:** 534; **Supp. I Part 2:** 539; **Supp. IV Part 2:** 626
Smart, Joyce H., **Supp. XI:** 169
"Smart Cookie, A" (Cisneros), **Supp. VII:** 64
"Smash"(Thompson), **Supp. XXIII:** 301, 302
"Smashup" (Thurber), **Supp. I Part 2:** 616
Smedly, Agnes, **Supp. XIII:** 295
"Smell of a God, The" (Peacock), **Supp. XIX:** 199
"Smelt Fishing" (Hayden), **Supp. II Part 1:** 367
"Smile of the Bathers, The" (Kees), **Supp. XV:** 145
"Smile on the Face of a Kouros, The" (Bronk), **Supp. XXI:** 31
"Smiles" (Dunn), **Supp. XI:** 151
Smiles, Samuel, **Supp. X:** 167
Smiley, Jane, **Supp. VI: 291–309; Supp. XII:** 73, 297; **Supp. XIII:** 127; **Supp. XIX:** 54
Smith, Adam, **II:** 9; **Supp. I Part 2:** 633, 634, 639; **Supp. XVII:** 235
Smith, Annick, **Supp. XIV:** 223; **Supp. XXVI:** 183, 186, 188
Smith, Barbara, **Supp. XXIII:** 194
Smith, Benjamin, **IV:** 148
Smith, Bernard, **I:** 260
Smith, Bessie, **Retro. Supp. I:** 343; **Supp. VIII:** 330; **Supp. XIX:** 147
Smith, Betty, **Supp. XXIII: 257–271**
Smith, Charlie, **Supp. X:** 177
Smith, Clark Ashton, **Supp. XXV:** 111
Smith, Dale, **Supp. XV:** 136, 138, 139
Smith, Dave, **Supp. V:** 333; **Supp. XI:** 152; **Supp. XII:** 178, 198; **Supp. XIX:** 277, 282
Smith, David, **Supp. XIII:** 246, 247
Smith, David Nichol, **Supp. XIV:** 2
Smith, Dinitia, **Supp. VIII:** 74, 82, 83; **Supp. XVIII:** 162; **Supp. XXIV:** 2–3
Smith, Elihu Hubbard, **Supp. I Part 1:** 126, 127, 130

Smith, Ernest J., **Supp. XXIII:** 111, 113, 117
Smith, George Adam, **III:** 199
Smith, Hannah Whitall, **Supp. XIV:** 333, 334, 338
Smith, Harrison, **II:** 61
Smith, Henry Nash, **IV:** 210; **Supp. I Part 1:** 233
Smith, Herbert F., **Supp. I Part 2:** 423
Smith, Iain Crichton, **Supp. XVIII:** 196
Smith, James, **II:** 111
Smith, Jedediah Strong, **Supp. IV Part 2:** 602
Smith, Jerome, **Supp. IV Part 1:** 369
Smith, Joe, **Supp. IV Part 2:** 584
Smith, John, **I:** 4, 131; **II:** 296
Smith, John Allyn, **I:** 168
Smith, Johnston (pseudonym). *See* Crane, Stephen
Smith, Katherine Capshaw, **Supp. XXII:** 10, 13–14
Smith, Kellogg, **Supp. I Part 2:** 660
Smith, Lamar, **II:** 585
Smith, Mrs. Lamar (Marguerite Walters), **II:** 585, 587
Smith, Lane, **Supp. XIX:** 231
Smith, Larry David, **Supp. XVIII:** 22
Smith, Lee, **Supp. XII:** 311; **Supp. XVIII:** 195; **Supp. XXII:** 206, 213
Smith, Lillian, **Supp. XXII:** 67
Smith, Logan Pearsall, **Supp. XIV: 333– 351**
Smith, Lula Carson. *See* McCullers, Carson
Smith, Mark, **Supp. XVIII:** 155
Smith, Martha Nell, **Retro. Supp. I:** 33, 43, 46, 47
Smith, Mary Rozet, **Supp. I Part 1:** 5, 22
Smith, Oliver, **II:** 586
Smith, Patricia Clark, **Supp. IV Part 1:** 397, 398, 402, 406, 408, 410; **Supp. IV Part 2:** 509; **Supp. XII:** 218
Smith, Patrick, **Supp. VIII:** 40, 41
Smith, Patti, **Supp. XII:** 136; **Supp. XIV:** 151
Smith, Porter, **III:** 572
Smith, Red, **II:** 417, 424
Smith, Robert McClure, **Supp. XV:** 270
Smith, Robert Pearsall, **Supp. XIV:** 333
Smith, Sarah A., **Supp. XVIII:** 99
Smith, Seba, **Supp. I Part 2:** 411
Smith, Sidonie, **Supp. IV Part 1:** 11; **Supp. XXII:** 70
Smith, Stevie, **Supp. V:** 84
Smith, Sydney, **II:** 295; **Supp. XIV:** 112
Smith, Thorne, **Supp. IX:** 194
Smith, Valerie, **Supp. XXII:** 146
Smith, Wendy, **Supp. XII:** 330, 335; **Supp. XVIII:** 89, 92
Smith, Wilford Bascom "Pitchfork", **Supp. XIII:** 168
Smith, William, **II:** 114
Smith, William Gardner, **Supp. XVI:** 142–143
Smith, William Jay, **Supp. XIII: 331– 350**
Smitherman, Geneva, **Supp. XXVI:** 13
"Smoke" (Di Piero), **Supp. XIX:** 38
Smoke (film), **Supp. XII:** 21

"Smoke" (Huddle), **Supp. XXVI:** 149

Smoke and Steel (Sandburg), **III:** 585–587, 592

Smoke Dancing (Gansworth), **Supp. XXVI:** 104–105

"Smokehouse" (Offutt), **Supp. XIX:** 166, 167

"Smokers" (Wolff), **Supp. VII:** 340–341

Smokey Bites the Dust (film, C. Griffith), **Supp. XVII:** 9

Smoking Mountain, The: Stories of Postwar Germany (Boyle), **Supp. XXIV:** 61

"Smoking My Prayers" (Ortiz), **Supp. IV Part 2:** 503

"Smoking Room, The" (Jackson), **Supp. IX:** 116

"Smoky Gold" (Leopold), **Supp. XIV:** 186

Smolan, Sandy, **Supp. XVI:** 36

Smollett, Tobias G., **I:** 134, 339, 343; **II:** 304–305; **III:** 61; **Supp. XVIII:** 7; **Supp. XXV:** 258

Smooding, Robert, **Supp. XXIII:** 294

Smuggler's Bible, A (McElroy), **Supp. IV Part 1:** 285

Smuggler's Handbook, The (Goldbarth), **Supp. XII:** 181, 183

Smugglers of Lost Soul's Rock, The (Gardner), **Supp. VI: 70**

Smyth, Albert Henry, **II:** 123

Smyth, Jacqui, **Supp. XXI:** 215

"Snack Firm Maps New Chip Push" (Keillor), **Supp. XVI:** 168, 169

"Snail, The" (Hay), **Supp. XIV:** 124

"Snake, The" (Berry), **Supp. X:** 31

"Snake, The" (Crane), **I:** 420

"Snakecharmer" (Plath), **Supp. I Part 2:** 538

"Snakes, Mongooses" (Moore), **III:** 207

"Snakeskin" (Kooser), **Supp. XIX:** 123

"Snakes of September, The" (Kunitz), **Supp. III Part 1:** 258

"Snapshot of 15th S.W., A" (Hugo), **Supp. VI:** 141

"Snapshot Rediscovered, A" (X. J. Kennedy), **Supp. XV:** 170

"Snapshots in an Album" (Espaillat), **Supp. XXI:** 111

"Snapshots of a Daughter-in-Law" (Rich), **Supp. I Part 2:** 553–554

Snapshots of a Daughter-in-Law: Poems, 1954–1962 (Rich), **Supp. I Part 2:** 550–551, 553–554; **Supp. XII:** 255

Snaring the Flightless Birds (Bierds), **Supp. XVII:** 26

Sneetches and Other Stories, The (Geisel), **Supp. XVI:** 109

"Sneeze, The" (Chekhov), **Supp. IV Part 2:** 585

Snell, Ebenezer, **Supp. I Part 1:** 151

Snell, Thomas, **Supp. I Part 1:** 153

Sniffen, Matthew, **Supp. XXV:** 283

"Snob, The" (Boulton), **Supp. XXII:** 23

"Snob, The" (Shapiro), **Supp. II Part 2:** 705

Snobbery: The America Version (Epstein), **Supp. XIV:** 102, 114–115

Snodgrass, Kathleen, **Supp. XVI:** 42

Snodgrass, W. D., **I:** 400; **Retro. Supp. II:** 179; **Supp. III Part 2:** 541; **Supp. V:** 337; **Supp. VI: 311–328; Supp. XI:** 141, 315; **Supp. XIII:** 312; **Supp. XV:** 92, 153; **Supp. XVII:** 239

"Snow" (C. Baxter), **Supp. XVII:** 19

"Snow" (Frost), **Retro. Supp. I:** 133

"Snow" (Haines), **Supp. XII:** 212

"Snow" (Sexton), **Supp. II Part 2:** 696

"Snow" (W. V. Davis), **Supp. XXI:** 89, 90, 93

Snow, C. P., **Supp. I Part 2:** 536

Snow, Dean, **Supp. XXVI:** 86

Snow, Hank, **Supp. V:** 335

Snow Angels (film), **Supp. XXV:** 153–154

Snow Angels (O'Nan), **Supp. XXV:** 142, 143, 150

Snow Ball, The (Gurney), **Supp. V:** 99

"Snow-Bound" (Whittier), **Supp. I Part 2:** 700–703

"Snow Bound at Eagle's" (Harte), **Supp. II Part 1:** 356

"Snowflakes" (Longfellow), **II:** 498

"Snow Goose, The" (Gallico), **Supp. XVI:** 238

Snow-Image and Other Twice Told Tales, The (Hawthorne), **II:** 237; **Retro. Supp. I:** 160

"Snowing in Greenwich Village" (Updike), **IV:** 226; **Retro. Supp. I:** 321

"Snow in New York" (Swenson), **Supp. IV Part 2:** 644

Snow Leopard, The (Matthiessen), **Supp. V:** 199, 207–211

"Snow Man, The" (Stevens), **IV:** 82–83; **Retro. Supp. I:** 299, 300, 302, 306, 307, 312; **Supp. XXI:** 60

"Snowmass Cycle, The" (Dunn), **Supp. XI:** 152

Snow: Meditations of a Cautious Man in Winter (Banks), **Supp. V:** 6

Snow Poems, The (Ammons), **Supp. VII:** 32–34

Snowshoe Trek to Otter River (Budbill), **Supp. XIX:** 11

Snow's Music, The (Skloot), **Supp. XX: 196, 204–205**

"Snows of Kilimanjaro, The" (Hemingway), **II:** 78, 257, 263, 264; **Retro. Supp. I:** 98, 182; **Supp. XII:** 249

"Snows of Studiofiftyfour, The" (Plimpton), **Supp. XVI:** 245

"Snow Songs" (Snodgrass), **Supp. VI:** 324

"Snowstorm, The" (Oates), **Supp. II Part 2:** 523

"Snowstorm as It Affects the American Farmer, A" (Crèvecoeur), **Supp. I Part 1:** 251

Snow White (Barthelme), **Supp. IV Part 1:** 40, 47, 48–49, 50, 52; **Supp. V:** 39

"Snowy Egret" (Weigl), **Supp. XIX:** 280–281

"Snowy Mountain Song, A" (Ortiz), **Supp. IV Part 2:** 506

Snyder, Gary, **Supp. III Part 1:** 350; **Supp. IV Part 2:** 502; **Supp. V:** 168–169; **Supp. VIII:** 39, **289–307; Supp. XVI:** 283; **Supp. XXII:** 276

Snyder, Mike, **Supp. XIV:** 36

"So-and-So Reclining on Her Couch" (Stevens), **IV:** 90

"Soapland" (Thurber), **Supp. I Part 2:** 619

Soares, Lota de Macedo, **Retro. Supp. II:** 44; **Supp. I Part 1:** 89, 94

"Sobbin' Women, The" (Benét), **Supp. XI:** 47

Sobin, Gustaf, **Supp. XVI: 281–298**

Sochen, June, **Supp. XXI:** 1

Social Ethics (Gilman), **Supp. XI:** 207

"Social Function of the Story Teller, The" (lecture, Murray), **Supp. XIX:** 153

"Socialism and the Negro" (McKay), **Supp. X:** 135

"Socialism of the Skin, A (Liberation, Honey!)" (Kushner), **Supp. IX:** 135

Social Thought in America: The Revolt against Formalism (White), **Supp. I Part 2:** 648, 650

"Society, Morality, and the Novel" (Ellison), **Retro. Supp. II:** 118, 123–124

"Society of Eros" (Kittredge), **Supp. XXVI:** 178, 184

"Sociological Habit Patterns in Linguistic Transmogrification" (Cowley), **Supp. II Part 1:** 143

"Sociological Poet, A" (Bourne), **I:** 228

Socrates, **I:** 136, 265; **II:** 8–9, 105, 106; **III:** 281, 419, 606; **Supp. I Part 2:** 458; **Supp. XII:** 98

Socrates Fortlow stories (Mosley), **Supp. XIII: 242–243**

So Forth (Brodsky), **Supp. VIII:** 32–33

"So Forth" (Brodsky), **Supp. VIII:** 33

"Soft Flame" (Skloot), **Supp. XX: 203**

"Soft-Hearted Sioux, The" (Zitkala-Ša), **Supp. XXV:** 274, 282

Soft Machine, The (Burroughs), **Supp. III Part 1:** 93, 103, 104

"Soft Mask" (Karr), **Supp. XI:** 243

Soft Side, The (James), **II:** 335; **Retro. Supp. I:** 229

"Soft Spring Night in Shillington, A" (Updike), **Retro. Supp. I:** 318, 319

"Soft Wood" (Lowell), **II:** 550–551

"So Help Me" (Algren), **Supp. IX:** 2

Soil and Survival: Land Stewardship and the Future of American Agriculture (C. Bly, J. Paddock and N. Paddock), **Supp. XVI:** 36–37

"Soirée in Hollywood" (H. Miller), **III:** 186

Sojourner, The (Rawlings), **Supp. X:** 233–234

"Sojourn in a Whale" (Moore), **III:** 211, 213

"Sojourns" (Didion), **Supp. IV Part 1:** 205

Sokolow, Jayme, **Supp. XIX:** 134

Solanus, Jane, **Supp. XVI:** 293

Solar Lottery (Dick), **Supp. XVIII:** 138

Solar Storms (Hogan), **Supp. IV Part 1:** 397, 410, 414–415

"Soldier, The" (Frost), **II:** 155

"Soldier Asleep at the Tomb" (Schnackenberg), **Supp. XV:** 262–263

Soldier Blue (film), **Supp. X:** 124

"Soldier of Fortune" (Wright), **Supp. XV:** 341

Soldier of the Great War, A (Helprin), **Supp. XXV:** 83–84, 86–87

"Soldier's Home" (Hemingway), **Retro. Supp. I:** 189

Soldier's Joy (Bell), **Supp. X:** 7, **7–8**, 10, 11; **Supp. XXIII:** 43

Soldiers of the Storm (film), **Supp. XIII:** 163

Soldiers' Pay (Faulkner), **I:** 117; **II:** 56, 68; **Retro. Supp. I:** 80, 81

"Soldier's Testament, The" (Mumford), **Supp. II Part 2:** 473

"Soliloquy: Man Talking to a Mirror" (Komunyakaa), **Supp. XIII:** 116–117

"Solipsism" (Monson), **Supp. XXIV:** 230

"Solitary Confinement" (X. J. Kennedy), **Supp. XV:** 157

"Solitary Pond, The" (Updike), **Retro. Supp. I:** 323

So Little Time (Marquand), **III:** 55, 59, 65, 67, 69

"Solitude" (Maupassant), **Supp. I Part 1:** 223

Solnit, Rebecca, **Supp. XXVI:** 45

Solo Faces (Salter), **Supp. IX: 259–260**

Solomon, Andy, **Supp. X:** 11

Solomon, Carl, **Supp. XIV:** 143, 150

Solomon, Charles, **Supp. VIII:** 82

Solomon, Deborah, **Supp. XXI:** 245

Solomon, Henry, Jr., **Supp. I Part 2:** 490

Solomons, Leon, **IV:** 26

So Long, See You Tomorrow (Maxwell), **Supp. VIII:** 156, 160, 162, **167–169; Supp. XVII:** 23

"So Long Ago" (Bausch), **Supp. VII:** 41–42

Solotaroff, Robert, **Retro. Supp. II:** 203

Solotaroff, Theodore, **III:** 452–453; **Retro. Supp. II:** 281; **Supp. I Part 2:** 440, 445; **Supp. X:** 79; **Supp. XI:** 340; **Supp. XII:** 291; **Supp. XIX:** 268; **Supp. XXVI:** 118

Solstice (Di Piero), **Supp. XIX:** 36

"Solstice" (Jeffers), **Supp. II Part 2:** 433, 435

"Solstice, The" (Merwin), **Supp. III Part 1:** 356

"Solus Rex" (Nabokov), **Retro. Supp. I:** 274

"Solutions" (McCarthy), **II:** 578

"Solving the Puzzle" (Dunn), **Supp. XI:** 152

Solzhenitsyn, Alexandr, **Retro. Supp. I:** 278; **Supp. VIII:** 241

"Some Afternoon" (Creeley), **Supp. IV Part 1:** 150–151

Some American People (Caldwell), **I:** 292, 294, 295, 296, 304, 309

"Some Ashes Drifting above Piedra, California" (Levis), **Supp. XI:** 264–265

"Some Aspects of the Grotesque in Southern Fiction" (O'Connor), **Retro. Supp. II:** 223, 224

"Some Birds on a Dun Field" (Bronk), **Supp. XXI:** 27

"Somebody Always Grabs the Purple" (H. Roth), **Supp. IX:** 234

Somebody Else, Somewhere Else: The Raymond Andrews Story (film, Freeman), **Supp. XXVI:** 11

Somebody in Boots (Algren), **Supp. IX:** 3, **5–7,** 12

Somebody's Darling (McMurtry), **Supp. V:** 225

Some Came Running (film), **Supp. XI:** 213

Some Came Running (Jones), **Supp. XI:** 214, 215, 220, **222–223,** 226, 227, 232

Some Can Whistle (McMurtry), **Supp. V:** 229

"Some Children of the Goddess" (Mailer), **Retro. Supp. II:** 204

Someday, Maybe (Stafford), **Supp. XI: 323–325; Supp. XIII:** 281

"Some Dreamers of the Golden Dream" (Didion), **Supp. IV Part 1:** 200

"Some Esoteric Aspects of the League of the Iroquois" (Hewitt), **Supp. XXVI:** 96

Some Faces in the Crowd (Schulberg), **Supp. XVIII:** 252

"Some Foreign Letters" (Sexton), **Supp. II Part 2:** 674

"Some General Instructions" (Koch), **Supp. XV:** 182

"Some Good News" (Olson), **Supp. II Part 2:** 575, 576, 577

"Some Grass along a Ditch Bank" (Levis), **Supp. XI:** 266

"Some Greek Writings" (Corso), **Supp. XII:** 130

Some Honorable Men: Political Conventions, 1960–1972 (Mailer), **Retro. Supp. II:** 208

Some Imagist Poets (Lowell), **III:** 511, 518, 520; **Supp. I Part 1:** 257, 261

"Some keep the Sabbath going to Church" (Dickinson), **Retro. Supp. I:** 30; **Supp. XVIII:** 301

"Some Laughed" (L. Michaels), **Supp. XVI:** 207

"Some Like Indians Endure" (Gunn Allen), **Supp. IV Part 1:** 330

"Some Like Them Cold" (Lardner), **II:** 427–428, 430, 431; **Supp. IX:** 202

"Some Lines from Whitman" (Jarrell), **IV:** 352

"Some Matters Concerning the Occupant" (Keillor), **Supp. XVI:** 167

"Some Musicians Play Chamber Music for Us" (Bronk), **Supp. XXI:** 27–28

"Some Negatives: X. at the Chateau" (Merrill), **Supp. III Part 1:** 322

"Some Neglected Points in the Theory of Socialism" (Veblen), **Supp. I Part 2:** 635

"Some Notes for an Autobiographical Lecture" (Trilling), **Supp. III Part 2:** 493, 497, 500

"Some Notes on French Poetry" (R. Bly), **Supp. IV Part 1:** 61

"Some Notes on Miss L." (West), **IV:** 290–291, 295; **Retro. Supp. II:** 322

"Some Notes on Organic Form" (Levertov), **Supp. III Part 1:** 272, 279

"Some Notes on Teaching: Probably Spoken" (Paley), **Supp. VI:** 225

"Some Notes on the Gazer Within" (Levis), **Supp. XI:** 270

"Some Notes on Violence" (West), **IV:** 304; **Retro. Supp. II:** 322, 323

"Some Observations Now" (Conroy), **Supp. XVI:** 75

Some Observations of a Stranger at Zuni in the Later Part of the Century (Major), **Supp. XXII:** 179–180

"Some Observations of a Stranger at Zuni in the Later Part of the Century" (Major), **Supp. XXII:** 179

Some of the Dharma (Kerouac), **Supp. III Part 1:** 225

"Some of Us Have Fewer" (Monson), **Supp. XXIV:** 240

"Someone Is Buried" (Salinas), **Supp. XIII:** 324

"Someone Puts a Pineapple Together" (Stevens), **IV:** 90–91

"Someone's Blood" (Dove), **Supp. IV Part 1:** 245

"Someone Talking" (Harjo), **Supp. XII:** 219–220

"Someone Talking to Himself" (Wilbur), **Supp. III Part 2:** 557

"Someone to Watch Over Me" (Stern), **Supp. IX:** 300

Someone to Watch Over Me: Stories (Bausch), **Supp. VII:** 53

Some People, Places, & Things That Will Not Appear in My Next Novel (Cheever), **Supp. I Part 1:** 184–185

"Some Poets' Criticism and the Age" (Yenser), **Supp. XV:** 113–114

Some Problems of Philosophy: A Beginning of an Introduction to Philosophy (James), **II:** 360–361

"Some Questions You Might Ask" (Oliver), **Supp. VII:** 238–239

"Some Remarks on Humor" (White), **Supp. I Part 2:** 672

"Some Remarks on Rhythm" (Roethke), **III:** 548–549

Somers, Fred, **I:** 196

Somerville, Jane, **Supp. IX:** 289, 296–297

"Some Secrets" (Stern), **Supp. IX:** 286, 287, 288, 289, 295

Some Sort of Epic Grandeur (Bruccoli), **Retro. Supp. I:** 115, 359

"Something" (Oliver), **Supp. VII:** 236

Something Happened (Heller), **Supp. IV Part 1:** 383, 386–388, 389, 392

"*Something Happened:* The Imaginary, the Symbolic, and the Discourse of the Family" (Mellard), **Supp. IV Part 1:** 387

Something in Common (Hughes), **Supp. I Part 1:** 329–330

Something Inside: Conversations with Gay Fiction Writers (Gambone), **Supp. XII:** 81

"Something Matters but We Don't " (Bronk), **Supp. XXI:** 32

"Something Might Be Gaining" (Mosher), **Supp. XXII:** 209
"Something New" (Stern), **Supp. IX:** 290
Some Things (Berrigan, Padgett, and Brainard), **Supp. XXIV:** 41
Something Said (Sorrentino), **Supp. XXI:** 226, 227, 229, 235
"Something's Going to Happen" (Zinberg), **Supp. XV:** 196
"Something Spurious from the Mindinao Deep" (Stegner), **Supp. IV Part 2:** 605
"Something That Needs Nothing" (July), **Supp. XXIV:** 203
"Something to Believe In" (Pitts), **Supp. XXII:** 280
Something to Declare (Alvarez), **Supp. VII:** 1, 2, 11, 17–19
Something to Remember Me By (Bellow), **Retro. Supp. II:** 32
"Something to Remember Me By" (Bellow), **Retro. Supp. II:** 32
"Something Wicked" (O'Nan), **Supp. XXV:** 148
Something Wicked This Way Comes (Bradbury), **Supp. IV Part 1:** 101, 110–111; **Supp. XXV:** 148
"Something Wild . . ." (T. Williams), **IV:** 381
"Some Thoughts" (McNally), **Supp. XIII:** 207
"Some Thoughts on the Line" (Oliver), **Supp. VII:** 238
"Sometimes, Reading" (Stafford), **Supp. XI:** 314
"Sometimes It Just Happens That Way, That's All" (Hinojosa), **Supp. XIX:** 101
"Sometimes I Wonder" (Hughes), **Supp. I Part 1:** 337
Sometimes Mysteriously (Salinas), **Supp. XIII:** 311, **326–328**
"Sometimes Mysteriously" (Salinas), **Supp. XIII:** 328
Some Trees (Ashbery), **Supp. III Part 1:** 3–7, 12
"Some Trees" (Ashbery), **Supp. III Part 1:** 2
"Some Truths About American Readers" (Atherton), **Supp. XXIV:** 24, 27
"Some Views on the Reading and Writing of Short Stories" (Welty), **Retro. Supp. I:** 351
"Somewhere" (Nemerov), **III:** 279–280
"Somewhere Else" (Paley), **Supp. VI:** 227
"Somewhere in Africa" (Sexton), **Supp. II Part 2:** 684–685
"Somewhere Is Such a Kingdom" (Ransom), **III:** 492
"Somewhere near Phu Bai" (Komunyakaa), **Supp. XIII:** 123–124
Some Words (Bronk), **Supp. XXI:** 32
"Some Words with a Mummy" (Poe), **III:** 425
"Some Yips and Barks in the Dark" (Snyder), **Supp. VIII:** 291
Sommers, Michael, **Supp. IV Part 2:** 581
Sommers, William, **I:** 387, 388

"Somnambulisma" (Stevens), **Retro. Supp. I:** 310
"So Much Summer" (Dickinson), **Retro. Supp. I:** 26, 44, 45
"So Much the Worse for Boston" (Lindsay), **Supp. I Part 2:** 398
"So Much Water So Close to Home" (Carver), **Supp. III Part 1:** 143, 146
Son, Cathy, **Supp. X:** 292
"Son, The" (Dove), **Supp. IV Part 1:** 245
"Son and Father" (Pickering), **Supp. XXI:** 197
"Sonata" (Schnackenberg), **Supp. XV:** 259
"Sonata for the Invisible" (Harjo), **Supp. XII:** 228
Sonata for Two Pianos (Bowles), **Supp. IV Part 1:** 83
Son at the Front, A (Wharton), **II:** 183; **IV:** 320; **Retro. Supp. I:** 378
Sondheim, Stephen, **Supp. XII:** 260; **Supp. XVI:** 194
Son Excellence Eugène Rougon (Zola), **III:** 322
Son from Sleep, A (Hadas), **Supp. XXIII: 114–115**
Song (B. Kelly), **Supp. XVII:** 123, **127–130**
"Song" (B. Kelly), **Supp. XVII:** 127
"Song" (Bogan), **Supp. III Part 1:** 57
"Song" (Bryant). *See* "Hunter of the West, The"
"Song" (Dunbar), **Supp. II Part 1:** 199
"Song" (Espaillat), **Supp. XXI:** 106–107
"Song" (Ginsberg), **Supp. II Part 1:** 317
"Song" (Kenyon), **Supp. VII:** 169
"Song" (Rich), **Supp. I Part 2:** 560
"Song" (Wylie), **Supp. I Part 2:** 729
"Song, A" (Creeley), **Supp. IV Part 1:** 145
"Song, The" (Gioia), **Supp. XV:** 117
"Song, The" (Very), **Supp. XXV:** 242
Song and Idea (Eberhart), **I:** 526, 529, 533, 539
"Song: Enlightenment" (X. J. Kennedy), **Supp. XV:** 169
"Song for a Lover Killed in Battle"(J. Schoolcraft), **Supp. XXIII:** 235
Song for Anninho (G. Jones), **Supp. XXIV:** 185, 195
Song for My Father, A: A Play in Two Acts (Budbill), **Supp. XIX:** 3, **15–16**
"Song for Myself and the Deer to Return On" (Harjo), **Supp. XII:** 225
"Song for My Sixtieth Year" (Carruth), **Supp. XVI:** 54
"Song for Occupations, A" (Whitman), **Retro. Supp. I:** 394
"Song for Simeon, A" (Eliot), **Retro. Supp. I:** 64
"Song for the Coming of Smallpox" (Wagoner), **Supp. IX:** 329, 330
"Song for the End of Time" (Gioia), **Supp. XV:** 126–127
"Song for the First People" (Wagoner), **Supp. IX:** 328
"Song for the Last Act" (Bogan), **Supp. III Part 1:** 64
"Song for the Middle of the Night, A" (Wright), **Supp. III Part 2:** 594

"Song for the Rainy Season" (Bishop), **Supp. I Part 1:** 93–94, 96
"Song for the Romeos, A" (Stern), **Supp. IX:** 296
"Song for Woody" (song, Dylan), **Supp. XVIII:** 24
"Song from a Courtyard Window" (Gioia), **Supp. XV:** 119
"Song III" (Taggard), **Supp. XXII:** 284
"Song in the Front Yard, A" (Brooks), **Supp. XVIII:** 181
"Songline of Dawn" (Harjo), **Supp. XII:** 229
"Song: Love in Whose Rich Honor" (Rukeyser), **Supp. VI:** 285
"Song: Now That She Is Here" (Carruth), **Supp. XVI:** 59
"Song of Advent, A" (Winters), **Supp. II Part 2:** 789
"Song of a Man Who Rushed at the Enemy" (Wagoner), **Supp. IX:** 329, 330
"Song of Courage, A" (Masters), **Supp. I Part 2:** 458
Song of God, The: Bhagavad-Gita (Isherwood and Prabhavananda, trans.), **Supp. XIV:** 156, 157, 164
Song of Hiawatha, The (Longfellow), **II:** 501, 503–504; **Retro. Supp. II:** 155, **159–161**, 162, 163; **Supp. XXIII:** 223, 234–235
"Song of Innocence, A" (Ellison), **Retro. Supp. II:** 126; **Supp. II Part 1:** 248
"Song of My Fiftieth Birthday, The" (Lindsay), **Supp. I Part 2:** 399
"Song of Myself" (Whitman), **II:** 544; **III:** 572, 584, 595; **IV:** 333, 334, 337–339, 340, 341, 342, 344, 348, 349, 351, 405; **Retro. Supp. I:** 388, 389, 395–399, 400; **Supp. IX:** 131, 136, 143, 328, 331; **Supp. V:** 122; **Supp. XIV:** 139; **Supp. XVIII:** 194, 304; **Supp. XXII:** 81
Song of Napalm (Weigl), **Supp. XIX:** 278–282
"Song of Napalm" (Weigl), **Supp. XIX:** 276–277
Song of Russia (film), **Supp. I Part 1:** 281, 294; **Supp. XVII:** 60–61
"Song of Self" (Huncke), **Supp. XIV:** 138–139, 145
Song of Solomon (biblical book), **III:** 118; **IV:** 150
Song of Solomon (Morrison), **Supp. III Part 1:** 364, 368, 369, 372, 379; **Supp. XVIII:** 55
Song of Songs (biblical book), **II:** 538; **IV:** 153–154; **Supp. XV:** 221
"Song of the Answerer" (Whitman), **Retro. Supp. I:** 393, 399
Song of the Cardinal, The (Stratton-Porter), **Supp. XX: 217, 218, 219**
"Song of the Chattahoochee, The" (Lanier), **Supp. I Part 1:** 365, 368
"Song of the Degrees, A" (Pound), **III:** 466
"Song of the Drunkard" (Ferry), **Supp. XXIV:** 153, 162
"Song of the Dryads" (Taggard), **Supp. XXII:** 272

"Song of the Exposition" (Whitman), **IV:** 332

"Song of the Gavilan" (Leopold), **Supp. XIV:** 189

"Song of the Gourd" (Wright), **Supp. XV:** 348–349

"Song of the Greek Amazon" (Bryant), **Supp. I Part 1:** 168

Song of the Lark, The (Cather), **I:** 312, 319–321, 323; **Retro. Supp. I:** 1, 3, 7, **9–11,** 13, 19, 20

"Song of the Okogis, or Frog in Spring"(J. Schoolcraft), **Supp. XXIII:** 232, 233, 235

"Song of the Open Road" (McGrath), **Supp. X:** 127

"Song of the Open Road" (Whitman), **IV:** 340–341; **Retro. Supp. I:** 400; **Supp. IX:** 265

"Song of the Redwood Tree" (Whitman), **IV:** 348

"Song of the Scullery" (McCarriston), **Supp. XIV:** 272

"Song of the Sky Loom" (traditional Tewa poem), **Supp. IV Part 1:** 325

"Song of the Son" (Toomer), **Supp. III Part 2:** 482–483; **Supp. IX:** 313

"Song of the Sower, The" (Bryant), **Supp. I Part 1:** 169

"Song of the Stars" (Bryant), **Supp. I Part 1:** 163

"Song of the Swamp-Robin, The" (Frederic), **II:** 138

"Song of the Vermonters, The" (Whittier), **Supp. I Part 2:** 692

"Song of Three Smiles" (Merwin), **Supp. III Part 1:** 344

"Song of Wandering Aengus, The" (Yeats), **IV:** 271; **Retro. Supp. I:** 342, 350

"Song of Welcome" (Brodsky), **Supp. VIII:** 32

"Song on Captain Barney's Victory" (Freneau), **Supp. II Part 1:** 261

"Song/Poetry and Language-Expression and Perception" (Ortiz), **Supp. IV Part 2:** 500, 508

"Song Rehearsal, The" (Stallings), **Supp. XXV:** 233

"Song: 'Rough Winds Do Shake the Darling Buds of May' " (Simpson), **Supp. IX:** 268

Songs (Boyce), **Supp. XXI:** 9

Songs and Satires (Masters), **Supp. I Part 2:** 465–466

Songs and Sonnets (L. P. Smith), **Supp. XIV:** 341

Songs and Sonnets (Masters), **Supp. I Part 2:** 455, 459, 461, 466

"Songs for a Colored Singer" (Bishop), **Supp. I Part 1:** 80, 85

Songs for a Summer's Day (A Sonnet Cycle) (MacLeish), **III:** 3

Songs for Eve (MacLeish), **III:** 3, 19

"Songs for Eve" (MacLeish), **III:** 19

"Songs for My Father" (Komunyakaa), **Supp. XIII:** 128

Songs for the Missing (O'Nan), **Supp. XXV:** 143, 148, 150

Songs for the Unborn Second Baby (Notley), **Supp. XXII:** 228

"Songs for Two Seasons" (C. Frost), **Supp. XV:** 95–96

Songs from This Earth on Turtle's Back: Contemporary American Indian Poetry (Bruchac, ed.), **Supp. IV Part 1:** 320, 328

"Songs of a Housewife" (Rawlings), **Supp. X:** 221–222

"Songs of Billy Bathgate, The" (Doctorow), **Supp. IV Part 1:** 230

Songs of Innocence (Blake), **Supp. I Part 2:** 708

Songs of Jamaica (McKay), **Supp. X:** 131, 133

"Songs of Maximus, The" (Olson), **Supp. II Part 2:** 567

"Songs of Parting" (Whitman), **IV:** 348

Songs of the Doomed (Thompson), **Supp. XXIV:** 283

Songs of the North: A Sigurd Olson Reader (Mosher, ed.), **Supp. XXII:** 218

Songs of the Sierras (J. Miller), **I:** 459

Songs of Three Centuries (Whittier and Larcom, eds.), **Supp. XIII:** 142

"Song to David" (Smart), **III:** 534

"Song to No Music, A" (Brodsky), **Supp. VIII:** 26

"Song V" (Taggard), **Supp. XXII:** 284

Song Yet Sung (McBride), **Supp. XXVI:** 194, 199–201, 204

Soniat, Katherine, **Supp. XXI:** 245

Sonneschein, Rosa, **Retro. Supp. II:** 65

"Sonnet" (Rukeyser), **Supp. VI:** 284

"Sonnet, A" (Very), **Supp. XXV:** 242

"Sonnet Crown for Two Voices" (Bierds), **Supp. XVII:** 35

"Sonnet"(J. Schoolcraft), **Supp. XXIII:** 229

"Sonnets" (Carruth), **Supp. XVI:** 56

Sonnets, The (Berrigan), **Supp. XXII:** 224; **Supp. XXIV:** 33, 34, 35, 37, 38–41, 45

"Sonnets at Christmas" (Tate), **IV:** 135

Sonnets to Orpheus (Rilke), **Supp. XV:** 222; **Supp. XXIV:** 38

"Sonnet to a Negro in Harlem" (H. Johnson), **Supp. XXVI:** 166, 167–170

"Sonnet-To Zante" (Poe), **III:** 421

"Sonnet XV" (Berrigan), **Supp. XXIV:** 38–39, 44

"Sonny's Blues" (Baldwin), **Retro. Supp. II:** 7, 8, 10, 14; **Supp. I Part 1:** 58–59, 63, 67; **Supp. XI:** 288

Son of Laughter, The: A Novel (Buechner), **Supp. XII:** 54

Son of Perdition, The (Cozzens), **I:** 359–360, 377, 378, 379

Son of the Circus, A (Irving), **Supp. VI:** 165, 166, **176–179**

Son of the Gamblin' Man: The Youth of an Artist (Sandoz), **Supp. XXIV:** 244, **256–257**

"Son of the Gods, A" (Bierce), **I:** 202

Son of the Morning (Oates), **Supp. II Part 2:** 518, 519, 520–522

Son of the Morning Star: Custer and the Little Bighorn (Connell), **Supp. XIV:** 80, 82, 97

"Son of the Romanovs, A" (Simpson), **Supp. IX:** 273–274

Son of the Wolf, The (London), **II:** 465, 469

"Son of the Wolfman" (Chabon), **Supp. XI:** 76

"Sonrisas" (Mora), **Supp. XIII:** 216, 219

Sons (Buck), **Supp. II Part 1:** 117–118

Sons and Lovers (Lawrence), **III:** 27

Sons of Kai, The: The Story the Indian Told (Beston), **Supp. XXVI:** 33

Sontag, Kate, **Supp. XV:** 104

Sontag, Susan, **IV:** 13, 14; **Retro. Supp. II:** 279; **Supp. I Part 2:** 423; **Supp. III Part 2:** 451–473; **Supp. VIII:** 75; **Supp. XIV:** 14, 15, 95–96, 167; **Supp. XVI:** 201, 204, 206; **Supp. XX: 205; Supp. XXI:** 243; **Supp. XXVI:** 45

"Soonest Mended" (Ashbery), **Supp. III Part 1:** 1, 13

"Sootfall and Fallout" (White), **Supp. I Part 2:** 671

Sophisticates, The (Atherton), **Supp. XXIV:** 20, 25

Sophocles, **I:** 274; **II:** 291, 385, 577; **III:** 145, 151, 152, 153, 159, 398, 476, 478, 609, 613; **IV:** 291, 363, 368, 370; **Supp. I Part 1:** 153, 284; **Supp. I Part 2:** 491; **Supp. V:** 97; **Supp. VIII:** 332; **Supp. XV:** 265, 266

"Sophronsiba" (Bourne), **I:** 221

Sorayam, Aram, **Supp. XXII:** 25

Sorby, Angela, **Supp. XXIII:** 132

Sorcerer's Apprentice, The: Tales and Conjurations (C. Johnson), **Supp. VI: 192–193,** 194

"Sorcerer's Eye, The" (Nemerov), **III:** 283

Sordello (Browning), **III:** 467, 469, 470

"Sordid? Good God!" (Williams), **Retro. Supp. II:** 334

So Red the Rose (Young), **Supp. XXII:** 190, 193

"Sorghum" (Mason), **Supp. VIII:** 146

Sorkin, Adam, **Supp. XXIV:** 178

Sorokin, Pitirim, **Supp. I Part 2:** 679

Sorrentino, Christopher, **Supp. XVIII:** 148

Sorrentino, Gilbert, **Retro. Supp. I:** 426; **Supp. IV Part 1:** 286; **Supp. XII:** 139; **Supp. XXI: 225–241; Supp. XXII:** 261; **Supp. XXVI:** 26

Sorrento (Notley), **Supp. XXII:** 231

"Sorrow" (Komunyakaa), **Supp. XIII:** 119

Sorrow Dance, The (Levertov), **Supp. III Part 1:** 279–280, 283

"Sorrowful Guest, A" (Jewett), **Retro. Supp. II:** 137

Sorrows of Fat City, The: A Selection of Literary Essays and Reviews (Garrett), **Supp. VII:** 111

Sorrows of Young Werther, The (Goethe), **Supp. XI:** 169; **Supp. XX: 234, 236**

Sorrows of Young Werther, The (Goethe; Bogan and Mayer, trans.), **Supp. III Part 1:** 63

"Sorry Fugu" (Boyle), **Supp. XX: 19**

"Sorting Facts; or, Nineteen Ways of Looking at Marker" (Howe), **Supp. IV Part 2:** 434, 436

"Sort of Song, A" (W. C. Williams), **Supp. XVII:** 243

"S O S" (Baraka), **Supp. II Part 1:** 50

"So Sassafras" (Olson), **Supp. II Part 2:** 574

"So There" (Creeley), **Supp. IV Part 1:** 157

"So This Is Nebraska" (Kooser), **Supp. XIX:** 120

Sotirov, Vasil, **Supp. IX:** 152

Soto, Gary, **Supp. IV Part 2:** 545; **Supp. V:** 180; **Supp. XI:** 270; **Supp. XIII:** 313, 315, 316, 320, 323; **Supp. XV:** 73; **Supp. XXV:** 130

"Soto Thinking of the Ocean" (Salinas), **Supp. XIII:** 321

"Sotto Voce" (Kunitz), **Supp. III Part 1:** 265

Sot-Weed Factor, The (Barth), **I:** 122, 123, 125, 129, 130, 131–134, 135; **Supp. XXII:** 259

"Soul" (Ferry), **Supp. XXIV:** 162

Soul, The (Brooks), **I:** 244

Soul and Body of John Brown, The (Rukeyser), **Supp. VI:** 273

Soul Barnacles: Ten More Years with Ray (Gallagher; Simon, ed.), **Supp. XXIV:** 166, 167, 171, 172

Soul Clap Hands and Sing (Marshall), **Supp. XI:** 276, 278, **280–282**

Soul Expeditions (Singer). *See* Shosha (Singer)

Soul Gone Home (Hughes), **Retro. Supp. I:** 203; **Supp. I Part 1:** 328

"Soul inside the Sentence, The" (Gass), **Supp. VI:** 88

Soul Is Here for Its Own Joy, The (Bly, ed.), **Supp. IV Part 1:** 74

Soul of Man under Socialism, The (Wilde), **Supp. IX:** 134–135

"Soul of Spain, The \[In the manner of Gertrude Stein\]" (Hemingway), **Supp. XX:** 74

Soul of the Far East, The (Lowell), **II:** 513

"Soul on Bench" (Halliday), **Supp. XIX:** 91

Soul on Ice (Cleaver), **Retro. Supp. II:** 12, 13

"Souls Belated" (Wharton), **Retro. Supp. I:** 364

"Soul selects her own Society, The" (Dickinson), **Retro. Supp. I:** 37

Souls of Black Folk, The (Du Bois), **Supp. II Part 1:** 33, 40, 160, 168–170, 176, 183; **Supp. IV Part 1:** 164; **Supp. IX:** 305, 306; **Supp. X:** 133; **Supp. XIII:** 185, 238, 243

Souls of Black Folk. The (Du Bois), **Supp. XX:** 102

"Sound, The" (Olds), **Supp. X:** 214

Sound and Beauty (Hwang), **Supp. XXI:** 146

"Sound and Fury" (O. Henry), **Supp. II Part 1:** 402

Sound and the Fury, The (Faulkner), **I:** 480; **II:** 55, 57, 58–60, 73; **III:** 237;

IV: 100, 101, 104; **Retro. Supp. I:** 73, 75, 77, 82, **83–84**, 86, 88, 89, 90, 91, 92; **Supp. IX:** 103; **Supp. VIII:** 215; **Supp. X:** 44; **Supp. XII:** 33; **Supp. XIV:** 12; **Supp. XVII:** 138; **Supp. XVIII:** 84

"Sound Bites" (Alvarez), **Supp. VII:** 11

Sound I Listened For, The (Francis), **Supp. IX: 78–79,** 87

"Soundless Trumpet, The" (Antin), **Supp. XX:** 12

"Sound Mind, Sound Body" (Lowell), **II:** 554

Sound of a Voice, The (Hwang), **Supp. XXI:** 146

"Sound of Distant Thunder, A" (Elkin), **Supp. VI: 42–43,** 44

"Sound of Light, The" (Merwin), **Supp. III Part 1:** 356

Sound of Mountain Water, The (Stegner), **Supp. IV Part 2:** 595, 596, 598, 600, 608

"Sound of Talking" (Purdy), **Supp. VII:** 270

Sounds of Poetry (television special, Moyers), **Supp. XXIII:** 139

Sounds of Poetry, The (Pinsky), **Supp. VI:** 236, 247, 248; **Supp. XXIII:** 124

Sound the Stars Make Rushing Through the Sky, The: The Writings of Jane Johnston Schoolcraft (Parker, ed.), **Supp. XXIII:** 223–224, 227, 228

Soupault, Philippe, **IV:** 288, 404; **Retro. Supp. II:** 85, 321, 324

Source (Doty), **Supp. XI:** 121, **134–137**

"Source" (Doty), **Supp. XI:** 136

"Source, The" (Olds), **Supp. X:** 211

"Source, The" (Porter), **III:** 443

Source of Light, The (Price), **Supp. VI: 262,** 266

"Sources of Soviet Conduct, The" (Kennan), **Supp. VIII:** 241

Sour Grapes (W. C. Williams), **Retro. Supp. I:** 418

"Sour Grapes"(Moraga), **Supp. XXIII:** 202

"Sourwood Nocturne" (Skloot), **Supp. XX: 202**

"South" (Levis), **Supp. XI:** 266

"South" (Trethewey), **Supp. XXI:** 247, 256

"South, The" (Hughes), **Supp. I Part 1:** 321

South American Journey (W. Frank), **Supp. XX: 79**

"Southampton Variations"(O'Hara), **Supp. XXIII:** 212

"Southbound on the Freeway" (Swenson), **Supp. IV Part 2:** 643

South Dakota Guidebook, The (C. Baxter), **Supp. XVII:** 15

Southern, Terry, **Supp. IV Part 1:** 379; **Supp. V:** 40, 201; **Supp. XI: 293–310;** **Supp. XVI:** 230

Southern Cross, The (Wright), **Supp. V:** 332, 342

"Southern Cross, The" (Wright), **Supp. V:** 338

"Southerner's Problem, The" (Du Bois), **Supp. II Part 1:** 168

"Southern Girl" (Zelda Fitzgerald), **Supp. IX:** 71

"Southern Gothic" (Trethewey), **Supp. XXI:** 256

"Southern History" (Trethewey), **Supp. XXI:** 256, 257

"Southern Mode of the Imagination, A" (Tate), **IV:** 120

"Southern Road, A" (H. Johnson), **Supp. XXVI:** 165, 167, 172, 174

"Southern Romantic, A" (Tate), **Supp. I Part 1:** 373

"Southern Sojourn, A" (Hoffman), **Supp. XVIII:** 87

Southern Terry, **Supp. XIV:** 82

Southern Writers: A New Biographical Dictionary (Flora, Vogel, and Giemza, eds.), **Supp. XXVI:** 148

Southey, Robert, **II:** 304, 502; **Supp. I Part 1:** 154; **Supp. XXIV:** 74

"South Lingers On, The" (R. Fisher), **Supp. XIX:** 69–70

South Moon Under (Rawlings), **Supp. X: 225–226,** 229, 233

South Pacific Affair (Lacy), **Supp. XV:** 206

Southpaw, The (Harris), **II:** 424–425

"South Sangamon" (Cisneros), **Supp. VII:** 66

"South State Street: Chicago" (Bodenheim), **Supp. XXV:** 22

South to a Very Old Place (Murray), **Supp. XIX: 151–153**

Southwell, Robert, **IV:** 151

Southwestern Homelands (Kittredge), **Supp. XXVI:** 188

Southwick, Marcia, **Supp. XI:** 259

Southworth, E. D. E. N, **Retro. Supp. I:** 246

Souvenir of the Ancient World, Selected Poems of Carlos Drummond de Andrade (Strand, trans.), **Supp. IV Part 2:** 630

Sovereign Bones: New Native American Writing (Gansworth, ed.), **Supp. XXVI:** 113

"Sow" (Plath), **Supp. I Part 2:** 537

"Sowing and Reaping in *Furors Die*" (Nostrandt), **Supp. XVIII:** 80–81

Soyinka, Wole, **Supp. XX: 100**

"Space" (Brockmeier), **Supp. XXII:** 51

Space between Our Footsteps, The: Poems and Paintings from the Middle East (Nye, ed.), **Supp. XIII:** 280

"Space Quale, The" (James), **II:** 349

"Spaces Between, The" (Kingsolver), **Supp. VII:** 209

"Space Where Sex Should Be, The: Toward a Definition of the Black Literary Tradition" (Nelson), **Supp. XVIII:** 172

Spack, Ruth, **Supp. XXV:** 278

Spackman, Peter, **Supp. XVI:** 221

Spacks, Patricia, **Supp. XVI:** 251

"Spain" (Auden), **Supp. II Part 1:** 12–13, 14

"Spain in Fifty-Ninth Street" (White), **Supp. I Part 2:** 677

Spanier, Sandra, **Supp. XXIV:** 51, 64

"Spanish-American War Play" (Crane), **I:** 422

Spanish Ballads (Merwin, trans.), **Supp. III Part 1:** 347

Spanish Bayonet (Benét), **Supp. XI:** 45, 47

Spanish Earth, The (film), **Retro. Supp. I:** 184

Spanish Love (Rinehart), **Supp. XXV:** 195

Spanish Papers and Other Miscellanies (Irving), **II:** 314

"Spanish Revolution, The" (Bryant), **Supp. I Part 1:** 153, 168

Spanish Student, The (Longfellow), **II:** 489, 506; **Retro. Supp. II:** 165

"Spanish Winter" (Egan), **Supp. XIX:** 52

Spanking the Maid (Coover), **Supp. V:** 47, 48, 49, 52

Spare Change (Parker), **Supp. XIX:** 186–187

Spargo, John, **Supp. I Part 1:** 13

"Spark, The" (Wharton), **Retro. Supp. I:** 381

"Sparkles from the Wheel" (Whitman), **IV:** 348

Sparks, Debra, **Supp. X:** 177

Sparks, Jared, **Supp. I Part 1:** 156; **Supp. XXIV:** 71

"Sparrow" (Berry), **Supp. X:** 31

Sparrow, Henry, **III:** 587

Sparrow, Mrs. Henry, **III:** 587

"Sparrow's Gate, The" (B. Kelly), **Supp. XVII:** 133

Spaulding, William, **Supp. XVI:** 106

"Spawning Run, The" (Humphrey), **Supp. IX:** 95

"Speak, Gay Memory" (Kirp), **Supp. XI:** 129

"Speak, Hoyt-Schermerhorn" (Lethem), **Supp. XVIII:** 148

Speak, Memory (Nabokov), **III:** 247–250, 252; **Retro. Supp. I:** 264, 265, 266, 267, 268, 277; **Supp. XVI:** 148

Speak, Memory (V. Nabakov), **Supp. XVII:** 47

Speaking and Language (Shapiro), **Supp. II Part 2:** 721

Speaking for Nature: How Literary Naturalists from Henry Thoreau to Rachel Carson Have Shaped America (Brooks), **Supp. IX:** 31

Speaking for Ourselves: American Ethnic Writing (Faderman and Bradshaw, eds.), **Supp. XIII:** 313

Speaking of Accidents (Everwine), **Supp. XV:** 75, 88

"Speaking of Accidents" (Everwine), **Supp. XV:** 88–89

"Speaking of Counterweights" (White), **Supp. I Part 2:** 669

Speaking of Literature and Society (Trilling), **Supp. III Part 2:** 494, 496, 499

"Speaking of Love" (Gioia), **Supp. XV:** 124–125

Speaking of Race, Speaking of Sex: Hate Speech, Civil Rights, and Civil Liberties (H. L. Gates, Griffin, Lively, and Strossen), **Supp. XX:** 111

Speaking on Stage (Kolin and Kullman, eds.), **Supp. IX:** 145

Speaking on Stage: Interviews with Contemporary American Playwrights (Balakian), **Supp. XV:** 327

"Speaking Passions" (Kitchen), **Supp. XV:** 215

Speak of the Devil (Holding), **Supp. XXII:** 127

Speak What We Feel (Not What We Ought to Say): Reflections on Literature and Faith (Buechner), **Supp. XII:** 57

Spear, Roberta, **Supp. V:** 180; **Supp. XV:** 73

"Special Kind of Fantasy, A: James Dickey on the Razor's Edge" (Niflis), **Supp. IV Part 1:** 175

"Special Pleading" (Lanier), **Supp. I Part 1:** 364

"Special Problems in Teaching Leslie Marmon Silko's *Ceremony*" (Gunn Allen), **Supp. IV Part 1:** 333

Special Providence, A (Yates), **Supp. XI:** 342, **344–345**

"Special Time, a Special School, A" (Knowles), **Supp. XII:** 236

Special View of History, The (Olson), **Supp. II Part 2:** 566, 569, 572

Specimen Days (Whitman), **IV:** 338, 347, 348, 350; **Retro. Supp. I:** 408

Specimens of the American Poets, **Supp. I Part 1:** 155

"Spectacles, The" (Poe), **III:** 425

Spectator Bird, The (Stegner), **Supp. IV Part 2:** 599, 604, 606, 611–612

Spector, Herman, **Supp. XXV:** 26; **Supp. XXVI:** 143

Spector, Robert, **Supp. XIII:** 87

Spectra: A Book of Poetic Experiments (Bynner and Ficke), **Supp. XV:** 43

"Spectre Bridegroom, The" (Irving), **II:** 304

"Spectre Pig, The" (Holmes), **Supp. I Part 1:** 302

"Speculating Woman" (X. J. Kennedy), **Supp. XV:** 168

"Speech Sounds" (O. Butler), **Supp. XIII:** 61, **70**

"Speech to a Crowd" (MacLeish), **III:** 16

"Speech to the Detractors" (MacLeish), **III:** 16

"Speech to the Young" (Brooks), **Supp. III Part 1:** 79, 86

"Speech to Those Who Say Comrade" (MacLeish), **III:** 16

Speedboat (Adler), **Supp. X:** 171

Speed of Darkness, The (Rukeyser), **Supp. VI:** 274, 281

Speed Queen, The (O'Nan), **Supp. XXV:** 142, 144

Speed-the-Plow (Mamet), **Supp. XIV:** 241, 246, 249, 250, 251

"Speedy Gonzales Was the Fastest Mouse in Mexico" (P. N. Warren as Kilina), **Supp. XX:** **262**

Speilberg, Steven, **Supp. XI:** 234

Speirs, Logan, **Supp. XIX:** 282

"Spell" (Francis), **Supp. IX:** 87

"Spell, The" (Peacock), **Supp. XIX:** 198, 200

"Spell for the Manufacture & Use of a Magic Carpet" (Hull), **Supp. XXI:** 132–133, 139, 141

Spelling Dictionary, A (Rowson), **Supp. XV:** 244

Spence, Thomas, **Supp. I Part 2:** 518

Spence + Lila (Mason), **Supp. VIII:** 133, **143–145**

Spencer, Edward, **Supp. I Part 1:** 357, 360

Spencer, Herbert, **I:** 515; **II:** 345, 462–463, 480, 483, 536; **III:** 102, 315; **IV:** 135; **Retro. Supp. II:** 60, 65, 93, 98; **Supp. I Part 1:** 368; **Supp. I Part 2:** 635

Spencer, Sharon, **Supp. X:** 185, 186, 195, 196

Spencer, Theodore, **I:** 433; **Supp. III Part 1:** 2

Spender, Natasha, **Supp. IV Part 1:** 119, 127, 134

Spender, Stephen, **II:** 371; **III:** 504, 527; **Retro. Supp. I:** 216; **Retro. Supp. II:** 243, 244; **Supp. I Part 2:** 536; **Supp. II Part 1:** 11; **Supp. IV Part 1:** 82, 134; **Supp. IV Part 2:** 440; **Supp. X:** 116

Spengler, Oswald, **I:** 255, 270; **II:** 7, 577; **III:** 172, 176; **Retro. Supp. II:** 324; **Supp. I Part 2:** 647

Spens, Sir Patrick, **Supp. I Part 2:** 404

Spenser, Edmund, **I:** 62; **III:** 77, 78, 89; **IV:** 155, 453; **Retro. Supp. I:** 62; **Supp. I Part 1:** 98, 152, 369; **Supp. I Part 2:** 422, 719; **Supp. XXIV:** 159

"Spenser's Ireland" (Moore), **III:** 211, 212

"Spermaceti Papers"(Lippard), **Supp. XXIII:** 178

Sperry, Margaret, **Supp. IV Part 1:** 169

Spheres of Existence (C. L. R. James), **Supp. XXI:** 172

Sphere: The Form of a Motion (Ammons), **Supp. VII:** 24, 32, 33, 35, 36

"Sphinx" (Hayden), **Supp. II Part 1:** 373

"Spiced Plums" (Ríos), **Supp. IV Part 2:** 553

Spickard, Paul, **Supp. XXI:** 149

"Spider and the Ghost of the Fly, The" (Lindsay), **Supp. I Part 2:** 375

Spider Bay (Van Vechten), **Supp. II Part 2:** 746

"Spider Heart, The" (Peacock), **Supp. XIX:** 200

"Spiders" (Schwartz), **Supp. II Part 2:** 665

Spider's House, The (Bowles), **Supp. IV Part 1:** 87–89, 90, 91

Spider Woman's Granddaughters: Traditional Tales and Contemporary Writing by Native American Women (Gunn Allen, ed.), **Supp. IV Part 1:** 320, 326, 332–333; **Supp. IV Part 2:** 567

Spiegel, Sam, **Supp. XVIII:** 251, 252

Spiegelman, Art, **Supp. XVII:** 48

Spiegelman, Willard, **Supp. XI:** 126

Spielberg, Steven, **Supp. XXI:** 154

Spillane, Mickey, **Supp. IV Part 2:** 469, 472; **Supp. XV:** 200; **Supp. XVIII:** 236, 237

Spiller, Robert E., **I:** 241; **Supp. I Part 1:** 104

Spillers, Hortense, **Supp. XX: 109**

"Spillikins: Gregor Mendel at the Table" (Bierds), **Supp. XVII:** 34–35

Spillville (Hampl), **Supp. XXII:** 98

Spillway (Barnes), **Supp. III Part 1:** 44

Spingarn, Amy, **Supp. I Part 1:** 325, 326

Spingarn, Joel, **I:** 266; **Supp. I Part 1:** 325

Spinoza, Baruch, **I:** 493; **II:** 590, 593; **III:** 600; **IV:** 5, 7, 11, 12, 17; **Retro. Supp. II:** 300; **Supp. I Part 1:** 274; **Supp. I Part 2:** 643; **Supp. XVI:** 184

"Spinoza of Market Street, The" (Singer), **IV:** 12–13; **Retro. Supp. II:** 307

"Spinster" (Plath), **Supp. I Part 2:** 536

"Spinster's Tale, A" (Taylor), **Supp. V:** 314–315, 316–317, 319, 323

Spiral of Memory, The: Interviews (Coltelli, ed.), **Supp. XII:** 215

Spires, Elizabeth, **Supp. X:** 8

"Spire Song" (Bowles), **Supp. IV Part 1:** 80

Spirit and Flame: An Anthology of African American Poetry (Gilyard, ed.), **Supp. XXI:** 246

Spirit and the Flesh, The: Sexual Diversity in American Indian Culture (W. L. Williams), **Supp. IV Part 1:** 330

"Spirit Birth" (Cullen), **Supp. IV Part 1:** 168

Spirit Brides (Gibran). *See Nymphs in the Valley*

Spirit in Man, The (Jung), **Supp. IV Part 1:** 68

"Spirit in Me, The" (Hoffman), **Supp. XVIII:** 87

"Spirit Made Visible" (art exhibit), **Supp. XXII:** 180

Spirit of Culver (West), **IV:** 287

Spirit of Labor, The (Hapgood), **Supp. XVII:** 96, 99, 101–102; **Supp. XXI:** 4

Spirit of Romance, The (Pound), **III:** 470; **Retro. Supp. I:** 286

Spirit of the Ghetto, The: Studies of the Jewish Quarter of New York (Hapgood), **Supp. XVII:** 96, 101, 103, 106

Spirit of Youth and the City Streets, The (Addams), **Supp. I Part 1:** 6–7, 12–13, 16, 17, 19

"Spirits" (Bausch), **Supp. VII:** 46–47

Spirits, and Other Stories (Bausch), **Supp. VII:** 46–47, 54

"Spirit Says, You Are Nothing, The" (Levis), **Supp. XI:** 265–266

Spirits Rebellious (al-Arwá&hudot; al-Mutamarrida) (Gibran), **Supp. XX: 115, 124, 125**

Spiritual Adventures (Symons), **Supp. XX:** 239

Spiritual Conflict, The (Scupoli), **IV:** 156

Spiritual Exercises, The (Loyola), **IV:** 151; **Supp. XI:** 162

"Spiritual Manifestation, A" (Whittier), **Supp. I Part 2:** 699

"Spirituals and Neo-Spirituals" (Hurston), **Supp. VI:** 152–153

Spits, Ellen Handler, **Supp. XII:** 166

"Spitzbergen Tales" (Crane), **I:** 409, 415, 423

Spitzer, Philip, **Supp. XIV:** 21

"Spleen" (Eliot), **I:** 569, 573–574

Spleen de Paris, Le (Baudelaire), **Supp. XIV:** 337

Splendid Drunken Twenties, The (Van Vechten), **Supp. II Part 2:** 739–744

Splendide-Hôtel (Sorrentino), **Supp. XXI:** 233

Splendid Table, The (radio show), **Supp. XXIII:** 138

Splendor in the Grass (screenplay, Inge), **Supp. XXV:** 93, 95, 102–103, 104

"Splinters" (Bukiet), **Supp. XVII:** 47

"Split Infinitive" (Pickering), **Supp. XXI:** 204

"Splitting an Order" (Kooser), **Supp. XIX:** 128–129

"Splittings" (Rich), **Supp. I Part 2:** 570–571

"Splitting Wood at Six Above" (Kumin), **Supp. IV Part 2:** 449

Spofford, Harriet Prescott, **Supp. XIII:** 143

Spoils of Poynton, The (James), **I:** 463; **Retro. Supp. I:** 229–230

Spoken Page, The (Nye), **Supp. XIII:** 274

"Spokes" (Auster), **Supp. XII:** 23

Spokesmen (Whipple), **II:** 456

Spook Sonata, The (Strindberg), **III:** 387, 392

Spooky Art, The: A Book about Writing (Mailer), **Retro. Supp. II:** 214

"Spoon, The" (Simic), **Supp. VIII:** 275

Spoon River Anthology (Masters), **I:** 106; **III:** 579; **Supp. I Part 2:** 454, 455, 456, 460–465, 466, 467, 471, 472, 473, 476; **Supp. IX:** 306; **Supp. XIV:** 282–283; **Supp. XIX:** 121; **Supp. XXII:** 282

Sport and a Pastime, A (Salter), **Supp. IX: 254–257; Supp. XVI:** 237

Sporting Club, The (McGuane), **Supp. VIII:** 43

Sport of the Gods, The (Dunbar), **Supp. II Part 1:** 193, 200, 207, 214–217

Sports Illustrated Training with Weights (Parker and Marsh), **Supp. XIX:** 187

"Sportsman Born and Bred, A" (Plimpton), **Supp. XVI:** 241

Sportsman's Sketches, A (Turgenev), **I:** 106; **IV:** 277

Sportswriter, The (Ford), **Supp. V:** 57, 58, 62–67

"Spotted Horses" (Faulkner), **IV:** 260

Sprague, Morteza, **Retro. Supp. II:** 115

Spratling, William, **II:** 56; **Retro. Supp. I:** 80

Sprawl trilogy (W. Gibson), **Supp. XVI:** 117, 122, 124

"Spray, The" (Lethem), **Supp. XVIII:** 148

"Spray Paint King, The" (Dove), **Supp. IV Part 1:** 252–253

Spreading Fires (Knowles), **Supp. XII:** 249

Sprigge, Elizabeth, **IV:** 31

"Spring" (Kooser), **Supp. XIX:** 126

"Spring" (Millay), **III:** 126

"Spring" (Mora), **Supp. XIII:** 217

"Spring 1967" (Carruth), **Supp. XVI:** 55

Spring and All (W. C. Williams), **Retro. Supp. I:** 412, 418, **418–420,** 427, 430, 431

"Spring and All" (W. C. Williams), **Retro. Supp. I:** 419

Spring Awakening (Wedeking, trans. Franzen), **Supp. XX:** 85

"Spring Break-Up" (Carruth), **Supp. XVI:** 56

"Spring Bulletin" (Allen), **Supp. XV:** 15

Springer's Progress (Markson), **Supp. XVII: 141–142,** 143, **146**

"Spring Evening" (Farrell), **II:** 45

"Spring Evening" (Kenyon), **Supp. VII:** 173

"Springfield Magical" (Lindsay), **Supp. I Part 2:** 379

Spring in New Hampshire and Other Poems (McKay), **Supp. X:** 131, 135

"Spring Notes from Robin Hill" (Carruth), **Supp. XVI:** 48

"Spring Pastoral" (Wylie), **Supp. I Part 2:** 707

"Spring Pools" (Frost), **II:** 155; **Retro. Supp. I:** 137

"Spring Snow" (Matthews), **Supp. IX:** 160

"SPRING SONG" (Baraka), **Supp. II Part 1:** 60

Springsteen, Bruce, **Supp. VIII:** 143

"Spring Strains" (W. C. Williams), **Retro. Supp. I:** 416

Spring Tides (Morison), **Supp. I Part 2:** 494

Springtime and Harvest (Sinclair), **Supp. V:** 280

"Springtime for You" (Halliday), **Supp. XIX:** 87

Spruance, Raymond, **Supp. I Part 2:** 479, 491

"Spruce Has No Taproot, The" (Clampitt), **Supp. IX:** 41–42

"Spunk" (Hurston), **Supp. VI:** 150, 151–152

Spunk: The Selected Stories (Hurston), **Supp. VI:** 150

Spurr, David, **Supp. XV:** 183

Spy, The (Cooper), **I:** 335, 336, 337, 339, 340; **Supp. I Part 1:** 155

"Spy, The" (Francis), **Supp. IX:** 81

Spy, The (Freneau), **Supp. II Part 1:** 260

Spyglass Tree, The (Murray), **Supp. XIX: 155–156**

Spy in the House of Love, A (Nin), **Supp. X:** 186

Squanto, **Supp. I Part 2:** 486

"Square Business" (Baraka), **Supp. II Part 1:** 49

Square Root of Wonderful, The (McCullers), **II:** 587–588

"Squash in Blossom" (Francis), **Supp. IX:** 81

"Squatter on Company Land, The" (Hugo), **Supp. VI:** 133

"Squatter's Children" (Bishop), **Retro. Supp. II:** 47

"Squeak, Memory" (Bukiet), **Supp. XVII:** 47

Squeeze Play (Auster), **Supp. XII:** 21

Squires, Radcliffe, **IV:** 127; **Supp. XV:** 118

Squirrels (Mamet), **Supp. XIV:** 240

S.S. Glencairn (O'Neill), **III:** 387, 388, 405

S.S. San Pedro (Cozzens), **I:** 360–362, 370, 378, 379

"Ssshh" (Olds), **Supp. X:** 215

"Stacking the Straw" (Clampitt), **Supp. IX:** 41

Stade, George, **Supp. IV Part 1:** 286

Staël, Madame de, **II:** 298

"Staff of Life, The" (H. Miller), **III:** 187

Stafford, Jean, **II:** 537; **Retro. Supp. II:** 177; **Supp. V:** 316

Stafford, William, **Supp. IV Part 1:** 72; **Supp. IV Part 2:** 642; **Supp. IX:** 273; **Supp. XI: 311–332; Supp. XIII:** 76, 274, 276, 277, 281, 283; **Supp. XIV:** 119, 123; **Supp. XX: 161; Supp. XXI:** 246

"Stage All Blood, The" (MacLeish), **III:** 18

"Staggerlee Wonders" (Baldwin), **Retro. Supp. II:** 15

Stained White Radiance, A (Burke), **Supp. XIV:** 28, 31

Stalin, Joseph, **I:** 261, 490; **II:** 39, 40, 49, 564; **III:** 30, 298; **IV:** 372; **Supp. V:** 290; **Supp. XXI:** 164, 165, 167

"Stalking" (J. W. Miller), **Supp. XX: 167**

"Stalking the Billion-Footed Beast: A Literary Manifesto for the New Social Novel" (Wolfe), **Supp. III Part 2:** 586

Stallings, A. E., **Supp. XXIII:** 111, 124; **Supp. XXV: 221–236**

Stallings, H. A., **Supp. XXII:** 194

Stallman, R. W., **I:** 405

Stamberg, Susan, **Supp. IV Part 1:** 201; **Supp. XII:** 193

Stamford, Anne Marie, **Supp. XII:** 162

Stanard, Mrs. Jane, **III:** 410, 413

Stand, The (King), **Supp. V:** 139, 140–141, 144–146, 148, 152

"Standard of Liberty, The" (Rowson), **Supp. XV:** 243

"Standard of Living, The" (Parker), **Supp. IX: 198–199**

Stander, Lionel, **Supp. I Part 1:** 289

"Standing and the Waiting, The" (M. F. K. Fisher), **Supp. XVII:** 83

Standing by Words (Berry), **Supp. X:** 22, 27, 28, 31, 32, 33, 35

Standing Fast (Swados), **Supp. XIX: 268–269**

"Standing Fast: Fox into Hedgehog" (Davison), **Supp. XXVI:** 72

"Standing Halfway Home" (Wagoner), **Supp. IX:** 324

"Standing Humbly Before Nature" (Gerber), **Supp. XXVI:** 187

"Standing In" (Caputo), **Supp. XIX:** 26

Standing Still and Walking in New York (O'Hara), **Supp. XXIII:** 220

Stand in the Mountains, A (Taylor), **Supp. V:** 324

Standish, Burt L. (pseudonym). *See* Patten, Gilbert

Standish, Miles, **I:** 471; **II:** 502–503

Standley, Fred L., **Retro. Supp. II:** 6

Stand Still Like the Hummingbird (H. Miller), **III:** 184

"Stand Up" (Salinas), **Supp. XIII:** 315

Stand with Me Here (Francis), **Supp. IX:** 76

Stanford, Ann, **Retro. Supp. I:** 41; **Supp. I Part 1:** 99, 100, 102, 103, 106, 108, 109, 113, 117; **Supp. IV Part 2:** 637

Stanford, Charles Villiers, **Supp. XX: 228**

Stanford, Donald E., **II:** 217

Stanford, Frank, **Supp. XV:** 338, 339, 341, 342–343, 343, 345, 348, 350

Stanford, Ginny (Crouch), **Supp. XV:** 339

Stanford, Leland, **I:** 196, 198

Stanislavsky, Konstantin, **Supp. XIV:** 240, 243

Stanley, Jodee, **Supp. XIX:** 52

"Stanley Kunitz" (Oliver), **Supp. VII:** 237

Stansell, Christine, **Supp. XVII:** 106; **Supp. XXI:** 4

Stanton, Frank L., **Supp. II Part 1:** 192

Stanton, Robert J., **Supp. IV Part 2:** 681

"Stanzas, Written in 1815 before going to hear my Father read religious services"(J. Schoolcraft), **Supp. XXIII:** 229

"Stanzas from the Grande Chartreuse" (Arnold), **Supp. I Part 2:** 417

Stanzas in Meditation (Stein), **Supp. III Part 1:** 13

Staples, Hugh, **Retro. Supp. II:** 187

Star, Alexander, **Supp. X:** 310

Starbuck, George, **Retro. Supp. II:** 53, 245; **Supp. I Part 2:** 538; **Supp. IV Part 2:** 440; **Supp. XIII:** 76; **Supp. XXVI:** 68

Star Child (Gunn Allen), **Supp. IV Part 1:** 324

"Star Dust" (Wrigley), **Supp. XVIII:** 296

Stardust Lounge, The (Digges), **Supp. XXIII:** 57

Stardust Memories (film; Allen), **Supp. XV:** 1, 4, **8,** 9, 13

"Stare, The" (Updike), **Retro. Supp. I:** 329

"Starfish, The" (R. Bly), **Supp. IV Part 1:** 72

"Staring at the Sea on the Day of the Death of Another" (Swenson), **Supp. IV Part 2:** 652

Star Is Born, A (film), **Supp. IV Part 1:** 198; **Supp. IX:** 198; **Supp. XVIII:** 242, 243

Stark, David, **Supp. XII:** 202

Stark, Heidi, **Supp. XXIII:** 228, 233

"Stark Boughs on the Family Tree" (Oliver), **Supp. VII:** 232

Starke, Aubrey Harrison, **Supp. I Part 1:** 350, 352, 356, 360, 362, 365, 370, 371

Starkey, David, **Supp. XII:** 180, 181

Star Ledger (Hull), **Supp. XXI:** 129, **136–138**

"Star Ledger" (Hull), **Supp. XXI:** 136

"Starlight" (Levine), **Supp. V:** 188

"Starlight Scope Myopia" (Komunyakaa), **Supp. XIII:** 123, 124

Starlight Wonder Book, The (Beston), **Supp. XXVI:** 33

Starna, William A., **Supp. XXVI:** 85, 86

Starnino, Carmine, **Supp. XVII:** 74

"Star of the Nativity" (Brodsky), **Supp. VIII:** 33

Starr, Ellen Gates, **Supp. I Part 1:** 4, 5, 11

Starr, Jean. *See* Untermeyer, Jean Starr

Starr, Kevin, **Supp. XXIV:** 17, 22

Starr, Ringo, **Supp. XI:** 309

Star Rover, The (London), **II:** 467

"Starry Night, The" (Sexton), **Supp. II Part 2:** 681

"Stars" (Frost), **II:** 153

Stars, the Snow, the Fire, The: Twenty-five Years in the Northern Wilderness (Haines), **Supp. XII: 199–201,** 206, 209

Star Shines over Mt. Morris Park, A (H. Roth), **Supp. IX:** 227, 236, **236–237**

"Stars of the Summer Night" (Longfellow), **II:** 493

"Stars over Harlem" (Hughes), **Retro. Supp. I:** 207

"Star-Spangled" (García), **Supp. XI:** 177, 178

Star-Spangled Girl, The (Simon), **Supp. IV Part 2:** 579

"Star-Splitter, The" (Frost), **Retro. Supp. I:** 123, 133

Stars Principal (McClatchy), **Supp. XII: 256–258**

"Start Again Somewhere" (Gallagher), **Supp. XXIV:** 169

"Star That Would Not Shine, The" (C. L. R. James), **Supp. XXI:** 160

"Starting from Paumanok" (Whitman), **IV:** 333

Starting from Troy (Hadas), **Supp. XXIII: 113**

Starting Out in the Thirties (Kazin), **Supp. VIII: 95–97; Supp. XXIV:** 223

Star Trek television series, **Supp. XXII:** 60

"Starved Lovers" (MacLeish), **III:** 19

Starved Rock (Masters), **Supp. I Part 2:** 465

"Starving Again" (Moore), **Supp. X:** 163, 172, 175

"Starving"(Strout), **Supp. XXIII:** 283, 285

"Star Watcher, The" (Davison), **Supp. XXVI:** 69

"State, The" (Bourne), **I:** 233

State and Main (Mamet), **Supp. XIV:** 241

"Statement of Principles" (Ransom), **III:** 496

"Statement of Randolph Carter, The" (Lovecraft), **Supp. XXV:** 114, 123

"Statement: Phillipa Allen" (Rukeyser), **Supp. VI:** 283–284

"Statements on Poetics" (Snyder), **Supp. VIII:** 291, 292

"Statement with Rhymes" (Kees), **Supp. XV:** 139

"State of the Art, The" (Elkin), **Supp. VI:** 52

"State of the Arts, The" (Wasserstein), **Supp. XV:** 332

State of the Nation (Dos Passos), **I:** 489

"State of the Union" (Vidal), **Supp. IV Part 2:** 678

State Versus Elinor Norton, The (Rinehart), **Supp. XXV:** 197, 200

Static Element, The: Selected Poems of Natan Zach (Everwine, trans.), **Supp. XV:** 73, 75, **85–88**

"Statue, The" (Berryman), **I:** 173

"Statue and Birds" (Bogan), **Supp. III Part 1:** 50

"Statue of an Unkown Soldier, The" (Kooser), **Supp. XIX:** 124

"Statues, The" (Schwartz), **Supp. II Part 2:** 654, 659

"Status Rerum" (Pound), **Supp. I Part 1:** 257

Stavans, Ilan, **Supp. XI:** 190

"Stave Church" (W. V. Davis), **Supp. XXI:** 93, 94

"Staying Afloat"(Strout), **Supp. XXIII:** 274

"Staying Alive" (Levertov), **Supp. III Part 1:** 281

Staying Alive (Wagoner), **Supp. IX:** 324, **326**

"Staying at Ed's Place" (Swenson), **Supp. IV Part 2:** 648

Staying Put : Making a Home in a Restless World (Sanders), **Supp. XVI:** 274–275

Stay Me, Oh Comfort Me: Journals and Stories, 1933–1941 (M. F. K. Fisher), **Supp. XVII:** 92

Stayton, Richard, **Supp. IX:** 133

Steadman, Goodman, **IV:** 147

Steadman, Ralph, **Supp. XXIV:** 288

"Steak" (Snyder), **Supp. VIII:** 301

Steal Away: Selected and New Poems (Wright), **Supp. XV:** 337, 340, 348, 350–351

Stealing Beauty (Minot), **Supp. VI:** 205

Stealing Buddha's Dinner (Nguyen), **Supp. XXVI:** 208, 209–212, 217, 218, 219–220

Stealing Glimpses (McQuade), **Supp. IX:** 151

Stealing the Language: The Emergence of Women's Poetry in America (Ostriker), **Supp. XV:** 251

"Stealing the Thunder: Future Visions for American Indian Women, Tribes, and Literary Studies" (Gunn Allen), **Supp. IV Part 1:** 331

"Steam Shovel Cut" (Masters), **Supp. I Part 2:** 468

Stearns, Harold, **I:** 245; **Supp. XVII:** 106

Stedman, Edmund Clarence, **Supp. I Part 1:** 372; **Supp. II Part 1:** 192; **Supp. XV:** 115, 269, 273, 274, 282, 286

Steel, Sharon, **Supp. XIX:** 61

Steele, Lloyd, **Supp. XXV:** 96

Steele, Margaret, **Supp. XXI:** 5

Steele, Max, **Supp. XIV:** 82

Steele, Sir Richard, **I:** 378; **II:** 105, 107, 300; **III:** 430

Steele, Timothy, **Supp. XV:** 251; **Supp. XVII:** 112; **Supp. XXIII:** 111

Steele, Wilbur Daniel, **Supp. XXI:** 5

"Steel Mills: South Chicago" (Bodenheim), **Supp. XXV:** 22

Steelwork (Sorrentino), **Supp. XXI:** 227, 230, 231, 232

Steenburgen, Mary, **Supp. IV Part 1:** 236

Steeple Bush (Frost), **II:** 155; **Retro. Supp. I:** 140; **Retro. Supp. II:** 42

"Steeple-Jack, The" (Moore), **III:** 212, 213, 215

"Steerage" (Goldbarth), **Supp. XII:** 187

Steers, Nina, **Retro. Supp. II:** 25

Stefans, Brian Kim, **Supp. XXII:** 226

Steffens, Lincoln, **II:** 577; **III:** 580; **Retro. Supp. I:** 202; **Retro. Supp. II:** 101; **Supp. I Part 1:** 7; **Supp. XVII:** 98, 101, 106–107; **Supp. XXI:** 2, 3, 5, 7, 10; **Supp. XXIII:** 162

Stegner, Page, **IV:** 114, 116; **Supp. IV Part 2:** 599

Stegner, Wallace, **Supp. IV Part 2: 595– 618; Supp. V:** 220, 224, 296; **Supp. X:** 23, 24; **Supp. XIV:** 82, 193, 230, 233; **Supp. XVIII:** 192; **Supp. XXII:** 204, 205, 208

"Stegner's Short Fiction" (Ahearn), **Supp. IV Part 2:** 604

Steichen, Edward, **III:** 580, 594–595

Steichen, Lillian. *See* Sandburg, Mrs. Carl (Lillian Steichen)

Steiger, Rod, **Supp. VIII:** 269; **Supp. XI:** 305

Stein, Edith, **Supp. XXII:** 92–93, 167

Stein, Gertrude, **I:** 103, 105, 476; **II:** 56, 251, 252, 257, 260, 262–263, 264, 289; **III:** 71, 454, 471–472, 600; **IV: 24–48,** 368, 375, 404, 415, 443, 477; **Retro. Supp. I:** 108, 170, 176, 177, 186, 418, 422; **Retro. Supp. II:** 85, 207, 326, 331; **Supp. I Part 1:** 292; **Supp. III Part 1:** 13, 37, 225, 226; **Supp. III Part 2:** 626; **Supp. IV Part 1:** 11, 79, 80, 81, 322; **Supp. IV Part 2:** 468; **Supp. IX:** 55, 57, 62, 66; **Supp. V:** 53; **Supp. XII:** 1, 139; **Supp. XIV:** 336; **Supp. XVI:** 187; **Supp. XVII:** 98, 105, 107; **Supp. XVIII:** 148; **Supp. XXI:** 7, 33; **Supp. XXII:** 158, 159; **Supp. XXIII:** 166, 207

Stein, Howard, **Supp. XXIV:** 116

Stein, Jean, **Supp. XVI:** 245

Stein, Karen F., **Supp. XIII:** 29, 30

Stein, Leo, **IV:** 26; **Supp. XIV:** 336; **Supp. XV:** 298

Stein, Lorin, **Supp. XII:** 254; **Supp. XVIII:** 137, 139

Steinbeck, John, **I:** 107, 288, 301, 378, 495, 519; **II:** 272; **III:** 382, 453, 454, 589; **IV: 49–72; Retro. Supp. II:** 19, 196; **Supp. IV Part 1:** 102, 225; **Supp. IV Part 2:** 502; **Supp. IX:** 33, 171; **Supp. V:** 290, 291; **Supp. VIII:** 10; **Supp. XI:** 169; **Supp. XIII:** 1, 17; **Supp. XIV:** 21, 181; **Supp. XIX:** 3;

Supp. XVII: 228; **Supp. XVIII:** 90, 102, 254

Steinbeck, Olive Hamilton, **IV:** 51

Steinberg, Saul, **Supp. VIII:** 272

Steinberg, Sybil, **Supp. XVII:** 165, 166; **Supp. XXIII:** 241; **Supp. XXVI:** 258

Steinem, Gloria, **Supp. IV Part 1:** 203; **Supp. XXIII:** 104, 105, 106

Steiner, George, **Retro. Supp. I:** 327; **Supp. IV Part 1:** 286; **Supp. XVI:** 230

Steiner, Michael, **Supp. XXII:** 205

Steiner, Nancy, **Supp. I Part 2:** 529

Steiner, Stan, **Supp. IV Part 2:** 505

Steinfels, Margaret, **Supp. XVII:** 170

Steinhoff, Eirik, **Supp. XVI:** 290

Steinman, Michael, **Supp. VIII:** 172

Steinmetz, Charles P., **Supp. XXIII:** 161

Steinmetz, Charles Proteus, **I:** 483

Steinway Quintet Plus Four, The (Epstein), **Supp. XII:** 159, **162–166**

Stekel, Wilhelm, **III:** 554

Stella (Goethe), **Supp. IX:** 133, 138

Stella (Kushner), **Supp. IX:** 133

Stella, Joseph, **I:** 387

"Stellaria" (Francis), **Supp. IX:** 83

Stelligery and Other Essays (Wendell), **Supp. I Part 2:** 414

St. Elmo (Evans), **Supp. XXII:** 120

Stendhal, **I:** 316; **III:** 465, 467; **Supp. I Part 1:** 293; **Supp. I Part 2:** 445

Stepanchev, Stephen, **Supp. XI:** 312

Stephen, Leslie, **IV:** 440

Stephen, Sir Leslie, **IV:** 440; **Supp. I Part 1:** 306

Stephen, Saint, **II:** 539; **IV:** 228

Stephen Crane (Berryman), **I:** 169–170, 405

Stephen King, The Second Decade: "Danse Macabre" to "The Dark Half" (Magistrale), **Supp. V:** 138, 146, 151

Stephen King: The Art of Darkness (Winter), **Supp. V:** 144

Stephens, Jack, **Supp. X:** 11, 14, 15, 17

Stephens, James, **Supp. XIX:** 204

Stephens, Uriah, **Supp. XXIII:** 187

Stephenson, Gregory, **Supp. XII:** 120, 123

Stephenson, Neal, **Supp. XXII:** 49

"Stepping Out" (Dunn), **Supp. XI:** 140, 141

Stepping Outside (Gallagher), **Supp. XXIV:** 165, 167

Steps (Kosinski), **Supp. VII:** 215, 221– 222, 225

"Steps" (Nye), **Supp. XIII:** 288

Steps to the Temple (Crashaw), **IV:** 145

"Steps Toward Poverty and Death" (R. Bly), **Supp. IV Part 1:** 60

Stepto, Robert B., **Retro. Supp. II:** 116, 120, 123

Sterile Cuckoo, The (Nichols), **Supp. XIII:** 258, **259–263,** 264

Sterling, Bruce, **Supp. XVI:** 118, 121, 123, 124, 128–129

Sterling, George, **I:** 199, 207, 208, 209; **II:** 440; **Supp. V:** 286; **Supp. XXII:** 276, 277

Sterling, Phillip, **Supp. XXIII:** 102

Stern, Bernhard J., **Supp. XIV:** 202, 213

Stern, Daniel, **Supp. VIII:** 238

Stern, Frederick C., **Supp. X:** 114, 115, 117

Stern, Gerald, **Supp. IX: 285–303; Supp. XI:** 139, 267; **Supp. XV:** 211, 212

Stern, Madeleine B., **Supp. I Part 1:** 35

Stern, Maurice, **IV:** 285

Stern, Philip Van Doren, **Supp. XIII:** 164

Stern, Richard, **Retro. Supp. II:** 291

Stern, Richard G., **Retro. Supp. II:** 204

Stern, Steven, **Supp. XVII:** 42, 48, 49; **Supp. XX: 178**

"Sterne" (Schwartz), **Supp. II Part 2:** 663

Sterne, Laurence, **II:** 302, 304–305, 308; **III:** 454; **IV:** 68, 211, 465; **Supp. I Part 2:** 714; **Supp. IV Part 1:** 299; **Supp. V:** 127; **Supp. X:** 324; **Supp. XV:** 232

Sterritt, David, **Supp. IV Part 2:** 574

Stetson, Caleb, **IV:** 178

Stetson, Charles Walter, **Supp. XI:** 195, 196, 197, 202, 204, 209

Steve Nelson, American Radical (Nelson), **Supp. XVIII:** 226

Stevens, Frances Simpson, **Supp. XXII:** 159, 162

Stevens, James, **Supp. XXIII:** 152

Stevens, Wallace, **I:** 60, 61, 266, 273, 462, 521, 528, 540–541; **II:** 56, 57, 530, 552, 556; **III:** 19, 23, 194, 216, 270–271, 272, 278, 279, 281, 453, 463, 493, 509, 521, 523, 600, 605, 613, 614; **IV: 73–96,** 140, 141, 332, 402, 415; **Retro. Supp. I:** 67, 89, 193, 284, 288, **295–315,** 335, 403, 411, 416, 417, 422; **Retro. Supp. II:** 40, 44, 326; **Supp. I Part 1:** 80, 82, 257; **Supp. II Part 1:** 9, 18; **Supp. III Part 1:** 2, 3, 12, 20, 48, 239, 318, 319, 344; **Supp. III Part 2:** 611; **Supp. IV Part 1:** 72, 393; **Supp. IV Part 2:** 619, 620, 621, 634; **Supp. IX:** 41; **Supp. V:** 337; **Supp. VIII:** 21, 102, 195, 271, 292; **Supp. X:** 58; **Supp. XI:** 123, 191, 312; **Supp. XIII:** 44, 45; **Supp. XIX:** 7, 40, 86, 87; **Supp. XV:** 39, 41, 92, 115, 250, 261, 298, 302, 306, 307; **Supp. XVI:** 64, 158, 202, 210, 288; **Supp. XVII:** 36, 42, 110, 129, 130, 240, 241; **Supp. XXI:** 19, 28, 60, 133; **Supp. XXII:** 162; **Supp. XXIII:** 53, 57, 65; **Supp. XXIV:** 41, 45; **Supp. XXVI:** 67

Stevens, Mrs. Wallace (Elsie Kachel), **IV:** 75

"Stevens and the Idea of the Hero" (Bromwich), **Retro. Supp. I:** 305

Stevens and the Interpersonal (Halliday), **Supp. XIX: 85–86**

Stevenson, Adlai, **II:** 49; **III:** 581

Stevenson, Anne, **Supp. XV:** 121; **Supp. XVII:** 74; **Supp. XXVI:** 66

Stevenson, Burton E., **Supp. XIV:** 120

Stevenson, David, **Supp. XI:** 230

Stevenson, Ellen Borden, **Supp. XXV:** 30

Stevenson, Robert Louis, **I:** 2, 53; **II:** 283, 290, 311, 338; **III:** 328; **IV:** 183–184, 186, 187; **Retro. Supp. I:** 224,

228; **Supp. I Part 1:** 49; **Supp. II Part 1:** 404–405; **Supp. IV Part 1:** 298, 314; **Supp. VIII:** 125; **Supp. XIII:** 75; **Supp. XIV:** 40; **Supp. XVII:** 69; **Supp. XXI:** 204

Stevick, Robert D., **III:** 509

Stewart, Dugald, **II:** 8, 9; **Supp. I Part 1:** 151, 159; **Supp. I Part 2:** 422

Stewart, Elinore Pruitt, **Supp. XXVI:** 183

Stewart, George, **Supp. XVIII:** 138

Stewart, Jeffrey C., **Supp. XIV:** 196, 209, 210

Stewart, Randall, **II:** 244; **Supp. XX: 164**

Stewart, Robert E., **Supp. XI:** 216

"St. Francis of Assisi" (Di Piero), **Supp. XIX:** 43

Stickeen (Muir), **Supp. IX:** 182

Sticks and Bones (Rabe), **Supp. XXIV:** 117

"Sticks and Stones" (L. Michaels), **Supp. XVI:** 205

Sticks and Stones (Mumford), **Supp. II Part 2:** 475, 483, 487–488

Sticks & Stones (Matthews), **Supp. IX:** 154, 155, 157, 158

Stieglitz, Alfred, **Retro. Supp. I:** 416; **Retro. Supp. II:** 103; **Supp. VIII:** 98; **Supp. XVII:** 96; **Supp. XX: 74, 75**

"Stigmata" (Oates), **Supp. II Part 2:** 520

Stiles, Ezra, **II:** 108, 122; **IV:** 144, 146, 148; **Supp. XXIV:** 68

Still, James, **Supp. XX: 163**

Still, William Grant, **Retro. Supp. I:** 203

Still Alice (Genova), **Supp. XXIII:** 127

"Stillborn" (Plath), **Supp. I Part 2:** 544

"Still Here" (Hughes), **Retro. Supp. I:** 211

"Still Just Writing" (Tyler), **Supp. IV Part 2:** 658

"Still Life" (Hecht), **Supp. X:** 68

"Still Life" (Malamud), **Supp. I Part 2:** 450

Still Life (Pickering), **Supp. XXI:** 198

"Still Life" (Pickering), **Supp. XXI:** 198

"Still Life" (Sandburg), **III:** 584

"Still Life" (Vaz), **Supp. XXVI:** 261

"Still Life: Moonlight Striking up on a Chess-Board" (Lowell), **II:** 528

"Still Life Or" (Creeley), **Supp. IV Part 1:** 141, 150, 158

Still Life with Oysters and Lemon (Doty), **Supp. XI:** 119, 121, **133–134**

Still Life with Woodpecker (Robbins), **Supp. X:** 260, **271–274,** 282

"Still Moment, A" (Welty), **IV:** 265; **Retro. Supp. I:** 347

Stillness (Gardner), **Supp. VI:** 74

"Stillness in the Air" (Dickinson), **Supp. XV:** 261

Stillness of Dancing, The (Bierds), **Supp. XVII: 27–28**

"Still Small Voices, The" (Fante), **Supp. XI:** 164

Still Such (Salter), **Supp. IX:** 246

"Still the Place Where Creation Does Some Work on Itself" (W. V. Davis), **Supp. IV Part 1:** 68

Stimpson, Catharine R., **Supp. IV Part 2:** 686

Stimson, Eleanor Kenyon. *See* Brooks, Mrs. Van Wyck

"Stimulants, Poultices, Goads" (Wright), **Supp. XV:** 349

"Stings" (Plath), **Retro. Supp. II:** 255; **Supp. I Part 2:** 541

"Stirling Street September" (Baraka), **Supp. II Part 1:** 51

Stirner, Max, **II:** 27

"Stirrup-Cup, The" (Lanier), **Supp. I Part 1:** 364

Stitt, Peter, **Supp. IV Part 1:** 68; **Supp. IV Part 2:** 628; **Supp. IX:** 152, 163, 291, 299; **Supp. XI:** 311, 317; **Supp. XIII:** 87; **Supp. XIX:** 121; **Supp. XV:** 98, 99

Stivers, Valerie, **Supp. X:** 311

St. John, David, **Supp. XV:** 73, 253

St. Louis Woman (Bontemps and Cullen), **Supp. XXII:** 6

St. Mark, Tyler, **Supp. XX: 260**

Stock, Noel, **III:** 479

Stockbroker, the Bitter Young Man, and the Beautiful Girl, The (Hayes), **Supp. XXVI:** 143

Stockton, Frank R., **I:** 201

Stoddard, Charles Warren, **I:** 193, 195, 196; **Supp. II Part 1:** 192, 341, 351

Stoddard, Elizabeth, **II:** 275; **Supp. XV: 269–291**

Stoddard, Richard, **Supp. I Part 1:** 372

Stoddard, Richard Henry, **Supp. XV:** 269, 271, 272, 273, 274, 278, 279, 286

Stoddard, Solomon, **I:** 545, 548; **IV:** 145, 148

Stoffman, Judy, **Supp. XVIII:** 97

Stoic, The (Dreiser), **I:** 497, 502, 508, 516; **Retro. Supp. II:** 95, 96, 101, 108

Stoker, Bram, **Supp. XXVI:** 58

Stokes, Geoffrey, **Supp. XV:** 256

Stokes, Olivia Egleston Phelps, **Supp. XVIII:** 261

"Stolen Calf, The" (Dunbar), **Supp. II Part 1:** 196

Stolen Jew, The (Neugeboren), **Supp. XVI: 222–224,** 225

Stolen Past, A (Knowles), **Supp. XII:** 249

Stolen Words: Forays into the Origins and Ravages of Plagiarism (Mallon), **Supp. XIX: 134–135**

Stollman, Aryeh Lev, **Supp. XVII:** 49; **Supp. XXIV:** 2, 8, 10–11

Stolmar, Thomas, **Supp. XVIII:** 138

Stomping the Blues (Murray), **Supp. XIX: 158–159**

"Stone" (Ozick), **Supp. XVII:** 50

Stone, Edward, **III:** 479

Stone, Herbert S., **Supp. XXI:** 2

Stone, I. F., **Supp. XIV:** 3

Stone, Irving, **II:** 463, 466, 467

Stone, Oliver, **Supp. XIV:** 48, 316

Stone, Phil, **II:** 55

Stone, Richard, **Supp. XIV:** 54

Stone, Robert, **Supp. V: 295–312; Supp. X:** 1; **Supp. XIX:** 54

Stone, Rosetta (pseudonym). *See* Geisel, Theodor Seuss (Dr. Seuss)

Stone, Wilmer, **Supp. I Part 1:** 49

Stone and the Shell, The (Hay), **Supp. XIV:** 122, 123, 127, 130

"Stone Bear, The" (Haines), **Supp. XII:** 206–207, 212

"Stone City" (Proulx), **Supp. VII:** 251–253

Stone Country (Sanders), **Supp. XVI:** 271–272

Stone Diaries, The (Shields), **Supp. VII:** 307, 315, 324–326, 327

"Stone Dreams" (Kingsolver), **Supp. VII:** 203

Stone Harp, The (Haines), **Supp. XII: 204,** 205, 206, 207

Stonemason, The (McCarthy), **Supp. VIII:** 175, 187

"Stones" (Hoffman), **Supp. XVIII:** 86

"Stones" (Kumin), **Supp. IV Part 2:** 447

Stones (lithograph series, O'Hara and Rivers), **Supp. XXIII:** 217

"Stones, The" (Plath), **Supp. I Part 2:** 535, 539

"Stones in My Passway, Hellhounds on My Trail" (Boyle), **Supp. VIII:** 15

Stones of Florence, The (McCarthy), **II:** 562

"Stone Walls" (Sarton), **Supp. VIII:** 259

"Stop" (Wilbur), **Supp. III Part 2:** 556

Stop-Loss (screenplay, Richard), **Supp. XIX:** 222

"Stop Me If You've Heard This One" (Lardner), **II:** 433

Stopover: Tokyo (Marquand), **III:** 53, 57, 61, 70

Stoppard, Tom, **Retro. Supp. I:** 189

Stopping by Home (Huddle), **Supp. XXVI:** 149

"Stopping by Woods" (Frost), **II:** 154

"Stopping by Woods on a Snowy Evening" (Frost), **Retro. Supp. I:** 129, 133, 134, 135, 139

Stopping Westward (Richards), **II:** 396

"Stop Player. Joke No. 4" (Gaddis), **Supp. IV Part 1:** 280

Stop-Time (Conroy), **Supp. XVI: 63–71,** 72, 75, 76–77

"Store, The" (E. P. Jones), **Supp. XXII:** 144–145

Store, The (Stribling), **Supp. VIII:** 126; **Supp. XXII:** 195

"*Store* and *Mockingbird:* Two Pulitzer Novels about Alabama" (Going), **Supp. VIII:** 126

Store of a Million Items, The (Cliff), **Supp. XXII:** 67, 74, 75

"Store of a Million Items, The" (Cliff), **Supp. XXII:** 75

Storer, Edward, **Supp. I Part 1:** 261, 262

Stories, Fables and Other Diversions (Nemerov), **III:** 268–269, 285

Stories: Elizabeth Stoddard, **Supp. XV:** 270

"Stories for Sale" (Kolba), **Supp. XVIII:** 257

Stories for the Sixties (Yates, ed.), **Supp. XI:** 343

Stories from Our Living Past (Prose), **Supp. XVI:** 251

Stories from the Italian Poets (Hunt), **Supp. XV:** 175

Stories from the Old Testament Retold (L. P. Smith), **Supp. XIV:** 342

Stories from World Literature, **Supp. IX:** 4

"Stories in the Snow" (Leopold), **Supp. XIV:** 183

Stories into Film (Kittredge and Krauzer), **Supp. XXVI:** 182

Stories of an Imaginary Childhood (Bukiet), **Supp. XVII: 41–44,** 45

Stories of F. Scott Fitzgerald, The (Cowley, ed.), **Retro. Supp. I:** 115

Stories of F. Scott Fitzgerald, The (Fitzgerald), **II:** 94

Stories of Modern America, **Supp. IX:** 4

Stories of Stephen Dixon, The (Dixon), **Supp. XII:** 152

Stories of the American Experience (Kriegel and Lass, eds.), **Supp. XXIV:** 214

Stories of the Spanish Civil War (Hemingway), **II:** 258

Stories Revived (James), **II:** 322

Stories that Could Be True (Stafford), **Supp. XI: 325–327**

Stories Toto Told Me (Rolfe), **Supp. XX: 235**

Storm, The (Buechner), **Supp. XII: 54–57**

"Storm, The" (Chopin), **Retro. Supp. II:** 60, 68; **Supp. I Part 1:** 218, 224

Storm, The (al-'Awásif) (Gibran), **Supp. XX: 116, 124, 125**

"Storm Fear" (Frost), **II:** 153; **Retro. Supp. I:** 127

"Storm Ship, The" (Irving), **II:** 309

"Storm Warnings" (Kingsolver), **Supp. VII:** 207–208

"Stormy Weather" (Ellison), **Supp. II Part 1:** 233

"Story" (Everwine), **Supp. XV:** 89

"Story, A" (Jarrell), **II:** 371

Story, Julian, **Supp. XX: 232**

Story, Richard David, **Supp. IV Part 2:** 575, 588

Story, William Wetmore, **Supp. XX: 228**

"Story about Chicken Soup, A" (Simpson), **Supp. IX: 272–273**

"Story about the Anteater, The" (Benét), **Supp. XI:** 53

"Story About the Body, A" (Hass), **Supp. VI: 107–108**

"Story for Teddy, A" (Swados), **Supp. XIX:** 266–267

Story for Teddy, A—and Others (Swados), **Supp. XIX: 266–268**

"Story Hearer, The" (Paley), **Supp. VI:** 230, 231

"Story Hour" (Hay), **Supp. XIV:** 124

"Story Hour" (Jarman), **Supp. XVII:** 116

Story Hour: A Second Look at Cinderella, Bluebeard, and Company (Hay), **Supp. XIV:** 119, 124, 125, 132, 133

Story of a Country Town, The (Howe), **I:** 106

Story of a Lover, The (Hapgood), **Supp. XVII:** 99, 100, 104; **Supp. XXI:** 3, 5, 7

"Story of America, The: A Tribalography" (Howe), **Supp. XXVI:** 84

Story of a Million Years, The (Huddle), **Supp. XXVI:** 147, 152, 157–158

Story of an American Family, The: Letters of the Hapgood Family, 1648–1917 (Boyce), **Supp. XVII:** 97; **Supp. XXI:** 9, 14

"Story of an Hour, The" (Chopin), **Retro. Supp. II:** 72; **Supp. I Part 1:** 212–213, 216

Story of a Novel, The (Wolfe), **IV:** 456, 458

"Story of a Proverb, The" (Lanier), **Supp. I Part 1:** 365

"Story of a Proverb, The: A Fairy Tale for Grown People" (Lanier), **Supp. I Part 1:** 365

Story of a Story and Other Stories, The: A Novel (Dixon), **Supp. XII:** 155

Story of a Wonder Man, The (Lardner), **II:** 433–434

"Story of a Year, The" (James), **Retro. Supp. I:** 218

Story of George Washington Carver, The (Bontemps), **Supp. XXII:** 13

Story of G.I. Joe, The (film, Wellman), **Supp. XVII:** 61, 62

"Story of Gus, The" (A. Miller), **III:** 147–148

"Story of How a Wall Stands, A" (Ortiz), **Supp. IV Part 2:** 499, 507

Story of Mist, The (Dybek), **Supp. XXIII: 74–75,** 78

"Story of Mist, The"(Dybek), **Supp. XXIII:** 74–75

Story of Mount Desert Island, Maine, The (Morison), **Supp. I Part 2:** 494

Story of My Boyhood and Youth, The (Muir), **Supp. IX: 172–174,** 176

Story of My Father, The: A Memoir (Miller), **Supp. XII:** 301

Story of O, The (Réage), **Supp. XII:** 9, 10

Story of Our Lives, The (Strand), **Supp. IV Part 2:** 620, 628–629, 629

"Story of Poppy Van Buster, The" (Briggs), **Supp. XVIII:** 8

Story of the Negro (Bontemps), **Supp. XXII:** 6, 12–13

Story of the Normans, The, Told Chiefly in Relation to Their Conquest of England (Jewett), **II:** 406

Story of the Telegraph, The (Briggs, and Maverick), **Supp. XVIII:** 4

"Story of Toby, The" (Melville), **III:** 76

"Story of To-day, A" (Davis). *See also Margret Howth*

"Story of To-day, A" (R. H. Davis), **Supp. XVI:** 88, 89

Story of Utopias, The (Mumford), **Supp. II Part 2:** 475, 483–486, 495

Story of Wine in California, The (M. F. K. Fisher), **Supp. XVII:** 88

Story on Page One, The (Odets), **Supp. II Part 2:** 546

Storyteller (Silko), **Supp. IV Part 2:** 558, 559, 560, 561, **566–570**

"Storyteller" (Silko), **Supp. IV Part 2:** 569

Storyteller: Grandmother Spider's Web (Danielson), **Supp. IV Part 2:** 569

"Storyteller's Notebook, A" (Carver), **Supp. III Part 1:** 142–143

Story Teller's Story, A: The Tale of an American Writer's Journey through His Own Imaginative World and through the World of Facts . . . (Anderson), **I:** 98, 101, 114, 117
"Story That Could Be True, A" (Stafford), **Supp. XI:** 326
Stothard, Peter, **Supp. XXV:** 221
"Stout Gentleman, The" (Irving), **II:** 309
Stover at Yale (Johnson), **III:** 321
Stowe, Calvin, **IV:** 445; **Supp. I Part 2:** 587, 588, 590, 596, 597
Stowe, Charles, **Supp. I Part 2:** 581, 582
Stowe, Eliza, **Supp. I Part 2:** 587
Stowe, Harriet Beecher, **II:** 274, 399, 403, 541; **Retro. Supp. I:** 34, 246; **Retro. Supp. II:** 4, 138, 156; **Supp. I Part 1:** 30, 206, 301; **Supp. I Part 2:** **579–601; Supp. III Part 1:** 154, 168, 171; **Supp. IX:** 33; **Supp. X:** 223, 246, 249, 250; **Supp. XI:** 193; **Supp. XIII:** 141, 295; **Supp. XV:** 278; **Supp. XVI:** 82, 85
Stowe, Samuel Charles, **Supp. I Part 2:** 587
Stowe, William, **Supp. IV Part 1:** 129
Strachey, Lytton, **I:** 5; **IV:** 436; **Retro. Supp. I:** 59; **Supp. I Part 2:** 485, 494; **Supp. XIV:** 342; **Supp. XVI:** 191
"Stradivari" (Bierds), **Supp. XVII:** 28
Straight Cut (Bell), **Supp. X:** 5, **6–7,** 10
Straight Man (Russo), **Supp. XII: 335– 339,** 340
Straits: Poems (Koch), **Supp. XV:** 184
Strand, Mark, **Supp. IV Part 2: 619–636; Supp. IX:** 155; **Supp. V:** 92, 332, 337, 338, 343; **Supp. XI:** 139, 145; **Supp. XII:** 254; **Supp. XIII:** 76; **Supp. XV:** 74; **Supp. XXIV:** 165
Strand, Paul, **Supp. VIII:** 272
Strandberg, Victor, **Supp. V:** 273
Strange, Sharan, **Supp. XXI:** 246
"Strange Beautiful Woman, A" (Nelson), **Supp. XVIII:** 173
Strange Bedfellows (Woods), **Supp. XXI:** 70
Strange Case of Dr. Jekyll and Mr. Hyde, The (Stevenson), **II:** 290
Strange Children, The (Gordon), **II:** 196, 197, 199, 211–213
Strange Commonplace, A (Sorrentino), **Supp. XXI:** 232, 237, 238
Strange Crime in Bermuda, The (Holding), **Supp. XXII: 124–125,** 127, 129
Strange Fire (Bukiet), **Supp. XVII: 46**
"Strange Fruit" (Harjo), **Supp. XII:** 224, 225
"Strange Fruit" (song), **Supp. I Part 1:** 80; **Supp. XVIII:** 228
Strange Interlude (O'Neill), **III:** 391, 397–398; **IV:** 61; **Supp. XXII:** 24
Stranger, The (Camus), **I:** 53, 292; **Supp. VIII:** 11; **Supp. XV:** 352
"Stranger, The" (Rich), **Supp. I Part 2:** 555, 560
"Stranger, The" (Salinger), **III:** 552–553
Strange Relation (Hadas), **Supp. XXIII:** 111, 113, 120, **127**

"Stranger in My Own Life, A: Alienation in American Indian Poetry and Prose" (Gunn Allen), **Supp. IV Part 1:** 322
Stranger in the Kingdom, A (Mosher), **Supp. XXII:** 204, 205, 206, 207, 208, 209, **212–213**
"Stranger in the Village" (Baldwin), **Retro. Supp. II:** 3; **Supp. I Part 1:** 54; **Supp. IV Part 1:** 10
"Stranger in Town" (Hughes), **Supp. I Part 1:** 334
"Strangers" (Howe), **Supp. VI:** 120
Strangers: A Book of Poems (Ferry), **Supp. XXIV: 149–150**
Strangers and Wayfarers (Jewett), **Retro. Supp. II:** 138
"Strangers from the Horizon" (Merwin), **Supp. III Part 1:** 356
"Stranger's Gift, The" (Very), **Supp. XXV:** 242
Strangers on a Train (Highsmith), **Supp. IV Part 1:** 132
"Strange Story, A" (Taylor), **Supp. V:** 323
"Strange Story, A" (Wylie), **Supp. I Part 2:** 723
Strange Things (Atwood), **Supp. XIII:** 35
"Strato in Plaster" (Merrill), **Supp. III Part 1:** 328
Stratton-Porter, Gene, **Supp. XX: 211– 225**
Straub, Peter, **Supp. XXV:** 145
Straus, Ralph, **Supp. XIII:** 168
Straus, Roger, **Supp. VIII:** 82; **Supp. XV:** 59
Strauss, Harold, **Supp. XV:** 137
Strauss, Helen, **Supp. XXIII:** 258
Strauss, Johann, **I:** 66
Strauss, Richard, **IV:** 316
Strauss, Robert, **Supp. XI:** 141, 142
Stravinsky (De Schloezer), **III:** 474
Stravinsky, Igor, **Retro. Supp. I:** 378; **Supp. IV Part 1:** 81; **Supp. XI:** 133; **Supp. XV:** 265
"Stravinsky's Three Pieces 'Grotesques,' for String Quartet" (Lowell), **II:** 523
Straw, The (O'Neill), **III:** 390
"Strawberry Milkshake" (Halliday), **Supp. XIX:** 92, 94
"Stray Document, A" (Pound), **II:** 517
"Strays" (Richard), **Supp. XIX:** 210–211, 220
Streaks of the Tulip, The: Selected Criticism (W. J. Smith), **Supp. XIII:** 333, 334, 344, **347–348**
Streamline Your Mind (Mursell), **Supp. I Part 2:** 608
Strecker, Trey, **Supp. XXI:** 238
"Street, Cloud" (Ríos), **Supp. IV Part 2:** 549
Street, The (Petry), **Supp. XVIII:** 286
Streetcar Named Desire, A (T. Williams), **IV:** 382, 383, 385, 386, 387, 389–390, 395, 398; **Supp. IV Part 1:** 359
Street in Bronzeville, A (Brooks), **Retro. Supp. I:** 208; **Supp. III Part 1:** 74–78
"Street Moths" (X. J. Kennedy), **Supp. XV:** 170
"Street Musicians" (Ashbery), **Supp. III Part 1:** 18

"Street of Crocodiles" (Hull), **Supp. XXI:** 130
"Street off Sunset, A" (Jarrell), **II:** 387
Street of Seven Stars, The (Rinehart), **Supp. XXV:** 193
"Streets" (Dixon), **Supp. XII: 145–146**
Streets in Their Own Ink (Dybek), **Supp. XXIII:** 78
Streets in the Moon (MacLeish), **III:** 5, 8–11, 15, 19
Streets of Laredo (McMurtry), **Supp. V:** 230
"Streets of Laredo" (screenplay) (McMurtry and Ossana), **Supp. V:** 226, 230
Streets of Night (Dos Passos), **I:** 478, 479–480, 481, 488
Streitfield, David, **Supp. XIII:** 234; **Supp. XVI:** 63
Strength of Fields, The (Dickey), **Supp. IV Part 1:** 178
"Strength of Fields, The" (Dickey), **Supp. IV Part 1:** 176, 184–185
"Strength of Gideon, The" (Dunbar), **Supp. II Part 1:** 212
Strength of Gideon and Other Stories, The (Dunbar), **Supp. II Part 1:** 211, 212
"Strenuous Artistry" (Zagarell), **Supp. XV:** 281
Strether, Lambert, **II:** 313
"Stretto" (Davison), **Supp. XXVI:** 77
Stribling, T. S., **Supp. VIII:** 126
Strickland, Barbara, **Supp. XIX:** 102
Strickland, Joe (pseudonym). *See* Arnold, George W.
"Strictly Bucolic" (Simic), **Supp. VIII:** 278
Strictly Business (O. Henry), **Supp. II Part 1:** 410
"Strike, The" (Olsen), **Supp. XIII:** 292, 297
Strike at Shane's, The (Skloot), **Supp. XX: 216**
"Strikers" (Untermeyer), **Supp. XV:** 296
Strindberg, August, **I:** 78; **III:** 145, 165, 387, 390, 391, 392, 393; **IV:** 17; **Supp. XVII:** 100; **Supp. XXII:** 23
"String, The" (Dickey), **Supp. IV Part 1:** 179
String Light (Wright), **Supp. XV: 345– 346**
"String Quartet, The" (Weigl), **Supp. XIX:** 278
"Strivings of the Negro People" (Du Bois), **Supp. II Part 1:** 167
Stroby, W. C., **Supp. XIV:** 26
Strohbach, Hermann, **Supp. XI:** 242
"Stroke of Good Fortune, A" (O'Connor), **III:** 344; **Retro. Supp. II:** 229, 232
Strom, Stephen, **Supp. XII:** 223
Strong, Anna Louise, **Supp. XVIII:** 238; **Supp. XXIII:** 166
Strong, George Templeton, **IV:** 321
Strong, Josiah, **Supp. XIV:** 64
"Strong Draughts of Their Refreshing Minds" (Dickinson), **Retro. Supp. I:** 46
Strong Motion (Franzen), **Supp. XX: 85, 88–89, 92, 95**

Strong Opinions (Nabokov), **Retro. Supp. I:** 263, 266, 270, 276

"Strong Room of the House, The" (Bronk), **Supp. XXI:** 32

"Strong Women" (Dorman), **Supp. XI:** 240

Strout, Elizabeth, **Supp. X:** 86; **Supp. XXIII:** 273–287

Structure of Nations and Empires, The (Niebuhr), **III:** 292, 308

"Structure of Rime, The" (Duncan), **Supp. XVI:** 287

Structuring the Void (Klinkowitz), **Supp. XXI:** 233

Struggle, The (film; Griffith), **Supp. XVI:** 191

"Strumpet Song" (Plath), **Retro. Supp. II:** 246; **Supp. I Part 2:** 536

Strunk, William, **Supp. I Part 2:** 652, 662, 670, 671, 672

Strunsky, Anna, **II:** 465

"Strut for Roethke, A" (Berryman), **I:** 188

Strychacz, Thomas F., **Supp. XVI:** 69–70

Stuart, Dabney, **Supp. XVIII:** 79

Stuart, Gilbert, **I:** 16

Stuart, J. E. B., **III:** 56

Stuart, Jesse, **Supp. XX: 162–163,** 165

Stuart, Michael, **Supp. XV:** 140

Stuart Little (White), **Supp. I Part 2:** 655–658

"Stubborn Kisses" (Gallagher), **Supp. XXIV:** 170

Stuckey, W. J., **Supp. XXII:** 191–192

"Student, The" (Moore), **III:** 212, 215

"Student of Clouds" (Collins), **Supp. XXI:** 60

"Student of Salmanaca, The" (Irving), **II:** 309

"Student's Wife, The" (Carver), **Supp. III Part 1:** 141

Studies in American Indian Literature: Critical Essays and Course Designs (Gunn Allen), **Supp. IV Part 1:** 324, 333

Studies in Classic American Literature (Lawrence), **II:** 102; **III:** 33; **IV:** 333; **Retro. Supp. I:** 421

Studies in Short Fiction (Edmonds), **Supp. XXIII:** 291

Studies in Short Fiction (Malin), **Supp. XVI:** 71

Studies in the Psychology of Sex (Ellis), **Supp. XX: 235**

"Studs" (Farrell), **II:** 25, 28, 31

Studs Lonigan: A Trilogy (Farrell), **II:** 25, 26, 27, 31–34, 37, 38, 41–42

"Study in Orange and White" (Collins), **Supp. XXI:** 60

"Study of Images" (Stevens), **IV:** 79

"Study of Lanier's Poems, A" (Kent), **Supp. I Part 1:** 373

Study of Milton's Prosody (Bridges), **II:** 537

"Study of the Negro Problems, The" (Du Bois), **Supp. II Part 1:** 165

Stuewe, Paul, **Supp. IV Part 1:** 68

Stuhlmann, Gunther, **Supp. X:** 182, 184, 185, 187

Stull, William L., **Supp. XXIV:** 177

Stultifera Navis (Brant), **III:** 447

"Stumps" (Davison), **Supp. XXVI:** 72

Sturak, John Thomas, **Supp. XIII:** 162, 163, 165, 168

Sturgeon, Theodore, **Supp. XVIII:** 145

Sturgis, George, **III:** 600

Sturgis, Howard, **IV:** 319; **Retro. Supp. I:** 367, 373

Sturgis, Howard Overing, **Supp. XX:** 227–242

Sturgis, Julian Russell, **Supp. XX: 228, 233, 238**

Sturgis, Susan, **III:** 600

Sturm, Margaret. See Millar, Margaret

Stuttaford, Genevieve, **Supp. IX:** 279

Stuyvesant, Peter, **II:** 301

"Style" (Nemerov), **III:** 275

Styles of Radical Will (Sontag), **Supp. III Part 2:** 451, 459, 460–463

"Stylist, The" (Egan), **Supp. XIX:** 51, 52

Styne, Jule, **Supp. XVI:** 193

Styron, William, **III:** 40; **IV:** 4, **97–119,** 216; **Supp. IX:** 208; **Supp. V:** 201; **Supp. X:** 15–16, 250; **Supp. XI:** 229, 231, 343; **Supp. XIV:** 82; **Supp. XVI:** 235–236; **Supp. XXIII:** 107, 109

Suares, J. C., **Supp. IV Part 1:** 234

Suarez, Ernest, **Supp. IV Part 1:** 175; **Supp. V:** 180

Suarez, Ray, **Supp. XXI:** 243

"Sub, The" (Dixon), **Supp. XII:** 146

Subjection of Women, The (Mill), **Supp. XI:** 196, 203

"Subjective Necessity for Social Settlements" (Addams), **Supp. I Part 1:** 4

"Subject of Childhood, A" (Paley), **Supp. VI:** 221; **Supp. XXI:** 118

"Submarginalia" (Howe), **Supp. IV Part 2:** 422

Substance and Shadow (James), **II:** 344

"Subterranean Homesick Blues" (song, Dylan), **Supp. XVIII:** 25

Subterraneans, The (Kerouac), **Supp. III Part 1:** 225, 227–231

"Subtitle" (Kees), **Supp. XV:** 139

Subtreasury of American Humor, A (White and White), **Supp. I Part 2:** 668

"Suburban Culture, Imaginative Wonder: The Fiction of Frederick Barthelme" (Brinkmeyer), **Supp. XI:** 38

Suburban Sketches (Howells), **II:** 274, 277

"Subversive Element, The" (Ryan as Quin), **Supp. XVIII:** 230

"Subverted Flower, The" (Frost), **Retro. Supp. I:** 139

"Subway, The" (Tate), **IV:** 128

"Subway Singer, The" (Clampitt), **Supp. IX:** 45

"Success" (Mora), **Supp. XIII:** 217

Successful Love and Other Stories (Schwartz), **Supp. II Part 2:** 661, 665

Successful Women (Taves), **Supp. XXV:** 198

Succession, The: A Novel of Elizabeth and James (Garrett), **Supp. VII:** 104–107, 108

"Success is counted sweetest" (Dickinson), **Retro. Supp. I:** 30, 31–32, 38; **Supp. XV:** 126

Success Stories (Banks), **Supp. V:** 14–15

"Success Story" (Banks), **Supp. V:** 15

"Such Counsels You Gave to Me" (Jeffers), **Supp. II Part 2:** 433

Such Silence (Milburn), **Supp. XI:** 242

"Such Things Happen Only in Books" (Wilder), **IV:** 365

Such Was the Season (Major), **Supp. XXII: 177–178,** 179, 182

"Sudden Journey" (Gallagher), **Supp. XXIV:** 169

Suddenly, Last Summer (film) (Vidal), **Supp. IV Part 2:** 683

Suddenly Last Summer (T. Williams), **I:** 73; **IV:** 382, 383, 385, 386, 387, 389, 390, 391, 392, 395–396, 397, 398

Suder (Everett), **Supp. XVIII: 54–55**

Sudermann, Hermann, **I:** 66

Sue, Eugène, **Supp. XXIII:** 182

Sugg, Richard P., **Supp. IV Part 1:** 68

"Suggestion from a Friend" (Kenyon), **Supp. VII:** 171

"Suicide" (Barnes), **Supp. III Part 1:** 33

"Suicide off Egg Rock" (Plath), **Supp. I Part 2:** 529, 538

Suicides and Jazzers (Carruth), **Supp. XVI:** 46

"Suicide's Note" (Hughes), **Retro. Supp. I:** 199

"Suitable Surroundings, The" (Bierce), **I:** 203

"Suitcase, The" (Ozick), **Supp. V:** 262, 264

"Suite for Augustus, A" (Dove), **Supp. IV Part 1:** 245

"Suite for Emily" (Hull), **Supp. XXI:** 139–140

"Suite for Lord Timothy Dexter" (Rukeyser), **Supp. VI:** 283, 285

"Suite from the Firebird" (Stravinsky), **Supp. XI:** 133

"Suitor, The" (Kenyon), **Supp. VII:** 164–165

Sukarno, **IV:** 490

Sukenick, Ronald, **Supp. V:** 39, 44, 46; **Supp. XII:** 139

Sula (Morrison), **Supp. III Part 1:** 362, 364, 367, 368, 379; **Supp. VIII:** 219

Sullivan, Andrew, **Supp. IX:** 135

Sullivan, Arthur, **Supp. XX:** 228

Sullivan, Frank, **Supp. IX:** 201

Sullivan, Harry Stack, **I:** 59

Sullivan, Jack, **Supp. X:** 86; **Supp. XII:** 331

Sullivan, Noel, **Retro. Supp. I:** 202; **Supp. I Part 1:** 329, 333

Sullivan, Patrick, **Supp. XXVI:** 158

Sullivan, Richard, **Supp. VIII:** 124

Sullivan, Walter, **Supp. VIII:** 168

"Sullivan County Sketches" (Crane), **I:** 407, 421

"Sumach and Goldenrod: An American Idyll" (Mumford), **Supp. II Part 2:** 475

Suma Genji (Play), **III:** 466

Sumerian Vistas (Ammons), **Supp. VII:** 34, 35

"Summa Lyrica" (Grossman), **Supp. XIX:** 86

"Summer" (Emerson), **II:** 10

Summer (Gioia), **Supp. XV:** 117
"Summer" (Lowell), **II:** 554
Summer (Wharton), **IV:** 317; **Retro. Supp. I:** 360, 367, 374, **378–379,** 382; **Supp. XXIII:** 275, 281
Summer, Bob, **Supp. X:** 1, 5, 6, 42
Summer and Smoke (T. Williams), **IV:** 382, 384, 385, 386, 387, 395, 397, 398; **Supp. IV Part 1:** 84
Summer Anniversaries, The (Justice), **Supp. VII:** 115, 117
Summer Blue (Skloot), **Supp. XX: 196, 207–208**
Summer Brave (Inge), **Supp. XXV:** 99
"Summer Commentary, A" (Winters), **Supp. II Part 2:** 808
"Summer Day" (O'Hara), **III:** 369
"Summer Days, The" (Oliver), **Supp. VII:** 239
"Summer Evening" (Boyle), **Supp. XXIV:** 61
"Summer Lake" (Huddle), **Supp. XXVI:** 150
Summer Lake: New and Selected Poems (Huddle), **Supp. XXVI:** 150
"Summer Love Overheated" (Díaz), **Supp. XXIV:** 89
"Summer Matures" (H. Johnson), **Supp. XXVI:** 174
Summer Never Ends (W. Frank), **Supp. XX: 78**
"Summer Night" (Hughes), **Supp. I Part 1:** 325
"Summer Night, A" (Auden), **Supp. II Part 1:** 8
"Summer Night—Broadway" (Untermeyer), **Supp. XV:** 296
"Summer Noon: 1941" (Winters), **Supp. II Part 2:** 811
"Summer of '82" (Merwin), **Supp. III Part 1:** 355–356
Summer on the Lakes in 1843 (Fuller), **Supp. II Part 1:** 279, 295–296
"Summer People" (Hemingway), **II:** 258–259
"Summer People, The" (Jackson), **Supp. IX:** 120
"Summer People, The" (Merrill), **Supp. III Part 1:** 325–326
"Summer Perdu" (Halliday), **Supp. XIX:** 89
"Summer Planning" (Halliday), **Supp. XIX:** 92
"Summer Ramble, A" (Bryant), **Supp. I Part 1:** 162, 164
Summers, Claude J., **Supp. IV Part 2:** 680–681; **Supp. XIV:** 161, 169
Summers, Robert, **Supp. IX:** 289
"Summer School" (Davison), **Supp. XXVI:** 69
"Summer Solstice, New York City" (Olds), **Supp. X:** 207
"Summer's Reading, A" (Malamud), **Supp. I Part 2:** 430–431, 442
"Summer Storm" (Gioia), **Supp. XV:** 127
"Summer Storm" (Simpson), **Supp. IX:** 268
"'Summertime and the Living . . .' " (Hayden), **Supp. II Part 1:** 363, 366

Summertime Island (Caldwell), **I:** 307–308
"Summer Tragedy" (Bontemps), **Supp. XXII:** 9
"Summer: West Side" (Updike), **Retro. Supp. I:** 320
"Summer with Tu Fu, A" (Carruth), **Supp. XVI:** 55, 58
"Summit Beach, 1921" (Dove), **Supp. IV Part 1:** 249
Summoning of Stones, A (Hecht), **Supp. X:** 57, 58, **58–59**
"Summons" (Gansworth), **Supp. XXVI:** 114
"Summons" (Untermeyer), **Supp. XV:** 296
Summons to Memphis, A (Taylor), **Supp. V:** 313, 314, 327
Summons to the Free, A (Benét), **Supp. XI:** 47
Sumner, Charles, **I:** 3, 15; **Supp. I Part 2:** 685, 687
Sumner, John, **Retro. Supp. II:** 95
Sumner, John B., **I:** 511
Sumner, William Graham, **III:** 102, 108; **Supp. I Part 2:** 640
"Sumptuous Destination" (Wilbur), **Supp. III Part 2:** 553
"Sun" (Moore), **III:** 215
"Sun" (Swenson), **Supp. IV Part 2:** 640
"Sun, Sea, and Sand" (Marquand), **III:** 60
Sun Also Rises, The (Hemingway), **I:** 107; **II:** 68, 90, 249, 251–252, 260, 600; **III:** 36; **IV:** 35, 297; **Retro. Supp. I:** 171, **177–180,** 181, 189; **Supp. I Part 2:** 614; **Supp. XIII:** 263; **Supp. XVIII:** 74
"Sun and Moon" (Kenyon), **Supp. VII:** 168
"Sun and the Still-born Stars, The" (Southern), **Supp. XI:** 295
Sun at Midnight (Soseki; Merwin and Shigematsu, trans.), **Supp. III Part 1:** 353
"Sun Crosses Heaven from West to East Bringing Samson Back to the Womb, The" (R. Bly), **Supp. IV Part 1:** 73
Sun Dance Land (Hanson), **Supp. XXV:** 280
Sun Dance Opera, The (Zitkala-Ša and Hanson), **Supp. XXV:** 279–280
"Sun Dance Shield" (Momaday), **Supp. IV Part 2:** 491
Sunday, Billy, **II:** 449
"Sunday Afternoons" (Komunyakaa), **Supp. XIII:** 127
Sunday after the War (H. Miller), **III:** 184
"Sunday at Home" (Hawthorne), **II:** 231–232
"Sunday Following Mother's Day, The" (E. P. Jones), **Supp. XXII:** 145
"Sunday Morning" (Stevens), **II:** 552; **III:** 278, 463, 509; **IV:** 92–93; **Retro. Supp. I:** 296, 300, 301, 304, 307, 313; **Supp. XIX:** 40; **Supp. XV:** 120; **Supp. XVI:** 210; **Supp. XVII:** 42; **Supp. XXI:** 28, 133; **Supp. XXIII:** 57

"Sunday Morning Apples" (Crane), **I:** 387
"Sunday Morning Prophecy" (Hughes), **Supp. I Part 1:** 334
"Sunday Morning with the Sensational Nightingales" (Collins), **Supp. XXI:** 60
"Sundays" (B. Kelly), **Supp. XVII:** 124–125
"Sundays" (Salter), **Supp. IX:** 257
"Sundays, They Sleep Late" (Rukeyser), **Supp. VI:** 278
"Sundays of Satin-Legs Smith, The" (Brooks), **Supp. III Part 1:** 74, 75
"Sundays Visiting" (Ríos), **Supp. IV Part 2:** 541
Sundial, The (Jackson), **Supp. IX: 126–127**
Sundog (Harrison), **Supp. VIII: 46–48**
Sun Dogs (R. O. Butler), **Supp. XII: 64–65**
Sun Do Move, The (Hughes), **Supp. I Part 1:** 339
Sundquist, Eric, **Supp. XIV:** 66, 71
"Sunfish" (C. Frost), **Supp. XV:** 100–101, 102
"Sunflower Sutra" (Ginsberg), **Supp. II Part 1:** 317, 321; **Supp. XV:** 215
Sunlight Dialogues, The (Gardner), **Supp. VI:** 63, **68,** 69, 70
"Sunlight Is Imagination" (Wilbur), **Supp. III Part 2:** 549
"Sunny Ridge, The" (Halliday), **Supp. XIX:** 92
Sun Out: Selected Poems, 1952–1954 (Koch), **Supp. XV:** 179
"Sunrise" (Lanier), **Supp. I Part 1:** 370
"Sunrise and the Bomb" (Halliday), **Supp. XIX:** 84, 85, 92
"Sunrise runs for Both, The" (Dickinson), **Retro. Supp. I:** 45
Sunrise with Seamonsters: Travels and Discoveries, 1964–1984 (Theroux), **Supp. VIII:** 311, 313, 323, 325
"Sun Rising" (Donne), **Supp. VIII:** 164
"Sunset" (Ransom), **III:** 484
"Sunset from Omaha Hotel Window" (Sandburg), **III:** 584
Sunset Gun (Parker), **Supp. IX:** 192
Sunset Limited (Burke), **Supp. XIV:** 32, 33
Sunset Limited (Harrison), **Supp. VIII:** 51
"Sunset Maker, The" (Justice), **Supp. VII:** 123
Sunset Maker, The: Poems, Stories, a Memoir (Justice), **Supp. VII:** 116, 118, 119, 123–124
Sunshine Boys, The (film), **Supp. IV Part 2:** 589
Sunshine Boys, The (Simon), **Supp. IV Part 2:** 575, 584–585
"Sunthin' in the Pastoral Line" (Lowell), **Supp. I Part 2:** 415–416
Sun to Sun (Hurston), **Supp. VI:** 154
Sun Tracks (Ortiz), **Supp. IV Part 2:** 499, 500
Sun Under Wood (Hass), **Supp. VI:** 103, 108–109
"Superb Lily, The" (Pinsky), **Supp. VI:** 250

"Super Goat Man" (Lethem), **Supp. XVIII:** 148

"Superman Comes to the Supermarket" (Mailer), **Retro. Supp. II:** 204

"Supermarket in California, A" (Ginsberg), **Supp. XI:** 135

"Supernatural Horror in Literature" (Lovecraft), **Supp. XXV:** 120

"Supernatural Love" (Schnackenberg), **Supp. XV:** 257, 259–260

Supernatural Love: Poems 1976–1992 (Schnackenberg), **Supp. XV:** 253, 256, 260, 263

Suplee, Curt, **Supp. XVI:** 202

"Supper After the Last, The" (Kinnell), **Supp. III Part 1:** 239

"Supposedly Fun Thing I'll Never Do Again, A" (Wallace), **Supp. X:** 315

Supposedly Fun Thing I'll Never Do Again, A: Essays and Arguments (Wallace), **Supp. X:** 314–316

Suppressed Desires (Glaspell and Cook), **Supp. III Part 1:** 178; **Supp. XXI:** 6

Suppression of the African Slave Trade to the United States of America, 1638–1870 (Du Bois), **Supp. II Part 1:** 157, 162

Supreme Fiction, The (Stevens), **Supp. XVI:** 158

"Supremes, The" (Jarman), **Supp. XVII:** 115

Sure Hand of God, The (Caldwell), **I:** 297, 302

Sure Signs: New and Selected Poems (Kooser), **Supp. XIX:** 116, 117, **121–122**

"Surety and Fidelity Claims" (Stevens), **Retro. Supp. I:** 296, 309

Surface of Earth, The (Price), **Supp. VI:** 261–262

"Surfaces" (Ammons), **Supp. VII:** 36

Surfaces and Masks (Major), **Supp. XXII:** 180

Surfacing (Atwood), **Supp. XIII:** 20, 21, **22–23,** 24, 33, 35

"Surgeon at 2 A.M." (Plath), **Supp. I Part 2:** 545

Summer Knowledge (Schwartz), **Supp. II Part 2:** 662, 665

"Surprise" (Kenyon), **Supp. VII:** 173

Surprised by Sin: The Reader in Paradise Lost (Fish), **Supp. XIV:** 15

Surreal South (eds. P. Benedict and L. Benedict), **Supp. XXIII:** 35

"Surround, The Imagining Herself as the Environment,/She Speaks to James Wright at Sundow" (Dickey), **Supp. IV Part 1:** 185

"Surrounded by Weasels" (Gray and Gallagher), **Supp. XXIV:** 178

"Survey of Literature" (Ransom), **III:** 480

"Survey of the Literature, A" (Saunders), **Supp. XIX:** 235

"Surveyor, The" (H. Roth), **Supp. IX:** 233, 234

Survival (Atwood), **Supp. XIII:** 20, 22, 35

"Survival, Infantry" (Oppen), **Supp. XXVI:** 232

"Survival as Tao, Beginning at 5:00 A.M." (Carruth), **Supp. XVI:** 56

Survival of the Bark Canoe, The (McPhee), **Supp. III Part 1:** 301, 302, 308, 313

Survival This Way: Interviews with American Indian Poets (Bruchac), **Supp. IV Part 2:** 506

"Surviving Love" (Berryman), **I:** 173

Survivor (O. Butler), **Supp. XIII:** 62, 63

Susan and Anna Warner (Foster), **Supp. XVIII:** 265

Susan and God (film; Cukor), **Supp. XVI:** 192

Susanna Moodie: Voice and Vision (Shields), **Supp. VII:** 313

Susan Warner ("Elizabeth Wetherell") (A. Warner), **Supp. XVIII:** 259, 260

Suspect in Poetry, The (Dickey), **Supp. IV Part 1:** 177

"Sustained by Fiction" (Hoffman), **Supp. X:** 90, 92

"Susto" (Ríos), **Supp. IV Part 2:** 553

Sutherland, Donald, **IV:** 38, 44; **Supp. IX:** 254

Sutherland, Efua, **Supp. IV Part 1:** 9, 16

Sutherland-Smith, James, **Supp. X:** 211, 212

Sut Lovingood (Harris), **II:** 70; **Supp. XXII:** 193

Sutton, Roger, **Supp. X:** 266

Sutton, Walter, **III:** 479

"Sutton Pie Safe, The" (P. Benedict), **Supp. XXIII:** 36

Suttree (McCarthy), **Supp. VIII: 178–180,** 189

Suvero, Mark di, **Supp. IX:** 251

Svevo, Italo, **Supp. XIV:** 112

Swados, Harvey, **Supp. XI:** 222; **Supp. XIX: 255–271**

Swales, Martin, **Supp. XIX:** 183

Swallow, Alan, **Supp. X:** 112, 115, 116, 120, 123

Swallow Barn (J. P. Kennedy), **II:** 313

Swallow Barn (Kennedy), **Supp. XXII:** 193

Swallow the Lake (Major), **Supp. XXII:** 174

"Swamp Boy" (Bass), **Supp. XVI:** 20

Swan, Barbara, **Supp. IV Part 2:** 447

Swan, Jon, **Supp. IV Part 1:** 176

Swan Lake (Helprin), **Supp. XXV:** 83, 87

Swan Lake (Tchaikovsky), **Supp. IX:** 51

Swan Lake Trilogy (Helprin), **Supp. XXV:** 81, 84, 87

"Swan Legs" (Stern), **Supp. IX:** 299

Swann (Shields), **Supp. VII:** 315, 318–323, 326

Swann, Brian, **Supp. IV Part 2:** 500

Swanson, Gloria, **II:** 429

Swanson, Stevenson, **Supp. XIV:** 111

Swanton, John Reed, **Supp. VIII:** 295

Swan Watch (Schulberg), **Supp. XVIII:** 254

Swanwick, John, **Supp. XV:** 237

Swanwick, Michael, **Supp. XVI:** 128

"Swarm, The" (Plath), **Retro. Supp. II:** 255

"Sway" (Simpson), **Supp. IX:** 276

Sweat (Hurston), **Supp. VI:** 152

Swedenborg, Emanuel, **II:** 5, 10, 321, 342, 343–344, 396

Sweeney Agonistes (Eliot), **I:** 580; **Retro. Supp. I:** 64, 65; **Retro. Supp. II:** 247

"Sweeney Among the Nightingales" (Eliot), **III:** 4

"Sweeper, The" (Kooser), **Supp. XIX:** 125

Sweet, Blanche, **Supp. I Part 2:** 391

Sweet, Timothy, **Supp. IV Part 1:** 330

Sweet and Lowdown (film; Allen), **Supp. XV:** 11

Sweet and Sour (O'Hara), **III:** 361

"Sweet Armageddon" (Hoffman), **Supp. XVIII:** 85, 86

Sweet Bird of Youth (T. Williams), **IV:** 382, 383, 385, 386, 387, 388, 389, 390, 391, 392, 395, 396, 398; **Supp. IV Part 1:** 84, 89

Sweet Charity (musical), **Supp. IV Part 2:** 575

Sweet Flypaper of Life, The (Hughes), **Supp. I Part 1:** 335–336

"Sweetgrass"(Kenny), **Supp. XXIII:** 148

"Sweetheart" (Notley), **Supp. XXII:** 231

"Sweetheart of the Song Tra Bong, The" (O'Brien), **Supp. V:** 243, 249

"Sweethearts" (Ford), **Supp. V:** 69

Sweet Hereafter, The (Banks), **Supp. V:** 15–16

Sweet Lorain (Weigl), **Supp. XIX:** 282

Sweet Machine (Doty), **Supp. XI:** 121, **131–132,** 135

Sweet Sue (Gurney), **Supp. V:** 105, 107–108

Sweet Sweetback's Baadasss Song (Peebles; film), **Supp. XI:** 17

Sweet Thursday (Steinbeck), **IV:** 50, 52, 64–65

Sweet Will (Levine), **Supp. V:** 178, 187, 189, 190

"Sweet Will" (Levine), **Supp. V:** 190

"Sweet Willy"(J. Schoolcraft), **Supp. XXIII:** 226, 231

"Sweet Words on Race" (Hughes), **Retro. Supp. I:** 211

Sweezy, Paul, **Supp. I Part 2:** 645

"Swell-Looking Girl, A" (Caldwell), **I:** 310

Swenson, May, **Retro. Supp. II:** 44; **Supp. IV Part 2: 637–655; Supp. XIX:** 123; **Supp. XXVI:** 66, 67

Swetman, Glenn R., **Supp. XXI:** 91

"Swift" (Schwartz), **Supp. II Part 2:** 663

Swift, Jonathan, **I:** 125, 194, 209, 441; **II:** 110, 302, 304–305, 577; **III:** 113; **IV:** 68; **Retro. Supp. I:** 66; **Supp. I Part 2:** 406, 523, 603, 656, 665, 708, 714; **Supp. IV Part 1:** 51; **Supp. IV Part 2:** 692; **Supp. XI:** 105, 209; **Supp. XII:** 276; **Supp. XV:** 258; **Supp. XVI:** 110; **Supp. XVIII:** 2, 12; **Supp. XXV:** 87

"Swimmer" (Francis), **Supp. IX:** 82

"Swimmer" (Skloot), **Supp. XX: 199, 200**

"Swimmer, The" (Cheever), **Supp. I Part 1:** 185, 187

"Swimmer, The" (Glück), **Supp. V:** 82

"Swimmers" (Untermeyer), **Supp. XV:** 300

"Swimmers, The" (Fitzgerald), **Retro. Supp. I:** 110, 111

"Swimmers, The" (Tate), **IV:** 136

"Swimming" (Harjo), **Supp. XII:** 218

Swimming Pool, The (Rinehart), **Supp. XXV:** 189, 198, 200, 202

"Swimming Pool, The"(Strout), **Supp. XXIII:** 284

"Swim Team, The" (July), **Supp. XXIV:** 201

Swinburne, Algernon C., **I:** 50, 384, 568; **II:** 3, 4, 129, 400, 524; **IV:** 135; **Retro. Supp. I:** 100; **Supp. I Part 1:** 79; **Supp. I Part 2:** 422, 552; **Supp. XIV:** 120, 344

"Swinburne as Poet" (Eliot), **I:** 576

Swinger of Birches, A: A Portrait of Robert Frost (Cox), **Retro. Supp. I:** 132

"Swinging an Arc Before Him As He Goes" (Espaillat), **Supp. XXI:** 108

"Swinging on a Birch-Tree" (Larcom), **Supp. XIII:** 147

Swiss, Tom, **Supp. XIX:** 40

Switch, The (Dixon), **Supp. XII:** 141

Swope, D. B., **Supp. IX:** 95

Sword Blades and Poppy Seed (Lowell), **II:** 518, 520, 522, 532

Sword of God, The: Jeanne D'Arc (Endore), **Supp. XVII:** 55

Sybil (Auchincloss), **Supp. IV Part 1:** 25

Sybil and Chryssa (S. and A. Warner), **Supp. XVIII:** 264

"Sycamore" (Stern), **Supp. IX:** 294

"Sycamore, The" (Moore), **III:** 216

"Sycamores, The" (Whittier), **Supp. I Part 2:** 699

Sylvester, Johnny, **Supp. I Part 2:** 438

Sylvester, Joshua, **I:** 178, 179; **II:** 18; **III:** 157; **Supp. I Part 1:** 98, 104, 114, 116

Sylvia (Gurney), **Supp. V:** 105

"Sylvia" (L. Michaels), **Supp. XVI:** 202, 213

"Sylvia" (Larcom), **Supp. XIII:** 144

"Sylvia" (Stern), **Supp. IX:** 297

Sylvia: A Fictional Memoir (L. Michaels), **Supp. XVI:** 202, 213

Sylvia Plath: Method and Madness (Butscher), **Supp. I Part 2:** 526

Sylvia Plath: Poetry and Existence (Holbrook), **Supp. I Part 2:** 526–527

"Sylvia's Death" (Sexton), **Supp. II Part 2:** 671, 684, 685

"Symbol and Image in the Shorter Poems of Herman Melville" (Dickey), **Supp. IV Part 1:** 176

Symbolist Movement in Literature, The (Symons), **I:** 50, 569; **Retro. Supp. I:** 55

Symonds, John Addington, **I:** 241, 242, 251, 259; **IV:** 334; **Supp. XIV:** 329, 335; **Supp. XX: 230**

Symons, Arthur, **I:** 50, 569; **Retro. Supp. I:** 55; **Supp. XX: 239**

Symons, Julian, **Supp. IV Part 1:** 343, 351

"Sympathy" (Dunbar), **Supp. IV Part 1:** 15

Sympathy of Souls, A (Goldbarth), **Supp. XII:** 175, 176, **186–187**

"Symphony, The" (Lanier), **Supp. I Part 1:** 352, 360–361, 364; **Supp. I Part 2:** 416

Symposium (Plato), **Retro. Supp. II:** 31; **Supp. IV Part 1:** 391

Symposium: To Kill a Mockingbird (Alabama Law Review), **Supp. VIII:** 127, 128

Symptoms and Madness (Major), **Supp. XXII:** 174

Symptoms of Being 35 (Lardner), **II:** 434

Synanon (Endore), **Supp. XVII:** 65

Synanon (film, Quine), **Supp. XVII:** 65

Synanon City (Endore), **Supp. XVII:** 65

Syncopated Cakewalk, The (Major), **Supp. XXII:** 174

Synge, John Millington, **I:** 434; **III:** 591–592; **Supp. III Part 1:** 34; **Supp. VIII:** 155

Synthetic Philosophy (Spencer), **II:** 462–463

"Syringa" (Ashbery), **Supp. III Part 1:** 19–21, 25

"Syrinx" (Clampitt), **Supp. IX:** 53

"Syrinx" (Merrill), **Supp. III Part 1:** 328

Syrkin, Marie, **Supp. XIV:** 279, 288, 291

"System, The" (Ashbery), **Supp. III Part 1:** 14, 15, 18, 21–22

System of Dante's Hell, The (Baraka), **Supp. II Part 1:** 39–41, 55

"System of Dante's Inferno, The" (Baraka), **Supp. II Part 1:** 40

"System of Doctor Tarr and Professor Fether, The" (Poe), **III:** 419, 425

System of General Geography, A (Brown), **Supp. I Part 1:** 146

Szaylay, Michael, **Supp. XXI:** 267

Sze, Mai-mai, **Supp. X:** 291

Szentgyorgyi, Tom, **Supp. IX:** 135, 136, 140, 141–142

Szilagyi, Anca, **Supp. XXVI:** 218

Szukalski, Stanislaus, **Supp. XXV:** 19, 23

Szulc, Tad, **Supp. XVI:** 154

Szymborka, Wislawa, **Supp. XI:** 267

Szymborska, Wislawa, **Supp. XVIII:** 29

T

"T-2 Tanker Blues" (Snyder), **Supp. VIII:** 294

Tabios, Eileen, **Supp. XV:** 214, 225, 226

"Table of Delectable Contents, The" (Simic), **Supp. VIII:** 276

Tabloid Dreams (R. O. Butler), **Supp. XII: 70–72,** 74

Tacey Cromwell (Richter), **Supp. XVIII:** **211,** 215, 217

Tacitus, Cornelius, **I:** 485; **II:** 113

Tadic, Novica, **Supp. VIII:** 272

Taft (Patchett), **Supp. XII:** 307, 312, **314–317**

"Tag" (Hughes), **Supp. I Part 1:** 341

Taggard, Genevieve, **IV:** 436; **Supp. XXII: 271–287; Supp. XXVI:** 144

Taggart, John, **Supp. IV Part 2:** 421

Tagore, Rabindranath, **I:** 383; **Supp. XX: 117**

"Taibele and Her Demon" (Singer), **Retro. Supp. II:** 307

Taibl, Erika, **Supp. XV:** 255

"Tailor Shop, The" (H. Miller), **III:** 175

"Tails" (Dixon), **Supp. XII:** 154

Taine, Hippolyte, **I:** 503; **II:** 271; **III:** 323; **IV:** 440, 444

"Tain't So" (Hughes), **Supp. I Part 1:** 330

"Taipei Tangle" (Halliday), **Supp. XIX:** 91

Takasago (play), **III:** 466

Takazauckas, Albert, **Supp. XXIII:** 203

Take Away the Darkness (Bynner), **Supp. XV:** 51

Take Heart (Peacock), **Supp. XIX: 197–199,** 206

Take Me Back: A Novel (Bausch), **Supp. VII:** 41, 43–45, 46, 49

"Take My Saddle from the Wall: A Valediction" (McMurtry), **Supp. V:** 219

"'Take No for an Answer' " (Didion), **Supp. IV Part 1:** 203

"Take Pity" (Malamud), **Supp. I Part 2:** 427, 428, 435, 436, 437

"Takers, The" (Olds), **Supp. X:** 205

"Take the I Out" (Olds), **Supp. X:** 213

Take the Money and Run (film; Allen), **Supp. XV: 3–4,** 6

"Taking a Stitch in a Dead Man's Arm" (Vaz), **Supp. XXVI:** 264

"Taking Away the Name of a Nephew" (Ríos), **Supp. IV Part 2:** 545–546

Taking Care of Mrs. Carroll (Monette), **Supp. X:** 153

Taking Care: Thoughts on Storytelling and Belief (Kittredge), **Supp. XXVI:** 181, 182, 183, 185

"Taking of Captain Ball, The" (Jewett), **Retro. Supp. II:** 134

"Taking Off Emily Dickinson's Clothes" (Collins), **Supp. XXI:** 59, 60

"Taking Out the Lawn Chairs" (Karr), **Supp. XI:** 241

"Taking the Bypass" (J. Epstein), **Supp. XIV:** 110; **Supp. XVI:** 230

"Taking the Forest" (Howe), **Supp. IV Part 2:** 433

"Taking the Lambs to Market" (Kumin), **Supp. IV Part 2:** 455

Talbot, Daniel, **Supp. XIX:** 264

"Tale, A" (Bogan), **Supp. III Part 1:** 50, 51

Taleb-Khyar, Mohamed, **Supp. IV Part 1:** 242, 243, 244, 247, 257

Talented Mr. Ripley, The (Highsmith), **Supp. XXII:** 119

"Tale of Jerusalem, A" (Poe), **III:** 411

Tale of Possessors Self-Dispossessed, A (O'Neill), **III:** 404

Tale of the Body Thief, The (Rice), **Supp. VII:** 290, 293–294, 297

Tale of Two Cities, A (film), **Supp. I Part 1:** 67

"Tale of Two Liars, A" (Singer), **IV:** 12

Tales (Baraka), **Supp. II Part 1:** 39, 55

Tales (Poe), **III:** 413

Tales and Stories for Black Folks (Bambara, ed.), **Supp. XI:** 1
Tales before Midnight (Benét), **Supp. XI:** 46, 53, 57
Talese, Gay, **Supp. XVI:** 273; **Supp. XVII:** 199–211; **Supp. XXIV:** 282
Tales of a Traveller (Irving), **II:** 309–310
Tales of a Wayside Inn (Longfellow), **II:** 489, 490, 501, 502, 504–505; **Retro. Supp. II:** 154, 162–165
Tales of Glauber-Spa (Bryant, ed.), **Supp. I Part 1:** 157
Tales of H. P. Lovecraft (Oates, ed.), **Supp. XXV:** 123
Tales of Manhattan (Auchincloss), **Supp. IV Part 1:** 23
Tales of Men and Ghosts (Wharton), **IV:** 315; **Retro. Supp. I:** 372
Tales of My People (Asch), **Supp. XXIII:** 7
Tales of Rhoda, The (Rice), **Supp. VII:** 288
Tales of Soldiers and Civilians (Bierce), **I:** 200–203, 204, 206, 208, 212
Tales of the Argonauts (Harte), **Supp. II Part 1:** 337, 348, 351
Tales of the Fish Patrol (London), **II:** 465
Tales of the Grotesque and Arabesque (Poe), **II:** 273; **III:** 412, 415; **Retro. Supp. I:** 270
Tales of the Jazz Age (Fitzgerald), **II:** 88; **Retro. Supp. I:** 105; **Supp. IX:** 57
Tales You Won't Believe (Stratton-Porter), **Supp. XX:** 217
Taliaferro, Frances, **Supp. XXII:** 210
"Talisman, A" (Moore), **III:** 195–196
Talisman, The (King), **Supp. V:** 140, 144, 152
"Talkin Bout Sonny" (Bambara), **Supp. XI:** 6–7
"Talking" (Merwin), **Supp. III Part 1:** 354
Talking All Morning (R. Bly), **Supp. IV Part 1:** 59, 60, 61, 62, 64, 65
Talking Dirty to the Gods (Komunyakaa), **Supp. XIII:** 130–131
Talking History (television program), **Supp. XXI:** 172
"Talking Horse" (Malamud), **Supp. I Part 2:** 435
Talking Soft Dutch (McCarriston), **Supp. XIV:** 260–263, 266, 270, 271
"Talking to Barr Creek" (Wagoner), **Supp. IX:** 328
"Talking to Sheep" (Sexton), **Supp. II Part 2:** 695
Talking to the Sun: An Illustrated Anthology of Poems for Young People (Koch and Farrell, eds.), **Supp. XV:** 188
"Talking Water" (Taggard), **Supp. XXII:** 276
"Talk of Heroes" (C. Bly), **Supp. XVI:** 34
"Talk of the Town" (*The New Yorker* column), **IV:** 215; **Supp. IV Part 1:** 53, 54
"Talk on Guadalcanal" (Wolfert), **Supp. XXI:** 264
Talk Talk (Boyle), **Supp. XX:** 24

"Talk with the Yellow Kid, A" (Bellow), **I:** 151
Tallent, Elizabeth, **Supp. IV Part 2:** 570
Tallman, Warren, **Supp. IV Part 1:** 154
TallMountain, Mary, **Supp. IV Part 1:** 324–325
Talma, Louise, **IV:** 357
Talmadge, Constance, **Supp. XVI:** 186, 187, 196
Talmadge, Norma, **Supp. XVI:** 186, 187, 196
Talmadge Girls, The (Loos), **Supp. XVI:** 186, 196
Talmey, Allene, **Supp. IV Part 1:** 197; **Supp. XIII:** 172
Talmud, **IV:** 8, 17
Taltos: Lives of the Mayfair Witches (Rice), **Supp. VII:** 299–300
"Tamar" (Jeffers), **Supp. II Part 2:** 427–428, 436
Tamar and Other Poems (Jeffers), **Supp. II Part 2:** 416, 419
"Tambourine Life" (Berrigan), **Supp. XXIV:** 42
Tambourines to Glory (Hughes), **Supp. I Part 1:** 338–339
"Tame Indians" (Jewett), **Retro. Supp. II:** 141
"Tamerlane" (Poe), **III:** 426
Tamerlane and Other Poems (Poe), **III:** 410
"Tammany Man, The" (Hapgood), **Supp. XVII:** 103
"Tam O'Shanter" (Burns), **II:** 306
Tamsen Donner: A Woman's Journey (Whitman), **Supp. XXI:** 246
Tan, Amy, **Supp. X:** 289–300
Tangential Views (Bierce), **I:** 209
"Tangier 1975" (Bowles), **Supp. IV Part 1:** 94
Tanguay, Pablo, **Supp. XXIII:** 299
"Tankas" (McClatchy), **Supp. XII:** 266
Tanner, Laura E., **Supp. X:** 209; **Supp. XXI:** 217
Tanner, Obour, **Supp. XX:** 281, 288
Tanner, Tony, **I:** 260, 261; **Retro. Supp. II:** 205; **Supp. IV Part 1:** 285; **Supp. XVI:** 65, 69
Tannhäuser (Wagner), **I:** 315
"Tan Ta Ra, Cries Mars...," (Wagoner), **Supp. IX:** 325
Tao of Physics, The (Capra), **Supp. X:** 261
Tao Teh Ching (Bynner, trans.), **Supp. XV:** 46, 47
Tapahonso, Luci, **Supp. IV Part 1:** 404; **Supp. IV Part 2:** 499, 508
Tape for the Turn of the Year (Ammons), **Supp. VII:** 31–33, 35
"Tapestry" (Ashbery), **Supp. III Part 1:** 22–23
"Tapestry" (E. P. Jones), **Supp. XXII:** 152
Tapestry Room Murder, The (Wells), **Supp. XXVI:** 282
"Tapiama" (Bowles), **Supp. IV Part 1:** 89–90
"Tapiola" (W. C. Williams), **Retro. Supp. I:** 429
Tappan, Arthur, **Supp. I Part 2:** 588

Tapping the White Cane of Solitude (F. Wright), **Supp. XVII:** 243
Taps at Reveille (Fitzgerald), **II:** 94, 96; **Retro. Supp. I:** 113
Taradash, Daniel, **Supp. XXV:** 95
Tar: A Midwest Childhood (Anderson), **I:** 98, 115; **II:** 27
Tarantino, Quentin, **Supp. IV Part 1:** 356
Tarantula (Dylan), **Supp. XVIII:** 21, 29, 31–32
Tar Baby (Morrison), **Supp. III Part 1:** 364, 369–372, 379; **Supp. IV Part 1:** 13
Tarbell, Ida, **III:** 322, 580; **Retro. Supp. II:** 101
"Target Practice" (Offutt), **Supp. XIX:** 171
"Target Study" (Baraka), **Supp. II Part 1:** 49–50, 54
Tarkington, Booth, **II:** 444; **III:** 70; **Retro. Supp. I:** 100; **Supp. XV:** 41
Tarnawsky, Yuriy (George) Orest, **Supp. XX:** 259
Tarpon (film), **Supp. VIII:** 42
Tarr, Rodger L., **Supp. X:** 222, 224, 226
Tárrega, Francisco, **Supp. XXI:** 100
Tartt, Donna, **Supp. XVIII:** 135
Tartuffe (Molière; Wilbur, trans.), **Supp. III Part 2:** 560
Tarumba, Selected Poems of Jaime Sabines (Levine and Trejo, trans.), **Supp. V:** 178
Tarzan Finds a Son (film, Weismuller), **Supp. XX:** 18
"Tarzan Is an Expatriate" (Theroux), **Supp. VIII:** 313
Tasis, Juan de, **Supp. XXI:** 104
Task, The (Cowper), **II:** 304
Tasker Street (Halliday), **Supp. XIX:** 82, 87–89
Tasso, Torquato, **I:** 276
Taste of Palestine, A: Menus and Memories (Shihab), **Supp. XIII:** 273
Tate, Alan, **Supp. XV:** 141
Tate, Allen, **I:** 48, 49, 50, 67, 69, 381, 382, 386, 390, 396, 397, 399, 402, 441, 468; **II:** 197–198, 367, 536, 537, 542, 551, 554; **III:** 424, 428, 454, 482, 483, 485, 493, 495, 496, 497, 499, 500, 517; **IV:** 120–143, 236, 237, 433; **Retro. Supp. I:** 37, 41, 90; **Retro. Supp. II:** 77, 79, 82, 83, 89, 176, 178, 179; **Supp. I Part 1:** 364, 371; **Supp. I Part 2:** 423; **Supp. II Part 1:** 90–91, 96, 98, 103–104, 136, 139, 144, 150, 151, 318; **Supp. II Part 2:** 643; **Supp. III Part 2:** 542; **Supp. V:** 315, 331; **Supp. X:** 1, 52; **Supp. XIV:** 2; **Supp. XXI:** 256; **Supp. XXII:** 277
Tate, Mrs. Allen (Caroline Gordon). *See* Gordon, Caroline
Tate, Mrs. Allen (Helen Heinz), **IV:** 127
Tate, Mrs. Allen (Isabella Gardner), **IV:** 127
Tate, Benjamin Lewis Bogan, **IV:** 127
Tate, Greg, **Supp. XIII:** 233, 237
Tate, James, **Supp. V:** 92, 338; **Supp. VIII:** 39, 279; **Supp. XV:** 250; **Supp. XVII:** 242
Tate, John Allen, **IV:** 127

Tate, Michael Paul, **IV:** 127
Tate, Nancy, **II:** 197
Tatonetti, Lisa, **Supp. XXIII:** 149–150
Tattooed Countess, The (Van Vechten), **I:** 295; **Supp. II Part 2:** 726–728, 738, 742
Tattooed Feet (Nye), **Supp. XIII:** 274
"Tattoos" (McClatchy), **Supp. XII:** 266–267, 268
"Tattoos" (Wright), **Supp. V:** 335, 340
Tatum, Anna, **I:** 516
Tatum, James, **Supp. IV Part 2:** 684
Taubman, Howard, **Supp. XXV:** 106
Taupin, René, **II:** 528, 529; **Supp. III Part 2:** 614, 615, 617, 621
Tavano, John, **Supp. XXI:** 99
Taves, Isabella, **Supp. XXV:** 198
Tawney, Richard Henry, **Supp. I Part 2:** 481
Taylor, Ann, **Supp. XXIII:** 231
Taylor, Bayard, **II:** 275; **Supp. I Part 1:** 350, 361, 362, 365, 366, 372; **Supp. XV:** 269
Taylor, Chuck, **Supp. XXIII:** 57
Taylor, Cora. *See* Howarth, Cora
Taylor, Deems, **III:** 138
Taylor, Edward, **III:** 493; **IV: 144–166;** **Supp. I Part 1:** 98; **Supp. I Part 2:** 375, 386, 546
Taylor, Mrs. Edward (Elizabeth Fitch), **IV:** 147, 165
Taylor, Mrs. Edward (Ruth Wyllys), **IV:** 148
Taylor, Eleanor Ross, **Supp. V:** 317, 318
Taylor, Elizabeth, **II:** 588
Taylor, Frank, **III:** 81
Taylor, Frederick Winslow, **Supp. I Part 2:** 644
Taylor, Graham, **Supp. I Part 1:** 5
Taylor, Henry, **Retro. Supp. I:** 212; **Supp. XI:** 317; **Supp. XIII:** 333
Taylor, Henry W., **IV:** 144
Taylor, Jeremy, **II:** 11; **III:** 487; **Supp. I Part 1:** 349; **Supp. XII:** 45; **Supp. XIV:** 344, 345
Taylor, John, **IV:** 149
Taylor, Katherine, **Supp. VIII:** 251
Taylor, Kezia, **IV:** 148
Taylor, Nathaniel W., **Supp. I Part 2:** 580
Taylor, Paul, **I:** 293
Taylor, Peter, **Retro. Supp. II:** 179; **Supp. V: 313–329; Supp. XIV:** 3
Taylor, Raynor, **Supp. XV:** 238
Taylor, Richard, **IV:** 146
Taylor, Robert, **Supp. I Part 1:** 294; **Supp. XV:** 135, 138; **Supp. XVI:** 277
Taylor, Samuel A., **Supp. XX: 253**
Taylor, Stephan, **Supp. XVI:** 203
Taylor, Thomas, **II:** 10
Taylor, William, **IV:** 145–146
Taylor, Zachary, **I:** 3; **II:** 433–434
Tchelitchew, Peter, **II:** 586
Tea and Sympathy (Anderson), **Supp. I Part 1:** 277; **Supp. V:** 108
"Tea at the Palaz of Hoon" (Stevens), **Retro. Supp. I:** 300, 302, 306
"Teacher's Pet" (Thurber), **Supp. I Part 2:** 605–606

"Teaching and Story Telling" (Maclean), **Supp. XIV:** 234
Teaching a Stone to Talk: Expeditions and Encounters (Dillard), **Supp. VI:** 23, 26, 28, 32, 33, 34–35
"Teaching Emily Dickenson"(Hadas), **Supp. XXIII:** 115
"Teaching Hanh the Blues" (Weigl), **Supp. XIX:** 287
Teachings of Don B., The (Barthelme), **Supp. IV Part 1:** 53
Teachout, Terry, **Supp. XIX:** 137
Teale, Edwin Way, **Supp. XIII:** 7
Teall, Dorothy, **I:** 221
"Team Blue/Team Square: Revisiting the Lyric and the Narrative" (Biss and Zapruder), **Supp. XXVI:** 54–55
"Team Players" (Biss), **Supp. XXVI:** 46
Team Team Team (film), **Supp. IX:** 251
"Tea on the Mountain" (Bowles), **Supp. IV Part 1:** 90
"Tea Party, The" (MacLeish), **III:** 11
Tear and a Smile, A (Dam'a wa Ibtisáma) (Gibran), **Supp. XX:** 116, 118, **124**
Teare, Brian, **Supp. XXII:** 236
"Tears, Idle Tears" (Lord Tennyson), **Supp. XIV:** 8
"Tears of the Pilgrims, The" (McClatchy), **Supp. XII:** 256
Teasdale, Sara, **Retro. Supp. I:** 133; **Supp. I Part 2:** 393, 707; **Supp. XIV:** 127; **Supp. XV:** 295, 297, 301, 305, 307, 308; **Supp. XVII:** 69, 75
"Tease" (Swados), **Supp. XIX:** 267
Tebeaux, Elizabeth, **Supp. IX:** 109
"Technical Manifesto of Futurist Literature" (Marinetti), **Supp. XXII:** 161
Technics and Civilization (Mumford), **Supp. I Part 2:** 638; **Supp. II Part 2:** 479, 493, 497
Technics and Human Development (Mumford), **Supp. I Part 2:** 638; **Supp. II Part 2:** 497
Technique of the Mystery Story, The (Wells), **Supp. XXVI:** 277, 280, 281–282
"Technology, The" (Egan), **Supp. XIX:** 61
"Teddy" (Salinger), **III:** 561–563, 571
"Te Deum" (Reznikoff), **Supp. XIV:** 281
Tedlock, Dennis, **Supp. IV Part 2:** 509
"Teeth Mother Naked at Last, The" (R. Bly), **Supp. IV Part 1:** 63, 68, 73
Teggart, Richard, **Supp. I Part 2:** 650
Tegnér, Esaias, **Retro. Supp. II:** 155
Teilhard de Chardin, Pierre, **Supp. I Part 1:** 314
Tekonwatonti/Molly Brant (Kenny), **Supp. XXIII:** 143, 147, 151, **152–153,** 154
Telephone, The (film), **Supp. XI:** 309
"Telephone Call, A" (Parker), **Supp. IX:** **202–203**
"Telephone Number of the Muse, The" (Justice), **Supp. VII:** 124–125
Telephone Poles and Other Poems (Updike), **IV:** 214, 215
"Television" (Beattie), **Supp. V:** 33
Teller, Edward, **I:** 137

"Tell Him About Brother John" (Muñoz), **Supp. XXV:** 136
"Telling" (Ortiz), **Supp. IV Part 2:** 509
"Telling It in Black and White: The Importance of the Africanist Presence in *To Kill a Mockingbird*" (Baecker), **Supp. VIII:** 128
Telling Secrets (Buechner), **Supp. XII:** 53–54
Telling Stories (Didion), **Supp. IV Part 1:** 197
"Telling Stories" (Didion), **Supp. IV Part 1:** 197
"Telling the Bees" (Whittier), **Supp. I Part 2:** 694–695
Telling the Little Secrets (J. Burstein), **Supp. XVII:** 44
Telling the Truth: The Gospel as Tragedy, Comedy, and Fairy Tale (Buechner), **Supp. XII:** 53
"Tell Me" (Hughes), **Supp. VIII:** 213
"Tell Me, Sir, ... What Is 'Black' Literature?" (H. L. Gates), **Supp. XX: 108**
Tell Me, Tell Me (Moore), **III:** 215
Tell Me Again (Notley), **Supp. XXII:** 224, 230–231
Tell Me Again How the White Heron Rises and Flies across the Nacreous River at Twilight toward the Distant Islands (Carruth), **Supp. XVI:**56
Tell Me a Riddle (film), **Supp. XIII:** 295
Tell Me a Riddle (Olsen), **Supp. XIII:** 294, 296, **298–302,** 303, 305
"Tell Me a Riddle" (Olsen), **Supp. XIII:** 294, 297, 298, **300–302,** 305
"Tell Me a Story" (McDermott), **Supp. XVIII:** 177
Tell Me How Long the Train's Been Gone (Baldwin), **Retro. Supp. II:** 9, **11–12,** 14; **Supp. I Part 1:** 48, 52, 63–65, 67
"Tell Me My Fortune" (Epstein), **Supp. XII:** 163
Tell Me True: Memoir, History, and Writing a Life (Hampl and May, eds.), **Supp. XXII:** 81–82, 84, **94–95**
Tell Me Your Answer True (Sexton), **Supp. II Part 2:** 683
Tell My Horse (Hurston), **Supp. VI:** 149, 156, 158
"Tell-Tale Heart, The" (Poe), **III:** 413, 414–415, 416; **Retro. Supp. II:** 267, 269, 270; **Supp. XXV:** 112
"Tell the Women We're Going" (Carver), **Supp. III Part 1:** 138, 144
"Telluride Blues—A Hatchet Job" (Abbey), **Supp. XIII:** 10
Telushkin, Dvorah, **Retro. Supp. II:** 317
Temblor (Howe), **Supp. IV Part 2:** 431
Temperamental People (Rinehart), **Supp. XXV:** 196
Tempering of Eugene O'Neill, The (D. Alexander), **Supp. XVII:** 99
"Temper of Steel, The" (Jones), **Supp. XI:** 218
Tempers, The (W. C. Williams), **Retro. Supp. I: 413–414,** 415, 416, 424
Tempest, The (Shakespeare), **I:** 394; **II:** 12; **III:** 40, 61, 263; **Retro. Supp. I:** 61; **Supp. IV Part 2:** 463; **Supp. V:** 302–303; **Supp. XII:** 54–57; **Supp.**

XV: 255, 256

Temple, Minnie, **II:** 323

Temple, The (Herbert), **IV:** 145, 153

Temple, William, **III:** 303

Temple House (E. Stoddard), **Supp. XV:** 273, **284–286**

Temple of My Familiar, The (Walker), **Supp. III Part 2:** 521, 527, 529, 535, 537; **Supp. IV Part 1:** 14

"Temple of the Holy Ghost, A" (O'Connor), **III:** 344, 352; **Retro. Supp. II:** 232

Templin, Charlotte, **Supp. V:** 116

Temporary Shelter (Gordon), **Supp. IV Part 1:** 299, 305–307

"Temporary Shelter" (Gordon), **Supp. IV Part 1:** 306

Temptation Game, The (Gardner), **Supp. VI:** 72

Temptation of Don Volpi, The (Hayes), **Supp. XXVI:** 135, 137

"Temptation of St. Anthony, The" (Barthelme), **Supp. IV Part 1:** 47

Temptations, The, **Supp. X:** 242

"10 Best Weathers of 1983, The" (Notley), **Supp. XXII:** 224

"10 Things I Do Every Day" (Berrigan), **Supp. XXII:** 224; **Supp. XXIV:** 41

"Tenancy, A" (Merrill), **Supp. III Part 1:** 322, 323

"Tenant" (Hoffman), **Supp. XVIII:** 86

Tenants, The (Malamud), **Supp. I Part 2:** 448–450

"Ten Best Issues of Comic Books, The" (Notley), **Supp. XXII:** 224

Ten Commandments (McClatchy), **Supp. XII: 262–265**

Ten Days That Shook the World (Reed), **II:** 577; **Supp. X:** 136; **Supp. XVIII:** 225

Tendencies in Modern American Poetry (Lowell), **II:** 529

"Tender, Hilarious Reminiscences of Life in Mythical Lake Wobegon" (MacDougall), **Supp. XVI:** 174

Tender Buttons (G. Stein), **I:** 103, 105; **IV:** 27, 42–43; **Retro. Supp. II:** 331; **Supp. XV:** 347

"Tenderfoot" (Haines), **Supp. XII:** 209

Tender Is the Night (Fitzgerald), **I:** 375; **II:** 79, 84, 91, 95–96, 97, 98, 420; **Retro. Supp. I:** 105, 108, 109, **110–112**, 114; **Supp. IX:** 59, 60, 61; **Supp. XV:** 197; **Supp. XXI:** 11

"Tenderloin" (Crane), **I:** 408

"Tenderly" (Dobyns), **Supp. XIII:** 86–87

"Tender Man, A" (Bambara), **Supp. XI:** 9–10

"Tenderness" (Dunn), **Supp. XI:** 149, 150

"Tender Offer, The" (Auchincloss), **Supp. IV Part 1:** 34

"Tender Organizations, The" (C. Bly), **Supp. XVI:** 40, 42

"Tenebrae" (Komunyakaa), **Supp. XIII:** 132

Tenenbaum, Joseph, **Supp. XX:** 253

"Ten Forty-Four" (Kingsolver), **Supp. VII:** 208

Ten Indians (Bell), **Supp. X:** 7, **12**

Ten Introductions: A Collection of Modern Verse (Taggard and Fitts, ed.), **Supp. XXII:** 281

Tennant, Agnieszka, **Supp. XX: 140**

"Ten Neglected American Writers Who Deserve to Be Better Known" (Cantor), **Supp. IV Part 1:** 285

Tennent, Gilbert, **I:** 546

Tennessee Day in St. Louis (Taylor), **Supp. V:** 324

"Tennessee's Partner" (Harte), **Supp. II Part 1:** 345, 348–350

"Tennis" (Pinsky), **Supp. VI:** 241, 242

Tennis Court Oath, The (Ashbery), **Supp. III Part 1:** 7, 9, 12, 14, 26

Ten North Frederick (O'Hara), **III:** 361

Tennyson, Alfred, Lord, **I:** 587–588; **II:** 18, 82, 273, 338, 404, 439, 604; **III:** 5, 409, 469, 485, 511, 521, 523; **Retro. Supp. I:** 100, 325; **Retro. Supp. II:** 135; **Supp. I Part 1:** 349, 356; **Supp. I Part 2:** 410, 416, 552; **Supp. IX:** 19; **Supp. X:** 157; **Supp. XIII:** 111; **Supp. XIV:** 40, 120; **Supp. XV:** 275; **Supp. XVIII:** 78

"Tenochtitlan" (Bronk), **Supp. XXI:** 31

"Ten O'Clock News" (Ortiz), **Supp. IV Part 2:** 503–504

"Te-Non-An-At-Che"(Kenny), **Supp. XXIII:** 151

Tenorman (Huddle), **Supp. XXVI:** 150, 151, 153, 156, 159

Ten Poems (Dove), **Supp. IV Part 1:** 244

Ten Poems of Francis Ponge Translated by Robert Bly and Ten Poems of Robert Bly Inspired by the Poems by Francis Ponge (R. Bly), **Supp. IV Part 1:** 71

"Tension in Poetry" (Tate), **IV:** 128, 129, 135

Tenth Muse, The (Bradstreet), **Supp. I Part 1:** 102, 103, 114

10,000 Days of Thunder: A History of the Vietnam War (Caputo), **Supp. XIX:** 29

Tenting Tonight (Rinehart), **Supp. XXV:** 195

"Tent on the Beach, The" (Whittier), **Supp. I Part 2:** 703

"Ten True Things" (July), **Supp. XXIV:** 205

"Teodoro Luna Confesses after Years to His Brother, Anselmo the Priest, Who Is Required to Understand, But Who Understands Anyway, More Than People Think" (Ríos), **Supp. IV Part 2:** 552

Teodoro Luna's Two Kisses (Ríos), **Supp. IV Part 2:** 550–552, 553

"Tepeyac" (Cisneros), **Supp. VII:** 69

"Terce" (Auden), **Supp. II Part 1:** 22

Terence, **IV:** 155, 363; **Supp. I Part 2:** 405

Terkel, Studs, **Supp. IV Part 1:** 364

"Term" (Merwin), **Supp. III Part 1:** 356–357

"Terminal Days at Beverly Farms" (Lowell), **Retro. Supp. II:** 189

Terminating, or Sonnet LXXV, or "Lass Meine Schmerzen nicht verloren sein,

or Ambivalence" (Kushner), *Supp. IX:* 132

Terminations (James), **Retro. Supp. I:** 229

"Terminus" (Emerson), **II:** 13, 19

"Terminus" (Wharton), **Retro. Supp. I:** 371

"Terms in Which I Think of Reality, The" (Ginsberg), **Supp. II Part 1:** 311

Terms of Endearment (film), **Supp. V:** 226

Terms of Endearment (McMurtry), **Supp. V:** 224–225

"Terrace, The" (Wilbur), **Supp. III Part 2:** 550

Terrarium (Sanders), **Supp. XVI:** 270

"Terrence McNally" (Bryer), **Supp. XIII:** 200

"Terrence McNally" (Di Gaetani), **Supp. XIII:** 200

Terrence McNally: A Casebook (Zinman), **Supp. XIII:** 209

"Terrestrial Cuckoo"(O'Hara), **Supp. XXIII:** 210

"Terrible Peacock, The" (Barnes), **Supp. III Part 1:** 33

Terrible Threes, The (Reed), **Supp. X:** 241, 253

Terrible Twos, The (Reed), **Supp. X:** 241, **252–253**

"Terrific Mother" (Moore), **Supp. X:** 178

Territory Ahead, The (Morris), **III:** 228–229, 236

Terrorism (Wright), **Supp. XV:** 341, 342

"Terrorism" (Wright), **Supp. XV:** 341

"Terrors of the Amazon" (Grossman), **Supp. XXV:** 66

Terry, Edward A., **II:** 128, 129

Terry, Rose, **Supp. I Part 2:** 420

Tertium Organum (Ouspensky), **I:** 383; **Supp. XX: 116**

Terzian, Peter, **Supp. XXV:** 12, 13

Tess of the d'Urbervilles (Hardy), **II:** 181; **Retro. Supp. II:** 100

"Testament" (Berry), **Supp. X:** 36

"Testament" (Carruth), **Supp. XVI:** 59

"Testament (Or, Homage to Walt Whitman)" (Jong), **Supp. V:** 130

"Testament of Flood" (Warren), **IV:** 253

Testament of François Villon, The (Pound, opera), **Retro. Supp. I:** 287

"Testament: Vermeer in December" (Bierds), **Supp. XVII:** 33

"Testimonia on the Question of Stesichoros' Blinding by Helen" (Carson), **Supp. XII:** 107

"Testimonies of a Roasted Chicken" (Jarman), **Supp. XVII:** 120

"Testimony" (Komunyakaa), **Supp. XIII:** 129

"Testimony of James Apthorp, The" (Kees), **Supp. XV:** 146

Testimony: The United States (1885–1890): Recitative (Reznikoff), **Supp. XIV:** 279, 280, 281, 285, **289–291**

Testimony: The United States (1891–1900): Recitative (Reznikoff), **Supp. XIV:** 291

Testing-Tree, The (Kunitz), **Supp. III Part 1:** 260, 263, 264, 267, 268

"Testing-Tree, The" (Kunitz), **Supp. III Part 1:** 269

Test of Poetry, A (Zukofsky), **Supp. III Part 2:** 618, 622

Teuton, Christopher, **Supp. XXVI:** 102, 110, 111

"Teutonic Scholar" (X. J. Kennedy), **Supp. XV:** 161

"Texas Moon, and Elsewhere, The" (McMurtry), **Supp. V:** 225

Texas Poets in Concert: A Quartet (Gwynn, ed.), **Supp. XIII:** 277

Texas Summer (Southern), **Supp. XI:** 309

Texasville (McMurtry), **Supp. V:** 228, 233

Thacher, Molly Day, **IV:** 381

Thackeray, William Makepeace, **I:** 194, 354; **II:** 182, 271, 282, 288, 316, 321, 322; **III:** 64, 70; **IV:** 326; **Retro. Supp. I:** 218; **Supp. I Part 1:** 307; **Supp. I Part 2:** 421, 495, 579; **Supp. IV Part 1:** 297; **Supp. IX:** 200; **Supp. XI:** 277; **Supp. XIV:** 306; **Supp. XX: 228**

Thaddeus, Janice Farrar, **Supp. IV Part 1:** 299

"Thailand" (Barthelme), **Supp. IV Part 1:** 41

Thalberg, Irving, **Retro. Supp. I:** 109, 110, 114; **Supp. XVI:** 191, 192

Thales, **I:** 480–481

Thalia Trilogy (McMurtry), **Supp. V:** 220–223, 234

Tham, Claire, **Supp. VIII:** 79

"Thanatopsis" (Bryant), **Supp. I Part 1:** 150, 154, 155, 170

Thanatos Syndrome, The (Percy), **Supp. III Part 1:** 385, 397–399

"Thanks Can Be Named to Death" (Peacock), **Supp. XIX:** 199

"Thanksgiving" (Davison), **Supp. XXVI:** 74

"Thanksgiving" (Glück), **Supp. V:** 83

"Thanksgiving, A" (Auden), **Supp. II Part 1:** 26

"Thanksgiving for a Habitat" (Auden), **Supp. II Part 1:** 24

Thanksgivings (Traherne), **Supp. XVI:** 288

"Thanksgiving Spirit" (Farrell), **II:** 45

Thanksgiving Visitor, The (Capote), **Supp. III Part 1:** 116, 118, 119

"Thank You, Esther Forbes" (Saunders), **Supp. XIX:** 235

Thank You, Fog (Auden), **Supp. II Part 1:** 24

"Thank You, Lord" (Angelou), **Supp. IV Part 1:** 15

Thank You, Mr. Moto (Marquand), **III:** 57, 58

Thank You and Other Poems (Koch), **Supp. XV:** 180–181

"Thank You in Arabic" (Nye), **Supp. XIII:** 273, 281

"Thar's More in the Man Than Thar Is in the Land" (Lanier), **Supp. I Part 1:** 352–353, 359–360

That Affair Next Door (Green), **Supp. XXVI:** 277

"That Evening Sun" (Faulkner), **II:** 72; **Retro. Supp. I:** 75, 83

That Horse (Hogan), **Supp. IV Part 1:** 397, 404, 405

"That House, This Room" (W. V. Davis), **Supp. XXI:** 90

"That I Had the Wings" (Ellison), **Supp. II Part 1:** 238

That Night (McDermott), **Supp. XVIII:** 155, **158–160**, 162, 166

"That's the Place Indians Talk About" (Ortiz), **Supp. IV Part 2:** 511

That Tantalus (Bronk), **Supp. XXI:** 31

"That the Soul May Wax Plump" (Swenson), **Supp. IV Part 2:** 650

"That the Universe Is Chrysalid" (Sobin), **Supp. XVI:** 284

"That Tree" (Porter), **III:** 434–435, 446, 451

That Was the Week That Was (television program), **Supp. XIV:** 125

"That Year" (Olds), **Supp. X:** 203

"Thaw" (C. Frost), **Supp. XV:** 93, 104, 105

Thaxter, Celia, **Retro. Supp. II:** 136, 147; **Supp. XIII:** 143, 153

Thayer, Abbott, **I:** 231

Thayer, Scofield, **I:** 231; **Retro. Supp. I:** 58

Thayer and Eldridge, **Retro. Supp. I:** 403

"Theater" (Toomer), **Supp. IX:** 309, 317–318

"Theater Chronicle" (McCarthy), **II:** 562

"Theater Problems? Call Dr. Chekhov" (Wasserstein), **Supp. XV:** 320

Theatricals (James), **Retro. Supp. I:** 228

The Blacker the Berry: A Novel of Negro Life (Thurman), **Supp. XIX:** 73; **Supp. XVIII:** 281

"Theft" (Porter), **III:** 434, 435

Theft, A (Bellow), **Retro. Supp. II:** 31–32, 34

The Harder They Fall (Schulberg), **Supp. XVIII: 247**, 253

The Harder They Fall: Celebrities Tell Their Real-Life Stories of Addiction and Recovery (F. Wright), **Supp. XVII:** 240

Their Dogs Came with Them (Viramontes), **Supp. XXV:** 130, 138

Their Eyes Were Watching God (Hurston), **Supp. VI:** 149, 152, 156–157; **Supp. XX: 107**

Their Heads Are Green and Their Hands Are Blue: Scenes from the Non-Christian World (Bowles), **Supp. IV Part 1:** 89

"Their Losses" (Taylor), **Supp. V:** 320

"Their Name is Macaroni" (Boyle), **Supp. XXIV:** 61

"Their Sleep" (W. V. Davis), **Supp. XXI:** 93

Their Wedding Journey (Howells), **II:** 277–278; **Retro. Supp. I:** 334

them (Oates), **Supp. II Part 2:** 503, 511–514

Theme Is Freedom, The (Dos Passos), **I:** 488–489, 492, 494

Theme Time Radio Hour (radio show, Dylan), **Supp. XVIII:** 28

"Theme with Variations" (Agee), **I:** 27

"Then" (Barthelme), **Supp. IV Part 1:** 48

"Then as Now" (Cliff), **Supp. XXII:** 76

"The Night Rhonda Ferguson Was Killed" (E. P. Jones), **Supp. XXII:** 144

"Then It All Came Down" (Capote), **Supp. III Part 1:** 125, 131

Theocritus, **II:** 169; **Retro. Supp. I:** 286; **Supp. XXIV:** 156

Theodore Roethke's Far Fields: The Evolution of His Poetry (Balakian), **Supp. XXIII:** 19

"Theodore the Poet" (Masters), **Supp. I Part 2:** 461

Theological Position, A (Coover), **Supp. V:** 44

Theophrastus, **I:** 58

"Theoretical and Scientific Conceptions of Race, The" (Locke), **Supp. XIV:** 209

"Theoretical Subject(s) of *This Bridge Called My Back*, The"(Alarcón), **Supp. XXIII:** 204–205

"Theories of Time and Space" (Trethewey), **Supp. XXI:** 255

"Theory" (Huddle), **Supp. XXVI:** 149

Theory and Practice of Rivers and Other Poems, The (Harrison), **Supp. VIII:** 47, 49

Theory of Business Enterprise, The (Veblen), **Supp. I Part 2:** 638, 641, 644

Theory of Flight (Rukeyser), **Supp. VI:** 272, 275, **277–278**, 284

"Theory of Flight" (Rukeyser), **Supp. VI:** 277–278

Theory of Moral Sentiments, The (A. Smith), **Supp. I Part 2:** 634

Theory of the Leisure Class, The (Veblen), **I:** 475–476; **Supp. I Part 2:** 629, 633, 641, 645; **Supp. IV Part 1:** 22

"There" (Taylor), **Supp. V:** 323

"There Are No Such Trees in Alpine California" (Haines), **Supp. XII:** 207

"There Goes (Varoom! Varoom!) That Kandy-Kolored Tangerine-Flake Streamline Baby" (Wolfe), **Supp. III Part 2:** 569–571

"There Have Been Changes" (Pickering), **Supp. XXI:** 202–203

"There Is a Lesson" (Olsen), **Supp. XIII:** 292, 297

"There is a Man" (Espaillat), **Supp. XXI:** 108–109

"There Is Only One of Everything" (Atwood), **Supp. XIII:** 34

There Is Something Out There (McNally). *See And Things That Go Bump in the Night* (McNally)

"There Must Be" (Peacock), **Supp. XIX:** 199

"There's a certain Slant of light" (Dickinson), **Retro. Supp. I:** 38

There's a Wocket in My Pocket! (Geisel), **Supp. XVI:** 111

Thérèse de Lisieux, Saint, **Supp. VIII:** 195

"There She Is She Is Taking Her Bath" (Anderson), **I:** 113, 114

"There Was a Child Went Forth" (Whitman), **IV:** 348; **Supp. XXVI:** 230

"There Was a Man, There Was a Woman" (Cisneros), **Supp. VII:** 70

"There Was an Old Woman She Had So Many Children She Didn't Know What to Do" (Cisneros), **Supp. VII:** 60

"There Was a Youth Whose Name Was Thomas Granger" (Olson), **Supp. II Part 2:** 558, 560, 563

There Were Giants in the Land (Benét), **Supp. XI:** 50

There You Are (Simpson), **Supp. IX:** 279–280

"There You Are" (Simpson), **Supp. IX:** 279

"Thermopylae" (Clampitt), **Supp. IX:** 43

Theroux, Alexander, **Supp. VIII:** 312

Theroux, Marcel, **Supp. VIII:** 325

Theroux, Paul, **Supp. V:** 122; **Supp. VIII:** 309–327

"These Are My People" (Hayden), **Supp. II Part 1:** 365

These Are My Same Hands (Schott), **Supp. XXIII:** 241, 242

"These are the days when Birds come back" (Dickinson), **Retro. Supp. I:** 30

"These Days" (Davison), **Supp. XXVI:** 79

"These Days" (Olds), **Supp. X:** 215

"These Flames and Generosities of the Heart: Emily Dickinson and the Illogic of Sumptuary Values" (Howe), **Supp. IV Part 2:** 431

"These Hands" (Brockmeier), **Supp. XXII:** 51, 52, 53

These Happy Golden Years (L. I. Wilder), **Supp. XXII:** 294, 297, 299

These Low Grounds (Turpin), **Supp. XVIII:** 283

"These Nerves" (Biss), **Supp. XXVI:** 50–51

"These saw Visions" (Dickinson), **Retro. Supp. I:** 46

These Thirteen (Faulkner), **II:** 72

These Three (film), **Supp. I Part 1:** 281

These Times (Untermeyer), **Supp. XV:** 299–300, 303

"These Times" (Untermeyer), **Supp. XV:** 300

"Thessalonica: A Roman Story" (Brown), **Supp. I Part 1:** 133

Thévenaz, Paul, **Supp. XV:** 42

Thew, Harvey, **Supp. XIII:** 166

"They Ain't the Men They Used To Be" (Farrell), **II:** 45

"They Burned the Books" (Benét), **Supp. XI:** 46

They Came Like Swallows (Maxwell), **Supp. VIII:** 155–159, 168, 169

"They Can't Turn Back" (Baldwin), **Supp. I Part 1:** 52

They Do Not: The Letters of a Non-Professional Lady Arranged for Public Consumption (Clements), **Supp. XVI:** 190

They Feed They Lion (Levine), **Supp. V:** 178, 179, 181, 184–185, 186

"They Feed They Lion" (Levine), **Supp. V:** 188

"They Lion Grow" (Levine), **Supp. V:** 184–185

"They're Not Your Husband" (Carver), **Supp. III Part 1:** 141, 143

They're Playing Our Song (musical), **Supp. IV Part 2:** 589

They Seek a City (Bontemps and Conroy), **Supp. XXII:** 5, 11

They Shall Inherit the Laughter (Jones), **Supp. XI:** 217, 218, 232

"They Shall Not Die" (Ryan as Quin), **Supp. XVIII:** 228–229

They Shoot Horses (film), **Supp. XIII:** 159

They Shoot Horses, Don't They? (McCoy), **Supp. XIII:** 159, **164–166,** 168, 171, 172, 174; **Supp. XXV:** 26

"They Sing, They Sing" (Roethke), **III:** 544

They Stooped to Folly (Glasgow), **II:** 175, 186–187

They Were Expendable (film), **Supp. XVIII:** 247

"They Weren't Going to Die" (Boyle), **Supp. XXIV:** 61

They Whisper (R. O. Butler), **Supp. XII:** 72–73

They Who Knock at Our Gates: A Complete Gospel of Immigration (Antin), **Supp. XX:** 2–3, 10–11, 12

"Thick and Thin"(Hadas), **Supp. XXIII:** 119

Thidwick the Big-Hearted Moose (Geisel), **Supp. XVI:** 104

Thief's Journal, The (Genet), **Supp. XXIV:** 210

"Thief's Philosophy of Life, The" (Hapgood), **Supp. XVII:** 103

"Thief's Wife, The" (B. Kelly), **Supp. XVII:** 125–126

"Thieves" (Yates), **Supp. XI:** 349

Thieves of Paradise (Komunyakaa), **Supp. XIII:** 113, **128–130,** 132

"Thimble, The" (Kenyon), **Supp. VII:** 164

"Thing and Its Relations, The" (James), **II:** 357

"Things" (Haines), **Supp. XII:** 207

"Things" (Kenyon), **Supp. VII:** 169

"Things, The" (Kinnell), **Supp. III Part 1:** 246

Things As They Are (Stein), **IV:** 34, 37, 40

"Things Can Be Named to Death" (Peacock), **Supp. XIX:** 199

"Things Don't Stop" (Nye), **Supp. XIII:** 287

Things Gone and Things Still Here (Bowles), **Supp. IV Part 1:** 91

"Things of August" (Stevens), **Retro. Supp. I:** 309

Things of This World (Wilbur), **Supp. III Part 2:** 552–555

Things That Fall from the Sky (Brockmeier), **Supp. XXII:** 50–53

"Things That Fall from the Sky" (Brockmeier), **Supp. XXII:** 51, 53

Things Themselves: Essays and Scenes (Price), **Supp. VI:** 261

Things They Carried, The (T. O'Brien), **Supp. V:** 238, 239, 240, 243, 248–250; **Supp. XVII:** 14; **Supp. XXI:** 122

"Things to Do in New York City" (Berrigan), **Supp. XXII:** 224

Things We Don't Understand and Definitely Are Not Going to Talk About (performance piece, July), **Supp. XXIV:** 200

"Thing That Killed My Father Off, The" (Carver), **Supp. III Part 1:** 143

Thingy World!: or, How We Got to Where We Are: A Satire in One Act (Budbill), **Supp. XIX:** 13–14

"Think about It" (Conroy), **Supp. XVI:** 75

Think Back on Us . . . (Cowley), **Supp. II Part 1:** 139, 140, 142

Think Fast, Mr. Moto (Marquand), **III:** 57, 58

"Thinking about Barbara Deming" (Paley), **Supp. VI:** 227

"Thinking about Being Called Simple by a Critic" (Stafford), **Supp. XI:** 328

Thinking about the Longstanding Problems of Virtue and Happiness: Essays, a Play, Two Poems, and a Prayer (Kushner), **Supp. IX:** 131, 134, 135

"Thinking about the Past" (Justice), **Supp. VII:** 123–124

"Thinking about Western Thinking" (Didion), **Supp. IV Part 1:** 204, 206

"'Thinking against Oneself': Reflections on Cioran" (Sontag), **Supp. III Part 2:** 459–460

"Thinking Back Through Our Mothers: Traditions in Canadian Women's Writing" (Shields), **Supp. VII:** 307–308

"Thinking for Berky" (Stafford), **Supp. XI:** 320

"Thinking in Subversion" (Gansworth), **Supp. XXVI:** 114

"Thinking like a Mountain" (Leopold), **Supp. XIV:** 188, 189

"Thinking of the Lost World" (Jarrell), **II:** 338–389

Thinking Out Loud (Quindlen), **Supp. XVII:** 167, **169–170**

Thin Man, The (film), **Supp. IV Part 1:** 342, 355

Thin Man, The (Hammett), **Supp. IV Part 1:** 354–355

"Thinnest Shadow, The" (Ashbery), **Supp. III Part 1:** 5

"Thin People, The" (Plath), **Supp. I Part 2:** 538, 547

Thin Red Line, The (film; Malick), **Supp. V:** 249; **Supp. XV:** 351

Thin Red Line, The (Jones), **Supp. XI:** 219, **224–225,** 229, 231, 232, 233, 234

"Thin Strips" (Sandburg), **III:** 587

"Third and Final Continent, The" (Lahiri), **Supp. XXI:** 178–180

"Third Avenue in Sunlight" (Hecht), **Supp. X:** 61

"Third Body, A" (R. Bly), **Supp. IV Part 1:** 71

Third Circle, The (Norris), **III:** 327

"Third Expedition, The" (Bradbury), **Supp. IV Part 1:** 103, 106

Third Generation, The (C. Himes), **Supp. XVI:** 135, **140–141**

Third Life of Grange Copeland, The (Walker), **Supp. III Part 2:** 520, 527–536

Third Mind, The (Burroughs), **Supp. XII:** 3

"Third Myth, The" (Muñoz), **Supp. XXV:** 134

Third Rose, The (Brinnin), **IV:** 26

"Third Sermon on the Warpland, The" (Brooks), **Supp. III Part 1:** 85

"Third Thing That Killed My Father Off, The" (Carver), **Supp. III Part 1:** 144

Third Violet, The (Crane), **I:** 408, 417–418

Thirlwall, John C., **Retro. Supp. I:** 430

"Thirst: Introduction to Kinds of Water" (Carson), **Supp. XII: 103**

"13, 1977, 21" (Lethem), **Supp. XVIII:** 148

13 by Shanley (Shanley), **Supp. XIV:** 316

13 Seconds: A Look Back at the Kent State Shootings (Caputo), **Supp. XIX:** 29

Thirteen Hands: A Play in Two Acts (Shields), **Supp. VII:** 322–323

Thirteen O'Clock (Benét), **Supp. XI:** 46

Thirteen Other Stories (Purdy), **Supp. VII:** 278

Thirteen Stories and Thirteen Epitaphs (Vollmann), **Supp. XVII:** 226

"Thirteenth and Pennsylvania" (Stafford), **Supp. XI:** 324

Thirteenth Month, The (Pedersen; Nelson, trans.), **Supp. XVIII:** 179–180

"Thirteen Ways of Looking at a Black-bird" (Stevens), **IV:** 94; **Supp. IX:** 47; **Supp. XVII:** 130; **Supp. XXIII:** 253

"Thirteen Ways of Looking at a Black-bird" (W. Stevens), **Supp. XI:** 328

Thirteen Ways of Looking at a Black Man (H. L. Gates), **Supp. XX:** 102, 110

30/6 (poetry chapbook), **Supp. V:** 5, 6

"30. Meditation. 2. Cor. 5.17. He Is a New Creature" (Taylor), **IV:** 144

30: Pieces of a Novel (Dixon), **Supp. XII:** 152, **153–154**

"Thirty Bob a Week" (Davidson), **Retro. Supp. I:** 55

"Thirty Delft Tiles" (Doty), **Supp. XI:** 131

"35/10" (Olds), **Supp. X:** 206

"35,000 Feet—The Lanterns" (Goldbarth), **Supp. XII:** 182

31 Letters and 13 Dreams (Hugo), **Supp. VI:** 141–144

Thirty Poems (Bryant), **Supp. I Part 1:** 157, 158

Thirty-Six Poems (Warren), **IV:** 236, 239, 240

"33" (Alvarez), **Supp. VII:** 4

"3275" (Monette), **Supp. X:** 148, 159

Thirty Years (Marquand), **III:** 56, 60–61

Thirty Years of Treason (Bentley), **Supp. I Part 1:** 297

This, My Letter (Hay), **Supp. XIV:** 121, 122, 129, 131

"This, That & the Other" (Nemerov), **III:** 269

This Body Is Made of Camphor and Go-pherwood (R. Bly), **Supp. IV Part 1:** 63–65, 66, 71; **Supp. XXI:** 85

This Boy's Life: A Memoir (T. Wolff), **Supp. VII:** 334–339, 340, 343; **Supp. XI:** 246, 247; **Supp. XXV:** 208

This Bridge Called My Back: Writings by Radical Women of Color (Moraga and Anzaldúa, eds.), **Supp. XXIII:** 193, 194, 196, **204–205**

"This Bright Dream" (Benét), **Supp. XI:** 55

This Coffin Has No Handles (McGrath), **Supp. X:** 117

"This Configuration" (Ashbery), **Supp. III Part 1:** 22

"This Corruptible" (Wylie), **Supp. I Part 2:** 727, 729

"This Crazy Wickedness, Little Nests of Light" (Notley), **Supp. XXII:** 228

"This Crutch That I Love" (Nye), **Supp. XIII:** 288

"This Gentile World" (H. Miller), **III:** 177

"This Hand" (Wylie), **Supp. I Part 2:** 713

"This Hour" (Olds), **Supp. X:** 212

"This House I Cannot Leave" (Kingsolver), **Supp. VII:** 208

This Hunger (Nin), **Supp. X:** 185

This in Which (Oppen), **Supp. XXVI:** 225, 230, 232–233, 234

"This Is a Photograph of Me" (Atwood), **Supp. XIII:** 33

"This Is a Poem, Good Afternoon" (Keillor), **Supp. XVI:** 167

This Is How You Lose Her (Díaz), **Supp. XXIV:** 83, 84, 86, 88, **92–93**

"This Is It" (Stern), **Supp. IX:** 290

"This Is Just to Say" (W. C. Williams), **Supp. XX:** 328

This Is My God: The Jewish Way of Life (Wouk), **Supp. XXV:** 253, 255–256, 263, 268

"This Is My Heart" (Harjo), **Supp. XII:** 230

This Is Not a Novel (Markson), **Supp. XVII:** 145–146

"This Is Not Who We Are" (Nye), **Supp. XIII:** 285, 286

This Is Our Time: Secular Cantata No. 1, Mixed Voice Chorus and Orchestra (Taggard, Schuman and Weissleder), **Supp. XXII:** 283

"This Is Us, Excellent" (Richard), **Supp. XIX:** 212

"This Is What I Said" (Salinas), **Supp. XIII:** 322

This Journey (Wright), **Supp. III Part 2:** 605–606

"This Lime-Tree Bower My Prison" (Coleridge), **Supp. XXI:** 52, 55

This Man and This Woman (Farrell), **II:** 42

"This Monkey, My Back" (Boyle), **Supp. XX:** 17

"This Morning" (Huddle), **Supp. XXVI:** 151

"This Morning" (Kenyon), **Supp. VII:** 164

"This Morning, This Evening, So Soon" (Baldwin), **Supp. I Part 1:** 63

"This Morning Again It Was in the Dusty Pines" (Oliver), **Supp. VII:** 240

This Music Crept by Me upon the Waters (MacLeish), **III:** 21

"This New England: Newport, Vermont" (Mosher), **Supp. XXII:** 209

This Old House (J. Davison), **Supp. XXVI:** 65

This People Israel: The Meaning of Jewish Existence (Baeck), **Supp. V:** 260

"This Person" (July), **Supp. XXIV:** 202

"This Personal Maze Is Not the Prize" (Selinger), **Supp. XI:** 248

"This Place in the Ways" (Rukeyser), **Supp. VI:** 273–274

This Property Is Condemned (T. Williams), **IV:** 378

This Proud Heart (Buck), **Supp. II Part 1:** 119–120

This Same Sky: A Collection of Poems from around the World (Nye, ed.), **Supp. XIII:** 280

"This Sandwich Has No Mayonnaise" (Salinger), **III:** 552–553

This Shape We're In (Lethem), **Supp. XVIII:** 145

"This Shape We're In" (Lethem), **Supp. XVIII:** 148

This Side of Paradise (Fitzgerald), **I:** 358; **II:** 77, 80, 81, 82–83, 84, 85–87, 88; **Retro. Supp. I:** 99–100, **101–102**, 103, 105, 106, 110, 111; **Supp. XVIII:** 248

This Singing World: An Anthology of Modern Poetry for Young People (Untermeyer, ed.), **Supp. XV:** 306

This Strange Joy: Selected Poems of Sandro Penna (Di Perio, trans.), **Supp. XIX:** 34

This Stubborn Self: Texas Autobiographies (Almon), **Supp. XIII:** 288

"This They Took with Them" (Boyle), **Supp. XXIV:** 61

This Thing Don't Lead to Heaven (Crews), **Supp. XI: 112**

This Time: New and Selected Poems (Stern), **Supp. IX:** 290–291, **299**

"Thistle Seed in the Wind" (Francis), **Supp. IX:** 81

"Thistles in Sweden, The" (Maxwell), **Supp. VIII:** 169

"This Tokyo" (Snyder), **Supp. VIII:** 298

This Tree Will Be Here for a Thousand Years (R. Bly), **Supp. IV Part 1:** 65–66, 71, 72

This Tree Will Be Here for a Thousand Years (revised edition) (R. Bly), **Supp. IV Part 1:** 66

This Very Earth (Caldwell), **I:** 297, 302

This Waiting for Love (Mitchell, ed.), **Supp. XXVI:** 165, 173

This Wheel's on Fire: Levon Helm and the Story of the Band (Helm), **Supp. XVIII:** 26

This Woman (di Donato), **Supp. XX:** 33, **41–42, 46**

Thoens, Karen, **Supp. V:** 147

Thomas, Brandon, **II:** 138

Thomas, Dave, **Supp. XXVI:** 18

Thomas, Debra, **Supp. XIII:** 114

Thomas, D. M., **Supp. VIII:** 5

Thomas, Dylan, **I:** 49, 64, 382, 432, 526, 533; **III:** 21, 521, 528, 532, 534; **IV:** 89, 93, 136; **Supp. I Part 1:** 263; **Supp. III Part 1:** 42, 47; **Supp. IX:** 114; **Supp. V:** 344; **Supp. VIII:** 21; **Supp. X:** 115; **Supp. XV:** 74; **Supp. XVII:** 135; **Supp. XX:** 199, 204; **Supp. XXIV:** 54

Thomas, Edna Lewis, **Supp. XVIII:** 281

Thomas, Edward, **II:** 154; **Retro. Supp. I:** 127, 131, 132; **Supp. I Part 1:** 263; **Supp. II Part 1:** 4

Thomas, Jacob ("Jake"), **Supp. XXVI:** 83

Thomas, James, **Supp. XVI:** 268

Thomas, Joseph, **Supp. XVIII:** 183

Thomas, J. Parnell, **Supp. I Part 1:** 286; **Supp. XV:** 198

Thomas, June, **Supp. XXV:** 2, 3

Thomas, Lewis, **Retro. Supp. I:** 323

Thomas, Lorenzo, **Supp. XXIV:** 37

Thomas, Louisa, **Supp. XXIII:** 280, 283

Thomas, Rob, **Supp. XVIII:** 100, 101

Thomas, R. S., **Supp. XXI:** 83, 86–87, 93, 95, 96

Thomas, William I., **Supp. I Part 2:** 641

Thomas-a-Kempis, **Retro. Supp. I:** 247

Thomas and Beulah (Dove), **Supp. IV Part 1:** 242, 247–248, 249; **Supp. XVIII:** 174; **Supp. XXI:** 249

Thomas Aquinas (Saint), **I:** 13, 14, 265, 267; **III:** 270; **Retro. Supp. II:** 222; **Supp. IV Part 2:** 526

"Thomas at the Wheel" (Dove), **Supp. IV Part 1:** 248

"Thomas Eakins and the Photograph of a Man in Motion" (Major), **Supp. XXII:** 183

"Thomas Eakins' Delaware River Paintings" (Major), **Supp. XXII:** 183

"Thomas McGrath: Words for a Vanished Age" (Vinz), **Supp. X:** 117

Thomas Merton on Peace, **Supp. VIII:** 208

Thomas Merton Studies Center, The, **Supp. VIII:** 208

Thompson, Barbara, **Supp. V:** 322

Thompson, Caroline, **Supp. XXIII:** 291

Thompson, Cy, **I:** 538

Thompson, Daniel, **Supp. XXIII:** 174

Thompson, Dorothy, **II:** 449–450, 451, 453; **Supp. XV:** 307

Thompson, Edward, **Supp. XXI:** 172

Thompson, E. P., **Supp. X:** 112, 117

Thompson, Francis, **Retro. Supp. I:** 55

Thompson, Frank, **II:** 20

Thompson, George, **Supp. I Part 2:** 686; **Supp. XXIII:** 182

Thompson, Hunter S., **Supp. VIII:** 42; **Supp. XI:** 105; **Supp. XIII:** 1, 17; **Supp. XVII:** 95, 102, 228; **Supp. XXIV:** 279–294

Thompson, James R., **Supp. IV Part 1:** 217

Thompson, Jean, **Supp. XXIII: 289–305**

Thompson, John, **Supp. V:** 323; **Supp. XXI:** 151

Thompson, Juliet, **Supp. XX: 117**

Thompson, Lawrance, **II:** 508

Thompson, Lawrance Roger, **Retro. Supp. I:** 138, 141

Thompson, Lisa B., **Supp. XXIII:** 202

Thompson, Morton, **Supp. XIII:** 170

Thompson, Theresa, **Supp. V:** 141

Thompson, William T., **Supp. I Part 2:** 411

Thomson, James, **II:** 304; **Supp. I Part 1:** 150, 151; **Supp. XXIV:** 159

Thomson, Virgil, **IV:** 45; **Supp. IV Part 1:** 81, 83, 84, 173; **Supp. XVI:** 195

"Thoreau" (Lowell), **Supp. I Part 2:** 420, 422

Thoreau, Henry David, **I:** 98, 104, 228, 236, 257, 258, 261, 305, 433; **II:** 7, 8, 13, 17, 101, 159, 224, 273–274, 295, 312–313, 321, 457–458, 540, 546–547; **III:** 171, 174, 186–187, 189, 208, 214–215, 453, 454, 507, 577; **IV:** 167–189, 191, 341; **Retro. Supp. I:** 51, 62, 122; **Retro. Supp. II:** 13, 96, 142, 158; **Supp. I Part 1:** 29, 34, 116, 188, 299, 358; **Supp. I Part 2:** 383, 400, 420, 421, 507, 540, 579, 580, 655, 659, 660, 664, 678; **Supp. III Part 1:** 340, 353; **Supp. IV Part 1:** 236, 392, 416; **Supp. IV Part 2:** 420, 430, 433, 439, 447; **Supp. IX:** 25, 90, 171; **Supp. V:** 200, 208; **Supp. VIII:** 40, 42, 103, 105, 198, 201, 204, 205, 292, 303; **Supp. X:** 21, 27, 28–29, 101, 102; **Supp. XII:** 155; **Supp. XIII:** 1, 17; **Supp. XIV:** 40, 54, 106, 177, 181; **Supp. XVIII:** 4; **Supp. XX: 116, 221; Supp. XXI:** 203, 217; **Supp. XXII:** 206; **Supp. XXIII:** 174; **Supp. XXVI:** 31, 34, 37

Thoreau, John, **IV:** 171, 182

Thoreau, Mrs. John, **IV:** 172

"Thoreau's Hound: On Hiddenness" (Hirshfield), **Supp. XXIII:** 137

"Thorn, The" (Gordon), **Supp. IV Part 1:** 314

Thorne, Francis, **Supp. XII:** 253

"Thorn Merchant, The" (Komunyakaa), **Supp. XIII:** 119–120

Thornton, Billy Bob, **Supp. VIII:** 175

Thornton, Lionel, **III:** 291

"Thorofare" (Minot), **Supp. VI: 209–210**

"Thorow" (Howe), **Supp. IV Part 2:** 419, 420, 421, 431, 433–434

Thorp, Willard, **Supp. XIII:** 101

Thorslev, Peter L., Jr., **I:** 524

Thorstein Veblen (Dowd), **Supp. I Part 2:** 650

Thorstein Veblen (Qualey, ed.), **Supp. I Part 2:** 650

Thorstein Veblen: A Chapter in American Economic Thought (Teggart), **Supp. I Part 2:** 650

Thorstein Veblen: A Critical Interpretation (Riesman), **Supp. I Part 2:** 649, 650

Thorstein Veblen: A Critical Reappraisal (Dowd, ed.), **Supp. I Part 2:** 650

Thorstein Veblen and His America (Dorfman), **Supp. I Part 2:** 631, 650

Thorstein Veblen and the Institutionalists: A Study in the Social Philosophy of Economics (Seckler), **Supp. I Part 2:** 650

"Those before Us" (Lowell), **II:** 550

"Those Being Eaten by America" (R. Bly), **Supp. IV Part 1:** 62

Those Bones Are Not My Child (Bambara), **Supp. XI:** 1, 14, 20–22

Those Extraordinary Twins (Twain), **IV:** 205–206

"Those Graves in Rome" (Levis), **Supp. XI:** 266

"Those of Us Who Think We Know" (Dunn), **Supp. XI:** 146

Those That Be in Bondage (Webber), **Supp. XXI:** 160

"Those Times . . ." (Sexton), **Supp. II Part 2:** 670, 684

"Those Various Scalpels" (Moore), **III:** 202

"Those Were the Days" (Levine), **Supp. V:** 190

"Those Who Don't" (Cisneros), **Supp. VII:** 60

"Those Who Thunder" (Hogan), **Supp. IV Part 1:** 406

"Thought, A" (Sarton), **Supp. VIII:** 262

Thought and Character of William James (Perry), **II:** 362

Thoughtbook of Francis Scott Key Fitzgerald (Fitzgerald), **Retro. Supp. I:** 99

"Thought Experiment" (Saunders), **Supp. XIX:** 235

"Thoughtful Roisterer Declines the Gambit, The" (Hecht), **Supp. X:** 63

"Thought of Heaven, The" (Stern), **Supp. IX:** 297

"Thoughts after Lambeth" (Eliot), **I:** 587; **Retro. Supp. I:** 324

Thoughts and Reflections (Lord Halifax), **II:** 111

Thoughts in Solitude (Merton), **Supp. VIII:** 207

"Thoughts on Being Bibliographed" (Wilson), **IV:** 435

"Thoughts on the Establishment of a Mint in the United States" (Paine), **Supp. I Part 2:** 512

"Thoughts on the Gifts of Art" (Kenyon), **Supp. VII:** 167

Thousand Acres, A (Smiley), **Supp. VI:** 292, 301–303

"Thousand and Second Night, The" (Merrill), **Supp. III Part 1:** 324

"Thousand Dollar Vagrant, The" (Olsen), **Supp. XIII:** 292, 297

"Thousand Faces of Danny Torrance, The" (Figliola), **Supp. V:** 143

"Thousand Genuflections, A" (McCarriston), **Supp. XIV:** 266

Thousand-Mile Walk to the Gulf, A (Muir), **Supp. IX: 177–178**

Thousand Plateaus, A (Deleuze and Guattari), **Supp. XXV:** 123

"Thou Shalt Not Steal" (McClatchy), **Supp. XII:** 264

"Thread, The" (Merwin), **Supp. III Part 1:** 351

Three (film), **Supp. IX:** 253

3-3-8 (Marquand), **III:** 58

"3 A.M. Kitchen: My Father Talking" (Gallagher), **Supp. XXIV:** 169

"Three Academic Pieces" (Stevens), **IV:** 90

"Three Agee Wards, The" (Morris), **III:** 220–221

"Three American Singers" (Cather), **Retro. Supp. I:** 10

"Three Around the Old Gentleman" (Berryman), **I:** 188

"Three Avilas, The" (Jeffers), **Supp. II Part 2:** 418

"Three Black Women Writers" (C. L. R. James), **Supp. XXI:** 172

Three Books of Song (Longfellow), **II:** 490

"Three Bushes" (Yeats), **Supp. I Part 1:** 80

Three Cantos (Pound), **Retro. Supp. I:** 290

Three Centuries of Harvard (Morison), **Supp. I Part 2:** 485

Three Changes (Silver), **Supp. XXIV:** 275

Three Circles of Light (di Donato), **Supp. XX:** 33, 42–43, 44, 46

Three Cities: A Trilogy (Asch), **Supp. XXIII:** 1, 5, **10–12**

Three Comrades (Remarque), **Retro. Supp. I:** 113

"Three Corollaries of Cultural Relativism" (Locke), **Supp. XIV:** 202

"Three-Day Blow, The" (Hemingway), **II:** 248

Three Essays on America (Brooks), **I:** 246

Three Farmers on Their Way to a Dance (Powers), **Supp. IX:** 211–212, **213–214,** 222

"Three Fates, The" (Benét), **Supp. XI:** 48–49, 50

"Three Generations of Secrets" (A. Finch), **Supp. XVII:** 73

"Three Gifts, The" (Gibran), **Supp. XX: 124**

Three Gospels (Price), **Supp. VI:** 267

365 Days (Boyle), **Supp. XXIV:** 50, 60

"Three Kings, The: Hemingway, Faulkner, and Fitzgerald" (Ford), **Supp. V:** 59

Three Lives (Auchincloss), **Supp. IV Part 1:** 25

Three Lives (Stein), **I:** 103; **IV:** 26, 27, 31, 35, 37–41, 42, 45, 46; **Supp. IX:** 306; **Supp. XXIII:** 166

"THREE MOVEMENTS AND A CODA" (Baraka), **Supp. II Part 1:** 50

Three One Act Plays (Riverside Drive, Old Saybrook, and *Central Park West)* (Allen), **Supp. XV:** 3

Three on the Tower: The Lives and Works of Ezra Pound, T. S. Eliot, and William Carlos Williams (Simpson), **Supp. IX:** 276

Three Papers on Fiction (Welty), **IV:** 261

Three-Penny Opera (Brecht), **I:** 301; **Supp. XIV:** 162

"Three Percent Own All the Wealth" (Ryan as Quin), **Supp. XVIII:** 231–232

Three Philosophical Poets (Santayana), **III:** 610–612

"Three Pigs in Five Days" (Prose), **Supp. XVI:** 257, 258

"Three Players of a Summer Game" (T. Williams), **IV:** 383

Three Poems (Ashbery), **Supp. III Part 1:** 2, 3, 14, 15, 18, 24–26

"Three Poems for my Daughter" (Di Piero), **Supp. XIX:** 40

"Three Pokes of a Thistle" (Nye), **Supp. XIII:** 281

Three Prophets of Religious Liberalism (Wright), **Supp. XXIV:** 71

Three Roads, The (Macdonald, under Millar), **Supp. IV Part 2:** 466, 467

Three Short Plays with Long Titles (Silver and Ann), **Supp. XXIV:** 264

"Three Silences of Molinos, The" (Longfellow), **Retro. Supp. II:** 169

Three Sisters, The (Chekhov), **Supp. XV:** 323

"Three Sisters, The" (Cisneros), **Supp. VII:** 64

Three Soldiers (Dos Passos), **I:** 477–478, 480, 482, 488, 493–494; **Supp. XXI:** 277

"Three Songs at the End of Summer" (Kenyon), **Supp. VII:** 169–170

"Three Steps to the Graveyard" (Wright), **Supp. III Part 2:** 593, 596

Three Stories and Ten Poems (Hemingway), **II:** 68, 263; **Supp. XVII:** 105

Three Tall Women (Albee), **Supp. XXIV:** 270

Three Taverns, The (Robinson), **III:** 510

"Three Taverns, The" (Robinson), **III:** 521, 522

Three Tenant Families (Agee), **I:** 37–38

Three Tenors, One Vehicle: A Book of Songs (X. J. Kennedy, Camp, and Waldrop), **Supp. XV:** 165

"Three Types of Poetry" (Tate), **IV:** 131

"Three Vagabonds of Trinidad" (Harte), **Supp. II Part 1:** 338

"Three Waterfalls, The" (Lanier), **Supp. I Part 1:** 350

"Three-Way Mirror" (Brooks), **Supp. III Part 1:** 69–70

Three Weeks in Spring (Parker and Parker), **Supp. XIX:** 187

"Three Women" (Plath), **Supp. I Part 2:** 539, 541, 544, 545, 546

Three Young Poets (Swallow, ed.), **Supp. X:** 116

Threnody (Emerson), **Supp. I Part 2:** 416

"Threnody" (Emerson), **II:** 7

"Threnody for a Brown Girl" (Cullen), **Supp. IV Part 1:** 166

"Threshing-Floor, The" (Baldwin), **Supp. I Part 1:** 50

"Threshing Wheat" (Huddle), **Supp. XXVI:** 148

Threshold (film), **Supp. IX:** 254

"Threshold" (Goldbarth), **Supp. XII:** 175

Threshold (Jackson), **Supp. IX:** 117

"Throat" (Goldbarth), **Supp. XII:** 177–178

Throne of Labdacus, The (Schnackenberg), **Supp. XV:** 260, **263–266**

Thrones (Pound), **Retro. Supp. I:** 293

Through Dooms of Love (Kumin), **Supp. IV Part 2:** 444

Through Glacier Park in 1915 (Rinehart), **Supp. XXV:** 195

"Through the Black Curtain" (Kingston), **Supp. V:** 169

Through the Forest: New and Selected Poems, 1977–1987 (Wagoner), **Supp. IX: 330–331**

"Through the Gates of the Silver Key" (Lovecraft and Price), **Supp. XXV:** 114, 123

"Through the Hills of Spain" (Salinas), **Supp. XIII:** 315

"Through the Hole in the Mundane Millstone" (West), **Retro. Supp. II:** 321, 322

Through the Ivory Gate (Dove), **Supp. IV Part 1:** 242, 243, 251, 252, 253–254, 254

"Through the Kitchen Window, Chiapas" (Nye), **Supp. XIII:** 277

Through the Safety Net (C. Baxter), **Supp. XVII:** 17, 22

"Through the Smoke Hole" (Snyder), **Supp. VIII:** 299

Throw Like a Girl (Thompson), **Supp. XXIII: 299–300**

"Throw Like a Girl"(Thompson), **Supp. XXIII:** 299, 300

"Thrush Relinquished, The" (Grossman), **Supp. XIX:** 83

Thucydides, **II:** 418; **IV:** 50; **Supp. I Part 2:** 488, 489, 492; **Supp. IV Part 1:** 391; **Supp. XIII:** 233

Thunderbolt and Lightfoot (film), **Supp. X:** 126

"Thunder from a Cloudless Sky" (Mosher), **Supp. XXII:** 209

"Thunderhead" (MacLeish), **III:** 19

Thurber, James, **I:** 487; **II:** 432; **IV:** 396; **Supp. I Part 2: 602–627,** 653, 654, 668, 672, 673, 679; **Supp. II Part 1:** 143; **Supp. IV Part 1:** 349; **Supp. IX:** 118; **Supp. XIV:** 104; **Supp. XVI:** 167; **Supp. XVII:** 4

Thurber, Mrs. James (Althea Adams), **Supp. I Part 2:** 613, 615, 617

Thurber, Mrs. James (Helen Muriel Wismer), **Supp. I Part 2:** 613, 617, 618

Thurber, Robert, **Supp. I Part 2:** 613, 617

Thurber, Rosemary, **Supp. I Part 2:** 616

Thurber, William, **Supp. I Part 2:** 602

Thurber Album, The (Thurber), **Supp. I Part 2:** 611, 619

Thurber Carnival, The (Thurber), **Supp. I Part 2:** 620; **Supp. XIV:** 104

Thurman, Judith, **Supp. IV Part 1:** 309; **Supp. XXV:** 2

Thurman, Wallace, **Retro. Supp. I:** 200; **Supp. I Part 1:** 325, 326, 328, 332; **Supp. IV Part 1:** 164; **Supp. X:** 136,

139; **Supp. XIX:** 78; **Supp. XVI:** 135; **Supp. XVIII:** 279, 281; **Supp. XXII:** 2

"Thursday" (Millay), **III:** 129

"Thurso's Landing" (Jeffers), **Supp. II Part 2:** 433

"Thus Do I Refute Gioia" (Junker), **Supp. XV:** 116

"Thus Far by Faith" (Nelson), **Supp. XVIII:** 177

Thus Spake Zarathustra (Nietzsche), **II:** 463; **Supp. IV Part 1:** 110; **Supp. IV Part 2:** 519

Thwaite, Lady Alicia. *See* Rawlings, Marjorie Kinnan

"Thyme" (Stallings), **Supp. XXV:** 232–233

Thy Neighbor's Wife (Talese), **Supp. XVII:** 204, 205–206, 207, 208, 210

"Tiara" (Doty), **Supp. XI:** 122

"Tibetan Time" (Prose), **Supp. XVI:** 255

Ticket for a Seamstitch, A (Harris), **II:** 424–425

Tickets for a Prayer Wheel (Dillard), **Supp. VI:** 22, 34

Ticket That Exploded, The (Burroughs), **Supp. III Part 1:** 93, 103, 104

Tickless Time (Glaspell), **Supp. III Part 1:** 179

Ticknor, George, **II:** 488; **Supp. I Part 1:** 313

Ticknor, William, **Supp. XVIII:** 258

"Ti Démon" (Chopin), **Supp. I Part 1:** 225

Tide of Time, The (Masters), **Supp. I Part 2:** 471

"Tide of Voices" (Hull), **Supp. XXI:** 132, 133–134, 136

"Tide Rises, the Tide Falls, The" (Longfellow), **I:** 498

"Tides" (Hoffman), **Supp. XVIII:** 86

Tidewater Blood (Hoffman), **Supp. XVIII:** 82–83

Tidyman, Ernest, **Supp. V:** 226

Tietjens, Eunice, **Supp. XV:** 47, 297

"Tiger" (Blake), **Supp. I Part 1:** 80; **Supp. VIII:** 26

Tiger (Bynner), **Supp. XV:** 42, 50

"Tiger, The" (Buechner), **Supp. XII:** 48

Tiger in the House, The (Van Vechten), **Supp. II Part 2:** 736

Tiger Joy (Benét), **Supp. XI:** 45

Tiger-Lilies (Lanier), **Supp. I Part 1:** 350–351, 357, 360, 371

Tiger Who Wore White Gloves, The: or, What You Are, You Are (Brooks), **Supp. III Part 1:** 86

Till, Emmett, **Supp. I Part 1:** 61

Till, Eric, **Supp. XXIII:** 103

Tillich, Paul, **II:** 244; **III:** 291, 292, 303, 309; **IV:** 226; **Retro. Supp. I:** 325, 326, 327; **Supp. V:** 267; **Supp. XIII:** 74, 91

Tillie Olsen: A Study of the Short Fiction (Frye), **Supp. XIII:** 292, 296, 298, 299, 302

Tillman, Lynne, **Supp. XII:** 4

Tillotson, John, **II:** 114

Tillotson, Kristen, **Supp. XVII:** 23

Tillstrom, Burr, **Supp. XIV:** 125

Till the Day I Die (Odets), **Supp. II Part 2:** 530, 533–536, 552

Tilton, Eleanor, **Supp. I Part 1:** 317

Tilton, Theodore, **Supp. XVIII:** 4

Timaeus (Plato), **II:** 10; **III:** 609

Tim: A Story of School Life (Sturgis), **Supp. XX: 227, 230, 232, 233–235**

Timber (Jonson), **II:** 16

Timberg, Scott, **Supp. XV:** 116

"Timberwolf" (Halliday), **Supp. XIX:** 91

Timbuktu (Auster), **Supp. XII:** 34, **35–36**

"Time" (Matthews), **Supp. IX: 165–166**

"Time" (Merrill), **Supp. III Part 1:** 325

"Time" (Very), **Supp. XXV:** 249

"Time and Again" (Sanders), **Supp. XVI:** 269

Time and a Place, A (Humphrey), **Supp. IX:** 95, 98, **100–102**

"Time and Distance Overcome" (Biss), **Supp. XXVI:** 55–56

"Time and the Garden" (Winters), **Supp. II Part 2:** 801, 809

"Time and the Liturgy" (Merton), **Supp. VIII:** 199

Time and the River (Edgell), **Supp. XXIII:** 84, 85, **91–93**

Time and Tide: A Walk through Nantucket (Conroy), **Supp. XVI:** 63, 71, **76–77**

"Time Exposure" (C. Baxter), **Supp. XVII:** 20–21

Time Exposures, by Search-Light (W. Frank), **Supp. XX:** 75

Time in the Rock (Aiken), **I:** 65

Time Is Noon, The (Buck), **Supp. II Part 1:** 129, 130–131

Time & Money (Matthews), **Supp. IX:** 155, **165–167**

"Time of Friendship, The" (Bowles), **Supp. IV Part 1:** 90–91

"Time of Her Time, The" (Mailer), **III:** 37, 45; **Retro. Supp. II:** 200

Time of Our Time, The (Mailer), **Retro. Supp. II:** 213–214

Time of the Assassins, The: A Study of Rimbaud (H. Miller), **III:** 189

"Time of the Missile" (Oppen), **Supp. XXVI:** 232

Time Out of Mind (album, Dylan), **Supp. XVIII:** 28

"Time Past" (Morris), **III:** 232

"Time Present" (Morris), **III:** 232

"Times" (Beattie), **Supp. V:** 31

"Times, The" (Emerson), **II:** 11–12

Times Are Never So Bad, The (Dubus), **Supp. VII:** 87–88

Time's Arrow (Amis), **Retro. Supp. I:** 278

"Time Shall Not Die" (Chandler), **Supp. IV Part 1:** 120

Times of Melville and Whitman, The (Brooks), **I:** 257

Times They Are A-Changin', The (album, Dylan), **Supp. XVIII:** 20, 25

"Times They Are A-Changin,' The" (song, Dylan), **Supp. XVIII:** 30

"Timesweep" (Sandburg), **III:** 595–596

Time to Act, A (MacLeish), **III:** 3

Time to Be Born, A (Powell), **Supp. XIX:** 143

Time to Go (Dixon), **Supp. XII:** 147

Time to Kill (film), **Supp. IV Part 1:** 130

Time to Speak, A (MacLeish), **III:** 3

Time Will Darken It (Maxwell), **Supp. VIII:** 159, **162–164,** 169

"Timing of Sin, The" (Dubus), **Supp. VII:** 91

Tim O'Brien (Herzog), **Supp. V:** 239

Timoleon (Melville), **III:** 93; **Retro. Supp. I:** 257

Timothy Dexter Revisited (Marquand), **III:** 55, 62, 63

Timothy Findley: Stories from a Life (Roberts), **Supp. XX:** 53

Timrod, Henry, **Supp. XVIII:** 31, 33

Tin Can, The (W. J. Smith), **Supp. XIII:** 334, **Supp. XIII:** 336, 337

"Tin Can, The" (W. J. Smith), **Supp. XIII: 337–339**

Tin Can Tree, The (Tyler), **Supp. IV Part 2:** 659–660

Tinguely, Jean, **Supp. XV:** 187

Tinker, Chauncey Brewster, **Supp. XIV:** 12

"Tinseled Bucks: A Historical Study of Indian Homosexuality"(Kenny), **Supp. XXIII:** 149

Tintern Abbey (Wordsworth), **Supp. I Part 2:** 673, 675

Tiny Alice (Albee), **I:** 81–86, 87, 88, 94

"Tiny Closet, The" (Inge), **Supp. XXV:** 105–106

"Tiny Mummies! The True Story of the Ruler of 43rd Street's Land of the Walking Dead" (Wolfe), **Supp. III Part 2:** 573, 574

Tip on a Dead Jockey and Other Stories (Shaw), **Supp. XIX:** 251

"Tip-Top Club, The" (Keillor), **Supp. XVI:** 172

"Tired" (Hughes), **Supp. I Part 1:** 331

"Tired and Unhappy, You Think of Houses" (Schwartz), **Supp. II Part 2:** 649

"Tiresias" (Garrett), **Supp. VII:** 96–97

'Tis (McCourt), **Supp. XII:** 271, **279–286**

Tisch (Dixon), **Supp. XII:** 141, **155–156**

" 'Tis Finished" (Very), **Supp. XXV:** 249

Tish (Rinehart), **Supp. XXV:** 194

Tish Marches On (Rinehart), **Supp. XXV:** 194

Tish Plays the Game (Rinehart), **Supp. XXV:** 194

Titan, The (Dreiser), **I:** 497, 501, 507–508, 509, 510; **Retro. Supp. II:** 94, 101, 102

Titian, **Supp. I Part 2:** 397, 714

"Tito's Goodbye" (García), **Supp. XI:** 190

"To a Bird, Seen Under My Window in the Garden"(J. Schoolcraft), **Supp. XXIII:** 230

To a Blossoming Pear Tree (Wright), **Supp. III Part 2:** 602–605

"To a Blossoming Pear Tree" (Wright), **Supp. III Part 2:** 604

"To Abolish Children" (Shapiro), **Supp. II Part 2:** 717

To Abolish Children and Other Essays (Shapiro), **Supp. II Part 2:** 703

"To a Calvinist in Bali" (Millay), **Supp. XXVI:** 170

"To a Caty-Did, the Precursor of Winter" (Freneau), **Supp. II Part 1:** 274–275

"To a Chameleon" (Moore), **III:** 195, 196, 215

"To a Conscript of 1940" (Read), **II:** 372–373, 377–378

"To a Contemporary Bunk Shooter" (Sandburg), **III:** 582

"To a Cough in the Street at Midnight" (Wylie), **Supp. I Part 2:** 727, 729–730

"To a Defeated Savior" (Wright), **Supp. III Part 2:** 593–594, 596

"To a Face in the Crowd" (Warren), **IV:** 239

"To a Fish Head Found on the Beach near Malaga" (Levine), **Supp. V:** 185

"To a Friend" (Nemerov), **III:** 272

"To a Friend"(O'Hara), **Supp. XXIII:** 212

"To a Friend Whose Work Has Come to Triumph" (Sexton), **Supp. II Part 2:** 683

To a God Unknown (Steinbeck), **I:** 107; **IV:** 51, 59–60, 67

"To a Greek Marble" (Aldington), **Supp. I Part 1:** 257

"To a Locomotive in Winter" (Whitman), **IV:** 348

"To a Mad Friend" (Davison), **Supp. XXVI:** 69

"To a Military Rifle" (Winters), **Supp. II Part 2:** 810, 811, 815

"To a Mouse" (Burns), **Supp. IX:** 173

"To an American Workman Dying of Starvation" (Taggard), **Supp. XXII:** 282

"To an Athlete Dying Young" (Houseman), **Supp. XVII:** 121

"To a Negro Jazz Band in a Parisian Cabaret" (Hughes), **Supp. I Part 1:** 325

"To an Old Philosopher in Rome" (Stevens), **III:** 605; **Retro. Supp. I:** 312

"To an Old Poet in Peru" (Ginsberg), **Supp. II Part 1:** 322

"To a Now-Type Poet" (X. J. Kennedy), **Supp. XV:** 161

"To Answer Your Question" (Jarman), **Supp. XVII:** 114–115

"To Any Would-Be Terrorists" (Nye), **Supp. XIII:** 285, 286

"To a Poet" (Rich), **Supp. I Part 2:** 571; **Supp. XIX:** 83

"To a Prize Bird" (Moore), **III:** 215

"To a Republican, with Mr. Paine's Rights of Man" (Freneau), **Supp. II Part 1:** 267

"To a Revolutionary Girl" (Bodenheim), **Supp. XXV:** 28

"To a Shade" (Yeats), **III:** 18

"To a Skylark" (Shelley), **Supp. I Part 2:** 720; **Supp. X:** 31

"Toast to Harlem, A" (Hughes), **Supp. I Part 1:** 338

"To Aunt Rose" (Ginsberg), **Supp. II Part 1:** 320

"To Autumn" (Keats), **Supp. IX:** 50

"To a Waterfowl" (Bryant), **Supp. I Part 1:** 154, 155, 162, 171

"To a Young Poet" (X. J. Kennedy), **Supp. XV:** 161

"To a Young Writer" (Stegner), **Supp. X:** 24

Tobacco Road (Caldwell), **I:** 288, 289, 290, 295–296, 297, 298, 302, 307, 309, 310; **IV:** 198; **Supp. XXII:** 196

"To Be a Monstrous Clever Fellow" (Fante), **Supp. XI:** 167

"To Become Music or Break" (Jauss), **Supp. XXI:** 133

To Bedlam and Part Way Back (Sexton), **Retro. Supp. II:** 245; **Supp. II Part 2:** 672–678; **Supp. IV Part 2:** 441; **Supp. XI:** 317

"To Beethoven" (Lanier), **Supp. I Part 1:** 364

To Begin Again: Stories and Memoirs, 1908–1929 (M. F. K. Fisher), **Supp. XVII:** 92

Tobey, Mark, **Supp. X:** 264

To Be Young, Gifted, and Black: Lorraine Hansberry in Her Own Words (Nemiroff), **Supp. IV Part 1:** 372, 374

"To Big Mary from an Ex-Catholic" (Mora), **Supp. XIII:** 217, 224, 228

Tobin, Jacqueline L., **Supp. XXVI:** 200

"Tobin's Palm" (O. Henry), **Supp. II Part 1:** 408; **Supp. XV:** 40

Tobit (apocryphal book), **I:** 89

"To Build a Fire" (London), **II:** 468

Toby Tyler: or, Ten Weeks with a Circus (Otis), **III:** 577

"To Change in a Good Way" (Ortiz), **Supp. IV Part 2:** 511

"To Charlotte Cushman" (Lanier), **Supp. I Part 1:** 364

"To Cole, the Painter, Departing for Europe" (Bryant), **Supp. I Part 1:** 157, 161

Tocqueville, Alexis de, **III:** 261; **IV:** 349; **Retro. Supp. I:** 235; **Supp. I Part 1:** 137; **Supp. I Part 2:** 659, 660; **Supp. II Part 1:** 281, 282, 284; **Supp. XIV:** 306, 312

"To Crispin O'Conner" (Freneau), **Supp. II Part 1:** 268

"To Da-Duh, In Memoriam" (Marshall), **Supp. XI:** 276

"TODAY" (Baraka), **Supp. II Part 1:** 55

"Today" (Ginsberg), **Supp. II Part 1:** 328

"Today Is a Good Day To Die" (Bell), **Supp. X:** 7

"Today"(O'Hara), **Supp. XXIII:** 210–211

"Today Will Be a Quiet Day" (Hempel), **Supp. XXI:** 117,Supp. XXI: 118

Todd, Mabel Loomis, **I:** 454, 470; **Retro. Supp. I:** 33, 34, 35, 39, 47

"To Death" (Levertov), **Supp. III Part 1:** 274

"To Delmore Schwartz" (Lowell), **II:** 547; **Retro. Supp. II:** 188

"to disembark" (Brooks), **Supp. III Part 1:** 86

"To Dorothy on Her Exclusion from The Guinness Book of Records" (X. J. Kennedy), **Supp. XV:** 166

"To Dream of Bears" (Gallagher), **Supp. XXIV:** 176

"To Dr. Thomas Shearer" (Lanier), **Supp. I Part 1:** 370

"To Earthward" (Frost), **II:** 154

"To Edward John Moreton Drax Plunkett, Eighteenth Baron Dunsany" (Lovecraft), **Supp. XXV:** 113

"To Edwin V. McKenzie" (Winters), **Supp. II Part 2:** 801

"To Eleonora Duse" (Lowell), **II:** 528

"To Elizabeth Ward Perkins" (Lowell), **II:** 516

"To Elsie" (W. C. Williams), **Retro. Supp. I:** 419

"To Emily Dickinson" (H. Crane), **Retro. Supp. II:** 76

"To E. T." (Frost), **Retro. Supp. I:** 132

To Feel These Things (L. Michaels), **Supp. XVI:** 205, **213–214**

"To Feel These Things" (L. Michaels), **Supp. XVI:** 214

Toffler, Alvin, **Supp. IV Part 2:** 517

"To Fill" (Moore), **Supp. X:** 168, 169

"To Gabriela, a Young Writer" (Mora), **Supp. XIII:** 220

"To George May" (Bodenheim), **Supp. XXV:** 25

To Have and Have Not (film), **Supp. XV:** 347

To Have and Have Not (Hemingway), **I:** 31; **II:** 253–254, 264; **Retro. Supp. I:** 182, **183,** 187

"To Helen" (Poe), **III:** 410, 411, 427; **Retro. Supp. II:** 102

"To Hell With Dying" (Walker), **Supp. III Part 2:** 523

"To His Coy Mistress"(Marvell), **Supp. XXIII:** 62

"To His Excellency General Washington" (Wheatley), **Supp. XX: 289**

"To His Father" (Jeffers), **Supp. II Part 2:** 415

Toilet, The (Baraka), **Supp. II Part 1:** 37, 40–42

"To James Russell Lowell" (Holmes), **Supp. I Part 1:** 311

To Jerusalem and Back (Bellow), **Retro. Supp. II:** 29

"To Jesus on His Birthday" (Millay), **III:** 136–137

"To John Keats" (Lowell), **II:** 516

"To Judge Faolain, Dead Long Enough: A Summons" (McCarriston), **Supp. XIV:** 264–265

"To Justify My Singing" (Wright), **Supp. III Part 2:** 590

"To Kill a Deer" (C. Frost), **Supp. XV:** 102

To Kill a Mockingbird (film), **Supp. VIII:** 128–129

To Kill a Mockingbird (Lee), **Supp. VIII: 113–129; Supp. XIX:** 142; **Supp. XVI:** 259

"To Kill a Mockingbird: Harper Lee's Tragic Vision" (Dave), **Supp. VIII:** 126

To Kill a Mockingbird: Threatening Boundaries (C. D. Johnson), **Supp. VIII:** 126

Toklas, Alice B., **IV:** 27; **Supp. IV Part 1:** 81, 91; **Supp. XVI:** 187
"Tokyo Story" (Wasserstein), **Supp. XV:** 328
"To Larry Rivers"(O'Hara), **Supp. XXIII:** 212
"To Light" (Hogan), **Supp. IV Part 1:** 402
"To Ligurinus" (Horace; Ferry, trans.), **Supp. XXIV:** 155
"To Ligurinus" (Horace; Howard, trans.), **Supp. XXIV:** 155
"To Live and Diet" (Wasserstein), **Supp. XV:** 328
Tolkien, J. R. R., **Supp. V:** 140
Tolkin, Michael, **Supp. XI:** 160
Toller, Ernst, **I:** 479
"To Lose the Earth" (Sexton), **Supp. II Part 2:** 684, 685
Tolson, Melvin, **Retro. Supp. I:** 208, 209, 210
Tolstoy, Leo, **I:** 6, 7, 58, 103, 312, 376; **II:** 191–192, 205, 271, 272, 275, 276, 281, 285, 286, 320, 407, 542, 559, 570, 579, 606; **III:** 37, 45, 61, 323, 467, 572; **IV:** 17, 21, 170, 285; **Retro. Supp. I:** 91, 225; **Retro. Supp. II:** 299; **Supp. I Part 1:** 2, 3, 6, 20; **Supp. IV Part 1:** 392; **Supp. IX:** 246; **Supp. V:** 277, 323; **Supp. XI:** 68; **Supp. XII:** 310, 322; **Supp. XIV:** 87, 97, 98; **Supp. XIX:** 241; **Supp. XXIII:** 4, 11, 275; **Supp. XXIV:** 132; **Supp. XXV:** 142
"To Lu Chi" (Nemerov), **III:** 275
"To Lydia" (Horace; Ferry, trans.), **Supp. XXIV:** 154
"To Lydia" (Horace; McHugh, trans.), **Supp. XXIV:** 154
Tom (Cummings), **I:** 430
"Tom" (Oliver), **Supp. VII:** 232
"Tom, Tom, the Piper's Son" (Ransom), **Supp. X:** 58
"To M, with a Rose" (Lanier), **Supp. I Part 1:** 364
To Make a Prairie (Kumin), **Supp. IV Part 2:** 440, 441
"To Make Words Disappear" (Simpson), **Supp. IX:** 265–266
Tomás and the Library Lady (Mora), **Supp. XIII:** 216, 221
"Tomatoes" (Francis), **Supp. IX:** 82
"Tom Ball's Barn" (Kooser), **Supp. XIX:** 119
"Tom Brown at Fisk" (Du Bois), **Supp. II Part 1:** 160
Tom Brown's School Days (Hughes), **Supp. I Part 2:** 406
"Tomb Stone" (Dickey), **Supp. IV Part 1:** 185
"Tombstone Blues" (song, Dylan), **Supp. XVIII:** 30
Tomcat in Love (O'Brien), **Supp. V:** 238, 240, 243, 252–254
"Tomcat's Wife, The" (C. Bly), **Supp. XVI:** 40
Tomcat's Wife and Other Stories, The (C. Bly), **Supp. XVI:** 40–41
"Tom Fool at Jamaica" (Moore), **III:** 215

To Mix with Time (Swenson), **Supp. IV Part 2:** 637, 643–645, 645
Tom Jones (Fielding), **I:** 131; **Supp. V:** 127
Tomlinson, Charles, **Supp. XVI:** 284
Tommy Gallagher's Crusade (Farrell), **II:** 44
Tommyknockers, The (King), **Supp. V:** 139, 144
"Tommy's Burglar" (Henry), **Supp. II Part 1:** 399, 401
"Tommy Stames" (Budbill), **Supp. XIX:** 8
Tomo Cheeki (pseudonym). *See* Freneau, Philip
Tomorrow Is Another Day (E. P. Jones), **Supp. XXII:** 252
Tomorrow is Another Day (film, Feist), **Supp. XVII:** 62
"Tomorrow the Moon" (Dos Passos), **I:** 493
Tomorrow Will Be Better (B. Smith), **Supp. XXIII:** 258, **264–267**
"Tom Outland's Story" (Cather), **I:** 325–326
Tompkins, Jane, **Supp. XVI:** 89; **Supp. XVIII:** 258, 259, 263
Tompson, Benjamin, **Supp. I Part 1:** 110, 111
"Tom-Rock Through Eels" (Hempel), **Supp. XXI:** 116, 118, **123–124**
Tom Sawyer (Twain). *See Adventures of Tom Sawyer, The* (Twain)
Tom Sawyer Abroad (Twain), **II:** 482; **IV:** 19, 204
Tom Sawyer Detective (Twain), **IV:** 204
Tom Sawyer (musical) (Gurney), **Supp. V:** 96
"Tom's Husband" (Jewett), **Retro. Supp. II:** 132, 141
Tom Swift (Stratemeyer), **III:** 146
Tom-Walker, The (Sandoz), **Supp. XXIV:** 244, **253–255**
"Tom Wolfe's Guide to Etiquette" (Wolfe), **Supp. III Part 2:** 578
"To My Brother Killed: Haumont Wood: October, 1918" (Bogan), **Supp. III Part 1:** 58
"To My Class, on Certain Fruits and Flowers Sent Me in Sickness" (Lanier), **Supp. I Part 1:** 370
"To my ever beloved & lamented son William Henry"(J. Schoolcraft), **Supp. XXIII:** 226, 231
"To My Father's Ghost" (Everwine), **Supp. XV:** 76
"To My Ghost Reflected in the Auxvasse River" (Levis), **Supp. XI:** 265
"To My Greek" (Merrill), **Supp. III Part 1:** 326
"To My Mother" (Berry), **Supp. X:** 23
"To My Sister—Ernestine Kealoha Taggard, 1900–1943" (Taggard), **Supp. XXII:** 284
"To My Small Son, at the Photographer's" (Hay), **Supp. XIV:** 121
"To My Small Son, on Certain Occasions" (Hay), **Supp. XIV:** 121
"To My Students" (Taggard), **Supp. XXII:** 280

"To Name is to Possess" (Kincaid), **Supp. VII:** 194
Tone, Aileen, **I:** 21–22
"Tongue Is, The" (Komunyakaa), **Supp. XIII:** 113
"Tongue of the Jews" (Bukiet), **Supp. XVII:** 47
Tongues (Shepard and Chaikin), **Supp. III Part 2:** 433
Tongues of Angels, The (Price), **Supp. VI:** 265
Tongues Untied (Riggs; film), **Supp. XI:** 19, 20
"Tonight" (Lowell), **II:** 538
"Tonight Is Part of the Struggle"(Le Sueur), **Supp. XXIII:** 172
Tonight Is the Night of the Prom (Jarman), **Supp. XVII:** 110, **112–113**
"Tonight Is the Night of the Prom" (Jarman), **Supp. XVII:** 113
Tony Kushner in Conversation (Vorlicky, ed.), **Supp. IX:** 132
"Too Anxious for Rivers" (Frost), **II:** 162
"Too Blue" (Hughes), **Retro. Supp. I:** 207
"Too Damn Close: Thresholds and Their Maintenance in Rick Bass's Work" (Kerridge), **Supp. XVI:** 26
"Too Early" (Leopold), **Supp. XIV:** 186
"Too Early Spring" (Benét), **Supp. XI:** 53
"Too Far from Home" (Bowles), **Supp. IV Part 1:** 94–95
Too Far from Home: Selected Writings of Paul Bowles (Halpern, ed.), **Supp. IV Part 1:** 94, 95
Too Far to Go: The Maples Stories (Updike), **Retro. Supp. I:** 321
"Too Good To Be True": The Life and Art of Leslie Fiedler (Winchell), **Supp. XIII:** 94, 98, 99, 101
Toohey, John Peter, **Supp. IX:** 190
Toolan, David, **Supp. IV Part 1:** 308
Too Late (Dixon), **Supp. XII: 143–144**
"Too Late" (Pickering), **Supp. XXI:** 197
"Too-Late Born, The" (Hemingway), **III:** 9
Toole, John Kennedy, **Supp. XIV:** 21; **Supp. XXVI: 239–254**
"Toolless" (Pickering), **Supp. XXI:** 204
Too Many Bottles (Holding), **Supp. XXII:** 126, **134–135**
Toomer, Jean, **Retro. Supp. II:** 79; **Supp. I Part 1:** 325, 332; **Supp. III Part 2: 475–491; Supp. IV Part 1:** 16, 164, 168; **Supp. IX: 305–322; Supp. XIII:** 305; **Supp. XVIII:** 122; **Supp. XX:** 73; **Supp. XXII:** 6
Toomer, Nathan Eugene Pinchback. *See* Toomer, Jean
Too Much Johnson (film), **Supp. IV Part 1:** 83
"To One Who Said Me Nay" (Cullen), **Supp. IV Part 1:** 166
"Tooth, The" (Jackson), **Supp. IX:** 122
Tooth and Claw (Boyle), **Supp. XX: 20**
Tooth of Crime, The (Shepard), **Supp. III Part 2:** 432, 441–445, 447
"Too Young" (O'Hara), **III:** 369
Topaz (film), **Supp. XX:** 253

Topaz (Uris), **Supp. XX: 247, 248, 253**

"Top Israeli Official Hints at 'Shared' Jerusalem" (Nye), **Supp. XIII:** 287

"To P. L., 1916–1937" (Levine), **Supp. V:** 185

"To Please a Shadow" (Brodsky), **Supp. VIII:** 30

"Top of the Food Chain" (Boyle), **Supp. XX: 20**

"Top of the Hill" (Jewett), **II:** 406

"Topography" (Olds), **Supp. X:** 208

Topper (T. Smith), **Supp. IX:** 194

To Praise the Music (Bronk), **Supp. XXI:** 31, 32

Torah, **IV:** 19

"Torch Songs" (Wrigley), **Supp. XVIII:** 296

Torday, Daniel, **Supp. XXII:** 151

"Toronto, More or Less, in Fifteen Years" (Gansworth), **Supp. XXVI:** 110

Torpedo 8: The Story of Swede Larsen's Bomber Squadron (Wolfert), **Supp. XXI:** 267

"Torquemada" (Bukiet), **Supp. XVII:** 44

"Torquemada" (Longfellow), **II:** 505; **Retro. Supp. II:** 164

Torrence, Ridgely, **III:** 507

Torrent and the Night Before, The (Robinson), **III:** 504

Torrents of Spring, The (Hemingway), **I:** 117; **II:** 250–251

Torres, Ben Fong, **Supp. XXVI:** 209

Torres, Héctor A., **Supp. XIII:** 225

Torres, Louis, **Supp. IV Part 2:** 529, 530

Torres-Saillant, Silvio, **Supp. XXI:** 104, 105, 108, 109

Torsney, Cheryl, **Retro. Supp. I:** 224

Tortilla Curtain, The (Boyle), **Supp. VIII: 9–10; Supp. XX: 28–29**

Tortilla Flat (Steinbeck), **IV:** 50, 51, 61, 64

Tortilla Flats (Steinbeck), **Supp. XX: 28**

Tortured Skins, and Other Fictions (Kenny), **Supp. XXIII:** 150, 156, 157

Tory Lover, The (Jewett), **II:** 406; **Retro. Supp. II:** 144–145

"Toscana" (Dixon), **Supp. XII:** 154

"To Sestius" (Horace; Ferry, trans.), **Supp. XXIV:** 155

"To Sestius" (Horace; Lasdun, trans.), **Supp. XXIV:** 154

"To Sir Toby" (Freneau), **Supp. II Part 1:** 269

"To Sophy, Expectant" (Mumford), **Supp. II Part 2:** 475

"To Speak of Woe That Is in Marriage" (Lowell), **II:** 550

"To Statecraft Embalmed" (Moore), **III:** 197

To Stay Alive (Levertov), **Supp. III Part 1:** 280–282

"Total Eclipse" (Dillard), **Supp. VI:** 28

"Total Eclipse of the Moon" (Crooker), **Supp. XXIII:** 55

Total Immersion (Goodman), **Supp. XXVI:** 118–121, 125

"Total Immersion" (Goodman), **Supp. XXVI:** 120

Total Recall (Paretsky), **Supp. XXV:** 172, 180, 181, 183–184

Toth, Emily, **Retro. Supp. II:** 71

Toth, Susan Allan, **Retro. Supp. II:** 138

"To the Americans of the United States" (Freneau), **Supp. II Part 1:** 271

"To the Apennines" (Bryant), **Supp. I Part 1:** 157, 164

"To the Bleeding Hearts Association of American Novelists" (Nemerov), **III:** 281

"To the Botequim & Back" (Bishop), **Retro. Supp. II:** 51

To the Bright and Shining Sun (Burke), **Supp. XIV:** 22, 25

"To the Citizens of the United States" (Paine), **Supp. I Part 2:** 519–520

"To the Dandelion" (Lowell), **Supp. I Part 2:** 424

"To the End" (Haines), **Supp. XII:** 212–213

To the Ends of the Earth: The Selected Travels of Paul Theroux, **Supp. VIII:** 324

"To the Fabulous Constellation" (Ferry), **Supp. XXIV:** 148–149

"To the Film Industry in Crisis" (O'Hara), **Supp. XXIII:** 214

To the Finland Station: A Study in the Writing and Acting of History (Wilson), **IV:** 429, 436, 443–444, 446

"To the Governor & Legislature of Massachusetts" (Nemerov), **III:** 287

To the Green Man (Jarman), **Supp. XVII:** 110, 120–121

"To the Harbormaster" (O'Hara), **Supp. XXIII:** 208, 212, 214; **Supp. XXIV:** 42

To the Holy Spirit (Winters), **Supp. II Part 2:** 810

"To the Keeper of the King's Water Works" (Freneau), **Supp. II Part 1:** 269

"To the Lacedemonians" (Tate), **IV:** 134

"To the Laodiceans" (Jarrell), **Retro. Supp. I:** 121, 140

To the Lighthouse (Woolf), **I:** 309; **II:** 600; **Retro. Supp. II:** 337; **Supp. VIII:** 155

"To the Man on Trail" (London), **II:** 466

"To the Memory of the Brave Americans Under General Greene" (Freneau), **Supp. II Part 1:** 262, 274

"To the Miscodeed" (J. Schoolcraft), **Supp. XXIII:** 230

"To the Muse" (Wright), **Supp. III Part 2:** 601

"To the Natural World: at 37" (Taggard), **Supp. XXII:** 279–280

"To the Nazi Leaders" (Hay), **Supp. XIV:** 121

"To the New World" (Jarrell), **II:** 371

"To the One of Fictive Music" (Stevens), **IV:** 89; **Retro. Supp. I:** 297, 300

"To the One Upstairs" (Simic), **Supp. VIII:** 283

"To the Peoples of the World" (Du Bois), **Supp. II Part 1:** 172

"To the Pine Tree on first seeing it on returning from Europe" (J. Schoolcraft), **Supp. XXIII:** 225, 228, 232–233

To the Place of Trumpets (B. Kelly), 132; **Supp. XVII: 123–127**

"To the Pliocene Skull" (Harte), **Supp. II Part 1:** 343–344

"To the Powers of Darkness" (Taggard), **Supp. XXII:** 279, 280

"To the Powers of Desolation" (Taggard), **Supp. XXII:** 280

"To the pure all things are pure" (Very), **Supp. XXV:** 242, 248

"To the Queen of Heaven" (Taggard), **Supp. XXII:** 280

"To the Reader" (Baudelaire), **II:** 544–545

"To The Reader" (Jarman), **Supp. XVII:** 115

"To the Reader" (Levertov), **Supp. III Part 1:** 277

"To the Republic" (Horace; Ferry, trans.), **Supp. XXIV:** 154

"To the Right Honourable William, Earl of Dartmouth" (Wheatley), **Supp. XX: 278, 284, 287–288**

"To the River Arve" (Bryant), **Supp. I Part 1:** 163

"To the Snake" (Levertov), **Supp. III Part 1:** 277

"To the Stone-Cutters" (Jeffers), **Supp. II Part 2:** 420

"To the Unseeable Animal" (Berry), **Supp. X:** 31

"To the Western World" (Simpson), **Supp. IX:** 269, 270

To the White Sea (Dickey), **Supp. IV Part 1:** 186, 190–191

"To the Young Who Want to Die" (Brooks), **Supp. III Part 1:** 85–86

"To Tlaoc of the Rain" (Everwine), **Supp. XV:** 77

"To Train a Writer" (Bierce), **I:** 199

"Touch, The" (Sexton), **Supp. II Part 2:** 687

Touch and Go (M. F. K. Fisher and D. Parrish), **Supp. XVII:** 84

"Touching the Tree" (Merwin), **Supp. III Part 1:** 355

Touching the World (Eakin), **Supp. VIII:** 167

Touch of Danger, A (Jones), **Supp. XI:** 226, **228–229**

Touch of the Poet, A (O'Neill), **III:** 385, 401, 404

Touchstone, The (Wharton), **Retro. Supp. I:** 365

Touchstone Anthology of Contemporary Nonfiction, The: Work from 1970 to the Present (Williford and Martone, eds.), **Supp. XXVI:** 53

"Touch-up Man" (Komunyakaa), **Supp. XIII:** 119

Tough Guys Don't Dance (Mailer), **Retro. Supp. II:** 211

"Tough People" (Offutt), **Supp. XIX:** 170–171

Toulet, Paul Jean, **IV:** 79

Tour (McNally), **Supp. XIII:** 197

"Tour 5" (Hayden), **Supp. II Part 1:** 381

To Urania (Brodsky), **Supp. VIII:** 22, 28–29

Tourgée, Albion W., **Supp. XIV:** 63

"Tour Guide" (Komunyakaa), **Supp. XIII:** 114

"Tourist Death" (MacLeish), **III:** 12

Tourmaline (J. Scott), **Supp. XVII: 192–194,** 195

Tour of Duty (Dos Passos), **I:** 489

"Tour of the Labyrinth" (Stallings), **Supp. XXV:** 229

Touron the Prairies, A (Irving), **II:** 312–313

Toussaint L'Ouverture, **Supp. XXI:** 166

Toussaint L'Ouverture (C. L. R. James), **Supp. XXI:** 167

Tovey, Donald Francis, **Supp. XIV:** 336

"To Virgil" (Horace; Ferry, trans.), **Supp. XXIV:** 155

"To Virgil" (Horace; Wright, trans.), **Supp. XXIV:** 155

To Walk a Crooked Mile (McGrath), **Supp. X:** 117

Toward a New Synthesis (Begiebing), **Retro. Supp. II:** 210

"Toward an Understanding of the Public Life" (Davison), **Supp. XXVI:** 73

"Toward Nightfall" (Simic), **Supp. VIII:** 277

Towards a Better Life (Burke), **I:** 270

"Towards a Chicano Poetics: The Making of the Chicano Subject, 1969–1982" (Saldívar), **Supp. IV Part 2:** 544

Towards an Enduring Peace (Bourne), **I:** 232

"Towards Morning" (Pedersen; Nelson, trans.), **Supp. XVIII:** 180

Toward the Blanched Alphabets (Sobin), **Supp. XVI:** 290

Toward the Gulf (Masters), **Supp. I Part 2:** 465–466

"Toward the Solstice" (Rich), **Supp. I Part 2:** 575–576

Toward Wholeness in Paule Marshall's Fiction (Pettis), **Supp. XI:** 276

"Tower" (Merwin), **Supp. III Part 1:** 343

"Tower Beyond Tragedy, The" (Jeffers), **Supp. II Part 2:** 429–430

Tower of Ivory (Atherton), **Supp. XXIV:** 21, 23

Tower of Ivory (MacLeish), **III:** 3–4

Towers, Robert, **Supp. IX:** 259; **Supp. XVI:** 211; **Supp. XXV:** 86

"To What Red Hell" (C. Himes), **Supp. XVI:** 137

"To Whistler, American" (Pound), **III:** 465–466

"To Wine" (Bogan), **Supp. III Part 1:** 57, 58

Towle, Tony, **Supp. XXIII:** 221

Town, Caren J., **Supp. XVIII:** 195, 199

Town, The (Faulkner), **II:** 57, 73; **Retro. Supp. I:** 74, 82

Town, The (Richter), **Supp. XVIII:** 207, **214–215,** 217

Town and the City, The (Kerouac), **Supp. III Part 1:** 222–224; **Supp. XIV:** 143

"Town Crier" (Bierce), **I:** 193, 194, 195, 196

"*Town Crier* Exclusive, Confessions of a Princess Manqué: 'How Royals Found Me "Unsuitable" to Marry Their Larry' " (Elkin), **Supp. VI:** 56

Town Down the River, The (Robinson), **III:** 508

"Town Dump, The" (Nemerov), **III:** 272, 275, 281

Towne, Robert, **Supp. XI:** 159, 172, 174

"Townhouse Interior with Cat" (Clampitt), **Supp. IX:** 40

Townie (Dubus III), **Supp. XXIV:** 98, **108–111**

"Townies" (Dubus), **Supp. VII:** 86

Town in the Forest, The: Life Story of Richmond, New Hampshire (Boyce; Faust, ed.), **Supp. XXI:** 8

"Town of the Sound of a Twig Breaking" (Carson), **Supp. XII: 102**

"Town Poor, The" (Jewett), **Retro. Supp. II:** 138, 139, 143

Townsend, Alison, **Supp. XIII:** 222; **Supp. XXIII:** 132, 139

Townsend, Ann, **Supp. V:** 77

Townsend, Jim, **Supp. XXII:** 243

"Towns in Colour" (Lowell), **II:** 523–524

Townsman, The (Sedges), **Supp. II Part 1:** 124–125

Town Smokes (P. Benedict), **Supp. XXIII: 35–39**

"Town Smokes" (P. Benedict), **Supp. XXIII:** 37

"To World War Two" (Koch), **Supp. XV:** 184

Toys in a Field (Komunyakaa), **Supp. XIII: 121–122**

"Toys in a Field" (Komunyakaa), **Supp. XIII:** 122

Toys in the Attic (Hellman), **Supp. I Part 1:** 289–290

Toyter mentsh, Der (The dead man) (Asch), **Supp. XXIII:** 9

Tracer (F. Barthelme), **Supp. XI:** 31–32, 33

Traces of Thomas Hariot, The (Rukeyser), **Supp. VI:** 273, 274, 283

"Tracing Life with a Finger" (Caldwell), **I:** 291

Tracker (Wagoner), **Supp. IX:** 329, **336–337**

"Tracking" (Wagoner), **Supp. IX:** 329

"Track Meet, The" (Schwartz), **Supp. II Part 2:** 665

Tracks (Erdrich), **Supp. IV Part 1:** 259, 262–263, 269, 272, 273–274, 274, 275

"Track-Workers" (Bodenheim), **Supp. XXV:** 22

"Tract" (W. C. Williams), **Retro. Supp. I:** 414

"Tract against Communism, A" (Twelve Southerners), **IV:** 125, 237

Tractatus (Wittgenstein), **Supp. XVII:** 143

Tracy, Benjamin, **Supp. XVIII:** 4

Tracy, D. H., **Supp. XVIII:** 178

Tracy, Lee, **IV:** 287, 288

Tracy, Steven, **Retro. Supp. I:** 195

"Trade, The" (Levine), **Supp. V:** 193

Trading Twelves (Callahan and Murray, eds.), **Retro. Supp. II:** 119

Trading Twelves: The Selected Letters of Ralph Ellison and Albert Murray (Murray and Callahan, eds.), **Supp. XIX:** 148, 158

Traditional History of the Confederacy of the Six Nations (Scott), **Supp. XXVI:** 87

" 'Traditional' Marriage: A Secular Affair" (P. N. Warren), **Supp. XX:** 273

"Tradition and Industrialization" (Wright), **IV:** 489–490

"Tradition and Mythology: Signatures of Landscape in Chicana Poetry" (Rebolledo), **Supp. XIII:** 214

"Tradition and the Individual Talent" (Eliot), **I:** 441, 574, 585; **Retro. Supp. I:** 59, 286

Tragedies, Life and Letters of James Gates Percival (Swinburne), **Supp. I Part 2:** 422

Tragedy of Bees, A (P. N. Warren), **Supp. XX: 261**

"Tragedy of Bees, A" (P. N. Warren), **Supp. XX: 272**

Tragedy of Don Ippolito, The (Howells), **II:** 279

"Tragedy of Error, A" (James), **II:** 322; **Retro. Supp. I:** 218

Tragedy of Pudd'nhead Wilson, The (Twain), **IV:** 206–207

Tragic America (Dreiser), **Retro. Supp. II:** 95

"Tragic Dialogue" (Wylie), **Supp. I Part 2:** 724

Tragic Ground (Caldwell), **I:** 297, 306

Tragic Muse, The (James), **Retro. Supp. I:** 227

Traherne, Thomas, **IV:** 151; **Supp. III Part 1:** 14; **Supp. V:** 208; **Supp. XV:** 212; **Supp. XVI:** 282, 288, 295

"Trail, The" (W. J. Smith), **Supp. XIII:** 342

Trailerpark (Banks), **Supp. V:** 12

"Trailing Arbutus, The" (Whittier), **Supp. I Part 2:** 691

Trail of the Lonesome Pine, The (Fox), **Supp. XIII:** 166

"Train, The" (O'Connor), **Retro. Supp. II:** 225

"Train Dreams" (Berrigan), **Supp. XXIV:** 45

"Train Ride" (Berrigan), **Supp. XXIV:** 42, 43–44

"Train Rising Out of the Sea" (Ashbery), **Supp. III Part 1:** 22

"Trains" (Banks), **Supp. V:** 8

"Train Tune" (Bogan), **Supp. III Part 1:** 64

Train Whistle Guitar (Murray), **Supp. XIX: 153–155,** 157

Traitor, The (Wouk), **Supp. XXV:** 256, 259

"Traits of Indian Character" (Irving), **II:** 303

Trakl, Georg, **Supp. XVII:** 241

Tramp Abroad, A (Twain), **IV:** 200

Tramping With a Poet in the Rockies (S. Graham), **Supp. I Part 2:** 397

Tramp's Excuse, The (Lindsay), **Supp. I Part 2:** 379, 380, 382

Tran, Sharon, **Supp. XXVI:** 216, 218

"Trance, The" (Taggard), **Supp. XXII:** 280

"Transaction" (Cliff), **Supp. XXII:** 75

"Transatlantic" (Toomer), **Supp. III Part 2:** 486

Transatlantic Sketches (James), **II:** 324; **Retro. Supp. I:** 219

"Transcendental Etude" (Rich), **Supp. I Part 2:** 576

"Transcontinental Highway" (Cowley), **Supp. II Part 1:** 141

"Transducer" (Ammons), **Supp. VII:** 28

"Transfiguration" (Jarman), **Supp. XVII:** 118, 119

"Transfigured Bird" (Merrill), **Supp. III Part 1:** 320–321

"Transformations" (Harjo), **Supp. XII:** 226

Transformations (Sexton), **Supp. II Part 2:** 689–691; **Supp. IV Part 2:** 447; **Supp. XIV:** 125

Transforming Madness: New Lives for People Living with Mental Illness (Neugeboren), **Supp. XVI:** 229

"Transit" (Conroy), **Supp. XVI:** 72

Transit to Narcissus, A (Mailer), **Retro. Supp. II:** 196

"Translation" (Espaillat), **Supp. XXI:** 107

"Translation and Transposition" (Carne-Ross), **Supp. I Part 1:** 268–269

"Translation of a Fragment of Simonides" (Bryant), **Supp. I Part 1:** 153, 155

"Translations" (Rich), **Supp. I Part 2:** 563

Translations of Ezra Pound, The (Kenner, ed.), **III:** 463

Translations of the Gospel Back into Tongues (Wright), **Supp. XV:** 342–343, 346

"Translator's Task, The" (Benjamin), **Supp. XXIII:** 28

"Trans-National America" (Bourne), **I:** 229, 230

"Transparency" (X. J. Kennedy), **Supp. XV:** 159–160

"Transparent Itineraries: 1983" (Sobin), **Supp. XVI:** 287

"Transparent Itineraries: 1984" (Sobin), **Supp. XVI:** 287

"Transparent Itineraries: 1992" (Sobin), **Supp. XVI:** 289

"Transparent Itineraries" poems (Sobin), **Supp. XVI:** 290

Transparent Man, The (Hecht), **Supp. X:** 57, **69–71**

"Transparent Man, The" (Hecht), **Supp. X: 69–70**

Transparent Things (Nabokov), **Retro. Supp. I:** 266, 270, 277

"Transport" (Simic), **Supp. VIII:** 282

Transport to Summer (Stevens), **IV:** 76, 93; **Retro. Supp. I:** 309–312

Tranströmer, Thomas, **Supp. IV Part 2:** 648

"Traps for the Unwary" (Bourne), **I:** 235

Trash Trilogy (McMurtry), **Supp. V:** 225–226, 231

Traub, James, **Supp. XXIV:** 221, 222

Traubel, Horace, **IV:** 350

"Travel: After a Death" (Kenyon), **Supp. VII:** 169

Travel Alarm (Nye), **Supp. XIII:** 277

"Traveled World, The" (Pickering), **Supp. XXI:** 203

"Traveler, The" (Haines), **Supp. XII:** 203–204, 210

"Traveler, The" (Stegner), **Supp. IV Part 2:** 605

Traveler at Forty, A (Dreiser), **I:** 515

Traveler from Altruria, a Romance A, (Howells), **II:** 285, 287

Traveler's Tree, The: New and Selected Poems (W. J. Smith), **Supp. XIII:** 332, 347

"Traveling" (Paley), **Supp. VI:** 230

"Traveling Light" (Wagoner), **Supp. IX:** 329

Traveling Mercies: Some Thoughts on Faith (Lamott), **Supp. XX: 132, 140–142**

"Traveling Onion, The" (Nye), **Supp. XIII:** 276

Traveling through the Dark (Stafford), **Supp. XI:** 311, 316, **318–321**

"Traveling through the Dark" (Stafford), **Supp. XI:** 318–320, 321, 323, 329

Travelling in Amherst: A Poet's Journal, 1931–1954, **Supp. IX: 88–89**

Travelling Standing Still: Poems, 1918–1928 (Taggard), **Supp. XXII:** 278

Travelling Thirds, The (Atherton), **Supp. XXIV:** 23

Travels in Alaska (Muir), **Supp. IX:** 182, 185–186

"Travels in Georgia" (McPhee), **Supp. III Part 1:** 293–294

"Travels in North America" (Kees), **Supp. XV:** 133–134

Travels in the Congo (Gide), **III:** 210

"Travels in the South" (Ortiz), **Supp. IV Part 2:** 506

Travels with Charley (Steinbeck), **IV:** 52

"Travel Writing: Why I Bother" (Theroux), **Supp. VIII:** 310

Travis, Merle, **Supp. V:** 335

Travisano, Thomas, **Retro. Supp. II:** 40

Treadway, Jessica, **Supp. XXIII:** 280

Treasure Hunt (Buechner), **Supp. XII:** 52

Treasure Island (Stevenson), **Supp. X:** 230

Treasure of the Humble, The (Maeterlinck), **Supp. XX: 116**

"Treasure of the Redwoods, A" (Harte), **Supp. II Part 1:** 337

Treasury of Art Masterpieces, A: From the Renaissance to the Present Day (Craven), **Supp. XII:** 44

Treasury of English Aphorisms, A (L. P. Smith), **Supp. XIV:** 344

Treasury of English Prose, A (L. P. Smith, ed.), **Supp. XIV:** 341

Treasury of the Theatre, A (Gassner), **Supp. I Part 1:** 292

Treasury of Yiddish Stories, A (Howe and Greenberg, eds.), **Supp. I Part 2:** 432; **Supp. XXIII:** 7

Treat 'Em Rough (Lardner), **II:** 422–423

Treatise Concerning Religious Affections (Edwards), **I:** 547, 552, 554, 555, 557, 558, 560, 562

Treatise Concerning the Lord's Supper (Doolittle), **IV:** 150

"Treatise on Poetry" (Milosz), **Supp. VIII:** 20

Treatise on Right and Wrong, A (Mencken), **III:** 110, 119

"Treatise on Tales of Horror, A" (Wilson), **IV:** 438

Treatise on the Gods, A (Mencken), **III:** 108–109, 119

"Treatment" (Wright), **Supp. XV:** 343

Trece poetas del mundo azteca (León-Portilla), **Supp. XV:** 77

Tre Croce (Tozzi), **Supp. III Part 2:** 616

"Tree, a Rock, a Cloud, A" (McCullers), **II:** 587

"Tree, The" (Pound), **Retro. Supp. I:** 286; **Supp. I Part 1:** 255

"Tree, the Bird, The" (Roethke), **III:** 548

"Tree at My Window" (Frost), **II:** 155

Tree Grows in Brooklyn, A (B. Smith), **Supp. XVII:** 9; **Supp. XXIII:** 257, **259–264**, 265, 271

Tree Grows in Brooklyn, A (film; Kazan), **Supp. XVI:** 193

"Tree House at Night, The" (Dickey), **Supp. IV Part 1:** 179

"Tree House" (Thompson), **Supp. XXIII:** 301

Tree Is Older Than You Are, The (Nye, ed.), **Supp. XIII:** 280

"Tree of Laughing Bells, The" (Lindsay), **Supp. I Part 2:** 376

"Tree of Life, The" (Swados), **Supp. XIX:** 268

"Tree of Night, A" (Capote), **Supp. III Part 1:** 114, 120

Tree of Night and Other Stories, A (Capote), **Supp. III Part 1:** 114

"Trees, The" (Rich), **Supp. I Part 2:** 555

Trees, The (Richter), **Supp. XVIII: 212–213**, 220

"Trees at Night" (H. Johnson), **Supp. XXVI:** 174

"Trees Listening to Bach" (Merrill), **Supp. III Part 1:** 336

Tree That Came to Stay, The (Quindlen), **Supp. XVII:** 167

Tree Where Man Was Born, The (Matthiessen), **Supp. V:** 199, 203, 204

Trejo, Ernesto, **Supp. V:** 178, 180; **Supp. XIII:** 313, 316; **Supp. XV:** 73

Trelawny, Edward John, **Supp. I Part 2:** 721

"Trellis for R., A" (Swenson), **Supp. IV Part 2:** 647

Tremblay, Bill, **Supp. XIII:** 112

Tremble (Wright), **Supp. XV: 348–349**

"Trespass" (Frost), **Retro. Supp. I:** 139

Trespassing (Pickering), **Supp. XXI:** 202

"Trespassing" (Pickering), **Supp. XXI:** 202

Trethewey, Eric, **Supp. XXI:** 243, 244

Trethewey, Natasha, **Supp. XXI: 243–259**

"Tretitoli, Where the Bomb Group Was" (Hugo), **Supp. VI:** 138

Trevelyan, Robert C., **Supp. XIV:** 334

Trevor-Roper, Hugh, **Supp. XIV:** 348

Trial, The (Kafka), **IV:** 113; **Retro. Supp. II:** 20

"Trial, The" (Rukeyser), **Supp. VI:** 278

"Trial by Existence, The" (Frost), **II:** 166

"Trial for Arson, The"(Hadas), **Supp. XXIII:** 114

Trial of a Poet, The (Shapiro), **Supp. II Part 2:** 710

Trial of the Hawk, The: A Comedy of the Seriousness of Life (Lewis), **II:** 441

"Trial path, The" (Zitkala-Ša), **Supp. XXV:** 274–275, 282

Trials of the Human Heart (Rowson), **Supp. XV:** 237, 239

Tribal Secrets: Recovering American Indian Intellectual Traditions (Warrior), **Supp. IV Part 1:** 329

"Tribute" (A. Finch), **Supp. XVII:** 72, 73–74

"Tribute, A" (Easton), **Supp. IV Part 2:** 461

"Tribute, The" (Doolittle), **Supp. I Part 1:** 267

"Tribute (To My Mother)" (Cullen), **Supp. IV Part 1:** 166

Tribute to Freud (Doolittle), **Supp. I Part 1:** 253, 254, 258, 259, 260, 268

Tribute to the Angels (Doolittle), **Supp. I Part 1:** 272

"Trick on the World, A" (Ríos), **Supp. IV Part 2:** 553

"Tricks" (Olds), **Supp. X:** 203–204

"Trick Scenery" (F. Barthelme), **Supp. XI:** 26

Trifler, The (Masters), **Supp. I Part 2:** 459–460

Trifles (Glaspell), **Supp. III Part 1:** 175, 178, 179, 182, 186, 187; **Supp. X:** 46; **Supp. XXI:** 12

Trifonov, Iurii V., **Retro. Supp. I:** 278

Triggering Town, The: Lectures and Essays on Poetry and Writing (Hugo), **Supp. VI:** 133, 140

Trilling, Diana, **II:** 587, 600; **Supp. I Part 1:** 297; **Supp. XII:** 126; **Supp. XXI:** 271, 275

Trilling, Lionel, **I:** 48; **II:** 579; **III:** 308, 310, 319, 327; **IV:** 201, 211; **Retro. Supp. I:** 19, 97, 121, 216, 227; **Supp. III Part 2:** 493–515; **Supp. IX:** 266, 287; **Supp. V:** 259; **Supp. VIII:** 93, 98, 190, 231, 236, 243; **Supp. XIII:** 100–101; **Supp. XIV:** 280, 288–289; **Supp. XV:** 20, 140, 152

Trilogy (Doolittle), **Supp. I Part 1:** 271, 272

Trilogy of Desire (Dreiser), **I:** 497, 508; **Retro. Supp. II:** 94, 96, **101–102**

Trimberger, Ellen Kay, **Supp. XVII:** 96, 106; **Supp. XXI:** 12

Trimmed Lamp, The (O. Henry), **Supp. II Part 1:** 410

"Trinc" (McGrath), **Supp. X:** 127

Trinity (Uris), **Supp. XX: 243, 244, 245, 246, 247, 248, 253, 254–255**

Trio (Baker), **Supp. I Part 1:** 277

Trio (Saroyan), **Supp. XXII:** 25

"Triolets for Triolet" (Nelson), **Supp. XVIII:** 179

"Trip" (F. Barthelme), *Supp. XI:* 26

Triple Thinkers, The: Ten Essays on Literature (Wilson), **IV:** 428, 431; **Supp. II Part 1:** 146

"Triplex" (Doolittle), **Supp. I Part 1:** 271

Tripmaster Monkey: His Fake Book (Kingston), **Supp. V:** 157, 158, 169, 170–173

Trippings in Authorland (Forrester), **Supp. XVIII:** 13

Trippings of Tom Pepper, The (Briggs), **Supp. XVIII:** 3, **13–14**

"Trip to Hanoi" (Sontag), **Supp. III Part 2:** 460–462

Trip to Parnassus, A; or, The Judgement of Apollo on Dramatic Authors and Performers (Rowson), **Supp. XV: 232–233**

"Triptych" (Eberhart), **I:** 522, 539

Tristam Shandy (Sterne), **Supp. XXII:** 267

Tristan and Iseult, **Retro. Supp. I:** 328, 329, 330, 331

Tristessa (Kerouac), **Supp. III Part 1:** 225, 227, 229

Tristram (Robinson), **III:** 521, 522, 523

Tristram Shandy (Sterne), **I:** 299; **IV:** 465–466; **Supp. V:** 127; **Supp. XVIII:** 60

"Triumph" (C. L. R. James), **Supp. XXI:** 160

"Triumphal March" (Eliot), **I:** 580; **III:** 17; **Retro. Supp. I:** 64

Triumph of Achilles, The (Glück), **Supp. V:** 79, 84–86, 92

"Triumph of a Modern, The, or, Send for the Lawyer" (Anderson), **I:** 113, 114

"Triumph of the Egg, The" (Anderson), **I:** 113

Triumph of the Egg, The: A Book of Impressions from American Life in Tales and Poems (Anderson), **I:** 112, 114

Triumph of the Spider Monkey, The (Oates), **Supp. II Part 2:** 522

Triumphs of the Reformed Religion in America (Mather), **Supp. II Part 2:** 453

Trivial Breath (Wylie), **Supp. I Part 2:** 709, 722–724

Trivia; or, the Art of Walking the Streets of London (Gay), **Supp. XIV:** 337

Trivia: Printed from the Papers of Anthony Woodhouse, Esq. (L. P. Smith), **Supp. XIV:** 336, **337–340**

"Trivia Tea" (Skloot), **Supp. XX: 205**

Trocchi, Alexander, **Supp. XI:** 294, 295, 301

Troilus and Criseyde (Chaucer), **Retro. Supp. I:** 426

Trois contes (Flaubert), **IV:** 31, 37

Trojan Horse, The: A Play (MacLeish), **III:** 21

"Trojan Women, The" (Maxwell), **Supp. VIII:** 169

Troll Garden, The (Cather), **I:** 313, 314–316, 322; **Retro. Supp. I:** 5, 6, 8, 14

"Trolling for Blues" (Wilbur), **Supp. III Part 2:** 563–564

Trollope, Anthony, **I:** 10, 375; **II:** 192, 237; **III:** 51, 70, 281, 382; **Retro.**

Supp. I: 361

Trombly, Albert Edmund, **Supp. I Part 2:** 403

Trombold, John, **Supp. XVIII:** 111

"Trompe L'Oeil" (Collins), **Supp. XXI:** 60

"Troop Train" (Shapiro), **Supp. II Part 2:** 707

"Tropes of the Text" (Gass), **Supp. VI:** 88

Tropic of Cancer (H. Miller), **III:** 170, 171, 174, 177, 178–180, 181, 182, 183, 187, 190; **Supp. V:** 119; **Supp. X:** 187; **Supp. XXII:** 230, 257

Tropic of Capricorn (H. Miller), **III:** 170, 176–177, 178, 182, 183, 184, 187, 188–189, 190

"Tropic of Cuba" (di Donato), **Supp. XX: 45**

Trotsky, Leon, **I:** 366; **II:** 562, 564; **IV:** 429; **Supp. XXI:** 161, 164, 165, 167, 168

Trotter, W., **I:** 249

"Trouble at the Home Office" (Huddle), **Supp. XXVI:** 156

Troubled Air, The (Shaw), **Supp. XIX: 249–250**

Troubled Island (opera; Hughes and Still), **Retro. Supp. I:** 203

Troubled Lovers in History (Goldbarth), **Supp. XII:** 176, **192–193**

Trouble Follows Me (Macdonald, under Millar), **Supp. IV Part 2:** 466

Trouble in July (Caldwell), **I:** 297, 304–305, 306, 309

Trouble Island (Hughes), **Supp. I Part 1:** 328

"Trouble of Marcie Flint, The" (Cheever), **Supp. I Part 1:** 186

Trouble with Francis, The: An Autobiography (Francis), **Supp. IX:** 76, 77, 82, **84–85**

Trouble with God, The (Francis), **Supp. IX:** 88

"Trouble with Poetry, The" (Collins), **Supp. XXI:** 57

Trouble with Poetry and Other Poems, The (Collins), **Supp. XXI:** 55, 57, 62

"Trouble with the Stars and Stripes" (Nye), **Supp. XIII:** 277

Trouillot, Michel-Rolphe, **Supp. X:** 14–15

Troupe, Quincy, **Retro. Supp. II:** 15, 111; **Supp. X:** 242

"Trout" (Hugo), **Supp. VI:** 135

Trout Fishing in America (Brautigan), **Supp. VIII:** 43

"Trouvée" (Bishop), **Retro. Supp. II:** 49

Troy (film), **Supp. XX: 273**

"Truce" (Taggard), **Supp. XXII:** 276–277

"Truce of the Bishop, The" (Frederic), **II:** 139–140

"Truck Stop: Minnesota" (Dunn), **Supp. XI:** 145–146

Trudeau, Garry, **Supp. XXIV:** 283

True Account, The: A Novel of the Lewis & Clark & Kinneson Expeditions (Mosher), **Supp. XXII:** 206, 207, 208, **214–215**

True and False: Heresy and Common Sense for the Actor (Mamet), **Supp. XIV:** 241, 243

True Blood (television series), **Supp. XIX:** 174

Trueblood, Valerie, **Supp. XIII:** 306

True Confessions (Dunne), **Supp. IV Part 1:** 198

True Confessions (film), **Supp. IV Part 1:** 198

"True Crime" (Gansworth), **Supp. XXVI:** 114

"True Feeling Leaves No Memory" (Davison), **Supp. XXVI:** 69

Trueheart, Charles, **Supp. XXI:** 238

True History of the Conquest of New Spain, The (Castillo), **III:** 13

True Intellectual System of the Universe, The (Cuddleworth), **II:** 10

"True Love" (Olds), **Supp. X:** 212

Trueman, Matthew (pseudonym). *See* Lowell, James Russell

"True Morality" (Bell), **Supp. X:** 13

"True Romance" (Everett), **Supp. XVIII:** 65

Truesdale, C. W., **Supp. XXI:** 246

True Stories (Atwood), **Supp. XIII:** 34–35

"True Stories" (Atwood), **Supp. XIII:** 34

"True Stories of Bitches" (Mamet), **Supp. XIV:** 246, 252

"Truest Sport, The: Jousting with Sam and Charlie" (Wolfe), **Supp. III Part 2:** 581–582

"True Vine" (Wylie), **Supp. I Part 2:** 723

True West (Shepard), **Supp. III Part 2:** 433, 441, 445, 447, 448

Truman, Harry, **III:** 3

Truman Capote: In Which Various Friends, Enemies, Acquaintances, and Detractors Recall His Turbulent Career (Plimpton), **Supp. XVI:** 245

Truman Show, The (film), **Supp. XVI:** 271

Trumbo, Dalton, **Supp. I Part 1:** 295; **Supp. XIII:** 6; **Supp. XVII:** 63; **Supp. XX:** 246; **Supp. XXI:** 45

Trumbull, John, **Supp. II Part 1:** 65, 69, 70, 268

Trump, Donald, **Supp. IV Part 1:** 393

Trumpener, Katie, **Retro. Supp. I:** 380

"Trumpet Player" (Hughes), **Supp. I Part 1:** 333

"Trumpet Player, 1963" (Halliday), **Supp. XIX:** 92

Trumpet Shall Sound, The (Wilder), **IV:** 356

Trumpet Unblown, The (Hoffman), **Supp. XVIII:** 71, **74–75**

Trunk Music (Connelly), **Supp. XXI: 72,** 75

"Truro Bear, The" (Oliver), **Supp. VII:** 234

Truscott, Lucian K., **Supp. IV Part 2:** 683

Trust (Ozick), **Supp. V:** 257–258, 259, 260–263, 270, 272

Trust Me (Updike), **Retro. Supp. I:** 322

"Trust Yourself" (Emerson), **II:** 10

"Truth" (Emerson), **II:** 6

"Truth, The" (Halliday), **Supp. XIX:** 87, 88, 94

"Truth, The" (Jarrell), **II:** 381–382

Truth About Celia, The (Brockmeier), **Supp. XXII: 53–55**

"Truth about God, The" (Carson), **Supp. XII: 105–106**

"Truth be told" (Trethewey), **Supp. XXI:** 255, 256

"Truthful James" (Harte), **IV:** 196

"Truth Is, The" (Hogan), **Supp. IV Part 1:** 401–402

"Truth Is Forced, The" (Swenson), **Supp. IV Part 2:** 652

"Truth of the Matter, The" (Nemerov), **III:** 270

Truth Serum (Cooper), **Supp. XI:** 129

"Truth the Dead Know, The" (Sexton), **Supp. II Part 2:** 681

"Trying to Evangelize a Cut Flower" (Peacock), **Supp. XIX:** 199

Trying to Find Chinatown (Hwang), **Supp. XXI:** 147

Trying to Save Piggy Sneed (Irving), **Supp. VI: 19–165**

"Trying to Talk with a Man" (Rich), **Supp. I Part 2:** 559

"Tryptich I" (Bell), **Supp. X:** 7

"Tryst, The" (Wharton), **Retro. Supp. I:** 378

"Try the Girl" (Chandler), **Supp. IV Part 1:** 125

Try! Try! (O'Hara), **Supp. XXIII:** 209, 210, 216

"Ts'ai Chih" (Pound), **III:** 466

T. S. Eliot and American Philosophy (Jain), **Retro. Supp. I:** 58

T. S. Eliot's Silent Voices (Mayer), **Retro. Supp. I:** 58

Tsuji, Shizuo, **Supp. XVII:** 90

Tsurikgekumen (The return) (Asch), **Supp. XXIII:** 5

Tsvetaeva, Marina, **Supp. VIII:** 30; **Supp. XXIII:** 168

"Tuberoses" (E. Stoddard), **Supp. XV:** 282

Tubert, Susana, **Supp. XXIII:** 203

Tuck, James A., **Supp. XXVI:** 83

Tucker, Benjamin R., **Supp. XXI:** 9

Tuckerman, Frederick Goddard, **IV:** 144; **Supp. XXV:** 241

Tucker's People (Wolfert), **Supp. XXI:** 261, 262, 263, 267, **267–275,** 278

"Tuesday, November 5th, 1940" (Benét), **Supp. XI:** 46, 52

"Tuesday April 25th 1966" (Olson), **Supp. II Part 2:** 585

"Tuesday Night at the Savoy Ballroom" (Komunyakaa), **Supp. XIII:** 132

Tuffield, Aviva, **Supp. XVI:** 147, 148

"Tuft of Flowers, The" (Frost), **II:** 153; **Retro. Supp. I:** 126, 127

Tufts, James Hayden, **Supp. I Part 2:** 632

Tu Fu, **II:** 526; **Supp. XV:** 47

Tu Fu (Ayscough), **II:** 527

Tugwell, Rexford Guy, **Supp. I Part 2:** 645

"Tulip" (Hammett), **Supp. IV Part 1:** 356

"Tulip Man, The" (McCarriston), **Supp. XIV:** 261

"Tulips" (Nye), **Supp. XIII:** 281

"Tulips" (Plath), **Retro. Supp. II:** 252–253; **Supp. I Part 2:** 540, 542, 544

"Tulips" (Snodgrass), **Supp. VI:** 325

Tulips and Chimneys (Cummings), **I:** 436, 437, 440, 445, 447

"Tulips"(Strout), **Supp. XXIII:** 283, 285

"Tulips"(theater performance, Strout), **Supp. XXIII:** 281

Tully, Jim, **III:** 103, 109

Tumble Home (Hempel), **Supp. XXI:** 115, **124–125**

"Tumble Home" (Hempel), **Supp. XXI:** 115, 116, **124–125,** 126

Tumble Tower (Modarressi and Tyler), **Supp. IV Part 2:** 657

"Tuned in Late One Night" (Stafford), **Supp. XI:** 327–328

Tunnel, The (Gass), **Supp. V:** 44; **Supp. VI: 89–91,** 94

"Tunnel, The" (Strand), **Supp. IV Part 2:** 622

"Tunnels" (Komunyakaa), **Supp. XIII:** 123

Tunnel Vision (Paretsky), **Supp. XXV:** 173–174, 177, 178, 181

Tuon, Bunkong, **Supp. XXVI:** 211, 220

Tuqan, Fadwa, **Supp. XIII:** 278

Tura, Cosimo, **III:** 474–475

Turandot and Other Poems (Ashbery), **Supp. III Part 1:** 3

Turco, Lewis, **Supp. XV:** 118

Turgenev, Ivan Sergeevich, **I:** 106; **II:** 263, 271, 275, 280, 281, 288, 319, 320, 324–325, 338, 407; **III:** 461; **IV:** 17, 277; **Retro. Supp. I:** 215, 222; **Supp. VIII:** 167

Turgot, Anne Robert Jacques, **II:** 103; **Supp. I Part 1:** 250

"Turkey and Bones and Eating and We Liked It" (Stein), **IV:** 44

Turman, Glynn, **Supp. IV Part 1:** 362

Turnbull, Dr. George, **II:** 113

Turnbull, Lawrence, **Supp. I Part 1:** 352

"Turned" (Gilman), **Supp. XI:** 207

Turner, Addie, **IV:** 123

Turner, Darwin, **Supp. I Part 1:** 339; **Supp. IV Part 1:** 165

Turner, Frederick Jackson, **Supp. I Part 2:** 480, 481, 632, 640; **Supp. IV Part 2:** 596

Turner, Nat, **IV:** 113–114, 115, 116, 117

Turner, Patricia A., **Supp. XIII:** 237; **Supp. XX: 110**

Turner, Russell. *See* Lacy, Ed

Turner, Victor, **Supp. IV Part 1:** 304

"Turning Away Variations on Estrangement" (Dickey), **Supp. IV Part 1:** 183

Turning Point, The (McCoy), **Supp. XIII:** 175

"Turning Thirty, I Contemplate Students Bicycling Home" (Dove), **Supp. IV Part 1:** 250

Turning Wind, A (Rukeyser), **Supp. VI:** 272–273, 279–280

Turn in the South, A (Naipaul), **Supp. XXII:** 240

Turn of the Screw, The (H. James), **Retro. Supp. I:** 219, 231; **Supp. IV Part 2:** 682

"Turn of the Screw, The" (H. James), **II:** 331–332; **Retro. Supp. I:** 228, 229, 231, 232; **Supp. XVII:** 143

Turns and Movies and Other Tales in Verse (Aiken), **I:** 65

"Turn with the Sun, A" (Knowles), **Supp. XII:** 237–238

"Turn Your Radio On" (J. W. Miller), **Supp. XX: 169**

Turow, Scott, **Supp. V:** 220; **Supp. XVII: 213–224**

"Turpentine" (Gallagher), **Supp. XXIV:** 174, 175, 176

Turpin, E. Walters, **Supp. XVIII:** 283

Turrinus, Lucius Mamilius, **IV:** 373

"Turtle" (Hogan), **Supp. IV Part 1:** 401

Turtle, Swan (Doty), **Supp. XI: 121–122**

"Turtle, Swan" (Doty), **Supp. XI:** 121–122

Turtle Island (Snyder), **Supp. VIII: 300–303**

Turtle Moon (Hoffman), **Supp. X:** 77, **87–88,** 89

"Turtle Shrine near Chittagong, The" (Nye), **Supp. XIII:** 277

Turtotte, James, **Supp. XXIII:** 125

Turturro, John, **Supp. XI:** 174

Tuscan Cities (Howells), **II:** 280

Tuskegee movement, **Supp. II Part 1:** 169, 172

Tuten, Frederic, **Supp. VIII:** 75, 76; **Supp. XIII:** 237, 249

Tuten, James, **Supp. XVIII:** 195

Tuthill, Louisa Cavolne, **Supp. I Part 2:** 684

"Tutored Child, The" (Kunitz), **Supp. III Part 1:** 264

Tuttleton, James W., **Supp. IV Part 1:** 166, 168

"T.V.A." (Agee), **I:** 35

Tvedten, Brother Benet, **Supp. IV Part 2:** 505

"TV Men" (Carson), **Supp. XII: 105, 112**

Twain, Mark, **I:** 57, 103, 107, 109, 190, 192, 193, 195, 197, 203, 209, 245, 246, 247–250, 255, 256, 257, 260, 261, 292, 342, 418, 469, 485; **II:** 70, 140, 259, 262, 266–268, 271, 272, 274–275, 276, 277, 280, 285–286, 287, 288, 289, 301, 304, 306, 307, 312, 415, 432, 434, 436, 446, 457, 467, 475, 476, 482; **III:** 65, 101, 102, 112–113, 114, 220, 347, 357, 409, 453, 454, 504, 507, 554, 558, 572, 575, 576; **IV: 190–213,** 333, 349, 451; **Retro. Supp. I:** 169, 194, 195; **Retro. Supp. II:** 123; **Supp. I Part 1:** 37, 39, 44, 247, 251, 313, 317; **Supp. I Part 2:** 377, 385, 393, 410, 455, 456, 457, 473, 475, 579, 602, 604, 618, 629, 651, 660; **Supp. II Part 1:** 193, 344, 354, 385; **Supp. IV Part 1:** 388; **Supp. IV Part 2:** 463, 468, 603, 607, 693; **Supp. IX:** 14, 171; **Supp. V:** 44, 113, 131; **Supp. VIII:** 40, 189; **Supp. X:** 51, 227; **Supp. XII:** 343; **Supp. XIII:** 1, 17; **Supp. XV:** 41;

Supp. XVI: 66, 208; **Supp. XVIII:** 1, 9, 13; **Supp. XXI:** 205; **Supp. XXII:** 89, 203, 205, 206; **Supp. XXIII:** 85

"Twa Sisters, The" (ballad), **Supp. I Part 2:** 696

Twelfth Night (Shakespeare), **Supp. IV Part 1:** 83; **Supp. IX:** 14; **Supp. XXII:** 229

Twelve (Blok), **Supp. XXVI:** 144

"12 O'Clock News" (Bishop), **Retro. Supp. II:** 48

Twelve Men (Dreiser), **Retro. Supp. II:** 94, 104

Twelve Moons (Oliver), **Supp. VII:** 231, 233–236, 238, 240

Twelve Southerners, **IV:** 125; **Supp. X:** 25

Twelve Years a Slave (Northup), **Supp. XIV:** 32

Twentieth Century Authors, **I:** 376, 527

"Twentieth Century Fiction and the Black Mask of Humanity" (Ellison), **Retro. Supp. II:** 118

Twentieth Century Pleasures (Hass), **Supp. VI:** 103, 106, 109

Twenty Drawings (Gibran), **Supp. XX: 116**

"28" (Levine), **Supp. V:** 187, 191

"Twenty-Four Poems" (Schwartz), **Supp. II Part 2:** 646, 649

"2433 Agnes, First Home, Last House in Missoula" (Hugo), **Supp. VI:** 139–140

"Twenty Hill Hollow" (Muir), **Supp. IX:** 178

Twenty Love Poems and a Song of Despair (Neruda), **Supp. XXIV:** 170

"Twenty Minutes" (Salter), **Supp. IX:** 260

"Twenty-One Love Poems" (Rich), **Supp. I Part 2:** 572–573

"Twenty-One Poems" (MacLeish), **III:** 19

Twenty Poems (Haines), **Supp. XII:** 204, **205–206**

Twenty Poems of Anna Akhmatova (Kenyon), **Supp. VII:** 165–166

Twenty Questions: (Posed by Poems) (McClatchy), **Supp. XII:** 254, **259–262**

27 Wagons Full of Cotton and Other One-Act Plays (T. Williams), **IV:** 381, 383

Twenty-seventh City, The (Franzen), **Supp. XX: 83–84, 84,** 85, **86–88, 88, 89, 91, 92, 95**

Twentysomething Essays by Twentysomething Writers (Kellogg and Quint, eds.), **Supp. XXVI:** 53

Twenty Thousand Leagues under the Sea (Verne), **I:** 480; **Supp. XI:** 63

"Twenty Years Ago" (Lindsay), **Supp. I Part 2:** 384, 399

Twenty Years at Hull-House (Addams), **Supp. I Part 1:** 3, 4, 11, 16

Twersky, David, **Supp. XX: 244**

Twice over Lightly: New York Ten and Now (Hayes and Loos), **Supp. XVI:** 195

Twice-Told Tales (Hawthorne), **I:** 354; **II:** 224; **III:** 412, 421; **Retro. Supp. I:** 154–155, 160

Twichell, Chase, **Supp. V:** 16; **Supp. XVII:** 110, 112

Twilight (Frost), **II:** 151

"Twilight's Last Gleaming" (Burroughs and Elvins), **Supp. III Part 1:** 93, 94, 101

Twilight Sleep (Wharton), **IV:** 320–322, 324–325, 327, 328; **Retro. Supp. I:** 381

"Twin, The" (Olds), **Supp. X:** 207

"Twin Beds in Rome" (Updike), **Retro. Supp. I:** 332

"Twins of Table Mountain, The" (Harte), **Supp. II Part 1:** 355

"Twist, The" (Olson), **Supp. II Part 2:** 570

Twitch and Shout (film), **Supp. XVIII:** 143

Twitchell-Waas, Jeffrey, **Supp. XVIII:** 99; **Supp. XXII:** 163

"Two" (Huddle), **Supp. XXVI:** 150

Two Admirals, The (Cooper), **I:** 350

Two against One (F. Barthelme), **Supp. XI:** 32, 33, 36

"Two and One"(Hadas), **Supp. XXIII:** 114–115

"Two Boys" (Moore), **Supp. X:** 173

"Two Brothers, The" (Jewett), **Retro. Supp. II:** 132

Two-Character Play, The (T. Williams), **IV:** 382, 386, 393, 398

Two Citizens (Wright), **Supp. III Part 2:** 602–604

"Two Deer" (Bass), **Supp. XVI:** 24

"Two Domains, The" (Goldbarth), **Supp. XII:** 192

"Two-Eleven All Around" (Offutt), **Supp. XIX:** 170

"Two Environments, The" (Trilling), **Supp. III Part 2:** 510

"Two-Fisted Self Pity" (Broyard), **Supp. XI:** 348

Two for Texas (Burke), **Supp. XIV:** 25, 34

"Two Friends" (Cather), **I:** 332

"Two Gardens in Linndale" (Robinson), **III:** 508

Two Gentlemen in Bonds (Ransom), **III:** 491–492

Two: Gertrude Stein and Her Brother (Stein), **IV:** 43

"Two Ghosts" (Francis), **Supp. IX:** 87

"Two Hangovers" (Wright), **Supp. III Part 2:** 596

Two-Headed Poems (Atwood), **Supp. XIII:** 34

Two Hot to Handle (Lacy), **Supp. XV:** 206

Two Hours to Doom (Bryant), **Supp. XI:** 302

"Two Hundred Years in an Hour" (Boyce), **Supp. XXI:** 8

"Two Kitchens in Provence" (M. F. K. Fisher), **Supp. XVII:** 88, 91

"Two Ladies in Retirement" (Taylor), **Supp. V:** 320

Two Letters to the Citizens of the United States, and One to General Washington (Barlow), **Supp. II Part 1:** 80

Two Little Women on a Holiday (Wells), **Supp. XXVI:** 277

"Two Lives, The" (Hogan), **Supp. IV Part 1:** 400, 402, 403, 406, 411

Two Long Poems (Stern), **Supp. IX:** 296

"Two Look at Two" (Frost), **Supp. XXI:** 26

"Two Lovers and a Beachcomber by the Real Sea" (Plath), **Supp. I Part 2:** 536

"Two Men" (McClatchy)", **Supp. XII:** 269

Two Men (E. Stoddard), **Supp. XV:** 272, 273, **283–284**

Two Men of Sandy Bar (Harte), **Supp. II Part 1:** 354

Twomey, Jay, **Supp. XVII:** 111

"Two Moods of Love" (Cullen), **Supp. IV Part 1:** 166

Two Moons (Mallon), **Supp. XIX:** 132, **138–141**

"Two Morning Monologues" (Bellow), **I:** 150; **Retro. Supp. II:** 20

"Two Nations of Black America, The" *(Frontline)*, **Supp. XX: 99**

Two-Ocean War, The (Morison), **Supp. I Part 2:** 491

"Two of Hearts" (Hogan), **Supp. IV Part 1:** 410

"Two on a Party" (T. Williams), **IV:** 388

"Two or Three Things I Dunno About John Cassavetes" (Lethem), **Supp. XVIII:** 148

"Two Pendants: For the Ears" (W. C. Williams), **Retro. Supp. I:** 423

"Two Poems of Going Home" (Dickey), **Supp. IV Part 1:** 182–183

"Two Portraits" (Chopin), **Supp. I Part 1:** 218

"Two Presences, The" (R. Bly), **Supp. IV Part 1:** 65

"Two Rivers" (Stegner), **Supp. IV Part 2:** 605

Tworkov, Jack, **Supp. XII:** 198

"Two Scenes" (Ashbery), **Supp. III Part 1:** 4

Two Serious Ladies (Jane Bowles), **Supp. IV Part 1:** 82

"Two Silences" (Carruth), **Supp. XVI:** 55

"Two Sisters" (Farrell), **II:** 45

Two Sisters: A Memoir in the Form of a Novel (Vidal), **Supp. IV Part 2:** 679

"Two Sisters of Persephone" (Plath), **Retro. Supp. II:** 246

"Two Songs on the Economy of Abundance" (Agee), **I:** 28

Two Sons, The (Boyce), **Supp. XXI:** 7, 13

"Two Tales of Clumsy" (Schnackenberg), **Supp. XV:** 258

"Two Temples, The" (Melville), **III:** 89–90

Two Thousand Seasons (Armah), **Supp. IV Part 1:** 373

Two Towns in Provence (M. F. K. Fisher), **Supp. XVII:** 91

Two Trains Running (Wilson), **Supp. VIII:** 345–348

"Two Tramps in Mudtime" (Frost), **II:** 164; **Retro. Supp. I:** 137; **Supp. IX:** 261

"Two Twilights for William Carlos Williams" (Boyle), **Supp. XXIV:** 63

"Two Views of a Cadaver Room" (Plath), **Supp. I Part 2:** 538

"Two Villages" (Paley), **Supp. VI:** 227

"Two Voices in a Meadow" (Wilbur), **Supp. III Part 2:** 555

Two Weeks in Another Town (Shaw), **Supp. XIX:** 251

"Two Witches" (Frost), **Retro. Supp. I:** 135

"Two Words" (Francis), **Supp. IX:** 81

Two Worlds Walking: A Mixed-Blood Anthology (Glancy and Truesdale, eds.), **Supp. XXI:** 246

Two Years Before the Mast (Dana), **I:** 351; **Supp. XXV:** 208

"Tyger, The" (Blake), **Supp. XVII:** 128

Tyler, Anne, **Supp. IV Part 2: 657–675; Supp. V:** 227, 326; **Supp. VIII:** 141; **Supp. X:** 1, 77, 83, 85; **Supp. XII:** 307; **Supp. XVI:** 37; **Supp. XVIII:** 157, 195; **Supp. XXIII:** 298

Tyler, Royall, **I:** 344; **Retro. Supp. I:** 377

Tymms, Ralph, **Supp. IX:** 105

Tyndale, William, **II:** 15

Tyndall, John, **Retro. Supp. II:** 93

Typee: A Peep at Polynesian Life (Melville), **III:** 75–77, 79, 84; **Retro. Supp. I:** 245–246, 249, 252, 256

Types From City Streets (Hapgood), **Supp. XVII:** 103

"Typewriter, The" (D. West), **Supp. XVIII:** 279; **Supp. XXVI:** 164

Typewriter Town (W. J. Smith), **Supp. XIII:** 332

"Typhus" (Simpson), **Supp. IX:** 277

Tyranny of the Normal (Fiedler), **Supp. XIII: 107–108**

"Tyranny of the Normal" (Fiedler), **Supp. XIII:** 107–108

"Tyrant of Syracuse" (MacLeish), **III:** 20

"Tyrian Businesses" (Olson), **Supp. II Part 2:** 567, 568, 569

Tytell, John, **Supp. XIV:** 140

Tzara, Tristan, **Supp. III Part 1:** 104, 105

U

U and I (Baker), **Supp. XIII: 45–47,** 48, 52, 55

Überdie Seelenfrage (Fechner), **II:** 358

Ubik (Dick), **Supp. XVIII:** 136

"*Ubi Sunt* Lament for the Eccentric Museums of My Childhood" (Stallings), **Supp. XXV:** 232

Ubu Roi (Jarry), **Supp. XV:** 178, 186

Ueland, Brenda, **Supp. XVII:** 13

Uhry, Alfred, **Supp. XX: 177**

ukanhavyrfuckinciti back (Phillips), **Supp. XXIII:** 174

Ukrainian Dumy (P. N. Warren as Kilina and Tarnawsky, trans.), **Supp. XX: 261**

"Ulalume" (Poe), **III:** 427; **Retro. Supp. II:** 264, 266

Ulin, David, **Supp. XIII:** 244; **Supp. XVI:** 74

Ullman, Leslie, **Supp. IV Part 2:** 550; **Supp. XVIII:** 175

Ultimate Good Luck, The (Ford), **Supp. V:** 57, 61–62

Ultimate Punishment: A Lawyer's Reflections on Dealing with the Death Penalty (Turow), **Supp. XVII:** 220–221

Ultima Thule (Longfellow), **II:** 490; **Retro. Supp. II:** 169

"Ultima Thule" (Nabokov), **Retro. Supp. I:** 274

Ultramarine (Carver), **Supp. III Part 1:** 137, 138, 147, 148

"Ultrasound" (Stallings), **Supp. XXV:** 225, 233, 234

Ulysses (Joyce), **I:** 395, 475–476, 478, 479, 481; **II:** 42, 264, 542; **III:** 170, 398; **IV:** 103, 418, 428, 455; **Retro. Supp. I:** 59, 63, 290, 291; **Retro. Supp. II:** 121; **Supp. I Part 1:** 57; **Supp. III Part 2:** 618, 619; **Supp. IV Part 1:** 285; **Supp. IV Part 2:** 424; **Supp. IX:** 102; **Supp. V:** 261; **Supp. X:** 114; **Supp. XIII:** 43, 191; **Supp. XV:** 305; **Supp. XVII:** 140, 227; **Supp. XXV:** 65

"*Ulysses,* Order and Myth" (Eliot), **Retro. Supp. I:** 63

"Umbrella, The" (Peacock), **Supp. XIX:** 203–204

Unaccountable Worth of the World, The (Price), **Supp. VI:** 267

Unaccustomed Earth (Lahiri), **Supp. XXI:** 176, **181–183,** 183, 188

"Unaccustomed Earth" (Lahiri), **Supp. XXI:** 186

Unamuno y Jugo, Miguel de, **III:** 310; **Supp. XV:** 79

"Unattached Smile, The" (Crews), **Supp. XI:** 101

"Unbelievable Thing Usually Goes to the Heart of the Story, The: Magic Realism in the Fiction of Rick Bass" (Dwyer), **Supp. XVI:** 16

"Unbeliever, The" (Bishop), **Retro. Supp. II:** 43

"Unborn Song" (Rukeyser), **Supp. VI:** 274

Unbought Spirit: A John Jay Chapman Reader (Stone, ed.), **Supp. XIV:** 54

Uncalled, The (Dunbar), **Supp. II Part 1:** 200, 211, 212

Uncentering the Earth: Copernicus and The Revolutions of the Heavenly Spheres (Vollmann), **Supp. XVII:** 226

Uncertain Certainty, The: Interviews, Essays, and Notes on Poetry (Simic), **Supp. VIII:** 270, 273, 274

Uncertainty and Plenitude: Five Contemporary Poets (Stitt), **Supp. IX:** 299

"Uncle" (Levine), **Supp. V:** 186

"Uncle Adler" (Kooser), **Supp. XIX:** 120

"Uncle Christmas" (Ríos), **Supp. IV Part 2:** 552

"Uncle Jim's Baptist Revival Hymn" (Lanier and Lanier), **Supp. I Part 1:** 353

"Uncle Lot" (Stowe), **Supp. I Part 2:** 585–586

Uncle Moses (Asch), **Supp. XXIII:** 14

"Uncle Moustapha's Eclipse" (McKnight), **Supp. XX: 148**

Uncle Remus Tales (Harris), **Supp. II Part 1:** 201

"Uncle Tomitudes" (Briggs), **Supp. XVIII:** 14

Uncle Tom's Cabin (Stowe), **II:** 291; **Supp. I Part 1:** 49; **Supp. I Part 2:** 410, 579, 582, 589–592; **Supp. II Part 1:** 170; **Supp. III Part 1:** 154, 171; **Supp. IX:** 19; **Supp. X:** 246, 249, 250; **Supp. XIII:** 95; **Supp. XVI:** 82, 85, 88; **Supp. XVIII:** 14

Uncle Tom's Children (Wright), **IV:** 476, 478, 488; **Supp. II Part 1:** 228, 235; **Supp. XVIII:** 283

"Uncle Wiggily in Connecticut" (Salinger), **III:** 559–560, 563

"Unclouded Day, The" (Proulx), **Supp. VII:** 254–255

"Uncommon Visage" (Brodsky), **Supp. VIII:** 31

"Uncommon Woman: An Interview with Wendy Wasserstein" (Cohen), **Supp. XV:** 323

Uncommon Women and Others (Wasserstein), **Supp. XV:** 320–321, **322–323; Supp. XXIV:** 117

Uncompromising Fictions of Cynthia Ozick (Pinsker), **Supp. V:** 272

"Unconscious Came a Beauty" (Swenson), **Supp. IV Part 2:** 646

"Uncreation, The" (Pinsky), **Supp. VI:** 245

"Undead, The" (Wilbur), **Supp. III Part 2:** 556

"Undefeated, The" (Hemingway), **II:** 250; **Retro. Supp. I:** 180

Under a Glass Bell (Nin), **Supp. X:** 186

"Under Ben Bulben" (Yeats), **Supp. V:** 220

Undercliff: Poems 1946–1953 (Eberhart), **I:** 528, 536–537

Under Cover (Goldbarth), **Supp. XII:** 177, 180, 193

Undercover Doctor (film), **Supp. XIII:** 170

"Under Cygnus" (Wilbur), **Supp. III Part 2:** 558

"Under Forty" (Trilling), **Supp. III Part 2:** 494

"Underground" (Hayes), **Supp. XXVI:** 144

Underground, The Story of a People (Tenenbaum), **Supp. XX:** 253

Underground Man, The (film), **Supp. IV Part 2:** 474

Underground Man, The (Macdonald), **Supp. IV Part 2:** 474, 475

Underground Woman, The (Boyle), **Supp. XXIV:** 62

"Under Libra: Weights and Measures" (Merrill), **Supp. III Part 1:** 328

Under Milk Wood (D. Thomas), **III:** 21

"Undersea" (Carson), **Supp. IX:** 21

Understanding Cynthia Ozick (Friedman), **Supp. V:** 273

Understanding Drama (Brooks and Heilman), **Supp. XIV:** 12

Understanding E. L. Doctorow (Fowler), **Supp. IV Part 1:** 226

Understanding Fiction (Brooks and Warren), **IV:** 279; **Supp. XIV:** 11

Understanding Fiction (Brooks and Warren, eds.), **Supp. XIX:** 246

Understanding Flannery O'Connor (Whitt), **Retro. Supp. II:** 226

Understanding Nicholson Baker (Saltzman), **Supp. XIII:** 48

Understanding Poetry: An Anthology for College Students (Brooks and Warren), **IV:** 236; **Retro. Supp. I:** 40, 41; **Supp. XIV:** 4–5

Understanding Robert Bly (W. V. Davis), **Supp. XXI: 84–85,** 88

"Understandings of Food as Culture" (Dusselier), **Supp. XXVI:** 210

Understanding Tim O'Brien (Kaplan), **Supp. V:** 241

Understanding To Kill a Mockingbird: A Student Casebook to Issues, Sources, and Documents (C. D. Johnson), **Supp. VIII:** 127

Under Stars (Gallagher), **Supp. XXIV:** 166, 167, 168–169, 170

Undertaker's Garland, The (Wilson and Bishop), **IV:** 427

Under Taos Mountain: The Terrible Quarrel of Magpie and Tía (Schott), **Supp. XXIII: 250–251**

Under the Banner of Heaven: A Story of Violent Faith (Krakauer), **Supp. XVIII:** 105, **114–116,** 117

"Under the Cedarcroft Chestnut" (Lanier), **Supp. I Part 1:** 364

Under the Feet of Jesus (Viramontes), **Supp. XXV:** 130

"Under the Harbour Bridge" (Komunyakaa), **Supp. XIII:** 125

"Under the Influence" (Sanders), **Supp. XVI:** 274, 277

"Under the Language Sea" (Davison), **Supp. XXVI:** 79

Under the Lilacs (Alcott), **Supp. I Part 1:** 42–43, 44

"Under the Maud Moon" (Kinnell), **Supp. III Part 1:** 246–247

Under the Mountain Wall: A Chronicle of Two Seasons in the Stone Age (Matthiessen), **Supp. V:** 202

Under the Red Flag (Jin), **Supp. XVIII:** 89, **94–95**

"Under the Roof of Memory" (Davison), **Supp. XXVI:** 78

"Under the Rose" (Pynchon), **Supp. II Part 2:** 620

Under the Sea-Wind: A Naturalist's Picture of Ocean Life (Carson), **Supp. IX:** 19, **22–23**

Under the Shadow (Sorrentino), **Supp. XXI:** 236–237

Under the Sign of Saturn (Sontag), **Supp. III Part 2:** 451, 452, 458, 470–471

"Under the Sign of Saturn" (Sontag), **Supp. III Part 2:** 470

"Under the Sky" (Bowles), **Supp. IV Part 1:** 87

"Under the Sun"(Schott), **Supp. XXIII:** 247, 248

" 'Under the Umbrella of Black Civilization': A Conversation with Reginald McKnight" (Ashe), **Supp. XX: 154**

Under the Volcano (M. Lowry), **Supp. XVII:** 135, 139, 140; **Supp. XXVI:** 28

"Under the Willows" (Lowell), **Supp. I Part 2:** 416

Under the Willows and Other Poems (Lowell), **Supp. I Part 2:** 424

"Undertow" (Boyce), **Supp. XXI:** 10

"Underwater Spring" (Huddle), **Supp. XXVI:** 153

Underwood, John Curtis, **Supp. XXIV:** 29

Underwood, Wilbur, **Retro. Supp. II:** 79

Underworld (DeLillo), **Supp. VI:** 2, 4–5, 6–7, 8, 9, 10, 11, **13–15;** **Supp. XI:** 68; **Supp. XX:** 91

Underworld, The (Wolfert). *See Tucker's World* (Wolfert)

"Undesirable, The" (Huddle), **Supp. XXVI:** 148, 153

Undine (La Motte-Fouqué), **II:** 212; **III:** 78

Undiscovered Country, The (Howells), **II:** 282

"Undressing, The" (C. Frost), **Supp. XV:** 98

"Undressing the Vanity Dolls" (Vaz), **Supp. XXVI:** 260–261

Uneasy Chair, The (Stegner), **Supp. IV Part 2:** 599

"Unemployed, Disabled, and Insane, The" (Haines), **Supp. XII:** 211–212

Unending Blues (Simic), **Supp. VIII: 278–279**

Unending Dialogue: Voices from an AIDS Poetry Workshop (Hadas, Barber, et al), **Supp. XXIII:** 118, **125–126**

"Unexpected Freedom" (Peacock), **Supp. XIX:** 199

"Unexpressed" (Dunbar), **Supp. II Part 1:** 199

"Unfinished Bronx, The" (Paley), **Supp. VI:** 228

Unfinished Crime, The (Holding), **Supp. XXII:** 120, **123–124,** 135, 136

"Unfinished Poems" (Eliot), **I:** 579

"Unfinished Song" (C. Frost), **Supp. XV:** 97

Unfinished Woman, An (Hellman), **Supp. I Part 1:** 292, 293, 294; **Supp. IV Part 1:** 12, 353–354; **Supp. IX:** 196, 200–201

Unforeseen Wilderness, The: An Essay on Kentucky's Red River Gorge (Berry), **Supp. X:** 28, 29, 30, 36

Unforgotten Years (L. P. Smith), **Supp. XIV:** 333, 334, 335, 336, 347

"Unfortunate Coincidence" (Parker), **Supp. IX:** 190

Unframed Originals (Merwin), **Supp. III Part 1:** 341

Ungar, Sanford, **Supp. XI:** 228

Ungaretti, Giuseppe, **Supp. V:** 337

Unguided Tour (Sontag), **Supp. III Part 2:** 452

"Unheimliche, Das" (The Uncanny) (Freud), **Supp. XVI:** 157–158

Unholy Sonnets (Jarman), **Supp. XVII:** 109, 110, **119–120; Supp. XVIII:** 178

"Unholy Sonnets" (Jarman), **Supp. XVII:** 118, 119–120

"Unidentified Flying Object" (Hayden), **Supp. II Part 1:** 368

"Unifying Principle, The" (Ammons), **Supp. VII:** 28

"Unimportant Man, An" (D. West), **Supp. XVIII:** 280

"Union" (Hughes), **Supp. I Part 1:** 331

"Union Street: San Francisco, Summer 1975" (Carver), **Supp. III Part 1:** 138

"Unitarian Christianity" (Channing), **Supp. XXIV: 71–73,** 77

Unitarians and the Universalists, The (Robinson), **Supp. XXIV:** 70

"United"(Kenny), **Supp. XXIII:** 149

United States Army in World War II (Morison), **Supp. I Part 2:** 490

United States Constitution, **I:** 6, 283

United States Essays, 1951–1991 (Vidal), **Supp. IV Part 2:** 678, 687

"United States of Huck, The: Introduction to *Adventures of Huckleberry Finn*" (Saunders), **Supp. XIX:** 235

United States of Poetry, The (television series), **Supp. XIII:** 274

"Unity through Diversity" (Locke), **Supp. XIV:** 212, 213

Universal Baseball Asociation, Inc., J. Henry Waugh, Prop., The (Coover), **Supp. V:** 39, 41–42, 44, 46

Universal Passion (Young), **III:** 111

"Universe of Death, The" (H. Miller), **III:** 184

Universe of Time, A (Anderson), **II:** 27, 28, 45, 46, 48, 49

"Universities" (Emerson), **II:** 6

"Universities: A Mirage? " (Mora), **Supp. XIII:** 219

"University" (Shapiro), **Supp. II Part 2:** 704–705, 717

"University Avenue" (Mora), **Supp. XIII:** 216

"University Days" (Thurber), **Supp. I Part 2:** 605

"University Hospital, Boston" (Oliver), **Supp. VII:** 235

"University's Peril, The" (Taggard), **Supp. XXII:** 273

"Unknowable, The" (Levine), **Supp. V:** 195

"Unknown Girl in the Maternity Ward" (Sexton), **Supp. II Part 2:** 676

"Unknown Love, The" (Chandler), **Supp. IV Part 1:** 120

Unknown Rilke, The (Rilke; F. Wright, trans.), **Supp. XVII:** 244

"Unknown War, The" (Sandburg), **III:** 594

Unkown Constellations, The (Swados), **Supp. XIX:** 256

Unleashed (anthology), **Supp. XI:** 132

Unleashed: Poems by Writers' Dogs (Hempel and Shepard, eds.), **Supp. XXI:** 115

"Unlighted Lamps" (Anderson), **I:** 112

Unlit Lamp, The (Holding), **Supp. XXII:** 121, 130

Unloved Wife, The (Alcott), **Supp. I Part 1:** 33

Unmarried Woman, An (film), **Supp. IV Part 1:** 303

"Unnatural Mother, The" (Gilman), **Supp. XI:** 207

"Unnatural State of the Unicorn" (Komunyakaa), **Supp. XIII:** 119

"Unparalleled Adventure of One Hans Pfaall, The" (Poe), **III:** 424

"Unpleasant Profession of Jonathan Hoag, The" (Heinlein), **Supp. XVIII:** 149

Unprecedented Era, The (Goebbels), **III:** 560

"Unprofitable Servant, The" (O. Henry), **Supp. II Part 1:** 403

Unpublished Poems of Emily Dickinson (Bianchi and Hampson, ed.), **Retro. Supp. I:** 35

Unpunished (Gilman), **Supp. XI:** 208

Unraveling Strangeness, The (Weigl), **Supp. XIX: 287–288**

"Unreal City" (Eliot), **Supp. XV:** 218

"Unreality of Modern Realism, The" (Rinehart), **Supp. XXV:** 201

"Unreasoning Heart" (Untermeyer), **Supp. XV:** 309

"Unsaid (Gioia), **Supp. XV:** 129

"Unseen, The" (Pinsky), **Supp. VI:** 243–244

"Unseen, The" (Singer), **Retro. Supp. II:** 307

Unseen Hand, The (Shepard), **Supp. III Part 2:** 439, 445–446

Unselected Poems (Levine), **Supp. V:** 179

Unsettling of America, The: Culture and Agriculture (Berry), **Supp. X:** 22, 26, 29, 32, 33, 35; **Supp. XIV:** 177, 179

Unspeakable Gentleman, The (Marquand), **III:** 53–54, 60, 63

Unspeakable Practices, Unnatural Acts (Barthelme), **Supp. IV Part 1:** 39

"Unspeakable Things Unspoken: The Afro-American Presence in American Literature" (Morrison), **Supp. III Part 1:** 375, 377–379

Unspoken and Other Poems, The (Bremer), **Supp. XXII:** 277

"Untelling, The" (Strand), **Supp. IV Part 2:** 629

Unterecker, John, **I:** 386

Untermeyer, Jean Starr, **II:** 530; **Supp. XV:** 294, 295, 303, 307, 308, 310

Untermeyer, Louis, **II:** 516–517, 530, 532; **III:** 268; **Retro. Supp. I:** 124, 133, 136; **Supp. III Part 1:** 2; **Supp. IX:** 76; **Supp. XIV:** 119, 123; **Supp. XV: 293–318; Supp. XXI:** 277; **Supp. XXV:** 21, 23

Untimely Papers (Bourne), **I:** 218, 233

"Untitled" (C. Frost), **Supp. XV:** 103

"Untitled Blues" (Komunyakaa), **Supp. XIII:** 117

Unto the Sons (Talese), **Supp. XVII:** 199–200, **206–207,** 208, 209, 210

"Untrustworthy Speaker, The" (Glück), **Supp. V:** 86

"Unused" (Anderson), **I:** 112, 113

Unvanquished, The (Faulkner), **II:** 55, 67–68, 71; **Retro. Supp. I:** 84; **Supp. I Part 2:** 450

"Unvexed Isles, The" (Warren), **IV:** 253

"Unwedded" (Larcom), **Supp. XIII:** 144

"Unweepables, The" (Karr), **Supp. XI:** 243

"Unwelcome Guest, An" (Papernick), **Supp. XVII:** 50

Unwelcome Man, The (W. Frank), **Supp. XX: 70, 76**

Unwelcome Words (Bowles), **Supp. IV Part 1:** 93, 94

"Unwelcome Words" (Bowles), **Supp. IV Part 1:** 94, 95

Unwin, T. Fisher, **Supp. XI:** 202

"Unwithered Garland, The" (Kunitz), **Supp. III Part 1:** 265

Unwobbling Pivot, The (Pound, trans.), **III:** 472

"Unwritten, The" (Merwin), **Supp. III Part 1:** 352

"Unwritten Law" (Glück), **Supp. V:** 91

Up (Sukenick), **Supp. V:** 39

Up Above the World (Bowles), **Supp. IV Part 1:** 82, 91, 92

"Up and Down" (Merrill), **Supp. III Part 1:** 328

Upanishads, **IV:** 183

Up Country: Poems of New England (Kumin), **Supp. IV Part 2:** 446, 447–448, 453

"Update" (Dunn), **Supp. XI:** 150–151

Updike, John, **I:** 54; **III:** 572; **IV: 214–235; Retro. Supp. I:** 116, **317–338; Retro. Supp. II:** 213, 279, 280; **Supp. I Part 1:** 186, 196; **Supp. IV Part 2:** 657; **Supp. IX:** 208; **Supp. V:** 23, 43, 95, 119; **Supp. VIII:** 151, 167, 236; **Supp. XI:** 65, 66, 99, 140; **Supp. XII:** 140, 296, 298, 310; **Supp. XIII:** 45–46, 47, 52; **Supp. XIV:** 79, 93, 111; **Supp. XVI:** 205, 207, 220; **Supp. XX:** 17; **Supp. XXI:** 116, 226; **Supp. XXIII:** 109

Updike, Mrs. Wesley, **IV:** 218, 220

Up from Slavery (Washington), **Supp. II Part 1:** 169; **Supp. IX:** 19

Upham, Thomas Goggswell, **II:** 487

"Upholsterers, The" (Lardner), **II:** 435

"Up in Michigan" (Hemingway), **II:** 263; **Supp. XIX:** 241

Upjohn, Richard, **IV:** 312

"Upon a Spider Catching a Fly" (Taylor), **IV:** 161

"Upon a Wasp Child with Cold" (Taylor), **IV:** 161

"Upon Meeting Don L. Lee, in a Dream" (Dove), **Supp. IV Part 1:** 244

"Upon My Dear and Loving Husband His Going into England, Jan. 16, 1661" (Bradstreet), **Supp. I Part 1:** 110

"Upon My Mother's Death"(Hadas), **Supp. XXIII:** 118

"Upon Returning to the Country Road" (Lindsay), **Supp. I Part 2:** 382

"Upon the Burning of Our House, July 10th, 1666" (Bradstreet), **Supp. I Part 1:** 107–108, 122

"Upon the Sweeping Flood" (Taylor), **IV:** 161

"Upon Wedlock, and Death of Children" (Taylor), **IV:** 144, 147, 161

"Upon Westminster Bridge" (Wordsworth), **Supp. XXIV:** 148

"Upset, An" (Merrill), **Supp. III Part 1:** 336

Upstairs and Downstairs (Vonnegut), **Supp. II Part 2:** 757

Upstate (Wilson), **IV:** 447

Upton, Lee, **Supp. X:** 209

"Upturned Face" (Crane), **I:** 423

Upward, Allen, **Supp. I Part 1:** 262

Upward, Edward, **Supp. XIV:** 159, 160

"Upward Moon and the Downward Moon, The" (R. Bly), **Supp. IV Part 1:** 71

Urania: A Rhymed Lesson (Holmes), **Supp. I Part 1:** 300

"Urban Convalescence, An" (Merrill), **Supp. III Part 1:** 322–324

"Urban Renewal" (Komunyakaa), **Supp. XIII:** 113

Urdang, Constance, **Supp. XV:** 74

"Urganda and Fatima" (Rowson), **Supp. XV:** 234

Urial Accosta: A Play (Reznikoff), **Supp. XIV:** 282, 288

Urich, Robert, **Supp. V:** 228

"Uriel" (Emerson), **II:** 19

Uris, Leon, **Supp. IV Part 1:** 285, 379; **Supp. XX: 243–258**

Uroff, Margaret D., **Supp. I Part 2:** 542

Ursu, Liliana, **Supp. XXIV:** 178

"Us" (Sexton), **Supp. II Part 2:** 687

U.S. 1 (Rukeyser), **Supp. VI:** 272, 278, 283, 285

U.S.A. (Dos Passos), **I:** 379, 475, 478, 482–488, 489, 490, 491, 492, 493, 494, 495; **Retro. Supp. II:** 197; **Supp. I Part 2:** 646; **Supp. III Part 1:** 104, 105; **Supp. XIV:** 24; **Supp. XXVI:** 23

"U.S.A. School of Writing, The" (Bishop), **Retro. Supp. II:** 43

"U.S. Commercial Orchid, The" (Agee), **I:** 35

"Used-Boy Raisers, The" (Paley), **Supp. VI:** 218, 228

"Used Cars on Oahu" (Nye), **Supp. XIII:** 282

"Used Side of the Sofa, The" (Ríos), **Supp. IV Part 2:** 551

Useless Servants, The (Hinojosa), **Supp. XIX:** 98, 103, 104, **109–110**

Use of Fire, The (Price), **Supp. VI:** 265

"Use of Force, The" (W. C. Williams), **Retro. Supp. I:** 424

Use of Poetry and the Use of Criticism, The (Eliot), **Retro. Supp. I:** 65

Uses of Enchantment, The: The Meaning and Importance of Fairy Tales (Bettelheim), **Supp. X:** 77; **Supp. XIV:** 126

"Uses of Hell, The" (E. Hoffman), **Supp. XVI:** 154

"Uses of Hell, The: An Exchange"(Novick, Katz, and Szulc), **Supp. XVI:** 154

Uses of Literacy, The (Hoggart), **Supp. XIV:** 299

Uses of Literature, The (Calvino), **Supp. XXII:** 263

"Uses of Poetry, The" (W. C. Williams), **Retro. Supp. I:** 412

"Uses of the Blues, The" (Baldwin), **Retro. Supp. II:** 8

"Use-Unuse of Us, The" (Bronk), **Supp. XXI:** 32

"USFS 1919: The Ranger, the Cook, and a Hole in the Sky" (Maclean), **Supp. XIV:** 230, 234

Ushant: An Essay (Aiken), **I:** 49, 54, 55, 56, 57

"Usher 11" (Bradbury), **Supp. I Part 2:** 622

U.S.I. (Kramer), **Supp. XXVI:** 26

"Using Parrots to Kill Mockingbirds: Yet Another Racial Prosecution and Wrongful Conviction in Maycomb" (Fair), **Supp. VIII:** 128

Ustedes y Nosotros: Nuevo Mensaje a Ibero-América (W. Frank), **Supp. XX: 79**

"Usual Objects"(Schott), **Supp. XXIII:** 248

Usual Star, The (Doolittle), **Supp. I Part 1:** 270

"Usurpation (Other People's Stories)" (Ozick), **Supp. V:** 268, 271

Utopia 14 (Vonnegut), **Supp. II Part 2:** 757

V

V. (Pynchon), **Supp. II Part 2:** 618, 620–622, 627–630; **Supp. IV Part 1:** 279

"Vacation" (Stafford), **Supp. XI:** 321, 322

Vacationland (Monson), **Supp. XXIV:** 230, 231, 234

"Vacation Trip" (Stafford), **Supp. XI:** 322

Vachel Lindsay: A Poet in America (Masters), **Supp. I Part 2:** 473, 474

"Vachel Lindsay: The Midwest as Utopia" (Whitney), **Supp. I Part 2:** 403

"Vachel Lindsay Writes to Floyd Dell" (Tanselle), **Supp. I Part 2:** 403

"Vacillation" (Yeats), **Supp. XV:** 253

Vadim, Roger, **Supp. XI:** 293, 307

"Vag" (Dos Passos), **I:** 487–488

Vagina Monologues, The (Ensler), **Supp. XIX:** 204–205

Vail, Laurence, **Supp. XXIV:** 50

Valdez, Luis, **Supp. XXIII:** 203

"Vale" (Stallings), **Supp. XXV:** 230, 231

Valediction (Parker), **Supp. XIX:** 185

Valentine, Jean, **Supp. V:** 92

Valentine, Saint, **IV:** 396

Valentines (Kooser), **Supp. XIX:** 116, 123, **128–129**

Valentino, Rudolph, **I:** 483

Valéry, Paul, **II:** 543, 544; **III:** 279, 409, 428, 609; **IV:** 79, 91, 92, 428, 443; **Retro. Supp. II:** 187

"Valhalla" (Francis), **Supp. IX:** 77

Valhalla and Other Poems (Francis), **Supp. IX:** 76

Valiant Runaways, The (Atherton), **Supp. XXIV:** 22

Validity in Interpretation (Hirsch), **Supp. XIV:** 15

Valitsky, Ken, **Supp. XII:** 7

Vallejo, César, **Supp. IX:** 271; **Supp. V:** 332; **Supp. XIII:** 114, 315, 323; **Supp. XXI:** 132

Valley, The (Asch), **Supp. XXVI:** 17, 21, 23–26

Valley, The (Bass), **Supp. XVI:** 20, 22

Valley, The (Hinojosa), **Supp. XIX:** 97, 99, **100–101**

"Valley Between, The" (Marshall), **Supp. XI:** 278

Valley of Decision, The (Wharton), **IV:** 311, 315; **Retro. Supp. I:** 365–367

"Valley of the Monsters, The" (Peacock), **Supp. XIX:** 198

Valley of the Moon, The (London), **II:** 467, 481

"Valley of Unrest, The" (Poe), **III:** 411

Valli, Alida, **Supp. IV Part 2:** 520

"Valor" (Bausch), **Supp. VII:** 54

Valparaiso (DeLillo), **Supp. VI:** 4, 12

"Value of a Place, The" (Bass), **Supp. XVI:** 18

"Values and Fictions" (Toomer), **Supp. III Part 2:** 485–486

"Values and Imperatives" (Locke), **Supp. XIV:** 199, 202, 212

Values of Veblen, The: A Critical Appraisal (Rosenberg), **Supp. I Part 2:** 650

"Vampire" (Karr), **Supp. XI:** 241

Vampire Armand, The (Rice), **Supp. VII:** 290, 294–295

Vampire Chronicles, The (Rice), **Supp. VII:** 290

Vampire Lestat, The (Rice), **Supp. VII:** 290–292, 298, 299

Van Aalst, Mariska, **Supp. XIX:** 50, 51

Van Arsdale, Sarah, **Supp. XXV:** 4

Van Buren, Martin, **II:** 134, 312; **III:** 473

Vande Kieft, Ruth M., **IV:** 260

Vanderbilt, Cornelius, **III:** 14

VanDerWerff, Todd, **Supp. XXV:** 75

Van Dine, S. S., **Supp. IV Part 1:** 341; **Supp. XXVI:** 283

Van Doren, Carl, **I:** 252–253, 423; **II:** 103, 111, 112; **Supp. I Part 2:** 474, 486, 707, 709, 717, 718, 727; **Supp. II Part 1:** 395; **Supp. VIII:** 96–97

Van Doren, Mark, **I:** 168; **III:** 4, 23, 589; **Supp. I Part 2:** 604; **Supp. III Part 2:** 626; **Supp. IX:** 266, 268; **Supp. VIII:** 231; **Supp. XV:** 152, 305, 307; **Supp. XXII:** 275

Vandover and the Brute (Norris), **III:** 314, 315, 316, 320–322, 328, 333, 334

Van Duyn, Mona, **Supp. IX:** 269

Van Dyke, Annette, **Supp. IV Part 1:** 327

Van Dyke, Henry, **I:** 223; **II:** 456

Van Gogh, Vincent, **I:** 27; **IV:** 290; **Supp. I Part 2:** 451; **Supp. IV Part 1:** 284; **Supp. XXII:** 171–172

Van Gogh Field and Other Stories, The (Kittredge), **Supp. XXVI:** 181, 182, 184

Van Gogh's Room at Arles (Elkin), **Supp. VI:** 56

"Vanilla Dunk" (Lethem), **Supp. XVIII:** 139

"Vanisher, The" (Whittier), **Supp. I Part 2:** 691

Vanishing of Betty Varian, The (Wells), **Supp. XXVI:** 278

Vanishing Point (Markson), **Supp. XVII:** 135, 137, 138, 145–146

"Vanishing Point, The" (Davison), **Supp. XXVI:** 76

"Vanishing Point: Former City" (Monson), **Supp. XXIV:** 238

"Vanishing Point for Solo Voice" (Monson), **Supp. XXIV:** 239

Vanishing Point: Not a Memoir (Monson), **Supp. XXIV:** 230, **236–239,** 241–242

"Vanishing Point: Panera" (Monson), **Supp. XXIV:** 238

"Vanishing Red, The" (Frost), **Retro. Supp. II:** 47

"Vanity" (B. Diop), **Supp. IV Part 1:** 16

Vanity Fair (Thackeray), **I:** 354; **II:** 91; **III:** 70; **Supp. IX:** 200

"Vanity of All Wordly Things, The" (Bradstreet), **Supp. I Part 1:** 102, 119

Vanity of Duluoz (Kerouac), **Supp. III Part 1:** 221, 222

"Vanity of Existence, The" (Freneau), **Supp. II Part 1:** 262

Van Matre, Lynn, **Supp. V:** 126

Vann, Barbara, **Supp. XV:** 187

Vanquished, The (Faulkner), **I:** 205

Van Rensselaer, Stephen, **I:** 351

Van Vechten, Carl, **I:** 295; **IV:** 76; **Retro. Supp. I:** 199; **Supp. I Part 1:** 324, 327, 332; **Supp. I Part 2:** 715; **Supp. II Part 2: 725–751; Supp. X:** 247; **Supp. XIX:** 76; **Supp. XVI:** 135; **Supp. XVII:** 96, 97, 101, 104; **Supp. XVIII:** 123, 131, 132, 279, 280; **Supp. XX: 69; Supp. XXI:** 5, 8; **Supp. XXII:** 5, 158, 160

Van Vliet, Don, **Supp. XXIII:** 174

Vanya and Sonia and Masha and Spike (Durang), **Supp. XXIV: 127–128**

Vanzetti, Bartolomeo, **I:** 482, 486, 490, 494; **II:** 38–39, 426; **III:** 139–140; **Supp. I Part 2:** 446, 610, 611; **Supp. IX:** 199; **Supp. V:** 288–289; **Supp. XXII:** 277

"Vapor Trail Reflected in the Frog Pond" (Kinnell), **Supp. III Part 1:** 242–243

"Vapor Trails" (Snyder), **Supp. VIII:** 298

"Variant Text" (Goodman), **Supp. XXVI:** 118

"Variation: Ode to Fear" (Warren), **IV:** 241

"Variation on a Sentence" (Bogan), **Supp. III Part 1:** 60

"Variation on Gaining a Son" (Dove), **Supp. IV Part 1:** 248

"Variation on Pain" (Dove), **Supp. IV Part 1:** 248

"Variations: The air is sweetest that a thistle guards" (Merrill), **Supp. III Part 1:** 321

"Variations: White Stag, Black Bear" (Merrill), **Supp. III Part 1:** 321

"Varick Street" (Bishop), **Supp. I Part 1:** 90, 92

Varieties of Metaphysical Poetry, The (Eliot), **Retro. Supp. I:** 65

Varieties of Religious Experience, The (William James), **II:** 344, 353, 354, 359–360, 362; **IV:** 28, 291; **Supp. IX:** 19

Variety (film), **Supp. XII:** 7

Variorum (Whitman), **Retro. Supp. I:** 406

Various Antidotes (J. Scott), **Supp. XVII: 188–189**

Various Miracles (Shields), **Supp. VII:** 318–320, 323, 324

"Various Miracles" (Shields), **Supp. VII:** 318–319, 324

Various Poems (Zach), **Supp. XV:** 86

"Various Tourists" (Connell), **Supp. XIV:** 79

"Varmint Question, The" (Leopold), **Supp. XIV:** 180–181

Varno, David, **Supp. XIX:** 205

Vasari, Giorgio, **Supp. I Part 2:** 450; **Supp. III Part 1:** 5

Vasquez, Robert, **Supp. V:** 180

Vassall Morton (Parkman), **Supp. II Part 2:** 595, 597–598

Vasse, W. W., **III:** 478

Vaudeville for a Princess (Schwartz), **Supp. II Part 2:** 661–662

"Vaudeville Moment" (Bodenheim), **Supp. XXV:** 22

Vaughan, Henry, **IV:** 151; **Supp. XV:** 251

Vaughn, Robert, **Supp. XI:** 343

Vaughn, Stephanie, **Supp. XXV:** 142

"Vaunting Oak" (Ransom), **III:** 490

Vaz, Katherine, **Supp. XXVI: 255–269**

Vazirani, Reetika, **Supp. XIII:** 133

Veblen (Hobson), **Supp. I Part 2:** 650

Veblen, Andrew, **Supp. I Part 2:** 640

Veblen, Oswald, **Supp. I Part 2:** 640

Veblen, Thorstein, **I:** 104, 283, 475–476, 483, 498, 511; **II:** 27, 272, 276, 287; **Supp. I Part 2: 628–650; Supp. IV Part 1:** 22

Veblen, Mrs. Thorstein (Ellen Rolfe), **Supp. I Part 2:** 641

Veblenism: A New Critique (Dobriansky), **Supp. I Part 2:** 648, 650

"Veblen's Attack on Culture" (Adorno), **Supp. I Part 2:** 650

Vecsey, Christopher, **Supp. XXVI:** 90

Vectors and Smoothable Curves (Bronk), **Supp. XXI: 24–26,** 32

Vedanta for Modern Man (Isherwood, ed.), **Supp. XIV:** 164

Vedanta for the Western World (Isherwood, ed.), **Supp. XIV:** 164

Vedas, **IV:** 183

Vega, Janine Pommy, **Supp. XIV:** 148

Vega, Lope de, **Retro. Supp. I:** 285; **Supp. III Part 1:** 341, 347

Vegetable, The (Fitzgerald), **Retro. Supp. I:** 105; **Supp. IX:** 57

Vegetable, The, or From President to Postman (Fitzgerald), **II:** 91

"Vegetable Love" (Apple), **Supp. XVII:** 4

"Vegetable Love"(Crooker), **Supp. XXIII:** 62

"Vegetable Wisdom" (Halliday), **Supp. XIX:** 88

Veg tsu zikh, Der (The road to one's self) (Asch), **Supp. XXIII:** 5, 11

Veil of Snows, A (Helprin), **Supp. XXV:** 84, 87

Veinberg, Jon, **Supp. V:** 180; **Supp. XIII:** 313; **Supp. XV:** 76–77, 86

Vein of Iron (Glasgow), **II:** 175, 186, 188–189, 191, 192, 194

Vein of Riches, A (Knowles), **Supp. XII:** 249

Vein of Words (J. W. Miller), **Supp. XX:** 165

Velie, Alan R., **Supp. IV Part 2:** 486

Velocities: New and Selected Poems, 1966–1992 (Dobyns), **Supp. XIII:** 86–87, 87, 88

"Velocity" (Collins), **Supp. XXI:** 61

"Velorio" (Cisneros), **Supp. VII:** 66

Velvet Gentleman, The (Skloot), **Supp. XX: 201**

"Velvet Shoes" (Wylie), **Supp. I Part 2:** 711, 714

Venant, Elizabeth, **Supp. XI:** 343

Vencloca, Thomas, **Supp. VIII:** 29

Vendler, Helen H., **Retro. Supp. I:** 297; **Retro. Supp. II:** 184, 191; **Supp. I Part 1:** 77, 78, 92, 95; **Supp. I Part 2:** 565; **Supp. IV Part 1:** 245, 247, 249, 254, 257; **Supp. IV Part 2:** 448; **Supp. V:** 78, 82, 189, 343; **Supp. XII:** 187, 189; **Supp. XV:** 20, 184

"Venetian Blind, The" (Jarrell), **II:** 382–383

Venetian Glass Nephew, The (Wylie), **Supp. I Part 2:** 707, 709, 714, 717–719, 721, 724

Venetian Life (Howells), **II:** 274, 277, 279

Venetian Vespers, The (Hecht), **Supp. X:** 57, 65–69

"Venetian Vespers, The" (Hecht), **Supp. X:** 65, 66–67

Venice Observed (McCarthy), **II:** 562

Ventadorn, Bernard de, **Supp. IV Part 1:** 146

"Ventriloquists' Conversations" (Gentry), **Supp. IV Part 1:** 236

Venturesome Voyages of Captain Voss, The (Voss), **Supp. XXV:** 217

"Venus, Cupid, Folly and Time" (Taylor), **Supp. V:** 322–323

Venus and Adonis (film), **Supp. IV Part 1:** 82

Venus and Don Juan (C. Frost), **Supp. XV:** 93, **102–103,** 104, 107

"Venus and Don Juan" (C. Frost), **Supp. XV:** 103

Venus Blue (Sobin), **Supp. XVI:** 293–294, 294

Venus in Sparta (Auchincloss), **Supp. IV Part 1:** 25

"Venus Pandemos" (Halliday), **Supp. XIX:** 85, 89, 90, 93

"Venus's-flytraps" (Komunyakaa), **Supp. XIII:** 126, 127

"Veracruz" (Hayden), **Supp. II Part 1:** 371, 373

Verducci, Tom, **Supp. XXII:** 209

"Verdun" (Beston), **Supp. XXVI:** 32

Verga, Giovanni, **II:** 271, 275

Verghese, Abraham, **Supp. X:** 160

Verhaeren, Emile, **I:** 476; **II:** 528, 529

Verlaine, Paul, **II:** 529, 543; **III:** 466; **IV:** 79, 80, 86, 286; **Retro. Supp. I:** 56, 62; **Retro. Supp. II:** 326

"Vermeer" (Nemerov), **III:** 275, 278, 280

Vermeer, Jan, **Retro. Supp. I:** 335

"Vermont" (Carruth), **Supp. XVI:** 54

"Vermont" (Huddle), **Supp. XXVI:** 161

Vermont Notebook, The (Ashbery), **Supp. III Part 1:** 1

"Vermont Tale, A" (Helprin), **Supp. XXV:** 85

Vermont Writers: A State of Mind (Daley), **Supp. XXII:** 216

"Vernal Ague, The" (Freneau), **Supp. II Part 1:** 258

Verne, Jules, **I:** 480; **Retro. Supp. I:** 270; **Supp. XI:** 63

Vernon, John, **Supp. X:** 15

Verplanck, Gulian C., **Supp. I Part 1:** 155, 156, 157, 158

Verrazano, Giovanni da, **Supp. I Part 2:** 496, 497

Verse (Zawacki), **Supp. VIII:** 272

"Verse for Urania" (Merrill), **Supp. III Part 1:** 329, 330

Verses (Wharton), **Retro. Supp. I:** 362

Verses, Printed for Her Friends (Jewett), **II:** 406

"Verses for Children" (Lowell), **II:** 516

"Verses Made at Sea in a Heavy Gale" (Freneau), **Supp. II Part 1:** 262

"Verses on the Death of T. S. Eliot" (Brodsky), **Supp. VIII:** 19

"Version of a Fragment of Simonides" (Bryant), **Supp. I Part 1:** 153, 155

"Vers Libre Epidemic, The" (Lovecraft), **Supp. XXV:** 120

Verulam, Baron. *See* Bacon, Francis

Very, Jones, **III:** 507; **Supp. XXV:** 237–252

"Very Hot Sun in Bermuda, The" (Jackson), **Supp. IX:** 126

Very Old Bones (W. Kennedy), **Supp. VII:** 133, 148, 150–153

"Very Old Man with Enormous Wings, A" (García Márquez), **Supp. XXIV:** 190

Very Persistent Gappers of Frip, The (Saunders), **Supp. XIX:** 229–230

"Very Proper Gander, The" (Thurber), **Supp. I Part 2:** 610

"Very Short Story, A" (Hemingway), **II:** 252; **Retro. Supp. I:** 173

"Vesalius in Zante" (Wharton), **Retro. Supp. I:** 372

Vesey, Denmark, **Supp. I Part 2:** 592

Vesey, Desmond, **Supp. XIV:** 162

"Vespers" (Auden), **Supp. II Part 1:** 23

"Vespers" (Glück), **Supp. V:** 88

"Vespers"(Dybek), **Supp. XXIII:** 78

Vestal Lady on Brattle, The (Corso), **Supp. XII:** 119, **120–121,** 134

Vested Interests and the Common Man, The (Veblen), **Supp. I Part 2:** 642

"Vesuvius at Home" (Rich), **Retro. Supp. I:** 42

"Veteran, The" (Crane), **I:** 413

"Veterans' Cemetery" (Gioia), **Supp. XV:** 117

"Veteran Sirens" (Robinson), **III:** 512, 524

"Veterinarian" (X. J. Kennedy), **Supp. XV:** 168

"Vetiver" (Ashbery), **Supp. III Part 1:** 26

Vetter, Lara, **Supp. XXII:** 166

"Via Dieppe-Newhaven" (H. Miller), **III:** 183

"Via Negativa" (Salter), **Supp. IX:** 257

Vicar of Wakefield, The (Goldsmith), **I:** 216

Vicious Circle, The (film, Wilder), **Supp. XVII:** 62

"Vicissitudes of the Avant-Garde, The" (Gass), **Supp. VI:** 91

Vicky Van (Wells), **Supp. XXVI:** 280

Vico, Giambattista, **Supp. XX: 38**

Victim, The (Bellow), **I:** 144, 145, 147, 149, 150, 151, 152, 153, 155, 156, 158, 159, 164; **IV:** 19; **Retro. Supp. II:** 21, 22, 34

"Victor" (Mumford), **Supp. II Part 2:** 476

Victoria (Rowson), **Supp. XV:** 231

Victorian in the Modern World, A (Hapgood), **Supp. XVII:** 95, 97, 100, 101, 103, 105, 106; **Supp. XXI:** 8

"Victoria's Secret" (Collins), **Supp. XXI:** 58–59

"Victories" (Untermeyer), **Supp. XV:** 300

"Victory at Sea" (television series), **Supp. I Part 2:** 490

"Victory comes late" (Dickinson), **Retro. Supp. I:** 45

"Victory of the Moon, The" (Crane), **I:** 420

Vida, Vendela, **Supp. XIX:** 49, 50, 53, 57, 58, 59, 61, 62

Vidal, Gore, **II:** 587; **IV:** 383; **Supp. IV Part 1:** 22, 35, 92, 95, 198; **Supp. IV Part 2: 677–696; Supp. IX:** 96; **Supp. X:** 186, 195; **Supp. XIV:** 156, 170, 338; **Supp. XIX:** 131, 132

Video Poems (Collins), **Supp. XXI:** 53

Viebahn, Fred, **Supp. IV Part 1:** 248

Viera, Joseph M., **Supp. XI:** 178, 186

Viereck, Peter, **Supp. I Part 2:** 403

Viertel, Berthold, **Supp. XIV:** 165

Viertel, Salka, **Supp. XVI:** 192

Viet Journal (Jones), **Supp. XI: 230–231**

Vietnam (McCarthy), **II:** 578–579

"Vietnam in Me, The" (O'Brien), **Supp. V:** 241, 252

Vietnamization of New Jersey, The (Durang), **Supp. XXIV:** 113, **117–118**

Vietnam Reader, The: The Definitive Collection of Fiction and Nonfiction on the War (O'Nan, ed.), **Supp. XXV:** 153

Vie unanime, La (Romains), **I:** 227

"View, The" (Roussel), **Supp. III Part 1:** 15, 16, 21

View from 80, The (Cowley), **Supp. II Part 1:** 141, 144, 153

"View from an Institution" (F. Wright), **Supp. XVII:** 244

"View from the Backyard" (W. V. Davis), **Supp. XXI:** 96

View from the Bridge, A (A. Miller), **III:** 147, 148, 156, 158, 159–160; **Supp. XXV:** 93

View from the Seventh Layer, The (Brockmeier), **Supp. XXII: 59–61**

"View from the Seventh Layer, The" (Brockmeier), **Supp. XXII:** 61

View of My Own, A: Essays in Literature and Society (Hardwick), **Supp. III Part 1:** 194, 200

"View of the Capital from the Library of Congress" (Bishop), **Retro. Supp. II:** 45

View of the Soil and Climate of the United States, A (Brown, trans.), **Supp. I Part 1:** 146

"View of the Woods, A" (O'Connor), **III:** 349, 351, 358; **Retro. Supp. II:** 237

"Viewpoint" (column, Siddons), **Supp. XXII:** 240, 245

"Views of the Mysterious Hill: The Appearance of Parnassus in American Poetry" (Strand), **Supp. IV Part 2:** 631

"Vigil" (Karr), **Supp. XI:** 241

"Vigil, The" (Dante), **III:** 542

"Vigil at Heiligenkreuz" (W. V. Davis), **Supp. XXI:** 93

"Vigil"(Dybek), **Supp. XXIII:** 78

"Vignette" (Trethewey), **Supp. XXI:** 253, 254

Vigny, Alfred Victor de, **II:** 543

Vildrac, Charles, **Supp. XV:** 50

Vile Bodies (Waugh), **Supp. I Part 2:** 607

Villa, Pancho, **I:** 210; **III:** 584

"Villa dei Pini" (Davison), **Supp. XXVI:** 79

"Village, The" (Huddle), **Supp. XXVI:** 156

"Village Blacksmith, The" (Longfellow), **Retro. Supp. II:** 167, 168; **Supp. I Part 2:** 409

Village Hymns, a Supplement to Dr. Watts's Psalms and Hymns (Nettleton), **I:** 458

"Village Improvement Parade, The" (Lindsay), **Supp. I Part 2:** 388, 389

Village Magazine, The (Lindsay), **Supp. I Part 2:** 379–380, 382

Village Virus, The (Lewis), **II:** 440

"Villanelle at Sundown" (Justice), **Supp. VII:** 119, 122–123

"Villanelle of Change" (Robinson), **III:** 524

Villard, Oswald, **Supp. I Part 1:** 332

"Villa Selene" (Simpson), **Supp. IX:** 279

Villon, François, **II:** 544; **III:** 9, 174, 592; **Retro. Supp. I:** 286; **Supp. I Part 1:** 261; **Supp. III Part 1:** 235, 243, 249, 253; **Supp. III Part 2:** 560; **Supp. IX:** 116

"Villonaud for This Yule" (Pound), **Retro. Supp. I:** 286
Vincent, Steven, **Supp. XXV:** 201
"Vincenzo Tailor" (Di Piero), **Supp. XIX:** 38
Vindication of the Rights of Woman (Wollstonecraft), **Supp. I Part 1:** 126; **Supp. XI:** 203
Vines, Lois Davis, **Retro. Supp. II:** 261
"Vineyard of Red Wine, The" (Beston), **Supp. XXVI:** 32
Vintage Book of Amnesia, The (Lethem, ed.), **Supp. XVIII:** 138
"Vintage Thunderbird, A" (Beattie), **Supp. V:** 27
Vinz, Mark, **Supp. X:** 117
Viol de Lucrèce, Le (Obey), **IV:** 356
Violence (Bausch), **Supp. VII:** 48–49, 54
Violent Bear It Away, The (O'Connor), **III:** 339, 345–348, 350, 351, 354, 355, 356, 357; **Retro. Supp. II:** 233, **234–236**
Violent Hero, Wilderness Heritage and Urban Reality, The: A Study of the Private Eye in the Novels of Dashiell Hammett, Raymond Chandler and Ross Macdonald (Parker), **Supp. XIX:** 177
"Violent Vet, The" (O'Brien), **Supp. V:** 238
Violin (Rice), **Supp. VII:** 302
Viorst, Judith, **Supp. X:** 153
Viper Run (Karr), **Supp. XI: 248–251**
Viramontes, Helene María, **Supp. XXV:** 130, 133, 138
Virgil, **I:** 312, 322, 587; **II:** 133, 542; **IV:** 137, 359; **Retro. Supp. I:** 135; **Supp. I Part 1:** 153; **Supp. I Part 2:** 494; **Supp. IV Part 2:** 631
"Virgin and Child with Music and Numbers" (Bronk), **Supp. XXI:** 30
"Virgin and the Dynamo" (Adams), **III:** 396
"Virgin Carrying a Lantern, The" (Stevens), **IV:** 80
Virgin Huntress, The (Holding), **Supp. XXII:** 119, 124, **135–136**
Virginia (Glasgow), **II:** 175, 178, 181–182, 193, 194
"Virginia" (Lindsay), **Supp. I Part 2:** 398
"Virginia Britannia" (Moore), **III:** 198, 208–209
"Virginians Are Coming Again, The" (Lindsay), **Supp. I Part 2:** 399
Virginia Reels (Hoffman), **Supp. XVIII:** 79, 86
Virgin Spain (W. Frank), **Supp. XX:** 76
"Virgins Plus Curtains Minus Dots" (Loy), **Supp. XXII:** 161
Virgin Suicides, The (Eugenides), **Supp. XXIV:** 134, **136–138**, 141, 142
Virgin Time: In Search of the Contemplative Life (Hampl), **Supp. XXII:** 82, 83–84, **90–92**
"Virgin Violeta" (Porter), **III:** 454
"Virility" (Ozick), **Supp. V:** 262, 265
Virtual Light (W. Gibson), **Supp. XVI:** 124, **129,** 130
Virtue of Selfishness, The: A New Concept of Egoism (Rand), **Supp. IV Part 2:**

527, 530–532
"Virtuoso" (Francis), **Supp. IX:** 82
Virtuous Girl, A (Bodenheim), **Supp. XXV:** 27
Virtuous Woman, A (Gibbons), **Supp. X: 44–45,** 46, 50
Visconti, Luchino, **Supp. V:** 51
Viscusi, Robert, **Supp. XX:** 46
Visible Saints: The History of a Puritan Idea (Morgan), **IV:** 149
"Vision, A" (Olds), **Supp. X:** 214
"Vision, A" (Winters), **Supp. II Part 2:** 785, 795
"Vision and Prayer" (D. Thomas), **I:** 432
"Visionary, The" (Poe), **III:** 411
Visionary Farms, The (Eberhart), **I:** 537–539
Visioning, The (Glaspell), **Supp. III Part 1:** 175–177, 180, 187, 188
Vision in Spring (Faulkner), **Retro. Supp. I:** 79
Vision of Columbus (Barlow), **Supp. I Part 1:** 124; **Supp. II Part 1:** 67, 68, 70–75, 77, 79
Vision of Sir Launfal, The (Lowell), **Supp. I Part 1:** 311; **Supp. I Part 2:** 406, 409, 410
"Vision of the World, A" (Cheever), **Supp. I Part 1:** 182, 192
"Visions and Voices" (Davison), **Supp. XXVI:** 71
"Visions of Budhardin"(Dybek), **Supp. XXIII:** 70–71
Visions of Cody (Kerouac), **Supp. III Part 1:** 225–227
Visions of Gerard (Kerouac), **Supp. III Part 1:** 219–222, 225, 227, 229
"Visions of the Daughters of Albion" (Blake), **III:** 540
"Visit" (Ammons), **Supp. VII:** 28–29
"Visit, The" (Kenyon), **Supp. VII:** 169
"Visitant, The" (Dunn), **Supp. XI:** 147
"Visitation, The/La Visitación" (Mora), **Supp. XIII:** 217, 224, 228
"Visitation"(Kenny), **Supp. XXIII:** 157
"Visit Home, A" (Stafford), **Supp. XI:** 318
Visit in 2001, The (musical, McNally), **Supp. XIII:** 207
"Visiting My Own House in Iowa City" (Stern), **Supp. IX:** 300
Visiting Villain, The (Wells), **Supp. XXVI:** 278, 280
"Visit of Charity, A" (Welty), **IV:** 262
"Visit of the Hawk" (Huddle), **Supp. XXVI:** 149
"Visitors" (J. W. Miller), **Supp. XX: 167**
"Visitors" (Salinas), **Supp. XIII:** 318
"Visitors, The/Los Visitantes" (Kingsolver), **Supp. VII:** 208
"Visits to St. Elizabeths" (Bishop), **Retro. Supp. II:** 47
Visit to a Small Planet: A Comedy Akin to Vaudeville (Vidal), **Supp. IV Part 2:** 682–683
"Visit to a Small Planet" (teleplay) (Vidal), **Supp. IV Part 2:** 682
"Visit to Avoyelles, A" (Chopin), **Supp. I Part 1:** 213

"Visit to Manafon, A" (W. V. Davis), **Supp. XXI:** 96
"Vissi d'Arte" (Moore), **Supp. X: 173–174**
Vistas of History (Morison), **Supp. I Part 2:** 492
"Vita" (Stafford), **Supp. XI:** 330
"Vita Brevis" (Hull), **Supp. XXI:** 138
Vital, David, **Supp. XVI:** 160
Vital Provisions (Price), **Supp. VI:** 262–263
"Vitamins" (Carver), **Supp. III Part 1:** 138
Vita Nova (Glück), **Supp. V:** 90–92
Vitruvius, **Supp. XVI:** 292
Vittorio, the Vampire (Rice), **Supp. VII:** 295–296
Viudas (Dorfman), **Supp. IX:** 138
"Vivaldi"(Dybek), **Supp. XXIII:** 68
"Viva Vargas!" (Allen), **Supp. XV:** 15
Viviparous Quadrupeds of North America, The (Audubon and Bachman), **Supp. XVI:** 10
Vivisections (Siegel), **Supp. XXII:** 257
Vizenor, Gerald, **Supp. IV Part 1:** 260, 262, 329, 404; **Supp. IV Part 2:** 502
Vladimir Nabokov: The American Years (Nabokov), **Retro. Supp. I:** 275
Vlag, Piet, **Supp. XV:** 295
"Vlemk, the Box Painter" (Gardner), **Supp. VI:** 73
"V-Letter" (Shapiro), **Supp. II Part 2:** 707
V-Letter and Other Poems (Shapiro), **Supp. II Part 2:** 702, 706
"Vocabulary of Dearness" (Nye), **Supp. XIII:** 284
"Vocation" (Stafford), **Supp. XI:** 312, 321
Vocation and a Voice, A (Chopin), **Retro. Supp. II:** 67, 72
"Vocation and a Voice, A" (Chopin), **Retro. Supp. II:** 72; **Supp. I Part 1:** 200, 220, 224, 225
Vogel, David, **Supp. XV:** 88
Vogel, Speed, **Supp. IV Part 1:** 390
"Vogue Vista" (Peacock), **Supp. XIX:** 200
"Voice" (F. Wright), **Supp. XVII:** 245
"Voice" (Notley), **Supp. XXII:** 230
"Voice, The" (Dunn), **Supp. XI:** 152
Voiced Connections of James Dickey, The (Dickey), **Supp. IV Part 1:** 177
"Voice from the Wilderness" (Ray), **Supp. XVIII:** 202
"Voice from the Woods, A" (Humphrey), **Supp. IX:** 101
"Voice from Under the Table, A" (Wilbur), **Supp. III Part 2:** 553, 554
Voice in the Mountain, A (Davison), **Supp. XXVI:** 65, 73–75, 77
"Voice of God, The" (Very), **Supp. XXV:** 243
Voice of Reason, The: Essays in Objectivist Thought (Rand), **Supp. IV Part 2:** 527, 528, 532
"Voice of Rock, The" (Ginsberg), **Supp. II Part 1:** 313
Voice of the Butterfly, The (Nichols), **Supp. XIII:** 270

Voice of the City, The (O. Henry), **Supp. II Part 1:** 410

"Voice of the Mountain, The" (Crane), **I:** 420

Voice of the Negro (Barber), **Supp. II Part 1:** 168

"Voice of the Past, The" (Skloot), **Supp. XX:** 207

Voice of the People, The (Glasgow), **II:** 175, 176

Voice of the Turtle: American Indian Literature 1900–1970 (Gunn Allen, ed.), **Supp. IV Part 1:** 332, 334

Voices from the Moon (Dubus), **Supp. VII:** 88–89

"Voices from the Other World" (Merrill), **Supp. III Part 1:** 331

Voices in the House (Sedges), **Supp. II Part 1:** 125

Voices of a Summer Day (Shaw), **Supp. XIX:** 251

Voices of the Night (Longfellow), **II:** 489, 493; **Retro. Supp. II:** 154, 157, 168

"Voices of Village Square, The" (Wolfe), **Supp. III Part 2:** 571–572

Voice That Is Great within Us, The (Caruth, ed.), **Supp. XIII:** 112

Void Moon (Connelly), **Supp. XXI:** 73, 74

Voigt, Ellen Bryan, **Supp. XIII:** 76

"Voir Dire" (Monson), **Supp. XXIV:** 237

Voix humaine, La (Cocteau), **Supp. XX:** 236

Volkening, Henry, **Retro. Supp. II:** 117; **Supp. XV:** 142

Vollmann, William T., **Supp. XIV:** 96; **Supp. XVII: 225–237; Supp. XX:** 93

Volney, Constantin François de Chasse-boeuf, **Supp. I Part 1:** 146

Voltaire, **I:** 194; **II:** 86, 103, 449; **III:** 420; **IV:** 18; **Retro. Supp. II:** 94; **Supp. I Part 1:** 288–289; **Supp. I Part 2:** 669, 717; **Supp. XV:** 258; **Supp. XX:** 285

Voltaire! Voltaire! (Endore), **Supp. XVII:** 65

Volunteer Poilu, A (Beston), **Supp. XXVI:** 32

Volunteers, The (Rowson and Reinagle), **Supp. XV:** 238

Volynsky, Akim (Chaim Flekser), **Supp. XXIII:** 11

Vonnegut, Kurt, **Retro. Supp. I:** 170; **Supp. II Part 2:** 557, 689, **753–784; Supp. IV Part 1:** 227, 392; **Supp. V:** 40, 42, 237, 244, 296; **Supp. X:** 260; **Supp. XI:** 104; **Supp. XII:** 139, 141; **Supp. XVIII:** 242, 252; **Supp. XXI:** 226; **Supp. XXIII:** 42, 101, 109

Vonnegut, Kurt, Jr., **Supp. XIX:** 223; **Supp. XVII:** 41, 135

"Voracities and Verities" (Moore), **III:** 214

Vore, Nellie, **I:** 199

Vorlicky, Robert, **Supp. IX:** 132, 135, 136, 141, 144, 147

Vorse, Mary Heaton, **Supp. XVII:** 99; **Supp. XX:** 76; **Supp. XXI:** 5, 6, 9, 13

Vortex, The (Coward), **Supp. XXIV:** 267

"Vorticism" (Pound), **Retro. Supp. I:** 288

Vosjoli, Philippe de, **Supp. XX:** 253

Voss, J. C., **Supp. XXV:** 217

Voss, Ralph E., **Supp. XXV:** 93

Voss, Richard, **I:** 199–200

"Vow, The" (Hecht), **Supp. X:** 64

"Vowels 2" (Baraka), **Supp. II Part 1:** 51

Vow of Conversation, A: Journal, 1964–1965 (Merton), **Supp. VIII:** 206

Vox (Baker), **Supp. XIII: 47–49,** 50, 52, 53

"Voyage" (MacLeish), **III:** 15

Voyage, The (Caputo), **Supp. XIX:** 25, 27–28

"Voyage, The" (Irving), **II:** 304

Voyage, The, and Other Versions of Poems by Baudelaire (Lowell), **Retro. Supp. II:** 187

Voyage dans la Haute Pennsylvanie et dans l'état de New-York (Crèvecoeur), **Supp. I Part 1:** 250–251

Voyage of the Beagle (Darwin), **Supp. IX:** 211

Voyage of the Dawn Treader (C. S. Lewis), **Supp. XXV:** 74

Voyage of the Destroyer *from New York to Brazil, The* (Slocum), **Supp. XXV:** 208, 212–213

Voyage of the Liberdade, The (Slocum), **Supp. XXV:** 208, 210–212

Voyage Out, The (Woolf), **Supp. XV:** 65

"Voyager, The" (Everwine), **Supp. XV:** 75

"Voyages" (H. Crane), **I:** 393–395; **Retro. Supp. II:** 78, 80, 81

"Voyages" (Levine), **Supp. V:** 190

Voyages and Discoveries of the Companions of Columbus (Irving), **II:** 310

Voyage to Pagany, A (W. C. Williams), **IV:** 404; **Retro. Supp. I:** 418–419, **420–421,** 423

Voyaging Portraits (Sobin), **Supp. XVI:** 282, 287

"Voyeur, The" (Gioia), **Supp. XV:** 125

"Voz de America" (column, W. Frank), **Supp. XX:** 80

Voznesensky, Andrei, **II:** 553; **Supp. III Part 1:** 268; **Supp. III Part 2:** 560

Vrbovska, Anca, **Supp. IV Part 2:** 639

V. S. Naipaul: An Introduction to His Work (Theroux), **Supp. VIII:** 314, 318

"V. S. Pritchett's Apprenticeship" (Maxwell), **Supp. VIII:** 172

Vukelich, James, **Supp. XXIII:** 228, 233

"Vulgarity in Literature" (Huxley), **III:** 429–430

"Vultures" (Oliver), **Supp. VII:** 235

"V. V." (Alcott), **Supp. I Part 1:** 37

W

W (Viva) (Cummings), **I:** 429, 433, 434, 436, 443, 444, 447

Wabash (R. O. Butler), **Supp. XII:** 61, **68–69**

Wade, Grace, **I:** 216

"Wading at Wellfleet" (Bishop), **Retro. Supp. II:** 42, 43; **Supp. I Part 1:** 80, 85, 86

Wadsworth, Charles, **I:** 454, 470; **Retro. Supp. I:** 32, 33

Wage, William, **Supp. XXVI:** 87

Wagenknecht, Edward, **II:** 508; **Supp. I Part 2:** 408, 584; **Supp. IV Part 2:** 681

"Wages of Poetry, The" (Wright), **Supp. XV:** 337

Wagner, Erica, **Supp. XXI:** 117

Wagner, Jean, **Supp. I Part 1:** 341, 346; **Supp. IV Part 1:** 165, 167, 171

Wagner, Richard, **I:** 284, 395; **II:** 425; **III:** 396, 507; **Supp. IV Part 1:** 392

Wagner, Robert, **Supp. IX:** 250

"Wagnerians, The" (Auchincloss), **Supp. IV Part 1:** 23

"Wagner Matinee, A" (Cather), **I:** 315–316; **Retro. Supp. I:** 5, 8

Wagoner, David, **Supp. IX: 323–340; Supp. XII:** 178; **Supp. XX:** 200

Wahlöö, Per, **Supp. XX:** 87

Waid, Candace, **Retro. Supp. I:** 360, 372, 373

Waif, The (Longfellow, ed.), **Retro. Supp. II:** 155

"Waif of the Plains, A" (Harte), **Supp. II Part 1:** 354

Wain, John, **Supp. XIV:** 166

"Wait" (Kinnell), **Supp. III Part 1:** 250

"Waiter in a California Vietnamese Restaurant" (Major), **Supp. XXII:** 182

"Waiting" (Dubus), **Supp. VII:** 87

Waiting (Jin), **Supp. XVIII:** 89, **96–97,** 99

"Waiting" (W. C. Williams), **Retro. Supp. I:** 418

"Waiting, The" (L.-Y. Lee), **Supp. XV:** 218

"Waiting, The" (Olds), **Supp. X:** 209

"Waiting between the Trees" (Tan), **Supp. X:** 290

"Waiting by the Gate" (Bryant), **Supp. I Part 1:** 171

Waiting for God (Weil), **I:** 298

Waiting for Godot (Beckett), **I:** 78, 91, 298; **Supp. IV Part 1:** 368–369; **Supp. XXIII:** 213

Waiting for Lefty (Odets), **Supp. I Part 1:** 277; **Supp. II Part 2:** 529, 530–533, 540; **Supp. V:** 109; **Supp. XIX:** 242

Waiting for Sweet Betty (Major), **Supp. XXII:** 183

Waiting for Teddy Williams (Mosher), **Supp. XXII:** 205, 206, 207, 208, 209, **215–216**

Waiting for the End of the World (Bell), **Supp. X: 4–5,** 11

"Waiting for the Ladies" (L. Brown), **Supp. XXI:** 44

Waiting for the Verdict (R. H. Davis), **Supp. XVI:** 85, 89, 90

"Waiting in a Rain Forest" (Wagoner), **Supp. IX:** 329

Waiting in the Wings (Loraga), **Supp. XXIII:** 195

Waiting Room, The (Kees), **Supp. XV:** 133, 148

Waiting to Exhale (McMillan), **Supp. XIII:** 184, 185, **189–190,** 191

"Waiting to Freeze" (Banks), **Supp. V:** 5, 6

Waiting to Freeze: Poems (Banks), **Supp. V:** 6, 8

Waits, Tom, **Supp. VIII:** 12

Wait until Spring, Bandini (Fante), **Supp. XI:** 160, 161, 164, 165, **166–167**

Wait until Spring, Bandini (film), **Supp. XI:** 173

"Wake, The" (Dove), **Supp. IV Part 1:** 250

"Wakefield" (Hawthorne), **Retro. Supp. I:** 154, 159

Wakefield, Dan, **Supp. VIII:** 43; **Supp. XIX:** 257, 258; **Supp. XVI:** 220

Wakefield, Richard, **Supp. IX:** 323

"Wake Island" (Rukeyser), **Supp. VI:** 273

"Wake"(Kenny), **Supp. XXIII:** 155

Wakeman, Frederic, **Supp. IX:** 247

Wake Up and Live! (Brande), **Supp. I Part 2:** 608

"Waking" (C. Frost), **Supp. XV:** 93

Waking, The (Roethke), **III:** 541

"Waking Early Sunday Morning" (Lowell), **II:** 552; **Retro. Supp. II:** 190

"Waking in the Blue" (Lowell), **II:** 547; **Retro. Supp. II:** 180

"Waking in the Dark" (Rich), **Supp. I Part 2:** 559

"Waking Up the Rake" (Hogan), **Supp. IV Part 1:** 415–416, 416

Wakoski, Diane, **Supp. V:** 79; **Supp. XII:** 184; **Supp. XV:** 252; **Supp. XVII:** 112; **Supp. XXIII:** 52; **Supp. XXIV:** 37

Walbridge, John, **Supp. XX: 125**

Walcott, Charles C., **II:** 49

Walcott, Derek, **Supp. VIII:** 28; **Supp. X:** 122, 131; **Supp. XV:** 256; **Supp. XXIV:** 86

Walcott, Jersey Joe, **Supp. V:** 182

Wald, Alan, **Supp. XV:** 202; **Supp. XVIII:** 223; **Supp. XXI:** 261, 262, 271, 275–276, 277, 278

Wald, Lillian, **Supp. I Part 1:** 12

Walden (Thoreau), **Supp. XIV:** 177, 227; **Supp. XV:** 275; **Supp. XVIII:** 14, 80, 189; **Supp. XXIV:** 73; **Supp. XXVI:** 34, 41, 43

Walden, Daniel, **Supp. IV Part 2:** 584, 591; **Supp. V:** 272

Walden; or, Life in the Woods (Thoreau), **I:** 219, 305; **II:** 8, 142, 159, 312–313, 458; **IV:** 168, 169, 170, 176, 177–178, 179–182, 183, 187; **Retro. Supp. I:** 62; **Supp. I Part 2:** 579, 655, 664, 672; **Supp. VIII:** 296; **Supp. X:** 27, 101; **Supp. XIII:** 152

Waldman, Anne, **Supp. XIV:** 150; **Supp. XXIII:** 221; **Supp. XXIV:** 33, 41, 45

Waldmeir, Joseph, **III:** 45

Waldmeir, Joseph J., **Supp. I Part 2:** 476

Waldo (Theroux), **Supp. VIII:** 313, 314, **314–315**

Waldo Frank: A Study (Munson), **Supp. XX: 74**

Waldron, Jeremy, **Supp. XVII:** 235

Waldron, Nan Turner, **Supp. XXVI:** 37

Waldrop, Keith, **Supp. XV:** 153, 165

Waley, Arthur, **II:** 526; **III:** 466; **Supp. V:** 340

"Walk, A" (Snyder), **Supp. VIII:** 297

Walkabout Year: Twelve Months in Australia (Pickering), **Supp. XXI:** 199, 200

"Walk at Sunset, A" (Bryant), **Supp. I Part 1:** 155

"Walk before Mass, A" (Agee), **I:** 28–29

Walker, Alice, **Retro. Supp. I:** 215; **Supp. I Part 2:** 550; **Supp. III Part 2:** 488, **517–540**; **Supp. IV Part 1:** 14; **Supp. IX:** 306, 311; **Supp. VIII:** 141, 214; **Supp. X:** 85, 228, 252, 325, 330; **Supp. XIII:** 179, 185, 291, 295; **Supp. XVI:** 39; **Supp. XVIII:** 200, 283; **Supp. XX: 84, 107, 108; Supp. XXI:** 172; **Supp. XXII:** 172

Walker, Cheryl, **Supp. XI:** 145

Walker, David, **Supp. V:** 189; **Supp. XVII:** 246

Walker, Franklin D., **III:** 321

Walker, Gue, **Supp. XII:** 207

Walker, Margaret, **Supp. XVIII:** 282; **Supp. XX: 106**

Walker, Marianne, **Supp. VIII:** 139

Walker, Obadiah, **II:** 113

Walker, Scott, **Supp. XV:** 92

Walker in the City, A (Kazin), **Supp. VIII:** 93–95, 99

Walk Hard (Blum and Hill), **Supp. XV:** 194

Walk Hard-Talk Loud (Zinberg), **Supp. XV:** 194, 202

"Walking" (Hogan), **Supp. IV Part 1:** 416

"Walking" (Thoreau), **Supp. IV Part 1:** 416; **Supp. IX:** 178

"Walking Along in Winter" (Kenyon), **Supp. VII:** 167

"Walking around the Block with a Three-Year-Old" (Wagoner), **Supp. IX:** 331–332

"Walking at Noon Near the Burlington Depot in Lincoln, Nebraska" (Kooser), **Supp. XIX:** 122

"Walking Backwards into the Future" (R. Williams), **Supp. IX:** 146

Walking Down the Stairs: Selections from Interviews (Kinnell), **Supp. III Part 1:** 235, 249

"Walking Home" (Schnackenberg). *See* "Laughing with One Eye" (Schnackenberg)

"Walking Home at Night" (Ginsberg), **Supp. II Part 1:** 313

"Walking Is Almost Falling" (Peacock), **Supp. XIX:** 196, 197

Walking Light (Dunn), **Supp. XI:** 140, 141, 153

"Walking Man of Rodin, The" (Sandburg), **III:** 583

"Walking Sticks and Paperweights and Water Marks" (Moore), **III:** 215

Walking Tall (Dunn), **Supp. XI:** 140

Walking the Black Cat (Simic), **Supp. VIII:** 280, **282–284**

Walking the Boundaries (Davison), **Supp. XXVI:** 65, 72–73, 74

"Walking the Boundaries" (Davison), **Supp. XXVI:** 73

Walking to Gatlinburg (Mosher), **Supp. XXII:** 204, 205, 206, 207, 208, 209, 215, **216–217**

Walking to Martha's Vineyard (F. Wright), **Supp. XVII:** 240, 241, 245, 246

Walking to Sleep (Wilbur), **Supp. III Part 2:** 557–560

"Walking to Sleep" (Wilbur), **Supp. III Part 2:** 544, 557, 559, 561, 562

"Walking Wounded" (Shaw), **Supp. XIX:** 248

Walkin' the Dog (Mosley), **Supp. XIII:** 242

"Walk in the Moonlight, A" (Anderson), **I:** 114

Walk Me to the Distance (Everett), **Supp. XVIII:** 55–56, 57

Walk on the Wild Side, A (Algren), **Supp. IX:** 3, **12–13**, 14; **Supp. V:** 4

"Walks in Rome" (Merrill), **Supp. III Part 1:** 337

Walk to the River, A (Hoffman), **Supp. XVIII:** 77–78

Walk with Tom Jefferson, A (Levine), **Supp. V:** 179, 187, 190–191

Wall, Cheryl, **Supp. XXVI:** 165, 166

"Wall, The" (Bronk), **Supp. XXI:** 31

"Wall, The" (Brooks), **Supp. III Part 1:** 70, 71, 84

Wall, The (Hersey), **IV:** 4; **Supp. XX: 251**

Wall, The (Rinehart), **Supp. XXV:** 197–198, 200

"Wall, The" (Roethke), **III:** 544

"Wall, The" (Sexton), **Supp. II Part 2:** 696

Wallace, Daniel, **Supp. XXII:** 49

Wallace, David, **Supp. XXI:** 277

Wallace, David Foster, **Retro. Supp. II:** 279; **Supp. X:** **301–318; Supp. XIX:** 223; **Supp. XVII:** 226; **Supp. XX: 91, 93; Supp. XXII:** 260, 261

Wallace, Henry, **I:** 489; **III:** 111, 475; **Supp. I Part 1:** 286; **Supp. I Part 2:** 645

Wallace, Jim, **Supp. XX: 143**

Wallace, Mike, **Supp. IV Part 1:** 364; **Supp. IV Part 2:** 526; **Supp. XX: 102**

Wallace, Paul, **Supp. XXVI:** 90, 96–97

Wallace, Richard, **Supp. XVIII:** 101–102

Wallace Stevens (Kermode), **Retro. Supp. I:** 301

Wallace Stevens: The Poems of our Climate (Bloom), **Retro. Supp. I:** 299

Wallace Stevens: Words Chosen out of Desire (Stevens), **Retro. Supp. I:** 297

Wallach, Eli, **III:** 161

Wallant, Edward Lewis, **Supp. XVI:** 220

Wallas, Graham, **Supp. I Part 2:** 643

"Walled City" (Oates), **Supp. II Part 2:** 524

Wallenstein, Anna. *See* Weinstein, Mrs. Max (Anna Wallenstein)

Waller, Edmund, **III:** 463

Waller, Fats, **IV:** 263

Waller, Nicole, **Supp. XXII:** 78

Walling, William English, **Supp. I Part 2:** 645; **Supp. XV:** 295

"Wall of Paintings, The" (Notley), **Supp. XXII:** 230

Wall of the Sky, the Wall of the Eye, The (Lethem), **Supp. XVIII:** 139

Walls Do Not Fall, The (Doolittle), **Supp. I Part 1:** 271, 272

Walls of Jericho, The (R. Fisher), **Supp. XIX:** 65, 67, 70, **72–77**, 78

"Wall Songs" (Hogan), **Supp. IV Part 1:** 413

Wall Writing (Auster), **Supp. XII:** 23–24

Walpole, Horace, **I:** 203; **Supp. I Part 2:** 410, 714

Walpole, Hugh, **Retro. Supp. I:** 231; **Supp. XX: 232**

Walpole, Robert, **IV:** 145

Walsh, David M., **Supp. XV:** 5

Walsh, Ed, **II:** 424

Walsh, Ernest, **Supp. XXIV:** 50

Walsh, George, **Supp. IV Part 2:** 528

Walsh, Keenan, **Supp. XXVI:** 152

Walsh, Raoul, **Supp. XIII:** 174

Walsh, Richard J., **Supp. II Part 1:** 119, 130

Walsh, William, **Supp. IV Part 1:** 242, 243, 246, 248, 252, 254, 257; **Supp. XXVI:** 4, 9

"Walt, the Wounded" (Di Piero), **Supp. XIX:** 37

"Walt and Will" (Apple), **Supp. XVII:** 6

Walter, Eugene, **Supp. XVI:** 230

Walter, Joyce, **Supp. XV:** 121

Walter Benjamin at the Dairy Queen: Reflections at Sixty and Beyond (McMurtry), **Supp. V:** 232

Walters, Barbara, **Supp. XIV:** 125

Walters, Marguerite. *See* Smith, Mrs. Lamar (Marguerite Walters)

"Walter T. Carriman" (O'Hara), **III:** 368

Walton, Izaak, **Supp. I Part 2:** 422

"Walt Whitman" (Kooser), **Supp. XIX:** 118

"Walt Whitman" (Masters), **Supp. I Part 2:** 458

"Walt Whitman at Bear Mountain" (Simpson), **Supp. IX:** 265

Walt Whitman Bathing (Wagoner), **Supp. IX: 331–332**

Walt Whitman Handbook (Allen), **IV:** 352

Walt Whitman Reconsidered (Chase), **IV:** 352

"Waltz, The" (Parker), **Supp. IX:** 204

"Waltzer in the House, The" (Kunitz), **Supp. III Part 1:** 258

Waltzing Matilda (Notley), **Supp. XXII:** 229–230

"Waltzing Matilda" (Notley), **Supp. XXII:** 230

Waltzing the Magpies: A Year in Australia (Pickering), **Supp. XXI:** 199, 200

Walzer, Kevin, **Supp. XII:** 202; **Supp. XV:** 118; **Supp. XVIII:** 174

Wambaugh, Joseph, **Supp. X:** 5; **Supp. XXI:** 67

Wampeters, Foma, & Granfalloons (Vonnegut), **Supp. II Part 2:** 758, 759–760, 776, 779

Wand, David Hsin-fu, **Supp. X:** 292

"Wanderer, The" (W. C. Williams), **Retro. Supp. I:** 414, 421

Wanderer, The: His Parables and His Sayings (Gibran), **Supp. XX: 116, 123–124**

"Wanderers, The" (Welty), **IV:** 273–274

"Wandering Jew, The" (Robinson), **III:** 505, 516–517

Wanderings of Oisin (Yeats), **Supp. I Part 1:** 79

Wang, Dorothy, **Supp. X:** 289

Wang Wei, **Supp. XV:** 47

Waniek, Marilyn Nelson, **Supp. IV Part 1:** 244. *See also* Nelson, Marilyn

Wanking 'Tards (Silver), **Supp. XXIV:** 265

"Wan Lee, the Pagan" (Harte), **Supp. II Part 1:** 351

"Want, The" (Olds), **Supp. X:** 210

Want Bone, The (Pinsky), **Supp. VI:** 236–237, 244–245, 247

"Wanted: An Ontological Critic" (Ransom), **III:** 498

"Wanting to Die" (Sexton), **Supp. II Part 2:** 684, 686; **Supp. XIV:** 132

"Wants" (Paley), **Supp. VI:** 219

Waples, Dorothy, **I:** 348

Wapshot Chronicle, The (Cheever), **Supp. I Part 1:** 174, 177–180, 181, 196

Wapshot Scandal, The (Cheever), **Supp. I Part 1:** 180–184, 187, 191, 196

"War" (Findley), **Supp. XX: 49**

"War" (H. Johnson), **Supp. XXVI:** 173

"War" (Jin), **Supp. XVIII:** 93

"War" (Kingston), **Supp. V:** 169

"War" (Simic), **Supp. VIII:** 282

"War, Response, and Contradiction" (Burke), **I:** 283

"War and Peace" (Sanders), **Supp. XVI:** 277

War and Peace (Tolstoy), **I:** 6, 7; **II:** 191, 205, 291; **IV:** 446; **Supp. V:** 277; **Supp. XI:** 68; **Supp. XIV:** 97; **Supp. XXIII:** 11

War and Remembrance (miniseries), **Supp. XXV:** 265

War and Remembrance (Wouk), **Supp. XX: 243; Supp. XXV:** 253, 254, 257, 258, 264–265

"War and the Small Nations" (Gibran), **Supp. XX: 127**

War and War (F. Barthelme), **Supp. XI:** 25

"War Between Men and Women, The" (Thurber), **Supp. I Part 2:** 615

War Bulletins (Lindsay), **Supp. I Part 2:** 378–379

Ward, Aileen, **II:** 531

Ward, Artemus (pseudonym). *See* Browne, Charles Farrar

Ward, Douglas Turner, **Supp. IV Part 1:** 362

Ward, Geoff, **Supp. XXIII:** 218

Ward, Henry, **Supp. I Part 2:** 588

Ward, Mrs. Humphry, **II:** 338

Ward, Leo R., **Supp. VIII:** 124

Ward, Lester F., **Supp. I Part 2:** 640; **Supp. XI:** 202, 203

Ward, Lynn, **I:** 31

Ward, Nathaniel, **Supp. I Part 1:** 99, 102, 111, 116

Ward, Susan, **Supp. XXIII:** 146

Ward, Theodora, **I:** 470; **Retro. Supp. I:** 28

Ward, William Hayes, **Supp. I Part 1:** 371

"War Debt, A" (Jewett), **Retro. Supp. II:** 138, 141

"War Diary" (Boyce), **Supp. XVII:** 104; **Supp. XXI:** 6

"War Diary, A" (Bourne), **I:** 229

War Dispatches of Stephen Crane, The (Crane), **I:** 422

"Ward Line, The" (Morris), **III:** 220

Ware, Amy, **Supp. XXVI:** 113

Warfel, Harry R., **Supp. I Part 1:** 366

War Games (Morris), **III:** 238

War Goes On, The (Asch), **Supp. XXIII:** 6

"Warhol / Blue Jackie"(Balakian), **Supp. XXIII:** 32

War in Heaven, The (Shepard and Chaikin), **Supp. III Part 2:** 433

War Is Kind (S. Crane), **I:** 409; **III:** 585

"War Is Kind" (S. Crane), **I:** 419; **Supp. XXVI:** 173

Warlock (Harrison), **Supp. VIII:** 45, **46**

Warm as Wool (Sanders), **Supp. XVI:** 269

"Warming" (Trethewey), **Supp. XXI:** 245

Warner, Anna, **Supp. XVIII:** 258–275

Warner, Charles Dudley, **II:** 405; **IV:** 198

Warner, Jack, **Supp. XII:** 160–161; **Supp. XVIII:** 249

Warner, John R., **III:** 193

Warner, Oliver, **I:** 548

Warner, Susan, **Retro. Supp. I:** 246; **Supp. XV:** 275; **Supp. XVIII:** 257–275

Warner, Sylvia Townsend, **Supp. VIII:** 151, 155, 164, 171

Warner, W. Lloyd, **III:** 60

Warner Family and the Warner Books, The (Baker), **Supp. XVIII:** 259, 267

"Warning" (Hughes), **Supp. I Part 1:** 343

"Warning" (Pound), **III:** 474

"Warning, The" (Creeley), **Supp. IV Part 1:** 150

"Warning, The" (Longfellow), **II:** 498

Warning Hill (Marquand), **III:** 55–56, 60, 68

"War of Eyes, A" (Coleman), **Supp. XI:** 93–94

War of Eyes and Other Stories, A (Coleman), **Supp. XI: 91–92**

War of the Classes (London), **II:** 466

"War of the Wall, The" (Bambara), **Supp. XI:** 15–16

"War of Vaslav Nijinsky, The" (Bidart), **Supp. XV:** 21–22, **27–29**

Warp (Grossman), **Supp. XXV:** 64, 65–66

"War Poems" (Sandburg), **III:** 581

Warren, Austin, **I:** 265, 268, 271; **Supp. I Part 2:** 423

Warren, David, **Supp. XXIV:** 269

Warren, Earl, **III:** 581

Warren, Gabriel, **IV:** 244

Warren, Mercy Otis, **Supp. XV:** 230

Warren, Patricia Nell, **Supp. XX: 259–276**

Warren, Robert Penn, **I:** 190, 211, 517; **II:** 57, 217, 228, 253; **III:** 134, 310, 382–383, 454, 482, 485, 490, 496,

497; **IV:** 121, 122, 123, 125, 126, **236–259**, 261, 262, 279, 340–341, 458; **Retro. Supp. I:** 40, 41, 73, 90; **Retro. Supp. II:** 220, 235; **Supp. I Part 1:** 359, 371; **Supp. I Part 2:** 386, 423; **Supp. II Part 1:** 139; **Supp. III Part 2:** 542; **Supp. IX:** 257; **Supp. V:** 261, 316, 318, 319, 333; **Supp. VIII:** 126, 176; **Supp. X:** 1, 25, 26; **Supp. XI:** 315; **Supp. XII:** 254, 255; **Supp. XIV:** 1, 2, 3, 4, 11, 14, 15; **Supp. XIX:** 246; **Supp. XVIII:** 77, 78–79; **Supp. XXI:** 256; **Supp. XXVI:** 63, 67, 78

Warren, Mrs. Robert Penn (Eleanor Clark), **IV:** 244

Warren, Rosanna, **IV:** 244; **Supp. XIX:** 34; **Supp. XV:** 251, 261, 262, 263

Warren, Vincent, **Supp. XXIII:** 218, 219

Warrington Poems, The (Ríos), **Supp. IV Part 2:** 540

Warrior, Robert Allen, **Supp. IV Part 1:** 329

"Warrior, The" (Gunn Allen), **Supp. IV Part 1:** 326

"Warrior: 5th Grade" (Olds), **Supp. X:** 214

"Warrior Road" (Harjo), **Supp. XII:** 217

"Warrior's Daughter, A" (Zitkala-Ša), **Supp. XXV:** 274, 275, 282

Wars, The (Findley), **Supp. XX:** 53–54

Warsh, Lewis, **Supp. XXIV:** 41

Warshavsky, Isaac (pseudonym). *See* Singer, Isaac Bashevis

Warshow, Robert, **Supp. I Part 1:** 51

Wars I Have Seen (Stein), **IV:** 27, 36, 477

Wartime (Fussell), **Supp. V:** 241

War Trash (Jin), **Supp. XVIII:** 89, **100–101**

"War Widow, The" (Frederic), **II:** 135–136

"Was" (Creeley), **Supp. IV Part 1:** 155

"Was" (Faulkner), **II:** 71

"Wash" (Faulkner), **II:** 72

Wash, Richard, **Supp. XII:** 14

"Washboard Wizard" (Nelson), **Supp. XVIII:** 182

Washburn, Keith, **Supp. XXVI:** 148–149

"Washed in the Rain" (Fante), **Supp. XI:** 165

"Washing of Hands, A" (Kooser), **Supp. XIX:** 115

Washington, Booker T., **Supp. I Part 2:** 393; **Supp. II Part 1:** 157, 160, 167, 168, 171, 225; **Supp. XIV:** 198, 199, 201; **Supp. XVIII:** 121–122

Washington, D.C. (Vidal), **Supp. IV Part 2:** 677, 684, 686–687, 690

Washington, George, **I:** 453; **II:** 313–314; **Supp. I Part 2:** 399, 485, 508, 509, 511, 513, 517, 518, 520, 599

Washington, Mary Helen, **Supp. XVIII:** 119, 284

Washington and His Generals (Lippard), **Supp. XXIII:** 178, **185–186,** 187

Washington Crossing the Delaware (Rivers), **Supp. XV:** 186

Washington Post Book World (Lesser), **Supp. IV Part 2:** 453; **Supp. VIII:** 80, 84, 241; **Supp. X:** 282

Washington Square (James), **II:** 327, 328; **Retro. Supp. I:** 215, 220, **222–223**

"Washington Square, 1946" (Ozick), **Supp. V:** 272

Washington Square Ensemble, The (Bell), **Supp. X:** 1, **3–4**

"Washman"(P. Benedict), **Supp. XXIII:** 40

"Was Lowell an Historical Critic?" (Altick), **Supp. I Part 2:** 423

Wasserman, Earl R., **Supp. I Part 2:** 439, 440

Wasserman, Jakob, **Supp. I Part 2:** 669

Wasserstein, Wendy, **Supp. IV Part 1:** 309; **Supp. XV: 319–336; Supp. XXIV:** 116, 117, 119, 128

Wasson, Ben, **Retro. Supp. I:** 79, 83

"Waste Carpet, The" (Matthews), **Supp. IX: 158–159**

Waste Land, The (T. S. Eliot), **I:** 107, 266, 298, 395, 396, 482, 570–571, 572, 574–575, 577–578, 580, 581, 584, 585, 586, 587; **III:** 6–8, 12, 196, 277–278, 453, 471, 492, 586; **IV:** 122, 123, 124, 140, 418, 419, 420; **Retro. Supp. I:** 51, 60, **60–62,** 63, 64, 66, 210, 290, 291, 299, 311, 420, 427; **Retro. Supp. II:** 85, 121, 190; **Supp. I Part 1:** 272; **Supp. I Part 2:** 439, 455, 614; **Supp. II Part 1:** 4, 5, 11, 96; **Supp. III Part 1:** 9, 10, 41, 63, 105; **Supp. IV Part 1:** 47, 284; **Supp. IX:** 158, 305; **Supp. V:** 338; **Supp. X:** 125; **Supp. XIII:** 341–342, 344, 346; **Supp. XIV:** 6, 284; **Supp. XIX:** 288; **Supp. XV:** 21, 181, 261, 306; **Supp. XVI:** 204; **Supp. XVII:** 140–141, 144, 227; **Supp. XVIII:** 78, 79–80; **Supp. XXIII:** 23, 25, 79, 165; **Supp. XXIV:** 140

"Waste Land, The": A Facsimile and Transcript of the Original Drafts Including the Annotations of Ezra Pound (Eliot, ed.), **Retro. Supp. I:** 58

Waste Land and Other Poems, The (T. S. Eliot), **Supp. XV:** 305

Wat, Alexander, **Supp. XVI:** 155, 161

Watch, The (Bass), **Supp. XVI: 16–17**

"Watch, The, — " (Bass), **Supp. XVI:** 17

Watch and Ward (James), **II:** 323; **Retro. Supp. I:** 218, **219,** 220

"Watcher" (Trethewey), **Supp. XXI:** 247

"Watcher, The" (R. Bly), **Supp. IV Part 1:** 71

"Watcher by the Dead, A" (Bierce), **I:** 203

Watchfires (Auchincloss), **Supp. IV Part 1:** 23

"Watching Crow, Looking toward the Manzano Mountains" (Harjo), **Supp. XII:** 219

"Watching the Oregon Whale" (A. Finch), **Supp. XVII:** 77

"Watching the Sunset" (Coleman), **Supp. XI:** 92

"Watching the Vulture at the Road Kill" (Stallings), **Supp. XXV:** 230

Watch on the Rhine (Hellman), **Supp. I Part 1:** 276, 278, 279–281, 283–284; **Supp. IV Part 1:** 83

"Watch Out for Landmines" (Biss), **Supp. XXVI:** 47, 51, 56

"Water" (Emerson), **II:** 19

"Water" (Komunyakaa), **Supp. XIII:** 132

"Water" (Lowell), **II:** 550

"Waterbird" (Swenson), **Supp. IV Part 2:** 651

"Water Borders" (Dillard), **Supp. VI:** 27

"Water Buffalo" (Komunyakaa), **Supp. XIII:** 122

"Watercolor of Grantchester Meadows" (Plath), **Supp. I Part 2:** 537

Water Cure, The (Everett), **Supp. XVIII: 64–66**

"Water Drum"(Kenny), **Supp. XXIII:** 144

"Waterfall, The" (Clampitt), **Supp. IX:** 44

Waterfront (Schulberg), **Supp. XVIII: 251–252**

"Water Hose Is on Fire, The" (Simic), **Supp. XV:** 185

Waterhouse, Keith, **Supp. VIII:** 124

"Waterlily Fire" (Rukeyser), **Supp. VI:** 285, 286

Waterlily Fire: Poems 1935–1962 (Rukeyser), **Supp. VI:** 274, 283, 285

Watermark (Brodsky), **Supp. VIII:** 29

Water-Method Man, The (Irving), **Supp. VI:** 163, **167–179,** 180

Water Music (Boyle), **Supp. VIII:** 1, 3–5, 8, 14; **Supp. XX: 20–22**

"Water Music for the Progress of Love in a Life-Raft Down the Sammamish Slough" (Wagoner), **Supp. IX:** 326

"Water People" (Burke), **Supp. XIV:** 21

"Water Picture" (Swenson), **Supp. IV Part 2:** 641

"Water Rising" (Hogan), **Supp. IV Part 1:** 400

Waters, Ethel, **II:** 587

Waters, Frank, **Supp. X:** 124

Waters, Muddy, **Supp. VIII:** 345

Watershed (Everett), **Supp. XVIII: 58–59,** 64

"Watershed" (Kingsolver), **Supp. VII:** 208

"Watershed" (Warren), **IV:** 239

"Watershed, The" (Auden), **Supp. II Part 1:** 5

Waters of Kronos, The (Richter), **Supp. XVIII:** 207, 208, **218–219,** 220

Waters of Siloe, The (Merton), **Supp. VIII:** 196, 208

Waterston, Sam, **Supp. IX:** 253

Water Street (Merrill), **Supp. III Part 1:** 321–323

"Water Walker" (Wilbur), **Supp. III Part 2:** 548, 560

Water-Witch, The (Cooper), **I:** 342–343

"Water Witch"(P. Benedict), **Supp. XXIII:** 38

Waterworks, The (Doctorow), **Supp. IV Part 1:** 218, 222, 223, 231–233, 234

"Water Works, The" (Doctorow), **Supp. IV Part 1:** 234

Watkin, E. I., **Retro. Supp. II:** 187

Watkins, Floyd C., **IV:** 452

Watkins, James T., **I:** 193, 194

Watkins, Maureen, **Supp. XVI:** 188

Watkins, Mel, **Supp. X:** 330; **Supp. XIII:** 246

Watman, Max, **Supp. XX: 92**

Watrous, Peter, **Supp. VIII:** 79

Watson, Brook, **Supp. XX: 284**

Watson, Burton, **Supp. XV:** 47

Watson, James Sibley, Jr., **I:** 261

Watson, Jay, **Supp. XVIII:** 195; **Supp. XXI:** 46

Watson, J. B., **II:** 361

Watson, Julia, **Supp. XXV:** 8

Watson, Richard, **Supp. I Part 2:** 516, 517

Watson, William, **II:** 114

Watsonville: Some Place Not Here (Moraga), **Supp. XXIII:** 195, 196, 202, 203

Watt, Ian, **Supp. VIII:** 4

Watteau, Jean Antoine, **III:** 275; **IV:** 79

Watts, Emily Stipes, **Supp. I Part 1:** 115

Waugh, Arthur, **Supp. XXIV:** 30

Waugh, Evelyn, **I:** 480; **III:** 281; **Supp. I Part 2:** 607; **Supp. IV Part 2:** 688; **Supp. XI:** 305, 306; **Supp. XIX:** 131; **Supp. XXV:** 70

Waugh, Robert H., **Supp. XXV:** 123

"Wave" (Snyder), **Supp. VIII:** 299

Wave, A (Ashbery), **Supp. III Part 1:** 1, 4, 24–26

"Wave, A" (Ashbery), **Supp. III Part 1:** 9, 19, 24–25

"Wave, The" (MacLeish), **III:** 19

"Wave, The" (Untermeyer), **Supp. XV:** 300

Wave Amplitude in the Mona Passage (Schott), **Supp. XXIII: 242–243**

"Wavemaker Falters, The" (Saunders), **Supp. XIX:** 225

"Waxwings" (Francis), **Supp. IX:** 82

Way, The (Steiner and Witt, eds.), **Supp. IV Part 2:** 505

"Way Down, The" (Kunitz), **Supp. III Part 1:** 263

"Way It Is, The" (Ellison), **Supp. II Part 1:** 245

"Way It Is, The" (Jones), **Supp. XI:** 229

Way It Is, The (Stafford), **Supp. XIII:** 274

"Way It Is, The" (Strand), **Supp. IV Part 2:** 627

"Wayland" (Sanders), **Supp. XVI:** 275

Wayne, John, **Supp. IV Part 1:** 200

Way of Chuang-Tzu, The (Merton), **Supp. VIII:** 208

"Way of Exchange in James Dickey's Poetry, The" (Weatherby), **Supp. IV Part 1:** 175

Way of Life According to Laotzu, The (Bynner), **Supp. XV:** 46, 48

Way Out, A (Frost), **Retro. Supp. I:** 133

Wayside Motor Inn, The (Gurney), **Supp. V:** 96, 105, 109

"Ways of Breaking: Lynda Hull's 'Ornithology' " (Jauss), **Supp. XXI:** 139

"Ways of Talking" (Jin), **Supp. XVIII:** 93

Ways of the Hour, The (Cooper), **I:** 354

Ways of White Folks, The (Hughes), **Retro. Supp. I:** 203, 204; **Supp. I**

Part 1: 329, 330, 332

Way Some People Die, The (Macdonald), **Supp. IV Part 2:** 470, 471, 472, 474

Way Some People Live, The (Cheever), **Supp. I Part 1:** 175

"Way the Cards Fall, The" (Komunyakaa), **Supp. XIII:** 117

"Way the Luck Runs, The" (Wolfert), **Supp. XXI:** 265

"Way Things Are, The" (Turow, unpub.), **Supp. XVII:** 215, 218

Way to Rainy Mountain, The (Momaday), **Supp. IV Part 2:** 485–486, 487–489, 491, 493

Way to Wealth, The (Franklin), **II:** 101–102, 110; **Supp. XX: 27**

Wayward and the Seeking, The: A Collection of Writings by Jean Toomer (Toomer), **Supp. III Part 2:** 478–481, 484, 487

Wayward Bus, The (Steinbeck), **IV:** 51, 64–65

"Way We Live Now, The" (Sontag), **Supp. III Part 2:** 467–468

"Way You'll Never Be, A" (Hemingway), **II:** 249

"W. D. Sees Himself Animated" (Snodgrass), **Supp. VI:** 327

"W. D. Sits in Kafka's Chair and Is Interrogated Concerning the Assumed Death of Cock Robin" (Snodgrass), **Supp. VI:** 319

"W. D. Tries to Warn Cock Robin" (Snodgrass), **Supp. VI:** 319

"We" (Alexander), **Supp. XVIII:** 185

Weaks, Mary Louise, **Supp. X:** 5

Weales, Gerald, **II:** 602

"Wealth," from *Conduct of Life, The* (Emerson), **II:** 2, 3–4

"Wealth," from *English Traits* (Emerson), **II:** 6

Wealth of Nations, The (A. Smith), **II:** 109

"We Are Looking at You, Agnes" (Caldwell), **I:** 309

We Are Not in This Together (Kittredge), **Supp. XXVI:** 182, 183, 184

We Are Still Married: Stories and Letters (Keillor), **Supp. XVI:** 176, 177

"We Are the Crazy Lady and Other Feisty Feminist Fables" (Ozick), **Supp. V:** 259

Weary Blues, The (Hughes), **Retro. Supp. I:** 195, 197, 198, 199, 200, 203, 205; **Supp. I Part 1:** 325

"Weary Blues, The" (Hughes), **Retro. Supp. I:** 198, 199; **Supp. I Part 1:** 324, 325

"Weary Kingdom" (Irving), **Supp. VI:** 163

Weasels and Wisemen: Ethics and Ethnicity in the Work of David Mamet (Kane), **Supp. XIV:** 250

Weather and the Women Treat Me Fair, The (Everett), **Supp. XVIII:** 66

Weatherby, H. L., **Supp. IV Part 1:** 175

Weather Central (Kooser), **Supp. XIX:** 116, **123–125**

"Weathering Out" (Dove), **Supp. IV Part 1:** 248

"Weather Report" (Huddle), **Supp. XXVI:** 152

"Weather Within, The" (M. F. K. Fisher), **Supp. XVII:** 88, 91

Weaver, Harriet, **III:** 471

Weaver, James, **Supp. XVIII:** 72

Weaver, Michael, **Supp. XVIII:** 176, 177

Weaver, Mike, **Retro. Supp. I:** 430

Weaver, Will, **Supp. XVI:** 39

"Weaving" (Larcom), **Supp. XIII:** 142, **Supp. XIII:** 144–145, 150, 151

"Web" (Oliver), **Supp. VII:** 236

Web and the Rock, The (Wolfe), **IV:** 451, 455, 457, 459–460, 462, 464, 467, 468

Webb, Beatrice, **Supp. I Part 1:** 5

Webb, Mary, **I:** 226

Webb, Phyllis, **Supp. XX: 56**

Webb, Sidney, **Supp. I Part 1:** 5

Webb, W. P., **Supp. V:** 225

Webber, A. R. F., **Supp. XXI:** 160

Weber, Brom, **I:** 383, 386

Weber, Carl, **Supp. IX:** 133, 138, 141

Weber, Max, **I:** 498; **Supp. I Part 2:** 637, 648

Weber, Sarah, **Supp. I Part 1:** 2

Weberman, A. J., **Supp. XVIII:** 27

Web of Earth, The (Wolfe), **IV:** 451–452, 456, 458, 464, 465

Web of Iniquity, The (Nickerson), **Supp. XXV:** 200

"Web of Life, The" (Nemerov), **III:** 282

Webster, Brenda, **Supp. XVI:** 157, 161

Webster, Daniel, **II:** 5, 9; **Supp. I Part 2:** 659, 687, 689, 690

Webster, John, **I:** 384; **Supp. I Part 2:** 422

Webster, Noah, **Supp. I Part 2:** 660; **Supp. II Part 1:** 77

Wector, Dixon, **II:** 103

Wedding, The (D. West), **Supp. XVIII:** 277, **287–289**; **Supp. XXVI:** 174

"Wedding, The" (Everwine), **Supp. XV:** 83

"Wedding, The" (Major), **Supp. XXII:** 185

Wedding, The (television miniseries), **Supp. XVIII:** 277, 289

"Wedding Cake" (Nye), **Supp. XIII:** 283

"Wedding Dance, The" (Di Piero), **Supp. XIX:** 47

"Wedding Day" (Boyle), **Supp. XXIV:** 56–57

Wedding Day and Other Stories (Boyle), **Supp. XXIV: 56–57**

"Wedding in Brownsville, A" (Singer), **IV:** 15

Wedding in Hell, A (Simic), **Supp. VIII:** 280, **282**

"Wedding of Henry Markowitz, The" (Goodman), **Supp. XXVI:** 121–122

"Wedding of the Rose and Lotus, The" (Lindsay), **Supp. I Part 2:** 387

"Wedding Supper, The" (Rowson), **Supp. XV:** 243

"Wedding Toast, A" (Wilbur), **Supp. III Part 2:** 561

Wedekind, Frank, **III:** 398; **Supp. XX: 85**; **Supp. XXII:** 23

Wedge, The (W. C. Williams), **Retro. Supp. I:** 424

"We Didn't"(Dybek), **Supp. XXIII:** 77–78

"Wednesday at the Waldorf" (Swenson), **Supp. IV Part 2:** 647

We Don't Live Here Anymore (Dubus), **Supp. XXIV:** 97

"We Don't Live Here Anymore" (Dubus), **Supp. VII:** 78–79, 85

"Weed" (McCarriston), **Supp. XIV:** 259, 273

"Weed, The" (Bishop), **Supp. I Part 1:** 80, 88–89

"Weed, The" (Taggard), **Supp. XXII:** 284

"Weeds, The" (McCarthy), **II:** 566

"Weekend" (Beattie), **Supp. V:** 27

"Weekend" (Hempel), **Supp. XXI:** 124

Weekend, The (Cameron), **Supp. XII:** 80, 81, **86–88**

"Weekend at Ellerslie, A" (Wilson), **IV:** 431

Weekend Edition (National Public Radio), **Supp. IX:** 299; **Supp. XVII:** 240, 242

Weekend in Dinlock (Sigal), **Supp. XXIII:** 166

"Week in the Word, A" (Hampl), **Supp. XXII:** 85

Week on the Concord and Merrimack Rivers, A (Thoreau), **IV:** 168, 169, 177, 182–183; **Supp. I Part 2:** 420; **Supp. XIV:** 227

Weeks, Edward, **III:** 64

Weeks, Jerome, **Supp. VIII:** 76

"Weeping Burgher" (Stevens), **IV:** 77

"Weeping Women" (Levertov), **Supp. III Part 1:** 282

We Fished All Night (W. Motley), **Supp. XVII: 155–158,** 159, 160

We Fly Away (Francis), **Supp. IX: 79–80,** 84

" ' We Had Some Good Times Anyway' " (Gansworth), **Supp. XXVI:** 114

We Happy Few (Hinojosa), **Supp. XIX:** 99, **111–112**

We Have Always Lived in the Castle (Jackson), **Supp. IX:** 121, 126, **127–128**

"We Have Our Arts So We Won't Die of Truth" (Bradbury), **Supp. IV Part 1:** 105

We Have Tomorrow (Bontemps), **Supp. XXII:** 6, 12

Weich, Dave, **Supp. XII:** 321; **Supp. XVIII:** 91

"Weighing In" (Espaillat), **Supp. XXI:** 111

"Weight" (Wideman), **Supp. X:** 321

"Weights" (C. Baxter), **Supp. XVII:** 16

Weigl, Bruce, **Supp. VIII:** 269, 274; **Supp. XIX: 273–290; Supp. XV:** 342

Weik, Alexa, **Supp. XXIV:** 64

Weil, Dorothy, **Supp. XV:** 231

Weil, James L., **Supp. XXI:** 23, 31

Weil, Robert, **Supp. IX:** 236

Weil, Simone, **I:** 298; **Supp. XV:** 259; **Supp. XXII:** 93; **Supp. XXVI:** 234

Weiland (C. B. Brown), **Supp. XIII:** 100

Weinauer, Ellen, **Supp. XV:** 270, 284

Weinberger, Eliot, **Supp. IV Part 1:** 66; **Supp. VIII:** 290, 292; **Supp. XVI:** 284

Weinberger, Eric, **Supp. XXII:** 264

Weinfield, Henry, **Supp. XXI:** 24, 28, 33

Weininger, Otto, **Retro. Supp. I:** 416

Weinraub, Judith, **Supp. XXI:** 39

Weinreb, Mindy, **Supp. X:** 24

Weinreich, Regina, **Supp. XIV:** 22

Weinstein, Cindy, **Supp. XVIII:** 261

Weinstein, Hinda, **IV:** 285

Weinstein, Max, **IV:** 285

Weinstein, Mrs. Max (Anna Wallenstein), **IV:** 285, 287

Weinstein, Nathan. *See* West, Nathanael

Weinstein, Selma, **Supp. XXI:** 170

Weir, Sybil, **Supp. XXIV:** 20

Weisheit, Rabbi, **IV:** 76

Weismuller, Johnny, **Supp. X:** 264; **Supp. XX: 18**

Weiss, David, **Supp. XVI:** 55

Weiss, Jane, **Supp. XVIII:** 267, 269

Weiss, Peter, **IV:** 117

Weiss, Theodore, **Supp. IV Part 2:** 440; **Supp. IX:** 96

Weissleder, Paul, **Supp. XXII:** 283

Weist, Dianne, **Supp. X:** 80

Weithas, Art, **Supp. XI:** 231

Welch, Dave, **Supp. XXI:** 118

Welch, Don, **Supp. XIX:** 119

Welch, James, **Supp. IV Part 1:** 404; **Supp. IV Part 2:** 503, 513, 557, 562; **Supp. XXIV:** 257; **Supp. XXVI:** 186, 188

Welch, Lew, **Supp. V:** 170; **Supp. VIII:** 303; **Supp. XXII:** 276

"Welcome from War" (Rukeyser), **Supp. VI:** 286

"Welcome Morning" (Sexton), **Supp. II Part 2:** 696

"Welcome the Wrath" (Kunitz), **Supp. III Part 1:** 261

Welcome to Hard Times (Doctorow), **Supp. IV Part 1:** 218, 219–220, 222, 224, 230, 238

Welcome to Hard Times (film), **Supp. IV Part 1:** 236

"Welcome to New Dork" (Leonard), **Supp. XVIII:** 148

Welcome to Our City (Wolfe), **IV:** 461

Welcome to the Castle (Hayes), **Supp. XXVI:** 144

Welcome to the Monkey House (Vonnegut), **Supp. II Part 2:** 758

Welcome to the Moon (Shanley), **Supp. XIV:** 318

Welcome to the Moon and Other Plays (Shanley), **Supp. XIV:** 315, **316–319**

Weld, Theodore, **Supp. I Part 2:** 587, 588

Weld, Tuesday, **Supp. XI:** 306

Welded (O'Neill), **III:** 390; **Supp. XXII:** 24

"Welfare Worker, Disenchanted, Contemplates Friday Afternoon, The" (Trethewey), **Supp. XXI:** 246

"Well, The" (Momaday), **Supp. IV Part 2:** 483

"Well Dressed Man with a Beard, The" (Stevens), **Retro. Supp. I:** 297

Wellek, René, **I:** 253, 261, 282; **II:** 320; **Supp. XIV:** 12, 14

Weller, George, **III:** 322

Welles, Gideon, **Supp. I Part 2:** 484

Welles, Orson, **IV:** 476; **Supp. I Part 1:** 67; **Supp. IV Part 1:** 82, 83; **Supp. V:** 251; **Supp. VIII:** 46; **Supp. XI:** 169, 307

"Wellfleet Whale, The" (Kunitz), **Supp. III Part 1:** 263, 269

Wellfleet Whale and Companion Poems, The (Kunitz), **Supp. III Part 1:** 263

Wellink, Yvonne, **Supp. XVIII:** 257

Wellman, Flora, **II:** 463–464, 465

Wellman, Rita, **Supp. XXV:** 20

"Well Rising, The" (Stafford), **Supp. XI:** 318

Wells, Carolyn, **Supp. XXVI: 271–287**

Wells, H. G., **I:** 103, 226, 241, 243, 253, 405, 409, 415; **II:** 82, 144, 276, 337, 338, 458; **III:** 456; **IV:** 340, 455; **Retro. Supp. I:** 100, 228, 231; **Supp. XVI:** 190; **Supp. XXI:** 8

Wellspring, The (Olds), **Supp. X: 211–212**

Well Wrought Urn, The: Studies in the Structure of Poetry (Brooks), **Supp. XIV:** 1, **8–9,** 14, 15, 16

Welsh, Mary, **Supp. XIX:** 248. *See also* Hemingway, Mrs. Ernest (Mary Welsh)

Welty, Eudora, **II:** 194, 217, 606; **IV: 260–284; Retro. Supp. I:** 339–358; **Retro. Supp. II:** 235; **Supp. IV Part 2:** 474; **Supp. V:** 59, 315, 336; **Supp. VIII:** 94, 151, 171; **Supp. X:** 42, 290; **Supp. XII:** 310, 322; **Supp. XIV:** 3; **Supp. XV:** 338; **Supp. XXIV:** 223; **Supp. XXVI:** 152

Welty, Eurora, **Supp. XIX:** 151

Weltzien, O. Alan, **Supp. XVI:** 20–21, 28

"We miss Her, not because We see—" (Dickinson), **Retro. Supp. I:** 46

We Must Dance My Darlings (Trilling), **Supp. I Part 1:** 297

Wendell, Barrett, **III:** 507; **Supp. I Part 2:** 414; **Supp. XIV:** 197

Wendell, Sarah. *See* Holmes, Mrs. Abiel (Sarah Wendell)

Wendy Wasserstein: A Casebook (Barnett), **Supp. XV:** 323, 330

"Wendy Wasserstein's Three Sisters: Squandered Privilege" (Brewer), **Supp. XV:** 330

Wenner, Jann S., **Supp. XXIV:** 280, 283

Wept of Wish-ton-Wish, The (Cooper), **I:** 339, 342, 350

Werbe, Peter, **Supp. XIII:** 236

"We Real Cool" (Brooks), **Supp. III Part 1:** 80

"We're All Pharaohs When We Die" (Gallagher), **Supp. XXIV:** 170

We're Back! A Dinosaur's Story (screenplay, Shanley), **Supp. XIV:** 316

"We're Friends Again" (O'Hara), **III:** 372–373

"Were the Whole Realm of Nature Mine" (Watts), **I:** 458

Werewolf (M. Sommers), **Supp. XVII:** 55

Were-Wolf, The (C. Housman), **Supp. XVII:** 55

Werewolf of Paris, The (Endore), **Supp. XVII:** 55–56

Werewolves in Their Youth (Chabon), **Supp. XI:** 66, **76–77**

Werlock, Abby, **Supp. XIII:** 293

Werthman, Michael, **Supp. V:** 115

"Wer-Trout, The" (Proulx), **Supp. VII:** 255–256

Wescott, Glenway, **I:** 288; **II:** 85; **III:** 448, 454; **Supp. VIII:** 156; **Supp. XIV:** 342; **Supp. XVI:** 195

"We Shall All Be Born Again But We Shall Not All Be Saved" (Matthews), **Supp. IX:** 162

West, Anthony, **Supp. IV Part 1:** 284

West, Benjamin, **Supp. I Part 2:** 511

West, Dorothy, **Supp. XIII:** 295; **Supp. XIX:** 72; **Supp. XVIII: 277–291; Supp. XXVI:** 164, 173, 174

West, James, **II:** 562

West, Nathanael, **I:** 97, 107, 190, 211, 298; **II:** 436; **III:** 357, 425; **IV: 285– 307; Retro. Supp. II: 321–341; Supp. IV Part 1:** 203; **Supp. VIII:** 97; **Supp. XI:** 85, 105, 159, 296; **Supp. XII:** 173, 310; **Supp. XIII:** 106, 170; **Supp. XIX:** 223; **Supp. XVIII:** 251, 253, 254

West, Ray, **Supp. XV:** 142

West, Rebecca, **II:** 412, 445; **Supp. XVI:** 152, 153

Westall, Julia Elizabeth. *See* Wolfe, Mrs. William Oliver (Julia Elizabeth Westall)

"We Stand United" (Benét), **Supp. XI:** 46

"West Authentic, The: Willa Cather" (Stegner), **Supp. IV Part 2:** 608

"West Coast, The: Region with a View" (Stegner), **Supp. IV Part 2:** 608–609

"West Coast Waterfront: End of an Era" (Swados), **Supp. XIX:** 264

Westcott, Edward N., **II:** 102

"Western Association of Writers" (Chopin), **Supp. I Part 1:** 217

"Western Ballad, A" (Ginsberg), **Supp. II Part 1:** 311

Western Borders, The (Howe), **Supp. IV Part 2:** 424–425

Western Canon (Bloom), **Supp. XXV:** 251

Western Canon: The Books and Schools of the Ages (Bloom), **Supp. IX:** 146

Western Lands, The (Burroughs), **Supp. III Part 1:** 106

"Western North Carolina" (Halliday), **Supp. XIX:** 85

Western Star (Benét), **Supp. XI:** 46, 47, 57

"Westland" (C. Baxter), **Supp. XVII:** 18, 19

"West Marginal Way" (Hugo), **Supp. VI:** 131, 135

West of Eden: Writers in Hollywood, 1928–1940 (Fine), **Supp. XVIII:** 248

West of Yesterday, East of Summer: New and Selected Poems, 1973–1993 (Monette), **Supp. X:** 159

West of Your City (Stafford), **Supp. XI:** 316, **317–318,** 321, 322

Weston, Jessie L., **II:** 540; **III:** 12; **Supp. I Part 2:** 438

"West Real" (Ríos), **Supp. IV Part 2:** 539, 540

West-running Brook (Frost), **II:** 155; **Retro. Supp. I:** 136, 137

"West-running Brook" (Frost), **II:** 150, 162–164

"West Wall" (Merwin), **Supp. III Part 1:** 355

"Westward Beach, A" (Jeffers), **Supp. II Part 2:** 418

Westward Ho (Harrison), **Supp. VIII:** 51, **52**

Westward the Course of Empire (Leutze), **Supp. X:** 307

"Westward the Course of Empire Takes Its Way" (Wallace), **Supp. X: 307– 308; Supp. XXII:** 260

"West Wind" (Oliver), **Supp. VII:** 246

"West Wind, The" (Bryant), **Supp. I Part 1:** 155

West Wind: Poems and Prose Poems (Oliver), **Supp. VII:** 243, 246–248

"Wet Casements" (Ashbery), **Supp. III Part 1:** 18–20

We the Living (film), **Supp. IV Part 2:** 520

We the Living (Rand), **Supp. IV Part 2:** 520–521

Wetherell, Elizabeth (pseudonym). *See* Warner, Susan

Wet Parade (Sinclair), **Supp. V:** 289

Wetzsteon, Ross, **Supp. XXI:** 12

"We've Adjusted Too Well" (O'Brien), **Supp. V:** 247

Wevill, David, **Retro. Supp. II:** 247, 249

"We Wear the Mask" (Dunbar), **Supp. II Part 1:** 199, 207, 209–210

We Will Be Citizens: New Essays on Gay and Lesbian Theatre (Fischer, ed.), **Supp. XXIV:** 263

Weybright, Victor, **Supp. XIII:** 172

Weyden, Rogier van der, **Supp. IV Part 1:** 284

Whalen, Marcella, **Supp. I Part 1:** 49

Whalen, Philip, **Supp. VIII:** 289; **Supp. XXII:** 226

Whalen-Bridge, John, **Retro. Supp. II:** 211–212

"Whales off Wales, The" (X. J. Kennedy), **Supp. XV:** 163

"Whales Weep" (Boyle), **Supp. XX: 19**

"Whales Weep Not!" (D. H. Lawrence), **Supp. XVII:** 77

Wharton, Edith, **I:** 12, 375; **II:** 96, 180, 183, 186, 189–190, 193, 283, 338, 444, 451; **III:** 69, 175, 576; **IV:** 8, 53, 58, **308–330; Retro. Supp. I:** 108, 232, **359–385; Supp. IV Part 1:** 23, 31, 35, 36, 80, 81, 310; **Supp. IX:** 57; **Supp. XII:** 308; **Supp. XIV:** 337, 347; **Supp. XVI:** 189; **Supp. XVIII:** 278; **Supp. XX: 227, 229, 232, 239, 240; Supp. XXIII:** 275; **Supp. XXIV:** 29, 64; **Supp. XXV:** 201; **Supp. XXVI:** 145, 276

Wharton, Edward Robbins, **IV:** 310, 313–314, 319

"What" (Dunn), **Supp. XI:** 144

What a Kingdom It Was (Kinnell), **Supp. III Part 1:** 235, 238, 239

"What America Would Be Like without Blacks" (Ellison), **Retro. Supp. II:** 123

What Are Masterpieces (Stein), **IV:** 30–31

What Are Years (Moore), **III:** 208–209, 210, 215

"What Are Years?" (Moore), **III:** 211, 213

What a Way to Go (Morris), **III:** 230–232

"What a Wonder among the Instruments Is the Walloping Trombone!" (Carruth), **Supp. XVI:** 51

"What Became of the Flappers?" (Zelda Fitzgerald), **Supp. IX:** 71

"What Can I Tell My Bones?" (Roethke), **III:** 546, 549

What Century? (O'Hara), **Supp. XXIII:** 216

"What Child Is This?" (Jarman), **Supp. XVII:** 113–114, 115

"What Do I Care for Morning" (H. Johnson), **Supp. XXVI:** 173

"What Do We Have Here" (Carson), **Supp. XII: 101**

"What Do We See" (Rukeyser), **Supp. VI:** 282

What Do Women Want? Bread Roses Sex Power (Jong), **Supp. V:** 115, 117, 129, 130

"What Do You Do in San Francisco?" (Carver), **Supp. III Part 1:** 143

What Dreams My Come (Atherton as Frank Lin), **Supp. XXIV:** 28

What D'Ya Know for Sure (Zinberg), **Supp. XV:** 196

Whatever Happened to Gloomy Gus of the Chicago Bears? (Coover), **Supp. V:** 51, 52

Whatever Happened to Jacy Farrow? (Cleveland), **Supp. V:** 222

"What Every Boy Should Know" (Maxwell), **Supp. VIII:** 169

"What Feels Like the World" (Bausch), **Supp. VII:** 46

"What Fort Sumter Did for Me" (E. Stoddard), **Supp. XV:** 282

"What Girls Read" (Salmon), **Supp. XVIII:** 258

"What God Is Like to Him I Serve" (Bradstreet), **Supp. I Part 1:** 106–107

"What Happened Here Before" (Snyder), **Supp. VIII:** 302

"What Happened to Georgia" (Ray), **Supp. XVIII:** 194

What Happens (Herrmann), **Supp. XXII:** 277

What Have I Ever Lost by Dying? (R. Bly), **Supp. IV Part 1:** 71–72

What Have You Lost? (Nye, ed.), **Supp. XIII:** 280

What I Believe (Asch), **Supp. XXIII:** 2

"What I Believe" (Mumford), **Supp. II Part 2:** 479

"What I Call What They Call Onanism" (Goldbarth), **Supp. XII:** 175

What I Did Last Summer (Gurney), **Supp. V:** 96, 100, 107, 108

"What if God" (Olds), **Supp. X:** 208

What I Have Done with Birds: Character Studies of Native American Birds (Stratton-Porter), **Supp. XX: 218**

"What I Have to Defend, What I Can't Bear Losing" (Stern), **Supp. IX:** 286, 287, 288, 298

"What I Knew" (Nelson), **Supp. XVIII:** 178

"What I Know about Being a Playwright" (McNally), **Supp. XIII:** 195, 207

"What I Mean" (Ortiz), **Supp. IV Part 2:** 497

"What Is an Emotion" (James), **II:** 350

What Is Art? (Tolstoy), **I:** 58

"What Is Civilization? Africa's Answer" (Du Bois), **Supp. II Part 1:** 176

"What Is College For?" (Bourne), **I:** 216

"What Is Exploitation?" (Bourne), **I:** 216

What Is Found There: Notebooks on Poetry and Politics (A. Rich), **Supp. XVII:** 74

"What Is It?" (Carver), **Supp. III Part 1:** 139

What Is Man? (Twain), **II:** 434; **IV:** 209

"What Is Poetry" (Ashbery), **Supp. III Part 1:** 19

"What Is Seized" (Moore), **Supp. X:** 164, 168, 169, 172, 175

"What Is the Earth?" (Olds), **Supp. X:** 213

"What Is This Poet" (Stern), **Supp. IX:** 295

What Is To Be Done? (Lenin), **Supp. XXI:** 164

"What I Think" (Hogan), **Supp. IV Part 1:** 406

What Maisie Knew (H. James), **II:** 332; **Retro. Supp. I:** 229, **230;** **Supp. XVIII:** 160

What Makes Sammy Run? (NBC broadcast, Schulberg and Schulberg), **Supp. XVIII:** 254

What Makes Sammy Run? (Schulberg), **Supp. XIII:** 170; **Supp. XVIII:** 241, **244–247,** 248, 249, 253

"What Makes Sammy Run?" (Schulberg), **Supp. XVIII:** 241

What Moon Drove Me to This? (Harjo), **Supp. XII: 218–220**

"What Must" (MacLeish), **III:** 18

What My Father Believed (Wrigley), **Supp. XVIII:** 298–300

"What My Father Believed" (Wrigley), **Supp. XVIII: 298–299**

What Price Hollywood? (film), **Supp. XVIII:** 243

"What Sally Said" (Cisneros), **Supp. VII:** 63

What Saves Us (Weigl), **Supp. XIX:** 282

"What's Happening in America" (Sontag), **Supp. III Part 2:** 460–461

"What She Couldn't Tell" (Hampl), **Supp. XXII:** 92

"What's in Alaska?" (Carver), **Supp. III Part 1:** 141, 143

"What's in a Name" (H. L. Gates), **Supp. XX: 101**

What's New, Pussycat? (film; Allen), **Supp. XI:** 307; **Supp. XV:** 1, 2, 14

"What's New in American and Canadian Poetry" (R. Bly), **Supp. IV Part 1:** 67

What's O'Clock (Lowell), **II:** 511, 527, 528

What's Up, Tiger Lily? (film; Allen), **Supp. XV:** 2, **3**

"What the Arts Need Now" (Baraka), **Supp. II Part 1:** 47

"What the Bed Knows"(Schott), **Supp. XXIII:** 249

"What the Body Can Say" (Trethewey), **Supp. XXI:** 255

"What the Brand New Freeway Won't Go By" (Hugo), **Supp. VI:** 132–133

"What the Gypsies Told My Grandmother While She Was Still a Young Girl" (Simic), **Supp. VIII:** 283

"What the Prose Poem Carries with It" (R. Bly), **Supp. IV Part 1:** 64

"What the Stone Says" (Huddle), **Supp. XXVI:** 151

"What They Wanted" (Dunn), **Supp. XI:** 151

What Thou Lovest Well (Hugo), **Supp. VI:** 140, 141

"What Thou Lovest Well Remains American" (Hugo), **Supp. VI:** 140, 141

What Time Collects (Farrell), **II:** 46, 47–48

What to Do? (Chernyshevsky), **Retro. Supp. I:** 269

"What to Keep, What to Discard" (Taggard), **Supp. XXII:** 280

"What to the Slave is Your Fourth of July?"(Douglass), **Supp. XXIII:** 167

What Use Are Flowers? (Hansberry), **Supp. IV Part 1:** 359, 368–369, 374

What Was Literature? (Fiedler), **Supp. XIII:** 96–97, **105–106**

What Was Mine (Beattie), **Supp. V:** 33, 35

What Was the Relationship of the Lone Ranger to the Means of Production? (Baraka), **Supp. II Part 1:** 58

"What We Came Through" (Goldbarth), **Supp. XII:** 179–180

"What Were the White Things?" (Hempel), **Supp. XXI:** 126

What We Talk About When We Talk About Love (Carver), **Supp. III Part 1:** 142–146; **Supp. XII:** 139; **Supp. XXIV:** 177

"What Why When How Who" (Pinsky), **Supp. VI:** 244

What Will Suffice: Contemporary American Poets on the Art of Poetry (Buckley and Young, eds.), **Supp. XIII:** 313

What Work Is (Levine), **Supp. V:** 181, 187, 192–193

"What You Hear from 'Em" (Taylor), **Supp. V:** 314, 320, 324

"What You Live For" (Huddle), **Supp. XXVI:** 150

What You See in the Dark (Muñoz), **Supp. XXV:** 127, 137–139

"What You Want" (O. Henry), **Supp. II Part 1:** 402

"What You Would Do" (Weigl), **Supp. XIX:** 288

Wheatley, Phillis, **Supp. XIII:** 111; **Supp. XVII:** 74–75; **Supp. XX: 106, 277–291**

Whedon, Tony, **Supp. XXI:** 131, 132

"Wheelchairs" (Kriegel), **Supp. XXIV:** 220

Wheeler, David, **Supp. XVI:** 277

Wheeler, John, **II:** 433

Wheeler, Monroe, **Supp. XV:** 295

Wheelock, John Hall, **IV:** 461; **Supp. IX:** 268; **Supp. XIV:** 120; **Supp. XV:** 301

Wheel of Life, The (Glasgow), **II:** 176, 178, 179, 183

Wheelwright, Philip, **Supp. XV:** 20

"When" (Olds), **Supp. X:** 207

When Boyhood Dreams Come True (Farrell), **II:** 45

"When Death Came April Twelve 1945" (Sandburg), **III:** 591, 593

"When Death Comes" (Oliver), **Supp. VII:** 241

"When De Co'n Pone's Hot" (Dunbar), **Supp. II Part 1:** 202–203

"When God First Said" (Zach; Everwine trans.), **Supp. XV:** 87

"When Grandma Died—1942" (Shields), **Supp. VII:** 311

"When Howitzers Began" (Carruth), **Supp. XVI:** 55

"When I Buy Pictures" (Moore), **III:** 205

"When I Came from Colchis" (Merwin), **Supp. III Part 1:** 343

"When I Have Fears I May Cease to Be" (Keats), **Supp. XIX:** 92

"When I Left Business for Literature" (Anderson), **I:** 101

"When I Love You" (Peacock), **Supp. XIX:** 199

"When in Rome—Apologia" (Komunyakaa), **Supp. XIII:** 120

"When It Comes" (Olds), **Supp. X:** 213

"When It's Clear and Hot" (Trethewey), **Supp. XXI:** 246

When I Was Alive (Notley), **Supp. XXII:** 228

"When I Was Alive" (Notley), **Supp. XXII:** 229

"When I Was Seventeen" (Kincaid), **Supp. VII:** 181

"When I Was Twenty-five" (Talese), **Supp. XVII:** 202

When Knighthood Was in Flower (Major), **III:** 320

"\[When\] Let by rain" (Taylor), **IV:** 160–161

"When Lilacs Last in the Dooryard Bloom'd" (Whitman), **IV:** 347–348, 351; **Retro. Supp. I:** 406; **Supp. IV Part 1:** 16; **Supp. XV:** 215

"When Malindy Sings" (Dunbar), **Supp. II Part 1:** 200, 204–205

When Peoples Meet: A Study of Race and Culture (Locke and Stern), **Supp. XIV:** 202, 213

When She Was Good (P. Roth), **Retro. Supp. II:** 282, 283, 284; **Supp. III Part 2:** 403, 405, 410–413

"When Sue Wears Red" (Hughes), **Retro. Supp. I:** 195, 204

"When the Acacia Blooms"(Crooker), **Supp. XXIII:** 60

"When the Dead Ask My Father about Me" (Olds), **Supp. X:** 210

"When the Frost Is on the Punkin" (Riley), **Supp. II Part 1:** 202

When the Jack Hollers (Hughes), **Retro. Supp. I:** 203; **Supp. I Part 1:** 328

"When the Last Riders" (Zach; Everwine, trans.), **Supp. XV:** 75, 86

"When the Light Gets Green" (Warren), **IV:** 252

"When the Model Does Not Show" (Major), **Supp. XXII:** 184

"When the Peace Corps Was Young" (Theroux), **Supp. VIII:** 314

When the Sun Tries to Go On (Koch), **Supp. XV:** 185

"When the Sun Tries to Go On" (Koch), **Supp. XV:** 179, 180

"When the World Ended as We Knew It" (Harjo), **Supp. XII:** 231

When Time Was Born (Farrell), **II:** 46, 47

"When We Dead Awaken: Writing as Re-Vision" (Rich), **Supp. I Part 2:** 552–553, 560

"When We Gonna Rise" (Baraka), **Supp. II Part 1:** 48

"When We Have To" (Salinas), **Supp. XIII:** 322–323

"WHEN WE'LL WORSHIP JESUS" (Baraka), **Supp. II Part 1:** 54

"When We Sold the Tent" (Espaillat), **Supp. XXI:** 102

"When we speak of God, is it God we speak of?" (J. Logan), **Supp. XVII:** 113

"When Women Throw Down Bundles: Strong Women Make Strong Nations" (Gunn Allen), **Supp. IV Part 1:** 328

"When You Come into Your Kingdom" (Muñoz), **Supp. XXV:** 136

"'When You Finally See Them': The Unconquered Eye in *To Kill a Mockingbird*" (Champion), **Supp. VIII:** 128

"When You Lie Down, the Sea Stands Up" (Swenson), **Supp. IV Part 2:** 643

"Where Blue Is Blue" (Richard), **Supp. XIX:** 221

Where Does One Go When There's No Place Left to Go? (Crews), **Supp. XI:** 103

"Where Go the Boats" (R. Stevenson), **Supp. XVII:** 69

Where Horizons Go (Espaillat), **Supp. XXI:** 99, 103, 104

"Where I Come from Is Like This" (Gunn Allen), **Supp. IV Part 1:** 319

"Where I'm Calling From" (Carver), **Supp. III Part 1:** 145

Where I'm Calling From: New and Selected Stories (Carver), **Supp. III Part 1:** 138, 148; **Supp. XXIV:** 178

"Where I Ought to Be" (Erdrich), **Supp. IV Part 1:** 265

Where Is My Wandering Boy Tonight? (Wagoner), **Supp. IX:** 335–336

"Where Is the Island?" (Francis), **Supp. IX:** 78

"Where Is the Voice Coming From?" (Welty), **IV:** 280; **Retro. Supp. I:** 355

Where Joy Resides (Isherwood), **Supp. XIV:** 156

"Where Knock Is Open Wide" (Roethke), **III:** 533–535

"Where My Sympathy Lies" (H. Roth), **Supp. IX:** 234

Where's Daddy? (Inge), **Supp. XXV:** 95, 105, 106

Where's My Money? (Shanley), **Supp. XIV:** 316, 328, **330–331**

Where the Bluebird Sings to the Lemonade Springs (Stegner), **Supp. IV Part 2:** 596, 597, 598, 600, 604, 606, 613; **Supp. XXII:** 205

"Where the Bones Move" (W. V. Davis), **Supp. XXI:** 92

Where the Cross Is Made (O'Neill), **III:** 388, 391

Where There's a Will (Rinehart), **Supp. XXV:** 193

Where the Rivers Flow North (Mosher), **Supp. XXII:** 205, 207, 208, **210–212**

"Where the Rivers Flow North" (Mosher), **Supp. XXII:** 204, 206, 207, 208, 209, **210–211**

Where the Sea Used to Be (Bass), **Supp. XVI:** 21

"Where the Sea Used to Be" (Bass), **Supp. XVI:** 20, 21

"*Where the Sea Used to Be:* Rick Bass and the Novel of Ecological Education" (Dixon), **Supp. XVI:** 21

"Where the Soft Air Lives" (Nye), **Supp. XIII:** 275

Where the Twilight Never Ends (Haines), **Supp. XII:** 211

Where the Wild Grape Grows: Selected Writings, 1930–1950 (D. West; Mitchell and Davis, eds.), **Supp. XVIII:** 283, 286

Where the Wild Things Are (Sendak), **Supp. IX:** 207

"Wherever Home Is" (Wright), **Supp. III Part 2:** 605, 606

"Wherever I Am Not" (Huddle), **Supp. XXVI:** 156–157

Where Water Comes Together With Other Water (Carver), **Supp. III Part 1:** 147, 148

"Where We Crashed" (Hugo), **Supp. VI:** 138

"Where We Must Look for Help" (R. Bly), **Supp. XXI:** 84

"Where You Are" (Doty), **Supp. XI:** 131

Where You'll Find Me, and Other Stories (Beattie), **Supp. V:** 30–31

Whicher, Stephen, **II:** 20

"Which Is More Than I Can Say for Some People" (Moore), **Supp. X:** 177, 178

Which Ones Are the Enemy? (Garrett), **Supp. VII:** 98

"Which Theatre Is the Absurd One?" (Albee), **I:** 71

"Which Way to the Future?" (Rehder), **Supp. IV Part 1:** 69

"While Hendrix Played a Solo: 'Burning of the Midnight Lamp' " (Gansworth),

Supp. XXVI: 112

While I Was Gone (Miller), **Supp. XII:** 290, **301–303**

"While Seated in a Plane" (Swenson), **Supp. IV Part 2:** 645

While the Messiah Tarries (Bukiet), **Supp. XVII:** 43, **46–47**

While We've Still Got Feet (Budbill), **Supp. XIX:** 5, 7, **10–11**, 15

Whilomville Stories (Crane), **I:** 414

"Whip, The" (Robinson), **III:** 513

Whipple, Thomas K., **II:** 456, 458; **IV:** 427

"Whippoorwill, The" (Francis), **Supp. IX:** 90

"Whip-poor-will, The" (Thurber), **Supp. I Part 2:** 616

Whirl Asunder, A (Atherton), **Supp. XXIV:** 22

Whirlpool (film, Preminger), **Supp. XVII:** 62

"Whisperer in Darkness, The" (Lovecraft), **Supp. XXV:** 114

"Whispering Gallery, The" (Komunyakaa), **Supp. XIII:** 132

"Whispering Leaves" (Glasgow), **II:** 190

Whispering to Fool the Wind (Ríos), **Supp. IV Part 2:** 540–541, 544, 545

"Whispers in the Next Room" (Simic), **Supp. VIII:** 278

"Whispers of Heavenly Death" (Whitman), **IV:** 348

"Whispers of Immortality" (Eliot), **Supp. XI:** 242

Whistle (Jones), **Supp. XI:** 219, 224, **231–234**

"Whistle, The" (Franklin), **II:** 121

"Whistle, The" (Komunyakaa), **Supp. XIII:** 111, 126

"Whistle, The" (Welty), **IV:** 262

Whistler, James, **I:** 484; **III:** 461, 465, 466; **IV:** 77, 369

Whistler, James Abbott McNeill, **Supp. XIV:** 335–336

"Whistling Dick's Christmas Stocking" (O. Henry), **Supp. II Part 1:** 390, 392

Whistling in the Dark (Garrett), **Supp. VII:** 111

Whistling in the Dark: True Stories and Other Fables (Garrett), **Supp. VII:** 95

Whitcher, Frances Miriam Berry, **Supp. XIII:** 152

"White" (Simic), **Supp. VIII: 275–276**

White, Barbara, **Retro. Supp. I:** 379

White, Dana, **Supp. XXII:** 251

White, E. B., **Retro. Supp. I:** 335; **Supp. I Part 2:** 602, 607, 608, 612, 619, 620, **651–681**; **Supp. II Part 1:** 143; **Supp. IX:** 20, 32; **Supp. VIII:** 171; **Supp. XVI:** 167

White, Elizabeth Wade, **Supp. I Part 1:** 100, 103, 111

White, Henry Kirke, **Supp. I Part 1:** 150

White, James L., **Supp. XI:** 123

White, Joel, **Supp. I Part 2:** 654, 678

White, Katharine. (Katharine Sergeant Angell), **Supp. I Part 2:** 610, 653, 655, 656, 669; **Supp. VIII:** 151, 171

White, Lillian, **Supp. I Part 2:** 651

White, Lucia, **I:** 258

White, Maria. *See* Lowell, Mrs. James Russell (Maria White)

White, Morton, **I:** 258; **Supp. I Part 2:** 647, 648, 650

White, Roberta, **Supp. XII:** 293

White, Stanford, **Supp. IV Part 1:** 223

White, Stanley, **Supp. I Part 2:** 651, 655

White, T. H., **III:** 522

White, T. W., **III:** 411, 415

White, Walter, **Supp. I Part 1:** 345; **Supp. XIX:** 73; **Supp. XVIII:** 123, 127

White, William, **Retro. Supp. II:** 326

White, William A., **I:** 252

White Album, The (Didion), **Supp. IV Part 1:** 198, 202, 205–207, 210

"White Album, The" (Didion), **Supp. IV Part 1:** 205, 206

"White Angel" (Cunningham), **Supp. XV:** 59

"White Apache" (Markson), **Supp. XVII:** 136

"White as Snow" (Boyle), **Supp. XXIV:** 58, 59

White Boys (McKnight), **Supp. XX: 155–157**

"White Boys, The" (McKnight), **Supp. XX: 155–157**

White Buildings (H. Crane), **I:** 385, 386, 390–395, 400; **Retro. Supp. II:** 77–78, **80–81,** 82, 83, 85

White Butterfly (Mosley), **Supp. XIII:** 237, 238, 240

White Center (Hugo), **Supp. VI:** 144–145

"White Center" (Hugo), **Supp. VI:** 144, 146

Whited, Stephen, **Supp. XI:** 135

White Deer, The (Thurber), **Supp. I Part 2:** 606

White Doves at Morning (Burke), **Supp. XIV:** 22–23, 32, 35–36

"White Eagle, The" (Chopin), **Retro. Supp. II:** 72

White Fang (London), **II:** 471–472, 481

Whitefield, George, **I:** 546; **Supp. XX: 280**

White-Footed Deer and Other Poems (Bryant), **Supp. I Part 1:** 157

White Goddess, The (Graves), **Supp. IV Part 1:** 280

White-Haired Lover (Shapiro), **Supp. II Part 2:** 703, 717

Whitehead, Alfred North, **III:** 605, 619, 620; **IV:** 88; **Supp. I Part 2:** 554, 647

Whitehead, Mrs. Catherine, **IV:** 116

Whitehead, Colson, **Supp. XIII:** 233, 241

Whitehead, James, **Supp. XV:** 339

Whitehead, Margaret, **IV:** 114, 115, 116

Whitehead, William, **Supp. XX: 50–51, 53**

White Heat (Walsh), **Supp. XIII:** 174

"White Heron, A" (Jewett), **II:** 409; **Retro. Supp. II:** 17

White Heron and Other Stories, A (Jewett), **II:** 396

White Horses (Hoffman), **Supp. X: 83–85,** 90, 92

"White Horses of Vienna, The" (Boyle), **Supp. XXIV: 59–60**

White Horses of Vienna, The, and Other Stories (Boyle), **Supp. XXIV:** 57, **58–59**

White House Diary, A (Lady Bird Johnson), **Supp. IV Part 1:** 22

White-Jacket; or, The World in a Man-of-War (Melville), **III:** 80, 81, 84, 94; **Retro Supp. I:** 248, 249, 254; **Supp. XVIII:** 7, 9

White Lantern, The (Connell), **Supp. XIV:** 97

"White Lies" (Trethewey), **Supp. XXI:** 244, 246, 251

"White Lights, The" (Robinson), **III:** 524

"White Lilies, The" (Glück), **Supp. V:** 88

White Man, Listen! (Wright), **IV:** 478, 488, 489, 494

White Morning, The (Atherton), **Supp. XXIV:** 24, 29

"White Mulberry Tree, The" (Cather), **I:** 319; **Retro. Supp. I:** 7, 9, 17

White Mule (W. C. Williams), **Retro. Supp. I:** 423

"White Negro, The" (Mailer), **III:** 36–37; **Retro. Supp. II:** 202

"Whiteness of the Whale, The" (Melville), **III:** 84, 86

"White Night" (Oliver), **Supp. VII:** 236

"White Nights" (Auster), **Supp. XII:** 23–24

White Noise (DeLillo), **Supp. VI:** 1, 3–4, 5–7, 10, 11–12, 16; **Supp. XVIII:** 140; **Supp. XX: 91**

White Oxen and Other Stories, The (Burke), **I:** 269, 271

White Paper on Contemporary American Poetry (McClatchy), **Supp. XII:** 253, **259–260**

"White Phosphorous" (Notley), **Supp. XXII:** 232, 233

"White Pine" (Oliver), **Supp. VII:** 244

White Pine: Poems and Prose Poems (Oliver), **Supp. VII:** 243–246

White Poems, The (Crooker), **Supp. XXIII: 54–55**

White Rat (G. Jones), **Supp. XXIV:** 185

White Roots of Peace (Wallace), **Supp. XXVI:** 90, 96–97

White Sail (Sorrentino), **Supp. XXI:** 228

"White Ship, The" (Lovecraft), **Supp. XXV:** 113

"White Silence, The" (London), **II:** 468

"White Silk" (Nye), **Supp. XIII:** 275

"White Snake, The" (Sexton), **Supp. II Part 2:** 691

"White Spot" (Anderson), **I:** 116

"White-Tailed Hornet, The" (Frost), **Retro. Supp. I:** 138

"White Trash Cowboys of *Father and Son,* The" (Bjerre), **Supp. XXI:** 41

"White Trees, Hammer Moon" (Dubus III), **Supp. XXIV:** 101, 104

Whitfield, Raoul, **Supp. IV Part 1:** 345

Whitfield, Stephen J., **Supp. XX: 243, 244**

Whitlock, Brand, **II:** 276

Whitman (Masters), **Supp. I Part 2:** 473, 475, 476

Whitman, George, **IV:** 346, 350

Whitman, Ruth, **Supp. XXI:** 246

Whitman, Sarah Wyman, **Retro. Supp. II:** 136

Whitman, Walt, **I:** 61, 68, 98, 103, 104, 109, 219, 220, 227, 228, 242, 246, 250, 251, 260, 261, 285, 381, 384, 386, 396, 397, 398, 402, 419, 430, 459, 460, 483, 485, 486, 577; **II:** 7, 8, 18, 127, 140, 273–274, 275, 289, 295, 301, 320, 321, 373, 445, 446, 451, 457, 494, 529, 530, 552; **III:** 171, 175, 177, 181–182, 189, 203, 234, 260, 426, 430, 453, 454, 461, 505, 507–508, 511, 528, 548, 552, 555, 559, 567, 572, 576, 577, 579, 584, 585, 595, 606, 609; **IV:** 74, 169, 191, 192, 202, **331–354,** 405, 409, 416, 444, 450–451, 457, 463, 464, 469, 470, 471; **Retro. Supp. I:** 8, 52, 194, 254, 283, 284, 333, **387–410,** 412, 417, 427; **Retro. Supp. II:** 40, 76, 93, 99, 155, 156, 158, 170, 262; **Supp. I Part 1:** 6, 79, 167, 311, 314, 325, 365, 368, 372; **Supp. I Part 2:** 374, 384, 385, 387, 389, 391, 393, 399, 416, 436, 455, 456, 458, 473, 474, 475, 525, 540, 579, 580, 582, 682, 691; **Supp. III Part 1:** 6, 20, 156, 239–241, 253, 340; **Supp. III Part 2:** 596; **Supp. IV Part 1:** 16, 169, 325; **Supp. IV Part 2:** 597, 625; **Supp. IX:** 8, 9, 15, 38, 41, 44, 48, 53, 131, 292, 298, 299, 308, 320; **Supp. V:** 113, 118, 122, 130, 170, 178, 183, 277, 279, 332; **Supp. VIII:** 42, 95, 105, 126, 198, 202, 269; **Supp. X:** 36, 112, 203, 204; **Supp. XI:** 83, 123, 132, 135, 203, 321; **Supp. XII:** 132, 185, 190, 256; **Supp. XIII:** 1, 77, 115, 153, 221, 304, 335; **Supp. XIV:** 89, 312, 334, 335, 338; **Supp. XIX:** 118, 276; **Supp. XV:** 41, 93, 181, 183, 212, 213, 218, 250, 275, 301, 302, 303, 309, 352; **Supp. XVI:** 209; **Supp. XVII:** 42, 71, 112, 133; **Supp. XVIII:** 4, 194, 196, 304; **Supp. XX: 69, 115, 116, 221; Supp. XXI:** 169, 217, 227, 256; **Supp. XXII:** 81, 82, 86, 92; **Supp. XXIII:** 19, 109, 166, 207; **Supp. XXVI:** 227, 230, 233, 234

"Whitman Pinch Hits, 1861" (Skloot), **Supp. XX: 203**

"Whitman: The Poet and the Mask" (Cowley), **Supp. II Part 1:** 143

Whitmarsh, Jason, **Supp. VIII:** 283

Whitmer, Peter, **Supp. X:** 264, 265

Whitney, Blair, **Supp. I Part 2:** 403

Whitney, Josiah, **Supp. IX:** 180, 181

Whitt, Margaret Earley, **Retro. Supp. II:** 226

Whittemore, Reed, **III:** 268; **Supp. XI:** 315

Whittier, Elizabeth, **Supp. I Part 2:** 700, 701, 703; **Supp. XIII:** 141, 142

Whittier, John Greenleaf, **I:** 216; **II:** 275; **III:** 52; **Retro. Supp. I:** 54; **Retro. Supp. II:** 155, 163, 169; **Supp. I Part 1:** 168, 299, 313, 317, 372; **Supp. I Part 2:** 420, 602, **682–707; Supp. VIII:** 202, 204; **Supp. XI:** 50; **Supp. XIII:** 140, 145; **Supp. XV:** 246; **Supp.**

XXIII: 156

Whittier, Mary, **Supp. I Part 2:** 683

"Whittier Birthday Speech" (Twain), **Supp. I Part 1:** 313

"Who" (Kenyon), **Supp. VII:** 174

"Who" (Sobin), **Supp. XVI:** 284–285

"Who Am I—Who I Am" (Corso), **Supp. XII:** 134

"Who Be Kind To" (Ginsberg), **Supp. II Part 1:** 323

Who Do You Love (Thompson), **Supp. XXIII:** 289, **295–296**

"Whoever Was Using This Bed" (Carver), **Supp. III Part 1:** 148

"Whoever You Are Holding Me Now in Hand" (Whitman), **IV:** 342; **Retro. Supp. I:** 52

Who Gathered and Whispered behind Me (Goldbarth), **Supp. XII:** 181, 182

"Who in One Lifetime" (Rukeyser), **Supp. VI:** 276, 279

Who Is Witter Bynner? (Kraft), **Supp. XV:** 40, 52

"Who Is Your Mother? Red Roots of White Feminism" (Gunn Allen), **Supp. IV Part 1:** 329

Whole Hog (Wagoner), **Supp. IX:** 337–338

"Whole Mess…Almost, The" (Corso), **Supp. XII:** 135

"Whole Moisty Night, The" (R. Bly), **Supp. IV Part 1:** 69

Whole New Life, A (Price), **Supp. VI:** 265, **266,** 267

"Whole Self, The" (Nye), **Supp. XIII:** 275

"Whole Soul, The" (Levine), **Supp. V:** 192

"Whole Story, The" (Strand), **Supp. IV Part 2:** 622

Whole Town's Talking, The (Loos), **Supp. XVI:** 187

"Whole World Knows, The" (Welty), **IV:** 272; **Retro. Supp. I:** 343

Who'll Stop the Rain (film), **Supp. V:** 301

Who Lost an American? (Algren), **Supp. IX:** **15–16**

Who Owns America? (symposium), **Supp. XIV:** 4

Who Owns the West? (Kittredge), **Supp. XXVI:** 185

"Who Puts Together" (Hogan), **Supp. IV Part 1:** 403, 405, 412–413

"Whore of Mensa, The" (Allen), **Supp. XV:** 15

Whores for Gloria (Vollmann), **Supp. XVII:** 226, 230

Whorf, Benjamin Lee, **Supp. XVI:** 283

Who's Afraid? (Holding), **Supp. XXII:** 120, **125–126**

Who's Afraid of Virginia Woolf? (Albee), **I:** 71, 77–81, 83, 85, 86, 87, 94; **IV:** 230

Who Shall Be the Sun? Poems Based on the Lore, Legends, and Myths of the Northwest Coast and Plateau Indians (Wagoner), **Supp. IX:** 328, **329–330,** 337

"Whosis Kid, The" (Hammett), **Supp. IV Part 1:** 344

"Who Sit Watch in Daylight" (Wright), **Supp. XV:** 342

"Who's Passing for Who?" (Hughes), **Supp. I Part 1:** 330

"Who Speak on the Page?" (Sanders), **Supp. XVI:** 278

Who We Are: On Being (and Not Being) a Jewish American Writer (Rubin, ed.), **Supp. XXIV:** 3

Who Will Run the Frog Hospital?: A Novel (Moore), **Supp. X:** 163, 165, 169, **175–177**

Who Wrote the Book of Love? (Siegel), **Supp. XXII: 265–267,** 267

Why Are We in Vietnam? (Mailer), **III:** 27, 29, 30, 33, 34–35, 39, 42, 44; **Retro. Supp. II:** 205–206

"Why Bother?" (Franzen). *See* "Perchance to Dream" (Franzen)

"Why China?" (Egan), **Supp. XIX:** 51, 52

"Why Did the Balinese Chicken Cross the Road?" (Walker), **Supp. III Part 2:** 527

"Why Do the Heathens Rage?" (O'Connor), **III:** 351

"Why Do They Prate?" (H. Johnson), **Supp. XXVI:** 174

"Why Do You Write About Russia?" (Simpson), **Supp. IX:** 277

"Why Have We Not More Great Novelists?" (Atherton), **Supp. XXIV:** 24

"Why I Am a Danger to the Public" (Kingsolver), **Supp. VII:** 204

"Why I Am a Pagan" (Zitkala-Ša), **Supp. XXV:** 276–277

Why I Am Not a Christian (Russell), **Supp. I Part 2:** 522

"Why I Am Not a Painter"(O'Hara), **Supp. XXIII:** 208

Why I Came to Judevine (Budbill), **Supp. XIX:** 2, **7–8,** 15

"Why I Do Not Wish to Float in Space"(Schott), **Supp. XXIII:** 251

"Why I Entered the Gurdjieff Work" (Toomer), **Supp. III Part 2:** 481

"Why I Like Laurel" (Patchett), **Supp. XII:** 309

"Why I Live at the P.O." (Welty), **IV:** 262; **Retro. Supp. I:** 345

"Why I Make Sam Go to Church" (Lamott), **Supp. XX: 141**

"Why Is American Literature Bourgeois?" (Atherton), **Supp. XXIV:** 24, 28

"Why Is Economics Not an Evolutionary Science?" (Veblen), **Supp. I Part 2:** 634

"Why I Write" (Didion), **Supp. IV Part 1:** 201, 203

"Why I Wrote *Phil:* An Exclusive Essay for Amazon.com" (Saunders), **Supp. XIX:** 230–231

Why Johnny Can't Read: And What You Can Do About It (Flesch), **Supp. XVI:** 105

"Why Negro Women Leave Home" (Brooks), **Supp. III Part 1:** 75

Why Poetry Matters (Parini), **Supp. XIX:** 120, 129

"Why Resign from the Human Race?" (Swados), **Supp. XIX:** 265

"Why the Little Frenchman Wears His Hand in a Sling" (Poe), **III:** 425

Why Torture Is Wrong, and the People Who Love Them (Durang), **Supp. XXIV: 126–127**

"Why We Are Forgiven" (Weigl), **Supp. XIX:** 282–283

Why We Behave Like Microbe Hunters (Thurber), **Supp. I Part 2:** 606

Why We Were in Vietnam (Podhoretz), **Supp. VIII:** 241

"Why Write?" (Updike), **Retro. Supp. I:** 317

"Wichita Vortex Sutra" (Ginsberg), **Supp. II Part 1:** 319, 321, 323–325, 327

Wickenden, Dorothy, **Supp. XXIII:** 291

Wickes, George, **Supp. XIV:** 165

Wickford Point (Marquand), **III:** 50, 58, 64–65, 69

Wicks, Robert Russell, **Supp. XII:** 49

Wide, Wide World, The (S. Warner as Wetherell), **Supp. XV:** 275; **Supp. XVIII:** 257, 260, **262–264,** 265

Wide Blue Yonder (Thompson), **Supp. XXIII:** 289, **296–298**

"Wide Empty Landscape with a Death in the Foreground" (Momaday), **Supp. IV Part 2:** 492

Wideman, Edgar, **Supp. XXV:** 146, 147

Wideman, John Edgar, **Retro. Supp. II:** 123; **Supp. X:** 239, 250, **319–336;** **Supp. XI:** 245; **Supp. XIII:** 247; **Supp. XVIII:** 89; **Supp. XXI:** 246; **Supp. XXIV:** 183

Widener, Jeff, **Supp. XVIII:** 91

"Wideness" (Pickering), **Supp. XXI:** 203

"Wide Net, The" (Welty), **IV:** 266

Wide Net and Other Stories, The (Welty), **IV:** 261, 264–266, 271; **Retro. Supp. I: 347–349,** 352, 355

Widening Spell of the Leaves, The (Levis), **Supp. XI:** 258, 259, 261, **268–269,** 271

"Wide Prospect, The" (Jarrell), **II:** 376–377

Wide Sargasso Sea (Rhys), **Supp. XVIII:** 131

"Widespread Enigma Concerning Blue-Star Woman" (Zitkala-Ša), **Supp. XXV:** 282–283

"Widow" (Peacock), **Supp. XIX:** 206

"Widower" (Robison), **Supp. XXI:** 118

Widow for One Year, A (Irving), **Supp. VI:** 165, **179–181**

Widow's Mite (Holding), **Supp. XXII: 136**

Widows of Thornton, The (Taylor), **Supp. V:** 320, 321

Widow's Story, A (Oates), **Supp. XXV:** 60

"Widow's Wish, The" (Briggs), **Supp. XVIII:** 15

Wieland; or, The Transformation. An American Tale (Brown), **Supp. I Part 1:** 128–132, 133, 137, 140

Wiene, Robert, **Retro. Supp. I:** 268

Wiener, John, **Supp. IV Part 1:** 153

Wieners, John, **Supp. II Part 1:** 32; **Supp. XXIII:** 215

Wiesel, Elie, **Supp. XVII:** 47, 48, 49

Wiest, Dianne, **Supp. XV:** 12

"Wife, Forty-five, Remembers Love, A" (Shields), **Supp. VII:** 310

"Wifebeater, The" (Sexton), **Supp. II Part 2:** 693

"Wife for Dino Rossi, A" (Fante), **Supp. XI:** 165

"Wife of His Youth, The" (Chesnutt), **Supp. XIV: 63–66**

Wife of His Youth and Other Stories of the Color Line, The (Chesnutt), **Supp. XIV:** 62, 63

"Wife of Jesus Speaks, The" (Karr), **Supp. XI:** 250–251

"Wife of Nashville, A" (Taylor), **Supp. V:** 320

"Wife's Story, The" (R. H. Davis), **Supp. XVI:** 85, 91, 92–93

Wife's Story, The (Shields), **Supp. VII:** 316. *See also* Happenstance

"Wife-Wooing" (Updike), **IV:** 226

Wigan, Gareth, **Supp. XI:** 306

Wiget, Andrew, **Supp. IV Part 2:** 509

Wigglesworth, Michael, **IV:** 147, 156; **Supp. I Part 1:** 110, 111

Wilbur, Richard, **III:** 527; **Retro. Supp. II:** 50; **Supp. III Part 1:** 64; **Supp. III Part 2: 541–565; Supp. IV Part 2:** 626, 634, 642; **Supp. V:** 337; **Supp. VIII:** 28; **Supp. X:** 58, 120; **Supp. XII:** 258; **Supp. XIII:** 76, 336; **Supp. XV:** 51, 251, 256; **Supp. XVII:** 26; **Supp. XVIII:** 178; **Supp. XX: 199; Supp. XXI:** 247; **Supp. XXIV:** 36, 45; **Supp. XXVI:** 64, 68

Wilcocks, Alexander, **Supp. I Part 1:** 125

Wilcox, Ella Wheeler, **Supp. II Part 1:** 197

Wilcox, Kirstin, **Supp. XX: 283, 284, 285**

Wild, John, **II:** 362, 363–364

Wild, Peter, **Supp. V:** 5

Wild, Robert, **IV:** 155

"Wild, The" (Berry), **Supp. X:** 30

Wild 90 (film) (Mailer), **Retro. Supp. II:** 205

Wild and Woolly (film), **Supp. XVI:** 185

Wild Boy of Aveyron, The (Itard). *See* De l'éducation d'un homme sauvage

Wild Boys, The: A Book of the Dead (Burroughs), **Supp. III Part 1:** 106–107

Wild Card Quilt: Taking A chance on Home (Ray), **Supp. XVIII:** 189, 192, 193, 196, 198, **200–202,** 204

Wilde, Oscar, **I:** 50, 66, 381, 384; **II:** 515; **IV:** 77, 350; **Retro. Supp. I:** 56, 102, 227; **Retro. Supp. II:** 76, 326; **Supp. IV Part 2:** 578, 679, 683; **Supp. IX:** 65, 66, 68, 189, 192; **Supp. V:** 106, 283; **Supp. X:** 148, 151, 188–189; **Supp. XIV:** 324, 334; **Supp. XV:** 350; **Supp. XXIV:** 263

Wilder, Amos Parker, **IV:** 356

Wilder, Mrs. Amos Parker (Isabella Thornton Niven), **IV:** 356

Wilder, Billy, **Supp. IV Part 1:** 130; **Supp. XI:** 307

Wilder, Isabel, **IV:** 357, 366, 375

Wilder, Laura Ingalls, **Supp. XXI:** 2; **Supp. XXII: 289–303; Supp. XXVI:** 217

Wilder, Thornton, **I:** 360, 482; **IV: 355–377,** 431; **Retro. Supp. I:** 109, 359; **Supp. I Part 2:** 609; **Supp. IV Part 2:** 586; **Supp. IX:** 140; **Supp. V:** 105; **Supp. XII:** 236–237; **Supp. XX: 50**

"Wilderness" (Leopold), **Supp. XIV:** 190

Wilderness (Parker), **Supp. XIX:** 177, **188–189**

"Wilderness" (Sandburg), **III:** 584, 595

Wilderness (Warren), **IV:** 256

"Wilderness, The" (Merwin), **Supp. III Part 1:** 340, 345

"Wilderness, The" (Robinson), **III:** 524

Wilderness of Vision, The: On the Poetry of John Haines (Bezner and Walzer, eds.), **Supp. XII:** 202

Wilderness Plots: Tales about the Settlement of the American Land (Sanders), **Supp. XVI:** 267–268, 269

"Wilderness"(Thompson), **Supp. XXIII:** 301

Wilderness World of Anne LaBastille, The (LaBastille), **Supp. X: 105,** 106

Wild Flag, The (White), **Supp. I Part 2:** 654

"Wildflower, The" (W. C. Williams), **Retro. Supp. I:** 420

"Wild Flowers" (Caldwell), **I:** 310

"Wildflowers" (Minot), **Supp. VI:** 208

"Wild Geese" (Oliver), **Supp. VII:** 237

"Wild Honey Suckle, The" (Freneau), **Supp. II Part 1:** 253, 264, 266

Wild in the Country (Odets), **Supp. II Part 2:** 546

"Wild in the Woods" (Skloot), **Supp. XX: 206**

Wild Iris, The (Glück), **Supp. V:** 79, 87–89, 91

Wildlife (Ford), **Supp. V:** 57, 69–71

Wildlife in America (Matthiessen), **Supp. V:** 199, 201, 204

"Wildlife in American Culture" (Leopold), **Supp. XIV:** 190, 191

"Wild Light" (Skloot), **Supp. XX: 200**

Wild Man, The (P. N. Warren), **Supp. XX: 260, 270–272**

"Wildness" (Sanders), **Supp. XVI:** 276

Wild Old Wicked Man, The (MacLeish), **III:** 3, 20

Wild Palms, The (Faulkner), **II:** 68–69; **Retro. Supp. I:** 85

"Wild Palms, The" (Faulkner), **II:** 68

"Wild Peaches" (Wylie), **Supp. I Part 2:** 707, 712

Wild Roses of Cape Ann and Other Poems (Larcom), **Supp. XIII:** 142, 147

Wild Seed (O. Butler), **Supp. XIII:** 62, 63

"Wild Swans at Coole, The " (W. B. Yeats), **Supp. XVI:** 48

"Wild Swans at Norfolk, The" (Carruth), **Supp. XVI:** 48

"Wild Thing" (L. Brown), **Supp. XXI:** 44

Wild Thorn (Hoffman), **Supp. XVIII: 84–85**

Wild to the Heart (Bass), **Supp. XVI:** 16

"Wild Turkeys: Dignity of the Damned" (B. Kelly), **Supp. XVII:** 129

"Wildwest" (MacLeish), **III:** 14

Wiley, Catherine, **Supp. XXIII:** 199

Wiley, Craig, **Supp. VIII:** 313

Wilhelm Meister (Goethe), **II:** 291

Wilkes, John, **Supp. I Part 2:** 503, 519, 522

Wilkie, Curtis, **Supp. V:** 11

Wilkins, Roy, **Supp. I Part 1:** 345

Wilkinson, Alec, **Supp. VIII:** 164, 168, 171

Wilkinson, Max, **Supp. IX:** 251

Will, The (Swados), **Supp. XIX: 265–266**

Willard, Nancy, **Supp. XIX:** 138

Willard, Samuel, **IV:** 150

Willard Gibbs (Rukeyser), **Supp. VI:** 273, 283, 284

Willcutts, Tim, **Supp. XVII:** 239, 241, 246

Willett, Ralph, **Supp. XIV:** 27

Willey, Basil, **Retro. Supp. II:** 243

"William Butler Yeats Among the Ghosts" (Skloot), **Supp. XX: 204–205**

William Carlos Williams (Koch), **Retro. Supp. I:** 428

William Carlos Williams: An American Artist (Breslin), **Retro. Supp. I:** 430

William Carlos Williams and Alterity (Ahearn), **Retro. Supp. I:** 415

William Carlos Williams and the Meanings of Measure (Cushman), **Retro. Supp. I:** 430

William Carlos Williams: The American Background (Weaver), **Retro. Supp. I:** 430

William Ellery Channing: An Intellectual Portrait (Edgell), **Supp. XXIV:** 71

William Ellery Channing: Selected Writings (Robinson, ed.), **Supp. XXIV:** 71

William Faulkner: A Critical Study (Howe), **Supp. VI:** 119–120, 125

William Faulkner: Early Prose and Poetry (Faulkner), **Retro. Supp. I:** 80

William Faulkner: First Encounters (Brooks), **Supp. XIV:** 13

"William Faulkner's Legend of the South" (Cowley), **Supp. II Part 1:** 143

"William Faulkner: The Stillness of *Light in August*" (Kazin), **Supp. VIII:** 104

William Faulkner: The Yoknapatawpha Country (Brooks), **Supp. XIV: 12–13,** 16

William Faulkner: Toward Yoknapatawpha and Beyond (Brooks), **Supp. XIV:** 13

"William Humphrey, 73, Writer of Novels about Rural Texas" (Gussow), **Supp. IX:** 93

William Humphrey, Destroyer of Myths (Almon), **Supp. IX:** 93

William Humphrey. Boise State University Western Writers Series (Winchell), **Supp. IX:** 109

"William Humphrey Remembered" (Masters), **Supp. IX:** 96

William Humphrey. Southwestern Series (Lee), **Supp. IX:** 109

William Inge and the Subversion of Gender (J. Johnson), **Supp. XXV:** 98

"William Ireland's Confession" (A. Miller), **III:** 147–148

William James and Phenomenology: A Study of the "Principles of Psychology" (Wilshire), **II:** 362

William Lloyd Garrison (Chapman), **Supp. XIV:** 46–51, 52, 53, 55

William Maxwell Portrait, A: Memories and Appreciations (C. Baxter, Collier, and Hirsch, eds.), **Supp. XVII:** 23

Williams, Annie Laurie, **Supp. IX:** 93

Williams, Blanch Colton, **Supp. XVIII:** 279

Williams, Cecil, **II:** 508

Williams, Charles, **Supp. II Part 1:** 15, 16

Williams, C. K., **Supp. XIII:** 114; **Supp. XVII:** 112

Williams, Cratis, **Supp. XX:** 163

Williams, Dakin, **IV:** 379

Williams, David Reichard, **Supp. XIII:** 162

Williams, Edward, **IV:** 404

Williams, Edwina Dakin, **IV:** 379

Williams, Eric, **Supp. XXI:** 166, 170, 171

Williams, Esther, **Supp. XII:** 165

Williams, Fannie Barrier, **Supp. XIV:** 201

Williams, Garth, **Supp. XXII:** 301

Williams, George, **Supp. V:** 220

Williams, Henry Sylvester, **Supp. XXI:** 166

Williams, Horace, **IV:** 453

Williams, Joan, **Supp. IX:** 95

Williams, John A., **Supp. XVI:** 143

Williams, John Alexander, **Supp. XXIII:** 39

Williams, John Sharp, **IV:** 378

Williams, Jonathan, **Supp. XXII:** 168

Williams, Kenny J., **Supp. XX:** 281, 286

Williams, Lyle, **Supp. XIV:** 22

Williams, Michael, **Supp. V:** 286

Williams, Miller, **Supp. XIV:** 126; **Supp. XV:** 339; **Supp. XVIII:** 177

Williams, Paul, **IV:** 404

Williams, Raymond, **Supp. IX:** 146

Williams, Roger, **Supp. I Part 2:** 699; **Supp. XXIII:** 15

Williams, Rose, **IV:** 379

Williams, Sherley Anne, **Supp. V:** 180

Williams, Solomon, **I:** 549

Williams, Stanley T., **II:** 301, 316; **Supp. I Part 1:** 251

Williams, Stephen, **IV:** 148

Williams, Ted, **IV:** 216; **Supp. IX:** 162

Williams, Ted. C., **Supp. XXVI:** 102

Williams, Tennessee, **I:** 73, 81, 113, 211; **II:** 190, 194; **III:** 145, 147; **IV:** 4, 378–401; **Supp. I Part 1:** 290, 291; **Supp. IV Part 1:** 79, 83, 84, 359; **Supp. IV Part 2:** 574, 682; **Supp. IX:** 133; **Supp. XI:** 103; **Supp. XIII:** 331; **Supp. XIV:** 250, 315; **Supp. XVI:** 194; **Supp. XXIV:** 113; **Supp. XXV:** 94, 96, 97

Williams, Terry Tempest, **Supp. XIII:** 16; **Supp. XVIII:** 189

Williams, Walter L., **Supp. IV Part 1:** 330, 331

Williams, William, **IV:** 404, 405

Williams, William Carlos, **I:** 61, 62, 229, 255, 256, 261, 285, 428, 438, 446, 539; **II:** 133, 536, 542, 543, 544, 545; **III:** 194, 196, 198, 214, 269, 409, 453, 457, 458, 464, 465, 591; **IV:** 30, 74, 75, 76, 94, 95, 286, 287, 402–425; **Retro. Supp. I:** 51, 52, 62, 209, 284, 285, 288, 296, 298, 411–433; **Retro. Supp. II:** 178, 181, 189, 250, 321, 322, 326, 327, 328, 334, 335; **Supp. I Part 1:** 254, 255, 259, 266; **Supp. II Part 1:** 9, 30, 308, 318; **Supp. II Part 2:** 421, 443; **Supp. III Part 1:** 9, 147, 239, 271, 275, 276, 278, 350; **Supp. III Part 2:** 542, 610, 613, 614, 615, 616, 617, 621, 622, 626, 628; **Supp. IV Part 1:** 151, 153, 246, 325; **Supp. IX:** 38, 268, 291; **Supp. V:** 180, 337; **Supp. VIII:** 195, 269, 272, 277, 292; **Supp. X:** 112, 120, 204; **Supp. XI:** 311, 328; **Supp. XII:** 198; **Supp. XIII:** 77, 90, 335; **Supp. XIV:** 280, 284, 285, 293; **Supp. XIX:** 1, 42, 117, 119, 121; **Supp. XV:** 42, 51, 182, 250, 306, 307; **Supp. XVI:** 48, 282; **Supp. XVII:** 36, 113, 227, 243; **Supp. XXI:** 226, 227, 230, 233; **Supp. XXII:** 162, 165, 168, 226, 227, 228; **Supp. XXIII:** 164, 207, 211; **Supp. XXIV:** 39, 41, 52, 63; **Supp. XXV:** 19; **Supp. XXVI:** 78, 143, 224, 226

Williams, Mrs. William Carlos (Florence Herman), **IV:** 404

Williams, Wirt, **Supp. XIV:** 24

Williamson, Alan, **Retro. Supp. II:** 185; **Supp. XIX:** 91

Williamson, J. W., **Supp. XX:** 164

William Styron's Nat Turner: Ten Black Writers Respond (Clarke, ed.), **IV:** 115

Williams-Walsh, Mary Ellen, **Supp. IV Part 2:** 611

William the Conqueror, **Supp. I Part 2:** 507

William Wetmore Story and His Friends (James), **Retro. Supp. I:** 235; **Supp. XX:** 228

William Wilson (Gardner), **Supp. VI:** 72

"William Wilson" (Poe), **II:** 475; **III:** 410, 412; **Retro. Supp. II:** 269; **Supp. IX:** 105

"Willie" (Angelou), **Supp. IV Part 1:** 15

Willie Masters' Lonesome Wife (Gass), **Supp. VI:** 77, 84–85, 86–87

"Willing" (Moore), **Supp. X:** 178

Willingly (Gallagher), **Supp. XXIV:** 166, 168, 169, 170, 176

Willis, Bruce, **Supp. IV Part 1:** 236

Willis, Dail, **Supp. XXIII:** 298

Willis, Gordon, **Supp. XV:** 7

Willis, Mary Hard, **Supp. V:** 290–291

Willis, Meredith, **Supp. XXVI:** 153

Willis, Nathaniel Parker, **II:** 313; **Supp. I Part 2:** 405; **Supp. XVIII:** 12

Williwaw (Vidal), **Supp. IV Part 2:** 677, 680, 681

Willow Field, The (Kittredge), **Supp. XXVI:** 184

"Willow Woman" (Francis), **Supp. IX:** 78

Wills, Garry, **Supp. I Part 1:** 294; **Supp. IV Part 1:** 355

Wills, Ridley, **IV:** 122

Wills, Ross B., **Supp. XI:** 169

"Will to Believe, The" (James), **II:** 352; **Supp. XIV:** 50

Will to Believe, The, and Other Essays in Popular Philosophy (James), **II:** 356; **IV:** 28

Will to Change, The: Poems, 1968–1970 (Rich), **Supp. I Part 2:** 551, 557–559

Will to Live On, The: This Is Our Heritage (Wouk), **Supp. XXV:** 257, 266

"Will We Plug Chips into Our Brains?" (W. Gibson), **Supp. XVI:** 117–118

Will You Please Be Quiet, Please? (Carver), **Supp. III Part 1:** 138, 140, 144

"Will You Please Be Quiet, Please?" (Carver), **Supp. III Part 1:** 137, 141

"Will You Tell Me?" (Barthelme), **Supp. IV Part 1:** 42, 47

Wilsdorf, Anne, **Supp. XVI:** 177

Wilsey, Sean, **Supp. XXV:** 1, 8

Wilshire, Bruce, **II:** 362, 364

Wilshire, Gaylord, **Supp. V:** 280

Wilson, Adrian, **Supp. XV:** 147

Wilson, Alexander, **Supp. XVI:** 4, 6

Wilson, Angus, **IV:** 430, 435

Wilson, August, **Supp. VIII:** 329–353; **Supp. XIX:** 132

Wilson, Augusta Jane Evans, **Retro. Supp. I:** 351

Wilson, Earl, **Supp. X:** 264

Wilson, Edmund, **I:** 67, 185, 236, 247, 260, 434, 482; **II:** 79, 80, 81, 86, 87, 91, 97, 98, 146, 276, 430, 530, 562, 587; **III:** 588; **IV:** 308, 310, 426–449; **Retro. Supp. I:** 1, 97, 100, 101, 103, 104, 105, 115, 274; **Retro. Supp. II:** 321, 327, 329; **Supp. I Part 1:** 372; **Supp. I Part 2:** 407, 646, 678, 709; **Supp. II Part 1:** 19, 90, 106, 136, 137, 143; **Supp. III Part 2:** 612; **Supp. IV Part 2:** 693; **Supp. IX:** 55, 65, 190; **Supp. VIII:** 93, 95, 96, 97, 98–99, 100, 101, 103, 105, 162; **Supp. X:** 186; **Supp. XI:** 160; **Supp. XIII:** 170; **Supp. XIV:** 338; **Supp. XV:** 142, 308; **Supp. XVI:** 194; **Supp. XX:** 76, 81; **Supp. XXII:** 278; **Supp. XXIII:** 104–105, 106; **Supp. XXIV:** 62, 217, 222, 281

Wilson, Edmund (father), **IV:** 441

Wilson, E. O., **Supp. X:** 35

Wilson, Harriet, **Supp. XX:** 105

Wilson, Henry, **Supp. XV:** 48

Wilson, Reuel, **II:** 562

Wilson, Robert, **Supp. XI:** 144

Wilson, Robley, **Supp. XXIII:** 290

Wilson, Sloan, **Supp. IV Part 1:** 387

Wilson, Thomas, **IV:** 153

Wilson, Tracy, **Supp. XVIII:** 101

Wilson, Victoria, **Supp. X:** 166

Wilson, Woodrow, **I:** 245, 246, 490; **II:** 183, 253; **III:** 105, 581; **Supp. I Part 1:** 21; **Supp. I Part 2:** 474, 643; **Supp. V:** 288

Wilton, David, **IV:** 147
Wiman, Christian, **Supp. XV:** 251, 253, 264; **Supp. XVII:** 74; **Supp. XVIII:** 173, 174
Wimberly, Lowry, **Supp. XV:** 136, 137
"Wimp, The" (Gallagher), **Supp. XXIV:** 174
Wimsatt, William K., **Supp. XIV:** 12
Winch, Terence, **Supp. XXIII:** 291
Winchell, Mark, **Supp. VIII:** 176, 189
Winchell, Mark Royden, **Supp. IX:** 97, 98, 109; **Supp. VIII:** 241; **Supp. XIII:** 94, 98, 99, 101; **Supp. XIV:** 103, 106, 111
Winchell, Walter, **Supp. XXV:** 29
Winckelmann, Johann Joachim, **Supp. XII:** 178
Wind, Sand, and Stars (Saint-Exupéry), **Supp. IX:** 247
Wind Across the Everglades (film, Ray), **Supp. XVIII:** 253
Wind Chrysalid's Rattle (Sobin), **Supp. XVI:** 283
"Windfall" (B. Kelly), **Supp. XVII:** 132
Windflower Home Almanac of Poetry, The (Kooser, ed.), **Supp. XIX:** 119
Windham, Donald, **IV:** 382
"Windhover" (Hopkins), **I:** 397; **II:** 539; **Supp. IX:** 43
Winding Stair and Other Poems, The (Yeats), **Supp. XV:** 253
"Winding Street, The" (Petry), **Supp. XI:** 6
"Window" (Pinsky), **Supp. VI:** 237, 247
"Window, The" (Hull), **Supp. XXI:** 140–141
Window at the White Cat, The (Rinehart), **Supp. XXV:** 192
Windows (Creeley), **Supp. IV Part 1:** 157, 158
"Windows" (Jarrell), **II:** 388, 389
"Window Seat, A" (Goldbarth), **Supp. XII:** 185
Wind Remains, The (opera) (Bowles), **Supp. IV Part 1:** 83
"Winds, The" (Welty), **IV:** 265; **Retro. Supp. I:** 348, 350
"Winds and Clouds over a Funeral" (Jin), **Supp. XVIII:** 94
Winds of War, The (miniseries), **Supp. XXV:** 265
Winds of War, The (Wouk), **Supp. XX:** 243; **Supp. XXV:** 254, 257, 258
"Wind up Sushi" (Goldbarth), **Supp. XII:** 186–187
Windy City Blues (Paretsky), **Supp. XXV:** 171
"Windy Day at the Reservoir, A" (Beattie), **Supp. V:** 33
Windy McPherson's Son (Anderson), **I:** 101, 102–103, 105, 111
"Wine" (Carver), **Supp. III Part 1:** 138
"Wine Menagerie, The" (H. Crane), **I:** 389, 391; **Retro. Supp. II:** 82
Wine of the Puritans, The: A Study of Present-Day America (Brooks), **I:** 240
"Wine of Wizardry, A" (Sterling), **I:** 208
Winer, Linda, **Supp. IV Part 2:** 580; **Supp. XV:** 332

Winesburg, Ohio: A Group of Tales of Ohio Small Town Life (Anderson), **I:** 97, 102, 103, 104, 105–108; **III:** 112, 113, 114, 116, 224, 579; **Supp. IX:** 306, 308; **Supp. V:** 12; **Supp. XI:** 164; **Supp. XVI:** 17; **Supp. XXII:** 282; **Supp. XXIV:** 281
Winfrey, Oprah, **Supp. XIX:** 194, 204; **Supp. XX:** 83, 93
Wing-and-Wing, The (Cooper), **I:** 350, 355
Winged Seed, The: A Remembrance (L.-Y. Lee), **Supp. XV:** 211, **220–223**
Winged Words: American Indian Writers Speak (Coltelli), **Supp. IV Part 2:** 493, 497
"Wingfield" (Wolff), **Supp. VII:** 341–342
"Wings, The" (Doty), **Supp. XI:** 124
Wings of the Dove, The (James), **I:** 436; **II:** 320, 323, 333, 334–335; **Retro. Supp. I:** 215, 216, 217, 232, **233–234**; **Supp. II Part 1:** 94–95; **Supp. IV Part 1:** 349
Winik, Marion, **Supp. XXVI:** 212
"Wink of the Zenith, The" (Skloot), **Supp. XX:** 207
Wink of the Zenith, The: The Shaping of a Writer's Life (Skloot), **Supp. XX:** **195, 196,** 207
"Winkte"(Kenny), **Supp. XXIII:** 148–149
"Winky" (Saunders), **Supp. XIX:** 228–229, 229
"Winner, The" (Davison), **Supp. XXVI:** 64
Winner Names the Age, The: A Collection of Works by Lillian Smith (Cliff, ed.), **Supp. XXII:** 67
Winner Take Nothing (Hemingway), **II:** 249; **Retro. Supp. I:** 170, 175, 176, 181
"Winnie" (Brooks), **Supp. III Part 1:** 86
Winokur, Maxine. *See* Kumin, Maxine
Winslow, Art, **Supp. XVIII:** 102
Winslow, Devereux, **II:** 547
Winslow, Harriet, **II:** 552–553
Winslow, Ola Elizabeth, **I:** 547
Winslow, Warren, **II:** 540
Winston, Andrew, **Supp. XII:** 189
Winston, Michael R., **Supp. XIV:** 197
Winter, Douglas, **Supp. V:** 144
Winter, Johnny and Edgar, **Supp. V:** 334
Winter, Kate, **Supp. X:** 104
"Winter Branch, A" (Irving), **Supp. VI:** 163
"Winter Burial, A" (Clampitt), **Supp. IX:** 48
Winter Carnival (film), **Retro. Supp. I:** 113
"Winter Concert"(Strout), **Supp. XXIII:** 283
"Winter Daybreak at Vence, A" (Wright), **Supp. III Part 1:** 249–250
Winter Diary, A (Van Doren), **I:** 168
"Winter Dreams" (Fitzgerald), **II:** 80, 94; **Retro. Supp. I:** 108
"Winter Drive, A" (Jewett), **Retro. Supp. II:** 147
"Winter Eden, A" (Frost), **Retro. Supp. I:** 137

"Winter Father, The" (Dubus), **Supp. VII:** 83, 87
Winter Hours: Prose, Prose Poems, and Poems (Oliver), **Supp. VII:** 230, 247
"Winter in Dunbarton" (Lowell), **II:** 547; **Retro. Supp. II:** 187
"Wintering" (Plath), **Retro. Supp. II:** 255
"Wintering Over" (Davison), **Supp. XXVI:** 76
Winter Insomnia (Carver), **Supp. III Part 1:** 138
Winter in the Blood (Welch), **Supp. IV Part 2:** 562
"Winter Landscape" (Berryman), **I:** 174; **Retro. Supp. I:** 430
Winter Light (W. V. Davis), **Supp. XXI:** **92,** 93
"Winter Light" (W. V. Davis), **Supp. XXI:** 90, 92
Winter Lightning (Nemerov), **III:** 269
Winter Morning Walks: One Hundred Postcards to Jim Harrison (Kooser), **Supp. XIX:** 116, **125–126**
Winter News (Haines), **Supp. XII:** 199, **201–204,** 207–208, 208
Winternitz, Mary. *See* Cheever, Mrs. John (Mary Winternitz)
Winter: Notes from Montana (Bass), **Supp. XVI:** 17–18
Winter of Our Discontent, The (Steinbeck), **IV:** 52, 65–66, 68
"Winter on Earth" (Toomer), **Supp. III Part 2:** 486
"Winter Piece, A" (Bryant), **Supp. I Part 1:** 150, 155
"Winter Rains, Cataluña" (Levine), **Supp. V:** 182
"Winter Remembered" (Ransom), **III:** 492–493
"Winter Roses" (W. V. Davis), **Supp. XXI:** 94
Winterrowd, Prudence, **I:** 217, 224
Winters, Jonathan, **Supp. XI:** 305
Winters, Yvor, **I:** 59, 63, 386, 393, 397, 398, 402, 471; **III:** 194, 498; **IV:** 153; **Retro. Supp. II:** 76, 77, 78, 82, 83, 85, 89; **Supp. I Part 1:** 268; **Supp. II Part 2:** 416, 666, **785–816**; **Supp. IV Part 2:** 480; **Supp. V:** 180, 191–192; **Supp. XIV:** 287; **Supp. XV:** 74, 341; **Supp. XXV:** 250
"Winter Sacrament" (Bronk), **Supp. XXI:** 33
"Winter Scenes" (Bryant). *See* "Winter Piece, A"
Winterset (Anderson), **III:** 159
"Winter Shrub, A" (Bronk), **Supp. XXI:** 28
"Winter Skyline Late" (F. Wright), **Supp. XVII:** 245
"Winter Sleep" (Wylie), **Supp. I Part 2:** 711, 729
Winter's Night (Boyce), **Supp. XXI:** 7, **12–13**
Winter's Tale (film, Goldsman), **Supp. XXV:** 86
Winter's Tale (Helprin), **Supp. XXV:** 79–80, 81, 82, 83, 86
Winter's Tale, The (Shakespeare), **Supp. XIII:** 219

Winter Stars (Levis), **Supp. XI:** 259, **266–268**

"Winter Stars" (Levis), **Supp. XI:** 267–268

Winter Stop-Over (Everwine), **Supp. XV:** 74, 76

"Winter Stop-Over" (Everwine), **Supp. XV:** 76

Winter Studies and Summer Rambles in Canada (Jameson), **Supp. XXIII:** 225, 226

"Winter Sunrise" (Davison), **Supp. XXVI:** 69

"Winter Swan" (Bogan), **Supp. III Part 1:** 52

"Winter Thunder" (Sandoz), **Supp. XXIV:** 255

Winter Thunder (X. J. Kennedy), **Supp. XV:** 167

"Winter Thunder" (X. J. Kennedy), **Supp. XV:** 169

"Winter Trees" (Pedersen; Nelson, trans.), **Supp. XVIII:** 180

Winter Trees (Plath), **Retro. Supp. II:** 257; **Supp. I Part 2:** 526, 539, 541

"Winter Walk" (W. V. Davis), **Supp. XXI:** 92

"Winter Weather Advisory" (Ashbery), **Supp. III Part 1:** 26

"Winter Wheat" (Hoffman), **Supp. XVIII:** 86, 87

"Winter without Snow, The" (C. Frost), **Supp. XV:** 96, 105–106

"Winter Words" (Levine), **Supp. V:** 192

Winthrop, John, **Supp. I Part 1:** 99, 100, 101, 102, 105; **Supp. I Part 2:** 484, 485

Winthrop Covenant, The (Auchincloss), **Supp. IV Part 1:** 23

"Wires of the Night, The" (Collins), **Supp. XXI:** 64

Wirt, William, **I:** 232

Wirth, Louis, **IV:** 475

Wisconsin Death Trip (Lesy), **Supp. XXV:** 146

Wisconsin Death Trip (Levy), **Supp. XIX:** 102

"Wisdom Cometh with the Years" (Cullen), **Supp. IV Part 1:** 166

Wisdom of the African World (McKnight, ed.), **Supp. XX: 157–158**

Wisdom of the Desert, The: Sayings from the Desert Fathers of the Fourth Century (Merton), **Supp. VIII:** 201

Wisdom of the Heart, The (H. Miller), **III:** 178, 184

Wise Blood (O'Connor), **III:** 337, 338, 339–343, 344, 345, 346, 350, 354, 356, 357; **Retro. Supp. II:** 219, 221, 222, 223, **225–228**

Wise Men, The (Price), **Supp. VI:** 254

"Wiser Than a God" (Chopin), **Retro. Supp. II:** 61; **Supp. I Part 1:** 208

Wishes, Lies, and Dreams: Teaching Children to Write Poetry (Koch), **Supp. XV:** 176, 189

"Wish for a Young Wife" (Roethke), **III:** 548

Wishful Thinking: A Theological ABC (Buechner), **Supp. XII:** 53

Wishing Tree, The: Christopher Isherwood on Mystical Religion (Adjemian, ed.), **Supp. XIV:** 164, 173

"Wish List" (Goodman), **Supp. XXVI:** 119–120

Wish You Were Here (O'Nan), **Supp. XXV:** 142, 147–148, 150, 152

Wismer, Helen Muriel. *See* Thurber, Mrs. James (Helen Muriel Wismer)

Wisse, Ruth, **Supp. XII:** 167, 168

Wister, Owen, **I:** 62; **Retro. Supp. II:** 72; **Supp. XIV:** 39

Wit (Edson), **Supp. XVIII:** 35–36, 37, **38–51**

"Witchbird" (Bambara), **Supp. XI:** 11

"Witch Burning" (Plath), **Supp. I Part 2:** 539

Witchcraft of Salem Village, The (Jackson), **Supp. IX:** 121

"Witch Doctor" (Hayden), **Supp. II Part 1:** 368, 380

Witches of Eastwick, The (Updike), **Retro. Supp. I:** 330, 331

Witch from Castile, The (Asch), **Supp. XXIII:** 6, 10

Witching Hour, The (Rice), **Supp. VII:** 299–300

"Witch of Coös, The" (Frost), **II:** 154–155; **Retro. Supp. I:** 135; **Retro. Supp. II:** 42

"Witch of Owl Mountain Springs, The: An Account of Her Remarkable Powers" (Taylor), **Supp. V:** 328

"Witch of Wenham, The" (Whittier), **Supp. I Part 2:** 694, 696

Witek, Terri, **Supp. XVII:** 117

"With a Little Help from My Friends" (Kushner), **Supp. IX:** 131

With Bold Knife and Fork (M. F. K. Fisher), **Supp. XVII:** 89, 91

"With Che at Kitty Hawk" (Banks), **Supp. V:** 6

"With Che at the Plaza" (Banks), **Supp. V:** 7

"With Che in New Hampshire" (Banks), **Supp. V:** 6

"With Child" (Taggard), **Supp. XXII:** 276, 278

"Withdrawal Symptoms" (Mora), **Supp. XIII:** 216

"Withered Leaf, A—Seen on a Poet's Table" (Very), **Supp. XXV:** 243

"Withered Skins of Berries" (Toomer), **Supp. III Part 2:** 485; **Supp. IX:** 320

Withers, Harry Clay, **Supp. XIII:** 161

Witherspoon, John, **Supp. I Part 2:** 504

With Eyes at the Back of Our Heads (Levertov), **Supp. III Part 1:** 276–277

With Her in Ourland (Gilman), **Supp. XI:** 208–209

With His Pistol in His Hand (Paredes), **Supp. XIII:** 225; **Supp. XIX:** 98

"Within the Words: An Apprenticeship" (Haines), **Supp. XII:** 197

"With Kit, Age 7, at the Beach" (Stafford), **Supp. XI:** 323

With Love to Lesbia (Kenny), **Supp. XXIII:** 145

"With Mercy for the Greedy" (Sexton), **Supp. II Part 2:** 680

With My Trousers Rolled (Epstein), **Supp. XIV:** 101, 105

Without a Hero (Boyle), **Supp. VIII:** 16; **Supp. XX:** 20

Without Feathers (Allen), **Supp. XV:** 3, 14, 15

Without Stopping (Bowles), **Supp. IV Part 1:** 79, 81, 85, 90, 91, 92

"Without Tradition and within Reason: Judge Horton and Atticus Finch in Court" (C. D. Johnson), **Supp. VIII:** 127

With Shuddering Fall (Oates), **Supp. II Part 2:** 504–506

"With the Dog at Sunrise" (Kenyon), **Supp. VII:** 170

With the Empress Dowager of China (Carl), **III:** 475

"With the Horse in the Winter Pasture" (McCarriston), **Supp. XIV:** 262

With the Old Breed: At Peleliu and Okinawa (Sledge), **Supp. V:** 249–250

"With the Violin" (Chopin), **Retro. Supp. II:** 61

"Witness" (Clampitt), **Supp. IX:** 42–43, 45, 46

"Witness" (Dubus), **Supp. VII:** 89

"Witness" (Harjo), **Supp. XII:** 227–228

Witness (McNally), **Supp. XIII:** 197

"Witness" (Nelson), **Supp. XVIII:** 186

"Witness, The" (Porter), **III:** 443–444

"Witness for Poetry, A" (Stafford), **Supp. XI:** 324

"Witness for the Defense" (Hay), **Supp. XIV:** 124

"Witnessing My Father's Will" (Karr), **Supp. XI:** 241

"Witnessing to a Shared World" (Sanders), **Supp. XVI:** 278

Witness to the Times! (McGrath), **Supp. X:** 118

Witness Tree, A (Frost), **II:** 155; **Retro. Supp. I:** 122, 137, 139

Wit's End: Days and Nights of the Algonquin Round Table (Gaines), **Supp. IX:** 190

Wits Recreations (Mennes and Smith), **II:** 111

Witt, Shirley Hill, **Supp. IV Part 2:** 505

Witte, John, **Supp. XX: 200**

Wittels, Anne F., **Supp. XV:** 59

Wittenberg, Judith Bryant, **Retro. Supp. II:** 146

Wittgenstein, Ludwig, **Retro. Supp. I:** 53; **Supp. III Part 2:** 626–627; **Supp. X:** 304; **Supp. XII:** 21; **Supp. XV:** 344, 346

Wittgensteins' Mistress (Markson), **Supp. XVII:** 135, 142, 143, 145

Wittliff, William, **Supp. V:** 227

"Witty War, A" (Simpson), **Supp. IX:** 268

Witz (Cohen), **Supp. XXII:** 268

"Wives and Mistresses" (Hardwick), **Supp. III Part 1:** 211–212

Wizard of Loneliness, The (Nichols), **Supp. XIII:** 259, 263, 264

Wizard of Oz, The (Baum), **Supp. IV Part 1:** 113

Wizard of Oz, The (film), **Supp. X:** 172, 214

Wizard's Tide, The: A Story (Buechner), **Supp. XII:** 54

"WLT (The Edgar Era)" (Keillor), **Supp. XVI:** 172

WLT: A Radio Romance (Keillor), **Supp. XVI:** 176

Wobegon Boy (Keillor), **Supp. XVI:** 177

Wodehouse, P. G., **Supp. IX:** 195; **Supp. XXI:** 204–205

Woiwode, Larry, **Supp. VIII:** 151; **Supp. XVI:** 206

Wojahn, David, **Supp. IX:** 161, 292, 293; **Supp. XXI:** 130, 131, 132, 138, 139, 141

Wolcott, James, **Supp. IX:** 259

Wolf, Christa, **Supp. IV Part 1:** 310, 314

Wolf, Daniel, **Retro. Supp. II:** 202

Wolf, Robert L., **Supp. XXII:** 274, 277, 279, 280

Wolf: A False Memoir (Harrison), **Supp. VIII:** 40, **41–42,** 45

Wolfe, Ben, **IV:** 454

Wolfe, Gregory, **Supp. XIV:** 307

Wolfe, James, **Supp. I Part 2:** 498

Wolfe, Linnie, **Supp. IX:** 176

Wolfe, Mabel, **IV:** 454

Wolfe, Thomas, **I:** 288, 289, 374, 478, 495; **II:** 457; **III:** 40, 108, 278, 334, 482; **IV:** 52, 97, 357, **450–473; Retro. Supp. I:** 382; **Supp. I Part 1:** 29; **Supp. IV Part 1:** 101; **Supp. IX:** 229; **Supp. X:** 225; **Supp. XI:** 213, 216, 217, 218; **Supp. XIII:** 17; **Supp. XIV:** 122; **Supp. XVIII:** 78; **Supp. XX:** 163

Wolfe, Tom, **Supp. III Part 2:** 567–588; **Supp. IV Part 1:** 35, 198; **Supp. V:** 296; **Supp. X:** 264; **Supp. XI:** 239; **Supp. XV:** 143; **Supp. XVII:** 202; **Supp. XVIII:** 72, 117; **Supp. XXIV:** 282, 283

Wolfe, William Oliver, **IV:** 454

Wolfe, Mrs. William Oliver (Julia Elizabeth Westall), **IV:** 454

"Wolfe Homo Scribens" (Cowley), **Supp. II Part 1:** 144

Wolfert, Ira, **Supp. XXI:** 261–279

Wolfert's Roost (Irving), **II:** 314

Wolff, Cynthia Griffin, **Retro. Supp. I:** 379; **Supp. IV Part 1:** 203

Wolff, Donald, **Supp. XIII:** 316, 317, 326

Wolff, Geoffrey, **Supp. II Part 1:** 97; **Supp. XI:** 239, 245, 246; **Supp. XXII:** 206, 211; **Supp. XXV:** 217

Wolff, Tobias, **Retro. Supp. I:** 190; **Supp. V:** 22; **Supp. VII:** **331–346; Supp. X:** 1; **Supp. XI:** 26, 239, 245, 246, 247; **Supp. XV:** 223; **Supp. XVI:** 39, 41, 63, 70, 77; **Supp. XXIII:** 289; **Supp. XXV:** 142, 208

"Wolf in the Bed, The"(Hadas), **Supp. XXIII:** 118

Wolfreys, Julian, **Supp. XVIII:** 61

Wolfson, P. J., **Supp. XIII:** 172

"Wolf Town" (Carson), **Supp. XII:** **102**

Wolf Willow: A History, a Story, and a Memory of the Last Plains Frontier (Stegner), **Supp. IV Part 2:** 595, 596, 597, 598, 599, 600, 601, 604, 606, 611, 613, 614

Wolitzer, Hilma, **Supp. XV:** 55; **Supp. XXIII:** 108

Wolitzer, Meg, **Supp. XV:** 65

Wolkomir, Richard, **Supp. XXII:** 218

Wollaston, William, **II:** 108

Wollstonecraft, Mary, **Supp. I Part 1:** 126; **Supp. I Part 2:** 512, 554

"Wolves in the Marsh" (Dubus III), **Supp. XXIV:** 99–100

Womack, Craig, **Supp. XXIII:** 147, 153, 154–155

"Woman" (Bogan), **Supp. X:** 102

"Woman, I Got the Blues" (Komunyakaa), **Supp. XIII:** 117

"Woman, Why Are You Weeping?" (Kenyon), **Supp. VII:** 174–175

"Woman, Young and Old, A" (Paley), **Supp. VI:** 222, 225

Woman Aroused, The (Lacy), **Supp. XV:** 199–200

Woman at the Washington Zoo, The (Jarrell), **II:** 367, 386, 387, 389

Woman Before an Aquarium (Hampl), **Supp. XXII:** 83, 86, 98

"Woman Before an Aquarium" (Hampl), **Supp. XXII:** 85, 98

"Womand and the Woman's Movement" (Briggs), **Supp. XVIII:** 14

"Woman Dead in Her Forties, A" (Rich), **Supp. I Part 2:** 574–575

Woman Driver, The (Thompson), **Supp. XXIII:** 291, **294–295**

"Woman Enough" (Gallagher), **Supp. XXIV:** 169

"Woman Hanging from the Thirteenth Floor Window, The" (Harjo), **Supp. XII:** 216, 221

"Woman Hollering Creek" (Cisneros), **Supp. VII:** 70

Woman Hollering Creek and Other Stories (Cisneros), **Supp. VII:** 58, 68–70

"Womanhood" (Brooks), **Supp. III Part 1:** 77

"Woman in Rain" (X. J. Kennedy), **Supp. XV:** 168

Woman in the Dark (Hammett), **Supp. IV Part 1:** 343

"Woman in the House, A" (Caldwell), **I:** 310

Woman in the Nineteenth Century (Fuller), **Retro. Supp. I:** 156; **Supp. II Part 1:** 279, 292, 294–296; **Supp. XI:** 197, 203; **Supp. XVIII:** 3, 11

"Woman in the Shoe, The" (Ryan as Quin), **Supp. XVIII:** 231

Woman in White, The (Collins), **Supp. I Part 1:** 35, 36

"Woman Is Talking to Death, A"(Grahn), **Supp. XXIII:** 195

"Womanizer, The" (Ford), **Supp. V:** 71, 72

"Woman Like Yourself, A" (C. Frost), **Supp. XV:** 107

Woman Lit by Fireflies, The (Harrison), **Supp. VIII:** 50–51

"Woman Loses Cookie Bake-Off, Sets Self on Fire" (R. O. Butler), **Supp. XII:** 72

Woman of Andros, The (Wilder), **IV:** 356, 363–364, 367, 368, 374

Woman of Means, A (Taylor), **Supp. V:** 319–320

"Woman of Tomorrow, The" (Atherton), **Supp. XXIV:** 29

Woman on the Edge of Time (Piercy), **Supp. XIII:** 29

Woman on the Porch, The (Gordon), **II:** 199, 209–211

"Woman on the Stair, The" (MacLeish), **III:** 15–16

"Woman's Dream, A" (E. Stoddard), **Supp. XV:** 278

Woman's Fiction: A Guide to Novels By and About Women in America, 1820–1870 (Baym), **Supp. XVIII:** 258

"Woman's Heartlessness" (Thaxter), **Retro. Supp. II:** 147

Woman's Honor (Glaspell), **Supp. III Part 1:** 179

"Woman Singing" (Ortiz), **Supp. IV Part 2:** 513

Woman's Place, A (C. L. R. James and Weinstein), **Supp. XXI:** 170

Woman's Share in Primitive Culture (Mason), **Supp. I Part 1:** 18

"Woman Struck by Car Turns into Nymphomaniac" (R. O. Butler), **Supp. XII:** 72

"Woman's Work" (Alvarez), **Supp. VII:** 4

"Woman Taken in Adultery, A"(Thompson), **Supp. XXIII:** 300

"Woman Uses Glass Eye to Spy on Philandering Husband" (R. O. Butler), **Supp. XII:** 70, 72

Woman Warrior (Kingston), **Supp. IV Part 1:** 12; **Supp. V:** 157, 158, 159, 160–164, 166, 169; **Supp. X:** 291–292; **Supp. XIV:** 162

Woman Warrior, The (Kingston), **Supp. XV:** 220

Woman Who Fell from the Sky, The (Harjo), **Supp. XII: 226–228**

"Woman Who Fell From the Sky, The" (Iroquois creation story), **Supp. IV Part 1:** 327

Woman Who Owned the Shadows, The (Gunn Allen), **Supp. IV Part 1:** 320, 322, 326, 327–328

"Woman Who Plays Trumpet Is Deported, A" (Cliff), **Supp. XXII:** 74

"Woman Who Prayed, The" (Gallagher), **Supp. XXIV:** 175

"Woman Who Raised Goats, The" (Gallagher), **Supp. XXIV:** 168

"Woman Who Went Backwards, The"(Schott), **Supp. XXIII:** 241

Woman Within, The (Glasgow), **II:** 183, 190–191

"Womanwork" (Gunn Allen), **Supp. IV Part 1:** 326

Women (Bukowski), **Supp. XI:** 172

"Women" (Didion), **Supp. IV Part 1:** 205

"Women" (Swenson), **Supp. IV Part 2:** 647

Women, The (Boyle), **Supp. XX: 24, 26–27**

Women, The (film), **Retro. Supp. I:** 113

Women, The (film; Cukor), **Supp. XVI:** 181, 192

"Women and Children First" (Prose), **Supp. XVI:** 254

Women and Children First: Stories (Prose), **Supp. XVI:** 254

Women and Economics (Gilman), **Supp. I Part 2:** 637; **Supp. V:** 284; **Supp. XI:** 200, **203–204,** 206

"Women and Poetry" (Notley), **Supp. XXII:** 236

Women and Thomas Harrow (Marquand), **III:** 50, 61, 62, 66, 68, 69–70, 71

Women and Vodka (Markson as Merrill, ed.), **Supp. XVII:** 136

Women and Wilderness (LaBastille), **Supp. X:** 97, **102–104**

"Women as They Are" (Rowson), **Supp. XV:** 243

Women at Point Sur, The (Jeffers), **Supp. II Part 2:** 430–431

Women Authors of Our Day in Their Homes (Halsey), **Supp. XXIV:** 20

Women in Love (Lawrence), **III:** 27, 34; **Supp. XXIV:** 58

Women in Praise of the Sacred: 43 Centuries of Spiritual Poetry by Women (Hirshfield, ed.), **Supp. XXIII:** 136, 137

"Women of Auschwitz, The" (Gallagher), **Supp. XXIV:** 171

Women of Belize: Gender and Change in Central America (McClaurin), **Supp. XXIII:** 84

Women of Brewster Place, The: A Novel in Seven Stories (Naylor), **Supp. VIII:** 213, **214–218**

Women of Manhattan: An Upper West Side Story (Shanley), **Supp. XIV:** 315, **326–327**

"Women of My Color" (Coleman), **Supp. XI:** 88–89

Women of Mystery: The Lives and Works of Notable Women Crime Novelists (DuBose), **Supp. XXV:** 199

Women of Trachis (Pound, trans.), **III:** 476

"Women on the Breadlines"(Le Sueur), **Supp. XXIII:** 166, 167

Women on the Wall, The (Stegner), **Supp. IV Part 2:** 599, 605, 606

Women Poets in English (Stanford, ed.), **Retro. Supp. I:** 41

"Women Reformers and American Culture, 1870–1930" (Conway), **Supp. I Part 1:** 19

"Women's Movement, The" (Didion), **Supp. IV Part 1:** 206

"Women Waiting" (Shields), **Supp. VII:** 320

"Women We Love Whom We Never See Again" (R. Bly), **Supp. IV Part 1:** 66

"Women We Never See Again" (R. Bly), **Supp. IV Part 1:** 66

Women Who Make Our Novels, The (Overton), **Supp. XXV:** 200

Women with Men (Ford), **Supp. V:** 57, 71–72

"Wonder" (Olds), **Supp. X:** 210

Wonder Boys (Chabon), **Supp. XI:** 67, **73–75,Supp. XI:** 78; **Supp. XVI:** 259

Wonder Boys (film), **Supp. XI:** 67

Wonderful O, The (Thurber), **Supp. I Part 2:** 612

"Wonderful Old Gentleman, The" (Parker), **Supp. IX:** 197

"Wonderful Pen, The" (Swenson), **Supp. IV Part 2:** 650

Wonderful Wizard of Oz, The (Baum), **Supp. XXV:** 129

Wonderful Words, Silent Truth: Essays on Poetry and a Memoir (Simic), **Supp. VIII:** 270

Wonderland (Oates), **Supp. II Part 2:** 511, 512, 514–515

Wonders Hidden (Sanders), **Supp. XVI:** 269

Wonders of the African World (television series), **Supp. XX: 99**

Wonders of the Invisible World, The (Mather), **Supp. II Part 2:** 456–459, 460, 467

Wonder-Working Providence (E. Johnson), **IV:** 157

Wong, Hertha, **Supp. IV Part 1:** 275

Wong, Jade Snow, **Supp. X:** 291

Wong, Nellie, **Supp. XVII:** 72

Wong, Shawn, **Supp. XV:** 221

Wong, Timothy, **Supp. XVIII:** 94

"Wood" (Nye), **Supp. XIII:** 276

Wood, Audrey, **IV:** 381

Wood, Charles Erskine Scott, **Supp. XV:** 301

Wood, Clement, **Supp. XV:** 298

Wood, Clement Biddle, **Supp. XI:** 307

Wood, Gaby, **Supp. XXIV:** 166

Wood, Harrison, **Supp. XXII:** 283

Wood, Mrs. Henry, **Supp. I Part 1:** 35

Wood, James, **Supp. XIV:** 95–96; **Supp. XIX:** 138

Wood, Mabel, **I:** 199

Wood, Michael, **Supp. IV Part 2:** 691

Wood, Norman Barton, **Supp. XIV:** 201

Wood, Susan, **Supp. XVI:** 123

Woodard, Calvin, **Supp. VIII:** 128

Woodard, Charles L., **Supp. IV Part 2:** 484, 493

Woodard, Deborah, **Supp. XIII:** 114

Woodberry, George Edward, **III:** 508

Woodbridge, Frederick, **I:** 217, 224

Woodbridge, John, **Supp. I Part 1:** 101, 102, 114

Woodbury, Hanni, **Supp. XXVI:** 8, 82, 87, 90, 95

"Wood-Choppers, The" (Chopin), **Retro. Supp. II:** 72

Woodcock, George, **Supp. XIII:** 33

Woodcome, Beth, **Supp. XVII:** 240

"Wood Dove at Sandy Spring, The" (MacLeish), **III:** 19

"Wooden Spring" (Rukeyser), **Supp. VI:** 285

"Wooden Umbrella, The" (Porter), **IV:** 26

Woodhull, Victoria, **Supp. XVIII:** 4

"Woodnotes" (Emerson), **II:** 7, 19

"Wood-Pile, The" (Frost), **Retro. Supp. I:** 128; **Supp. IV Part 2:** 445

Woodrow, James, **Supp. I Part 1:** 349, 366

"Woods, Books, and Truant Officers, The" (Maclean), **Supp. XIV:** 221, 225

"Woods, New York, The" (Bronk), **Supp. XXI:** 27

Woods, Paula L., **Supp. XXI:** 70

Woods, Robert A., **Supp. I Part 1:** 19

Woods, The (Mamet), **Supp. XIV:** 241, 254–255

Woodswoman (LaBastille), **Supp. X:** 95, **96–99,** 108

Woodswoman III: Book Three of the Woodswoman's Adventures (LaBastille), **Supp. X:** 95, **106–107**

"Wood Thrush" (Kenyon), **Supp. VII:** 172

Woodward, C. Vann, **IV:** 114, 470–471; **Retro. Supp. I:** 75, 76; **Supp. XIX:** 152; **Supp. XXII:** 194

"Woof: A Plea of Sorts" (Saunders), **Supp. XIX:** 235

"Wooing the Inanimate" (Brodsky), **Supp. VIII:** 32

Woolcott, Alexander, **Supp. IX:** 197

Wooley, Bryan, **Supp. V:** 225

Woolf, Douglas, **Supp. XXIII:** 174

Woolf, Leonard, **Supp. IX:** 95

Woolf, Virginia, **I:** 53, 79, 112, 309; **II:** 320, 415; **IV:** 59; **Retro. Supp. I:** 59, 75, 170, 215, 291, 359; **Supp. I Part 2:** 553, 714, 718; **Supp. IV Part 1:** 299; **Supp. IX:** 66, 109; **Supp. V:** 127; **Supp. VIII:** 5, 155, 251, 252, 263, 265; **Supp. XI:** 134, 193; **Supp. XII:** 81, 98, 289; **Supp. XIII:** 305; **Supp. XIV:** 341–342, 342, 343, 346, 348; **Supp. XIX:** 134; **Supp. XV:** 55, 65; **Supp. XXIII:** 275

Woollcott, Alexander, **IV:** 432; **Retro. Supp. II:** 327; **Supp. I Part 2:** 664; **Supp. IX:** 190, 194

Woolley, Leonard, **Supp. XXIII:** 33

Woollstonecraft, Mary, **Supp. XVI:** 184

"Woolly Mammoth" (X. J. Kennedy), **Supp. XV:** 163–164

Woolman, John, **Supp. VIII:** 202, 204, 205

Woolson, Constance Fenimore, **Retro. Supp. I:** 224, 228

Woolverton, Linda, **Supp. XXI:** 148

Wooster, David, **Supp. XX: 288**

Worcester, Samuel, **I:** 458

Word and Idioms: Studies in the English Language (L. P. Smith), **Supp. XIV:** 343

"Word by Word" (column, Lamott), **Supp. XX: 140**

"Wordless Winter" (Davison), **Supp. XXVI:** 75–76

Word of God and the Word of Man, The (Barth), **Retro. Supp. I:** 327

"Word out of the Sea, A" (Whitman), **IV:** 344

Words (Creeley), **Supp. IV Part 1:** 139, 150–153, 154, 155, 158

"Words" (Creeley), **Supp. IV Part 1:** 152

"Words" (Gioia), **Supp. XV:** 125

"Words" (Merwin), **Supp. III Part 1:** 352

"Words" (Plath), **Supp. I Part 2:** 547

"Words" (Shields), **Supp. VII:** 323

"Words, The" (Wagoner), **Supp. IX:** 326

"Words above a Narrow Entrance" (Wagoner), **Supp. IX:** 325

"Words for a Bike-Racing, Osprey-Chasing Wine-Drunk Squaw Man" (Gunn Allen), **Supp. IV Part 1:** 325

Words for Dr. Y (Sexton), **Supp. II Part 2:** 698

"Words for Hart Crane" (Lowell), **I:** 381; **II:** 547; **Retro. Supp. II:** 188

"Words for Love" (Berrigan), **Supp. XXIV:** 35

"Words for Maria" (Merrill), **Supp. III Part 1:** 327

"Words for My Father" (Davison), **Supp. XXVI:** 72

"Words for My Grandmother"(Balakian), **Supp. XXIII:** 19, 20

Words for the Chisel (Taggard), **Supp. XXII: 276–277**

"Words for the Unknown Makers" (Kunitz), **Supp. III Part 1:** 264

Words for the Wind (Roethke), **III:** 529, 533, 541, 543, 545

"Words for the Wind" (Roethke), **III:** 542–543

Words in the Mourning Time (Hayden), **Supp. II Part 1:** 361, 366, 367

"Words in the Mourning Time" (Hayden), **Supp. II Part 1:** 370–371

"Words into Fiction" (Welty), **IV:** 279

"Words into Worlds Won't Go" (Major), **Supp. XXII:** 174

"Words Like Freedom" (Hughes), **Retro. Supp. I:** 207

"Words of a Young Girl" (Lowell), **II:** 554

"Words of Prey" (Stallings), **Supp. XXV:** 230

Words under the Words: Selected Poems (Nye), **Supp. XIII:** 277

Wordsworth, Dorothy, **Supp. IX:** 38

Wordsworth, William, **I:** 283, 522, 524, 525, 588; **II:** 7, 11, 17, 18, 97, 169, 273, 303, 304, 532, 549, 552; **III:** 219, 263, 277, 278, 511, 521, 523, 528, 583; **IV:** 120, 331, 343, 453, 465; **Retro. Supp. I:** 121, 196; **Supp. I Part 1:** 150, 151, 154, 161, 163, 312, 313, 349, 365; **Supp. I Part 2:** 375, 409, 416, 422, 607, 621, 622, 673, 674, 675, 676, 677, 710–711, 729; **Supp. II Part 1:** 4; **Supp. III Part 1:** 12, 15, 73, 279; **Supp. IV Part 2:** 597, 601; **Supp. IX:** 38, 41, 265, 274; **Supp. V:** 258; **Supp. VIII:** 273; **Supp. X:** 22, 23, 65, 120; **Supp. XI:** 248, 251, 312; **Supp. XIII:** 214; **Supp. XIV:** 184; **Supp. XIX:** 1; **Supp. XV:** 93, 250; **Supp. XX: 108, 116; Supp. XXI:** 131; **Supp. XXIV:** 74, 159

" 'Word Which Made All Clear, The': The Silent Close of *The House of Mirth*" (Benstock), *Supp. XX:* 240

Work (Alcott), **Supp. I Part 1:** 32–33, 42

Work (Dixon), **Supp. XII:** 141, **143**

"Work" (Halliday), **Supp. XIX:** 85

"Work" (Huddle), **Supp. XXVI:** 149

"Work" (Oliver), **Supp. VII:** 243

Work and Love (Dunn), **Supp. XI: 147–148**

"Worker" (Coleman), **Supp. XI:** 89

Worker Writers (Le Sueur), **Supp. XXIII:** 165

Working a Passage; or, Life on a Liner (Briggs), **Supp. XVIII:** 2, **9–10**

Working Class Movement in America, The (E. Marx and E. Aveling), **Supp. XVI:** 85

Working Papers: Selected Essays and Reviews (Carruth), **Supp. XVI:** 46

"Working Roots: A Collection of Poetry and Prose" (Trethewey), **Supp. XXI:** 245

"Working the Landscape" (Dunn), **Supp. XI:** 151

Working Through: A Teacher's Journey in the Urban University (Kriegel), **Supp. XXIV: 222–223**

Workin' on the Chain Gang: Shaking Off the Dead Hand of History (Mosley), **Supp. XIII:** 247, 248

"Work Notes '66" (Baraka), **Supp. II Part 1:** 47

Work of Art (Lewis), **II:** 453–454

"Work of Shading, The" (Simic), **Supp. VIII:** 277–278

Work of Stephen Crane, The (Follett, ed.), **I:** 405

"Work on Red Mountain, The" (Harte), **Supp. II Part 1:** 339

Works and Days (Erga Kai Hēmerai) (Hesiod; Stallings, trans.), **Supp. XXV:** 221

"Workshop" (Espaillat), **Supp. XXI:** 105

Works of Love, The (Morris), **III:** 223–224, 225, 233

Works of Witter Bynner, The (Kraft, ed.), **Supp. XV:** 52

"World, The" (Bronk), **Supp. XXI:** 32

"World, The" (Simic), **Supp. VIII:** 282

"World, the Flesh, and the Devil, The"(P. Benedict), **Supp. XXIII:** 48

World, the Worldless, The (Bronk), **Supp. XXI: 29–31**

"World, World—" (Oppen), **Supp. XXVI:** 233

World According to Garp, The (Irving), **Supp. VI:** 163, 164, **170–173,** 181

World and Africa, The: An Inquiry into the Part Which Africa Has Played in World History (Du Bois), **Supp. II Part 1:** 184–185

"World and All Its Teeth, The" (Nye), **Supp. XIII:** 282

"World and the Door, The" (O. Henry), **Supp. II Part 1:** 402

"World and the Jug, The" (Ellison), **Retro. Supp. II:** 112, 119, 123

"World as We Know It, The" (Barresi), **Supp. XV:** 100

World Authors 1950–1970, **Supp. XIII:** 102

World Away, A (O'Nan), **Supp. XXV:** 141, 144–145, 149

World Below, The (Miller), **Supp. XII: 303–304**

World Below the Window, The: Poems 1937–1997 (W. J. Smith), **Supp. XIII:** 332, 340, 345

World Doesn't End, The (Simic), **Supp. VIII:** 272, **279–280**

World Elsewhere, A: The Place of Style in American Literature (Poirier), **I:** 239

"World Ends Here, The" (Harjo), **Supp. XII:** 227–228

World Enough and Time (Warren), **IV:** 243, 253–254

World Gone Wrong (album, Dylan), **Supp. XVIII:** 28

"World I Live In, The" (T. Williams), **IV:** 388

World I Never Made, A (Farrell), **II:** 34, 35, 424

World in the Attic, The (Morris), **III:** 222–223, 224

World in the Evening, The (Isherwood), **Supp. XIV:** 157, 164, 165, **166–167,** 170

World Is a Wedding, The (Schwartz), **Supp. II Part 2:** 643, 654–660

"World Is a Wedding, The" (Schwartz), **Supp. II Part 2:** 655–656, 657

"World Is Too Much with Us, The" (Wordsworth), **Supp. I Part 1:** 312

Worldly Hopes (Ammons), **Supp. VII:** 34

Worldly Philosophers, The (Heilbroner), **Supp. I Part 2:** 644, 650

World of Apples, The (Cheever), **Supp. I Part 1:** 191, 193

World of David Wagoner, The (McFarland), **Supp. IX:** 323

"World of Easy Rawlins, The" (Mosley), **Supp. XIII:** 234, 236

World of Gwendolyn Brooks, The (Brooks), **Supp. III Part 1:** 83, 84

World of H. G. Wells, The (Brooks), **I:** 240, 241, 242

World of Light, A (Skloot), **Supp. XX: 196, 205, 206–207**

"World of Light, A" (Skloot), **Supp. XX: 194, 207**

World of Light, A: Portraits and Celebrations (Sarton), **Supp. III Part 1:** 62; **Supp. VIII:** 249, 253, 262

World of Our Fathers: The Journey of the Eastern European Jews to America and the Life They Found and Made (Howe), **Supp. VI:** 113, 114, 116, 118, 119, **120–125; Supp. XIV:** 104; **Supp. XXIII:** 3; **Supp. XXIV:** 220–221

"World of Pure Experience, A" (James), **II:** 356–357

World of Raymond Chandler, The (Spender), **Supp. IV Part 1:** 119

World of Sex, The (H. Miller), **III:** 170, 178, 187

"World of the Perfect Tear, The" (McGrath), **Supp. X:** 116, 118

World of the Ten Thousand Things, The: Selected Poems (Wright), **Supp. V:** 333

"World of Tomorrow, The" (White), **Supp. I Part 2:** 663

World of Washington Irving, The (Brooks), **I:** 256–257

World Over, The (Wharton), **Retro. Supp. I:** 382

World Revolution (C. L. R. James), **Supp. XXI:** 167

"Worlds" (Goldbarth), **Supp. XII:** 183, 189

World's Body, The (Ransom), **III:** 497, 499; **Supp. II Part 1:** 146

World's End (Boyle), **Supp. VIII:** 11–12; **Supp. XX:** 22–23

World's End and Other Stories (Theroux), **Supp. VIII:** 322

"World's Fair" (Berryman), **I:** 173

World's Fair (Doctorow), **Supp. IV Part 1:** 217, 224, 227–229, 234, 236–237

World's Fair, The (Fitzgerald), **II:** 93

Worlds of Color (Du Bois), **Supp. II Part 1:** 185–186

"Worlds of Color" (Du Bois), **Supp. II Part 1:** 175

World So Wide (Lewis), **II:** 456

"World's Worst Boyfriends, The" (Wasserstein), **Supp. XV:** 328

"World-Telegram" (Berryman), **I:** 173

World to Come, The (D. Horn), **Supp. XVII:** 50

"World Trade Center / Mail runner / '73"(Balakian), **Supp. XXIII:** 32–33

World View on Race and Democracy: A Study Guide in Human Group Relations (Locke), **Supp. XIV:** 205, 206

World within the Word, The (Gass), **Supp. VI:** 77

"World Without Objects Is a Sensible Place, A" (Wilbur), **Supp. III Part 2:** 550

"World Without Rodrigo, The" (Cisneros), **Supp. VII:** 68

"Worm Moon" (Oliver), **Supp. VII:** 234

Wormser, Baron, **Supp. XXIII:** 57

"Worn Path, A" (Welty), **IV:** 262; **Retro. Supp. I:** 345–346

"Worsening Situation" (Ashbery), **Supp. III Part 1:** 17–18

"Worship" (Emerson), **II:** 2, 4–5

"Worship" (H. Johnson), **Supp. XXVI:** 172

"Worship and Church Bells" (Paine), **Supp. I Part 2:** 521

Worster, Donald, **Supp. IX:** 19

Worthington, Marjorie, **Supp. XII:** 13

Wouk, Herman, **Supp. XX:** 243; **Supp. XXV:** 253–270

Wouldn't Take Nothing for My Journey Now (Angelou), **Supp. IV Part 1:** 10, 12, 14, 15, 16

"Wound" (Pedersen; Nelson, trans.), **Supp. XVIII:** 180

Wound and the Bow, The: Seven Studies in Literature (Wilson), **IV:** 429; **Supp. XXIV:** 217

Wounded (Everett), **Supp. XVIII:** 54, **64**, 65

Wounds in the Rain (Crane), **I:** 409, 414, 423

Woven Stone (Ortiz), **Supp. IV Part 2:** 501, 514

Woven Stories (Ortiz), **Supp. IV Part 2:** 503

"Wraith, The" (Roethke), **III:** 542

"Wrath of God, The" (Fante), **Supp. XI:** 160, 164

"Wreath for a Bridal" (Plath), **Supp. I Part 2:** 537

"Wreath for Emmet Till, A" (Nelson), **Supp. XVIII:** 177

Wreath for Emmett Till, A (Nelson), **Supp. XVIII:** 171, 173, 175, 181, **183–185**

Wreath for Garibaldi and Other Stories, A (Garrett), **Supp. VII:** 99–101

"Wreath of Women" (Rukeyser), **Supp. VI:** 280

Wreckage (Jin), **Supp. XVIII:** **98–99**

Wreckage of Agathon, The (Gardner), **Supp. VI:** 63, **65–66**

Wrecking Crew (Levis), **Supp. XI:** 259–260

Wrecking Yard, The (Benedict), **Supp. XXIII:** 35, **39–41**

"Wrecking Yard, The (P. Benedict), **Supp. XXIII:** 39–40

"Wreck of Rivermouth, The" (Whittier), **Supp. I Part 2:** 694, 696–697

"Wreck of the Deutschland" (Hopkins), **Supp. X:** 61

"Wreck of the Hesperus, The" (Longfellow), **Retro. Supp. II:** 168, 169

Wrestler's Cruel Study, The (Dobyns), **Supp. XIII:** **82–83**

"Wrestler with Sharks, A" (Yates), **Supp. XI:** 341

"Wrestling with Augie March" (Kriegel), **Supp. XXIV:** 220

Wright, Bernie, **I:** 191, 193

Wright, C. D. (Carolyn Doris), **Supp. XV:** 337–355

Wright, Charles, **Supp. V:** 92, **331–346**; **Supp. VIII:** 272; **Supp. XIII:** 114; **Supp. XVII:** 71; **Supp. XXI:** 95, 255; **Supp. XXIV:** 155

Wright, Chauncey, **II:** 344

Wright, Conrad, **Supp. XXIV:** 71, 72

Wright, Frank Lloyd, **I:** 104, 483

Wright, Franz, **Supp. XVII:** **239–249**

Wright, George, **III:** 479

Wright, Harold Bell, **II:** 467–468

Wright, Holly, **Supp. VIII:** 272

Wright, James, **I:** 291; **Supp. III Part 1:** 249; **Supp. III Part 2:** 541, **589–607**; **Supp. IV Part 1:** 60, 72; **Supp. IV Part 2:** 557, 558, 561, 566, 571, 623; **Supp. IX:** 152, 155, 159, 265, 271, 290, 293, 296; **Supp. V:** 332; **Supp. X:** 69, 127; **Supp. XI:** 150; **Supp. XII:** 217; **Supp. XIII:** 76; **Supp. XIX:** 122, 273; **Supp. XV:** 79, 93, 212; **Supp. XVII:** 239, 241, 243, 244; **Supp. XXVI:** 68

Wright, Nathalia, **IV:** 155

Wright, Philip Green, **III:** 578, 579, 580

Wright, Richard, **II:** 586; **IV:** 40, **474–497**; **Retro. Supp. II:** 4, 111, 116, 120; **Supp. I Part 1:** 51, 52, 64, 332, 337; **Supp. II Part 1:** 17, 40, 221, 228, 235, 250; **Supp. IV Part 1:** 1, 11, 84, 374; **Supp. IX:** 316; **Supp. VIII:** 88; **Supp. X:** 131, 245, 254; **Supp. XI:** 85; **Supp. XII:** 316; **Supp. XIII:** 46, 233; **Supp. XIV:** 73; **Supp. XVI:** 135, 139, 141, 143; **Supp. XVIII:** 277, 282, 286; **Supp. XXI:** 169; **Supp. XXIII:** 166

Wright, Mrs. Richard (Ellen Poplar), **IV:** 476

Wright, Sarah, **Supp. IV Part 1:** 8; **Supp. XIII:** 295

Wright, William, **Retro. Supp. II:** 76, 77

Wrigley, Robert, **Supp. XVIII:** **293–308**

"Writer" (Sanders), **Supp. XVI:** 277

"Writer, The" (Wilbur), **Supp. III Part 2:** 561, 562

"Writer as Alaskan, The" (Haines), **Supp. XII:** 199

Writer in America, The (Brooks), **I:** 253, 254, 257

Writer in America, The (Stegner), **Supp. IV Part 2:** 597, 599, 607

"Writers" (Lowell), **II:** 554

Writer's Almanac, The (Keillor, radio program), **Supp. XIII:** 274; **Supp. XVI:** 178; **Supp. XXIII:** 138

Writer's America, A: Landscape in Literature (Kazin), **Supp. VIII:** 106

Writers and Their Craft (Delbanco, ed.), **Supp. XXII:** 204

"Writer's Bed, A" (Mirvis), **Supp. XX:** **179**

Writer's Capital, A (Auchincloss), **Supp. IV Part 1:** 21, 23, 24, 31

"Writer's Credo, A" (Abbey), **Supp. XIII:** 1, 17

Writer's Eye, A: Collected Book Reviews (Welty), **Retro. Supp. I:** 339, 354, 356

Writers in America (Schulberg), **Supp. XVIII:** 242, 243, 250, 254

Writers in Revolt (Southern, Seaver, and Trocchi, eds.), **Supp. XI:** 301

Writer's Life, A (Talese), **Supp. XVII:** 208–209, 210

Writer's Notebook, A (Maugham), **Supp. X:** 58

Writers on America (U.S. Department of State, ed.), **Supp. XIII:** 288

Writers on the Left (Aaron), **IV:** 429; **Supp. II Part 1:** 137

Writers on Writing (Prose), **Supp. XVI:** 259

"Writer's Prologue to a Play in Verse" (W. C. Williams), **Retro. Supp. I:** 424

"Writer's Quest for a Parnassus, A" (T. Williams), **IV:** 392

Writers' Workshop (University of Iowa), **Supp. V:** 42

"Writers Workshop, The" (Conroy), **Supp. XVI:** 76

"Writing" (Nemerov), **III:** 275

"Writing About the Universe" (Mosley), **Supp. XIII:** 247

"Writing American Fiction" (P. Roth), **Retro. Supp. II:** 279; **Supp. I Part 1:** 192; **Supp. I Part 2:** 431; **Supp. III Part 2:** 414, 420, 421; **Supp. V:** 45

"Writing and a Life Lived Well" (Patchett), **Supp. XII:** 308

"Writing and Writers: *Disjecta Membra*" (Sorrentino), *Supp. XXI:* 235

Writing a Woman's Life (Heilbrun), **Supp. IX:** 66

"Writing Between Worlds" (Mirvis), **Supp. XX: 177, 178, 179**

Writing Brave and Free: Encouraging Words for People Who Want to Start Writing (Kooser and Cox), **Supp. XIX:** 116, 128

Writing Chicago: Modernism, Ethnography, and the Novel (Cappetti), **Supp. IX:** 4, 8

Writing Creative Nonfiction: The Literature of Reality (Talese and Lounsberry, eds.), **Supp. XVII:** 208

Writing Dylan: The Songs of a Lonesome Traveler (Smith), **Supp. XVIII:** 22

Writing from the Center (Sanders), **Supp. XVI:** 266, 275–276

"Writing from the Inside Out: Style Is Not the Frosting; It's the Cake" (Robbins), **Supp. X:** 266

Writing Habit, The (Huddle), **Supp. XXVI:** 152, 160

"Writing Habit, The" (Huddle), **Supp. XXVI:** 160

"Writing here last autumn of my hopes of seeing a hoopoe" (Updike), **Retro. Supp. I:** 335

Writing Home (Crooker), **Supp. XXIII:** 54

Writing in an Age of Silence (Paretsky), **Supp. XXV:** 169, 181

Writing in Restaurants (Mamet), **Supp. XIV:** 246

"Writing Is Work" (Rinehart), **Supp. XXV:** 198

"Writing Lesson, The" (Gordon), **Supp. IV Part 1:** 306

Writing Life, The (Dillard), **Supp. VI:** 23, 31

"Writing of Apollinaire, The" (Zukofsky), **Supp. III Part 2:** 616, 617

"Writing of *Fearless Jones,* The" (Mosley), **Supp. XIII:** 242

Writing on the Wall, The, and Literary Essays (McCarthy), **II:** 579

Writings to an Unfinished Accompaniment (Merwin), **Supp. III Part 1:** 352

"Writing the Rez: Popular Obsessions in the Works of Eric Gansworth" (de la Paz and Purdy), **Supp. XXVI:** 102, 111

"Writing the Universe-Mind" (Tabios), **Supp. XV:** 225

Writing the World (Stafford), **Supp. XI:** 314

"Writing to Save Our Lives" (Milligan), **Supp. XIII:** 274

Writing Vietnam, Writing Life: Caputo, Heinemann, O'Brien, Butler (Herzog), **Supp. XXII:** 116

Writin' Is Fightin' (Reed), **Supp. X:** 241

"Writ on the Eve of My 32nd Birthday" (Corso), **Supp. XII:** 129–130

"Written History as an Act of Faith" (Beard), **Supp. I Part 2:** 492

"Written on the Land" (J. W. Miller), **Supp. XX: 170**

"Wrong Man, The" (Larsen), **Supp. XVIII:** 124

"Wrong Notes" (S. Kauffmann), **Supp. XVI:** 74

"Wrought Figure" (McCarriston), **Supp. XIV:** 272

Wrozynski, Henryk, **Supp. XXIII:** 64

"Wunderkind" (McCullers), **II:** 585

Wunderlich, Mark, **Supp. XI:** 119, 132

Wundt, Wilhelm, **II:** 345

Wurlitzer, Rudolph, **Supp. XXVI:** 26

Wurster, William Wilson, **Supp. IV Part 1:** 197

WUSA (film), **Supp. V:** 301

Wuthering Heights (E. Brontë), **Supp. V:** 305; **Supp. X:** 89

WWII (Jones), **Supp. XI:** 219, 231

Wyandotté (Cooper), **I:** 350, 355

Wyatt, Robert B., **Supp. V:** 14

Wyatt, Thomas, **Supp. I Part 1:** 369

Wyce, Marion, **Supp. XXVI:** 57

Wycherly Woman, The (Macdonald), **Supp. IV Part 2:** 473

Wych Hazel (S. and A. Warner), **Supp. XVIII:** 267, **268–269**

Wydra, Ewa. *See* Hoffman, Eva

Wyeth, Andrew, **Supp. XIX:** 117

Wyler, William, **Supp. XV:** 195

Wylie, Elinor, **IV:** 436; **Supp. I Part 2: 707–730; Supp. III Part 1:** 2, 63, 318–319; **Supp. XI:** 44; **Supp. XIV:** 127; **Supp. XV:** 307

Wylie, Horace, **Supp. I Part 2:** 708, 709

Wylie, Philip, **III:** 223

Wyllys, Ruth. *See* Taylor, Mrs. Edward (Ruth Wyllys)

"Wyoming Valley Tales" (Crane), **I:** 409

Wyzewa, Théodore de, **Supp. XIV:** 336

X

Xaipe (Cummings), **I:** 430, 432–433, 447

Xarque and Other Poems (G. Jones), **Supp. XXIV:** 194

Xenogenesis trilogy (O. Butler), **Supp. XIII: 63–66,** 69

Xenophon, **II:** 105

X Factor, The: A Quest for Excellence" (Plimpton), **Supp. XVI:** 241

X Files (television series), **Supp. XVI:** 125

Xiaojing, Zhou, **Supp. XV:** 214

Xicana Codex of Changing Consciousness, A: Writings, 2000–2010 (Moraga), **Supp. XXIII:** 197

Xingu and Other Stories (Wharton), **IV:** 314, 320; **Retro. Supp. I:** 378

Xionia (Wright), **Supp. V:** 333

XLI Poems (Cummings), **I:** 429, 432, 440, 443

Xu, Wenying, **Supp. XXVI:** 212

Y

Yabroff, Jennie, **Supp. XIX:** 50, 58, 61

Yacoubi, Ahmed, **Supp. IV Part 1:** 88, 92, 93

Yage Letters, The (Burroughs), **Supp. III Part 1:** 94, 98, 100

Yagoda, Ben, **Supp. VIII:** 151

Yamamoto, Isoroku, **Supp. I Part 2:** 491

Yancey's War (Hoffman), **Supp. XVIII:** 71, **75–76**

Yankee City (Warner), **III:** 60

Yankee Clipper (ballet) (Kirstein), **Supp. IV Part 1:** 82

Yankee in Canada, A (Thoreau), **IV:** 188

Yankey in London (Tyler), **I:** 344

"Yánnina" (Merrill), **Supp. III Part 1:** 329

"Yanosz Korczak's Last Walk" (Markowick-Olczakova), **Supp. X:** 70

Yarboro, Chelsea Quinn, **Supp. V:** 147

Yarbro-Bejarano, Yvonne, **Supp. XXIII:** 196, 201

Yardley, Jonathan, **Supp. V:** 326; **Supp. XI:** 67; **Supp. XXIII:** 97, 99, 103, 104, 107, 108, 109

"Yard Sale" (Kenyon), **Supp. VII:** 169

Yates, Richard, **Supp. XI: 333–350; Supp. XXIII:** 289; **Supp. XXIV:** 97; **Supp. XXV:** 154

"Year, The" (Sandburg), **III:** 584

Year at the Races, A (Parker and Parker), **Supp. XIX:** 187

Year Before Last (Boyle), **Supp. XXIV: 52–53**

"Year Between, The" (Neugeboren), **Supp. XVI:** 226

Year in Provence, A (Mayle), **Supp. XVI:** 295

Yearling, The (Rawlings), **Supp. X:** 219, **230–231,** 233, 234; **Supp. XXII:** 195

"Year of Grace" (Swados), **Supp. XIX:** 262–263

Year of Happy, A (Goldbarth), **Supp. XII:** 180

Year of Magical Thinking, The (Didion), **Supp. XXV:** 60, 208

"Year of Mourning, The" (Jeffers), **Supp. II Part 2:** 415

Year of Silence, The (Bell), **Supp. X:** 1, **5–6,** 7

"Year of Silence, The" (Brockmeier), **Supp. XXII:** 59

"Year of the Double Spring, The" (Swenson), **Supp. IV Part 2:** 647

Year's Best Fantasy and Horror, 2004, **Supp. XXII:** 55

Year's Best Science Fiction, The (Merril, ed.), **Supp. XVI:** 123

Year's Life, A (Lowell), **Supp. I Part 2:** 405

"Years of Birth" (Cowley), **Supp. II Part 1:** 149

Years of Conscience: The Muckrakers: An Anthology of Reform Journalism (Swados, ed.), **Supp. XIX:** 264

Years of My Youth (Howells), **II:** 276

"Years of Wonder" (White), **Supp. I Part 2:** 652, 653

"Years Without Understanding, The" (Weigl), **Supp. XIX:** 282–283

Years With Ross, The (Thurber), **Supp. I Part 2:** 619

Year We Left Home, The (Thompson), **Supp. XXIII:** 301, **302–303**

Yeats, Jack, **Supp. XVI:** 190

Yeats, Jack B., **Supp. XX: 201**

Yeats, John Butler, **III:** 458; **Supp. XX: 69**

Yeats, William Butler, **I:** 69, 172, 384, 389, 403, 434, 478, 494, 532; **II:** 168–169, 566, 598; **III:** 4, 5, 8, 18, 19, 20, 23, 29, 40, 205, 249, 269, 270–271, 272, 278, 279, 294, 347, 409, 457, 458–460, 472, 473, 476–477, 521,

523, 524, 527, 528, 533, 540, 541, 542, 543–544, 591–592; **IV:** 89, 93, 121, 126, 136, 140, 271, 394, 404; **Retro. Supp. I:** 59, 66, 127, 141, 270, 283, 285, 286, 288, 290, 311, 342, 350, 378, 413; **Retro. Supp. II:** 185, 331; **Supp. I Part 1:** 79, 80, 254, 257, 262; **Supp. I Part 2:** 388, 389; **Supp. II Part 1:** 1, 4, 9, 20, 26, 361; **Supp. III Part 1:** 59, 63, 236, 238, 253; **Supp. IV Part 1:** 81; **Supp. IV Part 2:** 634; **Supp. IX:** 43, 119; **Supp. V:** 220; **Supp. VIII:** 19, 21, 30, 155, 156, 190, 239, 262, 292; **Supp. X:** 35, 58, 119, 120; **Supp. XI:** 140; **Supp. XII:** 132, 198, 217, 266; **Supp. XIII:** 77, **Supp. XIII:** 87; **Supp. XIV:** 7; **Supp. XV:** 36, 41, 181, 186; **Supp. XVI:** 47–48, 159; **Supp. XVII:** 36; **Supp. XXI:** 61

Yee, Amy, **Supp. XVIII:** 93, 94

"Ye Have Your Closes" (Davison), **Supp. XXVI:** 78

Yellin, Jean Fagan, **Supp. XVI:** 88, 89

Yellow Back Radio Broke-Down (Reed), **Supp. X:** 240, 242, **243–245**

"Yellow Dog Café" (Komunyakaa), **Supp. XIII:** 126

Yellow Face (Hwang), **Supp. XXI:** 143, 148, **154–156**

"Yellow Girl" (Caldwell), **I:** 310

Yellow Glove (Nye), **Supp. XIII:** 275, **276–277**

"Yellow Glove" (Nye), **Supp. XIII:** 276

"Yellow Gown, The" (Anderson), **I:** 114

Yellow House on the Corner, The (Dove), **Supp. IV Part 1:** 244, 245, 246, 254

"Yellow Raft, The" (Connell), **Supp. XIV: 85–86**

"Yellow River" (Tate), **IV:** 141

Yellow Room, The (Rinehart), **Supp. XXV:** 198, 200

"Yellowstone, The"(Kenny), **Supp. XXIII:** 155

"Yellow Violet, The" (Bryant), **Supp. I Part 1:** 154, 155

"Yellow Wallpaper, The" (Gilman), **Supp. XI: 198–199,** 207; **Supp. XVI:** 84

"Yellow Woman" (Keres stories), **Supp. IV Part 1:** 327

"Yellow Woman" (Silko), **Supp. IV Part 2:** 567–568

Yelverton, Theresa, **Supp. IX:** 181

Yenser, Stephen, **Supp. X:** 207, 208; **Supp. XV:** 113–114

"Yentl the Yeshiva Boy" (Singer), **IV:** 15, 20

Yerkes, Charles E., **I:** 507, 512

Yerma (opera) (Bowles), **Supp. IV Part 1:** 89

Yertle the Turtle and Other Stories (Geisel), **Supp. XVI:** 109

"Yes" (Stafford), **Supp. XI:** 329

Yes, Mrs. Williams (W. C. Williams), **Retro. Supp. I:** 423

Yes, Yes, No, No (Kushner), **Supp. IX:** 133

"Yes and It's Hopeless" (Ginsberg), **Supp. II Part 1:** 326

"Yes"(Crooker), **Supp. XXIII:** 62

Yesenin, Sergey, **Supp. VIII:** 40

"Yes: I Mean So OK–Love" (Bronk), **Supp. XXI:** 31

"Yes! No!" (Oliver), **Supp. VII:** 243–244

Yesterday and Today: A Comparative Anthology of Poetry (Untermeyer, ed.), **Supp. XV:** 309

Yesterday's Self: Nostalgia and the Immigrant Identity (Ritivoi), **Supp. XVI:** 148

Yesterday Will Make You Cry (C. Himes), **Supp. XVI:** 137

"Yet Another Example of the Porousness of Certain Borders" (Wallace), **Supp. X:** 309

"Yet Do I Marvel" (Cullen), **Supp. IV Part 1:** 165, 169

Yet Other Waters (Farrell), **II:** 29, 38, 39, 40

"Yevtushenko" (Kooser), **Supp. XIX:** 124

Yevtushenko, Yevgeny, **Supp. III Part 1:** 268

Yezzi, David, **Supp. XII:** 193

Yiddish Policemen's Union, The (Chabon), **Supp. XXII:** 49

Yizkor Book, **Supp. XVI:** 154

...y no se lo tragó la tierra (Rivera), **Supp. XIX:** 99, 101

Y no se lo trago la tierra (And the Earth Did Not Cover Him) (Rivera), **Supp. XIII:** 216

¡Yo! (Alvarez), **Supp. VII:** 1, 15–17

"Yogurt of Vasirin Kefirovsky, The" (Apple), **Supp. XVII:** 3, 4

Yohannan, J. D., **II:** 20

"Yoke, The" (Bidart), **Supp. XV:** 33

Yonge, Charlotte, **II:** 174

"Yonnondio" (Whitman), **Supp. XIII:** 304

Yonnondio: From the Thirties (Olsen), **Supp. XIII:** 295, 295, **Supp. XIII:** 292, 296, **303–304,** 305

"Yore" (Nemerov), **III:** 283

York, Jake Adam, **Supp. XXI:** 257

York, Lorraine, **Supp. XX: 51**

"York Beach" (Toomer), **Supp. III Part 2:** 486

Yorke, Dorothy, **Supp. I Part 1:** 258

Yorke, Henry Vincent. *See* Green, Henry

"York Garrison, 1640" (Jewett), **Retro. Supp. II:** 141

Yosemite, The (Muir), **Supp. IX:** 185

"Yosemite Glaciers: Ice Streams of the Great Valley" (Muir), **Supp. IX:** 181

Yoshe Kalb (Singer), **IV:** 2

"You, Andrew Marvell" (MacLeish), **III:** 12–13

"You, Dr. Martin" (Sexton), **Supp. II Part 2:** 673

You, Emperors, and Others: Poems 1957–1960 (Warren), **IV:** 245

"You, Genoese Mariner" (Merwin), **Supp. III Part 1:** 343

"You, Reader" (Collins), **Supp. XXI:** 55

"You, Too, Will Have This Printed Word (World) of Your Own" (Gansworth), **Supp. XXVI:** 114

"You All Know the Story of the Other Woman" (Sexton), **Supp. II Part 2:** 688

"You Are Gorgeous and I'm Coming"(O'Hara), **Supp. XXIII:** 219

You Are Happy (Atwood), **Supp. XIII:** 34

"You Are Happy" (Atwood), **Supp. XIII:** 34

"You Are in Bear Country" (Kumin), **Supp. IV Part 2:** 453, 455

"You Are Not I" (Bowles), **Supp. IV Part 1:** 87

"You Begin" (Atwood), **Supp. XIII:** 34

You Bright and Risen Angels (Vollmann), **Supp. XVII:** 225, 226

"You Bring Out the Mexican in Me" (Cisneros), **Supp. VII:** 71

You Came Along (film), **Supp. IV Part 2:** 524

"You Can Go Home Again" (TallMountain), **Supp. IV Part 1:** 324–325

"You Can Have It" (Levine), **Supp. V:** 188–189

You Can't Go Home Again (Wolfe), **IV:** 450, 451, 454, 456, 460, 462, 468, 469, 470

You Can't Keep a Good Woman Down (Walker), **Supp. III Part 2:** 520, 525, 531

You Can't Pet a Possom (Bontemps), **Supp. XXII:** 4, 12

You Can't Take It with You (Kaufman and Hart), **Supp. XIV:** 327

"You Can't Tell a Man by the Song He Sings" (P. Roth), **Supp. III Part 2:** 406

"You Don't Know What Love Is" (Carver), **Supp. III Part 1:** 147

You Don't Love Me Yet (Lethem), **Supp. XVIII: 149–150**

"You Have Left Your Lotus Pods on the Bus" (Bowles), **Supp. IV Part 1:** 91

You Have Seen Their Faces (Caldwell), **I:** 290, 293–294, 295, 304, 309

You Know Me, Al: A Busher's Letters (Lardner), **Supp. XVI:** 189

You Know Me Al (comic strip), **II:** 423

You Know Me Al (Lardner), **II:** 26, 415, 419, 422, 431

"You Know More Than You Think You Do"(Hadas), **Supp. XXIII:** 124

"You Know What" (Beattie), **Supp. V:** 33

"You Know Who You Are" (Nye), **Supp. XIII:** 275

You Might As Well Live: The Life and Times of Dorothy Parker (Keats), **Supp. IX:** 190

"You Must Relax!" (J. Scott), **Supp. XVII:** 189

You Must Revise Your Life (Stafford), **Supp. XI:** 312–313, 313–314, 315

"Young" (Sexton), **Supp. II Part 2:** 680

Young, Al, **Supp. X:** 240; **Supp. XXVI:** 12

Young, Art, **IV:** 436

Young, Barbara, **Supp. XX: 119, 123**

Young, Brigham, **Supp. IV Part 2:** 603

Young, Courtland, **Supp. XXII:** 21
Young, David, **Supp. XIX:** 276
Young, Dianne, **Supp. XXII:** 252
Young, Edward, **II:** 111; **III:** 415, 503
Young, Gary, **Supp. XV:** 88
Young, Hershini Bhana, **Supp. XXIV:** 189
Young, Mary, **Supp. XIII:** 236, 238, 239, 240
Young, Philip, **II:** 306; **Retro. Supp. I:** 172
Young, Stark, **Supp. XXII:** 193
Young Adventure (Benét), **Supp. XI:** 44
"Young America" (Brooks), **Supp. XV:** 298
Youngblood Hawke (film), **Supp. XXV:** 263
Youngblood Hawke (Wouk), **Supp. XXV:** 256, 257, 258, 259, 263
"Young Child and His Pregnant Mother, A" (Schwartz), **Supp. II Part 2:** 650
Young Christian, The (Abbott), **Supp. I Part 1:** 38
"Young Dr. Gosse" (Chopin), **Supp. I Part 1:** 211, 216
Younger Choir, The (anthology), **Supp. XV:** 294
Younger Quire, The (Untermeyer), **Supp. XV:** 294, 297
"Young Folks, The" (Salinger), **III:** 551
Young Folk's Cyclopaedia of Persons and Places (Champlin), **III:** 577
"Young Girl's Lament, A" (Jin), **Supp. XVIII:** 99
"Young Goodman Brown" (Hawthorne), **II:** 229; **Retro. Supp. I:** 151–152, 153, 154; **Supp. XI:** 51; **Supp. XIV:** 48, 50
Young Harvard: First Poems of Witter Bynner (Bynner), **Supp. XV:** 41
Young Hearts Crying (Yates), **Supp. XI:** 348
"Young Housewife, The" (W. C. Williams), **Retro. Supp. I:** 415
Young Immigrants, The (Lardner), **II:** 426
"Young Lady's Friend, The: Verses, Addressed to a Young Lady, on Her Leaving School" (Rowson), **Supp. XV:** 234
"Young Lions" (E. P. Jones), **Supp. XXII:** 145
Young Lions, The (Shaw), **Supp. XIX:** **248–249**
Young Lonigan: A Boyhood in Chicago Streets (Farrell), **II:** 31, 41
Young Manhood of Studs Lonigan, The (Farrell), **II:** 31, 34
"Young Man on the Go" (column, Siddons), **Supp. XXII:** 244
Young Men and Fire (Maclean), **Supp. XIV:** 221, **231–233**
Young People's Pride (Benét), **Supp. XI:** 44
Young Poet's Primer (Brooks), **Supp. III Part 1:** 86
Youngren, J. Alan, **Supp. XVI:** 174
"Young Sammy's First Wild Oats" (Santayana), **III:** 607, 615
"Young Sor Juana, The" (Mora), **Supp. XIII:** 218

"Your Arkansas Traveler" (Schulberg), **Supp. XVIII:** 252
"Your Dailiness" (Notley), **Supp. XXII:** 227
"Your Death" (Dove), **Supp. IV Part 1:** 250
"You're History" (Hampl), **Supp. XXII:** 84, 95
You're Only Old Once! (Geisel), **Supp. XVI:** 111
"You're Ugly, Too" (Moore), **Supp. X:** 171
"Your Face on the Dog's Neck" (Sexton), **Supp. II Part 2:** 686
"Your Hand, Your Hand" (Hoffman), **Supp. XVIII:** 79
Your Job in Germany (film, Capra), **Supp. XVI:** 102
Your Job in Japan (film, Capra), **Supp. XVI:** 102
"Your Life" (Stafford), **Supp. XI:** 329
"Your Mother's Eyes" (Kingsolver), **Supp. VII:** 209
"You Take a Train through a Foreign Country" (Dobyns), **Supp. XIII:** 90
"Youth" (Hughes), **Supp. I Part 1:** 321; **Supp. XXII:** 12
"Youth" (Huncke), **Supp. XIV:** 145
Youth and Life (Bourne), **I:** 217–222, 232
Youth and the Bright Medusa (Cather), **I:** 322; **Retro. Supp. I:** 14
"Youthful Religious Experiences" (Corso), **Supp. XII:** 117
Youth of Parnassus, and Other Stories, The (L. P. Smith), **Supp. XIV:** 336
Youth's First Steps in Geography (Rowson), **Supp. XV:** 243
You Touched Me! (Williams and Windham), **IV:** 382, 385, 387, 390, 392–393
"You Touch Me" (X. J. Kennedy), **Supp. XV:** 166
You Went Away (Findley), **Supp. XX: 49**
"You Who Sleep Soundly Through Our Bleakest Hour" (Espaillat), **Supp. XXI:** 110
Yurchenco, Henrietta, **Supp. XVIII:** 20
Yurka, Blanche, **Supp. I Part 1:** 67
Yutang, Adet, **Supp. X:** 291
Yutang, Anor, **Supp. X:** 291
Yutang, Lin, **Supp. X:** 291; **Supp. XVI:** 190
Yutang, Mei-mei, **Supp. X:** 291
Yvernelle: A Legend of Feudal France (Norris), **III:** 314
Y & X (Olson), **Supp. II Part 2:** 556

Z

Zabel, Morton Dauwen, **II:** 431; **III:** 194, 215; **Supp. I Part 2:** 721
Zach, Natan, **Supp. XV:** 75, 82, 85
Zaehner, R. C., **Supp. XXII:** 258
Zagajewski, Adam, **Supp. XVII:** 241
Zagarell, Sandra, **Supp. XV:** 269, 270, 278, 281, 282
Zagarell, Sandra A., **Retro. Supp. II:** 140, 143
"Zagrowsky Tells" (Paley), **Supp. VI:** 229

Zaino, Nick, **Supp. XXII:** 207
Zakrzewska, Marie, **Retro. Supp. II:** 146
Zaleski, Jeff, **Supp. XI:** 143; **Supp. XIX:** 54; **Supp. XXVI:** 158
Zall, Paul, **Supp. XIV:** 156
Zaltzberg, Charlotte, **Supp. IV Part 1:** 374
"Zambesi and Ranee" (Swenson), **Supp. IV Part 2:** 647
Zamir, Israel, **Retro. Supp. II:** 303, 317
Zamora, Bernice, **Supp. IV Part 2:** 545
Zamoyski, Adam, **Supp. XV:** 257
Zangwill, Israel, **I:** 229; **Supp. XX:** 2
Zanita: A Tale of the Yosemite (Yelverton), **Supp. IX:** 181
Zanuck, Darryl F., **Supp. XI:** 170; **Supp. XII:** 165
Zapata, Emiliano, **Supp. XIII:** 324
"Zapatos" (Boyle), **Supp. VIII:** 15
Zapruder, Matthew, **Supp. XVI:** 55; **Supp. XXVI:** 54
Zarathustra, **III:** 602
Zawacki, Andrew, **Supp. VIII:** 272
"Zaydee" (Levine), **Supp. V:** 186
Zebra-Striped Hearse, The (Macdonald), **Supp. IV Part 2:** 473
Zechariah (biblical book), **IV:** 152
Zeidner, Lisa, **Supp. IV Part 2:** 453; **Supp. XXIII:** 297
"Zeitl and Rickel" (Singer), **IV:** 20
Zeke and Ned (McMurtry and Ossana), **Supp. V:** 232
Zeke Proctor, Cherokee Outlaw (Conley), **Supp. V:** 232
Zelazny, Roger, **Supp. XXV:** 73
Zelazo, Suzanne, **Supp. XXII:** 158, 167
Zelda: A Biography (Milford), **Supp. IX:** 60
"Zelda and Scott: The Beautiful and Damned" (National Portrait Gallery exhibit), **Supp. IX:** 65
Zelig (film; Allen), **Supp. XV:** 4, 6, **8–9**
Zeller, Maya Jewell, **Supp. XXIV:** 167
Zen and the Birds of Appetite (Merton), **Supp. VIII:** 205–206, 208
Zend-Avesta (Fechner), **II:** 358
"Zenith: Walker Creek" (Davison), **Supp. XXVI:** 74
Zeno, **Retro. Supp. I:** 247
Zero db and Other Stories (Bell), **Supp. X:** 1, 5, 6
"Zeus over Redeye" (Hayden), **Supp. II Part 1:** 380
Zevi, Sabbatai, **IV:** 6
Ziegfeld, Florenz, **II:** 427–428
Ziegler, Cyd, **Supp. XX: 273**
Ziegler, Heidi, **Supp. XXII:** 260
Ziggurat (Balakian), **Supp. XXIII:** 19, **32–33**
Zigrosser, Carl, **I:** 226, 228, 231
Zigzagger (Muñoz), **Supp. XXV:** 127, 132, 133, 134
"Zigzagger" (Muñoz), **Supp. XXV:** 134
Zilles, Klaus, **Supp. XIX:** 112
Zimmerman, Paul D., **Supp. IV Part 2:** 583, 589, 590

Zimmerman, Robert. *See* Dylan, Bob

Zimmerman, Robert Allen. *See* Dylan, Bob

Zinberg, Leonard S. *See* Lacy, Ed

Zinman, Toby Silverman, **Supp. XIII:** 207–208, 209

Zinn, Howard, **Supp. V:** 289; **Supp. XXIV:** 87

Zinovyev, Grigory, **Supp. XXI:** 167

Zinsser, Hans, **I:** 251, 385

Zip: A Novel of the Left and Right (Apple), **Supp. XVII:** 4–5

Zipes, Jack, **Supp. XIV:** 126

"Zipper, The" (L. Michaels), **Supp. XVI:** 214

Zitkala-Ša (Gertrude Simmons Bonnin), **Supp. XXV: 271–287**

"Zizi's Lament" (Corso), **Supp. XII:** 123

Zodiac, The (Dickey), **Supp. IV Part 1:** 178, 183–184, 185

"Zog-19: A Scientific Romance"(P. Benedict), **Supp. XXIII:** 49

Zola, Émile, **I:** 211, 411, 474, 500, 502, 518; **II:** 174, 175–176, 182, 194, 275, 276, 281, 282, 319, 325, 337, 338; **III:** 315, 316, 317–318, 319–320, 321, 322, 323, 393, 511, 583; **IV:** 326; **Retro. Supp. I:** 226, 235; **Retro. Supp. II:** 93; **Supp. I Part 1:** 207; **Supp. II Part 1:** 117

Zolotow, Maurice, **III:** 161

"Zone" (Bogan), **Supp. III Part 1:** 60–61

Zone Journals (Wright), **Supp. V:** 332–333, 342–343

"Zooey" (Salinger), **III:** 564–565, 566, 567, 569, 572

"Zoo Revisited" (White), **Supp. I Part 2:** 654

Zoo Story, The (Albee), **I:** 71, 72–74, 75, 77, 84, 93, 94; **III:** 281

Zorach, William, **I:** 260

Zuccotti, Susan, **Supp. XVI:** 154

Zuckerman Bound: A Trilogy and Epilogue (P. Roth), **Supp. III Part 2:** 423

Zuckerman Unbound (P. Roth), **Retro. Supp. II:** 283; **Supp. III Part 2:** 421–422

Zueblin, Charles, **Supp. I Part 1:** 5

Zuger, Abigail, **Supp. X:** 160

Zukofsky, Celia (Mrs. Louis), **Supp. III Part 2:** 619–621, 623, 625, 626–629, 631

Zukofsky, Louis, **IV:** 415; **Retro. Supp. I:** 422; **Supp. III Part 2: 619–636; Supp. IV Part 1:** 154; **Supp. XIV:** 279, 282, 285, 286–287; **Supp. XXVI:** 224, 226, 227, 229

Zukofsky, Paul, **Supp. III Part 2:** 622, 623–626, 627, 628

Zuleika Dobson (Beerbohm), **Supp. I Part 2:** 714

Zulus (Everett), **Supp. XVIII:** 54, **56–57**

"Zuni Potter: Drawing the Heartline" (Bierds), **Supp. XVII:** 26

Zverev, Aleksei, **Retro. Supp. I:** 278

Zwinger, Ann, **Supp. X:** 29

Zyda, Joan, **Retro. Supp. II:** 52